DIRECT-LINE DISTANCES
International Edition

by
Gary L. Fitzpatrick
and
Marilyn J. Modlin

The Scarecrow Press, Inc.
Metuchen, N.J., and London
1986

Library of Congress Cataloging-in-Publication Data

Fitzpatrick, Gary L., 1947-
    Direct-line distances: International edition.

    1. Distances--Tables, etc.   I. Modlin, Marilyn J.
II. Title.
G109.F53   1986   910'.212   85-27748
ISBN 0-8108-1872-8

C O N T E N T S

Introduction

Using the Book

Direct-Line Distances is a table of distances between 1001 cities, towns, islands, and other places around the world. This, the International edition, gives distances in kilometers.

To find the distance between two places, take the place which comes first alphabetically and locate the pages where it appears as a column heading. Then go down the left margin until the second place is found. The distance between the two places is given where the column for the first place and the line for the second place intersect.

The table consists of fifty sections of twenty columns each. In the first section, for example, the cities Abadan through Al Minya appear as column headings. The pages within this section list all cities which follow Abadan alphabetically. For ease of use, a guide in the upper margin of each page indicates the names of the first and last column headings on that page. Finding the section in which a city appears as a column heading can also be accomplished by looking up the name in the "List of Entries," beginning on page XV.

To determine whether a place you are interested in is included in the table, consult the maps which appear on pages XXXIII-XLIV. Even if a place you are interested in is not included in the table, by consulting the maps you can locate a nearby place which is found in Direct-Line Distances.

Scope

Direct-Line Distances includes the capitals of all countries. To complete the table, large cities and strategically located places were selected. In addition, some remote islands or towns were chosen to provide coverage for certain geographic areas. Where large towns or cities are in close proximity, only one place was selected: Dallas, Texas is found in the table while Fort Worth is not; Saint Paul, Minnesota, being the state capital, was chosen while the larger city across the river, Minneapolis, was not.

In addition to stating distances in kilometers, this edition differs from the United States edition in that the selection of cities is not weighted heavily with cities and towns of that country.

In selecting places for Direct-Line Distances, no hard-and-fast rules were adhered to in choosing smaller towns and islands. Small places near important borders, passes, and straits were selected in lieu of the physical feature itself. Thus, the town of Punta Arenas was selected to represent the Strait of Magellan and Kumzar, a town lying along the Strait of Hormuz, was chosen because of its proximity to that important body of water.

The selection of islands in the Pacific and Indian Oceans was frequently guided by the desire to have at least one place in major portions of the oceans included in Direct-Line Distances. Because few people are acquainted with the names of towns in the oceans, many entries for the Pacific and Indian

Oceans are listed alphabetically by the name of the island. In such cases, however, a town name is given in parentheses to indicate the specific location on the island to which distances were computed.

Nature of the Distances Given in the Table

This volume gives distances computed mathematically from a complex formula which yields what is known as a "geodesic" distance. In the science of geodesy, a "geodesic" is defined as the shortest distance between two points on the spheroid. The formula used, a slightly modified version of one developed by E. M. Sodano*, takes into account the flattening of the earth at the poles. It is capable of yielding results accurate to a fraction of a meter, though in this book all distances have been rounded off to the nearest kilometer.

The calculations for computing a "geodesic" are based on the geographic coordinates of two points -- the more accurate the coordinates, the more accurate the final result. Since Direct-Line Distances is intended as a general reference work for libraries, the coordinates used in the computations were taken from standard reference sources which round latitude and longitude to the nearest minute. At that level of precision for the coordinates, the results of the computations are best expressed to the lowest full unit. Rounding off the distances in this volume to the nearest kilometer, therefore, reflects the precision of the coordinates on which the calculations are based. The coordinates from which the distances in this volume were computed are given in the "List of Entries" beginning on page XV.

The distances in this volume should not be confused with "great circle distances." The latter type of distance can also be computed from geographic coordinates, but it is based on an assumption that the earth is a true sphere. The "great circle" computation is freqently used in both marine and aeronautical navigation, where the level of precision imparted through the computation of the "geodesic" is not required.

In general terms, the distances in this volume reflect what people frequently call the "air distance" between two places, thereby differentiating it from the highway distance. With that usage, people imply that they want to know the distance along the most direct line between two points. In that sense, the term "air distance" does convey some sense of what the "geodesic distance" is, but it is not truly correct. The "geodesic distance" is actually computed along the surface of, not above, a mathematically defined figure which approximates the shape of the earth.

Uses of Direct-Line Distances

This volume is intended to answer a variety of distance questions. This is a general reference work. Though the distances in the table were computed with a formula borrowed from the field of geodesy, in no way was this volume intended to aid geodesists.

The experience of the authors is that most people, when queried, are not sure what degree of accuracy is required to answer their distance questions. They usually have not considered the factors that influence the computation of a distance. When finding the distance between two cities, for instance, the results can vary considerably if calculations are based on airport-to-airport, city hall-to-city hall, or some other combination. The distance between cities as large in area as Los Angeles and Oklahoma City can vary as much as sixty miles or so depending on which points are used for the computation. Most people are satisfied with any reasonably accurate figure they are given.

The great expansion of air travel since the introduction of jets has generated numerous distance questions. The promotional use of bonuses based on the number of miles flown has prompted some concern for knowing distances between places. The distances traveled on specific flights can usually be obtained from travel agents, but the figures in this volume will be reasonably close to the figures listed in airline guides. It should be kept in mind, however, that the miles awarded for specific flights may not be the true distance -- it is the experience of the authors that mileages quoted in such bonus plans tend to be slightly higher than the actual distances.

Concern for geopolitical issues creates many questions about distances. Such events as the battle for the Falkland Islands and continuing problems in the Middle East and Central America have been responsible for many distance questions. Discussions about the range of jet fighters and bombers, cruise missiles, and various types of naval vessels often give rise to questions about distances between specific places. In that light, the distances given in this volume may often be surprising, for distances measured on commonly available maps are invariably greater than the true distance as measured on a globe or computed mathematically.

The business of telecommunications frequently involves questions about distances. The siting of transmitters and relay stations necessitates some concern for the distance between places. Also, the application of statutory regulations governing various aspects of the operation of radio and television stations may vary depending on distances between transmitters, competing stations, or listening markets of particular sizes. Shortwave or "ham" radio operators may be interested in knowing the direct-line distance to other operators with whom they have had contact.

Another important need for precise distances often occurs in the business world. When a store or service business is sold, the contract of sale may include a "restraint of trade" clause specifying that the seller cannot open a similar or competing operation within a given distance from the one that has just been sold. Most contracts of that type do not even specify how the distance is to be determined. Indeed, many probably do not even indicate whether road mileage or a direct-line type of distance is to be used in determining the distance between potentially competitive operations. While Direct-Line Distances probably will not be adequate for answering distance questions in these cases, some of the issues raised in this introduction may be of value in framing an acceptable "restraint of trade" clause or in seeking a resolution of a dispute arising from such a clause.

Computing Geodesic Distances Between Two Places

With some reluctance, it was decided not to include or demonstrate the formula used for computing the distances in Direct-Line Distances. The formula for computing a "geodesic," is extremely complex--the one developed by Sodano which was used in this book fills nearly a full page. Readers who wish to review the formula are directed to the journal in which Sodano presented his work. That article also includes substantial supporting information which explains the formula and provides detailed examples of two calculations. The authors believe that <u>Direct-Line Distances</u> is not the correct medium for introducing librarians or the general public to the complex mathematics of the field of geodesy.

Therefore, any librarian confronted with a demand for a distance accurate to a fraction of a meter should refer the patron to the article by Sodano, basic textbooks on geodesy, or introduce them to this section on computing distances.

The proliferation of personal computers now puts the capability of computing accurate distances into the hands of many people. However, doing such work requires some fair degree of programming skill and a computer with sufficient mathematical functions. The programming languages provided with many popular computers lack the full range of mathematical expressions and an acceptable level of mathematical precision to compute a geodesic distance. There is little sense in attempting to compute a sophisticated distance formula if the computer lacks at least "double precision," or numbers accurate to twelve decimal places.

There is one possible approach for people who do have a need for accurate distances. Programs are available from the National Geodetic Survey of the United States which compute accurate distances on Hewlett-Packard handheld calculators. The HP-41 series of calculators are extremely sophisticated devices with a full array of mathematical functions and ten digit level of precision. The software sold by the National Geodetic Survey is quite inexpensive. An HP-41, running the program for computing the "geodetic inverse" issued by the National Geodetic Survey, was used as an aid in developing the program for producing <u>Direct-Line Distances</u>. It was also used to calculate selected distances in this volume, thereby ensuring that information was fed correctly into the main program. While the price range of the HP-41 may be more than can be justified for occasional computation of distances, that model of calculator is extremely popular in the technical and engineering professions. If you have friends in those fields, you may be able to obtain the use of one and get help in running the programs from the National Geodetic Service. For information regarding programs for the HP-41 calculators, contact the

National Geodetic Information Center (N/CG174)
National Oceanic and Atmospheric Administration
6001 Executive Blvd.
Rockville, MD 20852

Computing Great Circle Distances

While the "great circle" formula does not provide the true distance between two places on the earth, it does yield an answer that is accurate enough for many purposes. Fortunately, the great circle formula is relatively simple and can be computed on any scientific calculator which has the basic trigonometric functions. This formula is found in various sources and in various forms of notations. The notation given here is slightly modified from that given in

The American Practical Navigator,** a standard reference book for marine navigation:

$$Cos\ D = (SinL1 \times Sin\ L2) + (CosL1 \times CosL2 \times CosDLo)$$

where L1 = the latitude of place A
L2 = the latitude of place B
DLo = the difference in longitude between places A and B
D = the arc distance (in degrees) between places A and B

This formula can easily be worked with any scientific calculator. Consult the instruction manual if you are unsure of the use of the trigonometric functions. Following is a step-by-step example of a great circle computation:

	Latitude		Longitude	
	Deg	Min	Deg	Min
Place A: Boston, USA	42	22 N	71	3 W
Place B: Nairobi, Kenya	1	17 S	36	49 E

Note: Scientific calculators have a method for converting minutes and seconds to a decimal expression. In this example, the decimal form of the coordinate, rounded to four places, is used in the formula.

L1 = +42.3667
L2 = -1.2833
DLo = (-71.0500 - +36.8167) = -107.8667

$$Cos\ D = (SinL1 \times SinL2) + (CosL1 \times CosL2 \times CosDLo)$$

then
Cos D=(Sin 42.3667 x Sin -1.2833) + (Cos 42.3667 x Cos -1.2833 x Cos -107.8667)
then

$$Cos\ D = (.673873 \times -.022395) + (.738847 \times .999749 \times -.306803)$$

then

$$Cos\ D = -.015091 + -.226624$$

then

$$Cos\ D = .241715$$

The value, .211535, in this example represents the cosine of the angular distance, expressed in degrees, between the two places. With this value in the calculator's display, push the button which returns the arc-cosine: it is usually labeled "arc-cos," "cos^{-1}," or is activated by pushing in sequence the buttons labeled "INV" (for "Inverse") and "cosine." After that, the calculator will display the number of degrees between the two places. Continuing our example:

$$D = 103.987783$$

To convert this value, 103.987783 degrees, to kilometers, multiply by the average value of a degree, which for most purposes can be taken as 111.3 kilometers.

Boston to Nairobi = 103.987783 x 111.3

then

Boston to Nairobi = 11,574.08 kilometers

Note that the longitude of Boston and the latitude of Nairobi are expressed as negative values. By adhering to certain conventions when using this formula, the possibility of error can be reduced: state northern latitudes as positive values and southern latitudes as negative values; state eastern longitudes as positive values and western longitudes as negative values. If this convention is followed, the calculator will take care of handling the negative numbers correctly.

---

* Sodano, E. M. "General non-iterative solution of the inverse and direct geodetic problems." Bulletin Geodesique : No. 75, March 1965. pp. 69-89.

** American Practical Navigator : Volume 1 : Washington, U. S. Defense Mapping Agency, 1977.

Acknowledgements

Janice Fitzpatrick made numerous contributions to this work. In addition to offering useful suggestions, proofreading several lists, and reading the introductory material, she helped man the computer and printer during the many weeks required to print the tables for both editions of Direct-Line Distances.

Jeanne Sexton contributed her considerable expertise by reading and editing the introductory material for Direct-Line Distances.

Dr. Ray Vondran, Dean of the School of Library and Information Science at The Catholic University of America, guided an independent study project to investigate the feasibility of developing Direct-Line Distances.

Arthur Kinnear, of the Defense Mapping Agency, gave encouraging support for the concept of Direct-Line Distances.

Thaddeus Vincenty, of the National Geodetic Survey, provided valuable advice concerning the computation of geodesic distances.

McArdle Printing Company provided technical assistance during a stage in the compilation of Direct-Line Distances.

Sources of Coordinates

The coordinates listed in the following pages were taken from a number of sources, the most important being the series of gazetteers of individual countries published by the Defense Mapping Agency. These works can be found in most map and research libraries. A sample citation of a recent volume from that series is:

United States. Defense Mapping Agency.
     Gazetteer of Iran : names approved by the United States
Board on Geographic Names. -- 2nd ed., November 1984. --
Washington, D. C. : Defense Mapping Agency.

For many large, well-known places in the world, conventional names approved by the Board on Geographic Names were used in Direct-Line Distances.

Coordinates for places in the United States were taken primarily from the gazetteer in the National Atlas of the United States (Washington : U. S. Geological Survey, 1970), a work which is commonly available in public and academic libraries.

Coordinates for places in Canada were taken principally from the Canada Gazetteer Atlas (Ottawa : Dept. of Energy, Mines and Resources, 1980.)

Several sources were consulted to find coordinates for places not found in the works mentioned above. A valuable tool proved to be the series of Sailing Directions issued by the Defense Mapping Agency. The Times Atlas of the World; Comprehensive Edition was used for locating the geographic coordinates of a few places. Coordinates for some places included in Direct-Line Distances could not be found in any gazetteers; consequently, coordinates for approximately a half dozen localities were determined by examining nautical charts and large scale topographic maps.

List of Entries

	Latitude Deg Min	Longitude Deg Min

Pages 1-10

Pages 11-20

Pages 21-30

	Latitude Deg Min	Longitude Deg Min

	Latitude Deg Min	Longitude Deg Min
Pages 60-68		
Bombay, India	18 58 N	72 50 E
Bonn, West Germany	50 44 N	7 6 E
Bora Bora (Vaitape)	16 31 S	151 45 W
Bordeaux, France	44 50 N	0 34 W
Boston, Massachusetts	42 22 N	71 3 W
Bouvet Island	54 26 S	3 24 E
Brasilia, Brazil	15 47 S	47 55 W
Braunschweig, West Germany	52 16 N	10 32 E
Brazzaville, Congo	4 16 S	15 17 E
Bremerhaven, West Germany	53 33 N	8 35 E
Brest, France	48 24 N	4 29 W
Brest, USSR	52 6 N	23 42 E
Bridgetown, Barbados	13 6 N	59 37 W
Brisbane, Australia	27 30 S	153 1 E
Bristol, United Kingdom	51 27 N	2 35 W
Brno, Czechoslovakia	49 12 N	16 38 E
Broken Hill, Australia	31 57 S	141 26 E
Brussels, Belgium	50 50 N	4 20 E
Bucharest, Romania	44 26 N	26 6 E
Budapest, Hungary	47 30 N	19 5 E
Pages 69-77		
Buenos Aires, Argentina	34 36 S	58 27 W
Buffalo, New York	42 53 N	78 53 W
Bujumbura, Burundi	3 23 S	29 22 E
Bulawayo, Zimbabwe	20 9 S	28 36 E
Burlington, Vermont	44 29 N	73 12 W
Cabinda, Angola	5 33 S	12 12 E
Cagliari, Italy	39 13 N	9 7 E
Cairns, Australia	16 55 S	145 46 E
Cairo, Egypt	30 3 N	31 15 E
Calais, France	50 57 N	1 50 E
Calcutta, India	22 32 N	88 22 E
Calgary, Canada	51 3 N	114 5 W
Cali, Colombia	3 27 N	76 31 W
Camaguey, Cuba	21 23 N	77 55 W
Cambridge Bay, Canada	69 7 N	105 3 W
Cambridge, United Kingdom	52 12 N	0 7 E
Campbellton, Canada	48 0 N	66 40 W
Campo Grande, Brazil	20 27 S	54 37 W
Canakkale, Turkey	40 9 N	26 24 E
Canberra, Australia	35 20 S	149 10 E
Pages 78-86		
Cancun, Mexico	21 8 N	86 45 W
Canton, China	23 7 N	113 15 E
Canton Atoll, Phoenix Islands	2 50 S	171 41 W
Cape Town, South Africa	33 55 S	18 25 E
Cape York, Australia	10 43 S	142 28 E
Caracas, Venezuela	10 30 N	66 55 W
Cardiff, United Kingdom	51 30 N	3 12 W
Carlisle, United Kingdom	54 53 N	2 56 W
Carnarvon, Australia	24 52 S	113 38 E
Carson City, Nevada	39 10 N	119 46 W
Casablanca, Morocco	33 37 N	7 35 W
Casper, Wyoming	42 51 N	106 19 W
Castries, Saint Lucia	14 1 N	61 0 W
Catbalogan, Philippines	11 46 N	124 53 E
Cayenne, French Guiana	4 56 N	52 20 W
Cayman Islands (Georgetown)	19 18 N	81 23 W
Cazombo, Angola	11 54 S	22 52 E
Cebu, Philippines	10 18 N	123 54 E
Cedar Rapids, Iowa	41 59 N	91 40 W
Changsha, China	28 12 N	112 58 E

	Latitude Deg Min	Longitude Deg Min

Pages 87-95

Channel-Port-aux-Basques, Canada	47 34 N	59 9 W
Charleston, South Carolina	32 46 N	79 56 W
Charleston, West Virginia	38 21 N	81 38 W
Charlotte, North Carolina	35 13 N	80 51 W
Charlotte Amalie, U. S. Virgin Islands	18 21 N	64 56 W
Charlottetown, Canada	46 14 N	63 8 W
Chatham, Canada	47 2 N	65 28 W
Chatham Islands (Waitangi)	43 57 S	176 32 W
Chengdu, China	30 40 N	104 4 E
Chesterfield Inlet, Canada	63 21 N	90 42 W
Cheyenne, Wyoming	41 8 N	104 49 W
Chiang Mai, Thailand	18 47 N	98 59 E
Chibougamau, Canada	49 55 N	74 22 W
Chicago, Illinois	41 53 N	87 38 W
Chiclayo, Peru	6 46 S	79 51 W
Chihuahua, Mexico	28 38 N	106 5 W
Chongqing, China	29 34 N	106 35 E
Christchurch, New Zealand	43 32 S	172 38 E
Christiansted, U. S. Virgin Islands	17 45 N	64 42 W
Christmas Island [Indian Ocean]	10 30 S	105 40 E

Pages 96-103

Christmas Island [Pacific Ocean]	1 59 N	157 32 W
Churchill, Canada	58 45 N	94 7 W
Cincinnati, Ohio	39 6 N	84 31 W
Ciudad Bolivia, Venezuela	8 21 N	70 34 W
Ciudad Juarez, Mexico	31 44 N	106 29 W
Ciudad Victoria, Mexico	23 44 N	99 8 W
Clarksburg, West Virginia	39 17 N	80 21 W
Cleveland, Ohio	41 30 N	81 42 W
Cocos (Keeling) Island	12 0 S	96 50 E
Colombo, Sri Lanka	6 56 N	79 51 E
Colon, Panama	9 22 N	79 54 W
Colorado Springs, Colorado	38 50 N	104 49 W
Columbia, South Carolina	34 0 N	81 3 W
Columbus, Georgia	32 28 N	84 59 W
Columbus, Ohio	39 58 N	83 0 W
Conakry, Guinea	9 31 N	13 43 W
Concepcion, Chile	36 50 S	73 3 W
Concord, New Hampshire	43 12 N	71 32 W
Constantine, Algeria	36 22 N	6 37 E
Copenhagen, Denmark	55 40 N	12 35 E

Pages 104-111

Coppermine, Canada	67 50 N	115 5 W
Coquimbo, Chile	29 58 S	71 21 W
Cordoba, Argentina	31 24 S	64 11 W
Cordoba, Spain	37 53 N	4 46 W
Cork, Ireland	51 54 N	8 28 W
Corner Brook, Canada	48 57 N	57 57 W
Corrientes, Argentina	27 28 S	58 50 W
Cosenza, Italy	39 18 N	16 15 E
Craiova, Romania	44 19 N	23 48 E
Cruzeiro do Sul, Brazil	7 38 S	72 36 W
Cuiaba, Brazil	15 35 S	56 5 W
Curitiba, Brazil	25 25 S	49 15 W
Cuzco, Peru	13 31 S	71 59 W
Dacca, Bangladesh	23 43 N	90 25 E
Dakar, Senegal	14 40 N	17 26 W
Dallas, Texas	32 47 N	96 49 W
Damascus, Syria	33 30 N	36 18 E
Danang, Vietnam	16 4 N	108 13 E
Dar es Salaam, Tanzania	6 48 S	39 17 E
Darwin, Australia	12 28 S	130 50 E

	Latitude Deg Min	Longitude Deg Min
Pages 112-119		
Davao, Philippines	7 4 N	125 36 E
David, Panama	8 26 N	82 26 W
Dawson, Canada	64 4 N	139 25 W
Dawson Creek, Canada	55 46 N	120 14 W
Denpasar, Indonesia	8 39 S	115 13 E
Denver, Colorado	39 44 N	104 59 W
Derby, Australia	17 18 S	123 38 E
Des Moines, Iowa	41 35 N	93 37 W
Detroit, Michigan	42 20 N	83 3 W
Dhahran, Saudi Arabia	26 18 N	50 8 E
Diego Garcia Island	7 20 S	72 25 E
Dijon, France	47 19 N	5 1 E
Dili, Indonesia	8 33 S	125 34 E
Djibouti, Djibouti	11 36 N	43 9 E
Dnepropetrovsk, USSR	48 27 N	34 59 E
Dobo, Indonesia	5 46 S	134 13 E
Doha, Qatar	25 17 N	51 32 E
Donetsk, USSR	48 0 N	37 48 E
Dover, Delaware	39 10 N	75 32 W
Dresden, East Germany	51 3 N	13 45 E
Pages 120-127		
Dubayy, United Arab Emirates	25 16 N	55 18 E
Dublin, Ireland	53 20 N	6 15 W
Duluth, Minnesota	46 47 N	92 7 W
Dunedin, New Zealand	45 52 S	170 30 E
Durango, Mexico	24 2 N	104 40 W
Durban, South Africa	29 51 S	31 1 E
Dushanbe, USSR	38 33 N	68 48 E
East London, South Africa	33 2 S	27 55 E
Easter Island (Hanga Roa)	27 9 S	109 26 W
Echo Bay, Canada	66 5 N	118 2 W
Edinburgh, United Kingdom	55 55 N	3 12 W
Edmonton, Canada	53 33 N	113 28 W
El Aaiun, Morocco	27 10 N	13 12 W
Elat, Israel	29 33 N	34 57 E
Elazig, Turkey	38 41 N	39 14 E
Eniwetok Atoll, Marshall Islands	11 30 N	162 15 E
Erfurt, East Germany	50 59 N	11 2 E
Erzurum, Turkey	39 55 N	41 17 E
Esfahan, Iran	32 40 N	51 38 E
Essen, West Germany	51 27 N	7 1 E
Pages 128-135		
Eucla, Australia	31 43 S	128 52 E
Fargo, North Dakota	46 53 N	96 48 W
Faroe Islands (Torshavn)	62 1 N	6 46 W
Florence, Italy	43 46 N	11 15 E
Florianopolis, Brazil	27 35 S	48 34 W
Fort George, Canada	53 50 N	79 0 W
Fort McMurray, Canada	56 44 N	111 23 W
Fort Nelson, Canada	58 49 N	122 43 W
Fort Severn, Canada	55 59 N	87 38 W
Fort Smith, Arkansas	35 23 N	94 25 W
Fort Vermilion, Canada	58 24 N	116 0 W
Fort Wayne, Indiana	41 4 N	85 9 W
Fort-Chimo, Canada	58 6 N	68 24 W
Fort-de-France, Martinique	14 36 N	61 5 W
Fortaleza, Brazil	3 43 S	38 30 W
Frankfort, Kentucky	38 12 N	84 52 W
Frankfurt am Main, West Germany	50 7 N	8 41 E
Fredericton, Canada	45 58 N	66 39 W
Freeport, Bahamas	26 31 N	78 47 W
Freetown, Sierra Leone	8 30 N	13 15 W

	Latitude Deg Min	Longitude Deg Min

Pages 136-124

Frobisher Bay, Canada	63 45 N	68 31 W
Frunze, USSR	42 54 N	74 36 E
Fukuoka, Japan	33 35 N	130 24 E
Funafuti Atoll, Tuvalu	8 31 S	179 8 E
Funchal, Madeira Island	32 38 N	16 54 W
Fuzhou, China	26 5 N	119 18 E
Gaborone, Botswana	24 40 S	25 54 E
Galapagos Islands (Santa Cruz)	0 38 S	90 23 W
Gander, Canada	48 57 N	54 37 W
Gangtok, India	27 20 N	88 37 E
Garyarsa, China	31 45 N	80 22 E
Gaspe, Canada	48 50 N	64 29 W
Gauhati, India	26 11 N	91 44 E
Gdansk, Poland	54 21 N	18 40 E
Geneva, Switzerland	46 12 N	6 10 E
Genoa, Italy	44 25 N	8 57 E
Georgetown, Guyana	6 48 N	58 10 W
Geraldton, Australia	28 46 S	114 36 E
Ghanzi, Botswana	21 34 S	21 47 E
Ghat, Libya	24 58 N	10 11 E

Pages 143-149

Gibraltar	36 8 N	5 21 W
Gijon, Spain	43 32 N	5 40 W
Gisborne, New Zealand	38 40 S	178 1 E
Glasgow, United Kingdom	55 50 N	4 15 W
Godthab, Greenland	64 15 N	51 35 W
Gomez Palacio, Mexico	25 34 N	103 30 W
Goose Bay, Canada	51 23 N	127 40 W
Gorki, USSR	56 20 N	44 0 E
Goteborg, Sweden	57 43 N	11 58 E
Granada, Spain	37 13 N	3 41 W
Grand Turk, Turks & Caicos	21 28 N	71 8 W
Graz, Austria	47 4 N	15 27 E
Green Bay, Wisconsin	44 31 N	88 0 W
Grenoble, France	45 10 N	5 43 E
Guadalajara, Mexico	20 40 N	103 20 W
Guam (Agana)	13 28 N	144 45 E
Guantanamo, Cuba	20 8 N	75 12 W
Guatemala City, Guatemala	14 38 N	90 31 W
Guayaquil, Ecuador	2 10 S	79 50 W
Guiyang, China	26 35 N	106 43 E

Pages 150-156

Gur'yev, USSR	47 7 N	51 53 E
Haifa, Israel	32 50 N	35 0 E
Haikou, China	20 3 N	110 19 E
Haiphong, Vietnam	20 52 N	106 41 E
Hakodate, Japan	41 45 N	140 43 E
Halifax, Canada	44 39 N	63 36 W
Hamburg, West Germany	53 33 N	10 0 E
Hamilton, Bermuda	32 17 N	64 46 W
Hamilton, New Zealand	37 47 S	175 17 E
Hangzhou, China	30 15 N	120 10 E
Hannover, West Germany	52 22 N	9 43 E
Hanoi, Vietnam	21 2 N	105 51 E
Harare, Zimbabwe	17 50 S	31 3 E
Harbin, China	45 45 N	126 39 E
Harrisburg, Pennsylvania	40 16 N	76 53 W
Hartford, Connecticut	41 46 N	72 41 W
Havana, Cuba	23 8 N	82 22 W
Helena, Montana	46 36 N	112 2 W
Helsinki, Finland	60 10 N	24 58 E
Hengyang, China	26 54 N	112 36 E

	Latitude Deg Min	Longitude Deg Min
Pages 157-163		
Herat, Afghanistan	34 20 N	62 12 E
Hermosillo, Mexico	29 4 N	110 58 W
Hiroshima, Japan	34 24 N	132 27 E
Hiva Oa (Atuona)	9 48 S	139 2 W
Ho Chi Minh City, Vietnam	10 45 N	106 40 E
Hobart, Australia	42 55 S	147 20 E
Hohhot, China	40 47 N	111 37 E
Hong Kong	22 15 N	114 10 E
Honiara, Solomon Islands	9 26 S	159 57 E
Honolulu, Hawaii	21 19 N	157 52 W
Houston, Texas	29 46 N	95 22 W
Huambo, Angola	12 44 S	15 47 E
Hubli, India	15 21 N	75 10 E
Hugh Town, United Kingdom	49 55 N	6 19 W
Hull, Canada	45 26 N	75 44 W
Hyderabad, India	17 23 N	78 28 E
Hyderabad, Pakistan	25 22 N	68 22 E
Igloolik, Canada	69 23 N	81 46 W
Iloilo, Philippines	10 42 N	122 34 E
Indianapolis, Indiana	39 46 N	86 9 W
Pages 164-170		
Innsbruck, Austria	47 16 N	11 24 E
Inuvik, Canada	68 21 N	133 43 W
Invercargill, New Zealand	46 24 S	168 21 E
Inverness, United Kingdom	57 28 N	4 14 W
Iquitos, Peru	3 46 S	73 15 W
Iraklion, Greece	35 20 N	25 8 E
Irkutsk, USSR	52 16 N	104 20 E
Islamabad, Pakistan	33 42 N	73 10 E
Istanbul, Turkey	41 1 N	28 58 E
Ivujivik, Canada	62 24 N	77 55 W
Iwo Jima Island, Japan	24 47 N	141 20 E
Izmir, Turkey	38 25 N	27 9 E
Jackson, Mississippi	32 18 N	90 12 W
Jaffna, Sri Lanka	9 40 N	80 0 E
Jakarta, Indonesia	6 10 S	106 48 E
Jamestown, St. Helena	15 56 S	5 43 W
Jamnagar, India	22 28 N	70 4 E
Jan Mayen Island	71 0 N	9 0 W
Jayapura, Indonesia	2 32 S	140 42 E
Jefferson City, Missouri	38 34 N	92 10 W
Pages 171-176		
Jerusalem, Israel	31 46 N	35 14 E
Jiggalong, Australia	23 24 S	120 47 E
Jinan, China	36 40 N	117 0 E
Jodhpur, India	26 17 N	73 2 E
Johannesburg, South Africa	26 12 S	28 5 E
Juazeiro do Norte, Brazil	7 12 S	39 20 W
Juneau, Alaska	58 18 N	134 24 W
Kabul, Afghanistan	34 31 N	69 12 E
Kalgoorlie, Australia	30 45 S	121 28 E
Kaliningrad, USSR	54 43 N	20 30 E
Kamloops, Canada	50 40 N	120 19 W
Kampala, Uganda	0 19 N	32 35 E
Kananga, Zaire	5 54 S	22 25 E
Kano, Nigeria	12 0 N	8 31 E
Kanpur, India	26 28 N	80 21 E
Kansas City, Missouri	39 6 N	94 35 W
Kaohsiung, Taiwan	22 38 N	120 17 E
Karachi, Pakistan	24 52 N	67 3 E
Karaganda, USSR	49 50 N	73 10 E
Karl-Marx-Stadt, East Germany	50 50 N	12 55 E

	Latitude Deg Min	Longitude Deg Min
Pages 177-182		
Kasanga, Tanzania	8 28 S	31 9 E
Kashgar, China	39 29 N	75 58 E
Kassel, West Germany	51 19 N	9 30 E
Kathmandu, Nepal	27 43 N	85 19 E
Kayes, Mali	14 27 N	11 26 W
Kazan, USSR	55 45 N	49 8 E
Kemi, Finland	65 49 N	24 32 E
Kenora, Canada	49 47 N	94 29 W
Kerguelen Island	49 30 S	69 30 E
Kerkira, Greece	39 36 N	19 55 E
Kermanshah, Iran	34 19 N	47 4 E
Khabarovsk, USSR	48 30 N	135 6 E
Kharkov, USSR	50 0 N	36 15 E
Khartoum, Sudan	15 36 N	32 32 E
Khon Kaen, Thailand	16 26 N	102 50 E
Kiev, USSR	50 26 N	30 31 E
Kigali, Rwanda	1 57 S	30 4 E
Kingston, Canada	44 14 N	76 30 W
Kingston, Jamaica	18 0 N	76 48 W
Kingstown, Saint Vincent	13 9 N	61 14 W
Pages 183-188		
Kinshasa, Zaire	4 18 S	15 18 E
Kirkwall, United Kingdom	58 58 N	2 57 W
Kirov, USSR	58 33 N	49 42 E
Kiruna, Sweden	67 51 N	20 13 E
Kisangani, Zaire	0 30 N	25 12 E
Kishinev, USSR	47 0 N	28 50 E
Kitchener, Canada	43 27 N	80 29 W
Knoxville, Tennessee	35 58 N	83 55 W
Kosice, Czechoslovakia	48 42 N	21 15 E
Kota Kinabalu, Malaysia	5 59 N	116 4 E
Krakow, Poland	50 5 N	19 55 E
Kralendijk, Bonaire	12 10 N	68 16 W
Krasnodar, USSR	45 2 N	39 0 E
Krasnoyarsk, USSR	56 1 N	92 50 E
Kristiansand, Norway	58 10 N	8 0 E
Kuala Lumpur, Malaysia	3 10 N	101 42 E
Kuching, Malaysia	1 33 N	110 20 E
Kumasi, Ghana	6 41 N	1 37 W
Kumzar, Oman	26 20 N	56 25 E
Kunming, China	25 4 N	102 41 E
Pages 189-194		
Kuqa Chang, China	41 11 N	83 28 E
Kurgan, USSR	55 26 N	65 18 E
Kuwait, Kuwait	29 23 N	47 58 E
Kuybyshev, USSR	53 12 N	50 9 E
Kyoto, Japan	35 0 N	135 45 E
Kzyl-Orda, USSR	44 48 N	65 28 E
L'vov, USSR	49 50 N	24 0 E
La Ceiba, Honduras	15 47 N	86 48 W
La Coruna, Spain	43 22 N	8 23 W
La Paz, Bolivia	16 30 S	68 9 W
La Paz, Mexico	24 10 N	110 18 W
La Ronge, Canada	55 6 N	105 17 W
Labrador City, Canada	52 57 N	66 55 W
Lagos, Nigeria	6 27 N	3 23 E
Lahore, Pakistan	31 35 N	74 18 E
Lambasa, Fiji	16 26 S	179 23 E
Lansing, Michigan	42 44 N	84 33 W
Lanzhou, China	36 3 N	103 41 E
Laoag, Philippines	18 12 N	120 36 E
Largeau, Chad	17 55 N	19 7 E

	Latitude Deg Min	Longitude Deg Min
Pages 211-215		
Maseru, Lesotho	29 19 S	27 29 E
Mashhad, Iran	36 18 N	59 36 E
Mazatlan, Mexico	23 13 N	106 25 W
Mbabane, Swaziland	26 19 S	31 8 E
Mbandaka, Zaire	0 4 N	18 16 E
McMurdo Sound, Antarctica	77 30 S	165 0 E
Mecca, Saudi Arabia	21 27 N	39 49 E
Medan, Indonesia	3 35 N	98 40 E
Medellin, Colombia	6 15 N	75 35 W
Medicine Hat, Canada	50 3 N	110 40 W
Medina, Saudi Arabia	24 28 N	39 36 E
Melbourne, Australia	37 50 S	145 0 E
Memphis, Tennessee	35 8 N	90 3 W
Merauke, Indonesia	8 28 S	140 20 E
Merida, Mexico	20 58 N	89 37 W
Meridian, Mississippi	32 22 N	88 42 W
Messina, Italy	38 11 N	15 34 E
Mexico City, Mexico	19 24 N	99 9 W
Miami, Florida	25 47 N	80 11 W
Midway Islands, USA	28 12 N	177 22 W
Pages 216-220		
Milan, Italy	45 28 N	9 12 E
Milford Sound, New Zealand	44 35 S	167 47 E
Milwaukee, Wisconsin	43 2 N	87 55 W
Minsk, USSR	53 54 N	27 34 E
Mogadiscio, Somalia	2 4 N	45 22 E
Mombasa, Kenya	4 3 S	39 40 E
Monclova, Mexico	26 54 N	101 25 W
Moncton, Canada	46 6 N	64 47 W
Monrovia, Liberia	6 19 N	10 48 W
Monte Carlo, Monaco	43 44 N	7 25 E
Monterrey, Mexico	25 40 N	100 19 W
Montevideo, Uruguay	34 53 S	56 11 W
Montgomery, Alabama	32 23 N	86 18 W
Montpelier, Vermont	44 16 N	72 35 W
Montpellier, France	43 36 N	3 53 E
Montreal, Canada	45 30 N	73 36 W
Moosonee, Canada	51 17 N	80 39 W
Moroni, Comoros	11 41 S	43 16 E
Moscow, USSR	55 45 N	37 35 E
Mosul, Iraq	36 20 N	43 8 E
Pages 221-225		
Mount Isa, Australia	20 44 S	139 30 E
Multan, Pakistan	30 11 N	71 29 E
Munich, West Germany	48 9 N	11 35 E
Murcia, Spain	37 59 N	1 7 W
Murmansk, USSR	68 58 N	33 5 E
Mururoa Atoll, French Polynesia	21 52 S	138 55 W
Muscat, Oman	23 37 N	58 35 E
Myitkyina, Burma	25 23 N	97 24 E
Naga, Philippines	13 38 N	123 11 E
Nagasaki, Japan	32 48 N	129 55 E
Nagoya, Japan	35 10 N	136 55 E
Nagpur, India	21 9 N	79 6 E
Nairobi, Kenya	1 17 S	36 49 E
Nanchang, China	28 41 N	115 53 E
Nancy, France	48 41 N	6 12 E
Nandi, Fiji	17 48 S	177 25 E
Nanjing, China	32 3 N	118 47 E
Nanning, China	22 49 N	108 19 E
Nantes, France	47 13 N	1 33 W
Naples, Italy	40 50 N	14 15 E

	Latitude Deg Min	Longitude Deg Min

	Latitude Deg Min	Longitude Deg Min

Pages 238-241

Ottawa, Canada	45 25 N	75 42 W
Ouagadougou, Bourkina Fasso	12 22 N	1 31 W
Oujda, Morocco	34 40 N	1 54 W
Oxford, United Kingdom	51 45 N	1 15 W
Pago Pago, American Samoa	14 16 S	170 42 W
Pakxe, Laos	15 7 N	105 47 E
Palembang, Indonesia	2 55 S	104 45 E
Palermo, Italy	38 7 N	13 22 E
Palma, Majorca	39 34 N	2 39 E
Palmerston North, New Zealand	40 21 S	175 37 E
Panama, Panama	8 58 N	79 32 W
Paramaribo, Suriname	5 50 N	55 10 W
Paris, France	48 52 N	2 20 E
Patna, India	25 36 N	85 7 E
Patrai, Greece	38 15 N	21 44 E
Peking, China	39 56 N	116 24 E
Penrhyn Island (Omoka)	9 0 S	158 4 W
Peoria, Illinois	40 42 N	89 36 W
Perm', USSR	58 0 N	56 15 E
Perth, Australia	31 56 S	115 50 E

Pages 242-245

Peshawar, Pakistan	34 1 N	71 33 E
Petropavlovsk-Kamchatskiy, USSR	53 1 N	158 39 E
Petrozavodsk, USSR	61 49 N	34 20 E
Pevek, USSR	69 42 N	170 17 E
Philadelphia, Pennsylvania	39 57 N	75 10 W
Phnom Penh, Kampuchea	11 33 N	104 55 E
Phoenix, Arizona	33 27 N	112 4 W
Pierre, South Dakota	44 22 N	100 21 W
Pinang, Malaysia	5 25 N	100 20 E
Pitcairn Island (Adamstown)	25 4 S	130 5 W
Pittsburgh, Pennsylvania	40 26 N	80 0 W
Plymouth, Montserrat	16 42 N	62 13 W
Plymouth, United Kingdom	50 24 N	4 7 W
Ponape Island	6 55 N	158 15 E
Ponce, Puerto Rico	18 1 N	66 37 W
Ponta Delgada, Azores	37 44 N	25 40 W
Pontianak, Indonesia	0 2 S	109 20 E
Port Augusta, Australia	32 30 S	137 46 E
Port Blair, India	11 36 N	92 45 E
Port Elizabeth, South Africa	33 58 S	25 35 E

Pages 246-248

Port Hedland, Australia	20 19 S	118 34 E
Port Louis, Mauritius	20 10 S	57 30 E
Port Moresby, Papua New Guinea	9 29 S	147 11 E
Port Said, Egypt	31 16 N	32 18 E
Port Sudan, Sudan	19 37 N	37 14 E
Port-au-Prince, Haiti	18 32 N	72 20 W
Port-of-Spain, Trinidad & Tobago	10 39 N	61 31 W
Port-Vila, Vanuatu	17 44 S	168 19 E
Portland, Maine	43 39 N	70 16 W
Portland, Oregon	45 32 N	122 37 W
Porto, Portugal	41 9 N	8 37 W
Porto Alegre, Brazil	30 4 S	51 11 W
Porto Alexandre, Angola	15 49 S	11 53 E
Porto Novo, Benin	6 29 N	2 37 E
Porto Velho, Brazil	8 46 S	63 54 W
Portsmouth, United Kingdom	50 46 N	1 5 W
Poznan, Poland	52 25 N	16 58 E
Prague, Czechoslovakia	50 5 N	14 28 E
Praia, Cape Verde Islands	14 55 N	23 31 W
Pretoria, South Africa	25 45 S	28 10 E

	Latitude Deg Min	Longitude Deg Min
Pages 249-251		
Prince Albert, Canada	53 12 N	105 46 W
Prince Edward Island	46 35 S	37 56 E
Prince George, Canada	53 55 N	122 45 W
Prince Rupert, Canada	54 19 N	130 19 W
Providence, Rhode Island	41 49 N	71 24 W
Provo, Utah	40 14 N	111 39 W
Puerto Aisen, Chile	45 24 S	72 42 W
Puerto Deseado, Argentina	47 45 S	65 54 W
Puerto Princesa, Philippines	9 44 N	118 44 E
Punta Arenas, Chile	53 9 S	70 55 W
Pusan, South Korea	35 6 N	129 3 E
Pyongyang, North Korea	39 1 N	125 45 E
Qamdo, China	31 10 N	97 14 E
Qandahar, Afghanistan	31 35 N	65 45 E
Qiqian, China	52 12 N	120 49 E
Qom, Iran	34 39 N	50 54 E
Quebec, Canada	46 49 N	71 14 W
Quetta, Pakistan	30 12 N	67 0 E
Quito, Ecuador	0 13 S	78 30 W
Rabaul, Papua New Guinea	4 12 S	152 11 E
Pages 252-254		
Raiatea (Uturoa)	16 44 S	151 26 W
Raleigh, North Carolina	35 46 N	78 38 W
Rangiroa (Avatoru)	14 56 S	147 42 W
Rangoon, Burma	16 47 N	96 10 E
Raoul Island, Kermandec Islands	29 16 S	177 54 W
Rarotonga (Avarua)	21 12 S	159 46 W
Rawson, Argentina	43 18 S	65 6 W
Recife, Brazil	8 3 S	34 54 W
Regina, Canada	50 27 N	104 37 W
Reykjavik, Iceland	64 9 N	21 57 W
Rhodes, Greece	36 26 N	28 13 E
Richmond, Virginia	37 33 N	77 27 W
Riga, USSR	56 57 N	24 6 E
Ringkobing, Denmark	56 5 N	8 15 E
Rio Branco, Brazil	9 58 S	67 48 W
Rio Cuarto, Argentina	33 8 S	64 21 W
Rio de Janeiro, Brazil	22 54 S	43 14 W
Rio Gallegos, Argentina	51 38 S	69 13 W
Rio Grande, Brazil	32 2 S	52 5 W
Riyadh, Saudi Arabia	24 38 N	46 43 E
Pages 255-257		
Road Town, British Virgin Islands	18 27 N	64 37 W
Roanoke, Virginia	37 16 N	79 56 W
Robinson Crusoe Island, Chile	33 38 S	78 52 W
Rochester, New York	43 9 N	77 36 W
Rockhampton, Australia	23 23 S	150 30 E
Rome, Italy	41 54 N	12 29 E
Rosario, Argentina	32 57 S	60 40 W
Roseau, Dominica	15 18 N	61 24 W
Rostock, East Germany	54 5 N	12 8 E
Rostov-na-Donu, USSR	47 14 N	39 42 E
Rotterdam, Netherlands	51 55 N	4 30 E
Rouyn, Canada	48 14 N	79 1 W
Sacramento, California	38 35 N	121 29 W
Saginaw, Michigan	43 26 N	83 56 W
Saint Denis, Reunion	20 52 S	55 27 E
Saint George's, Grenada	12 3 N	61 45 W
Saint John, Canada	45 16 N	66 3 W
Saint John's, Antigua	17 6 N	61 51 W
Saint John's, Canada	47 34 N	52 43 W
Saint Louis, Missouri	38 37 N	90 12 W

	Latitude	Longitude
	Deg Min	Deg Min

Pages 258-260

Saint Paul, Minnesota	44 57 N	93 6 W
Saint Peter Port, United Kingdom	49 27 N	2 32 W
Saipan (Susupe)	15 9 N	145 43 E
Salalah, Oman	17 0 N	54 6 E
Salem, Oregon	44 56 N	123 2 W
Salt Lake City, Utah	40 45 N	111 53 W
Salta, Argentina	24 47 S	65 25 W
Salto, Uruguay	31 23 S	57 58 W
Salvador, Brazil	12 59 S	38 31 W
Salzburg, Austria	47 48 N	13 2 E
Samsun, Turkey	41 17 N	36 20 E
San Antonio, Texas	29 25 N	98 30 W
San Cristobal, Venezuela	7 46 N	72 14 W
San Diego, California	32 43 N	117 9 W
San Francisco, California	37 47 N	122 25 W
San Jose, Costa Rica	9 56 N	84 5 W
San Juan, Argentina	31 32 S	68 31 W
San Juan, Puerto Rico	18 28 N	66 7 W
San Luis Potosi, Mexico	22 9 N	100 59 W
San Marino, San Marino	43 55 N	12 28 E

Pages 261-262

San Miguel de Tucuman, Argentina	26 49 S	65 13 W
San Salvador, El Salvador	13 42 N	89 12 W
Sanaa, Yemen	15 21 N	44 12 E
Santa Cruz, Bolivia	17 48 S	63 10 W
Santa Cruz, Tenerife	28 27 N	16 14 W
Santa Fe, New Mexico	35 41 N	105 57 W
Santa Rosa, Argentina	36 37 S	64 17 W
Santa Rosalia, Mexico	27 19 N	112 17 W
Santarem, Brazil	2 26 S	54 42 W
Santiago del Estero, Argentina	27 47 S	64 16 W
Santiago, Chile	33 27 S	70 40 W
Santo Domingo, Dominican Republic	18 28 N	69 54 W
Sao Paulo de Olivenca, Brazil	3 27 S	68 48 W
Sao Paulo, Brazil	23 32 S	46 37 W
Sao Tome, Sao Tome & Principe	0 20 N	6 44 E
Sapporo, Japan	43 3 N	141 21 E
Sarajevo, Yugoslavia	43 50 N	18 25 E
Saratov, USSR	51 34 N	46 2 E
Saskatoon, Canada	52 7 N	106 38 W
Schefferville, Canada	54 48 N	66 50 W

Pages 263-264

Seattle, Washington	47 36 N	122 20 W
Sendai, Japan	38 15 N	140 53 E
Seoul, South Korea	37 34 N	127 0 E
Sept-Iles, Canada	50 12 N	66 23 W
Sevastopol, USSR	44 36 N	33 32 E
Seville, Spain	37 23 N	5 59 W
Shanghai, China	31 7 N	121 22 E
Sheffield, United Kingdom	53 22 N	1 30 W
Shenyang, China	41 48 N	123 27 E
Shiraz, Iran	29 36 N	52 32 E
Sibiu, Romania	45 48 N	24 9 E
Singapore	1 17 N	103 51 E
Sioux Falls, South Dakota	43 33 N	96 44 W
Skelleftea, Sweden	64 46 N	20 57 E
Skopje, Yugoslavia	42 0 N	21 29 E
Socotra Island (Tamrida)	12 39 N	54 1 E
Sofia, Bulgaria	42 41 N	23 19 E
Songkhla, Thailand	7 12 N	100 36 E
Sorong, Indonesia	0 53 S	131 15 E
South Georgia Island	54 15 S	36 45 W

	Latitude Deg Min	Longitude Deg Min
Pages 265-266		
South Pole	90 0 S	0 0
South Sandwich Islands	57 45 S	26 30 W
Split, Yugoslavia	43 31 N	16 26 E
Spokane, Washington	47 40 N	117 24 W
Spoleto, Italy	42 44 N	12 44 E
Springbok, South Africa	29 40 S	17 53 E
Springfield, Illinois	39 48 N	89 39 W
Springfield, Massachusetts	42 6 N	72 35 W
Srinagar, India	34 5 N	74 49 E
Stanley, Falkland Islands	51 42 S	57 51 W
Stara Zagora, Bulgaria	42 25 N	25 38 E
Stockholm, Sweden	59 20 N	18 3 E
Stornoway, United Kingdom	58 13 N	6 22 W
Strasbourg, France	48 35 N	7 45 E
Stuttgart, West Germany	48 46 N	9 11 E
Subic, Philippines	14 53 N	120 14 E
Suchow, China	34 16 N	117 11 E
Sucre, Bolivia	19 2 S	65 17 W
Sudbury, Canada	46 30 N	81 0 W
Suez, Egypt	29 58 N	32 33 E
Pages 267-268		
Sundsvall, Sweden	62 23 N	17 18 E
Surabaya, Indonesia	7 15 S	112 45 E
Suva, Fiji	18 8 S	178 25 E
Sverdlovsk, USSR	56 51 N	60 36 E
Svobodnyy, USSR	51 24 N	128 8 E
Sydney, Australia	33 53 S	151 12 E
Sydney, Canada	46 9 N	60 11 W
Syktyvkar, USSR	61 40 N	50 48 E
Szeged, Hungary	46 16 N	20 10 E
Szombathely, Hungary	47 14 N	16 37 E
Tabriz, Iran	38 5 N	46 18 E
Tacheng, China	46 45 N	82 57 E
Tahiti (Papeete)	17 32 S	149 34 W
Taipei, Taiwan	25 3 N	121 30 E
Taiyuan, China	37 52 N	112 33 E
Tallahassee, Florida	30 27 N	84 17 W
Tallinn, USSR	59 25 N	24 45 E
Tamanrasset, Algeria	22 47 N	5 31 E
Tampa, Florida	27 57 N	82 27 W
Tampere, Finland	61 30 N	23 45 E
Pages 269-270		
Tanami, Australia	19 59 S	129 43 E
Tangier, Morocco	35 48 N	5 48 W
Tarawa (Betio)	1 21 N	172 56 E
Tashkent, USSR	41 20 N	69 18 E
Tbilisi, USSR	41 42 N	44 45 E
Tegucigalpa, Honduras	14 6 N	87 13 W
Tehran, Iran	35 40 N	51 26 E
Tel Aviv, Israel	32 4 N	34 46 E
Telegraph Creek, Canada	57 54 N	131 10 W
Teresina, Brazil	5 5 S	42 49 W
Ternate, Indonesia	0 48 N	127 24 E
The Valley, Anguilla	18 3 N	63 4 W
Thessaloniki, Greece	40 38 N	22 56 E
Thimphu, Bhutan	27 32 N	89 43 E
Thunder Bay, Canada	48 24 N	89 19 W
Tientsin, China	39 8 N	117 12 E
Tijuana, Mexico	32 32 N	117 1 W
Tiksi, USSR	71 36 N	128 48 E
Timbuktu, Mali	16 46 N	3 1 W
Tindouf, Algeria	27 42 N	8 9 W

	Latitude Deg Min	Longitude Deg Min

| | | Latitude | | Longitude | |
| | | Deg | Min | Deg | Min |

Page 274

	Latitude Deg	Latitude Min	Longitude Deg	Longitude Min
Watson Lake, Canada	60	7 N	128	48 W
Weimar, East Germany	50	59 N	11	19 E
Wellington, New Zealand	41	18 S	174	47 E
West Berlin, West Germany	52	31 N	13	24 E
Wewak, Papua New Guinea	3	33 S	143	38 E
Whangarei, New Zealand	35	43 S	174	20 E
Whitehorse, Canada	60	43 N	135	3 W
Wichita, Kansas	37	42 N	97	20 W
Willemstad, Curacao	12	7 N	68	57 W
Wiluna, Australia	26	36 S	120	13 E
Windhoek, Namibia	22	35 S	17	5 E
Windsor, Canada	42	18 N	83	1 W
Winnipeg, Canada	49	53 N	97	9 W
Winston-Salem, North Carolina	36	6 N	80	15 W
Wroclaw, Poland	51	6 N	17	2 E
Wuhan, China	30	35 N	114	16 E
Wyndham, Australia	15	28 S	128	6 E
Xi'an, China	34	16 N	108	54 E
Xining, China	36	37 N	101	46 E
Yakutsk, USSR	62	0 N	129	40 E

Page 275

	Latitude Deg	Latitude Min	Longitude Deg	Longitude Min
Yanji, China	42	53 N	129	31 E
Yaounde, Cameroon	3	52 N	11	32 E
Yap Island (Colonia)	9	31 N	138	8 E
Yaraka, Australia	24	53 S	144	5 E
Yarmouth, Canada	43	50 N	66	7 W
Yellowknife, Canada	62	27 N	114	21 W
Yerevan, USSR	40	11 N	44	30 E
Yinchuan, China	38	28 N	106	19 E
Yogyakarta, Indonesia	7	48 S	110	22 E
York, United Kingdom	53	50 N	1	10 W
Yumen, China	39	50 N	97	44 E
Yutian, China	36	52 N	81	42 E
Yuzhno-Sakhalinsk, USSR	46	57 N	142	44 E
Zagreb, Yugoslavia	45	48 N	16	0 E
Zahedan, Iran	29	30 N	60	52 E
Zamboanga, Philippines	6	54 N	122	4 E
Zanzibar, Tanzania	6	10 S	39	11 E
Zaragoza, Spain	41	38 N	0	53 W
Zashiversk, USSR	67	27 N	142	37 E
Zhengzhou, China	34	45 N	113	40 E
Zurich, Switzerland	47	22 N	8	22 E

SEE SEPARATE MAP OF THE UNITED STATES

1   New Glasgow

2   Truro

1

2

Barranquilla
Maracaibo
San Cristobal
Caracas
Ciudad Bolivia
Georgetown
Paramaribo
Cayenne
Medellin
Bogota
Cali
Boa Vista
do Rio Branco
Macapa
Quito
Belem
Manaus
Santarem
Guayaquil
Sao Paulo de Olivenca
Iquitos
Fortaleza
Chiclayo
Teresina
Natal
Cruzeiro do Sul
Juazeiro do Norte
Trujillo
Rio Branco
Porto Velho
Recife
Lima
Magdalena
Cuzco
Salvador
Arequipa
Cuiaba
Brasilia
La Paz
Santa Cruz
Uberlandia
Sucre
Belo Horizonte
Vitoria
Campo Grande
Antofagasta
Salta
Sao Paulo
Rio de Janeiro
San Miguel de Tucuman
Asuncion
Curitiba
Corrientes
Florianopolis
Santiago del Estero
Coquimbo
Porto Alegre
San Juan
Cordoba
Salto
Valparaiso
Rio Cuarto
Rosario
Rio Grande
Robinson Crusoe Island
Santiago
Buenos Aires
Montevideo
Santa Rosa
Concepcion
Bahia Blanca
Mar del Plata
Neuquen
Osorno
Rawson
Puerto Aisen
Puerto Deseado
Rio Gallegos
Stanley
Punta Arenas
Ushuaia
South Georgia Island

3

Angra do Heroismo
Ponta Delgada

Canakkale Istanbul Samsun
Ankara Elazig Erzurum
Izmir Adana Al Qamishli Tabriz Kermanshah
Nicosia Allepo Mosul Tehran Mashhad
Tangier Algiers Tunis Tripoli Baghdad Qom
Funchal Casablanca Oujda Oran Constantine Annaba Beirut Damascus Esfahan
Marrakech Bechar Banghazi Alexandria Haifa Amman Al Basrah Abadan Zahedan
Tel Aviv Jerusalem Kuwait Shiraz
Santa Cruz Tripoli Port Said Elat Suez Dhahran Doha Dubayy
El Aaiun Tindouf As Sallum Cairo Manama Kumzar
Ghat Al Minya Riyadh Abu Dhabi Muscat
Nouakchott Al Jawf Luxor Medina
Tamanrasset Aswan Mecca
Praia Nema Timbuktu Agadez Largeau Port Sudan Sanaa Salalah
Dakar Khartoum Asmera Socotra Island
Banjul Kayes Niamey Ndjamena Aden
Bamako Kano Nyala Djibouti
Bissau Ouagadougou Porto Novo Ogbomosho Abuja
Conakry Kumasi Lagos Addis Ababa
Freetown Lome Bangui
Monrovia Abidjan Accra Malabo Yaounde Kisangani Mogadiscio
Sao Tome Bata Kampala Nairobi
Libreville Mbandaka Kigali
Brazzaville Bujumbura Victoria
Ascension Island Cabinda Kinshasa Mombasa
Luanda Kananga Zanzibar
Lubumbashi Kasanga Dar es Salaam
Cazombo Moroni
Jamestown Porto Alexandre Huambo Lilongwe
Lusaka Blantyre
Harare Antananarivo
Ghanzi Bulawayo Beira Port Louis
Walvis Bay Windhoek Saint Denis
Gaborone
Tristan da Cunha Springbok Bloemfontein Pretoria Maputo
Johannesburg Mbabane
Maseru Durban
East London
Cape Town Port Elizabeth

Jan Mayen Island

Akureyri

Reykjavik

Faroe Islands

Lerwick

Stornoway
Kirkwall
Inverness
Aberdeen
Glasgow Edinburgh
Londonderry
Belfast Newcastle upon Tyne
Carlisle
York
Dublin
Limerick Liverpool
Sheffield
Nottingham
Cork Norwich
Birmingham
Oxford Amsterdam
Cardiff Cambridge Rotterdam
Bristol London
Portsmouth
Hugh Town Plymouth Calais
Brussels
Saint Peter Port Amiens
Le Havre
Brest Luxembourg

Paris

Nancy
Strasbourg
Dijon Zurich
Nantes Tours

Limoges
Bordeaux Lyon
Grenoble
Montpellier
Toulouse Marseilles
Gijon Monte Carlo
La Coruna
Bilbao
Leon
Porto Valladolid Andorra
Zaragoza
Barcelona
Madrid
Toledo
Lisbon Valencia
Palma
Cordoba Murcia
Seville
Granada
Gibraltar

Narvik
Bodo Kiruna

Kemi

Skelleftea

Sundsvall

Tampere

Trondheim

Helsinki

Bergen
Oslo Orebro
Stockholm
Kristiansand
Goteborg Visby

Ringkobing
Copenhagen
Odense
Gdansk
Bialystok
Hamburg Rostock
Bremerhaven West Berlin Poznan Warsaw
Hannover Magdeburg Lodz
Braunschweig
Kassel Leipzig Wroclaw
Essen Erfurt
Bonn Weimar Dresden Krakow
Karl-Marx-Stadt
Mannheim Frankfurt am Main Prague
Nuremberg Ostrava
Brno Kosice
Stuttgart
Munich Linz Vienna
Salzburg Budapest Oradea
Vaduz Innsbruck Szombathely
Bern Graz Szeged Sibiu
Geneva Bolzano
Milan Zagreb
Verona Venice Bucharest
Turin Belgrade Craiova
Bologna Varna
Genoa Split
Sarajevo Stara Zagora
San Marino Sofia
Florence
Spoleto Skopje
Alexandroupolis
Ajaccio Rome Tirane Thessaloniki
Bari
Naples Kerkira
Cagliari
Cosenza Patrai Athens
Messina Rhodes
Palermo
Iraklion
Valletta

Hanoi
Haiphong
Louangphrabang
Vientiane
Chiang Mai
Khon Kaen
Bangkok
Danang
Pakxe
Phnom Penh
Ho Chi Minh City
Songkhla
Pinang
Kuala Lumpur
Singapore
Medan
Palembang
Jakarta
Yogyakarta
Surabaya
Denpasar
Christmas Island
Cocos (Keeling) Island
Kuching
Pontianak
Bandar Seri Begawan
Kota Kinabalu
Banjarmasin
Balikpapan
Ujungpandang
Manado
Ternate
Ambon
Dobo
Sorong
Jayapura
Merauke
Dili
Zamboanga
Davao
Puerto Princesa
Iloilo
Cebu
Naga
Catbalogan
Manila
Subic
Baguio
Laoag

7

XXXIX

Duluth •

Saint Paul •

Green Bay •

Saginaw •

Madison • Milwaukee •

Lansing • Detroit •

Cedar Rapids •

Chicago •

Cleveland •

Des Moines •

Fort Wayne •

Peoria •

Columbus •

Springfield •

Indianapolis • Cincinnati •

Kansas City •

Jefferson City • Saint Louis •

Louisville • Frankfort •

Clarksburg •

Charleston •

Rochester •

Buffalo •

Harrisburg •

Pittsburgh •

Baltimore •

Washington •

Richmond •

Norfolk •

Augusta

Burlington • Portland •

Montpelier • Concord •

Manchester •

Albany • Springfield • Boston •

Hartford •

New Haven • Providence

New York •

Philadelphia •

Trenton •

Atlantic City •

Dover •

Annapolis

Roanoke •

Winston-Salem •

Knoxville • Raleigh •

Nashville • Charlotte •

Fort Smith •

Memphis •

Columbia •

Little Rock •

Charleston •

Atlanta •

Birmingham •

Columbus •

Meridian •

Montgomery •

Jackson •

Tallahasee •

Baton Rouge •

New Orleans •

Tampa •

Miami •

8

9

Pitcairn Island ●

Mangareva Island ●

Mururoa Atoll ●

Rangiroa ●

Hiva Oa ●

Tahiti ●
Bora Bora ●
Raiatea ●

Tubuai Island ●

Christmas Island ●

Penrhyn Island ●

Rarotonga ★

Honolulu

Nukunono Island ●

Niue ★

Pago Pago ●
Apia ★
Asau ★

Canton Atoll ●

Nuku'alofa ★

Chatham Islands

Midway Islands ●

Wallis Island ●

Funafuti Atoll ★

Lambasa ★
Suva ★
Nandi

Gisborne ●
Whangarei ●
Auckland ●
Palmerston North ●
Wellington ●
Christchurch ●

Raoul Island ●

Majuro Atoll ●

Tarawa ●

Hamilton ●
New Plymouth ●
Nelson ●
Dunedin ●
Invercargill ●

Milford Sound

Auckland Islands ●

Wake Island ●

Eniwetok Atoll ●

Ponape Island ●

Nauru Island ★

Port-Vila ★
Noumea ●

Norfolk Island ●

Lord Howe Island ●

Iwo Jima Island ●

Saipan ●

Guam ●

Truk Island ●

Honiara ★
Rabaul ●

Brisbane ●

Sydney ●
Canberra ★

Launceston ●
Hobart ●

Yap Island ●
Belau Islands ●

Mewak ●

Port Moresby ★
Cairns ●
Townsville ●

Rockhampton ●

Yaraka ●

Broken Hill ●

Melbourne ●
Ballarat ●

Cape York

Normanton ●
Mount Isa ●

Adelaide ●

Darwin ●
Wyndham ●

Newcastle Waters ●
Tanami ●
Alice Springs ●

Oodnadatta ●

Port Augusta ●

Derby ●

Port Hedland ●
Wiluna ●

Kalgoorlie ●
Eucla ●

Jiggalong ●

Geraldton ●

Perth ●
Albany ●

Carnarvon ●

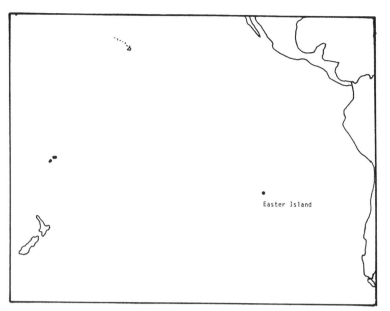

SOUTHEASTERN PACIFIC OCEAN

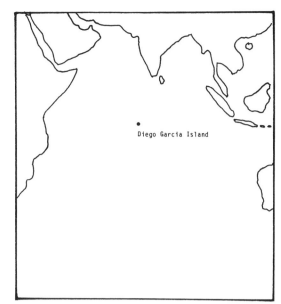

INDIAN OCEAN

ANTARCTIC REGION

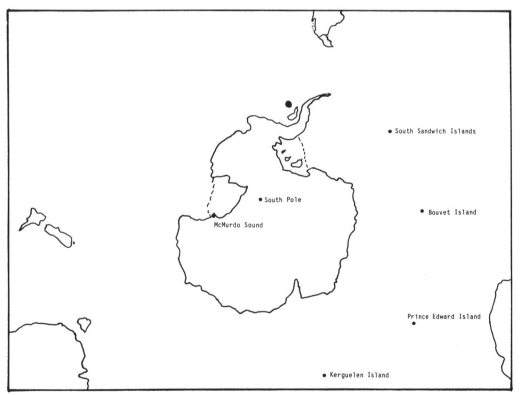

Distances in Kilometers	Abadan, Iran	Aberdeen, United Kingdom	Abidjan, Ivory Coast	Abu Dhabi, United Arab Emir.	Abuja, Nigeria	Acapulco, Mexico	Accra, Ghana	Adana, Turkey	Addis Ababa, Ethiopia	Adelaide, Australia	Aden, P.D.R. Yemen	Agadez, Niger	Aguascalientes, Mexico	Ahmadabad, India	Ajaccio, France	Akita, Japan	Akureyri, Iceland	Al Basrah, Iraq	Al Jawf, Libya	Al Minya, Egypt
Aberdeen, United Kingdom	4,866	0	5,750	5,747	5,382	8,912	5,724	3,542	6,385	16,184	6,327	4,537	8,583	6,970	1,860	8,705	1,271	4,823	4,188	4,125
Abidjan, Ivory Coast	6,127	5,750	0	6,579	1,310	10,471	424	5,319	4,735	14,974	5,447	1,838	10,647	8,421	4,248	13,820	6,788	6,088	3,595	4,456
Abu Dhabi, United Arab Emir.	887	5,747	6,579	0	5,276	14,657	6,186	2,288	2,384	11,037	1,627	4,880	14,295	1,866	4,608	7,970	6,751	932	3,146	2,389
Abuja, Nigeria	4,862	5,382	1,310	5,276	0	11,511	910	4,187	3,464	14,331	4,151	867	11,607	7,113	3,632	12,752	6,567	4,825	2,388	3,239
Acapulco, Mexico	13,778	8,912	10,471	14,657	11,511	0	10,867	12,426	14,648	13,921	14,963	11,285	611	15,519	10,240	11,194	7,937	13,735	12,367	12,742
Accra, Ghana	5,762	5,724	424	6,186	910	10,867	0	5,016	4,313	14,691	5,028	1,547	11,027	8,020	4,125	13,561	6,818	5,724	3,254	4,113
Adana, Turkey	1,411	3,542	5,319	2,288	4,187	12,426	5,016	0	3,118	13,301	2,856	3,482	12,121	3,888	2,340	8,565	4,664	1,362	1,825	1,077
Addis Ababa, Ethiopia	2,559	6,385	4,735	2,384	3,464	14,648	4,313	3,118	0	11,484	805	3,441	14,563	3,932	4,679	10,338	7,618	2,557	2,344	2,269
Adelaide, Australia	11,895	16,184	14,974	11,037	14,331	13,921	14,691	13,301	11,484	0	11,138	14,757	13,978	9,465	15,640	8,267	16,257	11,945	13,751	13,277
Aden, P.D.R. Yemen	1,974	6,327	5,447	1,627	4,151	14,963	5,028	2,856	805	11,138	0	4,007	14,782	3,130	4,767	9,544	7,503	1,984	2,614	2,254
Agadez, Niger	4,341	4,537	1,838	4,880	867	11,285	1,547	3,482	3,441	14,757	4,007	0	11,300	6,746	2,767	12,014	5,744	4,299	1,785	2,640
Aguascalientes, Mexico	13,431	8,583	10,647	14,295	11,607	611	11,027	12,121	14,563	13,978	14,782	11,300	0	15,005	10,018	10,615	7,545	13,391	12,236	12,533
Ahmadabad, India	2,549	6,970	8,421	1,866	7,113	15,519	8,020	3,888	3,932	9,465	3,130	6,746	15,005	0	6,209	6,528	7,728	2,598	5,008	4,224
Ajaccio, France	3,745	1,860	4,248	4,608	3,632	10,240	4,125	2,340	4,679	15,640	4,767	2,767	10,018	6,209	0	9,723	3,127	3,696	2,382	2,515
Akita, Japan	8,075	8,705	13,820	7,970	12,752	11,194	13,561	8,565	10,338	8,267	9,544	12,014	10,615	6,528	9,723	0	8,170	8,102	10,375	9,543
Akureyri, Iceland	5,895	1,271	6,788	6,751	6,567	7,937	6,818	4,664	7,618	16,257	7,503	5,744	7,545	7,728	3,127	8,170	0	5,857	5,456	5,349
Al Basrah, Iraq	50	4,823	6,088	932	4,825	13,735	5,724	1,362	2,557	11,945	1,984	4,299	13,391	2,598	3,696	8,102	5,857	0	2,515	1,675
Al Jawf, Libya	2,558	4,188	3,595	3,146	2,388	12,367	3,254	1,825	2,344	13,751	2,614	1,785	12,236	5,008	2,382	10,375	5,456	2,515	0	861
Al Minya, Egypt	1,719	4,125	4,456	2,389	3,239	12,742	4,113	1,077	2,269	13,277	2,254	2,640	12,533	4,224	2,515	9,543	5,349	1,675	861	0
Al Qamishli, Syria	988	3,879	5,783	1,873	4,611	12,790	5,464	528	3,112	12,821	2,715	3,946	12,451	3,380	2,831	8,152	4,928	945	2,225	1,395
Albany, Australia	10,271	14,974	13,237	9,389	12,477	15,772	12,914	11,677	9,613	1,888	9,310	12,871	15,863	8,008	13,968	8,586	15,551	10,318	11,910	11,505
Albany, New York	9,994	5,129	7,957	10,876	8,586	3,787	8,249	8,641	11,115	17,104	11,277	8,085	3,510	11,960	6,510	10,267	4,233	9,950	8,772	9,024
Albuquerque, New Mexico	12,304	7,604	10,815	13,119	11,532	2,128	11,139	11,110	13,922	14,184	13,930	11,039	1,523	13,572	9,244	9,269	6,447	12,270	11,596	11,709
Alexandria, Egypt	1,759	3,787	4,556	2,517	3,389	12,468	4,236	815	2,618	13,499	2,563	2,721	12,238	4,304	2,228	9,366	5,003	1,711	1,012	353
Alexandroupolis, Greece	2,331	2,698	4,937	3,209	3,965	11,528	4,695	921	3,746	14,215	3,630	3,156	11,245	4,773	1,436	8,883	3,887	2,283	1,862	1,483
Algiers, Algeria	4,220	2,294	3,559	5,043	3,087	10,013	3,475	2,861	4,727	16,041	4,950	2,249	9,856	6,745	751	10,468	3,497	4,170	2,384	2,765
Alice Springs, Australia	10,914	14,898	15,086	10,098	14,153	14,393	14,725	12,289	10,940	1,326	10,465	14,366	14,298	8,403	14,607	7,050	14,934	10,964	13,045	12,442
Allepo, Syria	1,221	3,717	5,418	2,098	4,261	12,609	5,104	190	3,013	13,112	2,712	3,580	12,299	3,704	2,529	8,495	4,825	1,172	1,881	1,083
Alma-Ata, USSR	2,913	5,510	8,878	2,932	7,680	13,343	8,551	3,579	5,304	10,679	4,559	7,042	12,793	2,278	5,439	5,163	5,942	2,939	5,298	4,441
Ambon, Indonesia	9,259	12,666	14,735	8,559	13,491	14,584	14,312	10,518	10,028	3,619	9,371	13,352	14,227	6,718	12,697	4,962	12,640	9,307	11,697	10,940
Amherst, Canada	9,181	4,326	7,304	10,066	7,843	4,610	7,568	7,817	10,279	17,747	10,436	7,302	4,349	11,226	5,670	10,225	3,511	9,137	7,935	8,184
Amiens, France	4,388	856	4,978	5,274	4,539	9,438	4,922	2,996	5,641	16,126	5,658	3,689	9,164	6,689	1,017	9,255	2,113	4,341	3,384	3,415
Amman, Jordan	1,189	4,028	5,096	1,987	3,893	12,853	4,762	565	2,553	13,015	2,319	3,269	12,580	3,738	2,649	8,886	5,186	1,140	1,508	657
Amsterdam, Netherlands	4,280	698	5,279	5,167	4,793	9,512	5,210	2,916	5,693	15,901	5,656	3,935	9,210	6,509	1,195	8,927	1,965	4,235	3,492	3,438
Anadyr, USSR	8,587	6,486	12,232	8,984	11,767	7,974	12,205	8,252	11,137	11,559	10,536	10,900	7,364	8,390	8,138	3,675	5,481	8,586	9,895	9,316
Anchorage, Alaska	9,725	6,584	12,062	10,260	11,948	6,294	12,152	9,106	12,180	12,445	11,698	11,118	5,684	9,922	8,410	5,198	5,381	9,714	10,517	10,105
Andorra, Andorra	4,344	1,648	4,156	5,207	3,735	9,665	4,097	2,938	5,185	16,239	5,322	2,897	9,460	6,799	599	9,992	2,852	4,295	2,852	3,078
Angra do Heroismo, Azores	6,801	2,753	4,371	7,657	4,737	7,372	4,567	5,396	7,301	18,694	7,598	4,178	7,263	9,248	3,056	11,232	3,063	6,751	4,995	5,429
Ankara, Turkey	1,758	3,157	5,323	2,643	4,255	12,050	5,046	387	3,472	13,619	3,238	3,500	11,739	4,171	2,038	8,516	4,277	1,711	1,962	1,327
Annaba, Algeria	3,799	2,366	3,699	4,624	3,072	10,396	3,566	2,444	4,387	15,632	4,570	2,209	10,222	6,326	563	10,227	3,616	3,749	2,045	2,362
Annapolis, Maryland	10,443	5,582	8,127	11,327	8,832	3,345	8,440	9,081	11,487	16,887	11,681	8,376	3,101	12,428	6,920	10,530	4,701	10,399	9,148	9,434
Antananarivo, Madagascar	5,450	9,601	6,254	4,857	5,408	16,581	5,892	6,323	3,239	8,927	3,515	5,872	16,871	5,383	7,828	11,548	10,848	5,468	5,446	5,507
Antofagasta, Chile	13,967	10,968	7,877	14,452	9,176	5,511	8,266	12,904	12,356	12,840	13,149	9,628	6,109	16,260	10,887	16,649	10,845	13,924	11,410	12,253
Antwerp, Belgium	4,277	783	5,149	5,164	4,670	9,526	5,081	2,900	5,629	15,955	5,612	3,813	9,236	6,539	1,085	9,052	2,055	4,232	3,407	3,383
Apia, Western Samoa	15,545	15,120	18,381	15,066	19,477	8,592	18,716	16,304	16,675	5,486	16,056	19,657	8,545	13,209	16,892	7,744	13,918	15,584	18,072	17,212
Arequipa, Peru	13,757	10,339	7,808	14,352	9,118	4,818	8,216	12,575	12,449	13,497	13,214	9,472	5,402	16,215	10,434	16,011	10,127	13,710	11,227	12,041
Arkhangel'sk, USSR	3,844	2,406	7,459	4,568	6,679	10,373	7,299	3,085	6,166	13,827	5,762	5,826	9,903	5,172	3,227	6,526	2,657	3,821	4,657	4,113
As Sallum, Egypt	2,209	3,527	4,208	2,969	3,099	12,079	3,910	1,112	2,862	13,929	2,910	2,371	11,873	4,756	1,857	9,660	4,774	2,160	836	664
Asau, Western Samoa	15,441	15,091	18,484	14,961	19,530	8,666	18,812	16,209	16,584	5,431	15,959	19,611	8,611	13,104	16,847	7,652	13,897	15,481	17,971	17,110
Ascension Island (Georgetown)	7,912	7,299	1,864	8,273	3,052	9,795	2,170	7,178	6,183	14,484	6,960	3,697	10,125	10,056	6,003	15,674	8,169	7,875	5,424	6,282
Ashkhabad, USSR	1,257	4,830	7,244	1,543	6,021	13,531	6,903	2,039	3,763	11,551	3,089	5,418	13,082	2,140	4,208	6,833	5,627	1,278	3,650	2,790
Asmera, Ethiopia	1,916	5,770	4,825	1,904	3,517	14,272	4,413	2,429	697	11,844	716	3,312	14,118	3,635	4,130	9,862	6,983	1,907	1,908	1,646
Astrakhan, USSR	1,778	3,572	6,746	2,493	5,656	12,306	6,464	1,480	4,231	12,752	3,734	4,919	11,882	3,400	3,152	7,101	4,378	1,760	3,305	2,530
Asuncion, Paraguay	12,838	10,501	6,711	13,241	7,989	6,534	7,082	11,904	11,076	13,126	11,874	8,510	7,104	15,001	10,091	17,710	10,630	12,798	10,293	11,150
Aswan, Egypt	1,672	4,618	4,462	2,180	3,191	13,182	4,092	1,452	1,777	12,883	1,790	2,709	12,992	4,045	2,982	9,690	5,843	1,636	974	494
Athens, Greece	2,407	2,849	4,582	3,260	3,598	11,567	4,334	1,028	3,541	14,297	3,501	2,792	11,316	4,914	1,352	9,239	4,077	2,358	1,529	1,276
Atlanta, Georgia	11,349	6,484	8,795	12,231	9,598	2,433	9,135	9,993	12,376	16,100	12,590	9,196	2,195	13,268	7,833	10,676	5,560	11,306	10,043	10,345
Atlantic City, New Jersey	10,288	5,431	7,958	11,172	8,654	3,508	8,268	8,921	11,309	17,064	11,508	8,196	3,275	12,301	6,749	10,572	4,573	10,243	8,970	9,262
Auckland, New Zealand	15,072	17,740	16,509	14,244	16,694	10,714	16,500	16,442	14,635	3,253	14,369	17,451	10,845	12,555	18,696	9,192	16,693	15,122	16,963	16,530
Auckland Islands, New Zealand	14,503	18,974	14,901	13,618	15,029	11,690	14,853	15,899	13,384	2,846	13,298	15,808	11,942	12,222	18,057	10,339	18,313	14,550	15,705	15,552
Augusta, Maine	9,631	4,768	7,680	10,514	8,267	4,153	7,959	8,273	10,749	17,388	10,906	7,746	3,881	11,627	6,139	10,229	3,900	9,587	8,405	8,653
Austin, Texas	12,398	7,558	10,074	13,260	10,911	1,504	10,425	11,099	13,649	14,782	13,804	10,513	1,036	14,016	9,038	10,228	6,510	12,358	11,306	11,550
Ayan, USSR	7,249	6,919	12,348	7,401	11,465	10,265	12,165	7,381	9,753	10,126	9,027	10,648	9,656	6,406	8,120	1,866	6,313	7,263	9,196	8,437
Baghdad, Iraq	495	4,378	5,887	1,381	4,659	13,289	5,541	924	2,756	12,377	2,281	4,068	12,952	2,983	3,264	8,168	5,427	449	2,292	1,431
Baguio, Philippines	7,438	10,301	13,482	6,908	12,174	14,253	13,081	8,522	8,880	5,993	8,108	11,768	13,710	5,062	10,515	3,201	10,272	7,482	9,993	9,156
Bahia Blanca, Argentina	13,731	12,021	7,717	13,930	8,910	7,295	8,039	13,033	11,587	11,573	12,387	9,555	7,901	15,429	11,458	18,092	12,183	13,699	11,292	12,148
Baku, USSR	1,124	4,121	6,618	1,815	5,445	12,943	6,300	1,318	3,645	12,322	3,097	4,781	12,535	2,875	3,423	7,326	5,006	1,112	3,058	2,217
Balikpapan, Indonesia	8,042	11,828	13,453	7,309	12,201	15,654	13,030	9,346	8,737	4,356	8,079	12,065	15,217	5,493	11,599	5,123	12,028	8,091	10,433	9,697
Balkhash, USSR	2,937	5,125	8,746	3,085	7,587	12,936	8,438	3,427	5,416	11,060	4,702	6,909	12,392	2,647	5,152	5,192	5,524	2,956	5,200	4,356
Ballarat, Australia	12,444	16,702	15,185	11,583	14,663	13,435	14,938	13,851	11,955	554	11,641	15,154	13,526	10,019	16,189	8,564	16,666	12,493	14,248	13,803
Baltimore, Maryland	10,426	5,564	8,141	11,310	8,841	3,360	8,453	9,066	11,483	16,878	11,672	8,380	3,110	12,404	6,910	10,495	4,677	10,382	9,143	9,424
Bamako, Mali	6,085	4,962	921	6,661	1,704	9,815	1,161	5,079	5,116	15,852	5,748	1,785	9,934	8,527	3,627	13,341	5,937	6,041	3,535	4,367
Bandar Seri Begawan, Brunei	7,504	11,131	13,159	6,816	11,872	15,503	12,737	8,767	8,424	5,057	7,721	11,651	15,002	4,967	10,976	4,614	11,314	7,553	9,961	9,191
Bangalore, India	3,573	8,182	8,980	2,752	7,681	16,694	8,561	4,971	4,268	8,333	3,533	7,462	16,148	1,230	7,310	6,756	8,958	3,623	5,827	5,127
Banghazi, Libya	2,687	3,257	3,885	3,454	2,868	11,641	3,620	1,498	3,198	14,398	3,328	2,074	11,457	5,235	1,481	9,943	4,524	2,637	933	1,121
Bangkok, Thailand	5,644	9,479	11,441	4,975	10,134	15,952	11,026	6,910	6,751	6,723	6,002	9,841	15,351	3,115	9,148	4,816	9,859	5,692	8,121	7,338
Bangui, Central African Rep.	4,239	6,128	2,511	4,430	1,367	12,878	2,089	3,998	2,283	13,009	3,052	1,812	12,971	6,157	4,273	12,315	7,384	4,214	2,252	2,926
Banjarmasin, Indonesia	7,955	11,899	13,223	7,196	11,988	15,977	12,800	9,286	8,529	4,289	7,892	11,892	15,548	5,409	11,569	5,435	12,164	8,004	10,297	9,584
Banjul, Gambia	6,868	5,001	1,645	7,498	2,636	8,896	1,997	5,756	6,045	16,572	6,662	2,666	9,034	9,360	3,991	13,647	5,799	6,822	4,352	5,152
Barcelona, Spain	4,285	1,778	4,043	5,142	3,603	9,760	3,977	2,884	5,069	16,179	5,220	2,763	9,564	6,757	549	10,071	2,987	4,235	2,732	2,982
Bari, Italy	3,063	2,238	4,480	3,929	3,668	10,880	4,292	1,657	4,157	14,958	4,169	2,811	10,634	5,530	683	9,376	3,495	3,014	1,972	1,923
Barranquilla, Colombia	12,411	7,945	7,809	13,253	8,959	2,788	8,221	11,011	12,346	15,726	12,883	8,908	3,168	14,846	8,671	13,340	7,414	12,362	10,328	10,932
Basse-Terre, Guadeloupe	10,948	6,709	6,403	11,771	7,497	4,073	6,804	9,563	10,843	17,101	11,366	7,402	4,310	13,439	7,231	13,436	6,388	10,898	8,810	9,428
Basseterre, St. Kitts & Nevis	10,951	6,646	6,518	11,783	7,593	3,954	6,915	9,559	10,916	17,140	11,422	7,476	4,173	13,424	7,222	13,265	6,289	10,901	8,852	9,453
Bata, Equatorial Guinea	5,141	6,220	1,578	5,407	858	12,046	1,180	4,694	3,303	13,596	4,070	1,683	12,205	7,165	4,439	13,189	7,418	5,110	2,871	3,665
Baton Rouge, Louisiana	12,033	7,169	9,445	12,910	10,295	1,748	9,798	10,694	13,114	15,379	13,323	9,918	1,460	13,841	8,560	10,609	6,192	11,991	10,781	11,075
Bear Lake, Canada	10,405	6,502	11,450	11,066	11,625	4,922	11,627	9,538	12,653	13,415	12,324	10,871	4,312	11,036	8,359	6,628	5,232	10,385	10,663	10,427
Bechar, Algeria	4,781	2,836	2,918	5,560	2,669	9,750	2,893	3,482	4,907	16,381	5,249	1,922	9,661	7,328	1,502	11,207	3,937	4,731	2,636	3,197
Beira, Mozambique	5,734	9,197	5,086	5,337	4,415	15,257	4,758	6,293	3,220	9,953	3,774	5,021	15,584	6,269	7,347	12,677	10,469	5,739	5,030	5,322
Beirut, Lebanon	1,267	3,829	5,160	2,106	3,985	12,677	4,838	348	2,771	13,143	2,530	3,325	12,393	3,805	2,505	8,777	4,977	1,217	1,599	785
Belau Islands (Koror)	9,245	11,851	15,220	8,684	13,911	13,475	14,806	10,334	10,522	4,698	9,782	13,560	13,044	6,822	12,271	3,631	11,603	9,290	11,794	10,964
Belem, Brazil	10,745	7,697	4,999	11,384	6,283	5,997	5,422	9,557	9,734	15,911	10,434	6,521	6,388	13,248	7,478	15,679	7,835	10,698	8,240	9,035
Belfast, United Kingdom	5,038	372	5,466	5,924	5,170	8,750	5,462	3,677	6,404	16,518	6,401	4,342	8,450	7,223	1,773	9,067	1,402	4,994	4,148	4,168
Belgrade, Yugoslavia	2,911	2,078	4,987	3,795	4,155	10,914	4,797	1,515	4,337	14,744	4,249	3,304	10,624	5,279	1,006	8,871	3,282	2,864	2,303	2,068
Belmopan, Belize	13,029	8,219	9,289	13,915	10,347	1,184	9,687	11,631	13,566	14,950	13,963	10,159	1,507	15,120	9,354	11,925	7,392	12,983	11,349	11,808
Belo Horizonte, Brazil	11,309	9,383	5,183	11,716	6,458	7,348	5,552	10,413	9,595	13,928	10,385	6,989	7,853	13,499	8,728	17,776	9,738	11,270	8,769	9,628
Bergen, Norway	4,596	562	6,160	5,462	5,685	9,204	6,101	3,350	6,334	15,652	6,193	4,825	8,836	6,562	2,068	8,171	1,314	4,557	4,252	4,066
Bern, Switzerland	3,942	1,310	4,741	4,825	4,184	9,918	4,643	2,538	5,135	15,771	5,157	3,322	9,656	6,307	565	9,325	2,581	3,895	2,888	2,911
Bhopal, India	2,991	7,238	8,910	2,347	7,602	15,557	8,510	4,292	4,410	9,120	3,611	7,227	15,009	491	6,590	6,104	7,919	3,040	5,481	4,686
Bhubaneswar, India	3,926	8,018	9,801	3,268	8,491	15,855	9,394	5,212	5,208	8,267	4,424	8,146	15,263	1,402	7,488	5,570	8,593	3,974	6,410	5,619

Distances in Kilometers

	Abadan, Iran	Aberdeen, United Kingdom	Abidjan, Ivory Coast	Abu Dhabi, United Arab Emir.	Abuja, Nigeria	Acapulco, Mexico	Accra, Ghana	Adana, Turkey	Addis Ababa, Ethiopia	Adelaide, Australia	Aden, P.D.R. Yemen	Agadez, Niger	Aguascalientes, Mexico	Ahmadabad, India	Ajaccio, France	Akita, Japan	Akureyri, Iceland	Al Basrah, Iraq	Al Jawf, Libya	Al Minya, Egypt
Bialystok, Poland	3,248	1,660	5,852	4,117	5,084	10,542	5,689	2,024	5,087	14,670	4,880	4,225	10,183	5,318	1,647	8,076	2,657	3,208	3,212	2,850
Big Trout Lake, Canada	9,854	5,175	9,269	10,680	9,660	4,193	9,499	8,658	11,548	15,723	11,492	9,014	3,696	11,327	6,891	8,587	3,994	9,819	9,271	9,299
Bilbao, Spain	4,712	1,546	4,204	5,578	3,904	9,292	4,186	3,304	5,538	16,604	5,691	3,093	9,091	7,153	971	10,097	2,665	4,663	3,199	3,451
Billings, Montana	11,257	6,729	10,700	12,036	11,201	3,306	10,967	10,147	13,114	14,365	13,001	10,587	2,710	12,384	8,478	8,338	5,508	11,226	10,860	10,851
Birmingham, Alabama	11,513	6,646	9,020	12,392	9,823	2,265	9,360	10,166	12,586	15,876	12,788	9,419	1,995	13,380	8,025	10,574	5,694	11,470	10,250	10,539
Birmingham, United Kingdom	4,734	520	5,231	5,621	4,872	9,069	5,204	3,358	6,050	16,351	6,056	4,034	8,780	6,974	1,421	9,155	1,727	4,689	3,793	3,818
Bismarck, North Dakota	10,916	6,269	10,094	11,727	10,607	3,323	10,362	9,743	12,639	14,970	12,583	10,009	2,768	12,242	7,975	8,684	5,081	10,882	10,352	10,392
Bissau, Guinea Bissau	6,854	5,155	1,462	7,461	2,509	9,047	1,828	5,777	5,943	16,367	6,577	2,602	9,199	9,327	4,084	13,771	5,978	6,809	4,321	5,136
Biysk, USSR	3,885	5,242	9,494	4,061	8,398	12,298	9,215	4,211	6,388	10,986	5,678	7,670	11,725	3,450	5,632	4,355	5,385	3,901	6,025	5,204
Blagoveshchensk, USSR	6,751	7,237	12,304	6,778	11,279	11,247	12,061	7,101	9,160	9,501	8,398	10,515	10,639	5,597	8,192	1,532	6,817	6,772	8,924	8,112
Blantyre, Malawi	5,297	8,779	4,894	4,925	4,125	15,226	4,542	5,844	2,775	10,212	3,345	4,682	15,497	5,935	6,935	12,401	10,051	5,301	4,602	4,877
Bloemfontein, South Africa	6,987	9,922	4,997	6,655	4,702	14,386	4,765	7,384	4,432	9,992	5,060	5,463	14,828	7,621	8,068	13,976	11,171	6,987	5,910	6,352
Bluefields, Nicaragua	13,070	8,392	8,780	13,941	9,909	1,823	9,190	11,660	13,255	15,061	13,746	9,814	2,255	15,361	9,333	12,712	7,692	13,022	11,152	11,698
Boa Vista do Rio Branco, Braz.	11,663	7,901	6,295	12,398	7,537	4,562	6,718	10,357	11,000	15,935	11,649	7,656	4,968	14,212	8,106	14,842	7,735	11,614	9,278	10,010
Bodo, Norway	4,679	1,410	7,020	5,490	6,475	9,282	6,942	3,618	6,719	14,989	6,459	5,609	8,849	6,317	2,844	7,295	1,442	4,647	4,828	4,495
Bogota, Colombia	12,782	8,497	7,765	13,589	8,980	3,128	8,186	11,405	12,427	15,266	13,033	9,026	3,594	15,286	9,077	13,985	8,041	12,732	10,555	11,220
Boise, Idaho	11,666	7,276	11,355	12,406	11,853	3,342	11,623	10,625	13,651	13,711	13,479	11,229	2,732	12,571	9,058	8,026	6,033	11,638	11,439	11,382
Bologna, Italy	3,587	1,690	4,592	4,464	3,934	10,306	4,459	2,177	4,732	15,459	4,754	3,067	10,052	5,999	355	9,368	2,959	3,539	2,499	2,507
Bolzano, Italy	3,643	1,497	4,800	4,526	4,159	10,206	4,675	2,240	4,899	15,472	4,891	3,292	9,935	6,007	553	9,186	2,761	3,595	2,696	2,655
Bombay, India	2,779	7,349	8,446	2,003	7,137	15,965	8,036	4,161	3,840	9,153	3,053	6,833	15,455	451	6,498	6,764	8,143	2,829	5,137	4,392
Bonn, West Germany	4,081	933	5,141	4,968	4,609	9,721	5,055	2,705	5,458	15,775	5,427	3,747	9,428	6,349	988	8,991	2,197	4,036	3,259	3,205
Bora Bora (Vaitape)	17,475	14,838	16,300	17,174	17,608	6,780	16,700	17,631	18,622	7,142	18,182	17,875	6,865	15,345	16,635	9,404	13,574	17,504	19,017	18,697
Bordeaux, France	4,526	1,373	4,392	5,399	4,023	9,421	4,353	3,115	5,470	16,402	5,583	3,192	9,200	6,940	820	9,851	2,553	4,477	3,145	3,333
Boston, Massachusetts	9,851	4,992	7,734	10,735	8,365	3,939	8,025	8,488	10,920	17,328	11,097	7,869	3,686	11,864	6,333	10,388	4,138	9,807	8,578	8,847
Bouvet Island	10,330	12,379	6,658	10,006	7,057	12,375	6,657	10,584	7,771	9,217	8,415	7,923	12,968	10,809	10,689	16,419	13,444	10,328	8,918	9,514
Brasilia, Brazil	11,467	9,121	5,369	11,947	6,671	6,754	5,761	10,468	9,929	14,350	10,705	7,125	7,249	13,775	8,632	17,242	9,371	11,424	8,909	9,759
Braunschweig, West Germany	3,918	976	5,375	4,803	4,789	9,865	5,273	2,572	5,431	15,522	5,352	3,923	9,550	6,127	1,159	8,713	2,188	3,874	3,299	3,164
Brazzaville, Congo	5,195	6,986	2,395	5,292	1,736	12,838	2,037	5,020	2,986	12,687	3,790	2,482	13,038	6,918	5,157	13,247	8,215	5,173	3,267	3,947
Bremerhaven, West Germany	4,095	785	5,470	4,979	4,924	9,685	5,382	2,758	5,625	15,637	5,545	4,060	9,364	6,273	1,294	8,677	1,995	4,052	3,484	3,358
Brest, France	4,854	985	4,775	5,736	4,485	9,018	4,767	3,449	5,939	16,643	6,020	3,666	8,773	7,194	1,262	9,640	2,082	4,806	3,626	3,766
Brest, USSR	3,145	1,746	5,780	4,017	4,992	10,641	5,610	1,907	4,967	14,623	4,762	4,136	10,287	5,246	1,599	8,129	2,768	3,104	3,097	2,729
Bridgetown, Barbados	10,941	6,860	6,157	11,742	7,291	4,348	6,565	9,575	10,682	16,979	11,239	7,248	4,621	13,462	7,261	13,813	6,616	10,891	8,721	9,374
Brisbane, Australia	12,824	16,177	16,565	12,033	15,907	12,516	16,290	14,166	12,871	1,599	12,424	16,256	12,498	10,286	16,415	7,561	15,717	12,874	15,010	14,396
Bristol, United Kingdom	4,759	633	5,116	5,646	4,773	9,057	5,093	3,374	6,019	16,426	6,043	3,939	8,779	7,026	1,365	9,276	1,812	4,713	3,746	3,799
Brno, Czechoslovakia	3,384	1,525	5,240	4,270	4,525	10,406	5,093	2,025	4,905	15,095	4,807	3,660	10,097	5,651	1,017	8,706	2,715	3,339	2,835	2,635
Broken Hill, Australia	11,993	16,068	15,374	11,152	14,685	13,668	15,080	13,388	11,740	423	11,354	15,068	13,688	9,518	15,724	7,936	16,009	12,043	13,966	13,443
Brussels, Belgium	4,272	818	5,106	5,158	4,627	9,537	5,038	2,890	5,604	15,967	5,593	3,771	9,249	6,544	1,047	9,091	2,089	4,226	3,376	3,361
Bucharest, Romania	2,496	2,411	5,236	3,383	4,313	11,301	5,014	1,131	4,107	14,300	3,946	3,487	10,990	4,835	1,437	8,592	3,557	2,450	2,259	1,859
Budapest, Hungary	3,137	1,786	5,170	4,024	4,395	10,660	5,001	1,767	4,649	14,896	4,545	3,536	10,355	5,438	1,027	8,727	2,974	3,091	2,612	2,380
Buenos Aires, Argentina	13,274	11,455	7,210	13,534	8,427	7,188	7,544	12,514	11,231	12,107	12,035	9,045	7,783	15,132	10,893	18,283	11,646	13,240	10,798	11,657
Buffalo, New York	10,273	5,409	8,376	11,149	9,004	3,509	8,669	8,940	11,487	16,684	11,620	8,495	3,185	12,146	6,855	10,053	4,445	10,230	9,143	9,367
Bujumbura, Burundi	4,239	7,282	3,837	4,100	2,826	14,299	3,435	4,515	1,720	11,535	2,487	3,254	14,428	5,530	5,434	12,021	8,553	4,230	3,122	3,487
Bulawayo, Zimbabwe	5,970	9,030	4,548	5,671	4,003	14,606	4,246	6,366	3,412	10,446	4,061	4,683	14,947	6,758	7,170	13,233	10,294	5,969	4,940	5,344
Burlington, Vermont	9,823	4,957	7,950	10,704	8,540	3,955	8,232	8,478	10,998	17,117	11,138	8,017	3,657	11,765	6,372	10,103	4,040	9,780	8,653	8,885
Cabinda, Angola	5,527	7,069	2,168	5,649	1,720	12,549	1,847	5,289	3,354	12,845	4,157	2,533	12,774	7,286	5,268	13,592	8,275	5,503	3,505	4,223
Cagliari, Italy	3,686	2,153	3,981	4,530	3,335	10,397	3,845	2,301	4,455	15,565	4,586	2,468	10,197	6,188	302	9,948	3,417	3,636	2,134	2,346
Cairns, Australia	11,650	14,805	16,500	10,916	15,471	13,072	16,120	12,928	12,113	2,120	11,549	15,547	12,918	9,102	15,090	6,297	14,459	11,699	14,019	13,305
Cairo, Egypt	1,638	3,962	4,602	2,367	3,408	12,649	4,270	859	2,453	13,328	2,382	2,774	12,420	4,172	2,409	9,359	5,174	1,590	1,020	222
Calais, France	4,446	735	5,088	5,332	4,659	9,367	5,037	3,061	5,743	16,139	5,747	3,810	9,085	6,720	1,134	9,173	1,994	4,400	3,495	3,509
Calcutta, India	4,071	7,959	10,038	3,471	8,730	15,557	9,637	5,305	5,500	8,281	4,708	8,348	14,958	1,618	7,539	5,210	8,468	4,118	6,592	5,782
Calgary, Canada	10,825	6,504	10,927	11,564	11,291	3,998	11,156	9,802	12,853	14,085	12,651	10,612	3,395	11,772	8,315	7,646	5,247	10,798	10,686	10,585
Cali, Colombia	13,074	8,749	8,044	13,885	9,267	2,956	8,466	11,694	12,718	14,993	13,328	9,322	3,452	15,571	9,363	13,944	8,258	13,024	10,853	11,518
Camaguey, Cuba	11,903	7,184	8,134	12,782	9,146	2,366	8,521	10,495	12,333	16,165	12,738	8,932	2,522	14,152	8,186	12,178	6,490	11,856	10,124	10,607
Cambridge Bay, Canada	8,764	4,704	9,890	9,494	9,913	5,818	10,013	7,795	10,893	14,624	10,624	9,128	5,253	9,784	6,563	6,823	3,437	8,738	8,862	8,647
Cambridge, United Kingdom	4,592	567	5,212	5,479	4,815	9,210	5,172	3,217	5,923	16,225	5,921	3,970	8,920	6,837	1,315	9,113	1,816	4,547	3,678	3,686
Campbellton, Canada	9,186	4,320	7,556	10,066	8,056	4,593	7,811	7,840	10,390	17,474	10,511	7,489	4,292	11,155	5,747	9,935	3,427	9,142	8,048	8,258
Campo Grande, Brazil	12,333	9,884	6,220	12,788	7,514	6,443	6,605	11,345	10,706	13,719	11,494	7,992	6,986	14,590	9,406	17,455	10,034	12,291	9,777	10,629
Canakkale, Turkey	2,260	2,787	4,915	3,135	3,925	11,611	4,667	849	3,657	14,149	3,540	3,124	11,331	4,716	1,496	8,905	3,977	2,211	1,792	1,395
Canberra, Australia	12,800	16,774	15,703	11,955	15,199	12,958	15,466	14,196	12,445	964	12,101	15,681	13,025	10,327	16,533	8,362	16,528	12,850	14,714	14,226
Cancun, Mexico	12,561	7,740	9,051	13,447	10,057	1,465	9,438	11,168	13,196	15,357	13,555	9,821	1,613	14,636	8,905	11,704	6,907	12,515	10,945	11,375
Canton, China	6,430	9,283	12,529	5,956	11,232	14,310	12,141	7,471	8,052	6,960	7,260	10,771	13,721	4,150	9,446	3,128	9,338	6,473	8,988	8,142
Canton Atoll, Phoenix Islands	14,835	13,913	18,638	14,541	19,294	8,174	19,041	15,329	16,605	6,236	15,847	18,441	8,018	12,767	15,675	6,806	12,727	14,866	17,154	16,344
Cape Town, South Africa	7,773	10,273	4,944	7,498	4,914	13,636	4,789	8,046	5,215	10,173	5,885	5,739	14,121	8,523	8,455	14,873	11,480	7,769	6,453	6,986
Cape York, Australia	11,009	14,034	16,298	10,313	15,134	13,280	15,888	12,245	11,695	2,711	11,075	15,077	13,048	8,472	14,353	5,589	13,726	11,057	13,449	12,695
Caracas, Venezuela	11,758	7,524	6,948	12,571	8,110	3,634	7,362	10,380	11,519	16,274	12,084	8,089	3,976	14,261	8,052	13,789	7,152	11,708	9,565	10,211
Cardiff, United Kingdom	4,802	631	5,121	5,689	4,789	9,014	5,102	3,417	6,056	16,466	6,084	3,957	8,737	7,069	1,399	9,291	1,790	4,756	3,781	3,839
Carlisle, United Kingdom	4,855	256	5,497	5,740	5,149	8,929	5,476	3,502	6,268	16,327	6,245	4,311	8,621	7,028	1,676	8,950	1,457	4,811	4,035	4,021
Carnarvon, Australia	9,267	13,840	13,053	8,401	12,095	16,439	12,680	10,678	8,941	2,647	8,529	12,337	16,354	6,906	13,008	7,661	14,356	9,316	11,141	10,633
Carson City, Nevada	12,212	7,852	11,805	12,934	12,365	3,135	12,092	11,193	14,226	13,260	14,044	11,765	2,536	13,000	9,631	8,094	6,609	12,186	12,012	11,957
Casablanca, Morocco	5,228	2,647	3,155	6,032	3,102	9,204	3,200	3,885	5,456	16,924	5,787	2,414	9,110	7,763	1,703	11,234	3,634	5,178	3,173	3,696
Casper, Wyoming	11,497	6,885	10,605	12,294	11,175	2,945	10,890	10,347	13,259	14,461	13,193	10,599	2,355	12,710	8,595	8,688	5,689	11,465	10,972	11,010
Castries, Saint Lucia	11,008	6,852	6,311	11,819	7,433	4,182	6,718	9,633	10,809	16,976	11,354	7,372	4,447	13,518	7,310	13,669	6,569	10,958	8,820	9,460
Catbalogan, Philippines	8,086	10,968	14,072	7,522	12,762	14,170	13,662	9,198	9,404	5,368	8,651	12,398	13,669	5,663	11,206	3,442	10,890	8,131	10,633	9,805
Cayenne, French Guiana	10,751	7,253	5,354	11,466	6,586	5,351	5,776	9,475	10,047	16,500	10,692	6,701	5,696	13,297	7,273	14,900	7,252	10,703	8,335	9,081
Cayman Islands (Georgetown)	12,324	7,582	8,496	13,204	9,535	1,980	8,889	10,917	12,752	15,736	13,165	9,342	2,198	14,544	8,612	12,187	6,851	12,276	10,552	11,036
Cazombo, Angola	5,408	7,989	3,535	5,283	2,905	13,859	3,202	5,569	2,903	11,503	3,664	3,588	14,117	6,657	6,132	13,175	9,244	5,397	3,994	4,506
Cebu, Philippines	8,069	11,066	14,010	7,483	12,702	14,347	13,597	9,208	9,321	5,241	8,576	12,363	13,852	5,620	11,251	3,633	11,019	8,114	10,607	9,787
Cedar Rapids, Iowa	11,011	6,202	9,424	11,865	10,059	2,894	9,723	9,740	12,441	15,629	12,506	9,538	2,439	12,629	7,771	9,562	5,116	10,973	10,104	10,262
Changsha, China	6,204	8,780	12,331	5,809	11,054	13,900	11,960	7,156	8,007	7,490	7,205	10,534	13,301	4,075	9,038	2,800	8,795	6,244	8,751	7,894
Channel-Port-aux-Basques, Can.	8,754	3,905	7,012	9,639	7,492	5,040	7,259	7,387	9,858	17,979	10,007	6,925	4,779	10,825	5,240	10,150	3,132	8,710	7,514	7,754
Charleston, South Carolina	11,153	6,305	8,377	12,039	9,200	2,672	8,720	9,776	12,050	16,475	12,303	8,821	2,513	13,181	7,568	10,986	5,453	11,108	9,730	10,072
Charleston, West Virginia	10,801	5,935	8,566	11,681	9,284	2,976	8,883	9,456	11,921	16,436	12,095	8,828	2,690	12,701	7,329	10,374	4,995	10,759	9,579	9,844
Charlotte, North Carolina	11,012	6,151	8,476	11,896	9,254	2,779	8,809	9,649	12,013	16,452	12,230	8,841	2,557	12,980	7,475	10,708	5,257	10,968	9,680	9,987
Charlotte Amalie, U.S.V.I.	11,073	6,679	6,761	11,916	7,821	3,711	7,156	9,673	11,120	17,057	11,608	7,682	3,918	13,520	7,333	13,074	6,264	11,023	9,025	9,606
Charlottetown, Canada	9,089	4,234	7,240	9,973	7,767	4,703	7,501	7,723	10,188	17,802	10,343	7,220	4,442	11,138	5,576	10,208	3,428	9,044	7,843	8,091
Chatham, Canada	9,179	4,316	7,438	10,062	7,955	4,602	7,697	7,825	10,336	17,602	10,473	7,399	4,320	11,184	5,706	10,067	3,459	9,136	7,991	8,220
Chatham Islands (Waitangi)	15,824	18,488	15,662	14,954	16,133	10,263	15,735	17,234	14,863	3,938	14,766	16,983	10,486	13,394	19,533	10,237	17,252	15,873	17,174	17,018
Chengdu, China	5,299	8,095	11,425	4,917	10,151	14,159	11,056	6,266	7,153	8,113	6,349	9,629	13,548	3,226	8,209	3,408	8,244	5,338	7,846	6,990
Chesterfield Inlet, Canada	9,008	4,557	9,314	9,800	9,492	5,213	9,482	7,902	10,917	15,414	10,758	8,760	4,688	10,318	6,374	7,730	3,302	8,977	8,740	8,648
Cheyenne, Wyoming	11,623	6,963	10,523	12,432	11,133	2,733	10,818	10,449	13,319	14,536	13,284	10,580	2,148	12,895	8,645	8,910	5,785	11,590	11,015	11,082
Chiang Mai, Thailand	5,251	8,921	11,190	4,643	9,880	15,560	10,784	6,465	6,576	7,272	5,801	9,523	14,951	2,779	8,660	4,566	9,281	5,298	7,772	6,963
Chibougamau, Canada	9,476	4,628	8,155	10,345	8,630	4,325	8,405	8,170	10,843	16,872	10,910	8,041	3,957	11,295	6,171	9,519	3,612	9,435	8,510	8,663
Chicago, Illinois	10,824	5,986	9,089	11,688	9,732	3,013	9,388	9,528	12,169	15,963	12,263	9,221	2,608	12,537	7,512	9,767	4,939	10,784	9,828	10,013
Chiclayo, Peru	14,027	9,902	8,529	14,777	9,813	3,421	8,951	12,691	13,264	13,887	13,961	10,006	4,006	16,573	10,393	14,614	9,445	13,978	11,655	12,388
Chihuahua, Mexico	12,938	8,167	10,902	13,770	11,737	1,450	11,254	11,699	14,389	13,965	14,477	11,324	839	14,286	9,735	9,813	7,051	12,901	12,046	12,232
Chongquing, China	5,565	8,328	11,691	5,171	10,413	14,140	11,319	6,538	7,387	7,891	6,584	9,898	13,532	3,456	8,473	3,251	8,444	5,605	8,114	7,259
Christchurch, New Zealand	14,954	18,448	15,758	14,087	15,946	11,082	15,739	16,363	14,153	3,065	13,983	16,727	11,273	12,523	18,694	9,783	17,454	15,003	16,496	16,219
Christiansted, U.S.V.I.	11,092	6,720	6,731	11,932	7,801	3,740	7,128	9,695	11,111	17,029	11,606	7,672	3,956	13,547	7,355	13,144	6,317	11,042	9,028	9,616
Christmas Is. [Indian Ocean]	7,619	12,052	12,277	6,783	11,121	17,182	11,864	9,017	7,726	4,296	7,180	11,162	16,793	5,170	11,356	6,601	12,565	7,669	9,727	9,113
Christmas Is. [Pacific Ocean]	15,511	13,092	16,980	15,501	17,930	6,512	17,379	15,490	17,853	7,789	17,049	17,385	6,364	13,931	14,951	7,531	11,829	15,528	17,106	16,562

Distances in Kilometers	Abadan, Iran	Aberdeen, United Kingdom	Abidjan, Ivory Coast	Abu Dhabi, United Arab Emir.	Abuja, Nigeria	Acapulco, Mexico	Accra, Ghana	Adana, Turkey	Addis Ababa, Ethiopia	Adelaide, Australia	Aden, P.D.R. Yemen	Agadez, Niger	Aguascalientes, Mexico	Ahmadabad, India	Ajaccio, France	Akita, Japan	Akureyri, Iceland	Al Basrah, Iraq	Al Jawf, Libya	Al Minya, Egypt
Churchill, Canada	9,538	5,012	9,510	10,336	9,786	4,676	9,708	8,409	11,393	15,373	11,263	9,089	4,146	10,859	6,799	8,001	3,777	9,505	9,177	9,125
Cincinnati, Ohio	10,902	6,040	8,820	11,777	9,521	2,885	9,134	9,573	12,102	16,196	12,250	9,051	2,551	12,729	7,484	10,171	5,056	10,860	9,758	9,997
Ciudad Bolivia, Venezuela	12,222	7,939	7,354	13,037	8,537	3,320	7,771	10,841	11,961	15,834	12,538	8,538	3,714	14,719	8,511	13,822	7,515	12,172	10,028	10,677
Ciudad Juarez, Mexico	12,639	7,902	10,874	13,463	11,653	1,777	11,213	11,423	14,179	14,065	14,225	11,200	1,168	13,943	9,507	9,542	6,765	12,604	11,841	11,990
Ciudad Victoria, Mexico	13,090	8,232	10,298	13,960	11,238	766	10,673	11,766	14,179	14,361	14,405	10,920	384	14,755	9,644	10,684	7,217	13,049	11,853	12,158
Clarksburg, West Virginia	10,650	5,784	8,462	11,530	9,162	3,128	8,774	9,304	11,775	16,556	11,945	8,696	2,841	12,559	7,179	10,341	4,848	10,607	9,432	9,693
Cleveland, Ohio	10,544	5,682	8,594	11,419	9,250	3,241	8,896	9,216	11,765	16,453	11,900	8,755	2,907	12,388	7,135	10,070	4,703	10,502	9,420	9,646
Cocos (Keeling) Island	6,997	11,658	11,320	6,129	10,190	18,150	10,911	8,408	6,840	4,913	6,344	10,281	17,719	4,689	10,737	7,266	12,344	7,046	8,934	8,382
Colombo, Sri Lanka	4,193	8,877	9,275	3,339	8,001	17,374	8,851	5,601	4,541	7,703	3,872	7,869	16,809	1,943	7,938	6,993	9,670	4,242	6,313	5,666
Colon, Panama	12,955	8,401	8,375	13,806	9,538	2,321	8,790	11,549	12,932	15,195	13,469	9,494	2,767	15,347	9,210	13,192	7,793	12,905	10,909	11,502
Colorado Springs, Colorado	11,858	7,170	10,573	12,672	11,227	2,483	10,880	10,668	13,508	14,468	13,495	10,699	1,894	13,151	8,829	9,091	6,005	11,823	11,191	11,282
Columbia, South Carolina	11,124	6,266	8,487	12,009	9,288	2,676	8,825	9,756	12,087	16,406	12,319	8,890	2,477	13,109	7,570	10,816	5,384	11,080	9,759	10,079
Columbus, Georgia	11,494	6,631	8,850	12,377	9,675	2,291	9,195	10,135	12,492	16,008	12,719	9,289	2,073	13,421	7,965	10,766	5,712	11,451	10,163	10,476
Columbus, Ohio	10,745	5,882	8,694	11,620	9,380	3,039	9,003	9,414	11,942	16,335	12,089	8,901	2,712	12,589	7,322	10,159	4,906	10,703	9,598	9,835
Conakry, Guinea	6,800	5,377	1,165	7,370	2,296	9,314	1,553	5,780	5,754	16,038	6,413	2,490	9,482	9,235	4,209	13,927	6,243	6,756	4,248	5,081
Concepcion, Chile	14,614	12,342	8,528	14,870	9,760	6,578	8,871	13,804	12,545	11,414	13,347	10,356	7,189	16,400	12,035	17,121	12,304	14,580	12,121	12,982
Concord, New Hampshire	9,818	4,956	7,791	10,701	8,405	3,965	8,078	8,461	10,924	17,275	11,088	7,898	3,697	11,809	6,322	10,287	4,081	9,774	8,580	8,836
Constantine, Algeria	3,904	2,398	3,607	4,723	3,013	10,326	3,483	2,555	4,435	15,719	4,638	2,154	10,161	6,434	643	10,334	3,638	3,854	2,091	2,444
Copenhagen, Denmark	3,969	919	5,777	4,845	5,180	9,812	5,674	2,687	5,657	15,351	5,521	4,313	9,465	6,053	1,554	8,333	1,983	3,928	3,603	3,390
Coppermine, Canada	9,032	5,105	10,324	9,733	10,342	5,767	10,448	8,117	11,228	14,228	10,923	9,552	5,184	9,909	6,965	6,559	3,843	9,008	9,243	8,997
Coquimbo, Chile	14,284	11,615	8,157	14,666	9,431	6,019	8,526	13,331	12,442	12,168	13,245	9,956	6,626	16,372	11,423	16,968	11,536	14,244	11,739	12,595
Cordoba, Argentina	13,674	11,401	7,557	14,008	8,812	6,564	7,914	12,803	11,753	12,287	12,558	9,376	7,163	15,679	11,023	17,644	11,464	13,637	11,151	12,012
Cordoba, Spain	4,899	2,149	3,607	5,733	3,400	9,318	3,611	3,519	5,396	16,744	5,646	2,632	9,175	7,406	1,237	10,697	3,210	4,849	3,061	3,468
Cork, Ireland	5,169	713	5,181	6,055	4,948	8,650	5,195	3,783	6,385	16,793	6,434	4,139	8,378	7,426	1,710	9,409	1,627	5,123	4,089	4,184
Corner Brook, Canada	8,597	3,741	6,994	9,481	7,437	5,192	7,230	7,234	9,740	17,946	9,873	6,851	4,918	10,652	5,106	10,023	2,955	8,553	7,397	7,620
Corrientes, Argentina	13,038	10,771	6,913	13,414	8,181	6,610	7,277	12,134	11,214	12,860	12,015	8,722	7,190	15,145	10,348	17,804	10,896	12,999	10,502	11,361
Cosenza, Italy	3,075	2,390	4,282	3,926	3,458	10,939	4,089	1,686	4,030	14,964	4,079	2,602	10,710	5,573	699	9,565	3,655	3,025	1,801	1,826
Craiova, Romania	2,650	2,295	5,104	3,535	4,213	11,162	4,893	1,264	4,167	14,476	4,040	3,376	10,863	5,011	1,253	8,732	3,470	2,603	2,232	1,903
Cruzeiro do Sul, Brazil	13,397	9,565	7,748	14,099	9,041	4,047	8,169	12,110	12,479	14,274	13,192	9,271	4,601	15,941	9,863	15,195	9,252	13,348	10,957	11,720
Cuiaba, Brazil	12,233	9,467	6,185	12,759	7,492	6,003	6,586	11,160	10,792	14,204	11,562	7,901	6,527	14,605	9,194	16,907	9,552	12,189	9,677	10,515
Curitiba, Brazil	12,072	10,155	5,953	12,432	7,210	7,212	6,310	11,216	10,238	13,274	11,038	7,774	7,759	14,167	9,544	18,199	10,443	12,034	9,547	10,408
Cuzco, Peru	13,655	10,089	7,791	14,289	9,099	4,551	8,204	12,434	12,474	13,753	13,225	9,413	5,128	16,155	10,253	15,743	9,842	13,608	11,149	11,948
Dacca, Bangladesh	4,222	7,972	10,232	3,656	8,926	15,380	9,835	5,422	5,725	8,245	4,930	8,524	14,777	1,820	7,625	4,962	8,433	4,269	6,759	5,940
Dakar, Senegal	6,888	4,888	1,795	7,536	2,748	8,773	2,137	5,750	6,134	16,733	6,737	2,733	8,902	9,394	3,931	13,553	5,664	6,842	4,389	5,177
Dallas, Texas	12,116	7,282	9,956	12,975	10,752	1,792	10,297	10,824	13,413	14,959	13,546	10,325	1,323	13,728	8,784	10,074	6,225	12,076	11,069	11,293
Damascus, Syria	1,184	3,907	5,205	2,021	4,019	12,761	4,879	401	2,720	13,058	2,461	3,372	12,475	3,726	2,590	8,748	5,049	1,134	1,632	800
Danang, Vietnam	6,267	9,693	12,210	5,669	10,900	15,244	11,801	7,451	7,564	6,494	6,800	10,549	14,659	3,805	9,594	4,052	9,907	6,313	8,795	7,982
Dar es Salaam, Tanzania	4,220	8,017	4,996	3,827	3,975	15,462	4,596	4,868	1,752	10,426	2,255	4,333	15,582	4,905	6,225	11,419	9,275	4,226	3,844	3,969
Darwin, Australia	10,007	13,658	15,016	9,251	13,874	14,561	14,608	11,324	10,461	2,609	9,876	13,880	14,313	7,459	13,573	5,856	13,649	10,057	12,339	11,638
Davao, Philippines	8,406	11,470	14,276	7,795	12,973	14,365	13,858	9,571	9,558	4,845	8,829	12,673	13,900	5,929	11,640	3,897	11,413	8,453	10,931	10,121
David, Panama	13,232	8,641	8,659	14,088	9,829	2,113	9,075	11,825	13,228	14,919	13,766	9,791	2,597	15,600	9,487	13,117	7,996	13,183	11,204	11,793
Dawson, Canada	9,518	6,081	11,472	10,117	11,413	6,035	11,576	8,789	11,897	13,067	11,477	10,596	5,426	9,957	7,926	5,677	4,852	9,502	10,105	9,751
Dawson Creek, Canada	10,402	6,316	11,108	11,100	11,339	4,650	11,300	9,465	12,564	13,800	12,287	10,608	4,044	11,189	8,163	7,012	5,045	10,379	10,498	10,313
Denpasar, Indonesia	8,342	12,439	13,321	7,550	12,136	16,120	12,904	9,702	8,706	3,762	8,116	12,120	15,759	5,815	12,013	5,939	12,743	8,392	10,599	9,926
Denver, Colorado	11,771	7,097	10,567	12,583	11,204	2,584	10,870	10,590	13,444	14,481	13,421	10,665	1,996	13,051	8,767	9,009	5,926	11,737	11,133	11,213
Derby, Australia	9,633	13,732	14,189	8,821	13,116	15,409	13,793	11,007	9,781	2,455	9,257	13,222	15,205	7,122	13,328	6,540	13,943	9,683	11,807	11,177
Des Moines, Iowa	11,136	6,340	9,588	11,986	10,227	2,808	9,888	9,875	12,596	15,464	12,651	9,705	2,332	12,712	7,924	9,497	5,241	11,098	10,261	10,410
Detroit, Michigan	10,547	5,692	8,712	11,419	9,351	3,249	9,009	9,230	11,819	16,343	11,936	8,843	2,891	12,350	7,175	9,933	4,688	10,506	9,475	9,683
Dhahran, Saudi Arabia	483	5,335	6,196	472	4,904	14,245	5,813	1,837	2,260	11,505	1,591	4,464	13,908	2,301	4,144	8,194	6,376	519	2,709	1,929
Diego Garcia Island	4,902	9,767	8,606	4,027	7,462	18,674	8,192	6,248	4,155	7,380	3,759	7,581	18,301	3,359	8,444	8,668	10,767	4,944	6,371	5,951
Dijon, France	4,133	1,194	4,735	5,016	4,234	9,729	4,656	2,729	5,301	15,955	5,336	3,377	9,471	6,493	668	9,392	2,459	4,086	3,035	3,087
Dili, Indonesia	9,289	13,002	14,460	8,540	13,268	15,022	14,043	10,603	9,825	3,210	9,213	13,219	14,707	6,741	12,855	5,550	13,079	9,339	11,642	10,929
Djibouti, Djibouti	2,141	6,346	5,236	1,852	3,945	14,885	4,816	2,923	564	11,236	241	3,835	14,733	3,369	4,737	9,783	7,542	2,147	2,518	2,238
Dnepropetrovsk, USSR	2,306	2,642	6,038	3,158	5,073	11,511	5,804	1,270	4,384	13,756	4,064	4,266	11,137	4,348	2,174	7,784	3,593	2,270	2,881	2,288
Dobo, Indonesia	9,948	13,163	15,412	9,259	14,183	14,019	14,991	11,189	10,722	3,261	10,072	14,056	13,706	7,413	13,328	5,072	13,015	9,996	12,399	11,637
Doha, Qatar	646	5,508	6,312	300	5,014	14,419	5,923	2,017	2,254	11,326	1,545	4,597	14,077	2,155	4,324	8,148	6,540	686	2,853	2,089
Donetsk, USSR	2,155	2,841	6,173	2,992	5,176	11,690	5,927	1,237	4,320	13,541	3,964	4,384	11,306	4,140	2,375	7,647	3,761	2,121	2,935	2,292
Dover, Delaware	10,369	5,510	8,046	11,254	8,748	3,422	8,358	9,005	11,402	16,971	11,599	8,291	3,184	12,368	6,839	10,550	4,640	10,325	9,063	9,352
Dresden, East Germany	3,660	1,234	5,333	4,545	4,683	10,125	5,208	2,311	5,190	15,306	5,098	3,816	9,810	5,888	1,085	8,682	2,428	3,615	3,091	2,921
Dubayy, United Arab Emir.	892	5,730	6,685	129	5,385	14,634	6,295	2,302	2,514	11,009	1,755	4,976	14,259	1,776	4,632	7,842	6,714	940	3,232	2,459
Dublin, Ireland	5,038	498	5,328	5,924	5,045	8,762	5,327	3,664	6,343	16,593	6,360	4,221	8,473	7,257	1,690	9,201	1,523	4,992	4,071	4,119
Duluth, Minnesota	10,587	5,830	9,436	11,428	9,973	3,397	9,708	9,351	12,147	15,630	12,155	9,397	2,911	12,123	7,469	9,117	4,698	10,550	9,831	9,930
Dunedin, New Zealand	14,793	18,654	15,480	13,918	15,639	11,304	15,449	16,204	13,885	2,942	13,742	16,417	11,515	12,406	18,495	9,952	17,740	14,842	16,224	15,988
Durango, Mexico	13,336	8,516	10,851	14,186	11,769	937	11,222	12,058	14,615	13,873	14,778	11,422	340	14,789	10,013	10,276	7,440	13,297	12,274	12,524
Durban, South Africa	6,907	10,129	5,398	6,508	5,016	14,851	5,144	7,415	4,381	9,579	4,949	5,740	15,300	7,352	8,269	13,609	11,391	6,911	6,038	6,413
Dushanbe, USSR	2,089	5,409	8,153	2,073	6,920	13,761	7,807	2,940	4,442	10,854	3,699	6,330	13,251	1,758	5,020	5,995	6,040	2,120	4,559	3,698
East London, South Africa	7,334	10,383	5,421	6,955	5,162	14,523	5,202	7,793	4,794	9,585	5,385	5,926	15,002	7,811	8,528	14,038	11,634	7,337	6,353	6,773
Easter Island (Hanga Roa)	17,827	13,534	11,808	18,381	13,107	4,975	12,197	16,544	16,122	10,101	16,924	13,536	5,479	19,509	14,244	13,568	12,782	17,779	15,302	16,117
Echo Bay, Canada	9,251	5,336	10,519	9,945	10,559	5,630	10,650	8,347	11,459	14,092	11,149	9,773	5,040	10,083	7,196	6,541	4,072	9,228	9,476	9,230
Edinburgh, United Kingdom	4,897	151	5,612	5,781	5,265	8,883	5,592	3,555	6,352	16,299	6,317	4,426	8,566	7,041	1,780	8,856	1,349	4,854	4,131	4,100
Edmonton, Canada	10,546	6,256	10,796	11,283	11,113	4,239	11,011	9,531	12,591	14,179	12,378	10,417	3,641	11,500	8,077	7,511	4,995	10,519	10,442	10,325
El Aaiun, Morocco	5,940	3,443	2,606	6,697	2,927	8,861	2,760	4,655	5,801	17,211	6,244	2,456	8,849	8,489	2,581	12,103	4,293	5,891	3,666	4,315
Elat, Israel	1,288	4,198	4,894	2,005	3,669	12,960	4,549	829	2,305	12,982	2,130	3,080	12,711	3,814	2,724	9,132	5,381	1,242	1,300	440
Elazig, Turkey	1,242	3,625	5,711	2,127	4,573	12,537	5,407	392	3,285	13,058	2,928	3,874	12,199	3,605	2,604	8,180	4,681	1,199	2,201	1,413
Eniwetok Atoll, Marshall Isls.	11,587	12,263	17,617	11,249	16,441	10,468	17,315	12,304	13,386	5,713	12,599	15,785	10,098	9,486	13,503	3,812	11,447	11,623	14,063	13,206
Erfurt, East Germany	3,831	1,096	5,253	4,717	4,650	9,960	5,144	2,469	5,298	15,497	5,231	3,783	9,653	6,075	1,023	8,806	2,324	3,786	3,154	3,033
Erzurum, Turkey	1,238	3,645	5,929	2,106	4,797	12,551	5,629	613	3,431	12,953	3,031	4,095	12,195	3,489	2,735	7,956	4,657	1,200	2,424	1,630
Esfahan, Iran	411	4,862	6,505	947	5,251	13,750	6,146	1,568	2,936	11,755	2,305	4,704	13,367	2,320	3,897	7,665	5,823	437	2,919	2,066
Essen, West Germany	4,112	866	5,216	4,998	4,689	9,684	5,133	2,743	5,520	15,772	5,480	3,827	9,384	6,360	1,068	8,929	2,126	4,067	3,330	3,264
Eucla, Australia	10,928	15,347	14,322	10,067	13,536	14,856	13,996	12,336	10,552	973	10,181	13,885	14,873	8,519	14,673	7,994	15,624	10,977	12,795	12,306
Fargo, North Dakota	10,766	6,064	9,792	11,591	10,316	3,342	10,062	9,563	12,415	15,273	12,388	9,727	2,817	12,190	7,741	8,882	4,899	10,730	10,113	10,180
Faroe Islands (Torshavn)	5,268	604	6,295	6,135	5,974	8,529	6,289	4,001	6,931	16,147	6,829	5,135	8,164	7,220	2,462	8,342	689	5,228	4,771	4,663
Florence, Italy	3,576	1,757	4,516	4,450	3,855	10,336	4,381	2,166	4,678	15,458	4,712	2,987	10,089	6,003	291	9,435	3,027	3,528	2,433	2,461
Florianopolis, Brazil	12,112	10,348	6,011	12,438	7,250	7,406	6,357	11,300	10,208	13,044	11,011	7,841	7,960	14,140	9,687	18,444	10,663	12,075	9,605	10,466
Fort George, Canada	9,395	4,614	8,548	10,247	8,941	4,486	8,776	8,140	10,940	16,422	10,939	8,307	4,056	11,064	6,264	8,985	3,500	9,357	8,634	8,715
Fort McMurray, Canada	10,168	5,897	10,559	10,908	10,821	4,530	10,757	9,154	12,219	14,359	12,000	10,107	3,940	11,158	7,726	7,404	4,632	10,141	10,085	9,953
Fort Nelson, Canada	10,090	6,123	11,091	10,771	11,247	5,019	11,260	9,190	12,301	13,732	11,993	10,490	4,413	10,825	7,979	6,712	4,852	10,068	10,288	10,065
Fort Severn, Canada	9,571	4,905	9,122	10,397	9,468	4,466	9,339	8,379	11,283	15,822	11,216	8,804	3,975	11,053	6,635	8,485	3,716	9,536	9,017	9,030
Fort Smith, Arkansas	11,753	6,918	9,709	12,614	10,464	2,125	10,039	10,460	13,064	15,255	13,186	10,013	1,682	13,397	8,426	9,991	5,864	11,714	10,720	10,933
Fort Vermilion, Canada	10,063	5,927	10,756	10,778	10,961	4,799	10,938	9,099	12,190	14,107	11,930	10,223	4,202	10,945	7,774	7,071	4,657	10,038	10,111	9,936
Fort Wayne, Indiana	10,767	5,913	8,880	11,637	9,542	3,037	9,184	9,452	12,040	16,163	12,159	9,046	2,670	12,547	7,398	9,958	4,901	10,725	9,696	9,906
Fort-Chimo, Canada	8,587	3,802	8,021	9,443	8,300	5,264	8,214	7,327	10,144	16,750	10,128	7,622	4,854	10,319	5,475	8,845	2,693	8,548	7,853	7,909
Fort-de-France, Martinique	10,979	6,802	6,324	11,793	7,437	4,163	6,728	9,601	10,806	17,023	11,344	7,366	4,420	13,484	7,276	13,605	6,511	10,929	8,804	9,438
Fortaleza, Brazil	9,912	7,499	3,961	10,476	5,265	7,122	4,378	8,833	8,680	15,716	9,407	5,598	7,495	12,339	6,946	16,015	7,873	9,867	7,362	8,192
Frankfort, Kentucky	10,998	6,135	8,847	11,874	9,566	2,786	9,166	9,666	12,178	16,153	12,334	9,106	2,461	12,832	7,567	10,238	5,157	10,956	9,834	10,081
Frankfurt am Main, W. Ger.	3,953	1,055	5,107	4,840	4,542	9,852	5,010	2,574	5,332	15,668	5,297	3,678	9,559	6,232	911	8,983	2,315	3,907	3,143	3,077
Fredericton, Canada	9,324	4,462	7,489	10,207	8,033	4,460	7,756	7,966	10,457	17,567	10,604	7,492	4,185	11,333	5,837	10,148	3,608	9,280	8,113	8,351
Freeport, Bahamas	11,571	6,779	8,236	12,456	9,167	2,430	8,605	10,172	12,218	16,350	12,555	8,877	2,440	13,724	7,900	11,642	6,015	11,524	9,947	10,368
Freetown, Sierra Leone	6,811	5,481	1,078	7,366	2,249	9,395	1,476	5,814	5,711	15,919	6,381	2,486	9,571	9,230	4,286	14,008	6,357	6,767	4,255	5,095
Frobisher Bay, Canada	8,211	3,555	8,243	9,046	8,394	5,733	8,398	7,012	9,941	16,307	9,852	7,664	5,283	9,808	5,329	8,259	2,349	8,175	7,708	7,679

Distances in Kilometers	Abadan, Iran	Aberdeen, United Kingdom	Abidjan, Ivory Coast	Abu Dhabi, United Arab Emir.	Abuja, Nigeria	Acapulco, Mexico	Accra, Ghana	Adana, Turkey	Addis Ababa, Ethiopia	Adelaide, Australia	Aden, P.D.R. Yemen	Agadez, Niger	Aguascalientes, Mexico	Ahmadabad, India	Ajaccio, France	Akita, Japan	Akureyri, Iceland	Al Basrah, Iraq	Al Jawf, Libya	Al Minya, Egypt
Frunze, USSR	2,720	5,403	8,684	2,760	7,485	13,366	8,356	3,389	5,125	10,794	4,386	6,849	12,825	2,211	5,278	5,357	5,876	2,746	5,103	4,246
Fukuoka, Japan	7,555	9,011	13,577	7,315	12,385	12,295	13,257	8,258	9,620	7,633	8,816	11,739	11,718	5,715	9,749	1,103	8,672	7,588	10,005	9,148
Funafuti Atoll, Tuvalu	14,387	14,610	19,523	13,919	19,149	9,337	19,670	15,199	15,686	5,057	15,000	18,681	9,202	12,069	16,187	6,683	13,523	14,427	16,924	16,063
Funchal, Madeira Island	6,097	2,948	3,307	6,906	3,590	8,382	3,463	4,741	6,266	17,749	6,636	3,043	8,322	8,626	2,483	11,653	3,675	6,047	4,023	4,571
Fuzhou, China	6,874	9,289	13,001	6,472	11,723	13,649	12,629	7,815	8,644	7,053	7,845	11,203	13,067	4,717	9,651	2,455	9,206	6,914	9,420	8,563
Gaborone, Botswana	6,538	9,437	4,639	6,243	4,259	14,358	4,380	6,898	3,979	10,336	4,633	5,000	14,754	7,301	7,581	13,742	10,690	6,536	5,414	5,862
Galapagos Islands (Santa Cruz)	14,558	9,962	9,621	15,404	10,861	2,199	10,044	13,153	14,320	13,591	14,936	10,929	2,807	16,930	10,813	13,327	9,265	14,508	12,441	13,074
Gander, Canada	8,387	3,542	6,776	9,272	7,201	5,410	7,006	7,018	9,500	18,113	9,639	6,610	5,148	10,477	4,872	10,076	2,813	8,342	7,156	7,387
Gangtok, India	3,932	7,541	10,008	3,436	8,710	15,031	9,620	5,075	5,612	8,669	4,809	8,263	14,435	1,680	7,240	4,907	7,994	3,976	6,486	5,651
Garyarsa, China	3,057	6,668	9,176	2,672	7,895	14,627	8,801	4,147	4,978	9,569	4,177	7,399	14,063	1,232	6,304	5,378	7,206	3,099	5,615	4,767
Gaspe, Canada	9,001	4,135	7,432	9,882	7,906	4,778	7,679	7,654	10,209	17,572	10,326	7,328	4,478	10,982	5,562	9,902	3,255	8,958	7,867	8,072
Gauhati, India	4,265	7,825	10,330	3,754	9,031	15,082	9,940	5,410	5,895	8,374	5,095	8,593	14,477	1,965	7,565	4,704	8,237	4,309	6,817	5,984
Gdansk, Poland	3,564	1,335	5,810	4,436	5,115	10,222	5,673	2,309	5,333	14,971	5,158	4,249	9,868	5,641	1,564	8,187	2,357	3,523	3,370	3,076
Geneva, Switzerland	4,023	1,342	4,636	4,903	4,106	9,858	4,547	2,615	5,152	15,871	5,195	3,246	9,606	6,406	518	9,447	2,609	3,975	2,883	2,944
Genoa, Italy	3,771	1,611	4,514	4,646	3,910	10,139	4,399	2,361	4,858	15,648	4,904	3,045	9,894	6,188	278	9,486	2,882	3,723	2,594	2,652
Georgetown, Guyana	11,191	7,380	5,992	11,945	7,201	4,673	6,412	[illegible]	10,650	16,453	11,270	7,264	5,022	13,738	7,602	14,525	7,231	11,141	8,845	9,557
Geraldton, Australia	9,607	14,242	13,084	8,733	12,196	16,265	12,728	11,017	9,143	2,366	8,774	12,496	16,253	7,288	13,336	8,029	14,790	9,655	11,388	10,920
Ghanzi, Botswana	6,404	9,002	4,096	6,194	3,755	13,914	3,842	6,638	3,857	10,879	4,568	4,521	14,281	7,397	7,156	13,906	10,243	6,398	5,066	5,579
Ghat, Libya	3,787	3,706	2,652	4,451	1,777	11,150	2,419	2,733	3,498	14,982	3,897	915	11,077	6,299	1,885	11,168	4,946	3,741	1,331	2,076
Gibraltar	4,976	2,347	3,415	5,798	3,245	9,323	3,427	3,612	5,365	16,773	5,646	2,499	9,199	7,498	1,376	10,895	3,391	4,926	3,045	3,500
Gijon, Spain	4,931	1,533	4,237	5,798	4,008	9,073	4,242	3,522	5,744	16,820	5,907	3,215	8,876	7,364	1,192	10,167	2,580	4,882	3,402	3,670
Gisborne, New Zealand	15,377	17,951	16,305	14,538	16,613	10,499	16,332	16,760	14,804	3,515	14,584	17,415	10,656	12,874	19,042	9,501	16,828	15,427	17,147	16,782
Glasgow, United Kingdom	4,959	196	5,602	5,843	5,273	8,821	5,588	3,614	6,399	16,363	6,369	4,437	8,507	7,107	1,811	8,895	1,324	4,916	4,169	4,149
Godthab, Greenland	7,465	2,738	7,548	8,317	7,618	6,392	7,675	6,227	9,121	16,672	9,053	6,868	5,982	9,208	4,501	8,433	1,571	7,427	6,880	6,863
Gomez Palacio, Mexico	13,131	8,309	10,707	13,982	11,604	1,034	11,073	11,851	14,417	14,054	14,573	11,243	426	14,611	9,808	10,235	7,236	13,092	12,075	12,319
Goose Bay, Canada	10,944	6,991	11,771	11,600	12,029	4,551	11,974	10,072	13,184	13,187	12,863	11,300	3,941	11,527	8,843	6,831	5,719	10,923	11,165	10,951
Gorki, USSR	2,908	2,769	7,054	3,638	6,131	11,226	6,840	2,244	5,267	13,423	4,835	5,312	10,779	4,372	2,984	6,790	3,358	2,886	3,944	3,308
Goteborg, Sweden	4,119	846	5,977	4,988	5,402	9,673	5,883	2,868	5,868	15,356	5,713	4,535	9,312	6,136	1,772	8,180	1,796	4,079	3,831	3,602
Granada, Spain	4,812	2,217	3,533	5,642	3,294	9,431	3,525	3,440	5,278	16,641	5,533	2,520	9,291	7,327	1,186	10,720	3,302	4,762	2,945	3,364
Grand Turk, Turks & Caicos	11,371	6,766	7,431	12,239	8,445	3,066	7,817	9,960	11,661	16,764	12,093	8,246	3,221	13,717	7,631	12,498	6,193	11,322	9,485	10,003
Graz, Austria	3,368	1,635	4,990	4,253	4,274	10,451	4,840	1,978	4,756	15,165	4,698	3,408	10,162	5,703	782	8,944	2,865	3,321	2,632	2,491
Green Bay, Wisconsin	10,609	5,793	9,121	11,466	9,711	3,264	9,406	9,332	12,035	15,946	12,096	9,168	2,832	12,271	7,363	9,510	4,716	10,570	9,701	9,852
Grenoble, France	4,038	1,437	4,516	4,914	3,992	9,871	4,428	2,627	5,101	15,906	5,164	3,134	9,630	6,443	436	9,562	2,699	3,989	2,816	2,911
Guadalajara, Mexico	13,601	8,754	10,773	14,464	11,748	555	11,156	12,293	14,728	13,820	14,953	11,452	172	15,150	10,189	10,639	7,714	13,561	12,403	12,704
Guam (Agana)	9,876	11,608	16,001	9,443	14,715	12,171	15,624	10,778	11,494	5,396	10,717	14,202	11,733	7,633	12,406	2,944	11,114	9,916	12,421	11,563
Guantanamo, Cuba	11,788	7,132	7,848	12,660	8,881	2,633	8,239	10,378	12,109	16,330	12,540	8,692	2,821	14,098	8,054	12,437	6,499	11,740	9,931	10,442
Guatemala City, Guatemala	13,365	8,559	9,493	14,251	10,581	1,037	9,896	11,966	13,846	14,640	14,266	10,424	1,481	15,456	9,683	12,037	7,728	13,319	11,652	12,127
Guayaquil, Ecuador	13,740	9,471	8,469	14,527	9,729	3,048	8,893	12,374	13,193	14,282	13,850	9,855	3,613	16,260	10,053	14,225	8,971	13,690	11,448	12,145
Guiyang, China	5,677	8,616	11,789	5,231	10,499	14,411	11,407	6,707	7,388	7,592	6,588	10,018	13,804	3,460	8,700	3,413	8,759	5,719	8,234	7,385
Gur'yev, USSR	1,889	3,751	7,048	2,523	5,950	12,383	6,764	1,766	4,402	12,527	3,862	5,220	11,938	3,251	3,434	6,804	4,485	1,878	3,590	2,799
Haifa, Israel	1,288	3,897	5,063	2,104	3,878	12,722	4,737	465	2,663	13,137	2,445	3,231	12,448	3,836	2,522	8,888	5,058	1,239	1,491	665
Haikou, China	6,283	9,425	12,327	5,750	11,020	14,765	11,928	7,395	7,763	6,780	6,982	10,609	14,176	3,909	9,458	3,582	9,564	6,328	8,835	8,002
Haiphong, Vietnam	5,899	9,154	11,937	5,361	10,630	14,931	11,538	7,026	7,382	7,037	6,598	10,222	14,332	3,520	9,117	3,801	9,352	5,944	8,449	7,618
Hakodate, Japan	8,025	8,509	13,692	7,954	12,653	11,030	13,446	8,467	10,330	8,494	9,542	11,900	10,446	6,559	9,563	231	7,955	8,050	10,284	9,460
Halifax, Canada	9,221	4,376	7,217	10,107	7,780	4,581	7,488	7,849	10,269	17,843	10,443	7,254	4,339	11,296	5,680	10,365	3,594	9,177	7,925	8,194
Hamburg, West Germany	4,009	864	5,498	4,892	4,929	9,770	5,403	2,678	5,566	15,544	5,475	4,063	9,446	6,180	1,297	8,621	2,052	3,966	3,444	3,297
Hamilton, Bermuda	10,128	5,432	6,958	11,008	7,780	3,925	7,297	8,721	10,726	17,844	11,053	7,427	3,875	12,398	6,422	11,632	4,840	10,080	8,446	8,873
Hamilton, New Zealand	15,130	17,845	16,408	14,296	16,620	10,699	16,406	16,508	14,635	3,287	14,386	17,390	10,840	12,621	18,784	9,303	16,784	15,180	16,970	16,563
Hangzhou, China	6,787	8,921	12,902	6,453	11,650	13,263	12,547	7,643	8,697	7,470	7,893	11,080	12,674	4,768	9,379	2,096	8,787	6,825	9,307	8,447
Hannover, West Germany	3,974	926	5,367	4,859	4,796	9,810	5,270	2,625	5,475	15,577	5,401	3,931	9,496	6,183	1,164	8,738	2,146	3,930	3,332	3,209
Hanoi, Vietnam	5,812	9,093	11,848	5,272	10,542	14,967	11,450	6,943	7,295	7,096	6,510	10,134	14,366	3,431	9,040	3,855	9,305	5,857	8,362	7,531
Harare, Zimbabwe	5,640	8,860	4,627	5,320	3,975	14,837	4,300	6,087	3,088	10,406	3,716	4,605	15,145	6,394	7,003	12,874	10,130	5,641	4,726	5,082
Harbin, China	6,810	7,653	12,548	6,757	11,465	11,645	12,280	7,278	9,139	9,016	8,358	10,733	11,040	5,444	8,516	1,288	7,284	6,835	9,087	8,256
Harrisburg, Pennsylvania	10,366	5,501	8,177	11,248	8,857	3,415	8,483	9,011	11,460	16,857	11,636	8,384	3,147	12,321	6,871	10,388	4,597	10,322	9,118	9,385
Hartford, Connecticut	9,995	5,134	7,852	10,878	8,498	3,793	8,148	8,633	11,069	17,203	11,246	8,009	3,536	11,994	6,482	10,394	4,266	9,951	8,727	8,996
Havana, Cuba	12,092	7,296	8,593	12,977	9,575	1,962	8,974	10,693	12,694	15,860	13,053	9,324	2,054	14,230	8,417	11,774	6,511	12,045	10,442	10,879
Helena, Montana	11,259	6,816	10,938	12,017	11,403	3,483	11,195	10,188	13,196	14,121	13,044	10,769	2,879	12,280	8,593	8,073	5,579	11,230	10,974	10,928
Helsinki, Finland	3,742	1,595	6,560	4,568	5,850	10,154	6,422	2,677	5,789	14,588	5,512	4,987	9,745	5,521	2,313	7,464	2,223	3,709	3,997	3,590
Hengyang, China	6,218	8,887	12,341	5,800	11,058	14,034	11,965	7,197	7,973	7,371	7,173	10,554	13,437	4,044	9,110	2,913	8,920	6,259	8,770	7,916
Herat, Afghanistan	1,383	5,358	7,503	1,331	6,245	14,035	7,142	2,445	3,689	11,041	2,954	5,701	13,572	1,612	4,686	6,736	6,147	1,420	3,918	3,062
Hermosillo, Mexico	13,074	8,385	11,358	13,878	12,163	1,763	11,705	11,891	14,690	13,552	14,712	11,720	1,179	14,227	10,014	9,437	7,227	13,041	12,356	12,487
Hiroshima, Japan	7,694	9,004	13,682	7,475	12,508	12,090	13,372	8,363	9,793	7,702	8,990	11,845	11,514	5,897	9,797	901	8,624	7,726	10,123	9,269
Hiva Oa (Atuona)	17,611	13,595	15,050	17,861	16,328	5,218	15,472	16,937	19,771	8,703	19,475	16,380	5,327	16,358	15,264	9,930	12,376	17,609	17,562	17,720
Ho Chi Minh City, Vietnam	6,390	10,112	12,154	5,720	10,852	15,792	11,737	7,648	7,442	6,074	6,708	10,579	15,218	3,862	9,868	4,603	10,405	6,439	8,866	8,084
Hobart, Australia	12,926	17,348	14,983	12,051	14,636	13,113	14,788	14,336	12,207	1,164	11,967	15,226	13,270	10,561	16,647	9,181	17,317	12,974	14,540	14,182
Hohhot, China	5,734	7,522	11,733	5,564	10,544	12,846	11,413	6,417	7,923	8,828	7,128	9,896	12,236	4,134	8,015	2,417	7,436	5,765	8,161	7,305
Hong Kong	6,554	9,413	12,647	6,071	11,348	14,317	12,257	7,601	8,151	6,835	7,361	10,894	13,733	4,257	9,580	3,125	9,459	6,597	9,112	8,267
Honiara, Solomon Islands	12,618	14,492	18,210	12,017	17,046	11,388	17,806	13,698	13,589	3,563	12,935	16,887	11,197	10,152	15,444	5,814	13,760	12,664	15,155	14,337
Honolulu, Hawaii	13,648	11,023	15,917	13,865	16,264	6,086	16,172	13,403	16,198	9,150	15,490	15,501	5,721	12,671	12,870	6,165	9,781	13,654	14,968	14,460
Houston, Texas	12,325	7,470	9,852	13,194	10,704	1,504	10,206	11,007	13,494	14,975	13,677	10,321	1,116	14,024	8,910	10,419	6,451	12,284	11,156	11,425
Huambo, Angola	5,901	7,917	2,965	5,875	2,602	13,126	2,687	5,874	3,495	12,013	4,286	3,395	13,414	7,348	6,094	13,830	9,138	5,885	4,167	4,797
Hubli, India	3,208	7,819	8,706	2,396	7,402	16,403	8,290	4,603	4,024	8,702	3,266	7,151	15,877	892	6,942	6,802	8,611	3,258	5,493	4,778
Hugh Town, United Kingdom	5,000	850	4,948	5,885	4,688	8,846	4,951	3,603	6,142	16,728	6,209	3,874	8,590	7,306	1,463	9,547	1,882	4,953	3,835	3,957
Hull, Canada	9,895	5,031	8,165	10,771	8,738	3,887	8,443	8,565	11,139	16,902	11,256	8,201	3,558	11,777	6,494	9,920	4,069	9,853	8,796	9,003
Hyderabad, India	3,379	7,833	9,048	2,622	7,740	16,214	8,635	4,745	4,399	8,592	3,628	7,451	15,660	874	7,074	6,384	8,556	3,429	5,758	5,010
Hyderabad, Pakistan	2,052	6,505	7,995	1,417	6,692	15,167	7,601	3,384	3,622	9,961	2,818	6,290	14,682	503	5,707	6,747	7,304	2,101	4,538	3,740
Igloolik, Canada	8,236	3,892	8,974	9,022	9,015	5,971	9,099	7,155	10,201	15,454	10,009	8,242	5,458	9,552	5,738	7,431	2,622	8,205	8,078	7,935
Iloilo, Philippines	7,919	10,961	13,858	7,332	12,549	14,447	13,445	9,064	9,170	5,326	8,424	12,212	13,943	5,467	11,119	3,653	10,939	7,965	10,456	9,638
Indianapolis, Indiana	10,933	6,078	8,963	11,804	9,650	2,868	9,273	9,617	12,187	16,064	12,316	9,167	2,505	12,713	7,553	10,031	5,069	10,892	9,843	10,063
Innsbruck, Austria	3,665	1,429	4,878	4,549	4,242	10,170	4,755	2,267	4,961	15,473	4,942	3,375	9,893	6,010	631	9,118	2,689	3,617	2,769	2,712
Inuvik, Canada	9,061	5,539	10,962	9,691	10,876	6,196	11,056	8,285	11,400	13,471	11,007	10,057	5,594	9,646	7,385	5,819	4,313	9,043	9,571	9,233
Invercargill, New Zealand	14,629	18,646	15,394	13,752	15,509	11,479	15,347	16,039	13,709	2,797	13,566	16,276	11,691	12,255	18,321	9,944	17,825	14,678	16,049	15,812
Inverness, United Kingdom	5,000	134	5,784	5,881	5,448	8,778	5,769	3,675	6,508	16,285	6,457	4,609	8,449	7,097	1,959	8,732	1,169	4,957	4,301	4,251
Iquitos, Peru	13,233	9,236	7,762	13,975	9,036	3,715	8,185	11,909	12,495	14,590	13,178	9,208	4,250	15,781	9,627	14,807	8,875	13,183	10,851	11,586
Iraklion, Greece	2,230	3,164	4,472	3,055	3,425	11,838	4,199	933	3,223	14,083	3,201	2,652	11,601	4,767	1,601	9,362	4,396	2,180	1,247	962
Irkutsk, USSR	5,127	6,162	10,773	5,198	9,692	11,999	10,503	5,505	7,569	10,219	6,824	8,957	11,394	4,220	6,809	3,061	6,045	5,147	7,320	6,498
Islamabad, Pakistan	2,376	6,072	8,503	2,092	7,233	14,363	8,136	3,439	4,460	10,207	3,675	6,711	13,835	1,183	5,614	5,881	6,701	2,416	4,926	4,074
Istanbul, Turkey	2,104	2,850	5,140	2,987	4,131	11,721	4,885	705	3,671	13,971	3,500	3,340	11,422	4,520	1,689	8,682	4,004	2,056	1,938	1,442
Ivujivik, Canada	8,669	4,051	8,657	9,494	8,856	5,342	8,828	7,490	10,436	16,042	10,336	8,139	4,867	10,182	5,827	8,185	2,833	8,634	8,206	8,172
Iwo Jima Island, Japan	8,937	10,306	15,007	8,627	13,792	11,942	14,676	9,693	10,854	6,616	10,052	13,170	11,425	6,922	11,164	1,660	9,824	8,972	11,422	10,562
Izmir, Turkey	2,133	2,980	4,833	2,997	3,806	11,780	4,570	735	3,454	14,028	3,347	3,023	11,508	4,622	1,613	8,993	4,176	2,083	1,618	1,192
Jackson, Mississippi	11,812	6,948	9,340	12,688	10,160	1,972	9,685	10,477	12,927	15,534	13,120	9,761	1,663	13,616	8,355	10,501	5,967	11,770	10,590	10,870
Jaffna, Sri Lanka	4,008	8,634	9,268	3,173	7,981	17,072	8,846	5,410	4,535	7,892	3,833	7,806	16,506	1,675	7,750	6,784	9,401	4,057	6,208	5,531
Jakarta, Indonesia	7,426	11,716	12,381	6,616	11,179	16,892	11,962	8,805	7,740	4,558	7,147	11,152	16,448	4,926	11,134	6,125	12,165	7,476	9,639	8,980
Jamestown, St. Helena	7,723	8,104	2,358	7,907	3,119	10,953	2,452	7,270	5,620	13,238	6,424	3,937	11,325	9,551	6,575	15,789	9,108	7,695	5,446	6,260
Jamnagar, India	2,338	6,866	8,158	1,618	6,849	15,522	7,756	3,702	3,664	9,623	2,862	6,493	15,030	269	6,034	6,780	7,669	2,388	4,765	3,992
Jan Mayen Island	5,677	1,580	7,301	6,497	6,959	8,278	7,294	4,561	7,624	15,560	7,416	6,111	7,841	7,299	3,387	7,481	702	5,644	5,596	5,367
Jayapura, Indonesia	10,390	13,123	16,110	9,761	14,842	13,225	15,686	11,549	11,381	3,594	10,697	14,625	12,904	7,897	13,550	4,679	12,801	10,437	12,904	12,103
Jefferson City, Missouri	11,348	6,517	9,485	12,208	10,185	2,523	9,800	10,058	12,695	15,530	12,796	9,703	2,088	13,004	8,043	9,836	5,457	11,308	10,352	10,546
Jerusalem, Israel	1,253	4,007	5,028	2,043	3,827	12,817	4,694	582	2,542	13,066	2,330	3,200	12,550	3,802	2,604	8,949	5,173	1,204	1,441	594

Distances in Kilometers	Abadan, Iran	Aberdeen, United Kingdom	Abidjan, Ivory Coast	Abu Dhabi, United Arab Emir.	Abuja, Nigeria	Acapulco, Mexico	Accra, Ghana	Adana, Turkey	Addis Ababa, Ethiopia	Adelaide, Australia	Aden, P.D.R. Yemen	Agadez, Niger	Aguascalientes, Mexico	Ahmadabad, India	Ajaccio, France	Akita, Japan	Akureyri, Iceland	Al Basrah, Iraq	Al Jawf, Libya	Al Minya, Egypt
Jiggalong, Australia	9,760	14,132	13,796	8,913	12,821	15,730	13,421	11,162	9,613	2,148	9,163	13,032	15,617	7,317	13,502	7,270	14,480	9,810	11,762	11,206
Jinan, China	6,290	8,155	12,342	6,053	11,131	12,933	12,011	7,036	8,376	8,237	7,574	10,507	12,329	4,502	8,669	2,047	8,021	6,324	8,757	7,898
Jodhpur, India	2,465	6,706	8,466	1,888	7,164	15,173	8,074	3,744	4,093	9,671	3,288	6,748	14,652	362	6,036	6,298	7,425	2,513	4,985	4,174
Johannesburg, South Africa	6,616	9,659	4,916	6,279	4,519	14,581	4,655	7,038	4,064	10,058	4,685	5,248	14,991	7,259	7,800	13,647	10,917	6,616	5,600	6,015
Juazeiro do Norte, Brazil	10,186	7,892	4,158	10,717	5,468	7,178	4,568	9,146	8,840	15,336	9,585	5,853	7,582	12,572	7,307	16,402	8,267	10,142	7,630	8,469
Juneau, Alaska	10,179	6,526	11,692	10,796	11,767	5,403	11,840	9,398	12,515	13,067	12,127	10,982	4,792	10,651	8,385	6,117	5,269	10,162	10,632	10,331
Kabul, Afghanistan	2,019	5,765	8,144	1,816	6,881	14,205	7,781	3,062	4,200	10,544	3,430	6,345	13,699	1,316	5,249	6,163	6,446	2,057	4,561	3,706
Kalgoorlie, Australia	10,274	14,826	13,685	9,405	12,850	15,569	13,344	11,685	9,839	1,667	9,473	13,178	15,579	7,913	14,012	8,036	15,261	10,323	12,087	11,613
Kaliningrad, USSR	3,495	1,431	5,905	4,363	5,188	10,298	5,761	2,268	5,318	14,853	5,122	4,325	9,936	5,539	1,665	8,075	2,409	3,455	3,396	3,071
Kamloops, Canada	10,962	6,789	11,350	11,666	11,681	4,170	11,572	10,003	13,088	13,650	12,835	10,984	3,559	11,743	8,621	7,313	5,522	10,938	10,977	10,829
Kampala, Uganda	3,714	7,014	4,107	3,557	2,980	14,489	3,691	4,073	1,179	11,491	1,944	3,266	14,554	5,005	5,192	11,483	8,282	3,707	2,826	3,081
Kananga, Zaire	4,866	7,333	3,191	4,826	2,373	13,647	2,816	4,936	2,448	11,968	3,242	2,986	13,838	6,327	5,475	12,785	8,592	4,852	3,331	3,867
Kano, Nigeria	4,567	5,089	1,566	5,017	346	11,539	1,156	3,851	3,319	14,402	3,967	553	11,600	6,866	3,315	12,416	6,292	4,529	2,064	2,921
Kanpur, India	3,163	7,130	9,196	2,618	7,895	15,212	8,804	4,383	4,791	9,153	3,987	7,470	14,648	870	6,627	5,663	7,730	3,209	5,702	4,880
Kansas City, Missouri	11,413	6,604	9,690	12,266	10,374	2,520	10,002	10,143	12,829	15,336	12,905	9,879	2,046	12,999	8,165	9,661	5,518	11,375	10,489	10,659
Kaohsiung, Taiwan	7,115	9,674	13,230	6,667	11,938	13,836	12,848	8,107	8,775	6,659	7,984	11,455	13,268	4,871	9,995	2,664	9,601	7,157	9,670	8,819
Karachi, Pakistan	1,948	6,469	7,860	1,284	6,555	15,180	7,464	3,299	3,478	10,030	2,675	6,162	14,707	602	5,629	6,889	7,293	1,997	4,414	3,624
Karaganda, USSR	3,005	4,801	8,641	3,253	7,519	12,587	8,350	3,335	5,533	11,382	4,847	6,809	12,049	2,975	4,922	5,235	5,170	3,019	5,140	4,313
Karl-Marx-Stadt, East Germany	3,703	1,205	5,287	4,589	4,650	10,085	5,167	2,347	5,204	15,365	5,123	3,783	9,774	5,942	1,042	8,737	2,414	3,658	3,088	2,937
Kasanga, Tanzania	4,667	7,878	4,193	4,431	3,296	14,653	3,811	5,053	2,109	11,037	2,805	3,797	14,838	5,704	6,029	12,231	9,149	4,664	3,713	4,046
Kashgar, China	2,714	5,757	8,780	2,622	7,549	13,754	8,436	3,540	5,006	10,453	4,242	6,954	13,209	1,851	5,539	5,385	6,262	2,745	5,185	4,325
Kassel, West Germany	3,944	994	5,252	4,830	4,679	9,847	5,153	2,581	5,395	15,602	5,337	3,813	9,542	6,186	1,047	8,841	2,233	3,899	3,234	3,132
Kathmandu, Nepal	3,605	7,314	9,679	3,109	8,382	15,042	9,292	4,764	5,303	8,915	4,499	7,935	14,456	1,378	6,951	5,168	7,818	3,650	6,158	5,324
Kayes, Mali	6,322	4,802	1,295	6,938	2,110	9,402	1,574	5,245	5,488	16,260	6,096	2,099	9,515	8,802	3,611	13,327	5,710	6,277	3,794	4,604
Kazan, USSR	2,825	3,089	7,293	3,500	6,330	11,453	7,064	2,329	5,262	13,100	4,782	5,527	10,990	4,114	3,278	6,536	3,633	2,807	4,089	3,405
Kemi, Finland	4,264	1,697	7,075	5,056	6,429	9,748	6,962	3,280	6,397	14,579	6,091	5,563	9,307	5,840	2,837	7,076	1,918	4,234	4,626	4,215
Kenora, Canada	10,400	5,710	9,594	11,225	10,063	3,686	9,848	9,202	12,072	15,455	12,032	9,450	3,171	11,840	7,405	8,747	4,538	10,365	9,781	9,830
Kerguelen Island	9,090	13,521	9,282	8,329	8,865	16,261	9,038	10,159	7,145	5,717	7,304	9,517	16,857	8,040	11,735	12,060	14,763	9,119	9,356	9,414
Kerkira, Greece	2,771	2,519	4,495	3,630	3,601	11,191	4,279	1,374	3,867	14,665	3,862	2,762	10,945	5,259	978	9,333	3,766	2,722	1,737	1,620
Kermanshah, Iran	456	4,450	6,154	1,301	4,927	13,357	5,809	1,106	2,928	12,214	2,396	4,334	12,996	2,782	3,435	7,907	5,454	429	2,559	1,698
Khabarovsk, USSR	7,333	7,650	12,848	7,348	11,847	10,961	12,617	7,675	9,732	9,248	8,964	11,073	10,358	6,115	8,697	1,055	7,138	7,354	9,499	8,692
Kharkov, USSR	2,405	2,622	6,219	3,239	5,264	11,449	5,989	1,445	4,548	13,715	4,206	4,454	11,061	4,349	2,298	7,607	3,517	2,371	3,076	2,476
Khartoum, Sudan	2,289	5,446	4,154	2,482	2,845	13,691	3,746	2,389	988	12,442	1,383	2,627	13,583	4,279	3,703	10,354	6,695	2,268	1,356	1,396
Khon Kaen, Thailand	5,731	9,359	11,637	5,110	10,328	15,567	11,227	6,950	6,987	6,827	6,223	9,990	14,966	3,244	9,139	4,431	9,671	5,779	8,246	7,442
Kiev, USSR	2,678	2,250	5,947	3,539	5,055	11,125	5,740	1,539	4,652	14,124	4,381	4,223	10,757	4,735	1,920	7,898	3,217	2,640	2,978	2,480
Kigali, Rwanda	4,062	7,156	3,876	3,929	2,820	14,320	3,468	4,348	1,547	11,568	2,319	3,203	14,427	5,377	5,313	11,858	8,428	4,054	2,984	3,326
Kingston, Canada	10,032	5,167	8,205	10,909	8,804	3,748	8,489	8,697	11,249	16,862	11,378	8,281	3,428	11,923	6,613	10,011	4,213	9,989	8,905	9,124
Kingston, Jamaica	12,071	7,422	8,014	12,941	9,075	2,458	8,410	10,660	12,341	16,057	12,791	8,913	2,701	14,388	8,334	12,561	6,783	12,022	10,185	10,710
Kingstown, Saint Vincent	11,083	6,947	6,333	11,890	7,465	4,174	6,741	9,711	10,853	16,884	11,406	7,418	4,453	13,597	7,391	13,751	6,668	11,033	8,880	9,527
Kinshasa, Zaire	5,196	6,990	2,398	5,293	1,740	12,841	2,040	5,023	2,986	12,683	3,790	2,486	13,041	6,918	5,161	13,248	8,219	5,174	3,270	3,950
Kirkwall, United Kingdom	4,971	210	5,952	5,847	5,592	8,809	5,930	3,670	6,555	16,142	6,476	4,748	8,466	7,018	2,063	8,549	1,079	4,930	4,377	4,290
Kirov, USSR	3,137	3,004	7,475	3,804	6,551	11,200	7,261	2,613	5,573	13,180	5,096	5,734	10,726	4,345	3,381	6,374	3,443	3,121	4,347	3,686
Kiruna, Sweden	4,559	1,640	7,178	5,352	6,587	9,462	7,085	3,558	6,673	14,733	6,379	5,720	9,016	6,115	2,968	7,073	1,677	4,529	4,856	4,476
Kisangani, Zaire	4,106	6,733	3,293	4,112	2,215	13,718	2,879	4,175	1,769	12,164	2,574	2,623	13,821	5,698	4,876	12,082	8,003	4,090	2,630	3,111
Kishinev, USSR	2,493	2,374	5,589	3,373	4,668	11,285	5,369	1,230	4,311	14,161	4,086	3,843	10,946	4,711	1,691	8,242	3,443	2,450	2,577	2,104
Kitchner, Canada	10,316	5,457	8,512	11,189	9,129	3,474	8,803	8,994	11,576	16,551	11,693	8,611	3,128	12,149	6,932	9,934	4,467	10,274	9,232	9,440
Knoxville, Tennessee	11,134	6,268	8,757	12,014	9,519	2,644	9,087	9,786	12,223	16,195	12,413	9,090	2,369	13,026	7,649	10,492	5,326	11,091	9,884	10,164
Kosice, Czechoslovakia	3,062	1,816	5,371	3,947	4,576	10,720	5,196	1,727	4,691	14,753	4,547	3,720	10,399	5,308	1,235	8,519	2,956	3,017	2,725	2,428
Kota Kinabalu, Malaysia	7,551	11,086	13,264	6,879	11,971	15,331	12,842	8,795	8,531	5,109	7,820	11,729	14,829	5,023	10,983	4,446	11,236	7,599	10,026	9,246
Krakow, Poland	3,225	1,645	5,445	4,109	4,687	10,554	5,284	1,904	4,872	14,865	4,728	3,826	10,227	5,438	1,252	8,474	2,775	3,182	2,888	2,608
Kralendijk, Bonaire	11,768	7,447	7,094	12,594	8,236	3,447	7,505	10,379	11,623	16,317	12,167	8,186	3,770	14,248	8,045	13,559	7,031	11,718	9,625	10,250
Krasnodar, USSR	1,822	3,117	6,060	2,670	5,011	11,998	5,793	943	3,990	13,345	3,622	4,246	11,625	3,902	2,459	7,768	4,081	1,787	2,712	2,016
Krasnoyarsk, USSR	4,489	5,345	9,947	4,685	8,898	11,842	9,689	4,722	7,005	10,971	6,300	8,142	11,256	4,020	5,951	3,874	5,321	4,502	6,546	5,744
Kristiansand, Norway	4,348	613	5,954	5,220	5,437	9,439	5,880	3,079	6,047	15,576	5,915	4,573	9,084	6,376	1,808	8,284	1,589	4,307	3,964	3,778
Kuala Lumpur, Malaysia	6,364	10,540	11,726	5,594	10,459	16,774	11,303	7,715	6,996	5,713	6,326	10,311	16,211	3,828	10,024	5,600	10,998	6,414	8,695	7,982
Kuching, Malaysia	7,263	11,193	12,701	6,523	11,435	16,133	12,277	8,582	7,973	4,999	7,302	11,281	15,632	4,715	10,855	5,192	11,499	7,313	9,645	8,912
Kumasi, Ghana	5,820	5,596	307	6,272	1,008	10,681	199	5,026	4,452	14,890	5,154	1,544	10,835	8,116	4,035	13,546	6,672	5,781	3,291	4,152
Kumzar, Oman	914	5,700	6,814	292	5,517	14,591	6,426	2,319	2,676	10,984	1,918	5,090	14,202	1,679	4,657	7,682	6,661	963	3,335	2,546
Kunming, China	5,349	8,542	11,435	4,860	10,136	14,766	11,046	6,436	6,977	7,645	6,181	9,687	14,157	3,060	8,502	3,843	8,773	5,393	7,906	7,065
Kuqa Chang, China	3,376	6,046	9,416	3,270	8,199	13,570	9,079	4,139	5,654	10,138	4,882	7,585	12,997	2,254	6,024	4,721	6,408	3,406	5,826	4,966
Kurgan, USSR	3,097	4,006	8,227	3,554	7,195	11,875	7,973	3,047	5,653	12,181	5,050	6,426	11,358	3,648	4,291	5,594	4,352	3,097	4,869	4,101
Kuwait, Kuwait	109	4,933	6,071	837	4,800	13,844	5,702	1,451	2,452	11,866	1,865	4,294	13,505	2,556	3,776	8,161	5,975	125	2,514	1,686
Kuybyshev, USSR	2,544	3,275	7,219	3,210	6,213	11,732	6,973	2,135	5,006	12,930	4,508	5,428	11,274	3,849	3,304	6,602	3,884	2,529	3,929	3,211
Kyoto, Japan	7,944	9,057	13,883	7,749	12,734	11,806	13,586	8,570	10,078	7,748	9,276	12,050	11,235	6,192	9,927	651	8,619	7,975	10,346	9,496
Kzyl-Orda, USSR	2,202	4,725	7,983	2,469	6,815	13,020	7,669	2,667	4,726	11,497	4,048	6,145	12,518	2,501	4,516	5,965	5,304	2,216	4,427	3,582
L'vov, USSR	2,969	1,898	5,591	3,849	4,771	10,809	5,408	1,688	4,725	14,571	4,537	3,920	10,469	5,148	1,472	8,289	2,976	2,927	2,846	2,480
La Ceiba, Honduras	13,004	8,229	9,086	13,886	10,165	1,406	9,487	11,599	13,427	15,042	13,855	10,005	1,766	15,167	9,301	12,180	7,445	12,956	11,243	11,730
La Coruna, Spain	5,151	1,594	4,237	6,018	4,081	8,864	4,266	3,742	5,932	17,041	6,111	3,310	8,676	7,583	1,411	10,275	2,554	5,102	3,588	3,878
La Paz, Bolivia	13,435	10,166	7,456	14,011	8,766	5,075	7,862	12,279	12,087	13,654	12,854	9,134	5,648	15,871	10,176	16,263	10,020	13,389	10,895	11,716
La Paz, Mexico	13,558	8,811	11,411	14,378	12,304	1,352	11,778	12,338	15,035	13,370	15,125	11,926	858	14,773	10,384	9,858	7,682	13,523	12,691	12,881
La Ronge, Canada	10,209	5,783	10,237	10,979	10,561	4,270	10,452	9,131	12,151	14,727	11,987	9,874	3,696	11,346	7,583	7,813	4,535	10,179	9,958	9,882
Labrador City, Canada	8,863	4,011	7,745	9,734	8,135	4,929	7,969	7,553	10,239	17,178	10,294	7,511	4,573	10,727	5,563	9,413	3,017	8,822	7,912	8,049
Lagos, Nigeria	5,378	5,642	831	5,784	516	11,214	411	4,684	3,905	14,463	4,618	1,267	11,352	7,613	3,965	13,246	6,783	5,341	2,896	3,750
Lahore, Pakistan	2,485	6,321	8,601	2,109	7,319	14,610	8,226	3,615	4,444	9,971	3,648	6,827	14,077	962	5,824	5,896	6,958	2,528	5,043	4,199
Lambasa, Fiji	14,843	15,486	18,722	14,262	18,854	9,587	18,800	15,823	15,695	4,536	15,112	19,116	9,531	12,396	17,044	7,432	14,384	14,887	17,394	16,561
Lansing, Michigan	10,592	5,744	8,837	11,460	9,466	3,219	9,132	9,285	11,903	16,221	12,007	8,951	2,840	12,357	7,251	9,830	4,719	10,551	9,561	9,755
Lanzhou, China	5,138	7,578	11,240	4,863	9,997	13,648	10,890	5,984	7,180	8,653	6,378	9,416	13,038	3,319	7,808	3,209	7,676	5,174	7,645	6,784
Laoag, Philippines	7,351	10,126	13,423	6,844	12,118	14,130	13,026	8,409	8,858	6,181	8,079	11,688	13,579	5,009	10,372	3,036	10,082	7,395	9,909	9,067
Largeau, Chad	3,253	4,697	2,878	3,721	1,613	12,321	2,508	2,644	2,334	13,799	2,836	1,187	12,273	5,581	2,838	11,181	5,965	3,215	820	1,639
Las Vegas, Nevada	12,443	7,924	11,530	13,204	12,180	2,617	11,839	11,350	14,307	13,509	14,204	11,633	2,014	13,401	9,652	8,620	6,710	12,413	12,030	12,049
Launceston, Australia	12,858	17,213	15,095	11,987	14,710	13,137	14,889	14,268	12,208	1,037	11,947	15,278	13,275	10,470	16,592	9,013	17,152	12,906	14,532	14,148
Le Havre, France	4,533	862	4,913	5,418	4,519	9,306	4,872	3,137	5,734	16,287	5,771	3,678	9,040	6,847	1,075	9,373	2,087	4,486	3,456	3,522
Leipzig, East Germany	3,761	1,140	5,319	4,647	4,696	10,024	5,204	2,409	5,271	15,404	5,188	3,828	9,712	5,990	1,079	8,722	2,348	3,717	3,152	3,003
Leningrad, USSR	3,554	1,891	6,716	4,359	5,952	10,396	6,560	2,572	5,690	14,293	5,373	5,096	9,974	5,250	2,486	7,253	2,481	3,522	4,004	3,536
Leon, Spain	4,926	1,635	4,133	5,789	3,908	9,108	4,139	3,519	5,688	16,820	5,866	3,120	8,921	7,374	1,181	10,257	2,683	4,877	3,345	3,635
Lerwick, United Kingdom	4,916	341	6,088	5,787	5,700	8,873	6,058	3,638	6,565	15,993	6,462	4,851	8,516	6,918	2,138	8,385	1,053	4,875	4,419	4,296
Lhasa, China	4,109	7,476	10,219	3,674	8,931	14,727	9,839	5,185	5,901	8,715	5,097	8,450	14,126	1,982	7,287	4,570	7,861	4,151	6,667	5,821
Libreville, Gabon	5,274	6,376	1,595	5,521	1,003	12,065	1,217	4,851	3,380	13,514	4,157	1,841	12,240	7,264	4,601	13,332	7,569	5,245	3,029	3,816
Lilongwe, Malawi	5,144	8,548	4,691	4,806	3,897	15,066	4,333	5,647	2,603	10,437	3,207	4,445	15,315	5,888	6,702	12,384	9,819	5,146	4,375	4,668
Lima, Peru	14,063	10,236	8,305	14,742	9,609	4,068	8,722	12,792	13,011	13,598	13,750	9,885	4,658	16,598	10,552	15,254	9,879	14,015	11,596	12,374
Limerick, Ireland	5,187	649	5,267	6,073	5,031	8,623	5,280	3,806	6,438	16,768	6,475	4,219	8,344	7,424	1,767	9,335	1,542	5,141	4,148	4,228
Limoges, France	4,394	1,278	4,519	5,270	4,103	9,519	4,466	2,984	5,419	16,253	5,504	3,262	9,284	6,788	742	9,684	2,496	4,345	3,110	3,251
Limon, Costa Rica	13,165	8,532	8,714	14,028	9,867	1,978	9,128	11,755	13,244	14,982	13,762	9,804	2,442	15,500	9,421	12,938	7,863	13,116	11,184	11,755
Lincoln, Nebraska	11,343	6,570	9,851	12,185	10,497	2,675	10,154	10,099	12,850	15,196	12,889	9,975	2,166	12,850	8,174	9,399	5,452	11,306	10,518	10,653
Linz, Austria	3,499	1,475	5,072	4,386	4,389	10,308	4,935	2,118	4,918	15,260	4,855	3,523	10,013	5,805	833	8,893	2,703	3,453	2,789	2,653
Lisbon, Portugal	5,266	2,111	3,735	6,108	3,657	8,925	3,782	3,876	5,783	17,131	6,039	2,930	8,785	7,758	1,557	10,774	3,054	5,216	3,452	3,858
Little Rock, Arkansas	11,704	6,854	9,519	12,571	10,291	2,124	9,853	10,393	12,944	15,424	13,091	9,855	1,729	13,415	8,325	10,167	5,827	11,663	10,601	10,837
Liverpool, United Kingdom	4,826	418	5,334	5,712	4,992	8,969	5,313	3,457	6,172	16,388	6,171	4,156	8,674	7,041	1,549	9,096	1,601	4,781	3,920	3,936
Lodz, Poland	3,353	1,514	5,586	4,233	4,853	10,425	5,435	2,058	5,051	14,910	4,895	3,990	10,087	5,514	1,363	8,361	2,610	3,311	3,076	2,790
Lome, Togo	5,595	5,664	589	6,015	739	10,998	171	4,864	4,147	14,619	4,860	1,407	11,147	7,848	4,033	13,417	6,778	5,557	3,093	3,951

Distances in Kilometers	Abadan, Iran	Aberdeen, United Kingdom	Abidjan, Ivory Coast	Abu Dhabi, United Arab Emir.	Abuja, Nigeria	Acapulco, Mexico	Accra, Ghana	Adana, Turkey	Addis Ababa, Ethiopia	Adelaide, Australia	Aden, P.D.R. Yemen	Agadez, Niger	Aguascalientes, Mexico	Ahmadabad, India	Ajaccio, France	Akita, Japan	Akureyri, Iceland	Al Basrah, Iraq	Al Jawf, Libya	Al Minya, Egypt
London, United Kingdom	4,592	640	5,133	5,478	4,741	9,219	5,094	3,209	5,886	16,259	5,896	3,898	8,936	6,855	1,260	9,189	1,878	4,546	3,630	3,656
Londonderry, United Kingdom	5,135	403	5,517	6,020	5,243	8,652	5,521	3,776	6,505	16,579	6,502	4,420	8,350	7,309	1,869	9,063	1,325	5,090	4,246	4,269
Longlac, Canada	10,075	5,301	9,021	10,922	9,503	3,847	9,277	8,827	11,617	16,025	11,625	8,904	3,392	11,681	6,938	9,092	4,181	10,037	9,302	9,398
Lord Howe Island, Australia	13,532	16,818	16,616	12,724	16,204	11,999	16,417	14,888	13,410	1,942	13,020	16,692	12,038	11,003	17,153	8,130	16,206	13,582	15,629	15,066
Los Angeles, California	12,739	8,271	11,871	13,481	12,540	2,643	12,186	11,675	14,656	13,156	14,531	12,000	2,065	13,583	10,010	8,553	7,049	12,711	12,390	12,394
Louangphrabang, Laos	5,506	8,998	11,495	4,930	10,186	15,290	11,092	6,682	6,907	7,186	6,128	9,805	14,684	3,075	8,833	4,235	9,290	5,552	8,043	7,223
Louisville, Kentucky	11,044	6,183	8,926	11,918	9,643	2,745	9,245	9,717	12,244	16,076	12,394	9,181	2,407	12,858	7,627	10,191	5,194	11,002	9,900	10,140
Luanda, Angola	5,725	7,442	2,472	5,787	2,097	12,754	2,179	5,570	3,444	12,515	4,248	2,908	13,008	7,361	5,634	13,755	8,651	5,704	3,811	4,497
Lubumbashi, Zaire	5,154	8,095	3,962	4,952	3,217	14,344	3,609	5,451	2,605	11,134	3,326	3,824	14,584	6,240	6,235	12,768	9,362	5,148	3,994	4,414
Lusaka, Zambia	5,497	8,518	4,237	5,244	3,579	14,508	3,906	5,850	2,938	10,804	3,621	4,219	14,792	6,435	6,658	12,952	9,785	5,494	4,416	4,822
Luxembourg, Luxembourg	4,112	1,000	5,001	4,998	4,484	9,708	4,919	2,723	5,416	15,855	5,409	3,624	9,426	6,413	877	9,134	2,271	4,065	3,190	3,174
Luxor, Egypt	1,618	4,451	4,509	2,193	3,254	13,055	4,148	1,282	1,951	12,987	1,930	2,729	12,853	4,051	2,837	9,587	5,671	1,579	958	328
Lynn Lake, Canada	9,922	5,459	9,941	10,704	10,243	4,441	10,149	8,825	11,833	14,990	11,681	9,550	3,884	11,133	7,256	7,872	4,215	9,891	9,632	9,564
Lyon, France	4,115	1,354	4,562	4,993	4,061	9,784	4,482	2,705	5,195	15,974	5,256	3,205	9,539	6,509	528	9,545	2,612	4,067	2,909	3,003
Macapa, Brazil	10,908	7,672	5,259	11,574	6,532	5,671	5,682	9,686	9,991	16,015	10,676	6,733	6,059	13,431	7,556	15,460	7,741	10,860	8,428	9,208
Madison, Wisconsin	10,804	5,986	9,233	11,662	9,851	3,073	9,526	9,526	12,218	15,827	12,286	9,322	2,637	12,459	7,549	9,576	4,911	10,765	9,881	10,041
Madras, India	3,803	8,336	9,271	3,001	7,972	16,694	8,853	5,190	4,561	8,125	3,824	7,745	16,127	1,367	7,527	6,520	9,070	3,853	6,098	5,384
Madrid, Spain	4,781	1,864	3,886	5,632	3,624	9,327	3,876	3,384	5,436	16,668	5,639	2,830	9,156	7,262	1,055	10,406	2,957	4,731	3,091	3,425
Madurai, India	3,830	8,495	9,059	2,986	7,772	17,035	8,638	5,236	4,327	8,065	3,624	7,599	16,485	1,564	7,575	6,923	9,289	3,880	6,006	5,336
Magadan, USSR	7,810	6,846	12,477	8,044	11,730	9,447	12,348	7,784	10,353	10,534	9,659	10,882	8,838	7,165	8,232	2,332	6,082	7,819	9,565	8,858
Magdalena, Bolivia	12,891	9,648	6,955	13,486	8,264	5,160	7,366	11,725	11,626	14,153	12,380	8,606	5,705	15,351	9,622	16,248	9,553	12,845	10,359	11,174
Magdeburg, East Germany	3,843	1,044	5,392	4,728	4,786	9,939	5,283	2,500	5,375	15,446	5,288	3,919	9,622	6,048	1,161	8,675	2,243	3,799	3,258	3,107
Majuro Atoll, Marshall Isls.	12,663	12,853	18,532	12,342	17,491	9,671	18,318	13,314	14,470	5,781	13,687	16,771	9,364	10,579	14,288	4,757	11,892	12,697	15,104	14,253
Malabo, Equatorial Guinea	5,085	5,998	1,433	5,393	625	11,877	1,018	4,572	3,359	13,815	4,109	1,465	12,021	7,178	4,228	13,102	7,190	5,052	2,748	3,562
Male, Maldives	3,938	8,766	8,595	3,053	7,344	17,589	8,171	5,339	3,884	8,038	3,276	7,280	17,105	2,108	7,638	7,740	9,674	3,985	5,819	5,248
Manado, Indonesia	8,644	11,985	14,304	7,974	13,026	14,716	13,881	9,874	9,570	4,279	8,878	12,815	14,293	6,118	12,026	4,508	11,989	8,692	11,120	10,341
Managua, Nicaragua	13,255	8,531	9,054	14,131	10,179	1,558	9,463	11,845	13,512	14,853	13,988	10,073	2,015	15,492	9,528	12,535	7,788	13,207	11,388	11,917
Manama, Bahrain	510	5,368	6,238	427	4,945	14,279	5,854	1,876	2,279	11,462	1,599	4,508	13,939	2,256	4,186	8,163	6,405	548	2,754	1,975
Manaus, Brazil	11,944	8,441	6,295	12,626	7,578	4,911	6,718	10,694	11,030	15,368	11,726	7,790	5,369	14,477	8,508	15,477	8,342	11,896	9,481	10,253
Manchester, New Hampshire	9,829	4,967	7,780	10,712	8,399	3,956	8,069	8,470	10,927	17,285	11,093	7,895	3,691	11,825	6,328	10,311	4,097	9,785	8,583	8,842
Mandalay, Burma	4,834	8,457	10,834	4,263	9,527	15,371	10,434	6,021	6,286	7,738	5,498	9,135	14,760	2,415	8,199	4,589	8,837	4,880	7,371	6,551
Mangareva Island, Fr.Polynesia	19,147	14,673	14,414	19,071	15,714	5,838	14,805	18,209	18,310	8,271	18,859	16,106	6,108	17,212	16,066	11,206	13,547	19,145	17,813	18,491
Manila, Philippines	7,568	10,501	13,581	7,017	12,272	14,342	13,176	8,674	8,946	5,787	8,182	11,888	13,810	5,163	10,691	3,352	10,479	7,613	10,118	9,287
Mannheim, West Germany	3,946	1,102	5,035	4,832	4,471	9,867	4,938	2,561	5,290	15,688	5,265	3,607	9,581	6,243	841	9,049	2,367	3,900	3,089	3,039
Maputo, Mozambique	6,451	9,765	5,253	6,053	4,760	15,030	4,969	6,977	3,929	9,726	4,492	5,445	15,436	6,930	7,906	13,254	11,033	6,456	5,640	5,986
Mar del Plata, Argentina	13,311	11,752	7,312	13,510	8,496	7,514	7,629	12,631	11,171	11,760	11,972	9,150	8,113	15,028	11,109	18,482	11,987	13,279	10,880	11,735
Maracaibo, Venezuela	12,160	7,785	7,462	12,990	8,619	3,133	7,875	10,767	12,016	15,947	12,567	8,581	3,498	14,628	8,430	13,542	7,317	12,110	10,027	10,650
Marrakech, Morocco	5,315	2,870	2,943	6,103	2,941	9,225	2,999	3,995	5,425	16,909	5,789	2,290	9,153	7,859	1,874	11,451	3,846	5,265	3,177	3,745
Marseilles, France	4,035	1,627	4,309	4,903	3,786	9,928	4,219	2,626	4,986	15,926	5,081	2,930	9,704	6,476	314	9,749	2,880	3,986	2,678	2,828
Maseru, Lesotho	6,960	9,975	5,103	6,610	4,783	14,513	4,865	7,388	4,411	9,882	5,023	5,533	14,956	7,544	8,119	13,875	11,229	6,961	5,939	6,363
Mashhad, Iran	1,244	5,038	7,310	1,404	6,071	13,743	6,960	2,168	3,687	11,360	2,988	5,493	13,291	1,933	4,379	6,831	5,840	1,272	3,716	2,856
Mazatlan, Mexico	13,496	8,689	11,042	14,339	11,967	979	11,415	12,229	14,810	13,673	14,964	11,622	448	14,887	10,200	10,215	7,601	13,458	12,469	12,711
Mbabane, Swaziland	6,529	9,759	5,161	6,150	4,703	14,885	4,886	7,024	3,996	9,814	4,578	5,404	15,296	7,056	7,899	13,395	11,024	6,533	5,653	6,022
Mbandaka, Zaire	4,615	6,584	2,546	4,735	1,588	13,007	2,142	4,452	2,473	12,743	3,270	2,183	13,149	6,399	4,733	12,675	7,833	4,592	2,725	3,376
McMurdo Sound, Antarctica	13,909	17,679	11,960	13,136	12,304	11,944	11,964	14,913	11,808	4,912	12,082	13,155	12,429	12,545	15,894	13,116	18,680	13,938	13,743	14,037
Mecca, Saudi Arabia	1,297	5,218	5,051	1,528	3,748	13,918	4,658	1,780	1,379	12,120	1,109	3,378	13,701	3,379	3,685	9,349	6,401	1,280	1,722	1,175
Medan, Indonesia	6,061	10,322	11,386	5,279	10,118	16,972	10,963	7,423	6,656	5,965	5,987	9,975	16,391	3,536	9,742	5,778	10,831	6,111	8,368	7,663
Medellin, Colombia	12,804	8,432	7,919	13,626	9,118	2,897	8,339	11,416	12,552	15,292	13,136	9,134	3,354	15,282	9,080	13,742	7,932	12,754	10,629	11,273
Medicine Hat, Canada	10,862	6,448	10,730	11,620	11,134	3,807	10,970	9,799	12,820	14,301	12,654	10,474	3,211	11,903	8,239	7,905	5,203	10,833	10,617	10,551
Medina, Saudi Arabia	1,075	4,919	5,120	1,496	3,833	13,679	4,740	1,451	1,711	12,308	1,415	3,388	13,438	3,362	3,438	9,150	6,088	1,049	1,654	971
Melbourne, Australia	12,550	16,788	15,241	11,689	14,741	13,333	15,001	13,957	12,055	658	11,744	15,242	13,428	10,123	16,295	8,602	16,721	12,599	14,350	13,909
Memphis, Tennessee	11,552	6,695	9,315	12,424	10,084	2,249	9,647	10,231	12,752	15,631	12,910	9,650	1,891	13,315	8,143	10,256	5,688	11,511	10,408	10,657
Merauke, Indonesia	10,682	13,713	16,085	9,997	14,886	13,448	15,668	11,910	11,433	2,936	10,796	14,788	13,185	8,150	14,011	5,334	13,441	10,731	13,138	12,374
Merida, Mexico	12,768	7,926	9,349	13,655	10,353	1,177	9,736	11,383	13,475	15,088	13,817	10,110	1,319	14,773	9,140	11,542	7,054	12,723	11,210	11,622
Meridian, Mississippi	11,722	6,856	9,199	12,600	10,021	2,057	9,545	10,379	12,803	15,670	13,005	9,626	1,777	13,562	8,243	10,577	5,892	11,679	10,467	10,757
Messina, Italy	3,117	2,474	4,146	3,958	3,322	10,948	3,951	1,744	3,975	14,992	4,052	2,465	10,732	5,630	715	9,699	3,743	3,067	1,715	1,801
Mexico City, Mexico	13,497	8,631	10,357	14,374	11,363	294	10,746	12,152	14,436	14,134	14,722	11,104	428	15,227	9,983	11,040	7,647	13,454	12,138	12,491
Miami, Florida	11,728	6,930	8,374	12,614	9,317	2,269	8,746	10,331	12,379	16,188	12,718	9,034	2,291	13,867	8,061	11,641	6,151	11,682	10,110	10,530
Midway Islands, USA	11,925	10,539	16,229	11,976	15,842	7,943	16,258	12,024	14,360	8,382	13,587	14,975	7,489	10,617	12,216	4,090	9,447	11,941	13,801	13,096
Milan, Italy	3,776	1,514	4,630	4,655	4,028	10,107	4,516	2,367	4,927	15,634	4,954	3,162	9,852	6,170	396	9,380	2,785	3,728	2,680	2,706
Milford Sound, New Zealand	14,573	18,444	15,582	13,701	15,662	11,486	15,526	15,984	13,751	2,702	13,577	16,412	11,679	12,167	18,300	9,740	17,630	14,622	16,095	15,814
Milwaukee, Wisconsin	10,736	5,907	9,113	11,596	9,733	3,118	9,406	9,449	12,119	15,947	12,198	9,208	2,699	12,424	7,454	9,648	4,846	10,696	9,780	9,950
Minsk, USSR	3,102	1,893	6,097	3,955	5,285	10,719	5,920	1,969	5,075	14,388	4,815	4,434	10,340	5,077	1,927	7,802	2,796	3,065	3,317	2,877
Mogadiscio, Somalia	3,144	7,398	5,498	2,661	4,299	15,680	5,077	4,005	1,067	10,440	1,184	4,410	15,622	3,746	5,731	10,273	8,609	3,157	3,411	3,274
Mombasa, Kenya	3,914	7,753	4,968	3,534	3,889	15,400	4,560	4,569	1,451	10,569	1,952	4,188	15,477	4,668	5,976	11,193	9,006	3,920	3,594	3,684
Monclova, Mexico	12,902	8,071	10,479	13,759	11,362	1,124	10,842	11,613	14,162	14,305	14,323	10,992	563	14,443	9,557	10,269	7,009	12,863	11,820	12,069
Moncton, Canada	9,200	4,342	7,356	10,084	7,891	4,588	7,620	7,838	10,315	17,694	10,466	7,347	4,320	11,232	5,699	10,182	3,513	9,156	7,970	8,214
Monrovia, Liberia	6,701	5,688	758	7,214	2,008	9,722	1,175	5,773	5,466	15,560	6,159	2,360	9,912	9,072	4,391	14,104	6,612	6,659	4,144	4,996
Monte Carlo, Monaco	3,879	1,633	4,402	4,751	3,831	10,059	4,296	2,469	4,894	15,765	4,965	2,968	9,825	6,312	229	9,619	2,899	3,831	2,607	2,712
Monterrey, Mexico	12,967	8,122	10,389	13,830	11,295	977	10,757	11,662	14,155	14,347	14,344	10,946	465	14,563	9,577	10,444	7,080	12,927	11,819	12,091
Montevideo, Uruguay	13,088	11,388	7,040	13,335	8,247	7,358	7,369	12,351	11,026	12,125	11,830	8,877	7,950	14,923	10,773	18,484	11,621	13,054	10,623	11,482
Montgomery, Alabama	11,581	6,715	8,974	12,462	9,799	2,200	9,320	10,227	12,606	15,886	12,825	9,410	1,962	13,479	8,068	10,704	5,780	11,537	10,274	10,580
Montpelier, Vermont	9,802	4,937	7,897	10,683	8,490	3,976	8,179	8,454	10,960	17,171	11,106	7,970	3,686	11,757	6,339	10,145	4,031	9,759	8,616	8,853
Montpellier, France	4,160	1,563	4,312	5,029	3,829	9,802	4,235	2,751	5,102	16,049	5,204	2,978	9,580	6,597	439	9,788	2,803	4,111	2,788	2,953
Montreal, Canada	9,769	4,903	8,002	10,647	8,571	4,010	8,278	8,431	10,983	17,064	11,109	8,035	3,696	11,685	6,345	9,986	3,965	9,726	8,639	8,855
Moosonee, Canada	9,679	4,877	8,619	10,535	9,070	4,185	8,864	8,412	11,174	16,402	11,196	8,461	3,763	11,368	6,495	9,175	3,785	9,640	8,856	8,963
Moroni, Comoros	4,680	8,685	5,565	4,177	4,611	16,027	5,178	5,455	2,346	9,757	2,711	5,011	16,202	4,998	6,907	11,416	9,936	4,693	4,525	4,604
Moscow, USSR	2,947	2,418	6,696	3,735	5,812	11,032	6,495	2,090	5,183	13,791	4,812	4,980	10,609	4,629	2,587	7,165	3,111	2,918	3,693	3,120
Mosul, Iraq	819	4,048	5,904	1,699	4,714	12,960	5,577	704	3,057	12,635	2,617	4,070	12,613	3,194	3,017	8,064	5,081	778	2,327	1,480
Mount Isa, Australia	11,263	14,900	15,739	10,481	14,767	13,789	15,371	12,602	11,486	1,576	10,969	14,926	13,665	8,723	14,869	6,962	14,755	11,313	13,511	12,856
Multan, Pakistan	2,230	6,272	8,327	1,806	7,039	14,720	7,947	3,421	4,134	10,070	3,338	6,565	14,205	800	5,674	6,207	6,971	2,275	4,786	3,950
Munich, West Germany	3,682	1,358	4,974	4,568	4,341	10,138	4,853	2,292	5,028	15,462	4,994	3,474	9,853	6,004	728	9,032	2,611	3,636	2,851	2,772
Murcia, Spain	4,578	2,130	3,630	5,412	3,299	9,621	3,593	3,201	5,114	16,426	5,343	2,493	9,466	7,089	947	10,539	3,270	4,528	2,772	3,153
Murmansk, USSR	4,407	2,165	7,574	5,147	6,901	9,789	7,454	3,558	6,668	14,195	6,300	6,037	9,315	5,749	3,331	6,574	2,167	4,382	5,020	4,547
Mururoa Atoll, Fr. Polynesia	18,834	14,768	14,843	18,642	16,144	6,036	15,235	18,237	18,563	7,994	18,919	16,522	6,263	16,791	16,274	10,802	13,596	18,846	18,193	18,774
Muscat, Oman	1,265	6,072	6,992	439	5,686	14,961	6,595	2,675	2,662	10,632	1,869	5,310	14,566	1,436	5,009	7,677	7,028	1,314	3,584	2,827
Myitkyina, Burma	4,833	8,220	10,906	4,329	9,606	14,974	10,515	5,953	6,449	7,965	5,651	9,166	14,363	2,528	8,068	4,268	8,542	4,878	7,388	6,552
Naga, Philippines	7,826	10,702	13,837	7,275	12,527	14,211	13,431	8,927	9,193	5,616	8,432	12,146	13,692	5,420	10,929	3,332	10,643	7,870	10,376	9,545
Nagasaki, Japan	7,547	9,072	13,586	7,293	12,385	12,385	13,262	8,270	9,589	7,553	8,784	11,748	11,808	5,676	9,787	1,194	8,747	7,581	10,008	9,150
Nagoya, Japan	8,033	9,079	13,954	7,846	12,813	11,708	13,661	8,645	10,178	7,762	9,376	12,123	11,138	6,296	9,975	579	8,620	8,063	10,426	9,577
Nagpur, India	3,245	7,531	9,094	2,562	7,785	15,800	8,689	4,564	4,530	8,831	3,738	7,439	15,242	701	6,870	6,089	8,206	3,294	5,707	4,925
Nairobi, Kenya	3,704	7,349	4,600	3,422	3,484	14,992	4,186	4,243	1,160	11,005	1,799	3,754	15,050	4,720	5,557	11,240	8,608	3,705	3,175	3,316
Nanchang, China	6,456	8,875	12,582	6,080	11,312	13,674	12,216	7,376	8,291	7,435	7,489	10,776	13,079	4,359	9,208	2,535	8,832	6,495	8,995	8,137
Nancy, France	4,081	1,092	4,904	4,966	4,382	9,752	4,819	2,685	5,341	15,858	5,346	3,522	9,479	6,405	778	9,216	2,363	4,034	3,103	3,106
Nandi, Fiji	14,720	15,638	18,615	14,110	18,598	9,834	18,626	15,755	15,470	4,278	14,905	18,909	9,783	12,246	17,126	7,453	14,566	14,766	17,254	16,440
Nanjing, China	6,597	8,682	12,700	6,286	11,458	13,210	12,352	7,428	8,555	7,699	7,750	10,874	12,615	4,633	9,144	2,099	8,558	6,633	9,106	8,245
Nanning, China	5,973	9,056	12,050	5,472	10,749	14,657	11,658	7,057	7,547	7,147	6,757	10,310	14,058	3,653	9,098	3,532	9,206	6,017	8,530	7,690
Nantes, France	4,623	1,104	4,650	5,503	4,298	9,266	4,619	3,216	5,683	16,451	5,765	3,467	9,025	6,990	1,006	9,656	2,277	4,575	3,373	3,512
Naples, Italy	3,271	2,160	4,337	4,132	3,577	10,706	4,166	1,869	4,270	15,166	4,319	2,713	10,473	5,747	477	9,541	3,428	3,222	2,028	2,065
Narvik, Norway	4,684	1,591	7,187	5,480	6,624	9,329	7,104	3,667	6,778	14,831	6,494	5,757	8,884	6,248	2,997	7,114	1,553	4,653	4,933	4,571

Distances in Kilometers	Abadan, Iran	Aberdeen, United Kingdom	Abidjan, Ivory Coast	Abu Dhabi, United Arab Emir.	Abuja, Nigeria	Acapulco, Mexico	Accra, Ghana	Adana, Turkey	Addis Ababa, Ethiopia	Adelaide, Australia	Aden, P.D.R. Yemen	Agadez, Niger	Aguascalientes, Mexico	Ahmadabad, India	Ajaccio, France	Akita, Japan	Akureyri, Iceland	Al Basrah, Iraq	Al Jawf, Libya	Al Minya, Egypt
Nashville, Tennessee	11,281	6,417	9,015	12,157	9,770	2,503	9,344	9,948	12,438	15,947	12,607	9,332	2,183	13,106	7,840	10,333	5,438	11,239	10,096	10,354
Nassau, Bahamas	11,579	6,819	8,086	12,462	9,042	2,513	8,460	10,175	12,140	16,413	12,502	8,776	2,570	13,780	7,885	11,851	6,094	11,532	9,890	10,335
Natal, Brazil	9,714	7,592	3,677	10,238	4,987	7,544	4,087	8,694	8,363	15,452	9,105	5,378	7,922	12,092	6,909	16,217	8,048	9,671	7,157	7,999
Natashquan, Canada	8,755	3,890	7,306	9,636	7,739	5,023	7,541	7,410	9,983	17,644	10,090	7,143	4,719	10,741	5,329	9,816	3,016	8,712	7,643	7,836
Nauru Island	12,772	13,653	18,896	12,319	17,594	10,370	18,502	13,623	14,225	4,812	13,489	17,087	10,118	10,482	14,931	5,226	12,767	12,812	15,313	14,453
Ndjamena, Chad	3,971	5,205	2,229	4,358	920	12,194	1,829	3,421	2,610	13,826	3,257	931	12,224	6,192	3,359	11,951	6,454	3,936	1,596	2,408
Nelson, New Zealand	14,994	18,211	16,012	14,138	16,195	10,968	15,994	16,396	14,312	3,101	14,110	16,969	11,139	12,528	18,735	9,578	17,199	15,043	16,656	16,327
Nema, Mauritania	5,814	4,518	1,298	6,435	1,769	9,765	1,445	4,743	5,047	16,073	5,631	1,624	9,842	8,298	3,193	12,914	5,508	5,768	3,290	4,096
Neuquen, Argentina	14,226	12,302	8,189	14,433	9,395	7,011	8,518	13,497	12,088	11,378	12,887	10,026	7,621	15,916	11,848	17,603	12,370	14,194	11,772	12,631
New Delhi, India	2,806	6,754	8,878	2,317	7,584	14,966	8,493	4,000	4,569	9,541	3,765	7,132	14,418	769	6,236	5,812	7,380	2,851	5,356	4,525
New Glasgow, Canada	9,100	4,252	7,180	9,986	7,719	4,698	7,445	7,730	10,170	17,868	10,335	7,181	4,448	11,168	5,570	10,288	3,466	9,056	7,826	8,084
New Haven, Connecticut	10,044	5,184	7,862	10,928	8,518	3,745	8,161	8,681	11,106	17,188	11,288	8,035	3,494	12,048	6,524	10,433	4,320	10,000	8,764	9,039
New Orleans, Louisiana	12,013	7,146	9,340	12,892	10,200	1,765	9,695	10,665	13,049	15,462	13,272	9,833	1,516	13,857	8,514	10,717	6,188	11,970	10,720	11,027
New Plymouth, New Zealand	15,041	17,977	16,262	14,198	16,448	10,838	16,249	16,430	14,479	3,171	14,245	17,214	10,989	12,546	18,743	9,385	16,944	15,091	16,819	16,438
New York, New York	10,156	5,296	7,942	11,040	8,611	3,632	8,245	8,794	11,216	17,101	11,400	8,135	3,382	12,153	6,637	10,453	4,425	10,112	8,874	9,151
Newcastle upon Tyne, UK	4,775	240	5,514	5,660	5,143	9,008	5,485	3,425	6,209	16,242	6,178	4,300	8,697	6,943	1,639	8,898	1,488	4,731	3,987	3,959
Newcastle Waters, Australia	10,523	14,270	15,213	9,742	14,154	14,380	14,822	11,863	10,809	2,010	10,267	14,248	14,201	7,983	14,139	6,361	14,247	10,573	12,787	12,121
Niamey, Niger	5,077	4,853	1,130	5,601	733	10,829	918	4,199	4,021	15,062	4,646	737	10,902	7,464	3,212	12,691	5,989	5,035	2,521	3,376
Nicosia, Cyprus	1,494	3,599	5,063	2,344	3,921	12,437	4,755	269	2,945	13,380	2,745	3,225	12,156	4,020	2,265	8,831	4,759	1,444	1,556	822
Niue (Alofi)	15,988	15,656	17,866	15,431	18,873	8,626	18,154	16,856	16,756	5,343	16,237	19,702	8,638	13,565	17,462	8,317	14,429	16,031	18,546	17,695
Norfolk, Virginia	10,596	5,744	8,081	11,481	8,828	3,211	8,405	9,224	11,563	16,887	11,785	8,400	3,006	12,622	7,034	10,748	4,894	10,551	9,231	9,544
Norfolk Island, Australia	14,260	16,788	17,250	13,489	17,039	11,108	17,127	15,561	14,299	2,839	13,887	17,580	11,141	11,712	17,663	8,139	15,910	14,310	16,483	15,864
Noril'sk, USSR	5,014	4,270	9,539	5,462	8,699	10,425	9,364	4,768	7,563	12,270	6,972	7,864	9,854	5,250	5,314	4,468	3,987	5,012	6,525	5,845
Norman Wells, Canada	9,396	5,656	10,918	10,054	10,926	5,742	11,041	8,558	11,676	13,679	11,323	10,129	5,141	10,073	7,514	6,211	4,403	9,376	9,761	9,474
Normanton, Australia	11,249	14,673	15,999	10,493	14,967	13,577	15,617	12,558	11,623	1,929	11,072	15,061	13,420	8,701	14,778	6,353	14,456	11,298	13,570	12,879
North Pole	6,646	3,669	9,416	7,296	8,990	8,138	9,390	5,905	9,005	13,868	8,592	8,127	7,581	7,455	5,362	5,603	2,718	6,628	7,327	6,894
Nottingham, United Kingdom	4,696	468	5,290	5,582	4,915	9,101	5,258	3,325	6,045	16,286	6,039	4,074	8,807	6,921	1,435	9,082	1,700	4,651	3,799	3,806
Norway House, Canada	10,112	5,539	9,782	10,913	10,154	4,124	10,009	8,969	11,924	15,209	11,820	9,493	3,583	11,423	7,298	8,243	4,321	10,079	9,680	9,662
Norwich, United Kingdom	4,525	546	5,269	5,412	4,850	9,270	5,222	3,156	5,893	16,135	5,877	4,000	8,974	6,755	1,316	9,031	1,812	4,480	3,663	3,649
Nouakchott, Mauritania	6,580	4,483	1,918	7,257	2,688	8,830	2,203	5,403	5,979	16,889	6,543	2,543	8,920	9,104	3,529	13,142	5,286	6,532	4,119	4,881
Noumea, New Caledonia	13,865	16,023	17,875	13,155	17,379	11,073	17,675	15,081	14,273	3,050	13,762	17,701	11,032	11,325	17,005	7,388	15,171	13,913	16,266	15,543
Novosibirsk, USSR	3,877	4,946	9,332	4,124	8,269	12,035	9,067	4,089	6,411	11,292	5,725	7,520	11,468	3,654	5,399	4,495	5,072	3,889	5,912	5,109
Nuku'alofa, Tonga	15,578	15,968	18,019	14,956	18,657	9,226	18,200	16,594	16,160	4,747	15,663	19,445	9,237	13,095	17,671	8,180	14,787	15,624	18,102	17,298
Nukunono Island, Tokelau Isls.	15,249	14,615	18,628	14,848	19,937	8,429	19,029	15,894	16,675	5,772	15,986	19,145	8,335	13,016	16,379	7,331	13,421	15,285	17,703	16,857
Nuremberg, West Germany	3,765	1,223	5,095	4,652	4,481	10,040	4,981	2,386	5,163	15,498	5,116	3,614	9,746	6,054	857	8,939	2,469	3,720	2,998	2,903
Nyala, Sudan	3,148	5,506	3,266	3,397	1,963	13,168	2,852	2,955	1,548	12,930	2,190	1,900	13,146	5,188	3,663	11,223	6,777	3,121	1,355	1,879
Oaxaca, Mexico	13,567	8,706	10,130	14,451	11,175	342	10,526	12,198	14,337	14,224	14,679	10,960	794	15,423	9,982	11,405	7,770	13,523	12,074	12,474
Ocean Falls, Canada	10,837	6,898	11,717	11,493	11,957	4,631	11,914	9,967	13,081	13,224	12,756	11,222	4,020	11,425	8,751	6,779	5,627	10,816	11,069	10,849
Odense, Denmark	4,077	796	5,701	4,955	5,136	9,702	5,609	2,776	5,714	15,493	5,597	4,270	9,362	6,185	1,504	8,442	1,910	4,035	3,623	3,444
Odessa, USSR	2,345	2,523	5,652	3,224	4,701	11,433	5,422	1,116	4,218	14,005	3,970	3,887	11,089	4,554	1,823	8,172	3,576	2,304	2,558	2,038
Ogbomosho, Nigeria	5,192	5,464	969	5,616	341	11,247	572	4,478	3,791	14,510	4,486	1,057	11,364	7,453	3,769	13,039	6,617	5,154	2,696	3,553
Okha, USSR	7,646	7,329	12,789	7,765	11,907	10,189	12,600	7,813	10,130	9,814	9,392	11,090	9,584	6,689	8,557	1,554	6,683	7,662	9,631	8,866
Okinawa (Naha)	7,638	9,647	13,758	7,276	12,499	13,007	13,400	8,504	9,475	6,866	8,674	11,940	12,447	5,544	10,205	1,892	9,408	7,676	10,165	9,304
Oklahoma City, Oklahoma	11,890	7,079	9,987	12,741	10,731	2,079	10,315	10,619	13,280	14,989	13,374	10,269	1,579	13,444	8,625	9,803	5,995	11,851	10,937	11,125
Old Crow, Canada	9,129	5,743	11,211	9,732	11,097	6,310	11,297	8,401	11,507	13,200	11,086	10,271	5,704	9,608	7,579	5,586	4,530	9,113	9,734	9,368
Olympia, Washington	11,389	7,231	11,691	12,080	12,073	3,959	11,929	10,444	13,533	13,344	13,272	11,392	3,349	12,090	9,059	7,379	5,965	11,366	11,419	11,274
Omaha, Nebraska	11,270	6,494	9,790	12,113	10,428	2,734	10,090	10,024	12,773	15,261	12,813	9,903	2,231	12,789	8,098	9,396	5,378	11,233	10,442	10,577
Omsk, USSR	3,389	4,464	8,724	3,735	7,669	12,018	8,462	3,498	5,945	11,737	5,296	6,915	11,476	3,550	4,809	5,100	4,715	3,396	5,323	4,532
Oodnadatta, Australia	11,259	15,343	15,088	10,427	14,246	14,245	14,750	12,647	11,139	871	10,706	14,533	14,203	8,770	14,979	7,462	15,387	11,309	13,307	12,744
Oradea, Romania	2,924	1,975	5,253	3,811	4,427	10,866	5,066	1,568	4,505	14,676	4,372	3,576	10,554	5,218	1,194	8,615	3,134	2,879	2,540	2,241
Oran, Algeria	4,561	2,385	3,382	5,376	3,044	9,743	3,339	3,209	4,958	16,345	5,223	2,244	9,609	7,091	1,066	10,739	3,526	4,511	2,628	3,071
Oranjestad, Aruba	11,898	7,519	7,286	12,731	8,423	3,251	7,696	10,504	11,801	16,214	12,337	8,362	3,577	14,361	8,166	13,440	7,064	11,848	9,785	10,398
Orebro, Sweden	4,063	1,043	6,209	4,919	5,602	9,756	6,105	2,866	5,916	15,142	5,722	4,735	9,376	5,995	1,983	7,924	1,833	4,025	3,948	3,663
Orel, USSR	2,697	2,453	6,417	3,513	5,505	11,203	6,205	1,768	4,872	13,811	4,524	4,681	10,799	4,528	2,377	7,425	3,266	2,666	3,365	2,791
Orsk, USSR	2,469	3,882	7,664	2,989	6,593	12,182	7,392	2,421	5,017	12,316	4,435	5,846	11,696	3,353	3,877	6,169	4,427	2,466	4,246	3,463
Osaka, Japan	7,939	9,083	13,888	7,737	12,734	11,846	13,588	8,574	10,063	7,712	9,260	12,054	11,275	6,173	9,943	694	8,651	7,970	10,347	9,496
Oslo, Norway	4,310	809	6,186	5,170	5,639	9,500	6,103	3,089	6,110	15,377	5,940	4,774	9,125	6,257	2,007	8,033	1,588	4,271	4,086	3,847
Osorno, Chile	14,685	12,691	8,660	14,864	9,862	6,934	8,987	13,968	12,504	11,038	13,299	10,496	7,544	16,277	12,299	17,204	12,693	14,653	12,241	13,099
Ostrava, Czechoslovakia	3,312	1,569	5,360	4,197	4,625	10,471	5,206	1,972	4,903	14,980	4,781	3,762	10,151	5,546	1,149	8,574	2,727	3,267	2,878	2,635
Ottawa, Canada	9,894	5,031	8,163	10,770	8,736	3,887	8,440	8,564	11,138	16,905	11,255	8,199	3,559	11,777	6,493	9,923	4,069	9,852	8,794	9,002
Ouagadougou, Bourkina Fasso	5,483	4,967	827	6,015	1,015	10,497	767	4,572	4,411	15,296	5,050	1,143	10,595	7,878	3,423	13,014	6,051	5,441	2,925	3,777
Oujda, Morocco	4,691	2,497	3,257	5,498	2,972	9,671	3,229	3,350	5,012	16,436	5,302	2,194	9,551	7,226	1,228	10,895	3,612	4,641	2,696	3,175
Oxford, United Kingdom	4,674	602	5,154	5,561	4,784	9,136	5,123	3,292	5,965	16,329	5,978	3,944	8,853	6,932	1,330	9,203	1,819	4,628	3,704	3,737
Pago Pago, American Samoa	15,665	15,151	18,262	15,187	19,400	8,505	18,602	16,413	16,781	5,551	16,170	19,680	8,467	13,330	16,940	7,851	13,939	15,705	18,189	17,329
Pakxe, Laos	6,079	9,648	11,974	5,456	10,665	15,493	11,563	7,293	7,310	6,535	6,551	10,336	14,903	3,590	9,472	4,308	9,918	6,127	8,593	7,790
Palembang, Indonesia	7,030	11,291	12,129	6,231	10,901	16,922	11,707	8,401	7,446	4,979	6,825	10,832	16,426	4,517	10,726	5,944	11,747	7,080	9,282	8,605
Palermo, Italy	3,308	2,400	4,038	4,147	3,266	10,782	3,860	1,937	4,101	15,178	4,206	2,402	10,576	5,823	578	9,825	3,671	3,258	1,808	1,961
Palma, Majorca	4,244	1,984	3,853	5,089	3,398	9,869	3,779	2,855	4,923	16,122	5,101	2,558	9,688	6,740	576	10,223	3,191	4,194	2,581	2,879
Palmerston North, New Zealand	15,183	18,131	16,124	14,333	16,368	10,751	16,128	16,580	14,534	3,297	14,329	17,156	10,918	12,702	18,909	9,571	17,057	15,233	16,878	16,541
Panama, Panama	12,953	8,416	8,337	13,802	9,505	2,375	8,753	11,548	12,905	15,195	13,448	9,468	2,825	15,356	9,209	13,252	7,818	12,903	10,892	11,492
Paramaribo, Suriname	10,967	7,312	5,664	11,701	6,884	5,022	6,085	9,667	10,341	16,490	10,974	6,974	5,369	13,516	7,432	14,725	7,239	10,918	8,583	9,313
Paris, France	4,363	966	4,864	5,247	4,425	9,480	4,807	2,964	5,565	16,139	5,597	3,575	9,215	6,689	920	9,352	2,218	4,316	3,295	3,349
Patna, India	3,648	7,491	9,678	3,099	8,375	15,277	9,284	4,851	5,231	8,755	4,430	7,957	14,691	1,300	7,071	5,305	8,022	3,694	6,188	5,365
Patrai, Greece	2,585	2,729	4,483	3,436	3,536	11,405	4,248	1,204	3,656	14,473	3,645	2,714	11,161	5,091	1,180	9,338	3,971	2,535	1,565	1,404
Peking, China	6,151	7,815	12,144	5,972	10,960	12,684	11,827	6,826	8,325	8,597	7,527	10,306	12,077	4,507	8,382	2,025	7,660	6,182	8,576	7,720
Penrhyn Island (Omoka)	16,407	14,278	17,141	16,186	18,416	7,010	17,562	16,625	18,194	7,017	17,479	18,278	6,980	14,421	16,137	8,331	13,010	16,433	18,316	17,702
Peoria, Illinois	11,028	6,194	9,255	11,890	9,919	2,824	9,560	9,736	12,379	15,786	12,474	9,418	2,405	12,715	7,723	9,780	5,140	10,988	10,037	10,224
Perm', USSR	3,135	3,384	7,792	3,727	6,829	11,425	7,565	2,791	5,637	12,803	5,108	6,027	10,932	4,099	3,746	6,039	3,765	3,124	4,573	3,867
Perth, Australia	9,914	14,589	13,133	9,035	12,307	16,059	12,793	11,322	9,346	2,138	9,011	12,654	16,103	7,627	13,627	8,320	15,159	9,962	11,620	11,185
Peshawar, Pakistan	2,229	5,949	8,355	1,973	7,088	14,304	7,990	3,285	4,350	10,342	3,570	6,561	13,784	1,222	5,466	5,997	6,599	2,268	4,776	3,923
Petropavlovsk-Kamchatskiy,USSR	8,597	7,668	13,339	8,769	12,605	9,270	13,218	8,637	11,115	9,936	10,394	11,757	8,674	7,736	9,098	2,042	6,839	8,608	10,429	9,708
Petrozavodsk, USSR	3,644	2,100	7,022	4,417	6,248	10,404	6,863	2,759	5,869	14,092	5,512	5,393	9,961	5,191	2,792	6,950	2,546	3,616	4,262	3,756
Pevek, USSR	7,983	5,921	11,670	8,409	11,159	8,252	11,624	7,621	10,526	11,886	9,941	10,292	7,642	7,914	7,535	3,775	4,969	7,980	9,263	8,684
Philadelphia, Pennsylvania	10,286	5,425	8,027	11,169	8,712	3,503	8,334	8,924	11,339	17,004	11,528	8,245	3,254	12,277	6,765	10,486	4,549	10,242	8,999	9,279
Phnom Penh, Kampuchea	6,180	9,937	11,951	5,509	10,648	15,855	11,534	7,441	7,244	6,252	6,506	10,370	15,272	3,651	9,667	4,661	10,256	6,229	8,656	7,874
Phoenix, Arizona	12,650	8,030	11,343	13,437	12,062	2,206	11,668	11,504	14,385	13,653	14,346	11,561	1,603	13,733	9,709	9,030	6,844	12,618	12,074	12,150
Pierre, South Dakota	11,142	6,455	10,101	11,961	10,665	3,052	10,383	9,950	12,807	14,966	12,779	10,093	2,501	12,507	8,133	8,905	5,286	11,107	10,503	10,572
Pinang, Malaysia	6,099	10,249	11,547	5,341	10,268	16,698	11,124	7,442	6,812	6,001	6,124	10,093	16,117	3,557	9,745	5,504	10,711	6,149	8,456	7,730
Pitcairn Island (Adamstown)	19,401	14,580	13,884	19,577	15,181	5,675	14,272	18,098	17,878	8,574	18,553	15,599	6,000	17,715	15,816	11,729	13,522	19,370	17,340	18,094
Pittsburgh, Pennsylvania	10,536	5,670	8,443	11,415	9,120	3,242	8,750	9,194	11,692	16,592	11,849	8,641	2,941	12,431	7,082	10,244	4,724	10,493	9,348	9,597
Plymouth, Montserrat	10,946	6,672	6,460	11,774	7,544	4,013	6,859	9,557	10,878	17,126	11,392	7,437	4,240	13,428	7,222	13,346	6,333	10,896	8,828	9,437
Plymouth, United Kingdom	4,849	761	4,998	5,735	4,689	8,985	4,985	3,455	6,039	16,562	6,088	3,864	8,720	7,144	1,366	9,430	1,880	4,803	3,747	3,838
Ponape Island	11,513	12,684	17,639	11,089	16,361	11,044	17,269	12,358	13,102	5,071	12,337	15,819	10,699	9,273	13,778	4,061	11,948	11,552	14,047	13,186
Ponce, Puerto Rico	11,237	6,809	6,936	12,084	8,001	3,536	7,332	9,836	11,302	16,901	11,789	7,864	3,752	13,673	7,496	13,041	6,363	11,188	9,204	9,780
Ponta Delgada, Azores	6,701	2,766	4,208	7,552	4,567	7,515	4,400	5,300	7,152	18,581	7,460	4,012	7,414	9,164	2,961	11,307	3,146	6,651	4,853	5,304
Pontianak, Indonesia	7,266	11,286	12,609	6,508	11,354	16,321	12,185	8,601	7,891	4,917	7,235	11,227	15,828	4,721	10,891	5,399	11,627	7,316	9,615	8,897
Port Augusta, Australia	11,708	15,921	15,046	10,858	14,337	14,012	14,745	13,109	11,396	281	11,021	14,718	14,038	9,255	15,449	7,999	15,976	11,758	13,634	13,128
Port Blair, India	5,028	9,223	10,637	4,289	9,338	16,568	10,217	6,363	5,919	7,062	5,189	9,098	15,958	2,482	8,667	5,593	9,763	5,078	7,422	6,676
Port Elizabeth, South Africa	7,506	10,426	5,349	7,148	5,155	14,297	5,148	7,923	4,957	9,684	5,567	5,938	14,783	8,037	8,577	14,278	11,667	7,507	6,442	6,891
Port Hedland, Australia	9,377	13,721	13,619	8,537	12,590	15,963	13,231	10,775	9,320	2,547	8,841	12,753	15,796	6,920	13,114	7,013	14,079	9,427	11,428	10,849

Distances in Kilometers	Abadan, Iran	Aberdeen, United Kingdom	Abidjan, Ivory Coast	Abu Dhabi, United Arab Emir.	Abuja, Nigeria	Acapulco, Mexico	Accra, Ghana	Adana, Turkey	Addis Ababa, Ethiopia	Adelaide, Australia	Aden, P.D.R. Yemen	Agadez, Niger	Aguascalientes, Mexico	Ahmadabad, India	Ajaccio, France	Akita, Japan	Akureyri, Iceland	Al Basrah, Iraq	Al Jawf, Libya	Al Minya, Egypt
Port Louis, Mauritius	5,675	10,190	7,293	4,950	6,395	17,623	6,923	6,745	3,831	7,969	3,891	6,794	17,927	5,053	8,509	10,814	11,390	5,702	6,151	6,067
Port Moresby, Papua New Guinea	11,394	14,098	16,827	10,730	15,645	12,746	16,414	12,584	12,194	2,951	11,556	15,545	12,516	8,875	14,601	5,496	13,666	11,441	13,876	13,097
Port Said, Egypt	1,530	3,900	4,756	2,295	3,570	12,642	4,428	695	2,549	13,294	2,429	2,925	12,397	4,076	2,406	9,194	5,097	1,482	1,183	382
Port Sudan, Sudan	1,626	5,266	4,740	1,847	3,434	13,840	4,343	1,938	1,182	12,247	1,125	3,103	13,659	3,682	3,650	9,686	6,476	1,606	1,526	1,148
Port-au-Prince, Haiti	11,675	7,104	7,542	12,537	8,599	2,929	7,937	10,266	11,872	16,473	12,333	8,441	3,149	14,045	7,931	12,734	6,540	11,626	9,733	10,276
Port-of-Spain, Trin. & Tobago	11,264	7,199	6,357	12,058	7,521	4,202	6,770	9,904	10,936	16,639	11,513	7,512	4,518	13,792	7,594	14,001	6,939	11,215	9,016	9,684
Port-Vila, Vanuatu	13,843	15,559	18,407	13,190	17,781	10,755	18,183	14,973	14,509	3,504	13,940	17,944	10,673	11,334	16,703	7,002	14,659	13,889	16,335	15,553
Portland, Maine	9,708	4,846	7,701	10,591	8,303	4,077	7,985	8,349	10,810	17,367	10,973	7,791	3,811	11,710	6,207	10,282	3,982	9,664	8,466	8,722
Portland, Oregon	11,553	7,364	11,744	12,247	12,157	3,818	11,991	10,598	13,681	13,304	13,430	11,489	3,210	12,257	9,186	7,489	6,101	11,529	11,551	11,419
Porto, Portugal	5,190	1,838	3,996	6,046	3,871	8,904	4,031	3,787	5,847	17,083	6,062	3,118	8,737	7,654	1,448	10,509	2,793	5,140	3,504	3,850
Porto Alegre, Brazil	12,457	10,703	6,370	12,760	7,599	7,365	6,710	11,667	10,501	12,737	11,305	8,203	7,935	14,429	10,062	18,530	10,987	12,421	9,962	10,822
Porto Alexandre, Angola	6,425	8,188	2,922	6,415	2,811	12,785	2,713	6,343	4,036	12,070	4,828	3,651	13,114	7,885	6,400	14,372	9,378	6,408	4,598	5,268
Porto Novo, Benin	5,445	5,633	748	5,859	585	11,133	330	4,735	3,989	14,529	4,700	1,299	11,273	7,690	3,972	13,294	6,765	5,408	2,954	3,810
Porto Velho, Brazil	12,629	9,194	6,824	13,274	8,126	4,873	7,243	11,410	11,542	14,625	12,271	8,405	5,392	15,138	9,251	15,835	9,064	12,581	10,130	10,923
Portsmouth, United Kingdom	4,643	712	5,046	5,529	4,675	9,179	5,013	3,254	5,889	16,344	5,915	3,836	8,905	6,926	1,238	9,293	1,923	4,596	3,618	3,670
Poznan, Poland	3,537	1,329	5,567	4,418	4,878	10,241	5,430	2,232	5,198	15,084	5,060	4,012	9,906	5,698	1,322	8,422	2,444	3,495	3,178	2,932
Prague, Czechoslovakia	3,568	1,343	5,256	4,454	4,586	10,221	5,125	2,209	5,073	15,255	4,986	3,719	9,912	5,821	1,010	8,732	2,545	3,523	2,973	2,804
Praia, Cape Verde Islands	7,460	5,021	2,382	8,136	3,400	8,131	2,752	6,269	6,788	17,166	7,383	3,377	8,275	9,986	4,304	13,725	5,651	7,413	4,996	5,762
Pretoria, South Africa	6,566	9,613	4,890	6,231	4,482	14,589	4,626	6,988	4,014	10,084	4,636	5,207	14,995	7,218	7,754	13,613	10,872	6,567	5,551	5,965
Prince Albert, Canada	10,416	5,962	10,314	11,189	10,675	4,065	10,540	9,329	12,338	14,683	12,185	10,003	3,489	11,558	7,751	7,931	4,720	10,386	10,129	10,069
Prince Edward Island	8,581	12,080	7,080	8,041	6,889	14,934	6,892	9,263	6,160	8,008	6,611	7,653	15,518	8,464	10,221	13,903	13,341	8,594	7,976	8,302
Prince George, Canada	10,631	6,577	11,344	11,316	11,593	4,562	11,542	9,712	12,814	13,592	12,526	10,866	3,953	11,353	8,424	6,980	5,306	10,608	10,758	10,568
Prince Rupert, Canada	10,625	6,794	11,749	11,265	11,929	4,910	11,928	9,792	12,909	13,138	12,558	11,174	4,300	11,159	8,653	6,523	5,526	10,606	10,947	10,695
Providence, Rhode Island	9,912	5,055	7,750	10,797	8,393	3,879	8,045	8,548	10,968	17,308	11,150	7,904	3,632	11,931	6,387	10,432	4,204	9,868	8,627	8,901
Provo, Utah	11,923	7,380	11,108	12,698	11,701	2,829	11,401	10,812	13,762	13,952	13,665	11,130	2,219	12,987	9,109	8,556	6,168	11,893	11,489	11,504
Puerto Aisen, Chile	14,693	13,110	8,795	14,771	9,950	7,422	9,098	14,112	12,389	10,569	13,169	10,631	8,032	16,023	12,594	17,274	13,176	14,666	12,337	13,185
Puerto Deseado, Argentina	14,192	13,029	8,409	14,224	9,520	7,917	8,692	13,704	11,840	10,528	12,613	10,235	8,527	15,441	12,344	17,755	13,227	14,167	11,903	12,739
Puerto Princesa, Philippines	7,602	10,863	13,474	6,984	12,168	14,855	13,058	8,787	8,768	5,369	8,031	11,862	14,341	5,118	10,902	3,941	10,926	7,649	10,121	9,315
Punta Arenas, Chile	14,562	13,725	8,974	14,483	10,034	8,240	9,234	14,218	12,113	9,838	12,857	10,782	8,848	15,475	12,990	17,235	13,918	14,543	12,399	13,214
Pusan, South Korea	7,377	8,807	13,381	7,154	12,198	12,286	13,065	8,062	9,474	7,816	8,670	11,543	11,702	5,582	9,540	1,105	8,480	7,409	9,814	8,959
Pyongyang, North Korea	6,954	8,288	12,900	6,783	11,740	12,217	12,596	7,583	9,132	8,294	8,334	11,064	11,620	5,292	9,020	1,239	7,987	6,984	9,353	8,502
Qamdo, China	4,650	7,683	10,776	4,262	9,497	14,387	10,403	5,653	6,511	8,503	5,706	8,986	13,778	2,595	7,662	3,968	7,945	4,691	7,202	6,348
Qandahar, Afghanistan	1,674	5,805	7,792	1,368	6,513	14,433	7,418	2,854	3,748	10,592	2,974	6,015	13,954	1,165	5,123	6,603	6,575	1,717	4,232	3,390
Qiqian, China	6,251	6,819	11,796	6,305	10,763	11,408	11,549	6,585	8,683	9,807	7,929	10,002	10,797	5,203	7,708	2,029	6,474	6,271	8,408	7,598
Qom, Iran	539	4,650	6,500	1,177	5,265	13,529	6,151	1,432	3,098	11,927	2,496	4,684	13,141	2,471	3,737	7,597	5,598	545	2,906	2,045
Quebec, Canada	9,535	4,669	7,854	10,414	8,391	4,243	8,121	8,197	10,759	17,203	10,878	7,839	3,930	11,463	6,115	9,929	3,739	9,492	8,416	8,625
Quetta, Pakistan	1,801	5,999	7,896	1,401	6,610	14,615	7,517	3,022	3,761	10,403	2,975	6,134	14,130	971	5,304	6,578	6,767	1,846	4,354	3,520
Quito, Ecuador	13,493	9,209	8,300	14,289	9,548	3,014	8,723	12,123	13,010	14,542	13,652	9,650	3,557	16,007	9,798	14,146	8,716	13,443	11,224	11,910
Rabaul, Papua New Guinea	11,586	13,716	17,397	11,000	16,130	12,058	16,973	12,667	12,671	3,680	11,983	15,879	11,792	9,134	14,483	5,017	13,140	11,631	14,129	13,306
Raiatea (Uturoa)	17,517	14,847	16,261	17,214	17,569	6,763	16,660	17,663	18,634	7,158	18,210	17,843	6,852	15,384	16,639	9,444	13,584	17,545	19,021	18,727
Raleigh, North Carolina	10,829	5,973	8,280	11,714	9,048	2,972	8,609	9,460	11,810	16,661	12,027	8,631	2,764	12,831	7,276	10,754	5,103	10,785	9,473	9,786
Rangiroa (Avatoru)	17,657	14,507	15,920	17,491	17,229	6,318	16,330	17,540	19,067	7,603	18,640	17,424	6,414	15,708	16,262	9,599	13,254	17,677	18,625	18,538
Rangoon, Burma	5,075	8,944	10,929	4,422	9,620	15,893	10,518	6,335	6,276	7,271	5,511	9,297	15,283	2,558	8,575	4,938	9,374	5,123	7,566	6,774
Raoul Is., Kermadec Islands	15,595	16,891	17,278	14,851	17,719	9,799	17,368	16,829	15,602	4,122	15,242	18,520	9,879	13,048	18,482	8,787	15,726	15,644	17,850	17,234
Rarotonga (Avarua)	17,050	15,620	16,872	16,519	18,090	7,770	17,219	17,736	17,632	6,151	17,237	18,660	7,853	14,653	17,471	9,185	14,349	17,090	19,560	18,713
Rawson, Argentina	14,066	12,579	8,146	14,185	9,303	7,549	8,450	13,463	11,812	11,015	12,600	9,981	8,159	15,547	11,976	17,888	12,741	14,037	11,690	12,540
Recife, Brazil	9,812	7,818	3,733	10,309	5,040	7,667	4,134	8,828	8,378	15,199	9,132	5,471	8,062	12,153	7,093	16,462	8,292	9,770	7,255	8,104
Regina, Canada	10,668	6,142	10,301	11,453	10,725	3,751	10,545	9,552	12,527	14,734	12,407	10,080	3,177	11,861	7,905	8,197	4,916	10,636	10,287	10,262
Reykjavik, Iceland	6,061	1,329	6,685	6,924	6,520	7,750	6,732	4,802	7,711	16,498	7,627	5,711	7,372	7,943	3,156	8,382	249	6,022	5,512	5,447
Rhodes, Greece	1,980	3,214	4,764	2,827	3,693	11,989	4,484	636	3,215	13,865	3,114	2,938	11,727	4,500	1,785	9,078	4,415	1,930	1,436	954
Richmond, Virginia	10,615	5,756	8,192	11,499	8,926	3,179	8,513	9,250	11,627	16,792	11,835	8,488	2,950	12,608	7,077	10,632	4,880	10,571	9,291	9,590
Riga, USSR	3,502	1,581	6,236	4,349	5,500	10,335	6,087	2,367	5,464	14,634	5,217	4,639	9,948	5,415	1,999	7,740	2,403	3,465	3,638	3,248
Ringkobing, Denmark	4,231	646	5,735	5,109	5,205	9,548	5,654	2,929	5,856	15,612	5,747	4,341	9,208	6,329	1,576	8,462	1,764	4,189	3,747	3,587
Rio Branco, Brazil	13,068	9,520	7,270	13,720	8,573	4,615	7,688	11,835	11,983	14,317	12,716	8,853	5,158	15,583	9,652	15,714	9,322	13,020	10,575	11,365
Rio Cuarto, Argentina	13,747	11,576	7,642	14,051	8,886	6,701	7,992	12,910	11,771	12,101	12,576	9,468	7,302	15,685	11,167	17,720	11,651	13,710	11,237	12,098
Rio de Janeiro, Brazil	11,400	9,665	5,284	11,764	6,538	7,576	5,639	10,559	9,587	13,601	10,384	7,108	8,095	13,511	8,948	18,114	10,050	11,362	8,879	9,739
Rio Gallegos, Argentina	14,451	13,521	8,802	14,405	9,878	8,151	9,069	14,064	12,027	10,039	12,780	10,616	8,760	15,465	12,798	17,401	13,717	14,430	12,249	13,071
Rio Grande, Brazil	12,620	10,937	6,553	12,897	7,770	7,435	6,887	11,860	10,615	12,509	11,419	8,389	8,012	14,534	10,284	18,627	11,219	12,585	10,140	11,000
Riyadh, Saudi Arabia	650	5,292	5,821	775	4,525	14,171	5,434	1,751	1,925	11,698	1,326	4,107	13,873	2,641	3,979	8,579	6,386	659	2,373	1,638
Road Town, Brit. Virgin Isls.	11,039	6,651	6,728	11,882	7,787	3,744	7,123	9,640	11,085	17,089	11,573	7,647	3,948	13,488	7,300	13,075	6,241	10,990	8,990	9,571
Roanoke, Virginia	10,789	5,925	8,409	11,672	9,148	2,995	8,731	9,431	11,840	16,570	12,037	8,709	2,745	12,740	7,276	10,552	5,019	10,745	9,502	9,790
Robinson Crusoe Island, Chile	15,071	12,345	8,948	15,401	10,210	6,017	9,309	14,148	13,114	11,474	13,918	10,757	6,628	17,006	12,231	16,503	12,173	15,033	12,538	13,396
Rochester, New York	10,179	5,314	8,277	11,057	8,899	3,600	8,568	8,843	11,381	16,786	11,517	8,388	3,284	12,071	6,751	10,076	4,362	10,137	9,036	9,264
Rockhampton, Australia	12,410	15,658	16,640	11,642	15,823	12,702	16,319	13,725	12,632	1,723	12,135	16,062	12,632	9,863	15,935	7,068	15,236	12,460	14,683	14,022
Rome, Italy	3,437	1,987	4,371	4,303	3,664	10,520	4,219	2,030	4,457	15,332	4,508	2,797	10,285	5,898	311	9,539	3,258	3,388	2,203	2,255
Rosario, Argentina	13,412	11,391	7,318	13,707	8,554	6,914	7,662	12,600	11,427	12,227	12,231	9,147	7,509	15,342	10,907	18,018	11,529	13,376	10,911	11,772
Roseau, Dominica	10,963	6,755	6,362	11,782	7,466	4,118	6,765	9,581	10,824	17,063	11,355	7,383	4,365	13,461	7,252	13,521	6,449	10,913	8,806	9,432
Rostock, East Germany	3,909	957	5,602	4,790	5,001	9,869	5,496	2,598	5,529	15,398	5,414	4,134	9,535	6,050	1,376	8,488	2,095	3,867	3,446	3,260
Rostov-na-Donu, USSR	2,015	3,007	6,241	2,842	5,217	11,848	5,985	1,191	4,235	13,379	3,854	4,439	11,460	3,974	2,512	7,581	3,916	1,983	2,942	2,262
Rotterdam, Netherlands	4,294	720	5,226	5,180	4,747	9,503	5,159	2,923	5,679	15,937	5,651	3,890	9,206	6,536	1,157	8,983	1,991	4,248	3,468	3,428
Rouyn, Canada	9,848	5,009	8,459	10,714	8,975	3,967	8,722	8,551	11,230	16,596	11,297	8,402	3,583	11,622	6,559	9,528	3,971	9,808	8,896	9,051
Sacramento, California	12,302	7,983	11,968	13,012	12,526	3,196	12,255	11,303	14,351	13,097	14,151	11,922	2,605	13,028	9,770	8,014	6,736	12,276	12,150	12,081
Saginaw, Michigan	10,501	5,654	8,791	11,369	9,407	3,312	9,082	9,195	11,821	16,271	11,920	8,884	2,932	12,267	7,166	9,791	4,627	10,460	9,480	9,669
Saint Denis, Reunion	5,717	10,159	7,110	5,017	6,238	17,403	6,745	6,747	3,781	8,111	3,891	6,661	17,725	5,202	8,451	11,028	11,374	5,743	6,082	6,035
Saint George's, Grenada	11,198	7,080	6,385	12,001	7,532	4,143	6,796	9,830	10,932	16,752	11,494	7,500	4,439	13,717	7,513	13,847	6,801	11,148	8,979	9,633
Saint John, Canada	9,335	4,477	7,422	10,219	7,980	4,454	7,693	7,972	10,436	17,638	10,594	7,447	4,191	11,366	5,827	10,237	3,645	9,291	8,091	8,342
Saint John's, Antigua	10,888	6,614	6,424	11,717	7,503	4,048	6,822	9,499	10,830	17,185	11,341	7,390	4,268	13,369	7,164	13,317	6,278	10,838	8,775	9,382
Saint John's, Canada	8,338	3,518	6,578	9,225	7,023	5,478	6,813	6,958	9,381	18,321	9,543	6,445	5,239	10,475	4,779	10,253	2,861	8,293	7,037	7,293
Saint Louis, Missouri	11,245	6,403	9,313	12,110	10,016	2,592	9,629	9,944	12,551	15,700	12,666	9,538	2,186	12,950	7,907	9,936	5,363	11,205	10,207	10,414
Saint Paul, Minnesota	10,799	6,031	9,522	11,642	10,095	3,180	9,805	9,557	12,333	15,545	12,355	9,536	2,693	12,339	7,655	9,230	4,908	10,762	10,010	10,124
Saint Peter Port, UK	4,723	856	4,894	5,608	4,557	9,123	4,871	3,325	5,885	16,478	5,940	3,726	8,864	7,040	1,211	9,471	2,019	4,676	3,591	3,688
Saipan (Susupe)	9,869	11,462	15,995	9,463	14,723	12,001	15,629	10,735	11,553	5,594	10,769	14,180	11,554	7,669	12,307	2,777	10,941	9,908	12,404	11,544
Salalah, Oman	1,591	6,419	6,457	827	5,149	15,311	6,044	2,886	1,887	10,592	1,084	4,899	15,001	2,047	5,112	8,489	7,481	1,627	3,301	2,691
Salem, Oregon	11,623	7,437	11,802	12,315	12,223	3,790	12,051	10,671	13,754	13,250	13,502	11,557	3,183	12,313	9,259	7,500	6,174	11,599	11,624	11,493
Salt Lake City, Utah	11,874	7,342	11,111	12,646	11,692	2,889	11,401	10,768	13,726	13,952	13,622	11,115	2,279	12,928	9,077	8,504	6,127	11,844	11,458	11,467
Salta, Argentina	13,542	10,822	7,427	13,987	8,717	5,936	7,809	12,536	11,853	12,930	12,649	9,201	6,524	15,771	10,603	17,117	10,803	13,500	10,986	11,837
Salto, Uruguay	13,115	11,118	7,014	13,425	8,254	6,970	7,361	12,292	11,162	12,463	11,967	8,841	7,557	15,087	10,604	18,144	11,291	13,078	10,608	11,469
Salvador, Brazil	10,430	8,463	4,317	10,891	5,615	7,515	4,705	9,481	8,876	14,693	9,648	6,092	7,959	12,716	7,767	17,039	8,886	10,389	7,877	8,731
Salzburg, Austria	3,567	1,455	4,982	4,453	4,318	10,252	4,850	2,177	4,930	15,352	4,887	3,451	9,965	5,893	737	8,996	2,701	3,521	2,772	2,670
Samsun, Turkey	1,621	3,245	5,650	2,505	4,569	12,157	5,369	482	3,581	13,398	3,271	3,823	11,819	3,934	2,292	8,194	4,305	1,578	2,248	1,549
San Antonio, Texas	12,517	7,677	10,158	13,378	11,007	1,400	10,512	11,219	13,764	14,679	13,923	10,617	918	14,123	9,156	10,252	6,628	12,477	11,422	11,669
San Cristobal, Venezuela	12,408	8,091	7,541	13,226	8,728	3,170	7,958	11,024	12,154	15,665	12,733	8,732	3,582	14,898	8,692	13,790	7,641	12,358	10,222	10,869
San Diego, California	12,861	8,348	11,821	13,613	12,523	2,468	12,144	11,775	14,729	13,186	14,630	12,003	1,894	13,749	10,068	8,727	7,136	12,832	12,444	12,473
San Francisco, California	12,403	8,101	12,078	13,107	12,643	3,197	12,367	11,414	14,466	12,986	14,260	12,042	2,613	13,094	9,890	8,003	6,853	12,378	12,270	12,197
San Jose, Costa Rica	13,254	8,602	8,830	14,120	9,982	1,877	9,243	11,844	13,357	14,889	13,871	9,916	2,353	15,571	9,512	12,876	7,916	13,205	11,290	11,855
San Juan, Argentina	14,072	11,622	7,950	14,418	9,211	6,318	8,311	13,172	12,165	12,122	12,969	9,762	6,923	16,089	11,335	17,290	11,608	14,034	11,541	12,401
San Juan, Puerto Rico	11,165	6,738	6,886	12,012	7,945	3,586	7,281	9,763	11,238	16,974	11,722	7,802	3,793	13,601	7,423	13,015	6,297	11,116	9,136	9,710
San Luis Potosi, Mexico	13,338	8,483	10,508	14,205	11,468	597	10,888	12,019	14,434	14,112	14,663	11,163	139	14,959	9,902	10,686	7,458	13,297	12,110	12,416
San Marino, San Marino	3,485	1,789	4,572	4,360	3,885	10,415	4,429	2,074	4,625	15,363	4,644	3,018	10,163	5,906	377	9,363	3,056	3,436	2,400	2,397
San Miguel de Tucuman, Argen.	13,603	11,009	7,478	14,016	8,760	6,116	7,853	12,636	11,841	12,728	12,641	9,269	6,708	15,770	10,744	17,276	11,011	13,563	11,053	11,908

Distances in Kilometers

	Abadan, Iran	Aberdeen, United Kingdom	Abidjan, Ivory Coast	Abu Dhabi, United Arab Emir.	Abuja, Nigeria	Acapulco, Mexico	Accra, Ghana	Adana, Turkey	Addis Ababa, Ethiopia	Adelaide, Australia	Aden, P.D.R. Yemen	Agadez, Niger	Aguascalientes, Mexico	Ahmadabad, India	Ajaccio, France	Akita, Japan	Akureyri, Iceland	Al Basrah, Iraq	Al Jawf, Libya	Al Minya, Egypt
San Salvador, El Salvador	13,348	8,565	9,358	14,231	10,460	1,202	9,764	11,944	13,751	14,698	14,192	10,322	1,657	15,490	9,648	12,206	7,763	13,301	11,581	12,075
Sanaa, Yemen	1,711	6,034	5,386	1,466	4,080	14,711	4,972	2,557	920	11,369	299	3,872	14,512	3,101	4,494	9,429	7,206	1,717	2,395	1,979
Santa Cruz, Bolivia	13,019	10,033	6,979	13,553	8,286	5,560	7,379	11,920	11,570	13,735	12,345	8,692	6,120	15,399	9,895	16,709	9,995	12,974	10,466	11,300
Santa Cruz, Tenerife	6,177	3,374	2,866	6,952	3,250	8,537	3,047	4,864	6,120	17,542	6,548	2,786	8,520	8,723	2,705	12,073	4,140	6,127	3,958	4,579
Santa Fe, New Mexico	12,218	7,513	10,739	13,035	11,448	2,170	11,060	11,020	13,830	14,266	13,840	10,951	1,570	13,504	9,152	9,268	6,357	12,184	11,504	11,618
Santa Rosa, Argentina	13,844	11,907	7,784	14,087	9,000	7,003	8,118	13,085	11,765	11,738	12,567	9,618	7,608	15,639	11,427	17,866	12,017	13,811	11,372	12,231
Santa Rosalia, Mexico	13,300	8,618	11,529	14,100	12,358	1,722	11,881	12,122	14,920	13,351	14,945	11,929	1,176	14,409	10,246	9,474	7,458	13,267	12,585	12,720
Santarem, Brazil	11,396	8,098	5,699	12,058	6,983	5,406	6,122	10,175	10,434	15,644	11,132	7,208	5,833	13,916	8,035	15,615	8,107	11,349	8,911	9,695
Santiago del Estero, Argentina	13,552	11,056	7,425	13,945	8,701	6,258	7,795	12,610	11,751	12,661	12,552	9,224	6,851	15,683	10,751	17,416	11,084	13,512	11,007	11,864
Santiago, Chile	14,323	11,909	8,208	14,639	9,461	6,375	8,563	13,449	12,359	11,846	13,163	10,027	6,984	16,266	11,627	17,198	11,877	14,286	11,802	12,662
Santo Domingo, Dominican Rep.	11,481	6,964	7,285	12,337	8,344	3,187	7,680	10,074	11,626	16,670	12,097	8,192	3,402	13,880	7,736	12,854	6,448	11,431	9,502	10,058
Sao Paulo de Olivenca, Brazil	12,796	8,952	7,267	13,519	8,543	4,092	7,690	11,495	12,001	14,890	12,687	8,727	4,600	15,345	9,239	15,051	8,675	12,747	10,385	11,133
Sao Paulo, Brazil	11,740	9,859	5,619	12,113	6,880	7,317	5,978	10,877	9,940	13,510	10,738	7,437	7,849	13,864	9,214	18,104	10,183	11,702	9,212	10,072
Sao Tome, Sao Tome & Principe	5,503	6,347	1,318	5,781	978	11,779	964	5,014	3,671	13,733	4,443	1,845	11,964	7,541	4,610	13,537	7,515	5,472	3,189	4,000
Sapporo, Japan	8,011	8,391	13,621	7,962	12,602	10,908	13,384	8,421	10,343	8,640	9,559	11,838	10,323	6,601	9,472	384	7,821	8,035	10,241	9,423
Sarajevo, Yugoslavia	3,024	2,060	4,801	3,904	3,993	10,835	4,618	1,616	4,328	14,888	4,280	3,137	10,561	5,428	819	9,065	3,293	2,976	2,223	2,065
Saratov, USSR	2,365	3,122	6,886	3,091	5,880	11,740	6,639	1,825	4,764	13,119	4,304	5,094	11,304	3,902	3,006	6,934	3,833	2,344	3,604	2,902
Saskatoon, Canada	10,550	6,091	10,398	11,322	10,779	3,957	10,630	9,463	12,469	14,614	12,319	10,114	3,376	11,680	7,877	7,968	4,851	10,520	10,256	10,200
Schefferville, Canada	8,734	3,897	7,808	9,601	8,156	5,072	8,020	7,438	10,170	17,059	10,202	7,511	4,698	10,559	5,491	9,222	2,865	8,693	7,853	7,963
Seattle, Washington	11,323	7,156	11,627	12,017	12,002	3,980	11,862	10,373	13,460	13,404	13,203	11,319	3,369	12,041	8,984	7,380	5,891	11,299	11,344	11,200
Sendai, Japan	8,206	8,880	13,983	8,083	12,904	11,225	13,719	8,717	10,443	8,106	9,647	12,173	10,652	6,610	9,895	176	8,341	8,233	10,524	9,688
Seoul, South Korea	7,109	8,481	13,078	6,918	11,909	12,246	12,770	7,759	9,257	8,116	8,457	11,242	11,653	5,395	9,212	1,166	8,171	7,140	9,523	8,670
Sept-Iles, Canada	9,020	4,155	7,612	9,897	8,062	4,760	7,852	7,688	10,297	17,376	10,390	7,468	4,435	10,948	5,635	9,713	3,222	8,977	7,959	8,138
Sevastopol, USSR	2,044	2,824	5,682	2,923	4,675	11,735	5,431	855	3,973	13,737	3,694	3,886	11,390	4,276	2,028	8,139	3,871	2,002	2,446	1,848
Seville, Spain	5,012	2,214	3,230	5,844	3,395	9,230	3,557	3,636	5,471	16,846	5,735	2,645	9,095	7,523	1,357	10,794	3,244	4,962	3,142	3,568
Shanghai, China	6,862	8,889	12,966	6,547	11,724	13,114	12,618	7,691	8,805	7,531	8,001	11,140	12,525	4,879	9,390	1,946	8,727	6,899	9,372	8,511
Sheffield, United Kingdom	4,727	421	5,333	5,613	4,964	9,066	5,303	3,360	6,090	16,295	6,081	4,122	8,770	6,942	1,484	9,054	1,650	4,682	3,847	3,849
Shenyang, China	6,677	7,924	12,572	6,548	11,431	12,138	12,277	7,260	8,914	8,636	8,121	10,740	11,534	5,127	8,660	1,424	7,638	6,706	9,043	8,197
Shiraz, Iran	420	5,181	6,506	597	5,229	14,082	6,133	1,800	2,695	11,502	2,019	4,736	13,707	2,130	4,139	7,788	6,162	469	2,957	2,129
Sibiu, Romania	2,706	2,195	5,248	3,593	4,372	11,087	5,043	1,347	4,306	14,483	4,158	3,532	10,775	5,020	1,310	8,595	3,346	2,661	2,398	2,049
Singapore	6,679	10,844	11,987	5,905	10,729	16,734	11,563	8,031	7,265	5,400	6,608	10,601	16,195	4,144	10,341	5,620	11,278	6,729	8,998	8,291
Sioux Falls, South Dakota	11,084	6,340	9,825	11,919	10,416	2,975	10,113	9,858	12,657	15,240	12,666	9,864	2,457	12,554	7,978	9,166	5,201	11,048	10,336	10,441
Skelleftea, Sweden	4,271	1,498	6,869	5,081	6,265	9,683	6,783	3,230	6,341	14,758	6,063	5,398	9,255	5,933	2,659	7,279	1,801	4,239	4,511	4,134
Skopje, Yugoslavia	2,719	2,373	4,786	3,596	3,899	11,156	4,574	1,309	4,024	14,601	3,960	3,059	10,883	5,154	1,056	9,048	3,594	2,671	1,981	1,756
Socotra Island (Tamrida)	2,046	6,824	6,423	1,309	5,128	15,675	6,003	3,282	1,722	10,324	978	4,968	15,401	2,278	5,439	8,794	7,914	2,078	3,477	2,961
Sofia, Bulgaria	2,607	2,407	4,941	3,488	4,034	11,237	4,723	1,201	4,020	14,472	3,920	3,201	10,951	5,016	1,204	8,888	3,604	2,559	2,050	1,752
Songkhla, Thailand	6,017	10,097	11,552	5,277	10,265	16,529	11,130	7,344	6,818	6,137	6,115	10,063	15,943	3,469	9,635	5,336	10,538	6,066	8,405	7,665
Sorong, Indonesia	9,390	12,534	15,045	8,730	13,775	14,159	14,621	10,601	10,314	3,846	9,631	13,574	13,785	6,872	12,710	4,586	12,416	9,438	11,876	11,092
South Georgia Island	12,378	12,741	7,269	12,249	8,142	9,882	7,447	12,227	9,887	10,113	10,622	8,961	10,487	13,305	11,503	18,372	13,394	12,363	10,411	11,172
South Pole	13,361	16,339	10,592	12,710	11,018	11,866	10,618	14,102	11,003	6,134	11,416	11,881	12,423	12,551	14,647	14,399	17,290	13,379	12,681	13,113
South Sandwich Islands	11,969	12,923	7,278	11,754	8,022	10,627	7,406	11,975	9,433	9,640	10,134	8,870	11,233	12,679	11,523	17,783	13,708	11,959	10,190	10,902
Split, Yugoslavia	3,164	1,996	4,685	4,042	3,911	10,716	4,513	1,754	4,390	15,040	4,371	3,050	10,452	5,584	655	9,196	3,245	3,116	2,233	2,138
Spokane, Washington	11,248	6,950	11,160	11,973	11,694	3,775	11,527	10,241	13,298	13,759	13,088	11,030	3,165	12,111	8,759	7,679	5,694	11,222	11,132	11,031
Spoleto, Italy	3,435	1,914	4,463	4,305	3,759	10,496	4,313	2,025	4,512	15,325	4,547	2,892	10,252	5,879	342	9,453	3,183	3,386	2,274	2,296
Springbok, South Africa	7,380	9,800	4,524	7,148	4,447	13,582	4,351	7,602	4,829	10,542	5,525	5,268	14,032	8,264	7,981	14,707	11,011	7,374	5,989	6,538
Springfield, Illinois	11,111	6,272	9,262	11,975	9,943	2,731	9,572	9,814	12,439	15,768	12,544	9,453	2,320	12,811	7,788	9,857	5,226	11,071	10,095	10,292
Springfield, Massachusetts	9,964	5,103	7,852	10,848	8,491	3,821	8,146	8,605	11,049	17,207	11,222	7,997	3,561	11,959	6,457	10,363	4,231	9,920	8,706	8,972
Srinagar, India	2,530	6,138	8,657	2,249	7,389	14,341	8,291	3,572	4,615	10,122	3,827	6,862	13,803	1,243	5,726	5,725	6,736	2,570	5,078	4,224
Stanley, Falkland Islands	13,668	13,094	8,111	13,622	9,145	8,619	8,359	13,324	11,243	10,274	11,999	9,905	9,230	14,744	12,199	18,091	13,450	13,648	11,502	12,314
Stara Zagora, Bulgaria	2,422	2,552	5,047	3,305	4,102	11,407	4,816	1,022	3,914	14,281	3,782	3,283	11,114	4,824	1,395	8,775	3,727	2,374	2,032	1,654
Stockholm, Sweden	3,942	1,204	6,283	4,792	5,641	9,891	6,167	2,774	5,846	14,981	5,630	4,774	9,504	5,843	2,042	7,810	1,959	3,905	3,924	3,604
Stornoway, United Kingdom	5,142	282	5,871	6,022	5,564	8,636	5,866	3,823	6,660	16,357	6,608	4,730	8,303	7,219	2,100	8,714	1,030	5,100	4,449	4,402
Strasbourg, France	3,968	1,157	4,924	4,853	4,370	9,861	4,829	2,574	5,252	15,745	5,247	3,507	9,584	6,291	745	9,161	2,428	3,921	3,031	3,011
Stuttgart, West Germany	3,872	1,198	4,976	4,758	4,394	9,948	4,872	2,482	5,196	15,639	5,175	3,529	9,666	6,186	762	9,083	2,462	3,826	2,994	2,946
Subic, Philippines	7,479	10,434	13,493	6,929	12,183	14,388	13,087	8,588	8,860	5,845	8,095	11,799	13,851	5,074	10,610	3,366	10,425	7,524	10,029	9,199
Suchow, China	6,379	8,395	12,465	6,101	11,235	13,126	12,123	7,177	8,397	7,979	7,593	10,634	12,525	4,493	8,865	2,123	8,279	6,415	8,872	8,012
Sucre, Bolivia	13,279	10,260	7,231	13,807	8,537	5,489	7,630	12,182	11,804	13,524	12,583	8,950	6,060	15,649	10,150	16,673	10,192	13,235	10,725	11,561
Sudbury, Canada	10,092	5,249	8,586	10,958	9,139	3,724	8,859	8,791	11,453	16,481	11,530	8,584	3,340	11,861	6,786	9,621	4,215	10,051	9,115	9,282
Suez, Egypt	1,514	4,035	4,708	2,242	3,502	12,752	4,371	823	2,404	13,210	2,298	2,884	12,516	4,047	2,512	9,273	5,237	1,467	1,117	271
Sundsvall, Sweden	4,201	1,231	6,571	5,036	5,963	9,676	6,469	3,081	6,170	14,978	5,933	5,096	9,271	5,996	2,347	7,594	1,744	4,166	4,266	3,936
Surabaya, Indonesia	8,030	12,165	13,044	7,237	11,847	16,328	12,625	9,393	8,409	4,049	7,811	11,817	15,936	5,505	11,707	5,914	12,506	8,080	10,288	9,613
Suva, Fiji	14,832	15,675	18,563	14,222	18,648	9,745	18,605	15,862	15,570	4,345	15,011	19,011	9,701	12,358	17,195	7,539	14,586	14,877	17,366	16,551
Sverdlovsk, USSR	3,099	3,675	7,991	3,631	6,994	11,639	7,751	2,894	5,634	12,512	5,070	6,207	11,135	3,880	3,996	5,831	4,039	3,093	4,702	3,964
Svobodnyy, USSR	6,763	7,145	12,260	6,811	11,252	11,129	12,024	7,081	9,191	9,619	8,434	10,480	10,520	5,664	8,128	1,596	6,707	6,783	8,905	8,101
Sydney, Australia	12,919	16,733	15,948	12,084	15,439	12,763	15,712	14,307	12,645	1,164	12,282	15,909	12,815	10,426	16,633	8,228	16,398	12,969	14,895	14,381
Sydney, Canada	8,907	4,064	7,024	9,793	7,540	4,896	7,281	7,534	9,969	18,004	10,133	6,992	4,649	10,993	5,369	10,282	3,307	8,862	7,625	7,883
Syktyvkar, USSR	3,488	2,961	7,698	4,142	6,816	10,925	7,502	2,946	5,925	13,244	5,448	5,987	10,438	4,603	3,540	6,185	3,266	3,471	4,654	4,015
Szeged, Hungary	3,002	1,942	5,102	3,888	4,294	10,804	4,921	1,622	4,489	14,796	4,387	3,439	10,505	5,332	1,034	8,772	3,134	2,956	2,464	2,220
Szombathely, Hungary	3,293	1,679	5,049	4,179	4,313	10,518	4,892	1,909	4,721	15,078	4,649	3,449	10,224	5,617	860	8,873	2,897	3,247	2,624	2,454
Tabriz, Iran	879	4,091	6,239	1,692	5,055	12,981	5,915	979	3,307	12,473	2,808	4,403	12,605	3,009	3,210	7,722	5,059	852	2,667	1,821
Tacheng, China	3,489	5,568	9,353	3,544	8,189	12,955	9,042	4,034	5,911	10,621	5,170	7,515	12,386	2,790	5,720	4,605	5,850	3,512	5,801	4,954
Tahiti (Papeete)	17,724	14,851	16,046	17,431	17,352	6,640	16,443	17,795	18,722	7,283	18,380	17,648	6,749	15,600	16,612	9,649	13,595	17,751	18,973	18,834
Taipei, Taiwan	7,122	9,493	13,249	6,714	11,969	13,565	12,876	8,063	8,874	6,880	8,077	11,452	12,993	4,951	9,886	2,381	9,377	7,162	9,669	8,812
Taiyuan, China	5,875	7,839	11,927	5,650	10,714	13,068	11,594	6,624	7,984	8,497	7,184	10,092	12,459	4,134	8,288	2,394	7,768	5,908	8,340	7,481
Tallahassee, Florida	11,621	6,764	8,782	12,506	9,643	2,189	9,136	10,250	12,533	16,005	12,790	9,286	2,032	13,597	8,052	10,990	5,876	11,576	10,216	10,557
Tallinn, USSR	3,685	1,585	6,484	4,515	5,768	10,197	6,344	2,604	5,713	14,600	5,443	4,906	9,792	5,494	2,239	7,528	2,261	3,650	3,913	3,510
Tamanrasset, Algeria	4,316	3,864	2,188	4,963	1,517	10,806	2,004	3,261	3,852	15,301	4,318	694	10,774	6,817	2,143	11,641	5,058	4,269	1,822	2,600
Tampa, Florida	11,708	6,873	8,662	12,595	9,507	2,174	8,966	10,322	12,490	16,077	12,789	9,188	2,112	13,765	8,086	11,318	6,037	11,663	10,194	10,577
Tampere, Finland	3,900	1,538	6,647	4,721	5,965	10,011	6,519	2,840	5,950	14,651	5,675	5,100	9,597	5,646	2,400	7,416	2,087	3,866	4,144	3,748
Tanami, Australia	10,334	14,322	14,775	9,527	13,756	14,797	14,392	11,703	10,461	1,873	9,953	13,901	14,644	7,816	14,015	6,697	14,418	10,384	12,511	11,884
Tangier, Morocco	5,022	2,388	3,380	5,842	3,230	9,295	3,398	3,660	5,388	16,807	5,677	2,493	9,175	7,546	1,430	10,946	3,420	4,972	3,073	3,538
Tarawa (Betio)	13,202	13,505	19,200	12,820	18,064	9,671	18,943	13,927	14,832	5,377	14,075	17,403	9,421	11,014	14,958	5,394	12,517	13,239	15,692	14,834
Tashkent, USSR	2,249	5,217	8,232	2,327	7,023	13,469	7,899	2,958	4,675	11,015	3,949	6,399	12,953	2,053	4,938	5,828	5,797	2,274	4,644	3,786
Tbilisi, USSR	1,300	3,711	6,283	2,108	5,150	12,579	5,982	965	3,668	12,771	3,207	4,446	12,194	3,315	2,971	7,603	4,650	1,272	2,776	1,973
Tegucigalpa, Honduras	13,170	8,409	9,141	14,051	10,241	1,396	9,546	11,763	13,535	14,899	13,982	10,104	1,813	15,353	9,459	12,302	7,633	13,122	11,373	11,875
Tehran, Iran	661	4,597	6,579	1,273	5,352	13,460	6,235	1,454	3,221	11,943	2,617	4,758	13,064	2,479	3,735	7,494	5,525	667	2,985	2,124
Tel Aviv, Israel	1,300	3,955	5,004	2,095	3,810	12,762	4,673	551	2,582	13,120	2,380	3,174	12,496	3,849	2,549	8,960	5,123	1,251	1,423	586
Telegraph Creek, Canada	10,227	6,473	11,566	10,863	11,676	5,237	11,724	9,410	12,529	13,229	12,165	10,901	4,626	10,768	8,333	6,311	5,210	10,208	10,603	10,327
Teresina, Brazil	10,402	7,814	4,462	10,975	5,767	6,732	4,879	9,303	9,178	15,573	9,908	6,096	7,132	12,839	7,364	16,157	8,102	10,357	7,856	8,682
Ternate, Indonesia	8,926	12,180	14,596	8,263	13,319	14,487	14,172	10,147	9,862	4,124	9,172	13,108	14,082	6,405	12,279	4,499	12,134	8,974	11,409	10,627
The Valley, Anguilla	10,933	6,597	6,561	11,769	7,626	3,911	6,957	9,537	10,935	17,174	11,432	7,495	4,118	13,397	7,199	13,175	6,224	10,883	8,855	9,447
Thessaloniki, Greece	2,555	2,568	4,749	3,426	3,818	11,342	4,521	1,145	3,832	14,446	3,766	2,992	11,074	5,015	1,197	9,074	3,786	2,506	1,823	1,564
Thimphu, Bhutan	4,031	7,587	10,113	3,544	8,817	14,987	9,726	5,163	5,723	8,617	4,920	8,365	14,388	1,791	7,315	4,801	8,019	4,076	6,587	5,750
Thunder Bay, Canada	10,320	5,554	9,222	11,164	9,730	3,630	9,485	9,077	11,871	15,837	11,879	9,141	3,161	11,892	7,193	9,100	4,428	10,282	9,556	9,653
Tientsin, China	6,239	7,927	12,244	6,047	11,054	12,711	11,924	6,927	8,393	8,491	7,594	10,406	12,104	4,559	8,493	1,969	7,765	6,270	8,672	7,816
Tijuana, Mexico	12,877	8,358	11,815	13,631	12,521	2,445	12,139	11,788	14,738	13,189	14,643	12,004	1,872	13,771	10,076	8,749	7,148	12,848	12,452	12,483
Tiksi, USSR	6,505	5,221	10,816	6,897	10,091	9,536	10,689	6,267	9,060	11,840	8,447	9,237	8,934	6,431	6,570	3,606	4,569	6,504	7,998	7,343
Timbuktu, Mali	5,400	4,481	1,271	6,002	1,389	10,191	1,278	4,375	4,599	15,720	5,179	1,172	10,251	7,867	3,005	12,682	5,546	5,355	2,861	3,681
Tindouf, Algeria	5,447	3,304	2,515	6,198	2,608	9,328	2,591	4,180	5,324	16,778	5,750	2,040	9,297	7,996	2,200	11,853	4,277	5,398	3,165	3,814
Tirane, Albania	2,827	2,354	4,642	3,698	3,775	11,082	4,437	1,417	4,032	14,718	4,001	2,930	10,822	5,282	927	9,195	3,592	2,778	1,927	1,773

Distances in Kilometers	Abadan, Iran	Aberdeen, United Kingdom	Abidjan, Ivory Coast	Abu Dhabi, United Arab Emir.	Abuja, Nigeria	Acapulco, Mexico	Accra, Ghana	Adana, Turkey	Addis Ababa, Ethiopia	Adelaide, Australia	Aden, P.D.R. Yemen	Agadez, Niger	Aguascalientes, Mexico	Ahmadabad, India	Ajaccio, France	Akita, Japan	Akureyri, Iceland	Al Basrah, Iraq	Al Jawf, Libya	Al Minya, Egypt
Tokyo, Japan	8,241	9,114	14,109	8,075	12,993	11,459	13,828	8,814	10,417	7,821	9,616	12,285	10,892	6,546	10,075	447	8,605	8,270	10,607	9,763
Toledo, Spain	4,813	1,925	3,827	5,661	3,578	9,317	3,820	3,420	5,434	16,694	5,647	2,791	9,153	7,300	1,097	10,471	3,008	4,764	3,090	3,441
Topeka, Kansas	11,468	6,668	9,784	12,317	10,467	2,495	10,096	10,205	12,907	15,243	12,975	9,968	2,005	13,025	8,239	9,605	5,572	11,429	10,568	10,731
Toronto, Canada	10,238	5,377	8,426	11,112	9,038	3,548	8,715	8,912	11,485	16,638	11,606	8,519	3,210	12,088	6,844	9,957	4,397	10,196	9,142	9,353
Toulouse, France	4,358	1,526	4,275	5,226	3,856	9,617	4,219	2,948	5,261	16,247	5,380	3,017	9,402	6,794	626	9,890	2,734	4,309	2,935	3,132
Tours, France	4,458	1,101	4,684	5,339	4,281	9,421	4,637	3,051	5,558	16,281	5,623	3,439	9,173	6,820	881	9,557	2,320	4,410	3,261	3,370
Townsville, Australia	11,865	15,086	16,512	11,117	15,547	13,009	16,149	13,160	12,237	1,917	11,697	15,678	12,884	9,316	15,346	6,564	14,731	11,914	14,199	13,504
Trenton, New Jersey	10,240	5,380	7,998	11,124	8,678	3,548	8,304	8,878	11,296	17,037	11,483	8,207	3,299	12,233	6,720	10,473	4,505	10,196	8,955	9,235
Tripoli, Lebanon	1,253	3,799	5,218	2,104	4,047	12,659	4,898	291	2,828	13,140	2,573	3,382	12,369	3,783	2,504	8,712	4,939	1,203	1,662	854
Tripoli, Libya	3,326	2,935	3,538	4,105	2,700	11,034	3,332	2,066	3,723	15,037	3,929	1,841	10,874	5,874	1,075	10,291	4,202	3,276	1,381	1,766
Tristan da Cunha (Edinburgh)	9,770	10,481	4,768	9,750	5,506	10,917	4,880	9,554	7,365	11,489	8,141	6,347	11,445	11,092	9,002	17,606	11,399	9,751	7,739	8,500
Trondheim, Norway	4,544	982	6,553	5,387	6,027	9,314	6,479	3,383	6,443	15,292	6,239	5,162	8,914	6,364	2,395	7,741	1,379	4,508	4,461	4,190
Trujillo, Peru	14,031	9,981	8,458	14,763	9,749	3,593	8,880	12,710	13,190	13,824	13,900	9,963	4,179	16,580	10,425	14,786	9,551	13,982	11,630	12,376
Truk Island (Moen)	10,889	12,467	17,005	10,430	15,706	11,692	16,615	11,804	12,403	4,892	11,643	15,222	11,323	8,599	13,386	3,764	11,855	10,930	13,439	12,583
Truro, Canada	9,153	4,304	7,218	10,039	7,764	4,644	7,484	7,784	10,223	17,835	10,389	7,228	4,394	11,218	5,624	10,297	3,513	9,109	7,879	8,138
Tsingtao, China	6,594	8,358	12,640	6,357	11,433	12,787	12,311	7,330	8,676	8,086	7,873	10,803	12,187	4,792	8,927	1,784	8,172	6,628	9,057	8,198
Tsitsihar, China	6,566	7,398	12,276	6,536	11,198	11,662	12,010	7,011	8,920	9,232	8,144	10,463	11,054	5,273	8,244	1,554	7,055	6,590	8,823	7,995
Tubuai Island (Mataura)	18,106	15,432	15,818	17,606	17,085	6,989	16,186	18,426	18,202	6,971	18,096	17,574	7,153	15,740	17,132	10,101	14,189	18,143	19,289	19,480
Tucson, Arizona	12,746	8,090	11,276	13,543	12,025	2,034	11,609	11,580	14,426	13,694	14,414	11,544	1,431	13,879	9,747	9,199	6,917	12,713	12,104	12,204
Tulsa, Oklahoma	11,752	6,933	9,836	12,607	10,572	2,176	10,161	10,474	13,121	15,147	13,221	10,107	1,699	13,344	8,469	9,839	5,858	11,713	10,777	10,971
Tunis, Tunisia	3,584	2,437	3,776	4,408	3,076	10,596	3,619	2,232	4,211	15,419	4,373	2,208	10,414	6,112	582	10,111	3,701	3,534	1,877	2,155
Tura, USSR	5,201	5,029	10,158	5,519	9,241	10,845	9,955	5,175	7,757	11,501	7,101	8,429	10,255	5,010	5,978	3,755	4,756	5,206	6,981	6,242
Turin, Italy	3,884	1,505	4,547	4,761	3,977	10,017	4,443	2,474	4,980	15,753	5,027	3,114	9,770	6,290	359	9,487	2,774	3,836	2,710	2,776
Uberlandia, Brazil	11,665	9,457	5,545	12,108	6,836	6,898	5,926	10,711	10,027	13,999	10,812	7,329	7,412	13,912	8,927	17,566	9,720	11,624	9,113	9,968
Ufa, USSR	2,779	3,527	7,635	3,363	6,624	11,751	7,388	2,519	5,294	12,659	4,753	5,843	11,267	3,784	3,694	6,186	4,013	2,770	4,326	3,589
Ujungpandang, Indonesia	8,510	12,338	13,769	7,760	12,546	15,556	13,348	9,830	9,090	3,847	8,459	12,461	15,173	5,962	12,096	5,400	12,518	8,560	10,866	10,149
Ulaanbaatar, Mongolia	5,288	6,656	11,102	5,262	9,974	12,354	10,811	5,795	7,647	9,705	6,877	9,271	11,746	4,100	7,230	2,799	6,561	5,312	7,589	6,749
Ulan-Ude, USSR	5,349	6,340	11,002	5,403	9,922	11,943	10,733	5,735	7,779	10,076	7,028	9,186	11,336	4,374	7,024	2,831	6,182	5,369	7,550	6,727
Uliastay, Mongolia	4,535	6,200	10,381	4,530	9,235	12,659	10,081	5,065	6,912	10,059	6,151	8,546	12,061	3,484	6,607	3,551	6,258	4,559	6,848	6,004
Uranium City, Canada	9,817	5,552	10,312	10,562	10,528	4,795	10,496	8,798	11,865	14,541	11,645	9,799	4,215	10,850	7,387	7,340	4,285	9,790	9,740	9,600
Urumqi, China	3,759	6,056	9,735	3,700	8,541	13,246	9,411	4,427	6,084	10,134	5,317	7,898	12,663	2,682	6,189	4,319	6,314	3,787	6,158	5,302
Ushuaia, Argentina	14,383	13,767	8,887	14,275	9,919	8,485	9,136	14,094	11,912	9,736	12,648	10,682	9,093	15,231	12,955	17,318	14,018	14,366	12,270	13,075
Vaduz, Liechtenstein	3,798	1,361	4,816	4,682	4,218	10,047	4,705	2,397	5,047	15,615	5,047	3,352	9,777	6,152	587	9,212	2,629	3,751	2,828	2,808
Valencia, Spain	4,503	1,969	3,800	5,347	3,440	9,629	3,757	3,114	5,137	16,379	5,337	2,622	9,458	6,999	815	10,363	3,128	4,453	2,793	3,125
Valladolid, Spain	4,860	1,732	4,026	5,718	3,784	9,204	4,024	3,457	5,577	16,755	5,766	2,994	9,024	7,323	1,117	10,321	2,802	4,811	3,233	3,541
Valletta, Malta	3,194	2,666	3,883	4,010	3,053	10,988	3,684	1,863	3,855	15,017	3,987	2,195	10,796	5,729	835	9,954	3,938	3,144	1,547	1,758
Valparaiso, Chile	14,399	11,918	8,280	14,726	9,537	6,287	8,638	13,509	12,451	11,850	13,256	10,096	6,896	16,362	11,666	17,097	11,864	14,362	11,873	12,733
Vancouver, Canada	11,149	7,030	11,599	11,836	11,936	4,160	11,824	10,215	13,310	13,410	13,037	11,238	3,549	11,849	8,866	7,231	5,761	11,126	11,217	11,055
Varna, Bulgaria	2,301	2,610	5,242	3,187	4,278	11,499	5,005	932	3,931	14,124	3,754	3,467	11,189	4,661	1,578	8,579	3,750	2,255	2,151	1,697
Venice, Italy	3,537	1,638	4,722	4,417	4,052	10,328	4,586	2,130	4,760	15,388	4,757	3,185	10,063	5,924	489	9,234	2,901	3,489	2,556	2,518
Veracruz, Mexico	13,338	8,474	10,045	14,220	11,061	478	10,435	11,974	14,171	14,398	14,487	10,817	708	15,177	9,772	11,266	7,528	13,294	11,890	12,271
Verona, Italy	3,639	1,583	4,680	4,519	4,038	10,234	4,553	2,231	4,829	15,493	4,840	3,171	9,974	6,029	433	9,298	2,851	3,591	2,605	2,596
Victoria, Canada	11,241	7,117	11,656	11,928	12,007	4,100	11,885	10,307	13,401	13,363	13,130	11,314	3,490	11,932	8,951	7,264	5,849	11,218	11,305	11,146
Victoria, Seychelles	3,943	8,566	6,704	3,220	5,568	17,021	6,290	5,062	2,395	9,097	2,242	5,739	16,956	3,583	6,989	9,882	9,725	3,971	4,723	4,486
Vienna, Austria	3,354	1,588	5,133	4,240	4,412	10,446	4,983	1,980	4,822	15,106	4,739	3,547	10,146	5,652	921	8,803	2,796	3,308	2,733	2,553
Vientiane, Laos	5,636	9,202	11,582	5,035	10,272	15,440	11,175	6,836	6,958	6,983	6,187	9,915	14,837	3,172	9,008	4,335	9,504	5,683	8,162	7,351
Villahermosa, Mexico	13,243	8,395	9,719	14,129	10,759	754	10,113	11,860	13,930	14,623	14,288	10,545	1,073	15,205	9,619	11,587	7,502	13,198	11,679	12,099
Vilnius, USSR	3,265	1,724	6,075	4,121	5,298	10,550	5,911	2,106	5,201	14,542	4,959	4,442	10,174	5,246	1,869	7,854	2,631	3,228	3,389	2,985
Visby, Sweden	3,808	1,224	6,121	4,666	5,461	10,005	5,998	2,611	5,670	14,982	5,467	4,595	9,629	5,769	1,875	7,937	2,088	3,769	3,735	3,423
Vitoria, Brazil	11,001	9,293	4,880	11,383	6,142	7,698	5,240	10,148	9,236	13,889	10,030	6,701	8,194	13,150	8,541	17,853	9,718	10,963	8,474	9,334
Vladivostok, USSR	7,296	8,096	13,057	7,213	11,972	11,527	12,789	7,785	9,589	8,672	8,801	11,242	10,930	5,832	9,009	784	7,667	7,322	9,592	8,759
Volgograd, USSR	2,071	3,193	6,629	2,832	5,593	11,931	6,369	1,499	4,435	13,110	3,990	4,822	11,515	3,781	2,870	7,195	4,000	2,046	3,293	2,575
Vologda, USSR	3,272	2,441	7,050	4,023	6,197	10,823	6,862	2,491	5,569	13,743	5,173	5,359	10,377	4,771	2,882	6,843	2,963	3,247	4,102	3,528
Vorkuta, USSR	4,263	3,422	8,538	4,829	7,699	10,559	8,363	3,840	6,761	12,927	6,236	6,861	10,029	4,978	4,323	5,420	3,382	4,252	5,557	4,912
Wake Island	11,442	11,472	17,102	11,236	16,146	9,756	16,910	11,962	13,518	6,694	12,714	15,373	9,339	9,588	12,860	3,403	10,577	11,472	13,777	12,946
Wallis Island	15,101	15,115	18,785	14,596	19,432	9,021	19,046	15,936	16,202	5,127	15,574	19,419	8,951	12,736	16,798	7,411	13,959	15,142	17,650	16,791
Walvis Bay, Namibia	6,913	9,009	3,721	6,788	3,641	13,185	3,536	6,987	4,413	11,310	5,165	4,472	13,577	8,090	7,206	14,615	10,208	6,901	5,303	5,912
Warsaw, Poland	3,299	1,576	5,689	4,176	4,940	10,481	5,532	2,030	5,055	14,808	4,878	4,079	10,135	5,427	1,475	8,248	2,635	3,258	3,120	2,801
Washington, D.C.	10,483	5,621	8,172	11,366	8,879	3,304	8,486	9,122	11,534	16,840	11,726	8,424	3,056	12,460	6,964	10,517	4,733	10,439	9,194	9,478
Watson Lake, Canada	9,977	6,191	11,315	10,626	11,403	5,335	11,464	9,141	12,259	13,436	11,907	10,624	4,727	10,586	8,052	6,339	4,929	9,957	10,322	10,051
Weimar, East Germany	3,812	1,111	5,260	4,699	4,652	9,977	5,150	2,452	5,286	15,477	5,216	3,785	9,670	6,056	1,027	8,794	2,336	3,768	3,146	3,020
Wellington, New Zealand	15,119	18,230	16,017	14,264	16,244	10,847	16,014	16,521	14,423	3,226	14,229	17,030	11,022	12,652	18,860	9,634	17,175	15,169	16,768	16,450
West Berlin, West Germany	3,754	1,118	5,472	4,637	4,840	10,025	5,355	2,425	5,338	15,326	5,231	3,973	9,700	5,938	1,230	8,571	2,283	3,710	3,253	3,068
Wewak, Papua New Guinea	10,728	13,346	16,444	10,104	15,182	12,948	16,021	11,876	11,721	3,513	11,039	14,969	12,647	8,240	13,847	4,804	12,963	10,775	13,247	12,443
Whangarei, New Zealand	15,015	17,609	16,634	14,196	16,792	10,716	16,619	16,375	14,650	3,232	14,363	17,534	10,834	12,489	18,595	9,060	16,574	15,065	16,967	16,502
Whitehorse, Canada	9,909	6,307	11,552	10,525	11,581	5,616	11,685	9,136	12,252	13,133	11,859	10,785	5,005	10,392	8,163	5,993	5,056	9,892	10,392	10,077
Wichita, Kansas	11,671	6,876	9,944	12,518	10,648	2,324	10,262	10,412	13,114	15,067	13,184	10,160	1,817	13,201	8,448	9,627	5,776	11,633	10,775	10,940
Willemstad, Curacao	11,831	7,492	7,169	12,659	8,311	3,376	7,579	10,441	11,697	16,263	12,240	8,259	3,703	14,307	8,105	13,532	7,063	11,781	9,695	10,318
Wiluna, Australia	9,914	14,387	13,673	9,054	12,755	15,760	13,311	11,322	9,628	1,983	9,216	13,018	15,701	7,511	13,659	7,627	14,789	9,963	11,826	11,309
Windhoek, Namibia	6,738	9,014	3,849	6,583	3,674	13,444	3,638	6,868	4,218	11,153	4,957	4,486	13,828	7,850	7,193	14,372	10,230	6,728	5,219	5,797
Windsor, Canada	10,548	5,693	8,709	11,420	9,348	3,248	9,006	9,231	11,818	16,346	11,936	8,841	2,890	12,352	7,175	9,937	4,689	10,507	9,475	9,683
Winnipeg, Canada	10,488	5,834	9,784	11,304	10,244	3,673	10,036	9,309	12,208	15,263	12,148	9,624	3,140	11,866	7,548	8,613	4,646	10,453	9,927	9,958
Winston-Salem, North Carolina	10,903	6,041	8,427	11,786	9,189	2,886	8,756	9,541	11,921	16,523	12,131	8,765	2,654	12,868	7,374	10,651	5,145	10,859	9,586	9,886
Wroclaw, Poland	3,459	1,413	5,439	4,342	4,737	10,321	5,298	2,131	5,070	15,076	4,945	3,871	9,996	5,662	1,202	8,528	2,561	3,415	3,034	2,802
Wuhan, China	6,240	8,615	12,362	5,889	11,101	13,615	12,002	7,135	8,129	7,688	7,326	10,549	13,015	4,201	8,949	2,552	8,584	6,278	8,771	7,911
Wyndham, Australia	9,927	13,804	14,687	9,141	13,589	14,910	14,287	11,276	10,218	2,398	9,667	13,655	14,692	7,392	13,567	6,235	13,890	9,977	12,182	11,517
Xi'an, China	5,643	8,004	11,752	5,342	10,505	13,583	11,400	6,499	7,635	8,262	6,830	9,930	12,973	3,736	8,301	2,829	8,032	5,680	8,157	7,296
Xining, China	4,958	7,429	11,057	4,693	9,816	13,667	10,709	5,801	7,019	8,793	6,218	9,233	13,057	3,176	7,633	3,353	7,552	4,994	7,463	6,602
Yakutsk, USSR	6,636	6,151	11,567	6,870	10,708	10,247	11,391	6,666	9,176	10,775	8,483	9,882	9,637	6,067	7,336	2,578	5,597	6,646	8,470	7,733
Yanji, China	7,121	8,040	12,920	7,026	11,819	11,693	12,645	7,635	9,400	8,667	8,611	11,100	11,094	5,636	8,906	954	7,650	7,148	9,436	8,599
Yaounde, Cameroon	4,844	6,029	1,735	5,122	758	12,162	1,317	4,401	3,058	13,589	3,813	1,500	12,293	6,893	4,224	12,891	7,243	4,813	2,580	3,368
Yap Island (Colonia)	9,474	11,778	15,527	8,956	14,218	13,009	15,123	10,501	10,875	4,920	10,121	13,811	12,575	7,107	12,337	3,352	11,440	9,517	12,031	11,188
Yaraka, Australia	11,891	15,527	15,992	11,095	15,150	13,369	15,659	13,243	11,982	1,233	11,507	15,402	13,305	9,358	15,522	7,163	15,300	11,941	14,081	13,458
Yarmouth, Canada	9,437	4,587	7,382	10,322	7,971	4,362	7,661	8,067	10,487	17,685	10,663	7,456	4,119	11,494	5,900	10,385	3,780	9,392	8,144	8,414
Yellowknife, Canada	9,604	5,523	10,509	10,318	10,639	5,188	10,667	8,650	11,747	14,243	11,475	9,880	4,599	10,509	7,377	6,900	4,251	9,579	9,696	9,498
Yerevan, USSR	1,145	3,815	6,191	1,972	5,040	12,701	5,882	875	3,499	12,717	3,038	4,353	12,325	3,253	2,991	7,716	4,779	1,115	2,659	1,841
Yinchuan, China	5,326	7,487	11,389	5,103	10,169	13,302	11,053	6,097	7,445	8,782	6,646	9,557	12,691	3,624	7,826	2,910	7,514	5,359	7,799	6,939
Yogyakarta, Indonesia	7,851	12,079	12,784	7,045	11,594	16,596	12,366	9,225	8,163	4,165	7,577	11,580	16,197	5,341	11,550	6,088	12,473	7,901	10,072	9,412
York, United Kingdom	4,717	372	5,386	5,603	5,010	9,072	5,354	3,355	6,105	16,258	6,088	4,167	8,771	6,918	1,515	8,998	1,615	4,672	3,871	3,861
Yumen, China	4,573	6,932	10,633	4,380	9,412	13,470	10,296	5,348	6,742	9,281	5,949	8,802	12,865	3,010	7,138	3,596	7,084	4,606	7,043	6,182
Yutian, China	3,169	6,307	9,282	2,943	8,030	14,057	8,926	4,091	5,311	9,892	4,523	7,468	13,488	1,764	6,118	5,029	6,758	3,206	5,689	4,829
Yuzhno-Sakhalinsk, USSR	7,928	8,018	13,362	7,944	12,400	10,587	13,149	8,243	10,329	9,078	9,559	11,611	9,993	6,685	9,167	831	7,409	7,949	10,068	9,268
Zagreb, Yugoslavia	3,278	1,770	4,887	4,162	4,147	10,558	4,728	1,878	4,616	15,109	4,570	3,283	10,278	5,644	726	9,025	3,008	3,231	2,485	2,355
Zahedan, Iran	1,220	5,689	7,298	853	6,012	14,480	6,920	2,515	3,237	10,828	2,473	5,540	14,042	1,374	4,836	7,123	6,555	1,267	3,763	2,936
Zamboanga, Philippines	8,075	11,311	13,898	7,444	12,598	14,714	13,479	9,269	9,174	4,945	8,451	12,317	14,234	5,579	11,383	4,059	11,329	8,122	10,586	9,786
Zanzibar, Tanzania	4,154	7,948	4,968	3,768	3,935	15,429	4,566	4,797	1,682	10,476	2,191	4,282	15,540	4,865	6,158	11,383	9,206	4,160	3,776	3,898
Zaragoza, Spain	4,541	1,726	4,035	5,399	3,684	9,510	3,998	3,138	5,299	16,435	5,466	2,863	9,320	7,008	800	10,174	2,884	4,492	2,957	3,233
Zashiversk, USSR	7,109	5,883	11,515	7,444	10,799	9,391	11,394	6,945	9,669	11,357	9,025	9,945	8,781	6,810	7,273	3,090	5,156	7,113	8,692	8,022
Zhengzhou, China	6,054	8,187	12,146	5,774	10,911	13,287	11,802	6,867	8,074	8,139	7,270	10,317	12,682	4,177	8,594	2,402	8,128	6,090	8,552	7,691
Zurich, Switzerland	3,888	1,298	4,809	4,772	4,236	9,959	4,707	2,487	5,123	15,702	5,130	3,372	9,691	6,240	606	9,245	2,568	3,841	2,892	2,889

Distances in Kilometers	Al Qamishli, Syria	Albany, Australia	Albany, New York	Albuquerque, New Mexico	Alexandria, Egypt	Alexandroupolis, Greece	Algiers, Algeria	Alice Springs, Australia	Allepo, Syria	Alma-Ata, USSR	Ambon, Indonesia	Amherst, Canada	Amiens, France	Amman, Jordan	Amsterdam, Netherlands	Anadyr, USSR	Anchorage, Alaska	Andorra, Andorra	Angra do Heroismo, Azores	Ankara, Turkey
Albany, Australia	11,241	0	18,701	15,998	11,757	12,598	14,257	1,993	11,488	9,613	3,627	18,793	14,649	11,320	14,502	12,208	13,461	14,559	16,905	12,028
Albany, New York	9,006	18,701	0	2,955	8,728	7,749	6,388	16,719	8,823	10,053	15,179	841	5,662	9,080	5,725	6,603	5,270	5,959	3,912	8,263
Albuquerque, New Mexico	11,361	15,998	2,955	0	11,381	10,301	9,241	14,106	11,272	11,322	13,408	3,743	8,296	11,623	8,278	5,880	4,203	8,744	6,862	10,723
Alexandria, Egypt	1,228	11,757	8,728	11,381	0	1,130	2,548	12,611	872	4,322	11,018	7,890	3,095	579	3,104	9,001	9,761	2,807	5,200	1,005
Alexandroupolis, Greece	1,396	12,598	7,749	10,301	1,130	0	2,026	13,173	1,111	4,171	11,319	6,919	2,090	1,336	2,039	8,038	8,684	2,029	4,486	603
Algiers, Algeria	3,380	14,257	6,388	9,241	2,548	2,026	0	15,134	3,041	6,143	13,345	5,552	1,459	3,057	1,736	8,738	8,869	648	2,665	2,617
Alice Springs, Australia	11,782	1,993	16,719	14,106	12,611	13,173	15,134	0	12,104	9,424	2,294	17,065	14,936	12,081	14,681	10,497	11,582	15,190	17,579	12,570
Allepo, Syria	375	11,488	8,823	11,272	872	1,111	3,041	12,104	0	3,465	10,348	8,000	3,183	485	3,097	8,292	9,188	3,127	5,585	560
Alma-Ata, USSR	3,096	9,613	10,053	11,322	4,322	4,171	6,143	9,424	3,465	0	7,303	9,419	5,530	3,790	5,261	6,216	7,680	5,940	8,162	3,651
Ambon, Indonesia	9,991	3,627	15,179	13,408	11,018	11,319	13,345	2,294	10,348	7,303	0	15,186	12,821	10,445	12,536	8,588	9,933	13,229	15,411	10,731
Amherst, Canada	8,194	18,793	841	3,743	7,890	6,919	5,552	17,065	8,000	9,419	15,186	0	4,830	8,248	4,904	6,635	5,484	5,118	3,125	7,442
Amiens, France	3,411	14,649	5,662	8,296	3,095	2,090	1,459	14,936	3,183	5,530	12,821	4,830	0	3,418	328	7,284	7,437	825	2,643	2,631
Amman, Jordan	745	11,320	9,080	11,623	579	1,336	3,057	12,081	485	3,790	10,445	8,248	3,418	0	3,375	8,777	9,665	3,244	5,679	928
Amsterdam, Netherlands	3,294	14,502	5,725	8,278	3,104	2,039	1,736	14,681	3,097	5,261	12,536	4,904	328	3,375	0	7,003	7,216	1,124	2,901	2,538
Anadyr, USSR	8,096	12,208	6,603	5,880	9,001	8,038	8,738	10,497	8,292	6,216	8,588	6,635	7,284	8,777	7,003	0	1,680	8,108	8,340	7,996
Anchorage, Alaska	9,068	13,461	5,270	4,203	9,761	8,684	8,869	11,582	9,188	7,680	9,933	5,484	7,437	9,665	7,216	1,680	0	8,221	7,789	8,790
Andorra, Andorra	3,425	14,559	5,959	8,744	2,807	2,029	648	15,190	3,127	5,940	13,229	5,118	825	3,244	1,124	8,108	8,221	0	2,458	2,629
Angra do Heroismo, Azores	5,881	16,905	3,912	6,862	5,200	4,486	2,665	17,579	5,585	8,162	15,411	3,125	2,643	5,679	2,901	8,340	7,789	2,458	0	5,084
Ankara, Turkey	797	12,028	8,263	10,723	1,005	603	2,617	12,570	560	3,651	10,731	7,442	2,631	928	2,538	7,996	8,790	2,629	5,084	0
Annaba, Algeria	2,965	13,865	6,736	9,553	2,133	1,627	421	14,713	2,623	5,774	12,942	5,897	1,510	2,637	1,731	8,700	8,942	820	3,070	2,210
Annapolis, Maryland	9,455	18,673	469	2,705	9,144	8,183	6,764	16,695	9,265	10,515	15,377	1,264	6,094	9,510	6,168	6,855	5,444	6,359	4,226	8,706
Antananarivo, Madagascar	6,228	7,070	13,957	16,910	5,857	6,985	7,734	8,835	6,197	7,513	8,904	13,169	8,824	5,763	8,905	13,729	15,113	8,276	10,049	6,690
Antofagasta, Chile	13,425	13,452	7,349	7,542	12,270	12,198	10,195	14,152	13,051	16,324	16,376	7,720	10,831	12,845	11,117	13,405	11,740	10,384	8,236	12,756
Antwerp, Belgium	3,294	14,520	5,743	8,328	3,053	2,009	1,607	14,750	3,084	5,336	12,621	4,917	210	3,345	131	7,131	7,331	994	2,830	2,527
Apia, Western Samoa	15,863	7,365	11,689	8,734	17,090	16,563	17,411	5,804	16,220	12,776	6,686	12,458	15,968	16,565	15,722	8,761	8,542	16,763	15,581	16,255
Arequipa, Peru	13,103	14,226	6,542	6,798	12,012	11,802	9,777	14,786	12,737	15,806	16,910	6,931	10,276	12,590	10,547	12,634	10,980	9,900	7,646	12,383
Arkhangel'sk, USSR	3,063	12,898	6,824	8,592	3,783	2,803	3,958	12,517	3,163	3,285	10,265	6,149	2,761	3,641	2,435	5,238	6,024	3,467	5,159	2,786
As Sallum, Egypt	1,597	12,167	8,366	11,078	454	1,032	2,113	13,060	1,224	4,686	11,467	7,526	2,783	1,022	2,833	9,059	9,711	2,416	4,774	1,160
Asau, Western Samoa	15,765	7,307	11,733	8,779	16,993	16,482	17,384	5,728	16,124	12,677	6,588	12,497	15,936	16,465	15,684	8,712	8,518	16,736	15,618	16,166
Ascension Island (Georgetown)	7,633	13,115	8,204	10,718	6,404	6,794	5,275	15,108	7,271	10,721	15,688	7,740	6,609	6,931	6,929	13,629	13,060	5,815	5,325	7,188
Ashkhabad, USSR	1,518	10,147	9,856	11,773	2,707	2,803	4,829	10,419	1,893	1,674	8,517	9,102	4,579	2,150	4,382	7,457	8,718	4,776	7,184	2,216
Asmera, Ethiopia	2,415	10,006	10,626	13,354	1,983	3,098	4,266	11,180	2,319	4,750	10,048	9,785	5,058	1,865	5,085	10,462	11,483	4,667	6,900	2,789
Astrakhan, USSR	1,179	11,403	8,601	10,637	2,295	1,885	3,845	11,572	1,447	2,299	9,554	7,841	3,375	1,906	3,155	6,931	7,971	3,677	6,011	1,423
Asuncion, Paraguay	12,409	13,314	7,699	8,441	11,208	11,293	9,361	14,447	12,034	15,461	16,737	7,901	10,209	11,772	10,520	14,149	12,552	9,649	7,755	11,810
Aswan, Egypt	1,642	11,082	9,488	12,197	842	1,971	3,175	12,108	1,405	4,538	10,724	8,648	3,901	922	3,930	9,696	10,547	3,532	5,835	1,758
Athens, Greece	1,549	12,618	7,807	10,440	941	367	1,833	13,312	1,210	4,465	11,534	6,971	2,158	1,298	2,164	8,387	8,994	1,950	4,397	820
Atlanta, Georgia	10,361	17,979	1,355	2,048	10,058	9,097	7,662	16,151	10,176	11,270	15,280	2,178	7,008	10,425	7,079	7,033	5,486	7,269	5,088	9,617
Atlantic City, New Jersey	9,300	18,828	371	2,881	8,974	8,020	6,587	16,840	9,105	10,416	15,450	1,106	5,931	9,345	6,010	6,900	5,519	6,186	4,045	8,547
Auckland, New Zealand	15,928	5,059	14,276	11,374	16,740	17,303	19,287	4,158	16,259	13,260	6,001	15,101	18,438	16,231	18,112	11,268	11,334	19,162	18,083	16,704
Auckland Islands, New Zealand	15,480	4,244	15,452	12,724	15,854	16,811	17,982	4,103	15,711	13,520	6,314	16,289	18,891	15,493	18,728	12,834	12,999	18,553	18,294	16,260
Augusta, Maine	8,642	18,789	371	3,293	8,357	7,380	6,022	16,875	8,456	9,760	15,177	471	5,292	8,710	5,359	6,589	5,333	5,589	3,569	7,897
Austin, Texas	11,420	16,662	2,537	990	11,246	10,232	8,922	14,896	11,275	11,845	14,378	3,376	8,160	11,568	8,193	6,761	5,100	8,494	6,389	10,715
Ayan, USSR	7,061	10,317	8,622	8,176	8,194	7,501	8,843	8,890	7,355	4,472	6,731	8,478	7,535	7,804	7,210	2,297	3,975	8,312	9,376	7,244
Baghdad, Iraq	501	10,764	9,504	11,854	1,387	1,842	3,763	11,375	735	3,027	9,663	8,690	3,893	811	3,787	8,392	9,443	3,862	6,320	1,263
Baguio, Philippines	8,000	5,701	13,303	12,443	9,150	9,223	11,217	4,667	8,374	5,076	2,379	13,094	10,512	8,573	10,214	6,825	8,395	11,002	13,053	8,669
Bahia Blanca, Argentina	13,499	11,839	9,085	9,362	12,272	12,545	10,712	12,894	13,135	16,589	15,186	9,367	11,676	12,800	11,994	15,237	13,565	11,063	9,287	13,006
Baku, USSR	836	10,873	9,208	11,310	2,064	2,024	4,050	11,202	1,201	2,264	9,295	8,430	3,816	1,560	3,635	7,493	8,601	3,991	6,406	1,446
Balikpapan, Indonesia	8,824	3,738	15,304	14,171	9,796	10,186	12,202	3,088	9,170	6,336	1,292	15,068	11,851	9,231	11,593	8,789	10,306	12,160	14,493	9,588
Balkhash, USSR	2,976	10,029	9,627	10,932	4,203	3,941	5,871	9,792	3,333	425	7,639	8,996	5,182	3,699	4,904	5,955	7,370	5,631	7,802	3,456
Ballarat, Australia	13,374	2,342	16,794	13,841	14,032	14,766	16,568	1,806	13,662	11,210	4,072	17,527	16,676	13,557	16,446	11,715	12,469	16,788	19,232	14,171
Baltimore, Maryland	9,438	18,653	444	2,695	9,134	8,169	6,759	16,672	9,249	10,485	15,343	1,250	6,080	9,497	6,152	6,820	5,410	6,351	4,227	8,691
Bamako, Mali	5,581	14,067	7,089	9,984	4,390	4,543	2,893	15,833	5,206	8,652	15,117	6,411	4,237	4,961	4,553	11,409	11,159	3,434	3,451	5,010
Bandar Seri Begawan, Brunei	8,240	4,429	14,669	13,816	9,263	9,581	11,606	3,773	8,596	5,655	1,755	14,386	11,181	8,690	10,916	8,242	9,811	11,526	13,817	8,989
Bangalore, India	4,489	6,805	13,190	14,666	5,269	5,881	7,788	7,348	4,782	3,355	5,892	12,454	7,862	4,734	7,699	9,173	10,788	7,908	10,366	5,286
Banghazi, Libya	2,013	12,618	7,959	10,724	938	1,099	1,645	13,544	1,638	5,067	11,941	7,119	2,463	1,498	2,560	9,087	9,620	2,001	4,309	1,441
Bangkok, Thailand	6,385	5,702	13,733	13,893	7,403	7,738	9,758	5,509	6,738	3,972	3,617	13,231	9,429	6,829	9,185	8,014	9,689	9,711	12,071	7,142
Bangui, Central African Rep.	4,293	11,138	9,876	12,831	3,198	4,106	3,925	12,786	4,006	7,152	12,225	9,104	5,275	3,550	5,467	12,144	12,664	4,550	5,980	4,193
Banjarmasin, Indonesia	8,768	3,526	15,572	14,508	9,700	10,144	12,147	3,064	9,106	6,390	1,514	15,294	11,875	9,142	11,629	9,094	10,626	12,141	14,517	9,543
Banjul, Gambia	6,275	14,879	6,336	9,171	5,131	5,112	3,241	16,722	5,901	9,280	16,018	5,718	4,393	5,709	4,721	11,252	10,770	3,661	2,983	5,634
Barcelona, Spain	3,378	14,476	6,066	8,864	2,719	1,984	516	15,155	3,072	5,951	13,228	5,226	947	3,170	1,237	8,231	8,355	136	2,516	2,586
Bari, Italy	2,151	13,301	7,125	9,789	1,607	759	1,288	13,931	1,846	4,861	12,064	6,288	1,493	1,983	1,541	8,144	8,596	1,281	3,739	1,362
Barranquilla, Colombia	11,496	17,052	3,511	4,183	10,752	10,101	8,211	16,682	11,200	13,354	17,373	3,992	8,159	11,267	8,351	9,729	8,145	8,074	5,616	10,698
Basse-Terre, Guadeloupe	10,062	17,896	3,169	4,932	9,259	8,667	6,731	18,185	9,749	12,215	18,277	3,316	6,809	9,786	7,032	9,768	8,363	6,640	4,197	9,268
Basseterre, St. Kitts & Nevis	10,053	18,039	2,999	4,765	9,276	8,657	6,740	18,161	9,746	12,144	18,099	3,167	6,771	9,796	6,987	9,596	8,186	6,628	4,177	9,257
Bata, Equatorial Guinea	5,059	11,779	9,341	12,264	3,879	4,614	3,929	13,553	4,737	8,037	13,192	8,623	5,372	4,318	5,616	12,549	12,797	4,577	5,543	4,822
Baton Rouge, Louisiana	11,047	17,266	2,058	1,535	10,783	9,806	8,399	15,526	10,875	11,755	14,940	2,894	7,720	11,138	7,779	7,049	5,425	8,001	5,824	10,315
Bear Lake, Canada	9,612	14,686	4,017	2,803	10,074	8,947	8,671	12,730	9,655	8,759	11,272	4,380	7,344	10,102	7,188	3,091	1,438	8,044	7,079	9,181
Bechar, Algeria	4,009	14,520	6,284	9,212	3,043	2,710	751	15,639	3,653	6,864	14,000	5,471	2,065	3,595	2,375	9,321	9,308	1,252	2,399	3,280
Beira, Mozambique	6,330	8,157	12,985	15,896	5,672	6,782	7,103	10,014	6,206	8,204	10,227	12,257	8,364	5,731	8,507	14,308	15,394	7,704	9,150	6,619
Beirut, Lebanon	627	11,473	8,899	11,418	604	1,150	2,954	12,180	299	3,718	10,492	8,069	3,239	218	3,184	8,581	9,452	3,103	5,551	711
Belau Islands (Koror)	9,813	5,003	13,779	12,086	10,963	11,017	12,990	3,434	10,187	6,852	1,407	13,831	12,172	10,386	11,859	7,205	8,526	12,728	14,577	10,472
Belem, Brazil	10,084	15,726	5,503	7,265	8,994	8,806	6,792	17,211	9,717	12,915	19,334	5,462	7,461	9,572	7,761	12,081	10,757	6,978	4,946	9,377
Belfast, United Kingdom	4,051	15,230	4,964	7,541	3,841	2,796	2,095	15,245	3,859	5,839	13,026	4,144	766	4,132	761	6,767	6,779	1,450	2,388	3,299
Belgrade, Yugoslavia	1,942	13,180	7,132	9,681	1,721	623	1,717	13,647	1,702	4,435	11,694	6,305	1,481	1,959	1,417	7,690	8,216	1,549	3,970	1,153
Belmopan, Belize	12,049	16,721	3,160	2,656	11,563	10,713	9,046	15,538	11,820	13,154	15,728	3,907	8,641	12,001	8,759	8,464	6,808	8,763	6,382	11,272
Belo Horizonte, Brazil	10,909	13,629	7,573	8,991	9,698	9,850	7,983	15,174	10,535	13,988	17,256	7,564	8,972	10,256	9,295	14,172	12,781	8,336	6,714	10,342
Bergen, Norway	3,622	14,537	5,449	7,760	3,716	2,590	2,629	14,354	3,512	4,999	12,112	4,676	1,183	3,874	895	6,109	6,352	2,006	3,312	2,964
Bern, Switzerland	2,978	14,213	6,149	8,802	2,593	1,620	1,183	14,639	2,727	5,303	12,606	5,314	506	2,935	632	7,592	7,845	680	2,955	2,186
Bhopal, India	3,775	7,739	12,132	13,533	4,750	5,158	7,153	8,017	4,113	2,217	6,267	11,430	7,014	4,179	6,816	8,154	9,731	7,173	9,607	4,555
Bhubaneswar, India	4,690	6,992	12,736	13,743	5,685	6,062	8,070	7,126	5,035	2,684	5,333	12,091	7,859	5,112	7,642	8,068	9,712	8,065	10,477	5,461
Bialystok, Poland	2,273	13,326	6,772	9,100	2,497	1,381	2,395	13,455	2,177	4,044	11,340	5,980	1,486	2,568	1,231	6,747	7,310	1,993	4,125	1,642
Big Trout Lake, Canada	8,906	17,001	1,725	2,456	8,962	7,865	6,993	15,070	8,818	9,175	13,461	2,043	5,909	9,177	5,861	4,912	3,546	6,438	4,945	8,271
Bilbao, Spain	3,784	14,935	5,594	8,399	3,182	2,390	882	15,529	3,494	6,219	13,521	4,754	842	3,619	1,170	8,030	8,046	376	2,097	2,987
Billings, Montana	10,347	15,969	2,777	1,198	10,508	9,395	8,590	13,978	10,297	10,128	12,836	3,399	7,487	10,683	7,421	4,807	3,161	8,034	6,465	9,763
Birmingham, Alabama	10,525	17,753	1,526	1,832	10,248	9,275	7,867	15,930	10,348	11,346	15,115	2,360	7,188	10,606	7,250	6,949	5,378	7,466	5,304	9,788
Birmingham, United Kingdom	3,750	14,966	5,285	7,891	3,494	2,465	1,786	15,113	3,542	5,690	12,938	4,459	410	3,800	465	7,005	7,084	1,138	2,480	2,985
Bismarck, North Dakota	9,978	16,553	2,178	1,392	10,055	8,957	8,050	14,560	9,901	10,026	13,318	2,794	6,998	10,266	6,954	5,071	3,487	7,510	5,870	9,357
Bissau, Guinea Bissau	6,292	14,686	6,536	9,361	5,130	5,162	3,333	16,548	5,917	9,321	15,946	5,922	4,527	5,707	4,854	11,440	10,974	3,779	3,185	5,670
Biysk, USSR	3,810	10,209	9,264	10,226	5,014	4,583	6,378	9,673	4,144	1,206	7,424	8,719	5,471	4,550	5,164	5,012	6,481	6,041	7,991	4,172
Blagoveshchensk, USSR	6,718	9,497	9,505	9,162	7,911	7,370	8,938	8,217	7,045	3,865	5,982	9,297	7,749	7,460	7,420	3,282	4,960	8,471	9,850	7,026
Blantyre, Malawi	5,882	8,385	12,712	15,653	5,227	6,340	6,716	10,193	5,758	7,812	10,249	11,960	7,952	5,283	8,087	13,880	14,945	7,308	8,840	6,172
Bloemfontein, South Africa	7,492	8,362	12,906	15,566	6,689	7,748	7,686	10,330	7,323	9,545	10,979	12,294	9,067	6,839	9,261	15,569	16,427	8,324	9,329	7,678
Bluefields, Nicaragua	12,115	16,658	3,532	3,446	11,488	10,739	8,941	15,853	11,850	13,582	16,399	4,182	8,717	11,971	8,872	9,219	7,575	8,734	6,293	11,322
Boa Vista do Rio Branco, Braz.	10,880	16,435	4,600	5,933	9,909	9,518	7,501	17,222	10,533	13,383	19,046	4,779	7,863	10,474	8,124	11,167	9,691	7,546	5,223	10,116
Bodo, Norway	3,767	14,116	5,647	7,630	4,142	3,025	3,469	13,668	3,749	4,503	11,389	4,947	2,051	4,177	1,742	5,293	5,691	2,866	4,089	3,251
Bogota, Colombia	11,907	16,420	4,215	4,755	11,072	10,513	8,562	16,355	11,591	13,964	17,562	4,668	8,645	11,610	8,858	10,406	8,801	8,487	6,044	11,115
Boise, Idaho	10,789	15,345	3,419	1,254	11,034	9,911	9,202	13,361	10,767	10,294	12,338	4,055	8,056	11,173	7,972	4,636	2,957	8,633	7,118	10,247
Bologna, Italy	2,640	13,851	6,544	9,207	2,191	1,256	1,104	14,374	2,367	5,129	12,409	5,708	911	2,549	995	7,833	8,165	824	3,249	1,843
Bolzano, Italy	2,677	13,913	6,432	9,054	2,329	1,325	1,282	14,350	2,428	5,043	12,339	5,599	771	2,648	799	7,608	7,943	901	3,250	1,886
Bombay, India	3,670	7,640	12,376	14,022	4,507	5,065	6,999	8,136	3,974	2,720	6,561	11,630	7,030	3,956	6,864	8,788	10,340	7,094	9,550	4,467

Distances in Kilometers	Al Qamishli, Syria	Albany, Australia	Albany, New York	Albuquerque, New Mexico	Alexandria, Egypt	Alexandroupolis, Greece	Algiers, Algeria	Alice Springs, Australia	Allepo, Syria	Alma-Ata, USSR	Ambon, Indonesia	Amherst, Canada	Amiens, France	Amman, Jordan	Amsterdam, Netherlands	Anadyr, USSR	Anchorage, Alaska	Andorra, Andorra	Angra do Heroismo, Azores	Ankara, Turkey
Bonn, West Germany	3,098	14,325	5,937	8,508	2,873	1,818	1,583	14,581	2,889	5,177	12,471	5,112	354	3,154	235	7,172	7,424	1,010	2,997	2,332
Bora Bora (Vaitape)	17,403	9,009	10,292	7,436	18,370	17,298	16,672	7,735	17,656	14,566	8,840	11,124	15,635	18,132	15,535	9,382	8,618	16,174	14,127	17,372
Bordeaux, France	3,583	14,777	5,693	8,455	3,047	2,196	944	15,298	3,305	5,966	13,269	4,853	603	3,458	928	7,853	7,928	309	2,309	2,786
Boston, Massachusetts	8,863	18,890	224	3,174	8,555	7,590	6,193	16,922	8,671	10,000	15,320	671	5,501	8,918	5,575	6,734	5,435	5,776	3,698	8,113
Bouvet Island	10,763	8,289	13,001	14,343	9,823	10,774	10,107	10,146	10,551	12,867	11,814	12,806	11,565	10,068	11,838	18,810	18,271	10,743	10,722	10,829
Brasilia, Brazil	10,979	14,186	6,990	8,371	9,795	9,837	7,901	15,632	10,604	14,007	17,807	7,018	8,780	10,365	9,096	13,593	12,172	8,198	6,400	10,361
Braunschweig, West Germany	2,931	14,122	6,078	8,578	2,821	1,723	1,818	14,312	2,750	4,898	12,187	5,263	634	3,052	383	6,979	7,302	1,279	3,268	2,189
Brazzaville, Congo	5,306	10,883	10,252	13,166	4,221	5,111	4,719	12,694	5,026	8,102	12,524	9,537	6,131	4,566	6,350	13,144	13,566	5,363	6,455	5,215
Bremerhaven, West Germany	3,107	14,277	5,899	8,385	3,015	1,916	1,912	14,408	2,934	4,986	12,257	5,087	594	3,243	280	6,850	7,137	1,335	3,177	2,374
Brest, France	3,887	15,124	5,263	7,984	3,465	2,531	1,429	15,457	3,638	6,048	13,333	4,425	522	3,837	799	7,457	7,464	806	2,121	3,097
Brest, USSR	2,166	13,252	6,867	9,212	2,376	1,261	2,350	13,419	2,062	4,021	11,322	6,071	1,516	2,449	1,280	6,852	7,427	1,976	4,160	1,525
Bridgetown, Barbados	10,084	17,562	3,547	5,303	9,225	8,694	6,723	18,178	9,759	12,369	18,670	3,655	6,902	9,766	7,141	10,150	8,755	6,678	4,266	9,297
Brisbane, Australia	13,646	3,430	15,505	12,594	14,550	15,012	17,026	1,965	13,986	11,021	3,725	16,170	16,497	14,005	16,192	10,445	11,089	16,955	18,768	14,414
Bristol, United Kingdom	3,778	15,008	5,278	7,915	3,480	2,472	1,690	15,200	3,559	5,777	13,037	4,448	386	3,802	526	7,119	7,179	1,042	2,387	3,005
Brno, Czechoslovakia	2,398	13,621	6,620	9,124	2,288	1,177	1,764	13,931	2,204	4,575	11,878	5,800	1,039	2,503	896	7,261	7,703	1,387	3,653	1,644
Broken Hill, Australia	12,893	2,210	16,713	13,817	13,644	14,289	16,191	1,178	13,201	10,601	3,418	17,331	16,108	13,138	15,858	11,170	12,027	16,317	18,749	13,688
Brussels, Belgium	3,290	14,520	5,754	8,349	3,033	1,996	1,564	14,767	3,075	5,357	12,645	4,927	178	3,331	174	7,174	7,371	951	2,812	2,519
Bucharest, Romania	1,516	12,756	7,514	9,995	1,506	399	2,118	13,200	1,310	4,025	11,260	6,694	1,895	1,629	1,789	7,645	8,287	1,993	4,416	749
Budapest, Hungary	2,154	13,388	6,874	9,387	2,031	916	1,775	13,758	1,949	4,452	11,744	6,053	1,261	2,241	1,149	7,418	7,911	1,488	3,836	1,390
Buenos Aires, Argentina	12,991	12,287	8,695	9,200	11,765	11,999	10,149	13,423	12,622	16,087	15,707	8,927	11,105	12,304	11,424	15,026	13,381	10,494	8,726	12,472
Buffalo, New York	9,286	18,330	420	2,544	9,063	8,060	6,762	16,337	9,120	10,165	14,913	1,213	5,981	9,395	6,026	6,378	4,980	6,315	4,318	8,559
Bujumbura, Burundi	4,640	9,664	11,339	14,293	3,828	4,911	5,218	11,338	4,456	7,024	10,974	10,555	6,451	3,972	6,592	12,737	13,588	5,805	7,432	4,810
Bulawayo, Zimbabwe	6,467	8,691	12,495	15,355	5,684	6,759	6,850	10,586	6,302	8,584	10,875	11,802	8,181	5,818	8,354	14,546	15,442	7,473	8,729	6,666
Burlington, Vermont	8,836	18,601	208	3,024	8,584	7,592	6,273	16,646	8,659	9,847	15,030	724	5,508	8,925	5,563	6,446	5,143	5,828	3,839	8,099
Cabinda, Angola	5,597	11,074	10,096	12,980	4,481	5,324	4,782	12,924	5,305	8,438	12,848	9,406	6,218	4,854	6,453	13,332	13,651	5,430	6,360	5,464
Cagliari, Italy	2,812	13,842	6,696	9,469	2,084	1,439	597	14,590	2,486	5,546	12,755	5,855	1,304	2,550	1,495	8,434	8,711	737	3,130	2,036
Cairns, Australia	12,401	3,418	15,318	12,657	13,406	13,728	15,754	1,450	12,757	9,661	2,412	15,773	15,109	12,839	14,803	9,448	10,344	15,601	17,503	13,142
Cairo, Egypt	1,207	11,580	8,910	11,559	182	1,293	2,716	12,453	877	4,280	10,890	8,071	3,275	494	3,282	9,095	9,888	2,986	5,373	1,106
Calais, France	3,464	14,696	5,587	8,200	3,185	2,162	1,577	14,932	3,247	5,516	12,797	4,758	121	3,495	264	7,169	7,316	940	2,649	2,692
Calcutta, India	4,778	7,093	12,559	13,435	5,824	6,128	8,148	7,101	5,134	2,528	5,214	11,945	7,851	5,247	7,620	7,722	9,373	8,105	10,486	5,531
Calgary, Canada	9,954	15,536	3,170	1,872	10,235	9,108	8,511	13,549	9,940	9,502	12,237	3,664	7,304	10,353	7,202	4,092	2,455	7,920	6,596	9,426
Cali, Colombia	12,194	16,209	4,351	4,682	11,368	10,799	8,854	16,064	11,880	14,193	17,292	4,847	8,916	11,905	9,124	10,411	8,785	8,772	6,325	11,401
Camaguey, Cuba	10,937	17,857	2,390	3,186	10,375	9,574	7,842	16,758	10,685	12,403	16,591	2,986	7,530	10,834	7,675	8,544	6,982	7,590	5,178	10,148
Cambridge Bay, Canada	7,913	15,397	3,455	3,788	8,294	7,164	6,902	13,660	7,923	7,542	11,771	3,444	5,550	8,355	5,388	3,192	2,216	6,267	5,578	7,428
Cambridge, United Kingdom	3,608	14,827	5,426	8,023	3,360	2,325	1,729	14,996	3,400	5,573	12,834	4,600	298	3,660	328	7,033	7,151	1,084	2,591	2,843
Campbellton, Canada	8,198	18,517	813	3,582	7,953	6,955	5,673	16,760	8,021	9,287	14,897	305	4,873	8,289	4,925	6,335	5,178	5,211	3,323	7,461
Campo Grande, Brazil	11,856	13,814	7,257	8,244	10,670	10,709	8,761	15,035	11,481	14,880	17,314	7,404	9,592	11,239	9,902	13,798	12,258	9,037	7,140	11,236
Canakkale, Turkey	1,336	12,522	7,833	10,390	1,042	90	2,066	13,118	1,039	4,158	11,281	7,003	2,173	1,250	2,127	8,104	8,763	2,092	4,550	552
Canberra, Australia	13,702	2,838	16,258	13,307	14,437	15,098	16,985	1,960	14,009	11,367	4,113	16,992	16,891	13,939	16,627	11,368	12,030	17,126	19,525	14,497
Cancun, Mexico	11,578	17,166	2,677	2,484	11,121	10,252	8,619	15,853	11,355	12,685	15,786	3,424	8,174	11,548	8,286	8,170	6,537	8,317	5,960	10,806
Canton, China	6,952	6,454	12,688	12,318	8,118	8,157	10,149	5,640	7,326	4,007	3,384	12,365	9,460	7,544	9,167	6,487	8,138	9,936	12,028	7,607
Canton Atoll, Phoenix Islands	14,950	8,054	10,873	7,954	16,142	15,444	16,207	6,287	15,279	11,948	6,681	11,586	14,757	15,688	14,506	7,550	7,346	15,559	14,658	15,214
Cape Town, South Africa	8,204	8,688	12,625	15,045	7,308	8,314	7,988	10,680	8,003	10,410	11,590	12,106	9,420	7,519	9,647	16,295	16,856	8,636	9,313	8,311
Cape York, Australia	11,717	3,668	15,034	12,589	12,768	13,017	15,036	1,701	12,080	8,915	1,755	15,369	14,339	12,194	14,031	8,867	9,886	14,849	16,747	12,440
Caracas, Venezuela	10,882	17,245	3,624	4,854	10,055	9,488	7,538	17,380	10,566	13,022	18,202	3,925	7,636	10,590	7,858	10,120	8,614	7,463	5,024	10,090
Cardiff, United Kingdom	3,821	15,051	5,235	7,876	3,520	2,514	1,708	15,237	3,602	5,814	13,070	4,405	427	3,845	566	7,113	7,162	1,062	2,351	3,048
Carlisle, United Kingdom	3,867	15,035	5,143	7,691	3,690	2,630	2,063	15,059	3,682	5,648	12,849	4,326	659	3,966	591	6,737	6,807	1,415	2,563	3,122
Carnarvon, Australia	10,213	1,199	17,921	16,007	10,851	11,597	13,395	2,058	10,488	8,425	2,813	17,670	13,592	10,372	13,415	11,332	12,740	13,608	16,050	11,009
Carson City, Nevada	11,347	14,965	3,848	1,249	11,609	10,485	9,765	13,005	11,332	10,724	12,165	4,534	8,631	11,742	8,548	4,873	3,206	9,201	7,629	10,816
Casablanca, Morocco	4,407	15,069	5,740	8,673	3,517	3,055	1,029	16,128	4,064	7,142	14,373	4,930	1,983	4,051	2,310	9,091	8,954	1,267	1,849	3,647
Casper, Wyoming	10,570	16,140	2,649	862	10,672	9,570	8,664	14,162	10,503	10,463	13,124	3,336	7,618	10,875	7,572	5,173	3,522	8,129	6,442	9,962
Castries, Saint Lucia	10,138	17,674	3,402	5,122	9,303	8,745	6,788	18,128	9,818	12,362	18,496	3,540	6,922	9,838	7,154	10,001	8,593	6,723	4,296	9,348
Catbalogan, Philippines	8,674	5,232	13,689	12,515	9,811	9,909	11,907	4,044	9,047	5,767	1,751	13,561	11,198	9,233	10,897	7,116	8,612	11,693	13,721	9,352
Cayenne, French Guiana	10,001	16,525	4,684	6,487	8,993	8,662	6,636	17,826	9,647	12,645	19,863	4,676	7,120	9,563	7,400	11,274	9,932	6,732	4,515	9,253
Cayman Islands (Georgetown)	11,355	17,442	2,687	3,039	10,803	9,995	8,271	16,355	11,106	12,735	16,382	3,340	7,945	11,260	8,085	8,597	6,995	8,016	5,607	10,568
Cazombo, Angola	5,748	9,712	11,437	14,341	4,828	5,848	5,775	11,557	5,532	8,207	11,597	10,725	7,135	5,048	7,324	13,820	14,499	6,406	7,637	5,831
Cebu, Philippines	8,682	5,057	13,874	12,706	9,804	9,936	11,944	3,915	9,053	5,813	1,622	13,736	11,273	9,225	10,976	7,307	8,807	11,748	13,818	9,372
Cedar Rapids, Iowa	10,039	17,347	1,476	1,510	9,943	8,894	7,739	15,369	9,911	10,497	14,218	2,237	6,849	10,228	6,856	5,923	4,372	7,256	5,360	9,354
Changsha, China	6,647	7,018	12,130	11,864	7,841	7,794	9,756	6,166	7,023	3,623	3,891	11,801	8,996	7,275	8,695	6,002	7,666	9,507	11,531	7,264
Channel-Port-aux-Basques, Can.	7,767	18,591	1,270	4,138	7,459	6,488	5,134	17,118	7,571	9,063	15,095	432	4,399	7,816	4,476	6,625	5,578	4,691	2,758	7,013
Charleston, South Carolina	10,166	18,363	1,224	2,477	9,796	8,869	7,358	16,577	9,962	11,266	15,668	1,979	6,781	10,187	6,873	7,323	5,815	6,994	4,750	9,406
Charleston, West Virginia	9,814	18,246	820	2,257	9,548	8,567	7,195	16,295	9,637	10,714	15,130	1,659	6,481	9,899	6,540	6,704	5,224	6,776	4,674	9,077
Charlotte, North Carolina	10,024	18,322	1,028	2,344	9,702	8,749	7,299	16,446	9,832	11,029	15,421	1,832	6,659	10,075	6,736	7,043	5,544	6,910	4,725	9,274
Charlotte Amalie, U.S.V.I.	10,160	18,136	2,820	4,505	9,418	8,765	6,875	17,990	9,862	12,157	17,858	3,049	6,844	9,929	7,048	9,400	7,967	6,737	4,279	9,363
Charlottetown, Canada	8,101	18,758	934	3,828	7,796	6,826	5,461	17,081	7,907	9,341	15,168	94	4,737	8,154	4,811	6,631	5,502	5,026	3,044	7,349
Chatham, Canada	8,191	18,644	816	3,657	7,920	6,933	5,613	16,900	8,007	9,344	15,029	165	4,847	8,265	4,909	6,472	5,319	5,163	3,227	7,448
Chatham Islands (Waitangi)	16,760	5,579	13,994	11,245	17,307	18,152	19,208	5,017	17,045	14,294	7,000	14,834	19,337	16,899	19,065	12,063	11,904	19,787	17,402	17,557
Chengdu, China	5,754	7,415	11,884	12,052	6,941	6,929	8,914	6,806	6,129	2,771	4,589	11,451	8,237	6,373	7,948	6,185	7,865	8,700	10,826	6,387
Chesterfield Inlet, Canada	8,094	16,299	2,551	3,330	8,300	7,176	6,602	14,522	8,049	8,136	12,676	2,558	5,360	8,445	5,254	4,091	2,972	5,996	4,947	7,521
Cheyenne, Wyoming	10,686	16,255	2,568	691	10,748	9,656	8,688	14,290	10,608	10,656	13,314	3,290	7,679	10,969	7,645	5,400	3,747	8,165	6,410	10,062
Chiang Mai, Thailand	5,938	6,282	13,163	13,461	7,002	7,266	9,292	6,038	6,298	3,410	4,055	12,652	8,898	6,425	8,646	7,588	9,267	9,212	11,541	6,676
Chibougamau, Canada	8,494	18,079	809	3,087	8,347	7,309	6,155	16,209	8,345	9,313	14,463	885	5,252	8,645	5,270	5,876	4,638	5,659	3,894	7,786
Chicago, Illinois	9,845	17,680	1,146	1,818	9,700	8,668	7,454	15,698	9,702	10,450	14,488	1,926	6,607	10,004	6,628	6,108	4,598	6,986	5,044	9,143
Chiclayo, Peru	13,207	15,021	5,507	5,419	12,280	11,823	9,831	15,042	12,872	15,374	16,708	6,031	10,021	12,840	10,245	11,283	9,616	9,812	7,397	12,426
Chihuahua, Mexico	11,979	15,839	3,287	717	11,914	10,863	9,667	14,071	11,868	12,039	13,672	4,116	8,820	12,195	8,826	6,525	4,845	9,209	7,179	11,312
Chongquing, China	6,025	7,248	12,008	12,050	7,211	7,199	9,180	6,578	6,400	3,037	4,346	11,603	8,487	6,643	8,196	6,171	7,851	8,960	11,066	6,658
Christchurch, New Zealand	15,886	4,730	14,764	11,933	16,485	17,279	18,856	4,161	16,174	13,508	6,205	15,603	18,991	16,046	18,672	12,013	12,095	19,289	18,273	16,684
Christiansted, U.S.V.I.	10,183	18,073	2,891	4,562	9,432	8,788	6,890	17,988	9,883	12,203	17,924	3,115	6,876	9,945	7,083	9,470	8,037	6,759	4,303	9,387
Christmas Is. [Indian Ocean]	8,529	2,987	16,441	15,764	9,289	9,924	11,826	3,330	8,828	6,628	2,598	15,972	11,853	8,770	11,656	10,212	11,796	11,952	14,409	9,325
Christmas Is. [Pacific Ocean]	15,274	9,646	9,353	6,402	16,250	15,249	15,271	7,935	15,514	12,634	8,287	10,112	13,942	15,992	13,763	7,249	6,603	14,651	13,234	15,245
Churchill, Canada	8,615	16,484	2,278	2,788	8,780	7,662	6,980	14,606	8,560	8,669	12,902	2,463	5,794	8,946	5,708	4,330	3,031	6,392	5,143	8,026
Cincinnati, Ohio	9,916	17,988	988	2,013	9,695	8,694	7,375	16,031	9,752	10,696	14,890	1,824	6,614	10,029	6,660	6,508	5,004	6,939	4,886	9,192
Ciudad Bolivia, Venezuela	11,342	16,928	3,813	4,718	10,521	9,947	8,003	16,916	11,027	13,420	17,897	4,199	8,077	11,055	8,292	10,182	8,625	7,920	5,476	10,549
Ciudad Juarez, Mexico	11,688	15,916	3,124	372	11,667	10,600	9,472	14,082	11,589	11,694	13,538	3,937	8,575	11,928	8,569	6,207	4,528	8,994	7,034	11,036
Ciudad Victoria, Mexico	12,106	16,247	3,140	1,453	11,866	10,883	9,475	14,659	11,945	12,577	14,489	3,977	8,799	12,217	8,852	7,333	5,656	9,083	6,879	11,385
Clarksburg, West Virginia	9,662	18,341	669	2,373	9,397	8,415	7,048	16,371	9,485	10,584	15,134	1,509	6,329	9,747	6,388	6,667	5,212	6,626	4,537	8,925
Cleveland, Ohio	9,559	18,169	669	2,287	9,343	8,337	7,039	16,181	9,395	10,379	14,875	1,488	6,259	9,673	6,303	6,397	4,948	6,594	4,581	8,834
Cocos (Keeling) Island	7,949	3,320	16,490	16,531	8,589	9,328	11,136	4,120	8,218	6,444	3,575	15,851	11,344	8,102	11,185	10,764	12,406	11,336	13,781	8,743
Colombo, Sri Lanka	5,136	6,124	13,902	15,305	5,838	6,519	8,379	6,777	5,412	4,034	5,500	13,162	8,531	5,324	8,378	9,674	11,319	8,537	10,992	5,931
Colon, Panama	12,025	16,643	3,737	3,938	11,315	10,634	8,770	16,105	11,738	13,727	16,868	4,311	8,660	11,822	8,838	9,661	8,032	8,611	6,154	11,228
Colorado Springs, Colorado	10,915	16,231	2,643	447	10,951	9,866	8,849	14,290	10,830	10,912	13,413	3,398	7,873	11,184	7,847	5,614	3,951	8,339	6,523	10,282
Columbia, South Carolina	10,136	18,288	1,152	2,347	9,798	8,854	7,381	16,453	9,940	11,165	15,500	1,943	6,764	10,177	6,846	7,155	5,643	7,001	4,792	9,383
Columbus, Georgia	10,506	17,894	1,502	2,023	10,192	9,237	7,784	16,109	10,318	11,422	15,321	2,318	7,148	10,564	7,222	7,133	5,570	7,399	5,197	9,760
Columbus, Ohio	9,759	18,103	829	2,152	9,533	8,533	7,215	16,131	9,593	10,572	14,920	1,663	6,453	9,868	6,500	6,490	5,010	6,778	4,733	9,033
Conakry, Guinea	6,287	14,367	6,861	9,676	5,101	5,213	3,461	16,247	5,911	9,347	15,780	6,251	4,716	5,674	5,041	11,715	11,286	3,946	3,498	5,698
Concepcion, Chile	14,294	11,969	8,802	8,689	13,075	13,229	11,306	12,737	13,922	17,381	15,009	9,199	12,116	13,623	12,420	14,550	12,871	11,585	9,591	13,733
Concord, New Hampshire	8,830	18,796	191	3,141	8,541	7,566	6,197	16,837	8,643	9,928	15,219	652	5,478	8,897	5,546	6,633	5,338	5,769	3,723	8,084
Constantine, Algeria	3,077	13,941	6,682	9,515	2,225	1,745	323	14,816	2,733	5,893	13,057	5,845	1,543	2,737	1,781	8,766	8,981	810	2,985	2,326
Copenhagen, Denmark	2,986	14,061	6,036	8,424	3,039	1,913	2,219	14,103	2,853	4,680	11,931	5,240	943	3,203	623	6,588	6,952	1,668	3,491	2,300
Coppermine, Canada	8,208	15,093	3,710	3,683	8,644	7,518	7,320	13,303	8,237	7,645	11,480	3,778	5,955	8,680	5,783	2,894	1,796	6,683	6,007	7,757

Distances in Kilometers	Al Qamishli, Syria	Albany, Australia	Albany, New York	Albuquerque, New Mexico	Alexandria, Egypt	Alexandroupolis, Greece	Algiers, Algeria	Alice Springs, Australia	Allepo, Syria	Alma-Ata, USSR	Ambon, Indonesia	Amherst, Canada	Amiens, France	Amman, Jordan	Amsterdam, Netherlands	Anadyr, USSR	Anchorage, Alaska	Andorra, Andorra	Angra do Heroismo, Azores	Ankara, Turkey
Coquimbo, Chile	13,841	12,745	8,044	8,096	12,648	12,683	10,711	13,487	13,465	16,851	15,742	8,425	11,434	13,214	11,729	13,976	12,299	10,945	8,871	13,218
Cordoba, Argentina	13,300	12,648	8,258	8,597	12,089	12,215	10,292	13,613	12,927	16,374	15,905	8,553	11,133	12,644	11,442	14,452	12,791	10,581	8,650	12,723
Cordoba, Spain	4,029	14,955	5,728	8,614	3,248	2,647	703	15,808	3,704	6,662	13,933	4,898	1,449	3,747	1,776	8,625	8,576	741	1,962	3,248
Cork, Ireland	4,188	15,415	4,874	7,540	3,871	2,878	1,909	15,541	3,969	6,121	13,341	4,042	789	4,206	917	7,058	7,004	1,288	2,070	3,415
Corner Brook, Canada	7,609	18,422	1,410	4,233	7,320	6,339	5,021	17,019	7,417	8,885	14,958	585	4,251	7,670	4,321	6,522	5,515	4,564	2,701	6,859
Corrientes, Argentina	12,635	13,078	7,913	8,557	11,428	11,538	9,616	14,182	12,260	15,700	16,474	8,135	10,476	11,988	10,787	14,314	12,698	9,911	8,025	12,048
Cosenza, Italy	2,197	13,271	7,201	9,902	1,530	838	1,191	13,974	1,871	4,992	12,155	6,361	1,612	1,955	1,692	8,353	8,792	1,289	3,731	1,427
Craiova, Romania	1,676	12,917	7,377	9,893	1,551	421	1,939	13,382	1,448	4,204	11,444	6,553	1,738	1,733	1,653	7,697	8,292	1,811	4,238	893
Cruzeiro do Sul, Brazil	12,634	15,157	5,569	5,928	11,639	11,275	9,257	15,511	12,284	15,075	17,401	5,981	9,588	12,209	9,837	11,707	10,072	9,299	6,945	11,872
Cuiaba, Brazil	11,681	14,367	6,697	7,741	10,526	10,471	8,485	15,528	11,307	14,628	17,820	6,850	9,226	11,102	9,529	13,242	11,715	8,717	6,715	11,020
Curitiba, Brazil	11,706	13,179	7,945	9,021	10,490	10,666	8,800	14,560	11,334	14,794	16,770	8,034	9,771	11,042	10,091	14,525	13,014	9,147	7,455	11,153
Cuzco, Peru	12,962	14,532	6,221	6,505	11,901	11,638	9,612	15,027	12,601	15,579	17,090	6,619	10,055	12,478	10,319	12,326	10,677	9,708	7,417	12,226
Dacca, Bangladesh	4,894	7,119	12,480	13,254	5,968	6,226	8,251	7,041	5,256	2,495	5,098	11,889	7,899	5,389	7,658	7,509	9,166	8,183	10,540	5,634
Dakar, Senegal	6,272	15,032	6,178	9,020	5,144	5,085	3,183	16,860	5,899	9,256	16,075	5,556	4,298	5,722	4,626	11,109	10,611	3,580	2,826	5,616
Dallas, Texas	11,139	16,824	2,299	945	10,985	9,961	8,686	15,000	10,999	11,562	14,347	3,134	7,895	11,298	7,922	6,563	4,916	8,245	6,180	10,439
Damascus, Syria	596	11,387	8,981	11,492	654	1,233	3,037	12,097	310	3,673	10,417	8,152	3,322	175	3,265	8,602	9,491	3,189	5,636	777
Danang, Vietnam	6,923	5,747	13,500	13,260	8,012	8,225	10,250	5,210	7,289	4,224	3,103	13,108	9,754	7,434	9,484	7,421	9,076	10,128	12,384	7,644
Dar es Salaam, Tanzania	4,856	8,545	12,400	15,336	4,322	5,452	6,125	10,181	4,765	6,720	9,851	11,595	7,227	4,303	7,320	12,789	13,919	6,666	8,490	5,216
Darwin, Australia	10,802	2,820	15,912	13,752	11,754	12,164	14,181	1,284	11,147	8,243	1,010	16,045	13,773	11,195	13,498	9,410	10,645	14,128	16,391	11,567
Davao, Philippines	9,044	4,730	14,163	12,829	10,150	10,314	12,327	3,521	9,413	6,204	1,227	14,065	11,674	9,571	11,378	7,570	9,027	12,142	14,222	9,744
David, Panama	12,296	16,412	3,885	3,847	11,602	10,908	9,056	15,811	12,014	13,916	16,607	4,498	8,920	12,105	9,092	9,638	7,991	8,888	6,433	11,499
Dawson, Canada	8,797	14,050	4,695	3,911	9,402	8,301	8,349	12,191	8,885	7,687	10,491	4,875	6,937	9,353	6,732	2,039	623	7,703	7,177	8,455
Dawson Creek, Canada	9,573	15,099	3,603	2,522	9,961	8,830	8,434	13,139	9,591	8,913	11,685	3,982	7,146	10,026	7,009	3,432	1,814	7,818	6,739	9,099
Denpasar, Indonesia	9,192	2,934	16,138	14,859	10,066	10,580	12,557	2,594	9,519	6,929	1,537	15,883	12,376	9,520	12,141	9,610	11,106	12,596	15,009	9,978
Denver, Colorado	10,832	16,228	2,625	537	10,880	9,792	8,797	14,276	10,750	10,811	13,361	3,367	7,806	11,108	7,776	5,521	3,862	8,281	6,491	10,203
Derby, Australia	10,501	2,046	16,752	14,693	11,337	11,893	13,853	1,282	10,822	8,225	1,583	16,759	13,696	10,803	13,456	10,171	11,489	13,913	16,331	11,290
Des Moines, Iowa	10,168	17,191	1,643	1,347	10,090	9,035	7,899	15,218	10,045	10,561	14,111	2,403	6,996	10,367	6,998	5,872	4,301	7,412	5,527	9,489
Detroit, Michigan	9,564	18,035	764	2,196	9,375	8,359	7,097	16,044	9,408	10,318	14,731	1,555	6,287	9,695	6,321	6,260	4,805	6,641	4,666	8,848
Dhahran, Saudi Arabia	1,457	9,843	10,458	12,787	2,046	2,756	4,572	10,570	1,649	3,069	9,012	9,642	4,832	1,516	4,737	8,945	10,138	4,743	7,189	2,202
Diego Garcia Island	5,888	5,559	14,888	16,930	6,217	7,146	8,698	6,787	6,065	5,620	6,191	14,064	9,236	5,823	9,163	11,452	13,090	9,023	11,354	6,625
Dijon, France	3,169	14,404	5,963	8,631	2,774	1,811	1,181	14,814	2,918	5,457	12,761	5,128	350	3,123	560	7,561	7,763	602	2,776	2,377
Dili, Indonesia	10,081	3,036	15,785	13,968	11,039	11,444	13,460	1,896	10,426	7,550	609	15,769	13,078	10,478	12,811	9,189	10,542	13,413	15,711	10,846
Djibouti, Djibouti	2,824	9,393	11,238	13,944	2,563	3,657	4,881	10,601	2,791	4,783	9,562	10,398	5,653	2,372	5,667	10,722	11,851	5,280	7,513	3,299
Dnepropetrovsk, USSR	1,366	12,353	7,749	10,003	1,963	1,110	2,894	12,584	1,372	3,268	10,555	6,961	2,370	1,834	2,165	7,040	7,838	2,676	5,000	961
Dobo, Indonesia	10,661	3,649	15,084	13,019	11,707	11,972	13,996	1,985	11,022	7,904	705	15,225	13,386	11,133	13,089	8,591	9,817	13,843	15,915	11,390
Doha, Qatar	1,629	9,663	10,633	12,941	2,218	2,935	4,748	10,395	1,828	3,052	8,856	9,818	5,010	1,693	4,914	9,002	10,225	4,922	7,368	2,380
Donetsk, USSR	1,250	12,147	7,937	10,149	1,982	1,236	3,088	12,369	1,312	3,064	10,345	7,153	2,584	1,789	2,377	7,025	7,876	2,885	5,215	979
Dover, Delaware	9,381	18,747	415	2,788	9,064	8,106	6,680	16,764	9,189	10,468	15,412	1,189	6,016	9,432	6,093	6,876	5,479	6,277	4,141	8,631
Dresden, East Germany	2,672	13,875	6,338	8,833	2,576	1,469	1,799	14,115	2,489	4,720	12,020	5,522	822	2,794	627	7,087	7,472	1,330	3,464	1,929
Dubayy, United Arab Emir.	1,867	9,380	10,858	13,061	2,572	3,223	5,085	10,051	2,112	2,804	8,482	10,053	5,276	2,030	5,160	8,867	10,154	5,232	7,686	2,648
Dublin, Ireland	4,052	15,258	4,978	7,592	3,797	2,772	1,976	15,332	3,848	5,916	13,125	4,153	704	4,106	760	6,905	6,903	1,335	2,286	3,290
Duluth, Minnesota	9,625	17,199	1,521	1,780	9,602	8,528	7,495	15,207	9,517	9,973	13,866	2,142	6,517	9,854	6,500	5,457	3,955	6,979	5,239	8,964
Dunedin, New Zealand	15,745	4,536	15,016	12,211	16,268	17,125	18,561	4,100	16,014	13,499	6,209	15,856	19,028	15,854	18,742	12,280	12,395	19,063	18,357	16,541
Durango, Mexico	12,364	15,761	3,509	1,240	12,219	11,198	9,890	14,114	12,231	12,553	13,936	4,349	9,131	12,534	9,159	7,040	5,361	9,467	7,334	11,672
Durban, South Africa	7,480	7,918	13,335	16,035	6,758	7,846	7,933	9,877	7,340	9,354	10,502	12,701	9,279	6,860	9,455	15,484	16,517	8,562	9,695	7,728
Dushanbe, USSR	2,425	9,589	10,252	11,839	3,621	3,654	5,676	9,666	2,800	862	7,678	9,551	5,278	3,062	5,047	7,004	8,406	5,566	7,917	3,085
East London, South Africa	7,879	7,995	13,290	15,862	7,113	8,183	8,150	9,975	7,725	9,810	10,746	12,704	9,529	7,242	9,721	15,919	16,867	8,788	9,769	8,095
Easter Island (Hanga Roa)	17,062	11,521	8,551	6,894	16,070	15,677	13,684	11,195	16,723	18,130	12,965	9,284	13,797	16,645	13,984	11,943	10,452	13,659	11,220	16,280
Echo Bay, Canada	8,434	15,030	3,745	3,529	8,877	7,751	7,545	13,204	8,466	7,814	11,435	3,866	6,185	8,910	6,015	2,866	1,648	6,909	6,187	7,988
Edinburgh, United Kingdom	3,909	15,048	5,097	7,616	3,766	2,694	2,178	15,021	3,734	5,621	12,798	4,286	764	4,028	662	6,621	6,692	1,530	2,617	3,173
Edmonton, Canada	9,678	15,555	3,146	2,121	9,974	8,845	8,293	13,580	9,667	9,232	12,178	3,580	7,064	10,084	6,954	3,917	2,314	7,694	6,445	9,156
El Aaiun, Morocco	5,183	15,326	5,668	8,620	4,190	3,875	1,865	16,707	4,825	8,008	15,173	4,916	2,850	4,751	3,178	9,773	9,463	2,162	1,824	4,452
Elat, Israel	1,015	11,250	9,204	11,801	519	1,500	3,066	12,094	766	4,012	10,532	8,367	3,549	282	3,531	9,058	9,935	3,310	5,716	1,168
Elazig, Turkey	254	11,490	8,752	11,118	1,189	1,169	3,176	12,004	331	3,188	10,179	7,940	3,160	805	3,041	7,975	8,900	3,194	5,647	566
Eniwetok Atoll, Marshall Isls.	11,851	6,955	11,750	9,386	13,079	12,689	14,237	4,970	12,212	8,766	4,129	12,148	12,929	12,555	12,606	6,029	6,732	13,713	14,367	12,293
Erfurt, East Germany	2,845	14,059	6,173	8,699	2,692	1,605	1,701	14,305	2,650	4,905	12,203	5,353	632	2,938	450	7,117	7,449	1,189	3,274	2,090
Erzurum, Turkey	320	11,422	8,773	11,075	1,412	1,312	3,335	11,873	548	2,974	10,012	7,969	3,229	1,007	3,088	7,791	8,749	3,317	5,759	719
Esfahan, Iran	1,067	10,195	9,985	12,172	2,058	2,462	4,426	10,722	1,385	2,502	8,985	9,188	4,455	1,479	4,316	8,233	9,418	4,491	6,947	1,864
Essen, West Germany	3,127	14,345	5,898	8,453	2,929	1,864	1,660	14,568	2,925	5,157	12,446	5,076	375	3,200	176	7,092	7,345	1,079	3,011	2,367
Eucla, Australia	11,861	1,086	17,684	14,915	12,525	13,252	15,069	1,017	12,146	9,843	3,100	18,082	15,202	12,043	14,998	11,495	12,598	15,272	17,722	12,659
Fargo, North Dakota	9,816	16,851	1,876	1,547	9,847	8,759	7,794	14,858	9,725	10,002	13,572	2,494	6,775	10,077	6,743	5,243	3,696	7,265	5,580	9,176
Faroe Islands (Torshavn)	4,290	15,166	4,777	7,110	4,318	3,205	2,888	14,827	4,168	5,578	12,550	4,010	1,460	4,514	1,283	5,938	5,984	2,240	2,950	3,614
Florence, Italy	2,637	13,834	6,579	9,257	2,151	1,246	1,042	14,387	2,356	5,167	12,439	5,742	964	2,523	1,064	7,913	8,243	804	3,246	1,839
Florianopolis, Brazil	11,783	12,930	8,194	9,240	10,561	10,778	8,940	14,324	11,413	14,878	16,524	8,282	9,944	11,107	10,266	14,772	13,253	9,304	7,662	11,252
Fort George, Canada	8,426	17,539	1,302	2,995	8,386	7,312	6,323	15,687	8,308	9,006	13,925	1,383	5,304	8,640	5,284	5,337	4,108	5,787	4,222	7,753
Fort McMurray, Canada	9,299	15,628	3,079	2,433	9,602	8,473	7,960	13,681	9,290	8,896	12,162	3,428	6,711	9,707	6,594	3,761	2,235	7,355	6,193	8,779
Fort Nelson, Canada	9,278	14,929	3,783	2,891	9,712	8,584	8,288	12,997	9,311	8,548	11,450	4,090	6,963	9,753	6,810	3,099	1,527	7,662	6,722	8,830
Fort Severn, Canada	8,624	16,981	1,786	2,737	8,691	7,591	6,755	15,094	8,539	8,912	13,395	1,982	5,647	8,900	5,593	4,817	3,525	6,192	4,774	7,993
Fort Smith, Arkansas	10,776	17,098	1,956	1,113	10,624	9,598	8,339	15,219	10,635	11,253	14,412	2,786	7,533	10,934	7,559	6,424	4,803	7,890	5,855	10,075
Fort Vermilion, Canada	9,219	15,322	3,390	2,683	9,583	8,453	8,046	13,388	9,228	8,675	11,836	3,703	6,756	9,658	6,621	3,432	1,905	7,429	6,385	8,731
Fort Wayne, Indiana	9,784	17,901	961	1,995	9,599	8,582	7,317	15,922	9,629	10,495	14,703	1,770	6,510	9,918	6,544	6,292	4,800	6,863	4,871	9,069
Fort-Chimo, Canada	7,616	17,399	1,759	3,803	7,578	6,500	5,571	15,795	7,495	8,323	13,802	1,394	4,503	7,827	4,475	5,300	4,306	5,016	3,651	6,940
Fort-de-France, Martinique	10,105	17,739	3,338	5,077	9,278	8,711	6,759	18,159	9,787	12,312	18,441	3,475	6,879	9,811	7,109	9,938	8,532	6,687	4,256	9,314
Fortaleza, Brazil	9,352	15,062	6,242	8,287	8,196	8,168	6,216	16,863	8,977	12,338	18,338	6,048	7,112	8,772	7,432	12,653	11,500	6,514	4,832	8,704
Frankfort, Kentucky	10,012	17,966	1,063	1,974	9,781	8,785	7,450	16,025	9,846	10,800	14,933	1,902	6,703	10,119	6,752	6,580	5,064	7,020	4,947	9,285
Frankfurt am Main, W. Ger.	2,971	14,202	6,068	8,638	2,743	1,686	1,549	14,486	2,758	5,093	12,393	5,242	458	3,022	362	7,230	7,514	1,010	3,094	2,202
Fredericton, Canada	8,336	18,733	676	3,555	8,054	7,073	5,732	16,929	8,149	9,490	15,108	191	4,986	8,404	5,052	6,537	5,351	5,290	3,315	7,590
Freeport, Bahamas	10,592	18,173	1,847	2,820	10,115	9,254	7,614	16,731	10,361	11,893	16,197	2,504	7,183	10,545	7,305	7,993	6,452	7,311	4,957	9,814
Freetown, Sierra Leone	6,317	14,257	6,976	9,783	5,124	5,265	3,540	16,147	5,942	9,386	15,740	6,370	4,812	5,694	5,135	11,832	11,409	4,035	3,621	5,741
Frobisher Bay, Canada	7,259	16,781	2,372	4,103	7,337	6,230	5,520	15,260	7,171	7,759	13,207	2,013	4,325	7,534	4,249	4,771	3,919	4,925	3,893	6,625
Frunze, USSR	2,904	9,686	10,017	11,368	4,129	3,995	5,976	9,549	3,274	195	7,449	9,367	5,395	3,595	5,133	6,346	7,786	5,787	8,033	3,469
Fukuoka, Japan	7,796	7,707	11,213	10,366	9,024	8,721	10,499	6,350	8,159	4,707	4,135	11,088	9,443	8,497	9,118	4,685	6,261	10,106	11,682	8,276
Funafuti Atoll, Tuvalu	14,737	6,862	12,048	9,142	15,964	15,563	16,849	5,098	15,101	11,642	5,659	12,741	15,407	15,424	15,116	8,127	8,190	16,232	15,762	15,189
Funchal, Madeira Island	5,258	15,868	5,043	7,997	4,393	3,887	1,881	17,004	4,922	7,895	15,178	4,268	2,488	4,924	2,808	9,136	8,771	1,955	1,147	4,485
Fuzhou, China	7,309	6,766	12,278	11,693	8,507	8,435	10,377	5,728	7,684	4,265	3,434	12,033	9,557	7,943	9,249	5,917	7,542	10,102	12,040	7,914
Gaborone, Botswana	7,016	8,651	12,587	15,345	6,197	7,253	7,212	10,594	6,840	9,154	11,083	11,941	8,583	6,356	8,773	15,106	15,931	7,847	8,930	7,188
Galapagos Islands (Santa Cruz)	13,629	15,092	5,075	4,301	12,901	12,239	10,361	14,540	13,342	15,120	15,718	5,754	10,256	13,417	10,425	10,170	8,490	10,215	7,757	12,832
Gander, Canada	7,399	18,343	1,639	4,477	7,090	6,118	4,779	17,106	7,202	8,753	14,984	801	4,029	7,446	4,107	6,620	5,668	4,327	2,465	6,644
Gangtok, India	4,548	7,559	12,049	12,913	5,656	5,855	7,881	7,453	4,915	2,056	5,464	11,451	7,484	5,078	7,238	7,239	8,879	7,790	10,127	5,270
Garyarsa, China	3,620	8,370	11,355	12,570	4,752	4,918	6,944	8,372	3,990	1,311	6,401	10,703	6,570	4,175	6,333	7,184	8,749	6,857	9,210	4,334
Gaspe, Canada	8,013	18,460	995	3,755	7,768	6,768	5,494	16,788	7,835	9,132	14,862	334	4,686	8,102	4,739	6,326	5,215	5,028	3,170	7,275
Gauhati, India	4,882	7,314	12,240	12,955	5,991	6,185	8,211	7,145	5,249	2,320	5,136	11,669	7,790	5,413	7,539	7,205	8,863	8,112	10,434	5,601
Gdansk, Poland	2,584	13,649	6,449	8,803	2,723	1,594	2,290	13,741	2,469	4,320	11,601	5,655	1,222	2,840	941	6,672	7,150	1,820	3,842	1,923
Geneva, Switzerland	3,066	14,292	6,098	8,777	2,634	1,694	1,078	14,751	2,805	5,426	12,728	5,261	502	2,996	690	7,679	7,903	553	2,849	2,271
Genoa, Italy	2,827	14,031	6,384	9,072	2,345	1,440	983	14,564	2,551	5,306	12,592	5,546	791	2,721	931	7,860	8,140	638	3,059	2,030
Georgetown, Guyana	10,389	16,853	4,258	5,854	9,443	9,019	7,009	17,743	10,047	12,862	19,248	4,365	7,344	10,003	7,603	10,857	9,440	7,037	4,702	9,619
Geraldton, Australia	10,564	761	18,295	16,092	11,153	11,938	13,685	2,004	10,827	8,854	3,124	18,108	13,960	10,690	13,796	11,692	13,054	13,933	16,349	11,357
Ghanzi, Botswana	6,800	9,192	12,043	14,814	5,903	6,923	6,752	11,130	6,596	9,126	11,554	11,399	8,146	6,111	8,351	14,888	15,554	7,393	8,399	6,905
Ghat, Libya	3,234	13,109	7,700	10,616	2,054	2,285	1,476	14,358	2,859	6,311	13,009	6,882	2,850	2,631	3,072	9,998	10,285	2,101	3,819	2,689
Gibraltar	4,128	14,954	5,776	8,683	3,296	2,758	756	15,890	3,794	6,814	14,066	4,953	1,650	3,812	1,975	8,818	8,747	921	1,952	3,356

Distances in Kilometers	Al Qamishli, Syria	Albany, Australia	Albany, New York	Albuquerque, New Mexico	Alexandria, Egypt	Alexandroupolis, Greece	Algiers, Algeria	Alice Springs, Australia	Allepo, Syria	Alma-Ata, USSR	Ambon, Indonesia	Amherst, Canada	Amiens, France	Amman, Jordan	Amsterdam, Netherlands	Anadyr, USSR	Anchorage, Alaska	Andorra, Andorra	Angra do Heroismo, Azores	Ankara, Turkey
Gijon, Spain	3,999	15,156	5,382	8,200	3,402	2,606	1,054	15,730	3,711	6,392	13,696	4,542	933	3,840	1,257	7,996	7,953	597	1,884	3,202
Gisborne, New Zealand	16,252	5,282	14,121	11,256	17,013	17,635	19,531	4,472	16,575	13,609	6,346	14,955	18,712	16,523	18,395	11,465	11,448	19,492	17,835	17,034
Glasgow, United Kingdom	3,971	15,114	5,035	7,564	3,817	2,750	2,188	15,083	3,793	5,686	12,857	4,223	793	4,085	713	6,630	6,681	1,540	2,559	3,233
Godthab, Greenland	6,499	16,678	2,787	4,884	6,524	5,425	4,702	15,481	6,392	7,268	13,288	2,194	3,498	6,740	3,428	5,148	4,532	4,101	3,268	5,840
Gomez Palacio, Mexico	12,158	15,941	3,307	1,097	12,013	10,991	9,691	14,264	12,025	12,385	14,008	4,147	8,924	12,327	8,952	6,946	5,266	9,264	7,143	11,466
Goose Bay, Canada	10,150	14,590	4,114	2,471	10,597	9,469	9,125	12,606	10,190	9,254	11,310	4,573	7,825	10,635	7,681	3,423	1,744	8,506	7,408	9,713
Gorki, USSR	2,156	12,275	7,588	9,502	3,001	2,166	3,734	12,160	2,296	2,744	9,991	6,865	2,835	2,781	2,545	6,009	6,912	3,374	5,436	1,997
Goteborg, Sweden	3,142	14,135	5,908	8,243	3,251	2,122	2,418	14,087	3,029	4,677	11,887	5,124	1,076	3,394	748	6,366	6,721	1,845	3,525	2,482
Granada, Spain	3,953	14,844	5,847	8,735	3,149	2,578	601	15,725	3,623	6,623	13,880	5,018	1,489	3,655	1,811	8,700	8,673	736	2,069	3,177
Grand Turk, Turks & Caicos	10,423	18,269	2,362	3,771	9,787	9,041	7,242	17,452	10,150	12,134	17,153	2,776	7,037	10,268	7,208	8,827	7,338	7,031	4,589	9,627
Graz, Austria	2,392	13,633	6,668	9,234	2,152	1,083	1,533	14,034	2,164	4,729	12,023	5,841	1,020	2,419	959	7,508	7,928	1,212	3,562	1,611
Green Bay, Wisconsin	9,635	17,579	1,168	1,902	9,533	8,484	7,340	15,586	9,504	10,169	14,273	1,870	6,439	9,818	6,446	5,844	4,358	6,851	4,994	8,946
Grenoble, France	3,089	14,300	6,120	8,824	2,608	1,706	958	14,806	2,817	5,505	12,803	5,281	586	2,989	801	7,796	8,008	449	2,805	2,293
Guadalajara, Mexico	12,621	15,703	3,682	1,630	12,410	11,417	10,025	14,161	12,470	12,928	14,151	4,520	9,336	12,752	9,382	7,434	5,756	9,631	7,427	11,910
Guam (Agana)	10,284	6,071	12,660	10,789	11,495	11,326	13,155	4,278	10,657	7,201	2,637	12,827	12,089	10,937	11,762	6,219	7,392	12,765	14,176	10,843
Guantanamo, Cuba	10,833	17,922	2,500	3,497	10,221	9,457	7,679	17,007	10,568	12,434	16,904	3,023	7,436	10,696	7,596	8,788	7,246	7,455	5,021	10,039
Guatemala City, Guatemala	12,386	16,391	3,496	2,782	11,887	11,047	9,363	15,275	12,154	13,470	15,620	4,246	8,977	12,331	9,097	8,640	6,972	9,090	6,698	11,608
Guayaquil, Ecuador	12,880	15,496	5,001	4,982	12,013	11,488	9,522	15,386	12,559	14,910	16,851	5,536	9,629	12,561	9,841	10,823	9,164	9,464	7,026	12,090
Guiyang, China	6,188	6,921	12,339	12,334	7,356	7,398	9,396	6,285	6,563	3,261	4,073	11,933	8,749	6,783	8,463	6,454	8,132	9,199	11,345	6,846
Gur'yev, USSR	1,422	11,228	8,717	10,652	2,578	2,188	4,136	11,328	1,719	2,007	9,282	7,974	3,609	2,163	3,374	6,739	7,836	3,948	6,251	1,726
Haifa, Israel	736	11,448	8,949	11,493	515	1,205	2,942	12,193	423	3,815	10,536	8,116	3,287	132	3,244	8,706	9,571	3,119	5,558	811
Haikou, China	6,870	6,149	13,050	12,768	8,003	8,126	10,139	5,474	7,242	4,032	3,276	12,688	9,544	7,426	9,262	6,927	8,583	9,971	12,150	7,559
Haiphong, Vietnam	6,500	6,299	12,972	12,888	7,624	7,771	9,789	5,745	6,871	3,711	3,593	12,562	9,238	7,046	8,962	7,017	8,687	9,639	11,859	7,199
Hakodate, Japan	8,067	8,816	10,041	9,084	9,273	8,758	10,306	7,280	8,403	5,113	5,192	9,994	9,074	8,804	8,746	3,453	4,991	9,819	11,018	8,405
Halifax, Canada	8,234	18,930	848	3,785	7,903	6,947	5,541	17,197	8,034	9,514	15,326	140	4,858	8,272	4,942	6,774	5,615	5,122	3,076	7,477
Hamburg, West Germany	3,021	14,184	5,984	8,457	2,953	1,846	1,940	14,317	2,853	4,895	12,169	5,174	669	3,168	367	6,841	7,155	1,380	3,267	2,294
Hamilton, Bermuda	9,160	19,622	1,397	3,868	8,626	7,799	6,114	17,963	8,910	10,781	16,569	1,505	5,753	9,070	5,903	7,983	6,666	5,828	3,456	8,372
Hamilton, New Zealand	15,997	5,076	14,284	11,394	16,783	17,378	19,328	4,220	16,324	13,355	6,087	15,113	18,549	16,283	18,223	11,369	11,419	19,269	18,057	16,777
Hangzhou, China	7,150	7,230	11,809	11,275	8,365	8,214	10,116	6,147	7,523	4,068	3,855	11,568	9,228	7,812	8,915	5,468	7,105	9,806	11,664	7,715
Hannover, West Germany	2,986	14,179	6,023	8,529	2,867	1,773	1,809	14,364	2,804	4,949	12,235	5,208	587	3,103	327	6,974	7,281	1,258	3,216	2,243
Hanoi, Vietnam	6,417	6,334	12,954	12,915	7,539	7,690	9,710	5,807	6,787	3,641	3,667	12,533	9,169	6,960	8,895	7,040	8,712	9,564	11,793	7,117
Harare, Zimbabwe	6,166	8,615	12,533	15,439	5,427	6,519	6,723	10,473	6,015	8,228	10,647	11,812	8,018	5,534	8,176	14,225	15,187	7,335	8,712	6,398
Harbin, China	6,865	8,990	10,007	9,581	8,078	7,615	9,266	7,725	7,207	3,899	5,482	9,803	8,128	7,599	7,801	3,712	5,380	8,827	10,300	7,234
Harrisburg, Pennsylvania	9,378	18,598	372	2,675	9,092	8,118	6,733	16,609	9,194	10,390	15,244	1,202	6,030	9,448	6,096	6,714	5,311	6,316	4,222	8,635
Hartford, Connecticut	9,006	18,831	133	3,037	8,704	7,737	6,342	16,846	8,817	10,112	15,310	817	5,648	9,065	5,720	6,732	5,402	5,925	3,841	8,258
Havana, Cuba	11,113	17,658	2,306	2,699	10,629	9,775	8,120	16,337	10,882	12,357	16,098	3,005	7,704	11,063	7,826	8,171	6,578	7,827	5,459	10,335
Helena, Montana	10,366	15,697	3,038	1,356	10,582	9,461	8,735	13,705	10,333	10,013	12,550	3,634	7,592	10,732	7,512	4,570	2,911	8,166	6,672	9,808
Helsinki, Finland	2,821	13,464	6,451	8,562	3,240	2,150	3,032	13,306	2,805	3,920	11,094	5,705	1,830	3,239	1,507	5,959	6,535	2,528	4,317	2,317
Hengyang, China	6,685	6,877	12,277	12,004	7,871	7,851	9,823	6,049	7,060	3,684	3,780	11,944	9,088	7,303	8,790	6,146	7,809	9,586	11,636	7,314
Herat, Afghanistan	1,918	9,619	10,378	12,233	3,034	3,265	5,283	9,927	2,281	1,615	8,074	9,628	5,095	2,458	4,904	7,682	9,023	5,263	7,687	2,667
Hermosillo, Mexico	12,136	15,412	3,646	782	12,160	11,083	9,990	13,610	12,052	11,957	13,198	4,459	9,073	12,404	9,058	6,251	4,577	9,506	7,555	11,504
Hiroshima, Japan	7,908	7,835	11,067	10,170	9,136	8,801	10,548	6,432	8,269	4,828	4,243	10,963	9,460	8,616	9,133	4,517	6,078	10,138	11,651	8,369
Hiva Oa (Atuona)	16,988	10,562	8,795	6,025	17,379	16,261	15,179	9,289	17,056	14,931	10,252	9,634	14,319	17,499	14,283	9,024	7,931	14,743	12,581	16,572
Ho Chi Minh City, Vietnam	7,122	5,203	14,092	13,846	8,149	8,466	10,490	4,827	7,477	4,605	2,873	13,672	10,110	7,575	9,855	8,024	9,674	10,423	12,752	7,872
Hobart, Australia	13,879	2,682	16,693	13,760	14,439	15,257	16,916	2,465	14,146	11,842	4,738	17,503	17,248	13,998	17,044	12,224	12,851	17,241	19,354	14,674
Hohhot, China	5,952	8,419	10,748	10,741	7,180	6,910	8,759	7,502	6,316	2,864	5,209	10,401	7,830	6,653	7,516	4,872	6,552	8,423	10,269	6,446
Hong Kong	7,082	6,352	12,774	12,344	8,245	8,291	10,283	5,514	7,457	4,142	3,253	12,464	9,594	7,671	9,300	6,531	8,174	10,070	12,159	7,740
Honiara, Solomon Islands	13,182	5,123	13,651	10,918	14,342	14,327	16,194	3,189	13,557	10,162	3,566	14,198	15,069	13,765	14,740	8,357	8,963	15,785	16,691	13,811
Honolulu, Hawaii	13,245	10,846	7,968	5,195	14,135	13,112	13,271	8,913	13,447	10,934	8,510	8,614	11,879	13,931	11,676	5,155	4,475	12,631	11,617	13,134
Houston, Texas	11,342	16,860	2,401	1,214	11,127	10,129	8,772	15,121	11,185	11,882	14,611	3,241	8,049	11,464	8,094	6,922	5,271	8,358	6,215	10,624
Huambo, Angola	6,120	10,282	10,922	13,761	5,090	6,023	5,641	12,181	5,864	8,767	12,347	10,255	7,063	5,391	7,286	14,061	14,500	6,287	7,234	6,093
Hubli, India	4,119	7,172	12,844	14,420	4,913	5,512	7,425	7,709	4,414	3,098	6,212	12,100	7,493	4,373	7,331	9,046	10,634	7,540	9,998	4,917
Hugh Town, United Kingdom	4,026	15,266	5,081	7,781	3,650	2,689	1,642	15,511	3,790	6,089	13,351	4,245	619	4,006	831	7,285	7,262	1,021	2,074	3,243
Hull, Canada	8,909	18,383	347	2,848	8,697	7,687	6,420	16,421	8,744	9,817	14,833	900	5,610	9,023	5,652	6,256	4,932	5,960	4,024	8,183
Hyderabad, India	4,243	7,142	12,778	14,173	5,119	5,638	7,594	7,544	4,559	2,871	5,940	12,063	7,563	4,563	7,382	8,692	10,299	7,667	10,118	5,037
Hyderabad, Pakistan	2,877	8,480	11,536	13,294	3,810	4,271	6,242	8,906	3,201	2,132	7,209	10,786	6,201	3,241	6,028	8,338	9,811	6,298	8,749	3,669
Igloolik, Canada	7,331	15,997	3,012	4,111	7,584	6,455	6,033	14,407	7,297	7,392	12,390	2,800	4,721	7,703	4,586	3,914	3,118	5,407	4,671	6,776
Iloilo, Philippines	8,538	5,086	13,869	12,775	9,656	9,797	11,808	4,000	8,908	5,682	1,712	13,707	11,154	9,077	10,860	7,322	8,840	11,620	13,712	9,231
Indianapolis, Indiana	9,950	17,839	1,087	1,882	9,757	8,744	7,462	15,876	9,794	10,655	14,735	1,911	6,670	10,080	6,707	6,373	4,858	7,015	4,997	9,234
Innsbruck, Austria	2,693	13,933	6,393	8,999	2,382	1,358	1,352	14,338	2,454	5,011	12,311	5,562	732	2,687	733	7,525	7,861	942	3,256	1,907
Inuvik, Canada	8,312	14,323	4,464	4,071	8,883	7,776	7,809	12,528	8,387	7,368	10,719	4,553	6,395	8,850	6,190	2,145	1,100	7,163	6,699	7,945
Invercargill, New Zealand	15,585	4,367	15,192	12,385	16,093	16,961	18,394	3,976	15,849	13,388	6,112	16,033	18,911	15,683	18,647	12,350	12,507	18,887	18,480	16,380
Inverness, United Kingdom	4,013	15,100	4,995	7,474	3,913	2,829	2,362	14,992	3,850	5,618	12,750	4,193	945	4,159	817	6,448	6,509	1,714	2,677	3,291
Iquitos, Peru	12,428	15,557	5,141	5,538	11,482	11,052	9,049	15,790	12,089	14,743	17,509	5,567	9,300	12,044	9,538	11,288	9,661	9,053	6,663	11,653
Iraklion, Greece	1,459	12,371	8,092	10,748	638	616	1,992	13,142	1,092	4,483	11,438	7,254	2,458	1,069	2,476	8,650	9,293	2,188	4,612	852
Irkutsk, USSR	5,103	9,761	9,486	9,871	6,309	5,845	7,560	8,893	5,439	2,266	6,600	9,079	6,524	5,843	6,202	4,209	5,823	7,166	8,898	5,457
Islamabad, Pakistan	2,912	8,923	10,906	12,390	4,048	4,217	6,244	9,036	3,281	1,110	7,102	10,213	5,921	3,473	5,698	7,305	8,788	6,174	8,552	3,630
Istanbul, Turkey	1,149	12,375	7,937	10,440	1,093	262	2,288	12,918	892	3,920	11,057	7,112	2,291	1,183	2,213	7,961	8,672	2,279	4,732	352
Ivujivik, Canada	7,725	16,769	2,215	3,636	7,829	6,719	6,010	15,092	7,647	8,079	13,147	2,041	4,823	8,018	4,745	4,606	3,599	5,419	4,289	7,105
Iwo Jima Island, Japan	9,224	7,068	11,721	10,266	10,451	10,161	11,915	5,424	9,590	6,130	3,458	11,772	10,801	9,916	10,473	5,141	6,489	11,496	12,883	9,717
Izmir, Turkey	1,250	12,375	8,007	10,584	839	292	2,130	13,024	921	4,172	11,232	7,174	2,345	1,074	2,313	8,278	8,958	2,212	4,668	522
Jackson, Mississippi	10,826	17,414	1,847	1,555	10,575	9,591	8,206	15,621	10,657	11,538	14,921	2,686	7,507	10,925	7,562	6,915	5,308	7,799	5,648	10,097
Jaffna, Sri Lanka	4,933	6,354	13,631	15,003	5,686	6,323	8,215	6,926	5,221	3,733	5,547	12,901	8,312	5,159	8,150	9,393	11,033	8,348	10,806	5,730
Jakarta, Indonesia	8,304	3,393	15,962	15,330	9,132	9,699	11,646	3,488	8,619	6,246	2,389	15,525	11,569	8,596	11,356	9,723	11,316	11,725	14,169	9,097
Jamestown, St. Helena	7,654	11,821	9,496	11,996	6,458	7,082	5,907	13,813	7,324	10,630	14,513	9,012	7,335	6,915	7,634	14,578	14,233	6,512	6,445	7,365
Jamnagar, India	3,203	8,123	11,901	13,626	4,085	4,599	6,551	8,588	3,516	2,391	6,949	11,150	6,551	3,524	6,383	8,558	10,064	6,628	9,083	3,999
Jan Mayen Island	4,749	14,957	4,686	6,628	5,014	3,884	3,873	14,239	4,704	5,391	11,946	4,028	2,422	5,110	2,192	4,932	5,024	3,227	3,751	4,183
Jayapura, Indonesia	11,023	4,303	14,407	12,228	12,135	12,268	14,261	2,454	11,394	8,118	1,396	14,634	13,462	11,557	13,148	8,043	9,167	14,016	15,823	11,710
Jefferson City, Missouri	10,371	17,327	1,619	1,347	10,233	9,200	7,975	15,389	10,232	10,877	14,399	2,432	7,140	10,536	7,161	6,222	4,639	7,514	5,530	9,673
Jerusalem, Israel	803	11,364	9,048	11,606	511	1,311	3,001	12,139	523	3,857	10,511	8,215	3,387	69	3,350	8,814	9,688	3,198	5,629	931
Jiggalong, Australia	10,676	1,320	17,489	15,285	11,403	12,071	13,949	1,338	10,973	8,636	2,320	17,476	13,990	10,898	13,781	10,907	12,222	14,099	16,557	11,473
Jinan, China	6,561	7,938	11,154	10,873	7,787	7,552	9,411	6,913	6,928	3,465	4,620	10,867	8,479	7,250	8,163	5,000	6,670	9,077	10,896	7,078
Jodhpur, India	3,224	8,268	11,651	13,212	4,222	4,605	6,603	8,571	3,566	1,916	6,800	10,930	6,465	3,647	6,271	8,047	9,568	6,620	9,053	4,002
Johannesburg, South Africa	7,134	8,374	12,865	15,616	6,355	7,427	7,449	10,320	6,972	9,170	10,841	12,218	8,807	6,489	8,990	15,201	16,111	8,081	9,201	7,338
Juazeiro do Norte, Brazil	9,661	14,759	6,529	8,453	8,489	8,504	6,572	16,509	9,286	12,675	18,186	6,374	7,496	9,063	7,817	12,997	11,798	6,886	5,229	9,031
Juneau, Alaska	9,431	14,248	4,462	3,294	9,979	8,864	8,751	12,315	9,502	8,382	10,789	4,768	7,379	9,963	7,198	2,588	926	8,113	7,335	9,053
Kabul, Afghanistan	2,535	9,216	10,669	12,288	3,674	3,847	5,872	9,389	2,904	1,179	7,474	9,955	5,582	3,100	5,367	7,388	8,820	5,813	8,205	3,257
Kalgoorlie, Australia	11,222	581	18,125	15,543	11,841	12,605	14,378	1,456	11,495	9,368	3,075	18,261	14,600	11,371	14,419	11,641	12,880	14,611	17,041	12,018
Kaliningrad, USSR	2,521	13,546	6,531	8,853	2,717	1,592	2,397	13,619	2,422	4,197	11,476	5,742	1,347	2,808	1,064	6,610	7,121	1,939	3,965	1,885
Kamloops, Canada	10,123	15,098	3,609	2,053	10,477	9,346	8,852	13,109	10,133	9,466	11,831	4,101	7,606	10,561	7,485	3,831	2,161	8,249	7,007	9,633
Kampala, Uganda	4,162	9,605	11,318	14,253	3,430	4,540	5,055	11,182	4,001	6,482	10,645	10,512	6,203	3,519	6,318	12,250	13,176	5,610	7,409	4,387
Kananga, Zaire	5,140	10,136	10,958	13,897	4,182	5,188	5,137	11,909	4,908	7,720	11,719	10,215	6,481	4,428	6,665	13,182	13,834	5,763	7,103	5,187
Kano, Nigeria	4,283	12,529	8,488	11,442	3,057	3,619	2,799	14,134	3,929	7,361	13,335	7,724	4,241	3,572	4,487	11,443	11,668	3,448	4,603	3,912
Kanpur, India	3,857	7,871	11,907	13,153	4,910	5,210	7,229	7,999	4,213	1,887	6,136	11,237	6,973	4,332	6,754	7,704	9,292	7,197	9,597	4,613
Kansas City, Missouri	10,442	17,119	1,794	1,161	10,342	9,296	8,118	15,175	10,314	10,845	14,191	2,590	7,248	10,630	7,258	6,063	4,464	7,644	5,703	9,757
Kaohsiung, Taiwan	7,594	6,387	12,635	11,933	8,779	8,754	10,715	5,333	7,970	4,583	3,039	12,409	9,927	8,209	9,622	6,215	7,818	10,457	12,426	8,221
Karachi, Pakistan	2,798	8,524	11,522	13,336	3,702	4,194	6,152	8,990	3,114	2,231	7,320	10,764	6,145	3,137	5,980	8,444	9,903	6,223	8,677	3,593
Karaganda, USSR	2,919	10,382	9,266	10,598	4,132	3,771	5,652	10,104	3,260	787	7,927	8,636	4,895	3,658	4,609	5,741	7,108	5,379	7,499	3,322
Karl-Marx-Stadt, East Germany	2,716	13,926	6,298	8,808	2,593	1,493	1,748	14,176	2,526	4,783	12,083	5,480	762	2,823	579	7,118	7,487	1,270	3,403	1,966
Kasanga, Tanzania	5,145	9,182	11,864	14,818	4,391	5,487	5,805	10,919	4,984	7,362	10,733	11,094	7,046	4,502	7,187	13,228	14,150	6,397	7,970	5,361

Distances in Kilometers	Al Qamishli, Syria	Albany, Australia	Albany, New York	Albuquerque, New Mexico	Alexandria, Egypt	Alexandroupolis, Greece	Algiers, Algeria	Alice Springs, Australia	Allepo, Syria	Alma-Ata, USSR	Ambon, Indonesia	Amherst, Canada	Amiens, France	Amman, Jordan	Amsterdam, Netherlands	Anadyr, USSR	Anchorage, Alaska	Andorra, Andorra	Angra do Heroismo, Azores	Ankara, Turkey
Kashgar, China	3,033	9,308	10,412	11,744	4,240	4,211	6,218	9,225	3,408	426	7,165	9,757	5,712	3,686	5,459	6,620	8,099	6,065	8,355	3,660
Kassel, West Germany	2,958	14,172	6,061	8,595	2,793	1,712	1,694	14,403	2,762	4,997	12,291	5,240	533	3,047	336	7,092	7,393	1,152	3,176	2,203
Kathmandu, Nepal	4,236	7,744	11,925	12,941	5,334	5,555	7,581	7,717	4,601	1,881	5,765	11,300	7,224	4,755	6,987	7,354	8,974	7,507	9,865	4,966
Kayes, Mali	5,759	14,486	6,678	9,566	4,596	4,643	2,862	16,252	5,384	8,795	15,450	6,011	4,125	5,173	4,448	11,190	10,854	3,348	3,098	5,143
Kazan, USSR	2,164	11,975	7,852	9,681	3,116	2,371	4,026	11,835	2,355	2,422	9,665	7,144	3,159	2,838	2,871	5,940	6,927	3,685	5,762	2,127
Kemi, Finland	3,381	13,647	6,125	8,063	3,867	2,780	3,519	13,265	3,397	4,034	11,001	5,426	2,185	3,844	1,858	5,356	5,905	2,960	4,439	2,929
Kenora, Canada	9,452	16,925	1,777	1,910	9,495	8,403	7,478	14,943	9,363	9,664	13,522	2,294	6,431	9,718	6,392	5,083	3,597	6,938	5,328	8,815
Kerguelen Island	9,982	4,217	17,108	18,373	9,761	10,883	11,577	6,208	10,015	10,302	7,479	16,572	12,739	9,615	12,824	15,621	17,252	12,154	13,583	10,539
Kerkira, Greece	1,881	12,995	7,436	10,089	1,299	525	1,508	13,662	1,561	4,692	11,839	6,599	1,797	1,675	1,825	8,271	8,791	1,577	4,030	1,109
Kermanshah, Iran	608	10,638	9,579	11,852	1,643	2,002	3,966	11,184	924	2,761	9,433	8,774	4,012	1,071	3,885	8,210	9,305	4,031	6,487	1,405
Khabarovsk, USSR	7,297	9,409	9,520	8,916	8,487	7,922	9,438	7,997	7,622	4,442	5,824	9,386	8,205	8,040	7,877	3,078	4,725	8,949	10,195	7,592
Kharkov, USSR	1,495	12,357	7,702	9,899	2,154	1,299	3,029	12,523	1,535	3,164	10,463	6,923	2,416	2,005	2,189	6,848	7,661	2,777	5,056	1,150
Khartoum, Sudan	2,526	10,581	10,127	12,942	1,748	2,872	3,740	11,832	2,328	5,198	10,735	9,291	4,679	1,843	4,749	10,616	11,486	4,200	6,327	2,697
Khon Kaen, Thailand	6,422	5,914	13,454	13,514	7,484	7,749	9,775	5,578	6,783	3,852	3,572	12,987	9,360	6,907	9,103	7,637	9,311	9,688	12,002	7,159
Kiev, USSR	1,717	12,742	7,359	9,644	2,137	1,125	2,662	12,935	1,669	3,569	10,871	6,569	2,005	2,101	1,785	6,918	7,625	2,377	4,645	1,181
Kigali, Rwanda	4,468	9,691	11,288	14,238	3,669	4,759	5,119	11,334	4,287	6,850	10,908	10,496	6,330	3,803	6,464	12,564	13,430	5,698	7,377	4,647
Kingston, Canada	9,045	18,418	283	2,760	8,820	7,817	6,526	16,438	8,877	9,963	14,909	984	5,737	9,152	5,783	6,342	4,992	6,075	4,103	8,317
Kingston, Jamaica	11,118	17,632	2,748	3,504	10,494	9,740	7,949	16,784	10,850	12,715	16,879	3,299	7,724	10,973	7,885	8,933	7,364	7,735	5,296	10,324
Kingstown, Saint Vincent	10,218	17,579	3,485	5,158	9,373	8,826	6,863	18,048	9,896	12,457	18,549	3,634	7,011	9,911	7,245	10,081	8,663	6,805	4,382	9,428
Kinshasa, Zaire	5,308	10,880	10,256	13,170	4,224	5,114	4,723	12,690	5,029	8,103	12,522	9,541	6,135	4,568	6,354	13,148	13,570	5,367	6,459	5,218
Kirkwall, United Kingdom	3,987	15,010	5,035	7,456	3,948	2,847	2,505	14,842	3,841	5,490	12,592	4,244	1,064	4,168	886	6,282	6,374	1,858	2,844	3,284
Kirov, USSR	2,471	12,132	7,640	9,398	3,389	2,586	4,132	11,896	2,649	2,532	9,693	6,950	3,163	3,133	2,859	5,643	6,614	3,747	5,721	2,391
Kiruna, Sweden	3,672	13,875	5,858	7,767	4,125	3,025	3,620	13,411	3,680	4,264	11,134	5,172	2,231	4,122	1,913	5,182	5,663	3,034	4,340	3,202
Kisangani, Zaire	4,369	10,290	10,707	13,661	3,434	4,469	4,620	11,939	4,141	6,978	11,467	9,924	5,892	3,660	6,051	12,426	13,147	5,220	6,801	4,436
Kishinev, USSR	1,507	12,687	7,502	9,889	1,757	724	2,406	13,019	1,384	3,749	11,022	6,695	1,978	1,777	1,816	7,318	8,007	2,208	4,575	850
Kitchner, Canada	9,331	18,185	555	2,429	9,133	8,119	6,855	16,192	9,172	10,143	14,781	1,316	6,045	9,455	6,083	6,259	4,848	6,397	4,433	8,611
Knoxville, Tennessee	10,146	18,050	1,147	2,060	9,871	8,895	7,500	16,157	9,968	11,021	15,158	1,982	6,808	10,227	6,871	6,837	5,312	7,092	4,955	9,408
Kosice, Czechoslovakia	2,074	13,283	6,934	9,392	2,076	945	1,984	13,595	1,901	4,262	11,560	6,120	1,381	2,231	1,224	7,257	7,792	1,680	3,992	1,342
Kota Kinabalu, Malaysia	8,268	4,544	14,529	13,641	9,309	9,597	11,623	3,812	8,626	5,631	1,723	14,265	11,160	8,734	10,889	8,081	9,643	11,525	13,789	9,008
Krakow, Poland	2,237	13,426	6,769	9,213	2,256	1,126	2,003	13,689	2,075	4,321	11,625	5,957	1,261	2,412	1,076	7,124	7,631	1,643	3,892	1,517
Kralendijk, Bonaire	10,875	17,398	3,420	4,622	10,082	9,480	7,553	17,362	10,567	12,929	17,990	3,752	7,592	10,608	7,804	9,893	8,381	7,451	5,001	10,081
Krasnodar, USSR	908	11,894	8,233	10,483	1,728	1,167	3,135	12,206	993	3,015	10,238	7,441	2,790	1,477	2,610	7,309	8,199	3,004	5,391	758
Krasnoyarsk, USSR	4,352	10,365	8,998	9,743	5,534	5,011	6,702	9,646	4,671	1,817	7,362	8,514	5,676	5,096	5,357	4,402	5,901	6,310	8,093	4,647
Kristiansand, Norway	3,368	14,374	5,671	8,031	3,429	2,304	2,405	14,299	3,244	4,899	12,084	4,885	992	3,597	676	6,342	6,627	1,801	3,327	2,692
Kuala Lumpur, Malaysia	7,203	4,554	14,910	14,848	8,102	8,591	10,573	4,583	7,532	5,070	3,045	14,402	10,413	7,548	10,192	9,016	10,671	10,608	13,032	7,988
Kuching, Malaysia	8,061	4,126	15,092	14,427	9,015	9,434	11,441	3,782	8,403	5,683	2,071	14,728	11,158	8,452	10,913	8,784	10,379	11,425	13,800	8,833
Kumasi, Ghana	5,485	13,113	8,051	10,939	4,258	4,666	3,367	14,920	5,122	8,579	14,467	7,371	4,805	4,794	5,099	12,082	11,991	3,980	4,378	5,039
Kumzar, Oman	1,861	9,379	10,825	12,979	2,638	3,237	5,131	10,003	2,129	2,642	8,395	10,027	5,271	2,084	5,145	8,716	10,015	5,256	7,713	2,652
Kunming, China	5,912	6,842	12,498	12,669	7,055	7,165	9,180	6,359	6,285	3,091	4,213	12,043	8,618	6,479	8,343	6,794	8,474	9,021	11,241	6,598
Kuqa Chang, China	3,646	9,144	10,443	11,497	4,865	4,753	6,728	8,869	4,018	585	6,728	9,847	6,097	4,321	5,823	6,137	7,678	6,522	8,723	4,226
Kurgan, USSR	2,734	11,200	8,470	9,946	3,862	3,291	5,037	10,892	3,019	1,593	8,686	7,826	4,158	3,473	3,859	5,491	6,707	4,702	6,727	2,940
Kuwait, Kuwait	1,055	10,226	10,058	12,391	1,748	2,372	4,234	10,900	1,262	3,001	9,273	9,243	4,439	1,187	4,339	8,696	9,834	4,375	6,829	1,808
Kuybyshev, USSR	1,925	11,751	8,112	9,971	2,939	2,282	4,044	11,682	2,144	2,259	9,545	7,392	3,277	2,622	3,003	6,171	7,194	3,747	5,904	1,972
Kyoto, Japan	8,125	7,973	10,900	9,907	9,352	8,976	10,678	6,500	8,482	5,061	4,358	10,832	9,547	8,841	9,219	4,318	5,848	10,247	11,665	8,561
Kzyl-Orda, USSR	2,205	10,301	9,509	11,122	3,433	3,235	5,212	10,273	2,566	936	8,202	8,815	4,663	2,925	4,411	6,515	7,828	5,029	7,306	2,720
L'vov, USSR	1,983	13,142	7,027	9,422	2,127	1,009	2,220	13,396	1,850	4,040	11,341	6,222	1,555	2,220	1,362	7,094	7,680	1,908	4,186	1,302
La Ceiba, Honduras	12,030	16,764	3,228	2,913	11,496	10,678	8,965	15,694	11,788	13,262	15,977	3,942	8,619	11,950	8,750	8,700	7,050	8,706	6,301	11,246
La Coruna, Spain	4,220	15,371	5,187	8,025	3,615	2,827	1,217	15,943	3,932	6,589	13,891	4,349	1,092	4,058	1,406	8,006	7,903	813	1,664	3,422
La Paz, Bolivia	12,806	14,266	6,574	7,009	11,697	11,526	9,505	14,960	12,438	15,584	17,148	6,914	10,062	12,276	10,340	12,801	11,165	9,654	7,448	12,100
La Paz, Mexico	12,607	15,254	3,925	1,260	12,563	11,507	10,310	13,559	12,504	12,504	13,372	4,758	9,468	12,838	9,472	6,759	5,093	9,857	7,802	11,951
La Ronge, Canada	9,310	16,043	2,662	2,227	9,534	8,411	7,770	14,086	9,276	9,103	12,584	3,042	6,574	9,676	6,480	4,160	2,656	7,181	5,886	8,751
Labrador City, Canada	7,880	17,979	1,253	3,685	7,731	6,691	5,570	16,317	7,728	8,799	14,374	816	4,637	8,027	4,652	5,842	4,764	5,060	3,413	7,169
Lagos, Nigeria	5,116	12,650	8,476	11,394	3,891	4,418	3,359	14,412	4,763	8,192	13,914	7,767	4,818	4,403	5,091	12,093	12,153	3,998	4,711	4,736
Lahore, Pakistan	3,087	8,670	11,164	12,624	4,193	4,417	6,441	8,812	3,452	1,316	6,909	10,470	6,155	3,615	5,937	7,466	8,973	6,389	8,781	3,824
Lambasa, Fiji	15,328	6,403	12,602	9,655	16,530	16,300	17,721	4,807	15,702	12,244	5,766	13,345	16,283	15,962	15,990	9,003	9,030	17,108	16,443	15,868
Lansing, Michigan	9,611	17,904	883	2,089	9,444	8,419	7,186	15,914	9,461	10,304	14,613	1,655	6,353	9,755	6,380	6,159	4,691	6,722	4,773	8,901
Lanzhou, China	5,488	8,006	11,286	11,528	6,701	6,584	8,530	7,337	5,861	2,417	5,089	10,855	7,767	6,148	7,469	5,690	7,365	8,273	10,323	6,069
Laoag, Philippines	7,890	5,898	13,110	12,292	9,050	9,095	11,080	4,855	8,264	4,938	2,564	12,897	10,350	8,475	10,050	6,645	8,224	10,852	12,878	8,547
Largeau, Chad	3,029	11,917	8,911	11,822	1,830	2,623	2,618	13,267	2,694	6,073	12,165	8,092	3,854	2,297	4,018	10,655	11,178	3,194	5,025	2,776
Las Vegas, Nevada	11,543	15,280	3,599	779	11,707	10,597	9,724	13,356	11,499	11,125	12,635	4,341	8,670	11,887	8,615	5,373	3,698	9,188	7,463	10,967
Launceston, Australia	13,804	2,643	16,666	13,721	14,397	15,188	16,897	2,319	14,078	11,714	4,584	17,462	17,151	13,945	16,935	12,065	12,712	17,189	19,447	14,600
Le Havre, France	3,559	14,799	5,534	8,196	3,208	2,225	1,432	15,098	3,324	5,691	12,980	4,700	163	3,548	462	7,334	7,441	785	2,481	2,776
Leipzig, East Germany	2,774	13,978	6,238	8,742	2,659	1,559	1,773	14,209	2,588	4,808	12,106	5,421	727	2,888	524	7,072	7,429	1,277	3,370	2,028
Leningrad, USSR	2,663	13,176	6,713	8,761	3,192	2,143	3,221	13,013	2,684	3,624	10,806	5,977	2,087	3,137	1,771	5,907	6,570	2,749	4,606	2,230
Leon, Spain	4,003	15,132	5,432	8,264	3,375	2,608	981	15,753	3,708	6,439	13,742	4,593	1,012	3,823	1,339	8,100	8,054	582	1,878	3,207
Lerwick, United Kingdom	3,935	14,897	5,108	7,476	3,951	2,838	2,616	14,688	3,805	5,354	12,433	4,327	1,162	4,147	946	6,150	6,280	1,972	3,008	3,251
Lhasa, China	4,661	7,692	11,851	12,603	5,804	5,928	7,950	7,469	5,033	1,966	5,410	11,283	7,470	5,228	7,212	6,897	8,543	7,822	10,111	5,355
Libreville, Gabon	5,211	11,711	9,426	12,338	4,036	4,778	4,084	13,508	4,891	8,176	13,215	8,718	5,530	4,468	5,776	12,714	12,950	4,732	5,651	4,983
Lilongwe, Malawi	5,701	8,603	12,483	15,428	5,017	6,125	6,479	10,396	5,566	7,712	10,395	11,728	7,719	5,088	7,856	13,731	14,753	7,071	8,606	5,969
Lima, Peru	13,317	14,563	6,066	6,079	12,304	11,962	9,943	14,824	12,965	15,745	16,735	6,539	10,275	12,877	10,521	11,943	10,276	9,990	7,633	12,559
Limerick, Ireland	4,203	15,420	4,843	7,490	3,912	2,906	1,987	15,506	3,991	6,092	13,297	4,013	820	4,238	918	6,973	6,921	1,361	2,116	3,435
Limoges, France	3,442	14,657	5,775	8,504	2,955	2,062	1,016	15,132	3,173	5,789	13,092	4,935	459	3,345	772	7,739	7,856	371	2,466	2,646
Limon, Costa Rica	12,220	16,522	3,729	3,669	11,555	10,836	9,007	15,831	11,945	13,771	16,517	4,358	8,832	12,050	8,997	9,453	7,807	8,822	6,371	11,424
Lincoln, Nebraska	10,380	16,938	1,912	1,082	10,330	9,267	8,160	14,975	10,267	10,671	13,938	2,673	7,238	10,597	7,234	5,805	4,202	7,667	5,797	9,712
Linz, Austria	2,519	13,756	6,524	9,076	2,312	1,234	1,575	14,110	2,302	4,768	12,070	5,699	893	2,570	805	7,384	7,780	1,188	3,478	1,746
Lisbon, Portugal	4,379	15,348	5,346	8,245	3,633	2,988	1,094	16,161	4,062	6,927	14,222	4,519	1,538	4,124	1,864	8,519	8,373	993	1,571	3,591
Little Rock, Arkansas	10,722	17,280	1,829	1,313	10,533	9,522	8,217	15,417	10,570	11,299	14,616	2,667	7,448	10,858	7,485	6,583	4,974	7,782	5,707	10,010
Liverpool, United Kingdom	3,840	15,041	5,184	7,773	3,610	2,570	1,907	15,135	3,640	5,715	12,942	4,361	536	3,906	546	6,900	6,962	1,259	2,470	3,081
Lodz, Poland	2,366	13,515	6,643	9,053	2,437	1,307	2,107	13,712	2,224	4,315	11,616	5,838	1,224	2,576	999	6,947	7,443	1,699	3,867	1,670
Lome, Togo	5,307	12,824	8,323	11,226	4,079	4,561	3,399	14,613	4,949	8,391	14,154	7,629	4,853	4,601	5,135	12,137	12,130	4,029	4,601	4,901
London, United Kingdom	3,609	14,837	5,437	8,054	3,333	2,311	1,654	15,039	3,394	5,618	12,887	4,609	247	3,644	359	7,111	7,222	1,008	2,544	2,839
Londonderry, United Kingdom	4,147	15,316	4,866	7,440	3,942	2,897	2,174	15,298	3,957	5,902	13,069	4,047	865	4,233	860	6,717	6,705	1,532	2,350	3,398
Longlac, Canada	9,109	17,442	1,262	2,311	9,071	7,999	6,973	15,477	8,994	9,573	13,949	1,722	5,985	9,327	5,970	5,417	4,020	6,451	4,766	8,440
Lord Howe Island, Australia	14,372	3,830	15,248	12,295	15,239	15,745	17,748	2,628	14,707	11,758	4,465	15,995	17,208	14,706	16,895	10,796	11,267	17,694	19,038	15,145
Los Angeles, California	11,854	14,942	3,956	1,070	12,051	10,936	10,089	13,037	11,821	11,306	12,408	4,705	9,024	12,217	8,963	5,426	3,768	9,551	7,828	11,294
Louangphrabang, Laos	6,154	6,300	13,070	13,211	7,247	7,458	9,484	5,925	6,519	3,499	3,864	12,600	9,021	6,668	8,758	7,331	9,009	9,373	11,659	6,875
Louisville, Kentucky	10,059	17,887	1,128	1,896	9,839	8,838	7,516	15,947	9,896	10,813	14,870	1,966	6,758	10,173	6,803	6,537	5,011	7,082	5,020	9,335
Luanda, Angola	5,855	10,766	10,423	13,284	4,770	5,648	5,157	12,644	5,576	8,626	12,688	9,747	6,589	5,116	6,822	13,673	14,025	5,804	6,718	5,762
Lubumbashi, Zaire	5,580	9,315	11,797	14,729	4,751	5,817	5,942	11,125	5,395	7,885	11,102	11,060	7,249	4,910	7,415	13,676	14,501	6,557	7,949	5,740
Lusaka, Zambia	5,962	9,009	12,135	15,044	5,161	6,234	6,356	10,857	5,789	8,172	10,969	11,414	7,672	5,305	7,839	14,053	14,918	6,974	8,316	6,146
Luxembourg, Luxembourg	3,133	14,371	5,927	8,535	2,848	1,821	1,445	14,677	2,909	5,285	12,584	5,098	278	3,154	318	7,302	7,533	866	2,902	2,356
Luxor, Egypt	1,499	11,201	9,347	12,037	668	1,795	3,061	12,185	1,243	4,447	10,750	8,506	3,743	765	3,765	9,530	10,370	3,395	5,725	1,581
Lynn Lake, Canada	9,014	16,225	2,494	2,456	9,217	8,095	7,442	14,296	8,972	8,909	12,706	2,800	6,248	9,367	6,156	4,201	2,778	6,853	5,582	8,444
Lyon, France	3,162	14,381	6,030	8,730	2,699	1,784	1,007	14,861	2,895	5,540	12,841	5,192	499	3,075	734	7,736	7,930	449	2,743	2,366
Macapa, Brazil	10,214	15,965	5,238	6,941	9,151	8,910	6,887	17,334	9,851	12,977	19,590	5,236	7,482	9,727	7,774	11,832	10,477	7,038	4,921	9,490
Madison, Wisconsin	9,830	17,511	1,277	1,732	9,723	8,676	7,515	15,524	9,698	10,347	14,292	2,020	6,628	10,011	6,638	5,920	4,403	7,033	5,145	9,140
Madras, India	4,698	6,641	13,292	14,624	5,517	6,094	8,023	7,111	5,002	3,359	5,612	12,576	8,048	4,974	7,873	9,038	10,671	8,123	10,579	5,495
Madrid, Spain	3,882	14,930	5,680	8,531	3,180	2,489	711	15,661	3,572	6,433	13,722	4,844	1,155	3,653	1,482	8,346	8,334	493	2,027	3,092
Madurai, India	4,765	6,503	13,522	14,997	5,496	6,152	8,030	7,115	5,047	3,694	5,755	12,780	8,155	4,973	7,999	9,454	11,081	8,174	10,631	5,561
Magadan, USSR	7,517	10,914	7,965	7,366	8,587	7,789	8,922	9,358	7,781	5,141	7,293	7,894	7,540	8,248	7,225	1,492	3,162	8,347	9,117	7,604

Distances in Kilometers	Al Qamishli, Syria	Albany, Australia	Albany, New York	Albuquerque, New Mexico	Alexandria, Egypt	Alexandroupolis, Greece	Algiers, Algeria	Alice Springs, Australia	Allepo, Syria	Alma-Ata, USSR	Ambon, Indonesia	Amherst, Canada	Amiens, France	Amman, Jordan	Amsterdam, Netherlands	Anadyr, USSR	Anchorage, Alaska	Andorra, Andorra	Angra do Heroismo, Azores	Ankara, Turkey
Magdalena, Bolivia	12,252	14,647	6,276	6,987	11,149	10,969	8,949	15,469	11,884	15,037	17,689	6,552	9,522	11,728	9,804	12,665	11,069	9,102	6,918	11,544
Magdeburg, East Germany	2,855	14,044	6,153	8,643	2,763	1,658	1,839	14,238	2,677	4,827	12,118	5,338	703	2,984	461	6,982	7,327	1,318	3,341	2,117
Majuro Atoll, Marshall Isls.	12,881	7,281	11,463	8,847	14,105	13,625	14,988	5,301	13,234	9,814	4,926	11,983	13,594	13,598	13,284	6,412	6,804	14,409	14,592	13,273
Malabo, Equatorial Guinea	4,955	11,989	9,120	12,048	3,759	4,452	3,705	13,743	4,624	7,966	13,309	8,396	5,152	4,218	5,400	12,350	12,570	4,353	5,311	4,684
Male, Maldives	4,919	6,339	13,881	15,678	5,461	6,259	8,006	7,227	5,150	4,362	6,148	13,092	8,326	4,990	8,211	10,265	11,877	8,235	10,660	5,696
Manado, Indonesia	9,347	4,107	14,775	13,314	10,401	10,660	12,685	2,953	9,708	6,622	685	14,688	12,136	9,825	11,851	8,176	9,608	12,553	14,727	10,077
Managua, Nicaragua	12,292	16,501	3,591	3,267	11,699	10,924	9,155	15,606	12,035	13,639	16,125	4,278	8,885	12,172	9,030	9,086	7,430	8,930	6,499	11,502
Manama, Bahrain	1,490	9,803	10,493	12,812	2,092	2,795	4,616	10,525	1,688	3,044	8,966	9,677	4,870	1,560	4,773	8,938	10,139	4,785	7,232	2,239
Manaus, Brazil	11,221	15,774	5,256	6,444	10,186	9,892	7,865	16,682	10,863	13,873	18,837	5,440	8,344	10,760	8,619	11,805	10,303	7,968	5,723	10,481
Manchester, New Hampshire	8,841	18,817	192	3,145	8,548	7,575	6,199	16,855	8,653	9,948	15,243	658	5,487	8,905	5,556	6,657	5,360	5,774	3,720	8,094
Mandalay, Burma	5,493	6,719	12,772	13,250	6,577	6,811	8,837	6,505	5,857	2,947	4,508	12,235	8,431	5,999	8,179	7,409	9,085	8,749	11,074	6,224
Mangareva Island, Fr.Polynesia	18,420	10,006	9,608	7,101	18,278	17,353	15,738	9,124	18,373	16,337	10,555	10,441	15,269	18,688	15,316	10,560	9,444	15,479	13,079	17,822
Manila, Philippines	8,151	5,501	13,492	12,569	9,289	9,387	11,388	4,461	8,523	5,251	2,174	13,294	10,704	8,712	10,407	6,993	8,550	11,183	13,253	8,828
Mannheim, West Germany	2,966	14,203	6,085	8,673	2,708	1,664	1,477	14,515	2,746	5,131	12,433	5,258	447	3,000	405	7,302	7,580	944	3,066	2,192
Maputo, Mozambique	7,032	8,005	13,210	16,014	6,333	7,430	7,604	9,932	6,898	8,908	10,399	12,536	8,921	6,420	9,084	15,027	16,083	8,224	9,480	7,295
Mar del Plata, Argentina	13,092	11,905	9,081	9,546	11,864	12,163	10,360	13,072	12,729	16,177	15,348	9,309	11,368	12,388	11,690	15,391	13,737	10,732	9,038	12,612
Maracaibo, Venezuela	11,260	17,142	3,550	4,458	10,480	9,864	7,947	16,964	10,955	13,241	17,716	3,961	7,957	11,003	8,162	9,901	8,345	7,835	5,381	10,464
Marrakech, Morocco	4,520	15,035	5,820	8,765	3,586	3,188	1,167	16,187	4,170	7,305	14,504	5,022	2,202	4,132	2,529	9,309	9,153	1,471	1,912	3,773
Marseilles, France	3,106	14,273	6,196	8,937	2,540	1,711	751	14,862	2,815	5,618	12,903	5,356	771	2,953	1,007	8,005	8,206	329	2,775	2,309
Maseru, Lesotho	7,484	8,242	13,021	15,693	6,703	7,770	7,750	10,208	7,323	9,490	10,849	12,404	9,121	6,839	9,311	15,547	16,454	8,385	9,427	7,687
Mashhad, Iran	1,641	9,941	10,069	11,975	2,798	2,964	4,987	10,239	2,012	1,670	8,363	9,314	4,774	2,230	4,583	7,580	8,870	4,952	7,371	2,370
Mazatlan, Mexico	12,528	15,561	3,701	1,316	12,403	11,375	10,085	13,920	12,402	12,637	13,781	4,540	9,312	12,711	9,336	7,037	5,361	9,658	7,533	11,843
Mbabane, Swaziland	7,092	8,108	13,117	15,900	6,367	7,456	7,579	10,043	6,949	9,016	10,537	12,454	8,911	6,468	9,081	15,113	16,126	8,204	9,412	7,336
Mbandaka, Zaire	4,727	10,894	10,172	13,120	3,658	4,582	4,358	12,617	4,452	7,524	12,234	9,421	5,728	3,989	5,928	12,619	13,133	4,990	6,304	4,657
McMurdo Sound, Antarctica	14,788	5,243	15,333	13,742	14,390	15,513	15,388	6,208	14,786	14,607	8,481	15,884	16,842	14,352	17,084	15,813	15,702	16,033	15,639	15,277
Mecca, Saudi Arabia	1,733	10,333	10,191	12,822	1,464	2,522	3,929	11,340	1,655	4,196	9,999	9,352	4,555	1,226	4,548	9,786	10,800	4,253	6,593	2,153
Medan, Indonesia	6,915	4,723	14,828	14,981	7,791	8,307	10,276	4,867	7,239	4,890	3,383	14,277	10,162	7,241	9,950	9,116	10,784	10,330	12,766	7,704
Medellin, Colombia	11,911	16,535	4,037	4,508	11,112	10,515	8,587	16,330	11,603	13,868	17,385	4,522	8,612	11,642	8,816	10,172	8,562	8,486	6,034	11,116
Medicine Hat, Canada	9,972	15,785	2,925	1,694	10,203	9,080	8,405	13,795	9,942	9,641	12,503	3,446	7,233	10,345	7,145	4,335	2,710	7,825	6,420	9,419
Medina, Saudi Arabia	1,402	10,549	9,930	12,521	1,211	2,221	3,733	11,477	1,322	3,987	10,044	9,093	4,277	904	4,256	9,473	10,469	4,018	6,396	1,827
Melbourne, Australia	13,479	2,443	16,711	13,757	14,138	14,871	16,673	1,891	13,768	11,302	4,147	17,455	16,777	13,663	16,544	11,721	12,448	16,894	19,338	14,276
Memphis, Tennessee	10,568	17,487	1,638	1,511	10,356	9,354	8,024	15,617	10,409	11,226	14,767	2,478	7,275	10,689	7,319	6,647	5,058	7,596	5,505	9,849
Merauke, Indonesia	11,382	3,728	14,974	12,643	12,441	12,677	14,696	1,821	11,745	8,574	1,442	15,250	14,004	11,866	13,698	8,686	9,770	14,508	16,439	12,101
Merida, Mexico	11,783	16,918	2,824	2,285	11,362	10,471	8,873	15,558	11,570	12,764	15,516	3,601	8,387	11,777	8,488	8,053	6,404	8,556	6,220	11,017
Meridian, Mississippi	10,735	17,552	1,741	1,688	10,465	9,490	8,085	15,761	10,560	11,505	15,037	2,576	7,403	10,821	7,463	6,976	5,381	7,683	5,518	10,000
Messina, Italy	2,263	13,277	7,225	9,951	1,522	933	1,117	14,027	1,926	5,100	12,238	6,384	1,676	1,977	1,778	8,484	8,908	1,284	3,702	1,508
Mexico City, Mexico	12,510	16,000	3,511	1,888	12,211	11,258	9,773	14,549	12,334	13,057	14,608	4,339	9,169	12,586	9,236	7,758	6,079	9,412	7,145	11,774
Miami, Florida	10,749	18,010	1,962	2,733	10,277	9,413	7,777	16,587	10,519	12,014	16,131	2,643	7,340	10,706	7,460	8,005	6,446	7,473	5,120	9,972
Midway Islands, USA	11,740	9,758	8,953	6,613	12,827	11,995	12,811	7,767	12,016	9,066	6,809	9,406	11,354	12,478	11,079	4,079	4,199	12,176	11,983	11,842
Milan, Italy	2,821	14,044	6,344	9,009	2,392	1,446	1,093	14,530	2,557	5,242	12,535	5,507	715	2,747	827	7,742	8,029	699	3,080	2,026
Milford Sound, New Zealand	15,516	4,332	15,168	12,327	16,082	16,903	18,467	3,846	15,794	13,242	5,953	16,007	18,771	15,651	18,487	12,152	12,333	18,889	18,609	16,313
Milwaukee, Wisconsin	9,759	17,630	1,157	1,841	9,635	8,594	7,412	15,641	9,622	10,329	14,387	1,906	6,540	9,929	6,555	5,987	4,485	6,935	5,030	9,063
Minsk, USSR	2,149	13,082	6,966	9,212	2,529	1,456	2,678	13,162	2,103	3,746	11,038	6,186	1,785	2,528	1,520	6,597	7,238	2,294	4,419	1,603
Mogadiscio, Somalia	3,895	8,562	12,182	14,972	3,612	4,722	5,794	9,957	3,873	5,532	9,238	11,346	6,678	3,453	6,712	11,644	12,866	6,246	8,359	4,380
Mombasa, Kenya	4,551	8,683	12,221	15,137	4,037	5,167	5,904	10,266	4,463	6,437	9,828	11,406	6,971	4,004	7,055	12,487	13,612	6,431	8,317	4,920
Monclova, Mexico	11,927	16,192	3,053	1,035	11,765	10,748	9,436	14,494	11,787	12,236	14,167	3,894	8,678	12,085	8,710	6,915	5,238	9,012	6,888	11,228
Moncton, Canada	8,212	18,756	811	3,700	7,918	6,943	5,589	17,014	8,021	9,413	15,144	54	4,854	8,272	4,925	6,588	5,432	5,150	3,171	7,463
Monrovia, Liberia	6,264	13,895	7,339	10,143	5,053	5,280	3,656	15,791	5,891	9,352	15,483	6,729	4,984	5,614	5,303	12,093	11,727	4,189	3,945	5,728
Monte Carlo, Monaco	2,944	14,129	6,315	9,030	2,414	1,552	856	14,694	2,659	5,450	12,733	5,476	789	2,811	976	7,945	8,192	499	2,938	2,147
Monterrey, Mexico	11,988	16,236	3,067	1,208	11,792	10,789	9,436	14,580	11,839	12,369	14,313	3,908	8,712	12,125	8,753	7,088	5,411	9,025	6,866	11,279
Montevideo, Uruguay	12,823	12,240	8,770	9,355	11,596	11,855	10,026	13,435	12,456	15,917	15,708	8,976	11,014	12,130	11,334	15,158	13,524	10,386	8,672	12,318
Montgomery, Alabama	10,593	17,771	1,587	1,905	10,293	9,331	7,894	15,986	10,409	11,459	15,224	2,412	7,243	10,660	7,312	7,082	5,507	7,504	5,314	9,850
Montpelier, Vermont	8,815	18,653	203	3,070	8,553	7,565	6,234	16,700	8,635	9,851	15,076	682	5,480	8,898	5,538	6,490	5,194	5,793	3,792	8,076
Montpellier, France	3,229	14,401	6,072	8,820	2,666	1,835	760	14,978	2,941	5,713	13,004	5,232	711	3,080	976	7,978	8,147	228	2,653	2,432
Montreal, Canada	8,782	18,498	317	3,012	8,551	7,549	6,262	16,555	8,611	9,752	14,916	733	5,469	8,884	5,516	6,331	5,037	5,807	3,858	8,051
Moosonee, Canada	8,707	17,673	1,093	2,750	8,638	7,574	6,524	15,761	8,582	9,310	14,092	1,353	5,548	8,905	5,540	5,511	4,213	6,004	4,335	8,025
Moroni, Comoros	5,397	7,881	13,088	16,029	4,956	6,086	6,819	9,563	5,338	6,980	9,384	12,286	7,904	4,891	7,988	13,154	14,404	7,356	9,177	5,815
Moscow, USSR	2,099	12,587	7,342	9,384	2,794	1,865	3,338	12,540	2,173	3,117	10,386	6,597	2,437	2,648	2,152	6,213	7,017	2,969	5,050	1,793
Mosul, Iraq	187	11,058	9,177	11,504	1,350	1,583	3,562	11,597	536	2,974	9,814	8,367	3,593	823	3,471	8,116	9,128	3,612	6,068	984
Mount Isa, Australia	12,083	2,643	16,081	13,440	12,996	13,455	15,463	666	12,422	9,536	2,246	16,488	15,062	12,446	14,781	10,019	11,018	15,427	17,652	12,855
Multan, Pakistan	2,895	8,705	11,195	12,778	3,962	4,252	6,268	8,942	3,251	1,529	7,097	10,478	6,059	3,383	5,855	7,725	9,208	6,249	8,666	3,653
Munich, West Germany	2,706	13,946	6,357	8,942	2,439	1,392	1,443	14,313	2,478	4,965	12,268	5,528	706	2,727	666	7,426	7,766	1,007	3,276	1,926
Murcia, Spain	3,713	14,649	6,003	8,868	2,928	2,336	392	15,489	3,385	6,387	13,638	5,169	1,352	3,426	1,664	8,615	8,651	549	2,276	2,936
Murmansk, USSR	3,589	13,389	6,270	8,004	4,206	3,159	4,022	12,872	3,655	3,801	10,593	5,618	2,691	4,122	2,364	4,909	5,559	3,467	4,880	3,232
Mururoa Atoll, Fr. Polynesia	18,323	9,768	9,773	7,165	18,500	17,466	16,012	8,796	18,373	15,950	10,162	10,611	15,418	18,781	15,433	10,303	9,262	15,701	13,347	17,859
Muscat, Oman	2,228	9,013	11,197	13,325	2,949	3,596	5,465	9,672	2,485	2,754	8,120	10,399	5,639	2,410	5,515	8,912	10,260	5,609	8,064	3,015
Myitkyina, Burma	5,427	7,027	12,418	12,852	6,552	6,707	8,730	6,705	5,797	2,718	4,629	11,903	8,240	5,974	7,977	7,015	8,690	8,602	10,878	6,131
Naga, Philippines	8,404	5,415	13,538	12,491	9,546	9,634	11,631	4,291	8,777	5,490	1,997	13,378	10,923	8,968	10,624	6,996	8,524	11,416	13,454	9,078
Nagasaki, Japan	7,803	7,613	11,310	10,461	9,031	8,745	10,537	6,267	8,168	4,711	4,046	11,181	9,495	8,500	9,171	4,783	6,358	10,151	11,750	8,294
Nagoya, Japan	8,203	8,019	10,843	9,817	9,429	9,040	10,726	6,523	8,558	5,145	4,400	10,787	9,580	8,921	9,252	4,254	5,771	10,286	11,671	8,631
Nagpur, India	4,050	7,447	12,415	13,752	5,002	5,437	7,425	7,737	4,384	2,459	6,018	11,718	7,304	4,434	7,107	8,288	9,886	7,456	9,893	4,834
Nairobi, Kenya	4,267	9,118	11,780	14,699	3,669	4,796	5,470	10,679	4,150	6,352	10,164	10,966	6,558	3,679	6,651	12,290	13,332	6,003	7,877	4,582
Nanchang, China	6,872	7,056	12,045	11,660	8,074	7,991	9,934	6,109	7,247	3,822	3,820	11,753	9,125	7,512	8,820	5,819	7,473	9,662	11,628	7,471
Nancy, France	3,107	14,347	5,976	8,603	2,784	1,776	1,347	14,695	2,873	5,318	12,620	5,144	314	3,104	418	7,404	7,634	778	2,888	2,324
Nandi, Fiji	15,251	6,145	12,860	9,913	16,434	16,286	17,831	4,564	15,626	12,183	5,584	13,601	16,417	15,859	16,116	9,153	9,230	17,239	16,694	15,825
Nanjing, China	6,938	7,426	11,635	11,194	8,156	7,987	9,882	6,375	7,310	3,850	4,082	11,374	8,989	7,606	8,675	5,357	7,008	9,568	11,427	7,493
Nanning, China	6,534	6,482	12,753	12,617	7,680	7,775	9,784	5,843	6,907	3,667	3,645	12,365	9,175	7,104	8,892	6,748	8,417	9,607	11,780	7,213
Nantes, France	3,663	14,893	5,516	8,239	3,213	2,295	1,219	15,296	3,405	5,912	13,211	4,677	412	3,592	736	7,589	7,652	577	2,287	2,869
Naples, Italy	2,368	13,493	6,964	9,661	1,765	979	1,071	14,150	2,057	5,074	12,285	6,124	1,372	2,173	1,464	8,208	8,602	1,075	3,530	1,581
Narvik, Norway	3,790	13,998	5,726	7,639	4,219	3,112	3,633	13,508	3,791	4,390	11,226	5,043	2,224	4,229	1,911	5,144	5,584	3,035	4,263	3,306
Nashville, Tennessee	10,295	17,794	1,331	1,801	10,056	9,064	7,711	15,899	10,127	11,058	14,943	2,171	6,982	10,399	7,033	6,693	5,141	7,289	5,186	9,567
Nassau, Bahamas	10,605	18,187	1,976	3,020	10,090	9,255	7,574	16,867	10,364	11,997	16,407	2,585	7,195	10,533	7,328	8,198	6,663	7,292	4,911	9,822
Natal, Brazil	9,206	14,687	6,627	8,715	8,025	8,073	6,168	16,538	8,830	12,239	17,908	6,400	7,151	8,598	7,475	12,970	11,870	6,510	4,988	8,590
Natashquan, Canada	7,768	18,320	1,241	3,967	7,530	6,526	5,276	16,767	7,591	8,907	14,768	517	4,446	7,861	4,495	6,277	5,228	4,800	3,004	7,031
Nauru Island	13,146	6,354	12,406	9,721	14,368	14,074	15,665	4,393	13,515	10,050	4,323	12,947	14,343	13,819	14,023	7,293	7,765	15,135	15,546	13,647
Ndjamena, Chad	3,801	11,940	9,012	11,963	2,607	3,355	2,985	13,472	3,470	6,827	12,623	8,223	4,350	3,065	4,554	11,354	11,767	3,613	5,102	3,545
Nelson, New Zealand	15,904	4,823	14,613	11,753	16,577	17,300	19,038	4,137	16,208	13,421	6,121	15,449	18,824	16,112	18,497	11,762	11,841	19,326	18,252	16,699
Nema, Mauritania	5,254	14,239	6,864	9,791	4,088	4,161	2,454	15,907	4,879	8,300	14,963	6,154	3,791	4,665	4,107	10,974	10,764	2,988	3,122	4,650
Neuquen, Argentina	13,972	11,790	9,055	9,108	12,745	12,979	11,108	12,705	13,604	17,067	14,997	9,399	12,009	13,280	12,322	14,984	13,304	11,429	9,552	13,455
New Delhi, India	3,473	8,239	11,576	12,944	4,543	4,821	6,841	8,390	3,831	1,626	6,518	10,891	6,585	3,964	6,368	7,634	9,185	6,807	9,207	4,225
New Glasgow, Canada	8,113	18,832	946	3,863	7,792	6,830	5,443	17,161	7,915	9,387	15,248	124	4,740	8,156	4,821	6,712	5,581	5,015	3,003	7,357
New Haven, Connecticut	9,056	18,845	165	3,015	8,748	7,783	6,380	16,856	8,865	10,167	15,343	864	5,694	9,111	5,768	6,768	5,430	5,966	3,869	8,306
New Orleans, Louisiana	11,025	17,350	2,025	1,656	10,739	9,773	8,340	15,633	10,847	11,791	15,060	2,855	7,685	11,103	7,750	7,148	5,530	7,951	5,753	10,287
New Plymouth, New Zealand	15,926	4,940	14,443	11,561	16,669	17,316	19,196	4,144	16,244	13,345	6,060	15,275	18,640	16,182	18,312	11,513	11,585	19,285	18,180	16,713
New York, New York	9,168	18,801	217	2,921	8,860	7,896	6,490	16,808	8,977	10,261	15,348	977	5,807	9,224	5,881	6,784	5,425	6,078	3,973	8,419
Newcastle upon Tyne, UK	3,787	14,950	5,221	7,756	3,625	2,558	2,056	14,977	3,605	5,564	12,770	4,407	626	3,893	522	6,723	6,820	1,409	2,641	3,045
Newcastle Waters, Australia	11,345	2,487	16,215	13,812	12,257	12,720	14,724	699	11,683	8,843	1,617	16,460	14,373	11,706	14,102	9,846	10,994	14,703	16,999	12,119
Niamey, Niger	4,672	13,204	7,853	10,799	3,450	3,809	2,579	14,844	4,303	7,768	14,016	7,112	4,035	4,003	4,315	11,317	11,360	3,213	4,011	4,194
Nicosia, Cyprus	738	11,714	8,659	11,194	546	911	2,729	12,406	363	3,824	10,690	7,829	2,999	429	2,949	8,496	9,317	2,864	5,314	531
Niue (Alofi)	16,393	7,231	11,913	8,967	17,618	17,162	17,922	5,816	16,759	13,297	6,927	12,710	16,510	17,069	16,279	9,350	9,072	17,280	15,824	16,832

Distances in Kilometers

	Al Qamishli, Syria	Albany, Australia	Albany, New York	Albuquerque, New Mexico	Alexandria, Egypt	Alexandroupolis, Greece	Algiers, Algeria	Alice Springs, Australia	Allepo, Syria	Alma-Ata, USSR	Ambon, Indonesia	Amherst, Canada	Amiens, France	Amman, Jordan	Amsterdam, Netherlands	Anadyr, USSR	Anchorage, Alaska	Andorra, Andorra	Angra do Heroismo, Azores	Ankara, Turkey
Norfolk, Virginia	9,608	18,733	679	2,735	9,261	8,320	6,850	16,795	9,408	10,732	15,572	1,418	6,231	9,642	6,316	7,073	5,643	6,466	4,277	8,852
Norfolk Island, Australia	15,035	4,727	14,376	11,421	16,003	16,354	18,371	3,439	15,389	12,231	5,045	15,144	17,394	15,447	17,065	10,430	10,703	18,085	18,260	15,773
Noril'sk, USSR	4,553	11,827	7,497	8,363	5,559	4,745	6,043	10,947	4,783	2,974	8,654	7,032	4,788	5,261	4,459	3,575	4,813	5,535	6,934	4,567
Norman Wells, Canada	8,614	14,649	4,108	3,618	9,121	8,002	7,892	12,803	8,668	7,795	11,071	4,264	6,510	9,123	6,326	2,540	1,234	7,251	6,595	8,207
Normanton, Australia	12,034	2,997	15,719	13,126	12,997	13,385	15,408	1,004	12,382	9,389	2,087	16,112	14,893	12,437	14,600	9,648	10,640	15,316	17,421	12,791
North Pole	5,903	13,880	5,279	6,118	6,551	5,480	5,932	12,623	5,996	5,212	10,412	4,925	4,474	6,467	4,202	2,817	3,211	5,297	5,724	5,582
Nottingham, United Kingdom	3,710	14,918	5,316	7,903	3,479	2,438	1,828	15,045	3,508	5,621	12,866	4,492	418	3,774	417	6,949	7,045	1,181	2,551	2,950
Norway House, Canada	9,185	16,538	2,168	2,210	9,319	8,208	7,437	14,584	9,122	9,218	13,057	2,551	6,302	9,501	6,232	4,574	3,123	6,867	5,450	8,584
Norwich, United Kingdom	3,540	14,750	5,485	8,061	3,319	2,271	1,767	14,904	3,338	5,481	12,740	4,662	312	3,607	248	6,983	7,126	1,127	2,684	2,780
Nouakchott, Mauritania	5,928	15,111	6,049	8,939	4,826	4,711	2,784	16,840	5,557	8,882	15,815	5,385	3,886	5,403	4,215	10,748	10,311	3,170	2,526	5,254
Noumea, New Caledonia	14,554	4,903	14,066	11,134	15,623	15,800	17,748	3,336	14,921	11,633	4,607	14,777	16,642	15,049	16,314	9,694	10,045	17,366	17,778	15,247
Novosibirsk, USSR	3,717	10,523	8,957	9,978	4,900	4,402	6,148	9,977	4,036	1,380	7,721	8,407	5,199	4,461	4,888	4,888	6,309	5,789	7,697	4,022
Nuku'alofa, Tonga	16,096	6,635	12,489	9,538	17,289	17,060	18,262	5,223	16,471	13,016	6,410	13,278	16,805	16,716	16,540	9,542	9,406	17,616	16,400	16,639
Nukunono Island, Tokelau Isls.	15,479	7,631	11,364	8,417	16,697	16,089	16,908	5,971	15,825	12,418	6,647	12,110	15,461	16,201	15,211	8,249	8,042	16,260	15,219	15,816
Nuremberg, West Germany	2,784	14,017	6,255	8,817	2,566	1,500	1,550	14,329	2,570	4,953	12,256	5,430	636	2,837	540	7,287	7,618	1,069	3,253	2,014
Nyala, Sudan	3,214	11,043	9,807	12,720	2,182	3,193	3,504	12,468	2,946	6,060	11,553	8,989	4,679	2,478	4,815	11,183	11,869	4,061	5,914	3,188
Oaxaca, Mexico	12,579	16,060	3,577	2,228	12,208	11,293	9,731	14,725	12,383	13,297	14,915	4,386	9,204	12,609	9,290	8,106	6,428	9,402	7,081	11,826
Ocean Falls, Canada	10,044	14,601	4,101	2,541	10,496	9,368	9,040	12,621	10,085	9,151	11,292	4,541	7,735	10,531	7,588	3,345	1,665	8,420	7,351	9,609
Odense, Denmark	3,091	14,193	5,922	8,340	3,096	1,977	2,143	14,245	2,946	4,822	12,071	5,122	820	3,283	494	6,634	6,957	1,572	3,350	2,389
Odessa, USSR	1,362	12,531	7,652	10,019	1,696	737	2,528	12,867	1,260	3,618	10,881	6,847	2,135	1,672	1,972	7,340	8,066	2,352	4,729	746
Ogbomosho, Nigeria	4,914	12,677	8,424	11,355	3,688	4,208	3,176	14,402	4,559	7,993	13,815	7,700	4,634	4,204	4,903	11,902	11,993	3,817	4,621	4,527
Okha, USSR	7,485	10,110	8,783	8,134	8,627	7,942	9,278	8,604	7,784	4,833	6,496	8,693	7,960	8,229	7,636	2,293	3,939	8,741	9,743	7,681
Okinawa (Naha)	8,011	6,857	12,071	11,144	9,225	9,065	10,947	5,563	8,384	4,927	3,312	11,937	10,006	8,671	9,687	5,533	7,088	10,614	12,365	8,572
Oklahoma City, Oklahoma	10,919	16,823	2,194	833	10,810	9,769	8,560	14,939	10,791	11,267	14,158	3,014	7,716	11,104	7,730	6,271	4,631	8,098	6,103	10,233
Old Crow, Canada	8,406	14,066	4,712	4,182	9,020	7,922	8,022	12,261	8,496	7,333	10,468	4,817	6,598	8,965	6,384	1,912	856	7,375	6,961	8,069
Olympia, Washington	10,559	14,875	3,851	1,898	10,921	9,791	9,278	12,882	10,573	9,814	11,739	4,404	8,044	11,003	7,927	4,016	2,337	8,680	7,374	10,076
Omaha, Nebraska	10,306	16,994	1,845	1,157	10,254	9,191	8,084	15,025	10,192	10,615	13,961	2,601	7,162	10,522	7,158	5,793	4,199	7,591	5,726	9,637
Omsk, USSR	3,145	10,841	8,746	10,023	4,311	3,794	5,555	10,436	3,453	1,332	8,210	8,141	4,655	3,890	4,352	5,251	6,569	5,216	7,202	3,418
Oodnadatta, Australia	12,148	1,865	16,897	14,148	12,930	13,543	15,471	455	12,461	9,857	2,748	17,344	15,354	12,414	15,108	10,858	11,877	15,569	17,993	12,941
Oradea, Romania	1,940	13,170	7,079	9,564	1,889	759	1,930	13,542	1,746	4,257	11,541	6,261	1,481	2,059	1,356	7,426	7,977	1,688	4,054	1,185
Oran, Algeria	3,730	14,533	6,168	9,055	2,871	2,378	352	15,472	3,389	6,487	13,697	5,339	1,595	3,391	1,901	8,867	8,907	777	2,375	2,969
Oranjestad, Aruba	10,995	17,388	3,359	4,450	10,224	9,600	7,688	17,217	10,692	12,982	17,800	3,734	7,689	10,745	7,894	9,782	8,252	7,571	5,116	10,199
Orebro, Sweden	3,099	13,975	6,011	8,264	3,310	2,181	2,652	13,863	3,018	4,468	11,650	5,242	1,332	3,409	1,004	6,166	6,579	2,092	3,761	2,484
Orel, USSR	1,810	12,523	7,477	9,612	2,464	1,548	3,124	12,588	1,860	3,179	10,478	6,712	2,352	2,329	2,095	6,543	7,338	2,806	4,992	1,464
Orsk, USSR	2,088	11,171	8,634	10,338	3,235	2,751	4,608	11,066	2,382	1,642	8,932	7,937	3,892	2,829	3,619	6,121	7,286	4,342	6,520	2,346
Osaka, Japan	8,127	7,931	10,942	9,949	9,354	8,985	10,694	6,462	8,484	5,059	4,317	10,873	9,569	8,841	9,241	4,362	5,892	10,266	11,695	8,567
Oslo, Norway	3,341	14,234	5,751	8,029	3,495	2,365	2,631	14,089	3,245	4,711	11,862	4,980	1,238	3,623	916	6,132	6,467	2,038	3,552	2,704
Osorno, Chile	14,442	11,558	9,217	9,052	13,216	13,445	11,561	12,363	14,075	17,537	14,644	9,612	12,431	13,749	12,739	14,892	13,218	11,870	9,938	13,925
Ostrava, Czechoslovakia	2,324	13,529	6,684	9,155	2,285	1,161	1,898	13,807	2,148	4,442	11,745	5,870	1,147	2,468	976	7,172	7,647	1,525	3,775	1,588
Ottawa, Canada	8,908	18,386	345	2,850	8,696	7,686	6,418	16,424	8,743	9,818	14,836	897	5,609	9,022	5,651	6,259	4,935	5,958	4,022	8,183
Ouagadougou, Bourkina Fasso	5,054	13,465	7,639	10,568	3,838	4,135	2,743	15,168	4,683	8,148	14,421	6,923	4,177	4,396	4,472	11,453	11,387	3,352	3,865	4,548
Oujda, Morocco	3,872	14,607	6,129	9,032	2,986	2,529	506	15,596	3,528	6,646	13,848	5,304	1,727	3,516	2,038	8,983	8,989	919	2,299	3,117
Oxford, United Kingdom	3,691	14,917	5,354	7,973	3,415	2,395	1,697	15,102	3,477	5,679	12,940	4,526	324	3,728	428	7,085	7,173	1,049	2,485	2,922
Pago Pago, American Samoa	15,976	7,434	11,636	8,681	17,203	16,654	17,435	5,894	16,332	12,892	6,801	12,411	16,002	16,681	15,762	8,819	8,569	16,788	15,536	16,358
Pakxe, Laos	6,765	5,696	13,609	13,486	7,832	8,087	10,113	5,271	7,127	4,152	3,232	13,181	9,673	7,254	9,411	7,629	9,293	10,017	12,312	7,499
Palembang, Indonesia	7,897	3,806	15,601	15,202	8,747	9,290	11,249	3,888	8,216	5,823	2,608	15,130	11,148	8,205	10,933	9,487	11,108	11,315	13,753	8,688
Palermo, Italy	2,455	13,453	7,071	9,821	1,695	1,116	924	14,220	2,119	5,275	12,428	6,231	1,578	2,163	1,713	8,516	8,890	1,117	3,517	1,697
Palma, Majorca	3,361	14,383	6,200	9,020	2,632	1,976	311	15,143	3,041	6,015	13,268	5,361	1,149	3,107	1,432	8,431	8,560	339	2,574	2,578
Palmerston North, New Zealand	16,082	5,036	14,391	11,532	16,785	17,475	19,261	4,303	16,393	13,532	6,243	15,226	18,825	16,312	18,497	11,653	11,684	19,472	18,057	16,872
Panama, Panama	12,027	16,624	3,775	3,997	11,307	10,635	8,763	16,119	11,738	13,754	16,915	4,341	8,667	11,816	8,848	9,718	8,090	8,610	6,153	11,229
Paramaribo, Suriname	10,191	16,695	4,472	6,179	9,213	8,836	6,815	17,809	9,842	12,756	19,588	4,518	7,227	9,778	7,497	11,074	9,694	6,878	4,598	9,432
Paris, France	3,390	14,631	5,709	8,367	3,034	2,051	1,344	14,966	3,152	5,572	12,870	4,875	115	3,373	428	7,399	7,550	710	2,614	2,605
Patna, India	4,324	7,548	12,145	13,176	5,392	5,664	7,687	7,574	4,683	2,094	5,667	11,511	7,377	4,814	7,147	7,571	9,197	7,635	10,013	5,070
Patrai, Greece	1,723	12,789	7,652	10,306	1,081	458	1,657	13,490	1,387	4,611	11,705	6,814	2,014	1,469	2,038	8,391	8,953	1,776	4,221	981
Peking, China	6,364	8,302	10,802	10,603	7,592	7,304	9,128	7,275	6,727	3,279	4,982	10,505	8,160	7,068	7,841	4,723	6,400	8,774	10,550	6,848
Penrhyn Island (Omoka)	16,348	8,905	10,221	7,278	17,415	16,455	16,392	7,388	16,626	13,494	8,168	11,021	15,122	17,088	14,958	8,430	7,818	15,796	14,133	16,412
Peoria, Illinois	10,050	17,537	1,334	1,621	9,911	8,877	7,663	15,568	9,910	10,610	14,443	2,129	6,818	10,213	6,838	6,135	4,593	7,197	5,241	9,351
Perm', USSR	2,578	11,794	7,929	9,567	3,590	2,872	4,497	11,515	2,801	2,182	9,306	7,260	3,551	3,280	3,248	5,522	6,590	4,126	6,107	2,612
Perth, Australia	10,878	393	18,552	16,094	11,428	12,244	13,945	1,995	11,133	9,220	3,381	18,461	14,283	10,979	14,128	11,967	13,282	14,222	16,607	11,668
Peshawar, Pakistan	2,758	9,040	10,812	12,353	3,895	4,067	6,093	9,179	3,128	1,127	7,253	10,110	5,784	3,320	5,564	7,341	8,804	6,028	8,412	3,479
Petropavlovsk-Kamchatskiy,USSR	8,354	10,522	8,281	7,272	9,444	8,662	9,781	8,831	8,628	5,840	6,904	8,319	8,384	9,090	8,073	1,686	3,156	9,197	9,833	8,467
Petrozavodsk, USSR	2,798	13,050	6,770	8,706	3,419	2,401	3,526	12,799	2,856	3,456	10,572	6,057	2,367	3,322	2,046	5,637	6,353	3,048	4,840	2,437
Pevek, USSR	7,472	12,361	6,515	6,131	8,369	7,407	8,150	10,757	7,663	5,698	8,736	6,451	6,703	8,148	6,414	633	2,024	7,528	7,904	7,364
Philadelphia, Pennsylvania	9,298	18,747	322	2,820	8,989	8,026	6,615	16,757	9,107	10,375	15,360	1,107	5,937	9,354	6,011	6,813	5,429	6,206	4,088	8,549
Phnom Penh, Kampuchea	6,915	5,334	14,002	13,872	7,939	8,262	10,285	5,015	7,270	4,427	3,082	13,557	9,921	7,365	9,669	8,026	9,685	10,225	12,564	7,668
Phoenix, Arizona	11,727	15,469	3,481	531	11,815	10,720	9,733	13,589	11,660	11,462	12,981	4,262	8,746	12,029	8,712	5,776	4,099	9,222	7,384	11,118
Pierre, South Dakota	10,197	16,618	2,149	1,163	10,239	9,150	8,179	14,630	10,111	10,295	13,481	2,825	7,168	10,466	7,135	5,311	3,708	7,654	5,933	9,563
Pinang, Malaysia	6,928	4,841	14,649	14,713	7,843	8,313	10,301	4,863	7,260	4,780	3,259	14,126	10,125	7,286	9,902	8,854	10,520	10,327	12,746	7,711
Pitcairn Island (Adamstown)	18,449	10,250	9,462	7,101	17,951	17,186	15,411	9,493	18,283	16,836	11,018	10,283	15,102	18,459	15,187	10,927	9,729	15,218	12,780	17,725
Pittsburgh, Pennsylvania	9,549	18,339	576	2,412	9,298	8,308	6,964	16,356	9,375	10,453	15,059	1,416	6,224	9,642	6,279	6,569	5,129	6,534	4,474	8,815
Plymouth, Montserrat	10,053	17,973	3,079	4,846	9,264	8,658	6,731	18,178	9,744	12,175	18,184	3,236	6,785	9,788	7,004	9,677	8,270	6,629	4,182	9,259
Plymouth, United Kingdom	3,872	15,111	5,213	7,887	3,526	2,545	1,618	15,346	3,643	5,924	13,190	4,379	462	3,869	665	7,235	7,259	978	2,238	3,092
Ponape Island	11,878	6,284	12,421	10,037	13,100	12,835	14,526	4,300	12,248	8,783	3,540	12,810	13,296	12,551	12,969	6,596	7,375	14,049	14,929	12,391
Ponce, Puerto Rico	10,320	18,069	2,813	4,376	9,590	8,925	7,045	17,810	10,024	12,273	17,760	3,093	6,991	10,098	7,191	9,365	7,909	6,898	4,440	9,522
Ponta Delgada, Azores	5,791	16,762	4,076	7,027	5,082	4,395	2,540	17,528	5,489	8,130	15,402	3,292	2,602	5,570	2,872	8,465	7,939	2,366	170	4,995
Pontianak, Indonesia	8,084	3,975	15,274	14,633	9,011	9,464	11,461	3,727	8,420	5,777	2,138	14,891	11,225	8,453	10,987	8,989	10,586	11,467	13,862	8,862
Port Augusta, Australia	12,622	1,860	17,040	14,159	13,338	14,017	15,885	1,047	12,921	10,423	3,339	17,623	15,892	12,842	15,659	11,321	12,248	16,046	18,502	13,418
Port Blair, India	5,849	5,802	13,843	14,451	6,777	7,234	9,223	5,941	6,182	3,825	4,275	13,240	9,064	6,216	8,850	8,597	10,276	9,250	11,676	6,632
Port Elizabeth, South Africa	8,026	8,128	13,169	15,681	7,227	8,284	8,174	10,114	7,861	10,018	10,942	12,605	9,570	7,377	9,772	16,093	16,957	8,816	9,712	8,216
Port Hedland, Australia	10,285	1,632	17,277	15,322	11,036	11,681	13,579	1,624	10,587	8,225	2,113	17,163	13,585	10,524	13,373	10,673	12,046	13,710	16,165	11,082
Port Louis, Mauritius	6,558	6,092	14,851	17,747	6,404	7,506	8,508	7,804	6,596	7,298	7,859	14,035	9,469	6,209	9,505	13,423	14,974	9,003	10,946	7,128
Port Moresby, Papua New Guinea	12,057	4,107	14,603	12,084	13,148	13,316	15,312	2,116	12,426	9,169	2,193	14,996	14,484	12,570	14,166	8,612	9,537	15,060	16,726	12,754
Port Said, Egypt	1,042	11,567	8,889	11,503	229	1,210	2,758	12,392	709	4,123	10,789	8,052	3,238	353	3,228	8,939	9,752	2,992	5,403	963
Port Sudan, Sudan	1,969	10,431	10,156	12,857	1,479	2,590	3,827	11,520	1,838	4,531	10,256	9,316	4,563	1,373	4,583	10,057	11,022	4,199	6,481	2,291
Port-au-Prince, Haiti	10,735	17,922	2,677	3,845	10,069	9,348	7,522	17,254	10,456	12,482	17,253	3,119	7,360	10,560	7,536	9,073	7,552	7,332	4,881	9,938
Port-of-Spain, Trin. & Tobago	10,415	17,303	3,740	5,300	9,541	9,027	7,049	17,841	10,087	12,709	18,708	3,908	7,243	10,086	7,482	10,327	8,889	7,013	4,606	9,629
Port-Vila, Vanuatu	14,453	5,322	13,601	10,690	15,587	15,616	17,454	3,638	14,826	11,449	4,640	14,288	16,225	15,009	15,900	9,179	9,507	16,991	17,247	15,096
Portland, Maine	8,720	18,826	305	3,248	8,427	7,453	6,083	16,890	8,531	9,843	15,225	538	5,365	8,783	5,434	6,637	5,365	5,655	3,615	7,973
Portland, Oregon	10,718	14,871	3,866	1,780	11,067	9,937	9,391	12,879	10,728	9,981	11,793	4,446	8,173	11,156	8,061	4,160	2,484	8,798	7,445	10,228
Porto, Portugal	4,278	15,355	5,269	8,138	3,604	2,882	1,120	16,042	3,976	6,739	14,042	4,435	1,291	4,070	1,613	8,252	8,131	855	1,612	3,483
Porto Alegre, Brazil	12,147	12,709	8,377	9,263	10,923	11,152	9,315	14,031	11,778	15,243	16,265	8,508	10,311	11,466	10,633	14,909	13,344	9,677	8,004	11,623
Porto Alexandre, Angola	6,611	10,410	10,838	13,592	5,548	6,438	5,895	12,353	6,343	9,301	12,700	10,216	7,340	5,876	7,582	14,462	14,759	6,544	7,277	6,544
Porto Novo, Benin	5,172	12,721	8,411	11,325	3,945	4,454	3,356	14,491	4,816	8,251	13,999	7,707	4,813	4,462	5,090	12,093	12,129	3,992	4,658	4,780
Porto Velho, Brazil	11,938	15,153	5,781	6,613	10,874	10,624	8,598	15,932	11,576	14,629	18,095	6,047	9,101	11,451	9,376	12,213	10,640	8,716	6,480	11,208
Portsmouth, United Kingdom	3,663	14,899	5,402	8,044	3,351	2,349	1,588	15,132	3,440	5,713	12,986	4,571	259	3,678	452	7,194	7,282	940	2,450	2,887
Poznan, Poland	2,550	13,700	6,458	8,882	2,581	1,453	2,051	13,876	2,401	4,469	11,764	5,652	1,062	2,743	820	6,904	7,351	1,598	3,703	1,845
Prague, Czechoslovakia	2,581	13,799	6,435	8,945	2,459	1,356	1,739	14,078	2,389	4,700	12,003	5,616	872	2,685	713	7,186	7,586	1,303	3,503	1,829
Praia, Cape Verde Islands	6,796	15,576	5,676	8,459	5,705	5,551	3,576	17,468	6,427	9,712	16,693	5,109	4,529	6,282	4,855	10,994	10,341	3,884	2,655	6,106
Pretoria, South Africa	7,083	8,394	12,841	15,603	6,305	7,377	7,406	10,336	6,922	9,124	10,840	12,191	8,761	6,439	8,943	15,151	16,061	8,037	9,169	7,288
Prince Albert, Canada	9,514	16,066	2,635	2,014	9,722	8,601	7,921	14,094	9,475	9,314	12,659	3,072	6,746	9,872	6,658	4,294	2,751	7,339	5,979	8,948

Distances in Kilometers	Al Qamishli, Syria	Albany, Australia	Albany, New York	Albuquerque, New Mexico	Alexandria, Egypt	Alexandroupolis, Greece	Algiers, Algeria	Alice Springs, Australia	Allepo, Syria	Alma-Ata, USSR	Ambon, Indonesia	Amherst, Canada	Amiens, France	Amman, Jordan	Amsterdam, Netherlands	Anadyr, USSR	Anchorage, Alaska	Andorra, Andorra	Angra do Heroismo, Azores	Ankara, Turkey
Prince Edward Island	9,267	6,575	14,751	16,805	8,652	9,759	9,870	8,566	9,169	10,669	9,733	14,267	11,229	8,700	11,406	16,850	18,300	10,504	11,449	9,596
Prince George, Canada	9,811	14,941	3,759	2,441	10,215	9,085	8,695	12,968	9,835	9,075	11,582	4,177	7,407	10,273	7,270	3,455	1,799	8,080	6,978	9,347
Prince Rupert, Canada	9,851	14,451	4,250	2,816	10,342	9,218	8,971	12,483	9,904	8,887	11,087	4,646	7,638	10,356	7,479	3,066	1,387	8,343	7,377	9,439
Providence, Rhode Island	8,924	18,910	215	3,142	8,611	7,649	6,242	16,932	8,731	10,067	15,359	731	5,559	8,976	5,636	6,775	5,464	5,829	3,736	8,173
Provo, Utah	11,014	15,670	3,152	722	11,163	10,054	9,191	13,709	10,963	10,718	12,808	3,859	8,126	11,347	8,070	5,161	3,483	8,650	6,971	10,428
Puerto Aisen, Chile	14,559	11,034	9,754	9,546	13,333	13,664	11,848	11,895	14,203	17,603	14,186	10,142	12,799	13,841	13,114	15,350	13,686	12,197	10,362	14,108
Puerto Deseado, Argentina	14,127	10,828	10,044	10,032	12,909	13,325	11,593	11,849	13,781	17,102	14,140	10,370	12,641	13,397	12,963	15,877	14,203	11,989	10,310	13,732
Puerto Princesa, Philippines	8,260	4,956	14,068	13,136	9,350	9,550	11,572	4,049	8,626	5,487	1,821	13,844	11,000	8,772	10,716	7,584	9,138	11,422	13,598	8,973
Punta Arenas, Chile	14,609	10,198	10,619	10,368	13,410	13,909	12,239	11,161	14,278	17,415	13,454	10,988	13,322	13,867	13,646	16,092	14,458	12,655	11,008	14,279
Pusan, South Korea	7,602	7,850	11,089	10,328	8,830	8,517	10,290	6,528	7,964	4,517	4,298	10,943	9,235	8,306	8,910	4,596	6,195	9,897	11,483	8,075
Pyongyang, North Korea	7,133	8,239	10,749	10,197	8,361	8,013	9,770	6,994	7,491	4,066	4,738	10,554	8,711	7,847	8,386	4,371	6,014	9,373	10,974	7,583
Qamdo, China	5,135	7,640	11,780	12,260	6,309	6,347	8,350	7,220	5,510	2,235	5,069	11,275	7,757	5,738	7,481	6,462	8,128	8,172	10,379	5,792
Qandahar, Afghanistan	2,329	9,171	10,808	12,583	3,395	3,696	5,706	9,486	2,683	1,628	7,665	10,065	5,545	2,816	5,355	7,821	9,226	5,703	8,133	3,095
Qiqian, China	6,203	9,668	9,402	9,296	7,396	6,860	8,456	8,504	6,530	3,380	6,236	9,131	7,298	6,945	6,970	3,444	5,119	8,004	9,475	6,511
Qom, Iran	912	10,391	9,768	11,942	1,997	2,302	4,291	10,872	1,258	2,439	9,091	8,975	4,262	1,424	4,115	8,052	9,213	4,328	6,780	1,699
Quebec, Canada	8,548	18,495	504	3,220	8,320	7,315	6,041	16,609	8,377	9,548	14,877	552	5,236	8,650	5,282	6,290	5,048	5,580	3,666	7,817
Quetta, Pakistan	2,499	8,977	11,000	12,748	3,539	3,874	5,879	9,304	2,848	1,696	7,503	10,258	5,736	2,961	5,548	7,909	9,339	5,886	8,320	3,272
Quito, Ecuador	12,627	15,751	4,772	4,881	11,773	11,234	9,274	15,638	12,308	14,653	17,036	5,291	9,368	12,317	9,580	10,689	9,041	9,209	6,768	11,836
Rabaul, Papua New Guinea	12,149	4,911	13,801	11,298	13,307	13,313	15,226	2,919	12,524	9,143	2,664	14,211	14,208	12,730	13,881	7,926	8,773	14,872	16,189	12,787
Raiatea (Uturoa)	17,439	9,024	10,284	7,433	18,397	17,319	16,667	7,759	17,690	14,607	8,873	11,117	15,641	18,167	15,545	9,413	8,642	16,173	14,114	17,400
Raleigh, North Carolina	9,841	18,526	872	2,537	9,503	8,558	7,093	16,627	9,645	10,912	15,521	1,648	6,468	9,881	6,551	7,082	5,613	6,708	4,515	9,088
Rangiroa (Avatoru)	17,404	9,466	9,859	7,030	18,187	17,067	16,246	8,203	17,600	14,752	9,279	10,694	15,280	18,085	15,204	9,313	8,444	15,774	13,674	17,233
Rangoon, Burma	5,810	6,177	13,344	13,783	6,833	7,163	9,183	6,072	6,163	3,452	4,189	12,795	8,871	6,259	8,632	7,919	9,599	9,140	11,511	6,567
Raoul Is., Kermadec Islands	16,302	5,989	13,248	10,321	17,352	17,513	19,166	4,814	16,670	13,344	6,340	14,061	17,714	16,784	17,431	10,430	10,345	18,535	17,137	16,983
Rarotonga (Avarua)	17,337	8,018	11,264	8,381	18,548	17,763	17,619	6,772	17,679	14,272	8,004	12,092	16,454	18,059	16,307	9,728	9,178	17,075	15,116	17,612
Rawson, Argentina	13,912	11,325	9,559	9,650	12,685	13,022	11,228	12,338	13,554	16,968	14,630	9,874	12,222	13,196	12,542	15,523	13,844	11,596	9,847	13,460
Recife, Brazil	9,335	14,451	6,859	8,895	8,143	8,230	6,348	16,290	8,959	12,387	17,744	6,644	7,362	8,712	7,687	13,222	12,109	6,708	5,231	8,736
Regina, Canada	9,754	16,207	2,499	1,715	9,918	8,803	8,041	14,220	9,702	9,622	12,874	3,013	6,908	10,089	6,836	4,578	3,004	7,473	6,002	9,169
Reykjavik, Iceland	5,087	15,793	4,024	6,310	5,105	4,000	3,473	15,176	4,968	6,181	12,883	3,288	2,139	5,313	2,026	5,617	5,439	2,836	2,858	4,415
Rhodes, Greece	1,164	12,186	8,222	10,817	601	531	2,245	12,891	804	4,179	11,151	7,388	2,563	867	2,543	8,472	9,180	2,383	4,830	563
Richmond, Virginia	9,627	18,622	649	2,626	9,303	8,349	6,909	16,673	9,433	10,692	15,446	1,434	6,260	9,675	6,338	6,957	5,519	6,513	4,352	8,876
Riga, USSR	2,553	13,405	6,594	8,809	2,896	1,795	2,733	13,378	2,505	3,957	11,206	5,825	1,638	2,924	1,334	6,319	6,890	2,268	4,217	1,996
Ringkobing, Denmark	3,245	14,336	5,769	8,189	3,240	2,124	2,181	14,354	3,100	4,935	12,165	4,970	795	3,434	469	6,572	6,857	1,586	3,249	2,543
Rio Branco, Brazil	12,363	14,989	5,858	6,448	11,311	11,037	9,010	15,605	12,003	14,993	17,692	6,190	9,465	11,887	9,732	12,161	10,550	9,108	6,831	11,625
Rio Cuarto, Argentina	13,402	12,455	8,446	8,746	12,185	12,341	10,433	13,427	13,029	16,487	15,720	8,745	11,296	12,736	11,606	14,611	12,945	10,733	8,826	12,840
Rio de Janeiro, Brazil	11,046	13,292	7,905	9,268	9,826	10,031	8,200	14,840	10,674	14,138	16,919	7,901	9,230	10,376	9,555	14,506	13,101	8,575	7,015	10,507
Rio Gallegos, Argentina	14,465	10,379	10,456	10,278	13,259	13,735	12,047	11,361	14,129	17,329	13,654	10,811	13,121	13,726	13,445	16,047	14,397	12,457	10,803	14,116
Rio Grande, Brazil	12,335	12,507	8,561	9,365	11,109	11,360	9,536	13,805	11,967	15,431	16,048	8,710	10,541	11,646	10,864	15,064	13,478	9,903	8,238	11,824
Riyadh, Saudi Arabia	1,471	9,989	10,388	12,828	1,806	2,643	4,353	10,813	1,575	3,443	9,328	9,561	4,732	1,332	4,666	9,234	10,372	4,574	6,998	2,135
Road Town, Brit. Virgin Isls.	10,127	18,151	2,819	4,527	9,384	8,732	6,841	18,025	9,828	12,131	17,872	3,037	6,813	9,895	7,018	9,402	7,974	6,704	4,246	9,330
Roanoke, Virginia	9,801	18,406	797	2,407	9,500	8,535	7,118	16,471	9,614	10,787	15,320	1,616	6,446	9,864	6,517	6,880	5,410	6,715	4,570	9,055
Robinson Crusoe Island, Chile	14,656	12,207	8,463	8,140	13,459	13,502	11,524	12,779	14,281	17,667	14,995	8,924	12,208	14,022	12,496	13,970	12,297	11,744	9,616	14,037
Rochester, New York	9,193	18,407	320	2,651	8,961	7,961	6,656	16,417	9,023	10,105	14,953	1,106	5,880	9,296	5,929	6,403	5,024	6,210	4,211	8,463
Rockhampton, Australia	13,202	3,405	15,435	12,593	14,153	14,551	16,576	1,696	13,550	10,520	3,239	16,029	15,979	13,597	15,672	10,044	10,780	16,460	18,298	13,958
Rome, Italy	2,520	13,672	6,775	9,473	1,954	1,125	991	14,296	2,220	5,159	12,399	5,936	1,188	2,352	1,294	8,108	8,463	908	3,366	1,727
Rosario, Argentina	13,087	12,477	8,477	8,930	11,866	12,052	10,167	13,549	12,715	16,179	15,841	8,732	11,075	12,413	11,389	14,765	13,115	10,488	8,649	12,541
Roseau, Dominica	10,083	17,817	3,254	5,005	9,268	8,688	6,744	18,175	9,767	12,263	18,360	3,396	6,843	9,798	7,070	9,853	8,448	6,663	4,225	9,290
Rostock, East Germany	2,922	14,057	6,086	8,522	2,911	1,792	2,046	14,167	2,769	4,745	12,017	5,281	819	3,101	519	6,766	7,121	1,506	3,418	2,211
Rostov-na-Donu, USSR	1,140	11,980	8,098	10,291	1,967	1,313	3,215	12,211	1,243	2,930	10,198	7,317	2,747	1,727	2,542	7,060	7,950	3,032	5,374	980
Rotterdam, Netherlands	3,308	14,524	5,718	8,285	3,096	2,040	1,686	14,722	3,106	5,304	12,583	4,895	273	3,377	56	7,053	7,256	1,071	2,859	2,548
Rouyn, Canada	8,868	17,989	744	2,703	8,734	7,693	6,538	16,043	8,725	9,601	14,435	1,155	5,639	9,029	5,654	5,861	4,533	6,046	4,241	8,166
Sacramento, California	11,447	14,804	4,011	1,378	11,732	10,606	9,913	12,846	11,440	10,753	12,031	4,696	8,767	11,855	8,680	4,846	3,188	9,345	7,789	10,928
Saginaw, Michigan	9,519	17,927	833	2,159	9,357	8,330	7,107	15,934	9,371	10,217	14,593	1,584	6,265	9,666	6,291	6,118	4,665	6,639	4,706	8,811
Saint Denis, Reunion	6,580	6,242	14,736	17,663	6,375	7,487	8,424	7,981	6,603	7,433	8,077	13,929	9,422	6,204	9,470	13,585	15,112	8,933	10,826	7,128
Saint George's, Grenada	10,338	17,459	3,585	5,185	9,484	8,947	6,979	17,927	10,014	12,591	18,592	3,752	7,141	10,024	7,375	10,174	8,742	6,928	4,509	9,550
Saint John, Canada	8,347	18,822	683	3,595	8,047	7,075	5,709	17,018	8,155	9,540	15,198	158	4,987	8,404	5,059	6,628	5,440	5,276	3,269	7,597
Saint John's, Antigua	9,995	18,017	3,050	4,854	9,208	8,599	6,674	10,233	9,686	12,117	18,173	3,194	6,726	9,731	6,945	9,650	8,251	6,571	4,123	9,201
Saint John's, Canada	7,353	18,413	1,737	4,622	7,003	6,052	4,655	17,293	7,144	8,801	15,144	898	3,964	7,374	4,059	6,816	5,876	4,223	2,286	6,589
Saint Louis, Missouri	10,266	17,499	1,458	1,517	10,104	9,080	7,827	15,559	10,120	10,846	14,538	2,278	7,013	10,416	7,041	6,306	4,741	7,374	5,368	9,560
Saint Paul, Minnesota	9,836	17,177	1,573	1,589	9,798	8,729	7,665	15,185	9,724	10,185	13,930	2,253	6,710	10,058	6,698	5,583	4,049	7,158	5,368	9,170
Saint Peter Port, UK	3,750	14,991	5,356	8,040	3,379	2,411	1,478	15,281	3,513	5,868	13,150	4,521	352	3,729	615	7,341	7,394	834	2,298	2,966
Saipan (Susupe)	10,247	6,285	12,446	10,591	11,465	11,258	13,058	4,486	10,619	7,157	2,843	12,615	11,961	10,911	11,634	6,011	7,179	12,651	14,004	10,787
Salalah, Oman	2,555	8,856	11,527	13,895	2,909	3,784	5,450	9,766	2,706	3,623	8,453	10,702	5,874	2,469	5,802	9,765	11,076	5,703	8,109	3,266
Salem, Oregon	10,790	14,828	3,913	1,770	11,141	10,011	9,463	12,838	10,801	10,037	11,774	4,501	8,246	11,229	8,135	4,193	2,519	8,870	7,508	10,301
Salt Lake City, Utah	10,967	15,659	3,154	779	11,125	10,014	9,166	13,694	10,919	10,659	12,772	3,852	8,092	11,304	8,033	5,102	3,424	8,621	6,960	10,385
Salta, Argentina	13,051	13,375	7,515	7,925	11,873	11,871	9,892	14,254	12,676	16,034	16,530	7,821	10,620	12,444	10,918	13,749	12,102	10,124	8,072	12,412
Salto, Uruguay	12,780	12,640	8,355	8,948	11,560	11,744	9,864	13,781	12,408	15,871	16,066	8,574	10,786	12,108	11,102	14,738	13,109	10,191	8,383	12,232
Salvador, Brazil	9,984	14,141	7,134	8,926	8,783	8,898	7,022	15,864	9,609	13,049	17,658	7,006	8,025	9,348	8,350	13,635	12,403	7,379	5,835	9,398
Salzburg, Austria	2,591	13,831	6,470	9,047	2,335	1,280	1,472	14,210	2,363	4,875	12,176	5,642	821	2,615	770	7,452	7,822	1,079	3,381	1,811
Samsun, Turkey	634	11,855	8,372	10,745	1,259	881	2,907	12,317	569	3,325	10,439	7,561	2,794	1,036	2,666	7,772	8,629	2,872	5,313	329
San Antonio, Texas	11,539	16,562	2,653	992	11,365	10,351	9,038	14,815	11,394	11,944	14,346	3,493	8,279	11,688	8,313	6,808	5,143	8,611	6,499	10,835
San Cristobal, Venezuela	11,523	16,816	3,868	4,634	10,710	10,127	8,189	16,729	11,211	13,559	17,730	4,289	8,245	11,243	8,456	10,168	8,593	8,099	5,652	10,729
San Diego, California	11,965	14,993	3,937	1,006	12,132	11,022	10,127	13,107	11,924	11,472	12,536	4,702	9,090	12,312	9,037	5,606	3,948	9,599	7,827	11,392
San Francisco, California	11,554	14,702	4,120	1,443	11,848	10,722	10,034	12,749	11,550	10,822	11,966	4,811	8,887	11,967	8,799	4,877	3,230	9,466	7,907	11,039
San Jose, Costa Rica	12,305	16,451	3,762	3,607	11,653	10,924	9,105	15,725	12,034	13,811	16,405	4,407	8,913	12,144	9,074	9,411	7,759	8,913	6,465	11,510
San Juan, Argentina	13,674	12,606	8,232	8,384	12,469	12,559	10,612	13,447	13,300	16,728	15,725	8,579	11,398	13,029	11,700	14,261	12,587	10,876	8,870	13,079
San Juan, Puerto Rico	10,247	18,128	2,777	4,393	9,519	8,853	6,973	17,876	9,952	12,204	17,763	3,040	6,919	10,026	7,119	9,340	7,892	6,826	4,368	9,450
San Luis Potosi, Mexico	12,355	15,996	3,397	1,536	12,124	11,139	9,732	14,437	12,198	12,760	14,352	4,235	9,055	12,473	9,106	7,400	5,721	9,342	7,133	11,637
San Marino, San Marino	2,542	13,746	6,654	9,316	2,081	1,153	1,124	14,288	2,264	5,070	12,340	5,818	1,019	2,440	1,092	7,886	8,242	903	3,343	1,744
San Miguel de Tucuman, Argen.	13,146	13,151	7,741	8,121	11,956	11,992	10,027	14,053	12,771	16,162	16,336	8,046	10,788	12,524	11,089	13,958	12,306	10,276	8,257	12,524
San Salvador, El Salvador	12,373	16,419	3,536	2,946	11,842	11,024	9,310	15,374	12,133	13,544	15,781	4,267	8,963	12,296	9,091	8,795	7,130	9,053	6,646	11,591
Sanaa, Yemen	2,420	9,556	11,003	13,637	2,280	3,336	4,701	10,658	2,413	4,385	9,484	10,163	5,373	2,021	5,366	10,292	11,425	5,055	7,357	2,939
Santa Cruz, Bolivia	12,444	14,156	6,780	7,440	11,302	11,206	9,202	15,058	12,071	15,334	17,324	7,047	9,859	11,879	10,151	13,157	11,551	9,396	7,287	11,766
Santa Cruz, Tenerife	5,389	15,657	5,340	8,292	4,438	4,053	2,027	17,003	5,038	8,144	15,371	4,594	2,853	4,990	3,178	9,604	9,227	2,233	1,521	4,640
Santa Fe, New Mexico	11,273	16,075	2,868	92	11,289	10,210	9,149	14,175	11,183	11,259	13,446	3,654	8,205	11,532	8,186	5,857	4,183	8,652	6,774	10,633
Santa Rosa, Argentina	13,563	12,069	8,831	9,070	12,339	12,558	10,686	13,063	13,195	16,660	15,357	9,132	11,599	12,878	11,913	14,946	13,273	11,012	9,162	13,038
Santa Rosalia, Mexico	12,365	15,219	3,864	1,014	12,393	11,315	10,217	13,444	12,283	12,135	13,111	4,681	9,306	12,637	9,291	6,358	4,692	9,736	7,770	11,735
Santarem, Brazil	10,703	15,786	5,348	6,816	9,640	9,395	7,371	16,970	10,340	13,446	19,258	5,428	7,937	10,216	8,224	11,949	10,521	7,511	5,352	9,977
Santiago del Estero, Argentina	13,117	13,048	7,859	8,263	11,920	11,982	10,029	13,987	12,742	16,153	16,275	8,152	10,817	12,485	11,121	14,097	12,446	10,291	8,303	12,507
Santiago, Chile	13,948	12,372	8,433	8,464	12,738	12,845	10,903	13,169	13,574	17,012	15,442	8,805	11,690	13,295	11,992	14,343	12,664	11,169	9,158	13,361
Santo Domingo, Dominican Rep.	10,549	18,018	2,706	4,060	9,858	9,159	7,310	17,497	10,263	12,382	17,465	3,080	7,190	10,355	7,376	9,183	7,689	7,137	4,681	9,752
Sao Paulo de Olivenca, Brazil	12,018	15,689	5,130	5,814	11,041	10,654	8,639	16,135	11,671	14,459	17,983	5,478	8,964	11,607	9,215	11,458	9,864	8,675	6,321	11,253
Sao Paulo, Brazil	11,368	13,321	7,840	9,063	10,152	10,328	8,469	14,779	10,995	14,455	16,939	7,885	9,457	10,706	9,779	14,440	12,979	8,824	7,175	10,814
Sao Tome, Sao Tome & Principe	5,394	11,950	9,208	12,103	4,200	4,886	4,054	13,772	5,064	8,393	13,517	8,516	5,509	4,655	5,768	12,745	12,894	4,700	5,477	5,124
Sapporo, Japan	8,028	8,970	9,888	8,951	9,229	8,691	10,212	7,430	8,361	5,102	5,346	9,841	8,966	8,768	8,638	3,302	4,847	9,717	10,884	8,350
Sarajevo, Yugoslavia	2,070	13,293	7,059	9,655	1,727	697	1,519	13,810	1,805	4,629	11,878	6,228	1,398	2,021	1,377	7,828	8,311	1,380	3,819	1,273
Saratov, USSR	1,659	11,867	8,065	10,043	2,621	1,949	3,740	11,893	1,847	2,487	9,790	7,323	3,047	2,330	2,790	6,449	7,420	3,471	5,687	1,644
Saskatoon, Canada	9,648	16,034	2,667	1,893	9,854	8,733	8,041	14,054	9,609	9,432	12,663	3,136	6,873	10,006	6,788	4,345	2,777	7,461	6,074	9,082
Schefferville, Canada	7,753	17,778	1,442	3,753	7,641	6,587	5,529	16,152	7,612	8,612	14,181	1,015	4,548	7,921	4,549	5,665	4,623	5,002	3,454	7,053
Seattle, Washington	10,490	14,924	3,798	1,904	10,848	9,718	9,204	12,931	10,502	9,764	11,768	4,343	7,970	10,932	7,853	3,995	2,315	8,605	7,306	10,004

Distances in Kilometers	Al Qamishli, Syria	Albany, Australia	Albany, New York	Albuquerque, New Mexico	Alexandria, Egypt	Alexandroupolis, Greece	Algiers, Algeria	Alice Springs, Australia	Allepo, Syria	Alma-Ata, USSR	Ambon, Indonesia	Amherst, Canada	Amiens, France	Amman, Jordan	Amsterdam, Netherlands	Anadyr, USSR	Anchorage, Alaska	Andorra, Andorra	Angra do Heroismo, Azores	Ankara, Turkey
Sendai, Japan	8,300	8,454	10,388	9,325	9,517	9,046	10,641	6,896	8,645	5,296	4,827	10,361	9,431	9,031	9,103	3,788	5,285	10,167	11,403	8,673
Seoul, South Korea	7,306	8,093	10,877	10,247	8,534	8,200	9,963	6,820	7,666	4,231	4,572	10,700	8,905	8,016	8,581	4,451	6,080	9,567	11,164	7,765
Sept-Iles, Canada	8,033	18,285	1,012	3,646	7,828	6,811	5,596	16,584	7,866	9,058	14,674	512	4,738	8,147	4,775	6,128	5,010	5,112	3,326	7,306
Sevastopol, USSR	1,061	12,240	7,953	10,312	1,521	753	2,700	12,618	982	3,449	10,669	7,147	2,418	1,420	2,266	7,482	8,270	2,581	4,988	521
Seville, Spain	4,147	15,045	5,660	8,558	3,353	2,766	806	15,923	3,820	6,782	14,054	4,833	1,541	3,857	1,868	8,678	8,598	856	1,866	3,367
Shanghai, China	7,203	7,331	11,692	11,128	8,422	8,245	10,129	6,211	7,575	4,113	3,923	11,465	9,215	7,872	8,899	5,329	6,962	9,806	11,626	7,754
Sheffield, United Kingdom	3,741	14,941	5,281	7,860	3,521	2,476	1,877	15,047	3,542	5,625	12,861	4,459	467	3,812	447	6,905	6,996	1,229	2,553	2,984
Shenyang, China	6,820	8,527	10,494	10,083	8,045	7,671	9,411	7,331	7,174	3,775	5,063	10,268	8,345	7,540	8,021	4,219	5,884	9,010	10,615	7,250
Shiraz, Iran	1,335	9,906	10,309	12,521	2,179	2,715	4,631	10,504	1,611	2,646	8,839	9,506	4,745	1,609	4,620	8,519	9,736	4,738	7,196	2,127
Sibiu, Romania	1,723	12,958	7,300	9,781	1,695	567	2,022	13,366	1,525	4,130	11,394	6,481	1,691	1,842	1,576	7,530	8,129	1,841	4,240	964
Singapore	7,520	4,278	15,133	14,889	8,415	8,908	10,889	4,266	7,849	5,362	2,765	14,655	10,726	7,862	10,503	9,105	10,745	10,924	13,347	8,305
Sioux Falls, South Dakota	10,127	16,915	1,867	1,268	10,113	9,038	7,993	14,930	10,023	10,371	13,778	2,574	7,028	10,364	7,011	5,551	3,970	7,484	5,693	9,471
Skelleftea, Sweden	3,364	13,787	6,027	8,039	3,783	2,680	3,332	13,448	3,357	4,180	11,190	5,312	1,984	3,792	1,658	5,510	6,008	2,765	4,244	2,869
Skopje, Yugoslavia	1,781	12,983	7,381	9,973	1,414	388	1,686	13,551	1,499	4,467	11,667	6,549	1,720	1,699	1,696	7,985	8,536	1,645	4,100	985
Socotra Island (Tamrida)	2,987	8,546	11,906	14,345	3,215	4,158	5,724	9,568	3,107	4,044	8,397	11,074	6,244	2,826	6,191	10,218	11,549	6,021	8,388	3,667
Sofia, Bulgaria	1,652	12,877	7,456	10,010	1,402	294	1,851	13,406	1,390	4,299	11,507	6,627	1,799	1,630	1,745	7,882	8,471	1,785	4,233	855
Songkhla, Thailand	6,827	5,015	14,455	14,527	7,767	8,207	10,205	4,978	7,165	4,615	3,296	13,940	9,992	7,205	9,764	8,663	10,331	10,213	12,621	7,605
Sorong, Indonesia	10,073	4,027	14,754	12,947	11,145	11,367	13,387	2,540	10,438	7,279	462	14,802	12,753	10,569	12,457	8,181	9,496	13,219	15,287	10,791
South Georgia Island	12,550	9,818	11,301	11,940	11,413	12,107	10,784	11,322	12,254	15,181	13,431	11,391	12,107	11,807	12,430	17,787	16,137	11,323	10,334	12,363
South Pole	14,104	6,123	14,727	13,886	13,457	14,528	14,077	7,379	14,012	14,793	9,590	15,081	15,534	13,540	15,807	17,184	16,791	14,711	14,284	14,426
South Sandwich Islands	12,247	9,198	11,962	12,688	11,171	11,964	10,835	10,796	11,980	14,667	12,825	11,999	12,222	11,514	12,536	18,518	16,883	11,413	10,684	12,152
Split, Yugoslavia	2,219	13,430	6,947	9,572	1,810	833	1,361	13,970	1,944	4,791	12,042	6,113	1,290	2,136	1,303	7,888	8,329	1,220	3,665	1,421
Spokane, Washington	10,386	15,294	3,430	1,659	10,681	9,553	8,946	13,301	10,378	9,834	12,125	3,990	7,749	10,794	7,648	4,222	2,549	8,359	6,981	9,867
Spoleto, Italy	2,506	13,683	6,742	9,423	1,987	1,110	1,059	14,272	2,215	5,102	12,355	5,905	1,130	2,367	1,219	8,014	8,375	920	3,375	1,710
Springbok, South Africa	7,775	8,998	12,299	14,838	6,855	7,851	7,517	10,985	7,565	10,074	11,755	11,745	8,947	7,081	9,173	15,854	16,384	8,165	8,895	7,860
Springfield, Illinois	10,132	17,541	1,367	1,590	9,981	8,952	7,719	15,583	9,989	10,709	14,499	2,176	6,889	10,288	6,913	6,218	4,667	7,258	5,279	9,429
Springfield, Massachusetts	8,976	18,815	114	3,046	8,678	7,709	6,322	16,833	8,788	10,075	15,282	790	5,620	9,038	5,691	6,702	5,378	5,902	3,827	8,229
Srinagar, India	3,047	8,869	10,928	12,346	4,193	4,338	6,364	8,939	3,418	1,034	6,981	10,246	6,009	3,619	5,780	7,197	8,696	6,281	8,646	3,755
Stanley, Falkland Islands	13,709	10,387	10,566	10,726	12,514	13,047	11,450	11,574	13,381	16,544	13,837	10,825	12,612	12,967	12,939	16,590	14,912	11,903	10,444	13,397
Stara Zagora, Bulgaria	1,462	12,692	7,624	10,151	1,301	175	2,031	13,214	1,209	4,129	11,321	6,798	1,974	1,476	1,904	7,872	8,509	1,977	4,425	666
Stockholm, Sweden	2,986	13,817	6,154	8,374	3,251	2,127	2,731	13,703	2,920	4,307	11,494	5,390	1,455	3,323	1,128	6,133	6,594	2,191	3,917	2,396
Stornoway, United Kingdom	4,156	15,217	4,855	7,323	4,065	2,980	2,481	15,054	3,997	5,706	12,801	4,057	1,084	4,309	968	6,362	6,388	1,833	2,643	3,438
Strasbourg, France	2,993	14,233	6,083	8,698	2,685	1,667	1,366	14,586	2,761	5,215	12,518	5,253	423	2,997	465	7,406	7,668	833	2,999	2,210
Stuttgart, West Germany	2,895	14,135	6,168	8,764	2,616	1,581	1,422	14,478	2,668	5,109	12,413	5,339	516	2,914	500	7,376	7,668	917	3,106	2,116
Subic, Philippines	8,064	5,530	13,477	12,598	9,201	9,303	11,306	4,519	8,436	5,170	2,237	13,266	10,629	8,624	10,334	6,996	8,562	11,104	13,184	8,743
Suchow, China	6,692	7,672	11,415	11,082	7,914	7,721	9,605	6,654	7,063	3,599	4,360	11,133	8,702	7,369	8,389	5,219	6,883	9,285	11,140	7,234
Sucre, Bolivia	12,705	14,012	6,885	7,414	11,564	11,465	9,459	14,844	12,333	15,587	17,095	7,184	10,102	12,141	10,391	13,185	11,558	9,648	7,519	12,026
Sudbury, Canada	9,111	17,985	716	2,492	8,967	7,931	6,751	16,008	8,966	9,828	14,495	1,297	5,873	9,267	5,892	5,947	4,569	6,268	4,413	8,406
Suez, Egypt	1,124	11,469	9,006	11,637	289	1,350	2,835	12,330	814	4,180	10,765	8,168	3,363	391	3,360	9,073	9,896	3,093	5,489	1,106
Sundsvall, Sweden	3,263	13,920	5,972	8,104	3,583	2,463	3,012	13,678	3,220	4,342	11,437	5,230	1,665	3,636	1,338	5,807	6,252	2,444	3,983	2,708
Surabaya, Indonesia	8,883	3,121	16,031	14,956	9,753	10,273	12,247	2,900	9,209	6,659	1,756	15,719	12,083	9,208	11,853	9,572	11,103	12,291	14,711	9,670
Suva, Fiji	15,358	6,218	12,801	9,852	16,544	16,383	17,890	4,656	15,733	12,288	5,694	13,549	16,464	15,970	16,166	9,190	9,238	17,287	16,652	15,927
Sverdlovsk, USSR	2,631	11,516	8,183	9,747	3,704	3,057	4,745	11,224	2,885	1,903	9,017	7,526	3,833	3,354	3,532	5,505	6,644	4,393	6,396	2,750
Svobodnyy, USSR	6,706	9,627	9,372	9,040	7,893	7,330	8,872	8,338	7,030	3,890	6,108	9,166	7,668	7,450	7,339	3,160	4,839	8,398	9,745	6,998
Sydney, Australia	13,805	3,050	16,020	13,070	14,580	15,198	17,126	2,028	14,120	11,388	4,104	16,747	16,917	14,071	16,639	11,173	11,804	17,218	19,458	14,596
Sydney, Canada	7,920	18,760	1,147	4,056	7,591	6,632	5,242	17,216	7,719	9,239	15,234	313	4,543	7,957	4,627	6,736	5,652	4,813	2,816	7,162
Syktyvkar, USSR	2,820	12,288	7,419	9,089	3,711	2,859	4,289	11,942	2,989	2,676	9,706	6,754	3,218	3,474	2,902	5,306	6,262	3,859	5,707	2,707
Szeged, Hungary	2,023	13,263	7,019	9,544	1,871	757	1,769	13,676	1,805	4,412	11,690	6,196	1,387	2,086	1,295	7,538	8,055	1,540	3,927	1,248
Szombathely, Hungary	2,315	13,555	6,734	9,282	2,111	1,025	1,611	13,945	2,093	4,639	11,932	5,908	1,096	2,361	1,015	7,477	7,920	1,301	3,651	1,538
Tabriz, Iran	463	10,952	9,213	11,439	1,683	1,781	3,796	11,397	838	2,639	9,558	8,417	3,703	1,164	3,553	7,840	8,900	3,795	6,239	1,180
Tacheng, China	3,579	9,709	9,839	10,891	4,807	4,534	6,447	9,330	3,938	612	7,134	9,258	5,692	4,297	5,402	5,636	7,134	6,181	8,284	4,061
Tahiti (Papeete)	17,603	9,138	10,203	7,380	18,490	17,384	16,591	7,916	17,835	14,812	9,070	11,039	15,628	18,317	15,548	9,545	8,729	16,124	14,005	17,511
Taipei, Taiwan	7,557	6,661	12,348	11,646	8,756	8,678	10,615	5,557	7,932	4,510	3,264	12,134	9,777	8,192	9,467	5,920	7,525	10,332	12,241	8,159
Taiyuan, China	6,146	8,090	11,065	10,977	7,371	7,151	9,027	7,171	6,514	3,050	4,879	10,728	8,131	6,834	7,819	5,098	6,777	8,709	10,589	6,670
Tallahasee, Florida	10,633	17,893	1,647	2,153	10,280	9,346	7,844	16,189	10,435	11,624	15,505	2,440	7,257	10,666	7,342	7,362	5,793	7,479	5,232	9,878
Tallinn, USSR	2,756	13,451	6,483	8,620	3,160	2,067	2,961	13,324	2,733	3,926	11,121	5,732	1,781	3,165	1,461	6,043	6,617	2,465	4,292	2,241
Tamanrasset, Algeria	3,765	13,414	7,478	10,422	2,587	2,766	1,570	14,777	3,389	6,835	13,519	6,678	3,022	3,163	3,282	10,276	10,436	2,218	3,567	3,201
Tampa, Florida	10,723	17,945	1,810	2,423	10,311	9,410	7,839	16,371	10,509	11,846	15,809	2,553	7,326	10,719	7,429	7,689	6,122	7,504	5,200	9,956
Tampere, Finland	2,982	13,568	6,319	8,406	3,398	2,302	3,105	13,359	2,967	3,999	11,132	5,581	1,851	3,402	1,524	5,831	6,382	2,580	4,280	2,478
Tanami, Australia	11,194	2,033	16,675	14,291	12,043	12,583	14,554	596	11,519	8,836	1,807	16,870	14,342	11,507	14,090	10,238	11,432	14,596	16,985	11,980
Tangier, Morocco	4,177	14,983	5,759	8,671	3,338	2,809	802	15,936	3,842	6,868	14,119	4,938	1,698	3,856	2,024	8,854	8,771	976	1,922	3,406
Tarawa (Betio)	13,479	6,992	11,791	9,055	14,707	14,274	15,657	5,052	13,838	10,394	5,009	12,371	14,256	14,184	13,948	7,044	7,345	15,073	15,123	13,904
Tashkent, USSR	2,460	9,805	9,994	11,533	3,679	3,611	5,616	9,802	2,833	666	7,763	9,307	5,133	3,138	4,889	6,710	8,099	5,468	7,777	3,064
Tbilisi, USSR	600	11,301	8,822	11,018	1,765	1,582	3,606	11,655	897	2,637	9,741	8,033	3,374	1,336	3,202	7,508	8,520	3,538	5,955	1,021
Tegucigalpa, Honduras	12,199	16,598	3,418	3,033	11,647	10,842	9,110	15,590	11,953	13,454	15,980	4,128	8,789	12,107	8,923	8,848	7,192	8,863	6,448	11,413
Tehran, Iran	928	10,428	9,708	11,850	2,058	2,301	4,305	10,872	1,288	2,341	9,063	8,919	4,231	1,491	4,075	7,930	9,093	4,322	6,768	1,699
Tel Aviv, Israel	809	11,419	8,993	11,554	472	1,258	2,948	12,191	509	3,877	10,556	8,160	3,332	111	3,297	8,794	9,657	3,143	5,575	889
Telegraph Creek, Canada	9,460	14,434	4,273	3,121	9,974	8,854	8,680	12,495	9,520	8,495	10,984	4,594	7,322	9,975	7,151	2,768	1,117	8,045	7,202	9,061
Teresina, Brazil	9,824	15,130	6,140	8,006	8,678	8,617	6,644	16,801	9,450	12,782	18,627	6,025	7,476	9,256	7,790	12,660	11,410	6,911	5,102	9,162
Ternate, Indonesia	9,619	4,089	14,750	13,154	10,683	10,923	12,946	2,800	9,982	6,860	507	14,715	12,360	10,106	12,070	8,148	9,538	12,798	14,930	10,343
The Valley, Anguilla	10,029	18,120	2,909	4,689	9,266	8,633	6,726	18,161	9,725	12,090	18,011	3,083	6,735	9,782	6,947	9,505	8,095	6,604	4,150	9,233
Thessaloniki, Greece	1,635	12,810	7,570	10,167	1,220	249	1,777	13,416	1,335	4,410	11,568	6,737	1,909	1,511	1,890	8,112	8,696	1,794	4,252	848
Thimphu, Bhutan	4,636	7,533	12,052	12,865	5,752	5,935	7,961	7,392	5,004	2,089	5,386	11,465	7,544	5,173	7,295	7,168	8,813	7,862	10,187	5,352
Thunder Bay, Canada	9,356	17,333	1,370	2,056	9,325	8,252	7,224	15,349	9,244	9,763	13,910	1,919	6,240	9,580	6,224	5,428	3,978	6,705	4,993	8,690
Tientsin, China	6,462	8,212	10,880	10,637	7,690	7,410	9,239	7,169	6,826	3,375	4,877	10,593	8,272	7,164	7,954	4,759	6,434	8,886	10,661	6,952
Tijuana, Mexico	11,980	14,998	3,935	1,000	12,143	11,034	10,133	13,116	11,938	11,494	12,552	4,702	9,099	12,325	9,048	5,630	3,971	9,606	7,827	11,405
Tiksi, USSR	6,062	11,857	7,208	7,411	7,049	6,182	7,261	10,577	6,288	4,192	8,359	6,939	5,889	6,768	5,571	2,089	3,492	6,691	7,631	6,049
Timbuktu, Mali	4,879	13,862	7,200	10,143	3,692	3,848	2,297	15,481	4,504	7,948	14,516	6,466	3,706	4,265	4,009	10,966	10,875	2,885	3,381	4,308
Tindouf, Algeria	4,708	14,890	6,047	9,001	3,694	3,427	1,457	16,209	4,347	7,584	14,693	5,270	2,620	4,258	2,945	9,744	9,564	1,861	2,146	3,992
Tirane, Albania	1,904	13,079	7,315	9,940	1,441	510	1,535	13,683	1,607	4,622	11,814	6,480	1,660	1,772	1,665	8,083	8,599	1,522	3,980	1,112
Tokyo, Japan	8,382	8,154	10,687	9,585	9,605	9,181	10,823	6,604	8,733	5,342	4,527	10,661	9,643	9,106	9,315	4,086	5,570	10,366	11,665	8,787
Toledo, Spain	3,921	14,945	5,682	8,542	3,201	2,529	706	15,702	3,607	6,488	13,775	4,847	1,221	3,679	1,547	8,405	8,383	549	2,001	3,131
Topeka, Kansas	10,498	17,024	1,885	1,070	10,412	9,361	8,199	15,081	10,375	10,860	14,113	2,677	7,318	10,695	7,324	6,018	4,410	7,722	5,792	9,818
Toronto, Canada	9,253	18,254	471	2,521	9,047	8,036	6,764	16,263	9,091	10,094	14,819	1,224	5,960	9,372	6,000	6,282	4,888	6,308	4,342	8,530
Toulouse, France	3,426	14,593	5,897	8,665	2,851	2,033	769	15,173	3,138	5,889	13,185	5,056	703	3,273	1,007	7,987	8,101	122	2,455	2,629
Tours, France	3,495	14,728	5,663	8,366	3,066	2,131	1,193	15,129	3,240	5,753	13,054	4,826	304	3,435	630	7,568	7,679	547	2,456	2,703
Townsville, Australia	12,634	3,339	15,423	12,696	13,617	13,972	15,998	1,426	12,987	9,925	2,654	15,920	15,384	13,054	15,079	9,676	10,529	15,865	17,780	13,383
Trenton, New Jersey	9,252	18,766	282	2,855	8,944	7,981	6,571	16,774	9,062	10,334	15,355	1,062	5,891	9,308	5,965	6,802	5,426	6,161	4,048	8,503
Tripoli, Lebanon	566	11,479	8,878	11,382	662	1,132	2,969	12,166	230	3,660	10,461	8,050	3,221	276	3,159	8,514	9,390	3,104	5,555	665
Tripoli, Libya	2,593	13,237	7,396	10,218	1,588	1,432	1,021	14,197	2,226	5,575	12,566	6,558	2,091	2,138	2,261	9,093	9,461	1,478	3,678	1,925
Tristan da Cunha (Edinburgh)	9,882	10,514	10,800	12,590	8,740	9,464	8,327	12,409	9,582	12,650	13,927	10,548	9,739	9,138	10,045	16,856	16,032	8,920	8,521	9,694
Trondheim, Norway	3,594	14,279	5,604	7,767	3,837	2,708	3,004	13,983	3,531	4,689	11,724	4,862	1,582	3,930	1,274	5,746	6,081	2,398	3,715	3,004
Trujillo, Peru	13,229	14,912	5,647	5,594	12,278	11,851	9,850	15,001	12,889	15,469	16,738	6,156	10,078	12,842	10,309	11,456	9,790	9,849	7,447	12,453
Truk Island (Moen)	11,310	5,902	12,800	10,575	12,520	12,342	14,137	3,961	11,683	8,227	2,904	13,107	13,007	11,959	12,679	6,674	7,626	13,716	14,902	11,866
Truro, Canada	8,166	18,853	893	3,814	7,846	6,884	5,495	17,151	7,968	9,431	15,258	89	4,794	8,210	4,874	6,713	5,570	5,069	3,051	7,411
Tsingtao, China	6,857	7,875	11,172	10,752	8,084	7,832	9,673	6,767	7,224	3,762	4,480	10,923	8,709	7,550	8,391	4,901	6,559	9,324	11,087	7,365
Tsitsihar, China	6,602	9,147	9,882	9,578	7,814	7,342	8,994	7,933	6,942	3,658	5,674	9,648	7,863	7,338	7,535	3,698	5,375	8,558	10,058	6,963
Tubuai Island (Mataura)	18,183	8,787	10,646	7,891	19,134	18,018	17,001	7,719	18,449	15,248	9,071	11,486	16,180	18,921	16,126	10,175	9,375	16,603	14,353	18,155
Tucson, Arizona	11,815	15,528	3,458	511	11,872	10,785	9,752	13,670	11,739	11,609	13,115	4,253	8,794	12,100	8,768	5,947	4,270	9,252	7,368	11,194
Tulsa, Oklahoma	10,779	16,977	2,032	980	10,657	9,620	8,400	15,081	10,646	11,181	14,252	2,853	7,563	10,955	7,581	6,281	4,655	7,940	5,941	10,088

Distances in Kilometers	Al Qamishli, Syria	Albany, Australia	Albany, New York	Albuquerque, New Mexico	Alexandria, Egypt	Alexandroupolis, Greece	Algiers, Algeria	Alice Springs, Australia	Allepo, Syria	Alma-Ata, USSR	Ambon, Indonesia	Amherst, Canada	Amiens, France	Amman, Jordan	Amsterdam, Netherlands	Anadyr, USSR	Anchorage, Alaska	Andorra, Andorra	Angra do Heroismo, Azores	Ankara, Turkey
Tunis, Tunisia	2,755	13,660	6,922	9,720	1,920	1,432	637	14,497	2,410	5,592	12,737	6,082	1,587	2,421	1,777	8,692	8,991	976	3,281	2,007
Tura, USSR	4,888	11,119	8,137	8,739	5,986	5,278	6,718	10,180	5,161	2,765	7,888	7,720	5,514	5,623	5,185	3,478	4,917	6,238	7,706	5,024
Turin, Italy	2,935	14,148	6,261	8,949	2,468	1,553	997	14,656	2,664	5,371	12,664	5,423	674	2,841	837	7,798	8,052	570	2,958	2,139
Uberlandia, Brazil	11,216	13,857	7,302	8,583	10,019	10,105	8,191	15,282	10,841	14,269	17,471	7,350	9,102	10,584	9,419	13,903	12,453	8,505	6,743	10,618
Ufa, USSR	2,264	11,568	8,210	9,915	3,329	2,698	4,439	11,390	2,512	1,986	9,219	7,521	3,606	2,983	3,317	5,852	6,948	4,118	6,208	2,377
Ujungpandang, Indonesia	9,310	3,316	15,650	14,253	10,259	10,679	12,689	2,577	9,652	6,847	989	15,479	12,361	9,698	12,104	9,075	10,540	12,661	15,003	10,079
Ulaanbaatar, Mongolia	5,364	9,253	9,971	10,227	6,586	6,202	7,979	8,379	5,714	2,377	6,087	9,582	6,991	6,092	6,672	4,460	6,111	7,611	9,398	5,779
Ulan-Ude, USSR	5,333	9,675	9,535	9,815	6,539	6,072	7,775	8,751	5,669	2,475	6,457	9,154	6,720	6,072	6,398	4,094	5,728	7,373	9,067	5,686
Uliastay, Mongolia	4,624	9,407	9,947	10,538	5,849	5,513	7,350	8,739	4,978	1,626	6,471	9,473	6,452	5,347	6,143	4,939	6,539	7,023	8,953	5,067
Uranium City, Canada	8,945	15,703	3,024	2,726	9,249	8,119	7,636	13,792	8,934	8,597	12,171	3,286	6,371	9,352	6,248	3,671	2,246	7,025	5,941	8,424
Urumqi, China	3,952	9,254	10,251	11,151	5,179	4,978	6,911	8,842	4,319	861	6,645	9,694	6,179	4,650	5,891	5,710	7,269	6,659	8,774	4,480
Ushuaia, Argentina	14,469	10,034	10,811	10,613	13,282	13,824	12,206	11,054	14,147	17,207	13,343	11,159	13,330	13,725	13,656	16,343	14,709	12,642	11,071	14,172
Vaduz, Liechtenstein	2,830	14,068	6,273	8,901	2,484	1,483	1,271	14,481	2,585	5,149	12,450	5,441	613	2,807	665	7,551	7,847	817	3,113	2,041
Valencia, Spain	3,619	14,630	5,979	8,822	2,885	2,232	422	15,401	3,300	6,245	13,512	5,142	1,178	3,365	1,489	8,449	8,509	372	2,317	2,834
Valladolid, Spain	3,947	15,044	5,541	8,381	3,287	2,552	861	15,713	3,646	6,434	13,733	4,703	1,066	3,746	1,394	8,207	8,176	524	1,940	3,153
Valletta, Malta	2,390	13,262	7,297	10,068	1,519	1,133	1,033	14,104	2,037	5,301	12,381	6,457	1,843	2,024	1,979	8,748	9,148	1,339	3,682	1,671
Valparaiso, Chile	14,011	12,405	8,383	8,379	12,804	12,895	10,945	13,171	13,637	17,065	15,438	8,766	11,713	13,363	12,012	14,257	12,578	11,201	9,169	13,416
Vancouver, Canada	10,323	14,886	3,826	2,071	10,702	9,572	9,103	12,895	10,342	9,572	11,672	4,339	7,850	10,775	7,725	3,816	2,137	8,498	7,260	9,848
Varna, Bulgaria	1,324	12,565	7,713	10,190	1,345	313	2,231	13,039	1,111	3,924	11,127	6,892	2,088	1,435	1,988	7,744	8,426	2,150	4,587	551
Venice, Italy	2,578	13,807	6,558	9,191	2,194	1,210	1,238	14,286	2,319	5,015	12,301	5,724	901	2,525	940	7,718	8,072	928	3,326	1,783
Veracruz, Mexico	12,350	16,250	3,344	2,042	12,000	11,072	9,537	14,850	12,158	13,054	14,922	4,159	8,982	12,392	9,063	7,921	6,246	9,195	6,895	11,601
Verona, Italy	2,682	13,908	6,467	9,114	2,277	1,310	1,170	14,391	2,420	5,113	12,402	5,632	819	2,619	887	7,729	8,055	828	3,220	1,887
Victoria, Canada	10,416	14,858	3,858	2,024	10,793	9,663	9,184	12,866	10,434	9,655	11,673	4,385	7,935	10,867	7,813	3,874	2,194	8,581	7,323	9,940
Victoria, Seychelles	4,841	7,221	13,484	16,167	4,804	5,868	7,106	8,633	4,904	5,726	8,075	12,644	7,898	4,545	7,898	11,938	13,378	7,528	9,695	5,448
Vienna, Austria	2,372	13,606	6,661	9,191	2,208	1,111	1,671	13,958	2,162	4,625	11,924	5,838	1,044	2,444	936	7,374	7,811	1,322	3,631	1,604
Vientiane, Laos	6,308	6,084	13,283	13,376	7,385	7,625	9,651	5,727	6,671	3,698	3,694	12,816	9,214	6,807	8,954	7,497	9,172	9,553	11,854	7,038
Villahermosa, Mexico	12,256	16,442	3,280	2,332	11,840	10,949	9,348	15,142	12,047	13,147	15,284	4,069	8,864	12,256	8,962	8,194	6,524	9,034	6,691	11,493
Vilnius, USSR	2,307	13,250	6,796	9,054	2,634	1,539	2,615	13,309	2,247	3,888	11,171	6,016	1,649	2,662	1,373	6,547	7,146	2,199	4,274	1,734
Visby, Sweden	2,843	13,762	6,253	8,521	3,069	1,943	2,576	13,719	2,761	4,303	11,530	5,478	1,356	3,155	1,036	6,317	6,784	2,056	3,885	2,230
Vitoria, Brazil	10,635	13,465	7,769	9,301	9,417	9,618	7,792	15,096	10,263	13,726	17,072	7,712	8,839	9,969	9,165	14,343	13,010	8,175	6,670	10,093
Vladivostok, USSR	7,369	8,772	10,165	9,511	8,585	8,123	9,759	7,403	7,713	4,383	5,202	10,022	8,597	8,102	8,269	3,706	5,336	9,308	10,707	7,743
Volgograd, USSR	1,327	11,781	8,220	10,288	2,301	1,704	3,585	11,915	1,515	2,572	9,863	7,459	3,024	1,997	2,792	6,782	7,746	3,370	5,665	1,342
Vologda, USSR	2,469	12,649	7,190	9,108	3,203	2,266	3,631	12,463	2,567	3,077	10,262	6,473	2,600	3,045	2,293	5,802	6,621	3,211	5,151	2,201
Vorkuta, USSR	3,680	12,229	7,285	8,603	4,612	3,754	5,059	11,603	3,873	2,808	9,319	6,709	3,855	4,357	3,527	4,420	5,463	4,572	6,154	3,610
Wake Island	11,556	7,917	10,786	8,515	12,767	12,218	13,566	5,938	11,896	8,543	4,918	11,168	12,189	12,289	11,875	5,115	5,752	12,997	13,432	11,893
Wallis Island	15,473	6,993	12,013	9,065	16,700	16,282	17,402	5,372	15,839	12,378	6,203	12,760	15,943	16,156	15,672	8,671	8,581	16,761	15,867	15,922
Walvis Bay, Namibia	7,208	9,711	11,566	14,221	6,213	7,160	6,720	11,682	6,968	9,716	12,259	10,979	8,159	6,490	8,393	15,198	15,588	7,368	8,089	7,218
Warsaw, Poland	2,316	13,432	6,703	9,081	2,448	1,320	2,221	13,603	2,191	4,202	11,501	5,903	1,332	2,560	1,095	6,873	7,397	1,818	3,975	1,644
Washington, D.C.	9,495	18,630	501	2,658	9,188	8,225	6,810	16,655	9,306	10,539	15,355	1,306	6,136	9,553	6,209	6,842	5,422	6,404	4,274	8,747
Watson Lake, Canada	9,198	14,580	4,138	3,209	9,698	8,577	8,401	12,662	9,252	8,309	11,082	4,413	7,041	9,706	6,869	2,734	1,155	7,765	6,957	8,789
Weimar, East Germany	2,826	14,040	6,191	8,714	2,679	1,589	1,709	14,285	2,633	4,886	12,184	5,371	651	2,922	468	7,115	7,452	1,202	3,294	2,073
Wellington, New Zealand	16,029	4,946	14,500	11,650	16,701	17,424	19,145	4,259	16,333	13,528	6,231	15,337	18,889	16,238	18,561	11,760	11,805	19,448	18,127	16,823
West Berlin, West Germany	2,766	13,938	6,240	8,703	2,721	1,605	1,927	14,115	2,600	4,703	11,993	5,429	828	2,920	577	6,928	7,307	1,425	3,465	2,040
Wewak, Papua New Guinea	11,351	4,383	14,319	12,031	12,471	12,583	14,565	2,464	11,723	8,424	1,715	14,602	13,720	11,892	13,402	8,067	9,120	14,298	16,010	12,030
Whangarei, New Zealand	15,857	5,056	14,247	11,334	16,701	17,223	19,234	4,102	16,193	13,156	5,910	15,068	18,304	16,182	17,979	11,141	11,223	19,037	18,089	16,626
Whitehorse, Canada	9,165	14,239	4,483	3,497	9,726	8,614	8,547	12,332	9,239	8,121	10,733	4,738	7,161	9,701	6,973	2,408	804	7,906	7,211	8,794
Wichita, Kansas	10,703	16,870	2,074	884	10,621	9,570	8,404	14,947	10,582	11,021	14,060	2,876	7,527	10,903	7,533	6,069	4,442	7,929	5,985	10,025
Willemstad, Curacao	10,935	17,376	3,416	4,569	10,148	9,540	7,617	17,296	10,628	12,968	17,926	3,765	7,645	10,673	7,855	9,869	8,349	7,511	5,059	10,140
Wiluna, Australia	10,848	961	17,825	15,488	11,521	12,238	14,068	1,414	11,132	8,910	2,672	17,835	14,199	11,032	14,004	11,258	12,555	14,258	16,711	11,645
Windhoek, Namibia	7,069	9,522	11,742	14,438	6,107	7,081	6,734	11,484	6,841	9,515	12,009	11,135	8,160	6,360	8,385	15,107	15,598	7,381	8,203	7,112
Windsor, Canada	9,565	18,038	762	2,198	9,375	8,359	7,097	16,048	9,409	10,321	14,735	1,554	6,287	9,695	6,322	6,265	4,809	6,641	4,664	8,848
Winnipeg, Canada	9,547	16,740	1,964	1,817	9,621	8,522	7,636	14,755	9,467	9,670	13,361	2,486	6,568	9,831	6,520	4,959	3,447	7,089	5,511	8,923
Winston-Salem, North Carolina	9,915	18,381	917	2,388	9,599	8,643	7,204	16,477	9,725	10,920	15,393	1,724	6,553	9,969	6,628	6,982	5,497	6,810	4,640	9,166
Wroclaw, Poland	2,470	13,655	6,535	8,991	2,452	1,327	1,940	13,886	2,304	4,495	11,797	5,724	1,052	2,631	848	7,047	7,497	1,517	3,693	1,745
Wuhan, China	6,634	7,273	11,855	11,574	7,841	7,740	9,676	6,362	7,009	3,573	4,075	11,541	8,863	7,282	8,557	5,710	7,375	9,401	11,367	7,224
Wyndham, Australia	10,761	2,396	16,348	14,181	11,657	12,142	14,136	1,095	11,095	8,331	1,300	16,449	13,849	11,109	13,590	9,819	11,078	14,140	16,491	11,540
Xi'an, China	6,002	7,729	11,483	11,487	7,215	7,092	9,027	6,939	6,376	2,929	4,666	11,107	8,229	6,661	7,926	5,611	7,291	8,756	10,756	6,581
Xining, China	5,304	8,106	11,215	11,542	6,518	6,404	8,353	7,480	5,678	2,236	5,241	10,766	7,604	6,965	7,308	5,728	7,397	8,102	10,170	5,887
Yakutsk, USSR	6,374	10,808	8,215	8,124	7,476	6,743	8,058	9,507	6,652	3,979	7,289	7,986	6,754	7,111	6,428	2,353	3,992	7,528	8,656	6,510
Yanji, China	7,212	8,709	10,251	9,665	8,431	7,991	9,657	7,386	7,559	4,209	5,163	10,084	8,520	7,942	8,192	3,838	5,481	9,219	10,676	7,601
Yaounde, Cameroon	4,762	11,748	9,336	12,277	3,586	4,341	3,747	13,474	4,441	7,739	13,005	8,598	5,176	4,020	5,410	12,306	12,612	4,394	5,495	4,535
Yap Island (Colonia)	9,987	5,372	13,387	11,624	11,164	11,138	13,071	3,704	10,362	6,968	1,832	13,484	12,158	10,591	11,839	6,849	8,121	12,761	14,462	10,613
Yaraka, Australia	12,727	2,757	16,047	13,245	13,612	14,103	16,103	1,044	13,061	10,192	2,895	16,584	15,715	13,070	15,431	10,347	11,213	16,083	18,277	13,503
Yarmouth, Canada	8,449	18,971	634	3,582	8,124	7,166	5,760	17,128	8,251	9,685	15,344	269	5,076	8,491	5,157	6,769	5,560	5,342	3,280	7,694
Yellowknife, Canada	8,763	15,312	3,432	3,091	9,145	8,015	7,678	13,432	8,776	8,243	11,752	3,635	6,360	9,209	6,212	3,228	1,854	7,053	6,145	8,283
Yerevan, USSR	451	11,217	8,935	11,164	1,652	1,578	3,604	11,621	779	2,705	9,742	8,140	3,444	1,195	3,286	7,674	8,689	3,568	6,001	992
Yinchuan, China	5,613	8,225	11,021	11,185	6,836	6,650	8,558	7,459	5,983	2,519	5,186	10,620	7,725	6,294	7,420	5,339	7,014	8,268	10,240	6,156
Yogyakarta, Indonesia	8,721	3,112	16,122	15,187	9,562	10,114	12,071	3,064	9,040	6,585	2,026	15,758	11,961	9,023	11,740	9,731	11,284	12,138	14,574	9,512
York, United Kingdom	3,730	14,921	5,286	7,850	3,531	2,477	1,923	15,006	3,537	5,585	12,815	4,466	498	3,813	440	6,853	6,952	1,276	2,598	2,977
Yumen, China	4,860	8,544	10,830	11,342	6,082	5,925	7,861	7,972	5,231	1,770	5,741	10,347	7,102	5,538	6,807	5,617	7,262	7,603	9,671	5,418
Yutian, China	3,577	8,797	10,856	11,992	4,767	4,784	6,795	8,654	3,952	816	6,585	10,231	6,285	4,203	6,028	6,627	8,178	6,645	8,926	4,226
Yuzhno-Sakhalinsk, USSR	7,875	9,414	9,450	8,594	9,056	8,456	9,900	7,874	8,195	5,040	5,792	9,395	8,620	8,619	8,293	2,878	4,453	9,386	10,471	8,147
Zagreb, Yugoslavia	2,310	13,548	6,779	9,365	2,018	970	1,473	13,999	2,066	4,734	12,016	5,949	1,120	2,302	1,087	7,642	8,073	1,213	3,609	1,521
Zahedan, Iran	2,006	9,316	10,771	12,738	2,974	3,400	5,374	9,777	2,333	2,093	8,048	9,998	5,348	2,398	5,186	8,223	9,573	5,428	7,880	2,798
Zamboanga, Philippines	8,741	4,662	14,290	13,117	9,826	10,033	12,054	3,621	9,107	5,963	1,357	14,131	11,468	9,248	11,181	7,731	9,233	11,900	14,054	9,456
Zanzibar, Tanzania	4,787	8,593	12,344	15,277	4,252	5,381	6,062	10,220	4,694	6,665	9,866	11,537	7,159	4,232	7,251	12,726	13,850	6,600	8,434	5,145
Zaragoza, Spain	3,631	14,731	5,827	8,643	2,974	2,235	637	15,403	3,327	6,160	13,450	4,988	951	3,428	1,269	8,209	8,265	221	2,259	2,837
Zashiversk, USSR	6,719	11,553	7,418	7,266	7,734	6,884	7,958	10,133	6,958	4,637	7,977	7,241	6,573	7,434	6,258	1,583	3,164	7,381	8,209	6,738
Zhengzhou, China	6,378	7,738	11,401	11,217	7,598	7,426	9,329	6,813	6,750	3,288	4,522	11,077	8,463	7,051	8,153	5,339	7,013	9,026	10,938	6,931
Zurich, Switzerland	2,920	14,158	6,186	8,821	2,567	1,572	1,254	14,564	2,675	5,221	12,524	5,353	528	2,895	607	7,537	7,809	764	3,028	2,131

Distances in Kilometers	Annaba, Algeria	Annapolis, Maryland	Antananarivo, Madagascar	Antofagasta, Chile	Antwerp, Belgium	Apia, Western Samoa	Arequipa, Peru	Arkhangel'sk, USSR	As Sallum, Egypt	Asau, Western Samoa	Ascension Island (Georgetown)	Ashkhabad, USSR	Asmera, Ethiopia	Astrakhan, USSR	Asuncion, Paraguay	Aswan, Egypt	Athens, Greece	Atlanta, Georgia	Atlantic City, New Jersey	Auckland, New Zealand
Annapolis, Maryland	7,123	0	14,233	6,962	6,181	11,415	6,152	7,292	8,773	11,465	8,234	10,323	11,019	9,066	7,377	9,891	8,231	915	181	13,920
Antananarivo, Madagascar	7,456	14,233	0	11,804	8,832	14,398	12,298	9,275	6,076	14,350	6,785	6,396	3,903	7,228	10,571	5,015	6,772	15,003	14,053	11,726
Antofagasta, Chile	10,576	6,962	11,804	0	11,031	10,525	812	13,353	11,849	10,630	6,204	14,943	12,626	14,037	1,303	12,327	11,936	6,523	6,987	10,454
Antwerp, Belgium	1,613	6,181	8,832	11,031	0	15,844	10,470	2,552	2,767	15,807	6,799	4,420	5,029	3,203	10,417	3,873	2,113	7,094	6,021	18,239
Apia, Western Samoa	17,449	11,415	14,398	10,525	15,844	0	10,642	13,857	17,404	105	16,547	14,422	16,730	14,845	11,673	17,206	16,929	10,615	11,595	2,884
Arequipa, Peru	10,175	6,152	12,298	812	10,470	10,642	0	12,690	11,573	10,746	6,270	14,598	12,627	13,577	1,745	12,179	11,572	5,715	6,179	10,912
Arkhangel'sk, USSR	3,763	7,292	9,275	13,353	2,552	13,857	12,690	0	3,821	13,790	9,229	3,186	5,469	2,080	12,902	4,533	3,158	8,104	7,179	15,710
As Sallum, Egypt	1,704	8,773	6,076	11,849	2,767	17,404	11,573	3,821	0	17,312	6,068	3,107	2,279	2,559	10,812	1,125	724	9,684	8,600	17,178
Asau, Western Samoa	17,406	11,465	14,350	10,630	15,807	105	10,746	13,790	17,312	0	16,645	14,320	16,630	14,753	11,777	17,101	16,848	10,672	11,645	2,883
Ascension Island (Georgetown)	5,476	8,234	6,785	6,204	6,799	16,547	6,270	9,229	6,068	16,645	0	9,070	6,422	8,610	4,969	6,240	6,442	8,687	8,092	14,955
Ashkhabad, USSR	4,425	10,323	6,396	14,943	4,420	14,422	14,598	3,186	3,107	14,320	9,070	0	3,152	1,263	13,915	2,865	3,027	11,187	10,189	14,505
Asmera, Ethiopia	3,896	11,019	3,903	12,626	5,029	16,730	12,627	5,469	2,279	16,630	6,422	3,152	0	3,542	11,379	1,157	2,921	11,923	10,844	15,063
Astrakhan, USSR	3,475	9,066	7,228	14,037	3,203	14,845	13,577	2,080	2,559	14,753	8,610	1,263	3,542	0	13,175	2,819	2,202	9,937	8,930	15,544
Asuncion, Paraguay	9,709	7,377	10,571	1,303	10,417	11,673	1,745	12,902	10,812	11,777	4,969	13,915	11,379	13,175	0	11,172	10,996	7,117	7,363	11,214
Aswan, Egypt	2,786	9,891	5,015	12,327	3,873	17,206	12,179	4,533	1,125	17,101	6,240	2,865	1,157	2,819	11,172	0	1,769	10,800	9,718	16,132
Athens, Greece	1,416	8,231	6,772	11,936	2,113	16,929	11,572	3,158	724	16,848	6,442	3,027	2,921	2,202	10,996	1,769	0	9,145	8,063	17,469
Atlanta, Georgia	8,027	915	15,003	6,523	7,094	10,615	5,715	8,104	9,684	10,672	8,687	11,187	11,923	9,937	7,117	10,800	9,145	0	1,084	13,034
Atlantic City, New Jersey	6,947	181	14,053	6,987	6,021	11,595	6,179	7,179	8,600	11,645	8,092	10,189	10,844	8,930	7,363	9,718	8,063	1,084	0	14,099
Auckland, New Zealand	18,868	13,920	11,726	10,454	18,239	2,884	10,912	15,710	17,178	2,883	14,955	14,505	15,063	15,544	11,214	16,132	17,469	13,034	14,099	0
Auckland Islands, New Zealand	17,733	15,030	10,278	10,070	18,760	4,534	10,683	16,568	16,204	4,540	13,512	14,346	13,928	15,576	10,545	15,078	16,775	14,115	15,196	1,669
Augusta, Maine	6,368	815	13,618	7,526	5,374	12,021	6,725	6,512	7,995	12,062	8,013	9,515	10,256	8,256	7,803	9,118	7,437	1,720	674	14,636
Austin, Texas	9,273	2,167	16,310	6,645	8,223	9,298	5,879	8,883	10,895	9,354	9,820	12,056	13,161	10,849	7,487	12,019	10,316	1,318	2,347	11,754
Ayan, USSR	8,657	8,938	11,779	15,692	7,338	9,062	14,909	4,894	8,403	8,983	14,118	6,004	9,156	5,908	16,315	8,694	7,868	9,235	8,953	10,903
Baghdad, Iraq	3,343	9,952	5,793	13,656	3,783	15,782	13,393	3,482	1,820	15,680	7,708	1,362	2,071	1,476	12,577	1,523	1,937	10,859	9,796	15,533
Baguio, Philippines	10,842	13,622	8,904	18,623	10,308	8,158	18,738	7,896	9,574	8,054	15,061	6,483	8,679	7,372	19,009	9,060	9,489	13,857	13,637	8,187
Bahia Blanca, Argentina	11,029	8,725	10,326	1,839	11,886	10,678	2,633	14,407	11,921	10,777	5,869	14,929	12,027	14,419	1,553	12,072	12,218	8,342	8,734	9,803
Baku, USSR	3,650	9,670	6,569	14,198	3,665	15,026	13,825	2,758	2,422	14,928	8,469	785	2,971	679	13,221	2,404	2,264	10,553	9,528	15,288
Balikpapan, Indonesia	11,788	15,618	7,795	17,139	11,664	7,978	17,849	9,482	10,248	7,880	14,530	7,391	8,758	8,503	17,009	9,459	10,372	15,792	15,637	7,117
Balkhash, USSR	5,517	10,090	7,785	16,007	4,985	12,888	15,448	2,869	4,539	12,790	10,604	1,680	4,826	2,056	15,226	4,502	4,254	10,847	9,991	13,556
Ballarat, Australia	16,163	16,519	9,289	12,346	16,504	5,109	12,984	14,322	14,458	5,062	14,490	12,104	12,341	13,302	12,699	13,399	14,843	15,684	16,699	2,733
Baltimore, Maryland	7,117	36	14,239	6,997	6,166	11,409	6,187	7,265	8,763	11,459	8,258	10,300	11,012	9,044	7,413	9,882	8,219	928	186	13,923
Bamako, Mali	3,114	7,282	7,020	7,887	4,422	18,269	7,695	6,850	3,985	18,366	2,384	7,091	5,070	6,416	6,827	4,484	4,214	7,991	7,109	17,308
Bandar Seri Begawan, Brunei	11,198	15,010	7,839	17,853	10,990	8,357	18,555	8,775	9,712	8,256	14,427	6,778	8,375	7,854	17,618	8,990	9,786	15,275	15,014	7,728
Bangalore, India	7,367	13,658	4,830	16,457	7,722	12,556	16,693	6,392	5,721	12,455	10,429	3,358	4,176	4,620	15,156	4,855	5,980	14,494	13,531	11,501
Banghazi, Libya	1,247	8,356	6,361	11,413	2,478	17,657	11,115	3,874	485	17,574	5,749	3,531	2,666	2,863	10,408	1,540	732	9,263	8,181	17,651
Bangkok, Thailand	9,347	14,160	6,843	18,563	9,248	10,140	19,131	7,223	7,851	10,037	12,911	4,941	6,617	6,064	17,412	7,154	7,933	14,722	14,103	9,566
Bangui, Central African Rep.	3,768	10,148	4,085	10,106	5,358	18,480	10,168	6,907	3,088	18,436	3,909	5,487	2,537	5,452	8,847	2,667	3,759	10,937	9,968	15,670
Banjarmasin, Indonesia	11,729	15,903	7,484	16,972	11,693	8,167	17,723	9,584	10,153	8,071	14,238	7,365	8,580	8,508	16,734	9,325	10,314	16,111	15,913	7,162
Banjul, Gambia	3,552	6,489	7,888	7,151	4,596	17,348	6,889	7,127	4,702	17,442	2,377	7,793	5,975	6,996	6,181	5,320	4,816	7,150	6,322	17,179
Barcelona, Spain	693	6,463	8,149	10,373	1,106	16,896	9,903	3,545	2,319	16,869	5,718	4,753	4,559	3,676	9,615	3,430	1,882	7,371	6,289	19,204
Bari, Italy	916	7,546	7,364	11,482	1,472	16,868	11,062	3,017	1,296	16,804	6,304	3,554	3,565	2,561	10,625	2,408	687	8,460	7,378	18,059
Barranquilla, Colombia	8,630	3,106	13,793	3,861	8,314	11,044	3,050	10,069	10,306	11,132	7,008	12,733	12,170	11,498	4,420	11,269	10,004	2,704	3,143	12,554
Basse-Terre, Guadeloupe	7,151	2,925	12,562	4,486	6,979	12,536	3,742	8,985	8,810	12,621	5,848	11,378	10,652	10,182	4,587	9,755	8,544	3,004	2,869	14,031
Basseterre, St. Kitts & Nevis	7,160	2,750	12,698	4,606	6,938	12,453	3,851	8,900	8,829	12,536	6,002	11,347	10,707	10,141	4,741	9,791	8,544	2,829	2,696	14,024
Bata, Equatorial Guinea	3,886	9,559	4,727	9,095	5,495	18,670	9,147	7,388	3,666	18,697	2,893	6,364	3,534	6,174	7,846	3,501	4,249	10,283	9,384	15,837
Baton Rouge, Louisiana	8,763	1,641	15,860	6,385	7,799	9,902	5,595	8,670	10,414	9,961	9,206	11,802	12,659	10,566	7,127	11,532	9,865	738	1,816	12,296
Bear Lake, Canada	8,836	4,124	15,839	10,315	7,284	8,808	9,548	6,567	9,925	8,808	12,116	9,560	11,968	8,629	11,114	10,906	9,205	4,075	4,221	11,691
Bechar, Algeria	1,089	6,619	7,710	9,489	2,244	17,770	9,104	4,686	2,591	17,772	4,565	5,494	4,540	4,565	8,624	3,540	2,468	7,487	6,438	19,364
Beira, Mozambique	6,895	13,196	1,333	10,603	8,414	15,289	11,042	9,370	5,782	15,262	5,466	6,853	3,915	7,449	9,338	4,863	6,505	13,881	13,022	12,456
Beirut, Lebanon	2,533	9,333	5,981	12,852	3,158	16,489	12,569	3,430	1,003	16,390	7,007	2,108	2,084	1,745	11,806	1,116	1,154	10,247	9,169	16,337
Belau Islands (Koror)	12,627	13,970	9,962	16,813	11,963	6,387	17,029	9,462	11,388	6,283	16,606	8,296	10,395	9,151	17,646	10,851	11,292	13,895	14,044	6,445
Belem, Brazil	7,179	5,315	10,597	3,409	7,666	13,553	3,021	10,103	8,553	13,655	3,845	11,588	9,783	10,629	2,814	9,205	8,561	5,413	5,239	13,863
Belfast, United Kingdom	2,227	5,408	9,590	10,614	790	15,319	9,996	2,773	3,544	15,297	6,974	5,087	5,813	3,839	10,132	4,656	2,901	6,318	5,250	18,035
Belgrade, Yugoslavia	1,386	7,569	7,573	11,893	1,390	16,380	11,431	2,523	1,527	16,313	6,811	3,228	3,702	2,146	11,078	2,561	807	8,482	7,407	17,690
Belmopan, Belize	9,446	2,692	15,418	4,944	8,755	9,735	4,172	9,975	11,148	9,813	8,639	13,007	13,254	11,746	5,786	12,217	10,703	1,884	2,820	11,703
Belo Horizonte, Brazil	8,305	7,350	9,461	2,764	9,182	13,200	2,945	11,726	9,311	13,304	3,446	12,404	9,866	11,734	1,530	9,643	9,537	7,327	7,290	12,529
Bergen, Norway	2,617	5,912	9,572	11,515	1,022	14,832	10,875	1,848	3,520	14,792	7,772	4,429	5,687	3,166	11,062	4,557	2,807	6,797	5,770	17,285
Bern, Switzerland	1,113	6,576	8,323	11,027	527	16,336	10,517	2,800	2,277	16,294	6,450	4,228	4,552	3,073	10,320	3,395	1,661	7,491	6,411	18,482
Bhopal, India	6,736	12,601	5,685	16,749	6,855	12,722	16,699	5,310	5,200	12,618	10,546	2,435	4,125	3,671	15,485	4,523	5,320	13,408	12,484	12,154
Bhubaneswar, India	7,654	13,198	6,019	17,551	7,690	11,815	17,608	5,942	6,134	11,711	11,384	3,295	4,987	4,488	16,253	5,447	6,238	13,942	13,099	11,243
Bialystok, Poland	2,164	7,230	8,320	12,308	1,295	15,452	11,762	1,610	2,401	15,388	7,639	3,180	4,417	1,934	11,634	3,328	1,684	8,125	7,082	17,170
Big Trout Lake, Canada	7,258	1,944	14,713	8,789	5,920	10,704	7,979	6,209	8,687	10,726	9,783	9,393	10,945	8,217	9,300	9,791	8,023	2,275	1,993	13,530
Bilbao, Spain	1,154	5,990	8,600	10,111	1,046	16,574	9,603	3,595	2,788	16,558	5,785	5,109	5,032	3,981	9,424	3,901	2,323	6,899	5,817	19,271
Billings, Montana	8,854	2,722	16,306	8,600	7,488	9,141	7,827	7,476	10,254	9,168	10,954	10,639	12,490	9,544	9,395	11,344	9,575	2,446	2,862	11,941
Birmingham, Alabama	8,229	1,107	15,229	6,561	7,269	10,391	5,756	8,210	9,879	10,447	8,894	11,316	12,125	10,072	7,200	10,997	9,331	226	1,281	12,824
Birmingham, United Kingdom	1,889	5,723	9,235	10,713	458	15,625	10,124	2,745	3,191	15,599	6,798	4,846	5,463	3,614	10,166	4,305	2,555	6,636	5,563	18,252
Bismarck, North Dakota	8,329	2,155	15,783	8,380	7,013	9,726	7,588	7,206	9,778	9,756	10,372	10,391	12,038	9,246	9,083	10,884	9,117	2,003	2,285	12,504
Bissau, Guinea Bissau	3,627	6,683	7,714	7,141	4,727	17,439	6,908	7,246	4,708	17,536	2,192	7,809	5,898	7,047	6,140	5,282	4,856	7,336	6,517	17,049
Biysk, USSR	6,064	9,710	8,718	16,195	5,264	12,097	15,509	2,844	5,307	12,004	11,358	2,636	5,788	2,751	15,678	5,396	4,925	10,389	9,634	13,124
Blagoveshchensk, USSR	8,695	9,843	10,919	16,671	7,543	9,229	15,880	5,004	8,180	9,141	14,149	5,494	8,615	5,625	17,194	8,304	7,729	10,184	9,847	10,707
Blantyre, Malawi	6,494	12,949	1,374	10,822	7,996	15,616	11,216	8,921	5,344	15,582	5,442	6,431	3,469	7,005	9,539	4,416	6,067	13,675	12,772	12,819
Bloemfontein, South Africa	7,558	13,011	2,443	9,362	9,153	14,880	9,864	10,463	6,719	14,883	4,848	8,149	5,108	8,646	8,130	5,932	7,434	13,530	12,855	12,001
Bluefields, Nicaragua	9,354	3,074	14,765	4,203	8,852	10,118	3,416	10,329	11,053	10,203	7,983	13,221	13,029	11,961	5,001	12,068	10,683	2,410	3,166	11,821
Boa Vista do Rio Branco, Braz.	7,915	4,314	12,034	3,112	8,052	12,367	2,438	10,258	9,457	12,465	5,273	12,314	10,966	11,207	3,124	10,252	9,331	4,218	4,280	13,226
Bodo, Norway	3,407	6,116	9,940	12,186	1,872	14,051	11,500	1,219	4,035	14,004	8,655	4,250	6,040	3,033	11,836	4,970	3,313	6,953	5,995	16,401
Bogota, Colombia	8,983	3,815	13,505	3,151	8,811	10,965	2,339	10,688	10,620	11,058	6,769	13,220	12,332	12,013	3,751	11,518	10,383	3,399	3,849	12,197
Boise, Idaho	9,453	3,335	16,877	8,796	8,045	8,494	8,052	7,840	10,802	8,520	11,566	10,955	13,007	9,919	9,687	11,875	10,111	2,956	3,483	11,310
Bologna, Italy	894	6,968	7,925	11,195	909	16,595	10,721	2,875	1,873	16,544	6,355	3,956	4,148	2,856	10,423	2,991	1,263	7,882	6,801	18,387
Bolzano, Italy	1,109	6,862	8,106	11,283	730	16,369	10,788	2,678	2,038	16,320	6,551	3,934	4,301	2,794	10,545	3,144	1,390	7,777	6,698	18,273
Bombay, India	6,578	12,844	5,021	16,193	6,888	13,150	16,251	5,607	4,961	13,047	10,014	2,528	3,624	3,791	14,905	4,164	5,179	13,694	12,713	12,294
Bonn, West Germany	1,538	6,376	8,670	11,178	196	15,911	10,629	2,473	2,598	15,869	6,823	4,233	4,852	3,023	10,539	3,697	1,932	7,288	6,216	18,182
Bora Bora (Vaitape)	16,988	9,930	15,561	8,436	15,616	2,167	8,496	14,588	18,309	2,269	14,608	16,236	18,884	16,228	9,642	19,045	17,586	9,047	10,109	3,990
Bordeaux, France	1,126	6,101	8,577	10,367	801	16,469	9,852	3,341	2,673	16,446	6,007	4,880	4,939	3,737	9,685	3,796	2,160	7,013	5,930	19,040
Boston, Massachusetts	6,547	594	13,739	7,309	5,588	11,908	6,506	6,752	8,187	11,953	7,994	9,750	10,440	8,490	7,613	9,307	7,639	1,508	440	14,478
Bouvet Island	10,128	12,834	5,426	6,864	11,711	12,426	7,568	13,575	9,755	12,473	5,397	11,504	8,431	11,936	5,902	9,146	10,424	12,845	12,755	9,855
Brasilia, Brazil	8,249	6,753	10,009	2,509	8,989	13,034	2,528	11,503	9,387	13,138	3,747	12,494	10,146	11,717	1,460	9,820	9,544	6,710	6,698	12,666
Braunschweig, West Germany	1,721	6,525	8,661	11,464	438	15,737	10,907	2,190	2,588	15,690	7,081	3,999	4,804	2,773	10,832	3,658	1,890	7,433	6,369	17,899
Brazzaville, Congo	4,624	10,462	3,860	9,388	6,235	17,862	9,547	7,914	4,101	17,865	3,312	6,450	3,391	6,470	8,099	3,671	4,758	11,171	10,288	14,982
Bremerhaven, West Germany	1,852	6,348	8,854	11,396	384	15,598	10,823	2,170	2,780	15,555	7,150	4,140	4,998	2,902	10,798	3,852	2,084	7,254	6,193	17,869
Brest, France	1,621	5,682	9,066	10,320	713	15,997	9,758	3,204	3,114	15,979	6,316	5,092	5,391	3,896	9,726	4,239	2,549	6,597	5,514	18,722
Brest, USSR	2,102	7,323	8,200	12,321	1,334	15,544	11,787	1,692	2,284	15,478	7,577	3,111	4,297	1,875	11,624	3,207	1,569	8,221	7,174	17,189
Bridgetown, Barbados	7,143	3,315	12,260	4,232	7,081	12,712	3,517	9,178	8,773	12,800	5,513	11,444	10,530	10,276	4,250	9,679	8,550	3,393	3,254	14,032
Brisbane, Australia	16,609	15,299	10,499	12,684	16,290	3,954	13,185	13,802	15,002	3,890	15,860	12,213	13,140	13,278	13,310	14,072	15,193	14,550	15,474	2,292
Bristol, United Kingdom	1,812	5,712	9,191	10,616	488	15,721	10,033	2,858	3,164	15,696	6,677	4,904	5,440	3,680	10,056	4,283	2,544	6,625	5,549	18,371
Brno, Czechoslovakia	1,543	7,064	8,140	11,755	899	16,009	11,242	2,220	2,084	15,951	7,015	3,544	4,268	2,359	11,035	3,128	1,370	7,974	6,906	17,781
Broken Hill, Australia	15,773	16,522	9,277	12,988	15,925	5,159	13,610	13,677	14,084	5,099	14,906	11,568	12,065	12,738	13,358	13,070	14,401	15,769	16,696	3,097
Brussels, Belgium	1,572	6,191	8,804	11,007	43	15,886	10,449	2,588	2,742	15,849	6,757	4,427	5,007	3,215	10,387	3,850	2,092	7,104	6,030	18,279
Bucharest, Romania	1,756	7,958	7,345	12,311	1,781	16,218	11,871	2,415	1,431	16,142	7,082	2,783	3,446	1,726	11,465	2,340	743	8,868	7,799	17,261
Budapest, Hungary	1,500	7,317	7,886	11,872	1,140	16,140	11,383	2,299	1,843	16,077	6,971	3,348	4,009	2,197	11,111	2,872	1,123	8,227	7,158	17,702
Buenos Aires, Argentina	10,470	8,356	10,216	1,678	11,315	11,177	2,403	13,838	11,403	11,278	5,376	14,446	11,632	13,879	1,037	11,607	11,677	8,036	8,352	10,372

Distances in Kilometers	Annaba, Algeria	Annapolis, Maryland	Antananarivo, Madagascar	Antofagasta, Chile	Antwerp, Belgium	Apia, Western Samoa	Arequipa, Peru	Arkhangel'sk, USSR	As Sallum, Egypt	Asau, Western Samoa	Ascension Island (Georgetown)	Ashkhabad, USSR	Asmera, Ethiopia	Astrakhan, USSR	Asuncion, Paraguay	Aswan, Egypt	Athens, Greece	Atlanta, Georgia	Atlantic City, New Jersey	Auckland, New Zealand
Buffalo, New York	7,102	478	14,367	7,418	6,051	11,275	6,607	6,982	8,712	11,319	8,593	10,069	10,981	8,823	7,853	9,837	8,135	1,122	540	13,888
Bujumbura, Burundi	4,990	11,619	2,618	10,859	6,499	17,015	11,074	7,593	3,894	16,965	4,874	5,468	2,323	5,809	9,558	3,062	4,617	12,412	11,439	14,297
Bulawayo, Zimbabwe	6,683	12,674	1,989	10,000	8,252	15,644	10,414	9,448	5,735	15,631	4,823	7,147	4,085	7,621	8,724	4,916	6,455	13,318	12,505	12,769
Burlington, Vermont	6,613	669	13,887	7,549	5,583	11,749	6,743	6,623	8,229	11,790	8,259	9,666	10,495	8,412	7,883	9,353	7,659	1,531	578	14,377
Cabinda, Angola	4,722	10,285	4,106	9,018	6,334	17,819	9,180	8,123	4,332	17,839	2,954	6,779	3,745	6,752	7,729	3,973	4,965	10,963	10,113	14,975
Cagliari, Italy	283	7,096	7,575	10,792	1,383	17,191	10,371	3,480	1,682	17,144	5,758	4,241	3,931	3,248	9,951	2,795	1,279	8,005	6,922	18,740
Cairns, Australia	15,352	15,259	10,249	14,052	14,902	4,567	14,514	12,418	13,858	4,481	16,508	10,927	12,254	11,939	14,698	13,048	13,946	14,703	15,410	3,606
Cairo, Egypt	2,304	9,326	5,692	12,360	3,232	17,057	12,121	3,892	607	16,957	6,440	2,644	1,809	2,322	11,279	681	1,120	10,239	9,156	16,573
Calais, France	1,631	6,022	8,932	10,856	183	15,848	10,291	2,693	2,882	15,816	6,709	4,602	5,154	3,387	10,256	3,996	2,246	6,936	5,860	18,344
Calcutta, India	7,738	13,017	6,385	17,856	7,675	11,596	17,819	5,811	6,268	11,491	11,661	3,332	5,245	4,477	16,569	5,640	6,325	13,729	12,926	11,176
Calgary, Canada	8,736	3,208	16,092	9,316	7,281	9,093	8,541	6,998	10,021	9,109	11,367	10,117	12,198	9,077	10,097	11,077	9,320	3,074	3,324	11,953
Cali, Colombia	9,275	3,934	13,716	3,071	9,079	10,672	2,262	10,911	10,916	10,766	7,010	13,494	12,628	12,278	3,774	11,816	10,674	3,453	3,982	11,905
Camaguey, Cuba	8,247	1,955	14,350	5,048	7,659	10,955	4,237	9,135	9,951	11,030	7,654	12,013	12,027	10,752	5,606	11,004	9,538	1,511	2,019	12,913
Cambridge Bay, Canada	7,048	3,763	14,118	10,660	5,485	10,543	9,849	4,929	8,131	10,535	10,849	8,054	10,217	7,009	11,139	9,131	7,412	4,141	3,779	13,408
Cambridge, United Kingdom	1,803	5,865	9,115	10,819	317	15,688	10,237	2,670	3,062	15,658	6,806	4,710	5,332	3,482	10,252	4,174	2,420	6,777	5,704	18,251
Campbellton, Canada	6,004	1,277	13,342	7,944	4,946	12,260	7,149	6,037	7,604	12,295	8,032	9,046	9,875	7,789	8,164	8,728	7,026	2,166	1,147	14,956
Campo Grande, Brazil	9,115	6,963	10,489	1,666	9,800	12,174	1,843	12,284	10,263	12,279	4,540	13,370	10,961	12,587	618	10,679	10,419	6,779	6,935	11,824
Canakkale, Turkey	1,661	8,267	6,896	12,222	2,095	16,600	11,836	2,867	959	16,518	6,775	2,765	3,008	1,881	11,304	1,882	333	9,181	8,103	17,256
Canberra, Australia	16,570	15,990	9,822	12,266	16,702	4,577	12,857	14,368	14,873	4,529	14,918	12,372	12,807	13,532	12,730	13,840	15,207	15,168	16,171	2,305
Cancun, Mexico	9,014	2,208	15,258	5,262	8,284	10,055	4,471	9,494	10,713	10,129	8,528	12,523	12,852	11,263	6,020	11,793	10,251	1,417	2,335	12,123
Canton, China	9,774	13,057	8,522	19,655	9,257	9,132	19,116	6,884	8,534	9,027	14,206	5,434	7,784	6,304	19,078	8,075	8,428	13,442	13,043	9,256
Canton Atoll, Phoenix Islands	16,232	10,659	15,109	11,038	14,629	1,217	11,009	12,685	16,374	1,179	17,241	13,621	16,401	13,848	12,275	16,486	15,811	9,937	10,833	4,016
Cape Town, South Africa	7,917	12,662	3,327	8,482	9,530	14,613	9,010	11,088	7,283	14,635	4,428	8,966	5,869	9,375	7,269	6,599	7,979	13,068	12,521	11,796
Cape York, Australia	14,645	15,053	10,148	14,799	14,132	4,988	15,226	11,645	13,216	4,893	16,736	10,225	11,765	11,202	15,471	12,475	13,252	14,626	15,185	4,345
Caracas, Venezuela	7,959	3,295	12,948	3,797	7,806	11,877	3,019	9,773	9,604	11,967	6,164	12,206	11,375	11,009	4,082	10,521	9,358	3,132	3,283	13,221
Cardiff, United Kingdom	1,839	5,669	9,226	10,582	531	15,703	9,997	2,883	3,203	15,679	6,673	4,946	5,480	3,721	10,028	4,323	2,585	6,583	5,506	18,371
Carlisle, United Kingdom	2,159	5,589	9,468	10,795	639	15,348	10,182	2,607	3,406	15,321	7,044	4,891	5,668	3,643	10,295	4,512	2,749	6,497	5,433	17,994
Carnarvon, Australia	12,984	18,179	6,801	14,619	13,446	7,849	15,405	11,706	11,283	7,776	13,328	9,035	9,241	10,279	14,380	10,248	11,659	18,020	18,232	5,897
Carson City, Nevada	10,021	3,708	17,453	8,645	8,621	7,967	7,934	8,376	11,379	7,996	11,889	11,463	13,581	10,455	9,617	12,450	10,687	3,207	3,869	10,761
Casablanca, Morocco	1,442	6,070	8,244	9,186	2,184	17,299	8,752	4,719	3,069	17,314	4,655	5,858	5,080	4,850	8,399	4,060	2,858	6,937	5,890	19,591
Casper, Wyoming	8,947	2,535	16,399	8,232	7,632	9,143	7,462	7,749	10,398	9,177	10,760	10,925	12,655	9,806	9,040	11,502	9,734	2,159	2,688	11,899
Castries, Saint Lucia	7,209	3,157	12,431	4,291	7,097	12,580	3,559	9,150	8,852	12,667	5,690	11,479	10,643	10,297	4,361	9,774	8,610	3,217	3,102	13,970
Catbalogan, Philippines	11,530	13,968	9,139	17,938	10,993	7,546	18,187	8,562	10,239	7,442	15,556	7,159	9,250	8,063	18,487	9,689	10,172	14,098	14,004	7,496
Cayenne, French Guiana	7,044	4,490	11,230	3,721	7,318	13,324	3,169	9,650	8,542	13,421	4,445	11,465	10,010	10,409	3,391	9,309	8,455	4,600	4,415	14,071
Cayman Islands (Georgetown)	8,676	2,231	14,677	4,899	8,071	10,552	4,093	9,484	10,380	10,629	7,934	12,407	12,453	11,144	5,559	11,433	9,964	1,629	2,320	12,483
Cazombo, Angola	5,628	11,641	2,754	9,819	7,217	16,742	10,111	8,610	4,816	16,730	4,109	6,645	3,494	6,925	8,517	4,127	5,522	12,330	11,468	13,863
Cebu, Philippines	11,561	14,158	8,980	17,902	11,069	7,592	18,228	8,661	10,237	7,488	15,451	7,170	9,185	8,103	18,340	9,656	10,191	14,292	14,192	7,447
Cedar Rapids, Iowa	8,059	1,328	15,406	7,589	6,896	10,226	6,786	7,481	9,619	10,268	9,557	10,650	11,898	9,443	8,226	10,743	9,005	1,115	1,482	12,884
Changsha, China	9,395	12,504	8,761	19,407	8,790	9,340	18,621	6,376	8,242	9,237	14,080	5,137	7,681	5,920	19,042	7,870	8,082	12,910	12,487	9,673
Channel-Port-aux-Basques, Can.	5,474	1,695	12,781	7,967	4,487	12,825	7,192	5,783	7,096	12,860	7,558	8,695	9,358	7,433	8,067	8,219	6,540	2,609	1,534	15,509
Charleston, South Carolina	7,733	756	14,598	6,325	6,879	11,000	5,513	8,048	9,409	11,059	8,259	11,070	11,624	9,811	6,843	10,516	8,897	429	881	13,354
Charleston, West Virginia	7,548	452	14,685	6,962	6,559	10,963	6,151	7,538	9,185	11,013	8,621	10,621	11,441	9,372	7,473	10,306	8,628	567	633	13,481
Charlotte, North Carolina	7,665	569	14,662	6,608	6,749	10,967	5,797	7,830	9,325	11,022	8,433	10,883	11,561	9,628	7,126	10,440	8,792	363	729	13,397
Charlotte Amalie, U.S.V.I.	7,294	2,545	12,953	4,684	7,005	12,237	3,911	8,894	8,975	12,319	6,263	11,422	10,893	10,202	4,889	9,955	8,665	2,580	2,503	13,890
Charlottetown, Canada	5,805	1,358	13,085	7,773	4,823	12,538	6,988	6,069	7,432	12,576	7,700	9,013	9,692	7,752	7,937	8,555	6,877	2,272	1,199	15,190
Chatham, Canada	5,950	1,266	13,260	7,843	4,927	12,355	7,051	6,084	7,563	12,391	7,897	9,067	9,830	7,808	8,045	8,687	6,996	2,170	1,122	15,028
Chatham Islands (Waitangi)	19,145	13,585	11,732	9,418	19,194	3,370	9,911	16,763	17,676	3,401	13,985	15,435	15,405	16,550	10,142	16,552	18,197	12,672	13,756	1,078
Chengdu, China	8,542	12,294	8,167	19,062	8,036	10,246	18,365	5,713	7,346	10,142	13,182	4,239	6,800	5,069	18,137	6,965	7,207	12,820	12,251	10,492
Chesterfield Inlet, Canada	6,807	2,873	14,151	9,808	5,334	10,928	8,996	5,262	8,076	10,933	10,113	8,446	10,273	7,312	10,244	9,141	7,379	3,321	2,880	13,810
Cheyenne, Wyoming	8,981	2,417	16,415	8,006	7,700	9,171	7,235	7,901	10,462	9,208	10,620	11,082	12,729	9,948	8,816	11,573	9,808	1,979	2,578	11,894
Chiang Mai, Thailand	8,886	13,594	7,001	18,802	8,713	10,430	18,994	6,648	7,445	10,326	12,758	4,463	6,375	5,547	17,520	6,817	7,479	14,180	13,533	10,045
Chibougamau, Canada	6,466	1,227	13,868	8,158	5,305	11,699	7,351	6,129	8,019	11,731	8,624	9,228	10,298	7,987	8,490	9,143	7,410	1,975	1,174	14,442
Chicago, Illinois	7,783	997	15,092	7,469	6,662	10,547	6,661	7,370	9,365	10,590	9,231	10,518	11,642	9,295	8,049	10,490	8,765	947	1,148	13,181
Chiclayo, Peru	10,249	5,076	13,597	2,124	10,193	10,042	1,397	12,096	11,827	10,142	7,218	14,579	13,300	13,396	3,124	12,629	11,664	4,510	5,136	10,914
Chihuahua, Mexico	10,003	2,953	17,139	6,936	8,867	8,479	6,217	9,274	11,586	8,534	10,595	12,459	13,864	11,303	7,900	12,711	10,976	2,140	3,134	10,989
Chongqing, China	8,810	12,410	8,302	19,288	8,285	9,980	18,534	5,939	7,617	9,876	13,440	4,510	7,047	5,336	18,402	7,229	7,478	12,903	12,374	10,230
Christchurch, New Zealand	18,539	14,374	11,122	10,185	18,782	3,615	10,716	16,240	16,882	3,621	14,261	14,578	14,648	15,724	10,825	15,773	17,342	13,467	14,548	762
Christiansted, U.S.V.I.	7,309	2,616	12,915	4,622	7,038	12,252	3,851	8,944	8,987	12,334	6,215	11,455	10,891	10,238	4,820	9,961	8,685	2,644	2,574	13,875
Christmas Is. [Indian Ocean]	11,406	16,843	6,306	16,203	11,696	8,953	17,014	9,911	9,735	8,865	13,090	7,276	7,892	8,506	15,660	8,782	10,027	17,237	16,808	7,462
Christmas Is. [Pacific Ocean]	15,442	9,099	16,715	9,812	13,867	2,349	9,651	12,476	16,281	2,385	15,896	14,256	17,383	14,095	11,103	16,912	15,578	8,335	9,277	5,168
Churchill, Canada	7,209	2,533	14,613	9,391	5,781	10,611	8,580	5,805	8,539	10,623	10,166	8,989	10,759	7,850	9,900	9,619	7,851	2,872	2,571	13,480
Cincinnati, Ohio	7,721	694	14,916	7,100	6,684	10,734	6,290	7,558	9,341	10,782	8,885	10,672	11,606	9,432	7,654	10,465	8,768	594	868	13,288
Ciudad Bolivia, Venezuela	8,424	3,444	13,265	3,540	8,244	11,436	2,739	10,153	10,070	11,527	6,485	12,652	11,831	11,446	3,973	10,986	9,821	3,150	3,456	12,758
Ciudad Juarez, Mexico	9,796	2,827	17,059	7,234	8,615	8,588	6,502	8,949	11,352	8,638	10,668	12,133	13,631	10,987	8,168	12,474	10,727	2,079	3,007	11,165
Ciudad Victoria, Mexico	9,842	2,724	16,540	6,093	8,875	8,921	5,358	9,618	11,497	8,986	9,834	12,786	13,738	11,572	7,027	12,615	10,947	1,815	2,897	11,228
Clarksburg, West Virginia	7,400	335	14,559	7,043	6,407	11,091	6,231	7,398	9,035	11,140	8,554	10,475	11,292	9,225	7,525	10,156	8,476	712	508	13,625
Cleveland, Ohio	7,380	524	14,626	7,306	6,328	11,020	6,495	7,219	8,992	11,066	8,751	10,322	11,260	9,080	7,796	10,116	8,414	892	659	13,615
Cocos (Keeling) Island	10,722	16,945	5,332	15,827	11,207	9,855	16,618	9,702	9,025	9,770	12,114	6,829	7,060	8,087	15,049	8,015	9,388	17,593	16,856	8,153
Colombo, Sri Lanka	7,960	14,371	4,556	16,350	8,397	12,185	16,749	7,105	6,285	12,087	10,591	4,061	4,557	5,324	15,083	5,353	6,595	15,208	14,243	10,909
Colon, Panama	9,188	3,298	14,280	3,796	8,808	10,460	2,995	10,447	10,871	10,548	7,509	13,217	12,756	11,970	4,527	11,847	10,550	2,739	3,366	11,995
Colorado Springs, Colorado	9,152	2,447	16,558	7,792	7,899	9,061	7,028	8,148	10,656	9,101	10,595	11,331	12,928	10,191	8,628	11,771	10,010	1,916	2,615	11,749
Columbia, South Carolina	7,751	687	14,692	6,478	6,856	10,924	5,667	7,962	9,417	10,981	8,403	11,008	11,645	9,752	7,009	10,529	8,891	310	836	13,322
Columbus, Georgia	8,152	1,054	15,074	6,400	7,235	10,528	5,594	8,257	9,814	10,587	8,697	11,339	12,048	10,089	7,016	10,929	9,282	154	1,218	12,917
Columbus, Ohio	7,560	570	14,769	7,163	6,524	10,881	6,351	7,419	9,179	10,928	8,794	10,525	11,445	9,283	7,685	10,303	8,607	700	736	13,446
Conakry, Guinea	3,726	7,004	7,418	7,174	4,912	17,593	6,984	7,405	4,692	17,694	1,931	7,799	5,748	7,095	6,124	5,195	4,894	7,646	6,839	16,859
Concepcion, Chile	11,653	8,402	11,248	1,483	12,323	9,855	2,269	14,746	12,699	9,957	6,708	15,771	12,966	15,114	1,945	12,945	12,924	7,902	8,437	9,276
Concord, New Hampshire	6,545	628	13,770	7,403	5,562	11,874	6,600	6,687	8,178	11,917	8,073	9,699	10,436	8,441	7,713	9,299	7,622	1,533	493	14,467
Constantine, Algeria	119	7,065	7,480	10,457	1,659	17,503	10,059	3,860	1,790	17,465	5,374	4,542	3,958	3,594	9,591	2,858	1,529	7,966	6,888	18,965
Copenhagen, Denmark	2,118	6,493	8,896	11,722	734	15,348	11,136	1,820	2,853	15,299	7,478	3,914	5,010	2,660	11,142	3,881	2,136	7,390	6,344	17,525
Coppermine, Canada	7,458	3,980	14,433	10,786	5,884	10,118	9,981	5,188	8,498	10,108	11,265	8,262	10,545	7,263	11,342	9,477	7,777	4,268	4,014	12,979
Coquimbo, Chile	11,077	7,651	11,528	706	11,638	10,227	1,503	14,012	12,246	10,331	6,400	15,352	12,786	14,552	1,446	12,617	12,399	7,185	7,681	9,907
Cordoba, Argentina	10,638	7,895	10,853	1,055	11,341	10,824	1,822	13,807	11,703	10,926	5,766	14,794	12,116	14,099	933	12,003	11,912	7,517	7,905	10,282
Cordoba, Spain	1,114	6,091	8,331	9,662	1,649	17,049	9,198	4,181	2,815	17,046	5,170	5,439	4,956	4,384	8,909	3,875	2,496	6,982	5,913	19,887
Cork, Ireland	2,100	5,305	9,533	10,304	896	15,527	9,700	3,102	3,541	15,512	6,654	5,298	5,820	4,065	9,800	4,665	2,939	6,220	5,142	18,315
Corner Brook, Canada	5,354	1,847	12,695	8,136	4,335	12,892	7,362	5,606	6,963	12,924	7,595	8,525	9,230	7,262	8,220	8,087	6,398	2,759	1,691	15,607
Corrientes, Argentina	9,961	7,581	10,578	1,236	10,684	11,469	1,794	13,171	11,037	11,573	5,146	14,135	11,539	13,422	270	11,369	11,236	7,293	7,573	10,953
Cosenza, Italy	790	7,614	7,220	11,364	1,613	17,078	10,964	3,225	1,177	17,013	6,112	3,639	3,456	2,695	10,482	2,302	668	8,528	7,444	18,125
Craiova, Romania	1,583	7,817	7,406	12,130	1,636	16,321	11,687	2,484	1,420	16,247	6,944	2,965	3,517	1,907	11,292	2,392	703	8,729	7,657	17,444
Cruzeiro do Sul, Brazil	9,670	5,176	12,837	1,788	9,772	10,794	977	11,860	11,188	10,895	6,412	14,070	12,544	12,949	2,515	11,929	11,085	4,746	5,205	11,469
Cuiaba, Brazil	8,856	6,403	10,835	1,745	9,432	12,238	1,658	11,874	10,104	12,343	4,612	13,198	10,988	12,329	1,085	10,608	10,200	6,231	6,374	12,136
Curitiba, Brazil	9,123	7,672	9,778	2,150	9,980	12,428	2,521	12,517	10,110	12,531	4,169	13,192	10,557	12,544	847	10,400	10,350	7,530	7,634	11,719
Cuzco, Peru	10,016	5,830	12,488	1,134	10,246	10,685	322	12,423	11,457	10,789	6,315	14,441	12,616	13,382	1,985	12,110	11,421	5,394	5,858	11,091
Dacca, Bangladesh	7,844	12,933	6,629	18,077	7,718	11,410	17,979	5,778	6,408	11,305	11,875	3,423	5,455	4,531	16,800	5,815	6,436	13,621	12,849	11,082
Dakar, Senegal	3,507	6,334	8,029	7,153	4,502	17,263	6,870	7,041	4,709	17,354	2,522	7,789	6,045	6,965	6,210	5,360	4,797	7,003	6,166	17,268
Dallas, Texas	9,031	1,954	16,159	6,846	7,955	9,474	6,070	8,593	10,640	9,528	9,782	11,766	12,911	10,560	7,648	11,765	10,052	1,162	2,135	11,979
Damascus, Syria	2,616	9,416	5,922	12,916	3,240	16,448	12,639	3,467	1,069	16,349	7,049	2,053	2,030	1,741	11,862	1,096	1,239	10,330	9,253	16,254
Danang, Vietnam	9,851	13,892	7,691	19,154	9,560	9,405	19,970	7,343	8,451	9,301	13,742	5,428	7,389	6,452	18,237	7,842	8,455	14,333	13,864	9,104
Dar es Salaam, Tanzania	5,846	12,707	1,610	11,690	7,242	15,910	11,999	7,916	4,504	15,851	5,926	5,336	2,448	5,951	10,390	3,487	5,214	13,527	12,526	13,324
Darwin, Australia	13,767	16,030	8,883	15,397	13,578	6,214	15,984	11,262	12,208	6,123	15,572	9,367	10,578	10,457	15,731	11,370	12,351	15,749	16,133	5,139
Davao, Philippines	11,940	14,424	9,028	17,510	11,470	7,299	17,896	9,064	10,587	7,196	15,625	7,537	9,457	8,489	17,962	9,973	10,562	14,499	14,469	7,057

Distances in Kilometers	Annaba, Algeria	Annapolis, Maryland	Antananarivo, Madagascar	Antofagasta, Chile	Antwerp, Belgium	Apia, Western Samoa	Arequipa, Peru	Arkhangel'sk, USSR	As Sallum, Egypt	Asau, Western Samoa	Ascension Island (Georgetown)	Ashkhabad, USSR	Asmera, Ethiopia	Astrakhan, USSR	Asuncion, Paraguay	Aswan, Egypt	Athens, Greece	Atlanta, Georgia	Atlantic City, New Jersey	Auckland, New Zealand
David, Panama	9,473	3,435	14,516	3,783	9,064	10,164	2,997	10,645	11,160	10,253	7,760	13,465	13,053	12,212	4,594	12,140	10,830	2,811	3,516	11,709
Dawson, Canada	8,446	4,894	14,962	11,383	6,842	9,066	10,603	5,734	9,317	9,048	12,438	8,587	11,200	7,745	12,113	10,210	8,595	5,004	4,959	11,890
Dawson Creek, Canada	8,621	3,708	15,788	9,979	7,099	9,079	9,202	6,558	9,786	9,084	11,721	9,619	11,888	8,634	10,743	10,799	9,071	3,676	3,805	11,962
Denpasar, Indonesia	12,137	16,450	7,369	16,380	12,199	7,970	17,138	10,148	10,519	7,879	14,154	7,829	8,819	9,001	16,175	9,635	10,728	16,584	16,471	6,740
Denver, Colorado	9,096	2,447	16,515	7,884	7,830	9,091	7,118	8,055	10,589	9,130	10,620	11,237	12,859	10,100	8,712	11,703	9,940	1,951	2,612	11,794
Derby, Australia	13,432	16,919	7,990	15,228	13,517	6,912	15,927	11,402	11,788	6,828	14,635	9,151	9,970	10,322	15,293	10,858	12,030	16,687	17,006	5,440
Des Moines, Iowa	8,217	1,482	15,572	7,609	7,040	10,059	6,810	7,576	9,769	10,100	9,704	10,752	12,048	9,553	8,277	10,893	9,150	1,190	1,640	12,721
Detroit, Michigan	7,432	668	14,714	7,420	6,350	10,927	6,609	7,179	9,031	10,971	8,888	10,298	11,304	9,061	7,926	10,156	8,444	960	796	13,547
Dhahran, Saudi Arabia	4,152	10,905	5,011	14,072	4,729	15,462	13,932	4,309	2,499	15,358	7,929	1,507	1,681	2,233	12,890	1,755	2,794	11,813	10,747	14,716
Diego Garcia Island	8,307	15,329	2,983	14,723	9,147	12,571	15,269	8,403	6,615	12,489	9,561	5,220	4,464	6,419	13,530	5,524	7,112	16,241	15,166	10,613
Dijon, France	1,179	6,389	8,477	10,878	436	16,280	10,357	2,868	2,448	16,243	6,414	4,409	4,726	3,243	10,194	3,569	1,845	7,304	6,223	18,576
Dili, Indonesia	13,046	15,986	8,461	16,048	12,886	6,856	16,673	10,621	11,492	6,762	15,234	8,648	9,909	9,747	16,247	10,670	11,630	15,872	16,058	5,859
Djibouti, Djibouti	4,512	11,634	3,409	12,913	5,616	16,243	12,988	5,884	2,882	16,147	6,730	3,290	616	3,880	11,637	1,757	3,504	12,538	11,459	14,449
Dnepropetrovsk, USSR	2,554	8,208	7,565	13,056	2,204	15,454	12,573	1,825	2,050	15,372	7,890	2,218	3,690	1,012	12,255	2,710	1,476	9,100	8,062	16,528
Dobo, Indonesia	13,598	15,213	9,465	15,805	13,182	5,984	16,273	10,757	12,155	5,887	16,235	9,174	10,751	10,177	16,342	11,426	12,199	14,979	15,311	5,368
Doha, Qatar	4,329	11,080	4,909	14,189	4,907	15,340	14,069	4,437	2,670	15,236	8,026	1,546	1,714	2,358	12,992	1,891	2,973	11,988	10,923	14,540
Donetsk, USSR	2,737	8,397	7,474	13,261	2,418	15,346	12,784	1,852	2,116	15,262	8,030	2,006	3,624	798	12,445	2,689	1,594	9,286	8,253	16,324
Dover, Delaware	7,040	86	14,148	6,973	6,105	11,500	6,164	7,238	8,691	11,550	8,167	10,259	10,936	9,001	7,370	9,809	8,151	994	95	14,005
Dresden, East Germany	1,643	6,784	8,423	11,625	653	15,848	11,088	2,161	2,359	15,795	7,074	3,767	4,557	2,554	10,954	3,414	1,651	7,693	6,628	17,833
Dubayy, United Arab Emir.	4,665	11,312	4,960	14,561	5,161	14,963	14,448	4,496	3,025	14,859	8,388	1,436	2,030	2,427	13,356	2,270	3,289	12,213	11,159	14,204
Dublin, Ireland	2,125	5,417	9,516	10,519	764	15,441	9,910	2,883	3,487	15,420	6,833	5,125	5,762	3,884	10,019	4,605	2,859	6,329	5,257	18,173
Duluth, Minnesota	7,793	1,538	15,220	8,100	6,549	10,346	7,295	6,992	9,299	10,380	9,722	10,172	11,575	8,981	8,699	10,417	8,661	1,588	1,653	13,088
Dunedin, New Zealand	18,269	14,616	10,830	10,169	18,831	3,924	10,729	16,350	16,650	3,929	14,026	14,490	14,396	15,670	10,754	15,532	17,152	13,705	14,789	1,061
Durango, Mexico	10,244	3,128	17,100	6,445	9,191	8,407	5,741	9,734	11,869	8,470	10,397	12,920	14,134	11,742	7,444	12,994	11,288	2,246	3,306	10,794
Durban, South Africa	7,778	13,456	2,062	9,754	9,352	14,596	10,281	10,500	6,826	14,590	5,318	8,028	5,071	8,612	8,542	5,971	7,547	13,995	13,297	11,712
Dushanbe, USSR	5,282	10,721	6,738	15,838	5,102	13,515	15,451	3,434	4,018	13,413	9,972	914	3,893	1,906	14,828	3,745	3,904	11,537	10,603	13,679
East London, South Africa	8,020	13,374	2,502	9,338	9,613	14,417	9,885	10,876	7,156	14,421	5,164	8,469	5,479	9,022	8,141	6,343	7,874	13,848	13,222	11,539
Easter Island (Hanga Roa)	14,100	8,082	14,339	3,931	13,950	6,601	4,077	15,334	15,623	6,705	10,109	18,362	16,508	17,105	5,141	16,245	15,516	7,241	8,209	7,059
Echo Bay, Canada	7,687	3,990	14,660	10,727	6,115	9,897	9,925	5,407	8,732	9,889	11,420	8,466	10,776	7,480	11,326	9,709	8,010	4,225	4,035	12,763
Edinburgh, United Kingdom	2,269	5,546	9,558	10,840	726	15,233	10,219	2,544	3,491	15,206	7,152	4,902	5,746	3,648	10,360	4,592	2,826	6,452	5,392	17,881
Edmonton, Canada	8,508	3,227	15,831	9,504	7,035	9,282	8,722	6,717	9,767	9,295	11,312	9,836	11,933	8,796	10,248	10,816	9,063	3,175	3,330	12,153
El Aaiun, Morocco	2,248	5,935	8,299	8,330	3,055	17,350	7,931	5,602	3,737	17,399	3,886	6,667	5,528	5,710	7,511	4,616	3,642	6,742	5,755	18,701
Elat, Israel	2,651	9,626	5,530	12,691	3,491	16,775	12,469	3,913	966	16,673	6,716	2,354	1,627	2,185	11,590	640	1,396	10,541	9,458	16,222
Elazig, Turkey	2,765	9,201	6,434	13,275	3,042	15,915	12,927	2,881	1,504	15,819	7,570	1,674	2,588	1,117	12,290	1,727	1,356	10,107	9,046	16,140
Eniwetok Atoll, Marshall Isls.	14,024	11,764	13,009	14,316	12,735	4,012	14,212	10,280	13,413	3,914	19,482	10,420	13,115	10,871	15,567	13,258	13,040	11,386	11,894	5,512
Erfurt, East Germany	1,586	6,617	8,524	11,444	464	15,877	10,901	2,280	2,450	15,829	6,972	3,956	4,676	2,745	10,786	3,526	1,757	7,527	6,459	17,980
Erzurum, Turkey	2,929	9,227	6,545	13,467	3,099	15,692	13,102	2,743	1,724	15,597	7,791	1,496	2,734	901	12,497	1,925	1,534	10,128	9,075	15,992
Esfahan, Iran	4,007	10,442	5,725	14,316	4,327	15,168	14,069	3,629	2,496	15,064	8,302	848	2,310	1,550	13,211	2,065	2,594	11,338	10,293	14,875
Essen, West Germany	1,618	6,340	8,735	11,206	183	15,831	10,649	2,415	2,661	15,790	6,893	4,238	4,910	3,020	10,580	3,756	1,989	7,251	6,181	18,121
Eucla, Australia	14,658	17,592	8,136	13,546	15,042	6,334	14,255	13,063	12,956	6,271	14,145	10,624	10,889	11,843	13,661	11,915	13,327	16,916	17,753	4,224
Fargo, North Dakota	8,082	1,868	15,527	8,249	6,797	10,011	7,450	7,104	9,558	10,042	10,073	10,291	11,826	9,124	8,905	10,670	8,907	1,794	1,992	12,773
Faroe Islands (Torshavn)	2,970	5,240	10,160	11,032	1,380	14,523	10,357	2,334	4,085	14,496	7,784	5,092	6,299	3,831	10,681	5,156	3,390	6,123	5,101	17,205
Florence, Italy	818	7,000	7,865	11,158	974	16,674	10,692	2,949	1,822	16,624	6,284	3,972	4,099	2,887	10,375	2,943	1,231	7,915	6,833	18,427
Florianopolis, Brazil	9,254	7,920	9,632	2,233	10,153	12,372	2,670	12,697	10,191	12,473	4,200	13,255	10,551	12,658	943	10,440	10,456	7,770	7,883	11,560
Fort George, Canada	6,605	1,662	14,056	8,624	5,333	11,416	7,814	5,896	8,087	11,440	9,106	9,046	10,360	7,830	9,001	9,203	7,445	2,272	1,646	14,225
Fort McMurray, Canada	8,165	3,216	15,458	9,702	6,677	9,586	8,909	6,341	9,401	9,595	11,166	9,468	11,558	8,420	10,387	10,444	8,694	3,276	3,301	12,465
Fort Nelson, Canada	8,454	3,928	15,505	10,323	6,905	9,189	9,542	6,246	9,556	9,188	11,808	9,280	11,619	8,316	11,059	10,547	8,837	3,965	4,012	12,071
Fort Severn, Canada	7,012	2,063	14,462	8,973	5,655	10,908	8,162	5,929	8,422	10,927	9,708	9,112	10,675	7,933	9,439	9,522	7,754	2,483	2,089	13,751
Fort Smith, Arkansas	8,679	1,638	15,869	7,008	7,591	9,777	6,219	8,250	10,281	9,828	9,623	11,417	12,554	10,206	7,749	11,407	9,690	938	1,818	12,320
Fort Vermilion, Canada	8,231	3,541	15,421	10,020	6,710	9,462	9,230	6,222	9,403	9,466	11,429	9,314	11,519	8,301	10,718	10,423	8,689	3,608	3,622	12,345
Fort Wayne, Indiana	7,653	774	14,918	7,326	6,573	10,728	6,516	7,376	9,254	10,773	9,006	10,504	11,527	9,271	7,874	10,379	8,667	815	929	13,331
Fort-Chimo, Canada	5,836	2,205	13,291	9,061	4,527	12,086	8,262	5,148	7,286	12,102	8,772	8,271	9,556	7,043	9,292	8,399	6,638	2,960	2,130	14,937
Fort-de-France, Martinique	7,180	3,095	12,456	4,351	7,053	12,582	3,617	9,096	8,827	12,668	5,723	11,439	10,632	10,254	4,426	9,755	8,579	3,164	3,039	14,001
Fortaleza, Brazil	6,569	6,127	9,466	4,076	7,322	14,517	3,876	9,854	7,773	14,621	2,707	10,870	8,782	10,042	3,145	8,307	7,884	6,354	6,025	14,351
Frankfort, Kentucky	7,799	734	14,966	7,011	6,776	10,682	6,202	7,662	9,424	10,732	8,882	10,774	11,687	9,533	7,578	10,548	8,856	496	913	13,218
Frankfurt am Main, W. Ger.	1,470	6,507	8,546	11,254	325	15,980	10,714	2,458	2,472	15,936	6,809	4,121	4,723	2,920	10,594	3,568	1,802	7,419	6,346	18,164
Fredericton, Canada	6,073	1,120	13,358	7,718	5,068	12,267	6,924	6,232	7,694	12,306	7,904	9,216	9,957	7,957	7,940	8,817	7,132	2,027	974	14,917
Freeport, Bahamas	8,008	1,398	14,489	5,624	7,299	10,979	4,812	8,643	9,706	11,048	7,919	11,592	11,854	10,329	6,162	10,788	9,247	966	1,479	13,126
Freetown, Sierra Leone	3,795	7,115	7,324	7,158	5,006	17,613	6,986	7,489	4,720	17,716	1,822	7,826	5,722	7,143	6,092	5,195	4,941	7,750	6,950	16,762
Frobisher Bay, Canada	5,741	2,807	13,148	9,690	4,317	12,026	8,890	4,642	7,081	12,031	9,143	7,804	9,320	6,601	9,914	8,172	6,403	3,512	2,743	14,908
Frunze, USSR	5,604	10,482	7,386	16,165	5,204	12,971	15,669	3,221	4,496	12,871	10,526	1,479	4,565	2,131	15,279	4,343	4,284	11,253	10,378	13,419
Fukuoka, Japan	10,202	11,508	10,524	17,718	9,234	8,070	17,111	6,684	9,370	7,971	15,427	6,365	9,218	6,857	18,807	9,218	9,055	11,717	11,535	9,057
Funafuti Atoll, Tuvalu	16,744	11,846	13,914	11,680	15,245	1,158	11,777	12,997	16,310	1,054	17,658	13,275	15,642	13,767	12,830	16,049	15,921	11,132	12,019	3,171
Funchal, Madeira Island	2,300	5,337	8,914	8,430	2,698	16,726	7,953	5,237	3,945	16,764	4,497	6,684	5,925	5,626	7,731	4,927	3,713	6,175	5,156	18,858
Fuzhou, China	10,024	12,619	9,217	19,014	9,350	8,670	18,466	6,884	8,905	8,567	14,744	5,801	8,336	6,555	19,712	8,539	8,729	12,928	12,622	9,071
Gaborone, Botswana	7,075	12,723	2,321	9,538	8,666	15,340	9,992	9,974	6,224	15,338	4,665	7,718	4,646	8,176	8,279	5,446	6,939	13,298	12,561	12,457
Galapagos Islands (Santa Cruz)	10,781	4,610	14,948	3,338	10,399	9,066	2,704	11,894	12,454	9,161	8,462	14,791	14,234	13,534	4,448	13,396	12,152	3,857	4,716	10,403
Gander, Canada	5,113	2,065	12,451	8,193	4,118	13,132	7,430	5,469	6,729	13,163	7,420	8,344	8,994	7,081	8,225	7,853	6,170	2,979	1,903	15,851
Gangtok, India	7,479	12,504	6,770	17,885	7,301	11,650	17,650	5,339	6,089	11,546	11,702	3,054	5,287	4,126	16,666	5,559	6,079	13,204	12,417	11,462
Garyarsa, China	6,543	11,819	6,613	17,019	6,391	12,492	16,717	4,555	5,177	12,388	10,925	2,119	4,570	3,201	15,884	4,714	5,145	12,581	11,716	12,399
Gaspe, Canada	5,822	1,456	13,174	8,049	4,760	12,417	7,259	5,874	7,419	12,451	7,955	8,869	9,691	7,611	8,235	8,544	6,840	2,350	1,320	15,129
Gauhati, India	7,810	12,689	6,910	18,206	7,605	11,324	17,984	5,588	6,424	11,220	12,011	3,386	5,591	4,442	16,966	5,887	6,412	13,359	12,610	11,135
Gdansk, Poland	2,112	6,906	8,571	12,051	1,021	15,419	11,487	1,667	2,583	15,362	7,563	3,502	4,672	2,252	11,418	3,562	1,860	7,803	6,758	17,345
Geneva, Switzerland	1,041	6,520	8,326	10,903	573	16,411	10,396	2,921	2,302	16,372	6,336	4,336	4,581	3,190	10,193	3,425	1,710	7,435	6,353	18,609
Genoa, Italy	841	6,804	8,034	11,017	828	16,614	10,538	2,975	2,008	16,569	6,255	4,145	4,286	3,039	10,260	3,131	1,428	7,719	6,636	18,557
Georgetown, Guyana	7,425	4,011	11,908	3,622	7,532	12,738	2,959	9,741	8,990	12,833	5,123	11,810	10,576	10,692	3,548	9,817	8,841	4,024	3,958	13,725
Geraldton, Australia	13,280	18,489	6,836	14,180	13,821	7,710	14,964	12,137	11,576	7,642	13,214	9,423	9,481	10,673	13,969	10,519	11,984	18,139	18,573	5,614
Ghanzi, Botswana	6,637	12,182	2,702	9,288	8,240	15,824	9,691	9,685	5,891	15,828	4,165	7,620	4,491	7,974	8,007	5,191	6,595	12,766	12,019	12,946
Ghat, Libya	1,343	8,039	6,319	10,216	2,955	18,757	9,970	4,913	1,638	18,698	4,513	4,745	3,181	4,109	9,175	2,300	1,930	8,907	7,859	18,045
Gibraltar	1,177	6,128	8,250	9,512	1,848	17,191	9,063	4,376	2,856	17,193	4,969	5,559	4,949	4,527	8,739	3,890	2,585	7,011	5,949	19,923
Gijon, Spain	1,358	5,775	8,787	9,945	1,142	16,457	9,423	3,692	3,006	16,447	5,768	5,311	5,245	4,169	9,286	4,117	2,544	6,683	5,601	19,263
Gisborne, New Zealand	19,144	13,747	11,815	10,106	18,525	2,931	10,566	16,025	17,440	2,943	14,689	14,842	15,267	15,892	10,867	16,364	17,782	12,851	13,925	349
Glasgow, United Kingdom	2,291	5,484	9,601	10,779	770	15,222	10,156	2,600	3,537	15,197	7,130	4,968	5,796	3,715	10,305	4,640	2,876	6,390	5,329	17,895
Godthab, Greenland	4,916	3,252	12,322	9,881	3,494	12,815	9,104	4,046	6,260	12,816	8,586	7,146	8,507	5,914	9,938	7,356	5,587	4,061	3,148	15,698
Gomez Palacio, Mexico	10,043	2,930	16,961	6,510	8,985	8,581	5,792	9,540	11,665	8,642	10,301	12,725	13,931	11,542	7,479	12,789	11,082	2,056	3,109	10,990
Goose Bay, Canada	9,306	4,156	16,378	10,014	7,774	8,387	9,267	7,106	10,439	8,393	12,300	10,090	12,501	9,167	10,887	11,432	9,721	3,979	4,273	11,270
Gorki, USSR	3,451	8,056	8,345	13,661	2,632	14,398	13,080	937	3,117	14,320	8,889	2,306	4,570	1,146	13,017	3,694	2,534	8,901	7,931	15,790
Goteborg, Sweden	2,335	6,368	9,107	11,761	872	15,125	11,154	1,698	3,076	15,077	7,660	3,998	5,215	2,736	11,223	4,092	2,356	7,259	6,223	17,367
Granada, Spain	1,018	6,210	8,210	9,702	1,682	17,160	9,250	4,198	2,713	17,155	5,122	5,376	4,842	4,338	8,930	3,766	2,414	7,100	6,031	19,881
Grand Turk, Turks & Caicos	7,654	2,008	13,656	4,992	7,180	11,648	4,189	8,849	9,355	11,725	6,995	11,584	11,379	10,334	5,371	10,384	8,980	1,884	2,008	13,519
Graz, Austria	1,295	7,106	7,983	11,596	927	16,260	11,105	2,469	1,910	16,203	6,770	3,621	4,135	2,476	10,845	2,985	1,216	8,019	6,944	17,972
Green Bay, Wisconsin	7,656	1,136	15,027	7,758	6,486	10,588	6,949	7,110	9,210	10,627	9,346	10,269	11,489	9,055	8,321	10,334	8,595	1,235	1,259	13,274
Grenoble, France	934	6,538	8,261	10,821	680	16,523	10,324	3,037	2,261	16,485	6,217	4,387	4,540	3,257	10,097	3,386	1,696	7,452	6,369	18,713
Guadalajara, Mexico	10,391	3,272	16,977	6,066	9,408	8,397	5,373	10,061	12,044	8,464	10,213	13,242	14,288	12,046	7,086	13,163	11,488	2,365	3,446	10,678
Guam (Agana)	12,848	12,800	11,241	16,166	11,880	5,669	16,122	9,328	11,881	5,565	17,676	8,789	11,267	9,444	17,341	11,539	11,644	12,644	12,892	6,399
Guantanamo, Cuba	8,089	2,093	14,050	4,872	7,573	11,206	4,061	9,153	9,791	11,283	7,342	11,960	11,827	10,704	5,369	10,827	9,405	1,761	2,132	13,081
Guatemala City, Guatemala	9,765	3,028	15,545	4,768	9,092	9,482	4,016	10,305	11,469	9,563	8,761	13,346	13,554	12,086	5,673	12,530	11,033	2,206	3,158	11,389
Guayaquil, Ecuador	9,943	4,568	13,819	2,585	9,794	10,166	1,817	11,626	11,560	10,264	7,276	14,205	13,166	12,996	3,491	12,418	11,349	4,004	4,630	11,232
Guiyang, China	9,018	12,739	8,137	19,581	8,549	9,876	18,864	6,235	7,771	9,772	13,500	4,670	7,083	5,552	18,461	7,329	7,666	13,226	12,704	9,999
Gur'yev, USSR	3,771	9,185	7,326	14,321	3,430	14,549	13,845	2,061	2,856	14,456	8,912	1,149	3,723	305	13,476	3,063	2,507	10,042	9,054	15,263

Distances in Kilometers	Annaba, Algeria	Annapolis, Maryland	Antananarivo, Madagascar	Antofagasta, Chile	Antwerp, Belgium	Apia, Western Samoa	Arequipa, Peru	Arkhangel'sk, USSR	As Sallum, Egypt	Asau, Western Samoa	Ascension Island (Georgetown)	Ashkhabad, USSR	Asmera, Ethiopia	Astrakhan, USSR	Asuncion, Paraguay	Aswan, Egypt	Athens, Greece	Atlanta, Georgia	Atlantic City, New Jersey	Auckland, New Zealand
Haifa, Israel	2,522	9,379	5,880	12,781	3,213	16,590	12,512	3,549	939	16,491	6,907	2,192	1,979	1,868	11,723	992	1,171	10,294	9,214	16,346
Haikou, China	9,752	13,432	8,095	19,600	9,346	9,317	19,561	7,046	8,432	9,213	13,942	5,357	7,536	6,306	18,665	7,901	8,378	13,851	13,410	9,238
Haiphong, Vietnam	9,398	13,372	7,808	19,588	9,042	9,706	19,480	6,795	8,055	9,602	13,557	4,991	7,148	5,967	18,356	7,513	8,015	13,848	13,338	9,579
Hakodate, Japan	10,074	10,307	11,647	16,510	8,871	7,850	15,848	6,356	9,555	7,760	15,537	6,777	9,836	6,997	17,524	9,623	9,116	10,464	10,347	9,370
Halifax, Canada	5,893	1,241	13,125	7,594	4,950	12,512	6,808	6,239	7,533	12,553	7,624	9,168	9,786	7,905	7,765	8,653	6,990	2,155	1,074	15,124
Hamburg, West Germany	1,859	6,434	8,797	11,483	460	15,596	10,913	2,106	2,728	15,550	7,192	4,047	4,935	2,808	10,877	3,791	2,026	7,340	6,280	17,813
Hamilton, Bermuda	6,511	1,294	13,174	6,219	5,884	12,407	5,436	7,496	8,212	12,470	6,950	10,259	10,353	9,003	6,413	9,289	7,773	1,838	1,174	14,627
Hamilton, New Zealand	18,916	13,922	11,697	10,360	18,351	2,948	10,824	15,821	17,216	2,951	14,845	14,584	15,076	15,635	11,111	16,156	17,532	13,032	14,101	112
Hangzhou, China	9,778	12,150	9,488	18,745	9,019	8,769	18,072	6,523	8,746	8,666	14,697	5,662	8,343	6,329	19,416	8,459	8,523	12,468	12,153	9,360
Hannover, West Germany	1,726	6,470	8,702	11,417	387	15,728	10,857	2,217	2,628	15,683	7,066	4,056	4,850	2,828	10,791	3,702	1,934	7,378	6,314	17,927
Hanoi, Vietnam	9,318	13,357	7,742	19,540	8,973	9,795	19,430	6,739	7,970	9,690	13,470	4,908	7,059	5,890	18,280	7,425	7,934	13,846	13,320	9,656
Harare, Zimbabwe	6,533	12,739	1,744	10,343	8,078	15,711	10,743	9,172	5,503	15,689	5,041	6,805	3,769	7,311	9,062	4,641	6,226	13,422	12,566	12,859
Harbin, China	9,003	10,341	10,685	17,117	7,921	9,030	16,341	5,370	8,374	8,937	14,409	5,562	8,630	5,816	17,700	8,410	7,967	10,665	10,347	10,343
Harrisburg, Pennsylvania	7,087	147	14,249	7,107	6,113	11,401	6,297	7,176	8,726	11,449	8,323	10,223	10,980	8,968	7,523	9,847	8,173	983	231	13,941
Hartford, Connecticut	6,696	449	13,879	7,246	5,734	11,770	6,441	6,872	8,336	11,816	8,079	9,883	10,589	8,625	7,581	9,456	7,787	1,360	308	14,330
Havana, Cuba	8,517	1,843	14,827	5,335	7,820	10,547	4,529	9,126	10,218	10,619	8,149	12,103	12,349	10,840	5,982	11,294	9,765	1,193	1,948	12,623
Helena, Montana	8,986	3,000	16,416	8,836	7,584	8,951	8,070	7,450	10,344	8,976	11,228	10,592	12,559	9,526	9,654	11,421	9,655	2,731	3,136	11,775
Helsinki, Finland	2,862	6,918	9,000	12,551	1,620	14,685	11,933	940	3,179	14,624	8,307	3,406	5,105	2,155	12,016	4,055	2,469	7,783	6,785	16,650
Hengyang, China	9,458	12,651	8,660	19,546	8,883	9,328	18,769	6,484	8,277	9,224	14,072	5,171	7,662	5,983	19,041	7,879	8,134	13,058	12,634	9,597
Herat, Afghanistan	4,872	10,846	6,095	15,303	4,939	14,169	15,018	3,669	3,459	14,066	9,295	528	3,141	1,791	14,210	3,055	3,460	11,705	10,713	14,038
Hermosillo, Mexico	10,311	3,345	17,571	7,274	9,107	8,071	6,578	9,333	11,853	8,122	11,074	12,504	14,131	11,391	8,283	12,973	11,219	2,573	3,525	10,643
Hiroshima, Japan	10,261	11,353	10,732	17,508	9,251	7,955	16,904	6,699	9,474	7,857	15,540	6,493	9,379	6,947	18,611	9,352	9,140	11,543	11,385	9,027
Hiva Oa (Atuona)	15,531	8,415	16,750	7,414	14,341	3,589	7,325	13,925	17,102	3,682	13,590	16,438	19,357	15,898	8,694	18,213	16,444	7,519	8,592	5,518
Ho Chi Minh City, Vietnam	10,081	14,490	7,273	18,545	9,923	9,409	19,353	7,803	8,597	9,307	13,566	5,664	7,337	6,760	17,715	7,898	8,668	14,944	14,457	8,840
Hobart, Australia	16,536	16,348	9,367	11,687	17,089	5,066	12,335	14,982	14,845	5,034	14,080	12,671	12,650	13,890	12,035	13,750	15,296	15,461	16,527	2,428
Hohhot, China	8,436	11,134	9,349	18,095	7,621	9,914	17,285	5,122	7,529	9,815	13,583	4,528	7,463	5,034	18,023	7,388	7,236	11,591	11,109	10,740
Hong Kong	9,908	13,137	8,562	19,537	9,391	9,012	19,135	7,013	8,663	8,907	14,313	5,564	7,892	6,438	19,132	8,196	8,560	13,505	13,127	9,121
Honiara, Solomon Islands	15,882	13,550	11,984	13,440	14,864	3,124	13,680	12,324	14,765	3,025	17,988	11,665	13,606	12,442	14,421	14,197	14,627	12,962	13,708	3,386
Honolulu, Hawaii	13,388	7,829	17,369	10,696	11,786	4,173	10,297	10,353	14,144	4,170	15,839	12,435	15,560	12,072	11,979	14,851	13,439	7,242	7,992	7,052
Houston, Texas	9,129	2,008	16,095	6,486	8,120	9,495	5,712	8,870	10,767	9,554	9,583	12,029	13,023	10,809	7,299	11,889	10,202	1,129	2,186	11,914
Huambo, Angola	5,558	11,087	3,463	9,074	7,170	16,954	9,345	8,823	5,003	16,967	3,348	7,155	4,018	7,296	7,771	4,478	5,675	11,723	10,919	14,093
Hubli, India	7,004	13,312	4,853	16,313	7,353	12,854	16,473	6,063	5,365	12,753	10,204	2,999	3,886	4,262	15,011	4,519	5,614	14,158	13,182	11,865
Hugh Town, United Kingdom	1,836	5,506	9,277	10,302	773	15,791	9,720	3,162	3,308	15,774	6,457	5,191	5,587	3,976	9,747	4,433	2,726	6,420	5,339	18,552
Hull, Canada	6,753	720	14,067	7,669	5,678	11,559	6,860	6,618	8,350	11,598	8,485	9,694	10,623	8,447	8,040	9,476	7,766	1,493	684	14,217
Hyderabad, India	7,174	13,247	5,253	16,719	7,413	12,537	16,842	5,961	5,572	12,434	10,582	3,006	4,223	4,262	15,419	4,785	5,768	14,063	13,126	11,701
Hyderabad, Pakistan	5,823	12,003	5,395	15,865	6,055	13,649	15,761	4,794	4,261	13,545	9,672	1,684	3,259	2,946	14,636	3,582	4,411	12,860	11,871	13,058
Igloolik, Canada	6,202	3,399	13,441	10,358	4,675	11,433	9,549	4,481	7,383	11,428	9,963	7,665	9,545	6,532	10,675	8,425	6,675	3,968	3,371	14,307
Iloilo, Philippines	11,423	14,164	8,860	18,033	10,951	7,744	18,380	8,557	10,090	7,641	15,305	7,027	9,033	7,969	18,392	9,505	10,049	14,325	14,192	7,579
Indianapolis, Indiana	7,802	837	15,037	7,209	6,735	10,612	6,400	7,542	9,410	10,659	9,042	10,672	11,680	9,439	7,784	10,535	8,827	686	1,006	13,192
Innsbruck, Austria	1,190	6,826	8,172	11,316	671	16,286	10,813	2,606	2,100	16,237	6,625	3,928	4,358	2,774	10,591	3,202	1,441	7,740	6,662	18,225
Inuvik, Canada	7,904	4,711	14,511	11,407	6,300	9,605	10,610	5,249	8,788	9,585	11,993	8,174	10,705	7,284	12,038	9,696	8,065	4,928	4,756	12,421
Invercargill, New Zealand	18,094	14,792	10,660	10,264	18,724	4,063	10,837	16,295	16,474	4,065	13,980	14,348	14,220	15,539	10,820	15,356	16,981	13,881	14,965	1,185
Inverness, United Kingdom	2,452	5,449	9,721	10,877	893	15,049	10,241	2,486	3,649	15,023	7,308	4,957	5,896	3,698	10,431	4,743	2,975	6,351	5,298	17,713
Iquitos, Peru	9,466	4,744	13,079	2,221	9,479	10,833	1,410	11,500	11,029	10,932	6,527	13,828	12,509	12,673	2,905	11,825	10,882	4,314	4,776	11,691
Iraklion, Greece	1,571	8,510	6,453	11,971	2,421	17,093	11,645	3,413	418	17,006	6,336	2,972	2,609	2,275	10,986	1,454	320	9,424	8,341	17,298
Irkutsk, USSR	7,273	9,895	9,603	16,797	6,314	10,806	16,009	3,779	6,598	10,714	12,636	3,870	7,004	4,040	16,648	6,678	6,194	10,438	9,853	11,996
Islamabad, Pakistan	5,840	11,374	6,428	16,318	5,749	13,169	16,011	4,083	4,471	13,065	10,276	1,415	3,993	2,546	15,214	4,044	4,439	12,181	11,259	13,093
Istanbul, Turkey	1,888	8,376	6,907	12,456	2,195	16,391	12,063	2,724	1,103	16,307	7,002	2,542	3,005	1,644	11,542	1,913	562	9,289	8,216	17,042
Ivujivik, Canada	6,236	2,607	13,646	9,562	4,815	11,555	8,754	5,037	7,577	11,563	9,469	8,216	9,812	7,032	9,883	8,665	6,896	3,218	2,575	14,433
Iwo Jima Island, Japan	11,630	11,929	11,247	16,813	10,593	6,650	16,490	8,043	10,805	6,549	16,843	7,774	10,515	8,298	18,115	10,607	10,496	11,930	11,995	7,672
Izmir, Turkey	1,716	8,437	6,694	12,237	2,277	16,714	11,875	3,040	782	16,628	6,696	2,724	2,807	1,926	11,289	1,679	303	9,351	8,272	17,176
Jackson, Mississippi	8,566	1,443	15,562	6,540	7,583	10,050	5,744	8,446	10,210	10,107	9,164	11,576	12,461	10,341	7,247	11,330	9,655	566	1,620	12,482
Jaffna, Sri Lanka	7,795	14,099	4,765	16,524	8,173	12,230	16,864	6,823	6,136	12,131	10,645	3,808	4,501	5,071	15,240	5,240	6,415	14,927	13,975	11,073
Jakarta, Indonesia	11,225	16,356	6,566	16,692	11,403	8,937	17,502	9,520	9,584	8,844	13,326	6,994	7,851	8,202	16,148	8,678	9,826	16,743	16,327	7,646
Jamestown, St. Helena	6,017	9,530	5,645	6,778	7,504	16,376	7,007	9,747	6,205	16,455	1,296	8,958	6,004	8,749	5,481	6,099	6,715	9,974	9,388	14,160
Jamnagar, India	6,130	12,368	5,194	15,992	6,408	13,467	15,958	5,152	4,538	13,362	9,788	2,048	3,367	3,310	14,732	3,798	4,724	13,224	12,236	12,745
Jan Mayen Island	3,920	5,153	10,861	11,507	2,307	13,546	10,776	2,138	4,849	13,515	8,767	5,253	6,959	4,042	11,326	5,854	4,130	5,970	5,042	16,199
Jayapura, Indonesia	13,888	14,496	10,262	15,579	13,253	5,377	15,910	10,744	12,572	5,276	17,037	9,511	11,355	10,417	16,355	11,940	12,529	14,207	14,607	5,160
Jefferson City, Missouri	8,309	1,361	15,573	7,253	7,196	10,076	6,454	7,850	9,897	10,123	9,506	11,014	12,173	9,800	7,930	11,022	9,298	881	1,535	12,669
Jerusalem, Israel	2,581	9,477	5,760	12,776	3,317	16,633	12,523	3,666	956	16,533	6,864	2,218	1,859	1,957	11,703	882	1,256	10,391	9,311	16,287
Jiggalong, Australia	13,532	17,638	7,545	14,662	13,827	7,141	15,404	11,877	11,844	7,066	14,045	9,411	9,878	10,626	14,618	10,845	12,167	17,319	17,734	5,338
Jinan, China	9,087	11,516	9,536	18,401	8,270	9,315	17,609	5,761	8,147	9,215	14,180	5,110	7,957	5,672	18,646	7,955	7,874	11,901	11,506	10,086
Jodhpur, India	6,187	12,120	5,711	16,340	6,308	13,183	16,212	4,845	4,669	13,079	10,150	1,889	3,738	3,135	15,115	4,039	4,771	12,948	11,997	12,705
Johannesburg, South Africa	7,302	13,000	2,152	9,668	8,885	15,089	10,146	10,120	6,400	15,085	4,924	7,774	4,743	8,283	8,422	5,588	7,119	13,569	12,838	12,205
Juazeiro do Norte, Brazil	6,917	6,390	9,431	3,784	7,706	14,282	3,650	10,243	8,073	14,386	2,751	11,178	8,981	10,384	2,792	8,561	8,213	6,565	6,297	13,980
Juneau, Alaska	8,885	4,595	15,629	10,820	7,302	8,688	10,056	6,369	9,865	8,680	12,474	9,271	11,821	8,402	11,627	10,799	9,142	4,580	4,683	11,555
Kabul, Afghanistan	5,467	11,137	6,344	15,944	5,414	13,528	15,635	3,861	4,096	13,425	9,928	1,044	3,699	2,213	14,852	3,690	4,064	11,964	11,016	13,461
Kalgoorlie, Australia	13,972	18,148	7,463	13,854	14,452	7,035	14,606	12,634	12,268	6,971	13,661	10,037	10,181	11,276	13,805	11,216	12,662	17,575	18,286	4,918
Kaliningrad, USSR	2,206	6,990	8,554	12,176	1,146	15,346	11,611	1,562	2,598	15,287	7,667	3,400	4,651	2,145	11,543	3,553	1,876	7,883	6,844	17,225
Kamloops, Canada	9,060	3,639	16,323	9,579	7,570	8,714	8,819	7,119	10,286	8,727	11,808	10,187	12,420	9,197	10,413	11,317	9,576	3,461	3,759	11,587
Kampala, Uganda	4,789	11,630	2,682	11,353	6,233	16,961	11,536	7,158	3,546	16,895	5,295	4,935	1,802	5,319	10,056	2,630	4,268	12,461	11,449	14,405
Kananga, Zaire	4,977	11,193	3,079	10,042	6,559	17,331	10,256	7,959	4,156	17,308	4,076	6,117	2,972	6,319	8,742	3,506	4,860	11,930	11,017	14,472
Kano, Nigeria	2,759	8,755	5,478	9,442	4,365	19,801	9,354	6,337	2,758	19,814	3,362	5,708	3,309	5,317	8,274	2,899	3,252	9,546	8,575	16,931
Kanpur, India	6,817	12,373	6,148	17,070	6,803	12,456	16,919	5,090	5,352	12,351	10,877	2,422	4,460	3,600	15,840	4,762	5,404	13,149	12,265	12,093
Kansas City, Missouri	8,444	1,563	15,750	7,389	7,296	9,895	6,595	7,864	10,015	9,940	9,723	11,038	12,293	9,837	8,095	11,139	9,404	1,089	1,734	12,516
Kaohsiung, Taiwan	10,355	12,966	9,149	18,933	9,721	8,436	18,607	7,268	9,186	8,331	14,926	6,080	8,504	6,880	19,655	8,770	9,040	13,243	12,975	8,720
Karachi, Pakistan	5,732	11,989	5,286	15,726	6,003	13,781	15,634	4,809	4,154	13,677	9,531	1,666	3,116	2,924	14,495	3,456	4,323	12,853	11,853	13,145
Karaganda, USSR	5,312	9,728	8,024	15,726	4,695	12,969	15,138	2,517	4,440	12,874	10,505	1,770	4,916	1,901	15,013	4,500	4,100	10,486	9,629	13,798
Karl-Marx-Stadt, East Germany	1,602	6,743	8,436	11,562	598	15,880	11,025	2,214	2,366	15,829	7,023	3,823	4,576	2,613	10,891	3,430	1,664	7,652	6,586	17,894
Kasanga, Tanzania	5,584	12,125	2,112	10,802	7,094	16,490	11,091	8,138	4,476	16,448	5,019	5,866	2,769	6,300	9,500	3,606	5,200	12,891	11,947	13,723
Kashgar, China	5,834	10,877	7,110	16,409	5,525	12,887	15,964	3,609	4,630	12,786	10,601	1,536	4,484	2,389	15,442	4,373	4,480	11,649	10,773	13,157
Kassel, West Germany	1,608	6,504	8,618	11,359	355	15,846	10,809	2,317	2,542	15,800	6,955	4,065	4,776	2,849	10,715	3,625	1,856	7,414	6,346	18,026
Kathmandu, Nepal	7,177	12,385	6,574	17,556	7,046	11,979	17,337	5,161	5,769	11,874	11,378	2,752	4,966	3,855	16,344	5,231	5,772	13,116	12,291	11,755
Kayes, Mali	3,133	6,866	7,441	7,675	4,319	17,909	7,437	6,805	4,174	18,000	2,497	7,276	5,408	6,527	6,667	4,759	4,332	7,570	6,693	17,447
Kazan, USSR	3,730	8,321	8,275	13,987	2,958	14,194	13,406	1,090	3,275	14,112	9,139	2,096	4,569	1,048	13,333	3,760	2,736	9,154	8,200	15,481
Kemi, Finland	3,397	6,594	9,593	12,602	1,985	14,104	11,932	760	3,809	14,048	8,775	3,783	5,709	2,581	12,193	4,676	3,097	7,428	6,474	16,254
Kenora, Canada	7,757	1,862	15,211	8,475	6,449	10,280	7,670	6,742	9,213	10,307	9,971	9,928	11,477	8,758	9,075	10,321	8,556	1,965	1,958	13,071
Kerguelen Island	11,334	17,093	3,920	10,987	12,751	10,799	11,766	12,896	9,994	10,778	8,904	9,749	7,786	10,821	10,220	8,921	10,685	17,248	16,970	7,957
Kerkira, Greece	1,104	7,857	7,085	11,673	1,765	16,933	11,279	3,084	1,009	16,861	6,341	3,322	3,265	2,400	10,776	2,108	377	8,772	7,689	17,809
Kermanshah, Iran	3,547	10,032	5,892	13,913	3,890	15,514	13,636	3,394	2,068	15,412	7,976	1,095	2,256	1,339	12,841	1,782	2,133	10,934	9,880	15,336
Khabarovsk, USSR	9,211	9,827	11,388	16,459	8,002	8,665	15,705	5,486	8,748	8,578	14,681	6,076	9,193	6,197	17,198	8,886	8,283	10,089	9,847	10,239
Kharkov, USSR	2,701	8,164	7,714	13,161	2,240	15,263	12,659	1,642	2,246	15,183	8,067	2,210	3,853	966	12,388	2,891	1,666	9,049	8,021	16,414
Khartoum, Sudan	3,399	10,501	4,156	11,990	4,678	17,417	11,962	5,472	1,921	17,316	5,794	3,546	687	3,702	10,762	940	2,627	11,393	10,323	15,618
Khon Kaen, Thailand	9,370	13,871	7,209	18,951	9,172	9,971	19,436	7,058	7,928	9,867	13,166	4,945	6,815	6,018	17,779	7,287	7,963	14,399	13,823	9,564
Kiev, USSR	2,355	7,818	7,861	12,758	1,832	15,477	12,249	1,680	2,142	15,403	7,780	2,601	3,966	1,372	12,008	2,932	1,484	8,712	7,671	16,806
Kigali, Rwanda	4,881	11,578	2,673	10,995	6,373	17,054	11,195	7,429	3,746	16,998	4,975	5,292	2,147	5,635	9,696	2,896	4,469	12,383	11,397	14,380
Kingston, Canada	6,863	584	14,151	7,542	5,807	11,485	6,733	6,765	8,470	11,526	8,481	9,839	10,740	8,590	7,932	9,595	7,892	1,348	568	14,119
Kingston, Jamaica	8,361	2,325	14,177	4,660	7,862	10,994	3,848	9,436	10,062	11,074	7,429	12,250	12,076	10,994	5,217	11,089	9,684	1,902	2,377	12,812
Kingstown, Saint Vincent	7,284	3,233	12,430	4,191	7,187	12,540	3,460	9,248	8,922	12,628	5,677	11,565	10,696	10,386	4,268	9,836	8,688	3,271	3,181	13,894
Kinshasa, Zaire	4,628	10,466	3,856	9,388	6,239	17,858	9,548	7,917	4,105	17,861	3,313	6,452	3,392	6,473	8,099	3,674	4,762	11,174	10,292	14,978

Distances in Kilometers	Annaba, Algeria	Annapolis, Maryland	Antananarivo, Madagascar	Antofagasta, Chile	Antwerp, Belgium	Apia, Western Samoa	Arequipa, Peru	Arkhangel'sk, USSR	As Sallum, Egypt	Asau, Western Samoa	Ascension Island (Georgetown)	Ashkhabad, USSR	Asmera, Ethiopia	Astrakhan, USSR	Asuncion, Paraguay	Aswan, Egypt	Athens, Greece	Atlanta, Georgia	Atlantic City, New Jersey	Auckland, New Zealand
Kirkwall, United Kingdom	2,574	5,493	9,778	11,028	981	14,910	10,384	2,328	3,702	14,881	7,487	4,880	5,931	3,618	10,599	4,783	3,014	6,388	5,346	17,542
Kirov, USSR	3,860	8,108	8,588	13,957	2,956	13,978	13,343	827	3,525	13,899	9,307	2,375	4,879	1,362	13,369	4,053	2,953	8,927	7,992	15,415
Kiruna, Sweden	3,531	6,326	9,877	12,442	2,043	13,943	11,755	980	4,048	13,891	8,841	4,071	5,987	2,875	12,089	4,942	3,331	7,153	6,210	16,210
Kisangani, Zaire	4,412	10,988	3,250	10,610	5,952	17,647	10,754	7,216	3,439	17,595	4,494	5,360	2,230	5,548	9,322	2,738	4,153	11,785	10,808	14,914
Kishinev, USSR	2,066	7,954	7,537	12,577	1,834	15,863	12,108	2,081	1,742	15,786	7,432	2,610	3,634	1,469	11,767	2,568	1,085	8,858	7,801	17,008
Kitchner, Canada	7,189	599	14,482	7,501	6,111	11,156	6,689	6,980	8,788	11,198	8,738	10,085	11,060	8,844	7,959	9,913	8,202	1,129	679	13,788
Knoxville, Tennessee	7,859	736	14,927	6,750	6,889	10,711	5,941	7,860	9,503	10,764	8,723	10,951	11,754	9,704	7,318	10,623	8,953	250	915	13,184
Kosice, Czechoslovakia	1,708	7,382	7,930	12,064	1,237	15,960	11,565	2,108	1,931	15,895	7,176	3,201	4,038	2,025	11,314	2,917	1,207	8,289	7,226	17,502
Kota Kinabalu, Malaysia	11,219	14,863	8,001	17,934	10,967	8,270	18,595	8,718	9,756	8,168	14,564	6,794	8,466	7,850	17,771	9,056	9,811	15,113	14,871	7,718
Krakow, Poland	1,759	7,218	8,111	12,010	1,101	15,849	11,494	2,016	2,102	15,786	7,235	3,320	4,219	2,118	11,291	3,097	1,378	8,124	7,064	17,526
Kralendijk, Bonaire	7,973	3,080	13,139	3,969	7,757	11,768	3,180	9,665	9,633	11,856	6,360	12,170	11,456	10,959	4,298	10,574	9,363	2,897	3,073	13,210
Krasnodar, USSR	2,760	8,691	7,134	13,330	2,638	15,502	12,893	2,177	1,918	15,413	7,924	1,794	3,293	720	12,456	2,389	1,492	9,585	8,544	16,238
Krasnoyarsk, USSR	6,417	9,430	9,327	16,160	5,467	11,608	15,414	2,947	5,799	11,518	11,805	3,246	6,398	3,244	15,846	5,963	5,365	10,055	9,368	12,852
Kristiansand, Norway	2,365	6,131	9,285	11,559	807	15,084	10,942	1,855	3,230	15,042	7,602	4,238	5,402	2,976	11,050	4,270	2,518	7,023	5,985	17,448
Kuala Lumpur, Malaysia	10,153	15,335	6,414	17,588	10,243	9,731	18,372	8,348	8,556	9,633	12,945	5,848	7,003	7,040	16,723	7,722	8,742	15,869	15,281	8,728
Kuching, Malaysia	11,025	15,464	7,228	17,558	10,976	8,756	18,350	8,897	9,468	8,658	13,872	6,650	7,976	7,791	17,087	8,671	9,609	15,808	15,449	7,871
Kumasi, Ghana	3,480	8,240	6,088	8,184	4,969	18,686	8,111	7,229	3,916	18,787	2,152	6,941	4,526	6,461	7,018	4,155	4,308	8,936	8,068	16,642
Kumzar, Oman	4,710	11,282	5,098	14,691	5,150	14,840	14,560	4,399	3,092	14,736	8,528	1,301	2,186	2,342	13,495	2,382	3,321	12,179	11,132	14,160
Kunming, China	8,791	12,915	7,706	19,312	8,422	10,223	18,881	6,194	7,480	10,119	13,115	4,398	6,693	5,351	18,053	6,986	7,416	13,453	12,867	10,194
Kuqa Chang, China	6,358	10,899	7,619	16,906	5,902	12,246	16,369	3,763	5,242	12,145	11,247	2,177	5,144	2,884	16,036	5,030	5,042	11,615	10,811	12,676
Kurgan, USSR	4,730	8,935	8,408	14,964	3,952	13,317	14,345	1,698	4,099	13,229	10,085	2,012	4,990	1,572	14,349	4,376	3,645	9,711	8,832	14,463
Kuwait, Kuwait	3,813	10,505	5,344	13,922	4,333	15,600	13,727	3,946	2,200	15,496	7,846	1,353	1,811	1,883	12,781	1,610	2,432	11,413	10,349	15,056
Kuybyshev, USSR	3,724	8,580	7,994	14,103	3,081	14,305	13,549	1,379	3,131	14,220	9,075	1,810	4,315	777	13,390	3,544	2,640	9,421	8,456	15,427
Kyoto, Japan	10,405	11,171	11,040	17,202	9,340	7,739	16,613	6,790	9,679	7,642	15,747	6,731	9,652	7,139	18,338	9,595	9,320	11,327	11,209	8,923
Kzyl-Orda, USSR	4,840	9,977	7,287	15,403	4,477	13,657	14,923	2,687	3,778	13,559	9,837	964	4,110	1,368	14,526	3,733	3,531	10,790	9,861	14,181
L'vov, USSR	1,940	7,480	7,960	12,288	1,393	15,765	11,780	1,908	2,031	15,697	7,403	3,027	4,058	1,825	11,548	2,960	1,317	8,382	7,327	17,270
La Ceiba, Honduras	9,370	2,760	15,180	4,713	8,740	9,901	3,934	10,052	11,074	9,981	8,397	13,040	13,142	11,777	5,533	12,127	10,653	2,005	2,875	11,789
La Coruna, Spain	1,549	5,576	8,948	9,754	1,300	16,369	9,222	3,832	3,215	16,365	5,714	5,527	5,443	4,378	9,117	4,322	2,762	6,481	5,400	19,237
La Paz, Bolivia	9,898	6,202	11,971	826	10,259	10,986	363	12,540	11,262	11,091	5,907	14,311	12,272	13,326	1,459	11,843	11,285	5,822	6,217	11,170
La Paz, Mexico	10,649	3,576	17,664	6,823	9,514	7,889	6,154	9,850	12,236	7,949	10,968	13,028	14,514	11,898	7,878	13,361	11,624	2,730	3,757	10,352
La Ronge, Canada	7,998	2,794	15,382	9,336	6,556	9,829	8,538	6,416	9,307	9,843	10,781	9,578	11,507	8,486	9,990	10,375	8,612	2,874	2,879	12,693
Labrador City, Canada	5,871	1,718	13,298	8,492	4,687	12,217	7,696	5,576	7,407	12,243	8,363	8,642	9,686	7,395	8,711	8,531	6,794	2,546	1,618	15,004
Lagos, Nigeria	3,402	8,689	5,595	8,668	4,964	19,038	8,626	7,085	3,586	19,123	2,537	6,535	4,003	6,145	7,475	3,706	4,053	9,413	8,514	16,526
Lahore, Pakistan	6,034	11,632	6,278	16,452	5,985	13,067	16,189	4,340	4,625	12,963	10,351	1,616	4,011	2,782	15,308	4,139	4,626	12,437	11,517	12,889
Lambasa, Fiji	17,594	12,353	13,463	11,243	16,120	997	11,441	13,833	16,926	922	16,918	13,825	15,805	14,450	12,310	16,441	16,644	11,576	12,531	2,309
Lansing, Michigan	7,517	796	14,822	7,492	6,412	10,816	6,681	7,186	9,105	10,858	9,019	10,318	11,380	9,087	8,018	10,231	8,510	997	927	13,451
Lanzhou, China	8,174	11,697	8,481	18,520	7,563	10,429	17,778	5,182	7,085	10,327	13,049	3,998	6,766	4,703	17,877	6,809	6,882	12,232	11,654	10,906
Laoag, Philippines	10,709	13,431	8,981	18,735	10,145	8,227	18,728	7,720	9,470	8,123	15,039	6,372	8,637	7,236	19,203	8,985	9,367	13,678	13,445	8,333
Largeau, Chad	2,380	9,248	5,123	10,750	3,917	18,785	10,634	5,426	1,630	18,681	4,665	4,410	2,133	4,125	9,588	1,585	2,269	10,112	9,067	16,842
Las Vegas, Nevada	10,007	3,403	17,458	8,123	8,678	8,118	7,409	8,636	11,445	8,156	11,492	11,771	13,690	10,712	9,092	12,542	10,773	2,811	3,573	10,846
Launceston, Australia	16,508	16,337	9,410	11,832	16,986	5,008	12,473	14,836	14,810	4,972	14,227	12,572	12,635	13,783	12,194	13,724	15,240	15,462	16,518	2,431
Le Havre, France	1,529	5,963	8,901	10,672	360	15,981	10,115	2,895	2,883	15,953	6,518	4,739	5,161	3,537	10,060	4,005	2,276	6,877	5,798	18,537
Leipzig, East Germany	1,641	6,683	8,501	11,542	552	15,833	10,998	2,197	2,431	15,783	7,047	3,868	4,642	2,652	10,882	3,496	1,730	7,592	6,527	17,889
Leningrad, USSR	3,020	7,181	8,877	12,841	1,878	14,584	12,227	743	3,174	14,518	8,489	3,148	4,999	1,910	12,289	3,986	2,483	8,039	7,051	16,419
Leon, Spain	1,304	5,821	8,714	9,894	1,221	16,554	9,381	3,773	2,972	16,545	5,667	5,333	5,198	4,204	9,219	4,077	2,530	6,726	5,645	19,367
Lerwick, United Kingdom	2,662	5,568	9,796	11,183	1,054	14,806	10,532	2,171	3,723	14,774	7,639	4,782	5,932	3,520	10,763	4,790	3,024	6,459	5,425	17,399
Lhasa, China	7,556	12,300	7,123	18,073	7,282	11,447	17,721	5,216	6,228	11,342	11,946	3,148	5,549	4,145	16,914	5,759	6,171	12,971	12,221	11,410
Libreville, Gabon	4,047	9,635	4,675	8,999	5,654	18,512	9,069	7,553	3,827	18,542	2,804	6,502	3,639	6,330	7,742	3,642	4,413	10,346	9,461	15,695
Lilongwe, Malawi	6,258	12,725	1,564	10,795	7,765	15,851	11,162	8,729	5,124	15,816	5,302	6,297	3,292	6,833	9,505	4,212	5,847	13,461	12,548	13,057
Lima, Peru	10,354	5,649	13,050	1,464	10,458	10,197	764	12,507	11,855	10,300	6,869	14,759	13,125	13,639	2,509	12,565	11,769	5,128	5,697	10,781
Limerick, Ireland	2,169	5,277	9,514	10,346	909	15,446	9,735	3,048	3,589	15,430	6,738	5,293	5,867	4,055	9,855	4,711	2,977	6,191	5,115	18,229
Limoges, France	1,131	6,189	8,553	10,546	643	16,397	10,027	3,169	2,596	16,369	6,157	4,719	4,871	3,566	9,865	3,722	2,050	7,103	6,020	18,876
Limon, Costa Rica	9,423	3,275	14,630	3,968	8,972	10,142	3,182	10,508	11,116	10,228	7,860	13,361	13,047	12,104	4,774	12,112	10,768	2,634	3,362	11,757
Lincoln, Nebraska	8,474	1,735	15,841	7,638	7,278	9,788	6,847	7,739	10,016	9,830	9,938	10,922	12,294	9,736	8,355	11,138	9,390	1,342	1,898	12,455
Linz, Austria	1,374	6,963	8,145	11,560	782	16,143	11,053	2,394	2,072	16,088	6,836	3,710	4,296	2,540	10,837	3,146	1,377	7,875	6,803	17,980
Lisbon, Portugal	1,500	5,705	8,690	9,400	1,747	16,766	8,907	4,299	3,203	16,773	5,193	5,762	5,348	4,670	8,701	4,268	2,859	6,593	5,526	19,620
Little Rock, Arkansas	8,564	1,481	15,698	6,864	7,513	9,942	6,071	8,254	10,182	9,994	9,417	11,408	12,449	10,186	7,580	11,307	9,604	735	1,662	12,451
Liverpool, United Kingdom	2,016	5,625	9,360	10,706	562	15,503	10,105	2,721	3,312	15,478	6,883	4,909	5,582	3,669	10,182	4,424	2,670	6,536	5,466	18,157
Lodz, Poland	1,890	7,096	8,290	12,028	1,045	15,682	11,493	1,873	2,289	15,622	7,363	3,384	4,395	2,158	11,342	3,278	1,566	7,998	6,944	17,464
Lome, Togo	3,472	8,523	5,784	8,437	5,007	18,870	8,387	7,190	3,760	18,963	2,331	6,740	4,242	6,317	7,252	3,924	4,198	9,232	8,350	16,539
London, United Kingdom	1,738	5,873	9,071	10,766	317	15,760	10,191	2,738	3,027	15,731	6,727	4,733	5,300	3,510	10,189	4,143	2,394	6,787	5,712	18,330
Londonderry, United Kingdom	2,316	5,310	9,689	10,565	891	15,242	9,940	2,809	3,645	15,222	7,006	5,171	5,915	3,920	10,101	4,757	3,002	6,220	5,153	17,983
Longlac, Canada	7,266	1,440	14,704	8,289	6,017	10,831	7,478	6,527	8,768	10,861	9,420	9,695	11,043	8,490	8,790	9,886	8,130	1,790	1,501	13,599
Lord Howe Island, Australia	17,328	14,979	10,834	11,950	17,000	3,564	12,446	14,481	15,688	3,516	15,582	12,949	13,733	14,018	12,609	14,716	15,916	14,163	15,159	1,559
Los Angeles, California	10,370	3,747	17,823	8,150	9,029	7,754	7,461	8,915	11,795	7,792	11,778	12,025	14,032	10,994	9,168	12,887	11,118	3,118	3,919	10,479
Louangphrabang, Laos	9,084	13,489	7,344	19,149	8,830	10,137	19,257	6,683	7,685	10,032	13,088	4,660	6,690	5,698	17,872	7,096	7,686	14,031	13,440	9,866
Louisville, Kentucky	7,863	811	15,042	7,037	6,828	10,607	6,229	7,686	9,484	10,656	8,958	10,806	11,749	9,569	7,618	10,608	8,912	514	989	13,149
Luanda, Angola	5,091	10,598	3,863	8,983	6,703	17,444	9,192	8,450	4,644	17,463	3,046	6,982	3,894	7,020	7,685	4,219	5,293	11,255	10,429	14,598
Lubumbashi, Zaire	5,758	12,024	2,296	10,287	7,315	16,489	10,597	8,525	4,790	16,463	4,610	6,368	3,243	6,747	8,986	3,998	5,510	12,742	11,848	13,643
Lusaka, Zambia	6,178	12,343	2,081	10,192	7,738	16,101	10,551	8,930	5,210	16,080	4,721	6,693	3,597	7,122	8,900	4,398	5,930	13,033	12,170	13,241
Luxembourg, Luxembourg	1,417	6,362	8,616	11,063	217	16,033	10,522	2,615	2,554	15,994	6,680	4,306	4,820	3,109	10,410	3,663	1,908	7,276	6,200	18,325
Luxor, Egypt	2,664	9,753	5,190	12,357	3,710	17,163	12,185	4,359	981	17,059	6,306	2,777	1,319	2,670	11,219	179	1,602	10,664	9,581	16,240
Lynn Lake, Canada	7,670	2,676	15,060	9,373	6,231	10,151	8,568	6,150	8,985	10,164	10,536	9,323	11,192	8,212	9,968	10,057	8,292	2,863	2,743	13,018
Lyon, France	1,013	6,449	8,355	10,789	609	16,452	10,283	3,019	2,354	16,416	6,249	4,444	4,633	3,302	10,081	3,479	1,783	7,364	6,281	18,716
Macapa, Brazil	7,283	5,033	10,921	3,353	7,684	13,326	2,893	10,078	8,706	13,427	4,159	11,705	10,015	10,707	2,888	9,398	8,679	5,103	4,964	13,790
Madison, Wisconsin	7,836	1,175	15,187	7,640	6,677	10,440	6,833	7,301	9,397	10,480	9,408	10,462	11,676	9,249	8,235	10,521	8,785	1,123	1,317	13,106
Madras, India	7,602	13,761	5,045	16,728	7,902	12,269	16,983	6,474	5,970	12,168	10,721	3,507	4,464	4,766	15,429	5,124	6,206	14,575	13,640	11,269
Madrid, Spain	1,069	6,060	8,437	9,892	1,355	16,842	9,408	3,894	2,764	16,832	5,464	5,258	4,962	4,169	9,167	3,854	2,374	6,961	5,884	19,592
Madurai, India	7,610	13,990	4,633	16,359	8,019	12,438	16,673	6,731	5,945	12,339	10,444	3,679	4,293	4,941	15,068	5,039	6,236	14,831	13,861	11,258
Magadan, USSR	8,787	8,254	12,548	14,897	7,355	8,806	14,125	5,057	8,746	8,735	14,142	6,590	9,726	6,342	15,608	9,159	8,155	8,494	8,282	10,914
Magdalena, Bolivia	9,342	5,932	11,731	1,319	9,720	11,505	867	12,035	10,712	11,609	5,464	13,756	11,779	12,772	1,485	11,312	10,729	5,636	5,930	11,724
Magdeburg, East Germany	1,724	6,600	8,607	11,533	512	15,742	10,979	2,149	2,538	15,693	7,108	3,921	4,745	2,696	10,892	3,601	1,835	7,508	6,445	17,855
Majuro Atoll, Marshall Isls.	14,835	11,397	13,814	13,224	13,415	2,990	13,144	11,073	14,415	2,883	19,411	11,478	14,209	11,857	14,473	14,331	13,985	10,890	11,547	4,887
Malabo, Equatorial Guinea	3,672	9,343	4,929	9,084	5,277	18,888	9,106	7,210	3,524	18,921	2,882	6,293	3,543	6,052	7,849	3,429	4,085	10,077	9,168	16,071
Male, Maldives	7,594	14,342	3,810	15,581	8,213	12,803	15,972	7,217	5,893	12,709	9,847	4,061	3,984	5,297	14,307	4,886	6,286	15,228	14,195	11,285
Manado, Indonesia	12,286	15,026	8,739	17,061	11,936	7,195	17,582	9,585	10,847	7,094	15,465	7,861	9,536	8,879	17,359	10,149	10,885	15,058	15,076	6,670
Managua, Nicaragua	9,566	3,126	15,036	4,321	9,014	9,855	3,550	10,410	11,268	9,939	8,256	13,356	13,272	12,093	5,175	12,296	10,880	2,400	3,232	11,605
Manama, Bahrain	4,196	10,940	5,004	14,115	4,766	15,419	13,977	4,323	2,544	15,315	7,968	1,494	1,708	2,245	12,931	1,799	2,836	11,848	10,783	14,672
Manaus, Brazil	8,270	4,960	11,742	2,530	8,540	12,270	1,936	10,822	9,738	12,371	5,078	12,695	11,070	11,644	2,462	10,452	9,678	4,818	4,931	12,837
Manchester, New Hampshire	6,549	615	13,766	7,380	5,571	11,879	6,576	6,705	8,183	11,923	8,057	9,714	10,440	8,456	7,689	9,305	7,629	1,523	476	14,466
Mandalay, Burma	8,434	13,211	6,959	18,634	8,245	10,803	18,589	6,197	7,016	10,699	12,455	4,009	6,042	5,081	17,334	6,425	7,030	13,835	13,143	10,503
Mangareva Island, Fr.Polynesia	16,148	9,178	15,347	6,538	15,344	4,006	6,638	15,387	17,850	4,111	12,705	17,935	18,940	17,413	7,738	18,787	17,404	8,264	9,344	5,024
Manila, Philippines	11,009	13,805	8,864	18,460	10,500	8,048	18,674	8,096	9,717	7,944	15,120	6,635	8,767	7,545	18,814	9,179	9,648	14,022	13,824	8,009
Mannheim, West Germany	1,399	6,522	8,500	11,211	347	16,051	10,678	2,523	2,429	16,007	6,739	4,137	4,686	2,945	10,542	3,530	1,767	7,435	6,361	18,227
Maputo, Mozambique	7,428	13,367	1,724	10,083	8,985	14,883	10,577	10,060	6,416	14,869	5,351	7,572	4,621	8,159	8,847	5,538	7,139	13,967	13,202	12,008
Mar del Plata, Argentina	10,666	8,741	9,987	2,006	11,578	11,087	2,759	14,117	11,519	11,186	5,459	14,513	11,607	14,030	1,412	11,654	11,831	8,415	8,738	10,133
Maracaibo, Venezuela	8,367	3,174	13,448	3,798	8,118	11,377	2,994	9,964	10,031	11,466	6,663	12,536	11,856	11,316	4,254	10,975	9,753	2,869	3,190	12,816
Marrakech, Morocco	1,563	6,137	8,147	9,029	2,402	17,439	8,614	4,931	3,134	17,461	4,432	5,988	5,078	5,009	8,218	4,088	2,972	6,991	5,956	19,374
Marseilles, France	739	6,606	8,122	10,706	883	16,727	10,228	3,227	2,170	16,691	6,017	4,447	4,442	3,349	9,955	3,295	1,655	7,519	6,435	18,864
Maseru, Lesotho	7,614	13,131	2,334	9,470	9,204	14,807	9,979	10,470	6,743	14,808	4,975	8,112	5,091	8,632	8,243	5,937	7,460	13,656	12,974	11,926

Distances in Kilometers	Annaba, Algeria	Annapolis, Maryland	Antananarivo, Madagascar	Antofagasta, Chile	Antwerp, Belgium	Apia, Western Samoa	Arequipa, Peru	Arkhangel'sk, USSR	As Sallum, Egypt	Asau, Western Samoa	Ascension Island (Georgetown)	Ashkhabad, USSR	Asmera, Ethiopia	Astrakhan, USSR	Asuncion, Paraguay	Aswan, Egypt	Athens, Greece	Atlanta, Georgia	Atlantic City, New Jersey	Auckland, New Zealand
Mashhad, Iran	4,579	10,535	6,242	15,059	4,618	14,360	14,742	3,392	3,211	14,258	9,122	213	3,098	1,474	14,001	2,894	3,173	11,399	10,401	14,340
Mazatlan, Mexico	10,437	3,323	17,286	6,485	9,370	8,207	5,797	9,865	12,057	8,270	10,564	13,051	14,325	11,884	7,512	13,182	11,470	2,445	3,502	10,597
Mbabane, Swaziland	7,413	13,265	1,871	9,937	8,980	14,927	10,429	10,108	6,437	14,917	5,221	7,662	4,685	8,226	8,700	5,580	7,160	13,852	13,101	12,047
Mbandaka, Zaire	4,219	10,420	3,824	9,883	5,818	18,136	10,000	7,381	3,561	18,112	3,733	5,870	2,831	5,895	8,605	3,090	4,236	11,179	10,242	15,272
McMurdo Sound, Antarctica	15,353	14,878	8,590	8,218	16,965	7,198	8,984	17,675	14,516	7,231	10,521	14,488	12,488	15,627	8,261	13,559	15,240	14,134	14,965	4,549
Mecca, Saudi Arabia	3,532	10,605	4,544	12,924	4,505	16,588	12,837	4,791	1,839	16,483	6,756	2,554	683	2,861	11,722	769	2,397	11,517	10,434	15,372
Medan, Indonesia	9,856	15,266	6,129	17,499	9,997	10,069	18,240	8,175	8,245	9,971	12,617	5,587	6,666	6,796	16,532	7,397	8,448	15,860	15,199	9,021
Medellin, Colombia	9,008	3,626	13,722	3,355	8,773	10,845	2,544	10,585	10,662	10,936	6,970	13,191	12,430	11,969	3,990	11,585	10,399	3,178	3,668	12,175
Medicine Hat, Canada	8,644	2,949	16,049	9,078	7,219	9,237	8,300	7,053	9,973	9,257	11,127	10,197	12,177	9,128	9,843	11,044	9,280	2,808	3,069	12,083
Medina, Saudi Arabia	3,326	10,350	4,876	12,994	4,218	16,541	12,860	4,457	1,622	16,437	6,869	2,324	1,014	2,543	11,821	683	2,123	11,265	10,181	15,560
Melbourne, Australia	16,268	16,429	9,375	12,263	16,602	5,023	12,896	14,403	14,564	4,978	14,509	12,206	12,444	13,401	12,632	13,503	14,949	15,589	16,610	2,629
Memphis, Tennessee	8,374	1,278	15,491	6,828	7,344	10,148	6,029	8,147	10,000	10,201	9,230	11,287	12,263	10,057	7,506	11,124	9,429	543	1,459	12,649
Merauke, Indonesia	14,305	15,028	10,009	15,141	13,797	5,261	15,564	11,319	12,887	5,165	16,691	9,887	11,480	10,861	15,800	12,165	12,914	14,662	15,150	4,687
Merida, Mexico	9,264	2,358	15,553	5,358	8,491	9,763	4,580	9,611	10,959	9,835	8,814	12,680	13,118	11,424	6,173	12,048	10,481	1,507	2,499	11,864
Meridian, Mississippi	8,447	1,324	15,422	6,497	7,482	10,187	5,698	8,391	10,096	10,245	9,030	11,509	12,343	10,269	7,179	11,215	9,547	431	1,499	12,607
Messina, Italy	704	7,633	7,149	11,265	1,692	17,214	10,876	3,362	1,142	17,149	5,978	3,723	3,416	2,806	10,369	2,267	717	8,545	7,461	18,185
Mexico City, Mexico	10,152	3,075	16,533	5,694	9,253	8,760	4,981	10,080	11,828	8,831	9,759	13,239	14,038	12,014	6,677	12,936	11,304	2,161	3,241	10,947
Miami, Florida	8,170	1,504	14,625	5,569	7,455	10,825	4,759	8,773	9,869	10,894	8,026	11,738	12,017	10,475	6,145	10,951	9,408	972	1,598	12,963
Midway Islands, USA	12,779	8,950	15,361	12,807	11,206	4,690	12,384	9,209	12,976	4,637	17,145	10,670	13,812	10,572	14,084	13,379	12,357	8,582	9,084	7,249
Milan, Italy	959	6,768	8,114	11,083	731	16,497	10,593	2,865	2,070	16,451	6,368	4,111	4,346	2,986	10,341	3,189	1,464	7,683	6,601	18,478
Milford Sound, New Zealand	18,135	14,779	10,740	10,425	18,575	3,923	10,985	16,108	16,477	3,921	14,184	14,244	14,242	15,418	11,002	15,367	16,949	13,873	14,954	1,040
Milwaukee, Wisconsin	7,735	1,060	15,075	7,599	6,592	10,555	6,791	7,260	9,305	10,597	9,291	10,414	11,583	9,195	8,173	10,430	8,697	1,076	1,199	13,214
Minsk, USSR	2,427	7,427	8,291	12,611	1,591	15,251	12,060	1,394	2,489	15,183	7,900	2,938	4,392	1,680	11,938	3,340	1,793	8,314	7,284	16,869
Mogadiscio, Somalia	5,452	12,553	2,333	12,728	6,655	15,750	12,953	6,946	3,895	15,668	6,729	4,190	1,629	4,914	11,426	2,782	4,549	13,440	12,375	13,570
Mombasa, Kenya	5,613	12,542	1,853	11,863	6,981	16,037	12,140	7,611	4,232	15,972	6,000	5,036	2,145	5,644	10,561	3,198	4,936	13,381	12,361	13,527
Monclova, Mexico	9,789	2,675	16,733	6,512	8,741	8,829	5,777	9,344	11,414	8,889	10,115	12,525	13,679	11,331	7,441	12,538	10,835	1,802	2,854	11,245
Moncton, Canada	5,931	1,243	13,213	7,745	4,939	12,411	6,955	6,147	7,556	12,450	7,794	9,110	9,817	7,849	7,936	8,678	6,997	2,155	1,089	15,062
Monrovia, Liberia	3,877	7,477	6,977	7,270	5,173	17,785	7,144	7,614	4,667	17,890	1,626	7,759	5,517	7,143	6,158	5,060	4,944	8,108	7,313	16,575
Monte Carlo, Monaco	759	6,730	8,052	10,874	862	16,689	10,397	3,103	2,059	16,648	6,131	4,278	4,337	3,179	10,116	3,184	1,513	7,644	6,561	18,702
Monterrey, Mexico	9,795	2,672	16,643	6,338	8,780	8,882	5,601	9,446	11,433	8,945	9,986	12,622	13,689	11,419	7,266	12,556	10,866	1,780	2,849	11,255
Montevideo, Uruguay	10,340	8,441	10,013	1,856	11,223	11,351	2,557	13,758	11,240	11,451	5,199	14,269	11,432	13,730	1,076	11,422	11,528	8,147	8,432	10,479
Montgomery, Alabama	8,260	1,150	15,199	6,427	7,327	10,406	5,623	8,310	9,918	10,464	8,814	11,405	12,156	10,158	7,068	11,035	9,380	235	1,319	12,804
Montpelier, Vermont	6,576	671	13,840	7,523	5,558	11,797	6,718	6,621	8,196	11,839	8,204	9,655	10,461	8,400	7,847	9,320	7,630	1,549	567	14,419
Montpellier, France	814	6,481	8,230	10,612	848	16,679	10,125	3,262	2,294	16,646	5,999	4,561	4,563	3,452	9,876	3,417	1,782	7,394	6,310	18,938
Montreal, Canada	6,597	763	13,901	7,664	5,540	11,726	6,858	6,536	8,201	11,765	8,340	9,592	10,472	8,341	8,001	9,326	7,623	1,597	687	14,379
Moosonee, Canada	6,819	1,406	14,255	8,361	5,585	11,271	7,550	6,199	8,329	11,300	9,090	9,346	10,606	8,126	8,774	9,449	7,697	1,971	1,411	14,047
Moroni, Comoros	6,536	13,387	921	11,824	7,914	15,242	12,214	8,458	5,162	15,187	6,332	5,716	3,026	6,445	10,542	4,115	5,863	14,195	13,207	12,629
Moscow, USSR	3,065	7,809	8,326	13,267	2,236	14,721	12,696	996	2,858	14,646	8,520	2,516	4,486	1,275	12,612	3,537	2,230	8,671	7,677	16,194
Mosul, Iraq	3,146	9,628	6,132	13,584	3,474	15,750	13,273	3,145	1,741	15,651	7,747	1,365	2,364	1,186	12,552	1,676	1,730	10,532	9,474	15,744
Mount Isa, Australia	15,046	16,038	9,485	14,130	14,864	5,223	14,690	12,494	13,449	5,142	15,753	10,662	11,683	11,757	14,591	12,554	13,630	15,486	16,186	3,849
Multan, Pakistan	5,856	11,664	6,010	16,193	5,896	13,339	15,973	4,387	4,400	13,234	10,062	1,482	3,707	2,706	15,026	3,868	4,442	12,490	11,542	13,051
Munich, West Germany	1,288	6,793	8,244	11,366	619	16,187	10,853	2,515	2,169	16,138	6,717	3,911	4,418	2,742	10,655	3,264	1,498	7,706	6,631	18,156
Murcia, Spain	795	6,375	8,094	9,940	1,534	17,175	9,492	4,013	2,498	17,161	5,268	5,134	4,658	4,099	9,157	3,566	2,177	7,272	6,198	19,639
Murmansk, USSR	3,888	6,737	9,815	12,975	2,492	13,634	12,279	589	4,191	13,575	9,281	3,776	5,972	2,655	12,631	4,989	3,495	7,536	6,629	15,747
Mururoa Atoll, Fr. Polynesia	16,412	9,356	15,440	6,968	15,473	3,582	7,060	15,260	18,111	3,686	13,135	17,581	19,249	17,217	8,169	19,155	17,576	8,442	9,526	4,742
Muscat, Oman	5,044	11,654	4,856	14,856	5,520	14,644	14,779	4,737	3,402	14,540	8,662	1,589	2,254	2,694	13,627	2,615	3,667	12,550	11,504	13,824
Myitkyina, Burma	8,334	12,852	7,293	18,781	8,050	10,750	18,502	5,920	6,982	10,645	12,581	3,920	6,159	4,926	17,525	6,461	6,946	13,457	12,789	10,629
Naga, Philippines	11,254	13,835	9,043	18,213	10,719	7,791	18,422	8,295	9,973	7,687	15,362	6,888	9,020	7,786	18,714	9,437	9,898	14,008	13,862	7,773
Nagasaki, Japan	10,236	11,605	10,452	17,793	9,286	8,065	17,198	6,737	9,382	7,966	15,432	6,364	9,195	6,877	18,902	9,212	9,076	11,815	11,632	9,011
Nagoya, Japan	10,457	11,108	11,148	17,096	9,373	7,662	16,512	6,826	9,752	7,566	15,818	6,817	9,749	7,208	18,241	9,681	9,386	11,253	11,149	8,885
Nagpur, India	7,007	12,883	5,612	16,886	7,146	12,524	16,900	5,591	5,453	12,420	10,694	2,726	4,285	3,964	15,601	4,742	5,592	13,684	12,768	11,879
Nairobi, Kenya	5,184	12,103	2,273	11,709	6,574	16,465	11,934	7,311	3,839	16,397	5,728	4,877	1,853	5,391	10,407	2,839	4,551	12,943	11,922	13,966
Nanchang, China	9,580	12,406	9,039	19,180	8,919	9,090	18,452	6,469	8,469	8,986	14,346	5,367	7,957	6,111	19,281	8,124	8,287	12,774	12,397	9,512
Nancy, France	1,315	6,408	8,535	11,024	309	16,135	10,492	2,693	2,480	16,096	6,589	4,307	4,751	3,123	10,355	3,594	1,846	7,322	6,244	18,402
Nandi, Fiji	17,662	12,611	13,205	11,351	16,246	1,242	11,578	13,901	16,845	1,172	16,881	13,739	15,604	14,417	12,388	16,289	16,619	11,833	12,789	2,129
Nanjing, China	9,546	11,985	9,454	18,720	8,780	8,968	17,988	6,284	8,533	8,866	14,508	5,457	8,182	6,102	19,181	8,268	8,299	12,329	11,983	9,597
Nanning, China	9,400	13,146	8,062	19,863	8,976	9,604	19,294	6,679	8,104	9,500	13,708	5,018	7,288	5,946	18,581	7,606	8,032	13,602	13,117	9,599
Nantes, France	1,379	5,933	8,814	10,436	622	16,193	9,895	3,171	2,859	16,170	6,240	4,902	5,135	3,724	9,800	3,984	2,301	6,847	5,764	18,817
Naples, Italy	712	7,379	7,456	11,265	1,380	16,957	10,842	3,133	1,418	16,898	6,146	3,775	3,697	2,775	10,418	2,542	875	8,293	7,209	18,280
Narvik, Norway	3,560	6,194	9,988	12,339	2,042	13,905	11,645	1,107	4,131	13,855	8,831	4,204	6,094	3,006	12,005	5,040	3,411	7,020	6,078	16,225
Nashville, Tennessee	8,064	960	15,177	6,841	7,056	10,465	6,035	7,934	9,696	10,517	8,975	11,053	11,956	9,814	7,456	10,819	9,133	346	1,141	12,964
Nassau, Bahamas	7,973	1,543	14,335	5,444	7,317	11,090	4,632	8,734	9,675	11,161	7,731	11,643	11,797	10,381	5,960	10,747	9,235	1,178	1,605	13,172
Natal, Brazil	6,501	6,527	9,048	4,254	7,360	14,761	4,131	9,909	7,614	14,865	2,311	10,721	8,500	9,957	3,221	8,084	7,775	6,775	6,421	14,355
Natashquan, Canada	5,598	1,701	12,974	8,224	4,517	12,596	7,439	5,643	7,184	12,626	7,897	8,626	9,458	7,368	8,369	8,310	6,600	2,595	1,562	15,335
Nauru Island	15,449	12,319	13,078	13,289	14,153	2,773	13,349	11,708	14,734	2,669	19,057	11,669	14,092	12,226	14,446	14,434	14,417	11,769	12,474	4,103
Ndjamena, Chad	2,841	9,307	4,947	10,094	4,442	19,275	10,036	6,147	2,390	19,190	3,944	5,158	2,606	4,901	8,898	2,302	2,993	10,127	9,126	16,604
Nelson, New Zealand	18,680	14,234	11,319	10,285	18,615	3,371	10,792	16,063	16,989	3,375	14,499	14,553	14,785	15,666	10,965	15,895	17,398	13,334	14,411	507
Nema, Mauritania	2,691	7,086	7,169	8,183	3,976	18,340	7,945	6,412	3,667	18,423	2,828	6,771	4,935	6,042	7,165	4,257	3,843	7,834	6,910	17,752
Neuquen, Argentina	11,437	8,672	10,752	1,711	12,218	10,201	2,522	14,705	12,386	10,301	6,349	15,417	12,530	14,860	1,804	12,565	12,659	8,223	8,695	9,436
New Delhi, India	6,431	12,044	6,151	16,754	6,416	12,781	16,555	4,753	4,982	12,677	10,590	2,031	4,194	3,214	15,559	4,428	5,019	12,838	11,931	12,482
New Glasgow, Canada	5,790	1,355	13,049	7,707	4,831	12,580	6,922	6,112	7,425	12,619	7,626	9,041	9,681	7,778	7,862	8,546	6,876	2,269	1,191	15,215
New Haven, Connecticut	6,735	400	13,903	7,195	5,781	11,746	6,390	6,927	8,378	11,793	8,073	9,936	10,629	8,678	7,536	9,498	7,832	1,314	253	14,295
New Orleans, Louisiana	8,707	1,595	15,585	6,294	7,767	9,991	5,501	8,686	10,365	10,051	9,089	11,805	12,603	10,565	7,022	11,482	9,825	682	1,765	12,360
New Plymouth, New Zealand	18,800	14,076	11,526	10,368	18,436	3,124	10,850	15,890	17,096	3,126	14,728	14,535	14,931	15,613	11,089	16,022	17,448	13,183	14,254	251
New York, New York	6,846	287	14,001	7,135	5,894	11,649	6,327	7,026	8,491	11,697	8,124	10,043	10,741	8,785	7,497	9,610	7,945	1,201	156	14,187
Newcastle upon Tyne, UK	2,134	5,668	9,414	10,875	582	15,358	10,265	2,534	3,348	15,330	7,076	4,805	5,605	3,557	10,368	4,450	2,685	6,576	5,513	17,970
Newcastle Waters, Australia	14,306	16,265	8,986	14,786	14,179	5,878	15,383	11,874	12,710	5,793	15,510	9,931	10,977	11,042	15,136	11,826	12,891	15,851	16,389	4,585
Niamey, Niger	2,651	8,101	6,137	8,894	4,187	19,370	8,751	6,382	3,087	19,466	2,995	6,152	3,971	5,616	7,774	3,438	3,452	8,872	7,922	17,318
Nicosia, Cyprus	2,308	9,093	6,170	12,691	2,921	16,567	12,386	3,306	862	16,471	6,920	2,254	2,267	1,749	11,671	1,229	917	10,007	8,929	16,565
Niue (Alofi)	18,010	11,605	14,161	10,103	16,398	606	10,277	14,462	17,966	680	16,005	14,919	16,942	15,414	11,208	17,608	17,527	10,768	11,786	2,480
Norfolk, Virginia	7,218	237	14,236	6,725	6,325	11,402	5,915	7,498	8,881	11,456	8,121	10,508	11,114	9,249	7,148	9,995	8,356	813	321	13,847
Norfolk Island, Australia	17,981	14,092	11,712	11,476	17,189	2,688	11,891	14,643	16,456	2,647	15,907	13,558	14,602	14,528	12,278	15,546	16,579	13,269	14,273	1,077
Noril'sk, USSR	5,848	7,927	10,302	14,729	4,584	11,834	13,956	2,087	5,702	11,759	11,316	3,920	6,890	3,376	14,617	6,182	5,112	8,557	7,867	13,657
Norman Wells, Canada	8,017	4,329	14,837	10,962	6,430	9,538	10,168	5,562	8,999	9,527	11,835	8,550	10,986	7,619	11,619	9,946	8,275	4,502	4,385	12,392
Normanton, Australia	14,997	15,692	9,752	14,306	14,691	5,062	14,824	12,268	13,451	4,977	16,112	10,583	11,781	11,640	14,843	12,604	13,582	15,174	15,836	3,924
North Pole	5,919	5,687	12,096	12,619	4,328	11,530	11,817	2,840	6,510	11,488	10,881	5,801	8,308	4,868	12,799	7,339	5,798	6,266	5,645	14,082
Nottingham, United Kingdom	1,916	5,756	9,237	10,785	429	15,584	10,194	2,669	3,184	15,556	6,864	4,791	5,452	3,555	10,240	4,295	2,539	6,668	5,597	18,188
Norway House, Canada	7,687	2,321	15,125	8,996	6,300	10,219	8,191	6,383	9,065	10,239	10,288	9,567	11,302	8,428	9,591	10,155	8,386	2,485	2,397	13,062
Norwich, United Kingdom	1,820	5,926	9,093	10,912	266	15,657	10,330	2,580	3,032	15,625	6,876	4,627	5,295	3,396	10,344	4,139	2,379	6,838	5,767	18,181
Nouakchott, Mauritania	3,119	6,238	8,057	7,505	4,091	17,402	7,189	6,630	4,384	17,484	2,884	7,442	5,840	6,587	6,591	5,093	4,433	6,950	6,065	17,680
Noumea, New Caledonia	17,405	13,837	11,971	12,045	16,439	2,488	12,395	13,904	16,071	2,420	16,663	13,046	14,474	13,931	12,923	15,295	16,066	13,075	14,014	1,806
Novosibirsk, USSR	5,846	9,405	8,854	15,888	4,991	12,235	15,197	2,544	5,170	12,145	11,194	2,648	5,791	2,613	15,408	5,330	4,752	10,093	9,327	13,373
Nuku'alofa, Tonga	18,234	12,190	13,595	10,494	16,666	888	10,721	14,515	17,694	894	16,173	14,589	16,374	15,220	11,544	17,132	17,409	11,360	12,371	1,996
Nukunono Island, Tokelau Isls.	16,936	11,116	14,698	10,763	15,334	513	10,820	13,359	16,974	477	16,891	14,081	16,616	14,421	11,952	16,921	16,457	10,348	11,294	3,347
Nuremberg, West Germany	1,420	6,695	8,383	11,385	514	16,046	10,858	2,416	2,308	15,998	6,824	3,948	4,548	2,757	10,699	3,396	1,627	7,607	6,534	18,093
Nyala, Sudan	3,242	10,139	4,231	11,077	4,723	18,223	11,065	5,955	2,161	18,130	4,879	4,391	1,562	4,384	9,846	1,577	2,875	10,997	9,959	15,944
Oaxaca, Mexico	10,120	3,124	16,247	5,335	9,299	8,922	4,617	10,256	11,811	8,997	9,463	13,387	13,981	12,147	6,312	12,905	11,317	2,223	3,288	11,002
Ocean Falls, Canada	9,218	4,156	16,271	10,083	7,681	8,463	9,332	6,999	10,341	8,468	12,275	9,983	12,396	9,060	10,943	11,330	9,622	4,004	4,269	11,347
Odense, Denmark	2,066	6,377	8,950	11,581	612	15,889	10,994	1,941	2,891	15,343	7,386	4,048	5,074	2,795	11,007	3,937	2,100	7,277	6,226	17,633
Odessa, USSR	2,176	8,105	7,435	12,710	1,991	15,827	12,250	2,102	1,722	15,747	7,502	2,456	3,536	1,329	11,884	2,491	1,104	9,007	7,952	16,873

Distances in Kilometers	Annaba, Algeria	Annapolis, Maryland	Antananarivo, Madagascar	Antofagasta, Chile	Antwerp, Belgium	Apia, Western Samoa	Arequipa, Peru	Arkhangel'sk, USSR	As Sallum, Egypt	Asau, Western Samoa	Ascension Island (Georgetown)	Ashkhabad, USSR	Asmera, Ethiopia	Astrakhan, USSR	Asuncion, Paraguay	Aswan, Egypt	Athens, Greece	Atlanta, Georgia	Atlantic City, New Jersey	Auckland, New Zealand
Ogbomosho, Nigeria	3,206	8,650	5,611	8,837	4,777	19,248	8,777	6,879	3,379	19,333	2,730	6,340	3,857	5,938	7,654	3,521	3,843	9,392	8,474	16,682
Okha, USSR	9,096	9,076	12,033	15,676	7,765	8,620	14,919	5,333	8,841	8,541	14,552	6,396	9,546	6,338	16,430	9,114	8,309	9,314	9,103	10,479
Okinawa (Naha)	10,617	12,365	9,992	18,186	9,796	7,913	17,760	7,270	9,607	7,810	15,539	6,522	9,152	7,180	19,486	9,309	9,377	12,559	12,393	8,549
Oklahoma City, Oklahoma	8,893	1,899	16,132	7,142	7,768	9,517	6,363	8,324	10,478	9,566	9,900	11,504	12,755	10,308	7,925	11,603	9,873	1,217	2,079	12,087
Old Crow, Canada	8,106	4,948	14,574	11,584	6,497	9,389	10,793	5,344	8,941	9,367	12,260	8,205	10,810	7,354	12,250	9,824	8,219	5,134	4,998	12,190
Olympia, Washington	9,493	3,828	16,766	9,434	8,011	8,311	8,695	7,545	10,730	8,327	12,050	10,589	12,863	9,620	10,334	11,762	10,021	3,541	3,962	11,175
Omaha, Nebraska	8,398	1,679	15,768	7,660	7,202	9,859	6,866	7,673	9,939	9,900	9,892	10,854	12,218	9,667	8,363	11,061	9,314	1,323	1,840	12,530
Omsk, USSR	5,247	9,205	8,550	15,432	4,449	12,837	14,786	2,097	4,571	12,747	10,586	2,208	5,303	2,018	14,857	4,774	4,144	9,945	9,113	13,949
Oodnadatta, Australia	15,051	16,809	8,869	13,701	15,173	5,663	14,343	12,968	13,375	5,594	14,924	10,813	11,421	11,983	13,995	12,389	13,665	16,171	16,968	3,817
Oradea, Romania	1,624	7,524	7,745	12,067	1,355	16,109	11,588	2,251	1,743	16,041	7,071	3,130	3,855	1,990	11,285	2,730	1,020	8,434	7,366	17,516
Oran, Algeria	766	6,530	7,893	9,847	1,771	17,427	9,426	4,216	2,428	17,415	5,041	5,181	4,528	4,190	9,027	3,463	2,182	7,418	6,351	19,592
Oranjestad, Aruba	8,108	3,000	13,335	4,001	7,851	11,587	3,203	9,708	9,777	11,675	6,555	12,268	11,624	11,048	4,390	10,729	9,491	2,766	3,005	13,076
Orebro, Sweden	2,546	6,474	9,153	11,994	1,128	14,928	11,377	1,442	3,169	14,877	7,905	3,862	5,252	2,600	11,473	4,148	2,446	7,356	6,334	17,113
Orel, USSR	2,826	7,942	8,034	13,165	2,162	15,026	12,628	1,322	2,531	14,948	8,253	2,392	4,177	1,129	12,452	3,212	1,914	8,818	7,803	16,366
Orsk, USSR	4,270	9,102	7,842	14,713	3,696	13,911	14,166	1,819	3,495	13,820	9,528	1,473	4,348	941	13,968	3,728	3,092	9,922	8,985	14,839
Osaka, Japan	10,419	11,214	11,008	17,236	9,361	7,736	16,652	6,811	9,683	7,639	15,751	6,728	9,641	7,145	18,379	9,591	9,329	11,370	11,252	8,903
Oslo, Norway	2,568	6,214	9,349	11,776	1,047	14,886	11,147	1,615	3,328	14,840	7,845	4,124	5,453	2,861	11,287	4,336	2,607	7,097	6,073	17,201
Osorno, Chile	11,896	8,815	11,021	1,894	12,639	9,731	2,683	15,097	12,858	9,831	6,817	15,883	12,964	15,328	2,224	13,027	13,127	8,309	8,851	8,994
Ostrava, Czechoslovakia	1,667	7,132	8,142	11,890	994	15,910	11,374	2,098	2,108	15,850	7,142	3,432	4,258	2,236	11,174	3,127	1,387	8,039	6,976	17,643
Ottawa, Canada	6,751	718	14,065	7,667	5,677	11,561	6,858	6,619	8,349	11,601	8,482	9,694	10,621	8,447	8,038	9,474	7,765	1,493	681	14,218
Ouagadougou, Bourkina Fasso	2,872	7,863	6,396	8,486	4,342	18,963	8,337	6,631	3,461	19,063	2,660	6,543	4,379	5,969	7,376	3,850	3,786	8,606	7,687	17,266
Oujda, Morocco	908	6,482	7,904	9,690	1,908	17,485	9,273	4,371	2,540	17,479	4,896	5,331	4,602	4,349	8,865	3,554	2,323	7,364	6,302	19,630
Oxford, United Kingdom	1,797	5,790	9,146	10,712	398	15,714	10,131	2,771	3,107	15,687	6,732	4,808	5,381	3,583	10,148	4,223	2,477	6,703	5,629	18,322
Pago Pago, American Samoa	17,492	11,355	14,453	10,404	15,883	121	10,521	13,934	17,510	226	16,432	14,539	16,846	14,951	11,553	17,327	17,021	10,549	11,536	2,890
Pakxe, Laos	9,710	14,012	7,412	18,983	9,483	9,628	19,711	7,325	8,275	9,524	13,482	5,284	7,150	6,343	17,966	7,634	8,305	14,491	13,975	9,229
Palembang, Indonesia	10,829	16,009	6,470	17,020	10,981	9,241	17,831	9,100	9,200	9,146	13,177	6,574	7,522	7,778	16,362	8,316	9,425	16,463	15,969	8,045
Palermo, Italy	513	7,475	7,253	11,083	1,617	17,268	10,688	3,440	1,298	17,209	5,857	3,912	3,560	2,978	10,199	2,417	910	8,386	7,302	18,377
Palma, Majorca	537	6,588	7,978	10,311	1,302	17,101	9,862	3,701	2,217	17,074	5,546	4,768	4,431	3,727	9,522	3,313	1,836	7,493	6,413	19,270
Palmerston North, New Zealand	18,899	14,013	11,537	10,179	18,623	3,187	10,668	16,081	17,203	3,195	14,561	14,706	15,006	15,796	10,895	16,113	17,590	13,113	14,190	394
Panama, Panama	9,181	3,338	14,229	3,743	8,816	10,489	2,940	10,473	10,863	10,577	7,460	13,229	12,735	11,983	4,468	11,832	10,547	2,789	3,404	12,002
Paramaribo, Suriname	7,227	4,253	11,559	3,658	7,420	13,040	3,050	9,695	8,760	13,136	4,774	11,636	10,286	10,549	3,451	9,557	8,643	4,318	4,188	13,906
Paris, France	1,401	6,138	8,739	10,779	301	16,082	10,234	2,849	2,711	16,050	6,502	4,588	4,989	3,397	10,140	3,832	2,101	7,052	5,973	18,540
Patna, India	7,278	12,606	6,389	17,547	7,202	11,971	17,404	5,367	5,832	11,866	11,347	2,864	4,925	4,003	16,300	5,248	5,868	13,344	12,509	11,641
Patrai, Greece	1,242	8,072	6,878	11,777	1,980	16,995	11,405	3,178	804	16,918	6,339	3,194	3,050	2,335	10,850	1,893	178	8,987	7,904	17,646
Peking, China	8,814	11,169	9,656	18,092	7,950	9,501	17,287	5,428	7,938	9,402	13,996	4,944	7,873	5,432	18,289	7,805	7,633	11,572	11,156	10,388
Penrhyn Island (Omoka)	16,604	9,915	15,846	9,384	15,058	1,584	9,370	13,667	17,484	1,663	15,587	15,161	18,055	15,183	10,624	17,979	16,789	9,086	10,096	4,127
Peoria, Illinois	7,993	1,136	15,289	7,395	6,873	10,354	6,590	7,553	9,576	10,399	9,352	10,709	11,853	9,490	8,015	10,701	8,976	898	1,299	12,975
Perm', USSR	4,212	8,396	8,562	14,343	3,345	13,695	13,722	1,111	3,766	13,612	9,636	2,235	4,951	1,410	13,756	4,201	3,236	9,196	8,286	15,036
Perth, Australia	13,547	18,657	6,915	13,818	14,149	7,567	14,599	12,505	11,844	7,504	13,141	9,764	9,713	11,018	13,637	10,772	12,276	18,127	18,775	5,361
Peshawar, Pakistan	5,689	11,281	6,389	16,165	5,613	13,316	15,858	3,993	4,318	13,213	10,133	1,264	3,869	2,410	15,066	3,898	4,287	12,096	11,163	13,243
Petropavlovsk-Kamchatskiy,USSR	9,654	8,518	13,077	14,782	8,203	7,930	14,066	5,931	9,613	7,860	14,966	7,359	10,509	7,184	15,697	9,995	9,028	8,635	8,570	10,080
Petrozavodsk, USSR	3,326	7,239	9,026	13,067	2,158	14,288	12,434	437	3,428	14,222	8,795	3,127	5,174	1,932	12,553	4,194	2,750	8,079	7,115	16,123
Pevek, USSR	8,098	6,810	13,200	13,568	6,543	9,372	12,774	4,606	8,427	9,319	13,138	6,874	9,847	6,310	14,179	9,067	7,757	7,087	6,835	11,823
Philadelphia, Pennsylvania	6,972	158	14,107	7,058	6,024	11,542	6,249	7,145	8,619	11,591	8,176	10,169	10,867	8,912	7,445	9,738	8,074	1,071	90	14,066
Phnom Penh, Kampuchea	9,875	14,409	7,143	18,580	9,736	9,617	19,357	7,643	8,387	9,514	13,379	5,462	7,132	6,566	17,642	7,687	8,462	14,896	14,369	9,043
Phoenix, Arizona	10,036	3,236	17,431	7,710	8,768	8,208	6,997	8,878	11,529	8,252	11,205	12,038	13,796	10,945	8,682	12,641	10,876	2,562	3,412	10,869
Pierre, South Dakota	8,470	2,066	15,911	8,126	7,190	9,651	7,337	7,455	9,951	9,686	10,300	10,641	12,219	9,487	8,851	11,062	9,299	1,811	2,211	12,396
Pinang, Malaysia	9,882	15,079	6,385	17,762	9,954	9,938	18,512	8,059	8,297	9,839	12,824	5,563	6,792	6,751	16,807	7,482	8,469	15,642	15,019	9,001
Pitcairn Island (Adamstown)	15,829	9,019	15,132	6,007	15,199	4,527	6,127	15,563	17,501	4,631	12,166	18,373	18,447	17,637	7,200	18,305	17,168	8,108	9,178	5,354
Pittsburgh, Pennsylvania	7,312	342	14,509	7,164	6,300	11,141	6,353	7,269	8,939	11,188	8,575	10,350	11,201	9,102	7,633	10,062	8,374	838	490	13,701
Plymouth, Montserrat	7,152	2,833	12,631	4,552	6,954	12,496	3,802	8,937	8,816	12,580	5,926	11,358	10,677	10,157	4,669	9,770	8,540	2,913	2,778	14,032
Plymouth, United Kingdom	1,775	5,642	9,192	10,462	608	15,798	9,884	3,017	3,194	15,777	6,539	5,027	5,473	3,811	9,898	4,318	2,596	6,556	5,477	18,498
Ponape Island	14,270	12,434	12,444	14,521	13,096	4,033	14,519	10,585	13,469	3,930	19,220	10,401	12,904	10,974	15,705	13,180	13,171	12,046	12,565	5,143
Ponce, Puerto Rico	7,463	2,512	13,119	4,628	7,150	12,056	3,845	9,002	9,147	12,138	6,414	11,569	11,073	10,343	4,886	10,132	8,831	2,484	2,483	13,720
Ponta Delgada, Azores	2,949	4,386	9,883	8,250	2,794	15,750	7,676	5,170	4,652	15,787	5,189	7,115	6,760	5,956	7,735	5,704	4,295	5,243	4,205	18,215
Pontianak, Indonesia	11,044	15,652	7,060	17,384	11,047	8,821	18,184	9,011	9,464	8,724	13,735	6,693	7,917	7,852	16,881	8,642	9,629	16,010	15,634	7,845
Port Augusta, Australia	15,471	16,863	8,929	13,113	15,717	5,510	13,764	13,555	13,774	5,450	14,654	11,327	11,731	12,517	13,407	12,747	14,114	16,118	17,036	3,404
Port Blair, India	8,805	14,296	6,003	17,797	8,897	10,908	18,257	7,107	7,231	10,806	12,055	4,493	5,828	5,695	16,569	6,449	7,391	14,977	14,212	10,080
Port Elizabeth, South Africa	8,060	13,235	2,740	9,097	9,662	14,408	9,646	11,001	7,254	14,417	5,009	8,655	5,637	9,177	7,903	6,471	7,968	13,683	13,087	11,540
Port Hedland, Australia	13,160	17,490	7,393	15,045	13,420	7,403	15,798	11,470	11,480	7,324	14,008	9,007	9,557	10,218	14,945	10,499	11,785	17,313	17,560	5,709
Port Louis, Mauritius	8,194	15,167	1,057	12,578	9,448	13,455	13,142	9,507	6,686	13,399	7,832	6,434	4,421	7,427	11,398	5,576	7,342	15,983	14,986	10,903
Port Moresby, Papua New Guinea	14,938	14,592	10,680	14,531	14,274	4,500	14,889	11,745	13,590	4,404	17,216	10,550	12,238	11,468	15,320	12,904	13,573	14,126	14,731	4,113
Port Said, Egypt	2,342	9,310	5,786	12,492	3,185	16,899	12,239	3,747	681	16,800	6,598	2,495	1,889	2,154	11,423	798	1,082	10,225	9,142	16,529
Port Sudan, Sudan	3,445	10,558	4,408	12,607	4,530	16,884	12,538	4,999	1,793	16,780	6,428	2,883	507	3,126	11,396	668	2,419	11,466	10,384	15,487
Port-au-Prince, Haiti	7,936	2,301	13,723	4,671	7,506	11,469	3,865	9,197	9,633	11,549	6,999	11,916	11,618	10,669	5,100	10,646	9,277	2,069	2,317	13,241
Port-of-Spain, Trin. & Tobago	7,469	3,473	12,385	3,916	7,422	12,461	3,189	9,511	9,089	12,551	5,609	11,782	10,807	10,616	3,995	9,979	8,878	3,461	3,429	13,704
Port-Vila, Vanuatu	17,162	13,395	12,389	12,174	16,029	2,180	12,458	13,528	16,021	2,098	17,150	12,935	14,641	13,731	13,132	15,362	15,913	12,664	13,569	2,213
Portland, Maine	6,431	736	13,663	7,452	5,449	11,979	6,651	6,595	8,063	12,022	8,009	9,596	10,321	8,338	7,739	9,185	7,508	1,645	592	14,580
Portland, Oregon	9,613	3,821	16,917	9,304	8,143	8,219	8,572	7,709	10,870	8,236	12,053	10,758	13,014	9,784	10,221	11,908	10,163	3,493	3,961	11,074
Porto, Portugal	1,492	5,644	8,815	9,594	1,500	16,568	9,081	4,047	3,188	16,569	5,467	5,624	5,382	4,502	8,927	4,278	2,786	6,543	5,467	19,452
Porto Alegre, Brazil	9,630	8,082	9,777	2,034	10,520	12,015	2,568	13,061	10,557	12,116	4,547	13,612	10,865	13,031	832	10,786	10,829	7,880	8,055	11,188
Porto Alexandre, Angola	5,851	10,965	3,796	8,557	7,461	16,702	8,851	9,240	5,432	16,731	2,992	7,681	4,551	7,782	7,254	4,969	6,083	11,544	10,803	13,905
Porto Novo, Benin	3,409	8,620	5,670	8,594	4,962	18,995	8,546	7,106	3,634	19,084	2,473	6,597	4,083	6,193	7,404	3,774	4,089	9,340	8,446	16,548
Porto Velho, Brazil	8,999	5,444	11,910	1,787	9,296	11,681	1,184	11,569	10,430	11,784	5,448	13,424	11,641	12,392	1,942	11,095	10,400	5,180	5,438	12,095
Portsmouth, United Kingdom	1,694	5,835	9,062	10,667	389	15,823	10,095	2,844	3,034	15,796	6,630	4,809	5,311	3,592	10,085	4,154	2,416	6,749	5,672	18,426
Poznan, Poland	1,869	6,910	8,438	11,884	875	15,656	11,337	1,907	2,409	15,599	7,322	3,566	4,549	2,335	11,222	3,423	1,688	7,813	6,758	17,565
Prague, Czechoslovakia	1,560	6,879	8,306	11,638	721	15,945	11,112	2,220	2,240	15,891	7,010	3,707	4,441	2,508	10,945	3,298	1,533	7,789	6,722	17,859
Praia, Cape Verde Islands	3,937	5,798	8,636	6,650	4,738	16,609	6,314	7,289	5,262	16,699	2,719	8,305	6,688	7,412	5,787	5,970	5,286	6,425	5,636	16,982
Pretoria, South Africa	7,257	12,980	2,129	9,697	8,838	15,129	10,170	10,070	6,351	15,124	4,918	7,726	4,693	8,233	8,448	5,537	7,070	13,556	12,818	12,246
Prince Albert, Canada	8,158	2,730	15,563	9,174	6,732	9,704	8,380	6,628	9,488	9,721	10,799	9,791	11,698	8,697	9,855	10,562	8,797	2,746	2,828	12,558
Prince Edward Island	9,726	14,744	3,192	9,429	11,304	12,689	10,117	12,326	8,750	12,693	6,551	9,583	6,858	10,344	8,418	7,842	9,473	15,023	14,615	9,810
Prince George, Canada	8,882	3,836	16,032	9,950	7,360	8,822	9,184	6,787	10,044	8,828	11,915	9,825	12,137	8,859	10,757	11,052	9,328	3,741	3,942	11,705
Prince Rupert, Canada	9,133	4,332	16,071	10,356	7,576	8,505	9,602	6,797	10,203	8,504	12,385	9,747	12,220	8,847	11,203	11,171	9,481	4,227	4,438	11,387
Providence, Rhode Island	6,597	535	13,773	7,249	5,648	11,875	6,445	6,819	8,241	11,921	7,989	9,815	10,492	8,556	7,561	9,360	7,696	1,449	376	14,432
Provo, Utah	9,469	3,003	16,924	8,265	8,133	8,613	7,520	8,134	10,900	8,647	11,191	11,288	13,147	10,205	9,155	11,997	10,228	2,521	3,164	11,368
Puerto Aisen, Chile	12,162	9,353	10,685	2,422	13,008	9,617	3,217	15,510	13,002	9,714	6,934	15,930	12,895	15,528	2,609	13,067	13,331	8,844	9,389	8,669
Puerto Deseado, Argentina	11,882	9,664	10,105	2,704	12,850	10,028	3,515	15,393	12,601	10,122	6,544	15,441	12,363	15,153	2,598	12,592	12,980	9,214	9,686	8,873
Puerto Princesa, Philippines	11,178	14,388	8,431	18,193	10,801	8,109	18,690	8,470	9,790	8,006	14,883	6,760	8,651	7,751	18,245	9,162	9,787	14,612	14,403	7,794
Punta Arenas, Chile	12,514	10,222	10,092	3,275	13,531	9,495	4,078	16,080	13,131	9,586	7,115	15,819	12,681	15,690	3,288	13,023	13,555	9,716	10,255	8,204
Pusan, South Korea	9,995	11,394	10,464	17,754	9,026	8,262	17,104	6,476	9,173	8,163	15,235	6,180	9,058	6,655	18,744	9,037	8,852	11,629	11,416	9,266
Pyongyang, North Korea	9,478	11,076	10,344	17,728	8,502	8,730	16,993	5,952	8,693	8,632	14,761	5,737	8,684	6,161	18,447	8,601	8,352	11,373	11,087	9,790
Qamdo, China	7,969	12,212	7,677	18,545	7,561	10,895	18,021	5,345	6,721	10,791	12,527	3,617	6,147	4,511	17,486	6,314	6,612	12,817	12,151	11,035
Qandahar, Afghanistan	5,293	11,276	5,918	15,642	5,390	13,878	15,404	4,060	3,831	13,774	9,551	976	3,263	2,235	14,501	3,329	3,877	12,128	11,145	13,609
Qiqian, China	8,204	9,765	10,564	16,696	7,090	9,744	15,887	4,542	7,664	9,655	13,646	4,994	8,125	5,109	17,012	7,793	7,218	10,173	9,754	11,168
Qom, Iran	3,875	10,226	5,939	14,267	4,129	15,170	13,986	3,401	2,421	15,068	8,316	765	2,453	1,321	13,193	2,100	2,459	11,120	10,079	15,016
Quebec, Canada	6,372	971	13,700	7,804	5,306	11,916	7,001	6,321	7,971	11,953	8,252	9,366	10,243	8,113	8,099	9,096	7,391	1,827	870	14,592
Quetta, Pakistan	5,464	11,468	5,822	15,761	5,582	13,770	15,551	4,242	3,980	13,665	9,637	1,170	3,305	2,429	14,598	3,436	4,048	12,317	11,338	13,433
Quito, Ecuador	9,695	4,345	13,771	2,736	9,533	10,362	1,946	11,370	11,320	10,458	7,159	13,945	12,962	12,734	3,564	12,192	11,099	3,810	4,401	11,482
Rabaul, Papua New Guinea	14,892	13,788	11,402	14,475	13,999	4,102	14,707	11,447	13,730	4,000	18,019	10,631	12,635	11,431	15,434	13,176	13,605	13,335	13,927	4,290
Raiatea (Uturoa)	16,986	9,920	15,556	8,396	15,625	2,203	8,458	14,616	18,327	2,305	14,567	16,277	18,915	16,264	9,601	19,082	17,604	9,036	10,100	4,000

Distances in Kilometers

	Annaba, Algeria	Annapolis, Maryland	Antananarivo, Madagascar	Antofagasta, Chile	Antwerp, Belgium	Apia, Western Samoa	Arequipa, Peru	Arkhangel'sk, USSR	As Sallum, Egypt	Asau, Western Samoa	Ascension Island (Georgetown)	Ashkhabad, USSR	Asmera, Ethiopia	Astrakhan, USSR	Asuncion, Paraguay	Aswan, Egypt	Athens, Greece	Atlanta, Georgia	Atlantic City, New Jersey	Auckland, New Zealand
Raleigh, North Carolina	7,460	403	14,456	6,634	6,561	11,175	5,822	7,694	9,124	11,230	8,268	10,724	11,356	9,467	7,107	10,237	8,596	572	542	13,606
Rangiroa (Avatoru)	16,580	9,489	15,911	8,092	15,277	2,594	8,113	14,457	18,028	2,693	14,289	16,400	19,322	16,228	9,322	18,990	17,317	8,601	9,668	4,433
Rangoon, Burma	8,772	13,785	6,630	18,432	8,692	10,672	18,724	6,725	7,281	10,568	12,456	4,367	6,105	5,500	17,159	6,602	7,357	14,412	13,715	10,140
Raoul Is., Kermadec Islands	19,013	12,915	12,793	10,307	17,560	1,823	10,646	15,257	17,804	1,834	15,528	14,793	15,954	15,629	11,236	16,922	17,803	12,049	13,095	1,085
Rarotonga (Avarua)	17,895	10,910	14,673	9,034	16,403	1,509	9,191	14,960	18,760	1,612	15,050	15,926	17,952	16,256	10,167	18,693	18,115	10,032	11,090	3,012
Rawson, Argentina	11,533	9,184	10,295	2,233	12,432	10,265	3,044	14,961	12,353	10,362	6,285	15,294	12,295	14,881	2,112	12,430	12,686	8,755	9,202	9,269
Recife, Brazil	6,673	6,749	8,937	4,159	7,571	14,683	4,087	10,122	7,739	14,787	2,258	10,845	8,542	10,115	3,077	8,169	7,924	6,975	6,646	14,156
Regina, Canada	8,293	2,545	15,732	8,872	6,905	9,637	8,081	6,900	9,669	9,660	10,698	10,071	11,899	8,962	9,575	10,756	8,987	2,482	2,657	12,468
Reykjavik, Iceland	3,621	4,491	10,930	10,596	2,104	13,955	9,879	2,896	4,856	13,939	8,019	5,833	7,088	4,578	10,388	5,940	4,171	5,359	4,359	16,771
Rhodes, Greece	1,826	8,649	6,454	12,272	2,502	16,818	11,939	3,236	610	16,729	6,628	2,672	2,568	1,982	11,290	1,440	434	9,564	8,483	17,050
Richmond, Virginia	7,272	180	14,332	6,813	6,350	11,310	6,003	7,471	8,928	11,363	8,246	10,502	11,168	9,245	7,254	10,044	8,393	756	329	13,782
Riga, USSR	2,538	7,058	8,687	12,447	1,431	15,036	11,861	1,227	2,822	14,974	8,002	3,280	4,785	2,017	11,847	3,718	2,109	7,939	6,918	16,898
Ringkobing, Denmark	2,133	6,224	9,091	11,485	598	15,317	10,887	1,988	3,026	15,274	7,396	4,189	5,219	2,935	10,935	4,080	2,319	7,124	6,074	17,643
Rio Branco, Brazil	9,415	5,493	12,249	1,539	9,657	11,233	820	11,873	10,865	11,335	5,869	13,839	12,088	12,783	2,004	11,541	10,821	5,147	5,503	11,692
Rio Cuarto, Argentina	10,773	8,082	10,777	1,206	11,504	10,739	1,990	13,980	11,806	10,841	5,835	14,885	12,153	14,226	1,087	12,075	12,032	7,695	8,093	10,131
Rio de Janeiro, Brazil	8,510	7,677	9,289	2,777	9,439	13,097	3,050	11,989	9,452	13,200	3,497	12,526	9,893	11,911	1,490	9,729	9,709	7,637	7,619	12,288
Rio Gallegos, Argentina	12,325	10,064	10,087	3,108	13,330	9,657	3,914	15,877	12,972	9,748	6,941	15,708	12,583	15,531	3,087	12,892	13,383	9,574	10,093	8,402
Rio Grande, Brazil	9,847	8,257	9,780	2,025	10,751	11,835	2,620	13,293	10,749	11,935	4,719	13,789	10,997	13,235	927	10,951	11,033	8,031	8,235	10,961
Riyadh, Saudi Arabia	3,937	10,825	4,819	13,698	4,646	15,832	13,579	4,460	2,250	15,727	7,543	1,844	1,312	2,413	12,507	1,404	2,630	11,739	10,663	14,935
Road Town, Brit. Virgin Isls.	7,259	2,548	12,923	4,700	6,974	12,272	3,929	8,870	8,940	12,354	6,237	11,392	10,857	10,172	4,895	9,920	8,632	2,596	2,504	13,924
Roanoke, Virginia	7,479	356	14,554	6,817	6,532	11,088	6,006	7,588	9,129	11,141	8,438	10,645	11,375	9,392	7,305	10,247	8,585	562	532	13,568
Robinson Crusoe Island, Chile	11,893	8,043	11,885	1,381	12,409	9,434	2,045	14,721	13,061	9,537	7,166	16,165	13,504	15,367	2,250	13,400	13,219	7,481	8,093	9,103
Rochester, New York	6,996	474	14,260	7,434	5,952	11,382	6,623	6,911	8,608	11,425	8,511	9,988	10,876	8,740	7,847	9,733	8,034	1,199	498	13,996
Rockhampton, Australia	16,165	15,283	10,447	13,189	15,772	4,110	13,673	13,281	14,606	4,036	16,177	11,748	12,849	12,789	13,831	13,726	14,750	14,599	15,451	2,762
Rome, Italy	688	7,191	7,638	11,172	1,205	16,868	10,731	3,088	1,608	16,814	6,161	3,902	3,887	2,864	10,352	2,732	1,054	8,105	7,022	18,400
Rosario, Argentina	10,499	8,130	10,480	1,403	11,284	11,065	2,135	13,787	11,493	11,167	5,502	14,561	11,809	13,936	900	11,741	11,737	7,790	8,130	10,378
Roseau, Dominica	7,165	3,011	12,508	4,419	7,016	12,560	3,679	9,040	8,818	12,646	5,784	11,408	10,642	10,218	4,506	9,755	8,561	3,084	2,954	14,017
Rostock, East Germany	1,939	6,539	8,765	11,636	612	15,526	11,064	1,967	2,708	15,478	7,310	3,914	4,889	2,670	11,028	3,752	1,996	7,441	6,387	17,677
Rostov-na-Donu, USSR	2,856	8,560	7,368	13,399	2,582	15,300	12,932	1,931	2,136	15,214	8,102	1,841	3,538	645	12,565	2,639	1,660	9,447	8,416	16,185
Rotterdam, Netherlands	1,688	6,159	8,887	11,070	78	15,767	10,503	2,490	2,818	15,730	6,874	4,412	5,075	3,188	10,468	3,919	2,155	7,070	6,000	18,168
Rouyn, Canada	6,852	1,048	14,242	8,007	5,690	11,344	7,197	6,451	8,407	11,378	8,845	9,573	10,686	8,339	8,415	9,531	7,796	1,670	1,052	14,066
Sacramento, California	10,165	3,869	17,584	8,708	8,754	7,808	8,007	8,461	11,508	7,837	12,043	11,530	13,700	10,540	9,700	12,574	10,813	3,358	4,030	10,608
Saginaw, Michigan	7,435	796	14,753	7,556	6,323	10,880	6,745	7,095	9,020	10,922	8,998	10,226	11,296	8,994	8,068	10,145	8,423	1,076	912	13,527
Saint Denis, Reunion	8,120	15,037	858	12,361	9,409	13,595	12,920	9,558	6,642	13,542	7,617	6,518	4,392	7,481	11,176	5,542	7,311	15,834	14,857	11,000
Saint George's, Grenada	7,400	3,321	12,452	4,060	7,317	12,463	3,326	9,382	9,032	12,553	5,686	11,691	10,786	10,515	4,152	9,938	8,805	3,326	3,275	13,777
Saint John, Canada	6,054	1,109	13,316	7,644	5,072	12,316	6,851	6,276	7,683	12,356	7,821	9,245	9,943	7,984	7,857	8,805	7,128	2,022	954	14,947
Saint John's, Antigua	7,095	2,811	12,603	4,603	6,895	12,541	3,855	8,881	8,760	12,625	5,908	11,299	10,627	10,098	4,709	9,716	8,483	2,910	2,752	14,089
Saint John's, Canada	4,999	2,142	12,298	8,084	4,062	13,302	7,330	5,516	6,633	13,336	7,211	8,338	8,889	7,076	8,081	7,754	6,090	3,056	1,973	15,992
Saint Louis, Missouri	8,164	1,190	15,407	7,196	7,073	10,243	6,393	7,787	9,762	10,290	9,341	10,940	12,036	9,718	7,843	10,888	9,171	751	1,364	12,823
Saint Paul, Minnesota	7,969	1,524	15,379	7,938	6,745	10,213	7,135	7,210	9,490	10,250	9,748	10,389	11,767	9,198	8,567	10,610	8,857	1,450	1,656	12,931
Saint Peter Port, UK	1,623	5,782	9,037	10,503	532	15,935	9,938	3,023	3,043	15,911	6,462	4,931	5,322	3,726	9,910	4,167	2,452	6,697	5,616	18,590
Saipan (Susupe)	12,760	12,587	11,394	16,135	11,754	5,677	16,045	9,203	11,842	5,574	17,725	8,762	11,304	9,380	17,347	11,537	11,582	12,437	12,679	6,515
Salalah, Oman	5,040	11,966	4,038	14,224	5,785	15,114	14,257	5,382	3,337	15,012	8,026	2,359	1,632	3,303	12,955	2,344	3,766	12,879	11,804	13,842
Salem, Oregon	9,686	3,861	16,991	9,283	8,217	8,151	8,554	7,779	10,944	8,170	12,094	10,823	13,087	9,853	10,210	11,982	10,236	3,516	4,002	11,005
Salt Lake City, Utah	9,441	3,014	16,897	8,322	8,098	8,626	7,575	8,082	10,865	8,659	11,212	11,233	13,108	10,153	9,208	11,960	10,191	2,548	3,173	11,389
Salta, Argentina	10,260	7,152	11,300	522	10,824	10,966	1,127	13,226	11,462	11,070	5,721	14,568	12,141	13,735	784	11,887	11,592	6,782	7,162	10,727
Salto, Uruguay	10,194	8,022	10,322	1,496	10,995	11,369	2,156	13,508	11,186	11,470	5,203	14,257	11,531	13,628	679	11,443	11,429	7,725	8,015	10,675
Salvador, Brazil	7,346	6,974	9,147	3,561	8,235	14,078	3,574	10,784	8,387	14,182	2,696	11,489	9,086	10,783	2,426	8,775	8,589	7,096	6,889	13,485
Salzburg, Austria	1,285	6,907	8,151	11,453	730	16,213	10,948	2,491	2,075	16,160	6,739	3,804	4,316	2,642	10,727	3,163	1,395	7,820	6,745	18,090
Samsun, Turkey	2,507	8,822	6,764	13,070	2,670	15,937	12,682	2,605	1,470	15,846	7,514	1,924	2,887	1,096	12,135	1,934	1,141	9,728	8,668	16,428
San Antonio, Texas	9,389	2,279	16,400	6,598	8,343	9,196	5,839	8,996	11,013	9,254	9,875	12,170	13,278	10,965	7,460	12,138	10,435	1,421	2,459	11,640
San Cristobal, Venezuela	8,610	3,483	13,421	3,481	8,410	11,243	2,674	10,285	10,260	11,334	6,647	12,822	12,026	11,610	3,981	11,179	10,005	3,137	3,506	12,572
San Diego, California	10,416	3,707	17,855	7,972	9,100	7,758	7,286	9,046	11,867	7,799	11,678	12,168	14,115	11,124	8,996	12,966	11,197	3,044	3,881	10,455
San Francisco, California	10,286	3,972	17,701	8,706	8,873	7,689	8,013	8,561	11,626	7,718	12,131	11,620	13,814	10,639	9,715	12,690	10,930	3,444	4,134	10,487
San Jose, Costa Rica	9,520	3,305	14,738	4,003	9,051	10,028	3,223	10,556	11,215	10,115	7,971	13,432	13,155	12,173	4,835	12,216	10,860	2,638	3,397	11,659
San Juan, Argentina	10,968	7,850	11,206	893	11,604	10,431	1,704	14,027	12,077	10,534	6,168	15,176	12,528	14,439	1,269	12,402	12,264	7,416	7,872	9,983
San Juan, Puerto Rico	7,391	2,405	13,078	4,602	7,077	12,116	3,902	8,935	9,076	12,197	6,384	11,497	11,006	10,271	4,924	10,063	8,759	2,483	2,451	13,792
San Luis Potosi, Mexico	10,100	2,983	16,735	6,053	9,130	8,683	5,337	9,839	11,755	8,749	9,995	13,013	13,996	11,806	7,029	12,873	11,204	2,073	3,156	10,972
San Marino, San Marino	875	7,077	7,821	11,255	1,012	16,646	10,791	2,888	1,764	16,593	6,349	3,873	4,039	2,789	10,467	2,881	1,153	7,992	6,910	18,330
San Miguel de Tucuman, Argen.	10,389	7,377	11,178	629	10,993	10,908	1,326	13,414	11,553	11,012	5,743	14,659	12,153	13,864	775	11,941	11,706	7,003	7,388	10,580
San Salvador, El Salvador	9,715	3,067	15,384	4,611	9,082	9,592	3,854	10,356	11,419	9,674	8,601	13,368	13,478	12,106	5,504	12,470	10,999	2,274	3,189	11,445
Sanaa, Yemen	4,315	11,412	3,808	13,161	5,323	16,165	13,183	5,473	2,640	16,064	6,958	2,867	566	3,456	11,902	1,529	3,215	12,324	11,240	14,610
Santa Cruz, Bolivia	9,583	6,437	11,431	993	10,062	11,445	906	12,432	10,876	11,549	5,387	13,959	11,778	13,044	1,004	11,400	10,946	6,134	6,435	11,445
Santa Cruz, Tenerife	2,430	5,605	8,629	8,183	3,062	17,020	7,751	5,613	3,984	17,070	4,030	6,854	5,833	5,855	7,416	4,897	3,841	6,411	5,425	18,628
Santa Fe, New Mexico	9,461	2,624	16,822	7,559	8,236	8,820	6,810	8,512	10,986	8,865	10,660	11,695	13,262	10,555	8,443	12,105	10,348	1,982	2,799	11,465
Santa Rosa, Argentina	11,015	8,463	10,590	1,553	11,808	10,604	2,352	14,306	11,975	10,704	5,950	15,020	12,183	14,440	1,407	12,178	12,239	8,065	8,476	9,854
Santa Rosalia, Mexico	10,540	3,553	17,764	7,215	9,340	7,867	6,537	9,549	12,086	7,920	11,191	12,715	14,363	11,610	8,255	13,206	11,452	2,761	3,734	10,420
Santarem, Brazil	7,769	5,101	11,213	2,893	8,137	12,860	2,407	10,499	9,195	12,961	4,505	12,192	10,479	11,184	2,547	9,880	9,167	5,073	5,049	13,312
Santiago del Estero, Argentina	10,386	7,499	11,045	767	11,024	10,959	1,467	13,462	11,521	11,063	5,674	14,626	12,074	13,859	714	11,886	11,690	7,134	7,507	10,567
Santiago, Chile	11,257	8,041	11,270	1,086	11,896	10,173	1,891	14,313	12,351	10,276	6,413	15,444	12,742	14,727	1,552	12,651	12,548	7,576	8,070	9,690
Santo Domingo, Dominican Rep.	7,726	2,361	13,469	4,660	7,342	11,721	3,861	9,100	9,418	11,802	6,755	11,759	11,381	10,520	5,017	10,421	9,078	2,223	2,356	13,454
Sao Paulo de Olivenca, Brazil	9,053	4,764	12,638	2,242	9,149	11,320	1,464	11,265	10,588	11,420	6,041	13,447	12,022	12,324	2,692	11,359	10,469	4,431	4,775	12,090
Sao Paulo, Brazil	8,790	7,588	9,596	2,425	9,666	12,762	2,722	12,208	9,772	12,865	3,844	12,855	10,245	12,212	1,137	10,070	10,012	7,497	7,540	12,042
Sao Tome, Sao Tome & Principe	4,050	9,403	4,938	8,720	5,644	18,502	8,777	7,634	3,964	18,552	2,519	6,720	3,909	6,494	7,470	3,855	4,518	10,097	9,231	15,778
Sapporo, Japan	9,987	10,155	11,727	16,399	8,764	7,906	15,725	6,258	9,503	7,817	15,457	6,759	9,837	6,946	17,388	9,597	9,051	10,317	10,195	9,475
Sarajevo, Yugoslavia	1,186	7,491	7,556	11,701	1,332	16,543	11,253	2,690	1,484	16,478	6,619	3,397	3,710	2,336	10,880	2,558	789	8,405	7,327	17,878
Saratov, USSR	3,411	8,533	7,809	13,848	2,858	14,639	13,321	1,483	2,802	14,554	8,743	1,796	4,069	599	13,097	3,251	2,306	9,392	8,402	15,712
Saskatoon, Canada	8,280	2,740	15,693	9,104	6,861	9,596	8,313	6,760	9,618	9,615	10,851	9,921	11,831	8,829	9,807	10,694	8,928	2,709	2,845	12,445
Schefferville, Canada	5,818	1,903	13,263	8,698	4,590	12,208	7,902	5,400	7,327	12,231	8,479	8,483	9,605	7,241	8,914	8,448	6,701	2,710	1,810	15,023
Seattle, Washington	9,418	3,782	16,694	9,445	7,937	8,383	8,703	7,479	10,656	8,399	12,000	10,529	12,791	9,554	10,334	11,689	9,947	3,512	3,915	11,248
Sendai, Japan	10,398	10,643	11,576	16,647	9,227	7,589	16,036	6,700	9,815	7,497	15,839	6,968	9,978	7,257	17,755	9,828	9,401	10,769	10,688	9,017
Seoul, South Korea	9,670	11,196	10,387	17,753	8,696	8,556	17,045	6,146	8,871	8,459	14,937	5,899	8,821	6,344	18,573	8,761	8,537	11,470	11,211	9,596
Sept-Iles, Canada	5,914	1,480	13,299	8,189	4,802	12,271	7,395	5,816	7,489	12,302	8,156	8,848	9,765	7,594	8,403	8,614	6,895	2,346	1,363	15,011
Sevastopol, USSR	2,326	8,406	7,175	12,895	2,280	15,846	12,461	2,265	1,621	15,762	7,542	2,199	3,284	1,150	12,027	2,277	1,100	9,309	8,253	16,670
Seville, Spain	1,222	6,018	8,380	9,541	1,743	17,043	9,077	4,283	2,918	17,045	5,093	5,559	5,042	4,504	8,793	3,970	2,611	6,905	5,839	19,929
Shanghai, China	9,798	12,029	9,633	18,596	9,006	8,702	17,924	6,497	8,797	8,600	14,774	5,723	8,440	6,360	19,350	8,534	8,558	12,336	12,034	9,358
Sheffield, United Kingdom	1,966	5,722	9,284	10,788	469	15,536	10,193	2,654	3,229	15,508	6,902	4,810	5,495	3,571	10,253	4,339	2,581	6,634	5,564	18,148
Shenyang, China	9,123	10,835	10,282	17,623	8,136	9,046	16,849	5,586	8,369	8,950	14,436	5,448	8,442	5,828	18,168	8,312	8,012	11,171	10,838	10,154
Shiraz, Iran	4,211	10,764	5,395	14,364	4,625	15,163	14,170	3,978	2,629	15,059	8,271	1,072	2,107	1,900	13,215	2,043	2,811	11,663	10,612	14,662
Sibiu, Romania	1,685	7,744	7,545	12,197	1,571	16,162	11,737	2,319	1,582	16,090	7,082	2,947	3,650	1,843	11,383	2,534	869	8,654	7,586	17,387
Singapore	10,469	15,547	6,549	17,455	10,555	9,449	18,261	8,633	8,869	9,351	13,154	6,164	7,290	7,352	16,702	8,027	9,058	16,033	15,502	8,411
Sioux Falls, South Dakota	8,296	1,765	15,709	7,912	7,060	9,888	7,117	7,454	9,810	9,925	9,999	10,639	12,086	9,461	8,602	10,928	9,172	1,525	1,913	12,601
Skelleftea, Sweden	3,221	6,496	9,552	12,421	1,786	14,266	11,759	932	3,703	14,213	8,580	3,852	5,657	2,628	11,997	4,603	2,985	7,342	6,371	16,454
Skopje, Yugoslavia	1,307	7,812	7,257	11,879	1,654	16,636	11,460	2,789	1,203	16,563	6,627	3,159	3,397	2,168	11,013	2,250	486	8,727	7,648	17,664
Socotra Island (Tamrida)	5,323	12,336	3,564	14,062	6,167	15,083	14,170	5,858	3,621	14,985	7,904	2,836	1,656	3,778	12,773	2,562	4,108	13,251	12,170	13,576
Sofia, Bulgaria	1,476	7,891	7,258	12,045	1,716	16,499	11,622	2,668	1,244	16,425	6,786	3,004	3,379	2,000	11,182	2,243	523	8,805	7,729	17,506
Songkhla, Thailand	9,788	14,884	6,500	17,952	9,818	9,957	18,689	7,890	8,220	9,857	12,873	5,442	6,773	6,617	16,967	7,431	8,372	15,442	14,826	9,102
Sorong, Indonesia	12,995	14,937	9,326	16,433	12,550	6,438	16,874	10,128	11,590	6,337	16,102	8,577	10,292	9,558	16,959	10,907	11,604	14,820	15,015	5,986
South Georgia Island	10,963	11,007	7,954	4,398	12,301	11,351	5,158	14,726	11,204	11,429	5,511	13,627	10,475	13,701	3,653	10,919	11,740	10,768	10,981	9,468
South Pole	14,090	14,319	7,911	7,386	15,680	8,471	8,189	17,167	13,498	8,513	9,127	14,205	11,700	15,139	7,208	12,668	14,210	13,738	14,360	5,919

Distances in Kilometers	Annaba, Algeria	Annapolis, Maryland	Antananarivo, Madagascar	Antofagasta, Chile	Antwerp, Belgium	Apia, Western Samoa	Arequipa, Peru	Arkhangel'sk, USSR	As Sallum, Egypt	Asau, Western Samoa	Ascension Island (Georgetown)	Ashkhabad, USSR	Asmera, Ethiopia	Astrakhan, USSR	Asuncion, Paraguay	Aswan, Egypt	Athens, Greece	Atlanta, Georgia	Atlantic City, New Jersey	Auckland, New Zealand
South Sandwich Islands	10,968	11,688	7,301	5,146	12,405	11,458	5,903	14,695	11,008	11,528	5,624	13,195	10,054	13,420	4,370	10,605	11,598	11,486	11,653	9,333
Split, Yugoslavia	1,040	7,375	7,607	11,538	1,245	16,624	11,089	2,787	1,532	16,563	6,494	3,559	3,785	2,499	10,722	2,629	870	8,289	7,209	18,041
Spokane, Washington	9,176	3,412	16,537	9,191	7,726	8,679	8,436	7,412	10,468	8,698	11,631	10,511	12,642	9,492	10,042	11,522	9,767	3,156	3,545	11,530
Spoleto, Italy	774	7,162	7,701	11,226	1,134	16,773	10,776	2,995	1,655	16,719	6,250	3,867	3,933	2,812	10,418	2,777	1,072	8,077	6,994	18,355
Springbok, South Africa	7,444	12,365	3,224	8,594	9,057	15,083	9,075	10,632	6,821	15,104	4,143	8,590	5,468	8,950	7,348	6,160	7,514	12,824	12,217	12,257
Springfield, Illinois	8,052	1,136	15,324	7,303	6,946	10,323	6,499	7,647	9,643	10,369	9,330	10,801	11,918	9,580	7,931	10,768	9,047	819	1,305	12,926
Springfield, Massachusetts	6,674	479	13,868	7,283	5,705	11,780	6,478	6,835	8,312	11,825	8,090	9,849	10,566	8,591	7,615	9,433	7,761	1,389	344	14,348
Srinagar, India	5,963	11,395	6,541	16,462	5,834	13,015	16,138	4,104	4,613	12,911	10,433	1,540	4,151	2,635	15,368	4,199	4,567	12,190	11,283	12,978
Stanley, Falkland Islands	11,702	10,208	9,390	3,294	12,819	10,378	4,100	15,366	12,244	10,467	6,260	14,925	11,797	14,800	2,934	12,121	12,689	9,815	10,216	8,944
Stara Zagora, Bulgaria	1,647	8,062	7,153	12,222	1,882	16,428	11,806	2,640	1,205	16,350	6,900	2,815	3,261	1,832	11,344	2,141	518	8,975	7,901	17,319
Stockholm, Sweden	2,602	6,618	9,079	12,152	1,247	14,891	11,537	1,307	3,132	14,837	7,997	3,712	5,175	2,451	11,621	4,085	2,409	7,497	6,480	17,002
Stornoway, United Kingdom	2,586	5,310	9,871	10,816	1,042	14,930	10,169	2,539	3,800	14,905	7,369	5,080	6,048	3,819	10,397	4,895	3,127	6,210	5,161	17,629
Strasbourg, France	1,298	6,516	8,454	11,123	378	16,151	10,596	2,635	2,391	16,109	6,626	4,194	4,657	3,013	10,442	3,500	1,746	7,430	6,353	18,336
Stuttgart, West Germany	1,323	6,603	8,405	11,228	437	16,130	10,703	2,558	2,334	16,085	6,692	4,087	4,593	2,906	10,542	3,437	1,675	7,517	6,441	18,247
Subic, Philippines	10,926	13,796	8,801	18,543	10,426	8,137	18,761	8,030	9,629	8,033	15,036	6,549	8,679	7,462	18,835	9,090	9,563	14,028	13,811	8,090
Suchow, China	9,272	11,774	9,430	18,623	8,494	9,200	17,846	5,996	8,285	9,098	14,287	5,222	8,002	5,837	18,895	8,050	8,036	12,148	11,767	9,879
Sucre, Bolivia	9,841	6,527	11,574	737	10,303	11,189	726	12,655	11,138	11,293	5,622	14,221	12,024	13,300	1,045	11,657	11,207	6,183	6,533	11,191
Sudbury, Canada	7,070	913	14,438	7,842	5,927	11,168	7,030	6,689	8,636	11,205	8,906	9,815	10,915	8,583	8,288	9,761	8,031	1,445	956	13,865
Suez, Egypt	2,421	9,425	5,642	12,478	3,314	16,955	12,244	3,887	730	16,855	6,541	2,536	1,747	2,261	11,391	653	1,205	10,339	9,256	16,454
Sundsvall, Sweden	2,910	6,440	9,397	12,191	1,466	14,567	11,548	1,176	3,472	14,516	8,258	3,884	5,494	2,634	11,727	4,414	2,750	7,304	6,308	16,774
Surabaya, Indonesia	11,826	16,372	7,155	16,569	11,909	8,269	17,347	9,894	10,206	8,176	13,936	7,529	8,513	8,708	16,263	9,323	10,418	16,589	16,377	7,050
Suva, Fiji	17,736	12,546	13,271	11,240	16,296	1,156	11,466	13,974	16,954	1,091	16,801	13,847	15,712	14,517	12,281	16,401	16,718	11,761	12,725	2,107
Sverdlovsk, USSR	4,449	8,649	8,485	14,632	3,627	13,525	14,013	1,383	3,910	13,439	9,843	2,108	4,957	1,452	14,032	4,270	3,417	9,439	8,542	14,771
Svobodnyy, USSR	8,636	9,710	11,001	16,542	7,463	9,259	15,750	4,931	8,154	9,172	14,099	5,506	8,636	5,603	17,062	8,302	7,691	10,052	9,714	10,784
Sydney, Australia	16,707	15,759	10,056	12,272	16,721	4,294	12,839	14,329	15,021	4,294	15,136	12,446	12,991	13,584	12,787	14,006	15,325	14,946	15,939	2,161
Sydney, Canada	5,589	1,554	12,858	7,798	4,635	12,766	7,021	5,959	7,223	12,803	7,516	8,862	9,479	7,600	7,913	8,344	6,676	2,469	1,388	15,414
Syktyvkar, USSR	4,043	7,886	8,937	13,927	3,009	13,716	13,280	610	3,825	13,640	9,514	2,690	5,230	1,714	13,418	4,391	3,226	8,687	7,776	15,304
Szeged, Hungary	1,463	7,460	7,726	11,913	1,279	16,242	11,440	2,387	1,687	16,176	6,916	3,258	3,849	2,137	11,124	2,712	966	8,372	7,300	17,671
Szombathely, Hungary	1,360	7,173	7,953	11,686	991	16,222	11,195	2,411	1,886	16,162	6,836	3,533	4,094	2,386	10,932	2,947	1,181	8,085	7,012	17,884
Tabriz, Iran	3,386	9,670	6,311	13,882	3,568	15,412	13,546	2,971	2,060	15,313	8,085	1,060	2,623	930	12,871	2,007	1,976	10,566	9,521	15,523
Tacheng, China	6,101	10,292	8,095	16,518	5,490	12,283	15,906	3,228	5,146	12,186	11,209	2,235	5,349	2,655	15,808	5,085	4,856	11,000	10,208	12,997
Tahiti (Papeete)	16,928	9,830	15,566	8,179	15,622	2,410	8,245	14,726	18,364	2,512	14,350	16,480	19,094	16,424	9,384	19,239	17,648	8,939	10,009	4,096
Taipei, Taiwan	10,265	12,675	9,371	18,815	9,569	8,422	18,363	7,090	9,153	8,319	14,987	6,050	8,574	6,797	19,943	8,787	8,975	12,948	12,686	8,839
Taiyuan, China	8,696	11,446	9,253	18,404	7,922	9,732	17,593	5,436	7,734	9,631	13,763	4,693	7,554	5,268	18,337	7,540	7,469	11,886	11,424	10,457
Tallahassee, Florida	8,220	1,184	15,026	6,167	7,351	10,543	5,360	8,441	9,894	10,605	8,567	11,502	12,110	10,247	6,787	11,002	9,378	367	1,334	12,868
Tallinn, USSR	2,786	6,950	8,926	12,527	1,571	14,767	11,917	1,003	3,096	14,706	8,236	3,374	5,030	2,118	11,977	3,976	2,385	7,819	6,815	16,709
Tamanrasset, Algeria	1,580	7,789	6,491	9,683	3,157	18,975	9,441	5,296	2,171	18,954	4,033	5,277	3,604	4,616	8,645	2,796	2,421	8,633	7,608	18,140
Tampa, Florida	8,224	1,341	14,856	5,854	7,431	10,656	5,046	8,633	9,913	10,721	8,314	11,651	12,098	10,391	6,460	11,010	9,424	669	1,464	12,888
Tampere, Finland	2,955	6,787	9,162	12,506	1,643	14,570	11,875	912	3,329	14,511	8,378	3,540	5,267	2,295	12,003	4,215	2,616	7,647	6,656	16,608
Tanami, Australia	14,133	16,740	8,532	14,712	14,157	6,246	15,364	11,954	12,494	6,165	15,027	9,824	10,668	10,977	14,936	11,564	12,728	16,333	16,861	4,741
Tangier, Morocco	1,223	6,108	8,259	9,457	1,897	17,200	9,010	4,428	2,896	17,205	4,924	5,611	4,978	4,581	8,684	3,924	2,633	6,989	5,929	19,879
Tarawa (Betio)	15,504	11,681	13,776	12,785	14,079	2,384	12,781	11,742	15,035	2,285	18,930	12,046	14,646	12,484	13,994	14,874	14,631	11,101	11,840	4,235
Tashkent, USSR	5,232	10,462	7,039	15,808	4,951	13,428	15,368	3,170	4,057	13,327	10,068	1,009	4,103	1,791	14,861	3,873	3,883	11,268	10,348	13,758
Tbilisi, USSR	3,209	9,281	6,717	13,773	3,227	15,339	13,383	2,559	2,075	15,244	8,143	1,238	2,976	580	12,827	2,242	1,841	10,172	9,135	15,738
Tegucigalpa, Honduras	9,517	2,951	15,185	4,560	8,912	9,811	3,788	10,242	11,221	9,892	8,400	13,223	13,267	11,961	5,408	12,266	10,811	2,195	3,065	11,646
Tehran, Iran	3,891	10,167	6,055	14,322	4,093	15,088	14,024	3,297	2,473	14,987	8,402	670	2,574	1,220	13,263	2,198	2,476	11,058	10,021	15,008
Tel Aviv, Israel	2,529	9,422	5,803	12,741	3,263	16,654	12,482	3,636	912	16,554	6,844	2,245	1,901	1,951	11,673	904	1,201	10,336	9,256	16,340
Telegraph Creek, Canada	8,824	4,401	15,675	10,638	7,252	8,772	9,871	6,403	9,847	8,767	12,311	9,345	11,838	8,449	11,435	10,800	9,124	4,383	4,492	11,647
Teresina, Brazil	7,008	5,984	9,871	3,601	7,685	14,016	3,377	10,195	8,252	14,120	3,156	11,341	9,285	10,483	2,739	8,804	8,342	6,131	5,896	13,950
Ternate, Indonesia	12,550	14,975	8,981	16,840	12,158	6,901	17,322	9,775	11,128	6,800	15,729	8,128	9,830	9,129	17,244	10,439	11,153	14,950	15,036	6,417
The Valley, Anguilla	7,146	2,659	12,753	4,681	6,900	12,424	3,922	8,840	8,820	12,510	6,069	11,312	10,716	10,101	4,828	9,790	8,525	2,744	2,605	14,038
Thessaloniki, Greece	1,380	7,999	7,067	11,953	1,847	16,714	11,553	2,895	1,026	16,638	6,600	3,052	3,203	2,118	11,057	2,057	302	8,914	7,834	17,551
Thimphu, Bhutan	7,561	12,505	6,864	17,990	7,359	11,546	17,736	5,366	6,183	11,441	11,811	3,137	5,397	4,192	16,776	5,663	6,164	13,194	12,421	11,385
Thunder Bay, Canada	7,519	1,468	14,953	8,200	6,272	10,598	7,391	6,748	9,023	10,629	9,567	9,922	11,298	8,724	8,748	10,140	8,384	1,678	1,556	13,354
Tientsin, China	8,924	11,244	9,676	18,147	8,062	9,403	17,348	5,540	8,039	9,304	14,094	5,037	7,949	5,537	18,395	7,895	7,738	11,636	11,233	10,276
Tijuana, Mexico	10,423	3,703	17,859	7,949	9,110	7,758	7,263	9,063	11,877	7,800	11,665	12,187	14,126	11,141	8,974	12,976	11,207	3,035	3,877	10,451
Tiksi, USSR	7,126	7,579	11,683	14,537	5,701	10,445	13,725	3,413	7,167	10,378	12,498	5,368	8,393	4,886	14,836	7,689	6,545	8,035	7,563	12,558
Timbuktu, Mali	2,471	7,443	6,795	8,580	3,879	18,780	8,367	6,231	3,283	18,857	3,006	6,390	4,484	5,717	7,530	3,822	3,515	8,213	7,265	17,767
Tindouf, Algeria	1,809	6,337	7,910	8,771	2,817	17,728	8,397	5,328	3,241	17,763	4,000	6,203	5,034	5,284	7,906	4,113	3,176	7,166	6,157	18,953
Tirane, Albania	1,152	7,742	7,257	11,726	1,612	16,760	11,311	2,905	1,183	16,690	6,480	3,303	3,419	2,323	10,857	2,265	500	8,656	7,575	17,807
Tokyo, Japan	10,568	10,939	11,413	16,831	9,438	7,490	16,256	6,900	9,918	7,395	15,972	7,016	9,977	7,366	17,992	9,880	9,531	11,056	10,986	8,811
Toledo, Spain	1,080	6,059	8,421	9,836	1,421	16,883	9,356	3,959	2,780	16,875	5,399	5,303	4,967	4,221	9,106	3,865	2,406	6,958	5,881	19,657
Topeka, Kansas	8,523	1,658	15,840	7,423	7,364	9,804	6,632	7,899	10,088	9,848	9,815	11,077	12,367	9,881	8,145	11,212	9,474	1,169	1,829	12,431
Toronto, Canada	7,099	574	14,390	7,510	6,027	11,247	6,699	6,921	8,700	11,289	8,666	10,018	10,972	8,774	7,949	9,825	8,117	1,183	631	13,879
Toulouse, France	918	6,302	8,367	10,438	876	16,642	9,942	3,367	2,471	16,615	5,927	4,754	4,733	3,637	9,720	3,592	1,976	7,214	6,130	19,074
Tours, France	1,302	6,084	8,706	10,592	505	16,219	10,057	3,055	2,721	16,191	6,306	4,732	4,999	3,557	9,941	3,846	2,147	6,999	5,916	18,742
Townsville, Australia	15,593	15,334	10,260	13,786	15,178	4,457	14,262	12,698	14,070	4,374	16,370	11,169	12,406	12,196	14,419	13,232	14,181	14,735	15,491	3,351
Trenton, New Jersey	6,928	203	14,071	7,086	5,978	11,579	6,277	7,103	8,574	11,627	8,159	10,125	10,823	8,867	7,464	9,693	8,029	1,117	101	14,108
Tripoli, Lebanon	2,548	9,314	6,032	12,896	3,136	16,428	12,605	3,366	1,049	16,330	7,067	2,059	2,138	1,676	11,857	1,183	1,158	10,228	9,152	16,324
Tripoli, Libya	665	7,779	6,799	10,844	2,156	17,836	10,511	3,986	1,137	17,773	5,383	4,103	3,245	3,309	9,886	2,157	1,111	8,679	7,602	18,289
Tristan da Cunha (Edinburgh)	8,445	10,681	6,113	5,691	9,914	13,978	6,215	12,169	8,538	14,050	3,232	11,027	7,900	11,028	4,473	8,259	9,096	10,825	10,583	11,789
Trondheim, Norway	2,955	6,072	9,679	11,887	1,404	14,497	11,228	1,466	3,691	14,452	8,188	4,252	5,777	3,000	11,470	4,675	2,968	6,937	5,939	16,868
Trujillo, Peru	10,267	5,220	13,448	1,950	10,253	10,094	1,225	12,197	11,826	10,194	7,115	14,622	13,247	13,453	2,957	12,604	11,683	4,668	5,276	10,891
Truk Island (Moen)	13,845	12,859	11,789	15,179	12,801	4,659	15,213	10,256	12,907	4,555	18,523	9,813	12,222	10,463	16,321	12,547	12,664	12,548	12,978	5,455
Truro, Canada	5,843	1,301	13,097	7,677	4,884	12,534	6,891	6,157	7,478	12,573	7,650	9,091	9,734	7,829	7,842	8,599	6,930	2,216	1,137	15,164
Tsingtao, China	9,355	11,519	9,774	18,294	8,500	9,016	17,535	5,975	8,441	8,915	14,480	5,411	8,261	5,955	18,792	8,259	8,157	11,863	11,518	9,839
Tsitsihar, China	8,729	10,229	10,558	17,084	7,655	9,298	16,290	5,103	8,106	9,206	14,136	5,315	8,399	5,547	17,548	8,156	7,694	10,587	10,228	10,611
Tubuai Island (Mataura)	17,375	10,253	14,980	7,955	16,192	2,571	8,103	15,369	18,959	2,676	14,034	16,920	18,767	17,015	9,107	19,778	18,263	9,348	10,428	3,730
Tucson, Arizona	10,062	3,193	17,415	7,539	8,821	8,233	6,826	8,991	11,577	8,280	11,095	12,159	13,850	11,053	8,514	12,693	10,932	2,484	3,370	10,863
Tulsa, Oklahoma	8,734	1,740	15,972	7,143	7,617	9,678	6,358	8,210	10,322	9,727	9,772	11,385	12,599	10,183	7,898	11,448	9,721	1,085	1,919	12,249
Tunis, Tunisia	216	7,314	7,308	10,766	1,666	17,453	10,376	3,685	1,495	17,403	5,578	4,223	3,706	3,295	9,883	2,586	1,206	8,220	7,139	18,652
Tura, USSR	6,495	8,553	10,264	15,438	5,308	11,285	14,650	2,771	6,181	11,205	11,971	4,017	7,113	3,717	15,385	6,530	5,644	9,129	8,506	12,942
Turin, Italy	905	6,682	8,153	10,954	727	16,543	10,464	2,967	2,131	16,501	6,271	4,236	4,410	3,114	10,215	3,254	1,550	7,596	6,514	18,603
Uberlandia, Brazil	8,531	7,052	9,930	2,349	9,311	12,845	2,481	11,834	9,620	12,949	3,857	12,724	10,277	11,989	1,193	10,006	9,804	6,976	7,003	12,360
Ufa, USSR	4,128	8,678	8,199	14,434	3,404	13,893	13,851	1,390	3,537	13,807	9,490	1,875	4,612	1,086	13,767	3,900	3,055	9,494	8,563	15,050
Ujungpandang, Indonesia	12,274	15,930	7,928	16,652	12,174	7,602	17,344	9,987	10,713	7,506	14,708	7,889	9,149	9,009	16,628	9,894	10,857	16,003	15,967	6,625
Ulaanbaatar, Mongolia	7,676	10,374	9,464	17,301	6,781	10,509	16,506	4,262	6,901	10,414	12,966	4,039	7,119	4,357	17,153	6,891	6,542	10,890	10,337	11,551
Ulan-Ude, USSR	7,492	9,936	9,757	16,872	6,511	10,576	16,073	3,969	6,828	10,483	12,864	4,091	7,219	4,270	16,805	6,906	6,422	10,452	9,900	11,790
Uliastay, Mongolia	7,028	10,375	8,868	17,103	6,245	11,243	16,370	3,795	6,175	11,147	12,243	3,286	6,373	3,647	16,661	6,139	5,845	10,977	10,318	12,142
Uranium City, Canada	7,833	3,213	15,104	9,861	6,333	9,889	9,061	5,994	9,051	9,895	10,998	9,130	11,203	8,072	10,489	10,090	8,343	3,374	3,279	12,772
Urumqi, China	6,558	10,699	8,056	17,008	5,978	11,917	16,392	3,706	5,537	11,817	11,581	2,531	5,561	3,094	16,267	5,396	5,286	11,379	10,621	12,522
Ushuaia, Argentina	12,466	10,421	9,848	3,463	13,538	9,602	4,270	16,090	13,018	9,691	7,035	15,638	12,491	15,572	3,394	12,868	13,466	9,932	10,449	8,212
Vaduz, Liechtenstein	1,149	6,704	8,248	11,180	584	16,307	10,673	2,691	2,186	16,261	6,546	4,071	4,453	2,915	10,465	3,296	1,546	7,618	6,539	18,346
Valencia, Spain	767	6,361	8,156	10,080	1,358	17,043	9,619	3,838	2,465	17,025	5,444	5,020	4,661	3,963	9,313	3,553	2,096	7,263	6,185	19,504
Valladolid, Spain	1,198	5,926	8,593	9,894	1,272	16,679	9,394	3,822	2,878	16,670	5,579	5,298	5,094	4,186	9,198	3,978	2,458	6,829	5,750	19,472
Valletta, Malta	615	7,695	6,993	11,085	1,883	17,483	10,720	3,632	1,096	17,419	5,721	3,879	3,329	3,018	10,162	2,197	853	8,603	7,521	18,254
Valparaiso, Chile	11,302	7,988	11,371	1,047	11,918	10,101	1,843	14,320	12,414	10,204	6,491	15,511	12,830	14,774	1,606	12,728	12,601	7,512	8,019	9,655
Vancouver, Canada	9,308	3,835	16,538	9,614	7,812	8,459	8,866	7,304	10,519	8,472	12,029	10,344	12,637	9,378	10,486	11,542	9,807	3,610	3,961	11,332
Varna, Bulgaria	1,851	8,156	7,166	12,424	1,978	16,250	12,001	2,506	1,316	16,170	7,097	2,629	3,264	1,626	11,550	2,171	680	9,066	7,997	17,127
Venice, Italy	1,024	6,986	7,965	11,309	869	16,479	10,828	2,743	1,898	16,427	6,489	3,866	4,164	2,749	10,548	3,007	1,257	7,901	6,821	18,267

Distances in Kilometers	Annaba, Algeria	Annapolis, Maryland	Antananarivo, Madagascar	Antofagasta, Chile	Antwerp, Belgium	Apia, Western Samoa	Arequipa, Peru	Arkhangel'sk, USSR	As Sallum, Egypt	Asau, Western Samoa	Ascension Island (Georgetown)	Ashkhabad, USSR	Asmera, Ethiopia	Astrakhan, USSR	Asuncion, Paraguay	Aswan, Egypt	Athens, Greece	Atlanta, Georgia	Atlantic City, New Jersey	Auckland, New Zealand
Veracruz, Mexico	9,922	2,895	16,215	5,503	9,075	9,054	4,770	10,010	11,607	9,126	9,443	13,144	13,795	11,905	6,446	12,707	11,103	1,989	3,054	11,191
Verona, Italy	987	6,893	8,027	11,212	805	16,490	10,727	2,795	1,968	16,441	6,435	3,972	4,240	2,851	10,458	3,083	1,343	7,808	6,727	18,359
Victoria, Canada	9,392	3,856	16,630	9,565	7,899	8,386	8,822	7,397	10,608	8,399	12,062	10,434	12,729	9,470	10,450	11,633	9,897	3,607	3,985	11,256
Victoria, Seychelles	6,749	13,870	1,802	13,376	7,854	14,437	13,754	7,772	5,134	14,359	7,732	4,722	2,861	5,693	12,093	4,009	5,743	14,766	13,693	12,245
Vienna, Austria	1,438	7,102	8,054	11,702	924	16,122	11,200	2,326	1,991	16,064	6,913	3,556	4,191	2,389	10,966	3,046	1,282	8,014	6,943	17,853
Vientiane, Laos	9,248	13,701	7,275	19,059	9,025	10,037	19,387	6,894	7,826	9,933	13,141	4,823	6,766	5,880	17,836	7,208	7,845	14,234	13,652	9,693
Villahermosa, Mexico	9,740	2,818	15,862	5,215	8,967	9,338	4,467	10,035	11,436	9,414	9,084	13,129	13,586	11,878	6,122	12,522	10,960	1,943	2,964	11,391
Vilnius, USSR	2,387	7,257	8,424	12,480	1,451	15,238	11,919	1,389	2,568	15,172	7,863	3,107	4,522	1,848	11,829	3,455	1,860	8,144	7,114	16,963
Visby, Sweden	2,432	6,716	8,905	12,120	1,146	15,071	11,523	1,415	2,944	15,016	7,849	3,632	5,002	2,370	11,554	3,905	2,221	7,601	6,574	17,125
Vitoria, Brazil	8,100	7,568	9,090	3,120	9,048	13,501	3,321	11,600	9,041	13,604	3,110	12,119	9,522	11,498	1,859	9,331	9,296	7,591	7,499	12,686
Vladivostok, USSR	9,501	10,473	10,985	17,038	8,390	8,522	16,309	5,845	8,883	8,429	14,917	6,052	9,097	6,325	17,843	8,906	8,475	10,729	10,493	9,865
Volgograd, USSR	3,234	8,685	7,501	13,752	2,846	14,921	13,263	1,776	2,502	14,833	8,490	1,645	3,740	382	12,942	2,919	2,049	9,558	8,548	15,832
Vologda, USSR	3,386	7,658	8,687	13,387	2,393	14,337	12,778	597	3,266	14,264	8,859	2,709	4,872	1,531	12,810	3,941	2,629	8,500	7,534	15,951
Vorkuta, USSR	4,852	7,740	9,678	14,225	3,647	12,834	13,507	1,106	4,728	12,761	10,325	3,307	6,072	2,530	13,907	5,278	4,120	8,469	7,653	14,607
Wake Island	13,405	10,816	13,664	14,137	12,005	4,363	13,885	9,644	13,047	4,275	18,744	10,217	13,139	10,490	15,437	13,081	12,581	10,481	10,941	6,273
Wallis Island	17,361	11,761	14,054	10,982	15,799	483	11,115	13,660	17,047	385	16,923	14,006	16,246	14,501	12,111	16,751	16,643	10,986	11,940	2,763
Walvis Bay, Namibia	6,662	11,661	3,456	8,534	8,275	15,880	8,926	9,960	6,139	15,905	3,509	8,154	5,002	8,387	7,248	5,570	6,814	12,181	11,506	13,070
Warsaw, Poland	1,997	7,158	8,293	12,144	1,149	15,596	11,605	1,770	2,322	15,534	7,471	3,293	4,393	2,060	11,461	3,286	1,600	8,058	7,007	17,345
Washington, D.C.	7,169	48	14,280	6,958	6,223	11,368	6,147	7,320	8,817	11,418	8,273	10,357	11,065	9,101	7,383	9,936	8,274	872	229	13,873
Watson Lake, Canada	8,543	4,295	15,420	10,679	6,970	9,040	9,901	6,145	9,568	9,041	12,104	9,115	11,569	8,199	11,430	10,525	8,845	4,338	4,375	11,920
Weimar, East Germany	1,590	6,635	8,513	11,463	484	15,875	10,921	2,268	2,439	15,827	6,981	3,936	4,662	2,725	10,803	3,514	1,745	7,545	6,477	17,965
Wellington, New Zealand	18,798	14,119	11,415	10,180	18,683	3,313	10,681	16,132	17,112	3,320	14,473	14,672	14,902	15,780	10,874	16,015	17,523	13,217	14,295	492
West Berlin, West Germany	1,791	6,690	8,573	11,657	635	15,690	11,103	2,045	2,515	15,638	7,201	3,808	4,700	2,578	11,014	3,561	1,803	7,595	6,536	17,743
Wewak, Papua New Guinea	14,198	14,378	10,533	15,262	13,510	5,032	15,574	10,985	12,906	4,931	17,282	9,837	11,699	10,724	16,084	12,284	12,850	14,035	14,498	4,872
Whangarei, New Zealand	18,814	13,899	11,775	10,558	18,106	2,797	11,006	15,580	17,143	2,792	15,088	14,421	15,062	15,445	11,330	16,115	17,402	13,020	14,079	133
Whitehorse, Canada	8,669	4,644	15,359	10,998	7,079	8,882	10,225	6,102	9,619	8,871	12,403	9,000	11,558	8,132	11,768	10,543	8,896	4,685	4,723	11,738
Wichita, Kansas	8,730	1,823	16,031	7,353	7,573	9,616	6,568	8,086	10,296	9,662	9,929	11,267	12,575	10,077	8,110	11,421	9,682	1,249	1,998	12,229
Willemstad, Curacao	8,037	3,068	13,210	3,960	7,809	11,694	3,167	9,700	9,700	11,782	6,429	12,224	11,528	11,010	4,313	10,643	9,425	2,864	3,066	13,146
Wiluna, Australia	13,654	17,942	7,420	14,330	10,443	7,174	15,082	12,169	11,956	7,103	13,813	9,624	9,929	10,853	14,261	10,930	12,314	17,535	18,051	5,222
Windhoek, Namibia	6,656	11,852	3,190	8,796	8,269	15,865	9,193	9,872	6,054	15,883	3,739	7,972	4,824	8,248	7,512	5,439	6,740	12,393	11,694	13,023
Windsor, Canada	7,432	663	14,713	7,416	6,351	10,929	6,605	7,181	9,031	10,973	8,885	10,299	11,304	9,063	7,922	10,156	8,444	957	792	12,904
Winnipeg, Canada	7,909	2,032	15,365	8,563	6,580	10,102	7,761	6,797	9,346	10,129	10,161	9,983	11,604	8,828	9,193	10,450	8,683	2,076	2,135	12,904
Winston-Salem, North Carolina	7,568	460	14,597	6,694	6,641	11,038	5,882	7,718	9,224	11,092	8,417	10,771	11,464	9,516	7,195	10,341	8,688	459	625	13,489
Wroclaw, Poland	1,741	6,985	8,308	11,846	882	15,797	11,313	2,025	2,270	15,740	7,205	3,539	4,425	2,324	11,159	3,293	1,550	7,891	6,830	17,445
Wuhan, China	9,325	12,224	8,998	19,115	8,656	9,310	18,329	6,208	8,232	9,207	14,143	5,135	7,776	5,858	19,033	7,910	8,038	12,621	12,210	9,772
Wyndham, Australia	13,717	16,473	8,504	15,238	13,661	6,463	15,880	11,430	12,110	6,376	15,151	9,364	10,376	10,496	15,456	11,221	12,304	16,187	16,574	5,167
Xi'an, China	8,676	11,876	8,765	18,826	8,023	9,918	18,025	5,600	7,599	9,816	13,555	4,512	7,242	5,210	18,385	7,315	7,393	12,349	11,846	10,418
Xining, China	7,996	11,633	8,381	18,388	7,400	10,611	17,671	5,037	6,901	10,509	12,868	3,815	6,597	4,524	17,696	6,629	6,700	12,189	11,584	11,079
Yakutsk, USSR	7,874	8,567	11,443	15,483	6,557	9,822	14,675	4,111	7,665	9,745	13,333	5,413	8,552	5,206	15,886	8,015	7,111	8,960	8,563	11,684
Yanji, China	9,391	10,568	10,792	17,202	8,312	8,670	16,460	5,762	8,736	8,576	14,783	5,880	8,913	6,181	17,945	8,738	8,341	10,847	10,583	9,951
Yaounde, Cameroon	3,678	9,574	4,679	9,368	5,291	18,848	9,402	7,124	3,381	18,856	3,164	6,066	3,259	5,880	8,125	3,203	3,977	10,323	9,396	15,973
Yap Island (Colonia)	12,725	13,558	10,420	16,616	11,949	6,110	16,729	9,417	11,576	6,006	17,012	8,471	10,713	9,258	17,604	11,106	11,430	13,452	13,640	6,403
Yaraka, Australia	15,684	15,922	9,779	13,482	15,516	4,778	14,034	13,121	14,064	4,705	15,699	11,315	12,223	12,415	13,987	13,137	14,270	15,262	16,086	3,202
Yarmouth, Canada	6,112	1,021	13,328	7,485	5,167	12,313	6,692	6,418	7,754	12,356	7,737	9,369	10,006	8,107	7,700	8,874	7,210	1,935	854	14,908
Yellowknife, Canada	7,847	3,642	14,972	10,305	6,306	9,799	9,506	5,762	8,976	9,797	11,295	8,856	11,072	7,841	10,935	9,983	8,259	3,821	3,701	12,680
Yerevan, USSR	3,200	9,392	6,550	13,743	3,304	15,442	13,375	2,725	1,986	15,345	8,047	1,226	2,807	743	12,771	2,091	1,809	10,287	9,244	15,728
Yinchuan, China	8,216	11,424	8,827	18,333	7,518	10,272	17,550	5,082	7,205	10,171	13,220	4,150	7,007	4,765	17,916	6,992	6,961	11,934	11,387	10,902
Yogyakarta, Indonesia	11,650	16,484	6,886	16,524	11,791	8,513	17,320	9,843	10,014	8,421	13,666	7,392	8,282	8,588	16,127	9,112	10,248	16,762	16,477	7,222
York, United Kingdom	2,004	5,730	9,304	10,834	478	15,491	10,235	2,602	3,244	15,462	6,958	4,784	5,507	3,543	10,304	4,351	2,590	6,640	5,572	18,093
Yumen, China	7,508	11,258	8,333	17,898	6,898	11,029	17,211	4,546	6,454	10,928	12,463	3,393	6,280	4,041	17,217	6,236	6,228	11,855	11,200	11,576
Yutian, China	6,409	11,316	7,142	16,981	6,097	12,390	16,544	4,101	5,169	12,287	11,081	2,063	4,842	2,969	15,975	4,841	5,046	12,055	11,221	12,577
Yuzhno-Sakhalinsk, USSR	9,694	9,723	11,913	16,097	8,421	8,117	15,388	5,943	9,306	8,032	15,170	6,671	9,790	6,763	17,005	9,473	8,820	9,905	9,760	9,818
Zagreb, Yugoslavia	1,203	7,213	7,841	11,590	1,045	16,388	11,114	2,574	1,766	16,329	6,679	3,580	4,000	2,463	10,814	2,847	1,079	8,127	7,050	17,992
Zahedan, Iran	4,955	11,235	5,546	15,166	5,208	14,367	14,976	4,151	3,420	14,263	9,042	965	2,741	2,177	14,001	2,839	3,542	12,112	11,095	13,928
Zamboanga, Philippines	11,660	14,579	8,656	17,732	11,268	7,642	18,209	8,912	10,267	7,561	15,234	7,242	9,084	8,232	17,972	9,624	10,269	14,718	14,611	7,313
Zanzibar, Tanzania	5,781	12,653	1,675	11,711	7,174	15,958	12,012	7,846	4,434	15,898	5,922	5,274	2,378	5,883	10,411	3,416	5,143	13,477	12,472	13,385
Zaragoza, Spain	912	6,219	8,352	10,164	1,140	16,001	9,680	3,653	2,570	16,782	6,660	4,992	4,800	3,897	9,435	3,676	2,139	7,126	6,044	19,363
Zashiversk, USSR	7,830	7,754	12,148	14,634	6,389	9,737	13,828	4,121	7,864	9,670	13,176	5,935	9,013	5,540	15,115	8,354	7,249	8,115	7,758	11,880
Zhengzhou, China	8,990	11,775	9,170	18,715	8,255	9,520	17,908	5,782	7,973	9,419	13,963	4,902	7,676	5,541	18,672	7,725	7,737	12,193	11,733	10,141
Zurich, Switzerland	1,164	6,616	8,319	11,110	516	16,286	10,597	2,720	2,262	16,243	6,525	4,156	4,533	2,995	10,405	3,376	1,630	7,530	6,451	18,398

Distances in Kilometers	Auckland Islands, New Zealand	Augusta, Maine	Austin, Texas	Ayan, USSR	Baghdad, Iraq	Baguio, Philippines	Bahia Blanca, Argentina	Baku, USSR	Balikpapan, Indonesia	Balkhash, USSR	Ballarat, Australia	Baltimore, Maryland	Bamako, Mali	Bandar Seri Begawan, Brunei	Bangalore, India	Banghazi, Libya	Bangkok, Thailand	Bangui, Central African Rep.	Banjarmasin, Indonesia	Banjul, Gambia
Augusta, Maine	15,823	0	2,906	8,536	9,140	13,198	9,227	8,857	15,194	9,335	17,114	796	6,799	14,536	12,857	7,589	13,501	9,544	15,444	6,072
Austin, Texas	12,932	2,906	0	9,051	11,921	13,414	8,478	11,500	15,161	11,435	14,373	2,169	9,291	14,797	15,191	10,494	14,758	12,254	15,498	8,433
Ayan, USSR	12,158	8,536	9,051	0	7,207	4,684	17,529	6,297	6,684	4,337	10,430	8,902	11,734	6,077	7,022	8,598	5,717	11,354	6,964	11,913
Baghdad, Iraq	14,998	9,140	11,921	7,207	0	7,763	13,568	918	8,466	2,979	12,927	9,935	5,772	7,908	4,047	2,281	6,046	4,181	8,392	6,517
Baguio, Philippines	8,675	13,198	13,414	4,684	7,763	0	17,518	7,227	2,001	5,371	6,451	13,585	13,524	1,418	4,640	10,012	2,178	11,158	2,282	14,274
Bahia Blanca, Argentina	9,021	9,227	8,478	17,529	13,568	17,518	0	14,335	15,575	16,457	11,148	8,761	8,004	16,247	15,152	11,568	16,768	9,524	15,338	7,477
Baku, USSR	15,097	8,857	11,500	6,297	918	7,227	14,335	0	8,176	2,142	12,876	9,649	6,397	7,561	4,068	2,814	5,725	5,072	8,150	7,062
Balikpapan, Indonesia	7,185	15,194	15,161	6,684	8,466	2,001	15,575	8,176	0	6,709	4,877	15,582	13,826	714	4,613	10,728	2,451	10,945	338	14,731
Balkhash, USSR	13,894	9,335	11,435	4,337	2,979	5,371	16,457	2,142	6,709	0	11,586	10,060	8,465	6,019	3,759	4,890	4,370	7,151	6,774	9,051
Ballarat, Australia	2,310	17,114	14,373	10,430	12,927	6,451	11,148	12,876	4,877	11,586	0	16,514	16,090	5,571	8,885	14,923	7,263	13,373	4,823	16,713
Baltimore, Maryland	15,042	796	2,169	8,902	9,935	13,585	8,761	9,649	15,582	10,060	16,514	0	7,295	14,973	13,634	8,348	14,126	10,154	15,867	6,504
Bamako, Mali	15,759	6,799	9,291	11,734	5,772	13,524	8,004	6,397	13,826	8,465	16,090	7,295	0	13,432	9,238	3,585	11,625	3,064	13,636	935
Bandar Seri Begawan, Brunei	7,875	14,536	14,797	6,077	7,908	1,418	16,247	7,561	714	6,019	5,571	14,973	13,432	0	4,199	10,185	1,861	10,680	909	14,305
Bangalore, India	11,038	12,857	15,191	7,022	4,047	4,640	15,152	4,068	4,613	3,759	8,885	13,634	9,238	4,199	0	6,206	2,485	6,549	4,470	10,127
Banghazi, Libya	16,581	7,589	10,494	8,598	2,281	10,012	11,568	2,814	10,728	4,890	14,923	8,348	3,585	10,185	6,206	0	8,324	3,076	10,636	4,263
Bangkok, Thailand	9,569	13,501	14,758	5,717	6,046	2,178	16,768	5,725	2,451	4,370	7,263	14,126	11,625	1,861	2,485	8,324	0	9,033	2,446	12,473
Bangui, Central African Rep.	14,069	9,544	12,254	11,354	4,181	11,158	9,524	5,072	10,945	7,151	13,373	10,154	3,064	10,680	6,549	3,076	9,033	0	10,712	3,991
Banjarmasin, Indonesia	7,132	15,444	15,498	6,964	8,392	2,282	15,338	8,150	338	6,774	4,823	15,867	13,636	909	4,470	10,636	2,446	10,712	0	14,553
Banjul, Gambia	15,868	6,072	8,433	11,913	6,517	14,274	7,477	7,062	14,731	9,051	16,713	6,504	935	14,305	10,127	4,263	12,473	3,991	14,553	0
Barcelona, Spain	18,426	5,697	8,602	8,404	3,806	11,020	11,016	3,968	12,143	5,650	16,724	6,455	3,335	11,515	7,854	1,894	9,692	4,415	12,116	3,591
Bari, Italy	17,458	6,754	9,639	7,875	2,581	9,932	11,935	2,771	10,942	4,601	15,507	7,534	3,977	10,332	6,628	1,041	8,493	4,076	10,903	4,462
Barranquilla, Colombia	12,955	3,725	3,193	11,938	11,934	16,540	5,653	11,975	18,349	12,937	15,173	3,141	7,262	17,954	15,982	9,824	17,222	10,295	18,687	6,327
Basse-Terre, Guadeloupe	14,261	3,229	3,990	11,765	10,481	16,410	6,057	10,602	18,370	11,820	16,552	2,960	5,794	17,667	14,519	8,326	16,187	8,850	18,549	4,861
Basseterre, St. Kitts & Nevis	14,311	3,068	3,828	11,603	10,480	16,258	6,201	10,575	18,232	11,744	16,587	2,785	5,890	17,538	14,524	8,347	16,115	8,951	18,433	4,960
Bata, Equatorial Guinea	14,171	9,034	11,583	12,065	5,021	12,178	8,592	5,874	11,924	7,998	13,891	9,570	2,293	11,684	7,568	3,521	10,053	1,021	11,679	3,171
Baton Rouge, Louisiana	13,395	2,429	631	9,314	11,547	13,810	8,224	11,198	15,640	11,336	14,952	1,650	8,666	15,216	15,052	9,997	14,958	11,644	15,974	7,804
Bear Lake, Canada	13,338	4,145	3,670	5,384	10,048	9,828	12,147	9,297	11,721	8,407	13,332	4,092	10,529	11,242	12,010	9,731	11,100	12,594	12,045	9,982
Bechar, Algeria	17,696	5,930	8,784	9,556	4,351	11,930	9,963	4,725	12,816	6,604	16,862	6,618	2,182	12,248	8,311	2,106	10,390	3,718	12,736	2,490
Beira, Mozambique	10,880	12,676	15,146	12,637	5,972	10,193	9,251	6,845	9,128	8,409	10,253	13,208	5,913	9,165	5,923	5,962	8,091	3,216	8,816	6,731
Beirut, Lebanon	15,666	8,530	11,377	7,652	829	8,570	12,875	1,462	9,293	3,603	13,689	9,319	4,983	8,737	4,837	1,454	6,876	3,708	9,214	5,704
Belau Islands (Koror)	7,127	13,791	10,490	5,457	9,576	1,814	16,147	9,034	2,180	7,120	5,063	13,936	15,328	2,181	6,255	11,825	3,781	12,800	2,506	16,088
Belem, Brazil	13,350	5,493	6,289	13,877	10,372	17,973	4,360	10,823	18,375	12,608	15,506	5,348	4,737	18,155	13,958	8,093	16,359	7,488	18,079	3,888
Belfast, United Kingdom	19,340	4,598	7,435	7,273	4,546	10,665	11,650	4,357	12,168	5,460	17,045	5,392	4,655	11,474	8,425	3,229	9,800	5,991	12,230	4,657
Belgrade, Yugoslavia	17,412	6,763	9,609	7,369	2,416	9,511	12,414	2,445	10,611	4,155	15,298	7,554	4,477	9,980	6,422	1,412	8,162	4,488	10,593	4,937
Belmopan, Belize	12,504	3,494	1,709	10,749	12,534	15,095	6,781	12,334	16,714	12,731	14,435	2,716	8,646	16,446	16,350	10,689	16,432	11,710	17,048	7,723
Belo Horizonte, Brazil	11,639	7,583	8,002	15,945	11,057	18,352	2,731	11,731	16,871	13,790	13,592	7,384	5,336	17,195	13,770	8,922	16,192	7,342	16,536	4,754
Bergen, Norway	18,413	5,099	7,802	6,405	4,122	9,744	12,582	3,759	11,296	4,605	16,160	5,891	5,410	10,595	7,786	3,324	8,971	6,315	11,377	5,508
Bern, Switzerland	18,428	5,779	8,656	7,668	3,449	10,348	11,742	3,452	11,576	4,982	16,325	6,563	4,066	10,925	7,457	1,963	9,134	4,835	11,577	4,336
Bhopal, India	11,913	11,813	14,057	6,094	3,406	4,572	15,852	3,203	5,060	2,622	9,673	12,574	9,006	4,513	1,138	5,675	2,654	6,644	4,994	9,831
Bhubaneswar, India	11,090	12,441	14,402	5,870	4,334	3,693	16,342	4,076	4,135	3,109	8,818	13,169	9,928	3,579	1,191	6,608	1,719	7,475	4,082	10,762
Bialystok, Poland	17,507	6,415	9,150	6,497	2,773	9,050	13,056	2,461	10,368	3,700	15,215	7,211	5,270	9,696	6,525	2,348	7,954	5,423	10,399	5,622
Big Trout Lake, Canada	15,036	1,807	2,690	7,020	9,400	11,694	10,594	8,883	13,684	8,761	15,578	1,908	8,358	13,096	12,508	8,367	12,450	10,820	13,977	7,723
Bilbao, Spain	18,864	5,224	8,130	8,372	4,228	11,260	10,868	4,327	12,480	5,896	17,155	5,982	3,426	11,835	8,271	2,366	10,034	4,803	12,472	3,552
Billings, Montana	13,439	3,026	1,959	7,094	10,829	11,539	10,436	10,221	13,398	9,740	14,132	2,697	9,810	12,948	13,468	9,949	12,800	12,398	13,727	9,098
Birmingham, Alabama	13,929	1,896	1,094	9,173	11,024	13,766	8,389	10,696	15,677	10,924	15,464	1,115	8,217	15,184	14,602	9,462	14,717	11,163	16,001	7,375
Birmingham, United Kingdom	19,190	4,917	7,770	7,392	4,240	10,597	11,663	4,100	12,026	5,324	16,892	5,709	4,450	11,342	8,164	2,874	9,629	5,657	12,070	4,521
Bismarck, North Dakota	13,966	2,420	1,853	7,322	10,470	11,877	10,218	9,919	13,791	9,624	14,735	2,128	9,205	13,294	13,381	9,453	12,971	11,820	14,112	8,493
Bissau, Guinea Bissau	15,696	6,275	8,613	12,057	6,517	14,280	7,404	7,089	14,655	9,103	16,505	6,699	830	14,252	10,062	4,280	12,434	3,852	14,466	208
Biysk, USSR	13,737	9,007	10,822	3,369	3,881	5,065	17,090	2,997	6,657	976	11,478	9,678	9,120	5,946	4,444	5,609	4,515	8,061	6,780	9,614
Blagoveshchensk, USSR	11,781	9,392	10,034	985	6,784	3,806	18,510	5,907	5,803	3,817	9,859	9,807	11,809	5,167	6,115	8,441	4,732	10,965	6,068	12,131
Blantyre, Malawi	11,266	12,391	14,967	12,264	5,529	10,050	9,543	6,405	9,104	8,004	10,538	12,959	5,684	9,091	5,666	5,535	7,915	2,870	8,802	6,534
Bloemfontein, South Africa	10,346	12,653	14,656	13,990	7,179	11,307	7,929	8,076	10,011	9,707	10,188	13,031	5,904	10,157	7,227	6,810	9,282	3,795	9,682	6,581
Bluefields, Nicaragua	12,423	3,823	2,487	11,493	12,581	15,888	6,042	12,501	17,468	13,157	14,519	3,105	8,207	17,237	16,569	10,579	17,119	11,255	17,795	7,273
Boa Vista do Rio Branco, Braz.	13,119	4,684	4,946	13,217	11,238	17,873	4,602	11,529	19,705	13,015	15,423	4,350	5,901	19,032	15,102	8,977	17,254	8,805	19,509	4,991
Bodo, Norway	17,601	5,324	7,817	5,519	4,246	9,011	13,374	3,693	10,669	4,087	15,462	6,090	6,288	9,958	7,546	3,929	8,438	6,991	10,783	6,394
Bogota, Colombia	12,443	4,420	3,775	12,633	12,321	17,184	4,948	12,447	18,768	13,554	14,714	3,850	7,311	18,570	16,341	10,135	17,892	10,275	19,065	6,384
Boise, Idaho	12,834	3,677	2,204	6,931	11,259	11,211	10,612	10,597	12,994	9,926	13,475	3,312	10,466	12,598	13,584	10,519	12,644	13,038	13,329	9,749
Bologna, Italy	18,038	6,173	9,055	7,769	3,097	10,200	11,803	3,172	11,337	4,831	16,012	6,956	3,981	10,703	7,128	1,569	8,888	4,501	11,321	4,342
Bolzano, Italy	18,136	6,062	8,930	7,569	3,149	10,101	11,945	3,156	11,294	4,731	16,026	6,849	4,172	10,648	7,156	1,763	8,849	4,722	11,289	4,502
Bombay, India	11,872	12,039	14,463	6,758	3,241	5,061	15,190	3,233	5,306	3,095	9,705	12,820	8,618	4,827	835	5,444	3,010	6,105	5,195	9,479
Bonn, West Germany	18,567	5,569	8,414	7,302	3,587	10,170	11,994	3,475	11,497	4,832	16,325	6,361	4,441	10,828	7,529	2,327	9,075	5,251	11,521	4,656
Bora Bora (Vaitape)	5,301	10,655	7,765	10,352	17,545	10,284	8,836	16,647	10,129	14,575	6,667	9,933	16,111	10,524	14,721	18,094	12,303	18,308	10,304	15,211
Bordeaux, France	18,851	5,322	8,224	8,138	4,038	11,001	11,128	4,100	12,239	5,640	16,956	6,091	3,637	11,590	8,072	2,277	9,796	4,858	12,237	3,796
Boston, Massachusetts	15,621	240	2,729	8,716	9,359	13,389	9,023	9,088	15,387	9,575	17,014	580	6,864	14,738	13,094	7,775	13,733	9,657	15,645	6,113
Bouvet Island	8,250	12,941	13,384	17,195	10,491	13,230	5,119	11,401	11,381	13,081	9,136	12,867	7,511	11,830	10,176	9,722	11,699	6,668	11,054	7,756
Brasilia, Brazil	11,918	7,015	7,381	15,462	11,174	18,805	2,904	11,782	17,494	13,766	13,975	6,788	5,405	17,798	14,165	8,971	16,633	7,653	17,159	4,728
Braunschweig, West Germany	18,345	5,713	8,528	7,039	3,427	9,881	12,287	3,253	11,225	4,549	16,069	6,509	4,697	10,552	7,318	2,368	8,811	5,362	11,255	4,937
Brazzaville, Congo	13,328	9,947	12,462	12,365	5,172	11,785	8,638	6,073	11,290	8,126	12,977	10,474	3,183	11,127	7,146	4,058	9,616	1,023	11,022	4,030
Bremerhaven, West Germany	18,476	5,535	8,341	6,978	3,605	9,934	12,270	3,403	11,320	4,626	16,180	6,331	4,768	10,641	7,471	2,552	8,917	5,529	11,359	4,970
Brest, France	19,318	4,892	7,784	7,880	4,360	11,014	11,210	4,325	12,373	5,697	17,195	5,671	3,977	11,702	8,357	2,741	9,951	5,351	12,397	4,033
Brest, USSR	17,451	6,509	9,254	6,568	2,667	9,046	13,033	2,380	10,335	3,686	15,170	7,304	5,213	9,668	6,448	2,239	7,914	5,313	10,360	5,585
Bridgetown, Barbados	14,135	3,593	4,351	12,123	10,485	16,740	5,743	10,663	18,643	11,984	16,443	3,349	5,593	17,929	14,494	8,288	16,326	8,631	18,758	4,658
Brisbane, Australia	2,814	15,793	13,235	9,407	13,270	5,988	11,811	12,997	4,826	11,344	1,407	15,288	17,451	5,439	9,281	15,487	7,274	14,565	4,880	18,120
Bristol, United Kingdom	19,248	4,908	7,774	7,514	4,265	10,701	11,550	4,152	12,112	5,415	16,971	5,698	4,331	11,432	8,210	2,832	9,709	5,577	12,151	4,399
Brno, Czechoslovakia	17,863	6,254	9,076	7,113	2,891	9,622	12,439	2,778	10,858	4,254	15,647	7,048	4,642	10,202	6,826	1,919	8,422	4,973	10,867	4,993
Broken Hill, Australia	2,927	16,985	14,452	9,800	12,467	5,796	11,807	12,347	4,265	10,969	659	16,510	16,241	4,950	8,421	14,561	6,679	13,348	4,233	16,983
Brussels, Belgium	18,762	5,386	8,239	7,379	3,777	10,335	11,853	3,670	11,682	5,007	16,516	6,177	4,380	11,010	7,724	2,448	9,263	5,320	11,709	4,557
Bucharest, Romania	16,996	7,148	9,968	7,161	2,002	9,099	12,768	1,999	10,168	3,761	14,854	7,942	4,788	9,541	5,984	1,465	7,718	4,500	10,148	5,300
Budapest, Hungary	17,632	6,507	9,336	7,177	2,643	9,517	12,485	2,574	10,698	4,147	15,450	7,301	4,614	10,051	6,603	1,710	8,254	4,780	10,696	5,016
Buenos Aires, Argentina	9,585	8,814	8,281	17,271	13,085	17,988	571	13,824	16,002	15,927	11,692	8,392	7,464	16,645	14,999	11,038	16,885	9,108	15,744	6,917
Buffalo, New York	15,116	751	2,184	8,462	9,787	13,145	9,191	9,446	15,141	9,740	16,378	442	7,508	14,536	13,372	8,315	13,733	10,289	15,427	6,752
Bujumbura, Burundi	12,766	11,001	13,728	11,468	4,363	10,255	9,922	5,277	9,729	7,131	11,907	11,624	4,496	9,560	5,628	4,050	8,078	1,474	9,467	5,406
Bulawayo, Zimbabwe	11,147	12,202	14,557	13,052	6,155	10,834	8,712	7,054	9,784	8,756	10,712	12,689	5,407	9,821	6,496	5,855	8,717	2,925	9,471	6,187
Burlington, Vermont	15,596	274	2,667	8,442	9,335	13,119	9,279	9,024	15,119	9,422	16,840	642	7,071	14,478	12,994	7,829	13,526	9,815	15,383	6,340
Cabinda, Angola	13,309	9,803	12,239	12,658	5,485	12,153	8,282	6,378	11,626	8,450	13,106	10,298	3,008	11,478	7,514	4,251	9,982	1,306	11,352	3,813
Cagliari, Italy	17,838	6,326	9,230	8,374	3,216	10,620	11,287	3,460	11,624	5,278	16,106	7,087	3,393	11,020	7,259	1,265	9,177	3,976	11,578	3,810
Cairns, Australia	4,176	15,514	13,462	8,161	12,065	4,607	13,192	11,704	3,610	9,973	2,294	15,238	17,174	4,161	8,194	14,336	6,021	14,111	3,724	18,100
Cairo, Egypt	15,672	8,539	11,428	8,230	1,300	9,056	12,309	2,038	9,660	4,180	13,860	9,315	4,473	9,137	5,117	1,091	7,279	3,140	9,558	5,234
Calais, France	18,939	5,218	8,077	7,442	3,951	10,478	11,732	3,846	11,845	5,162	16,687	6,008	4,340	11,170	7,900	2,571	9,430	5,395	11,875	4,479
Calcutta, India	11,120	12,277	14,124	5,512	4,453	3,444	16,708	4,117	4,060	2,950	8,828	12,986	10,123	3,462	1,556	6,735	1,610	7,754	4,039	10,934
Calgary, Canada	13,530	3,356	2,675	6,378	10,421	10,846	11,152	9,755	12,732	9,125	13,921	3,179	10,017	12,259	12,822	9,759	12,084	12,403	13,057	9,373
Cali, Colombia	12,179	4,575	3,716	12,663	12,611	17,124	4,893	12,724	18,533	13,779	14,439	3,969	7,602	18,455	16,637	10,431	18,075	10,555	18,805	6,676
Camaguey, Cuba	13,614	2,651	2,214	10,742	11,411	15,366	6,850	11,298	17,276	11,979	15,640	1,989	7,452	16,784	15,365	9,486	16,115	10,513	17,602	6,538
Cambridge Bay, Canada	15,074	3,407	4,345	5,176	8,371	9,860	12,463	7,687	11,859	7,147	14,677	3,726	8,977	11,248	10,896	7,930	10,595	10,815	12,140	8,556
Cambridge, United Kingdom	19,057	5,058	7,909	7,364	4,098	10,501	11,741	3,962	11,909	5,211	16,769	5,850	4,447	11,228	8,025	2,754	9,506	5,570	11,948	4,550
Campbellton, Canada	16,225	475	3,293	8,201	8,697	12,834	9,615	8,394	14,817	8,863	17,289	1,255	6,657	14,144	12,385	7,211	13,049	9,297	15,053	5,984
Campo Grande, Brazil	11,161	7,336	7,268	15,871	12,048	19,347	2,155	12,659	17,430	14,631	13,302	6,999	6,280	17,954	14,887	9,848	17,288	8,446	17,127	5,602
Canakkale, Turkey	16,730	7,464	10,318	7,540	1,773	9,200	12,542	1,989	10,140	3,936	14,699	8,253	4,538	9,540	5,816	1,057	7,694	4,040	10,095	5,123
Canberra, Australia	2,202	16,578	13,853	10,224	13,275	6,473	11,193	13,153	5,040	11,725	536	15,985	16,613	5,712	9,228	15,347	7,469	13,907	5,024	17,197
Cancun, Mexico	12,970	3,010	1,496	10,437	12,066	14,900	7,100	11,853	16,650	12,260	14,855	2,233	8,366	16,291	15,866	10,260	16,066	11,424	16,987	7,454

Distances in Kilometers	Auckland Islands, New Zealand	Augusta, Maine	Austin, Texas	Ayan, USSR	Baghdad, Iraq	Baguio, Philippines	Bahia Blanca, Argentina	Baku, USSR	Balikpapan, Indonesia	Balkhash, USSR	Ballarat, Australia	Baltimore, Maryland	Bamako, Mali	Bandar Seri Begawan, Brunei	Bangalore, India	Banghazi, Libya	Bangkok, Thailand	Bangui, Central African Rep.	Banjarmasin, Indonesia	Banjul, Gambia
Canton, China	9,698	12,532	13,238	4,222	6,733	1,069	18,225	6,169	2,727	4,305	7,441	13,021	12,504	2,026	3,927	8,964	1,697	10,304	2,930	13,226
Canton Atoll, Phoenix Islands	5,684	11,178	8,638	7,971	14,970	7,740	11,483	14,129	7,954	11,998	5,941	10,647	17,929	8,206	12,337	16,541	9,855	18,884	8,195	17,052
Cape Town, South Africa	10,127	12,415	14,085	14,871	7,927	12,122	7,024	8,838	10,712	10,583	10,294	12,686	5,865	10,916	8,130	7,311	10,144	4,237	10,377	6,421
Cape York, Australia	4,945	15,175	13,465	7,455	11,405	3,848	13,964	10,996	3,020	9,218	2,976	15,027	16,811	3,505	7,633	13,686	5,365	13,812	3,185	17,736
Caracas, Venezuela	13,437	3,758	3,870	12,233	11,296	16,917	5,470	11,430	18,909	12,622	15,724	3,332	6,418	18,292	15,323	9,119	16,992	9,439	19,196	5,483
Cardiff, United Kingdom	19,291	4,866	7,732	7,525	4,308	10,732	11,524	4,194	12,150	5,451	17,010	5,655	4,331	11,468	8,253	2,869	9,747	5,603	12,190	4,389
Carlisle, United Kingdom	19,161	4,777	7,604	7,170	4,363	10,492	11,807	4,163	11,979	5,271	16,856	5,572	4,706	11,287	8,231	3,109	9,607	5,927	12,038	4,748
Carnarvon, Australia	5,316	17,826	16,884	9,303	9,755	4,629	12,953	9,781	2,632	8,838	3,185	18,145	13,776	3,294	5,732	11,754	4,503	10,728	2,385	14,675
Carson City, Nevada	12,269	4,133	2,237	7,147	11,813	11,237	10,428	11,133	12,926	10,368	12,993	3,690	10,931	12,591	13,959	11,093	12,817	13,576	13,263	10,181
Casablanca, Morocco	18,051	5,387	8,235	9,514	4,780	12,218	9,798	5,078	13,230	6,854	17,410	6,070	2,323	12,635	8,783	2,586	10,787	4,224	13,170	2,412
Casper, Wyoming	13,347	2,931	1,589	7,462	11,058	11,888	10,067	10,481	13,728	10,071	14,192	2,514	9,730	13,293	13,810	10,073	13,170	12,410	14,059	8,985
Castries, Saint Lucia	14,131	3,461	4,170	11,996	10,547	16,634	5,839	10,700	18,577	11,972	16,433	3,192	5,732	17,868	14,571	8,367	16,329	8,778	18,732	4,797
Catbalogan, Philippines	8,006	13,621	13,502	5,088	8,424	692	16,937	7,908	1,696	6,062	5,808	13,933	14,167	1,334	5,139	10,683	2,654	11,687	2,022	14,941
Cayenne, French Guiana	13,788	4,685	5,521	13,134	10,340	17,522	4,940	10,684	18,765	12,302	16,040	4,523	4,945	18,242	14,153	8,066	16,385	7,865	18,574	4,035
Cayman Islands (Georgetown)	13,199	2,976	2,049	10,835	11,831	15,388	6,724	11,700	17,207	12,310	15,211	2,263	7,837	16,797	15,763	9,915	16,343	10,900	17,543	6,916
Cazombo, Angola	12,232	11,134	13,606	12,648	5,505	11,198	8,777	6,423	10,421	8,312	11,789	11,653	4,359	10,354	6,639	4,880	9,026	1,860	10,129	5,180
Cebu, Philippines	7,910	13,802	13,694	5,267	8,418	765	16,798	7,927	1,501	6,119	5,691	14,122	14,140	1,156	5,053	10,686	2,574	11,602	1,827	14,934
Cedar Rapids, Iowa	14,203	1,795	1,407	8,141	10,539	12,745	9,419	10,096	14,679	10,081	15,322	1,306	8,562	14,163	13,822	9,247	13,710	11,338	14,996	7,794
Changsha, China	10,196	11,970	12,762	3,718	6,469	1,522	18,761	5,842	3,289	3,887	7,960	12,468	12,227	2,589	4,034	8,654	2,055	10,217	3,494	12,898
Channel-Port-aux-Basques, Can.	16,720	899	3,803	8,364	8,262	12,918	9,563	8,015	14,862	8,642	17,838	1,681	6,108	14,166	12,051	6,692	12,921	8,732	15,066	5,456
Charleston, South Carolina	14,354	1,555	1,712	9,486	10,660	14,144	8,122	10,408	16,109	10,841	16,037	783	7,581	15,555	14,411	8,976	14,857	10,547	16,417	6,732
Charleston, West Virginia	14,631	1,191	1,728	8,852	10,313	13,517	8,760	9,991	15,493	10,290	16,067	448	7,727	14,925	13,927	8,775	14,233	10,600	15,795	6,925
Charlotte, North Carolina	14,467	1,383	1,672	9,202	10,521	13,861	8,406	10,236	15,830	10,605	16,044	587	7,661	15,272	14,210	8,902	14,583	10,589	16,137	6,831
Charlotte Amalie, U.S.V.I.	14,255	2,914	3,566	11,440	10,596	16,112	6,323	10,657	18,107	11,752	16,503	2,580	6,119	17,435	14,644	8,494	16,117	9,182	18,343	5,192
Charlottetown, Canada	16,383	563	3,469	8,452	8,597	13,057	9,410	8,340	15,024	8,918	17,597	1,344	6,345	14,339	12,366	7,026	13,164	9,024	15,246	5,660
Chatham, Canada	16,261	452	3,332	8,326	8,689	12,952	9,503	8,406	14,931	8,920	17,402	1,248	6,541	14,253	12,413	7,164	13,130	9,205	15,162	5,859
Chatham Islands (Waitangi)	1,479	14,365	11,464	11,907	16,311	9,235	8,725	16,219	8,058	14,605	3,386	13,594	16,368	8,697	12,271	18,061	10,506	15,377	8,071	16,127
Chengdu, China	10,894	11,678	12,878	3,900	5,566	2,305	18,485	4,956	3,786	3,070	8,612	12,260	11,329	3,073	3,350	7,764	1,908	9,337	3,925	12,018
Chesterfield Inlet, Canada	15,432	2,501	3,710	6,074	8,577	10,757	11,593	7,987	12,757	7,725	15,406	2,837	8,393	12,138	11,481	7,812	11,402	10,520	13,034	7,886
Cheyenne, Wyoming	13,309	2,869	1,363	7,689	11,177	12,109	9,841	10,622	13,939	10,262	14,246	2,399	9,657	13,512	14,008	10,125	13,396	12,388	14,271	8,894
Chiang Mai, Thailand	10,117	12,926	14,290	5,295	5,628	2,308	17,158	5,244	2,957	3,803	7,807	13,560	11,301	2,317	2,378	7,909	581	8,852	2,984	12,116
Chibougamau, Canada	15,803	713	2,929	7,839	8,995	12,512	9,890	8,618	14,512	8,889	16,693	1,194	7,254	13,867	12,520	7,647	12,934	9,852	14,773	6,586
Chicago, Illinois	14,464	1,475	1,575	8,293	10,346	12,932	9,288	9,939	14,890	10,030	15,649	975	8,228	14,347	13,745	8,983	13,789	11,017	15,201	7,459
Chiclayo, Peru	11,050	5,747	4,523	13,574	13,589	17,561	3,955	13,798	17,976	14,963	13,338	5,110	8,232	18,387	17,468	11,345	19,231	11,006	18,073	7,341
Chihuahua, Mexico	12,241	3,649	829	8,817	12,476	12,943	8,735	11,972	14,557	11,648	13,569	2,952	10,120	14,275	15,383	11,206	14,518	13,076	14,894	9,261
Chongquing, China	10,656	11,815	12,900	3,876	5,836	2,042	18,575	5,227	3,584	3,329	8,384	12,375	11,600	2,870	3,509	8,035	1,860	9,584	3,739	12,289
Christchurch, New Zealand	919	15,132	12,227	11,542	15,440	8,491	9,356	15,359	7,222	13,841	2,513	14,381	16,581	7,875	11,398	17,311	9,664	14,977	7,222	16,557
Christiansted, U.S.V.I.	14,219	2,984	3,620	11,510	10,617	16,182	6,256	10,688	18,176	11,799	16,475	2,651	6,098	17,501	14,664	8,505	16,167	9,160	18,408	5,169
Christmas Is. [Indian Ocean]	7,072	16,232	16,753	8,003	8,094	3,401	14,416	8,037	1,601	7,042	4,850	16,807	12,816	1,987	4,047	10,218	2,742	9,788	1,264	13,751
Christmas Is. [Pacific Ocean]	6,761	9,679	7,023	8,272	15,473	9,087	10,606	14,557	9,538	12,575	7,441	9,091	16,296	9,727	13,727	16,222	11,256	19,189	9,797	15,396
Churchill, Canada	15,062	2,306	3,176	6,418	9,101	11,095	11,198	8,525	13,087	8,260	15,295	2,497	8,591	12,494	12,018	8,255	11,860	10,873	13,378	8,019
Cincinnati, Ohio	14,485	1,354	1,555	8,681	10,417	13,330	8,911	10,062	15,293	10,273	15,842	682	7,976	14,744	13,949	8,940	14,131	10,831	15,602	7,181
Ciudad Bolivia, Venezuela	13,007	3,986	3,728	12,356	11,758	17,007	5,281	11,879	18,889	13,013	15,282	3,480	6,851	18,424	15,788	9,585	17,374	9,856	19,226	5,918
Ciudad Juarez, Mexico	12,466	3,476	850	8,502	12,184	12,695	9,043	11,658	14,366	11,304	13,694	2,821	10,067	14,048	15,038	10,984	14,212	12,975	14,703	9,229
Ciudad Victoria, Mexico	12,312	3,510	739	9,629	12,607	13,824	7,909	12,217	15,422	12,170	13,910	2,734	9,571	15,155	15,927	11,078	15,346	12,601	15,758	8,678
Clarksburg, West Virginia	14,783	1,040	1,874	8,795	10,161	13,468	8,832	9,843	15,453	10,160	16,198	322	7,616	14,871	13,786	8,626	14,134	10,473	15,750	6,824
Cleveland, Ohio	14,836	1,022	1,904	8,524	10,059	13,197	9,099	9,708	15,182	9,955	16,127	496	7,735	14,600	13,611	8,595	13,884	10,545	15,478	6,964
Cocos (Keeling) Island	7,554	16,204	17,493	8,492	7,486	4,089	13,989	7,553	2,506	6,868	5,455	16,914	11,891	2,739	3,486	9,501	2,877	8,845	2,179	12,826
Colombo, Sri Lanka	10,365	13,569	15,879	7,460	4,678	4,556	14,841	4,758	4,208	4,445	8,251	14,346	9,619	3,891	714	6,768	2,384	6,789	4,023	10,531
Colon, Panama	12,466	3,994	2,966	11,919	12,473	16,380	5,628	12,472	17,974	13,305	14,644	3,331	7,843	17,743	16,513	10,391	17,448	10,869	18,298	6,908
Colorado Springs, Colorado	13,133	2,962	1,149	7,906	11,408	12,285	9,624	10,864	14,086	10,518	14,155	2,432	9,720	13,680	14,263	10,310	13,619	12,502	14,420	8,936
Columbia, South Carolina	14,366	1,501	1,626	9,322	10,632	13,976	8,280	10,357	15,939	10,740	15,985	708	7,681	15,389	14,339	8,990	14,718	10,628	16,248	6,842
Columbus, Georgia	13,978	1,864	1,236	9,346	11,004	13,953	8,223	10,704	15,874	10,999	15,581	1,069	8,057	15,371	14,648	9,390	14,858	11,020	16,196	7,206
Columbus, Ohio	14,646	1,194	1,716	8,642	10,259	13,304	8,965	9,910	15,279	10,148	15,989	553	7,845	14,713	13,811	8,779	14,047	10,684	15,582	7,057
Conakry, Guinea	15,442	6,602	8,916	12,251	6,484	14,238	7,333	7,098	14,488	9,148	16,178	7,020	714	14,121	9,922	4,284	12,328	3,613	14,283	536
Concepcion, Chile	8,704	8,993	7,864	16,827	14,412	17,379	971	15,121	15,664	17,168	10,940	8,437	8,729	16,375	16,078	12,314	17,370	10,447	15,489	8,118
Concord, New Hampshire	15,638	188	2,727	8,615	9,327	13,289	9,121	9,043	15,288	9,504	16,976	608	6,917	14,640	13,039	7,770	13,647	9,691	15,547	6,175
Constantine, Algeria	17,754	6,315	9,218	8,754	3,451	10,960	10,913	3,767	11,901	5,635	16,247	7,058	3,007	11,313	7,469	1,324	9,461	3,749	11,839	3,436
Copenhagen, Denmark	18,197	5,678	8,435	6,644	3,487	9,599	12,617	3,201	11,016	4,312	15,887	6,474	5,094	10,331	7,264	2,681	8,628	5,714	11,065	5,314
Coppermine, Canada	14,645	3,700	4,329	4,980	8,655	9,651	12,610	7,938	11,641	7,262	14,264	3,944	9,411	11,054	10,983	8,313	10,516	11,226	11,934	8,983
Coquimbo, Chile	9,428	8,227	7,231	16,273	14,021	18,083	1,278	14,644	16,440	16,574	11,685	7,686	8,262	17,152	16,317	11,833	18,029	10,249	16,267	7,585
Cordoba, Argentina	9,646	8,403	7,693	16,730	13,442	18,278	830	14,121	16,386	16,153	11,837	7,931	7,725	17,068	15,620	11,310	17,513	9,581	16,158	7,103
Cordoba, Spain	18,428	5,365	8,255	8,984	4,433	11,732	10,323	4,655	12,830	6,362	17,271	6,087	2,814	12,212	8,471	2,348	10,380	4,405	12,791	2,949
Cork, Ireland	19,639	4,504	7,377	7,611	4,675	10,987	11,314	4,551	12,457	5,749	17,330	5,292	4,354	11,769	8,614	3,189	10,070	5,833	12,508	4,326
Corner Brook, Canada	16,860	1,041	3,932	8,227	8,105	12,763	9,721	7,848	14,699	8,464	17,852	1,832	6,085	14,001	11,879	6,565	12,744	8,662	14,900	5,457
Corrientes, Argentina	10,275	8,026	7,614	16,515	12,790	18,780	1,288	13,452	16,790	15,475	12,430	7,617	7,055	17,421	15,231	10,639	17,397	9,003	16,525	6,426
Cosenza, Italy	17,377	6,830	9,724	8,077	2,602	10,054	11,772	2,861	11,014	4,745	15,509	7,604	3,797	10,415	6,647	868	8,568	3,876	10,964	4,308
Craiova, Romania	17,153	7,010	9,844	7,274	2,155	9,279	12,604	2,181	10,352	3,935	15,029	7,802	4,635	9,725	6,154	1,393	7,902	4,456	10,330	5,132
Cruzeiro do Sul, Brazil	11,431	5,760	4,982	13,963	12,983	18,293	3,595	13,285	18,584	14,687	13,741	5,211	7,489	19,147	16,719	10,711	19,010	10,213	18,563	6,616
Cuiaba, Brazil	11,580	6,777	6,759	15,312	11,912	19,667	2,634	12,460	17,988	14,344	13,767	6,439	6,148	18,479	15,037	9,668	17,508	8,513	17,680	5,406
Curitiba, Brazil	10,876	8,000	8,045	16,507	11,838	18,569	1,917	12,532	16,698	14,604	12,902	7,708	6,144	17,185	14,311	9,728	16,616	8,021	16,384	5,572
Cuzco, Peru	10,925	6,408	5,578	14,595	13,273	18,644	2,951	13,662	18,109	15,209	13,232	5,865	7,629	18,797	16,740	10,991	19,224	10,192	18,009	6,798
Dacca, Bangladesh	11,090	12,208	13,967	5,287	4,589	3,252	16,953	4,206	3,977	2,910	8,788	12,902	10,294	3,355	1,801	6,869	1,532	7,972	3,978	11,091
Dakar, Senegal	15,996	5,912	8,288	11,804	6,528	14,272	7,530	7,051	14,794	9,017	16,876	6,349	1,045	14,350	10,184	4,262	12,509	4,108	14,625	163
Dallas, Texas	13,189	2,665	290	8,846	11,640	13,271	8,683	11,212	15,066	11,152	14,568	1,953	9,153	14,667	14,906	10,246	14,539	12,084	15,402	8,312
Damascus, Syria	15,582	8,612	11,458	7,644	755	8,506	12,917	1,426	9,214	3,568	13,603	9,402	5,041	8,661	4,753	1,527	6,800	3,712	9,134	5,770
Danang, Vietnam	9,313	13,316	14,177	5,144	6,632	1,324	17,331	6,202	2,140	4,583	7,010	13,857	12,326	1,438	3,316	8,910	867	9,846	2,257	13,134
Dar es Salaam, Tanzania	11,887	12,051	14,845	11,180	4,477	9,310	10,537	5,335	8,626	6,907	10,823	12,710	5,656	8,504	4,767	4,765	7,137	2,611	8,352	6,568
Darwin, Australia	5,327	15,969	14,667	7,668	10,439	3,387	14,178	10,151	1,979	8,594	3,066	16,000	15,567	2,603	6,518	12,690	4,427	12,539	2,055	16,502
Davao, Philippines	7,506	14,110	13,819	5,588	8,767	1,169	16,412	8,299	1,342	6,515	5,291	14,389	14,456	1,205	5,297	11,042	2,842	11,831	1,680	15,274
David, Panama	12,211	4,161	2,897	11,913	12,749	16,279	5,622	12,727	17,757	13,492	14,369	3,467	8,136	17,600	16,781	10,680	17,530	11,156	18,069	7,201
Dawson, Canada	13,559	4,741	4,747	4,309	9,200	8,855	13,221	8,396	10,800	7,348	13,091	4,859	10,563	10,272	10,904	9,191	10,012	12,198	11,112	10,155
Dawson Creek, Canada	13,592	3,736	3,340	5,714	10,023	10,209	11,816	9,309	12,117	8,546	13,699	3,677	10,189	11,625	12,207	9,565	11,419	12,358	12,438	9,615
Denpasar, Indonesia	6,608	16,023	15,844	7,518	8,794	2,835	14,755	8,611	834	7,321	4,306	16,414	13,819	1,497	4,800	11,004	2,962	10,820	592	14,751
Denver, Colorado	13,192	2,937	1,239	7,813	11,324	12,205	9,717	10,773	14,017	10,417	14,178	2,430	9,709	13,603	14,162	10,248	13,525	12,471	14,350	8,933
Derby, Australia	5,299	16,760	15,602	8,285	10,093	3,744	13,774	9,931	1,922	8,608	2,991	16,886	14,820	2,633	6,070	12,272	4,272	11,759	1,834	15,750
Des Moines, Iowa	14,050	1,962	1,308	8,107	10,667	12,687	9,444	10,210	14,605	10,148	15,155	1,462	8,727	14,105	13,896	9,401	13,710	11,505	14,926	7,957
Detroit, Michigan	14,799	1,097	1,873	8,396	10,065	13,065	9,219	9,694	15,047	9,895	16,030	639	7,848	14,471	13,570	8,640	13,784	10,637	15,346	7,084
Dhahran, Saudi Arabia	14,062	10,094	12,876	7,494	957	7,308	13,669	1,562	7,769	3,158	12,049	10,889	6,237	7,265	3,224	2,984	5,417	4,144	7,661	7,059
Diego Garcia Island	9,670	14,521	17,268	9,239	5,388	5,921	13,100	5,768	4,973	6,003	7,882	15,314	9,164	4,912	2,318	7,061	3,883	6,119	4,693	10,098
Dijon, France	18,617	5,593	8,473	7,710	3,640	10,489	11,631	3,634	11,744	5,129	16,509	6,376	4,031	11,089	7,646	2,117	9,306	4,935	11,750	4,259
Dili, Indonesia	5,993	15,775	14,926	7,297	9,719	2,815	14,710	9,433	1,258	7,909	3,702	15,952	14,941	1,897	5,815	11,974	3,707	11,957	1,346	15,869
Djibouti, Djibouti	13,322	10,868	13,773	9,247	2,412	8,336	12,147	3,257	8,270	4,917	11,730	11,626	5,560	7,927	3,746	3,279	6,222	2,822	8,076	6,480
Dnepropetrovsk, USSR	16,564	7,394	10,102	6,393	1,852	8,341	13,578	1,481	9,514	2,979	14,307	8,189	5,603	8,863	5,548	2,205	7,076	5,129	9,520	6,105
Dobo, Indonesia	5,811	15,141	13,961	6,906	10,345	2,875	14,797	9,948	1,994	8,222	3,653	15,182	15,819	2,446	6,597	12,625	4,304	12,902	2,195	16,722
Doha, Qatar	13,883	10,269	13,044	7,500	1,129	7,182	13,732	1,682	7,608	3,166	11,870	11,064	6,375	7,112	3,052	3,155	5,268	4,212	7,496	7,206
Donetsk, USSR	16,352	7,583	10,270	6,296	1,719	8,140	13,751	1,280	9,300	2,783	14,092	8,377	5,762	8,651	5,344	2,312	6,861	5,172	9,305	6,285
Dover, Delaware	15,109	746	2,252	8,945	9,878	13,629	8,729	9,603	15,628	10,043	16,604	95	7,200	15,012	13,598	8,273	14,133	10,063	15,908	6,409
Dresden, East Germany	18,109	5,973	8,788	7,044	3,168	9,734	12,387	3,013	11,033	4,382	15,856	6,768	4,691	10,366	7,073	2,166	8,608	5,195	11,054	4,985
Dubayy, United Arab Emir.	13,615	10,498	13,224	7,274	1,384	6,805	14,056	1,752	7,239	2,960	11,557	11,294	6,754	6,736	2,704	3,510	4,890	4,552	7,132	7,584

Distances in Kilometers	Auckland Islands, New Zealand	Augusta, Maine	Austin, Texas	Ayan, USSR	Baghdad, Iraq	Baguio, Philippines	Bahia Blanca, Argentina	Baku, USSR	Balikpapan, Indonesia	Balkhash, USSR	Ballarat, Australia	Baltimore, Maryland	Bamako, Mali	Bandar Seri Begawan, Brunei	Bangalore, India	Banghazi, Libya	Bangkok, Thailand	Bangui, Central African Rep.	Banjarmasin, Indonesia	Banjul, Gambia
Dublin, Ireland	19,435	4,610	7,464	7,410	4,544	10,769	11,533	4,386	12,250	5,541	17,126	5,402	4,516	11,559	8,453	3,158	9,871	5,883	12,305	4,518
Duluth, Minnesota	14,494	1,760	1,895	7,647	10,123	12,281	9,925	9,642	14,240	9,559	15,385	1,508	8,550	13,696	13,306	8,950	13,184	11,207	14,549	7,832
Dunedin, New Zealand	611	15,386	12,481	11,735	15,284	8,528	9,263	15,264	7,180	13,847	2,388	14,625	16,320	7,847	11,259	17,063	9,609	14,669	7,163	16,350
Durango, Mexico	11,958	3,879	974	9,329	12,864	13,372	8,232	12,403	14,899	12,159	13,441	3,132	10,112	14,670	15,902	11,468	15,017	13,127	15,233	9,226
Durban, South Africa	10,074	13,072	15,131	13,753	7,136	10,867	8,268	8,015	9,540	9,571	9,795	13,475	6,295	9,698	6,885	6,955	8,871	4,012	9,211	7,001
Dushanbe, USSR	13,690	9,932	12,258	5,329	2,267	5,587	15,817	1,640	6,599	1,049	11,402	10,694	8,003	5,960	2,963	4,436	4,157	6,322	6,602	8,695
East London, South Africa	9,883	13,050	14,922	14,213	7,549	11,236	7,824	8,436	9,836	10,023	9,764	13,395	6,334	10,030	7,330	7,258	9,275	4,255	9,503	6,986
Easter Island (Hanga Roa)	7,321	8,883	6,476	13,844	17,426	14,757	4,539	17,613	14,159	17,788	9,547	8,107	11,768	14,721	18,279	15,151	16,582	13,971	14,220	10,964
Echo Bay, Canada	14,428	3,759	4,213	5,010	8,878	9,663	12,558	8,154	11,644	7,436	14,108	3,954	9,603	11,072	11,142	8,546	10,598	11,454	11,942	9,156
Edinburgh, United Kingdom	19,111	4,733	7,545	7,070	4,407	10,436	11,877	4,182	11,946	5,239	16,823	5,529	4,818	11,251	8,248	3,203	9,586	6,037	12,012	4,851
Edmonton, Canada	13,747	3,303	2,880	6,188	10,144	10,707	11,343	9,474	12,618	8,853	14,042	3,196	9,881	12,123	12,558	9,513	11,880	12,197	12,939	9,265
El Aaiun, Morocco	17,395	5,343	8,060	10,354	5,518	13,083	8,903	5,895	13,981	7,731	17,584	5,941	1,696	13,421	9,442	3,255	11,562	4,214	13,890	1,559
Elat, Israel	15,379	8,833	11,709	8,076	993	8,720	12,579	1,811	9,299	3,940	13,517	9,615	4,804	8,780	4,756	1,451	6,922	3,278	9,196	5,580
Elazig, Turkey	15,731	8,388	11,168	7,025	754	8,151	13,426	931	9,027	3,035	13,611	9,184	5,467	8,433	4,728	1,883	6,582	4,337	8,979	6,133
Eniwetok Atoll, Marshall Isls.	6,899	11,911	10,318	5,402	11,782	4,526	14,690	11,015	5,219	8,879	5,760	11,737	17,129	5,259	9,166	13,732	6,694	15,643	5,526	17,242
Erfurt, East Germany	18,297	5,807	8,634	7,146	3,338	9,911	12,229	3,201	11,221	4,564	16,046	6,601	4,588	10,554	7,259	2,223	8,798	5,215	11,244	4,850
Erzurum, Turkey	15,665	8,413	11,161	6,808	781	7,958	13,645	732	8,875	2,814	13,507	9,209	5,678	8,271	4,637	2,092	6,426	4,551	8,836	6,332
Esfahan, Iran	14,439	9,627	12,331	6,848	678	7,098	14,134	871	7,791	2,529	12,308	10,423	6,429	7,230	3,424	2,960	5,369	4,650	7,723	7,189
Essen, West Germany	18,581	5,531	8,368	7,234	3,618	10,138	12,040	3,485	11,482	4,807	16,320	6,324	4,512	10,810	7,544	2,397	9,065	5,329	11,510	4,718
Eucla, Australia	3,733	17,872	15,608	9,809	11,412	5,399	12,122	11,387	3,598	10,238	1,516	17,574	15,146	4,312	7,373	13,427	5,871	12,186	3,480	15,964
Fargo, North Dakota	14,210	2,117	1,844	7,469	10,311	12,065	10,083	9,791	14,001	9,594	15,034	1,839	8,904	13,483	13,352	9,221	13,073	11,539	14,317	8,189
Faroe Islands (Torshavn)	18,677	4,428	7,131	6,519	4,791	10,171	12,224	4,431	11,815	5,173	16,622	5,219	5,481	11,106	8,446	3,839	9,542	6,733	11,917	5,448
Florence, Italy	18,004	6,209	9,095	7,843	3,088	10,240	11,748	3,187	11,358	4,873	16,010	6,989	3,911	10,727	7,125	1,506	8,908	4,424	11,337	4,282
Florianopolis, Brazil	10,679	8,249	8,267	16,754	11,896	18,352	1,774	12,614	16,454	14,707	12,680	7,956	6,243	16,953	14,225	9,820	16,476	8,014	16,142	5,703
Fort George, Canada	15,688	1,253	3,020	7,320	8,926	12,000	10,380	8,480	14,001	8,583	16,296	1,627	7,636	13,369	12,276	7,744	12,516	10,115	14,271	7,011
Fort McMurray, Canada	14,076	3,194	3,126	6,001	9,765	10,582	11,540	9,099	12,525	8,512	14,256	3,183	9,640	12,000	12,234	9,154	11,656	11,875	12,839	9,058
Fort Nelson, Canada	13,719	3,883	3,693	5,369	9,721	9,901	12,162	8,989	11,829	8,183	13,669	3,895	10,171	11,319	11,837	9,356	11,065	12,212	12,146	9,641
Fort Severn, Canada	15,279	1,810	2,964	6,876	9,118	11,559	10,765	8,599	13,556	8,496	15,712	2,027	8,206	12,950	12,239	8,108	12,240	10,605	13,840	7,600
Fort Smith, Arkansas	13,548	2,318	646	8,689	11,277	13,192	8,847	10,856	15,046	10,839	14,881	1,633	8,888	14,602	14,586	9,890	14,345	11,785	15,377	8,064
Fort Vermilion, Canada	13,979	3,490	3,422	5,679	9,675	10,251	11,859	8,978	12,192	8,298	14,029	3,508	9,836	11,669	11,997	9,178	11,348	11,970	12,506	9,284
Fort Wayne, Indiana	14,575	1,307	1,650	8,459	10,285	13,112	9,136	9,907	15,080	10,073	15,835	752	8,024	14,524	13,763	8,863	13,908	10,837	15,386	7,247
Fort-Chimo, Canada	16,458	1,537	3,818	7,085	8,116	11,705	10,745	7,686	13,687	7,898	16,744	2,174	7,101	13,016	11,540	6,954	11,977	9,420	13,925	6,558
Fort-de-France, Martinique	14,178	3,396	4,129	11,930	10,517	16,569	5,903	10,661	18,515	11,920	16,478	3,130	5,736	17,807	14,544	8,343	16,281	8,785	18,675	4,801
Fortaleza, Brazil	13,526	6,167	7,328	14,149	9,583	17,345	4,564	10,138	17,237	12,085	15,430	6,158	3,828	17,086	12,939	7,339	15,399	6,412	16,942	3,077
Frankfort, Kentucky	14,399	1,432	1,474	8,762	10,512	13,404	8,825	10,162	15,361	10,378	15,788	727	8,010	14,819	14,053	9,021	14,227	10,881	15,672	7,206
Frankfurt am Main, W. Ger.	18,445	5,700	8,546	7,311	3,459	10,103	12,038	3,359	11,405	4,754	16,219	6,492	4,425	10,740	7,409	2,210	8,978	5,156	11,424	4,670
Fredericton, Canada	16,127	307	3,203	8,420	8,833	13,058	9,390	8,555	15,042	9,066	17,337	1,102	6,598	14,370	12,563	7,291	13,268	9,295	15,279	5,899
Freeport, Bahamas	13,962	2,134	1,902	10,176	11,076	14,818	7,423	10,900	16,759	11,468	15,856	1,431	7,498	16,234	14,949	9,254	15,549	10,532	17,077	6,608
Freetown, Sierra Leone	15,329	6,719	9,016	12,344	6,504	14,248	7,280	7,132	14,448	9,194	16,056	7,131	735	14,097	9,898	4,320	12,315	3,550	14,237	658
Frobisher Bay, Canada	16,519	2,165	4,253	6,479	7,754	11,082	11,373	7,259	13,060	7,335	16,383	2,774	7,324	12,387	11,020	6,788	11,360	9,430	13,296	6,861
Frunze, USSR	13,638	9,718	11,864	4,641	2,832	5,241	16,395	2,073	6,461	436	11,328	10,453	8,465	5,786	3,328	4,880	4,075	6,959	6,506	9,100
Fukuoka, Japan	9,984	11,141	11,320	2,610	7,727	2,141	18,748	6,960	4,113	4,832	7,998	11,472	13,263	3,559	5,793	9,716	3,733	11,739	4,412	13,740
Funafuti Atoll, Tuvalu	4,817	12,344	9,834	8,120	14,632	7,011	11,806	13,901	6,949	11,772	4,787	11,834	19,124	7,279	11,472	16,624	9,026	17,837	7,164	18,232
Funchal, Madeira Island	17,983	4,707	7,487	9,857	5,644	12,951	9,188	5,900	14,073	7,582	18,191	5,340	2,392	13,459	9,657	3,462	11,624	4,838	14,026	2,125
Fuzhou, China	9,684	12,155	12,632	3,697	7,137	1,079	18,596	6,498	3,040	4,508	7,497	12,582	12,890	2,392	4,589	9,312	2,389	10,870	3,294	13,545
Gaborone, Botswana	10,809	12,317	14,480	13,619	6,714	11,224	8,192	7,617	10,052	9,328	10,559	12,741	5,532	10,143	6,979	6,315	9,144	3,308	9,730	6,251
Galapagos Islands (Santa Cruz)	10,877	5,382	3,509	12,463	14,077	16,209	5,099	14,060	17,001	14,695	13,040	4,639	9,206	17,184	18,116	11,971	18,135	12,130	17,225	8,282
Gander, Canada	17,090	1,267	4,167	8,262	7,894	12,749	9,741	7,657	14,660	8,334	18,061	2,051	5,864	13,955	11,701	6,328	12,642	8,420	14,847	5,253
Gangtok, India	11,515	11,774	13,593	5,062	4,270	3,507	17,043	3,831	4,377	2,470	9,210	12,473	10,017	3,736	1,961	6,542	1,947	7,821	4,392	10,787
Garyarsa, China	12,410	11,056	13,136	5,174	3,365	4,398	16,564	2,894	5,306	1,735	10,114	11,790	9,132	4,672	2,098	5,623	2,863	7,101	5,308	9,879
Gaspe, Canada	16,410	646	3,478	8,148	8,512	12,760	9,701	8,214	14,734	8,708	17,417	1,435	6,529	14,053	12,212	7,027	12,917	9,138	14,961	5,873
Gauhati, India	11,220	11,976	13,676	4,986	4,606	3,176	17,226	4,161	4,064	2,724	8,912	12,657	10,349	3,414	2,080	6,877	1,654	8,120	4,090	11,122
Gdansk, Poland	17,814	6,092	8,836	6,556	3,085	9,291	12,866	2,786	10,653	3,965	15,513	6,887	5,182	9,975	6,849	2,473	8,250	5,542	10,692	5,479
Geneva, Switzerland	18,485	5,727	8,612	7,784	3,531	10,473	11,614	3,557	11,692	5,106	16,425	6,508	3,951	11,043	7,550	1,966	9,249	4,789	11,690	4,211
Genoa, Italy	18,199	6,013	8,902	7,864	3,282	10,373	11,651	3,362	11,525	5,003	16,200	6,793	3,874	10,888	7,316	1,673	9,076	4,537	11,510	4,203
Georgetown, Guyana	13,641	4,308	4,880	12,837	10,758	17,433	5,057	11,025	19,195	12,494	15,944	4,046	5,535	18,511	14,672	8,508	16,748	8,500	19,141	4,611
Geraldton, Australia	4,939	18,237	16,900	9,702	10,098	5,041	12,527	10,161	3,051	9,269	2,883	18,457	13,851	3,724	6,099	12,040	4,942	10,834	2,815	14,723
Ghanzi, Botswana	11,290	11,774	13,963	13,595	6,536	11,561	8,047	7,450	10,488	9,265	11,098	12,199	4,992	10,540	7,194	5,944	9,440	2,890	10,171	5,707
Ghat, Libya	16,510	7,344	10,205	9,750	3,441	11,203	10,319	4,051	11,755	6,140	15,448	8,038	2,347	11,264	7,155	1,249	9,413	2,450	11,625	3,082
Gibraltar	18,265	5,417	8,295	9,184	4,518	11,888	10,143	4,776	12,944	6,520	17,286	6,126	2,615	12,337	8,544	2,380	10,496	4,288	12,896	2,753
Gijon, Spain	19,020	5,013	7,918	8,419	4,446	11,416	10,745	4,530	12,672	6,062	17,372	5,768	3,430	12,021	8,487	2,580	10,229	4,952	12,669	3,494
Gisborne, New Zealand	1,612	14,486	11,588	11,190	15,845	8,537	9,463	15,627	7,452	13,905	2,982	13,753	17,062	8,068	11,804	17,900	9,902	15,679	7,491	16,867
Glasgow, United Kingdom	19,169	4,671	7,487	7,104	4,469	10,494	11,825	4,247	12,010	5,303	16,886	5,467	4,802	11,314	8,314	3,243	9,651	6,059	12,076	4,821
Godthab, Greenland	17,332	2,495	4,946	6,592	6,998	11,036	11,454	6,557	12,955	6,843	16,863	3,224	6,636	12,255	10,433	5,961	11,037	8,620	13,154	6,250
Gomez Palacio, Mexico	12,163	3,676	771	9,240	12,659	13,357	8,311	12,203	14,936	11,987	13,628	2,934	9,957	14,677	15,738	11,265	14,943	12,959	15,271	9,077
Goose Bay, Canada	12,900	4,287	3,401	5,716	10,586	10,027	11,829	9,835	11,862	8,909	13,057	4,127	10,853	11,428	12,469	10,232	11,426	13,049	12,192	10,254
Gorki, USSR	16,261	7,257	9,751	5,337	2,554	7,678	14,433	1,824	9,076	2,368	13,952	8,032	6,557	8,388	5,602	3,265	6,710	6,188	9,134	6,975
Goteborg, Sweden	18,190	5,554	8,279	6,470	3,643	9,540	12,715	3,306	11,007	4,298	15,884	6,348	5,279	10,315	7,354	2,911	8,640	5,945	11,068	5,468
Granada, Spain	18,322	5,484	8,374	9,021	4,350	11,697	10,332	4,593	12,764	6,329	17,164	6,206	2,755	12,153	8,383	2,243	10,315	4,288	12,720	2,929
Grand Turk, Turks & Caicos	14,095	2,537	2,832	10,944	10,883	15,625	6,726	10,843	17,614	11,716	16,223	2,044	6,750	17,017	14,899	8,882	16,005	9,811	17,908	5,835
Graz, Austria	17,871	6,300	9,149	7,362	2,873	9,791	12,231	2,844	10,976	4,421	15,719	7,091	4,400	10,330	6,859	1,706	8,532	4,742	10,973	4,772
Green Bay, Wisconsin	14,610	1,449	1,796	8,014	10,135	12,664	9,573	9,704	14,631	9,751	15,667	1,108	8,246	14,077	13,474	8,840	13,496	10,973	14,938	7,503
Grenoble, France	18,462	5,749	8,640	7,902	3,548	10,560	11,512	3,605	11,755	5,191	16,460	6,527	3,832	11,111	7,578	1,907	9,309	4,691	11,747	4,099
Guadalajara, Mexico	11,770	4,053	1,204	9,721	13,122	13,709	7,845	12,701	15,169	12,530	13,364	3,281	10,069	14,980	16,281	11,627	15,400	13,114	15,497	9,166
Guam (Agana)	7,414	12,720	11,769	4,803	10,134	2,617	16,156	9,461	3,486	7,390	5,648	12,768	15,852	3,408	7,255	12,268	4,780	13,768	3,816	16,396
Guantanamo, Cuba	13,702	2,728	2,528	10,963	11,298	15,613	6,652	11,229	17,551	12,012	15,794	2,128	7,183	17,028	15,295	9,321	16,228	10,246	17,872	6,263
Guatemala City, Guatemala	12,168	3,832	1,884	10,933	12,871	15,174	6,597	12,674	16,680	13,048	14,120	3,052	8,877	16,483	16,686	11,007	16,643	11,939	17,007	7,948
Guayaquil, Ecuador	11,461	5,245	4,064	13,107	13,285	17,289	4,424	13,431	18,143	14,494	13,729	4,602	8,102	18,369	17,271	11,075	18,723	10,971	18,318	7,191
Guiyang, China	10,374	12,146	13,198	4,158	5,973	1,824	18,320	5,406	3,269	3,574	8,091	12,704	11,744	2,556	3,392	8,201	1,561	9,615	3,417	12,463
Gur'yev, USSR	15,363	8,380	10,910	5,641	1,654	7,083	14,724	766	8,250	1,753	13,074	9,162	6,721	7,594	4,480	3,167	5,820	5,713	8,266	7,298
Haifa, Israel	15,624	8,579	11,436	7,774	881	8,639	12,775	1,567	9,328	3,709	13,679	9,366	4,904	8,780	4,846	1,405	6,919	3,584	9,243	5,638
Haikou, China	9,566	12,878	13,683	4,652	6,616	1,159	17,819	6,114	2,465	4,363	7,280	13,397	12,368	1,751	3,574	8,877	1,255	10,033	2,628	13,133
Haiphong, Vietnam	9,847	12,779	13,775	4,724	6,238	1,548	17,766	5,753	2,688	4,058	7,548	13,337	11,983	1,981	3,215	8,504	1,024	9,648	2,812	12,755
Hakodate, Japan	10,542	10,000	10,037	1,645	8,101	3,405	18,043	7,245	5,339	5,122	8,787	10,271	13,187	4,820	6,836	9,826	4,961	12,263	5,650	13,467
Halifax, Canada	16,270	493	3,381	8,617	8,729	13,229	9,234	8,488	15,200	9,091	17,598	1,230	6,329	14,517	12,523	7,120	13,342	9,052	15,424	5,623
Hamburg, West Germany	18,383	5,621	8,421	6,932	3,520	9,850	12,344	3,311	11,229	4,537	16,087	6,417	4,808	10,550	7,379	2,514	8,824	5,509	11,267	5,026
Hamilton, Bermuda	15,389	1,405	3,136	9,937	9,635	14,586	7,865	9,532	16,569	10,364	17,357	1,322	6,157	15,891	13,600	7,756	14,677	9,131	16,799	5,313
Hamilton, New Zealand	1,592	14,647	11,758	11,014	15,595	8,284	9,696	15,368	7,194	13,654	2,760	13,926	17,201	7,810	11,557	17,684	9,644	15,619	7,234	17,067
Hangzhou, China	10,054	11,687	12,202	3,234	7,016	1,533	19,040	6,326	3,508	4,273	7,901	12,114	12,719	2,861	4,770	9,134	2,722	10,879	3,764	13,322
Hannover, West Germany	18,402	5,658	8,475	7,056	3,482	9,926	12,249	3,310	11,277	4,598	16,123	6,453	4,682	10,603	7,375	2,400	8,864	5,384	11,308	4,911
Hanoi, Vietnam	9,910	12,755	13,795	4,745	6,152	1,636	17,745	5,672	2,743	3,991	7,609	13,322	11,896	2,039	3,133	8,419	985	9,561	2,859	12,670
Harare, Zimbabwe	11,263	12,227	14,688	12,693	5,840	10,518	9,073	6,733	9,527	8,405	10,700	12,751	5,457	9,537	6,144	5,650	8,388	2,811	9,220	6,272
Harbin, China	11,352	9,897	10,473	1,434	6,888	3,301	18,940	6,039	5,299	3,909	9,386	10,305	12,109	4,669	5,857	8,666	4,314	11,048	5,567	12,487
Harrisburg, Pennsylvania	15,087	738	2,189	8,792	9,876	13,476	8,871	9,578	15,473	9,965	16,509	111	7,324	14,863	13,551	8,315	14,019	10,164	15,757	6,543
Hartford, Connecticut	15,473	368	2,580	8,742	9,503	13,421	8,975	9,225	15,422	9,687	16,878	433	6,988	14,782	13,224	7,924	13,819	9,795	15,687	6,227
Havana, Cuba	13,441	2,616	1,721	10,402	11,598	14,973	7,160	11,416	16,833	11,932	15,356	1,872	7,890	16,388	15,458	9,762	15,913	10,942	17,165	6,984
Helena, Montana	13,302	3,275	2,191	6,862	10,842	11,273	10,668	10,204	13,121	9,633	13,904	2,974	10,041	12,679	13,337	10,055	12,576	12,576	13,451	9,345
Helsinki, Finland	17,404	6,111	8,710	5,811	3,302	8,745	13,500	2,791	10,233	3,530	15,108	6,895	5,924	9,537	6,749	3,139	7,891	6,214	10,305	6,187
Hengyang, China	10,091	12,116	12,906	3,864	6,494	1,425	18,613	5,886	3,151	3,959	7,846	12,616	12,260	2,449	3,958	8,695	1,924	10,196	3,352	12,947
Herat, Afghanistan	13,825	10,039	12,551	6,074	1,648	6,116	15,104	1,282	6,922	1,755	11,594	10,822	7,419	6,326	2,830	3,907	4,475	5,588	6,882	8,161

Distances in Kilometers

	Auckland Islands, New Zealand	Augusta, Maine	Austin, Texas	Ayan, USSR	Baghdad, Iraq	Baguio, Philippines	Bahia Blanca, Argentina	Baku, USSR	Balikpapan, Indonesia	Balkhash, USSR	Ballarat, Australia	Baltimore, Maryland	Bamako, Mali	Bandar Seri Begawan, Brunei	Bangalore, India	Banghazi, Libya	Bangkok, Thailand	Bangui, Central African Rep.	Banjarmasin, Indonesia	Banjul, Gambia
Hermosillo, Mexico	11,958	3,998	1,287	8,529	12,628	12,535	9,048	12,066	14,103	11,580	13,175	3,340	10,564	13,845	15,263	11,492	14,192	13,491	14,439	9,715
Hiroshima, Japan	9,999	11,004	11,126	2,489	7,853	2,317	18,622	7,072	4,274	4,937	8,053	11,317	13,339	3,735	5,995	9,810	3,943	11,893	4,577	13,786
Hiva Oa (Atuona)	6,710	9,164	6,259	10,469	17,373	11,418	8,189	16,506	11,544	14,802	8,221	8,420	14,687	11,866	16,028	16,740	13,546	17,492	11,747	13,760
Ho Chi Minh City, Vietnam	8,915	13,897	14,773	5,752	6,790	1,632	16,720	6,448	1,743	4,987	6,605	14,455	12,364	1,119	3,177	9,069	747	9,720	1,787	13,217
Hobart, Australia	1,691	17,047	14,181	11,046	13,416	7,116	10,485	13,432	5,520	12,224	665	16,350	15,903	6,219	9,399	15,290	7,882	13,417	5,452	16,396
Hohhot, China	11,452	10,578	11,578	2,591	5,888	2,836	19,451	5,116	4,688	2,993	9,275	11,098	11,450	3,990	4,522	7,883	3,185	9,953	4,895	11,988
Hong Kong	9,567	12,623	13,272	4,276	6,860	935	18,149	6,300	2,619	4,439	7,313	13,101	12,631	1,923	4,005	9,095	1,723	10,408	2,830	13,357
Honiara, Solomon Islands	4,612	13,883	11,717	7,573	12,955	5,192	13,121	12,388	4,858	10,386	3,509	13,531	18,671	5,239	9,435	15,195	7,048	15,733	5,060	19,435
Honolulu, Hawaii	8,707	8,238	6,044	6,464	13,513	8,514	11,931	12,599	9,581	10,792	8,925	7,811	15,022	9,532	12,879	14,088	10,634	17,138	9,897	14,304
Houston, Texas	13,054	2,771	237	9,207	11,843	13,612	8,323	11,453	15,380	11,469	14,555	2,013	9,075	15,002	15,215	10,358	14,900	12,052	15,717	8,212
Huambo, Angola	12,429	10,640	12,969	13,141	5,937	11,968	8,107	6,851	11,186	8,835	12,251	11,102	3,844	11,128	7,390	4,984	9,793	1,916	10,890	4,598
Hubli, India	11,407	12,508	14,899	6,947	3,680	4,857	15,133	3,702	4,940	3,489	9,254	13,288	8,932	4,501	370	5,850	2,736	6,306	4,809	9,811
Hugh Town, United Kingdom	19,500	4,710	7,596	7,768	4,506	11,014	11,246	4,432	12,423	5,728	17,275	5,493	4,136	11,744	8,481	2,944	10,015	5,565	12,459	4,151
Hull, Canada	15,479	487	2,550	8,279	9,409	12,961	9,417	9,068	14,962	9,392	16,639	686	7,283	14,332	13,004	7,959	13,440	10,004	15,234	6,559
Hyderabad, India	11,349	12,454	14,715	6,563	3,832	4,481	15,548	3,749	4,687	3,280	9,146	13,221	9,236	4,206	496	6,055	2,398	6,677	4,581	10,099
Hyderabad, Pakistan	12,705	11,197	13,672	6,462	2,481	5,491	15,197	2,394	5,991	2,452	10,515	11,980	8,066	5,456	1,677	4,738	3,598	5,795	5,911	8,886
Igloolik, Canada	15,967	2,874	4,467	5,680	7,809	10,326	12,094	7,208	12,320	6,977	15,549	3,364	8,061	11,666	10,726	7,145	10,782	9,957	12,574	7,652
Iloilo, Philippines	8,016	13,787	13,760	5,252	8,271	667	16,864	7,786	1,469	5,992	5,785	14,128	13,989	1,059	4,902	10,540	2,422	11,451	1,786	14,786
Indianapolis, Indiana	14,419	1,444	1,490	8,558	10,451	13,198	9,026	10,075	15,154	10,233	15,721	821	8,115	14,613	13,929	9,015	14,040	10,953	15,465	7,325
Innsbruck, Austria	18,165	6,023	8,886	7,495	3,170	10,063	11,998	3,152	11,276	4,694	16,027	6,812	4,244	10,626	7,166	1,836	8,834	4,804	11,276	4,563
Inuvik, Canada	14,089	4,467	4,830	4,310	8,727	8,948	13,243	7,944	10,925	7,011	13,528	4,675	10,059	10,360	10,647	8,655	9,945	11,656	11,225	9,682
Invercargill, New Zealand	494	15,562	12,657	11,742	15,121	8,444	9,319	15,119	7,061	13,743	2,244	14,801	16,247	7,734	11,102	16,886	9,482	14,516	7,036	16,323
Inverness, United Kingdom	19,041	4,635	7,424	6,935	4,512	10,381	11,956	4,251	11,929	5,229	16,797	5,431	4,983	11,229	8,311	3,371	9,588	6,219	12,004	4,995
Iquitos, Peru	11,744	5,337	4,582	13,537	12,801	17,960	4,027	13,044	18,778	14,346	14,048	4,780	7,439	19,121	16,668	10,548	18,714	10,254	18,850	6,543
Iraklion, Greece	16,491	7,721	10,608	8,049	1,785	9,455	12,157	2,238	10,250	4,302	14,624	8,499	4,170	9,684	5,796	590	7,824	3,494	10,176	4,826
Irkutsk, USSR	12,815	9,288	10,611	2,224	5,158	4,228	18,182	4,286	6,050	2,191	10,663	9,860	10,362	5,343	4,969	6,890	4,286	9,337	6,237	10,800
Islamabad, Pakistan	13,036	10,590	12,859	5,454	2,662	5,102	16,020	2,195	5,987	1,465	10,756	11,347	8,433	5,366	2,338	4,915	3,537	6,502	5,974	9,173
Istanbul, Turkey	16,603	7,569	10,403	7,338	1,611	8,965	12,778	1,762	9,925	3,699	14,523	8,361	4,774	9,319	5,638	1,267	7,477	4,190	9,885	5,360
Ivujivik, Canada	16,031	2,081	3,847	6,460	8,218	11,118	11,296	7,697	13,114	7,659	16,056	2,573	7,736	12,463	11,380	7,286	11,561	9,913	13,370	7,231
Iwo Jima Island, Japan	8,717	11,727	11,255	3,526	9,135	2,348	17,315	8,389	3,912	6,269	6,905	11,894	14,703	3,580	6,787	11,156	4,443	13,052	4,248	15,150
Izmir, Turkey	16,566	7,637	10,499	7,664	1,654	9,188	12,495	1,962	10,073	3,971	14,576	8,424	4,494	9,485	5,701	950	7,632	3,870	10,017	5,112
Jackson, Mississippi	13,604	2,218	753	9,167	11,326	13,701	8,376	10,973	15,565	11,118	15,120	1,449	8,546	15,114	14,829	9,797	14,784	11,502	15,896	7,696
Jaffna, Sri Lanka	10,588	13,301	15,578	7,193	4,486	4,459	15,077	4,520	4,259	4,145	8,443	14,074	9,571	3,892	452	6,621	2,281	6,804	4,096	10,473
Jakarta, Indonesia	7,376	15,765	16,315	7,508	7,889	2,924	14,911	7,766	1,238	6,655	5,111	16,320	12,856	1,520	3,864	10,069	2,309	9,874	919	13,786
Jamestown, St. Helena	12,588	9,297	11,082	14,582	7,621	14,311	6,032	8,473	13,440	10,598	13,288	9,554	3,171	13,444	9,709	5,986	12,135	3,494	13,128	3,463
Jamnagar, India	12,353	11,562	14,025	6,613	2,788	5,325	15,176	2,751	5,712	2,738	10,176	12,345	8,276	5,201	1,317	5,019	3,357	5,888	5,617	9,116
Jan Mayen Island	17,727	4,377	6,809	5,630	5,235	9,584	12,879	4,702	11,367	4,968	15,964	5,126	6,482	10,653	8,524	4,669	9,254	7,653	11,516	6,414
Jayapura, Indonesia	5,860	14,499	13,164	6,543	10,752	3,046	14,870	10,265	2,659	8,398	3,891	14,467	16,409	2,981	7,180	13,025	4,787	13,604	2,905	17,255
Jefferson City, Missouri	13,932	1,969	1,052	8,461	10,872	13,031	9,088	10,449	14,936	10,461	15,185	1,349	8,643	14,448	14,199	9,512	14,065	11,489	15,260	7,845
Jerusalem, Israel	15,528	8,678	11,541	7,859	880	8,642	12,733	1,624	9,295	3,763	13,607	9,464	4,892	8,756	4,792	1,433	6,895	3,497	9,204	5,641
Jiggalong, Australia	4,951	17,496	16,144	8,998	10,238	4,405	13,121	10,178	2,484	9,035	2,702	17,607	14,509	3,193	6,191	12,323	4,665	11,454	2,318	15,414
Jinan, China	10,820	11,010	11,759	2,709	6,472	2,272	19,770	5,727	4,202	3,622	8,670	11,480	12,086	3,526	4,719	8,512	3,023	10,473	4,435	12,639
Jodhpur, India	12,457	11,324	13,669	6,095	2,865	5,025	15,653	2,652	5,604	2,285	10,225	12,094	8,519	5,044	1,547	5,141	3,183	6,274	5,544	9,326
Johannesburg, South Africa	10,564	12,595	14,742	13,619	6,814	11,050	8,271	7,708	9,828	9,361	10,283	13,018	5,808	9,940	6,892	6,510	8,994	3,534	9,504	6,529
Juazeiro do Norte, Brazil	13,131	6,472	7,481	14,538	9,873	17,621	4,183	10,457	17,226	12,434	15,040	6,422	4,103	17,178	13,108	7,649	15,587	6,560	16,910	3,397
Juneau, Alaska	13,219	4,565	4,177	4,884	9,847	9,316	12,649	9,060	11,215	8,044	13,022	4,562	10,773	10,730	11,586	9,707	10,601	12,653	11,537	10,278
Kabul, Afghanistan	13,363	10,344	12,703	5,631	2,289	5,478	15,710	1,827	6,350	1,450	11,095	11,112	8,061	5,735	2,531	4,538	3,899	6,186	6,330	8,796
Kalgoorlie, Australia	4,310	18,211	16,285	9,791	10,763	5,220	12,304	10,788	3,298	9,775	2,191	18,124	14,482	4,004	6,742	12,734	5,411	11,494	3,120	15,330
Kaliningrad, USSR	17,697	6,175	8,903	6,455	3,020	9,166	12,989	2,692	10,531	3,841	15,393	6,970	5,288	9,852	6,751	2,511	8,131	5,586	10,572	5,595
Kamloops, Canada	13,187	3,797	2,940	6,127	10,578	10,514	11,406	9,872	12,368	9,103	13,494	3,610	10,437	11,920	12,743	10,046	11,845	12,761	12,696	9,805
Kampala, Uganda	12,946	10,969	13,777	10,930	3,861	9,796	10,458	4,769	9,380	6,593	11,897	11,633	4,682	9,168	5,158	3,758	7,626	1,620	9,132	5,610
Kananga, Zaire	12,859	10,640	13,232	12,114	4,926	11,073	9,145	5,844	10,493	7,795	12,289	11,203	3,941	10,352	6,448	4,215	8,895	1,213	10,221	4,813
Kano, Nigeria	15,276	8,159	10,863	11,120	4,346	11,924	9,228	5,118	12,042	7,259	14,764	8,761	1,798	11,682	7,484	2,522	9,917	1,393	11,844	2,730
Kanpur, India	11,979	11,601	13,721	5,632	3,535	4,299	16,294	3,206	4,976	2,307	9,704	12,344	9,236	4,384	1,520	5,816	2,530	6,994	4,944	10,031
Kansas City, Missouri	13,811	2,135	1,020	8,315	10,942	12,859	9,226	10,493	14,750	10,432	15,002	1,549	8,844	14,275	14,182	9,638	13,949	11,670	15,076	8,051
Kaohsiung, Taiwan	9,300	12,522	12,886	4,030	7,400	689	18,205	6,794	2,672	4,844	7,105	12,929	13,168	2,047	4,635	9,604	2,307	11,026	2,939	13,854
Karachi, Pakistan	12,757	11,180	13,692	6,587	2,389	5,625	15,055	2,351	6,094	2,536	10,583	11,966	7,940	5,568	1,719	4,634	3,714	5,652	6,008	8,765
Karaganda, USSR	14,207	8,974	11,085	4,244	2,985	5,629	16,316	2,101	7,027	362	11,903	9,698	8,313	6,332	4,106	4,763	4,712	7,165	7,102	8,861
Karl-Marx-Stadt, East Germany	18,163	5,932	8,754	7,095	3,210	9,798	12,325	3,067	11,095	4,445	15,915	6,727	4,640	10,429	7,126	2,160	8,669	5,178	11,115	4,927
Kasanga, Tanzania	12,177	11,533	14,202	11,832	4,836	10,222	9,725	5,740	9,523	7,503	11,388	12,133	4,920	9,416	5,656	4,643	8,047	1,990	9,242	5,806
Kashgar, China	13,299	10,111	12,254	4,817	2,894	5,012	16,444	2,227	6,140	818	10,992	10,848	8,615	5,476	2,941	5,038	3,730	6,938	6,170	9,288
Kassel, West Germany	18,408	5,694	8,524	7,166	3,451	9,991	12,166	3,311	11,318	4,652	16,150	6,488	4,570	10,648	7,371	2,301	8,898	5,273	11,343	4,810
Kathmandu, Nepal	11,758	11,638	13,578	5,223	3,949	3,834	16,788	3,533	4,654	2,304	9,460	12,355	9,690	4,027	1,819	6,224	2,209	7,501	4,653	10,464
Kayes, Mali	15,983	6,393	8,869	11,657	5,983	13,746	7,911	6,558	14,164	8,583	16,480	6,878	422	13,740	9,560	3,748	11,913	3,475	13,988	567
Kazan, USSR	15,937	7,528	9,968	5,137	2,516	7,355	14,735	1,710	8,751	2,043	13,628	8,296	6,825	8,062	5,341	3,463	6,390	6,314	8,812	7,267
Kemi, Finland	17,280	5,803	8,276	5,354	3,848	8,627	13,718	3,249	10,240	3,621	15,067	6,568	6,392	9,531	7,068	3,760	7,981	6,836	10,343	6,577
Kenora, Canada	14,538	1,963	2,183	7,270	9,946	11,906	10,301	9,426	13,869	9,253	15,251	1,829	8,695	13,321	13,009	8,883	12,816	11,261	14,177	8,011
Kerguelen Island	6,408	16,903	17,619	13,340	9,507	8,860	9,150	10,142	6,975	10,686	5,904	17,121	10,186	7,446	6,967	10,277	7,639	7,716	6,649	10,855
Kerkira, Greece	17,148	7,065	9,949	7,889	2,294	9,747	12,047	2,546	10,696	4,454	15,213	7,845	4,054	10,098	6,341	830	8,251	3,905	10,647	4,597
Kermanshah, Iran	14,880	9,218	11,962	6,971	268	7,508	13,835	717	8,247	2,721	12,766	10,014	6,032	7,679	3,881	2,522	5,819	4,433	8,182	6,769
Khabarovsk, USSR	11,391	9,440	9,825	909	7,367	3,796	18,247	6,489	5,792	4,400	9,571	9,791	12,322	5,200	6,562	9,000	4,992	11,548	6,078	12,598
Kharkov, USSR	16,541	7,350	10,025	6,202	1,968	8,228	13,730	1,507	9,445	2,858	14,264	8,143	5,769	8,786	5,560	2,396	7,015	5,324	9,461	6,253
Khartoum, Sudan	14,365	9,761	12,662	9,505	2,302	9,336	11,493	3,218	9,445	5,223	12,923	10,497	4,383	9,060	4,861	2,223	7,294	1,969	9,266	5,288
Khon Kaen, Thailand	9,668	13,237	14,389	5,342	6,111	1,897	17,147	5,726	2,491	4,235	7,358	13,836	11,771	1,838	2,744	8,392	388	9,269	2,540	12,593
Kiev, USSR	16,944	7,004	9,723	6,427	2,212	8,625	13,374	1,872	9,857	3,254	14,673	7,799	5,453	9,197	5,938	2,210	7,427	5,227	9,873	5,899
Kigali, Rwanda	12,868	10,946	13,701	11,292	4,188	10,135	10,082	5,101	9,655	6,956	11,951	11,583	4,506	9,468	5,502	3,915	7,961	1,456	9,397	5,424
Kingston, Canada	15,358	537	2,426	8,385	9,545	13,069	9,298	9,211	15,069	9,538	16,578	549	7,329	14,447	13,150	8,075	13,577	10,079	15,346	6,590
Kingston, Jamaica	13,413	2,991	2,519	11,134	11,582	15,753	6,458	11,519	17,642	12,293	15,517	2,360	7,373	17,171	15,584	9,589	16,481	10,437	17,973	6,448
Kingstown, Saint Vincent	14,038	3,549	4,200	12,085	10,624	16,728	5,742	10,785	18,676	12,068	16,342	3,268	5,767	17,967	14,642	8,437	16,423	8,806	18,830	4,831
Kinshasa, Zaire	13,324	9,951	12,465	12,368	5,174	11,785	8,637	6,075	11,288	8,128	12,973	10,478	3,187	11,125	7,145	4,062	9,615	1,026	11,020	4,033
Kirkwall, United Kingdom	18,865	4,678	7,437	6,752	4,487	10,220	12,128	4,188	11,787	5,097	16,648	5,473	5,157	11,085	8,237	3,445	9,462	6,334	11,869	5,177
Kirov, USSR	15,996	7,323	9,708	4,916	2,829	7,357	14,809	2,021	8,825	2,131	13,698	8,082	6,970	8,127	5,567	3,684	6,500	6,584	8,901	7,370
Kiruna, Sweden	17,358	5,540	7,987	5,313	4,140	8,755	13,626	3,544	10,414	3,847	15,206	6,300	6,466	9,703	7,342	3,975	8,191	7,048	10,530	6,601
Kisangani, Zaire	13,362	10,369	13,103	11,349	4,155	10,579	9,828	5,072	10,202	7,040	12,538	10,993	3,903	9,985	5,939	3,541	8,418	851	9,954	4,823
Kishinev, USSR	16,926	7,141	9,916	6,805	2,007	8,824	13,093	1,840	9,962	3,465	14,714	7,936	5,128	9,320	5,888	1,813	7,516	4,826	9,957	5,618
Kitchner, Canada	15,042	865	2,114	8,358	9,832	13,038	9,283	9,473	15,030	9,719	16,253	564	7,642	14,434	13,372	8,397	13,670	10,409	15,320	6,891
Knoxville, Tennessee	14,307	1,516	1,434	9,023	10,645	13,662	8,563	10,324	15,614	10,598	15,802	742	7,936	15,078	14,251	9,090	14,482	10,848	15,927	7,113
Kosice, Czechoslovakia	17,524	6,570	9,374	6,978	2,570	9,322	12,693	2,436	10,527	3,951	15,305	7,365	4,821	9,875	6,485	1,844	8,087	4,920	10,531	5,225
Kota Kinabalu, Malaysia	7,913	14,404	14,623	5,926	7,946	1,256	16,375	7,574	808	5,987	5,616	14,827	13,513	175	4,291	10,226	1,908	10,794	1,043	14,375
Krakow, Poland	17,660	6,405	9,201	6,903	2,735	9,365	12,691	2,563	10,613	3,998	15,416	7,201	4,869	9,953	6,624	1,995	8,180	5,069	10,625	5,239
Kralendijk, Bonaire	13,496	3,566	3,639	12,018	11,299	16,699	5,667	11,399	18,682	12,524	15,764	3,116	6,538	18,087	15,340	9,149	16,888	9,575	18,981	5,603
Krasnodar, USSR	16,123	7,877	10,590	6,488	1,378	8,083	13,708	1,027	9,157	2,775	13,898	8,672	5,704	8,523	5,089	2,176	6,709	4,926	9,146	6,277
Krasnoyarsk, USSR	13,629	8,766	10,390	2,761	4,458	4,984	17,351	3,558	6,714	1,600	11,435	9,397	9,513	6,001	4,952	6,070	4,736	8,630	6,871	9,941
Kristiansand, Norway	18,397	5,316	8,052	6,546	3,869	9,729	12,553	3,546	11,223	4,516	16,099	6,111	5,228	10,528	7,595	3,036	8,866	6,038	11,289	5,373
Kuala Lumpur, Malaysia	8,544	14,678	15,772	6,735	6,810	2,535	15,749	6,627	1,754	5,481	6,263	15,301	12,072	1,482	2,868	9,039	1,178	9,229	1,604	12,977
Kuching, Malaysia	7,844	14,924	15,404	6,576	7,693	1,993	15,822	7,435	788	6,071	5,536	15,428	13,046	630	3,825	9,949	1,729	10,200	718	13,947
Kumasi, Ghana	15,006	7,761	10,228	12,108	5,583	13,177	8,014	6,321	13,181	8,453	15,134	8,253	962	12,872	8,686	3,604	11,143	2,253	12,957	1,802
Kumzar, Oman	13,620	10,467	13,166	7,112	1,395	6,683	14,213	1,673	7,160	2,801	11,533	11,263	6,864	6,646	2,660	3,575	4,794	4,703	7,061	7,685
Kunming, China	10,462	12,284	13,507	4,501	5,668	2,094	17,945	5,153	3,291	3,439	8,160	12,880	11,432	2,589	2,954	7,921	1,273	9,218	3,395	12,181
Kuqa Chang, China	12,971	10,166	12,091	4,225	3,540	4,491	17,103	2,821	5,786	923	10,663	10,868	9,218	5,097	3,177	5,633	3,461	7,603	5,854	9,858

Distances in Kilometers	Auckland Islands, New Zealand	Augusta, Maine	Austin, Texas	Ayan, USSR	Baghdad, Iraq	Baguio, Philippines	Bahia Blanca, Argentina	Baku, USSR	Balikpapan, Indonesia	Balkhash, USSR	Ballarat, Australia	Baltimore, Maryland	Bamako, Mali	Bandar Seri Begawan, Brunei	Bangalore, India	Banghazi, Libya	Bangkok, Thailand	Bangui, Central African Rep.	Banjarmasin, Indonesia	Banjul, Gambia
Kurgan, USSR	14,990	8,172	10,371	4,336	2,940	6,356	15,750	2,023	7,825	1,172	12,695	8,906	7,805	7,125	4,829	4,353	5,528	7,022	7,909	8,276
Kuwait, Kuwait	14,453	9,694	12,473	7,350	554	7,479	13,654	1,232	8,048	3,034	12,413	10,489	6,046	7,519	3,555	2,681	5,661	4,154	7,955	6,839
Kuybyshev, USSR	15,774	7,783	10,250	5,272	2,252	7,262	14,752	1,425	8,594	1,906	13,464	8,555	6,791	7,914	5,079	3,356	6,209	6,133	8,642	7,275
Kyoto, Japan	9,959	10,852	10,870	2,391	8,088	2,552	18,367	7,290	4,474	5,149	8,076	11,135	13,500	3,963	6,304	10,001	4,244	12,158	4,786	13,905
Kzyl-Orda, USSR	14,342	9,191	11,519	5,048	2,211	6,005	15,699	1,370	7,188	774	12,038	9,950	7,727	6,523	3,710	4,144	4,775	6,389	7,217	8,345
L'vov, USSR	17,370	6,666	9,440	6,760	2,484	9,093	12,929	2,273	10,321	3,723	15,122	7,462	5,052	9,664	6,337	1,995	7,887	5,065	10,332	5,462
La Ceiba, Honduras	12,526	3,547	1,956	10,980	12,510	15,355	6,552	12,350	16,978	12,838	14,517	2,788	8,462	16,711	16,395	10,609	16,642	11,525	17,312	7,534
La Coruna, Spain	19,108	4,819	7,724	8,508	4,666	11,599	10,589	4,746	12,880	6,254	17,593	5,569	3,405	12,225	8,708	2,782	10,439	5,071	12,881	3,408
La Paz, Bolivia	10,867	6,736	6,071	15,051	13,082	19,101	2,528	13,545	17,965	15,243	13,154	6,238	7,361	18,678	16,330	10,809	18,779	9,807	17,791	6,568
La Paz, Mexico	11,592	4,289	1,415	9,025	13,102	12,901	8,572	12,570	14,361	12,126	12,958	3,577	10,660	14,165	15,808	11,855	14,648	13,656	14,692	9,781
La Ronge, Canada	14,271	2,789	2,822	6,379	9,788	10,984	11,171	9,164	12,936	8,709	14,599	2,761	9,322	12,402	12,455	9,033	12,001	11,662	13,247	8,711
Labrador City, Canada	16,408	983	3,546	7,663	8,381	12,286	10,166	8,019	14,267	8,374	17,091	1,690	6,831	13,593	11,955	7,041	12,518	9,321	14,502	6,222
Lagos, Nigeria	14,860	8,173	10,715	11,914	5,173	12,674	8,398	5,952	12,629	8,093	14,747	8,700	1,425	12,328	8,150	3,328	10,615	1,700	12,404	2,321
Lahore, Pakistan	12,795	10,847	13,106	5,561	2,807	4,960	16,029	2,401	5,775	1,692	10,521	11,605	8,566	5,165	2,087	5,077	3,324	6,538	5,753	9,324
Lambasa, Fiji	3,969	12,922	10,260	8,942	15,152	7,405	11,166	14,506	7,052	12,414	4,193	12,345	19,130	7,473	11,657	17,305	9,292	17,541	7,224	18,286
Lansing, Michigan	14,724	1,205	1,814	8,308	10,112	12,971	9,297	9,725	14,948	9,882	15,915	768	7,971	14,380	13,573	8,719	13,730	10,748	15,250	7,211
Lanzhou, China	11,403	11,080	12,330	3,432	5,353	2,745	18,748	4,666	4,352	2,659	9,141	11,663	11,063	3,639	3,654	7,478	2,491	9,289	4,505	11,696
Laoag, Philippines	8,849	13,003	13,259	4,493	7,665	197	17,714	7,108	2,194	5,223	6,635	13,395	13,433	1,597	4,639	9,902	2,204	11,131	2,472	14,165
Largeau, Chad	15,372	8,554	11,413	10,016	3,049	10,627	10,520	3,856	10,879	5,995	14,250	9,248	2,967	10,465	6,275	1,576	8,663	1,500	10,709	3,853
Las Vegas, Nevada	12,287	3,913	1,746	7,655	12,022	11,761	9,912	11,391	13,431	10,757	13,202	3,389	10,679	13,109	14,403	11,128	13,337	13,442	13,768	9,891
Launceston, Australia	1,809	17,014	14,171	10,879	13,346	6,962	10,645	13,338	5,385	12,093	514	16,338	16,014	6,082	9,318	15,262	7,760	13,473	5,324	16,531
Le Havre, France	19,035	5,164	8,040	7,639	4,039	10,668	11,532	3,975	12,014	5,342	16,838	5,950	4,154	11,343	8,017	2,544	9,592	5,297	12,038	4,280
Leipzig, East Germany	18,211	5,872	8,691	7,071	3,269	9,814	12,323	3,115	11,125	4,466	15,954	6,667	4,663	10,457	7,176	2,223	8,703	5,235	11,148	4,937
Leningrad, USSR	17,113	6,377	8,940	5,637	3,131	8,461	13,764	2,563	9,938	3,235	14,814	7,157	6,111	9,242	6,480	3,181	7,595	6,242	10,009	6,410
Leon, Spain	18,928	5,064	7,969	8,514	4,443	11,473	10,672	4,551	12,704	6,113	17,370	5,814	3,328	12,058	8,488	2,538	10,258	4,863	12,696	3,401
Lerwick, United Kingdom	18,699	4,754	7,485	6,590	4,436	10,060	12,293	4,104	11,640	4,957	16,493	5,548	5,302	10,936	8,140	3,486	9,325	6,411	11,726	5,336
Lhasa, China	11,558	11,588	13,384	4,711	4,418	3,346	17,384	3,909	4,382	2,360	9,248	12,268	10,186	3,715	2,313	6,669	2,010	8,086	4,426	10,929
Libreville, Gabon	14,027	9,124	11,640	12,225	5,164	12,260	8,461	6,022	11,955	8,142	13,796	9,646	2,356	11,733	7,639	3,686	10,124	1,107	11,703	3,214
Lilongwe, Malawi	11,504	12,160	14,758	12,176	5,359	10,118	9,567	6,244	9,233	7,890	10,768	12,735	5,470	9,197	5,677	5,307	7,969	2,634	8,936	6,327
Lima, Peru	10,752	6,285	5,182	14,233	13,658	18,070	3,297	13,975	17,893	15,351	13,061	5,683	8,100	18,490	17,279	11,382	19,702	10,731	17,883	7,246
Limerick, Ireland	19,609	4,473	7,339	7,534	4,693	10,938	11,372	4,551	12,425	5,716	17,301	5,263	4,439	11,734	8,616	3,244	10,046	5,908	12,480	4,408
Limoges, France	18,799	5,403	8,299	7,980	3,903	10,821	11,307	3,940	12,069	5,461	16,807	6,179	3,781	11,416	7,929	2,221	9,627	4,893	12,070	3,963
Limon, Costa Rica	12,303	4,012	2,715	11,728	12,678	16,106	5,807	12,630	17,632	13,346	14,436	3,307	8,169	17,440	16,694	10,638	17,350	11,203	17,952	7,234
Lincoln, Nebraska	13,798	2,233	1,174	8,062	10,878	12,597	9,477	10,398	14,487	10,262	14,885	1,717	8,994	14,013	14,019	9,652	13,710	11,776	14,813	8,218
Linz, Austria	17,999	6,156	8,998	7,288	3,005	9,818	12,241	2,938	11,042	4,449	15,814	6,948	4,460	10,389	6,972	1,862	8,603	4,886	11,047	4,799
Lisbon, Portugal	18,634	4,985	7,870	9,019	4,795	11,978	10,148	4,977	13,151	6,610	17,661	5,701	2,890	12,519	8,839	2,738	10,700	4,725	13,125	2,894
Little Rock, Arkansas	13,645	2,196	713	8,839	11,223	13,368	8,702	10,829	15,236	10,882	15,039	1,480	8,705	14,781	14,616	9,783	14,471	11,618	15,566	7,874
Liverpool, United Kingdom	19,234	4,816	7,662	7,322	4,332	10,593	11,687	4,169	12,051	5,344	16,924	5,609	4,544	11,363	8,236	2,999	9,665	5,784	12,101	4,593
Lodz, Poland	17,730	6,282	9,059	6,766	2,867	9,335	12,762	2,642	10,628	3,978	15,458	7,078	4,989	9,961	6,709	2,181	8,205	5,253	10,651	5,330
Lome, Togo	14,883	8,027	10,528	12,043	5,378	12,910	8,199	6,143	12,869	8,282	14,882	8,535	1,242	12,570	8,392	3,480	10,856	1,935	12,643	2,112
London, United Kingdom	19,077	5,069	7,928	7,442	4,097	10,558	11,675	3,980	11,952	5,259	16,805	5,859	4,367	11,273	8,039	2,710	9,544	5,506	11,988	4,472
Londonderry, United Kingdom	19,374	4,500	7,335	7,261	4,642	10,704	11,624	4,445	12,226	5,519	17,101	5,294	4,699	11,530	8,513	3,328	9,867	6,078	12,292	4,680
Longlac, Canada	15,022	1,407	2,361	7,530	9,608	12,204	10,089	9,146	14,193	9,154	15,823	1,405	8,123	13,606	12,881	8,419	12,933	10,716	14,487	7,440
Lord Howe Island, Australia	2,210	15,572	12,847	9,950	13,985	6,713	11,130	13,733	5,559	12,076	1,546	14,973	17,536	6,177	9,973	16,172	8,009	14,919	5,604	17,953
Los Angeles, California	11,925	4,274	1,976	7,685	12,327	11,653	9,911	11,673	13,257	10,950	12,841	3,734	11,028	12,974	14,538	11,484	13,319	13,807	13,594	10,230
Louangphrabang, Laos	10,022	12,851	14,065	5,035	5,865	1,990	17,441	5,435	2,837	3,874	7,713	13,455	11,577	2,162	2,727	8,142	698	9,179	2,905	12,373
Louisville, Kentucky	14,341	1,496	1,411	8,727	10,559	13,362	8,854	10,200	15,313	10,391	15,713	803	8,089	14,778	14,076	9,083	14,212	10,957	15,626	7,285
Luanda, Angola	12,932	10,137	12,516	12,913	5,714	12,135	8,149	6,618	11,492	8,660	12,762	10,613	3,338	11,385	7,511	4,586	9,957	1,572	11,208	4,113
Lubumbashi, Zaire	12,046	11,482	14,033	12,350	5,297	10,707	9,189	6,208	9,921	8,016	11,447	12,034	4,752	9,852	6,170	4,909	8,538	2,028	9,630	5,601
Lusaka, Zambia	11,634	11,829	14,306	12,643	5,663	10,732	9,004	6,568	9,825	8,323	11,098	12,355	5,061	9,803	6,273	5,333	8,580	2,435	9,524	5,882
Luxembourg, Luxembourg	18,614	5,558	8,418	7,446	3,617	10,292	11,860	3,541	11,597	4,945	16,407	6,348	4,298	10,932	7,584	2,261	9,169	5,149	11,615	4,514
Luxor, Egypt	15,227	8,976	11,874	8,559	1,421	9,040	12,154	2,281	9,494	4,395	13,508	9,744	4,491	9,009	4,900	1,418	7,165	2,796	9,368	5,309
Lynn Lake, Canada	14,599	2,583	2,963	6,372	9,495	11,017	11,200	8,889	12,989	8,508	14,883	2,642	9,024	12,430	12,264	8,708	11,931	11,336	13,293	8,430
Lyon, France	18,553	5,659	8,549	7,873	3,624	10,587	11,505	3,664	11,803	5,220	16,528	6,438	3,865	11,156	7,649	2,001	9,360	4,775	11,800	4,110
Macapa, Brazil	13,374	5,244	5,963	13,688	10,521	17,974	4,442	10,933	18,682	12,654	15,581	5,067	4,952	18,384	14,189	8,239	16,546	7,758	18,397	4,080
Madison, Wisconsin	14,426	1,584	1,601	8,112	10,331	12,744	9,462	9,899	14,698	9,929	15,531	1,150	8,365	14,160	13,659	9,024	13,633	11,124	15,010	7,608
Madras, India	10,859	12,968	15,202	6,856	4,269	4,350	15,370	4,239	4,337	3,772	8,678	13,735	9,522	3,912	293	6,454	2,192	6,842	4,203	10,408
Madrid, Spain	18,637	5,313	8,215	8,689	4,306	11,492	10,594	4,473	12,646	6,122	17,209	6,054	3,104	12,016	8,353	2,315	10,196	4,573	12,621	3,241
Madurai, India	10,742	13,187	15,556	7,276	4,312	4,653	14,956	4,376	4,466	4,099	8,615	13,966	9,363	4,100	342	6,430	2,476	6,597	4,301	10,265
Magadan, USSR	12,303	7,909	8,252	822	7,716	5,380	16,727	6,798	7,366	4,959	10,783	8,218	11,777	6,790	7,826	8,886	6,527	11,782	7,661	11,832
Magdalena, Bolivia	11,389	6,409	6,022	14,857	12,532	19,413	2,818	12,989	18,385	14,703	13,664	5,968	6,828	19,065	15,890	10,257	18,374	9,343	18,156	6,023
Magdeburg, East Germany	18,267	5,788	8,599	7,010	3,352	9,815	12,342	3,175	11,152	4,479	15,993	6,583	4,724	10,480	7,240	2,329	8,736	5,338	11,181	4,978
Majuro Atoll, Marshall Isls.	6,422	11,679	9,719	6,185	12,839	5,595	13,639	12,046	6,110	9,904	5,707	11,375	17,813	6,231	10,231	14,697	7,750	16,735	6,396	17,573
Malabo, Equatorial Guinea	14,404	8,810	11,381	11,927	4,941	12,213	8,647	5,778	12,033	7,911	14,117	9,354	2,093	11,770	7,627	3,354	10,107	1,090	11,796	2,988
Male, Maldives	10,565	13,527	16,099	8,105	4,433	5,328	14,126	4,675	4,860	4,747	8,573	14,322	8,996	4,603	1,092	6,367	3,161	6,092	4,645	9,921
Manado, Indonesia	6,997	14,729	14,302	6,210	9,034	1,716	15,819	8,636	943	6,955	4,745	14,991	14,597	1,164	5,362	11,315	3,003	11,811	1,260	15,467
Managua, Nicaragua	12,258	3,899	2,150	11,371	12,763	15,691	6,159	12,649	17,211	13,214	14,316	3,155	8,476	17,014	16,713	10,796	17,046	11,526	17,535	7,542
Manama, Bahrain	14,023	10,129	12,906	7,475	990	7,264	13,703	1,573	7,723	3,138	12,007	10,924	6,282	7,220	3,179	3,029	5,371	4,179	7,615	7,105
Manaus, Brazil	12,592	5,345	5,454	13,876	11,546	18,534	3,947	11,915	19,415	13,523	14,876	4,996	6,010	19,441	15,245	9,266	17,589	8,782	19,084	5,136
Manchester, New Hampshire	15,631	200	2,724	8,640	9,338	13,313	9,097	9,057	15,312	9,523	16,982	597	6,908	14,664	13,055	7,774	13,669	9,686	15,571	6,163
Mandalay, Burma	10,583	12,523	14,035	5,135	5,197	2,648	17,246	4,788	3,423	3,344	8,274	13,178	10,905	2,778	2,201	7,475	1,027	8,547	3,451	11,702
Mangareva Island, Fr.Polynesia	5,852	9,978	7,123	11,932	18,869	12,163	6,979	18,039	11,819	16,264	7,738	9,191	14,323	12,287	16,419	17,375	14,116	16,503	11,950	13,473
Manila, Philippines	8,475	13,393	13,545	4,870	7,902	207	17,311	7,385	1,814	5,553	6,247	13,769	13,652	1,262	4,691	10,160	2,213	11,228	2,104	14,419
Mannheim, West Germany	18,446	5,717	8,569	7,380	3,451	10,149	11,982	3,372	11,437	4,796	16,240	6,507	4,355	10,774	7,415	2,157	9,006	5,091	11,452	4,605
Maputo, Mozambique	10,390	12,927	15,162	13,322	6,684	10,609	8,647	7,560	9,380	9,120	9,975	13,384	6,129	9,491	6,507	6,564	8,566	3,680	9,056	6,881
Mar del Plata, Argentina	9,283	9,199	8,637	17,649	13,153	17,606	421	13,928	15,617	16,057	11,357	8,777	7,620	16,260	14,800	11,173	16,563	9,103	15,358	7,120
Maracaibo, Venezuela	13,142	3,733	3,468	12,077	11,689	16,726	5,552	11,770	18,623	12,830	15,393	3,210	6,923	18,143	15,733	9,548	17,171	9,951	18,957	5,988
Marrakech, Morocco	17,843	5,474	8,297	9,736	4,877	12,381	9,604	5,212	13,340	7,025	17,372	6,138	2,102	12,759	8,855	2,649	10,905	4,102	13,268	2,196
Marseilles, France	18,368	5,825	8,725	8,101	3,550	10,684	11,355	3,663	11,831	5,313	16,476	6,596	3,633	11,197	7,592	1,788	9,381	4,505	11,812	3,921
Maseru, Lesotho	10,275	12,765	14,785	13,925	7,162	11,186	8,023	8,055	9,883	9,689	10,083	13,151	6,008	10,032	7,131	6,844	9,169	3,847	9,554	6,693
Mashhad, Iran	14,146	9,727	12,266	6,067	1,425	6,365	14,966	965	7,223	1,731	11,913	10,513	7,188	6,619	3,148	3,648	4,774	5,483	7,190	7,909
Mazatlan, Mexico	11,772	4,070	1,164	9,319	13,027	13,285	8,256	12,549	14,769	12,248	13,241	3,327	10,308	14,563	15,977	11,658	14,982	13,326	15,100	9,419
Mbabane, Swaziland	10,420	12,840	15,037	13,441	6,752	10,757	8,509	7,634	9,524	9,222	10,054	13,282	6,044	9,638	6,646	6,573	8,714	3,655	9,199	6,784
Mbandaka, Zaire	13,649	9,850	12,489	11,785	4,589	11,332	9,197	5,491	10,973	7,544	13,078	10,429	3,216	10,758	6,696	3,553	9,178	477	10,722	4,118
McMurdo Sound, Antarctica	2,992	15,600	13,442	14,981	14,321	10,804	6,718	14,951	8,936	15,031	4,563	14,909	12,786	9,643	11,342	14,661	10,896	11,642	8,754	12,885
Mecca, Saudi Arabia	14,390	9,820	12,710	8,542	1,394	8,434	12,494	2,304	8,726	4,234	12,640	10,594	5,163	8,279	4,114	2,286	6,462	2,972	8,581	6,027
Medan, Indonesia	8,781	14,577	15,875	6,824	6,513	2,787	15,666	6,361	2,092	5,307	6,517	15,233	11,734	1,812	2,542	8,729	1,143	8,890	1,929	12,641
Medellin, Colombia	12,489	4,255	3,529	12,406	12,336	16,940	5,164	12,425	18,549	13,454	14,738	3,661	7,438	18,323	16,375	10,178	17,752	10,426	18,863	6,507
Medicine Hat, Canada	13,636	3,123	2,448	6,614	10,447	11,104	10,916	9,807	12,995	9,257	14,119	2,921	9,824	12,518	12,976	9,694	12,311	12,274	13,320	9,162
Medina, Saudi Arabia	14,654	9,559	12,437	8,279	1,091	8,386	12,662	2,008	8,784	3,998	12,836	10,339	5,166	8,308	4,187	2,091	6,471	3,165	8,655	6,003
Melbourne, Australia	2,218	17,036	14,279	10,468	13,033	6,525	11,082	12,979	4,968	11,676	106	16,425	16,150	5,660	8,990	15,029	7,359	13,458	4,918	16,753
Memphis, Tennessee	13,824	2,008	898	8,888	11,069	13,452	8,662	10,694	15,346	10,807	15,244	1,278	8,498	14,869	14,524	9,597	14,483	11,412	15,672	7,670
Merauke, Indonesia	5,264	15,090	13,545	7,198	11,074	3,507	14,285	10,657	2,723	8,877	3,241	15,000	16,542	3,183	7,332	13,356	5,039	13,583	2,906	17,454
Merida, Mexico	12,754	3,170	1,315	10,335	12,274	14,726	7,196	12,027	16,420	12,341	14,593	2,380	8,664	16,100	16,001	10,511	16,010	11,720	16,757	7,752
Meridian, Mississippi	13,713	2,111	891	9,218	11,234	13,776	8,331	10,896	15,657	11,085	15,253	1,333	8,406	15,191	14,780	9,680	14,809	11,364	15,985	7,556
Messina, Italy	17,344	6,854	9,753	8,214	2,652	10,156	11,650	2,950	11,086	4,859	15,534	7,623	3,668	10,494	6,690	788	8,643	3,758	11,030	4,192
Mexico City, Mexico	11,955	3,879	1,214	10,053	13,010	14,139	7,495	12,653	15,627	12,648	13,658	3,089	9,675	15,427	16,405	11,396	15,760	12,730	15,956	8,763
Miami, Florida	13,804	2,261	1,795	10,206	11,234	14,828	7,379	11,049	16,747	11,589	15,693	1,535	7,644	16,246	15,094	9,417	15,631	10,682	17,070	6,750
Midway Islands, USA	8,879	9,135	7,571	4,691	11,898	6,458	14,003	10,988	7,728	8,991	8,328	8,925	15,344	7,575	10,768	13,081	8,542	16,021	8,059	14,958
Milan, Italy	18,238	5,973	8,855	7,751	3,284	10,303	11,741	3,330	11,481	4,933	16,188	6,756	3,986	10,839	7,308	1,754	9,035	4,645	11,472	4,302

Distances in Kilometers	Auckland Islands, New Zealand	Augusta, Maine	Austin, Texas	Ayan, USSR	Baghdad, Iraq	Baguio, Philippines	Bahia Blanca, Argentina	Baku, USSR	Balikpapan, Indonesia	Balkhash, USSR	Ballarat, Australia	Baltimore, Maryland	Bamako, Mali	Bandar Seri Begawan, Brunei	Bangalore, India	Banghazi, Libya	Bangkok, Thailand	Bangui, Central African Rep.	Banjarmasin, Indonesia	Banjul, Gambia
Milford Sound, New Zealand	683	15,536	12,631	11,536	15,061	8,274	9,506	15,020	6,925	13,590	2,148	14,786	16,442	7,591	11,028	16,905	9,355	14,637	6,910	16,529
Milwaukee, Wisconsin	14,521	1,466	1,663	8,166	10,260	12,809	9,417	9,841	14,771	9,910	15,649	1,034	8,245	14,224	13,629	8,928	13,659	11,008	15,080	7,488
Minsk, USSR	17,230	6,613	9,305	6,251	2,642	8,745	13,355	2,244	10,074	3,398	14,930	7,407	5,540	9,400	6,293	2,493	7,667	5,553	10,110	5,912
Mogadiscio, Somalia	12,328	11,816	14,716	9,990	3,465	8,376	11,684	4,268	7,963	5,728	10,901	12,549	5,995	7,734	3,749	4,253	6,201	2,988	7,725	6,930
Mombasa, Kenya	12,122	11,867	14,695	10,904	4,170	9,179	10,764	5,029	8,584	6,617	10,982	12,544	5,586	8,428	4,596	4,508	7,002	2,523	8,320	6,508
Monclova, Mexico	12,413	3,423	519	9,212	12,427	13,418	8,328	11,988	15,054	11,833	13,882	2,679	9,720	14,761	15,591	11,012	14,927	12,714	15,391	8,845
Moncton, Canada	16,262	440	3,343	8,439	8,709	13,060	9,398	8,442	15,037	8,990	17,476	1,228	6,463	14,357	12,460	7,151	13,215	9,150	15,265	5,771
Monrovia, Liberia	15,082	7,080	9,371	12,495	6,420	14,119	7,278	7,089	14,197	9,182	15,707	7,494	765	13,880	9,688	4,292	12,130	3,264	13,973	1,012
Monte Carlo, Monaco	18,263	5,944	8,839	7,987	3,392	10,517	11,509	3,494	11,661	5,147	16,317	6,719	3,749	11,027	7,432	1,699	9,212	4,498	11,643	4,064
Monterrey, Mexico	12,388	3,438	571	9,384	12,489	13,591	8,154	12,071	15,216	11,964	13,912	2,678	9,643	14,931	15,723	11,024	15,100	12,653	15,552	8,760
Montevideo, Uruguay	9,648	8,878	8,427	17,374	12,906	17,934	691	13,657	15,936	15,772	11,724	8,477	7,314	16,561	14,792	10,881	16,708	8,911	15,667	6,789
Montgomery, Alabama	13,880	1,953	1,112	9,306	11,091	13,897	8,255	10,778	15,803	11,036	15,463	1,162	8,181	15,315	14,702	9,497	14,849	11,144	16,128	7,331
Montpelier, Vermont	15,627	224	2,700	8,479	9,313	13,154	9,248	9,009	15,154	9,426	16,891	646	7,018	14,510	12,987	7,794	13,543	9,767	15,416	6,286
Montpellier, France	18,486	5,701	8,602	8,122	3,675	10,773	11,287	3,777	11,941	5,403	16,601	6,472	3,615	11,304	7,716	1,905	9,492	4,581	11,926	3,872
Montreal, Canada	15,627	329	2,695	8,324	9,282	13,001	9,396	8,957	15,001	9,327	16,805	733	7,118	14,360	12,914	7,807	13,417	9,837	15,266	6,399
Moosonee, Canada	15,468	1,122	2,727	7,543	9,207	12,226	10,130	8,774	14,226	8,888	16,231	1,370	7,715	13,607	12,581	7,976	12,799	10,273	14,504	7,055
Moroni, Comoros	11,197	12,741	15,512	11,382	4,985	9,060	10,520	5,804	8,198	7,209	10,143	13,391	6,270	8,142	4,670	5,441	6,917	3,259	7,908	7,168
Moscow, USSR	16,635	7,003	9,575	5,671	2,545	8,079	14,029	1,931	9,453	2,753	14,325	7,786	6,177	8,769	5,857	2,960	7,070	5,945	9,503	6,578
Mosul, Iraq	15,299	8,815	11,580	7,018	351	7,841	13,616	739	8,643	2,876	13,187	9,610	5,726	8,063	4,302	2,171	6,206	4,341	8,585	6,433
Mount Isa, Australia	4,076	16,259	14,237	8,553	11,706	4,599	13,045	11,447	3,271	9,880	1,911	16,016	16,461	3,903	7,731	13,934	5,721	13,401	3,316	17,366
Multan, Pakistan	12,874	10,869	13,217	5,854	2,581	5,208	15,719	2,261	5,935	1,871	10,622	11,638	8,316	5,346	2,006	4,861	3,491	6,236	5,895	9,091
Munich, West Germany	18,185	5,988	8,842	7,402	3,188	10,009	12,069	3,139	11,244	4,643	16,015	6,778	4,335	10,590	7,167	1,919	8,805	4,898	11,249	4,644
Murcia, Spain	18,294	5,637	8,535	8,861	4,114	11,461	10,548	4,350	12,522	6,096	16,956	6,370	2,889	11,911	8,151	2,034	10,073	4,227	12,479	3,120
Murmansk, USSR	16,823	5,966	8,297	4,847	4,026	8,214	14,167	3,334	9,887	3,378	14,665	6,709	6,898	9,175	6,965	4,182	7,692	7,252	10,009	7,082
Mururoa Atoll, Fr. Polynesia	5,679	10,144	7,259	11,584	18,692	11,736	7,396	17,794	11,433	15,901	7,471	9,366	14,737	11,885	16,043	17,656	13,705	16,918	11,574	13,877
Muscat, Oman	13,252	10,839	13,531	7,219	1,754	6,491	14,247	2,032	6,870	2,963	11,180	11,635	7,093	6,378	2,324	3,887	4,539	4,791	6,759	7,934
Myitkyina, Burma	10,802	12,178	13,638	4,746	5,165	2,605	17,607	4,686	3,618	3,096	8,492	12,819	10,919	2,941	2,490	7,430	1,329	8,685	3,679	11,683
Naga, Philippines	8,274	13,456	13,473	4,921	8,159	415	17,174	7,635	1,792	5,785	6,064	13,799	13,910	1,325	4,934	10,414	2,451	11,475	2,103	14,674
Nagasaki, Japan	9,921	11,236	11,415	2,704	7,726	2,043	18,739	6,968	4,016	4,845	7,921	11,569	13,287	3,461	5,734	9,733	3,652	11,720	4,314	13,778
Nagoya, Japan	9,942	10,800	10,782	2,368	8,172	2,636	18,273	7,368	4,545	5,227	8,083	11,073	13,557	4,044	6,412	10,070	4,348	12,251	4,858	13,947
Nagpur, India	11,621	12,098	14,304	6,182	3,670	4,395	15,859	3,492	4,798	2,871	9,385	12,856	9,221	4,267	918	5,931	2,415	6,786	4,723	10,059
Nairobi, Kenya	12,550	11,426	14,257	10,823	3,916	9,394	10,713	4,800	8,905	6,500	11,420	12,104	5,185	8,714	4,770	4,097	7,218	2,122	8,651	6,113
Nanchang, China	10,099	11,901	12,573	3,551	6,709	1,442	18,879	6,059	3,318	4,064	7,891	12,370	12,453	2,636	4,324	8,873	2,293	10,494	3,546	13,102
Nancy, France	18,584	5,606	8,473	7,535	3,587	10,337	11,797	3,538	11,619	4,983	16,411	6,394	4,205	10,958	7,570	2,176	9,186	5,051	11,631	4,434
Nandi, Fiji	3,773	13,179	10,517	9,007	15,049	7,288	11,202	14,437	6,864	12,370	3,935	12,603	19,206	7,304	11,475	17,250	9,135	17,284	7,028	18,457
Nanjing, China	10,292	11,504	12,109	3,098	6,814	1,741	19,259	6,111	3,695	4,046	8,133	11,949	12,501	3,034	4,696	8,916	2,751	10,716	3,941	13,093
Nanning, China	9,936	12,569	13,507	4,457	6,293	1,469	18,033	5,768	2,822	3,995	7,648	13,111	12,057	2,108	3,425	8,544	1,298	9,803	2,972	12,805
Nantes, France	19,062	5,145	8,038	7,921	4,131	10,914	11,264	4,129	12,220	5,572	17,005	5,922	3,880	11,557	8,143	2,485	9,787	5,127	12,233	3,997
Naples, Italy	17,617	6,592	9,485	8,011	2,792	10,147	11,740	2,992	11,163	4,809	15,714	7,368	3,803	10,553	6,839	1,098	8,714	4,063	11,123	4,264
Narvik, Norway	17,422	5,409	7,854	5,339	4,262	8,848	13,546	3,673	10,522	3,971	15,298	6,168	6,461	9,810	7,475	4,043	8,310	7,112	10,641	6,574
Nashville, Tennessee	14,124	1,701	1,211	8,904	10,795	13,516	8,665	10,444	15,447	10,636	15,562	960	8,192	14,934	14,324	9,290	14,428	11,096	15,766	7,371
Nassau, Bahamas	13,951	2,241	2,089	10,373	11,085	15,022	7,235	10,939	16,970	11,573	15,905	1,577	7,364	16,437	15,000	9,217	15,702	10,408	17,286	6,466
Natal, Brazil	13,414	6,538	7,758	14,355	9,408	17,144	4,554	10,008	16,832	12,011	15,206	6,557	3,636	16,728	12,631	7,197	15,108	6,085	16,530	2,961
Natashquan, Canada	16,645	889	3,716	8,040	8,266	12,622	9,850	7,969	14,582	8,483	17,540	1,681	6,396	13,893	11,971	6,797	12,714	8,954	14,799	5,769
Nauru Island	5,556	12,633	10,557	6,827	13,022	5,421	13,383	12,314	5,577	10,201	4,734	12,299	18,557	5,813	9,961	15,087	7,487	16,493	5,832	18,527
Ndjamena, Chad	15,010	8,670	11,444	10,788	3,800	11,254	9,773	4,625	11,331	6,761	14,223	9,311	2,507	10,976	6,779	2,274	9,221	941	11,132	3,436
Nelson, New Zealand	1,167	14,979	12,078	11,323	15,473	8,378	9,513	15,337	7,172	13,742	2,556	14,240	16,829	7,813	11,426	17,435	9,621	15,207	7,187	16,777
Nema, Mauritania	16,187	6,559	9,145	11,292	5,475	13,238	8,386	6,058	13,681	8,097	16,360	7,096	446	13,243	9,071	3,245	11,410	3,130	13,514	1,063
Neuquen, Argentina	8,745	9,223	8,259	17,276	14,055	17,371	503	14,806	15,522	16,911	10,929	8,707	8,447	16,220	15,582	12,022	16,999	10,026	15,315	7,886
New Delhi, India	12,363	11,263	13,466	5,638	3,163	4,637	16,138	2,815	5,365	2,031	10,092	12,016	8,889	4,768	1,730	5,443	2,917	6,731	5,334	9,670
New Glasgow, Canada	16,384	580	3,482	8,530	8,607	13,131	9,337	8,362	15,096	8,965	17,650	1,342	6,287	14,410	12,396	7,015	13,221	8,983	15,316	5,596
New Haven, Connecticut	15,428	421	2,543	8,786	9,552	13,466	8,927	9,277	15,467	9,742	16,855	386	7,001	14,829	13,278	7,965	13,873	9,819	15,733	6,235
New Orleans, Louisiana	13,435	2,393	741	9,408	11,524	13,918	8,132	11,192	15,756	11,371	15,028	1,606	8,566	15,326	15,073	9,944	15,038	11,552	16,089	7,700
New Plymouth, New Zealand	1,420	14,807	11,914	11,113	15,512	8,283	9,657	15,320	7,145	13,654	2,638	14,081	17,071	7,771	11,468	17,556	9,595	15,442	7,175	16,981
New York, New York	15,315	530	2,434	8,822	9,665	13,504	8,876	9,387	15,505	9,836	16,757	273	7,085	14,875	13,383	8,076	13,949	9,916	15,777	6,311
Newcastle upon Tyne, UK	19,080	4,856	7,677	7,124	4,284	10,416	11,877	4,078	11,896	5,187	16,773	5,652	4,731	11,205	8,146	3,059	9,522	5,901	11,954	4,790
Newcastle Waters, Australia	4,716	16,323	14,674	8,196	10,966	3,995	13,583	10,716	2,543	9,198	2,456	16,237	15,858	3,193	6,994	13,195	4,992	12,797	2,577	16,787
Niamey, Niger	15,651	7,534	10,187	11,253	4,804	12,499	8,834	5,505	12,725	7,625	15,395	8,109	1,101	12,340	8,142	2,755	10,547	2,073	12,535	2,024
Nicosia, Cyprus	15,907	8,290	11,142	7,649	1,037	8,733	12,780	1,560	9,501	3,684	13,926	9,079	4,844	8,936	5,067	1,278	7,076	3,735	9,429	5,541
Niue (Alofi)	4,082	12,259	9,455	9,663	16,268	8,556	10,149	15,558	8,209	13,429	4,918	11,603	17,972	8,641	12,819	18,251	10,462	18,147	8,372	17,121
Norfolk, Virginia	14,901	994	2,116	9,168	10,103	13,850	8,490	9,845	15,845	10,307	16,489	272	7,252	15,241	13,852	8,456	14,394	10,157	16,132	6,438
Norfolk Island, Australia	2,405	14,708	11,953	9,882	14,689	7,155	10,878	14,332	6,223	12,511	2,426	14,088	18,144	6,794	10,740	16,940	8,651	15,792	6,306	18,219
Noril'sk, USSR	14,735	7,271	8,948	2,809	4,823	6,295	16,170	3,919	8,130	2,611	12,691	7,894	8,936	7,421	6,303	5,844	6,236	8,757	8,310	9,180
Norman Wells, Canada	14,060	4,140	4,375	4,746	9,044	9,362	12,799	8,286	11,328	7,432	13,694	4,294	10,004	10,777	11,088	8,835	10,397	11,784	11,633	9,567
Normanton, Australia	4,301	15,889	13,947	8,217	11,678	4,388	13,308	11,365	3,213	9,719	2,220	15,669	16,670	3,805	7,756	13,933	5,651	13,607	3,298	17,596
North Pole	15,616	5,094	6,651	3,742	6,312	8,186	14,290	5,531	10,143	4,816	14,158	5,652	8,605	9,462	8,567	6,449	8,481	9,521	10,370	8,517
Nottingham, United Kingdom	19,129	4,948	7,794	7,321	4,202	10,524	11,738	4,048	11,958	5,254	16,826	5,741	4,513	11,273	8,113	2,876	9,564	5,684	12,004	4,592
Norway House, Canada	14,601	2,291	2,633	6,751	9,672	11,393	10,822	9,102	13,363	8,813	15,064	2,287	8,870	12,807	12,572	8,765	12,301	11,294	13,668	8,238
Norwich, United Kingdom	18,971	5,118	7,961	7,287	4,032	10,407	11,832	3,882	11,816	5,118	16,678	5,911	4,512	11,135	7,946	2,736	9,415	5,582	11,857	4,628
Nouakchott, Mauritania	16,385	5,764	8,253	11,397	6,203	13,921	7,929	6,694	14,551	8,635	17,096	6,250	1,045	14,071	9,940	3,927	12,218	4,054	14,404	519
Noumea, New Caledonia	3,152	14,372	11,760	9,119	14,258	6,579	11,567	13,803	5,846	11,888	2,750	13,828	18,795	6,361	10,440	16,540	8,221	16,039	5,971	18,980
Novosibirsk, USSR	14,031	8,698	10,552	3,380	3,830	5,356	16,852	2,926	6,968	1,069	11,780	9,373	8,924	6,256	4,688	5,450	4,828	7,997	7,093	9,388
Nuku'alofa, Tonga	3,647	12,831	10,045	9,643	15,906	8,146	10,394	15,276	7,682	13,187	4,330	12,187	18,371	8,142	12,294	18,077	9,981	17,637	7,831	17,607
Nukunono Island, Tokelau Isls.	5,009	11,684	9,034	8,592	15,443	7,954	11,035	14,646	7,938	12,504	5,431	11,107	18,235	8,265	12,455	17,188	10,000	18,756	8,150	17,302
Nuremberg, West Germany	18,261	5,887	8,731	7,293	3,271	9,981	12,128	3,182	11,252	4,622	16,051	6,680	4,441	10,592	7,227	2,065	8,820	5,047	11,265	4,725
Nyala, Sudan	14,496	9,451	12,302	10,271	3,085	10,241	10,598	3,980	10,260	6,055	13,369	10,140	3,575	9,911	5,719	2,276	8,175	1,097	10,062	4,501
Oaxaca, Mexico	11,931	3,938	1,469	10,402	13,076	14,503	7,141	12,772	15,965	12,883	13,730	3,142	9,477	15,784	16,625	11,366	16,114	12,540	16,291	8,557
Ocean Falls, Canada	12,981	4,265	3,460	5,640	10,480	9,977	11,902	9,727	11,824	8,805	13,103	4,126	10,798	11,381	12,372	10,137	11,353	12,965	12,153	10,209
Odense, Denmark	18,338	5,562	8,334	6,741	3,592	9,738	12,487	3,328	11,158	4,454	16,029	6,358	5,004	10,473	7,393	2,696	8,770	5,707	11,207	5,205
Odessa, USSR	16,769	7,291	10,058	6,765	1,863	8,694	13,194	1,684	9,814	3,344	14,559	8,087	5,214	9,174	5,731	1,836	7,367	4,811	9,806	5,724
Ogbomosho, Nigeria	15,014	8,114	10,700	11,704	4,978	12,515	8,596	5,750	12,526	7,890	14,813	8,660	1,433	12,206	8,018	3,118	10,474	1,638	12,308	2,354
Okha, USSR	11,762	8,721	9,039	443	7,619	4,557	17,484	6,713	6,543	4,721	10,096	9,040	12,167	5,968	7,234	9,039	5,768	11,777	6,837	12,328
Okinawa (Naha)	9,334	11,996	12,111	3,462	7,874	1,309	18,342	7,186	3,258	5,124	7,259	12,329	13,579	2,723	5,420	9,994	3,149	11,688	3,560	14,167
Oklahoma City, Oklahoma	13,350	2,550	578	8,550	11,419	13,003	8,981	10,966	14,828	10,858	14,624	1,892	9,163	14,406	14,615	10,095	14,236	12,047	15,161	8,342
Old Crow, Canada	13,855	4,724	4,977	4,118	8,810	8,731	13,423	8,007	10,700	6,987	13,259	4,912	10,311	10,145	10,578	8,824	9,786	11,846	11,004	9,944
Olympia, Washington	12,762	4,069	2,850	6,306	11,011	10,565	11,244	10,293	12,360	9,461	13,158	3,802	10,785	11,955	13,052	10,488	12,011	13,179	12,694	10,121
Omaha, Nebraska	13,874	2,163	1,231	8,044	10,805	12,593	9,497	10,328	14,492	10,205	14,954	1,660	8,930	14,009	13,961	9,576	13,681	11,705	14,817	8,158
Omsk, USSR	14,522	8,464	10,518	3,920	3,295	5,865	16,267	2,380	7,387	917	12,242	9,175	8,317	6,681	4,676	4,843	5,144	7,436	7,487	8,793
Oodnadatta, Australia	3,664	17,097	14,879	9,311	11,728	5,122	12,441	11,593	3,521	10,229	1,359	16,790	15,889	4,213	7,686	13,857	5,925	12,885	3,480	16,732
Oradea, Romania	17,413	6,714	9,531	7,100	2,431	9,328	12,641	2,354	10,486	3,961	15,230	7,508	4,729	9,843	6,383	1,668	8,041	4,743	10,481	5,165
Oran, Algeria	18,051	5,805	8,694	9,080	4,108	11,562	10,394	4,402	12,553	6,210	16,861	6,526	2,658	11,958	8,125	1,951	10,110	3,992	12,495	2,938
Oranjestad, Aruba	13,410	3,525	3,465	11,929	11,426	16,601	5,728	11,502	18,558	12,572	15,660	3,037	6,723	18,006	15,471	9,293	16,922	9,764	18,875	5,788
Orebro, Sweden	17,961	5,662	8,341	6,220	3,597	9,298	12,969	3,197	10,788	4,082	15,664	6,453	5,523	10,093	7,219	3,041	8,437	6,098	10,856	5,723
Orel, USSR	16,654	7,130	9,764	5,967	2,273	8,204	13,836	1,741	9,501	2,841	14,354	7,920	5,926	8,829	5,749	2,646	7,091	5,617	9,534	6,364
Orsk, USSR	15,160	8,315	10,685	4,976	2,292	6,660	15,288	1,378	7,978	1,294	12,850	9,076	7,293	7,297	4,573	3,779	5,598	6,379	8,028	7,820
Osaka, Japan	9,931	10,894	10,913	2,430	8,086	2,509	18,376	7,291	4,431	5,151	8,042	11,178	13,512	3,920	6,276	10,008	4,208	12,149	4,742	13,923
Oslo, Norway	18,175	5,401	8,090	6,298	3,839	9,501	12,795	3,457	11,021	4,321	15,893	6,193	5,469	10,323	7,481	3,166	8,682	6,198	11,095	5,623
Osorno, Chile	8,357	9,407	8,244	17,144	14,521	17,022	954	15,277	15,262	17,380	10,572	8,850	8,916	15,971	15,835	12,493	16,970	10,472	15,081	8,347
Ostrava, Czechoslovakia	17,766	6,320	9,127	6,990	2,820	9,485	12,578	2,672	10,732	4,118	15,532	7,115	4,772	10,073	6,728	1,973	8,298	5,040	10,744	5,130
Ottawa, Canada	15,480	484	2,551	8,281	9,408	12,964	9,415	9,068	14,964	9,393	16,641	685	7,280	14,335	13,005	7,958	13,442	10,002	15,236	6,556

Distances in Kilometers	Auckland Islands, New Zealand	Augusta, Maine	Austin, Texas	Ayan, USSR	Baghdad, Iraq	Baguio, Philippines	Bahia Blanca, Argentina	Baku, USSR	Balikpapan, Indonesia	Balkhash, USSR	Ballarat, Australia	Baltimore, Maryland	Bamako, Mali	Bandar Seri Begawan, Brunei	Bangalore, India	Banghazi, Libya	Bangkok, Thailand	Bangui, Central African Rep.	Banjarmasin, Indonesia	Banjul, Gambia
Ouagadougou, Bourkina Fasso	15,621	7,332	9,916	11,521	5,201	12,910	8,465	5,884	13,129	7,992	15,591	7,873	705	12,751	8,553	3,107	10,961	2,382	12,934	1,639
Oujda, Morocco	17,998	5,769	8,648	9,229	4,243	11,722	10,232	4,553	12,696	6,371	16,942	6,479	2,515	12,106	8,249	2,059	10,255	3,965	12,633	2,777
Oxford, United Kingdom	19,154	4,985	7,845	7,448	4,180	10,606	11,639	4,057	12,014	5,317	16,873	5,776	4,379	11,334	8,118	2,786	9,611	5,565	12,053	4,465
Pago Pago, American Samoa	4,531	11,970	9,231	9,154	15,900	8,280	10,563	15,140	8,092	13,000	5,165	11,350	18,155	8,475	12,673	17,751	10,260	18,524	8,279	17,238
Pakxe, Laos	9,369	13,409	14,390	5,343	6,458	1,594	17,144	6,063	2,184	4,526	7,060	13,977	12,117	1,512	3,053	8,739	588	9,592	2,259	12,941
Palembang, Indonesia	7,801	15,387	16,170	7,242	7,488	2,759	15,208	7,348	1,356	6,233	5,531	15,974	12,559	1,424	3,480	9,685	1,902	9,619	1,094	13,483
Palermo, Italy	17,483	6,701	9,603	8,313	2,845	10,336	11,494	3,137	11,278	5,027	15,718	7,466	3,528	10,685	6,881	903	8,835	3,775	11,223	4,027
Palma, Majorca	18,249	5,831	8,736	8,573	3,773	11,090	10,903	3,984	12,159	5,726	16,661	6,581	3,161	11,543	7,817	1,773	9,709	4,216	12,120	3,454
Palmerston North, New Zealand	1,348	14,757	11,856	11,292	15,659	8,474	9,463	15,491	7,318	13,844	2,756	14,019	16,915	7,949	11,612	17,653	9,768	15,408	7,343	16,798
Panama, Panama	12,457	4,029	3,026	11,975	12,472	16,439	5,573	12,481	18,029	13,333	14,643	3,372	7,811	17,803	16,515	10,381	17,492	10,833	18,352	6,876
Paramaribo, Suriname	13,721	4,496	5,209	12,994	10,545	17,501	4,987	10,852	19,009	12,400	16,004	4,287	5,230	18,403	14,409	8,280	16,573	8,174	18,866	4,312
Paris, France	18,862	5,339	8,215	7,638	3,869	10,571	11,600	3,821	11,885	5,230	16,692	6,125	4,128	11,220	7,855	2,379	9,457	5,168	11,903	4,295
Patna, India	11,593	11,854	13,813	5,423	4,014	3,814	16,646	3,649	4,528	2,519	9,302	12,576	9,723	3,920	1,604	6,294	2,077	7,454	4,511	10,516
Patrai, Greece	16,931	7,281	10,166	7,935	2,115	9,647	12,090	2,426	10,547	4,391	15,019	8,061	4,086	9,958	6,158	697	8,106	3,766	10,490	4,669
Peking, China	11,162	10,653	11,472	2,427	6,304	2,638	19,836	5,528	4,564	3,400	9,027	11,133	11,846	3,885	4,827	8,287	3,291	10,367	4,794	12,365
Penrhyn Island (Omoka)	5,649	10,568	7,770	9,287	16,468	9,385	9,890	15,575	9,458	13,497	6,606	9,912	16,740	9,774	13,949	17,438	11,477	19,384	9,670	15,806
Peoria, Illinois	14,252	1,673	1,370	8,344	10,551	12,959	9,222	10,136	14,899	10,192	15,460	1,118	8,401	14,377	13,918	9,194	13,888	11,211	15,215	7,620
Perm', USSR	15,612	7,620	9,926	4,641	2,881	6,968	15,189	2,012	8,447	1,771	13,318	8,368	7,315	7,748	5,309	3,962	6,139	6,787	8,529	7,738
Perth, Australia	4,612	18,548	16,833	10,019	10,406	5,374	12,181	10,496	3,394	9,636	2,630	18,629	13,933	4,076	6,429	12,302	5,313	10,954	3,169	14,778
Peshawar, Pakistan	13,168	10,492	12,800	5,528	2,510	5,256	15,893	2,046	6,134	1,451	10,892	11,255	8,281	5,515	2,408	4,761	3,683	6,371	6,118	9,019
Petropavlovsk-Kamchatskiy,USSR	11,515	8,274	8,214	1,368	8,531	5,240	16,526	7,615	7,161	5,699	10,136	8,483	12,618	6,655	8,269	9,759	6,685	12,634	7,476	12,626
Petrozavodsk, USSR	16,886	6,443	8,932	5,330	3,246	8,216	14,039	2,605	9,737	3,054	14,604	7,213	6,417	9,036	6,421	3,458	7,424	6,507	9,820	6,710
Pevek, USSR	13,354	6,458	6,957	2,148	7,776	6,815	15,406	6,882	8,808	5,415	12,087	6,774	10,869	8,218	8,764	8,459	7,803	11,513	9,097	10,766
Philadelphia, Pennsylvania	15,186	658	2,312	8,872	9,794	13,556	8,810	9,514	15,555	9,950	16,649	145	7,175	14,935	13,507	8,203	14,043	10,022	15,833	6,393
Phnom Penh, Kampuchea	9,095	13,795	14,785	5,743	6,581	1,777	16,742	6,246	1,937	4,814	6,786	14,374	12,155	1,327	2,977	8,859	536	9,523	1,963	13,007
Phoenix, Arizona	12,251	3,815	1,400	8,062	12,214	12,164	9,501	11,622	13,811	11,086	13,313	3,226	10,514	13,505	14,765	11,189	13,748	13,357	14,148	9,698
Pierre, South Dakota	13,821	2,424	1,581	7,571	10,691	12,102	9,965	10,157	13,998	9,892	14,702	2,043	9,222	13,518	13,650	9,613	13,233	11,903	14,323	8,485
Pinang, Malaysia	8,834	14,409	15,615	6,565	6,541	2,524	15,925	6,343	1,979	5,192	6,551	15,045	11,862	1,620	2,634	8,779	922	9,061	1,857	12,759
Pitcairn Island (Adamstown)	6,038	9,828	7,030	12,397	18,949	12,685	6,445	18,306	12,268	16,734	8,032	9,034	13,821	12,761	16,833	17,016	14,603	15,968	12,383	12,988
Pittsburgh, Pennsylvania	14,883	945	1,960	8,685	10,048	13,362	8,949	9,721	15,350	10,028	16,249	317	7,590	14,761	13,658	8,535	14,006	10,424	15,644	6,809
Plymouth, Montserrat	14,291	3,143	3,907	11,679	10,477	16,329	6,134	10,585	18,296	11,777	16,575	2,868	5,840	17,597	14,518	8,333	16,146	8,900	18,487	4,909
Plymouth, United Kingdom	19,353	4,843	7,721	7,662	4,355	10,857	11,391	4,269	12,258	5,565	17,109	5,629	4,201	11,580	8,321	2,844	9,849	5,528	12,293	4,251
Ponape Island	6,429	12,579	10,959	5,770	11,755	4,229	14,643	11,047	4,689	8,939	5,145	12,408	17,370	4,801	8,840	13,829	6,355	15,384	4,983	17,683
Ponce, Puerto Rico	14,114	2,931	3,428	11,434	10,759	16,116	6,296	10,807	18,117	11,865	16,348	2,548	6,299	17,466	14,806	8,666	16,222	9,361	18,375	5,371
Ponta Delgada, Azores	18,279	3,735	6,546	9,457	6,223	13,056	9,259	6,335	14,451	7,776	19,101	4,388	3,287	13,783	10,271	4,184	12,019	5,812	14,464	2,837
Pontianak, Indonesia	7,763	15,099	15,610	6,776	7,704	2,200	15,630	7,477	846	6,172	5,459	15,616	12,983	827	3,788	9,947	1,808	10,103	689	13,892
Port Augusta, Australia	3,098	17,299	14,802	9,856	12,186	5,714	11,853	12,102	4,093	10,800	788	16,851	15,904	4,791	8,139	14,249	6,475	12,998	4,035	16,667
Port Blair, India	9,882	13,568	15,238	6,312	5,465	3,053	16,124	5,270	3,021	4,246	7,614	14,265	10,879	2,553	1,657	7,712	876	8,197	2,928	11,755
Port Elizabeth, South Africa	9,878	12,939	14,731	14,434	7,708	11,469	7,586	8,601	10,050	10,223	9,844	13,257	6,266	10,255	7,568	7,338	9,514	4,306	9,716	6,890
Port Hedland, Australia	5,360	17,235	16,228	8,703	9,852	4,069	13,469	9,776	2,114	8,625	3,101	17,456	14,289	2,816	5,805	11,961	4,255	11,226	1,928	15,210
Port Louis, Mauritius	9,558	14,497	17,300	11,297	6,083	7,997	10,973	6,750	6,776	7,624	8,362	15,170	8,037	6,862	4,276	7,028	6,021	5,047	6,459	8,919
Port Moresby, Papua New Guinea	4,899	14,769	12,947	7,355	11,771	4,096	13,863	11,309	3,481	9,449	3,127	14,568	17,303	3,915	8,084	14,051	5,760	14,334	3,668	18,211
Port Said, Egypt	15,694	8,518	11,397	8,062	1,164	8,926	12,467	1,876	9,568	4,017	13,831	9,299	4,609	9,034	5,047	1,163	7,174	3,306	9,473	5,357
Port Sudan, Sudan	14,410	9,786	12,688	8,861	1,680	8,742	12,157	2,598	8,975	4,563	12,756	10,549	4,886	8,548	4,364	2,203	6,746	2,635	8,819	5,763
Port-au-Prince, Haiti	13,768	2,869	2,877	11,221	11,190	15,891	6,423	11,170	17,857	12,064	15,926	2,337	6,897	17,297	15,218	9,157	16,350	9,961	18,167	5,972
Port-of-Spain, Trin. & Tobago	13,794	3,815	4,330	12,350	10,812	17,002	5,465	11,000	18,954	12,322	16,102	3,508	5,830	18,244	14,809	8,604	16,667	8,848	19,095	4,896
Port-Vila, Vanuatu	3,657	13,895	11,356	8,691	14,202	6,453	11,842	13,667	5,913	11,675	3,245	13,383	19,327	6,374	10,526	16,464	8,219	16,418	6,069	19,314
Portland, Maine	15,752	83	2,842	8,596	9,217	13,262	9,158	8,937	15,259	9,418	17,079	719	6,824	14,604	12,939	7,655	13,580	9,586	15,513	6,089
Portland, Oregon	12,650	4,097	2,747	6,447	11,172	10,668	11,109	10,458	12,443	9,629	13,104	3,796	10,842	12,052	13,215	10,621	12,146	13,282	12,778	10,162
Porto, Portugal	18,883	4,904	7,802	8,748	4,711	11,772	10,386	4,841	13,001	6,413	17,627	5,639	3,159	12,357	8,758	2,739	10,553	4,895	12,989	3,166
Porto Alegre, Brazil	10,327	8,451	8,302	16,984	12,252	18,283	1,399	12,979	16,313	15,079	12,358	8,118	6,615	16,865	14,446	10,190	16,604	8,331	16,014	6,079
Porto Alexandre, Angola	12,236	10,578	12,749	13,653	6,446	12,453	7,566	7,357	11,578	9,362	12,262	10,983	3,835	11,561	7,903	5,376	10,284	2,351	11,273	4,505
Porto Novo, Benin	14,885	8,110	10,641	11,945	5,235	12,751	8,338	6,007	12,713	8,148	14,807	8,632	1,350	12,412	8,233	3,367	10,696	1,785	12,488	2,240
Porto Velho, Brazil	11,838	5,908	5,636	14,379	12,246	19,035	3,322	12,648	18,890	14,280	14,126	5,480	6,620	19,559	15,803	9,964	18,246	9,268	18,657	5,778
Portsmouth, United Kingdom	19,142	5,033	7,901	7,544	4,148	10,660	11,570	4,052	12,044	5,356	16,891	5,821	4,274	11,368	8,105	2,703	9,633	5,462	12,077	4,370
Poznan, Poland	17,910	6,096	8,878	6,798	3,050	9,471	12,656	2,827	10,791	4,125	15,630	6,892	4,942	10,120	6,895	2,269	8,373	5,329	10,818	5,250
Prague, Czechoslovakia	18,039	6,069	8,892	7,111	3,075	9,730	12,366	2,947	11,000	4,369	15,806	6,863	4,630	10,338	7,001	2,049	8,569	5,082	11,015	4,944
Praia, Cape Verde Islands	15,939	5,434	7,695	11,915	7,080	14,773	7,179	7,550	15,423	9,447	17,209	5,815	1,696	14,952	10,810	4,801	13,099	4,756	15,265	766
Pretoria, South Africa	10,606	12,570	14,735	13,574	6,763	11,030	8,307	7,658	9,821	9,313	10,312	12,998	5,780	9,926	6,858	6,462	8,969	3,489	9,497	6,506
Prince Albert, Canada	14,120	2,789	2,628	6,532	9,993	11,113	11,011	9,375	13,051	8,920	14,532	2,699	9,402	12,531	12,665	9,207	12,175	11,799	13,366	8,769
Prince Edward Island	8,156	14,562	15,817	14,691	8,877	10,773	7,687	9,706	9,058	10,961	8,132	14,771	8,000	9,416	7,693	8,899	9,133	5,958	8,722	8,885
Prince George, Canada	13,332	3,912	3,306	5,749	10,258	10,181	11,782	9,532	12,063	8,716	13,476	3,805	10,425	11,593	12,346	9,825	11,465	12,619	12,388	9,837
Prince Rupert, Canada	13,035	4,394	3,726	5,362	10,279	9,724	12,178	9,511	11,586	8,546	13,044	4,302	10,828	11,131	12,097	10,016	11,077	12,894	11,914	10,271
Providence, Rhode Island	15,564	307	2,681	8,767	9,421	13,441	8,966	9,152	15,441	9,642	16,984	523	6,884	14,794	13,160	7,827	13,797	9,690	15,701	6,126
Provo, Utah	12,825	3,447	1,676	7,457	11,496	11,739	10,083	10,883	13,504	10,340	13,671	2,985	10,240	13,122	14,037	10,585	13,172	12,941	13,840	9,480
Puerto Aisen, Chile	7,937	9,942	8,756	17,550	14,583	16,562	1,136	15,395	14,749	17,535	10,117	9,388	9,122	15,455	15,455	12,667	16,439	10,454	14,559	8,612
Puerto Deseado, Argentina	8,007	10,207	9,211	18,116	14,114	16,479	1,045	14,956	14,566	17,091	10,107	9,700	8,798	15,253	14,887	12,294	16,032	9,955	14,345	8,353
Puerto Princesa, Philippines	8,123	13,959	14,116	5,451	7,971	767	16,792	7,529	1,236	5,819	5,853	14,352	13,644	681	4,502	10,249	2,034	11,046	1,516	14,467
Punta Arenas, Chile	7,310	10,801	9,602	18,124	14,541	15,807	1,735	15,421	13,928	17,500	9,413	10,257	9,412	14,627	14,756	12,853	15,569	10,361	13,724	9,006
Pusan, South Korea	10,187	11,007	11,272	2,472	7,540	2,234	18,937	6,766	4,224	4,635	8,188	11,358	13,058	3,647	5,703	9,516	3,712	11,573	4,515	13,531
Pyongyang, North Korea	10,703	10,645	11,114	2,143	7,093	2,554	19,327	6,297	4,555	4,158	8,678	11,040	12,551	3,935	5,532	9,024	3,739	11,176	4,827	13,011
Qamdo, China	11,323	11,543	13,023	4,225	4,929	2,877	17,979	4,351	4,147	2,577	9,020	12,179	10,699	3,449	2,848	7,147	1,958	8,684	4,239	11,408
Qandahar, Afghanistan	13,374	10,471	12,941	6,088	2,012	5,767	15,287	1,731	6,496	1,867	11,146	11,252	7,757	5,913	2,389	4,291	4,056	5,768	6,449	8,525
Qiqian, China	12,184	9,262	10,129	1,220	6,275	3,970	18,487	5,394	5,939	3,314	10,192	9,729	11,316	5,274	5,804	7,929	4,633	10,456	6,182	11,666
Qom, Iran	14,634	9,412	12,105	6,721	616	7,154	14,168	643	7,914	2,428	12,480	10,207	6,386	7,338	3,604	2,872	5,480	4,727	7,856	7,123
Quebec, Canada	15,858	301	2,926	8,237	9,048	12,903	9,516	8,726	14,900	9,123	16,974	944	6,963	14,246	12,692	7,579	13,247	9,645	15,154	6,263
Quetta, Pakistan	13,181	10,664	13,120	6,129	2,163	5,639	15,331	1,920	6,324	1,970	10,957	11,444	7,885	5,749	2,196	4,445	3,890	5,826	6,272	8,665
Quito, Ecuador	11,722	5,008	3,943	12,963	13,036	17,266	4,574	13,172	18,323	14,238	13,989	4,379	7,907	18,454	17,037	10,835	18,504	10,807	18,528	6,990
Rabaul, Papua New Guinea	5,322	13,972	12,177	6,843	11,920	4,157	14,086	11,359	3,943	9,379	3,790	13,764	17,660	4,262	8,460	14,162	6,042	14,888	4,178	18,421
Raiatea (Uturoa)	5,301	10,648	7,755	10,390	17,584	10,323	8,795	16,685	10,162	14,615	6,682	9,924	16,077	10,559	14,756	18,102	12,340	18,268	10,336	15,178
Raleigh, North Carolina	14,662	1,211	1,882	9,213	10,337	13,886	8,417	10,068	15,869	10,487	16,254	429	7,459	15,289	14,061	8,699	14,523	10,381	16,167	6,635
Rangiroa (Avatoru)	5,695	10,224	7,326	10,433	17,634	10,654	8,596	16,716	10,569	14,721	7,124	9,493	15,677	10,947	15,146	17,741	12,706	18,121	10,751	14,767
Rangoon, Burma	10,116	13,091	14,590	5,632	5,473	2,606	16,805	5,152	3,024	3,860	7,814	13,753	11,081	2,434	2,043	7,752	575	8,556	3,009	11,917
Raoul Is., Kermadec Islands	2,712	13,602	10,750	10,364	16,001	8,316	9,955	15,543	7,556	13,573	3,648	12,915	17,896	8,095	12,107	18,281	9,957	16,755	7,656	17,416
Rarotonga (Avarua)	4,396	11,625	8,744	10,370	17,288	9,634	9,184	16,505	9,281	14,363	5,677	10,913	16,885	9,725	13,893	18,795	11,550	18,134	9,433	16,037
Rawson, Argentina	8,462	9,716	8,803	17,810	13,943	16,976	561	14,747	15,063	16,887	10,587	9,220	8,480	15,748	15,116	12,019	16,455	9,831	14,840	7,988
Recife, Brazil	13,182	6,776	7,931	14,602	9,521	17,215	4,365	10,145	16,732	12,171	14,955	6,780	3,754	16,683	12,645	7,331	15,128	6,096	16,419	3,123
Regina, Canada	13,995	2,691	2,312	6,828	10,237	11,388	10,711	9,639	13,310	9,227	14,548	2,515	9,397	12,805	12,974	9,372	12,484	11,885	13,629	8,730
Reykjavik, Iceland	18,424	3,685	6,337	6,522	5,587	10,517	11,942	5,197	12,276	5,764	16,899	4,468	5,820	11,562	9,173	4,583	10,104	7,384	12,413	5,645
Rhodes, Greece	16,356	7,852	10,722	7,796	1,518	9,154	12,457	1,935	9,973	4,001	14,410	8,637	4,473	9,399	5,553	890	7,541	3,685	9,906	5,129
Richmond, Virginia	14,867	990	2,037	9,062	10,123	13,743	8,586	9,847	15,734	10,267	16,405	207	7,358	15,138	13,838	8,508	14,323	10,250	16,025	6,550
Riga, USSR	17,477	6,246	8,912	6,121	3,045	8,880	13,304	2,614	10,292	3,587	15,167	7,037	5,623	9,606	6,637	2,777	7,913	5,852	10,345	5,926
Ringkobing, Denmark	18,455	5,410	8,180	6,741	3,746	9,823	12,425	3,475	11,270	4,562	16,145	6,206	5,019	10,581	7,539	2,817	8,890	5,809	11,324	5,188
Rio Branco, Brazil	11,502	6,014	5,487	14,381	12,679	18,868	3,232	13,060	18,664	14,631	13,804	5,529	7,068	19,374	16,248	10,398	18,694	9,706	18,511	6,223
Rio Cuarto, Argentina	9,471	8,594	7,851	16,896	13,529	18,089	647	14,227	16,193	16,282	11,654	8,118	7,835	16,876	15,568	11,420	17,375	9,621	15,967	7,231
Rio de Janeiro, Brazil	11,350	7,919	8,280	16,278	11,170	18,190	2,519	11,874	16,578	13,962	13,273	7,711	5,497	16,943	13,707	9,076	16,081	7,358	16,245	4,961
Rio Gallegos, Argentina	7,514	10,632	9,494	18,157	14,413	16,003	1,534	15,283	14,112	17,384	9,615	10,099	9,228	14,808	14,793	12,685	15,704	10,235	13,903	8,811
Rio Grande, Brazil	10,093	8,643	8,413	17,179	12,427	18,128	1,186	13,168	16,139	15,278	12,127	8,294	6,819	16,713	14,494	10,388	16,576	8,467	15,848	6,297
Riyadh, Saudi Arabia	14,171	10,020	12,849	7,847	992	7,674	13,279	1,771	8,072	3,074	12,236	10,811	5,886	7,589	3,489	2,732	5,750	3,755	7,951	6,723
Road Town, Brit. Virgin Isls.	14,285	2,908	3,591	11,436	10,563	16,107	6,333	10,626	18,099	11,726	16,535	2,584	6,085	17,423	14,610	8,459	16,093	9,148	18,330	5,158

Distances in Kilometers	Auckland Islands, New Zealand	Augusta, Maine	Austin, Texas	Ayan, USSR	Baghdad, Iraq	Baguio, Philippines	Bahia Blanca, Argentina	Baku, USSR	Balikpapan, Indonesia	Balkhash, USSR	Ballarat, Australia	Baltimore, Maryland	Bamako, Mali	Bandar Seri Begawan, Brunei	Bangalore, India	Banghazi, Libya	Bangkok, Thailand	Bangui, Central African Rep.	Banjarmasin, Indonesia	Banjul, Gambia
Roanoke, Virginia	14,675	1,159	1,818	9,016	10,298	13,687	8,607	10,003	15,668	10,362	16,184	367	7,578	15,092	13,969	8,712	14,357	10,472	15,968	6,766
Robinson Crusoe Island, Chile	8,691	8,681	7,348	16,226	14,825	17,290	1,592	15,463	15,809	17,375	10,974	8,077	9,076	16,520	16,714	12,650	17,801	10,971	15,679	8,404
Rochester, New York	15,219	643	2,287	8,469	9,693	13,153	9,199	9,360	15,151	9,680	16,483	438	7,407	14,538	13,298	8,211	13,701	10,183	15,433	6,656
Rockhampton, Australia	3,330	15,691	13,301	8,922	12,843	5,475	12,333	12,530	4,379	10,837	1,694	15,268	17,465	4,970	8,896	15,090	6,818	14,459	4,455	18,272
Rome, Italy	17,806	6,404	9,296	7,978	2,954	10,235	11,697	3,117	11,293	4,881	15,881	7,180	3,801	10,674	7,001	1,277	8,842	4,202	11,260	4,221
Rosario, Argentina	9,654	8,606	8,015	17,023	13,203	18,169	656	13,915	16,206	15,991	11,798	8,166	7,531	16,864	15,251	11,115	17,160	9,278	15,958	6,950
Roseau, Dominica	14,220	3,313	4,060	11,848	10,498	16,490	5,980	10,631	18,443	11,870	16,516	3,045	5,763	17,737	14,531	8,334	16,234	8,817	18,613	4,830
Rostock, East Germany	18,240	5,725	8,508	6,810	3,422	9,698	12,493	3,185	11,079	4,386	15,940	6,521	4,926	10,400	7,253	2,521	8,677	5,544	11,119	5,161
Rostov-na-Donu, USSR	16,186	7,746	10,424	6,267	1,592	8,006	13,852	1,115	9,145	2,661	13,930	8,539	5,854	8,499	5,178	2,365	6,704	5,165	9,147	6,396
Rotterdam, Netherlands	18,757	5,350	8,191	7,266	3,800	10,263	11,941	3,661	11,635	4,949	16,484	6,143	4,498	10,959	7,723	2,537	9,224	5,430	11,668	4,665
Rouyn, Canada	15,415	834	2,552	7,901	9,369	12,585	9,773	8,976	14,585	9,177	16,376	1,012	7,565	13,966	12,842	8,035	13,139	10,212	14,863	6,870
Sacramento, California	12,123	4,296	2,360	7,108	11,909	11,143	10,480	11,216	12,809	10,404	12,831	3,851	11,094	12,487	13,964	11,229	12,758	13,733	13,147	10,344
Saginaw, Michigan	14,810	1,141	1,904	8,256	10,020	12,924	9,356	9,632	14,905	9,795	15,975	766	7,921	14,330	13,483	8,636	13,657	10,684	15,204	7,168
Saint Denis, Reunion	9,624	14,387	17,149	11,481	6,113	8,223	10,770	6,805	7,000	7,749	8,492	15,042	7,867	7,089	4,459	6,971	6,241	4,898	6,682	8,741
Saint George's, Grenada	13,906	3,658	4,221	12,193	10,741	16,846	5,620	10,910	18,804	12,201	16,212	3,356	5,836	18,098	14,753	8,547	16,555	8,867	18,964	4,901
Saint John, Canada	16,132	313	3,219	8,507	8,843	13,141	9,309	8,577	15,124	9,116	17,396	1,094	6,534	14,449	12,595	7,276	13,331	9,247	15,358	5,828
Saint John's, Antigua	14,350	3,108	3,920	11,643	10,419	16,288	6,179	10,526	18,249	11,720	16,634	2,846	5,799	17,548	14,461	8,277	16,088	8,859	18,435	4,869
Saint John's, Canada	17,168	1,369	4,274	8,431	7,845	12,887	9,605	7,638	14,778	8,385	18,264	2,131	5,668	14,070	11,695	6,223	12,714	8,254	14,955	5,049
Saint Louis, Missouri	14,067	1,813	1,155	8,531	10,767	13,124	9,026	10,363	15,046	10,428	15,351	1,178	8,472	14,542	14,154	9,373	14,102	11,322	15,367	7,672
Saint Paul, Minnesota	14,312	1,845	1,678	7,794	10,335	12,407	9,768	9,858	14,351	9,772	15,277	1,497	8,644	13,825	13,521	9,135	13,362	11,345	14,666	7,907
Saint Peter Port, UK	19,222	4,985	7,867	7,719	4,229	10,829	11,392	4,168	12,196	5,515	17,028	5,769	4,112	11,522	8,210	2,690	9,777	5,380	12,223	4,194
Saipan (Susupe)	7,568	12,507	11,573	4,628	10,114	2,693	16,233	9,420	3,663	7,332	5,837	12,555	15,796	3,555	7,333	12,218	4,868	13,819	3,994	16,298
Salalah, Oman	13,029	11,159	13,972	8,086	2,055	7,055	13,452	2,624	7,171	3,826	11,124	11,951	6,676	6,757	2,563	3,810	4,985	4,119	7,014	7,564
Salem, Oregon	12,579	4,149	2,744	6,477	11,243	10,674	11,083	10,527	12,438	9,687	13,045	3,836	10,901	12,053	13,264	10,694	12,170	13,352	12,773	10,216
Salt Lake City, Utah	12,854	3,443	1,727	7,398	11,448	11,688	10,141	10,832	13,459	10,280	13,677	2,995	10,240	13,073	13,976	10,552	13,114	12,926	13,795	9,485
Salta, Argentina	10,223	7,664	7,002	16,009	13,253	18,896	1,573	13,845	17,111	15,753	12,460	7,188	7,483	17,802	15,935	11,040	18,107	9,613	16,894	6,783
Salto, Uruguay	9,924	8,468	8,016	16,953	12,899	18,341	904	13,608	16,348	15,683	12,046	8,059	7,223	16,980	15,054	10,806	17,080	8,996	16,083	6,644
Salvador, Brazil	12,548	7,090	7,943	15,173	10,155	17,755	3,691	10,799	16,883	12,839	14,406	7,007	4,403	16,983	13,124	7,986	15,603	6,597	16,551	3,795
Salzburg, Austria	18,070	6,101	8,953	7,383	3,073	9,927	12,132	3,030	11,144	4,558	15,906	6,892	4,360	10,493	7,054	1,840	8,703	4,843	11,146	4,692
Samsun, Turkey	16,098	8,009	10,788	6,948	1,134	8,353	13,335	1,143	9,312	3,126	13,952	8,805	5,339	8,702	5,078	1,769	6,862	4,456	9,277	5,957
San Antonio, Texas	12,813	3,023	120	9,101	12,040	13,432	8,429	11,617	15,154	11,536	14,266	2,282	9,380	14,807	15,294	10,612	14,814	12,353	15,492	8,518
San Cristobal, Venezuela	12,846	4,057	3,645	12,364	11,942	16,986	5,248	12,051	18,792	13,150	15,112	3,519	7,043	18,403	15,976	9,775	17,497	10,044	19,128	6,111
San Diego, California	11,877	4,263	1,861	7,866	12,443	11,819	9,731	11,802	13,404	11,113	12,857	3,695	10,988	13,132	14,713	11,546	13,497	13,806	13,741	10,177
San Francisco, California	12,002	4,408	2,417	7,131	12,014	11,119	10,469	11,314	12,763	10,476	12,716	3,954	11,206	12,454	14,014	11,348	12,762	13,853	13,101	10,451
San Jose, Costa Rica	12,224	4,052	2,662	11,691	12,766	16,034	5,841	12,706	17,528	13,387	14,344	3,336	8,283	17,355	16,772	10,738	17,338	11,318	17,846	7,348
San Juan, Argentina	9,424	8,400	7,506	16,556	13,830	18,099	978	14,490	16,329	16,483	11,654	7,885	8,094	17,033	15,998	11,676	17,746	9,992	16,132	7,448
San Juan, Puerto Rico	14,186	2,886	3,450	11,399	10,687	16,078	6,342	10,734	18,078	11,797	16,420	2,520	6,243	17,419	14,734	8,596	16,156	9,306	18,329	5,317
San Luis Potosi, Mexico	12,055	3,768	957	9,695	12,856	13,797	7,854	12,455	15,329	12,357	13,658	2,992	9,795	15,101	16,115	11,337	15,400	12,833	15,662	8,895
San Marino, San Marino	17,928	6,283	9,166	7,782	2,995	10,144	11,835	3,088	11,259	4,778	15,915	7,065	3,980	10,628	7,030	1,468	8,809	4,423	11,238	4,366
San Miguel de Tucuman, Argen.	10,038	7,890	7,206	16,225	13,331	18,712	1,348	13,949	16,888	15,896	12,263	7,413	7,568	17,577	15,864	11,138	17,946	9,619	16,669	6,890
San Salvador, El Salvador	12,183	3,863	2,035	11,086	12,854	15,347	6,444	12,685	16,852	13,120	14,172	3,093	8,756	16,659	16,719	10,954	16,789	11,815	17,177	7,825
Sanaa, Yemen	13,576	10,632	13,526	8,840	1,994	8,129	12,485	2,828	8,195	4,505	11,878	11,403	5,635	7,809	3,610	3,069	6,055	3,056	8,020	6,537
Santa Cruz, Bolivia	11,011	6,910	6,484	15,360	12,689	19,602	2,320	13,210	17,894	15,024	13,261	6,473	6,933	18,561	15,795	10,434	18,230	9,294	17,654	6,174
Santa Cruz, Tenerife	17,527	5,017	7,729	10,292	5,743	13,219	8,842	6,076	14,208	7,851	17,912	5,611	1,947	13,627	9,702	3,500	11,773	4,543	14,131	1,661
Santa Fe, New Mexico	12,816	3,205	972	8,153	11,767	12,448	9,382	11,227	14,192	10,867	13,927	2,613	9,905	13,826	14,606	10,632	13,871	12,745	14,529	9,096
Santa Rosa, Argentina	9,138	8,980	8,188	17,239	13,658	17,716	292	14,396	15,807	16,493	11,300	8,499	8,028	16,490	15,410	11,606	17,060	9,665	15,580	7,464
Santa Rosalia, Mexico	11,726	4,218	1,456	8,624	12,856	12,540	8,971	12,286	14,054	11,762	12,966	3,549	10,746	13,826	15,422	11,724	14,255	13,692	14,388	9,888
Santarem, Brazil	12,946	5,391	5,829	13,906	11,010	18,378	4,091	11,418	19,005	13,116	15,186	5,136	5,424	18,853	14,654	8,729	17,032	8,187	18,678	4,561
Santiago del Estero, Argentina	9,991	8,003	7,346	16,360	13,290	18,654	1,227	13,926	16,786	15,900	12,203	7,535	7,536	17,469	15,746	11,112	17,805	9,538	16,559	6,874
Santiago, Chile	9,137	8,612	7,608	16,638	14,093	17,812	954	14,767	16,081	16,774	11,373	8,077	8,370	16,790	16,088	11,954	17,651	10,210	15,897	7,734
Santo Domingo, Dominican Rep.	13,930	2,866	3,101	11,299	10,998	15,981	6,380	11,006	17,971	11,968	16,120	2,397	6,642	17,369	15,037	8,941	16,292	9,705	18,263	5,716
Sao Paulo de Olivenca, Brazil	12,049	5,291	4,839	13,661	12,375	18,251	3,961	12,662	19,208	14,076	14,360	4,800	6,953	19,590	16,189	10,110	18,385	9,758	19,172	6,063
Sao Paulo, Brazil	11,168	7,875	8,080	16,329	11,503	18,475	2,244	12,194	16,736	14,266	13,156	7,623	5,805	17,159	14,053	9,389	16,409	7,711	16,410	5,238
Sao Tome, Sao Tome & Principe	14,109	8,913	11,385	12,366	5,372	12,549	8,227	6,214	12,257	8,345	13,996	9,416	2,121	12,034	7,934	3,787	10,419	1,391	12,005	2,952
Sapporo, Japan	10,666	9,847	9,901	1,508	8,074	3,548	17,981	7,211	5,489	5,096	8,930	10,119	13,097	4,965	6,909	9,765	5,073	12,245	5,798	13,359
Sarajevo, Yugoslavia	17,508	6,690	9,553	7,551	2,532	9,705	12,214	2,612	10,785	4,352	15,441	7,477	4,281	10,159	6,558	1,309	8,335	4,373	10,762	4,737
Saratov, USSR	15,963	7,728	10,273	5,601	2,028	7,531	14,439	1,277	8,806	2,161	13,660	8,510	6,466	8,135	5,131	3,022	6,397	5,818	8,839	6,963
Saskatoon, Canada	14,000	2,838	2,533	6,596	10,127	11,157	10,943	9,507	13,083	9,040	14,450	2,709	9,489	12,575	12,781	9,335	12,255	11,911	13,402	8,843
Schefferville, Canada	16,472	1,185	3,666	7,465	8,254	12,082	10,371	7,872	14,062	8,187	17,007	1,874	6,891	13,387	11,786	6,972	12,316	9,319	14,297	6,307
Seattle, Washington	12,836	4,012	2,848	6,288	10,942	10,570	11,259	10,228	12,375	9,410	13,223	3,756	10,719	11,963	13,011	10,413	11,997	13,105	12,709	10,060
Sendai, Japan	10,164	10,357	10,290	2,033	8,308	3,128	18,008	7,471	5,025	5,335	8,398	10,607	13,511	4,534	6,803	10,103	4,810	12,443	5,342	13,822
Seoul, South Korea	10,511	10,781	11,175	2,258	7,258	2,427	19,202	6,470	4,427	4,333	8,496	11,160	12,739	3,822	5,590	9,206	3,720	11,322	4,707	13,204
Sept-Iles, Canada	16,340	703	3,422	7,968	8,533	12,594	9,859	8,207	14,575	8,633	17,238	1,456	6,705	13,900	12,178	7,107	12,806	9,280	14,809	6,061
Sevastopol, USSR	16,481	7,592	10,359	6,796	1,562	8,518	13,296	1,418	9,579	3,201	14,291	8,388	5,295	8,950	5,445	1,813	7,130	4,691	9,562	5,850
Seville, Spain	18,415	5,298	8,183	9,072	4,548	11,851	10,211	4,775	12,950	6,481	17,368	6,014	2,747	12,333	8,584	2,447	10,500	4,430	12,910	2,853
Shanghai, China	10,087	11,576	12,058	3,104	7,080	1,630	19,101	6,375	3,618	4,304	7,953	11,992	12,762	2,981	4,905	9,178	2,871	10,975	3,880	13,346
Sheffield, United Kingdom	19,140	4,914	7,756	7,289	4,234	10,516	11,754	4,070	11,961	5,256	16,833	5,707	4,553	11,275	8,136	2,923	9,572	5,734	12,010	4,624
Shenyang, China	11,066	10,376	10,979	1,942	6,798	2,827	19,422	5,985	4,818	3,844	9,028	10,799	12,204	4,176	5,453	8,691	3,817	10,912	5,078	12,651
Shiraz, Iran	14,146	9,949	12,672	7,061	876	7,036	14,054	1,221	7,622	2,724	12,052	10,745	6,490	7,085	3,172	3,106	5,225	4,535	7,537	7,281
Sibiu, Romania	17,201	6,934	9,752	7,122	2,212	9,206	12,713	2,167	10,321	3,849	15,037	7,728	4,762	9,685	6,178	1,559	7,872	4,623	10,308	5,237
Singapore	8,234	14,915	15,836	6,841	7,126	2,485	15,628	6,943	1,473	5,769	5,950	15,512	12,355	1,295	3,172	9,353	1,427	9,483	1,299	13,265
Sioux Falls, South Dakota	13,987	2,157	1,474	7,795	10,624	12,359	9,749	10,126	14,272	9,962	14,960	1,742	8,952	13,777	13,719	9,458	13,424	11,671	14,594	8,203
Skelleftea, Sweden	17,478	5,698	8,221	5,552	3,841	8,818	13,518	3,285	10,413	3,770	15,252	6,471	6,199	9,706	7,163	3,631	8,137	6,705	10,511	6,375
Skopje, Yugoslavia	17,189	7,012	9,875	7,593	2,230	9,536	12,306	2,376	10,550	4,213	15,153	7,799	4,326	9,936	6,268	1,104	8,100	4,179	10,514	4,842
Socotra Island (Tamrida)	12,669	11,536	14,381	8,486	2,492	7,158	13,160	3,100	7,106	4,268	10,845	12,323	6,720	6,744	2,558	4,079	5,034	4,003	6,925	7,629
Sofia, Bulgaria	17,099	7,087	9,938	7,447	2,114	9,369	12,474	2,220	10,396	4,044	15,025	7,877	4,491	9,778	6,141	1,207	7,945	4,271	10,365	5,011
Songkhla, Thailand	8,976	14,219	15,423	6,372	6,450	2,404	16,118	6,225	2,033	5,024	6,685	14,850	11,839	1,607	2,601	8,702	725	9,079	1,942	12,726
Sorong, Indonesia	6,440	14,768	13,918	6,387	9,773	2,243	15,409	9,346	1,605	7,594	4,261	14,904	15,355	1,923	6,119	12,054	3,756	12,542	1,874	16,226
South Georgia Island	8,176	11,363	11,037	19,607	12,411	15,377	2,587	13,319	13,389	15,300	9,833	11,043	7,896	13,967	12,745	11,010	14,186	8,258	13,096	7,741
South Pole	4,385	14,692	13,353	16,260	13,695	11,817	5,716	14,476	9,860	15,190	5,843	14,353	11,403	10,541	11,439	13,559	11,523	10,487	9,633	11,492
South Sandwich Islands	7,927	12,003	11,783	19,076	12,055	14,673	3,333	12,972	12,699	14,836	9,405	11,724	7,985	13,257	12,054	10,867	13,438	7,977	12,399	7,944
Split, Yugoslavia	17,630	6,577	9,449	7,663	2,674	9,867	12,063	2,774	10,948	4,511	15,592	7,362	4,146	10,323	6,708	1,305	8,498	4,343	10,923	4,586
Spokane, Washington	13,095	3,650	2,560	6,519	10,850	10,876	11,017	10,170	12,707	9,467	13,566	3,386	10,380	12,276	13,125	10,204	12,236	12,827	13,038	9,707
Spoleto, Italy	17,841	6,371	9,259	7,887	2,949	10,178	11,771	3,082	11,258	4,819	15,876	7,151	3,887	10,635	6,992	1,344	8,807	4,290	11,230	4,296
Springbok, South Africa	10,588	12,072	13,904	14,546	7,514	12,108	7,224	8,429	10,810	10,227	10,686	12,387	5,445	10,963	7,952	6,842	10,067	3,767	10,480	6,037
Springfield, Illinois	14,187	1,715	1,287	8,432	10,633	13,040	9,131	10,225	14,974	10,290	15,431	1,121	8,413	14,458	14,015	9,256	13,984	11,242	15,292	7,625
Springfield, Massachusetts	15,499	336	2,600	8,709	9,473	13,387	9,011	9,192	15,387	9,650	16,887	462	6,985	14,747	13,189	7,901	13,781	9,785	15,652	6,229
Srinagar, India	12,958	10,616	12,838	5,321	2,809	4,960	16,177	2,314	5,880	1,414	10,669	11,367	8,580	5,251	2,354	5,053	3,433	6,660	5,875	9,314
Stanley, Falkland Islands	7,916	10,701	9,883	18,843	13,640	16,088	1,484	14,519	14,111	16,604	9,895	10,244	8,590	14,772	14,161	11,979	15,375	9,459	13,864	8,242
Stara Zagora, Bulgaria	16,920	7,256	10,097	7,367	1,928	9,194	12,620	2,031	10,206	3,884	14,834	8,047	4,625	9,591	5,950	1,244	7,756	4,273	10,173	5,167
Stockholm, Sweden	17,803	5,807	8,468	6,123	3,481	9,144	13,111	3,057	10,627	3,921	15,504	6,597	5,613	9,933	7,068	3,029	8,276	6,097	10,695	5,837
Stornoway, United Kingdom	19,049	4,496	7,277	6,905	4,656	10,427	11,930	4,381	12,002	5,313	16,860	5,292	5,058	11,300	8,436	3,520	9,677	6,354	12,085	5,042
Strasbourg, France	18,471	5,714	8,577	7,493	3,473	10,242	11,877	3,424	11,511	4,884	16,298	6,503	4,242	10,852	7,455	2,101	9,076	5,008	11,522	4,494
Stuttgart, West Germany	18,375	5,799	8,656	7,426	3,378	10,139	11,972	3,318	11,404	4,779	16,192	6,589	4,307	10,745	7,353	2,062	8,969	5,001	11,414	4,576
Subic, Philippines	8,543	13,372	13,572	4,858	7,814	174	17,352	7,299	1,827	5,474	6,308	13,759	13,563	1,249	4,607	10,073	2,130	11,142	2,109	14,331
Suchow, China	10,579	11,274	11,979	2,937	6,582	2,007	19,509	5,862	3,935	3,782	8,416	11,738	12,243	3,366	4,635	8,661	2,826	10,530	4,171	12,821
Sucre, Bolivia	10,781	7,029	6,471	15,418	12,951	19,342	2,201	13,471	17,746	15,273	13,043	6,563	7,194	18,439	16,012	10,696	18,407	9,531	17,531	6,436
Sudbury, Canada	15,189	911	2,309	8,027	9,612	12,710	9,622	9,220	14,705	9,405	16,230	877	7,700	14,101	13,080	8,260	13,330	10,391	14,991	6,982
Suez, Egypt	15,577	8,635	11,520	8,168	1,186	8,936	12,409	1,948	9,534	4,089	13,744	9,414	4,591	9,012	4,993	1,215	7,154	3,192	9,432	5,357
Sundsvall, Sweden	17,744	5,634	8,235	5,873	3,752	9,071	13,238	3,268	10,623	3,943	15,484	6,416	5,877	9,921	7,225	3,371	8,312	6,438	10,709	6,058

Distances in Kilometers

	Auckland Islands, New Zealand	Augusta, Maine	Austin, Texas	Ayan, USSR	Baghdad, Iraq	Baguio, Philippines	Bahia Blanca, Argentina	Baku, USSR	Balikpapan, Indonesia	Balkhash, USSR	Ballarat, Australia	Baltimore, Maryland	Bamako, Mali	Bandar Seri Begawan, Brunei	Bangalore, India	Banghazi, Libya	Bangkok, Thailand	Bangui, Central African Rep.	Banjarmasin, Indonesia	Banjul, Gambia
Surabaya, Indonesia	6,891	15,890	15,945	7,435	8,483	2,757	14,890	8,309	800	7,055	4,595	16,336	13,524	1,363	4,487	10,691	2,687	10,538	478	14,454
Suva, Fiji	3,761	13,123	10,444	9,080	15,159	7,399	11,102	14,544	6,974	12,472	3,993	12,538	19,104	7,415	11,585	17,355	9,247	17,354	7,137	18,345
Sverdlovsk, USSR	15,322	7,879	10,137	4,495	2,889	6,683	15,451	1,990	8,156	1,488	13,027	8,621	7,540	7,457	5,079	4,135	5,853	6,890	8,239	7,986
Svobodnyy, USSR	11,878	9,260	9,909	865	6,785	3,938	18,381	5,901	5,936	3,827	9,973	9,674	11,749	5,300	6,206	8,407	4,855	10,966	6,201	12,055
Sydney, Australia	2,242	16,336	13,630	10,085	13,388	6,444	11,259	13,229	5,081	11,737	779	15,753	16,859	5,740	9,346	15,499	7,523	14,141	5,083	17,432
Sydney, Canada	16,584	780	3,684	8,505	8,414	13,076	9,402	8,178	15,025	8,818	17,818	1,543	6,126	14,331	12,219	6,813	13,096	8,796	15,233	5,451
Syktyvkar, USSR	16,020	7,111	9,428	4,663	3,181	7,348	14,894	2,369	8,892	2,259	13,748	7,859	7,157	8,187	5,816	3,957	6,616	6,898	8,987	7,511
Szeged, Hungary	17,504	6,652	9,487	7,249	2,507	9,484	12,479	2,479	10,626	4,119	15,350	7,445	4,571	9,987	6,488	1,571	8,179	4,645	10,617	5,004
Szombathely, Hungary	17,795	6,366	9,208	7,301	2,799	9,702	12,314	2,757	10,886	4,332	15,632	7,158	4,470	10,240	6,777	1,704	8,442	4,754	10,883	4,851
Tabriz, Iran	15,194	8,855	11,569	6,690	552	7,544	13,953	399	8,408	2,535	13,027	9,651	6,044	7,812	4,160	2,473	5,962	4,674	8,364	6,734
Tacheng, China	13,429	9,568	11,473	3,860	3,564	4,828	17,064	2,744	6,266	607	11,134	10,261	9,068	5,564	3,777	5,497	4,010	7,721	6,357	9,643
Tahiti (Papeete)	5,345	10,569	7,669	10,570	17,773	10,538	8,583	16,867	10,357	14,813	6,797	9,835	15,875	10,762	14,957	18,090	12,549	18,072	10,526	14,982
Taipei, Taiwan	9,481	12,239	12,597	3,738	7,386	960	18,449	6,746	2,957	4,748	7,314	12,639	13,138	2,339	4,789	9,560	2,529	11,106	3,228	13,790
Taiyuan, China	11,135	10,900	11,833	2,803	6,055	2,505	19,563	5,313	4,357	3,215	8,948	11,410	11,680	3,661	4,424	8,102	2,925	10,065	4,566	12,247
Tallahasee, Florida	13,876	1,998	1,293	9,578	11,128	14,180	7,990	10,854	16,091	11,200	15,558	1,205	8,006	15,598	14,826	9,462	15,088	10,996	16,416	7,142
Tallinn, USSR	17,425	6,141	8,757	5,883	3,241	8,776	13,455	2,747	10,247	3,540	15,124	6,927	5,853	9,553	6,722	3,054	7,895	6,129	10,314	6,126
Tamanrasset, Algeria	16,502	7,131	9,944	10,169	3,974	11,736	9,805	4,579	12,255	6,656	15,733	7,791	1,818	11,779	7,647	1,769	9,932	2,476	12,115	2,553
Tampa, Florida	13,814	2,138	1,509	9,901	11,214	14,509	7,673	10,983	16,419	11,421	15,604	1,368	7,850	15,927	14,995	9,471	15,380	10,868	16,744	6,969
Tampere, Finland	17,446	5,982	8,562	5,740	3,462	8,775	13,500	2,939	10,295	3,603	15,164	6,763	5,994	9,595	6,876	3,277	7,970	6,353	10,374	6,231
Tanami, Australia	4,686	16,765	15,146	8,507	10,792	4,148	13,388	10,607	2,499	9,207	2,380	16,713	15,455	3,191	6,775	12,979	4,914	12,392	2,469	16,375
Tangier, Morocco	18,243	5,401	8,275	9,233	4,565	11,942	10,089	4,828	12,995	6,575	17,317	6,106	2,574	12,389	8,589	2,418	10,547	4,287	12,945	2,701
Tarawa (Betio)	5,797	12,035	9,875	6,852	13,408	5,971	13,061	12,643	6,251	10,505	5,246	11,662	18,453	6,457	10,565	15,337	8,082	17,114	6,513	18,069
Tashkent, USSR	13,859	9,679	11,965	5,081	2,366	5,612	15,933	1,640	6,722	761	11,558	10,435	8,036	6,066	3,243	4,454	4,297	6,488	6,742	8,696
Tbilisi, USSR	15,533	8,467	11,158	6,469	927	7,650	13,992	453	8,628	2,465	13,325	9,261	6,016	8,010	4,496	2,432	6,177	4,886	8,603	6,654
Tegucigalpa, Honduras	12,356	3,736	2,092	11,133	12,677	15,464	6,397	12,529	17,027	13,029	14,369	2,978	8,538	16,800	16,580	10,754	16,811	11,597	17,356	7,607
Tehran, Iran	14,668	9,353	12,028	6,603	694	7,100	14,260	542	7,898	2,318	12,497	10,148	6,448	7,313	3,631	2,916	5,457	4,834	7,846	7,174
Tel Aviv, Israel	15,583	8,623	11,487	7,857	916	8,678	12,712	1,637	9,342	3,778	13,661	9,409	4,859	8,801	4,843	1,387	6,940	3,501	9,253	5,602
Telegraph Creek, Canada	13,306	4,382	3,993	5,062	9,884	9,510	12,469	9,112	11,410	8,150	13,173	4,369	10,646	10,925	11,722	9,675	10,779	12,592	11,732	10,134
Teresina, Brazil	13,223	6,100	7,033	14,307	10,065	17,824	4,212	10,601	17,665	12,515	15,235	6,016	4,322	17,570	13,439	7,812	15,902	6,907	17,354	3,551
Ternate, Indonesia	6,798	14,727	14,137	6,246	9,313	1,882	15,693	8,900	1,199	7,185	4,571	14,941	14,890	1,458	5,655	11,594	3,290	12,100	1,498	15,758
The Valley, Anguilla	14,353	2,979	3,757	11,514	10,459	16,171	6,284	10,543	18,150	11,689	16,621	2,694	5,923	17,459	14,506	8,338	16,059	8,986	18,357	4,995
Thessaloniki, Greece	17,004	7,200	10,067	7,656	2,069	9,467	12,324	2,273	10,434	4,173	14,997	7,986	4,327	9,830	6,114	979	7,986	4,041	10,391	4,878
Thimphu, Bhutan	11,462	11,781	13,558	4,980	4,365	3,407	17,147	3,911	4,312	2,498	9,155	12,473	10,117	3,664	2,047	6,633	1,894	7,931	4,334	10,882
Thunder Bay, Canada	14,769	1,566	2,136	7,581	9,854	12,240	10,013	9,382	14,216	9,346	15,613	1,434	8,329	13,650	13,084	8,674	13,053	10,953	14,518	7,629
Tientsin, China	11,051	10,736	11,515	2,464	6,397	2,539	19,950	5,627	4,475	3,502	8,919	11,208	11,952	3,800	4,849	8,390	3,255	10,449	4,710	12,475
Tijuana, Mexico	11,870	4,263	1,847	7,890	12,458	11,841	9,708	11,820	13,423	11,135	12,858	3,691	10,984	13,153	14,736	11,554	13,520	13,806	13,760	10,171
Tiksi, USSR	13,885	7,064	8,144	1,745	6,329	6,156	16,290	5,421	8,136	3,899	12,164	7,544	10,123	7,472	7,344	7,271	6,700	10,242	8,380	10,221
Timbuktu, Mali	16,130	6,884	9,529	11,125	5,076	12,835	8,703	5,693	13,232	7,763	16,045	7,452	704	12,802	8,624	2,882	10,976	2,728	13,064	1,503
Tindouf, Algeria	17,415	5,710	8,481	10,155	5,032	12,649	9,259	5,438	13,489	7,322	17,193	6,341	1,666	12,939	8,940	2,761	11,078	3,834	13,392	1,805
Tirane, Albania	17,264	6,945	9,819	7,728	2,341	9,690	12,151	2,521	10,691	4,369	15,269	7,729	4,174	10,081	6,386	1,023	8,242	4,097	10,652	4,686
Tokyo, Japan	9,921	10,657	10,555	2,310	8,366	2,860	18,044	7,549	4,737	5,408	8,121	10,904	13,677	4,258	6,675	10,224	4,610	12,468	5,055	14,027
Toledo, Spain	18,599	5,316	8,216	8,755	4,340	11,550	10,531	4,518	12,693	6,180	17,233	6,053	3,041	12,065	8,386	2,327	10,243	4,541	12,666	3,176
Topeka, Kansas	13,736	2,223	991	8,277	10,998	12,805	9,262	10,539	14,686	10,448	14,910	1,644	8,938	14,219	14,202	9,714	13,924	11,761	15,014	8,146
Toronto, Canada	15,129	773	2,199	8,367	9,753	13,049	9,285	9,401	15,045	9,670	16,343	538	7,554	14,440	13,312	8,308	13,647	10,317	15,331	6,807
Toulouse, France	18,640	5,526	8,429	8,202	3,872	10,942	11,144	3,971	12,131	5,573	16,799	6,293	3,548	11,490	7,914	2,069	9,683	4,663	12,118	3,760
Tours, France	18,920	5,292	8,182	7,839	3,965	10,764	11,397	3,959	12,055	5,415	16,835	6,072	3,935	11,394	7,974	2,361	9,620	5,067	12,065	4,091
Townsville, Australia	3,895	15,637	13,471	8,427	12,288	4,877	12,912	11,949	3,824	10,240	2,048	15,315	17,242	4,395	8,383	14,551	6,250	14,181	3,921	18,145
Trenton, New Jersey	15,231	613	2,354	8,853	9,749	13,537	8,834	9,469	15,537	9,909	16,687	190	7,144	14,913	13,463	8,159	14,010	9,985	15,813	6,365
Tripoli, Lebanon	15,680	8,510	11,351	7,584	801	8,527	12,934	1,402	9,267	3,542	13,686	9,300	5,032	8,707	4,825	1,491	6,846	3,777	9,192	5,747
Tripoli, Libya	17,075	7,028	9,932	8,833	2,904	10,582	11,114	3,357	11,366	5,364	15,556	7,773	3,111	10,811	6,858	653	8,950	3,208	11,280	3,709
Tristan da Cunha (Edinburgh)	10,287	10,709	11,600	16,935	9,765	14,877	4,346	10,664	13,283	12,707	11,390	10,712	5,520	13,594	10,861	8,364	12,941	5,593	12,945	5,608
Trondheim, Norway	18,001	5,265	7,878	5,978	4,087	9,351	12,996	3,629	10,944	4,284	15,787	6,048	5,819	10,238	7,593	3,546	8,654	6,586	11,039	5,935
Trujillo, Peru	10,982	5,881	4,696	13,747	13,601	17,709	3,782	13,839	17,984	15,061	13,278	5,254	8,185	18,451	17,422	11,345	19,380	10,924	18,052	7,302
Truk Island (Moen)	6,590	12,923	11,520	5,568	11,156	3,543	15,148	10,486	4,008	8,411	5,049	12,831	16,876	4,097	8,138	13,293	5,653	14,685	4,309	17,373
Truro, Canada	16,330	528	3,429	8,544	8,661	13,152	9,313	8,414	15,121	9,008	17,609	1,289	6,326	14,436	12,446	7,068	13,259	9,030	15,343	5,630
Tsingtao, China	10,620	11,045	11,658	2,633	6,774	2,177	19,639	6,023	4,151	3,911	8,504	11,483	12,371	3,497	4,972	8,801	3,166	10,778	4,402	12,907
Tsitsihar, China	11,603	9,759	10,450	1,401	6,634	3,446	18,922	5,779	5,434	3,655	9,612	10,192	11,835	4,787	5,740	8,394	4,316	10,801	5,691	12,216
Tubuai Island (Mataura)	4,843	11,016	8,110	11,122	18,269	10,719	8,193	17,401	10,338	15,291	6,461	10,260	15,797	10,801	14,947	18,604	12,633	17,549	10,477	14,958
Tucson, Arizona	12,218	3,800	1,277	8,234	12,304	12,329	9,329	11,729	13,962	11,231	13,341	3,184	10,459	13,665	14,921	11,228	13,920	13,332	14,300	9,631
Tulsa, Oklahoma	13,507	2,388	674	8,551	11,279	13,040	8,982	10,838	14,889	10,770	14,785	1,732	9,008	14,449	14,523	9,938	14,219	11,886	15,220	8,192
Tunis, Tunisia	17,581	6,552	9,458	8,572	3,129	10,653	11,184	3,450	11,578	5,343	15,952	7,306	3,233	10,991	7,152	1,045	9,139	3,693	11,517	3,713
Tura, USSR	13,970	7,933	9,404	2,225	5,086	5,537	16,938	4,168	7,400	2,480	11,918	8,519	9,604	6,696	5,960	6,373	5,611	9,168	7,593	9,896
Turin, Italy	18,322	5,890	8,778	7,847	3,394	10,431	11,619	3,454	11,609	5,061	16,306	6,670	3,887	10,968	7,424	1,792	9,162	4,632	11,598	4,187
Uberlandia, Brazil	11,579	7,337	7,596	15,806	11,391	18,824	2,576	12,028	17,251	14,043	13,625	7,087	5,635	17,629	14,225	9,214	16,658	7,764	16,921	4,993
Ufa, USSR	15,493	7,894	10,255	4,870	2,541	6,911	15,151	1,658	8,308	1,600	13,185	8,652	7,203	7,618	5,002	3,770	5,957	6,515	8,372	7,675
Ujungpandang, Indonesia	6,675	15,571	15,238	7,036	8,942	2,385	15,149	8,674	511	7,219	4,367	15,895	14,201	1,212	5,039	11,194	2,951	11,258	570	15,120
Ulaanbaatar, Mongolia	12,320	9,781	11,003	2,315	5,369	3,712	18,667	4,533	5,536	2,394	10,153	10,339	10,740	4,831	4,729	7,220	3,834	9,525	5,727	11,220
Ulan-Ude, USSR	12,640	9,348	10,578	2,043	5,385	4,094	18,353	4,515	5,951	2,414	10,511	9,901	10,585	5,249	5,080	7,118	4,272	9,563	6,149	11,013
Uliastay, Mongolia	12,775	9,721	11,241	2,942	4,618	4,101	18,055	3,790	5,770	1,648	10,538	10,341	10,056	5,056	4,249	6,508	3,786	8,772	5,919	10,580
Uranium City, Canada	14,395	3,097	3,356	5,864	9,412	10,493	11,695	8,751	12,459	8,207	14,472	3,178	9,391	11,907	11,944	8,808	11,467	11,557	12,765	8,841
Urumqi, China	12,940	9,990	11,784	3,779	3,888	4,345	17,450	3,118	5,781	1,041	10,646	10,667	9,489	5,077	3,547	5,907	3,552	7,996	5,877	10,090
Ushuaia, Argentina	7,259	10,985	9,840	18,348	14,381	15,678	1,844	15,271	13,770	17,317	9,323	10,456	9,356	14,462	14,505	12,756	15,348	10,202	13,555	8,984
Vaduz, Liechtenstein	18,294	5,903	8,773	7,572	3,304	10,197	11,880	3,295	11,418	4,829	16,169	6,691	4,162	10,767	7,305	1,897	8,976	4,822	11,418	4,458
Valencia, Spain	18,398	5,612	8,515	8,683	4,032	11,317	10,712	4,235	12,411	5,948	16,916	6,355	3,065	11,791	8,076	2,013	9,961	4,331	12,376	3,293
Valladolid, Spain	18,801	5,173	8,077	8,589	4,381	11,481	10,640	4,514	12,678	6,115	17,301	5,919	3,230	12,039	8,428	2,438	10,230	4,736	12,663	3,330
Valletta, Malta	17,239	6,927	9,832	8,481	2,746	10,339	11,420	3,116	11,206	5,074	15,550	7,687	3,425	10,630	6,757	662	8,773	3,517	11,137	3,980
Valparaiso, Chile	9,127	8,567	7,528	16,551	14,163	17,799	1,053	14,827	16,105	16,816	11,372	8,024	8,431	16,816	16,190	12,013	17,729	10,297	15,927	7,785
Vancouver, Canada	12,934	4,025	3,000	6,111	10,773	10,425	11,431	10,051	12,250	9,218	13,247	3,808	10,687	11,824	12,819	10,285	11,824	13,015	12,582	10,048
Varna, Bulgaria	16,803	7,346	10,167	7,188	1,807	8,991	12,826	1,844	10,020	3,677	14,678	8,140	4,830	9,400	5,801	1,412	7,570	4,402	9,993	5,374
Venice, Italy	18,017	6,187	9,060	7,637	3,044	10,082	11,932	3,084	11,240	4,712	15,940	6,973	4,114	10,600	7,063	1,623	8,792	4,592	11,228	4,474
Veracruz, Mexico	12,150	3,707	1,238	10,218	12,847	14,392	7,319	12,532	15,925	12,640	13,913	2,912	9,369	15,702	16,380	11,167	15,935	12,428	16,256	8,455
Verona, Italy	18,112	6,096	8,973	7,687	3,147	10,178	11,849	3,190	11,344	4,807	16,047	6,881	4,056	10,703	7,168	1,674	8,896	4,612	11,333	4,398
Victoria, Canada	12,854	4,064	2,964	6,167	10,865	10,456	11,379	10,143	12,268	9,302	13,192	3,829	10,746	11,850	12,896	10,373	11,876	13,093	12,601	10,099
Victoria, Seychelles	11,070	13,115	16,021	9,985	4,360	7,535	12,038	5,015	6,832	6,014	9,561	13,864	7,272	6,697	3,127	5,527	5,377	4,219	6,567	8,204
Vienna, Austria	17,849	6,294	9,128	7,219	2,860	9,680	12,360	2,785	10,892	4,310	15,660	7,087	4,542	10,240	6,819	1,813	8,451	4,863	10,895	4,906
Vientiane, Laos	9,821	13,065	14,242	5,200	6,007	1,922	17,285	5,601	2,639	4,077	7,511	13,666	11,692	1,974	2,738	8,287	517	9,236	2,698	12,503
Villahermosa, Mexico	12,276	3,632	1,447	10,488	12,749	14,731	7,043	12,488	16,289	12,727	14,122	2,838	9,062	16,055	16,427	10,987	16,202	12,124	16,621	8,142
Vilnius, USSR	17,387	6,443	9,139	6,213	2,802	8,868	13,261	2,415	10,221	3,534	15,083	7,236	5,493	9,543	6,462	2,541	7,820	5,612	10,261	5,838
Visby, Sweden	17,821	5,902	8,594	6,269	3,340	9,193	13,031	2,955	10,636	3,927	15,512	6,695	5,465	9,946	6,990	2,839	8,264	5,908	10,693	5,713
Vitoria, Brazil	11,714	7,758	8,311	15,991	10,765	17,976	2,931	11,463	16,571	13,548	13,585	7,602	5,084	16,853	13,398	8,664	15,815	6,992	16,234	4,552
Vladivostok, USSR	10,921	10,082	10,434	1,547	7,385	3,150	18,732	6,542	5,145	4,408	9,017	10,437	12,610	4,556	6,158	9,174	4,428	11,535	5,432	12,970
Volgograd, USSR	15,942	7,875	10,480	5,905	1,710	7,645	14,240	1,024	8,837	2,286	13,657	8,663	6,244	8,179	5,002	2,749	6,406	5,496	8,852	6,779
Vologda, USSR	16,564	6,862	9,348	5,303	2,895	7,925	14,264	2,208	9,388	2,685	14,263	7,633	6,499	8,692	6,000	3,356	7,048	6,354	9,459	6,856
Vorkuta, USSR	15,557	7,013	9,055	3,810	4,005	6,940	15,439	3,140	8,646	2,389	13,391	7,709	7,949	7,933	6,136	4,850	6,532	7,801	8,785	8,231
Wake Island	7,748	10,938	9,469	4,756	11,563	4,878	14,866	10,729	5,898	8,593	6,729	10,789	16,425	5,826	9,452	13,302	7,047	15,658	6,221	16,367
Wallis Island	4,432	12,334	9,670	8,808	15,360	7,693	11,069	14,638	7,495	12,509	4,781	11,754	18,751	7,874	12,073	17,354	9,660	18,130	7,686	17,825
Walvis Bay, Namibia	11,401	11,323	13,328	14,158	6,993	12,327	7,342	7,911	11,223	9,823	11,475	11,682	4,640	11,295	7,939	6,123	10,205	3,054	10,903	5,262
Warsaw, Poland	17,635	6,343	9,104	6,661	2,817	9,218	12,881	2,559	10,519	3,863	15,355	7,139	5,100	9,850	6,627	2,238	8,099	5,313	10,544	5,447
Washington, D.C.	14,986	853	2,120	8,932	9,992	13,615	8,725	9,706	15,610	10,114	16,471	57	7,328	15,005	13,690	8,401	14,172	10,195	15,897	6,534
Watson Lake, Canada	13,581	4,225	4,040	5,013	9,627	9,529	12,516	8,864	11,455	7,956	13,398	4,261	10,395	10,947	11,567	9,393	10,719	12,311	11,773	9,901

Distances in Kilometers	Auckland Islands, New Zealand	Augusta, Maine	Austin, Texas	Ayan, USSR	Baghdad, Iraq	Baguio, Philippines	Bahia Blanca, Argentina	Baku, USSR	Balikpapan, Indonesia	Balkhash, USSR	Ballarat, Australia	Baltimore, Maryland	Bamako, Mali	Bandar Seri Begawan, Brunei	Bangalore, India	Banghazi, Libya	Bangkok, Thailand	Bangui, Central African Rep.	Banjarmasin, Indonesia	Banjul, Gambia
Weimar, East Germany	18,277	5,825	8,651	7,136	3,319	9,893	12,244	3,181	11,202	4,545	16,027	6,619	4,597	10,535	7,239	2,215	8,778	5,212	11,224	4,863
Wellington, New Zealand	1,221	14,867	11,965	11,367	15,598	8,479	9,430	15,457	7,290	13,846	2,681	14,125	16,818	7,927	11,551	17,556	9,739	15,282	7,307	16,730
West Berlin, West Germany	18,152	5,877	8,675	6,917	3,264	9,692	12,461	3,065	11,029	4,355	15,872	6,672	4,817	10,356	7,132	2,329	8,613	5,359	11,058	5,086
Wewak, Papua New Guinea	5,645	14,435	12,950	6,670	11,087	3,362	14,626	10,587	2,991	8,696	3,765	14,350	16,754	3,325	7,524	13,356	5,131	13,936	3,228	17,596
Whangarei, New Zealand	1,776	14,605	11,733	10,770	15,471	8,081	9,925	15,203	7,038	13,447	2,722	13,901	17,439	7,642	11,449	17,621	9,485	15,742	7,089	17,311
Whitehorse, Canada	13,406	4,562	4,354	4,697	9,579	9,186	12,833	8,789	11,108	7,780	13,114	4,611	10,636	10,603	11,339	9,469	10,411	12,435	11,426	10,171
Wichita, Kansas	13,527	2,418	824	8,341	11,203	12,828	9,192	10,737	14,681	10,612	14,724	1,812	9,105	14,237	14,370	9,922	14,014	11,949	15,011	8,303
Willemstad, Curacao	13,447	3,570	3,585	12,004	11,361	16,682	5,670	11,454	18,654	12,561	15,710	3,104	6,612	18,078	15,404	9,216	16,921	9,650	18,963	5,677
Wiluna, Australia	4,724	17,848	16,306	9,357	10,398	4,759	12,769	10,382	2,825	9,315	2,530	17,913	14,424	3,530	6,359	12,429	4,947	11,389	2,644	15,308
Windhoek, Namibia	11,355	11,490	13,557	13,971	6,836	12,058	7,585	7,754	10,963	9,634	11,337	11,871	4,762	11,029	7,680	6,062	9,938	2,986	10,644	5,420
Windsor, Canada	14,799	1,096	1,873	8,401	10,066	13,070	9,214	9,696	15,051	9,898	16,032	635	7,846	14,475	13,572	8,640	13,788	10,635	15,350	7,081
Winnipeg, Canada	14,386	2,155	2,177	7,166	10,039	11,784	10,394	9,498	13,736	9,263	15,062	2,000	8,884	13,201	13,022	9,024	12,748	11,434	14,047	8,203
Winston-Salem, North Carolina	14,572	1,273	1,751	9,129	10,412	13,795	8,487	10,124	15,771	10,495	16,124	477	7,605	15,203	14,097	8,804	14,487	10,520	16,074	6,783
Wroclaw, Poland	17,884	6,172	8,970	6,919	2,968	9,519	12,580	2,788	10,804	4,161	15,626	6,968	4,827	10,139	6,851	2,123	8,378	5,182	10,824	5,155
Wuhan, China	10,360	11,701	12,470	3,425	6,481	1,696	19,051	5,817	3,537	3,808	8,147	12,188	12,214	2,846	4,237	8,631	2,337	10,313	3,754	12,852
Wyndham, Australia	5,198	16,394	15,085	8,025	10,375	3,621	13,911	10,149	1,998	8,698	2,898	16,443	15,292	2,678	6,392	12,595	4,434	12,239	1,999	16,226
Xi'an, China	10,972	11,302	12,335	3,318	5,865	2,297	19,089	5,181	4,022	3,159	8,735	11,841	11,577	3,312	3,942	7,992	2,425	9,772	4,204	12,205
Xining, China	11,555	11,002	12,326	3,490	5,171	2,909	18,600	4,483	4,476	2,482	9,285	11,598	10,880	3,763	3,561	7,295	2,536	9,116	4,619	11,515
Yakutsk, USSR	12,911	8,091	8,934	785	6,554	5,112	17,290	5,637	7,103	3,785	11,109	8,531	10,949	6,454	6,820	7,842	5,837	10,658	7,359	11,137
Yanji, China	10,968	10,158	10,581	1,630	7,218	3,054	18,924	6,382	5,054	4,245	9,025	10,532	12,495	4,449	5,964	9,036	4,260	11,360	5,335	12,879
Yaounde, Cameroon	14,317	9,020	11,632	11,776	4,723	11,920	8,887	5,576	11,728	7,699	13,910	9,583	2,359	11,465	7,326	3,252	9,807	785	11,491	3,267
Yap Island (Colonia)	7,210	13,418	12,606	5,206	9,780	2,048	16,190	9,189	2,646	7,209	5,244	13,525	15,552	2,612	6,609	11,998	4,125	13,158	2,974	16,247
Yaraka, Australia	3,448	16,281	13,968	9,029	12,341	5,232	12,451	12,100	3,924	10,534	1,405	15,905	16,799	4,561	8,343	14,549	6,375	13,786	3,960	17,635
Yarmouth, Canada	16,050	298	3,162	8,661	8,944	13,299	9,151	8,694	15,282	9,262	17,411	1,010	6,501	14,608	12,722	7,341	13,486	9,251	15,517	5,777
Yellowknife, Canada	14,330	3,481	3,772	5,417	9,217	10,048	12,139	8,518	12,017	7,862	14,213	3,607	9,588	11,462	11,577	8,764	11,031	11,602	12,321	9,085
Yerevan, USSR	15,456	8,578	11,289	6,611	758	7,682	13,907	455	8,611	2,556	13,271	9,373	5,949	8,003	4,418	2,364	6,162	4,743	8,577	6,608
Yinchuan, China	11,488	10,828	11,997	3,077	5,512	2,814	19,032	4,783	4,532	2,709	9,255	11,389	11,165	3,820	4,002	7,582	2,798	9,515	4,706	11,759
Yogyakarta, Indonesia	6,997	15,958	16,178	7,564	8,311	2,906	14,800	8,168	1,017	6,988	4,715	16,448	13,276	1,491	4,293	10,499	2,620	10,280	680	14,208
York, United Kingdom	19,104	4,920	7,755	7,232	4,224	10,468	11,806	4,047	11,921	5,214	16,794	5,714	4,608	11,233	8,115	2,945	9,535	5,771	11,972	4,681
Yumen, China	12,053	10,601	12,080	3,458	4,755	3,411	18,299	4,032	4,951	1,991	9,778	11,224	10,422	4,239	3,571	6,837	2,903	8,775	5,081	11,037
Yutian, China	12,737	10,568	12,571	4,670	3,400	4,442	16,866	2,786	5,567	1,236	10,428	11,286	9,153	4,900	2,678	5,588	3,172	7,343	5,605	9,846
Yuzhno-Sakhalinsk, USSR	11,055	9,404	9,531	1,103	7,956	3,953	17,791	7,072	5,911	4,994	9,360	9,687	12,792	5,371	7,083	9,542	5,373	12,137	6,217	13,006
Zagreb, Yugoslavia	17,777	6,410	9,267	7,462	2,784	9,805	12,184	2,799	10,952	4,437	15,663	7,199	4,316	10,314	6,790	1,559	8,505	4,598	10,941	4,714
Zahedan, Iran	13,553	10,423	13,013	6,565	1,619	6,229	14,765	1,569	6,846	2,279	11,382	11,214	7,297	6,293	2,515	3,892	4,432	5,246	6,775	8,087
Zamboanga, Philippines	7,671	14,210	14,106	5,675	8,448	1,065	16,454	8,012	1,076	6,290	5,416	14,544	14,101	821	4,918	10,728	2,477	11,445	1,404	14,936
Zanzibar, Tanzania	11,953	11,994	14,794	11,128	4,408	9,300	10,573	5,269	8,637	6,849	10,876	12,656	5,619	8,507	4,746	4,697	7,125	2,569	8,365	6,534
Zaragoza, Spain	18,617	5,458	8,364	8,477	4,062	11,221	10,855	4,208	12,379	5,850	16,982	6,212	3,286	11,746	8,109	2,137	9,929	4,561	12,357	3,474
Zashiversk, USSR	13,252	7,314	8,071	1,247	6,963	5,887	16,456	6,048	7,887	4,388	11,643	7,717	10,810	7,257	7,626	7,976	6,699	10,931	8,156	10,875
Zhengzhou, China	10,787	11,242	12,093	3,043	6,261	2,146	19,444	5,550	4,002	3,485	8,592	11,739	11,939	3,310	4,357	8,354	2,676	10,203	4,217	12,534
Zurich, Switzerland	18,383	5,816	8,687	7,592	3,394	10,264	11,826	3,381	11,498	4,898	16,256	6,603	4,141	10,845	7,394	1,963	9,058	4,865	11,501	4,418

Distances in Kilometers

	Barcelona, Spain	Bari, Italy	Barranquilla, Colombia	Basse-Terre, Guadeloupe	Basseterre, St. Kitts & Nevis	Bata, Equatorial Guinea	Baton Rouge, Louisiana	Bear Lake, Canada	Bechar, Algeria	Beira, Mozambique	Beirut, Lebanon	Belau Islands (Koror)	Belem, Brazil	Belfast, United Kingdom	Belgrade, Yugoslavia	Belmopan, Belize	Belo Horizonte, Brazil	Bergen, Norway	Bern, Switzerland	Bhopal, India
Bari, Italy	1,228	0	9,354	7,911	7,904	4,409	9,182	8,691	2,004	7,002	1,830	11,713	8,080	2,249	507	10,019	9,216	2,283	988	5,917
Barranquilla, Colombia	8,128	9,354	0	1,519	1,479	9,384	2,742	6,712	7,737	12,469	11,153	16,204	3,222	7,661	9,571	1,661	4,809	8,409	8,540	15,167
Basse-Terre, Guadeloupe	6,683	7,911	1,519	0	178	7,980	3,397	7,009	6,231	11,279	9,683	16,876	2,418	6,392	8,167	2,889	4,425	7,216	7,151	13,804
Basseterre, St. Kitts & Nevis	6,676	7,904	1,479	178	0	8,094	3,231	6,831	6,258	11,422	9,688	16,698	2,596	6,335	8,146	2,772	4,600	7,146	7,125	13,778
Bata, Equatorial Guinea	4,444	4,409	9,384	7,980	8,094	0	10,958	12,479	3,527	3,644	4,445	13,816	6,492	6,018	4,878	10,865	6,333	6,503	4,998	7,654
Baton Rouge, Louisiana	8,104	9,182	2,742	3,397	3,231	10,958	0	3,988	8,223	14,515	10,956	13,603	5,738	7,017	9,188	1,486	7,526	7,456	8,207	13,938
Bear Lake, Canada	8,180	8,691	6,712	7,009	6,831	12,479	3,988	0	8,963	15,692	9,884	9,868	9,423	6,609	8,399	5,376	11,398	6,413	7,812	10,908
Bechar, Algeria	1,153	2,004	7,737	6,231	6,258	3,527	8,223	8,963	0	6,934	3,524	13,716	6,098	2,569	2,457	8,714	7,235	3,246	1,890	7,756
Beira, Mozambique	7,570	7,002	12,469	11,279	11,422	3,644	14,515	15,692	6,934	0	5,945	11,294	9,266	9,113	7,308	14,106	8,163	9,282	7,888	6,638
Beirut, Lebanon	3,036	1,830	11,153	9,683	9,688	4,445	10,956	9,884	3,524	5,945	0	10,385	9,547	3,944	1,769	11,846	10,299	3,665	2,763	4,233
Belau Islands (Koror)	12,758	11,713	16,204	16,876	16,698	13,816	13,603	9,868	13,716	11,294	10,385	0	19,282	12,222	11,275	14,548	18,602	11,290	12,059	6,337
Belem, Brazil	6,965	8,080	3,222	2,418	2,596	6,492	5,738	9,423	6,098	9,266	9,547	19,282	0	7,330	8,484	4,881	2,102	8,258	7,628	13,718
Belfast, United Kingdom	1,585	2,249	7,661	6,392	6,335	6,018	7,017	6,609	2,569	9,113	3,944	12,222	7,330	0	2,175	8,009	9,012	933	1,270	7,510
Belgrade, Yugoslavia	1,536	507	9,571	8,167	8,146	4,878	9,188	8,399	2,457	7,308	1,769	11,275	8,484	2,175	0	10,120	9,689	2,002	1,037	5,638
Belmopan, Belize	8,846	10,019	1,661	2,889	2,772	10,865	1,486	5,376	8,714	14,106	11,846	14,548	4,881	8,009	10,120	0	6,397	8,583	9,094	15,284
Belo Horizonte, Brazil	8,286	9,216	4,809	4,425	4,600	6,333	7,526	11,398	7,235	8,163	10,299	18,602	2,102	9,012	9,689	6,397	0	9,940	9,016	13,986
Bergen, Norway	2,125	2,283	8,409	7,216	7,146	6,503	7,456	6,413	3,246	9,282	3,665	11,290	8,258	933	2,002	8,583	9,940	0	1,505	6,803
Bern, Switzerland	746	988	8,540	7,151	7,125	4,998	8,207	7,812	1,890	7,888	2,763	12,059	7,628	1,270	1,037	9,094	9,016	1,505	0	6,654
Bhopal, India	7,138	5,917	15,167	13,804	13,778	7,654	13,938	10,908	7,756	6,638	4,233	6,337	13,718	7,510	5,638	15,284	13,986	6,803	6,654	0
Bhubaneswar, India	8,036	6,821	15,961	14,667	14,628	8,493	14,387	10,998	8,684	7,107	5,163	5,429	14,649	8,310	6,520	15,821	14,800	7,552	7,522	935
Bialystok, Poland	2,042	1,416	9,564	8,262	8,215	5,818	8,794	7,579	3,141	8,162	2,353	10,747	8,923	1,907	943	9,878	10,328	1,349	1,315	5,605
Big Trout Lake, Canada	6,566	7,391	4,941	4,862	4,688	10,482	2,599	2,343	7,102	14,034	8,970	12,058	7,224	5,145	7,249	4,065	9,283	5,308	6,414	11,378
Bilbao, Spain	472	1,650	7,711	6,288	6,272	4,757	7,632	7,797	1,293	7,985	3,476	12,958	6,715	1,279	1,883	8,387	8,153	1,987	916	7,519
Billings, Montana	8,162	8,959	5,007	5,444	5,268	12,004	2,271	1,723	8,685	15,605	10,471	11,450	7,858	6,721	8,788	3,657	9,753	6,812	7,990	12,336
Birmingham, Alabama	7,569	8,647	2,780	3,177	3,003	10,509	535	3,956	7,702	14,105	10,425	13,739	5,575	6,489	8,658	1,816	7,461	6,945	7,674	13,504
Birmingham, United Kingdom	1,271	1,898	7,888	6,579	6,531	5,715	7,342	6,950	2,316	8,765	3,615	12,205	7,384	356	1,847	8,300	8,990	987	915	7,278
Bismarck, North Dakota	7,636	8,483	4,664	4,959	4,781	11,405	1,995	2,072	8,115	15,018	10,058	11,920	7,377	6,235	8,342	3,462	9,328	6,394	7,504	12,242
Bissau, Guinea Bissau	3,703	4,530	6,451	4,999	5,103	3,007	7,983	10,189	2,583	6,545	5,711	16,093	3,925	4,816	5,013	7,871	4,690	5,654	4,449	9,802
Biysk, USSR	6,083	5,163	12,711	11,773	11,674	8,868	10,801	7,595	7,127	9,379	4,430	6,704	12,918	5,603	4,678	12,253	14,360	4,688	5,365	3,320
Blagoveshchensk, USSR	8,547	7,847	12,882	12,609	12,453	11,777	10,287	6,369	9,679	11,866	7,334	4,803	14,581	7,604	7,342	11,729	16,555	6,692	7,801	5,247
Blantyre, Malawi	7,175	6,574	12,445	11,189	11,324	3,395	14,338	15,264	6,581	448	5,497	11,248	9,276	8,705	6,871	14,054	8,302	8,851	7,471	6,322
Bloemfontein, South Africa	8,189	7,839	11,661	10,667	10,828	3,850	14,050	16,327	7,364	1,355	7,044	12,188	8,446	9,773	8,211	13,321	7,078	10,102	8,630	7,983
Bluefields, Nicaragua	8,803	10,012	983	2,418	2,339	10,357	2,182	6,139	8,529	13,437	11,837	15,289	4,174	8,144	10,174	793	5,612	8,805	9,137	15,603
Boa Vista do Rio Branco, Braz.	7,563	8,762	1,802	1,463	1,617	7,834	4,434	8,293	6,887	10,704	10,411	18,003	1,437	7,558	9,095	3,461	3,111	8,437	8,133	14,644
Bodo, Norway	2,977	2,915	8,851	7,779	7,690	7,270	7,553	5,937	4,115	9,807	3,959	10,488	9,022	1,776	2,526	8,806	10,776	887	2,303	6,489
Bogota, Colombia	8,529	9,756	710	1,848	1,874	9,319	3,378	7,365	8,030	12,173	11,515	16,596	2,925	8,195	10,014	2,127	4,271	8,982	8,996	15,650
Boise, Idaho	8,763	9,513	5,375	5,956	5,781	12,659	2,647	1,591	9,321	16,250	10,958	10,973	8,350	7,291	9,314	3,901	10,172	7,321	8,556	12,471
Bologna, Italy	822	585	8,858	7,443	7,426	4,726	8,602	8,181	1,853	7,513	2,384	11,945	7,786	1,672	728	9,463	9,072	1,814	405	6,363
Bolzano, Italy	931	743	8,840	7,447	7,423	4,952	8,490	7,974	2,023	7,719	2,472	11,830	7,878	1,513	735	9,391	9,215	1,593	301	6,357
Bombay, India	7,044	5,816	15,165	13,723	13,719	7,122	14,278	11,474	7,549	5,966	4,045	6,775	13,354	7,590	5,596	15,532	13,434	6,957	6,630	672
Bonn, West Germany	1,106	1,305	8,502	7,160	7,121	5,424	7,992	7,417	2,258	8,277	2,966	11,843	7,802	979	1,197	8,951	9,281	1,080	425	6,668
Bora Bora (Vaitape)	16,297	17,068	8,999	10,514	10,452	17,428	8,309	8,388	16,523	15,920	17,952	8,537	11,386	14,870	16,783	7,847	11,170	14,800	16,133	14,855
Bordeaux, France	444	1,476	7,915	6,506	6,485	4,869	7,742	7,736	1,474	8,013	3,305	12,697	6,973	1,151	1,661	8,544	8,412	1,774	665	7,298
Boston, Massachusetts	5,881	6,955	3,496	3,055	2,889	9,117	2,228	4,205	6,076	12,762	8,740	13,926	5,356	4,814	6,975	3,258	7,437	5,330	5,984	12,053
Bouvet Island	10,618	10,667	10,242	9,923	10,100	6,266	12,983	16,918	9,549	4,672	10,259	13,222	7,519	12,116	11,120	11,688	5,520	12,732	11,239	11,105
Brasilia, Brazil	8,161	9,165	4,188	3,829	4,004	6,635	6,903	10,783	7,163	8,698	10,387	19,036	1,587	8,749	9,618	5,784	622	9,682	8,872	14,266
Braunschweig, West Germany	1,365	1,327	8,734	7,412	7,368	5,589	8,127	7,364	2,517	8,329	2,854	11,550	8,092	1,122	1,105	9,130	9,573	959	635	6,433
Brazzaville, Congo	5,228	5,030	10,117	8,765	8,888	915	11,833	13,347	4,383	2,735	4,727	13,300	7,095	6,812	5,463	11,654	6,639	7,221	5,722	7,394
Bremerhaven, West Germany	1,435	1,513	8,597	7,293	7,245	5,732	7,945	7,179	2,586	8,513	3,044	11,581	8,041	956	1,298	8,962	9,566	786	742	6,570
Brest, France	940	1,864	7,652	6,290	6,255	5,336	7,319	7,243	1,873	8,510	3,670	12,651	6,962	695	1,945	8,182	8,523	1,475	912	7,526
Brest, USSR	2,018	1,326	9,627	8,311	8,267	5,720	8,894	7,699	3,099	8,042	2,234	10,754	8,928	1,978	842	9,965	10,303	1,457	1,306	5,540
Bridgetown, Barbados	6,712	7,935	1,670	394	572	7,735	3,767	7,402	6,183	10,963	9,675	17,270	2,025	6,531	8,219	3,166	4,036	7,381	7,219	13,850
Brisbane, Australia	16,952	15,767	14,719	16,232	16,197	15,192	13,848	11,925	17,591	11,550	14,089	4,340	16,070	16,549	15,416	13,624	14,453	15,618	16,324	9,873
Bristol, United Kingdom	1,177	1,876	7,829	6,506	6,461	5,618	7,336	7,023	2,203	8,699	3,622	12,316	7,279	415	1,859	8,271	8,873	1,109	888	7,338
Brno, Czechoslovakia	1,424	897	9,197	7,837	7,804	5,288	8,671	7,843	2,510	7,857	2,305	11,341	8,355	1,656	567	9,652	9,709	1,437	728	5,978
Broken Hill, Australia	16,271	15,043	15,644	17,088	17,100	13,970	15,061	12,993	16,602	10,331	13,254	4,410	16,165	16,419	14,788	14,736	14,237	15,520	15,796	9,150
Brussels, Belgium	1,063	1,446	8,307	6,967	6,927	5,453	7,811	7,320	2,202	8,380	3,146	11,994	7,639	809	1,378	8,759	9,148	1,065	492	6,863
Bucharest, Romania	1,975	840	10,014	8,613	8,592	4,985	9,566	8,568	2,843	7,172	1,423	10,875	8,905	2,550	446	10,534	10,053	2,248	1,474	5,192
Budapest, Hungary	1,503	729	9,407	8,030	8,001	5,138	8,927	8,083	2,526	7,623	2,044	11,258	8,465	1,910	316	9,894	9,755	1,687	882	5,777
Buenos Aires, Argentina	10,447	11,378	5,332	5,611	5,762	8,152	7,978	11,947	9,401	9,077	12,370	16,711	3,813	11,084	11,854	6,573	2,166	12,017	11,172	15,581
Buffalo, New York	6,425	7,457	3,558	3,398	3,223	9,760	1,761	3,682	6,681	13,404	9,209	13,506	5,777	5,266	7,440	2,997	7,821	5,697	6,474	12,289
Bujumbura, Burundi	5,672	5,091	11,637	10,238	10,350	2,258	13,117	13,779	5,117	1,915	4,175	11,734	8,660	7,202	5,413	13,121	8,142	7,373	5,972	5,986
Bulawayo, Zimbabwe	7,338	6,892	11,819	10,651	10,797	3,187	13,928	15,517	6,606	657	6,024	11,951	8,612	8,910	7,242	13,460	7,520	9,171	7,725	7,150
Burlington, Vermont	5,938	6,979	3,715	3,337	3,169	9,308	2,216	3,921	6,194	12,949	8,741	13,635	5,648	4,801	6,973	3,357	7,727	5,267	5,999	11,932
Cabinda, Angola	5,296	5,191	9,808	8,482	8,610	862	11,609	13,337	4,389	2,919	5,007	13,654	6,755	6,875	5,642	11,366	6,269	7,335	5,831	7,763
Cagliari, Italy	636	692	8,727	7,265	7,265	4,139	8,737	8,647	1,329	7,066	2,426	12,395	7,388	2,048	1,129	9,478	8,561	2,369	866	6,586
Cairns, Australia	15,611	14,470	15,611	17,099	17,006	14,940	14,092	11,394	16,410	11,452	12,894	2,956	17,452	15,177	14,084	14,246	15,797	14,244	14,954	8,662
Cairo, Egypt	2,897	1,789	10,914	9,417	9,437	3,860	10,965	10,226	3,194	5,533	585	10,868	9,107	4,021	1,893	11,739	9,762	3,883	2,774	4,625
Calais, France	1,064	1,589	8,132	6,796	6,755	5,493	7,644	7,225	2,173	8,481	3,312	12,123	7,497	661	1,547	8,585	9,034	1,073	609	7,037
Calcutta, India	8,084	6,883	15,873	14,651	14,599	8,768	14,141	10,674	8,786	7,468	5,282	5,213	14,815	8,265	6,556	15,597	15,093	7,476	7,539	1,128
Calgary, Canada	8,053	8,740	5,695	6,040	5,862	12,123	2,970	1,018	8,691	15,611	10,137	10,839	8,458	6,543	8,519	4,372	10,401	6,519	7,798	11,696
Cali, Colombia	8,816	10,044	854	2,132	2,149	9,592	3,364	7,347	8,327	12,385	11,808	16,390	3,166	8,453	10,295	2,030	4,401	9,226	9,274	15,927
Camaguey, Cuba	7,666	8,860	1,198	1,807	1,659	9,701	1,664	5,558	7,489	13,080	10,689	15,267	4,079	6,942	8,997	1,233	5,879	7,595	7,962	14,394
Cambridge Bay, Canada	6,403	6,890	6,810	6,620	6,452	10,771	4,392	1,801	7,244	13,891	8,137	10,396	8,892	4,823	6,605	5,876	10,988	4,614	6,013	9,758
Cambridge, United Kingdom	1,213	1,768	8,023	6,707	6,661	5,653	7,482	7,046	2,294	8,662	3,475	12,123	7,478	482	1,706	8,441	9,057	966	792	7,144
Campbellton, Canada	5,324	6,347	4,174	3,578	3,424	8,848	2,854	4,084	5,633	12,471	8,104	13,535	5,756	4,163	6,335	3,965	7,857	4,636	5,365	11,338
Campo Grande, Brazil	9,006	10,030	4,120	4,106	4,268	7,433	6,859	10,830	8,027	9,214	11,263	18,263	2,205	9,515	10,478	5,595	1,118	10,446	9,707	15,085
Canakkale, Turkey	2,043	815	10,166	8,726	8,718	4,563	9,891	9,034	2,737	6,698	1,066	10,998	8,836	2,883	711	10,791	9,854	2,680	1,699	5,105
Canberra, Australia	17,080	15,852	14,838	16,279	16,291	14,426	14,440	12,841	17,345	10,789	14,058	4,968	15,542	17,138	15,595	13,989	13,737	16,216	16,597	9,958
Cancun, Mexico	8,403	9,565	1,700	2,698	2,560	10,618	1,124	5,099	8,315	13,976	11,389	14,529	4,857	7,534	9,654	484	6,508	8,100	8,632	14,804
Canton, China	9,952	8,864	16,133	15,644	15,512	11,315	13,532	9,571	10,863	9,744	7,531	2,865	16,912	9,642	8,442	14,946	17,645	8,730	9,285	3,661
Canton Atoll, Phoenix Islands	15,691	15,678	10,830	12,238	12,126	19,835	9,264	7,696	16,636	16,188	15,568	6,085	13,699	14,124	15,202	9,355	13,795	13,616	15,119	12,277
Cape Town, South Africa	8,502	8,311	10,981	10,114	10,282	4,062	13,509	16,390	7,570	2,254	7,715	12,868	7,802	10,080	8,724	12,630	6,290	10,520	9,020	8,888
Cape York, Australia	14,865	13,748	15,965	17,351	17,221	14,720	14,087	11,032	15,720	11,412	12,234	2,183	18,208	14,405	13,347	14,464	16,546	13,473	14,195	8,018
Caracas, Venezuela	7,504	8,731	864	828	879	8,522	3,345	7,207	7,016	11,630	10,492	16,940	2,432	7,211	8,993	2,477	4,203	8,024	7,978	14,631
Cardiff, United Kingdom	1,197	1,916	7,787	6,466	6,421	5,635	7,293	6,996	2,210	8,729	3,664	12,343	7,248	389	1,902	8,228	8,850	1,122	928	7,380
Carlisle, United Kingdom	1,548	2,111	7,857	6,586	6,530	5,992	7,193	6,686	2,586	9,023	3,774	12,065	7,499	196	2,007	8,197	9,156	786	1,147	7,314
Carnarvon, Australia	13,540	12,329	18,236	18,916	19,090	11,504	17,509	14,085	13,776	8,019	10,505	4,219	16,521	14,118	12,152	17,554	14,492	13,379	13,188	6,607
Carson City, Nevada	9,330	10,089	5,425	6,160	5,990	13,156	2,774	1,965	9,865	16,777	11,527	10,837	8,511	7,865	9,889	3,860	10,232	7,895	9,131	12,868
Casablanca, Morocco	1,219	2,310	7,239	5,742	5,761	3,954	7,673	8,526	550	7,435	3,962	13,970	5,778	2,333	2,707	8,176	7,070	3,121	1,948	8,177
Casper, Wyoming	8,254	9,102	4,665	5,163	4,987	11,958	1,924	2,086	8,715	15,590	10,665	11,749	7,567	6,855	8,957	3,290	9,431	7,001	8,124	12,675
Castries, Saint Lucia	6,761	7,987	1,537	233	407	7,890	3,586	7,234	6,265	11,137	9,742	17,100	2,198	6,529	8,258	3,000	4,193	7,367	7,251	13,895
Catbalogan, Philippines	11,712	10,621	16,692	16,850	16,685	12,707	13,957	10,026	12,618	10,456	9,237	1,162	18,658	11,334	10,203	15,124	18,526	10,409	11,038	5,176
Cayenne, French Guiana	6,738	7,913	2,564	1,598	1,776	6,906	4,953	8,598	5,994	9,909	9,511	18,459	826	6,896	8,273	4,199	2,898	7,805	7,348	13,741
Cayman Islands (Georgetown)	8,093	9,284	1,160	2,116	1,985	10,069	1,582	5,560	7,916	13,387	11,114	15,111	4,266	7,347	9,415	817	5,959	7,982	8,382	14,768
Cazombo, Angola	6,270	5,904	11,089	9,811	9,945	2,102	12,976	14,445	5,509	1,555	5,241	12,530	7,954	7,850	6,287	12,682	7,166	8,164	6,693	7,099
Cebu, Philippines	11,763	10,656	16,885	17,032	16,868	12,620	14,151	10,220	12,646	10,300	9,236	1,210	18,727	11,430	10,246	15,311	18,339	10,509	11,100	5,136
Cedar Rapids, Iowa	7,373	8,340	3,808	4,059	3,881	10,817	1,280	2,969	7,702	14,461	10,031	12,821	6,477	6,106	8,271	2,758	8,429	6,417	7,352	12,695
Changsha, China	9,531	8,480	15,590	15,081	14,949	11,211	13,029	9,092	10,484	9,935	7,245	3,234	16,456	9,143	8,041	14,465	17,512	8,224	8,845	3,598
Channel-Port-aux-Basques, Can.	4,800	5,856	4,313	3,509	3,373	8,287	3,326	4,563	5,074	11,907	7,638	13,778	5,529	3,716	5,874	4,319	7,627	4,267	4,883	11,042

Distances in Kilometers	Barcelona, Spain	Bari, Italy	Barranquilla, Colombia	Basse-Terre, Guadeloupe	Basseterre, St. Kitts & Nevis	Bata, Equatorial Guinea	Baton Rouge, Louisiana	Bear Lake, Canada	Bechar, Algeria	Beira, Mozambique	Beirut, Lebanon	Belau Islands (Koror)	Belem, Brazil	Belfast, United Kingdom	Belgrade, Yugoslavia	Belmopan, Belize	Belo Horizonte, Brazil	Bergen, Norway	Bern, Switzerland	Bhopal, India
Charleston, South Carolina	7,090	8,210	2,468	2,610	2,433	9,874	1,098	4,423	7,148	13,460	10,016	14,275	5,026	6,115	8,261	1,939	6,975	6,651	7,253	13,356
Charleston, West Virginia	6,882	7,945	3,107	3,150	2,972	10,007	1,239	3,858	7,064	13,640	9,717	13,726	5,565	5,779	7,949	2,444	7,557	6,238	6,969	12,844
Charlotte, North Carolina	7,011	8,106	2,753	2,856	2,678	9,950	1,102	4,161	7,124	13,562	9,898	14,022	5,274	5,976	8,136	2,145	7,241	6,477	7,140	13,140
Charlotte Amalie, U.S.V.I.	6,790	8,016	1,339	428	262	8,335	2,970	6,601	6,416	11,680	9,814	16,464	2,836	6,378	8,241	2,532	4,814	7,167	7,213	13,857
Charlottetown, Canada	5,133	6,194	4,061	3,355	3,209	8,550	2,988	4,417	5,385	12,182	7,975	13,821	5,475	4,051	6,211	3,996	7,577	4,587	5,221	11,346
Chatham, Canada	5,273	6,315	4,092	3,459	3,307	8,741	2,873	4,221	5,554	12,370	8,084	13,670	5,622	4,148	6,316	3,940	7,723	4,648	5,336	11,377
Chatham Islands (Waitangi)	19,703	18,880	11,789	13,209	13,226	15,300	11,944	12,036	18,550	12,255	17,050	7,512	12,822	18,645	18,663	11,142	11,451	18,172	19,558	13,028
Chengdu, China	8,716	7,630	15,394	14,624	14,513	10,324	13,052	9,248	9,631	9,270	6,346	4,088	15,678	8,448	7,206	14,532	16,607	7,548	8,051	2,764
Chesterfield Inlet, Canada	6,130	6,793	5,948	5,713	5,546	10,343	3,658	2,146	6,842	13,700	8,231	11,296	7,990	4,601	6,580	5,125	10,084	4,586	5,852	10,346
Cheyenne, Wyoming	8,289	9,168	4,448	4,978	4,804	11,903	1,706	2,312	8,711	15,544	10,762	11,945	7,375	6,919	9,039	3,064	9,223	7,099	8,185	12,871
Chiang Mai, Thailand	9,200	8,015	16,644	15,623	15,545	9,871	14,450	10,659	9,946	8,199	6,455	4,043	15,995	9,247	7,665	15,934	16,144	8,407	8,620	2,296
Chibougamau, Canada	5,778	6,742	4,317	3,931	3,766	9,431	2,580	3,498	6,163	13,042	8,452	13,078	6,206	4,515	6,686	3,852	8,297	4,884	5,754	11,435
Chicago, Illinois	7,101	8,094	3,646	3,790	3,612	10,486	1,308	3,219	7,397	14,130	9,811	13,085	6,207	5,873	8,045	2,737	8,187	6,228	7,107	12,630
Chiclayo, Peru	9,844	11,064	2,041	3,214	3,262	9,999	4,292	8,192	9,246	12,305	12,768	16,245	3,531	9,596	11,355	2,829	4,142	10,392	10,352	16,981
Chihuahua, Mexico	9,322	10,310	3,796	4,749	4,594	12,413	1,457	3,476	9,566	15,965	11,996	12,414	6,976	8,077	10,240	2,173	8,570	8,361	9,322	14,250
Chongquing, China	8,978	7,898	15,515	14,811	14,695	10,575	13,103	9,250	9,900	9,431	6,618	3,818	15,936	8,684	7,471	14,574	16,871	7,779	8,309	2,985
Christchurch, New Zealand	19,201	18,016	12,662	14,077	14,096	15,089	12,733	12,421	18,609	11,777	16,189	6,820	13,567	18,771	17,799	11,992	12,054	17,947	18,798	12,162
Christiansted, U.S.V.I.	6,811	8,038	1,321	371	216	8,307	3,027	6,670	6,424	11,638	9,832	16,532	2,770	6,417	8,268	2,559	4,744	7,211	7,241	13,889
Christmas Is. [Indian Ocean]	11,900	10,673	19,946	18,537	18,565	10,703	17,201	13,229	12,309	7,630	8,880	3,754	16,878	12,341	10,448	18,300	15,286	11,583	11,477	4,841
Christmas Is. [Pacific Ocean]	14,786	15,196	9,183	10,578	10,464	18,558	7,643	6,608	15,472	17,623	15,809	7,560	12,144	13,216	14,815	7,693	12,559	12,932	14,393	13,460
Churchill, Canada	6,524	7,249	5,544	5,438	5,266	10,627	3,153	1,964	7,166	14,079	8,733	11,504	7,778	5,029	7,059	4,631	9,851	5,076	6,292	10,882
Cincinnati, Ohio	7,048	8,089	3,261	3,388	3,210	10,252	1,137	3,624	7,268	13,890	9,843	13,489	5,805	5,899	8,073	2,461	7,781	6,319	7,107	12,850
Ciudad Bolivia, Venezuela	7,963	9,191	548	1,280	1,306	8,923	3,254	7,200	7,483	11,938	10,956	16,752	2,680	7,634	9,446	2,207	4,277	8,429	8,427	15,081
Ciudad Juarez, Mexico	9,111	10,068	3,983	4,840	4,678	12,357	1,465	3,145	9,406	15,959	11,726	12,247	7,123	7,826	9,979	2,402	8,782	8,078	9,080	13,904
Ciudad Victoria, Mexico	9,186	10,264	2,939	3,997	3,854	11,849	1,083	4,252	9,276	15,276	12,033	13,265	6,143	8,091	10,264	1,296	7,692	8,498	9,289	14,791
Clarksburg, West Virginia	6,733	7,794	3,183	3,153	2,975	9,892	1,391	3,863	6,924	13,530	9,565	13,727	5,561	5,627	7,797	2,579	7,570	6,088	6,817	12,706
Cleveland, Ohio	6,705	7,736	3,448	3,415	3,238	9,998	1,493	3,610	6,951	13,641	9,486	13,469	5,818	5,543	7,717	2,776	7,835	5,963	6,754	12,519
Cocos (Keeling) Island	11,269	10,058	19,117	17,679	17,756	9,743	17,805	13,843	11,555	6,658	8,234	4,684	15,920	11,910	9,890	19,184	14,461	11,239	10,927	4,439
Colombo, Sri Lanka	8,476	7,256	16,590	15,094	15,114	7,795	15,760	12,593	8,863	5,748	5,443	6,032	14,273	9,112	7,076	17,062	13,808	8,490	8,113	1,826
Colon, Panama	8,670	9,892	587	2,104	2,056	9,947	2,612	6,594	8,311	12,950	11,702	15,795	3,683	8,132	10,092	1,297	5,102	8,845	9,057	15,639
Colorado Springs, Colorado	8,461	9,364	4,287	4,892	4,719	11,982	1,555	2,523	8,848	15,626	10,978	12,058	7,271	7,115	9,247	2,857	9,081	7,319	8,379	13,127
Columbia, South Carolina	7,100	8,205	2,627	2,778	2,600	9,973	1,033	4,252	7,192	13,573	10,003	14,105	5,195	6,087	8,242	2,013	7,147	6,599	7,242	13,272
Columbus, Georgia	7,499	8,596	2,598	2,971	2,797	10,350	630	4,152	7,596	13,932	10,387	13,945	5,370	6,461	8,623	1,732	7,260	6,947	7,629	13,562
Columbus, Ohio	6,887	7,927	3,311	3,362	3,184	10,116	1,291	3,648	7,112	13,756	9,682	13,515	5,775	5,739	7,913	2,582	7,770	6,165	6,946	12,717
Conakry, Guinea	3,861	4,614	6,683	5,252	5,363	2,732	8,286	10,516	2,720	6,236	5,692	16,042	4,041	5,046	5,107	8,134	4,644	5,862	4,605	9,716
Concepcion, Chile	11,554	12,569	5,296	5,967	6,089	9,495	7,685	11,492	10,568	10,204	13,679	15,720	4,661	11,979	13,023	6,207	3,392	12,899	12,251	16,820
Concord, New Hampshire	5,876	6,939	3,585	3,156	2,991	9,164	2,243	4,115	6,094	12,808	8,717	13,826	5,457	4,785	6,950	3,311	7,539	5,285	5,964	11,991
Constantine, Algeria	677	1,034	8,532	7,050	7,060	3,835	8,702	8,848	971	6,894	2,637	12,745	7,061	2,242	1,501	9,365	8,189	2,672	1,174	6,847
Copenhagen, Denmark	1,760	1,646	8,844	7,570	7,516	5,972	8,066	7,073	2,913	8,627	2,995	11,237	8,378	1,184	1,329	9,137	9,916	677	1,036	6,330
Coppermine, Canada	6,819	7,272	6,965	6,878	6,707	11,199	4,443	1,430	7,674	14,272	8,462	10,092	9,192	5,236	6,971	5,926	11,278	4,990	6,411	9,851
Coquimbo, Chile	10,924	11,991	4,546	5,190	5,311	9,260	7,009	10,891	9,988	10,395	13,244	16,338	3,976	11,256	12,424	5,546	2,975	12,168	11,601	16,841
Cordoba, Argentina	10,547	11,554	4,825	5,252	5,391	8,602	7,416	11,363	9,554	9,702	12,690	16,719	3,704	11,034	12,009	5,989	2,392	11,962	11,251	16,143
Cordoba, Spain	712	1,889	7,520	6,049	6,053	4,257	7,721	8,241	733	7,617	3,635	13,466	6,253	1,858	2,240	8,343	7,598	2,602	1,419	7,802
Cork, Ireland	1,422	2,264	7,436	6,132	6,082	5,802	6,932	6,762	2,310	8,991	4,028	12,559	7,003	343	2,267	7,861	8,671	1,271	1,279	7,731
Corner Brook, Canada	4,675	5,716	4,490	3,671	3,537	8,241	3,469	4,540	4,985	11,848	7,489	13,653	5,659	3,560	5,723	4,487	7,753	4,097	4,739	10,867
Corrientes, Argentina	9,875	10,876	4,590	4,819	4,971	8,009	7,274	11,260	8,877	9,368	12,028	17,379	3,084	10,402	11,332	5,908	1,732	11,332	10,583	15,623
Cosenza, Italy	1,216	210	9,337	7,879	7,878	4,200	9,254	8,865	1,876	6,827	1,820	11,844	7,969	2,376	708	10,051	9,059	2,465	1,106	5,971
Craiova, Romania	1,791	670	9,840	8,434	8,414	4,904	9,432	8,531	2,668	7,192	1,535	11,052	8,723	2,414	268	10,380	9,885	2,170	1,304	5,371
Cruzeiro do Sul, Brazil	9,318	10,519	2,073	2,875	2,964	9,202	4,658	8,634	8,634	11,532	12,154	17,048	2,761	9,236	10,848	3,276	3,377	10,082	9,877	16,387
Cuiaba, Brazil	8,694	9,768	3,590	3,548	3,709	7,492	6,332	10,291	7,767	9,536	11,107	18,555	1,772	9,101	10,195	5,105	1,374	10,027	9,376	15,095
Curitiba, Brazil	9,099	10,034	4,888	4,778	4,946	7,027	7,629	11,592	8,052	8,525	11,092	17,965	2,653	9,783	10,507	6,373	818	10,714	9,826	14,648
Cuzco, Peru	9,716	10,892	2,727	3,454	3,557	9,172	5,282	9,243	8,954	11,214	12,445	17,060	2,912	9,750	11,252	3,869	3,070	10,619	10,313	16,630
Dacca, Bangladesh	8,167	6,977	15,847	14,678	14,618	8,983	14,008	10,481	8,903	7,715	5,415	5,036	14,961	8,286	6,634	15,476	15,313	7,477	7,603	1,330
Dakar, Senegal	3,515	4,421	6,226	4,751	4,846	3,307	7,660	9,819	2,434	6,881	5,710	16,084	3,858	4,540	4,888	7,602	4,801	5,400	4,258	9,862
Dallas, Texas	8,356	9,378	3,301	3,988	3,820	11,445	593	3,480	8,570	15,040	11,106	13,013	6,330	7,166	9,339	1,902	8,101	7,519	8,393	13,772
Damascus, Syria	3,121	1,915	11,237	9,766	9,772	4,464	11,038	9,938	3,603	5,904	85	10,320	9,618	4,025	1,851	11,931	10,352	3,736	2,847	4,156
Danang, Vietnam	10,126	8,965	16,995	16,293	16,184	10,066	14,450	10,508	10,923	8,951	7,456	3,018	17,004	10,036	8,591	15,883	17,057	9,157	9,512	3,321
Dar es Salaam, Tanzania	6,539	5,781	12,784	11,399	11,511	3,418	14,243	14,392	6,124	1,519	4,520	10,685	9,753	7,992	6,020	14,283	9,055	8,021	6,728	5,315
Darwin, Australia	14,114	12,920	17,239	18,623	18,480	13,438	15,276	11,912	14,787	10,163	11,264	2,227	18,464	14,015	12,580	15,744	16,378	13,107	13,527	7,035
Davao, Philippines	12,155	11,038	17,008	17,331	17,162	12,844	14,306	10,425	13,022	10,357	9,589	982	19,118	11,834	10,634	15,386	18,200	10,912	11,496	5,451
David, Panama	8,949	10,169	884	2,401	2,352	10,229	2,602	6,556	8,603	13,184	11,983	15,581	3,923	8,378	10,360	1,192	5,256	9,074	9,324	15,876
Dawson, Canada	7,838	8,156	7,693	7,819	7,643	12,267	5,012	1,117	8,757	15,072	9,137	9,087	10,195	6,255	7,803	6,440	12,243	5,888	7,363	9,811
Dawson Creek, Canada	7,953	8,530	6,331	6,597	6,419	12,189	3,621	416	8,690	15,510	9,808	10,280	9,010	6,398	8,264	5,035	10,993	6,266	7,625	11,090
Denpasar, Indonesia	12,562	11,339	18,907	19,131	19,023	11,752	16,366	12,509	13,109	8,690	9,608	2,774	17,903	12,763	11,055	17,263	16,116	11,926	12,056	5,424
Denver, Colorado	8,404	9,296	4,361	4,938	4,765	11,965	1,623	2,431	8,807	15,609	10,901	12,001	7,325	7,047	9,174	2,946	9,149	7,239	8,312	13,025
Derby, Australia	13,876	12,651	17,925	19,443	19,360	12,614	16,214	12,795	14,373	9,253	10,899	2,975	17,762	14,064	12,375	16,590	15,672	13,207	13,378	6,740
Des Moines, Iowa	7,529	8,488	3,857	4,167	3,990	10,984	1,255	2,885	7,866	14,628	10,169	12,718	6,584	6,250	8,412	2,740	8,517	6,546	7,499	12,766
Detroit, Michigan	6,753	7,768	3,566	3,558	3,381	10,105	1,505	3,465	7,026	13,749	9,506	13,324	5,963	5,563	7,737	2,838	7,978	5,958	6,784	12,470
Dhahran, Saudi Arabia	4,675	3,466	12,782	11,299	11,311	5,094	12,503	10,859	5,089	5,364	1,640	9,096	10,947	5,497	3,351	13,468	11,361	5,075	4,375	2,773
Diego Garcia Island	8,932	7,799	16,413	14,956	15,044	7,034	16,935	14,328	9,004	4,280	5,997	7,079	13,403	9,924	7,760	17,715	12,440	9,487	8,758	3,428
Dijon, France	697	1,167	8,353	6,969	6,941	5,059	8,021	7,691	1,849	8,015	2,953	12,187	7,485	1,114	1,227	8,903	8,910	1,455	191	6,837
Dili, Indonesia	13,398	12,200	17,787	18,876	18,699	12,891	15,503	11,879	14,068	9,771	10,544	2,016	18,725	13,352	11,865	16,190	16,656	12,458	12,820	6,314
Djibouti, Djibouti	5,173	4,160	12,732	11,217	11,279	3,842	13,274	12,434	5,146	3,593	2,588	10,000	10,229	6,403	4,270	13,857	10,150	6,236	5,148	3,849
Dnepropetrovsk, USSR	2,683	1,643	10,516	9,178	9,140	5,702	9,763	8,283	3,633	7,563	1,618	10,099	9,647	2,877	1,177	10,860	10,858	2,307	2,062	4,651
Dobo, Indonesia	13,851	12,709	16,791	17,951	17,784	13,857	14,553	11,091	14,667	10,774	11,174	1,449	19,156	13,530	12,322	15,186	17,157	12,603	13,203	6,958
Doha, Qatar	4,854	3,646	12,959	11,474	11,487	5,175	12,676	10,975	5,260	5,307	1,819	8,964	11,093	5,673	3,530	13,648	11,464	5,242	4,554	2,632
Donetsk, USSR	2,889	1,823	10,728	9,393	9,355	5,780	9,942	8,367	3,822	7,518	1,579	9,903	9,852	3,084	1,373	11,055	11,037	2,489	2,276	4,439
Dover, Delaware	6,380	7,466	3,123	2,898	2,723	9,476	1,724	4,169	6,533	13,113	9,255	14,005	5,278	5,333	7,492	2,752	7,321	5,844	6,498	12,545
Dresden, East Germany	1,393	1,128	8,967	7,629	7,589	5,466	8,387	7,576	2,526	8,119	2,595	11,427	8,239	1,379	855	9,384	9,663	1,164	650	6,202
Dubayy, United Arab Emir.	5,170	3,951	13,290	11,816	11,824	5,527	12,886	10,976	5,615	5,458	2,138	8,585	11,472	5,915	3,801	13,916	11,830	5,432	4,833	2,253
Dublin, Ireland	1,471	2,197	7,614	6,327	6,274	5,895	7,035	6,713	2,434	9,017	3,922	12,340	7,222	141	2,154	7,999	8,887	1,053	1,210	7,553
Duluth, Minnesota	7,101	8,009	4,291	4,418	4,240	10,762	1,815	2,595	7,520	14,388	9,652	12,460	6,828	5,762	7,907	3,293	8,827	6,008	7,023	12,176
Dunedin, New Zealand	18,953	17,837	12,788	14,171	14,201	14,782	12,974	12,730	18,305	11,471	16,008	6,895	13,524	19,003	17,681	12,186	11,938	18,121	18,713	12,061
Durango, Mexico	9,575	10,612	3,474	4,562	4,418	12,396	1,511	4,002	9,733	15,840	12,342	12,732	6,689	8,402	10,575	1,816	8,185	8,742	9,628	14,767
Durban, South Africa	8,426	7,993	12,135	11,143	11,303	4,174	14,523	16,604	7,657	1,176	7,070	11,716	8,921	10,003	8,339	13,795	7,527	10,272	8,825	7,691
Dushanbe, USSR	5,556	4,389	13,354	12,079	12,031	7,230	12,090	9,402	6,362	7,370	3,022	7,397	12,460	5,703	4,021	13,407	13,318	4,949	4,978	1,881
East London, South Africa	8,652	8,290	11,853	10,935	11,100	4,308	14,331	16,787	7,826	1,617	7,450	12,000	8,658	10,236	8,656	13,506	7,178	10,558	9,089	8,148
Easter Island (Hanga Roa)	13,696	14,919	5,638	7,023	7,044	12,982	6,664	9,382	13,077	13,547	16,598	12,965	7,083	13,275	15,190	5,391	6,665	13,946	14,168	19,213
Echo Bay, Canada	7,045	7,505	6,928	6,904	6,731	11,417	4,360	1,197	7,890	14,506	8,692	10,039	9,244	5,464	7,205	5,837	11,319	5,224	6,643	10,012
Edinburgh, United Kingdom	1,663	2,196	7,858	6,604	6,544	6,107	7,143	6,580	2,701	9,126	3,834	11,995	7,559	229	2,071	8,167	9,235	706	1,243	7,318
Edmonton, Canada	7,828	8,490	5,833	6,102	5,924	11,952	3,132	907	8,494	15,395	9,867	10,774	8,517	6,305	8,260	4,563	10,493	6,259	7,555	11,430
El Aaiun, Morocco	2,113	3,152	6,661	5,144	5,187	3,721	7,462	8,867	1,174	7,342	4,690	14,851	4,931	3,102	3,577	7,765	6,174	3,950	2,843	8,923
Elat, Israel	3,226	2,081	11,270	9,776	9,794	4,063	11,261	10,348	3,555	5,464	483	10,530	9,458	4,281	2,120	12,072	10,068	4,075	3,056	4,269
Elazig, Turkey	3,152	1,928	11,259	9,834	9,822	5,063	10,793	9,408	3,824	6,493	629	9,960	9,914	3,797	1,696	11,797	10,802	3,373	2,733	3,989
Eniwetok Atoll, Marshall Isls.	13,805	13,187	13,252	14,308	14,145	16,649	10,916	7,773	14,957	14,340	12,477	3,083	16,463	12,598	12,681	11,599	17,080	11,777	13,068	8,999
Erfurt, East Germany	1,265	1,183	8,778	7,438	7,399	5,447	8,225	7,508	2,412	8,184	2,744	11,596	8,062	1,209	983	9,207	9,509	1,105	522	6,391
Erzurum, Turkey	3,283	2,068	11,362	9,953	9,936	5,284	10,804	9,295	3,999	6,648	845	9,765	10,095	3,837	1,791	11,846	11,014	3,359	2,823	3,856
Esfahan, Iran	4,443	3,215	12,562	11,127	11,119	5,547	12,002	10,157	5,026	6,078	1,508	8,910	11,049	5,064	3,000	13,072	11,686	4,546	4,036	2,732
Essen, West Germany	1,178	1,372	8,495	7,162	7,121	5,504	7,952	7,343	2,329	8,351	3,009	11,802	7,836	935	1,241	8,924	9,331	1,000	505	6,673
Eucla, Australia	15,208	13,991	16,675	17,967	18,035	12,855	16,226	13,732	15,429	9,240	12,173	4,363	16,323	15,658	13,792	15,911	14,240	14,842	14,825	8,188

Distances in Kilometers	Barcelona, Spain	Bari, Italy	Barranquilla, Colombia	Basse-Terre, Guadeloupe	Basseterre, St. Kitts & Nevis	Bata, Equatorial Guinea	Baton Rouge, Louisiana	Bear Lake, Canada	Bechar, Algeria	Beira, Mozambique	Beirut, Lebanon	Belau Islands (Koror)	Belem, Brazil	Belfast, United Kingdom	Belgrade, Yugoslavia	Belmopan, Belize	Belo Horizonte, Brazil	Bergen, Norway	Bern, Switzerland	Bhopal, India
Fargo, North Dakota	7,389	8,264	4,486	4,707	4,529	11,109	1,886	2,304	7,841	14,729	9,872	12,169	7,124	6,015	8,141	3,371	9,097	6,213	7,281	12,215
Faroe Islands (Torshavn)	2,372	2,808	7,794	6,655	6,574	6,817	6,781	5,905	3,395	9,791	4,308	11,629	7,867	829	2,597	7,916	9,659	674	1,908	7,447
Florence, Italy	790	546	8,859	7,437	7,422	4,646	8,636	8,252	1,792	7,444	2,362	11,990	7,749	1,728	747	9,484	9,017	1,891	459	6,372
Florianopolis, Brazil	9,253	10,161	5,120	5,027	5,195	7,032	7,860	11,828	8,190	8,395	11,165	17,741	2,892	9,977	10,640	6,588	971	10,906	9,984	14,616
Fort George, Canada	5,912	6,795	4,768	4,458	4,291	9,761	2,777	3,010	6,401	13,327	8,439	12,539	6,746	4,547	6,691	4,151	8,835	4,805	5,810	11,168
Fort McMurray, Canada	7,489	8,127	5,967	6,129	5,952	11,666	3,317	953	8,185	15,059	9,490	10,755	8,530	5,954	7,890	4,777	10,545	5,889	7,199	11,102
Fort Nelson, Canada	7,797	8,317	6,641	6,840	6,663	12,102	3,951	382	8,584	15,316	9,535	10,043	9,242	6,227	8,030	5,381	11,254	6,040	7,433	10,721
Fort Severn, Canada	6,320	7,126	5,115	4,952	4,781	10,298	2,851	2,408	6,886	13,820	8,692	11,999	7,284	4,882	6,977	4,304	9,359	5,029	6,152	11,111
Fort Smith, Arkansas	8,002	9,017	3,352	3,892	3,719	11,175	625	3,366	8,238	14,794	10,742	13,051	6,274	6,803	8,975	2,089	8,113	7,157	8,031	13,456
Fort Vermilion, Canada	7,564	8,144	6,297	6,458	6,280	11,812	3,635	698	8,308	15,121	9,440	10,429	8,856	6,008	7,882	5,087	10,876	5,883	7,236	10,870
Fort Wayne, Indiana	6,975	7,992	3,485	3,577	3,399	10,288	1,298	3,432	7,238	13,931	9,728	13,299	5,992	5,785	7,960	2,667	7,981	6,176	7,007	12,658
Fort-Chimo, Canada	5,143	5,993	5,256	4,706	4,553	9,137	3,532	3,433	5,702	12,635	7,625	12,465	6,836	3,743	5,880	4,840	8,937	3,994	5,009	10,449
Fort-de-France, Martinique	6,727	7,954	1,542	170	346	7,902	3,542	7,176	6,242	11,165	9,713	17,043	2,254	6,480	8,221	2,980	4,255	7,315	7,211	13,859
Fortaleza, Brazil	6,475	7,485	4,338	3,362	3,533	5,404	6,751	10,246	5,482	8,137	8,776	19,157	1,138	7,127	7,933	5,991	1,887	8,056	7,189	12,823
Frankfort, Kentucky	7,128	8,176	3,178	3,344	3,166	10,290	1,038	3,675	7,333	13,923	9,934	13,535	5,762	5,991	8,165	2,357	7,725	6,418	7,195	12,955
Frankfurt am Main, W. Ger.	1,094	1,183	8,616	7,266	7,229	5,350	8,123	7,527	2,245	8,166	2,834	11,788	7,870	1,110	1,065	9,078	9,319	1,162	367	6,556
Fredericton, Canada	5,399	6,450	3,954	3,354	3,200	8,813	2,734	4,222	5,658	12,448	8,223	13,741	5,548	4,291	6,457	3,790	7,648	4,797	5,473	11,526
Freeport, Bahamas	7,396	8,562	1,770	2,115	1,946	9,779	1,289	5,040	7,323	13,269	10,388	14,831	4,490	6,559	8,661	1,459	6,368	7,163	7,635	13,934
Freetown, Sierra Leone	3,948	4,677	6,748	5,328	5,441	2,652	8,386	10,639	2,803	6,133	5,718	16,046	4,062	5,152	5,172	8,213	4,603	5,962	4,691	9,713
Frobisher Bay, Canada	5,057	5,788	5,878	5,328	5,178	9,245	4,033	3,238	5,744	12,623	7,326	11,888	7,420	3,560	5,619	5,395	9,518	3,662	4,825	9,912
Frunze, USSR	5,794	4,692	13,280	12,112	12,045	7,842	11,755	8,839	6,693	8,050	3,525	7,024	12,756	5,726	4,273	13,136	13,801	4,901	5,156	2,193
Fukuoka, Japan	10,164	9,306	14,403	14,370	14,205	12,688	11,685	7,698	11,250	11,703	8,420	2,937	16,446	9,382	8,818	13,021	18,393	8,456	9,426	5,260
Funafuti Atoll, Tuvalu	16,351	15,995	11,940	13,383	13,279	18,640	10,459	8,709	17,443	15,008	15,360	5,255	14,639	14,876	15,489	10,512	14,357	14,226	15,676	11,581
Funchal, Madeira Island	1,950	3,131	6,363	4,866	4,885	4,402	6,905	8,164	1,389	8,003	4,830	14,651	5,026	2,587	3,485	7,330	6,489	3,487	2,603	9,032
Fuzhou, China	10,133	9,109	15,633	15,347	15,200	11,869	12,962	8,980	11,112	10,434	7,909	2,626	16,987	9,657	8,660	14,339	18,181	8,729	9,433	4,235
Gaborone, Botswana	7,711	7,344	11,592	10,512	10,667	3,413	13,860	15,871	6,910	1,068	6,559	12,230	8,370	9,294	7,715	13,250	7,140	9,610	8,141	7,683
Galapagos Islands (Santa Cruz)	10,273	11,496	2,151	3,647	3,625	11,149	3,441	7,104	9,877	13,650	13,302	15,003	4,665	9,707	11,694	1,982	5,489	10,382	10,658	17,180
Gander, Canada	4,437	5,487	4,607	3,711	3,586	8,008	3,695	4,733	4,742	11,610	7,268	13,707	5,616	3,348	5,504	4,678	7,701	3,915	4,513	10,704
Gangtok, India	7,779	6,600	15,407	14,249	14,186	8,821	13,610	10,162	8,547	7,797	5,090	5,314	14,632	7,858	6,244	15,068	15,148	7,042	7,199	1,215
Garyarsa, China	6,844	5,663	14,592	13,361	13,308	8,076	13,063	9,925	7,613	7,493	4,175	6,212	13,704	6,973	5,309	14,465	14,353	6,187	6,272	985
Gaspe, Canada	5,141	6,161	4,305	3,650	3,501	8,704	3,040	4,161	5,465	12,320	7,918	13,515	5,781	3,977	6,149	4,139	7,883	4,456	5,179	11,171
Gauhati, India	8,102	6,929	15,645	14,533	14,464	9,125	13,730	10,178	8,880	7,978	5,425	4,980	14,966	8,147	6,567	15,203	15,457	7,318	7,514	1,485
Gdansk, Poland	1,888	1,476	9,247	7,957	7,907	5,877	8,475	7,355	3,021	8,364	2,628	10,963	8,682	1,587	1,067	9,553	10,146	1,043	1,143	5,923
Geneva, Switzerland	624	1,028	8,443	7,046	7,022	4,926	8,155	7,841	1,772	7,864	2,829	12,186	7,503	1,265	1,129	9,020	8,889	1,579	128	6,758
Genoa, Italy	647	742	8,670	7,254	7,236	4,716	8,440	8,113	1,723	7,587	2,560	12,112	7,610	1,556	917	9,286	8,921	1,793	301	6,553
Georgetown, Guyana	7,057	8,262	1,887	1,089	1,263	7,554	4,327	8,071	6,410	10,587	9,933	17,918	1,411	7,037	8,587	3,523	3,341	7,917	7,619	14,160
Geraldton, Australia	13,859	12,660	17,812	18,543	18,707	11,562	17,530	14,365	14,021	8,011	10,831	4,529	16,212	14,510	12,506	17,315	14,149	13,792	13,542	7,004
Ghanzi, Botswana	7,257	6,960	11,133	10,012	10,163	2,903	13,340	15,380	6,418	1,376	6,307	12,660	7,917	8,842	7,354	12,784	6,794	9,204	7,719	7,806
Ghat, Libya	1,965	1,897	9,007	7,488	7,535	2,558	9,643	10,144	1,421	5,631	2,639	13,017	6,960	3,547	2,393	10,088	7,680	3,952	2,448	6,762
Gibraltar	876	2,005	7,457	5,975	5,985	4,103	7,750	8,385	579	7,503	3,710	13,633	6,103	2,051	2,382	8,327	7,415	2,803	1,602	7,902
Gijon, Spain	688	1,869	7,496	6,079	6,061	4,864	7,417	7,660	1,357	8,146	3,696	13,096	6,557	1,229	2,088	8,166	8,039	2,015	1,096	7,726
Gisborne, New Zealand	19,550	18,393	12,258	13,724	13,722	15,758	12,113	11,727	19,222	12,481	16,639	6,793	13,514	18,211	18,037	11,459	12,191	17,536	18,815	12,479
Glasgow, United Kingdom	1,674	2,242	7,791	6,539	6,478	6,117	7,083	6,552	2,695	9,158	3,891	12,048	7,503	176	2,127	8,103	9,188	758	1,281	7,385
Godthab, Greenland	4,234	4,965	6,185	5,414	5,283	8,474	4,656	4,008	4,956	11,803	6,534	12,050	7,293	2,732	4,810	5,929	9,354	2,881	3,999	9,356
Gomez Palacio, Mexico	9,373	10,406	3,425	4,457	4,309	12,244	1,326	3,888	9,541	15,725	12,135	12,779	6,627	8,196	10,369	1,781	8,173	8,537	9,422	14,601
Goose Bay, Canada	8,641	9,195	6,532	6,967	6,789	12,877	3,790	539	9,382	16,188	10,417	9,918	9,384	7,082	8,914	5,107	11,292	6,921	8,300	11,381
Gorki, USSR	3,417	2,586	10,680	9,478	9,413	6,770	9,501	7,501	4,485	8,483	2,579	9,364	10,294	3,095	2,082	10,748	11,702	2,273	2,699	4,566
Goteborg, Sweden	1,945	1,877	8,791	7,549	7,488	6,198	7,925	6,850	3,096	8,853	3,184	11,150	8,442	1,162	1,549	9,028	10,028	483	1,240	6,396
Granada, Spain	685	1,822	7,612	6,136	6,142	4,151	7,838	8,352	636	7,498	3,547	13,441	6,293	1,938	2,192	8,451	7,603	2,654	1,416	7,728
Grand Turk, Turks & Caicos	7,099	8,310	1,224	1,161	997	8,997	2,236	5,946	6,852	12,396	10,134	15,778	3,536	6,497	8,483	1,914	5,452	7,214	7,446	14,004
Graz, Austria	1,232	669	9,143	7,758	7,731	5,041	8,725	8,034	2,283	7,661	2,232	11,527	8,190	1,713	463	9,661	9,500	1,621	607	6,047
Green Bay, Wisconsin	6,969	7,930	3,926	4,011	3,833	10,483	1,586	3,003	7,318	14,123	9,622	12,867	6,421	5,696	7,861	3,028	8,423	6,013	6,942	12,355
Grenoble, France	509	1,009	8,410	7,002	6,982	4,815	8,175	7,930	1,654	7,781	2,829	12,281	7,418	1,337	1,165	9,017	8,785	1,694	237	6,802
Guadalajara, Mexico	9,734	10,806	3,233	4,416	4,283	12,335	1,630	4,399	9,824	15,678	12,566	12,991	6,454	8,622	10,796	1,577	7,875	9,005	9,828	15,144
Guam (Agana)	12,824	11,943	14,891	15,647	15,470	14,786	12,313	8,676	13,906	12,570	10,894	1,313	18,050	11,975	11,462	13,236	18,855	11,061	12,085	7,143
Guantanamo, Cuba	7,526	8,732	1,013	1,497	1,353	9,419	1,971	5,830	7,297	12,774	10,558	15,573	3,768	6,875	8,891	1,470	5,590	7,563	7,855	14,365
Guatemala City, Guatemala	9,171	10,349	1,753	3,092	2,988	11,071	1,753	5,549	9,017	14,221	12,177	14,501	4,961	8,347	10,455	340	6,373	8,922	9,428	15,613
Guayaquil, Ecuador	9,504	10,730	1,557	2,829	2,858	9,980	3,806	7,734	8,970	12,505	12,474	16,189	3,489	9,174	10,995	2,359	4,369	9,948	9,979	16,633
Guiyang, China	9,212	8,110	15,845	15,133	15,019	10,617	13,414	9,540	10,106	9,298	6,769	3,628	16,176	8,969	7,694	14,880	16,946	8,069	8,555	2,978
Gur'yev, USSR	3,952	2,856	11,694	10,406	10,358	6,454	10,654	8,553	4,860	7,608	2,014	8,857	10,913	4,035	2,429	11,874	12,038	3,316	3,331	3,490
Haifa, Israel	3,046	1,855	11,150	9,673	9,681	4,327	11,007	9,991	3,493	5,828	125	10,453	9,492	4,001	1,827	11,873	10,212	3,748	2,804	4,271
Haikou, China	9,978	8,851	16,527	15,925	15,805	11,050	13,965	10,014	10,836	9,331	7,430	2,962	16,931	9,777	8,452	15,390	17,342	8,880	9,335	3,419
Haiphong, Vietnam	9,642	8,502	16,478	15,737	15,629	10,665	14,016	10,107	10,478	9,023	7,054	3,346	16,576	9,500	8,111	15,470	16,969	8,615	9,012	3,029
Hakodate, Japan	9,900	9,233	13,135	13,210	13,039	13,117	10,408	6,424	11,041	12,750	8,688	3,862	15,448	8,870	8,727	11,738	17,545	7,980	9,156	6,147
Halifax, Canada	5,227	6,305	3,883	3,181	3,034	8,553	2,881	4,500	5,439	12,192	8,096	13,971	5,322	4,183	6,335	3,846	7,424	4,739	5,337	11,509
Hamburg, West Germany	1,473	1,473	8,691	7,387	7,339	5,731	8,029	7,219	2,626	8,474	2,968	11,503	8,124	1,047	1,232	9,052	9,637	812	760	6,476
Hamilton, Bermuda	5,909	7,091	2,515	1,830	1,673	8,449	2,515	5,391	5,825	12,044	8,921	15,173	5,176	5,820	7,220	2,937	6,189	5,867	6,186	12,666
Hamilton, New Zealand	19,304	18,136	12,502	13,973	13,969	15,763	12,293	11,757	19,286	12,408	16,394	6,547	13,769	18,135	17,780	11,675	12,421	17,394	18,589	12,224
Hangzhou, China	9,844	8,864	15,172	14,883	14,734	11,860	12,517	8,541	10,858	10,670	7,762	2,945	16,603	9,290	8,401	13,911	18,056	8,359	9,131	4,299
Hannover, West Germany	1,348	1,361	8,678	7,357	7,313	5,600	8,072	7,331	2,500	8,362	2,906	11,591	8,048	1,066	1,153	9,073	9,537	932	628	6,489
Hanoi, Vietnam	9,566	8,423	16,462	15,693	15,587	10,577	14,026	10,129	10,397	8,953	6,969	3,433	16,495	9,438	8,034	15,485	16,883	8,556	8,939	2,941
Harare, Zimbabwe	7,200	6,691	12,049	10,836	10,977	3,193	14,057	15,362	6,524	459	5,743	11,683	8,859	8,758	7,021	13,676	7,835	8,973	7,551	6,788
Harbin, China	8,896	8,134	13,367	13,115	12,959	11,907	10,746	6,802	10,013	11,698	7,489	4,324	15,074	8,023	7,632	12,175	17,014	7,102	8,151	5,061
Harrisburg, Pennsylvania	6,421	7,490	3,251	3,063	2,888	9,594	1,692	4,001	6,608	13,235	9,268	13,837	5,446	5,335	7,502	2,801	7,487	5,820	6,516	12,486
Hartford, Connecticut	6,030	7,103	3,417	3,043	2,874	9,246	2,079	4,149	6,222	12,890	8,887	13,910	5,372	4,959	7,122	3,126	7,444	5,467	6,131	12,176
Havana, Cuba	7,911	9,081	1,566	2,302	2,150	10,153	1,193	5,146	7,812	13,567	10,907	14,785	4,569	7,078	9,182	938	6,332	7,674	8,156	14,429
Helena, Montana	8,296	9,053	5,278	5,731	5,554	12,215	2,537	1,479	8,858	15,790	10,518	11,165	8,144	6,827	8,861	3,898	10,034	6,872	8,093	12,210
Helsinki, Finland	2,608	2,190	9,489	8,296	8,227	6,599	8,412	6,864	3,753	8,912	3,021	10,359	9,237	1,939	1,732	9,604	10,802	1,083	1,864	5,740
Hengyang, China	9,608	8,544	15,739	15,219	15,089	11,195	13,176	9,236	10,547	9,846	7,278	3,169	16,548	9,248	8,111	14,609	17,515	8,331	8,928	3,563
Herat, Afghanistan	5,234	4,022	13,253	11,884	11,857	6,513	12,312	9,936	5,926	6,657	2,457	7,930	11,997	5,613	3,721	13,532	12,684	4,956	4,733	1,921
Hermosillo, Mexico	9,624	10,565	4,255	5,228	5,073	12,856	1,917	3,266	9,928	16,432	12,199	11,951	7,446	8,320	10,463	2,615	9,007	8,541	9,578	14,145
Hiroshima, Japan	10,201	9,371	14,223	14,230	14,064	12,832	11,498	7,513	11,298	11,908	8,534	3,004	16,356	9,374	8,878	12,825	18,362	8,451	9,459	5,446
Hiva Oa (Atuona)	14,856	15,809	7,473	8,980	8,911	16,472	6,781	7,401	14,968	16,661	17,281	9,773	10,052	13,560	15,658	6,283	10,176	13,671	14,825	15,882
Ho Chi Minh City, Vietnam	10,409	9,219	17,596	16,787	16,694	10,736	15,066	11,108	11,130	8,561	7,619	3,080	17,100	10,444	8,875	16,482	16,723	9,589	9,834	3,400
Hobart, Australia	17,157	15,976	14,630	15,951	16,001	13,822	14,723	13,591	17,065	10,230	14,146	5,715	14,844	17,681	15,819	14,041	12,953	16,814	16,855	10,236
Hohhot, China	8,467	7,528	14,236	13,681	13,548	10,875	11,778	7,938	9,506	10,369	6,576	4,345	15,214	7,891	7,052	13,248	16,741	6,961	7,746	3,736
Hong Kong	10,087	8,998	16,202	15,750	15,617	11,420	13,579	9,609	10,997	9,795	7,660	2,734	17,047	9,773	8,577	14,980	17,745	8,859	9,419	3,768
Honiara, Solomon Islands	15,852	14,972	14,043	15,458	15,342	16,632	12,347	9,855	16,945	13,197	13,762	3,379	16,659	14,844	14,497	12,571	15,847	13,973	15,109	9,675
Honolulu, Hawaii	12,766	13,070	8,868	9,993	9,842	17,116	6,667	4,639	13,602	18,697	13,735	7,410	12,083	11,181	12,678	7,218	13,198	10,823	12,307	12,264
Houston, Texas	8,464	9,522	2,978	3,754	3,592	11,367	410	3,836	8,614	14,918	11,278	13,299	6,057	7,334	9,509	1,542	7,785	7,732	8,542	14,086
Huambo, Angola	6,153	5,965	10,345	9,104	9,244	1,745	12,339	14,223	5,271	2,184	5,566	13,303	7,190	7,736	6,393	11,956	6,400	8,159	6,658	7,802
Hubli, India	7,486	6,260	15,613	14,155	14,158	7,327	14,732	11,815	7,956	5,882	4,472	6,517	13,663	8,059	6,052	16,002	13,585	7,428	7,088	907
Hugh Town, United Kingdom	1,155	2,044	7,544	6,206	6,165	5,541	7,139	7,029	2,061	8,725	3,834	12,623	6,966	520	2,090	8,030	8,577	1,377	1,072	7,626
Hull, Canada	6,073	7,090	3,820	3,516	3,346	9,512	2,139	3,699	6,364	13,151	8,835	13,434	5,847	4,892	7,066	3,357	7,920	5,318	6,106	11,928
Hyderabad, India	7,622	6,394	15,720	14,305	14,294	7,697	14,598	11,514	8,157	6,297	4,644	6,172	13,972	8,093	6,152	15,935	13,979	7,415	7,181	661
Hyderabad, Pakistan	6,255	5,028	14,352	12,938	12,925	6,791	13,458	10,853	6,828	6,176	3,304	7,270	12,773	6,750	4,782	14,690	13,118	6,112	5,812	946
Igloolik, Canada	5,543	6,114	6,505	6,093	5,935	9,873	4,372	2,638	6,347	13,086	7,487	11,053	8,249	3,977	5,871	5,817	10,350	3,869	5,200	9,595
Iloilo, Philippines	11,633	10,520	16,945	17,015	16,855	12,470	14,205	10,259	12,507	10,178	9,090	1,362	18,597	11,324	10,113	15,392	18,255	10,405	10,974	4,984
Indianapolis, Indiana	7,126	8,150	3,381	3,543	3,365	10,387	1,131	3,472	7,371	14,027	9,891	13,334	5,961	5,948	8,122	2,513	7,930	6,343	7,166	12,822
Innsbruck, Austria	983	808	8,836	7,451	7,424	5,035	8,451	7,898	2,089	7,794	2,507	11,785	7,914	1,459	754	9,366	9,269	1,512	301	6,355

Distances in Kilometers	Barcelona, Spain	Bari, Italy	Barranquilla, Colombia	Basse-Terre, Guadeloupe	Basseterre, St. Kitts & Nevis	Bata, Equatorial Guinea	Baton Rouge, Louisiana	Bear Lake, Canada	Bechar, Algeria	Beira, Mozambique	Beirut, Lebanon	Belau Islands (Koror)	Belem, Brazil	Belfast, United Kingdom	Belgrade, Yugoslavia	Belmopan, Belize	Belo Horizonte, Brazil	Bergen, Norway	Bern, Switzerland	Bhopal, India
Inuvik, Canada	7,298	7,619	7,632	7,625	7,452	11,729	5,024	1,398	8,224	14,555	8,633	9,325	9,957	5,715	7,271	6,488	12,037	5,348	6,822	9,533
Invercargill, New Zealand	18,777	17,666	12,939	14,310	14,344	14,652	13,150	12,871	18,178	11,314	15,839	6,833	13,603	19,011	17,524	12,356	11,978	18,097	18,560	11,916
Inverness, United Kingdom	1,846	2,357	7,825	6,599	6,533	6,290	7,035	6,401	2,877	9,303	3,961	11,914	7,623	338	2,208	8,087	9,333	639	1,416	7,362
Iquitos, Peru	9,080	10,294	1,640	2,527	2,602	9,255	4,240	8,223	8,453	11,760	11,976	16,940	2,766	8,915	10,600	2,882	3,649	9,744	9,611	16,202
Iraklion, Greece	2,108	969	10,199	8,722	8,730	4,034	10,147	9,522	2,567	6,192	964	11,266	8,626	3,207	1,126	10,951	9,506	3,127	1,955	5,190
Irkutsk, USSR	7,223	6,387	12,996	12,323	12,197	10,159	10,718	7,102	8,310	10,415	5,724	5,690	13,835	6,533	5,892	12,203	15,494	5,600	6,486	3,951
Islamabad, Pakistan	6,156	4,966	14,017	12,728	12,684	7,456	12,717	9,865	6,907	7,184	3,469	6,917	12,995	6,362	4,624	14,056	13,685	5,615	5,603	1,228
Istanbul, Turkey	2,238	1,018	10,347	8,918	8,906	4,749	9,991	8,993	2,969	6,764	980	10,762	9,066	2,974	810	10,929	10,091	2,694	1,839	4,901
Ivujivik, Canada	5,551	6,285	5,713	5,306	5,147	9,704	3,679	2,798	6,217	13,112	7,808	11,792	7,502	4,058	6,110	5,089	9,604	4,143	5,323	10,260
Iwo Jima Island, Japan	11,561	10,739	14,448	14,852	14,675	14,033	11,729	7,863	12,665	12,525	9,847	2,064	17,220	10,673	10,247	12,870	19,255	9,761	10,818	6,444
Izmir, Turkey	2,153	932	10,281	8,828	8,825	4,421	10,065	9,237	2,771	6,498	904	10,993	8,864	3,066	902	10,942	9,823	2,881	1,862	5,024
Jackson, Mississippi	7,903	8,972	2,840	3,392	3,222	10,839	226	3,873	8,046	14,421	10,741	13,566	5,762	6,801	8,973	1,677	7,594	7,232	7,996	13,717
Jaffna, Sri Lanka	8,292	7,067	16,419	14,944	14,954	7,817	15,468	12,297	8,723	5,926	5,268	5,999	14,264	8,877	6,869	16,791	13,919	8,236	7,905	1,530
Jakarta, Indonesia	11,682	10,455	19,447	18,365	18,341	10,821	16,733	12,751	12,173	7,897	8,693	3,418	17,162	12,018	10,199	17,934	15,710	11,230	11,217	4,564
Jamestown, St. Helena	6,398	6,733	8,171	7,095	7,254	2,601	10,476	13,375	5,275	4,313	7,035	15,600	4,956	7,813	7,234	9,824	4,065	8,517	7,085	10,025
Jamnagar, India	6,581	5,353	14,694	13,264	13,256	6,897	13,819	11,144	7,119	6,045	3,602	7,080	13,003	7,108	5,122	15,055	13,230	6,476	6,155	758
Jan Mayen Island	3,357	3,628	7,991	7,033	6,927	7,794	6,555	5,076	4,401	10,623	4,894	10,902	8,535	1,836	3,323	7,837	10,438	1,347	2,822	7,449
Jayapura, Indonesia	14,044	12,977	16,006	17,154	16,991	14,582	13,760	10,392	14,976	11,574	11,573	1,291	18,920	13,495	12,550	14,388	17,471	12,562	13,349	7,424
Jefferson City, Missouri	7,628	8,627	3,511	3,883	3,707	10,919	906	3,215	7,900	14,557	10,343	13,015	6,294	6,406	8,578	2,390	8,199	6,751	7,640	13,074
Jerusalem, Israel	3,122	1,942	11,212	9,729	9,740	4,257	11,106	10,111	3,533	5,710	236	10,455	9,504	4,106	1,934	11,958	10,187	3,864	2,900	4,244
Jiggalong, Australia	14,044	12,819	17,873	19,147	19,243	12,243	16,771	13,515	14,385	8,763	11,017	3,712	17,024	14,441	12,596	16,874	14,937	13,634	13,624	6,977
Jinan, China	9,121	8,177	14,589	14,174	14,031	11,420	12,018	8,090	10,159	10,634	7,182	3,702	15,833	8,525	7,704	13,458	17,392	7,593	8,399	4,066
Jodhpur, India	6,585	5,364	14,622	13,251	13,226	7,270	13,507	10,674	7,214	6,560	3,694	6,813	13,208	6,972	5,084	14,811	13,596	6,282	6,102	554
Johannesburg, South Africa	7,945	7,544	11,825	10,768	10,924	3,677	14,125	16,117	7,163	990	6,696	12,008	8,604	9,525	7,903	13,485	7,322	9,817	8,359	7,627
Juazeiro do Norte, Brazil	6,844	7,833	4,414	3,561	3,736	5,543	6,922	10,514	5,832	8,098	9,076	19,355	1,198	7,520	8,288	6,075	1,492	8,449	7,563	13,060
Juneau, Alaska	8,249	8,667	7,224	7,495	7,317	12,625	4,500	512	9,098	15,646	9,745	9,383	9,905	6,666	8,341	5,884	11,896	6,385	7,828	10,500
Kabul, Afghanistan	5,793	4,598	13,707	12,390	12,352	7,127	12,527	9,838	6,533	7,028	3,092	7,292	12,619	6,046	4,264	13,828	13,326	5,324	5,252	1,480
Kalgoorlie, Australia	14,541	13,334	17,256	18,340	18,458	12,190	16,909	14,108	14,720	8,599	11,508	4,437	16,288	15,114	13,162	16,617	14,187	14,351	14,198	7,606
Kaliningrad, USSR	2,004	1,534	9,357	8,074	8,022	5,942	8,550	7,357	3,132	8,373	2,594	10,839	8,807	1,696	1,099	9,643	10,268	1,102	1,260	5,816
Kamloops, Canada	8,383	9,017	6,036	6,446	6,268	12,519	3,297	753	9,061	15,953	10,343	10,438	8,864	6,849	8,770	4,649	10,781	6,769	8,093	11,633
Kampala, Uganda	5,481	4,791	11,910	10,470	10,571	2,547	13,183	13,471	5,041	2,243	3,728	11,328	9,026	6,965	5,074	13,327	8,619	7,061	5,712	5,467
Kananga, Zaire	5,627	5,239	10,928	9,574	9,696	1,648	12,607	13,807	4,907	2,047	4,614	12,530	7,888	7,202	5,622	12,463	7,323	7,501	6,034	6,789
Kano, Nigeria	3,314	3,329	9,051	7,568	7,656	1,131	10,255	11,398	2,436	4,554	3,656	13,683	6,474	4,891	3,815	10,388	6,744	5,376	3,872	7,354
Kanpur, India	7,173	5,966	15,075	13,781	13,741	7,994	13,642	10,492	7,865	7,097	4,363	6,093	13,904	7,421	5,650	15,033	14,324	6,669	6,643	463
Kansas City, Missouri	7,760	8,738	3,681	4,093	3,917	11,115	1,008	3,034	8,061	14,756	10,433	12,810	6,501	6,507	8,673	2,489	8,394	6,820	7,750	13,051
Kaohsiung, Taiwan	10,484	9,440	15,943	15,725	15,575	12,036	13,243	9,256	11,444	10,397	8,186	2,276	17,371	10,041	8,999	14,587	18,368	9,114	9,792	4,382
Karachi, Pakistan	6,176	4,949	14,287	12,860	12,851	6,649	13,461	10,927	6,728	6,050	3,207	7,400	12,653	6,707	4,716	14,670	12,977	6,088	5,748	1,067
Karaganda, USSR	5,406	4,399	12,583	11,483	11,405	7,974	10,979	8,107	6,393	8,590	3,542	7,353	12,345	5,142	3,936	12,370	13,613	4,274	4,720	2,971
Karl-Marx-Stadt, East Germany	1,336	1,120	8,911	7,570	7,531	5,437	8,349	7,576	2,472	8,118	2,626	11,490	8,175	1,336	875	9,338	9,602	1,164	591	6,258
Kasanga, Tanzania	6,264	5,684	11,926	10,580	10,702	2,635	13,581	14,373	5,682	1,320	4,710	11,597	8,854	7,797	5,999	13,469	8,146	7,965	6,568	6,137
Kashgar, China	6,065	4,930	13,658	12,464	12,402	7,854	12,150	9,185	6,920	7,834	3,639	6,812	13,009	6,072	4,533	13,533	13,938	5,263	5,450	1,803
Kassel, West Germany	1,238	1,265	8,668	7,333	7,293	5,483	8,113	7,430	2,390	8,262	2,854	11,667	7,982	1,097	1,090	9,094	9,450	1,042	511	6,500
Kathmandu, Nepal	7,492	6,304	15,222	14,013	13,957	8,499	13,557	10,223	8,240	7,563	4,771	5,640	14,316	7,623	5,958	14,993	14,823	6,826	6,926	936
Kayes, Mali	3,263	4,027	6,873	5,394	5,486	2,714	8,244	10,172	2,121	6,331	5,177	15,559	4,446	4,478	4,516	8,236	5,207	5,278	4,006	9,276
Kazan, USSR	3,725	2,848	10,985	9,797	9,729	6,940	9,740	7,587	4,777	8,483	2,647	9,047	10,618	3,419	2,349	11,012	12,004	2,585	3,013	4,287
Kemi, Finland	3,057	2,789	9,320	8,225	8,140	7,194	8,023	6,259	4,210	9,537	3,626	10,154	9,385	2,069	2,349	9,284	11,074	1,136	2,336	6,010
Kenora, Canada	7,064	7,918	4,668	4,767	4,590	10,870	2,165	2,263	7,551	14,466	9,512	12,115	7,171	5,669	7,786	3,649	9,184	5,852	6,937	11,874
Kerguelen Island	12,023	11,284	14,626	14,278	14,455	8,043	17,346	18,688	11,434	4,500	9,829	8,876	11,859	13,504	11,481	15,931	9,921	13,472	12,240	8,097
Kerkira, Greece	1,514	311	9,641	8,189	8,185	4,306	9,493	8,936	2,185	6,761	1,527	11,540	8,281	2,548	583	10,326	9,342	2,524	1,295	5,655
Kermanshah, Iran	3,982	2,754	12,103	10,665	10,657	5,283	11,610	9,958	4,572	6,131	1,068	9,322	10,615	4,638	2,548	12,643	11,323	4,162	3,585	3,189
Khabarovsk, USSR	9,030	8,378	12,793	12,669	12,507	12,356	10,127	6,157	10,172	12,380	7,912	4,564	14,780	8,012	7,871	11,532	16,832	7,116	8,286	5,745
Kharkov, USSR	2,792	1,799	10,534	9,219	9,176	5,896	9,702	8,130	3,773	7,736	1,791	9,974	9,755	2,878	1,317	10,828	11,005	2,253	2,143	4,634
Khartoum, Sudan	4,082	3,209	11,504	9,988	10,048	2,927	12,131	11,819	3,941	3,928	2,047	11,067	9,098	5,445	3,433	12,638	9,240	5,434	4,175	4,769
Khon Kaen, Thailand	9,677	8,497	16,961	16,043	15,956	10,289	14,606	10,726	10,430	8,445	6,939	3,587	16,476	9,691	8,142	16,073	16,503	8,838	9,091	2,765
Kiev, USSR	2,398	1,478	10,135	8,811	8,769	5,730	9,377	8,002	3,411	7,795	1,883	10,361	9,355	2,488	975	10,468	10,645	1,923	1,735	5,032
Kigali, Rwanda	5,566	4,956	11,684	10,270	10,377	2,300	13,095	13,646	5,043	2,046	4,007	11,638	8,740	7,084	5,268	13,145	8,269	7,236	5,848	5,836
Kingston, Canada	6,186	7,214	3,689	3,426	3,254	9,569	2,002	3,734	6,456	13,211	8,966	13,507	5,775	5,023	7,196	3,210	7,839	5,459	6,231	12,074
Kingston, Jamaica	7,804	9,013	806	1,619	1,496	9,589	2,005	5,937	7,554	12,883	10,838	15,589	3,776	7,165	9,177	1,276	5,521	7,853	8,140	14,655
Kingstown, Saint Vincent	6,842	8,068	1,496	320	486	7,911	3,623	7,300	6,333	11,131	9,817	17,162	2,142	6,623	8,342	2,994	4,119	7,463	7,337	13,978
Kinshasa, Zaire	5,232	5,033	10,120	8,768	8,891	919	11,837	13,351	4,388	2,731	4,730	13,298	7,097	6,816	5,467	11,656	6,640	7,225	5,726	7,394
Kirkwall, United Kingdom	1,989	2,418	7,928	6,725	6,655	6,430	7,063	6,304	3,040	9,393	3,966	11,741	7,790	521	2,231	8,146	9,511	492	1,509	7,271
Kirov, USSR	3,797	3,004	10,834	9,689	9,614	7,183	9,498	7,277	4,882	8,794	2,939	9,013	10,619	3,349	2,498	10,795	12,083	2,476	3,067	4,492
Kiruna, Sweden	3,140	2,981	9,091	8,031	7,940	7,369	7,740	5,980	4,286	9,797	3,904	10,239	9,275	2,010	2,563	9,015	11,018	1,098	2,443	6,275
Kisangani, Zaire	5,086	4,578	11,101	9,674	9,780	1,726	12,494	13,235	4,493	2,484	3,849	12,140	8,205	6,634	4,933	12,545	7,858	6,858	5,424	6,172
Kishinev, USSR	2,208	1,158	10,136	8,768	8,738	5,333	9,541	8,344	3,144	7,426	1,561	10,586	9,168	2,562	689	10,570	10,371	2,130	1,621	5,041
Kitchner, Canada	6,510	7,526	3,640	3,524	3,348	9,890	1,726	3,542	6,788	13,533	9,267	13,374	5,910	5,323	7,498	3,013	7,948	5,731	6,542	12,281
Knoxville, Tennessee	7,196	8,269	2,916	3,120	2,942	10,224	912	3,915	7,350	13,842	10,046	13,764	5,537	6,109	8,278	2,133	7,483	6,571	7,295	13,162
Kosice, Czechoslovakia	1,702	909	9,540	8,179	8,146	5,307	8,981	8,008	2,735	7,710	2,026	11,057	8,659	1,978	434	9,983	9,962	1,650	1,050	5,635
Kota Kinabalu, Malaysia	11,519	10,345	17,785	17,562	17,426	11,802	15,045	11,074	12,277	9,326	8,775	2,042	18,248	11,433	9,983	16,272	17,369	10,546	10,915	4,562
Krakow, Poland	1,678	1,023	9,415	8,069	8,032	5,432	8,812	7,831	2,752	7,883	2,205	11,085	8,611	1,820	585	9,829	9,961	1,468	984	5,755
Kralendijk, Bonaire	7,498	8,726	725	823	824	8,671	3,110	6,972	7,053	11,826	10,504	16,708	2,656	7,143	8,971	2,280	4,439	7,938	7,949	14,602
Krasnodar, USSR	2,993	1,849	10,949	9,584	9,554	5,578	10,250	8,707	3,849	7,195	1,274	9,867	9,926	3,339	1,457	11,336	11,017	2,795	2,436	4,226
Krasnoyarsk, USSR	6,365	5,536	12,491	11,678	11,564	9,407	10,416	7,060	7,452	10,003	4,963	6,516	13,039	5,714	5,038	11,888	14,642	4,784	5,630	3,850
Kristiansand, Norway	1,911	1,995	8,555	7,322	7,259	6,247	7,692	6,702	3,051	8,993	3,389	11,317	8,259	947	1,713	8,789	9,882	290	1,252	6,635
Kuala Lumpur, Malaysia	10,573	9,350	18,394	17,222	17,178	10,224	16,044	12,103	11,143	7,729	7,628	3,662	16,716	10,846	9,069	17,479	15,864	10,052	10,077	3,434
Kuching, Malaysia	11,402	10,192	18,511	17,882	17,788	11,191	15,800	11,815	12,042	8,557	8,518	2,754	17,681	11,521	9,877	17,068	16,566	10,676	10,859	4,290
Kumasi, Ghana	3,863	4,234	8,048	6,622	6,731	1,370	9,600	11,444	2,761	4,957	4,862	14,920	5,284	5,326	4,740	9,502	5,489	5,987	4,543	8,605
Kumzar, Oman	5,198	3,974	13,325	11,860	11,864	5,673	12,843	10,855	5,678	5,613	2,178	8,470	11,572	5,896	3,802	13,903	11,967	5,387	4,838	2,146
Kunming, China	9,025	7,892	16,007	15,161	15,061	10,225	13,687	9,867	9,874	8,861	6,477	3,908	15,971	8,886	7,496	15,166	16,559	8,006	8,393	2,573
Kuqa Chang, China	6,534	5,445	13,816	12,735	12,656	8,516	12,055	8,842	7,448	8,413	4,262	6,268	13,499	6,382	5,020	13,491	14,552	5,524	5,882	2,066
Kurgan, USSR	4,742	3,835	11,766	10,670	10,589	7,740	10,229	7,579	5,787	8,823	3,316	8,032	11,618	4,354	3,344	11,594	13,019	3,471	4,029	3,709
Kuwait, Kuwait	4,313	3,095	12,435	10,965	10,970	5,063	12,101	10,509	4,782	5,624	1,282	9,282	10,720	5,098	2,960	13,080	11,252	4,673	3,988	3,007
Kuybyshev, USSR	3,776	2,823	11,201	9,982	9,921	6,794	10,014	7,874	4,791	8,224	2,440	8,982	10,713	3,592	2,338	11,272	12,025	2,792	3,086	4,039
Kyoto, Japan	10,314	9,525	13,991	14,068	13,899	13,085	11,257	7,278	11,427	12,217	8,752	3,066	16,265	9,425	9,027	12,563	18,333	8,510	9,570	5,745
Kzyl-Orda, USSR	5,035	3,928	12,655	11,426	11,368	7,226	11,344	8,752	5,930	7,802	2,832	7,787	11,994	5,034	3,510	12,662	13,062	4,246	4,406	2,624
L'vov, USSR	1,934	1,116	9,707	8,363	8,326	5,487	9,064	7,947	2,971	7,791	2,007	10,824	8,885	2,096	615	10,103	10,199	1,662	1,264	5,462
La Ceiba, Honduras	8,785	9,972	1,404	2,683	2,575	10,663	1,685	5,615	8,607	13,862	11,801	14,810	4,625	8,006	10,093	266	6,131	8,611	9,062	15,359
La Coruna, Spain	897	2,089	7,276	5,860	5,841	4,938	7,216	7,561	1,413	8,276	3,915	13,263	6,373	1,260	2,306	7,951	7,894	2,106	1,305	7,944
La Paz, Bolivia	9,651	10,793	3,127	3,663	3,786	8,786	5,752	9,728	8,820	10,705	12,261	17,369	2,724	9,815	11,182	4,363	2,587	10,709	10,282	16,357
La Paz, Mexico	9,970	10,959	4,026	5,135	4,991	12,948	2,013	3,804	10,195	16,413	12,638	12,187	7,246	8,725	10,885	2,365	8,690	8,995	9,971	14,692
La Ronge, Canada	7,313	8,020	5,573	5,708	5,530	11,397	2,959	1,358	7,952	14,869	9,461	11,177	8,108	5,811	7,814	4,433	10,125	5,821	7,071	11,318
Labrador City, Canada	5,180	6,127	4,708	4,125	3,973	8,953	3,181	3,769	5,613	12,528	7,834	13,026	6,270	3,898	6,068	4,400	8,372	4,275	5,139	10,886
Lagos, Nigeria	3,872	4,068	8,597	7,164	7,270	871	10,090	11,718	2,847	4,510	4,490	14,395	5,829	5,403	4,566	10,038	5,945	5,986	4,502	8,103
Lahore, Pakistan	6,368	5,170	14,266	12,964	12,923	7,507	12,971	10,074	7,093	7,077	3,624	6,771	13,168	6,608	4,841	14,314	13,778	5,867	5,829	971
Lambasa, Fiji	17,226	16,800	12,029	13,527	13,447	18,042	10,871	9,476	18,315	14,438	15,934	5,600	14,416	15,747	16,293	10,733	13,810	15,102	16,544	11,918
Lansing, Michigan	6,835	7,838	3,643	3,674	3,496	10,224	1,486	3,343	7,126	13,868	9,564	13,206	6,081	5,623	7,797	2,858	8,090	5,999	6,851	12,467
Lanzhou, China	8,298	7,258	14,796	14,044	13,930	10,247	12,482	8,727	9,262	9,517	6,099	4,463	15,228	7,937	6,813	13,966	16,396	7,026	7,612	2,899
Laoag, Philippines	10,873	9,797	16,367	16,213	16,061	12,149	13,644	9,659	11,799	10,261	8,467	1,926	17,810	10,490	9,371	14,947	18,396	9,567	10,194	4,518
Largeau, Chad	3,062	2,583	10,054	8,540	8,603	2,051	10,847	11,197	2,629	4,516	2,406	12,403	7,703	4,597	2,988	11,232	8,058	4,842	3,389	6,066
Las Vegas, Nevada	9,314	10,149	4,919	5,710	5,544	12,940	2,313	2,395	9,763	16,584	11,674	11,325	8,034	7,905	9,988	3,339	9,721	8,015	9,175	13,296

Distances in Kilometers	Barcelona, Spain	Bari, Italy	Barranquilla, Colombia	Basse-Terre, Guadeloupe	Basseterre, St. Kitts & Nevis	Bata, Equatorial Guinea	Baton Rouge, Louisiana	Bear Lake, Canada	Bechar, Algeria	Beira, Mozambique	Beirut, Lebanon	Belau Islands (Koror)	Belem, Brazil	Belfast, United Kingdom	Belgrade, Yugoslavia	Belmopan, Belize	Belo Horizonte, Brazil	Bergen, Norway	Bern, Switzerland	Bhopal, India
Launceston, Australia	17,112	15,915	14,723	16,067	16,112	13,904	14,724	13,476	17,089	10,298	14,087	5,550	15,004	17,552	15,740	14,086	13,120	16,673	16,774	10,137
Le Havre, France	916	1,601	8,000	6,647	6,610	5,360	7,592	7,308	1,996	8,411	3,372	12,320	7,306	702	1,623	8,497	8,834	1,256	616	7,174
Leipzig, East Germany	1,348	1,182	8,866	7,530	7,490	5,486	8,287	7,512	2,491	8,182	2,690	11,500	8,159	1,277	941	9,282	9,602	1,101	603	6,302
Leningrad, USSR	2,821	2,285	9,780	8,591	8,522	6,677	8,658	6,971	3,954	8,849	2,920	10,089	9,519	2,232	1,801	9,871	11,056	1,377	2,075	5,461
Leon, Spain	656	1,863	7,494	6,066	6,051	4,765	7,461	7,753	1,255	8,061	3,684	13,162	6,500	1,333	2,106	8,190	7,963	2,112	1,136	7,742
Lerwick, United Kingdom	2,100	2,451	8,050	6,863	6,790	6,534	7,125	6,249	3,173	9,444	3,942	11,576	7,952	683	2,230	8,233	9,678	360	1,577	7,161
Lhasa, China	7,818	6,663	15,264	14,179	14,105	9,077	13,349	9,839	8,634	8,144	5,225	5,160	14,732	7,804	6,284	14,819	15,386	6,963	7,211	1,537
Libreville, Gabon	4,599	4,574	9,382	7,994	8,111	166	11,013	12,613	3,669	3,562	4,598	13,876	6,452	6,171	5,043	10,882	6,235	6,664	5,159	7,751
Lilongwe, Malawi	6,938	6,347	12,294	11,014	11,146	3,178	14,130	15,038	6,343	658	5,300	11,363	9,144	8,471	6,650	13,888	8,235	8,626	7,239	6,288
Lima, Peru	10,008	11,207	2,559	3,531	3,609	9,713	4,940	8,852	9,312	11,782	12,829	16,539	3,364	9,911	11,539	3,485	3,643	10,747	10,567	17,055
Limerick, Ireland	1,496	2,307	7,444	6,152	6,100	5,885	6,901	6,686	2,395	9,063	4,056	12,500	7,055	278	2,292	7,846	8,736	1,210	1,319	7,723
Limoges, France	500	1,363	8,062	6,663	6,639	4,943	7,828	7,706	1,606	8,025	3,185	12,516	7,152	1,099	1,509	8,660	8,590	1,641	493	7,141
Limon, Costa Rica	8,886	10,102	908	2,402	2,340	10,288	2,417	6,371	8,572	13,299	11,922	15,452	4,033	8,276	10,280	1,013	5,414	8,957	9,243	15,760
Lincoln, Nebraska	7,786	8,731	3,942	4,343	4,167	11,253	1,253	2,772	8,134	14,897	10,397	12,554	6,754	6,489	8,645	2,724	8,655	6,761	7,743	12,883
Linz, Austria	1,226	822	9,040	7,668	7,638	5,166	8,579	7,875	2,318	7,819	2,380	11,540	8,159	1,563	612	9,531	9,511	1,463	536	6,141
Lisbon, Portugal	1,009	2,229	7,147	5,687	5,685	4,512	7,332	7,968	1,008	7,941	4,005	13,680	5,998	1,780	2,540	7,952	7,437	2,614	1,630	8,145
Little Rock, Arkansas	7,891	8,926	3,173	3,685	3,513	10,994	487	3,539	8,097	14,606	10,669	13,252	6,071	6,726	8,900	1,973	7,920	7,110	7,943	13,493
Liverpool, United Kingdom	1,393	2,017	7,829	6,536	6,484	5,836	7,239	6,822	2,423	8,893	3,719	12,184	7,392	232	1,950	8,213	9,026	926	1,038	7,338
Lodz, Poland	1,748	1,197	9,350	8,025	7,982	5,605	8,681	7,645	2,851	8,070	2,367	11,038	8,638	1,718	773	9,721	10,034	1,298	1,023	5,817
Lome, Togo	3,906	4,177	8,367	6,941	7,049	1,059	9,902	11,642	2,844	4,672	4,681	14,636	5,587	5,411	4,679	9,820	5,721	6,029	4,559	8,338
London, United Kingdom	1,138	1,735	8,000	6,674	6,630	5,580	7,495	7,106	2,215	8,606	3,461	12,187	7,419	519	1,696	8,439	8,988	1,045	751	7,167
Londonderry, United Kingdom	1,668	2,350	7,582	6,323	6,264	6,093	6,918	6,520	2,629	9,206	4,044	12,247	7,296	101	2,275	7,915	8,998	962	1,370	7,591
Longlac, Canada	6,574	7,478	4,436	4,364	4,189	10,305	2,182	2,756	7,015	13,912	9,126	12,543	6,739	5,231	7,378	3,618	8,788	5,489	6,491	11,760
Lord Howe Island, Australia	17,691	16,501	14,059	15,558	15,537	15,417	13,439	11,959	18,256	11,790	14,798	5,036	15,346	17,186	16,155	13,066	13,807	16,267	17,058	10,597
Los Angeles, California	9,677	10,500	5,094	5,964	5,801	13,295	2,574	2,547	10,131	16,939	12,003	11,124	8,252	8,259	10,330	3,476	9,873	8,350	9,528	13,449
Louangphrabang, Laos	9,367	8,201	16,576	15,668	15,577	10,197	14,259	10,413	10,154	8,548	6,689	3,755	16,235	9,333	7,832	15,735	16,487	8,472	8,765	2,586
Louisville, Kentucky	7,191	8,233	3,212	3,407	3,229	10,368	998	3,617	7,404	14,002	9,986	13,473	5,825	6,043	8,217	2,349	7,781	6,460	7,251	12,974
Luanda, Angola	5,670	5,541	9,990	8,702	8,836	1,240	11,886	13,711	4,766	2,629	5,278	13,566	6,884	7,250	5,984	11,575	6,259	7,702	6,198	7,830
Lubumbashi, Zaire	6,422	5,947	11,580	10,286	10,416	2,465	13,405	14,593	5,742	1,202	5,112	12,028	8,454	7,985	6,296	13,164	7,654	8,226	6,787	6,671
Lusaka, Zambia	6,839	6,371	11,725	10,482	10,620	2,795	13,675	15,014	6,140	853	5,509	11,964	8,555	8,405	6,718	13,338	7,622	8,650	7,211	6,848
Luxembourg, Luxembourg	964	1,259	8,434	7,078	7,042	5,303	7,985	7,500	2,115	8,198	2,971	11,972	7,681	994	1,208	8,917	9,145	1,202	314	6,740
Luxor, Egypt	3,296	2,250	11,193	9,682	9,714	3,603	11,395	10,728	3,457	5,041	950	10,838	9,197	4,495	2,389	12,106	9,692	4,383	3,238	4,523
Lynn Lake, Canada	6,985	7,697	5,566	5,601	5,426	11,082	3,032	1,580	7,628	14,542	9,153	11,301	7,982	5,484	7,496	4,517	10,026	5,506	6,745	11,126
Lyon, France	531	1,097	8,342	6,940	6,917	4,887	8,086	7,842	1,683	7,870	2,912	12,299	7,389	1,246	1,230	8,935	8,780	1,629	240	6,864
Macapa, Brazil	7,032	8,174	2,893	2,120	2,298	6,770	5,415	9,129	6,211	9,591	9,693	18,996	329	7,309	8,561	4,552	2,339	8,230	7,675	13,894
Madison, Wisconsin	7,150	8,119	3,826	3,987	3,809	10,614	1,410	3,023	7,481	14,257	9,815	12,889	6,403	5,887	8,054	2,867	8,382	6,209	7,131	12,537
Madras, India	8,073	6,845	16,193	14,750	14,748	7,861	15,103	11,925	8,560	6,165	5,069	5,962	14,247	8,590	6,622	16,449	14,056	7,924	7,655	1,168
Madrid, Spain	506	1,732	7,630	6,180	6,174	4,480	7,698	8,043	984	7,773	3,526	13,212	6,487	1,586	2,036	8,385	7,872	2,309	1,153	7,644
Madurai, India	8,115	6,892	16,239	14,755	14,769	7,611	15,394	12,322	8,530	5,771	5,086	6,204	14,055	8,731	6,704	16,681	13,731	8,107	7,741	1,478
Magadan, USSR	8,451	8,074	11,196	11,130	10,963	12,401	8,536	4,582	9,599	13,343	8,079	5,958	13,348	7,179	7,578	9,955	15,448	6,371	7,739	6,873
Magdalena, Bolivia	9,098	10,237	2,936	3,255	3,392	8,323	5,645	9,632	8,264	10,436	11,710	17,891	2,168	9,294	10,627	4,332	2,273	10,196	9,734	15,834
Magdeburg, East Germany	1,398	1,288	8,812	7,488	7,445	5,580	8,200	7,406	2,547	8,288	2,785	11,490	8,158	1,198	1,043	9,207	9,626	994	658	6,355
Majuro Atoll, Marshall Isls.	14,516	14,056	12,454	13,662	13,515	17,743	10,340	7,639	15,659	15,119	13,507	4,054	15,590	13,158	13,549	10,837	15,987	12,415	13,805	10,091
Malabo, Equatorial Guinea	4,220	4,219	9,240	7,820	7,929	236	10,757	12,244	3,293	3,866	4,335	13,881	6,397	5,792	4,694	10,699	6,328	6,289	4,785	7,667
Male, Maldives	8,160	6,965	16,145	14,626	14,671	7,086	15,862	13,081	8,426	4,977	5,136	6,765	13,578	8,964	6,848	16,967	13,032	8,432	7,877	2,173
Manado, Indonesia	12,555	11,401	17,453	17,944	17,772	12,805	14,818	10,991	13,353	10,071	9,863	1,249	19,296	12,343	11,022	15,797	17,636	11,431	11,925	5,656
Managua, Nicaragua	9,002	10,204	1,259	2,684	2,599	10,632	2,088	5,998	8,759	13,707	12,033	15,032	4,441	8,294	10,350	623	5,840	8,930	9,315	15,708
Manama, Bahrain	4,718	3,508	12,826	11,344	11,356	5,131	12,537	10,870	5,135	5,370	1,682	9,052	10,992	5,533	3,389	13,507	11,401	5,105	4,414	2,728
Manaus, Brazil	7,973	9,145	2,263	2,125	2,279	7,783	4,978	8,892	7,212	10,410	10,717	18,363	1,296	8,090	9,508	3,881	2,550	8,986	8,581	14,935
Manchester, New Hampshire	5,881	6,946	3,562	3,132	2,967	9,156	2,236	4,134	6,093	12,800	8,725	13,849	5,434	4,795	6,960	3,295	7,515	5,298	5,972	12,008
Mandalay, Burma	8,738	7,558	16,225	15,162	15,088	9,562	14,149	10,449	9,498	8,107	6,021	4,426	15,568	8,782	7,202	15,634	15,880	7,946	8,154	1,924
Mangareva Island, Fr.Polynesia	15,563	16,717	7,559	9,066	9,038	15,550	7,549	8,822	15,296	15,128	18,500	10,391	9,592	14,557	16,732	6,717	9,266	14,861	15,755	16,728
Manila, Philippines	11,200	10,102	16,692	16,609	16,455	12,248	13,955	9,980	12,096	10,164	8,715	1,677	18,160	10,864	9,686	15,215	18,325	9,944	10,533	4,675
Mannheim, West Germany	1,025	1,136	8,604	7,245	7,210	5,280	8,142	7,585	2,176	8,109	2,814	11,840	7,824	1,137	1,047	9,083	9,261	1,230	295	6,572
Maputo, Mozambique	8,088	7,604	12,272	11,199	11,353	3,937	14,540	16,264	7,367	719	6,631	11,559	9,050	9,655	7,935	13,931	7,766	9,886	8,457	7,281
Mar del Plata, Argentina	10,679	11,567	5,713	5,993	6,145	8,171	8,346	12,306	9,610	8,884	12,467	16,401	4,152	11,380	12,052	6,931	2,398	12,312	11,412	15,459
Maracaibo, Venezuela	7,884	9,112	350	1,222	1,209	9,036	2,983	6,921	7,453	12,126	10,897	16,516	2,891	7,488	9,348	1,992	4,544	8,265	8,323	14,971
Marrakech, Morocco	1,413	2,455	7,189	5,683	5,710	3,787	7,725	8,697	549	7,305	4,054	14,145	5,625	2,555	2,871	8,177	6,874	3,344	2,150	8,281
Marseilles, France	340	975	8,390	6,963	6,949	4,612	8,247	8,106	1,460	7,613	2,804	12,419	7,299	1,501	1,220	9,048	8,625	1,901	434	6,847
Maseru, Lesotho	8,250	7,877	11,790	10,796	10,957	3,933	14,178	16,403	7,440	1,289	7,046	12,059	8,575	9,832	8,242	13,450	7,201	10,145	8,679	7,900
Mashhad, Iran	4,926	3,719	12,932	11,567	11,539	6,381	12,014	9,737	5,641	6,736	2,208	8,179	11,725	5,291	3,408	13,219	12,483	4,640	4,416	2,240
Mazatlan, Mexico	9,766	10,796	3,616	4,737	4,596	12,590	1,711	4,025	9,932	16,016	12,517	12,596	6,836	8,581	10,752	1,955	8,293	8,906	9,811	14,846
Mbabane, Swaziland	8,068	7,612	12,130	11,067	11,222	3,873	14,417	16,248	7,325	813	6,679	11,703	8,909	9,640	7,952	13,790	7,618	9,892	8,453	7,411
Mbandaka, Zaire	4,854	4,550	10,352	8,946	9,057	968	11,869	13,027	4,105	2,850	4,154	12,911	7,432	6,436	4,964	11,828	7,123	6,782	5,296	6,880
McMurdo Sound, Antarctica	15,904	15,696	11,893	12,701	12,824	11,472	13,618	15,546	14,857	8,735	14,570	9,608	11,005	17,424	16,040	12,250	9,031	17,956	16,458	12,455
Mecca, Saudi Arabia	4,158	3,071	12,037	10,522	10,559	3,914	12,245	11,310	4,310	4,599	1,442	10,201	9,899	5,294	3,140	12,975	10,194	5,093	4,055	3,866
Medan, Indonesia	10,291	9,065	18,244	16,963	16,934	9,886	16,097	12,207	10,834	7,436	7,326	3,990	16,377	10,618	8,797	17,566	15,589	9,846	9,813	3,160
Medellin, Colombia	8,534	9,762	531	1,856	1,858	9,481	3,137	7,124	8,077	12,390	11,539	16,371	3,130	8,139	10,002	1,882	4,515	8,906	8,978	15,626
Medicine Hat, Canada	7,956	8,685	5,436	5,774	5,596	11,958	2,718	1,277	8,556	15,489	10,130	11,105	8,192	6,469	8,483	4,135	10,136	6,490	7,732	11,845
Medina, Saudi Arabia	3,929	2,805	11,899	10,391	10,420	4,070	11,987	10,976	4,162	4,928	1,117	10,172	9,888	5,008	2,843	12,769	10,291	4,778	3,783	3,841
Melbourne, Australia	16,830	15,613	15,068	16,451	16,485	13,963	14,856	13,291	16,961	10,328	13,795	5,118	15,442	17,134	15,402	14,330	13,545	16,244	16,428	9,776
Memphis, Tennessee	7,704	8,750	3,088	3,526	3,352	10,787	529	3,630	7,896	14,401	10,502	13,393	5,923	6,559	8,733	1,988	7,800	6,963	7,768	13,409
Merauke, Indonesia	14,524	13,407	16,174	17,494	17,350	14,514	14,159	10,958	15,381	11,293	11,903	1,864	18,550	14,084	13,005	14,629	16,831	13,152	13,855	7,693
Merida, Mexico	8,644	9,795	1,931	2,992	2,856	10,916	1,062	4,969	8,585	14,267	11,613	14,280	5,119	7,732	9,868	424	6,723	8,269	8,852	14,915
Meridian, Mississippi	7,787	8,864	2,764	3,269	3,098	10,698	318	3,950	7,917	14,281	10,640	13,676	5,648	6,702	8,872	1,678	7,497	7,149	7,890	13,674
Messina, Italy	1,199	346	9,298	7,831	7,834	4,067	9,274	8,962	1,777	6,732	1,855	11,949	7,875	2,442	845	10,044	8,940	2,572	1,175	6,036
Mexico City, Mexico	9,510	10,618	2,773	3,980	3,851	11,926	1,464	4,691	9,531	15,225	12,408	13,450	5,995	8,475	10,642	1,120	7,429	8,918	9,651	15,270
Miami, Florida	7,558	8,723	1,733	2,201	2,036	9,921	1,197	5,026	7,485	13,395	10,548	14,778	4,551	6,712	8,819	1,301	6,397	7,309	7,794	14,070
Midway Islands, USA	12,301	12,191	10,648	11,544	11,375	16,595	8,148	5,034	13,365	16,634	12,315	5,556	13,846	10,796	11,717	8,992	15,236	10,184	11,672	10,191
Milan, Italy	727	785	8,682	7,277	7,256	4,833	8,401	8,014	1,827	7,684	2,580	12,034	7,677	1,479	891	9,269	9,011	1,680	209	6,527
Milford Sound, New Zealand	18,796	17,628	13,025	14,418	14,445	14,805	13,139	12,729	18,328	11,427	15,799	6,648	13,777	18,806	17,446	12,389	12,173	17,899	18,471	11,817
Milwaukee, Wisconsin	7,051	8,029	3,773	3,894	3,716	10,495	1,427	3,115	7,371	14,138	9,735	12,983	6,308	5,802	7,971	2,864	8,297	6,139	7,042	12,512
Minsk, USSR	2,340	1,629	9,825	8,541	8,490	5,997	8,971	7,579	3,426	8,199	2,310	10,442	9,228	2,165	1,130	10,091	10,626	1,517	1,618	5,349
Mogadiscio, Somalia	6,132	5,187	13,257	11,779	11,865	3,963	14,178	13,507	5,962	2,680	3,669	9,892	10,453	7,437	5,330	14,569	10,022	7,309	6,172	4,176
Mombasa, Kenya	6,306	5,515	12,776	11,360	11,466	3,392	14,105	14,099	5,937	1,822	4,221	10,606	9,802	7,737	5,741	14,231	9,196	7,743	6,470	5,091
Monclova, Mexico	9,120	10,158	3,299	4,267	4,115	12,009	1,074	3,837	9,286	15,516	11,893	12,912	6,479	7,952	10,126	1,685	8,079	8,306	9,174	14,452
Moncton, Canada	5,259	6,315	4,007	3,350	3,199	8,672	2,868	4,326	5,513	12,306	8,093	13,786	5,506	4,164	6,327	3,897	7,607	4,686	5,340	11,432
Monrovia, Liberia	4,093	4,734	7,052	5,651	5,769	2,334	8,740	10,984	2,940	5,777	5,653	15,893	4,275	5,370	5,236	8,539	4,646	6,150	4,827	9,558
Monte Carlo, Monaco	503	828	8,551	7,128	7,113	4,645	8,369	8,131	1,588	7,576	2,656	12,256	7,466	1,545	1,050	9,191	8,778	1,858	354	6,680
Monterrey, Mexico	9,131	10,187	3,139	4,140	3,991	11,928	1,042	4,008	9,265	15,405	11,937	13,068	6,329	7,994	10,168	1,515	7,911	8,371	9,206	14,585
Montevideo, Uruguay	10,336	11,245	5,443	5,662	5,816	7,959	8,110	12,088	9,277	8,870	12,200	16,767	3,787	11,016	11,725	6,719	2,050	11,949	11,066	15,372
Montgomery, Alabama	7,605	8,695	2,647	3,073	2,900	10,474	511	4,083	7,713	14,056	10,481	13,854	5,464	6,551	8,716	1,699	7,339	7,023	7,726	13,609
Montpelier, Vermont	5,903	6,949	3,695	3,296	3,129	9,256	2,241	3,975	6,150	12,898	8,715	13,682	5,601	4,777	6,947	3,363	7,682	5,251	5,970	11,930
Montpellier, France	283	1,101	8,267	6,843	6,828	4,661	8,122	8,022	1,434	7,704	2,931	12,500	7,206	1,413	1,333	8,921	8,559	1,870	464	6,965
Montreal, Canada	5,918	6,945	3,828	3,454	3,287	9,345	2,265	3,826	6,200	12,984	8,698	13,522	5,760	4,756	6,929	3,440	7,841	5,202	5,963	11,846
Moosonee, Canada	6,127	7,041	4,501	4,261	4,091	9,877	2,472	3,037	6,569	13,474	8,706	12,696	6,586	4,797	6,952	3,848	8,663	5,085	6,053	11,473
Moroni, Comoros	7,229	6,447	13,289	11,955	12,076	3,999	14,903	14,993	6,817	1,274	5,110	10,313	10,177	8,670	6,666	14,843	9,292	8,668	7,403	5,364
Moscow, USSR	3,014	2,218	10,355	9,122	9,062	6,479	9,294	7,513	4,088	8,379	2,435	9,768	9,893	2,731	1,711	10,496	11,300	1,950	2,294	4,854
Mosul, Iraq	3,565	2,337	11,682	10,248	10,239	5,135	11,215	9,707	4,185	6,277	747	9,655	10,253	4,227	2,126	12,228	11,046	3,779	3,163	3,591
Mount Isa, Australia	15,412	14,212	16,213	17,731	17,666	14,195	14,868	12,121	16,039	10,676	12,526	3,153	17,405	15,264	13,879	14,951	15,493	14,342	14,826	8,310

Distances in Kilometers	Barcelona, Spain	Bari, Italy	Barranquilla, Colombia	Basse-Terre, Guadeloupe	Basseterre, St. Kitts & Nevis	Bata, Equatorial Guinea	Baton Rouge, Louisiana	Bear Lake, Canada	Bechar, Algeria	Beira, Mozambique	Beirut, Lebanon	Belau Islands (Koror)	Belem, Brazil	Belfast, United Kingdom	Belgrade, Yugoslavia	Belmopan, Belize	Belo Horizonte, Brazil	Bergen, Norway	Bern, Switzerland	Bhopal, India
Multan, Pakistan	6,221	5,010	14,204	12,860	12,829	7,210	13,050	10,277	6,903	6,784	3,406	7,015	12,953	6,545	4,705	14,354	13,496	5,839	5,711	966
Munich, West Germany	1,056	884	8,841	7,466	7,437	5,134	8,414	7,813	2,175	7,879	2,542	11,724	7,966	1,409	777	9,347	9,341	1,420	339	6,342
Murcia, Spain	472	1,580	7,841	6,370	6,374	4,152	8,009	8,385	713	7,425	3,314	13,212	6,531	1,881	1,953	8,656	7,818	2,532	1,216	7,487
Murmansk, USSR	3,564	3,243	9,570	8,547	8,452	7,652	8,092	6,024	4,716	9,849	3,906	9,700	9,817	2,537	2,782	9,412	11,549	1,611	2,839	5,873
Mururoa Atoll, Fr. Polynesia	15,794	16,897	7,886	9,400	9,365	15,976	7,717	8,725	15,618	15,343	18,568	9,969	10,002	14,683	16,845	6,967	9,697	14,907	15,915	16,304
Muscat, Oman	5,547	4,328	13,670	12,195	12,204	5,783	13,213	11,146	5,992	5,453	2,517	8,258	11,820	6,267	4,167	14,274	12,108	5,758	5,202	1,922
Myitkyina, Burma	8,599	7,443	15,895	14,904	14,819	9,692	13,759	10,052	9,411	8,413	5,980	4,414	15,507	8,554	7,065	15,245	16,026	7,698	7,989	2,042
Naga, Philippines	11,435	10,345	16,646	16,684	16,523	12,496	13,905	9,947	12,342	10,350	8,970	1,419	18,385	11,066	9,926	15,123	18,491	10,143	10,762	4,932
Nagasaki, Japan	10,208	9,337	14,500	14,465	14,301	12,674	11,781	7,795	11,288	11,638	8,427	2,859	16,530	9,444	8,851	13,115	18,456	8,516	9,471	5,218
Nagoya, Japan	10,356	9,581	13,910	14,012	13,842	13,173	11,174	7,199	11,473	12,325	8,830	3,092	16,231	9,446	9,082	12,473	18,313	8,534	9,611	5,850
Nagpur, India	7,419	6,195	15,458	14,090	14,066	7,801	14,202	11,094	8,019	6,615	4,495	6,138	13,946	7,803	5,923	15,563	14,123	7,095	6,941	293
Nairobi, Kenya	5,877	5,113	12,407	10,972	11,073	3,033	13,669	13,742	5,496	2,063	3,895	10,883	9,493	7,323	5,358	13,830	9,001	7,358	6,059	5,165
Nanchang, China	9,692	8,665	15,470	15,054	14,915	11,485	12,862	8,904	10,668	10,220	7,475	3,066	16,570	9,241	8,217	14,280	17,764	8,316	8,995	3,884
Nancy, France	871	1,186	8,440	7,072	7,040	5,201	8,034	7,594	2,023	8,106	2,925	12,027	7,636	1,064	1,171	8,949	9,079	1,304	218	6,740
Nandi, Fiji	17,352	16,829	12,253	13,756	13,679	17,796	11,127	9,706	18,474	14,183	15,845	5,477	14,570	15,912	16,324	10,975	13,873	15,234	16,648	11,772
Nanjing, China	9,608	8,633	15,030	14,687	14,541	11,689	12,404	8,441	10,625	10,613	7,553	3,184	16,367	9,052	8,168	13,816	17,835	8,121	8,894	4,171
Nanning, China	9,616	8,496	16,251	15,578	15,462	10,815	13,756	9,838	10,485	9,267	7,101	3,284	16,575	9,408	8,092	15,205	17,141	8,511	8,969	3,163
Nantes, France	713	1,614	7,856	6,476	6,447	5,144	7,571	7,468	1,733	8,273	3,428	12,581	7,059	875	1,722	8,420	8,560	1,532	685	7,332
Naples, Italy	1,015	221	9,143	7,696	7,690	4,341	9,018	8,646	1,795	7,047	2,028	11,924	7,862	2,137	677	9,829	9,017	2,260	868	6,136
Narvik, Norway	3,145	3,039	8,967	7,918	7,825	7,413	7,607	5,875	4,286	9,890	4,011	10,314	9,191	1,956	2,634	8,882	10,954	1,066	2,461	6,406
Nashville, Tennessee	7,396	8,452	3,039	3,337	3,161	10,479	755	3,730	7,578	14,100	10,214	13,556	5,750	6,272	8,445	2,109	7,672	6,701	7,473	13,221
Nassau, Bahamas	7,374	8,552	1,584	1,912	1,745	9,637	1,486	5,253	7,259	13,101	10,381	15,044	4,278	6,587	8,669	1,473	6,154	7,218	7,638	14,008
Natal, Brazil	6,461	7,415	4,762	3,787	3,958	5,070	7,179	10,639	5,423	7,717	8,615	18,885	1,550	7,222	7,880	6,417	1,826	8,144	7,190	12,580
Natashquan, Canada	4,914	5,923	4,509	3,794	3,651	8,546	3,284	4,232	5,266	12,147	7,675	13,440	5,863	3,734	5,906	4,381	7,964	4,211	4,940	10,934
Nauru Island	15,230	14,601	13,115	14,426	14,291	17,495	11,184	8,611	16,382	14,341	13,764	3,707	16,090	13,977	14,097	11,552	15,971	13,182	14,495	9,992
Ndjamena, Chad	3,477	3,220	9,749	8,259	8,342	1,277	10,848	11,655	2,793	4,148	3,181	12,995	7,180	5,058	3,664	11,055	7,369	5,416	3,923	6,682
Nelson, New Zealand	19,279	18,053	12,640	14,079	14,089	15,338	12,597	12,179	18,862	12,001	16,244	6,682	13,681	18,525	17,780	11,907	12,223	17,727	18,724	12,153
Nema, Mauritania	2,891	3,568	7,300	5,804	5,887	2,477	8,527	10,185	1,738	6,121	4,670	15,051	4,950	4,215	4,064	8,612	5,694	4,964	3,624	8,770
Neuquen, Argentina	11,389	12,348	5,572	6,118	6,251	9,090	8,048	11,909	10,362	9,708	13,350	15,844	4,606	11,933	12,819	6,582	3,133	12,863	12,105	16,329
New Delhi, India	6,782	5,577	14,699	13,393	13,354	7,720	13,355	10,337	7,482	7,031	3,988	6,440	13,535	7,041	5,259	14,718	14,033	6,299	6,253	591
New Glasgow, Canada	5,121	6,192	4,006	3,281	3,136	8,499	2,991	4,491	5,354	12,134	7,979	13,902	5,394	4,062	6,217	3,972	7,496	4,612	5,222	11,381
New Haven, Connecticut	6,071	7,148	3,365	3,004	2,834	9,263	2,036	4,169	6,254	12,906	8,933	13,942	5,340	5,008	7,169	3,073	7,408	5,519	6,177	12,231
New Orleans, Louisiana	8,052	9,141	2,630	3,277	3,111	10,857	121	4,093	8,152	14,406	10,923	13,723	5,617	6,988	9,156	1,418	7,409	7,443	8,169	13,965
New Plymouth, New Zealand	19,286	18,075	12,596	14,056	14,057	15,590	12,444	11,932	19,116	12,232	16,301	6,563	13,773	18,280	17,751	11,803	12,376	17,508	18,622	12,158
New York, New York	6,183	7,261	3,295	2,984	2,812	9,351	1,923	4,146	6,359	12,993	9,046	13,944	5,338	5,120	7,282	2,967	7,398	5,628	6,290	12,332
Newcastle upon Tyne, UK	1,539	2,053	7,943	6,672	6,616	5,982	7,271	6,720	2,598	8,984	3,700	11,995	7,573	283	1,935	8,280	9,220	728	1,100	7,228
Newcastle Waters, Australia	14,684	13,478	16,912	18,414	18,323	13,642	15,299	12,199	15,300	10,225	11,786	2,738	17,910	14,625	13,154	15,558	15,867	13,719	14,115	7,571
Niamey, Niger	3,088	3,379	8,339	6,854	6,941	1,540	9,573	10,954	2,053	5,146	4,054	14,285	5,823	4,610	3,884	9,675	6,254	5,209	3,737	7,948
Nicosia, Cyprus	2,798	1,589	10,919	9,454	9,457	4,425	10,717	9,709	3,316	6,089	242	10,547	9,365	3,707	1,532	11,604	10,173	3,449	2,521	4,441
Niue (Alofi)	17,416	17,471	10,941	12,453	12,387	18,105	10,040	9,260	18,153	14,936	17,014	6,759	13,245	15,830	16,985	9,735	12,726	15,396	16,901	13,085
Norfolk, Virginia	6,566	7,669	2,869	2,721	2,544	9,537	1,551	4,305	6,675	13,162	9,468	14,165	5,122	5,557	7,709	2,500	7,143	6,088	6,707	12,804
Norfolk Island, Australia	18,134	17,083	13,245	14,759	14,723	16,222	12,543	11,263	19,040	12,628	15,516	5,391	14,881	17,125	16,664	12,187	13,605	16,287	17,405	11,283
Noril'sk, USSR	5,619	5,072	10,996	10,246	10,123	9,356	8,940	5,796	6,767	10,745	5,079	7,649	11,817	4,639	4,568	10,402	13,640	3,722	4,877	5,171
Norman Wells, Canada	7,387	7,795	7,204	7,252	7,077	11,783	4,577	1,012	8,259	14,780	8,905	9,671	9,611	5,802	7,473	6,037	11,674	5,512	6,956	9,971
Normanton, Australia	15,313	14,137	16,100	17,598	17,509	14,437	14,577	11,748	16,028	10,966	12,504	2,859	17,651	15,041	13,778	14,751	15,812	14,112	14,692	8,272
North Pole	5,421	5,449	8,788	8,234	8,090	9,800	6,632	3,770	6,505	12,198	6,253	9,190	10,164	3,953	5,038	8,098	12,207	3,307	4,806	7,429
Nottingham, United Kingdom	1,312	1,889	7,945	6,642	6,592	5,756	7,371	6,928	2,373	8,782	3,587	12,130	7,458	362	1,818	8,342	9,065	916	914	7,222
Norway House, Canada	6,996	7,771	5,188	5,243	5,067	10,981	2,668	1,855	7,576	14,509	9,290	11,650	7,634	5,536	7,599	4,154	9,667	5,627	6,804	11,434
Norwich, United Kingdom	1,252	1,736	8,107	6,796	6,748	5,684	7,540	7,044	2,352	8,659	3,419	12,031	7,571	525	1,650	8,512	9,147	898	775	7,059
Nouakchott, Mauritania	3,106	4,034	6,367	4,868	4,949	3,333	7,630	9,578	2,038	6,958	5,380	15,726	4,169	4,139	4,495	7,675	5,199	4,993	3,848	9,565
Noumea, New Caledonia	17,431	16,489	13,421	14,937	14,873	16,637	12,373	10,699	18,491	12,994	15,086	4,783	15,414	16,361	16,034	12,204	14,298	15,523	16,689	10,873
Novosibirsk, USSR	5,836	4,953	12,399	11,460	11,359	8,772	10,517	7,381	6,898	9,460	4,327	6,973	12,633	5,309	4,462	11,961	14,122	4,391	5,111	3,557
Nuku'alofa, Tonga	17,746	17,518	11,520	13,035	12,973	17,807	10,634	9,696	18,656	14,425	16,697	6,335	13,720	16,184	17,012	10,333	13,039	15,645	17,134	12,624
Nukunono Island, Tokelau Isls.	16,392	16,364	10,978	12,441	12,345	19,173	9,650	8,347	17,308	15,670	16,105	6,222	13,653	14,820	15,881	9,593	13,482	14,320	15,823	12,526
Nuremberg, West Germany	1,134	1,028	8,793	7,434	7,400	5,277	8,311	7,666	2,271	8,026	2,648	11,681	7,993	1,296	879	9,265	9,403	1,271	389	6,382
Nyala, Sudan	3,931	3,317	10,799	9,298	9,374	2,015	11,730	12,001	3,523	3,692	2,648	11,955	8,244	5,435	3,658	12,054	8,325	5,600	4,197	5,679
Oaxaca, Mexico	9,493	10,630	2,459	3,732	3,613	11,705	1,587	5,031	9,449	14,927	12,439	13,786	5,674	8,530	10,684	843	7,072	9,019	9,677	15,500
Ocean Falls, Canada	8,555	9,098	6,576	6,985	6,807	12,807	3,836	432	9,306	16,095	10,313	9,897	9,403	6,993	8,815	5,167	11,325	6,824	8,208	11,282
Odense, Denmark	1,670	1,656	8,707	7,430	7,376	5,938	7,957	7,043	2,822	8,653	3,078	11,370	8,240	1,046	1,377	9,014	9,789	630	965	6,465
Odessa, USSR	2,347	1,262	10,293	8,922	8,893	5,348	9,688	8,435	3,260	7,354	1,454	10,462	9,302	2,716	817	10,724	10,478	2,265	1,774	4,886
Ogbomosho, Nigeria	3,690	3,862	8,662	7,212	7,313	923	10,079	11,593	2,686	4,562	4,287	14,252	5,950	5,231	4,359	10,076	6,124	5,798	4,309	7,943
Okha, USSR	8,835	8,317	12,015	11,946	11,780	12,501	9,341	5,371	9,988	12,948	8,080	5,183	14,133	7,679	7,811	10,746	16,224	6,822	8,102	6,353
Okinawa (Naha)	10,658	9,705	15,232	15,226	15,062	12,681	12,501	8,520	11,693	11,233	8,623	2,211	17,234	10,018	9,236	13,800	18,914	9,086	9,936	5,064
Oklahoma City, Oklahoma	8,212	9,205	3,554	4,153	3,982	11,448	813	3,193	8,478	15,071	10,908	12,806	6,525	6,978	9,146	2,201	8,337	7,297	8,217	13,479
Old Crow, Canada	7,509	7,792	7,836	7,867	7,693	11,948	5,199	1,432	8,453	14,688	8,749	9,072	10,210	5,930	7,431	6,651	12,284	5,531	7,015	9,476
Olympia, Washington	8,813	9,460	6,015	6,545	6,369	12,904	3,280	1,054	9,470	16,380	10,785	10,363	8,952	7,287	9,215	4,548	10,804	7,213	8,533	11,957
Omaha, Nebraska	7,710	8,655	3,947	4,319	4,142	11,186	1,278	2,772	8,060	14,830	10,321	12,573	6,733	6,413	8,569	2,756	8,645	6,687	7,667	12,826
Omsk, USSR	5,257	4,350	12,114	11,079	10,991	8,189	10,423	7,540	6,305	9,061	3,747	7,525	12,112	4,819	3,861	11,828	13,536	3,918	4,540	3,539
Oodnadatta, Australia	15,527	14,299	16,371	17,837	17,840	13,596	15,504	12,970	15,929	10,001	12,523	3,861	16,768	15,687	14,035	15,357	14,752	14,802	15,041	8,398
Oradea, Romania	1,694	774	9,628	8,249	8,221	5,147	9,130	8,196	2,678	7,522	1,856	11,078	8,658	2,116	272	10,110	9,913	1,832	1,099	5,557
Oran, Algeria	677	1,638	7,882	6,395	6,408	3,898	8,157	8,630	476	7,197	3,295	13,330	6,443	2,138	2,055	8,754	7,663	2,778	1,417	7,502
Oranjestad, Aruba	7,621	8,848	547	975	948	8,864	2,947	6,837	7,202	12,021	10,636	16,535	2,839	7,222	9,082	2,084	4,588	8,001	8,056	14,703
Orebro, Sweden	2,188	2,022	8,966	7,750	7,684	6,387	8,008	6,767	3,340	8,951	3,194	10,898	8,688	1,383	1,647	9,148	10,284	567	1,469	6,238
Orel, USSR	2,837	1,952	10,395	9,117	9,066	6,161	9,458	7,808	3,874	8,060	2,115	9,922	9,771	2,737	1,449	10,619	11,105	2,037	2,144	4,785
Orsk, USSR	4,365	3,358	11,789	10,591	10,527	7,114	10,488	8,089	5,349	8,203	2,678	8,396	11,316	4,203	2,892	11,790	12,574	3,387	3,689	3,499
Osaka, Japan	10,333	9,538	14,034	14,111	13,942	13,079	11,300	7,322	11,443	12,188	8,753	3,029	16,304	9,451	9,041	12,605	18,369	8,535	9,589	5,724
Oslo, Norway	2,145	2,132	8,710	7,505	7,437	6,441	7,752	6,598	3,290	9,106	3,410	11,077	8,491	1,164	1,801	8,887	10,129	305	1,463	6,499
Osorno, Chile	11,833	12,808	5,710	6,373	6,497	9,545	8,080	11,854	10,818	10,027	13,820	15,423	4,996	12,325	13,275	6,599	3,596	13,250	12,542	16,664
Ostrava, Czechoslovakia	1,563	973	9,304	7,954	7,918	5,379	8,732	7,818	2,645	7,888	2,265	11,203	8,491	1,728	581	9,734	9,847	1,431	864	5,867
Ottawa, Canada	6,071	7,089	3,818	3,513	3,344	9,509	2,140	3,702	6,362	13,148	8,834	13,437	5,844	4,891	7,065	3,356	7,917	5,318	6,105	11,928
Ouagadougou, Bourkina Fasso	3,236	3,656	7,965	6,492	6,585	1,702	9,296	10,891	2,133	5,346	4,440	14,698	5,411	4,699	4,164	9,333	5,861	5,359	3,922	8,362
Oujda, Morocco	827	1,794	7,766	6,274	6,290	3,829	8,103	8,678	340	7,177	3,425	13,491	6,286	2,235	2,216	8,667	7,501	2,907	1,571	7,641
Oxford, United Kingdom	1,182	1,815	7,925	6,604	6,559	5,626	7,412	7,042	2,238	8,673	3,545	12,226	7,372	444	1,779	8,357	8,958	1,044	830	7,242
Pago Pago, American Samoa	16,923	16,940	10,942	12,437	12,356	18,630	9,832	8,808	17,760	15,319	16,602	6,508	13,434	15,341	16,456	9,645	13,080	14,875	16,380	12,843
Pakxe, Laos	10,008	8,833	17,117	16,304	16,207	10,613	14,648	10,719	10,773	8,669	7,285	3,247	16,824	9,985	8,473	16,092	16,779	9,121	9,413	3,112
Palembang, Indonesia	11,274	10,047	19,111	17,951	17,919	10,585	16,532	12,546	11,790	7,802	8,296	3,492	17,020	11,593	9,784	17,853	15,772	10,805	10,800	4,147
Palermo, Italy	1,024	449	9,108	7,640	7,643	4,033	9,117	8,900	1,594	6,797	2,045	12,126	7,690	2,341	954	9,868	8,778	2,540	1,090	6,229
Palma, Majorca	206	1,218	8,169	6,709	6,708	4,239	8,228	8,378	986	7,380	2,984	12,844	6,902	1,789	1,582	8,933	8,172	2,323	905	7,132
Palmerston North, New Zealand	19,458	18,232	12,453	13,903	13,909	15,511	12,376	11,990	19,017	12,207	16,439	6,756	13,583	18,418	17,928	11,696	12,183	17,678	18,815	12,320
Panama, Panama	8,668	9,892	565	2,084	2,041	9,908	2,669	6,652	8,298	12,898	11,698	15,850	3,632	8,144	10,095	1,357	5,042	8,863	9,061	15,653
Paramaribo, Suriname	6,891	8,082	2,235	1,334	1,512	7,221	4,648	8,342	6,194	10,238	9,717	18,208	1,096	6,961	8,425	3,871	3,103	7,858	7,478	13,950
Paris, France	832	1,427	8,156	6,793	6,759	5,258	7,768	7,446	1,953	8,265	3,198	12,242	7,401	854	1,452	8,668	8,891	1,296	441	7,022
Patna, India	7,615	6,417	15,416	14,178	14,128	8,459	13,790	10,453	8,333	7,403	4,840	5,606	14,385	7,794	6,085	15,223	14,792	7,011	7,066	824
Patrai, Greece	1,706	527	9,827	8,366	8,366	4,212	9,709	9,127	2,301	6,574	1,330	11,448	8,397	2,764	738	10,533	9,399	2,718	1,512	5,496
Peking, China	8,822	7,909	14,251	13,810	13,668	11,292	11,710	7,810	9,878	10,711	6,989	4,037	15,479	8,186	7,428	13,163	17,108	7,253	8,095	4,094
Penrhyn Island (Omoka)	15,930	16,410	9,480	10,962	10,875	18,465	8,362	7,778	16,483	16,520	16,924	7,697	12,144	14,381	16,031	8,152	12,141	14,139	15,586	13,931
Peoria, Illinois	7,311	8,305	3,598	3,834	3,656	10,666	1,146	3,193	7,600	14,309	10,020	13,046	6,252	6,083	8,255	2,603	8,205	6,432	7,318	12,798
Perm', USSR	4,174	3,340	11,173	10,054	9,976	7,432	9,744	7,339	5,247	8,850	3,098	8,626	11,008	3,732	2,838	11,073	12,460	2,849	3,448	4,212
Perth, Australia	14,143	12,956	17,445	18,223	18,377	11,640	17,455	14,557	14,244	8,047	11,126	4,776	15,961	14,850	12,820	17,055	13,878	14,148	13,855	7,352
Peshawar, Pakistan	6,009	4,817	13,893	12,592	12,551	7,320	12,644	9,858	6,755	7,116	3,315	7,070	12,842	6,235	4,478	13,967	13,538	5,498	5,461	1,321

Distances in Kilometers	Barcelona, Spain	Bari, Italy	Barranquilla, Colombia	Basse-Terre, Guadeloupe	Basseterre, St. Kitts & Nevis	Bata, Equatorial Guinea	Baton Rouge, Louisiana	Bear Lake, Canada	Bechar, Algeria	Beira, Mozambique	Beirut, Lebanon	Belau Islands (Koror)	Belem, Brazil	Belfast, United Kingdom	Belgrade, Yugoslavia	Belmopan, Belize	Belo Horizonte, Brazil	Bergen, Norway	Bern, Switzerland	Bhopal, India
Petropavlovsk-Kamchatskiy, USSR	9,304	8,948	11,300	11,439	11,265	13,273	8,574	4,589	10,447	13,991	8,927	5,519	13,767	7,993	8,453	9,920	15,854	7,209	8,598	7,400
Petrozavodsk, USSR	3,122	2,583	9,914	8,766	8,690	6,965	8,678	6,815	4,259	9,051	3,107	9,822	9,770	2,455	2,093	9,930	11,340	1,559	2,376	5,373
Pevek, USSR	7,647	7,524	9,790	9,679	9,512	11,931	7,183	3,330	8,753	13,714	7,951	7,387	11,912	6,214	7,065	8,637	14,014	5,523	6,995	7,710
Philadelphia, Pennsylvania	6,310	7,390	3,210	2,957	2,783	9,446	1,795	4,131	6,477	13,087	9,176	13,954	5,328	5,250	7,412	2,843	7,378	5,756	6,420	12,453
Phnom Penh, Kampuchea	10,209	9,016	17,512	16,627	16,541	10,541	15,051	11,115	10,922	8,422	7,410	3,279	16,890	10,266	8,676	16,489	16,575	9,419	9,639	3,190
Phoenix, Arizona	9,344	10,235	4,539	5,388	5,225	12,795	1,999	2,771	9,724	16,426	11,821	11,689	7,681	7,986	10,105	2,941	9,332	8,156	9,252	13,648
Pierre, South Dakota	7,778	8,657	4,437	4,797	4,619	11,448	1,742	2,279	8,215	15,080	10,260	12,090	7,213	6,407	8,532	3,200	9,136	6,600	7,674	12,512
Pinang, Malaysia	10,293	9,072	18,115	16,933	16,888	10,064	15,853	11,945	10,880	7,686	7,361	3,783	16,546	10,554	8,786	17,312	15,845	9,761	9,791	3,156
Pitcairn Island (Adamstown)	15,290	16,489	7,201	8,692	8,675	15,011	7,413	9,010	14,913	14,780	18,319	10,904	9,101	14,426	16,582	6,475	8,729	14,827	15,566	17,237
Pittsburgh, Pennsylvania	6,642	7,693	3,303	3,234	3,057	9,859	1,500	3,795	6,854	13,501	9,458	13,651	5,635	5,518	7,689	2,709	7,656	5,968	6,715	12,577
Plymouth, Montserrat	6,675	7,903	1,500	93	85	8,037	3,312	6,916	6,241	11,351	9,682	16,783	2,511	6,358	8,152	2,830	4,517	7,176	7,133	13,787
Plymouth, United Kingdom	1,114	1,919	7,707	6,372	6,330	5,538	7,272	7,067	2,092	8,670	3,693	12,475	7,122	482	1,941	8,180	8,715	1,260	936	7,462
Ponape Island	14,130	13,395	13,833	14,946	14,787	16,404	11,562	8,438	15,267	13,766	12,496	2,626	17,009	13,032	12,897	12,193	17,234	12,175	13,385	8,783
Ponce, Puerto Rico	6,953	8,179	1,176	566	421	8,511	2,840	6,530	6,592	11,841	9,981	16,379	2,930	6,513	8,397	2,355	4,873	7,290	7,367	14,004
Ponta Delgada, Azores	2,417	3,644	5,711	4,276	4,262	5,373	5,979	7,243	2,247	8,980	5,446	14,610	4,933	2,398	3,893	6,513	6,662	3,327	2,889	9,531
Pontianak, Indonesia	11,439	10,223	18,714	17,992	17,911	11,086	16,008	12,022	12,047	8,391	8,526	2,909	17,563	11,608	9,921	17,271	16,369	10,776	10,913	4,309
Port Augusta, Australia	15,992	14,766	15,926	17,334	17,362	13,627	15,411	13,258	16,270	9,991	12,963	4,422	16,191	16,260	14,533	15,071	14,201	15,385	15,554	8,900
Port Blair, India	9,215	7,993	17,160	15,870	15,835	9,214	15,333	11,649	9,809	7,232	6,287	4,603	15,610	9,518	7,711	16,813	15,315	8,752	8,721	2,077
Port Elizabeth, South Africa	8,681	8,364	11,642	10,750	10,917	4,298	14,147	16,766	7,823	1,815	7,582	12,209	8,456	10,266	8,742	13,291	6,950	10,620	9,140	8,378
Port Hedland, Australia	13,658	12,431	18,260	19,526	19,649	12,051	16,843	13,378	14,038	8,643	10,637	3,520	17,221	14,030	12,199	17,132	15,167	13,223	13,224	6,573
Port Louis, Mauritius	8,883	7,980	14,836	13,619	13,754	5,750	16,689	15,988	8,567	2,367	6,421	8,952	11,628	10,229	8,118	16,470	10,390	10,082	8,963	5,268
Port Moresby, Papua New Guinea	15,091	14,028	15,438	16,816	16,687	15,251	13,571	10,628	16,025	11,940	12,597	2,333	17,911	14,469	13,601	13,930	16,536	13,541	14,390	8,411
Port Said, Egypt	2,909	1,764	10,967	9,478	9,493	4,028	10,946	10,114	3,268	5,661	418	10,739	9,222	3,974	1,823	11,755	9,909	3,798	2,742	4,522
Port Sudan, Sudan	4,095	3,070	11,851	10,332	10,377	3,580	12,199	11,472	4,153	4,372	1,590	10,499	9,622	5,315	3,196	12,856	9,870	5,180	4,058	4,171
Port-au-Prince, Haiti	7,396	8,612	877	1,161	1,028	9,117	2,317	6,144	7,107	12,440	10,431	15,916	3,421	6,831	8,797	1,751	5,264	7,556	7,761	14,340
Port-of-Spain, Trin. & Tobago	7,046	8,268	1,453	592	747	7,931	3,770	7,513	6,498	11,074	9,999	17,355	1,968	6,871	8,555	3,033	3,892	7,719	7,557	14,184
Port-Vila, Vanuatu	17,072	16,256	13,214	14,713	14,632	17,097	11,977	10,168	18,202	13,456	15,019	4,639	15,472	15,886	15,776	11,909	14,563	15,079	16,327	10,868
Portland, Maine	5,762	6,825	3,647	3,170	3,007	9,065	2,357	4,161	5,982	12,708	8,604	13,836	5,448	4,673	6,838	3,412	7,535	5,179	5,851	11,896
Portland, Oregon	8,931	9,596	5,925	6,496	6,321	12,983	3,198	1,223	9,568	16,491	10,938	10,425	8,896	7,413	9,358	4,436	10,724	7,356	8,664	12,122
Porto, Portugal	905	2,130	7,224	5,785	5,775	4,728	7,280	7,761	1,203	8,107	3,939	13,455	6,202	1,507	2,396	7,961	7,682	2,344	1,436	8,027
Porto Alegre, Brazil	9,626	10,536	5,200	5,221	5,385	7,357	7,925	11,910	8,566	8,569	11,527	17,421	3,180	10,332	11,015	6,607	1,341	11,262	10,357	14,898
Porto Alexandre, Angola	6,411	6,326	9,997	8,819	8,966	1,968	12,124	14,339	5,461	2,475	6,044	13,723	6,806	7,982	6,772	11,631	5,908	8,467	6,962	8,337
Porto Novo, Benin	3,867	4,091	8,513	7,081	7,187	943	10,016	11,677	2,828	4,577	4,545	14,476	5,746	5,389	4,590	9,956	5,874	5,984	4,505	8,180
Porto Velho, Brazil	8,718	9,881	2,496	2,750	2,886	8,254	5,228	9,207	7,932	10,595	11,418	18,005	1,890	8,844	10,253	3,971	2,478	9,737	9,334	15,608
Portsmouth, United Kingdom	1,073	1,747	7,925	6,591	6,549	5,517	7,460	7,142	2,129	8,577	3,498	12,292	7,317	536	1,738	8,386	8,882	1,143	759	7,244
Poznan, Poland	1,659	1,254	9,169	7,850	7,806	5,645	8,497	7,517	2,785	8,190	2,536	11,160	8,502	1,532	882	9,535	9,932	1,138	918	5,998
Prague, Czechoslovakia	1,357	1,012	9,029	7,679	7,643	5,364	8,486	7,695	2,475	8,001	2,488	11,435	8,244	1,472	740	9,470	9,639	1,283	625	6,142
Praia, Cape Verde Islands	3,839	4,851	5,570	4,098	4,195	3,930	7,065	9,445	2,848	7,457	6,255	16,564	3,292	4,658	5,293	6,957	4,454	5,560	4,563	10,446
Pretoria, South Africa	7,901	7,496	11,830	10,764	10,919	3,641	14,116	16,074	7,123	950	6,645	12,000	8,608	9,480	7,855	13,489	7,340	9,770	8,313	7,587
Prince Albert, Canada	7,470	8,199	5,435	5,626	5,448	11,506	2,790	1,394	8,083	15,011	9,658	11,253	8,035	5,981	8,001	4,257	10,033	6,011	7,244	11,528
Prince Edward Island	10,368	9,939	12,625	12,019	12,195	6,034	15,330	18,512	9,554	2,980	8,915	11,099	9,619	11,949	10,271	14,169	7,817	12,220	10,777	8,696
Prince George, Canada	8,215	8,790	6,361	6,696	6,518	12,442	3,631	365	8,947	15,772	10,055	10,180	9,114	6,660	8,521	5,012	11,068	6,523	7,886	11,238
Prince Rupert, Canada	8,479	8,976	6,824	7,190	7,012	12,783	4,086	304	9,267	15,977	10,138	9,687	9,608	6,906	8,675	5,434	11,553	6,695	8,104	11,010
Providence, Rhode Island	5,933	7,012	3,433	3,008	2,841	9,141	2,173	4,224	6,118	12,785	8,798	13,962	5,320	4,875	7,035	3,192	7,398	5,395	6,041	12,119
Provo, Utah	8,776	9,605	4,859	5,499	5,327	12,479	2,147	2,094	9,247	16,116	11,135	11,458	7,875	7,361	9,445	3,369	9,663	7,474	8,631	12,913
Puerto Aisen, Chile	12,151	13,066	6,248	6,889	7,016	9,566	8,605	12,344	11,099	9,755	13,933	15,047	5,416	12,741	13,548	7,122	3,867	13,671	12,875	16,367
Puerto Deseado, Argentina	11,931	12,770	6,565	7,073	7,211	9,093	9,023	12,835	10,843	9,172	13,502	15,130	5,399	12,658	13,264	7,549	3,669	13,590	12,669	15,786
Puerto Princesa, Philippines	11,426	10,285	17,277	17,158	17,011	12,063	14,537	10,567	12,254	9,747	8,795	1,754	18,342	11,218	9,896	15,771	17,851	10,312	10,790	4,640
Punta Arenas, Chile	12,593	13,388	7,116	7,712	7,845	9,550	9,468	13,153	11,490	9,268	13,991	14,432	6,094	13,353	13,888	7,983	4,354	14,285	13,334	15,755
Pusan, South Korea	9,955	9,099	14,324	14,237	14,075	12,514	11,620	7,633	11,041	11,622	8,227	3,125	16,271	9,178	8,610	12,978	18,190	8,251	9,217	5,134
Pyongyang, North Korea	9,432	8,586	14,077	13,865	13,709	12,094	11,420	7,448	10,521	11,447	7,760	3,617	15,804	8,660	8,094	12,822	17,671	7,731	8,693	4,865
Qamdo, China	8,180	7,063	15,264	14,326	14,233	9,669	13,128	9,467	9,056	8,729	5,719	4,683	15,140	8,026	6,656	14,612	15,956	7,149	7,538	2,147
Qandahar, Afghanistan	5,671	4,454	13,703	12,330	12,305	6,723	12,723	10,205	6,336	6,576	2,837	7,576	12,383	6,063	4,165	13,965	12,971	5,398	5,181	1,474
Qiqian, China	8,076	7,348	12,847	12,445	12,298	11,262	10,334	6,493	9,200	11,457	6,819	5,129	14,292	7,189	6,844	11,801	16,188	6,268	7,330	4,879
Qom, Iran	4,286	3,060	12,390	10,968	10,955	5,598	11,781	9,936	4,911	6,264	1,419	8,968	10,964	4,858	2,819	12,865	11,673	4,326	3,854	2,863
Quebec, Canada	5,692	6,713	3,987	3,529	3,366	9,174	2,499	3,884	5,993	12,806	8,464	13,493	5,791	4,522	6,695	3,659	7,883	4,971	5,730	11,630
Quetta, Pakistan	5,852	4,633	13,895	12,517	12,493	6,793	12,909	10,342	6,500	6,519	2,991	7,444	12,533	6,256	4,350	14,157	13,068	5,592	5,369	1,288
Quito, Ecuador	9,250	10,477	1,305	2,571	2,598	9,825	3,650	7,606	8,729	12,448	12,227	16,292	3,344	8,912	10,738	2,235	4,352	9,688	9,721	16,374
Rabaul, Papua New Guinea	14,925	13,977	14,804	16,102	15,960	15,854	12,797	9,836	15,971	12,683	12,727	2,344	17,653	14,081	13,514	13,238	16,817	13,174	14,191	8,654
Raiatea (Uturoa)	16,296	17,079	8,972	10,488	10,427	17,387	8,298	8,403	16,508	15,902	17,985	8,575	11,350	14,876	16,800	7,827	11,129	14,814	16,140	14,895
Raleigh, North Carolina	6,808	7,910	2,773	2,759	2,581	9,748	1,310	4,249	6,914	13,365	9,707	14,117	5,175	5,791	7,946	2,289	7,168	6,310	6,946	13,003
Rangiroa (Avatoru)	15,893	16,745	8,534	10,049	9,986	17,160	7,863	8,120	16,065	16,149	17,881	8,930	10,967	14,514	16,510	7,381	10,843	14,510	15,783	15,217
Rangoon, Burma	9,120	7,919	16,780	15,652	15,589	9,577	14,720	10,980	9,815	7,831	6,303	4,292	15,805	9,260	7,591	16,205	15,812	8,445	8,568	2,088
Raoul Is., Kermadec Islands	18,660	18,140	11,869	13,383	13,347	16,866	11,313	10,627	19,533	13,541	16,830	6,510	13,666	17,120	17,646	10,848	12,668	16,538	17,992	12,605
Rarotonga (Avarua)	17,204	17,772	9,939	11,458	11,404	17,587	9,295	9,119	17,513	15,197	17,962	7,842	12,157	15,701	17,383	8,831	11,693	15,499	16,930	14,173
Rawson, Argentina	11,545	12,433	6,091	6,575	6,714	8,931	8,590	12,451	10,477	9,294	13,285	15,588	4,921	12,208	12,919	7,125	3,260	13,141	12,276	15,931
Recife, Brazil	6,655	7,585	4,895	3,978	4,151	5,076	7,361	10,867	5,600	7,604	8,737	18,864	1,674	7,450	8,055	6,555	1,635	8,368	7,388	12,643
Regina, Canada	7,603	8,376	5,155	5,406	5,228	11,544	2,487	1,605	8,166	15,100	9,877	11,470	7,822	6,143	8,198	3,948	9,795	6,219	7,411	11,837
Reykjavik, Iceland	2,971	3,567	7,173	6,140	6,041	7,375	6,002	5,215	3,869	10,502	5,108	11,836	7,597	1,394	3,387	7,179	9,512	1,465	2,625	8,143
Rhodes, Greece	2,315	1,116	10,433	8,969	8,971	4,275	10,281	9,473	2,849	6,267	721	10,964	8,921	3,292	1,137	11,135	9,809	3,121	2,073	4,915
Richmond, Virginia	6,615	7,707	2,954	2,844	2,667	9,641	1,491	4,178	6,748	13,270	9,499	14,039	5,247	5,578	7,736	2,512	7,265	6,089	6,740	12,780
Riga, USSR	2,336	1,835	9,525	8,280	8,221	6,242	8,588	7,191	3,467	8,568	2,706	10,535	9,095	1,888	1,371	9,732	10,588	1,150	1,591	5,666
Ringkobing, Denmark	1,693	1,776	8,571	7,305	7,248	6,015	7,803	6,916	2,838	8,777	3,229	11,439	8,157	914	1,519	8,864	9,738	509	1,021	6,604
Rio Branco, Brazil	9,115	10,290	2,443	2,949	3,067	8,690	5,124	9,112	8,354	10,945	11,850	17,568	2,336	9,176	10,651	3,792	2,789	10,055	9,716	16,051
Rio Cuarto, Argentina	10,697	11,688	5,007	5,444	5,584	8,651	7,584	11,521	9,692	9,646	12,788	16,559	3,880	11,208	12,149	6,149	2,499	12,137	11,405	16,140
Rio de Janeiro, Brazil	8,520	9,416	5,088	4,752	4,927	6,361	7,816	11,711	7,450	8,007	10,430	18,265	2,440	9,294	9,896	6,655	338	10,219	9,255	13,995
Rio Gallegos, Argentina	12,397	13,204	6,958	7,528	7,662	9,409	9,344	13,071	11,297	9,230	13,844	14,636	5,891	13,149	13,703	7,861	4,152	14,081	13,137	15,765
Rio Grande, Brazil	9,851	10,751	5,340	5,414	5,576	7,504	8,053	12,041	8,786	8,593	11,713	17,188	3,406	10,566	11,233	6,711	1,570	11,496	10,583	14,995
Riyadh, Saudi Arabia	4,496	3,314	12,556	11,058	11,079	4,704	12,444	11,028	4,830	5,084	1,495	9,455	10,609	5,427	3,257	13,333	10,978	5,075	4,257	3,121
Road Town, Brit. Virgin Isls.	6,757	7,983	1,372	409	238	8,302	2,993	6,611	6,381	11,651	9,780	16,476	2,822	6,349	8,209	2,565	4,808	7,140	7,181	13,827
Roanoke, Virginia	6,819	7,901	2,957	2,961	2,783	9,862	1,285	4,048	6,966	13,489	9,685	13,915	5,375	5,756	7,920	2,387	7,371	6,245	6,930	12,898
Robinson Crusoe Island, Chile	11,727	12,806	4,956	5,786	5,892	9,999	7,211	10,940	10,803	10,839	14,056	15,522	4,766	11,992	13,234	5,725	3,768	12,890	12,394	17,441
Rochester, New York	6,320	7,355	3,576	3,367	3,194	9,657	1,854	3,741	6,573	13,301	9,110	13,547	5,735	5,168	7,341	3,065	7,788	5,608	6,373	12,220
Rockhampton, Australia	16,464	15,301	15,045	16,564	16,508	15,173	13,925	11,698	17,191	11,562	13,668	3,819	16,584	16,030	14,932	13,842	14,968	15,098	15,819	9,438
Rome, Italy	860	374	8,981	7,542	7,533	4,444	8,829	8,482	1,735	7,213	2,203	12,002	7,765	1,953	727	9,649	8,969	2,113	686	6,279
Rosario, Argentina	10,447	11,412	5,088	5,418	5,565	8,310	7,719	11,682	9,422	9,331	12,470	16,772	3,713	11,021	11,879	6,307	2,202	11,952	11,164	15,800
Roseau, Dominica	6,704	7,932	1,529	85	262	7,940	3,470	7,093	6,235	11,222	9,697	16,960	2,335	6,436	8,193	2,934	4,339	7,265	7,180	13,831
Rostock, East Germany	1,594	1,482	8,828	7,531	7,482	5,795	8,125	7,223	2,746	8,474	2,897	11,352	8,276	1,173	1,192	9,167	9,783	812	863	6,340
Rostov-na-Donu, USSR	3,032	1,940	10,893	9,555	9,518	5,801	10,101	8,472	3,943	7,443	1,524	9,776	9,990	3,250	1,506	11,220	11,145	2,650	2,431	4,274
Rotterdam, Netherlands	1,184	1,524	8,321	6,996	6,953	5,571	7,772	7,218	2,320	8,479	3,187	11,911	7,711	756	1,418	8,742	9,241	944	596	6,846
Rouyn, Canada	6,164	7,129	4,149	3,909	3,738	9,766	2,229	3,314	6,534	13,390	8,835	13,035	6,247	4,900	7,070	3,554	8,317	5,253	6,141	11,745
Sacramento, California	9,475	10,221	5,540	6,301	6,132	13,318	2,910	1,998	10,020	16,937	11,639	10,710	8,643	8,002	10,014	3,960	10,343	8,017	9,266	12,882
Saginaw, Michigan	6,753	7,751	3,703	3,698	3,521	10,169	1,577	3,330	7,053	13,812	9,474	13,186	6,100	5,534	7,707	2,943	8,118	5,907	6,764	12,378
Saint Denis, Reunion	8,811	7,938	14,617	13,415	13,553	5,576	16,530	16,077	8,458	2,151	6,418	9,176	11,406	10,185	8,095	16,257	10,163	10,071	8,916	5,432
Saint George's, Grenada	6,964	8,188	1,428	437	590	7,962	3,653	7,370	6,442	11,147	9,932	17,221	2,093	6,755	8,467	2,967	4,039	7,596	7,463	14,101
Saint John, Canada	5,383	6,445	3,891	3,270	3,117	8,755	2,737	4,307	5,622	12,393	8,225	13,831	5,458	4,298	6,460	3,762	7,558	4,821	5,471	11,565
Saint John's, Antigua	6,617	7,845	1,553	122	95	8,000	3,321	6,901	6,186	11,327	9,624	16,769	2,522	6,299	8,093	2,865	4,539	7,118	7,074	13,728
Saint John's, Canada	4,329	5,405	4,553	3,598	3,479	7,824	3,781	4,939	4,590	11,435	7,201	13,882	5,446	3,305	5,443	4,705	7,525	3,915	4,439	10,716
Saint Louis, Missouri	7,486	8,497	3,423	3,741	3,564	10,748	911	3,326	7,742	14,385	10,224	13,149	6,155	6,284	8,457	2,376	8,078	6,650	7,511	13,034
Saint Paul, Minnesota	7,278	8,202	4,151	4,349	4,171	10,874	1,618	2,662	7,671	14,510	9,856	12,527	6,766	5,957	8,108	3,101	8,740	6,217	7,215	12,390

Distances in Kilometers	Barcelona, Spain	Bari, Italy	Barranquilla, Colombia	Basse-Terre, Guadeloupe	Basseterre, St. Kitts & Nevis	Bata, Equatorial Guinea	Baton Rouge, Louisiana	Bear Lake, Canada	Bechar, Algeria	Beira, Mozambique	Beirut, Lebanon	Belau Islands (Koror)	Belem, Brazil	Belfast, United Kingdom	Belgrade, Yugoslavia	Belmopan, Belize	Belo Horizonte, Brazil	Bergen, Norway	Bern, Switzerland	Bhopal, India
Saint Peter Port, UK	969	1,772	7,807	6,457	6,419	5,403	7,414	7,216	1,981	8,517	3,556	12,467	7,146	617	1,813	8,307	8,703	1,315	794	7,366
Saipan (Susupe)	12,714	11,861	14,707	15,439	15,262	14,833	12,113	8,464	13,808	12,720	10,862	1,500	17,846	11,827	11,375	13,054	18,877	10,919	11,973	7,180
Salalah, Oman	5,622	4,452	13,612	12,099	12,133	5,133	13,581	11,893	5,876	4,585	2,636	8,763	11,404	6,564	4,397	14,466	11,460	6,177	5,399	2,530
Salem, Oregon	9,003	9,670	5,927	6,518	6,343	13,047	3,207	1,281	9,637	16,562	11,011	10,410	8,914	7,486	9,431	4,426	10,729	7,430	8,737	12,174
Salt Lake City, Utah	8,748	9,569	4,905	5,532	5,359	12,474	2,188	2,033	9,228	16,108	11,092	11,419	7,912	7,327	9,406	3,422	9,708	7,432	8,596	12,853
Salta, Argentina	10,103	11,174	4,086	4,529	4,665	8,607	6,702	10,668	9,171	10,089	12,463	17,155	3,159	10,460	11,604	5,294	2,275	11,378	10,781	16,257
Salto, Uruguay	10,148	11,106	5,021	5,259	5,411	8,022	7,691	11,672	9,118	9,147	12,164	17,050	3,460	10,747	11,575	6,307	1,894	11,680	10,867	15,552
Salvador, Brazil	7,328	8,257	4,806	4,100	4,277	5,578	7,407	11,094	6,274	7,819	9,381	19,035	1,684	8,093	8,729	6,458	961	9,016	8,059	13,206
Salzburg, Austria	1,117	800	8,953	7,574	7,546	5,102	8,527	7,891	2,214	7,802	2,429	11,649	8,050	1,519	663	9,462	9,402	1,486	432	6,233
Samsun, Turkey	2,840	1,631	10,918	9,508	9,490	5,118	10,413	9,086	3,586	6,768	825	10,154	9,684	3,421	1,346	11,424	10,670	2,995	2,380	4,301
San Antonio, Texas	8,719	9,758	3,196	4,037	3,878	11,673	715	3,718	8,895	15,222	11,497	13,050	6,317	7,555	9,729	1,675	8,004	7,921	8,775	14,158
San Cristobal, Venezuela	8,144	9,372	454	1,461	1,476	9,107	3,195	7,162	7,673	12,092	11,142	16,627	2,827	7,791	9,622	2,080	4,358	8,576	8,601	15,254
San Diego, California	9,724	10,571	4,949	5,851	5,690	13,265	2,472	2,716	10,148	16,902	12,100	11,264	8,119	8,326	10,413	3,321	9,717	8,441	9,595	13,621
San Francisco, California	9,596	10,339	5,586	6,374	6,206	13,433	2,978	2,075	10,140	17,055	11,751	10,654	8,705	8,122	10,130	3,992	10,383	8,132	9,386	12,939
San Jose, Costa Rica	8,979	10,193	1,023	2,514	2,449	10,404	2,388	6,325	8,675	13,407	12,014	15,350	4,141	8,350	10,365	954	5,501	9,021	9,328	15,822
San Juan, Argentina	10,848	11,883	4,752	5,310	5,439	9,011	7,266	11,172	9,880	10,076	13,069	16,428	3,940	11,258	12,329	5,814	2,773	12,179	11,540	16,551
San Juan, Puerto Rico	6,881	8,106	1,248	540	383	8,460	2,858	6,519	6,523	11,804	9,909	16,376	2,929	6,442	8,324	2,407	4,888	7,220	7,294	13,932
San Luis Potosi, Mexico	9,444	10,522	3,049	4,175	4,037	12,066	1,342	4,336	9,530	15,451	12,288	13,160	6,267	8,345	10,519	1,389	7,754	8,744	9,545	14,977
San Marino, San Marino	888	476	8,966	7,636	7,519	4,668	8,712	8,274	1,875	7,420	2,276	11,896	7,846	1,780	648	9,570	9,104	1,894	514	6,274
San Miguel de Tucuman, Argen.	10,251	11,304	4,308	4,752	4,888	8,620	6,914	10,874	9,300	9,985	12,551	17,021	3,328	10,645	11,742	5,498	2,303	11,566	10,937	16,252
San Salvador, El Salvador	9,131	10,318	1,594	2,965	2,867	10,937	1,866	5,704	8,946	14,057	12,147	14,673	4,795	8,345	10,438	391	6,197	8,940	9,407	15,666
Sanaa, Yemen	4,955	3,887	12,705	11,186	11,236	4,066	13,054	12,032	5,028	4,024	2,232	9,834	10,348	6,113	3,956	13,734	10,398	5,895	4,873	3,589
Santa Cruz, Bolivia	9,383	10,489	3,431	3,742	3,883	8,274	6,125	10,113	8,496	10,159	11,879	17,790	2,418	9,673	10,901	4,784	2,039	10,586	10,043	15,889
Santa Cruz, Tenerife	2,203	3,312	6,373	4,858	4,896	4,035	7,131	8,589	1,396	7,664	4,918	14,960	4,774	3,020	3,710	7,448	6,125	3,902	2,906	9,148
Santa Fe, New Mexico	8,772	9,697	4,164	4,886	4,718	12,183	1,493	2,774	9,122	15,818	11,328	12,118	7,229	7,450	9,591	2,657	8,973	7,671	8,710	13,471
Santa Rosa, Argentina	10,970	11,926	5,383	5,830	5,970	8,716	7,938	11,856	9,940	9,498	12,943	16,250	4,220	11,538	12,397	6,492	2,711	12,469	11,688	16,073
Santa Rosalia, Mexico	9,854	10,798	4,314	5,344	5,193	13,039	2,084	3,413	10,148	16,587	12,431	11,890	7,522	8,553	10,696	2,660	9,029	8,772	9,811	14,313
Santarem, Brazil	7,508	8,657	2,675	2,181	2,353	7,189	5,314	9,139	6,699	9,881	10,182	18,877	700	7,738	9,040	4,329	2,261	8,652	8,143	14,381
Santiago del Estero, Argentina	10,263	11,302	4,437	4,852	4,991	8,543	7,051	11,013	9,298	9,858	12,517	17,013	3,365	10,691	11,745	5,638	2,243	11,615	10,955	16,161
Santiago, Chile	11,141	12,173	4,937	5,554	5,679	9,238	7,395	11,262	10,170	10,172	13,339	16,135	4,232	11,546	12,620	5,929	3,040	12,465	11,833	16,715
Santo Domingo, Dominican Rep.	7,197	8,418	982	910	772	8,860	2,526	6,293	6,881	12,189	10,231	16,107	3,218	6,681	8,616	2,007	5,106	7,428	7,582	14,190
Sao Paulo de Olivenca, Brazil	8,695	9,898	1,729	2,288	2,390	8,760	4,443	8,428	8,024	11,312	11,548	17,422	2,270	8,620	10,224	3,171	3,257	9,474	9,252	15,781
Sao Paulo, Brazil	8,774	9,699	4,899	4,672	4,845	6,712	7,638	11,570	7,720	8,324	10,755	18,208	2,452	9,487	10,174	6,431	487	10,417	9,503	14,348
Sao Tome, Sao Tome & Principe	4,569	4,632	9,086	7,706	7,825	375	10,756	12,489	3,589	3,794	4,775	14,175	6,150	6,125	5,113	10,595	5,958	6,661	5,162	8,029
Sapporo, Japan	9,800	9,154	12,991	13,057	12,887	13,085	10,267	6,281	10,944	12,813	8,648	4,014	15,295	8,750	8,647	11,604	17,393	7,864	9,057	6,196
Sarajevo, Yugoslavia	1,357	326	9,429	8,013	7,996	4,729	9,118	8,451	2,258	7,247	1,843	11,472	8,293	2,122	200	10,016	9,489	2,039	923	5,795
Saratov, USSR	3,493	2,505	11,067	9,807	9,753	6,466	10,007	8,040	4,484	7,984	2,140	9,268	10,447	3,419	2,027	11,222	11,716	2,672	2,821	4,131
Saskatoon, Canada	7,592	8,328	5,387	5,618	5,440	11,606	2,719	1,391	8,195	15,126	9,792	11,258	8,032	6,108	8,133	4,178	10,015	6,144	7,372	11,645
Schefferville, Canada	5,125	6,041	4,911	4,328	4,177	8,982	3,326	3,675	5,604	12,532	7,725	12,840	6,459	3,801	5,964	4,575	8,561	4,139	5,053	10,710
Seattle, Washington	8,739	9,386	6,004	6,515	6,338	12,834	3,266	1,006	9,397	16,306	10,714	10,388	8,924	7,212	9,141	4,549	10,788	7,140	8,459	11,913
Sendai, Japan	10,245	9,545	13,420	13,555	13,384	13,328	10,683	6,710	11,380	12,725	8,925	3,485	15,820	9,242	9,040	11,981	17,921	8,347	9,499	6,180
Seoul, South Korea	9,626	8,776	14,173	14,006	13,848	12,249	11,497	7,517	10,714	11,512	7,932	3,433	15,979	8,852	8,285	12,883	17,864	7,924	8,887	4,960
Sept-Iles, Canada	5,228	6,221	4,417	3,817	3,664	8,866	3,014	3,962	5,592	12,471	7,959	13,321	5,973	4,015	6,190	4,172	8,075	4,451	5,236	11,123
Sevastopol, USSR	2,566	1,414	10,569	9,185	9,160	5,283	9,990	8,683	3,415	7,136	1,202	10,301	9,491	3,014	1,032	11,022	10,595	2,562	2,035	4,619
Seville, Spain	832	2,008	7,409	5,936	5,941	4,252	7,643	8,236	727	7,645	3,748	13,583	6,133	1,912	2,361	8,247	7,487	2,680	1,531	7,920
Shanghai, China	9,848	8,885	15,040	14,781	14,630	11,951	12,377	8,399	10,874	10,810	7,818	2,966	16,554	9,259	8,417	13,767	18,095	8,327	9,130	4,414
Sheffield, United Kingdom	1,361	1,933	7,928	6,631	6,580	5,804	7,335	6,879	2,417	8,831	3,624	12,116	7,467	321	1,855	8,313	9,084	884	961	7,239
Shenyang, China	9,069	8,234	13,871	13,583	13,431	11,812	11,255	7,309	10,162	11,341	7,447	3,971	15,464	8,296	7,740	12,682	17,307	7,367	8,330	4,719
Shiraz, Iran	4,682	3,457	12,810	11,355	11,355	5,465	12,334	10,498	5,199	5,789	1,680	8,839	11,160	5,372	3,276	13,378	11,685	4,880	4,312	2,572
Sibiu, Romania	1,834	785	9,826	8,437	8,425	5,069	9,351	8,380	2,761	7,348	1,638	10,970	8,788	2,336	306	10,326	9,990	2,040	1,288	5,367
Singapore	10,890	9,667	18,640	17,534	17,486	10,471	16,153	12,182	11,456	7,873	7,943	3,464	16,959	11,152	9,385	17,542	15,961	10,351	10,392	3,751
Sioux Falls, South Dakota	7,605	8,520	4,183	4,499	4,322	11,190	1,534	2,551	8,001	14,830	10,161	12,383	6,917	6,273	8,418	3,013	8,853	6,513	7,534	12,583
Skelleftea, Sweden	2,864	2,643	9,180	8,062	7,980	7,039	7,950	6,312	4,016	9,455	3,574	10,354	9,190	1,869	2,219	9,187	10,871	936	2,149	6,119
Skopje, Yugoslavia	1,605	398	9,715	8,284	8,273	4,599	9,440	8,723	2,397	6,983	1,523	11,319	8,478	2,444	325	10,330	9,593	2,322	1,240	5,533
Socotra Island (Tamrida)	5,932	4,795	13,801	12,282	12,329	5,023	13,964	12,374	6,098	4,161	3,009	8,812	11,411	6,952	4,778	14,768	11,307	6,605	5,760	2,766
Sofia, Bulgaria	1,751	563	9,845	8,423	8,409	4,721	9,513	8,694	2,565	7,022	1,443	11,151	8,643	2,502	329	10,430	9,762	2,314	1,337	5,389
Songkhla, Thailand	10,184	8,966	17,932	16,796	16,742	10,087	15,655	11,754	10,797	7,793	7,274	3,741	16,548	10,407	8,669	17,117	15,956	9,604	9,668	3,053
Sorong, Indonesia	13,229	12,100	16,944	17,821	17,644	13,527	14,478	10,824	14,071	10,652	10,600	977	19,745	12,900	11,704	15,290	17,646	11,975	12,575	6,407
South Georgia Island	11,229	11,738	8,066	8,138	8,305	7,542	10,738	14,706	10,076	7,051	11,957	14,743	5,951	12,392	12,243	9,330	3,859	13,247	11,961	13,636
South Pole	14,587	14,560	11,217	11,773	11,917	10,209	13,372	16,232	13,504	7,810	13,755	10,812	9,843	16,055	14,971	11,907	7,800	16,701	15,202	12,577
South Sandwich Islands	11,307	11,679	8,789	8,793	8,963	7,352	11,475	15,450	10,161	6,472	11,681	14,177	6,538	12,592	12,174	10,075	4,436	13,393	12,018	12,984
Split, Yugoslavia	1,194	267	9,277	7,856	7,841	4,663	9,005	8,430	2,103	7,263	1,966	11,632	8,130	2,032	357	9,884	9,337	2,020	799	5,954
Spokane, Washington	8,491	9,186	5,683	6,156	5,979	12,519	2,942	1,148	9,111	16,040	10,578	10,741	8,568	6,987	8,965	4,268	10,451	6,965	8,244	12,010
Spoleto, Italy	885	385	8,991	7,560	7,548	4,538	8,799	8,404	1,807	7,290	2,211	11,940	7,817	1,894	667	9,636	9,042	2,027	624	6,255
Springbok, South Africa	8,031	7,839	10,868	9,915	10,079	3,594	13,309	15,973	7,108	2,030	7,274	12,984	7,659	9,610	8,254	12,527	6,273	10,046	8,546	8,650
Springfield, Illinois	7,372	8,374	3,513	3,778	3,601	10,684	1,047	3,261	7,645	14,325	10,096	13,105	6,196	6,157	8,330	2,504	8,138	6,515	7,388	12,896
Springfield, Massachusetts	6,007	7,077	3,455	3,074	2,906	9,241	2,105	4,130	6,206	12,885	8,859	13,883	5,399	4,930	7,093	3,161	7,472	5,434	6,105	12,140
Srinagar, India	6,266	5,084	14,080	12,812	12,764	7,615	12,713	9,793	7,034	7,316	3,610	6,775	13,127	6,435	4,732	14,070	13,840	5,672	5,702	1,225
Stanley, Falkland Islands	11,832	12,558	7,134	7,509	7,658	8,649	9,667	13,529	10,707	8,485	13,092	14,958	5,638	12,724	13,062	8,205	3,730	13,644	12,577	15,074
Stara Zagora, Bulgaria	1,943	744	10,037	8,616	8,601	4,765	9,680	8,774	2,736	6,957	1,281	10,981	8,822	2,664	494	10,611	9,914	2,426	1,521	5,197
Stockholm, Sweden	2,280	2,026	9,126	7,912	7,846	6,416	8,144	6,823	3,433	8,908	3,107	10,752	8,839	1,542	1,622	9,296	10,420	721	1,549	6,082
Stornoway, United Kingdom	1,967	2,508	7,717	6,509	6,440	6,409	6,891	6,260	2,973	9,446	4,111	11,937	7,586	405	2,359	7,955	9,325	708	1,562	7,478
Strasbourg, France	912	1,095	8,555	7,185	7,153	5,182	8,141	7,653	2,063	8,043	2,817	11,939	7,731	1,157	1,059	9,062	9,155	1,323	187	6,626
Stuttgart, West Germany	988	1,041	8,659	7,292	7,260	5,200	8,225	7,679	2,132	8,015	2,731	11,839	7,835	1,226	967	9,157	9,248	1,316	243	6,520
Subic, Philippines	11,120	10,019	16,706	16,582	16,430	12,162	13,973	9,994	12,012	10,098	8,627	1,765	18,083	10,796	9,605	15,247	18,261	9,878	10,455	4,586
Suchow, China	9,326	8,360	14,841	14,440	14,298	11,492	12,251	8,309	10,349	10,557	7,310	3,471	16,082	8,765	7,892	13,682	17,571	7,834	8,610	4,043
Sucre, Bolivia	9,636	10,747	3,480	3,895	4,029	8,513	6,138	10,120	8,756	10,316	12,141	17,528	2,672	9,903	11,156	4,764	2,242	10,811	10,292	16,139
Sudbury, Canada	6,384	7,362	3,981	3,825	3,651	9,920	1,987	3,301	6,729	13,554	9,074	13,090	6,192	5,137	7,308	3,326	8,246	5,497	6,374	11,980
Suez, Egypt	3,006	1,882	11,036	9,540	9,559	3,936	11,062	10,260	3,319	5,516	516	10,747	9,231	4,103	1,960	11,851	9,873	3,939	2,864	4,500
Sundsvall, Sweden	2,543	2,365	9,040	7,877	7,802	6,745	7,934	6,492	3,695	9,245	3,419	10,633	8,927	1,596	1,964	9,127	10,575	676	1,830	6,209
Surabaya, Indonesia	12,256	11,032	19,104	18,874	18,794	11,480	16,437	12,521	12,797	8,482	9,296	2,902	17,736	12,484	10,752	17,443	16,074	11,658	11,756	5,118
Suva, Fiji	17,403	16,915	12,151	13,656	13,581	17,829	11,052	9,691	18,510	14,233	15,954	5,588	14,458	15,942	16,409	10,882	13,768	15,281	16,708	11,885
Sverdlovsk, USSR	4,436	3,564	11,451	10,343	10,263	7,570	9,973	7,452	5,496	8,832	3,184	8,350	11,292	4,022	3,067	11,319	12,720	3,140	3,717	3,971
Svobodnyy, USSR	8,475	7,795	12,750	12,477	12,322	11,765	10,158	6,245	9,611	11,930	7,320	4,921	14,459	7,511	7,289	11,602	16,443	6,602	7,729	5,322
Sydney, Australia	17,182	15,956	14,714	16,179	16,180	14,670	14,221	12,600	17,531	11,032	14,182	4,891	15,590	17,101	15,674	13,811	13,840	16,171	16,657	10,045
Sydney, Canada	4,920	5,992	4,137	3,346	3,208	8,325	3,192	4,600	5,158	11,955	7,781	13,905	5,397	3,869	6,020	4,156	7,498	4,433	5,023	11,213
Syktyvkar, USSR	3,921	3,219	10,679	9,587	9,504	7,471	9,238	6,932	5,034	9,145	3,276	8,959	10,638	3,320	2,711	10,563	12,183	2,412	3,180	4,722
Szeged, Hungary	1,541	630	9,514	8,124	8,099	5,025	9,074	8,239	2,516	7,468	1,891	11,237	8,504	2,056	161	10,027	9,751	1,847	975	5,680
Szombathely, Hungary	1,319	678	9,228	7,846	7,818	5,072	8,789	8,048	2,362	7,649	2,170	11,439	8,279	1,774	402	9,736	9,583	1,636	695	5,960
Tabriz, Iran	3,759	2,540	11,841	10,433	10,415	5,475	11,232	9,537	4,444	6,521	1,079	9,356	10,531	4,297	2,271	12,304	11,371	3,777	3,302	3,379
Tacheng, China	6,207	5,186	13,240	12,213	12,125	8,585	11,435	8,261	7,185	8,811	4,206	6,553	13,146	5,915	4,730	12,873	14,389	5,031	5,522	2,653
Tahiti (Papeete)	16,242	17,088	8,802	10,320	10,263	17,175	8,201	8,444	16,390	15,843	18,126	8,787	11,144	14,862	16,841	7,688	10,912	14,844	16,131	15,110
Taipei, Taiwan	10,365	9,349	15,648	15,450	15,297	12,108	12,950	8,963	11,351	10,604	8,158	2,398	17,185	9,862	8,898	14,300	18,428	8,932	9,662	4,467
Taiyuan, China	8,748	7,785	14,544	14,012	13,878	11,008	12,052	8,178	9,773	10,316	6,767	4,041	15,535	8,208	7,316	13,514	16,999	7,278	8,034	3,711
Tallahassee, Florida	7,576	8,692	2,368	2,798	2,627	10,298	663	4,371	7,629	13,853	10,494	14,139	5,182	6,583	8,736	1,535	7,051	7,095	7,732	13,750
Tallinn, USSR	2,542	2,107	9,497	8,291	8,225	6,515	8,453	6,941	3,685	8,832	2,947	10,400	9,204	1,921	1,648	9,634	10,752	1,088	1,798	5,722
Tamanrasset, Algeria	2,086	2,295	8,566	7,048	7,104	2,361	9,363	10,178	1,242	5,692	3,172	13,549	6,435	3,658	2,801	9,714	7,153	4,176	2,683	7,284
Tampa, Florida	7,596	8,737	2,041	2,510	2,342	10,136	893	4,699	7,585	13,650	10,553	14,451	4,875	6,674	8,807	1,356	6,727	7,229	7,791	13,942
Tampere, Finland	2,666	2,313	9,390	8,218	8,145	6,722	8,271	6,703	3,817	9,070	3,183	10,367	9,214	1,894	1,867	9,476	10,814	1,003	1,928	5,856
Tanami, Australia	14,564	13,342	17,223	18,742	18,689	13,212	15,773	12,659	15,080	9,760	11,601	3,066	17,626	14,665	13,052	15,966	15,538	13,783	14,044	7,426

Distances in Kilometers	Barcelona, Spain	Bari, Italy	Barranquilla, Colombia	Basse-Terre, Guadeloupe	Basseterre, St. Kitts & Nevis	Bata, Equatorial Guinea	Baton Rouge, Louisiana	Bear Lake, Canada	Bechar, Algeria	Beira, Mozambique	Beirut, Lebanon	Belau Islands (Koror)	Belem, Brazil	Belfast, United Kingdom	Belgrade, Yugoslavia	Belmopan, Belize	Belo Horizonte, Brazil	Bergen, Norway	Bern, Switzerland	Bhopal, India
Tangier, Morocco	931	2,057	7,415	5,930	5,942	4,087	7,727	8,397	571	7,502	3,756	13,688	6,048	2,088	2,436	8,294	7,361	2,848	1,656	7,951
Tarawa (Betio)	15,182	14,720	12,418	13,728	13,593	18,132	10,504	8,088	16,321	15,031	14,105	4,317	15,429	13,803	14,213	10,852	15,523	13,075	14,473	10,523
Tashkent, USSR	5,466	4,328	13,150	11,912	11,857	7,372	11,809	9,090	6,319	7,648	3,075	7,410	12,408	5,522	3,933	13,143	13,368	4,741	4,859	2,141
Tbilisi, USSR	3,515	2,323	11,532	10,152	10,126	5,633	10,831	9,126	4,290	6,888	1,189	9,452	10,387	3,934	1,992	11,930	11,352	3,377	3,001	3,653
Tegucigalpa, Honduras	8,939	10,132	1,393	2,747	2,648	10,720	1,856	5,760	8,739	13,861	11,961	14,850	4,604	8,182	10,261	384	6,051	8,794	9,228	15,549
Tehran, Iran	4,283	3,060	12,372	10,961	10,945	5,699	11,713	9,824	4,936	6,386	1,470	8,915	11,004	4,813	2,801	12,815	11,747	4,261	3,832	2,856
Tel Aviv, Israel	3,067	1,887	11,159	9,677	9,688	4,250	11,052	10,071	3,484	5,743	213	10,492	9,463	4,052	1,881	11,903	10,159	3,814	2,846	4,289
Telegraph Creek, Canada	8,181	8,634	7,030	7,300	7,122	12,533	4,309	323	9,007	15,628	9,758	9,578	9,710	6,601	8,320	5,699	11,700	6,351	7,779	10,628
Teresina, Brazil	6,880	7,922	3,964	3,127	3,304	5,896	6,476	10,105	5,918	8,539	9,255	19,635	747	7,442	8,360	5,625	1,646	8,375	7,581	13,323
Ternate, Indonesia	12,803	11,660	17,249	17,900	17,723	13,092	14,670	10,902	13,622	10,313	10,140	1,068	19,574	12,542	11,273	15,589	17,694	11,623	12,163	5,941
The Valley, Anguilla	6,654	7,882	1,486	268	91	8,136	3,156	6,741	6,254	11,481	9,671	16,609	2,684	6,289	8,118	2,730	4,691	7,093	7,094	13,745
Thessaloniki, Greece	1,743	516	9,867	8,427	8,419	4,496	9,629	8,903	2,464	6,807	1,341	11,259	8,559	2,637	507	10,506	9,621	2,509	1,424	5,403
Thimphu, Bhutan	7,852	6,679	15,431	14,296	14,229	8,930	13,587	10,106	8,632	7,898	5,182	5,216	14,720	7,907	6,317	15,051	15,257	7,084	7,265	1,326
Thunder Bay, Canada	6,827	7,732	4,363	4,386	4,209	10,526	1,999	2,665	7,258	14,143	9,378	12,503	6,782	5,485	7,631	3,459	8,808	5,737	6,746	11,958
Tientsin, China	8,934	8,018	14,320	13,901	13,758	11,378	11,762	7,848	9,988	10,745	7,087	3,925	15,588	8,297	7,538	13,209	17,220	7,365	8,207	4,139
Tijuana, Mexico	9,730	10,581	4,930	5,836	5,676	13,261	2,459	2,738	10,150	16,897	12,113	11,282	8,102	8,335	10,425	3,302	9,697	8,453	9,604	13,644
Tiksi, USSR	6,793	6,426	10,676	10,255	10,105	10,792	8,268	4,670	7,943	12,219	6,583	7,148	12,215	5,565	5,936	9,752	14,241	4,729	6,078	6,257
Timbuktu, Mali	2,774	3,306	7,748	6,249	6,329	2,163	8,916	10,385	1,647	5,792	4,282	14,645	5,383	4,204	3,810	9,044	6,040	4,889	3,480	8,342
Tindouf, Algeria	1,787	2,724	7,162	5,645	5,687	3,438	7,893	9,069	720	7,009	4,202	14,436	5,385	2,991	3,172	8,245	6,528	3,772	2,532	8,434
Tirane, Albania	1,474	251	9,596	8,158	8,149	4,489	9,373	8,751	2,242	6,947	1,608	11,474	8,326	2,400	393	10,238	9,437	2,340	1,166	5,667
Tokyo, Japan	10,440	9,702	13,698	13,854	13,682	13,378	10,958	6,992	11,567	12,590	9,009	3,187	16,119	9,478	9,200	12,240	18,219	8,575	9,694	6,103
Toledo, Spain	551	1,770	7,598	6,143	6,140	4,435	7,695	8,081	930	7,744	3,556	13,272	6,430	1,642	2,085	8,368	7,809	2,373	1,214	7,686
Topeka, Kansas	7,838	8,809	3,735	4,173	3,998	11,209	1,038	2,977	8,148	14,850	10,497	12,735	6,578	6,575	8,739	2,510	8,462	6,877	7,821	13,069
Toronto, Canada	6,420	7,440	3,649	3,493	3,318	9,800	1,800	3,595	6,695	13,444	9,184	13,413	5,870	5,240	7,415	3,064	7,916	5,656	6,456	12,225
Toulouse, France	254	1,297	8,069	6,646	6,630	4,698	7,943	7,932	1,368	7,810	3,126	12,659	7,035	1,333	1,526	8,729	8,420	1,886	600	7,161
Tours, France	677	1,462	8,026	6,646	6,616	5,121	7,720	7,534	1,768	8,193	3,268	12,441	7,209	925	1,554	8,582	8,686	1,478	517	7,162
Townsville, Australia	15,871	14,718	15,482	16,988	16,910	14,974	14,101	11,543	16,638	11,437	13,116	3,236	17,181	15,457	14,341	14,174	15,519	14,524	15,222	8,883
Trenton, New Jersey	6,265	7,345	3,240	2,967	2,794	9,414	1,840	4,135	6,436	13,055	9,130	13,950	5,332	5,205	7,366	2,887	7,386	5,711	6,374	12,410
Tripoli, Lebanon	3,039	1,826	11,161	9,695	9,698	4,511	10,935	9,829	3,550	6,007	69	10,341	9,584	3,920	1,747	11,837	10,352	3,625	2,749	4,207
Tripoli, Libya	1,355	970	9,172	7,674	7,694	3,456	9,416	9,434	1,457	6,275	2,075	12,391	7,492	2,839	1,468	10,060	8,427	3,109	1,630	6,308
Tristan da Cunha (Edinburgh)	8,810	9,153	8,410	7,830	8,008	4,872	11,100	14,804	7,674	4,939	9,286	15,316	5,414	10,171	9,650	10,002	3,607	10,919	9,507	11,507
Trondheim, Norway	2,510	2,515	8,683	7,540	7,461	6,831	7,570	6,241	3,646	9,472	3,714	10,875	8,660	1,353	2,165	8,759	10,365	431	1,846	6,575
Trujillo, Peru	9,877	11,093	2,164	3,279	3,336	9,914	4,461	8,366	9,252	12,161	12,776	16,340	3,466	9,669	11,394	3,001	3,999	10,477	10,399	17,003
Truk Island (Moen)	13,783	12,947	14,477	15,507	15,340	15,705	12,109	8,785	14,888	13,118	11,919	1,919	17,683	12,828	12,460	12,825	17,829	11,935	13,039	8,108
Truro, Canada	5,175	6,246	3,967	3,259	3,113	8,542	2,937	4,469	5,404	12,178	8,033	13,907	5,388	4,115	6,271	3,921	7,490	4,663	5,275	11,429
Tsingtao, China	9,371	8,448	14,563	14,238	14,089	11,725	11,943	7,988	10,422	10,893	7,480	3,494	16,004	8,729	7,970	13,364	17,655	7,796	8,645	4,351
Tsitsihar, China	8,625	7,860	13,281	12,964	12,812	11,650	10,699	6,785	9,741	11,539	7,226	4,549	14,865	7,768	7,358	12,144	16,770	6,845	7,881	4,905
Tubuai Island (Mataura)	16,712	17,664	8,967	10,484	10,444	16,749	8,613	9,071	16,680	15,203	18,746	8,930	11,074	15,417	17,457	7,979	10,637	15,456	16,686	15,261
Tucson, Arizona	9,372	10,285	4,388	5,267	5,106	12,745	1,890	2,936	9,722	16,363	11,893	11,833	7,543	8,036	10,167	2,781	9,175	8,231	9,300	13,801
Tulsa, Oklahoma	8,054	9,051	3,506	4,050	3,877	11,292	771	3,217	8,316	14,919	10,761	12,891	6,434	6,827	8,997	2,213	8,272	7,157	8,064	13,390
Tunis, Tunisia	858	751	8,846	7,367	7,376	3,870	8,954	8,931	1,278	6,784	2,317	12,444	7,375	2,329	1,244	9,653	8,466	2,645	1,146	6,524
Tura, USSR	6,316	5,679	11,648	10,971	10,842	9,846	9,455	6,053	7,454	10,856	5,460	6,876	12,589	5,399	5,172	10,935	14,407	4,476	5,570	4,855
Turin, Italy	603	864	8,564	7,155	7,135	4,790	8,318	8,007	1,720	7,696	2,678	12,160	7,549	1,438	1,012	9,168	8,890	1,713	208	6,650
Uberlandia, Brazil	8,464	9,446	4,406	4,135	4,307	6,750	7,138	11,051	7,449	8,634	10,616	18,688	1,934	9,086	9,906	5,969	471	10,018	9,181	14,402
Ufa, USSR	4,154	3,232	11,397	10,230	10,159	7,195	10,057	7,703	5,188	8,502	2,810	8,610	11,062	3,860	2,742	11,364	12,421	3,014	3,449	3,922
Ujungpandang, Indonesia	12,641	11,436	18,339	18,795	18,638	12,216	15,763	11,932	13,290	9,255	9,767	2,169	18,500	12,678	11,112	16,680	16,698	11,804	12,082	5,539
Ulaanbaatar, Mongolia	7,662	6,779	13,479	12,836	12,708	10,390	11,140	7,436	8,730	10,358	5,990	5,200	14,340	7,026	6,291	12,625	15,947	6,094	6,931	3,779
Ulan-Ude, USSR	7,432	6,609	13,041	12,420	12,289	10,389	10,707	7,032	8,525	10,595	5,954	5,513	13,994	6,711	6,112	12,192	15,693	5,779	6,693	4,087
Uliastay, Mongolia	7,063	6,120	13,447	12,630	12,518	9,639	11,307	7,791	8,097	9,695	5,250	5,721	13,891	6,565	5,643	12,788	15,332	5,643	6,348	3,217
Uranium City, Canada	7,160	7,780	6,078	6,138	5,962	11,377	3,490	1,141	7,880	14,727	9,135	10,765	8,517	5,617	7,538	4,968	10,563	5,536	6,856	10,808
Urumqi, China	6,682	5,642	13,683	12,688	12,598	8,893	11,782	8,462	7,644	8,859	4,575	6,082	13,630	6,404	5,194	13,239	14,822	5,517	6,003	2,462
Ushuaia, Argentina	12,575	13,329	7,315	7,869	8,006	9,411	9,697	13,400	11,459	9,038	13,856	14,365	6,183	13,396	13,832	8,213	4,384	14,324	13,319	15,507
Vaduz, Liechtenstein	869	890	8,694	7,308	7,281	5,021	8,332	7,851	1,995	7,843	2,630	11,913	7,780	1,360	889	9,234	9,152	1,496	158	6,497
Valencia, Spain	304	1,473	7,909	6,449	6,448	4,290	7,999	8,270	887	7,518	3,243	13,059	6,671	1,732	1,819	8,683	7,983	2,360	1,043	7,389
Valladolid, Spain	577	1,800	7,554	6,116	6,105	4,641	7,565	7,880	1,136	7,935	3,612	13,184	6,495	1,441	2,070	8,276	7,924	2,194	1,133	7,698
Valletta, Malta	1,233	615	9,244	7,762	7,773	3,802	9,336	9,167	1,619	6,531	1,927	12,140	7,709	2,604	1,114	10,053	8,719	2,801	1,357	6,148
Valparaiso, Chile	11,176	12,217	4,883	5,527	5,650	9,322	7,322	11,179	10,214	10,273	13,405	16,099	4,252	11,556	12,661	5,853	3,107	12,473	11,863	16,813
Vancouver, Canada	8,632	9,254	6,138	6,607	6,430	12,774	3,397	813	9,316	16,203	10,557	10,286	9,021	7,095	9,000	4,705	10,909	7,000	8,335	11,720
Varna, Bulgaria	2,123	942	10,192	8,782	8,764	4,925	9,765	8,735	2,940	7,017	1,228	10,776	9,022	2,749	621	10,728	10,121	2,439	1,657	5,025
Venice, Italy	938	603	8,928	7,523	7,502	4,837	8,616	8,113	1,986	7,580	2,352	11,822	7,902	1,650	644	9,503	9,201	1,725	411	6,281
Veracruz, Mexico	9,289	10,416	2,464	3,663	3,535	11,615	1,342	4,838	9,272	14,909	12,220	13,752	5,686	8,303	10,461	806	7,153	8,781	9,458	15,255
Verona, Italy	844	674	8,822	7,417	7,396	4,832	8,525	8,072	1,914	7,622	2,449	11,914	7,805	1,576	750	9,403	9,119	1,704	318	6,387
Victoria, Canada	8,715	9,342	6,114	6,608	6,431	12,843	3,374	896	9,391	16,285	10,649	10,290	9,020	7,180	9,090	4,666	10,893	7,089	8,422	11,800
Victoria, Seychelles	7,418	6,407	14,511	13,065	13,161	5,133	15,504	14,280	7,300	2,795	4,750	8,878	11,551	8,643	6,489	15,894	10,821	8,412	7,395	3,899
Vienna, Austria	1,351	786	9,194	7,822	7,792	5,175	8,715	7,941	2,419	7,757	2,250	11,408	8,298	1,769	490	9,677	9,629	1,530	684	5,987
Vientiane, Laos	9,545	8,370	16,790	15,879	15,790	10,256	14,449	10,583	10,313	8,498	6,833	3,651	16,378	9,536	8,009	15,920	16,508	8,679	8,951	2,688
Villahermosa, Mexico	9,122	10,273	2,099	3,324	3,202	11,293	1,392	5,104	9,050	14,551	12,091	14,117	5,321	8,205	10,345	445	6,797	8,729	9,330	15,323
Vilnius, USSR	2,253	1,631	9,661	8,384	8,331	6,026	8,802	7,455	3,360	8,306	2,444	10,552	9,105	2,001	1,149	9,921	10,536	1,347	1,520	5,515
Visby, Sweden	2,139	1,838	9,168	7,927	7,866	6,232	8,257	7,005	3,289	8,722	2,940	10,824	8,786	1,537	1,432	9,384	10,328	804	1,399	6,023
Vitoria, Brazil	8,118	9,004	5,121	4,648	4,826	5,988	7,819	11,649	7,042	7,790	10,020	18,468	2,267	8,923	9,486	6,727	377	9,844	8,855	13,636
Vladivostok, USSR	9,380	8,636	13,431	13,312	13,150	12,405	10,752	6,773	10,504	12,051	7,994	3,975	15,387	8,464	8,134	12,142	17,401	7,550	8,635	5,428
Volgograd, USSR	3,379	2,319	11,126	9,824	9,779	6,161	10,190	8,344	4,318	7,655	1,809	9,406	10,343	3,466	1,869	11,365	11,531	2,784	2,747	4,046
Vologda, USSR	3,270	2,572	10,312	9,139	9,068	6,877	9,098	7,153	4,377	8,773	2,835	9,572	10,052	2,782	2,066	10,350	11,544	1,923	2,531	4,957
Vorkuta, USSR	4,650	4,068	10,698	9,765	9,661	8,368	8,947	6,254	5,791	9,976	4,164	8,431	11,094	3,794	3,564	10,351	12,796	2,862	3,905	5,004
Wake Island	13,101	12,629	12,507	13,446	13,278	16,580	10,050	6,796	14,249	14,992	12,179	3,718	15,723	11,790	12,123	10,846	16,829	11,015	12,383	9,115
Wallis Island	16,888	16,674	11,510	12,994	12,907	18,587	10,283	8,954	17,886	15,021	16,095	5,914	14,035	15,346	16,172	10,174	13,633	14,777	16,262	12,251
Walvis Bay, Namibia	7,235	7,099	10,415	9,348	9,505	2,792	12,715	15,162	6,296	2,138	6,672	13,401	7,194	8,810	7,530	12,073	6,028	9,273	7,769	8,512
Warsaw, Poland	1,867	1,275	9,443	8,126	8,082	5,684	8,735	7,627	2,966	8,098	2,348	10,919	8,756	1,798	826	9,793	10,153	1,321	1,142	5,724
Washington, D.C.	6,508	7,589	3,100	2,944	2,768	9,605	1,597	4,097	6,666	13,242	9,375	13,948	5,337	5,448	7,611	2,661	7,368	5,948	6,619	12,629
Watson Lake, Canada	7,901	8,352	7,012	7,210	7,033	12,260	4,315	451	8,734	15,348	9,488	9,675	9,609	6,320	8,041	5,735	11,626	6,070	7,497	10,462
Weimar, East Germany	1,277	1,175	8,797	7,458	7,418	5,448	8,243	7,516	2,422	8,176	2,727	11,579	8,080	1,227	968	9,226	9,524	1,111	533	6,372
Wellington, New Zealand	19,404	18,178	12,515	13,955	13,965	15,387	12,481	12,117	18,898	12,081	16,370	6,774	13,579	18,527	17,900	11,783	12,145	17,763	18,827	12,275
West Berlin, West Germany	1,500	1,292	8,927	7,608	7,564	5,627	8,284	7,416	2,644	8,281	2,718	11,368	8,281	1,298	1,001	9,305	9,743	1,006	755	6,240
Wewak, Papua New Guinea	14,331	13,285	15,718	16,931	16,776	14,907	13,556	10,303	15,287	11,836	11,906	1,575	18,576	13,717	12,850	14,118	17,283	12,788	13,627	7,766
Whangarei, New Zealand	19,087	17,974	12,600	14,085	14,074	15,935	12,281	11,599	19,456	12,527	16,281	6,333	13,967	17,908	17,590	11,718	12,652	17,152	18,357	12,083
Whitehorse, Canada	8,042	8,430	7,354	7,561	7,383	12,438	4,648	693	8,914	15,396	9,484	9,325	9,959	6,456	8,097	6,055	11,977	6,150	7,604	10,247
Wichita, Kansas	8,045	9,018	3,718	4,237	4,063	11,382	984	3,004	8,347	15,019	10,705	12,693	6,628	6,783	8,947	2,419	8,478	7,082	8,030	13,234
Willemstad, Curacao	7,558	8,786	650	890	883	8,746	3,061	6,937	7,120	11,896	10,567	16,655	2,715	7,190	9,028	2,210	4,480	7,980	8,005	14,657
Wiluna, Australia	14,196	12,977	17,679	18,814	18,934	12,140	16,936	13,830	14,461	8,608	11,160	4,058	16,676	14,684	12,780	16,866	14,584	13,901	13,813	7,189
Windhoek, Namibia	7,247	7,054	10,670	9,585	9,740	2,818	12,941	15,257	6,341	1,870	6,547	13,139	7,450	8,828	7,473	12,326	6,296	9,257	7,757	8,268
Windsor, Canada	6,753	7,768	3,561	3,554	3,376	10,102	1,504	3,469	7,024	13,746	9,506	13,329	5,958	5,563	7,737	2,835	7,973	5,960	6,784	12,473
Winnipeg, Canada	7,216	8,051	4,778	4,924	4,747	11,054	2,215	2,093	7,722	14,643	9,623	11,954	7,333	5,804	7,907	3,700	9,335	5,959	7,073	11,885
Winston-Salem, North Carolina	6,911	8,003	2,836	2,885	2,707	9,893	1,195	4,124	7,038	13,512	9,792	13,991	5,303	5,868	8,029	2,256	7,284	6,366	7,034	13,029
Wroclaw, Poland	1,569	1,108	9,194	7,859	7,819	5,502	8,580	7,656	2,680	8,049	2,427	11,221	8,455	1,588	743	9,596	9,853	1,264	839	5,973
Wuhan, China	9,431	8,410	15,305	14,833	14,696	11,296	12,737	8,800	10,412	10,153	7,241	3,327	16,309	8,980	7,959	14,172	17,538	8,055	8,734	3,733
Wyndham, Australia	14,115	12,901	17,506	18,980	18,862	13,110	15,699	12,354	14,700	9,771	11,192	2,618	18,097	14,151	12,591	16,093	15,996	13,263	13,569	6,987
Xi'an, China	8,785	7,760	14,982	14,355	14,230	10,739	12,539	8,687	9,762	9,854	6,613	3,973	15,685	8,368	7,310	14,009	16,911	7,448	8,090	3,292
Xining, China	8,126	7,080	14,724	13,930	13,820	10,072	12,459	8,745	9,084	9,397	5,915	4,639	15,064	7,786	6,637	13,944	16,213	6,878	7,443	2,766
Yakutsk, USSR	7,619	7,099	11,638	11,300	11,146	11,331	9,125	5,325	8,771	12,182	6,950	6,079	13,286	6,508	6,594	10,596	15,305	5,631	6,883	5,810
Yanji, China	9,288	8,519	13,551	13,385	13,225	12,239	10,887	6,915	10,404	11,855	7,838	3,969	15,411	8,409	8,018	12,289	17,386	7,490	8,543	5,232

Distances in Kilometers	Barcelona, Spain	Bari, Italy	Barranquilla, Colombia	Basse-Terre, Guadeloupe	Basseterre, St. Kitts & Nevis	Bata, Equatorial Guinea	Baton Rouge, Louisiana	Bear Lake, Canada	Bechar, Algeria	Beira, Mozambique	Beirut, Lebanon	Belau Islands (Koror)	Belem, Brazil	Belfast, United Kingdom	Belgrade, Yugoslavia	Belmopan, Belize	Belo Horizonte, Brazil	Bergen, Norway	Bern, Switzerland	Bhopal, India
Yaounde, Cameroon	4,259	4,162	9,537	8,110	8,217	298	11,011	12,356	3,392	3,659	4,149	13,579	6,703	5,841	4,623	10,986	6,608	6,292	4,787	7,382
Yap Island (Colonia)	12,802	11,810	15,735	16,445	16,267	14,177	13,144	9,444	13,810	11,751	10,575	469	18,864	12,150	11,354	14,079	18,834	11,220	12,085	6,618
Yaraka, Australia	16,067	14,861	15,653	17,169	17,129	14,506	14,594	12,213	16,653	10,907	13,157	3,713	16,797	15,893	14,535	14,503	14,974	14,966	15,484	8,952
Yarmouth, Canada	5,447	6,525	3,736	3,113	2,959	8,736	2,660	4,404	5,650	12,378	8,315	13,973	5,315	4,398	6,553	3,641	7,413	4,942	5,556	11,699
Yellowknife, Canada	7,189	7,726	6,525	6,566	6,391	11,495	3,929	992	7,975	14,720	8,992	10,348	8,933	5,620	7,452	5,402	10,990	5,456	6,833	10,446
Yerevan, USSR	3,539	2,331	11,593	10,198	10,176	5,505	10,952	9,293	4,273	6,719	1,062	9,489	10,369	4,026	2,031	12,030	11,285	3,497	3,054	3,607
Yinchuan, China	8,301	7,302	14,529	13,849	13,727	10,458	12,163	8,382	9,299	9,848	6,232	4,461	15,175	7,851	6,842	13,644	16,498	6,930	7,599	3,217
Yogyakarta, Indonesia	12,098	10,871	19,360	18,770	18,724	11,217	16,651	12,709	12,603	8,213	9,117	3,157	17,471	12,389	10,606	17,704	15,857	11,581	11,620	4,968
York, United Kingdom	1,407	1,948	7,956	6,665	6,613	5,849	7,339	6,846	2,470	8,861	3,623	12,064	7,516	322	1,855	8,327	9,138	828	983	7,212
Yumen, China	7,628	6,592	14,327	13,470	13,365	9,709	12,169	8,566	8,595	9,278	5,478	5,133	14,562	7,288	6,144	13,653	15,758	6,383	6,942	2,653
Yutian, China	6,645	5,507	14,170	13,016	12,949	8,287	12,516	9,345	7,494	7,972	4,171	6,248	13,587	6,629	5,113	13,937	14,457	5,803	6,028	1,563
Yuzhno-Sakhalinsk, USSR	9,474	8,883	12,590	12,618	12,449	12,932	9,878	5,890	10,623	12,941	8,487	4,461	14,848	8,373	8,375	11,238	16,946	7,500	8,734	6,304
Zagreb, Yugoslavia	1,217	523	9,205	7,806	7,784	4,908	8,837	8,181	2,224	7,514	2,120	11,552	8,181	1,834	369	9,754	9,453	1,768	668	5,997
Zahedan, Iran	5,384	4,157	13,488	12,067	12,055	6,205	12,743	10,481	5,970	6,131	2,447	8,032	11,964	5,918	3,917	13,903	12,471	5,324	4,949	1,786
Zamboanga, Philippines	11,906	10,767	17,299	17,438	17,278	12,457	14,571	10,646	12,736	9,983	9,274	1,372	18,820	11,669	10,377	15,707	17,933	10,757	11,266	5,105
Zanzibar, Tanzania	6,474	5,712	12,763	11,370	11,481	3,390	14,195	14,321	6,066	1,583	4,450	10,688	9,744	7,924	5,950	14,252	9,068	7,951	6,660	5,279
Zaragoza, Spain	258	1,482	7,873	6,432	6,422	4,534	7,860	8,037	1,118	7,739	3,293	12,943	6,759	1,487	1,768	8,590	8,130	2,129	887	7,386
Zashiversk, USSR	7,486	7,135	10,804	10,540	10,381	11,496	8,265	4,470	8,633	12,781	7,255	6,702	12,630	6,220	6,644	9,734	14,703	5,405	6,775	6,585
Zhengzhou, China	9,063	8,075	14,866	14,367	14,232	11,164	12,335	8,427	10,071	10,276	6,995	3,710	15,884	8,555	7,613	13,786	17,273	7,627	8,354	3,732
Zurich, Switzerland	827	968	8,606	7,222	7,195	5,045	8,245	7,795	1,967	7,901	2,719	11,975	7,711	1,282	978	9,145	9,100	1,462	85	6,584

Distances in Kilometers	Bhubaneswar, India	Bialystok, Poland	Big Trout Lake, Canada	Bilbao, Spain	Billings, Montana	Birmingham, Alabama	Birmingham, United Kingdom	Bismarck, North Dakota	Bissau, Guinea Bissau	Biysk, USSR	Blagoveshchensk, USSR	Blantyre, Malawi	Bloemfontein, South Africa	Bluefields, Nicaragua	Boa Vista do Rio Branco, Braz.	Bodo, Norway	Bogota, Colombia	Boise, Idaho	Bologna, Italy	Bolzano, Italy
Bialystok, Poland	6,417	0	6,644	2,213	8,122	8,279	1,684	7,725	5,723	4,050	6,545	7,720	9,118	10,046	9,347	1,646	10,084	8,605	1,292	1,120
Big Trout Lake, Canada	11,789	6,644	0	6,119	1,598	2,272	5,499	1,093	7,930	8,202	7,946	13,680	14,262	4,673	6,257	5,191	5,647	2,220	6,817	6,650
Bilbao, Spain	8,403	2,213	6,119	0	7,717	7,097	1,028	7,183	3,687	6,255	8,589	7,598	8,550	8,363	7,228	2,870	8,135	8,325	1,156	1,187
Billings, Montana	12,553	8,122	1,598	7,717	0	2,295	7,076	606	9,300	9,028	8,076	15,266	15,677	4,416	6,644	6,583	5,648	657	8,391	8,216
Birmingham, Alabama	14,006	8,279	2,272	7,097	2,295	0	6,811	1,890	7,560	10,437	10,130	13,901	13,740	2,403	4,351	7,073	3,462	2,779	8,068	7,958
Birmingham, United Kingdom	8,100	1,684	5,499	1,028	7,076	6,811	0	6,589	4,669	5,534	7,669	8,355	9,444	8,407	7,694	1,873	8,400	7,646	1,318	1,165
Bismarck, North Dakota	12,551	7,725	1,093	7,183	606	1,890	6,589	0	8,695	8,977	8,293	14,690	15,073	4,177	6,221	6,240	5,335	1,261	7,907	7,742
Bissau, Guinea Bissau	10,729	5,723	7,930	3,687	9,300	7,560	4,669	8,695	0	9,691	12,250	6,355	6,378	7,404	5,072	6,541	6,485	9,950	4,437	4,604
Biysk, USSR	3,589	4,050	8,202	6,255	9,028	10,437	5,534	8,977	9,691	0	2,910	8,977	10,710	12,774	13,091	4,012	13,378	9,151	5,289	5,152
Blagoveshchensk, USSR	4,945	6,545	7,946	8,589	8,076	10,130	7,669	8,293	12,250	2,910	0	11,521	13,219	12,468	14,071	5,829	13,583	7,916	7,837	7,657
Blantyre, Malawi	6,839	7,720	13,680	7,598	15,266	13,901	8,355	14,690	6,355	8,977	11,521	0	1,734	13,424	10,711	9,365	12,199	15,900	7,092	7,296
Bloemfontein, South Africa	8,416	9,118	14,262	8,550	15,677	13,740	9,444	15,073	6,378	10,710	13,219	1,734	0	12,582	9,860	10,736	11,259	16,324	8,290	8,509
Bluefields, Nicaragua	16,264	10,046	4,673	8,363	4,416	2,403	8,407	4,177	7,404	12,774	12,468	13,424	12,582	0	2,739	9,129	1,342	4,687	9,483	9,438
Boa Vista do Rio Branco, Braz.	15,568	9,347	6,257	7,228	6,644	4,351	7,694	6,221	5,072	13,091	14,071	10,711	9,860	2,739	0	9,079	1,502	7,079	8,369	8,414
Bodo, Norway	7,151	1,646	5,191	2,870	6,583	7,073	1,873	6,240	6,541	4,012	5,829	9,365	10,736	9,129	9,079	0	9,470	7,024	2,545	2,319
Bogota, Colombia	16,500	10,084	5,647	8,135	5,648	3,462	8,400	5,335	6,485	13,378	13,583	12,199	11,259	1,342	1,502	9,470	0	5,977	9,291	9,293
Boise, Idaho	12,587	8,605	2,220	8,325	657	2,779	7,646	1,261	9,950	9,151	7,916	15,900	16,324	4,687	7,079	7,024	5,977	0	8,953	8,771
Bologna, Italy	7,248	1,292	6,817	1,156	8,391	8,068	1,318	7,907	4,437	5,289	7,837	7,092	8,290	9,483	8,369	2,545	9,291	8,953	0	226
Bolzano, Italy	7,229	1,120	6,650	1,187	8,216	7,958	1,165	7,742	4,604	5,152	7,657	7,296	8,509	9,438	8,414	2,319	9,293	8,771	226	0
Bombay, India	1,371	5,691	11,774	7,454	12,834	13,811	7,329	12,693	9,431	3,882	5,918	5,652	7,311	15,734	14,402	6,741	15,560	13,015	6,307	6,329
Bonn, West Germany	7,508	1,133	6,094	1,129	7,656	7,463	653	7,187	4,781	5,139	7,475	7,856	9,044	9,045	8,217	1,887	8,994	8,208	764	564
Bora Bora (Vaitape)	13,964	15,918	9,747	15,835	8,157	8,835	15,225	8,668	15,284	13,664	10,762	16,357	14,949	8,120	10,220	14,277	8,853	7,579	16,525	16,334
Bordeaux, France	8,175	1,953	6,136	261	7,731	7,206	855	7,211	3,927	5,995	8,340	7,616	8,629	8,544	7,469	2,651	8,353	8,328	944	947
Boston, Massachusetts	12,681	6,643	1,891	5,409	2,996	1,693	5,130	2,396	6,313	9,243	9,584	12,490	12,684	3,583	4,501	5,563	4,194	3,640	6,376	6,269
Bouvet Island	11,339	12,062	14,725	10,842	15,247	12,970	11,860	14,847	7,560	14,050	16,281	5,081	3,355	10,900	8,626	13,531	9,617	15,587	10,988	11,213
Brasilia, Brazil	15,127	10,187	8,691	7,983	9,132	6,842	8,759	8,712	4,693	14,237	16,158	8,814	7,652	5,002	2,492	10,489	3,660	9,550	8,966	9,092
Braunschweig, West Germany	7,261	857	6,145	1,420	7,687	7,601	847	7,238	5,058	4,847	7,194	7,901	9,145	9,252	8,490	1,686	9,240	8,221	868	642
Brazzaville, Congo	8,165	6,404	11,391	5,573	12,917	11,396	6,493	12,319	3,854	9,051	11,943	2,505	2,982	11,098	8,487	7,938	9,987	13,573	5,414	5,639
Bremerhaven, West Germany	7,387	970	5,951	1,426	7,493	7,420	714	7,044	5,097	4,884	7,165	8,086	9,317	9,098	8,398	1,562	9,114	8,027	1,028	807
Brest, France	8,377	2,005	5,648	584	7,241	6,784	488	6,726	4,182	5,961	8,151	8,113	9,115	8,230	7,342	2,361	8,129	7,834	1,288	1,211
Brest, USSR	6,362	121	6,757	2,214	8,239	8,377	1,740	7,840	5,682	4,065	6,597	7,599	9,002	10,121	9,378	1,766	10,138	8,724	1,246	1,089
Bridgetown, Barbados	14,739	8,372	5,248	6,336	5,836	3,563	6,696	5,352	4,783	11,992	12,951	10,891	10,313	2,625	1,143	7,983	1,847	6,342	7,492	7,510
Brisbane, Australia	8,956	15,037	14,182	17,240	12,775	14,324	16,545	13,380	17,912	11,028	8,974	11,802	11,571	13,893	15,518	14,787	14,435	12,120	16,134	16,063
Bristol, United Kingdom	8,167	1,756	5,535	912	7,117	6,804	122	6,623	4,547	5,640	7,789	8,293	9,361	8,363	7,606	1,995	8,333	7,693	1,293	1,157
Brno, Czechoslovakia	6,830	631	6,687	1,644	8,222	8,144	1,352	7,780	5,093	4,658	7,176	7,423	8,728	9,749	8,852	2,018	9,677	8,747	662	494
Broken Hill, Australia	8,273	14,630	15,302	16,668	13,959	15,543	16,291	14,564	16,779	10,833	9,210	10,579	10,402	14,913	16,044	14,807	15,240	13,308	15,512	15,502
Brussels, Belgium	7,701	1,314	5,945	1,008	7,514	7,280	469	7,037	4,687	5,293	7,581	7,963	9,115	8,850	8,033	1,915	8,800	8,074	879	706
Bucharest, Romania	6,074	991	7,548	2,329	9,060	9,039	2,239	8,638	5,365	4,336	7,069	6,729	8,146	10,605	9,537	2,637	10,460	9,563	1,174	1,173
Budapest, Hungary	6,641	690	6,949	1,784	8,481	8,399	1,597	8,041	5,105	4,605	7,195	7,186	8,517	9,978	9,011	2,220	9,874	9,003	687	597
Buenos Aires, Argentina	16,179	12,486	10,258	10,297	10,225	8,100	11,094	9,962	6,849	16,526	18,199	9,340	7,787	5,809	4,148	12,816	4,639	10,454	11,237	11,377
Buffalo, New York	12,844	7,034	1,466	5,954	2,371	1,250	5,596	1,779	6,952	9,319	9,371	13,129	13,317	3,455	4,792	5,831	4,268	3,008	6,873	6,752
Bujumbura, Burundi	6,695	6,291	12,198	6,098	13,792	12,637	6,853	13,230	5,252	8,100	10,878	1,504	2,870	12,612	10,043	7,929	11,540	14,416	5,598	5,805
Bulawayo, Zimbabwe	7,671	8,136	13,662	7,727	15,190	13,539	8,571	14,590	5,996	9,732	12,333	832	1,025	12,784	10,049	9,766	11,517	15,846	7,369	7,584
Burlington, Vermont	12,531	6,594	1,600	5,466	2,758	1,690	5,127	2,154	6,542	9,056	9,318	12,664	12,919	3,738	4,777	5,449	4,419	3,408	6,396	6,279
Cabinda, Angola	8,535	6,585	11,305	5,617	12,801	11,188	6,567	12,198	3,628	9,365	12,266	2,736	2,996	10,791	8,156	8,082	9,657	13,458	5,542	5,768
Cagliari, Italy	7,497	1,881	7,139	1,106	8,730	8,202	1,700	8,218	3,891	5,804	8,417	6,657	7,771	9,422	8,080	3,141	9,105	9,318	613	831
Cairns, Australia	7,731	13,656	13,735	15,866	12,553	14,484	15,159	13,144	17,947	9,639	7,654	11,615	11,774	14,682	16,744	13,430	15,479	11,927	14,789	14,702
Cairo, Egypt	5,560	2,647	9,138	3,361	10,681	10,430	3,674	10,231	5,227	5,014	7,919	5,087	6,572	11,657	10,046	4,290	11,224	11,203	2,373	2,509
Calais, France	7,874	1,477	5,806	930	7,381	7,113	309	6,896	4,616	5,428	7,670	8,068	9,188	8,674	7,871	1,948	8,627	7,947	1,011	856
Calcutta, India	366	6,389	11,543	8,433	12,251	13,781	8,072	12,271	10,912	3,344	4,582	7,196	8,780	16,090	15,644	7,027	16,456	12,264	7,283	7,250
Calgary, Canada	11,873	7,786	1,658	7,629	716	2,946	6,896	1,081	9,579	8,378	7,360	15,227	15,920	5,128	7,292	6,193	6,346	842	8,190	8,001
Cali, Colombia	16,763	10,347	5,720	8,418	5,625	3,496	8,664	5,345	6,775	13,565	13,625	12,426	11,434	1,237	1,761	9,692	299	5,919	9,573	9,572
Camaguey, Cuba	15,077	8,840	3,745	7,216	3,878	1,604	7,211	3,494	6,695	11,652	11,684	12,976	12,461	1,210	2,775	7,929	1,903	4,304	8,318	8,262
Cambridge Bay, Canada	10,057	5,806	1,870	6,037	2,606	4,123	5,160	2,496	8,760	6,481	6,086	13,464	14,587	6,524	8,054	4,178	7,517	2,912	6,380	6,172
Cambridge, United Kingdom	7,969	1,555	5,625	1,021	7,199	6,952	142	6,716	4,693	5,441	7,620	8,250	9,361	8,547	7,810	1,852	8,531	7,764	1,192	1,031
Campbellton, Canada	11,968	5,960	1,755	4,853	3,159	2,328	4,490	2,557	6,190	8,547	9,031	12,162	12,552	4,297	5,040	4,849	4,862	3,816	5,764	5,644
Campo Grande, Brazil	15,914	11,020	8,901	8,809	9,127	6,881	9,547	8,771	5,570	15,062	16,691	9,376	8,072	4,802	2,658	11,224	3,494	9,471	9,816	9,935
Canakkale, Turkey	6,013	1,464	7,955	2,456	9,485	9,359	2,550	9,047	5,169	4,594	7,395	6,256	7,670	10,810	9,563	3,110	10,571	10,001	1,330	1,406
Canberra, Australia	9,077	15,407	15,061	17,477	13,600	14,946	17,046	14,203	16,990	11,535	9,718	11,074	10,709	14,126	15,279	15,449	14,432	12,943	16,320	16,306
Cancun, Mexico	15,359	9,398	3,640	7,941	3,377	1,372	7,829	3,118	7,612	11,804	11,410	13,884	13,294	1,060	3,476	8,323	2,285	3,693	9,005	8,928
Canton, China	2,851	7,992	11,192	10,198	11,292	13,389	9,559	11,543	13,242	4,041	3,259	9,539	10,964	15,707	17,063	8,029	16,838	11,064	9,132	9,035
Canton Atoll, Phoenix Islands	11,429	14,265	9,716	15,391	8,201	9,712	14,422	8,801	17,215	11,140	8,234	16,439	15,994	9,859	12,367	12,836	10,887	7,545	15,381	15,155
Cape Town, South Africa	9,320	9,655	14,137	8,818	15,383	13,263	9,772	14,799	6,214	11,559	14,119	2,608	907	11,866	9,184	11,226	10,528	15,989	8,712	8,936
Cape York, Australia	7,083	12,892	13,369	15,104	12,332	14,417	14,386	12,900	17,638	8,868	6,910	11,522	11,896	14,996	17,332	12,664	15,951	11,735	14,044	13,949
Caracas, Venezuela	15,495	9,087	5,226	7,113	5,551	3,259	7,403	5,135	5,601	12,532	13,129	11,593	10,873	1,845	1,094	8,560	1,025	5,987	8,269	8,274
Cardiff, United Kingdom	8,208	1,796	5,498	917	7,082	6,762	139	6,586	4,538	5,670	7,807	8,323	9,384	8,320	7,569	2,006	8,292	7,659	1,332	1,198
Carlisle, United Kingdom	8,114	1,711	5,281	1,294	6,849	6,666	277	6,373	4,901	5,428	7,476	8,610	9,716	8,338	7,746	1,655	8,391	7,410	1,543	1,369
Carnarvon, Australia	5,827	12,212	16,241	13,978	15,612	17,824	13,879	16,120	14,508	9,011	8,434	8,169	8,480	17,704	17,491	12,925	17,618	15,070	12,851	12,887
Carson City, Nevada	12,913	9,175	2,774	8,889	1,180	3,008	8,221	1,760	10,379	9,558	8,125	16,445	16,714	4,653	7,182	7,586	5,979	576	9,528	9,347
Casablanca, Morocco	9,096	3,258	6,600	1,142	8,174	7,152	2,143	7,598	2,544	7,301	9,721	7,093	7,803	8,010	6,473	4,007	7,559	8,815	2,026	2,150
Casper, Wyoming	12,911	8,326	1,711	7,800	370	1,991	7,209	620	9,184	9,374	8,445	15,279	15,542	4,053	6,325	6,818	5,297	809	8,527	8,361
Castries, Saint Lucia	14,773	8,385	5,094	6,376	5,660	3,385	6,705	5,181	4,927	11,952	12,835	11,061	10,493	2,477	1,239	7,949	1,774	6,164	7,533	7,545
Catbalogan, Philippines	4,273	9,739	12,025	11,949	11,705	13,981	11,275	12,096	14,938	5,741	4,276	10,356	11,483	15,910	18,282	9,660	17,251	11,317	10,891	10,793
Cayenne, French Guiana	14,673	8,604	6,403	6,434	7,042	4,768	6,992	6,555	4,115	12,493	13,888	9,881	9,169	3,544	956	8,516	2,413	7,546	7,554	7,618
Cayman Islands (Georgetown)	15,417	9,240	3,903	7,642	3,850	1,664	7,622	3,526	7,068	11,939	11,794	13,305	12,698	847	2,898	8,287	1,809	4,217	8,740	8,682
Cazombo, Angola	7,756	7,206	12,564	6,648	14,102	12,555	7,517	13,505	4,996	9,279	12,060	1,380	1,939	12,070	9,381	8,809	10,878	14,756	6,352	6,571
Cebu, Philippines	4,223	9,807	12,215	12,013	11,899	14,176	11,362	12,290	14,923	5,830	4,444	10,209	11,312	16,096	18,471	9,772	17,438	11,510	10,942	10,849
Cedar Rapids, Iowa	13,113	7,766	1,324	6,905	1,414	1,032	6,450	902	7,992	9,525	9,099	14,184	14,337	3,410	5,324	6,410	4,494	2,009	7,755	7,615
Changsha, China	2,887	7,541	10,651	9,753	10,808	12,865	9,075	11,035	12,930	3,542	2,743	9,697	11,200	15,210	16,507	7,503	16,299	10,611	8,715	8,606
Channel-Port-aux-Basques, Can.	11,724	5,561	2,268	4,328	3,718	2,791	4,029	3,118	5,663	8,406	9,145	11,597	12,009	4,563	4,961	4,573	4,972	4,374	5,276	5,168
Charleston, South Carolina	13,949	7,959	2,474	6,621	2,835	647	6,421	2,357	6,916	10,443	10,419	13,262	13,101	2,332	3,876	6,870	3,177	3,367	7,638	7,545
Charleston, West Virginia	13,390	7,570	1,836	6,409	2,359	711	6,103	1,824	7,118	9,852	9,782	13,398	13,423	2,927	4,475	6,385	3,815	2,947	7,364	7,251
Charlotte, North Carolina	13,710	7,798	2,189	6,539	2,603	580	6,291	2,103	7,019	10,186	10,134	13,345	13,263	2,588	4,148	6,664	3,461	3,158	7,530	7,427
Charlotte Amalie, U.S.V.I.	14,687	8,270	4,488	6,376	5,023	2,750	6,588	4,544	5,339	11,639	12,307	11,579	11,090	2,139	1,780	7,679	1,818	5,529	7,525	7,512
Charlottetown, Canada	12,011	5,889	2,086	4,661	3,466	2,454	4,366	2,862	5,865	8,650	9,263	11,882	12,233	4,264	4,817	4,865	4,733	4,123	5,614	5,506
Chatham, Canada	12,021	5,964	1,888	4,802	3,270	2,342	4,470	2,667	6,065	8,622	9,151	12,067	12,432	4,246	4,921	4,889	4,775	3,927	5,733	5,618
Chatham Islands (Waitangi)	12,143	18,247	13,580	19,497	11,988	12,479	18,979	12,501	16,010	14,199	11,760	12,659	11,590	11,148	12,276	17,327	11,362	11,398	19,391	19,336
Chengdu, China	2,163	6,763	10,545	8,965	10,926	12,810	8,349	11,071	12,043	2,875	2,924	8,997	10,577	15,211	15,965	6,887	16,097	10,818	7,895	7,800
Chesterfield Inlet, Canada	10,734	5,879	1,061	5,720	2,252	3,329	4,953	1,945	8,094	7,146	6,970	13,301	14,193	5,727	7,151	4,331	6,658	2,735	6,243	6,054
Cheyenne, Wyoming	13,122	8,432	1,792	7,830	596	1,802	7,271	708	9,091	9,577	8,671	15,250	15,427	3,828	6,120	6,946	5,076	978	8,590	8,429
Chiang Mai, Thailand	1,389	7,418	11,914	9,526	12,339	14,185	9,086	12,476	12,093	3,935	4,313	7,984	9,443	16,587	16,753	7,863	17,311	12,223	8,388	8,339
Chibougamau, Canada	11,994	6,228	1,158	5,312	2,573	2,089	4,856	1,977	6,792	8,486	8,709	12,721	13,152	4,292	5,378	4,983	5,023	3,228	6,157	6,020
Chicago, Illinois	13,095	7,575	1,340	6,631	1,729	932	6,212	1,181	7,656	9,517	9,239	13,858	14,003	3,333	5,094	6,269	4,344	2,337	7,509	7,376
Chiclayo, Peru	17,874	11,474	6,783	9,472	6,480	4,518	9,791	6,285	7,406	14,749	14,556	12,434	11,186	2,120	2,379	10,877	1,411	6,673	10,628	10,645
Chihuahua, Mexico	14,450	9,708	3,090	8,852	1,915	1,914	8,421	2,069	9,440	10,942	9,801	15,795	15,404	2,961	5,590	8,281	4,300	1,893	9,726	9,586
Chongquing, China	2,332	7,016	10,628	9,222	10,943	12,883	8,593	11,113	12,315	3,095	2,893	9,171	10,725	15,275	16,176	7,102	16,223	10,807	8,157	8,060
Christchurch, New Zealand	11,283	17,539	14,177	19,664	12,580	13,267	18,934	13,125	16,406	13,522	11,276	12,155	11,265	12,017	13,107	17,061	12,229	11,962	18,522	18,511
Christiansted, U.S.V.I.	14,724	8,307	4,559	6,400	5,088	2,813	6,624	4,612	5,314	11,695	12,376	11,541	11,037	2,145	1,709	7,729	1,778	5,592	7,550	7,540
Christmas Is. [Indian Ocean]	4,034	10,440	15,002	12,313	14,934	17,161	12,118	15,276	13,630	7,255	7,060	7,652	8,439	18,995	18,299	11,130	19,352	14,569	11,164	11,178
Christmas Is. [Pacific Ocean]	12,702	13,895	8,372	14,391	6,798	8,109	13,554	7,379	15,555	11,627	8,772	17,965	16,975	8,207	10,769	12,293	9,275	6,156	14,741	14,523

Distances in Kilometers	Bhubaneswar, India	Bialystok, Poland	Big Trout Lake, Canada	Bilbao, Spain	Billings, Montana	Birmingham, Alabama	Birmingham, United Kingdom	Bismarck, North Dakota	Bissau, Guinea Bissau	Biysk, USSR	Blagoveshchensk, USSR	Blantyre, Malawi	Bloemfontein, South Africa	Bluefields, Nicaragua	Boa Vista do Rio Branco, Braz.	Bodo, Norway	Bogota, Colombia	Boise, Idaho	Bologna, Italy	Bolzano, Italy
Churchill, Canada	11,251	6,385	604	6,098	1,738	2,858	5,384	1,401	8,227	7,663	7,343	13,696	14,461	5,260	6,846	4,858	6,251	2,264	6,689	6,507
Cincinnati, Ohio	13,361	7,660	1,690	6,576	2,099	653	6,229	1,575	7,374	9,800	9,621	13,641	13,686	3,004	4,688	6,425	3,964	2,683	7,506	7,385
Ciudad Bolivia, Venezuela	15,934	9,519	5,337	7,568	5,508	3,248	7,835	5,138	6,030	12,876	13,280	11,926	11,114	1,500	1,254	8,936	569	5,898	8,723	8,724
Ciudad Juarez, Mexico	14,107	9,421	2,786	8,643	1,569	1,854	8,173	1,743	9,414	10,596	9,487	15,752	15,506	3,195	5,760	7,973	4,522	1,571	9,484	9,338
Ciudad Victoria, Mexico	15,111	9,843	3,428	8,714	2,588	1,619	8,418	2,564	8,845	11,542	10,615	15,166	14,588	2,081	4,739	8,542	3,422	2,703	9,684	9,570
Clarksburg, West Virginia	13,263	7,419	1,775	6,260	2,409	863	5,950	1,855	7,018	9,734	9,717	13,280	13,341	3,041	4,503	6,242	3,893	3,012	7,213	7,099
Cleveland, Ohio	13,051	7,302	1,504	6,233	2,204	994	5,873	1,631	7,161	9,507	9,448	13,375	13,510	3,275	4,772	6,078	4,157	2,824	7,153	7,030
Cocos (Keeling) Island	3,763	10,006	15,325	11,707	15,566	17,594	11,650	15,810	12,695	7,239	7,518	6,674	7,505	19,973	17,354	10,905	18,732	15,292	10,583	10,625
Colombo, Sri Lanka	1,607	7,218	13,204	8,905	14,108	15,314	8,843	14,052	10,449	5,084	6,518	5,546	6,995	17,248	15,520	8,259	16,868	14,179	7,773	7,812
Colon, Panama	16,383	10,038	5,014	8,245	4,872	2,766	8,374	4,598	7,029	12,998	12,886	12,951	12,074	512	2,246	9,234	831	5,170	9,385	9,358
Colorado Springs, Colorado	13,373	8,656	2,012	7,999	829	1,721	7,466	945	9,130	9,831	8,890	15,352	15,427	3,631	5,988	7,184	4,899	1,092	8,783	8,627
Columbia, South Carolina	13,846	7,916	2,315	6,629	2,669	536	6,399	2,187	7,028	10,323	10,258	13,365	13,241	2,451	4,048	6,793	3,333	3,209	7,630	7,531
Columbus, Georgia	14,093	8,273	2,408	7,028	2,499	206	6,778	2,083	7,389	10,537	10,299	13,737	13,545	2,270	4,149	7,106	3,287	2,985	8,019	7,916
Columbus, Ohio	13,242	7,504	1,630	6,415	2,171	792	6,069	1,624	7,252	9,690	9,574	13,501	13,580	3,099	4,690	6,280	4,018	2,772	7,344	7,224
Conakry, Guinea	10,636	5,856	8,259	3,881	9,627	7,869	4,881	9,023	329	9,775	12,398	6,055	6,050	7,645	5,246	6,748	6,684	10,277	4,564	4,742
Concepcion, Chile	17,264	13,561	10,177	11,348	9,816	7,918	12,044	9,669	8,069	17,579	17,793	10,505	8,874	5,520	4,573	13,614	4,588	9,920	12,365	12,483
Concord, New Hampshire	12,611	6,602	1,795	5,404	2,928	1,710	5,104	2,326	6,376	9,162	9,485	12,530	12,750	3,653	4,602	5,502	4,284	3,575	6,359	6,248
Constantine, Algeria	7,766	2,265	7,237	1,120	8,834	8,169	1,911	8,303	3,512	6,180	8,802	6,498	7,534	9,264	7,803	3,475	8,878	9,438	986	1,195
Copenhagen, Denmark	7,126	741	5,975	1,774	7,487	7,548	1,012	7,063	5,440	4,544	6,818	8,193	9,484	9,308	8,705	1,298	9,379	7,998	1,247	1,021
Coppermine, Canada	10,090	6,149	2,043	6,460	2,485	4,226	5,569	2,481	9,188	6,544	5,918	13,840	15,007	6,609	8,292	4,509	7,666	2,697	6,772	6,562
Coquimbo, Chile	17,492	12,899	9,457	10,690	9,189	7,212	11,339	9,002	7,555	16,856	17,258	10,654	9,103	4,830	3,802	12,861	3,836	9,343	11,743	11,846
Cordoba, Argentina	16,790	12,564	9,766	10,353	9,645	7,568	11,080	9,409	7,056	16,604	17,698	9,955	8,420	5,237	3,805	12,714	4,120	9,850	11,356	11,477
Cordoba, Spain	8,709	2,733	6,432	615	8,024	7,191	1,636	7,467	3,079	6,781	9,184	7,250	8,088	8,240	6,875	3,485	7,887	8,651	1,533	1,637
Cork, Ireland	8,550	2,133	5,183	1,046	6,773	6,400	452	6,265	4,488	5,923	7,947	8,594	9,593	7,958	7,266	2,119	7,950	7,361	1,680	1,558
Corner Brook, Canada	11,547	5,396	2,275	4,204	3,764	2,936	3,877	3,170	5,664	8,230	8,997	11,530	11,989	4,738	5,119	4,396	5,148	4,418	5,134	5,022
Corrientes, Argentina	16,356	11,897	9,495	9,689	9,537	7,368	10,435	9,244	6,380	15,944	17,417	9,586	8,134	5,129	3,357	12,106	3,908	9,807	10,682	10,806
Cosenza, Italy	6,884	1,625	7,520	1,665	9,096	8,719	2,021	8,610	4,370	5,331	8,038	6,402	7,646	10,019	8,690	3,116	9,720	9,658	705	895
Craiova, Romania	6,256	982	7,452	2,148	8,977	8,903	2,094	8,544	5,200	4,495	7,206	6,751	8,137	10,440	9,354	2,617	10,281	9,491	992	1,002
Cruzeiro do Sul, Brazil	17,317	11,067	7,005	8,976	6,911	4,795	9,397	6,644	6,669	14,633	14,925	11,647	10,449	2,498	1,757	10,653	1,363	7,176	10,122	10,162
Cuiaba, Brazil	15,975	10,679	8,342	8,467	8,596	6,338	9,156	8,227	5,396	14,689	16,144	9,667	8,448	4,313	2,097	10,780	2,986	8,957	9,513	9,617
Curitiba, Brazil	15,406	11,139	9,615	8,956	9,895	7,638	9,775	9,527	5,507	15,176	17,233	8,713	7,346	5,580	3,359	11,536	4,270	10,246	9,888	10,029
Cuzco, Peru	17,557	11,540	7,657	9,401	7,521	5,437	9,889	7,274	6,829	15,227	15,564	11,369	10,064	3,107	2,196	11,226	2,017	7,758	10,531	10,588
Dacca, Bangladesh	611	6,427	11,413	8,504	12,076	13,664	8,105	12,114	11,075	3,232	4,350	7,444	9,027	16,004	15,729	6,997	16,456	12,071	7,360	7,318
Dakar, Senegal	10,794	5,552	7,561	3,456	8,938	7,227	4,413	8,332	371	9,560	12,043	6,678	6,742	7,166	4,925	6,285	6,301	9,589	4,278	4,433
Dallas, Texas	14,132	8,868	2,401	7,884	1,757	937	7,503	1,594	8,496	10,548	9,827	14,837	14,630	2,659	5,018	7,528	3,913	2,074	8,794	8,665
Damascus, Syria	5,086	2,419	9,043	3,561	10,540	10,508	3,697	10,130	5,774	4,405	7,313	5,456	7,014	11,923	10,489	4,018	11,598	11,023	2,469	2,556
Danang, Vietnam	2,411	8,268	12,068	10,426	12,228	14,293	9,907	12,464	13,115	4,525	4,172	8,780	10,124	16,637	17,593	8,533	17,705	12,006	9,307	9,241
Dar es Salaam, Tanzania	5,907	6,814	13,104	6,990	14,698	13,751	7,636	14,173	6,415	7,880	10,462	1,098	2,830	13,763	11,157	8,455	12,658	15,282	6,333	6,521
Darwin, Australia	6,113	12,287	14,190	14,438	13,360	15,555	13,911	13,893	16,383	8,419	6,957	10,256	10,730	16,276	18,366	12,396	17,159	12,803	13,304	13,251
Davao, Philippines	4,527	10,206	12,481	12,410	12,079	14,369	11,765	12,496	15,252	6,233	4,793	10,293	11,310	16,155	18,717	10,173	17,490	11,659	11,333	11,243
David, Panama	16,588	10,285	5,081	8,521	4,833	2,813	8,627	4,597	7,320	13,145	12,888	13,198	12,273	420	2,487	9,437	1,016	5,093	9,657	9,625
Dawson, Canada	9,882	6,921	2,971	7,510	2,788	4,913	6,571	3,032	10,360	6,508	5,290	14,626	15,989	7,186	9,178	5,282	8,367	2,707	7,699	7,480
Dawson Creek, Canada	11,233	7,476	1,941	7,555	1,381	3,564	6,745	1,675	9,823	7,770	6,695	15,095	16,037	5,787	7,891	5,849	6,992	1,382	8,003	7,802
Denpasar, Indonesia	4,535	10,910	14,512	12,937	14,161	16,454	12,589	14,581	14,641	7,358	6,636	8,719	9,460	17,927	19,227	11,352	18,911	13,723	11,782	11,763
Denver, Colorado	13,272	8,575	1,932	7,944	730	1,763	7,399	856	9,129	9,730	8,797	15,327	15,443	3,717	6,052	7,096	4,979	1,028	8,717	8,558
Derby, Australia	5,856	12,225	15,029	14,257	14,284	16,495	13,901	14,805	15,607	8,579	7,494	9,365	9,791	17,030	18,337	12,591	17,637	13,736	13,101	13,085
Des Moines, Iowa	13,160	7,895	1,388	7,063	1,285	1,079	6,596	814	8,154	9,572	9,070	14,351	14,493	3,417	5,409	6,520	4,535	1,863	7,904	7,761
Detroit, Michigan	12,985	7,302	1,378	6,282	2,066	1,033	5,897	1,490	7,283	9,429	9,324	13,476	13,639	3,362	4,911	6,049	4,274	2,692	7,184	7,057
Dhahran, Saudi Arabia	3,702	3,726	10,337	5,115	11,737	11,980	5,187	11,399	7,029	4,128	6,933	4,936	6,647	13,477	11,938	5,161	13,117	12,140	4,009	4,077
Diego Garcia Island	3,385	8,144	14,612	9,398	15,743	16,412	9,605	15,582	9,968	6,749	8,290	4,180	5,406	17,371	14,816	9,452	16,317	15,898	8,371	8,469
Dijon, France	7,702	1,441	6,252	772	7,833	7,488	759	7,340	4,379	5,486	7,873	7,602	8,729	8,947	7,966	2,288	8,813	8,404	582	492
Dili, Indonesia	5,392	11,593	14,069	13,728	13,431	15,701	13,233	13,921	15,768	7,778	6,519	9,822	10,458	16,804	19,084	11,779	17,820	12,922	12,590	12,541
Djibouti, Djibouti	4,656	4,940	11,520	5,645	13,048	12,740	6,055	12,613	6,390	5,892	8,628	3,159	4,863	13,609	11,460	6,539	12,859	13,545	4,744	4,891
Dnepropetrovsk, USSR	5,489	982	7,550	2,972	8,980	9,251	2,629	8,617	6,174	3,522	6,266	7,114	8,638	11,021	10,195	2,401	11,014	9,425	1,861	1,786
Dobo, Indonesia	6,023	11,917	13,362	14,118	12,565	14,794	13,472	13,087	16,649	7,937	6,242	10,826	11,436	15,808	18,351	11,839	16,898	12,024	13,029	12,946
Doha, Qatar	3,557	3,894	10,494	5,294	11,882	12,154	5,364	11,552	7,172	4,140	6,915	4,884	6,604	13,656	12,099	5,312	13,289	12,275	4,188	4,257
Donetsk, USSR	5,274	1,182	7,699	3,185	9,111	9,434	2,840	8,761	6,349	3,357	6,135	7,070	8,622	11,226	10,409	2,528	11,228	9,542	2,068	1,998
Dover, Delaware	13,152	7,160	1,965	5,908	2,788	1,189	5,647	2,215	6,604	9,674	9,845	12,865	12,937	3,117	4,297	6,058	3,830	3,404	6,888	6,784
Dresden, East Germany	7,039	684	6,397	1,530	7,933	7,861	1,091	7,489	5,095	4,727	7,156	7,688	8,965	9,498	8,680	1,809	9,462	8,461	752	534
Dubayy, United Arab Emir.	3,178	4,092	10,629	5,601	11,969	12,370	5,617	11,670	7,551	3,936	6,649	5,047	6,778	13,961	12,468	5,438	13,640	12,329	4,479	4,533
Dublin, Ireland	8,364	1,949	5,209	1,147	6,791	6,505	307	6,297	4,676	5,705	7,735	8,613	9,660	8,117	7,474	1,908	8,139	7,368	1,614	1,469
Duluth, Minnesota	12,580	7,355	798	6,640	1,266	1,541	6,112	661	8,034	8,992	8,598	14,075	14,412	3,936	5,740	5,949	4,987	1,919	7,427	7,275
Dunedin, New Zealand	11,199	17,543	14,475	19,423	12,877	13,509	19,092	13,417	16,190	13,582	11,429	11,851	10,956	12,178	13,141	17,246	12,328	12,263	18,381	18,413
Durango, Mexico	14,978	10,091	3,528	9,103	2,437	2,031	8,740	2,551	9,395	11,465	10,311	15,727	15,134	2,579	5,276	8,711	3,920	2,415	10,028	9,901
Durban, South Africa	8,075	9,225	14,639	8,807	16,096	14,206	9,666	15,491	6,800	10,538	12,938	1,610	477	13,052	10,334	10,860	11,725	16,749	8,471	8,686
Dushanbe, USSR	2,609	3,817	9,569	5,881	10,660	11,640	5,501	10,494	8,716	2,009	4,724	6,971	8,705	13,728	13,109	4,608	13,897	10,891	4,743	4,694
East London, South Africa	8,520	9,557	14,690	9,013	16,067	14,052	9,907	15,466	6,781	10,991	13,395	2,040	464	12,747	10,053	11,181	11,411	16,704	8,747	8,966
Easter Island (Hanga Roa)	18,294	15,182	9,166	13,311	8,077	7,127	13,520	8,236	10,985	16,932	14,603	13,908	12,192	5,144	6,191	14,193	5,176	7,866	14,466	14,467
Echo Bay, Canada	10,226	6,382	2,046	6,682	2,332	4,170	5,798	2,377	9,362	6,699	5,961	14,074	15,232	6,535	8,303	4,741	7,624	2,504	7,005	6,794
Edinburgh, United Kingdom	8,109	1,723	5,199	1,409	6,763	6,618	393	6,292	5,005	5,375	7,388	8,712	9,828	8,322	7,781	1,562	8,400	7,319	1,635	1,454
Edmonton, Canada	11,623	7,518	1,544	7,410	935	3,063	6,657	1,174	9,472	8,115	7,167	15,002	15,774	5,306	7,390	5,919	6,498	1,123	7,944	7,752
El Aaiun, Morocco	9,853	4,153	6,768	2,009	8,284	6,966	2,963	7,686	1,714	8,195	10,598	7,048	7,513	7,501	5,723	4,835	6,908	8,938	2,913	3,044
Elat, Israel	5,203	2,791	9,364	3,686	10,887	10,727	3,941	10,456	5,567	4,807	7,717	5,016	6,561	12,006	10,407	4,415	11,585	11,389	2,660	2,779
Elazig, Turkey	4,897	2,024	8,662	3,550	10,112	10,271	3,497	9,737	6,158	3,826	6,723	6,045	7,629	11,869	10,677	3,538	11,681	10,562	2,401	2,431
Eniwetok Atoll, Marshall Isls.	8,178	11,862	10,116	13,760	9,045	11,188	12,758	9,610	17,411	8,123	5,340	14,322	15,081	12,290	15,025	10,891	13,548	8,458	13,150	12,957
Erfurt, East Germany	7,230	864	6,271	1,363	7,818	7,698	909	7,364	4,966	4,893	7,283	7,757	8,998	9,313	8,492	1,825	9,272	8,356	723	497
Erzurum, Turkey	4,754	2,012	8,622	3,665	10,048	10,287	3,550	9,690	6,361	3,603	6,500	6,200	7,803	11,946	10,829	3,466	11,801	10,482	2,510	2,522
Esfahan, Iran	3,658	3,213	9,736	4,851	11,090	11,490	4,778	10,780	7,184	3,481	6,341	5,647	7,350	13,170	11,912	4,545	12,971	11,468	3,705	3,735
Essen, West Germany	7,507	1,114	6,035	1,181	7,593	7,423	624	7,128	4,844	5,100	7,415	7,929	9,122	9,028	8,233	1,810	8,993	8,142	839	634
Eucla, Australia	7,357	13,774	16,075	15,640	14,913	16,690	15,457	15,507	15,772	10,253	9,082	9,461	9,435	16,034	16,655	14,262	16,175	14,279	14,501	14,524
Fargo, North Dakota	12,568	7,553	912	6,933	909	1,707	6,367	304	8,391	8,983	8,431	14,409	14,769	4,056	5,997	6,102	5,169	1,563	7,685	7,526
Faroe Islands (Torshavn)	8,174	2,019	4,664	2,103	6,191	6,271	1,102	5,754	5,614	5,163	6,916	9,370	10,526	8,156	7,929	1,161	8,386	6,721	2,277	2,075
Florence, Italy	7,261	1,360	6,872	1,150	8,449	8,102	1,373	7,962	4,375	5,343	7,904	7,024	8,214	9,494	8,348	2,625	9,285	9,014	80	306
Florianopolis, Brazil	15,343	11,294	9,863	9,123	10,128	7,876	9,959	9,766	5,630	15,317	17,465	8,597	7,194	5,796	3,606	11,736	4,494	10,470	10,033	10,180
Fort George, Canada	11,671	6,153	724	5,457	2,284	2,341	4,898	1,727	7,218	8,121	8,203	12,982	13,539	4,659	5,899	4,799	5,477	2,923	6,214	6,059
Fort McMurray, Canada	11,325	7,142	1,390	7,078	1,235	3,188	6,306	1,322	9,266	7,793	6,971	14,658	15,507	5,499	7,460	5,541	6,647	1,499	7,586	7,392
Fort Nelson, Canada	10,862	7,219	2,076	7,414	1,737	3,865	6,569	1,977	9,849	7,401	6,348	14,890	15,948	6,126	8,164	5,582	7,311	1,749	7,803	7,597
Fort Severn, Canada	11,537	6,364	283	5,879	1,844	2,498	5,237	1,366	7,808	7,954	7,788	13,457	14,103	4,891	6,369	4,908	5,825	2,448	6,554	6,384
Fort Smith, Arkansas	13,849	8,505	2,079	7,531	1,655	730	7,140	1,375	8,253	10,261	9,663	14,570	14,468	2,805	5,010	7,174	3,999	2,077	8,432	8,302
Fort Vermilion, Canada	11,062	7,103	1,683	7,167	1,493	3,518	6,356	1,644	9,492	7,553	6,651	14,706	15,661	5,817	7,793	5,482	6,975	1,645	7,615	7,415
Fort Wayne, Indiana	13,154	7,520	1,465	6,504	1,955	852	6,120	1,405	7,443	9,588	9,397	13,667	13,783	3,224	4,895	6,254	4,188	2,561	7,408	7,281
Fort-Chimo, Canada	11,004	5,343	1,423	4,697	3,020	3,062	4,096	2,500	6,766	7,506	7,904	12,270	12,967	5,278	6,168	4,021	5,955	3,634	5,414	5,255
Fort-de-France, Martinique	14,733	8,340	5,032	6,340	5,606	3,334	6,659	5,124	4,933	11,894	12,770	11,085	10,532	2,472	1,304	7,893	1,804	6,113	7,496	7,506
Fortaleza, Brazil	13,735	8,504	7,959	6,306	8,776	6,535	7,112	8,256	3,066	12,554	14,682	8,139	7,358	5,301	2,572	8,889	4,063	9,310	7,280	7,406
Frankfort, Kentucky	13,464	7,757	1,782	6,656	2,122	549	6,320	1,615	7,399	9,903	9,705	13,681	13,694	2,905	4,627	6,528	3,878	2,692	7,593	7,474
Frankfurt am Main, W. Ger.	7,401	1,054	6,223	1,171	7,782	7,594	783	7,316	4,789	5,085	7,462	7,743	8,947	9,167	8,308	1,939	9,102	8,331	657	447
Fredericton, Canada	12,168	6,110	1,880	4,927	3,212	2,202	4,610	2,606	6,104	8,763	9,254	12,151	12,478	4,098	4,816	5,038	4,640	3,868	5,868	5,756
Freeport, Bahamas	14,575	8,439	3,171	6,935	3,390	1,095	6,845	2,968	6,778	11,108	11,114	13,122	12,761	1,689	3,258	7,448	2,477	3,860	8,005	7,932
Freetown, Sierra Leone	10,629	5,933	8,380	3,979	9,744	7,973	4,983	9,139	450	9,834	12,478	5,958	5,934	7,714	5,289	6,848	6,736	10,393	4,641	4,822
Frobisher Bay, Canada	10,432	4,997	1,648	4,638	3,173	3,593	3,915	2,732	7,067	6,907	7,284	12,232	13,095	5,868	6,791	3,568	6,579	3,731	5,224	5,045

Distances in Kilometers	Bhubaneswar, India	Bialystok, Poland	Big Trout Lake, Canada	Bilbao, Spain	Billings, Montana	Birmingham, Alabama	Birmingham, United Kingdom	Bismarck, North Dakota	Bissau, Guinea Bissau	Biysk, USSR	Blagoveshchensk, USSR	Blantyre, Malawi	Bloemfontein, South Africa	Bluefields, Nicaragua	Boa Vista do Rio Branco, Braz.	Bodo, Norway	Bogota, Colombia	Boise, Idaho	Bologna, Italy	Bolzano, Italy
Frunze, USSR	2,724	3,910	9,185	6,072	10,176	11,335	5,567	10,057	9,139	1,336	4,050	7,655	9,388	13,541	13,256	4,435	13,878	10,362	4,972	4,892
Fukuoka, Japan	4,628	8,124	9,571	10,271	9,415	11,626	9,412	9,739	13,828	4,146	1,868	11,459	12,965	13,806	15,813	7,617	15,062	9,120	9,399	9,243
Funafuti Atoll, Tuvalu	10,683	14,607	10,823	16,150	9,344	10,907	15,130	9,948	18,382	11,017	8,194	15,246	14,939	10,981	13,387	13,380	11,938	8,688	15,850	15,636
Funchal, Madeira Island	9,946	3,908	6,080	1,695	7,610	6,395	2,512	7,017	2,306	7,948	10,179	7,694	8,211	7,141	5,631	4,358	6,687	8,263	2,771	2,853
Fuzhou, China	3,478	8,122	10,714	10,334	10,703	12,858	9,612	10,987	13,583	4,086	2,776	10,223	11,659	15,115	16,807	7,971	16,320	10,442	9,321	9,204
Gaborone, Botswana	8,172	8,623	13,874	8,080	15,339	13,513	8,963	14,733	6,052	10,303	12,888	1,367	496	12,538	9,800	10,241	11,237	15,994	7,799	8,018
Galapagos Islands (Santa Cruz)	17,799	11,612	6,038	9,849	5,442	3,798	9,960	5,353	8,378	14,234	13,446	13,765	12,538	1,578	3,327	10,700	1,903	5,535	10,989	10,960
Gander, Canada	11,403	5,200	2,494	3,965	4,000	3,141	3,660	3,468	5,461	8,134	9,008	11,289	11,768	4,899	5,145	4,254	5,250	4,653	4,907	4,798
Gangtok, India	836	6,008	11,011	8,105	11,726	13,253	7,683	11,740	10,782	2,816	4,157	7,500	9,129	15,577	15,332	6,557	16,018	11,752	6,967	6,918
Garyarsa, China	1,388	5,102	10,478	7,174	11,372	12,657	6,783	11,304	9,882	2,346	4,374	7,149	8,847	14,879	14,402	5,764	15,164	11,491	6,033	5,988
Gaspe, Canada	11,810	5,777	1,852	4,671	3,300	2,513	4,304	2,701	6,079	8,409	8,963	12,005	12,429	4,456	5,113	4,682	4,986	3,955	5,578	5,457
Gauhati, India	894	6,310	11,138	8,422	11,778	13,396	7,980	11,825	11,116	2,979	4,053	7,697	9,297	15,752	15,647	6,806	16,276	11,769	7,288	7,235
Gdansk, Poland	6,728	325	6,350	1,998	7,843	7,958	1,380	7,434	5,590	4,260	6,660	7,924	9,277	9,722	9,064	1,459	9,774	8,338	1,218	1,013
Geneva, Switzerland	7,631	1,443	6,402	794	7,983	7,621	910	7,490	4,326	5,493	7,924	7,451	8,583	9,051	8,017	2,396	8,892	8,556	448	402
Genoa, Italy	7,437	1,420	6,696	966	8,276	7,906	1,201	7,784	4,304	5,443	7,957	7,171	8,331	9,299	8,182	2,566	9,101	8,847	190	300
Georgetown, Guyana	15,079	8,827	5,950	6,715	6,469	4,178	7,173	6,009	4,707	12,576	13,658	10,559	9,832	2,867	521	8,565	1,780	6,947	7,860	7,902
Geraldton, Australia	6,241	12,603	16,584	14,307	15,822	17,924	14,261	16,361	14,545	9,452	8,847	8,190	8,379	17,360	17,090	13,356	17,180	15,247	13,194	13,241
Ghanzi, Botswana	8,361	8,276	13,340	7,611	14,796	12,983	8,518	14,190	5,508	10,240	12,932	1,533	947	12,091	9,353	9,871	10,810	15,451	7,391	7,612
Ghat, Libya	7,696	3,311	8,439	2,357	10,033	9,123	3,219	9,479	3,076	6,850	9,654	5,251	6,226	9,849	7,955	4,713	9,224	10,656	2,168	2,394
Gibraltar	8,815	2,913	6,536	816	8,124	7,223	1,835	7,560	2,880	6,958	9,379	7,144	7,943	8,199	6,760	3,686	7,806	8,756	1,689	1,807
Gijon, Spain	8,606	2,366	5,939	221	7,536	6,882	1,032	6,997	3,639	6,393	8,668	7,765	8,678	8,143	7,037	2,902	7,926	8,149	1,365	1,380
Gisborne, New Zealand	11,573	17,509	13,476	19,489	11,880	12,645	18,471	12,429	16,746	13,467	11,021	12,859	11,953	11,547	12,890	16,661	11,884	11,260	18,736	18,618
Glasgow, United Kingdom	8,175	1,789	5,151	1,403	6,718	6,557	405	6,244	4,978	5,433	7,430	8,745	9,848	8,257	7,718	1,602	8,334	7,277	1,676	1,499
Godthab, Greenland	9,951	4,227	2,440	3,820	3,994	4,176	3,088	3,533	6,451	6,527	7,306	11,409	12,320	6,314	6,856	2,897	6,861	4,558	4,398	4,222
Gomez Palacio, Mexico	14,839	9,886	3,332	8,900	2,287	1,839	8,533	2,369	9,249	11,308	10,224	15,593	15,071	2,561	5,225	8,510	3,903	2,311	9,822	9,695
Goose Bay, Canada	11,428	8,104	2,536	8,246	1,539	3,834	7,427	2,016	10,461	8,079	6,700	15,767	16,722	5,887	8,183	6,466	7,157	1,218	8,675	8,471
Gorki, USSR	5,284	1,384	7,096	3,595	8,400	9,022	2,956	8,113	7,065	2,667	5,261	8,036	9,620	11,037	10,647	1,950	11,255	8,774	2,634	2,488
Goteborg, Sweden	7,172	871	5,790	1,918	7,290	7,411	1,059	6,876	5,600	4,476	6,673	8,418	9,716	9,225	8,718	1,073	9,342	7,793	1,473	1,247
Granada, Spain	8,638	2,724	6,552	673	8,144	7,309	1,700	7,587	3,051	6,768	9,202	7,131	7,978	8,340	6,940	3,535	7,971	8,771	1,498	1,616
Grand Turk, Turks & Caicos	14,762	8,404	3,932	6,661	4,329	2,040	6,743	3,877	5,992	11,491	11,850	12,281	11,825	1,704	2,353	7,631	1,893	4,815	7,786	7,748
Graz, Austria	6,915	870	6,810	1,505	8,360	8,195	1,383	7,903	4,866	4,862	7,413	7,230	8,507	9,727	8,732	2,252	9,603	8,897	430	318
Green Bay, Wisconsin	12,808	7,363	1,047	6,502	1,614	1,226	6,040	1,026	7,703	9,228	8,956	13,831	14,073	3,627	5,341	6,024	4,627	2,251	7,346	7,205
Grenoble, France	7,681	1,544	6,460	726	8,046	7,641	985	7,546	4,212	5,592	8,038	7,370	8,485	9,033	7,953	2,515	8,849	8,623	451	464
Guadalajara, Mexico	15,373	10,353	3,852	9,262	2,825	2,165	8,953	2,909	9,328	11,849	10,703	15,606	14,881	2,299	5,027	9,013	3,629	2,812	10,224	10,107
Guam (Agana)	6,293	10,784	10,937	12,922	10,202	12,477	12,034	10,698	16,474	6,784	4,371	12,498	13,497	13,981	16,691	10,199	15,298	9,701	12,057	11,903
Guantanamo, Cuba	15,090	8,780	3,948	7,083	4,164	1,875	7,131	3,760	6,416	11,732	11,894	12,676	12,146	1,283	2,481	7,940	1,723	4,604	8,201	8,156
Guatemala City, Guatemala	16,128	10,218	4,349	8,715	3,843	2,124	8,638	3,693	8,090	12,549	11,917	14,196	13,369	789	3,527	9,141	2,116	4,036	9,796	9,726
Guayaquil, Ecuador	17,483	11,065	6,278	9,115	6,016	4,016	9,382	5,800	7,273	14,250	14,086	12,599	11,446	1,625	2,201	10,407	984	6,236	10,271	10,276
Guiyang, China	2,244	7,273	10,952	9,470	11,240	13,203	8,867	11,422	12,478	3,395	3,173	9,056	10,572	15,590	16,485	7,407	16,553	11,088	8,390	8,300
Gur'yev, USSR	4,276	2,144	8,254	4,243	9,536	10,169	3,828	9,265	7,350	2,452	5,335	7,168	8,831	12,122	11,461	3,101	12,226	9,886	3,131	3,058
Haifa, Israel	5,203	2,446	9,049	3,493	10,558	10,475	3,668	10,138	5,641	4,544	7,450	5,380	6,922	11,849	10,377	4,061	11,500	11,050	2,419	2,517
Haikou, China	2,558	8,063	11,591	10,251	11,734	13,807	9,671	11,973	13,132	4,207	3,681	9,139	10,535	16,144	17,295	8,218	17,237	11,514	9,156	9,075
Haiphong, Vietnam	2,174	7,753	11,576	9,928	11,818	13,820	9,379	12,021	12,751	3,972	3,742	8,817	10,251	16,197	17,051	7,982	17,186	11,636	8,821	8,746
Hakodate, Japan	5,648	7,917	8,363	9,916	8,137	10,365	8,965	8,475	13,596	4,260	1,389	12,460	14,063	12,523	14,620	7,100	13,786	7,837	9,209	9,023
Halifax, Canada	12,181	6,033	2,159	4,754	3,483	2,346	4,492	2,877	5,827	8,829	9,433	11,902	12,203	4,098	4,644	5,033	4,554	4,138	5,727	5,625
Hamburg, West Germany	7,293	876	6,019	1,490	7,556	7,505	808	7,111	5,151	4,804	7,106	8,045	9,293	9,190	8,489	1,548	9,208	8,085	1,013	788
Hamilton, Bermuda	13,409	7,080	3,122	5,453	4,013	2,063	5,438	3,449	5,499	10,165	10,781	11,839	11,756	2,969	3,290	6,278	3,215	4,616	6,545	6,486
Hamilton, New Zealand	11,316	17,276	13,572	19,381	11,980	12,823	18,359	12,539	16,938	13,229	10,818	12,776	11,933	11,780	13,148	16,511	12,135	11,352	18,483	18,376
Hangzhou, China	3,617	7,816	10,247	10,021	10,264	12,402	9,262	10,536	13,376	3,767	2,307	10,433	11,929	14,680	16,344	7,581	15,864	10,021	9,042	8,913
Hannover, West Germany	7,316	910	6,097	1,385	7,642	7,546	791	7,190	5,033	4,888	7,221	7,935	9,170	9,195	8,439	1,681	9,184	8,178	885	662
Hanoi, Vietnam	2,087	7,684	11,572	9,855	11,837	13,822	9,314	12,032	12,664	3,922	3,761	8,743	10,185	16,205	16,993	7,929	17,169	11,664	8,746	8,673
Harare, Zimbabwe	7,315	7,899	13,616	7,605	15,174	13,646	8,414	14,582	6,086	9,380	11,970	478	1,347	13,022	10,296	9,538	11,776	15,824	7,185	7,396
Harbin, China	4,671	6,872	8,437	8,965	8,518	10,605	8,070	8,755	12,595	3,068	507	11,377	13,041	12,924	14,577	6,251	14,064	8,330	8,162	7,991
Harrisburg, Pennsylvania	13,073	7,144	1,802	5,949	2,631	1,158	5,655	2,054	6,739	9,576	9,696	12,979	13,083	3,204	4,457	6,006	3,960	3,253	6,910	6,800
Hartford, Connecticut	12,795	6,783	1,857	5,558	2,894	1,544	5,276	2,299	6,426	9,339	9,621	12,623	12,792	3,470	4,478	5,687	4,120	3,533	6,524	6,417
Havana, Cuba	15,041	8,956	3,468	7,451	3,445	1,229	7,366	3,101	7,146	11,533	11,360	13,453	12,959	1,241	3,243	7,939	2,236	3,840	8,525	8,453
Helena, Montana	12,390	8,166	1,756	7,857	287	2,578	7,182	860	9,548	8,894	7,847	15,436	15,926	4,665	6,925	6,599	5,912	467	8,491	8,310
Helsinki, Finland	6,474	791	6,115	2,659	7,527	7,917	1,854	7,174	6,307	3,681	5,944	8,467	9,898	9,863	9,495	947	10,065	7,972	1,968	1,761
Hengyang, China	2,824	7,627	10,800	9,838	10,953	13,013	9,174	11,182	12,974	3,646	2,890	9,615	11,102	15,357	16,640	7,619	16,447	10,751	8,790	8,685
Herat, Afghanistan	2,802	3,707	9,877	5,604	11,083	11,831	5,369	10,858	8,163	2,730	5,478	6,250	7,982	13,749	12,782	4,760	13,729	11,371	4,448	4,437
Hermosillo, Mexico	14,262	9,879	3,234	9,157	1,868	2,347	8,669	2,159	9,896	10,825	9,507	16,247	15,880	3,395	6,052	8,396	4,737	1,681	9,983	9,832
Hiroshima, Japan	4,827	8,164	9,413	10,292	9,228	11,449	9,415	9,560	13,880	4,219	1,807	11,661	13,173	13,612	15,664	7,603	14,876	8,925	9,445	9,284
Hiva Oa (Atuona)	15,089	14,941	8,422	14,384	6,870	7,312	13,912	7,329	13,859	13,828	11,084	17,101	15,417	6,573	8,796	13,322	7,377	6,350	15,230	15,070
Ho Chi Minh City, Vietnam	2,466	8,628	12,677	10,739	12,829	14,905	10,291	13,074	13,175	5,022	4,782	8,423	9,684	17,243	17,967	9,008	18,305	12,593	9,600	9,553
Hobart, Australia	9,402	15,817	15,727	17,616	14,198	15,252	17,501	14,789	16,191	12,138	10,502	10,550	10,026	14,045	14,773	16,127	14,132	13,546	16,513	16,554
Hohhot, China	3,340	6,431	9,319	8,629	9,623	11,565	7,861	9,787	12,057	2,384	1,624	10,057	11,708	13,952	15,114	6,194	14,946	9,505	7,673	7,536
Hong Kong	2,945	8,126	11,263	10,332	11,332	13,448	9,691	11,593	13,371	4,171	3,321	9,597	11,003	15,748	17,177	8,154	16,904	11,090	9,266	9,170
Honiara, Solomon Islands	8,749	13,817	12,162	15,910	10,875	12,741	14,960	11,474	19,473	9,820	7,322	13,354	13,481	13,077	15,484	13,090	14,049	10,236	15,095	14,937
Honolulu, Hawaii	11,712	11,757	6,675	12,411	5,216	7,025	11,506	5,822	14,503	9,817	7,132	18,541	19,053	7,909	10,647	10,160	9,188	4,562	12,637	12,416
Houston, Texas	14,471	9,078	2,709	7,992	2,115	911	7,665	1,949	8,390	10,884	10,188	14,745	14,419	2,305	4,720	7,782	3,574	2,404	8,939	8,820
Huambo, Angola	8,490	7,332	12,177	6,486	13,654	11,945	7,421	13,048	4,404	9,786	12,632	2,100	2,110	11,325	8,621	8,875	10,115	14,310	6,352	6,577
Hubli, India	1,253	6,161	12,210	7,902	13,225	14,272	7,796	13,109	9,753	4,224	6,067	5,600	7,208	16,202	14,771	7,205	15,983	13,374	6,759	6,786
Hugh Town, United Kingdom	8,464	2,061	5,437	784	7,029	6,605	418	6,517	4,306	5,952	8,069	8,328	9,327	8,098	7,294	2,254	8,037	7,621	1,463	1,364
Hull, Canada	12,499	6,655	1,386	5,602	2,539	1,628	5,223	1,934	6,761	8,994	9,166	12,859	13,139	3,783	4,945	5,460	4,527	3,191	6,506	6,381
Hyderabad, India	838	6,186	12,038	8,022	12,975	14,161	7,846	12,896	10,050	3,949	5,672	6,017	7,620	16,220	15,020	7,132	16,150	13,088	6,869	6,881
Hyderabad, Pakistan	1,879	4,848	10,987	6,653	12,120	12,982	6,493	11,938	8,859	3,337	5,710	5,815	7,531	14,893	13,713	5,910	14,784	12,353	5,500	5,512
Igloolik, Canada	10,017	5,135	1,783	5,160	3,021	4,003	4,322	2,726	7,856	6,436	6,520	12,671	13,705	6,375	7,552	3,564	7,214	3,471	5,581	5,382
Iloilo, Philippines	4,071	9,684	12,224	11,888	11,947	14,214	11,249	12,326	14,773	5,721	4,411	10,080	11,204	16,180	18,469	9,677	17,519	11,570	10,811	10,721
Indianapolis, Indiana	13,311	7,687	1,590	6,654	1,939	697	6,281	1,418	7,520	9,740	9,503	13,772	13,840	3,086	4,833	6,422	4,080	2,525	7,566	7,441
Innsbruck, Austria	7,222	1,061	6,590	1,211	8,153	7,919	1,116	7,683	4,668	5,101	7,590	7,370	8,590	9,424	8,433	2,236	9,296	8,705	309	83
Inuvik, Canada	9,675	6,396	2,767	6,973	2,895	4,863	6,030	3,030	9,884	6,214	5,271	14,110	15,449	7,206	9,023	4,753	8,323	2,938	7,159	6,940
Invercargill, New Zealand	11,060	17,429	14,641	19,248	13,043	13,686	19,037	13,586	16,157	13,504	11,409	11,691	10,818	12,339	13,257	17,236	12,470	12,427	18,216	18,258
Inverness, United Kingdom	8,138	1,791	5,049	1,584	6,605	6,513	576	6,142	5,153	5,327	7,274	8,887	10,011	8,264	7,802	1,446	8,381	7,156	1,802	1,615
Iquitos, Peru	17,115	10,769	6,572	8,720	6,500	4,366	9,091	6,221	6,611	14,246	14,496	11,848	10,725	2,095	1,576	10,287	930	6,782	9,873	9,900
Iraklion, Greece	6,117	1,984	8,337	2,564	9,892	9,613	2,859	9,430	4,851	5,022	7,866	5,753	7,137	10,904	9,454	3,621	10,552	10,429	1,553	1,694
Irkutsk, USSR	3,899	5,182	8,169	7,342	8,697	10,440	6,524	8,769	10,892	1,295	1,627	10,040	11,767	12,842	13,740	4,813	13,701	8,692	6,458	6,301
Islamabad, Pakistan	1,948	4,470	10,172	6,498	11,201	12,277	6,154	11,068	9,178	2,308	4,743	6,811	8,536	14,392	13,719	5,267	14,554	11,391	5,351	5,315
Istanbul, Turkey	5,803	1,416	7,994	2,636	9,506	9,463	2,653	9,084	5,406	4,363	7,175	6,319	7,772	10,972	9,779	3,057	10,765	10,006	1,491	1,539
Ivujivik, Canada	10,733	5,471	1,187	5,128	2,679	3,273	4,413	2,255	7,438	7,171	7,312	12,725	13,551	5,614	6,764	4,005	6,421	3,233	5,721	5,542
Iwo Jima Island, Japan	5,695	9,528	10,004	11,638	9,502	11,794	10,736	9,932	15,248	5,583	3,069	12,357	13,654	13,658	16,145	8,897	14,997	9,082	10,811	10,648
Izmir, Turkey	5,940	1,664	8,151	2,582	9,684	9,533	2,729	9,243	5,149	4,663	7,492	6,055	7,479	10,944	9,630	3,310	10,670	10,202	1,480	1,575
Jackson, Mississippi	14,176	8,572	2,393	7,431	2,171	344	7,127	1,846	7,879	10,593	10,136	14,227	14,012	2,343	4,490	7,327	3,496	2,594	8,391	8,277
Jaffna, Sri Lanka	1,326	6,977	12,905	8,713	13,806	15,028	8,615	13,749	10,399	4,781	6,259	5,703	7,195	17,021	15,462	7,984	16,751	13,882	7,573	7,603
Jakarta, Indonesia	3,714	10,130	14,507	12,077	14,463	16,672	11,814	14,791	13,680	6,821	6,564	7,887	8,775	18,703	18,598	10,737	19,814	14,118	10,922	10,920
Jamestown, St. Helena	10,774	8,138	11,054	6,559	12,250	10,178	7,587	11,666	3,259	11,464	14,369	4,354	3,575	9,130	6,393	9,374	7,861	12,862	6,910	7,125
Jamnagar, India	1,653	5,208	11,338	6,986	12,446	13,345	6,848	12,278	9,079	3,584	5,822	5,702	7,399	15,252	13,994	6,273	15,107	12,660	5,836	5,854
Jan Mayen Island	8,067	2,543	4,184	3,108	5,599	6,082	2,096	5,239	6,586	4,753	6,117	10,190	11,445	8,199	8,403	1,010	8,638	6,064	3,154	2,936
Jayapura, Indonesia	6,494	12,037	12,698	14,249	11,815	14,016	13,488	12,352	17,221	7,995	5,985	11,618	12,236	15,025	17,660	11,745	16,167	11,258	13,228	13,117
Jefferson City, Missouri	13,492	8,100	1,704	7,158	1,565	741	6,746	1,154	8,037	9,904	9,426	14,306	14,329	3,060	5,089	6,769	4,184	2,088	8,042	7,909
Jerusalem, Israel	5,178	2,565	9,163	3,573	10,675	10,574	3,771	10,253	5,638	4,611	7,520	5,262	6,808	11,921	10,410	4,181	11,551	11,169	2,512	2,616

Distances in Kilometers	Bhubaneswar, India	Bialystok, Poland	Big Trout Lake, Canada	Bilbao, Spain	Billings, Montana	Birmingham, Alabama	Birmingham, United Kingdom	Bismarck, North Dakota	Bissau, Guinea Bissau	Biysk, USSR	Blagoveshchensk, USSR	Blantyre, Malawi	Bloemfontein, South Africa	Bluefields, Nicaragua	Boa Vista do Rio Branco, Braz.	Bodo, Norway	Bogota, Colombia	Boise, Idaho	Bologna, Italy	Bolzano, Italy
Jiggalong, Australia	6,139	12,556	15,765	14,461	14,966	17,113	14,239	15,503	15,249	9,094	8,187	8,913	9,201	17,143	17,722	13,086	17,393	14,397	13,312	13,324
Jinan, China	3,530	7,084	9,648	9,281	9,803	11,854	8,503	10,023	12,705	3,038	1,731	10,353	11,946	14,199	15,627	6,812	15,295	9,622	8,327	8,190
Jodhpur, India	1,470	5,065	10,980	6,965	12,023	13,054	6,735	11,887	9,304	3,092	5,308	6,213	7,915	15,088	14,099	6,004	15,097	12,208	5,809	5,804
Johannesburg, South Africa	8,079	8,802	14,146	8,321	15,616	13,784	9,190	15,010	6,329	10,334	12,855	1,358	376	12,764	10,030	10,429	11,455	16,271	8,010	8,227
Juazeiro do Norte, Brazil	13,958	8,878	8,252	6,685	9,002	6,737	7,502	8,499	3,369	12,926	15,078	8,130	7,249	5,356	2,618	9,284	4,075	9,516	7,644	7,775
Juneau, Alaska	10,548	7,485	2,758	7,891	2,234	4,464	6,997	2,577	10,486	7,202	5,869	15,205	16,438	6,649	8,794	5,839	7,877	2,061	8,182	7,968
Kabul, Afghanistan	2,277	4,145	10,014	6,142	11,109	12,071	5,827	10,942	8,802	2,376	4,968	6,640	8,373	14,123	13,355	5,022	14,224	11,335	4,992	4,962
Kalgoorlie, Australia	6,808	13,210	16,420	14,983	15,426	17,351	14,883	16,001	15,144	9,879	8,994	8,802	8,875	16,699	16,905	13,849	16,689	14,814	13,859	13,897
Kaliningrad, USSR	6,615	248	6,398	2,122	7,879	8,036	1,499	7,479	5,705	4,135	6,548	7,932	9,306	9,822	9,186	1,437	9,888	8,365	1,315	1,116
Kamloops, Canada	11,745	8,003	2,084	7,969	1,030	3,320	7,201	1,495	10,012	8,314	7,112	15,554	16,337	5,421	7,670	6,385	6,672	843	8,479	8,283
Kampala, Uganda	6,198	5,920	12,045	5,925	13,642	12,683	6,611	13,105	5,472	7,564	10,335	1,800	3,330	12,873	10,381	7,565	11,865	14,242	5,325	5,521
Kananga, Zaire	7,512	6,542	11,996	6,015	13,558	12,156	6,866	12,970	4,643	8,751	11,585	1,756	2,602	11,909	9,288	8,144	10,789	14,206	5,690	5,908
Kano, Nigeria	8,254	4,745	9,492	3,636	11,051	9,771	4,585	10,464	2,625	8,061	10,938	4,237	4,931	9,986	7,689	6,154	9,109	11,699	3,611	3,836
Kanpur, India	889	5,528	11,060	7,530	11,955	13,230	7,211	11,889	10,015	2,927	4,784	6,776	8,443	15,419	14,728	6,290	15,612	12,064	6,377	6,352
Kansas City, Missouri	13,437	8,169	1,674	7,291	1,362	933	6,850	994	8,245	9,848	9,285	14,498	14,544	3,188	5,283	6,804	4,345	1,873	8,153	8,014
Kaohsiung, Taiwan	3,574	8,484	11,049	10,697	10,976	13,164	9,990	11,283	13,883	4,459	3,131	10,211	11,584	15,373	17,187	8,362	16,617	10,687	9,669	9,557
Karachi, Pakistan	1,997	4,810	11,011	6,580	12,169	12,980	6,445	11,974	8,735	3,436	5,843	5,686	7,404	14,850	13,610	5,909	14,704	12,415	5,430	5,448
Karaganda, USSR	3,471	3,422	8,407	5,631	9,409	10,564	5,019	9,280	8,923	896	3,806	8,176	9,903	12,795	12,700	3,735	13,205	9,611	4,592	4,479
Karl-Marx-Stadt, East Germany	7,098	747	6,374	1,467	7,915	7,822	1,041	7,467	5,039	4,789	7,212	7,688	8,953	9,446	8,618	1,834	9,404	8,447	716	493
Kasanga, Tanzania	6,776	6,868	12,776	6,687	14,366	13,118	7,448	13,797	5,639	8,478	11,182	911	2,346	12,908	10,266	8,510	11,768	14,996	6,194	6,399
Kashgar, China	2,334	4,230	9,578	6,363	10,550	11,731	5,900	10,441	9,315	1,619	4,156	7,451	9,182	13,933	13,574	4,820	14,245	10,721	5,245	5,177
Kassel, West Germany	7,336	953	6,169	1,298	7,720	7,585	795	7,262	4,930	4,963	7,321	7,836	9,060	9,201	8,396	1,799	9,165	8,261	772	551
Kathmandu, Nepal	831	5,756	10,959	7,827	11,747	13,177	7,436	11,729	10,457	2,759	4,345	7,253	8,903	15,457	15,053	6,377	15,808	11,808	6,684	6,641
Kayes, Mali	10,204	5,257	7,974	3,293	9,409	7,796	4,301	8,803	534	9,190	11,799	6,105	6,292	7,810	5,558	6,163	6,945	10,065	3,965	4,142
Kazan, USSR	4,983	1,700	7,298	3,913	8,559	9,269	3,282	8,296	7,352	2,358	5,012	8,037	9,656	11,322	10,972	2,206	11,567	8,907	2,932	2,794
Kemi, Finland	6,675	1,415	5,635	3,026	6,993	7,546	2,092	6,671	6,712	3,593	5,580	9,091	10,528	9,608	9,503	479	9,933	7,411	2,507	2,288
Kenora, Canada	12,249	7,190	546	6,611	1,139	1,915	6,023	572	8,216	8,661	8,221	14,130	14,588	4,304	6,105	5,736	5,364	1,790	7,341	7,178
Kerguelen Island	7,891	12,182	18,524	12,457	19,566	17,377	13,149	19,235	10,650	11,409	12,359	4,866	4,285	15,181	13,030	13,750	13,971	19,222	11,843	12,026
Kerkira, Greece	6,567	1,524	7,684	1,949	9,247	8,958	2,199	8,777	4,652	5,066	7,811	6,328	7,637	10,311	9,007	3,100	10,031	9,793	893	1,036
Kermanshah, Iran	4,113	2,817	9,404	4,391	10,801	11,093	4,344	10,463	6,772	3,633	6,532	5,690	7,359	12,721	11,456	4,225	12,509	11,210	3,248	3,283
Khabarovsk, USSR	5,379	7,052	7,899	9,047	7,879	10,016	8,101	8,146	12,726	3,492	583	12,048	13,728	12,295	14,118	6,240	13,478	7,663	8,342	8,156
Kharkov, USSR	5,453	971	7,450	3,058	8,862	9,195	2,649	8,511	6,327	3,364	6,085	7,288	8,822	11,013	10,266	2,279	11,047	9,295	1,973	1,879
Khartoum, Sudan	5,648	4,245	10,587	4,551	12,165	11,602	5,089	11,675	5,211	6,159	9,039	3,482	4,997	12,378	10,279	5,891	11,651	12,721	3,774	3,951
Khon Kaen, Thailand	1,845	7,877	12,124	9,999	12,431	14,384	9,539	12,615	12,567	4,296	4,357	8,257	9,650	16,779	17,222	8,266	17,654	12,264	8,865	8,812
Kiev, USSR	5,859	590	7,188	2,650	8,639	8,864	2,247	8,262	5,980	3,716	6,370	7,348	8,824	10,631	9,855	2,080	10,642	9,099	1,585	1,477
Kigali, Rwanda	6,557	6,139	12,108	5,997	13,704	12,608	6,734	13,149	5,275	7,924	10,707	1,623	3,037	12,656	10,113	7,780	11,606	14,321	5,470	5,674
Kingston, Canada	12,645	6,794	1,449	5,715	2,512	1,486	5,352	1,911	6,791	9,137	9,279	12,927	13,166	3,640	4,845	5,606	4,398	3,159	6,630	6,508
Kingston, Jamaica	15,375	9,070	4,136	7,363	4,247	1,988	7,420	3,877	6,594	11,998	12,076	12,805	12,199	999	2,432	8,224	1,512	4,652	8,485	8,441
Kingstown, Saint Vincent	14,859	8,476	5,172	6,460	5,716	3,435	6,797	5,242	4,958	12,050	12,928	11,062	10,469	2,449	1,144	8,047	1,699	6,212	7,616	7,630
Kinshasa, Zaire	8,165	6,408	11,395	5,578	12,921	11,400	6,497	12,323	3,857	9,053	11,945	2,502	2,978	11,101	8,489	7,942	9,989	13,577	5,418	5,642
Kirkwall, United Kingdom	8,033	1,737	5,018	1,749	6,561	6,545	727	6,111	5,335	5,171	7,093	8,973	10,128	8,344	7,946	1,266	8,495	7,101	1,881	1,682
Kirov, USSR	5,151	1,755	7,030	3,948	8,268	9,036	3,245	8,017	7,465	2,309	4,844	8,348	9,960	11,132	10,905	2,003	11,433	8,607	3,029	2,872
Kiruna, Sweden	6,921	1,647	5,342	3,062	6,698	7,267	2,084	6,376	6,744	3,757	5,597	9,352	10,765	9,353	9,334	256	9,714	7,119	2,653	2,430
Kisangani, Zaire	6,944	5,837	11,585	5,502	13,175	12,010	6,289	12,609	4,677	7,991	10,841	2,099	3,281	12,068	9,559	7,459	11,045	13,804	5,062	5,274
Kishinev, USSR	5,902	794	7,434	2,519	8,916	9,020	2,279	8,517	5,688	4,004	6,718	6,980	8,436	10,685	9,746	2,408	10,611	9,397	1,387	1,333
Kitchner, Canada	12,817	7,072	1,348	6,039	2,228	1,233	5,657	1,635	7,091	9,278	9,272	13,254	13,459	3,500	4,909	5,840	4,350	2,866	6,942	6,816
Knoxville, Tennessee	13,692	7,903	2,041	6,724	2,328	380	6,432	1,847	7,302	10,140	9,966	13,619	13,554	2,655	4,381	6,712	3,617	2,873	7,689	7,578
Kosice, Czechoslovakia	6,489	511	6,946	1,962	8,461	8,456	1,685	8,036	5,314	4,398	6,988	7,271	8,634	10,089	9,183	2,106	10,019	8,970	892	781
Kota Kinabalu, Malaysia	3,627	9,675	12,944	11,828	12,777	15,018	11,310	13,129	14,329	5,882	5,025	9,247	10,326	17,062	18,971	9,893	18,395	12,425	10,703	10,642
Krakow, Poland	6,598	407	6,765	1,899	8,280	8,289	1,540	7,855	5,335	4,404	6,943	7,445	8,796	9,947	9,099	1,941	9,905	8,788	899	747
Kralendijk, Bonaire	15,446	9,030	5,005	7,096	5,315	3,023	7,347	4,901	5,728	12,400	12,920	11,780	11,090	1,686	1,330	8,449	1,054	5,752	8,250	8,247
Krasnodar, USSR	5,086	1,462	8,032	3,326	9,451	9,738	3,075	9,096	6,328	3,436	6,272	6,747	8,315	11,480	10,550	2,868	11,427	9,884	2,181	2,145
Krasnoyarsk, USSR	4,015	4,324	7,824	6,490	8,547	10,084	5,690	8,538	10,034	625	2,381	9,602	11,335	12,460	13,055	4,027	13,180	8,632	5,600	5,443
Kristiansand, Norway	7,407	1,103	5,581	1,826	7,093	7,177	892	6,669	5,512	4,665	6,788	8,562	9,821	8,985	8,504	1,066	9,110	7,607	1,540	1,316
Kuala Lumpur, Malaysia	2,556	8,964	13,594	10,951	13,823	15,849	10,648	14,049	12,901	5,683	5,758	7,632	8,786	18,226	17,966	9,566	19,034	13,595	9,795	9,782
Kuching, Malaysia	3,372	9,683	13,585	11,755	13,529	15,733	11,356	13,852	13,875	6,115	5,639	8,496	9,531	17,860	18,922	10,103	19,177	13,201	10,605	10,572
Kumasi, Ghana	9,498	5,620	9,306	4,054	10,770	9,162	5,076	10,165	1,637	9,211	12,036	4,740	4,957	9,013	6,564	6,836	8,025	11,426	4,374	4,587
Kumzar, Oman	3,077	4,054	10,555	5,622	11,875	12,332	5,604	11,588	7,656	3,776	6,486	5,204	6,936	13,974	12,546	5,365	13,692	12,224	4,491	4,537
Kunming, China	1,811	7,133	11,179	9,308	11,552	13,445	8,762	11,704	12,185	3,388	3,519	8,618	10,138	15,846	16,443	7,388	16,704	11,430	8,204	8,128
Kuqa Chang, China	2,334	4,613	9,458	6,798	10,299	11,674	6,245	10,249	9,896	1,273	3,519	8,042	9,766	13,973	13,938	4,980	14,449	10,409	5,712	5,623
Kurgan, USSR	4,269	2,715	7,683	4,926	8,772	9,798	4,251	8,598	8,356	1,342	4,089	8,390	10,084	11,995	11,906	2,917	12,386	9,027	3,948	3,811
Kuwait, Kuwait	3,942	3,324	9,939	4,745	11,350	11,579	4,790	11,004	6,821	3,985	6,845	5,188	6,878	13,107	11,657	4,770	12,794	11,763	3,628	3,689
Kuybyshev, USSR	4,761	1,795	7,583	3,998	8,850	9,539	3,432	8,585	7,351	2,340	5,089	7,780	9,413	11,565	11,125	2,468	11,770	9,198	2,967	2,848
Kyoto, Japan	5,134	8,286	9,228	10,384	8,987	11,225	9,483	9,335	14,010	4,396	1,822	11,970	13,482	13,353	15,484	7,650	14,633	8,667	9,574	9,406
Kzyl-Orda, USSR	3,309	3,182	8,829	5,321	9,953	10,893	4,855	9,767	8,388	1,685	4,576	7,384	9,107	12,996	12,525	3,869	13,222	10,209	4,213	4,137
L'vov, USSR	6,304	372	6,969	2,180	8,464	8,544	1,827	8,055	5,550	4,162	6,757	7,348	8,749	10,233	9,389	2,017	10,199	8,956	1,128	1,008
La Ceiba, Honduras	15,941	9,889	4,231	8,332	3,893	1,964	8,288	3,676	7,678	12,394	11,958	13,821	13,061	533	3,201	8,870	1,861	4,155	9,424	9,361
La Coruna, Spain	8,821	2,554	5,789	440	7,385	6,682	1,120	6,838	3,561	6,563	8,787	7,902	8,769	7,923	6,830	2,989	7,708	8,005	1,584	1,593
La Paz, Bolivia	17,257	11,545	8,067	9,366	8,005	5,879	9,927	7,735	6,581	15,378	16,006	10,870	9,542	3,590	2,289	11,367	2,423	8,261	10,471	10,547
La Paz, Mexico	14,794	10,339	3,704	9,499	2,403	2,508	9,069	2,652	9,953	11,372	9,999	16,294	15,685	3,108	5,826	8,888	4,442	2,224	10,375	10,234
La Ronge, Canada	11,592	7,109	999	6,888	1,061	2,796	6,166	975	8,918	8,030	7,342	14,486	15,216	5,138	7,045	5,543	6,258	1,500	7,465	7,279
Labrador City, Canada	11,483	5,617	1,532	4,718	3,077	2,678	4,239	2,502	6,430	8,026	8,485	12,191	12,733	4,784	5,587	4,410	5,401	3,723	5,543	5,404
Lagos, Nigeria	8,985	5,479	9,655	4,125	11,157	9,639	5,125	10,556	2,168	8,892	11,761	4,265	4,633	9,560	7,116	6,805	8,579	11,814	4,285	4,506
Lahore, Pakistan	1,705	4,712	10,421	6,719	11,432	12,533	6,395	11,309	9,322	2,494	4,815	6,715	8,432	14,649	13,930	5,525	14,795	11,610	5,568	5,538
Lambasa, Fiji	10,994	15,439	11,507	17,023	9,979	11,350	16,005	10,575	18,340	11,720	8,957	14,731	14,206	11,110	13,298	14,253	11,925	9,325	16,701	16,491
Lansing, Michigan	12,964	7,345	1,298	6,365	1,936	1,043	5,960	1,360	7,409	9,400	9,241	13,592	13,768	3,407	5,016	6,068	4,349	2,562	7,253	7,122
Lanzhou, China	2,471	6,308	9,959	8,520	10,386	12,227	7,856	10,509	11,738	2,338	2,482	9,215	10,850	14,630	15,409	6,338	15,499	10,307	7,483	7,373
Laoag, Philippines	3,656	8,893	11,507	11,104	11,373	13,590	10,428	11,703	14,178	4,894	3,611	10,105	11,396	15,738	17,676	8,828	17,021	11,055	10,054	9,951
Largeau, Chad	6,978	3,923	9,611	3,494	11,208	10,329	4,251	10,665	3,788	6,836	9,739	4,115	5,261	10,938	8,842	5,495	10,199	11,819	3,034	3,251
Las Vegas, Nevada	13,385	9,325	2,762	8,860	1,204	2,600	8,260	1,679	10,085	9,977	8,635	16,301	16,339	4,132	6,688	7,777	5,461	831	9,577	9,407
Launceston, Australia	9,295	15,705	15,638	17,563	14,125	15,249	17,387	14,720	16,325	11,992	10,336	10,610	10,124	14,115	14,912	15,973	14,239	13,471	16,442	16,473
Le Havre, France	8,020	1,647	5,822	734	7,406	7,059	360	6,909	4,418	5,622	7,871	8,004	9,084	8,564	7,701	2,137	8,484	7,983	1,017	900
Leipzig, East Germany	7,138	766	6,308	1,458	7,849	7,761	988	7,401	5,051	4,797	7,198	7,752	9,013	9,395	8,588	1,784	9,363	8,381	762	537
Leningrad, USSR	6,185	872	6,323	2,904	7,704	8,169	2,136	7,370	6,524	3,400	5,727	8,402	9,876	10,142	9,789	1,131	10,358	8,128	2,134	1,939
Leon, Spain	8,627	2,424	6,016	224	7,613	6,927	1,131	7,070	3,543	6,459	8,756	7,682	8,582	8,153	7,004	2,999	7,914	8,229	1,379	1,411
Lerwick, United Kingdom	7,912	1,670	5,030	1,884	6,558	6,611	857	6,121	5,491	5,015	6,927	9,020	10,206	8,448	8,096	1,099	8,624	7,086	1,933	1,725
Lhasa, China	1,170	5,986	10,755	8,123	11,421	13,010	7,647	11,454	10,934	2,590	3,804	7,843	9,478	15,364	15,333	6,434	15,902	11,430	7,000	6,937
Libreville, Gabon	8,581	5,984	10,594	4,907	12,105	10,572	5,870	11,505	3,043	9,018	11,927	3,329	3,719	10,358	7,808	7,434	9,298	12,761	4,889	5,115
Lilongwe, Malawi	6,839	7,506	13,442	7,360	15,028	13,687	8,121	14,453	6,151	8,865	11,457	238	1,852	13,275	10,575	9,150	12,069	15,662	6,862	7,066
Lima, Peru	17,989	11,751	7,403	9,667	7,139	5,147	10,078	6,935	7,288	15,242	15,214	11,941	10,620	2,761	2,446	11,294	1,870	7,333	10,812	10,852
Limerick, Ireland	8,536	2,121	5,124	1,128	6,713	6,369	455	6,209	4,570	5,875	7,877	8,663	9,672	7,954	7,299	2,048	7,965	7,298	1,722	1,592
Limoges, France	8,013	1,773	6,161	441	7,753	7,293	773	7,242	4,090	5,814	8,170	7,622	8,675	8,678	7,641	2,509	8,509	8,341	806	784
Limon, Costa Rica	16,449	10,181	4,901	8,453	4,649	2,632	8,532	4,412	7,358	12,983	12,703	13,301	12,412	235	2,595	9,303	1,154	4,913	9,582	9,545
Lincoln, Nebraska	13,240	8,108	1,531	7,320	1,104	1,194	6,836	742	8,414	9,655	9,034	14,622	14,742	3,436	5,544	6,705	4,605	1,638	8,147	8,001
Linz, Austria	7,000	823	6,650	1,451	8,198	8,050	1,240	7,743	4,900	4,857	7,363	7,389	8,658	9,609	8,667	2,114	9,511	8,735	482	297
Lisbon, Portugal	9,044	2,935	6,097	723	7,684	6,803	1,627	7,119	3,045	6,978	9,277	7,584	8,359	7,856	6,555	3,500	7,530	8,317	1,817	1,884
Little Rock, Arkansas	13,917	8,456	2,128	7,419	1,839	523	7,059	1,517	8,061	10,329	9,809	14,388	14,262	2,663	4,814	7,159	3,829	2,280	8,343	8,218
Liverpool, United Kingdom	8,151	1,735	5,376	1,131	6,952	6,710	128	6,467	4,744	5,529	7,618	8,483	9,571	8,333	7,672	1,805	8,351	7,520	1,440	1,281
Lodz, Poland	6,646	294	6,603	1,925	8,109	8,160	1,462	7,691	5,433	4,343	6,831	7,632	8,984	9,860	9,085	1,753	9,854	8,613	1,008	829
Lome, Togo	9,223	5,580	9,542	4,133	11,025	9,458	5,145	10,421	1,952	9,067	11,921	4,443	4,729	9,332	6,877	6,862	8,341	11,681	4,362	4,580

Distances in Kilometers	Bhubaneswar, India	Bialystok, Poland	Big Trout Lake, Canada	Bilbao, Spain	Billings, Montana	Birmingham, Alabama	Birmingham, United Kingdom	Bismarck, North Dakota	Bissau, Guinea Bissau	Biysk, USSR	Blagoveshchensk, USSR	Blantyre, Malawi	Bloemfontein, South Africa	Bluefields, Nicaragua	Boa Vista do Rio Branco, Braz.	Bodo, Norway	Bogota, Colombia	Boise, Idaho	Bologna, Italy	Bolzano, Italy
London, United Kingdom	7,998	1,590	5,663	942	7,240	6,964	164	6,753	4,615	5,500	7,694	8,195	9,296	8,534	7,766	1,930	8,502	7,810	1,155	1,005
Londonderry, United Kingdom	8,386	1,991	5,044	1,344	6,621	6,391	455	6,134	4,841	5,645	7,608	8,799	9,856	8,057	7,502	1,781	8,121	7,192	1,773	1,614
Longlac, Canada	12,213	6,836	510	6,115	1,699	1,807	5,580	1,106	7,645	8,635	8,454	13,586	14,015	4,198	5,751	5,457	5,144	2,354	6,896	6,743
Lord Howe Island, Australia	9,684	15,763	14,112	17,972	12,616	13,941	17,222	13,216	17,757	11,737	9,582	12,082	11,653	13,272	14,783	15,411	13,738	11,960	16,874	16,800
Los Angeles, California	13,481	9,651	3,119	9,224	1,543	2,901	8,614	2,041	10,422	10,141	8,658	16,664	16,624	4,263	6,881	8,087	5,603	1,075	9,930	9,758
Louangphrabang, Laos	1,705	7,536	11,757	9,677	12,108	14,022	9,189	12,273	12,358	3,912	4,049	8,335	9,787	16,422	16,882	7,889	17,268	11,965	8,551	8,490
Louisville, Kentucky	13,473	7,801	1,763	6,719	2,052	534	6,373	1,553	7,478	9,906	9,673	13,759	13,772	2,915	4,680	6,558	3,910	2,618	7,650	7,529
Luanda, Angola	8,569	6,927	11,662	5,993	13,145	11,478	6,941	12,540	3,923	9,591	12,476	2,489	2,626	10,972	8,301	8,440	9,802	13,801	5,904	6,130
Lubumbashi, Zaire	7,300	7,192	12,837	6,823	14,403	12,968	7,642	13,816	5,423	8,990	11,713	933	1,939	12,563	9,880	8,820	11,378	15,050	6,428	6,642
Lusaka, Zambia	7,427	7,611	13,225	7,236	14,779	13,257	8,064	14,186	5,698	9,299	11,967	721	1,534	12,703	9,990	9,242	11,478	15,430	6,852	7,066
Luxembourg, Luxembourg	7,589	1,245	6,133	992	7,702	7,454	648	7,224	4,637	5,268	7,618	7,779	8,944	8,995	8,116	2,024	8,916	8,261	692	519
Luxor, Egypt	5,453	3,149	9,625	3,767	11,175	10,860	4,146	10,718	5,279	5,277	8,187	4,595	6,105	11,977	10,215	4,791	11,459	11,702	2,834	2,983
Lynn Lake, Canada	11,439	6,801	776	6,560	1,335	2,812	5,839	1,118	8,638	7,861	7,322	14,158	14,909	5,193	6,971	5,249	6,262	1,819	7,140	6,955
Lyon, France	7,739	1,554	6,366	681	7,952	7,551	895	7,452	4,227	5,604	8,023	7,460	8,568	8,957	7,905	2,462	8,787	8,530	529	511
Macapa, Brazil	14,828	8,956	6,954	6,759	7,549	5,262	7,383	7,076	4,131	12,911	14,429	9,596	8,775	3,848	1,115	8,970	2,611	8,034	7,854	7,934
Madison, Wisconsin	12,979	7,558	1,198	6,682	1,548	1,085	6,230	989	7,807	9,395	9,062	13,974	14,165	3,486	5,288	6,218	4,522	2,167	7,534	7,395
Madras, India	988	6,685	12,533	8,483	13,427	14,671	8,338	13,371	10,346	4,402	5,933	5,920	7,457	16,727	15,375	7,646	16,584	13,508	7,334	7,354
Madrid, Spain	8,542	2,467	6,299	322	7,895	7,165	1,348	7,349	3,372	6,517	8,894	7,395	8,293	8,319	7,059	3,191	8,025	8,513	1,314	1,392
Madurai, India	1,409	6,836	12,850	8,540	13,799	14,941	8,464	13,719	10,191	4,772	6,353	5,538	7,053	16,870	15,255	7,881	16,554	13,901	7,404	7,439
Magadan, USSR	6,682	6,664	6,317	8,358	6,299	8,420	7,345	6,551	11,995	3,983	1,801	12,952	14,686	10,709	12,562	5,490	11,881	6,117	7,892	7,680
Magdalena, Bolivia	16,747	11,003	7,838	8,818	7,915	5,716	9,397	7,598	6,041	14,879	15,775	10,570	9,332	3,541	1,826	10,876	2,268	8,225	9,919	9,997
Magdeburg, East Germany	7,183	784	6,207	1,474	7,746	7,675	926	7,300	5,097	4,786	7,154	7,858	9,117	9,330	8,563	1,691	9,317	8,276	855	629
Majuro Atoll, Marshall Isls.	9,263	12,680	9,945	14,393	8,691	10,678	13,366	9,285	17,777	9,108	6,257	15,171	15,627	11,475	14,168	11,544	12,669	8,064	13,943	13,736
Malabo, Equatorial Guinea	8,522	5,631	10,249	4,527	11,774	10,303	5,490	11,176	2,830	8,765	11,669	3,606	4,085	10,208	7,719	7,065	9,196	12,429	4,520	4,746
Male, Maldives	2,241	7,113	13,413	8,609	14,487	15,368	8,668	14,348	9,825	5,493	7,186	4,769	6,239	16,946	14,881	8,311	16,304	14,643	7,512	7,578
Manado, Indonesia	4,722	10,656	13,085	12,841	12,622	14,917	12,253	13,060	15,417	6,743	5,413	10,046	10,940	16,535	19,248	10,718	17,824	12,175	11,734	11,661
Managua, Nicaragua	16,322	10,189	4,635	8,557	4,279	2,366	8,566	4,076	7,675	12,789	12,351	13,698	12,836	276	3,005	9,220	1,581	4,516	9,668	9,616
Manama, Bahrain	3,657	3,757	10,362	5,156	11,758	12,014	5,224	11,422	7,074	4,109	6,908	4,943	6,657	13,519	11,983	5,184	13,163	12,157	4,049	4,116
Manaus, Brazil	15,870	9,829	6,901	7,667	7,219	4,938	8,203	6,821	5,189	13,665	14,733	10,460	9,476	3,114	662	9,660	1,783	7,624	8,790	8,853
Manchester, New Hampshire	12,630	6,615	1,817	5,408	2,941	1,702	5,113	2,340	6,364	9,183	9,509	12,524	12,737	3,634	4,577	5,519	4,261	3,588	6,366	6,256
Mandalay, Burma	1,082	6,950	11,583	9,061	12,100	13,854	8,619	12,199	11,686	3,517	4,166	7,864	9,388	16,244	16,287	7,413	16,877	12,030	7,925	7,874
Mangareva Island, Fr.Polynesia	15,813	16,197	9,554	15,103	8,085	8,082	14,888	8,472	13,517	15,300	12,474	15,566	13,882	6,797	8,535	14,657	7,283	7,633	16,144	16,040
Manila, Philippines	3,781	9,238	11,874	11,446	11,686	13,925	10,793	12,035	14,418	5,263	4,002	10,035	11,252	16,008	18,072	9,215	17,320	11,344	10,379	10,283
Mannheim, West Germany	7,422	1,099	6,262	1,118	7,825	7,611	800	7,354	4,723	5,138	7,528	7,687	8,883	9,164	8,275	2,010	9,084	8,377	597	394
Maputo, Mozambique	7,697	8,810	14,418	8,483	15,932	14,184	9,313	15,329	6,685	10,088	12,524	1,155	723	13,212	10,477	10,451	11,904	16,589	8,095	8,307
Mar del Plata, Argentina	15,989	12,721	10,642	10,550	10,586	8,477	11,375	10,333	7,040	16,730	18,584	9,166	7,574	6,172	4,531	13,126	5,017	10,800	11,456	11,605
Maracaibo, Venezuela	15,799	9,383	5,059	7,478	5,232	2,968	7,702	4,858	6,110	12,660	13,004	12,098	11,336	1,333	1,487	8,746	724	5,628	8,630	8,622
Marrakech, Morocco	9,205	3,455	6,735	1,363	8,300	7,209	2,366	7,719	2,325	7,492	9,935	6,972	7,636	7,982	6,363	4,230	7,486	8,945	2,207	2,341
Marseilles, France	7,737	1,705	6,593	679	8,183	7,712	1,155	7,675	4,029	5,743	8,223	7,206	8,296	9,038	7,875	2,724	8,810	8,769	494	591
Maseru, Lesotho	8,321	9,144	14,364	8,617	15,791	13,866	9,501	15,186	6,491	10,661	13,141	1,685	130	12,710	9,989	10,767	11,386	16,439	8,336	8,554
Mashhad, Iran	3,113	3,386	9,600	5,290	10,836	11,528	5,047	10,594	7,919	2,701	5,523	6,319	8,044	13,429	12,481	4,462	13,411	11,145	4,135	4,120
Mazatlan, Mexico	15,019	10,255	3,668	9,294	2,510	2,230	8,919	2,666	9,588	11,534	10,298	15,912	15,276	2,702	5,416	8,857	4,038	2,435	10,212	10,082
Mbabane, Swaziland	7,836	8,836	14,354	8,456	15,852	14,068	9,301	15,248	6,586	10,192	12,652	1,233	581	13,069	10,335	10,473	11,759	16,509	8,095	8,308
Mbandaka, Zaire	7,677	5,900	11,191	5,230	12,755	11,405	6,106	12,168	3,961	8,468	11,361	2,541	3,339	11,325	8,790	7,465	10,279	13,402	4,968	5,190
McMurdo Sound, Antarctica	11,928	16,886	16,125	16,150	14,839	14,051	17,163	15,130	12,709	15,404	14,412	9,175	7,860	11,804	11,282	18,527	11,215	14,432	16,142	16,364
Mecca, Saudi Arabia	4,774	3,793	10,386	4,626	11,904	11,709	4,951	11,477	5,976	5,182	8,046	4,152	5,786	12,837	10,988	5,397	12,276	12,398	3,654	3,786
Medan, Indonesia	2,309	8,726	13,590	10,678	13,918	15,859	10,409	14,107	12,563	5,570	5,841	7,328	8,520	18,261	17,631	9,393	18,807	13,727	9,522	9,516
Medellin, Colombia	16,449	10,036	5,435	8,130	5,407	3,233	8,355	5,101	6,615	13,240	13,361	12,406	11,492	1,100	1,696	9,366	247	5,731	9,283	9,276
Medicine Hat, Canada	12,053	7,777	1,476	7,525	501	2,682	6,824	815	9,368	8,533	7,594	15,118	15,728	4,884	7,026	6,205	6,092	831	8,127	7,943
Medina, Saudi Arabia	4,764	3,470	10,078	4,393	11,587	11,452	4,668	11,168	5,965	4,931	7,815	4,481	6,103	12,669	10,926	5,067	12,172	12,074	3,386	3,507
Melbourne, Australia	8,919	15,313	15,523	17,261	14,064	15,370	16,988	14,667	16,546	11,559	9,909	10,617	10,246	14,413	15,334	15,536	14,612	13,407	16,117	16,130
Memphis, Tennessee	13,863	8,307	2,079	7,232	1,954	349	6,890	1,577	7,857	10,279	9,852	14,182	14,073	2,639	4,690	7,036	3,759	2,430	8,167	8,046
Merauke, Indonesia	6,758	12,553	13,283	14,765	12,319	14,460	14,057	12,874	17,372	8,534	6,624	11,380	11,844	15,196	17,626	12,351	16,208	11,739	13,703	13,608
Merida, Mexico	15,420	9,581	3,648	8,180	3,247	1,418	8,034	3,040	7,910	11,844	11,314	14,180	13,563	1,173	3,724	8,456	2,470	3,517	9,230	9,146
Meridian, Mississippi	14,155	8,485	2,387	7,315	2,259	218	7,025	1,905	7,738	10,577	10,183	14,087	13,878	2,312	4,390	7,262	3,430	2,703	8,284	8,173
Messina, Italy	6,953	1,761	7,582	1,660	9,162	8,739	2,086	8,669	4,250	5,457	8,172	6,309	7,533	9,994	8,618	3,239	9,669	9,731	784	988
Mexico City, Mexico	15,587	10,258	3,901	9,040	3,050	1,986	8,796	3,044	8,921	12,021	11,038	15,165	14,422	1,841	4,568	8,990	3,175	3,122	10,042	9,938
Miami, Florida	14,697	8,590	3,220	7,097	3,356	1,070	7,001	2,959	6,919	11,212	11,151	13,256	12,862	1,570	3,288	7,582	2,432	3,805	8,165	8,091
Midway Islands, USA	9,606	10,778	7,363	12,073	6,230	8,390	11,058	6,799	15,163	8,040	5,202	16,430	17,731	9,741	12,449	9,372	11,069	5,644	11,908	11,684
Milan, Italy	7,406	1,321	6,623	1,000	8,200	7,867	1,124	7,713	4,406	5,356	7,851	7,265	8,438	9,297	8,226	2,448	9,124	8,765	201	204
Milford Sound, New Zealand	10,951	17,286	14,546	19,264	12,952	13,673	18,852	13,503	16,362	13,330	11,208	11,797	10,963	12,400	13,397	17,033	12,573	12,328	18,156	18,173
Milwaukee, Wisconsin	12,970	7,488	1,210	6,582	1,663	1,062	6,143	1,097	7,686	9,391	9,111	13,857	14,045	3,463	5,208	6,166	4,472	2,286	7,445	7,308
Minsk, USSR	6,147	305	6,757	2,518	8,204	8,462	1,963	7,829	6,010	3,747	6,270	7,753	9,200	10,283	9,642	1,649	10,356	8,664	1,573	1,413
Mogadiscio, Somalia	4,834	6,020	12,573	6,602	14,117	13,651	7,085	13,666	6,808	6,699	9,276	2,280	4,014	14,197	11,791	7,621	13,263	14,624	5,767	5,926
Mombasa, Kenya	5,715	6,524	12,864	6,761	14,454	13,602	7,382	13,941	6,363	7,592	10,201	1,395	3,121	13,748	11,189	8,162	12,686	15,026	6,073	6,256
Monclova, Mexico	14,732	9,655	3,135	8,647	2,187	1,584	8,288	2,210	9,019	11,178	10,197	15,370	14,911	2,476	5,091	8,298	3,811	2,284	9,574	9,449
Moncton, Canada	12,087	5,994	1,989	4,786	3,347	2,334	4,481	2,742	5,976	8,705	9,261	12,008	12,347	4,183	4,812	4,947	4,686	4,004	5,734	5,624
Monrovia, Liberia	10,464	6,035	8,735	4,164	10,105	8,331	5,181	9,501	807	9,863	12,572	5,608	5,572	8,023	5,547	7,032	7,012	10,755	4,746	4,936
Monte Carlo, Monaco	7,568	1,558	6,669	841	8,255	7,834	1,192	7,754	4,167	5,587	8,090	7,164	8,292	9,191	8,045	2,655	8,976	8,832	324	438
Monterrey, Mexico	14,884	9,719	3,242	8,658	2,348	1,569	8,326	2,346	8,932	11,321	10,369	15,274	14,768	2,306	4,935	8,386	3,642	2,458	9,604	9,483
Montevideo, Uruguay	15,970	12,378	10,355	10,199	10,365	8,218	11,015	10,088	6,715	16,403	18,270	9,131	7,582	5,949	4,200	12,760	4,756	10,608	11,119	11,264
Montgomery, Alabama	14,123	8,354	2,401	7,133	2,415	134	6,870	2,020	7,513	10,558	10,264	13,862	13,661	2,272	4,229	7,166	3,329	2,887	8,117	8,011
Montpelier, Vermont	12,535	6,577	1,652	5,431	2,813	1,712	5,101	2,209	6,488	9,068	9,352	12,614	12,864	3,732	4,739	5,444	4,397	3,463	6,366	6,251
Montpellier, France	7,852	1,769	6,484	556	8,076	7,587	1,076	7,564	3,986	5,815	8,264	7,300	8,369	8,912	7,766	2,710	8,690	8,665	605	672
Montreal, Canada	12,436	6,534	1,498	5,447	2,700	1,745	5,084	2,094	6,601	8,952	9,200	12,692	12,979	3,836	4,894	5,368	4,532	3,353	6,361	6,240
Moosonee, Canada	11,974	6,434	694	5,667	2,132	2,036	5,145	1,548	7,261	8,419	8,440	13,143	13,616	4,366	5,687	5,098	5,211	2,784	6,458	6,309
Moroni, Comoros	5,848	7,433	13,792	7,682	15,385	14,419	8,314	14,865	7,006	8,169	10,595	1,002	2,623	14,272	11,602	9,064	13,100	15,959	7,006	7,189
Moscow, USSR	5,606	979	6,952	3,190	8,313	8,803	2,573	7,992	6,671	3,072	5,634	7,930	9,468	10,750	10,267	1,762	10,915	8,721	2,236	2,085
Mosul, Iraq	4,508	2,431	9,050	3,971	10,478	10,695	3,929	10,119	6,445	3,735	6,645	5,831	7,461	12,300	11,061	3,895	12,093	10,909	2,826	2,862
Mount Isa, Australia	7,395	13,578	14,464	15,738	13,326	15,266	15,183	13,912	17,198	9,661	7,952	10,847	10,993	15,328	17,069	13,590	15,984	12,704	14,604	14,551
Multan, Pakistan	1,815	4,640	10,527	6,588	11,592	12,596	6,316	11,443	9,082	2,729	5,119	6,417	8,137	14,643	13,769	5,548	14,702	11,796	5,432	5,416
Munich, West Germany	7,203	986	6,527	1,255	8,086	7,883	1,073	7,620	4,750	5,034	7,504	7,453	8,683	9,416	8,466	2,137	9,309	8,633	408	182
Murcia, Spain	8,397	2,512	6,646	605	8,242	7,478	1,611	7,694	3,233	6,548	9,016	7,047	7,955	8,560	7,182	3,403	8,207	8,861	1,267	1,397
Murmansk, USSR	6,476	1,839	5,620	3,531	6,892	7,637	2,585	6,617	7,217	3,230	5,084	9,401	10,893	9,789	9,865	797	10,206	7,265	2,996	2,780
Mururoa Atoll, Fr. Polynesia	15,395	16,216	9,607	15,327	8,098	8,252	15,025	8,516	13,926	14,949	12,094	15,788	14,141	7,093	8,921	14,624	7,640	7,613	16,314	16,188
Muscat, Oman	2,836	4,425	10,910	5,977	12,210	12,702	5,974	11,936	7,896	3,928	6,545	5,058	6,792	14,335	12,837	5,723	14,018	12,542	4,851	4,901
Myitkyina, Burma	1,317	6,755	11,200	8,902	11,702	13,471	8,408	11,805	11,681	3,186	3,780	8,153	9,710	15,867	16,101	7,130	16,564	11,633	7,781	7,716
Naga, Philippines	4,036	9,463	11,896	11,673	11,641	13,901	11,004	12,011	14,675	5,470	4,082	10,233	11,414	15,914	18,138	9,400	17,244	11,277	10,614	10,516
Nagasaki, Japan	4,573	8,166	9,668	10,320	9,511	11,724	9,469	9,836	13,863	4,175	1,950	11,399	12,894	13,901	15,909	7,680	15,159	9,215	9,438	9,285
Nagoya, Japan	5,242	8,332	9,165	10,491	8,904	11,148	9,509	9,258	14,055	4,462	1,842	12,078	13,589	13,263	15,421	7,670	14,548	8,579	9,621	9,451
Nagpur, India	709	5,897	11,632	7,803	12,554	13,775	7,570	12,479	10,024	3,527	5,307	6,316	7,950	15,893	14,906	6,774	15,937	12,666	6,647	6,644
Nairobi, Kenya	5,849	6,164	12,440	6,330	14,033	13,165	6,968	13,512	5,973	7,476	10,169	1,616	3,283	13,373	10,860	7,808	12,349	14,614	5,665	5,852
Nanchang, China	3,177	7,685	10,530	9,897	10,625	12,720	9,188	10,872	13,141	3,656	2,590	9,985	11,479	15,038	16,500	7,572	16,172	10,406	8,879	8,763
Nancy, France	7,595	1,287	6,207	931	7,781	7,502	712	7,298	4,555	5,324	7,698	7,688	8,845	9,014	8,092	2,123	8,913	8,343	610	457
Nandi, Fiji	10,844	15,498	11,754	17,183	10,231	11,608	16,158	10,828	18,485	11,705	8,983	14,473	13,970	11,341	13,487	14,374	12,132	9,577	16,776	16,574
Nanjing, China	3,528	7,578	10,095	9,783	10,162	12,270	9,023	10,416	13,149	3,529	2,149	10,362	11,890	14,576	16,145	7,345	15,729	9,940	8,807	8,677
Nanning, China	2,345	7,695	11,333	9,885	11,551	13,569	9,301	11,761	12,810	3,842	3,476	9,052	10,505	15,938	16,932	7,854	16,961	11,364	8,794	8,710
Nantes, France	8,193	1,872	5,899	455	7,492	7,036	585	6,979	4,136	5,879	8,153	7,873	8,902	8,453	7,492	2,416	8,319	8,082	1,044	987
Naples, Italy	7,041	1,523	7,281	1,448	8,858	8,483	1,782	8,370	4,337	5,354	8,010	6,624	7,843	9,810	8,541	2,944	9,540	9,422	471	673
Narvik, Norway	7,050	1,731	5,211	3,046	6,573	7,134	2,053	6,247	6,720	3,864	5,648	9,447	10,843	9,223	9,229	181	9,593	6,999	2,690	2,465

Distances in Kilometers	Bhubaneswar, India	Bialystok, Poland	Big Trout Lake, Canada	Bilbao, Spain	Billings, Montana	Birmingham, Alabama	Birmingham, United Kingdom	Bismarck, North Dakota	Bissau, Guinea Bissau	Biysk, USSR	Blagoveshchensk, USSR	Blantyre, Malawi	Bloemfontein, South Africa	Bluefields, Nicaragua	Boa Vista do Rio Branco, Braz.	Bodo, Norway	Bogota, Colombia	Boise, Idaho	Bologna, Italy	Bolzano, Italy
Nashville, Tennessee	13,715	8,040	1,980	6,924	2,108	294	6,600	1,658	7,560	10,144	9,857	13,874	13,809	2,694	4,564	6,806	3,729	2,634	7,870	7,753
Nassau, Bahamas	14,674	8,478	3,361	6,917	3,604	1,309	6,866	3,181	6,633	11,239	11,307	12,965	12,568	1,597	3,044	7,532	2,293	4,072	8,002	7,937
Natal, Brazil	13,477	8,502	8,338	6,328	9,190	6,957	7,181	8,664	2,920	12,540	14,819	7,728	6,929	5,721	2,987	8,995	4,471	9,731	7,251	7,391
Natashquan, Canada	11,582	5,531	1,963	4,445	3,461	2,758	4,061	2,870	5,976	8,202	8,835	11,824	12,301	4,686	5,253	4,446	5,184	4,114	5,339	5,217
Nauru Island	9,108	13,289	10,911	15,168	9,630	11,552	14,156	10,228	18,724	9,493	6,756	14,452	14,716	12,133	14,734	12,298	13,239	8,995	14,577	14,385
Ndjamena, Chad	7,572	4,606	9,893	3,862	11,478	10,350	4,726	10,907	3,335	7,610	10,515	3,788	4,718	10,677	8,401	6,126	9,818	12,113	3,605	3,829
Nelson, New Zealand	11,262	17,425	13,967	19,638	12,372	13,130	18,711	12,924	16,632	13,385	11,079	12,374	11,509	11,964	13,162	16,840	12,232	11,750	18,508	18,459
Nema, Mauritania	9,700	4,840	8,060	2,980	9,546	8,060	4,005	8,944	1,042	8,725	11,383	5,862	6,207	8,222	6,038	5,841	7,403	10,203	3,548	3,736
Neuquen, Argentina	16,770	13,420	10,494	11,216	10,217	8,253	11,970	10,041	7,823	17,470	18,255	10,011	8,376	5,871	4,686	13,622	4,861	10,348	12,188	12,320
New Delhi, India	1,274	5,144	10,789	7,139	11,748	12,928	6,827	11,651	9,660	2,743	4,835	6,690	8,384	15,072	14,339	5,944	15,226	11,893	5,987	5,962
New Glasgow, Canada	12,054	5,908	2,158	4,649	3,522	2,456	4,373	2,917	5,801	8,706	9,339	11,838	12,172	4,226	4,742	4,905	4,675	4,179	5,613	5,508
New Haven, Connecticut	12,850	6,834	1,886	5,599	2,895	1,501	5,323	2,302	6,433	9,394	9,667	12,642	12,795	3,415	4,435	5,742	4,067	3,531	6,569	6,463
New Orleans, Louisiana	14,433	8,779	2,651	7,581	2,379	500	7,310	2,086	7,878	10,851	10,379	14,233	13,932	2,093	4,316	7,558	3,272	2,764	8,562	8,454
New Plymouth, New Zealand	11,256	17,307	13,747	19,482	12,154	12,975	18,484	12,712	16,843	13,257	10,894	12,600	11,758	11,891	13,195	16,622	12,214	11,527	18,469	18,385
New York, New York	12,945	6,944	1,887	5,710	2,835	1,388	5,436	2,248	6,509	9,478	9,710	12,734	12,863	3,321	4,405	5,844	4,000	3,466	6,682	6,576
Newcastle upon Tyne, UK	8,028	1,625	5,341	1,311	6,906	6,744	283	6,434	4,941	5,351	7,420	8,569	9,693	8,424	7,828	1,606	8,477	7,463	1,491	1,310
Newcastle Waters, Australia	6,658	12,887	14,519	15,022	13,549	15,642	14,519	14,110	16,641	9,031	7,517	10,359	10,671	15,996	17,791	13,006	16,717	12,958	13,880	13,835
Niamey, Niger	8,862	4,772	8,944	3,332	10,476	9,097	4,335	9,881	1,931	8,364	11,178	4,858	5,381	9,272	7,003	6,039	8,408	11,130	3,543	3,760
Nicosia, Cyprus	5,367	2,152	8,749	3,236	10,259	10,186	3,376	9,839	5,555	4,477	7,369	5,641	7,157	11,598	10,203	3,775	11,290	10,755	2,142	2,231
Niue (Alofi)	12,163	16,055	11,053	17,056	9,468	10,547	16,150	10,039	17,170	12,664	9,812	15,297	14,407	10,050	12,142	14,633	10,795	8,833	17,178	16,952
Norfolk, Virginia	13,415	7,397	2,164	6,094	2,851	1,027	5,867	2,302	6,630	9,938	10,076	12,931	12,923	2,852	4,094	6,315	3,578	3,446	7,095	6,996
Norfolk Island, Australia	10,356	16,094	13,328	18,235	11,796	13,047	17,273	12,390	18,068	12,051	9,646	12,937	12,401	12,424	14,128	15,400	12,975	11,143	17,332	17,203
Noril'sk, USSR	5,459	3,687	6,341	5,629	7,165	8,593	4,698	7,103	9,309	1,874	2,971	10,311	11,995	10,960	11,659	2,866	11,689	7,321	4,962	4,765
Norman Wells, Canada	10,126	6,625	2,392	7,036	2,440	4,430	6,130	2,582	9,773	6,651	5,712	14,341	15,574	6,759	8,632	4,979	7,892	2,501	7,309	7,095
Normanton, Australia	7,347	13,418	14,091	15,608	12,974	14,957	14,985	13,557	17,443	9,451	7,642	11,121	11,327	15,180	17,137	13,335	15,939	12,358	14,495	14,426
North Pole	7,764	4,114	4,035	5,214	4,930	6,293	4,189	4,816	8,694	4,176	4,431	11,750	13,228	8,675	9,692	2,538	9,494	5,171	5,076	4,850
Nottingham, United Kingdom	8,040	1,623	5,504	1,089	7,077	6,842	75	6,595	4,739	5,460	7,595	8,370	9,474	8,456	7,763	1,802	8,461	7,643	1,314	1,151
Norway House, Canada	11,775	6,946	515	6,559	1,189	2,435	5,891	825	8,445	8,190	7,700	14,144	14,773	4,821	6,603	5,432	5,884	1,767	7,204	7,028
Norwich, United Kingdom	7,882	1,466	5,655	1,090	7,224	7,011	219	6,747	4,769	5,348	7,535	8,244	9,376	8,624	7,903	1,780	8,618	7,785	1,168	995
Nouakchott, Mauritania	10,499	5,145	7,359	3,045	8,782	7,176	4,005	8,177	693	9,161	11,632	6,727	6,913	7,285	5,162	5,878	6,492	9,438	3,875	4,026
Noumea, New Caledonia	9,939	15,392	12,858	17,483	11,383	12,850	16,509	11,986	18,833	11,373	8,901	13,262	12,911	12,537	14,508	14,637	13,240	10,726	16,660	16,511
Novosibirsk, USSR	3,871	3,797	7,919	5,993	8,780	10,145	5,250	8,712	9,472	315	3,012	9,049	10,778	12,472	12,781	3,703	13,064	8,924	5,052	4,907
Nuku'alofa, Tonga	11,694	16,125	11,572	17,450	9,998	11,138	16,480	10,577	17,627	12,485	9,700	14,768	13,993	10,638	12,672	14,832	11,353	9,356	17,347	17,127
Nukunono Island, Tokelau Isls.	11,640	14,949	10,300	16,083	8,756	10,122	15,122	9,348	17,429	11,684	8,797	15,969	15,346	10,029	12,399	13,539	10,957	8,104	16,082	15,857
Nuremberg, West Germany	7,233	935	6,396	1,279	7,951	7,781	971	7,489	4,836	4,983	7,414	7,600	8,832	9,351	8,459	1,995	9,273	8,495	552	327
Nyala, Sudan	6,549	4,560	10,493	4,374	12,091	11,215	5,083	11,554	4,404	6,966	9,868	3,274	4,559	11,713	9,471	6,183	10,884	12,694	3,821	4,027
Oaxaca, Mexico	15,871	10,348	4,123	9,027	3,369	2,076	8,842	3,321	8,707	12,290	11,388	14,889	14,084	1,505	4,241	9,139	2,827	3,472	10,060	9,968
Ocean Falls, Canada	11,336	8,002	2,500	8,163	1,574	3,864	7,337	2,028	10,417	7,978	6,624	15,672	16,655	5,945	8,215	6,363	7,207	1,292	8,582	8,377
Odense, Denmark	7,265	868	5,895	1,658	7,418	7,437	870	6,985	5,333	4,680	6,932	8,221	9,486	9,178	8,563	1,341	9,239	7,938	1,216	991
Odessa, USSR	5,749	920	7,564	2,667	9,037	9,168	2,436	8,645	5,790	3,909	6,652	6,907	8,385	10,842	9,894	2,505	10,766	9,510	1,529	1,483
Ogbomosho, Nigeria	8,832	5,274	9,563	3,955	11,080	9,619	4,948	10,481	2,214	8,685	11,552	4,299	4,746	9,618	7,215	6,611	8,666	11,736	4,086	4,308
Okha, USSR	6,063	6,937	7,141	8,795	7,093	9,237	7,808	7,363	12,476	3,761	1,119	12,589	14,303	11,508	13,382	5,935	12,697	6,881	8,208	8,006
Okinawa (Naha)	4,315	8,621	10,427	10,813	10,230	12,462	10,015	10,572	14,226	4,576	2,670	11,035	12,430	14,591	16,671	8,277	15,876	9,907	9,864	9,727
Oklahoma City, Oklahoma	13,827	8,646	2,120	7,742	1,471	1,006	7,319	1,286	8,531	10,245	9,529	14,842	14,746	2,948	5,241	7,275	4,182	1,838	8,620	8,484
Old Crow, Canada	9,579	6,542	3,006	7,194	3,026	5,060	6,239	3,205	10,147	6,164	5,088	14,240	15,630	7,381	9,256	4,907	8,522	3,011	7,345	7,124
Olympia, Washington	12,019	8,447	2,430	8,395	1,113	3,377	7,639	1,679	10,326	8,647	7,290	15,987	16,688	5,334	7,704	6,827	6,622	647	8,920	8,725
Omaha, Nebraska	13,192	8,034	1,465	7,244	1,125	1,185	6,760	723	8,355	9,605	9,014	14,553	14,689	3,458	5,534	6,635	4,614	1,678	8,071	7,925
Omsk, USSR	3,999	3,225	7,844	5,433	8,834	10,017	4,733	8,708	8,873	826	3,609	8,639	10,354	12,278	12,351	3,301	12,754	9,039	4,464	4,326
Oodnadatta, Australia	7,519	13,879	15,313	15,917	14,125	15,946	15,546	14,719	16,544	10,125	8,655	10,209	10,223	15,599	16,781	14,122	15,990	13,491	14,761	14,748
Oradea, Romania	6,423	680	7,120	1,994	8,641	8,603	1,810	8,211	5,247	4,449	7,084	7,082	8,450	10,197	9,222	2,293	10,093	9,153	872	809
Oran, Algeria	8,420	2,685	6,861	862	8,455	7,628	1,866	7,901	3,041	6,697	9,213	6,825	7,707	8,627	7,150	3,643	8,222	9,079	1,409	1,564
Oranjestad, Aruba	15,532	9,116	4,910	7,212	5,167	2,883	7,434	4,767	5,916	12,417	12,843	11,975	11,278	1,493	1,487	8,490	982	5,592	8,364	8,355
Orebro, Sweden	6,995	842	5,808	2,174	7,280	7,501	1,308	6,886	5,853	4,233	6,416	8,512	9,851	9,372	8,939	893	9,530	7,764	1,668	1,444
Orel, USSR	5,574	867	7,168	3,057	8,561	8,957	2,540	8,221	6,449	3,255	5,897	7,612	9,141	10,835	10,214	1,982	10,931	8,986	2,035	1,907
Orsk, USSR	4,180	2,408	8,001	4,603	9,187	10,029	4,048	8,966	7,886	1,833	4,686	7,767	9,450	12,118	11,741	2,991	12,369	9,487	3,549	3,442
Osaka, Japan	5,108	8,303	9,271	10,406	9,030	11,269	9,507	9,378	14,027	4,404	1,850	11,942	13,450	13,395	15,528	7,676	14,675	8,709	9,590	9,423
Oslo, Norway	7,251	1,071	5,574	2,074	7,061	7,243	1,139	6,656	5,761	4,438	6,537	8,671	9,970	9,110	8,709	840	9,278	7,556	1,718	1,492
Osorno, Chile	17,005	13,857	10,584	11,648	10,191	8,321	12,376	10,059	8,286	17,902	18,081	10,347	8,683	5,921	4,969	13,984	5,002	10,275	12,636	12,764
Ostrava, Czechoslovakia	6,713	499	6,711	1,779	8,235	8,207	1,438	7,803	5,228	4,520	7,043	7,452	8,781	9,844	8,979	1,956	9,791	8,751	794	633
Ottawa, Canada	12,500	6,655	1,390	5,600	2,542	1,628	5,222	1,937	6,758	8,996	9,169	12,856	13,136	3,782	4,943	5,460	4,525	3,194	6,505	6,380
Ouagadougou, Bourkina Fasso	9,277	5,025	8,809	3,426	10,311	8,832	4,448	9,709	1,532	8,709	11,492	5,086	5,472	8,907	6,601	6,211	8,016	10,967	3,765	3,975
Oujda, Morocco	8,561	2,845	6,869	957	8,459	7,576	1,978	7,899	2,882	6,860	9,370	6,812	7,653	8,524	7,008	3,777	8,095	9,088	1,571	1,725
Oxford, United Kingdom	8,070	1,658	5,585	954	7,164	6,881	92	6,674	4,611	5,546	7,712	8,264	9,353	8,455	7,704	1,931	8,430	7,735	1,234	1,087
Pago Pago, American Samoa	11,936	15,524	10,677	16,587	9,108	10,325	15,653	9,690	17,325	12,205	9,332	15,655	14,875	10,019	12,254	14,105	10,855	8,464	16,649	16,424
Pakxe, Laos	2,189	8,188	12,219	10,324	12,435	14,461	9,842	12,653	12,914	4,533	4,364	8,499	9,846	16,830	17,535	8,526	17,824	12,232	9,194	9,137
Palembang, Indonesia	3,291	9,706	14,202	11,664	14,268	16,414	11,390	14,556	13,388	6,416	6,284	7,761	8,748	18,646	18,419	10,318	19,789	13,967	10,508	10,503
Palermo, Italy	7,145	1,831	7,468	1,491	9,054	8,581	1,986	8,553	4,090	5,607	8,295	6,380	7,563	9,810	8,425	3,246	9,476	9,631	727	947
Palma, Majorca	8,038	2,168	6,740	623	8,337	7,694	1,476	7,805	3,558	6,190	8,696	6,988	7,987	8,866	7,546	3,169	8,550	8,943	902	1,048
Palmerston North, New Zealand	11,422	17,501	13,754	19,664	12,158	12,909	18,645	12,707	16,663	13,451	11,082	12,583	11,693	11,764	13,020	16,794	12,059	11,538	18,651	18,574
Panama, Panama	16,405	10,051	5,063	8,245	4,930	2,819	8,384	4,654	6,996	13,035	12,941	12,901	12,018	571	2,194	9,259	772	5,229	9,387	9,362
Paramaribo, Suriname	14,877	8,712	6,181	6,568	6,763	4,480	7,077	6,289	4,401	12,539	13,783	10,210	9,491	3,215	697	8,539	2,102	7,255	7,702	7,755
Paris, France	7,874	1,530	5,988	747	7,570	7,235	500	7,076	4,426	5,539	7,843	7,855	8,959	8,729	7,827	2,162	8,633	8,143	843	726
Patna, India	599	5,916	11,192	7,961	11,982	13,407	7,599	11,964	10,501	2,994	4,532	7,103	8,737	15,676	15,177	6,580	15,988	12,039	6,812	6,778
Patrai, Greece	6,413	1,658	7,898	2,150	9,458	9,174	2,415	8,991	4,714	5,040	7,822	6,140	7,474	10,508	9,157	3,264	10,205	10,001	1,110	1,252
Peking, China	3,637	6,782	9,312	8,968	9,514	11,531	8,173	9,715	12,439	2,751	1,441	10,411	12,040	13,892	15,262	6,463	14,959	9,357	8,037	7,894
Penrhyn Island (Omoka)	13,077	15,109	9,414	15,510	7,820	8,863	14,726	8,378	15,920	12,587	9,684	16,915	15,761	8,544	10,879	13,509	9,439	7,197	15,943	15,728
Peoria, Illinois	13,243	7,780	1,461	6,841	1,632	834	6,423	1,127	7,816	9,660	9,299	14,044	14,146	3,231	5,101	6,461	4,289	2,215	7,720	7,587
Perm', USSR	4,831	2,134	7,238	4,334	8,416	9,295	3,633	8,196	7,828	1,922	4,514	8,408	10,056	11,439	11,284	2,324	11,783	8,721	3,396	3,246
Perth, Australia	6,600	12,945	16,827	14,597	15,939	17,903	14,593	16,502	14,592	9,822	9,178	8,251	8,336	17,035	16,761	13,723	16,810	15,338	13,499	13,554
Peshawar, Pakistan	2,078	4,339	10,111	6,354	11,167	12,197	6,022	11,020	9,024	2,333	4,836	6,737	8,466	14,286	13,572	5,168	14,422	11,372	5,205	5,172
Petropavlovsk-Kamchatskiy,USSR	7,092	7,537	6,578	9,194	6,304	8,532	8,174	6,642	12,797	4,727	2,158	13,626	15,346	10,700	12,817	6,333	11,952	6,021	8,760	8,546
Petrozavodsk, USSR	6,062	1,174	6,286	3,192	7,622	8,199	2,388	7,314	6,825	3,151	5,425	8,603	10,108	10,236	9,996	1,127	10,510	8,022	2,440	2,245
Pevek, USSR	7,697	6,122	4,880	7,466	5,000	7,027	6,439	5,188	10,947	4,493	3,106	13,280	14,955	9,365	11,113	4,692	10,485	4,915	7,225	7,001
Philadelphia, Pennsylvania	13,058	7,073	1,905	5,837	2,779	1,260	5,566	2,199	6,589	9,582	9,768	12,833	12,933	3,210	4,365	5,966	3,917	3,402	6,811	6,706
Phnom Penh, Kampuchea	2,256	8,441	12,624	10,543	12,833	14,867	10,108	13,056	12,966	4,879	4,766	8,273	9,564	17,233	17,771	8,851	18,215	12,618	9,401	9,357
Phoenix, Arizona	13,769	9,484	2,856	8,883	1,402	2,343	8,339	1,764	9,887	10,328	9,043	16,184	16,050	3,733	6,318	7,971	5,067	1,184	9,657	9,497
Pierre, South Dakota	12,824	7,937	1,293	7,320	661	1,678	6,760	273	8,685	9,250	8,545	14,771	15,053	3,923	6,026	6,472	5,100	1,274	8,078	7,918
Pinang, Malaysia	2,269	8,674	13,368	10,669	13,658	15,632	10,357	13,859	12,689	5,408	5,583	7,569	8,783	18,028	17,734	9,278	18,743	13,459	9,513	9,498
Pitcairn Island (Adamstown)	16,313	16,176	9,554	14,845	8,144	7,938	14,741	8,488	13,023	15,762	12,972	15,208	13,496	6,488	8,086	14,723	6,883	7,736	15,938	15,861
Pittsburgh, Pennsylvania	13,131	7,302	1,667	6,170	2,381	978	5,844	1,813	7,005	9,603	9,604	13,243	13,345	3,172	4,598	6,115	4,014	2,996	7,111	6,995
Plymouth, Montserrat	14,644	8,233	4,770	6,275	5,352	3,087	6,550	4,866	5,050	11,718	12,526	11,258	10,750	2,379	1,545	7,729	1,863	5,866	7,430	7,430
Plymouth, United Kingdom	8,298	1,895	5,525	800	7,114	6,739	276	6,609	4,402	5,797	7,945	8,268	9,302	8,256	7,459	2,143	8,203	7,698	1,335	1,221
Ponape Island	7,921	12,132	10,782	14,137	9,715	11,846	13,162	10,281	17,823	8,253	5,589	13,781	14,442	12,861	15,578	11,289	14,084	9,125	13,424	13,245
Ponce, Puerto Rico	14,824	8,410	4,455	6,536	4,930	2,646	6,730	4,466	5,517	11,729	12,315	11,746	11,231	1,958	1,802	7,785	1,692	5,423	7,683	7,667
Ponta Delgada, Azores	10,410	4,087	5,114	2,012	6,634	5,460	2,464	6,040	3,038	7,991	9,909	8,671	9,162	6,406	5,262	4,124	6,123	7,288	3,168	3,181
Pontianak, Indonesia	3,403	9,756	13,782	11,802	13,737	15,937	11,434	14,057	13,812	6,247	5,837	8,340	9,349	18,063	18,883	10,221	19,385	13,408	10,649	10,623
Port Augusta, Australia	8,037	14,428	15,583	16,406	14,275	15,893	16,104	14,879	16,466	10,713	9,223	10,234	10,088	15,225	16,202	14,713	15,491	13,626	15,254	15,257
Port Blair, India	1,208	7,625	12,750	9,593	13,305	15,012	9,308	13,398	11,700	4,593	5,334	7,046	8,445	17,367	16,685	8,323	17,708	13,226	8,437	8,426
Port Elizabeth, South Africa	8,758	9,652	14,610	9,030	15,943	13,883	9,942	15,347	6,685	11,194	13,625	2,225	539	12,528	9,843	11,266	11,190	16,569	8,807	9,027
Port Hedland, Australia	5,731	12,147	15,568	14,069	14,898	17,123	13,830	15,407	15,056	8,694	7,868	8,766	9,162	17,477	18,067	12,680	17,803	14,359	12,917	12,925

Distances in Kilometers	Bhubaneswar, India	Bialystok, Poland	Big Trout Lake, Canada	Bilbao, Spain	Billings, Montana	Birmingham, Alabama	Birmingham, United Kingdom	Bismarck, North Dakota	Bissau, Guinea Bissau	Biysk, USSR	Blagoveshchensk, USSR	Blantyre, Malawi	Bloemfontein, South Africa	Bluefields, Nicaragua	Boa Vista do Rio Branco, Braz.	Bodo, Norway	Bogota, Colombia	Boise, Idaho	Bologna, Italy	Bolzano, Italy
Port Louis, Mauritius	5,432	8,769	15,366	9,348	16,892	16,207	9,876	16,459	8,749	8,494	10,376	2,430	3,312	15,801	13,064	10,325	14,519	17,341	8,558	8,719
Port Moresby, Papua New Guinea	7,478	13,076	12,972	15,283	11,870	13,915	14,488	12,448	18,133	9,028	6,889	12,055	12,395	14,466	16,867	12,702	15,449	11,262	14,277	14,162
Port Said, Egypt	5,456	2,539	9,073	3,368	10,605	10,412	3,632	10,165	5,354	4,847	7,752	5,214	6,716	11,694	10,137	4,177	11,294	11,118	2,345	2,468
Port Sudan, Sudan	5,070	3,913	10,441	4,567	11,984	11,664	4,966	11,534	5,705	5,505	8,377	3,923	5,524	12,677	10,741	5,539	12,059	12,500	3,654	3,803
Port-au-Prince, Haiti	15,106	8,737	4,201	6,963	4,492	2,198	7,072	4,072	6,120	11,837	12,139	12,350	11,798	1,423	2,153	7,979	1,553	4,944	8,096	8,063
Port-of-Spain, Trin. & Tobago	15,076	8,713	5,416	6,673	5,906	3,615	7,037	5,449	5,012	12,320	13,199	11,024	10,362	2,431	871	8,314	1,539	6,385	7,828	7,849
Port-Vila, Vanuatu	9,935	15,061	12,345	17,060	10,889	12,438	16,058	11,494	19,239	11,097	8,527	13,704	13,426	12,296	14,440	14,193	13,097	10,233	16,350	16,180
Portland, Maine	12,524	6,495	1,830	5,289	3,011	1,823	4,992	2,407	6,290	9,088	9,457	12,428	12,667	3,740	4,622	5,407	4,343	3,660	6,245	6,135
Portland, Oregon	12,177	8,597	2,501	8,509	1,099	3,321	7,766	1,687	10,366	8,814	7,430	16,106	16,740	5,224	7,630	6,981	6,522	551	9,052	8,860
Porto, Portugal	8,916	2,721	5,942	522	7,535	6,747	1,357	6,979	3,317	6,752	9,015	7,741	8,567	7,901	6,707	3,229	7,632	8,161	1,669	1,709
Porto Alegre, Brazil	15,588	11,667	10,020	9,493	10,196	7,974	10,320	9,863	6,006	15,692	17,759	8,791	7,334	5,818	3,777	12,085	4,547	10,505	10,408	10,553
Porto Alexandre, Angola	9,014	7,715	12,191	6,714	13,603	11,761	7,681	12,998	4,303	10,307	13,165	2,476	2,078	10,968	8,243	9,218	9,725	14,253	6,677	6,903
Porto Novo, Benin	9,064	5,499	9,602	4,110	11,098	9,566	5,115	10,496	2,086	8,941	11,805	4,337	4,679	9,476	7,032	6,808	8,494	11,755	4,295	4,515
Porto Velho, Brazil	16,539	10,586	7,360	8,419	7,499	5,270	8,959	7,158	5,813	14,409	15,284	10,696	9,552	3,178	1,330	10,399	1,861	7,837	9,537	9,604
Portsmouth, United Kingdom	8,079	1,679	5,664	848	7,246	6,928	198	6,752	4,513	5,604	7,799	8,169	9,248	8,470	7,672	2,030	8,421	7,821	1,163	1,030
Poznan, Poland	6,823	425	6,434	1,798	7,949	7,975	1,280	7,524	5,359	4,458	6,894	7,754	9,078	9,674	8,924	1,662	9,677	8,459	975	771
Prague, Czechoslovakia	6,988	690	6,510	1,530	8,049	7,959	1,171	7,603	5,051	4,740	7,204	7,569	8,850	9,573	8,712	1,916	9,516	8,578	666	458
Praia, Cape Verde Islands	11,380	5,877	7,142	3,701	8,451	6,648	4,583	7,849	924	9,922	12,252	7,275	7,229	6,511	4,292	6,431	5,651	9,095	4,639	4,770
Pretoria, South Africa	8,045	8,752	14,113	8,278	15,589	13,771	9,146	14,984	6,307	10,287	12,814	1,312	424	12,771	10,036	10,380	11,464	16,245	7,964	8,180
Prince Albert, Canada	11,793	7,306	1,046	7,040	849	2,655	6,336	796	8,975	8,236	7,500	14,636	15,305	4,972	6,940	5,747	6,114	1,314	7,640	7,457
Prince Edward Island	8,826	11,140	16,301	10,737	17,447	15,194	11,614	16,898	8,378	11,874	13,740	3,426	2,191	13,376	10,896	12,783	12,054	17,969	10,422	10,636
Prince George, Canada	11,347	7,728	2,135	7,816	1,363	3,614	7,007	1,742	10,045	7,920	6,734	15,356	16,287	5,777	7,960	6,097	7,009	1,241	8,264	8,063
Prince Rupert, Canada	11,057	7,845	2,604	8,098	1,817	4,094	7,246	2,233	10,479	7,710	6,347	15,545	16,631	6,209	8,443	6,201	7,462	1,570	8,470	8,262
Providence, Rhode Island	12,749	6,706	1,919	5,461	2,991	1,638	5,190	2,393	6,325	9,309	9,638	12,517	12,693	3,516	4,451	5,630	4,131	3,632	6,433	6,328
Provo, Utah	13,071	8,788	2,218	8,324	668	2,329	7,716	1,141	9,678	9,594	8,442	15,809	16,010	4,156	6,580	7,250	5,451	533	9,033	8,863
Puerto Aisen, Chile	16,596	14,190	11,119	11,997	10,696	8,854	12,771	10,579	8,536	18,226	18,415	10,097	8,402	6,453	5,472	14,434	5,540	10,759	12,939	13,080
Puerto Deseado, Argentina	16,041	13,972	11,486	11,818	11,163	9,239	12,653	11,011	8,262	17,903	18,998	9,517	7,819	6,851	5,625	14,399	5,855	11,259	12,695	12,852
Puerto Princesa, Philippines	3,716	9,520	12,460	11,706	12,270	14,515	11,121	12,624	14,442	5,626	4,567	9,647	10,783	16,563	18,615	9,620	17,890	11,917	10,605	10,528
Punta Arenas, Chile	15,848	14,628	11,990	12,495	11,532	9,724	13,343	11,434	8,907	18,417	18,706	9,642	7,916	7,322	6,276	15,097	6,407	11,563	13,343	13,508
Pusan, South Korea	4,529	7,915	9,462	10,062	9,354	11,545	9,205	9,661	13,619	3,939	1,689	11,368	12,900	13,758	15,688	7,414	14,994	9,078	9,190	9,034
Pyongyang, North Korea	4,343	7,392	9,162	9,538	9,171	11,304	8,683	9,438	13,101	3,432	1,258	11,164	12,758	13,587	15,326	6,899	14,766	8,943	8,669	8,512
Qamdo, China	1,664	6,273	10,562	8,454	11,098	12,833	7,900	11,183	11,426	2,569	3,285	8,436	10,055	15,227	15,583	6,547	15,942	11,054	7,358	7,277
Qandahar, Afghanistan	2,366	4,156	10,258	6,047	11,418	12,248	5,819	11,219	8,519	2,815	5,424	6,186	7,919	14,196	13,207	5,176	14,177	11,676	4,891	4,883
Qiqian, China	4,657	6,061	7,909	8,135	8,173	10,137	7,236	8,342	11,778	2,397	516	11,099	12,812	12,513	13,906	5,418	13,555	8,066	7,353	7,177
Qom, Iran	3,780	2,997	9,507	4,683	10,861	11,271	4,578	10,550	7,126	3,363	6,245	5,830	7,524	12,979	11,789	4,315	12,814	11,240	3,532	3,552
Quebec, Canada	12,232	6,302	1,541	5,222	2,847	1,978	4,851	2,242	6,468	8,767	9,097	12,505	12,843	4,035	4,981	5,147	4,686	3,503	6,129	6,007
Quetta, Pakistan	2,191	4,350	10,435	6,231	11,578	12,437	6,012	11,389	8,654	2,897	5,437	6,137	7,867	14,390	13,379	5,365	14,364	11,825	5,075	5,071
Quito, Ecuador	17,221	10,804	6,085	8,859	5,884	3,833	9,121	5,644	7,078	14,009	13,937	12,523	11,427	1,470	2,011	10,151	725	6,132	10,014	10,017
Rabaul, Papua New Guinea	7,733	12,883	12,179	15,039	11,066	13,126	14,150	11,644	18,437	8,851	6,482	12,773	13,187	13,822	16,383	12,306	14,903	10,460	14,140	13,997
Raiatea (Uturoa)	14,002	15,938	9,750	15,833	8,161	8,824	15,231	8,669	15,250	13,703	10,802	16,341	14,923	8,096	10,187	14,297	8,823	7,585	16,534	16,343
Raleigh, North Carolina	13,595	7,624	2,193	6,337	2,735	790	6,103	2,211	6,824	10,094	10,134	13,142	13,089	2,683	4,091	6,518	3,483	3,309	7,335	7,235
Rangiroa (Avatoru)	14,344	15,691	9,374	15,426	7,793	8,391	14,870	8,288	14,848	13,782	10,906	16,595	15,085	7,653	9,777	14,046	8,398	7,232	16,183	16,003
Rangoon, Burma	1,156	7,401	12,159	9,465	12,646	14,430	9,080	12,762	11,884	4,084	4,653	7,620	9,072	16,821	16,681	7,944	17,413	12,552	8,318	8,282
Raoul Is., Kermadec Islands	11,673	16,851	12,446	18,390	10,859	11,833	17,407	11,426	17,358	12,979	10,319	13,903	13,058	11,056	12,798	15,698	11,605	10,226	18,133	17,930
Rarotonga (Avarua)	13,251	16,452	10,639	16,757	9,042	9,819	16,051	9,574	16,082	13,535	10,636	15,611	14,399	9,081	11,072	14,867	9,754	8,442	17,297	17,085
Rawson, Argentina	16,294	13,586	11,022	11,409	10,760	8,788	12,217	10,583	7,907	17,596	18,780	9,615	7,950	6,411	5,127	13,936	5,381	10,888	12,324	12,472
Recife, Brazil	13,528	8,697	8,573	6,535	9,398	7,154	7,402	8,879	3,069	12,725	15,051	7,633	6,775	5,844	3,105	9,224	4,570	9,930	7,438	7,582
Regina, Canada	12,109	7,528	1,067	7,163	594	2,378	6,498	494	8,935	8,549	7,800	14,742	15,298	4,669	6,693	5,991	5,828	1,162	7,810	7,633
Reykjavik, Iceland	8,826	2,814	3,866	2,619	5,404	5,499	1,738	4,957	5,828	5,634	7,043	10,091	11,159	7,464	7,486	1,678	7,798	5,947	3,014	2,826
Rhodes, Greece	5,838	1,898	8,387	2,756	9,923	9,747	2,952	9,480	5,155	4,733	7,588	5,823	7,261	11,116	9,730	3,543	10,805	10,441	1,683	1,792
Richmond, Virginia	13,376	7,405	2,051	6,143	2,723	959	5,892	2,173	6,743	9,882	9,975	13,034	13,045	2,899	4,210	6,295	3,664	3,320	7,130	7,027
Riga, USSR	6,437	429	6,355	2,437	7,799	8,082	1,738	7,425	6,038	3,833	6,213	8,124	9,541	9,949	9,429	1,255	10,076	8,262	1,648	1,452
Ringkobing, Denmark	7,398	1,015	5,745	1,636	7,272	7,283	774	6,836	5,322	4,761	6,958	8,348	9,594	9,033	8,453	1,288	9,109	7,795	1,309	1,086
Rio Branco, Brazil	16,984	10,951	7,374	8,804	7,392	5,216	9,307	7,090	6,260	14,697	15,320	11,064	9,862	3,002	1,619	10,686	1,755	7,689	9,931	9,990
Rio Cuarto, Argentina	16,748	12,719	9,948	10,510	9,805	7,743	11,249	9,577	7,179	16,765	17,870	9,909	8,352	5,403	3,998	12,895	4,301	9,999	11,502	11,628
Rio de Janeiro, Brazil	14,775	10,562	9,612	8,404	10,055	7,766	9,261	9,639	4,885	14,574	16,864	8,167	6,884	5,866	3,418	11,064	4,528	10,461	9,296	9,445
Rio Gallegos, Argentina	15,905	14,434	11,849	12,295	11,432	9,588	13,140	11,318	8,714	18,273	18,833	9,596	7,876	7,188	6,088	14,892	6,249	11,483	13,151	13,313
Rio Grande, Brazil	15,652	11,893	10,191	9,722	10,322	8,118	10,553	10,004	6,221	15,911	17,979	8,830	7,338	5,927	3,963	12,320	4,676	10,612	10,630	10,778
Riyadh, Saudi Arabia	4,043	3,730	10,372	4,949	11,817	11,915	5,103	11,448	6,686	4,478	7,306	4,649	6,343	13,290	11,636	5,235	12,858	12,251	3,876	3,966
Road Town, Brit. Virgin Isls.	14,658	8,241	4,491	6,343	5,037	2,768	6,558	4,556	5,305	11,618	12,301	11,549	11,065	2,174	1,782	7,655	1,846	5,547	7,492	7,480
Roanoke, Virginia	13,468	7,569	1,997	6,346	2,548	751	6,074	2,015	6,958	9,949	9,941	13,255	13,248	2,826	4,294	6,423	3,667	3,131	7,322	7,215
Robinson Crusoe Island, Chile	17,899	13,682	9,750	11,480	9,288	7,479	12,094	9,176	8,374	17,552	17,177	11,135	9,510	5,077	4,464	13,541	4,262	9,358	12,547	12,644
Rochester, New York	12,785	6,943	1,495	5,849	2,460	1,337	5,496	1,865	6,855	9,271	9,371	13,024	13,224	3,504	4,773	5,754	4,286	3,101	6,772	6,651
Rockhampton, Australia	8,514	14,525	14,000	16,733	12,668	14,373	16,024	13,272	18,072	10,509	8,467	11,781	11,696	14,175	15,970	14,271	14,815	12,019	15,644	15,563
Rome, Italy	7,179	1,482	7,095	1,275	8,674	8,295	1,598	8,184	4,303	5,393	8,008	6,793	7,990	9,638	8,412	2,828	9,388	9,242	302	521
Rosario, Argentina	16,425	12,479	10,022	10,278	9,961	7,850	11,045	9,706	6,891	16,529	17,968	9,587	8,047	5,546	3,959	12,733	4,391	10,184	11,246	11,378
Roseau, Dominica	14,700	8,300	4,947	6,313	5,526	3,256	6,618	5,042	4,965	11,834	12,690	11,137	10,599	2,444	1,383	7,836	1,825	6,035	7,469	7,476
Rostock, East Germany	7,152	736	6,078	1,633	7,603	7,603	953	7,169	5,283	4,652	6,970	8,042	9,318	9,317	8,639	1,476	9,349	8,123	1,069	843
Rostov-na-Donu, USSR	5,111	1,348	7,844	3,337	9,244	9,593	3,005	8,901	6,455	3,269	6,076	6,995	8,566	11,392	10,563	2,664	11,392	9,667	2,212	2,150
Rotterdam, Netherlands	7,676	1,269	5,872	1,114	7,436	7,243	443	6,965	4,798	5,214	7,476	8,060	9,225	8,849	8,082	1,795	8,825	7,990	969	781
Rouyn, Canada	12,274	6,600	989	5,698	2,245	1,760	5,242	1,641	7,074	8,735	8,798	13,079	13,449	4,041	5,330	5,323	4,859	2,902	6,544	6,406
Sacramento, California	12,901	9,288	2,924	9,036	1,335	3,156	8,357	1,919	10,542	9,581	8,083	16,601	16,873	4,752	7,305	7,692	6,083	712	9,663	9,479
Saginaw, Michigan	12,879	7,253	1,239	6,283	1,960	1,129	5,872	1,374	7,368	9,317	9,185	13,531	13,732	3,484	5,053	5,976	4,410	2,594	7,166	7,034
Saint Denis, Reunion	5,623	8,770	15,329	9,272	16,882	16,060	9,831	16,420	8,568	8,632	10,568	2,232	3,085	15,580	12,842	10,344	14,294	17,368	8,513	8,679
Saint George's, Grenada	14,985	8,607	5,263	6,584	5,771	3,484	6,928	5,308	5,023	12,184	13,043	11,087	10,459	2,395	1,028	8,181	1,588	6,257	7,740	7,756
Saint John, Canada	12,216	6,129	1,964	4,911	3,278	2,203	4,614	2,672	6,032	8,823	9,338	12,100	12,408	4,053	4,732	5,078	4,573	3,933	5,865	5,756
Saint John's, Antigua	14,585	8,174	4,745	6,217	5,347	3,087	6,491	4,856	5,011	11,663	12,486	11,230	10,736	2,425	1,585	7,673	1,922	5,865	7,371	7,371
Saint John's, Canada	11,435	5,178	2,691	3,857	4,180	3,246	3,605	3,585	5,256	8,215	9,164	11,120	11,572	4,890	5,018	4,298	5,182	4,835	4,828	4,729
Saint Louis, Missouri	13,477	7,997	1,692	7,015	1,703	643	6,621	1,255	7,865	9,892	9,491	14,136	14,160	3,017	4,969	6,691	4,105	2,245	7,913	7,783
Saint Paul, Minnesota	12,786	7,565	1,013	6,816	1,209	1,380	6,306	631	8,108	9,198	8,751	14,209	14,479	3,759	5,642	6,166	4,839	1,846	7,620	7,470
Saint Peter Port, UK	8,211	1,827	5,680	690	7,269	6,880	338	6,764	4,339	5,776	7,978	8,115	9,158	8,371	7,520	2,202	8,292	7,853	1,189	1,086
Saipan (Susupe)	6,346	10,677	10,724	12,798	9,994	12,272	11,895	10,488	16,387	6,699	4,226	12,636	13,672	13,805	16,504	10,052	15,129	9,496	11,956	11,797
Salalah, Oman	3,363	4,828	11,445	6,079	12,836	13,053	6,243	12,506	7,500	4,794	7,399	4,189	5,922	14,389	12,547	6,267	13,855	13,221	5,017	5,108
Salem, Oregon	12,220	8,670	2,565	8,581	1,141	3,342	7,839	1,734	10,420	8,867	7,458	16,178	16,796	5,216	7,640	7,054	6,519	564	9,126	8,933
Salt Lake City, Utah	13,010	8,744	2,187	8,298	622	2,359	7,682	1,117	9,683	9,534	8,383	15,795	16,023	4,208	6,622	7,202	5,501	479	8,998	8,827
Salta, Argentina	17,037	12,081	9,026	9,870	8,946	6,838	10,533	8,690	6,760	16,063	16,966	10,303	8,856	4,530	3,096	12,095	3,384	9,179	10,922	11,025
Salto, Uruguay	16,214	12,183	9,934	9,985	9,949	7,796	10,765	9,667	6,584	16,231	17,859	9,389	7,882	5,534	3,796	12,471	4,334	10,201	10,945	11,079
Salvador, Brazil	14,068	9,370	8,858	7,201	9,541	7,258	8,056	9,057	3,736	13,399	15,681	7,895	6,874	5,708	3,009	9,864	4,387	10,030	8,112	8,256
Salzburg, Austria	7,096	930	6,629	1,345	8,184	7,996	1,185	7,722	4,794	4,966	7,466	7,374	8,621	9,531	8,565	2,171	9,418	8,728	391	191
Samsun, Turkey	5,196	1,648	8,290	3,220	9,750	9,891	3,124	9,368	5,996	3,847	6,710	6,319	7,866	11,509	10,393	3,188	11,355	10,210	2,065	2,079
San Antonio, Texas	14,491	9,269	2,797	8,247	2,015	1,199	7,890	1,940	8,696	10,915	10,085	15,051	14,704	2,460	4,961	7,932	3,763	2,227	9,175	9,050
San Cristobal, Venezuela	16,097	9,680	5,353	7,746	5,459	3,221	7,997	5,109	6,222	12,987	13,299	12,089	11,246	1,347	1,392	9,068	406	5,829	8,900	8,899
San Diego, California	13,660	9,751	3,181	9,267	1,629	2,824	8,680	2,093	10,367	10,310	8,839	16,648	16,517	4,105	6,740	8,198	5,447	1,213	9,998	9,829
San Francisco, California	12,940	9,401	3,045	9,157	1,455	3,240	8,477	2,037	10,648	9,645	8,102	16,721	16,968	4,784	7,358	7,801	6,118	833	9,782	9,598
San Jose, Costa Rica	16,493	10,254	4,898	8,543	4,604	2,626	8,609	4,476	7,473	13,005	12,668	13,412	12,510	231	2,704	9,354	1,252	4,854	9,670	9,629
San Juan, Argentina	17,177	12,847	9,682	10,634	9,464	7,452	11,323	9,261	7,409	16,857	17,540	10,338	8,782	5,084	3,891	12,902	4,042	9,634	11,662	11,775
San Juan, Puerto Rico	14,752	8,338	4,428	6,463	4,928	2,649	6,658	4,458	5,464	11,666	12,275	11,704	11,207	2,023	1,830	7,718	1,762	5,428	7,610	7,594
San Luis Potosi, Mexico	15,258	10,090	3,637	8,972	2,709	1,877	8,674	2,735	9,060	11,706	10,679	15,360	14,710	2,148	4,850	8,774	3,489	2,764	9,941	9,826
San Marino, San Marino	7,162	1,291	6,924	1,247	8,496	8,178	1,426	8,015	4,456	5,256	7,831	6,997	8,209	9,586	8,447	2,604	9,382	9,057	110	302
San Miguel de Tucuman, Argen.	16,993	12,242	9,249	10,029	9,153	7,056	10,711	8,904	6,860	16,244	17,186	10,211	8,736	4,739	3,315	12,293	3,605	9,376	11,068	11,176

Distances in Kilometers	Bhubaneswar, India	Bialystok, Poland	Big Trout Lake, Canada	Bilbao, Spain	Billings, Montana	Birmingham, Alabama	Birmingham, United Kingdom	Bismarck, North Dakota	Bissau, Guinea Bissau	Biysk, USSR	Blagoveshchensk, USSR	Blantyre, Malawi	Bloemfontein, South Africa	Bluefields, Nicaragua	Boa Vista do Rio Branco, Braz.	Bodo, Norway	Bogota, Colombia	Boise, Idaho	Bologna, Italy	Bolzano, Italy
San Salvador, El Salvador	16,213	10,225	4,453	8,678	3,993	2,208	8,630	3,827	7,964	12,644	12,069	14,040	13,196	621	3,359	9,182	1,941	4,199	9,770	9,706
Sanaa, Yemen	4,436	4,581	11,196	5,426	12,702	12,518	5,769	12,286	6,462	5,479	8,241	3,589	5,290	13,546	11,528	6,160	12,884	13,180	4,472	4,605
Santa Cruz, Bolivia	16,764	11,331	8,341	9,128	8,392	6,209	9,757	8,087	6,172	15,274	16,280	10,322	9,007	3,998	2,297	11,292	2,753	8,684	10,205	10,296
Santa Cruz, Tenerife	10,073	4,221	6,463	2,027	7,968	6,635	2,918	7,369	1,839	8,271	10,585	7,374	7,809	7,199	5,496	4,781	6,641	8,624	3,020	3,130
Santa Fe, New Mexico	13,694	9,011	2,368	8,307	1,142	1,769	7,800	1,309	9,286	10,168	9,139	15,571	15,508	3,445	5,906	7,546	4,745	1,245	9,115	8,962
Santa Rosa, Argentina	16,600	13,003	10,323	10,802	10,146	8,109	11,567	9,933	7,401	17,052	18,221	9,782	8,184	5,756	4,381	13,242	4,675	10,319	11,767	11,901
Santa Rosalia, Mexico	14,397	10,109	3,465	9,386	2,076	2,535	8,902	2,387	10,067	10,993	9,598	16,422	15,967	3,426	6,115	8,622	4,767	1,843	10,216	10,065
Santarem, Brazil	15,315	9,416	7,041	7,227	7,509	5,214	7,825	7,070	4,607	13,340	14,699	9,913	8,996	3,588	883	9,370	2,292	7,956	8,329	8,405
Santiago del Estero, Argentina	16,884	12,264	9,377	10,051	9,292	7,190	10,749	9,040	6,839	16,283	17,318	10,088	8,604	4,878	3,408	12,352	3,735	9,517	11,078	11,190
Santiago, Chile	17,277	13,140	9,848	10,927	9,566	7,602	11,614	9,387	7,691	17,147	17,622	10,450	8,862	5,218	4,149	13,181	4,227	9,707	11,955	12,068
Santo Domingo, Dominican Rep.	14,979	8,586	4,288	6,770	4,663	2,369	6,913	4,222	5,863	11,779	12,202	12,096	11,564	1,650	2,002	7,881	1,600	5,135	7,909	7,883
Sao Paulo de Olivenca, Brazil	16,707	10,444	6,648	8,351	6,714	4,508	8,776	6,390	6,127	14,061	14,594	11,387	10,312	2,378	1,138	10,064	1,067	7,041	9,497	9,536
Sao Paulo, Brazil	15,127	10,815	9,530	8,638	9,893	7,616	9,470	9,500	5,171	14,847	16,995	8,494	7,178	5,639	3,290	11,247	4,311	10,273	9,559	9,702
Sao Tome, Sao Tome & Principe	8,866	6,047	10,421	4,851	11,911	10,323	5,835	11,308	2,775	9,204	12,109	3,582	3,861	10,063	7,506	7,453	8,997	12,568	4,912	5,137
Sapporo, Japan	5,719	7,827	8,212	9,808	7,997	10,219	8,850	8,329	13,491	4,219	1,324	12,515	14,134	12,388	14,468	6,983	13,645	7,703	9,117	8,930
Sarajevo, Yugoslavia	6,685	1,091	7,235	1,725	8,787	8,585	1,782	8,328	4,813	4,878	7,535	6,814	8,118	10,050	8,920	2,622	9,860	9,325	571	629
Saratov, USSR	4,896	1,562	7,629	3,737	8,946	9,520	3,232	8,653	7,035	2,658	5,423	7,538	9,149	11,475	10,909	2,458	11,614	9,321	2,677	2,570
Saskatoon, Canada	11,899	7,440	1,131	7,160	718	2,609	6,463	727	9,050	8,349	7,567	14,754	15,393	4,901	6,916	5,882	6,061	1,185	7,769	7,586
Schefferville, Canada	11,296	5,486	1,505	4,667	3,082	2,832	4,147	2,523	6,515	7,828	8,282	12,185	12,784	4,974	5,791	4,243	5,605	3,718	5,458	5,312
Seattle, Washington	11,985	8,375	2,363	8,321	1,075	3,351	7,564	1,630	10,265	8,601	7,272	15,913	16,623	5,333	7,685	6,756	6,616	650	8,845	8,651
Sendai, Japan	5,621	8,248	8,700	10,273	8,414	10,662	9,331	8,772	13,946	4,508	1,703	12,459	14,011	12,771	14,950	7,471	14,056	8,086	9,540	9,359
Seoul, South Korea	4,405	7,586	9,274	9,732	9,240	11,396	8,877	9,522	13,293	3,619	1,412	11,239	12,812	13,655	15,465	7,090	14,856	8,993	8,862	8,705
Sept-Iles, Canada	11,740	5,784	1,663	4,760	3,139	2,496	4,349	2,546	6,268	8,307	8,793	12,149	12,608	4,524	5,279	4,636	5,106	3,793	5,637	5,508
Sevastopol, USSR	5,493	1,214	7,856	2,911	9,320	9,470	2,728	8,935	5,905	3,830	6,630	6,688	8,199	11,131	10,127	2,767	11,031	9,785	1,759	1,738
Seville, Spain	8,828	2,846	6,397	700	7,986	7,115	1,706	7,424	2,987	6,896	9,283	7,283	8,091	8,136	6,755	3,566	7,772	8,617	1,653	1,754
Shanghai, China	3,746	7,815	10,121	10,014	10,122	12,267	9,239	10,399	13,405	3,766	2,188	10,570	12,073	14,538	16,243	7,539	15,729	9,875	9,050	8,917
Sheffield, United Kingdom	8,054	1,637	5,458	1,130	7,031	6,806	104	6,550	4,772	5,452	7,569	8,419	9,524	8,433	7,760	1,770	8,447	7,595	1,360	1,194
Shenyang, China	4,263	7,030	8,938	9,173	9,026	11,113	8,318	9,264	12,743	3,088	992	11,039	12,669	13,433	15,046	6,536	14,570	8,831	8,309	8,150
Shiraz, Iran	3,506	3,540	10,084	5,103	11,441	11,819	5,079	11,130	7,264	3,693	6,509	5,363	7,078	13,449	12,082	4,893	13,192	11,817	3,968	4,011
Sibiu, Romania	6,242	819	7,335	2,164	8,851	8,824	2,028	8,425	5,310	4,381	7,068	6,907	8,301	10,406	9,386	2,460	10,283	9,358	1,018	990
Singapore	2,870	9,274	13,763	11,268	13,905	15,997	10,957	14,163	13,185	5,941	5,873	7,797	8,889	18,320	18,256	9,851	19,318	13,641	10,112	10,098
Sioux Falls, South Dakota	12,939	7,858	1,246	7,143	965	1,408	6,623	482	8,402	9,353	8,763	14,533	14,763	3,712	5,744	6,433	4,855	1,570	7,938	7,786
Skelleftea, Sweden	6,804	1,302	5,600	2,824	6,989	7,465	1,888	6,648	6,511	3,775	5,784	9,011	10,420	9,490	9,326	409	9,784	7,425	2,336	2,114
Skopje, Yugoslavia	6,433	1,244	7,549	2,003	9,095	8,908	2,105	8,642	4,904	4,798	7,523	6,547	7,891	10,351	9,155	2,847	10,131	9,627	869	950
Socotra Island (Tamrida)	3,494	5,257	11,891	6,397	13,302	13,432	6,623	12,959	7,549	5,228	7,766	3,778	5,508	14,626	12,619	6,725	13,986	13,697	5,370	5,475
Sofia, Bulgaria	6,284	1,162	7,576	2,136	9,112	8,982	2,172	8,669	5,073	4,631	7,365	6,583	7,957	10,467	9,309	2,791	10,270	9,633	987	1,039
Songkhla, Thailand	2,149	8,534	13,168	10,551	13,466	15,432	10,217	13,662	12,663	5,221	5,390	7,663	8,910	17,829	17,675	9,108	18,578	13,273	9,397	9,376
Sorong, Indonesia	5,473	11,286	13,032	13,490	12,377	14,654	12,839	12,864	16,176	7,305	5,679	10,661	11,430	15,979	18,693	11,218	17,191	11,876	12,407	12,321
South Georgia Island	13,913	13,121	12,943	11,272	12,985	10,844	12,261	12,717	7,593	16,263	18,857	7,414	5,696	8,570	6,702	14,134	7,384	13,192	11,852	12,054
South Pole	12,241	15,894	15,970	14,795	15,073	13,712	15,820	15,188	11,315	15,829	15,572	8,258	6,780	11,330	10,315	17,470	10,511	14,832	14,932	15,158
South Sandwich Islands	13,210	13,089	13,630	11,406	13,728	11,569	12,422	13,448	7,779	15,812	18,134	6,856	5,124	9,312	7,375	14,272	8,113	13,940	11,862	12,075
Split, Yugoslavia	6,845	1,178	7,163	1,569	8,724	8,472	1,685	8,255	4,665	5,028	7,665	6,834	8,106	9,906	8,757	2,649	9,703	9,271	423	520
Spokane, Washington	12,135	8,228	2,037	8,065	712	3,001	7,341	1,260	9,912	8,690	7,504	15,662	16,280	5,045	7,344	6,629	6,308	460	8,636	8,447
Spoleto, Italy	7,151	1,391	7,038	1,280	8,613	8,264	1,539	8,128	4,381	5,319	7,922	6,868	8,075	9,637	8,447	2,735	9,407	9,177	225	434
Springbok, South Africa	9,137	9,187	13,761	8,350	15,073	13,027	9,301	14,478	5,831	11,202	13,843	2,330	806	11,782	9,067	10,753	10,456	15,699	8,238	8,462
Springfield, Illinois	13,343	7,863	1,560	6,901	1,675	743	6,495	1,190	7,819	9,759	9,388	14,067	14,135	3,135	5,032	6,552	4,201	2,242	7,790	7,658
Springfield, Massachusetts	12,758	6,751	1,832	5,535	2,888	1,570	5,247	2,291	6,428	9,301	9,586	12,616	12,796	3,507	4,511	5,652	4,157	3,529	6,498	6,389
Srinagar, India	1,881	4,550	10,155	6,601	11,154	12,281	6,234	11,035	9,321	2,216	4,598	6,947	8,670	14,427	13,827	5,298	14,630	11,328	5,458	5,416
Stanley, Falkland Islands	15,314	13,845	12,074	11,773	11,841	9,855	12,675	11,661	8,129	17,516	19,606	8,840	7,130	7,486	6,047	14,496	6,427	11,960	12,553	12,730
Stara Zagora, Bulgaria	6,093	1,206	7,710	2,329	9,235	9,150	2,339	8,802	5,224	4,495	7,257	6,515	7,922	10,656	9,499	2,850	10,463	9,747	1,178	1,221
Stockholm, Sweden	6,835	759	5,919	2,293	7,377	7,639	1,456	6,993	5,963	4,080	6,297	8,467	9,833	9,526	9,100	905	9,691	7,851	1,714	1,494
Stornoway, United Kingdom	8,244	1,924	4,897	1,682	6,454	6,370	699	5,990	5,204	5,383	7,268	9,032	10,143	8,142	7,732	1,452	8,281	7,006	1,951	1,765
Strasbourg, France	7,483	1,193	6,296	1,020	7,865	7,609	809	7,388	4,611	5,238	7,639	7,623	8,801	9,128	8,200	2,117	9,027	8,424	532	356
Stuttgart, West Germany	7,376	1,093	6,355	1,121	7,919	7,694	886	7,448	4,690	5,140	7,559	7,592	8,792	9,229	8,307	2,083	9,133	8,472	504	299
Subic, Philippines	3,693	9,162	11,868	11,368	11,703	13,935	10,722	12,045	14,330	5,194	3,980	9,965	11,194	16,040	18,044	9,153	17,344	11,369	10,298	10,204
Suchow, China	3,452	7,295	9,900	9,497	10,025	12,097	8,736	10,258	12,881	3,245	1,967	10,290	11,854	14,430	15,894	7,060	15,545	9,829	8,526	8,395
Sucre, Bolivia	17,005	11,577	8,413	9,377	8,397	6,248	9,993	8,115	6,434	15,499	16,359	10,492	9,141	3,986	2,469	11,505	2,786	8,664	10,458	10,547
Sudbury, Canada	12,497	6,843	1,037	5,917	2,116	1,524	5,477	1,510	7,185	8,949	8,937	13,253	13,563	3,833	5,226	5,566	4,691	2,769	6,777	6,641
Suez, Egypt	5,434	2,685	9,209	3,469	10,745	10,528	3,759	10,302	5,348	4,934	7,841	5,069	6,576	11,776	10,171	4,323	11,349	11,260	2,465	2,594
Sundsvall, Sweden	6,928	1,086	5,652	2,506	7,085	7,438	1,586	6,718	6,192	4,013	6,094	8,804	10,175	9,394	9,111	563	9,627	7,546	2,029	1,806
Surabaya, Indonesia	4,234	10,622	14,451	12,634	14,198	16,476	12,303	14,589	14,349	7,123	6,531	8,494	9,296	18,150	19,150	11,104	19,222	13,790	11,478	11,463
Suva, Fiji	10,956	15,574	11,718	17,217	10,187	11,536	16,195	10,783	18,373	11,801	9,067	14,530	13,992	11,242	13,377	14,426	12,026	9,534	16,847	16,642
Sverdlovsk, USSR	4,565	2,401	7,447	4,608	8,584	9,533	3,921	8,386	8,072	1,649	4,313	8,393	10,065	11,701	11,575	2,600	12,066	8,866	3,649	3,506
Svobodnyy, USSR	5,040	6,481	7,814	8,509	7,950	9,999	7,582	8,163	12,177	2,906	133	11,580	13,284	12,340	13,939	5,735	13,451	7,796	7,773	7,590
Sydney, Australia	9,154	15,432	14,815	17,555	13,354	14,723	17,039	13,957	17,226	11,509	9,609	11,314	10,955	13,975	15,246	15,379	14,335	12,697	16,401	16,372
Sydney, Canada	11,899	5,722	2,282	4,447	3,687	2,657	4,177	3,083	5,657	8,582	9,295	11,655	12,019	4,390	4,802	4,748	4,797	4,344	5,414	5,310
Syktyvkar, USSR	5,337	1,894	6,743	4,031	7,949	8,787	3,255	7,713	7,615	2,284	4,653	8,699	10,306	10,932	10,844	1,828	11,297	8,275	3,185	3,012
Szeged, Hungary	6,553	793	7,108	1,855	8,641	8,545	1,737	8,200	5,086	4,611	7,241	7,032	8,372	10,099	9,081	2,364	9,970	9,163	719	677
Szombathely, Hungary	6,827	805	6,853	1,595	8,398	8,260	1,449	7,946	4,944	4,778	7,341	7,217	8,512	9,808	8,822	2,237	9,690	8,930	511	408
Tabriz, Iran	4,281	2,441	8,994	4,145	10,382	10,720	4,016	10,049	6,752	3,396	6,306	6,078	7,731	12,419	11,296	3,810	12,280	10,787	2,990	3,001
Tacheng, China	2,953	4,223	8,838	6,432	9,692	11,057	5,806	9,633	9,699	668	3,268	8,422	10,155	13,365	13,467	4,436	13,887	9,818	5,392	5,281
Tahiti (Papeete)	14,215	16,004	9,723	15,775	8,141	8,730	15,217	8,638	15,051	13,894	10,997	16,286	14,821	7,937	9,993	14,359	8,639	7,577	16,530	16,347
Taipei, Taiwan	3,694	8,349	10,757	10,559	10,683	12,869	9,824	10,989	13,829	4,306	2,847	10,403	11,811	15,084	16,913	8,163	16,323	10,399	9,555	9,435
Taiyuan, China	3,234	6,718	9,617	8,923	9,875	11,854	8,171	10,058	12,309	2,669	1,820	10,021	11,642	14,231	15,447	6,518	15,254	9,734	7,949	7,817
Tallahassee, Florida	14,299	8,414	2,639	7,106	2,703	415	6,893	2,306	7,320	10,753	10,532	13,675	13,415	2,043	3,940	7,280	3,055	3,168	8,118	8,022
Tallinn, USSR	6,464	707	6,170	2,604	7,590	7,955	1,821	7,232	6,244	3,714	6,006	8,387	9,814	9,883	9,480	1,016	10,067	8,039	1,892	1,687
Tamanrasset, Algeria	8,216	3,686	8,344	2,401	9,925	8,853	3,355	9,353	2,544	7,346	10,119	5,340	6,156	9,433	7,457	4,984	8,753	10,562	2,465	2,685
Tampa, Florida	14,528	8,530	2,940	7,129	3,027	744	6,974	2,634	7,142	11,005	10,852	13,493	13,157	1,771	3,617	7,456	2,732	3,478	8,1/1	8,085
Tampere, Finland	6,576	932	5,960	2,688	7,367	7,779	1,838	7,016	6,356	3,710	5,902	8,625	10,048	9,746	9,436	786	9,974	7,810	2,061	1,848
Tanami, Australia	6,532	12,862	14,968	14,934	14,028	16,122	14,525	14,586	16,219	9,113	7,784	9,903	10,190	16,351	17,803	13,118	16,937	13,439	13,780	13,755
Tangier, Morocco	8,865	2,967	6,535	862	8,121	7,201	1,877	7,555	2,830	7,012	9,431	7,146	7,930	8,161	6,709	3,732	7,760	8,755	1,744	1,862
Tarawa (Betio)	9,663	13,348	10,352	15,048	9,016	10,882	14,021	9,618	18,277	9,733	6,904	15,150	15,346	11,436	14,053	12,207	12,555	8,373	14,612	14,405
Tashkent, USSR	2,813	3,658	9,276	5,770	10,353	11,365	5,336	10,192	8,727	1,734	4,514	7,244	8,976	13,488	12,989	4,359	13,714	10,580	4,647	4,583
Tbilisi, USSR	4,529	2,053	8,574	3,874	9,959	10,322	3,667	9,627	6,688	3,250	6,149	6,443	8,072	12,074	11,077	3,388	11,997	10,366	2,719	2,705
Tegucigalpa, Honduras	16,133	10,069	4,415	8,488	4,041	2,151	8,461	3,841	7,746	12,583	12,113	13,836	13,022	442	3,172	9,060	1,783	4,281	9,587	9,528
Tehran, Iran	3,766	2,939	9,420	4,673	10,763	11,205	4,539	10,459	7,181	3,248	6,134	5,952	7,646	12,944	11,806	4,229	12,808	11,137	3,519	3,531
Tel Aviv, Israel	5,223	2,520	9,112	3,518	10,626	10,519	3,717	10,203	5,602	4,619	7,527	5,295	6,834	11,867	10,363	4,139	11,500	11,122	2,457	2,561
Telegraph Creek, Canada	10,697	7,478	2,575	7,813	2,046	4,268	6,936	2,381	10,341	7,322	6,047	15,191	16,363	6,462	8,598	5,832	7,685	1,898	8,139	7,927
Teresina, Brazil	14,236	8,895	7,865	6,685	8,572	6,299	7,451	8,077	3,549	12,941	14,916	8,562	7,700	4,909	2,171	9,187	3,638	9,078	7,692	7,809
Ternate, Indonesia	5,007	10,884	13,043	13,079	12,506	14,799	12,464	12,964	15,709	6,939	5,482	10,299	11,150	16,310	19,048	10,892	17,573	12,038	11,982	11,902
The Valley, Anguilla	14,589	8,173	4,597	6,246	5,182	2,921	6,489	4,693	5,141	11,608	12,366	11,379	10,900	2,321	1,705	7,629	1,911	5,698	7,399	7,392
Thessaloniki, Greece	6,309	1,390	7,743	2,159	9,288	9,096	2,297	8,836	4,932	4,794	7,555	6,369	7,731	10,517	9,270	3,012	10,272	9,819	1,043	1,138
Thimphu, Bhutan	900	6,065	10,990	8,173	11,681	13,238	7,737	11,705	10,879	2,804	4,069	7,603	9,228	15,575	15,398	6,585	16,052	11,696	7,038	6,986
Thunder Bay, Canada	12,388	7,084	606	6,367	1,482	1,667	5,835	879	7,833	8,803	8,519	13,822	14,209	4,069	5,744	5,691	5,066	2,138	7,151	6,998
Tientsin, China	3,658	6,894	9,379	9,081	9,557	11,591	8,285	9,767	12,549	2,861	1,481	10,450	12,069	13,944	15,355	6,573	15,027	9,389	8,148	8,005
Tijuana, Mexico	13,683	9,764	3,190	9,274	1,642	2,815	8,689	2,102	10,360	10,333	8,862	16,646	16,503	4,085	6,722	8,214	5,427	1,232	10,007	9,839
Tiksi, USSR	6,337	5,013	5,761	6,714	6,231	8,019	5,710	6,304	10,376	2,990	2,378	11,791	13,491	10,419	11,717	3,843	11,386	6,254	6,232	6,018
Timbuktu, Mali	9,269	4,634	8,324	2,936	9,841	8,439	3,962	9,243	1,460	8,430	11,152	5,512	5,970	8,666	6,487	5,751	7,855	10,496	3,355	3,557
Tindouf, Algeria	9,365	3,819	7,052	1,787	8,598	7,388	2,799	8,008	1,918	7,832	10,332	6,694	7,275	7,996	6,216	4,657	7,411	9,249	2,546	2,699
Tirane, Albania	6,570	1,335	7,526	1,887	9,082	8,840	2,055	8,619	4,749	4,952	7,669	6,514	7,829	10,245	9,013	2,908	10,003	9,623	777	890

Distances in Kilometers	Bhubaneswar, India	Bialystok, Poland	Big Trout Lake, Canada	Bilbao, Spain	Billings, Montana	Birmingham, Alabama	Birmingham, United Kingdom	Bismarck, North Dakota	Bissau, Guinea Bissau	Biysk, USSR	Blagoveshchensk, USSR	Blantyre, Malawi	Bloemfontein, South Africa	Bluefields, Nicaragua	Boa Vista do Rio Branco, Braz.	Bodo, Norway	Bogota, Colombia	Boise, Idaho	Bologna, Italy	Bolzano, Italy
Tokyo, Japan	5,504	8,429	8,997	10,484	8,691	10,946	9,556	9,057	14,143	4,616	1,896	12,341	13,855	13,031	15,244	7,703	14,326	8,351	9,720	9,544
Toledo, Spain	8,585	2,529	6,321	386	7,916	7,162	1,410	7,367	3,307	6,579	8,959	7,369	8,253	8,294	7,012	3,256	7,987	8,537	1,365	1,449
Topeka, Kansas	13,440	8,226	1,699	7,370	1,292	1,005	6,919	957	8,339	9,853	9,249	14,591	14,637	3,221	5,352	6,848	4,394	1,788	8,224	8,084
Toronto, Canada	12,771	6,996	1,371	5,949	2,306	1,298	5,573	1,710	7,007	9,240	9,276	13,163	13,377	3,535	4,888	5,776	4,360	2,947	6,856	6,731
Toulouse, France	8,047	1,915	6,346	358	7,941	7,408	1,017	7,421	3,881	5,965	8,372	7,411	8,440	8,715	7,576	2,748	8,494	8,537	799	846
Tours, France	8,023	1,716	6,011	541	7,600	7,185	595	7,094	4,223	5,738	8,048	7,788	8,851	8,620	7,657	2,352	8,489	8,184	886	818
Townsville, Australia	7,955	13,928	13,878	16,136	12,648	14,513	15,438	13,244	17,973	9,916	7,930	11,619	11,699	14,573	16,528	13,710	15,310	12,014	15,050	14,967
Trenton, New Jersey	13,018	7,028	1,897	5,793	2,797	1,305	5,521	2,215	6,561	9,545	9,746	12,799	12,909	3,250	4,380	5,923	3,947	3,423	6,766	6,660
Tripoli, Lebanon	5,135	2,308	8,932	3,475	10,428	10,405	3,593	10,019	5,756	4,364	7,268	5,558	7,109	11,838	10,437	3,908	11,530	10,911	2,374	2,456
Tripoli, Libya	7,238	2,385	7,914	1,819	9,509	8,883	2,490	8,988	3,746	6,012	8,769	5,867	7,001	9,933	8,338	3,825	9,483	10,102	1,296	1,520
Tristan da Cunha (Edinburgh)	12,042	10,562	12,511	8,943	13,271	10,982	9,969	12,786	5,424	13,643	16,515	5,206	3,671	9,215	6,666	11,786	7,875	13,742	9,339	9,553
Trondheim, Norway	7,288	1,362	5,312	2,404	6,766	7,073	1,416	6,384	6,080	4,309	6,262	9,035	10,353	9,028	8,794	469	9,277	7,243	2,108	1,882
Trujillo, Peru	17,913	11,539	6,942	9,513	6,653	4,680	9,857	6,454	7,362	14,875	14,729	12,298	11,032	2,285	2,369	10,979	1,510	6,847	10,667	10,690
Truk Island (Moen)	7,235	11,751	11,115	13,847	10,163	12,357	12,918	10,708	17,469	7,784	5,258	13,111	13,870	13,514	16,246	11,058	14,761	9,600	13,034	12,872
Truro, Canada	12,099	5,960	2,132	4,702	3,484	2,402	4,426	2,878	5,835	8,745	9,357	11,883	12,208	4,178	4,721	4,952	4,638	4,140	5,667	5,562
Tsingtao, China	3,786	7,331	9,627	9,518	9,708	11,805	8,720	9,954	12,978	3,295	1,681	10,620	12,195	14,119	15,699	6,998	15,262	9,499	8,583	8,442
Tsitsihar, China	4,563	6,600	8,342	8,698	8,492	10,536	7,810	8,704	12,323	2,801	416	11,207	12,887	12,881	14,427	5,998	13,984	8,332	7,890	7,719
Tubuai Island (Mataura)	14,338	16,642	10,273	16,240	8,705	9,147	15,771	9,182	14,998	14,405	11,496	15,647	14,177	8,153	10,015	14,996	8,735	8,158	17,089	16,921
Tucson, Arizona	13,933	9,564	2,924	8,908	1,521	2,261	8,388	1,838	9,818	10,481	9,215	16,138	15,933	3,572	6,172	8,067	4,908	1,346	9,704	9,548
Tulsa, Oklahoma	13,760	8,506	2,017	7,583	1,502	882	7,168	1,250	8,381	10,174	9,527	14,685	14,615	2,942	5,169	7,150	4,148	1,917	8,466	8,332
Tunis, Tunisia	7,444	2,076	7,405	1,329	8,998	8,420	1,982	8,481	3,779	5,914	8,580	6,377	7,487	9,568	8,125	3,402	9,198	9,590	859	1,084
Tura, USSR	5,010	4,334	6,876	6,354	7,545	9,146	5,445	7,551	10,017	1,563	2,236	10,439	12,160	11,539	12,398	3,631	12,350	7,624	5,623	5,436
Turin, Italy	7,530	1,439	6,575	873	8,157	7,783	1,083	7,663	4,294	5,480	7,960	7,282	8,426	9,187	8,099	2,507	9,002	8,729	297	331
Uberlandia, Brazil	15,235	10,496	8,994	8,298	9,383	7,100	9,089	8,979	4,948	14,546	16,509	8,773	7,541	5,181	2,762	10,830	3,843	9,780	9,265	9,395
Ufa, USSR	4,583	2,141	7,571	4,354	8,769	9,600	3,729	8,540	7,754	1,939	4,673	8,061	9,720	11,703	11,416	2,574	11,989	9,081	3,353	3,223
Ujungpandang, Indonesia	4,620	10,878	13,987	12,984	13,570	15,865	12,537	14,003	15,030	7,157	6,186	9,266	10,054	17,377	19,750	11,170	18,541	13,123	11,839	11,799
Ulaanbaatar, Mongolia	3,608	5,620	8,616	7,801	9,069	10,883	7,006	9,173	11,303	1,620	1,526	10,004	11,713	13,286	14,256	5,318	14,186	9,024	6,883	6,734
Ulan-Ude, USSR	3,985	5,392	8,178	7,543	8,650	10,446	6,711	8,744	11,107	1,525	1,403	10,225	11,949	12,849	13,849	4,979	13,749	8,622	6,672	6,512
Uliastay, Mongolia	3,209	5,033	8,728	7,239	9,353	10,997	6,508	9,390	10,651	983	2,248	9,327	11,049	13,387	13,992	4,929	14,138	9,379	6,266	6,132
Uranium City, Canada	11,063	6,787	1,300	6,755	1,534	3,310	5,967	1,511	9,049	7,510	6,821	14,322	15,225	5,667	7,505	5,186	6,770	1,849	7,241	7,045
Urumqi, China	2,619	4,708	9,183	6,915	9,955	11,425	6,295	9,934	10,139	990	3,081	8,488	10,212	13,764	13,954	4,909	14,340	10,038	5,865	5,759
Ushuaia, Argentina	15,597	14,600	12,206	12,496	11,773	9,944	13,370	11,668	8,877	18,261	18,831	9,415	7,687	7,544	6,425	15,154	6,606	11,811	13,310	13,481
Vaduz, Liechtenstein	7,365	1,176	6,501	1,071	8,071	7,799	1,010	7,593	4,567	5,223	7,686	7,422	8,614	9,286	8,291	2,258	9,153	8,629	330	159
Valencia, Spain	8,294	2,345	6,571	473	8,168	7,466	1,450	7,627	3,408	6,386	8,841	7,134	8,077	8,609	7,294	3,228	8,291	8,781	1,117	1,234
Valladolid, Spain	8,588	2,438	6,139	229	7,736	7,031	1,221	7,192	3,468	6,482	8,814	7,557	8,456	8,226	7,028	3,080	7,963	8,353	1,342	1,394
Valletta, Malta	7,072	2,031	7,725	1,705	9,313	8,802	2,250	8,808	4,030	5,695	8,429	6,114	7,301	9,969	8,497	3,492	9,590	9,893	991	1,208
Valparaiso, Chile	17,378	13,168	9,786	10,955	9,486	7,536	11,630	9,313	7,746	17,159	17,534	10,550	8,963	5,147	4,132	13,179	4,173	9,621	11,991	12,101
Vancouver, Canada	11,795	8,223	2,331	8,221	1,164	3,457	7,446	1,682	10,254	8,408	7,096	15,800	16,589	5,486	7,801	6,598	6,759	820	8,719	8,522
Varna, Bulgaria	5,915	1,158	7,742	2,494	9,250	9,237	2,436	8,831	5,431	4,291	7,063	6,573	8,013	10,793	9,685	2,799	10,629	9,748	1,339	1,356
Venice, Italy	7,160	1,158	6,789	1,243	8,357	8,083	1,300	7,881	4,570	5,160	7,703	7,156	8,377	9,538	8,467	2,434	9,370	8,912	134	141
Veracruz, Mexico	15,637	10,113	3,880	8,821	3,160	1,837	8,617	3,091	8,611	12,053	11,203	14,847	14,121	1,548	4,262	8,895	2,888	3,294	9,844	9,748
Verona, Italy	7,266	1,226	6,719	1,139	8,291	7,991	1,223	7,810	4,497	5,245	7,768	7,201	8,401	9,435	8,364	2,439	9,264	8,850	111	122
Victoria, Canada	11,866	8,314	2,387	8,302	1,164	3,450	7,531	1,701	10,304	8,489	7,151	15,885	16,649	5,450	7,788	6,690	6,729	770	8,806	8,609
Victoria, Seychelles	4,312	7,080	13,719	7,891	15,188	14,973	8,298	14,805	8,070	6,931	9,145	2,555	4,110	15,473	12,942	8,606	14,439	15,608	6,992	7,132
Vienna, Austria	6,847	728	6,759	1,597	8,300	8,186	1,381	7,852	5,003	4,735	7,272	7,324	8,621	9,761	8,818	2,128	9,665	8,829	566	421
Vientiane, Laos	1,781	7,730	11,959	9,861	12,284	14,222	9,387	12,460	12,482	4,127	4,215	8,299	9,718	16,619	17,077	8,101	17,483	12,127	8,730	8,674
Villahermosa, Mexico	15,775	10,047	3,986	8,658	3,403	1,825	8,509	3,277	8,293	12,187	11,473	14,498	13,755	1,187	3,896	8,894	2,529	3,586	9,708	9,624
Vilnius, USSR	6,309	224	6,599	2,405	8,053	8,293	1,809	7,673	5,941	3,851	6,323	7,862	9,287	10,114	9,496	1,518	10,195	8,520	1,514	1,338
Visby, Sweden	6,795	587	6,065	2,182	7,536	7,748	1,407	7,144	5,834	4,134	6,418	8,281	9,643	9,594	9,088	1,094	9,720	8,018	1,540	1,324
Vitoria, Brazil	14,438	10,160	9,488	8,010	10,027	7,733	8,880	9,584	4,474	14,164	16,516	7,926	6,716	5,947	3,388	10,696	4,604	10,466	8,890	9,042
Vladivostok, USSR	4,968	7,364	8,545	9,436	8,496	10,653	8,525	8,777	13,082	3,576	860	11,748	13,378	12,911	14,763	6,688	14,112	8,257	8,655	8,481
Volgograd, USSR	4,851	1,565	7,858	3,660	9,207	9,694	3,249	8,896	6,841	2,879	5,694	7,208	8,816	11,581	10,874	2,669	11,649	9,599	2,557	2,477
Vologda, USSR	5,657	1,236	6,696	3,397	8,013	8,620	2,676	7,717	6,959	2,871	5,311	8,325	9,873	10,650	10,340	1,548	10,899	8,398	2,527	2,355
Vorkuta, USSR	5,473	2,689	6,374	4,693	7,427	8,540	3,808	7,264	8,351	2,020	3,900	9,533	11,170	10,814	11,113	2,073	11,360	7,683	3,970	3,778
Wake Island	8,374	11,250	9,139	13,000	8,106	10,290	11,980	8,661	16,552	7,753	4,867	14,902	15,891	11,574	14,306	10,138	12,879	7,535	12,514	12,308
Wallis Island	11,340	15,269	10,941	16,622	9,403	10,760	15,630	9,997	17,921	11,751	8,915	15,319	14,737	10,577	12,850	13,959	11,442	8,750	16,476	16,256
Walvis Bay, Namibia	9,098	8,470	12,979	7,545	14,342	12,392	8,506	13,740	5,057	10,789	13,562	2,292	1,353	11,364	8,625	10,005	10,069	14,983	7,474	7,699
Warsaw, Poland	6,547	175	6,628	2,043	8,124	8,216	1,555	7,714	5,549	4,223	6,717	7,658	9,029	9,942	9,195	1,713	9,953	8,619	1,120	945
Washington, D.C.	13,222	7,267	1,931	6,035	2,685	1,062	5,765	2,120	6,728	9,728	9,840	12,996	13,053	3,053	4,326	6,146	3,810	3,295	7,011	6,905
Watson Lake, Canada	10,566	7,201	2,421	7,535	2,082	4,237	6,655	2,348	10,108	7,147	5,995	14,912	16,085	6,486	8,537	5,556	7,680	2,023	7,857	7,646
Weimar, East Germany	7,210	845	6,284	1,379	7,831	7,715	928	7,378	4,979	4,876	7,271	7,748	8,994	9,333	8,512	1,824	9,292	8,367	723	497
Wellington, New Zealand	11,383	17,521	13,878	19,727	12,282	13,014	18,739	12,830	16,590	13,475	11,140	12,457	11,567	11,838	13,046	16,877	12,108	11,662	18,627	18,570
West Berlin, West Germany	7,065	660	6,261	1,594	7,791	7,760	1,038	7,353	5,202	4,665	7,048	7,848	9,130	9,437	8,687	1,646	9,435	8,314	906	683
Wewak, Papua New Guinea	6,837	12,312	12,629	14,519	11,674	13,838	13,728	12,225	17,565	8,264	6,160	11,896	12,449	14,735	17,334	11,956	15,849	11,100	13,519	13,402
Whangarei, New Zealand	11,168	17,048	13,465	19,138	11,880	12,807	18,120	12,447	17,182	13,004	10,576	12,884	12,094	11,854	13,307	16,268	12,256	11,245	18,277	18,156
Whitehorse, Canada	10,313	7,233	2,763	7,692	2,399	4,581	6,783	2,691	10,378	6,944	5,681	14,953	16,227	6,812	8,887	5,588	8,018	2,280	7,953	7,737
Wichita, Kansas	13,584	8,430	1,879	7,577	1,290	1,060	7,128	1,050	8,495	10,001	9,318	14,769	14,764	3,152	5,373	7,045	4,361	1,722	8,433	8,293
Willemstad, Curacao	15,497	9,080	4,987	7,155	5,274	2,985	7,396	4,866	5,803	12,426	12,911	11,851	11,153	1,611	1,374	8,484	1,005	5,705	8,308	8,303
Wiluna, Australia	6,374	12,787	16,100	14,626	15,241	17,320	14,466	15,792	15,134	9,406	8,545	8,780	8,982	17,042	17,371	13,382	17,142	14,656	13,487	13,512
Windhoek, Namibia	8,842	8,409	13,117	7,573	14,514	12,606	8,513	13,910	5,216	10,604	13,349	2,027	1,164	11,621	8,883	9,967	10,331	15,161	7,449	7,674
Windsor, Canada	12,988	7,303	1,382	6,282	2,070	1,031	5,897	1,494	7,279	9,433	9,329	13,474	13,636	3,359	4,906	6,051	4,269	2,695	7,184	7,057
Winnipeg, Canada	12,233	7,292	660	6,766	963	2,007	6,158	435	8,408	8,648	8,123	14,302	14,779	4,377	6,247	5,814	5,468	1,609	7,476	7,310
Winston-Salem, North Carolina	13,601	7,687	2,111	6,440	2,593	665	6,183	2,077	6,973	10,081	10,057	13,287	13,239	2,693	4,199	6,552	3,545	3,162	7,425	7,321
Wroclaw, Poland	6,810	476	6,547	1,741	8,069	8,056	1,313	7,638	5,259	4,526	6,999	7,613	8,933	9,719	8,909	1,809	9,692	8,584	850	658
Wuhan, China	3,071	7,423	10,365	9,635	10,516	12,575	8,926	10,743	12,894	3,394	2,450	9,903	11,432	14,918	16,270	7,315	16,012	10,321	8,620	8,503
Wyndham, Australia	6,080	12,366	14,624	14,468	13,804	15,990	14,020	14,337	16,091	8,588	7,281	9,879	10,305	16,573	18,316	12,591	17,322	13,244	13,319	13,284
Xi'an, China	2,752	6,782	10,076	8,995	10,378	12,326	8,302	10,549	12,249	2,768	2,336	9,572	11,168	14,714	15,759	6,729	15,691	10,247	7,972	7,857
Xining, China	2,387	6,141	9,919	8,352	10,390	12,190	7,669	10,496	11,557	2,194	2,557	9,088	10,735	14,593	15,279	6,202	15,422	10,329	7,309	7,201
Yakutsk, USSR	5,722	5,715	6,698	7,593	6,983	8,924	6,618	7,134	11,278	2,810	1,313	11,785	13,519	11,301	12,762	4,747	12,346	6,910	6,986	6,785
Yanji, China	4,774	7,263	8,647	9,357	8,637	10,776	8,460	8,907	12,986	3,430	835	11,552	13,183	13,053	14,841	6,636	14,237	8,411	8,553	8,382
Yaounde, Cameroon	8,230	5,565	10,416	4,592	11,959	10,550	5,529	11,365	3,115	8,570	11,480	3,377	3,972	10,504	8,024	7,042	9,499	12,611	4,500	4,726
Yap Island (Colonia)	5,728	10,770	11,663	12,966	11,006	13,292	12,160	11,486	16,277	6,720	4,623	11,697	12,656	14,822	17,535	10,392	16,133	10,520	12,000	11,871
Yaraka, Australia	8,041	14,233	14,542	16,396	13,271	15,036	15,827	13,871	17,443	10,296	8,483	11,118	11,090	14,810	16,413	14,192	15,373	12,628	15,260	15,209
Yarmouth, Canada	12,359	6,242	2,061	4,975	3,321	2,125	4,709	2,715	5,980	8,977	9,495	12,095	12,358	3,913	4,575	5,216	4,417	3,974	5,947	5,844
Yellowknife, Canada	10,668	6,660	1,709	6,804	1,893	3,756	5,964	1,940	9,293	7,135	6,376	14,298	15,339	6,108	7,943	5,033	7,216	2,100	7,206	7,002
Yerevan, USSR	4,497	2,163	8,717	3,912	10,112	10,440	3,750	9,774	6,636	3,368	6,273	6,273	7,905	12,156	11,093	3,536	12,045	10,525	2,755	2,755
Yinchuan, China	2,822	6,287	9,659	8,499	10,048	11,922	7,791	10,183	11,812	2,257	2,127	9,539	11,186	14,322	15,244	6,209	15,236	9,960	7,493	7,371
Yogyakarta, Indonesia	4,103	10,511	14,584	12,487	14,399	16,662	12,195	14,771	14,099	7,102	6,644	8,224	9,035	18,419	18,895	11,058	19,420	14,008	11,331	11,324
York, United Kingdom	8,023	1,608	5,443	1,184	7,013	6,811	160	6,535	4,829	5,404	7,514	8,448	9,562	8,454	7,801	1,713	8,479	7,574	1,379	1,207
Yumen, China	2,452	5,640	9,600	7,851	10,169	11,871	7,199	10,234	11,084	1,707	2,595	8,944	10,628	14,264	14,798	5,719	15,015	10,156	6,812	6,702
Yutian, China	1,887	4,801	9,924	6,942	10,794	12,123	6,465	10,734	9,868	1,767	3,917	7,612	9,327	14,387	14,148	5,319	14,777	10,911	5,825	5,757
Yuzhno-Sakhalinsk, USSR	5,894	7,530	7,780	9,469	7,611	9,813	8,487	7,926	13,146	4,077	1,178	12,619	14,282	12,016	14,037	6,615	13,254	7,341	8,815	8,621
Zagreb, Yugoslavia	6,874	965	6,945	1,530	8,498	8,305	1,497	8,038	4,803	4,907	7,493	7,083	8,362	9,805	8,755	2,394	9,653	9,039	395	367
Zahedan, Iran	2,716	4,029	10,356	5,783	11,600	12,249	5,651	11,356	8,072	3,248	5,927	5,730	7,463	14,058	12,857	5,199	13,913	11,903	4,632	4,648
Zamboanga, Philippines	4,177	9,990	12,638	12,182	12,323	14,601	11,581	12,716	14,906	6,069	4,835	9,912	10,957	16,486	18,890	10,048	17,827	11,928	11,085	11,005
Zanzibar, Tanzania	5,880	6,743	13,038	6,925	14,632	13,700	7,569	14,108	6,382	7,824	10,415	1,158	2,887	13,740	11,143	8,384	12,644	15,215	6,265	6,452
Zaragoza, Spain	8,280	2,203	6,367	248	7,965	7,325	1,207	7,431	3,598	6,252	8,657	7,350	8,315	8,545	7,327	3,002	8,278	8,573	1,043	1,120
Zashiversk, USSR	6,553	5,721	5,863	7,392	6,121	8,073	6,380	6,273	11,035	3,435	2,089	12,364	14,084	10,444	11,998	4,523	11,508	6,058	6,936	6,722
Zhengzhou, China	3,170	7,040	9,930	9,248	10,135	12,154	8,512	10,339	12,588	2,994	2,059	10,000	11,583	14,517	15,805	6,873	15,575	9,968	8,258	8,132
Zurich, Switzerland	7,449	1,231	6,425	998	7,997	7,712	930	7,516	4,530	5,280	7,720	7,482	8,658	9,196	8,212	2,245	9,067	8,559	394	247

Distances in Kilometers	Bombay, India	Bonn, West Germany	Bora Bora (Vaitape)	Bordeaux, France	Boston, Massachusetts	Bouvet Island	Brasilia, Brazil	Braunschweig, West Germany	Brazzaville, Congo	Bremerhaven, West Germany	Brest, France	Brest, USSR	Bridgetown, Barbados	Brisbane, Australia	Bristol, United Kingdom	Brno, Czechoslovakia	Broken Hill, Australia	Brussels, Belgium	Bucharest, Romania	Budapest, Hungary
Bonn, West Germany	6,696	0	15,769	871	5,782	11,662	9,104	293	6,145	329	876	1,162	7,256	16,158	683	704	15,754	195	1,586	944
Bora Bora (Vaitape)	15,310	15,769	0	15,877	10,491	11,798	10,939	15,745	17,308	15,557	15,393	16,037	10,647	5,786	15,272	16,231	6,895	15,646	16,903	16,468
Bordeaux, France	7,250	871	15,877	0	5,514	11,007	8,243	1,162	5,663	1,175	497	1,956	6,564	16,984	751	1,391	16,447	761	2,107	1,542
Boston, Massachusetts	12,275	5,782	10,491	5,514	0	12,836	6,861	5,932	10,028	5,756	5,092	6,735	3,426	15,729	5,118	6,471	16,937	5,598	7,364	6,723
Bouvet Island	10,445	11,662	11,798	11,007	12,836	0	6,136	11,846	5,666	11,980	11,421	11,958	9,530	10,472	11,750	11,553	9,625	11,668	11,166	11,393
Brasilia, Brazil	13,756	9,104	10,939	8,243	6,861	6,136	0	9,397	7,020	9,372	8,308	10,174	3,444	14,715	8,647	9,583	14,630	8,958	10,005	9,653
Braunschweig, West Germany	6,484	293	15,745	1,162	5,932	11,846	9,397	0	6,281	194	1,150	900	7,517	15,867	907	549	15,487	459	1,441	811
Brazzaville, Congo	6,807	6,145	17,308	5,663	10,028	5,666	7,020	6,281	0	6,438	6,144	6,297	8,496	14,285	6,404	5,925	13,065	6,195	5,501	5,747
Bremerhaven, West Germany	6,637	329	15,557	1,175	5,756	11,980	9,372	194	6,438	0	1,079	1,030	7,409	15,912	793	740	15,585	419	1,627	1,002
Brest, France	7,528	876	15,393	497	5,092	11,421	8,308	1,150	6,144	1,079	0	2,038	6,381	16,988	366	1,549	16,630	692	2,376	1,756
Brest, USSR	5,613	1,162	16,037	1,956	6,735	11,958	10,174	900	6,297	1,030	2,038	0	8,415	15,029	1,806	594	14,592	1,349	871	610
Bridgetown, Barbados	13,720	7,256	10,647	6,564	3,426	9,530	3,444	7,517	8,496	7,409	6,381	8,415	0	16,282	6,617	7,920	17,023	7,066	8,665	8,100
Brisbane, Australia	10,049	16,158	5,786	16,984	15,729	10,472	14,715	15,867	14,285	15,912	16,988	15,029	16,282	0	16,657	15,596	1,224	16,319	14,979	15,469
Bristol, United Kingdom	7,377	683	15,272	751	5,118	11,750	8,647	907	6,404	793	366	1,806	6,617	16,657	0	1,387	16,378	489	2,263	1,624
Brno, Czechoslovakia	5,993	704	16,231	1,391	6,471	11,553	9,583	549	5,925	740	1,549	594	7,920	15,596	1,387	0	15,095	899	895	262
Broken Hill, Australia	9,227	15,754	6,895	16,447	16,937	9,625	14,630	15,487	13,065	15,585	16,630	14,592	17,023	1,224	16,378	15,095	0	15,941	14,341	14,914
Brussels, Belgium	6,891	195	15,646	761	5,598	11,668	8,958	459	6,195	419	692	1,349	7,066	16,319	489	899	15,941	0	1,775	1,135
Bucharest, Romania	5,156	1,586	16,903	2,107	7,364	11,166	10,005	1,441	5,501	1,627	2,376	871	8,665	14,979	2,263	895	14,341	1,775	0	641
Budapest, Hungary	5,772	944	16,468	1,542	6,723	11,393	9,653	811	5,747	1,002	1,756	610	8,100	15,469	1,624	262	14,914	1,135	641	0
Buenos Aires, Argentina	14,937	11,423	9,281	10,557	8,619	5,187	2,336	11,716	8,256	11,699	10,639	12,465	5,281	12,379	10,981	11,871	12,352	11,282	12,213	11,920
Buffalo, New York	12,572	6,243	9,912	6,042	644	13,294	7,226	6,370	10,671	6,187	5,600	7,132	3,785	15,085	5,595	6,916	16,294	6,064	7,810	7,173
Bujumbura, Burundi	5,363	6,362	17,800	6,113	11,121	6,130	8,555	6,418	1,567	6,601	6,610	6,172	9,993	13,091	6,789	5,955	11,874	6,465	5,306	5,726
Bulawayo, Zimbabwe	6,482	8,130	15,949	7,781	12,271	4,362	8,049	8,212	2,274	8,389	8,275	8,018	10,328	12,045	8,495	7,772	10,835	8,215	7,156	7,552
Burlington, Vermont	12,183	5,776	10,402	5,557	292	13,128	7,149	5,912	10,221	5,731	5,120	6,691	3,711	15,521	5,123	6,455	16,716	5,596	7,350	6,711
Cabinda, Angola	7,177	6,255	17,003	5,724	9,872	5,478	6,653	6,409	370	6,558	6,195	6,481	8,202	14,444	6,472	6,081	13,233	6,293	5,708	5,915
Cagliari, Italy	6,458	1,290	16,885	1,015	6,513	10,391	8,491	1,455	4,856	1,594	1,492	1,821	7,274	16,450	1,636	1,260	15,679	1,344	1,522	1,223
Cairns, Australia	8,913	14,772	6,633	15,608	15,531	11,333	16,093	14,480	14,105	14,523	15,599	13,652	17,275	1,389	15,269	14,226	1,722	14,931	13,656	14,113
Cairo, Egypt	4,363	3,051	18,476	3,228	8,737	9,735	9,875	2,995	4,162	3,189	3,647	2,526	9,377	14,397	3,661	2,459	13,478	3,212	1,660	2,201
Calais, France	7,067	372	15,525	703	5,429	11,682	8,832	620	6,252	544	537	1,517	6,898	16,456	314	1,075	16,107	176	1,949	1,310
Calcutta, India	1,664	7,498	13,728	8,198	12,517	11,700	15,390	7,241	8,471	7,358	8,372	6,342	14,752	8,885	8,145	6,833	8,262	7,689	6,112	6,657
Calgary, Canada	12,219	7,436	8,335	7,612	3,376	15,916	9,783	7,434	13,026	7,241	7,116	7,906	6,433	12,529	6,951	7,952	13,668	7,311	8,752	8,205
Cali, Colombia	15,852	9,264	8,557	8,634	4,344	9,668	3,801	9,506	10,247	9,377	8,401	10,403	2,144	14,139	8,599	9,950	14,957	9,070	10,740	10,150
Camaguey, Cuba	14,531	7,853	9,080	7,386	2,413	11,373	5,257	8,053	10,520	7,897	7,051	8,918	2,149	14,857	7,171	8,558	15,965	7,659	9,423	8,790
Cambridge Bay, Canada	10,234	5,616	10,186	5,961	3,566	16,176	10,423	5,563	11,610	5,378	5,473	5,927	6,993	13,304	5,238	6,047	14,213	5,521	6,791	6,289
Cambridge, United Kingdom	7,191	512	15,342	821	5,271	11,824	8,838	711	6,420	589	535	1,607	6,820	16,463	204	1,211	16,174	330	2,097	1,456
Campbellton, Canada	11,568	5,139	10,999	4,936	715	13,112	7,306	5,273	9,762	5,092	4,491	6,055	3,925	15,913	4,487	5,817	17,055	4,959	6,712	6,073
Campo Grande, Brazil	14,546	9,922	10,100	9,069	7,157	6,126	877	10,215	7,757	10,181	9,108	11,012	3,751	13,928	9,438	10,424	13,961	9,770	10,870	10,504
Canakkale, Turkey	5,002	1,904	17,379	2,266	7,673	10,708	9,850	1,812	5,048	2,005	2,609	1,344	8,749	14,967	2,555	1,267	14,228	2,081	476	1,006
Canberra, Australia	10,036	16,537	6,180	17,252	16,479	9,533	14,069	16,264	13,512	16,351	17,412	15,375	16,224	942	17,140	15,891	809	16,721	15,148	15,716
Cancun, Mexico	15,048	8,480	8,227	8,091	2,774	11,902	5,888	8,655	11,436	8,487	7,721	9,486	3,016	13,979	7,802	9,180	15,121	8,289	10,065	9,425
Canton, China	4,213	9,116	11,219	9,940	12,742	13,343	17,895	8,827	11,016	8,887	9,966	7,984	15,925	7,045	9,660	8,557	6,793	9,283	8,030	8,450
Canton Atoll, Phoenix Islands	12,799	14,694	2,655	15,271	11,097	13,641	13,513	14,521	18,918	14,382	14,810	14,361	12,481	4,641	14,521	14,806	5,863	14,671	15,079	14,948
Cape Town, South Africa	8,216	9,443	14,328	8,930	12,411	2,564	6,882	9,578	3,299	9,737	9,398	9,543	9,742	11,699	9,678	9,208	10,593	9,490	8,711	9,018
Cape York, Australia	8,314	14,003	7,119	14,845	15,232	11,832	16,863	13,711	13,953	13,752	14,826	12,891	17,617	2,161	14,496	13,469	2,354	14,161	12,926	13,364
Caracas, Venezuela	14,536	7,987	9,803	7,332	3,554	9,714	3,583	8,238	9,253	8,118	7,118	9,137	846	15,450	7,332	8,665	16,262	7,795	9,439	8,857
Cardiff, United Kingdom	7,419	726	15,237	767	5,076	11,758	8,621	948	6,425	831	357	1,846	6,578	16,684	43	1,430	16,415	532	2,306	1,667
Carlisle, United Kingdom	7,396	818	14,986	1,131	4,996	12,133	8,904	937	6,769	765	729	1,783	6,722	16,399	383	1,477	16,235	665	2,372	1,734
Carnarvon, Australia	6,562	13,255	9,706	13,792	18,018	9,004	15,087	13,032	10,658	13,175	14,090	12,145	18,528	3,932	13,933	12,554	2,826	13,450	11,715	12,335
Carson City, Nevada	13,438	8,784	7,005	8,896	4,072	15,502	9,612	8,796	14,070	8,603	8,404	9,294	6,536	11,661	8,267	9,322	12,865	8,649	10,135	9,578
Casablanca, Morocco	8,005	2,246	15,973	1,384	5,530	9,812	6,943	2,530	4,835	2,557	1,662	3,236	5,715	18,049	2,022	2,643	17,130	2,144	3,127	2,713
Casper, Wyoming	13,160	7,805	8,048	7,830	2,872	14,907	8,809	7,852	12,873	7,659	7,346	8,441	5,551	12,863	7,243	8,393	14,065	7,656	9,247	8,654
Castries, Saint Lucia	13,787	7,275	10,530	6,600	3,287	9,695	3,597	7,532	8,658	7,418	6,402	8,431	181	16,202	6,629	7,945	16,994	7,084	8,705	8,131
Catbalogan, Philippines	5,626	10,857	9,691	11,691	13,796	13,076	19,132	10,567	12,249	10,617	11,696	9,735	17,211	5,300	11,380	10,312	5,149	11,020	9,789	10,209
Cayenne, French Guiana	13,468	7,471	11,176	6,684	4,542	8,345	2,342	7,754	7,587	7,679	6,605	8,624	1,207	16,353	6,896	8,075	16,692	7,295	8,710	8,214
Cayman Islands (Georgetown)	14,930	8,266	8,658	7,810	2,736	11,402	5,338	8,462	10,872	8,302	7,471	9,320	2,424	14,439	7,584	8,970	15,538	8,072	9,839	9,205
Cazombo, Angola	6,458	7,106	16,807	6,713	11,214	5,019	7,630	7,207	1,188	7,378	7,204	7,091	9,517	13,101	7,436	6,796	11,884	7,179	6,247	6,590
Cebu, Philippines	5,566	10,930	9,746	11,755	13,979	12,881	18,952	10,640	12,140	10,696	11,776	9,800	17,388	5,230	11,465	10,372	5,035	11,095	9,828	10,262
Cedar Rapids, Iowa	13,073	7,082	8,935	6,971	1,700	13,949	7,814	7,177	11,728	6,987	6,509	7,873	4,452	14,030	6,464	7,726	15,243	6,914	8,612	7,987
Changsha, China	4,202	8,656	11,371	9,494	12,181	13,754	17,624	8,365	10,991	8,415	9,494	7,541	15,367	7,502	9,179	8,122	7,308	8,818	7,641	8,029
Channel-Port-aux-Basques, Can.	11,224	4,682	11,540	4,423	1,102	12,737	7,105	4,836	9,201	4,661	3,994	5,650	3,822	16,448	4,017	5,372	17,556	4,497	6,265	5,624
Charleston, South Carolina	13,594	7,075	9,378	6,749	1,321	12,496	6,362	7,236	10,757	7,062	6,350	8,050	3,002	14,945	6,403	7,769	16,158	6,887	8,660	8,018
Charleston, West Virginia	13,126	6,753	9,492	6,512	1,002	13,070	6,949	6,890	10,909	6,709	6,083	7,667	3,544	14,850	6,097	7,433	16,074	6,571	8,328	7,689
Charlotte, North Carolina	13,400	6,944	9,410	6,656	1,162	12,760	6,630	7,094	10,843	6,917	6,243	7,892	3,249	14,893	6,278	7,632	16,114	6,758	8,526	7,885
Charlotte Amalie, U.S.V.I.	13,830	7,190	10,259	6,582	2,725	10,325	4,211	7,430	9,136	7,301	6,332	8,327	814	16,025	6,524	7,880	16,982	6,996	8,684	8,084
Charlottetown, Canada	11,541	5,018	11,214	4,759	764	12,793	7,036	5,170	9,464	4,994	4,331	5,979	3,688	16,233	4,354	5,707	17,384	4,833	6,600	5,959
Chatham, Canada	11,593	5,121	11,060	4,892	682	12,971	7,175	5,263	9,656	5,084	4,455	6,057	3,802	16,034	4,463	5,804	17,184	4,938	6,698	6,058
Chatham Islands (Waitangi)	13,091	19,204	3,834	19,684	14,172	9,102	11,592	18,945	14,536	18,875	19,227	18,264	13,161	3,275	19,059	18,853	3,879	19,237	18,217	18,744
Chengdu, China	3,398	7,890	12,268	8,708	11,903	13,385	16,733	7,603	10,138	7,668	8,746	6,753	14,860	8,276	8,448	7,323	7,973	8,060	6,795	7,214
Chesterfield Inlet, Canada	10,767	5,489	10,282	5,687	2,659	15,347	9,516	5,490	11,222	5,297	5,190	5,996	6,086	14,007	5,011	6,013	14,995	5,364	6,829	6,269
Cheyenne, Wyoming	13,346	7,877	8,008	7,870	2,792	14,688	8,601	7,934	12,816	7,741	7,390	8,546	5,365	12,936	7,301	8,478	14,146	7,723	9,340	8,740
Chiang Mai, Thailand	2,753	8,544	12,575	9,284	13,159	12,043	16,505	8,275	9,507	8,376	9,420	7,382	15,778	7,756	9,168	7,902	7,212	8,730	7,225	7,743
Chibougamau, Canada	11,723	5,493	10,524	5,373	878	13,640	7,727	5,600	10,345	5,412	4,909	6,331	4,299	15,312	4,867	6,148	16,453	5,322	7,039	6,408
Chicago, Illinois	12,976	6,851	9,218	6,706	1,369	13,705	7,576	6,958	11,396	6,770	6,251	7,680	4,184	14,364	6,221	7,507	15,578	6,679	8,397	7,767
Chiclayo, Peru	16,780	10,373	7,879	9,699	5,513	8,963	3,621	10,625	10,529	10,505	9,502	11,525	3,136	13,193	9,720	11,047	13,893	10,181	11,801	11,233
Chihuahua, Mexico	14,737	9,053	7,008	8,929	3,491	13,785	7,956	9,143	13,290	8,952	8,474	9,818	5,095	12,410	8,435	9,692	13,629	8,885	10,574	9,954
Chongquing, China	3,607	8,142	12,011	8,964	12,037	13,455	17,004	7,854	10,373	7,916	8,994	7,008	15,059	8,021	8,692	7,581	7,741	8,310	7,062	7,475
Christchurch, New Zealand	12,217	18,660	4,498	19,458	14,952	9,100	12,254	18,368	14,247	18,398	19,422	17,527	14,019	2,504	19,056	18,077	3,012	18,813	17,353	17,918
Christiansted, U.S.V.I.	13,853	7,223	10,264	6,608	2,794	10,255	4,141	7,465	9,103	7,337	6,363	8,363	750	16,023	6,558	7,912	16,963	7,029	8,712	8,114
Christmas Is. [Indian Ocean]	4,859	11,508	11,004	12,107	16,460	9,846	15,907	11,273	9,975	11,408	12,362	10,379	18,407	5,290	12,179	10,815	4,374	11,703	10,005	10,608
Christmas Is. [Pacific Ocean]	14,056	13,984	2,143	14,342	9,574	13,937	12,178	13,889	19,198	13,716	13,848	14,010	10,826	6,216	13,630	14,306	7,438	13,905	14,851	14,512
Churchill, Canada	11,309	5,943	9,841	6,084	2,423	15,246	9,265	5,961	11,522	5,768	5,588	6,501	5,821	13,889	5,434	6,492	14,950	5,809	7,324	6,750
Cincinnati, Ohio	13,161	6,877	9,304	6,669	1,191	13,299	7,169	7,003	11,156	6,819	6,231	7,760	3,781	14,606	6,229	7,549	15,828	6,698	8,443	7,806
Ciudad Bolivia, Venezuela	14,999	8,426	9,349	7,785	3,769	9,739	3,655	8,673	9,631	8,549	7,561	9,572	1,308	14,984	7,766	9,109	15,808	8,233	9,892	9,305
Ciudad Juarez, Mexico	14,394	8,798	7,201	8,709	3,336	14,065	8,165	8,878	13,249	8,686	8,245	9,533	5,199	12,490	8,192	9,426	13,713	8,635	10,303	9,688
Ciudad Victoria, Mexico	15,202	9,067	7,249	8,825	3,311	12,921	7,080	9,195	12,692	9,012	8,402	9,945	4,322	12,875	8,415	9,741	14,068	8,888	10,636	9,999
Clarksburg, West Virginia	12,983	6,601	9,637	6,361	855	13,075	6,966	6,738	10,796	6,557	5,932	7,516	3,545	14,966	5,945	7,281	16,188	6,419	8,176	7,537
Cleveland, Ohio	12,817	6,520	9,636	6,322	887	13,335	7,232	6,645	10,907	6,461	5,880	7,402	3,807	14,855	5,874	7,191	16,071	6,342	8,085	7,449
Cocos (Keeling) Island	4,321	11,013	11,853	11,523	16,444	9,153	15,073	10,804	9,002	10,957	11,833	9,932	17,475	6,081	11,695	10,310	5,061	11,208	9,457	10,083
Colombo, Sri Lanka	1,533	8,203	14,327	8,715	13,805	9,764	14,265	8,000	7,280	8,157	9,019	7,138	15,031	8,731	8,885	7,498	7,814	8,397	6,643	7,270
Colon, Panama	15,687	8,999	8,412	8,442	3,757	10,418	4,491	9,221	10,663	9,077	8,160	10,107	2,252	14,141	8,321	9,698	15,091	8,803	10,531	9,916
Colorado Springs, Colorado	13,602	8,078	7,836	8,046	2,866	14,516	8,458	8,143	12,892	7,950	7,571	8,769	5,273	12,870	7,492	8,689	14,087	7,922	9,556	8,950
Columbia, South Carolina	13,527	7,052	9,338	6,750	1,274	12,667	6,533	7,206	10,861	7,030	6,343	8,009	3,170	14,860	6,384	7,742	16,078	6,866	8,635	7,994
Columbus, Georgia	13,847	7,430	8,933	7,145	1,648	12,772	6,641	7,577	11,232	7,399	6,733	8,368	3,357	14,471	6,766	8,117	15,686	7,246	9,011	8,370
Columbus, Ohio	13,019	6,716	9,463	6,508	1,036	13,283	7,163	6,844	11,022	6,660	6,070	7,603	3,755	14,741	6,068	7,389	15,962	6,538	8,284	7,647
Conakry, Guinea	9,318	4,954	15,426	4,113	6,639	7,267	4,695	5,224	3,560	5,276	4,397	5,808	5,020	17,585	4,760	5,225	16,451	4,872	5,439	5,219
Concepcion, Chile	16,156	12,453	7,938	11,609	8,772	5,949	3,405	12,745	9,583	12,700	11,621	13,557	5,704	11,415	11,939	12,971	11,592	12,294	13,409	13,052
Concord, New Hampshire	12,222	5,756	10,483	5,504	102	12,934	6,963	5,901	10,076	5,723	5,076	6,696	3,528	15,676	5,095	6,441	16,879	5,573	7,335	6,695
Constantine, Algeria	6,683	1,597	16,951	1,119	6,491	10,065	8,131	1,794	4,588	1,916	1,616	2,206	7,038	16,719	1,828	1,641	15,869	1,618	1,874	1,608
Copenhagen, Denmark	6,430	660	15,461	1,522	5,904	12,235	9,719	402	6,648	350	1,417	831	7,699	15,571	1,106	770	15,280	769	1,575	1,013
Coppermine, Canada	10,357	6,009	9,814	6,378	3,841	16,561	10,700	5,945	12,033	5,762	5,892	6,270	7,257	12,884	5,650	6,417	13,814	5,920	7,138	6,655

Distances in Kilometers	Bombay, India	Bonn, West Germany	Bora Bora (Vaitape)	Bordeaux, France	Boston, Massachusetts	Bouvet Island	Brasilia, Brazil	Braunschweig, West Germany	Brazzaville, Congo	Bremerhaven, West Germany	Brest, France	Brest, USSR	Bridgetown, Barbados	Brisbane, Australia	Bristol, United Kingdom	Brno, Czechoslovakia	Broken Hill, Australia	Brussels, Belgium	Bucharest, Romania	Budapest, Hungary
Coquimbo, Chile	16,217	11,777	8,208	10,948	8,008	6,395	2,862	12,067	9,456	12,010	10,930	12,904	4,929	12,095	11,238	12,327	12,333	11,611	12,828	12,427
Cordoba, Argentina	15,514	11,465	8,849	10,614	8,198	5,814	2,391	11,758	8,768	11,721	10,646	12,556	4,948	12,392	10,972	11,967	12,495	11,311	12,394	12,043
Cordoba, Spain	7,674	1,709	16,019	848	5,528	10,259	7,458	1,993	5,106	2,020	1,169	2,717	6,056	17,651	1,517	2,126	16,885	1,609	2,673	2,215
Cork, Ireland	7,780	1,091	14,929	979	4,712	11,838	8,412	1,299	6,619	1,164	482	2,191	6,256	16,889	410	1,795	16,718	898	2,673	2,034
Corner Brook, Canada	11,053	4,529	11,651	4,292	1,254	12,813	7,238	4,678	9,154	4,502	3,855	5,486	3,978	16,451	3,868	5,216	17,524	4,346	6,110	5,469
Corrientes, Argentina	15,026	10,805	9,461	9,949	7,833	5,791	1,716	11,098	8,230	11,066	9,994	11,887	4,489	13,041	10,325	11,297	13,090	10,654	11,716	11,369
Cosenza, Italy	5,844	1,459	17,228	1,518	7,026	10,459	9,023	1,507	4,825	1,688	1,940	1,535	7,890	15,839	1,989	1,101	15,068	1,584	996	939
Craiova, Romania	5,328	1,441	16,894	1,929	7,224	11,113	9,831	1,319	5,448	1,510	2,210	866	8,484	15,163	2,112	770	14,521	1,627	184	509
Cruzeiro do Sul, Brazil	16,093	9,943	8,627	9,215	5,538	8,416	2,835	10,210	9,723	10,107	9,066	11,104	2,705	13,761	9,315	10,591	14,337	9,756	11,292	10,757
Cuiaba, Brazil	14,608	9,565	10,116	8,726	6,597	6,652	876	9,856	7,895	9,809	8,730	10,680	3,196	14,305	9,050	10,100	14,426	9,404	10,603	10,197
Curitiba, Brazil	14,061	10,084	10,440	9,216	7,832	5,354	1,076	10,376	7,257	10,365	9,313	11,117	4,407	13,686	9,660	10,523	13,556	9,947	10,870	10,571
Cuzco, Peru	16,232	10,409	8,527	9,648	6,188	7,851	2,603	10,684	9,613	10,593	9,535	11,570	3,244	13,375	9,802	11,035	13,849	10,227	11,689	11,185
Dacca, Bangladesh	1,897	7,545	13,531	8,265	12,446	11,931	15,594	7,282	8,701	7,392	8,420	6,384	14,799	8,792	8,183	6,890	8,210	7,733	6,192	6,723
Dakar, Senegal	9,523	4,569	15,142	3,704	5,954	7,907	4,752	4,852	4,173	4,878	3,926	5,519	4,557	18,283	4,291	4,926	17,144	4,463	5,260	4,957
Dallas, Texas	14,174	8,144	7,993	7,972	2,498	13,530	7,478	8,254	12,333	8,066	7,527	8,973	4,359	13,395	7,509	8,802	14,617	7,971	9,693	9,063
Damascus, Syria	3,963	3,047	17,961	3,390	8,823	10,242	10,446	2,933	4,730	3,122	3,754	2,301	9,757	14,008	3,704	2,384	13,169	3,228	1,499	2,123
Danang, Vietnam	3,765	9,401	11,553	10,177	13,535	12,403	17,481	9,123	10,461	9,207	10,272	8,243	16,517	6,827	9,997	8,787	6,387	9,581	8,157	8,645
Dar es Salaam, Tanzania	4,655	7,085	17,160	6,968	12,187	6,179	9,516	7,092	2,674	7,283	7,457	6,693	11,148	11,962	7,589	6,584	10,752	7,213	5,826	6,335
Darwin, Australia	7,250	13,421	8,308	14,192	16,080	11,107	16,877	13,141	12,671	13,220	14,290	12,263	18,900	2,848	14,006	12,804	2,415	13,599	12,139	12,655
Davao, Philippines	5,851	11,330	9,461	12,153	14,278	12,685	18,820	11,041	12,318	11,098	12,178	10,198	17,703	4,831	11,868	10,768	4,634	11,497	10,213	10,655
David, Panama	15,950	9,256	8,115	8,714	3,921	10,496	4,653	9,474	10,936	9,327	8,423	10,355	2,547	13,846	8,577	9,958	14,806	9,061	10,797	10,178
Dawson, Canada	10,390	6,947	8,997	7,405	4,852	17,679	11,643	6,845	13,064	6,673	6,932	7,040	8,208	11,709	6,661	7,273	12,650	6,881	7,908	7,492
Dawson Creek, Canada	11,633	7,241	8,539	7,509	3,793	16,513	10,379	7,206	13,070	7,018	7,013	7,597	6,990	12,293	6,812	7,702	13,378	7,132	8,459	7,948
Denpasar, Indonesia	5,565	12,023	10,067	12,710	16,220	10,600	16,735	11,764	11,037	11,875	12,897	10,865	19,274	4,485	12,666	11,356	3,740	12,213	10,608	11,174
Denver, Colorado	13,502	8,008	7,893	7,987	2,848	14,595	8,526	8,069	12,877	7,876	7,510	8,688	5,322	12,882	7,427	8,614	14,097	7,853	9,479	8,876
Derby, Australia	6,855	13,342	8,929	14,031	16,900	10,263	16,232	13,081	11,814	13,189	14,217	12,183	19,435	3,219	13,980	12,678	2,418	13,532	11,928	12,496
Des Moines, Iowa	13,158	7,225	8,776	7,126	1,866	14,035	7,900	7,316	11,895	7,125	6,662	8,003	4,559	13,865	6,611	7,865	15,079	7,059	8,748	8,126
Detroit, Michigan	12,783	6,541	9,575	6,365	987	13,480	7,374	6,659	11,015	6,473	5,917	7,403	3,951	14,744	5,901	7,206	15,957	6,365	8,099	7,465
Dhahran, Saudi Arabia	2,466	4,533	17,519	4,939	10,312	10,001	11,564	4,380	5,054	4,560	5,286	3,621	11,271	12,503	5,207	3,841	11,623	4,722	2,949	3,590
Diego Garcia Island	2,909	8,953	14,497	9,262	14,735	7,997	12,978	8,811	6,333	8,992	9,659	8,044	14,750	8,717	9,617	8,269	7,606	9,137	7,374	8,014
Dijon, France	6,818	409	15,983	512	5,797	11,278	8,751	679	5,803	738	721	1,444	7,041	16,472	718	887	15,974	394	1,663	1,060
Dili, Indonesia	6,538	12,725	8,976	13,484	15,923	11,206	17,221	12,448	12,170	12,534	13,598	11,565	19,265	3,568	13,324	12,099	3,067	12,906	11,423	11,944
Djibouti, Djibouti	3,286	5,436	18,335	5,549	11,054	8,216	10,475	5,375	3,550	5,569	5,996	4,821	11,080	12,554	6,036	4,833	11,464	5,595	3,988	4,572
Dnepropetrovsk, USSR	4,714	2,020	16,411	2,726	7,622	11,782	10,795	1,782	6,147	1,925	2,888	900	9,266	14,279	2,687	1,347	13,749	2,213	815	1,190
Dobo, Indonesia	7,262	13,042	8,136	13,862	15,252	11,936	17,610	12,753	13,159	12,809	13,889	11,907	18,309	3,122	13,576	12,475	2,995	13,208	11,894	12,355
Doha, Qatar	2,303	4,711	17,425	5,119	10,488	9,960	11,681	4,555	5,102	4,734	5,466	3,790	11,443	12,332	5,385	4,017	11,446	4,899	3,126	3,767
Donetsk, USSR	4,510	2,234	16,407	2,940	7,813	11,804	10,985	1,994	6,193	2,134	3,103	1,106	9,481	14,070	2,899	1,562	13,534	2,428	985	1,401
Dover, Delaware	12,782	6,300	10,015	6,020	519	12,797	6,727	6,451	10,380	6,274	5,602	7,252	3,285	15,382	5,634	6,989	16,604	6,115	7,882	7,241
Dresden, East Germany	6,239	469	15,964	1,270	6,192	11,732	9,510	260	6,131	449	1,344	699	7,724	15,721	1,139	291	15,286	662	1,180	553
Dubayy, United Arab Emir.	1,937	4,965	17,061	5,417	10,721	10,128	12,054	4,793	5,419	4,967	5,745	3,994	11,794	11,979	5,645	4,265	11,116	5,157	3,382	4,021
Dublin, Ireland	7,618	959	14,946	1,032	4,823	11,979	8,631	1,136	6,695	984	563	2,014	6,457	16,671	326	1,654	16,508	776	2,543	1,902
Duluth, Minnesota	12,569	6,730	9,196	6,686	1,737	14,339	8,218	6,805	11,676	6,613	6,210	7,465	4,811	14,038	6,135	7,353	15,225	6,570	8,229	7,615
Dunedin, New Zealand	12,085	18,675	4,775	19,312	15,200	8,823	12,166	18,395	13,938	18,462	19,541	17,515	14,091	2,556	19,208	18,027	2,932	18,854	17,240	17,838
Durango, Mexico	15,240	9,381	6,804	9,198	3,698	13,306	7,579	9,489	13,246	9,301	8,758	10,198	4,885	12,360	8,745	10,038	13,564	9,207	10,928	10,298
Durban, South Africa	7,020	9,232	14,866	8,869	13,113	3,513	8,107	9,314	3,281	9,491	9,361	9,106	10,789	11,167	9,589	8,871	9,985	9,315	8,241	8,650
Dushanbe, USSR	2,205	4,925	15,386	5,640	10,171	12,041	13,404	4,668	7,258	4,786	5,800	3,768	12,181	11,396	5,573	4,265	10,832	5,115	3,583	4,098
East London, South Africa	7,478	9,502	14,521	9,092	13,071	3,059	7,769	9,600	3,445	9,773	9,579	9,440	10,571	11,155	9,823	9,177	9,998	9,575	8,581	8,963
Easter Island (Hanga Roa)	19,071	14,140	4,508	13,529	8,646	8,935	6,439	14,367	13,149	14,223	13,288	15,252	6,984	9,342	13,465	14,835	10,065	13,944	15,636	15,042
Echo Bay, Canada	10,530	6,241	9,580	6,604	3,887	16,670	10,732	6,178	12,255	5,995	6,116	6,503	7,288	12,720	5,877	6,651	13,675	6,151	7,371	6,889
Edinburgh, United Kingdom	7,414	895	14,891	1,247	4,954	12,248	8,976	984	6,882	802	841	1,802	6,748	16,324	499	1,531	16,194	755	2,425	1,791
Edmonton, Canada	11,948	7,188	8,582	7,386	3,343	16,013	9,879	7,179	12,849	6,987	6,889	7,638	6,496	12,642	6,715	7,693	13,759	7,066	8,487	7,946
El Aaiun, Morocco	8,696	3,130	15,608	2,261	5,447	9,180	6,053	3,417	4,634	3,435	2,475	4,131	5,065	18,667	2,840	3,537	17,520	3,017	3,984	3,600
Elat, Israel	4,002	3,304	18,412	3,541	9,035	9,786	10,198	3,223	4,291	3,416	3,944	2,671	9,738	14,036	3,935	2,677	13,125	3,474	1,827	2,416
Elazig, Turkey	3,906	2,846	17,329	3,345	8,609	10,872	10,851	2,677	5,357	2,853	3,639	1,916	9,863	13,852	3,526	2,145	13,122	3,038	1,266	1,902
Eniwetok Atoll, Marshall Isls.	9,547	12,703	5,937	13,532	11,953	14,894	16,740	12,440	16,310	12,378	13,243	11,922	14,664	4,429	12,879	12,489	5,295	12,777	12,404	12,526
Erfurt, East Germany	6,425	278	15,888	1,102	6,024	11,706	9,346	147	6,136	331	1,154	886	7,534	15,899	951	447	15,476	471	1,341	702
Erzurum, Turkey	3,808	2,904	17,125	3,451	8,636	11,062	11,054	2,716	5,569	2,885	3,721	1,911	9,994	13,701	3,586	2,200	13,003	3,098	1,349	1,969
Esfahan, Iran	2,603	4,131	17,066	4,648	9,853	10,700	11,825	3,943	5,606	4,110	4,941	3,119	11,143	12,602	4,814	3,427	11,828	4,325	2,565	3,193
Essen, West Germany	6,710	80	15,700	926	5,746	11,741	9,147	259	6,224	257	892	1,151	7,264	16,123	667	728	15,743	200	1,618	977
Eucla, Australia	8,196	14,856	8,080	15,445	17,897	9,130	14,737	14,616	11,963	14,743	15,712	13,718	17,772	2,380	15,523	14,165	1,189	15,051	13,351	13,957
Fargo, North Dakota	12,640	6,975	8,909	6,968	2,093	14,617	8,484	7,037	12,024	6,844	6,487	7,665	5,101	13,683	6,397	7,582	14,868	6,820	8,449	7,844
Faroe Islands (Torshavn)	7,620	1,514	14,260	1,954	4,661	12,944	9,349	1,499	7,589	1,306	1,523	2,124	6,844	15,890	1,204	2,031	15,967	1,417	2,885	2,290
Florence, Italy	6,306	835	16,589	950	6,409	10,908	8,917	947	5,335	1,105	1,318	1,310	7,480	16,162	1,342	731	15,520	943	1,190	738
Florianopolis, Brazil	14,013	10,252	10,420	9,382	8,081	5,125	1,308	10,544	7,223	10,538	9,493	11,268	4,657	13,491	9,843	10,674	13,332	10,119	10,994	10,714
Fort George, Canada	11,502	5,514	10,387	5,490	1,404	14,174	8,263	5,590	10,670	5,398	5,009	6,262	4,830	14,897	4,923	6,138	15,999	5,354	7,016	6,400
Fort McMurray, Canada	11,607	6,827	8,942	7,046	3,262	16,049	9,938	6,813	12,556	6,622	6,549	7,262	6,521	12,851	6,366	7,324	13,936	6,709	8,113	7,576
Fort Nelson, Canada	11,267	7,039	8,760	7,354	3,961	16,762	10,645	6,990	12,966	6,804	6,861	7,340	7,233	12,263	6,642	7,473	13,309	6,940	8,207	7,714
Fort Severn, Canada	11,499	5,827	10,001	5,888	1,928	14,751	8,776	5,872	11,202	5,679	5,397	6,477	5,333	14,308	5,276	6,414	15,399	5,680	7,271	6,675
Fort Smith, Arkansas	13,842	7,781	8,337	7,615	2,162	13,593	7,491	7,890	12,071	7,702	7,168	8,610	4,274	13,677	7,147	8,439	14,901	7,608	9,329	8,699
Fort Vermilion, Canada	11,392	6,853	8,924	7,120	3,568	16,375	10,269	6,821	12,689	6,632	6,624	7,224	6,850	12,623	6,423	7,320	13,684	6,744	8,084	7,567
Fort Wayne, Indiana	12,982	6,764	9,357	6,588	1,179	13,496	7,372	6,881	11,197	6,695	6,141	7,622	3,971	14,566	6,124	7,428	15,783	6,588	8,321	7,687
Fort-Chimo, Canada	10,751	4,706	11,166	4,714	1,761	14,038	8,402	4,777	10,036	4,585	4,227	5,450	5,048	15,342	4,126	5,325	16,333	4,549	6,203	5,587
Fort-de-France, Martinique	13,757	7,231	10,539	6,562	3,223	9,754	3,659	7,487	8,675	7,373	6,359	8,387	230	16,225	6,584	7,904	17,033	7,040	8,667	8,091
Fortaleza, Brazil	12,396	7,431	12,363	6,566	6,068	6,774	1,687	7,723	5,972	7,706	6,651	8,490	2,985	16,339	6,997	7,898	16,057	7,289	8,325	7,967
Frankfort, Kentucky	13,264	6,968	9,231	6,752	1,260	13,245	7,112	7,096	11,192	6,913	6,316	7,857	3,737	14,567	6,318	7,642	15,790	6,789	8,536	7,899
Frankfurt am Main, W. Ger.	6,576	132	15,888	911	5,913	11,599	9,154	272	6,059	382	976	1,073	7,356	16,090	807	583	15,656	319	1,457	817
Fredericton, Canada	11,742	5,262	10,943	5,022	533	12,933	7,094	5,406	9,727	5,228	4,588	6,203	3,703	15,985	4,602	5,946	17,153	5,079	6,841	6,200
Freeport, Bahamas	14,120	7,495	9,210	7,087	1,894	11,882	5,749	7,678	10,631	7,514	6,723	8,523	2,492	14,926	6,814	8,197	16,095	7,303	9,077	8,438
Freetown, Sierra Leone	9,305	5,044	15,447	4,208	6,754	7,147	4,671	5,313	3,468	5,367	4,499	5,883	5,090	17,462	4,862	5,302	16,333	4,965	5,498	5,292
Frobisher Bay, Canada	10,247	4,484	11,310	4,617	2,386	14,486	8,995	4,516	10,123	4,322	4,120	5,110	5,666	15,008	3,964	5,054	15,903	4,345	5,906	5,314
Frunze, USSR	2,659	5,042	14,760	5,820	9,958	12,719	13,828	4,766	7,911	4,859	5,915	3,883	12,256	11,171	5,652	4,429	10,726	5,224	3,858	4,298
Fukuoka, Japan	5,898	9,143	9,933	10,014	11,316	15,322	18,026	8,853	12,595	8,850	9,882	8,157	14,731	7,170	9,529	8,750	7,346	9,269	8,481	8,725
Funafuti Atoll, Tuvalu	12,030	15,267	3,282	15,980	12,272	13,017	14,189	15,044	17,742	14,939	15,570	14,684	13,604	3,458	15,242	15,210	4,677	15,289	15,256	15,293
Funchal, Madeira Island	8,875	2,810	15,161	1,955	4,826	9,842	6,294	3,103	5,313	3,082	2,037	3,907	4,844	18,898	2,393	3,329	17,990	2,665	3,920	3,443
Fuzhou, China	4,820	9,224	10,706	10,073	12,353	13,987	18,272	8,931	11,624	8,970	10,045	8,128	15,668	6,943	9,720	8,715	6,839	9,379	8,269	8,634
Gaborone, Botswana	7,013	8,554	15,442	8,153	12,364	3,793	7,691	8,653	2,528	8,825	8,641	8,506	10,172	11,926	8,881	8,233	10,739	8,628	7,651	8,021
Galapagos Islands (Santa Cruz)	17,286	10,591	6,950	10,046	5,142	10,196	4,954	10,807	11,753	10,657	9,759	11,684	3,720	12,587	9,911	11,293	13,494	10,395	12,132	11,514
Gander, Canada	10,872	4,313	11,894	4,057	1,472	12,677	7,200	4,469	8,920	4,295	3,624	5,288	4,002	16,655	3,647	5,004	17,694	4,127	5,896	5,255
Gangtok, India	1,861	7,130	13,738	7,862	12,013	12,137	15,376	6,864	8,598	6,970	8,006	5,968	14,379	9,175	7,762	6,482	8,624	7,317	5,805	6,321
Garyarsa, China	1,605	6,216	14,525	6,934	11,296	12,039	14,524	5,955	7,944	6,069	7,091	5,057	13,472	10,111	6,858	5,559	9,540	6,405	4,869	5,392
Gaspe, Canada	11,393	4,953	11,178	4,752	883	13,085	7,342	5,088	9,618	4,907	4,306	5,872	3,988	16,030	4,301	5,631	17,150	4,773	6,526	5,887
Gauhati, India	2,099	7,436	13,421	8,179	12,214	12,229	15,700	7,167	8,879	7,270	8,312	6,274	14,675	8,850	8,062	6,795	8,320	7,622	6,129	6,639
Gdansk, Poland	6,015	881	15,726	1,738	6,318	12,141	9,981	589	6,504	667	1,733	419	8,076	15,278	1,460	590	14,918	1,045	1,226	763
Geneva, Switzerland	6,725	509	16,135	547	5,929	11,156	8,744	746	5,662	836	841	1,433	7,109	16,448	867	853	15,904	533	1,571	995
Genoa, Italy	6,495	716	16,425	756	6,213	10,967	8,805	881	5,429	1,016	1,122	1,385	7,302	16,317	1,161	791	15,702	793	1,363	856
Georgetown, Guyana	13,947	7,698	10,611	6,956	4,140	8,852	2,741	7,970	8,253	7,877	6,822	8,860	715	16,015	7,085	8,336	16,566	7,514	9,030	8,497
Geraldton, Australia	6,932	13,628	9,490	14,131	18,415	8,697	14,732	13,414	10,693	13,562	14,449	12,533	18,173	3,760	14,309	12,925	2,597	13,823	12,074	12,700
Ghanzi, Botswana	7,143	8,137	15,734	7,695	11,820	3,963	7,323	8,252	2,039	8,419	8,179	8,163	9,678	12,469	8,432	7,854	11,282	8,201	7,321	7,654
Ghat, Libya	6,451	2,872	17,930	2,408	7,494	8,821	7,749	3,031	3,281	3,176	2,901	3,222	7,392	16,320	3,135	2,748	15,231	2,915	2,595	2,621
Gibraltar	7,755	1,904	16,058	1,047	5,573	10,070	7,285	2,186	4,962	2,218	1,364	2,892	5,967	17,770	1,716	2,299	16,940	1,808	2,808	2,375

Distances in Kilometers	Bombay, India	Bonn, West Germany	Bora Bora (Vaitape)	Bordeaux, France	Boston, Massachusetts	Bouvet Island	Brasilia, Brazil	Braunschweig, West Germany	Brazzaville, Congo	Bremerhaven, West Germany	Brest, France	Brest, USSR	Bridgetown, Barbados	Brisbane, Australia	Bristol, United Kingdom	Brno, Czechoslovakia	Broken Hill, Australia	Brussels, Belgium	Bucharest, Romania	Budapest, Hungary
Gijon, Spain	7,668	1,254	15,636	433	5,195	10,890	7,852	1,546	5,697	1,527	549	2,376	6,133	17,403	910	1,820	16,876	1,109	2,535	1,974
Gisborne, New Zealand	12,604	18,489	3,832	19,310	14,317	9,676	12,321	18,214	14,933	18,167	18,905	17,532	13,713	2,630	18,583	18,125	3,386	18,566	17,606	18,051
Glasgow, United Kingdom	7,480	944	14,852	1,251	4,892	12,244	8,925	1,044	6,898	864	827	1,867	6,683	16,373	500	1,590	16,255	797	2,484	1,849
Godthab, Greenland	9,636	3,663	12,137	3,793	2,734	13,980	8,879	3,705	9,339	3,511	3,296	4,337	5,713	15,561	3,136	4,248	16,302	3,521	5,111	4,509
Gomez Palacio, Mexico	15,062	9,174	7,000	8,994	3,497	13,360	7,563	9,282	13,102	9,094	8,553	9,992	4,789	12,531	8,539	9,831	13,739	9,001	10,721	10,091
Goose Bay, Canada	11,960	7,912	7,878	8,198	4,317	16,773	10,671	7,868	13,761	7,682	7,702	8,225	7,360	11,654	7,496	8,356	12,766	7,808	9,092	8,598
Gorki, USSR	4,793	2,492	15,391	3,334	7,496	12,822	11,570	2,202	7,208	2,265	3,342	1,399	9,625	13,666	3,049	1,994	13,338	2,658	1,826	1,960
Goteborg, Sweden	6,523	839	15,237	1,673	5,783	12,458	9,812	614	6,878	510	1,506	976	7,692	15,490	1,167	997	15,263	912	1,771	1,233
Granada, Spain	7,589	1,729	16,138	885	5,647	10,178	7,476	2,008	4,996	2,047	1,244	2,703	6,136	17,589	1,584	2,109	16,791	1,642	2,620	2,184
Grand Turk, Turks & Caicos	14,068	7,372	9,744	6,845	2,317	10,972	4,838	7,590	9,819	7,444	6,543	8,473	1,534	15,529	6,693	8,074	16,601	7,177	8,918	8,296
Graz, Austria	6,030	735	16,420	1,264	6,512	11,306	9,389	678	5,687	871	1,498	817	7,825	15,747	1,396	253	15,189	914	878	279
Green Bay, Wisconsin	12,712	6,672	9,336	6,565	1,390	13,933	7,815	6,768	11,396	6,578	6,102	7,469	4,404	14,347	6,054	7,317	15,549	6,504	8,203	7,578
Grenoble, France	6,755	628	16,201	497	5,948	11,040	8,647	865	5,558	955	857	1,527	7,058	16,526	930	940	15,952	638	1,611	1,060
Guadalajara, Mexico	15,601	9,600	6,700	9,371	3,857	12,930	7,275	9,721	13,160	9,536	8,944	10,457	4,719	12,348	8,951	10,269	13,534	9,422	11,162	10,527
Guam (Agana)	7,664	11,795	7,731	12,666	12,827	14,360	18,647	11,507	14,396	11,498	12,512	10,816	16,037	4,620	12,153	11,409	5,038	11,917	11,110	11,380
Guantanamo, Cuba	14,461	7,767	9,296	7,263	2,495	11,095	4,969	7,977	10,229	7,826	6,948	8,853	1,834	15,081	7,085	8,470	16,157	7,572	9,323	8,697
Guatemala City, Guatemala	15,870	9,288	7,560	8,874	3,596	11,570	5,768	9,468	11,837	9,301	8,516	10,304	3,342	13,344	8,608	9,990	14,437	9,096	10,871	10,232
Guayaquil, Ecuador	16,517	9,978	8,020	9,335	5,010	9,375	3,810	10,223	10,569	10,096	9,113	11,121	2,800	13,489	9,316	10,662	14,260	9,784	11,442	10,857
Guiyang, China	3,569	8,402	11,943	9,214	12,368	13,214	17,143	8,116	10,369	8,184	9,260	7,260	15,375	7,770	8,965	7,827	7,452	8,573	7,278	7,711
Gur'yev, USSR	3,659	3,256	15,981	3,996	8,616	12,144	12,017	2,995	6,728	3,113	4,131	2,096	10,511	13,007	3,900	2,609	12,499	3,445	2,018	2,462
Haifa, Israel	4,063	3,023	18,077	3,330	8,786	10,134	10,309	2,921	4,604	3,112	3,707	2,327	9,657	14,112	3,671	2,372	13,256	3,199	1,501	2,111
Haikou, China	3,928	9,195	11,437	9,997	13,093	12,888	17,682	8,911	10,704	8,983	10,058	8,047	16,178	6,989	9,767	8,607	6,643	9,369	8,028	8,482
Haiphong, Vietnam	3,544	8,886	11,827	9,676	13,001	12,723	17,293	8,605	10,330	8,684	9,754	7,732	15,964	7,316	9,472	8,285	6,920	9,064	7,683	8,152
Hakodate, Japan	6,812	8,816	9,460	9,672	10,160	16,604	17,011	8,540	13,212	8,499	9,451	7,973	13,586	7,771	9,087	8,547	8,161	8,911	8,458	8,575
Halifax, Canada	11,696	5,145	11,140	4,861	654	12,672	6,878	5,304	9,467	5,130	4,441	6,122	3,518	16,257	4,477	5,838	17,431	4,959	6,730	6,088
Hamburg, West Germany	6,544	371	15,602	1,235	5,843	11,986	9,449	147	6,427	94	1,164	936	7,501	15,831	885	668	15,494	491	1,548	930
Hamilton, Bermuda	12,766	6,078	10,702	5,616	1,249	11,605	5,614	6,283	9,334	6,129	5,275	7,154	2,189	16,360	5,396	6,783	17,562	5,884	7,646	7,014
Hamilton, New Zealand	12,354	18,293	3,994	19,151	14,484	9,757	12,562	18,010	14,915	17,980	18,825	17,294	13,967	2,371	18,477	17,885	3,144	18,391	17,348	17,801
Hangzhou, China	4,917	8,901	10,744	9,760	11,883	14,390	18,003	8,608	11,683	8,637	9,706	7,830	15,208	7,284	9,373	8,421	7,241	9,050	8,024	8,355
Hannover, West Germany	6,540	257	15,709	1,128	5,877	11,853	9,358	57	6,298	152	1,100	954	7,463	15,911	852	601	15,540	410	1,494	862
Hanoi, Vietnam	3,457	8,817	11,916	9,603	12,979	12,683	17,205	8,536	10,244	8,617	9,686	7,662	15,913	7,391	9,406	8,212	6,983	8,995	7,606	8,078
Harare, Zimbabwe	6,120	7,949	16,193	7,644	12,309	4,700	8,353	8,016	2,281	8,197	8,140	7,780	10,525	12,004	8,344	7,560	10,786	8,043	6,913	7,334
Harbin, China	5,732	7,843	10,675	8,712	10,088	15,959	16,644	7,557	11,999	7,539	8,548	6,917	13,457	8,539	8,190	7,504	8,733	7,958	7,335	7,506
Harrisburg, Pennsylvania	12,740	6,307	9,953	6,053	540	12,965	6,892	6,450	10,500	6,271	5,627	7,239	3,451	15,263	5,647	6,991	16,483	6,124	7,885	7,245
Hartford, Connecticut	12,406	5,928	10,343	5,663	149	12,868	6,862	6,077	10,156	5,899	5,240	6,875	3,420	15,604	5,265	6,615	16,817	5,744	7,509	6,868
Havana, Cuba	14,631	8,016	8,730	7,606	2,376	11,802	5,710	8,199	10,984	8,033	7,244	9,041	2,647	14,478	7,335	8,718	15,624	7,824	9,598	8,959
Helena, Montana	12,728	7,747	8,044	7,861	3,256	15,519	9,412	7,765	13,127	7,571	7,367	8,284	6,122	12,536	7,228	8,294	13,712	7,612	9,117	8,551
Helsinki, Finland	5,928	1,534	15,151	2,404	6,347	12,851	10,600	1,250	7,195	1,236	2,292	902	8,454	14,698	1,961	1,331	14,480	1,655	1,752	1,461
Hengyang, China	4,155	8,746	11,376	9,579	12,327	13,622	17,664	8,456	10,955	8,509	9,589	7,624	15,501	7,412	9,277	8,203	7,196	8,910	7,706	8,105
Herat, Afghanistan	2,002	4,751	16,108	5,380	10,274	11,329	12,819	4,521	6,512	4,665	5,606	3,636	11,940	11,748	5,425	4,058	11,067	4,946	3,275	3,856
Hermosillo, Mexico	14,674	9,288	6,683	9,219	3,858	14,137	8,397	9,359	13,741	9,167	8,752	9,992	5,574	11,983	8,690	9,906	13,205	9,128	10,776	10,168
Hiroshima, Japan	6,088	9,166	9,788	10,037	11,175	15,519	17,942	8,877	12,762	8,868	9,889	8,201	14,596	7,186	9,533	8,792	7,405	9,287	8,552	8,776
Hiva Oa (Atuona)	16,457	14,516	1,565	14,464	8,987	12,068	9,843	14,557	16,785	14,363	14,003	15,062	9,134	7,347	13,939	15,091	8,460	14,365	15,911	15,350
Ho Chi Minh City, Vietnam	3,746	9,755	11,575	10,497	14,119	11,832	17,227	9,485	10,257	9,580	10,631	8,593	16,971	6,549	10,375	9,115	6,003	9,941	8,434	8,956
Hobart, Australia	10,227	16,903	6,418	17,449	16,900	8,688	13,322	16,662	12,912	16,786	17,754	15,764	15,816	1,786	17,569	16,210	1,324	17,098	15,382	15,998
Hohhot, China	4,406	7,506	11,744	8,368	10,792	14,662	16,610	7,213	10,854	7,238	8,306	6,449	13,972	8,685	7,972	7,042	8,617	7,653	6,693	6,989
Hong Kong	4,311	9,250	11,105	10,074	12,831	13,328	18,015	8,961	11,110	9,020	10,099	8,118	16,037	6,911	9,792	8,692	6,664	9,416	8,164	8,585
Honiara, Solomon Islands	10,054	14,797	5,287	15,662	13,870	12,595	15,874	14,514	15,831	14,487	15,448	13,852	15,701	2,128	15,082	14,445	3,141	14,903	14,135	14,419
Honolulu, Hawaii	12,928	11,889	4,238	12,328	8,191	16,007	12,669	11,776	17,982	11,609	11,843	11,871	10,326	7,558	11,592	12,176	8,748	11,825	12,714	12,378
Houston, Texas	14,467	8,312	7,925	8,094	2,583	13,189	7,164	8,435	12,242	8,251	7,661	9,180	4,115	13,439	7,664	8,982	14,653	8,134	9,876	9,240
Huambo, Angola	7,173	7,081	16,496	6,585	10,698	4,752	6,857	7,219	938	7,376	7,061	7,223	8,797	13,609	7,329	6,861	12,410	7,129	6,416	6,679
Hubli, India	471	7,160	15,021	7,703	12,744	10,248	13,950	6,951	6,946	7,105	7,988	6,083	14,137	9,637	7,842	6,457	8,787	7,356	5,614	6,234
Hugh Town, United Kingdom	7,649	958	15,184	712	4,914	11,602	8,342	1,206	6,353	1,103	215	2,105	6,311	16,963	314	1,656	16,688	764	2,511	1,879
Hull, Canada	12,201	5,869	10,252	5,684	507	13,339	7,337	5,994	10,425	5,810	5,237	6,754	3,895	15,308	5,225	6,540	16,498	5,692	7,434	6,798
Hyderabad, India	621	7,223	14,701	7,812	12,693	10,632	14,329	6,999	7,340	7,144	8,069	6,116	14,317	9,445	7,900	6,525	8,650	7,418	5,708	6,313
Hyderabad, Pakistan	845	5,863	15,763	6,442	11,432	10,792	13,362	5,646	6,601	5,797	6,703	4,772	12,959	10,789	6,543	5,163	10,019	6,059	4,339	4,947
Igloolik, Canada	10,001	4,819	10,954	5,099	3,072	15,330	9,815	4,796	10,723	4,605	4,606	5,254	6,445	14,193	4,391	5,305	15,052	4,708	6,099	5,557
Iloilo, Philippines	5,413	10,810	9,898	11,631	13,968	12,836	18,855	10,521	11,994	10,580	11,659	9,676	17,362	5,353	11,351	10,246	5,130	10,977	9,693	10,133
Indianapolis, Indiana	13,148	6,926	9,213	6,741	1,299	13,449	7,318	7,045	11,293	6,860	6,297	7,789	3,936	14,471	6,284	7,592	15,691	6,750	8,486	7,851
Innsbruck, Austria	6,337	497	16,263	964	6,232	11,296	9,139	560	5,722	727	1,194	1,036	7,520	16,032	1,115	444	15,495	651	1,182	581
Inuvik, Canada	10,086	6,406	9,524	6,865	4,602	17,328	11,452	6,305	12,523	6,133	6,393	6,515	8,008	12,162	6,121	6,738	13,059	6,339	7,385	6,959
Invercargill, New Zealand	11,929	18,557	4,949	19,139	15,376	8,740	12,222	18,286	13,800	18,368	19,433	17,395	14,222	2,493	19,144	17,890	2,803	18,743	17,085	17,692
Inverness, United Kingdom	7,478	1,052	14,723	1,428	4,859	12,425	9,060	1,107	7,066	918	1,009	1,878	6,755	16,230	678	1,656	16,159	925	2,544	1,918
Iquitos, Peru	15,978	9,654	8,673	8,953	5,113	8,806	3,075	9,915	9,826	9,804	8,779	10,813	2,398	13,976	9,013	10,316	14,626	9,464	11,046	10,492
Iraklion, Greece	5,009	2,243	17,897	2,419	7,920	10,162	9,544	2,209	4,503	2,402	2,829	1,866	8,711	15,052	2,843	1,690	14,207	2,399	1,014	1,442
Irkutsk, USSR	4,597	6,213	12,389	7,083	9,510	15,026	15,280	5,922	10,316	5,929	6,981	5,215	12,601	10,025	6,637	5,808	10,005	6,348	5,576	5,787
Islamabad, Pakistan	1,633	5,569	15,160	6,263	10,829	11,819	13,833	5,317	7,383	5,440	6,441	4,417	12,818	10,803	6,223	4,899	10,197	5,761	4,182	4,722
Istanbul, Turkey	4,818	2,000	17,288	2,434	7,783	10,854	10,087	1,876	5,204	2,065	2,750	1,296	8,950	14,751	2,668	1,327	14,038	2,185	446	1,067
Ivujivik, Canada	10,625	4,980	10,812	5,111	2,275	14,749	9,056	5,008	10,589	4,814	4,615	5,586	5,663	14,660	4,461	5,544	15,626	4,842	6,390	5,804
Iwo Jima Island, Japan	7,038	10,515	8,576	11,384	11,864	15,245	18,632	10,228	13,838	10,212	11,216	9,566	15,243	5,919	10,855	10,157	6,278	10,630	9,918	10,143
Izmir, Turkey	4,895	2,088	17,575	2,404	7,844	10,536	9,839	2,006	4,882	2,200	2,767	1,544	8,840	14,896	2,730	1,464	14,121	2,261	674	1,203
Jackson, Mississippi	14,053	7,776	8,493	7,537	2,023	13,076	6,972	7,908	11,722	7,726	7,110	8,671	3,770	13,987	7,122	8,453	15,205	7,596	9,348	8,710
Jaffna, Sri Lanka	1,287	7,979	14,387	8,516	13,530	10,022	14,352	7,770	7,341	7,923	8,806	6,900	14,905	8,868	8,661	7,276	7,987	8,175	6,431	7,052
Jakarta, Indonesia	4,648	11,220	11,036	11,860	15,989	10,312	16,327	10,974	10,136	11,100	12,085	10,076	18,355	5,419	11,881	10,537	4,592	11,414	9,753	10,340
Jamestown, St. Helena	9,427	7,490	14,845	6,749	9,284	4,344	4,512	7,717	2,635	7,819	7,126	8,056	6,746	14,685	7,471	7,544	13,661	7,461	7,423	7,448
Jamnagar, India	483	6,215	15,608	6,779	11,797	10,614	13,509	6,002	6,650	6,154	7,050	5,131	13,273	10,487	6,896	5,513	9,690	6,411	4,681	5,294
Jan Mayen Island	7,729	2,403	13,464	2,950	4,617	13,950	10,072	2,305	8,542	2,129	2,529	2,663	7,276	15,038	2,203	2,768	15,308	2,348	3,516	3,007
Jayapura, Indonesia	7,792	13,134	7,543	13,988	14,587	12,576	17,774	12,841	13,919	12,871	13,939	12,044	17,506	3,058	13,601	12,630	3,257	13,284	12,143	12,542
Jefferson City, Missouri	13,447	7,384	8,697	7,236	1,834	13,711	7,580	7,490	11,823	7,301	6,783	8,205	4,273	13,939	6,754	8,038	15,161	7,212	8,928	8,299
Jerusalem, Israel	4,017	3,127	18,178	3,415	8,884	10,028	10,296	3,031	4,514	3,223	3,800	2,446	9,706	14,066	3,771	2,483	13,193	3,302	1,616	2,221
Jiggalong, Australia	7,007	13,642	9,050	14,255	17,638	9,531	15,501	13,399	11,401	13,525	14,503	12,501	18,864	3,265	14,306	12,954	2,242	13,836	12,152	12,751
Jinan, China	4,721	8,157	11,200	9,020	11,215	14,695	17,259	7,864	11,341	7,887	8,952	7,103	14,485	8,042	8,615	7,696	8,011	8,302	7,341	7,642
Jodhpur, India	811	6,120	15,288	6,745	11,562	11,132	13,835	5,888	7,074	6,028	6,976	4,998	13,297	10,422	6,793	5,428	9,703	6,315	4,638	5,226
Johannesburg, South Africa	6,955	8,769	15,279	8,387	12,642	3,731	7,883	8,859	2,785	9,034	8,878	8,684	10,424	11,649	9,111	8,428	10,461	8,847	7,824	8,212
Juazeiro do Norte, Brazil	12,604	7,811	12,145	6,945	6,363	6,473	1,333	8,104	6,055	8,090	7,039	8,861	3,174	15,945	7,386	8,268	15,671	7,672	8,673	8,330
Juneau, Alaska	11,083	7,421	8,444	7,809	4,642	17,415	11,283	7,343	13,464	7,164	7,323	7,605	7,889	11,619	7,078	7,798	12,644	7,339	8,476	8,027
Kabul, Afghanistan	1,760	5,232	15,493	5,909	10,582	11,689	13,463	4,985	7,087	5,114	6,100	4,087	12,471	11,170	5,892	4,554	10,544	5,425	3,820	4,371
Kalgoorlie, Australia	7,572	14,262	8,792	14,800	18,309	8,870	14,733	14,036	11,308	14,176	15,099	13,146	18,047	3,082	14,939	13,562	1,902	14,457	12,725	13,344
Kaliningrad, USSR	5,917	1,006	15,714	1,862	6,404	12,201	10,105	715	6,555	789	1,857	361	8,195	15,152	1,581	669	14,797	1,170	1,212	809
Kamloops, Canada	12,185	7,719	8,051	7,940	3,816	16,277	10,160	7,699	13,417	7,509	7,443	8,123	6,839	12,098	7,261	8,206	13,231	7,602	8,981	8,455
Kampala, Uganda	4,854	6,084	18,153	5,914	11,106	6,632	9,010	6,115	1,990	6,303	6,407	5,800	10,249	13,007	6,557	5,628	11,806	6,201	4,929	5,389
Kananga, Zaire	6,174	6,445	17,446	6,070	10,736	5,647	7,738	6,544	811	6,715	6,564	6,428	9,307	13,557	6,788	6,130	12,334	6,521	5,587	5,924
Kano, Nigeria	6,910	4,297	17,848	3,741	8,268	7,377	6,934	4,470	1,949	4,609	4,213	4,652	7,382	15,952	4,489	4,192	14,739	4,323	3,968	4,058
Kanpur, India	1,133	6,622	14,558	7,299	11,841	11,566	14,565	6,373	7,777	6,498	7,492	5,474	13,862	9,802	7,279	5,946	9,153	6,814	5,204	5,762
Kansas City, Missouri	13,445	7,483	8,554	7,362	2,013	13,899	7,774	7,579	12,021	7,390	6,903	8,276	4,482	13,742	6,862	8,128	14,962	7,314	9,015	8,390
Kaohsiung, Taiwan	4,937	9,591	10,507	10,437	12,715	13,756	18,573	9,300	11,739	9,342	10,420	8,487	16,052	6,570	10,097	9,071	6,447	9,749	8,601	8,983
Karachi, Pakistan	885	5,811	15,900	6,373	11,414	10,675	13,226	5,599	6,457	5,753	6,644	4,731	12,873	10,882	6,491	5,108	10,095	6,006	4,274	4,888
Karaganda, USSR	3,425	4,549	14,560	5,372	9,214	13,257	13,553	4,262	8,156	4,330	5,406	3,416	11,656	11,615	5,114	3,995	11,280	4,719	3,561	3,905
Karl-Marx-Stadt, East Germany	6,292	410	15,962	1,207	6,150	11,702	9,447	230	6,110	423	1,283	762	7,664	15,784	1,085	322	15,347	604	1,217	582
Kasanga, Tanzania	5,489	6,958	17,223	6,705	11,644	5,665	8,601	7,011	1,815	7,195	7,202	6,749	10,311	12,611	7,384	6,544	11,389	7,060	5,880	6,313

Distances in Kilometers	Bombay, India	Bonn, West Germany	Bora Bora (Vaitape)	Bordeaux, France	Boston, Massachusetts	Bouvet Island	Brasilia, Brazil	Braunschweig, West Germany	Brazzaville, Congo	Bremerhaven, West Germany	Brest, France	Brest, USSR	Bridgetown, Barbados	Brisbane, Australia	Bristol, United Kingdom	Brno, Czechoslovakia	Broken Hill, Australia	Brussels, Belgium	Bucharest, Romania	Budapest, Hungary
Kashgar, China	2,294	5,358	14,764	6,115	10,351	12,486	14,008	5,087	7,863	5,189	6,233	4,196	12,596	10,890	5,981	4,726	10,400	5,543	4,106	4,581
Kassel, West Germany	6,537	180	15,803	1,039	5,911	11,735	9,278	127	6,184	256	1,055	984	7,432	15,978	840	560	15,576	366	1,454	814
Kathmandu, Nepal	1,601	6,871	14,065	7,588	11,878	11,971	15,047	6,610	8,288	6,722	7,746	5,711	14,126	9,465	7,512	6,214	8,885	7,060	5,517	6,046
Kayes, Mali	8,915	4,357	15,778	3,521	6,454	7,761	5,224	4,626	3,603	4,680	3,819	5,210	5,203	17,856	4,180	4,626	16,653	4,278	4,857	4,623
Kazan, USSR	4,542	2,816	15,305	3,653	7,767	12,906	11,883	2,526	7,337	2,591	3,668	1,709	9,948	13,343	3,376	2,301	13,012	2,983	2,057	2,251
Kemi, Finland	6,266	1,952	14,522	2,786	6,042	13,456	10,818	1,701	7,811	1,625	2,572	1,529	8,419	14,482	2,212	1,907	14,418	2,026	2,382	2,065
Kenora, Canada	12,288	6,625	9,239	6,639	1,980	14,689	8,578	6,682	11,783	6,488	6,154	7,302	5,160	13,878	6,055	7,226	15,041	6,472	8,090	7,487
Kerguelen Island	7,591	12,589	11,648	12,460	16,897	4,407	10,539	12,576	7,134	12,769	12,954	12,063	13,884	7,287	13,100	12,049	6,131	12,723	11,228	11,792
Kerkira, Greece	5,534	1,591	17,324	1,783	7,266	10,538	9,318	1,582	4,880	1,773	2,175	1,420	8,203	15,522	2,182	1,098	14,761	1,742	742	880
Kermanshah, Iran	3,063	3,694	17,294	4,191	9,441	10,687	11,436	3,516	5,418	3,688	4,492	2,717	10,681	13,062	4,376	2,991	12,289	3,887	2,118	2,752
Khabarovsk, USSR	6,417	7,945	10,179	8,802	9,618	16,664	16,366	7,670	12,526	7,629	8,586	7,109	13,029	8,605	8,222	7,681	8,933	8,041	7,613	7,713
Kharkov, USSR	4,727	2,062	16,222	2,807	7,581	11,975	10,929	1,808	6,342	1,937	2,937	909	9,318	14,185	2,715	1,417	13,693	2,253	986	1,290
Khartoum, Sudan	4,292	4,514	19,565	4,487	9,933	8,237	9,497	4,509	2,905	4,701	4,960	4,124	9,857	13,783	5,053	3,997	12,682	4,651	3,254	3,749
Khon Kaen, Thailand	3,191	9,006	12,124	9,755	13,465	12,086	16,908	8,734	9,890	8,831	9,881	7,844	16,219	7,276	9,623	8,370	6,755	9,190	7,703	8,215
Kiev, USSR	5,104	1,652	16,237	2,398	7,231	11,895	10,550	1,403	6,235	1,539	2,526	510	8,907	14,591	2,309	1,007	14,105	1,843	745	897
Kigali, Rwanda	5,219	6,233	17,953	6,005	11,072	6,305	8,672	6,283	1,663	6,467	6,501	6,020	10,033	13,113	6,673	5,813	11,900	6,340	5,153	5,582
Kingston, Canada	12,347	6,000	10,147	5,801	488	13,279	7,252	6,127	10,482	5,944	5,358	6,892	3,808	15,264	5,352	6,673	16,464	5,821	7,567	6,930
Kingston, Jamaica	14,750	8,055	9,056	7,545	2,755	11,001	4,899	8,267	10,383	8,116	7,234	9,143	1,920	14,841	7,374	8,758	15,896	7,860	9,610	8,984
Kingstown, Saint Vincent	13,862	7,364	10,480	6,685	3,374	9,626	3,520	7,622	8,670	7,510	6,491	8,521	175	16,133	6,720	8,033	16,908	7,174	8,789	8,218
Kinshasa, Zaire	6,806	6,148	17,306	5,667	10,032	5,662	7,021	6,285	4	6,442	6,148	6,301	8,499	14,281	6,408	5,929	13,061	6,199	5,504	5,750
Kirkwall, United Kingdom	7,405	1,119	14,652	1,581	4,906	12,586	9,233	1,127	7,195	933	1,180	1,832	6,889	16,052	837	1,670	16,004	1,018	2,544	1,931
Kirov, USSR	4,780	2,830	15,018	3,688	7,562	13,196	11,931	2,537	7,606	2,579	3,657	1,785	9,857	13,335	3,346	2,379	13,070	2,985	2,248	2,364
Kiruna, Sweden	6,544	2,038	14,273	2,834	5,780	13,635	10,737	1,813	8,011	1,709	2,571	1,765	8,238	14,545	2,206	2,087	14,551	2,085	2,630	2,267
Kisangani, Zaire	5,584	5,824	18,203	5,529	10,489	6,410	8,226	5,899	1,223	6,078	6,026	5,721	9,444	13,715	6,220	5,459	12,500	5,916	4,868	5,241
Kishinev, USSR	5,055	1,641	16,624	2,280	7,363	11,494	10,307	1,441	5,833	1,609	2,486	678	8,840	14,747	2,322	940	14,175	1,836	356	740
Kitchner, Canada	12,579	6,302	9,818	6,122	779	13,428	7,351	6,422	10,802	6,237	5,674	7,173	3,913	14,951	5,660	6,969	16,158	6,125	7,863	7,228
Knoxville, Tennessee	13,453	7,083	9,195	6,831	1,317	13,004	6,869	7,222	11,119	7,041	6,406	8,000	3,512	14,625	6,425	7,764	15,848	6,901	8,659	8,019
Kosice, Czechoslovakia	5,652	1,044	16,379	1,715	6,789	11,553	9,857	857	5,897	1,036	1,891	416	8,258	15,282	1,725	343	14,757	1,239	602	209
Kota Kinabalu, Malaysia	4,898	10,807	10,437	11,580	14,603	12,002	17,971	10,529	11,259	10,613	11,679	9,649	17,842	5,433	11,402	10,191	4,987	10,987	9,546	10,046
Krakow, Poland	5,790	913	16,207	1,645	6,626	11,687	9,839	699	6,039	870	1,779	347	8,157	15,341	1,588	257	14,856	1,108	783	294
Kralendijk, Bonaire	14,540	7,941	9,717	7,309	3,357	9,949	3,818	8,186	9,418	8,060	7,077	9,085	945	15,411	7,279	8,626	16,278	7,747	9,416	8,825
Krasnodar, USSR	4,255	2,448	16,689	3,092	8,104	11,526	10,998	2,229	5,949	2,384	3,301	1,371	9,655	13,959	3,125	1,752	13,359	2,643	1,023	1,555
Krasnoyarsk, USSR	4,441	5,362	13,090	6,231	8,997	14,674	14,448	5,070	9,629	5,082	6,141	4,357	11,929	10,856	5,802	4,950	10,779	5,500	4,731	4,929
Kristiansand, Norway	6,763	829	15,090	1,595	5,545	12,491	9,649	676	6,952	515	1,365	1,203	7,470	15,657	1,009	1,147	15,473	850	1,969	1,399
Kuala Lumpur, Malaysia	3,595	10,062	11,883	10,727	14,910	10,831	16,423	9,812	9,648	9,933	10,932	8,912	17,285	6,461	10,718	9,385	5,720	10,255	8,622	9,196
Kuching, Malaysia	4,520	10,804	10,911	11,519	15,139	11,237	17,168	10,539	10,592	10,645	11,680	9,643	18,051	5,585	11,437	10,149	4,950	10,992	9,432	9,978
Kumasi, Ghana	8,145	4,950	16,605	4,229	7,826	6,790	5,676	5,175	2,235	5,278	4,632	5,544	6,388	16,489	4,964	5,015	15,279	4,926	4,974	4,934
Kumzar, Oman	1,872	4,955	16,923	5,432	10,692	10,284	12,183	4,774	5,576	4,944	5,747	3,959	11,849	11,921	5,636	4,252	11,080	5,147	3,377	4,012
Kunming, China	3,148	8,266	12,314	9,056	12,512	12,826	16,803	7,985	9,954	8,066	9,135	7,112	15,371	7,935	8,854	7,665	7,535	8,444	7,070	7,534
Kuqa Chang, China	2,663	5,746	14,101	6,543	10,405	13,031	14,586	5,465	8,526	5,546	6,614	4,594	12,904	10,442	6,336	5,153	10,047	5,923	4,609	5,034
Kurgan, USSR	4,097	3,819	14,669	4,665	8,412	13,421	12,900	3,527	8,038	3,579	4,658	2,726	10,849	12,339	4,351	3,318	12,065	3,980	3,018	3,264
Kuwait, Kuwait	2,770	4,137	17,556	4,563	9,912	10,222	11,418	3,980	5,103	4,159	4,900	3,219	10,951	12,819	4,813	3,443	11,971	4,326	2,552	3,193
Kuybyshev, USSR	4,273	2,927	15,512	3,740	8,021	12,685	11,933	2,644	7,156	2,727	3,793	1,784	10,120	13,245	3,519	2,362	12,860	3,102	2,004	2,280
Kyoto, Japan	6,389	9,262	9,534	10,131	11,016	15,777	17,845	8,977	13,040	8,959	9,962	8,328	14,442	7,152	9,603	8,917	7,435	9,377	8,714	8,912
Kzyl-Orda, USSR	2,945	4,309	15,338	5,071	9,431	12,462	13,072	4,039	7,371	4,142	5,185	3,147	11,551	11,926	4,934	3,681	11,448	4,494	3,094	3,542
L'vov, USSR	5,503	1,206	16,289	1,928	6,889	11,716	10,092	981	6,053	1,141	2,073	253	8,451	15,061	1,879	538	14,563	1,401	621	445
La Ceiba, Honduras	15,568	8,936	7,977	8,497	3,308	11,433	5,518	9,124	11,439	8,961	8,150	9,973	2,944	13,762	8,254	9,639	14,848	8,743	10,514	9,877
La Coruna, Spain	7,889	1,429	15,458	646	4,998	10,896	7,690	1,720	5,787	1,682	636	2,569	5,917	17,586	999	2,023	17,093	1,270	2,753	2,186
La Paz, Bolivia	15,895	10,412	8,846	9,619	6,524	7,339	2,165	10,695	9,184	10,619	9,546	11,564	3,406	13,428	9,833	11,010	13,791	10,236	11,610	11,141
La Paz, Mexico	15,221	9,700	6,367	9,578	4,126	13,682	8,090	9,787	13,806	9,595	9,123	10,450	5,457	11,836	9,084	10,335	13,048	9,533	11,215	10,597
La Ronge, Canada	11,796	6,715	9,062	6,874	2,848	15,627	9,519	6,722	12,297	6,529	6,377	7,227	6,100	13,197	6,218	7,247	14,305	6,586	8,063	7,503
Labrador City, Canada	11,149	4,875	11,117	4,770	1,217	13,548	7,831	4,982	9,863	4,795	4,301	5,718	4,468	15,686	4,252	5,530	16,755	4,705	6,422	5,791
Lagos, Nigeria	7,626	4,921	17,104	4,271	8,252	6,748	6,165	5,122	1,776	5,244	4,709	5,394	6,936	16,060	5,019	4,900	14,839	4,921	4,753	4,789
Lahore, Pakistan	1,405	5,804	15,098	6,486	11,087	11,687	13,952	5,555	7,395	5,681	6,674	4,656	13,047	10,597	6,462	5,129	9,968	5,997	4,396	4,947
Lambasa, Fiji	12,295	16,138	3,080	16,856	12,824	12,143	13,727	15,910	17,135	15,810	16,442	15,509	13,693	2,978	16,116	16,052	4,193	16,163	16,024	16,118
Lansing, Michigan	12,793	6,602	9,486	6,443	1,107	13,596	7,484	6,714	11,135	6,527	5,991	7,447	4,066	14,622	5,967	7,262	15,833	6,428	8,154	7,522
Lanzhou, China	3,564	7,426	12,370	8,261	11,305	13,800	16,421	7,135	10,146	7,189	8,269	6,307	14,291	8,732	7,959	6,888	8,495	7,589	6,418	6,796
Laoag, Philippines	5,027	10,010	10,339	10,845	13,194	13,388	18,782	9,719	11,783	9,769	10,849	8,891	16,543	6,148	10,533	9,469	5,978	10,172	8,962	9,370
Largeau, Chad	5,653	3,794	19,051	3,502	8,704	8,155	8,241	3,885	2,489	4,058	3,999	3,814	8,404	15,205	4,183	3,477	14,068	3,880	3,012	3,281
Las Vegas, Nevada	13,845	8,849	6,989	8,889	3,823	14,977	9,103	8,886	13,851	8,692	8,404	9,442	6,080	11,911	8,297	9,423	13,128	8,703	10,264	9,683
Launceston, Australia	10,144	16,803	6,415	17,383	16,878	8,838	13,486	16,555	12,992	16,673	17,663	15,655	15,943	1,635	17,461	16,115	1,167	16,996	15,300	15,909
Le Havre, France	7,186	517	15,561	522	5,370	11,524	8,634	793	6,134	739	360	1,679	6,740	16,650	290	1,197	16,270	335	2,043	1,414
Leipzig, East Germany	6,342	373	15,897	1,198	6,091	11,749	9,441	164	6,164	357	1,249	790	7,628	15,801	1,037	385	15,381	563	1,279	647
Leningrad, USSR	5,663	1,775	15,184	2,646	6,614	12,902	10,866	1,485	7,237	1,494	2,564	960	8,749	14,424	2,240	1,477	14,187	1,911	1,745	1,562
Leon, Spain	7,673	1,322	15,699	473	5,243	10,786	7,782	1,615	5,601	1,605	650	2,428	6,113	17,457	1,009	1,864	16,890	1,186	2,553	2,007
Lerwick, United Kingdom	7,310	1,169	14,617	1,705	4,984	12,712	9,399	1,135	7,286	943	1,325	1,771	7,033	15,885	973	1,663	15,848	1,093	2,519	1,923
Lhasa, China	2,195	7,116	13,504	7,876	11,825	12,489	15,575	6,843	8,886	6,939	7,991	5,955	14,334	9,134	7,732	6,488	8,646	7,300	5,851	6,341
Libreville, Gabon	7,210	5,585	17,296	5,022	9,202	6,102	6,550	5,752	828	5,894	5,487	5,885	7,741	15,112	5,772	5,453	13,893	5,612	5,150	5,303
Lilongwe, Malawi	5,623	7,626	16,578	7,380	12,262	5,208	8,733	7,674	2,298	7,859	7,877	7,386	10,723	12,024	8,058	7,200	10,801	7,731	6,515	6,965
Lima, Peru	16,718	10,629	8,032	9,905	6,056	8,310	3,173	10,895	10,174	10,790	9,753	11,791	3,383	13,073	9,998	11,280	13,652	10,442	11,982	11,447
Limerick, Ireland	7,782	1,105	14,870	1,052	4,684	11,924	8,472	1,298	6,699	1,153	558	2,183	6,282	16,826	435	1,807	16,682	916	2,691	2,050
Limoges, France	7,105	696	15,908	181	5,600	11,114	8,424	985	5,721	1,007	520	1,776	6,727	16,805	685	1,215	16,287	601	1,953	1,374
Limon, Costa Rica	15,861	9,165	8,114	8,641	3,772	10,675	4,808	9,378	11,010	9,228	8,340	10,254	2,576	13,866	8,484	9,868	14,853	8,970	10,715	10,092
Lincoln, Nebraska	13,298	7,462	8,516	7,380	2,135	14,161	8,035	7,546	12,163	7,354	6,912	8,218	4,734	13,598	6,855	8,094	14,813	7,298	8,975	8,356
Linz, Austria	6,141	587	16,259	1,201	6,369	11,432	9,385	516	5,824	709	1,389	792	7,744	15,789	1,260	199	15,271	773	1,003	368
Lisbon, Portugal	8,036	1,846	15,635	983	5,145	10,391	7,261	2,139	5,382	2,131	1,139	2,933	5,706	17,947	1,505	2,357	17,259	1,712	2,982	2,478
Little Rock, Arkansas	13,857	7,704	8,464	7,512	2,026	13,408	7,298	7,822	11,887	7,636	7,071	8,559	4,068	13,854	7,062	8,369	15,077	7,528	9,262	8,628
Liverpool, United Kingdom	7,402	753	15,099	971	5,031	11,970	8,784	919	6,618	768	568	1,798	6,662	16,522	221	1,442	16,313	578	2,333	1,692
Lodz, Poland	5,874	870	16,020	1,666	6,505	11,864	9,895	616	6,220	763	1,746	294	8,125	15,320	1,522	348	14,884	1,059	951	474
Lome, Togo	7,865	4,975	16,871	4,292	8,099	6,716	5,933	5,186	1,941	5,300	4,716	5,499	6,708	16,218	5,036	4,989	15,002	4,964	4,886	4,891
London, United Kingdom	7,205	512	15,388	742	5,280	11,747	8,773	738	6,351	633	466	1,637	6,782	16,525	171	1,216	16,216	320	2,095	1,455
Londonderry, United Kingdom	7,678	1,079	14,771	1,229	4,717	12,171	8,726	1,217	6,893	1,047	760	2,065	6,467	16,565	506	1,754	16,470	910	2,648	2,009
Longlac, Canada	12,124	6,199	9,723	6,157	1,449	14,253	8,192	6,277	11,219	6,085	5,680	6,945	4,752	14,450	5,604	6,825	15,611	6,039	7,703	7,087
Lord Howe Island, Australia	10,754	16,875	5,224	17,715	15,468	10,197	14,032	16,583	14,503	16,618	17,683	15,759	15,580	740	17,338	16,330	1,671	17,030	15,718	16,207
Los Angeles, California	14,021	9,198	6,629	9,251	4,179	15,014	9,260	9,230	14,204	9,036	8,765	9,769	6,327	11,559	8,652	9,764	12,779	9,055	10,597	10,023
Louangphrabang, Laos	3,075	8,667	12,272	9,430	13,080	12,341	16,832	8,392	9,848	8,484	9,541	7,506	15,853	7,584	9,276	8,041	7,102	8,850	7,396	7,894
Louisville, Kentucky	13,291	7,020	9,164	6,813	1,329	13,302	7,167	7,146	11,270	6,962	6,375	7,901	3,800	14,489	6,373	7,692	15,712	6,842	8,586	7,950
Luanda, Angola	7,224	6,622	16,761	6,099	10,199	5,136	6,676	6,771	550	6,923	6,571	6,822	8,409	14,113	6,846	6,434	12,909	6,663	6,036	6,263
Lubumbashi, Zaire	6,022	7,190	16,886	6,865	11,574	5,195	8,125	7,268	1,572	7,446	7,361	7,074	9,997	12,727	7,570	6,826	11,505	7,279	6,214	6,606
Lusaka, Zambia	6,188	7,614	16,473	7,283	11,911	4,835	8,120	7,692	1,883	7,870	7,778	7,493	10,178	12,402	7,990	7,249	11,183	7,702	6,631	7,028
Luxembourg, Luxembourg	6,752	144	15,833	733	5,769	11,534	8,973	428	6,033	471	788	1,265	7,166	16,279	651	763	15,847	188	1,617	983
Luxor, Egypt	4,190	3,532	18,897	3,654	9,168	9,309	9,852	3,488	3,808	3,682	4,091	3,029	9,616	14,145	4,126	2,956	13,165	3,688	2,163	2,699
Lynn Lake, Canada	11,584	6,391	9,387	6,545	2,666	15,493	9,427	6,402	11,979	6,209	6,049	6,919	5,991	13,478	5,891	6,929	14,567	6,261	7,751	7,186
Lyon, France	6,825	579	16,108	437	5,859	11,104	8,633	835	5,636	908	767	1,545	7,000	16,561	837	966	16,011	567	1,674	1,106
Macapa, Brazil	13,559	7,828	11,161	7,015	5,099	7,804	1,783	8,116	7,392	8,054	6,975	8,968	1,727	16,036	7,281	8,404	16,239	7,659	8,989	8,526
Madison, Wisconsin	12,901	6,864	9,158	6,748	1,501	13,901	7,771	6,961	11,526	6,771	6,287	7,664	4,380	14,228	6,243	7,510	15,437	6,695	8,397	7,771
Madras, India	1,029	7,710	14,436	8,278	13,207	10,351	14,455	7,491	7,435	7,640	8,549	6,612	14,740	9,034	8,389	7,010	8,199	7,906	6,180	6,793
Madrid, Spain	7,545	1,421	15,962	555	5,487	10,530	7,720	1,708	5,312	1,729	891	2,458	6,206	17,447	1,231	1,873	16,772	1,316	2,478	1,981
Madurai, India	1,150	7,825	14,595	8,347	13,423	9,930	14,157	7,620	7,142	7,776	8,645	6,757	14,709	9,061	8,507	7,121	8,168	8,020	6,269	6,894
Magadan, USSR	7,531	7,346	9,886	8,140	8,075	17,975	14,912	7,104	12,804	7,017	7,827	6,748	11,501	9,651	7,466	7,255	10,179	7,398	7,424	7,354

Distances in Kilometers

	Bombay, India	Bonn, West Germany	Bora Bora (Vaitape)	Bordeaux, France	Boston, Massachusetts	Bouvet Island	Brasilia, Brazil	Braunschweig, West Germany	Brazzaville, Congo	Bremerhaven, West Germany	Brest, France	Brest, USSR	Bridgetown, Barbados	Brisbane, Australia	Bristol, United Kingdom	Brno, Czechoslovakia	Broken Hill, Australia	Brussels, Belgium	Bucharest, Romania	Budapest, Hungary
Magdalena, Bolivia	15,401	9,871	9,354	9,071	6,207	7,362	1,768	10,155	8,765	10,083	9,008	11,020	2,966	13,978	9,300	10,462	14,307	9,697	11,055	10,590
Magdeburg, East Germany	6,405	355	15,790	1,215	6,008	11,841	9,455	78	6,263	258	1,222	823	7,593	15,802	985	482	15,413	530	1,369	744
Majuro Atoll, Marshall Isls.	10,634	13,412	4,848	14,189	11,679	14,649	15,669	13,170	17,351	13,083	13,837	12,752	13,984	4,305	13,485	13,292	5,359	13,458	13,313	13,362
Malabo, Equatorial Guinea	7,153	5,210	17,473	4,643	8,896	6,468	6,606	5,381	1,144	5,521	5,108	5,535	7,583	15,408	5,393	5,092	14,185	5,236	4,817	4,948
Male, Maldives	1,657	8,017	14,906	8,440	13,755	9,099	13,497	7,842	6,536	8,012	8,789	7,021	14,514	9,192	8,696	7,316	8,195	8,208	6,433	7,073
Manado, Indonesia	5,989	11,787	9,360	12,588	14,895	12,118	18,241	11,502	12,203	11,571	12,648	10,639	18,321	4,402	12,351	11,197	4,093	11,960	10,591	11,066
Managua, Nicaragua	15,880	9,209	7,871	8,733	3,659	11,077	5,235	9,408	11,375	9,250	8,405	10,269	2,898	13,650	8,526	9,913	14,690	9,015	10,778	10,146
Manama, Bahrain	2,421	4,570	17,481	4,980	10,347	10,012	11,606	4,415	5,084	4,594	5,325	3,652	11,316	12,458	5,245	3,877	11,579	4,759	2,985	3,627
Manaus, Brazil	14,614	8,696	10,104	7,916	5,160	8,033	1,928	8,977	8,363	8,897	7,827	9,852	1,796	15,117	8,109	9,307	15,515	8,518	9,944	9,449
Manchester, New Hampshire	12,237	5,765	10,481	5,510	78	12,912	6,939	5,912	10,068	5,734	5,083	6,708	3,504	15,685	5,104	6,451	16,890	5,582	7,345	6,705
Mandalay, Burma	2,446	8,076	12,931	8,818	12,758	12,138	16,188	7,807	9,247	7,908	8,952	6,914	15,312	8,216	8,701	7,435	7,680	8,262	6,763	7,278
Mangareva Island, Fr.Polynesia	17,113	15,535	1,904	15,250	9,771	10,540	9,045	15,647	15,590	15,458	14,856	16,312	9,127	7,167	14,885	16,196	8,117	15,357	17,083	16,457
Manila, Philippines	5,143	10,361	10,185	11,188	13,581	13,091	18,837	10,071	11,828	10,127	11,207	9,232	16,942	5,799	10,896	9,805	5,592	10,526	9,271	9,697
Mannheim, West Germany	6,583	170	15,939	857	5,928	11,528	9,100	342	5,992	453	955	1,111	7,331	16,136	814	594	15,683	331	1,451	814
Maputo, Mozambique	6,609	8,858	15,282	8,532	12,986	3,962	8,330	8,929	3,028	9,109	9,027	8,691	10,858	11,323	9,240	8,475	10,122	8,949	7,823	8,248
Mar del Plata, Argentina	14,801	11,679	9,257	10,809	9,004	4,867	2,637	11,971	8,218	11,962	10,913	12,694	5,660	12,089	11,260	12,099	12,016	11,544	12,396	12,135
Maracaibo, Venezuela	14,928	8,304	9,318	7,688	3,513	10,016	3,922	8,544	9,767	8,414	7,445	9,441	1,335	15,011	7,637	8,993	15,892	8,110	9,793	9,196
Marrakech, Morocco	8,088	2,460	16,004	1,602	5,608	9,598	6,760	2,742	4,677	2,774	1,885	3,430	5,639	18,135	2,245	2,835	17,143	2,362	3,282	2,894
Marseilles, France	6,775	836	16,340	507	6,019	10,832	8,501	1,068	5,361	1,164	953	1,679	7,004	16,628	1,087	1,085	15,994	841	1,664	1,167
Maseru, Lesotho	7,228	9,091	14,933	8,691	12,800	3,396	7,777	9,188	3,057	9,361	9,179	9,027	10,442	11,463	9,419	8,763	10,290	9,166	8,168	8,549
Mashhad, Iran	2,317	4,430	16,231	5,064	9,962	11,399	12,593	4,200	6,432	4,343	5,286	3,314	11,627	12,048	5,103	3,738	11,383	4,625	2,962	3,538
Mazatlan, Mexico	15,337	9,559	6,607	9,387	3,891	13,349	7,691	9,663	13,436	9,474	8,944	10,363	5,055	12,161	8,926	10,212	13,364	9,387	11,100	10,473
Mbabane, Swaziland	6,739	8,857	15,256	8,512	12,894	3,859	8,182	8,934	2,968	9,112	9,005	8,717	10,725	11,409	9,226	8,487	10,213	8,943	7,851	8,264
Mbandaka, Zaire	6,311	5,714	17,889	5,296	9,951	6,194	7,474	5,831	583	5,996	5,787	5,790	8,703	14,323	6,023	5,447	13,099	5,779	4,976	5,256
McMurdo Sound, Antarctica	12,101	16,881	7,185	16,308	15,363	5,308	9,438	17,004	10,737	17,170	16,730	16,765	12,423	5,598	17,055	16,578	5,206	16,924	15,896	16,353
Mecca, Saudi Arabia	3,455	4,320	18,695	4,504	10,017	9,098	10,419	4,244	3,905	4,437	4,929	3,675	10,441	13,304	4,940	3,699	12,302	4,486	2,844	3,437
Medan, Indonesia	3,285	9,813	12,220	10,458	14,813	10,672	16,134	9,568	9,315	9,696	10,678	8,670	16,998	6,764	10,475	9,130	5,991	10,007	8,351	8,934
Medellin, Colombia	15,577	8,959	8,751	8,342	4,026	9,862	3,904	9,198	10,166	9,067	8,100	10,095	1,908	14,389	8,292	9,648	15,242	8,764	10,447	9,851
Medicine Hat, Canada	12,352	7,380	8,402	7,519	3,134	15,651	9,518	7,390	12,866	7,197	7,023	7,896	6,167	12,734	6,873	7,916	13,886	7,248	8,733	8,172
Medina, Saudi Arabia	3,484	4,031	18,549	4,258	9,760	9,404	10,485	3,944	4,128	4,136	4,668	3,351	10,329	13,436	4,663	3,396	12,472	4,201	2,531	3,134
Melbourne, Australia	10,151	16,424	6,567	17,060	16,931	9,144	13,919	16,167	13,049	16,276	17,296	15,268	16,348	1,369	17,068	15,748	729	16,616	14,958	15,553
Memphis, Tennessee	13,753	7,536	8,660	7,328	1,831	13,303	7,179	7,660	11,681	7,475	6,891	8,408	3,912	14,061	6,890	8,206	15,284	7,358	9,100	8,464
Merauke, Indonesia	8,001	13,667	7,406	14,506	15,164	11,964	17,176	13,375	13,776	13,418	14,494	12,551	17,795	2,494	14,166	13,129	2,603	13,825	12,584	13,022
Merida, Mexico	15,196	8,687	7,950	8,324	2,940	12,070	6,106	8,854	11,734	8,682	7,943	9,671	3,304	13,692	8,012	9,384	14,842	8,498	10,273	9,632
Meridian, Mississippi	13,996	7,676	8,619	7,424	1,910	12,990	6,875	7,813	11,581	7,631	7,001	8,584	3,650	14,126	7,019	8,356	15,343	7,494	9,251	8,612
Messina, Italy	5,892	1,546	17,307	1,532	7,046	10,328	8,911	1,613	4,700	1,790	1,974	1,671	7,834	15,909	2,047	1,227	15,109	1,661	1,121	1,074
Mexico City, Mexico	15,673	9,448	6,993	9,164	3,668	12,548	6,827	9,587	12,738	9,406	8,755	10,357	4,274	12,700	8,786	10,130	13,867	9,264	11,025	10,385
Miami, Florida	14,266	7,651	9,048	7,248	2,021	11,901	5,776	7,833	10,769	7,667	6,882	8,674	2,570	14,770	6,971	8,353	15,935	7,459	9,233	8,594
Midway Islands, USA	10,847	11,250	5,666	11,911	9,160	17,090	14,672	11,058	17,042	10,930	11,491	10,876	11,915	6,928	11,167	11,320	7,959	11,249	11,617	11,461
Milan, Italy	6,484	606	16,342	771	6,176	11,085	8,887	762	5,542	900	1,090	1,292	7,333	16,260	1,094	698	15,677	698	1,336	791
Milford Sound, New Zealand	11,851	18,419	4,895	19,099	15,357	8,933	12,410	18,139	13,944	18,207	19,286	17,259	14,343	2,308	18,965	17,776	2,681	18,597	17,002	17,592
Milwaukee, Wisconsin	12,864	6,779	9,260	6,652	1,381	13,813	7,687	6,881	11,407	6,692	6,193	7,593	4,287	14,348	6,155	7,430	15,557	6,609	8,319	7,691
Minsk, USSR	5,460	1,434	15,856	2,258	6,844	12,213	10,490	1,153	6,548	1,250	2,303	328	8,659	14,732	2,042	920	14,338	1,611	1,058	929
Mogadiscio, Somalia	3,529	6,479	17,560	6,529	11,987	7,353	10,432	6,433	3,419	6,627	6,993	5,901	11,588	11,862	7,059	5,895	10,709	6,632	5,063	5,636
Mombasa, Kenya	4,437	6,820	17,414	6,730	12,011	6,474	9,638	6,820	2,707	7,012	7,217	6,403	11,125	12,083	7,338	6,306	10,883	6,952	5,538	6,056
Monclova, Mexico	14,893	8,931	7,255	8,743	3,243	13,338	7,464	9,042	12,873	8,855	8,303	9,761	4,608	12,777	8,292	9,591	13,988	8,756	10,482	9,851
Moncton, Canada	11,637	5,133	11,086	4,883	651	12,857	7,060	5,282	9,587	5,105	4,452	6,085	3,691	16,118	4,471	5,820	17,278	4,949	6,714	6,073
Monrovia, Liberia	9,123	5,197	15,635	4,382	7,116	6,862	4,766	5,457	3,126	5,524	4,703	5,978	5,401	17,113	5,061	5,407	15,973	5,131	5,538	5,377
Monte Carlo, Monaco	6,614	779	16,410	649	6,141	10,885	8,660	977	5,374	1,095	1,055	1,526	7,172	16,458	1,139	932	15,828	823	1,495	1,000
Monterrey, Mexico	15,012	8,972	7,267	8,760	3,250	13,162	7,297	9,090	12,784	8,905	8,328	9,823	4,475	12,835	8,327	9,638	14,039	8,795	10,531	9,897
Montevideo, Uruguay	14,727	11,327	9,471	10,458	8,687	5,017	2,271	11,619	8,053	11,608	10,555	12,353	5,323	12,451	10,900	11,758	12,382	11,190	12,077	11,800
Montgomery, Alabama	13,907	7,522	8,818	7,248	1,742	12,845	6,719	7,665	11,356	7,486	6,832	8,450	3,457	14,347	6,860	8,206	15,563	7,338	9,101	8,461
Montpelier, Vermont	12,174	5,751	10,441	5,524	244	13,078	7,105	5,889	10,169	5,709	5,088	6,672	3,669	15,574	5,096	6,431	16,770	5,570	7,326	6,687
Montpellier, France	6,898	830	16,231	381	5,894	10,864	8,425	1,083	5,423	1,159	839	1,750	6,888	16,729	999	1,159	16,114	805	1,778	1,261
Montreal, Canada	12,105	5,732	10,411	5,533	404	13,235	7,264	5,862	10,259	5,680	5,089	6,632	3,827	15,471	5,084	6,407	16,658	5,553	7,302	6,664
Moosonee, Canada	11,806	5,768	10,170	5,711	1,230	14,060	8,082	5,853	10,790	5,663	5,236	6,541	4,640	14,845	5,166	6,402	15,983	5,605	7,285	6,664
Moroni, Comoros	4,693	7,753	16,482	7,657	12,874	5,888	9,793	7,749	3,190	7,941	8,145	7,313	11,684	11,306	8,270	7,233	10,090	7,885	6,452	6,981
Moscow, USSR	5,036	2,091	15,579	2,930	7,239	12,606	11,165	1,803	6,959	1,874	2,947	996	9,259	14,067	2,663	1,591	13,718	2,260	1,499	1,568
Mosul, Iraq	3,483	3,278	17,370	3,770	9,036	10,753	11,128	3,106	5,348	3,280	4,071	2,326	10,269	13,464	3,958	2,576	12,707	3,470	1,698	2,335
Mount Isa, Australia	8,491	14,711	7,217	15,491	16,290	10,690	15,886	14,429	13,345	14,502	15,577	13,557	17,828	1,564	15,282	14,102	1,258	14,887	13,438	13,954
Multan, Pakistan	1,250	5,711	15,388	6,361	11,108	11,407	13,687	5,472	7,087	5,607	6,574	4,577	12,924	10,761	6,378	5,025	10,086	5,905	4,259	4,831
Munich, West Germany	6,337	434	16,184	1,002	6,199	11,395	9,205	464	5,818	637	1,191	970	7,542	15,985	1,082	390	15,474	604	1,190	566
Murcia, Spain	7,354	1,559	16,292	762	5,807	10,249	7,701	1,828	4,975	1,884	1,189	2,485	6,374	17,347	1,501	1,891	16,564	1,491	2,380	1,954
Murmansk, USSR	6,187	2,458	14,168	3,292	6,207	13,901	11,275	2,204	8,240	2,132	3,068	1,943	8,762	14,013	2,705	2,377	14,010	2,533	2,761	2,514
Mururoa Atoll, Fr. Polynesia	16,710	15,660	1,473	15,454	9,945	10,820	9,475	15,743	15,988	15,551	15,036	16,334	9,477	6,833	15,032	16,290	7,820	15,491	17,154	16,552
Muscat, Oman	1,565	5,324	16,770	5,791	11,064	10,123	12,356	5,146	5,619	5,316	6,112	4,331	12,173	11,601	6,005	4,622	10,737	5,516	3,744	4,381
Myitkyina, Burma	2,627	7,887	12,847	8,654	12,411	12,515	16,275	7,612	9,428	7,703	8,761	6,727	15,079	8,353	8,495	7,264	7,883	8,069	6,632	7,120
Naga, Philippines	5,396	10,582	9,929	11,415	13,637	13,141	19,047	10,292	12,064	10,344	11,423	9,459	17,032	5,575	11,108	10,036	5,407	10,746	9,513	9,932
Nagasaki, Japan	5,852	9,192	9,946	10,063	11,412	15,228	18,107	8,901	12,567	8,901	9,938	8,197	14,826	7,107	9,586	8,791	7,269	9,320	8,510	8,762
Nagoya, Japan	6,495	9,299	9,444	10,167	10,962	15,865	17,805	9,014	13,137	8,993	9,990	8,376	14,388	7,140	9,630	8,963	7,445	9,411	8,773	8,962
Nagpur, India	699	6,959	14,671	7,584	12,337	11,013	14,430	6,724	7,502	6,862	7,816	5,832	14,131	9,602	7,630	6,268	8,865	7,154	5,477	6,066
Nairobi, Kenya	4,531	6,417	17,828	6,304	11,571	6,632	9,415	6,426	2,417	6,617	6,792	6,044	10,748	12,512	6,921	5,921	11,315	6,544	5,175	5,674
Nanchang, China	4,491	8,790	11,104	9,637	12,106	13,983	17,828	8,498	11,276	8,540	9,617	7,689	15,357	7,372	9,295	8,275	7,235	8,947	7,825	8,192
Nancy, France	6,740	237	15,918	671	5,814	11,432	8,914	503	5,932	566	789	1,298	7,154	16,324	700	766	15,861	274	1,592	968
Nandi, Fiji	12,130	16,252	3,280	17,001	13,082	11,981	13,819	16,013	16,886	15,923	16,606	15,563	13,914	2,722	16,271	16,120	3,936	16,289	16,030	16,169
Nanjing, China	4,802	8,663	10,922	9,522	11,704	14,447	17,765	8,370	11,538	8,398	9,467	7,592	15,005	7,523	9,134	8,184	7,474	8,811	7,794	8,120
Nanning, China	3,708	8,826	11,706	9,631	12,788	12,997	17,419	8,542	10,510	8,613	9,688	7,680	15,822	7,355	9,397	8,241	7,012	9,000	7,670	8,119
Nantes, France	7,315	744	15,646	276	5,343	11,275	8,369	1,034	5,938	1,006	256	1,891	6,554	16,901	477	1,366	16,461	589	2,159	1,555
Naples, Italy	6,030	1,232	16,996	1,288	6,790	10,607	8,958	1,302	4,995	1,476	1,702	1,445	7,717	15,988	1,749	948	15,257	1,350	1,050	835
Narvik, Norway	6,677	2,050	14,186	2,825	5,649	13,677	10,663	1,838	8,068	1,722	2,540	1,850	8,128	14,608	2,175	2,143	14,642	2,085	2,719	2,333
Nashville, Tennessee	13,539	7,248	8,975	7,024	1,518	13,190	7,055	7,378	11,376	7,195	6,591	8,140	3,728	14,372	6,597	7,923	15,596	7,069	8,818	8,180
Nassau, Bahamas	14,168	7,512	9,284	7,077	2,002	11,668	5,535	7,704	10,481	7,543	6,726	8,559	2,285	15,028	6,830	8,216	16,178	7,319	9,089	8,453
Natal, Brazil	12,123	7,457	12,627	6,587	6,448	6,409	1,774	7,748	5,601	7,745	6,710	8,479	3,412	16,219	7,064	7,885	15,814	7,326	8,255	7,935
Natashquan, Canada	11,151	4,710	11,398	4,520	1,124	13,089	7,435	4,843	9,459	4,662	4,071	5,626	4,119	16,139	4,060	5,387	17,221	4,530	6,281	5,643
Nauru Island	10,468	14,126	4,864	14,946	12,624	13,728	15,797	13,865	16,840	13,800	14,637	13,347	14,718	3,334	14,276	13,916	4,391	14,194	13,805	13,949
Ndjamena, Chad	6,220	4,343	18,528	3,920	8,796	7,456	7,590	4,472	1,812	4,632	4,412	4,502	8,081	15,336	4,644	4,115	14,141	4,403	3,735	3,941
Nelson, New Zealand	12,237	18,518	4,328	19,378	14,807	9,355	12,403	18,225	14,492	18,232	19,195	17,424	14,041	2,400	18,832	17,995	3,011	18,651	17,335	17,863
Nema, Mauritania	8,416	3,996	16,251	3,191	6,640	7,937	5,726	4,254	3,389	4,323	3,534	4,786	5,634	17,664	3,887	4,210	16,441	3,934	4,389	4,190
Neuquen, Argentina	15,663	12,336	8,339	11,477	9,010	5,470	3,234	12,629	9,140	12,600	11,529	13,405	5,828	11,506	11,860	12,813	11,586	12,187	13,186	12,874
New Delhi, India	1,156	6,234	14,858	6,908	11,504	11,577	14,245	5,987	7,547	6,114	7,103	5,088	13,472	10,191	6,894	5,557	9,543	6,427	4,814	5,372
New Glasgow, Canada	11,569	5,026	11,235	4,752	763	12,712	6,956	5,182	9,413	5,008	4,328	5,997	3,612	16,293	4,359	5,717	17,451	4,840	6,609	5,968
New Haven, Connecticut	12,460	5,976	10,307	5,706	194	12,841	6,825	6,126	10,171	5,949	5,284	6,926	3,382	15,590	5,312	6,664	16,805	5,791	7,558	6,917
New Orleans, Louisiana	14,291	7,961	8,376	7,695	2,186	12,872	6,787	8,101	11,730	7,920	7,277	8,876	3,647	13,940	7,301	8,643	15,149	7,778	9,538	8,898
New Plymouth, New Zealand	12,270	18,361	4,152	19,232	14,642	9,606	12,535	18,072	14,740	18,058	18,961	17,317	14,038	2,335	18,605	17,902	3,048	18,475	17,311	17,797
New York, New York	12,566	6,089	10,198	5,818	307	12,847	6,810	6,238	10,258	6,061	5,397	7,037	3,366	15,505	5,425	6,776	16,722	5,904	7,670	7,029
Newcastle upon Tyne, UK	7,311	753	15,035	1,133	5,076	12,140	8,973	857	6,752	682	761	1,698	6,807	16,332	401	1,401	16,153	611	2,295	1,659
Newcastle Waters, Australia	7,751	14,020	7,916	14,779	16,403	10,749	16,331	13,742	12,828	13,825	14,892	12,860	18,556	2,304	14,613	13,394	1,804	14,200	12,711	13,239
Niamey, Niger	7,537	4,152	17,207	3,481	7,632	7,530	6,390	4,364	2,446	4,478	3,916	4,694	6,670	16,633	4,229	4,175	15,413	4,144	4,115	4,085
Nicosia, Cyprus	4,270	2,729	17,878	3,063	8,499	10,335	10,242	2,623	4,757	2,814	3,428	2,033	9,452	14,306	3,382	2,074	13,486	2,907	1,201	1,812
Niue (Alofi)	13,465	16,476	1,945	16,978	12,127	11,842	12,601	16,315	17,368	16,170	16,493	16,148	12,592	3,892	16,240	16,606	5,053	16,439	16,822	16,742

Distances in Kilometers	Bombay, India	Bonn, West Germany	Bora Bora (Vaitape)	Bordeaux, France	Boston, Massachusetts	Bouvet Island	Brasilia, Brazil	Braunschweig, West Germany	Brazzaville, Congo	Bremerhaven, West Germany	Brest, France	Brest, USSR	Bridgetown, Barbados	Brisbane, Australia	Bristol, United Kingdom	Brno, Czechoslovakia	Broken Hill, Australia	Brussels, Belgium	Bucharest, Romania	Budapest, Hungary
Norfolk, Virginia	13,033	6,520	9,860	6,214	759	12,639	6,543	6,678	10,435	6,503	5,807	7,488	3,112	15,315	5,851	7,213	16,539	6,333	8,104	7,463
Norfolk Island, Australia	11,496	17,116	4,340	17,984	14,594	10,639	13,734	16,829	15,313	16,810	17,761	16,116	14,821	1,474	17,395	16,710	2,560	17,227	16,254	16,645
Noril'sk, USSR	5,694	4,529	12,873	5,384	7,500	15,311	13,328	4,255	9,780	4,211	5,180	3,759	10,520	11,922	4,818	4,305	12,032	4,623	4,386	4,369
Norman Wells, Canada	10,515	6,549	9,311	6,948	4,259	17,070	11,081	6,470	12,609	6,291	6,465	6,745	7,639	12,306	6,214	6,927	13,261	6,468	7,616	7,158
Normanton, Australia	8,493	14,547	7,110	15,355	15,926	11,067	16,177	14,260	13,606	14,320	15,399	13,404	17,757	1,639	15,089	13,964	1,583	14,716	13,342	13,831
North Pole	7,905	4,382	11,827	5,038	5,311	16,038	11,749	4,211	10,476	4,068	4,641	4,229	8,554	13,044	4,302	4,552	13,537	4,370	5,082	4,741
Nottingham, United Kingdom	7,279	621	15,220	906	5,163	11,913	8,834	795	6,529	653	559	1,682	6,762	16,470	195	1,312	16,222	447	2,202	1,561
Norway House, Canada	11,873	6,467	9,337	6,562	2,352	15,152	9,065	6,498	11,887	6,304	6,069	7,062	5,634	13,667	5,935	7,034	14,789	6,327	7,876	7,293
Norwich, United Kingdom	7,112	453	15,359	878	5,333	11,870	8,930	629	6,442	498	624	1,521	6,910	16,370	297	1,141	16,082	290	2,032	1,391
Nouakchott, Mauritania	9,254	4,157	15,344	3,292	5,824	8,245	5,132	4,440	4,228	4,467	3,518	5,114	4,705	18,483	3,883	4,520	17,283	4,052	4,874	4,556
Noumea, New Caledonia	11,152	16,376	4,423	17,239	14,290	11,354	14,383	16,094	15,724	16,064	16,997	15,423	15,061	1,475	16,631	16,017	2,694	16,478	15,649	15,978
Novosibirsk, USSR	4,093	4,872	13,721	5,763	8,934	14,130	13,975	4,579	8,999	4,609	5,683	3,818	11,680	11,305	5,357	4,413	11,133	5,021	4,136	4,373
Nuku'alofa, Tonga	12,968	16,714	2,521	17,331	12,704	11,631	12,968	16,514	16,975	16,392	16,869	16,204	13,163	3,293	16,580	16,720	4,453	16,709	16,769	16,813
Nukunono Island, Tokelau Isls.	12,996	15,399	2,330	15,969	11,585	12,939	13,268	15,224	18,323	15,086	15,503	15,042	12,647	4,202	15,220	15,500	5,422	15,375	15,735	15,635
Nuremberg, West Germany	6,395	319	16,039	1,020	6,101	11,537	9,254	316	5,965	488	1,145	936	7,519	15,965	994	404	15,496	506	1,269	630
Nyala, Sudan	5,186	4,585	19,402	4,367	9,599	7,641	8,588	4,643	2,094	4,825	4,862	4,443	9,134	14,377	5,024	4,189	13,214	4,689	3,591	3,968
Oaxaca, Mexico	15,862	9,495	7,087	9,164	3,717	12,185	6,472	9,649	12,496	9,472	8,772	10,444	4,007	12,838	8,825	10,186	13,981	9,308	11,079	10,437
Ocean Falls, Canada	11,859	7,818	7,976	8,111	4,301	16,818	10,705	7,772	13,687	7,586	7,616	8,123	7,378	11,699	7,407	8,257	12,802	7,716	8,991	8,499
Odense, Denmark	6,559	564	15,430	1,409	5,787	12,193	9,587	349	6,629	237	1,282	950	7,557	15,706	966	810	15,422	649	1,654	1,065
Odessa, USSR	4,898	1,798	16,676	2,431	7,514	11,476	10,424	1,596	5,823	1,763	2,642	808	8,992	14,605	2,479	1,097	14,022	1,993	427	893
Ogbomosho, Nigeria	7,477	4,730	17,268	4,094	8,200	6,934	6,331	4,927	1,838	5,052	4,539	5,187	6,996	16,100	4,844	4,697	14,877	4,734	4,544	4,584
Okha, USSR	7,022	7,732	9,934	8,563	8,891	17,397	15,708	7,471	12,785	7,407	8,295	7,009	12,314	9,034	7,930	7,553	9,475	7,806	7,603	7,619
Okinawa (Naha)	5,656	9,688	9,910	10,553	12,173	14,536	18,766	9,395	12,457	9,412	10,471	8,640	15,585	6,535	10,128	9,234	6,601	9,829	8,867	9,179
Oklahoma City, Oklahoma	13,892	7,955	8,113	7,819	2,405	13,794	7,715	8,054	12,346	7,865	7,364	8,753	4,533	13,407	7,330	8,603	14,630	7,785	9,490	8,864
Old Crow, Canada	10,044	6,597	9,375	7,080	4,854	17,598	11,696	6,486	12,729	6,317	6,613	6,661	8,252	11,896	6,333	6,905	12,789	6,537	7,528	7,122
Olympia, Washington	12,527	8,161	7,609	8,371	4,065	16,234	10,182	8,143	13,808	7,953	7,874	8,567	6,935	11,773	7,698	8,650	12,930	8,043	9,425	8,900
Omaha, Nebraska	13,236	7,386	8,592	7,303	2,069	14,156	8,025	7,470	12,097	7,279	6,836	8,143	4,710	13,662	6,778	8,019	14,876	7,222	8,899	8,281
Omsk, USSR	4,000	4,321	14,272	5,172	8,704	13,708	13,401	4,028	8,445	4,072	5,150	3,240	11,275	11,841	4,836	3,833	11,604	4,477	3,530	3,782
Oodnadatta, Australia	8,487	15,000	7,514	15,693	17,112	9,832	15,197	14,735	12,714	14,837	15,876	13,839	17,778	1,732	15,630	14,340	755	15,189	13,589	14,159
Oradea, Romania	5,552	1,159	16,568	1,756	6,931	11,384	9,826	1,004	5,724	1,190	1,977	574	8,317	15,267	1,840	460	14,697	1,352	437	221
Oran, Algeria	7,340	1,782	16,459	1,014	5,968	9,994	7,568	2,042	4,726	2,110	1,446	2,649	6,380	17,375	1,757	2,056	16,512	1,728	2,464	2,092
Oranjestad, Aruba	14,664	8,036	9,545	7,422	3,309	10,088	3,966	8,277	9,613	8,147	7,177	9,173	1,133	15,259	7,370	8,726	16,156	7,842	9,526	8,929
Orebro, Sweden	6,391	1,083	15,140	1,928	5,894	12,653	10,065	834	7,046	758	1,762	960	7,902	15,238	1,419	1,126	15,037	1,167	1,809	1,336
Orel, USSR	4,920	1,999	15,909	2,799	7,364	12,277	10,998	1,724	6,632	1,826	2,872	845	9,235	14,185	2,618	1,420	13,764	2,181	1,194	1,350
Orsk, USSR	3,791	3,541	15,317	4,346	8,554	12,779	12,508	3,259	7,394	3,344	4,409	2,392	10,734	12,638	4,135	2,961	12,243	3,718	2,522	2,863
Osaka, Japan	6,367	9,283	9,540	10,152	11,058	15,735	17,886	8,997	13,027	8,980	9,986	8,345	14,484	7,124	9,627	8,934	7,400	9,398	8,725	8,927
Oslo, Norway	6,652	1,048	14,984	1,841	5,633	12,696	9,891	852	7,128	721	1,615	1,183	7,663	15,415	1,257	1,251	15,260	1,089	2,007	1,485
Osorno, Chile	15,993	12,762	7,883	11,908	9,187	5,666	3,672	13,055	9,573	13,019	11,944	13,846	6,103	11,094	12,269	13,255	11,227	12,609	13,647	13,323
Ostrava, Czechoslovakia	5,895	803	16,203	1,524	6,539	11,640	9,722	607	6,001	787	1,663	456	8,040	15,461	1,482	139	14,974	998	843	266
Ottawa, Canada	12,201	5,869	10,254	5,683	504	13,336	7,334	5,993	10,423	5,809	5,236	6,754	3,892	15,310	5,224	6,539	16,501	5,691	7,434	6,797
Ouagadougou, Bourkina Fasso	7,951	4,326	16,796	3,600	7,416	7,417	5,984	4,556	2,615	4,655	4,005	4,953	6,296	16,888	4,336	4,413	15,665	4,299	4,423	4,344
Oujda, Morocco	7,469	1,928	16,411	1,135	5,926	9,885	7,406	2,192	4,671	2,254	1,540	2,810	6,251	17,513	1,865	2,217	16,618	1,865	2,623	2,254
Oxford, United Kingdom	7,284	594	15,314	771	5,197	11,778	8,736	810	6,403	694	439	1,708	6,715	16,566	98	1,297	16,280	403	2,178	1,537
Pago Pago, American Samoa	13,270	15,955	2,049	16,492	11,854	12,372	12,912	15,788	17,854	15,646	16,015	15,618	12,608	4,031	15,746	16,073	5,230	15,924	16,305	16,211
Pakxe, Laos	3,529	9,319	11,783	10,078	13,633	12,162	17,214	9,045	10,194	9,137	10,194	8,158	16,501	6,944	9,929	8,691	6,449	9,502	8,035	8,540
Palembang, Indonesia	4,251	10,798	11,362	11,445	15,616	10,477	16,375	10,551	9,936	10,676	11,664	9,652	17,971	5,802	11,458	10,116	5,004	10,991	9,338	9,921
Palermo, Italy	6,084	1,487	17,210	1,379	6,890	10,299	8,740	1,588	4,696	1,754	1,838	1,750	7,641	16,101	1,938	1,259	15,298	1,583	1,275	1,142
Palma, Majorca	7,014	1,289	16,456	642	6,011	10,416	8,064	1,536	5,023	1,618	1,135	2,134	6,723	16,981	1,382	1,541	16,237	1,259	2,009	1,589
Palmerston North, New Zealand	12,419	18,553	4,105	19,422	14,585	9,476	12,341	18,265	14,675	18,247	19,110	17,510	13,876	2,518	18,763	18,094	3,192	18,662	17,486	17,984
Panama, Panama	15,691	9,007	8,435	8,443	3,792	10,358	4,432	9,231	10,620	9,088	8,165	10,118	2,223	14,156	8,330	9,706	15,096	8,811	10,535	9,922
Paramaribo, Suriname	13,705	7,579	10,901	6,813	4,341	8,589	2,521	7,858	7,911	7,774	6,708	8,738	940	16,197	6,985	8,201	16,644	7,399	8,866	8,351
Paris, France	7,024	401	15,722	500	5,545	11,450	8,707	693	6,019	679	505	1,552	6,879	16,559	454	1,045	16,135	262	1,876	1,252
Patna, India	1,462	7,024	14,079	7,725	12,094	11,772	15,046	6,768	8,216	6,885	7,898	5,868	14,278	9,350	7,672	6,359	8,736	7,215	5,642	6,184
Patrai, Greece	5,356	1,804	17,515	1,991	7,482	10,419	9,396	1,784	4,754	1,976	2,390	1,547	8,372	15,369	2,399	1,283	14,578	1,957	778	1,050
Peking, China	4,760	7,842	11,327	8,708	10,860	14,903	16,932	7,549	11,264	7,566	8,626	6,805	14,119	8,374	8,285	7,399	8,367	7,983	7,077	7,355
Penrhyn Island (Omoka)	14,445	15,182	1,078	15,487	10,435	12,764	11,863	15,097	18,369	14,922	14,990	15,223	11,150	5,520	14,796	15,521	6,710	15,094	16,057	15,728
Peoria, Illinois	13,156	7,061	9,009	6,917	1,555	13,725	7,590	7,167	11,574	6,979	6,463	7,885	4,227	14,189	6,432	7,716	15,406	6,890	8,606	7,976
Perm', USSR	4,541	3,218	14,854	4,073	7,860	13,340	12,316	2,925	7,810	2,968	4,046	2,157	10,229	12,946	3,734	2,752	12,687	3,373	2,557	2,723
Perth, Australia	7,264	13,955	9,280	14,431	18,701	8,471	14,450	13,747	10,756	13,899	14,765	12,872	17,869	3,614	14,637	13,251	2,415	14,150	12,391	13,022
Peshawar, Pakistan	1,672	5,433	15,298	6,120	10,732	11,763	13,681	5,183	7,260	5,308	6,303	4,284	12,678	10,952	6,090	4,759	10,337	5,625	4,035	4,580
Petropavlovsk-Kamchatskiy,USSR	8,069	8,201	9,050	8,982	8,417	18,383	15,268	7,964	13,654	7,872	8,653	7,623	11,824	8,936	8,294	8,126	9,560	8,246	8,299	8,227
Petrozavodsk, USSR	5,614	2,065	14,952	2,936	6,682	13,173	11,138	1,777	7,508	1,773	2,830	1,257	8,939	14,161	2,496	1,783	13,968	2,192	2,008	1,863
Pevek, USSR	8,326	6,576	10,014	7,280	6,624	18,180	13,466	6,376	12,515	6,253	6,899	6,226	10,050	10,868	6,554	6,644	11,512	6,586	7,015	6,796
Philadelphia, Pennsylvania	12,691	6,219	10,076	5,946	436	12,845	6,786	6,368	10,353	6,190	5,526	7,166	3,343	15,411	5,555	6,906	16,631	6,034	7,800	7,159
Phnom Penh, Kampuchea	3,537	9,567	11,782	10,302	14,021	11,790	17,062	9,298	10,073	9,398	10,443	8,404	16,797	6,752	10,191	8,923	6,189	9,753	8,234	8,761
Phoenix, Arizona	14,180	8,945	6,952	8,929	3,701	14,565	8,716	9,000	13,697	8,807	8,452	9,599	5,751	12,063	8,367	9,543	13,286	8,791	10,401	9,804
Pierre, South Dakota	12,957	7,367	8,520	7,358	2,372	14,649	8,518	7,428	12,362	7,234	6,878	8,050	5,189	13,369	6,789	7,972	14,568	7,213	8,838	8,234
Pinang, Malaysia	3,339	9,774	12,097	10,443	14,643	10,944	16,381	9,522	9,516	9,643	10,644	8,623	17,004	6,729	10,428	9,098	6,005	9,966	8,340	8,910
Pitcairn Island (Adamstown)	17,574	15,394	2,442	15,014	9,612	10,142	8,515	15,539	15,068	15,358	14,656	16,283	8,730	7,553	14,724	16,082	8,449	15,208	16,976	16,335
Pittsburgh, Pennsylvania	12,856	6,493	9,716	6,267	778	13,153	7,054	6,627	10,766	6,445	5,833	7,399	3,625	14,997	5,840	7,171	16,217	6,313	8,066	7,427
Plymouth, Montserrat	13,718	7,135	10,485	6,491	2,967	10,016	3,921	7,385	8,827	7,264	6,268	8,284	487	16,218	6,479	7,816	17,099	6,943	8,598	8,011
Plymouth, United Kingdom	7,488	795	15,271	674	5,049	11,641	8,488	1,040	6,337	939	224	1,939	6,478	16,815	159	1,495	16,523	600	2,356	1,722
Ponape Island	9,290	13,045	6,085	13,897	12,623	14,277	17,017	12,770	15,925	12,726	13,650	12,181	15,294	3,849	13,284	12,763	4,657	13,136	12,583	12,772
Ponce, Puerto Rico	13,989	7,336	10,078	6,739	2,732	10,391	4,264	7,574	9,309	7,441	6,481	8,469	927	15,846	6,667	8,029	16,815	7,142	8,839	8,236
Ponta Delgada, Azores	9,459	2,955	14,277	2,235	3,861	10,585	6,365	3,232	6,285	3,150	2,082	4,117	4,330	18,863	2,366	3,597	18,681	2,774	4,339	3,771
Pontianak, Indonesia	4,506	10,872	10,968	11,571	15,316	11,030	16,975	10,611	10,468	10,721	11,746	9,713	18,128	5,566	11,512	10,209	4,886	11,061	9,475	10,032
Port Augusta, Australia	8,952	15,540	7,236	16,195	17,263	9,430	14,628	15,282	12,724	15,392	16,412	14,383	17,232	1,571	16,183	14,867	351	15,731	14,088	14,675
Port Blair, India	2,287	8,714	13,075	9,369	13,807	11,006	15,762	8,468	8,752	8,595	9,581	7,570	15,927	7,805	9,375	8,033	7,078	8,908	7,264	7,841
Port Elizabeth, South Africa	7,707	9,557	14,411	9,118	12,951	2,858	7,544	9,665	3,457	9,834	9,601	9,536	10,382	11,241	9,855	9,255	10,100	9,623	8,682	9,046
Port Hedland, Australia	6,616	13,236	9,359	13,860	17,401	9,702	15,750	12,991	11,232	13,116	14,099	12,093	19,184	3,585	13,898	12,550	2,617	13,430	11,755	12,350
Port Louis, Mauritius	4,641	9,272	14,851	9,294	14,641	5,907	10,959	9,223	4,899	9,416	9,767	8,652	13,316	9,518	9,848	8,682	8,302	9,425	7,834	8,421
Port Moresby, Papua New Guinea	8,741	14,162	6,648	15,022	14,808	12,155	16,761	13,869	14,487	13,891	14,948	13,085	17,085	2,086	14,603	13,674	2,557	14,307	13,194	13,590
Port Said, Egypt	4,282	2,999	18,322	3,224	8,719	9,892	10,013	2,928	4,328	3,122	3,628	2,418	9,448	14,327	3,624	2,386	13,432	3,166	1,559	2,125
Port Sudan, Sudan	3,736	4,350	19,021	4,464	9,975	8,816	10,104	4,299	3,571	4,493	4,907	3,792	10,234	13,485	4,947	3,762	12,449	4,508	2,940	3,503
Port-au-Prince, Haiti	14,389	7,697	9,521	7,153	2,645	10,777	4,644	7,919	9,916	7,775	6,861	8,805	1,488	15,304	7,019	8,398	16,335	7,502	9,235	8,617
Port-of-Spain, Trin. & Tobago	14,042	7,597	10,374	6,902	3,635	9,408	3,285	7,858	8,667	7,750	6,722	8,756	341	15,964	6,958	8,260	16,683	7,407	9,002	8,439
Port-Vila, Vanuatu	11,198	15,985	4,244	16,828	13,825	11,881	14,587	15,712	16,191	15,664	16,542	15,104	14,877	1,906	16,179	15,693	3,127	16,069	15,421	15,683
Portland, Maine	12,121	5,644	10,597	5,390	158	12,908	6,964	5,790	9,978	5,612	4,962	6,587	3,537	15,769	4,982	6,330	16,967	5,460	7,224	6,583
Portland, Oregon	12,694	8,295	7,474	8,490	4,083	16,123	10,101	8,282	13,890	8,091	7,993	8,717	6,884	11,726	7,823	8,792	12,893	8,175	9,573	9,043
Porto, Portugal	7,946	1,613	15,558	773	5,074	10,653	7,492	1,906	5,586	1,885	869	2,728	5,824	17,757	1,235	2,164	17,171	1,467	2,842	2,305
Porto Alegre, Brazil	14,280	10,621	10,085	9,752	8,274	5,082	1,617	10,913	7,516	10,905	9,857	11,642	4,861	13,137	10,205	11,048	13,014	10,486	11,370	11,089
Porto Alexandre, Angola	7,705	7,387	16,009	6,833	10,615	4,347	6,383	7,544	1,331	7,692	7,296	7,610	8,495	13,649	7,583	7,217	12,478	7,420	6,826	7,049
Porto Novo, Benin	7,706	4,923	17,028	4,261	8,187	6,752	6,090	5,128	1,843	5,247	4,694	5,415	6,852	16,127	5,008	4,915	14,908	4,919	4,785	4,809
Porto Velho, Brazil	15,237	9,452	9,516	8,669	5,708	7,758	1,903	9,733	8,759	9,653	8,584	10,608	2,464	14,370	8,866	10,060	14,762	9,275	10,687	10,199
Portsmouth, United Kingdom	7,272	577	15,400	661	5,241	11,668	8,668	823	6,296	730	360	1,721	6,694	16,629	130	1,279	16,308	382	2,148	1,511
Poznan, Poland	6,060	709	15,901	1,537	6,319	11,911	9,779	439	6,284	577	1,582	461	7,955	15,459	1,345	359	15,050	891	1,114	568
Prague, Czechoslovakia	6,167	528	16,083	1,272	6,286	11,631	9,497	367	6,023	559	1,389	684	7,768	15,712	1,210	185	15,246	724	1,080	444
Praia, Cape Verde Islands	10,133	4,830	14,499	3,959	5,456	8,097	4,328	5,121	4,776	5,121	4,103	5,857	3,901	18,568	4,463	5,263	17,588	4,702	5,690	5,326
Pretoria, South Africa	6,916	8,722	15,329	8,344	12,618	3,779	7,899	8,812	2,747	8,987	8,835	8,635	10,421	11,676	9,066	8,380	10,486	8,801	7,774	8,163
Prince Albert, Canada	12,008	6,894	8,889	7,032	2,830	15,548	9,423	6,907	12,410	6,713	6,537	7,424	6,019	13,136	6,386	7,434	14,264	6,761	8,256	7,691

Distances in Kilometers

	Bombay, India	Bonn, West Germany	Bora Bora (Vaitape)	Bordeaux, France	Boston, Massachusetts	Bouvet Island	Brasilia, Brazil	Braunschweig, West Germany	Brazzaville, Congo	Bremerhaven, West Germany	Brest, France	Brest, USSR	Bridgetown, Barbados	Brisbane, Australia	Bristol, United Kingdom	Brno, Czechoslovakia	Broken Hill, Australia	Brussels, Belgium	Bucharest, Romania	Budapest, Hungary
Prince Edward Island	8,062	11,183	12,950	10,810	14,543	2,570	8,438	11,262	5,173	11,440	11,299	11,020	11,631	9,537	11,535	10,811	8,429	11,267	10,150	10,584
Prince George, Canada	11,794	7,501	8,280	7,771	3,956	16,585	10,451	7,465	13,325	7,277	7,275	7,849	7,090	12,071	7,074	7,960	13,170	7,394	8,712	8,205
Prince Rupert, Canada	11,591	7,706	8,109	8,036	4,444	17,062	10,935	7,648	13,650	7,465	7,543	7,966	7,584	11,637	7,321	8,123	12,715	7,612	8,836	8,360
Providence, Rhode Island	12,341	5,843	10,444	5,568	67	12,807	6,819	5,994	10,051	5,818	5,148	6,798	3,381	15,708	5,177	6,531	16,920	5,658	7,425	6,784
Provo, Utah	13,435	8,304	7,530	8,350	3,376	15,056	9,041	8,342	13,393	8,148	7,864	8,905	5,880	12,353	7,753	8,879	13,561	8,159	9,722	9,139
Puerto Aisen, Chile	15,698	13,121	7,873	12,257	9,723	5,283	4,019	13,414	9,518	13,391	12,325	14,169	6,611	10,706	12,660	13,574	10,774	12,976	13,897	13,621
Puerto Deseado, Argentina	15,116	12,947	8,362	12,076	9,996	4,711	3,911	13,238	9,001	13,234	12,190	13,938	6,768	10,810	12,537	13,345	10,767	12,816	13,586	13,367
Puerto Princesa, Philippines	5,041	10,651	10,270	11,453	14,151	12,510	18,435	10,366	11,572	10,437	11,512	9,503	17,473	5,535	11,218	10,062	5,208	10,824	9,468	9,934
Punta Arenas, Chile	15,104	13,623	7,947	12,752	10,583	4,666	4,609	13,912	9,377	13,915	12,877	14,589	7,419	10,115	13,227	13,999	10,072	13,496	14,190	14,007
Pusan, South Korea	5,778	8,934	10,107	9,805	11,187	15,355	17,844	8,644	12,442	8,642	9,675	7,948	14,593	7,373	9,322	8,541	7,534	9,061	8,275	8,516
Pyongyang, North Korea	5,525	8,410	10,523	9,281	10,834	15,438	17,358	8,120	12,074	8,118	9,152	7,426	14,209	7,890	8,800	8,019	8,023	8,537	7,765	7,996
Qamdo, China	2,799	7,406	12,924	8,201	11,776	12,997	16,103	7,124	9,494	7,204	8,274	6,254	14,523	8,787	7,992	6,810	8,397	7,583	6,235	6,684
Qandahar, Afghanistan	1,568	5,201	15,891	5,825	10,707	11,241	13,141	4,972	6,653	5,115	6,056	4,086	12,381	11,321	5,875	4,508	10,623	5,396	3,719	4,304
Qiqian, China	5,545	7,015	11,270	7,883	9,465	15,975	15,845	6,731	11,439	6,710	7,714	6,110	12,770	9,370	7,356	6,693	9,537	7,128	6,564	6,704
Qom, Iran	2,777	3,934	16,998	4,475	9,639	10,868	11,789	3,739	5,698	3,903	4,754	2,904	10,995	12,735	4,617	3,230	11,989	4,129	2,380	3,001
Quebec, Canada	11,881	5,498	10,631	5,304	495	13,228	7,316	5,628	10,088	5,445	4,858	6,399	3,893	15,620	4,850	6,173	16,790	5,320	7,067	6,430
Quetta, Pakistan	1,377	5,393	15,812	6,011	10,900	11,174	13,255	5,165	6,693	5,309	6,246	4,280	12,564	11,147	6,068	4,698	10,437	5,588	3,904	4,494
Quito, Ecuador	16,272	9,717	8,225	9,077	4,775	9,464	3,775	9,962	10,437	9,834	8,853	10,860	2,552	13,733	9,055	10,401	14,517	9,523	11,184	10,598
Rabaul, Papua New Guinea	9,052	13,912	6,268	14,783	14,007	12,896	16,892	13,622	15,153	13,616	14,630	12,908	16,404	2,580	14,270	13,503	3,271	14,035	13,137	13,457
Raiatea (Uturoa)	15,348	15,779	41	15,878	10,482	11,766	10,899	15,758	17,270	15,569	15,395	16,058	10,619	5,808	15,277	16,247	6,913	15,655	16,925	16,485
Raleigh, North Carolina	13,246	6,756	9,619	6,456	982	12,680	6,560	6,911	10,642	6,735	6,047	7,716	3,153	15,098	6,088	7,447	16,320	6,570	8,340	7,698
Rangiroa (Avatoru)	15,703	15,439	468	15,484	10,055	11,848	10,583	15,440	17,185	15,248	15,008	15,812	10,185	6,254	14,909	15,948	7,360	15,305	16,683	16,195
Rangoon, Burma	2,483	8,517	12,829	9,229	13,327	11,686	16,200	8,256	9,186	8,366	9,393	7,358	15,773	7,849	9,157	7,859	7,238	8,706	7,147	7,687
Raoul Is., Kermadec Islands	12,851	17,585	3,021	18,261	13,456	10,731	12,692	17,358	16,039	17,257	17,808	16,912	13,450	2,850	17,511	17,475	3,888	17,603	17,312	17,514
Rarotonga (Avarua)	14,551	16,534	991	16,770	11,466	11,473	11,539	16,458	17,137	16,281	16,276	16,562	11,571	4,814	16,113	16,882	5,908	16,438	17,373	17,085
Rawson, Argentina	15,260	12,537	8,503	11,669	9,507	4,965	3,460	12,829	8,908	12,816	11,760	13,560	6,270	11,256	12,103	12,966	11,247	12,399	13,260	13,003
Recife, Brazil	12,165	7,663	12,568	6,792	6,682	6,168	1,655	7,954	5,567	7,955	6,927	8,671	3,597	15,981	7,283	8,077	15,561	7,536	8,423	8,120
Regina, Canada	12,311	7,071	8,730	7,168	2,705	15,315	9,181	7,098	12,454	6,904	6,676	7,645	5,799	13,165	6,542	7,631	14,319	6,932	8,467	7,890
Reykjavik, Iceland	8,354	2,261	13,512	2,530	3,922	13,331	9,137	2,283	8,189	2,090	2,045	2,921	6,368	15,915	1,809	2,823	16,244	2,135	3,685	3,084
Rhodes, Greece	4,756	2,315	17,798	2,591	8,057	10,345	9,848	2,242	4,702	2,436	2,971	1,777	8,968	14,786	2,949	1,701	13,972	2,485	906	1,441
Richmond, Virginia	13,023	6,545	9,793	6,258	764	12,764	6,663	6,696	10,541	6,520	5,844	7,498	3,236	15,214	5,878	7,234	16,438	6,359	8,127	7,486
Riga, USSR	5,808	1,310	15,504	2,177	6,478	12,490	10,414	1,017	6,833	1,054	2,134	541	8,416	14,860	1,832	996	14,556	1,460	1,399	1,105
Ringkobing, Denmark	6,705	600	15,301	1,397	5,635	12,260	9,522	450	6,721	283	1,216	1,101	7,438	15,778	879	952	15,531	639	1,806	1,210
Rio Branco, Brazil	15,685	9,818	9,068	9,051	5,804	7,898	2,251	10,095	9,180	10,008	8,946	10,978	2,707	13,975	9,218	10,440	14,428	9,637	11,088	10,587
Rio Cuarto, Argentina	15,501	11,626	8,791	10,771	8,388	5,685	2,536	11,919	8,790	11,885	10,811	12,709	5,141	12,225	11,140	12,119	12,312	11,474	12,528	12,189
Rio de Janeiro, Brazil	13,419	9,533	11,111	8,662	7,771	5,208	929	9,823	6,612	9,823	8,790	10,534	4,365	14,163	9,143	9,939	13,915	9,404	10,249	9,975
Rio Gallegos, Argentina	15,107	13,423	8,074	12,552	10,416	4,662	4,404	13,713	9,259	13,714	12,674	14,396	7,231	10,320	13,024	13,805	10,275	13,295	14,010	13,817
Rio Grande, Brazil	14,366	10,851	9,931	9,981	8,463	4,979	1,849	11,142	7,633	11,135	10,089	11,866	5,059	12,903	10,437	11,272	12,782	10,717	11,583	11,310
Riyadh, Saudi Arabia	2,768	4,452	17,907	4,739	10,232	9,691	11,190	4,323	4,669	4,509	5,164	3,619	11,011	12,761	5,114	3,776	11,838	4,635	2,882	3,518
Road Town, Brit. Virgin Isls.	13,797	7,160	10,294	6,549	2,720	10,316	4,206	7,400	9,104	7,271	6,301	8,298	798	16,060	6,493	7,849	17,016	6,965	8,652	8,053
Roanoke, Virginia	13,161	6,726	9,579	6,457	946	12,882	6,764	6,872	10,761	6,694	6,037	7,663	3,355	14,993	6,064	7,412	16,216	6,542	8,306	7,666
Robinson Crusoe Island, Chile	16,781	12,555	7,449	11,737	8,453	6,571	3,680	12,842	10,137	12,776	11,699	13,692	5,561	11,312	11,996	13,121	11,612	12,385	13,642	13,229
Rochester, New York	12,495	6,144	10,019	5,938	543	13,248	7,196	6,274	10,568	6,091	5,498	7,041	3,753	15,186	5,495	6,819	16,393	5,965	7,714	7,076
Rockhampton, Australia	9,646	15,642	6,056	16,475	15,658	10,829	15,236	15,350	14,285	15,393	16,467	14,519	16,658	522	16,135	15,091	1,303	15,801	14,499	14,972
Rome, Italy	6,187	1,065	16,818	1,105	6,602	10,710	8,892	1,162	5,120	1,327	1,513	1,416	7,571	16,113	1,562	873	15,413	1,173	1,141	812
Rosario, Argentina	15,163	11,399	9,130	10,538	8,407	5,461	2,295	11,692	8,445	11,667	10,599	12,463	5,097	12,432	10,934	11,871	12,458	11,252	12,250	11,932
Roseau, Dominica	13,739	7,195	10,527	6,533	3,139	9,838	3,744	7,449	8,719	7,332	6,324	8,348	310	16,230	6,544	7,870	17,062	7,003	8,639	8,060
Rostock, East Germany	6,418	506	15,611	1,377	5,948	12,056	9,598	229	6,474	241	1,317	805	7,649	15,679	1,034	626	15,344	641	1,473	880
Rostov-na-Donu, USSR	4,344	2,398	16,441	3,094	7,976	11,774	11,105	2,159	6,187	2,300	3,265	1,272	9,641	13,923	3,065	1,721	13,374	2,591	1,100	1,553
Rotterdam, Netherlands	6,889	224	15,557	872	5,565	11,789	9,043	415	6,309	330	751	1,315	7,103	16,242	492	910	15,898	121	1,800	1,158
Rouyn, Canada	12,055	5,878	10,139	5,760	902	13,737	7,733	5,981	10,680	5,793	5,297	6,704	4,289	15,015	5,254	6,530	16,184	5,708	7,420	6,791
Sacramento, California	13,462	8,915	6,868	9,040	4,235	15,571	9,725	8,924	14,232	8,731	8,547	9,408	6,675	11,498	8,405	9,446	12,702	8,783	10,253	9,702
Saginaw, Michigan	12,702	6,513	9,566	6,359	1,057	13,618	7,515	6,624	11,081	6,437	5,906	7,356	4,090	14,672	5,879	7,172	15,879	6,339	8,064	7,432
Saint Denis, Reunion	4,797	9,236	14,924	9,227	14,523	5,718	10,731	9,197	4,715	9,391	9,706	8,652	13,108	9,671	9,798	8,660	8,451	9,384	7,823	8,401
Saint George's, Grenada	13,977	7,494	10,392	6,810	3,478	9,553	3,435	7,752	8,711	7,641	6,620	8,651	259	16,023	6,850	8,161	16,781	7,303	8,913	8,345
Saint John, Canada	11,772	5,267	10,968	5,010	516	12,843	7,005	5,416	9,669	5,240	4,582	6,220	3,618	16,052	4,604	5,954	17,226	5,082	6,848	6,207
Saint John's, Antigua	13,660	7,076	10,535	6,432	2,934	10,032	3,946	7,326	8,794	7,205	6,209	8,225	504	16,272	6,420	7,757	17,158	6,883	8,539	7,952
Saint John's, Canada	10,863	4,258	12,020	3,960	1,554	12,472	7,032	4,426	8,737	4,257	3,542	5,262	3,875	16,860	3,585	4,955	17,902	4,069	5,843	5,202
Saint Louis, Missouri	13,391	7,263	8,846	7,097	1,671	13,595	7,461	7,374	11,652	7,187	6,649	8,101	4,132	14,110	6,627	7,922	15,332	7,089	8,813	8,182
Saint Paul, Minnesota	12,786	6,928	9,019	6,867	1,795	14,260	8,128	7,007	11,788	6,816	6,394	7,674	4,742	13,948	6,327	7,555	15,146	6,766	8,434	7,817
Saint Peter Port, UK	7,379	703	15,426	534	5,190	11,527	8,491	970	6,196	895	185	1,863	6,553	16,803	223	1,390	16,456	514	2,236	1,607
Saipan (Susupe)	7,716	11,674	7,711	12,544	12,613	14,574	18,571	11,387	14,478	11,372	12,376	10,713	15,830	4,784	12,015	11,305	5,232	11,790	11,032	11,283
Salalah, Oman	1,995	5,591	17,281	5,925	11,372	9,256	11,764	5,455	4,873	5,638	6,305	4,721	12,021	11,729	6,255	4,910	10,752	5,775	4,015	4,654
Salem, Oregon	12,749	8,369	7,401	8,562	4,131	16,112	10,107	8,356	13,955	8,165	8,065	8,791	6,905	11,670	7,896	8,866	12,840	8,248	9,647	9,117
Salt Lake City, Utah	13,375	8,268	7,560	8,321	3,377	15,109	9,085	8,303	13,388	8,109	7,834	8,861	5,914	12,353	7,720	8,840	13,559	8,123	9,681	9,100
Salta, Argentina	15,686	10,962	8,901	10,129	7,457	6,444	2,079	11,252	8,879	11,198	10,119	12,084	4,238	12,911	10,430	11,507	13,113	10,798	12,010	11,606
Salto, Uruguay	14,926	11,108	9,422	10,245	8,275	5,412	2,007	11,401	8,178	11,379	10,314	12,165	4,925	12,711	10,652	11,572	12,705	10,964	11,944	11,630
Salvador, Brazil	12,698	8,330	11,996	7,460	6,973	5,868	1,060	8,621	5,989	8,619	7,584	9,344	3,707	15,358	7,938	8,750	15,032	8,200	9,095	8,794
Salzburg, Austria	6,224	541	16,269	1,096	6,313	11,367	9,275	528	5,772	712	1,304	901	7,647	15,897	1,196	308	15,368	716	1,076	456
Samsun, Turkey	4,250	2,475	17,153	3,006	8,230	11,061	10,685	2,299	5,479	2,474	3,281	1,538	9,550	14,136	3,156	1,772	13,448	2,668	906	1,534
San Antonio, Texas	14,571	8,534	7,651	8,342	2,844	13,361	7,384	8,648	12,548	8,461	7,903	9,374	4,394	13,138	7,893	9,196	14,353	8,358	10,088	9,455
San Cristobal, Venezuela	15,184	8,593	9,155	7,961	3,835	9,789	3,738	8,838	9,809	8,711	7,730	9,736	1,502	14,793	7,931	9,279	15,629	8,400	10,067	9,477
San Diego, California	14,189	9,272	6,576	9,301	4,158	14,836	9,105	9,311	14,169	9,117	8,818	9,868	6,209	11,593	8,715	9,848	12,815	9,125	10,689	10,108
San Francisco, California	13,526	9,034	6,748	9,161	4,344	15,571	9,767	9,041	14,348	8,848	8,667	9,520	6,746	11,387	8,525	9,563	12,593	8,902	10,367	9,818
San Jose, Costa Rica	15,938	9,244	8,003	8,729	3,812	10,737	4,897	9,455	11,125	9,303	8,423	10,328	2,691	13,760	8,563	9,948	14,755	9,049	10,798	10,174
San Juan, Argentina	15,919	11,736	8,443	10,894	8,186	6,083	2,722	12,027	9,180	11,980	10,901	12,845	5,030	12,134	11,219	12,261	12,307	11,576	12,723	12,349
San Juan, Puerto Rico	13,916	7,264	10,143	6,667	2,690	10,404	4,282	7,501	9,262	7,369	6,409	8,397	915	15,914	6,595	7,956	16,887	7,069	8,767	8,163
San Luis Potosi, Mexico	15,407	9,322	6,994	9,083	3,569	12,905	7,148	9,448	12,899	9,264	8,659	10,193	4,488	12,635	8,671	9,994	13,824	9,143	10,889	10,252
San Marino, San Marino	6,210	859	16,626	1,043	6,486	10,933	9,009	939	5,344	1,108	1,397	1,234	7,579	16,063	1,402	668	15,422	983	1,091	651
San Miguel de Tucuman, Argen.	15,660	11,127	8,868	10,289	7,683	6,260	2,167	11,418	8,860	11,369	10,290	12,242	4,457	12,744	10,606	11,660	12,918	10,966	12,143	11,754
San Salvador, El Salvador	15,896	9,278	7,647	8,843	3,225	11,402	5,593	9,465	11,695	9,300	8,495	10,309	3,203	13,433	8,597	9,981	14,509	9,085	10,857	10,220
Sanaa, Yemen	3,069	5,138	18,323	5,312	10,826	8,643	10,692	5,059	3,856	5,251	5,743	4,463	11,074	12,622	5,759	4,512	11,573	5,305	3,649	4,250
Santa Cruz, Bolivia	15,395	10,205	9,322	9,385	6,710	6,904	1,641	10,493	8,650	10,431	9,352	11,341	3,440	13,664	9,657	10,771	13,911	10,036	11,318	10,884
Santa Cruz, Tenerife	8,944	3,156	15,295	2,287	5,119	9,375	5,966	3,448	4,950	3,445	2,434	4,208	4,795	18,968	2,797	3,619	17,848	3,026	4,131	3,705
Santa Fe, New Mexico	13,955	8,417	7,528	8,362	3,088	14,345	8,351	8,487	13,086	8,295	7,891	9,124	5,259	12,675	7,823	9,034	13,897	8,257	9,905	9,296
Santa Rosa, Argentina	15,417	11,923	8,714	11,063	8,773	5,407	2,820	12,217	8,800	12,190	11,122	12,987	5,525	11,910	11,456	12,394	11,958	11,776	12,764	12,453
Santa Rosalia, Mexico	14,854	9,521	6,456	9,450	4,074	14,077	8,424	9,592	13,917	9,400	8,984	10,222	5,681	11,789	8,923	10,139	13,010	9,361	11,008	10,401
Santarem, Brazil	14,038	8,285	10,693	7,481	5,228	7,780	1,653	8,571	7,778	8,504	7,426	9,431	1,802	15,569	7,725	8,871	15,840	8,113	9,469	8,999
Santiago del Estero, Argentina	15,561	11,154	8,934	10,311	7,798	6,117	2,146	11,446	8,767	11,401	10,323	12,261	4,551	12,714	10,643	11,677	12,859	10,995	12,141	11,764
Santiago, Chile	16,068	12,029	8,207	11,187	8,395	6,067	3,009	12,320	9,379	12,272	11,193	13,138	5,283	11,842	11,509	12,555	12,025	11,868	13,013	12,642
Santo Domingo, Dominican Rep.	14,212	7,531	9,762	6,966	2,652	10,625	4,490	7,759	9,659	7,620	6,687	8,650	1,251	15,541	6,856	8,229	16,551	7,336	9,056	8,443
Sao Paulo de Olivenca, Brazil	15,520	9,318	9,158	8,590	5,079	8,551	2,663	9,587	9,335	9,486	8,442	10,481	2,093	14,381	8,693	9,966	14,960	9,132	10,668	10,131
Sao Paulo, Brazil	13,772	9,767	10,764	8,898	7,716	5,356	869	10,059	6,965	10,051	9,005	10,791	4,293	13,980	9,354	10,196	13,806	9,632	10,535	10,241
Sao Tome, Sao Tome & Principe	7,495	5,586	17,063	4,982	8,984	6,079	6,262	5,767	1,078	5,902	5,435	5,953	7,448	15,333	5,733	5,498	14,119	5,601	5,247	5,362
Sapporo, Japan	6,863	8,712	9,480	9,565	10,007	16,734	16,858	8,438	13,204	8,394	9,337	7,885	13,433	7,902	8,972	8,456	8,305	8,804	8,385	8,489
Sarajevo, Yugoslavia	5,736	1,147	16,839	1,515	6,898	10,983	9,419	1,105	5,336	1,298	1,834	1,000	8,057	15,597	1,782	612	14,944	1,315	618	411
Saratov, USSR	4,311	2,694	15,812	3,482	7,964	12,398	11,639	2,419	6,841	2,520	3,568	1,535	9,929	13,503	3,312	2,093	13,069	2,876	1,678	1,990
Saskatoon, Canada	12,130	7,023	8,762	7,155	2,868	15,535	9,403	7,038	12,512	6,844	6,660	7,558	6,012	13,058	6,512	7,566	14,196	6,849	8,389	7,823
Schefferville, Canada	10,984	4,776	11,172	4,708	1,417	13,701	8,023	4,871	9,888	4,682	4,232	5,589	4,669	15,600	4,165	5,420	16,638	4,609	6,308	5,682
Seattle, Washington	12,479	8,087	7,683	8,297	4,011	16,231	10,165	8,069	13,737	7,879	7,800	8,495	6,905	11,836	7,623	8,577	12,990	7,969	9,353	8,826

Distances in Kilometers	Bombay, India	Bonn, West Germany	Bora Bora (Vaitape)	Bordeaux, France	Boston, Massachusetts	Bouvet Island	Brasilia, Brazil	Braunschweig, West Germany	Brazzaville, Congo	Bremerhaven, West Germany	Brest, France	Brest, USSR	Bridgetown, Barbados	Brisbane, Australia	Bristol, United Kingdom	Brno, Czechoslovakia	Broken Hill, Australia	Brussels, Belgium	Bucharest, Romania	Budapest, Hungary
Sendai, Japan	6,836	9,166	9,271	10,026	10,513	16,357	17,372	8,888	13,367	8,852	9,816	8,300	13,935	7,388	9,452	8,879	7,772	9,266	8,758	8,898
Seoul, South Korea	5,614	8,604	10,370	9,475	10,967	15,411	17,541	8,314	12,211	8,312	9,346	7,619	14,354	7,698	8,994	8,212	7,841	8,731	7,954	8,189
Sept-Iles, Canada	11,365	4,993	11,079	4,830	942	13,289	7,530	5,117	9,779	4,933	4,375	5,881	4,160	15,844	4,352	5,663	16,953	4,817	6,557	5,921
Sevastopol, USSR	4,613	2,086	16,852	2,682	7,815	11,340	10,568	1,892	5,711	2,062	2,918	1,106	9,245	14,388	2,768	1,382	13,765	2,281	591	1,162
Seville, Spain	7,788	1,811	15,948	944	5,458	10,213	7,342	2,097	5,110	2,118	1,230	2,832	5,940	17,772	1,586	2,242	16,995	1,704	2,794	2,334
Shanghai, China	5,038	8,892	10,659	9,754	11,770	14,539	17,995	8,598	11,790	8,622	9,688	7,831	15,111	7,306	9,351	8,424	7,294	9,037	8,046	8,364
Sheffield, United Kingdom	7,302	658	15,173	951	5,129	11,958	8,850	820	6,578	670	591	1,699	6,754	16,456	226	1,343	16,225	489	2,235	1,594
Shenyang, China	5,386	8,045	10,798	8,916	10,571	15,489	17,006	7,755	11,830	7,752	8,787	7,065	13,918	8,254	8,435	7,658	8,372	8,171	7,416	7,638
Shiraz, Iran	2,368	4,429	17,156	4,910	10,173	10,433	11,859	4,251	5,462	4,422	5,221	3,443	11,354	12,409	5,110	3,726	11,591	4,621	2,850	3,486
Sibiu, Romania	5,348	1,375	16,735	1,933	7,151	11,280	9,923	1,225	5,615	1,411	2,180	701	8,497	15,118	2,055	680	14,514	1,567	216	431
Singapore	3,908	10,375	11,595	11,043	15,144	10,799	16,541	10,123	9,870	10,243	11,245	9,223	17,602	6,146	11,029	9,699	5,404	10,567	8,939	9,511
Sioux Falls, South Dakota	13,003	7,241	8,692	7,192	2,091	14,370	8,235	7,315	12,103	7,123	6,718	7,969	4,892	13,641	6,646	7,863	14,846	7,081	8,738	8,125
Skelleftea, Sweden	6,353	1,758	14,618	2,586	5,937	13,305	10,618	1,514	7,672	1,430	2,368	1,420	8,249	14,684	2,007	1,752	14,605	1,827	2,286	1,926
Skopje, Yugoslavia	5,451	1,468	17,108	1,808	7,219	10,824	9,553	1,408	5,162	1,602	2,148	1,135	8,317	15,373	2,104	885	14,672	1,637	462	640
Socotra Island (Tamrida)	2,132	5,974	17,228	6,258	11,743	8,824	11,650	5,853	4,675	6,040	6,657	5,148	12,175	11,533	6,628	5,305	10,509	6,154	4,413	5,046
Sofia, Bulgaria	5,320	1,524	17,067	1,931	7,298	10,928	9,722	1,432	5,262	1,626	2,248	1,047	8,461	15,216	2,180	890	14,534	1,703	297	630
Songkhla, Thailand	3,274	9,640	12,121	10,322	14,452	11,121	16,476	9,385	9,562	9,502	10,512	8,485	16,886	6,822	10,290	8,969	6,128	9,831	8,223	8,786
Sorong, Indonesia	6,747	12,410	8,603	13,233	14,903	12,254	18,159	12,121	12,893	12,177	13,256	11,277	18,213	3,751	12,943	11,847	3,601	12,576	11,279	11,731
South Georgia Island	12,968	12,332	10,060	11,503	11,193	2,576	4,377	12,592	7,248	12,658	11,774	13,048	7,771	10,899	12,139	12,506	10,453	12,260	12,448	12,438
South Pole	12,101	15,627	8,174	14,971	14,695	3,970	8,258	15,797	9,532	15,940	15,367	15,779	11,452	6,958	15,706	15,456	6,464	15,638	14,926	15,267
South Sandwich Islands	12,322	12,412	10,372	11,622	11,843	1,881	4,988	12,653	6,955	12,741	11,940	13,004	8,418	10,558	12,301	12,498	10,001	12,362	12,328	12,399
Split, Yugoslavia	5,887	1,069	16,812	1,365	6,782	10,925	9,262	1,067	5,293	1,256	1,704	1,097	7,897	15,761	1,675	632	15,101	1,223	782	489
Spokane, Washington	12,554	7,882	7,890	8,052	3,645	15,924	9,830	7,880	13,426	7,688	7,555	8,348	6,547	12,185	7,394	8,398	13,346	7,757	9,196	8,651
Spoleto, Italy	6,175	987	16,750	1,094	6,571	10,804	8,958	1,073	5,211	1,241	1,480	1,327	7,595	16,073	1,509	780	15,397	1,104	1,095	728
Springbok, South Africa	7,980	8,969	14,776	8,460	12,082	2,987	6,846	9,105	2,825	9,263	8,930	9,076	9,553	12,088	9,207	8,736	10,959	9,016	8,248	8,547
Springfield, Illinois	13,251	7,135	8,954	6,980	1,585	13,657	7,522	7,244	11,590	7,056	6,529	7,967	4,171	14,173	6,503	7,792	15,393	6,963	8,683	8,053
Springfield, Massachusetts	12,372	5,900	10,362	5,639	130	12,893	6,891	6,047	10,151	5,869	5,214	6,844	3,450	15,607	5,237	6,586	16,818	5,716	7,480	6,839
Srinagar, India	1,686	5,657	15,002	6,363	10,856	11,942	13,982	5,400	7,541	5,519	6,530	4,501	12,911	10,689	6,305	4,993	10,103	5,847	4,291	4,821
Stanley, Falkland Islands	14,407	12,893	8,848	12,025	10,500	3,986	4,081	13,177	8,478	13,199	12,196	13,796	7,181	10,729	12,555	13,214	10,549	12,781	13,342	13,202
Stara Zagora, Bulgaria	5,128	1,688	17,123	2,122	7,469	10,939	9,885	1,576	5,275	1,767	2,432	1,086	8,654	15,028	2,352	1,027	14,341	1,871	227	765
Stockholm, Sweden	6,241	1,183	15,180	2,042	6,040	12,682	10,209	916	7,056	868	1,902	879	8,064	15,092	1,565	1,132	14,878	1,285	1,745	1,319
Stornoway, United Kingdom	7,604	1,203	14,574	1,541	4,721	12,521	9,039	1,258	7,193	1,067	1,100	2,014	6,674	16,236	791	1,806	16,215	1,072	2,693	2,068
Strasbourg, France	6,625	244	15,994	760	5,923	11,425	8,999	455	5,901	556	904	1,198	7,265	16,227	805	655	15,750	351	1,478	853
Stuttgart, West Germany	6,522	265	16,035	862	6,010	11,451	9,096	401	5,905	534	1,008	1,094	7,372	16,123	892	547	15,643	418	1,379	750
Subic, Philippines	5,055	10,286	10,274	11,111	13,563	13,069	18,759	9,997	11,746	10,054	11,133	9,155	16,910	5,875	10,824	9,727	5,655	10,452	9,188	9,618
Suchow, China	4,688	8,377	11,125	9,237	11,478	14,520	17,480	8,084	11,374	8,111	9,180	7,310	14,752	7,811	8,846	7,902	7,758	8,525	7,521	7,840
Sucre, Bolivia	15,635	10,448	9,071	9,633	6,823	6,932	1,879	10,735	8,872	10,671	9,593	11,588	3,608	13,417	9,894	11,020	13,690	10,278	11,575	11,136
Sudbury, Canada	12,295	6,115	9,923	5,984	915	13,703	7,654	6,221	10,834	6,034	5,524	6,947	4,211	14,889	5,487	6,770	16,075	5,944	7,660	7,030
Suez, Egypt	4,238	3,130	18,454	3,331	8,835	9,761	9,991	3,065	4,212	3,258	3,744	2,564	9,502	14,273	3,749	2,524	13,358	3,295	1,703	2,264
Sundsvall, Sweden	6,405	1,437	14,840	2,266	5,870	13,011	10,335	1,197	7,394	1,109	2,060	1,207	8,050	14,970	1,704	1,468	14,844	1,506	2,077	1,661
Surabaya, Indonesia	5,252	11,731	10,373	12,409	16,097	10,581	16,697	11,474	10,781	11,589	12,603	10,575	18,968	4,798	12,378	11,060	4,039	11,922	10,305	10,875
Suva, Fiji	12,242	16,307	3,173	17,042	13,023	11,951	13,711	16,073	16,923	15,978	16,637	15,640	13,810	2,799	16,307	16,193	4,009	16,339	16,122	16,248
Sverdlovsk, USSR	4,326	3,497	14,778	4,348	8,120	13,378	12,588	3,204	7,911	3,252	4,331	2,418	10,519	12,664	4,022	3,012	12,397	3,655	2,762	2,970
Svobodnyy, USSR	5,992	7,399	10,760	8,261	9,452	16,378	16,038	7,119	11,950	7,086	8,065	6,536	12,820	9,074	7,702	7,111	9,325	7,501	7,024	7,136
Sydney, Australia	10,147	16,565	5,983	17,319	16,241	9,745	14,149	16,285	13,756	16,360	17,434	15,407	16,150	729	17,140	15,940	938	16,743	15,228	15,777
Sydney, Canada	11,391	4,830	11,435	4,550	964	12,653	6,969	4,990	9,240	4,817	4,128	5,810	3,664	16,446	4,162	5,523	17,584	4,644	6,415	5,773
Syktyvkar, USSR	5,044	2,902	14,686	3,772	7,352	13,529	11,997	2,610	7,918	2,625	3,692	1,944	9,774	13,297	3,362	2,525	13,108	3,041	2,503	2,544
Szeged, Hungary	5,659	1,084	16,623	1,622	6,866	11,272	9,665	966	5,618	1,159	1,870	698	8,186	15,415	1,758	420	14,826	1,271	508	160
Szombathely, Hungary	5,947	797	16,436	1,354	6,579	11,336	9,475	711	5,707	904	1,581	744	7,914	15,657	1,467	219	15,100	982	799	189
Tabriz, Iran	3,330	3,374	17,042	3,931	9,081	11,041	11,441	3,177	5,677	3,342	4,198	2,347	10,471	13,234	4,056	2,670	12,524	3,569	1,828	2,443
Tacheng, China	3,217	5,347	14,003	6,174	9,806	13,469	14,348	5,059	8,684	5,122	6,200	4,218	12,403	10,814	5,903	4,797	10,504	5,515	4,346	4,705
Tahiti (Papeete)	15,558	15,783	258	15,834	10,398	11,628	10,682	15,778	17,085	15,587	15,358	16,124	10,443	5,959	15,257	16,280	7,049	15,651	16,995	16,525
Taipei, Taiwan	5,044	9,446	10,462	10,299	12,431	14,042	18,514	9,153	11,851	9,188	10,262	8,357	15,782	6,726	9,933	8,945	6,654	9,599	8,509	8,868
Taiyuan, China	4,374	7,803	11,613	8,662	11,112	14,502	16,905	7,510	10,941	7,540	8,611	6,733	14,305	8,377	8,280	7,325	8,290	7,953	6,947	7,263
Tallahassee, Florida	14,018	7,547	8,895	7,232	1,772	12,557	6,430	7,702	11,171	7,527	6,830	8,506	3,180	14,494	6,877	8,238	15,701	7,360	9,131	8,489
Tallinn, USSR	5,899	1,477	15,234	2,348	6,376	12,767	10,556	1,190	7,110	1,186	2,251	817	8,445	14,737	1,925	1,252	14,499	1,605	1,670	1,377
Tamanrasset, Algeria	6,958	3,105	17,552	2,508	7,265	8,557	7,216	3,301	3,175	3,425	2,977	3,607	6,933	16,722	3,257	3,090	15,582	3,115	3,050	2,998
Tampa, Florida	14,177	7,627	8,939	7,268	1,902	12,230	6,106	7,796	10,996	7,625	6,884	8,619	2,885	14,609	6,951	8,325	15,798	7,437	9,212	8,571
Tampere, Finland	6,057	1,575	14,997	2,437	6,219	12,980	10,596	1,301	7,330	1,263	2,292	1,047	8,384	14,708	1,950	1,440	14,530	1,680	1,906	1,586
Tanami, Australia	7,556	13,988	8,236	14,702	16,857	10,316	16,040	13,719	12,383	13,818	14,864	12,826	18,771	2,512	14,610	13,336	1,768	14,174	12,606	13,162
Tangier, Morocco	7,801	1,956	16,036	1,097	5,555	10,037	7,230	2,239	4,951	2,269	1,404	2,947	5,921	17,821	1,758	2,354	16,979	1,858	2,862	2,430
Tarawa (Betio)	11,031	14,079	4,354	14,849	12,012	14,043	15,276	13,839	17,532	13,750	14,487	13,420	14,018	3,839	14,138	13,962	4,961	14,122	13,969	14,029
Tashkent, USSR	2,502	4,779	15,232	5,523	9,919	12,320	13,420	4,514	7,442	4,622	5,655	3,618	12,030	11,487	5,413	4,137	10,975	4,967	3,505	3,986
Tbilisi, USSR	3,662	3,035	16,803	3,648	8,695	11,357	11,380	2,822	5,902	2,978	3,880	1,965	10,210	13,447	3,715	2,336	12,799	3,231	1,546	2,126
Tegucigalpa, Honduras	15,751	9,108	7,861	8,657	3,497	11,310	5,443	9,299	11,481	9,137	8,316	10,151	2,987	13,647	8,425	9,811	14,716	8,914	10,683	10,048
Tehran, Iran	2,800	3,899	16,892	4,461	9,581	10,991	11,853	3,697	5,810	3,858	4,727	2,851	10,995	12,722	4,581	3,195	11,996	4,094	2,358	2,972
Tel Aviv, Israel	4,067	3,074	18,164	3,360	8,829	10,046	10,263	2,979	4,519	3,171	3,745	2,400	9,656	14,116	3,717	2,431	13,246	3,248	1,566	2,169
Telegraph Creek, Canada	11,203	7,376	8,463	7,739	4,455	17,219	11,086	7,307	13,382	7,126	7,250	7,598	7,693	11,768	7,014	7,772	12,806	7,288	8,469	8,005
Teresina, Brazil	12,898	7,803	11,861	6,946	5,981	6,862	1,308	8,096	6,445	8,068	7,001	8,886	2,738	16,023	7,339	8,298	15,882	7,654	8,760	8,379
Ternate, Indonesia	6,280	12,013	9,067	12,824	14,881	12,200	18,272	11,726	12,481	11,790	12,868	10,871	18,290	4,161	12,565	11,434	3,915	12,183	10,845	11,310
The Valley, Anguilla	13,697	7,083	10,440	6,457	2,800	10,190	4,094	7,328	8,936	7,203	6,220	8,227	661	16,195	6,421	7,769	17,122	6,890	8,562	7,969
Thessaloniki, Greece	5,301	1,661	17,284	1,973	7,407	10,698	9,600	1,601	5,033	1,795	2,329	1,276	8,451	15,260	2,294	1,073	14,528	1,830	496	823
Thimphu, Bhutan	1,968	7,189	13,630	7,930	12,020	12,222	15,481	6,922	8,709	7,025	8,066	6,027	14,433	9,100	7,817	6,547	8,565	7,376	5,879	6,389
Thunder Bay, Canada	12,336	6,454	9,469	6,411	1,575	14,302	8,206	6,530	11,440	6,338	5,935	7,194	4,777	14,252	5,859	7,078	15,427	6,293	7,955	7,340
Tientsin, China	4,802	7,954	11,242	8,821	10,941	14,895	17,044	7,662	11,339	7,678	8,738	6,917	14,213	8,262	8,398	7,511	8,259	8,095	7,186	7,466
Tijuana, Mexico	14,211	9,282	6,569	9,308	4,157	14,812	9,086	9,322	14,165	9,128	8,826	9,881	6,194	11,597	8,724	9,859	12,819	9,135	10,702	10,119
Tiksi, USSR	6,853	5,688	11,369	6,491	7,268	16,820	13,799	5,443	11,263	5,359	6,196	5,101	10,587	11,151	5,831	5,597	11,527	5,743	5,807	5,703
Timbuktu, Mali	7,977	3,875	16,703	3,120	6,978	7,912	6,105	4,115	3,077	4,204	3,511	4,571	6,084	17,292	3,848	4,012	16,072	3,836	4,105	3,965
Tindouf, Algeria	8,197	2,863	16,093	2,017	5,830	9,167	6,446	3,139	4,341	3,183	2,320	3,785	5,567	18,173	2,678	3,192	17,061	2,776	3,563	3,227
Tirane, Albania	5,572	1,433	17,139	1,701	7,149	10,727	9,397	1,405	5,071	1,597	2,065	1,232	8,185	15,516	2,046	909	14,797	1,592	617	688
Tokyo, Japan	6,751	9,371	9,234	10,235	10,812	16,087	17,672	9,089	13,367	9,060	10,040	8,477	14,234	7,133	9,677	9,060	7,491	9,476	8,904	9,069
Toledo, Spain	7,580	1,486	15,968	620	5,487	10,473	7,658	1,773	5,271	1,795	949	2,518	6,166	17,499	1,292	1,932	16,806	1,381	2,526	2,036
Topeka, Kansas	13,472	7,550	8,473	7,438	2,105	13,962	7,841	7,643	12,115	7,453	6,978	8,333	4,562	13,648	6,933	8,192	14,868	7,383	9,077	8,454
Toronto, Canada	12,516	6,218	9,909	6,033	694	13,386	7,322	6,341	10,712	6,157	5,587	7,095	3,880	15,039	5,575	6,887	16,244	6,041	7,781	7,146
Toulouse, France	7,096	901	16,088	211	5,716	10,865	8,272	1,177	5,481	1,224	703	1,905	6,693	16,909	923	1,321	16,310	833	1,973	1,441
Tours, France	7,146	599	15,757	299	5,493	11,287	8,505	892	5,898	885	402	1,732	6,722	16,751	511	1,198	16,293	467	1,990	1,385
Townsville, Australia	9,115	15,046	6,486	15,878	15,639	11,131	15,812	14,755	14,119	14,800	15,876	13,922	17,131	1,113	15,548	14,494	1,506	15,206	13,910	14,376
Trenton, New Jersey	12,647	6,173	10,119	5,902	391	12,847	6,795	6,322	10,320	6,145	5,481	7,121	3,351	15,443	5,509	6,861	16,663	5,989	7,754	7,114
Tripoli, Lebanon	4,030	2,943	17,883	3,300	8,721	10,327	10,435	2,825	4,796	3,014	3,658	2,190	9,691	14,069	3,603	2,276	13,245	3,124	1,390	2,016
Tripoli, Libya	6,092	2,043	17,652	1,778	7,205	9,722	8,436	2,162	4,119	2,323	2,268	2,296	7,637	16,138	2,426	1,833	15,209	2,119	1,700	1,696
Tristan da Cunha (Edinburgh)	10,844	9,909	12,718	9,145	10,622	2,275	4,224	10,141	4,593	10,238	9,497	10,478	7,438	12,697	9,850	9,972	11,895	9,871	9,818	9,872
Trondheim, Norway	6,773	1,426	14,619	2,182	5,501	13,083	10,099	1,242	7,518	1,104	1,903	1,481	7,721	15,196	1,538	1,627	15,140	1,447	2,336	1,851
Trujillo, Peru	16,765	10,431	7,928	9,743	5,648	8,789	3,489	10,687	10,427	10,571	9,558	11,587	3,180	13,175	9,783	11,099	13,843	10,240	11,840	11,280
Truk Island (Moen)	8,602	12,729	6,750	13,596	12,991	14,086	17,687	12,445	15,219	12,422	13,403	11,789	15,871	3,867	13,040	12,381	4,497	12,839	12,118	12,364
Truro, Canada	11,619	5,079	11,183	4,805	709	12,721	6,947	5,235	9,456	5,061	4,382	6,050	3,594	16,256	4,412	5,770	17,420	4,894	6,663	6,022
Tsingtao, China	5,002	8,392	10,895	9,258	11,243	14,863	17,478	8,099	11,643	8,116	9,174	7,353	14,563	7,828	8,833	7,948	7,845	8,532	7,614	7,900
Tsitsihar, China	5,577	7,575	10,924	8,444	9,956	15,889	16,424	7,289	11,759	7,273	8,286	6,644	13,298	8,789	7,929	7,231	8,957	7,691	7,061	7,232
Tubuai Island (Mataura)	15,628	16,361	795	16,328	10,832	11,004	10,463	16,377	16,535	16,184	15,870	16,763	10,570	5,753	15,801	16,892	6,773	16,217	17,634	17,142
Tucson, Arizona	14,326	9,000	6,927	8,961	3,676	14,395	8,560	9,063	13,642	8,869	8,488	9,678	5,625	12,110	8,413	9,607	13,334	8,843	10,471	9,869
Tulsa, Oklahoma	13,790	7,805	8,273	7,662	2,243	13,748	7,650	7,907	12,191	7,718	7,209	8,613	4,432	13,564	7,178	8,456	14,787	7,634	9,344	8,717

Distances in Kilometers	Bombay, India	Bonn, West Germany	Bora Bora (Vaitape)	Bordeaux, France	Boston, Massachusetts	Bouvet Island	Brasilia, Brazil	Braunschweig, West Germany	Brazzaville, Congo	Bremerhaven, West Germany	Brest, France	Brest, USSR	Bridgetown, Barbados	Brisbane, Australia	Bristol, United Kingdom	Brno, Czechoslovakia	Broken Hill, Australia	Brussels, Belgium	Bucharest, Romania	Budapest, Hungary
Tunis, Tunisia	6,362	1,568	17,147	1,270	6,734	10,130	8,423	1,719	4,577	1,866	1,757	2,005	7,358	16,396	1,916	1,473	15,558	1,627	1,587	1,396
Tura, USSR	5,437	5,240	12,515	6,104	8,156	15,516	14,102	4,960	10,187	4,929	5,923	4,394	11,256	11,156	5,564	4,962	11,259	5,346	4,943	5,000
Turin, Italy	6,601	633	16,308	650	6,091	11,032	8,762	830	5,515	948	999	1,415	7,208	16,389	1,040	821	15,800	689	1,458	920
Uberlandia, Brazil	13,865	9,422	10,781	8,558	7,178	5,871	351	9,715	7,085	9,695	8,634	10,480	3,754	14,381	8,976	9,888	14,280	9,279	10,286	9,951
Ufa, USSR	4,222	3,261	15,149	4,094	8,134	13,021	12,314	2,972	7,536	3,038	4,115	2,144	10,386	12,898	3,823	2,732	12,567	3,429	2,417	2,668
Ujungpandang, Indonesia	5,757	12,007	9,735	12,745	15,752	11,178	17,312	11,736	11,536	11,831	12,883	10,845	19,115	4,337	12,623	11,366	3,755	12,192	10,669	11,203
Ulaanbaatar, Mongolia	4,443	6,674	12,197	7,541	10,001	14,882	15,765	6,381	10,479	6,397	7,457	5,646	13,116	9,540	7,118	6,240	9,494	6,814	5,955	6,204
Ulan-Ude, USSR	4,741	6,414	12,163	7,285	9,567	15,183	15,460	6,123	10,540	6,126	7,173	5,428	12,707	9,842	6,826	6,020	9,852	6,545	5,800	6,003
Uliastay, Mongolia	3,861	6,122	12,951	6,978	9,951	14,292	15,220	5,829	9,727	5,864	6,939	5,047	12,873	10,049	6,615	5,639	9,888	6,274	5,287	5,581
Uranium City, Canada	11,300	6,482	9,289	6,716	3,190	16,025	9,964	6,463	12,259	6,273	6,220	6,907	6,527	13,065	6,029	6,972	14,118	6,366	7,759	7,223
Urumqi, China	3,079	5,834	13,717	6,657	10,227	13,473	14,807	5,546	8,933	5,611	6,689	4,701	12,884	10,329	6,392	5,277	10,015	6,003	4,802	5,180
Ushuaia, Argentina	14,857	13,622	8,106	12,751	10,770	4,424	4,672	13,909	9,210	13,921	12,898	14,555	7,568	10,071	13,252	13,969	9,982	13,502	14,117	13,965
Vaduz, Liechtenstein	6,477	434	16,198	822	6,111	11,275	9,015	572	5,726	713	1,057	1,160	7,377	16,170	999	575	15,638	557	1,322	724
Valencia, Spain	7,273	1,382	16,255	596	5,787	10,411	7,858	1,651	5,102	1,706	1,046	2,321	6,465	17,230	1,343	1,728	16,497	1,316	2,252	1,802
Valladolid, Spain	7,615	1,357	15,814	488	5,350	10,675	7,755	1,649	5,475	1,653	750	2,436	6,153	17,455	1,102	1,861	16,840	1,235	2,515	1,990
Valletta, Malta	5,972	1,752	17,470	1,616	7,113	10,066	8,706	1,846	4,447	2,015	2,086	1,941	7,748	16,015	2,199	1,487	15,158	1,849	1,365	1,343
Valparaiso, Chile	16,167	12,053	8,125	11,215	8,349	6,162	3,058	12,343	9,470	12,292	11,213	13,168	5,263	11,819	11,526	12,586	12,023	11,890	13,057	12,677
Vancouver, Canada	12,287	7,958	7,814	8,190	4,036	16,376	10,287	7,934	13,672	7,744	7,693	8,343	6,999	11,854	7,507	8,437	12,993	7,844	9,204	8,685
Varna, Bulgaria	4,975	1,782	17,044	2,279	7,562	11,069	10,092	1,640	5,410	1,826	2,563	1,037	8,827	14,839	2,458	1,094	14,174	1,971	199	839
Venice, Italy	6,239	705	16,474	1,017	6,393	11,102	9,092	770	5,515	941	1,320	1,113	7,578	16,027	1,287	528	15,431	844	1,090	565
Veracruz, Mexico	15,616	9,270	7,256	8,953	3,488	12,335	6,546	9,420	12,423	9,242	8,556	10,209	3,956	12,986	8,602	9,959	14,143	9,084	10,852	10,211
Verona, Italy	6,344	655	16,420	912	6,301	11,093	9,003	759	5,523	918	1,222	1,188	7,473	16,127	1,203	596	15,536	777	1,195	661
Victoria, Canada	12,369	8,046	7,725	8,272	4,070	16,346	10,271	8,023	13,743	7,833	7,775	8,435	6,999	11,801	7,592	8,527	12,946	7,931	9,295	8,775
Victoria, Seychelles	3,231	7,670	16,227	7,800	13,296	7,226	11,303	7,591	4,458	7,783	8,248	6,966	12,850	10,524	8,283	7,044	9,366	7,835	6,173	6,781
Vienna, Austria	5,988	728	16,329	1,349	6,509	11,440	9,512	614	5,814	808	1,542	680	7,897	15,646	1,406	113	15,118	918	858	218
Vientiane, Laos	3,142	8,860	12,183	9,615	13,294	12,206	16,887	8,586	9,879	8,681	9,735	7,698	16,060	7,407	9,473	8,229	6,905	9,043	7,572	8,077
Villahermosa, Mexico	15,634	9,162	7,492	8,802	3,404	12,021	6,189	9,327	12,089	9,153	8,422	10,139	3,608	13,251	8,488	9,859	14,387	8,974	10,748	10,107
Vilnius, USSR	5,630	1,303	15,762	2,145	6,673	12,262	10,386	1,016	6,600	1,099	2,163	307	8,505	14,856	1,891	853	14,486	1,474	1,141	910
Visby, Sweden	6,159	1,058	15,367	1,927	6,134	12,497	10,132	777	6,868	762	1,828	706	8,067	15,160	1,508	945	14,895	1,180	1,565	1,129
Vitoria, Brazil	13,075	9,138	11,498	8,267	7,623	5,275	945	9,428	6,274	9,432	8,406	10,129	4,256	14,524	8,762	9,535	14,218	9,013	9,837	9,567
Vladivostok, USSR	6,096	8,318	10,185	9,185	10,262	16,127	16,973	8,034	12,476	8,011	9,006	7,411	13,669	8,114	8,645	7,995	8,371	8,428	7,841	8,002
Volgograd, USSR	4,173	2,670	16,143	3,412	8,109	12,065	11,482	2,412	6,518	2,535	3,546	1,513	9,926	13,586	3,318	2,023	13,085	2,860	1,479	1,882
Vologda, USSR	5,194	2,273	15,170	3,137	7,100	13,016	11,377	1,980	7,367	2,013	3,091	1,286	9,299	13,899	2,777	1,867	13,638	2,422	1,892	1,888
Vorkuta, USSR	5,429	3,575	13,792	4,441	7,251	14,423	12,543	3,294	8,822	3,267	4,279	2,758	9,998	12,756	3,925	3,311	12,735	3,685	3,389	3,367
Wake Island	9,717	11,995	6,034	12,788	10,985	15,853	16,350	11,749	16,504	11,666	12,457	11,323	13,817	5,381	12,099	11,863	6,275	12,048	11,896	11,933
Wallis Island	12,670	15,843	2,650	16,484	12,234	12,499	13,488	15,641	17,696	15,520	16,038	15,352	13,179	3,566	15,734	15,856	4,783	15,842	15,963	15,959
Walvis Bay, Namibia	7,855	8,194	15,392	7,660	11,346	3,616	6,560	8,341	2,069	8,494	8,126	8,362	9,003	12,872	8,409	7,994	11,724	8,234	7,554	7,816
Warsaw, Poland	5,792	978	15,989	1,784	6,568	11,937	10,014	714	6,286	847	1,854	185	8,230	15,203	1,620	458	14,777	1,164	947	546
Washington, D.C.	12,877	6,417	9,883	6,145	635	12,857	6,770	6,565	10,509	6,388	5,726	7,361	3,334	15,252	5,754	7,104	16,475	6,233	7,998	7,357
Watson Lake, Canada	11,024	7,094	8,742	7,460	4,312	17,129	11,018	7,026	13,106	6,844	6,971	7,322	7,602	11,996	6,734	7,492	13,014	7,007	8,192	7,726
Weimar, East Germany	6,406	298	15,897	1,119	6,012	11,708	9,362	153	6,134	341	1,173	867	7,554	15,880	971	429	15,457	491	1,323	685
Wellington, New Zealand	12,362	18,598	4,220	19,468	14,693	9,365	12,315	18,307	14,549	18,302	19,214	17,523	13,919	2,507	18,859	18,100	3,136	18,720	17,455	17,975
West Berlin, West Germany	6,298	479	15,805	1,333	6,098	11,891	9,576	197	6,295	343	1,346	703	7,714	15,679	1,102	433	15,290	654	1,296	690
Wewak, Papua New Guinea	8,136	13,397	7,198	14,258	14,509	12,610	17,525	13,104	14,228	13,127	14,186	12,323	17,265	2,832	13,843	12,912	3,152	13,542	12,448	12,832
Whangarei, New Zealand	12,236	18,051	3,972	18,907	14,452	9,978	12,784	17,769	15,074	17,736	18,592	17,069	14,095	2,212	18,240	17,663	3,060	18,146	17,165	17,591
Whitehorse, Canada	10,826	7,194	8,691	7,603	4,654	17,478	11,368	7,109	13,265	6,932	7,121	7,354	7,953	11,717	6,868	7,557	12,712	7,116	8,224	7,783
Wichita, Kansas	13,649	7,759	8,268	7,646	2,292	13,959	7,856	7,851	12,286	7,661	7,186	8,539	4,621	13,476	7,142	8,400	14,698	7,592	9,285	8,662
Willemstad, Curacao	14,602	7,994	9,644	7,367	3,358	9,986	3,859	8,237	9,491	8,110	7,131	9,135	1,020	15,343	7,330	8,680	16,218	7,800	9,473	8,880
Wiluna, Australia	7,184	13,855	9,019	14,431	17,982	9,198	15,145	13,621	11,280	13,755	14,705	12,727	18,510	3,246	14,527	13,160	2,141	14,050	12,339	12,949
Windhoek, Namibia	7,608	8,180	15,514	7,678	11,521	3,717	6,828	8,316	2,036	8,474	8,151	8,298	9,243	12,727	8,424	7,951	11,563	8,228	7,477	7,764
Windsor, Canada	12,785	6,541	9,576	6,365	985	13,475	7,369	6,659	11,012	6,474	5,917	7,404	3,946	14,747	5,901	7,207	15,959	6,366	8,100	7,466
Winnipeg, Canada	12,315	6,754	9,092	6,788	2,169	14,847	8,726	6,803	11,967	6,609	6,302	7,406	5,317	13,687	6,193	7,345	14,849	6,605	8,203	7,606
Winston-Salem, North Carolina	13,288	6,836	9,500	6,554	1,054	12,800	6,675	6,985	10,788	6,808	6,139	7,781	3,279	14,956	6,171	7,524	16,179	6,651	8,418	7,777
Wroclaw, Poland	6,017	699	16,041	1,482	6,393	11,766	9,711	468	6,137	637	1,574	475	7,954	15,503	1,365	213	15,057	892	1,004	427
Wuhan, China	4,356	8,528	11,304	9,375	11,910	14,035	17,574	8,236	11,115	8,278	9,355	7,428	15,127	7,635	9,033	8,014	7,492	8,685	7,569	7,933
Wyndham, Australia	7,153	13,495	8,515	14,230	16,512	10,675	16,521	13,223	12,320	13,316	14,371	12,333	19,161	2,897	14,108	12,854	2,272	13,680	12,146	12,689
Xi'an, China	3,944	7,891	11,874	8,735	11,519	13,987	16,925	7,600	10,611	7,646	8,725	6,785	14,625	8,268	8,407	7,370	8,083	8,051	6,920	7,285
Xining, China	3,435	7,261	12,547	8,094	11,228	13,726	16,241	6,972	9,980	7,028	8,108	6,139	14,168	8,897	7,800	6,718	8,642	7,427	6,240	6,623
Yakutsk, USSR	6,452	6,518	11,030	7,356	8,287	16,844	14,870	6,254	11,677	6,194	7,106	5,788	11,639	10,139	6,740	6,331	10,467	6,597	6,396	6,398
Yanji, China	5,900	8,235	10,357	9,104	10,342	15,956	16,991	7,949	12,296	7,931	8,938	7,307	13,737	8,157	8,579	7,894	8,375	8,349	7,716	7,894
Yaounde, Cameroon	6,860	5,212	17,723	4,691	9,114	6,506	6,897	5,366	991	5,515	5,166	5,464	7,879	15,174	5,436	5,048	13,951	5,250	4,716	4,889
Yap Island (Colonia)	7,089	11,841	8,239	12,706	13,542	13,631	19,065	11,548	13,701	11,565	12,620	10,786	16,838	4,399	12,275	11,378	4,602	11,982	10,969	11,314
Yaraka, Australia	9,114	15,366	6,692	16,149	16,267	10,448	15,323	15,082	13,623	15,151	16,228	14,213	17,219	939	15,928	14,759	825	15,540	14,093	14,612
Yarmouth, Canada	11,897	5,362	10,923	5,081	434	12,719	6,856	5,518	9,649	5,344	4,662	6,332	3,463	16,090	4,695	6,054	17,280	5,176	6,946	6,305
Yellowknife, Canada	10,957	6,443	9,345	6,745	3,589	16,422	10,394	6,401	12,357	6,213	6,251	6,781	6,954	12,811	6,035	6,892	13,822	6,340	7,644	7,136
Yerevan, USSR	3,586	3,111	16,954	3,692	8,804	11,193	11,329	2,908	5,756	3,070	3,944	2,070	10,246	13,436	3,793	2,408	12,757	3,306	1,585	2,187
Yinchuan, China	3,886	7,390	12,163	8,238	11,049	14,155	16,458	7,098	10,395	7,140	8,217	6,294	14,113	8,772	7,897	6,881	8,603	7,547	6,462	6,805
Yogyakarta, Indonesia	5,072	11,610	10,606	12,267	16,173	10,384	16,479	11,360	10,514	11,481	12,479	10,460	18,787	4,988	12,266	10,932	4,181	11,803	10,160	10,740
York, United Kingdom	7,280	661	15,150	1,002	5,136	12,009	8,902	803	6,620	644	647	1,673	6,792	16,404	282	1,334	16,183	502	2,228	1,588
Yumen, China	3,323	6,759	12,912	7,592	10,832	13,737	15,757	6,470	9,671	6,526	7,606	5,638	13,697	9,399	7,299	6,218	9,137	6,924	5,752	6,126
Yutian, China	2,165	5,931	14,333	6,693	10,808	12,564	14,556	5,658	8,233	5,756	6,806	4,769	13,158	10,310	6,549	5,304	9,830	6,115	4,685	5,161
Yuzhno-Sakhalinsk, USSR	6,975	8,377	9,589	9,221	9,567	17,070	16,412	8,109	13,119	8,055	8,975	7,595	12,993	8,310	8,609	8,155	8,739	8,461	8,135	8,202
Zagreb, Yugoslavia	5,963	858	16,566	1,301	6,620	11,172	9,356	822	5,546	1,013	1,577	898	7,864	15,742	1,502	381	15,146	1,029	809	302
Zahedan, Iran	1,683	5,014	16,405	5,575	10,655	10,803	12,659	4,806	6,131	4,963	5,845	3,946	12,089	11,654	5,696	4,311	10,889	5,210	3,475	4,090
Zamboanga, Philippines	5,487	11,120	9,829	11,927	14,391	12,456	18,553	10,834	11,927	10,901	11,979	9,976	17,785	5,058	11,680	10,537	4,766	11,292	9,950	10,412
Zanzibar, Tanzania	4,621	7,016	17,228	6,902	12,132	6,238	9,524	7,022	2,658	7,213	7,391	6,622	11,123	12,008	7,522	6,514	10,799	7,144	5,756	6,265
Zaragoza, Spain	7,298	1,183	16,079	356	5,640	10,653	7,985	1,464	5,341	1,501	804	2,190	6,465	17,175	1,099	1,603	16,524	1,098	2,211	1,709
Zashiversk, USSR	7,212	6,381	10,698	7,174	7,502	17,438	14,215	6,141	11,953	6,052	6,863	5,809	10,892	10,564	6,501	6,304	11,022	6,431	6,511	6,411
Zhengzhou, China	4,381	8,133	11,452	8,988	11,452	14,331	17,224	7,840	11,049	7,875	8,948	7,050	14,662	8,040	8,620	7,641	7,935	8,285	7,236	7,571
Zurich, Switzerland	6,566	386	16,131	745	6,023	11,292	8,957	567	5,760	688	967	1,221	7,293	16,241	914	646	15,722	485	1,411	808

Distances in Kilometers	Buenos Aires, Argentina	Buffalo, New York	Bujumbura, Burundi	Bulawayo, Zimbabwe	Burlington, Vermont	Cabinda, Angola	Cagliari, Italy	Cairns, Australia	Cairo, Egypt	Calais, France	Calcutta, India	Calgary, Canada	Cali, Colombia	Camaguey, Cuba	Cambridge Bay, Canada	Cambridge, United Kingdom	Campbellton, Canada	Campo Grande, Brazil	Canakkale, Turkey	Canberra, Australia
Buffalo, New York	8,829	0	11,749	12,914	490	10,516	7,051	14,923	9,245	5,900	12,645	2,798	4,375	2,386	3,287	5,735	1,110	7,441	8,146	15,842
Bujumbura, Burundi	9,602	11,749	0	1,857	11,271	1,920	5,154	12,696	3,705	6,567	7,019	13,725	11,804	11,944	11,977	6,749	10,738	9,259	4,830	12,439
Bulawayo, Zimbabwe	8,508	12,914	1,857	0	12,475	2,400	6,878	12,032	5,562	8,301	8,028	15,288	11,728	12,456	13,731	8,479	12,032	8,580	6,679	11,246
Burlington, Vermont	8,883	490	11,271	12,475	0	10,076	6,564	15,267	8,766	5,430	12,353	3,108	4,557	2,598	3,283	5,267	638	7,434	7,677	16,304
Cabinda, Angola	7,894	10,516	1,920	2,400	10,076	0	4,967	14,351	4,433	6,339	8,841	12,954	9,914	10,252	11,633	6,501	9,642	7,387	5,265	13,638
Cagliari, Italy	10,726	7,051	5,154	6,878	6,564	4,967	0	15,161	2,262	1,423	7,566	8,585	9,395	8,294	6,853	1,601	5,946	9,353	1,484	16,484
Cairns, Australia	13,758	14,923	12,696	12,032	15,267	14,351	15,161	0	13,270	15,067	7,624	12,160	15,181	15,426	12,508	15,074	15,476	15,317	13,691	2,068
Cairo, Egypt	11,811	9,245	3,705	5,562	8,766	4,433	2,262	13,270	0	3,365	5,708	10,401	11,521	10,548	8,450	3,540	8,135	10,748	1,204	14,269
Calais, France	11,161	5,900	6,567	8,301	5,430	6,339	1,423	15,067	3,365	0	7,859	7,192	8,896	7,483	5,431	183	4,794	9,638	2,247	16,882
Calcutta, India	16,535	12,645	7,019	8,028	12,353	8,841	7,566	7,624	5,708	7,859	0	11,563	16,701	14,926	9,784	7,945	11,807	16,200	6,084	9,059
Calgary, Canada	10,937	2,798	13,725	15,288	3,108	12,954	8,585	12,160	10,401	7,192	11,563	0	6,331	4,545	2,070	7,009	3,390	9,813	9,197	13,403
Cali, Colombia	4,617	4,375	11,804	11,728	4,557	9,914	9,395	15,181	11,521	8,896	16,701	6,331	0	1,990	7,590	8,796	5,026	3,565	10,858	14,148
Camaguey, Cuba	6,529	2,386	11,944	12,456	2,598	10,252	8,294	15,426	10,548	7,483	14,926	4,545	1,990	0	5,615	7,351	3,120	5,277	9,648	15,209
Cambridge Bay, Canada	12,115	3,287	11,977	13,731	3,283	11,633	6,853	12,508	8,450	5,431	9,784	2,070	7,590	5,615	0	5,252	3,144	10,712	7,252	14,245
Cambridge, United Kingdom	11,171	5,735	6,749	8,479	5,267	6,501	1,601	15,074	3,540	183	7,945	7,009	8,796	7,351	5,252	0	4,630	9,633	2,411	16,936
Campbellton, Canada	9,185	1,110	10,738	12,032	638	9,642	5,946	15,476	8,135	4,794	11,807	3,390	5,026	3,120	3,144	4,630	0	7,676	7,040	16,758
Campo Grande, Brazil	1,613	7,441	9,259	8,580	7,434	7,387	9,353	15,317	10,748	9,638	16,200	9,813	3,565	5,277	10,712	9,633	7,676	0	10,723	13,344
Canakkale, Turkey	11,999	8,146	4,830	6,679	7,677	5,265	1,484	13,691	1,204	2,247	6,084	9,197	10,858	9,648	7,252	2,411	7,040	10,723	0	15,037
Canberra, Australia	11,751	15,842	12,439	11,246	16,304	13,638	16,484	2,068	14,269	16,882	9,059	13,403	14,148	15,209	14,245	16,936	16,758	13,344	15,037	0
Cancun, Mexico	6,857	2,522	12,860	13,344	2,874	11,165	9,037	14,509	11,299	8,115	15,145	4,084	2,248	917	5,476	7,970	3,481	5,778	10,330	14,394
Canton, China	18,505	12,592	9,538	10,356	12,492	11,387	9,552	5,669	8,031	9,429	2,552	10,579	16,884	14,937	9,324	9,459	12,129	18,743	8,136	7,497
Canton Atoll, Phoenix Islands	11,935	10,454	17,595	16,646	10,904	18,988	15,974	4,905	16,153	14,637	11,160	8,071	10,611	10,521	9,392	14,480	11,359	12,703	15,492	5,406
Cape Town, South Africa	6,891	13,019	3,566	1,827	12,669	3,206	8,154	12,096	7,208	9,541	9,684	15,767	10,682	11,871	14,795	9,705	12,385	7,245	8,242	10,791
Cape York, Australia	14,529	14,666	12,463	12,026	14,951	14,237	14,440	773	12,642	14,295	6,952	11,869	15,660	15,568	11,994	14,301	15,064	16,090	12,985	2,810
Caracas, Venezuela	5,071	3,772	10,774	10,983	3,814	8,946	8,080	16,434	10,209	7,623	15,475	6,203	1,316	1,683	7,057	7,532	4,157	3,679	9,546	15,454
Cardiff, United Kingdom	10,955	5,553	6,820	8,522	5,081	6,490	1,667	15,297	3,701	357	8,185	6,918	8,558	7,128	5,212	241	4,445	9,410	2,598	17,175
Carlisle, United Kingdom	11,240	5,439	7,109	8,838	4,978	6,844	1,961	15,021	3,869	542	8,070	6,652	8,648	7,135	4,893	361	4,339	9,677	2,717	16,962
Carnarvon, Australia	13,371	17,706	9,280	8,617	17,744	10,904	12,921	3,448	10,681	13,626	5,912	15,041	17,402	18,786	14,466	13,743	17,437	14,834	11,527	3,594
Carson City, Nevada	10,319	3,430	14,971	16,334	3,860	13,936	9,889	11,559	11,778	8,522	12,577	1,393	5,889	4,432	3,448	8,339	4,310	9,454	10,575	12,458
Casablanca, Morocco	9,229	6,138	5,642	7,082	5,653	4,811	1,618	16,779	3,676	2,072	9,178	8,207	7,854	6,953	6,842	2,155	5,099	7,791	3,095	17,887
Casper, Wyoming	9,861	2,232	13,832	15,133	2,658	12,734	8,838	12,724	10,847	7,516	12,612	1,086	5,267	3,553	2,926	7,336	3,120	8,782	9,660	13,657
Castries, Saint Lucia	5,387	3,630	10,148	10,503	3,570	8,367	7,332	17,147	9,457	6,914	14,773	6,262	2,067	1,969	6,853	6,830	3,805	3,876	8,802	16,189
Catbalogan, Philippines	17,454	13,490	10,695	11,108	13,516	12,611	11,310	3,917	9,712	11,161	4,051	11,036	17,121	15,581	10,234	11,181	13,287	19,042	9,885	5,807
Cayenne, French Guiana	4,423	4,953	9,132	9,262	4,832	7,267	7,224	17,649	9,125	7,141	14,780	7,636	2,690	3,307	8,090	7,099	4,965	2,819	8,702	15,987
Cayman Islands (Georgetown)	6,440	2,626	12,320	12,752	2,893	10,595	8,722	15,052	10,977	7,896	15,246	4,542	1,832	429	5,769	7,762	3,450	5,278	10,070	14,780
Cazombo, Angola	8,482	11,857	1,183	1,100	11,408	1,367	5,836	12,987	4,728	7,255	8,093	14,189	11,118	11,596	12,673	7,431	10,949	8,272	5,774	12,324
Cebu, Philippines	17,303	13,680	10,581	10,954	13,700	12,500	11,347	3,854	9,700	11,239	4,016	11,231	17,301	15,775	10,419	11,264	13,464	18,871	9,910	5,708
Cedar Rapids, Iowa	9,132	1,057	12,792	13,967	1,522	11,570	7,986	13,931	10,124	6,759	12,863	1,982	4,527	2,622	3,121	6,585	2,072	7,894	8,982	14,786
Changsha, China	18,938	12,041	9,565	10,525	11,933	11,360	9,162	6,116	7,768	8,959	2,549	10,093	16,360	14,396	8,782	8,979	11,565	18,500	7,779	7,995
Channel-Port-aux-Basques, Can.	9,101	1,629	10,174	11,472	1,140	9,085	5,428	15,919	7,640	4,327	11,591	3,920	5,166	3,358	3,459	4,170	565	7,546	6,572	17,312
Charleston, South Carolina	7,788	1,127	12,020	12,893	1,425	10,544	7,726	15,131	9,976	6,715	13,761	3,437	3,265	1,277	4,341	6,563	2,026	6,476	8,951	15,530
Charleston, West Virginia	8,424	555	12,071	13,113	978	10,727	7,513	14,850	9,730	6,405	13,186	2,901	3,900	1,914	3,703	6,243	1,617	7,094	8,651	15,538
Charlotte, North Carolina	8,073	868	12,063	13,011	1,217	10,643	7,645	14,996	9,883	6,589	13,513	3,184	3,546	1,560	4,057	6,432	1,841	6,756	8,832	15,525
Charlotte Amalie, U.S.V.I.	5,900	3,021	10,589	11,056	2,998	8,861	7,388	16,777	9,582	6,822	14,638	5,625	2,076	1,400	6,275	6,720	3,293	4,437	8,829	16,176
Charlottetown, Canada	8,965	1,302	10,473	11,731	813	9,337	5,762	15,807	7,978	4,664	11,868	3,717	4,915	3,066	3,443	4,507	332	7,434	6,909	17,063
Chatham, Canada	9,069	1,152	10,651	11,924	666	9,531	5,899	15,613	8,101	4,771	11,867	3,517	4,946	3,059	3,281	4,610	140	7,552	7,018	16,870
Chatham Islands (Waitangi)	9,294	13,647	14,163	12,461	14,131	14,453	19,307	4,634	17,126	19,217	12,110	12,126	11,079	12,303	13,822	19,055	14,754	10,755	18,084	3,070
Chengdu, China	18,332	11,855	8,750	9,829	11,679	10,505	8,317	6,903	6,865	8,209	1,802	10,213	16,229	14,241	8,688	8,245	11,243	17,609	6,910	8,698
Chesterfield Inlet, Canada	11,228	2,402	11,797	13,438	2,377	11,197	6,647	13,316	8,468	5,247	10,484	1,947	6,747	4,760	907	5,064	2,254	9,808	7,266	14,939
Cheyenne, Wyoming	9,635	2,149	13,825	15,063	2,595	12,664	8,881	12,846	10,925	7,580	12,826	1,312	5,043	3,345	3,115	7,400	3,091	8,563	9,745	13,709
Chiang Mai, Thailand	17,184	13,173	8,003	8,804	12,956	9,877	8,704	6,467	6,888	8,895	1,181	11,625	17,498	15,549	10,069	8,965	12,472	17,262	7,227	7,994
Chibougamau, Canada	9,493	855	11,278	12,617	611	10,232	6,388	14,892	8,528	5,164	11,802	2,787	5,154	3,182	2,696	4,992	603	8,034	7,396	16,165
Chicago, Illinois	8,978	729	12,476	13,633	1,205	11,235	7,719	14,263	9,881	6,520	12,861	2,257	4,399	2,449	3,198	6,350	1,781	7,693	8,755	15,113
Chiclayo, Peru	3,784	5,499	12,092	11,661	5,714	10,172	10,395	14,368	12,420	10,009	17,861	7,197	1,189	3,121	8,641	9,920	6,203	3,115	11,876	13,090
Chihuahua, Mexico	8,607	2,905	14,551	15,366	3,394	13,065	9,942	12,641	12,095	8,730	14,137	2,578	4,190	2,947	4,502	8,557	3,999	7,751	10,951	13,045
Chongquing, China	18,508	11,963	8,968	10,002	11,806	10,741	8,584	6,645	7,135	8,458	1,979	10,227	16,336	14,347	8,763	8,490	11,388	17,880	7,180	8,458
Christchurch, New Zealand	9,927	14,398	13,649	12,059	14,887	14,226	18,564	3,888	16,306	18,933	11,261	12,637	11,948	13,165	14,155	18,895	15,494	11,443	17,212	2,206
Christiansted, U.S.V.I.	5,831	3,092	10,562	11,012	3,068	8,826	7,407	16,799	9,594	6,855	14,680	5,693	2,041	1,443	6,345	6,756	3,360	4,367	8,851	16,156
Christmas Is. [Indian Ocean]	14,742	16,389	8,452	8,281	16,238	10,285	11,305	4,388	9,128	11,878	4,113	14,247	19,191	18,744	13,133	11,984	15,786	15,966	9,860	5,181
Christmas Is. [Pacific Ocean]	10,971	8,937	19,254	17,890	9,406	18,828	15,245	6,565	16,341	13,822	12,392	6,786	9,008	8,861	8,394	13,645	9,912	11,441	15,322	6,906
Churchill, Canada	10,862	2,055	12,195	13,771	2,132	11,470	7,064	13,322	8,951	5,684	10,994	1,532	6,321	4,348	1,270	5,501	2,160	9,496	7,752	14,800
Cincinnati, Ohio	8,590	634	12,299	13,367	1,112	10,979	7,676	14,587	9,876	6,534	13,142	2,654	4,030	2,063	3,560	6,369	1,742	7,291	8,779	15,310
Ciudad Bolivia, Venezuela	4,922	3,912	11,166	11,286	4,011	9,315	8,542	15,982	10,676	8,060	15,898	6,185	853	1,644	7,194	7,965	4,411	3,633	10,006	14,999
Ciudad Juarez, Mexico	8,899	2,725	14,446	15,385	3,213	13,042	9,724	12,640	11,847	8,483	13,796	2,235	4,430	3,057	4,159	8,307	3,799	7,996	10,689	13,164
Ciudad Victoria, Mexico	7,756	2,826	14,062	14,648	3,292	12,435	9,820	13,267	12,048	8,722	14,823	3,294	3,309	2,196	5,060	8,558	3,929	6,870	10,968	13,409
Clarksburg, West Virginia	8,485	419	11,943	13,009	827	10,619	7,363	14,931	9,579	6,253	13,063	2,923	3,987	1,998	3,633	6,091	1,465	7,134	8,499	15,667
Cleveland, Ohio	8,755	280	12,008	13,139	767	10,743	7,330	14,751	9,524	6,179	12,843	2,685	4,246	2,258	3,364	6,013	1,389	7,406	8,423	15,593
Cocos (Keeling) Island	14,230	16,557	7,488	7,311	16,283	9,309	10,652	5,291	8,420	11,385	3,930	14,855	18,821	18,832	13,472	11,511	15,731	15,259	9,257	5,849
Colombo, Sri Lanka	14,770	14,086	5,724	6,359	13,707	7,641	7,869	7,716	5,678	8,574	1,953	13,443	17,167	16,053	11,559	8,703	13,097	14,906	6,450	8,616
Colon, Panama	5,366	3,716	12,195	12,295	3,944	10,348	9,276	15,025	11,479	8,627	16,255	5,578	754	1,347	6,880	8,511	4,460	4,306	10,701	14,289
Colorado Springs, Colorado	9,430	2,224	13,952	15,120	2,689	12,726	9,060	12,841	11,129	7,775	13,075	1,539	4,855	3,214	3,371	7,597	3,216	8,392	9,955	13,619
Columbia, South Carolina	7,951	1,005	12,102	13,013	1,345	10,655	7,736	15,004	9,979	6,695	13,650	3,267	3,414	1,431	4,184	6,540	1,964	6,645	8,936	15,471
Columbus, Georgia	7,925	1,276	12,494	13,360	1,680	11,018	8,134	14,665	10,373	7,076	13,878	3,144	3,331	1,413	4,270	6,919	2,314	6,689	9,320	15,069
Columbus, Ohio	8,633	474	12,151	13,241	951	10,849	7,514	14,691	9,715	6,373	13,029	2,696	4,096	2,116	3,499	6,208	1,581	7,308	8,619	15,457
Conakry, Guinea	6,786	7,277	4,987	5,679	6,869	3,323	3,998	17,665	5,187	4,811	10,835	9,908	6,971	6,971	9,075	4,897	6,519	5,571	5,214	16,666
Concepcion, Chile	1,343	8,848	10,889	9,675	9,005	9,223	11,896	12,803	13,129	12,156	17,629	10,529	4,474	6,464	12,040	12,139	9,418	2,549	13,237	10,906
Concord, New Hampshire	8,718	599	11,152	12,324	195	9,924	6,506	15,452	8,723	5,404	12,442	3,294	4,432	2,492	3,465	5,245	654	7,258	7,650	16,440
Constantine, Algeria	10,353	7,052	4,995	6,670	6,563	4,676	385	15,468	2,394	1,665	7,852	8,729	9,172	8,163	7,065	1,832	5,957	8,996	1,778	16,662
Copenhagen, Denmark	12,046	6,304	6,724	8,536	5,861	6,785	1,847	14,182	3,206	887	7,083	7,196	9,636	8,102	5,278	904	5,225	10,524	2,003	16,035
Coppermine, Canada	12,293	3,501	12,363	14,135	3,552	12,062	7,257	12,118	8,796	5,835	9,800	1,871	7,718	5,766	435	5,658	3,474	10,942	7,604	13,824
Coquimbo, Chile	1,318	8,103	10,857	9,823	8,245	9,088	11,307	13,477	12,722	11,467	17,844	9,906	3,739	5,725	11,326	11,439	8,648	1,985	12,700	11,629
Cordoba, Argentina	643	8,362	10,157	9,124	8,452	8,402	10,882	13,781	12,150	11,177	17,140	10,360	4,073	6,022	11,633	11,169	8,797	1,544	12,224	11,841
Cordoba, Spain	9,754	6,110	5,768	7,312	5,621	5,120	1,218	16,322	3,417	1,543	8,770	7,998	8,178	7,138	6,514	1,636	5,035	8,299	2,697	17,684
Cork, Ireland	10,747	5,196	7,090	8,757	4,721	6,663	1,958	15,514	4,052	724	8,519	6,637	8,213	6,764	4,994	589	4,087	9,182	2,961	17,455
Corner Brook, Canada	9,255	1,750	10,095	11,428	1,265	9,048	5,300	15,860	7,502	4,177	11,413	3,933	5,343	3,534	3,372	4,018	653	7,694	6,423	17,336
Corrientes, Argentina	792	8,056	9,666	8,764	8,099	7,861	10,205	14,429	11,494	10,523	16,685	10,244	3,912	5,782	11,343	10,520	8,395	888	11,547	12,460
Cosenza, Italy	11,218	7,541	4,914	6,705	7,059	4,983	616	14,565	1,712	1,715	6,958	8,893	10,010	8,879	7,064	1,897	6,432	9,891	875	15,874
Craiova, Romania	12,048	7,679	5,312	7,155	7,216	5,644	1,343	13,839	1,714	1,799	6,295	8,687	10,563	9,261	6,746	1,953	6,578	10,695	510	15,328
Cruzeiro do Sul, Brazil	3,319	5,630	11,286	10,883	5,771	9,366	9,836	15,007	11,769	9,590	17,401	7,621	1,301	3,262	8,876	9,518	6,190	2,401	11,320	13,553
Cuiaba, Brazil	2,120	6,881	9,430	8,891	6,874	7,528	9,081	15,693	10,618	9,265	16,222	9,276	3,082	4,734	10,151	9,248	7,120	561	10,492	13,776
Curitiba, Brazil	1,349	8,150	8,711	7,903	8,115	6,887	9,379	15,050	10,548	9,830	15,724	10,577	4,343	6,034	11,398	9,847	8,316	778	10,669	13,009
Cuzco, Peru	2,704	6,285	11,156	10,578	6,423	9,248	10,202	14,681	12,018	10,065	17,725	8,234	1,942	3,915	9,527	10,006	6,834	2,001	11,676	13,085
Dacca, Bangladesh	16,782	12,550	7,257	8,276	12,273	9,071	7,664	7,510	5,857	7,901	248	11,383	16,688	14,859	9,634	7,980	11,740	16,415	6,185	9,001
Dakar, Senegal	6,967	6,594	5,534	6,341	6,180	3,962	3,760	18,219	5,252	4,381	10,958	9,211	6,594	6,411	8,397	4,446	5,822	5,624	5,099	17,359
Dallas, Texas	8,468	1,931	13,558	14,469	2,418	12,124	8,981	13,556	11,166	7,810	13,859	2,471	3,875	2,254	4,076	7,641	3,037	7,405	10,048	14,043
Damascus, Syria	12,415	9,290	4,147	5,993	8,823	5,014	2,511	12,817	612	3,395	5,208	10,201	11,891	10,775	8,196	3,556	8,186	11,322	1,150	13,974
Danang, Vietnam	17,565	13,437	8,932	9,580	13,299	10,829	9,657	5,504	7,902	9,739	2,203	11,513	17,786	15,809	10,198	9,793	12,891	18,155	8,191	7,144
Dar es Salaam, Tanzania	10,291	12,802	1,163	1,874	12,317	3,000	5,969	11,534	4,167	7,336	6,254	14,521	12,914	13,106	12,616	7,519	11,755	10,159	5,364	11,349
Darwin, Australia	14,705	15,595	11,180	10,788	15,788	12,960	13,603	1,681	11,613	13,756	6,037	12,825	16,862	16,821	12,602	13,803	15,746	16,316	12,119	3,134
Davao, Philippines	16,928	13,948	10,752	11,013	13,995	12,672	11,730	3,459	10,041	11,641	4,340	11,426	17,313	15,955	10,712	11,667	13,788	18,524	10,285	5,304

Distances in Kilometers	Buenos Aires, Argentina	Buffalo, New York	Bujumbura, Burundi	Bulawayo, Zimbabwe	Burlington, Vermont	Cabinda, Angola	Cagliari, Italy	Cairns, Australia	Cairo, Egypt	Calais, France	Calcutta, India	Calgary, Canada	Cali, Colombia	Camaguey, Cuba	Cambridge Bay, Canada	Cambridge, United Kingdom	Campbellton, Canada	Campo Grande, Brazil	Canakkale, Turkey	Canberra, Australia
David, Panama	5,392	3,833	12,473	12,528	4,093	10,616	9,558	14,729	11,767	8,885	16,438	5,546	856	1,513	6,936	8,765	4,631	4,414	10,976	14,006
Dawson, Canada	12,989	4,424	13,210	15,044	4,560	13,126	8,225	10,965	9,539	6,815	9,557	2,072	8,373	6,512	1,599	6,645	4,569	11,781	8,384	12,650
Dawson Creek, Canada	11,595	3,267	13,596	15,281	3,510	13,040	8,445	11,794	10,119	7,029	10,918	665	6,984	5,168	1,671	6,848	3,689	10,444	8,918	13,201
Denpasar, Indonesia	15,172	15,972	9,507	9,339	15,953	11,350	12,003	3,436	9,916	12,382	4,525	13,512	18,612	18,028	12,693	12,464	15,639	16,602	10,526	4,543
Denver, Colorado	9,519	2,205	13,915	15,113	2,663	12,717	9,000	12,829	11,058	7,708	12,974	1,442	4,938	3,277	3,270	7,529	3,178	8,470	9,881	13,641
Derby, Australia	14,257	16,466	10,359	9,870	16,609	12,087	13,308	2,355	11,182	13,700	5,845	13,730	17,345	17,726	13,354	13,778	16,474	15,825	11,837	3,221
Des Moines, Iowa	9,170	1,224	12,959	14,132	1,690	11,735	8,141	13,778	10,270	6,905	12,903	1,885	4,556	2,682	3,137	6,730	2,235	7,958	9,123	14,619
Detroit, Michigan	8,881	348	12,097	13,254	832	10,856	7,376	14,617	9,557	6,203	12,769	2,540	4,356	2,372	3,244	6,035	1,430	7,541	8,445	15,495
Dhahran, Saudi Arabia	13,245	10,743	3,974	5,641	10,290	5,400	4,061	11,378	1,898	4,894	3,886	11,298	13,413	12,325	9,234	5,045	9,652	12,416	2,679	12,425
Diego Garcia Island	13,080	15,174	4,790	4,929	14,722	6,660	8,295	8,016	6,038	9,306	3,733	15,121	16,569	16,483	13,142	9,464	14,084	13,471	7,063	8,344
Dijon, France	11,060	6,291	6,101	7,837	5,814	5,899	959	15,095	2,955	466	7,713	7,654	9,090	7,771	5,895	648	5,182	9,580	1,890	16,773
Dili, Indonesia	15,210	15,521	10,644	10,412	15,634	12,478	12,882	2,378	10,900	13,066	5,317	12,840	17,528	17,137	12,368	13,120	15,484	16,797	11,398	3,817
Djibouti, Djibouti	11,794	11,591	2,253	3,857	11,106	3,917	4,543	11,713	2,385	5,746	4,943	12,724	13,154	12,627	10,713	5,922	10,484	11,260	3,567	12,200
Dnepropetrovsk, USSR	13,021	8,004	5,769	7,624	7,570	6,382	2,304	12,928	2,067	2,387	5,487	8,592	11,283	9,817	6,560	2,493	6,936	11,655	1,147	14,544
Dobo, Indonesia	15,345	14,772	11,622	11,414	14,960	13,472	13,401	1,762	11,582	13,353	5,892	12,014	16,618	16,160	11,781	13,376	14,924	16,951	11,937	3,615
Doha, Qatar	13,319	10,916	3,974	5,606	10,464	5,453	4,240	11,216	2,067	5,072	3,751	11,433	13,586	12,505	9,366	5,222	9,826	12,528	2,859	12,247
Donetsk, USSR	13,198	8,185	5,752	7,603	7,755	6,439	2,494	12,722	2,070	2,601	5,272	8,706	11,497	10,021	6,663	2,705	7,123	11,847	1,260	14,329
Dover, Delaware	8,354	500	11,533	12,594	621	10,203	7,013	15,331	9,245	5,945	12,974	3,262	3,956	1,984	3,769	5,788	1,214	6,949	8,189	16,076
Dresden, East Germany	11,817	6,630	6,213	8,020	6,172	6,273	1,364	14,340	2,748	836	7,029	7,669	9,731	8,302	5,778	951	5,534	10,339	1,558	16,072
Dubayy, United Arab Emir.	13,658	11,125	4,230	5,796	10,684	5,775	4,564	10,847	2,427	5,331	3,373	11,487	13,935	12,795	9,418	5,475	10,047	12,899	3,151	11,920
Dublin, Ireland	10,966	5,289	7,109	8,804	4,820	6,752	1,957	15,295	3,977	613	8,326	6,628	8,399	6,918	4,932	448	4,183	9,401	2,857	17,239
Duluth, Minnesota	9,623	1,131	12,636	13,943	1,493	11,548	7,699	13,798	9,781	6,421	12,328	1,672	5,033	3,096	2,590	6,244	1,917	8,344	8,617	14,851
Dunedin, New Zealand	9,832	14,658	13,347	11,750	15,145	13,919	18,326	3,945	16,087	19,005	11,194	12,943	12,052	13,341	14,463	19,018	15,759	11,372	17,052	2,141
Durango, Mexico	8,120	3,158	14,594	15,212	3,641	12,994	10,204	12,713	12,401	9,047	14,665	3,106	3,785	2,760	5,012	8,877	4,267	7,324	11,285	12,930
Durban, South Africa	8,155	13,749	2,935	1,102	13,341	3,337	7,976	11,324	6,629	9,399	8,440	16,291	11,896	12,937	14,826	9,576	12,952	8,505	7,764	10,321
Dushanbe, USSR	15,347	10,416	6,162	7,735	10,053	7,598	5,081	10,080	3,556	5,285	2,573	10,074	14,155	12,522	8,055	5,372	9,457	14,281	3,624	11,626
East London, South Africa	7,724	13,698	3,286	1,429	13,313	3,452	8,231	11,412	6,991	9,649	8,886	16,348	11,569	12,711	15,051	9,823	12,967	8,130	8,104	10,281
Easter Island (Hanga Roa)	4,894	8,363	14,458	13,100	8,746	12,786	14,250	10,564	16,189	13,769	18,162	8,674	4,895	6,353	10,681	13,656	9,356	5,593	15,731	9,257
Echo Bay, Canada	12,260	3,512	12,596	14,366	3,596	12,279	7,488	11,990	9,029	6,065	9,930	1,689	7,665	5,731	646	5,888	3,561	10,943	7,837	13,659
Edinburgh, United Kingdom	11,311	5,386	7,212	8,946	4,929	6,958	2,068	14,950	3,944	646	8,057	6,556	8,655	7,117	4,785	467	4,290	9,743	2,782	16,909
Edmonton, Canada	11,110	2,795	13,498	15,099	3,066	12,791	8,350	12,213	10,139	6,951	11,318	281	6,495	4,668	1,788	6,768	3,296	9,944	8,934	13,531
El Aaiun, Morocco	8,334	6,083	5,684	6,908	5,616	4,537	2,463	17,582	4,332	2,931	9,959	8,418	7,206	6,532	7,284	2,994	5,131	6,906	3,906	18,119
Elat, Israel	12,092	9,529	3,693	5,541	9,054	4,583	2,595	12,910	362	3,633	5,357	10,575	11,882	10,888	8,592	3,803	8,421	11,069	1,411	13,919
Elazig, Turkey	12,906	9,033	4,767	6,606	8,582	5,636	2,599	12,591	1,206	3,213	4,973	9,730	11,966	10,689	7,696	3,355	7,944	11,728	1,116	13,932
Eniwetok Atoll, Marshall Isls.	15,181	11,377	14,766	14,994	11,677	16,676	13,743	3,629	13,045	12,832	7,891	8,581	13,324	12,516	8,925	12,743	11,848	15,975	12,707	5,364
Erfurt, East Germany	11,658	6,471	6,273	8,065	6,009	6,265	1,316	14,515	2,867	646	7,220	7,571	9,541	8,119	5,707	768	5,371	10,170	1,693	16,261
Erzurum, Turkey	13,123	9,043	4,947	6,779	8,599	5,851	2,750	12,423	1,425	3,274	4,816	9,646	12,084	10,757	7,601	3,409	7,962	11,931	1,269	13,812
Esfahan, Iran	13,672	10,243	4,630	6,338	9,807	5,938	3,868	11,388	1,958	4,501	3,775	10,626	13,259	11,984	8,558	4,637	9,172	12,695	2,401	12,637
Essen, West Germany	11,469	6,200	6,436	8,207	5,736	6,335	1,369	14,736	3,107	366	7,492	7,368	9,262	7,834	5,542	483	5,098	9,962	1,951	16,521
Eucla, Australia	12,624	17,284	10,714	9,777	17,632	12,158	14,592	2,366	12,354	15,225	7,394	14,524	15,912	17,133	14,669	15,325	17,776	14,220	13,184	1,924
Fargo, North Dakota	9,806	1,480	12,958	14,293	1,850	11,899	7,979	13,444	10,024	6,676	12,301	1,344	5,195	3,302	2,520	6,497	2,262	8,573	8,849	14,501
Faroe Islands (Torshavn)	11,668	5,022	7,875	9,632	4,593	7,668	2,757	14,556	4,490	1,339	8,081	5,936	8,622	6,947	4,105	1,169	3,964	10,071	3,295	16,596
Florence, Italy	11,183	6,912	5,528	7,296	6,433	5,463	536	14,824	2,333	1,068	7,302	8,254	9,568	8,333	6,451	1,250	5,802	9,770	1,316	16,328
Florianopolis, Brazil	1,221	8,398	8,652	7,781	8,364	6,854	9,514	14,847	10,613	10,006	15,671	10,812	4,559	6,272	11,647	10,028	8,565	1,001	10,778	12,797
Fort George, Canada	9,996	1,217	11,510	12,943	1,122	10,582	6,500	14,396	8,565	5,207	11,458	2,381	5,591	3,603	2,162	5,029	1,081	8,556	7,401	15,782
Fort McMurray, Canada	11,280	2,761	13,154	14,789	2,975	12,513	8,002	12,347	9,766	6,597	11,028	657	6,664	4,784	1,415	6,414	3,133	10,053	8,562	13,756
Fort Nelson, Canada	11,929	3,472	13,402	15,135	3,672	12,960	8,266	11,686	9,866	6,845	10,548	1,025	7,313	5,467	1,427	6,665	3,790	10,743	8,671	13,184
Fort Severn, Canada	10,412	1,586	11,968	13,468	1,636	11,129	6,886	13,794	8,867	5,543	11,297	1,825	5,910	3,925	1,702	5,361	1,682	9,022	7,681	15,204
Fort Smith, Arkansas	8,603	1,577	13,256	14,244	2,066	11,876	8,626	13,770	10,805	7,448	13,588	2,348	3,988	2,235	3,810	7,278	2,680	7,472	9,685	14,353
Fort Vermilion, Canada	11,605	3,082	13,207	14,894	3,279	12,666	8,055	12,071	9,742	6,640	10,758	827	6,988	5,115	1,307	6,458	3,404	10,386	8,541	13,538
Fort Wayne, Indiana	8,813	557	12,299	13,426	1,046	11,031	7,598	14,485	9,780	6,427	12,931	2,477	4,256	2,287	3,334	6,259	1,652	7,506	8,668	15,300
Fort-Chimo, Canada	10,315	1,843	10,782	12,295	1,552	9,977	5,719	14,643	7,757	4,404	10,814	2,993	6,103	4,149	2,143	4,225	1,130	8,798	6,589	16,268
Fort-de-France, Martinique	5,452	3,568	10,160	10,533	3,505	8,386	7,301	17,149	9,433	6,870	14,729	6,205	2,095	1,933	6,788	6,785	3,739	3,941	8,769	16,227
Fortaleza, Brazil	3,993	6,564	7,539	7,484	6,359	5,628	6,808	17,676	8,290	7,169	13,946	9,328	4,303	5,116	9,482	7,184	6,353	2,546	8,184	15,609
Frankfort, Kentucky	8,509	726	12,351	13,394	1,197	11,009	7,757	14,578	9,963	6,624	13,245	2,696	3,941	1,980	3,650	6,460	1,831	7,221	8,870	15,259
Frankfurt am Main, W. Ger.	11,467	6,375	6,251	8,027	5,908	6,177	1,212	14,708	2,921	494	7,396	7,557	9,374	7,977	5,726	642	5,270	9,978	1,773	16,444
Fredericton, Canada	8,961	1,031	10,745	11,991	541	9,595	6,027	15,615	8,235	4,911	12,013	3,488	4,808	2,913	3,345	4,751	226	7,455	7,157	16,802
Freeport, Bahamas	7,096	1,816	11,990	12,666	2,055	10,386	8,031	15,325	10,293	7,128	14,406	4,035	2,564	575	5,041	6,987	2,608	5,814	9,332	15,386
Freetown, Sierra Leone	6,736	7,391	4,910	5,572	6,986	3,224	4,069	17,573	5,205	4,907	10,834	10,028	7,021	7,056	9,198	4,996	6,638	5,546	5,263	16,543
Frobisher Bay, Canada	10,939	2,415	10,730	12,344	2,166	10,100	5,593	14,188	7,511	4,216	10,230	2,995	6,722	4,759	1,706	4,034	1,757	9,413	6,320	15,949
Frunze, USSR	15,894	10,142	6,845	8,421	9,813	8,246	5,379	9,817	4,086	5,385	2,593	9,561	14,113	12,353	7,582	5,448	9,244	14,702	3,980	11,497
Fukuoka, Japan	19,203	11,030	11,244	12,288	11,038	12,957	9,937	5,822	8,987	9,377	4,278	8,716	15,034	13,226	7,759	9,348	10,811	18,470	8,728	7,876
Funafuti Atoll, Tuvalu	12,316	11,628	16,429	15,496	12,071	17,893	16,463	3,735	15,918	15,293	10,453	9,168	11,654	11,694	10,328	15,160	12,502	13,332	15,588	4,256
Funchal, Madeira Island	8,617	5,453	6,296	7,587	4,978	5,228	2,449	17,555	4,552	2,546	10,013	7,726	6,981	6,102	6,585	2,571	4,470	7,115	3,933	18,706
Fuzhou, China	19,037	12,146	10,173	11,042	12,089	11,994	9,785	5,553	8,436	9,513	3,157	9,995	16,326	14,437	8,859	9,523	11,778	19,138	8,422	7,490
Gaborone, Botswana	8,010	13,003	2,384	572	12,587	2,573	7,284	12,043	6,082	8,703	8,533	15,526	11,431	12,317	14,114	8,878	12,189	8,172	7,176	11,086
Galapagos Islands (Santa Cruz)	5,015	4,956	13,320	13,003	5,279	11,406	10,876	13,579	13,061	10,219	17,578	6,150	1,608	2,788	7,820	10,098	5,857	4,466	12,305	12,689
Gander, Canada	9,262	1,989	9,852	11,194	1,501	8,819	5,063	16,006	7,271	3,958	11,280	4,153	5,455	3,691	3,499	3,801	896	7,686	6,202	17,553
Gangtok, India	16,795	12,125	7,201	8,331	11,842	8,966	7,291	7,873	5,555	7,484	532	11,042	16,248	14,425	9,252	7,559	11,305	16,224	5,818	9,411
Garyarsa, China	16,199	11,474	6,644	7,966	11,150	8,305	6,353	8,810	4,659	6,574	1,292	10,724	15,413	13,689	8,811	6,656	10,582	15,390	4,882	10,332
Gaspe, Canada	9,261	1,295	10,573	11,891	824	9,505	5,763	15,539	7,949	4,607	11,655	3,501	5,159	3,271	3,140	4,444	186	7,736	6,854	16,891
Gauhati, India	17,026	12,297	7,460	8,529	12,033	9,248	7,619	7,543	5,890	7,787	529	11,084	16,494	14,626	9,349	7,859	11,511	16,542	6,149	9,102
Gdansk, Poland	12,295	6,714	6,476	8,309	6,272	6,666	1,830	13,891	2,882	1,197	6,694	7,526	10,035	8,516	5,571	1,257	5,637	10,802	1,681	15,687
Geneva, Switzerland	11,045	6,429	5,950	7,688	5,951	5,763	812	15,079	2,816	617	7,651	7,806	9,171	7,880	6,045	799	5,319	9,580	1,771	16,708
Genoa, Italy	11,084	6,718	5,672	7,424	6,239	5,544	578	14,968	2,527	901	7,472	8,093	9,383	8,136	6,314	1,084	5,609	9,651	1,512	16,510
Georgetown, Guyana	4,582	4,485	9,791	9,939	4,423	7,936	7,583	17,198	9,584	7,351	15,141	7,089	2,068	2,669	7,706	7,289	4,637	3,039	9,067	15,799
Geraldton, Australia	12,953	18,034	9,371	8,588	18,132	10,920	13,232	3,444	10,979	14,000	6,336	15,292	16,970	18,521	14,849	14,122	17,867	14,438	11,866	3,327
Ghanzi, Botswana	7,820	12,460	2,173	726	12,044	2,051	6,857	12,580	5,801	8,268	8,715	14,995	11,016	11,818	13,648	8,439	11,649	7,855	6,849	11,624
Ghat, Libya	9,789	8,094	3,760	5,375	7,606	3,383	1,583	15,348	2,153	2,972	7,856	9,980	9,523	8,857	8,368	3,141	7,034	8,625	2,263	15,943
Gibraltar	9,574	6,165	5,671	7,182	5,676	4,965	1,320	16,465	3,462	1,744	8,886	8,117	8,098	7,114	6,670	1,837	5,101	8,130	2,804	17,726
Gijon, Spain	10,174	5,745	6,269	7,873	5,256	5,726	1,324	16,021	3,581	1,000	8,630	7,465	8,208	6,995	5,914	1,056	4,646	8,669	2,673	17,683
Gisborne, New Zealand	10,032	13,744	14,352	12,759	14,234	14,897	19,061	3,953	16,841	18,608	11,512	11,933	11,594	12,658	13,474	18,492	14,829	11,477	17,584	2,584
Glasgow, United Kingdom	11,259	5,326	7,244	8,971	4,868	6,970	2,096	15,001	3,995	677	8,123	6,517	8,589	7,051	4,759	495	4,230	9,689	2,838	16,967
Godthab, Greenland	10,975	2,939	9,906	11,541	2,583	9,333	4,766	14,586	6,699	3,390	9,782	3,821	7,040	5,146	2,342	3,207	2,026	9,394	5,515	16,498
Gomez Palacio, Mexico	8,181	2,953	14,430	15,105	3,437	12,858	10,001	12,853	12,195	8,840	14,533	2,969	3,783	2,650	4,843	8,671	4,062	7,338	11,078	13,114
Goose Bay, Canada	11,670	3,746	14,273	15,973	4,044	13,727	9,127	11,226	10,751	7,708	11,095	948	7,114	5,416	2,309	7,527	4,289	10,647	9,556	12,550
Gorki, USSR	13,864	7,780	6,752	8,598	7,392	7,448	3,179	12,281	3,087	2,806	5,202	7,932	11,499	9,830	5,864	2,846	6,784	12,403	2,210	14,090
Goteborg, Sweden	12,145	6,165	6,951	8,766	5,729	7,014	2,068	14,102	3,415	999	7,114	6,986	9,595	8,016	5,056	974	5,095	10,605	2,211	15,999
Granada, Spain	9,763	6,230	5,648	7,197	5,741	5,014	1,142	16,276	3,317	1,588	8,705	8,115	8,262	7,244	6,621	1,691	5,155	8,321	2,625	17,586
Grand Turk, Turks & Caicos	6,349	2,482	11,241	11,778	2,559	9,554	7,719	16,129	9,957	7,001	14,658	4,954	2,077	703	5,770	6,881	2,971	4,973	9,111	15,823
Graz, Austria	11,665	6,977	5,753	7,560	6,510	5,837	1,012	14,389	2,328	1,084	6,934	8,112	9,880	8,545	6,234	1,243	5,873	10,236	1,169	15,991
Green Bay, Wisconsin	9,257	758	12,420	13,651	1,176	11,251	7,580	14,166	9,714	6,349	12,572	2,072	4,687	2,728	2,907	6,175	1,685	7,955	8,572	15,131
Grenoble, France	10,943	6,457	5,867	7,596	5,976	5,654	718	15,163	2,790	705	7,708	7,880	9,130	7,868	6,135	884	5,347	9,485	1,779	16,758
Guadalajara, Mexico	7,743	3,357	14,566	15,035	3,829	12,890	10,367	12,791	12,591	9,257	15,061	3,500	3,475	2,641	5,386	9,092	4,464	6,987	11,503	12,865
Guam (Agana)	16,711	12,352	12,852	13,226	12,535	14,762	12,586	3,362	11,430	12,018	6,022	9,619	15,105	13,974	9,391	11,978	12,523	17,831	11,324	5,421
Guantanamo, Cuba	6,312	2,546	11,668	12,147	2,706	9,957	8,148	15,704	10,393	7,395	14,962	4,821	1,851	315	5,812	7,270	3,185	5,018	9,528	15,384
Guatemala City, Guatemala	6,418	3,324	13,329	13,569	3,691	11,539	9,803	14,019	12,062	8,922	15,891	4,559	1,973	1,528	6,139	8,779	4,302	5,521	11,124	13,681
Guayaquil, Ecuador	4,220	4,991	12,136	11,853	5,208	10,221	10,073	14,598	12,161	9,611	17,423	6,731	722	2,613	8,139	9,514	5,704	3,405	11,545	13,452
Guiyang, China	18,348	12,292	8,929	9,884	12,136	10,738	8,799	6,402	7,271	8,724	1,910	10,524	16,664	14,674	9,085	8,762	11,718	18,008	7,376	8,180
Gur'yev, USSR	14,184	8,923	6,014	7,807	8,525	7,016	3,540	11,659	2,596	3,614	4,246	9,044	12,487	10,912	6,975	3,699	7,909	12,885	2,185	13,287

Distances in Kilometers	Buenos Aires, Argentina	Buffalo, New York	Bujumbura, Burundi	Bulawayo, Zimbabwe	Burlington, Vermont	Cabinda, Angola	Cagliari, Italy	Cairns, Australia	Cairo, Egypt	Calais, France	Calcutta, India	Calgary, Canada	Cali, Colombia	Camaguey, Cuba	Cambridge Bay, Canada	Cambridge, United Kingdom	Campbellton, Canada	Campo Grande, Brazil	Canakkale, Turkey	Canberra, Australia
Haifa, Israel	12,273	9,264	4,052	5,903	8,794	4,884	2,429	12,933	471	3,364	5,331	10,232	11,794	10,709	8,239	3,529	8,157	11,184	1,118	14,058
Haikou, China	18,058	12,973	9,201	9,950	12,851	11,074	9,543	5,634	7,906	9,522	2,292	11,020	17,302	15,335	9,721	9,563	12,462	18,460	8,098	7,375
Haiphong, Vietnam	17,909	12,923	8,836	9,634	12,770	10,700	9,193	5,973	7,524	9,220	1,903	11,101	17,293	15,304	9,707	9,268	12,349	18,086	7,741	7,668
Hakodate, Japan	18,169	9,829	12,025	13,291	9,875	13,550	9,794	6,516	9,272	8,989	5,284	7,442	13,752	11,968	6,595	8,926	9,705	17,243	8,782	8,579
Halifax, Canada	8,792	1,244	10,509	11,727	763	9,329	5,858	15,893	8,085	4,788	12,041	3,768	4,737	2,897	3,583	4,634	441	7,266	7,030	17,062
Hamburg, West Germany	11,773	6,270	6,564	8,359	5,815	6,553	1,595	14,442	3,125	628	7,264	7,296	9,471	7,989	5,419	682	5,177	10,260	1,936	16,261
Hamilton, Bermuda	7,433	1,710	10,603	11,488	1,539	9,126	6,542	16,515	8,802	5,708	13,304	4,498	3,420	1,777	4,809	5,578	1,753	5,935	7,874	16,882
Hamilton, New Zealand	10,265	13,900	14,259	12,711	14,390	14,900	18,809	3,697	16,613	18,455	11,254	12,004	11,844	12,881	13,482	18,359	14,975	11,722	17,328	2,346
Hangzhou, China	19,507	11,677	10,280	11,261	11,620	12,050	9,530	5,897	8,306	9,179	3,274	9,554	15,880	13,975	8,391	9,179	11,311	18,804	8,208	7,870
Hannover, West Germany	11,678	6,316	6,450	8,240	5,857	6,422	1,462	14,524	3,042	568	7,296	7,393	9,450	7,997	5,529	655	5,219	10,174	1,862	16,315
Hanoi, Vietnam	17,866	12,911	8,753	9,561	12,750	10,614	9,115	6,051	7,438	9,152	1,815	11,120	17,284	15,295	9,705	9,202	12,323	18,000	7,660	7,734
Harare, Zimbabwe	8,863	12,953	1,609	364	12,501	2,460	6,716	11,910	5,298	8,137	7,672	15,213	11,995	12,634	13,564	8,316	12,031	8,904	6,437	11,236
Harbin, China	18,695	9,867	10,845	12,201	9,820	12,336	8,728	7,203	8,072	8,055	4,306	7,803	14,097	12,169	6,581	8,014	9,537	17,196	7,634	9,261
Harrisburg, Pennsylvania	8,502	335	11,632	12,724	557	10,330	7,052	15,180	9,273	5,956	12,888	3,097	4,078	2,096	3,616	5,796	1,184	7,107	8,202	15,977
Hartford, Connecticut	8,580	526	11,260	12,393	304	9,995	6,662	15,441	8,885	5,575	12,624	3,297	4,262	2,313	3,579	5,417	839	7,135	7,820	16,344
Havana, Cuba	6,872	2,214	12,386	12,946	2,511	10,723	8,545	14,972	10,806	7,649	14,855	4,128	2,267	498	5,334	7,507	3,091	5,685	9,852	14,897
Helena, Montana	10,470	2,638	13,949	15,401	3,011	13,023	8,852	12,285	10,752	7,484	12,080	518	5,881	4,157	2,538	7,301	3,384	9,396	9,551	13,375
Helsinki, Finland	12,930	6,668	7,057	8,908	6,260	7,372	2,580	13,310	3,380	1,769	6,393	7,140	10,308	8,653	5,119	1,764	5,641	11,398	2,229	15,208
Hengyang, China	18,808	12,189	9,514	10,441	12,079	11,324	9,228	6,029	7,794	9,053	2,495	10,237	16,509	14,545	8,930	9,077	11,709	18,541	7,834	7,889
Herat, Afghanistan	14,656	10,586	5,409	7,002	10,187	6,856	4,703	10,485	2,945	5,121	2,866	10,539	14,006	12,541	8,485	5,232	9,569	13,691	3,219	11,874
Hermosillo, Mexico	8,951	3,248	14,963	15,840	3,736	13,524	10,234	12,175	12,339	8,978	13,934	2,455	4,613	3,425	4,470	8,801	4,318	8,160	11,172	12,646
Hiroshima, Japan	19,027	10,875	11,427	12,491	10,894	13,122	9,992	5,852	9,104	9,390	4,475	8,531	14,842	13,050	7,612	9,355	10,682	18,314	8,811	7,913
Hiva Oa (Atuona)	8,542	8,431	18,075	16,430	8,919	16,417	15,477	8,141	17,551	14,221	14,796	7,159	7,085	7,515	9,144	14,042	9,532	9,064	16,350	7,740
Ho Chi Minh City, Vietnam	16,968	14,039	8,703	9,203	13,889	10,619	9,905	5,280	8,025	10,105	2,344	12,116	18,397	16,416	10,807	10,172	13,464	17,756	8,424	6,782
Hobart, Australia	11,031	16,296	11,977	10,638	16,782	13,000	16,523	2,886	14,261	17,272	9,429	14,077	13,866	15,208	15,065	17,371	17,324	12,639	15,185	857
Hohhot, China	18,906	10,678	9,604	10,885	10,549	11,206	8,180	7,298	7,143	7,779	2,975	8,908	15,038	13,053	7,450	7,778	10,168	17,406	6,912	9,263
Hong Kong	18,463	12,671	9,623	10,411	12,579	11,480	9,686	5,535	8,158	9,562	2,654	10,620	16,938	15,005	9,397	9,591	12,224	18,853	8,269	7,366
Honiara, Solomon Islands	13,682	13,243	14,374	13,775	13,623	16,089	15,624	1,745	14,245	14,987	8,563	10,537	13,762	13,717	11,177	14,924	13,916	14,998	14,317	3,071
Honolulu, Hawaii	12,160	7,552	17,876	19,348	7,968	17,966	13,169	7,464	14,239	11,757	11,357	5,020	8,981	8,186	6,374	11,586	8,365	12,134	13,186	8,398
Houston, Texas	8,111	2,069	13,525	14,325	2,543	12,015	9,095	13,689	11,308	7,970	14,204	2,830	3,526	1,980	4,421	7,804	3,177	7,067	10,215	14,039
Huambo, Angola	7,784	11,341	1,818	1,595	10,912	887	5,792	13,625	5,016	7,184	8,821	13,830	10,351	10,901	12,513	7,350	10,498	7,510	5,957	12,779
Hubli, India	14,936	13,036	5,455	6,432	12,650	7,316	6,893	8,534	4,763	7,532	1,600	12,594	16,278	15,000	10,636	7,657	12,037	14,702	5,448	9,595
Hugh Town, United Kingdom	10,677	5,413	6,825	8,490	4,934	6,400	1,702	15,577	3,832	590	8,447	6,901	8,306	6,912	5,261	517	4,303	9,129	2,769	17,453
Hull, Canada	9,033	378	11,455	12,684	226	10,286	6,695	15,041	8,878	5,529	12,309	2,882	4,652	2,675	3,109	5,362	749	7,603	7,773	16,103
Hyderabad, India	15,354	12,943	5,860	6,850	12,579	7,710	7,045	8,295	4,978	7,594	1,182	12,326	16,437	15,010	10,407	7,709	11,980	15,096	5,579	9,460
Hyderabad, Pakistan	14,853	11,739	5,276	6,623	11,344	6,966	5,685	9,598	3,681	6,235	2,058	11,537	15,070	13,688	9,514	6,355	10,727	14,199	4,213	10,828
Igloolik, Canada	11,688	2,955	11,171	12,881	2,816	10,734	6,022	13,334	7,749	4,604	9,781	2,654	7,329	5,341	916	4,423	2,521	10,196	6,544	15,135
Iloilo, Philippines	17,356	13,686	10,437	10,830	13,692	12,355	11,211	3,981	9,551	11,123	3,865	11,272	17,395	15,817	10,416	11,150	13,439	18,887	9,770	5,814
Indianapolis, Indiana	8,713	701	12,419	13,511	1,190	11,119	7,750	14,433	9,939	6,588	13,084	2,498	4,138	2,184	3,455	6,420	1,806	7,428	8,830	15,188
Innsbruck, Austria	11,430	6,709	5,881	7,663	6,238	5,851	913	14,667	2,561	809	7,238	7,932	9,573	8,244	6,097	980	5,602	9,980	1,441	16,296
Inuvik, Canada	12,962	4,234	12,682	14,510	4,311	12,588	7,683	11,356	9,023	6,274	9,364	2,199	8,355	6,437	1,153	6,104	4,249	11,662	7,860	13,105
Invercargill, New Zealand	9,887	14,834	13,184	11,602	15,322	13,789	18,150	3,878	15,913	18,904	11,062	13,100	12,196	13,507	14,594	18,944	15,935	11,439	16,887	2,022
Inverness, United Kingdom	11,393	5,275	7,388	9,126	4,823	7,142	2,248	14,865	4,090	826	8,075	6,388	8,631	7,056	4,605	649	4,186	9,815	2,918	16,852
Iquitos, Peru	3,741	5,198	11,393	11,107	5,343	9,476	9,619	15,169	11,620	9,296	17,149	7,207	877	2,828	8,442	9,216	5,771	2,736	11,102	13,831
Iraklion, Greece	11,626	8,425	4,309	6,152	7,947	4,724	1,482	13,845	820	2,549	6,224	9,640	10,846	9,774	7,730	2,726	7,316	10,421	546	15,009
Irkutsk, USSR	17,616	9,457	9,289	10,829	9,282	10,639	7,003	8,645	6,309	6,464	3,572	8,000	13,829	11,843	6,328	6,449	8,860	16,037	5,862	10,637
Islamabad, Pakistan	15,607	11,061	6,162	7,607	10,706	7,738	5,655	9,512	3,960	5,932	1,936	10,590	14,815	13,186	8,603	6,024	10,115	14,703	4,179	10,995
Istanbul, Turkey	12,235	8,239	4,917	6,772	7,776	5,433	1,700	13,466	1,234	2,356	5,867	9,194	11,051	9,800	7,223	2,512	7,138	10,960	238	14,847
Ivujivik, Canada	10,893	2,172	11,223	12,822	2,018	10,555	6,090	13,933	8,002	4,714	10,512	2,502	6,541	4,556	1,434	4,531	1,750	9,412	6,809	15,594
Iwo Jima Island, Japan	17,827	11,460	12,391	13,157	11,573	14,207	11,361	4,638	10,408	10,727	5,376	8,856	14,877	13,376	8,333	10,683	11,474	18,324	10,169	6,705
Izmir, Turkey	11,958	8,324	4,634	6,485	7,852	5,107	1,566	13,643	1,002	2,423	6,024	9,399	10,960	9,789	7,455	2,591	7,217	10,714	203	14,929
Jackson, Mississippi	8,116	1,540	12,976	13,847	2,000	11,507	8,535	14,179	10,757	7,430	13,935	2,855	3,498	1,715	4,202	7,267	2,637	6,959	9,676	14,603
Jaffna, Sri Lanka	14,980	13,805	5,798	6,524	13,434	7,706	7,692	7,811	5,530	8,351	1,681	13,143	17,049	15,817	11,256	8,476	12,828	15,028	6,257	8,792
Jakarta, Indonesia	15,237	15,899	8,590	8,553	15,760	10,460	11,105	4,404	8,979	11,587	3,757	13,769	19,550	18,249	12,639	11,683	15,327	16,437	9,640	5,401
Jamestown, St. Helena	5,629	9,887	4,084	3,657	9,547	2,269	6,297	15,222	6,451	7,446	11,090	12,653	8,078	8,895	12,018	7,569	9,300	5,179	7,044	13,747
Jamnagar, India	14,869	12,103	5,268	6,522	11,709	7,018	6,002	9,322	3,948	6,587	1,882	11,851	15,396	14,048	9,841	6,709	11,092	14,327	4,538	10,499
Jan Mayen Island	12,345	4,848	8,718	10,517	4,485	8,639	3,687	13,764	5,174	2,301	7,917	5,243	8,842	7,012	3,283	2,145	3,903	10,732	3,972	15,832
Jayapura, Indonesia	15,438	14,071	12,370	12,215	14,298	14,242	13,664	1,685	12,026	13,412	6,321	11,288	15,900	15,358	11,208	13,409	14,329	16,971	12,244	3,735
Jefferson City, Missouri	8,817	1,219	12,954	14,032	1,708	11,645	8,248	13,941	10,415	7,054	13,240	2,205	4,202	2,344	3,487	6,883	2,305	7,619	9,288	14,652
Jerusalem, Israel	12,236	9,366	3,939	5,788	8,894	4,799	2,499	12,903	426	3,465	5,314	10,351	11,846	10,787	8,359	3,632	8,259	11,169	1,224	13,992
Jiggalong, Australia	13,585	17,194	10,013	9,359	17,347	11,649	13,442	2,704	11,237	14,010	6,176	14,436	17,130	18,096	14,089	14,108	17,197	15,128	12,007	3,042
Jinan, China	19,550	11,050	10,025	11,186	10,960	11,700	8,832	6,657	7,742	8,427	3,167	9,087	15,350	13,392	7,779	8,422	10,619	18,035	7,552	8,639
Jodhpur, India	15,322	11,826	5,732	7,030	11,454	7,440	6,035	9,200	4,103	6,490	1,609	11,410	15,375	13,878	9,425	6,599	10,850	14,675	4,553	10,511
Johannesburg, South Africa	8,113	13,281	2,529	672	12,865	2,842	7,506	11,769	6,234	8,927	8,442	15,796	11,642	12,572	14,348	9,103	12,465	8,338	7,347	10,811
Juazeiro do Norte, Brazil	3,612	6,837	7,621	7,442	6,655	5,702	7,161	17,280	8,576	7,555	14,187	9,576	4,296	5,269	9,815	7,573	6,677	2,206	8,518	15,214
Juneau, Alaska	12,457	4,144	13,752	15,551	4,353	13,487	8,680	11,010	10,123	7,258	10,218	1,531	7,859	6,067	1,855	7,083	4,467	11,341	8,949	12,548
Kabul, Afghanistan	15,278	10,842	5,913	7,421	10,471	7,437	5,285	9,885	3,588	5,597	2,292	10,520	14,491	12,914	8,503	5,695	9,869	14,334	3,807	11,345
Kalgoorlie, Australia	12,771	17,768	10,025	9,155	18,020	11,517	13,917	2,901	11,669	14,633	6,875	14,970	16,449	17,831	14,833	14,747	17,970	14,324	12,534	2,628
Kaliningrad, USSR	12,418	6,790	6,492	8,331	6,352	6,724	1,923	13,766	2,872	1,321	6,577	7,549	10,147	8,615	5,578	1,377	5,718	10,927	1,678	15,564
Kamloops, Canada	11,222	3,235	14,050	15,667	3,548	13,357	8,897	11,719	10,638	7,491	11,423	441	6,640	4,908	2,211	7,309	3,825	10,155	9,435	12,979
Kampala, Uganda	10,128	11,720	544	2,305	11,234	2,357	4,926	12,492	3,294	6,316	6,515	13,507	12,139	12,123	11,674	6,499	10,672	9,737	4,456	12,421
Kananga, Zaire	8,808	11,376	820	1,713	10,914	1,132	5,180	13,310	4,088	6,601	7,833	13,598	11,046	11,323	12,026	6,777	10,425	8,440	5,115	12,826
Kano, Nigeria	8,738	8,902	2,867	4,182	8,431	1,983	3,016	15,403	3,083	4,362	8,482	11,107	9,399	9,173	9,665	4,522	7,925	7,786	3,580	15,298
Kanpur, India	16,001	12,038	6,399	7,603	11,704	8,144	6,648	8,545	4,798	6,986	922	11,302	15,874	14,220	9,396	7,081	11,126	15,405	5,165	9,954
Kansas City, Missouri	8,968	1,384	13,132	14,237	1,868	11,847	8,376	13,727	10,523	7,158	13,175	2,019	4,351	2,527	3,399	6,985	2,445	7,796	9,384	14,467
Kaohsiung, Taiwan	18,673	12,491	10,254	11,020	12,449	12,109	10,121	5,181	8,700	9,886	3,276	10,273	16,599	14,754	9,203	9,899	12,151	19,448	8,738	7,103
Karachi, Pakistan	14,709	11,734	5,133	6,491	11,332	6,822	5,600	9,703	3,571	6,182	2,187	11,595	14,992	13,649	9,563	6,306	10,712	14,061	4,134	10,904
Karaganda, USSR	15,769	9,379	7,236	8,908	9,060	8,470	5,064	10,236	4,126	4,870	3,309	8,803	13,427	11,618	6,811	4,911	8,501	14,408	3,774	12,026
Karl-Marx-Stadt, East Germany	11,755	6,593	6,210	8,012	6,133	6,248	1,325	14,403	2,766	779	7,089	7,658	9,674	8,251	5,776	900	5,495	10,276	1,583	16,134
Kasanga, Tanzania	9,448	12,278	596	1,322	11,805	2,118	5,749	12,310	4,262	7,163	7,116	14,315	12,019	12,326	12,572	7,344	11,286	9,254	5,405	11,922
Kashgar, China	15,976	10,538	6,722	8,235	10,208	8,207	5,621	9,551	4,180	5,707	2,216	9,927	14,486	12,743	7,961	5,778	9,637	14,885	4,188	11,180
Kassel, West Germany	11,595	6,359	6,349	8,134	5,897	6,306	1,345	14,593	2,969	538	7,323	7,481	9,434	8,006	5,629	655	5,259	10,099	1,800	16,358
Kathmandu, Nepal	16,509	12,022	6,908	8,083	11,719	8,655	6,993	8,176	5,231	7,229	651	11,075	16,051	14,283	9,234	7,310	11,166	15,896	5,516	9,677
Kayes, Mali	7,359	7,097	4,914	5,818	6,664	3,421	3,403	17,577	4,693	4,221	10,383	9,632	7,238	7,038	8,657	4,312	6,262	6,101	4,647	16,996
Kazan, USSR	14,169	8,032	6,800	8,631	7,655	7,591	3,462	11,959	3,185	3,131	4,893	8,065	11,808	10,117	5,996	3,172	7,053	12,719	2,406	13,764
Kemi, Finland	13,153	6,306	7,687	9,538	5,928	7,980	3,119	13,108	4,003	2,098	6,556	6,574	10,159	8,407	4,533	2,040	5,328	11,578	2,859	15,092
Kenora, Canada	10,000	1,421	12,664	14,057	1,712	11,674	7,646	13,555	9,672	6,330	11,990	1,396	5,409	3,473	2,228	6,150	2,038	8,716	8,493	14,723
Kerguelen Island	9,373	17,490	6,360	4,862	17,158	7,224	11,474	7,610	9,591	12,848	8,194	19,706	13,983	15,777	17,800	13,031	16,836	10,508	10,793	6,428
Kerkira, Greece	11,496	7,766	4,857	6,676	7,289	5,061	931	14,249	1,480	1,889	6,641	9,013	10,320	9,163	7,138	2,066	6,657	10,189	558	15,569
Kermanshah, Iran	13,352	9,849	4,567	6,337	9,405	5,735	3,407	11,839	1,563	4,062	4,219	10,370	12,797	11,541	8,309	4,202	8,769	12,310	1,939	13,098
Khabarovsk, USSR	18,104	9,350	11,448	12,867	9,342	12,849	8,930	7,322	8,497	8,121	5,013	7,166	13,489	11,600	6,068	8,060	9,108	16,775	7,950	9,390
Kharkov, USSR	13,170	7,946	5,952	7,807	7,519	6,577	2,445	12,824	2,255	2,423	5,436	8,459	11,313	9,806	6,418	2,516	6,889	11,784	1,339	14,482
Khartoum, Sudan	11,071	10,498	2,128	3,978	10,009	3,240	3,473	12,932	1,606	4,784	5,895	11,942	11,947	11,406	10,034	4,966	9,402	10,323	2,785	13,405
Khon Kaen, Thailand	17,272	13,434	8,366	9,066	13,248	10,258	9,186	5,983	7,369	9,354	1,661	11,714	17,804	15,821	10,262	9,420	12,793	17,613	7,710	7,531
Kiev, USSR	12,811	7,617	5,964	7,820	7,181	6,448	2,089	13,226	2,264	2,015	5,846	8,271	10,908	9,427	6,257	2,113	6,547	11,401	1,187	14,894
Kigali, Rwanda	9,756	11,695	177	2,020	11,215	2,024	5,037	12,677	3,544	6,445	6,878	13,617	11,874	11,959	11,845	6,627	10,672	9,387	4,677	12,481
Kingston, Canada	8,919	243	11,535	12,734	264	10,334	6,810	15,043	9,002	5,657	12,454	2,890	4,518	2,538	3,211	5,492	867	7,501	7,902	16,041
Kingston, Jamaica	6,137	2,766	11,844	12,248	2,955	10,101	8,425	15,521	10,664	7,684	15,242	4,922	1,610	392	6,005	7,559	3,453	4,894	9,811	15,117
Kingstown, Saint Vincent	5,293	3,707	10,168	10,495	3,655	8,376	7,410	17,104	9,527	7,004	14,863	6,323	1,995	1,992	6,938	6,922	3,897	3,786	8,882	16,104
Kinshasa, Zaire	8,256	10,675	1,566	2,270	10,225	371	4,860	14,102	4,164	6,256	8,471	13,030	10,249	10,523	11,614	6,424	9,766	7,757	5,051	13,508

Distances in Kilometers	Buenos Aires, Argentina	Buffalo, New York	Bujumbura, Burundi	Bulawayo, Zimbabwe	Burlington, Vermont	Cabinda, Angola	Cagliari, Italy	Cairns, Australia	Cairo, Egypt	Calais, France	Calcutta, India	Calgary, Canada	Cali, Colombia	Camaguey, Cuba	Cambridge Bay, Canada	Cambridge, United Kingdom	Campbellton, Canada	Campo Grande, Brazil	Canakkale, Turkey	Canberra, Australia
Kirkwall, United Kingdom	11,565	5,302	7,478	9,232	4,858	7,279	2,358	14,690	4,122	943	7,962	6,322	8,741	7,135	4,504	778	4,223	9,984	2,937	16,687
Kirov, USSR	14,240	7,806	7,100	8,936	7,440	7,852	3,585	11,946	3,466	3,122	5,039	7,765	11,667	9,932	5,696	3,145	6,848	12,752	2,628	13,804
Kiruna, Sweden	13,066	6,031	7,936	9,783	5,659	8,168	3,259	13,184	4,266	2,134	6,791	6,282	9,934	8,157	4,245	2,051	5,065	11,476	3,106	15,198
Kisangani, Zaire	9,463	11,117	632	2,314	10,640	1,592	4,590	13,277	3,333	6,010	7,249	13,131	11,318	11,355	11,437	6,190	10,108	8,975	4,393	13,070
Kishinev, USSR	12,535	7,780	5,582	7,436	7,331	6,048	1,816	13,404	1,893	2,013	5,918	8,576	10,886	9,490	6,584	2,139	6,693	11,167	786	14,976
Kitchner, Canada	8,928	145	11,866	13,048	595	10,649	7,132	14,778	9,315	5,963	12,611	2,653	4,449	2,459	3,187	5,796	1,186	7,554	8,206	15,717
Knoxville, Tennessee	8,248	882	12,322	13,295	1,311	10,924	7,828	14,707	10,052	6,733	13,479	2,927	3,680	1,719	3,910	6,572	1,949	6,966	8,980	15,279
Kosice, Czechoslovakia	12,128	7,222	5,824	7,660	6,766	6,075	1,431	13,921	2,238	1,415	6,496	8,164	10,293	8,895	6,221	1,545	6,128	10,706	1,034	15,555
Kota Kinabalu, Malaysia	16,787	14,388	9,693	9,980	14,340	11,612	11,034	4,135	9,186	11,146	3,493	12,091	18,281	16,621	11,100	11,198	14,018	18,123	9,558	5,738
Krakow, Poland	12,124	7,053	5,993	7,826	6,599	6,209	1,477	13,970	2,419	1,283	6,595	7,982	10,176	8,751	6,043	1,401	5,961	10,680	1,215	15,648
Kralendijk, Bonaire	5,279	3,555	10,927	11,182	3,612	9,116	8,084	16,334	10,240	7,574	15,406	5,967	1,325	1,448	6,842	7,477	3,976	3,905	9,540	15,468
Krasnodar, USSR	13,164	8,490	5,448	7,295	8,055	6,207	2,538	12,634	1,796	2,819	5,107	9,048	11,702	10,280	7,005	2,937	7,420	11,868	1,166	14,162
Krasnoyarsk, USSR	16,780	9,016	8,714	10,356	8,791	9,936	6,147	9,471	5,547	5,620	3,736	7,880	13,342	11,384	6,048	5,610	8,319	15,229	5,032	11,438
Kristiansand, Norway	11,984	5,931	7,085	8,886	5,493	7,074	2,109	14,272	3,596	896	7,346	6,807	9,361	7,776	4,903	832	4,859	10,432	2,394	16,198
Kuala Lumpur, Malaysia	15,971	14,904	8,080	8,380	14,704	9,997	10,014	5,328	7,958	10,427	2,581	13,108	19,249	17,289	11,730	10,518	14,225	16,823	8,537	6,526
Kuching, Malaysia	16,167	14,998	9,026	9,213	14,894	10,937	10,869	4,394	8,877	11,159	3,322	12,833	19,085	17,317	11,722	11,234	14,507	17,362	9,385	5,741
Kumasi, Ghana	7,510	8,470	3,619	4,444	8,033	2,046	3,761	16,310	4,301	4,918	9,733	10,964	8,307	8,331	9,842	5,049	7,615	6,527	4,642	15,661
Kumzar, Oman	13,810	11,084	4,393	5,956	10,648	5,931	4,599	10,770	2,500	5,323	3,259	11,383	13,985	12,798	9,314	5,463	10,013	13,031	3,167	11,886
Kunming, China	17,921	12,479	8,503	9,446	12,293	10,324	8,583	6,588	6,962	8,600	1,485	10,838	16,848	14,865	9,322	8,650	11,843	17,648	7,137	8,286
Kuqa Chang, China	16,623	10,527	7,367	8,838	10,236	8,871	6,131	9,079	4,814	6,080	2,118	9,645	14,664	12,818	7,753	6,132	9,698	15,460	4,738	10,805
Kurgan, USSR	15,184	8,598	7,301	9,065	8,266	8,323	4,466	10,953	3,894	4,122	4,121	8,201	12,608	10,811	6,166	4,149	7,699	13,734	3,312	12,797
Kuwait, Kuwait	13,203	10,341	4,134	5,862	9,889	5,437	3,708	11,658	1,618	4,500	4,096	10,923	13,088	11,946	8,863	4,649	9,251	12,282	2,298	12,776
Kuybyshev, USSR	14,191	8,299	6,566	8,388	7,916	7,420	3,465	11,868	2,995	3,259	4,686	8,356	12,017	10,357	6,287	3,315	7,309	12,782	2,306	13,625
Kyoto, Japan	18,728	10,693	11,721	12,800	10,732	13,397	10,133	5,843	9,326	9,473	4,782	8,296	14,586	12,829	7,449	9,429	10,546	18,106	8,989	7,910
Kzyl-Orda, USSR	15,179	9,669	6,429	8,107	9,309	7,690	4,615	10,577	3,407	4,659	3,234	9,384	13,471	11,792	7,347	4,731	8,716	13,944	3,222	12,228
L'vov, USSR	12,364	7,304	5,919	7,765	6,855	6,241	1,665	13,696	2,280	1,575	6,301	8,141	10,470	9,034	6,171	1,689	6,218	10,939	1,093	15,356
La Ceiba, Honduras	6,332	3,098	12,921	13,215	3,429	11,146	9,414	14,434	11,671	8,567	15,734	4,607	1,769	1,124	6,062	8,429	4,021	5,333	10,754	14,086
La Coruna, Spain	10,018	5,555	6,411	7,985	5,066	5,801	1,533	16,200	3,793	1,143	8,843	7,335	7,989	6,777	5,833	1,169	4,461	8,500	2,894	17,899
La Paz, Bolivia	2,227	6,666	10,712	10,073	6,771	8,816	10,101	14,776	11,803	10,082	17,482	8,715	2,391	4,324	9,935	10,036	7,145	1,494	11,557	13,055
La Paz, Mexico	8,501	3,548	15,128	15,785	4,038	13,560	10,591	12,150	12,743	9,378	14,462	3,002	4,290	3,333	5,009	9,204	4,646	7,795	11,596	12,438
La Ronge, Canada	10,896	2,339	12,985	14,553	2,564	12,234	7,850	12,738	9,703	6,463	11,306	741	6,285	4,384	1,562	6,280	2,753	9,646	8,500	14,089
Labrador City, Canada	9,734	1,428	10,729	12,136	1,049	9,773	5,784	15,104	7,912	4,548	11,309	3,188	5,558	3,628	2,660	4,375	551	8,218	6,778	16,583
Lagos, Nigeria	7,912	8,896	3,086	4,035	8,447	1,649	3,675	15,782	3,915	4,935	9,230	11,305	8,860	8,859	10,056	5,081	7,999	7,005	4,383	15,280
Lahore, Pakistan	15,643	11,318	6,129	7,520	10,963	7,753	5,855	9,320	4,096	6,169	1,716	10,814	15,058	13,443	8,838	6,264	10,372	14,816	4,375	10,769
Lambasa, Fiji	11,699	12,185	16,067	14,861	12,648	17,202	17,311	3,582	16,451	16,169	10,803	9,865	11,631	11,951	11,139	16,036	13,129	12,853	16,314	3,657
Lansing, Michigan	8,966	464	12,206	13,377	935	10,979	7,455	14,487	9,626	6,268	12,742	2,413	4,424	2,447	3,168	6,098	1,513	7,640	8,506	15,379
Lanzhou, China	18,396	11,259	8,832	10,045	11,081	10,507	7,936	7,348	6,642	7,733	2,106	9,676	15,632	13,646	8,107	7,758	10,646	17,289	6,573	9,202
Laoag, Philippines	18,185	12,955	10,264	10,897	12,925	12,152	10,484	4,763	8,961	10,313	3,393	10,677	16,974	15,189	9,669	10,333	12,637	19,468	9,074	6,649
Largeau, Chad	10,040	9,304	2,611	4,336	8,816	2,704	2,551	14,385	1,822	3,972	7,192	11,115	10,496	9,999	9,401	4,152	8,241	9,097	2,562	14,755
Las Vegas, Nevada	9,796	3,180	14,878	16,078	3,639	13,685	9,896	11,906	11,881	8,566	13,055	1,655	5,367	3,956	3,718	8,385	4,144	8,932	10,687	12,665
Launceston, Australia	11,192	16,263	12,025	10,718	16,745	13,089	16,481	2,719	14,221	17,169	9,315	13,984	13,970	15,266	14,927	17,260	17,267	12,799	15,118	698
Le Havre, France	10,962	5,859	6,500	8,212	5,383	6,210	1,346	15,261	3,389	202	8,013	7,241	8,755	7,379	5,519	300	4,750	9,442	2,306	17,053
Leipzig, East Germany	11,752	6,531	6,272	8,073	6,072	6,299	1,366	14,418	2,832	736	7,126	7,592	9,631	8,199	5,712	849	5,434	10,267	1,648	16,165
Leningrad, USSR	13,193	6,921	7,019	8,875	6,521	7,431	2,737	13,035	3,320	2,035	6,101	7,292	10,600	8,933	5,251	2,041	5,906	11,671	2,215	14,919
Leon, Spain	10,101	5,799	6,188	7,782	5,310	5,627	1,291	16,080	3,552	1,086	8,657	7,549	8,197	7,012	6,011	1,149	4,703	8,603	2,672	17,699
Lerwick, United Kingdom	11,730	5,364	7,529	9,299	4,928	7,379	2,437	14,524	4,123	1,041	7,834	6,299	8,867	7,238	4,448	889	4,295	10,148	2,928	16,525
Lhasa, China	17,113	11,908	7,512	8,673	11,644	9,252	7,355	7,807	5,713	7,463	834	10,731	16,114	14,238	8,973	7,528	11,124	16,438	5,897	9,421
Libreville, Gabon	8,028	9,846	2,255	3,085	9,398	724	4,300	14,908	4,014	5,650	8,861	12,239	9,568	9,728	10,913	5,809	8,947	7,339	4,727	14,330
Lilongwe, Malawi	9,343	12,900	1,269	877	12,433	2,543	6,423	11,813	4,880	7,835	7,193	14,989	12,302	12,793	13,237	8,017	11,928	9,320	6,041	11,304
Lima, Peru	3,127	6,086	11,721	11,148	6,271	9,809	10,524	14,330	12,430	10,275	18,090	7,855	1,715	3,699	9,267	10,201	6,730	2,568	12,007	12,865
Limerick, Ireland	10,807	5,160	7,159	8,833	4,688	6,745	2,020	15,454	4,093	745	8,500	6,569	8,226	6,757	4,916	596	4,052	9,238	2,990	17,410
Limoges, France	10,737	6,116	6,118	7,812	5,634	5,794	978	15,428	3,137	571	8,031	7,613	8,788	7,512	5,922	713	5,007	9,250	2,136	17,090
Limon, Costa Rica	5,576	3,667	12,538	12,644	3,936	10,696	9,500	14,709	11,722	8,793	16,288	5,361	1,021	1,373	6,754	8,670	4,484	4,586	10,906	14,058
Lincoln, Nebraska	9,224	1,494	13,229	14,397	1,960	12,001	8,394	13,531	10,510	7,146	12,971	1,756	4,607	2,789	3,188	6,970	2,502	8,058	9,356	14,349
Linz, Austria	11,673	6,829	5,911	7,714	6,363	5,969	1,092	14,422	2,488	946	7,010	7,950	9,786	8,423	6,075	1,098	5,726	10,226	1,322	16,070
Lisbon, Portugal	9,577	5,732	6,112	7,613	5,243	5,453	1,580	16,583	3,804	1,609	9,093	7,683	7,818	6,749	6,270	1,661	4,664	8,086	3,043	18,063
Little Rock, Arkansas	8,446	1,471	13,091	14,049	1,954	11,687	8,519	13,969	10,715	7,365	13,665	2,521	3,829	2,041	3,906	7,198	2,580	7,293	9,608	14,513
Liverpool, United Kingdom	11,119	5,490	6,981	8,699	5,023	6,689	1,828	15,139	3,790	430	8,116	6,769	8,612	7,134	5,032	250	4,386	9,564	2,657	17,055
Lodz, Poland	12,193	6,920	6,181	8,014	6,471	6,387	1,607	13,942	2,599	1,229	6,630	7,804	10,121	8,659	5,859	1,327	5,833	10,729	1,395	15,668
Lome, Togo	7,707	8,742	3,301	4,176	8,300	1,777	3,749	15,995	4,111	4,969	9,466	11,196	8,622	8,646	10,007	5,108	7,866	6,775	4,531	15,413
London, United Kingdom	11,105	5,751	6,693	8,417	5,281	6,430	1,542	15,136	3,513	149	7,978	7,059	8,769	7,341	5,313	80	4,644	9,571	2,396	16,984
Londonderry, United Kingdom	11,060	5,166	7,296	8,998	4,703	6,951	2,142	15,199	4,122	762	8,337	6,446	8,377	6,853	4,737	583	4,064	9,485	2,983	17,177
Longlac, Canada	9,750	966	12,132	13,492	1,168	11,106	7,170	14,107	9,250	5,889	11,979	1,952	5,222	3,242	2,374	5,712	1,466	8,393	8,088	15,293
Lord Howe Island, Australia	11,700	14,832	13,451	12,231	15,298	14,612	17,181	2,107	15,081	17,159	9,619	12,456	13,444	14,297	13,472	17,151	15,773	13,227	15,697	1,012
Los Angeles, California	9,828	3,538	15,245	16,417	4,000	14,031	10,256	11,588	12,223	8,920	13,141	1,918	5,489	4,187	3,987	8,738	4,511	9,042	11,026	12,305
Louangphrabang, Laos	17,506	13,056	8,350	9,154	12,865	10,218	8,892	6,270	7,139	9,011	1,459	11,392	17,421	15,441	9,900	9,072	12,406	17,605	7,423	7,871
Louisville, Kentucky	8,544	778	12,427	13,473	1,256	11,088	7,819	14,500	10,020	6,678	13,249	2,634	3,967	2,015	3,627	6,513	1,886	7,267	8,923	15,183
Luanda, Angola	7,787	10,842	1,883	2,076	10,409	377	5,333	14,081	4,712	6,711	8,886	13,314	10,049	10,487	12,010	6,874	9,988	7,377	5,587	13,291
Lubumbashi, Zaire	8,916	12,216	940	947	11,756	1,811	5,946	12,544	4,634	7,368	7,642	14,430	11,619	12,061	12,799	7,547	11,271	8,756	5,738	11,984
Lusaka, Zambia	8,762	12,555	1,336	525	12,102	2,069	6,368	12,290	5,041	7,791	7,778	14,831	11,707	12,275	13,221	7,969	11,633	8,708	6,154	11,634
Luxembourg, Luxembourg	11,289	6,242	6,282	8,039	5,771	6,138	1,178	14,895	3,028	341	7,586	7,498	9,188	7,808	5,700	512	5,135	9,794	1,906	16,636
Luxor, Egypt	11,679	9,691	3,235	5,090	9,208	4,102	2,661	13,092	503	3,837	5,634	10,902	11,757	10,899	8,953	4,014	8,582	10,716	1,706	13,941
Lynn Lake, Canada	10,899	2,207	12,657	14,231	2,376	11,922	7,522	12,973	9,386	6,137	11,164	1,069	6,307	4,370	1,382	5,954	2,504	9,598	8,185	14,379
Lyon, France	10,935	6,365	5,958	7,682	5,886	5,729	806	15,192	2,880	620	7,761	7,788	9,066	7,790	6,048	796	5,256	9,468	1,859	16,816
Macapa, Brazil	3,911	5,499	8,954	8,937	5,389	7,056	7,482	17,396	9,271	7,512	14,974	8,157	2,858	3,755	8,650	7,482	5,525	2,299	8,944	15,575
Madison, Wisconsin	9,158	858	12,575	13,772	1,310	11,373	7,763	14,093	9,904	6,539	12,737	2,062	4,571	2,631	3,038	6,366	1,850	7,883	8,764	14,994
Madras, India	15,240	13,455	5,914	6,748	13,093	7,803	7,485	7,927	5,368	8,082	1,351	12,765	16,877	15,518	10,877	8,201	12,494	15,172	6,031	9,007
Madrid, Spain	10,024	6,053	5,902	7,492	5,563	5,341	1,103	16,093	3,355	1,248	8,589	7,838	8,312	7,194	6,299	1,343	4,963	8,554	2,546	17,580
Madurai, India	14,839	13,709	5,602	6,363	13,327	7,507	7,512	8,014	5,339	8,196	1,772	13,147	16,852	15,673	11,232	8,324	12,715	14,842	6,085	8,972
Magadan, USSR	16,513	7,776	12,049	13,715	7,793	13,067	8,505	8,489	8,643	7,437	6,327	5,584	11,896	10,004	4,510	7,337	7,605	15,216	7,838	10,519
Magdalena, Bolivia	2,424	6,404	10,311	9,792	6,467	8,400	9,545	15,330	11,257	9,545	16,952	8,614	2,306	4,125	9,691	9,504	6,798	1,283	11,001	13,584
Magdeburg, East Germany	11,772	6,443	6,379	8,178	5,985	6,396	1,453	14,417	2,935	695	7,165	7,486	9,584	8,131	5,605	789	5,347	10,276	1,748	16,191
Majuro Atoll, Marshall Isls.	14,113	11,062	15,788	15,751	11,424	17,708	14,552	3,863	14,084	13,487	8,981	8,326	12,424	11,856	9,018	13,374	11,699	14,886	13,652	5,240
Malabo, Equatorial Guinea	8,194	9,539	2,422	3,418	9,084	1,096	3,928	15,117	3,751	5,272	8,787	11,888	9,473	9,524	10,537	5,431	8,619	7,418	4,404	14,652
Male, Maldives	14,024	14,119	4,973	5,584	13,699	6,893	7,534	8,273	5,290	8,383	2,605	13,862	16,597	15,824	11,891	8,527	13,068	14,128	6,183	8,980
Manado, Indonesia	16,323	14,551	10,638	10,727	14,610	12,544	12,092	3,069	10,280	12,111	4,581	11,984	17,597	16,479	11,328	12,149	14,410	17,906	10,625	4,797
Managua, Nicaragua	5,951	3,481	12,888	13,053	3,795	11,067	9,626	14,416	11,870	8,839	16,125	4,995	1,444	1,356	6,468	8,707	4,374	5,002	10,997	13,910
Manama, Bahrain	13,281	10,776	3,994	5,653	10,325	5,432	4,105	11,332	1,944	4,931	3,842	11,315	13,458	12,366	9,250	5,082	9,686	12,458	2,719	12,381
Manaus, Brazil	3,488	5,438	9,930	9,754	5,435	8,017	8,455	16,426	10,310	8,362	15,997	7,883	1,975	3,341	8,709	8,313	5,702	2,003	9,930	14,780
Manchester, New Hampshire	8,694	605	11,148	12,314	216	9,915	6,511	15,469	8,730	5,413	12,462	3,311	4,409	2,471	3,489	5,254	670	7,234	7,659	16,447
Mandalay, Burma	17,175	12,802	7,775	8,692	12,564	9,618	8,248	6,918	6,468	8,427	797	11,393	17,079	15,162	9,758	8,498	12,064	16,991	6,773	8,462
Mangareva Island, Fr.Polynesia	7,401	9,293	16,622	14,900	9,762	15,246	16,195	8,226	18,452	15,192	15,602	8,467	6,985	7,904	10,508	15,028	10,399	8,200	17,439	7,329
Manila, Philippines	17,787	13,327	10,288	10,809	13,309	12,194	10,791	4,421	9,192	10,670	3,547	10,997	17,243	15,528	10,045	10,695	13,032	19,216	9,363	6,273
Mannheim, West Germany	11,411	6,396	6,194	7,966	5,927	6,108	1,142	14,755	2,887	501	7,421	7,606	9,356	7,976	5,783	661	5,290	9,927	1,750	16,474
Maputo, Mozambique	8,509	13,628	2,522	762	13,199	3,131	7,617	11,382	6,200	9,039	8,061	16,049	12,091	13,004	14,469	9,218	12,773	8,776	7,347	10,507
Mar del Plata, Argentina	386	9,214	9,512	8,334	9,269	7,862	10,929	13,459	11,898	11,429	16,352	11,300	4,989	6,910	12,500	11,447	9,569	1,966	12,158	11,433
Maracaibo, Venezuela	5,199	3,639	11,288	11,477	3,750	9,459	8,474	15,941	10,639	7,936	15,740	5,906	964	1,364	6,918	7,834	4,165	3,913	9,926	15,083
Marrakech, Morocco	9,036	6,224	5,536	6,935	5,741	4,640	1,763	16,915	3,739	2,293	9,297	8,354	7,782	6,949	7,028	2,378	5,202	7,612	3,224	17,870
Marseilles, France	10,786	6,542	5,702	7,416	6,058	5,453	550	15,279	2,721	892	7,776	8,035	9,094	7,885	6,315	1,065	5,434	9,345	1,777	16,803
Maseru, Lesotho	7,888	13,434	2,877	1,022	13,033	3,083	7,823	11,653	6,582	9,242	8,685	16,021	11,560	12,590	14,652	9,417	12,659	8,191	7,691	10,605

Distances in Kilometers

	Buenos Aires, Argentina	Buffalo, New York	Bujumbura, Burundi	Bulawayo, Zimbabwe	Burlington, Vermont	Cabinda, Angola	Cagliari, Italy	Cairns, Australia	Cairo, Egypt	Calais, France	Calcutta, India	Calgary, Canada	Cali, Colombia	Camaguey, Cuba	Cambridge Bay, Canada	Cambridge, United Kingdom	Campbellton, Canada	Campo Grande, Brazil	Canakkale, Turkey	Canberra, Australia
Mashhad, Iran	14,497	10,282	5,401	7,049	9,879	6,767	4,403	10,774	2,723	4,800	3,164	10,308	13,687	12,221	8,247	4,911	9,258	13,467	2,921	12,188
Mazatlan, Mexico	8,163	3,345	14,792	15,383	3,830	13,182	10,394	12,523	12,584	9,227	14,699	3,159	3,891	2,939	5,103	9,057	4,453	7,411	11,462	12,730
Mbabane, Swaziland	8,367	13,535	2,545	730	13,111	3,055	7,607	11,493	6,238	9,030	8,200	15,994	11,945	12,872	14,460	9,208	12,695	8,627	7,375	10,584
Mbandaka, Zaire	8,803	10,589	1,293	2,504	10,123	917	4,435	13,986	3,592	5,849	7,973	12,795	10,550	10,655	11,258	6,023	9,627	8,237	4,515	13,614
McMurdo Sound, Antarctica	7,227	15,240	10,627	8,806	15,540	10,631	15,592	6,820	14,239	16,963	12,117	15,269	11,039	12,951	17,303	17,116	16,061	8,834	15,427	4,758
Mecca, Saudi Arabia	12,066	10,527	2,974	4,761	10,048	4,243	3,521	12,299	1,282	4,642	4,993	11,579	12,575	11,767	9,574	4,815	9,417	11,261	2,432	13,075
Medan, Indonesia	15,844	14,852	7,748	8,085	14,621	9,666	9,724	5,652	7,645	10,180	2,373	13,201	19,071	17,218	11,738	10,277	14,115	16,582	8,251	6,799
Medellin, Colombia	4,867	4,072	11,712	11,734	4,242	9,841	9,120	15,384	11,268	8,590	16,379	6,106	326	1,693	7,305	8,488	4,704	3,740	10,576	14,433
Medicine Hat, Canada	10,692	2,546	13,622	15,136	2,870	12,780	8,502	12,398	10,372	7,123	11,750	266	6,081	4,283	2,146	6,940	3,179	9,553	9,170	13,597
Medina, Saudi Arabia	12,215	10,257	3,293	5,078	9,781	4,456	3,274	12,379	1,032	4,361	4,960	11,252	12,470	11,573	9,243	4,531	9,148	11,340	2,132	13,256
Melbourne, Australia	11,629	16,296	11,993	10,782	16,762	13,173	16,212	2,319	13,966	16,786	8,927	13,865	14,337	15,534	14,660	16,865	17,223	13,237	14,805	465
Memphis, Tennessee	8,390	1,294	12,885	13,847	1,772	11,482	8,333	14,168	10,537	7,195	13,621	2,616	3,775	1,930	3,894	7,029	2,403	7,201	9,439	14,719
Merauke, Indonesia	14,848	14,621	12,263	11,918	14,878	14,073	14,099	1,105	12,318	13,962	6,621	11,826	15,922	15,691	11,840	13,970	14,945	16,418	12,646	3,109
Merida, Mexico	6,978	2,629	13,158	13,633	3,014	11,463	9,280	14,211	11,541	8,325	15,187	3,961	2,402	1,216	5,454	8,176	3,636	5,959	10,551	14,124
Meridian, Mississippi	8,060	1,452	12,838	13,707	1,901	11,367	8,420	14,319	10,647	7,327	13,921	2,933	3,445	1,619	4,217	7,166	2,539	6,880	9,574	14,737
Messina, Italy	11,097	7,570	4,817	6,599	7,087	4,854	573	14,650	1,702	1,784	7,034	8,972	9,960	8,864	7,160	1,966	6,462	9,781	961	15,913
Mexico City, Mexico	7,366	3,225	14,169	14,581	3,676	12,460	10,146	13,200	12,392	9,096	15,295	3,749	3,028	2,226	5,540	8,937	4,314	6,558	11,341	13,173
Miami, Florida	7,065	1,902	12,137	12,788	2,168	10,521	8,193	15,189	10,455	7,284	14,521	4,015	2,501	539	5,090	7,142	2,736	5,813	9,491	15,224
Midway Islands, USA	14,261	8,571	16,073	17,251	8,891	17,306	12,511	6,379	12,882	11,237	9,254	5,785	10,895	9,785	6,406	11,095	9,114	14,208	12,051	7,862
Milan, Italy	11,173	6,673	5,768	7,527	6,195	5,659	694	14,903	2,573	819	7,433	8,007	9,404	8,128	6,214	1,001	5,563	9,731	1,522	16,483
Milford Sound, New Zealand	10,075	14,800	13,285	11,731	15,289	13,943	18,160	3,696	15,903	18,749	10,943	12,986	12,296	13,555	14,436	18,770	15,894	11,621	16,833	1,887
Milwaukee, Wisconsin	9,105	737	12,462	13,652	1,193	11,253	7,666	14,212	9,815	6,452	12,735	2,164	4,528	2,575	3,068	6,280	1,743	7,813	8,682	15,113
Minsk, USSR	12,787	7,213	6,351	8,205	6,784	6,744	2,147	13,351	2,666	1,771	6,110	7,837	10,616	9,075	5,827	1,839	6,152	11,324	1,531	15,111
Mogadiscio, Somalia	11,409	12,553	1,880	3,065	12,064	3,783	5,514	11,192	3,438	6,776	5,166	13,806	13,543	13,340	11,795	6,955	11,455	11,138	4,632	11,398
Mombasa, Kenya	10,501	12,617	1,147	2,148	12,130	3,051	5,725	11,592	3,879	7,079	6,056	14,253	12,950	13,035	12,329	7,262	11,556	10,307	5,079	11,503
Monclova, Mexico	8,175	2,703	14,186	14,904	3,185	12,635	9,748	13,077	11,947	8,595	14,436	2,888	3,710	2,461	4,700	8,426	3,812	7,274	10,835	13,367
Moncton, Canada	8,960	1,175	10,600	11,852	685	9,457	5,887	15,720	8,099	4,781	11,938	3,610	4,861	2,990	3,397	4,622	255	7,441	7,026	16,942
Monrovia, Liberia	6,746	7,753	4,592	5,212	7,347	2,873	4,157	17,224	5,121	5,085	10,684	10,385	7,292	7,393	9,521	5,185	6,996	5,633	5,272	16,201
Monte Carlo, Monaco	10,941	6,655	5,662	7,397	6,174	5,479	521	15,111	2,596	906	7,606	8,088	9,259	8,034	6,335	1,087	5,546	9,507	1,620	16,637
Monterrey, Mexico	8,000	2,732	14,121	14,787	3,208	12,539	9,762	13,172	11,974	8,632	14,591	3,052	3,538	2,333	4,841	8,465	3,841	7,102	10,876	13,403
Montevideo, Uruguay	210	8,916	9,394	8,299	8,955	7,692	10,600	13,824	11,638	11,073	16,326	11,075	4,746	6,638	12,203	11,088	9,239	1,607	11,852	11,800
Montgomery, Alabama	7,967	1,337	12,617	13,483	1,759	11,142	8,239	14,543	10,474	7,170	13,901	3,072	3,362	1,475	4,254	7,011	2,396	6,751	9,415	14,949
Montpelier, Vermont	8,850	531	11,224	12,423	55	10,023	6,530	15,323	8,735	5,403	12,360	3,163	4,538	2,585	3,324	5,241	617	7,395	7,650	16,355
Montpellier, France	10,718	6,419	5,796	7,497	5,935	5,507	654	15,373	2,847	832	7,888	7,936	8,974	7,758	6,235	997	5,312	9,265	1,902	16,922
Montreal, Canada	9,001	512	11,288	12,519	118	10,120	6,542	15,186	8,733	5,389	12,254	3,028	4,668	2,704	3,166	5,224	598	7,552	7,635	16,269
Moosonee, Canada	9,759	943	11,685	13,064	939	10,686	6,724	14,429	8,817	5,454	11,758	2,318	5,316	3,327	2,368	5,278	1,072	8,344	7,662	15,706
Moroni, Comoros	10,331	13,492	1,787	1,827	13,008	3,484	6,654	10,942	4,794	8,012	6,207	15,183	13,341	13,698	13,239	8,195	12,449	10,373	5,997	10,671
Moscow, USSR	13,461	7,554	6,598	8,453	7,151	7,184	2,790	12,683	2,899	2,411	5,541	7,881	11,165	9,540	5,826	2,459	6,532	11,998	1,920	14,477
Mosul, Iraq	13,114	9,454	4,624	6,436	9,006	5,647	2,996	12,224	1,308	3,645	4,601	10,072	12,381	11,121	8,023	3,787	8,368	12,005	1,522	13,516
Mount Isa, Australia	13,595	15,691	11,965	11,250	16,020	13,581	14,891	784	12,847	15,041	7,331	12,914	15,686	16,153	13,143	15,080	16,186	15,200	13,407	1,874
Multan, Pakistan	15,338	11,368	5,818	7,219	10,997	7,447	5,690	9,507	3,857	6,079	1,883	10,990	14,974	13,433	8,990	6,183	10,395	14,546	4,206	10,892
Munich, West Germany	11,500	6,668	5,966	7,753	6,199	5,949	1,012	14,615	2,617	770	7,213	7,857	9,585	8,233	6,012	933	5,562	10,042	1,477	16,272
Murcia, Spain	9,980	6,380	5,555	7,147	5,890	5,013	901	16,036	3,099	1,460	8,463	8,186	8,498	7,454	6,634	1,583	5,295	8,550	2,384	17,364
Murmansk, USSR	13,606	6,416	8,033	9,890	6,067	8,423	3,609	12,648	4,330	2,602	6,328	6,423	10,418	8,603	4,358	2,539	5,492	12,018	3,232	14,656
Mururoa Atoll, Fr. Polynesia	7,824	9,441	16,939	15,165	9,918	15,649	16,430	7,853	18,682	15,333	15,177	8,436	7,341	8,171	10,450	15,161	10,550	8,631	17,555	7,043
Muscat, Oman	13,875	11,454	4,354	5,833	11,020	5,981	4,943	10,477	2,801	5,692	3,049	11,703	14,314	13,164	9,636	5,833	10,385	13,190	3,525	11,541
Myitkyina, Burma	17,490	12,436	7,988	8,984	12,211	9,798	8,135	7,026	6,454	8,230	972	10,995	16,749	14,806	9,369	8,291	11,724	17,115	6,675	8,652
Naga, Philippines	17,676	13,357	10,519	10,999	13,361	12,429	11,034	4,193	9,449	10,888	3,805	10,962	17,142	15,505	10,085	10,908	13,109	19,217	9,611	6,073
Nagasaki, Japan	19,226	11,127	11,204	12,227	11,134	12,930	9,972	5,755	8,991	9,430	4,225	8,813	15,129	13,323	7,855	9,403	10,905	18,567	8,750	7,805
Nagoya, Japan	18,622	10,631	11,824	12,908	10,677	13,494	10,184	5,840	9,406	9,504	4,889	8,216	14,498	12,753	7,396	9,458	10,500	18,029	9,054	7,908
Nagpur, India	15,626	12,566	6,062	7,147	12,214	7,872	6,862	8,405	4,872	7,328	970	11,904	16,215	14,684	9,989	7,435	11,623	15,232	5,383	9,673
Nairobi, Kenya	10,416	12,177	861	2,271	11,690	2,775	5,302	11,989	3,518	6,668	6,178	13,853	12,620	12,626	11,959	6,851	11,117	10,117	4,709	11,941
Nanchang, China	19,167	11,938	9,855	10,812	11,851	11,645	9,341	5,983	8,006	9,084	2,840	9,911	16,213	14,272	8,663	9,097	11,508	18,694	7,979	7,901
Nancy, France	11,227	6,295	6,190	7,942	5,822	6,037	1,077	14,943	2,964	403	7,599	7,583	9,188	7,831	5,795	583	5,187	9,740	1,859	16,655
Nandi, Fiji	11,742	12,443	15,810	14,611	12,905	16,963	17,379	3,361	16,344	16,306	10,664	10,110	11,837	12,196	11,355	16,180	13,383	12,942	16,293	3,399
Nanjing, China	19,633	11,514	10,157	11,192	11,444	11,904	9,297	6,136	8,101	8,939	3,178	9,449	15,760	13,832	8,233	8,939	11,122	18,567	7,982	8,107
Nanning, China	18,183	12,693	9,032	9,873	12,552	10,880	9,187	5,996	7,587	9,152	2,049	10,834	17,053	15,069	9,463	9,194	12,146	18,248	7,749	7,745
Nantes, France	10,693	5,855	6,369	8,050	5,373	6,000	1,239	15,515	3,394	483	8,199	7,358	8,595	7,280	5,690	567	4,746	9,183	2,371	17,256
Naples, Italy	11,181	7,302	5,132	6,913	6,821	5,140	473	14,690	1,947	1,477	7,104	8,661	9,828	8,663	6,845	1,659	6,193	9,822	1,032	16,066
Narvik, Norway	12,988	5,898	8,022	9,865	5,527	8,218	3,291	13,254	4,363	2,122	6,917	6,164	9,811	8,028	4,132	2,029	4,934	11,394	3,194	15,277
Nashville, Tennessee	8,368	1,009	12,569	13,554	1,474	11,181	8,026	14,449	10,238	6,903	13,488	2,729	3,773	1,850	3,834	6,740	2,110	7,123	9,150	15,037
Nassau, Bahamas	6,901	1,980	11,859	12,492	2,184	10,230	8,006	15,478	10,267	7,143	14,518	4,248	2,395	414	5,228	7,007	2,711	5,606	9,331	15,450
Natal, Brazil	3,986	6,958	7,168	7,063	6,738	5,251	6,751	17,492	8,110	7,216	13,707	9,733	4,704	5,545	9,818	7,244	6,705	2,651	8,083	15,431
Natashquan, Canada	9,399	1,535	10,381	11,733	1,069	9,356	5,533	15,571	7,712	4,366	11,432	3,621	5,363	3,496	3,107	4,201	430	7,858	6,611	17,024
Nauru Island	13,906	12,001	15,297	14,946	12,374	17,148	15,168	2,944	14,313	14,244	8,864	9,285	12,973	12,636	9,981	14,148	12,665	14,944	14,087	4,271
Ndjamena, Chad	9,305	9,420	2,334	3,865	8,940	1,979	3,059	14,709	2,596	4,471	7,810	11,465	10,109	9,833	9,880	4,644	8,403	8,431	3,300	14,750
Nelson, New Zealand	10,084	14,239	13,863	12,294	14,728	14,475	18,659	3,772	16,401	18,749	11,225	12,413	11,947	13,094	13,907	18,687	15,326	11,581	17,239	2,202
Nema, Mauritania	7,838	7,283	4,594	5,648	6,833	3,255	2,967	17,160	4,185	3,894	9,876	9,716	7,698	7,399	8,597	4,001	6,387	6,603	4,162	16,893
Neuquen, Argentina	984	9,129	10,420	9,181	9,254	8,785	11,690	12,894	12,788	12,058	17,136	10,932	4,774	6,757	12,364	12,055	9,633	2,423	12,980	10,937
New Delhi, India	15,800	11,721	6,216	7,509	11,375	7,911	6,260	8,928	4,436	6,600	1,307	11,113	15,491	13,868	9,167	6,695	10,788	15,098	4,777	10,345
New Glasgow, Canada	8,890	1,328	10,435	11,678	840	9,282	5,752	15,883	7,973	4,670	11,915	3,783	4,860	3,024	3,524	4,514	408	7,357	6,913	17,116
New Haven, Connecticut	8,534	524	11,285	12,406	353	10,008	6,703	15,446	8,929	5,622	12,680	3,309	4,208	2,258	3,620	5,465	893	7,093	7,867	16,322
New Orleans, Louisiana	7,880	1,747	13,024	13,816	2,189	11,503	8,687	14,201	10,921	7,611	14,193	3,074	3,264	1,544	4,460	7,450	2,828	6,749	9,857	14,519
New Plymouth, New Zealand	10,227	14,062	14,084	12,535	14,552	14,728	18,726	3,684	16,497	18,554	11,204	12,181	11,925	13,002	13,656	18,474	15,140	11,702	17,261	2,243
New York, New York	8,490	472	11,383	12,487	423	10,091	6,815	15,389	9,042	5,735	12,771	3,269	4,135	2,174	3,650	5,577	998	7,062	7,980	16,225
Newcastle upon Tyne, UK	11,309	5,515	7,070	8,807	5,055	6,832	1,929	14,951	3,803	506	7,984	6,700	8,735	7,220	4,924	332	4,417	9,750	2,646	16,883
Newcastle Waters, Australia	14,116	15,863	11,390	10,827	16,116	13,090	14,155	1,317	12,109	14,358	6,600	13,066	16,419	16,720	13,025	14,409	16,155	15,729	12,671	2,527
Niamey, Niger	8,319	8,271	3,543	4,720	7,808	2,385	2,930	16,117	3,508	4,152	9,072	10,583	8,700	8,463	9,274	4,295	7,327	7,256	3,786	15,932
Nicosia, Cyprus	12,264	8,971	4,288	6,143	8,503	5,023	2,193	13,096	601	3,073	5,476	9,938	11,582	10,448	7,951	3,236	7,866	11,119	826	14,292
Niue (Alofi)	10,661	11,508	16,762	15,230	11,991	17,278	17,764	4,688	17,563	16,388	11,968	9,476	10,499	10,966	11,021	16,222	12,535	11,732	17,197	4,400
Norfolk, Virginia	8,123	706	11,630	12,625	886	10,245	7,201	15,350	9,443	6,162	13,239	3,370	3,699	1,722	3,993	6,008	1,467	6,738	8,402	15,968
Norfolk Island, Australia	11,447	13,963	14,330	13,040	14,436	15,390	17,774	2,634	15,856	17,311	10,256	11,684	12,677	13,420	12,871	17,245	14,938	12,885	16,321	1,900
Noril'sk, USSR	15,630	7,514	9,181	10,973	7,290	10,030	5,565	10,573	5,627	4,705	5,202	6,530	11,844	9,882	4,607	4,650	6,828	14,020	4,794	12,616
Norman Wells, Canada	12,529	3,854	12,882	14,679	3,967	12,645	7,809	11,579	9,268	6,389	9,817	1,747	7,917	6,013	1,028	6,214	3,959	11,258	8,087	13,246
Normanton, Australia	13,865	15,334	12,191	11,552	15,653	13,856	14,824	505	12,856	14,863	7,260	12,550	15,640	15,930	12,766	14,889	15,809	15,458	13,343	2,115
North Pole	13,834	5,252	10,378	12,233	5,076	10,618	5,661	11,872	6,678	4,358	7,509	4,344	9,621	7,637	2,331	4,218	4,684	12,266	5,558	13,912
Nottingham, United Kingdom	11,169	5,622	6,868	8,595	5,155	6,606	1,719	15,084	3,659	305	8,009	6,888	8,724	7,259	5,136	122	4,518	9,622	2,524	16,974
Norway House, Canada	10,520	1,858	12,653	14,155	2,066	11,808	7,555	13,234	9,492	6,195	11,507	1,148	5,930	3,992	1,727	6,013	2,266	9,224	8,297	14,548
Norwich, United Kingdom	11,262	5,790	6,745	8,485	5,324	6,530	1,608	14,981	3,498	191	7,855	7,024	8,883	7,427	5,247	94	4,686	9,726	2,358	16,842
Nouakchott, Mauritania	7,365	6,468	5,509	6,447	6,036	4,050	3,366	18,090	4,943	3,970	10,649	9,016	6,788	6,464	8,103	4,037	5,639	6,000	4,729	17,604
Noumea, New Caledonia	12,133	13,647	14,566	13,462	14,098	15,855	17,162	2,247	15,497	16,556	9,805	11,200	12,941	13,431	12,238	16,484	14,541	13,520	15,779	2,217
Novosibirsk, USSR	16,283	9,017	8,112	9,786	8,749	9,303	5,581	9,916	4,912	5,152	3,637	8,141	13,253	11,344	6,218	5,160	8,236	14,790	4,419	11,829
Nuku'alofa, Tonga	10,926	12,081	16,208	14,762	12,561	16,947	17,959	4,126	17,202	16,686	11,519	9,971	11,056	11,565	11,428	16,533	13,093	12,092	17,077	3,808
Nukunono Island, Tokelau Isls.	11,517	10,947	17,290	16,068	11,411	18,314	16,678	4,661	16,684	15,340	11,398	8,672	10,670	10,794	10,065	15,182	11,898	12,425	16,132	4,895
Nuremberg, West Germany	11,558	6,561	6,114	7,901	6,095	6,094	1,148	14,588	2,743	681	7,233	7,716	9,546	8,162	5,865	830	5,457	10,085	1,587	16,288
Nyala, Sudan	10,166	10,201	1,777	3,585	9,713	2,400	3,389	13,661	2,099	4,794	6,803	11,973	11,176	10,825	10,200	4,977	9,138	9,410	3,117	13,879
Oaxaca, Mexico	7,005	3,326	13,959	14,277	3,754	12,208	10,130	13,412	12,387	9,137	15,591	4,075	2,671	2,033	5,814	8,983	4,389	6,193	11,374	13,260
Ocean Falls, Canada	11,735	3,739	14,180	15,890	4,026	13,658	9,036	11,250	10,649	7,617	11,004	950	7,169	5,452	2,210	7,436	4,255	10,694	9,455	12,600
Odense, Denmark	11,916	6,196	6,745	8,547	5,748	6,758	1,802	14,317	3,266	755	7,224	7,141	9,498	7,972	5,244	763	5,112	10,389	2,067	16,176
Odessa, USSR	12,639	7,927	5,524	7,380	7,480	6,046	1,934	13,268	1,823	2,170	5,767	8,686	11,041	9,647	6,683	2,296	6,842	11,287	785	14,824

Distances in Kilometers	Buenos Aires, Argentina	Buffalo, New York	Bujumbura, Burundi	Bulawayo, Zimbabwe	Burlington, Vermont	Cabinda, Angola	Cagliari, Italy	Cairns, Australia	Cairo, Egypt	Calais, France	Calcutta, India	Calgary, Canada	Cali, Colombia	Camaguey, Cuba	Cambridge Bay, Canada	Cambridge, United Kingdom	Campbellton, Canada	Campo Grande, Brazil	Canakkale, Turkey	Canberra, Australia
Ogbomosho, Nigeria	8,107	8,842	3,064	4,110	8,387	1,751	3,477	15,747	3,715	4,753	9,071	11,207	8,950	8,885	9,914	4,901	7,925	7,176	4,173	15,348
Okha, USSR	17,317	8,598	11,849	13,389	8,610	13,082	8,813	7,814	8,660	7,866	5,700	6,380	12,704	10,825	5,329	7,784	8,408	16,038	7,981	9,868
Okinawa (Naha)	18,913	11,887	11,010	11,850	11,895	12,826	10,365	5,158	9,165	9,950	3,993	9,538	15,826	14,065	8,617	9,939	11,662	19,328	9,061	7,179
Oklahoma City, Oklahoma	8,757	1,801	13,516	14,523	2,291	12,153	8,832	13,490	10,991	7,628	13,553	2,180	4,155	2,467	3,770	7,456	2,889	7,668	9,857	14,094
Old Crow, Canada	13,159	4,472	12,833	14,673	4,563	12,804	7,879	11,085	9,155	6,477	9,261	2,317	8,545	6,645	1,424	6,309	4,513	11,887	8,004	12,838
Olympia, Washington	11,096	3,457	14,483	16,070	3,811	13,733	9,333	11,468	11,082	7,930	11,688	782	6,566	4,929	2,650	7,748	4,140	10,116	9,880	12,636
Omaha, Nebraska	9,239	1,426	13,157	14,335	1,890	11,937	8,318	13,583	10,434	7,069	12,925	1,760	4,622	2,786	3,144	6,894	2,428	8,060	9,280	14,417
Omsk, USSR	15,701	8,845	7,625	9,347	8,540	8,742	4,984	10,453	4,330	4,616	3,814	8,229	12,963	11,115	6,236	4,636	7,995	14,242	3,811	12,323
Oodnadatta, Australia	12,972	16,496	11,421	10,549	16,851	12,920	14,944	1,584	12,768	15,355	7,507	13,743	15,705	16,589	13,996	15,426	17,043	14,585	13,484	1,560
Oradea, Romania	12,079	7,374	5,636	7,474	6,914	5,907	1,356	13,918	2,053	1,527	6,442	8,348	10,370	9,009	6,409	1,669	6,276	10,680	849	15,499
Oran, Algeria	9,829	6,552	5,337	6,908	6,062	4,759	946	16,106	3,035	1,706	8,500	8,415	8,515	7,542	6,884	1,834	5,476	8,424	2,418	17,297
Oranjestad, Aruba	5,356	3,472	11,120	11,377	3,555	9,311	8,212	16,155	10,384	7,668	15,476	5,828	1,231	1,291	6,759	7,566	3,947	4,018	9,662	15,347
Orebro, Sweden	12,399	6,251	7,060	8,888	5,826	7,193	2,273	13,851	3,468	1,256	6,926	6,948	9,778	8,162	4,983	1,229	5,198	10,855	2,269	15,763
Orel, USSR	13,271	7,708	6,271	8,127	7,290	6,859	2,558	12,810	2,570	2,343	5,534	8,148	11,189	9,626	6,103	2,415	6,664	11,842	1,599	14,540
Orsk, USSR	14,735	8,800	6,655	8,429	8,434	7,682	4,020	11,265	3,259	3,875	4,089	8,651	12,612	10,915	6,592	3,931	7,840	13,364	2,761	13,008
Osaka, Japan	18,749	10,736	11,702	12,772	10,775	13,386	10,147	5,811	9,327	9,495	4,756	8,339	14,629	12,872	7,492	9,453	10,587	18,149	8,998	7,879
Oslo, Norway	12,227	5,994	7,206	9,021	5,567	7,260	2,305	14,032	3,657	1,145	7,179	6,746	9,524	7,900	4,806	1,082	4,938	10,669	2,454	15,973
Osorno, Chile	1,455	9,261	10,821	9,521	9,419	9,221	12,146	12,483	13,257	12,475	17,366	10,903	4,886	6,876	12,444	12,466	9,832	2,840	13,447	10,555
Ostrava, Czechoslovakia	12,010	6,974	5,992	7,818	6,517	6,164	1,384	14,090	2,452	1,174	6,712	7,950	10,063	8,649	6,026	1,298	5,879	10,562	1,250	15,767
Ottawa, Canada	9,031	379	11,452	12,681	223	10,283	6,693	15,044	8,877	5,528	12,310	2,885	4,651	2,673	3,112	5,361	748	7,600	7,772	16,105
Ouagadougou, Bourkina Fasso	7,942	8,058	3,835	4,880	7,606	2,496	3,155	16,479	3,903	4,290	9,485	10,461	8,307	8,131	9,256	4,420	7,152	6,852	4,118	16,126
Oujda, Morocco	9,666	6,517	5,333	6,872	6,028	4,691	1,103	16,257	3,148	1,834	8,646	8,437	8,389	7,451	6,944	1,955	5,451	8,262	2,567	17,394
Oxford, United Kingdom	11,069	5,668	6,761	8,479	5,198	6,477	1,608	15,178	3,595	233	8,048	6,987	8,696	7,261	5,252	106	4,561	9,529	2,479	17,042
Pago Pago, American Samoa	11,061	11,224	17,071	15,658	11,699	17,790	17,240	4,669	17,172	15,881	11,717	9,073	10,563	10,866	10,552	15,719	12,218	12,053	16,694	4,635
Pakxe, Laos	17,339	13,565	8,661	9,299	13,405	10,561	9,523	5,643	7,717	9,664	2,009	11,720	17,936	15,947	10,350	9,725	12,974	17,874	8,049	7,219
Palembang, Indonesia	15,499	15,562	8,377	8,459	15,396	10,270	10,702	4,743	8,597	11,164	3,331	13,563	19,881	17,942	12,331	11,259	14,942	16,590	9,233	5,813
Palermo, Italy	10,939	7,422	4,882	6,644	6,937	4,836	389	14,839	1,873	1,691	7,226	8,882	9,768	8,683	7,100	1,874	6,315	9,608	1,148	16,102
Palma, Majorca	10,336	6,565	5,486	7,140	6,076	5,091	558	15,665	2,807	1,267	8,099	8,239	8,840	7,743	6,604	1,418	5,467	8,916	2,027	17,024
Palmerston North, New Zealand	10,033	14,016	14,075	12,491	14,506	14,649	18,862	3,872	16,611	18,734	11,375	12,207	11,771	12,888	13,729	18,644	15,104	11,509	17,418	2,384
Panama, Panama	5,310	3,759	12,154	12,243	3,982	10,304	9,272	15,053	11,470	8,635	16,283	5,636	695	1,385	6,930	8,520	4,493	4,246	10,701	14,293
Paramaribo, Suriname	4,489	4,722	9,453	9,591	4,629	7,592	7,397	17,440	9,348	7,241	14,963	7,370	2,383	2,996	7,903	7,189	4,800	2,908	8,879	15,905
Paris, France	11,029	6,034	6,353	8,077	5,558	6,105	1,201	15,172	3,215	234	7,873	7,396	8,906	7,547	5,654	403	4,925	9,523	2,132	16,924
Patna, India	16,398	12,247	6,809	7,934	11,939	8,585	7,103	8,078	5,282	7,385	474	11,308	16,237	14,496	9,469	7,471	11,382	15,881	5,621	9,533
Patrai, Greece	11,545	7,983	4,676	6,504	7,506	4,948	1,101	14,116	1,263	2,106	6,497	9,218	10,496	9,366	7,330	2,283	6,874	10,270	455	15,385
Peking, China	19,265	10,705	9,999	11,241	10,607	11,617	8,554	6,992	7,557	8,104	3,271	8,797	15,025	13,057	7,442	8,095	10,259	17,684	7,307	8,987
Penrhyn Island (Omoka)	10,319	9,817	18,415	16,700	10,301	18,077	16,425	6,138	17,485	15,003	12,812	7,881	9,151	9,371	9,574	14,824	10,851	11,049	16,526	6,083
Peoria, Illinois	8,927	923	12,672	13,802	1,406	11,407	7,930	14,127	10,092	6,731	13,002	2,207	4,329	2,408	3,293	6,560	1,990	7,676	8,965	14,925
Perm', USSR	14,620	8,077	7,216	9,031	7,727	8,071	3,941	11,557	3,650	3,512	4,703	7,883	12,011	10,246	5,822	3,533	7,145	13,140	2,906	13,418
Perth, Australia	12,616	18,239	9,483	8,604	18,410	10,965	13,512	3,444	11,252	14,326	6,700	15,452	16,601	18,223	15,142	14,453	18,208	14,120	12,169	3,101
Peshawar, Pakistan	15,472	10,975	6,056	7,527	10,613	7,613	5,505	9,664	3,808	5,797	2,079	10,565	14,685	13,078	8,565	5,891	10,017	14,552	4,028	11,136
Petropavlovsk-Kamchatskiy,USSR	16,458	8,043	12,826	14,418	8,127	13,926	9,373	7,846	9,495	8,279	6,728	5,607	11,924	10,136	4,878	8,172	8,020	15,413	8,710	9,831
Petrozavodsk, USSR	13,468	6,958	7,243	9,100	6,574	7,709	3,043	12,773	3,538	2,308	5,959	7,182	10,745	9,031	5,125	2,302	5,969	11,934	2,470	14,685
Pevek, USSR	15,122	6,332	12,112	13,930	6,342	12,707	7,829	9,799	8,463	6,589	7,363	4,286	10,520	8,593	3,060	6,460	6,161	13,769	7,473	11,774
Philadelphia, Pennsylvania	8,431	450	11,491	12,574	528	10,181	6,942	15,329	9,171	5,865	12,881	3,236	4,045	2,075	3,696	5,707	1,123	7,019	8,110	16,118
Phnom Penh, Kampuchea	16,954	13,965	8,522	9,060	13,798	10,436	9,701	5,488	7,815	9,918	2,137	12,117	18,338	16,349	10,755	9,987	13,357	17,632	8,220	6,972
Phoenix, Arizona	9,384	3,068	14,816	15,878	3,545	13,508	9,942	12,141	11,992	8,647	13,443	1,961	4,966	3,612	3,992	8,468	4,091	8,529	10,810	12,779
Pierre, South Dakota	9,718	1,736	13,331	14,624	2,152	12,226	8,369	13,200	10,416	7,068	12,544	1,267	5,101	3,280	2,769	6,889	2,610	8,552	9,239	14,167
Pinang, Malaysia	16,113	14,655	7,951	8,333	14,442	9,871	9,740	5,575	7,702	10,137	2,290	12,942	18,967	17,034	11,509	10,228	13,953	16,849	8,260	6,810
Pitcairn Island (Adamstown)	6,863	9,171	16,163	14,501	9,628	14,719	15,909	8,662	18,107	15,036	16,116	8,577	6,586	7,630	10,639	14,882	10,266	7,667	17,265	7,650
Pittsburgh, Pennsylvania	8,598	288	11,891	12,990	717	10,596	7,271	14,922	9,480	6,147	12,931	2,869	4,112	2,122	3,518	5,984	1,354	7,236	8,393	15,717
Plymouth, Montserrat	5,691	3,306	10,293	10,725	3,248	8,546	7,261	17,055	9,424	6,770	14,621	5,947	2,143	1,731	6,531	6,679	3,495	4,192	8,718	16,290
Plymouth, United Kingdom	10,822	5,539	6,764	8,450	5,063	6,395	1,620	15,428	3,707	425	8,281	6,967	8,471	7,068	5,289	357	4,430	9,279	2,627	17,290
Ponape Island	15,171	12,048	14,359	14,414	12,346	16,278	13,995	2,973	13,045	13,207	7,659	9,252	13,845	13,146	9,556	13,134	12,510	16,185	12,843	4,773
Ponce, Puerto Rico	5,887	2,991	10,766	11,215	2,998	9,031	7,555	16,597	9,754	6,967	14,765	5,545	1,940	1,242	6,262	6,863	3,326	4,452	8,990	16,011
Ponta Delgada, Azores	8,696	4,484	7,266	8,560	4,005	6,191	3,021	17,553	5,253	2,615	10,428	6,765	6,407	5,303	5,730	2,569	3,492	7,118	4,457	19,487
Pontianak, Indonesia	15,968	15,188	8,904	9,047	15,075	10,809	10,895	4,410	8,870	11,230	3,376	13,040	19,277	17,518	11,917	11,310	14,676	17,155	9,413	5,684
Port Augusta, Australia	12,387	16,623	11,524	10,502	17,033	12,898	15,389	1,905	13,169	15,901	8,042	13,962	15,213	16,297	14,411	15,981	17,337	14,000	13,954	1,099
Port Blair, India	16,149	13,912	7,208	7,853	13,636	9,117	8,661	6,631	6,640	9,081	1,297	12,597	17,971	16,218	10,943	9,177	13,098	16,414	7,181	7,884
Port Elizabeth, South Africa	7,484	13,572	3,409	1,560	13,199	3,436	8,279	11,545	7,111	9,691	9,123	16,263	11,344	12,518	15,064	9,863	12,874	7,895	8,207	10,356
Port Hedland, Australia	13,919	17,025	9,804	9,255	17,116	11,496	13,062	2,892	10,873	13,603	5,765	14,329	17,537	18,315	13,835	13,700	16,898	15,435	11,618	3,423
Port Louis, Mauritius	10,936	15,247	3,573	3,018	14,759	5,155	8,280	9,207	6,228	9,568	5,793	16,500	14,716	15,405	14,436	9,748	14,178	11,377	7,416	8,888
Port Moresby, Papua New Guinea	14,434	14,223	12,995	12,550	14,534	14,771	14,716	837	13,031	14,429	7,324	11,433	15,161	15,036	11,685	14,415	14,695	15,934	13,291	2,870
Port Said, Egypt	11,966	9,217	3,847	5,703	8,741	4,601	2,279	13,178	168	3,324	5,595	10,310	11,589	10,573	8,345	3,496	8,108	10,888	1,120	14,228
Port Sudan, Sudan	11,730	10,505	2,686	4,499	10,021	3,908	3,462	12,527	1,304	4,657	5,298	11,692	12,357	11,637	9,716	4,834	9,397	10,942	2,500	13,207
Port-au-Prince, Haiti	6,061	2,770	11,371	11,809	2,878	9,638	8,010	15,997	10,238	7,326	15,005	5,140	1,730	664	6,054	7,209	3,309	4,726	9,417	15,545
Port-of-Spain, Trin. & Tobago	5,019	3,949	10,184	10,431	3,913	8,363	7,604	17,007	9,692	7,239	15,093	6,528	1,838	2,116	7,195	7,161	4,169	3,522	9,081	15,885
Port-Vila, Vanuatu	12,400	13,181	14,955	13,945	13,623	16,344	16,898	2,397	15,479	16,131	9,773	10,687	12,800	13,122	11,700	16,044	14,044	13,713	15,606	2,718
Portland, Maine	8,748	704	11,045	12,229	253	9,830	6,392	15,518	8,609	5,292	12,360	3,358	4,496	2,570	3,459	5,132	558	7,276	7,537	16,543
Portland, Oregon	10,970	3,465	14,603	16,159	3,835	13,805	9,458	11,457	11,229	8,060	11,844	881	6,459	4,855	2,807	7,877	4,188	10,015	10,026	12,578
Porto, Portugal	9,815	5,646	6,257	7,799	5,156	5,590	1,523	16,378	3,779	1,354	8,951	7,507	7,917	6,772	6,045	1,396	4,562	8,310	2,944	17,980
Porto Alegre, Brazil	849	8,560	8,917	7,968	8,552	7,149	9,889	14,500	10,972	10,371	15,927	10,891	4,586	6,372	11,831	10,391	8,784	1,120	11,151	12,460
Porto Alexandre, Angola	7,246	11,252	2,358	1,833	10,845	1,136	6,099	13,802	5,484	7,461	9,348	13,849	9,950	10,625	12,691	7,621	10,474	7,010	6,376	12,780
Porto Novo, Benin	7,850	8,830	3,167	4,095	8,383	1,704	3,684	15,863	3,973	4,930	9,308	11,254	8,775	8,778	10,024	5,074	7,940	6,931	4,421	15,340
Porto Velho, Brazil	2,915	5,918	10,321	9,943	5,970	8,401	9,190	15,695	10,991	9,118	16,698	8,189	1,946	3,670	9,206	9,070	6,294	1,633	10,660	14,024
Portsmouth, United Kingdom	10,999	5,722	6,666	8,377	5,248	6,369	1,512	15,240	3,532	206	8,063	7,077	8,690	7,280	5,354	180	4,613	9,466	2,432	17,079
Poznan, Poland	12,086	6,736	6,293	8,118	6,286	6,439	1,587	14,076	2,746	1,057	6,803	7,655	9,943	8,473	5,725	1,147	5,649	10,606	1,542	15,830
Prague, Czechoslovakia	11,797	6,731	6,095	7,903	6,270	6,168	1,279	14,336	2,632	900	6,985	7,787	9,787	8,380	5,896	1,030	5,632	10,332	1,446	16,037
Praia, Cape Verde Islands	6,610	6,088	6,171	6,896	5,697	4,545	4,170	18,866	5,823	4,598	11,529	8,772	5,945	5,774	8,129	4,636	5,389	5,184	5,573	17,630
Pretoria, South Africa	8,146	13,258	2,478	622	12,840	2,809	7,460	11,785	6,184	8,881	8,407	15,762	11,654	12,568	14,304	9,058	12,437	8,360	7,298	10,840
Prince Albert, Canada	10,748	2,290	13,138	14,675	2,552	12,336	8,015	12,726	9,892	6,636	11,505	617	6,132	4,253	1,774	6,453	2,791	9,525	8,690	14,016
Prince Edward Island	7,751	15,132	4,858	3,053	14,810	5,176	9,927	9,959	8,513	11,349	9,181	17,917	12,140	13,668	16,771	11,526	14,549	8,575	9,675	8,635
Prince George, Canada	11,584	3,407	13,857	15,541	3,677	13,291	8,707	11,607	10,372	7,291	11,026	669	6,988	5,214	1,922	7,109	3,889	10,480	9,173	12,973
Prince Rupert, Canada	12,005	3,902	14,066	15,816	4,164	13,641	8,942	11,132	10,492	7,520	10,725	1,153	7,430	5,689	2,091	7,341	4,353	10,944	9,304	12,549
Providence, Rhode Island	8,565	627	11,155	12,290	330	9,892	6,565	15,533	8,792	5,488	12,584	3,383	4,280	2,347	3,612	5,331	782	7,108	7,732	16,449
Provo, Utah	9,922	2,733	14,364	15,647	3,173	13,247	9,355	12,264	11,337	8,022	12,755	1,217	5,390	3,810	3,239	7,841	3,648	8,945	10,144	13,135
Puerto Aisen, Chile	1,704	9,799	10,682	9,281	9,956	9,176	12,422	12,093	13,357	12,851	16,947	11,405	5,424	7,414	12,977	12,853	10,365	3,226	13,658	10,126
Puerto Deseado, Argentina	1,587	10,122	10,127	8,703	10,242	8,665	12,151	12,183	12,921	12,703	16,397	11,876	5,766	7,750	13,354	12,724	10,610	3,195	13,311	10,165
Puerto Princesa, Philippines	17,236	13,911	10,012	10,399	13,883	11,931	10,976	4,189	9,239	10,976	3,533	11,584	17,791	16,118	10,627	11,015	13,588	18,629	9,518	5,927
Punta Arenas, Chile	2,284	10,669	10,393	8,851	10,820	9,058	12,786	11,486	13,406	13,387	16,183	12,235	6,295	8,285	13,845	13,412	11,217	3,889	13,889	9,467
Pusan, South Korea	19,339	10,917	11,111	12,199	10,911	12,801	9,729	6,022	8,796	9,169	4,175	8,650	14,978	13,140	7,638	9,140	10,669	18,343	8,524	8,073
Pyongyang, North Korea	19,396	10,601	10,800	11,996	10,565	12,428	9,211	6,533	8,333	8,645	3,980	8,459	14,782	12,881	7,314	8,618	10,288	17,946	8,023	8,578
Qamdo, China	17,726	11,795	8,125	9,268	11,573	9,860	7,753	7,431	6,229	7,739	1,300	10,395	16,117	14,167	8,736	7,788	11,091	16,976	6,323	9,148
Qandahar, Afghanistan	14,873	11,007	5,459	6,964	10,615	7,007	5,131	10,074	3,292	5,572	2,451	10,851	14,454	12,987	8,813	5,683	10,000	14,005	3,647	11,430
Qiqian, China	18,048	9,300	10,403	11,902	9,208	11,759	7,927	8,029	7,404	7,223	4,302	7,458	13,625	11,653	6,039	7,181	8,878	16,459	6,885	10,082
Qom, Iran	13,692	10,022	4,776	6,508	9,589	6,023	3,724	11,499	1,915	4,305	3,877	10,398	13,100	11,788	8,330	4,437	8,955	12,663	2,246	12,798
Quebec, Canada	9,108	745	11,091	12,354	302	9,958	6,315	15,271	8,501	5,156	12,057	3,129	4,833	2,885	3,107	4,990	369	7,634	7,401	16,440
Quetta, Pakistan	14,933	11,196	5,462	6,925	10,806	7,050	5,306	9,910	3,431	5,764	2,291	11,004	14,642	13,181	8,972	5,876	10,192	14,115	3,823	11,245
Quito, Ecuador	4,341	4,774	12,003	11,793	4,978	10,094	9,822	14,822	11,922	9,350	17,163	6,597	462	2,390	7,950	9,252	5,464	3,431	11,291	13,709
Rabaul, Papua New Guinea	14,654	13,419	13,622	13,305	13,734	15,458	14,643	1,572	13,211	14,137	7,537	10,631	14,629	14,301	10,944	14,097	13,911	16,020	13,300	3,461
Raiatea (Uturoa)	9,239	9,905	17,778	15,925	10,395	16,963	16,887	6,662	18,506	15,532	13,767	8,344	8,526	9,060	10,200	15,349	10,994	10,060	17,401	6,196

Distances in Kilometers	Buenos Aires, Argentina	Buffalo, New York	Bujumbura, Burundi	Bulawayo, Zimbabwe	Burlington, Vermont	Cabinda, Angola	Cagliari, Italy	Cairns, Australia	Cairo, Egypt	Calais, France	Calcutta, India	Calgary, Canada	Cali, Colombia	Camaguey, Cuba	Cambridge Bay, Canada	Cambridge, United Kingdom	Campbellton, Canada	Campo Grande, Brazil	Canakkale, Turkey	Canberra, Australia
Raleigh, North Carolina	8,068	790	11,855	12,818	1,071	10,446	7,443	15,178	9,684	6,399	13,409	3,289	3,585	1,596	4,049	6,244	1,678	6,718	8,641	15,735
Rangiroa (Avatoru)	9,017	9,484	17,954	16,103	9,974	16,850	16,498	7,093	18,327	15,174	14,093	8,007	8,102	8,613	9,907	14,992	10,578	9,758	17,153	6,640
Rangoon, Burma	16,815	13,379	7,670	8,438	13,137	9,554	8,602	6,595	6,711	8,875	1,036	11,935	17,630	15,734	10,330	8,955	12,630	16,928	7,119	8,032
Raoul Is., Kermadec Islands	10,509	12,851	15,377	13,847	13,338	16,005	18,732	3,946	17,214	17,597	11,548	10,869	11,307	12,077	12,366	17,453	13,901	11,819	17,501	3,159
Rarotonga (Avarua)	9,675	10,879	17,112	15,342	11,368	16,921	17,748	5,726	18,543	16,338	13,053	9,165	9,456	10,062	10,919	16,156	11,956	10,675	17,825	5,189
Rawson, Argentina	1,124	9,645	10,117	8,790	9,756	8,562	11,797	12,635	12,710	12,280	16,658	11,476	5,303	7,281	12,893	12,293	10,116	2,716	13,014	10,632
Recife, Brazil	3,801	7,184	7,131	6,949	6,972	5,211	6,927	17,242	8,221	7,429	13,770	9,951	4,793	5,717	10,066	7,462	6,949	2,527	8,237	15,184
Regina, Canada	10,456	2,128	13,254	14,727	2,439	12,361	8,162	12,828	10,090	6,801	11,821	671	5,839	3,981	2,080	6,619	2,748	9,257	8,893	14,024
Reykjavik, Iceland	11,407	4,249	8,589	10,304	3,834	8,235	3,438	14,677	5,279	2,023	8,706	5,176	8,016	6,260	3,432	1,841	3,214	9,794	4,090	16,744
Rhodes, Greece	11,928	8,544	4,409	6,263	8,070	4,938	1,706	13,561	762	2,645	5,938	9,639	11,096	9,972	7,693	2,815	7,436	10,725	442	14,778
Richmond, Virginia	8,225	606	11,723	12,738	848	10,355	7,249	15,228	9,485	6,189	13,192	3,241	3,776	1,792	3,890	6,033	1,456	6,851	8,432	15,881
Riga, USSR	12,733	6,833	6,706	8,554	6,410	7,012	2,255	13,471	3,040	1,598	6,381	7,436	10,329	8,739	5,432	1,629	5,781	11,229	1,876	15,308
Ringkobing, Denmark	11,855	6,042	6,867	8,662	5,595	6,841	1,876	14,390	3,410	712	7,351	7,001	9,366	7,827	5,116	684	4,958	10,317	2,214	16,276
Rio Branco, Brazil	2,889	5,960	10,738	10,298	6,054	8,820	9,600	15,282	11,430	9,478	17,132	8,095	1,771	3,640	9,237	9,421	6,422	1,829	11,075	13,672
Rio Cuarto, Argentina	570	8,547	10,156	9,077	8,641	8,426	11,020	13,614	12,241	11,342	17,105	10,521	4,247	6,203	11,816	11,336	8,989	1,704	12,347	11,663
Rio de Janeiro, Brazil	1,968	8,149	8,087	7,372	8,060	6,242	8,771	15,494	9,882	9,296	15,083	10,710	4,644	6,177	11,324	9,325	8,194	1,209	10,031	13,429
Rio Gallegos, Argentina	2,080	10,514	10,307	8,798	10,656	8,935	12,597	11,690	13,260	13,185	16,248	12,139	6,143	8,133	13,711	13,209	11,044	3,686	13,716	9,671
Rio Grande, Brazil	657	8,735	9,009	8,002	8,739	7,268	10,107	14,266	11,154	10,603	15,998	11,022	4,701	6,521	12,013	10,623	8,983	1,308	11,357	12,226
Riyadh, Saudi Arabia	12,855	10,691	3,624	5,329	10,228	5,014	3,870	11,674	1,642	4,803	4,242	11,413	13,155	12,162	9,361	4,963	9,590	12,038	2,560	12,633
Road Town, Brit. Virgin Isls.	5,907	3,024	10,556	11,028	2,995	8,830	7,355	16,811	9,547	6,791	14,610	5,637	2,106	1,429	6,273	6,691	3,283	4,439	8,796	16,210
Roanoke, Virginia	8,262	630	11,945	12,953	980	10,573	7,452	15,024	9,681	6,374	13,273	3,092	3,762	1,772	3,857	6,215	1,609	6,919	8,619	15,659
Robinson Crusoe Island, Chile	1,884	8,473	11,480	10,304	8,669	9,774	12,120	12,687	13,528	12,235	18,264	9,996	4,112	6,089	11,595	12,199	9,123	2,804	13,519	10,886
Rochester, New York	8,828	108	11,642	12,814	383	10,414	6,946	15,008	9,143	5,801	12,592	2,871	4,400	2,415	3,293	5,636	1,008	7,426	8,047	15,947
Rockhampton, Australia	12,901	15,020	12,998	12,092	15,426	14,479	15,990	870	14,008	15,936	8,428	12,365	14,517	15,065	12,985	15,941	15,752	14,450	14,510	1,331
Rome, Italy	11,135	7,113	5,298	7,068	6,632	5,254	412	14,797	2,135	1,294	7,233	8,483	9,675	8,487	6,681	1,477	6,003	9,751	1,185	16,222
Rosario, Argentina	275	8,600	9,814	8,756	8,668	8,081	10,751	13,817	11,919	11,126	16,778	10,674	4,362	6,286	11,883	11,128	8,986	1,509	12,055	11,834
Roseau, Dominica	5,531	3,483	10,199	10,591	3,421	8,433	7,282	17,126	9,425	6,832	14,690	6,123	2,113	1,870	6,704	6,745	3,659	4,023	8,747	16,254
Rostock, East Germany	11,922	6,364	6,568	8,374	5,914	6,609	1,668	14,291	3,081	780	7,120	7,326	9,611	8,113	5,425	830	5,277	10,411	1,882	16,110
Rostov-na-Donu, USSR	13,302	8,344	5,698	7,545	7,916	6,442	2,619	12,580	2,042	2,765	5,112	8,829	11,661	10,187	6,780	2,870	7,285	11,970	1,327	14,171
Rotterdam, Netherlands	11,370	6,022	6,564	8,321	5,556	6,410	1,456	14,853	3,275	214	7,656	7,222	9,091	7,654	5,418	302	4,918	9,850	2,127	16,671
Rouyn, Canada	9,400	594	11,646	12,949	612	10,557	6,775	14,681	8,914	5,550	12,067	2,528	4,969	2,981	2,726	5,378	919	7,986	7,781	15,844
Sacramento, California	10,385	3,593	15,123	16,497	4,023	14,098	10,030	11,400	11,900	8,658	12,561	1,502	5,986	4,564	3,539	8,475	4,471	9,550	10,696	12,296
Saginaw, Michigan	9,021	416	12,138	13,328	868	10,928	7,372	14,513	9,538	6,179	12,659	2,414	4,490	2,508	3,107	6,010	1,433	7,683	8,417	15,439
Saint Denis, Reunion	10,724	15,138	3,424	2,799	14,652	4,964	8,215	9,392	6,202	9,524	5,986	16,534	14,489	15,207	14,481	9,705	14,082	11,151	7,397	9,021
Saint George's, Grenada	5,175	3,797	10,218	10,507	3,757	8,412	7,529	17,023	9,636	7,134	14,992	6,387	1,885	2,007	7,039	7,053	4,012	3,679	9,002	15,979
Saint John, Canada	8,878	1,060	10,701	11,930	572	9,533	6,013	15,699	8,229	4,914	12,064	3,565	4,745	2,863	3,436	4,755	308	7,369	7,159	16,860
Saint John's, Antigua	5,733	3,282	10,257	10,702	3,217	8,515	7,203	17,097	9,368	6,711	14,562	5,937	2,202	1,753	6,500	6,620	3,455	4,228	8,660	16,349
Saint John's, Canada	9,119	2,108	9,692	11,011	1,618	8,630	4,960	16,212	7,184	3,897	11,324	4,349	5,396	3,680	3,704	3,746	1,045	7,535	6,135	17,752
Saint Louis, Missouri	8,743	1,066	12,789	13,860	1,556	11,473	8,108	14,111	10,286	6,928	13,234	2,323	4,135	2,243	3,510	6,759	2,162	7,519	9,167	14,819
Saint Paul, Minnesota	9,478	1,163	12,783	14,047	1,573	11,648	7,881	13,762	9,977	6,615	12,531	1,699	4,875	2,961	2,776	6,439	2,048	8,226	8,818	14,741
Saint Peter Port, UK	10,822	5,685	6,611	8,301	5,208	6,259	1,465	15,414	3,560	354	8,202	7,121	8,563	7,187	5,436	358	4,575	9,292	2,492	17,234
Saipan (Susupe)	16,780	12,139	12,946	13,375	12,322	14,846	12,496	3,547	11,406	11,887	6,065	9,408	14,943	13,775	9,180	11,843	12,311	17,801	11,260	5,599
Salalah, Oman	13,113	11,825	3,532	4,965	11,365	5,241	4,991	10,725	2,736	5,944	3,635	12,379	14,154	13,284	10,311	6,102	10,726	12,565	3,702	11,537
Salem, Oregon	10,951	3,510	14,675	16,225	3,885	13,867	9,531	11,413	11,303	8,133	11,885	951	6,452	4,866	2,879	7,950	4,245	10,011	10,099	12,519
Salt Lake City, Utah	9,978	2,735	14,345	15,645	3,170	13,246	9,325	12,250	11,298	7,988	12,694	1,157	5,441	3,850	3,183	7,806	3,637	8,995	10,104	13,141
Salta, Argentina	1,279	7,619	10,342	9,482	7,710	8,509	10,489	14,294	11,954	10,655	17,350	9,659	3,346	5,284	10,892	10,631	8,062	1,209	11,889	12,425
Salto, Uruguay	360	8,497	9,567	8,560	8,542	7,812	10,446	14,094	11,614	10,839	16,560	10,658	4,328	6,215	11,784	10,844	8,835	1,257	11,747	12,097
Salvador, Brazil	3,127	7,429	7,536	7,163	7,265	5,624	7,601	16,665	8,856	8,090	14,330	10,138	4,577	5,744	10,449	8,119	7,308	1,904	8,904	14,597
Salzburg, Austria	11,564	6,780	5,890	7,685	6,312	5,911	1,005	14,531	2,512	884	7,109	7,948	9,694	8,347	6,090	1,045	5,675	10,116	1,365	16,168
Samsun, Turkey	12,801	8,653	4,997	6,848	8,202	5,739	2,318	12,848	1,328	2,843	5,252	9,380	11,638	10,324	7,357	2,983	7,564	11,559	848	14,257
San Antonio, Texas	8,242	2,302	13,827	14,627	2,785	12,321	9,348	13,385	11,547	8,196	14,209	2,731	3,694	2,250	4,435	8,028	3,412	7,253	10,438	13,747
San Cristobal, Venezuela	4,909	3,945	11,347	11,439	4,069	9,490	8,726	15,788	10,866	8,226	16,050	6,144	673	1,626	7,217	8,129	4,491	3,669	10,187	14,820
San Diego, California	9,650	3,521	15,255	16,359	3,991	13,986	10,310	11,660	12,306	8,987	13,321	2,052	5,327	4,064	4,121	8,806	4,518	8,877	11,112	12,322
San Francisco, California	10,384	3,702	15,244	16,610	4,135	14,211	10,151	11,302	12,015	8,777	12,598	1,615	6,015	4,626	3,643	8,594	4,588	9,576	10,811	12,181
San Jose, Costa Rica	5,622	3,687	12,653	12,751	3,969	10,810	9,594	14,595	11,820	8,873	16,322	5,318	1,101	1,429	6,744	8,748	4,525	4,659	10,994	13,962
San Juan, Argentina	999	8,308	10,565	9,507	8,430	8,814	11,205	13,522	12,535	11,436	17,532	10,181	3,963	5,941	11,553	11,418	8,811	1,853	12,571	11,626
San Juan, Puerto Rico	5,929	2,963	10,714	11,179	2,959	8,986	7,483	16,652	9,683	6,895	14,695	5,538	2,011	1,277	6,228	6,791	3,276	4,484	8,918	16,083
San Luis Potosi, Mexico	7,725	3,079	14,289	14,816	3,548	12,636	10,078	13,057	12,306	8,978	14,960	3,403	3,356	2,385	5,227	8,814	4,184	6,899	11,224	13,158
San Marino, San Marino	11,270	6,984	5,505	7,282	6,506	5,478	592	14,727	2,263	1,118	7,202	8,291	9,665	8,422	6,473	1,299	5,874	9,862	1,225	16,230
San Miguel de Tucuman, Argen.	1,079	7,844	10,302	9,387	7,936	8,490	10,622	14,130	12,032	10,825	17,321	9,866	3,563	5,506	11,116	10,806	8,287	1,290	12,008	12,239
San Salvador, El Salvador	6,257	3,384	13,195	13,405	3,734	11,393	9,760	14,139	12,016	8,910	15,988	4,710	1,797	1,468	6,257	8,771	4,336	5,347	11,099	13,744
Sanaa, Yemen	12,112	11,342	2,639	4,282	10,862	4,219	4,320	11,704	2,099	5,461	4,703	12,353	13,182	12,514	10,327	5,634	10,233	11,498	3,247	12,330
Santa Cruz, Bolivia	1,919	6,909	10,172	9,526	6,971	8,282	9,799	15,038	11,398	9,889	17,016	9,095	2,770	4,623	10,196	9,858	7,296	946	11,231	13,212
Santa Cruz, Tenerife	8,272	5,756	6,014	7,222	5,291	4,843	2,620	17,781	4,586	2,922	10,166	8,117	6,939	6,215	7,035	2,965	4,813	6,805	4,090	18,447
Santa Fe, New Mexico	9,213	2,456	14,205	15,281	2,935	12,903	9,377	12,726	11,468	8,109	13,389	1,828	4,679	3,151	3,721	7,931	3,491	8,237	10,300	13,392
Santa Rosa, Argentina	574	8,928	10,116	8,950	9,026	8,440	11,268	13,297	12,385	11,649	16,964	10,862	4,614	6,578	12,192	11,650	9,376	2,023	12,560	11,323
Santa Rosalia, Mexico	8,893	3,469	15,166	15,981	3,957	13,692	10,465	12,016	12,572	9,211	14,063	2,639	4,628	3,537	4,672	9,034	4,544	8,156	11,405	12,439
Santarem, Brazil	3,582	5,575	9,344	9,224	5,512	7,434	7,965	16,917	9,759	7,963	15,463	8,146	2,513	3,652	8,794	7,928	5,708	1,993	9,430	15,147
Santiago del Estero, Argentina	937	7,967	10,199	9,263	8,053	8,398	10,623	14,102	11,992	10,857	17,217	10,005	3,697	5,635	11,242	10,842	8,396	1,273	11,995	12,191
Santiago, Chile	1,135	8,494	10,736	9,617	8,633	9,015	11,496	13,229	12,800	11,728	17,640	10,282	4,130	6,117	11,717	11,709	9,030	2,143	12,857	11,339
Santo Domingo, Dominican Rep.	5,997	2,837	11,114	11,561	2,900	9,382	7,807	16,253	10,024	7,160	14,896	5,297	1,811	899	6,124	7,048	3,289	4,617	9,226	15,755
Sao Paulo de Olivenca, Brazil	3,611	5,231	10,902	10,657	5,326	8,986	9,217	15,612	11,174	8,967	16,779	7,410	1,149	2,921	8,510	8,897	5,704	2,430	10,701	14,178
Sao Paulo, Brazil	1,680	8,064	8,437	7,693	8,003	6,595	9,046	15,334	10,211	9,518	15,436	10,561	4,408	6,017	11,281	9,539	8,172	894	10,331	13,282
Sao Tome, Sao Tome & Principe	7,783	9,628	2,552	3,289	9,186	890	4,313	15,182	4,190	5,629	9,142	12,073	9,267	9,449	10,818	5,782	8,753	7,058	4,839	14,527
Sapporo, Japan	18,068	9,677	12,044	13,345	9,722	13,538	9,706	6,655	9,233	8,880	5,354	7,300	13,614	11,822	6,441	8,814	9,551	17,095	8,718	8,716
Sarajevo, Yugoslavia	11,654	7,376	5,343	7,160	6,905	5,505	929	14,272	1,905	1,476	6,728	8,539	10,143	8,880	6,653	1,645	6,269	10,280	777	15,752
Saratov, USSR	13,881	8,273	6,291	8,125	7,874	7,101	3,156	12,134	2,684	3,039	4,846	8,479	11,869	10,265	6,411	3,109	7,257	12,492	1,973	13,845
Saskatoon, Canada	10,689	2,310	13,258	14,780	2,595	12,433	8,140	12,676	10,024	6,764	11,608	530	6,071	4,211	1,896	6,581	2,861	9,487	8,823	13,931
Schefferville, Canada	9,938	1,588	10,712	12,159	1,236	9,810	5,721	14,968	7,821	4,456	11,117	3,144	5,761	3,825	2,493	4,281	757	8,418	6,675	16,511
Seattle, Washington	11,104	3,406	14,409	15,998	3,755	13,664	9,259	11,521	11,010	7,856	11,655	711	6,564	4,910	2,580	7,673	4,077	10,109	9,807	12,702
Sendai, Japan	18,248	10,166	12,118	13,291	10,226	13,714	10,120	6,128	9,507	9,348	5,263	7,727	14,005	12,266	6,950	9,289	10,070	17,540	9,068	8,192
Seoul, South Korea	19,429	10,720	10,915	12,071	10,695	12,566	9,403	6,343	8,504	8,840	4,045	8,530	14,860	12,980	7,434	8,812	10,431	18,101	8,208	8,390
Sept-Iles, Canada	9,426	1,254	10,707	12,053	818	9,673	5,844	15,335	8,009	4,655	11,574	3,317	5,269	3,354	2,940	4,487	246	7,911	6,897	16,716
Sevastopol, USSR	12,748	8,229	5,331	7,187	7,781	5,950	2,103	13,067	1,627	2,457	5,524	8,958	11,309	9,939	6,943	2,588	7,144	11,437	767	14,570
Seville, Spain	9,641	6,046	5,807	7,328	5,556	5,114	1,335	16,442	3,522	1,630	8,890	7,973	8,063	7,039	6,520	1,714	4,976	8,182	2,816	17,790
Shanghai, China	19,618	11,555	10,398	11,398	11,505	12,157	9,546	5,921	8,367	9,163	3,401	9,412	15,740	13,844	8,268	9,159	11,206	18,759	8,240	7,910
Sheffield, United Kingdom	11,185	5,585	6,917	8,645	5,119	6,655	1,769	15,071	3,701	353	8,020	6,840	8,709	7,234	5,086	170	4,482	9,635	2,562	16,972
Shenyang, China	19,189	10,363	10,600	11,868	10,306	12,178	8,854	6,895	8,023	8,280	3,897	8,310	14,605	12,673	7,078	8,252	10,007	17,630	7,682	8,935
Shiraz, Iran	13,615	10,573	4,407	6,074	10,133	5,804	4,090	11,230	2,055	4,797	3,655	10,975	13,484	12,272	8,906	4,937	9,497	12,721	2,647	12,399
Sibiu, Romania	12,154	7,595	5,472	7,317	7,135	5,810	1,432	13,782	1,854	1,742	6,269	8,550	10,561	9,221	6,598	1,886	6,497	10,783	654	15,319
Singapore	15,889	15,105	8,304	8,527	14,928	10,215	10,331	5,022	8,270	10,738	2,887	13,194	19,480	17,490	11,894	10,828	14,468	16,863	8,854	6,210
Sioux Falls, South Dakota	9,485	1,450	13,111	14,358	1,883	11,958	8,206	13,497	10,292	6,932	12,670	1,549	4,869	3,012	2,888	6,755	2,375	8,289	9,127	14,424
Skelleftea, Sweden	12,953	6,221	7,591	9,437	5,832	7,833	2,945	13,308	3,926	1,896	6,694	6,592	10,014	8,286	4,566	1,836	5,224	11,381	2,762	15,286
Skopje, Yugoslavia	11,753	7,699	5,089	6,920	7,227	5,349	1,090	14,072	1,589	1,799	6,490	8,835	10,417	9,187	6,929	1,967	6,592	10,420	461	15,481
Socotra Island (Tamrida)	12,853	12,217	3,252	4,573	11,750	5,045	5,297	10,602	3,036	6,320	3,796	12,854	14,283	13,563	10,787	6,483	11,113	12,421	4,073	11,279
Sofia, Bulgaria	11,921	7,766	5,138	6,978	7,298	5,459	1,254	13,909	1,571	1,870	6,336	8,834	10,554	9,297	6,905	2,032	6,661	10,589	382	15,343
Songkhla, Thailand	16,297	14,458	7,999	8,436	14,248	9,919	9,638	5,641	7,630	10,002	2,145	12,749	18,786	16,839	11,310	10,089	13,764	16,982	8,156	6,931
Sorong, Indonesia	15,950	14,476	11,334	11,304	14,611	13,225	12,791	2,383	11,027	12,720	5,322	11,784	16,936	16,131	11,371	12,743	14,508	17,562	11,335	4,242
South Georgia Island	2,761	11,485	8,170	6,617	11,474	6,953	11,246	12,116	11,379	12,201	14,275	13,698	7,375	9,257	14,756	12,284	11,676	4,046	12,067	10,063
South Pole	6,173	14,753	9,630	7,776	14,930	9,390	14,347	8,130	13,330	15,651	12,495	15,659	10,384	12,368	17,672	15,790	15,322	7,741	14,450	6,089

Distances in Kilometers	Buenos Aires, Argentina	Buffalo, New York	Bujumbura, Burundi	Bulawayo, Zimbabwe	Burlington, Vermont	Cabinda, Angola	Cagliari, Italy	Cairns, Australia	Cairo, Egypt	Calais, France	Calcutta, India	Calgary, Canada	Cali, Colombia	Camaguey, Cuba	Cambridge Bay, Canada	Cambridge, United Kingdom	Campbellton, Canada	Campo Grande, Brazil	Canakkale, Turkey	Canberra, Australia
South Sandwich Islands	3,503	12,167	7,731	6,085	12,128	6,690	11,249	11,699	11,116	12,325	13,569	14,439	8,112	9,975	15,409	12,427	12,291	4,731	11,915	9,681
Split, Yugoslavia	11,502	7,270	5,354	7,158	6,795	5,451	776	14,436	1,989	1,376	6,890	8,492	9,987	8,741	6,630	1,551	6,161	10,121	908	15,910
Spokane, Washington	10,839	3,037	14,162	15,696	3,391	13,340	9,027	11,888	10,846	7,637	11,815	446	6,269	4,573	2,484	7,454	3,728	9,798	9,642	13,041
Spoleto, Italy	11,208	7,076	5,375	7,150	6,597	5,347	495	14,749	2,169	1,233	7,199	8,415	9,692	8,480	6,603	1,415	5,967	9,815	1,176	16,206
Springbok, South Africa	7,048	12,702	3,151	1,509	12,332	2,736	7,680	12,416	6,759	9,068	9,498	15,408	10,629	11,697	14,343	9,233	12,018	7,274	7,779	11,192
Springfield, Illinois	8,840	964	12,706	13,810	1,452	11,418	7,992	14,138	10,162	6,803	13,101	2,268	4,238	2,326	3,390	6,633	2,048	7,598	9,039	14,897
Springfield, Massachusetts	8,615	524	11,250	12,392	269	9,993	6,638	15,432	8,860	5,547	12,587	3,284	4,299	2,351	3,547	5,388	804	7,168	7,792	16,353
Srinagar, India	15,765	11,073	6,313	7,746	10,726	7,896	5,773	9,390	4,107	6,017	1,842	10,534	14,886	13,225	8,561	6,105	10,141	14,853	4,302	10,898
Stanley, Falkland Islands	1,900	10,675	9,523	8,035	10,759	8,157	11,979	12,067	12,507	12,686	15,670	12,556	6,363	8,329	13,944	12,730	11,081	3,479	13,022	10,011
Stara Zagora, Bulgaria	12,070	7,930	5,086	6,934	7,464	5,483	1,436	13,726	1,461	2,040	6,146	8,941	10,747	9,483	6,992	2,198	6,827	10,754	260	15,150
Stockholm, Sweden	12,541	6,390	7,025	8,862	5,968	7,212	2,325	13,705	3,404	1,386	6,765	7,030	9,938	8,316	5,048	1,371	5,341	11,002	2,213	15,607
Stornoway, United Kingdom	11,368	5,131	7,532	9,264	4,682	7,263	2,387	14,882	4,242	966	8,175	6,239	8,528	6,933	4,466	786	4,045	9,783	3,069	16,890
Strasbourg, France	11,307	6,400	6,128	7,890	5,928	6,013	1,046	14,849	2,865	501	7,488	7,658	9,301	7,945	5,853	675	5,292	9,828	1,750	16,545
Stuttgart, West Germany	11,402	6,481	6,100	7,873	6,011	6,025	1,061	14,746	2,795	581	7,380	7,702	9,407	8,044	5,878	748	5,375	9,927	1,665	16,438
Subic, Philippines	17,817	13,319	10,207	10,742	13,293	12,112	10,708	4,499	9,103	10,597	3,459	11,012	17,277	15,536	10,034	10,623	13,006	19,195	9,278	6,341
Suchow, China	19,624	11,307	10,023	11,122	11,222	11,737	9,021	6,423	7,863	8,652	3,094	9,310	15,593	13,643	8,033	8,652	10,885	18,279	7,717	8,393
Sucre, Bolivia	1,852	6,996	10,384	9,689	7,078	8,503	10,056	14,787	11,660	10,130	17,266	9,105	2,775	4,678	10,276	10,096	7,425	1,129	11,491	12,981
Sudbury, Canada	9,263	435	11,834	13,097	649	10,700	6,998	14,620	9,148	5,785	12,286	2,462	4,790	2,800	2,853	5,614	1,096	7,876	8,018	15,695
Suez, Egypt	11,914	9,338	3,706	5,562	8,860	4,491	2,373	13,145	126	3,450	5,584	10,454	11,645	10,663	8,491	3,623	8,228	10,863	1,261	14,150
Sundsvall, Sweden	12,671	6,189	7,366	9,203	5,782	7,546	2,636	13,589	3,734	1,579	6,836	6,721	9,865	8,186	4,724	1,527	5,163	11,109	2,548	15,544
Surabaya, Indonesia	15,282	15,897	9,242	9,134	15,840	11,100	11,693	3,744	9,603	12,092	4,233	13,532	18,924	18,076	12,609	12,177	15,487	16,649	10,218	4,844
Suva, Fiji	11,641	12,385	15,880	14,650	12,850	16,987	17,453	3,465	16,455	16,351	10,776	10,078	11,730	12,105	11,352	16,222	13,335	12,834	16,391	3,457
Sverdlovsk, USSR	14,883	8,322	7,248	9,042	7,980	8,183	4,181	11,276	3,751	3,795	4,429	8,034	12,292	10,512	5,982	3,820	7,405	13,417	3,084	13,128
Svobodnyy, USSR	18,066	9,238	10,910	12,389	9,185	12,269	8,357	7,760	7,905	7,588	4,679	7,234	13,494	11,552	5,953	7,534	8,900	16,562	7,358	9,826
Sydney, Australia	11,821	15,602	12,671	11,491	16,062	13,883	16,604	1,957	14,415	16,898	9,122	13,157	14,048	15,036	14,020	16,937	16,512	13,403	15,141	246
Sydney, Canada	8,945	1,526	10,245	11,508	1,037	9,115	5,550	15,979	7,773	4,473	11,767	3,923	4,990	3,184	3,558	4,319	533	7,396	6,715	17,286
Syktyvkar, USSR	14,323	7,567	7,444	9,282	7,217	8,156	3,764	11,908	3,794	3,165	5,202	7,435	11,520	9,740	5,368	3,166	6,637	12,799	2,908	13,818
Szeged, Hungary	11,917	7,321	5,574	7,404	6,858	5,794	1,195	14,071	2,041	1,444	6,578	8,365	10,248	8,915	6,447	1,596	6,220	10,520	847	15,630
Szombathely, Hungary	11,748	7,039	5,745	7,559	6,573	5,863	1,078	14,300	2,285	1,154	6,845	8,140	9,967	8,624	6,250	1,308	5,936	10,323	1,113	15,902
Tabriz, Iran	13,448	9,473	4,912	6,707	9,036	5,980	3,217	11,970	1,647	3,745	4,353	9,947	12,563	11,227	7,886	3,876	8,401	12,318	1,733	13,333
Tacheng, China	16,532	9,915	7,631	9,196	9,632	9,014	5,857	9,434	4,781	5,664	2,731	9,045	14,092	12,219	7,137	5,700	9,102	15,206	4,536	11,240
Tahiti (Papeete)	9,025	9,830	17,688	15,831	10,320	16,771	16,848	6,842	18,616	15,521	13,982	8,349	8,342	8,919	10,235	15,339	10,925	9,843	17,468	6,319
Taipei, Taiwan	18,946	12,200	10,389	11,219	12,163	12,221	10,024	5,337	8,685	9,731	3,380	9,980	16,307	14,459	8,913	9,737	11,873	19,369	8,667	7,291
Taiyuan, China	19,137	10,988	9,644	10,852	10,867	11,298	8,444	6,989	7,326	8,083	2,868	9,159	15,337	13,356	7,747	8,085	10,493	17,718	7,149	8,942
Tallahassee, Florida	7,693	1,462	12,467	13,268	1,836	10,946	8,212	14,754	10,460	7,189	14,090	3,360	3,098	1,189	4,502	7,035	2,460	6,465	9,428	15,056
Tallinn, USSR	12,885	6,706	6,975	8,825	6,294	7,288	2,503	13,348	3,300	1,724	6,389	7,209	10,313	8,673	5,191	1,727	5,672	11,359	2,146	15,233
Tamanrasset, Algeria	9,271	7,882	3,886	5,371	7,398	3,218	1,854	15,832	2,684	3,142	8,383	9,931	9,052	8,481	8,434	3,298	6,853	8,093	2,752	16,249
Tampa, Florida	7,370	1,688	12,333	13,052	2,010	10,759	8,232	14,952	10,490	7,264	14,333	3,687	2,784	860	4,808	7,116	2,611	6,137	9,491	15,117
Tampere, Finland	12,930	6,530	7,212	9,061	6,127	7,502	2,674	13,321	3,539	1,781	6,487	6,978	10,214	8,538	4,956	1,759	5,511	11,385	2,382	15,245
Tanami, Australia	13,903	16,331	10,969	10,357	16,568	12,638	14,004	1,728	11,888	14,339	6,505	13,537	16,643	17,154	13,427	14,407	16,568	15,507	12,528	2,555
Tangier, Morocco	9,519	6,150	5,676	7,176	5,661	4,949	1,371	16,518	3,502	1,791	8,937	8,120	8,053	7,080	6,687	1,881	5,089	8,075	2,854	17,763
Tarawa (Betio)	13,555	11,381	15,980	15,628	11,771	17,846	15,221	3,603	14,674	14,148	9,401	8,708	12,292	11,940	9,548	14,032	12,098	14,451	14,298	4,754
Tashkent, USSR	15,441	10,148	6,393	7,998	9,793	7,775	5,019	10,152	3,630	5,133	2,743	9,764	13,964	12,286	7,747	5,211	9,204	14,296	3,589	11,760
Tbilisi, USSR	13,468	9,073	5,230	7,047	8,641	6,189	3,014	12,148	1,773	3,407	4,569	9,526	12,275	10,874	7,467	3,528	8,009	12,256	1,552	13,605
Tegucigalpa, Honduras	6,189	3,290	12,978	13,210	3,620	11,181	9,567	14,358	11,820	8,738	15,924	4,756	1,664	1,273	6,240	8,602	4,211	5,228	10,917	13,947
Tehran, Iran	13,778	9,956	4,897	6,631	9,527	6,133	3,732	11,474	1,985	4,270	3,851	10,294	13,092	11,750	8,226	4,399	8,894	12,728	2,249	12,805
Tel Aviv, Israel	12,213	9,311	3,965	5,816	8,840	4,802	2,445	12,950	403	3,411	5,356	10,306	11,795	10,733	8,316	3,578	8,204	11,137	1,170	14,046
Telegraph Creek, Canada	12,270	3,952	13,724	15,503	4,168	13,394	8,625	11,182	10,121	7,203	10,370	1,339	7,669	5,872	1,778	7,025	4,294	11,146	8,939	12,693
Teresina, Brazil	3,644	6,436	8,012	7,883	6,273	6,096	7,239	17,399	8,776	7,527	14,444	9,156	3,865	4,821	9,469	7,531	6,326	2,126	8,636	15,360
Ternate, Indonesia	16,214	14,504	10,917	10,967	14,593	12,819	12,352	2,811	10,563	12,331	4,860	11,884	17,335	16,334	11,320	12,363	14,430	17,820	10,889	4,596
The Valley, Anguilla	5,847	3,132	10,390	10,859	3,079	8,661	7,247	16,973	9,428	6,716	14,554	5,774	2,182	1,599	6,362	6,620	3,338	4,358	8,695	16,314
Thessaloniki, Greece	11,775	7,890	4,918	6,755	7,417	5,230	1,190	13,977	1,395	1,990	6,376	9,025	10,559	9,357	7,111	2,160	6,782	10,471	299	15,337
Thimphu, Bhutan	16,904	12,121	7,312	8,435	11,845	9,076	7,369	7,793	5,652	7,542	570	10,993	16,276	14,433	9,220	7,614	11,314	16,331	5,900	9,349
Thunder Bay, Canada	9,692	1,017	12,375	13,711	1,310	11,320	7,424	13,959	9,504	6,144	12,145	1,801	5,129	3,165	2,463	5,967	1,678	8,371	8,341	15,081
Tientsin, China	19,378	10,778	10,061	11,282	10,686	11,694	8,665	6,880	7,654	8,216	3,293	8,840	15,086	13,124	7,510	8,207	10,345	17,793	7,414	8,876
Tijuana, Mexico	9,627	3,519	15,257	16,351	3,991	13,980	10,318	11,669	12,317	8,996	13,344	2,071	5,307	4,048	4,139	8,815	4,520	8,855	11,124	12,323
Tiksi, USSR	15,865	7,119	10,690	12,473	7,013	11,499	6,845	9,903	7,123	5,789	6,024	5,539	11,476	9,490	3,897	5,695	6,682	14,315	6,237	11,968
Timbuktu, Mali	8,164	7,618	4,201	5,350	7,158	2,983	2,753	16,712	3,780	3,817	9,453	9,971	8,150	7,826	8,744	3,941	6,686	6,981	3,842	16,581
Tindouf, Algeria	8,694	6,458	5,292	6,610	5,982	4,280	2,045	17,096	3,834	2,715	9,479	8,686	7,709	7,013	7,424	2,806	5,468	7,308	3,453	17,717
Tirane, Albania	11,597	7,639	5,046	6,867	7,165	5,249	941	14,221	1,620	1,746	6,631	8,839	10,290	9,086	6,954	1,920	6,531	10,265	570	15,607
Tokyo, Japan	18,365	10,463	12,071	13,171	10,525	13,721	10,292	5,858	9,587	9,564	5,150	8,007	14,268	12,550	7,250	9,510	10,370	17,817	9,198	7,924
Toledo, Spain	9,961	6,057	5,879	7,458	5,567	5,297	1,130	16,150	3,375	1,313	8,635	7,866	8,275	7,174	6,341	1,407	4,970	8,494	2,585	17,613
Topeka, Kansas	9,011	1,474	13,223	14,332	1,955	11,942	8,453	13,633	10,593	7,228	13,175	1,960	4,394	2,589	3,393	7,054	2,528	7,853	9,450	14,375
Toronto, Canada	8,924	96	11,774	12,961	503	10,561	7,043	14,853	9,228	5,879	12,569	2,718	4,464	2,475	3,192	5,712	1,097	7,537	8,122	15,807
Toulouse, France	10,574	6,248	5,908	7,585	5,763	5,550	805	15,546	3,032	818	8,080	7,819	8,777	7,563	6,153	961	5,142	9,107	2,099	17,119
Tours, France	10,826	5,998	6,284	7,985	5,518	5,972	1,135	15,367	3,247	405	8,031	7,450	8,765	7,446	5,748	537	4,889	9,324	2,209	17,089
Townsville, Australia	13,478	15,019	12,747	12,001	15,384	14,349	15,408	280	13,478	15,344	7,857	12,281	15,012	15,373	12,708	15,352	15,627	15,038	13,933	1,797
Trenton, New Jersey	8,453	453	11,454	12,545	489	10,150	6,898	15,349	9,126	5,819	12,842	3,246	4,077	2,110	3,678	5,662	1,079	7,035	8,064	16,155
Tripoli, Lebanon	12,427	9,185	4,241	6,089	8,720	5,076	2,434	12,865	651	3,292	5,249	10,089	11,822	10,685	8,085	3,453	8,082	11,311	1,050	14,050
Tripoli, Libya	10,570	7,764	4,363	6,096	7,275	4,257	791	14,969	1,743	2,209	7,353	9,374	9,780	8,850	7,638	2,389	6,667	9,311	1,429	15,990
Tristan da Cunha (Edinburgh)	4,138	11,123	5,654	4,374	10,911	4,287	8,725	13,607	8,706	9,846	12,401	13,866	7,995	9,439	13,902	9,961	10,853	4,478	9,419	11,766
Trondheim, Norway	12,432	5,823	7,577	9,399	5,414	7,650	2,694	13,826	3,995	1,479	7,191	6,424	9,512	7,820	4,456	1,387	4,795	10,854	2,795	15,816
Trujillo, Peru	3,610	5,648	11,987	11,519	5,854	10,068	10,419	14,374	12,415	10,070	17,929	7,370	1,309	3,265	8,802	9,984	6,334	2,961	11,902	13,044
Truk Island (Moen)	15,697	12,448	13,653	13,770	12,706	15,573	13,579	2,776	12,453	12,928	6,982	9,653	14,529	13,726	9,751	12,874	12,802	16,834	12,343	4,742
Truro, Canada	8,869	1,277	10,483	11,719	791	9,323	5,805	15,862	8,027	4,724	11,958	3,752	4,821	2,978	3,523	4,568	392	7,341	6,967	17,073
Tsingtao, China	19,814	11,048	10,319	11,453	10,982	12,003	9,097	6,448	8,042	8,653	3,426	8,993	15,296	13,365	7,765	8,643	10,667	18,207	7,834	8,452
Tsitsihar, China	18,573	9,758	10,631	12,026	9,692	12,093	8,454	7,446	7,809	7,790	4,199	7,775	14,032	12,083	6,477	7,752	9,388	17,016	7,361	9,499
Tubuai Island (Mataura)	8,663	10,288	17,043	15,186	10,775	16,245	17,339	6,756	19,261	16,079	14,141	8,943	8,436	9,198	10,858	15,898	11,393	9,603	18,104	6,011
Tucson, Arizona	9,213	3,050	14,797	15,800	3,532	13,444	9,975	12,225	12,050	8,696	13,609	2,107	4,803	3,482	4,122	8,518	4,093	8,365	10,874	12,808
Tulsa, Oklahoma	8,745	1,640	13,355	14,375	2,130	12,001	8,674	13,632	10,838	7,476	13,493	2,199	4,133	2,394	3,710	7,305	2,730	7,626	9,708	14,254
Tunis, Tunisia	10,627	7,283	4,873	6,594	6,795	4,693	284	15,148	2,092	1,707	7,530	8,861	9,491	8,457	7,137	1,885	6,182	9,292	1,461	16,355
Tura, USSR	16,402	8,122	9,434	11,157	7,933	10,464	6,214	9,803	6,030	5,436	4,721	6,875	12,487	10,506	5,070	5,390	7,502	14,790	5,316	11,843
Turin, Italy	11,051	6,595	5,782	7,526	6,116	5,623	659	15,031	2,650	787	7,560	7,978	9,283	8,021	6,209	969	5,485	9,605	1,626	16,607
Uberlandia, Brazil	2,005	7,528	8,778	7,991	7,464	6,715	8,778	15,755	10,092	9,156	15,517	10,045	3,960	5,505	10,743	9,166	7,636	683	10,115	13,724
Ufa, USSR	14,587	8,373	6,892	8,696	8,010	7,808	3,865	11,516	3,375	3,578	4,477	8,243	12,226	10,503	6,179	3,619	7,419	13,156	2,722	13,317
Ujungpandang, Indonesia	15,603	15,453	9,989	9,906	15,475	11,860	12,115	3,157	10,119	12,355	4,557	12,929	18,261	17,426	12,195	12,419	15,217	17,103	10,631	4,530
Ulaanbaatar, Mongolia	18,096	9,929	9,361	10,812	9,769	10,814	7,412	8,156	6,570	6,935	3,263	8,363	14,304	12,315	6,762	6,927	9,359	16,538	6,212	10,135
Ulan-Ude, USSR	17,793	9,491	9,499	11,020	9,333	10,864	7,221	8,466	6,539	6,658	3,648	7,948	13,866	11,876	6,326	6,639	8,928	16,199	6,089	10,471
Uliastay, Mongolia	17,497	9,955	8,630	10,124	9,741	10,061	6,771	8,659	5,828	6,408	2,898	8,666	14,295	12,330	6,919	6,417	9,276	16,044	5,518	10,574
Uranium City, Canada	11,408	2,743	12,819	14,477	2,899	12,229	7,665	12,494	9,412	6,256	10,775	1,009	6,804	4,885	1,078	6,073	2,984	10,127	8,208	13,982
Urumqi, China	16,940	10,309	7,800	9,284	10,043	9,274	6,318	8,951	5,140	6,152	2,360	9,289	14,537	12,638	7,439	6,189	9,528	15,671	4,971	10,751
Ushuaia, Argentina	2,371	10,872	10,193	8,630	11,012	8,897	12,742	11,432	13,271	13,399	15,933	12,478	6,501	8,490	14,067	13,432	11,395	3,984	13,799	9,397
Vaduz, Liechtenstein	11,310	6,594	5,928	7,697	6,120	5,846	884	14,801	2,664	701	7,380	7,863	9,430	8,108	6,050	878	5,485	9,853	1,564	16,439
Valencia, Spain	10,144	6,350	5,637	7,255	5,860	5,149	818	15,902	3,059	1,288	8,351	8,094	8,580	7,490	6,510	1,416	5,257	8,704	2,285	17,302
Valladolid, Spain	10,069	5,910	6,063	7,656	5,421	5,503	1,203	16,087	3,464	1,149	8,626	7,676	8,248	7,092	6,136	1,229	4,817	8,583	2,613	17,650
Valletta, Malta	10,871	7,653	4,616	6,379	7,167	4,595	602	14,791	1,691	1,956	7,168	9,147	9,883	8,858	7,367	2,139	6,548	9,579	1,144	15,954
Valparaiso, Chile	1,232	8,439	10,832	9,718	8,585	9,106	11,538	13,205	12,869	11,749	17,741	10,202	4,071	6,059	11,653	11,727	8,989	2,188	12,908	11,329
Vancouver, Canada	11,269	3,444	14,297	15,922	3,772	13,611	9,143	11,496	10,862	7,735	11,466	675	6,714	5,030	2,420	7,552	4,065	10,250	9,660	12,730
Varna, Bulgaria	12,276	8,009	5,163	7,016	7,549	5,628	1,634	13,530	1,491	2,145	5,961	8,935	10,912	9,613	6,964	2,294	6,910	10,960	363	14,982
Venice, Italy	11,366	6,880	5,666	7,448	6,406	5,649	742	14,676	2,375	991	7,190	8,142	9,651	8,367	6,311	1,168	5,772	9,940	1,289	16,237

Distances in Kilometers	Buenos Aires, Argentina	Buffalo, New York	Bujumbura, Burundi	Bulawayo, Zimbabwe	Burlington, Vermont	Cabinda, Angola	Cagliari, Italy	Cairns, Australia	Cairo, Egypt	Calais, France	Calcutta, India	Calgary, Canada	Cali, Colombia	Camaguey, Cuba	Cambridge Bay, Canada	Cambridge, United Kingdom	Campbellton, Canada	Campo Grande, Brazil	Canakkale, Turkey	Canberra, Australia
Veracruz, Mexico	7,166	3,086	13,861	14,265	3,519	12,144	9,925	13,510	12,180	8,914	15,362	3,871	2,755	1,917	5,581	8,758	4,155	6,303	11,154	13,435
Verona, Italy	11,282	6,792	5,707	7,480	6,317	5,650	710	14,774	2,458	914	7,294	8,085	9,545	8,265	6,271	1,094	5,683	9,849	1,388	16,342
Victoria, Canada	11,224	3,471	14,381	15,996	3,809	13,678	9,228	11,461	10,953	7,821	11,536	729	6,680	5,015	2,512	7,638	4,115	10,222	9,751	12,674
Victoria, Seychelles	11,872	13,842	2,900	3,378	13,356	4,796	6,791	9,903	4,623	7,989	4,674	14,766	14,703	14,671	12,701	8,163	12,735	11,911	5,779	10,056
Vienna, Austria	11,793	6,962	5,853	7,668	6,499	5,968	1,155	14,282	2,382	1,093	6,858	8,038	9,940	8,573	6,143	1,239	5,861	10,356	1,200	15,917
Vientiane, Laos	17,386	13,265	8,366	9,112	13,078	10,248	9,061	6,104	7,273	9,206	1,570	11,568	17,634	15,651	10,099	9,269	12,621	17,624	7,588	7,678
Villahermosa, Mexico	6,868	3,063	13,545	13,905	3,466	11,805	9,758	13,826	12,019	8,801	15,520	4,119	2,405	1,616	5,744	8,651	4,093	5,963	11,029	13,659
Vilnius, USSR	12,691	7,044	6,447	8,297	6,614	6,786	2,105	13,471	2,777	1,628	6,268	7,695	10,454	8,906	5,695	1,688	5,982	11,214	1,618	15,255
Visby, Sweden	12,460	6,499	6,837	8,673	6,070	7,026	2,153	13,770	3,224	1,300	6,736	7,199	9,972	8,384	5,226	1,308	5,440	10,936	2,030	15,640
Vitoria, Brazil	2,381	8,035	7,771	7,146	7,915	5,904	8,361	15,833	9,475	8,907	14,736	10,662	4,745	6,163	11,151	8,940	8,009	1,489	9,618	13,765
Vladivostok, USSR	18,711	9,996	11,285	12,578	9,986	12,818	9,225	6,798	8,576	8,520	4,602	7,786	14,115	12,240	6,714	8,473	9,746	17,418	8,142	8,865
Volgograd, USSR	13,689	8,444	5,958	7,791	8,032	6,782	2,992	12,233	2,358	3,030	4,829	8,757	11,912	10,372	6,694	3,118	7,408	12,344	1,717	13,873
Vologda, USSR	13,694	7,379	7,003	8,857	6,994	7,589	3,106	12,510	3,307	2,557	5,564	7,556	11,138	9,444	5,492	2,576	6,388	12,192	2,323	14,373
Vorkuta, USSR	14,876	7,372	8,318	10,145	7,078	9,060	4,569	11,383	4,692	3,781	5,277	6,856	11,552	9,664	4,820	3,745	6,547	13,293	3,805	13,381
Wake Island	15,283	10,419	15,069	15,647	10,707	16,870	13,122	4,610	12,762	12,085	8,055	7,621	12,682	11,681	7,950	11,979	10,868	15,721	12,249	6,321
Wallis Island	11,580	11,596	16,657	15,428	12,061	17,729	17,087	4,106	16,650	15,825	11,125	9,307	11,150	11,387	10,648	15,677	12,548	12,623	16,310	4,246
Walvis Bay, Namibia	7,091	11,975	2,693	1,492	11,587	1,941	6,904	13,125	6,132	8,280	9,448	14,633	10,269	11,151	13,526	8,442	11,246	7,089	7,094	11,986
Warsaw, Poland	12,312	6,974	6,216	8,054	6,529	6,459	1,714	13,824	2,605	1,332	6,527	7,806	10,218	8,739	5,846	1,422	5,892	10,848	1,407	15,559
Washington, D.C.	8,359	470	11,666	12,720	697	10,330	7,141	15,218	9,370	6,064	13,038	3,177	3,925	1,943	3,757	5,906	1,312	6,973	8,309	15,943
Watson Lake, Canada	12,292	3,835	13,443	15,221	4,021	13,122	8,344	11,372	9,846	6,921	11,245	1,365	7,678	5,840	1,499	6,744	4,111	11,116	8,662	12,925
Weimar, East Germany	11,674	6,488	6,265	8,059	6,027	6,265	1,319	14,498	2,854	666	7,200	7,582	9,561	8,138	5,715	787	5,388	10,187	1,678	16,242
Wellington, New Zealand	10,001	14,128	13,950	12,364	14,618	14,525	18,784	3,874	16,525	18,806	11,344	12,333	11,823	12,969	13,855	18,729	15,218	11,489	17,364	2,326
West Berlin, West Germany	11,890	6,525	6,375	8,184	6,071	6,436	1,515	14,294	2,891	817	7,045	7,518	9,701	8,237	5,619	904	5,433	10,398	1,695	16,067
Wewak, Papua New Guinea	15,197	13,968	12,685	12,472	14,223	14,544	13,969	1,497	12,364	13,665	6,661	11,173	15,577	15,126	11,205	13,654	14,297	16,696	12,561	3,565
Whangarei, New Zealand	10,494	13,856	14,356	12,851	14,344	15,074	18,662	3,509	16,536	18,210	11,095	11,878	12,163	12,933	13,308	18,118	14,915	11,939	17,178	2,277
Whitehorse, Canada	12,621	4,184	13,510	15,321	4,363	13,301	8,459	11,056	9,868	7,040	9,987	1,684	8,011	6,185	1,674	6,866	4,435	11,461	8,698	12,651
Wichita, Kansas	8,957	1,668	13,413	14,490	2,153	12,106	8,661	13,497	10,802	7,436	13,311	1,986	4,346	2,600	3,528	7,263	2,732	7,838	9,658	14,191
Willemstad, Curacao	5,288	3,542	11,001	11,251	3,610	9,189	8,146	16,261	10,307	7,626	15,452	5,930	1,270	1,401	6,830	7,528	3,984	3,929	9,601	15,409
Wiluna, Australia	13,230	17,513	9,933	9,188	17,690	11,512	13,582	2,845	11,352	14,226	6,429	14,734	16,893	18,099	14,443	14,332	17,556	14,770	12,370	2,918
Windhoek, Namibia	7,343	12,154	2,504	1,224	11,756	1,957	6,891	12,931	6,018	8,282	9,194	14,775	10,533	11,389	13,584	8,447	11,396	7,357	7,012	11,854
Windsor, Canada	8,876	346	12,095	13,251	830	10,853	7,375	14,621	9,557	6,204	12,773	2,545	4,352	2,368	3,248	6,036	1,430	7,536	8,446	15,497
Winnipeg, Canada	10,106	1,601	12,831	14,241	1,902	11,861	7,793	13,365	9,797	6,465	11,965	1,207	5,502	3,587	2,185	6,284	2,227	8,846	8,612	14,535
Winston-Salem, North Carolina	8,148	763	11,993	12,967	1,105	10,593	7,546	15,028	9,781	6,482	13,406	3,157	3,635	1,647	3,976	6,325	1,730	6,816	8,726	15,603
Wroclaw, Poland	12,011	6,821	6,151	7,973	6,367	6,294	1,458	14,126	2,619	1,065	6,799	7,784	9,961	8,521	5,862	1,175	5,728	10,545	1,417	15,844
Wuhan, China	19,206	11,760	9,717	10,733	11,659	11,482	9,085	6,246	7,776	8,821	2,723	9,800	16,070	14,110	8,496	8,835	11,301	18,436	7,729	8,161
Wyndham, Australia	14,421	16,035	10,853	10,389	16,220	12,597	13,573	1,895	11,508	13,843	6,036	13,269	17,024	17,211	13,011	13,904	16,153	16,021	12,091	3,042
Xi'an, China	18,865	11,425	9,265	10,404	11,282	10,974	8,436	6,880	7,156	8,190	2,388	9,663	15,792	13,804	8,208	8,208	10,882	17,788	7,082	8,770
Xining, China	18,223	11,200	8,678	9,916	11,010	10,339	7,759	7,515	6,459	7,571	2,026	9,682	15,566	13,585	8,075	7,599	10,562	17,110	6,392	9,355
Yakutsk, USSR	16,905	8,099	10,874	12,540	8,025	11,955	7,591	8,863	7,521	6,663	5,381	6,272	12,413	10,443	4,829	6,588	7,723	15,378	6,786	10,931
Yanji, China	18,862	10,092	11,094	12,382	10,069	12,639	9,116	6,827	8,419	8,446	4,408	7,925	14,249	12,357	6,806	8,404	9,812	17,488	8,009	8,889
Yaounde, Cameroon	8,444	9,754	2,140	3,246	9,294	1,044	3,923	14,835	3,565	5,297	8,500	12,044	9,777	9,805	10,624	5,461	8,813	7,703	4,288	14,446
Yap Island (Colonia)	16,760	13,100	12,140	12,408	13,250	14,059	12,482	3,042	11,078	12,102	5,490	10,405	15,932	14,807	10,040	12,087	13,184	18,195	11,125	5,098
Yaraka, Australia	13,008	15,636	12,325	11,448	16,021	13,826	15,537	899	13,459	15,692	7,983	12,931	15,077	15,729	13,391	15,726	16,295	14,600	14,054	1,257
Yarmouth, Canada	8,720	1,039	10,711	11,904	571	9,505	6,079	15,788	8,305	5,006	12,211	3,638	4,590	2,718	3,577	4,851	465	7,214	7,249	16,874
Yellowknife, Canada	11,855	3,168	12,804	14,527	3,297	12,354	7,662	12,167	9,303	6,242	10,372	1,270	7,250	5,331	855	6,062	3,330	10,570	8,103	13,741
Yerevan, USSR	13,388	9,193	5,066	6,880	8,757	6,048	3,017	12,152	1,647	3,482	4,552	9,685	12,325	10,961	7,628	3,610	8,122	12,206	1,539	13,565
Yinchuan, China	18,596	10,980	9,114	10,367	10,818	10,752	7,970	7,384	6,788	7,684	2,459	9,337	15,355	13,365	7,799	7,698	10,402	17,306	6,645	9,287
Yogyakarta, Indonesia	15,168	16,014	8,977	8,865	15,926	10,831	11,526	3,973	9,409	11,975	4,125	13,723	19,127	18,266	12,730	12,066	15,540	16,481	10,057	4,990
York, United Kingdom	11,237	5,587	6,947	8,680	5,123	6,699	1,802	15,019	3,709	380	7,987	6,815	8,740	7,254	5,051	201	4,485	9,685	2,564	16,927
Yumen, China	17,839	10,837	8,429	9,765	10,623	10,024	7,269	8,016	6,031	7,069	2,113	9,472	15,176	13,213	7,778	7,098	10,154	16,622	5,916	9,854
Yutian, China	16,438	10,957	7,009	8,419	10,660	8,586	6,198	8,972	4,697	6,278	1,714	10,144	15,008	13,214	8,239	6,345	10,096	15,432	4,759	10,606
Yuzhno-Sakhalinsk, USSR	17,775	9,245	12,044	13,442	9,282	13,440	9,412	7,079	9,071	8,530	5,528	6,908	13,235	11,413	6,000	8,456	9,106	16,676	8,488	9,136
Zagreb, Yugoslavia	11,619	7,093	5,606	7,413	6,623	5,700	924	14,395	2,195	1,193	6,902	8,235	9,933	8,628	6,381	1,359	5,986	10,208	1,054	15,952
Zahedan, Iran	14,353	11,000	4,952	6,494	10,585	6,484	4,815	10,447	2,857	5,386	2,851	11,068	14,199	12,859	9,009	5,511	9,958	13,517	3,342	11,698
Zamboanga, Philippines	16,937	14,101	10,362	10,639	14,114	12,281	11,459	3,707	9,713	11,442	4,005	11,656	17,669	16,200	10,836	11,477	13,863	18,465	10,001	5,471
Zanzibar, Tanzania	10,322	12,745	1,132	1,924	12,259	2,989	5,902	11,567	4,096	7,268	6,225	14,452	12,902	13,071	12,545	7,451	11,695	10,174	5,293	11,401
Zaragoza, Spain	10,285	6,190	5,851	7,485	5,702	5,392	889	15,821	3,151	1,056	8,322	7,876	8,564	7,409	6,273	1,177	5,092	8,822	2,296	17,333
Zashiversk, USSR	16,109	7,812	11,326	13,076	7,232	12,195	7,549	9,359	7,803	6,471	6,218	5,410	11,566	9,607	3,998	6,371	6,967	14,643	6,938	11,410
Zhengzhou, China	19,305	11,314	9,706	10,833	11,204	11,411	8,742	6,650	7,545	8,418	2,808	9,418	15,646	13,674	8,059	8,424	10,839	18,055	7,421	8,591
Zurich, Switzerland	11,257	6,508	5,986	7,747	6,034	5,874	908	14,870	2,747	621	7,463	7,796	9,343	8,018	5,995	800	5,399	9,792	1,653	16,523

Distances in Kilometers	Cancun, Mexico	Canton, China	Canton Atoll, Phoenix Islands	Cape Town, South Africa	Cape York, Australia	Caracas, Venezuela	Cardiff, United Kingdom	Carlisle, United Kingdom	Carnarvon, Australia	Carson City, Nevada	Casablanca, Morocco	Casper, Wyoming	Castries, Saint Lucia	Catbalogan, Philippines	Cayenne, French Guiana	Cayman Islands (Georgetown)	Cazombo, Angola	Cebu, Philippines	Cedar Rapids, Iowa	Changsha, China
Canton, China	14,655	0	8,617	11,834	4,914	16,286	9,692	9,465	5,309	11,187	11,149	11,657	15,850	1,760	16,535	15,053	10,567	1,815	12,358	564
Canton Atoll, Phoenix Islands	9,604	8,617	0	15,803	5,137	11,691	14,505	14,145	8,338	7,052	16,222	8,251	12,327	7,201	13,300	10,152	17,730	7,284	9,397	8,733
Cape Town, South Africa	12,655	11,834	15,803	0	12,320	10,232	9,696	10,049	8,961	16,269	7,954	15,181	9,923	12,250	8,564	12,067	2,480	12,072	13,982	12,088
Cape York, Australia	14,661	4,914	5,137	12,320	0	16,823	14,524	14,249	3,423	11,424	16,052	12,543	17,459	3,157	18,281	15,237	12,902	3,103	13,740	5,351
Caracas, Venezuela	2,425	16,286	11,691	10,232	16,823	0	7,292	7,406	18,413	6,103	6,540	5,231	752	17,225	1,722	1,834	10,232	17,418	4,242	15,723
Cardiff, United Kingdom	7,759	9,692	14,505	9,696	14,524	7,292	0	377	13,975	8,232	2,018	7,206	6,589	11,410	6,862	7,541	7,461	11,496	6,424	9,210
Carlisle, United Kingdom	7,722	9,465	14,145	10,049	14,249	7,406	377	0	13,922	7,986	2,391	6,992	6,722	11,164	7,075	7,539	7,787	11,257	6,266	8,970
Carnarvon, Australia	17,904	5,309	8,338	8,961	3,423	18,413	13,975	13,922	0	14,816	14,306	15,874	18,684	4,233	17,347	18,363	9,543	4,047	17,015	5,872
Carson City, Nevada	3,725	11,187	7,052	16,269	11,424	6,103	8,232	7,986	14,816	0	9,353	1,202	6,356	11,280	7,727	4,286	15,258	11,471	2,388	10,765
Casablanca, Morocco	7,772	11,149	16,222	7,954	16,052	6,540	2,018	2,391	14,306	9,353	0	8,193	5,788	12,909	5,607	7,382	5,983	12,953	7,164	10,739
Casper, Wyoming	3,019	11,657	8,251	15,181	12,543	5,231	7,206	6,992	15,874	1,202	8,193	0	5,374	12,039	6,757	3,505	14,060	12,233	1,208	11,175
Castries, Saint Lucia	2,841	15,850	12,327	9,923	17,459	752	6,589	6,722	18,684	6,356	5,788	5,374	0	17,082	1,383	2,250	9,685	17,263	4,280	15,289
Catbalogan, Philippines	14,999	1,760	7,201	12,250	3,157	17,225	11,410	11,164	4,233	11,280	12,909	12,039	17,082	0	18,133	15,534	11,571	195	12,985	2,202
Cayenne, French Guiana	4,126	16,535	13,300	8,564	18,281	1,722	6,862	7,075	17,347	7,727	5,607	6,757	1,383	18,133	0	3,529	8,528	18,271	5,656	16,018
Cayman Islands (Georgetown)	596	15,053	10,152	12,067	15,237	1,834	7,541	7,539	18,363	4,286	7,382	3,505	2,250	15,534	3,529	0	11,927	15,727	2,696	14,529
Cazombo, Angola	12,505	10,567	17,730	2,480	12,902	10,232	7,461	7,787	9,543	15,258	5,983	14,060	9,685	11,571	8,528	11,927	0	11,438	12,913	10,641
Cebu, Philippines	15,190	1,815	7,284	12,072	3,103	17,418	11,496	11,257	4,047	11,471	12,953	12,233	17,263	195	18,271	15,727	11,438	0	13,179	2,288
Cedar Rapids, Iowa	2,357	12,358	9,397	13,982	13,740	4,242	6,424	6,266	17,015	2,388	7,164	1,208	4,280	12,985	5,656	2,696	12,913	13,179	0	11,835
Changsha, China	14,153	564	8,733	12,088	5,351	15,723	9,210	8,970	5,872	10,765	10,739	11,175	15,289	2,202	16,018	14,529	10,641	2,288	11,835	0
Channel-Port-aux-Basques, Can.	3,838	12,140	11,919	11,872	15,449	4,174	3,974	3,899	17,407	4,873	4,538	3,684	3,724	13,421	4,770	3,726	10,387	13,588	2,628	11,577
Charleston, South Carolina	1,455	13,665	10,348	12,645	15,054	2,803	6,360	6,300	18,438	3,633	6,597	2,564	2,828	14,422	4,208	1,499	11,911	14,615	1,456	13,122
Charleston, West Virginia	1,971	13,027	10,211	13,042	14,682	3,416	6,054	5,956	17,940	3,291	6,516	2,140	3,377	13,814	4,741	2,111	12,085	14,006	945	12,484
Charlotte, North Carolina	1,664	13,381	10,270	12,838	14,879	3,080	6,235	6,157	18,215	3,457	6,574	2,351	3,078	14,146	4,453	1,765	12,008	14,339	1,203	12,838
Charlotte Amalie, U.S.V.I.	2,306	15,413	11,886	10,541	16,966	894	6,482	6,574	19,269	5,732	5,910	4,737	638	16,506	2,020	1,736	10,199	16,693	3,643	14,849
Charlottetown, Canada	3,514	12,316	11,659	12,056	15,388	3,977	4,311	4,233	17,617	4,606	4,845	3,410	3,578	13,532	4,694	3,423	10,652	13,704	2,320	11,752
Chatham, Canada	3,456	12,235	11,466	12,255	15,204	4,052	4,421	4,327	17,544	4,415	5,017	3,220	3,684	13,412	4,833	3,400	10,843	13,587	2,147	11,671
Chatham Islands (Waitangi)	11,594	10,301	4,580	11,250	5,387	12,384	19,032	18,706	6,557	10,827	18,520	11,881	13,120	8,544	13,080	11,879	13,517	8,487	12,724	10,732
Chengdu, China	14,158	1,237	9,624	11,479	6,150	15,350	8,481	8,267	6,230	11,047	9,912	11,296	14,811	2,997	15,341	14,445	9,857	3,049	11,802	906
Chesterfield Inlet, Canada	4,699	10,192	9,836	14,258	12,840	6,163	4,980	4,706	15,371	3,310	6,390	2,494	5,946	11,139	7,186	4,944	12,347	11,324	2,379	9,644
Cheyenne, Wyoming	2,796	11,883	8,309	15,030	12,689	5,026	7,263	7,061	16,045	1,291	8,183	227	5,187	12,252	6,569	3,287	14,003	12,446	1,099	11,402
Chiang Mai, Thailand	15,546	1,559	10,048	10,326	5,782	16,421	9,206	9,055	5,083	12,435	10,321	12,708	15,773	2,885	15,928	15,792	9,013	2,841	13,190	1,766
Chibougamau, Canada	3,375	11,881	10,774	12,987	14,508	4,424	4,826	4,679	17,140	3,736	5,637	2,558	4,163	12,919	5,398	3,454	11,529	13,102	1,600	11,322
Chicago, Illinois	2,302	12,496	9,728	13,658	14,061	4,023	6,180	6,038	17,297	2,724	6,857	1,540	4,015	13,202	5,383	2,573	12,581	13,396	336	11,963
Chiclayo, Peru	3,177	17,727	10,185	10,355	14,961	2,388	9,679	9,791	16,217	6,539	8,810	6,112	3,102	17,264	3,320	2,888	11,237	17,394	5,530	17,282
Chihuahua, Mexico	2,119	12,903	7,809	14,773	12,668	4,544	8,394	8,236	16,075	1,719	9,019	1,577	4,916	12,951	6,236	2,711	14,431	13,138	1,971	12,472
Chongquing, China	14,217	976	9,371	11,623	5,889	15,517	8,725	8,505	6,070	11,014	10,176	11,313	15,003	2,734	15,580	14,531	10,063	2,791	11,866	641
Christchurch, New Zealand	12,437	9,548	4,768	11,039	4,657	13,251	19,067	18,703	5,688	11,403	18,904	12,511	13,983	7,804	13,882	12,738	13,147	7,734	13,433	10,004
Christiansted, U.S.V.I.	2,344	15,478	11,913	10,484	17,004	837	6,517	6,613	19,199	5,791	5,920	4,801	572	16,577	1,955	1,769	10,162	16,764	3,711	14,914
Christmas Is. [Indian Ocean]	18,248	3,809	9,158	9,118	4,025	19,225	12,221	12,145	1,799	14,523	12,804	15,278	18,533	3,253	17,533	18,783	9,007	3,060	16,133	4,353
Christmas Is. [Pacific Ocean]	7,944	9,851	1,662	16,445	6,791	10,046	13,604	13,287	9,990	5,621	14,971	6,795	10,670	8,621	11,684	8,490	18,907	8,727	7,884	9,863
Churchill, Canada	4,219	10,589	9,560	14,436	12,907	5,824	5,400	5,146	15,662	2,840	6,691	1,960	5,671	11,436	6,961	4,500	12,673	11,625	1,874	10,049
Cincinnati, Ohio	2,003	12,875	9,965	13,306	14,418	3,618	6,187	6,072	17,695	3,029	6,722	1,876	3,612	13,607	4,982	2,215	12,335	13,800	685	12,338
Ciudad Bolivia, Venezuela	2,241	16,499	11,288	10,433	16,402	466	7,726	7,829	18,125	5,963	7,005	5,172	1,218	17,211	2,051	1,682	10,578	17,405	4,264	15,943
Ciudad Juarez, Mexico	2,286	12,615	7,863	14,924	12,621	4,696	8,152	7,980	16,044	1,459	8,863	1,234	5,018	12,734	6,363	2,864	14,409	12,923	1,738	12,173
Ciudad Victoria, Mexico	1,306	13,759	8,374	13,919	13,373	3,716	8,373	8,264	16,711	2,591	8,726	2,221	4,146	13,830	5,427	1,902	13,787	14,016	2,138	13,313
Clarksburg, West Virginia	2,103	12,955	10,325	12,980	14,741	3,456	5,902	5,804	17,947	3,377	6,376	2,209	3,381	13,782	4,735	2,217	11,975	13,974	1,003	12,408
Cleveland, Ohio	2,307	12,688	10,218	13,179	14,531	3,727	5,832	5,715	17,687	3,219	6,407	2,032	3,644	13,512	4,992	2,461	12,090	13,703	831	12,143
Cocos (Keeling) Island	18,928	4,277	10,115	8,216	4,978	18,255	11,738	11,715	2,271	15,323	12,072	15,928	17,622	4,064	16,555	19,176	8,028	3,879	16,583	4,776
Colombo, Sri Lanka	16,578	3,997	12,096	7,884	7,208	15,873	8,928	8,919	5,078	14,518	9,354	14,457	15,124	4,971	14,564	16,458	6,643	4,860	14,521	4,205
Colon, Panama	1,495	16,141	10,265	11,354	15,394	1,429	8,278	8,327	17,781	5,154	7,807	4,514	2,123	16,420	3,083	1,111	11,608	16,607	3,793	15,626
Colorado Springs, Colorado	2,615	12,089	8,232	14,983	12,718	4,897	7,454	7,261	16,105	1,294	8,315	463	5,094	12,406	6,473	3,128	14,076	12,600	1,168	11,615
Columbia, South Carolina	1,532	13,507	10,248	12,797	14,910	2,974	6,341	6,269	18,278	3,486	6,641	2,404	2,997	14,251	4,376	1,628	12,021	14,444	1,285	12,966
Columbus, Georgia	1,267	13,558	9,872	13,060	14,612	3,059	6,723	6,641	18,024	3,209	7,046	2,197	3,179	14,178	4,562	1,502	12,385	14,372	1,210	13,029
Columbus, Ohio	2,118	12,822	10,100	13,219	14,502	3,631	6,026	5,913	17,732	3,138	6,566	1,969	3,589	13,599	4,950	2,296	12,203	13,792	763	12,281
Conakry, Guinea	7,888	13,217	17,488	5,886	17,424	5,827	4,753	5,122	14,218	10,703	2,742	9,509	5,170	14,880	4,293	7,337	4,690	14,851	8,315	12,934
Concepcion, Chile	6,576	18,371	10,593	7,967	13,572	5,278	11,909	12,152	13,140	9,682	10,340	9,446	5,769	16,706	5,101	6,274	9,747	16,614	8,930	18,899
Concord, New Hampshire	2,827	12,645	11,049	12,488	15,144	3,652	5,053	4,965	17,917	4,015	5,549	2,814	3,389	13,694	4,643	2,807	11,262	13,878	1,655	12,085
Constantine, Algeria	8,937	9,893	16,288	7,877	14,762	7,856	1,853	2,184	13,073	10,004	1,331	8,920	7,105	11,649	6,929	8,592	5,608	11,679	8,017	9,514
Copenhagen, Denmark	8,657	8,555	14,134	9,942	13,410	8,392	1,140	988	12,937	8,572	2,903	7,672	7,703	10,281	8,002	8,501	7,549	10,362	7,061	8,079
Coppermine, Canada	5,551	9,174	8,962	15,229	11,624	7,269	5,625	5,300	14,219	3,203	7,275	2,830	7,111	9,991	8,381	5,888	13,086	10,179	3,201	8,642
Coquimbo, Chile	5,890	19,125	10,852	8,205	14,238	4,503	11,206	11,433	13,914	9,151	9,721	8,820	4,992	17,394	4,363	5,557	9,761	17,323	8,234	19,562
Cordoba, Argentina	6,293	19,054	11,501	7,527	14,553	4,646	10,943	11,201	13,774	9,699	9,331	9,279	5,037	17,644	4,213	5,904	9,057	17,527	8,599	19,565
Cordoba, Spain	7,918	10,664	15,903	8,303	15,577	6,863	1,518	1,895	14,098	9,204	538	8,075	6,115	12,423	6,037	7,568	6,219	12,475	7,106	10,242
Cork, Ireland	7,392	9,958	14,348	9,862	14,742	6,956	367	495	14,331	7,932	2,032	6,886	6,261	11,659	6,584	7,176	7,684	11,752	6,078	9,465
Corner Brook, Canada	4,005	11,975	11,962	11,878	15,365	4,344	3,825	3,742	17,234	4,929	4,454	3,749	3,884	13,273	4,908	3,901	10,338	13,439	2,724	11,412
Corrientes, Argentina	6,161	19,093	12,104	7,261	15,202	4,290	10,297	10,565	14,158	9,715	8,658	9,178	4,596	18,225	3,652	5,717	8,603	18,083	8,397	19,219
Cosenza, Italy	9,603	8,988	15,888	8,109	13,855	8,695	2,027	2,248	12,324	10,234	2,220	9,230	7,948	10,742	7,827	9,306	5,709	10,772	8,442	8,615
Craiova, Romania	9,912	8,210	15,165	8,681	13,108	9,260	2,155	2,241	11,884	10,065	2,945	9,156	8,525	9,970	8,526	9,679	6,226	10,009	8,496	7,818
Cruzeiro do Sul, Brazil	3,538	18,184	10,978	9,638	15,647	2,102	9,277	9,427	16,347	7,104	8,228	6,550	2,716	18,064	2,645	3,131	10,435	18,199	5,827	17,656
Cuiaba, Brazil	5,265	18,628	12,661	7,648	16,460	3,122	9,020	9,270	15,394	8,963	7,491	8,255	3,318	19,571	2,306	4,750	8,501	19,420	7,346	18,220
Curitiba, Brazil	6,554	18,238	13,086	6,504	15,813	4,411	9,636	9,932	14,147	10,232	7,882	9,553	4,545	18,377	3,374	6,048	7,672	18,187	8,644	18,237
Cuzco, Peru	4,159	18,813	10,993	9,223	15,373	2,714	9,765	9,938	15,715	7,654	8,584	7,157	3,277	18,194	2,980	3,773	10,226	18,269	6,367	18,302
Dacca, Bangladesh	15,033	2,332	10,947	9,931	6,824	15,496	8,222	8,092	5,930	12,372	9,280	12,439	14,810	3,874	14,887	15,164	8,336	3,848	12,729	2,309
Dakar, Senegal	7,326	13,219	16,916	6,584	17,810	5,387	4,280	4,636	14,809	10,024	2,322	8,826	4,693	14,945	3,971	6,794	5,328	14,946	7,638	12,878
Dallas, Texas	1,630	13,049	8,776	14,101	13,519	3,931	7,468	7,332	16,942	2,181	8,022	1,394	4,178	13,391	5,546	2,143	13,491	13,584	1,117	12,563
Damascus, Syria	11,474	7,469	15,545	7,693	12,160	10,575	3,747	3,854	10,420	11,591	4,044	10,737	9,825	9,171	9,587	11,199	5,223	9,168	10,109	7,188
Danang, Vietnam	15,581	942	9,048	10,976	4,797	17,019	10,033	9,849	4,566	12,127	11,275	12,593	16,476	1,862	16,860	15,956	9,891	1,815	13,264	1,430
Dar es Salaam, Tanzania	14,021	8,690	16,433	3,692	11,307	11,921	7,624	7,875	8,123	15,856	6,664	14,789	11,305	9,695	10,261	13,483	1,889	9,567	13,825	8,791
Darwin, Australia	15,925	4,378	6,419	11,231	1,283	18,088	14,041	13,834	2,271	12,547	15,209	13,609	18,742	2,759	19,106	16,508	11,634	2,632	14,773	4,894
Davao, Philippines	15,308	2,214	7,053	12,035	2,713	17,629	11,899	11,661	3,764	11,584	13,339	12,402	17,565	526	18,659	15,866	11,559	404	13,393	2,691
David, Panama	1,480	16,125	9,982	11,532	15,105	1,719	8,534	8,574	17,525	5,042	8,097	4,470	2,419	16,267	3,350	1,208	11,864	16,448	3,826	15,630
Dawson, Canada	6,134	8,521	7,884	16,326	10,499	8,113	6,641	6,295	13,286	3,057	8,385	3,157	8,050	9,113	9,373	6,558	14,051	9,306	3,890	8,027
Dawson Creek, Canada	4,739	9,919	7,993	16,035	11,442	6,808	6,783	6,487	14,498	1,846	8,237	1,751	6,823	10,421	8,184	5,184	14,194	10,616	2,566	9,430
Denpasar, Indonesia	17,296	3,521	8,113	10,103	2,998	19,712	12,705	12,570	1,803	13,610	13,569	14,480	19,292	2,499	18,599	17,883	10,075	2,306	15,476	4,084
Denver, Colorado	2,695	11,999	8,248	15,017	12,693	4,959	7,388	7,192	16,069	1,272	8,275	362	5,143	12,334	6,524	3,201	14,062	12,528	1,149	11,523
Derby, Australia	16,816	4,612	7,236	10,291	2,159	18,661	14,019	13,872	1,334	13,488	14,853	14,541	19,410	3,218	18,571	17,383	10,745	3,053	15,693	5,164
Des Moines, Iowa	2,358	12,327	9,230	14,126	13,598	4,322	6,571	6,408	16,897	2,228	7,329	1,057	4,386	12,910	5,765	2,729	13,080	13,104	167	11,811
Detroit, Michigan	2,376	12,568	10,110	13,317	14,390	3,862	5,859	5,732	17,543	3,097	6,484	1,904	3,788	13,374	5,137	2,559	12,200	13,566	714	12,025
Dhahran, Saudi Arabia	13,005	6,333	14,865	7,460	10,767	12,099	5,250	5,316	8,866	12,682	5,560	11,979	11,347	7,934	11,009	12,748	5,155	7,903	11,491	6,154
Diego Garcia Island	17,314	5,576	12,829	6,261	7,696	15,554	9,660	9,746	4,791	16,276	9,544	16,068	14,895	6,181	13,920	16,905	5,456	6,030	15,862	5,868
Dijon, France	8,441	9,428	15,065	9,096	14,333	7,797	756	1,008	13,378	8,979	1,854	7,960	7,071	11,178	7,190	8,191	6,795	11,243	7,175	8,982
Dili, Indonesia	16,296	3,751	6,973	11,038	1,870	18,649	13,360	13,168	2,206	12,731	14,488	13,714	19,086	2,248	19,550	16,892	11,188	2,093	14,820	4,286
Djibouti, Djibouti	13,461	7,495	16,073	5,678	11,256	11,923	6,076	6,253	8,643	14,114	5,688	13,227	11,199	8,873	10,504	13,053	3,432	8,795	12,499	7,444
Dnepropetrovsk, USSR	10,380	7,273	14,349	9,271	12,183	10,006	2,728	2,683	11,251	9,985	3,877	9,206	9,290	9,033	9,404	10,220	6,791	9,081	8,709	6,865
Dobo, Indonesia	15,301	3,926	6,012	11,984	1,061	17,650	13,607	13,361	3,049	11,796	15,019	12,826	18,129	2,197	19,306	15,896	12,190	2,113	13,973	4,397
Doha, Qatar	13,184	6,218	14,779	7,429	10,611	12,272	5,428	5,492	8,686	12,813	5,733	12,129	11,520	7,802	11,168	12,928	5,157	7,767	11,657	6,054
Donetsk, USSR	10,575	7,071	14,264	9,277	11,979	10,221	2,941	2,889	11,041	10,098	4,078	9,344	9,505	8,831	9,615	10,422	6,797	8,877	8,874	6,669
Dover, Delaware	2,268	13,051	10,741	12,595	15,116	3,288	5,592	5,514	18,206	3,784	5,985	2,607	3,130	13,986	4,454	2,272	11,559	14,174	1,400	12,496
Dresden, East Germany	8,911	8,676	14,636	9,423	13,576	8,456	1,181	1,196	12,794	9,037	2,597	8,103	7,744	10,423	7,926	8,712	7,030	10,491	7,436	8,225
Dubayy, United Arab Emir.	13,445	5,846	14,423	7,623	10,237	12,619	5,688	5,729	8,378	12,854	6,080	12,232	11,868	7,424	11,540	13,215	5,412	7,388	11,825	5,692

Distances in Kilometers	Cancun, Mexico	Canton, China	Canton Atoll, Phoenix Islands	Cape Town, South Africa	Cape York, Australia	Caracas, Venezuela	Cardiff, United Kingdom	Carlisle, United Kingdom	Carnarvon, Australia	Carson City, Nevada	Casablanca, Morocco	Casper, Wyoming	Castries, Saint Lucia	Catbalogan, Philippines	Cayenne, French Guiana	Cayman Islands (Georgetown)	Cazombo, Angola	Cebu, Philippines	Cedar Rapids, Iowa	Changsha, China
Dublin, Ireland	7,527	9,742	14,249	9,957	14,523	7,149	291	277	14,159	7,941	2,193	6,918	6,459	11,441	6,799	7,326	7,741	11,534	6,146	9,247
Duluth, Minnesota	2,887	11,856	9,446	14,146	13,536	4,672	6,096	5,912	16,679	2,394	6,994	1,203	4,645	12,553	6,003	3,202	12,864	12,746	535	11,328
Dunedin, New Zealand	12,639	9,575	5,074	10,735	4,718	13,343	19,231	18,902	5,532	11,702	18,635	12,802	14,065	7,845	13,883	12,918	12,838	7,765	13,707	10,047
Durango, Mexico	1,869	13,383	7,827	14,443	12,809	4,267	8,703	8,569	16,160	2,200	9,183	2,092	4,709	13,338	5,982	2,463	14,348	13,522	2,325	12,965
Durban, South Africa	13,771	10,561	15,664	1,273	11,430	11,349	9,614	9,934	8,011	17,164	8,115	15,980	10,969	11,026	9,646	13,175	2,159	10,854	14,779	10,818
Dushanbe, USSR	12,926	4,532	12,747	9,561	9,363	12,904	5,613	5,507	8,433	11,355	6,699	10,977	12,199	6,268	12,293	12,890	7,345	6,287	10,871	4,224
East London, South Africa	13,515	10,969	15,537	888	11,572	11,091	9,847	10,179	8,175	17,053	8,261	15,909	10,752	11,363	9,406	12,924	2,397	11,186	14,701	11,242
Easter Island (Hanga Roa)	5,875	15,724	7,134	11,301	11,219	6,198	13,422	13,471	12,635	7,420	12,659	7,757	6,936	14,127	7,087	5,964	13,301	14,153	7,868	15,867
Echo Bay, Canada	5,475	9,220	8,747	15,436	11,516	7,265	5,853	5,529	14,197	2,997	7,485	2,685	7,137	9,980	8,428	5,834	13,314	10,170	3,139	8,696
Edinburgh, United Kingdom	7,690	9,414	14,029	10,164	14,178	7,421	492	116	13,924	7,895	2,501	6,910	6,744	11,105	7,123	7,519	7,897	11,202	6,200	8,915
Edmonton, Canada	4,254	10,402	8,238	15,680	11,889	6,306	6,683	6,409	14,990	1,669	8,019	1,302	6,328	10,923	7,693	4,689	14,001	11,117	2,065	9,906
El Aaiun, Morocco	7,401	12,014	16,481	7,540	16,892	5,906	2,830	3,189	14,742	9,441	896	8,249	5,158	13,773	4,823	6,952	5,819	13,808	7,137	11,617
Elat, Israel	11,627	7,703	15,937	7,237	12,285	10,570	3,977	4,121	10,335	11,961	4,034	11,068	9,818	9,372	9,484	11,316	4,766	9,356	10,386	7,454
Elazig, Turkey	11,326	7,095	14,955	8,320	11,896	10,656	3,569	3,613	10,456	11,123	4,205	10,332	9,914	8,829	9,808	11,105	5,853	8,843	9,789	6,773
Eniwetok Atoll, Marshall Isls.	11,670	5,340	3,292	15,593	3,290	14,074	12,886	12,519	6,636	8,181	14,898	9,267	14,484	4,072	15,792	12,267	15,612	4,192	10,457	5,441
Erfurt, East Germany	8,735	8,854	14,662	9,433	13,749	8,265	994	1,032	12,982	8,932	2,451	7,980	7,553	10,599	7,741	8,530	7,060	10,668	7,290	8,399
Erzurum, Turkey	11,371	6,900	14,733	8,507	11,721	10,778	3,629	3,650	10,369	11,038	4,364	10,278	10,040	8,639	9,971	11,170	6,044	8,657	9,773	6,569
Esfahan, Iran	12,596	6,076	14,431	8,150	10,727	11,946	4,857	4,875	9,152	12,003	5,447	11,347	11,200	7,755	11,017	12,398	5,804	7,746	10,932	5,832
Essen, West Germany	8,452	9,085	14,614	9,522	13,966	7,989	709	766	13,266	8,718	2,306	7,746	7,280	10,823	7,495	8,245	7,184	10,898	7,032	8,621
Eucla, Australia	16,306	6,292	6,979	9,730	2,714	17,157	15,564	15,463	1,674	13,885	15,967	15,067	17,807	4,831	17,037	16,704	10,795	4,680	16,271	6,842
Fargo, North Dakota	2,997	11,689	9,097	14,499	13,193	4,918	6,359	6,159	16,381	2,049	7,320	874	4,932	12,308	6,300	3,366	13,210	12,502	680	11,171
Faroe Islands (Torshavn)	7,432	9,188	13,320	10,873	13,797	7,450	1,191	825	13,993	7,297	3,158	6,366	6,817	10,819	7,355	7,327	8,592	10,932	5,750	8,663
Florence, Italy	9,027	9,171	15,461	8,633	14,082	8,261	1,381	1,604	12,843	9,589	1,981	8,582	7,523	10,931	7,527	8,756	6,276	10,979	7,801	8,758
Florianopolis, Brazil	6,779	18,136	13,072	6,341	15,605	4,655	9,820	10,122	13,898	10,445	8,037	9,783	4,794	18,129	3,621	6,279	7,591	17,939	8,885	18,213
Fort George, Canada	3,689	11,399	10,437	13,429	13,988	4,925	4,885	4,696	16,623	3,464	5,892	2,343	4,691	12,394	5,937	3,838	11,846	12,578	1,618	10,844
Fort McMurray, Canada	4,440	10,222	8,519	15,479	11,982	6,389	6,335	6,055	14,973	2,048	7,721	1,586	6,358	10,836	7,705	4,840	13,695	11,029	2,162	9,713
Fort Nelson, Canada	5,073	9,583	8,073	16,035	11,296	7,088	6,615	6,305	14,261	2,195	8,149	2,107	7,069	10,137	8,417	5,502	14,063	10,331	2,850	9,087
Fort Severn, Canada	3,870	11,021	9,897	14,021	13,394	5,358	5,239	5,015	16,145	3,011	6,392	1,980	5,185	11,915	6,467	4,106	12,369	12,103	1,585	10,475
Fort Smith, Arkansas	1,748	12,907	9,044	13,990	13,689	3,916	7,106	6,969	17,095	2,279	7,691	1,319	4,094	13,356	5,474	2,195	13,240	13,551	769	12,406
Fort Vermilion, Canada	4,759	9,899	8,368	15,694	11,687	6,722	6,393	6,098	14,645	2,156	7,859	1,857	6,687	10,503	8,031	5,167	13,808	10,696	2,494	9,394
Fort Wayne, Indiana	2,216	12,650	9,927	13,433	14,287	3,831	6,083	5,954	17,515	2,940	6,695	1,762	3,803	13,396	5,167	2,440	12,380	13,589	554	12,113
Fort-Chimo, Canada	4,365	11,003	11,053	12,958	14,137	5,283	4,088	3,889	16,310	4,194	5,214	3,120	4,932	12,167	6,060	4,437	11,195	12,341	2,424	10,441
Fort-de-France, Martinique	2,811	15,788	12,316	9,967	17,443	779	6,544	6,674	18,746	6,309	5,762	5,321	65	17,017	1,436	2,222	9,709	17,198	4,224	15,226
Fortaleza, Brazil	5,936	16,304	14,779	6,759	18,405	3,520	6,973	7,273	15,651	9,520	5,257	8,511	3,165	17,995	1,812	5,340	6,816	17,958	7,369	15,962
Frankfort, Kentucky	1,901	12,960	9,928	13,298	14,426	3,553	6,276	6,165	17,731	3,020	6,786	1,884	3,566	13,672	4,940	2,122	12,368	13,865	716	12,425
Frankfurt am Main, W. Ger.	8,608	9,046	14,764	9,358	13,942	8,093	851	949	13,137	8,907	2,266	7,934	7,378	10,791	7,552	8,391	7,008	10,860	7,214	8,592
Fredericton, Canada	3,307	12,355	11,397	12,280	15,229	3,931	4,560	4,470	17,663	4,344	5,118	3,146	3,582	13,508	4,753	3,252	10,915	13,685	2,047	11,791
Freeport, Bahamas	1,007	14,364	10,444	12,228	15,365	2,168	6,771	6,749	18,772	4,045	6,778	3,082	2,312	15,064	3,690	842	11,747	15,258	2,080	13,822
Freetown, Sierra Leone	7,973	13,235	17,567	5,764	17,361	5,890	4,856	5,225	14,125	10,816	2,841	9,623	5,241	14,884	4,337	7,419	4,590	14,849	8,427	12,962
Frobisher Bay, Canada	4,927	10,374	10,933	13,183	13,636	5,912	3,930	3,681	15,681	4,306	5,292	3,341	5,553	11,554	6,657	5,032	11,252	11,726	2,846	9,811
Frunze, USSR	12,663	4,173	12,143	10,248	9,075	12,924	5,689	5,534	8,503	10,802	6,980	10,507	12,254	5,932	12,503	12,694	8,028	5,973	10,504	3,800
Fukuoka, Japan	12,788	2,038	7,281	13,848	5,067	14,796	9,551	9,241	6,708	9,196	11,373	9,769	14,601	2,481	15,732	13,256	12,356	2,663	10,604	1,768
Funafuti Atoll, Tuvalu	10,779	7,976	1,195	14,890	4,030	12,794	15,234	14,859	7,152	8,212	17,143	9,413	13,458	6,410	14,337	11,317	16,560	6,464	10,573	8,183
Funchal, Madeira Island	6,938	11,887	15,796	8,243	16,798	5,666	2,374	2,704	15,164	8,776	876	7,589	4,914	13,641	4,790	6,529	6,493	13,701	6,500	11,448
Fuzhou, China	14,079	695	8,073	12,529	4,782	15,903	9,749	9,490	5,670	10,540	11,347	11,063	15,568	1,690	16,458	14,513	11,224	1,813	11,827	670
Gaborone, Botswana	13,180	10,805	16,426	1,256	12,110	10,779	8,905	9,234	8,687	16,429	7,361	15,235	10,350	11,453	9,061	12,583	1,449	11,290	14,041	11,003
Galapagos Islands (Santa Cruz)	2,440	16,455	9,048	11,702	14,054	2,875	9,868	9,901	16,190	5,330	9,385	5,073	3,622	15,949	4,276	2,414	12,532	16,094	4,721	16,081
Gander, Canada	4,198	11,933	12,194	11,674	15,481	4,414	3,604	3,533	17,144	5,167	4,210	3,990	3,918	13,279	4,883	4,068	10,103	13,440	2,968	11,371
Gangtok, India	14,619	2,521	11,119	10,035	7,173	15,064	7,800	7,664	6,370	12,078	8,909	12,086	14,385	4,156	14,512	14,735	8,313	4,148	12,331	2,398
Garyarsa, China	13,995	3,374	11,876	9,746	8,107	14,184	6,897	6,778	7,196	11,884	7,972	11,717	13,487	5,062	13,575	14,032	7,799	5,063	11,801	3,159
Gaspe, Canada	3,655	12,033	11,501	12,285	15,100	4,256	4,259	4,153	17,340	4,459	4,933	3,274	3,874	13,229	5,000	3,610	10,803	13,403	2,247	11,469
Gauhati, India	14,767	2,202	10,812	10,202	6,840	15,342	8,100	7,954	6,120	12,068	9,238	12,142	14,676	3,822	14,838	14,918	8,556	3,813	12,450	2,113
Gdansk, Poland	9,073	8,239	14,216	9,780	13,123	8,781	1,498	1,391	12,530	8,910	3,085	8,039	8,084	9,977	8,338	8,916	7,352	10,051	7,457	7,776
Geneva, Switzerland	8,560	9,410	15,195	8,958	14,321	7,873	904	1,159	13,279	9,130	1,821	8,110	7,143	11,164	7,227	8,301	6,648	11,225	7,318	8,972
Genoa, Italy	8,829	9,306	15,397	8,728	14,220	8,079	1,199	1,442	13,036	9,421	1,861	8,404	7,343	11,065	7,370	8,559	6,393	11,117	7,612	8,884
Georgetown, Guyana	3,462	16,568	12,654	9,208	17,726	1,046	7,048	7,224	17,828	7,100	5,983	6,169	856	17,925	678	2,867	9,204	18,100	5,107	16,018
Geraldton, Australia	17,717	5,743	8,276	8,806	3,522	17,976	14,352	14,314	443	14,946	14,561	16,056	18,311	4,619	17,034	18,093	9,553	4,437	17,236	6,307
Ghanzi, Botswana	12,692	11,072	16,940	1,408	12,631	10,307	8,454	8,792	9,209	15,886	6,856	14,692	9,855	11,832	8,586	12,097	1,076	11,676	13,498	11,228
Ghat, Libya	9,704	10,170	17,548	6,575	14,764	8,237	3,158	3,493	12,415	11,212	1,970	10,087	7,494	11,863	7,017	9,281	4,305	11,853	9,106	9,881
Gibraltar	7,910	10,819	16,062	8,139	15,729	6,782	1,716	2,092	14,132	9,304	346	8,164	6,032	12,579	5,908	7,544	6,087	12,626	7,173	10,404
Gijon, Spain	7,720	10,358	15,291	8,919	15,255	6,905	905	1,278	14,197	8,711	1,113	7,612	6,171	12,105	6,255	7,421	6,788	12,173	6,703	9,905
Gisborne, New Zealand	11,889	9,605	4,104	11,699	4,694	12,909	18,575	18,200	6,162	10,702	19,261	11,817	13,656	7,845	13,728	12,229	13,844	7,796	12,761	10,022
Glasgow, United Kingdom	7,626	9,474	14,021	10,176	14,230	7,356	487	135	13,991	7,853	2,482	6,862	6,679	11,162	7,063	7,453	7,920	11,259	6,144	8,973
Godthab, Greenland	5,448	10,230	11,698	12,462	13,961	6,087	3,102	2,856	15,499	5,133	4,524	4,148	5,625	11,570	6,583	5,468	10,453	11,729	3,548	9,668
Gomez Palacio, Mexico	1,780	13,328	7,979	14,406	12,928	4,198	8,497	8,362	16,301	2,142	8,991	1,934	4,611	13,349	5,905	2,377	14,217	13,535	2,120	12,898
Goose Bay, Canada	4,873	9,849	7,306	16,672	10,922	7,090	7,468	7,167	14,106	1,491	8,927	1,868	7,186	10,171	8,565	5,372	14,886	10,365	2,910	9,393
Gorki, USSR	10,264	6,625	13,282	10,290	11,514	10,291	3,084	2,905	11,108	9,312	4,636	8,666	9,621	8,365	9,944	10,201	7,812	8,438	8,344	6,164
Goteborg, Sweden	8,546	8,505	13,910	10,172	13,329	8,366	1,195	973	12,995	8,366	3,056	7,481	7,689	10,217	8,040	8,409	7,780	10,305	6,897	8,018
Granada, Spain	8,028	10,628	16,007	8,202	15,538	6,947	1,588	1,965	13,996	9,324	534	8,196	6,197	12,388	6,093	7,673	6,105	12,436	7,227	10,213
Grand Turk, Turks & Caicos	1,620	15,050	11,224	11,274	16,256	1,295	6,650	6,693	19,406	5,002	6,324	4,031	1,354	15,939	2,732	1,096	10,902	16,131	2,977	14,492
Graz, Austria	9,194	8,725	15,055	8,974	13,638	8,586	1,439	1,549	12,592	9,473	2,446	8,520	7,858	10,483	7,935	8,962	6,572	10,537	7,815	8,300
Green Bay, Wisconsin	2,596	12,212	9,729	13,774	13,925	4,279	6,014	5,856	17,086	2,686	6,783	1,485	4,239	12,949	5,596	2,863	12,583	13,142	410	11,677
Grenoble, France	8,560	9,495	15,307	8,851	14,408	7,828	965	1,244	13,301	9,197	1,715	8,166	7,095	11,251	7,155	8,291	6,551	11,309	7,358	9,062
Guadalajara, Mexico	1,725	13,755	7,887	14,155	12,938	4,054	8,909	8,793	16,219	2,584	9,274	2,475	4,547	13,646	5,776	2,301	14,227	13,826	2,604	13,346
Guam (Agana)	13,220	3,489	5,138	14,179	2,686	15,637	12,172	11,846	5,422	9,542	14,031	10,487	15,861	2,166	17,244	13,804	13,736	2,298	11,594	3,672
Guantanamo, Cuba	1,209	15,134	10,802	11,557	15,869	1,388	7,042	7,070	18,977	4,742	6,768	3,844	1,655	15,855	2,993	655	11,297	16,050	2,876	14,586
Guatemala City, Guatemala	823	15,100	9,147	12,643	14,276	2,604	8,565	8,537	17,262	3,945	8,482	3,473	3,183	15,150	4,317	1,101	12,835	15,333	3,033	14,639
Guayaquil, Ecuador	2,685	17,299	10,213	10,641	15,138	2,003	9,275	9,369	16,685	6,132	8,512	5,649	2,743	17,106	3,158	2,381	11,350	17,260	5,032	16,824
Guiyang, China	14,531	764	9,321	11,464	5,654	15,845	8,998	8,787	5,741	11,278	10,401	11,609	15,323	2,512	15,860	14,854	10,000	2,552	12,183	644
Gur'yev, USSR	11,389	6,014	13,565	9,579	10,919	11,231	3,939	3,839	10,089	10,411	5,136	9,811	10,527	7,774	10,676	11,296	7,145	7,817	9,503	5,624
Haifa, Israel	11,420	7,605	15,684	7,590	12,281	10,479	3,713	3,834	10,494	11,621	3,942	10,747	9,727	9,303	9,470	11,135	5,116	9,298	10,097	7,326
Haikou, China	15,089	456	8,873	11,399	4,898	16,612	9,801	9,595	4,982	11,642	11,155	12,100	16,120	1,808	16,662	15,471	10,202	1,813	12,777	942
Haiphong, Vietnam	15,137	722	9,260	11,126	5,247	16,466	9,507	9,315	5,115	11,797	10,809	12,186	15,921	2,187	16,357	15,476	9,852	2,183	12,797	1,032
Hakodate, Japan	11,508	3,283	6,884	14,965	5,812	13,571	9,101	8,756	7,886	7,919	11,055	8,490	13,443	3,663	14,670	11,984	13,189	3,854	9,349	2,927
Halifax, Canada	3,365	12,494	11,658	12,000	15,498	3,798	4,434	4,368	17,796	4,607	4,895	3,407	3,405	13,699	4,536	3,259	10,654	13,873	2,285	11,930
Hamburg, West Germany	8,576	8,801	14,380	9,725	13,672	8,211	923	855	13,081	8,661	2,615	7,725	7,512	10,534	7,767	8,394	7,355	10,612	7,064	8,332
Hamilton, Bermuda	2,505	13,870	11,772	11,375	16,346	2,422	5,353	5,371	19,169	4,959	5,279	3,810	2,059	15,024	3,293	2,196	10,492	15,204	2,607	13,306
Hamilton, New Zealand	12,100	9,352	4,093	11,716	4,439	13,160	18,476	18,099	5,933	10,800	19,480	11,931	13,908	7,592	13,986	12,452	13,804	7,542	12,903	9,772
Hangzhou, China	13,637	1,048	8,093	12,814	5,124	15,433	9,400	9,129	6,139	10,140	11,063	10,627	15,105	2,104	16,031	14,060	11,367	2,243	11,370	736
Hannover, West Germany	8,599	8,873	14,512	9,596	13,754	8,183	892	881	13,089	8,754	2,502	7,806	7,478	10,611	7,705	8,405	7,231	10,686	7,125	8,409
Hanoi, Vietnam	15,145	798	9,348	11,062	5,327	16,430	9,441	9,252	5,148	11,832	10,730	12,206	15,873	2,274	16,286	15,475	9,772	2,267	12,801	1,072
Harare, Zimbabwe	13,534	10,016	16,639	2,182	11,861	11,205	8,372	8,677	8,475	16,340	7,017	15,148	10,698	10,811	9,486	12,947	1,098	10,661	14,009	10,175
Harbin, China	11,870	2,788	8,091	13,947	6,451	13,630	8,209	7,888	7,930	8,512	10,087	8,885	13,342	3,771	14,390	12,268	12,018	3,938	9,573	2,290
Harrisburg, Pennsylvania	2,318	12,911	10,622	12,752	14,954	3,441	5,604	5,514	18,041	3,643	6,060	2,459	3,295	13,825	4,622	2,363	11,682	14,014	1,255	12,357
Hartford, Connecticut	2,642	12,796	10,969	12,502	15,164	3,510	5,222	5,140	18,044	3,954	5,675	2,758	3,276	13,812	4,553	2,624	11,340	13,997	1,574	12,237
Havana, Cuba	503	14,619	10,069	12,365	15,085	2,157	7,292	7,268	18,394	3,947	7,269	3,107	2,467	15,146	3,803	437	12,073	15,340	2,262	14,093
Helena, Montana	3,634	11,048	7,987	15,656	12,053	5,831	7,194	6,948	15,326	1,039	8,355	615	5,946	11,429	7,328	4,118	14,308	11,624	1,698	10,571
Helsinki, Finland	9,120	7,712	13,489	10,445	12,537	9,105	1,990	1,756	12,299	8,533	3,779	7,757	8,443	9,422	8,831	9,032	7,991	9,510	7,307	7,223
Hengyang, China	14,299	424	8,746	11,986	5,266	15,866	9,309	9,073	5,729	10,901	10,813	11,319	15,426	2,112	16,132	14,677	10,580	2,188	11,983	149
Herat, Afghanistan	13,048	5,086	13,458	8,829	9,800	12,711	5,467	5,418	8,511	11,864	6,312	11,379	11,980	6,780	11,915	12,935	6,593	6,779	11,146	4,833

Distances in Kilometers	Cancun, Mexico	Canton, China	Canton Atoll, Phoenix Islands	Cape Town, South Africa	Cape York, Australia	Caracas, Venezuela	Cardiff, United Kingdom	Carlisle, United Kingdom	Carnarvon, Australia	Carson City, Nevada	Casablanca, Morocco	Casper, Wyoming	Castries, Saint Lucia	Catbalogan, Philippines	Cayenne, French Guiana	Cayman Islands (Georgetown)	Cazombo, Angola	Cebu, Philippines	Cedar Rapids, Iowa	Changsha, China
Hermosillo, Mexico	2,590	12,548	7,365	15,236	12,192	5,014	8,651	8,470	15,603	1,382	9,385	1,585	5,394	12,516	6,711	3,184	14,891	12,701	2,252	12,138
Hiroshima, Japan	12,599	2,247	7,140	14,057	5,104	14,635	9,554	9,237	6,854	8,995	11,403	9,580	14,462	2,622	15,622	13,073	12,545	2,807	10,430	1,974
Hiva Oa (Atuona)	6,662	12,244	3,691	14,616	8,575	8,295	13,900	13,702	11,271	5,776	14,420	6,711	9,009	10,892	9,750	7,094	16,893	10,975	7,494	12,285
Ho Chi Minh City, Vietnam	16,189	1,537	9,165	10,513	4,619	17,552	10,413	10,254	4,012	12,695	11,519	13,194	16,952	1,992	17,123	16,568	9,598	1,887	13,875	2,041
Hobart, Australia	14,485	8,104	6,012	10,042	3,600	15,128	17,610	17,489	3,667	13,029	17,608	14,210	15,818	6,473	15,375	14,783	11,732	6,356	15,268	8,625
Hohhot, China	12,893	1,965	9,101	12,614	6,525	14,325	7,999	7,729	7,271	9,737	9,685	9,992	13,891	3,468	14,687	13,219	10,762	3,587	10,545	1,401
Hong Kong	14,701	134	8,510	11,867	4,779	16,380	9,824	9,596	5,213	11,202	11,283	11,695	15,959	1,626	16,663	15,110	10,642	1,681	12,416	670
Honiara, Solomon Islands	12,801	6,232	3,222	13,730	1,921	14,901	15,095	14,743	5,186	9,842	17,043	11,022	15,549	4,534	16,438	13,361	14,729	4,551	12,226	6,548
Honolulu, Hawaii	7,311	9,003	3,067	18,562	7,421	9,694	11,570	11,233	10,842	4,125	13,163	5,320	10,149	8,241	11,416	7,906	18,960	8,396	6,513	8,846
Houston, Texas	1,289	13,407	8,855	13,850	13,700	3,641	7,622	7,506	17,117	2,463	8,064	1,750	3,934	13,715	5,287	1,827	13,382	13,907	1,395	12,923
Huambo, Angola	11,802	11,316	18,102	2,361	13,595	9,493	7,349	7,697	10,201	14,770	5,697	13,569	8,969	12,347	7,781	11,217	776	12,214	12,389	11,370
Hubli, India	15,517	4,083	12,585	8,115	7,959	14,962	7,884	7,865	6,102	13,775	8,423	13,559	14,211	5,385	13,827	15,401	6,504	5,310	13,517	4,139
Hugh Town, United Kingdom	7,565	9,974	14,607	9,602	14,804	7,033	282	599	14,210	8,191	1,813	7,137	6,326	11,692	6,582	7,329	7,417	11,778	6,312	9,492
Hull, Canada	2,878	12,360	10,699	12,895	14,727	3,962	5,183	5,064	17,575	3,650	5,826	2,449	3,749	13,342	5,029	2,945	11,613	13,528	1,339	11,804
Hyderabad, India	15,453	3,680	12,219	8,526	7,693	15,124	7,942	7,897	6,033	13,465	8,606	13,318	14,378	5,029	14,088	15,394	6,918	4,963	13,356	3,724
Hyderabad, Pakistan	14,206	4,544	13,150	8,422	8,961	13,759	6,585	6,555	7,391	12,811	7,261	12,433	13,015	6,109	12,803	14,086	6,430	6,074	12,273	4,422
Igloolik, Canada	5,373	9,676	10,294	13,883	12,779	6,625	4,363	4,063	14,952	4,040	5,934	3,273	6,321	10,767	7,473	5,566	11,808	10,944	3,105	9,118
Iloilo, Philippines	15,257	1,694	7,435	11,973	3,234	17,441	11,383	11,149	4,052	11,543	12,819	12,284	17,244	279	18,189	15,785	11,302	153	13,211	2,181
Indianapolis, Indiana	2,067	12,759	9,830	13,464	14,260	3,760	6,243	6,118	17,538	2,876	6,826	1,718	3,766	13,465	5,138	2,315	12,473	13,658	526	12,225
Innsbruck, Austria	8,901	8,999	15,072	9,019	13,911	8,278	1,157	1,310	12,898	9,281	2,201	8,301	7,551	10,754	7,644	8,662	6,652	10,813	7,565	8,565
Inuvik, Canada	6,146	8,528	8,420	15,790	10,852	7,984	6,101	5,754	13,477	3,357	7,861	3,262	7,858	9,259	9,143	6,526	13,510	9,449	3,831	8,011
Invercargill, New Zealand	12,810	9,486	5,201	10,614	4,651	13,482	19,174	18,883	5,372	11,867	18,545	12,972	14,200	7,764	13,982	13,084	12,692	7,680	13,882	9,965
Inverness, United Kingdom	7,608	9,369	13,846	10,347	14,096	7,411	668	299	13,961	7,732	2,663	6,759	6,744	11,045	7,166	7,453	8,080	11,146	6,069	8,862
Iquitos, Peru	3,124	17,755	10,934	9,936	15,764	1,727	8,974	9,109	16,752	6,729	8,025	6,141	2,387	17,847	2,517	2,702	10,597	18,007	5,398	17,223
Iraklion, Greece	10,504	8,402	16,015	7,698	13,172	9,530	2,883	3,059	11,439	11,005	2,998	10,048	8,779	10,131	8,560	10,201	5,233	10,140	9,306	8,079
Irkutsk, USSR	11,803	3,324	9,846	12,647	7,873	13,000	6,662	6,376	8,592	9,016	8,434	9,062	12,527	4,856	13,295	12,057	10,473	4,979	9,449	2,767
Islamabad, Pakistan	13,576	4,071	12,504	9,419	8,813	13,555	6,264	6,167	7,769	11,828	7,272	11,528	12,843	5,769	12,879	13,552	7,336	5,772	11,484	3,828
Istanbul, Turkey	10,464	7,901	15,301	8,367	12,756	9,741	2,711	2,801	11,360	10,578	3,316	9,693	8,999	9,651	8,923	10,220	5,892	9,677	9,052	7,542
Ivujivik, Canada	4,633	10,474	10,478	13,601	13,428	5,828	4,428	4,178	15,746	3,808	5,755	2,857	5,536	11,548	6,715	4,794	11,726	11,727	2,448	9,915
Iwo Jima Island, Japan	12,750	2,860	5,922	14,462	3,929	15,052	10,874	10,545	6,252	9,028	12,758	9,823	15,082	2,254	16,404	13,296	13,426	2,443	10,832	2,847
Izmir, Turkey	10,485	8,128	15,628	8,059	12,949	9,645	2,772	2,903	11,397	10,776	3,157	9,857	8,898	9,870	8,757	10,213	5,588	9,888	9,169	7,786
Jackson, Mississippi	1,283	13,389	9,383	13,502	14,141	3,397	7,080	6,976	17,562	2,768	7,496	1,838	3,590	13,875	4,967	1,688	12,875	14,069	1,082	12,878
Jaffna, Sri Lanka	16,307	3,838	12,081	8,089	7,274	15,740	8,704	8,683	5,284	14,228	9,203	14,155	14,988	4,911	14,507	16,214	6,756	4,810	14,224	4,011
Jakarta, Indonesia	17,810	3,315	9,047	9,486	3,957	19,185	11,922	11,823	2,194	14,098	12,646	14,810	18,434	2,818	17,722	18,311	9,220	2,629	15,642	3,860
Jamestown, St. Helena	9,749	13,621	17,429	3,133	15,444	7,349	7,474	7,851	12,047	13,179	5,487	12,056	6,925	14,687	5,630	9,152	3,119	14,549	10,853	13,622
Jamnagar, India	14,571	4,418	13,035	8,298	8,703	14,082	6,938	6,914	7,041	13,106	7,564	12,764	13,335	5,921	13,071	14,448	6,400	5,875	12,628	4,343
Jan Mayen Island	7,356	8,664	12,336	11,837	13,027	7,779	2,193	1,820	13,758	6,633	4,160	5,823	7,221	10,196	7,943	7,353	9,506	10,328	5,402	8,116
Jayapura, Indonesia	14,497	4,114	5,295	12,768	926	16,859	13,627	13,342	3,813	11,012	15,252	12,063	17,327	2,359	18,565	15,092	12,977	2,341	13,228	4,513
Jefferson City, Missouri	2,002	12,682	9,298	13,913	13,805	3,998	6,714	6,571	17,158	2,387	7,356	1,284	4,097	13,240	5,480	2,377	13,002	13,435	380	12,167
Jerusalem, Israel	11,507	7,613	15,751	7,481	12,260	10,531	3,814	3,941	10,421	11,739	3,992	10,862	9,779	9,302	9,498	11,214	5,009	9,293	10,205	7,345
Jiggalong, Australia	17,188	5,211	7,599	9,652	2,695	18,367	14,347	14,246	745	14,113	14,901	15,205	18,950	3,916	17,835	17,691	10,288	3,743	16,380	5,771
Jinan, China	13,141	1,545	8,547	12,849	5,884	14,768	8,642	8,365	6,820	9,799	10,339	10,171	14,391	2,869	15,269	13,518	11,159	3,002	10,823	1,012
Jodhpur, India	14,327	4,069	12,671	8,812	8,546	14,077	6,834	6,776	7,147	12,639	7,629	12,350	13,342	5,651	13,204	14,260	6,878	5,622	12,286	3,943
Johannesburg, South Africa	13,427	10,667	16,161	1,264	11,843	11,019	9,136	9,460	8,420	16,706	7,619	15,513	10,603	11,256	9,304	12,831	1,675	11,091	14,318	10,885
Juazeiro do Norte, Brazil	6,055	16,606	14,628	6,606	18,014	3,630	7,363	7,665	15,416	9,696	5,625	8,723	3,352	18,230	1,971	5,463	6,836	18,160	7,604	16,295
Juneau, Alaska	5,611	9,062	7,540	16,629	10,614	7,711	7,055	6,726	13,602	2,373	8,689	2,596	7,722	9,519	9,079	6,072	14,513	9,713	3,470	8,587
Kabul, Afghanistan	13,345	4,444	12,838	9,243	9,188	13,218	5,933	5,850	8,075	11,795	6,901	11,426	12,500	6,146	12,508	13,290	7,093	6,149	11,314	4,190
Kalgoorlie, Australia	17,018	6,025	7,646	9,233	3,103	17,604	14,981	14,918	1,010	14,459	15,260	15,617	18,135	4,719	17,075	17,401	10,150	4,550	16,823	6,586
Kaliningrad, USSR	9,163	8,113	14,148	9,822	12,998	8,897	1,619	1,500	12,423	8,936	3,205	8,081	8,203	9,852	8,463	9,013	7,385	9,926	7,519	7,650
Kamloops, Canada	4,393	10,298	7,671	16,206	11,431	6,578	7,230	6,949	14,627	1,279	8,587	1,375	6,666	10,675	8,044	4,877	14,569	10,869	2,389	9,827
Kampala, Uganda	13,030	9,047	17,323	4,069	12,199	11,052	6,590	6,857	9,127	14,811	5,581	13,718	10,397	10,262	9,452	12,515	1,726	10,157	12,742	9,055
Kananga, Zaire	12,240	10,356	18,188	3,129	13,143	10,064	6,814	7,135	9,865	14,730	5,397	13,545	9,469	11,505	8,394	11,680	665	11,388	12,432	10,376
Kano, Nigeria	10,077	10,963	18,991	5,189	15,014	8,211	4,507	4,862	12,082	12,224	2,900	11,044	7,517	12,527	6,734	9,572	3,082	12,475	9,953	10,768
Kanpur, India	14,559	3,339	11,944	9,348	7,872	14,609	7,320	7,225	6,712	12,446	8,258	12,300	13,892	4,931	13,858	14,574	7,526	4,908	12,383	3,224
Kansas City, Missouri	2,128	12,536	9,101	14,130	13,588	4,191	6,822	6,667	16,943	2,171	7,520	1,071	4,305	13,054	5,689	2,536	13,202	13,249	403	12,027
Kaohsiung, Taiwan	14,351	724	7,897	12,436	4,412	16,258	10,127	9,873	5,304	10,756	11,695	11,332	15,948	1,298	16,853	14,808	11,270	1,418	12,136	960
Karachi, Pakistan	14,187	4,603	13,291	8,293	9,073	13,679	6,534	6,514	7,447	12,881	7,168	12,477	12,932	6,239	12,695	14,051	6,289	6,202	12,289	4,564
Karaganda, USSR	11,899	4,569	12,031	10,731	9,475	12,281	5,149	4,955	9,190	10,064	6,618	9,736	11,639	6,319	12,009	11,949	8,410	6,384	9,727	4,127
Karl-Marx-Stadt, East Germany	8,865	8,739	14,667	9,404	13,639	8,397	1,127	1,156	12,848	9,023	2,536	8,082	7,684	10,486	7,863	8,662	7,017	10,554	7,405	8,288
Kasanga, Tanzania	13,243	9,583	17,206	3,106	12,137	11,063	7,415	7,705	8,869	15,546	6,200	14,393	10,473	10,611	9,384	12,685	984	10,483	13,328	9,662
Kashgar, China	13,059	3,948	12,121	10,056	8,820	13,280	6,020	5,879	8,128	11,150	7,233	10,884	12,600	5,698	12,795	13,087	7,904	5,727	10,898	3,616
Kassel, West Germany	8,621	8,936	14,629	9,482	13,826	8,160	883	921	13,092	8,837	2,404	7,879	7,450	10,678	7,651	8,417	7,122	10,750	7,182	8,477
Kathmandu, Nepal	14,533	2,850	11,442	9,810	7,482	14,834	7,551	7,428	6,563	12,158	8,610	12,102	14,141	4,481	14,217	14,611	8,030	4,470	12,282	2,715
Kayes, Mali	7,951	12,708	17,507	6,218	17,172	6,034	4,175	4,546	14,195	10,523	2,158	9,322	5,339	14,405	4,602	7,425	4,776	14,391	8,150	12,400
Kazan, USSR	10,529	6,301	13,104	10,576	11,193	10,608	3,411	3,229	10,803	9,434	4,943	8,836	9,941	8,042	10,270	10,483	7,887	8,114	8,563	5,842
Kemi, Finland	8,801	7,627	12,899	11,070	12,337	9,014	2,231	1,918	12,459	7,966	4,167	7,240	8,390	9,286	8,910	8,765	8,620	9,391	6,870	7,111
Kenora, Canada	3,252	11,480	9,334	14,378	13,257	5,042	6,017	5,810	16,334	2,315	7,037	1,191	4,996	12,185	6,346	3,577	12,966	12,378	895	10,952
Kerguelen Island	16,229	9,133	11,792	4,489	7,880	14,120	13,135	13,386	4,679	18,646	11,930	19,200	14,056	8,670	12,681	15,777	5,960	8,476	18,336	9,623
Kerkira, Greece	9,874	8,682	15,769	8,141	13,541	9,006	2,222	2,404	12,031	10,369	2,537	9,396	8,260	10,434	8,144	9,588	5,709	10,461	8,645	8,315
Kermanshah, Iran	12,171	6,474	14,707	8,124	11,171	11,483	4,419	4,451	9,605	11,757	4,988	11,043	10,738	8,172	10,566	11,957	5,720	8,169	10,571	6,205
Khabarovsk, USSR	11,247	3,413	7,657	14,633	6,599	13,122	8,237	7,895	8,403	7,826	10,186	8,243	12,901	4,182	14,041	11,671	12,628	4,362	8,986	2,948
Kharkov, USSR	10,346	7,160	14,155	9,461	12,074	10,046	2,755	2,682	11,240	9,852	3,997	9,095	9,337	8,919	9,491	10,204	6,981	8,972	8,627	6,742
Khartoum, Sudan	12,251	8,420	17,023	5,681	12,451	10,701	5,090	5,316	9,866	13,297	4,488	12,295	9,973	9,918	9,323	11,830	3,223	9,858	11,455	8,290
Khon Kaen, Thailand	15,721	1,318	9,624	10,517	5,298	16,823	9,661	9,500	4,717	12,432	10,803	12,800	16,203	2,435	16,410	16,026	9,341	2,379	13,370	1,668
Kiev, USSR	9,988	7,559	14,333	9,419	12,472	9,638	2,351	2,294	11,635	9,664	3,610	8,856	8,927	9,316	9,082	9,829	6,945	9,372	8,333	7,133
Kigali, Rwanda	12,872	9,404	17,559	3,741	12,422	10,822	6,704	6,988	9,276	14,881	5,573	13,755	10,185	10,587	9,195	12,340	1,357	10,477	12,733	9,421
Kingston, Canada	2,731	12,482	10,643	12,899	14,752	3,851	5,310	5,196	17,671	3,603	5,915	2,401	3,659	13,440	4,954	2,802	11,669	13,627	1,258	11,927
Kingston, Jamaica	1,100	15,328	10,631	11,578	15,732	1,351	7,331	7,360	18,703	4,753	7,029	3,914	1,747	15,952	3,029	505	11,428	16,146	3,010	14,787
Kingstown, Saint Vincent	2,851	15,949	12,306	9,888	17,442	685	6,681	6,815	18,604	6,395	5,860	5,425	99	17,169	1,335	2,257	9,689	17,351	4,341	15,388
Kinshasa, Zaire	11,439	11,016	18,914	3,295	13,950	9,256	6,429	6,773	10,655	14,074	4,839	12,877	8,661	12,248	7,590	10,875	1,184	12,138	11,732	10,992
Kirkwall, United Kingdom	7,665	9,212	13,703	10,483	13,922	7,533	831	455	13,860	7,677	2,839	6,726	6,875	10,881	7,323	7,527	8,194	10,984	6,070	8,702
Kirov, USSR	10,313	6,314	12,866	10,652	11,176	10,492	3,378	3,165	10,950	9,131	5,013	8,550	9,842	8,039	10,235	10,289	8,179	8,120	8,306	5,837
Kiruna, Sweden	8,532	7,772	12,732	11,285	12,417	8,810	2,219	1,880	12,682	7,675	4,203	6,945	8,202	9,405	8,772	8,509	8,848	9,517	6,580	7,247
Kisangani, Zaire	12,268	9,795	18,141	3,875	13,008	10,240	6,249	6,551	9,881	14,355	5,015	13,208	9,594	11,062	8,632	11,738	1,395	10,961	12,161	9,770
Kishinev, USSR	10,095	7,755	14,728	9,022	12,663	9,596	2,365	2,374	11,614	9,966	3,394	9,119	8,871	9,515	8,941	9,901	6,550	9,561	8,541	7,352
Kitchner, Canada	2,542	12,502	10,323	13,164	14,521	3,880	5,618	5,494	17,581	3,293	6,247	2,094	3,756	13,374	5,085	2,679	11,988	13,563	931	11,954
Knoxville, Tennessee	1,667	13,222	9,996	13,126	14,589	3,302	6,382	6,287	17,939	3,166	6,801	2,067	3,339	13,923	4,718	1,864	12,288	14,117	946	12,686
Kosice, Czechoslovakia	9,510	8,255	14,775	9,155	13,169	9,007	1,768	1,793	12,212	9,543	2,915	8,645	8,285	10,013	8,396	9,307	6,714	10,068	8,013	7,830
Kota Kinabalu, Malaysia	16,118	1,920	8,090	11,088	3,460	18,153	11,438	11,248	3,423	12,416	12,652	13,122	17,770	1,161	18,256	16,627	10,501	986	13,999	2,481
Krakow, Poland	9,354	8,301	14,655	9,306	13,212	8,896	1,631	1,633	12,344	9,362	2,897	8,464	8,180	10,056	8,327	9,160	6,872	10,116	7,837	7,865
Kralendijk, Bonaire	2,205	16,098	11,544	10,458	16,681	236	7,238	7,338	18,585	5,871	6,565	4,995	814	16,993	1,927	1,611	10,413	17,187	4,008	15,536
Krasnodar, USSR	10,857	7,015	14,457	8,987	11,904	10,412	3,168	3,146	10,808	10,441	4,149	9,682	9,687	8,773	9,730	10,686	6,511	8,808	9,196	6,638
Krasnoyarsk, USSR	11,456	4,018	10,609	12,183	8,698	12,399	5,828	5,552	9,176	9,017	7,577	8,901	11,870	5,635	12,541	11,641	9,891	5,745	9,137	3,481
Kristiansand, Norway	8,307	8,701	13,868	10,251	13,499	8,137	1,031	765	13,232	8,181	2,968	7,278	7,464	10,402	7,839	8,169	7,884	10,494	6,674	8,207
Kuala Lumpur, Malaysia	17,166	2,534	9,661	9,590	4,771	18,050	10,758	10,650	3,359	13,694	11,589	14,189	17,327	2,728	17,012	17,497	8,877	2,576	14,828	3,018
Kuching, Malaysia	16,892	2,407	8,692	10,287	3,808	18,639	11,475	11,329	2,944	13,209	12,467	13,880	18,043	1,964	17,977	17,374	9,778	1,786	14,704	2,963
Kumasi, Ghana	9,248	12,222	18,852	4,965	16,062	7,189	4,971	5,347	12,873	11,893	3,045	10,692	6,539	13,769	5,618	8,702	3,402	13,710	9,524	12,024
Kumzar, Oman	13,430	5,715	14,279	7,783	10,149	12,669	5,679	5,708	8,360	12,743	6,134	12,144	11,918	7,308	11,623	13,216	5,575	7,275	11,764	5,552
Kunming, China	14,794	1,096	9,709	11,032	5,857	15,914	8,889	8,700	5,649	11,643	10,197	11,922	15,337	2,762	15,737	15,077	9,567	2,774	12,437	1,081
Kuqa Chang, China	13,033	3,423	11,461	10,650	8,332	13,532	6,372	6,193	7,949	10,801	7,726	10,646	12,890	5,183	13,217	13,130	8,546	5,229	10,782	3,042

Distances in Kilometers

	Cancun, Mexico	Canton, China	Canton Atoll, Phoenix Islands	Cape Town, South Africa	Cape York, Australia	Caracas, Venezuela	Cardiff, United Kingdom	Carlisle, United Kingdom	Carnarvon, Australia	Carson City, Nevada	Casablanca, Morocco	Casper, Wyoming	Castries, Saint Lucia	Catbalogan, Philippines	Cayenne, French Guiana	Cayman Islands (Georgetown)	Cazombo, Angola	Cebu, Philippines	Cedar Rapids, Iowa	Changsha, China
Kurgan, USSR	11,119	5,309	12,286	10,859	10,185	11,465	4,384	4,171	10,008	9,511	5,961	9,084	10,829	7,040	11,242	11,148	8,444	7,118	8,993	4,838
Kuwait, Kuwait	12,614	6,477	14,910	7,666	11,025	11,772	4,856	4,917	9,233	12,310	5,236	11,587	11,021	8,122	10,741	12,368	5,304	8,102	11,089	6,260
Kuybyshev, USSR	10,788	6,200	13,243	10,128	11,108	10,799	3,555	3,399	10,587	9,725	4,991	9,127	10,121	7,952	10,397	10,729	7,667	8,015	8,844	5,760
Kyoto, Japan	12,350	2,547	6,893	14,365	5,109	14,436	9,621	9,295	7,025	8,723	11,507	9,336	14,301	2,798	15,505	12,836	12,844	2,989	10,212	2,284
Kzyl-Orda, USSR	12,180	4,936	12,771	9,929	9,837	12,245	4,973	4,840	9,134	10,690	6,217	10,262	11,558	6,695	11,754	12,155	7,604	6,736	10,128	4,559
L'vov, USSR	9,626	8,028	14,590	9,293	12,941	9,191	1,921	1,905	12,054	9,527	3,149	8,660	8,474	9,785	8,612	9,441	6,839	9,842	8,067	7,599
La Ceiba, Honduras	592	15,186	9,555	12,365	14,678	2,232	8,211	8,197	17,674	4,123	8,074	3,529	2,781	15,390	3,953	694	12,453	15,577	2,941	14,697
La Coruna, Spain	7,506	10,544	15,223	8,981	15,430	6,686	985	1,340	14,418	8,563	1,085	7,451	5,954	12,286	6,056	7,203	6,895	12,358	6,523	10,085
La Paz, Bolivia	4,632	19,259	11,369	8,698	15,503	2,989	9,798	9,999	15,424	8,169	8,485	7,643	3,466	18,531	2,941	4,217	9,753	18,556	6,911	18,704
La Paz, Mexico	2,441	12,982	7,274	14,969	12,237	4,830	9,043	8,882	15,598	1,887	9,646	2,104	5,281	12,831	6,548	3,034	14,916	13,011	2,620	12,594
La Ronge, Canada	4,077	10,599	8,794	15,129	12,389	5,977	6,185	5,924	15,394	2,075	7,471	1,365	5,937	11,249	7,283	4,456	13,454	11,442	1,765	10,083
Labrador City, Canada	3,918	11,578	11,246	12,644	14,639	4,708	4,211	4,061	16,886	4,255	5,098	3,106	4,351	12,747	5,489	3,938	11,040	12,921	2,213	11,015
Lagos, Nigeria	9,775	11,740	19,348	4,741	15,511	7,740	5,031	5,401	12,359	12,301	3,214	11,101	7,085	13,252	6,172	9,235	2,962	13,186	9,952	11,568
Lahore, Pakistan	13,834	3,945	12,447	9,322	8,630	13,791	6,503	6,412	7,519	12,039	7,470	11,763	13,075	5,617	13,077	13,809	7,295	5,612	11,735	3,735
Lambasa, Fiji	11,050	8,421	1,794	14,081	4,040	12,855	16,108	15,733	6,854	8,819	17,980	10,011	13,566	6,761	14,253	11,549	15,955	6,787	11,130	8,689
Lansing, Michigan	2,404	12,490	9,990	13,447	14,260	3,961	5,926	5,790	17,426	2,970	6,586	1,776	3,902	13,271	5,256	2,615	12,321	13,463	593	11,950
Lanzhou, China	13,582	1,705	9,715	11,757	6,584	14,760	7,990	7,760	6,823	10,563	9,508	10,755	14,236	3,431	14,831	13,856	9,973	3,507	11,225	1,234
Laoag, Philippines	14,740	939	7,773	12,222	4,000	16,727	10,563	10,319	4,824	11,094	12,075	11,724	16,437	848	17,334	15,219	11,230	944	12,567	1,355
Largeau, Chad	10,865	9,654	17,972	5,737	13,893	9,248	4,213	4,512	11,275	12,383	3,178	11,277	8,521	11,243	7,887	10,418	3,323	11,200	10,313	9,454
Las Vegas, Nevada	3,219	11,712	7,274	15,822	11,818	5,615	8,260	8,039	15,232	526	9,236	1,060	5,899	11,794	7,261	3,790	15,035	11,984	2,123	11,287
Launceston, Australia	14,524	7,954	5,929	10,159	3,432	15,241	17,501	17,362	3,592	12,962	17,636	14,148	15,940	6,316	15,528	14,840	11,809	6,202	15,226	8,473
Le Havre, France	8,031	9,617	14,775	9,415	14,490	7,475	325	635	13,748	8,557	1,875	7,530	6,760	11,352	6,960	7,796	7,157	11,429	6,739	9,150
Leipzig, East Germany	8,809	8,756	14,619	9,459	13,652	8,357	1,079	1,095	12,896	8,957	2,541	8,016	7,646	10,502	7,838	8,609	7,076	10,571	7,341	8,302
Leningrad, USSR	9,386	7,425	13,401	10,456	12,263	9,400	2,271	2,048	12,009	8,684	4,011	7,945	8,739	9,140	9,120	9,309	7,988	9,226	7,535	6,940
Leon, Spain	7,747	10,413	15,391	8,819	15,316	6,891	1,006	1,379	14,189	8,789	1,013	7,684	6,154	12,162	6,212	7,438	6,696	12,228	6,764	9,965
Lerwick, United Kingdom	7,751	9,055	13,596	10,579	13,756	7,669	972	596	13,739	7,662	2,987	6,733	7,016	10,720	7,480	7,626	8,269	10,824	6,109	8,543
Lhasa, China	14,381	2,321	10,868	10,385	7,089	14,982	7,769	7,612	6,496	11,745	8,972	11,783	14,328	4,014	14,554	14,529	8,634	4,022	12,069	2,135
Libreville, Gabon	10,646	11,411	19,712	3,911	14,715	8,519	5,789	6,147	11,465	13,252	4,087	12,052	7,898	12,777	6,886	10,091	2,011	12,686	10,902	11,319
Lilongwe, Malawi	13,705	9,573	16,657	2,698	11,701	11,438	8,089	8,377	8,365	16,208	6,856	15,043	10,891	10,446	9,731	13,130	1,207	10,303	13,954	9,711
Lima, Peru	3,821	18,378	10,457	9,771	14,986	2,734	9,959	10,104	15,761	7,193	8,914	6,771	3,383	17,648	3,319	3,500	10,799	17,741	6,166	17,942
Limerick, Ireland	7,375	9,913	14,265	9,945	14,683	6,975	393	448	14,328	7,869	2,118	6,829	6,284	11,609	6,626	7,167	7,761	11,704	6,033	9,416
Limoges, France	8,204	9,761	15,191	9,000	14,665	7,490	710	1,049	13,655	8,912	1,551	7,862	6,760	11,511	6,859	7,934	6,751	11,576	7,029	9,314
Limon, Costa Rica	1,295	15,940	9,925	11,681	15,058	1,766	8,441	8,471	17,609	4,869	8,060	4,286	2,439	16,109	3,433	1,044	11,958	16,293	3,643	15,445
Lincoln, Nebraska	2,377	12,283	8,962	14,354	13,369	4,453	6,815	6,644	16,702	1,974	7,598	830	4,558	12,792	5,940	2,796	13,348	12,986	438	11,776
Linz, Austria	9,062	8,754	14,934	9,116	13,666	8,496	1,303	1,395	12,703	9,311	2,444	8,359	7,773	10,509	7,884	8,838	6,722	10,568	7,660	8,320
Lisbon, Portugal	7,526	10,914	15,658	8,530	15,824	6,504	1,494	1,857	14,484	8,864	583	7,723	5,759	12,668	5,739	7,178	6,516	12,729	6,736	10,474
Little Rock, Arkansas	1,603	13,060	9,226	13,782	13,895	3,720	7,020	6,895	17,302	2,487	7,549	1,512	3,888	13,544	5,269	2,021	13,052	13,739	804	12,552
Liverpool, United Kingdom	7,740	9,561	14,302	9,895	14,366	7,359	214	163	13,943	8,095	2,230	7,087	6,666	11,268	6,985	7,542	7,644	11,358	6,336	9,071
Lodz, Poland	9,245	8,275	14,484	9,491	13,179	8,851	1,564	1,526	12,418	9,186	2,964	8,298	8,142	10,025	8,331	9,065	7,059	10,090	7,688	7,828
Lome, Togo	9,563	11,970	19,164	4,789	15,742	7,508	5,046	5,419	12,563	12,159	3,176	10,957	6,858	13,491	5,933	9,019	3,118	13,427	9,798	11,791
London, United Kingdom	7,969	9,513	14,553	9,635	14,364	7,500	214	421	13,761	8,384	2,076	7,373	6,795	11,239	7,048	7,754	7,366	11,321	6,610	9,037
Londonderry, United Kingdom	7,440	9,686	14,051	10,155	14,429	7,141	477	282	14,199	7,767	2,376	6,754	6,463	11,371	6,850	7,257	7,936	11,469	6,005	9,183
Longlac, Canada	3,179	11,698	9,900	13,816	13,784	4,717	5,565	5,381	16,741	2,865	6,495	1,700	4,596	12,532	5,916	3,413	12,403	12,722	955	11,155
Lord Howe Island, Australia	13,450	7,774	4,415	11,673	2,872	14,759	17,362	17,052	4,491	11,464	18,756	12,660	15,511	6,024	15,613	13,872	13,317	5,959	13,778	8,223
Los Angeles, California	3,405	11,667	6,920	16,054	11,525	5,823	8,616	8,390	14,947	583	9,604	1,425	6,146	11,648	7,493	3,989	15,386	11,835	2,481	11,264
Louangphrabang, Laos	15,368	1,206	9,724	10,667	5,566	16,441	9,313	9,144	5,103	12,157	10,510	12,478	15,832	2,593	16,105	15,655	9,364	2,565	13,013	1,436
Louisville, Kentucky	1,899	12,930	9,850	13,373	14,350	3,603	6,331	6,216	17,663	2,942	6,857	1,809	3,628	13,622	5,004	2,142	12,447	13,816	652	12,396
Luanda, Angola	11,396	11,416	18,612	2,832	14,011	9,131	6,865	7,217	10,643	14,269	5,185	13,067	8,577	12,559	7,433	10,818	1,109	12,438	11,893	11,424
Lubumbashi, Zaire	12,974	10,095	17,368	2,630	12,431	10,722	7,598	7,907	9,096	15,575	6,238	14,390	10,165	11,073	9,022	12,400	502	10,938	13,272	10,186
Lusaka, Zambia	13,179	10,178	17,037	2,277	12,224	10,874	8,018	8,329	8,850	15,943	6,629	14,750	10,349	11,057	9,160	12,596	703	10,913	13,611	10,306
Luxembourg, Luxembourg	8,450	9,235	14,817	9,330	14,129	7,906	694	853	13,314	8,837	2,104	7,844	7,189	10,979	7,360	8,223	7,007	11,050	7,097	8,779
Luxor, Egypt	11,678	8,043	16,391	6,766	12,504	10,457	4,166	4,349	10,347	12,277	3,968	11,336	9,707	9,676	9,278	11,328	4,291	9,649	10,589	7,822
Lynn Lake, Canada	4,136	10,581	9,108	14,852	12,595	5,920	5,857	5,599	15,503	2,395	7,150	1,602	5,833	11,314	7,158	4,476	13,133	11,506	1,785	10,053
Lyon, France	8,477	9,523	15,238	8,928	14,434	7,767	871	1,156	13,375	9,104	1,714	8,072	7,036	11,277	7,114	8,212	6,636	11,338	7,265	9,085
Macapa, Brazil	4,528	16,941	13,425	8,130	18,119	2,103	7,249	7,483	16,808	8,187	5,865	7,254	1,896	18,628	560	3,938	8,268	18,739	6,175	16,452
Madison, Wisconsin	2,445	12,320	9,599	13,836	13,879	4,215	6,203	6,048	17,101	2,573	6,944	1,379	4,212	13,009	5,579	2,741	12,712	13,203	223	11,790
Madras, India	15,967	3,652	12,044	8,358	7,357	15,561	8,432	8,395	5,545	13,860	9,025	13,776	14,810	4,846	14,429	15,905	6,916	4,760	13,854	3,777
Madrid, Spain	7,949	10,427	15,674	8,536	15,340	7,000	1,234	1,611	14,024	9,072	829	7,962	6,256	12,184	6,241	7,623	6,405	12,240	7,028	9,995
Madurai, India	16,196	4,010	12,287	7,951	7,481	15,546	8,550	8,538	5,448	14,265	9,013	14,143	14,795	5,112	14,300	16,076	6,572	5,014	14,164	4,164
Magadan, USSR	9,658	4,998	7,656	15,542	7,827	11,543	7,471	7,101	9,957	6,326	9,487	6,665	11,363	5,724	12,569	10,075	13,214	5,910	7,389	4,510
Magdalena, Bolivia	4,544	18,889	11,840	8,518	16,059	2,654	9,266	9,476	15,772	8,186	7,929	7,562	3,044	19,041	2,405	4,075	9,398	19,095	6,743	18,332
Magdeburg, East Germany	8,732	8,761	14,527	9,559	13,649	8,315	1,026	1,012	12,954	8,852	2,575	7,914	7,608	10,502	7,824	8,540	7,179	10,574	7,246	8,301
Majuro Atoll, Marshall Isls.	10,969	6,431	2,199	15,942	3,747	13,305	13,484	13,108	7,170	7,707	15,491	8,862	13,810	5,107	15,018	11,560	16,522	5,212	10,070	6,534
Malabo, Equatorial Guinea	10,441	11,326	19,898	4,290	14,869	8,379	5,410	5,768	11,690	12,929	3,718	11,732	7,735	12,759	6,783	9,898	2,329	12,679	10,596	11,202
Male, Maldives	16,497	4,772	12,799	7,134	7,816	15,359	8,740	8,776	5,391	15,038	8,940	14,816	14,626	5,726	13,930	16,250	5,870	5,609	14,698	4,964
Manado, Indonesia	15,772	2,702	7,079	11,620	2,372	18,162	12,385	12,165	3,157	12,065	13,711	12,935	18,177	1,137	19,234	16,349	11,358	981	13,960	3,216
Managua, Nicaragua	995	15,568	9,584	12,109	14,721	2,122	8,483	8,487	17,500	4,454	8,236	3,913	2,749	15,683	3,818	949	12,346	15,866	3,346	15,087
Manama, Bahrain	13,043	6,291	14,828	7,473	10,721	12,144	5,288	5,352	8,823	12,698	5,605	12,002	11,392	7,890	11,055	12,789	5,176	7,858	11,521	6,114
Manaus, Brazil	3,963	17,681	12,406	8,752	17,104	1,691	8,074	8,273	16,833	7,688	6,837	6,890	1,900	18,915	1,235	3,410	9,173	19,109	5,931	17,134
Manchester, New Hampshire	2,811	12,669	11,057	12,472	15,163	3,628	5,061	4,975	17,941	4,026	5,548	2,825	3,365	13,718	4,619	2,788	11,254	13,902	1,662	12,109
Mandalay, Burma	15,223	1,769	10,364	10,284	6,224	15,965	8,739	8,590	5,521	12,279	9,866	12,469	15,309	3,264	15,471	15,428	8,825	3,237	12,877	1,834
Mangareva Island, Fr.Polynesia	7,162	13,117	4,550	13,096	8,803	8,287	14,843	14,726	10,918	7,074	14,795	7,872	9,037	11,551	9,478	7,475	15,447	11,593	8,472	13,275
Manila, Philippines	15,036	1,248	7,665	12,054	3,666	17,099	10,927	10,691	4,437	11,355	12,393	12,032	16,834	524	17,728	15,535	11,207	569	12,908	1,721
Mannheim, West Germany	8,615	9,090	14,834	9,290	13,990	8,073	857	982	13,145	8,953	2,203	7,973	7,355	10,838	7,514	8,391	6,945	10,905	7,242	8,639
Maputo, Mozambique	13,866	10,245	15,897	1,623	11,431	11,462	9,268	9,578	8,008	17,058	7,843	15,857	11,036	10,809	9,745	13,269	1,860	10,643	14,675	10,477
Mar del Plata, Argentina	7,223	18,141	11,902	6,671	14,226	5,457	11,236	11,531	12,985	10,649	9,465	10,221	5,769	17,088	4,784	6,815	8,372	16,933	9,509	18,614
Maracaibo, Venezuela	1,989	16,231	11,177	10,671	16,310	515	7,596	7,684	18,341	5,705	6,963	4,898	1,213	16,936	2,218	1,419	10,740	17,131	3,983	15,676
Marrakech, Morocco	7,783	11,312	16,393	7,767	16,203	6,471	2,241	2,614	14,318	9,477	223	8,308	5,719	13,071	5,483	7,376	5,835	13,110	7,259	10,912
Marseilles, France	8,597	9,617	15,518	8,653	14,530	7,787	1,118	1,422	13,302	9,341	1,558	8,295	7,048	11,375	7,060	8,310	6,365	11,428	7,461	9,193
Maseru, Lesotho	13,423	10,853	15,909	1,000	11,770	11,003	9,443	9,773	8,353	16,836	7,885	15,661	10,622	11,358	9,299	12,828	1,987	11,187	14,456	11,094
Mashhad, Iran	12,735	5,323	13,597	8,873	10,081	12,394	5,145	5,096	8,833	11,648	6,016	11,125	11,664	7,036	11,623	12,616	6,582	7,041	10,860	5,045
Mazatlan, Mexico	2,040	13,332	7,633	14,566	12,629	4,421	8,885	8,745	15,969	2,173	9,382	2,177	4,880	13,230	6,140	2,631	14,533	13,411	2,490	12,928
Mbabane, Swaziland	13,730	10,392	15,962	1,485	11,553	11,323	9,252	9,567	8,130	16,965	7,794	15,766	10,903	10,957	9,608	13,133	1,816	10,790	14,578	10,622
Mbandaka, Zaire	11,572	10,524	18,887	3,762	13,752	9,490	6,047	6,378	10,561	13,927	4,593	12,746	8,857	11,827	7,867	11,029	1,418	11,729	11,644	10,473
McMurdo Sound, Antarctica	12,721	11,662	8,410	7,439	7,534	12,003	17,065	17,437	6,430	13,877	15,106	14,579	12,498	10,227	11,650	12,647	9,797	10,082	14,838	12,221
Mecca, Saudi Arabia	12,546	7,484	16,045	6,534	11,746	11,285	4,981	5,137	9,482	12,968	4,828	12,089	10,538	9,041	10,040	12,196	4,128	8,997	11,400	7,324
Medan, Indonesia	17,209	2,672	10,000	9,337	5,104	17,790	10,516	10,422	3,539	13,858	11,288	14,286	17,052	3,028	16,676	17,473	8,559	2,884	14,853	3,118
Medellin, Colombia	2,040	16,619	10,727	10,767	15,821	1,064	8,250	8,335	17,728	5,732	7,595	5,054	1,813	17,006	2,580	1,575	11,077	17,193	4,266	16,085
Medicine Hat, Canada	3,836	10,822	8,239	15,538	12,120	5,938	6,840	6,585	15,306	1,406	8,063	867	5,996	11,299	7,370	4,285	14,037	11,494	1,716	10,331
Medina, Saudi Arabia	12,331	7,410	15,901	6,839	11,797	11,168	4,705	4,847	9,663	12,643	4,666	11,778	10,418	9,010	9,986	12,002	4,415	8,976	11,113	7,222
Melbourne, Australia	14,751	7,520	5,869	10,338	3,015	15,624	17,107	16,947	3,291	12,921	17,511	14,119	16,335	5,878	15,964	15,105	11,862	5,764	15,243	8,037
Memphis, Tennessee	1,584	13,109	9,443	13,607	14,083	3,597	6,848	6,730	17,481	2,665	7,348	1,645	3,733	13,651	5,116	1,951	12,847	13,846	773	12,592
Merauke, Indonesia	14,796	4,573	5,348	12,313	342	17,037	14,195	13,925	3,365	11,455	15,711	12,547	17,627	2,816	18,582	15,382	12,757	2,761	13,733	5,013
Merida, Mexico	299	14,539	9,306	12,907	14,365	2,690	7,969	7,918	17,611	3,511	8,041	2,883	3,130	14,791	4,400	880	12,801	14,981	2,338	14,052
Meridian, Mississippi	1,260	13,439	9,523	13,376	14,277	3,296	6,977	6,878	17,696	2,893	7,367	1,935	3,470	13,963	4,849	1,622	12,734	14,158	1,098	12,923
Messina, Italy	9,600	9,090	16,022	7,988	13,946	8,644	2,084	2,321	12,348	10,306	2,144	9,290	7,895	10,842	7,747	9,291	5,596	10,869	8,483	8,724
Mexico City, Mexico	1,309	14,141	8,296	13,703	13,372	3,598	8,744	8,653	16,605	2,954	8,983	2,685	4,104	14,093	5,320	1,866	13,789	14,275	2,601	13,714
Miami, Florida	844	14,406	10,301	12,312	15,248	2,194	6,927	6,902	18,637	3,968	6,940	3,039	2,389	15,051	3,759	727	11,880	15,245	2,083	13,870
Midway Islands, USA	8,989	6,896	3,487	18,393	6,102	11,414	11,158	10,784	9,437	5,387	13,079	6,453	11,735	6,252	13,092	9,580	17,249	6,421	7,641	6,734
Milan, Italy	8,810	9,237	15,280	8,840	14,151	8,103	1,134	1,356	13,034	9,340	1,945	8,333	7,370	10,995	7,424	8,549	6,500	11,050	7,556	8,810

Distances in Kilometers	Cancun, Mexico	Canton, China	Canton Atoll, Phoenix Islands	Cape Town, South Africa	Cape York, Australia	Caracas, Venezuela	Cardiff, United Kingdom	Carlisle, United Kingdom	Carnarvon, Australia	Carson City, Nevada	Casablanca, Morocco	Casper, Wyoming	Castries, Saint Lucia	Catbalogan, Philippines	Cayenne, French Guiana	Cayman Islands (Georgetown)	Cazombo, Angola	Cebu, Philippines	Cedar Rapids, Iowa	Changsha, China
Milford Sound, New Zealand	12,837	9,320	5,046	10,778	4,469	13,590	18,991	18,684	5,306	11,773	18,725	12,892	14,315	7,592	14,139	13,130	12,824	7,511	13,830	9,794
Milwaukee, Wisconsin	2,432	12,368	9,718	13,719	13,993	4,140	6,114	5,964	17,198	2,694	6,833	1,499	4,120	13,085	5,484	2,703	12,593	13,278	331	11,834
Minsk, USSR	9,609	7,687	14,078	9,769	12,587	9,365	2,080	1,969	11,955	9,229	3,557	8,422	8,668	9,434	8,905	9,471	7,305	9,502	7,912	7,236
Mogadiscio, Somalia	14,220	7,666	15,917	4,882	10,837	12,409	7,097	7,294	7,932	15,195	6,512	14,283	11,726	8,830	10,853	13,751	2,929	8,722	13,500	7,716
Mombasa, Kenya	13,946	8,523	16,467	3,972	11,330	11,913	7,373	7,616	8,209	15,601	6,481	14,559	11,277	9,589	10,279	13,422	2,044	9,468	13,628	8,602
Monclova, Mexico	1,622	13,340	8,213	14,274	13,132	4,047	8,251	8,120	16,522	2,181	8,736	1,824	4,429	13,441	5,742	2,215	13,997	13,629	1,894	12,894
Moncton, Canada	3,414	12,337	11,536	12,160	15,316	3,951	4,428	4,345	17,644	4,484	4,973	3,286	3,575	13,524	4,718	3,340	10,774	13,699	2,192	11,774
Monrovia, Liberia	8,310	13,130	17,881	5,413	17,055	6,190	5,058	5,432	13,777	11,178	3,041	9,985	5,556	14,734	4,603	7,750	4,237	14,686	8,790	12,889
Monte Carlo, Monaco	8,738	9,450	15,473	8,671	14,363	7,953	1,174	1,447	13,147	9,406	1,717	8,375	7,215	11,209	7,230	8,458	6,357	11,261	7,562	9,029
Monterrey, Mexico	1,474	13,516	8,294	14,119	13,247	3,897	8,285	8,164	16,620	2,355	8,715	1,983	4,297	13,609	5,599	2,069	13,897	13,796	1,975	13,068
Montevideo, Uruguay	6,991	18,355	12,124	6,687	14,592	5,149	10,876	11,168	13,306	10,485	9,120	10,002	5,436	17,442	4,426	6,562	8,273	17,282	9,249	18,753
Montgomery, Alabama	1,247	13,523	9,747	13,170	14,495	3,136	6,817	6,730	17,910	3,099	7,163	2,105	3,278	14,108	4,659	1,531	12,509	14,302	1,166	12,999
Montpelier, Vermont	2,879	12,521	10,956	12,614	15,006	3,781	5,053	4,954	17,782	3,913	5,608	2,711	3,529	13,556	4,786	2,887	11,356	13,739	1,571	11,961
Montpellier, France	8,470	9,707	15,467	8,710	14,621	7,667	1,026	1,348	13,428	9,236	1,489	8,184	6,930	11,465	6,957	8,183	6,441	11,520	7,342	9,278
Montreal, Canada	2,958	12,375	10,865	12,744	14,858	3,932	5,042	4,930	17,627	3,815	5,661	2,615	3,687	13,398	4,946	2,993	11,447	13,582	1,504	11,816
Moosonee, Canada	3,388	11,652	10,325	13,457	14,060	4,693	5,126	4,951	16,832	3,305	6,051	2,148	4,495	12,599	5,770	3,549	11,973	12,785	1,332	11,100
Moroni, Comoros	14,615	8,537	15,845	3,526	10,763	12,428	8,305	8,548	7,508	16,534	7,356	15,482	11,847	9,386	10,737	14,059	2,223	9,244	14,519	8,698
Moscow, USSR	10,012	7,025	13,582	10,101	11,917	9,940	2,699	2,537	11,432	9,271	4,232	8,562	9,259	8,767	9,552	9,922	7,622	8,838	8,169	6,567
Mosul, Iraq	11,757	6,796	14,868	8,190	11,544	11,068	4,002	4,042	10,027	11,464	4,588	10,707	10,324	8,513	10,179	11,537	5,747	8,517	10,196	6,501
Mount Isa, Australia	15,240	5,626	5,647	11,330	1,153	16,986	15,315	15,089	2,691	12,341	16,486	13,503	17,732	3,935	17,849	15,764	12,215	3,834	14,710	6,121
Multan, Pakistan	13,871	4,208	12,742	9,024	8,831	13,688	6,419	6,349	7,573	12,240	7,297	11,915	12,961	5,856	12,896	13,812	6,984	5,843	11,831	4,019
Munich, West Germany	8,880	8,946	14,973	9,115	13,856	8,294	1,125	1,252	12,899	9,209	2,271	8,238	7,571	10,700	7,685	8,649	6,744	10,761	7,514	8,508
Murcia, Spain	8,228	10,393	15,997	8,213	15,300	7,182	1,511	1,884	13,779	9,419	759	8,306	6,434	12,153	6,335	7,883	6,062	12,199	7,363	9,981
Murmansk, USSR	8,932	7,235	12,436	11,472	11,879	9,318	2,723	2,397	12,192	7,806	4,673	7,162	8,722	8,863	9,312	8,942	9,006	8,975	6,895	6,707
Mururoa Atoll, Fr. Polynesia	7,399	12,687	4,121	13,384	8,414	8,634	14,991	14,843	10,637	7,045	15,103	7,907	9,381	11,128	9,867	7,742	15,780	11,172	8,578	12,844
Muscat, Oman	13,801	5,554	14,159	7,657	9,874	12,999	6,048	6,080	8,002	13,053	6,459	12,486	12,247	7,098	11,905	13,582	5,528	7,056	12,127	5,428
Myitkyina, Burma	14,839	1,628	10,242	10,610	6,310	15,691	8,532	8,364	5,828	11,887	9,753	12,071	15,063	3,259	15,334	15,059	9,065	3,257	12,489	1,578
Naga, Philippines	14,968	1,483	7,416	12,201	3,433	17,117	11,139	10,895	4,384	11,266	12,632	11,982	16,913	277	17,894	15,486	11,423	377	12,893	1,929
Nagasaki, Japan	12,884	1,956	7,292	13,775	4,997	14,894	9,608	9,300	6,612	9,288	11,418	9,865	14,697	2,385	15,822	13,354	12,310	2,567	10,702	1,703
Nagoya, Japan	12,264	2,652	6,806	14,472	5,112	14,367	9,647	9,318	7,084	8,629	11,544	9,252	14,245	2,863	15,463	12,754	12,949	3,054	10,138	2,392
Nagpur, India	15,083	3,522	12,124	8,857	7,772	14,916	7,671	7,607	6,315	13,047	8,447	12,898	14,179	4,981	13,995	15,056	7,153	4,932	12,952	3,504
Nairobi, Kenya	13,533	8,686	16,833	4,090	11,702	11,548	6,956	7,206	8,625	15,188	6,041	14,130	10,897	9,837	9,937	13,018	1,937	9,725	13,189	8,727
Nanchang, China	13,985	671	8,461	12,365	5,213	15,659	9,324	9,072	5,930	10,543	10,905	10,990	15,268	2,094	16,080	14,383	10,932	2,200	11,688	291
Nancy, France	8,483	9,278	14,919	9,229	14,178	7,900	741	933	13,302	8,919	2,027	7,918	7,180	11,026	7,328	8,248	6,909	11,093	7,160	8,827
Nandi, Fiji	11,297	8,316	2,039	13,867	3,846	13,073	16,265	15,889	6,607	9,073	18,185	10,266	13,789	6,635	14,440	11,792	15,704	6,653	11,387	8,603
Nanjing, China	13,526	1,130	8,268	12,782	5,363	15,257	9,161	8,890	6,323	10,079	10,826	10,527	14,907	2,332	15,806	13,933	11,260	2,465	11,238	704
Nanning, China	14,878	507	9,114	11,383	5,256	16,283	9,431	9,225	5,307	11,523	10,797	11,919	15,769	2,141	16,292	15,229	10,064	2,161	12,544	758
Nantes, France	7,961	9,859	14,996	9,205	14,746	7,304	491	858	13,874	8,653	1,593	7,599	6,581	11,601	6,733	7,701	6,983	11,673	6,765	9,399
Naples, Italy	9,379	9,079	15,754	8,288	13,967	8,515	1,787	2,012	12,532	9,998	2,090	8,990	7,770	10,837	7,692	9,089	5,905	10,873	8,201	8,691
Narvik, Norway	8,400	7,871	12,691	11,349	12,489	8,694	2,186	1,836	12,804	7,557	4,184	6,818	8,091	9,494	8,677	8,379	8,921	9,607	6,447	7,342
Nashville, Tennessee	1,666	13,116	9,740	13,373	14,338	3,477	6,555	6,446	17,704	2,914	7,030	1,831	3,553	13,752	4,935	1,942	12,545	13,947	772	12,588
Nassau, Bahamas	1,057	14,552	10,586	12,025	15,543	1,955	6,787	6,779	18,923	4,251	6,717	3,296	2,105	15,275	3,480	763	11,588	15,470	2,291	14,007
Natal, Brazil	6,365	16,140	15,104	6,330	18,163	3,948	7,043	7,358	15,237	9,947	5,244	8,929	3,593	17,749	2,242	5,770	6,415	17,681	7,780	15,850
Natashquan, Canada	3,897	11,869	11,656	12,189	15,097	4,427	4,018	3,909	17,166	4,630	4,739	3,456	4,014	13,109	5,096	3,842	10,641	13,279	2,463	11,306
Nauru Island	11,731	6,367	2,393	14,982	2,932	13,978	14,281	13,909	6,328	8,615	16,298	9,786	14,551	4,843	15,646	12,311	15,831	4,913	10,993	6,568
Ndjamena, Chad	10,729	10,314	18,749	5,107	14,305	8,914	4,669	4,998	11,430	12,658	3,310	11,503	8,213	11,844	7,445	10,238	2,793	11,786	10,459	10,145
Nelson, New Zealand	12,344	9,440	4,517	11,291	4,533	13,256	18,838	18,467	5,741	11,194	19,150	12,313	13,996	7,688	13,961	12,666	13,385	7,625	13,258	9,884
Nema, Mauritania	8,305	12,201	17,736	6,220	16,698	6,472	3,887	4,263	13,853	10,687	1,884	9,487	5,763	13,896	5,084	7,797	4,576	13,883	8,340	11,899
Neuquen, Argentina	6,930	18,245	10,987	7,470	13,667	5,475	11,832	12,098	12,938	10,130	10,170	9,847	5,909	16,735	5,122	6,596	9,270	16,618	9,275	18,809
New Delhi, India	14,241	3,651	12,225	9,284	8,250	14,221	6,934	6,845	7,087	12,300	7,871	12,086	13,502	5,280	13,474	14,231	7,363	5,264	12,108	3,492
New Glasgow, Canada	3,491	12,386	11,710	11,987	15,468	3,910	4,316	4,246	17,682	4,658	4,812	3,460	3,503	13,609	4,614	3,387	10,601	13,781	2,357	11,822
New Haven, Connecticut	2,588	12,845	10,953	12,497	15,177	3,463	5,269	5,189	18,086	3,946	5,707	2,752	3,237	13,854	4,520	2,569	11,355	14,039	1,562	12,286
New Orleans, Louisiana	1,033	13,628	9,365	13,389	14,203	3,226	7,259	7,166	17,624	2,895	7,602	2,035	3,466	14,071	4,832	1,471	12,869	14,265	1,341	13,121
New Plymouth, New Zealand	12,231	9,349	4,264	11,546	4,436	13,239	18,607	18,232	5,818	10,975	19,383	12,103	13,984	7,592	14,017	12,574	13,627	7,536	13,069	9,780
New York, New York	2,483	12,899	10,865	12,551	15,138	3,419	5,382	5,301	18,113	3,871	5,812	2,681	3,217	13,881	4,516	2,476	11,441	14,067	1,483	12,342
Newcastle upon Tyne, UK	7,805	9,387	14,152	10,036	14,178	7,492	404	86	13,835	8,039	2,422	7,053	6,807	11,088	7,154	7,624	7,761	11,181	6,336	8,893
Newcastle Waters, Australia	15,804	4,990	6,206	11,090	1,227	17,711	14,648	14,444	2,210	12,651	15,746	13,766	18,446	3,359	18,496	16,358	11,737	3,237	14,960	5,505
Niamey, Niger	9,368	11,506	18,648	5,527	15,714	7,502	4,240	4,611	12,789	11,637	2,433	10,445	6,804	13,123	6,046	8,859	3,626	13,084	9,326	11,271
Nicosia, Cyprus	11,147	7,687	15,598	7,805	12,426	10,266	3,424	3,539	10,744	11,325	3,743	10,448	9,516	9,405	9,309	10,873	5,326	9,409	9,799	7,385
Niue (Alofi)	10,088	9,558	1,801	14,081	5,191	11,748	16,218	15,875	7,823	8,288	17,633	9,441	12,474	7,921	13,095	10,551	16,313	7,951	10,474	9,800
Norfolk, Virginia	2,015	13,293	10,682	12,543	15,180	3,067	5,808	5,741	18,383	3,791	6,126	2,640	2,951	14,189	4,296	2,008	11,607	14,379	1,440	12,740
Norfolk Island, Australia	12,563	8,224	3,613	12,339	3,337	13,984	17,405	17,042	5,367	10,631	19,352	11,819	14,734	6,465	15,016	12,997	14,135	6,427	12,914	8,624
Noril'sk, USSR	9,963	5,405	10,699	12,748	9,813	10,938	4,836	4,507	10,647	7,758	6,768	7,508	10,448	6,903	11,235	10,139	10,300	7,036	7,661	4,848
Norman Wells, Canada	5,700	8,967	8,376	15,820	11,112	7,581	6,190	5,858	13,852	2,942	7,866	2,806	7,484	9,652	8,792	6,089	13,644	9,844	3,398	8,454
Normanton, Australia	15,013	5,434	5,409	11,684	783	16,912	15,120	14,873	2,952	12,008	16,438	13,160	17,637	3,711	17,992	15,557	12,495	3,625	14,366	5,910
North Pole	7,665	7,444	10,314	13,759	11,186	8,842	4,296	3,920	12,753	5,664	6,283	5,256	8,453	8,700	9,458	7,868	11,320	8,862	5,353	6,881
Nottingham, United Kingdom	7,869	9,486	14,379	9,811	14,311	7,466	214	243	13,825	8,217	2,210	7,214	6,769	11,201	7,064	7,668	7,545	11,288	6,468	9,001
Norway House, Canada	3,766	10,959	9,214	14,650	12,887	5,547	5,900	5,662	15,861	2,335	7,081	1,386	5,474	11,684	6,809	4,098	13,056	11,876	1,411	10,431
Norwich, United Kingdom	8,040	9,365	14,446	9,732	14,208	7,620	333	375	13,661	8,360	2,229	7,366	6,920	11,087	7,193	7,837	7,442	11,170	6,630	8,886
Nouakchott, Mauritania	7,372	12,861	16,887	6,814	17,568	5,546	3,872	4,230	14,782	9,894	1,911	8,693	4,831	14,600	4,216	6,860	5,403	14,610	7,520	12,505
Noumea, New Caledonia	12,538	7,643	3,195	12,931	2,856	14,215	16,640	16,278	5,366	10,244	18,622	11,444	14,950	5,895	15,437	13,022	14,537	5,877	12,590	8,011
Novosibirsk, USSR	11,509	4,341	11,243	11,610	9,144	12,217	5,386	5,137	9,325	9,346	7,054	9,123	11,639	6,028	12,194	11,635	9,284	6,121	9,242	3,834
Nuku'alofa, Tonga	10,688	9,173	2,060	13,745	4,662	12,318	16,564	16,203	7,224	8,820	18,172	9,986	13,050	7,493	13,619	11,149	15,858	7,510	11,041	9,452
Nukunono Island, Tokelau Isls.	9,884	8,892	704	15,111	5,002	11,827	15,203	14,845	8,028	7,590	16,867	8,779	12,505	7,370	13,351	10,405	17,167	7,431	9,892	9,064
Nuremberg, West Germany	8,796	8,920	14,831	9,263	13,825	8,262	1,037	1,131	12,956	9,071	2,336	8,107	7,543	10,670	7,692	8,576	6,893	10,736	7,396	8,474
Nyala, Sudan	11,706	9,333	17,938	5,133	13,237	9,970	5,056	5,337	10,447	13,261	4,070	12,168	9,262	10,811	8,516	11,237	2,658	10,746	11,210	9,205
Oaxaca, Mexico	1,142	14,504	8,515	13,351	13,622	3,299	8,782	8,712	16,767	3,317	8,904	3,001	3,841	14,450	5,018	1,641	13,520	14,630	2,805	14,073
Ocean Falls, Canada	4,925	9,784	7,375	16,630	10,933	7,122	7,379	7,076	14,093	1,587	8,855	1,912	7,205	10,131	8,582	5,417	14,806	10,326	2,926	9,323
Odense, Denmark	8,536	8,695	14,173	9,926	13,545	8,251	999	850	13,073	8,513	2,792	7,596	7,561	10,418	7,861	8,373	7,549	10,501	6,965	8,217
Odessa, USSR	10,249	7,625	14,708	8,988	12,530	9,750	2,522	2,527	11,458	10,077	3,524	9,244	9,024	9,386	9,083	10,057	6,512	9,428	8,680	7,228
Ogbomosho, Nigeria	9,799	11,570	19,279	4,888	15,441	7,809	4,857	5,224	12,345	12,233	3,073	11,036	7,141	13,103	6,266	9,268	3,024	13,042	9,900	11,388
Okha, USSR	10,461	4,200	7,533	15,196	7,123	12,367	7,940	7,581	9,138	7,056	9,937	7,457	12,178	4,906	13,366	10,889	13,031	5,091	8,207	3,730
Okinawa (Naha)	13,593	1,498	7,265	13,283	4,389	15,651	10,153	9,865	5,850	9,950	11,876	10,579	15,457	1,626	16,558	14,079	12,058	1,806	11,445	1,472
Oklahoma City, Oklahoma	1,906	12,758	8,771	14,259	13,411	4,149	7,290	7,140	16,821	2,009	7,934	1,115	4,353	13,144	5,730	2,393	13,516	13,338	880	12,268
Old Crow, Canada	6,323	8,340	8,198	16,009	10,583	8,209	6,314	5,963	13,236	3,395	8,099	3,395	8,100	9,027	9,394	6,719	13,693	9,218	4,029	7,830
Olympia, Washington	4,337	10,421	7,291	16,475	11,225	6,611	7,666	7,388	14,503	911	8,988	1,386	6,758	10,678	8,141	4,855	14,970	10,872	2,527	9,973
Omaha, Nebraska	2,399	12,265	9,028	14,311	13,413	4,443	6,739	6,568	16,733	2,029	7,525	870	4,535	12,796	5,917	2,805	13,282	12,991	369	11,756
Omsk, USSR	11,361	4,827	11,831	11,159	9,684	11,860	4,867	4,639	9,644	9,495	6,476	9,161	11,246	6,546	11,714	11,433	8,787	6,629	9,166	4,344
Oodnadatta, Australia	15,709	6,094	6,240	10,516	2,002	17,014	15,667	15,500	2,199	13,100	16,440	14,280	17,749	4,497	17,371	16,171	11,554	4,370	15,486	6,621
Oradea, Romania	9,639	8,260	14,931	8,976	13,172	9,077	1,884	1,937	12,114	9,727	2,893	8,822	8,350	10,020	8,419	9,423	6,531	10,069	8,176	7,846
Oran, Algeria	8,335	10,494	16,252	7,958	15,386	7,199	1,767	2,139	13,704	9,634	678	8,511	6,448	12,253	6,284	7,971	5,820	12,292	7,547	10,096
Oranjestad, Aruba	2,019	16,047	11,352	10,639	16,489	407	7,328	7,418	18,586	5,699	6,708	4,843	993	16,863	2,119	1,428	10,609	17,057	3,880	15,488
Orebro, Sweden	8,665	8,267	13,715	10,333	13,078	8,563	1,446	1,200	12,822	8,335	3,311	7,486	7,895	9,972	8,274	8,549	7,921	10,063	6,949	7,775
Orel, USSR	10,135	7,141	13,896	9,771	12,050	9,941	2,656	2,541	11,388	9,540	4,054	8,800	9,245	8,894	9,468	10,016	7,292	8,956	8,362	6,702
Orsk, USSR	11,308	5,596	12,907	10,216	10,508	11,405	4,172	4,011	9,999	9,992	5,575	9,482	10,732	7,351	11,012	11,277	7,796	7,411	9,287	5,166
Osaka, Japan	12,393	2,511	6,897	14,332	5,076	14,480	9,646	9,320	6,982	8,764	11,527	9,379	14,344	2,755	15,546	12,879	12,823	2,945	10,256	2,253
Oslo, Norway	8,404	8,478	13,670	10,423	13,259	8,315	1,278	993	13,079	8,129	3,217	7,259	7,652	10,172	8,059	8,287	8,035	10,266	6,702	7,979
Osorno, Chile	6,974	17,981	10,528	7,777	13,255	5,690	12,240	12,494	12,727	10,019	10,615	9,822	6,172	16,362	5,469	6,682	9,661	16,259	9,330	18,526
Ostrava, Czechoslovakia	9,260	8,421	14,711	9,277	13,332	8,781	1,525	1,543	12,452	9,325	2,781	8,414	8,064	10,176	8,206	9,060	6,853	10,236	7,769	7,984
Ottawa, Canada	2,877	12,362	10,702	12,891	14,731	3,960	5,182	5,063	17,578	3,653	5,824	2,452	3,747	13,345	5,026	2,944	11,610	13,531	1,341	11,806

Distances in Kilometers	Cancun, Mexico	Canton, China	Canton Atoll, Phoenix Islands	Cape Town, South Africa	Cape York, Australia	Caracas, Venezuela	Cardiff, United Kingdom	Carlisle, United Kingdom	Carnarvon, Australia	Carson City, Nevada	Casablanca, Morocco	Casper, Wyoming	Castries, Saint Lucia	Catbalogan, Philippines	Cayenne, French Guiana	Cayman Islands (Georgetown)	Cazombo, Angola	Cebu, Philippines	Cedar Rapids, Iowa	Changsha, China
Ouagadougou, Bourkina Fasso	9,042	11,913	18,509	5,541	16,106	7,122	4,343	4,718	13,110	11,457	2,433	10,258	6,434	13,536	5,645	8,521	3,803	13,498	9,115	11,670
Oujda, Morocco	8,254	10,653	16,327	7,882	15,542	7,074	1,873	2,248	13,801	9,639	537	8,505	6,322	12,412	6,136	7,880	5,780	12,449	7,522	10,257
Oxford, United Kingdom	7,887	9,565	14,510	9,683	14,405	7,430	138	366	13,839	8,309	2,078	7,295	6,727	11,286	6,992	7,673	7,425	11,370	6,528	9,085
Pago Pago, American Samoa	9,969	9,253	1,269	14,586	5,098	11,772	15,727	15,376	7,935	7,932	17,277	9,104	12,478	7,667	13,210	10,462	16,753	7,713	10,177	9,461
Pakxe, Laos	15,771	1,183	9,298	10,700	4,953	17,062	9,966	9,796	4,505	12,368	11,141	12,803	16,475	2,101	16,745	16,119	9,613	2,038	13,436	1,627
Palembang, Indonesia	17,644	3,024	9,289	9,495	4,253	18,777	11,499	11,398	2,609	13,993	12,255	14,624	18,035	2,757	17,483	18,077	9,068	2,577	15,382	3,554
Palermo, Italy	9,426	9,270	16,064	7,992	14,133	8,452	1,973	2,233	12,533	10,205	1,952	9,173	7,703	11,024	7,556	9,111	5,624	11,052	8,346	8,898
Palma, Majorca	8,496	10,022	15,897	8,297	14,929	7,525	1,402	1,753	13,476	9,508	1,128	8,423	6,779	11,782	6,704	8,171	6,070	11,827	7,524	9,612
Palmerston North, New Zealand	12,131	9,539	4,348	11,457	4,626	13,083	18,762	18,385	5,941	10,980	19,208	12,095	13,827	7,783	13,836	12,460	13,578	7,725	13,037	9,972
Panama, Panama	1,553	16,196	10,304	11,296	15,429	1,395	8,287	8,340	17,770	5,214	7,797	4,572	2,097	16,480	3,038	1,161	11,560	16,666	3,846	15,681
Paramaribo, Suriname	3,803	16,567	12,986	8,876	18,020	1,394	6,950	7,145	17,590	7,422	5,786	6,471	1,108	18,058	329	3,207	8,856	18,218	5,388	16,032
Paris, France	8,203	9,517	14,871	9,307	14,404	7,621	492	761	13,587	8,717	1,883	7,697	6,902	11,258	7,074	7,964	7,028	11,330	6,913	9,057
Patna, India	14,761	2,863	11,476	9,644	7,397	15,002	7,712	7,599	6,372	12,385	8,716	12,337	14,299	4,444	14,322	14,829	7,917	4,422	12,516	2,776
Patrai, Greece	10,082	8,584	15,854	7,997	13,419	9,181	2,439	2,619	11,835	10,577	2,683	9,609	8,432	10,331	8,283	9,792	5,553	10,352	8,863	8,232
Peking, China	12,833	1,888	8,684	12,947	6,220	14,411	8,311	8,029	7,179	9,556	10,040	9,883	14,026	3,231	14,906	13,194	11,151	3,366	10,503	1,339
Penrhyn Island (Omoka)	8,474	10,271	1,654	15,240	6,516	10,323	14,767	14,464	9,430	6,640	15,950	7,772	11,013	8,830	11,830	8,968	17,691	8,904	8,786	10,382
Peoria, Illinois	2,185	12,558	9,550	13,774	13,950	4,020	6,391	6,248	17,239	2,572	7,059	1,408	4,055	13,206	5,431	2,497	12,757	13,400	225	12,032
Perm', USSR	10,594	5,926	12,610	10,781	10,787	10,852	3,766	3,549	10,607	9,230	5,391	8,711	10,211	7,650	10,622	10,594	8,323	7,731	8,532	5,448
Perth, Australia	17,484	6,098	8,196	8,716	3,607	17,615	14,680	14,655	812	14,998	14,790	16,144	17,995	4,931	16,775	17,802	9,599	4,752	17,346	6,662
Peshawar, Pakistan	13,486	4,223	12,642	9,344	8,965	13,419	6,130	6,039	7,891	11,819	7,122	11,490	12,705	5,923	12,728	13,449	7,233	5,925	11,418	3,976
Petropavlovsk-Kamchatskiy,USSR	9,677	5,052	6,782	16,234	7,228	11,753	8,297	7,924	9,664	6,138	10,315	6,658	11,672	5,472	12,958	10,149	14,003	5,666	7,520	4,630
Petrozavodsk, USSR	9,446	7,188	13,111	10,708	12,000	9,568	2,525	2,277	11,871	8,571	4,307	7,877	8,921	8,891	9,350	9,396	8,234	8,981	7,525	6,694
Pevek, USSR	8,306	6,364	8,163	15,666	9,176	10,103	6,551	6,174	11,407	5,216	8,546	5,370	9,912	7,174	11,125	8,690	13,189	7,360	5,994	5,848
Philadelphia, Pennsylvania	2,359	12,969	10,770	12,604	15,098	3,363	5,512	5,431	18,145	3,794	5,930	2,610	3,190	13,919	4,505	2,365	11,533	14,107	1,406	12,413
Phnom Penh, Kampuchea	16,174	1,556	9,362	10,403	4,829	17,408	10,229	10,075	4,138	12,740	11,314	13,199	16,786	2,177	16,917	16,524	9,432	2,079	13,842	2,025
Phoenix, Arizona	2,843	12,124	7,423	15,482	12,094	5,254	8,329	8,129	15,517	937	9,188	1,158	5,570	12,186	6,919	3,422	14,871	12,375	2,025	11,699
Pierre, South Dakota	2,866	11,790	8,761	14,728	12,991	4,936	6,751	6,551	16,268	1,710	7,690	510	5,015	12,303	6,395	3,291	13,550	12,497	754	11,287
Pinang, Malaysia	16,970	2,400	9,825	9,605	4,999	17,760	10,468	10,359	3,647	13,586	11,320	14,026	17,042	2,790	16,787	17,264	8,785	2,653	14,618	2,853
Pitcairn Island (Adamstown)	6,934	13,649	5,089	12,682	9,264	7,898	14,681	14,605	11,217	7,191	14,434	7,905	8,650	12,065	9,020	7,205	14,981	12,101	8,409	13,813
Pittsburgh, Pennsylvania	2,234	12,837	10,357	13,003	14,711	3,559	5,797	5,693	17,869	3,379	6,308	2,199	3,464	13,685	4,809	2,347	11,948	13,876	992	12,289
Plymouth, Montserrat	2,628	15,573	12,183	10,200	17,286	854	6,439	6,553	19,008	6,072	5,748	5,071	324	16,763	1,690	2,049	9,879	16,945	3,966	15,010
Plymouth, United Kingdom	7,713	9,815	14,605	9,600	14,655	7,199	138	505	14,049	8,270	1,886	7,230	6,492	11,537	6,743	7,483	7,384	11,621	6,425	9,336
Ponape Island	12,286	5,134	3,511	14,929	2,620	14,670	13,295	12,937	5,978	8,839	15,279	9,934	15,115	3,702	16,392	12,882	15,111	3,798	11,125	5,310
Ponce, Puerto Rico	2,139	15,454	11,709	10,669	16,799	832	6,626	6,709	19,246	5,609	6,084	4,637	746	16,481	2,124	1,564	10,366	16,670	3,564	14,891
Ponta Delgada, Azores	6,096	12,023	14,827	9,151	16,789	5,101	2,332	2,565	15,934	7,798	1,697	6,611	4,366	13,729	4,530	5,727	7,468	13,821	5,527	11,534
Pontianak, Indonesia	17,099	2,596	8,794	10,097	3,852	18,779	11,551	11,415	2,786	13,413	12,483	14,087	18,137	2,158	17,927	17,581	9,633	1,977	14,907	3,148
Port Augusta, Australia	15,462	6,684	6,206	10,304	2,460	16,506	16,222	16,070	2,499	13,193	16,804	14,391	17,220	5,087	16,780	15,869	11,545	4,961	15,576	7,212
Port Blair, India	16,383	2,519	10,688	9,319	6,027	16,698	9,416	9,322	4,628	13,459	10,244	13,673	15,969	3,502	15,755	16,528	8,149	3,406	14,056	2,795
Port Elizabeth, South Africa	13,311	11,208	15,552	662	11,729	10,887	9,878	10,216	8,344	16,890	8,245	15,767	10,563	11,588	9,211	12,721	2,460	11,410	14,561	11,482
Port Hedland, Australia	17,398	4,839	7,795	9,663	2,771	18,777	13,939	13,835	715	14,117	14,545	15,161	19,306	3,616	18,046	17,942	10,146	3,437	16,301	5,402
Port Louis, Mauritius	16,314	7,717	14,089	4,136	9,092	13,997	9,886	10,087	5,760	17,882	9,111	17,075	13,487	8,179	12,276	15,734	3,809	8,013	16,247	8,014
Port Moresby, Papua New Guinea	14,128	5,164	4,608	12,789	535	16,298	14,627	14,325	3,938	10,933	16,302	12,068	16,925	3,408	17,823	14,703	13,434	3,382	13,271	5,563
Port Said, Egypt	11,309	7,896	15,986	7,361	12,539	10,276	3,665	3,817	10,647	11,692	3,737	10,779	9,524	9,586	9,222	11,001	4,882	9,577	10,080	7,625
Port Sudan, Sudan	12,440	7,802	16,377	6,252	11,995	11,080	4,986	5,167	9,623	13,074	4,684	12,151	10,338	9,342	9,789	12,065	3,825	9,292	11,409	7,652
Port-au-Prince, Haiti	1,537	15,358	11,104	11,207	16,194	1,063	6,976	7,027	19,083	5,090	6,587	4,178	1,310	16,165	2,644	957	10,971	16,359	3,180	14,803
Port-of-Spain, Trin. & Tobago	2,935	16,227	12,282	9,755	17,414	591	6,919	7,063	18,353	6,544	6,037	5,606	377	17,429	1,194	2,339	9,658	17,614	4,547	15,666
Port-Vila, Vanuatu	12,215	7,502	2,736	13,464	2,893	14,037	16,185	15,815	5,693	9,763	18,199	10,964	14,751	5,782	15,389	12,724	15,007	5,784	12,125	7,832
Portland, Maine	2,928	12,603	11,147	12,417	15,193	3,688	4,939	4,854	17,891	4,108	5,438	2,906	3,402	13,680	4,637	2,894	11,165	13,862	1,756	12,042
Portland, Oregon	4,239	10,545	7,214	16,482	11,234	6,538	7,791	7,518	14,540	745	9,081	1,335	6,706	10,767	8,089	4,767	15,059	10,960	2,508	10,103
Porto, Portugal	7,525	10,712	15,437	8,761	15,612	6,608	1,223	1,584	14,442	8,714	841	7,588	5,868	12,460	5,912	7,200	6,706	12,527	6,632	10,262
Porto Alegre, Brazil	6,827	18,297	12,740	6,463	15,264	4,795	10,181	10,480	13,715	10,445	8,410	9,844	4,990	17,939	3,875	6,350	7,834	17,759	8,994	18,475
Porto Alexandre, Angola	11,511	11,830	17,906	2,110	13,844	9,156	7,600	7,958	10,425	14,672	5,848	13,483	8,670	12,805	7,435	10,919	1,264	12,665	12,284	11,897
Porto Novo, Benin	9,694	11,814	19,278	4,772	15,596	7,656	5,020	5,390	12,437	12,240	3,183	11,039	7,001	13,332	6,087	9,153	3,027	13,267	9,887	11,639
Porto Velho, Brazil	4,145	18,389	11,922	8,768	16,397	2,157	8,831	9,028	16,274	7,830	7,572	7,151	2,540	19,016	1,986	3,649	9,471	19,163	6,292	17,829
Portsmouth, United Kingdom	7,918	9,614	14,619	9,574	14,468	7,417	169	475	13,832	8,395	1,977	7,373	6,709	11,341	6,949	7,695	7,321	11,422	6,593	9,139
Poznan, Poland	9,058	8,414	14,450	9,565	13,311	8,676	1,386	1,339	12,601	9,033	2,865	8,133	7,970	10,159	8,179	8,879	7,148	10,229	7,510	7,960
Prague, Czechoslovakia	8,998	8,668	14,736	9,313	13,575	8,507	1,253	1,293	12,726	9,154	2,569	8,217	7,790	10,420	7,946	8,791	6,915	10,484	7,543	8,224
Praia, Cape Verde Islands	6,691	13,708	16,293	6,997	18,443	4,732	4,445	4,778	15,432	9,504	2,621	8,476	4,038	15,458	3,343	6,511	5,912	15,476	7,116	13,331
Pretoria, South Africa	13,427	10,640	16,196	1,305	11,854	11,021	9,092	9,415	8,430	16,685	7,581	15,490	10,600	11,241	9,305	12,830	1,631	11,077	14,297	10,854
Prince Albert, Canada	3,912	10,753	8,688	15,177	12,402	5,865	6,352	6,098	15,472	1,890	7,595	1,152	5,853	11,360	7,210	4,308	13,575	11,553	1,632	10,242
Prince Edward Island	14,322	10,791	13,812	2,165	10,238	11,986	11,560	11,884	6,978	18,029	9,986	17,182	11,809	10,720	10,426	13,775	4,098	10,528	16,034	11,188
Prince George, Canada	4,739	9,934	7,742	16,259	11,276	6,871	7,045	6,749	14,391	1,655	8,492	1,723	6,920	10,367	8,290	5,206	14,453	10,562	2,644	9,457
Prince Rupert, Canada	5,183	9,514	7,392	16,686	10,788	7,353	7,294	6,981	13,895	1,863	8,830	2,165	7,413	9,892	8,785	5,666	14,746	10,086	3,135	9,050
Providence, Rhode Island	2,708	12,800	11,073	12,410	15,246	3,498	5,135	5,057	18,069	4,056	5,571	2,859	3,241	13,843	4,504	2,669	11,236	14,027	1,678	12,240
Provo, Utah	3,170	11,596	7,731	15,588	12,121	5,491	7,716	7,494	15,499	705	8,725	532	5,701	11,833	7,079	3,704	14,581	12,026	1,686	11,142
Puerto Aisen, Chile	7,504	17,475	10,488	7,501	12,866	6,218	12,633	12,904	12,197	10,481	10,933	10,328	6,685	15,923	5,931	7,218	9,507	15,807	9,861	18,033
Puerto Deseado, Argentina	7,909	17,270	10,949	6,919	12,951	6,453	12,514	12,809	11,962	11,004	10,722	10,793	6,858	15,891	5,985	7,585	8,949	15,753	10,259	17,832
Puerto Princesa, Philippines	15,610	1,592	7,838	11,561	3,467	17,684	11,252	11,038	3,868	11,913	12,593	12,614	17,378	709	18,113	16,118	10,870	570	13,498	2,132
Punta Arenas, Chile	8,370	16,652	10,474	7,034	12,254	7,063	13,204	13,503	11,351	11,257	11,389	11,164	7,502	15,205	6,670	8,090	9,209	15,072	10,727	17,216
Pusan, South Korea	12,730	2,027	7,458	13,791	5,264	14,688	9,344	9,035	6,833	9,173	11,164	9,711	14,467	2,619	15,571	13,185	12,233	2,796	10,519	1,704
Pyongyang, North Korea	12,540	2,124	7,886	13,660	5,772	14,369	8,822	8,515	7,184	9,083	10,640	9,535	14,092	3,020	15,135	12,962	11,946	3,187	10,273	1,684
Qamdo, China	14,202	1,818	10,280	10,961	6,691	15,097	8,027	7,839	6,442	11,333	9,361	11,465	14,495	3,562	14,877	14,418	9,245	3,593	11,855	1,557
Qandahar, Afghanistan	13,481	4,756	13,236	8,787	9,400	13,157	5,917	5,867	8,060	12,151	6,523	11,724	12,423	6,420	12,330	13,378	6,639	6,409	11,540	4,541
Qiqian, China	11,453	3,292	8,750	13,706	7,273	13,018	7,375	7,054	8,566	8,317	9,261	8,543	12,667	4,499	13,640	11,798	11,586	4,655	9,112	2,744
Qom, Iran	12,388	6,120	14,386	8,312	10,825	11,790	4,660	4,668	9,336	11,776	5,317	11,117	11,047	7,818	10,905	12,199	5,942	7,817	10,705	5,853
Quebec, Canada	3,176	12,247	11,035	12,638	14,908	4,046	4,809	4,695	17,531	3,982	5,456	2,785	3,760	13,322	4,985	3,190	11,276	13,503	1,709	11,686
Quetta, Pakistan	13,673	4,640	13,162	8,743	9,243	13,343	6,110	6,061	7,867	12,293	6,906	11,888	12,608	6,285	12,495	13,573	6,636	6,270	11,721	4,446
Quito, Ecuador	2,527	17,176	10,372	10,640	15,344	1,746	9,014	9,108	16,942	6,054	8,267	5,520	2,490	17,149	2,965	2,182	11,251	17,313	4,857	16,679
Rabaul, Papua New Guinea	13,404	5,198	4,017	13,592	1,292	15,667	14,288	13,958	4,714	10,137	16,139	11,266	16,235	3,500	17,316	13,988	14,149	3,522	12,468	5,523
Raiatea (Uturoa)	8,208	11,259	2,697	14,298	7,151	9,774	15,242	14,993	9,727	7,011	15,959	8,049	10,503	9,730	11,143	8,637	16,777	9,783	8,931	11,412
Raleigh, North Carolina	1,805	13,369	10,472	12,682	15,041	3,039	6,045	5,974	18,330	3,627	6,364	2,500	2,986	14,196	4,350	1,845	11,810	14,388	1,323	12,821
Rangiroa (Avatoru)	7,762	11,563	2,953	14,404	7,567	9,342	14,872	14,640	10,173	6,656	15,517	7,668	10,067	10,077	10,734	8,191	16,864	10,139	8,521	11,686
Rangoon, Burma	15,798	1,919	10,337	9,955	5,935	16,468	9,196	9,066	4,982	12,778	10,212	13,016	15,785	3,145	15,810	16,004	8,665	3,083	13,450	2,138
Raoul Is., Kermadec Islands	11,240	9,375	2,999	12,805	4,596	12,610	17,497	17,131	6,713	9,679	18,985	10,823	13,360	7,636	13,711	11,651	14,938	7,622	11,832	9,723
Rarotonga (Avarua)	9,214	10,625	2,408	13,902	6,260	10,725	16,081	15,796	8,724	7,874	16,963	8,957	11,462	9,004	12,022	9,639	16,332	9,038	9,887	10,846
Rawson, Argentina	7,471	17,761	11,127	7,044	13,406	5,960	12,078	12,364	12,456	10,663	10,329	10,390	6,360	16,381	5,494	7,129	8,950	16,246	9,812	18,320
Recife, Brazil	6,521	16,242	15,089	6,153	17,909	4,098	7,263	7,583	15,029	10,133	5,441	9,132	3,778	17,782	2,410	5,927	6,338	17,694	7,992	15,982
Regina, Canada	3,611	11,049	8,656	15,106	12,539	5,611	6,507	6,268	15,684	1,728	7,666	855	5,631	11,616	6,997	4,020	13,630	11,810	1,369	10,542
Reykjavik, Iceland	6,694	9,586	12,777	11,433	13,949	6,905	1,782	1,481	14,600	6,523	3,536	5,570	6,320	11,132	7,008	6,625	9,241	11,263	4,952	9,042
Rhodes, Greece	10,681	8,099	15,766	7,854	12,881	9,781	2,990	3,133	11,226	11,016	3,263	10,094	9,031	9,831	8,843	10,397	5,379	9,842	9,397	7,776
Richmond, Virginia	2,028	13,198	10,578	12,670	15,053	3,176	5,836	5,760	18,258	3,670	6,199	2,514	3,074	14,073	4,422	2,058	11,715	14,264	1,313	12,647
Riga, USSR	9,249	7,833	13,843	10,083	12,701	9,098	1,866	1,695	12,261	8,828	3,532	8,018	8,416	9,563	8,727	9,128	7,631	9,642	7,516	7,361
Ringkobing, Denmark	8,385	8,786	14,100	10,019	13,617	8,125	909	719	13,211	8,370	2,778	7,447	7,439	10,501	7,764	8,226	7,656	10,588	6,812	8,301
Rio Branco, Brazil	4,016	18,545	11,483	9,055	15,970	2,265	9,181	9,363	16,148	7,642	7,982	7,036	2,757	18,636	2,378	3,564	9,864	18,754	6,247	17,985
Rio Cuarto, Argentina	6,460	18,871	11,446	7,454	14,387	4,836	11,112	11,374	13,582	9,836	9,479	9,438	5,230	17,462	4,400	6,079	9,044	17,341	8,774	19,405
Rio de Janeiro, Brazil	6,784	17,625	13,755	6,075	16,235	4,508	9,122	9,434	14,165	10,503	7,308	9,728	4,520	18,258	3,234	6,244	7,075	18,065	8,742	17,572
Rio Gallegos, Argentina	8,240	16,832	10,620	6,988	12,459	6,887	13,001	13,299	11,526	11,192	11,191	11,064	7,316	15,405	6,471	7,947	9,124	15,270	10,597	17,396
Rio Grande, Brazil	6,947	18,272	12,587	6,457	15,029	4,965	10,414	10,713	13,529	10,534	8,636	9,967	5,184	17,739	4,091	6,483	7,910	17,564	9,143	18,527
Riyadh, Saudi Arabia	12,879	6,708	15,255	7,139	11,082	11,847	5,156	5,253	9,052	12,804	5,318	12,041	11,095	8,293	10,700	12,589	4,801	8,257	11,484	6,538
Road Town, Brit. Virgin Isls.	2,336	15,401	11,918	10,520	16,996	914	6,452	6,545	19,273	5,752	5,875	4,754	625	16,506	2,005	1,769	10,169	16,693	3,655	14,837

Distances in Kilometers

	Cancun, Mexico	Canton, China	Canton Atoll, Phoenix Islands	Cape Town, South Africa	Cape York, Australia	Caracas, Venezuela	Cardiff, United Kingdom	Carlisle, United Kingdom	Carnarvon, Australia	Carson City, Nevada	Casablanca, Morocco	Casper, Wyoming	Castries, Saint Lucia	Catbalogan, Philippines	Cayenne, French Guiana	Cayman Islands (Georgetown)	Cazombo, Angola	Cebu, Philippines	Cedar Rapids, Iowa	Changsha, China
Roanoke, Virginia	1,906	13,180	10,357	12,858	14,867	3,241	6,021	5,936	18,131	3,466	6,417	2,323	3,188	13,993	4,551	1,997	11,934	14,185	1,134	12,634
Robinson Crusoe Island, Chile	6,118	18,356	10,102	8,603	13,443	5,046	11,963	12,174	13,397	9,097	10,528	8,919	5,604	16,599	5,102	5,864	10,349	16,541	8,474	18,744
Rochester, New York	2,586	12,583	10,557	12,935	14,740	3,765	5,453	5,342	17,735	3,528	6,031	2,329	3,600	13,510	4,912	2,669	11,754	13,698	1,161	12,030
Rockhampton, Australia	14,165	6,535	4,663	11,896	1,641	15,814	16,162	15,879	3,740	11,592	17,605	12,788	16,560	4,786	16,833	14,659	13,117	4,720	13,979	6,986
Rome, Italy	9,197	9,166	15,658	8,417	14,066	8,363	1,599	1,832	12,703	9,816	1,986	8,804	7,621	10,926	7,573	8,912	6,051	10,967	8,012	8,767
Rosario, Argentina	6,596	18,768	11,785	7,153	14,590	4,854	10,907	11,181	13,578	10,046	9,228	9,596	5,198	17,593	4,284	6,188	8,705	17,454	8,882	19,213
Roseau, Dominica	2,755	15,716	12,278	10,040	17,399	800	6,504	6,629	18,831	6,235	5,751	5,243	148	16,934	1,516	2,169	9,759	17,115	4,142	15,154
Rostock, East Germany	8,690	8,649	14,312	9,769	13,520	8,355	1,071	979	12,947	8,698	2,752	7,780	7,658	10,382	7,919	8,517	7,382	10,459	7,143	8,180
Rostov-na-Donu, USSR	10,739	6,937	14,238	9,237	11,841	10,383	3,106	3,055	10,875	10,221	4,213	9,482	9,666	8,697	9,764	10,588	6,760	8,740	9,025	6,542
Rotterdam, Netherlands	8,270	9,215	14,552	9,605	14,082	7,823	534	594	13,442	8,566	2,254	7,583	7,117	10,947	7,355	8,064	7,288	11,025	6,858	8,745
Rouyn, Canada	3,085	12,009	10,441	13,240	14,345	4,334	5,213	5,063	17,187	3,391	6,004	2,201	4,142	12,955	5,428	3,217	11,867	13,142	1,212	11,456
Sacramento, California	3,840	11,117	6,890	16,413	11,271	6,229	8,371	8,120	14,667	163	9,509	1,365	6,495	11,172	7,863	4,408	15,419	11,362	2,550	10,704
Saginaw, Michigan	2,487	12,431	10,044	13,426	14,273	4,004	5,838	5,701	17,404	3,015	6,514	1,816	3,927	13,233	5,275	2,687	12,267	13,424	654	11,888
Saint Denis, Reunion	16,113	7,936	14,262	3,912	9,292	13,781	9,836	10,048	5,943	17,926	9,000	17,040	13,280	8,407	12,060	15,529	3,612	8,240	16,154	8,228
Saint George's, Grenada	2,846	16,077	12,253	9,864	17,390	590	6,811	6,948	18,508	6,427	5,973	5,475	232	17,273	1,301	2,250	9,717	17,457	4,406	15,516
Saint John, Canada	3,279	12,432	11,455	12,202	15,317	3,854	4,561	4,480	17,741	4,404	5,080	3,204	3,497	13,594	4,664	3,209	10,856	13,771	2,091	11,869
Saint John's, Antigua	2,655	15,524	12,219	10,194	17,315	913	6,380	6,494	19,032	6,077	5,692	5,069	353	16,729	1,700	2,080	9,850	16,910	3,956	14,962
Saint John's, Canada	4,229	12,052	12,380	11,470	15,680	4,320	3,542	3,493	17,216	5,343	4,054	4,159	3,799	13,429	4,725	4,069	9,922	13,586	3,112	11,492
Saint Louis, Missouri	1,966	12,750	9,469	13,751	13,969	3,882	6,586	6,451	17,310	2,555	7,198	1,438	3,957	13,350	5,339	2,304	12,830	13,545	394	12,228
Saint Paul, Minnesota	2,705	12,010	9,337	14,176	13,530	4,565	6,288	6,110	16,739	2,288	7,141	1,086	4,573	12,660	5,942	3,044	12,975	12,854	350	11,486
Saint Peter Port, UK	7,843	9,782	14,737	9,464	14,642	7,284	233	605	13,941	8,425	1,807	7,385	6,571	11,512	6,788	7,604	7,237	11,591	6,576	9,310
Saipan (Susupe)	13,029	3,519	5,098	14,366	2,883	15,442	12,033	11,702	5,633	9,343	13,915	10,281	15,654	2,286	17,036	13,612	13,855	2,428	11,385	3,669
Salalah, Oman	14,017	6,185	14,792	6,788	10,190	12,864	6,297	6,387	7,946	13,755	6,385	13,084	12,118	7,618	11,594	13,712	4,693	7,553	12,594	6,122
Salem, Oregon	4,238	10,563	7,151	16,522	11,197	6,549	7,864	7,591	14,513	696	9,149	1,361	6,726	10,765	8,109	4,771	15,126	10,957	2,543	10,125
Salt Lake City, Utah	3,218	11,541	7,736	15,614	12,100	5,532	7,684	7,459	15,472	696	8,708	518	5,735	11,787	7,114	3,749	14,576	11,979	1,692	11,084
Salta, Argentina	5,580	19,785	11,520	7,982	15,057	3,907	10,399	10,635	14,510	9,058	8,900	8,582	4,319	18,211	3,580	5,175	9,298	18,131	7,870	19,597
Salto, Uruguay	6,574	18,755	12,076	6,996	14,866	4,732	10,626	10,906	13,716	10,090	8,929	9,587	5,034	17,813	4,063	6,141	8,471	17,662	8,827	19,082
Salvador, Brazil	6,484	16,846	14,572	6,176	17,381	4,074	7,917	8,230	14,850	10,175	6,112	9,249	3,881	18,227	2,502	5,903	6,658	18,096	8,158	16,624
Salzburg, Austria	8,995	8,862	15,001	9,067	13,775	8,402	1,239	1,358	12,786	9,304	2,335	8,339	7,677	10,618	7,779	8,764	6,684	10,676	7,623	8,429
Samsun, Turkey	10,952	7,290	14,914	8,527	12,138	10,333	3,199	3,236	10,810	10,773	3,935	9,964	9,595	9,038	9,541	10,739	6,049	9,062	9,411	6,941
San Antonio, Texas	1,496	13,278	8,549	14,117	13,402	3,891	7,852	7,723	16,816	2,229	8,346	1,646	4,213	13,505	5,556	2,063	13,687	13,696	1,522	12,808
San Cristobal, Venezuela	2,150	16,537	11,103	10,551	16,212	658	7,890	7,986	18,015	5,874	7,194	5,118	1,409	17,145	2,224	1,614	10,746	17,338	4,246	15,987
San Diego, California	3,266	11,842	6,952	15,920	11,618	5,688	8,678	8,460	15,041	754	9,616	1,473	6,028	11,805	7,368	3,853	15,346	11,991	2,468	11,442
San Francisco, California	3,888	11,113	6,775	16,487	11,182	6,286	8,491	8,239	14,585	278	9,629	1,477	6,565	11,134	7,929	4,460	15,535	11,323	2,656	10,707
San Jose, Costa Rica	1,272	15,896	9,810	11,775	14,942	1,882	8,520	8,545	17,522	4,797	8,161	4,239	2,553	16,022	3,546	1,076	12,071	16,204	3,627	15,408
San Juan, Argentina	6,144	19,057	11,094	7,884	14,290	4,654	11,188	11,431	13,759	9,452	9,637	9,096	5,104	17,427	4,386	5,791	9,460	17,334	8,478	19,612
San Juan, Puerto Rico	2,180	15,404	11,760	10,652	16,841	886	6,554	6,638	19,295	5,623	6,014	4,639	736	16,453	2,118	1,611	10,325	16,641	3,556	14,840
San Luis Potosi, Mexico	1,477	13,784	8,157	14,013	13,185	3,850	8,629	8,518	16,493	2,597	8,980	2,348	4,314	13,769	5,569	2,064	13,981	13,952	2,364	13,355
San Marino, San Marino	9,112	9,075	15,435	8,640	13,985	8,359	1,442	1,647	12,750	9,632	2,076	8,634	7,622	10,835	7,626	8,845	6,270	10,883	7,865	8,664
San Miguel de Tucuman, Argen.	5,791	19,570	11,500	7,854	14,897	4,133	10,575	10,818	14,285	9,244	9,043	8,788	4,541	18,040	3,777	5,393	9,239	17,947	8,088	19,784
San Salvador, El Salvador	863	15,262	9,281	12,468	14,414	2,451	8,553	8,536	17,334	4,116	8,415	3,624	3,047	15,326	4,159	1,039	12,682	15,508	3,143	14,796
Sanaa, Yemen	13,317	7,249	15,863	6,100	11,205	11,920	5,799	5,955	8,747	13,745	5,561	12,895	11,183	8,692	10,572	12,942	3,822	8,625	12,219	7,165
Santa Cruz, Bolivia	5,017	19,316	11,875	8,171	15,789	3,157	9,624	9,850	15,272	8,623	8,194	8,036	3,527	18,931	2,782	4,562	9,205	18,892	7,238	18,790
Santa Cruz, Tenerife	7,079	12,150	16,169	7,809	17,057	5,632	2,781	3,126	15,059	9,123	1,004	7,928	4,882	13,911	4,614	6,637	6,136	13,956	6,810	11,734
Santa Fe, New Mexico	2,469	12,306	8,035	15,000	12,649	4,823	7,784	7,599	16,064	1,282	8,584	796	5,078	12,530	6,447	3,016	14,263	12,722	1,420	11,847
Santa Rosa, Argentina	6,815	18,490	11,367	7,280	14,070	5,223	11,429	11,700	13,196	10,137	9,751	9,777	5,615	17,105	4,765	6,445	8,981	16,977	9,138	19,038
Santa Rosalia, Mexico	2,677	12,595	7,183	15,289	12,055	5,094	8,884	8,703	15,455	1,487	9,603	1,806	5,503	12,494	6,802	3,273	15,057	12,676	2,481	12,200
Santarem, Brazil	4,358	17,380	13,001	8,306	17,632	1,969	7,692	7,915	16,736	8,065	6,347	7,196	1,948	18,971	856	3,782	8,609	19,122	6,170	16,872
Santiago del Estero, Argentina	5,929	19,436	11,573	7,720	14,871	4,245	10,613	10,861	14,174	9,386	9,052	8,927	4,638	17,997	3,840	5,526	9,128	17,894	8,222	19,754
Santiago, Chile	6,277	18,800	10,861	7,959	13,997	4,880	11,479	11,719	13,535	9,501	9,929	9,196	5,352	17,137	4,667	5,948	9,616	17,047	8,624	19,333
Santo Domingo, Dominican Rep.	1,789	15,392	11,361	10,987	16,449	938	6,814	6,877	19,213	5,300	6,365	4,358	1,071	16,294	2,427	1,213	10,717	16,486	3,324	14,832
Sao Paulo de Olivenca, Brazil	3,351	17,818	11,430	9,544	16,230	1,557	8,655	8,811	16,861	7,031	7,612	6,363	2,115	18,262	2,053	2,869	10,121	18,436	5,537	17,259
Sao Paulo, Brazil	6,584	17,975	13,405	6,355	16,091	4,366	9,331	9,633	14,245	10,289	7,557	9,558	4,439	18,431	3,210	6,059	7,418	18,237	8,608	17,922
Sao Tome, Sao Tome & Principe	10,366	11,690	19,686	3,983	15,006	8,223	5,747	6,112	11,735	13,046	3,977	11,844	7,607	13,072	6,586	9,807	2,238	12,983	10,682	11,586
Sapporo, Japan	11,369	3,402	6,921	15,039	5,955	13,421	8,986	8,639	8,038	7,793	10,948	8,350	13,290	3,814	14,516	11,841	13,213	4,005	9,202	3,031
Sarajevo, Yugoslavia	9,554	8,636	15,356	8,610	13,538	8,837	1,824	1,965	12,282	9,901	2,515	8,945	8,100	10,396	8,091	9,301	6,188	10,438	8,228	8,238
Saratov, USSR	10,737	6,466	13,572	9,847	11,379	10,629	3,351	3,224	10,719	9,858	4,703	9,209	9,937	8,222	10,158	10,647	7,378	8,280	8,866	6,039
Saskatoon, Canada	3,843	10,816	8,589	15,242	12,367	5,836	6,478	6,226	15,475	1,760	7,703	1,031	5,844	11,390	7,207	4,252	13,681	11,584	1,595	10,310
Schefferville, Canada	4,094	11,372	11,214	12,725	14,483	4,914	4,125	3,959	16,681	4,262	5,097	3,136	4,553	12,547	5,682	4,129	11,060	12,721	2,307	10,809
Seattle, Washington	4,331	10,414	7,360	16,422	11,271	6,591	7,592	7,314	14,537	959	8,916	1,361	6,729	10,691	8,111	4,844	14,899	10,885	2,488	9,961
Sendai, Japan	11,772	3,115	6,664	14,903	5,423	13,889	9,467	9,126	7,544	8,139	11,410	8,761	13,789	3,337	15,035	12,263	13,265	3,530	9,654	2,817
Seoul, South Korea	12,614	2,072	7,727	13,710	5,583	14,491	9,016	8,709	7,051	9,117	10,834	9,601	14,234	2,866	15,299	13,048	12,052	3,036	10,366	1,671
Sept-Iles, Canada	3,688	11,884	11,337	12,477	14,895	4,402	4,311	4,187	17,193	4,306	5,065	3,130	4,043	13,053	5,188	3,677	10,963	13,229	2,145	11,320
Sevastopol, USSR	10,547	7,450	14,763	8,829	12,339	10,012	2,811	2,826	11,175	10,350	3,715	9,532	9,282	9,208	9,301	10,350	6,349	9,243	8,979	7,070
Seville, Spain	7,825	10,784	15,912	8,289	15,697	6,748	1,584	1,959	14,200	9,166	442	8,030	5,999	12,543	5,916	7,469	6,233	12,595	7,048	10,360
Shanghai, China	13,496	1,196	8,005	12,959	5,149	15,316	9,378	9,100	6,250	9,991	11,066	10,484	15,004	2,173	15,960	13,923	11,492	2,320	11,235	875
Sheffield, United Kingdom	7,840	9,481	14,331	9,860	14,298	7,454	238	193	13,844	8,170	2,247	7,169	6,760	11,192	7,067	7,642	7,594	11,281	6,427	8,994
Shenyang, China	12,378	2,279	8,174	13,576	6,132	14,118	8,457	8,151	7,450	9,003	10,276	9,392	13,808	3,331	14,812	12,776	11,759	3,491	10,081	1,784
Shiraz, Iran	12,906	6,036	14,502	7,894	10,590	12,168	5,153	5,185	8,883	12,350	5,642	11,698	11,419	7,679	11,171	12,690	5,588	7,658	11,274	5,827
Sibiu, Romania	9,856	8,137	15,003	8,847	13,043	9,264	2,098	2,158	11,910	9,931	3,012	9,035	8,533	9,897	8,571	9,636	6,391	9,941	8,396	7,735
Singapore	17,275	2,620	9,411	9,671	4,477	18,361	11,069	10,957	3,080	13,707	11,905	14,267	17,643	2,596	17,300	17,659	9,066	2,432	14,968	3,133
Sioux Falls, South Dakota	2,652	12,017	9,021	14,426	13,294	4,656	6,607	6,423	16,569	1,981	7,470	782	4,719	12,576	6,097	3,047	13,291	12,771	449	11,505
Skelleftea, Sweden	8,703	7,813	13,058	10,942	12,537	8,855	2,027	1,716	12,603	7,985	3,966	7,226	8,224	9,479	8,723	8,651	8,503	9,582	6,815	7,300
Skopje, Yugoslavia	9,869	8,468	15,474	8,412	13,350	9,107	2,147	2,285	11,985	10,203	2,708	9,258	8,365	10,225	8,309	9,609	5,969	10,259	8,550	8,088
Socotra Island (Tamrida)	14,334	6,343	14,888	6,386	10,110	13,021	6,671	6,780	7,686	14,233	6,621	13,543	12,283	7,687	11,663	13,992	4,383	7,607	13,017	6,327
Sofia, Bulgaria	9,966	8,301	15,348	8,497	13,186	9,247	2,223	2,336	11,864	10,208	2,870	9,283	8,507	10,058	8,468	9,717	6,044	10,093	8,600	7,920
Songkhla, Thailand	16,771	2,222	9,806	9,741	5,045	17,619	10,330	10,213	3,819	13,409	11,228	13,834	16,914	2,713	16,740	17,066	8,859	2,586	14,419	2,664
Sorong, Indonesia	15,335	3,294	6,353	12,049	1,650	17,757	12,974	12,730	3,261	11,704	14,406	12,664	18,037	1,566	19,420	15,928	11,998	1,481	13,763	3,764
South Georgia Island	9,617	15,745	12,445	4,806	12,805	7,717	12,129	12,489	10,792	13,014	10,131	12,620	7,906	15,024	6,718	9,192	6,988	14,839	11,874	16,220
South Pole	12,340	12,559	9,687	6,250	8,816	11,164	15,712	16,089	7,250	14,338	13,725	14,748	11,553	11,303	10,549	12,137	8,688	11,140	14,651	13,122
South Sandwich Islands	10,357	15,002	12,608	4,258	12,350	8,409	12,296	12,667	10,129	13,758	10,279	13,364	8,560	14,359	7,327	9,922	6,562	14,170	12,596	15,472
Split, Yugoslavia	9,424	8,798	15,428	8,577	13,701	8,680	1,717	1,883	12,428	9,847	2,352	8,874	7,942	10,558	7,928	9,163	6,171	10,601	8,135	8,398
Spokane, Washington	4,025	10,681	7,679	16,055	11,641	6,250	7,362	7,097	14,901	964	8,620	1,021	6,371	11,018	7,754	4,523	14,597	11,212	2,120	10,215
Spoleto, Italy	9,181	9,109	15,563	8,507	14,014	8,383	1,547	1,767	12,702	9,752	2,040	8,748	7,642	10,869	7,615	8,904	6,137	10,913	7,967	8,706
Springbok, South Africa	12,514	11,741	16,269	474	12,594	10,090	9,226	9,578	9,199	16,030	7,500	14,898	9,734	12,289	8,395	11,920	2,034	12,118	13,691	11,956
Springfield, Illinois	2,088	12,647	9,533	13,748	13,976	3,948	6,462	6,323	17,287	2,580	7,102	1,433	3,998	13,280	5,376	2,407	12,771	13,474	296	12,123
Springfield, Massachusetts	2,677	12,759	10,973	12,512	15,148	3,545	5,195	5,110	18,011	3,954	5,660	2,756	3,307	13,780	4,581	2,661	11,336	13,965	1,577	12,200
Srinagar, India	13,592	3,925	12,346	9,555	8,686	13,637	6,345	6,239	7,708	11,757	7,392	11,485	12,931	5,630	12,996	13,585	7,486	5,635	11,471	3,675
Stanley, Falkland Islands	8,546	16,742	11,372	6,235	12,820	6,946	12,536	12,859	11,483	11,719	10,647	11,471	7,287	15,569	6,298	8,192	8,340	15,411	10,882	17,286
Stara Zagora, Bulgaria	10,146	8,127	15,297	8,485	13,005	9,439	2,395	2,493	11,675	10,320	3,053	9,414	8,700	9,883	8,655	9,903	6,021	9,915	8,752	7,752
Stockholm, Sweden	8,812	8,111	13,682	10,334	12,932	8,724	1,593	1,358	12,663	8,420	3,425	7,589	8,056	9,820	8,431	8,701	7,908	9,909	7,073	7,622
Stornoway, United Kingdom	7,475	9,422	13,730	10,469	14,115	7,319	775	427	14,070	7,582	2,736	6,607	6,659	11,087	7,112	7,327	8,214	11,191	5,920	8,910
Strasbourg, France	8,596	9,182	14,934	9,199	14,085	8,013	848	1,016	13,187	8,999	2,094	8,007	7,292	10,931	7,431	8,362	6,863	10,997	7,259	8,734
Stuttgart, West Germany	8,690	9,078	14,913	9,204	13,983	8,120	935	1,075	13,084	9,048	2,183	8,066	7,399	10,829	7,537	8,460	6,854	10,893	7,332	8,632
Subic, Philippines	15,059	1,170	7,752	12,001	3,746	17,091	10,856	10,622	4,455	11,388	12,312	12,051	16,805	610	17,669	15,552	11,132	645	12,915	1,654
Suchow, China	13,374	1,294	8,470	12,752	5,650	15,031	8,873	8,602	6,555	9,991	10,544	10,392	14,658	2,612	15,530	13,761	11,142	2,741	11,066	783
Sucre, Bolivia	5,022	19,530	11,633	8,292	15,536	3,271	9,861	10,081	15,146	8,579	8,450	8,037	3,686	18,670	3,007	4,590	9,400	18,639	7,280	18,975
Sudbury, Canada	2,862	12,163	10,290	13,318	14,319	4,208	5,447	5,301	17,278	3,238	6,195	2,039	4,057	13,057	5,369	3,017	12,022	13,246	989	11,614
Suez, Egypt	11,409	7,914	16,073	7,226	12,517	10,334	3,790	3,948	10,563	11,834	3,799	10,917	9,582	9,591	9,250	11,092	4,748	9,578	10,209	7,655
Sundsvall, Sweden	8,643	8,054	13,356	10,675	12,817	8,680	1,725	1,432	12,748	8,112	3,647	7,307	8,032	9,738	8,481	8,561	8,250	9,836	6,834	7,550

Distances in Kilometers	Cancun, Mexico	Canton, China	Canton Atoll, Phoenix Islands	Cape Town, South Africa	Cape York, Australia	Caracas, Venezuela	Cardiff, United Kingdom	Carlisle, United Kingdom	Carnarvon, Australia	Carson City, Nevada	Casablanca, Morocco	Casper, Wyoming	Castries, Saint Lucia	Catbalogan, Philippines	Cayenne, French Guiana	Cayman Islands (Georgetown)	Cazombo, Angola	Cebu, Philippines	Cedar Rapids, Iowa	Changsha, China
Surabaya, Indonesia	17,425	3,360	8,386	9,966	3,289	19,644	12,417	12,290	1,952	13,708	13,257	14,527	19,006	2,496	18,366	17,995	9,841	2,301	15,474	3,922
Suva, Fiji	11,209	8,426	2,008	13,869	3,955	12,969	16,300	15,924	6,695	9,026	18,191	10,217	13,687	6,746	14,330	11,700	15,746	6,765	11,330	8,711
Sverdlovsk, USSR	10,841	5,638	12,464	10,814	10,507	11,139	4,054	3,839	10,326	9,364	5,655	8,888	10,500	7,366	10,911	10,855	8,374	7,445	8,749	5,163
Svobodnyy, USSR	11,281	3,391	8,250	14,182	7,020	12,996	7,719	7,385	8,567	8,010	9,644	8,319	12,704	4,405	13,762	11,663	12,093	4,574	8,968	2,872
Sydney, Australia	14,206	7,480	5,162	11,034	2,716	15,360	17,172	16,934	3,759	12,214	18,065	13,413	16,103	5,770	15,991	14,608	12,569	5,679	14,546	7,966
Sydney, Canada	3,676	12,306	11,883	11,856	15,534	4,003	4,119	4,053	17,580	4,831	4,618	3,635	3,563	13,571	4,630	3,555	10,427	13,739	2,548	11,742
Syktyvkar, USSR	10,084	6,323	12,585	10,991	11,135	10,378	3,391	3,144	11,097	8,795	5,126	8,237	9,749	8,023	10,214	10,086	8,515	8,114	8,031	5,826
Szeged, Hungary	9,559	8,416	15,058	8,882	13,327	8,951	1,801	1,883	12,220	9,738	2,735	8,814	8,221	10,176	8,272	9,332	6,448	10,224	8,141	8,005
Szombathely, Hungary	9,268	8,635	15,020	8,990	13,549	8,673	1,510	1,605	12,509	9,506	2,533	8,562	7,946	10,394	8,026	9,040	6,579	10,448	7,869	8,212
Tabriz, Iran	11,827	6,493	14,527	8,477	11,277	11,257	4,099	4,107	9,892	11,334	4,825	10,626	10,518	8,219	10,429	11,638	6,048	8,230	10,173	6,185
Tacheng, China	12,416	3,769	11,408	11,021	8,673	12,996	5,936	5,731	8,511	10,225	7,418	10,037	12,378	5,517	12,798	12,524	8,815	5,584	10,162	3,325
Tahiti (Papeete)	8,077	11,476	2,912	14,171	7,343	9,598	15,221	14,987	9,868	7,001	15,843	8,017	10,330	9,943	10,948	8,495	16,647	9,995	8,870	11,629
Taipei, Taiwan	14,059	866	7,832	12,672	4,565	15,969	9,961	9,697	5,588	10,475	11,580	11,040	15,674	1,513	16,622	14,514	11,429	1,652	11,841	918
Taiyuan, China	13,171	1,637	8,961	12,548	6,216	14,650	8,308	8,043	6,945	9,355	9,967	10,244	14,223	3,142	15,017	13,512	10,788	3,258	10,829	1,073
Tallahassee, Florida	1,061	13,791	9,924	12,905	14,735	2,848	6,834	6,766	18,158	3,364	7,079	2,391	3,000	14,396	4,380	1,269	12,313	14,590	1,440	13,263
Tallinn, USSR	9,150	7,739	13,571	10,360	12,576	9,103	1,956	1,736	12,291	8,602	3,720	7,818	8,437	9,455	8,806	9,054	7,907	9,541	7,355	7,254
Tamanrasset, Algeria	9,348	10,703	17,777	6,422	15,271	7,779	3,275	3,633	12,793	11,105	1,756	9,949	7,042	12,395	6,513	8,900	4,278	12,383	8,915	10,412
Tampa, Florida	872	14,110	10,086	12,623	14,974	2,524	6,908	6,861	18,391	3,651	7,037	2,709	2,704	14,723	4,079	964	12,122	14,918	1,767	13,579
Tampere, Finland	8,991	7,749	13,369	10,587	12,548	9,023	1,976	1,718	12,398	8,371	3,819	7,599	8,369	9,447	8,789	8,913	8,138	9,540	7,158	7,252
Tanami, Australia	16,237	5,092	6,633	10,616	1,709	17,958	14,648	14,477	1,740	13,133	15,558	14,248	18,710	3,552	18,325	16,776	11,280	3,410	15,440	5,628
Tangier, Morocco	7,879	10,874	16,079	8,119	15,783	6,737	1,757	2,132	14,169	9,301	292	8,158	5,986	12,634	5,856	7,509	6,080	12,681	7,160	10,459
Tarawa (Betio)	11,033	6,870	1,773	15,538	3,628	13,281	14,136	13,759	7,013	7,973	16,134	9,155	13,851	5,428	14,956	11,612	16,529	5,513	10,358	7,021
Tashkent, USSR	12,663	4,547	12,613	9,825	9,422	12,733	5,452	5,327	8,639	11,043	6,631	10,671	12,041	6,299	12,200	12,646	7,576	6,329	10,582	4,204
Tbilisi, USSR	11,451	6,588	14,383	8,796	11,435	10,979	3,758	3,741	10,219	10,914	4,632	10,203	10,248	8,334	10,236	11,281	6,345	8,357	9,760	6,244
Tegucigalpa, Honduras	780	15,330	9,498	12,308	14,630	2,243	8,382	8,373	17,540	4,227	8,209	3,675	2,830	15,471	3,956	847	12,475	15,656	3,119	14,849
Tehran, Iran	12,336	6,062	14,288	8,434	10,793	11,785	4,624	4,622	9,363	11,670	5,332	11,023	11,044	7,769	10,929	12,159	6,062	7,770	10,626	5,784
Tel Aviv, Israel	11,451	7,647	15,759	7,502	12,304	10,480	3,754	3,887	10,476	11,693	3,941	10,813	9,728	9,339	9,452	11,159	5,028	9,332	10,152	7,375
Telegraph Creek, Canada	5,421	9,248	7,636	16,509	10,795	7,515	6,989	6,667	13,797	2,240	8,588	2,409	7,527	9,715	8,885	5,879	14,451	9,909	3,274	8,769
Teresina, Brazil	5,604	16,770	14,284	7,056	18,165	3,179	7,313	7,596	15,835	9,250	5,666	8,289	2,915	18,488	1,532	5,013	7,257	18,459	7,180	16,401
Ternate, Indonesia	15,590	2,905	6,791	11,810	2,099	18,006	12,597	12,367	3,204	11,905	13,969	12,810	18,130	1,244	19,370	16,175	11,620	1,120	13,865	3,400
The Valley, Anguilla	2,506	15,433	12,085	10,360	17,166	933	6,381	6,484	19,181	5,911	5,753	4,903	498	16,595	1,863	1,936	9,999	16,779	3,793	14,870
Thessaloniki, Greece	10,048	8,401	15,570	8,267	13,265	9,247	2,336	2,479	11,822	10,394	2,806	9,452	8,503	10,154	8,413	9,781	5,816	10,182	8,743	8,034
Thimphu, Bhutan	14,607	2,416	11,009	10,135	7,088	15,108	7,856	7,714	6,341	12,015	8,988	12,042	14,436	4,060	14,588	14,736	8,422	4,054	12,308	2,288
Thunder Bay, Canada	3,034	11,772	9,680	13,979	13,665	4,692	5,820	5,636	16,718	2,635	6,735	1,458	4,616	12,541	5,957	3,306	12,626	12,733	738	11,236
Tientsin, China	12,885	1,815	8,596	12,975	6,108	14,494	8,423	8,140	7,094	9,579	10,152	9,925	14,118	3,126	15,009	13,255	11,209	3,263	10,562	1,274
Tijuana, Mexico	3,248	11,865	6,956	15,903	11,629	5,671	8,687	8,470	15,052	777	9,619	1,481	6,013	11,825	7,352	3,836	15,341	12,011	2,468	11,466
Tiksi, USSR	9,367	5,481	9,276	14,256	9,190	10,821	5,839	5,475	10,763	6,616	7,849	6,596	10,478	6,652	11,511	9,664	11,810	6,817	7,011	4,925
Timbuktu, Mali	8,728	11,809	18,039	6,053	16,248	6,923	3,853	4,230	13,432	10,996	1,922	9,801	6,211	13,486	5,533	8,228	4,262	13,465	8,674	11,525
Tindouf, Algeria	7,873	11,582	16,751	7,373	16,425	6,409	2,675	3,049	14,261	9,768	658	8,586	5,661	13,336	5,308	7,434	5,513	13,362	7,504	11,204
Tirane, Albania	9,781	8,622	15,589	8,333	13,502	8,979	2,087	2,249	12,094	10,199	2,559	9,237	8,235	10,379	8,163	9,510	5,902	10,412	8,505	8,244
Tokyo, Japan	12,041	2,913	6,606	14,737	5,145	14,179	9,693	9,357	7,246	8,390	11,617	9,035	14,087	3,046	15,335	12,539	13,202	3,239	9,942	2,657
Toledo, Spain	7,934	10,484	15,720	8,489	15,398	6,962	1,295	1,672	14,048	9,094	763	7,979	6,217	12,241	6,189	7,602	6,370	12,297	7,037	10,054
Topeka, Kansas	2,162	12,497	9,008	14,219	13,497	4,259	6,893	6,734	16,858	2,078	7,608	989	4,384	12,992	5,768	2,586	13,296	13,186	469	11,991
Toronto, Canada	2,591	12,499	10,413	13,090	14,587	3,868	5,533	5,412	17,611	3,379	6,155	2,179	3,725	13,395	5,046	2,708	11,899	13,584	1,022	11,948
Toulouse, France	8,279	9,878	15,438	8,756	14,790	7,471	945	1,294	13,625	9,106	1,356	8,040	6,734	11,633	6,773	7,989	6,520	11,692	7,180	9,443
Tours, France	8,122	9,707	15,014	9,177	14,600	7,474	537	872	13,705	8,756	1,679	7,715	6,750	11,451	6,893	7,866	6,926	11,522	6,899	9,251
Townsville, Australia	14,459	5,938	4,867	11,984	1,053	16,286	15,576	15,301	3,471	11,626	17,027	12,804	17,016	4,189	17,413	14,986	12,982	4,123	14,009	6,390
Trenton, New Jersey	2,403	12,944	10,803	12,587	15,111	3,383	5,466	5,386	18,134	3,820	5,889	2,633	3,200	13,905	4,509	2,404	11,502	14,092	1,431	12,387
Tripoli, Lebanon	11,379	7,486	15,502	7,782	12,201	10,506	3,645	3,748	10,504	11,480	3,981	10,625	9,757	9,195	9,540	11,110	5,308	9,196	10,001	7,195
Tripoli, Libya	9,637	9,525	16,638	7,416	14,304	8,467	2,457	2,750	12,396	10,672	1,934	9,607	7,715	11,261	7,435	9,279	5,064	11,273	8,724	9,189
Tristan da Cunha (Edinburgh)	10,110	14,631	15,106	2,797	14,101	7,756	9,850	10,226	11,127	13,835	7,839	12,973	7,612	14,920	6,232	9,552	4,480	14,732	11,888	14,867
Trondheim, Norway	8,275	8,347	13,281	10,813	13,057	8,337	1,551	1,215	13,104	7,813	3,542	6,979	7,699	10,011	8,188	8,194	8,419	10,115	6,479	7,834
Trujillo, Peru	3,344	17,900	10,266	10,196	14,985	2,458	9,743	9,864	16,109	6,713	8,826	6,285	3,156	17,384	3,297	3,043	11,114	17,506	5,694	17,456
Truk Island (Moen)	12,890	4,476	4,205	14,426	2,261	15,298	13,055	12,713	5,473	9,355	14,975	10,406	15,691	2,999	17,015	13,487	14,425	3,092	11,577	4,688
Truro, Canada	3,439	12,413	11,668	12,017	15,455	3,880	4,370	4,299	17,713	4,616	4,862	3,417	3,482	13,625	4,605	3,339	10,643	13,798	2,309	11,849
Tsingtao, China	13,066	1,589	8,243	13,094	5,676	14,795	8,858	8,573	6,781	9,652	10,589	10,074	14,460	2,731	15,403	13,468	11,448	2,877	10,773	1,114
Tsitsihar, China	11,822	2,855	8,351	13,792	6,691	13,506	7,949	7,631	8,066	8,538	9,818	8,860	13,188	3,948	14,200	12,201	11,808	4,109	9,505	2,332
Tubuai Island (Mataura)	8,393	11,702	3,300	13,537	7,320	9,725	15,763	15,553	9,598	7,582	16,151	8,562	10,471	10,092	10,960	8,770	16,016	10,126	9,360	11,907
Tucson, Arizona	2,696	12,295	7,474	15,345	12,197	5,113	8,374	8,183	15,620	1,107	9,183	1,249	5,445	12,344	6,787	3,280	14,809	12,532	2,021	11,870
Tulsa, Oklahoma	1,889	12,767	8,927	14,145	13,541	4,075	7,137	6,990	16,941	2,125	7,772	1,161	4,253	13,200	5,633	2,348	13,364	13,394	742	12,269
Tunis, Tunisia	9,220	9,587	16,239	7,875	14,446	8,175	1,946	2,245	12,772	10,160	1,653	9,100	7,424	11,341	7,250	8,886	5,552	11,368	8,231	9,215
Tura, USSR	10,516	4,673	10,194	12,971	9,041	11,641	5,583	5,262	9,952	8,013	7,486	7,901	11,177	6,137	11,999	10,737	10,589	6,272	8,178	4,112
Turin, Italy	8,711	9,365	15,327	8,812	14,279	7,981	1,077	1,329	13,147	9,303	1,822	8,283	7,247	11,123	7,295	8,444	6,490	11,178	7,489	8,937
Uberlandia, Brazil	6,100	18,061	13,386	6,745	16,522	3,844	8,950	9,239	14,783	9,817	7,246	9,053	3,902	18,940	2,677	5,563	7,633	18,747	8,085	17,860
Ufa, USSR	10,882	5,855	12,838	10,458	10,751	11,038	3,857	3,671	10,389	9,592	5,372	9,061	10,377	7,599	10,717	10,861	8,011	7,669	8,856	5,400
Ujungpandang, Indonesia	16,694	3,194	7,655	10,706	2,617	19,107	12,660	12,490	2,271	13,004	13,715	13,884	19,019	1,963	19,121	17,279	10,610	1,776	14,901	3,751
Ulaanbaatar, Mongolia	12,238	2,809	9,604	12,608	7,383	13,505	7,144	6,866	8,089	9,317	8,877	9,437	13,041	4,345	13,810	12,515	10,542	4,465	9,881	2,251
Ulan-Ude, USSR	11,802	3,224	9,617	12,834	7,695	13,079	6,850	6,558	8,517	8,929	8,640	9,017	12,627	4,709	13,434	12,076	10,682	4,837	9,446	2,662
Uliastay, Mongolia	12,368	3,099	10,354	11,936	7,888	13,356	6,644	6,393	8,217	9,721	8,282	9,715	12,819	4,770	13,440	12,577	9,812	4,866	10,030	2,581
Uranium City, Canada	4,607	10,080	8,804	15,250	12,091	6,450	5,999	5,713	14,966	2,402	7,426	1,867	6,370	10,781	7,694	4,973	13,386	10,973	2,278	9,560
Urumqi, China	12,792	3,284	11,090	11,096	8,192	13,465	6,426	6,220	8,055	10,415	7,890	10,308	12,856	5,035	13,287	12,928	8,980	5,099	10,504	2,850
Ushuaia, Argentina	8,595	16,485	10,605	6,809	12,196	7,237	13,231	13,540	11,176	11,507	11,380	11,405	7,656	15,094	6,784	8,304	9,011	14,953	10,952	17,048
Vaduz, Liechtenstein	8,771	9,133	15,091	9,024	14,044	8,136	1,040	1,221	13,037	9,205	2,082	8,212	7,408	10,887	7,505	8,527	6,676	10,947	7,459	8,696
Valencia, Spain	8,249	10,249	15,855	8,352	15,160	7,266	1,355	1,725	13,733	9,343	915	8,242	6,520	12,008	6,458	7,919	6,175	12,057	7,321	9,831
Valladolid, Spain	7,836	10,418	15,514	8,696	15,327	6,939	1,101	1,477	14,117	8,913	927	7,806	6,199	12,171	6,225	7,519	6,569	12,233	6,880	9,976
Valletta, Malta	9,617	9,277	16,289	7,740	14,103	8,568	2,234	2,498	12,370	10,466	2,035	9,428	7,817	11,023	7,612	9,287	5,363	11,043	8,587	8,923
Valparaiso, Chile	6,206	18,810	10,778	8,060	13,971	4,844	11,495	11,731	13,573	9,411	9,966	9,116	5,328	17,118	4,670	5,884	9,714	17,034	8,555	19,321
Vancouver, Canada	4,474	10,250	7,417	16,439	11,224	6,708	7,477	7,192	14,456	1,152	8,843	1,478	6,824	10,562	8,205	4,977	14,824	10,756	2,561	9,793
Varna, Bulgaria	10,260	7,924	15,132	8,596	12,806	9,607	2,501	2,571	11,531	10,320	3,250	9,439	8,870	9,680	8,847	10,030	6,125	9,714	8,810	7,547
Venice, Italy	9,041	9,014	15,267	8,811	13,928	8,349	1,328	1,508	12,791	9,488	2,149	8,500	7,616	10,774	7,660	8,788	6,439	10,826	7,749	8,594
Veracruz, Mexico	1,004	14,348	8,606	13,413	13,688	3,283	8,559	8,484	16,902	3,172	8,726	2,791	3,786	14,371	5,005	1,550	13,471	14,554	2,560	13,904
Verona, Italy	8,943	9,111	15,276	8,821	14,024	8,244	1,244	1,441	12,895	9,426	2,060	8,430	7,511	10,869	7,558	8,686	6,462	10,923	7,667	8,687
Victoria, Canada	4,444	10,294	7,349	16,478	11,200	6,695	7,561	7,278	14,449	1,069	8,915	1,463	6,823	10,582	8,205	4,954	14,898	10,776	2,571	9,841
Victoria, Seychelles	15,558	6,985	14,730	5,016	9,599	13,651	8,323	8,487	6,598	16,148	7,850	15,406	12,996	7,896	12,031	15,077	3,676	7,765	14,747	7,147
Vienna, Austria	9,207	8,615	14,919	9,098	13,528	8,650	1,449	1,524	12,550	9,405	2,569	8,467	7,926	10,372	8,031	8,988	6,688	10,429	7,784	8,185
Vientiane, Laos	15,562	1,248	9,661	10,591	5,409	16,656	9,510	9,346	4,887	12,305	10,679	12,653	16,042	2,492	16,281	15,860	9,359	2,449	13,209	1,552
Villahermosa, Mexico	735	14,650	8,928	13,051	14,027	2,922	8,445	8,390	17,181	3,498	8,507	3,033	3,440	14,726	4,644	1,225	13,125	14,910	2,662	14,191
Vilnius, USSR	9,439	7,813	14,054	9,839	12,705	9,206	1,929	1,805	12,121	9,087	3,466	8,268	8,513	9,555	8,768	9,301	7,382	9,627	7,747	7,355
Visby, Sweden	8,902	8,152	13,864	10,145	12,998	8,744	1,540	1,345	12,618	8,587	3,304	7,743	8,065	9,873	8,399	8,775	7,718	9,956	7,204	7,671
Vitoria, Brazil	6,821	17,288	14,134	5,939	16,558	4,482	8,741	9,059	14,274	10,545	6,908	9,713	4,419	18,187	3,085	6,263	6,790	18,007	8,683	17,190
Vladivostok, USSR	11,869	2,807	7,590	14,284	6,059	13,768	8,663	8,335	7,758	8,394	10,564	8,858	13,542	3,542	14,665	12,304	12,450	3,720	9,623	2,373
Volgograd, USSR	10,881	6,577	13,874	9,514	11,487	10,650	3,358	3,270	10,653	10,142	4,573	9,462	9,943	8,337	10,094	10,763	7,045	8,385	9,075	6,172
Vologda, USSR	9,866	6,883	13,187	10,511	11,739	9,946	2,809	2,597	11,475	8,941	4,478	8,275	9,288	8,606	9,666	9,812	8,031	8,688	7,941	6,404
Vorkuta, USSR	9,886	5,971	11,691	11,875	10,613	10,515	3,947	3,643	11,030	8,173	5,821	7,741	9,949	7,587	10,584	9,971	9,405	7,700	7,693	5,437
Wake Island	10,870	5,531	3,407	16,491	4,249	13,294	12,102	11,728	7,539	7,289	14,119	8,342	13,636	4,546	14,987	11,464	16,073	4,696	9,520	5,519
Wallis Island	10,482	8,677	1,258	14,558	4,509	12,347	15,721	15,354	7,425	8,239	17,480	9,428	13,044	7,074	13,806	10,990	16,526	7,117	10,541	8,900
Walvis Bay, Namibia	12,006	11,830	17,076	1,274	13,244	9,602	8,427	8,783	9,824	15,362	6,684	14,195	9,182	12,593	7,885	11,410	1,511	12,435	12,988	11,973
Warsaw, Poland	9,315	8,158	14,403	9,549	13,061	8,952	1,661	1,604	12,328	9,191	3,083	8,319	8,246	9,907	8,444	9,143	7,110	9,973	7,728	7,710
Washington, D.C.	2,177	13,058	10,612	12,700	15,016	3,302	5,711	5,629	18,161	3,666	6,118	2,494	3,175	13,956	4,512	2,212	11,687	14,146	1,287	12,505
Watson Lake, Canada	5,435	9,221	7,907	16,253	10,962	7,462	6,709	6,386	13,892	2,415	8,319	2,451	7,439	9,763	8,784	5,871	14,170	9,957	3,224	8,730

Distances in Kilometers	Cancun, Mexico	Canton, China	Canton Atoll, Phoenix Islands	Cape Town, South Africa	Cape York, Australia	Caracas, Venezuela	Cardiff, United Kingdom	Carlisle, United Kingdom	Carnarvon, Australia	Carson City, Nevada	Casablanca, Morocco	Casper, Wyoming	Castries, Saint Lucia	Catbalogan, Philippines	Cayenne, French Guiana	Cayman Islands (Georgetown)	Cazombo, Angola	Cebu, Philippines	Cedar Rapids, Iowa	Changsha, China
Weimar, East Germany	8,754	8,836	14,660	9,431	13,732	8,285	1,014	1,049	12,962	8,943	2,465	7,993	7,573	10,581	7,760	8,549	7,056	10,650	7,306	8,382
Wellington, New Zealand	12,221	9,543	4,471	11,334	4,633	13,133	18,861	18,485	5,866	11,104	19,128	12,217	13,873	7,789	13,850	12,541	13,452	7,728	13,153	9,983
West Berlin, West Germany	8,829	8,637	14,477	9,588	13,526	8,434	1,143	1,108	12,842	8,889	2,687	7,965	7,729	10,378	7,948	8,644	7,195	10,450	7,315	8,178
Wewak, Papua New Guinea	14,249	4,426	4,967	12,945	803	16,577	13,867	13,571	3,986	10,830	15,545	11,908	17,089	2,679	18,259	14,842	13,262	2,670	13,088	4,809
Whangarei, New Zealand	12,133	9,150	3,916	11,902	4,242	13,279	18,240	17,864	5,871	10,700	19,721	11,845	14,030	7,390	14,160	12,504	13,947	7,344	12,844	9,563
Whitehorse, Canada	5,765	8,895	7,722	16,469	10,632	7,811	6,845	6,511	13,541	2,621	8,516	2,766	7,790	9,414	9,134	6,209	14,295	9,608	3,571	8,410
Wichita, Kansas	2,101	12,556	8,835	14,317	13,384	4,279	7,102	6,942	16,771	1,961	7,805	953	4,443	12,990	5,824	2,560	13,464	13,185	678	12,059
Willemstad, Curacao	2,143	16,100	11,470	10,516	16,606	285	7,289	7,386	18,568	5,818	6,631	4,952	887	16,961	1,993	1,551	10,485	17,155	3,976	15,539
Wiluna, Australia	17,224	5,552	7,699	9,400	2,924	18,076	14,569	14,488	688	14,346	14,989	15,464	18,606	4,275	17,482	17,675	10,146	4,102	16,654	6,113
Windhoek, Namibia	12,251	11,566	17,039	1,263	13,026	9,853	8,443	8,793	9,603	15,559	6,747	14,381	9,422	12,325	8,134	11,655	1,332	12,169	13,176	11,714
Windsor, Canada	2,373	12,573	10,112	13,313	14,394	3,857	5,860	5,733	17,548	3,100	6,482	1,908	3,783	13,379	5,133	2,555	12,198	13,571	716	12,029
Winnipeg, Canada	3,319	11,382	9,149	14,570	13,072	5,177	6,156	5,941	16,174	2,143	7,211	1,052	5,152	12,048	6,508	3,671	13,148	12,241	976	10,860
Winston-Salem, North Carolina	1,775	13,300	10,327	12,829	14,893	3,138	6,129	6,049	18,198	3,478	6,488	2,354	3,110	14,091	4,479	1,865	11,957	14,284	1,184	12,755
Wroclaw, Poland	9,121	8,458	14,593	9,419	13,363	8,686	1,407	1,400	12,568	9,159	2,783	8,249	7,974	10,208	8,150	8,930	7,002	10,274	7,609	8,012
Wuhan, China	13,860	833	8,655	12,324	5,476	15,457	9,062	8,811	6,137	10,480	10,645	10,883	15,044	2,354	15,827	14,239	10,811	2,457	11,544	293
Wyndham, Australia	16,304	4,564	6,742	10,794	1,644	18,315	14,145	13,965	1,833	12,983	15,154	14,051	19,042	3,033	18,839	16,877	11,258	2,887	15,217	5,099
Xi'an, China	13,655	1,306	9,219	12,072	6,113	15,031	8,438	8,195	6,564	10,461	9,998	10,748	14,556	2,973	15,244	13,978	10,390	3,063	11,306	776
Xining, China	13,551	1,860	9,891	11,641	6,752	14,658	7,833	7,608	6,919	10,600	9,334	10,758	14,118	3,597	14,681	13,807	9,824	3,669	11,195	1,406
Yakutsk, USSR	10,242	4,496	8,713	14,367	8,139	11,838	6,752	6,400	9,735	7,197	8,735	7,353	11,526	5,589	12,580	10,584	12,043	5,757	7,898	3,953
Yanji, China	12,007	2,657	7,754	14,089	6,080	13,863	8,598	8,276	7,676	8,558	10,479	9,001	13,614	3,478	14,706	12,431	12,258	3,652	9,745	2,207
Yaounde, Cameroon	10,720	11,043	19,660	4,244	14,572	8,678	5,455	5,806	11,418	13,123	3,845	11,932	8,029	12,460	7,087	10,182	2,148	12,379	10,811	10,929
Yap Island (Colonia)	14,062	3,047	5,731	13,336	2,288	16,476	12,299	12,002	4,641	10,375	14,020	11,300	16,665	1,471	18,041	14,645	12,965	1,563	12,386	3,349
Yaraka, Australia	14,833	6,268	5,330	11,338	1,577	16,389	15,960	15,723	3,071	12,219	17,119	13,408	17,141	4,559	17,196	15,321	12,461	4,467	14,607	6,754
Yarmouth, Canada	3,159	12,591	11,475	12,131	15,427	3,699	4,652	4,582	17,900	4,431	5,106	3,229	3,341	13,748	4,517	3,071	10,837	13,926	2,089	12,028
Yellowknife, Canada	5,048	9,634	8,678	15,451	11,734	6,892	6,008	5,701	14,538	2,616	7,544	2,244	6,798	10,342	8,112	5,419	13,452	10,533	2,724	9,115
Yerevan, USSR	11,553	6,624	14,507	8,631	11,448	11,024	3,836	3,835	10,148	11,074	4,632	10,353	10,288	8,363	10,240	11,370	6,184	8,381	9,893	6,294
Yinchuan, China	13,269	1,825	9,511	12,092	6,614	14,539	7,927	7,680	7,052	10,211	9,517	10,418	14,048	3,485	14,723	13,560	10,265	3,579	10,913	1,295
Yogyakarta, Indonesia	17,665	3,434	8,648	9,714	3,540	19,599	12,306	12,194	1,920	13,942	13,074	14,734	18,858	2,695	18,097	18,223	9,571	2,501	15,648	3,993
York, United Kingdom	7,853	9,434	14,285	9,904	14,246	7,488	294	164	13,818	8,150	2,303	7,154	6,796	11,144	7,112	7,661	7,632	11,233	6,421	8,946
Yumen, China	13,240	2,361	10,262	11,531	7,253	14,213	7,332	7,109	7,350	10,464	8,838	10,534	13,652	4,099	14,184	13,458	9,593	4,171	10,895	1,904
Yutian, China	13,472	3,383	11,679	10,219	8,242	13,827	6,586	6,436	7,610	11,304	7,812	11,140	13,158	5,126	13,375	13,541	8,180	5,152	11,248	3,074
Yuzhno-Sakhalinsk, USSR	10,987	3,730	7,086	15,189	6,387	12,997	8,621	8,268	8,475	7,458	10,602	7,968	12,851	4,246	14,070	11,446	13,223	4,435	8,792	3,319
Zagreb, Yugoslavia	9,289	8,737	15,186	8,832	13,649	8,633	1,544	1,676	12,520	9,615	2,419	8,655	7,901	10,497	7,946	9,047	6,427	10,546	7,940	8,321
Zahedan, Iran	13,422	5,236	13,752	8,320	9,795	12,888	5,739	5,726	8,245	12,402	6,395	11,888	12,144	6,871	11,957	13,265	6,134	6,851	11,607	5,043
Zamboanga, Philippines	15,601	2,028	7,439	11,699	2,984	17,845	11,713	11,492	3,631	11,878	13,075	12,655	17,667	621	18,562	16,145	11,172	427	13,606	2,545
Zanzibar, Tanzania	13,985	8,671	16,463	3,745	11,333	11,899	7,556	7,806	8,161	15,789	6,607	14,725	11,279	9,691	10,244	13,450	1,902	9,565	13,766	8,766
Zaragoza, Spain	8,148	10,155	15,611	8,595	15,068	7,253	1,111	1,481	13,798	9,137	1,068	8,047	6,512	11,912	6,512	7,836	6,408	11,968	7,147	9,724
Zashiversk, USSR	9,384	5,330	8,570	14,882	8,670	11,040	6,507	6,138	10,516	6,360	8,522	6,490	10,769	6,321	11,888	9,736	12,462	6,497	7,045	4,795
Zhengzhou, China	13,457	1,290	8,797	12,485	5,878	14,996	8,649	8,388	6,598	10,155	10,280	10,503	14,578	2,787	15,376	13,816	10,830	2,901	11,126	729
Zurich, Switzerland	8,681	9,201	15,070	9,059	14,111	8,050	955	1,148	13,126	9,134	2,032	8,136	7,323	10,955	7,429	8,437	6,721	11,016	7,377	8,761

Distances in Kilometers

	Channel-Port-aux-Basques, Can.	Charleston, South Carolina	Charleston, West Virginia	Charlotte, North Carolina	Charlotte Amalie, U.S.V.I.	Charlottetown, Canada	Chatham, Canada	Chatham Islands (Waitangi)	Chengdu, China	Chesterfield Inlet, Canada	Cheyenne, Wyoming	Chiang Mai, Thailand	Chibougamau, Canada	Chicago, Illinois	Chiclayo, Peru	Chihuahua, Mexico	Chongquing, China	Christchurch, New Zealand	Christiansted, U.S.V.I.	Christmas Island [Indian Ocean]
Charleston, South Carolina	2,401	0	639	285	2,191	2,071	2,003	12,936	12,971	3,484	2,393	14,299	1,960	1,219	4,375	2,540	13,072	13,751	2,257	17,475
Charleston, West Virginia	2,090	639	0	354	2,745	1,753	1,634	13,175	12,342	2,847	2,005	13,680	1,409	644	4,998	2,504	12,438	13,951	2,815	16,836
Charlotte, North Carolina	2,262	285	354	0	2,442	1,925	1,835	13,029	12,694	3,202	2,192	14,028	1,716	946	4,648	2,488	12,792	13,828	2,510	17,190
Charlotte Amalie, U.S.V.I.	3,283	2,191	2,745	2,442	0	3,097	3,182	13,124	14,456	5,371	4,552	15,541	3,602	3,382	3,225	4,332	14,626	13,997	71	18,689
Charlottetown, Canada	338	2,071	1,753	1,925	3,097	0	200	14,927	11,392	2,563	3,368	12,584	931	2,012	6,101	4,206	11,547	15,695	3,162	15,905
Chatham, Canada	481	2,003	1,634	1,835	3,182	200	0	14,796	11,336	2,393	3,184	12,552	731	1,847	6,126	4,054	11,484	15,549	3,248	15,870
Chatham Islands (Waitangi)	15,264	12,936	13,175	13,029	13,124	14,927	14,796	0	11,536	14,059	11,837	11,010	14,324	12,987	10,025	10,763	11,276	873	13,099	8,232
Chengdu, China	11,180	12,971	12,342	12,694	14,456	11,392	11,336	11,536	0	9,501	11,521	1,413	11,077	11,883	17,328	12,709	271	10,777	14,515	4,558
Chesterfield Inlet, Canada	2,611	3,484	2,847	3,202	5,371	2,563	2,393	14,059	9,501	0	2,639	10,860	1,789	2,397	7,830	4,015	9,592	14,524	5,441	13,996
Cheyenne, Wyoming	3,655	2,393	2,005	2,192	4,552	3,368	3,184	11,837	11,521	2,639	0	12,933	2,549	1,435	5,885	1,392	11,539	12,488	4,615	15,495
Chiang Mai, Thailand	12,340	14,299	13,680	14,028	15,541	12,584	12,552	11,010	1,413	10,860	12,933	0	12,367	13,254	18,669	14,112	1,421	10,178	15,592	3,321
Chibougamau, Canada	1,147	1,960	1,409	1,716	3,602	931	731	14,324	11,077	1,789	2,549	12,367	0	1,359	6,302	3,569	11,200	15,020	3,672	15,634
Chicago, Illinois	2,328	1,219	644	946	3,382	2,012	1,847	12,987	11,883	2,397	1,435	13,254	1,359	0	5,445	2,223	11,961	13,713	3,451	16,296
Chiclayo, Peru	6,354	4,375	4,998	4,648	3,225	6,101	6,126	10,025	17,328	7,830	5,885	18,669	6,302	5,445	0	4,824	17,394	10,884	3,182	18,003
Chihuahua, Mexico	4,533	2,540	2,504	2,488	4,332	4,206	4,054	10,763	12,709	4,015	1,392	14,112	3,569	2,223	4,824	0	12,694	11,496	4,381	16,157
Chongquing, China	11,344	13,072	12,438	12,792	14,626	11,547	11,484	11,276	271	9,592	11,539	1,421	11,200	11,961	17,394	12,694	0	10,523	14,687	4,434
Christchurch, New Zealand	16,026	13,751	13,951	13,828	13,997	15,695	15,549	873	10,777	14,524	12,488	10,178	15,020	13,713	10,884	11,496	10,523	0	13,972	7,359
Christiansted, U.S.V.I.	3,346	2,257	2,815	2,510	71	3,162	3,248	13,099	14,515	5,441	4,615	15,592	3,672	3,451	3,182	4,381	14,687	13,972	0	18,712
Christmas Is. [Indian Ocean]	15,657	17,475	16,836	17,190	18,689	15,905	15,870	8,232	4,558	13,996	15,495	3,321	15,634	16,296	18,003	16,157	4,434	7,359	18,712	0
Christmas Is. [Pacific Ocean]	10,477	8,735	8,647	8,677	10,223	10,191	10,007	5,429	10,706	8,672	6,823	11,364	9,351	8,208	8,685	6,196	10,476	5,856	10,251	10,803
Churchill, Canada	2,608	3,077	2,439	2,792	5,072	2,489	2,300	13,650	9,953	545	2,098	11,328	1,608	1,930	7,375	3,471	10,031	14,169	5,143	14,398
Cincinnati, Ohio	2,248	815	264	540	2,977	1,916	1,778	13,019	12,230	2,729	1,741	13,587	1,445	406	5,101	2,300	12,317	13,779	3,046	16,681
Ciudad Bolivia, Venezuela	4,479	2,870	3,504	3,155	1,263	4,258	4,315	11,929	15,650	6,314	4,959	16,796	4,622	4,076	1,964	4,344	15,798	12,798	1,219	19,552
Ciudad Juarez, Mexico	4,345	2,498	2,375	2,407	4,416	4,025	3,864	10,987	12,388	3,687	1,054	13,794	3,337	2,018	5,115	346	12,378	11,698	4,469	15,967
Ciudad Victoria, Mexico	4,408	2,129	2,319	2,177	3,596	4,071	3,952	10,861	13,500	4,446	2,002	14,911	3,615	2,278	3,972	881	13,502	11,652	3,638	17,018
Clarksburg, West Virginia	1,939	724	152	453	2,756	1,602	1,482	13,325	12,247	2,765	2,086	13,577	1,273	680	5,098	2,643	12,349	14,099	2,826	16,762
Cleveland, Ohio	1,907	982	350	701	3,022	1,578	1,431	13,367	11,993	2,502	1,930	13,331	1,095	495	5,347	2,628	12,091	14,119	3,092	16,496
Cocos (Keeling) Island	15,475	17,682	17,082	17,423	17,952	15,770	15,784	8,827	4,784	14,273	16,154	3,413	15,724	16,665	17,898	17,014	4,717	7,958	17,948	979
Colombo, Sri Lanka	12,757	15,123	14,641	14,923	15,253	13,074	13,124	11,633	3,645	12,169	14,661	2,452	13,233	14,452	17,794	16,019	3,757	10,762	15,269	3,450
Colon, Panama	4,664	2,591	3,215	2,865	1,897	4,387	4,393	11,258	15,555	6,054	4,289	16,889	4,525	3,682	1,784	3,470	15,642	12,131	1,887	19,413
Colorado Springs, Colorado	3,778	2,340	2,016	2,164	4,463	3,480	3,301	11,657	11,752	2,886	256	13,164	2,696	1,497	5,669	1,137	11,765	12,327	4,525	15,657
Columbia, South Carolina	2,370	171	486	137	2,360	2,036	1,952	12,934	12,828	3,333	2,236	14,164	1,851	1,049	4,513	2,450	12,924	13,739	2,427	17,316
Columbus, Georgia	2,749	476	721	490	2,544	2,412	2,315	12,539	12,953	3,458	2,008	14,318	2,129	1,071	4,375	2,065	13,032	13,340	2,607	17,343
Columbus, Ohio	2,087	845	215	560	2,958	1,755	1,616	13,180	12,151	2,652	1,847	13,498	1,297	444	5,184	2,458	12,244	13,940	3,028	16,631
Conakry, Guinea	5,992	7,224	7,437	7,333	5,603	6,194	6,394	15,847	12,038	8,416	9,414	12,011	7,121	7,979	7,552	9,742	12,309	16,186	5,575	13,401
Concepcion, Chile	9,450	7,738	8,371	8,018	6,167	9,254	9,320	8,209	19,273	11,216	9,221	17,861	9,611	8,842	3,401	8,028	19,198	8,915	6,105	14,764
Concord, New Hampshire	1,083	1,372	1,007	1,196	2,825	746	639	14,182	11,813	2,558	2,741	13,074	777	1,328	5,597	3,478	11,945	14,954	2,895	16,370
Constantine, Algeria	5,423	7,667	7,492	7,603	7,196	5,753	5,901	19,123	8,661	6,806	8,950	9,002	6,428	7,738	10,140	9,955	8,929	18,585	7,211	11,505
Copenhagen, Denmark	4,821	7,220	6,837	7,061	7,562	5,149	5,226	18,551	7,342	5,263	7,766	8,080	5,508	6,860	10,777	9,014	7,586	18,050	7,601	11,157
Coppermine, Canada	3,825	4,506	3,872	4,221	6,517	3,784	3,613	13,411	8,609	1,220	3,036	10,008	2,987	3,322	8,728	4,400	8,666	13,727	6,588	12,977
Coquimbo, Chile	8,673	7,002	7,638	7,284	5,390	8,479	8,548	8,852	19,581	10,485	8,593	18,437	8,853	8,129	2,718	7,462	19,824	9,591	5,328	15,516
Cordoba, Argentina	8,760	7,293	7,931	7,578	5,506	8,598	8,687	9,211	18,905	10,763	9,052	17,827	9,063	8,463	3,178	7,991	19,119	9,901	5,439	15,245
Cordoba, Spain	4,486	6,670	6,527	6,619	6,182	4,808	4,967	19,048	9,428	6,128	8,084	9,895	5,539	6,813	9,179	9,013	9,689	19,342	6,199	12,515
Cork, Ireland	3,611	5,994	5,693	5,871	6,137	3,948	4,060	18,759	8,758	4,709	6,936	9,523	4,479	5,830	9,343	8,048	8,997	19,071	6,174	12,570
Corner Brook, Canada	178	2,564	2,230	2,416	3,452	493	600	15,396	11,008	2,544	3,730	12,164	1,193	2,434	6,531	4,649	11,174	16,145	3,514	15,481
Corrientes, Argentina	8,310	7,030	7,663	7,314	5,112	8,173	8,277	9,880	18,328	10,452	8,954	17,566	8,708	8,230	3,190	7,997	18,584	10,559	5,043	15,487
Cosenza, Italy	5,931	8,266	8,021	8,171	7,998	6,268	6,394	18,838	7,757	6,946	9,290	8,101	6,842	8,189	11,010	10,410	8,026	18,000	8,018	10,694
Craiova, Romania	6,123	8,514	8,193	8,385	8,509	6,460	6,561	18,398	6,975	6,756	9,244	7,408	6,917	8,276	11,620	10,462	7,241	17,532	8,536	10,180
Cruzeiro do Sul, Brazil	6,257	4,538	5,176	4,821	2,995	6,040	6,096	10,526	17,432	8,020	6,325	18,482	6,378	5,693	806	5,387	17,575	11,364	2,939	17,990
Cuiaba, Brazil	7,001	5,922	6,538	6,201	3,877	6,882	6,998	11,080	17,398	9,248	8,038	17,361	7,474	7,140	2,770	7,272	17,665	11,804	3,806	16,498
Curitiba, Brazil	8,143	7,214	7,826	7,492	5,131	8,057	8,187	10,641	17,349	10,491	9,334	16,681	8,706	8,433	3,852	8,527	17,603	11,259	5,061	15,199
Cuzco, Peru	6,885	5,191	5,829	5,474	3,609	6,676	6,720	10,108	18,064	8,674	6,931	18,899	7,030	6,340	1,140	5,935	18,221	10,925	3,550	17,336
Dacca, Bangladesh	11,545	13,671	13,085	13,418	14,643	11,814	11,805	12,035	1,555	10,353	12,655	1,043	11,712	12,739	17,867	13,950	1,733	11,195	14,688	4,133
Dakar, Senegal	5,293	6,586	6,772	6,681	5,074	5,498	5,697	16,207	12,003	7,725	8,737	12,139	6,424	7,302	7,285	9,117	12,274	16,666	5,053	13,851
Dallas, Texas	3,557	1,580	1,506	1,498	3,560	3,226	3,082	11,717	12,649	3,426	1,169	14,059	2,654	1,296	4,731	999	12,679	12,469	3,617	16,643
Damascus, Syria	7,721	10,100	9,799	9,982	9,899	8,058	8,166	16,965	6,288	8,298	10,835	6,382	8,531	9,890	12,848	12,073	6,559	16,104	9,917	8,796
Danang, Vietnam	12,846	14,533	13,895	14,249	16,126	13,051	12,988	10,099	1,671	11,049	12,820	1,026	12,691	13,387	18,665	13,844	1,504	9,291	16,186	2,952
Dar es Salaam, Tanzania	11,198	13,145	13,158	13,173	11,751	11,509	11,678	13,339	8,041	12,574	14,811	7,134	12,268	13,521	13,112	15,657	8,232	12,731	11,724	7,306
Darwin, Australia	16,004	16,168	15,714	15,959	18,220	16,039	15,883	6,095	5,567	13,495	13,776	4,916	15,261	15,074	16,022	13,890	5,330	5,273	18,264	2,754
Davao, Philippines	13,935	14,842	14,247	14,571	16,969	14,038	13,914	8,093	3,445	11,619	12,611	3,159	13,404	13,625	17,225	13,220	3,189	7,334	17,040	2,942
David, Panama	4,864	2,706	3,315	2,970	2,187	4,577	4,572	10,984	15,623	6,131	4,244	16,990	4,660	3,741	1,705	3,338	15,692	11,856	2,179	19,117
Dawson, Canada	4,960	5,310	4,703	5,033	7,432	4,890	4,710	12,411	8,146	2,351	3,384	9,558	4,039	4,090	9,267	4,591	8,157	12,648	7,502	12,248
Dawson Creek, Canada	4,179	4,017	3,447	3,753	6,191	4,021	3,825	12,250	9,549	1,849	1,977	10,961	3,098	2,809	7,861	3,218	9,563	12,679	6,260	13,610
Denpasar, Indonesia	15,658	16,919	16,312	16,644	18,931	15,836	15,750	7,609	4,511	13,591	14,684	3,519	15,345	15,700	17,633	15,177	4,329	6,749	18,998	1,068
Denver, Colorado	3,741	2,372	2,022	2,186	4,511	3,447	3,266	11,717	11,655	2,793	156	13,067	2,648	1,482	5,762	1,236	11,669	12,379	4,573	15,583
Derby, Australia	16,638	17,104	16,629	16,887	19,119	16,736	16,604	6,289	5,706	14,259	14,711	4,818	16,046	15,985	16,311	14,818	5,500	5,427	19,149	2,081
Des Moines, Iowa	2,792	1,558	1,084	1,318	3,748	2,486	2,312	12,570	11,802	2,429	937	13,197	1,753	500	5,535	1,828	11,859	13,274	3,815	16,083
Detroit, Michigan	1,965	1,097	459	813	3,164	1,643	1,485	13,325	11,889	2,391	1,811	13,235	1,076	382	5,447	2,570	11,983	14,066	3,234	16,378
Dhahran, Saudi Arabia	9,213	11,608	11,269	11,473	11,445	9,548	9,643	15,414	5,254	9,489	12,106	5,065	9,951	11,301	14,315	13,420	5,513	14,550	11,461	7,254
Diego Garcia Island	13,634	16,009	15,701	15,895	15,260	13,971	14,072	11,094	5,393	13,642	16,250	4,105	14,371	15,706	16,579	17,642	5,481	10,270	15,246	3,672
Dijon, France	4,696	7,064	6,783	6,952	7,027	5,034	5,151	19,613	8,196	5,710	8,018	8,788	5,576	6,927	10,173	9,145	8,452	18,964	7,056	11,663
Dili, Indonesia	15,657	16,266	15,735	16,023	18,451	15,747	15,614	6,807	4,910	13,274	13,900	4,202	15,063	15,093	16,739	14,196	4,683	5,979	18,515	2,195
Djibouti, Djibouti	9,970	12,239	12,055	12,177	11,470	10,305	10,441	14,797	6,589	10,815	13,309	6,030	10,900	12,247	13,759	14,468	6,823	14,033	11,466	7,334
Dnepropetrovsk, USSR	6,542	8,940	8,581	8,776	9,209	6,869	6,942	17,554	6,036	6,728	9,325	6,558	7,190	8,529	12,390	10,631	6,299	16,736	9,242	9,492
Dobo, Indonesia	15,201	15,390	14,911	15,168	17,524	15,222	15,062	6,390	5,154	12,671	13,000	4,724	14,433	14,268	16,004	13,214	4,900	5,623	17,580	3,188
Doha, Qatar	9,389	11,785	11,443	11,649	11,622	9,724	9,818	15,235	5,157	9,637	12,258	4,927	10,121	11,469	14,477	13,580	5,414	14,371	11,638	7,078
Donetsk, USSR	6,737	9,132	8,726	8,964	9,422	7,062	7,132	17,344	5,834	6,859	9,468	6,344	7,366	8,701	12,605	10,786	6,099	16,522	9,456	9,280
Dover, Delaware	1,618	813	538	644	2,524	1,282	1,197	13,666	12,274	2,875	2,493	13,565	1,199	1,067	5,104	3,039	12,393	14,457	2,594	16,827
Dresden, East Germany	5,095	7,494	7,150	7,353	7,657	5,429	5,523	18,908	7,446	5,728	8,187	8,078	5,860	7,218	10,842	9,401	7,700	18,223	7,691	11,042
Dubayy, United Arab Emir.	9,628	12,029	11,660	11,881	11,952	9,961	10,046	14,934	4,799	9,738	12,373	4,547	10,315	11,654	14,845	13,719	5,054	14,065	11,970	6,743
Dublin, Ireland	3,723	6,116	5,795	5,985	6,323	4,059	4,163	18,746	8,543	4,690	6,977	9,321	4,551	5,907	9,535	8,118	8,781	18,912	6,361	12,389
Duluth, Minnesota	2,482	1,869	1,270	1,593	4,015	2,213	2,021	13,017	11,275	1,846	1,195	12,659	1,357	651	6,054	2,353	11,344	13,682	4,085	15,649
Dunedin, New Zealand	16,283	13,977	14,199	14,064	14,115	15,949	15,810	1,045	10,796	14,832	12,776	10,135	15,299	13,981	10,964	11,760	10,547	310	14,086	7,235
Durango, Mexico	4,776	2,602	2,696	2,609	4,160	4,442	4,307	10,490	13,225	4,490	1,897	14,624	3,890	2,531	4,345	529	13,204	11,255	4,202	16,485
Durban, South Africa	12,402	13,565	13,874	13,722	11,565	12,637	12,835	11,367	10,227	14,498	15,874	9,055	13,549	14,444	11,619	15,881	10,364	10,990	11,513	7,965
Dushanbe, USSR	9,166	11,476	10,971	11,263	12,081	9,467	9,496	14,655	3,329	8,563	11,156	3,646	9,562	10,784	15,292	12,548	3,600	13,820	12,120	6,643
East London, South Africa	12,430	13,421	13,775	13,597	11,361	12,645	12,844	11,128	10,668	14,649	15,779	9,476	13,569	14,369	11,237	15,655	10,799	10,802	11,306	8,247
Easter Island (Hanga Roa)	9,685	7,330	7,808	7,530	6,957	9,372	9,327	6,186	16,751	10,167	7,575	16,981	9,213	7,966	3,855	6,183	16,503	7,054	6,928	14,387
Echo Bay, Canada	3,938	4,483	3,854	4,199	6,534	3,877	3,701	13,183	8,695	1,327	2,897	10,100	3,050	3,283	8,651	4,244	8,743	13,509	6,605	13,013
Edinburgh, United Kingdom	3,861	6,262	5,907	6,115	6,583	4,193	4,282	18,593	8,222	4,610	6,983	9,031	4,618	5,977	9,803	8,169	8,458	18,596	6,623	12,142
Edmonton, Canada	3,810	3,518	2,952	3,255	5,694	3,627	3,428	12,357	9,998	1,704	1,524	11,411	2,696	2,312	7,392	2,832	10,021	12,847	5,763	14,107
El Aaiun, Morocco	4,568	6,366	6,387	6,388	5,366	4,840	5,029	17,625	10,779	6,723	8,206	11,120	5,711	6,812	8,090	8,874	11,045	18,116	5,366	13,393
Elat, Israel	7,936	10,288	10,024	10,187	9,937	8,273	8,392	16,815	6,549	8,656	11,155	6,538	8,796	10,153	12,781	12,357	6,818	15,980	9,950	8,771
Elazig, Turkey	7,513	9,912	9,560	9,770	9,925	7,847	7,937	16,995	5,886	7,860	10,445	6,124	8,241	9,593	12,992	11,732	6,157	16,122	9,950	8,763
Eniwetok Atoll, Marshall Isls.	12,293	11,809	11,400	11,614	13,884	12,180	11,987	6,506	6,333	9,701	9,423	6,816	11,269	10,774	13,202	9,570	6,078	6,185	13,937	6,716
Erfurt, East Germany	4,925	7,322	6,987	7,185	7,467	5,260	5,357	19,043	7,626	5,627	8,059	8,267	5,708	7,067	10,651	9,258	7,879	18,402	7,501	11,232
Erzurum, Turkey	7,545	9,947	9,576	9,796	10,032	7,877	7,961	16,882	5,686	7,796	10,398	5,958	8,241	9,587	13,127	11,702	5,957	16,011	10,058	8,657
Esfahan, Iran	8,766	11,167	10,781	11,010	11,226	9,096	9,175	15,694	4,926	8,853	11,485	4,950	9,428	10,762	14,257	12,826	5,194	14,820	11,250	7,462
Essen, West Germany	4,646	7,042	6,713	6,908	7,187	4,982	5,082	19,131	7,861	5,421	7,819	8,531	5,445	6,804	10,376	9,002	8,112	18,622	7,221	11,514
Eucla, Australia	18,120	17,320	17,161	17,248	17,989	18,097	17,917	4,900	7,384	15,537	15,176	6,435	17,221	16,606	14,776	14,780	7,180	4,028	17,952	3,350

Distances in Kilometers	Channel-Port-aux-Basques, Can.	Charleston, South Carolina	Charleston, West Virginia	Charlotte, North Carolina	Charlotte Amalie, U.S.V.I.	Charlottetown, Canada	Chatham, Canada	Chatham Islands (Waitangi)	Chengdu, China	Chesterfield Inlet, Canada	Cheyenne, Wyoming	Chiang Mai, Thailand	Chibougamau, Canada	Chicago, Illinois	Chiclayo, Peru	Chihuahua, Mexico	Chongquing, China	Christchurch, New Zealand	Christiansted, U.S.V.I.	Christmas Island [Indian Ocean]
Fargo, North Dakota	2,824	2,122	1,559	1,857	4,297	2,563	2,369	12,740	11,166	1,873	904	12,564	1,688	917	6,174	2,180	11,221	13,382	4,366	15,454
Faroe Islands (Torshavn)	3,605	5,982	5,563	5,805	6,579	3,921	3,979	17,887	8,038	3,991	6,456	8,971	4,210	5,556	9,797	7,700	8,257	17,947	6,626	12,194
Florence, Italy	5,311	7,666	7,400	7,561	7,524	5,648	5,769	19,396	7,934	6,307	8,642	8,412	6,202	7,552	10,615	9,770	8,198	18,523	7,549	11,164
Florianopolis, Brazil	8,390	7,458	8,071	7,736	5,380	8,306	8,436	10,483	17,351	10,740	9,564	16,580	8,956	8,677	4,025	8,736	17,594	11,083	5,309	14,966
Fort George, Canada	1,559	2,342	1,733	2,074	4,120	1,411	1,220	14,218	10,638	1,255	2,381	11,957	540	1,475	6,716	3,559	10,749	14,852	4,190	15,180
Fort McMurray, Canada	3,620	3,586	2,989	3,312	5,732	3,466	3,269	12,702	9,762	1,359	1,798	11,171	2,545	2,367	7,603	3,150	9,797	13,170	5,801	13,973
Fort Nelson, Canada	4,250	4,288	3,698	4,016	6,442	4,121	3,928	12,418	9,189	1,779	2,332	10,602	3,215	3,070	8,210	3,589	9,207	12,802	6,511	13,299
Fort Severn, Canada	2,157	2,648	2,011	2,365	4,592	2,013	1,821	13,832	10,340	838	2,070	11,697	1,115	1,568	6,992	3,373	10,430	14,410	4,663	14,829
Fort Smith, Arkansas	3,206	1,367	1,186	1,233	3,464	2,877	2,729	12,075	12,443	3,121	1,110	13,846	2,290	932	4,909	1,331	12,488	12,821	3,525	16,589
Fort Vermilion, Canada	3,872	3,919	3,321	3,645	6,062	3,736	3,542	12,640	9,458	1,469	2,076	10,869	2,826	2,700	7,916	3,395	9,488	13,065	6,132	13,643
Fort Wayne, Indiana	2,183	1,032	427	751	3,172	1,859	1,704	13,103	12,006	2,506	1,649	13,365	1,292	226	5,324	2,350	12,092	13,845	3,241	16,457
Fort-Chimo, Canada	1,325	2,947	2,396	2,706	4,422	1,368	1,247	15,000	10,143	1,341	3,176	11,405	990	2,253	7,265	4,373	10,279	15,596	4,490	14,699
Fort-de-France, Martinique	3,660	2,773	3,318	3,021	584	3,513	3,619	13,157	14,752	5,882	5,135	15,722	4,098	3,957	3,143	4,879	14,943	14,022	521	18,524
Fortaleza, Brazil	6,030	5,947	6,432	6,172	3,790	6,043	6,213	13,276	15,091	8,606	8,333	15,118	6,867	7,075	4,595	8,048	15,362	13,919	3,730	15,762
Frankfort, Kentucky	2,329	751	283	488	2,930	1,995	1,862	12,936	12,325	2,825	1,739	13,684	1,547	472	5,005	2,233	12,409	13,701	2,997	16,764
Frankfurt am Main, W. Ger.	4,812	7,204	6,884	7,074	7,302	5,149	5,252	19,217	7,817	5,610	8,006	8,450	5,625	6,983	10,478	9,184	8,071	18,594	7,334	11,395
Fredericton, Canada	600	1,854	1,496	1,689	3,067	274	149	14,666	11,467	2,450	3,100	12,690	724	1,739	5,987	3,935	11,612	15,427	3,134	16,007
Freeport, Bahamas	2,899	701	1,339	985	1,687	2,589	2,560	12,598	13,669	4,185	2,886	14,987	2,625	1,887	3,684	2,700	13,772	13,443	1,745	18,173
Freetown, Sierra Leone	6,113	7,327	7,546	7,439	5,684	6,314	6,513	15,758	12,064	8,540	9,526	12,009	7,241	8,092	7,581	9,841	12,335	16,081	5,655	13,336
Frobisher Bay, Canada	1,891	3,536	2,958	3,284	5,050	1,979	1,871	15,119	9,518	1,098	3,437	10,791	1,580	2,729	7,879	4,727	9,651	15,616	5,117	14,076
Frunze, USSR	9,005	11,235	10,693	11,003	12,066	9,288	9,297	14,446	2,939	8,154	10,697	3,522	9,289	10,447	15,289	12,084	3,207	13,651	12,111	6,704
Fukuoka, Japan	10,966	12,007	11,384	11,726	14,033	11,061	10,936	10,132	2,499	8,663	9,992	3,522	10,439	10,793	15,715	10,915	2,299	9,557	14,104	5,538
Funafuti Atoll, Tuvalu	13,057	11,543	11,400	11,463	13,044	12,810	12,615	3,949	9,089	10,855	9,480	9,294	11,910	10,906	11,111	9,004	8,822	3,931	13,068	8,052
Funchal, Madeira Island	3,905	5,816	5,788	5,815	5,036	4,188	4,373	17,848	10,652	6,020	7,556	11,142	5,040	6,181	7,951	8,289	10,911	18,543	5,045	13,680
Fuzhou, China	11,847	13,183	12,548	12,898	15,068	11,993	11,893	10,138	1,576	9,746	11,288	2,239	11,479	11,989	17,069	12,258	1,310	9,437	15,136	4,308
Gaborone, Botswana	11,638	12,869	13,148	13,013	10,929	11,876	12,073	12,072	10,334	13,749	15,139	9,263	12,785	13,705	11,276	15,261	10,498	11,727	10,880	8,508
Galapagos Islands (Santa Cruz)	6,139	3,856	4,409	4,091	3,488	5,837	5,812	9,654	16,352	7,098	4,851	17,758	5,807	4,717	1,352	3,646	16,339	10,527	3,472	17,865
Gander, Canada	370	2,767	2,459	2,631	3,519	708	837	15,631	10,937	2,699	3,973	12,062	1,432	2,676	6,644	4,890	11,111	16,386	3,579	15,369
Gangtok, India	11,106	13,245	12,664	12,994	14,208	11,376	11,369	12,431	1,549	9,952	12,299	1,422	11,285	12,332	17,429	13,617	1,775	11,599	14,253	4,573
Garyarsa, China	10,337	12,572	12,024	12,338	13,347	10,623	10,634	13,363	2,257	9,433	11,917	2,356	10,622	11,760	16,569	13,287	2,518	12,526	13,388	5,397
Gaspe, Canada	421	2,201	1,802	2,022	3,382	306	213	14,939	11,126	2,266	3,252	12,339	727	1,961	6,339	4,181	11,276	15,674	3,448	15,658
Gauhati, India	11,334	13,422	12,828	13,164	14,475	11,596	11,580	12,112	1,306	10,078	12,359	1,108	11,465	12,468	17,682	13,649	1,508	11,284	14,523	4,330
Gdansk, Poland	5,236	7,635	7,248	7,475	7,959	5,564	5,640	18,416	7,015	5,606	8,140	7,708	5,912	7,261	11,168	9,404	7,265	17,779	7,996	10,755
Geneva, Switzerland	4,829	7,191	6,918	7,082	7,113	5,167	5,287	19,683	8,176	5,862	8,167	8,737	5,719	7,069	10,243	9,288	8,434	18,912	7,141	11,576
Genoa, Italy	5,115	7,469	7,204	7,364	7,336	5,453	5,575	19,580	8,070	6,148	8,462	8,575	6,012	7,361	10,438	9,581	8,331	18,711	7,361	11,352
Georgetown, Guyana	4,519	3,651	4,218	3,910	1,474	4,396	4,513	12,787	15,451	6,799	5,974	16,238	5,013	4,853	2,837	5,578	15,666	13,622	1,404	18,210
Geraldton, Australia	17,850	18,569	18,180	18,401	18,850	18,056	17,977	6,221	6,672	15,756	16,209	5,523	17,538	17,541	15,782	16,074	6,512	5,358	18,782	2,226
Ghanzi, Botswana	11,099	12,337	12,608	12,477	10,424	11,335	11,532	12,515	10,513	13,246	14,596	9,517	12,246	13,162	10,934	14,754	10,693	12,209	10,377	8,967
Ghat, Libya	6,479	8,565	8,484	8,545	7,715	6,794	6,960	17,814	8,984	8,077	10,096	9,037	7,549	8,806	10,334	10,985	9,255	17,406	7,715	11,050
Gibraltar	4,547	6,689	6,568	6,648	6,122	4,864	5,028	18,866	9,582	6,263	8,167	10,020	5,618	6,875	9,080	9,063	9,846	19,166	6,136	12,581
Gijon, Spain	4,117	6,402	6,196	6,323	6,162	4,450	4,593	19,285	9,128	5,568	7,638	9,716	5,113	6,426	9,269	8,645	9,382	19,885	6,186	12,527
Gisborne, New Zealand	15,372	13,155	13,316	13,213	13,596	15,046	14,892	743	10,842	13,822	11,800	10,385	14,339	13,048	10,588	10,840	10,579	704	13,579	7,759
Glasgow, United Kingdom	3,798	6,199	5,846	6,053	6,517	4,130	4,220	18,575	8,283	4,572	6,933	9,095	4,561	5,920	9,737	8,114	8,518	18,619	6,557	12,208
Godthab, Greenland	1,914	4,007	3,494	3,785	5,197	2,128	2,096	15,946	9,269	1,900	4,231	10,458	2,087	3,383	8,222	5,480	9,431	16,421	5,259	13,779
Gomez Palacio, Mexico	4,573	2,421	2,496	2,418	4,049	4,239	4,102	10,694	13,129	4,303	1,731	14,534	3,683	2,324	4,398	426	13,116	11,457	4,093	16,531
Goose Bay, Canada	4,800	4,358	3,840	4,113	6,549	4,620	4,421	11,565	9,608	2,541	2,084	11,010	3,689	3,197	7,891	3,102	9,593	11,987	6,615	13,411
Gorki, USSR	6,475	8,809	8,334	8,609	9,439	6,780	6,817	16,866	5,404	6,174	8,812	6,153	6,933	8,213	12,664	10,176	5,653	16,169	9,482	9,311
Goteborg, Sweden	4,709	7,102	6,702	6,935	7,524	5,033	5,103	18,365	7,301	5,059	7,581	8,086	5,357	6,705	10,747	8,843	7,541	17,937	7,565	11,206
Granada, Spain	4,606	6,785	6,646	6,736	6,275	4,928	5,087	19,051	9,391	6,243	8,205	9,836	5,660	6,934	9,254	9,133	9,654	19,240	6,291	12,424
Grand Turk, Turks & Caicos	3,089	1,524	2,125	1,795	735	2,842	2,882	12,849	14,213	4,880	3,840	15,425	3,170	2,741	3,265	3,602	14,352	13,718	790	18,746
Graz, Austria	5,411	7,799	7,486	7,672	7,818	5,748	5,853	19,022	7,488	6,168	8,597	8,022	6,227	7,586	10,959	9,785	7,749	18,195	7,847	10,873
Green Bay, Wisconsin	2,246	1,480	867	1,199	3,610	1,950	1,769	13,131	11,590	2,104	1,422	12,960	1,193	294	5,738	2,381	11,669	13,833	3,680	16,015
Grenoble, France	4,850	7,201	6,940	7,098	7,078	5,188	5,312	19,791	8,260	5,938	8,219	8,801	5,758	7,104	10,193	9,325	8,519	18,964	7,104	11,610
Guadalajara, Mexico	4,951	2,677	2,861	2,727	4,030	4,614	4,492	10,315	13,619	4,837	2,274	15,015	4,128	2,777	3,976	925	13,594	11,103	4,066	16,731
Guam (Agana)	12,842	13,037	12,519	12,797	15,224	12,831	12,662	7,472	4,577	10,269	10,676	4,918	12,016	11,875	15,099	11,103	4,311	6,920	15,288	5,066
Guantanamo, Cuba	3,371	1,476	2,112	1,761	1,097	3,098	3,112	12,429	14,383	4,942	3,640	15,654	3,305	2,681	3,019	3,261	14,502	13,297	1,137	18,935
Guatemala City, Guatemala	4,659	2,277	2,769	2,477	2,760	4,336	4,278	10,813	14,757	5,409	3,247	16,167	4,179	3,033	2,644	2,231	14,784	11,665	2,780	18,218
Guayaquil, Ecuador	5,867	3,866	4,490	4,140	2,796	5,608	5,629	10,381	16,824	7,324	5,422	18,162	5,795	4,941	509	4,413	16,898	11,248	2,759	18,482
Guiyang, China	11,672	13,399	12,765	13,119	14,953	11,876	11,814	11,036	521	9,918	11,836	1,173	11,531	12,283	17,706	12,968	331	10,268	15,014	4,104
Gur'yev, USSR	7,574	9,935	9,476	9,743	10,411	7,887	7,935	16,282	4,778	7,322	9,961	5,294	8,080	9,370	13,619	11,330	5,045	15,469	10,449	8,306
Haifa, Israel	7,685	10,056	9,768	9,943	9,812	8,023	8,134	17,026	6,426	8,321	10,841	6,507	8,514	9,872	12,739	12,064	6,697	16,172	9,829	8,885
Haikou, China	12,443	14,060	13,422	13,776	15,726	12,635	12,564	10,262	1,333	10,579	12,326	1,198	12,241	12,905	18,181	13,357	1,119	9,480	15,789	3,417
Haiphong, Vietnam	12,295	14,029	13,393	13,747	15,572	12,504	12,444	10,592	1,117	10,546	12,413	839	12,164	12,904	18,298	13,503	964	9,797	15,632	3,471
Hakodate, Japan	9,919	10,770	10,155	10,491	12,849	9,977	9,836	10,408	3,486	7,502	8,712	4,688	9,290	9,551	14,450	9,638	3,345	9,971	12,920	6,806
Halifax, Canada	473	1,932	1,656	1,803	2,919	180	302	14,825	11,571	2,695	3,353	12,763	1,002	1,967	5,923	4,135	11,726	15,606	2,985	16,084
Hamburg, West Germany	4,749	7,150	6,794	7,003	7,395	5,082	5,170	18,837	7,582	5,353	7,810	8,283	5,492	6,850	10,599	9,028	7,830	18,322	7,431	11,314
Hamilton, Bermuda	1,762	1,424	1,671	1,524	1,544	1,555	1,639	14,072	12,939	3,903	3,676	14,097	2,114	2,285	4,608	3,965	13,099	14,927	1,610	17,404
Hamilton, New Zealand	15,525	13,345	13,486	13,395	13,839	15,203	15,043	971	10,588	13,871	11,923	10,127	14,468	13,197	10,844	10,998	10,326	677	13,823	7,514
Hangzhou, China	11,386	12,718	12,082	12,433	14,600	11,528	11,427	10,434	1,546	9,277	10,853	2,488	11,010	11,527	16,679	11,856	1,313	9,763	14,668	4,769
Hannover, West Germany	4,780	7,180	6,835	7,039	7,375	5,115	5,208	18,963	7,650	5,449	7,887	8,327	5,547	6,905	10,570	9,092	7,900	18,410	7,410	11,329
Hanoi, Vietnam	12,261	14,020	13,386	13,739	15,535	12,474	12,417	10,666	1,082	10,539	12,432	761	12,146	12,903	18,315	13,535	948	9,868	15,594	3,488
Harare, Zimbabwe	11,467	13,001	13,183	13,103	11,234	11,738	11,928	12,613	9,472	13,325	15,096	8,462	12,606	13,677	11,971	15,509	9,647	12,167	11,193	8,049
Harbin, China	9,650	10,908	10,272	10,623	12,811	9,769	9,657	11,407	2,575	7,469	9,112	3,927	9,212	9,721	14,994	10,205	2,508	10,884	12,881	6,575
Harrisburg, Pennsylvania	1,634	876	461	660	2,686	1,296	1,187	13,633	12,151	2,726	2,352	13,454	1,091	920	5,216	2,959	12,265	14,412	2,757	16,697
Hartford, Connecticut	1,249	1,187	853	1,018	2,698	911	819	14,023	11,978	2,673	2,671	13,247	915	1,241	5,424	3,345	12,106	14,803	2,769	16,536
Havana, Cuba	3,408	1,094	1,688	1,347	1,890	3,092	3,052	12,080	14,012	4,511	2,894	15,365	3,053	2,136	3,319	2,449	14,096	12,928	1,936	18,375
Helena, Montana	3,938	3,122	2,642	2,890	5,309	3,698	3,501	11,865	10,714	2,288	838	12,126	2,791	2,009	6,713	2,060	10,723	12,429	5,374	14,664
Helsinki, Finland	5,307	7,666	7,218	7,477	8,249	5,618	5,665	17,701	6,511	5,275	7,881	7,330	5,833	7,148	11,474	9,204	6,750	17,165	8,293	10,502
Hengyang, China	11,716	13,271	12,632	12,986	14,991	11,894	11,815	10,652	932	9,792	11,546	1,660	11,469	12,112	17,424	12,610	660	9,915	15,056	4,205
Herat, Afghanistan	9,222	11,594	11,138	11,404	11,938	9,539	9,592	14,943	3,928	8,913	11,543	4,020	9,742	11,023	15,075	12,928	4,196	14,079	11,969	6,758
Hermosillo, Mexico	4,866	2,984	2,893	2,910	4,811	4,547	4,385	10,478	12,429	4,079	1,451	13,817	3,847	2,538	5,181	479	12,396	11,181	4,860	15,700
Hiroshima, Japan	10,853	11,840	11,220	11,560	13,886	10,939	10,810	10,098	2,689	8,518	9,803	3,731	10,299	10,624	15,509	10,713	2,496	9,545	13,957	5,718
Hiva Oa (Atuona)	10,058	7,836	7,985	7,882	8,711	9,726	9,583	5,231	13,135	9,085	6,642	13,722	9,094	7,758	6,521	5,535	12,903	5,969	8,718	12,527
Ho Chi Minh City, Vietnam	13,395	15,139	14,502	14,856	16,659	13,612	13,557	9,797	2,222	11,655	13,420	1,214	13,283	13,998	19,187	14,414	2,083	8,964	16,715	2,353
Hobart, Australia	17,889	15,772	15,907	15,825	15,941	17,588	17,413	2,904	9,269	15,718	14,234	8,434	16,765	15,577	12,741	13,409	9,043	2,049	15,907	5,396
Hohhot, China	10,175	11,776	11,139	11,494	13,449	10,352	10,273	11,817	1,313	8,292	10,218	2,721	9,939	10,647	16,070	11,396	1,326	11,161	13,514	5,711
Hong Kong	12,244	13,736	13,098	13,451	15,512	12,416	12,332	10,166	1,371	10,269	11,921	1,629	11,967	12,560	17,738	12,919	1,110	9,414	15,578	3,740
Honiara, Solomon Islands	14,416	13,388	13,130	13,260	15,097	14,247	14,048	4,449	7,433	11,899	11,133	7,383	13,316	12,561	13,165	10,897	7,161	3,974	15,128	5,946
Honolulu, Hawaii	8,915	7,671	7,402	7,532	9,581	8,678	8,481	7,473	9,559	6,773	5,415	10,557	7,768	6,849	9,057	5,252	9,379	7,788	9,628	11,099
Houston, Texas	3,671	1,505	1,582	1,490	3,330	3,334	3,207	11,593	13,010	3,749	1,524	14,419	2,849	1,514	4,370	1,050	13,041	12,369	3,383	16,968
Huambo, Angola	9,945	11,298	11,522	11,416	9,501	10,188	10,384	13,606	10,565	12,084	13,487	9,767	11,092	12,053	10,461	13,784	10,780	13,348	9,460	9,752
Hubli, India	11,695	14,063	13,590	13,867	14,276	12,012	12,063	12,641	3,398	11,194	13,751	2,562	12,185	13,428	17,147	15,136	3,580	11,767	14,297	4,414
Hugh Town, United Kingdom	3,813	6,182	5,901	6,068	6,232	4,151	4,270	19,017	8,762	4,975	7,184	9,477	4,711	6,057	9,420	8,278	9,006	19,291	6,265	12,467
Hull, Canada	1,292	1,452	926	1,214	3,166	982	811	14,006	11,577	2,206	2,394	12,874	509	1,036	5,796	3,250	11,696	14,745	3,236	16,130
Hyderabad, India	11,669	14,002	13,498	13,790	14,393	11,978	12,015	12,524	2,980	11,005	13,517	2,176	12,088	13,290	17,397	14,890	3,162	11,652	14,419	4,297
Hyderabad, Pakistan	10,379	12,752	12,293	12,561	13,023	10,697	10,750	13,894	3,545	9,999	12,608	3,235	10,893	12,162	16,071	14,000	3,789	13,022	13,050	5,666
Igloolik, Canada	2,728	4,075	3,454	3,802	5,788	2,779	2,647	14,669	8,900	781	3,420	10,226	2,205	3,081	8,450	4,795	9,011	15,048	5,857	13,444
Iloilo, Philippines	13,549	14,640	14,025	14,361	16,690	13,674	13,561	8,615	2,923	11,319	12,499	2,689	13,091	13,421	17,533	13,219	2,668	7,855	16,760	2,999
Indianapolis, Indiana	2,329	957	422	689	3,131	2,001	1,853	12,948	12,136	2,641	1,587	13,501	1,459	265	5,193	2,205	12,217	13,697	3,199	16,560
Innsbruck, Austria	5,131	7,512	7,212	7,391	7,510	5,468	5,578	19,297	7,764	5,985	8,371	8,320	5,972	7,328	10,653	9,536	8,023	18,497	7,539	11,181

Distances in Kilometers	Channel-Port-aux-Basques, Can.	Charleston, South Carolina	Charleston, West Virginia	Charlotte, North Carolina	Charlotte Amalie, U.S.V.I.	Charlottetown, Canada	Chatham, Canada	Chatham Islands (Waitangi)	Chengdu, China	Chesterfield Inlet, Canada	Cheyenne, Wyoming	Chiang Mai, Thailand	Chibougamau, Canada	Chicago, Illinois	Chiclayo, Peru	Chihuahua, Mexico	Chongquing, China	Christchurch, New Zealand	Christiansted, U.S.V.I.	Christmas Island [Indian Ocean]
Inuvik, Canada	4,597	5,196	4,570	4,914	7,255	4,559	4,388	12,952	8,051	1,996	3,483	9,462	3,755	3,990	9,314	4,775	8,085	13,180	7,326	12,309
Invercargill, New Zealand	16,460	14,151	14,376	14,240	14,263	16,126	15,986	1,217	10,701	14,982	12,947	10,013	15,473	14,157	11,100	11,936	10,455	464	14,233	7,085
Inverness, United Kingdom	3,772	6,172	5,802	6,018	6,563	4,101	4,183	18,409	8,186	4,441	6,835	9,028	4,495	5,853	9,787	8,036	8,417	18,439	6,605	12,172
Iquitos, Peru	5,852	4,104	4,742	4,388	2,611	5,628	5,679	10,779	17,014	7,587	5,916	18,147	5,949	5,261	803	5,019	17,149	11,630	2,558	18,423
Iraklion, Greece	6,822	9,167	8,912	9,069	8,861	7,160	7,282	17,937	7,193	7,698	10,120	7,390	7,709	9,062	11,805	11,277	7,465	17,101	8,877	9,837
Irkutsk, USSR	8,830	10,576	9,949	10,300	12,113	9,024	8,958	13,072	2,399	7,117	9,281	3,745	8,679	9,509	14,945	10,567	2,528	12,470	12,176	6,955
Islamabad, Pakistan	9,829	12,130	11,616	11,912	12,739	10,129	10,156	14,043	2,923	9,152	11,716	3,049	10,207	11,409	15,941	13,105	3,189	13,196	12,777	5,980
Istanbul, Turkey	6,682	9,071	8,753	8,944	9,011	7,018	7,121	17,909	6,674	7,274	9,786	7,004	7,475	8,834	12,081	11,016	6,944	17,036	9,035	9,677
Ivujivik, Canada	2,026	3,298	2,687	3,030	4,995	2,029	1,882	14,623	9,687	658	2,962	11,001	1,407	2,372	7,672	4,277	9,803	15,132	5,064	14,237
Iwo Jima Island, Japan	11,735	12,286	11,711	12,022	14,456	11,764	11,610	8,740	3,715	9,232	10,031	4,413	11,014	11,078	15,215	10,697	3,471	8,214	14,525	5,498
Izmir, Turkey	6,743	9,115	8,826	9,001	8,942	7,080	7,192	17,950	6,909	7,467	9,941	7,176	7,581	8,939	11,959	11,139	7,180	17,084	8,963	9,748
Jackson, Mississippi	3,117	965	1,027	924	2,964	2,779	2,660	12,149	12,876	3,453	1,630	14,269	2,355	1,088	4,460	1,578	12,934	12,932	3,023	17,101
Jaffna, Sri Lanka	12,500	14,853	14,360	14,648	15,080	12,814	12,858	11,829	3,409	11,869	14,358	2,281	12,952	14,160	17,794	15,717	3,536	10,956	15,099	3,613
Jakarta, Indonesia	15,227	16,980	16,341	16,695	18,395	15,461	15,416	8,470	4,086	13,504	15,030	2,890	15,154	15,801	18,402	15,763	3,954	7,601	18,436	495
Jamestown, St. Helena	8,812	9,546	9,916	9,726	7,516	8,968	9,166	13,309	12,773	11,328	11,914	12,086	9,896	10,527	8,120	11,841	13,007	13,418	7,465	11,929
Jamnagar, India	10,743	13,117	12,657	12,926	13,361	11,062	11,115	13,559	3,493	10,343	12,943	3,037	11,256	12,521	16,364	14,335	3,723	12,687	13,386	5,328
Jan Mayen Island	3,680	5,909	5,403	5,692	6,887	3,951	3,954	16,916	7,591	3,347	5,946	8,674	3,996	5,265	10,031	7,274	7,784	16,945	6,942	11,982
Jayapura, Indonesia	14,664	14,624	14,171	14,413	16,729	14,642	14,469	6,223	5,347	12,079	12,232	5,140	13,804	13,531	15,415	12,411	5,081	5,530	16,783	3,970
Jefferson City, Missouri	2,843	1,280	920	1,075	3,460	2,520	2,363	12,456	12,158	2,758	1,118	13,551	1,891	533	5,179	1,695	12,215	13,189	3,525	16,430
Jerusalem, Israel	7,783	10,150	9,867	10,040	9,875	8,121	8,234	16,941	6,443	8,439	10,955	6,492	8,620	9,978	12,777	12,173	6,713	16,091	9,890	8,825
Jiggalong, Australia	17,323	17,746	17,323	17,555	19,204	17,447	17,324	6,084	6,244	14,994	15,364	5,233	16,783	16,683	15,993	15,332	6,055	5,211	19,171	2,148
Jinan, China	10,667	12,121	11,482	11,836	13,912	10,823	10,731	11,163	1,370	8,649	10,398	2,652	10,349	10,955	16,282	11,495	1,250	10,512	13,979	5,354
Jodhpur, India	10,535	12,874	12,381	12,667	13,308	10,844	10,883	13,582	3,068	9,966	12,537	2,790	10,973	12,201	16,428	13,927	3,311	12,715	13,339	5,388
Johannesburg, South Africa	11,914	13,140	13,424	13,286	11,186	12,153	12,349	11,844	10,242	14,004	15,416	9,134	13,060	13,982	11,449	15,517	10,396	11,481	11,136	8,275
Juazeiro do Norte, Brazil	6,373	6,166	6,676	6,402	3,987	6,373	6,538	12,903	15,412	8,932	8,538	15,347	7,178	7,320	4,476	8,174	15,684	13,534	3,923	15,686
Juneau, Alaska	4,919	4,921	4,346	4,655	7,091	4,798	4,606	11,983	8,760	2,393	2,822	10,168	3,896	3,711	8,696	3,953	8,755	12,300	7,160	12,717
Kabul, Afghanistan	9,563	11,892	11,397	11,684	12,415	9,869	9,905	14,401	3,285	9,011	11,605	3,420	9,989	11,222	15,601	12,997	3,553	13,549	12,450	6,295
Kalgoorlie, Australia	18,137	17,992	17,750	17,888	18,492	18,241	18,103	5,550	7,042	15,731	15,745	5,986	17,503	17,151	15,279	15,455	6,859	4,682	18,440	2,774
Kaliningrad, USSR	5,325	7,721	7,327	7,558	8,072	5,651	5,724	18,298	6,890	5,637	8,186	7,588	5,983	7,329	11,284	9,460	7,140	17,654	8,110	10,644
Kamloops, Canada	4,350	3,838	3,319	3,592	6,028	4,153	3,953	11,807	9,999	2,253	1,597	11,408	3,222	2,676	7,455	2,724	9,998	12,284	6,095	13,906
Kampala, Uganda	10,115	12,087	12,081	12,105	10,801	10,426	10,595	14,382	8,230	11,563	13,734	7,525	11,189	12,438	12,502	14,583	8,452	13,801	10,779	8,174
Kananga, Zaire	9,861	11,522	11,643	11,595	9,943	10,139	10,326	14,168	9,552	11,728	13,506	8,823	10,994	12,104	11,289	14,061	9,774	13,770	9,911	9,164
Kano, Nigeria	7,360	9,158	9,207	9,197	7,876	7,645	7,830	16,431	9,863	9,277	11,013	9,642	8,490	9,631	9,996	11,684	10,128	16,194	7,859	11,025
Kanpur, India	10,862	13,127	12,590	12,898	13,798	11,155	11,174	13,014	2,362	10,017	12,501	2,093	11,184	12,337	16,993	13,869	2,597	12,159	13,835	4,922
Kansas City, Missouri	2,993	1,495	1,128	1,292	3,669	2,677	2,512	12,332	12,045	2,710	901	13,444	1,996	665	5,301	1,572	12,094	13,051	3,733	16,260
Kaohsiung, Taiwan	12,230	13,512	12,880	13,228	15,436	12,371	12,268	9,782	1,841	10,095	11,556	2,257	11,840	12,309	17,240	12,473	1,569	9,069	15,505	3,997
Karachi, Pakistan	10,354	12,735	12,286	12,549	12,954	10,674	10,732	13,966	3,688	10,032	12,649	3,361	10,891	12,171	15,974	14,040	3,932	13,093	12,979	5,734
Karaganda, USSR	8,284	10,479	9,929	10,243	11,407	8,559	8,559	14,859	3,342	7,375	9,924	4,141	8,527	9,673	14,612	11,313	3,594	14,117	11,455	7,396
Karl-Marx-Stadt, East Germany	5,052	7,450	7,111	7,312	7,600	5,387	5,482	18,967	7,509	5,715	8,164	8,140	5,826	7,185	10,782	9,372	7,763	18,286	7,633	11,099
Kasanga, Tanzania	10,721	12,490	12,577	12,550	10,948	11,014	11,195	13,569	8,887	12,391	14,376	8,029	11,836	13,006	12,196	15,030	9,089	13,065	10,917	8,167
Kashgar, China	9,392	11,630	11,090	11,399	12,430	9,678	9,689	14,164	2,729	8,544	11,076	3,187	9,685	10,843	15,655	12,461	3,001	13,351	12,473	6,329
Kassel, West Germany	4,812	7,209	6,875	7,072	7,359	5,147	5,245	19,073	7,710	5,535	7,956	8,365	5,598	6,957	10,546	9,150	7,962	18,482	7,393	11,341
Kathmandu, Nepal	10,943	13,133	12,567	12,890	13,991	11,222	11,224	12,712	1,850	9,904	12,311	1,711	11,175	12,265	17,216	13,652	2,087	11,872	14,034	4,764
Kayes, Mali	5,717	7,160	7,310	7,240	5,712	5,946	6,144	16,445	11,511	8,045	9,246	11,564	6,860	7,815	7,908	9,698	11,783	16,758	5,692	13,204
Kazan, USSR	6,759	9,076	8,587	8,869	9,752	7,060	7,090	16,555	5,078	6,352	8,990	5,832	7,182	8,444	12,977	10,364	5,328	15,846	9,796	9,004
Kemi, Finland	5,050	7,349	6,861	7,141	8,136	5,343	5,368	17,253	6,466	4,747	7,375	7,407	5,457	6,735	11,342	8,723	6,688	16,855	8,185	10,662
Kenora, Canada	2,590	2,241	1,631	1,962	4,370	2,354	2,156	13,072	10,907	1,528	1,253	12,295	1,443	1,026	6,424	2,546	10,973	13,696	4,440	15,272
Kerguelen Island	16,293	16,882	17,412	17,133	14,693	16,515	16,714	7,835	9,517	18,058	18,978	8,104	17,437	18,055	13,103	17,658	9,497	7,290	14,626	5,459
Kerkira, Greece	6,167	8,521	8,256	8,417	8,303	6,505	6,625	18,574	7,453	7,067	9,465	7,785	7,048	8,402	11,326	10,616	7,722	17,716	8,323	10,388
Kermanshah, Iran	8,349	10,750	10,382	10,601	10,767	8,681	8,767	16,152	5,303	8,553	11,170	5,389	9,045	10,389	13,797	12,490	5,573	15,279	10,790	7,922
Khabarovsk, USSR	9,272	10,356	9,725	10,072	12,339	9,361	9,234	11,278	3,284	6,969	8,470	4,624	8,741	9,153	14,336	9,527	3,209	10,837	12,410	7,148
Kharkov, USSR	6,509	8,901	8,489	8,730	9,237	6,833	6,900	17,458	5,924	6,610	9,219	6,489	7,124	8,456	12,433	10,537	6,185	16,660	9,272	9,471
Khartoum, Sudan	8,870	11,073	10,934	11,030	10,240	9,199	9,347	15,842	7,399	9,997	12,348	7,037	9,859	11,182	12,613	13,401	7,652	15,141	10,235	8,561
Khon Kaen, Thailand	12,694	14,553	13,923	14,275	15,934	12,924	12,880	10,535	1,581	11,082	13,026	484	12,650	13,460	18,898	14,135	1,504	9,708	15,988	2,995
Kiev, USSR	6,151	8,549	8,155	8,386	8,833	6,478	6,552	17,859	6,323	6,388	8,970	6,901	6,807	8,149	12,024	10,264	6,583	17,071	8,868	9,871
Kigali, Rwanda	10,110	11,997	12,030	12,032	10,614	10,413	10,588	14,277	8,600	11,683	13,754	7,874	11,206	12,420	12,192	14,519	8,820	13,744	10,589	8,403
Kingston, Canada	1,393	1,308	782	1,068	3,067	1,072	914	13,888	11,710	2,312	2,334	13,012	652	942	5,658	3,141	11,827	14,636	3,138	16,260
Kingston, Jamaica	3,653	1,665	2,304	1,949	1,256	3,375	3,383	12,148	14,619	5,148	3,703	15,910	3,547	2,841	2,760	3,207	14,729	13,016	1,282	19,136
Kingstown, Saint Vincent	3,821	2,887	3,444	3,140	699	3,672	3,778	13,037	14,910	6,031	5,236	15,868	4,250	4,081	3,015	4,937	15,103	13,898	630	18,578
Kinshasa, Zaire	9,205	10,760	10,913	10,847	9,139	9,468	9,660	14,532	10,139	11,226	12,820	9,506	10,349	11,400	10,531	13,294	10,373	14,243	9,106	9,972
Kirkwall, United Kingdom	3,828	6,223	5,835	6,061	6,678	4,153	4,226	18,278	8,035	4,375	6,809	8,899	4,508	5,863	9,904	8,031	8,264	18,261	6,722	12,066
Kirov, USSR	6,575	8,864	8,361	8,650	9,625	6,868	6,890	16,493	5,106	6,071	8,707	5,934	6,953	8,197	12,844	10,086	5,347	15,831	9,672	9,151
Kiruna, Sweden	4,804	7,082	6,586	6,870	7,927	5,091	5,109	17,168	6,631	4,452	7,080	7,614	5,180	6,449	11,120	8,429	6,846	16,851	7,978	10,888
Kisangani, Zaire	9,544	11,396	11,440	11,435	10,014	9,842	10,020	14,736	8,921	11,216	13,197	8,292	10,652	11,844	11,689	13,923	9,153	14,253	9,990	8,985
Kishinev, USSR	6,270	8,671	8,309	8,523	8,817	6,603	6,689	18,017	6,519	6,672	9,223	7,008	6,988	8,341	11,972	10,490	6,783	17,179	8,848	9,877
Kitchner, Canada	1,723	1,187	575	915	3,143	1,403	1,242	13,569	11,785	2,310	2,016	13,114	857	611	5,561	2,814	11,888	14,309	3,214	16,305
Knoxville, Tennessee	2,413	511	333	290	2,701	2,075	1,962	12,855	12,582	3,081	1,904	13,937	1,731	731	4,749	2,234	12,668	13,639	2,768	17,025
Kosice, Czechoslovakia	5,693	8,092	7,745	7,951	8,223	6,027	6,119	18,555	7,019	6,235	8,738	7,571	6,444	7,801	11,387	9,973	7,280	17,749	8,254	10,472
Kota Kinabalu, Malaysia	14,054	15,398	14,770	15,115	17,311	14,220	14,130	8,700	3,007	11,992	13,340	2,332	13,730	14,188	18,275	14,100	2,794	7,887	17,378	2,157
Krakow, Poland	5,531	7,932	7,578	7,787	8,103	5,865	5,954	18,596	7,067	6,053	8,557	7,656	6,271	7,628	11,280	9,796	7,325	17,827	8,136	10,595
Kralendijk, Bonaire	4,016	2,573	3,189	2,851	772	3,808	3,874	12,402	15,195	5,951	4,791	16,311	4,223	3,792	2,455	4,322	15,354	13,272	727	19,347
Krasnodar, USSR	7,021	9,420	9,029	9,259	9,632	7,350	7,425	17,215	5,782	7,199	9,804	6,208	7,678	9,018	12,788	11,116	6,050	16,366	9,663	9,063
Krasnoyarsk, USSR	8,231	10,144	9,535	9,878	11,504	8,452	8,405	13,929	2,951	6,763	9,110	4,165	8,203	9,155	14,504	10,456	3,133	13,316	11,564	7,467
Kristiansand, Norway	4,470	6,864	6,467	6,698	7,292	4,794	4,865	18,393	7,503	4,872	7,373	8,309	5,127	6,477	10,516	8,624	7,741	18,064	7,333	11,442
Kuala Lumpur, Malaysia	14,083	16,024	15,396	15,747	17,218	14,334	14,304	9,595	3,054	12,554	14,415	1,753	14,111	14,928	19,576	15,412	2,967	8,732	17,261	1,574
Kuching, Malaysia	14,468	16,058	15,421	15,773	17,745	14,673	14,607	8,788	3,290	12,597	14,101	2,273	14,284	14,868	18,762	14,900	3,126	7,940	17,803	1,429
Kumasi, Ghana	7,063	8,522	8,684	8,610	6,970	7,304	7,500	15,846	11,119	9,300	10,619	10,887	8,210	9,189	8,815	11,057	11,384	15,883	6,943	12,037
Kumzar, Oman	9,603	12,005	11,623	11,850	11,986	9,934	10,015	14,916	4,656	9,652	12,289	4,437	10,268	11,600	14,919	13,644	4,912	14,045	12,006	6,706
Kunming, China	11,758	13,599	12,971	13,322	15,020	11,981	11,932	11,210	635	10,133	12,148	794	11,694	12,517	17,962	13,318	630	10,417	15,077	3,948
Kuqa Chang, China	9,507	11,643	11,069	11,395	12,656	9,773	9,763	13,713	2,186	8,404	10,850	2,889	9,683	10,761	15,852	12,213	2,453	12,933	12,705	6,159
Kurgan, USSR	7,470	9,688	9,150	9,458	10,589	7,748	7,753	15,538	4,099	6,670	9,262	4,956	7,744	8,921	13,793	10,654	4,341	14,841	10,638	8,214
Kuwait, Kuwait	8,815	11,211	10,867	11,074	11,096	9,150	9,243	15,789	5,355	9,100	11,712	5,278	9,548	10,898	14,026	13,021	5,621	14,921	11,114	7,598
Kuybyshev, USSR	7,003	9,334	8,854	9,131	9,952	7,307	7,343	16,492	4,969	6,641	9,280	5,658	7,450	8,721	13,177	10,652	5,224	15,745	9,995	8,791
Kyoto, Japan	10,740	11,635	11,020	11,356	13,712	10,811	10,676	9,988	2,992	8,356	9,557	4,039	10,143	10,416	15,221	10,439	2,802	9,467	13,783	5,950
Kzyl-Orda, USSR	8,434	10,733	10,224	10,517	11,404	8,732	8,757	15,201	3,702	7,831	10,437	4,236	8,815	10,038	14,627	11,828	3,970	14,396	11,446	7,337
L'vov, USSR	5,798	8,199	7,833	8,049	8,396	6,129	6,214	18,329	6,793	6,225	8,760	7,365	6,512	7,865	11,575	10,018	7,052	17,539	8,429	10,303
La Ceiba, Honduras	4,345	2,005	2,551	2,233	2,344	4,029	3,986	11,191	14,736	5,291	3,303	16,130	3,949	2,894	2,609	2,439	14,787	12,049	2,365	18,559
La Coruna, Spain	3,926	6,195	6,000	6,120	5,941	4,257	4,404	19,065	9,317	5,454	7,472	9,924	4,938	6,242	9,053	8,458	9,569	19,937	5,966	12,747
La Paz, Bolivia	7,152	5,594	6,232	5,879	3,871	6,965	7,041	10,154	18,253	9,066	7,417	18,646	7,382	6,767	1,668	6,450	18,464	10,943	3,807	16,943
La Paz, Mexico	5,177	3,111	3,131	3,087	4,733	4,849	4,699	10,114	12,923	4,589	1,950	14,298	4,218	2,872	4,758	649	12,879	10,850	4,775	15,935
La Ronge, Canada	3,258	3,174	2,571	2,898	5,311	3,085	2,887	12,862	10,098	1,235	1,553	11,503	2,157	1,954	7,251	2,941	10,144	13,378	5,381	14,368
Labrador City, Canada	815	2,473	1,979	2,255	3,843	795	666	14,929	10,700	1,799	3,118	11,943	618	1,977	6,730	4,183	10,842	15,606	3,911	15,250
Lagos, Nigeria	7,440	9,005	9,137	9,080	7,506	7,696	7,889	15,849	10,665	9,573	11,041	10,375	8,586	9,620	9,359	11,544	10,927	15,765	7,481	11,487
Lahore, Pakistan	10,086	12,388	11,873	12,170	12,982	10,386	10,413	13,824	2,832	9,398	11,952	2,853	10,464	11,663	16,176	13,340	3,094	12,973	13,019	5,733
Lambasa, Fiji	13,692	11,968	11,901	11,923	13,233	13,421	13,231	3,075	9,590	11,620	10,056	9,625	12,551	11,457	10,945	9,436	9,319	3,072	13,247	7,970
Lansing, Michigan	2,058	1,178	546	894	3,276	1,741	1,577	13,249	11,830	2,329	1,686	13,184	1,117	271	5,502	2,487	11,919	13,980	3,346	16,299
Lanzhou, China	10,587	12,378	11,749	12,101	13,866	10,797	10,739	11,965	598	8,912	10,979	1,968	10,480	11,299	16,742	12,199	769	11,235	13,927	5,157
Laoag, Philippines	12,721	13,960	13,332	13,677	15,917	12,859	12,755	9,386	2,167	10,565	11,946	2,282	12,318	12,750	17,475	12,804	1,900	8,651	15,987	3,573
Largeau, Chad	7,687	9,764	9,693	9,750	8,800	8,004	8,168	16,771	8,549	9,187	11,293	8,360	8,749	10,015	11,193	12,195	8,814	16,240	8,793	10,012
Las Vegas, Nevada	4,709	3,240	2,967	3,090	5,283	4,420	4,236	10,823	11,554	3,451	1,054	12,948	3,600	2,454	6,015	1,193	11,527	11,451	5,340	15,030

Distances in Kilometers	Channel-Port-aux-Basques, Can.	Charleston, South Carolina	Charleston, West Virginia	Charlotte, North Carolina	Charlotte Amalie, U.S.V.I.	Charlottetown, Canada	Chatham, Canada	Chatham Islands (Waitangi)	Chengdu, China	Chesterfield Inlet, Canada	Cheyenne, Wyoming	Chiang Mai, Thailand	Chibougamau, Canada	Chicago, Illinois	Chiclayo, Peru	Chihuahua, Mexico	Chongquing, China	Christchurch, New Zealand	Christiansted, U.S.V.I.	Christmas Island [Indian Ocean]
Launceston, Australia	17,832	15,784	15,893	15,825	16,043	17,544	17,362	2,967	9,126	15,595	14,179	8,308	16,697	15,540	12,854	13,390	8,897	2,102	16,010	5,301
Le Havre, France	4,269	6,644	6,354	6,527	6,684	4,606	4,721	19,340	8,395	5,301	7,586	9,060	5,141	6,493	9,859	8,709	8,644	19,134	6,716	12,012
Leipzig, East Germany	4,993	7,392	7,050	7,252	7,557	5,328	5,422	18,958	7,528	5,649	8,098	8,171	5,763	7,121	10,744	9,307	7,781	18,305	7,591	11,143
Leningrad, USSR	5,582	7,932	7,473	7,738	8,543	5,891	5,933	17,484	6,221	5,455	8,076	7,034	6,081	7,385	11,768	9,413	6,461	16,904	8,588	10,211
Leon, Spain	4,170	6,440	6,244	6,365	6,157	4,501	4,647	19,274	9,181	5,657	7,707	9,750	5,177	6,484	9,248	8,701	9,437	19,837	6,180	12,531
Lerwick, United Kingdom	3,915	6,304	5,901	6,135	6,809	4,237	4,303	18,176	7,882	4,355	6,822	8,760	4,560	5,910	10,034	8,062	8,110	18,109	6,854	11,942
Lhasa, China	10,951	13,033	12,439	12,775	14,109	11,211	11,194	12,405	1,254	9,694	11,999	1,445	11,076	12,083	17,303	13,303	1,499	11,589	14,158	4,709
Libreville, Gabon	8,388	9,933	10,081	10,016	8,355	8,646	8,839	15,143	10,435	10,474	11,992	9,955	9,533	10,570	9,947	12,469	10,685	14,944	8,325	10,707
Lilongwe, Malawi	11,363	13,050	13,175	13,128	11,399	11,649	11,833	12,894	8,990	13,066	15,017	8,015	12,485	13,628	12,354	15,587	9,171	12,393	11,362	7,803
Lima, Peru	6,838	4,969	5,599	5,247	3,616	6,603	6,645	9,835	17,940	8,442	6,544	19,154	6,869	6,069	660	5,480	18,030	10,674	3,565	17,493
Limerick, Ireland	3,582	5,971	5,661	5,844	6,151	3,920	4,028	18,695	8,716	4,639	6,882	9,496	4,435	5,788	9,361	8,004	8,953	18,985	6,188	12,561
Limoges, France	4,505	6,848	6,594	6,748	6,731	4,842	4,968	19,739	8,529	5,679	7,908	9,113	5,429	6,770	9,861	8,993	8,785	19,291	6,759	11,958
Limon, Costa Rica	4,731	2,541	3,143	2,802	2,159	4,439	4,428	11,055	15,442	5,953	4,060	16,813	4,498	3,561	1,887	3,169	15,508	11,926	2,157	19,082
Lincoln, Nebraska	3,061	1,738	1,320	1,520	3,920	2,756	2,581	12,318	11,808	2,537	685	13,211	2,008	767	5,544	1,601	11,853	13,014	3,985	15,998
Linz, Austria	5,269	7,660	7,340	7,530	7,719	5,605	5,708	19,051	7,519	6,006	8,438	8,086	6,075	7,433	10,875	9,630	7,778	18,264	7,749	10,974
Lisbon, Portugal	4,111	6,279	6,142	6,230	5,809	4,430	4,592	18,817	9,680	5,840	7,726	10,204	5,178	6,439	8,837	8,633	9,938	19,451	5,827	12,885
Little Rock, Arkansas	3,092	1,164	1,033	1,044	3,257	2,759	2,620	12,177	12,565	3,183	1,308	13,963	2,229	890	4,777	1,472	12,617	12,936	3,318	16,768
Liverpool, United Kingdom	3,932	6,327	6,000	6,193	6,536	4,267	4,368	18,853	8,356	4,826	7,151	9,117	4,744	6,101	9,746	8,307	8,597	18,861	6,573	12,175
Lodz, Poland	5,414	7,816	7,449	7,665	8,046	5,746	5,830	18,541	7,044	5,879	8,395	7,674	6,130	7,484	11,238	9,643	7,299	17,820	8,081	10,657
Lome, Togo	7,311	8,820	8,969	8,903	7,288	7,560	7,754	15,809	10,887	9,496	10,890	10,612	8,458	9,464	9,117	11,357	11,150	15,777	7,261	11,718
London, United Kingdom	4,179	6,567	6,256	6,440	6,694	4,516	4,622	19,125	8,298	5,115	7,435	9,005	5,015	6,371	9,888	8,582	8,544	18,969	6,728	12,008
Londonderry, United Kingdom	3,620	6,019	5,680	5,879	6,304	3,954	4,050	18,555	8,497	4,505	6,818	9,311	4,414	5,772	9,524	7,976	8,731	18,729	6,344	12,418
Longlac, Canada	2,020	1,968	1,329	1,683	3,985	1,782	1,584	13,547	11,032	1,531	1,715	12,391	874	882	6,299	2,873	11,121	14,203	4,056	15,507
Lord Howe Island, Australia	16,334	14,533	14,526	14,519	15,384	16,069	15,879	2,537	9,007	14,091	12,706	8,494	15,189	14,103	12,471	12,035	8,750	1,785	15,375	5,954
Los Angeles, California	5,075	3,547	3,306	3,411	5,540	4,784	4,602	10,462	11,582	3,773	1,421	12,959	3,967	2,810	6,064	1,303	11,539	11,086	5,594	14,858
Louangphrabang, Laos	12,307	14,176	13,549	13,900	15,551	12,537	12,493	10,853	1,212	10,712	12,704	352	12,268	13,095	18,540	13,848	1,165	10,036	15,605	3,381
Louisville, Kentucky	2,391	806	361	553	2,991	2,058	1,921	12,875	12,308	2,812	1,662	13,673	1,582	434	5,021	2,163	12,389	13,637	3,059	16,729
Luanda, Angola	9,433	10,833	11,037	10,942	9,090	9,679	9,874	14,081	10,587	11,570	12,991	9,886	10,580	11,558	10,241	13,338	10,815	13,849	9,052	10,105
Lubumbashi, Zaire	10,706	12,329	12,472	12,413	10,669	10,983	11,171	13,387	9,418	12,543	14,349	8,539	11,840	12,943	11,735	14,862	9,618	12,951	10,633	8,515
Lusaka, Zambia	11,070	12,613	12,788	12,712	10,876	11,340	11,530	12,967	9,570	12,955	14,698	8,620	12,209	13,280	11,741	15,129	9,757	12,542	10,836	8,372
Luxembourg, Luxembourg	4,667	7,053	6,746	6,929	7,117	5,005	5,112	19,346	8,007	5,551	7,910	8,642	5,504	6,860	10,289	9,069	8,260	18,783	7,149	11,578
Luxor, Egypt	8,077	10,387	10,166	10,305	9,873	8,413	8,543	16,696	6,917	8,968	11,409	6,814	8,990	10,339	12,594	12,559	7,183	15,905	9,880	8,855
Lynn Lake, Canada	2,989	3,127	2,503	2,844	5,217	2,837	2,641	13,190	10,023	923	1,768	11,418	1,920	1,921	7,312	3,160	10,083	13,705	5,287	14,375
Lyon, France	4,760	7,114	6,850	7,009	7,011	5,098	5,221	19,781	8,289	5,846	8,125	8,848	5,665	7,012	10,135	9,232	8,547	19,022	7,038	11,678
Macapa, Brazil	5,325	4,722	5,271	4,974	2,532	5,253	5,393	12,767	15,719	7,745	7,060	16,148	5,957	5,911	3,286	6,647	15,969	13,537	2,465	17,207
Madison, Wisconsin	2,407	1,413	839	1,141	3,578	2,103	1,928	12,947	11,726	2,259	1,292	13,103	1,378	196	5,603	2,192	11,799	13,656	3,647	16,115
Madras, India	12,181	14,516	14,010	14,304	14,858	12,490	12,529	12,062	3,123	11,495	13,979	2,098	12,601	13,795	17,748	15,339	3,269	11,189	14,882	3,830
Madrid, Spain	4,424	6,665	6,489	6,599	6,292	4,752	4,903	19,307	9,191	5,947	7,982	9,701	5,446	6,744	9,338	8,957	9,451	19,550	6,312	12,399
Madurai, India	12,374	14,742	14,264	14,544	14,900	12,691	12,742	12,000	3,534	11,823	14,342	2,451	12,857	14,087	17,585	15,714	3,672	11,128	14,918	3,796
Magadan, USSR	7,821	8,765	8,137	8,482	10,783	7,876	7,736	11,858	4,721	5,417	6,892	6,113	7,201	7,559	12,774	8,000	4,693	11,602	10,854	8,744
Magdalena, Bolivia	6,763	5,371	6,005	5,656	3,505	6,597	6,687	10,704	17,743	8,804	7,340	18,129	7,078	6,571	1,869	6,476	17,974	11,487	3,439	17,143
Magdeburg, East Germany	4,912	7,312	6,964	7,169	7,508	5,245	5,337	18,911	7,536	5,544	7,998	8,201	5,670	7,028	10,702	9,211	7,787	18,305	7,543	11,195
Majuro Atoll, Marshall Isls.	12,199	11,320	10,994	11,160	13,254	12,030	11,831	5,792	7,426	9,702	8,990	7,894	11,100	10,401	12,194	8,928	7,172	5,615	13,300	7,520
Malabo, Equatorial Guinea	8,058	9,670	9,792	9,742	8,167	8,323	8,514	15,521	10,308	10,107	11,679	9,905	9,201	10,265	9,917	12,210	10,564	15,321	8,141	10,846
Male, Maldives	12,670	15,071	14,666	14,909	14,841	13,000	13,076	11,914	4,361	12,418	15,003	3,221	13,284	14,578	17,065	16,393	4,492	11,056	14,845	3,913
Manado, Indonesia	14,556	15,414	14,832	15,149	17,569	14,661	14,537	7,677	3,904	12,235	13,138	3,410	14,022	14,203	17,234	13,660	3,661	6,888	17,640	2,504
Managua, Nicaragua	4,671	2,373	2,939	2,613	2,392	4,363	4,331	10,958	15,141	5,695	3,686	16,536	4,328	3,298	2,210	2,749	15,189	11,823	2,401	18,719
Manama, Bahrain	9,249	11,645	11,303	11,509	11,489	9,584	9,678	15,373	5,214	9,511	12,130	5,020	9,983	11,332	14,361	13,447	5,473	14,509	11,505	7,210
Manaus, Brazil	5,617	4,494	5,104	4,770	2,437	5,477	5,583	11,846	16,534	7,806	6,679	17,157	6,038	5,713	2,236	6,047	16,760	12,651	2,366	17,833
Manchester, New Hampshire	1,090	1,357	1,002	1,184	2,801	752	651	14,176	11,836	2,582	2,750	13,095	801	1,334	5,576	3,478	11,968	14,951	2,871	16,393
Mandalay, Burma	11,913	13,930	13,320	13,664	15,091	12,165	12,139	11,474	1,247	10,525	12,691	467	11,984	12,922	18,265	13,922	1,345	10,644	15,140	3,744
Mangareva Island, Fr.Polynesia	10,872	8,507	8,789	8,615	8,885	10,534	10,422	4,435	14,171	10,336	7,766	14,433	10,048	8,690	6,158	6,510	13,914	5,276	8,875	12,453
Manila, Philippines	13,121	14,316	13,692	14,034	16,305	13,257	13,150	9,053	2,484	10,944	12,251	2,392	12,704	13,101	17,596	13,054	2,224	8,302	16,375	3,249
Mannheim, West Germany	4,827	7,216	6,903	7,089	7,286	5,164	5,270	19,285	7,861	5,659	8,043	8,481	5,651	7,009	10,455	9,214	8,115	18,637	7,317	11,409
Maputo, Mozambique	12,215	13,538	13,798	13,674	11,614	12,467	12,662	11,716	9,856	14,197	15,774	8,721	13,362	14,339	11,889	15,946	10,003	11,300	11,566	7,829
Mar del Plata, Argentina	9,479	8,170	8,807	8,455	6,285	9,346	9,452	9,056	18,150	11,614	9,994	16,901	9,879	9,358	4,127	8,942	18,283	9,660	6,216	14,361
Maracaibo, Venezuela	4,255	2,591	3,225	2,876	1,114	4,024	4,073	12,020	15,408	6,041	4,685	16,591	4,359	3,796	2,133	4,102	15,549	12,892	1,082	19,739
Marrakech, Morocco	4,638	6,642	6,586	6,630	5,868	4,938	5,115	18,316	10,076	6,557	8,291	10,449	5,750	6,947	8,714	9,090	10,342	18,683	5,875	12,858
Marseilles, France	4,926	7,256	7,015	7,162	7,054	5,263	5,393	19,847	8,380	6,097	8,342	8,883	5,861	7,200	10,140	9,423	8,641	18,989	7,078	11,634
Maseru, Lesotho	12,114	13,227	13,545	13,387	11,219	12,342	12,540	11,533	10,479	14,275	15,548	9,336	13,259	14,122	11,305	15,534	10,625	11,193	11,166	8,310
Mashhad, Iran	8,907	11,282	10,833	11,096	11,618	9,225	9,280	15,255	4,144	8,649	11,284	4,307	9,440	10,730	14,762	12,663	4,414	14,394	11,649	7,079
Mazatlan, Mexico	4,967	2,802	2,890	2,807	4,339	4,633	4,495	10,302	13,218	4,610	1,993	14,608	4,066	2,708	4,400	601	13,187	11,063	4,380	16,345
Mbabane, Swaziland	12,140	13,423	13,693	13,564	11,484	12,386	12,582	11,731	9,996	14,163	15,677	8,866	13,287	14,242	11,740	15,816	10,144	11,333	11,435	7,970
Mbandaka, Zaire	9,062	10,777	10,872	10,838	9,297	9,343	9,529	14,929	9,609	10,934	12,711	9,037	10,193	11,318	10,917	13,317	9,848	14,563	9,270	9,735
McMurdo Sound, Antarctica	16,173	14,132	14,691	14,374	12,896	15,949	15,985	3,830	12,658	17,071	14,433	11,475	16,090	14,926	9,859	13,064	12,489	3,800	12,835	8,155
Mecca, Saudi Arabia	8,921	11,247	11,011	11,160	10,724	9,258	9,383	15,849	6,427	9,669	12,177	6,158	9,806	11,161	13,359	13,371	6,684	15,043	10,730	8,014
Medan, Indonesia	13,941	15,979	15,362	15,709	16,996	14,204	14,187	9,869	3,051	12,539	14,513	1,682	14,039	14,930	19,622	15,575	2,995	9,002	17,033	1,740
Medellin, Colombia	4,839	2,970	3,607	3,253	1,769	4,590	4,622	11,368	15,919	6,454	4,832	17,174	4,842	4,124	1,515	4,055	16,035	12,239	1,737	19,517
Medicine Hat, Canada	3,719	3,171	2,636	2,918	5,359	3,503	3,303	12,212	10,432	1,904	1,090	11,844	2,578	1,992	6,963	2,409	10,453	12,753	5,427	14,505
Medina, Saudi Arabia	8,661	11,006	10,750	10,909	10,575	8,999	9,118	16,097	6,319	9,348	11,870	6,136	9,523	10,881	13,305	13,083	6,581	15,274	10,584	8,148
Melbourne, Australia	17,777	15,939	15,978	15,949	16,399	17,527	17,334	3,281	8,696	15,376	14,169	7,902	16,630	15,567	13,239	13,478	8,466	2,408	16,371	4,954
Memphis, Tennessee	2,905	972	833	839	3,099	2,571	2,437	12,360	12,574	3,139	1,453	13,963	2,080	780	4,759	1,676	12,636	13,125	3,162	16,853
Merauke, Indonesia	15,299	15,087	14,677	14,895	17,090	15,263	15,085	5,728	5,809	12,702	12,704	5,449	14,406	14,046	15,267	12,763	5,548	4,993	17,134	3,812
Merida, Mexico	4,022	1,621	2,074	1,797	2,602	3,692	3,621	11,361	14,108	4,709	2,657	15,510	3,482	2,327	3,248	1,866	14,152	12,197	2,639	18,022
Meridian, Mississippi	3,008	825	923	792	2,841	2,670	2,556	12,262	12,900	3,448	1,733	14,286	2,282	1,060	4,431	1,717	12,964	13,049	2,901	17,177
Messina, Italy	5,955	8,276	8,044	8,187	7,959	6,291	6,421	18,818	7,862	7,026	9,345	8,183	6,883	8,226	10,947	10,448	8,131	18,006	7,977	10,735
Mexico City, Mexico	4,770	2,420	2,697	2,512	3,602	4,432	4,327	10,521	13,938	4,924	2,469	15,345	4,037	2,721	3,585	1,242	13,930	11,332	3,635	17,191
Miami, Florida	3,043	775	1,401	1,049	1,774	2,729	2,693	12,437	13,742	4,246	2,837	15,074	2,726	1,913	3,600	2,580	13,838	13,281	1,830	18,208
Midway Islands, USA	9,597	9,003	8,585	8,802	11,116	9,447	9,249	7,989	7,461	7,080	6,612	8,448	8,521	7,959	11,103	6,870	7,274	8,008	11,174	9,310
Milan, Italy	5,076	7,440	7,164	7,330	7,350	5,414	5,532	19,535	8,001	6,061	8,394	8,528	5,957	7,309	10,468	9,526	8,261	18,689	7,377	11,338
Milford Sound, New Zealand	16,429	14,156	14,356	14,234	14,355	16,098	15,951	1,252	10,540	14,850	12,875	9,881	15,412	14,112	11,213	11,897	10,292	406	14,327	6,998
Milwaukee, Wisconsin	2,297	1,338	743	1,061	3,488	1,990	1,817	13,042	11,753	2,268	1,412	13,124	1,288	130	5,575	2,282	11,831	13,758	3,557	16,169
Minsk, USSR	5,772	8,164	7,755	7,994	8,540	6,096	6,163	17,946	6,459	5,953	8,537	7,127	6,396	7,733	11,752	9,836	6,712	17,235	8,578	10,176
Mogadiscio, Somalia	10,924	13,109	12,988	13,077	12,081	11,254	11,401	13,808	6,928	11,892	14,355	6,126	11,901	13,232	13,938	15,454	7,133	13,087	12,066	6,822
Mombasa, Kenya	11,003	13,009	12,992	13,023	11,700	11,319	11,484	13,582	7,832	12,307	14,591	6,971	12,057	13,330	13,211	15,496	8,031	12,952	11,676	7,312
Monclova, Mexico	4,321	2,171	2,241	2,163	3,854	3,986	3,851	10,945	13,086	4,126	1,610	14,496	3,443	2,085	4,391	498	13,085	11,711	3,901	16,654
Moncton, Canada	460	1,966	1,631	1,812	3,078	128	116	14,804	11,430	2,509	3,243	12,637	831	1,884	6,044	4,079	11,580	15,569	3,144	15,957
Monrovia, Liberia	6,467	7,685	7,908	7,799	6,014	6,672	6,871	15,611	11,985	8,877	9,889	11,850	7,598	8,454	7,805	10,195	12,254	15,867	5,983	13,035
Monte Carlo, Monaco	5,045	7,387	7,135	7,288	7,216	5,382	5,508	19,704	8,214	6,145	8,427	8,713	5,961	7,306	10,308	9,528	8,475	18,830	7,240	11,472
Monterrey, Mexico	4,337	2,128	2,249	2,143	3,731	4,001	3,873	10,926	13,255	4,247	1,766	14,666	3,495	2,143	4,217	659	13,257	11,703	3,776	16,815
Montevideo, Uruguay	9,137	7,889	8,523	8,173	5,964	9,011	9,120	9,401	18,122	11,311	9,777	16,991	9,563	9,086	3,947	8,770	18,300	10,016	5,894	14,633
Montgomery, Alabama	2,843	600	786	595	2,645	2,506	2,403	12,437	12,942	3,457	1,911	14,315	2,184	1,061	4,386	1,940	13,015	13,233	2,707	17,293
Montpelier, Vermont	1,103	1,427	1,002	1,228	2,961	773	634	14,164	11,701	2,417	2,647	12,972	643	1,252	5,698	3,434	11,829	14,923	3,031	16,259
Montpellier, France	4,802	7,130	6,891	7,037	6,931	5,139	5,270	19,961	8,472	6,002	8,229	8,991	5,742	7,080	10,023	9,303	8,732	19,114	6,956	11,757
Montreal, Canada	1,130	1,515	1,036	1,296	3,116	816	649	14,157	11,567	2,259	2,561	12,847	494	1,198	5,822	3,406	11,692	14,902	3,186	16,125
Moosonee, Canada	1,607	2,058	1,440	1,785	3,908	1,401	1,201	13,992	10,915	1,470	2,164	12,243	470	1,173	6,432	3,290	11,021	14,652	3,979	15,446
Moroni, Comoros	11,891	13,806	13,839	13,844	12,323	12,201	12,371	12,653	8,009	13,238	15,506	6,981	12,963	14,213	13,414	16,331	8,177	12,037	12,291	6,805
Moscow, USSR	6,197	8,558	8,105	8,368	9,097	6,510	6,557	17,271	5,800	6,069	8,697	6,519	6,716	8,021	12,320	10,041	6,051	16,571	9,138	9,639
Mosul, Iraq	7,941	10,341	9,984	10,197	10,347	8,275	8,363	16,573	5,604	8,226	10,827	5,763	8,657	10,006	13,391	12,129	5,876	15,700	10,370	8,342
Mount Isa, Australia	16,592	15,913	15,632	15,780	17,459	16,514	16,325	4,795	6,835	13,981	13,628	6,215	15,615	15,041	14,757	13,414	6,591	3,975	17,471	3,791

Distances in Kilometers	Channel-Port-aux-Basques, Can.	Charleston, South Carolina	Charleston, West Virginia	Charlotte, North Carolina	Charlotte Amalie, U.S.V.I.	Charlottetown, Canada	Chatham, Canada	Chatham Islands (Waitangi)	Chengdu, China	Chesterfield Inlet, Canada	Cheyenne, Wyoming	Chiang Mai, Thailand	Chibougamau, Canada	Chicago, Illinois	Chiclayo, Peru	Chihuahua, Mexico	Chongquing, China	Christchurch, New Zealand	Christiansted, U.S.V.I.	Christmas Island [Indian Ocean]
Multan, Pakistan	10,085	12,418	11,923	12,210	12,901	10,393	10,430	13,958	3,120	9,517	12,099	3,049	10,515	11,744	16,060	13,490	3,378	13,098	12,934	5,802
Munich, West Germany	5,098	7,484	7,175	7,359	7,519	5,435	5,541	19,233	7,712	5,910	8,311	8,287	5,924	7,282	10,672	9,485	7,970	18,465	7,549	11,174
Murcia, Spain	4,752	6,966	6,807	6,909	6,503	5,078	5,232	19,243	9,156	6,293	8,324	9,594	5,785	7,076	9,494	9,284	9,419	19,202	6,520	12,194
Murmansk, USSR	5,265	7,492	6,970	7,269	8,431	5,540	5,545	16,747	6,102	4,674	7,313	7,114	5,561	6,789	11,606	8,685	6,313	16,357	8,483	10,406
Mururoa Atoll, Fr. Polynesia	11,042	8,707	8,952	8,799	9,202	10,705	10,582	4,231	13,741	10,338	7,815	14,012	10,169	8,812	6,548	6,607	13,484	5,048	9,195	12,124
Muscat, Oman	9,975	12,377	11,994	12,222	12,331	10,306	10,387	14,559	4,546	9,996	12,635	4,215	10,637	11,966	15,215	13,996	4,794	13,689	12,349	6,364
Myitkyina, Burma	11,592	13,563	12,949	13,295	14,806	11,835	11,803	11,625	879	10,143	12,293	749	11,625	12,539	17,924	13,525	1,019	10,813	14,858	4,070
Naga, Philippines	13,222	14,317	13,700	14,038	16,359	13,345	13,231	8,821	2,720	10,988	12,199	2,647	12,759	13,099	17,401	12,953	2,457	8,079	16,429	3,297
Nagasaki, Japan	11,058	12,105	11,482	11,823	14,130	11,154	11,030	10,087	2,455	8,759	10,088	3,451	10,535	10,891	15,804	11,007	2,248	9,504	14,200	5,440
Nagoya, Japan	10,703	11,564	10,952	11,287	13,651	10,769	10,631	9,948	3,099	8,303	9,473	4,147	10,091	10,345	15,122	10,345	2,910	9,438	13,722	6,031
Nagpur, India	11,331	13,639	13,120	13,420	14,148	11,633	11,663	12,744	2,707	10,595	13,097	2,096	11,711	12,894	17,256	14,468	2,911	11,876	14,179	4,550
Nairobi, Kenya	10,563	12,574	12,551	12,585	11,304	10,879	11,045	14,005	7,926	11,906	14,158	7,147	11,621	12,890	12,946	15,056	8,138	13,386	11,282	7,678
Nanchang, China	11,545	13,003	12,365	12,718	14,800	11,708	11,618	10,577	1,164	9,537	11,217	2,039	11,240	11,829	17,077	12,256	910	9,870	14,867	4,473
Nancy, France	4,713	7,093	6,795	6,973	7,119	5,050	5,162	19,440	8,048	5,637	7,982	8,663	5,564	6,919	10,281	9,131	8,303	18,824	7,150	11,574
Nandi, Fiji	13,946	12,224	12,159	12,180	13,468	13,676	13,486	2,955	9,499	11,852	10,312	9,483	12,804	11,714	11,125	9,694	9,228	2,889	13,481	7,747
Nanjing, China	11,184	12,568	11,931	12,283	14,413	11,333	11,236	10,672	1,408	9,113	10,753	2,468	10,833	11,385	16,612	11,790	1,199	10,002	14,481	4,912
Nanning, China	12,110	13,792	13,155	13,510	15,393	12,310	12,244	10,626	967	10,308	12,145	1,069	11,944	12,657	18,031	13,229	768	9,847	15,454	3,697
Nantes, France	4,246	6,596	6,336	6,493	6,531	4,583	4,708	19,480	8,633	5,428	7,645	9,263	5,165	6,507	9,683	8,730	8,885	19,402	6,560	12,160
Naples, Italy	5,694	8,035	7,784	7,937	7,804	6,031	6,156	19,068	7,844	6,714	9,050	8,237	6,601	7,949	10,845	10,169	8,111	18,217	7,826	10,886
Narvik, Norway	4,676	6,950	6,453	6,738	7,809	4,962	4,979	17,161	6,737	4,325	6,952	7,733	5,047	6,316	10,998	8,298	6,949	16,882	7,861	11,012
Nashville, Tennessee	2,600	733	517	547	2,915	2,264	2,137	12,664	12,521	3,036	1,661	13,893	1,827	639	4,807	1,994	12,597	13,435	2,980	16,902
Nassau, Bahamas	2,966	888	1,525	1,173	1,484	2,667	2,654	12,610	13,833	4,365	3,099	15,136	2,768	2,090	3,534	2,876	13,943	13,463	1,541	18,360
Natal, Brazil	6,360	6,365	6,841	6,587	4,215	6,390	6,565	13,277	14,959	8,953	8,753	14,866	7,232	7,483	4,939	8,478	15,231	13,872	4,156	15,338
Natashquan, Canada	352	2,444	2,047	2,268	3,544	452	443	15,171	10,940	2,260	3,445	12,135	898	2,187	6,548	4,409	11,096	15,896	3,609	15,456
Nauru Island	13,169	12,197	11,907	12,054	14,035	12,995	12,796	5,081	7,473	10,674	9,904	7,719	12,065	11,326	12,577	9,749	7,207	4,797	14,074	6,866
Ndjamena, Chad	7,840	9,751	9,758	9,772	8,557	8,139	8,317	16,308	9,244	9,578	11,492	8,961	8,947	10,145	10,705	12,255	9,505	15,917	8,542	10,326
Nelson, New Zealand	15,867	13,631	13,805	13,696	13,978	15,540	15,388	886	10,673	14,289	12,297	10,124	14,837	13,545	10,905	11,334	10,416	256	13,956	7,380
Nema, Mauritania	5,830	7,433	7,536	7,494	6,104	6,083	6,277	16,813	11,008	8,042	9,427	11,057	6,977	8,009	8,397	9,972	11,279	17,020	6,088	12,773
Neuquen, Argentina	9,624	8,034	8,671	8,317	6,351	9,414	9,528	8,360	18,847	11,517	9,621	17,449	9,864	9,168	3,756	8,460	18,858	9,025	6,286	14,492
New Delhi, India	10,510	12,799	12,275	12,577	13,415	10,808	10,832	13,405	2,606	9,756	12,281	2,468	10,867	12,047	16,604	13,661	2,855	12,550	13,451	5,300
New Glasgow, Canada	347	2,055	1,761	1,919	3,028	81	270	14,934	11,455	2,644	3,413	12,641	1,000	2,045	6,046	4,228	11,612	15,710	3,092	15,961
New Haven, Connecticut	1,295	1,134	815	968	2,656	958	871	13,980	12,030	2,715	2,660	13,301	964	1,227	5,369	3,313	12,158	14,763	2,726	16,589
New Orleans, Louisiana	3,286	1,012	1,211	1,042	2,850	2,949	2,840	11,990	13,131	3,712	1,819	14,525	2,578	1,341	4,209	1,562	13,186	12,786	2,906	17,312
New Plymouth, New Zealand	15,688	13,491	13,642	13,546	13,935	15,364	15,207	952	10,585	14,047	12,093	10,087	14,638	13,361	10,908	11,159	10,325	511	13,916	7,421
New York, New York	1,408	1,028	706	856	2,626	1,071	981	13,867	12,100	2,748	2,582	13,379	1,024	1,147	5,291	3,208	12,224	14,652	2,697	16,657
Newcastle upon Tyne, UK	3,980	6,381	6,033	6,237	6,660	4,314	4,406	18,724	8,187	4,753	7,124	8,971	4,752	6,110	9,877	8,305	8,426	18,664	6,699	12,058
Newcastle Waters, Australia	16,470	16,280	15,903	16,105	18,090	16,465	16,295	5,515	6,177	13,903	13,915	5,496	15,632	15,278	15,496	13,867	5,941	4,683	18,114	3,089
Niamey, Niger	6,764	8,477	8,552	8,526	7,161	7,036	7,225	16,629	10,366	8,813	10,401	10,243	7,904	8,999	9,330	11,012	10,635	16,558	7,144	11,737
Nicosia, Cyprus	7,398	9,775	9,478	9,658	9,581	7,735	7,844	17,291	6,491	8,024	10,541	6,645	8,218	9,576	12,553	11,766	6,763	16,429	9,600	9,112
Niue (Alofi)	13,098	11,133	11,155	11,126	12,187	12,795	12,619	2,833	10,705	11,352	9,449	10,791	11,996	10,785	9,782	8,652	10,436	3,171	12,195	9,061
Norfolk, Virginia	1,842	563	501	450	2,332	1,510	1,441	13,470	12,530	3,106	2,505	13,827	1,460	1,125	4,842	2,924	12,646	14,274	2,402	17,079
Norfolk Island, Australia	15,503	13,637	13,640	13,626	14,553	15,222	15,037	2,154	9,460	13,409	11,854	9,100	14,367	13,235	11,769	11,145	9,194	1,662	14,550	6,764
Noril'sk, USSR	6,765	8,641	8,034	8,376	10,047	6,972	6,918	14,691	4,419	5,282	7,708	5,667	6,700	7,666	13,003	9,080	4,579	14,245	10,109	8,961
Norman Wells, Canada	4,346	4,784	4,164	4,503	6,873	4,278	4,099	12,849	8,505	1,738	3,027	9,916	3,435	3,571	8,864	4,324	8,537	13,144	6,944	12,736
Normanton, Australia	16,214	15,603	15,295	15,457	17,281	16,137	15,949	4,912	6,578	13,603	13,290	6,121	15,240	14,695	14,780	13,129	6,406	4,123	17,302	3,900
North Pole	4,733	6,376	5,756	6,104	7,973	4,881	4,792	14,869	6,608	2,975	5,446	7,924	4,471	5,364	10,751	6,833	6,730	14,823	8,040	11,163
Nottingham, United Kingdom	4,063	6,458	6,132	6,324	6,648	4,399	4,500	18,947	8,277	4,943	7,279	9,019	4,876	6,233	9,853	8,439	8,520	18,862	6,684	12,061
Norway House, Canada	2,782	2,751	2,131	2,469	4,854	2,597	2,398	13,163	10,393	1,121	1,520	11,784	1,667	1,543	6,940	2,894	10,455	13,726	4,924	14,753
Norwich, United Kingdom	4,233	6,628	6,301	6,494	6,807	4,569	4,669	19,026	8,151	5,078	7,434	8,873	5,040	6,398	10,008	8,602	8,396	18,810	6,842	11,899
Nouakchott, Mauritania	5,097	6,542	6,682	6,618	5,165	5,322	5,522	16,617	11,639	7,462	8,617	11,828	6,239	7,186	7,536	9,082	11,909	17,073	5,150	13,704
Noumea, New Caledonia	15,096	13,470	13,387	13,420	14,674	14,847	14,653	2,869	8,870	12,834	11,504	8,631	13,949	12,921	12,129	10,936	8,601	2,427	14,682	6,582
Novosibirsk, USSR	8,093	10,140	9,553	9,886	11,325	8,338	8,311	14,451	3,184	6,864	9,322	4,248	8,182	9,227	14,437	10,695	3,401	13,793	11,380	7,568
Nuku'alofa, Tonga	13,658	11,728	11,739	11,717	12,777	13,360	13,182	2,533	10,351	11,815	10,003	10,338	12,544	11,356	10,300	9,239	10,080	2,729	12,783	8,483
Nukunono Island, Tokelau Isls.	12,462	10,745	10,664	10,692	12,118	12,187	11,999	3,877	9,966	10,478	8,820	10,250	11,325	10,218	10,123	8,208	9,704	4,090	12,138	9,015
Nuremberg, West Germany	5,000	7,392	7,072	7,262	7,476	5,337	5,439	19,168	7,685	5,770	8,182	8,296	5,809	7,167	10,644	9,366	7,944	18,461	7,507	11,219
Nyala, Sudan	8,585	10,643	10,586	10,636	9,582	8,901	9,066	15,923	8,313	10,035	12,187	7,937	9,645	10,912	11,771	13,089	8,567	15,352	9,571	9,274
Oaxaca, Mexico	4,814	2,423	2,781	2,555	3,371	4,479	4,389	10,520	14,279	5,163	2,781	15,690	4,161	2,886	3,222	1,602	14,277	11,349	3,399	17,509
Ocean Falls, Canada	4,760	4,378	3,850	4,129	6,568	4,586	4,387	11,653	9,528	2,465	2,132	10,932	3,657	3,206	7,959	3,181	9,516	12,067	6,635	13,366
Odense, Denmark	4,700	7,101	6,726	6,946	7,423	5,030	5,111	18,640	7,482	5,203	7,687	8,222	5,405	6,760	10,637	8,923	7,727	18,178	7,461	11,295
Odessa, USSR	6,422	8,824	8,457	8,674	8,973	6,754	6,839	17,871	6,389	6,790	9,352	6,862	7,132	8,484	12,126	10,626	6,655	17,028	9,004	9,720
Ogbomosho, Nigeria	7,363	8,988	9,100	9,054	7,546	7,627	7,819	16,035	10,484	9,450	10,983	10,221	8,508	9,569	9,480	11,529	10,747	15,923	7,523	11,420
Okha, USSR	8,604	9,588	8,960	9,305	11,603	8,673	8,538	11,476	4,018	6,234	7,684	5,383	8,016	8,381	13,553	8,751	3,963	11,127	11,674	7,925
Okinawa (Naha)	11,805	12,857	12,236	12,576	14,891	11,908	11,786	9,626	2,359	9,521	10,800	3,057	11,296	11,641	16,398	11,663	2,106	8,986	14,962	4,709
Oklahoma City, Oklahoma	3,427	1,647	1,447	1,512	3,725	3,103	2,947	11,873	12,343	3,133	895	13,753	2,464	1,113	5,030	1,110	12,376	12,604	3,785	16,389
Old Crow, Canada	4,866	5,414	4,793	5,133	7,493	4,825	4,652	12,746	7,902	2,262	3,620	9,314	4,013	4,202	9,481	4,876	7,926	12,950	7,563	12,105
Olympia, Washington	4,680	3,940	3,472	3,714	6,121	4,462	4,263	11,373	10,201	2,687	1,585	11,601	3,538	2,839	7,313	2,511	10,182	11,864	6,186	13,929
Omaha, Nebraska	2,987	1,711	1,272	1,485	3,897	2,684	2,508	12,395	11,777	2,480	738	13,178	1,932	702	5,570	1,675	11,825	13,090	3,963	15,994
Omsk, USSR	7,802	9,953	9,392	9,711	10,976	8,067	8,058	15,025	3,631	6,808	9,350	4,566	7,996	9,119	14,152	10,738	3,866	14,340	11,028	7,860
Oodnadatta, Australia	17,450	16,586	16,384	16,490	17,705	17,372	17,182	4,630	7,256	14,839	14,391	6,462	16,467	15,820	14,648	14,049	7,030	3,766	17,692	3,644
Oradea, Romania	5,832	8,229	7,893	8,092	8,305	6,167	6,264	18,540	7,023	6,418	8,912	7,532	6,603	7,961	11,451	10,140	7,286	17,703	8,335	10,387
Oran, Algeria	4,927	7,102	6,966	7,055	6,548	5,249	5,408	19,026	9,258	6,531	8,523	9,644	5,978	7,254	9,484	9,454	9,524	18,967	6,561	12,157
Oranjestad, Aruba	4,017	2,459	3,084	2,741	846	3,794	3,851	12,286	15,185	5,873	4,636	16,342	4,166	3,675	2,393	4,138	15,334	13,158	815	19,512
Orebro, Sweden	4,833	7,215	6,795	7,039	7,713	5,153	5,212	18,123	7,068	5,037	7,594	7,878	5,432	6,769	10,938	8,879	7,306	17,679	7,755	11,028
Orel, USSR	6,304	8,685	8,281	8,505	9,114	6,623	6,681	17,433	5,909	6,311	8,928	6,552	6,878	8,200	12,327	10,257	6,165	16,682	9,153	9,605
Orsk, USSR	7,557	9,858	9,356	9,645	10,553	7,854	7,880	15,895	4,362	7,022	9,648	5,044	7,947	9,185	13,778	11,035	4,620	15,135	10,597	8,200
Osaka, Japan	10,781	11,678	11,064	11,400	13,755	10,853	10,717	9,969	2,970	8,399	9,600	4,007	10,185	10,460	15,261	10,481	2,777	9,444	13,826	5,907
Oslo, Norway	4,572	6,954	6,537	6,779	7,461	4,891	4,951	18,162	7,287	4,824	7,363	8,121	5,177	6,517	10,687	8,638	7,521	17,813	7,505	11,284
Osorno, Chile	9,861	8,149	8,781	8,428	6,578	9,666	9,733	7,921	18,879	11,625	9,598	17,478	10,025	9,247	3,803	8,383	18,784	8,603	6,515	14,350
Ostrava, Czechoslovakia	5,443	7,842	7,495	7,701	7,990	5,777	5,869	18,715	7,187	6,016	8,503	7,775	6,198	7,555	11,165	9,731	7,445	17,947	8,023	10,707
Ottawa, Canada	1,290	1,451	926	1,214	3,163	980	809	14,008	11,579	2,209	2,397	12,875	510	1,038	5,794	3,252	11,698	14,747	3,234	16,132
Ouagadougou, Bourkina Fasso	6,593	8,204	8,312	8,267	6,810	6,851	7,044	16,472	10,766	8,745	10,201	10,657	7,739	8,784	8,921	10,744	11,035	16,505	6,791	12,112
Oujda, Morocco	4,897	7,040	6,922	7,001	6,435	5,216	5,379	18,879	9,418	6,568	8,511	9,793	5,964	7,225	9,347	9,416	9,684	18,917	6,446	12,275
Oxford, United Kingdom	4,095	6,484	6,172	6,357	6,620	4,432	4,539	19,071	8,351	5,044	7,356	9,070	4,933	6,289	9,817	8,500	8,596	18,986	6,655	12,083
Pago Pago, American Samoa	12,783	10,930	10,903	10,901	12,142	12,492	12,310	3,337	10,366	10,921	9,127	10,551	11,661	10,496	9,926	8,415	10,100	3,613	12,155	9,056
Pakxe, Laos	12,903	14,672	14,036	14,391	16,168	13,121	13,067	10,208	1,731	11,189	13,029	830	12,801	13,546	18,905	14,082	1,602	9,386	16,225	2,833
Palembang, Indonesia	14,822	16,665	16,028	16,383	17,970	15,064	15,026	8,883	3,717	13,181	14,848	2,482	14,795	15,517	18,824	15,690	3,600	8,015	18,010	845
Palermo, Italy	5,802	8,111	7,889	8,027	7,770	6,137	6,271	18,963	8,040	6,938	9,223	8,373	6,746	8,084	10,754	10,307	8,308	18,178	7,787	10,925
Palma, Majorca	4,937	7,203	7,012	7,132	6,830	5,268	5,413	19,513	8,785	6,321	8,453	9,226	5,933	7,247	9,848	9,466	9,049	19,075	6,849	11,863
Palmerston North, New Zealand	15,645	13,412	13,583	13,476	13,792	15,317	15,165	762	10,775	14,092	12,078	10,264	14,616	13,323	10,744	11,112	10,515	431	13,772	7,565
Panama, Panama	4,691	2,635	3,261	2,910	1,888	4,417	4,425	11,257	15,602	6,102	4,348	16,931	4,565	3,733	1,740	3,529	15,691	12,130	1,876	19,439
Paramaribo, Suriname	4,641	3,934	4,484	4,186	1,744	4,542	4,671	12,940	15,406	6,996	6,280	16,090	5,207	5,123	3,076	5,916	15,634	13,759	1,677	17,862
Paris, France	4,444	6,819	6,529	6,702	6,837	4,782	4,896	19,452	8,290	5,454	7,755	8,930	5,314	6,667	10,003	8,883	8,542	19,061	6,868	11,857
Patna, India	11,150	13,355	12,793	13,114	14,170	11,432	11,438	12,581	1,942	10,138	12,546	1,615	11,399	12,496	17,389	13,886	2,161	11,734	14,210	4,573
Patrai, Greece	6,383	8,734	8,472	8,632	8,488	6,721	6,842	18,365	7,361	7,273	9,680	7,649	7,266	8,619	11,487	10,834	7,631	17,515	8,507	10,204
Peking, China	10,302	11,783	11,144	11,499	13,551	10,460	10,370	11,465	1,519	8,306	10,110	2,879	9,995	10,626	15,992	11,240	1,458	10,832	13,618	5,692
Penrhyn Island (Omoka)	11,412	9,458	9,465	9,442	10,656	11,106	10,933	4,266	11,270	9,800	7,772	11,692	10,320	9,095	8,613	6,963	11,018	4,766	10,672	10,515
Peoria, Illinois	2,534	1,231	732	979	3,418	2,216	2,053	12,775	11,980	2,522	1,282	13,361	1,568	211	5,349	2,012	12,050	13,503	3,486	16,342
Perm', USSR	6,894	9,151	8,632	8,930	9,981	7,180	7,194	16,114	4,719	6,253	8,877	5,570	7,222	8,439	13,193	10,264	4,960	15,443	10,029	8,809
Perth, Australia	18,218	18,543	18,283	18,438	18,498	18,415	18,324	5,924	7,039	16,049	16,280	5,893	17,838	17,668	15,413	16,004	6,877	5,068	18,433	2,594
Peshawar, Pakistan	9,723	12,037	11,530	11,823	12,609	10,026	10,056	14,188	3,071	9,097	11,675	3,199	10,121	11,337	15,805	13,066	3,338	13,339	12,646	6,106

Distances in Kilometers	Channel-Port-aux-Basques, Can.	Charleston, South Carolina	Charleston, West Virginia	Charlotte, North Carolina	Charlotte Amalie, U.S.V.I.	Charlottetown, Canada	Chatham, Canada	Chatham Islands (Waitangi)	Chengdu, China	Chesterfield Inlet, Canada	Cheyenne, Wyoming	Chiang Mai, Thailand	Chibougamau, Canada	Chicago, Illinois	Chiclayo, Peru	Chihuahua, Mexico	Chongquing, China	Christchurch, New Zealand	Christiansted, U.S.V.I.	Christmas Island [Indian Ocean]
Petropavlovsk-Kamchatskiy,USSR	8,299	8,950	8,343	8,674	11,063	8,313	8,157	11,004	5,011	5,777	6,881	6,341	7,561	7,730	12,676	7,852	4,932	10,782	11,133	8,641
Petrozavodsk, USSR	5,674	7,993	7,512	7,789	8,701	5,973	6,004	17,184	5,995	5,383	8,017	6,857	6,110	7,391	11,921	9,371	6,230	16,626	8,748	10,072
Pevek, USSR	6,394	7,341	6,708	7,056	9,334	6,437	6,293	12,650	5,927	3,966	5,596	7,340	5,750	6,145	11,466	6,806	5,944	12,559	9,405	10,151
Philadelphia, Pennsylvania	1,538	905	587	727	2,588	1,201	1,110	13,739	12,186	2,799	2,503	13,475	1,109	1,071	5,195	3,091	12,306	14,526	2,659	16,741
Phnom Penh, Kampuchea	13,270	15,074	14,440	14,793	16,518	13,495	13,446	9,995	2,119	11,593	13,426	1,023	13,195	13,952	19,276	14,458	2,002	9,159	16,572	2,440
Phoenix, Arizona	4,650	2,989	2,788	2,868	4,964	4,345	4,171	10,775	11,960	3,642	1,068	13,356	3,579	2,341	5,603	782	11,935	11,443	5,018	15,412
Pierre, South Dakota	3,175	2,187	1,698	1,948	4,377	2,899	2,710	12,349	11,335	2,200	512	12,742	2,053	1,070	6,026	1,819	11,374	12,997	4,444	15,503
Pinang, Malaysia	13,802	15,779	15,155	15,505	16,927	14,056	14,030	9,878	2,822	12,322	14,253	1,486	13,853	14,705	19,855	15,303	2,753	9,016	16,969	1,857
Pitcairn Island (Adamstown)	10,712	8,321	8,649	8,451	8,536	10,376	10,278	4,674	14,710	10,393	7,781	14,942	9,957	8,605	5,708	6,474	14,453	5,536	8,522	12,814
Pittsburgh, Pennsylvania	1,843	852	271	584	2,843	1,508	1,379	13,421	12,121	2,645	2,088	13,448	1,142	659	5,226	2,714	12,225	14,187	2,913	16,642
Plymouth, Montserrat	3,435	2,518	3,057	2,763	341	3,276	3,377	13,222	14,564	5,625	4,888	15,580	3,843	3,697	3,241	4,670	14,747	14,091	289	18,550
Plymouth, United Kingdom	3,948	6,324	6,033	6,206	6,397	4,286	4,401	19,093	8,601	5,033	7,282	9,311	4,826	6,176	9,586	8,394	8,846	19,204	6,430	12,303
Ponape Island	12,946	12,471	12,069	12,279	14,525	12,840	12,649	6,178	6,215	10,347	10,087	6,537	11,933	11,444	13,620	10,200	5,950	5,772	14,577	6,138
Ponce, Puerto Rico	3,348	2,109	2,684	2,369	182	3,146	3,220	12,965	14,527	5,361	4,446	15,644	3,606	3,314	3,103	4,183	14,690	13,838	205	18,844
Ponta Delgada, Azores	2,927	4,901	4,835	4,881	4,373	3,212	3,395	17,485	10,813	5,108	6,579	11,496	4,063	5,210	7,464	7,339	11,057	18,349	4,394	14,317
Pontianak, Indonesia	14,622	16,256	15,618	15,970	17,886	14,834	14,773	8,742	3,443	12,788	14,309	2,369	14,465	15,069	18,759	15,101	3,289	7,888	17,942	1,227
Port Augusta, Australia	17,813	16,509	16,417	16,463	17,263	17,669	17,471	4,140	7,842	15,220	14,478	7,019	16,740	15,911	14,123	13,979	7,618	3,268	17,239	4,094
Port Blair, India	12,888	15,035	14,445	14,780	15,895	13,164	13,161	10,953	2,413	11,689	13,895	1,039	13,076	14,083	19,054	15,119	2,452	10,090	15,932	2,831
Port Elizabeth, South Africa	12,344	13,257	13,629	13,440	11,177	12,549	12,749	11,091	10,906	14,621	15,629	9,716	13,477	14,232	11,000	15,430	11,039	10,796	11,121	8,458
Port Hedland, Australia	16,975	17,726	17,229	17,501	19,599	17,126	17,019	6,477	5,851	14,742	15,335	4,824	16,529	16,585	16,404	15,438	5,667	5,604	19,576	1,758
Port Louis, Mauritius	13,628	15,593	15,618	15,631	14,009	13,947	14,109	11,035	7,513	14,645	17,148	6,250	14,660	15,956	14,490	18,117	7,615	10,354	13,971	5,263
Port Moresby, Papua New Guinea	15,115	14,556	14,208	14,390	16,433	15,024	14,834	5,179	6,399	12,506	12,207	6,146	14,122	13,596	14,517	12,145	6,132	4,507	16,471	4,550
Port Said, Egypt	7,620	9,971	9,709	9,870	9,632	7,958	8,077	17,133	6,724	8,383	10,863	6,774	8,488	9,844	12,507	12,052	6,994	16,297	9,646	9,072
Port Sudan, Sudan	8,887	11,178	10,974	11,105	10,551	9,223	9,355	15,884	6,756	9,765	12,227	6,457	9,809	11,158	13,104	13,378	7,012	15,108	10,553	8,206
Port-au-Prince, Haiti	3,437	1,750	2,374	2,031	782	3,187	3,223	12,543	14,547	5,172	3,976	15,771	3,486	2,967	2,917	3,608	14,681	13,415	812	19,092
Port-of-Spain, Trin. & Tobago	4,099	3,091	3,665	3,352	928	3,947	4,050	12,824	15,183	6,289	5,411	16,118	4,512	4,297	2,800	5,043	15,377	13,681	857	18,634
Port-Vila, Vanuatu	14,595	13,068	12,947	13,000	14,417	14,355	14,159	3,236	8,712	12,300	11,033	8,592	13,448	12,459	12,070	10,528	8,441	2,889	14,432	6,784
Portland, Maine	969	1,474	1,122	1,305	2,850	631	531	14,297	11,755	2,552	2,838	13,005	763	1,432	5,667	3,591	11,891	15,069	2,919	16,310
Portland, Oregon	4,734	3,899	3,452	3,681	6,071	4,507	4,308	11,250	10,344	2,813	1,521	11,742	3,589	2,827	7,186	2,373	10,322	11,756	6,134	14,020
Porto, Portugal	4,018	6,243	6,075	6,180	5,886	4,344	4,498	18,982	9,480	5,642	7,601	10,047	5,058	6,343	8,960	8,550	9,736	19,723	5,908	12,804
Porto Alegre, Brazil	8,635	7,586	8,208	7,867	5,557	8,535	8,658	10,111	17,654	10,927	9,622	16,767	9,151	8,801	3,954	8,729	17,883	10,717	5,486	14,883
Porto Alexandre, Angola	9,933	11,115	11,388	11,254	9,227	10,155	10,353	13,332	11,100	12,193	13,381	10,277	11,075	11,949	9,999	13,548	11,312	13,148	9,182	10,102
Porto Novo, Benin	7,382	8,931	9,067	9,008	7,424	7,636	7,830	15,852	10,735	9,531	10,977	10,453	8,528	9,554	9,276	11,470	10,998	15,786	7,399	11,571
Porto Velho, Brazil	6,257	4,901	5,531	5,184	3,001	6,092	6,182	11,095	17,283	8,315	6,931	17,873	6,580	6,109	1,773	6,136	17,501	11,897	2,934	17,588
Portsmouth, United Kingdom	4,140	6,523	6,221	6,400	6,615	4,477	4,588	19,175	8,398	5,136	7,431	9,096	4,995	6,349	9,804	8,564	8,644	19,075	6,649	12,084
Poznan, Poland	5,228	7,629	7,264	7,479	7,867	5,560	5,645	18,640	7,186	5,724	8,226	7,839	5,949	7,304	11,064	9,468	7,439	17,962	7,903	10,838
Prague, Czechoslovakia	5,188	7,585	7,248	7,448	7,715	5,523	5,619	18,937	7,436	5,846	8,300	8,044	5,964	7,323	10,890	9,510	7,692	18,207	7,748	10,982
Praia, Cape Verde Islands	4,885	6,003	6,226	6,114	4,426	5,059	5,258	15,904	12,478	7,401	8,213	12,707	5,990	6,780	6,662	8,521	12,747	16,484	4,404	14,506
Pretoria, South Africa	11,884	13,127	13,406	13,271	11,181	12,125	12,322	11,888	10,207	13,965	15,395	9,106	13,031	13,961	11,470	15,513	10,363	11,522	11,132	8,270
Prince Albert, Canada	3,313	3,064	2,478	2,793	5,223	3,120	2,921	12,699	10,276	1,428	1,343	11,683	2,190	1,847	7,080	2,728	10,317	13,234	5,293	14,505
Prince Edward Island	14,037	14,621	15,090	14,845	12,445	14,219	14,418	9,420	10,825	16,367	16,995	9,474	15,149	15,726	11,514	16,316	10,888	9,074	12,381	7,469
Prince George, Canada	4,390	4,099	3,550	3,842	6,284	4,221	4,023	11,988	9,612	2,106	1,949	11,022	3,293	2,907	7,827	3,118	9,615	12,420	6,352	13,580
Prince Rupert, Canada	4,841	4,590	4,045	4,335	6,777	4,685	4,488	11,739	9,249	2,449	2,387	10,654	3,762	3,402	8,232	3,461	9,238	12,118	6,845	13,117
Providence, Rhode Island	1,161	1,256	953	1,101	2,673	824	748	14,117	11,966	2,705	2,774	13,223	929	1,345	5,448	3,449	12,098	14,901	2,743	16,523
Provo, Utah	4,213	2,943	2,586	2,758	5,071	3,935	3,747	11,363	11,337	2,920	587	12,745	3,089	2,022	6,141	1,384	11,332	11,983	5,132	15,086
Puerto Aisen, Chile	10,385	8,687	9,319	8,966	7,103	10,195	10,265	7,591	18,346	12,162	10,105	16,956	10,562	9,782	4,337	8,868	18,246	8,236	7,040	13,812
Puerto Deseado, Argentina	10,581	9,027	9,664	9,310	7,321	10,416	10,502	7,798	17,927	12,511	10,568	16,514	10,853	10,158	4,732	9,366	17,887	8,386	7,255	13,499
Puerto Princesa, Philippines	13,654	14,906	14,281	14,624	16,873	13,803	13,703	8,810	2,772	11,523	12,832	2,352	13,275	13,692	17,964	13,602	2,534	8,024	16,942	2,665
Punta Arenas, Chile	11,217	9,558	10,190	9,837	7,942	11,038	11,115	7,132	17,475	13,033	10,943	16,093	11,428	10,652	5,207	9,679	17,377	7,701	7,878	12,945
Pusan, South Korea	10,812	11,910	11,283	11,627	13,909	10,915	10,793	10,341	2,382	8,539	9,935	3,469	10,310	10,700	15,707	10,891	2,197	9,765	13,979	5,616
Pyongyang, North Korea	10,402	11,629	10,995	11,344	13,558	10,521	10,408	10,865	2,182	8,207	9,761	3,418	9,958	10,433	15,614	10,794	2,046	10,288	13,628	5,864
Qamdo, China	10,972	12,922	12,308	12,654	14,206	11,209	11,173	12,060	655	9,504	11,686	1,383	10,985	11,901	17,287	12,943	916	11,274	14,261	4,698
Qandahar, Afghanistan	9,662	12,026	11,560	11,832	12,387	9,977	10,026	14,500	3,637	9,277	11,895	3,619	10,159	11,427	15,516	13,285	3,901	13,635	12,418	6,308
Qiqian, China	8,949	10,378	9,740	10,094	12,169	9,090	8,992	12,229	2,756	6,901	8,768	4,168	8,597	9,227	14,626	9,958	2,774	11,716	12,237	7,097
Qom, Iran	8,554	10,954	10,563	10,794	11,057	8,883	8,960	15,863	4,950	8,623	11,254	5,043	9,205	10,537	14,119	12,597	5,220	14,990	11,082	7,631
Quebec, Canada	919	1,726	1,268	1,519	3,210	625	440	14,386	11,411	2,201	2,745	12,674	416	1,414	5,996	3,630	11,543	15,125	3,279	15,968
Quetta, Pakistan	9,856	12,218	11,760	12,023	12,577	10,170	10,219	14,315	3,545	9,449	12,062	3,465	10,348	11,612	15,697	13,453	3,805	13,449	12,608	6,117
Quito, Ecuador	5,617	3,654	4,282	3,930	2,534	5,362	5,387	10,638	16,624	7,124	5,294	17,933	5,570	4,752	740	4,338	16,713	11,506	2,497	18,737
Rabaul, Papua New Guinea	14,347	13,764	13,406	13,593	15,701	14,242	14,050	5,367	6,403	11,745	11,407	6,359	13,333	12,793	14,129	11,384	6,132	4,800	15,744	5,178
Raiatea (Uturoa)	11,534	9,365	9,483	9,399	10,235	11,207	11,054	3,832	12,309	10,291	8,008	12,614	10,521	9,212	7,845	7,001	12,052	4,502	10,239	11,031
Raleigh, North Carolina	2,075	354	391	210	2,355	1,741	1,662	13,228	12,645	3,177	2,352	13,961	1,609	1,033	4,710	2,696	12,752	14,031	2,425	17,173
Rangiroa (Avatoru)	11,113	8,926	9,055	8,964	9,792	10,785	10,635	4,219	12,574	9,953	7,618	12,955	10,115	8,797	7,449	6,580	12,322	4,916	9,797	11,468
Rangoon, Burma	12,467	14,506	13,898	14,241	15,608	12,724	12,703	11,076	1,734	11,101	13,239	372	12,558	13,498	18,819	14,444	1,770	10,230	15,654	3,194
Raoul Is., Kermadec Islands	14,459	12,391	12,469	12,411	13,180	14,148	13,979	1,634	10,595	12,735	10,825	10,377	13,374	12,136	10,425	9,966	10,325	1,794	13,175	8,141
Rarotonga (Avarua)	12,504	10,366	10,470	10,395	11,218	12,181	12,023	2,961	11,752	11,102	8,931	11,878	11,465	10,177	8,704	7,977	11,485	3,557	11,220	10,066
Rawson, Argentina	10,083	8,557	9,195	8,841	6,826	9,920	10,007	8,192	18,313	12,039	10,164	16,908	10,367	9,701	4,298	8,998	18,314	8,809	6,760	13,975
Recife, Brazil	6,608	6,568	7,055	6,795	4,406	6,635	6,809	13,079	15,083	9,198	8,953	14,916	7,472	7,698	4,962	8,638	15,354	13,656	4,345	15,205
Regina, Canada	3,290	2,820	2,256	2,556	4,997	3,070	2,871	12,555	10,587	1,660	1,035	11,995	2,146	1,615	6,774	2,425	10,626	13,124	5,065	14,785
Reykjavik, Iceland	2,902	5,240	4,795	5,051	6,017	3,203	3,241	17,251	8,492	3,229	5,657	9,526	3,425	4,764	9,202	6,900	8,693	17,533	6,070	12,806
Rhodes, Greece	6,956	9,321	9,042	9,212	9,095	7,294	7,409	17,765	6,890	7,706	10,176	7,100	7,807	9,164	12,074	11,368	7,161	16,908	9,113	9,599
Richmond, Virginia	1,863	576	378	400	2,452	1,527	1,442	13,427	12,452	3,007	2,383	13,759	1,397	996	4,911	2,837	12,564	14,223	2,523	16,993
Riga, USSR	5,416	7,799	7,377	7,623	8,259	5,736	5,796	17,968	6,617	5,549	8,133	7,362	6,010	7,342	11,480	9,436	6,863	17,355	8,299	10,472
Ringkobing, Denmark	4,549	6,949	6,572	6,793	7,292	4,878	4,958	18,614	7,578	5,061	7,537	8,340	5,251	6,606	10,509	8,770	7,820	18,226	7,331	11,429
Rio Branco, Brazil	6,430	4,901	5,538	5,186	3,148	6,242	6,317	10,707	17,566	8,362	6,812	18,300	6,665	6,088	1,373	5,931	17,759	11,520	3,084	17,631
Rio Cuarto, Argentina	8,953	7,475	8,113	7,760	5,698	8,791	8,879	9,058	18,899	10,948	9,211	17,720	9,252	8,641	3,330	8,133	19,076	9,739	5,631	15,062
Rio de Janeiro, Brazil	7,965	7,290	7,877	7,558	5,138	7,915	8,061	11,212	16,678	10,420	9,518	16,085	8,632	8,504	4,308	8,827	16,934	11,791	5,067	15,005
Rio Gallegos, Argentina	11,035	9,408	10,042	9,688	7,764	10,860	10,940	7,329	17,612	12,888	10,842	16,217	11,265	10,514	5,070	9,595	17,530	7,903	7,699	13,103
Rio Grande, Brazil	8,844	7,746	8,372	8,029	5,741	8,739	8,859	9,884	17,759	11,111	9,743	16,781	9,341	8,958	4,015	8,815	17,972	10,486	5,671	14,741
Riyadh, Saudi Arabia	9,130	11,511	11,205	11,392	11,224	9,468	9,573	15,567	5,639	9,564	12,155	5,416	9,920	11,277	14,015	13,436	5,898	14,716	11,236	7,486
Road Town, Brit. Virgin Isls.	3,268	2,204	2,754	2,453	35	3,084	3,171	13,156	14,438	5,369	4,569	15,518	3,598	3,392	3,252	4,358	14,609	14,029	78	18,656
Roanoke, Virginia	2,047	500	191	243	2,558	1,710	1,609	13,229	12,472	2,991	2,183	13,799	1,474	835	4,875	2,615	12,575	14,018	2,628	16,987
Robinson Crusoe Island, Chile	9,207	7,350	7,974	7,625	5,940	8,986	9,034	8,056	19,585	10,802	8,696	18,346	9,265	8,410	2,977	7,466	19,332	8,810	5,882	15,097
Rochester, New York	1,523	1,172	633	925	2,998	1,195	1,047	13,751	11,828	2,400	2,250	13,138	791	835	5,533	3,011	11,941	14,504	3,069	16,372
Rockhampton, Australia	16,258	15,010	14,845	14,927	16,313	16,081	15,881	3,773	7,768	13,731	12,880	7,286	15,150	14,315	13,619	12,471	7,511	3,019	16,319	4,961
Rome, Italy	5,505	7,849	7,595	7,750	7,644	5,842	5,967	19,251	7,930	6,537	8,862	8,357	6,412	7,759	10,703	9,980	8,195	18,390	7,666	11,045
Rosario, Argentina	8,919	7,549	8,186	7,834	5,695	8,773	8,871	9,302	18,562	11,002	9,370	17,456	9,278	8,733	3,513	8,334	18,757	9,960	5,627	14,984
Roseau, Dominica	3,584	2,692	3,235	2,939	506	3,434	3,539	13,184	14,688	5,798	5,057	15,673	4,015	3,874	3,178	4,814	14,877	14,050	445	18,532
Rostock, East Germany	4,858	7,259	6,892	7,108	7,535	5,189	5,273	18,717	7,429	5,388	7,870	8,135	5,578	6,934	10,743	9,102	7,677	18,172	7,572	11,176
Rostov-na-Donu, USSR	6,901	9,295	8,887	9,126	9,587	7,226	7,295	17,195	5,701	6,994	9,609	6,190	7,523	8,855	12,767	10,932	5,966	16,367	9,621	9,115
Rotterdam, Netherlands	4,465	6,860	6,533	6,727	7,016	4,801	4,902	19,116	7,995	5,275	7,654	8,686	5,270	6,628	10,210	8,829	8,243	18,726	7,051	11,687
Rouyn, Canada	1,483	1,720	1,118	1,454	3,552	1,221	1,026	13,936	11,261	1,829	2,179	12,580	388	977	6,093	3,181	11,370	14,636	3,623	15,799
Sacramento, California	5,034	3,785	3,451	3,612	5,873	4,768	4,576	10,686	11,007	3,434	1,453	12,388	3,896	2,886	6,610	1,802	10,967	11,254	5,931	14,409
Saginaw, Michigan	1,982	1,235	597	950	3,304	1,669	1,500	13,333	11,759	2,259	1,736	13,110	1,026	348	5,574	2,570	11,851	14,061	3,374	16,240
Saint Denis, Reunion	13,528	15,437	15,489	15,487	13,809	13,842	14,009	11,096	7,716	14,649	17,096	6,463	14,580	15,855	14,265	17,974	7,822	10,434	13,769	5,482
Saint George's, Grenada	3,945	2,950	3,518	3,209	776	3,792	3,894	12,913	15,043	6,133	5,282	16,001	4,355	4,152	2,889	4,945	15,235	13,773	706	18,652
Saint John, Canada	589	1,831	1,502	1,678	2,987	251	201	14,677	11,537	2,540	3,153	12,753	811	1,777	5,926	3,961	11,684	15,446	3,054	16,072
Saint John's, Antigua	3,388	2,511	3,043	2,753	355	3,233	3,336	13,280	14,510	5,593	4,887	15,522	3,810	3,685	3,300	4,687	14,695	14,150	311	18,495
Saint John's, Canada	484	2,818	2,553	2,701	3,426	807	965	15,725	11,035	2,907	4,135	12,134	1,608	2,811	6,584	5,013	11,215	16,501	3,483	15,426
Saint Louis, Missouri	2,694	1,132	747	914	3,320	2,368	2,215	12,593	12,194	2,752	1,280	13,580	1,774	423	5,137	1,839	12,259	13,334	3,386	16,518
Saint Paul, Minnesota	2,612	1,766	1,202	1,499	3,939	2,329	2,142	12,834	11,454	2,054	1,043	12,843	1,512	558	5,879	2,144	11,517	13,511	4,008	15,790

Distances in Kilometers	Channel-Port-aux-Basques, Can.	Charleston, South Carolina	Charleston, West Virginia	Charlotte, North Carolina	Charlotte Amalie, U.S.V.I.	Charlottetown, Canada	Chatham, Canada	Chatham Islands (Waitangi)	Chengdu, China	Chesterfield Inlet, Canada	Cheyenne, Wyoming	Chiang Mai, Thailand	Chibougamau, Canada	Chicago, Illinois	Chiclayo, Peru	Chihuahua, Mexico	Chongquing, China	Christchurch, New Zealand	Christiansted, U.S.V.I.	Christmas Island [Indian Ocean]
Saint Peter Port, UK	4,089	6,460	6,176	6,345	6,491	4,427	4,544	19,246	8,563	5,187	7,436	9,244	4,976	6,325	9,669	8,544	8,811	19,254	6,523	12,205
Saipan (Susupe)	12,633	12,829	12,308	12,588	15,016	12,620	12,450	7,585	4,573	10,057	10,471	4,980	11,803	11,664	14,979	10,914	4,309	7,053	15,081	5,249
Salalah, Oman	10,271	12,653	12,342	12,532	12,292	10,608	10,711	14,431	5,266	10,592	13,213	4,748	11,044	12,398	14,905	14,528	5,500	13,586	12,300	6,438
Salem, Oregon	4,793	3,925	3,487	3,710	6,092	4,563	4,365	11,178	10,376	2,886	1,540	11,771	3,647	2,865	7,166	2,349	10,351	11,686	6,155	14,018
Salt Lake City, Utah	4,202	2,969	2,601	2,779	5,104	3,927	3,738	11,394	11,278	2,873	597	12,686	3,074	2,028	6,198	1,445	11,273	12,008	5,165	15,040
Salta, Argentina	8,037	6,552	7,191	6,837	4,772	7,868	7,953	9,673	18,799	10,020	8,356	18,286	8,321	7,727	2,518	7,341	19,070	10,407	4,706	15,985
Salto, Uruguay	8,745	7,467	8,101	7,751	5,553	8,611	8,717	9,598	18,314	10,894	9,362	17,322	9,150	8,664	3,552	8,373	18,533	10,248	5,484	15,055
Salvador, Brazil	7,013	6,709	7,241	6,955	4,519	7,006	7,169	12,408	15,720	9,561	9,057	15,449	7,799	7,884	4,580	8,599	15,990	12,997	4,453	15,294
Salzburg, Austria	5,212	7,599	7,288	7,473	7,629	5,549	5,655	19,160	7,627	6,002	8,414	8,188	6,034	7,392	10,778	9,594	7,886	18,366	7,659	11,063
Samsun, Turkey	7,135	9,535	9,180	9,391	9,587	7,469	7,558	17,327	6,067	7,500	10,075	6,386	7,861	9,214	12,684	11,355	6,338	16,457	9,613	9,102
San Antonio, Texas	3,920	1,807	1,843	1,778	3,616	3,586	3,450	11,346	12,941	3,813	1,420	14,353	3,049	1,694	4,475	744	12,958	12,110	3,667	16,752
San Cristobal, Venezuela	4,583	2,880	3,517	3,165	1,413	4,351	4,400	11,752	15,734	6,345	4,901	16,917	4,677	4,073	1,816	4,235	15,872	12,621	1,374	19,636
San Diego, California	5,081	3,471	3,261	3,348	5,428	4,783	4,604	10,409	11,763	3,875	1,441	13,139	3,987	2,792	5,889	1,152	11,719	11,049	5,480	15,005
San Francisco, California	5,151	3,872	3,550	3,705	5,946	4,884	4,692	10,565	11,026	3,551	1,557	12,401	4,014	2,992	6,616	1,825	10,981	11,133	6,003	14,364
San Jose, Costa Rica	4,785	2,564	3,157	2,819	2,265	4,489	4,473	10,966	15,429	5,953	4,013	16,811	4,523	3,557	1,905	3,092	15,489	11,836	2,265	18,967
San Juan, Argentina	8,811	7,217	7,855	7,501	5,533	8,629	8,707	8,919	19,315	10,700	8,869	18,127	9,040	8,362	2,985	7,757	19,507	9,633	5,469	15,313
San Juan, Puerto Rico	3,289	2,101	2,668	2,358	126	3,092	3,169	13,037	14,468	5,326	4,451	15,578	3,566	3,301	3,172	4,212	14,633	13,910	170	18,771
San Luis Potosi, Mexico	4,666	2,384	2,577	2,435	3,781	4,328	4,209	10,602	13,581	4,642	2,136	14,988	3,862	2,519	3,943	882	13,571	11,394	3,821	16,911
San Marino, San Marino	5,386	7,747	7,474	7,639	7,620	5,724	5,843	19,300	7,838	6,344	8,698	8,313	6,267	7,619	10,714	9,836	8,102	18,427	7,645	11,068
San Miguel de Tucuman, Argen.	8,260	6,776	7,414	7,061	4,997	8,092	8,178	9,520	18,897	10,245	8,561	18,179	8,547	7,948	2,707	7,530	19,167	10,242	4,931	15,762
San Salvador, El Salvador	4,674	2,312	2,831	2,527	2,645	4,355	4,306	10,845	14,896	5,514	3,398	16,303	4,238	3,127	2,488	2,404	14,929	11,702	2,662	18,379
Sanaa, Yemen	9,733	12,045	11,823	11,965	11,415	10,070	10,197	15,039	6,294	10,459	12,988	5,822	10,625	11,980	13,865	14,190	6,536	14,246	11,415	7,355
Santa Cruz, Bolivia	7,250	5,873	6,508	6,158	4,003	7,091	7,184	10,404	18,094	9,309	7,813	18,145	7,581	7,071	2,184	6,908	18,347	11,162	3,936	16,647
Santa Cruz, Tenerife	4,251	6,035	6,057	6,057	5,068	4,518	4,708	17,559	10,914	6,449	7,883	11,316	5,396	6,485	7,851	8,543	11,177	18,156	5,070	13,679
Santa Fe, New Mexico	4,048	2,412	2,178	2,273	4,458	3,739	3,567	11,338	12,022	3,250	614	13,433	2,996	1,730	5,435	782	12,024	12,025	4,516	15,782
Santa Rosa, Argentina	9,338	7,851	8,490	8,136	6,084	9,177	9,266	8,778	18,757	11,327	9,550	17,449	9,637	9,012	3,665	8,443	18,862	9,436	6,018	14,685
Santa Rosalia, Mexico	5,090	3,166	3,101	3,105	4,932	4,770	4,609	10,247	12,522	4,300	1,679	13,899	4,077	2,763	5,140	627	12,479	10,953	4,978	15,644
Santarem, Brazil	5,556	4,715	5,296	4,980	2,558	5,455	5,581	12,295	16,172	7,887	6,993	16,637	6,100	5,926	2,831	6,469	16,417	13,076	2,488	17,424
Santiago del Estero, Argentina	8,361	6,903	7,541	7,188	5,105	8,197	8,286	9,503	18,850	10,368	8,701	18,046	8,664	8,079	2,849	7,672	19,114	10,215	5,038	15,634
Santiago, Chile	9,047	7,393	8,029	7,675	5,765	8,857	8,929	8,625	19,437	10,877	8,970	18,088	9,242	8,520	3,103	7,821	19,508	9,341	5,701	15,125
Santo Domingo, Dominican Rep.	3,373	1,875	2,480	2,148	525	3,142	3,194	12,734	14,530	5,232	4,162	15,711	3,512	3,093	2,997	3,845	14,677	13,607	556	19,009
Sao Paulo de Olivenca, Brazil	5,730	4,177	4,813	4,462	2,448	5,532	5,602	11,151	16,902	7,633	6,142	17,861	5,937	5,370	1,279	5,338	17,074	11,990	2,388	18,349
Sao Paulo, Brazil	7,974	7,165	7,765	7,438	5,043	7,904	8,041	10,964	17,026	10,374	9,343	16,430	8,585	8,383	4,008	8,598	17,284	11,571	4,972	15,192
Sao Tome, Sao Tome & Principe	8,196	9,682	9,847	9,772	8,071	8,446	8,641	15,162	10,698	10,344	11,776	10,243	9,343	10,349	9,646	12,213	10,950	15,020	8,040	11,003
Sapporo, Japan	9,766	10,620	10,005	10,341	12,697	9,824	9,683	10,509	3,561	7,348	8,573	4,787	9,137	9,403	14,328	9,511	3,430	10,085	12,768	6,949
Sarajevo, Yugoslavia	5,796	8,174	7,878	8,056	8,096	6,134	6,245	18,822	7,400	6,595	9,021	7,843	6,637	7,994	11,192	10,199	7,665	17,951	8,121	10,593
Saratov, USSR	6,924	9,283	8,825	9,091	9,796	7,236	7,283	16,766	5,230	6,716	9,353	5,857	7,431	8,727	13,014	10,713	5,490	15,994	9,836	8,930
Saskatoon, Canada	3,391	3,041	2,468	2,775	5,212	3,188	2,989	12,575	10,360	1,561	1,228	11,769	2,259	1,830	7,004	2,608	10,396	13,117	5,281	14,554
Schefferville, Canada	966	2,656	2,142	2,430	4,049	988	869	14,996	10,495	1,652	3,164	11,741	747	2,092	6,930	4,277	10,636	15,646	4,116	15,047
Seattle, Washington	4,616	3,908	3,431	3,678	6,091	4,400	4,201	11,447	10,179	2,612	1,565	11,582	3,475	2,796	7,323	2,530	10,164	11,938	6,156	13,940
Sendai, Japan	10,294	11,085	10,477	10,809	13,188	10,346	10,203	10,063	3,462	7,856	8,981	4,582	9,645	9,866	14,642	9,856	3,294	9,607	13,258	6,521
Seoul, South Korea	10,555	11,735	11,103	11,451	13,691	10,668	10,552	10,670	2,243	8,330	9,827	3,427	10,089	10,534	15,656	10,832	2,087	10,094	13,761	5,768
Sept-Iles, Canada	606	2,235	1,787	2,036	3,536	503	359	14,863	10,998	2,063	3,119	12,230	572	1,877	6,444	4,100	11,142	15,577	3,603	15,543
Sevastopol, USSR	6,722	9,124	8,759	8,975	9,245	7,055	7,140	17,633	6,217	7,071	9,642	6,634	7,433	8,784	12,381	10,922	6,485	16,776	9,275	9,446
Seville, Spain	4,424	6,588	6,456	6,542	6,072	4,744	4,905	18,935	9,547	6,116	8,035	10,016	5,488	6,752	9,061	8,946	9,809	19,312	6,088	12,626
Shanghai, China	11,290	12,590	11,955	12,305	14,490	11,427	11,323	10,434	1,653	9,157	10,710	2,633	10,896	11,395	16,530	11,708	1,431	9,776	14,559	4,901
Sheffield, United Kingdom	4,030	6,426	6,096	6,291	6,633	4,365	4,465	18,898	8,274	4,895	7,235	9,025	4,836	6,194	9,841	8,398	8,516	18,831	6,670	12,077
Shenyang, China	10,101	11,410	10,773	11,125	13,290	10,231	10,125	11,228	2,128	7,962	9,619	3,446	9,696	10,227	15,499	10,701	2,036	10,654	13,359	6,070
Shiraz, Iran	9,082	11,484	11,109	11,332	11,472	9,414	9,497	15,438	4,922	9,203	11,835	4,836	9,763	11,101	14,445	13,174	5,186	14,565	11,493	7,218
Sibiu, Romania	6,052	8,448	8,113	8,312	8,500	6,387	6,484	18,378	6,901	6,624	9,127	7,371	6,823	8,181	11,632	10,359	7,165	17,525	8,529	10,190
Singapore	14,347	16,216	15,581	15,935	17,517	14,589	14,552	9,279	3,252	12,734	14,492	2,007	14,328	15,087	19,283	15,420	3,144	8,416	17,562	1,319
Sioux Falls, South Dakota	2,939	1,891	1,394	1,647	4,082	2,651	2,467	12,510	11,520	2,238	717	12,921	1,842	768	5,826	1,853	11,569	13,182	4,148	15,758
Skelleftea, Sweden	4,929	7,249	6,774	7,048	7,982	5,228	5,259	17,446	6,645	4,738	7,355	7,565	5,376	6,670	11,195	8,690	6,870	17,059	8,030	10,804
Skopje, Yugoslavia	6,118	8,493	8,201	8,377	8,379	6,456	6,567	18,540	7,235	6,894	9,336	7,619	6,959	8,317	11,449	10,520	7,503	17,666	8,403	10,309
Socotra Island (Tamrida)	10,642	13,005	12,725	12,899	12,503	10,980	11,091	14,096	5,499	11,054	13,667	4,855	11,452	12,810	14,939	14,965	5,721	13,270	12,505	6,257
Sofia, Bulgaria	6,197	8,580	8,274	8,458	8,511	6,534	6,641	18,410	7,068	6,898	9,367	7,461	7,015	8,374	11,595	10,569	7,335	17,537	8,535	10,178
Songkhla, Thailand	13,621	15,581	14,957	15,307	16,770	13,871	13,843	9,994	2,623	12,123	14,061	1,293	13,658	14,506	19,953	15,124	2,554	9,136	16,815	2,036
Sorong, Indonesia	14,736	15,211	14,680	14,967	17,400	14,789	14,642	7,015	4,525	12,272	12,853	4,145	14,055	14,037	16,479	13,217	4,269	6,254	17,465	3,024
South Georgia Island	11,480	10,494	11,123	10,778	8,481	11,412	11,547	8,475	15,947	13,850	12,394	14,576	12,069	11,702	6,522	11,321	15,997	8,816	8,411	12,012
South Pole	15,274	13,629	14,249	13,901	12,033	15,125	15,214	5,132	13,396	17,030	14,558	12,080	15,534	14,641	9,254	13,170	13,274	5,178	11,966	8,841
South Sandwich Islands	12,056	11,201	11,824	11,482	9,150	12,013	12,158	8,396	15,211	14,502	13,138	13,833	12,713	12,414	7,270	12,068	15,254	8,639	9,079	11,290
Split, Yugoslavia	5,681	8,051	7,767	7,938	7,943	6,019	6,134	18,977	7,562	6,546	8,944	8,006	6,540	7,896	11,032	10,106	7,827	18,104	7,968	10,745
Spokane, Washington	4,272	3,547	3,060	3,314	5,734	4,049	3,850	11,684	10,393	2,393	1,236	11,802	3,128	2,427	7,067	2,329	10,391	12,206	5,799	14,259
Spoleto, Italy	5,473	7,825	7,563	7,722	7,655	5,811	5,933	19,259	7,873	6,468	8,809	8,318	6,368	7,718	10,729	9,936	8,138	18,388	7,678	11,034
Springbok, South Africa	11,493	12,397	12,760	12,576	10,340	11,691	11,891	11,723	11,300	13,831	14,762	10,208	12,620	13,362	10,388	14,631	11,460	11,502	10,285	9,232
Springfield, Illinois	2,586	1,170	712	929	3,360	2,264	2,106	12,711	12,076	2,621	1,293	13,458	1,644	287	5,253	1,951	12,145	13,446	3,427	16,427
Springfield, Massachusetts	1,222	1,222	875	1,048	2,731	884	787	14,047	11,940	2,641	2,672	13,209	880	1,245	5,461	3,362	12,069	14,825	2,802	16,499
Srinagar, India	9,868	12,150	11,627	11,928	12,813	10,163	10,185	13,938	2,769	9,128	11,676	2,934	10,218	11,405	16,025	13,062	3,037	13,096	12,852	5,915
Stanley, Falkland Islands	11,001	9,603	10,241	9,887	7,790	10,864	10,965	7,885	17,241	13,076	11,245	15,832	11,370	10,761	5,377	10,069	17,233	8,391	7,722	12,934
Stara Zagora, Bulgaria	6,367	8,755	8,441	8,629	8,703	6,704	6,808	18,217	6,895	7,012	9,502	7,274	7,171	8,530	11,787	10,719	7,164	17,345	8,728	9,986
Stockholm, Sweden	4,983	7,361	6,935	7,182	7,874	5,301	5,358	18,030	6,910	5,129	7,701	7,717	5,566	6,898	11,099	8,997	7,149	17,547	7,917	10,868
Stornoway, United Kingdom	3,637	6,036	5,659	5,879	6,464	3,965	4,044	18,280	8,248	4,292	6,684	9,115	4,348	5,705	9,690	7,886	8,476	18,370	6,508	12,278
Strasbourg, France	4,821	7,204	6,902	7,082	7,233	5,159	5,268	19,398	7,951	5,711	8,074	8,555	5,665	7,021	10,393	9,230	8,206	18,723	7,264	11,459
Stuttgart, West Germany	4,908	7,294	6,986	7,170	7,339	5,245	5,353	19,318	7,847	5,754	8,136	8,447	5,740	7,097	10,500	9,303	8,102	18,617	7,370	11,354
Subic, Philippines	13,088	14,316	13,690	14,034	16,286	13,228	13,124	9,132	2,405	10,931	12,271	2,304	12,686	13,104	17,662	13,090	2,146	8,378	16,355	3,235
Suchow, China	10,934	12,373	11,735	12,088	14,177	11,089	10,996	10,955	1,295	8,905	10,619	2,489	10,611	11,202	16,499	11,694	1,129	10,289	14,245	5,102
Sucre, Bolivia	7,401	5,940	6,578	6,225	4,135	7,231	7,316	10,154	18,339	9,398	7,812	18,377	7,689	7,126	2,081	6,861	18,586	10,916	4,069	16,593
Sudbury, Canada	1,660	1,528	907	1,253	3,453	1,372	1,186	13,711	11,444	1,971	1,997	12,775	622	737	5,901	2,950	11,546	14,421	3,524	15,965
Suez, Egypt	7,737	10,080	9,827	9,983	9,703	8,075	8,196	17,024	6,751	8,525	10,998	6,765	8,614	9,970	12,546	12,180	7,021	16,197	9,716	9,006
Sundsvall, Sweden	4,835	7,189	6,739	6,999	7,816	5,144	5,188	17,767	6,872	4,834	7,426	7,745	5,354	6,671	11,038	8,738	7,103	17,369	7,862	10,949
Surabaya, Indonesia	15,471	16,895	16,272	16,614	18,752	15,666	15,592	7,912	4,297	13,500	14,738	3,252	15,229	15,679	17,932	15,315	4,127	7,050	18,812	858
Suva, Fiji	13,899	12,150	12,094	12,110	13,371	13,625	13,437	2,901	9,608	11,835	10,259	9,595	12,759	11,656	11,014	9,622	9,337	2,868	13,383	7,849
Sverdlovsk, USSR	7,164	9,404	8,876	9,178	10,266	7,447	7,456	15,847	4,430	6,448	9,060	5,282	7,467	8,666	13,475	10,450	4,671	15,164	10,314	8,530
Svobodnyy, USSR	9,016	10,287	9,649	10,002	12,174	9,132	9,020	11,832	3,037	6,838	8,546	4,430	8,576	9,107	14,430	9,682	3,012	11,361	12,244	7,192
Sydney, Australia	17,066	15,315	15,307	15,302	16,051	16,818	16,624	2,990	8,693	14,703	13,467	8,038	15,919	14,874	13,014	12,818	8,448	2,141	16,035	5,302
Sydney, Canada	176	2,246	1,962	2,117	3,114	228	417	15,136	11,352	2,695	3,596	12,516	1,135	2,239	6,178	4,428	11,515	15,911	3,177	15,833
Syktyvkar, USSR	6,391	8,642	8,122	8,420	9,501	6,674	6,686	16,378	5,136	5,768	8,399	6,043	6,713	7,933	12,705	9,782	5,368	15,773	9,550	9,301
Szeged, Hungary	5,766	8,158	7,835	8,027	8,188	6,102	6,203	18,684	7,179	6,429	8,898	7,674	6,561	7,919	11,321	10,109	7,442	17,836	8,216	10,503
Szombathely, Hungary	5,478	7,869	7,550	7,740	7,904	5,815	5,918	18,932	7,399	6,198	8,642	7,931	6,284	7,643	11,047	9,838	7,660	18,105	7,933	10,788
Tabriz, Iran	7,995	10,396	10,010	10,238	10,512	8,325	8,404	16,402	5,292	8,135	10,756	5,503	8,660	9,998	13,603	12,082	5,563	15,532	10,538	8,177
Tacheng, China	8,927	11,033	10,455	10,783	12,112	9,186	9,170	14,057	2,546	7,785	10,239	3,431	9,073	10,142	15,281	11,607	2,795	13,317	12,164	6,732
Tahiti (Papeete)	11,459	9,259	9,397	9,302	10,075	11,130	10,981	3,869	12,527	10,295	7,968	12,827	10,465	9,145	7,645	6,927	12,269	4,569	10,078	11,202
Taipei, Taiwan	11,962	13,218	12,586	12,934	15,153	12,097	11,991	9,908	1,824	9,806	11,264	2,424	11,555	12,014	16,978	12,193	1,558	9,216	15,223	4,292
Taiyuan, China	10,506	12,080	11,442	11,796	13,777	10,680	10,599	11,531	1,116	8,596	10,470	2,492	10,256	10,940	16,342	11,621	1,073	10,861	13,842	5,402
Tallahassee, Florida	2,866	486	910	619	2,370	2,532	2,450	12,452	13,184	3,687	2,194	14,546	2,316	1,304	4,145	2,120	13,265	13,265	2,431	17,573
Tallinn, USSR	5,331	7,697	7,254	7,511	8,251	5,644	5,694	17,765	6,535	5,338	7,940	7,336	5,873	7,193	11,476	9,258	6,775	17,212	8,294	10,495
Tamanrasset, Algeria	6,291	8,273	8,239	8,274	7,294	6,594	6,769	17,649	9,516	8,070	9,939	9,564	7,394	8,604	9,833	10,743	9,788	17,420	7,290	11,495
Tampa, Florida	2,969	586	1,156	820	2,082	2,643	2,584	12,416	13,481	3,980	2,508	14,831	2,534	1,616	3,852	2,316	13,568	13,246	2,140	17,899
Tampere, Finland	5,186	7,537	7,081	7,345	8,161	5,495	5,538	17,644	6,557	5,115	7,724	7,405	5,692	7,002	11,385	9,049	6,791	17,153	8,207	10,599
Tanami, Australia	16,843	16,762	16,304	16,587	18,403	16,060	16,706	5,611	6,241	14,314	14,397	5,445	16,065	15,756	16,636	14,336	6,018	4,756	18,495	2,784

Distances in Kilometers	Channel-Port-aux-Basques, Can.	Charleston, South Carolina	Charleston, West Virginia	Charlotte, North Carolina	Charlotte Amalie, U.S.V.I.	Charlottetown, Canada	Chatham, Canada	Chatham Islands (Waitangi)	Chengdu, China	Chesterfield Inlet, Canada	Cheyenne, Wyoming	Chiang Mai, Thailand	Chibougamau, Canada	Chicago, Illinois	Chiclayo, Peru	Chihuahua, Mexico	Chongquing, China	Christchurch, New Zealand	Christiansted, U.S.V.I.	Christmas Island [Indian Ocean]
Tangier, Morocco	4,534	6,664	6,549	6,626	6,081	4,850	5,015	18,812	9,637	6,273	8,158	10,072	5,610	6,861	9,031	9,046	9,900	19,136	6,094	12,624
Tarawa (Betio)	12,619	11,529	11,261	11,395	13,338	12,425	12,225	5,126	7,922	10,190	9,264	8,278	11,496	10,693	11,940	9,063	7,661	4,971	13,377	7,562
Tashkent, USSR	8,928	11,218	10,703	10,999	11,896	9,224	9,247	14,759	3,324	8,265	10,852	3,766	9,293	10,501	15,117	12,244	3,595	13,940	11,937	6,843
Tbilisi, USSR	7,614	10,012	9,614	9,849	10,210	7,942	8,015	16,672	5,367	7,712	10,334	5,693	8,255	9,589	13,346	11,663	5,637	15,811	10,240	8,482
Tegucigalpa, Honduras	4,529	2,195	2,743	2,425	2,427	4,215	4,174	11,032	14,908	5,475	3,448	16,306	4,141	3,080	2,447	2,527	14,953	11,892	2,443	18,578
Tehran, Iran	8,500	10,899	10,498	10,735	11,042	8,828	8,901	15,873	4,883	8,528	11,162	5,011	9,135	10,463	14,125	12,509	5,153	15,002	11,068	7,647
Tel Aviv, Israel	7,728	10,095	9,813	9,985	9,822	8,066	8,179	16,996	6,474	8,391	10,904	6,534	8,566	9,925	12,729	12,120	6,744	16,147	9,837	8,878
Telegraph Creek, Canada	4,753	4,725	4,150	4,459	6,896	4,626	4,433	12,045	8,930	2,255	2,636	10,340	3,718	3,515	8,515	3,789	8,930	12,387	6,965	12,911
Teresina, Brazil	6,049	5,736	6,257	5,977	3,551	6,029	6,189	12,881	15,546	8,578	8,101	15,618	6,810	6,901	4,104	7,723	15,816	13,558	3,487	16,136
Ternate, Indonesia	14,608	15,321	14,756	15,063	17,502	14,694	14,560	7,434	4,123	12,226	13,008	3,686	14,016	14,121	16,940	13,472	3,874	6,656	17,571	2,712
The Valley, Anguilla	3,293	2,346	2,883	2,590	200	3,126	3,222	13,252	14,443	5,456	4,720	15,488	3,677	3,523	3,307	4,527	14,621	14,123	176	18,552
Thessaloniki, Greece	6,306	8,677	8,390	8,563	8,530	6,643	6,756	18,379	7,172	7,085	9,530	7,515	7,152	8,509	11,578	10,714	7,441	17,509	8,552	10,159
Thimphu, Bhutan	11,125	13,243	12,656	12,989	14,246	11,391	11,380	12,361	1,438	9,930	12,256	1,355	11,283	12,314	17,461	13,567	1,664	11,533	14,292	4,546
Thunder Bay, Canada	2,239	1,906	1,277	1,622	3,995	1,984	1,789	13,293	11,147	1,667	1,464	12,518	1,102	736	6,181	2,624	11,226	13,953	4,065	15,578
Tientsin, China	10,394	11,852	11,213	11,567	13,638	10,549	10,456	11,353	1,521	8,378	10,152	2,859	10,075	10,689	16,037	11,268	1,440	10,719	13,705	5,623
Tijuana, Mexico	5,083	3,462	3,256	3,341	5,413	4,784	4,606	10,401	11,787	3,889	1,445	13,162	3,991	2,791	5,866	1,134	11,742	11,043	5,466	15,023
Tiksi, USSR	6,772	8,214	7,577	7,931	9,972	6,901	6,797	13,516	4,792	4,730	6,814	6,182	6,401	7,094	12,537	8,113	4,867	13,229	10,040	9,270
Timbuktu, Mali	6,125	7,819	7,895	7,868	6,543	6,391	6,582	16,930	10,629	8,239	9,752	10,633	7,268	8,346	8,843	10,353	10,900	17,009	6,529	12,324
Tindouf, Algeria	4,903	6,800	6,789	6,808	5,863	5,190	5,373	17,928	10,351	6,924	8,557	10,645	6,033	7,185	8,587	9,287	10,619	18,246	5,864	12,892
Tirane, Albania	6,049	8,415	8,135	8,304	8,259	6,387	6,502	18,651	7,390	6,895	9,310	7,765	6,910	8,266	11,314	10,476	7,658	17,781	8,281	10,430
Tokyo, Japan	10,592	11,376	10,770	11,101	13,484	10,646	10,502	9,866	3,357	8,156	9,254	4,412	9,945	10,157	14,868	10,104	3,171	9,385	13,555	6,244
Toledo, Spain	4,428	6,657	6,489	6,595	6,260	4,756	4,908	19,248	9,248	5,981	7,997	9,750	5,458	6,751	9,296	8,961	9,508	19,517	6,279	12,433
Topeka, Kansas	3,078	1,580	1,223	1,382	3,748	2,763	2,597	12,257	12,022	2,724	813	13,424	2,069	751	5,329	1,503	12,067	12,970	3,812	16,206
Toronto, Canada	1,631	1,211	620	947	3,117	1,311	1,151	13,657	11,766	2,308	2,104	13,088	793	703	5,585	2,904	11,873	14,400	3,188	16,297
Toulouse, France	4,628	6,945	6,715	6,855	6,734	4,963	5,097	19,853	8,643	5,891	8,080	9,179	5,582	6,914	9,828	9,137	8,902	19,312	6,758	11,955
Tours, France	4,394	6,752	6,484	6,645	6,701	4,732	4,854	19,570	8,479	5,514	7,765	9,098	5,298	6,645	9,852	8,866	8,732	19,255	6,730	11,990
Townsville, Australia	16,090	15,159	14,915	15,041	16,692	15,960	15,763	4,369	7,171	13,500	12,917	6,707	15,036	14,343	14,161	12,645	6,914	3,615	16,708	4,520
Trenton, New Jersey	1,492	948	628	772	2,602	1,155	1,064	13,784	12,155	2,780	2,530	13,440	1,078	1,095	5,229	3,131	12,277	14,570	2,673	16,711
Tripoli, Lebanon	7,619	10,001	9,696	9,880	9,822	7,956	8,063	17,054	6,298	8,186	10,724	6,421	8,424	9,783	12,790	11,964	6,569	16,190	9,841	8,871
Tripoli, Libya	6,135	8,379	8,206	8,317	7,843	6,466	6,612	18,522	8,310	7,437	9,643	8,522	7,131	8,447	10,702	10,666	8,581	17,876	7,854	10,871
Tristan da Cunha (Edinburgh)	10,466	10,440	10,966	10,685	8,250	10,531	10,713	10,895	14,203	13,077	12,775	13,113	11,397	11,610	7,572	12,176	14,370	11,067	8,183	11,686
Trondheim, Norway	4,467	6,820	6,372	6,631	7,468	4,776	4,820	17,793	7,179	4,519	7,092	8,085	4,990	6,312	10,687	8,393	7,404	17,518	7,515	11,304
Trujillo, Peru	6,472	4,525	5,151	4,800	3,312	6,224	6,255	9,985	17,488	7,987	6,058	18,806	6,445	5,605	174	4,998	17,560	10,840	3,266	17,883
Truk Island (Moen)	13,195	12,965	12,521	12,756	15,080	13,127	12,943	6,519	5,593	10,584	10,573	5,849	12,248	11,884	14,327	10,785	5,325	6,021	15,136	5,491
Truro, Canada	400	2,002	1,707	1,865	3,000	97	251	14,881	11,488	2,640	3,369	12,679	974	1,996	6,007	4,176	11,644	15,656	3,065	16,000
Tsingtao, China	10,741	12,100	11,463	11,815	13,957	10,883	10,783	10,916	1,624	8,647	10,300	2,837	10,371	10,918	16,172	11,359	1,472	10,282	14,025	5,379
Tsitsihar, China	9,482	10,815	10,177	10,530	12,673	9,611	9,506	11,677	2,516	7,356	9,087	3,899	9,082	9,641	14,972	10,216	2,478	11,147	12,742	6,661
Tubuai Island (Mataura)	11,913	9,644	9,831	9,710	10,274	11,579	11,440	3,365	12,812	10,887	8,501	12,966	10,961	9,622	7,640	7,399	12,548	4,121	10,270	11,041
Tucson, Arizona	4,649	2,907	2,742	2,801	4,843	4,338	4,168	10,740	12,131	3,743	1,132	13,528	3,597	2,327	5,432	615	12,107	11,423	4,896	15,564
Tulsa, Oklahoma	3,267	1,514	1,288	1,366	3,622	2,942	2,787	12,030	12,320	3,045	951	13,726	2,312	957	5,040	1,269	12,361	12,764	3,683	16,436
Tunis, Tunisia	5,656	7,931	7,736	7,858	7,509	5,989	6,131	19,034	8,357	6,925	9,139	8,681	6,635	7,959	10,463	10,181	8,626	18,353	7,525	11,190
Tura, USSR	7,473	9,246	8,626	8,974	10,755	7,665	7,599	13,992	3,747	5,817	8,112	5,055	7,333	8,214	13,621	9,451	3,885	13,506	10,818	8,305
Turin, Italy	4,992	7,348	7,081	7,242	7,232	5,330	5,451	19,664	8,130	6,034	8,340	8,656	5,889	7,238	10,344	9,457	8,390	18,812	7,258	11,457
Uberlandia, Brazil	7,444	6,638	7,234	6,909	4,507	7,370	7,506	11,284	16,957	9,836	8,841	16,592	8,047	7,855	3,671	8,142	17,226	11,932	4,437	15,687
Ufa, USSR	7,145	9,434	8,928	9,219	10,177	7,439	7,461	16,121	4,632	6,596	9,225	5,395	7,519	8,754	13,400	10,609	4,882	15,402	10,222	8,590
Ujungpandang, Indonesia	15,298	16,353	15,760	16,083	18,470	15,442	15,336	7,555	4,283	13,100	14,087	3,465	14,875	15,137	17,519	14,575	4,075	6,716	18,540	1,627
Ulaanbaatar, Mongolia	9,339	11,043	10,412	10,765	12,621	9,528	9,458	12,628	1,930	7,571	9,658	3,310	9,163	9,955	15,399	10,912	2,037	12,001	12,684	6,472
Ulan-Ude, USSR	8,918	10,604	9,973	10,326	12,196	9,102	9,029	12,865	2,369	7,133	9,238	3,744	8,726	9,517	14,961	10,505	2,474	12,275	12,260	6,909
Uliastay, Mongolia	9,191	11,081	10,466	10,812	12,462	9,411	9,363	13,217	1,995	7,669	9,930	3,219	9,149	10,065	15,451	11,242	2,186	12,540	12,521	6,511
Uranium City, Canada	3,440	3,653	3,034	3,372	5,753	3,315	3,123	13,036	9,564	1,039	2,067	10,968	2,416	2,440	7,782	3,443	9,612	13,485	5,823	13,862
Urumqi, China	9,372	11,432	10,842	11,176	12,578	9,623	9,600	13,578	2,057	8,124	10,516	2,972	9,475	10,502	15,724	11,865	2,309	12,832	12,631	6,286
Ushuaia, Argentina	11,378	9,766	10,400	10,046	8,111	11,208	11,289	7,145	17,256	13,245	11,184	15,865	11,621	10,870	5,426	9,926	17,172	7,685	8,046	12,746
Vaduz, Liechtenstein	5,009	7,386	7,093	7,269	7,368	5,347	5,459	19,423	7,898	5,916	8,278	8,462	5,864	7,219	10,509	9,431	8,157	18,639	7,397	11,323
Valencia, Spain	4,721	6,967	6,789	6,901	6,571	5,050	5,199	19,419	9,012	6,190	8,266	9,475	5,735	7,039	9,591	9,254	9,274	19,278	6,589	12,122
Valladolid, Spain	4,281	6,538	6,351	6,468	6,216	4,611	4,759	19,304	9,184	5,784	7,827	9,727	5,295	6,598	9,289	8,813	9,442	19,712	6,238	12,473
Valletta, Malta	6,030	8,320	8,114	8,243	7,908	6,364	6,501	18,717	8,053	7,203	9,475	8,327	6,988	8,321	10,844	10,545	8,323	17,970	7,923	10,793
Valparaiso, Chile	9,014	7,335	7,970	7,616	5,731	8,820	8,889	8,594	19,538	10,817	8,890	18,176	9,192	8,455	3,030	7,734	19,588	9,317	5,668	15,178
Vancouver, Canada	4,595	3,997	3,500	3,760	6,186	4,392	4,192	11,560	9,999	2,502	1,691	11,404	3,463	2,860	7,490	2,710	9,987	12,031	6,252	13,805
Varna, Bulgaria	6,463	8,857	8,527	8,724	8,860	6,799	6,897	18,053	6,691	7,016	9,534	7,083	7,238	8,596	11,963	10,772	6,959	17,184	8,887	9,828
Venice, Italy	5,292	7,664	7,377	7,550	7,597	5,630	5,744	19,298	7,778	6,194	8,567	8,288	6,153	7,508	10,714	9,720	8,040	18,443	7,623	11,092
Veracruz, Mexico	4,588	2,206	2,544	2,327	3,287	4,252	4,158	10,731	14,082	4,921	2,568	15,494	3,918	2,641	3,382	1,454	14,088	11,553	3,320	17,499
Verona, Italy	5,200	7,569	7,287	7,456	7,491	5,538	5,654	19,401	7,874	6,138	8,494	8,391	6,070	7,424	10,609	9,638	8,135	18,548	7,518	11,198
Victoria, Canada	4,648	3,999	3,513	3,766	6,186	4,440	4,240	11,476	10,058	2,585	1,671	11,461	3,512	2,875	7,443	2,651	10,043	11,952	6,251	13,829
Victoria, Seychelles	12,218	14,445	14,297	14,403	13,385	12,552	12,690	12,545	6,475	12,936	15,510	5,429	13,149	14,499	14,912	16,718	6,636	11,791	13,367	5,574
Vienna, Austria	5,409	7,802	7,476	7,670	7,873	5,745	5,845	18,915	7,379	6,097	8,549	7,936	6,202	7,561	11,028	9,752	7,639	18,113	7,903	10,820
Vientiane, Laos	12,523	14,384	13,755	14,107	15,765	12,752	12,708	10,671	1,415	10,916	12,880	393	12,480	13,296	18,739	14,003	1,347	9,849	15,820	3,166
Villahermosa, Mexico	4,492	2,091	2,510	2,252	2,958	4,161	4,084	10,882	14,326	5,041	2,807	15,737	3,911	2,697	3,091	1,788	14,346	11,719	2,988	17,864
Vilnius, USSR	5,602	7,993	7,585	7,823	8,379	5,925	5,992	18,040	6,588	5,804	8,381	7,277	6,228	7,567	11,593	9,675	6,839	17,359	8,417	10,340
Visby, Sweden	5,067	7,454	7,041	7,281	7,902	5,388	5,452	18,171	6,942	5,291	7,851	7,711	5,682	7,022	11,125	9,136	7,185	17,637	7,943	10,829
Vitoria, Brazil	7,750	7,227	7,795	7,488	5,049	7,720	7,873	11,612	16,290	10,252	9,508	15,774	8,471	8,431	4,515	8,898	16,550	12,178	4,980	14,975
Vladivostok, USSR	9,898	11,000	10,370	10,716	12,984	9,995	9,871	10,925	2,821	7,615	9,084	4,098	9,385	9,795	14,926	10,105	2,709	10,422	13,054	6,510
Volgograd, USSR	7,051	9,430	8,993	9,248	9,836	7,370	7,426	16,861	5,340	6,968	9,600	5,880	7,610	8,923	13,038	10,947	5,604	16,054	9,872	8,876
Vologda, USSR	6,087	8,412	7,933	8,209	9,086	6,389	6,422	17,027	5,675	5,781	8,418	6,485	6,531	7,810	12,309	9,778	5,917	16,392	9,131	9,676
Vorkuta, USSR	6,389	8,484	7,917	8,239	9,622	6,638	6,617	15,657	4,862	5,346	7,921	5,951	6,525	7,642	12,739	9,313	5,064	15,156	9,678	9,270
Wake Island	11,311	10,899	10,465	10,693	13,018	11,199	11,007	7,209	6,366	8,720	8,507	7,074	10,291	9,832	12,729	8,753	6,133	6,982	13,076	7,455
Wallis Island	13,112	11,379	11,310	11,332	12,687	12,836	12,648	3,398	9,806	11,092	9,470	9,957	11,973	10,868	10,526	8,846	9,538	3,519	12,704	8,487
Walvis Bay, Namibia	10,713	11,751	12,071	11,911	9,767	10,922	11,122	12,513	11,240	13,018	14,075	10,274	11,848	12,654	10,169	14,097	11,428	12,313	9,717	9,685
Warsaw, Poland	5,481	7,882	7,506	7,727	8,143	5,811	5,892	18,422	6,928	5,887	8,419	7,566	6,178	7,530	11,339	9,679	7,182	17,704	8,178	10,563
Washington, D.C.	1,737	729	405	531	2,560	1,400	1,305	13,540	12,303	2,870	2,375	13,607	1,243	958	5,063	2,906	12,417	14,328	2,631	16,848
Watson Lake, Canada	4,552	4,661	4,070	4,390	6,813	4,440	4,250	12,326	8,852	2,014	2,677	10,264	3,546	3,444	8,562	3,895	8,863	12,662	6,883	12,928
Weimar, East Germany	4,943	7,340	7,005	7,203	7,487	5,278	5,375	19,031	7,608	5,638	8,073	8,248	5,724	7,083	10,671	9,274	7,861	18,384	7,520	11,212
Wellington, New Zealand	15,757	13,511	13,691	13,579	13,853	15,428	15,278	770	10,777	14,219	12,198	10,240	14,735	13,437	10,784	11,224	10,519	305	13,831	7,505
West Berlin, West Germany	5,004	7,405	7,049	7,259	7,625	5,337	5,425	18,807	7,411	5,579	8,053	8,078	5,746	7,103	10,821	9,278	7,663	18,182	7,660	11,080
Wewak, Papua New Guinea	14,663	14,458	14,033	14,258	16,514	14,617	14,437	5,941	5,656	12,060	12,068	5,480	13,754	13,399	15,071	12,183	5,388	5,271	16,564	4,261
Whangarei, New Zealand	15,471	13,346	13,458	13,383	13,935	15,156	14,990	1,201	10,387	13,724	11,845	9,958	14,393	13,144	10,985	10,961	10,123	880	13,921	7,415
Whitehorse, Canada	4,864	5,011	4,420	4,740	7,164	4,763	4,575	12,196	8,555	2,292	2,993	9,966	3,878	3,794	8,877	4,169	8,559	12,488	7,233	12,587
Wichita, Kansas	3,280	1,673	1,379	1,501	3,809	2,963	2,798	12,048	12,118	2,888	748	13,525	2,278	952	5,247	1,294	12,155	12,765	3,872	16,224
Willemstad, Curacao	4,036	2,546	3,167	2,826	813	3,822	3,885	12,343	15,213	5,940	4,746	16,343	4,221	3,765	2,412	4,261	15,368	13,214	773	19,420
Wiluna, Australia	17,677	17,965	17,599	17,802	18,956	17,806	17,683	5,914	6,566	15,347	15,613	5,520	17,134	16,967	15,733	15,483	6,383	5,042	18,908	2,348
Windhoek, Namibia	10,857	11,964	12,268	12,117	10,002	11,076	11,274	12,509	10,989	13,112	14,269	10,010	11,997	12,842	10,437	14,334	11,173	12,271	9,953	9,430
Windsor, Canada	1,964	1,093	454	809	3,159	1,642	1,484	13,326	11,893	2,395	1,813	13,239	1,077	384	5,443	2,571	11,987	14,067	3,229	16,382
Winnipeg, Canada	2,778	2,374	1,778	2,099	4,523	2,545	2,347	12,925	10,840	1,549	1,140	12,235	1,631	1,155	6,496	2,478	10,898	13,536	4,592	15,162
Winston-Salem, North Carolina	2,155	371	278	112	2,477	1,818	1,725	13,131	12,600	3,114	2,203	13,930	1,607	905	4,745	2,560	12,701	13,927	2,545	17,108
Wroclaw, Poland	5,298	7,699	7,345	7,554	7,886	5,631	5,721	18,723	7,227	5,849	8,339	7,849	6,041	7,398	11,072	9,570	7,483	18,002	7,920	10,814
Wuhan, China	11,324	12,837	12,198	12,552	14,589	11,494	11,409	10,838	978	9,361	11,110	2,021	11,047	11,674	16,991	12,185	749	10,132	14,655	4,638
Wyndham, Australia	16,383	16,608	16,159	16,401	18,610	16,438	16,288	6,074	5,717	13,909	14,216	4,953	15,683	15,518	16,082	14,299	5,493	5,229	18,646	2,494
Xi'an, China	10,863	12,528	11,892	12,246	14,145	11,053	10,983	11,483	605	9,045	10,974	1,977	10,674	11,406	16,832	12,135	565	10,769	14,209	4,966
Xining, China	10,490	12,322	11,697	12,047	13,763	10,705	10,653	12,136	694	8,868	10,980	1,995	10,411	11,260	16,695	12,220	902	11,400	13,823	5,231
Yakutsk, USSR	7,832	9,170	8,531	8,885	11,005	7,951	7,841	12,691	3,945	5,698	7,577	5,357	7,414	8,014	13,417	8,800	3,979	12,316	11,074	8,305
Yanji, China	9,948	11,109	10,477	10,825	13,066	10,054	9,935	11,015	2,630	7,703	9,227	3,919	9,464	9,909	15,084	10,266	2,523	10,493	13,136	6,390

Distances in Kilometers	Channel-Port-aux-Basques, Can.	Charleston, South Carolina	Charleston, West Virginia	Charlotte, North Carolina	Charlotte Amalie, U.S.V.I.	Charlottetown, Canada	Chatham, Canada	Chatham Islands (Waitangi)	Chengdu, China	Chesterfield Inlet, Canada	Cheyenne, Wyoming	Chiang Mai, Thailand	Chibougamau, Canada	Chicago, Illinois	Chiclayo, Peru	Chihuahua, Mexico	Chongquing, China	Christchurch, New Zealand	Christiansted, U.S.V.I.	Christmas Island [Indian Ocean]
Yaounde, Cameroon	8,250	9,920	10,024	9,984	8,454	8,523	8,711	15,494	10,040	10,230	11,887	9,612	9,388	10,482	10,222	12,461	10,292	15,235	8,429	10,548
Yap Island (Colonia)	13,457	13,837	13,300	13,589	16,027	13,479	13,321	7,479	4,234	10,934	11,494	4,339	12,707	12,657	15,842	11,946	3,963	6,833	16,094	4,222
Yaraka, Australia	16,768	15,676	15,489	15,585	16,948	16,627	16,429	4,138	7,483	14,184	13,509	6,872	15,699	14,943	14,116	13,139	7,236	3,318	16,949	4,356
Yarmouth, Canada	683	1,719	1,436	1,583	2,828	355	359	14,604	11,695	2,678	3,167	12,908	922	1,766	5,772	3,920	11,843	15,387	2,895	16,227
Yellowknife, Canada	3,752	4,097	3,476	3,815	6,185	3,656	3,470	13,025	9,130	1,200	2,455	10,536	2,784	2,886	8,221	3,807	9,174	13,412	6,256	13,415
Yerevan, USSR	7,719	10,119	9,731	9,960	10,267	8,048	8,126	16,635	5,410	7,863	10,481	5,688	8,380	9,718	13,381	11,805	5,681	15,769	10,295	8,423
Yinchuan, China	10,367	12,092	11,460	11,813	13,650	10,564	10,499	11,972	890	8,617	10,642	2,294	10,213	10,996	16,440	11,852	988	11,270	13,712	5,421
Yogyakarta, Indonesia	15,487	17,047	16,415	16,763	18,736	15,700	15,638	8,060	4,309	13,613	14,948	3,195	15,315	15,838	18,046	15,564	4,154	7,193	18,787	597
York, United Kingdom	4,038	6,436	6,101	6,298	6,664	4,373	4,470	18,856	8,229	4,870	7,222	8,987	4,833	6,191	9,875	8,392	8,470	18,775	6,701	12,048
Yumen, China	10,058	11,963	11,347	11,694	13,319	10,284	10,240	12,636	1,168	8,541	10,753	2,336	10,032	10,939	16,334	12,036	1,396	11,902	13,376	5,632
Yutian, China	9,878	12,065	11,503	11,824	12,967	10,154	10,155	13,584	2,177	8,875	11,341	2,620	10,108	11,217	16,187	12,709	2,448	12,773	13,012	5,812
Yuzhno-Sakhalinsk, USSR	9,320	10,201	9,581	9,920	12,262	9,378	9,237	10,836	3,762	6,907	8,192	5,050	8,695	8,985	13,997	9,173	3,658	10,447	12,333	7,350
Zagreb, Yugoslavia	5,518	7,901	7,597	7,779	7,876	5,856	5,964	19,010	7,500	6,310	8,730	8,001	6,349	7,707	11,000	9,910	7,763	18,158	7,903	10,813
Zahedan, Iran	9,584	11,975	11,548	11,799	12,156	9,908	9,973	14,763	4,141	9,411	12,047	4,031	10,164	11,468	15,205	13,424	4,402	13,890	12,182	6,532
Zamboanga, Philippines	13,970	15,042	14,432	14,765	17,110	14,097	13,985	8,332	3,233	11,739	12,867	2,824	13,513	13,822	17,615	13,535	2,988	7,551	17,181	2,647
Zanzibar, Tanzania	11,139	13,097	13,104	13,122	11,720	11,451	11,620	13,405	8,010	12,505	14,749	7,115	12,207	13,463	13,115	15,605	8,203	12,794	11,693	7,327
Zaragoza, Spain	4,563	6,841	6,641	6,765	6,535	4,895	5,038	19,577	8,919	5,965	8,077	9,431	5,556	6,871	9,599	9,091	9,179	19,448	6,556	12,155
Zashiversk, USSR	7,119	8,337	7,699	8,052	10,226	7,213	7,091	12,823	4,807	4,881	6,715	6,220	6,625	7,169	12,557	7,946	4,840	12,565	10,296	9,139
Zhengzhou, China	10,859	12,398	11,760	12,114	14,126	11,030	10,946	11,213	1,007	8,918	10,730	2,288	10,593	11,247	16,614	11,846	881	10,529	14,192	5,079
Zurich, Switzerland	4,922	7,298	7,006	7,180	7,280	5,259	5,372	19,474	7,968	5,849	8,200	8,542	5,780	7,135	10,425	9,348	8,225	18,720	7,309	11,410

Distances in Kilometers	Christmas Island [Pacific Ocean]	Churchill, Canada	Cincinnati, Ohio	Ciudad Bolivia, Venezuela	Ciudad Juarez, Mexico	Ciudad Victoria, Mexico	Clarksburg, West Virginia	Cleveland, Ohio	Cocos (Keeling) Island	Colombo, Sri Lanka	Colon, Panama	Colorado Springs, Colorado	Columbia, South Carolina	Columbus, Georgia	Columbus, Ohio	Conakry, Guinea	Concepcion, Chile	Concord, New Hampshire	Constantine, Algeria	Copenhagen, Denmark
Churchill, Canada	8,316	0	2,290	5,940	3,144	3,909	2,377	2,107	14,736	12,703	5,610	2,344	2,918	3,001	2,233	8,554	10,772	2,324	7,200	5,752
Cincinnati, Ohio	8,411	2,290	0	3,681	2,149	2,193	360	358	16,999	14,661	3,326	1,757	646	738	161	7,694	8,490	1,179	7,668	6,933
Ciudad Bolivia, Venezuela	9,653	5,940	3,681	0	4,527	3,487	3,563	3,833	18,596	16,338	1,033	4,807	3,036	3,057	3,714	6,247	5,008	3,863	8,320	8,816
Ciudad Juarez, Mexico	6,277	3,144	2,149	4,527	0	1,144	2,504	2,456	16,782	15,674	3,696	802	2,388	2,027	2,300	9,723	8,351	3,313	9,753	8,737
Ciudad Victoria, Mexico	6,724	3,909	2,193	3,487	1,144	0	2,471	2,550	17,894	16,610	2,591	1,759	2,094	1,691	2,352	9,132	7,242	3,325	9,780	9,121
Clarksburg, West Virginia	8,770	2,377	360	3,563	2,504	2,471	0	272	16,969	14,500	3,314	2,112	590	865	240	7,338	8,461	857	7,345	6,686
Cleveland, Ohio	8,687	2,107	358	3,833	2,456	2,550	272	0	16,733	14,324	3,564	1,986	835	1,044	203	7,484	8,719	858	7,330	6,575
Cocos (Keeling) Island	11,766	14,736	16,999	18,596	16,782	17,894	16,969	16,733	0	2,814	19,563	16,349	17,559	17,731	16,906	12,455	14,497	16,371	10,814	10,742
Colombo, Sri Lanka	13,586	12,703	14,661	16,338	15,674	16,610	14,500	14,324	2,814	0	17,145	14,915	15,052	15,361	14,524	10,281	15,712	13,751	8,057	7,958
Colon, Panama	8,625	5,610	3,326	1,033	3,696	2,591	3,314	3,564	19,563	17,145	0	4,102	2,730	2,610	3,403	7,256	5,164	3,837	9,091	9,310
Colorado Springs, Colorado	6,717	2,344	1,757	4,807	802	1,759	2,112	1,986	16,349	14,915	4,102	0	2,192	1,925	1,879	9,451	8,990	2,822	9,117	7,984
Columbia, South Carolina	8,645	2,918	646	3,036	2,388	2,094	590	835	17,559	15,052	2,730	2,192	0	405	685	7,339	7,885	1,314	7,687	7,178
Columbus, Georgia	8,260	3,001	738	3,057	2,027	1,691	865	1,044	17,731	15,361	2,610	1,925	405	0	851	7,697	7,771	1,676	8,089	7,538
Columbus, Ohio	8,554	2,233	161	3,714	2,300	2,352	240	203	16,906	14,524	3,403	1,879	685	851	0	7,573	8,564	1,021	7,508	6,776
Conakry, Guinea	15,826	8,554	7,694	6,247	9,723	9,132	7,338	7,484	12,455	10,281	7,256	9,451	7,339	7,697	7,573	0	8,035	6,702	3,614	5,613
Concepcion, Chile	9,653	10,772	8,490	5,008	8,351	7,242	8,461	8,719	14,497	15,712	5,164	8,990	7,885	7,771	8,564	8,035	0	8,865	11,535	13,038
Concord, New Hampshire	9,536	2,324	1,179	3,863	3,313	3,325	857	858	16,371	13,751	3,837	2,822	1,314	1,676	1,021	6,702	8,865	0	6,491	5,865
Constantine, Algeria	15,456	7,200	7,668	8,320	9,753	9,780	7,345	7,330	10,814	8,057	9,091	9,117	7,687	8,089	7,508	3,614	11,535	6,491	0	2,193
Copenhagen, Denmark	13,551	5,752	6,933	8,816	8,737	9,121	6,686	6,575	10,742	7,958	9,310	7,984	7,178	7,538	6,776	5,613	13,038	5,865	2,193	0
Coppermine, Canada	7,987	1,446	3,704	7,375	4,054	5,023	3,818	3,546	13,383	11,627	6,992	3,289	4,343	4,387	3,662	9,504	12,126	3,739	7,478	5,647
Coquimbo, Chile	9,756	10,056	7,767	4,241	7,773	6,643	7,723	7,984	15,193	16,076	4,448	8,371	7,153	7,058	7,835	7,554	778	8,102	10,958	12,342
Cordoba, Argentina	10,447	10,369	8,084	4,451	8,289	7,148	8,002	8,269	14,796	15,409	4,813	8,841	7,452	7,400	8,136	7,028	1,015	8,295	10,520	12,063
Cordoba, Spain	14,784	6,468	6,715	7,325	8,831	8,792	6,382	6,385	11,837	9,071	8,075	8,234	6,698	7,102	6,557	3,268	10,846	5,536	1,025	2,365
Cork, Ireland	13,366	5,111	5,829	7,386	7,810	8,012	5,541	5,475	12,100	9,291	7,922	7,122	5,976	6,359	5,668	4,724	11,657	4,690	2,097	1,443
Corner Brook, Canada	10,543	2,577	2,377	4,653	4,451	4,550	2,079	2,030	15,298	12,586	4,842	3,863	2,528	2,901	2,216	5,993	9,619	1,227	5,306	4,656
Corrientes, Argentina	10,976	10,097	7,838	4,160	8,274	7,130	7,720	7,991	14,917	15,115	4,666	8,759	7,195	7,188	7,874	6,356	1,693	7,932	9,843	11,410
Cosenza, Italy	15,390	7,394	8,171	9,157	10,174	10,337	7,870	7,821	10,053	7,262	9,883	9,481	8,267	8,661	8,010	4,444	12,423	7,013	908	1,840
Craiova, Romania	14,874	7,244	8,313	9,713	10,196	10,505	8,041	7,956	9,623	6,810	10,360	9,456	8,493	8,871	8,153	5,280	13,236	7,197	1,701	1,493
Cruzeiro do Sul, Brazil	9,489	7,608	5,318	1,782	5,653	4,513	5,255	5,519	17,546	16,995	2,047	6,128	4,693	4,628	5,377	6,799	3,234	5,631	9,557	10,402
Cuiaba, Brazil	11,305	8,936	6,737	3,092	7,505	6,391	6,577	6,848	15,753	15,139	3,809	7,873	6,092	6,144	6,753	5,434	2,891	6,698	8,737	10,147
Curitiba, Brazil	11,946	10,203	8,029	4,392	8,774	7,647	7,858	8,129	14,481	14,258	5,084	9,166	7,385	7,444	8,040	5,456	2,588	7,933	9,007	10,713
Cuzco, Peru	9,588	8,259	5,969	2,423	6,215	5,071	5,909	6,172	16,930	16,867	2,678	6,726	5,345	5,273	6,029	6,923	2,585	6,281	9,900	10,900
Dacca, Bangladesh	12,160	10,856	13,031	15,906	13,612	14,656	12,966	12,739	4,012	2,174	16,199	12,902	13,555	13,769	12,922	11,007	17,869	12,369	7,959	7,109
Dakar, Senegal	15,265	7,856	7,026	5,827	9,082	8,543	6,669	6,807	12,932	10,602	6,809	8,781	6,694	7,060	6,902	699	8,151	6,016	3,390	5,225
Dallas, Texas	7,179	2,894	1,311	3,824	918	1,028	1,647	1,651	17,322	15,596	3,121	987	1,472	1,110	1,471	8,805	8,093	2,490	8,979	8,155
Damascus, Syria	15,821	8,802	9,924	11,039	11,802	12,115	9,647	9,567	8,149	5,358	11,787	11,052	10,086	10,470	9,764	5,752	13,728	8,799	2,720	3,069
Danang, Vietnam	10,412	11,467	13,757	17,301	13,557	14,701	13,814	13,551	3,348	3,251	17,056	13,028	14,379	14,455	13,695	13,037	17,700	13,442	9,968	8,895
Dar es Salaam, Tanzania	18,095	13,020	13,375	12,304	15,523	15,212	13,024	13,069	6,337	4,754	13,335	14,964	13,220	13,616	13,223	6,149	11,505	12,211	5,870	7,348
Darwin, Australia	8,074	13,664	15,458	17,650	13,817	14,627	15,747	15,509	3,697	6,035	16,661	13,834	16,011	15,757	15,517	16,151	14,006	15,983	13,879	12,901
Davao, Philippines	8,541	11,898	14,031	17,547	13,025	14,090	14,224	13,955	3,819	5,053	16,666	12,751	14,670	14,570	14,032	15,163	16,210	14,177	12,058	10,765
David, Panama	8,346	5,670	3,403	1,307	3,585	2,456	3,423	3,664	19,603	17,425	297	4,044	2,834	2,674	3,493	7,545	5,106	3,997	9,378	9,553
Dawson, Canada	7,044	2,434	4,494	8,154	4,258	5,354	4,679	4,411	12,798	11,479	7,623	3,608	5,139	5,099	4,488	10,674	12,595	4,753	8,478	6,511
Dawson Creek, Canada	6,836	1,600	3,215	6,811	2,879	3,955	3,449	3,195	14,196	12,814	6,232	2,203	3,846	3,758	3,235	10,150	11,193	3,703	8,626	6,935
Denpasar, Indonesia	9,749	13,918	16,105	19,400	15,020	16,011	16,278	16,007	2,047	4,286	18,373	14,814	16,748	16,655	16,098	14,427	14,897	16,120	12,244	11,590
Denver, Colorado	6,745	2,251	1,761	4,877	899	1,858	2,113	1,974	16,264	14,813	4,185	102	2,221	1,968	1,877	9,450	9,087	2,802	9,063	7,906
Derby, Australia	8,898	14,478	16,376	18,197	14,754	15,532	16,652	16,404	2,943	5,511	17,340	14,774	16,944	16,697	16,426	15,346	13,764	16,800	13,536	12,898
Des Moines, Iowa	7,717	1,909	821	4,326	1,584	2,045	1,154	994	16,574	14,591	3,816	1,001	1,389	1,269	914	8,477	8,933	1,822	8,176	7,193
Detroit, Michigan	8,590	1,982	380	3,959	2,382	2,542	409	146	16,643	14,282	3,666	1,878	942	1,109	263	7,607	8,826	947	7,385	6,578
Dhahran, Saudi Arabia	15,702	10,019	11,373	12,565	13,122	13,564	11,117	11,016	6,595	3,809	13,336	12,341	11,583	11,958	11,216	6,949	14,587	10,281	4,251	4,443
Diego Garcia Island	14,467	14,186	15,803	15,955	17,301	17,984	15,549	15,445	2,728	1,780	16,981	16,505	15,999	16,383	15,646	9,731	13,944	14,709	8,382	8,870
Dijon, France	14,286	6,143	6,923	8,245	8,905	9,103	6,632	6,570	11,117	8,303	8,868	8,209	7,053	7,441	6,762	4,548	12,120	5,778	1,223	1,066
Dili, Indonesia	8,611	13,507	15,494	18,261	14,081	14,990	15,741	15,484	3,169	5,354	17,236	13,991	16,099	15,907	15,526	15,562	14,622	15,822	13,158	12,221
Djibouti, Djibouti	17,290	11,312	12,218	12,373	14,228	14,353	11,905	11,871	6,482	4,062	13,318	13,514	12,261	12,663	12,057	6,219	13,106	11,049	4,574	5,561
Dnepropetrovsk, USSR	14,288	7,250	8,627	10,446	10,335	10,804	8,393	8,270	9,032	6,238	11,002	9,556	8,895	9,249	8,472	6,253	14,200	7,581	2,671	1,723
Dobo, Indonesia	7,635	12,835	14,657	17,285	13,112	13,994	14,937	14,694	4,166	6,201	16,253	13,073	15,229	14,998	14,709	16,476	14,509	15,154	13,715	12,475
Doha, Qatar	15,671	10,169	11,545	12,738	13,279	13,734	11,291	11,188	6,415	3,631	13,514	12,495	11,760	12,133	11,388	7,085	14,660	10,456	4,427	4,614
Donetsk, USSR	14,272	7,386	8,806	10,661	10,485	10,977	8,577	8,450	8,826	6,036	11,211	9,702	9,084	9,435	8,652	6,420	14,390	7,770	2,855	1,922
Dover, Delaware	9,183	2,549	776	3,449	2,912	2,806	416	585	16,904	14,310	3,329	2,527	756	1,131	648	6,926	8,418	560	6,981	6,422
Dresden, East Germany	14,070	6,204	7,263	8,895	9,135	9,456	6,998	6,906	10,559	7,752	9,460	8,397	7,465	7,837	7,104	5,246	12,879	6,161	1,728	520
Dubayy, United Arab Emir.	15,373	10,276	11,751	13,085	13,408	13,929	11,509	11,394	6,107	3,307	13,839	12,615	11,995	12,360	11,595	7,464	14,995	10,685	4,766	4,823
Dublin, Ireland	13,321	5,109	5,922	7,575	7,872	8,111	5,643	5,567	11,939	9,135	8,093	7,169	6,093	6,471	5,762	4,906	11,875	4,797	2,135	1,243
Duluth, Minnesota	7,998	1,338	1,054	4,727	2,074	2,633	1,268	1,018	16,059	14,002	4,306	1,361	1,699	1,702	1,057	8,362	9,455	1,665	7,760	6,664
Dunedin, New Zealand	6,163	14,475	14,035	12,897	11,970	11,892	14,349	14,379	7,798	10,609	12,269	12,610	13,972	13,575	14,196	15,956	8,864	15,206	18,306	18,125
Durango, Mexico	6,184	3,945	2,529	4,022	872	564	2,844	2,878	17,395	16,545	3,091	1,641	2,544	2,140	2,690	9,686	7,510	3,699	10,188	9,384
Durban, South Africa	16,793	14,801	14,136	11,588	15,981	15,064	13,788	13,950	7,034	6,616	12,543	15,883	13,703	14,012	14,026	6,474	9,198	13,176	7,761	9,636
Dushanbe, USSR	13,489	9,106	10,987	13,334	12,208	12,997	10,832	10,651	6,310	3,674	13,793	11,411	11,394	11,691	10,851	8,710	16,679	10,110	5,399	4,519
East London, South Africa	16,521	14,908	14,039	11,305	15,768	14,791	13,700	13,880	7,336	7,046	12,236	15,759	13,567	13,853	13,940	6,453	8,749	13,140	7,996	9,936
Easter Island (Hanga Roa)	6,078	9,625	7,778	5,744	6,524	5,738	7,951	8,120	14,836	17,566	5,146	7,320	7,401	7,088	7,919	11,055	3,578	8,701	13,990	14,449
Echo Bay, Canada	7,758	1,468	3,673	7,353	3,899	4,894	3,809	3,538	13,455	11,776	6,931	3,147	4,317	4,338	3,642	9,680	12,043	3,787	7,705	5,881
Edinburgh, United Kingdom	13,178	5,055	6,019	7,840	7,909	8,211	5,755	5,661	11,729	8,939	8,321	7,185	6,228	6,597	5,860	5,229	12,207	4,921	2,296	988
Edmonton, Canada	6,992	1,328	2,717	6,311	2,487	3,522	2,960	2,710	14,678	13,186	5,744	1,764	3,346	3,257	2,742	9,801	10,744	3,256	8,504	6,935
El Aaiun, Morocco	15,020	6,951	6,617	6,371	8,762	8,468	6,260	6,334	12,588	9,967	7,243	8,304	6,435	6,834	6,471	1,954	9,454	5,484	2,130	3,783
Elat, Israel	16,274	9,151	10,163	11,036	12,098	12,343	9,872	9,808	8,071	5,320	11,833	11,366	10,285	10,677	10,002	5,518	13,419	9,018	2,744	3,400
Elazig, Turkey	15,188	8,379	9,663	11,114	11,443	11,853	9,409	9,305	8,194	5,380	11,785	10,673	9,882	10,252	9,506	6,167	14,194	8,576	2,880	2,734
Eniwetok Atoll, Marshall Isls.	4,563	9,694	11,138	13,788	9,468	10,367	11,454	11,241	7,683	9,042	12,779	9,470	11,657	11,389	11,216	17,639	13,847	11,867	14,127	12,046
Erfurt, East Germany	14,036	6,095	7,104	8,704	8,996	9,297	6,835	6,747	10,744	7,935	9,272	8,266	7,295	7,670	6,945	5,126	12,707	5,994	1,662	531
Erzurum, Turkey	14,988	8,320	9,670	11,233	11,407	11,855	9,425	9,313	8,115	5,301	11,879	10,629	9,911	10,275	9,514	6,375	14,406	8,600	3,045	2,739
Esfahan, Iran	15,104	9,389	10,866	12,406	12,517	13,039	10,631	10,509	6,892	4,078	13,089	11,725	11,127	11,486	10,712	7,143	15,009	9,814	4,117	3,949
Essen, West Germany	13,906	5,878	6,834	8,426	8,745	9,026	6,561	6,477	11,030	8,221	8,988	8,022	7,017	7,393	6,674	5,020	12,490	5,718	1,676	597
Eucla, Australia	8,585	15,621	16,903	16,738	14,842	15,252	17,258	17,100	3,941	6,735	16,157	15,147	17,226	16,845	17,021	15,452	12,082	17,818	14,747	14,477
Fargo, North Dakota	7,663	1,334	1,320	4,944	1,874	2,576	1,578	1,344	15,934	14,035	4,455	1,107	1,950	1,889	1,353	8,719	9,570	2,022	8,053	6,877
Faroe Islands (Torshavn)	12,489	4,463	5,645	7,841	7,422	7,825	5,414	5,288	11,886	9,153	8,213	6,671	5,927	6,273	5,491	5,854	12,454	4,614	3,001	1,315
Florence, Italy	14,816	6,750	7,544	8,717	9,531	9,719	7,248	7,191	10,574	7,765	9,389	8,835	7,661	8,051	7,383	4,499	12,318	6,393	911	1,327
Florianopolis, Brazil	11,985	10,452	8,273	4,629	8,987	7,856	8,105	8,375	14,263	14,140	5,303	9,393	7,628	7,683	8,285	5,564	2,516	8,183	9,138	10,887
Fort George, Canada	9,078	1,081	1,690	5,101	3,289	3,742	1,621	1,386	15,350	12,986	4,932	2,569	2,210	2,422	1,571	7,547	10,062	1,302	6,577	5,455
Fort McMurray, Canada	7,315	1,049	2,773	6,426	2,804	3,797	2,977	2,715	14,488	12,874	5,918	2,048	3,415	3,372	2,775	9,593	10,979	3,169	8,165	6,564
Fort Nelson, Canada	6,990	1,642	3,476	7,111	3,249	4,319	3,688	3,426	13,859	12,443	6,563	2,563	4,116	4,054	3,484	10,174	11,553	3,867	8,466	6,703
Fort Severn, Canada	8,586	497	1,891	5,492	3,069	3,703	1,934	1,668	15,110	12,937	5,215	2,292	2,496	2,622	1,814	8,136	10,378	1,828	6,994	5,697
Fort Smith, Arkansas	7,466	2,598	970	3,855	1,190	1,370	1,318	1,299	17,181	15,283	3,237	1,000	1,234	930	1,127	8,566	8,296	2,147	8,629	7,792
Fort Vermilion, Canada	7,225	1,268	3,105	6,758	3,050	4,077	3,306	3,043	14,169	12,624	6,241	2,320	3,748	3,703	3,106	9,818	11,283	3,474	8,237	6,554
Fort Wayne, Indiana	8,395	2,065	225	3,901	2,169	2,323	454	292	16,777	14,474	3,551	1,696	865	956	219	7,766	8,714	1,148	7,605	6,798
Fort-Chimo, Canada	9,770	1,495	2,410	5,522	4,101	4,531	2,262	2,072	14,740	12,253	5,496	3,373	2,842	3,113	2,271	7,090	10,530	1,671	5,814	4,642
Fort-de-France, Martinique	10,657	5,608	3,554	1,244	4,978	4,115	3,321	3,584	17,627	15,103	2,128	5,045	2,941	3,128	3,529	5,179	5,830	3,324	7,076	7,655
Fortaleza, Brazil	13,258	8,472	6,685	3,802	8,173	7,234	6,405	6,647	14,795	13,199	4,815	8,252	6,109	6,330	6,633	3,114	5,090	6,164	6,451	8,054
Frankfort, Kentucky	8,365	2,380	104	3,605	2,095	2,100	410	455	17,097	14,765	3,232	1,739	580	637	253	7,717	8,396	1,254	7,745	7,029
Frankfurt am Main, W. Ger.	14,084	6,067	7,008	8,535	8,929	9,199	6,732	6,652	10,892	8,080	9,116	8,208	7,182	7,561	6,848	4,953	12,514	5,887	1,537	671
Fredericton, Canada	9,922	2,323	1,649	4,186	3,752	3,815	1,344	1,308	15,932	13,273	4,249	3,208	1,805	2,171	1,488	6,432	9,193	495	6,022	5,373
Freeport, Bahamas	8,797	3,775	1,494	2,190	2,749	2,073	1,423	1,683	18,335	15,652	1,902	2,784	857	892	1,542	7,071	7,038	1,964	7,931	7,699
Freetown, Sierra Leone	15,905	8,676	7,804	6,306	9,826	9,224	7,449	7,597	12,386	10,245	7,319	9,561	7,443	7,799	7,684	124	7,995	6,818	3,685	5,703
Frobisher Bay, Canada	9,761	1,470	2,940	6,151	4,430	4,983	2,833	2,620	14,146	11,729	6,104	3,659	3,420	3,664	2,813	7,384	11,157	2,295	5,734	4,331

Distances in Kilometers	Christmas Island [Pacific Ocean]	Churchill, Canada	Cincinnati, Ohio	Ciudad Bolivia, Venezuela	Ciudad Juarez, Mexico	Ciudad Victoria, Mexico	Clarksburg, West Virginia	Cleveland, Ohio	Cocos (Keeling) Island	Colombo, Sri Lanka	Colon, Panama	Colorado Springs, Colorado	Columbia, South Carolina	Columbus, Georgia	Columbus, Ohio	Conakry, Guinea	Concepcion, Chile	Concord, New Hampshire	Constantine, Algeria	Copenhagen, Denmark
Frunze, USSR	12,821	8,690	10,683	13,329	11,740	12,599	10,561	10,361	6,488	4,018	13,668	10,953	11,138	11,405	10,556	9,161	17,193	9,889	5,722	4,559
Fukuoka, Japan	8,233	8,975	11,193	14,867	10,643	11,785	11,340	11,069	6,173	5,970	14,280	10,179	11,839	11,813	11,170	13,920	17,866	11,215	10,317	8,500
Funafuti Atoll, Tuvalu	2,838	10,623	11,152	12,373	9,057	9,561	11,512	11,397	8,992	11,148	11,365	9,412	11,442	11,067	11,285	18,620	11,002	12,221	16,830	14,643
Funchal, Madeira Island	14,379	6,252	6,008	6,131	8,158	7,938	5,655	5,712	12,942	10,230	6,932	7,665	5,873	6,275	5,858	2,581	9,653	4,856	2,193	3,430
Fuzhou, China	9,236	10,111	12,378	16,051	11,979	13,123	12,488	12,218	4,866	4,686	15,573	11,485	13,019	13,036	12,338	13,595	18,347	12,254	10,143	8,628
Gaborone, Botswana	17,468	14,040	13,409	11,050	15,325	14,485	13,057	13,210	7,554	6,812	12,037	15,163	13,001	13,324	13,294	5,727	9,149	12,425	7,053	8,990
Galapagos Islands (Santa Cruz)	7,480	6,593	4,440	2,413	3,964	2,857	4,537	4,747	18,404	18,739	1,604	4,613	3,955	3,707	4,558	8,567	4,388	5,208	10,683	10,877
Gander, Canada	10,784	2,769	2,613	4,742	4,694	4,778	2,308	2,268	15,141	12,405	4,981	4,107	2,739	3,119	2,451	5,789	9,676	1,452	5,065	4,460
Gangtok, India	12,251	10,462	12,616	15,471	13,276	14,294	12,542	12,320	4,441	2,441	15,762	12,549	13,131	13,353	12,504	10,731	18,001	11,936	7,595	6,683
Garyarsa, China	12,876	9,962	12,007	14,606	12,941	13,864	11,893	11,690	5,150	2,748	14,998	12,172	12,473	12,733	11,883	9,845	17,523	11,227	6,659	5,792
Gaspe, Canada	10,068	2,217	1,928	4,524	3,977	4,115	1,650	1,575	15,574	12,923	4,606	3,384	2,143	2,497	1,767	6,408	9,527	830	5,777	5,041
Gauhati, India	11,976	10,577	12,767	15,738	13,312	14,360	12,711	12,481	4,260	2,476	15,970	12,605	13,301	13,505	12,662	11,064	18,157	12,134	7,926	6,977
Gdansk, Poland	13,750	6,105	7,341	9,210	9,121	9,526	7,097	6,983	10,330	7,543	9,718	8,361	7,592	7,951	7,185	5,741	13,334	6,279	2,203	416
Geneva, Switzerland	14,433	6,294	7,061	8,323	9,050	9,237	6,766	6,708	11,014	8,201	8,963	8,357	7,183	7,572	6,899	4,485	12,124	5,912	1,093	1,145
Genoa, Italy	14,694	6,584	7,350	8,533	9,344	9,523	7,053	6,998	10,768	7,959	9,198	8,652	7,463	7,854	7,188	4,442	12,200	6,198	915	1,278
Georgetown, Guyana	11,027	6,528	4,447	1,379	5,716	4,758	4,229	4,494	17,232	15,131	2,412	5,864	3,822	3,973	4,432	4,905	5,073	4,241	7,314	8,183
Geraldton, Australia	9,912	16,018	17,921	17,682	16,084	16,626	18,215	17,973	2,617	5,431	17,386	16,240	18,431	18,109	17,985	14,243	12,699	18,313	13,364	13,333
Ghanzi, Botswana	17,837	13,521	12,868	10,595	14,805	13,998	12,515	12,667	8,003	7,077	11,597	14,623	12,467	12,796	12,752	5,184	9,015	11,881	6,608	8,602
Ghat, Libya	16,746	8,448	8,685	8,699	10,819	10,693	8,343	8,365	10,239	7,644	9,590	10,242	8,611	9,016	8,529	3,054	11,071	7,510	1,309	3,415
Gibraltar	14,901	6,591	6,763	7,246	8,890	8,815	6,425	6,438	11,880	9,132	8,018	8,310	6,723	7,127	6,606	3,067	10,679	5,585	1,075	2,562
Gijon, Spain	14,239	5,933	6,365	7,358	8,439	8,498	6,047	6,023	11,927	9,123	8,028	7,803	6,412	6,811	6,204	3,850	11,202	5,192	1,315	1,876
Gisborne, New Zealand	5,152	13,464	13,133	12,447	11,031	11,038	13,462	13,468	8,427	11,200	11,706	11,643	13,132	12,729	13,293	16,573	8,929	14,312	19,222	17,829
Glasgow, United Kingdom	13,153	5,013	5,959	7,774	7,856	8,152	5,694	5,602	11,795	9,005	8,255	7,134	6,165	6,535	5,800	5,204	12,149	4,859	2,315	1,055
Godthab, Greenland	10,572	2,298	3,528	6,384	5,197	5,661	3,353	3,182	13,710	11,147	6,486	4,444	3,917	4,214	3,384	6,759	11,364	2,661	4,911	3,541
Gomez Palacio, Mexico	6,342	3,759	2,325	3,973	743	486	2,643	2,673	17,414	16,391	3,072	1,476	2,357	1,955	2,487	9,543	7,609	3,497	9,988	9,178
Goose Bay, Canada	6,146	2,266	3,590	7,040	2,787	3,922	3,868	3,633	14,092	13,031	6,362	2,259	4,190	4,037	3,639	10,789	11,128	4,233	9,314	7,586
Gorki, USSR	13,254	6,714	8,375	10,701	9,856	10,480	8,190	8,028	9,002	6,315	11,104	9,057	8,737	9,054	8,230	7,177	14,942	7,438	3,562	1,945
Goteborg, Sweden	13,320	5,553	6,790	8,783	8,560	8,972	6,552	6,433	10,823	8,054	9,244	7,801	7,055	7,408	6,634	5,782	13,102	5,741	2,406	231
Granada, Spain	14,901	6,585	6,835	7,410	8,951	8,908	6,501	6,505	11,737	8,978	8,169	8,355	6,814	7,218	6,676	3,230	10,870	5,656	924	2,388
Grand Turk, Turks & Caicos	9,564	4,530	2,335	1,453	3,681	2,885	2,161	2,433	18,368	15,559	1,635	3,741	1,696	1,834	2,339	6,268	6,456	2,411	7,564	7,674
Graz, Austria	14,528	6,637	7,611	9,035	9,528	9,801	7,334	7,255	10,335	7,521	9,656	8,802	7,779	8,160	7,451	4,991	12,785	6,487	1,395	977
Green Bay, Wisconsin	8,242	1,638	668	4,348	2,144	2,518	861	614	16,372	14,179	3,973	1,532	1,312	1,363	653	8,029	9,134	1,330	7,616	6,655
Grenoble, France	14,527	6,364	7,088	8,281	9,092	9,258	6,789	6,736	11,034	8,223	8,936	8,406	7,196	7,588	6,926	4,368	12,032	5,933	980	1,264
Guadalajara, Mexico	6,231	4,293	2,723	3,775	1,266	550	3,013	3,080	17,675	16,932	2,808	2,019	2,645	2,241	2,884	9,608	7,115	3,869	10,330	9,636
Guam (Agana)	6,476	10,413	12,273	15,440	10,941	11,953	12,535	12,286	5,992	7,130	14,488	10,779	12,870	12,683	12,313	16,538	15,463	12,729	12,963	11,148
Guantanamo, Cuba	9,140	4,551	2,285	1,396	3,372	2,501	2,179	2,447	18,780	15,966	1,294	3,516	1,641	1,678	2,321	6,687	6,309	2,581	8,001	8,046
Guatemala City, Guatemala	7,488	4,906	2,774	2,283	2,495	1,354	2,907	3,097	19,185	17,399	1,294	3,027	2,347	2,053	2,901	8,345	5,984	3,648	9,683	9,477
Guayaquil, Ecuador	8,660	6,872	4,594	1,553	4,691	3,547	4,590	4,839	18,397	17,722	1,275	5,213	4,005	3,871	4,676	7,443	3,901	5,094	9,837	10,357
Guiyang, China	10,490	10,354	12,641	16,129	12,658	13,787	12,677	12,418	4,401	3,581	15,964	12,059	13,251	13,354	12,570	12,457	18,868	12,275	9,137	7,858
Gur'yev, USSR	13,859	7,864	9,524	11,662	11,008	11,639	9,330	9,175	7,923	5,189	12,151	10,208	9,869	10,195	9,378	7,399	15,416	8,563	3,890	2,851
Haifa, Israel	15,935	8,820	9,897	10,943	11,798	12,085	9,616	9,541	8,224	5,442	11,703	11,055	10,046	10,433	9,737	5,615	13,587	8,765	2,623	3,075
Haikou, China	10,167	10,989	13,278	16,862	13,068	14,212	13,344	13,080	3,841	3,594	16,567	12,534	13,905	13,971	13,220	13,082	18,117	12,999	9,870	8,661
Haiphong, Vietnam	10,540	10,977	13,266	16,759	13,201	14,340	13,307	13,047	3,792	3,276	16,585	12,630	13,879	13,975	13,197	12,697	18,235	12,908	9,516	8,368
Hakodate, Japan	7,550	7,777	9,954	13,612	9,362	10,505	10,120	9,850	7,456	7,099	12,999	8,897	10,600	10,555	9,940	13,760	17,079	10,059	10,179	8,156
Halifax, Canada	10,169	2,592	1,836	4,079	3,967	3,964	1,507	1,512	15,938	13,229	4,214	3,451	1,907	2,292	1,678	6,156	9,074	657	5,837	5,293
Hamburg, West Germany	13,742	5,828	6,902	8,643	8,760	9,094	6,642	6,544	10,864	8,065	9,171	8,020	7,117	7,485	6,743	5,325	12,782	5,809	1,928	289
Hamilton, Bermuda	10,158	3,669	1,605	2,717	3,917	3,494	1,605	1,818	17,086	14,281	2,978	3,673	1,529	1,900	1,845	5,811	7,700	1,355	6,403	6,345
Hamilton, New Zealand	5,218	13,533	13,296	12,697	11,180	11,223	13,630	13,626	8,194	10,958	11,947	11,773	13,317	12,913	13,455	16,748	9,174	14,476	19,006	17,636
Hangzhou, China	9,164	9,644	11,915	15,584	11,569	12,713	12,021	11,751	5,302	4,935	15,129	11,054	12,555	12,578	11,873	13,413	18,595	11,784	9,896	8,292
Hannover, West Germany	13,864	5,918	6,949	8,618	8,828	9,141	6,683	6,591	10,861	8,056	9,165	8,094	7,150	7,522	6,790	5,203	12,702	5,846	1,795	413
Hanoi, Vietnam	10,625	10,975	13,262	16,731	13,231	14,367	13,297	13,039	3,785	3,205	16,585	12,651	13,871	13,974	13,191	12,610	18,250	12,887	9,435	8,302
Harare, Zimbabwe	18,023	13,685	13,433	11,523	15,500	14,830	13,073	13,187	7,074	6,022	12,541	15,173	13,114	13,473	13,301	5,777	10,036	12,357	6,527	8,328
Harbin, China	8,754	7,834	10,107	13,773	9,898	11,034	10,210	9,940	7,060	6,212	13,353	9,326	10,746	10,777	10,063	12,725	18,102	9,988	9,113	7,191
Harrisburg, Pennsylvania	9,076	2,389	667	3,591	2,816	2,775	316	428	16,814	14,264	3,436	2,397	788	1,130	523	7,062	8,546	552	7,031	6,408
Hartford, Connecticut	9,438	2,408	1,046	3,708	3,193	3,163	706	752	16,554	13,936	3,659	2,736	1,133	1,502	893	6,751	8,704	185	6,640	6,045
Havana, Cuba	8,412	4,064	1,782	2,065	2,561	1,714	1,800	2,037	18,770	16,164	1,546	2,749	1,211	1,065	1,867	7,428	6,709	2,440	8,439	8,215
Helena, Montana	6,616	1,804	2,383	5,782	1,717	2,787	2,690	2,479	15,316	13,961	5,128	1,044	2,956	2,783	2,453	9,876	10,027	3,185	8,970	7,549
Helsinki, Finland	13,109	5,799	7,278	9,512	8,900	9,426	7,071	6,925	10,179	7,459	9,918	8,116	7,603	7,935	7,128	6,469	13,897	6,294	2,953	887
Hengyang, China	9,904	10,197	12,486	16,090	12,312	13,453	12,557	12,291	4,629	4,107	15,774	11,758	13,114	13,178	12,429	12,969	18,785	12,231	9,577	8,175
Herat, Afghanistan	14,242	9,458	11,185	13,161	12,597	13,284	10,993	10,837	6,301	3,535	13,742	11,795	11,530	11,858	11,039	8,132	15,997	10,222	4,987	4,442
Hermosillo, Mexico	5,767	3,542	2,670	4,803	522	1,319	3,024	2,978	16,580	15,858	3,906	1,223	2,883	2,509	2,822	10,202	8,301	3,836	10,269	9,205
Hiroshima, Japan	8,060	8,820	11,025	14,693	10,443	11,585	11,179	10,908	6,367	6,178	14,089	9,987	11,671	11,637	11,006	13,985	17,707	11,074	10,374	8,519
Hiva Oa (Atuona)	2,430	8,600	7,810	7,850	5,757	5,710	8,133	8,152	13,400	15,745	6,886	6,446	7,804	7,400	7,971	14,042	7,230	8,986	15,477	14,348
Ho Chi Minh City, Vietnam	10,612	12,076	14,367	17,871	14,135	15,279	14,419	14,157	2,741	2,979	17,667	13,625	14,987	15,066	14,303	13,063	17,115	14,027	10,195	9,283
Hobart, Australia	7,415	15,531	15,709	14,697	13,572	13,652	16,050	16,027	5,931	8,743	14,125	14,112	15,746	15,343	15,865	15,874	10,276	16,884	16,606	16,509
Hohhot, China	9,941	8,720	11,009	14,560	11,075	12,190	11,056	10,794	6,039	4,899	14,329	10,446	11,624	11,718	10,941	12,123	19,417	10,697	8,553	6,893
Hong Kong	9,759	10,659	12,942	16,581	12,636	13,780	13,029	12,761	4,235	4,052	16,190	12,123	13,577	13,619	12,892	13,344	18,249	12,734	10,027	8,688
Honiara, Solomon Islands	4,881	11,816	12,869	14,484	10,895	11,539	13,218	13,054	6,896	9,066	13,472	11,115	13,265	12,921	12,980	19,342	12,485	13,800	15,998	14,141
Honolulu, Hawaii	2,139	6,496	7,142	9,405	5,202	6,005	7,495	7,344	12,064	12,998	8,403	5,387	7,541	7,212	7,258	14,828	10,963	8,131	13,417	11,428
Houston, Texas	7,233	3,222	1,436	3,509	1,087	766	1,732	1,792	17,677	15,912	2,773	1,329	1,432	1,033	1,596	8,693	7,732	2,589	9,072	8,356
Huambo, Angola	18,615	12,354	11,778	9,828	13,793	13,097	11,421	11,559	8,773	7,412	10,855	13,534	11,418	11,766	11,655	4,086	9,072	10,755	5,519	7,586
Hubli, India	13,925	11,734	13,620	15,427	14,792	15,637	13,447	13,279	3,854	1,062	16,144	14,007	13,995	14,311	13,480	9,623	16,082	12,691	7,107	6,900
Hugh Town, United Kingdom	13,633	5,374	6,044	7,470	8,046	8,221	5,750	5,692	11,962	9,149	8,043	7,366	6,170	6,558	5,883	4,531	11,627	4,896	1,831	1,420
Hull, Canada	9,213	1,932	1,009	4,140	3,054	3,201	782	651	16,233	13,718	4,017	2,499	1,349	1,646	850	7,089	9,115	416	6,706	5,926
Hyderabad, India	13,529	11,540	13,508	15,585	14,544	15,449	13,359	13,175	3,826	1,166	16,220	13,772	13,921	14,217	13,374	9,934	16,492	12,633	7,281	6,919
Hyderabad, Pakistan	14,231	10,544	12,334	14,218	13,662	14,409	12,148	11,988	5,160	2,378	14,861	12,863	12,688	13,013	12,190	8,777	16,162	11,380	5,931	5,586
Igloolik, Canada	9,244	1,324	3,375	6,826	4,468	5,205	3,352	3,105	13,631	11,421	6,666	3,667	3,938	4,112	3,276	8,168	11,800	2,974	6,212	4,545
Iloilo, Philippines	8,873	11,631	13,824	17,455	12,998	14,099	13,988	13,717	3,795	4,714	16,689	12,658	14,469	14,409	13,811	14,700	16,718	13,867	11,541	10,247
Indianapolis, Indiana	8,284	2,185	160	3,811	2,037	2,157	502	423	16,914	14,639	3,425	1,610	786	818	271	7,841	8,588	1,277	7,752	6,964
Innsbruck, Austria	14,443	6,441	7,343	8,727	9,285	9,530	7,060	6,987	10,639	7,825	9,350	8,571	7,496	7,880	7,182	4,809	12,527	6,210	1,274	938
Inuvik, Canada	7,584	2,187	4,384	8,065	4,433	5,483	4,528	4,257	12,782	11,253	7,616	3,724	5,029	5,037	4,357	10,195	12,690	4,501	7,936	5,974
Invercargill, New Zealand	6,317	14,632	14,211	13,039	12,145	12,068	14,525	14,555	7,636	10,449	12,424	12,782	14,147	13,751	14,372	15,912	8,942	15,382	18,133	18,041
Inverness, United Kingdom	12,997	4,892	5,906	7,824	7,772	8,098	5,650	5,548	11,786	9,007	8,277	7,041	6,133	6,497	5,748	5,382	12,260	4,822	2,480	1,050
Iquitos, Peru	9,399	7,175	4,885	1,373	5,274	4,140	4,822	5,085	17,954	17,036	1,629	5,724	4,259	4,197	4,944	6,765	3,662	5,205	9,355	10,090
Iraklion, Greece	15,864	8,170	9,057	9,994	11,032	11,231	8,761	8,705	9,170	6,393	10,753	10,320	9,166	9,558	8,896	4,865	12,898	7,905	1,674	2,455
Irkutsk, USSR	10,389	7,584	9,846	13,271	10,229	11,283	9,852	9,599	7,157	5,502	13,164	9,525	10,434	10,575	9,762	10,998	18,277	9,418	7,385	5,580
Islamabad, Pakistan	13,411	9,691	11,624	13,989	12,762	13,597	11,478	11,292	5,646	3,043	14,460	11,971	12,045	12,334	11,490	9,146	16,948	10,767	5,956	5,179
Istanbul, Turkey	15,198	7,769	8,873	10,199	10,746	11,065	8,601	8,516	9,094	6,282	10,876	10,001	9,051	9,430	8,713	5,451	13,475	7,756	2,006	2,021
Ivujivik, Canada	9,276	973	2,630	6,028	3,971	4,583	2,577	2,339	14,394	12,085	5,888	3,190	3,166	3,367	2,520	7,760	11,008	2,176	6,228	4,816
Iwo Jima Island, Japan	7,019	9,443	11,484	14,978	10,480	11,577	11,701	11,437	6,317	6,818	14,167	10,174	12,115	11,996	11,497	15,353	16,498	11,763	11,743	9,863
Izmir, Turkey	15,506	7,952	8,957	10,107	10,880	11,144	8,674	8,602	9,126	6,325	10,822	10,149	9,104	9,490	8,797	5,180	13,213	7,823	1,829	2,204
Jackson, Mississippi	7,774	2,955	913	3,338	1,539	1,293	1,179	1,269	17,647	15,538	2,752	1,509	874	490	1,068	8,186	7,858	2,034	8,507	7,844
Jaffna, Sri Lanka	13,530	12,402	14,375	16,206	15,372	16,309	14,220	14,041	3,035	303	16,958	14,613	14,778	15,080	14,240	10,245	15,965	13,482	7,895	7,715
Jakarta, Indonesia	10,669	13,903	16,186	19,646	15,552	16,637	16,268	16,002	1,271	3,326	19,212	15,200	16,821	16,851	16,136	13,474	15,245	15,898	11,329	10,835
Jamestown, St. Helena	16,576	11,415	10,180	7,634	11,932	11,053	9,850	10,046	10,964	9,756	8,639	11,885	9,693	9,980	10,090	2,950	6,962	9,363	5,932	8,118
Jamnagar, India	14,198	10,887	12,697	14,543	13,996	14,763	12,512	12,351	4,803	2,014	15,210	13,198	13,053	13,377	12,553	8,983	16,146	11,745	6,237	5,947
Jan Mayen Island	11,587	3,867	5,432	8,126	6,967	7,535	5,262	5,089	11,830	9,238	8,338	6,181	5,824	6,124	5,290	6,836	12,976	4,550	3,962	1,997
Jayapura, Indonesia	6,892	12,197	13,913	16,514	12,314	13,191	14,207	13,974	4,949	6,841	15,482	12,295	14,466	14,220	13,975	17,102	14,431	14,493	14,006	12,526
Jefferson City, Missouri	7,748	2,248	667	3,986	1,506	1,773	1,027	950	16,930	14,900	3,460	1,100	1,120	940	806	8,356	8,577	1,808	8,262	7,388
Jerusalem, Israel	16,037	8,937	9,999	10,997	11,909	12,186	9,715	9,644	8,152	5,379	11,760	11,168	10,141	10,529	9,839	5,605	13,555	8,864	2,680	3,191

Distances in Kilometers	Christmas Island [Pacific Ocean]	Churchill, Canada	Cincinnati, Ohio	Ciudad Bolivia, Venezuela	Ciudad Juarez, Mexico	Ciudad Victoria, Mexico	Clarksburg, West Virginia	Cleveland, Ohio	Cocos (Keeling) Island	Colombo, Sri Lanka	Colon, Panama	Colorado Springs, Colorado	Columbia, South Carolina	Columbus, Georgia	Columbus, Ohio	Conakry, Guinea	Concepcion, Chile	Concord, New Hampshire	Constantine, Algeria	Copenhagen, Denmark
Jiggalong, Australia	9,255	15,216	17,065	17,956	15,307	15,971	17,358	17,119	2,830	5,574	17,331	15,406	17,597	17,308	17,127	14,961	13,183	17,537	13,627	13,258
Jinan, China	9,477	9,045	11,332	14,960	11,189	12,325	11,410	11,143	5,787	5,003	14,614	10,613	11,962	12,019	11,278	12,765	19,129	11,117	9,204	7,540
Jodhpur, India	13,761	10,507	12,402	14,529	13,584	14,407	12,241	12,064	4,958	2,260	15,104	12,793	12,797	13,101	12,264	9,231	16,621	11,504	6,298	5,795
Johannesburg, South Africa	17,260	14,304	13,685	11,282	15,590	14,731	13,333	13,487	7,326	6,683	12,261	15,439	13,273	13,594	13,570	6,004	9,221	12,702	7,283	9,190
Juazeiro do Norte, Brazil	13,160	8,778	6,924	3,869	8,318	7,340	6,658	6,906	14,736	13,324	4,858	8,444	6,332	6,531	6,881	3,390	4,736	6,461	6,799	8,439
Juneau, Alaska	6,566	2,313	4,117	7,709	3,628	4,747	4,344	4,087	13,332	12,150	7,106	3,029	4,750	4,659	4,134	10,809	11,979	4,548	8,906	7,029
Kabul, Afghanistan	13,691	9,553	11,419	13,658	12,657	13,442	11,257	11,080	5,919	3,244	14,165	11,860	11,814	12,117	11,280	8,774	16,621	10,523	5,583	4,863
Kalgoorlie, Australia	9,267	15,904	17,487	17,233	15,496	15,956	17,826	17,630	3,277	6,087	16,776	15,742	17,883	17,517	17,586	14,832	12,373	18,215	14,057	13,931
Kaliningrad, USSR	13,717	6,141	7,415	9,324	9,174	9,598	7,176	7,058	10,228	7,447	9,825	8,409	7,676	8,032	7,260	5,852	13,459	6,362	2,300	515
Kamloops, Canada	6,428	1,896	3,068	6,538	2,393	3,504	3,348	3,115	14,560	13,336	5,886	1,792	3,669	3,522	3,118	10,341	10,741	3,735	9,059	7,442
Kampala, Uganda	18,882	11,990	12,295	11,462	14,442	14,177	11,945	11,987	7,226	5,299	12,480	13,883	12,155	12,555	12,142	5,229	11,423	11,129	4,808	6,398
Kananga, Zaire	19,571	12,073	11,885	10,440	14,002	13,487	11,525	11,620	8,191	6,536	11,472	13,600	11,620	11,998	11,746	4,356	10,108	10,778	4,961	6,884
Kano, Nigeria	17,837	9,591	9,438	8,648	11,582	11,226	9,081	9,155	10,111	7,835	9,634	11,120	9,237	9,630	9,293	2,447	10,067	8,304	2,706	4,857
Kanpur, India	13,068	10,547	12,579	15,046	13,523	14,450	12,457	12,257	4,614	2,163	15,509	12,756	13,033	13,302	12,452	9,949	17,264	11,774	6,931	6,237
Kansas City, Missouri	7,562	2,186	870	4,166	1,353	1,757	1,228	1,126	16,800	14,876	3,604	888	1,336	1,137	999	8,564	8,693	1,980	8,400	7,464
Kaohsiung, Taiwan	9,129	10,448	12,702	16,382	12,206	13,347	12,825	12,554	4,607	4,666	15,845	11,744	13,346	13,346	12,668	13,878	17,984	12,616	10,473	9,002
Karachi, Pakistan	14,375	10,577	12,334	14,139	13,704	14,427	12,141	11,986	5,205	2,408	14,804	12,903	12,674	13,005	12,188	8,650	16,019	11,364	5,840	5,550
Karaganda, USSR	12,513	7,912	9,913	12,668	10,970	11,821	9,798	9,594	7,230	4,797	12,946	10,180	10,378	10,638	9,788	8,984	16,956	9,142	5,430	4,008
Karl-Marx-Stadt, East Germany	14,082	6,189	7,226	8,837	9,107	9,419	6,959	6,869	10,611	7,803	9,405	8,373	7,422	7,796	7,067	5,191	12,816	6,120	1,684	538
Kasanga, Tanzania	18,826	12,784	12,812	11,433	14,949	14,484	12,453	12,531	7,192	5,666	12,466	14,492	12,581	12,965	12,668	5,357	10,696	11,679	5,587	7,313
Kashgar, China	12,899	9,079	11,079	13,692	12,116	12,988	10,957	10,757	6,096	3,626	14,054	11,332	11,534	11,802	10,952	9,319	17,307	10,283	5,952	4,898
Kassel, West Germany	13,972	5,999	6,993	8,598	8,890	9,185	6,723	6,636	10,856	8,048	9,161	8,162	7,182	7,557	6,833	5,097	12,631	5,882	1,677	526
Kathmandu, Nepal	12,556	10,422	12,533	15,252	13,308	14,292	12,441	12,227	4,567	2,372	15,607	12,563	13,026	13,266	12,416	10,404	17,756	11,805	7,292	6,443
Kayes, Mali	15,875	8,224	7,560	6,473	9,647	9,151	7,200	7,322	12,288	9,965	7,456	9,306	7,260	7,635	7,429	600	8,592	6,508	3,020	5,016
Kazan, USSR	13,163	6,895	8,619	11,015	10,039	10,701	8,445	8,276	8,715	6,055	11,401	9,238	8,999	9,308	8,477	7,455	15,262	7,707	3,843	2,271
Kemi, Finland	12,481	5,281	6,897	9,396	8,409	9,004	6,718	6,552	10,427	7,782	9,709	7,616	7,271	7,582	6,754	6,898	14,010	5,981	3,479	1,300
Kenora, Canada	7,936	998	1,425	5,103	2,240	2,919	1,615	1,354	15,689	13,697	4,680	1,467	2,071	2,078	1,416	8,545	9,824	1,898	7,731	6,517
Kerguelen Island	13,123	18,532	17,660	14,137	18,004	16,980	17,384	17,616	4,857	6,332	14,735	18,738	17,052	17,178	17,614	10,321	9,757	16,976	11,347	12,795
Kerkira, Greece	15,393	7,530	8,399	9,467	10,372	10,575	8,105	8,046	9,760	6,963	10,184	9,663	8,516	8,907	8,237	4,714	12,715	7,250	1,221	1,867
Kermanshah, Iran	15,242	9,083	10,476	11,944	12,189	12,660	10,231	10,119	7,342	4,529	12,633	11,405	10,716	11,081	10,320	6,744	14,680	9,406	3,658	3,545
Khabarovsk, USSR	8,192	7,299	9,546	13,227	9,226	10,365	9,674	9,402	7,688	6,921	12,739	8,676	10,190	10,195	9,514	12,891	17,393	9,517	9,315	7,286
Kharkov, USSR	14,096	7,136	8,565	10,481	10,236	10,733	8,340	8,210	9,038	6,256	11,010	9,453	8,851	9,199	8,412	6,413	14,332	7,537	2,817	1,705
Khartoum, Sudan	17,774	10,457	11,114	11,155	13,193	13,200	10,787	10,776	7,713	5,243	12,090	12,531	11,106	11,511	10,954	5,062	12,412	9,936	3,447	4,762
Khon Kaen, Thailand	10,983	11,530	13,810	17,171	13,831	14,967	13,828	13,574	3,213	2,714	17,136	13,247	14,409	14,531	13,733	12,479	17,709	13,377	9,485	8,530
Kiev, USSR	14,146	6,904	8,241	10,075	9,972	10,421	8,005	7,884	9,421	6,629	10,617	9,198	8,504	8,860	8,086	6,080	13,950	7,191	2,469	1,331
Kigali, Rwanda	19,193	12,089	12,254	11,221	14,403	14,057	11,899	11,957	7,444	5,617	12,247	13,888	12,075	12,469	12,104	5,018	11,048	11,100	4,889	6,583
Kingston, Canada	9,142	2,013	877	4,018	2,954	3,069	636	522	16,376	13,864	3,878	2,425	1,202	1,501	717	7,118	8,985	416	6,815	6,064
Kingston, Jamaica	8,969	4,739	2,455	1,263	3,348	2,406	2,383	2,646	19,067	16,253	1,012	3,561	1,822	1,800	2,507	6,857	6,082	2,838	8,271	8,336
Kingstown, Saint Vincent	10,651	5,752	3,676	1,150	5,047	4,157	3,452	3,716	17,650	15,188	2,080	5,138	3,057	3,229	3,656	5,196	5,670	3,475	7,179	7,795
Kinshasa, Zaire	19,198	11,526	11,160	9,634	13,252	12,695	10,800	10,910	8,999	7,279	10,666	12,896	10,865	11,236	11,026	3,563	9,582	10,080	4,592	6,652
Kirkwall, United Kingdom	12,888	4,838	5,930	7,941	7,760	8,120	5,684	5,573	11,703	8,937	8,371	7,019	6,179	6,536	5,774	5,562	12,420	4,865	2,607	1,003
Kirov, USSR	12,877	6,615	8,384	10,888	9,758	10,444	8,221	8,044	8,902	6,281	11,232	8,956	8,781	9,081	8,244	7,583	15,278	7,499	3,970	2,242
Kiruna, Sweden	12,254	4,985	6,617	9,183	8,115	8,716	6,444	6,274	10,679	8,056	9,467	7,321	7,001	7,306	6,475	6,944	13,870	5,717	3,606	1,414
Kisangani, Zaire	19,613	11,599	11,667	10,646	13,815	13,452	11,311	11,376	8,032	6,108	11,668	13,321	11,476	11,869	11,519	4,425	10,781	10,520	4,410	6,222
Kishinev, USSR	14,543	7,179	8,410	10,042	10,207	10,600	8,157	8,052	9,373	6,564	10,638	9,446	8,637	9,004	8,253	5,772	13,712	7,328	2,183	1,481
Kitchner, Canada	8,815	1,943	589	4,008	2,623	2,775	463	239	16,509	14,085	3,777	2,098	1,051	1,282	440	7,416	8,923	726	7,141	6,346
Knoxville, Tennessee	8,411	2,641	352	3,346	2,135	1,995	484	643	17,349	14,964	2,974	1,874	342	401	451	7,617	8,138	1,331	7,801	7,170
Kosice, Czechoslovakia	14,388	6,726	7,854	9,451	9,701	10,047	7,593	7,497	9,970	7,160	10,040	8,953	8,062	8,434	7,696	5,429	13,255	6,757	1,816	974
Kota Kinabalu, Malaysia	9,598	12,343	14,586	18,263	13,873	14,981	14,719	14,447	2,914	4,007	17,569	13,508	15,231	15,207	14,558	14,207	16,466	14,504	11,334	10,299
Krakow, Poland	14,230	6,544	7,684	9,337	9,522	9,877	7,426	7,327	10,109	7,303	9,909	8,773	7,900	8,269	7,526	5,461	13,227	6,593	1,862	793
Kralendijk, Bonaire	9,893	5,604	3,388	492	4,469	3,501	3,232	3,504	18,415	15,916	1,309	4,662	2,743	2,823	3,403	5,963	5,447	3,454	7,872	8,326
Krasnodar, USSR	14,547	7,724	9,114	10,859	10,818	11,292	8,878	8,757	8,575	5,773	11,446	10,037	9,377	9,734	8,959	6,379	14,394	8,064	2,878	2,201
Krasnoyarsk, USSR	11,030	7,264	9,461	12,709	10,111	11,096	9,425	9,186	7,547	5,563	12,727	9,362	10,014	10,199	9,361	10,143	17,626	8,911	6,530	4,734
Kristiansand, Norway	13,213	5,359	6,557	8,552	8,345	8,742	6,317	6,200	11,063	8,294	9,006	7,590	6,817	7,172	6,401	5,706	12,915	5,503	2,426	394
Kuala Lumpur, Malaysia	11,203	12,999	15,282	18,479	15,136	16,280	15,300	15,047	1,762	2,458	18,608	14,623	15,881	16,000	15,205	12,738	16,239	14,825	10,261	9,663
Kuching, Malaysia	10,250	12,982	15,257	18,906	14,667	15,781	15,355	15,086	2,115	3,435	18,363	14,278	15,896	15,913	15,213	13,715	16,083	15,044	11,136	10,352
Kumasi, Ghana	17,192	9,520	8,934	7,603	11,015	10,480	8,575	8,696	11,087	8,992	8,618	10,680	8,627	8,998	8,804	1,370	8,830	7,880	3,393	5,577
Kumzar, Oman	15,213	10,191	11,706	13,134	13,329	13,877	11,472	11,350	6,092	3,283	13,867	12,533	11,967	12,327	11,552	7,576	15,148	10,654	4,813	4,789
Kunming, China	10,908	10,587	12,862	16,237	13,001	14,120	12,875	12,622	4,149	3,152	16,185	12,377	13,456	13,587	12,782	12,146	18,640	12,423	8,909	7,750
Kuqa Chang, China	12,241	8,926	11,031	13,916	11,867	12,813	10,945	10,727	6,047	3,811	14,156	11,104	11,532	11,765	10,915	9,916	17,940	10,329	6,477	5,234
Kurgan, USSR	12,550	7,212	9,146	11,849	10,315	11,110	9,016	8,820	8,032	5,532	12,134	9,517	9,592	9,864	9,016	8,449	16,272	8,342	4,844	3,246
Kuwait, Kuwait	15,609	9,628	10,971	12,236	12,725	13,161	10,716	10,613	6,962	4,163	12,982	11,945	11,185	11,558	10,814	6,760	14,544	9,881	3,916	4,040
Kuybyshev, USSR	13,371	7,184	8,890	11,213	10,328	10,982	8,710	8,545	8,475	5,792	11,630	9,527	9,260	9,574	8,747	7,437	15,330	7,963	3,840	2,423
Kyoto, Japan	7,776	8,639	10,819	14,473	10,174	11,314	10,986	10,715	6,625	6,487	13,836	9,736	11,465	11,416	10,806	14,131	17,428	10,914	10,516	8,610
Kzyl-Orda, USSR	13,312	8,374	10,239	12,664	11,490	12,257	10,085	9,904	7,040	4,422	13,077	10,691	10,649	10,944	10,103	8,418	16,453	9,368	4,959	3,856
L'vov, USSR	14,261	6,726	7,933	9,632	9,738	10,123	7,681	7,576	9,823	7,019	10,199	8,980	8,163	8,529	7,776	5,663	13,488	6,853	2,049	1,006
La Ceiba, Honduras	7,895	4,807	2,594	1,948	2,665	1,562	2,679	2,892	19,445	17,101	1,032	3,102	2,098	1,856	2,705	7,935	6,000	3,368	9,286	9,149
La Coruna, Spain	14,118	5,804	6,173	7,140	8,258	8,296	5,851	5,833	12,147	9,344	7,808	7,632	6,208	6,608	6,012	3,787	11,026	4,997	1,497	2,029
La Paz, Bolivia	10,014	8,671	6,386	2,761	6,726	5,582	6,304	6,571	16,452	16,395	3,140	7,219	5,753	5,708	6,438	6,649	2,304	6,620	9,781	10,938
La Paz, Mexico	5,639	4,048	2,937	4,572	919	1,137	3,273	3,271	16,866	16,395	3,618	1,707	3,036	2,639	3,096	10,247	7,801	4,116	10,600	9,652
La Ronge, Canada	7,527	791	2,359	6,023	2,598	3,520	2,556	2,293	14,851	13,113	5,544	1,809	3,003	2,975	2,357	9,246	10,640	2,757	7,990	6,498
Labrador City, Canada	9,875	1,807	2,045	4,957	3,945	4,227	1,834	1,689	15,239	12,669	4,973	3,282	2,387	2,698	1,892	6,758	9,965	1,136	5,836	4,894
Lagos, Nigeria	17,716	9,829	9,383	8,155	11,487	10,992	9,022	9,131	10,539	8,445	9,169	11,116	9,103	9,480	9,247	1,915	9,245	8,300	3,329	5,519
Lahore, Pakistan	13,415	9,936	11,880	14,229	12,996	13,844	11,735	11,548	5,389	2,789	14,713	12,208	12,302	12,591	11,747	9,280	16,977	11,024	6,149	5,424
Lambasa, Fiji	3,254	11,354	11,665	12,409	9,529	9,904	12,024	11,938	8,863	11,247	11,443	9,962	11,885	11,494	11,807	18,416	10,419	12,784	17,685	15,509
Lansing, Michigan	8,476	1,901	404	4,048	2,287	2,500	521	272	16,596	14,284	3,725	1,761	1,017	1,141	334	7,733	8,888	1,061	7,471	6,625
Lanzhou, China	10,674	9,370	11,642	15,054	11,872	12,969	11,654	11,400	5,367	4,036	14,964	11,214	12,235	12,367	11,560	11,761	19,719	11,215	8,292	6,855
Laoag, Philippines	9,089	10,907	13,148	16,827	12,550	13,683	13,281	13,010	4,240	4,588	16,225	12,125	13,793	13,776	13,119	14,147	17,552	13,094	10,828	9,433
Largeau, Chad	17,774	9,586	9,896	9,702	12,029	11,889	9,553	9,576	9,154	6,687	10,641	11,444	9,814	10,218	9,739	3,665	11,373	8,720	2,385	4,226
Las Vegas, Nevada	5,771	2,941	2,710	5,460	939	2,066	3,068	2,945	15,844	14,985	4,635	959	3,104	2,795	2,837	10,404	9,178	3,777	9,980	8,690
Launceston, Australia	7,356	15,423	15,687	14,806	13,543	13,659	16,032	15,998	5,860	8,669	14,210	14,064	15,752	15,347	15,841	16,006	10,427	16,856	16,583	16,388
Le Havre, France	13,913	5,724	6,492	7,916	8,470	8,673	6,202	6,138	11,497	8,684	8,504	7,775	6,630	7,016	6,330	4,616	11,963	5,350	1,551	1,085
Leipzig, East Germany	14,023	6,122	7,164	8,796	9,042	9,357	6,898	6,807	10,662	7,855	9,358	8,307	7,363	7,736	7,005	5,208	12,804	6,060	1,720	486
Leningrad, USSR	13,107	5,985	7,526	9,806	9,104	9,661	7,327	7,175	9,899	7,191	10,204	8,314	7,865	8,191	7,378	6,674	14,179	6,560	3,117	1,148
Leon, Spain	14,327	6,018	6,417	7,346	8,499	8,541	6,096	6,077	11,918	9,119	8,030	7,870	6,453	6,853	6,256	3,751	11,140	5,241	1,254	1,954
Lerwick, United Kingdom	12,817	4,829	5,990	8,072	7,786	8,174	5,751	5,633	11,597	8,843	8,486	7,037	6,255	6,608	5,834	5,715	12,579	4,941	2,702	952
Lhasa, China	11,956	10,196	12,380	15,369	12,963	13,998	12,323	12,093	4,649	2,777	15,582	12,246	12,912	13,118	12,274	10,899	18,348	11,746	7,673	6,640
Libreville, Gabon	18,565	10,750	10,328	8,913	12,423	11,888	9,968	10,080	9,742	7,848	9,940	12,065	10,036	10,409	10,194	2,758	9,370	9,251	3,995	6,136
Lilongwe, Malawi	18,200	13,458	13,416	11,780	15,534	14,978	13,056	13,147	6,824	5,590	12,808	15,122	13,151	13,526	13,276	5,854	10,533	12,301	6,262	7,970
Lima, Peru	9,029	7,999	5,715	2,367	5,773	4,631	5,693	5,948	17,262	17,438	2,389	6,329	5,113	4,998	5,791	7,401	2,774	6,144	10,241	11,081
Limerick, Ireland	13,291	5,045	5,794	7,402	7,763	7,979	5,509	5,439	12,103	9,297	7,925	7,070	5,950	6,332	5,633	4,807	11,706	4,660	2,169	1,418
Limoges, France	14,313	6,089	6,746	7,941	8,766	8,911	6,444	6,396	11,388	8,577	8,584	8,090	6,845	7,238	6,584	4,271	11,789	5,587	1,143	1,352
Limon, Costa Rica	8,281	5,490	3,227	1,382	3,411	2,288	3,255	3,492	19,783	17,355	351	3,861	2,665	2,495	3,319	7,590	5,288	3,845	9,330	9,447
Lincoln, Nebraska	7,446	2,002	1,057	4,428	1,337	1,909	1,402	1,258	16,551	14,705	3,859	730	1,575	1,396	1,165	8,736	8,931	2,092	8,435	7,414
Linz, Austria	14,378	6,475	7,463	8,942	9,371	9,654	7,188	7,106	10,451	7,638	9,548	8,643	7,638	8,017	7,303	5,035	12,773	6,343	1,467	828
Lisbon, Portugal	14,465	6,159	6,333	6,965	8,455	8,402	5,998	6,006	12,220	9,447	7,698	7,871	6,308	6,712	6,175	3,267	10,626	5,155	1,414	2,481
Little Rock, Arkansas	7,639	2,672	843	3,669	1,364	1,390	1,174	1,191	17,325	15,319	3,081	1,207	1,036	722	1,004	8,374	8,171	2,020	8,511	7,736
Liverpool, United Kingdom	13,426	5,258	6,123	7,787	8,057	8,314	5,848	5,767	11,722	8,919	8,309	7,347	6,302	6,679	5,963	4,963	12,050	5,004	2,037	1,037
Lodz, Poland	14,043	6,373	7,550	9,288	9,366	9,740	7,297	7,192	10,195	7,394	9,835	8,612	7,779	8,145	7,393	5,568	13,272	6,469	1,989	629
Lome, Togo	17,507	9,735	9,217	7,921	11,309	10,790	8,857	8,973	10,768	8,687	8,937	10,958	8,922	9,296	9,085	1,689	9,035	8,149	3,393	5,586

Distances in Kilometers	Christmas Is. [Pacific Ocean]	Churchill, Canada	Cincinnati, Ohio	Ciudad Bolivia, Venezuela	Ciudad Juarez, Mexico	Ciudad Victoria, Mexico	Clarksburg, West Virginia	Cleveland, Ohio	Cocos (Keeling) Island	Colombo, Sri Lanka	Colon, Panama	Colorado Springs, Colorado	Columbia, South Carolina	Columbus, Georgia	Columbus, Ohio	Conakry, Guinea	Concepcion, Chile	Concord, New Hampshire	Constantine, Algeria	Copenhagen, Denmark
London, United Kingdom	13,707	5,547	6,385	7,936	8,335	8,573	6,104	6,029	11,524	8,714	8,492	7,629	6,547	6,928	6,224	4,818	12,080	5,255	1,764	958
Londonderry, United Kingdom	13,127	4,931	5,800	7,561	7,725	7,991	5,528	5,443	11,996	9,201	8,049	7,014	5,990	6,363	5,640	5,076	11,939	4,687	2,329	1,262
Longlac, Canada	8,485	1,112	1,198	4,828	2,601	3,092	1,265	995	15,804	13,585	4,523	1,891	1,811	1,928	1,126	7,973	9,686	1,360	7,235	6,141
Lord Howe Island, Australia	5,895	13,898	14,298	14,293	12,152	12,420	14,655	14,581	6,701	9,403	13,488	12,610	14,469	14,068	14,444	17,456	10,700	15,431	17,435	16,272
Los Angeles, California	5,407	3,274	3,053	5,640	1,130	2,182	3,412	3,298	15,712	15,087	4,772	1,314	3,417	3,091	3,183	10,739	9,141	4,136	10,344	9,026
Louangphrabang, Laos	11,023	11,165	13,441	16,785	13,536	14,663	13,452	13,200	3,572	2,800	16,764	12,929	14,035	14,165	13,360	12,289	18,068	12,992	9,201	8,179
Louisville, Kentucky	8,288	2,358	144	3,646	2,020	2,050	484	501	17,086	14,788	3,253	1,660	635	646	305	7,796	8,415	1,320	7,810	7,075
Luanda, Angola	18,756	11,837	11,291	9,484	13,331	12,679	10,933	11,064	9,127	7,593	10,516	13,044	10,948	11,303	11,165	3,609	9,103	10,254	5,047	7,145
Lubumbashi, Zaire	18,807	12,901	12,716	11,072	14,820	14,246	12,356	12,457	7,537	6,154	12,103	14,440	12,433	12,804	12,579	5,124	10,160	11,618	5,749	7,590
Lusaka, Zambia	18,392	13,305	13,037	11,205	15,112	14,469	12,677	12,790	7,395	6,200	12,229	14,775	12,724	13,086	12,904	5,390	9,973	11,959	6,168	8,014
Luxembourg, Luxembourg	14,079	5,997	6,875	8,348	8,819	9,063	6,594	6,520	11,066	8,253	8,937	8,108	7,035	7,417	6,715	4,810	12,328	5,745	1,471	803
Luxor, Egypt	16,756	9,448	10,320	10,922	12,318	12,478	10,015	9,971	8,105	5,417	11,767	11,610	10,396	10,794	10,159	5,204	13,014	9,158	2,742	3,707
Lynn Lake, Canada	7,853	463	2,314	5,995	2,822	3,681	2,469	2,199	14,799	12,934	5,577	2,022	2,959	2,978	2,290	8,966	10,711	2,570	7,662	6,182
Lyon, France	14,441	6,271	6,997	8,218	8,999	9,169	6,699	6,645	11,109	8,297	8,864	8,312	7,108	7,499	6,835	4,390	12,012	5,843	1,053	1,229
Macapa, Brazil	11,853	7,516	5,507	2,352	6,796	5,814	5,271	5,531	16,246	14,531	3,360	6,952	4,891	5,057	5,482	4,267	4,670	5,200	7,166	8,385
Madison, Wisconsin	8,096	1,775	602	4,263	1,961	2,324	867	658	16,510	14,362	3,847	1,379	1,242	1,239	635	8,131	9,002	1,450	7,794	6,849
Madras, India	13,437	12,026	14,018	16,025	14,994	15,931	13,872	13,687	3,322	682	16,708	14,233	14,435	14,729	13,885	10,209	16,279	13,148	7,705	7,421
Madrid, Spain	14,617	6,306	6,667	7,459	8,761	8,776	6,342	6,330	11,755	8,969	8,176	8,141	6,683	7,085	6,507	3,563	11,100	5,489	1,004	2,075
Madurai, India	13,730	12,359	14,289	16,012	15,368	16,268	14,122	13,950	3,189	383	16,785	14,598	14,672	14,985	14,150	10,036	15,860	13,370	7,709	7,576
Magadan, USSR	7,763	5,721	7,954	11,634	7,688	8,819	8,089	7,818	9,274	8,277	11,147	7,105	8,599	8,599	7,924	12,223	16,005	7,974	8,874	6,703
Magdalena, Bolivia	10,437	8,440	6,179	2,501	6,729	5,597	6,063	6,333	16,514	16,030	3,056	7,157	5,536	5,533	6,215	6,118	2,751	6,306	9,224	10,407
Magdeburg, East Germany	13,918	6,018	7,075	8,750	8,945	9,268	6,812	6,718	10,726	7,922	9,299	8,207	7,281	7,652	6,916	5,259	12,808	5,976	1,800	394
Majuro Atoll, Marshall Isls.	3,515	9,602	10,731	12,971	8,874	9,666	11,071	10,888	8,498	10,072	11,942	8,997	11,181	10,870	10,831	18,085	12,773	11,604	14,928	12,769
Malabo, Equatorial Guinea	18,384	10,392	10,036	8,787	12,148	11,661	9,676	9,778	9,892	7,879	9,807	11,762	9,767	10,146	9,899	2,567	9,536	8,942	3,618	5,767
Male, Maldives	14,325	12,961	14,729	15,814	16,050	16,835	14,517	14,377	3,134	778	16,727	15,259	15,028	15,379	14,580	9,637	15,027	13,714	7,683	7,851
Manado, Indonesia	8,636	12,506	14,609	18,001	13,487	14,514	14,815	14,548	3,438	5,030	17,037	13,265	15,243	15,120	14,618	15,284	15,685	14,793	12,402	11,245
Managua, Nicaragua	7,932	5,213	2,991	1,772	2,998	1,868	3,063	3,283	19,697	17,407	763	3,479	2,477	2,253	3,099	7,918	5,596	3,724	9,477	9,450
Manama, Bahrain	15,675	10,042	11,406	12,610	13,148	13,596	11,151	11,049	6,552	3,765	13,380	12,365	11,619	11,993	11,249	6,993	14,623	10,316	4,296	4,475
Manaus, Brazil	10,866	7,493	5,308	1,728	6,244	5,177	5,138	5,409	16,968	15,569	2,603	6,532	4,664	4,740	5,318	5,322	3,963	5,261	8,155	9,214
Manchester, New Hampshire	9,542	2,347	1,178	3,840	3,315	3,319	852	861	16,391	13,767	3,816	2,829	1,301	1,666	1,020	6,690	8,842	24	6,495	5,878
Mandalay, Burma	11,619	11,007	13,241	16,350	13,594	14,686	13,211	12,971	3,762	2,413	16,508	12,929	13,800	13,977	13,145	11,618	18,062	12,675	8,550	7,614
Mangareva Island, Fr.Polynesia	3,703	9,820	8,659	7,822	6,785	6,471	8,941	9,015	13,177	15,898	6,988	7,543	8,514	8,126	8,820	13,617	6,059	9,791	16,060	15,522
Manila, Philippines	9,044	11,276	13,501	17,172	12,813	13,935	13,646	13,374	3,968	4,573	16,506	12,422	14,147	14,115	13,478	14,366	17,179	13,480	11,128	9,793
Mannheim, West Germany	14,146	6,113	7,029	8,516	8,961	9,219	6,751	6,673	10,896	8,084	9,107	8,244	7,196	7,576	6,869	4,886	12,465	5,903	1,465	742
Maputo, Mozambique	17,143	14,532	14,056	11,728	16,006	15,171	13,701	13,844	6,878	6,272	12,710	15,813	13,667	13,997	13,937	6,363	9,588	13,043	7,418	9,242
Mar del Plata, Argentina	11,024	11,245	8,972	5,306	9,240	8,098	8,869	9,139	13,864	14,526	5,736	9,786	8,333	8,303	9,015	6,957	1,377	9,104	10,551	12,311
Maracaibo, Venezuela	9,532	5,662	3,400	281	4,275	3,255	3,286	3,556	18,767	16,316	919	4,537	2,756	2,776	3,435	6,339	5,260	3,606	8,267	8,672
Marrakech, Morocco	15,098	6,845	6,797	6,937	8,944	8,769	6,449	6,489	12,102	9,411	7,762	8,415	6,693	7,097	6,644	2,519	10,161	5,631	1,447	3,118
Marseilles, France	14,709	6,514	7,170	8,243	9,198	9,330	6,865	6,822	11,031	8,227	8,924	8,524	7,257	7,652	7,009	4,179	11,894	6,008	777	1,469
Maseru, Lesotho	16,934	14,553	13,808	11,243	15,635	14,718	13,462	13,629	7,377	6,889	12,202	15,550	13,366	13,671	13,701	6,163	8,964	12,865	7,592	9,522
Mashhad, Iran	14,294	9,193	10,884	12,843	12,336	12,997	10,687	10,535	6,622	3,850	13,420	11,534	11,221	11,552	10,737	7,898	15,831	9,911	4,694	4,121
Mazatlan, Mexico	5,988	4,066	2,718	4,162	944	746	3,037	3,065	17,272	16,602	3,213	1,738	2,744	2,340	2,880	9,877	7,513	3,891	10,382	9,552
Mbabane, Swaziland	17,160	14,486	13,953	11,586	15,882	15,034	13,599	13,747	7,021	6,417	12,565	15,709	13,554	13,880	13,835	6,263	9,452	12,952	7,400	9,253
Mbandaka, Zaire	19,512	11,271	11,109	9,889	13,240	12,788	10,750	10,837	8,775	6,879	10,915	12,811	10,869	11,253	10,968	3,695	10,135	9,990	4,195	6,186
McMurdo Sound, Antarctica	9,115	16,530	14,703	11,696	13,387	12,704	14,821	15,026	8,189	10,634	11,606	14,187	14,239	13,982	14,831	12,450	6,735	15,443	15,307	17,342
Mecca, Saudi Arabia	16,808	10,168	11,159	11,748	13,117	13,328	10,860	10,806	7,246	4,592	12,615	12,387	11,253	11,650	10,997	5,866	13,408	10,004	3,610	4,419
Medan, Indonesia	11,537	13,001	15,268	18,239	15,285	16,428	15,258	15,012	1,735	2,118	18,564	14,730	15,845	15,997	15,180	12,399	16,228	14,731	9,963	9,434
Medellin, Colombia	9,105	6,037	3,748	601	4,275	3,177	3,690	3,952	18,977	16,937	588	4,655	3,123	3,062	3,807	6,824	4,777	4,114	8,906	9,323
Medicine Hat, Canada	6,916	1,440	2,389	5,923	2,064	3,088	2,661	2,426	15,099	13,610	5,329	1,329	3,001	2,880	2,433	9,697	10,310	3,054	8,632	7,167
Medina, Saudi Arabia	16,550	9,850	10,890	11,634	12,822	13,069	10,598	10,536	7,411	4,705	12,471	12,083	11,007	11,399	10,729	5,876	13,557	9,744	3,411	4,106
Melbourne, Australia	7,359	15,253	15,755	15,180	13,606	13,812	16,110	16,044	5,562	8,357	14,539	14,075	15,889	15,485	15,903	16,220	10,863	16,895	16,353	15,981
Memphis, Tennessee	7,846	2,643	661	3,570	1,571	1,538	977	1,016	17,352	15,232	3,034	1,376	836	554	822	8,170	8,159	1,829	8,320	7,583
Merauke, Indonesia	6,991	12,799	14,416	16,635	12,697	13,497	14,726	14,504	4,777	6,925	15,613	12,747	14,936	14,659	14,490	17,182	13,908	15,072	14,422	13,077
Merida, Mexico	7,646	4,211	2,069	2,477	2,059	1,027	2,215	2,395	18,807	16,714	1,653	2,458	1,672	1,354	2,198	8,136	6,630	2,985	9,189	8,841
Meridian, Mississippi	7,913	2,961	837	3,252	1,679	1,401	1,075	1,189	17,681	15,491	2,703	1,624	736	349	986	8,046	7,832	1,926	8,387	7,755
Messina, Italy	15,502	7,467	8,199	9,107	10,218	10,357	7,893	7,850	10,079	7,297	9,848	9,533	8,281	8,677	8,037	4,319	12,309	7,036	819	1,956
Mexico City, Mexico	6,635	4,388	2,598	3,316	1,551	480	2,849	2,955	18,133	17,090	2,351	2,222	2,414	2,022	2,754	9,195	6,802	3,692	10,084	9,529
Miami, Florida	8,652	3,822	1,532	2,181	2,644	1,928	1,498	1,749	18,449	15,799	1,816	2,721	915	876	1,595	7,209	6,970	2,088	8,094	7,849
Midway Islands, USA	3,587	6,991	8,323	11,196	6,729	7,711	8,639	8,429	10,233	10,893	10,250	6,669	8,848	8,593	8,401	15,480	13,032	9,078	12,846	10,664
Milan, Italy	14,589	6,502	7,305	8,555	9,285	9,483	7,012	6,952	10,769	7,957	9,205	8,586	7,431	7,820	7,144	4,547	12,279	6,158	1,034	1,159
Milford Sound, New Zealand	6,199	14,515	14,183	13,142	12,096	12,058	14,504	14,522	7,576	10,384	12,501	12,717	14,145	13,746	14,343	16,116	9,116	15,359	18,186	17,872
Milwaukee, Wisconsin	8,213	1,800	522	4,200	2,061	2,377	759	540	16,535	14,335	3,812	1,495	1,168	1,202	534	8,011	8,973	1,331	7,693	6,776
Minsk, USSR	13,792	6,469	7,834	9,793	9,542	10,008	7,605	7,478	9,766	6,991	10,291	8,766	8,114	8,464	7,681	6,136	13,866	6,800	2,532	982
Mogadiscio, Somalia	17,449	12,384	13,169	12,834	15,237	15,238	12,842	12,831	5,900	3,863	13,837	14,551	13,149	13,554	13,009	6,588	12,655	11,991	5,501	6,632
Mombasa, Kenya	18,112	12,762	13,202	12,310	15,343	15,101	12,854	12,887	6,352	4,627	13,337	14,753	13,076	13,476	13,047	6,109	11,734	12,030	5,641	7,069
Monclova, Mexico	6,581	3,584	2,074	3,846	727	419	2,389	2,423	17,499	16,259	2,982	1,361	2,104	1,703	2,235	9,316	7,655	3,244	9,734	8,944
Moncton, Canada	10,065	2,411	1,790	4,220	3,897	3,950	1,480	1,451	15,849	13,169	4,319	3,352	1,925	2,297	1,629	6,304	9,223	625	5,880	5,255
Monrovia, Liberia	16,227	9,024	8,166	6,597	10,183	9,567	7,811	7,959	12,077	10,006	7,617	9,923	7,802	8,156	8,047	478	8,032	7,180	3,772	5,853
Monte Carlo, Monaco	14,725	6,573	7,285	8,408	9,297	9,452	6,984	6,935	10,877	8,070	9,083	8,613	7,385	7,778	7,124	4,308	12,056	6,128	821	1,378
Monterrey, Mexico	6,654	3,707	2,099	3,687	903	245	2,399	2,453	17,670	16,398	2,812	1,520	2,074	1,670	2,260	9,225	7,486	3,256	9,737	9,002
Montevideo, Uruguay	11,175	10,957	8,695	5,019	9,059	7,915	8,580	8,851	14,092	14,569	5,498	9,576	8,053	8,040	8,733	6,643	1,537	8,787	10,224	11,957
Montgomery, Alabama	8,136	2,989	763	3,118	1,904	1,582	935	1,091	17,725	15,416	2,633	1,819	522	124	892	7,820	7,786	1,766	8,198	7,620
Montpelier, Vermont	9,455	2,180	1,146	3,984	3,256	3,319	850	806	16,290	13,700	3,931	2,738	1,353	1,697	985	6,815	8,981	144	6,525	5,842
Montpellier, France	14,628	6,413	7,047	8,123	9,079	9,205	6,741	6,699	11,157	8,352	8,800	8,409	7,131	7,526	6,886	4,144	11,812	5,884	836	1,479
Montreal, Canada	9,380	2,021	1,145	4,128	3,215	3,335	886	791	16,183	13,627	4,050	2,665	1,427	1,748	984	6,929	9,119	303	6,549	5,803
Moosonee, Canada	8,926	1,193	1,387	4,850	3,030	3,445	1,334	1,091	15,642	13,291	4,648	2,336	1,921	2,120	1,271	7,590	9,790	1,131	6,786	5,730
Moroni, Comoros	17,497	13,694	14,060	12,788	16,209	15,842	13,707	13,757	5,827	4,544	13,820	15,659	13,886	14,279	13,909	6,727	11,476	12,899	6,562	7,992
Moscow, USSR	13,459	6,603	8,160	10,356	9,730	10,297	7,959	7,810	9,293	6,567	10,795	8,937	8,494	8,823	8,012	6,788	14,538	7,186	3,175	1,563
Mosul, Iraq	15,258	8,750	10,083	11,528	11,835	12,271	9,832	9,725	7,764	4,950	12,211	11,058	10,310	10,678	9,926	6,434	14,425	9,002	3,258	3,150
Mount Isa, Australia	7,302	14,026	15,369	16,522	13,420	14,021	15,711	15,527	4,646	7,202	15,627	13,625	15,788	15,446	15,471	16,903	12,780	16,208	15,155	14,176
Multan, Pakistan	13,725	10,059	11,944	14,134	13,148	13,955	11,783	11,606	5,401	2,718	14,673	12,354	12,341	12,643	11,806	9,030	16,669	11,049	5,970	5,365
Munich, West Germany	14,351	6,370	7,302	8,741	9,232	9,491	7,023	6,946	10,645	7,831	9,350	8,512	7,465	7,847	7,142	4,895	12,588	6,175	1,371	839
Murcia, Spain	14,964	6,654	6,990	7,645	9,093	9,084	6,661	6,656	11,517	8,750	8,396	8,481	6,990	7,393	6,831	3,397	11,098	5,811	710	2,217
Murmansk, USSR	12,090	5,216	6,984	9,682	8,360	9,032	6,833	6,648	10,240	7,678	9,927	7,560	7,402	7,689	6,847	7,405	14,409	6,138	3,973	1,805
Mururoa Atoll, Fr. Polynesia	3,326	9,835	8,809	8,170	6,866	6,634	9,104	9,162	12,881	15,554	7,309	7,602	8,704	8,309	8,970	14,033	6,482	9,959	16,332	15,579
Muscat, Oman	15,197	10,537	12,076	13,464	13,678	14,244	11,844	11,720	5,733	2,929	14,217	12,880	12,339	12,698	11,923	7,800	15,200	11,026	5,146	5,161
Myitkyina, Burma	11,432	10,621	12,864	16,055	13,197	14,288	12,843	12,600	4,136	2,766	16,149	12,531	13,431	13,598	12,771	11,633	18,452	12,327	8,452	7,398
Naga, Philippines	8,807	11,302	13,502	17,147	12,723	13,834	13,662	13,391	4,062	4,798	16,419	12,362	14,147	14,095	13,486	14,624	16,976	13,536	11,373	10,008
Nagasaki, Japan	8,265	9,073	11,291	14,965	10,736	11,878	11,438	11,167	6,078	5,901	14,376	10,274	11,937	11,911	11,268	13,949	17,883	11,311	10,351	8,552
Nagoya, Japan	7,676	8,579	10,749	14,396	10,082	11,220	10,920	10,649	6,715	6,595	13,748	9,649	11,394	11,341	10,738	14,182	17,329	10,860	10,568	8,645
Nagpur, India	13,359	11,128	13,122	15,368	14,123	15,035	12,984	12,794	4,148	1,575	15,932	13,352	13,552	13,837	12,991	9,928	16,819	12,275	7,117	6,623
Nairobi, Kenya	18,439	12,352	12,761	11,954	14,902	14,672	12,414	12,447	6,727	4,866	12,975	14,317	12,639	13,040	12,607	5,728	11,683	11,590	5,210	6,687
Nanchang, China	9,576	9,926	12,210	15,850	11,962	13,105	12,296	12,028	4,946	4,485	15,470	11,424	12,844	12,889	12,159	13,156	18,785	12,009	9,699	8,200
Nancy, France	14,176	6,079	6,928	8,345	8,885	9,114	6,643	6,573	11,048	8,234	8,948	8,178	7,078	7,461	6,767	4,724	12,277	5,793	1,369	891
Nandi, Fiji	3,512	11,593	11,923	12,623	9,787	10,158	12,282	12,196	8,632	11,049	11,666	10,219	12,142	11,751	12,066	18,512	10,480	13,041	17,761	15,612
Nanjing, China	9,302	9,491	11,770	15,426	11,497	12,639	11,865	11,596	5,407	4,898	15,013	10,960	12,407	12,442	11,723	13,191	18,814	11,606	9,664	8,053
Nanning, China	10,357	10,732	13,022	16,555	12,929	14,068	13,072	12,810	4,050	3,520	16,335	12,361	13,640	13,727	12,957	12,771	18,445	12,695	9,518	8,291
Nantes, France	14,075	5,833	6,485	7,751	8,502	8,654	6,185	6,135	11,611	8,798	8,372	7,826	6,591	6,982	6,324	4,334	11,711	5,329	1,381	1,355
Naples, Italy	15,191	7,158	7,933	8,975	9,933	10,101	7,633	7,582	10,261	7,463	9,684	9,240	8,034	8,427	7,771	4,430	12,363	6,776	829	1,654
Narvik, Norway	12,181	4,858	6,484	9,064	7,985	8,583	6,311	6,141	10,809	8,188	9,340	7,192	6,869	7,173	6,342	6,926	13,773	5,586	3,631	1,444

Distances in Kilometers	Christmas Is. [Pacific Ocean]	Churchill, Canada	Cincinnati, Ohio	Ciudad Bolivia, Venezuela	Ciudad Juarez, Mexico	Ciudad Victoria, Mexico	Clarksburg, West Virginia	Cleveland, Ohio	Cocos (Keeling) Island	Colombo, Sri Lanka	Colon, Panama	Colorado Springs, Colorado	Columbia, South Carolina	Columbus, Georgia	Columbus, Ohio	Conakry, Guinea	Concepcion, Chile	Concord, New Hampshire	Constantine, Algeria	Copenhagen, Denmark
Nashville, Tennessee	8,160	2,568	382	3,492	1,883	1,819	664	738	17,304	15,036	3,049	1,620	576	442	536	7,875	8,205	1,520	8,009	7,312
Nassau, Bahamas	8,933	3,965	1,694	1,987	2,939	2,212	1,599	1,864	18,437	15,696	1,760	2,994	1,050	1,106	1,732	6,921	6,868	2,079	7,893	7,738
Natal, Brazil	13,620	8,840	7,096	4,224	8,602	7,663	6,810	7,049	14,373	12,858	5,233	8,676	6,526	6,752	7,040	2,924	5,157	6,543	6,384	8,094
Natashquan, Canada	10,248	2,271	2,169	4,710	4,198	4,358	1,895	1,814	15,345	12,681	4,825	3,586	2,388	2,743	2,008	6,305	9,704	1,074	5,555	4,795
Nauru Island	3,965	10,574	11,644	13,604	9,722	10,441	11,990	11,817	7,840	9,704	12,572	9,897	12,066	11,738	11,751	19,009	12,604	12,552	15,553	13,470
Ndjamena, Chad	18,250	9,935	9,980	9,353	12,129	11,846	9,626	9,681	9,420	7,124	10,333	11,618	9,821	10,220	9,830	3,158	10,644	8,824	2,816	4,836
Nelson, New Zealand	5,628	13,943	13,626	12,799	11,527	11,520	13,952	13,962	8,011	10,803	12,098	12,141	13,612	13,210	13,786	16,419	9,044	14,804	18,743	17,882
Nema, Mauritania	16,168	8,263	7,779	6,918	9,897	9,471	7,418	7,521	11,875	9,492	7,885	9,505	7,524	7,909	7,641	1,053	9,083	6,687	2,582	4,650
Neuquen, Argentina	10,104	11,094	8,804	5,243	8,777	7,657	8,753	9,016	14,152	15,229	5,488	9,395	8,186	8,098	8,870	7,766	497	9,105	11,320	12,944
New Delhi, India	13,284	10,291	12,275	14,660	13,316	14,201	12,139	11,947	4,964	2,414	15,143	12,537	12,710	12,991	12,144	9,603	17,105	11,439	6,545	5,857
New Glasgow, Canada	10,235	2,567	1,933	4,196	4,053	4,075	1,611	1,601	15,810	13,102	4,340	3,520	2,026	2,408	1,773	6,130	9,187	755	5,736	5,168
New Haven, Connecticut	9,417	2,443	1,017	3,658	3,166	3,119	671	735	16,609	13,989	3,605	2,721	1,082	1,454	866	6,758	8,652	240	6,678	6,096
New Orleans, Louisiana	7,740	3,214	1,134	3,140	1,581	1,135	1,363	1,485	17,895	15,784	2,514	1,673	962	557	1,282	8,180	7,605	2,206	8,645	8,047
New Plymouth, New Zealand	5,394	13,709	13,456	12,778	11,343	11,371	13,787	13,787	8,084	10,859	12,046	11,942	13,466	13,062	13,615	16,641	9,158	14,635	18,880	17,710
New York, New York	9,323	2,455	916	3,601	3,065	3,007	565	653	16,701	14,095	3,521	2,635	971	1,341	769	6,832	8,587	344	6,789	6,207
Newcastle upon Tyne, UK	13,316	5,199	6,148	7,915	8,048	8,341	5,882	5,791	11,629	8,834	8,414	7,326	6,349	6,720	5,989	5,157	12,228	5,044	2,164	902
Newcastle Waters, Australia	7,868	14,024	15,640	17,249	13,835	14,540	15,958	15,741	3,977	6,474	16,326	13,945	16,137	15,835	15,720	16,374	13,395	16,311	14,416	13,508
Niamey, Niger	17,199	9,089	8,789	7,940	10,923	10,530	8,430	8,517	10,826	8,518	8,922	10,494	8,562	8,951	8,647	1,783	9,625	7,672	2,571	4,763
Nicosia, Cyprus	15,740	8,522	9,605	10,729	11,499	11,795	9,326	9,249	8,473	5,679	11,467	10,756	9,762	10,146	9,445	5,549	13,561	8,477	2,415	2,776
Niue (Alofi)	2,689	11,005	10,939	11,294	8,791	9,020	11,290	11,244	9,923	12,391	10,354	9,320	11,071	10,670	11,091	17,261	9,353	12,102	18,053	15,931
Norfolk, Virginia	9,102	2,758	765	3,209	2,826	2,624	447	696	17,168	14,563	3,066	2,511	536	934	681	6,947	8,165	813	7,155	6,658
Norfolk Island, Australia	5,031	13,165	13,416	13,518	11,268	11,523	13,771	13,707	7,549	10,202	12,667	11,748	13,573	13,172	13,565	17,837	10,336	14,561	18,098	16,463
Noril'sk, USSR	10,732	5,794	7,965	11,230	8,734	9,668	7,923	7,685	9,048	6,954	11,224	7,963	8,512	8,703	7,862	9,480	16,212	7,412	5,946	3,869
Norman Wells, Canada	7,437	1,836	3,970	7,647	3,981	5,027	4,130	3,860	13,228	11,700	7,175	3,269	4,616	4,607	3,950	10,090	12,237	4,159	8,040	6,158
Normanton, Australia	7,070	13,649	15,031	16,455	13,120	13,767	15,369	15,177	4,794	7,258	15,514	13,296	15,472	15,142	15,129	17,164	12,995	15,842	15,111	13,987
North Pole	9,781	3,487	5,673	9,080	6,489	7,376	5,653	5,407	11,329	9,236	8,967	5,702	6,240	6,409	5,577	8,952	14,081	5,217	5,978	3,833
Nottingham, United Kingdom	13,529	5,379	6,256	7,896	8,188	8,446	5,980	5,899	11,600	8,794	8,428	7,476	6,433	6,810	6,096	4,950	12,118	5,136	1,942	942
Norway House, Canada	7,896	578	1,937	5,618	2,566	3,360	2,101	1,833	15,172	13,250	5,201	1,766	2,583	2,599	1,916	8,774	10,341	2,260	7,671	6,302
Norwich, United Kingdom	13,637	5,521	6,424	8,053	8,349	8,615	6,149	6,067	11,432	8,626	8,593	7,633	6,603	6,980	6,263	4,970	12,232	5,305	1,855	810
Nouakchott, Mauritania	15,270	7,623	6,932	5,996	9,025	8,553	6,572	6,693	12,812	10,389	6,953	8,677	6,640	7,018	6,800	980	8,535	5,879	3,001	4,813
Noumea, New Caledonia	4,744	12,636	13,146	13,756	11,020	11,407	13,506	13,408	7,437	9,958	12,835	11,424	13,385	12,996	13,285	18,594	10,978	14,243	17,523	15,719
Novosibirsk, USSR	11,651	7,386	9,506	12,561	10,349	11,276	9,433	9,209	7,542	5,341	12,690	9,577	10,022	10,242	9,393	9,567	17,288	8,853	5,960	4,266
Nuku'alofa, Tonga	3,201	11,492	11,520	11,861	9,370	9,618	11,873	11,819	9,335	11,841	10,933	9,881	11,664	11,263	11,671	17,663	9,648	12,677	18,307	16,117
Nukunono Island, Tokelau Isls.	2,017	10,179	10,427	11,400	8,294	8,704	10,786	10,699	9,944	12,137	10,400	8,724	10,658	10,270	10,569	17,641	10,183	11,545	16,992	14,835
Nuremberg, West Germany	14,202	6,232	7,195	8,705	9,109	9,386	6,920	6,838	10,709	7,897	9,296	8,386	7,370	7,749	7,035	4,989	12,627	6,075	1,498	699
Nyala, Sudan	18,431	10,449	10,790	10,413	12,926	12,763	10,446	10,472	8,382	6,053	11,384	12,341	10,697	11,101	10,635	4,228	11,508	9,616	3,257	4,956
Oaxaca, Mexico	6,853	4,634	2,716	2,995	1,902	782	2,931	3,067	18,469	17,326	2,010	2,540	2,444	2,075	2,864	8,973	6,462	3,750	10,046	9,613
Ocean Falls, Canada	6,231	2,208	3,602	7,081	2,863	3,993	3,873	3,634	14,035	12,938	6,416	2,315	4,209	4,066	3,646	10,745	11,209	4,216	9,227	7,488
Odense, Denmark	13,549	5,686	6,825	8,676	8,649	9,015	6,575	6,468	10,874	8,086	9,175	7,901	7,061	7,424	6,668	5,512	12,900	5,750	2,135	142
Odessa, USSR	14,577	7,300	8,556	10,197	10,341	10,745	8,306	8,199	9,216	6,407	10,795	9,576	8,788	9,154	8,399	5,866	13,829	7,479	2,294	1,624
Ogbomosho, Nigeria	17,721	9,720	9,342	8,231	11,460	11,000	8,982	9,082	10,481	8,330	9,238	11,066	9,082	9,464	9,204	1,984	9,437	8,245	3,136	5,323
Okha, USSR	7,868	6,544	8,776	12,457	8,446	9,585	8,913	8,641	8,475	7,632	11,953	7,891	9,421	9,417	8,748	12,676	16,685	8,790	9,193	7,075
Okinawa (Naha)	8,402	9,832	12,042	15,708	11,405	12,541	12,195	11,923	5,387	5,491	15,077	10,978	12,688	12,652	12,022	14,270	17,737	12,072	10,734	9,064
Oklahoma City, Oklahoma	7,200	2,598	1,218	4,067	931	1,313	1,574	1,528	17,035	15,300	3,401	748	1,515	1,203	1,369	8,845	8,398	2,384	8,846	7,941
Old Crow, Canada	7,405	2,434	4,600	8,278	4,538	5,611	4,756	4,485	12,605	11,168	7,801	3,854	5,246	5,238	4,579	10,456	12,840	4,754	8,141	6,146
Olympia, Washington	6,010	2,305	3,212	6,534	2,201	3,341	3,519	3,306	14,645	13,621	5,816	1,728	3,776	3,583	3,282	10,655	10,534	3,990	9,490	7,887
Omaha, Nebraska	7,516	1,947	1,008	4,428	1,413	1,968	1,348	1,196	16,529	14,649	3,875	799	1,546	1,385	1,109	8,677	8,961	2,024	8,359	7,339
Omsk, USSR	12,178	7,343	9,368	12,230	10,395	11,252	9,264	9,054	7,744	5,362	12,451	9,606	9,847	10,097	9,246	8,964	16,772	8,629	5,361	3,735
Oodnadatta, Australia	7,866	14,883	16,124	16,557	14,092	14,575	16,476	16,313	4,375	7,093	15,808	14,368	16,479	16,111	16,238	16,228	12,282	17,035	15,150	14,537
Oradea, Romania	14,570	6,907	8,007	9,525	9,870	10,199	7,741	7,649	9,863	7,050	10,137	9,126	8,203	8,577	7,847	5,350	13,228	6,901	1,737	1,155
Oran, Algeria	15,198	6,884	7,156	7,664	9,272	9,226	6,822	6,826	11,452	8,708	8,444	8,674	7,132	7,536	6,997	3,189	10,971	5,977	657	2,437
Oranjestad, Aruba	9,699	5,511	3,274	465	4,290	3,312	3,135	3,406	18,607	16,062	1,133	4,501	2,628	2,685	3,297	6,153	5,471	3,404	8,008	8,406
Orebro, Sweden	13,181	5,543	6,871	8,974	8,589	9,044	6,646	6,516	10,673	7,923	9,407	7,819	7,161	7,506	6,718	6,033	13,346	5,848	2,623	433
Orel, USSR	13,789	6,840	8,322	10,368	9,952	10,478	8,106	7,968	9,212	6,453	10,854	9,165	8,628	8,969	8,171	6,552	14,390	7,316	2,939	1,553
Orsk, USSR	13,200	7,567	9,377	11,815	10,702	11,423	9,216	9,038	7,918	5,286	12,204	9,900	9,776	10,076	9,238	7,956	15,912	8,492	4,387	3,038
Osaka, Japan	7,791	8,683	10,863	14,516	10,216	11,355	11,029	10,758	6,583	6,456	13,879	9,778	11,508	11,460	10,849	14,145	17,442	10,957	10,531	8,631
Oslo, Norway	13,065	5,323	6,615	8,724	8,351	8,791	6,387	6,259	10,935	8,185	9,148	7,586	6,901	7,247	6,462	5,954	13,143	5,587	2,635	486
Osorno, Chile	9,680	11,177	8,898	5,422	8,710	7,610	8,872	9,129	14,095	15,422	5,572	9,364	8,295	8,177	8,974	8,233	415	9,280	11,778	13,361
Ostrava, Czechoslovakia	14,249	6,502	7,606	9,223	9,461	9,799	7,344	7,248	10,214	7,405	9,801	8,717	7,812	8,184	7,447	5,358	13,109	6,508	1,767	754
Ottawa, Canada	9,216	1,935	1,009	4,138	3,055	3,202	782	652	16,234	13,718	4,016	2,501	1,348	1,646	851	7,086	9,113	413	6,704	5,926
Ouagadougou, Bourkina Fasso	16,939	8,990	8,555	7,557	10,672	10,227	8,195	8,297	11,191	8,921	8,547	10,281	8,296	8,679	8,417	1,370	9,240	7,462	2,781	4,957
Oujda, Morocco	15,224	6,908	7,116	7,539	9,241	9,167	6,778	6,791	11,556	8,825	8,332	8,657	7,075	7,480	6,958	3,034	10,809	5,938	795	2,585
Oxford, United Kingdom	13,646	5,473	6,302	7,864	8,254	8,489	6,020	5,946	11,603	8,794	8,415	7,549	6,464	6,844	6,141	4,819	12,033	5,172	1,819	1,010
Pago Pago, American Samoa	2,311	10,595	10,676	11,330	8,529	8,844	11,033	10,967	9,954	12,298	10,356	9,013	10,856	10,460	10,824	17,475	9,738	11,822	17,542	15,402
Pakxe, Laos	10,679	11,620	13,909	17,379	13,790	14,932	13,950	13,690	3,157	2,972	17,227	13,242	14,522	14,617	13,840	12,825	17,596	13,541	9,825	8,832
Palembang, Indonesia	10,888	13,600	15,890	19,225	15,451	16,571	15,945	15,683	1,331	2,974	19,136	15,034	16,513	16,582	15,829	13,196	15,598	15,527	10,934	10,410
Palermo, Italy	15,468	7,370	8,049	8,915	10,083	10,199	7,739	7,701	10,264	7,485	9,660	9,407	8,119	8,516	7,887	4,168	12,141	6,882	629	1,952
Palma, Majorca	14,983	6,709	7,184	7,987	9,261	9,308	6,864	6,843	11,208	8,427	8,718	8,621	7,218	7,619	7,023	3,705	11,464	6,009	498	1,935
Palmerston North, New Zealand	5,425	13,739	13,403	12,624	11,305	11,299	13,730	13,739	8,210	10,996	11,908	11,920	13,392	12,990	13,563	16,468	8,965	14,582	18,964	17,900
Panama, Panama	8,665	5,661	3,375	989	3,756	2,650	3,359	3,611	19,503	17,140	60	4,161	2,776	2,662	3,451	7,221	5,115	3,873	9,084	9,323
Paramaribo, Suriname	11,365	6,749	4,720	1,724	6,049	5,102	4,486	4,747	16,884	14,843	2,756	6,177	4,104	4,274	4,695	4,589	5,077	4,442	7,114	8,089
Paris, France	14,047	5,882	6,667	8,064	8,642	8,848	6,377	6,313	11,333	8,519	8,663	7,946	6,805	7,191	6,506	4,612	12,053	5,525	1,432	1,029
Patna, India	12,637	10,657	12,762	15,428	13,542	14,527	12,666	12,454	4,349	2,140	15,814	12,798	13,250	13,494	12,643	10,436	17,607	12,022	7,393	6,612
Patrai, Greece	15,549	7,739	8,616	9,643	10,589	10,791	8,321	8,263	9,564	6,772	10,373	9,879	8,731	9,122	8,454	4,760	12,782	7,466	1,355	2,054
Peking, China	9,536	8,710	10,999	14,612	10,927	12,056	11,070	10,804	6,095	5,160	14,296	10,330	11,626	11,693	10,941	12,514	19,128	10,762	8,930	7,218
Penrhyn Island (Omoka)	1,216	9,413	9,247	9,890	7,099	7,359	9,599	9,552	11,429	13,654	8,898	7,635	9,391	8,991	9,400	16,121	8,977	10,410	16,606	14,764
Peoria, Illinois	8,019	2,034	469	4,048	1,810	2,082	805	669	16,764	14,623	3,600	1,319	1,060	1,002	566	8,138	8,749	1,520	7,948	7,066
Perm', USSR	12,713	6,798	8,642	11,242	9,931	10,664	8,494	8,308	8,592	6,020	11,557	9,129	9,063	9,350	8,507	7,938	15,667	7,794	4,324	2,631
Perth, Australia	9,812	16,280	18,019	17,312	16,048	16,483	18,348	18,133	2,943	5,753	17,033	16,284	18,435	18,067	18,108	14,281	12,336	18,600	13,626	13,678
Peshawar, Pakistan	13,528	9,638	11,544	13,856	12,724	13,538	11,391	11,209	5,753	3,118	14,343	11,930	11,954	12,249	11,408	8,994	16,814	10,670	5,805	5,051
Petropavlovsk-Kamchatskiy,USSR	6,942	6,004	8,135	11,780	7,564	8,708	8,316	8,046	9,280	8,646	11,170	7,070	8,779	8,723	8,128	13,038	15,672	8,316	9,740	7,562
Petrozavodsk, USSR	12,857	5,920	7,551	9,964	9,055	9,660	7,369	7,205	9,801	7,134	10,321	8,259	7,918	8,232	7,407	6,978	14,427	6,623	3,424	1,424
Pevek, USSR	7,881	4,280	6,534	10,211	6,475	7,574	6,655	6,383	10,622	9,303	9,780	5,825	7,176	7,198	6,497	11,211	14,815	6,523	8,167	5,982
Philadelphia, Pennsylvania	9,220	2,484	809	3,530	2,955	2,879	451	578	16,811	14,219	3,421	2,546	843	1,211	670	6,911	8,505	471	6,914	6,336
Phnom Penh, Kampuchea	10,797	12,025	14,314	17,749	14,171	15,315	14,351	14,093	2,753	2,800	17,632	13,636	14,925	15,023	14,244	12,855	17,197	13,931	9,989	9,102
Phoenix, Arizona	5,873	3,113	2,544	5,083	558	1,660	2,904	2,814	16,243	15,363	4,238	884	2,865	2,528	2,683	10,201	8,773	3,666	10,001	8,826
Pierre, South Dakota	7,303	1,655	1,439	4,921	1,502	2,292	1,750	1,552	16,063	14,323	4,352	719	2,019	1,877	1,511	9,011	9,405	2,311	8,440	7,265
Pinang, Malaysia	11,342	12,775	15,051	18,188	15,015	16,158	15,055	14,806	1,965	2,273	18,370	14,468	15,640	15,775	14,969	12,537	16,462	14,559	9,991	9,372
Pitcairn Island (Adamstown)	4,210	9,864	8,540	7,431	6,769	6,348	8,801	8,898	13,487	16,263	6,642	7,548	8,342	7,965	8,698	13,111	5,522	9,641	15,733	15,465
Pittsburgh, Pennsylvania	8,813	2,267	413	3,676	2,560	2,575	132	185	16,839	14,371	3,442	2,130	721	991	260	7,327	8,586	768	7,259	6,570
Plymouth, Montserrat	10,521	5,347	3,295	1,294	4,757	3,924	3,060	3,322	17,717	15,101	2,081	4,802	2,685	2,881	3,269	5,307	6,034	3,068	7,051	7,538
Plymouth, United Kingdom	13,675	5,444	6,172	7,636	8,157	8,353	5,882	5,818	11,804	8,991	8,204	7,469	6,310	6,695	6,011	4,619	11,782	5,029	1,781	1,260
Ponape Island	4,936	10,352	11,806	14,360	10,109	10,980	12,124	11,912	7,113	8,652	13,339	10,131	12,320	12,046	11,886	17,987	13,872	12,537	14,380	12,385
Ponce, Puerto Rico	10,047	5,045	2,908	1,152	4,277	3,435	2,705	2,973	18,133	15,422	1,725	4,350	2,279	2,440	2,899	5,779	6,108	2,831	7,367	7,697
Ponta Delgada, Azores	13,402	5,309	5,049	5,556	7,197	7,030	4,699	4,745	13,669	10,889	6,256	6,690	4,946	5,351	4,896	3,348	9,587	3,888	2,862	3,472
Pontianak, Indonesia	10,368	13,178	15,457	19,085	14,871	15,982	15,549	15,281	1,913	3,364	18,568	14,485	16,094	16,117	15,411	13,642	15,916	15,222	11,153	10,435
Port Augusta, Australia	7,786	15,206	16,169	16,059	14,060	14,418	16,529	16,406	4,749	7,520	15,384	14,424	16,428	16,037	16,301	16,139	11,691	17,201	15,563	15,099
Port Blair, India	12,119	12,182	14,385	17,141	14,794	15,891	14,327	14,099	2,649	1,508	17,551	14,134	14,917	15,123	14,280	11,570	16,874	13,731	8,914	8,334
Port Elizabeth, South Africa	16,449	14,855	13,893	11,093	15,574	14,580	13,558	13,746	7,554	7,286	12,017	15,597	13,406	13,682	13,799	6,356	8,513	13,023	8,032	10,009
Port Hedland, Australia	9,457	15,000	16,982	18,367	15,380	16,133	17,241	16,986	2,497	5,200	17,703	15,402	17,564	17,326	17,022	14,782	13,563	17,300	13,257	12,848

Distances in Kilometers	Christmas Is. [Pacific Ocean]	Churchill, Canada	Cincinnati, Ohio	Ciudad Bolivia, Venezuela	Ciudad Juarez, Mexico	Ciudad Victoria, Mexico	Clarksburg, West Virginia	Cleveland, Ohio	Cocos (Keeling) Island	Colombo, Sri Lanka	Colon, Panama	Colorado Springs, Colorado	Columbia, South Carolina	Columbus, Georgia	Columbus, Ohio	Conakry, Guinea	Concepcion, Chile	Concord, New Hampshire	Constantine, Algeria	Copenhagen, Denmark
Port Louis, Mauritius	15,723	15,154	15,831	14,303	17,972	17,590	15,482	15,517	4,294	3,870	15,309	17,338	15,674	16,067	15,677	8,459	11,847	14,661	8,232	9,409
Port Moresby, Papua New Guinea	6,259	12,535	13,944	15,885	12,106	12,842	14,274	14,074	5,507	7,685	14,870	12,226	14,415	14,107	14,034	17,940	13,388	14,723	15,056	13,543
Port Said, Egypt	16,182	8,872	9,850	10,741	11,797	12,028	9,557	9,496	8,382	5,622	11,528	11,070	9,968	10,360	9,688	5,321	13,281	8,703	2,436	3,121
Port Sudan, Sudan	17,131	10,252	11,133	11,541	13,138	13,281	10,824	10,785	7,409	4,810	12,433	12,429	11,194	11,594	10,972	5,583	13,072	9,967	3,514	4,503
Port-au-Prince, Haiti	9,441	4,803	2,565	1,143	3,721	2,838	2,426	2,697	18,658	15,867	1,302	3,857	1,919	1,996	2,587	6,385	6,129	2,737	7,844	8,010
Port-of-Spain, Trin. & Tobago	10,636	5,999	3,891	1,026	5,171	4,239	3,680	3,947	17,669	15,330	2,020	5,303	3,262	3,410	3,879	5,236	5,393	3,736	7,362	8,039
Port-Vila, Vanuatu	4,334	12,110	12,701	13,588	10,594	11,042	13,061	12,950	7,677	10,088	12,628	10,964	12,974	12,592	12,835	19,071	11,196	13,774	17,277	15,325
Portland, Maine	9,640	2,342	1,293	3,912	3,424	3,440	972	968	16,286	13,651	3,913	2,924	1,421	1,788	1,134	6,617	8,918	115	6,377	5,757
Portland, Oregon	5,907	2,413	3,190	6,448	2,071	3,214	3,507	3,303	14,754	13,780	5,711	1,643	3,737	3,527	3,268	10,695	10,389	4,011	9,608	8,031
Porto, Portugal	14,293	5,978	6,257	7,065	8,361	8,356	5,928	5,922	12,172	9,381	7,765	7,754	6,263	6,665	6,097	3,541	10,844	5,078	1,424	2,234
Porto Alegre, Brazil	11,698	10,615	8,401	4,730	8,994	7,854	8,251	8,522	14,235	14,316	5,338	9,440	7,755	7,786	8,422	5,938	2,161	8,375	9,514	11,254
Porto Alexandre, Angola	18,096	12,420	11,649	9,469	13,588	12,815	11,297	11,454	9,128	7,900	10,487	13,403	11,245	11,575	11,535	3,977	8,532	10,679	5,802	7,921
Porto Novo, Benin	17,637	9,782	9,314	8,071	11,415	10,914	8,954	9,064	10,623	8,529	9,085	11,050	9,030	9,407	9,180	1,831	9,181	8,236	3,334	5,526
Porto Velho, Brazil	10,452	7,961	5,712	2,032	6,372	5,255	5,584	5,856	16,886	16,036	2,677	6,759	5,067	5,083	5,743	5,919	3,243	5,807	8,882	9,971
Portsmouth, United Kingdom	13,748	5,561	6,355	7,854	8,321	8,540	6,069	6,000	11,589	8,777	8,421	7,622	6,505	6,889	6,194	4,719	11,977	5,219	1,714	1,061
Poznan, Poland	13,954	6,214	7,367	9,111	9,193	9,558	7,113	7,009	10,380	7,580	9,652	8,442	7,593	7,959	7,209	5,505	13,145	6,284	1,960	462
Prague, Czechoslovakia	14,185	6,321	7,364	8,948	9,245	9,557	7,096	7,006	10,485	7,675	9,527	8,510	7,558	7,932	7,205	5,195	12,875	6,256	1,650	634
Praia, Cape Verde Islands	14,634	7,483	6,485	5,173	8,501	7,921	6,132	6,286	13,587	11,244	6,153	8,242	6,119	6,475	6,368	1,222	7,731	5,524	3,819	5,471
Pretoria, South Africa	17,306	14,268	13,666	11,287	15,581	14,731	13,314	13,466	7,319	6,654	12,269	15,421	13,259	13,582	13,551	5,982	9,258	12,678	7,238	9,142
Prince Albert, Canada	7,391	952	2,254	5,895	2,385	3,319	2,475	2,218	15,016	13,320	5,387	1,599	2,893	2,840	2,265	9,304	10,463	2,743	8,147	6,688
Prince Edward Island	14,842	16,589	15,348	12,093	16,570	15,439	15,047	15,267	6,686	7,231	12,877	16,882	14,784	14,988	15,282	8,049	8,495	14,624	9,707	11,579
Prince George, Canada	6,575	1,835	3,309	6,853	2,785	3,888	3,563	3,317	14,205	12,938	6,234	2,158	3,929	3,813	3,342	10,373	11,129	3,869	8,888	7,192
Prince Rupert, Canada	6,310	2,252	3,803	7,324	3,141	4,269	4,060	3,813	13,771	12,659	6,676	2,578	4,420	4,294	3,838	10,806	11,488	4,356	9,146	7,352
Providence, Rhode Island	9,544	2,459	1,151	3,709	3,298	3,257	808	858	16,511	13,871	3,691	2,841	1,212	1,588	998	6,650	8,711	155	6,540	5,968
Provo, Utah	6,264	2,403	2,324	5,386	1,052	2,174	2,671	2,517	15,822	14,652	4,641	608	2,792	2,533	2,433	10,001	9,402	3,323	9,444	8,148
Puerto Aisen, Chile	9,763	11,711	9,434	5,957	9,199	8,111	9,410	9,667	13,562	14,994	6,108	9,868	8,833	8,712	9,511	8,458	952	9,816	12,046	13,737
Puerto Deseado, Argentina	10,294	12,085	9,796	6,231	9,692	8,587	9,746	10,009	13,170	14,447	6,476	10,337	9,179	9,086	9,862	8,158	1,347	10,092	11,769	13,584
Puerto Princesa, Philippines	9,294	11,861	14,091	17,762	13,371	14,483	14,234	13,962	3,413	4,292	17,067	13,000	14,737	14,705	14,068	14,351	16,780	14,051	11,295	10,112
Punta Arenas, Chile	9,957	12,581	10,305	6,815	10,015	8,944	10,281	10,538	12,693	14,241	6,980	10,703	9,704	9,582	10,382	8,788	1,821	10,677	12,403	14,265
Pusan, South Korea	8,380	8,864	11,097	14,776	10,612	11,756	11,235	10,963	6,222	5,907	14,225	10,127	11,742	11,729	11,070	13,713	18,028	11,086	10,109	8,292
Pyongyang, North Korea	8,726	8,560	10,823	14,498	10,499	11,642	10,937	10,667	6,396	5,803	14,032	9,965	11,465	11,481	10,785	13,200	18,357	10,734	9,592	7,768
Qamdo, China	11,345	9,985	12,223	15,445	12,610	13,686	12,201	11,959	4,777	3,236	15,509	11,927	12,790	12,958	12,130	11,410	18,925	11,691	8,087	6,888
Qandahar, Afghanistan	14,134	9,821	11,600	13,608	12,949	13,677	11,416	11,254	5,853	3,098	14,192	12,148	11,959	12,281	11,456	8,471	16,214	10,654	5,406	4,890
Qiqian, China	9,265	7,307	9,597	13,209	9,634	10,743	9,665	9,399	7,477	6,253	12,903	8,997	10,222	10,296	9,538	11,917	17,985	9,367	8,312	6,362
Qom, Iran	14,989	9,159	10,644	12,248	12,287	12,815	10,412	10,288	7,082	4,269	12,910	11,495	10,912	11,269	10,490	7,098	15,023	9,599	3,987	3,735
Quebec, Canada	9,568	2,018	1,379	4,264	3,432	3,569	1,118	1,024	15,987	13,405	4,232	2,861	1,647	1,977	1,218	6,796	9,267	402	6,326	5,569
Quetta, Pakistan	14,108	9,993	11,788	13,795	13,116	13,857	11,606	11,443	5,659	2,905	14,386	12,316	12,151	12,470	11,645	8,600	16,270	10,846	5,576	5,084
Quito, Ecuador	8,800	6,681	4,397	1,293	4,604	3,463	4,378	4,631	18,563	17,519	1,071	5,091	3,796	3,681	4,473	7,257	4,093	4,860	9,589	10,096
Rabaul, Papua New Guinea	5,636	11,754	13,142	15,287	11,332	12,106	13,471	13,270	6,151	8,131	14,256	11,430	13,621	13,321	13,231	18,368	13,492	13,923	15,010	13,266
Raiatea (Uturoa)	2,176	9,848	9,296	9,320	7,196	7,236	9,628	9,629	11,878	14,359	8,385	7,835	9,326	8,921	9,455	15,390	7,897	10,475	16,948	15,477
Raleigh, North Carolina	8,883	2,795	638	3,146	2,610	2,382	418	689	17,333	14,774	2,927	2,338	296	692	603	7,139	8,059	1,026	7,398	6,886
Rangiroa (Avatoru)	2,162	9,496	8,871	8,890	6,784	6,798	9,200	9,207	12,321	14,773	7,948	7,438	8,890	8,485	9,031	15,002	7,676	10,050	16,535	15,181
Rangoon, Burma	11,687	11,581	13,818	16,871	14,121	15,227	13,788	13,549	3,184	2,083	17,081	13,474	14,378	14,554	13,722	11,787	17,547	13,246	8,885	8,083
Raoul Is., Kermadec Islands	4,083	12,397	12,265	12,145	10,126	10,263	12,609	12,582	8,917	11,577	11,291	10,686	12,345	11,941	12,421	17,276	9,298	13,439	19,116	16,957
Rarotonga (Avarua)	2,576	10,689	10,277	10,266	8,159	8,238	10,613	10,604	10,892	13,442	9,354	8,770	10,325	9,920	10,435	16,175	8,349	11,455	17,876	16,126
Rawson, Argentina	10,359	11,624	9,333	5,746	9,318	8,199	9,274	9,538	13,614	14,729	6,022	9,938	8,711	8,631	9,396	7,821	987	9,603	11,419	13,165
Recife, Brazil	13,646	9,079	7,308	4,353	8,773	7,813	7,028	7,269	14,249	12,842	5,349	8,869	6,731	6,948	7,256	3,048	5,000	6,778	6,556	8,305
Regina, Canada	7,307	1,144	2,019	5,625	2,084	3,003	2,268	2,024	15,317	13,632	5,092	1,291	2,648	2,568	2,048	9,264	10,153	2,624	8,277	6,894
Reykjavik, Iceland	11,822	3,683	4,866	7,270	6,621	7,037	4,647	4,511	12,573	9,884	7,557	5,871	5,176	5,511	4,713	6,099	12,057	3,868	3,635	2,116
Rhodes, Greece	15,711	8,191	9,177	10,244	11,112	11,361	8,890	8,822	8,955	6,164	10,981	10,384	9,313	9,701	9,016	5,169	13,202	8,038	1,934	2,444
Richmond, Virginia	9,004	2,648	641	3,307	2,727	2,571	318	571	17,119	14,550	3,131	2,393	511	889	552	7,061	8,247	804	7,211	6,667
Riga, USSR	13,469	6,065	7,451	9,517	9,140	9,619	7,228	7,096	10,097	7,341	9,976	8,363	7,745	8,089	7,298	6,187	13,753	6,432	2,633	726
Ringkobing, Denmark	13,440	5,540	6,671	8,547	8,497	8,861	6,421	6,314	11,018	8,233	9,035	7,750	6,909	7,271	6,514	5,510	12,818	5,597	2,195	275
Rio Branco, Brazil	10,027	7,978	5,701	2,049	6,186	5,052	5,605	5,873	17,050	16,460	2,524	6,626	5,063	5,038	5,746	6,367	3,023	5,900	9,299	10,319
Rio Cuarto, Argentina	10,431	10,551	8,264	4,638	8,434	7,296	8,186	8,453	14,629	15,327	4,984	8,998	7,633	7,577	8,318	7,142	894	8,485	10,656	12,228
Rio de Janeiro, Brazil	12,588	10,183	8,098	4,563	9,049	7,947	7,893	8,159	14,204	13,700	5,358	9,370	7,462	7,566	8,091	4,818	3,249	7,872	8,395	10,173
Rio Gallegos, Argentina	10,064	12,444	10,162	6,647	9,928	8,846	10,130	10,389	12,828	14,299	6,836	10,604	9,556	9,443	10,236	8,600	1,672	10,511	12,214	14,064
Rio Grande, Brazil	11,587	10,788	8,560	4,882	9,088	7,945	8,419	8,690	14,122	14,331	5,454	9,555	7,914	7,933	8,585	6,148	1,995	8,564	9,731	11,485
Riyadh, Saudi Arabia	16,077	10,086	11,325	12,313	13,151	13,517	11,053	10,967	6,786	4,036	13,120	12,383	11,496	11,879	11,165	6,595	14,197	10,207	4,030	4,424
Road Town, Brit. Virgin Isls.	10,256	5,074	2,988	1,289	4,441	3,625	2,763	3,028	17,917	15,219	1,932	4,482	2,373	2,562	2,967	5,570	6,183	2,821	7,162	7,533
Roanoke, Virginia	8,782	2,599	449	3,340	2,505	2,368	226	493	17,187	14,683	3,091	2,184	378	706	400	7,275	8,236	971	7,420	6,833
Robinson Crusoe Island, Chile	9,088	10,336	8,074	4,729	7,794	6,702	8,074	8,324	14,934	16,334	4,760	8,459	7,489	7,344	8,160	8,370	637	8,541	11,774	13,102
Rochester, New York	9,043	2,074	734	3,918	2,833	2,923	488	384	16,510	14,012	3,751	2,329	1,060	1,352	573	7,181	8,871	494	6,946	6,212
Rockhampton, Australia	6,287	13,659	14,591	15,350	12,522	13,001	14,948	14,810	5,799	8,374	14,460	12,837	14,909	14,535	14,715	17,746	11,933	15,594	16,279	15,051
Rome, Italy	15,042	6,978	7,743	8,822	9,744	9,913	7,444	7,392	10,432	7,630	9,519	9,053	7,847	8,240	7,582	4,410	12,297	6,588	796	1,531
Rosario, Argentina	10,775	10,626	8,349	4,690	8,628	7,485	8,251	8,520	14,491	15,035	5,108	9,164	7,711	7,677	8,394	6,844	1,210	8,505	10,382	12,012
Roseau, Dominica	10,618	5,524	3,471	1,260	4,909	4,056	3,237	3,500	17,653	15,098	2,115	4,969	2,860	3,050	3,446	5,215	5,899	3,241	7,062	7,612
Rostock, East Germany	13,717	5,870	6,995	8,785	8,830	9,186	6,741	6,637	10,736	7,941	9,304	8,083	7,222	7,588	6,837	5,452	12,934	5,912	2,015	179
Rostov-na-Donu, USSR	14,300	7,522	8,964	10,824	10,629	11,132	8,737	8,608	8,660	5,871	11,378	9,844	9,246	9,596	8,811	6,519	14,508	7,932	2,974	2,087
Rotterdam, Netherlands	13,797	5,726	6,655	8,258	8,574	8,847	6,381	6,299	11,208	8,401	8,811	7,855	6,836	7,213	6,495	4,985	12,370	5,538	1,736	676
Rouyn, Canada	8,995	1,534	1,107	4,492	2,949	3,247	1,001	778	15,969	13,555	4,309	2,317	1,590	1,822	973	7,403	9,441	806	6,812	5,883
Sacramento, California	5,464	2,974	3,188	6,081	1,562	2,681	3,537	3,381	15,224	14,508	5,256	1,448	3,639	3,357	3,299	10,865	9,719	4,178	10,149	8,694
Saginaw, Michigan	8,538	1,842	484	4,100	2,366	2,592	550	283	16,520	14,194	3,795	1,821	1,077	1,221	393	7,693	8,957	1,005	7,390	6,534
Saint Denis, Reunion	15,884	15,147	15,710	14,083	17,859	17,398	15,357	15,405	4,514	4,071	15,086	17,272	15,525	15,912	15,559	8,275	11,650	14,547	8,154	9,395
Saint George's, Grenada	10,602	5,845	3,746	1,049	5,064	4,152	3,531	3,798	17,705	15,291	2,007	5,179	3,121	3,278	3,732	5,255	5,539	3,580	7,294	7,927
Saint John, Canada	9,971	2,412	1,667	4,114	3,785	3,820	1,351	1,333	15,978	13,304	4,195	3,255	1,790	2,163	1,507	6,360	9,120	494	6,001	5,390
Saint John's, Antigua	10,558	5,321	3,283	1,353	4,770	3,948	3,043	3,304	17,670	15,046	2,133	4,805	2,678	2,882	3,254	5,269	6,084	3,036	6,994	7,479
Saint John's, Canada	10,953	2,975	2,722	4,664	4,828	4,865	2,403	2,385	15,154	12,394	4,948	4,261	2,802	3,191	2,562	5,584	9,565	1,547	4,946	4,437
Saint Louis, Missouri	7,917	2,257	496	3,887	1,665	1,855	856	792	16,976	14,859	3,400	1,271	968	830	638	8,184	8,538	1,648	8,116	7,280
Saint Paul, Minnesota	7,865	1,537	962	4,600	1,871	2,416	1,226	1,001	16,234	14,216	4,142	1,185	1,595	1,553	997	8,434	9,279	1,733	7,934	6,871
Saint Peter Port, UK	13,824	5,599	6,317	7,725	8,309	8,496	6,025	5,964	11,690	8,876	8,310	7,622	6,447	6,834	6,156	4,548	11,806	5,171	1,631	1,233
Saipan (Susupe)	6,394	10,200	12,062	15,255	10,748	11,768	12,323	12,073	6,168	7,231	14,314	10,576	12,662	12,478	12,102	16,470	15,505	12,516	12,875	11,023
Salalah, Oman	15,969	11,124	12,457	13,328	14,231	14,650	12,190	12,099	5,691	3,013	14,187	13,448	12,638	13,020	12,298	7,364	14,416	11,347	5,127	5,538
Salem, Oregon	5,837	2,484	3,224	6,453	2,052	3,196	3,544	3,344	14,761	13,824	5,706	1,652	3,764	3,548	3,305	10,748	10,357	4,060	9,680	8,104
Salt Lake City, Utah	6,277	2,359	2,337	5,431	1,112	2,232	2,683	2,523	15,770	14,591	4,692	641	2,817	2,563	2,444	10,007	9,461	3,322	9,417	8,107
Salta, Argentina	10,322	9,630	7,346	3,708	7,629	6,485	7,260	7,528	15,508	15,837	4,092	8,151	6,712	6,668	7,396	6,772	1,521	7,554	10,142	11,533
Salto, Uruguay	11,038	10,536	8,273	4,597	8,657	7,513	8,159	8,430	14,508	14,877	5,080	9,163	7,631	7,618	8,311	6,535	1,515	8,374	10,077	11,725
Salvador, Brazil	13,213	9,394	7,484	4,258	8,767	7,744	7,231	7,484	14,378	13,259	5,200	8,948	6,877	7,052	7,449	3,703	4,335	7,072	7,229	8,969
Salzburg, Austria	14,414	6,465	7,414	8,849	9,338	9,604	7,136	7,058	10,531	7,717	9,463	8,617	7,580	7,961	7,254	4,932	12,663	6,288	1,375	876
Samsun, Turkey	15,014	8,015	9,283	10,788	11,069	11,473	9,029	8,925	8,552	5,738	11,436	10,301	9,504	9,873	9,125	6,026	14,060	8,197	2,624	2,353
San Antonio, Texas	6,929	3,276	1,673	3,735	808	634	1,990	2,023	17,518	15,978	2,948	1,195	1,727	1,333	1,834	8,998	7,801	2,844	9,334	8,554
San Cristobal, Venezuela	9,471	5,956	3,682	195	4,429	3,370	3,584	3,852	18,746	16,531	862	4,741	3,042	3,036	3,724	6,436	4,938	3,927	8,507	8,974
San Diego, California	5,417	3,367	3,013	5,496	1,011	2,025	3,373	3,273	15,869	15,266	4,616	1,304	3,347	3,008	3,149	10,681	8,961	4,119	10,387	9,116
San Francisco, California	5,344	3,093	3,289	6,128	1,603	2,706	3,639	3,487	15,192	14,547	5,290	1,541	3,729	3,439	3,402	10,971	9,696	4,289	10,270	8,809
San Jose, Costa Rica	8,166	5,483	3,231	1,496	3,341	2,211	3,272	3,505	19,760	17,441	463	3,810	2,683	2,496	3,329	7,706	5,304	3,883	9,427	9,518
San Juan, Argentina	10,036	10,284	7,993	4,419	8,065	6,931	7,935	8,199	14,943	15,754	4,686	8,650	7,371	7,292	8,056	7,392	721	8,281	10,849	12,318
San Juan, Puerto Rico	10,098	5,017	2,895	1,218	4,300	3,472	2,685	2,952	18,067	15,350	1,796	4,358	2,271	2,443	2,882	5,728	6,164	2,790	7,295	7,626
San Luis Potosi, Mexico	6,503	4,101	2,446	3,596	1,194	258	2,728	2,803	17,826	16,786	2,660	1,885	2,352	1,949	2,606	9,343	7,158	3,583	10,038	9,370
San Marino, San Marino	14,825	6,792	7,616	8,815	9,594	9,794	7,323	7,263	10,481	7,672	9,484	8,892	7,740	8,129	7,455	4,575	12,411	6,469	975	1,307
San Miguel de Tucuman, Argen.	10,345	9,853	7,568	3,933	7,821	6,678	7,484	7,752	15,297	15,728	4,306	8,354	6,936	6,887	7,619	6,860	1,334	7,780	10,271	11,706

Distances in Kilometers	Christmas Is. [Pacific Ocean]	Churchill, Canada	Cincinnati, Ohio	Ciudad Bolivia, Venezuela	Ciudad Juarez, Mexico	Ciudad Victoria, Mexico	Clarksburg, West Virginia	Cleveland, Ohio	Cocos (Keeling) Island	Colombo, Sri Lanka	Colon, Panama	Colorado Springs, Colorado	Columbia, South Carolina	Columbus, Georgia	Columbus, Ohio	Conakry, Guinea	Concepcion, Chile	Concord, New Hampshire	Constantine, Algeria	Copenhagen, Denmark
San Salvador, El Salvador	7,624	5,017	2,852	2,119	2,664	1,525	2,965	3,165	19,353	17,429	1,122	3,181	2,394	2,122	2,973	8,214	5,844	3,682	9,631	9,484
Sanaa, Yemen	16,958	10,964	11,973	12,378	13,935	14,137	11,672	11,622	6,541	3,998	13,289	13,201	12,056	12,454	11,812	6,313	13,437	10,815	4,386	5,224
Santa Cruz, Bolivia	10,547	8,944	6,680	3,005	7,171	6,032	6,567	6,837	16,053	15,846	3,523	7,625	6,038	6,029	6,718	6,219	2,321	6,809	9,464	10,762
Santa Cruz, Tenerife	14,693	6,661	6,287	6,098	8,432	8,139	5,930	6,006	12,889	10,242	6,952	7,978	6,104	6,503	6,142	2,112	9,352	5,157	2,315	3,795
Santa Fe, New Mexico	6,487	2,707	1,931	4,697	441	1,478	2,291	2,200	16,533	15,249	3,932	364	2,279	1,963	2,069	9,602	8,719	3,054	9,423	8,334
Santa Rosa, Argentina	10,434	10,926	8,637	5,021	8,751	7,617	8,564	8,830	14,274	15,117	5,346	9,333	8,008	7,945	8,693	7,346	783	8,870	10,898	12,536
Santa Rosalia, Mexico	5,574	3,765	2,884	4,862	745	1,379	3,235	3,197	16,549	15,999	3,938	1,454	3,071	2,690	3,038	10,369	8,203	4,054	10,498	9,437
Santarem, Brazil	11,455	7,619	5,520	2,127	6,643	5,614	5,312	5,579	16,500	14,973	3,085	6,866	4,887	5,011	5,510	4,733	4,249	5,329	7,652	8,831
Santiago del Estero, Argentina	10,439	9,980	7,697	4,055	7,963	6,820	7,610	7,878	15,159	15,597	4,442	8,495	7,063	7,019	7,747	6,830	1,299	7,895	10,268	11,740
Santiago, Chile	9,844	10,447	8,159	4,626	8,136	7,011	8,114	8,375	14,805	15,794	4,838	8,746	7,544	7,449	8,227	7,670	434	8,489	11,139	12,609
Santo Domingo, Dominican Rep.	9,698	4,886	2,687	1,122	3,948	3,087	2,518	2,789	18,436	15,673	1,476	4,054	2,046	2,164	2,695	6,128	6,130	2,747	7,632	7,864
Sao Paulo de Olivenca, Brazil	9,892	7,252	4,980	1,320	5,572	4,456	4,877	5,146	17,686	16,541	1,878	5,966	4,339	4,327	5,021	6,276	3,722	5,174	8,941	9,783
Sao Paulo, Brazil	12,236	10,111	7,978	4,386	8,831	7,717	7,789	8,058	14,427	14,033	5,135	9,186	7,336	7,418	7,979	5,118	2,927	7,818	8,673	10,400
Sao Tome, Sao Tome & Principe	18,268	10,600	10,097	8,615	12,176	11,615	9,737	9,857	10,037	8,149	9,643	11,841	9,788	10,156	9,966	2,483	9,126	9,035	3,989	6,158
Sapporo, Japan	7,547	7,624	9,805	13,465	9,233	10,376	9,970	9,699	7,592	7,187	12,861	8,759	10,451	10,409	9,790	13,662	17,025	9,906	10,091	8,052
Sarajevo, Yugoslavia	14,914	7,064	8,010	9,292	9,945	10,197	7,726	7,655	10,016	7,204	9,956	9,224	8,160	8,545	7,849	4,908	12,825	6,876	1,302	1,380
Saratov, USSR	13,669	7,256	8,875	11,053	10,395	10,999	8,680	8,526	8,568	5,841	11,514	9,597	9,217	9,544	8,729	7,116	15,041	7,911	3,527	2,237
Saskatoon, Canada	7,278	1,080	2,236	5,855	2,264	3,215	2,473	2,223	15,085	13,433	5,324	1,483	2,870	2,798	2,257	9,379	10,381	2,783	8,268	6,821
Schefferville, Canada	9,874	1,712	2,191	5,162	4,027	4,359	2,000	1,839	15,047	12,499	5,171	3,339	2,563	2,863	2,042	6,842	10,171	1,334	5,787	4,768
Seattle, Washington	6,084	2,232	3,173	6,520	2,216	3,352	3,476	3,260	14,646	13,585	5,813	1,718	3,743	3,556	3,240	10,594	10,557	3,935	9,415	7,813
Sendai, Japan	7,420	8,118	10,271	13,909	9,591	10,730	10,448	10,178	7,207	7,020	13,256	9,157	10,915	10,855	10,262	14,100	17,039	10,411	10,505	8,508
Seoul, South Korea	8,598	8,673	10,926	14,606	10,543	11,687	11,050	10,778	6,327	5,837	14,108	10,027	11,570	11,575	10,892	13,390	18,247	10,866	9,783	7,962
Sept-Iles, Canada	9,923	2,014	1,886	4,656	3,882	4,079	1,637	1,528	15,502	12,891	4,696	3,262	2,162	2,497	1,727	6,597	9,664	871	5,872	5,052
Sevastopol, USSR	14,730	7,584	8,858	10,462	10,635	11,046	8,607	8,500	8,928	6,117	11,077	9,868	9,089	9,455	8,701	5,963	13,967	7,780	2,444	1,925
Seville, Spain	14,759	6,446	6,647	7,211	8,769	8,712	6,311	6,320	11,942	9,181	7,966	8,182	6,618	7,023	6,489	3,183	10,729	5,468	1,128	2,465
Shanghai, China	9,053	9,518	11,785	15,458	11,422	12,566	11,896	11,625	5,444	5,078	14,989	10,910	12,426	12,444	11,745	13,451	18,550	11,671	9,915	8,276
Sheffield, United Kingdom	13,480	5,332	6,219	7,883	8,146	8,410	5,944	5,862	11,622	8,819	8,408	7,433	6,400	6,776	6,059	4,985	12,126	5,101	1,992	945
Shenyang, China	8,954	8,334	10,611	14,272	10,397	11,534	10,710	10,440	6,552	5,773	13,862	9,831	11,249	11,284	10,566	12,847	18,499	10,471	9,236	7,403
Shiraz, Iran	15,280	9,739	11,198	12,631	12,866	13,376	10,959	10,841	6,616	3,805	13,348	12,075	11,448	11,811	11,043	7,204	14,958	10,137	4,316	4,273
Sibiu, Romania	14,709	7,116	8,228	9,714	10,088	10,420	7,961	7,870	9,655	6,841	10,339	9,342	8,422	8,797	8,068	5,399	13,328	7,121	1,801	1,364
Singapore	10,973	13,163	15,453	18,781	15,160	16,298	15,493	15,234	1,661	2,736	18,759	14,690	16,067	16,157	15,385	13,015	16,056	15,056	10,577	9,970
Sioux Falls, South Dakota	7,540	1,702	1,134	4,656	1,565	2,208	1,447	1,254	16,276	14,404	4,124	856	1,722	1,602	1,208	8,727	9,218	2,035	8,262	7,171
Skelleftea, Sweden	12,599	5,266	6,820	9,243	8,381	8,945	6,630	6,471	10,546	7,876	9,579	7,592	7,176	7,494	6,674	6,699	13,822	5,878	3,300	1,113
Skopje, Yugoslavia	15,133	7,369	8,333	9,565	10,265	10,519	8,049	7,977	9,716	6,907	10,247	9,541	8,480	8,866	8,172	4,977	12,955	7,198	1,426	1,651
Socotra Island (Tamrida)	16,188	11,583	12,851	13,479	14,675	15,042	12,573	12,494	5,459	2,902	14,384	13,899	13,000	13,389	12,691	7,389	14,130	11,723	5,403	5,956
Sofia, Bulgaria	15,057	7,380	8,400	9,703	10,308	10,590	8,122	8,044	9,598	6,787	10,373	9,575	8,563	8,946	8,240	5,144	13,124	7,274	1,594	1,638
Songkhla, Thailand	11,301	12,576	14,852	18,033	14,832	15,975	14,858	14,608	2,164	2,293	18,172	14,277	15,442	15,576	14,770	12,521	16,661	14,367	9,898	9,227
Sorong, Indonesia	7,933	12,480	14,438	17,478	13,080	14,041	14,687	14,431	3,994	5,774	16,460	12,952	15,043	14,860	14,471	16,040	15,141	14,802	13,112	11,842
South Georgia Island	12,134	13,539	11,306	7,626	11,627	10,489	11,170	11,442	11,469	12,339	8,126	12,186	10,661	10,664	11,335	7,391	3,375	11,295	10,867	12,989
South Pole	10,220	16,517	14,332	10,926	13,514	12,628	14,352	14,598	8,675	10,769	11,038	14,302	13,766	13,596	14,428	11,057	5,925	14,788	14,030	16,176
South Sandwich Islands	12,492	14,221	12,015	8,338	12,374	11,237	11,865	12,136	10,728	11,624	8,863	12,931	11,369	11,386	12,037	7,546	4,100	11,945	10,880	13,054
Split, Yugoslavia	14,929	7,007	7,903	9,136	9,857	10,086	7,615	7,548	10,160	7,350	9,806	9,144	8,040	8,427	7,742	4,766	12,667	6,763	1,154	1,379
Spokane, Washington	6,362	1,968	2,805	6,193	1,998	3,111	3,106	2,890	14,935	13,724	5,516	1,414	3,381	3,205	2,871	10,240	10,346	3,570	9,168	7,641
Spoleto, Italy	14,957	6,913	7,708	8,840	9,698	9,881	7,411	7,356	10,432	7,626	9,525	9,001	7,821	8,212	7,547	4,492	12,362	6,556	880	1,438
Springbok, South Africa	16,903	14,032	13,024	10,321	14,752	13,802	12,689	12,875	8,304	7,756	11,274	14,736	12,544	12,828	12,929	5,502	8,181	12,154	7,404	9,468
Springfield, Illinois	7,992	2,131	449	3,968	1,762	1,992	801	698	16,860	14,720	3,508	1,311	1,001	916	569	8,140	8,654	1,555	8,005	7,147
Springfield, Massachusetts	9,447	2,380	1,062	3,745	3,207	3,188	727	760	16,516	13,901	3,697	2,741	1,165	1,531	907	6,753	8,741	150	6,618	6,013
Srinagar, India	13,255	9,666	11,628	14,067	12,718	13,574	11,491	11,300	5,607	3,051	14,511	11,931	12,061	12,343	11,497	9,293	17,107	10,791	6,080	5,251
Stanley, Falkland Islands	10,849	12,677	10,388	6,764	10,391	9,276	10,314	10,581	12,540	13,721	7,089	11,018	9,760	9,694	10,445	7,989	2,041	10,598	11,594	13,547
Stara Zagora, Bulgaria	15,077	7,501	8,563	9,896	10,453	10,755	8,289	8,206	9,410	6,597	10,563	9,714	8,736	9,116	8,403	5,287	13,284	7,443	1,766	1,749
Stockholm, Sweden	13,194	5,640	7,007	9,135	8,703	9,175	6,786	6,652	10,519	7,774	9,565	7,929	7,305	7,648	6,855	6,136	13,499	5,992	2,684	523
Stornoway, United Kingdom	12,860	4,741	5,761	7,726	7,621	7,953	5,508	5,404	11,906	9,134	8,163	6,889	5,995	6,357	5,604	5,439	12,211	4,683	2,610	1,184
Strasbourg, France	14,225	6,159	7,033	8,458	8,982	9,220	6,750	6,678	10,933	8,119	9,063	8,271	7,187	7,570	6,873	4,773	12,368	5,900	1,360	854
Stuttgart, West Germany	14,238	6,208	7,115	8,565	9,051	9,303	6,834	6,759	10,832	8,018	9,166	8,336	7,276	7,657	6,954	4,848	12,469	5,986	1,393	802
Subic, Philippines	9,126	11,269	13,502	17,178	12,846	13,971	13,642	13,370	3,937	4,494	16,535	12,445	14,148	14,123	13,477	14,277	17,245	13,462	11,044	9,721
Suchow, China	9,456	9,296	11,581	15,218	11,393	12,532	11,665	11,397	5,555	4,881	14,853	10,832	12,214	12,265	11,530	12,930	19,055	11,380	9,390	7,766
Sucre, Bolivia	10,325	9,017	6,740	3,084	7,134	5,991	6,643	6,912	16,059	16,031	3,527	7,617	6,102	6,073	6,785	6,480	2,114	6,921	9,723	10,999
Sudbury, Canada	8,821	1,621	871	4,344	2,726	3,003	804	559	16,175	13,792	4,117	2,120	1,389	1,595	744	7,513	9,264	832	7,029	6,126
Suez, Egypt	16,312	9,013	9,970	10,800	11,928	12,145	9,675	9,617	8,301	5,555	11,600	11,205	10,080	10,473	9,809	5,305	13,235	8,820	2,512	3,262
Sundsvall, Sweden	12,852	5,352	6,799	9,079	8,438	8,950	6,592	6,446	10,646	7,935	9,459	7,658	7,124	7,456	6,649	6,378	13,572	5,817	2,987	795
Surabaya, Indonesia	10,015	13,851	16,080	19,649	15,138	16,167	16,225	15,954	1,824	3,976	18,624	14,882	16,726	16,672	16,059	14,141	15,088	15,999	11,933	11,308
Suva, Fiji	3,450	11,568	11,860	12,518	9,720	10,077	12,218	12,136	8,731	11,158	11,564	10,162	12,070	11,677	12,003	18,405	10,376	12,984	17,833	15,672
Sverdlovsk, USSR	12,644	6,992	8,879	11,527	10,114	10,875	8,740	8,549	8,328	5,787	11,828	9,313	9,312	9,592	8,747	8,174	15,949	8,052	4,562	2,917
Svobodnyy, USSR	8,753	7,210	9,489	13,147	9,367	10,493	9,585	9,315	7,647	6,619	12,756	8,766	10,125	10,168	9,442	12,331	17,685	9,352	8,742	6,741
Sydney, Australia	6,669	14,557	15,076	14,900	12,932	13,198	15,434	15,355	5,999	8,747	14,157	13,378	15,251	14,850	15,221	16,903	10,937	16,201	16,804	16,034
Sydney, Canada	10,419	2,657	2,134	4,306	4,250	4,275	1,813	1,800	15,648	12,923	4,489	3,707	2,222	2,606	1,974	5,986	9,281	957	5,535	4,981
Syktyvkar, USSR	12,547	6,313	8,134	10,761	9,452	10,165	7,985	7,799	9,099	6,528	11,055	8,650	8,553	8,841	7,998	7,749	15,295	7,285	4,149	2,279
Szeged, Hungary	14,655	6,910	7,955	9,402	9,845	10,147	7,683	7,598	9,963	7,149	10,028	9,108	8,136	8,514	7,795	5,189	13,068	6,839	1,576	1,172
Szombathely, Hungary	14,522	6,671	7,673	9,122	9,578	9,864	7,398	7,316	10,254	7,440	9,740	8,849	7,847	8,227	7,513	5,065	12,872	6,553	1,463	979
Tabriz, Iran	14,943	8,666	10,096	11,712	11,779	12,273	9,860	9,740	7,641	4,829	12,357	10,992	10,355	10,714	9,942	6,749	14,755	9,043	3,500	3,177
Tacheng, China	12,039	8,307	10,414	13,365	11,261	12,196	10,332	10,112	6,653	4,423	13,561	10,494	10,920	11,149	10,299	9,749	17,753	9,728	6,219	4,796
Tahiti (Papeete)	2,329	9,841	9,216	9,142	7,132	7,132	9,543	9,553	12,037	14,548	8,216	7,788	9,226	8,821	9,376	15,185	7,682	10,394	16,882	15,513
Taipei, Taiwan	9,012	10,155	12,408	16,088	11,923	13,065	12,532	12,261	4,896	4,860	15,554	11,454	13,052	13,051	12,375	13,843	18,114	12,331	10,383	8,845
Taiyuan, China	9,871	9,016	11,306	14,878	11,305	12,429	11,361	11,098	5,759	4,755	14,619	10,695	11,926	12,010	11,242	12,362	19,516	11,017	8,814	7,196
Tallahassee, Florida	8,298	3,233	960	2,832	2,120	1,648	1,044	1,248	17,959	15,539	2,378	2,094	498	233	1,062	7,623	7,539	1,812	8,153	7,676
Tallinn, USSR	13,193	5,861	7,317	9,513	8,956	9,471	7,107	6,964	10,160	7,431	9,931	8,173	7,635	7,970	7,167	6,403	13,865	6,325	2,878	838
Tamanrasset, Algeria	16,714	8,405	8,453	8,238	10,601	10,392	8,103	8,147	10,658	8,116	9,152	10,069	8,331	8,734	8,300	2,522	10,546	7,289	1,509	3,697
Tampa, Florida	8,447	3,539	1,251	2,504	2,355	1,735	1,271	1,504	18,237	15,707	2,075	2,396	683	556	1,333	7,439	7,238	1,956	8,153	7,790
Tampere, Finland	12,963	5,640	7,137	9,425	8,744	9,280	6,935	6,786	10,294	7,587	9,811	7,959	7,471	7,797	6,989	6,526	13,869	6,165	3,042	916
Tanami, Australia	8,294	14,460	16,121	17,492	14,309	14,990	16,436	16,216	3,622	6,219	16,640	14,427	16,619	16,315	16,199	15,940	13,280	16,763	14,238	13,515
Tangier, Morocco	14,903	6,596	6,746	7,201	8,875	8,791	6,407	6,422	11,919	9,175	7,977	8,300	6,699	7,104	6,588	3,020	10,624	5,568	1,119	2,613
Tarawa (Betio)	3,287	10,050	10,999	12,910	9,044	9,746	11,349	11,187	8,537	10,342	11,878	9,246	11,402	11,066	11,111	18,604	12,226	11,944	15,598	13,437
Tashkent, USSR	13,285	8,807	10,712	13,154	11,903	12,703	10,565	10,379	6,547	3,952	13,573	11,107	11,132	11,421	10,578	8,738	16,754	9,856	5,351	4,342
Tbilisi, USSR	14,674	8,243	9,695	11,429	11,358	11,866	9,464	9,339	7,983	5,179	12,034	10,571	9,967	10,321	9,541	6,710	14,744	8,654	3,327	2,794
Tegucigalpa, Honduras	7,840	4,989	2,783	1,925	2,769	1,645	2,870	3,083	19,533	17,284	954	3,241	2,290	2,046	2,895	7,997	5,830	3,558	9,432	9,328
Tehran, Iran	14,873	9,066	10,576	12,241	12,198	12,741	10,349	10,220	7,114	4,304	12,887	11,404	10,854	11,207	10,423	7,159	15,106	9,540	4,004	3,679
Tel Aviv, Israel	16,022	8,889	9,945	10,945	11,857	12,131	9,661	9,590	8,207	5,432	11,715	11,117	10,086	10,474	9,784	5,571	13,530	8,809	2,628	3,141
Telegraph Creek, Canada	6,620	2,145	3,921	7,514	3,460	4,572	4,149	3,893	13,520	12,296	6,916	2,846	4,553	4,463	3,938	10,665	11,810	4,362	8,843	7,002
Teresina, Brazil	12,779	8,402	6,502	3,420	7,869	6,889	6,244	6,495	15,183	13,690	4,414	8,003	5,903	6,093	6,464	3,609	4,674	6,079	6,889	8,413
Ternate, Indonesia	8,355	12,473	14,526	17,795	13,311	14,316	14,749	14,486	3,664	5,322	16,805	13,125	15,151	15,004	14,544	15,578	15,500	14,780	12,667	11,460
The Valley, Anguilla	10,422	5,175	3,121	1,346	4,606	3,795	2,885	3,147	17,772	15,104	2,057	4,638	2,514	2,715	3,094	5,404	6,165	2,901	7,047	7,471
Thessaloniki, Greece	15,285	7,561	8,523	9,706	10,459	10,709	8,238	8,168	9,552	6,747	10,404	9,735	8,666	9,052	8,362	4,990	12,996	7,386	1,497	1,836
Thimphu, Bhutan	12,140	10,436	12,604	15,508	13,226	14,254	12,537	12,311	4,441	2,507	15,773	12,505	13,126	13,341	12,495	10,831	18,102	11,942	7,677	6,734
Thunder Bay, Canada	8,250	1,194	1,103	4,777	2,349	2,871	1,242	974	15,929	13,784	4,416	1,636	1,741	1,807	1,064	8,161	9,578	1,494	7,487	6,391
Tientsin, China	9,465	8,776	11,064	14,687	10,958	12,090	11,140	10,873	6,042	5,166	14,354	10,371	11,694	11,755	11,009	12,621	19,089	10,843	9,040	7,331
Tijuana, Mexico	5,418	3,380	3,009	5,477	997	2,005	3,369	3,271	15,890	15,289	4,595	1,305	3,339	2,999	3,146	10,674	8,937	4,118	10,394	9,128
Tiksi, USSR	9,226	5,164	7,450	11,019	7,772	8,815	7,494	7,232	9,576	7,925	10,774	7,059	8,062	8,165	7,380	10,591	15,936	7,170	7,213	5,042
Timbuktu, Mali	16,541	8,492	8,132	7,369	10,265	9,878	7,773	7,863	11,430	9,041	8,334	9,842	7,904	8,294	7,991	1,410	9,432	7,020	2,371	4,516
Tindouf, Algeria	15,380	7,191	7,011	6,874	9,160	8,914	6,657	6,716	12,092	9,464	7,743	8,668	6,862	7,263	6,861	2,096	9,851	5,860	1,691	3,523
Tirane, Albania	15,200	7,362	8,272	9,438	10,226	10,455	7,983	7,918	9,824	7,019	10,132	9,511	8,406	8,794	8,111	4,823	12,799	7,131	1,271	1,679

Distances in Kilometers	Christmas Island [Pacific Ocean]	Churchill, Canada	Cincinnati, Ohio	Ciudad Bolivia, Venezuela	Ciudad Juarez, Mexico	Ciudad Victoria, Mexico	Clarksburg, West Virginia	Cleveland, Ohio	Cocos (Keeling) Island	Colombo, Sri Lanka	Colon, Panama	Colorado Springs, Colorado	Columbia, South Carolina	Columbus, Georgia	Columbus, Ohio	Conakry, Guinea	Concepcion, Chile	Concord, New Hampshire	Constantine, Algeria	Copenhagen, Denmark
Tokyo, Japan	7,439	8,416	10,562	14,192	9,845	10,981	10,742	10,472	6,946	6,860	13,521	9,427	11,205	11,140	10,555	14,284	17,089	10,711	10,677	8,714
Toledo, Spain	14,649	6,335	6,669	7,422	8,769	8,771	6,342	6,334	11,781	8,999	8,146	8,154	6,678	7,081	6,509	3,497	11,040	5,491	1,009	2,141
Topeka, Kansas	7,470	2,193	965	4,225	1,273	1,730	1,323	1,217	16,766	14,893	3,645	793	1,423	1,210	1,093	8,659	8,717	2,071	8,480	7,524
Toronto, Canada	8,906	1,959	664	4,006	2,714	2,855	494	307	16,476	14,026	3,801	2,189	1,083	1,337	510	7,332	8,938	637	7,051	6,269
Toulouse, France	14,540	6,291	6,874	7,926	8,918	9,026	6,565	6,528	11,354	8,550	8,602	8,257	6,949	7,345	6,713	4,053	11,653	5,708	917	1,561
Tours, France	14,141	5,929	6,629	7,920	8,633	8,803	6,332	6,278	11,444	8,630	8,541	7,950	6,745	7,135	6,468	4,412	11,857	5,477	1,318	1,234
Townsville, Australia	6,521	13,485	14,653	15,828	12,661	13,241	15,003	14,835	5,400	7,887	14,895	12,900	15,041	14,689	14,764	17,671	12,527	15,565	15,708	14,459
Trenton, New Jersey	9,255	2,472	845	3,556	2,993	2,923	490	601	16,772	14,175	3,456	2,576	888	1,257	703	6,884	8,534	426	6,870	6,290
Tripoli, Lebanon	15,741	8,691	9,819	10,970	11,692	12,010	9,544	9,462	8,233	5,438	11,708	10,942	9,985	10,368	9,659	5,740	13,733	8,697	2,654	2,958
Tripoli, Libya	16,024	7,851	8,382	8,933	10,461	10,493	8,059	8,042	10,147	7,421	9,740	9,816	8,400	8,803	8,221	3,785	11,813	7,205	714	2,530
Tristan da Cunha (Edinburgh)	14,748	13,004	11,211	7,872	12,388	11,297	10,950	11,197	10,856	10,664	8,706	12,653	10,608	10,777	11,172	5,157	5,314	10,717	8,360	10,542
Trondheim, Norway	12,681	5,030	6,434	8,731	8,097	8,590	6,225	6,081	11,012	8,304	9,097	7,321	6,756	7,089	6,284	6,284	13,288	5,449	3,020	872
Trujillo, Peru	8,784	7,535	5,258	2,049	5,289	4,147	5,249	5,500	17,735	17,704	1,936	5,843	4,665	4,535	5,339	7,499	3,238	5,734	10,156	10,849
Truk Island (Moen)	5,643	10,646	12,262	15,012	10,672	11,588	12,563	12,336	6,459	7,945	14,001	10,636	12,808	12,561	12,328	17,555	14,438	12,900	13,959	12,074
Truro, Canada	10,189	2,551	1,880	4,162	4,002	4,021	1,558	1,549	15,857	13,152	4,297	3,473	1,972	2,354	1,720	6,164	9,157	702	5,789	5,220
Tsingtao, China	9,178	9,024	11,302	14,959	11,060	12,201	11,398	11,129	5,865	5,227	14,552	10,510	11,939	11,976	11,256	13,045	18,826	11,145	9,471	7,768
Tsitsihar, China	8,983	7,738	10,021	13,670	9,902	11,031	10,110	9,842	7,106	6,125	13,295	9,306	10,655	10,703	9,971	12,451	18,193	9,856	8,839	6,924
Tubuai Island (Mataura)	2,938	10,420	9,664	9,262	7,624	7,533	9,980	10,009	11,821	14,461	8,387	8,310	9,625	9,223	9,825	15,087	7,327	10,836	17,311	16,129
Tucson, Arizona	5,907	3,209	2,504	4,933	427	1,495	2,863	2,789	16,404	15,524	4,078	921	2,790	2,440	2,648	10,129	8,602	3,646	10,025	8,898
Tulsa, Oklahoma	7,359	2,515	1,057	4,011	1,093	1,412	1,413	1,366	17,043	15,214	3,381	842	1,375	1,085	1,207	8,696	8,419	2,223	8,687	7,798
Tunis, Tunisia	15,529	7,338	7,905	8,639	9,969	10,035	7,587	7,562	10,508	7,744	9,403	9,314	7,946	8,346	7,744	3,864	11,825	6,731	323	2,105
Tura, USSR	10,395	6,304	8,536	11,913	9,107	10,103	8,523	8,276	8,464	6,569	11,837	8,363	9,109	9,270	8,444	10,174	16,918	8,066	6,599	4,583
Turin, Italy	14,594	6,467	7,226	8,434	9,221	9,400	6,930	6,874	10,880	8,069	9,090	8,529	7,342	7,732	7,065	4,440	12,152	6,075	968	1,231
Uberlandia, Brazil	12,113	9,573	7,449	3,883	8,363	7,262	7,256	7,525	14,890	14,275	4,672	8,690	6,809	6,901	7,448	4,931	3,125	7,279	8,413	10,042
Ufa, USSR	13,012	7,140	8,947	11,440	10,278	10,992	8,788	8,609	8,331	5,715	11,800	9,476	9,351	9,648	8,809	7,846	15,701	8,070	4,243	2,717
Ujungpandang, Indonesia	9,270	13,399	15,544	18,876	14,415	15,416	15,736	15,467	2,597	4,592	17,854	14,212	16,181	16,068	15,546	14,841	15,186	15,651	12,385	11,527
Ulaanbaatar, Mongolia	10,264	8,026	10,300	13,767	10,578	11,656	10,319	10,064	6,711	5,214	13,625	9,898	10,898	11,024	10,221	11,393	18,773	9,909	7,791	6,049
Ulan-Ude, USSR	10,170	7,588	9,862	13,334	10,169	11,238	9,881	9,625	7,148	5,591	13,186	9,479	10,459	10,586	9,782	11,217	18,337	9,474	7,604	5,777
Uliastay, Mongolia	11,010	8,157	10,383	13,668	10,900	11,929	10,360	10,117	6,618	4,802	13,670	10,178	10,948	11,119	10,288	10,723	18,540	9,864	7,144	5,522
Uranium City, Canada	7,636	832	2,838	6,516	3,098	4,049	3,003	2,734	14,323	12,594	6,067	2,321	3,484	3,483	2,820	9,375	11,174	3,094	7,835	6,211
Urumqi, China	11,822	8,637	10,789	13,826	11,520	12,496	10,724	10,497	6,250	4,154	13,984	10,768	11,313	11,526	10,680	10,178	18,207	10,147	6,676	5,286
Ushuaia, Argentina	10,138	12,800	10,519	7,002	10,261	9,186	10,488	10,747	12,472	13,990	7,193	10,944	9,914	9,800	10,594	8,747	2,030	10,865	12,357	14,270
Vaduz, Liechtenstein	14,416	6,365	7,227	8,584	9,184	9,412	6,941	6,872	10,777	7,963	9,209	8,475	7,372	7,757	7,066	4,715	12,399	6,090	1,223	969
Valencia, Spain	14,862	6,562	6,965	7,727	9,055	9,077	6,641	6,628	11,465	8,686	8,459	8,428	6,985	7,387	6,805	3,574	11,253	5,788	704	2,040
Valladolid, Spain	14,454	6,144	6,526	7,396	8,614	8,644	6,204	6,188	11,846	9,052	8,094	7,989	6,554	6,955	6,366	3,668	11,124	5,350	1,142	2,002
Valletta, Malta	15,731	7,633	8,278	9,032	10,325	10,418	7,964	7,932	10,107	7,345	9,803	9,657	8,332	8,731	8,116	4,086	12,097	7,108	713	2,202
Valparaiso, Chile	9,751	10,384	8,096	4,581	8,050	6,927	8,057	8,317	14,874	15,894	4,774	8,664	7,485	7,384	8,166	7,729	441	8,442	11,183	12,628
Vancouver, Canada	6,175	2,152	3,245	6,649	2,391	3,523	3,537	3,312	14,493	13,394	5,962	1,860	3,830	3,661	3,303	10,584	10,738	3,956	9,308	7,672
Varna, Bulgaria	14,969	7,513	8,642	10,062	10,499	10,835	8,375	8,285	9,270	6,456	10,712	9,751	8,833	9,209	8,483	5,493	13,491	7,534	1,970	1,768
Venice, Italy	14,657	6,647	7,514	8,802	9,474	9,697	7,226	7,159	10,527	7,714	9,450	8,765	7,652	8,039	7,353	4,698	12,489	6,373	1,118	1,137
Veracruz, Mexico	6,945	4,394	2,473	3,009	1,733	590	2,694	2,826	18,426	17,081	2,060	2,332	2,218	1,843	2,623	8,883	6,660	3,519	9,851	9,379
Verona, Italy	14,631	6,586	7,425	8,696	9,394	9,606	7,135	7,071	10,630	7,818	9,345	8,689	7,558	7,946	7,264	4,631	12,398	6,282	1,074	1,142
Victoria, Canada	6,096	2,225	3,256	6,629	2,337	3,473	3,553	3,333	14,529	13,467	5,928	1,830	3,833	3,655	3,319	10,633	10,678	3,992	9,391	7,762
Victoria, Seychelles	16,361	13,456	14,467	14,056	16,467	16,573	14,149	14,121	4,626	2,997	15,079	15,728	14,480	14,884	14,305	7,829	12,983	13,294	6,806	7,745
Vienna, Austria	14,413	6,572	7,596	9,096	9,490	9,788	7,324	7,239	10,300	7,487	9,701	8,757	7,779	8,156	7,436	5,130	12,904	6,481	1,538	870
Vientiane, Laos	10,993	11,366	13,645	17,001	13,696	14,829	13,660	13,407	3,374	2,754	16,969	13,103	14,241	14,366	13,566	12,403	17,872	13,205	9,364	8,378
Villahermosa, Mexico	7,265	4,527	2,478	2,643	2,045	907	2,655	2,817	18,787	17,139	1,699	2,583	2,131	1,790	2,617	8,561	6,416	3,445	9,664	9,308
Vilnius, USSR	13,718	6,318	7,666	9,632	9,382	9,841	7,435	7,309	9,935	7,161	10,124	8,609	7,944	8,294	7,512	6,077	13,751	6,630	2,489	818
Visby, Sweden	13,384	5,799	7,120	9,161	8,846	9,296	6,891	6,764	10,453	7,692	9,618	8,077	7,402	7,751	6,967	6,000	13,446	6,088	2,517	413
Vitoria, Brazil	12,924	10,045	8,025	4,583	9,102	8,023	7,801	8,063	14,130	13,431	5,435	9,374	7,398	7,529	8,007	4,404	3,659	7,724	7,985	9,782
Vladivostok, USSR	8,290	7,945	10,189	13,870	9,811	10,954	10,319	10,047	7,071	6,462	13,363	9,285	10,834	10,833	10,158	13,219	17,789	10,161	9,610	7,663
Volgograd, USSR	14,000	7,504	9,055	11,084	10,635	11,200	8,846	8,703	8,467	5,706	11,593	9,841	9,371	9,709	8,905	6,907	14,887	8,060	3,352	2,284
Vologda, USSR	13,049	6,320	7,972	10,349	9,460	10,077	7,789	7,626	9,388	6,714	10,727	8,662	8,338	8,653	7,828	7,091	14,712	7,042	3,492	1,675
Vorkuta, USSR	11,650	5,885	7,790	10,856	8,973	9,792	7,790	7,578	9,205	6,829	11,007	8,176	8,376	8,620	7,769	8,510	15,674	7,173	4,952	2,920
Wake Island	4,345	8,712	10,204	13,052	8,624	9,580	10,512	10,292	8,400	9,431	12,077	8,569	10,743	10,494	10,276	16,819	13,946	10,899	13,500	11,348
Wallis Island	2,663	10,807	11,074	11,909	8,938	9,323	11,433	11,348	9,397	11,702	10,926	9,373	11,295	10,905	11,217	18,076	10,269	12,195	17,434	15,244
Walvis Bay, Namibia	17,534	13,230	12,335	9,874	14,177	13,311	11,990	12,163	8,728	7,838	10,865	14,074	11,890	12,198	12,230	4,728	8,312	11,414	6,618	8,713
Warsaw, Poland	13,992	6,386	7,602	9,387	9,398	9,791	7,355	7,245	10,111	7,315	9,924	8,639	7,842	8,205	7,446	5,682	13,391	6,531	2,097	670
Washington, D.C.	9,051	2,523	648	3,445	2,780	2,680	290	491	16,965	14,403	3,283	2,402	652	1,013	527	7,048	8,395	665	7,110	6,531
Watson Lake, Canada	6,901	1,952	3,850	7,484	3,559	4,649	4,058	3,796	13,498	12,157	6,927	2,902	4,490	4,427	3,856	10,431	11,890	4,216	8,562	6,722
Weimar, East Germany	14,041	6,107	7,121	8,724	9,012	9,314	6,853	6,764	10,725	7,916	9,292	8,280	7,313	7,688	6,962	5,138	12,724	6,012	1,667	528
Wellington, New Zealand	5,551	13,865	13,514	12,675	11,420	11,402	13,838	13,851	8,137	10,929	11,973	12,039	13,494	13,092	13,674	16,386	8,949	14,691	18,858	17,953
West Berlin, West Germany	13,905	6,060	7,157	8,869	9,008	9,349	6,897	6,799	10,618	7,816	9,411	8,265	7,372	7,741	6,998	5,360	12,931	6,064	1,872	355
Wewak, Papua New Guinea	6,575	12,148	13,772	16,215	12,100	12,944	14,078	13,854	5,239	7,181	15,182	12,119	14,304	14,039	13,843	17,446	14,148	14,417	14,317	12,779
Whangarei, New Zealand	5,096	13,402	13,261	12,815	11,131	11,218	13,600	13,584	8,120	10,864	12,038	11,703	13,310	12,905	13,418	16,992	9,390	14,438	18,918	17,393
Whitehorse, Canada	6,790	2,275	4,200	7,829	3,839	4,945	4,409	4,146	13,171	11,912	7,259	3,209	4,840	4,772	4,206	10,698	12,185	4,558	8,694	6,789
Wichita, Kansas	7,286	2,352	1,130	4,221	1,067	1,558	1,490	1,405	16,832	15,055	3,593	667	1,526	1,266	1,268	8,812	8,623	2,262	8,686	7,730
Willemstad, Curacao	9,818	5,587	3,362	453	4,411	3,437	3,213	3,485	18,489	15,983	1,236	4,614	2,716	2,786	3,381	6,037	5,435	3,455	7,936	8,373
Wiluna, Australia	9,343	15,559	17,337	17,693	15,484	16,067	17,647	17,419	2,932	5,721	17,170	15,639	17,828	17,507	17,411	14,834	12,848	17,883	13,745	13,500
Windhoek, Namibia	17,654	13,346	12,530	10,130	14,405	13,557	12,183	12,349	8,471	7,572	11,124	14,277	12,100	12,415	12,422	4,888	8,554	11,587	6,617	8,681
Windsor, Canada	8,592	1,986	377	3,955	2,383	2,541	404	141	16,647	14,284	3,662	1,881	938	1,106	260	7,603	8,821	944	7,384	6,579
Winnipeg, Canada	7,761	1,006	1,560	5,224	2,160	2,907	1,773	1,517	15,614	13,703	4,768	1,370	2,203	2,181	1,565	8,736	9,895	2,088	7,885	6,628
Winston-Salem, North Carolina	8,741	2,715	503	3,227	2,466	2,274	353	612	17,319	14,811	2,961	2,188	245	595	492	7,288	8,109	1,086	7,507	6,951
Wroclaw, Poland	14,100	6,335	7,453	9,125	9,299	9,645	7,193	7,095	10,337	7,532	9,685	8,553	7,667	8,036	7,294	5,399	13,088	6,360	1,835	588
Wuhan, China	9,731	9,762	12,050	15,666	11,885	13,024	12,124	11,858	5,068	4,442	15,335	11,323	12,679	12,740	11,994	12,915	19,047	11,813	9,444	7,938
Wyndham, Australia	8,403	14,091	15,902	17,854	14,237	15,016	16,191	15,953	3,401	5,869	16,920	14,272	16,452	16,191	15,961	15,839	13,808	16,413	13,826	13,009
Xi'an, China	10,219	9,478	11,766	15,288	11,818	12,939	11,806	11,546	5,277	4,249	15,088	11,200	12,378	12,478	11,696	12,275	19,676	11,426	8,794	7,308
Xining, China	10,836	9,334	11,596	14,964	11,890	12,976	11,598	11,348	5,406	3,970	14,912	11,218	12,182	12,325	11,511	11,579	19,563	11,139	8,114	6,696
Yakutsk, USSR	8,920	6,096	8,385	12,011	8,470	9,564	8,459	8,192	8,689	7,329	11,689	7,811	9,013	9,082	8,328	11,469	16,797	8,188	7,971	5,860
Yanji, China	8,476	8,046	10,301	13,980	9,970	11,112	10,422	10,151	6,929	6,272	13,499	9,432	10,944	10,954	10,266	13,114	17,985	10,241	9,501	7,582
Yaounde, Cameroon	18,653	10,535	10,264	9,088	12,388	11,930	9,904	9,998	9,596	7,574	10,106	11,978	10,013	10,396	10,124	2,860	9,787	9,156	3,634	5,745
Yap Island (Colonia)	7,165	11,119	13,059	16,283	11,781	12,797	13,307	13,051	5,152	6,421	15,328	11,603	13,668	13,497	13,091	16,264	15,659	13,443	12,843	11,217
Yaraka, Australia	6,958	14,161	15,232	15,923	13,183	13,674	15,588	15,438	5,163	7,793	15,073	13,476	15,571	15,201	15,352	17,123	12,148	16,197	15,792	14,823
Yarmouth, Canada	9,973	2,530	1,620	3,956	3,757	3,744	1,288	1,302	16,120	13,429	4,046	3,257	1,689	2,072	1,463	6,308	8,961	444	6,057	5,502
Yellowknife, Canada	7,598	1,177	3,283	6,962	3,461	4,451	3,441	3,171	13,881	12,215	6,511	2,706	3,929	3,930	3,261	9,616	11,609	3,491	7,858	6,124
Yerevan, USSR	14,830	8,393	9,816	11,477	11,502	11,993	9,581	9,460	7,902	5,093	12,103	10,717	10,078	10,436	9,662	6,648	14,677	8,765	3,317	2,900
Yinchuan, China	10,412	9,065	11,345	14,812	11,526	12,628	11,369	11,112	5,673	4,392	14,671	10,876	11,946	12,066	11,268	11,854	19,817	10,957	8,334	6,800
Yogyakarta, Indonesia	10,280	13,982	16,235	19,910	15,380	16,422	16,359	16,088	1,555	3,759	18,893	15,099	16,880	16,853	16,204	13,886	15,051	16,077	11,755	11,208
York, United Kingdom	13,444	5,310	6,220	7,915	8,138	8,412	5,949	5,863	11,601	8,799	8,433	7,422	6,408	6,783	6,061	5,041	12,175	5,107	2,033	907
Yumen, China	11,124	9,024	11,261	14,537	11,699	12,754	11,242	10,997	5,739	4,059	14,552	10,997	11,830	11,995	11,168	11,116	19,151	10,745	7,626	6,195
Yutian, China	12,559	9,401	11,476	14,230	12,363	13,296	11,376	11,165	5,637	3,320	14,541	11,596	11,960	12,207	11,356	9,861	17,780	10,735	6,527	5,460
Yuzhno-Sakhalinsk, USSR	7,595	7,191	9,386	13,055	8,886	10,030	9,543	9,272	7,964	7,406	12,482	8,385	10,032	10,000	9,367	13,331	16,878	9,465	9,795	7,718
Zagreb, Yugoslavia	14,673	6,777	7,726	9,085	9,656	9,915	7,445	7,371	10,259	7,445	9,724	8,934	7,884	8,267	7,566	4,919	12,757	6,597	1,309	1,123
Zahedan, Iran	14,653	9,954	11,609	13,347	13,098	13,741	11,400	11,257	5,999	3,194	14,005	12,296	11,922	12,263	11,460	8,011	15,693	10,608	5,065	4,770
Zamboanga, Philippines	8,932	12,046	14,227	17,825	13,327	14,410	14,399	14,128	3,489	4,664	16,998	13,018	14,871	14,798	14,218	14,805	16,356	14,290	11,778	10,574
Zanzibar, Tanzania	18,124	12,952	13,320	12,285	15,467	15,169	12,970	13,012	6,360	4,744	13,316	14,903	13,170	13,567	13,168	6,119	11,542	12,154	5,805	7,278
Zaragoza, Spain	14,634	6,345	6,811	7,712	8,884	8,941	6,492	6,469	11,527	8,733	8,414	8,244	6,853	7,253	6,650	3,775	11,369	5,637	873	1,842
Zashiversk, USSR	8,558	5,260	7,545	11,192	7,614	8,703	7,631	7,363	9,546	8,158	10,838	6,949	8,177	8,235	7,493	11,260	15,934	7,402	7,916	5,739
Zhengzhou, China	9,779	9,328	11,618	15,214	11,537	12,670	11,683	11,418	5,471	4,634	14,919	10,949	12,243	12,315	11,558	12,629	19,374	11,356	9,107	7,532
Zurich, Switzerland	14,368	6,294	7,141	8,498	9,102	9,325	6,854	6,787	10,867	8,053	9,120	8,396	7,284	7,669	6,980	4,684	12,336	6,002	1,230	968

Distances in Kilometers

	Coppermine, Canada	Coquimbo, Chile	Cordoba, Argentina	Cordoba, Spain	Cork, Ireland	Corner Brook, Canada	Corrientes, Argentina	Cosenza, Italy	Craiova, Romania	Cruzeiro do Sul, Brazil	Cuiaba, Brazil	Curitiba, Brazil	Cuzco, Peru	Dacca, Bangladesh	Dakar, Senegal	Dallas, Texas	Damascus, Syria	Danang, Vietnam	Dar es Salaam, Tanzania	Darwin, Australia
Coquimbo, Chile	11,435	0	705	10,213	10,940	8,842	1,253	11,859	12,650	2,476	2,230	2,234	1,823	18,091	7,603	7,446	13,302	18,465	11,591	14,747
Cordoba, Argentina	11,785	705	0	9,841	10,706	8,921	678	11,408	12,221	2,773	1,936	1,605	2,135	17,386	7,135	7,889	12,743	18,144	10,887	14,895
Cordoba, Spain	6,942	10,213	9,841	0	1,584	4,382	9,171	1,834	2,490	8,632	7,983	8,408	9,016	8,860	2,860	8,026	3,719	10,830	6,729	14,806
Cork, Ireland	5,415	10,940	10,706	1,584	0	3,463	10,070	2,364	2,522	8,959	8,775	9,443	9,460	8,549	4,207	7,114	4,111	10,331	7,926	14,324
Corner Brook, Canada	3,748	8,842	8,921	4,382	3,463	0	8,464	5,795	5,971	6,430	7,150	8,282	7,056	11,367	5,294	3,681	7,572	12,675	11,105	15,880
Corrientes, Argentina	11,535	1,253	678	9,171	10,070	8,464	0	10,730	11,543	2,632	1,346	982	2,062	16,922	6,458	7,785	12,082	18,182	10,465	15,466
Cosenza, Italy	7,450	11,859	11,408	1,834	2,364	5,795	10,730	0	838	10,446	9,642	9,877	10,802	7,060	4,273	9,467	1,905	9,063	5,629	12,993
Craiova, Romania	7,101	12,650	12,221	2,490	2,522	5,971	11,543	838	0	11,108	10,424	10,703	11,506	6,376	5,090	9,571	1,614	8,341	5,871	12,323
Cruzeiro do Sul, Brazil	9,014	2,476	2,773	8,632	8,959	6,430	2,632	10,446	11,108	0	2,003	3,165	654	17,480	6,570	5,156	12,231	19,068	12,308	16,608
Cuiaba, Brazil	10,382	2,230	1,936	7,983	8,775	7,150	1,346	9,642	10,424	2,003	0	1,301	1,728	16,415	5,410	6,886	11,171	18,353	10,388	16,812
Curitiba, Brazil	11,648	2,234	1,605	8,408	9,443	8,282	982	9,877	10,703	3,165	1,301	0	2,720	15,957	5,619	8,179	11,143	17,469	9,548	15,814
Cuzco, Peru	9,660	1,823	2,135	9,016	9,460	7,056	2,062	10,802	11,506	654	1,728	2,720	0	17,856	6,770	5,764	12,518	19,722	12,114	16,198
Dacca, Bangladesh	9,638	18,091	17,386	8,860	8,549	11,367	16,922	7,060	6,376	17,480	16,415	15,957	17,856	0	11,109	13,706	5,343	2,045	6,499	5,947
Dakar, Senegal	8,823	7,603	7,135	2,860	4,207	5,294	6,458	4,273	5,090	6,570	5,410	5,619	6,770	11,109	0	8,164	5,777	13,154	6,695	16,596
Dallas, Texas	4,074	7,446	7,889	8,026	7,114	3,681	7,785	9,467	9,571	5,156	6,886	8,179	5,764	13,706	8,164	0	11,185	13,984	14,658	14,693
Damascus, Syria	8,517	13,302	12,743	3,719	4,111	7,572	12,082	1,905	1,614	12,231	11,171	11,143	12,518	5,343	5,777	11,185	0	7,386	4,471	11,185
Danang, Vietnam	10,068	18,465	18,144	10,830	10,331	12,675	18,182	9,063	8,341	19,068	18,353	17,469	19,722	2,045	13,154	13,984	7,386	0	8,002	4,020
Dar es Salaam, Tanzania	12,963	11,591	10,887	6,729	7,926	11,105	10,465	5,629	5,871	12,308	10,388	9,548	12,114	6,499	6,695	14,658	4,471	8,002	0	10,024
Darwin, Australia	12,281	14,747	14,895	14,806	14,324	15,880	15,466	12,993	12,323	16,608	16,812	15,814	16,198	5,947	16,596	14,693	11,185	4,020	10,024	0
Davao, Philippines	10,456	16,921	17,128	12,866	12,156	13,789	17,700	11,150	10,395	18,027	19,046	17,903	17,980	4,184	15,293	13,729	9,520	2,139	9,707	2,236
David, Panama	7,026	4,412	4,818	8,360	8,176	5,041	4,717	10,163	10,627	2,085	3,937	5,191	2,688	16,365	7,103	3,076	12,068	17,057	13,609	16,370
Dawson, Canada	1,175	11,977	12,424	8,023	6,465	4,895	12,275	8,347	7,898	9,670	11,230	12,524	10,292	9,364	9,996	4,537	9,182	9,451	13,648	11,231
Dawson Creek, Canada	1,371	10,571	11,022	7,975	6,531	4,162	10,895	8,697	8,411	8,277	9,901	11,202	8,894	10,734	9,452	3,133	9,866	10,852	14,281	12,328
Denpasar, Indonesia	12,471	15,675	15,572	13,221	13,031	15,492	15,958	11,387	10,789	18,012	17,162	15,882	17,430	4,483	14,839	15,780	9,526	2,840	8,366	1,760
Denver, Colorado	3,187	8,466	8,933	8,187	7,059	3,822	8,845	9,416	9,381	6,214	7,949	9,243	6,815	12,801	8,778	1,065	10,974	12,938	14,916	13,798
Derby, Australia	13,062	14,536	14,552	14,526	14,341	16,491	15,045	12,693	12,109	16,729	16,367	15,217	16,195	5,799	15,864	15,634	10,816	4,060	9,197	941
Des Moines, Iowa	3,194	8,247	8,628	7,268	6,228	2,887	8,443	8,592	8,635	5,857	7,414	8,713	6,493	12,763	7,801	1,018	10,246	13,240	13,990	14,645
Detroit, Michigan	3,417	8,095	8,390	6,450	5,505	2,079	8,119	7,857	7,973	5,634	6,983	8,266	6,287	12,661	6,927	1,610	9,586	13,437	13,148	15,364
Dhahran, Saudi Arabia	9,495	14,328	13,688	5,262	5,617	9,057	13,075	3,459	3,095	13,648	12,360	12,097	13,857	4,060	7,092	12,594	1,554	6,089	3,845	9,716
Diego Garcia Island	13,265	14,359	13,722	9,398	10,024	13,482	13,517	7,745	7,512	15,812	13,814	12,753	15,468	3,953	10,206	16,979	5,914	4,718	3,660	6,421
Dijon, France	6,298	11,460	11,124	1,318	1,098	4,553	10,459	1,272	1,494	9,706	9,238	9,717	10,149	7,774	4,174	8,211	3,037	9,673	6,878	13,690
Dili, Indonesia	12,083	15,379	15,465	14,087	13,654	15,514	15,992	12,272	11,606	17,328	17,329	16,206	16,900	5,230	15,949	14,910	10,466	3,327	9,501	721
Djibouti, Djibouti	11,023	13,005	12,317	5,571	6,421	9,841	11,776	4,059	4,072	12,984	11,334	10,800	13,004	5,166	6,559	13,521	2,524	7,025	2,079	10,045
Dnepropetrovsk, USSR	6,868	13,598	13,186	3,394	3,081	6,377	12,509	1,809	974	11,937	11,368	11,676	12,373	5,544	6,060	9,817	1,664	7,456	6,135	11,467
Dobo, Indonesia	11,455	15,210	15,456	14,560	13,856	15,083	16,072	12,809	12,077	16,705	17,391	16,535	16,430	5,767	16,780	13,964	11,099	3,747	10,486	829
Doha, Qatar	9,620	14,425	13,776	5,440	5,795	9,233	13,172	3,638	3,273	13,803	12,485	12,192	14,000	3,931	7,241	12,761	1,734	5,952	3,789	9,551
Donetsk, USSR	6,960	13,796	13,375	3,600	3,292	6,570	12,698	1,980	1,154	12,152	11,568	11,855	12,586	5,329	6,244	9,985	1,615	7,245	6,072	11,254
Dover, Delaware	3,995	7,665	7,900	6,007	5,228	1,773	7,577	7,534	7,741	5,189	6,389	7,654	5,843	12,893	6,254	2,040	9,339	13,879	12,621	16,080
Dresden, East Germany	6,153	12,215	11,883	2,065	1,541	4,937	11,218	1,320	1,061	10,409	9,995	10,472	10,871	7,077	4,907	8,514	2,673	8,942	6,862	12,962
Dubayy, United Arab Emir.	9,651	14,784	14,128	5,771	6,055	9,468	13,531	3,956	3,538	14,177	12,862	12,550	14,380	3,554	7,619	12,938	2,053	5,573	3,949	9,187
Dublin, Ireland	5,348	11,157	10,924	1,721	219	3,570	10,289	2,313	2,400	9,161	8,993	9,661	9,668	8,352	4,401	7,197	4,004	10,121	7,915	14,110
Duluth, Minnesota	2,686	8,753	9,102	6,890	5,763	2,546	8,878	8,123	8,122	6,330	7,791	9,084	6,975	12,193	7,672	1,606	9,728	12,754	13,617	14,492
Dunedin, New Zealand	14,035	9,557	9,836	19,038	19,330	16,408	10,485	17,796	17,413	11,412	11,754	11,153	10,950	11,140	16,467	12,728	15,923	9,274	12,439	5,255
Durango, Mexico	4,921	6,956	7,498	9,219	8,349	4,906	7,529	10,699	10,807	4,941	6,863	8,098	5,468	14,479	9,089	1,237	12,421	14,320	15,736	14,062
Durban, South Africa	15,234	9,466	8,793	8,372	9,842	12,374	8,535	7,807	8,245	10,891	8,894	7,771	10,490	8,685	7,160	15,101	7,034	9,705	2,695	10,257
Dushanbe, USSR	8,204	16,265	15,706	6,257	5,949	8,990	15,049	4,492	3,767	14,855	14,098	14,104	15,272	2,625	8,687	11,970	2,967	4,576	5,875	8,561
East London, South Africa	15,470	9,032	8,364	8,551	10,056	12,415	8,125	8,098	8,576	10,525	8,536	7,385	10,103	9,130	7,148	14,919	7,417	10,100	3,133	10,438
Easter Island (Hanga Roa)	10,542	3,723	4,392	13,034	13,067	9,857	4,972	14,865	15,457	4,443	5,638	5,955	4,172	18,001	10,940	6,766	16,674	15,961	14,972	12,183
Echo Bay, Canada	234	11,365	11,737	7,160	5,639	3,870	11,511	7,683	7,335	8,964	10,385	11,661	9,606	9,762	8,996	3,966	8,747	10,125	13,196	12,212
Edinburgh, United Kingdom	5,191	11,484	11,263	2,008	565	3,701	10,630	2,339	2,299	9,453	9,330	10,008	9,971	8,075	4,737	7,272	3,913	9,813	7,968	13,788
Edmonton, Canada	1,594	10,106	10,543	7,794	6,408	3,810	10,403	8,646	8,424	7,791	9,401	10,701	8,412	11,142	9,102	2,661	9,930	11,331	14,270	12,804
El Aaiun, Morocco	7,718	8,848	8,443	1,427	2,775	4,520	7,769	3,038	3,804	7,465	6,620	6,986	7,780	10,077	1,452	7,878	4,767	12,095	6,785	15,945
Elat, Israel	8,923	13,036	12,451	3,766	4,334	7,794	11,801	2,025	1,912	12,127	10,952	10,847	12,370	5,510	5,601	11,443	456	7,554	4,049	11,251
Elazig, Turkey	7,999	13,713	13,192	3,813	3,936	7,355	12,522	1,987	1,429	12,433	11,534	11,606	12,777	5,081	6,124	10,888	633	7,099	5,035	11,006
Eniwetok Atoll, Marshall Isls.	8,520	14,143	14,784	14,375	12,924	12,241	15,396	13,377	12,544	14,008	15,867	16,376	14,149	7,672	17,110	10,330	12,436	5,850	13,756	4,368
Erfurt, East Germany	6,090	12,038	11,714	1,916	1,356	4,770	11,051	1,361	1,209	10,220	9,821	10,315	10,683	7,267	4,769	8,362	2,823	9,128	6,953	13,148
Erzurum, Turkey	7,893	13,916	13,402	3,957	3,994	7,384	12,731	2,144	1,523	12,586	11,728	11,819	12,945	4,916	6,320	10,878	839	6,924	5,176	10,853
Esfahan, Iran	8,806	14,658	14,060	5,087	5,222	8,603	13,417	3,253	2,732	13,659	12,575	12,455	13,951	3,912	7,202	12,045	1,433	5,956	4,560	9,766
Essen, West Germany	5,934	11,809	11,505	1,769	1,070	4,492	10,846	1,529	1,480	9,954	9,600	10,132	10,426	7,536	4,628	8,098	3,090	9,381	7,153	13,399
Eucla, Australia	14,317	12,854	12,886	15,771	15,907	18,009	13,404	13,993	13,524	15,094	14,744	13,679	14,532	7,375	16,117	15,755	12,087	5,729	9,581	2,141
Fargo, North Dakota	2,557	8,886	9,267	7,201	6,032	2,881	9,075	8,386	8,349	6,495	8,025	9,323	7,133	12,154	8,029	1,565	9,946	12,601	13,919	14,170
Faroe Islands (Torshavn)	4,503	11,703	11,555	2,688	1,131	3,433	10,950	2,970	2,790	9,530	9,622	10,405	10,089	8,069	5,325	6,849	4,382	9,676	8,587	13,557
Florence, Italy	6,845	11,701	11,308	1,497	1,723	5,170	10,633	648	1,007	10,102	9,471	9,833	10,505	7,381	4,221	8,834	2,447	9,336	6,271	13,327
Florianopolis, Brazil	11,897	2,237	1,571	8,567	9,636	8,528	1,014	9,999	10,830	3,360	1,539	250	2,887	15,908	5,757	8,406	11,213	17,316	9,458	15,573
Fort George, Canada	2,447	9,313	9,551	5,743	4,555	1,556	9,215	6,912	6,908	6,838	7,996	9,236	7,492	11,353	6,848	2,733	8,515	12,230	12,446	14,722
Fort McMurray, Canada	1,251	10,321	10,730	7,478	6,068	3,604	10,555	8,286	8,052	7,963	9,503	10,799	8,595	10,859	8,895	2,888	9,553	11,143	13,905	12,838
Fort Nelson, Canada	1,074	10,923	11,363	7,860	6,380	4,217	11,218	8,489	8,166	8,609	10,196	11,494	9,231	10,364	9,479	3,479	9,591	10,512	14,033	12,131
Fort Severn, Canada	1,926	9,648	9,935	6,207	4,929	2,143	9,641	7,258	7,177	7,186	8,462	9,723	7,839	11,172	7,437	2,675	8,765	11,884	12,854	14,161
Fort Smith, Arkansas	3,840	7,627	8,041	7,683	6,753	3,326	7,899	9,107	9,207	5,284	6,941	8,240	5,907	13,444	7,914	364	10,821	13,834	14,342	14,827
Fort Vermilion, Canada	1,052	10,634	11,051	7,591	6,142	3,845	10,883	8,310	8,033	8,288	9,836	11,132	8,917	10,583	9,121	3,192	9,500	10,822	13,902	12,523
Fort Wayne, Indiana	3,480	7,992	8,309	6,667	5,728	2,300	8,059	8,081	8,195	5,543	6,952	8,242	6,194	12,817	7,091	1,386	9,809	13,532	13,358	15,298
Fort-Chimo, Canada	2,525	9,763	9,926	5,021	3,766	1,229	9,524	6,114	6,095	7,297	8,244	9,425	7,944	10,728	6,396	3,533	7,702	11,779	11,682	14,689
Fort-de-France, Martinique	7,047	5,053	5,101	6,084	6,215	3,820	4,660	7,916	8,488	2,768	3,383	4,609	3,334	14,764	4,695	4,133	9,796	16,418	11,319	18,724
Fortaleza, Brazil	9,826	4,516	4,077	5,773	6,786	6,132	3,402	7,347	8,150	3,801	2,331	2,662	3,836	14,121	3,088	7,344	8,840	16,144	8,622	17,871
Frankfort, Kentucky	3,787	7,676	7,999	6,787	5,917	2,462	7,759	8,256	8,405	5,231	6,669	7,963	5,880	13,133	7,053	1,239	10,015	13,846	13,434	15,482
Frankfurt am Main, W. Ger.	6,116	11,846	11,522	1,730	1,217	4,660	10,859	1,342	1,311	10,038	9,629	10,125	10,498	7,446	4,586	8,276	2,916	9,316	6,964	13,336
Fredericton, Canada	3,666	8,422	8,571	5,080	4,198	735	8,170	6,527	6,703	5,966	6,899	8,098	6,609	11,949	5,738	2,957	8,306	13,116	11,782	15,945
Freeport, Bahamas	5,198	6,301	6,595	6,914	6,404	3,072	6,344	8,598	8,921	3,837	5,266	6,564	4,490	14,328	6,472	1,875	10,473	15,234	13,142	16,565
Freetown, Sierra Leone	9,627	7,527	6,990	3,365	4,832	6,115	6,320	4,503	5,341	6,822	5,422	5,412	6,932	11,009	821	8,907	5,776	13,034	6,071	16,083
Frobisher Bay, Canada	2,125	10,392	10,554	5,033	3,642	1,767	10,147	5,929	5,815	7,924	8,861	10,028	8,572	10,136	6,701	3,963	7,398	11,151	11,552	14,114
Frunze, USSR	7,698	16,678	16,189	6,505	6,002	8,827	15,516	4,819	4,038	14,961	14,459	14,605	15,450	2,578	9,078	11,579	3,480	4,361	6,560	8,381
Fukuoka, Japan	7,529	17,933	18,637	10,840	9,724	10,826	18,905	9,476	8,640	16,294	17,909	19,099	16,846	4,032	13,676	11,159	8,379	2,953	10,531	5,096
Funafuti Atoll, Tuvalu	9,894	11,384	11,976	16,729	15,145	13,089	12,625	16,196	15,382	11,880	13,387	13,580	11,808	10,263	18,103	9,971	15,315	8,272	15,267	5,299
Funchal, Madeira Island	7,019	8,998	8,659	1,247	2,247	3,847	7,996	3,062	3,736	7,388	6,773	7,284	7,769	10,106	1,991	7,290	4,913	12,075	7,370	16,051
Fuzhou, China	8,677	18,895	19,331	10,840	9,986	11,690	19,780	9,249	8,443	17,613	18,751	18,881	18,193	2,924	13,519	12,457	7,853	1,597	9,356	4,444
Gaborone, Botswana	14,530	9,328	8,634	7,630	9,120	11,609	8,304	7,152	7,641	10,516	8,514	7,472	10,172	8,780	6,409	14,426	6,531	10,000	2,438	10,908
Galapagos Islands (Santa Cruz)	7,834	3,821	4,383	9,670	9,509	6,314	4,490	11,484	11,962	2,120	4,115	5,198	2,479	17,449	8,202	3,759	13,386	17,362	14,387	15,257
Gander, Canada	3,888	8,898	8,950	4,138	3,241	244	8,474	5,562	5,754	6,510	7,149	8,254	7,128	11,242	5,090	3,919	7,351	12,607	10,861	15,928
Gangtok, India	9,271	18,052	17,357	8,477	8,124	10,928	16,821	6,692	5,988	17,072	16,163	15,840	17,492	440	10,798	13,327	5,021	2,376	6,515	6,337
Garyarsa, China	8,888	17,324	16,678	7,540	7,229	10,160	16,071	5,755	5,053	16,149	15,277	15,093	16,555	1,331	9,884	12,856	4,109	3,310	6,101	7,271
Gaspe, Canada	3,486	8,754	8,887	4,860	3,901	479	8,469	6,246	6,392	6,305	7,183	8,362	6,946	11,592	5,710	3,221	8,000	12,780	11,583	15,734
Gauhati, India	9,346	18,316	17,613	8,802	8,420	11,157	17,108	7,022	6,313	17,377	16,494	16,132	17,818	304	11,133	13,417	5,356	2,043	6,735	6,017
Gdansk, Poland	5,925	12,656	12,345	2,552	1,825	5,071	11,684	1,683	1,176	10,775	10,445	10,953	11,259	6,726	5,400	8,555	2,698	8,543	7,045	12,559
Geneva, Switzerland	6,447	11,475	11,124	1,291	1,240	4,688	10,456	1,125	1,397	9,762	9,249	9,699	10,194	7,717	4,132	8,351	2,914	9,633	6,726	13,646
Genoa, Italy	6,712	11,571	11,192	1,358	1,534	4,975	10,520	830	1,182	9,934	9,341	9,735	10,346	7,548	4,135	8,642	2,645	9,490	6,436	13,490
Georgetown, Guyana	7,967	4,306	4,276	6,374	6,744	4,672	3,792	8,195	8,847	2,262	2,486	3,693	2,717	15,219	4,533	4,919	10,012	17,072	10,926	18,858
Geraldton, Australia	14,585	13,474	13,345	14,388	14,712	17,677	13,743	12,645	12,240	15,905	14,997	13,767	15,274	6,360	14,865	17,000	10,746	5,008	8,223	2,468
Ghanzi, Botswana	14,071	9,131	8,430	7,143	8,655	11,072	8,053	6,762	7,298	10,158	8,165	7,182	9,852	8,962	5,866	13,900	6,286	10,304	2,493	11,417
Ghat, Libya	8,783	10,608	10,070	2,013	3,382	6,383	9,402	1,688	2,476	9,649	8,472	8,483	9,872	8,009	3,102	9,989	2,700	10,054	4,722	13,669
Gibraltar	7,100	10,054	9,672	201	1,769	4,450	9,000	1,932	2,625	8,517	7,824	8,227	8,888	8,982	2,665	8,071	3,793	10,965	6,655	14,922

Distances in Kilometers

	Coppermine, Canada	Coquimbo, Chile	Cordoba, Argentina	Cordoba, Spain	Cork, Ireland	Corner Brook, Canada	Corrientes, Argentina	Cosenza, Italy	Craiova, Romania	Cruzeiro do Sul, Brazil	Cuiaba, Brazil	Curitiba, Brazil	Cuzco, Peru	Dacca, Bangladesh	Dakar, Senegal	Dallas, Texas	Damascus, Syria	Danang, Vietnam	Dar es Salaam, Tanzania	Darwin, Australia
Gijon, Spain	6,339	10,533	10,212	632	954	3,996	9,552	1,886	2,355	8,782	8,315	8,838	9,217	8,697	3,391	7,674	3,781	10,607	7,177	14,623
Gisborne, New Zealand	13,049	9,558	9,935	19,764	18,452	15,482	10,607	18,446	17,789	11,133	11,788	11,379	10,748	11,421	16,949	11,822	16,555	9,448	13,422	5,476
Glasgow, United Kingdom	5,167	11,424	11,207	1,996	518	3,638	10,575	2,381	2,357	9,389	9,273	9,959	9,908	8,140	4,706	7,215	3,971	9,876	8,008	13,848
Godthab, Greenland	2,776	10,587	10,661	4,236	2,816	1,746	10,187	5,103	5,013	8,164	8,860	9,942	8,796	9,714	6,094	4,660	6,609	10,934	10,724	14,252
Gomez Palacio, Mexico	4,764	7,038	7,565	9,021	8,143	4,702	7,573	10,493	10,600	4,968	6,865	8,114	5,511	14,351	8,938	1,030	12,214	14,269	15,564	14,171
Goose Bay, Canada	1,957	10,560	11,068	8,668	7,220	4,797	11,014	9,365	9,051	8,382	10,122	11,419	8,971	10,894	10,091	3,244	10,472	10,790	14,918	11,880
Gorki, USSR	6,124	14,269	13,947	4,114	3,381	6,300	13,281	2,777	1,950	12,331	12,056	12,516	12,841	5,206	6,913	9,461	2,606	6,951	7,011	10,957
Goteborg, Sweden	5,423	12,393	12,138	2,521	1,457	4,541	11,492	2,071	1,701	10,398	10,214	10,820	10,911	7,130	5,374	7,997	3,255	8,877	7,566	12,867
Granada, Spain	7,048	10,245	9,863	121	1,674	4,503	9,190	1,756	2,437	8,697	8,015	8,415	9,073	8,798	2,845	8,145	3,631	10,778	6,608	14,742
Grand Turk, Turks & Caicos	5,975	5,691	5,897	6,540	6,292	3,266	5,574	8,315	8,750	3,223	4,416	5,701	3,871	14,625	5,709	2,827	10,219	15,852	12,403	17,492
Graz, Austria	6,612	12,154	11,777	1,942	1,805	5,260	11,105	865	718	10,479	9,925	10,316	10,906	7,001	4,708	8,879	2,314	8,924	6,414	12,934
Green Bay, Wisconsin	3,039	8,419	8,747	6,713	5,669	2,334	8,505	8,033	8,087	5,979	7,400	8,690	6,628	12,448	7,344	1,510	9,700	13,099	13,438	14,896
Grenoble, France	6,540	11,388	11,029	1,190	1,284	4,712	10,359	1,085	1,432	9,702	9,160	9,596	10,125	7,778	4,022	8,382	2,914	9,705	6,659	13,714
Guadalajara, Mexico	5,306	6,568	7,118	9,342	8,550	5,090	7,165	10,882	11,034	4,594	6,538	7,757	5,105	14,876	9,035	1,490	12,647	14,689	15,722	14,207
Guam (Agana)	9,049	15,894	16,463	13,497	12,318	12,740	17,126	12,106	11,274	15,902	17,779	18,046	16,063	5,812	16,335	11,721	10,841	3,939	11,861	3,253
Guantanamo, Cuba	5,982	5,559	5,823	6,976	6,681	3,549	5,554	8,742	9,157	3,084	4,470	5,769	3,739	14,912	6,140	2,562	10,644	15,983	12,831	17,128
Guatemala City, Guatemala	6,170	5,346	5,820	8,660	8,198	4,827	5,779	10,379	10,716	3,159	5,052	6,297	3,723	15,761	7,833	2,108	12,263	16,042	14,488	15,560
Guayaquil, Ecuador	8,233	3,205	3,630	8,855	8,932	6,044	3,584	10,688	11,263	1,004	2,999	4,167	1,524	17,404	7,122	4,261	12,555	18,240	13,201	16,275
Guiyang, China	8,983	19,590	18,989	9,923	9,277	11,502	18,595	8,230	7,459	17,906	17,866	17,625	18,552	1,673	12,456	12,982	6,707	1,175	8,148	5,047
Gur'yev, USSR	7,210	14,846	14,401	4,662	4,276	7,401	13,723	2,994	2,197	13,196	12,621	12,854	13,643	4,289	7,266	10,620	2,003	6,183	6,101	10,196
Haifa, Israel	8,567	13,163	12,602	3,630	4,075	7,538	11,942	1,831	1,602	12,115	11,037	11,002	12,394	5,469	5,647	11,166	142	7,512	4,410	11,295
Haikou, China	9,584	18,894	18,636	10,688	10,084	12,275	18,646	8,962	8,210	18,597	18,508	17,852	19,244	2,094	13,139	13,491	7,363	494	8,318	4,241
Haiphong, Vietnam	9,596	18,978	18,534	10,350	9,799	12,124	18,385	8,608	7,866	18,538	18,119	17,520	19,180	1,705	12,764	13,568	6,987	555	7,972	4,536
Hakodate, Japan	6,333	16,868	17,527	10,519	9,211	9,792	17,635	9,425	8,594	15,012	16,692	17,978	15,573	5,037	13,370	9,879	8,662	4,214	11,461	6,088
Halifax, Canada	3,915	8,300	8,422	4,879	4,069	644	8,000	6,374	6,586	5,860	6,713	7,895	6,497	11,989	5,462	3,147	8,180	13,231	11,559	16,184
Hamburg, West Germany	5,799	12,094	11,801	2,078	1,258	4,589	11,145	1,654	1,436	10,199	9,891	10,437	10,684	7,299	4,937	8,146	3,045	9,117	7,232	13,131
Hamilton, Bermuda	5,089	6,925	7,049	5,414	4,990	1,937	6,643	7,118	7,484	4,495	5,377	6,595	5,126	13,273	5,165	3,000	9,006	14,603	11,736	17,302
Hamilton, New Zealand	13,054	9,808	10,179	19,995	18,409	15,627	10,849	18,193	17,531	11,391	12,038	11,612	11,006	11,163	17,157	11,986	16,310	9,190	13,299	5,217
Hangzhou, China	8,212	18,920	19,592	10,546	9,623	11,231	19,683	9,014	8,195	17,175	18,337	18,854	17,779	3,031	13,284	12,021	7,711	1,988	9,523	4,863
Hannover, West Germany	5,913	12,021	11,716	1,964	1,243	4,623	11,057	1,537	1,371	10,157	9,812	10,340	10,633	7,336	4,824	8,201	2,985	9,173	7,131	13,190
Hanoi, Vietnam	9,600	18,978	18,498	10,274	9,735	12,089	18,319	8,528	7,789	18,513	18,031	17,441	19,144	1,616	12,679	13,584	6,901	604	7,894	4,604
Harare, Zimbabwe	13,958	10,177	9,477	7,216	8,622	11,413	9,108	6,509	6,921	11,187	9,202	8,237	10,899	7,919	6,422	14,581	5,708	9,253	1,513	10,608
Harbin, China	6,403	17,663	18,162	9,550	8,366	9,503	17,920	8,317	7,480	15,397	16,650	17,719	16,028	4,066	12,407	10,274	7,460	3,713	10,344	6,461
Harrisburg, Pennsylvania	3,836	7,796	8,042	6,066	5,242	1,779	7,728	7,563	7,748	5,321	6,547	7,815	5,975	12,801	6,387	1,963	9,351	13,747	12,710	15,911
Hartford, Connecticut	3,838	7,943	8,148	5,676	4,859	1,399	7,797	7,175	7,370	5,470	6,575	7,820	6,121	12,550	6,069	2,351	8,969	13,601	12,330	16,045
Havana, Cuba	5,452	5,993	6,339	7,419	6,926	3,579	6,144	9,115	9,443	3,566	5,151	6,451	4,209	14,764	6,854	1,775	10,993	15,520	13,546	16,330
Helena, Montana	2,372	9,414	9,884	8,186	6,895	3,975	9,792	9,196	9,042	7,162	8,867	10,166	7,766	11,898	9,184	2,007	10,585	11,986	14,817	13,075
Helsinki, Finland	5,440	13,187	12,932	3,242	2,247	5,133	12,285	2,400	1,765	11,157	11,009	11,599	11,684	6,394	6,102	8,422	3,078	8,098	7,531	12,078
Hengyang, China	8,791	19,504	19,423	10,319	9,568	11,552	19,180	8,675	7,884	17,804	18,303	18,211	18,451	2,259	12,930	12,708	7,219	1,282	8,722	4,781
Herat, Afghanistan	8,674	15,656	15,056	5,911	5,821	9,051	14,416	4,093	3,456	14,539	13,559	13,452	14,879	2,977	8,167	12,261	2,391	5,008	5,153	8,900
Hermosillo, Mexico	4,319	7,770	8,326	9,351	8,313	4,971	8,367	10,676	10,674	5,780	7,694	8,935	6,306	13,735	9,569	1,413	12,273	13,484	16,045	13,411
Hiroshima, Japan	7,374	17,735	18,438	10,868	9,717	10,715	18,698	9,545	8,707	16,096	17,755	18,996	16,641	4,229	13,715	10,969	8,494	3,160	10,727	5,190
Hiva Oa (Atuona)	8,821	7,329	8,018	14,501	13,564	10,180	8,557	15,927	15,841	7,303	8,981	9,532	7,302	14,570	13,675	6,501	17,338	12,733	18,160	9,800
Ho Chi Minh City, Vietnam	10,680	17,867	17,535	11,102	10,726	13,222	17,623	9,299	8,618	19,652	18,090	17,013	19,671	2,242	13,255	14,587	7,544	612	7,714	3,705
Hobart, Australia	14,639	11,023	11,172	17,601	17,948	17,958	11,766	15,951	15,551	13,111	13,102	12,251	12,589	9,400	16,555	14,403	14,060	7,657	10,943	3,731
Hohhot, China	7,344	18,776	18,900	9,164	8,223	10,011	18,293	7,688	6,858	16,309	16,973	17,558	16,963	2,738	11,940	11,355	6,534	2,759	9,039	6,219
Hong Kong	9,239	18,995	18,978	10,799	10,089	12,080	19,108	9,121	8,344	18,237	18,760	18,307	18,849	2,438	13,350	13,088	7,598	927	8,762	4,249
Honiara, Solomon Islands	10,759	13,015	13,499	16,505	15,180	14,394	14,177	15,127	14,302	13,909	15,185	15,029	13,758	8,399	19,366	11,812	13,698	6,360	13,214	3,199
Honolulu, Hawaii	5,952	10,850	11,552	12,877	11,367	8,942	11,932	13,267	12,736	9,835	11,827	12,805	10,137	11,110	14,146	6,108	13,757	9,771	17,576	8,640
Houston, Texas	4,429	7,084	7,530	8,099	7,264	3,806	7,432	9,601	9,747	4,802	6,554	7,843	5,407	14,055	8,069	362	11,359	14,343	14,649	14,903
Huambo, Angola	12,940	9,045	8,343	6,000	7,533	9,914	7,867	5,760	6,369	9,659	7,729	6,925	9,456	9,061	4,753	12,876	5,561	10,658	2,659	12,340
Hubli, India	10,742	16,244	15,540	8,106	8,246	11,524	15,106	6,281	5,784	16,421	14,816	14,164	16,491	1,847	9,864	14,612	4,389	3,540	4,655	6,861
Hugh Town, United Kingdom	5,681	10,924	10,662	1,343	267	3,672	10,016	2,132	2,351	9,007	8,738	9,360	9,490	8,488	4,038	7,336	3,918	10,310	7,669	14,320
Hull, Canada	3,363	8,361	8,588	5,777	4,827	1,400	8,252	7,177	7,305	5,886	7,042	8,292	6,539	12,221	6,399	2,290	8,916	13,183	12,488	15,577
Hyderabad, India	10,490	16,662	15,958	8,263	8,298	11,495	15,519	6,430	5,884	16,714	15,189	14,571	16,838	1,429	10,144	14,431	4,563	3,173	5,072	6,636
Hyderabad, Pakistan	9,666	16,043	15,366	6,903	6,944	10,208	14,798	5,070	4,514	15,448	14,176	13,816	15,685	2,239	8,916	13,382	3,225	4,260	4,752	7,960
Igloolik, Canada	1,350	11,050	11,268	5,619	4,124	2,614	10,899	6,277	6,034	8,574	9,639	10,834	9,227	9,661	7,494	4,180	7,552	10,494	11,887	13,278
Iloilo, Philippines	10,184	17,438	17,612	12,344	11,644	13,397	18,143	10,633	9,875	18,335	19,447	18,168	18,422	3,698	14,799	13,644	9,021	1,663	9,428	2,720
Indianapolis, Indiana	3,585	7,871	8,200	6,808	5,887	2,450	7,965	8,237	8,359	5,431	6,876	8,170	6,079	12,968	7,171	1,231	9,972	13,647	13,486	15,298
Innsbruck, Austria	6,485	11,884	11,523	1,682	1,520	4,983	10,853	968	1,017	10,178	9,657	10,082	10,611	7,302	4,492	8,619	2,590	9,216	6,589	13,229
Inuvik, Canada	775	12,032	12,427	7,491	5,928	4,517	12,220	7,809	7,371	9,656	11,105	12,382	10,293	9,184	9,524	4,598	8,681	9,441	13,152	11,508
Invercargill, New Zealand	14,164	9,644	9,907	18,906	19,352	16,584	10,551	17,622	17,256	11,535	11,831	11,200	11,063	11,013	16,445	12,904	15,754	9,164	12,270	5,149
Inverness, United Kingdom	5,009	11,529	11,327	2,178	677	3,608	10,701	2,505	2,427	9,458	9,392	10,099	9,988	8,085	4,878	7,149	4,039	9,791	8,134	13,746
Iquitos, Peru	8,583	2,907	3,203	8,405	8,648	6,026	3,038	10,232	10,864	434	2,290	3,511	1,087	17,196	6,484	4,747	12,056	18,635	12,450	16,815
Iraklion, Greece	8,093	12,406	11,892	2,679	3,233	6,683	11,220	902	1,004	11,201	10,228	10,314	11,509	6,347	4,818	10,347	1,046	8,380	4,894	12,224
Irkutsk, USSR	6,288	17,503	17,508	7,902	6,869	8,663	16,918	6,565	5,727	15,048	15,585	16,294	15,694	3,383	10,734	10,362	5,699	4,031	8,957	7,610
Islamabad, Pakistan	8,725	16,660	16,042	6,848	6,603	9,654	15,413	5,054	4,365	15,473	14,574	14,442	15,856	2,012	9,177	12,572	3,403	4,015	5,733	7,959
Istanbul, Turkey	7,564	12,937	12,462	2,906	3,077	6,530	11,785	1,099	560	11,536	10,727	10,906	11,900	5,964	5,336	10,129	1,057	7,964	5,399	11,904
Ivujivik, Canada	1,815	10,255	10,470	5,511	4,138	1,938	10,106	6,426	6,303	7,779	8,854	10,063	8,433	10,403	7,069	3,556	7,879	11,289	12,050	14,010
Iwo Jima Island, Japan	8,027	16,757	17,423	12,221	11,016	11,617	17,995	10,912	10,074	15,953	17,944	18,963	16,323	5,142	15,075	11,154	9,803	3,578	11,546	4,276
Izmir, Turkey	7,807	12,696	12,203	2,784	3,133	6,596	11,528	951	713	11,385	10,500	10,635	11,724	6,134	5,095	10,231	989	8,152	5,161	12,052
Jackson, Mississippi	4,268	7,173	7,564	7,532	6,719	3,257	7,402	9,047	9,215	4,798	6,426	7,726	5,429	13,805	7,550	624	10,823	14,308	14,093	15,306
Jaffna, Sri Lanka	11,324	16,294	15,615	8,902	9,065	12,328	15,288	7,082	6,601	17,014	15,228	14,406	16,953	1,909	10,537	15,296	5,183	3,140	4,869	6,131
Jakarta, Indonesia	12,482	16,001	15,740	12,322	12,264	15,051	15,979	10,490	9,931	18,477	16,960	15,665	17,824	3,755	13,872	16,187	8,610	2,464	7,462	2,729
Jamestown, St. Helena	12,444	6,821	6,134	5,958	7,519	8,838	5,601	6,527	7,314	7,320	5,384	4,635	7,111	11,323	3,621	11,057	7,059	12,997	5,004	14,304
Jamnagar, India	9,983	16,105	15,412	7,220	7,298	10,573	14,876	5,387	4,854	15,711	14,342	13,898	15,906	2,088	9,153	13,735	3,521	4,062	4,662	7,671
Jan Mayen Island	3,650	12,203	12,151	3,694	2,129	3,502	11,591	3,812	3,464	9,881	10,246	11,144	10,484	7,866	6,285	6,519	4,959	9,260	9,335	12,955
Jayapura, Indonesia	10,859	15,064	15,427	14,753	13,833	14,565	16,088	13,100	12,322	16,170	17,294	16,735	16,009	6,169	17,278	13,173	11,504	4,124	11,246	1,546
Jefferson City, Missouri	3,549	7,890	8,272	7,328	6,363	2,956	8,093	8,721	8,808	5,502	7,077	8,377	6,138	13,104	7,691	768	10,422	13,596	14,019	14,891
Jerusalem, Israel	8,687	13,145	12,576	3,693	4,174	7,638	11,919	1,909	1,713	12,144	11,033	10,973	12,411	5,457	5,654	11,272	217	7,502	4,290	11,258
Jiggalong, Australia	13,800	13,960	13,917	14,645	14,689	17,167	14,376	12,834	12,328	16,280	15,679	14,499	15,694	6,160	15,545	16,212	10,932	4,575	8,853	1,610
Jinan, China	7,633	18,942	19,411	9,817	8,860	10,508	18,915	8,336	7,507	16,647	17,572	18,210	17,291	2,920	12,592	11,556	7,137	2,442	9,376	5,629
Jodhpur, India	9,547	16,521	15,841	7,250	7,187	10,361	15,276	5,420	4,817	15,847	14,642	14,294	16,120	1,776	9,350	13,381	3,618	3,811	5,165	7,581
Johannesburg, South Africa	14,760	9,431	8,743	7,880	9,358	11,883	8,436	7,355	7,820	10,698	8,695	7,626	10,336	8,689	6,687	14,693	6,664	9,843	2,454	10,648
Juazeiro do Norte, Brazil	10,150	4,188	3,721	6,145	7,179	6,480	3,044	7,690	8,500	3,672	2,048	2,275	3,640	14,372	3,420	7,515	9,137	16,368	8,675	17,579
Juneau, Alaska	1,431	11,389	11,870	8,368	6,846	4,880	11,772	8,850	8,454	9,146	10,801	12,101	9,752	10,020	10,116	3,990	9,794	10,000	14,266	11,454
Kabul, Afghanistan	8,650	16,299	15,693	6,482	6,278	9,389	15,056	4,682	4,003	15,111	14,199	14,090	15,483	2,379	8,800	12,414	3,028	4,391	5,551	8,324
Kalgoorlie, Australia	14,521	13,150	13,100	15,082	15,335	17,983	13,562	13,325	12,894	15,503	14,871	13,712	14,902	6,878	15,478	16,414	11,422	5,371	8,885	2,242
Kaliningrad, USSR	5,927	12,781	12,471	2,672	1,942	5,159	11,809	1,743	1,181	10,895	10,571	11,075	11,382	6,607	5,518	8,621	2,661	8,420	7,039	12,435
Kamloops, Canada	1,934	10,146	10,630	8,359	6,962	4,358	10,549	9,178	8,926	7,918	9,626	10,924	8,518	11,231	9,643	2,765	10,403	11,237	14,789	12,400
Kampala, Uganda	12,044	11,374	10,676	5,650	6,881	10,022	10,172	4,626	4,951	11,699	9,884	9,210	11,603	6,750	5,727	13,583	3,694	8,472	1,083	10,923
Kananga, Zaire	12,435	10,052	9,353	5,606	7,045	9,801	8,853	5,044	5,563	10,483	8,613	7,895	10,340	8,070	4,952	13,091	4,600	9,751	1,869	11,861
Kano, Nigeria	10,091	9,718	9,110	3,158	4,682	7,297	8,471	3,120	3,869	9,235	7,743	7,506	9,321	8,672	2,825	10,691	3,694	10,665	3,990	13,773
Kanpur, India	9,470	17,232	16,543	7,855	7,661	10,685	15,995	6,039	5,387	16,485	15,369	15,014	16,808	1,060	10,050	13,441	4,290	3,104	5,761	6,955
Kansas City, Missouri	3,437	8,017	8,415	7,478	6,475	3,098	8,252	8,838	8,899	5,650	7,257	8,558	6,280	13,032	7,897	730	10,511	13,457	14,185	14,675
Kaohsiung, Taiwan	9,008	18,606	18,942	11,194	10,368	12,075	19,463	9,575	8,777	17,859	19,141	18,922	18,381	3,055	13,836	12,724	8,127	1,460	9,388	4,050
Karachi, Pakistan	9,724	15,900	15,222	6,818	6,895	10,184	14,655	4,985	4,447	15,339	14,042	13,673	15,563	2,373	8,797	13,401	3,127	4,387	4,619	8,059
Karaganda, USSR	6,936	16,320	15,944	6,115	5,439	8,106	15,268	4,554	3,730	14,355	14,095	14,430	14,890	3,264	8,820	10,801	3,515	4,894	7,078	8,892
Karl-Marx-Stadt, East Germany	6,154	12,151	11,820	2,004	1,489	4,896	11,155	1,308	1,091	10,348	9,932	10,410	10,809	7,138	4,849	8,480	2,705	9,005	6,870	13,025
Kasanga, Tanzania	12,956	10,735	10,030	6,344	7,683	10,648	9,584	5,508	5,892	11,392	9,474	8,655	11,201	7,359	5,942	14,047	4,676	8,912	916	10,856

Distances in Kilometers	Coppermine, Canada	Coquimbo, Chile	Cordoba, Argentina	Cordoba, Spain	Cork, Ireland	Corner Brook, Canada	Corrientes, Argentina	Cosenza, Italy	Craiova, Romania	Cruzeiro do Sul, Brazil	Cuiaba, Brazil	Curitiba, Brazil	Cuzco, Peru	Dacca, Bangladesh	Dakar, Senegal	Dallas, Texas	Damascus, Syria	Danang, Vietnam	Dar es Salaam, Tanzania	Darwin, Australia
Kashgar, China	8,069	16,870	16,329	6,772	6,340	9,214	15,667	5,045	4,289	15,296	14,679	14,728	15,761	2,216	9,275	11,970	3,586	4,064	6,364	8,078
Kassel, West Germany	6,015	11,957	11,642	1,867	1,243	4,657	10,981	1,435	1,320	10,121	9,743	10,255	10,589	7,368	4,725	8,252	2,934	9,221	7,042	13,240
Kathmandu, Nepal	9,275	17,743	17,055	8,186	7,881	10,765	16,504	6,391	5,700	16,803	15,835	15,522	17,193	677	10,477	13,306	4,701	2,688	6,251	6,623
Kayes, Mali	9,089	8,086	7,580	2,679	4,163	5,699	6,905	3,861	4,695	7,181	5,930	6,023	7,354	10,544	647	8,732	5,240	12,585	6,073	15,949
Kazan, USSR	6,235	14,593	14,264	4,426	3,706	6,583	13,596	3,032	2,196	12,653	12,378	12,820	13,166	4,892	7,209	9,677	2,664	6,625	6,992	10,631
Kemi, Finland	4,840	13,268	13,087	3,633	2,407	4,873	12,464	2,998	2,394	11,100	11,152	11,850	11,663	6,529	6,479	7,987	3,679	8,101	8,144	12,003
Kenora, Canada	2,311	9,125	9,479	6,898	5,695	2,629	9,255	8,043	7,992	6,706	8,162	9,453	7,351	11,849	7,850	1,899	9,586	12,379	13,601	14,175
Kerguelen Island	17,947	10,390	9,945	12,114	13,429	16,268	10,071	11,138	11,303	12,691	11,045	9,745	12,074	8,370	11,017	17,833	9,763	8,201	5,512	6,904
Kerkira, Greece	7,512	12,161	11,700	2,148	2,572	6,026	11,022	317	615	10,764	9,947	10,158	11,119	6,743	4,566	9,687	1,612	8,748	5,511	12,675
Kermanshah, Iran	8,580	14,285	13,709	4,625	4,785	8,189	13,056	2,791	2,282	13,206	12,168	12,105	13,510	4,349	6,777	11,678	999	6,389	4,624	10,223
Khabarovsk, USSR	5,856	16,970	17,513	9,649	8,355	9,134	17,382	8,572	7,745	14,785	16,215	17,415	15,400	4,774	12,502	9,636	7,892	4,351	11,001	6,766
Kharkov, USSR	6,719	13,716	13,320	3,504	3,100	6,341	12,644	1,972	1,134	12,001	11,486	11,823	12,452	5,484	6,205	9,739	1,833	7,370	6,300	11,387
Khartoum, Sudan	10,389	12,184	11,528	4,411	5,412	8,752	10,932	3,069	3,289	11,859	10,330	9,951	11,942	6,098	5,359	12,425	2,019	8,056	2,587	11,258
Khon Kaen, Thailand	10,170	18,396	17,899	10,375	9,973	12,519	17,776	8,584	7,887	18,918	17,778	16,969	19,384	1,527	12,619	14,175	6,866	577	7,453	4,440
Kiev, USSR	6,579	13,321	12,940	3,109	2,699	5,985	12,266	1,668	848	11,589	11,092	11,462	12,041	5,895	5,844	9,439	1,940	7,780	6,397	11,798
Kigali, Rwanda	12,227	11,005	10,306	5,682	6,980	10,027	9,808	4,781	5,163	11,386	9,547	8,849	11,270	7,114	5,548	13,523	3,978	8,812	1,155	11,141
Kingston, Canada	3,452	8,233	8,468	5,878	4,953	1,510	8,141	7,298	7,436	5,757	6,941	8,197	6,411	12,364	6,431	2,171	9,047	13,311	12,579	15,632
Kingston, Jamaica	6,159	5,340	5,630	7,247	6,970	3,830	5,391	9,020	9,443	2,872	4,355	5,655	3,526	15,188	6,329	2,587	10,923	16,197	13,006	17,007
Kingstown, Saint Vincent	7,193	4,893	4,940	6,192	6,354	3,981	4,501	8,026	8,609	2,620	3,228	4,460	3,179	14,902	4,730	4,215	9,899	16,575	11,323	18,724
Kinshasa, Zaire	12,037	9,455	8,768	5,110	6,623	9,158	8,230	4,828	5,451	9,725	7,895	7,257	9,614	8,701	4,177	12,337	4,732	10,460	2,671	12,669
Kirkwall, United Kingdom	4,903	11,685	11,492	2,348	860	3,661	10,869	2,577	2,437	9,590	9,557	10,275	10,127	7,966	5,061	7,159	4,042	9,648	8,199	13,590
Kirov, USSR	5,929	14,584	14,295	4,486	3,653	6,398	13,635	3,196	2,371	12,558	12,387	12,894	13,092	5,023	7,304	9,418	2,959	6,689	7,305	10,672
Kiruna, Sweden	4,559	13,118	12,969	3,676	2,352	4,626	12,359	3,187	2,629	10,904	11,035	11,782	11,479	6,756	6,496	7,697	3,959	8,279	8,417	12,140
Kisangani, Zaire	11,833	10,674	9,985	5,153	6,507	9,467	9,452	4,392	4,856	10,887	9,098	8,479	10,809	7,478	4,945	12,929	3,833	9,255	1,760	11,729
Kishinev, USSR	6,917	13,113	12,698	2,917	2,728	6,110	12,021	1,331	493	11,494	10,884	11,189	11,915	5,985	5,572	9,636	1,626	7,920	6,048	11,923
Kitchner, Canada	3,389	8,183	8,453	6,208	5,263	1,835	8,158	7,614	7,735	5,713	6,994	8,267	6,367	12,510	6,733	1,853	9,348	13,356	12,911	15,454
Knoxville, Tennessee	4,049	7,416	7,737	6,827	6,020	2,557	7,499	8,342	8,523	4,970	6,415	7,710	5,619	13,372	6,962	1,237	10,128	14,107	13,423	15,676
Kosice, Czechoslovakia	6,578	12,624	12,246	2,412	2,132	5,535	11,573	1,118	525	10,925	10,395	10,778	11,362	6,555	5,166	9,098	2,101	8,464	6,396	12,478
Kota Kinabalu, Malaysia	10,901	17,240	17,191	12,219	11,732	13,891	17,568	10,433	9,730	19,061	18,652	17,356	18,808	3,375	14,415	14,495	8,700	1,406	8,646	2,614
Krakow, Poland	6,402	12,583	12,223	2,382	1,990	5,372	11,553	1,233	705	10,835	10,357	10,775	11,284	6,648	5,174	8,924	2,280	8,536	6,575	12,554
Kralendijk, Bonaire	7,048	4,674	4,841	6,869	6,897	4,189	4,502	8,697	9,239	2,242	3,350	4,641	2,870	15,415	5,501	3,698	10,588	16,859	12,079	17,959
Krasnodar, USSR	7,301	13,836	13,380	3,695	3,526	6,857	12,702	1,977	1,206	12,301	11,616	11,832	12,709	5,179	6,246	10,305	1,301	7,135	5,741	11,124
Krasnoyarsk, USSR	6,076	16,856	16,740	7,046	6,047	8,059	16,116	5,717	4,879	14,488	14,804	15,446	15,113	3,592	9,875	10,124	4,944	4,622	8,505	8,370
Kristiansand, Norway	5,279	12,198	11,960	2,439	1,258	4,302	11,319	2,180	1,885	10,175	10,031	10,667	10,695	7,359	5,272	7,771	3,462	9,090	7,731	13,070
Kuala Lumpur, Malaysia	11,627	16,951	16,552	11,232	11,096	13,907	16,622	9,399	8,803	19,223	17,234	16,058	18,674	2,578	13,041	15,579	7,547	1,595	7,023	3,657
Kuching, Malaysia	11,554	16,855	16,651	12,080	11,795	14,297	16,917	10,256	9,615	19,264	17,868	16,586	18,658	3,260	14,008	15,263	8,439	1,622	7,947	2,745
Kumasi, Ghana	10,276	8,464	7,862	3,470	5,053	7,036	7,219	4,033	4,847	8,038	6,490	6,258	8,090	9,926	1,941	10,099	4,906	11,907	4,781	14,784
Kumzar, Oman	9,539	14,926	14,275	5,812	6,045	9,442	13,673	3,988	3,537	14,265	12,984	12,693	14,483	3,434	7,717	12,879	2,094	5,462	4,106	9,116
Kunming, China	9,244	19,218	18,559	9,734	9,184	11,585	18,167	8,002	7,253	18,013	17,580	17,209	18,614	1,253	12,183	13,280	6,412	1,151	7,712	5,156
Kuqa Chang, China	7,816	17,435	16,942	7,245	6,672	9,329	16,271	5,576	4,788	15,606	15,212	15,352	16,132	2,043	9,836	11,815	4,213	3,662	6,964	7,676
Kurgan, USSR	6,331	15,588	15,279	5,443	4,660	7,292	14,612	4,009	3,171	13,544	13,384	13,835	14,090	4,082	8,220	10,084	3,310	5,687	7,305	9,665
Kuwait, Kuwait	9,133	14,227	13,611	4,917	5,223	8,658	12,979	3,099	2,701	13,385	12,191	12,010	13,632	4,254	6,862	12,192	1,198	6,296	4,110	10,009
Kuybyshev, USSR	6,524	14,687	14,323	4,484	3,866	6,827	13,649	2,996	2,158	12,824	12,462	12,843	13,320	4,697	7,224	9,959	2,450	6,481	6,728	10,497
Kyoto, Japan	7,195	17,428	18,129	10,970	9,768	10,608	18,404	9,704	8,865	15,826	17,556	18,843	16,357	4,535	13,827	10,720	8,715	3,451	11,032	5,279
Kzyl-Orda, USSR	7,514	15,917	15,443	5,745	5,297	8,258	14,767	4,057	3,274	14,248	13,696	13,871	14,715	3,253	8,320	11,229	2,795	5,106	6,287	9,123
L'vov, USSR	6,517	12,853	12,480	2,643	2,278	5,637	11,807	1,321	614	11,127	10,625	11,015	11,573	6,355	5,402	9,161	2,077	8,249	6,447	12,266
La Ceiba, Honduras	6,127	5,327	5,754	8,262	7,845	4,516	5,658	9,996	10,355	3,026	4,841	6,111	3,628	15,625	7,417	2,136	11,887	16,120	14,081	15,961
La Coruna, Spain	6,261	10,349	10,041	681	949	3,809	9,384	2,103	2,574	8,572	8,136	8,687	9,012	8,907	3,296	7,483	4,001	10,808	7,340	14,826
La Paz, Bolivia	10,089	1,527	1,699	8,942	9,511	7,319	1,548	10,688	11,427	1,094	1,295	2,196	528	17,655	6,554	6,249	12,330	19,644	11,642	16,190
La Paz, Mexico	4,865	7,294	7,870	9,652	8,697	5,295	7,948	11,059	11,105	5,398	7,351	8,563	5,894	14,258	9,642	1,627	12,714	13,910	16,255	13,489
La Ronge, Canada	1,508	9,967	10,356	7,257	5,899	3,254	10,163	8,169	7,990	7,585	9,094	10,388	8,222	11,145	8,548	2,568	9,528	11,512	13,798	13,258
Labrador City, Canada	3,016	9,196	9,348	4,970	3,866	771	8,943	6,230	6,299	6,735	7,664	8,849	7,380	11,234	6,059	3,272	7,913	12,344	11,693	15,246
Lagos, Nigeria	10,489	8,916	8,296	3,578	5,156	7,400	7,666	3,861	4,643	8,579	6,993	6,694	8,615	9,430	2,451	10,574	4,527	11,391	4,248	14,236
Lahore, Pakistan	8,954	16,749	16,108	7,055	6,845	9,910	15,496	5,250	4,579	15,686	14,713	14,519	16,047	1,811	9,333	12,820	3,556	3,837	5,647	7,751
Lambasa, Fiji	10,706	10,873	11,419	17,594	16,010	13,743	12,085	16,994	16,163	11,674	12,982	13,007	11,514	10,634	18,221	10,426	15,877	8,600	14,939	5,242
Lansing, Michigan	3,328	8,162	8,468	6,543	5,573	2,165	8,208	7,930	8,030	5,708	7,083	8,369	6,359	12,629	7,053	1,543	9,644	13,365	13,250	15,238
Lanzhou, China	8,039	19,194	18,788	9,008	8,254	10,416	18,117	7,398	6,594	16,835	16,987	17,190	17,472	1,870	11,668	12,094	6,047	2,259	8,214	6,081
Laoag, Philippines	9,464	18,238	18,468	11,584	10,814	12,566	18,977	9,924	9,141	18,177	19,566	18,705	18,588	3,192	14,158	13,110	8,404	1,338	9,341	3,573
Largeau, Chad	9,800	11,033	10,422	3,210	4,479	7,589	9,785	2,386	2,960	10,456	9,040	8,818	10,585	7,376	3,917	11,199	2,433	9,386	3,519	12,710
Las Vegas, Nevada	3,523	8,635	9,177	9,130	7,943	4,784	9,190	10,281	10,180	6,578	8,444	9,709	7,128	12,855	9,737	1,723	11,743	12,652	15,849	12,973
Launceston, Australia	14,503	11,171	11,328	17,591	17,830	17,889	11,925	15,900	15,472	13,239	13,260	12,416	12,724	9,282	16,691	14,387	14,002	7,520	10,977	3,579
Le Havre, France	5,929	11,278	10,983	1,349	663	4,124	10,327	1,706	1,884	9,426	9,073	9,630	9,894	8,061	4,181	7,777	3,456	9,915	7,299	13,933
Leipzig, East Germany	6,091	12,135	11,811	2,007	1,438	4,836	11,147	1,368	1,155	10,315	9,918	10,409	10,780	7,172	4,857	8,417	2,769	9,031	6,935	13,051
Leningrad, USSR	5,556	13,474	13,209	3,475	2,537	5,408	12,557	2,494	1,789	11,453	11,290	11,857	11,979	6,100	6,330	8,651	2,970	7,804	7,440	11,787
Leon, Spain	6,437	10,476	10,147	528	1,057	4,052	9,485	1,868	2,372	8,752	8,256	8,763	9,179	8,728	3,299	7,727	3,770	10,648	7,106	14,661
Lerwick, United Kingdom	4,840	11,841	11,654	2,490	1,024	3,746	11,033	2,618	2,423	9,732	9,718	10,441	10,273	7,834	5,220	7,204	4,016	9,500	8,226	13,433
Lhasa, China	8,978	18,334	17,654	8,523	8,083	10,774	17,086	6,766	6,034	17,040	16,330	16,104	17,523	661	10,931	13,045	5,160	2,307	6,849	6,316
Libreville, Gabon	11,343	9,149	8,486	4,401	5,952	8,346	7,901	4,365	5,070	9,147	7,412	6,918	9,101	9,079	3,354	11,508	4,616	10,944	3,408	13,432
Lilongwe, Malawi	13,616	10,653	9,951	7,012	8,357	11,295	9,561	6,173	6,535	11,561	9,593	8,672	11,305	7,440	6,470	14,622	5,262	8,835	997	10,430
Lima, Peru	9,367	2,069	2,517	9,320	9,639	7,013	2,554	11,133	11,799	691	2,299	3,273	574	18,170	7,207	5,387	12,905	19,302	12,687	15,920
Limerick, Ireland	5,336	10,986	10,758	1,670	86	3,433	10,125	2,412	2,543	8,986	8,826	9,506	9,493	8,527	4,287	7,075	4,139	10,296	7,988	14,283
Limoges, France	6,335	11,128	10,794	1,014	980	4,369	10,130	1,426	1,778	9,384	8,907	9,395	9,821	8,096	3,873	8,044	3,271	10,002	6,946	14,018
Limon, Costa Rica	6,842	4,596	5,003	8,309	8,081	4,908	4,899	10,102	10,547	2,267	4,103	5,363	2,873	16,208	7,131	2,892	12,007	16,872	13,682	16,331
Lincoln, Nebraska	3,206	8,261	8,668	7,533	6,474	3,153	8,511	8,838	8,864	5,905	7,520	8,820	6,533	12,822	8,062	893	10,473	13,205	14,257	14,439
Linz, Austria	6,453	12,130	11,769	1,927	1,670	5,116	11,098	1,012	854	10,410	9,903	10,325	10,848	7,071	4,730	8,727	2,461	8,976	6,576	12,992
Lisbon, Portugal	6,701	9,971	9,631	393	1,466	4,012	8,966	2,192	2,799	8,310	7,747	8,238	8,715	9,174	2,787	7,643	4,090	11,121	7,093	15,120
Little Rock, Arkansas	3,956	7,492	7,891	7,554	6,664	3,219	7,734	9,011	9,136	5,127	6,758	8,058	5,756	13,528	7,725	473	10,749	13,981	14,187	15,034
Liverpool, United Kingdom	5,442	11,338	11,092	1,732	406	3,778	10,452	2,144	2,193	9,365	9,164	9,806	9,866	8,144	4,482	7,393	3,801	9,926	7,763	13,922
Lodz, Poland	6,216	12,614	12,273	2,439	1,914	5,253	11,606	1,406	887	10,812	10,392	10,845	11,276	6,675	5,259	8,780	2,440	8,537	6,758	12,557
Lome, Togo	10,441	8,695	8,080	3,568	5,152	7,277	7,445	3,972	4,769	8,337	6,757	6,477	8,375	9,664	2,248	10,394	4,720	11,630	4,464	14,465
London, United Kingdom	5,721	11,384	11,108	1,557	579	4,028	10,458	1,857	1,947	9,478	9,189	9,779	9,961	8,017	4,369	7,661	3,544	9,840	7,473	13,852
Londonderry, United Kingdom	5,151	11,212	11,000	1,913	353	3,463	10,371	2,476	2,513	9,173	9,066	9,765	9,692	8,355	4,560	7,065	4,124	10,092	8,090	14,061
Longlac, Canada	2,553	8,960	9,260	6,376	5,231	2,066	8,985	7,592	7,595	6,503	7,834	9,109	7,156	11,858	7,278	2,071	9,202	12,569	13,097	14,653
Lord Howe Island, Australia	13,041	11,370	11,686	18,388	17,529	16,375	12,342	16,568	15,902	13,026	13,588	13,023	12,635	9,529	18,102	13,033	14,716	7,567	12,358	3,582
Los Angeles, California	3,763	8,633	9,200	9,497	8,301	5,151	9,252	10,635	10,517	6,665	8,571	9,818	7,191	12,933	10,077	1,995	12,070	12,601	16,214	12,702
Louangphrabang, Laos	9,818	18,714	18,146	10,070	9,620	12,132	17,915	8,296	7,580	18,541	17,677	17,033	19,076	1,284	12,390	13,843	6,618	769	7,485	4,762
Louisville, Kentucky	3,756	7,699	8,029	6,855	5,973	2,521	7,797	8,315	8,456	5,259	6,716	8,011	5,907	13,134	7,132	1,171	10,068	13,819	13,508	15,411
Luanda, Angola	12,439	9,012	8,317	5,497	7,039	9,400	7,802	5,334	5,978	9,435	7,552	6,839	9,279	9,121	4,266	12,412	5,280	10,813	2,881	12,743
Lubumbashi, Zaire	13,198	10,206	9,501	6,433	7,843	10,647	9,064	5,761	6,210	10,934	8,994	8,143	10,718	7,887	5,745	13,905	5,086	9,404	1,405	11,158
Lusaka, Zambia	13,622	10,067	9,363	6,837	8,260	11,016	8,960	6,185	6,630	10,949	8,980	8,064	10,692	8,024	6,031	14,193	5,480	9,447	1,533	10,963
Luxembourg, Luxembourg	6,098	11,657	11,338	1,567	1,060	4,518	10,676	1,397	1,463	9,847	9,441	9,949	10,306	7,637	4,426	8,151	3,054	9,508	7,025	13,528
Luxor, Egypt	9,298	12,666	12,061	3,763	4,511	7,943	11,421	2,151	2,216	11,907	10,629	10,457	12,106	5,802	5,344	11,618	936	7,837	3,665	11,418
Lynn Lake, Canada	1,416	10,019	10,378	6,931	5,571	2,975	10,151	7,845	7,675	7,605	9,042	10,327	8,249	11,013	8,268	2,695	9,221	11,481	13,473	13,419
Lyon, France	6,454	11,362	11,012	1,182	1,190	4,622	10,344	1,177	1,498	9,651	9,136	9,589	10,081	7,828	4,029	8,290	2,997	9,746	6,752	13,759
Macapa, Brazil	8,939	3,957	3,745	6,323	6,988	5,461	3,155	8,072	8,806	2,538	1,814	2,823	2,752	15,106	4,039	6,007	9,766	17,134	10,056	18,615
Madison, Wisconsin	3,148	8,295	8,638	6,884	5,857	2,502	8,413	8,220	8,280	5,867	7,331	8,626	6,513	12,610	7,451	1,314	9,893	13,216	13,605	14,882
Madras, India	10,945	16,558	15,867	8,701	8,790	12,007	15,497	6,872	6,353	17,008	15,328	14,586	17,033	1,590	10,463	14,920	4,986	3,026	5,039	6,255
Madrid, Spain	6,724	10,455	10,098	295	1,330	4,310	9,430	1,707	2,294	8,814	8,227	8,680	9,217	8,670	3,150	7,978	3,611	10,620	6,830	14,616
Madurai, India	11,315	16,156	15,470	8,719	8,913	12,203	15,124	6,904	6,437	16,806	15,032	14,231	16,755	2,009	10,330	15,248	5,002	3,332	4,687	6,334
Magadan, USSR	4,275	15,461	15,944	8,973	7,507	7,696	15,786	8,281	7,518	13,194	14,656	15,907	13,816	6,103	11,708	8,055	8,081	5,930	11,858	8,184

Distances in Kilometers

	Coppermine, Canada	Coquimbo, Chile	Cordoba, Argentina	Cordoba, Spain	Cork, Ireland	Corner Brook, Canada	Corrientes, Argentina	Cosenza, Italy	Craiova, Romania	Cruzeiro do Sul, Brazil	Cuiaba, Brazil	Curitiba, Brazil	Cuzco, Peru	Dacca, Bangladesh	Dakar, Senegal	Dallas, Texas	Damascus, Syria	Danang, Vietnam	Dar es Salaam, Tanzania	Darwin, Australia
Magdalena, Bolivia	9,877	1,986	2,001	8,389	8,986	6,926	1,659	10,132	10,872	1,121	903	2,054	850	17,114	6,006	6,174	11,780	19,155	11,284	16,716
Magdeburg, East Germany	5,985	12,132	11,819	2,039	1,378	4,754	11,158	1,473	1,252	10,284	9,920	10,431	10,757	7,207	4,895	8,324	2,863	9,051	7,042	13,070
Majuro Atoll, Marshall Isls.	8,592	13,051	13,697	15,002	13,462	12,178	14,303	14,255	13,439	13,000	14,802	15,284	13,097	8,763	17,415	9,773	13,472	6,916	14,727	4,966
Malabo, Equatorial Guinea	10,966	9,274	8,626	4,024	5,572	8,010	8,021	4,009	4,730	9,125	7,456	7,040	9,118	8,998	3,119	11,237	4,360	10,909	3,585	13,590
Male, Maldives	12,007	15,338	14,659	8,707	9,106	12,507	14,345	6,946	6,588	16,259	14,370	13,481	16,096	2,842	10,003	15,809	5,050	4,028	3,982	6,601
Manado, Indonesia	11,066	16,423	16,562	13,262	12,657	14,410	17,103	11,498	10,774	17,983	18,442	17,283	17,744	4,453	15,509	14,232	9,789	2,435	9,548	1,679
Managua, Nicaragua	6,532	4,928	5,366	8,453	8,119	4,844	5,291	10,217	10,615	2,661	4,525	5,780	3,248	16,021	7,434	2,524	12,118	16,506	14,039	16,002
Manama, Bahrain	9,509	14,367	13,726	5,306	5,654	9,093	13,114	3,502	3,132	13,693	12,404	12,136	13,902	4,016	7,138	12,624	1,597	6,045	3,852	9,670
Manaus, Brazil	8,940	3,202	3,159	7,271	7,786	5,774	2,696	9,056	9,761	1,480	1,443	2,722	1,747	16,114	5,092	5,551	10,792	18,094	11,004	17,914
Manchester, New Hampshire	3,763	8,079	8,271	5,537	4,699	1,236	7,908	7,020	7,206	5,608	6,674	7,909	6,257	12,390	6,004	2,488	8,808	13,465	12,209	16,005
Mandalay, Burma	9,721	18,487	17,808	9,435	9,057	11,736	17,427	7,648	6,947	18,016	17,019	16,486	18,450	612	11,720	13,791	5,950	1,435	6,963	5,379
Mangareva Island, Fr.Polynesia	10,217	6,305	6,952	15,036	14,481	11,018	7,559	16,765	16,965	6,860	8,234	8,538	6,694	15,415	13,429	7,394	18,580	13,408	16,637	9,902
Manila, Philippines	9,831	17,892	18,071	11,911	11,185	12,967	18,578	10,221	9,451	18,358	19,700	18,444	18,629	3,364	14,422	13,409	8,649	1,382	9,321	3,182
Mannheim, West Germany	6,175	11,800	11,471	1,668	1,223	4,676	10,807	1,289	1,299	10,009	9,581	10,068	10,464	7,474	4,522	8,301	2,896	9,352	6,915	13,372
Maputo, Mozambique	14,867	9,826	9,143	8,072	9,509	12,175	8,855	7,422	7,833	11,142	9,139	8,057	10,771	8,307	7,037	15,102	6,593	9,412	2,238	10,224
Mar del Plata, Argentina	12,675	1,553	951	9,994	11,041	9,632	1,174	11,400	12,235	3,689	2,488	1,600	3,066	16,599	7,178	8,829	12,508	17,208	10,146	14,351
Maracaibo, Venezuela	7,097	4,496	4,722	7,262	7,251	4,430	4,439	9,087	9,617	2,027	3,371	4,671	2,675	15,734	5,890	3,557	10,980	17,048	12,435	17,581
Marrakech, Morocco	7,462	9,552	9,150	754	2,251	4,562	8,476	2,351	3,102	8,115	7,324	7,687	8,453	9,406	2,110	8,091	4,134	11,413	6,580	15,316
Marseilles, France	6,722	11,262	10,887	1,049	1,410	4,793	10,215	1,010	1,482	9,629	9,032	9,438	10,037	7,854	3,848	8,471	2,890	9,801	6,517	13,799
Maseru, Lesotho	15,068	9,204	8,523	8,162	9,658	12,092	8,245	7,685	8,162	10,570	8,570	7,463	10,181	8,931	6,853	14,757	7,015	10,009	2,783	10,602
Mashhad, Iran	8,450	15,444	14,867	5,607	5,499	8,736	14,215	3,796	3,143	14,238	13,314	13,263	14,594	3,265	7,910	11,976	2,147	5,284	5,222	9,201
Mazatlan, Mexico	4,995	6,979	7,536	9,415	8,532	5,095	7,589	10,885	10,982	5,019	6,960	8,182	5,530	14,506	9,283	1,418	12,595	14,265	15,935	13,886
Mbabane, Swaziland	14,863	9,684	9,000	8,035	9,487	12,103	8,708	7,427	7,857	10,993	8,990	7,909	10,623	8,446	6,941	14,982	6,643	9,560	2,327	10,352
Mbandaka, Zaire	11,672	9,982	9,301	4,808	6,267	9,000	8,746	4,349	4,932	10,115	8,343	7,768	10,047	8,198	4,248	12,336	4,154	10,010	2,455	12,470
McMurdo Sound, Antarctica	16,975	7,513	7,485	15,566	17,138	16,346	8,002	15,505	15,926	9,917	9,345	8,363	9,289	12,198	13,019	13,732	14,512	10,990	10,073	7,483
Mecca, Saudi Arabia	9,892	13,155	12,510	4,632	5,334	8,784	11,902	2,991	2,934	12,642	11,233	10,922	12,788	5,183	6,076	12,448	1,380	7,183	3,125	10,619
Medan, Indonesia	11,658	16,904	16,447	10,942	10,859	13,763	16,454	9,108	8,530	18,966	16,963	15,830	18,515	2,398	12,706	15,666	7,245	1,732	6,698	3,976
Medellin, Colombia	7,446	4,033	4,339	7,905	7,904	5,016	4,143	9,733	10,271	1,571	3,233	4,516	2,222	16,363	6,418	3,669	11,623	17,502	12,839	17,055
Medicine Hat, Canada	1,996	9,676	10,120	7,873	6,548	3,740	9,993	8,832	8,660	7,374	9,015	10,315	7,991	11,574	9,000	2,233	10,196	11,754	14,460	13,087
Medina, Saudi Arabia	9,559	13,263	12,634	4,436	5,061	8,520	12,011	2,740	2,628	12,610	11,281	11,037	12,793	5,138	6,042	12,171	1,051	7,161	3,459	10,704
Melbourne, Australia	14,243	11,605	11,766	17,376	17,424	17,798	12,363	15,615	15,134	13,647	13,698	12,848	13,142	8,886	16,916	14,477	13,710	7,099	10,913	3,143
Memphis, Tennessee	3,969	7,467	7,846	7,359	6,490	3,037	7,667	8,831	8,971	5,076	6,661	7,962	5,712	13,492	7,520	676	10,583	14,022	13,982	15,210
Merauke, Indonesia	11,483	14,578	14,885	15,236	14,419	15,205	15,531	13,515	12,766	15,967	16,797	16,117	15,707	6,490	17,516	13,582	11,829	4,460	11,115	1,130
Merida, Mexico	5,502	5,966	6,400	8,174	7,602	4,185	6,302	9,839	10,124	3,670	5,456	6,736	4,274	15,061	7,624	1,490	11,698	15,474	14,319	15,631
Meridian, Mississippi	4,298	7,138	7,515	7,408	6,615	3,152	7,339	8,936	9,116	4,745	6,343	7,644	5,381	13,797	7,409	763	10,722	14,353	13,956	15,436
Messina, Italy	7,549	11,752	11,294	1,782	2,411	5,821	10,616	137	969	10,373	9,538	9,757	10,719	7,141	4,159	9,499	1,939	9,151	5,553	13,064
Mexico City, Mexico	5,498	6,223	6,749	9,082	8,380	4,919	6,766	10,681	10,888	4,173	6,100	7,331	4,704	15,124	8,636	1,500	12,491	15,080	15,330	14,646
Miami, Florida	5,233	6,240	6,552	7,077	6,561	3,215	6,320	8,760	9,079	3,786	5,269	6,569	4,437	14,437	6,615	1,789	10,633	15,288	13,291	16,461
Midway Islands, USA	5,977	12,956	13,659	12,649	11,066	9,568	14,042	12,400	11,692	11,859	13,862	14,901	12,208	9,007	14,797	7,557	12,313	7,684	15,501	7,166
Milan, Italy	6,610	11,643	11,273	1,433	1,479	4,934	10,602	897	1,159	9,976	9,414	9,825	10,396	7,504	4,231	8,593	2,665	9,436	6,519	13,442
Milford Sound, New Zealand	14,005	9,812	10,086	19,042	19,146	16,545	10,733	17,603	17,177	11,667	12,006	11,392	11,206	10,887	16,652	12,873	15,713	9,018	12,347	4,999
Milwaukee, Wisconsin	3,194	8,259	8,591	6,777	5,766	2,395	8,355	8,128	8,200	5,822	7,260	8,552	6,470	12,612	7,330	1,380	9,813	13,257	13,495	14,988
Minsk, USSR	6,153	13,204	12,868	3,035	2,409	5,604	12,201	1,835	1,100	11,356	10,984	11,439	11,836	6,142	5,845	9,020	2,369	7,970	6,816	11,988
Mogadiscio, Somalia	12,101	12,691	11,987	6,462	7,433	10,805	11,523	5,070	5,140	13,134	11,307	10,578	13,030	5,408	7,033	14,480	3,606	7,053	1,191	9,575
Mombasa, Kenya	12,672	11,793	11,088	6,523	7,682	10,904	10,646	5,368	5,587	12,404	10,513	9,716	12,241	6,300	6,629	14,497	4,171	7,864	307	10,049
Monclova, Mexico	4,643	7,061	7,567	8,766	7,896	4,451	7,546	10,244	10,359	4,926	6,789	8,052	5,488	14,263	8,705	789	11,973	14,282	15,316	14,366
Moncton, Canada	3,729	8,450	8,583	4,869	4,066	604	8,189	6,390	6,574	6,002	6,887	8,074	6,642	11,880	5,609	3,099	8,175	13,085	11,637	15,999
Monrovia, Liberia	9,951	7,601	7,038	3,549	5,058	6,467	6,376	4,550	5,388	7,033	5,549	5,443	7,108	10,869	1,174	9,265	5,707	12,875	5,749	15,772
Monte Carlo, Monaco	6,738	11,427	11,048	1,214	1,491	4,909	10,376	886	1,313	9,798	9,197	9,592	10,207	7,684	3,994	8,582	2,742	9,631	6,450	13,629
Monterrey, Mexico	4,794	6,889	7,393	8,760	7,928	4,473	7,371	10,267	10,405	4,751	6,618	7,879	5,313	14,421	8,622	858	12,018	14,458	15,261	14,489
Montevideo, Uruguay	12,394	1,525	840	9,648	10,678	9,288	860	11,082	11,914	3,453	2,138	1,243	2,851	16,573	6,843	8,608	12,244	17,413	10,081	14,713
Montgomery, Alabama	4,359	7,079	7,434	7,214	6,454	2,993	7,235	8,763	8,963	4,661	6,209	7,509	5,304	13,787	7,185	987	10,564	14,427	13,739	15,645
Montpelier, Vermont	3,596	8,220	8,422	5,580	4,693	1,233	8,065	7,028	7,191	5,747	6,835	8,074	6,398	12,282	6,126	2,454	8,797	13,324	12,272	15,839
Montpellier, France	6,645	11,173	10,808	967	1,304	4,670	10,138	1,137	1,597	9,518	8,945	9,370	9,931	7,964	3,795	8,349	3,016	9,904	6,622	13,906
Montreal, Canada	3,437	8,360	8,569	5,616	4,684	1,243	8,217	7,030	7,170	5,886	6,991	8,232	6,538	12,172	6,238	2,440	8,780	13,184	12,324	15,681
Moosonee, Canada	2,618	9,046	9,301	5,927	4,790	1,637	8,982	7,152	7,172	6,573	7,783	9,037	7,228	11,651	6,892	2,441	8,783	12,494	12,648	14,855
Moroni, Comoros	13,571	11,648	10,950	7,424	8,612	11,799	10,588	6,301	6,506	12,621	10,652	9,714	12,361	6,454	7,301	15,335	5,055	7,783	695	9,482
Moscow, USSR	6,112	13,869	13,542	3,710	3,005	6,024	12,876	2,414	1,604	11,963	11,653	12,113	12,463	5,557	6,513	9,286	2,475	7,335	6,935	11,346
Mosul, Iraq	8,311	13,988	13,437	4,214	4,368	7,782	12,775	2,381	1,860	12,814	11,838	11,839	13,136	4,720	6,433	11,298	699	6,752	4,791	10,621
Mount Isa, Australia	12,768	13,501	13,711	16,100	15,583	16,514	14,321	14,278	13,621	15,313	15,646	14,813	14,899	7,245	17,498	14,336	12,446	5,316	10,805	1,300
Multan, Pakistan	9,123	16,462	15,812	6,898	6,768	9,911	15,209	5,079	4,440	15,525	14,463	14,229	15,850	2,009	9,106	12,929	3,335	4,051	5,345	7,914
Munich, West Germany	6,398	11,939	11,586	1,748	1,491	4,948	10,917	1,052	1,033	10,207	9,713	10,153	10,648	7,273	4,570	8,574	2,625	9,176	6,665	13,192
Murcia, Spain	7,058	10,479	10,090	321	1,650	4,642	9,416	1,517	2,197	8,939	8,249	8,632	9,315	8,556	3,043	8,301	3,398	10,536	6,487	14,500
Murmansk, USSR	4,630	13,653	13,511	4,140	2,878	5,087	12,901	3,453	2,796	11,416	11,577	12,317	11,999	6,281	6,982	8,006	3,951	7,755	8,420	11,600
Mururoa Atoll, Fr. Polynesia	10,138	6,736	7,380	15,309	14,636	11,181	7,989	16,970	17,058	7,261	8,662	8,968	7,110	14,988	13,829	7,523	18,635	12,986	16,828	9,533
Muscat, Oman	9,851	15,040	14,370	6,151	6,415	9,814	13,792	4,335	3,904	14,538	13,176	12,810	14,722	3,241	7,973	13,243	2,433	5,241	3,966	8,814
Myitkyina, Burma	9,327	18,807	18,106	9,304	8,840	11,416	17,653	7,545	6,816	17,778	17,066	16,685	18,296	731	11,690	13,395	5,913	1,526	7,223	5,539
Naga, Philippines	9,855	17,670	17,901	12,146	11,390	13,072	18,459	10,467	9,693	18,184	19,779	18,486	18,395	3,622	14,676	13,349	8,904	1,633	9,540	3,007
Nagasaki, Japan	7,626	17,985	18,689	10,886	9,785	10,916	18,992	9,506	8,670	16,388	18,006	19,182	16,936	3,980	13,716	11,255	8,384	2,866	10,479	5,010
Nagoya, Japan	7,136	17,320	18,021	11,007	9,789	10,572	18,301	9,761	8,923	15,732	17,484	18,778	16,258	4,642	13,866	10,635	8,794	3,553	11,139	5,311
Nagpur, India	10,069	16,914	16,210	8,079	8,023	11,155	15,724	6,246	5,656	16,640	15,272	14,758	16,851	1,199	10,094	14,021	4,417	3,119	5,337	6,769
Nairobi, Kenya	12,313	11,687	10,984	6,085	7,260	10,465	10,508	4,961	5,214	12,140	10,291	9,560	12,016	6,418	6,230	14,057	3,851	8,072	669	10,424
Nanchang, China	8,507	19,312	19,703	10,400	9,567	11,384	19,493	8,805	8,000	17,514	18,342	18,512	18,144	2,599	13,075	12,382	7,420	1,604	9,082	4,829
Nancy, France	6,193	11,612	11,284	1,491	1,102	4,566	10,620	1,316	1,432	9,828	9,393	9,884	10,280	7,654	4,349	8,208	3,009	9,537	6,942	13,557
Nandi, Fiji	10,921	10,958	11,486	17,769	16,186	13,995	12,157	17,015	16,178	11,843	13,094	13,063	11,661	10,501	18,410	10,684	15,785	8,461	14,683	5,030
Nanjing, China	8,066	19,034	19,737	10,309	9,385	11,027	19,451	8,785	7,964	17,060	18,110	18,644	17,683	2,932	13,053	11,919	7,503	2,068	9,431	5,091
Nanning, China	9,344	19,212	18,808	10,326	9,714	11,940	18,635	8,611	7,852	18,322	18,205	17,736	18,975	1,833	12,806	13,302	7,037	747	8,191	4,611
Nantes, France	6,106	11,034	10,725	1,070	722	4,109	10,067	1,686	1,989	9,227	8,822	9,359	9,680	8,255	3,898	7,782	3,513	10,134	7,207	14,154
Naples, Italy	7,234	11,779	11,348	1,668	2,123	5,557	10,670	241	874	10,298	9,554	9,835	10,670	7,198	4,219	9,228	2,113	9,186	5,863	13,141
Narvik, Norway	4,451	13,017	12,880	3,661	2,299	4,499	12,275	3,243	2,711	10,790	10,947	11,712	11,368	6,880	6,465	7,564	4,067	8,388	8,520	12,234
Nashville, Tennessee	3,946	7,496	7,842	7,044	6,195	2,736	7,629	8,530	8,686	5,070	6,576	7,874	5,715	13,370	7,220	995	10,296	14,014	13,664	15,436
Nassau, Bahamas	5,393	6,125	6,406	6,872	6,421	3,141	6,145	8,581	8,931	3,656	5,056	6,353	4,310	14,448	6,332	2,076	10,467	15,413	13,016	16,756
Natal, Brazil	10,173	4,636	4,142	5,772	6,879	6,454	3,465	7,267	8,084	4,137	2,524	2,638	4,120	13,893	2,995	7,771	8,676	15,886	8,236	17,476
Natashquan, Canada	3,473	8,930	9,042	4,649	3,661	312	8,608	6,011	6,148	6,492	7,308	8,467	7,128	11,374	5,606	3,456	7,757	12,600	11,377	15,665
Nauru Island	9,556	12,999	13,586	15,783	14,295	13,150	14,238	14,787	13,951	13,368	14,979	15,188	13,357	8,668	18,372	10,632	13,716	6,703	14,167	4,198
Ndjamena, Chad	10,294	10,338	9,709	3,469	4,893	7,762	9,086	3,014	3,666	9,941	8,413	8,111	10,013	8,006	3,527	11,257	3,206	9,981	3,402	13,069
Nelson, New Zealand	13,479	9,705	10,037	19,595	18,817	15,979	10,700	18,064	17,517	11,411	11,927	11,422	10,991	11,150	16,881	12,315	16,159	9,218	12,925	5,210
Nema, Mauritania	9,031	8,588	8,074	2,369	3,916	5,796	7,400	3,394	4,232	7,677	6,438	6,507	7,860	10,035	1,113	8,991	4,733	12,078	5,741	15,502
Neuquen, Argentina	12,476	1,041	909	10,689	11,603	9,788	1,535	12,192	13,018	3,499	2,842	2,315	2,844	17,377	7,931	8,479	13,394	17,443	11,016	13,986
New Delhi, India	9,263	16,979	16,309	7,465	7,277	10,334	15,729	5,651	4,996	16,096	15,033	14,747	16,432	1,427	9,686	13,182	3,917	3,470	5,647	7,343
New Glasgow, Canada	3,865	8,413	8,527	4,785	3,952	516	8,098	6,263	6,467	5,977	6,806	7,979	6,612	11,863	5,434	3,244	8,062	13,116	11,477	16,120
New Haven, Connecticut	3,876	7,892	8,099	5,712	4,906	1,448	7,751	7,218	7,417	5,418	6,532	7,780	6,070	12,605	6,078	2,317	9,016	13,652	12,358	16,070
New Orleans, Louisiana	4,522	6,923	7,322	7,659	6,896	3,433	7,172	9,209	9,402	4,560	6,220	7,518	5,187	14,064	7,557	714	11,005	14,551	14,154	15,394
New Plymouth, New Zealand	13,226	9,804	10,158	19,847	18,565	15,793	10,825	18,114	17,495	11,439	12,031	11,570	11,040	11,119	17,079	12,145	16,217	9,162	13,129	5,172
New York, New York	3,894	7,830	8,047	5,821	5,019	1,560	7,709	7,331	7,530	5,354	6,501	7,756	6,007	12,693	6,154	2,211	9,129	13,715	12,460	16,055
Newcastle upon Tyne, UK	5,329	11,512	11,275	1,918	572	3,822	10,637	2,195	2,166	9,512	9,345	9,999	10,022	8,006	4,680	7,405	3,780	9,767	7,824	13,754
Newcastle Waters, Australia	12,682	14,136	14,290	15,366	14,934	16,359	14,870	13,541	12,894	16,041	16,213	15,259	15,605	6,520	16,902	14,738	11,705	4,619	10,228	612
Niamey, Niger	9,706	9,219	8,642	2,785	4,362	6,712	7,986	3,176	3,988	8,581	7,170	7,041	8,700	9,251	2,114	10,024	4,103	11,269	4,683	14,481
Nicosia, Cyprus	8,283	13,103	12,565	3,405	3,787	7,250	11,898	1,584	1,304	11,950	10,946	10,973	12,255	5,603	5,540	10,871	327	7,640	4,686	11,475
Niue (Alofi)	10,602	9,764	10,337	17,473	16,015	13,179	10,993	17,681	16,926	10,506	11,835	11,938	10,345	11,795	17,066	9,652	16,966	9,765	15,731	6,364

Distances in Kilometers	Coppermine, Canada	Coquimbo, Chile	Cordoba, Argentina	Cordoba, Spain	Cork, Ireland	Corner Brook, Canada	Corrientes, Argentina	Cosenza, Italy	Craiova, Romania	Cruzeiro do Sul, Brazil	Cuiaba, Brazil	Curitiba, Brazil	Cuzco, Peru	Dacca, Bangladesh	Dakar, Senegal	Dallas, Texas	Damascus, Syria	Danang, Vietnam	Dar es Salaam, Tanzania	Darwin, Australia
Norfolk, Virginia	4,204	7,414	7,660	6,170	5,442	2,003	7,350	7,731	7,961	4,939	6,179	7,452	5,593	13,158	6,286	1,928	9,552	14,129	12,733	16,195
Norfolk Island, Australia	12,436	10,950	11,346	18,821	17,448	15,560	12,019	17,192	16,434	12,380	13,180	12,794	12,049	10,143	18,323	12,143	15,437	8,130	13,249	4,253
Noril'sk, USSR	4,680	15,434	15,438	6,231	4,982	6,595	14,883	5,276	4,488	13,012	13,538	14,388	13,648	5,073	9,085	8,675	5,089	6,082	9,227	9,663
Norman Wells, Canada	594	11,582	11,987	7,527	5,990	4,281	11,794	7,977	7,590	9,218	10,703	11,988	9,852	9,638	9,408	4,144	8,956	9,884	13,423	11,829
Normanton, Australia	12,391	13,699	13,947	16,015	15,369	16,137	14,573	14,218	13,525	15,383	15,879	15,110	15,013	7,160	17,715	14,034	12,425	5,188	11,029	1,243
North Pole	2,474	13,319	13,478	5,810	4,252	4,579	13,043	5,652	5,095	10,847	11,727	12,816	11,498	7,378	8,382	6,374	6,296	8,225	10,756	11,380
Nottingham, United Kingdom	5,543	11,412	11,154	1,699	510	3,909	10,510	2,019	2,061	9,463	9,230	9,850	9,958	8,041	4,485	7,525	3,668	9,837	7,641	13,840
Norway House, Canada	1,791	9,645	10,000	6,895	5,597	2,789	9,773	7,909	7,791	7,227	8,669	9,956	7,872	11,360	8,076	2,358	9,360	11,858	13,522	13,747
Norwich, United Kingdom	5,650	11,533	11,262	1,706	671	4,079	10,613	1,873	1,892	9,609	9,342	9,937	10,098	7,890	4,526	7,691	3,500	9,700	7,501	13,709
Nouakchott, Mauritania	8,533	7,972	7,520	2,448	3,807	5,084	6,842	3,892	4,702	6,843	5,766	6,016	7,076	10,792	412	8,111	5,450	12,835	6,662	16,418
Noumea, New Caledonia	11,805	11,557	11,992	18,084	16,687	15,127	12,669	16,626	15,823	12,794	13,774	13,482	12,525	9,671	19,075	11,922	15,013	7,633	13,435	3,927
Novosibirsk, USSR	6,295	16,555	16,328	6,529	5,632	7,917	15,675	5,128	4,289	14,319	14,405	14,935	14,914	3,532	9,330	10,275	4,309	4,838	7,951	8,719
Nuku'alofa, Tonga	11,001	10,109	10,649	17,937	16,404	13,732	11,317	17,719	16,901	11,005	12,237	12,235	10,809	11,358	17,573	10,238	16,638	9,317	15,151	5,806
Nukunono Island, Tokelau Isls.	9,637	10,510	11,130	16,579	15,037	12,518	11,760	16,574	15,831	10,896	12,446	12,732	10,838	11,201	17,191	9,195	16,072	9,232	16,146	6,262
Nuremberg, West Germany	6,250	11,968	11,630	1,806	1,404	4,848	10,963	1,200	1,123	10,195	9,746	10,213	10,646	7,288	4,647	8,461	2,729	9,172	6,806	13,191
Nyala, Sudan	10,587	11,269	10,616	4,107	5,338	8,487	10,017	3,137	3,578	11,003	9,427	9,036	11,056	7,008	4,587	12,092	2,644	8,951	2,624	12,009
Oaxaca, Mexico	5,792	5,871	6,390	9,034	8,416	4,971	6,401	10,681	10,935	3,808	5,738	6,966	4,339	15,429	8,434	1,742	12,523	15,444	15,122	14,902
Ocean Falls, Canada	1,854	10,635	11,136	8,590	7,134	4,752	11,073	9,270	8,951	8,442	10,166	11,465	9,034	10,805	10,046	3,296	10,367	10,725	14,816	11,876
Odense, Denmark	5,620	12,202	11,927	2,255	1,301	4,537	11,276	1,842	1,560	10,260	10,010	10,585	10,758	7,250	5,112	8,055	3,153	9,037	7,393	13,042
Odessa, USSR	7,010	13,239	12,814	3,055	2,884	6,261	12,136	1,423	593	11,643	11,011	11,295	12,060	5,837	5,683	9,778	1,515	7,778	5,961	11,777
Ogbomosho, Nigeria	10,346	9,098	8,483	3,418	4,991	7,318	7,848	3,654	4,434	8,706	7,152	6,880	8,759	9,267	2,474	10,551	4,325	11,241	4,223	14,173
Okha, USSR	5,098	16,206	16,730	9,408	8,016	8,474	16,604	8,519	7,717	13,999	15,478	16,720	14,614	5,467	12,217	8,850	8,070	5,137	11,515	7,407
Okinawa (Naha)	8,386	18,117	18,735	11,354	10,356	11,661	19,370	9,859	9,035	17,048	18,767	19,708	17,538	3,759	14,124	11,963	8,572	2,307	10,186	4,293
Oklahoma City, Oklahoma	3,766	7,747	8,183	7,911	6,941	3,540	8,067	9,301	9,373	5,442	7,144	8,440	6,055	13,399	8,191	308	10,986	13,691	14,592	14,555
Old Crow, Canada	1,042	12,198	12,613	7,720	6,151	4,786	12,426	7,985	7,521	9,846	11,331	12,614	10,478	9,074	9,787	4,753	8,794	9,259	13,258	11,249
Olympia, Washington	2,358	9,972	10,489	8,774	7,394	4,700	10,453	9,620	9,371	7,823	9,600	10,891	8,403	11,488	9,960	2,714	10,845	11,363	15,234	12,247
Omaha, Nebraska	3,171	8,287	8,687	7,458	6,398	3,078	8,522	8,762	8,789	5,921	7,519	8,820	6,552	12,778	8,002	947	10,398	13,186	14,182	14,474
Omsk, USSR	6,362	16,071	15,785	5,956	5,132	7,625	15,122	4,522	3,685	13,954	13,881	14,352	14,520	3,748	8,738	10,234	3,733	5,247	7,544	9,196
Oodnadatta, Australia	13,625	13,034	13,158	16,158	15,978	17,368	13,729	14,331	13,769	15,088	15,074	14,122	14,590	7,456	16,882	15,009	12,439	5,651	10,275	1,738
Oradea, Romania	6,767	12,613	12,217	2,405	2,250	5,677	11,541	978	338	10,970	10,383	10,730	11,393	6,510	5,112	9,257	1,933	8,441	6,208	12,446
Oran, Algeria	7,309	10,369	9,959	441	1,905	4,823	9,284	1,543	2,284	8,906	8,141	8,479	9,260	8,603	2,871	8,466	3,377	10,602	6,290	14,532
Oranjestad, Aruba	6,952	4,703	4,900	7,001	6,983	4,191	4,586	8,824	9,350	2,246	3,467	4,764	2,887	15,473	5,685	3,531	10,720	16,838	12,273	17,769
Orebro, Sweden	5,337	12,632	12,386	2,775	1,692	4,663	11,742	2,224	1,764	10,607	10,460	11,075	11,129	6,934	5,630	8,056	3,261	8,654	7,632	12,634
Orel, USSR	6,400	13,745	13,385	3,544	2,985	6,134	12,713	2,141	1,314	11,932	11,519	11,921	12,407	5,566	6,307	9,476	2,157	7,402	6,624	11,422
Orsk, USSR	6,792	15,287	14,900	5,076	4,481	7,381	14,223	3,517	2,688	13,438	13,058	13,392	13,937	4,092	7,777	10,395	2,668	5,864	6,687	9,881
Osaka, Japan	7,238	17,454	18,156	10,990	9,794	10,648	18,441	9,716	8,877	15,868	17,600	18,886	16,397	4,510	13,846	10,763	8,716	3,413	11,008	5,240
Oslo, Norway	5,170	12,420	12,194	2,686	1,488	4,401	11,556	2,325	1,944	10,366	10,263	10,912	10,895	7,183	5,523	7,807	3,480	8,884	7,813	12,851
Osorno, Chile	12,523	1,187	1,298	11,129	11,999	10,029	1,959	12,654	13,478	3,649	3,224	2,779	3,000	17,595	8,389	8,477	13,864	17,286	11,373	13,638
Ostrava, Czechoslovakia	6,390	12,464	12,106	2,265	1,886	5,285	11,435	1,182	742	10,716	10,237	10,661	11,164	6,766	5,063	8,852	2,342	8,656	6,596	12,674
Ottawa, Canada	3,366	8,359	8,586	5,775	4,826	1,398	8,250	7,176	7,304	5,884	7,039	8,289	6,537	12,222	6,396	2,291	8,915	13,185	12,486	15,580
Ouagadougou, Bourkina Fasso	9,691	8,820	8,251	2,845	4,429	6,553	7,592	3,460	4,287	8,169	6,759	6,653	8,286	9,664	1,741	9,765	4,492	11,683	4,988	14,863
Oujda, Morocco	7,371	10,209	9,797	440	1,985	4,799	9,121	1,692	2,443	8,762	7,981	8,317	9,110	8,751	2,709	8,424	3,507	10,754	6,307	14,674
Oxford, United Kingdom	5,661	11,333	11,064	1,565	498	3,945	10,416	1,936	2,030	9,413	9,143	9,746	9,900	8,085	4,360	7,578	3,627	9,900	7,548	13,909
Pago Pago, American Samoa	10,128	10,107	10,704	17,048	15,542	12,852	11,350	17,150	16,404	10,676	12,117	12,309	10,565	11,531	17,155	9,411	16,563	9,526	15,978	6,320
Pakxe, Laos	10,236	18,335	17,939	10,708	10,273	12,730	17,923	8,923	8,219	19,160	18,089	17,189	19,726	1,872	12,967	14,190	7,213	281	7,724	4,114
Palembang, Indonesia	12,196	16,342	16,032	11,920	11,839	14,646	16,216	10,087	9,517	18,803	17,082	15,812	18,153	3,331	13,562	16,015	8,214	2,134	7,270	3,062
Palermo, Italy	7,496	11,576	11,125	1,590	2,288	5,672	10,448	283	1,112	10,181	9,359	9,596	10,529	7,331	3,990	9,352	2,129	9,339	5,651	13,257
Palma, Majorca	7,021	10,849	10,454	671	1,617	4,817	9,780	1,170	1,826	9,303	8,619	8,987	9,684	8,190	3,385	8,494	3,069	10,166	6,367	14,135
Palmerston North, New Zealand	13,303	9,613	9,965	19,729	18,684	15,756	10,632	18,258	17,670	11,266	11,840	11,377	10,860	11,294	16,892	12,092	16,354	9,344	13,144	5,348
Panama, Panama	7,044	4,396	4,757	8,069	7,932	4,869	4,608	9,880	10,363	1,990	3,750	5,024	2,623	16,230	6,778	3,180	11,783	17,110	13,293	16,694
Paramaribo, Suriname	8,180	4,322	4,230	6,197	6,658	4,786	3,706	8,005	8,682	2,443	2,371	3,516	2,835	15,057	4,241	5,241	9,795	16,980	10,584	19,033
Paris, France	6,060	11,376	11,066	1,348	838	4,299	10,406	1,536	1,714	9,559	9,164	9,691	10,017	7,925	4,202	7,952	3,282	9,795	7,139	13,815
Patna, India	9,510	17,665	16,966	8,303	8,046	10,973	16,445	6,496	5,825	16,933	15,854	15,467	17,284	576	10,534	13,541	4,768	2,620	6,117	6,503
Patrai, Greece	7,701	12,248	11,769	2,318	2,790	6,243	11,093	490	696	10,911	10,043	10,214	11,252	6,607	4,646	9,904	1,415	8,622	5,308	12,525
Peking, China	7,307	18,699	19,056	9,514	8,522	10,143	18,556	8,073	7,240	16,317	17,211	17,922	16,966	3,028	12,311	11,262	6,948	2,762	9,407	5,990
Penrhyn Island (Omoka)	9,175	9,206	9,864	15,843	14,509	11,498	10,457	16,601	16,087	9,393	11,016	11,439	9,367	12,601	15,706	7,963	16,923	10,685	17,423	7,765
Peoria, Illinois	3,391	8,046	8,400	7,020	6,041	2,642	8,188	8,400	8,485	5,627	7,127	8,425	6,271	12,874	7,465	1,089	10,099	13,459	13,723	14,992
Perm', USSR	6,028	14,972	14,683	4,866	4,038	6,716	14,022	3,526	2,693	12,927	12,776	13,273	13,468	4,676	7,675	9,636	3,108	6,310	7,345	10,286
Perth, Australia	14,861	13,112	12,995	14,647	15,042	18,046	13,407	12,933	12,555	15,536	14,677	13,465	14,907	6,726	14,926	16,966	11,041	5,373	8,348	2,646
Peshawar, Pakistan	8,698	16,512	15,899	6,700	6,472	9,548	15,267	4,903	4,218	15,327	14,421	14,298	15,705	2,160	9,023	12,512	3,250	4,168	5,654	8,107
Petropavlovsk-Kamchatskiy,USSR	4,576	15,252	15,833	9,807	8,314	8,190	15,827	9,156	8,393	13,195	14,866	16,163	13,777	6,491	12,496	8,049	8,925	5,993	12,545	7,726
Petrozavodsk, USSR	5,412	13,710	13,467	3,770	2,771	5,498	12,821	2,791	2,065	11,637	11,542	12,137	12,178	5,946	6,627	8,642	3,152	7,598	7,621	11,560
Pevek, USSR	2,837	14,183	14,592	8,067	6,516	6,276	14,371	7,733	7,068	11,820	13,209	14,456	12,457	7,162	10,627	6,737	7,973	7,278	12,196	9,612
Philadelphia, Pennsylvania	3,928	7,751	7,980	5,944	5,148	1,690	7,653	7,459	7,660	5,275	6,458	7,720	5,928	12,800	6,237	2,093	9,259	13,794	12,573	16,043
Phnom Penh, Kampuchea	10,642	17,930	17,543	10,900	10,545	13,096	17,572	9,094	8,418	19,502	17,932	16,907	19,626	2,042	13,044	14,588	7,335	614	7,546	3,906
Phoenix, Arizona	3,829	8,225	8,765	9,116	8,000	4,740	8,779	10,357	10,307	6,170	8,046	9,306	6,717	13,247	9,547	1,425	11,893	13,064	15,844	13,276
Pierre, South Dakota	2,752	8,744	9,159	7,581	6,424	3,242	9,007	8,778	8,739	6,399	8,012	9,313	7,025	12,387	8,326	1,323	10,334	12,715	14,304	14,020
Pinang, Malaysia	11,419	17,153	16,712	10,956	10,805	13,625	16,728	9,124	8,520	19,216	17,220	16,100	18,790	2,287	12,818	15,410	7,281	1,459	6,916	3,912
Pitcairn Island (Adamstown)	10,376	5,766	6,412	14,716	14,315	10,866	7,020	16,506	16,835	6,387	7,711	7,999	6,194	15,936	12,951	7,310	18,404	13,916	16,299	10,329
Pittsburgh, Pennsylvania	3,711	7,846	8,119	6,303	5,438	1,978	7,830	7,772	7,932	5,376	6,678	7,956	6,030	12,834	6,653	1,723	9,540	13,692	12,963	15,694
Plymouth, Montserrat	6,787	5,256	5,327	6,047	6,102	3,698	4,900	7,874	8,420	2,924	3,634	4,067	3,510	14,644	4,797	3,901	9,765	16,234	11,455	18,551
Plymouth, United Kingdom	5,705	11,082	10,814	1,392	347	3,803	10,167	2,017	2,200	9,172	8,892	9,501	9,655	8,322	4,142	7,459	3,777	10,146	7,587	14,158
Ponape Island	9,157	14,259	14,854	14,744	13,366	12,889	15,503	13,574	12,735	14,425	16,171	16,457	14,493	7,453	17,572	10,979	12,447	5,538	13,297	3,715
Ponce, Puerto Rico	6,492	5,334	5,474	6,351	6,278	3,519	5,102	8,163	8,665	2,912	3,892	5,160	3,537	14,764	5,254	3,432	10,065	16,193	11,928	18,061
Ponta Delgada, Azores	6,160	8,876	8,637	1,837	2,070	2,870	8,005	3,627	4,160	6,994	6,705	7,413	7,453	10,487	2,682	6,340	5,531	12,354	8,327	16,370
Pontianak, Indonesia	11,753	16,684	16,460	12,110	11,877	14,449	16,714	10,281	9,657	19,132	17,663	16,379	18,499	3,329	13,959	15,471	8,446	1,785	7,814	2,744
Port Augusta, Australia	14,023	12,444	12,567	16,585	16,542	17,762	13,141	14,782	14,265	14,529	14,485	13,552	14,016	8,001	16,826	14,965	12,878	6,229	10,401	2,329
Port Blair, India	10,917	17,401	16,791	9,877	9,758	12,710	16,579	8,045	7,445	18,369	16,637	15,756	18,364	1,364	11,805	14,991	6,207	1,743	6,260	4,979
Port Elizabeth, South Africa	15,489	8,792	8,124	8,552	10,076	12,336	7,885	8,169	8,671	10,292	8,305	7,148	9,866	9,368	7,053	14,737	7,552	10,338	3,322	10,611
Port Hedland, Australia	13,567	14,341	14,274	14,270	14,280	16,813	14,710	12,452	11,931	16,684	15,991	14,778	16,091	5,749	15,333	16,263	10,553	4,181	8,642	1,571
Port Louis, Mauritius	14,682	12,223	11,578	9,143	10,216	13,525	11,376	7,859	7,921	13,761	11,760	10,639	13,359	6,027	9,057	17,119	6,352	6,842	2,461	7,826
Port Moresby, Papua New Guinea	11,300	14,013	14,390	15,799	14,811	15,048	15,056	14,150	13,373	15,232	16,243	15,758	15,009	7,182	18,264	13,009	12,526	5,140	11,840	1,817
Port Said, Egypt	8,686	12,864	12,299	3,456	4,021	7,479	11,640	1,707	1,628	11,867	10,749	10,698	12,129	5,740	5,371	11,133	451	7,785	4,278	11,528
Port Sudan, Sudan	10,047	12,826	12,178	4,525	5,330	8,756	11,573	2,969	3,010	12,374	10,924	10,593	12,499	5,493	5,820	12,433	1,541	7,481	2,931	10,846
Port-au-Prince, Haiti	6,243	5,368	5,594	6,822	6,620	3,614	5,294	8,611	9,065	2,894	4,173	5,467	3,545	14,973	5,853	2,909	10,517	16,177	12,533	17,461
Port-of-Spain, Trin. & Tobago	7,443	4,616	4,662	6,386	6,597	4,259	4,227	8,219	8,820	2,366	2,963	4,206	2,912	15,140	4,802	4,363	10,080	16,845	11,332	18,674
Port-Vila, Vanuatu	11,267	11,731	12,210	17,674	16,203	14,618	12,888	16,415	15,587	12,774	13,917	13,745	12,560	9,622	19,326	11,504	14,952	7,577	13,807	4,065
Portland, Maine	3,745	8,153	8,334	5,423	4,577	1,114	7,961	6,899	7,085	5,684	6,716	7,944	6,333	12,290	5,929	2,604	8,686	13,390	12,101	16,006
Portland, Oregon	2,521	9,835	10,359	8,877	7,514	4,761	10,336	9,754	9,516	7,708	9,504	10,792	8,282	11,642	10,001	2,624	10,999	11,487	15,374	12,278
Porto, Portugal	6,475	10,178	9,853	491	1,195	3,910	9,193	2,119	2,660	8,457	7,958	8,480	8,880	9,024	3,057	7,568	4,025	10,948	7,211	14,960
Porto Alegre, Brazil	12,061	1,943	1,253	8,938	9,991	8,778	801	10,374	11,206	3,342	1,680	549	2,816	16,169	6,132	8,456	11,574	17,412	9,684	15,293
Porto Alexandre, Angola	13,123	8,513	7,810	6,194	7,757	9,916	7,343	6,118	6,768	9,202	7,250	6,409	8,972	9,590	4,665	12,680	6,043	11,150	3,149	12,617
Porto Novo, Benin	10,457	8,846	8,229	3,557	5,138	7,344	7,596	3,884	4,672	8,496	6,915	6,626	8,534	9,506	2,371	10,502	4,583	11,471	4,329	14,320
Porto Velho, Brazil	9,401	2,472	2,506	8,014	8,541	6,420	2,137	9,787	10,503	967	1,136	2,409	1,027	16,831	5,746	5,772	11,491	18,844	11,342	17,157
Portsmouth, United Kingdom	5,764	11,282	11,004	1,461	530	3,992	10,353	1,859	1,994	9,388	9,086	9,673	9,867	8,105	4,266	7,636	3,581	9,935	7,461	13,950
Poznan, Poland	6,089	12,477	12,151	2,334	1,733	5,067	11,486	1,459	1,032	10,647	10,260	10,741	11,117	6,844	5,174	8,600	2,610	8,693	6,895	12,712
Prague, Czechoslovakia	6,272	12,219	11,876	2,043	1,616	5,032	11,208	1,207	953	10,446	9,996	10,450	10,899	7,037	4,871	8,618	2,567	8,918	6,743	12,937
Praia, Cape Verde Islands	8,546	7,140	6,719	3,145	4,316	4,906	6,044	4,721	5,513	5,963	4,921	5,263	6,196	11,669	655	7,583	6,326	13,711	7,333	17,250
Pretoria, South Africa	14,715	9,464	8,775	7,839	9,315	11,853	8,464	7,307	7,771	10,717	8,714	7,650	10,359	8,654	6,664	14,683	6,614	9,820	2,407	10,654
Prince Albert, Canada	1,704	9,798	10,200	7,395	6,061	3,321	10,022	8,345	8,181	7,432	8,976	10,273	8,065	11,342	8,606	2,379	9,725	11,672	13,972	13,305

Distances in Kilometers

	Coppermine, Canada	Coquimbo, Chile	Cordoba, Argentina	Cordoba, Spain	Cork, Ireland	Corner Brook, Canada	Corrientes, Argentina	Cosenza, Italy	Craiova, Romania	Cruzeiro do Sul, Brazil	Cuiaba, Brazil	Curitiba, Brazil	Cuzco, Peru	Dacca, Bangladesh	Dakar, Senegal	Dallas, Texas	Damascus, Syria	Danang, Vietnam	Dar es Salaam, Tanzania	Darwin, Australia
Prince Edward Island	17,183	8,963	8,382	10,279	11,778	14,042	8,328	9,755	10,166	10,929	9,068	7,797	10,390	9,405	8,748	15,913	8,871	9,857	4,411	9,233
Prince George, Canada	1,603	10,526	10,999	8,234	6,793	4,381	10,900	8,957	8,666	8,273	9,944	11,245	8,880	10,835	9,674	3,117	10,112	10,871	14,536	12,194
Prince Rupert, Canada	1,705	10,912	11,409	8,545	7,062	4,822	11,338	9,152	8,803	8,706	10,413	11,712	9,303	10,525	10,108	3,555	10,191	10,455	14,654	11,698
Providence, Rhode Island	3,881	7,948	8,141	5,575	4,771	1,316	7,779	7,081	7,284	5,477	6,547	7,786	6,127	12,513	5,968	2,454	8,882	13,596	12,225	16,109
Provo, Utah	3,079	8,816	9,319	8,605	7,401	4,279	9,275	9,737	9,637	6,644	8,435	9,721	7,225	12,567	9,323	1,563	11,205	12,538	15,314	13,228
Puerto Aisen, Chile	13,049	1,717	1,721	11,457	12,409	10,552	2,339	12,901	13,735	4,185	3,654	3,052	3,535	17,163	8,665	8,994	13,969	16,751	11,150	13,176
Puerto Deseado, Argentina	13,459	2,029	1,821	11,254	12,319	10,742	2,334	12,594	13,433	4,492	3,680	2,878	3,838	16,621	8,420	9,438	13,533	16,450	10,573	13,133
Puerto Princesa, Philippines	10,417	17,537	17,587	12,135	11,529	13,496	18,026	10,388	9,651	18,768	19,161	17,864	18,792	3,382	14,491	13,987	8,724	1,339	8,997	2,796
Punta Arenas, Chile	13,909	2,575	2,476	11,924	13,014	11,382	3,022	13,206	14,044	5,050	4,366	3,571	4,398	16,382	9,078	9,845	14,014	15,889	10,724	12,446
Pusan, South Korea	7,419	18,031	18,727	10,631	9,520	10,669	18,885	9,270	8,433	16,254	17,784	18,919	16,826	3,928	13,466	11,104	8,187	2,958	10,423	5,268
Pyongyang, North Korea	7,123	18,161	18,780	10,106	9,001	10,253	18,657	8,759	7,921	16,078	17,402	18,427	16,691	3,733	12,944	10,928	7,722	3,064	10,180	5,724
Qamdo, China	8,703	18,926	18,261	8,891	8,322	10,796	17,673	7,180	6,417	17,197	16,811	16,693	17,767	1,065	11,401	12,776	5,658	2,010	7,454	6,017
Qandahar, Afghanistan	8,981	15,944	15,314	6,343	6,271	9,490	14,693	4,518	3,899	14,962	13,905	13,719	15,281	2,578	8,538	12,650	2,765	4,620	5,095	8,475
Qiqian, China	5,912	17,343	17,659	8,724	7,532	8,794	17,258	7,536	6,703	14,915	15,933	16,917	15,565	4,080	11,583	9,906	6,798	4,160	10,028	7,229
Qom, Iran	8,581	14,637	14,057	4,941	5,024	8,390	13,405	3,109	2,551	13,542	12,522	12,453	13,856	4,001	7,129	11,818	1,353	6,039	4,748	9,892
Quebec, Canada	3,402	8,503	8,691	5,400	4,451	1,020	8,321	6,799	6,936	6,033	7,075	8,300	6,682	11,980	6,102	2,669	8,546	13,040	12,116	15,676
Quetta, Pakistan	9,133	16,037	15,393	6,520	6,464	9,684	14,784	4,693	4,083	15,132	14,032	13,805	15,436	2,428	8,682	12,830	2,918	4,473	5,052	8,303
Quito, Ecuador	8,058	3,379	3,767	8,604	8,671	5,794	3,676	10,437	11,005	1,049	2,993	4,202	1,637	17,148	6,917	4,127	12,309	18,108	13,085	16,502
Rabaul, Papua New Guinea	10,550	14,041	14,507	15,608	14,424	14,289	15,185	14,124	13,309	14,893	16,220	16,003	14,775	7,370	18,397	12,228	12,663	5,334	12,483	2,521
Raiatea (Uturoa)	9,830	8,167	8,808	16,010	14,932	11,646	9,420	17,237	16,914	8,591	10,077	10,399	8,490	13,570	15,110	7,985	17,996	11,592	17,152	8,338
Raleigh, North Carolina	4,235	7,317	7,587	6,412	5,680	2,233	7,302	7,973	8,197	4,846	6,161	7,445	5,500	13,321	6,485	1,704	9,790	14,222	12,963	16,095
Rangiroa (Avatoru)	9,549	7,901	8,558	15,581	14,553	11,229	9,153	16,888	16,651	8,206	9,747	10,135	8,131	13,888	14,693	7,560	17,910	11,939	17,484	8,765
Rangoon, Burma	10,285	18,081	17,458	9,806	9,523	12,290	17,198	7,993	7,330	18,438	17,067	16,325	18,710	974	11,949	14,351	6,227	1,289	6,782	5,001
Raoul Is., Kermadec Islands	11,941	9,842	10,313	18,864	17,345	14,549	10,990	18,308	17,474	11,065	12,044	11,851	10,778	11,418	17,444	10,963	16,756	9,382	14,383	5,601
Rarotonga (Avarua)	10,525	8,720	9,315	16,989	15,800	12,609	9,961	17,963	17,420	9,421	10,759	10,919	9,257	12,878	15,988	8,967	17,931	10,852	16,283	7,407
Rawson, Argentina	13,013	1,581	1,323	10,857	11,871	10,244	1,845	12,265	13,101	4,019	3,190	2,453	3,367	16,893	8,046	9,022	13,322	16,921	10,645	13,622
Recife, Brazil	10,419	4,507	3,988	5,971	7,107	6,704	3,312	7,431	8,254	4,157	2,452	2,452	4,096	13,964	3,167	7,954	8,795	15,929	8,179	17,251
Regina, Canada	2,020	9,492	9,902	7,492	6,204	3,315	9,737	8,515	8,385	7,138	8,712	10,011	7,767	11,658	8,568	2,065	9,946	11,971	14,130	13,486
Reykjavik, Iceland	3,848	11,288	11,218	3,137	1,573	2,726	10,654	3,717	3,587	9,005	9,309	10,210	9,594	8,674	5,506	6,055	5,182	10,156	9,346	13,892
Rhodes, Greece	8,043	12,710	12,196	2,919	3,349	6,812	11,524	1,099	952	11,481	10,530	10,617	11,799	6,057	5,120	10,455	806	8,087	4,923	11,950
Richmond, Virginia	4,093	7,500	7,756	6,232	5,471	2,018	7,454	7,773	7,986	5,026	6,292	7,568	5,680	13,107	6,397	1,838	9,582	14,042	12,820	16,066
Riga, USSR	5,764	13,063	12,771	2,997	2,164	5,246	12,113	2,045	1,406	11,121	10,862	11,393	11,624	6,399	5,848	8,627	2,767	8,170	7,201	12,175
Ringkobing, Denmark	5,496	12,113	11,851	2,244	1,187	4,385	11,204	1,957	1,708	10,143	9,929	10,529	10,648	7,373	5,091	7,901	3,305	9,144	7,529	13,142
Rio Branco, Brazil	9,405	2,245	2,402	8,415	8,882	6,598	2,154	10,201	10,904	588	1,415	2,601	602	17,257	6,190	5,645	11,924	19,213	11,742	16,793
Rio Cuarto, Argentina	11,963	751	193	9,993	10,878	9,114	822	11,539	12,357	2,949	2,115	1,696	2,307	17,352	7,268	8,051	12,838	17,975	10,858	14,709
Rio de Janeiro, Brazil	11,612	2,903	2,275	7,839	8,952	8,091	1,650	9,253	10,085	3,566	1,574	672	3,206	15,312	5,018	8,387	10,479	16,947	8,960	16,040
Rio Gallegos, Argentina	13,787	2,413	2,285	11,725	12,810	11,198	2,821	13,024	13,862	4,888	4,167	3,367	4,235	16,454	8,882	9,732	13,869	16,052	10,672	12,645
Rio Grande, Brazil	12,234	1,852	1,148	9,166	10,225	8,989	826	10,587	11,420	3,437	1,867	784	2,884	16,243	6,353	8,576	11,758	17,356	9,745	15,071
Riyadh, Saudi Arabia	9,642	13,942	13,300	5,051	5,521	8,980	12,689	3,284	3,013	13,328	11,994	11,710	13,514	4,423	6,762	12,573	1,411	6,442	3,570	10,003
Road Town, Brit. Virgin Isls.	6,518	5,406	5,516	6,148	6,108	3,436	5,118	7,965	8,477	3,015	3,879	5,131	3,627	14,617	5,040	3,582	9,865	16,108	11,718	18,247
Roanoke, Virginia	4,038	7,497	7,777	6,444	5,658	2,197	7,498	7,970	8,167	5,029	6,363	7,647	5,683	13,179	6,614	1,616	9,768	14,040	13,042	15,905
Robinson Crusoe Island, Chile	11,650	819	1,400	11,015	11,684	9,380	2,036	12,676	13,463	2,950	3,039	3,000	2,335	18,500	8,422	7,588	14,112	17,936	12,127	14,018
Rochester, New York	3,519	8,122	8,369	6,003	5,095	1,646	8,053	7,438	7,582	5,647	6,866	8,129	6,301	12,500	6,497	2,036	9,192	13,420	12,695	15,651
Rockhampton, Australia	12,574	12,608	12,912	17,171	16,369	16,236	13,563	15,385	14,683	14,216	14,823	14,205	13,853	8,325	18,430	13,437	13,589	6,342	11,849	2,404
Rome, Italy	7,074	11,698	11,283	1,538	1,934	5,368	10,607	430	959	10,169	9,470	9,787	10,553	7,322	4,168	9,038	2,288	9,297	6,043	13,268
Rosario, Argentina	12,053	1,067	374	9,747	10,687	9,075	633	11,258	12,081	3,062	1,979	1,388	2,440	17,025	6,992	8,204	12,518	17,832	10,527	14,834
Roseau, Dominica	6,963	5,121	5,176	6,065	6,173	3,745	4,740	7,897	8,460	2,821	3,465	4,693	3,394	14,721	4,721	4,061	9,780	16,356	11,358	18,676
Rostock, East Germany	5,799	12,247	11,952	2,214	1,399	4,696	11,295	1,673	1,376	10,348	10,043	10,585	10,834	7,153	5,074	8,230	2,972	8,966	7,210	12,979
Rostov-na-Donu, USSR	7,070	13,926	13,493	3,741	3,458	6,734	12,815	2,087	1,276	12,308	11,699	11,963	12,737	5,172	6,358	10,138	1,552	7,096	5,985	11,102
Rotterdam, Netherlands	5,815	11,681	11,391	1,720	891	4,312	10,736	1,671	1,660	9,797	9,479	10,038	10,276	7,696	4,570	7,921	3,269	9,527	7,299	13,543
Rouyn, Canada	2,969	8,695	8,943	5,917	4,867	1,551	8,623	7,229	7,300	6,221	7,426	8,682	6,875	11,967	6,709	2,274	8,914	12,847	12,646	15,179
Sacramento, California	3,279	9,202	9,760	9,356	8,074	5,089	9,793	10,367	10,186	7,189	9,065	10,327	7,730	12,352	10,186	2,317	11,702	12,055	15,994	12,400
Saginaw, Michigan	3,276	8,228	8,528	6,466	5,486	2,086	8,259	7,844	7,940	5,770	7,125	8,408	6,422	12,547	7,010	1,632	9,554	13,302	13,177	15,234
Saint Denis, Reunion	14,744	12,015	11,366	9,049	10,160	13,430	11,157	7,810	7,905	13,534	11,533	10,415	13,135	6,221	8,881	16,982	6,351	7,065	2,336	8,029
Saint George's, Grenada	7,288	4,762	4,815	6,311	6,485	4,107	4,383	8,144	8,733	2,486	3,119	4,361	3,045	15,033	4,802	4,245	10,014	16,708	11,370	18,667
Saint John, Canada	3,756	8,348	8,492	5,052	4,198	738	8,087	6,519	6,708	5,895	6,813	8,011	6,537	12,004	5,667	2,978	8,308	13,188	11,745	16,036
Saint John's, Antigua	6,759	5,307	5,373	5,990	6,043	3,550	4,942	7,817	8,361	2,980	3,670	4,898	3,565	14,585	4,755	3,910	9,708	16,180	11,418	18,574
Saint John's, Canada	4,095	8,788	8,832	4,003	3,176	418	8,332	5,473	5,697	6,421	7,002	8,090	7,032	11,294	4,886	4,033	7,284	12,707	10,714	16,099
Saint Louis, Missouri	3,595	7,841	8,207	7,176	6,233	2,811	8,011	8,588	8,690	5,435	6,974	8,273	6,075	13,104	7,519	882	10,304	13,657	13,858	15,047
Saint Paul, Minnesota	2,851	8,584	8,947	7,051	5,951	2,688	8,740	8,314	8,325	6,175	7,677	8,973	6,816	12,393	7,748	1,389	9,933	12,915	13,780	14,522
Saint Peter Port, UK	5,850	11,114	10,830	1,298	500	3,946	10,178	1,866	2,075	9,241	8,915	9,495	9,714	8,247	4,089	7,607	3,640	10,092	7,432	14,109
Saipan (Susupe)	8,837	15,902	16,494	13,379	12,170	12,532	17,146	12,028	11,193	15,778	17,696	18,094	15,970	5,850	16,229	11,522	10,811	4,017	11,974	3,467
Salalah, Oman	10,556	14,329	13,640	6,152	6,662	10,120	13,098	4,414	4,150	14,163	12,613	12,120	14,248	3,853	7,624	13,693	2,553	5,759	3,097	9,044
Salem, Oregon	2,591	9,808	10,338	8,947	7,586	4,822	10,322	9,827	9,590	7,696	9,503	10,788	8,266	11,682	10,055	2,629	11,072	11,505	15,448	12,248
Salt Lake City, Utah	3,020	8,875	9,376	8,583	7,369	4,266	9,329	9,703	9,597	6,698	8,483	9,771	7,281	12,506	9,328	1,607	11,162	12,482	15,287	13,201
Salta, Argentina	11,049	821	743	9,392	10,141	8,200	722	11,044	11,832	2,046	1,409	1,631	1,425	17,578	6,796	7,189	12,524	18,843	11,168	15,526
Salto, Uruguay	11,973	1,291	591	9,450	10,412	8,898	442	10,952	11,776	3,037	1,760	1,080	2,443	16,805	6,687	8,193	12,213	17,815	10,308	15,063
Salvador, Brazil	10,778	3,866	3,325	6,642	7,750	7,122	2,653	8,102	8,927	3,777	1,917	1,778	3,625	14,535	3,841	7,998	9,437	16,438	8,532	16,959
Salzburg, Austria	6,473	12,021	11,659	1,818	1,605	5,061	10,989	979	918	10,308	9,793	10,216	10,744	7,171	4,622	8,684	2,511	9,082	6,575	13,096
Samsun, Turkey	7,670	13,540	13,050	3,518	3,565	6,976	12,375	1,718	1,078	12,150	11,337	11,481	12,519	5,347	5,937	10,508	864	7,345	5,333	11,289
San Antonio, Texas	4,410	7,176	7,649	8,369	7,496	4,050	7,582	9,843	9,964	4,951	6,749	8,031	5,540	14,048	8,375	405	11,577	14,218	14,947	14,612
San Cristobal, Venezuela	7,385	4,176	4,418	7,510	7,547	4,758	4,157	9,340	9,890	1,703	3,137	4,436	2,354	16,051	6,020	3,755	11,226	17,368	12,483	17,456
San Diego, California	3,909	8,453	9,022	9,525	8,359	5,163	9,078	10,701	10,605	6,495	8,409	9,651	7,017	13,112	10,026	1,904	12,169	12,776	16,252	12,807
San Francisco, California	3,376	9,191	9,757	9,477	8,194	5,207	9,802	10,486	10,301	7,207	9,096	10,352	7,740	12,386	10,294	2,387	11,814	12,048	16,113	12,320
San Jose, Costa Rica	6,823	4,621	5,043	8,405	8,159	4,961	4,954	10,194	10,631	2,323	4,183	5,436	2,918	16,235	7,246	2,847	12,100	16,832	13,796	16,216
San Juan, Argentina	11,677	322	412	10,139	10,936	8,976	1,041	11,744	12,548	2,680	2,171	2,001	2,027	17,779	7,474	7,715	13,123	18,261	11,282	14,720
San Juan, Puerto Rico	6,462	5,388	5,522	6,279	6,206	3,461	5,142	8,091	8,592	2,973	3,924	5,187	3,596	14,694	5,198	3,448	9,993	16,136	11,877	18,097
San Luis Potosi, Mexico	5,171	6,582	7,108	9,049	8,269	4,807	7,121	10,595	10,759	4,521	6,434	7,674	5,058	14,784	8,762	1,247	12,369	14,724	15,443	14,447
San Marino, San Marino	6,863	11,796	11,400	1,595	1,790	5,244	10,725	602	908	10,201	9,566	9,921	10,604	7,282	4,306	8,904	2,361	9,237	6,231	13,228
San Miguel de Tucuman, Argen.	11,270	695	518	9,541	10,323	8,423	637	11,170	11,966	2,262	1,563	1,603	1,633	17,557	6,909	7,396	12,609	18,641	11,099	15,329
San Salvador, El Salvador	6,299	5,197	5,661	8,606	8,187	4,844	5,612	10,342	10,700	2,989	4,876	6,124	3,559	15,865	7,712	2,250	12,233	16,203	14,351	15,697
Sanaa, Yemen	10,628	13,295	12,616	5,400	6,151	9,597	12,054	3,803	3,745	13,109	11,539	11,073	13,176	4,917	6,605	13,265	2,162	6,833	2,509	10,025
Santa Cruz, Bolivia	10,379	1,583	1,510	8,672	9,357	7,411	1,159	10,371	11,137	1,520	794	1,668	1,057	17,209	6,172	6,645	11,944	19,097	11,094	16,326
Santa Cruz, Tenerife	7,468	8,723	8,348	1,494	2,683	4,207	7,678	3,216	3,949	7,246	6,493	6,929	7,586	10,274	1,531	7,547	4,997	12,277	7,116	16,182
Santa Fe, New Mexico	3,624	8,120	8,613	8,523	7,448	4,142	8,563	9,810	9,802	5,932	7,731	9,014	6,515	13,210	8,944	901	11,402	13,248	15,245	13,804
Santa Rosa, Argentina	12,332	988	579	10,271	11,205	9,499	1,137	11,770	12,596	3,319	2,468	1,894	2,672	17,211	7,509	8,394	12,989	17,612	10,762	14,347
Santa Rosalia, Mexico	4,509	7,692	8,263	9,576	8,545	5,197	8,330	10,909	10,907	5,765	7,702	8,927	6,273	13,858	9,744	1,608	12,506	13,526	16,259	13,288
Santarem, Brazil	9,058	3,518	3,358	6,800	7,422	5,702	2,805	8,558	9,286	2,066	1,462	2,609	2,263	15,595	4,523	5,899	10,255	17,620	10,427	18,251
Santiago del Estero, Argentina	11,401	732	401	9,554	10,366	8,522	537	11,164	11,965	2,397	1,593	1,518	1,771	17,456	6,897	7,535	12,573	18,501	10,984	15,266
Santiago, Chile	11,825	392	651	10,432	11,225	9,214	1,315	12,032	12,838	2,866	2,464	2,255	2,212	17,887	7,761	7,826	13,392	18,076	11,417	14,439
Santo Domingo, Dominican Rep.	6,331	5,361	5,552	6,612	6,460	3,548	5,220	8,411	8,884	2,902	4,059	5,345	3,545	14,877	5,597	3,119	10,316	16,179	12,276	17,713
Sao Paulo de Olivenca, Brazil	8,682	2,947	3,132	8,010	8,340	5,900	2,861	9,828	10,484	625	1,935	3,207	1,167	16,854	6,008	4,980	11,625	18,573	11,966	17,229
Sao Paulo, Brazil	11,550	2,556	1,939	8,085	9,146	8,107	1,302	9,541	10,369	3,285	1,326	339	2,893	15,665	5,287	8,200	10,806	17,273	9,301	16,013
Sao Tome, Sao Tome & Principe	11,250	8,885	8,229	4,322	5,890	8,161	7,635	4,423	5,157	8,847	7,122	6,653	8,806	9,358	3,096	11,259	4,798	11,236	3,700	13,723
Sapporo, Japan	6,181	16,780	17,427	10,413	9,091	9,640	17,506	9,347	8,519	14,879	16,542	17,827	15,446	5,108	13,259	9,740	8,624	4,337	11,505	6,240
Sarajevo, Yugoslavia	7,026	12,228	11,811	2,055	2,186	5,649	11,134	535	435	10,675	10,000	10,307	11,071	6,810	4,689	9,285	1,927	8,775	5,988	12,757
Saratov, USSR	6,669	14,416	14,030	4,203	3,676	6,751	13,354	2,673	1,837	12,627	12,187	12,534	13,102	4,873	6,916	9,983	2,156	6,709	6,499	10,729
Saskatoon, Canada	1,810	9,722	10,135	7,510	6,185	3,404	9,969	8,474	8,314	7,371	8,940	10,239	8,000	11,442	8,681	2,290	9,859	11,739	14,100	13,291
Schefferville, Canada	2,860	9,402	9,554	4,945	3,787	892	9,147	6,150	6,190	6,940	7,865	9,045	7,586	11,039	6,144	3,387	7,804	12,139	11,654	15,063
Seattle, Washington	2,291	9,989	10,500	8,701	7,319	4,634	10,456	9,545	9,297	7,825	9,591	10,884	8,408	11,457	9,898	2,705	10,774	11,355	15,160	12,286

Distances in Kilometers	Coppermine, Canada	Coquimbo, Chile	Cordoba, Argentina	Cordoba, Spain	Cork, Ireland	Corner Brook, Canada	Corrientes, Argentina	Cosenza, Italy	Craiova, Romania	Cruzeiro do Sul, Brazil	Cuiaba, Brazil	Curitiba, Brazil	Cuzco, Peru	Dacca, Bangladesh	Dakar, Senegal	Dallas, Texas	Damascus, Syria	Danang, Vietnam	Dar es Salaam, Tanzania	Darwin, Australia
Sendai, Japan	6,678	16,930	17,618	10,873	9,584	10,169	17,829	9,733	8,898	15,243	16,999	18,298	15,776	5,015	13,729	10,142	8,895	4,029	11,491	5,711
Seoul, South Korea	7,233	18,130	18,788	10,301	9,194	10,409	18,763	8,948	8,111	16,151	17,550	18,613	16,751	3,798	13,138	10,995	7,893	3,014	10,269	5,553
Sept-Iles, Canada	3,283	8,893	9,041	4,973	3,957	625	8,635	6,313	6,428	6,436	7,356	8,545	7,079	11,505	5,898	3,157	8,040	12,645	11,702	15,538
Sevastopol, USSR	7,262	13,403	12,952	3,264	3,175	6,562	12,274	1,545	775	11,880	11,181	11,412	12,280	5,603	5,817	10,078	1,255	7,567	5,722	11,549
Seville, Spain	6,950	10,094	9,725	121	1,625	4,324	9,055	1,950	2,610	8,512	7,864	8,296	8,896	8,980	2,760	7,956	3,831	10,951	6,782	14,926
Shanghai, China	8,084	18,803	19,500	10,547	9,594	11,136	19,600	9,039	8,215	17,033	18,265	18,906	17,633	3,157	13,305	11,878	7,769	2,136	9,653	4,928
Sheffield, United Kingdom	5,493	11,418	11,165	1,739	499	3,875	10,522	2,065	2,096	9,457	9,239	9,868	9,955	8,050	4,516	7,486	3,705	9,838	7,689	13,838
Shenyang, China	6,907	18,147	18,670	9,742	8,637	9,950	18,401	8,409	7,570	15,906	17,098	18,070	16,537	3,653	12,583	10,781	7,411	3,204	10,030	6,056
Shiraz, Iran	9,152	14,659	14,036	5,306	5,519	8,921	13,409	3,477	3,011	13,817	12,634	12,437	14,072	3,810	7,303	12,386	1,599	5,853	4,270	9,588
Sibiu, Romania	6,950	12,729	12,314	2,541	2,465	5,897	11,637	970	167	11,138	10,501	10,808	11,548	6,343	5,190	9,477	1,714	8,292	6,018	12,287
Singapore	11,771	16,790	16,445	11,549	11,405	14,171	16,577	9,716	9,119	19,207	17,314	16,089	18,579	2,874	13,333	15,661	7,862	1,704	7,228	3,347
Sioux Falls, South Dakota	2,914	8,542	8,937	7,381	6,272	3,016	8,764	8,634	8,632	6,169	7,745	9,045	6,801	12,522	8,045	1,195	10,237	12,935	14,110	14,324
Skelleftea, Sweden	4,888	13,083	12,893	3,433	2,206	4,752	12,267	2,850	2,283	10,937	10,958	11,648	11,494	6,674	6,276	7,932	3,631	8,273	8,082	12,190
Skopje, Yugoslavia	7,295	12,384	11,940	2,280	2,508	5,971	11,262	534	319	10,912	10,163	10,411	11,288	6,582	4,805	9,608	1,607	8,568	5,699	12,526
Socotra Island (Tamrida)	11,035	14,105	13,407	6,426	7,032	10,496	12,897	4,740	4,539	14,169	12,514	11,930	14,191	4,027	7,701	14,106	2,927	5,843	2,699	8,924
Sofia, Bulgaria	7,265	12,553	12,109	2,435	2,587	6,047	11,431	703	186	11,066	10,330	10,580	11,448	6,425	4,974	9,667	1,525	8,406	5,714	12,371
Songkhla, Thailand	11,220	17,350	16,901	10,853	10,663	13,444	16,898	9,024	8,404	19,285	17,328	16,243	18,952	2,127	12,780	15,216	7,195	1,285	6,983	3,990
Sorong, Indonesia	11,068	15,842	16,082	13,940	13,225	14,606	16,690	12,205	11,462	17,224	18,018	17,094	17,010	5,185	16,265	13,885	10,528	3,150	10,225	1,282
South Georgia Island	14,985	3,863	3,345	10,659	12,056	11,610	3,477	11,535	12,336	6,079	4,606	3,364	5,464	14,507	7,853	11,228	11,966	14,809	8,490	12,520
South Pole	17,529	6,686	6,528	14,199	15,756	15,427	6,964	14,356	14,913	9,159	8,280	7,191	8,508	12,626	11,626	13,630	13,712	11,779	9,252	8,622
South Sandwich Islands	15,667	4,608	4,092	10,791	12,266	12,175	4,205	11,471	12,234	6,819	5,289	4,018	6,207	13,797	8,069	11,971	11,681	14,064	7,948	11,951
Split, Yugoslavia	7,010	12,067	11,653	1,892	2,074	5,536	10,977	469	598	10,513	9,839	10,154	10,907	6,973	4,536	9,184	2,051	8,939	6,030	12,920
Spokane, Washington	2,249	9,754	10,244	8,423	7,077	4,297	10,173	9,339	9,132	7,541	9,273	10,570	8,136	11,625	9,545	2,396	10,641	11,621	14,967	12,653
Spoleto, Italy	6,994	11,758	11,349	1,579	1,889	5,334	10,673	482	911	10,203	9,529	9,859	10,595	7,284	4,241	8,999	2,296	9,252	6,109	13,231
Springbok, South Africa	14,775	8,366	7,675	7,841	9,396	11,492	7,362	7,637	8,214	9,646	7,644	6,555	9,269	9,746	6,200	13,895	7,256	10,914	3,381	11,462
Springfield, Illinois	3,484	7,953	8,310	7,071	6,110	2,699	8,103	8,467	8,561	5,537	7,050	8,349	6,180	12,973	7,470	1,010	10,175	13,550	13,765	15,033
Springfield, Massachusetts	3,808	7,980	8,184	5,657	4,832	1,370	7,831	7,150	7,341	5,507	6,608	7,851	6,158	12,512	6,070	2,369	8,942	13,564	12,317	16,022
Srinagar, India	8,674	16,814	16,199	6,962	6,682	9,691	15,568	5,175	4,475	15,578	14,717	14,599	15,975	1,903	9,316	12,552	3,546	3,889	5,872	7,848
Stanley, Falkland Islands	14,080	2,659	2,314	11,185	12,381	11,154	2,692	12,370	13,203	5,070	4,010	3,008	4,421	15,895	8,325	10,103	13,114	15,864	9,909	12,847
Stara Zagora, Bulgaria	7,344	12,722	12,269	2,624	2,761	6,216	11,592	863	258	11,255	10,503	10,731	11,634	6,236	5,134	9,825	1,361	8,222	5,623	12,182
Stockholm, Sweden	5,393	12,787	12,536	2,888	1,848	4,812	11,890	2,232	1,716	10,768	10,611	11,214	11,290	6,773	5,746	8,183	3,172	8,494	7,571	12,477
Stornoway, United Kingdom	4,873	11,474	11,287	2,264	716	3,472	10,668	2,655	2,577	9,375	9,352	10,085	9,912	8,180	4,921	7,001	4,189	9,863	8,284	13,800
Strasbourg, France	6,248	11,707	11,372	1,560	1,211	4,673	10,707	1,235	1,318	9,937	9,486	9,963	10,386	7,544	4,412	8,311	2,900	9,433	6,864	13,452
Stuttgart, West Germany	6,269	11,810	11,472	1,651	1,301	4,759	10,805	1,193	1,223	10,045	9,588	10,057	10,493	7,437	4,497	8,388	2,813	9,326	6,820	13,345
Subic, Philippines	9,825	17,965	18,122	11,831	11,116	12,932	18,608	10,137	9,369	18,415	19,632	18,417	18,709	3,275	14,335	13,431	8,561	1,296	9,245	3,243
Suchow, China	7,880	19,087	19,665	10,026	9,097	10,775	19,165	8,514	7,690	16,892	17,830	18,386	17,531	2,847	12,779	11,781	7,262	2,207	9,335	5,370
Sucre, Bolivia	10,444	1,358	1,374	8,925	9,589	7,565	1,143	10,631	11,394	1,489	1,050	1,796	941	17,463	6,434	6,643	12,206	19,265	11,288	16,104
Sudbury, Canada	3,067	8,524	8,792	6,123	5,098	1,744	8,491	7,459	7,539	6,054	7,316	8,583	6,708	12,181	6,822	2,033	9,153	13,015	12,848	15,203
Suez, Egypt	8,832	12,835	12,259	3,535	4,143	7,597	11,605	1,814	1,770	11,894	10,737	10,656	12,142	5,735	5,375	11,257	529	7,779	4,132	11,488
Sundsvall, Sweden	5,063	12,843	12,630	3,114	1,927	4,660	11,996	2,569	2,054	10,748	10,697	11,358	11,290	6,829	5,960	7,948	3,481	8,484	7,900	12,431
Surabaya, Indonesia	12,408	15,863	15,715	12,912	12,748	15,301	16,060	11,078	10,486	18,259	17,201	15,905	17,651	4,199	14,540	15,860	9,214	2,627	8,108	2,065
Suva, Fiji	10,918	10,850	11,381	17,794	16,210	13,951	12,051	17,103	16,267	11,731	12,984	12,960	11,549	10,613	18,299	10,614	15,894	8,573	14,760	5,136
Sverdlovsk, USSR	6,169	15,259	14,961	5,133	4,328	6,986	14,297	3,745	2,907	13,216	13,059	13,534	13,759	4,396	7,927	9,848	3,186	6,019	7,319	9,996
Svobodnyy, USSR	5,786	17,136	17,567	9,106	7,854	8,869	17,284	7,987	7,158	14,794	16,014	17,112	15,433	4,448	11,965	9,700	7,300	4,301	10,515	7,080
Sydney, Australia	13,597	11,648	11,886	17,817	17,429	17,090	12,516	15,990	15,409	13,505	13,819	13,097	13,058	9,054	17,594	13,816	14,098	7,164	11,576	3,145
Sydney, Canada	3,913	8,504	8,598	4,585	3,754	354	8,153	6,062	6,271	6,084	6,849	8,002	6,713	11,721	5,288	3,445	7,865	13,017	11,282	16,130
Syktyvkar, USSR	5,592	14,576	14,334	4,592	3,639	6,213	13,686	3,418	2,611	12,462	12,410	12,986	13,017	5,168	7,436	9,138	3,299	6,752	7,657	10,697
Szeged, Hungary	6,811	12,456	12,056	2,251	2,168	5,613	11,381	837	358	10,831	10,226	10,568	11,248	6,649	4,950	9,215	1,971	8,589	6,176	12,590
Szombathely, Hungary	6,623	12,243	11,864	2,030	1,877	5,326	11,191	882	646	10,569	10,014	10,399	10,996	6,911	4,789	8,937	2,251	8,834	6,389	12,843
Tabriz, Iran	8,157	14,303	13,763	4,428	4,463	7,832	13,097	2,606	2,002	13,052	12,139	12,167	13,398	4,460	6,729	11,284	1,036	6,480	5,022	10,387
Tacheng, China	7,208	17,121	16,739	6,917	6,219	8,750	16,061	5,335	4,518	15,088	14,897	15,204	15,646	2,641	9,606	11,197	4,169	4,126	7,330	8,107
Tahiti (Papeete)	9,873	7,950	8,591	15,921	14,903	11,576	9,203	17,235	16,971	8,387	9,861	10,182	8,279	13,786	14,917	7,905	18,144	11,805	17,146	8,520
Taipei, Taiwan	8,715	18,646	19,117	11,071	10,192	11,809	19,735	9,491	8,683	17,574	18,928	19,099	18,116	3,150	13,762	12,432	8,102	1,703	9,555	4,272
Taiyuan, China	7,629	19,061	19,231	9,449	8,538	10,342	18,605	7,940	7,115	16,617	17,299	17,816	17,270	2,624	12,203	11,616	6,722	2,453	9,026	5,889
Tallahassee, Florida	4,621	6,825	7,167	7,156	6,469	3,025	6,957	8,750	8,987	4,395	5,922	7,222	5,040	13,985	6,998	1,216	10,578	14,688	13,601	15,904
Tallinn, USSR	5,516	13,159	12,896	3,183	2,223	5,158	12,245	2,317	1,681	11,149	10,975	11,551	11,671	6,394	6,042	8,470	3,005	8,114	7,454	12,101
Tamanrasset, Algeria	8,859	10,076	9,543	1,941	3,447	6,210	8,874	2,095	2,916	9,137	7,939	7,959	9,348	8,538	2,578	9,744	3,234	10,582	4,923	14,150
Tampa, Florida	4,937	6,517	6,848	7,144	6,541	3,135	6,631	8,785	9,063	4,077	5,593	6,894	4,725	14,237	6,830	1,479	10,638	15,002	13,479	16,169
Tampere, Finland	5,278	13,150	12,914	3,282	2,212	5,012	12,272	2,523	1,912	11,085	10,986	11,606	11,621	6,482	6,141	8,274	3,241	8,157	7,692	12,121
Tanami, Australia	13,096	14,038	14,130	15,222	14,956	16,720	14,675	13,388	12,788	16,105	16,020	14,981	15,612	6,446	16,499	15,215	11,518	4,630	9,806	840
Tangier, Morocco	7,118	9,999	9,617	249	1,801	4,439	8,945	1,982	2,679	8,466	7,769	8,172	8,835	9,033	2,613	8,053	3,838	11,018	6,666	14,973
Tarawa (Betio)	9,117	12,554	13,177	15,654	14,102	12,614	13,806	14,918	14,098	12,738	14,430	14,779	12,766	9,194	17,906	9,957	14,065	7,275	14,858	4,897
Tashkent, USSR	7,894	16,280	15,760	6,173	5,780	8,751	15,092	4,444	3,688	14,722	14,081	14,166	15,171	2,770	8,680	11,677	3,027	4,661	6,146	8,669
Tbilisi, USSR	7,741	14,238	13,737	4,204	4,118	7,449	13,064	2,420	1,728	12,833	12,040	12,159	13,215	4,656	6,637	10,872	1,176	6,644	5,399	10,602
Tegucigalpa, Honduras	6,299	5,165	5,604	8,407	8,017	4,701	5,526	10,152	10,524	2,896	4,745	6,006	3,486	15,813	7,494	2,286	12,047	16,268	14,135	15,913
Tehran, Iran	8,473	14,705	14,134	4,946	4,987	8,335	13,479	3,118	2,533	13,561	12,577	12,530	13,888	3,968	7,177	11,741	1,408	6,001	4,870	9,876
Tel Aviv, Israel	8,646	13,114	12,548	3,640	4,119	7,583	11,890	1,854	1,662	12,098	10,997	10,947	12,368	5,498	5,614	11,218	214	7,542	4,328	11,306
Telegraph Creek, Canada	1,368	11,212	11,687	8,279	6,771	4,719	11,582	8,814	8,441	8,957	10,605	11,906	9,566	10,174	9,971	3,803	9,809	10,185	14,277	11,645
Teresina, Brazil	9,792	4,069	3,670	6,172	7,104	6,164	3,003	7,790	8,583	3,307	1,858	2,353	3,334	14,616	3,552	7,069	9,320	16,644	9,082	17,944
Ternate, Indonesia	11,042	16,223	16,408	13,512	12,861	14,468	16,981	11,761	11,028	17,690	18,327	17,258	17,470	4,727	15,798	14,081	10,068	2,699	9,821	1,515
The Valley, Anguilla	6,616	5,387	5,473	6,037	6,040	3,459	5,057	7,859	8,386	3,028	3,798	5,036	3,620	14,568	4,878	3,744	9,755	16,114	11,552	18,416
Thessaloniki, Greece	7,475	12,442	11,981	2,400	2,696	6,160	11,303	590	415	11,027	10,228	10,438	11,389	6,475	4,848	9,800	1,426	8,474	5,513	12,413
Thimphu, Bhutan	9,232	18,163	17,468	8,552	8,177	10,947	16,931	6,773	6,063	17,132	16,264	15,951	17,568	429	10,892	13,294	5,114	2,291	6,622	6,267
Thunder Bay, Canada	2,602	8,863	9,187	6,623	5,486	2,294	8,936	7,847	7,847	6,420	7,814	9,099	7,069	12,018	7,468	1,845	9,454	12,657	13,347	14,577
Tientsin, China	7,368	18,730	19,138	9,626	8,633	10,235	18,661	8,182	7,349	16,382	17,315	18,033	17,028	3,048	12,422	11,307	7,045	2,702	9,454	5,885
Tijuana, Mexico	3,928	8,429	8,998	9,529	8,367	5,165	9,055	10,710	10,617	6,473	8,388	9,630	6,995	13,136	10,020	1,893	12,182	12,799	16,257	12,820
Tiksi, USSR	3,827	15,215	15,465	7,329	5,899	6,622	15,074	6,635	5,890	12,749	13,772	14,868	13,403	5,845	10,105	7,896	6,595	6,320	10,700	9,328
Timbuktu, Mali	9,178	8,963	8,429	2,346	3,927	6,078	7,759	3,120	3,957	8,119	6,838	6,847	8,289	9,617	1,562	9,365	4,342	11,656	5,336	15,051
Tindouf, Algeria	7,858	9,268	8,837	1,173	2,687	4,840	8,160	2,595	3,387	7,953	7,047	7,345	8,254	9,602	1,734	8,288	4,279	11,629	6,370	15,447
Tirane, Albania	7,326	12,229	11,784	2,140	2,443	5,905	11,106	379	464	10,770	10,008	10,255	11,142	6,726	4,649	9,555	1,693	8,716	5,687	12,669
Tokyo, Japan	6,977	17,058	17,758	11,079	9,821	10,466	18,041	9,886	9,049	15,491	17,283	18,584	16,007	4,903	13,939	10,413	8,975	3,809	11,398	5,413
Toledo, Spain	6,767	10,397	10,038	230	1,381	4,317	9,369	1,739	2,342	8,767	8,169	8,616	9,167	8,718	3,084	7,980	3,641	10,672	6,814	14,665
Topeka, Kansas	3,418	8,046	8,453	7,562	6,547	3,180	8,300	8,910	8,963	5,692	7,316	8,617	6,319	13,028	7,991	704	10,575	13,420	14,272	14,589
Toronto, Canada	3,405	8,194	8,455	6,117	5,177	1,745	8,151	7,527	7,653	5,722	6,977	8,246	6,376	12,472	6,648	1,940	9,265	13,346	12,819	15,506
Toulouse, France	6,568	11,006	10,652	822	1,182	4,498	9,983	1,325	1,791	9,327	8,779	9,229	9,745	8,154	3,676	8,178	3,211	10,087	6,758	14,093
Tours, France	6,160	11,185	10,867	1,145	829	4,255	10,207	1,545	1,821	9,393	8,969	9,488	9,844	8,088	3,997	7,923	3,353	9,973	7,101	13,993
Townsville, Australia	12,311	13,205	13,503	16,580	15,794	16,041	14,150	14,808	14,094	14,781	15,418	14,770	14,437	7,748	18,279	13,580	13,038	5,754	11,586	1,866
Trenton, New Jersey	3,915	7,779	8,005	5,901	5,103	1,644	7,674	7,414	7,614	5,303	6,474	7,733	5,956	12,762	6,209	2,134	9,213	13,765	12,534	16,047
Tripoli, Lebanon	8,408	13,294	12,743	3,646	4,010	7,470	12,080	1,825	1,508	12,182	11,151	11,146	12,479	5,380	5,751	11,078	112	7,420	4,578	11,240
Tripoli, Libya	8,039	11,294	10,801	1,719	2,741	6,017	10,126	762	1,566	10,079	9,103	9,241	10,377	7,480	3,694	9,692	2,152	9,514	5,190	13,333
Tristan da Cunha (Edinburgh)	14,287	5,456	4,763	8,333	9,862	10,539	4,466	8,946	9,718	6,879	4,918	3,721	6,435	12,648	5,750	11,684	9,296	13,769	6,192	13,312
Trondheim, Norway	4,812	12,548	12,363	3,018	1,695	4,293	11,740	2,711	2,290	10,413	10,427	11,136	10,965	7,179	5,829	7,592	3,780	8,804	8,159	12,725
Trujillo, Peru	8,894	2,548	3,003	9,205	9,411	6,649	3,019	11,033	11,658	711	2,631	3,692	975	17,953	7,251	4,903	12,855	18,838	12,994	16,015
Truk Island (Moen)	9,372	14,876	15,438	14,437	13,169	13,119	16,102	13,114	12,279	15,132	16,858	17,023	15,195	6,781	17,296	11,520	11,866	4,843	12,597	3,203
Truro, Canada	3,860	8,382	8,502	4,837	4,005	567	8,078	6,317	6,520	5,944	6,788	7,966	6,580	11,906	5,469	3,191	8,116	13,148	11,526	16,123
Tsingtao, China	7,598	18,740	19,349	10,063	9,066	10,586	19,048	8,609	7,778	16,597	17,708	18,470	17,225	3,179	12,855	11,464	7,436	2,520	9,655	5,484
Tsitsihar, China	6,319	17,674	18,104	9,282	8,111	9,331	17,783	8,043	7,206	15,331	16,480	17,497	15,972	3,963	12,138	10,242	7,198	3,761	10,161	6,662
Tubuai Island (Mataura)	10,501	7,662	8,273	16,306	15,430	12,039	8,909	17,791	17,602	8,345	9,675	9,877	8,170	13,965	14,915	8,358	18,753	11,940	16,537	8,436
Tucson, Arizona	3,971	8,053	8,593	9,126	8,041	4,745	8,609	10,402	10,374	6,002	7,884	9,142	6,547	13,414	9,482	1,331	11,966	13,234	15,846	13,390
Tulsa, Oklahoma	3,725	7,758	8,179	7,750	6,787	3,381	8,045	9,146	9,226	5,426	7,096	8,394	6,047	13,344	8,040	384	10,839	13,696	14,430	14,672

Distances in Kilometers	Coppermine, Canada	Coquimbo, Chile	Cordoba, Argentina	Cordoba, Spain	Cork, Ireland	Corner Brook, Canada	Corrientes, Argentina	Cosenza, Italy	Craiova, Romania	Cruzeiro do Sul, Brazil	Cuiaba, Brazil	Curitiba, Brazil	Cuzco, Peru	Dacca, Bangladesh	Dakar, Senegal	Dallas, Texas	Damascus, Syria	Danang, Vietnam	Dar es Salaam, Tanzania	Darwin, Australia
Tunis, Tunisia	7,541	11,259	10,809	1,329	2,229	5,533	10,132	600	1,421	9,879	9,042	9,284	10,220	7,639	3,674	9,213	2,400	9,650	5,700	13,556
Tura, USSR	5,080	16,144	16,192	6,948	5,742	7,306	15,650	5,877	5,063	13,692	14,304	15,161	14,336	4,565	9,808	9,141	5,458	5,389	9,342	8,896
Turin, Italy	6,609	11,515	11,147	1,306	1,411	4,852	10,476	953	1,280	9,849	9,286	9,703	10,268	7,632	4,114	8,518	2,763	9,565	6,554	13,571
Uberlandia, Brazil	11,012	2,630	2,110	7,764	8,747	7,579	1,433	9,298	10,114	2,910	907	725	2,600	15,732	5,026	7,706	10,672	17,522	9,521	16,530
Ufa, USSR	6,389	15,038	14,699	4,858	4,151	6,968	14,029	3,407	2,568	13,091	12,820	13,238	13,610	4,467	7,621	9,965	2,814	6,180	6,994	10,184
Ujungpandang, Indonesia	11,954	15,959	15,946	13,325	12,968	15,140	16,394	11,503	10,852	18,080	17,663	16,414	17,599	4,481	15,194	15,176	9,688	2,647	8,863	1,497
Ulaanbaatar, Mongolia	6,699	18,006	18,023	8,350	7,360	9,172	17,423	6,950	6,113	15,539	16,096	16,756	16,189	3,055	11,161	10,761	5,958	3,534	8,939	7,097
Ulan-Ude, USSR	6,267	17,575	17,639	8,107	7,049	8,752	17,074	6,788	5,950	15,104	15,733	16,486	15,754	3,450	10,945	10,334	5,929	3,968	9,146	7,467
Uliastay, Mongolia	6,912	17,789	17,585	7,763	6,889	9,018	16,927	6,283	5,451	15,447	15,663	16,149	16,071	2,727	10,531	10,983	5,216	3,666	8,250	7,473
Uranium City, Canada	974	10,497	10,876	7,167	5,738	3,408	10,667	7,940	7,698	8,104	9,572	10,859	8,744	10,612	8,678	3,103	9,198	10,989	13,555	12,891
Urumqi, China	7,480	17,604	17,193	7,393	6,708	9,195	16,515	5,785	4,976	15,562	15,376	15,633	16,129	2,243	10,057	11,513	4,532	3,641	7,410	7,617
Ushuaia, Argentina	14,140	2,769	2,620	11,916	13,055	11,540	3,132	13,142	13,977	5,245	4,478	3,618	4,591	16,133	9,061	10,080	13,875	15,696	10,501	12,337
Vaduz, Liechtenstein	6,443	11,752	11,396	1,558	1,400	4,863	10,727	1,030	1,154	10,035	9,525	9,963	10,470	7,444	4,383	8,508	2,714	9,356	6,659	13,370
Valencia, Spain	6,932	10,626	10,245	421	1,517	4,606	9,573	1,430	2,068	9,050	8,396	8,796	9,437	8,440	3,215	8,276	3,328	10,409	6,548	14,386
Valladolid, Spain	6,562	10,468	10,127	418	1,175	4,165	9,462	1,793	2,333	8,780	8,244	8,728	9,197	8,701	3,232	7,837	3,698	10,635	6,985	14,642
Valletta, Malta	7,761	11,556	11,083	1,730	2,542	5,903	10,406	407	1,223	10,248	9,351	9,535	10,573	7,284	3,955	9,584	2,009	9,306	5,390	13,182
Valparaiso, Chile	11,755	341	725	10,466	11,237	9,182	1,376	12,079	12,881	2,814	2,489	2,328	2,162	17,988	7,810	7,749	13,458	18,125	11,517	14,438
Vancouver, Canada	2,118	10,163	10,668	8,613	7,211	4,606	10,613	9,417	9,152	7,981	9,727	11,023	8,569	11,269	9,886	2,845	10,616	11,192	15,020	12,214
Varna, Bulgaria	7,306	12,927	12,476	2,812	2,868	6,308	11,798	1,069	353	11,441	10,707	10,938	11,827	6,048	5,341	9,892	1,302	8,026	5,657	11,995
Venice, Italy	6,699	11,862	11,481	1,650	1,685	5,147	10,807	755	913	10,218	9,633	10,017	10,634	7,262	4,410	8,796	2,436	9,200	6,380	13,203
Veracruz, Mexico	5,567	6,055	6,558	8,842	8,194	4,742	6,545	10,471	10,711	3,934	5,835	7,079	4,484	15,205	8,329	1,506	12,304	15,290	15,023	14,963
Verona, Italy	6,662	11,768	11,391	1,555	1,596	5,056	10,718	808	1,018	10,114	9,538	9,933	10,532	7,366	4,331	8,710	2,533	9,302	6,437	13,306
Victoria, Canada	2,211	10,109	10,620	8,690	7,294	4,662	10,574	9,504	9,243	7,942	9,702	10,996	8,527	11,337	9,936	2,817	10,708	11,236	15,110	12,202
Victoria, Seychelles	12,951	13,190	12,496	7,783	8,670	12,091	12,141	6,310	6,275	14,109	12,170	11,263	13,890	4,922	8,316	15,772	4,676	6,244	1,807	8,322
Vienna, Austria	6,516	12,267	11,898	2,058	1,816	5,255	11,226	989	717	10,561	10,038	10,444	10,997	6,919	4,841	8,856	2,330	8,829	6,493	12,843
Vientiane, Laos	10,011	18,545	18,020	10,245	9,820	12,348	17,852	8,461	7,756	18,754	17,748	17,010	19,262	1,418	12,525	14,025	6,761	634	7,474	4,577
Villahermosa, Mexico	5,758	5,788	6,268	8,648	8,078	4,654	6,230	10,318	10,600	3,608	5,487	6,740	4,174	15,377	8,019	1,685	12,176	15,591	14,708	15,306
Vilnius, USSR	6,028	13,080	12,758	2,938	2,252	5,434	12,094	1,840	1,158	11,206	10,865	11,346	11,691	6,297	5,767	8,855	2,506	8,111	6,937	12,127
Visby, Sweden	5,575	12,746	12,474	2,766	1,823	4,897	11,822	2,044	1,530	10,772	10,556	11,126	11,282	6,752	5,626	8,310	3,007	8,508	7,391	12,506
Vitoria, Brazil	11,458	3,291	2,678	7,441	8,580	7,868	2,039	8,841	9,673	3,746	1,746	1,073	3,447	14,960	4,611	8,399	10,070	16,681	8,678	16,254
Vladivostok, USSR	6,502	17,490	18,091	10,026	8,807	9,758	18,020	8,821	7,985	15,407	16,859	18,036	16,011	4,357	12,886	10,252	7,965	3,749	10,736	6,157
Volgograd, USSR	6,962	14,292	13,872	4,090	3,699	6,880	13,194	2,472	1,651	12,610	12,063	12,348	13,058	4,875	6,739	10,192	1,823	6,766	6,174	10,781
Vologda, USSR	5,764	14,014	13,733	3,947	3,084	5,911	13,076	2,774	1,984	12,003	11,821	12,351	12,530	5,558	6,784	9,058	2,871	7,254	7,319	11,241
Vorkuta, USSR	4,987	14,912	14,787	5,284	4,133	6,212	14,177	4,272	3,487	12,616	12,853	13,576	13,218	5,196	8,144	8,770	4,183	6,528	8,473	10,327
Wake Island	7,543	14,099	14,786	13,614	12,105	11,259	15,319	12,830	12,019	13,520	15,487	16,284	13,766	7,820	16,223	9,459	12,151	6,182	14,184	5,269
Wallis Island	10,218	10,665	11,248	17,153	15,585	13,166	11,901	16,880	16,082	11,276	12,702	12,851	11,163	10,943	17,734	9,835	16,049	8,931	15,524	5,742
Walvis Bay, Namibia	13,959	8,396	7,693	7,029	8,589	10,705	7,300	6,893	7,508	9,394	7,399	6,420	9,086	9,695	5,424	13,289	6,662	11,069	3,200	12,063
Warsaw, Poland	6,197	12,731	12,392	2,558	2,007	5,318	11,725	1,485	906	10,920	10,510	10,964	11,387	6,570	5,377	8,824	2,418	8,424	6,770	12,444
Washington, D.C.	3,970	7,646	7,895	6,138	5,347	1,888	7,586	7,658	7,858	5,171	6,413	7,685	5,825	12,953	6,379	1,907	9,458	13,897	12,754	16,001
Watson Lake, Canada	1,086	11,271	11,722	8,005	6,493	4,510	11,586	8,532	8,163	8,973	10,569	11,868	9,592	10,056	9,739	3,833	9,540	10,153	14,005	11,774
Weimar, East Germany	6,098	12,056	11,732	1,930	1,375	4,787	11,068	1,354	1,193	10,239	9,839	10,331	10,703	7,247	4,782	8,379	2,807	9,109	6,942	13,129
Wellington, New Zealand	13,428	9,605	9,945	19,623	18,801	15,871	10,609	18,190	17,638	11,294	11,829	11,341	10,878	11,267	16,829	12,203	16,284	9,330	13,023	5,325
West Berlin, West Germany	5,992	12,256	11,941	2,152	1,491	4,844	11,279	1,485	1,191	10,407	10,043	10,548	10,880	7,085	5,005	8,399	2,795	8,927	7,016	12,945
Wewak, Papua New Guinea	10,842	14,764	15,152	15,038	14,058	14,575	15,820	13,413	12,626	15,825	16,989	16,516	15,668	6,506	17,615	12,973	11,838	4,462	11,554	1,720
Whangarei, New Zealand	12,877	10,015	10,397	19,753	18,193	15,565	11,069	18,052	17,348	11,550	12,246	11,841	11,180	10,998	17,399	11,954	16,198	9,011	13,369	5,059
Whitehorse, Canada	1,241	11,580	12,044	8,182	6,646	4,814	11,922	8,616	8,205	9,304	10,916	12,215	9,918	9,791	10,010	4,155	9,533	9,829	14,004	11,430
Wichita, Kansas	3,530	7,965	8,390	7,765	6,756	3,384	8,258	9,119	9,171	5,639	7,307	8,606	6,258	13,159	8,150	548	10,783	13,485	14,469	14,500
Willemstad, Curacao	7,030	4,664	4,842	6,932	6,946	4,209	4,514	8,759	9,296	2,221	3,376	4,670	2,855	15,456	5,576	3,647	10,651	16,872	12,153	17,885
Wiluna, Australia	14,149	13,626	13,569	14,769	14,918	17,519	14,021	12,981	12,512	15,976	15,321	14,140	15,377	6,425	15,447	16,399	11,075	4,896	8,780	1,918
Windhoek, Namibia	14,014	8,651	7,948	7,073	8,619	10,842	7,561	6,851	7,439	9,662	7,668	6,686	9,354	9,441	5,581	13,511	6,533	10,801	2,953	11,833
Windsor, Canada	3,421	8,091	8,385	6,449	5,505	2,078	8,114	7,857	7,973	5,630	6,979	8,262	6,283	12,665	6,924	1,610	9,587	13,441	13,147	15,369
Winnipeg, Canada	2,232	9,205	9,575	7,063	5,839	2,814	9,368	8,179	8,109	6,802	8,294	9,588	7,443	11,819	8,041	1,900	9,696	12,289	13,755	14,000
Winston-Salem, North Carolina	4,149	7,372	7,658	6,526	5,765	2,308	7,386	8,069	8,277	4,907	6,260	7,548	5,560	13,312	6,632	1,565	9,875	14,163	13,098	15,954
Wroclaw, Poland	6,228	12,430	12,089	2,257	1,764	5,139	11,422	1,313	908	10,639	10,208	10,664	11,098	6,847	5,082	8,694	2,503	8,716	6,761	12,736
Wuhan, China	8,353	19,485	19,849	10,139	9,306	11,162	19,269	8,552	7,744	17,367	18,081	18,310	18,012	2,478	12,823	12,270	7,187	1,722	8,976	5,083
Wyndham, Australia	12,698	14,566	14,657	14,788	14,447	16,251	15,197	12,958	12,329	16,593	16,540	15,473	16,121	5,966	16,333	15,121	11,111	4,116	9,692	444
Xi'an, China	8,106	19,527	19,303	9,494	8,690	10,696	18,629	7,903	7,094	17,051	17,455	17,703	17,704	2,142	12,175	12,114	6,561	2,017	8,598	5,669
Xining, China	8,020	19,038	18,605	8,836	8,100	10,317	17,934	7,219	6,416	16,745	16,818	17,007	17,372	1,797	11,488	12,085	5,864	2,365	8,077	6,230
Yakutsk, USSR	4,698	16,132	16,460	8,203	6,848	7,685	16,116	7,302	6,506	13,703	14,831	15,939	14,353	5,175	11,031	8,705	6,947	5,373	10,689	8,256
Yanji, China	6,605	17,672	18,257	9,942	8,752	9,804	18,139	8,701	7,863	15,545	16,932	18,064	16,158	4,164	12,799	10,394	7,807	3,597	10,540	6,130
Yaounde, Cameroon	11,049	9,544	8,889	4,116	5,638	8,196	8,292	3,953	4,640	9,430	7,750	7,310	9,418	8,712	3,394	11,481	4,168	10,613	3,302	13,294
Yap Island (Colonia)	9,722	16,214	16,673	13,502	12,490	13,340	17,349	11,952	11,143	16,649	18,348	18,084	16,723	5,300	16,223	12,553	10,514	3,324	11,109	2,562
Yaraka, Australia	12,995	12,861	13,093	16,750	16,218	16,723	13,716	14,923	14,276	14,659	15,027	14,259	14,241	7,900	17,788	14,100	13,075	5,973	11,176	1,958
Yarmouth, Canada	3,891	8,189	8,333	5,096	4,288	847	7,930	6,594	6,803	5,737	6,658	7,859	6,378	12,153	5,617	2,930	8,398	13,347	11,767	16,172
Yellowknife, Canada	601	10,937	11,322	7,251	5,770	3,704	11,114	7,896	7,596	8,550	10,014	11,299	9,189	10,204	8,924	3,526	9,050	10,545	13,467	12,493
Yerevan, USSR	7,905	14,191	13,674	4,219	4,198	7,555	13,003	2,413	1,764	12,850	12,004	12,089	13,215	4,648	6,596	11,004	1,041	6,652	5,229	10,589
Yinchuan, China	7,720	19,039	18,849	9,007	8,175	10,198	18,174	7,451	6,633	16,588	16,946	17,309	17,235	2,224	11,722	11,764	6,185	2,489	8,526	6,189
Yogyakarta, Indonesia	12,544	15,822	15,629	12,743	12,643	15,314	15,935	10,910	10,339	18,268	17,026	15,726	17,633	4,107	14,297	16,081	9,035	2,650	7,841	2,301
York, United Kingdom	5,457	11,465	11,215	1,794	536	3,882	10,573	2,084	2,093	9,495	9,288	9,921	9,996	8,015	4,572	7,485	3,704	9,796	7,711	13,794
Yumen, China	7,753	18,536	18,140	8,338	7,601	9,884	17,463	6,735	5,927	16,311	16,318	16,564	16,922	1,915	11,007	11,828	5,430	2,824	7,904	6,727
Yutian, China	8,310	17,415	16,839	7,352	6,903	9,700	16,190	5,619	4,868	15,862	15,245	15,234	16,338	1,680	9,836	12,293	4,114	3,485	6,546	7,500
Yuzhno-Sakhalinsk, USSR	5,746	16,538	17,145	10,069	8,712	9,193	17,145	9,080	8,261	14,513	16,119	17,394	15,099	5,285	12,900	9,361	8,468	4,672	11,581	6,687
Zagreb, Yugoslavia	6,759	12,137	11,746	1,928	1,908	5,369	11,068	722	636	10,505	9,907	10,270	10,921	6,975	4,655	8,999	2,203	8,915	6,270	12,916
Zahedan, Iran	9,207	15,440	14,802	6,033	6,100	9,417	14,188	4,199	3,648	14,601	13,440	13,211	14,874	3,003	8,108	12,723	2,370	5,047	4,634	8,820
Zamboanga, Philippines	10,600	17,097	17,217	12,615	11,984	13,817	17,726	10,871	10,132	18,416	19,024	17,762	18,327	3,859	14,963	14,002	9,202	1,818	9,317	2,351
Zanzibar, Tanzania	12,892	11,620	10,916	6,668	7,860	11,045	10,488	5,560	5,800	12,310	10,396	9,568	12,124	6,471	6,660	14,606	4,401	7,990	71	10,050
Zaragoza, Spain	6,693	10,726	10,366	533	1,278	4,442	9,697	1,473	2,028	9,081	8,498	8,940	9,488	8,402	3,388	8,120	3,378	10,349	6,742	14,347
Zashiversk, USSR	3,848	15,274	15,629	8,007	6,549	6,981	15,330	7,343	6,596	12,861	14,087	15,262	13,508	6,017	10,754	7,843	7,263	6,220	11,267	8,915
Zhengzhou, China	7,929	19,305	19,588	9,767	8,884	10,696	18,937	8,226	7,406	16,935	17,652	18,082	17,586	2,561	12,496	11,884	6,946	2,140	9,033	5,532
Zurich, Switzerland	6,390	11,685	11,336	1,503	1,313	4,776	10,668	1,100	1,244	9,954	9,460	9,911	10,392	7,526	4,340	8,423	2,803	9,432	6,728	13,448

Distances in Kilometers

	Davao, Philippines	David, Panama	Dawson, Canada	Dawson Creek, Canada	Denpasar, Indonesia	Denver, Colorado	Derby, Australia	Des Moines, Iowa	Detroit, Michigan	Dhahran, Saudi Arabia	Diego Garcia Island	Dijon, France	Dili, Indonesia	Djibouti, Djibouti	Dnepropetrovsk, USSR	Dobo, Indonesia	Doha, Qatar	Donetsk, USSR	Dover, Delaware	Dresden, East Germany
David, Panama	16,478	0	7,606	6,206	18,094	4,131	17,043	3,835	3,757	13,619	17,262	9,135	16,955	13,615	11,252	15,979	13,797	11,461	3,473	9,715
Dawson, Canada	9,546	7,606	0	1,407	11,612	3,513	12,058	3,835	4,270	9,952	13,222	7,270	11,099	11,611	7,519	10,402	10,054	7,576	4,924	7,029
Dawson Creek, Canada	10,827	6,206	1,407	0	12,910	2,107	13,210	2,489	3,050	10,866	14,518	7,495	12,292	12,381	8,226	11,506	10,991	8,323	3,754	7,428
Denpasar, Indonesia	2,085	18,094	11,612	12,910	0	14,751	1,322	15,394	15,870	8,020	4,719	12,233	1,139	8,285	10,011	2,122	7,850	9,795	16,461	11,554
Denver, Colorado	12,684	4,131	3,513	2,107	14,751	0	14,736	982	1,862	12,254	16,406	8,144	13,942	13,442	9,472	13,031	12,407	9,616	2,525	8,323
Derby, Australia	2,704	17,043	12,058	13,210	1,322	14,736	0	15,569	16,259	9,293	5,662	13,555	990	9,407	11,332	1,719	9,120	11,117	16,961	12,874
Des Moines, Iowa	13,309	3,835	3,835	2,489	15,394	982	15,569	0	880	11,617	15,970	7,324	14,709	12,648	8,832	13,850	11,781	8,994	1,557	7,574
Detroit, Michigan	13,815	3,757	4,270	3,050	15,870	1,862	16,259	880	0	11,021	15,446	6,602	15,339	11,912	8,265	14,549	11,192	8,442	726	6,919
Dhahran, Saudi Arabia	8,223	13,619	9,952	10,866	8,020	12,254	9,293	11,617	11,021	0	4,432	4,566	9,004	1,785	2,789	9,710	180	2,638	10,830	4,121
Diego Garcia Island	6,116	17,262	13,222	14,518	4,719	16,406	5,662	15,970	15,446	4,432	0	8,946	5,858	3,858	7,181	6,832	4,259	7,007	15,252	8,551
Dijon, France	11,641	9,135	7,270	7,495	12,233	8,144	13,555	7,324	6,602	4,566	8,946	0	12,985	5,324	2,231	13,351	4,745	2,445	6,310	759
Dili, Indonesia	1,727	16,955	11,099	12,292	1,139	13,942	990	14,709	15,339	9,004	5,858	12,985	0	9,390	10,758	1,004	8,840	10,545	16,021	12,264
Djibouti, Djibouti	9,043	13,615	11,611	12,381	8,285	13,442	9,407	12,648	11,912	1,785	3,858	5,324	9,390	0	4,156	10,262	1,753	4,066	11,551	5,124
Dnepropetrovsk, USSR	9,472	11,252	7,519	8,226	10,011	9,472	11,332	8,832	8,265	2,789	7,181	2,231	10,758	4,156	0	11,169	2,950	215	8,139	1,552
Dobo, Indonesia	1,712	15,979	10,402	11,506	2,122	13,031	1,719	13,850	14,549	9,710	6,832	13,351	1,004	10,262	11,169	0	9,555	10,961	15,260	12,600
Doha, Qatar	8,082	13,797	10,054	10,991	7,850	12,407	9,120	11,781	11,192	180	4,259	4,745	8,840	1,753	2,950	9,555	0	2,794	11,006	4,296
Donetsk, USSR	9,267	11,461	7,576	8,323	9,795	9,616	11,117	8,994	8,442	2,638	7,007	2,445	10,545	4,066	215	10,961	2,794	0	8,329	1,766
Dover, Delaware	14,446	3,473	4,924	3,754	16,461	2,525	16,961	1,557	726	10,830	15,252	6,310	16,021	11,551	8,139	15,260	11,006	8,329	0	6,710
Dresden, East Germany	10,890	9,715	7,029	7,428	11,554	8,323	12,874	7,574	6,919	4,121	8,551	759	12,264	5,124	1,552	12,600	4,296	1,766	6,710	0
Dubayy, United Arab Emir.	7,703	14,118	10,019	11,016	7,495	12,525	8,773	11,944	11,390	531	4,055	5,024	8,474	1,981	3,125	9,180	379	2,953	11,239	4,536
Dublin, Ireland	11,938	8,343	6,375	6,496	12,833	7,103	14,139	6,293	5,591	5,492	9,912	1,043	13,442	6,356	2,909	13,638	5,669	3,118	5,341	1,386
Duluth, Minnesota	12,980	4,349	3,440	2,181	15,052	1,303	15,387	590	873	11,069	15,392	6,852	14,473	12,165	8,280	13,676	11,230	8,438	1,591	7,062
Dunedin, New Zealand	7,363	12,000	12,951	12,989	6,671	12,664	5,349	13,549	14,330	14,376	10,051	18,898	5,950	13,784	16,681	5,652	14,196	16,466	14,698	18,213
Durango, Mexico	13,577	2,929	5,118	3,747	15,463	1,742	14,969	2,200	2,844	13,816	18,131	9,446	14,430	14,747	11,032	13,433	13,981	11,194	3,212	9,749
Durban, South Africa	10,843	12,738	16,141	16,347	8,984	15,896	9,318	14,937	14,076	6,540	4,989	8,935	9,981	4,768	8,681	10,960	6,482	8,649	13,381	9,121
Dushanbe, USSR	6,661	14,017	8,361	9,518	7,098	11,312	8,417	10,954	10,607	2,212	5,093	5,149	7,848	3,922	2,918	8,320	2,191	2,704	10,665	4,456
East London, South Africa	11,154	12,417	16,445	16,490	9,245	15,783	9,497	14,853	14,012	6,975	5,392	9,190	10,206	5,198	9,052	11,168	6,923	9,029	13,302	9,418
Easter Island (Hanga Roa)	13,823	4,897	10,446	9,244	13,789	7,419	12,473	7,783	8,157	17,998	16,184	13,984	12,904	16,684	16,148	12,280	18,120	16,357	8,142	14,603
Echo Bay, Canada	10,436	6,954	1,025	1,156	12,470	3,046	13,013	3,119	3,404	9,713	13,434	6,529	12,040	11,251	7,096	11,384	9,836	7,186	4,010	6,387
Edinburgh, United Kingdom	11,605	8,564	6,182	6,384	12,548	7,114	13,846	6,341	5,675	5,362	9,794	1,112	13,127	6,329	2,701	13,301	5,536	2,904	5,473	1,244
Edmonton, Canada	11,327	5,725	1,880	501	13,411	1,664	13,695	1,988	2,564	11,018	14,852	7,414	12,784	12,454	8,317	11,986	11,152	8,429	3,275	7,412
El Aaiun, Morocco	14,188	7,539	8,868	8,540	14,240	8,279	15,472	7,304	6,431	6,230	9,953	2,744	15,229	6,113	4,752	15,841	6,397	4,949	5,850	3,491
Elat, Israel	9,694	12,121	9,615	10,263	9,555	11,291	10,822	10,529	9,836	1,536	5,721	3,241	10,538	2,162	2,098	11,225	1,705	2,063	9,547	2,968
Elazig, Turkey	9,211	12,055	8,613	9,360	9,411	10,590	10,724	9,918	9,311	1,710	6,142	2,923	10,285	3,026	1,138	10,843	1,883	1,042	9,127	2,418
Eniwetok Atoll, Marshall Isls.	4,054	12,543	7,355	8,177	5,664	9,437	5,309	10,317	11,100	11,583	10,161	13,112	4,627	12,832	11,595	3,645	11,490	11,453	11,826	12,439
Erfurt, East Germany	11,068	9,528	6,992	7,349	11,745	8,193	13,064	7,430	6,763	4,288	8,715	599	12,451	5,250	1,742	12,779	4,464	1,956	6,542	191
Erzurum, Turkey	9,028	12,144	8,477	9,258	9,280	10,545	10,596	9,898	9,314	1,719	6,133	3,011	10,133	3,143	1,073	10,671	1,884	940	9,155	2,462
Esfahan, Iran	8,092	13,359	9,237	10,176	8,135	11,636	9,440	11,049	10,503	721	4,945	4,226	9,046	2,489	2,239	9,666	818	2,062	10,371	3,689
Essen, West Germany	11,299	9,243	6,869	7,168	12,016	7,951	13,334	7,174	6,496	4,567	8,991	482	12,707	5,492	2,022	13,010	4,744	2,235	6,264	472
Eucla, Australia	4,306	15,884	13,207	14,139	2,919	15,145	1,682	16,113	16,970	10,534	6,427	15,012	2,588	10,285	12,838	2,926	10,354	12,624	17,669	14,389
Fargo, North Dakota	12,720	4,474	3,210	1,896	14,801	1,033	15,074	640	1,200	11,249	15,504	7,114	14,177	12,409	8,461	13,359	11,406	8,611	1,925	7,291
Faroe Islands (Torshavn)	11,333	8,435	5,477	5,727	12,479	6,594	13,735	5,881	5,285	5,745	10,161	1,798	12,937	6,862	2,982	12,994	5,913	3,163	5,174	1,742
Florence, Italy	11,370	9,662	7,775	8,072	11,793	8,769	13,112	7,950	7,225	3,992	8,342	626	12,612	4,698	1,899	13,063	4,172	2,103	6,921	831
Florianopolis, Brazil	17,654	5,403	12,767	11,440	15,636	9,471	14,969	8,953	8,512	12,117	12,599	9,880	15,958	10,771	11,804	16,303	12,205	11,979	7,902	10,632
Fort George, Canada	12,874	5,044	3,505	2,621	14,835	2,504	15,508	1,742	1,313	9,876	14,248	5,640	14,525	10,949	7,091	13,895	10,040	7,255	1,652	5,846
Fort McMurray, Canada	11,259	5,919	1,728	559	13,333	1,946	13,706	2,112	2,571	10,641	14,515	7,061	12,771	12,077	7,939	12,013	10,776	8,051	3,255	7,044
Fort Nelson, Canada	10,555	6,545	1,061	371	12,632	2,466	12,995	2,786	3,282	10,549	14,149	7,311	12,059	12,096	7,941	11,305	10,670	8,031	3,967	7,204
Fort Severn, Canada	12,382	5,294	2,931	2,022	14,388	2,211	14,973	1,659	1,554	10,054	14,332	5,992	14,000	11,247	7,267	13,332	10,211	7,416	2,073	6,123
Fort Smith, Arkansas	13,720	3,225	4,386	2,996	15,795	1,051	15,767	692	1,251	12,231	16,624	7,850	14,991	13,163	9,456	14,071	12,399	9,625	1,723	8,150
Fort Vermilion, Canada	10,927	6,237	1,396	390	13,000	2,219	13,384	2,441	2,899	10,531	14,294	7,106	12,445	12,019	7,867	11,696	10,659	7,969	3,579	7,045
Fort Wayne, Indiana	13,825	3,626	4,283	3,020	15,895	1,688	16,207	712	223	11,241	15,663	6,825	15,309	12,135	8,482	14,490	11,411	8,657	846	7,141
Fort-Chimo, Canada	12,672	5,640	3,683	3,088	14,510	3,304	15,369	2,552	2,032	9,067	13,454	4,843	14,379	10,141	6,285	13,880	9,232	6,452	2,168	5,034
Fort-de-France, Martinique	17,500	2,425	7,989	6,764	19,241	5,093	19,441	4,330	3,727	11,321	14,899	7,031	19,035	11,191	9,247	18,090	11,495	9,462	3,067	7,701
Fortaleza, Brazil	18,236	5,059	10,906	9,831	16,810	8,298	16,975	7,491	6,792	10,061	12,267	7,071	17,797	9,193	9,111	18,692	10,194	9,302	6,079	7,830
Frankfort, Kentucky	14,091	3,306	4,561	3,268	16,169	1,749	16,406	837	484	11,469	15,900	7,011	15,535	12,300	8,725	14,687	11,641	8,905	818	7,357
Frankfurt am Main, W. Ger.	11,260	9,375	7,043	7,355	11,921	8,138	13,242	7,357	6,673	4,404	8,822	412	12,637	5,306	1,913	12,971	4,581	2,127	6,431	373
Fredericton, Canada	14,007	4,426	4,746	3,821	15,865	3,177	16,688	2,214	1,370	9,787	14,214	5,287	15,698	10,569	7,090	15,120	9,962	7,280	1,049	5,666
Freeport, Bahamas	15,461	2,038	5,967	4,642	17,547	2,835	17,503	2,154	1,797	12,009	16,311	7,444	16,774	12,465	9,421	15,839	12,189	9,620	1,435	7,932
Freetown, Sierra Leone	15,154	7,607	10,797	10,273	14,369	9,562	15,266	8,589	7,720	6,950	9,665	4,638	15,505	6,183	6,312	16,432	7,083	6,477	7,037	5,329
Frobisher Bay, Canada	12,062	6,239	3,300	2,947	13,882	3,579	14,763	2,952	2,561	8,694	13,018	4,674	13,776	9,886	5,905	13,316	8,853	6,059	2,775	4,764
Frunze, USSR	6,362	13,865	7,776	8,981	7,037	10,852	8,339	10,573	10,304	2,884	5,567	5,313	7,683	4,609	3,112	8,057	2,872	2,905	10,433	4,582
Fukuoka, Japan	2,977	14,213	6,714	8,073	4,942	10,095	5,677	10,547	10,935	7,598	7,605	9,522	4,691	9,057	7,667	4,374	7,527	7,502	11,521	8,777
Funafuti Atoll, Tuvalu	6,185	11,076	8,766	9,033	7,027	9,424	6,082	10,407	11,286	14,309	11,719	15,668	5,892	15,204	14,458	4,968	14,190	14,328	11,928	15,102
Funchal, Madeira Island	14,096	7,223	8,172	7,839	14,437	7,635	15,727	6,667	5,801	6,434	10,386	2,467	15,331	6,527	4,630	15,798	6,609	4,838	5,251	3,226
Fuzhou, China	2,208	15,529	7,956	9,341	3,868	11,398	4,823	11,785	12,091	6,822	6,271	9,562	3,891	8,083	7,483	3,875	6,720	7,291	12,620	8,803
Gaborone, Botswana	11,320	12,253	15,498	15,598	9,551	15,169	9,976	14,201	13,333	6,212	5,303	8,243	10,587	4,428	8,148	11,580	6,178	8,135	12,647	8,472
Galapagos Islands (Santa Cruz)	15,980	1,335	8,210	6,812	17,015	4,712	15,806	4,867	4,815	14,933	17,929	10,469	15,921	14,761	12,583	15,030	15,109	12,790	4,660	11,049
Gander, Canada	13,799	5,189	5,046	4,362	15,438	4,065	16,490	3,131	2,320	8,845	13,264	4,326	15,526	9,605	6,182	15,147	9,021	6,378	1,988	4,727
Gangtok, India	4,500	15,933	9,046	10,400	4,907	12,447	6,219	12,371	12,244	3,812	4,214	7,368	5,624	5,048	5,137	6,120	3,697	4,923	12,463	6,663
Garyarsa, China	5,424	15,200	8,827	10,112	5,808	12,070	7,126	11,861	11,629	2,996	4,407	6,443	6,556	4,418	4,213	7,056	2,903	3,998	11,770	5,748
Gaspe, Canada	13,735	4,784	4,602	3,772	15,550	3,343	16,431	2,409	1,613	9,467	13,898	4,996	15,442	10,299	6,754	14,917	9,641	6,942	1,390	5,348
Gauhati, India	4,165	16,124	9,062	10,433	4,616	12,505	5,921	12,481	12,400	4,138	4,256	7,681	5,306	5,333	5,452	5,789	4,019	5,239	12,652	6,970
Gdansk, Poland	10,452	9,963	6,737	7,237	11,209	8,281	12,522	7,587	6,984	4,040	8,463	1,236	11,870	5,209	1,307	12,164	4,209	1,506	6,836	495
Geneva, Switzerland	11,621	9,232	7,414	7,646	12,165	8,292	13,487	7,468	6,741	4,450	8,818	152	12,937	5,181	2,180	13,327	4,630	2,393	6,441	776
Genoa, Italy	11,510	9,470	7,661	7,924	11,971	8,587	13,291	7,762	7,032	4,189	8,540	444	12,777	4,887	2,040	13,208	4,369	2,248	6,724	820
Georgetown, Guyana	18,417	2,683	8,903	7,662	19,277	5,920	18,828	5,206	4,637	11,480	14,580	7,450	19,577	11,090	9,680	18,663	11,645	9,894	3,985	8,162
Geraldton, Australia	4,137	17,144	13,615	14,780	2,228	16,215	1,570	17,103	17,828	9,193	5,018	13,733	2,516	8,875	11,636	3,279	9,013	11,428	18,531	13,171
Ghanzi, Botswana	11,730	11,823	15,082	15,091	10,019	14,628	10,489	13,659	12,790	6,116	5,654	7,812	11,074	4,349	7,865	12,071	6,100	7,869	12,105	8,082
Ghat, Libya	12,193	9,886	9,787	9,910	11,930	10,197	13,131	9,269	8,437	3,999	7,626	2,522	12,970	3,773	3,390	13,709	4,153	3,521	7,954	2,911
Gibraltar	13,016	8,306	8,190	8,112	13,312	8,266	14,609	7,336	6,507	5,327	9,404	1,509	14,202	5,562	3,547	14,703	5,502	3,749	6,043	2,251
Gijon, Spain	12,572	8,303	7,407	7,408	13,140	7,749	14,461	6,861	6,075	5,335	9,618	935	13,916	5,859	3,158	14,282	5,514	3,372	5,693	1,682
Gisborne, New Zealand	7,406	11,422	11,988	11,980	7,060	11,693	5,753	12,600	13,408	15,008	10,840	18,893	6,195	14,651	16,877	5,715	14,831	16,673	13,832	18,165
Glasgow, United Kingdom	11,663	8,498	6,166	6,352	12,613	7,064	13,910	6,286	5,617	5,423	9,854	1,143	13,189	6,380	2,767	13,358	5,598	2,970	5,410	1,304
Godthab, Greenland	12,092	6,656	3,929	3,741	13,746	4,368	14,778	3,671	3,152	7,947	12,325	3,846	13,818	9,080	5,161	13,498	8,110	5,326	3,202	3,957
Gomez Palacio, Mexico	13,605	2,928	5,001	3,618	15,528	1,578	15,086	1,996	2,638	13,611	17,942	9,240	14,516	14,543	10,827	13,524	13,776	10,991	3,015	9,542
Goose Bay, Canada	10,541	6,297	1,571	692	12,622	2,178	12,789	2,800	3,488	11,397	14,785	8,174	11,910	12,971	8,819	11,071	11,512	8,905	4,211	8,085
Gorki, USSR	8,839	11,325	6,648	7,495	9,671	8,965	10,969	8,447	7,999	3,372	7,523	2,823	10,277	4,964	1,069	10,551	3,502	1,019	7,997	2,064
Goteborg, Sweden	10,708	9,481	6,280	6,716	11,602	7,722	12,902	7,027	6,431	4,597	9,015	1,248	12,197	5,759	1,841	12,414	4,765	2,030	6,299	751
Granada, Spain	12,825	8,455	8,124	8,089	13,142	8,308	14,443	7,389	6,570	5,170	9,287	1,330	14,022	5,456	3,356	14,514	5,347	3,559	6,125	2,065
Grand Turk, Turks & Caicos	16,365	1,884	6,826	5,541	18,437	3,792	18,415	3,069	2,568	11,774	15,816	7,257	17,732	11,973	9,369	16,790	11,953	9,578	2,006	7,831
Graz, Austria	10,931	9,921	7,488	7,882	11,449	8,730	12,771	7,957	7,276	3,812	8,223	791	12,223	4,712	1,469	12,632	3,990	1,680	7,029	460
Green Bay, Wisconsin	13,380	4,035	3,836	2,589	15,448	1,497	15,794	561	469	11,088	15,473	6,765	14,881	12,090	8,308	14,082	11,254	8,475	1,193	7,027
Grenoble, France	11,704	9,207	7,515	7,729	12,216	8,342	13,537	7,509	6,772	4,457	8,808	245	13,003	5,143	2,249	13,409	4,637	2,461	6,458	885
Guadalajara, Mexico	13,861	2,623	5,515	4,143	15,686	2,120	15,091	2,494	3,063	14,078	18,463	9,643	14,619	14,903	11,305	13,616	14,247	11,474	3,354	9,982
Guam (Agana)	2,213	14,282	7,979	9,091	4,079	10,725	4,119	11,482	12,140	9,811	8,318	12,179	3,229	10,947	10,300	2,425	9,702	10,126	12,844	11,436
Guantanamo, Cuba	16,243	1,511	6,763	5,435	18,324	3,576	18,024	2,946	2,570	12,198	16,264	7,664	17,452	12,421	9,751	16,474	12,377	9,958	2,109	8,222
Guatemala City, Guatemala	15,375	1,117	6,631	5,224	17,154	3,120	16,372	3,002	3,153	13,803	18,001	9,237	16,048	14,153	11,200	15,046	13,982	11,395	3,089	9,723
Guayaquil, Ecuador	17,164	1,207	8,798	7,394	17,972	5,303	16,666	5,042	4,939	14,058	16,778	9,797	16,975	13,661	11,998	16,151	14,227	12,212	4,597	10,446
Guiyang, China	2,943	16,008	8,452	9,859	4,005	11,964	5,188	12,174	12,309	5,595	5,272	8,703	4,388	6,826	6,529	4,648	5,486	6,325	12,723	7,955
Gur'yev, USSR	8,206	12,387	7,637	8,578	8,769	10,115	10,087	9,607	9,149	2,315	6,363	3,496	9,490	4,022	1,273	9,898	2,423	1,063	9,123	2,788

Distances in Kilometers	Davao, Philippines	David, Panama	Dawson, Canada	Dawson Creek, Canada	Denpasar, Indonesia	Denver, Colorado	Derby, Australia	Des Moines, Iowa	Detroit, Michigan	Dhahran, Saudi Arabia	Diego Garcia Island	Dijon, France	Dili, Indonesia	Djibouti, Djibouti	Dnepropetrovsk, USSR	Dobo, Indonesia	Doha, Qatar	Donetsk, USSR	Dover, Delaware	Dresden, East Germany
Haifa, Israel	9,648	11,986	9,252	9,910	9,628	10,979	10,914	10,237	9,563	1,633	5,954	2,993	10,577	2,495	1,734	11,221	1,811	1,701	9,301	2,663
Haikou, China	2,188	16,564	8,958	10,358	3,220	12,444	4,380	12,751	12,963	6,148	5,138	9,488	3,578	7,213	7,296	3,873	6,023	7,088	13,422	8,744
Haiphong, Vietnam	2,546	16,616	9,031	10,437	3,396	12,537	4,610	12,782	12,937	5,760	4,876	9,168	3,854	6,830	6,963	4,211	5,634	6,754	13,356	8,431
Hakodate, Japan	4,123	12,930	5,462	6,805	6,158	8,814	6,770	9,287	9,713	8,161	8,793	9,218	5,780	9,779	7,654	5,303	8,122	7,522	10,326	8,515
Halifax, Canada	14,204	4,406	5,008	4,099	16,013	3,424	16,898	2,453	1,590	9,678	14,093	5,149	15,908	10,400	7,015	15,364	9,855	7,209	1,161	5,562
Hamburg, West Germany	11,014	9,420	6,697	7,064	11,782	7,946	13,096	7,201	6,555	4,475	8,907	778	12,444	5,501	1,832	12,725	4,649	2,041	6,361	378
Hamilton, Bermuda	15,515	3,210	6,091	4,976	17,388	3,687	18,148	2,754	1,961	10,553	14,810	5,995	17,172	10,964	8,053	16,477	10,733	8,260	1,236	6,529
Hamilton, New Zealand	7,151	11,662	11,971	12,023	6,806	11,820	5,502	12,741	13,561	14,767	10,634	18,686	5,937	14,461	16,623	5,458	14,590	16,418	14,007	17,942
Hangzhou, China	2,629	15,096	7,507	8,897	4,337	10,966	5,275	11,331	11,625	6,775	6,577	9,252	4,332	8,133	7,226	4,258	6,686	7,041	12,151	8,493
Hannover, West Germany	11,087	9,418	6,820	7,170	11,818	8,021	13,135	7,264	6,605	4,435	8,865	655	12,499	5,422	1,838	12,799	4,611	2,050	6,396	315
Hanoi, Vietnam	2,629	16,624	9,049	10,456	3,440	12,558	4,664	12,789	12,930	5,672	4,817	9,096	3,919	6,743	6,889	4,289	5,546	6,679	13,340	8,361
Harare, Zimbabwe	10,735	12,781	14,819	15,153	9,113	15,158	9,702	14,176	13,296	5,301	4,631	7,671	10,203	3,517	7,352	11,206	5,261	7,322	12,657	7,816
Harbin, China	4,288	13,344	5,738	7,140	6,132	9,233	6,989	9,540	9,815	6,952	7,968	8,233	6,015	8,593	6,523	5,755	6,917	6,379	10,344	7,503
Harrisburg, Pennsylvania	14,283	3,569	4,757	3,585	16,305	2,391	16,792	1,415	565	10,830	15,259	6,330	15,853	11,594	8,121	15,091	11,005	8,307	169	6,710
Hartford, Connecticut	14,289	3,816	4,827	3,735	16,255	2,722	16,884	1,740	861	10,456	14,881	5,944	15,915	11,203	7,762	15,217	10,632	7,951	377	6,336
Havana, Cuba	15,499	1,627	6,132	4,765	17,555	2,816	17,244	2,299	2,130	12,530	16,812	7,964	16,640	12,957	9,938	15,662	12,710	10,136	1,891	8,452
Helena, Montana	11,799	5,080	2,568	1,169	13,880	952	13,998	1,571	2,340	11,735	15,633	7,940	13,145	13,103	9,001	12,279	11,875	9,123	3,064	8,007
Helsinki, Finland	9,913	10,142	6,162	6,788	10,849	8,029	12,138	7,423	6,907	4,225	8,560	1,929	11,413	5,595	1,454	11,619	4,380	1,587	6,854	1,233
Hengyang, China	2,590	15,776	8,172	9,575	3,943	11,667	5,033	11,958	12,174	6,154	5,755	9,067	4,165	7,411	6,936	4,300	6,050	6,738	12,643	8,311
Herat, Afghanistan	7,135	13,991	8,932	10,018	7,334	11,699	8,653	11,244	10,809	1,461	4,736	4,916	8,180	3,174	2,740	8,743	1,437	2,531	10,782	4,286
Hermosillo, Mexico	12,771	3,757	4,380	3,056	14,708	1,305	14,340	2,094	2,904	13,557	17,573	9,405	13,719	14,723	10,776	12,735	13,709	10,919	3,430	9,615
Hiroshima, Japan	3,107	14,017	6,540	7,892	5,100	9,904	5,797	10,370	10,773	7,750	7,815	9,550	4,809	9,230	7,737	4,450	7,682	7,576	11,368	8,809
Hiva Oa (Atuona)	10,736	6,590	8,191	7,473	11,558	6,513	10,464	7,341	8,102	17,945	16,062	14,655	10,444	19,713	15,684	9,556	17,968	15,759	8,499	14,803
Ho Chi Minh City, Vietnam	2,121	17,662	10,057	11,456	2,345	13,536	3,621	13,851	14,045	6,163	4,290	10,002	2,990	6,923	7,772	3,558	6,013	7,558	14,475	9,290
Hobart, Australia	5,956	13,861	13,467	13,934	4,920	14,148	3,618	15,102	15,951	12,510	8,231	17,045	4,361	12,034	14,885	4,314	12,330	14,672	16,433	16,437
Hohhot, China	3,985	14,370	6,839	8,243	5,486	10,350	6,549	10,535	10,682	5,810	6,667	7,862	5,647	7,367	5,884	5,648	5,753	5,708	11,122	7,104
Hong Kong	2,081	16,164	8,568	9,962	3,420	12,035	4,495	12,382	12,640	6,452	5,606	9,562	3,627	7,595	7,407	3,792	6,335	7,205	13,133	8,809
Honiara, Solomon Islands	4,224	13,185	9,584	10,238	4,916	11,108	4,022	12,069	12,925	12,447	9,617	15,191	3,781	13,128	13,329	2,868	12,306	13,150	13,625	14,459
Honolulu, Hawaii	8,342	8,175	4,944	4,927	10,046	5,382	9,566	6,352	7,221	13,940	14,419	12,214	8,988	15,709	12,173	7,990	13,957	12,171	7,906	11,947
Houston, Texas	14,039	2,720	4,898	3,493	16,072	1,413	15,838	1,321	1,778	12,799	17,218	8,357	15,162	13,637	10,037	14,198	12,970	10,211	2,092	8,696
Huambo, Angola	12,334	11,107	13,990	13,927	10,819	13,531	11,435	12,552	11,677	5,699	6,227	6,737	11,921	4,048	7,037	12,925	5,721	7,072	11,007	7,069
Hubli, India	5,571	16,411	10,718	11,993	5,154	13,906	6,430	13,597	13,242	2,866	2,527	7,277	6,155	3,488	5,183	6,916	2,696	4,979	13,250	6,705
Hugh Town, United Kingdom	12,181	8,302	6,726	6,798	12,970	7,304	14,286	6,463	5,727	5,440	9,829	883	13,637	6,190	2,977	13,889	5,619	3,191	5,427	1,425
Hull, Canada	13,816	4,151	4,353	3,287	15,796	2,468	16,409	1,504	681	10,366	14,796	5,923	15,439	11,232	7,625	14,748	10,538	7,807	697	6,254
Hyderabad, India	5,240	16,471	10,409	11,711	4,963	13,671	6,263	13,426	13,128	3,083	2,814	7,367	5,922	3,855	5,219	6,641	2,921	5,010	13,190	6,761
Hyderabad, Pakistan	6,393	15,119	9,799	10,978	6,318	12,764	7,624	12,364	11,958	1,830	3,644	5,999	7,241	3,059	3,873	7,901	1,694	3,667	11,941	5,404
Igloolik, Canada	11,267	6,768	2,508	2,425	13,150	3,574	13,959	3,171	3,013	8,716	12,866	5,070	12,969	10,075	5,964	12,474	8,862	6,091	3,385	5,025
Iloilo, Philippines	522	16,540	9,330	10,651	2,290	12,584	3,099	13,140	13,581	7,751	5,904	11,119	2,155	8,644	8,950	2,232	7,615	8,745	14,178	10,368
Indianapolis, Indiana	13,885	3,491	4,354	3,064	15,962	1,611	16,217	662	386	11,407	15,830	6,984	15,338	12,290	8,649	14,498	11,578	8,825	916	7,305
Innsbruck, Austria	11,208	9,615	7,399	7,729	11,755	8,501	13,077	7,710	7,012	4,104	8,504	483	12,521	4,945	1,763	12,913	4,283	1,976	6,748	454
Inuvik, Canada	9,714	7,625	542	1,562	11,750	3,624	12,299	3,800	4,122	9,505	12,961	6,728	11,323	11,133	7,017	10,682	9,613	7,082	4,731	6,491
Invercargill, New Zealand	7,277	12,157	13,070	13,136	6,537	12,836	5,217	13,724	14,506	14,209	9,877	18,747	5,838	13,607	16,547	5,568	14,029	16,332	14,874	18,090
Inverness, United Kingdom	11,550	8,515	5,998	6,208	12,547	6,968	13,836	6,208	5,558	5,464	9,901	1,291	13,095	6,474	2,773	13,238	5,642	2,971	5,377	1,366
Iquitos, Peru	17,917	1,691	9,250	7,861	18,351	5,809	17,039	5,431	5,200	13,514	16,028	9,435	17,534	12,980	11,662	16,804	13,675	11,877	4,759	10,122
Iraklion, Greece	10,503	11,036	8,902	9,390	10,571	10,251	11,862	9,453	8,737	2,584	6,844	2,136	11,504	3,197	1,667	12,113	2,762	1,754	8,430	1,971
Irkutsk, USSR	5,375	13,248	5,985	7,350	6,829	9,425	7,930	9,463	9,499	5,325	7,267	6,587	7,037	7,049	4,762	7,026	5,316	4,611	9,875	5,837
Islamabad, Pakistan	6,132	14,683	8,796	10,010	6,457	11,871	7,779	11,560	11,244	2,363	4,542	5,778	7,241	3,911	3,553	7,760	2,290	3,338	11,320	5,100
Istanbul, Turkey	10,054	11,148	8,310	8,893	10,324	9,924	11,638	9,190	8,532	2,541	6,953	2,030	11,183	3,543	953	11,710	2,720	1,045	8,300	1,616
Ivujivik, Canada	12,043	6,000	2,976	2,485	13,945	3,107	14,724	2,539	2,258	9,152	13,436	5,171	13,734	10,375	6,366	13,195	9,308	6,514	2,590	5,255
Iwo Jima Island, Japan	2,579	14,021	7,036	8,270	4,660	10,106	5,036	10,741	11,294	8,943	8,264	10,904	4,065	10,291	9,103	3,467	8,858	8,940	11,960	10,168
Izmir, Turkey	10,259	11,100	8,582	9,121	10,437	10,076	11,742	9,311	8,626	2,536	6,896	2,051	11,331	3,369	1,281	11,896	2,716	1,369	8,359	1,754
Jackson, Mississippi	14,240	2,761	4,875	3,496	16,314	1,566	16,247	1,075	1,280	12,283	16,714	7,810	15,496	13,076	9,539	14,564	12,455	9,718	1,527	8,169
Jaffna, Sri Lanka	5,027	17,228	11,184	12,515	4,398	14,511	5,651	14,293	13,995	3,644	2,059	8,094	5,438	4,035	6,000	6,251	3,470	5,796	14,040	7,524
Jakarta, Indonesia	2,550	18,986	11,760	13,128	969	15,123	2,207	15,595	15,883	7,087	3,803	11,400	2,088	7,317	9,200	3,036	6,915	8,986	16,343	10,752
Jamestown, St. Helena	14,647	8,871	13,617	12,987	12,979	11,911	13,364	11,000	10,184	7,637	8,532	7,087	14,018	6,184	8,191	15,005	7,701	8,294	9,463	7,659
Jamnagar, India	6,180	15,471	10,077	11,282	6,007	13,099	7,306	12,718	12,320	2,064	3,306	6,343	6,954	3,101	4,231	7,646	1,912	4,027	12,305	5,758
Jan Mayen Island	10,719	8,525	4,545	4,947	12,100	6,094	13,274	5,510	5,055	6,160	10,460	2,741	12,395	7,482	3,383	12,315	6,314	3,522	5,100	2,505
Jayapura, Indonesia	1,985	15,216	9,766	10,807	2,902	12,256	2,480	13,099	13,829	10,196	7,586	13,478	1,803	10,898	11,376	804	10,051	11,178	14,549	12,718
Jefferson City, Missouri	13,630	3,478	4,183	2,825	15,715	1,115	15,824	357	878	11,826	16,218	7,460	14,993	12,779	9,050	14,110	11,993	9,218	1,443	7,749
Jerusalem, Israel	9,639	12,052	9,371	10,030	9,581	11,092	10,861	10,345	9,667	1,571	5,859	3,088	10,541	2,377	1,853	11,199	1,747	1,816	9,398	2,774
Jiggalong, Australia	3,411	17,047	12,794	13,931	1,737	15,376	738	16,248	16,973	9,383	5,458	13,809	1,721	9,290	11,623	2,425	9,205	11,409	17,685	13,174
Jinan, China	3,393	14,619	7,018	8,423	5,020	10,521	6,014	10,798	11,024	6,331	6,731	8,515	5,085	7,815	6,534	5,028	6,261	6,356	11,511	7,757
Jodhpur, India	5,949	15,347	9,597	10,827	5,977	12,693	7,294	12,366	12,022	2,284	3,720	6,285	6,860	3,529	4,106	7,486	2,157	3,895	12,061	5,655
Johannesburg, South Africa	11,108	12,471	15,701	15,853	9,312	15,446	9,714	14,478	13,611	6,273	5,133	8,465	10,338	4,489	8,296	11,327	6,229	8,275	12,924	8,672
Juazeiro do Norte, Brazil	18,373	5,086	11,212	10,099	16,705	8,495	16,721	7,720	7,051	10,314	12,291	7,449	17,604	9,365	9,465	18,408	10,441	9,654	6,346	8,206
Juneau, Alaska	9,923	7,066	696	904	12,006	2,938	12,325	3,391	3,942	10,620	13,903	7,720	11,397	12,253	8,131	10,629	10,725	8,199	4,636	7,542
Kabul, Afghanistan	6,509	14,398	8,791	9,961	6,804	11,761	8,126	11,398	11,039	2,041	4,644	5,429	7,606	3,661	3,212	8,135	1,985	2,998	11,080	4,763
Kalgoorlie, Australia	4,208	16,516	13,470	14,522	2,532	15,730	1,506	16,673	17,490	9,869	5,717	14,387	2,495	9,575	12,255	3,070	9,689	12,043	18,214	13,800
Kaliningrad, USSR	10,327	10,067	6,719	7,247	11,090	8,328	12,402	7,647	7,056	3,973	8,389	1,358	11,747	5,179	1,219	12,038	4,141	1,412	6,920	610
Kamloops, Canada	11,051	5,835	1,868	568	13,135	1,704	13,310	2,280	2,971	11,428	15,059	7,956	12,431	12,923	8,771	11,592	11,554	8,873	3,695	7,927
Kampala, Uganda	10,348	12,766	12,832	13,321	9,213	13,837	10,140	12,907	12,065	3,436	4,503	5,853	10,352	1,709	5,339	11,311	3,433	5,308	11,544	5,897
Kananga, Zaire	11,549	11,744	13,388	13,569	10,227	13,577	11,007	12,599	11,722	4,652	5,529	6,139	11,359	3,003	6,145	12,349	4,672	6,158	11,110	6,365
Kano, Nigeria	12,759	9,928	11,144	11,125	12,021	11,091	13,051	10,121	9,250	4,631	7,389	3,929	13,144	3,772	4,727	14,033	4,747	4,830	8,670	4,357
Kanpur, India	5,243	15,724	9,389	10,687	5,412	12,655	6,734	12,445	12,200	3,008	3,836	6,821	6,234	4,227	4,603	6,812	2,885	4,389	12,322	6,153
Kansas City, Missouri	13,438	3,607	4,024	2,650	15,521	899	15,609	288	1,037	11,894	16,255	7,572	14,783	12,896	9,110	13,896	12,058	9,274	1,644	7,838
Kaohsiung, Taiwan	1,814	15,779	8,252	9,626	3,504	11,660	4,433	12,087	12,425	7,035	6,179	9,925	3,497	8,219	7,823	3,489	6,925	7,627	12,970	9,166
Karachi, Pakistan	6,518	15,066	9,880	11,044	6,406	12,805	7,708	12,384	11,959	1,706	3,609	5,936	7,341	2,915	3,831	8,014	1,565	3,629	11,925	5,354
Karaganda, USSR	6,783	13,131	7,061	8,234	7,654	10,080	8,933	9,795	9,534	3,275	6,334	4,860	8,215	5,054	2,760	8,494	3,302	2,576	9,681	4,106
Karl-Marx-Stadt, East Germany	10,953	9,662	7,039	7,424	11,614	8,299	12,934	7,544	6,884	4,162	8,590	697	12,326	5,145	1,610	12,664	4,337	1,824	6,668	63
Kasanga, Tanzania	10,620	12,733	13,788	14,192	9,232	14,461	10,002	13,495	12,626	4,360	4,550	6,697	10,361	2,586	6,316	11,354	4,339	6,289	12,041	6,804
Kashgar, China	6,109	14,254	8,112	9,339	6,692	11,231	8,001	10,965	10,700	2,809	5,196	5,613	7,373	4,472	3,391	7,789	2,772	3,180	10,827	4,893
Kassel, West Germany	11,150	9,417	6,929	7,266	11,847	8,089	13,166	7,322	6,653	4,401	8,827	551	12,545	5,353	1,849	12,862	4,578	2,063	6,429	299
Kathmandu, Nepal	4,819	15,796	9,111	10,443	5,154	12,461	6,472	12,331	12,158	3,484	4,119	7,097	5,906	4,739	4,867	6,427	3,368	4,652	12,340	6,403
Kayes, Mali	14,723	7,750	10,250	9,823	14,193	9,296	15,223	8,315	7,436	6,503	9,562	3,951	15,306	5,916	5,669	16,155	6,647	5,840	6,784	4,646
Kazan, USSR	8,515	11,617	6,696	7,604	9,350	9,144	10,646	8,661	8,241	3,272	7,315	3,142	9,950	4,926	1,261	10,226	3,389	1,160	8,263	2,383
Kemi, Finland	9,793	9,914	5,536	6,197	10,908	7,526	12,160	6,976	6,521	4,744	8,994	2,361	11,370	6,184	2,028	11,477	4,890	2,132	6,537	1,755
Kenora, Canada	12,616	4,719	3,072	1,848	14,684	1,389	15,057	914	1,209	10,883	15,144	6,772	14,130	12,056	8,096	13,354	11,040	8,246	1,906	6,935
Kerguelen Island	8,281	14,762	17,648	19,053	6,196	18,838	5,995	18,437	17,760	8,613	4,682	12,390	6,878	7,243	11,348	7,712	8,473	11,225	17,035	12,335
Kerkira, Greece	10,838	10,462	8,369	8,787	11,073	9,594	12,380	8,792	8,077	3,166	7,488	1,476	11,954	3,856	1,553	12,494	3,346	1,709	7,777	1,360
Kermanshah, Iran	8,521	12,904	9,083	9,950	8,596	11,319	9,902	10,694	10,118	936	5,327	3,775	9,503	2,547	1,862	10,111	1,090	1,704	9,960	3,260
Khabarovsk, USSR	4,679	12,712	5,116	6,508	6,625	8,586	7,376	8,943	9,272	7,511	8,676	8,348	6,389	9,196	6,814	6,012	7,489	6,690	9,836	7,645
Kharkov, USSR	9,366	11,255	7,351	8,081	9,961	9,367	11,280	8,747	8,200	2,888	7,250	2,303	10,683	4,305	196	11,068	3,043	250	8,096	1,594
Khartoum, Sudan	10,135	12,388	11,145	11,696	9,499	12,470	10,636	11,611	10,831	2,176	5,077	4,335	10,593	1,231	3,650	11,438	2,250	3,626	10,417	4,276
Khon Kaen, Thailand	2,686	17,195	9,643	11,049	3,091	13,153	4,374	13,363	13,470	5,537	4,258	9,257	3,729	6,448	7,029	4,239	5,397	6,815	13,848	8,542
Kiev, USSR	9,767	10,866	7,278	7,926	10,371	9,115	11,691	8,459	7,881	3,159	7,564	1,893	11,094	4,459	392	11,471	3,323	595	7,748	1,183
Kigali, Rwanda	10,656	12,528	13,060	13,472	9,453	13,848	10,333	12,899	12,043	3,798	4,734	5,980	10,592	2,084	5,604	11,563	3,800	5,585	11,492	6,074
Kingston, Canada	13,908	4,009	4,421	3,320	15,903	2,400	16,479	1,426	572	10,502	14,933	6,048	15,516	11,350	7,765	14,805	10,674	7,947	569	6,388
Kingston, Jamaica	16,311	1,222	6,899	5,549	18,363	3,627	17,866	3,066	2,762	12,477	16,494	7,950	17,395	12,666	10,041	16,400	12,657	10,248	2,349	8,510
Kingstown, Saint Vincent	17,648	2,375	8,125	6,889	19,386	5,189	19,326	4,444	3,859	11,419	14,925	7,158	19,126	11,248	9,378	18,149	11,591	9,593	3,207	7,833
Kinshasa, Zaire	12,317	10,938	13,068	13,074	11,035	12,880	11,811	11,898	11,019	5,055	6,331	5,806	12,167	3,550	6,150	13,156	5,103	6,196	10,384	6,135

Distances in Kilometers	Davao, Philippines	David, Panama	Dawson, Canada	Dawson Creek, Canada	Denpasar, Indonesia	Denver, Colorado	Derby, Australia	Des Moines, Iowa	Detroit, Michigan	Dhahran, Saudi Arabia	Diego Garcia Island	Dijon, France	Dili, Indonesia	Djibouti, Djibouti	Dnepropetrovsk, USSR	Dobo, Indonesia	Doha, Qatar	Donetsk, USSR	Dover, Delaware	Dresden, East Germany
Kirkwall, United Kingdom	11,387	8,605	5,873	6,122	12,418	6,945	13,700	6,206	5,577	5,444	9,873	1,400	12,945	6,501	2,717	13,072	5,615	2,909	5,423	1,378
Kirov, USSR	8,522	11,439	6,383	7,297	9,451	8,862	10,732	8,400	8,005	3,583	7,583	3,181	10,004	5,239	1,483	10,232	3,698	1,413	8,053	2,423
Kiruna, Sweden	9,918	9,667	5,279	5,912	11,100	7,231	12,336	6,685	6,240	5,039	9,285	2,445	11,522	6,469	2,315	11,586	5,185	2,423	6,271	1,905
Kisangani, Zaire	11,161	11,951	12,732	13,032	10,029	13,286	10,931	12,327	11,465	3,911	5,313	5,544	11,168	2,333	5,396	12,131	3,941	5,402	10,902	5,706
Kishinev, USSR	9,950	10,897	7,647	8,255	10,434	9,365	11,756	8,672	8,058	2,964	7,394	1,799	11,210	4,149	489	11,643	3,136	684	7,881	1,189
Kitchner, Canada	13,827	3,885	4,295	3,126	15,860	2,076	16,330	1,098	244	10,789	15,216	6,360	15,390	11,669	8,038	14,632	10,960	8,217	631	6,683
Knoxville, Tennessee	14,337	3,053	4,815	3,510	16,418	1,896	16,607	1,047	711	11,601	16,032	7,109	15,757	12,368	8,876	14,890	11,775	9,060	821	7,482
Kosice, Czechoslovakia	10,462	10,299	7,387	7,886	11,017	8,876	12,339	8,148	7,508	3,524	7,956	1,219	11,770	4,587	1,012	12,165	3,699	1,227	7,308	599
Kota Kinabalu, Malaysia	1,061	17,426	10,109	11,458	1,621	13,431	2,706	13,940	14,317	7,324	5,067	11,077	1,922	8,028	8,856	2,399	7,173	8,644	14,867	10,348
Krakow, Poland	10,512	10,165	7,220	7,707	11,119	8,696	12,440	7,972	7,336	3,691	8,123	1,137	11,850	4,768	1,110	12,219	3,865	1,325	7,145	450
Kralendijk, Bonaire	17,393	1,605	7,882	6,574	19,476	4,724	18,630	4,087	3,637	12,122	15,694	7,765	18,468	12,013	9,961	17,465	12,297	10,175	3,076	8,409
Krasnodar, USSR	9,192	11,701	7,908	8,665	9,619	9,952	10,941	9,319	8,753	2,305	6,693	2,616	10,409	3,727	488	10,871	2,464	342	8,621	1,986
Krasnoyarsk, USSR	6,146	12,848	5,961	7,257	7,459	9,261	8,623	9,171	9,098	4,745	7,269	5,732	7,766	6,514	3,919	7,823	4,761	3,775	9,401	4,981
Kristiansand, Norway	10,898	9,242	6,169	6,556	11,827	7,512	13,123	6,805	6,200	4,824	9,246	1,224	12,406	5,955	2,078	12,600	4,993	2,268	6,061	874
Kuala Lumpur, Malaysia	2,684	18,646	11,044	12,446	1,990	14,533	3,306	14,814	14,943	6,060	3,454	10,257	2,949	6,520	8,044	3,748	5,894	7,829	15,310	9,593
Kuching, Malaysia	1,801	18,229	10,821	12,190	1,251	14,198	2,545	14,656	14,963	6,984	4,324	11,032	2,026	7,497	8,803	2,776	6,822	8,588	15,458	10,336
Kumasi, Ghana	13,980	8,905	11,410	11,114	13,072	10,671	13,978	9,689	8,810	5,889	8,365	4,548	14,210	4,946	5,772	15,150	6,005	5,901	8,159	5,120
Kumzar, Oman	7,596	14,143	9,888	10,903	7,436	12,441	8,723	11,880	11,343	627	4,106	5,028	8,401	2,144	3,080	9,091	503	2,901	11,210	4,519
Kunming, China	3,149	16,258	8,769	10,173	3,970	12,280	5,209	12,438	12,519	5,240	4,859	8,548	4,471	6,418	6,345	4,826	5,123	6,137	12,892	7,811
Kuqa Chang, China	5,621	14,326	7,745	9,031	6,403	11,002	7,686	10,833	10,656	3,472	5,490	6,033	6,988	5,114	3,852	7,323	3,431	3,649	10,857	5,292
Kurgan, USSR	7,520	12,324	6,583	7,666	8,466	9,418	9,737	9,070	8,766	3,462	6,988	4,155	8,998	5,232	2,204	9,231	3,532	2,055	8,886	3,395
Kuwait, Kuwait	8,435	13,261	9,625	10,504	8,334	11,859	9,620	11,216	10,619	403	4,834	4,179	9,293	2,031	2,390	9,965	575	2,243	10,431	3,721
Kuybyshev, USSR	8,414	11,851	6,974	7,893	9,171	9,434	10,475	8,944	8,513	2,987	7,030	3,228	9,808	4,656	1,189	10,124	3,102	1,046	8,521	2,477
Kyoto, Japan	3,263	13,754	6,326	7,663	5,292	9,655	5,928	10,147	10,578	8,013	8,119	9,653	4,938	9,516	7,900	4,515	7,950	7,745	11,189	8,921
Kzyl-Orda, USSR	7,124	13,293	7,739	8,846	7,735	10,593	9,046	10,213	9,860	2,470	5,816	4,567	8,420	4,251	2,354	8,816	2,503	2,145	9,922	3,845
L'vov, USSR	10,237	10,454	7,292	7,840	10,825	8,901	12,146	8,199	7,581	3,440	7,871	1,424	11,561	4,590	815	11,942	3,612	1,030	7,407	740
La Ceiba, Honduras	15,651	942	6,671	5,269	17,513	3,189	16,786	2,934	2,965	13,433	17,583	8,871	16,427	13,739	10,871	15,424	13,613	11,070	2,814	9,377
La Coruna, Spain	12,758	8,082	7,347	7,299	13,356	7,580	14,678	6,683	5,887	5,554	9,829	1,136	14,122	6,058	3,366	14,470	5,734	3,580	5,493	1,872
La Paz, Bolivia	18,202	3,175	10,763	9,371	17,199	7,306	16,052	6,945	6,691	13,597	14,948	10,127	16,856	12,628	12,330	16,538	13,730	12,539	6,209	10,866
La Paz, Mexico	13,049	3,438	4,916	3,602	14,903	1,798	14,397	2,474	3,217	14,041	18,120	9,794	13,861	15,117	11,253	12,862	14,197	11,403	3,662	10,044
La Ronge, Canada	11,676	5,557	2,136	947	13,747	1,708	14,128	1,729	2,149	10,687	14,703	6,924	13,193	12,048	7,944	12,434	10,829	8,069	2,833	6,961
Labrador City, Canada	13,250	5,132	4,146	3,394	15,088	3,227	15,944	2,362	1,685	9,337	13,761	4,962	14,954	10,287	6,582	14,432	9,507	6,761	1,669	5,242
Lagos, Nigeria	13,447	9,456	11,594	11,408	12,520	11,101	13,440	10,119	9,239	5,416	7,816	4,532	13,657	4,406	5,528	14,597	5,524	5,640	8,606	5,037
Lahore, Pakistan	5,965	14,938	8,998	10,228	6,228	12,108	7,550	11,809	11,500	2,422	4,311	6,005	7,032	3,887	3,786	7,574	2,332	3,571	11,577	5,335
Lambasa, Fiji	6,468	11,147	9,595	9,781	7,001	9,985	5,920	10,962	11,838	14,689	11,576	16,541	5,899	15,286	15,213	5,061	14,550	15,067	12,437	15,959
Lansing, Michigan	13,708	3,806	4,162	2,929	15,768	1,741	16,136	760	130	11,068	15,485	6,671	15,220	11,987	8,304	14,424	11,237	8,478	856	6,974
Lanzhou, China	3,910	15,040	7,617	9,014	5,093	11,116	6,268	11,230	11,298	5,153	5,810	7,749	5,443	6,618	5,636	5,620	5,077	5,442	11,677	6,992
Laoag, Philippines	1,346	16,135	8,677	10,037	3,028	12,045	3,941	12,511	12,879	7,235	5,999	10,333	3,009	8,310	8,198	3,044	7,114	7,998	13,438	9,577
Largeau, Chad	11,501	10,938	10,730	10,995	10,951	11,397	12,084	10,476	9,647	3,323	6,488	3,506	12,040	2,678	3,679	12,869	3,445	3,744	9,162	3,707
Las Vegas, Nevada	12,089	4,518	3,506	2,212	14,099	976	13,914	1,956	2,836	12,920	16,721	9,013	13,192	14,251	10,177	12,241	13,061	10,303	3,483	9,134
Launceston, Australia	5,801	13,942	13,329	13,824	4,799	14,097	3,491	15,059	15,916	12,449	8,201	16,962	4,216	12,020	14,783	4,153	12,269	14,569	16,423	16,334
Le Havre, France	11,830	8,765	6,930	7,100	12,538	7,710	13,858	6,888	6,168	4,974	9,369	435	13,240	5,760	2,531	13,542	5,152	2,746	5,885	984
Leipzig, East Germany	10,971	9,613	6,979	7,359	11,651	8,233	12,970	7,480	6,821	4,221	8,651	692	12,354	5,211	1,652	12,682	4,397	1,865	6,609	103
Leningrad, USSR	9,629	10,426	6,225	6,915	10,553	8,226	11,842	7,647	7,153	4,034	8,328	2,157	11,120	5,468	1,312	11,336	4,183	1,414	7,119	1,429
Leon, Spain	12,626	8,306	7,507	7,499	13,161	7,817	14,480	6,923	6,131	5,324	9,586	985	13,952	5,813	3,195	14,335	5,503	3,408	5,738	1,740
Lerwick, United Kingdom	11,227	8,715	5,789	6,080	12,277	6,960	13,554	6,241	5,632	5,392	9,814	1,484	12,791	6,494	2,642	12,909	5,561	2,829	5,500	1,375
Lhasa, China	4,390	15,735	8,723	10,085	4,964	12,145	6,260	12,103	12,012	4,027	4,555	7,374	5,612	5,337	5,151	6,047	3,922	4,939	12,263	6,653
Libreville, Gabon	12,900	10,220	12,416	12,317	11,760	12,051	12,595	11,069	10,189	5,217	7,042	5,218	12,899	3,926	5,865	13,872	5,294	5,942	9,552	5,630
Lilongwe, Malawi	10,401	13,062	14,419	14,863	8,871	15,095	9,547	14,121	13,247	4,795	4,285	7,369	9,981	3,012	6,916	10,984	4,752	6,877	12,641	7,463
Lima, Peru	17,490	2,342	9,925	8,519	17,352	6,421	16,052	6,177	6,053	14,298	16,026	10,396	16,638	13,533	12,626	16,047	14,448	12,841	5,671	11,096
Limerick, Ireland	12,107	8,176	6,382	6,458	13,008	7,006	14,314	6,182	5,466	5,638	10,051	1,142	13,616	6,466	3,077	13,805	5,815	3,287	5,200	1,545
Limoges, France	11,974	8,854	7,343	7,490	12,547	8,029	13,869	7,182	6,435	4,814	9,161	332	13,312	5,478	2,554	13,683	4,994	2,768	6,109	1,090
Limon, Costa Rica	16,336	185	7,421	6,021	18,027	3,948	17,041	3,651	3,583	13,561	17,320	9,054	16,892	13,618	11,153	15,905	13,740	11,360	3,316	9,621
Lincoln, Nebraska	13,176	3,856	3,766	2,389	15,260	716	15,370	271	1,148	11,825	16,142	7,569	14,532	12,891	9,037	13,654	11,987	9,195	1,812	7,803
Linz, Austria	10,964	9,810	7,336	7,721	11,531	8,571	12,853	7,802	7,126	3,948	8,366	703	12,285	4,871	1,528	12,670	4,126	1,742	6,887	308
Lisbon, Portugal	13,125	7,982	7,806	7,688	13,568	7,826	14,880	6,899	6,073	5,638	9,791	1,494	14,405	5,963	3,667	14,830	5,816	3,877	5,620	2,253
Little Rock, Arkansas	13,914	3,083	4,544	3,163	15,991	1,255	15,975	760	1,163	12,180	16,594	7,760	15,197	13,061	9,414	14,279	12,349	9,587	1,567	8,082
Liverpool, United Kingdom	11,762	8,559	6,446	6,617	12,626	7,279	13,934	6,481	5,789	5,282	9,705	885	13,249	6,172	2,693	13,465	5,458	2,902	5,549	1,171
Lodz, Poland	10,489	10,087	7,032	7,524	11,154	8,534	12,473	7,821	7,198	3,824	8,254	1,154	11,859	4,939	1,167	12,199	3,996	1,378	7,023	405
Lome, Togo	13,689	9,224	11,561	11,322	12,754	10,946	13,660	9,964	9,084	5,643	8,046	4,579	13,892	4,648	5,671	14,835	5,753	5,790	8,441	5,113
London, United Kingdom	11,723	8,748	6,714	6,904	12,499	7,562	13,815	6,757	6,054	5,041	9,455	596	13,167	5,893	2,516	13,433	5,219	2,729	5,797	968
Londonderry, United Kingdom	11,873	8,294	6,177	6,306	12,829	6,946	14,126	6,149	5,462	5,594	10,022	1,212	13,404	6,505	2,964	13,565	5,770	3,170	5,236	1,475
Longlac, Canada	12,985	4,600	3,458	2,344	15,021	1,830	15,509	1,064	871	10,556	14,909	6,320	14,557	11,634	7,769	13,826	10,719	7,931	1,466	6,534
Lord Howe Island, Australia	5,562	13,197	11,875	12,300	5,191	12,635	3,903	13,611	14,485	13,196	9,277	17,202	4,302	13,134	15,018	3,855	13,022	14,809	15,064	16,447
Los Angeles, California	11,919	4,634	3,638	2,417	13,894	1,338	13,641	2,314	3,192	13,213	16,852	9,369	12,951	14,585	10,488	11,986	13,349	10,609	3,828	9,475
Louangphrabang, Laos	2,903	16,835	9,321	10,727	3,465	12,834	4,736	13,011	13,098	5,341	4,433	8,928	4,059	6,358	6,705	4,514	5,209	6,493	13,466	8,205
Louisville, Kentucky	14,037	3,319	4,514	3,212	16,117	1,671	16,336	767	509	11,516	15,945	7,068	15,471	12,361	8,767	14,617	11,688	8,945	895	7,406
Luanda, Angola	12,587	10,778	13,503	13,411	11,173	13,038	11,853	12,058	11,180	5,567	6,519	6,269	12,291	4,007	6,692	13,292	5,608	6,741	10,518	6,631
Lubumbashi, Zaire	11,057	12,362	14,098	14,374	9,583	14,419	10,278	13,439	12,562	4,865	4,954	6,903	10,700	3,103	6,700	11,701	4,851	6,687	11,940	7,074
Lusaka, Zambia	11,006	12,477	14,521	14,791	9,439	14,760	10,065	13,778	12,898	5,186	4,890	7,326	10,540	3,408	7,105	11,543	5,161	7,087	12,261	7,498
Luxembourg, Luxembourg	11,449	9,198	7,049	7,316	12,111	8,039	13,432	7,243	6,544	4,557	8,966	267	12,829	5,410	2,101	13,161	4,736	2,316	6,285	566
Luxor, Egypt	9,973	12,060	10,031	10,622	9,692	11,540	10,927	10,737	10,008	1,751	5,643	3,414	10,714	1,910	2,535	11,451	1,898	2,518	9,672	3,243
Lynn Lake, Canada	11,757	5,609	2,218	1,190	13,811	1,924	14,267	1,779	2,061	10,402	14,483	6,597	13,315	11,737	7,648	12,591	10,547	7,777	2,707	6,643
Lyon, France	11,734	9,134	7,434	7,640	12,273	8,249	13,595	7,416	6,681	4,538	8,895	175	13,050	5,236	2,292	13,441	4,718	2,505	6,369	883
Macapa, Brazil	19,142	3,603	9,922	8,717	18,232	7,008	18,011	6,279	5,675	11,130	13,711	7,526	18,995	10,476	9,714	19,157	11,280	9,921	5,000	8,273
Madison, Wisconsin	13,430	3,898	3,899	2,613	15,507	1,353	15,792	385	526	11,284	15,667	6,954	14,897	12,278	8,504	14,074	11,450	8,671	1,241	7,220
Madras, India	5,005	16,966	10,813	12,139	4,549	14,132	5,831	13,920	13,638	3,471	2,420	7,842	5,549	4,039	5,714	6,317	3,301	5,507	13,704	7,250
Madrid, Spain	12,635	8,457	7,790	7,790	13,068	8,090	14,382	7,188	6,387	5,163	9,375	1,038	13,901	5,578	3,169	14,336	5,342	3,378	5,977	1,793
Madurai, India	5,234	17,060	11,213	12,528	4,597	14,496	5,843	14,238	13,910	3,458	2,011	7,930	5,642	3,827	5,857	6,459	3,282	5,655	13,929	7,373
Magadan, USSR	6,203	11,128	3,524	4,922	8,197	7,013	8,869	7,346	7,685	8,095	10,056	7,755	7,879	9,871	6,701	7,391	8,118	6,632	8,267	7,147
Magdalena, Bolivia	18,756	3,144	10,628	9,259	17,572	7,239	16,512	6,793	6,461	13,065	14,712	9,580	17,363	12,158	11,778	17,092	13,202	11,986	5,930	10,323
Magdeburg, East Germany	10,975	9,552	6,874	7,252	11,688	8,133	13,005	7,384	6,731	4,306	8,737	721	12,376	5,313	1,704	12,687	4,481	1,916	6,526	190
Majuro Atoll, Marshall Isls.	5,035	11,686	7,419	8,020	6,453	8,979	5,889	9,917	10,754	12,671	11,083	13,820	5,353	13,919	12,517	4,349	12,581	12,392	11,468	13,205
Malabo, Equatorial Guinea	12,916	10,092	12,037	11,953	11,888	11,744	12,781	10,763	9,884	5,062	7,174	4,841	13,027	3,886	5,547	13,982	5,152	5,633	9,260	5,264
Male, Maldives	5,784	17,023	11,981	13,262	4,841	15,159	5,994	14,791	14,356	3,504	1,259	8,068	5,948	3,445	6,133	6,840	3,324	5,945	14,272	7,586
Manado, Indonesia	623	16,814	10,137	11,397	1,549	13,203	2,082	13,869	14,407	8,419	5,904	12,079	1,112	9,080	9,877	1,314	8,268	9,668	15,050	11,336
Managua, Nicaragua	15,909	589	7,062	5,658	17,651	3,568	16,767	3,339	3,360	13,671	17,640	9,124	16,528	13,857	11,168	15,532	13,851	11,371	3,176	9,657
Manama, Bahrain	8,178	13,663	9,958	10,879	7,974	12,278	9,248	11,646	11,054	46	4,398	4,605	8,958	1,796	2,816	9,664	141	2,663	10,866	4,156
Manaus, Brazil	19,267	2,798	9,803	8,495	18,603	6,601	17,710	6,007	5,545	12,178	14,627	8,421	18,578	11,523	10,638	18,165	12,330	10,850	4,946	9,153
Manchester, New Hampshire	14,200	3,977	4,776	3,722	16,144	2,809	16,823	1,829	952	10,292	14,718	5,786	15,846	11,053	7,594	15,176	10,467	7,783	546	6,171
Mandalay, Burma	3,573	16,634	9,339	10,733	3,982	12,830	5,284	12,895	12,881	4,671	4,147	8,322	4,667	5,731	6,092	5,169	4,540	5,878	13,179	7,611
Mangareva Island, Fr.Polynesia	11,286	6,698	9,673	8,851	11,628	7,623	10,387	8,335	8,995	19,400	15,522	15,567	10,604	18,715	17,058	9,852	19,328	17,171	9,257	15,907
Manila, Philippines	972	16,392	9,018	10,364	2,648	12,344	3,538	12,847	13,242	7,424	5,886	10,675	2,608	8,408	8,519	2,682	7,295	8,316	13,814	9,922
Mannheim, West Germany	11,304	9,367	7,107	7,410	11,945	8,174	13,267	7,386	6,696	4,394	8,807	351	12,671	5,271	1,935	13,015	4,572	2,150	6,445	415
Maputo, Mozambique	10,659	12,920	15,731	16,038	8,868	15,814	9,292	14,838	13,964	6,083	4,697	8,574	9,901	4,311	8,245	10,893	6,026	8,208	13,289	8,729
Mar del Plata, Argentina	16,564	5,754	13,357	11,960	14,787	9,876	13,882	9,544	9,264	13,247	12,808	11,307	14,841	11,732	13,209	15,010	13,311	13,378	8,740	12,059
Maracaibo, Venezuela	17,285	1,213	7,873	6,531	19,252	4,606	18,228	4,045	3,682	12,518	16,067	8,138	18,136	12,411	10,323	17,140	12,693	10,536	3,181	8,771
Marrakech, Morocco	13,493	8,055	8,579	8,401	13,651	8,379	14,920	7,425	6,571	5,632	9,539	2,064	14,595	5,681	4,046	15,160	5,803	4,244	6,051	2,800
Marseilles, France	11,821	9,199	7,708	7,899	12,269	8,462	13,587	7,614	6,862	4,441	8,755	447	13,084	5,050	2,351	13,520	4,621	2,559	6,525	1,068
Maseru, Lesotho	11,182	12,400	16,032	16,121	9,331	15,565	9,663	14,613	13,757	6,613	5,291	8,781	10,329	4,830	8,645	11,307	6,566	8,625	13,057	9,004

Distances in Kilometers	Davao, Philippines	David, Panama	Dawson, Canada	Dawson Creek, Canada	Denpasar, Indonesia	Denver, Colorado	Derby, Australia	Des Moines, Iowa	Detroit, Michigan	Dhahran, Saudi Arabia	Diego Garcia Island	Dijon, France	Dili, Indonesia	Djibouti, Djibouti	Dnepropetrovsk, USSR	Dobo, Indonesia	Doha, Qatar	Donetsk, USSR	Dover, Delaware	Dresden, East Germany
Mashhad, Iran	7,403	13,670	8,753	9,803	7,647	11,439	8,967	10,961	10,510	1,427	5,012	4,598	8,481	3,196	2,419	9,026	1,444	2,209	10,472	3,965
Mazatlan, Mexico	13,454	3,037	5,142	3,789	15,313	1,837	14,787	2,360	3,028	13,977	18,243	9,629	14,267	14,936	11,190	13,267	14,140	11,350	3,408	9,922
Mbabane, Swaziland	10,805	12,775	15,754	16,008	9,007	15,712	9,419	14,740	13,868	6,169	4,845	8,566	10,036	4,392	8,289	11,027	6,116	8,258	13,188	8,738
Mbandaka, Zaire	11,933	11,196	12,659	12,779	10,785	12,786	11,652	11,811	10,936	4,483	6,066	5,391	11,924	3,032	5,598	12,893	4,537	5,637	10,336	5,666
McMurdo Sound, Antarctica	9,701	11,448	16,158	15,634	8,163	14,279	7,067	14,749	15,083	13,432	9,274	16,530	7,992	11,995	16,146	8,172	13,290	16,037	14,920	16,824
Mecca, Saudi Arabia	9,298	12,909	10,524	11,244	8,877	12,313	10,092	11,545	10,839	1,179	4,777	4,237	9,925	1,147	3,027	10,704	1,270	2,951	10,524	3,990
Medan, Indonesia	3,010	18,670	11,130	12,537	2,281	14,637	3,586	14,851	14,917	5,747	3,156	9,995	3,274	6,180	7,793	4,085	5,579	7,579	15,235	9,345
Medellin, Colombia	17,253	794	8,132	6,754	18,815	4,734	17,607	4,303	4,065	13,154	16,499	8,793	17,689	12,970	10,977	16,739	13,329	11,191	3,645	9,426
Medicine Hat, Canada	11,692	5,303	2,305	903	13,777	1,230	13,994	1,619	2,282	11,339	15,260	7,582	13,106	12,716	8,607	12,277	11,478	8,728	3,005	7,630
Medina, Saudi Arabia	9,291	12,762	10,190	10,912	8,978	12,008	10,217	11,255	10,564	1,079	5,006	3,967	10,001	1,473	2,692	10,746	1,209	2,616	10,270	3,688
Melbourne, Australia	5,363	14,264	13,069	13,655	4,403	14,099	3,087	15,075	15,949	12,156	7,986	16,612	3,787	11,832	14,407	3,716	11,976	14,193	16,515	15,955
Memphis, Tennessee	14,033	3,057	4,608	3,244	16,115	1,415	16,149	782	1,005	12,026	16,450	7,585	15,353	12,876	9,270	14,446	12,197	9,445	1,364	7,920
Merauke, Indonesia	2,371	15,330	10,375	11,372	2,765	12,716	2,057	13,596	14,361	10,448	7,481	13,994	1,626	10,982	11,842	739	10,294	11,638	15,086	13,237
Merida, Mexico	15,081	1,587	6,026	4,623	17,035	2,544	16,518	2,317	2,448	13,219	17,571	8,661	16,015	13,728	10,561	15,017	13,397	10,752	2,425	9,111
Meridian, Mississippi	14,336	2,728	4,937	3,567	16,415	1,677	16,377	1,113	1,213	12,190	16,623	7,704	15,615	12,958	9,456	14,689	12,364	9,637	1,407	8,073
Messina, Italy	11,245	10,130	8,458	8,787	11,445	9,469	12,745	8,635	7,890	3,489	7,739	1,330	12,343	4,023	1,936	12,897	3,667	2,102	7,552	1,437
Mexico City, Mexico	14,316	2,173	5,799	4,406	16,144	2,323	15,518	2,515	2,961	13,966	18,398	9,463	15,071	14,653	11,225	14,068	14,139	11,403	3,154	9,848
Miami, Florida	15,435	1,934	5,973	4,633	17,517	2,777	17,395	2,145	1,855	12,168	16,474	7,603	16,699	12,628	9,572	15,750	12,347	9,770	1,547	8,087
Midway Islands, USA	6,423	10,056	4,807	5,425	8,307	6,632	8,105	7,502	8,288	12,133	12,379	11,638	7,357	13,821	10,926	6,410	12,116	10,866	9,014	11,159
Milan, Italy	11,444	9,475	7,553	7,830	11,941	8,520	13,262	7,704	6,983	4,201	8,570	382	12,730	4,944	1,981	13,146	4,381	2,191	6,689	707
Milford Sound, New Zealand	7,109	12,230	12,901	13,002	6,421	12,768	5,099	13,670	14,467	14,162	9,866	18,653	5,694	13,628	16,429	5,398	13,982	16,214	14,862	17,957
Milwaukee, Wisconsin	13,511	3,872	3,972	2,703	15,584	1,472	15,894	497	406	11,214	15,610	6,863	14,993	12,186	8,438	14,178	11,381	8,607	1,124	7,140
Minsk, USSR	9,901	10,532	6,874	7,497	10,625	8,683	11,939	8,035	7,471	3,584	7,976	1,746	11,296	4,891	797	11,612	3,746	972	7,359	989
Mogadiscio, Somalia	8,912	14,128	12,658	13,461	7,840	14,484	8,841	13,654	12,884	2,730	3,179	6,342	8,975	1,082	5,236	9,915	2,653	5,142	12,469	6,185
Mombasa, Kenya	9,626	13,617	13,345	13,997	8,363	14,701	9,244	13,791	12,961	3,542	3,645	6,624	9,502	1,773	5,834	10,477	3,490	5,769	12,457	6,587
Monclova, Mexico	13,716	2,861	4,942	3,546	15,675	1,462	15,288	1,779	2,391	13,381	17,745	8,992	14,687	14,291	10,602	13,701	13,548	10,768	2,760	9,302
Moncton, Canada	14,027	4,503	4,824	3,928	15,854	3,321	16,718	2,359	1,515	9,661	14,086	5,154	15,728	10,430	6,974	15,178	9,837	7,166	1,169	5,541
Monrovia, Liberia	14,972	7,902	11,119	10,622	14,078	9,924	14,936	8,951	8,082	6,811	9,363	4,788	15,217	5,954	6,352	16,165	6,937	6,507	7,399	5,455
Monte Carlo, Monaco	11,653	9,357	7,704	7,934	12,101	8,550	13,420	7,713	6,972	4,291	8,622	440	12,914	4,941	2,183	13,351	4,471	2,390	6,650	943
Monterrey, Mexico	13,880	2,688	5,110	3,712	15,826	1,620	15,405	1,870	2,432	13,444	17,838	9,022	14,826	14,304	10,672	13,836	13,613	10,841	2,756	9,351
Montevideo, Uruguay	16,919	5,533	13,118	11,730	15,103	9,664	14,229	9,291	8,978	13,050	12,887	10,959	15,194	11,589	12,888	15,376	13,123	13,061	8,437	11,712
Montgomery, Alabama	14,493	2,682	5,045	3,693	16,576	1,866	16,586	1,210	1,141	12,046	16,475	7,538	15,808	12,772	9,328	14,892	12,220	9,512	1,229	7,925
Montpelier, Vermont	14,036	4,084	4,609	3,564	15,988	2,713	16,656	1,738	876	10,268	14,700	5,785	15,679	11,072	7,553	15,010	10,443	7,739	618	6,149
Montpellier, France	11,914	9,074	7,642	7,809	12,386	8,348	13,705	7,496	6,741	4,568	8,882	422	13,192	5,172	2,450	13,616	4,748	2,659	6,400	1,113
Montreal, Canada	13,878	4,195	4,451	3,416	15,835	2,635	16,496	1,670	836	10,238	14,670	5,779	15,520	11,081	7,507	14,852	10,411	7,691	722	6,122
Moosonee, Canada	13,071	4,754	3,624	2,634	15,060	2,277	15,670	1,464	1,012	10,159	14,543	5,881	14,697	11,200	7,378	14,026	10,324	7,544	1,405	6,111
Moroni, Comoros	9,347	14,082	14,185	14,910	7,872	15,611	8,627	14,683	13,839	4,267	3,235	7,556	8,996	2,575	6,711	9,993	4,187	6,633	13,302	7,514
Moscow, USSR	9,239	11,024	6,714	7,479	10,032	8,848	11,337	8,280	7,788	3,425	7,693	2,419	10,661	4,922	831	10,950	3,569	862	7,746	1,660
Mosul, Iraq	8,877	12,482	8,872	9,678	9,007	10,974	10,315	10,322	9,728	1,296	5,721	3,353	9,900	2,740	1,502	10,487	1,464	1,368	9,555	2,848
Mount Isa, Australia	3,430	15,330	11,634	12,526	2,931	13,612	1,712	14,558	15,391	10,950	7,349	14,988	2,015	11,119	12,766	1,751	10,781	12,554	16,108	14,256
Multan, Pakistan	6,188	14,911	9,212	10,417	6,350	12,255	7,670	11,913	11,564	2,136	4,153	5,891	7,193	3,577	3,692	7,772	2,038	3,479	11,606	5,243
Munich, West Germany	11,157	9,614	7,307	7,647	11,733	8,442	13,055	7,658	6,969	4,127	8,536	501	12,486	5,002	1,730	12,864	4,305	1,944	6,716	359
Murcia, Spain	12,587	8,681	8,114	8,134	12,904	8,430	14,207	7,524	6,716	4,941	9,090	1,151	13,780	5,273	3,120	14,274	5,119	3,322	6,291	1,865
Murmansk, USSR	9,376	10,116	5,231	5,999	10,584	7,466	11,808	6,989	6,604	4,876	8,992	2,867	10,986	6,412	2,288	11,044	5,009	2,350	6,685	2,246
Mururoa Atoll, Fr. Polynesia	10,870	7,016	9,527	8,782	11,271	7,677	10,049	8,435	9,132	18,984	15,318	15,732	10,230	18,848	17,006	9,458	18,898	17,091	9,436	15,999
Muscat, Oman	7,363	14,496	10,159	11,208	7,117	12,788	8,394	12,241	11,713	903	3,740	5,393	8,102	2,107	3,451	8,820	738	3,271	11,582	4,890
Myitkyina, Burma	3,618	16,263	8,941	10,335	4,231	12,432	5,512	12,504	12,507	4,713	4,519	8,151	4,838	5,888	5,931	5,266	4,594	5,719	12,822	7,425
Naga, Philippines	773	16,286	9,009	10,337	2,617	12,287	3,422	12,825	13,255	7,682	6,071	10,902	2,467	8,657	8,756	2,468	7,553	8,554	13,848	10,147
Nagasaki, Japan	2,884	14,307	6,812	8,170	4,845	10,191	5,584	10,645	11,033	7,582	7,527	9,570	4,599	9,025	7,697	4,292	7,508	7,529	11,618	8,822
Nagoya, Japan	3,320	13,663	6,255	7,585	5,360	9,569	5,974	10,071	10,512	8,107	8,225	9,691	4,984	9,617	7,959	4,540	8,045	7,807	11,128	8,962
Nagpur, India	5,235	16,168	9,990	11,289	5,144	13,251	6,458	13,019	12,742	3,002	3,234	7,125	6,049	3,973	4,943	6,713	2,853	4,731	12,828	6,493
Nairobi, Kenya	9,902	13,259	13,032	13,622	8,721	14,266	9,637	13,352	12,521	3,371	4,006	6,210	9,860	1,588	5,513	10,824	3,340	5,461	12,017	6,198
Nanchang, China	2,602	15,456	7,852	9,250	4,131	11,334	5,156	11,657	11,907	6,418	6,134	9,126	4,249	7,728	7,039	4,739	6,321	6,847	12,402	8,367
Nancy, France	11,492	9,211	7,149	7,407	12,122	8,110	13,444	7,306	6,600	4,522	8,922	176	12,855	5,343	2,112	13,203	4,701	2,327	6,330	603
Nandi, Fiji	6,324	11,370	9,802	10,016	6,790	10,242	5,690	11,220	12,096	14,545	11,339	16,659	5,696	15,074	15,216	4,879	14,401	15,061	12,695	16,045
Nanjing, China	2,855	14,995	7,392	8,789	4,520	10,870	5,485	11,204	11,473	6,597	6,572	9,014	4,551	7,991	6,993	4,494	6,513	6,810	11,984	8,255
Nanning, China	2,543	16,358	8,765	10,170	3,561	12,269	4,741	12,526	12,698	5,858	5,139	9,121	3,947	6,991	6,933	4,236	5,739	6,727	13,132	8,376
Nantes, France	12,073	8,638	7,130	7,245	12,722	7,765	14,043	6,918	6,172	5,050	9,412	497	13,455	5,741	2,713	13,785	5,230	2,928	5,853	1,192
Naples, Italy	11,256	9,962	8,147	8,472	11,558	9,175	12,869	8,351	7,618	3,667	7,975	1,031	12,421	4,299	1,842	12,929	3,847	2,027	7,299	1,136
Narvik, Norway	10,008	9,538	5,189	5,800	11,213	7,103	12,443	6,553	6,107	5,164	9,417	2,453	11,622	6,581	2,430	11,670	5,311	2,543	6,139	1,947
Nashville, Tennessee	14,154	3,103	4,662	3,331	16,239	1,646	16,371	845	757	11,752	16,183	7,288	15,538	12,569	9,008	14,657	11,924	9,187	1,046	7,638
Nassau, Bahamas	15,675	1,920	6,175	4,854	17,760	3,047	17,690	2,367	1,984	12,010	16,261	7,446	16,982	12,404	9,458	16,040	12,190	9,660	1,570	7,955
Natal, Brazil	17,911	5,472	11,270	10,224	16,382	8,720	16,566	7,904	7,194	9,836	11,870	7,084	17,369	8,886	9,054	18,285	9,962	9,238	6,477	7,837
Natashquan, Canada	13,620	5,009	4,610	3,853	15,390	3,542	16,323	2,623	1,847	9,222	13,654	4,757	15,337	10,066	6,508	14,858	9,396	6,697	1,634	5,103
Nauru Island	4,667	12,299	8,382	8,990	5,802	9,885	5,091	10,837	11,686	12,700	10,510	14,535	4,671	13,707	12,992	3,681	12,585	12,842	12,393	13,866
Ndjamena, Chad	12,062	10,628	11,284	11,417	11,315	11,581	12,363	10,626	9,768	3,992	6,703	4,014	12,435	3,061	4,432	13,322	4,098	4,506	9,221	4,319
Nelson, New Zealand	7,228	11,819	12,395	12,443	6,731	12,191	5,413	13,098	13,903	14,605	10,377	18,866	5,922	14,170	16,673	5,521	14,426	16,462	14,318	18,108
Nema, Mauritania	14,216	8,181	10,175	9,856	13,743	9,488	14,817	8,507	7,627	5,998	9,158	3,587	14,843	5,458	5,203	15,668	6,143	5,369	7,003	4,253
Neuquen, Argentina	16,219	5,452	13,003	11,597	14,724	9,491	13,661	9,287	9,128	14,170	13,467	11,985	14,562	12,647	13,991	14,552	14,234	14,170	8,683	12,744
New Delhi, India	5,607	15,366	9,246	10,512	5,802	12,435	7,124	12,177	11,895	2,682	4,009	6,431	6,623	4,006	4,215	7,191	2,570	4,000	11,990	5,765
New Glasgow, Canada	14,116	4,534	4,971	4,095	15,906	3,490	16,815	2,524	1,672	9,558	13,976	5,034	15,826	10,294	6,890	15,303	9,735	7,084	1,276	5,440
New Haven, Connecticut	14,328	3,761	4,857	3,754	16,300	2,709	16,915	1,727	850	10,505	14,929	5,990	15,950	11,244	7,813	15,243	10,681	8,003	326	6,385
New Orleans, Louisiana	14,423	2,513	5,109	3,723	16,485	1,739	16,333	1,329	1,509	12,480	16,912	7,982	15,624	13,219	9,750	14,674	12,654	9,932	1,675	8,361
New Plymouth, New Zealand	7,142	11,763	12,141	12,200	6,735	11,990	5,425	12,907	13,723	14,668	10,498	18,739	5,889	14,315	16,610	5,442	14,490	16,402	14,161	17,983
New York, New York	14,350	3,672	4,858	3,730	16,339	2,626	16,914	1,646	776	10,617	15,041	6,103	15,956	11,355	7,923	15,230	10,793	8,113	216	6,497
Newcastle upon Tyne, UK	11,584	8,660	6,314	6,526	12,485	7,255	13,788	6,478	5,807	5,237	9,667	971	13,087	6,188	2,597	13,285	5,412	2,803	5,594	1,117
Newcastle Waters, Australia	2,839	16,029	11,594	12,612	2,195	13,919	1,038	14,819	15,599	10,212	6,700	14,281	1,296	10,423	12,053	1,290	10,042	11,840	16,324	13,559
Niamey, Niger	13,386	9,217	10,804	10,655	12,727	10,471	13,766	9,494	8,618	5,192	8,103	3,757	13,845	4,459	4,913	14,718	5,321	5,045	8,016	4,293
Nicosia, Cyprus	9,767	11,747	8,986	9,622	9,829	10,679	11,125	9,939	9,269	1,879	6,238	2,711	10,755	2,791	1,481	11,367	2,058	1,472	9,015	2,365
Niue (Alofi)	7,636	10,057	9,579	9,509	8,123	9,358	6,990	10,308	11,161	15,854	12,602	16,832	7,037	16,396	16,052	6,222	15,717	15,939	11,691	16,436
Norfolk, Virginia	14,640	3,208	5,101	3,891	16,675	2,521	17,097	1,583	841	11,053	15,465	6,518	16,180	11,729	8,378	15,384	11,230	8,569	265	6,936
Norfolk Island, Australia	6,045	12,372	11,293	11,582	5,940	11,776	4,691	12,747	13,615	13,958	10,157	17,503	4,972	14,009	15,490	4,384	13,789	15,292	14,178	16,756
Noril'sk, USSR	7,427	11,346	4,745	5,939	8,902	7,861	10,011	7,703	7,600	5,384	8,591	4,933	9,109	7,152	3,656	9,038	5,452	3,591	7,899	4,244
Norman Wells, Canada	10,098	7,179	614	1,119	12,149	3,169	12,645	3,361	3,722	9,848	13,399	6,850	11,679	11,438	7,296	11,000	9,963	7,373	4,354	6,670
Normanton, Australia	3,222	15,217	11,266	12,154	2,972	13,280	1,853	14,216	15,040	10,959	7,515	14,845	1,960	11,232	12,642	1,514	10,793	12,432	15,760	14,100
North Pole	9,220	9,070	2,893	3,819	10,958	5,601	11,915	5,396	5,314	7,093	10,814	4,762	10,947	8,721	4,635	10,639	7,206	4,685	5,666	4,346
Nottingham, United Kingdom	11,691	8,680	6,536	6,728	12,524	7,408	13,835	6,612	5,921	5,151	9,573	768	13,163	6,041	2,574	13,398	5,328	2,784	5,681	1,044
Norway House, Canada	12,123	5,237	2,578	1,445	14,182	1,673	14,609	1,413	1,692	10,594	14,758	6,649	13,666	11,862	7,820	12,921	10,744	7,958	2,355	6,745
Norwich, United Kingdom	11,573	8,846	6,626	6,851	12,373	7,564	13,687	6,774	6,088	4,981	9,404	648	13,027	5,882	2,410	13,282	5,157	2,621	5,851	875
Nouakchott, Mauritania	14,968	7,250	9,701	9,222	14,659	8,667	15,755	7,685	6,807	6,806	10,096	3,763	15,743	6,377	5,670	16,515	6,960	5,856	6,156	4,498
Noumea, New Caledonia	5,510	12,538	10,647	11,039	5,672	11,442	4,506	12,423	13,302	13,614	10,123	16,772	4,625	13,913	14,858	3,917	13,454	14,670	13,921	16,039
Novosibirsk, USSR	6,525	12,840	6,307	7,542	7,671	9,476	8,890	9,293	9,133	4,153	6,981	5,226	8,083	5,932	3,321	8,225	4,180	3,168	9,368	4,468
Nuku'alofa, Tonga	7,179	10,636	9,940	9,966	7,561	9,916	6,408	10,874	11,734	15,396	12,005	17,100	6,490	15,814	15,964	5,707	15,249	15,825	12,276	16,595
Nukunono Island, Tokelau Isls.	7,162	10,108	8,573	8,630	8,001	8,748	7,015	9,724	10,600	15,216	12,672	15,769	6,870	16,192	14,984	5,955	15,108	14,886	11,200	15,336
Nuremberg, West Germany	11,134	9,556	7,158	7,502	11,757	8,314	13,079	7,539	6,858	4,216	8,634	508	12,489	5,128	1,747	12,843	4,393	1,962	6,619	260
Nyala, Sudan	11,011	11,680	11,460	11,821	10,252	12,292	11,325	11,373	10,544	3,079	5,681	4,329	11,368	1,991	4,143	12,251	3,161	4,163	10,054	4,442
Oaxaca, Mexico	14,663	1,819	6,135	4,736	16,451	2,639	15,750	2,736	3,090	14,027	18,425	9,487	15,359	14,592	11,323	14,355	14,204	11,508	3,198	9,908
Ocean Falls, Canada	10,507	6,357	1,471	618	12,590	2,231	12,780	2,821	3,489	11,289	14,689	8,083	11,894	12,865	8,714	11,064	11,404	8,799	4,209	7,988
Odense, Denmark	10,904	9,419	6,505	6,895	11,731	7,825	13,039	7,100	6,473	4,548	8,979	973	12,363	5,632	1,848	12,613	4,720	2,049	6,305	534
Odessa, USSR	9,816	11,054	7,719	8,354	10,282	9,495	11,604	8,810	8,203	2,819	7,247	1,953	11,064	4,039	389	11,506	2,989	561	8,032	1,345

Distances in Kilometers	Davao, Philippines	David, Panama	Dawson, Canada	Dawson Creek, Canada	Denpasar, Indonesia	Denver, Colorado	Derby, Australia	Des Moines, Iowa	Detroit, Michigan	Dhahran, Saudi Arabia	Diego Garcia Island	Dijon, France	Dili, Indonesia	Djibouti, Djibouti	Dnepropetrovsk, USSR	Dobo, Indonesia	Doha, Qatar	Donetsk, USSR	Dover, Delaware	Dresden, East Germany
Ogbomosho, Nigeria	13,311	9,527	11,441	11,291	12,443	11,047	13,397	10,066	9,188	5,241	7,754	4,344	13,578	4,279	5,318	14,504	5,352	5,430	8,567	4,838
Okha, USSR	5,389	11,926	4,332	5,722	7,374	7,800	8,067	8,162	8,509	7,877	9,401	8,141	7,076	9,616	6,834	6,626	7,876	6,736	9,089	7,480
Okinawa (Naha)	2,131	14,989	7,555	8,902	4,086	10,898	4,834	11,384	11,789	7,611	7,025	10,049	3,853	8,913	8,064	3,609	7,516	7,882	12,379	9,292
Oklahoma City, Oklahoma	13,495	3,367	4,241	2,839	15,561	811	15,496	756	1,463	12,370	16,723	8,038	14,733	13,360	9,586	13,805	12,535	9,750	1,984	8,313
Old Crow, Canada	9,477	7,801	391	1,660	11,522	3,756	12,046	3,990	4,348	9,564	12,896	6,928	11,074	11,221	7,131	10,422	9,666	7,187	4,971	6,665
Olympia, Washington	11,028	5,740	2,148	988	13,100	1,656	13,173	2,397	3,166	11,852	15,370	8,394	12,330	13,363	9,210	11,454	11,975	9,309	3,891	8,372
Omaha, Nebraska	13,185	3,878	3,754	2,385	15,270	780	15,402	203	1,082	11,752	16,075	7,492	14,556	12,815	8,964	13,685	11,914	9,123	1,755	7,728
Omsk, USSR	7,032	12,625	6,503	7,662	8,053	9,505	9,306	9,231	8,990	3,707	6,909	4,663	8,540	5,492	2,715	8,740	3,754	2,560	9,161	3,904
Oodnadatta, Australia	3,975	15,518	12,493	13,373	2,985	14,364	1,663	15,328	16,182	10,899	6,986	15,218	2,347	10,829	12,994	2,415	10,723	12,779	16,884	14,533
Oradea, Romania	10,461	10,399	7,575	8,074	10,957	9,050	12,279	8,313	7,663	3,381	7,809	1,280	11,734	4,407	989	12,158	3,557	1,197	7,449	744
Oran, Algeria	12,675	8,732	8,369	8,374	12,901	8,626	14,193	7,709	6,891	4,905	8,979	1,373	13,811	5,143	3,231	14,347	5,080	3,427	6,445	2,058
Oranjestad, Aruba	17,246	1,430	7,763	6,441	19,309	4,565	18,470	3,953	3,536	12,260	15,883	7,871	18,273	12,185	10,055	17,269	12,436	10,268	3,002	8,504
Orebro, Sweden	10,466	9,638	6,156	6,651	11,397	7,737	12,690	7,073	6,508	4,544	8,940	1,492	11,970	5,780	1,761	12,170	4,708	1,935	6,408	921
Orel, USSR	9,354	11,092	7,026	7,763	10,049	9,077	11,363	8,478	7,953	3,179	7,507	2,288	10,726	4,626	503	11,063	3,330	560	7,876	1,542
Orsk, USSR	7,808	12,417	7,128	8,147	8,560	9,804	9,862	9,378	8,998	2,855	6,620	3,835	9,191	4,609	1,717	9,516	2,939	1,537	9,046	3,088
Osaka, Japan	3,221	13,796	6,370	7,706	5,249	9,698	5,887	10,191	10,621	8,004	8,084	9,673	4,896	9,501	7,911	4,477	7,940	7,755	11,232	8,939
Oslo, Norway	10,670	9,378	6,025	6,468	11,640	7,505	12,928	6,828	6,253	4,790	9,194	1,451	12,194	5,992	2,013	12,368	4,955	2,191	6,147	1,005
Osorno, Chile	15,857	5,508	12,963	11,565	14,489	9,462	13,369	9,330	9,235	14,615	13,644	12,418	14,240	13,060	14,449	14,167	14,673	14,631	8,832	13,177
Ostrava, Czechoslovakia	10,633	10,058	7,226	7,686	11,236	8,641	12,557	7,905	7,260	3,774	8,205	1,017	11,970	4,814	1,226	12,340	3,949	1,441	7,058	349
Ottawa, Canada	13,818	4,150	4,356	3,290	15,799	2,471	16,412	1,507	683	10,365	14,796	5,922	15,442	11,230	7,625	14,752	10,537	7,806	695	6,254
Ouagadougou, Bourkina Fasso	13,800	8,840	10,814	10,574	13,113	10,263	14,124	9,282	8,403	5,604	8,465	3,923	14,236	4,860	5,230	15,121	5,734	5,371	7,779	4,508
Oujda, Morocco	12,832	8,621	8,444	8,414	13,033	8,612	14,318	7,686	6,859	5,026	9,060	1,519	13,953	5,214	3,393	14,500	5,201	3,588	6,396	2,214
Oxford, United Kingdom	11,773	8,670	6,661	6,837	12,568	7,482	13,882	6,675	5,971	5,124	9,538	670	13,226	5,974	2,591	13,482	5,302	2,803	5,714	1,045
Pago Pago, American Samoa	7,419	10,061	9,086	9,073	8,078	9,045	7,011	10,010	10,876	15,584	12,667	16,319	6,965	16,354	15,546	6,098	15,462	15,442	11,441	15,905
Pakxe, Laos	2,339	17,250	9,652	11,056	2,827	13,150	4,086	13,419	13,580	5,885	4,441	9,577	3,408	6,775	7,352	3,895	5,743	7,139	13,995	8,857
Palembang, Indonesia	2,566	19,023	11,526	12,912	1,321	14,951	2,606	15,348	15,571	6,701	3,617	10,982	2,388	7,003	8,778	3,286	6,530	8,564	15,991	10,330
Palermo, Italy	11,430	9,942	8,426	8,715	11,637	9,345	12,938	8,499	7,744	3,677	7,908	1,228	12,536	4,170	2,085	13,085	3,855	2,259	7,393	1,438
Palma, Majorca	12,216	9,000	8,043	8,148	12,553	8,566	13,861	7,682	6,896	4,619	8,830	882	13,416	5,046	2,750	13,903	4,798	2,951	6,505	1,541
Palmerston North, New Zealand	7,331	11,627	12,231	12,248	6,896	11,971	5,582	12,876	13,681	14,802	10,592	18,933	6,064	14,391	16,796	5,629	14,623	16,587	14,097	18,176
Panama, Panama	16,724	325	7,680	6,290	18,414	4,244	17,360	3,871	3,713	13,331	16,942	8,873	17,276	13,295	11,012	16,296	13,509	11,222	3,369	9,469
Paramaribo, Suriname	18,576	3,025	9,145	7,930	18,928	6,230	18,730	5,492	4,891	11,240	14,241	7,314	19,696	10,790	9,539	18,999	11,402	9,752	4,221	8,039
Paris, France	11,731	8,926	7,047	7,245	12,398	7,880	13,719	7,061	6,343	4,801	9,194	264	13,117	5,587	2,387	13,442	4,981	2,602	6,059	853
Patna, India	4,759	16,009	9,340	10,675	4,999	12,696	6,319	12,565	12,386	3,494	3,894	7,240	5,784	4,669	5,013	6,339	3,369	4,798	12,560	6,555
Patrai, Greece	10,725	10,653	8,541	8,983	10,906	9,810	12,208	9,010	8,295	2,969	7,275	1,693	11,804	3,640	1,557	12,367	3,149	1,692	7,992	1,555
Peking, China	3,755	14,312	6,726	8,133	5,380	10,236	6,380	10,483	10,686	6,224	6,912	8,206	5,450	7,767	6,266	5,380	6,165	6,094	11,163	7,450
Penrhyn Island (Omoka)	8,652	8,605	8,254	7,984	9,513	7,676	8,489	8,620	9,470	16,488	14,151	15,469	8,385	17,695	15,465	7,476	16,413	15,433	10,001	15,282
Peoria, Illinois	13,616	3,644	4,106	2,789	15,698	1,313	15,914	352	576	11,506	15,905	7,138	15,044	12,459	8,732	14,195	11,674	8,901	1,213	7,427
Perm', USSR	8,134	11,756	6,401	7,387	9,083	9,033	10,358	8,619	8,263	3,554	7,388	3,565	9,621	5,267	1,761	9,843	3,653	1,655	8,343	2,807
Perth, Australia	4,439	16,799	13,857	14,973	2,579	16,270	1,802	17,200	17,990	9,492	5,253	14,046	2,778	9,102	11,974	3,472	9,312	11,766	18,714	13,502
Peshawar, Pakistan	6,286	14,570	8,797	9,994	6,597	11,831	7,919	11,498	11,164	2,228	4,577	5,637	7,389	3,804	3,415	7,912	2,161	3,200	11,225	4,963
Petropavlovsk-Kamchatskiy,USSR	5,909	11,110	3,641	4,970	7,971	6,985	8,486	7,454	7,907	8,855	10,403	8,609	7,507	10,613	7,571	6,909	8,865	7,498	8,543	8,013
Petrozavodsk, USSR	9,385	10,533	6,031	6,778	10,372	8,169	11,649	7,630	7,175	4,120	8,339	2,453	10,903	5,619	1,489	11,088	4,261	1,554	7,180	1,732
Pevek, USSR	7,654	9,785	2,220	3,622	9,640	5,728	10,315	5,964	6,253	8,351	11,069	6,971	9,325	10,122	6,407	8,808	8,414	6,393	6,821	6,476
Philadelphia, Pennsylvania	14,382	3,566	4,870	3,715	16,389	2,541	16,916	1,566	713	10,747	15,171	6,232	15,969	11,482	8,052	15,221	10,923	8,241	93	6,627
Phnom Penh, Kampuchea	2,325	17,654	10,052	11,455	2,508	13,545	3,797	13,824	13,984	5,952	4,161	9,808	3,189	6,722	7,578	3,768	5,803	7,363	14,391	9,101
Phoenix, Arizona	12,470	4,115	3,887	2,558	14,462	942	14,215	1,859	2,720	13,131	17,076	9,085	13,527	14,375	10,362	12,563	13,278	10,499	3,319	9,252
Pierre, South Dakota	12,693	4,343	3,272	1,894	14,778	642	14,942	630	1,418	11,625	15,841	7,506	14,080	12,801	8,840	13,223	11,780	8,987	2,134	7,681
Pinang, Malaysia	2,802	18,444	10,873	12,278	2,269	14,376	3,589	14,612	14,706	5,805	3,406	9,971	3,199	6,324	7,756	3,964	5,641	7,541	15,051	9,305
Pitcairn Island (Adamstown)	11,787	6,357	9,915	9,005	12,034	7,633	10,768	8,282	8,889	19,867	15,679	15,375	11,039	18,358	17,103	10,318	19,867	17,249	9,094	15,800
Pittsburgh, Pennsylvania	14,132	3,554	4,589	3,380	16,178	2,125	16,589	1,151	330	11,004	15,436	6,530	15,667	11,813	8,274	14,879	11,178	8,457	409	6,887
Plymouth, Montserrat	17,242	2,377	7,727	6,504	19,074	4,849	19,409	4,075	3,465	11,302	14,999	6,951	18,784	11,246	9,155	17,865	11,477	9,369	2,806	7,604
Plymouth, United Kingdom	12,024	8,463	6,733	6,846	12,804	7,405	14,120	6,575	5,850	5,292	9,690	752	13,473	6,074	2,812	13,732	5,471	3,026	5,564	1,261
Ponape Island	3,607	13,091	7,997	8,844	5,076	10,099	4,656	10,985	11,770	11,456	9,659	13,448	4,010	12,563	11,768	3,016	11,348	11,610	12,496	12,742
Ponce, Puerto Rico	16,929	2,014	7,383	6,122	18,951	4,400	18,945	3,663	3,113	11,613	15,442	7,180	18,340	11,651	9,354	17,389	11,791	9,567	2,497	7,803
Ponta Delgada, Azores	14,225	6,537	7,328	6,904	14,944	6,659	16,266	5,694	4,831	7,083	11,218	2,714	15,680	7,372	4,944	15,926	7,261	5,159	4,300	3,419
Pontianak, Indonesia	1,970	18,425	11,027	12,397	1,155	14,405	2,471	14,861	15,160	6,973	4,177	11,089	2,032	7,425	8,863	2,837	6,808	8,647	15,644	10,403
Port Augusta, Australia	4,565	15,102	12,869	13,650	3,518	14,432	2,203	15,412	16,288	11,328	7,269	15,736	2,935	11,127	13,524	2,983	11,150	13,309	16,945	15,071
Port Blair, India	3,641	17,728	10,541	11,936	3,347	14,035	4,664	14,080	14,018	4,748	3,075	8,901	4,262	5,402	6,695	4,978	4,588	6,480	14,257	8,246
Port Elizabeth, South Africa	11,373	12,194	16,504	16,448	9,448	15,626	9,670	14,711	13,880	7,157	5,632	9,235	10,396	5,375	9,176	11,351	7,109	9,160	13,165	9,489
Port Hedland, Australia	3,125	17,414	12,601	13,792	1,340	15,362	630	16,182	16,841	9,008	5,172	13,409	1,504	8,976	11,216	2,335	8,831	11,002	17,524	12,768
Port Louis, Mauritius	8,035	15,534	14,967	16,048	6,323	17,274	6,936	16,407	15,590	5,202	2,146	9,130	7,408	3,849	7,923	8,412	5,070	7,802	15,081	8,972
Port Moresby, Papua New Guinea	3,013	14,584	10,155	11,034	3,514	12,205	2,690	13,124	13,935	11,176	8,222	14,514	2,379	11,743	12,427	1,488	11,025	12,229	14,658	13,755
Port Said, Egypt	9,923	11,814	9,411	10,015	9,842	10,997	11,116	10,224	9,525	1,824	6,039	2,926	10,812	2,447	1,921	11,478	1,997	1,916	9,230	2,676
Port Sudan, Sudan	9,586	12,728	10,723	11,387	9,095	12,359	10,286	11,558	10,824	1,515	4,874	4,234	10,159	1,090	3,205	10,961	1,599	3,149	10,475	4,051
Port-au-Prince, Haiti	16,566	1,562	7,057	5,745	18,652	3,916	18,338	3,258	2,827	12,070	16,022	7,572	17,801	12,204	9,700	16,821	12,249	9,909	2,307	8,158
Port-of-Spain, Trin. & Tobago	17,897	2,309	8,358	7,105	19,607	5,358	19,094	4,644	4,089	11,588	14,962	7,381	19,223	11,348	9,606	18,219	11,758	9,821	3,451	8,065
Port-Vila, Vanuatu	5,438	12,332	10,108	10,511	5,825	10,977	4,734	11,959	12,839	13,635	10,391	16,389	4,734	14,109	14,613	3,936	13,485	14,436	13,477	15,683
Portland, Maine	14,166	4,078	4,776	3,751	16,090	2,902	16,807	1,924	1,052	10,170	14,597	5,664	15,825	10,934	7,474	15,177	10,345	7,663	665	6,050
Portland, Oregon	11,108	5,627	2,312	1,150	13,172	1,579	13,207	2,371	3,165	12,016	15,533	8,523	12,380	13,519	9,367	11,491	12,140	9,468	3,887	8,513
Porto, Portugal	12,925	8,044	7,569	7,490	13,449	7,705	14,767	6,793	5,983	5,578	9,799	1,284	14,249	5,998	3,494	14,635	5,757	3,706	5,560	2,037
Porto Alegre, Brazil	17,437	5,415	12,884	11,531	15,483	9,521	14,734	9,053	8,656	12,449	12,721	10,251	15,718	11,065	12,179	15,998	12,533	12,354	8,069	11,004
Porto Alexandre, Angola	12,764	10,729	14,217	14,013	11,164	13,410	11,695	12,444	11,579	6,233	6,648	7,026	12,244	4,589	7,478	13,246	6,258	7,523	10,888	7,409
Porto Novo, Benin	13,529	9,372	11,567	11,364	12,604	11,035	13,523	10,053	9,174	5,488	7,900	4,531	13,742	4,488	5,564	14,682	5,597	5,679	8,538	5,047
Porto Velho, Brazil	18,972	2,800	10,182	8,826	18,076	6,837	17,007	6,348	5,985	12,837	14,871	9,175	17,828	12,057	11,389	17,451	12,983	11,600	5,441	9,909
Portsmouth, United Kingdom	11,825	8,679	6,768	6,934	12,586	7,556	13,903	6,740	6,028	5,089	9,495	588	13,262	5,907	2,593	13,535	5,267	2,807	5,757	1,042
Poznan, Poland	10,628	9,903	6,927	7,386	11,325	8,365	12,643	7,645	7,016	4,007	8,438	1,028	12,017	5,099	1,350	12,339	4,179	1,560	6,838	269
Prague, Czechoslovakia	10,881	9,785	7,145	7,547	11,509	8,436	12,830	7,682	7,022	4,026	8,453	760	12,236	5,010	1,499	12,591	4,202	1,714	6,804	119
Praia, Cape Verde Islands	15,840	6,447	9,719	9,063	15,492	8,245	16,515	7,276	6,412	7,686	10,860	4,456	16,596	7,209	6,470	17,395	7,840	6,664	5,721	5,209
Pretoria, South Africa	11,097	12,480	15,653	15,813	9,309	15,427	9,721	14,458	13,589	6,224	5,111	8,419	10,340	4,440	8,246	11,330	6,181	8,224	12,904	8,624
Prince Albert, Canada	11,778	5,392	2,259	978	13,855	1,497	14,188	1,579	2,073	10,895	14,916	7,095	13,266	12,243	8,148	12,484	11,038	8,274	2,775	7,148
Prince Edward Island	10,398	12,987	18,051	18,189	8,344	16,941	8,309	16,162	15,409	8,164	5,453	10,886	9,145	6,465	10,533	10,027	8,076	10,480	14,683	11,065
Prince George, Canada	10,758	6,193	1,473	262	12,844	2,067	13,089	2,551	3,171	11,091	14,663	7,756	12,186	12,624	8,468	11,377	11,213	8,562	3,886	7,686
Prince Rupert, Canada	10,276	6,622	1,202	664	12,361	2,492	12,592	3,038	3,668	11,073	14,413	7,985	11,691	12,675	8,532	10,881	11,184	8,610	4,382	7,858
Providence, Rhode Island	14,324	3,855	4,884	3,811	16,273	2,826	16,937	1,844	965	10,373	14,794	5,854	15,963	11,106	7,686	15,281	10,549	7,877	457	6,253
Provo, Utah	12,166	4,561	3,207	1,839	14,219	572	14,167	1,524	2,397	12,403	16,338	8,470	13,385	13,709	9,648	12,465	12,547	9,778	3,079	8,590
Puerto Aisen, Chile	15,408	6,041	13,457	12,065	13,967	9,966	12,869	9,858	9,772	14,570	13,214	12,762	13,758	12,934	14,709	13,741	14,609	14,879	9,370	13,519
Puerto Deseado, Argentina	15,366	6,433	13,941	12,540	13,756	10,434	12,738	10,267	10,121	14,043	12,667	12,570	13,667	12,380	14,401	13,759	14,073	14,556	9,674	13,318
Puerto Princesa, Philippines	812	16,935	9,608	10,953	2,070	12,923	3,038	13,436	13,830	7,413	5,472	10,943	2,159	8,247	8,746	2,426	7,271	8,538	14,396	10,200
Punta Arenas, Chile	14,681	6,911	14,269	12,890	13,132	10,802	12,076	10,721	10,644	14,359	12,469	13,241	12,993	12,632	15,002	13,063	14,366	15,145	10,237	13,984
Pusan, South Korea	3,124	14,169	6,632	8,002	5,056	10,042	5,827	10,467	10,831	7,430	7,566	9,314	4,845	8,911	7,461	4,556	7,361	7,296	11,405	8,567
Pyongyang, North Korea	3,539	14,004	6,409	7,801	5,388	9,876	6,238	10,232	10,539	7,033	7,516	8,789	5,266	8,574	6,950	5,034	6,975	6,789	11,081	8,044
Qamdo, China	3,978	15,622	8,353	9,738	4,806	11,828	6,061	11,873	11,866	4,599	5,014	7,692	5,333	5,947	5,498	5,671	4,502	5,251	12,183	6,952
Qandahar, Afghanistan	6,756	14,441	9,174	10,309	6,892	12,051	8,211	11,633	11,223	1,629	4,365	5,364	7,754	3,207	3,191	8,341	1,556	2,981	11,214	4,737
Qiqian, China	5,023	12,932	5,390	6,794	6,763	8,901	7,704	9,097	9,281	6,446	8,034	7,408	6,747	8,157	5,758	6,548	6,432	5,625	9,760	6,683
Qom, Iran	8,170	13,177	9,024	9,951	8,281	11,405	9,592	10,822	10,281	929	5,169	4,042	9,171	2,671	2,020	9,766	1,040	1,839	10,156	3,488
Quebec, Canada	13,810	4,386	4,452	3,479	15,730	2,826	16,460	1,874	1,061	10,004	14,436	5,547	15,475	10,852	7,275	14,848	10,177	7,459	920	5,888
Quetta, Pakistan	6,611	14,635	9,302	10,455	6,710	12,218	8,027	11,812	11,410	1,709	4,193	5,552	7,582	3,211	3,384	8,182	1,618	3,174	11,406	4,929
Quito, Ecuador	17,255	1,051	8,657	7,257	18,218	5,179	16,920	4,874	4,735	13,819	16,701	9,538	17,194	13,468	11,737	16,341	13,989	11,951	4,371	10,185
Rabaul, Papua New Guinea	3,206	13,980	9,394	10,240	4,117	11,407	3,435	12,322	13,131	11,424	8,832	14,291	2,983	12,185	12,340	2,000	11,286	12,154	13,854	13,543
Raiatea (Uturoa)	9,498	8,088	9,018	8,551	10,097	7,892	8,955	8,772	9,569	17,560	14,517	15,989	9,007	18,360	16,439	8,169	17,466	16,437	10,005	15,978

Distances in Kilometers	Davao, Philippines	David, Panama	Dawson, Canada	Dawson Creek, Canada	Denpasar, Indonesia	Denver, Colorado	Derby, Australia	Des Moines, Iowa	Detroit, Michigan	Dhahran, Saudi Arabia	Diego Garcia Island	Dijon, France	Dili, Indonesia	Djibouti, Djibouti	Dnepropetrovsk, USSR	Dobo, Indonesia	Doha, Qatar	Donetsk, USSR	Dover, Delaware	Dresden, East Germany
Raleigh, North Carolina	14,633	3,052	5,087	3,838	16,693	2,355	17,014	1,452	822	11,288	15,704	6,758	16,126	11,972	8,604	15,295	11,465	8,794	465	7,170
Rangiroa (Avatoru)	9,866	7,650	8,788	8,246	10,525	7,498	9,395	8,364	9,151	17,784	14,964	15,625	9,428	18,802	16,280	8,576	17,716	16,303	9,574	15,670
Rangoon, Burma	3,376	17,211	9,874	11,273	3,509	13,376	4,825	13,465	13,459	4,858	3,735	8,741	4,281	5,736	6,512	4,874	4,712	6,297	13,752	8,049
Raoul Is., Kermadec Islands	7,258	10,997	10,880	10,889	7,308	10,729	6,067	11,667	12,507	15,317	11,493	17,985	6,314	15,352	16,500	5,657	15,151	16,328	13,000	17,400
Rarotonga (Avarua)	8,724	9,057	9,616	9,309	9,160	8,822	7,986	9,726	10,539	16,939	13,514	16,803	8,092	17,366	16,711	7,300	16,804	16,646	10,996	16,645
Rawson, Argentina	15,857	5,992	13,547	12,141	14,252	10,034	13,236	9,826	9,653	13,962	12,958	12,169	14,163	12,363	14,074	14,235	14,009	14,240	9,193	12,922
Recife, Brazil	17,883	5,579	11,511	10,451	16,235	8,916	16,352	8,113	7,415	9,917	11,793	7,286	17,184	8,909	9,226	18,069	10,038	9,408	6,700	8,036
Regina, Canada	12,024	5,089	2,539	1,198	14,107	1,191	14,383	1,300	1,879	11,148	15,217	7,256	13,479	12,455	8,387	12,671	11,294	8,519	2,597	7,343
Reykjavik, Iceland	11,656	7,764	4,893	5,008	12,991	5,795	14,191	5,082	4,501	6,540	10,947	2,488	13,325	7,656	3,766	13,252	6,707	3,941	4,428	2,533
Rhodes, Greece	10,206	11,262	8,810	9,360	10,312	10,311	11,610	9,541	8,849	2,360	6,688	2,260	11,229	3,133	1,445	11,824	2,540	1,506	8,570	1,991
Richmond, Virginia	14,521	3,263	4,980	3,764	16,563	2,401	16,969	1,458	715	11,075	15,496	6,552	16,054	11,783	8,384	15,255	11,251	8,574	246	6,955
Riga, USSR	10,044	10,210	6,509	7,103	10,875	8,279	12,179	7,638	7,086	3,984	8,365	1,680	11,495	5,290	1,195	11,755	4,145	1,358	6,992	943
Ringkobing, Denmark	10,991	9,278	6,396	6,763	11,852	7,674	13,157	6,946	6,319	4,702	9,132	1,000	12,468	5,780	1,996	12,698	4,874	2,196	6,153	668
Rio Branco, Brazil	18,526	2,602	10,122	8,743	17,920	6,709	16,742	6,290	5,996	13,282	15,225	9,553	17,489	12,501	11,776	17,029	13,429	11,988	5,497	10,279
Rio Cuarto, Argentina	16,944	4,983	12,587	11,184	15,380	9,090	14,360	8,800	8,572	13,743	13,622	11,281	15,275	12,335	13,325	15,279	13,826	13,511	8,087	12,040
Rio de Janeiro, Brazil	17,893	5,500	12,569	11,307	15,808	9,440	15,336	8,827	8,301	11,426	12,272	9,155	16,321	10,147	11,059	16,822	11,521	11,233	7,649	9,904
Rio Gallegos, Argentina	14,880	6,775	14,186	12,798	13,312	10,703	12,267	10,595	10,497	14,263	12,521	13,043	13,188	12,552	14,823	13,266	14,277	14,970	10,078	13,787
Rio Grande, Brazil	17,230	5,519	13,032	11,667	15,307	9,639	14,527	9,197	8,823	12,598	12,704	10,479	15,507	11,179	12,394	15,769	12,676	12,566	8,247	11,231
Riyadh, Saudi Arabia	8,570	13,408	10,157	11,011	8,288	12,300	9,543	11,617	10,982	390	4,504	4,447	9,296	1,491	2,837	10,029	492	2,709	10,748	4,063
Road Town, Brit. Virgin Isls.	16,972	2,222	7,438	6,200	18,920	4,529	19,151	3,762	3,170	11,411	15,225	6,996	18,468	11,435	9,178	17,546	11,588	9,392	2,526	7,627
Roanoke, Virginia	14,430	3,204	4,884	3,636	16,490	2,195	16,820	1,270	622	11,252	15,679	6,743	15,926	11,989	8,545	15,102	11,427	8,732	439	7,132
Robinson Crusoe Island, Chile	16,144	4,671	12,051	10,657	15,096	8,558	13,887	8,465	8,423	15,088	14,559	12,248	14,676	13,678	14,405	14,433	15,174	14,606	8,067	12,999
Rochester, New York	13,972	3,877	4,461	3,326	15,984	2,309	16,513	1,328	455	10,649	15,081	6,190	15,561	11,487	7,914	14,826	10,822	8,096	477	6,534
Rockhampton, Australia	4,323	14,163	11,402	12,080	4,097	12,840	2,880	13,817	14,689	12,110	8,482	15,963	3,124	12,279	13,784	2,617	11,942	13,576	15,363	15,209
Rome, Italy	11,353	9,795	8,000	8,302	11,703	8,988	13,017	8,162	7,428	3,840	8,161	844	12,549	4,488	1,904	13,035	4,020	2,099	7,111	1,022
Rosario, Argentina	17,068	5,128	12,730	11,334	15,380	9,253	14,425	8,917	8,644	13,403	13,352	11,045	15,365	11,991	13,053	15,443	13,484	13,235	8,130	11,804
Roseau, Dominica	17,416	2,412	7,904	6,681	19,188	5,016	19,449	4,249	3,643	11,310	14,927	6,999	18,957	11,203	9,212	18,022	11,484	9,427	2,983	7,664
Rostock, East Germany	10,861	9,551	6,675	7,078	11,636	8,007	12,949	7,278	6,645	4,379	8,810	904	12,293	5,448	1,704	12,572	4,551	1,910	6,466	355
Rostov-na-Donu, USSR	9,128	11,627	7,664	8,436	9,635	9,757	10,956	9,145	8,599	2,498	6,851	2,603	10,391	3,964	378	10,819	2,651	166	8,491	1,930
Rotterdam, Netherlands	11,427	9,066	6,769	7,035	12,178	7,785	13,495	7,001	6,319	4,748	9,171	513	12,854	5,659	2,194	13,138	4,925	2,407	6,083	649
Rouyn, Canada	13,424	4,424	3,954	2,904	15,419	2,273	16,009	1,366	728	10,325	14,737	5,963	15,041	11,287	7,557	14,350	10,494	7,731	1,046	6,241
Sacramento, California	11,468	5,136	3,073	1,913	13,484	1,430	13,341	2,390	3,259	12,769	16,275	9,116	12,593	14,226	10,088	11,653	12,898	10,198	3,945	9,162
Saginaw, Michigan	13,674	3,881	4,129	2,915	15,728	1,798	16,125	821	142	10,976	15,393	6,584	15,201	11,902	8,212	14,417	11,146	8,386	848	6,884
Saint Denis, Reunion	8,262	15,309	15,079	16,114	6,540	17,215	7,133	16,317	15,483	5,250	2,362	9,081	7,621	3,835	7,943	8,624	5,123	7,828	14,952	8,949
Saint George's, Grenada	17,744	2,300	8,208	6,961	19,517	5,232	19,200	4,505	3,939	11,530	14,985	7,285	19,141	11,333	9,506	18,145	11,701	9,722	3,298	7,962
Saint John, Canada	14,094	4,376	4,836	3,905	15,945	3,226	16,777	2,258	1,404	9,796	14,220	5,285	15,787	10,555	7,109	15,211	9,971	7,301	1,035	5,676
Saint John's, Antigua	17,212	2,429	7,705	6,489	19,020	4,850	19,452	4,067	3,448	11,245	14,955	6,892	18,776	11,196	9,096	17,873	11,421	9,310	2,782	7,545
Saint John's, Canada	13,951	5,166	5,254	4,567	15,544	4,223	16,631	3,276	2,447	8,791	13,197	4,251	15,677	9,502	6,160	15,325	8,969	6,359	2,061	4,683
Saint Louis, Missouri	13,749	3,433	4,271	2,929	15,834	1,283	15,978	440	733	11,722	16,129	7,331	15,135	12,644	8,952	14,261	11,891	9,124	1,272	7,634
Saint Paul, Minnesota	13,076	4,175	3,555	2,253	15,155	1,136	15,429	376	860	11,281	15,610	7,042	14,535	12,361	8,493	13,713	11,443	8,652	1,585	7,264
Saint Peter Port, UK	11,993	8,571	6,871	6,998	12,726	7,559	14,045	6,726	5,997	5,162	9,552	607	13,418	5,924	2,722	13,704	5,341	2,936	5,703	1,173
Saipan (Susupe)	2,370	14,114	7,766	8,879	4,272	10,521	4,331	11,273	11,928	9,820	8,457	12,061	3,437	11,002	10,220	2,638	9,716	10,050	12,631	11,323
Salalah, Oman	7,826	14,479	10,942	11,924	7,299	13,362	8,513	12,722	12,110	1,108	3,363	5,589	8,355	1,323	3,897	9,158	955	3,746	11,889	5,194
Salem, Oregon	11,101	5,618	2,363	1,220	13,162	1,591	13,180	2,404	3,207	12,086	15,580	8,596	12,360	13,592	9,439	11,465	12,209	9,540	3,927	8,586
Salt Lake City, Utah	12,122	4,614	3,147	1,778	14,178	597	14,139	1,533	2,401	12,353	16,278	8,436	13,350	13,668	9,601	12,435	12,496	9,730	3,089	8,551
Salta, Argentina	17,728	4,113	11,714	10,317	16,305	8,240	15,248	7,903	7,649	13,621	14,235	10,642	16,132	12,412	12,777	16,020	13,731	12,976	7,156	11,397
Salto, Uruguay	17,288	5,120	12,698	11,312	15,516	9,251	14,615	8,869	8,557	13,113	13,228	10,751	15,570	11,727	12,747	15,697	13,198	12,929	8,019	11,509
Salvador, Brazil	18,174	5,403	11,825	10,679	16,261	9,004	16,131	8,267	7,629	10,513	12,075	7,956	17,055	9,419	9,899	17,785	10,628	10,080	6,934	8,707
Salzburg, Austria	11,072	9,727	7,370	7,730	11,628	8,546	12,950	7,766	7,080	4,012	8,422	605	12,388	4,897	1,630	12,777	4,190	1,844	6,830	365
Samsun, Turkey	9,437	11,703	8,319	9,025	9,724	10,219	11,041	9,541	8,931	2,091	6,522	2,568	10,569	3,356	804	11,091	2,263	755	8,749	2,042
San Antonio, Texas	13,812	2,866	4,802	3,395	15,823	1,289	15,545	1,420	1,993	12,995	17,384	8,592	14,888	13,890	10,220	13,917	13,163	10,388	2,365	8,908
San Cristobal, Venezuela	17,453	1,127	8,134	6,778	19,210	4,815	18,009	4,300	3,975	12,754	16,137	8,418	18,074	12,568	10,613	17,106	12,927	10,827	3,493	9,062
San Diego, California	12,068	4,472	3,811	2,573	14,031	1,341	13,744	2,301	3,173	13,337	17,029	9,432	13,073	14,677	10,599	12,102	13,476	10,724	3,789	9,559
San Francisco, California	11,422	5,163	3,136	2,007	13,428	1,528	13,261	2,495	3,367	12,870	16,320	9,235	12,525	14,337	10,196	11,579	12,996	10,304	4,049	9,279
San Jose, Costa Rica	16,239	246	7,382	5,980	17,912	3,898	16,930	3,630	3,592	13,653	17,435	9,138	16,777	13,728	11,227	15,791	13,833	11,433	3,348	9,699
San Juan, Argentina	16,930	4,665	12,252	10,845	15,540	8,744	14,449	8,496	8,313	14,094	14,040	11,406	15,325	12,729	13,506	15,230	14,184	13,700	7,860	12,164
San Juan, Puerto Rico	16,907	2,084	7,363	6,110	18,909	4,407	18,993	3,658	3,093	11,541	15,381	7,108	18,350	11,586	9,281	17,410	11,719	9,494	2,467	7,730
San Luis Potosi, Mexico	14,007	2,500	5,446	4,057	15,883	1,987	15,342	2,263	2,792	13,813	18,224	9,360	14,836	14,611	11,048	13,836	13,983	11,219	3,065	9,709
San Marino, San Marino	11,273	9,756	7,781	8,100	11,695	8,825	13,013	8,013	7,294	3,903	8,262	693	12,512	4,634	1,803	12,965	4,083	2,006	6,998	799
San Miguel de Tucuman, Argen.	17,544	4,321	11,925	10,526	16,080	8,444	15,032	8,119	7,872	13,663	14,094	10,801	15,925	12,403	12,918	15,843	13,766	13,114	7,382	11,558
San Salvador, El Salvador	15,550	941	6,781	5,374	17,312	3,273	16,494	3,120	3,228	13,779	17,903	9,216	16,199	14,073	11,207	15,199	13,959	11,405	3,125	9,718
Sanaa, Yemen	8,893	13,585	11,194	11,990	8,268	13,125	9,435	12,363	11,656	1,360	3,998	5,054	9,351	430	3,767	10,188	1,339	3,668	11,331	4,804
Santa Cruz, Bolivia	18,495	3,593	11,119	9,743	17,074	7,708	16,052	7,285	6,964	13,153	14,411	9,897	16,939	12,116	12,065	16,784	13,279	12,270	6,435	10,648
Santa Cruz, Tenerife	14,344	7,247	8,626	8,255	14,502	7,954	15,753	6,978	6,104	6,483	10,268	2,788	15,462	6,422	4,878	16,022	6,652	5,080	5,520	3,546
Santa Fe, New Mexico	12,851	3,849	3,878	2,483	14,888	458	14,745	1,256	2,108	12,701	16,861	8,539	14,010	13,852	9,916	13,067	12,856	10,063	2,707	8,743
Santa Rosa, Argentina	16,584	5,335	12,932	11,526	14,994	9,426	13,980	9,161	8,948	13,806	13,382	11,569	14,901	12,327	13,569	14,936	13,877	13,749	8,469	12,328
Santa Rosalia, Mexico	12,730	3,773	4,523	3,224	14,632	1,534	14,210	2,324	3,127	13,783	17,739	9,638	13,620	14,956	11,004	12,629	13,933	11,146	3,639	9,848
Santarem, Brazil	19,491	3,305	9,990	8,732	18,360	6,928	17,815	6,261	5,721	11,615	14,064	7,990	18,790	10,928	10,187	18,679	11,764	10,396	5,076	8,734
Santiago del Estero, Argentina	17,492	4,459	12,062	10,665	15,973	8,584	14,945	8,254	7,999	13,600	13,957	10,822	15,849	12,313	12,922	15,801	13,700	13,117	7,503	11,581
Santiago, Chile	16,643	4,800	12,353	10,947	15,304	8,841	14,188	8,635	8,486	14,329	14,053	11,699	15,053	12,922	13,797	14,940	14,413	13,990	8,055	12,457
Santo Domingo, Dominican Rep.	16,716	1,752	7,180	5,890	18,792	4,108	18,595	3,412	2,924	11,868	15,773	7,394	18,027	11,965	9,541	17,058	12,047	9,752	2,357	7,994
Sao Paulo de Olivenca, Brazil	18,391	2,004	9,420	8,052	18,598	6,045	17,342	5,585	5,270	13,062	15,565	9,081	17,950	12,488	11,312	17,279	13,220	11,526	4,768	9,785
Sao Paulo, Brazil	18,007	5,262	12,467	11,173	15,940	9,259	15,366	8,685	8,198	11,772	12,578	9,397	16,357	10,500	11,342	16,762	11,869	11,520	7,565	10,150
Sao Tome, Sao Tome & Principe	13,201	9,922	12,345	12,180	12,058	11,830	12,879	10,848	9,969	5,465	7,340	5,208	13,196	4,213	5,984	14,172	5,548	6,072	9,321	5,660
Sapporo, Japan	4,275	12,796	5,314	6,660	6,308	8,676	6,924	9,141	9,562	8,159	8,891	9,116	5,934	9,795	7,585	5,454	8,124	7,457	10,174	8,418
Sarajevo, Yugoslavia	10,825	10,226	7,884	8,304	11,217	9,153	12,535	8,372	7,679	3,452	7,840	1,114	12,040	4,290	1,376	12,510	3,632	1,569	7,413	876
Saratov, USSR	8,675	11,746	7,173	8,040	9,356	9,506	10,669	8,973	8,502	2,826	6,997	2,972	10,032	4,440	864	10,382	2,955	713	8,471	2,234
Saskatoon, Canada	11,801	5,321	2,306	979	13,882	1,382	14,182	1,530	2,077	11,029	15,038	7,222	13,269	12,376	8,282	12,473	11,171	8,408	2,789	7,279
Schefferville, Canada	13,051	5,326	4,003	3,310	14,883	3,280	15,748	2,450	1,823	9,210	13,626	4,879	14,759	10,201	6,445	14,251	9,379	6,620	1,857	5,131
Seattle, Washington	11,046	5,741	2,108	920	13,120	1,643	13,209	2,360	3,119	11,786	15,330	8,320	12,361	13,293	9,140	11,490	11,910	9,240	3,845	8,298
Sendai, Japan	3,782	13,172	5,776	7,098	5,836	9,077	6,408	9,586	10,039	8,315	8,676	9,567	5,420	9,886	7,949	4,922	8,265	7,810	10,664	8,856
Seoul, South Korea	3,381	14,070	6,490	7,876	5,261	9,939	6,083	10,321	10,649	7,178	7,531	8,984	5,107	8,697	7,139	4,855	7,117	6,977	11,203	8,238
Sept-Iles, Canada	13,556	4,864	4,397	3,575	15,396	3,217	16,248	2,303	1,549	9,490	13,921	5,054	15,257	10,371	6,756	14,719	9,662	6,940	1,423	5,377
Sevastopol, USSR	9,627	11,338	7,941	8,612	10,028	9,786	11,349	9,108	8,504	2,518	6,946	2,219	10,833	3,772	442	11,305	2,688	501	8,333	1,639
Seville, Spain	12,986	8,251	8,040	7,964	13,338	8,136	14,641	7,211	6,387	5,373	9,490	1,425	14,207	5,656	3,514	14,681	5,550	3,720	5,933	2,176
Shanghai, China	2,699	14,953	7,368	8,757	4,449	10,822	5,363	11,194	11,498	6,861	6,725	9,247	4,412	8,241	7,244	4,305	6,775	7,062	12,031	8,489
Sheffield, United Kingdom	11,684	8,659	6,486	6,679	12,533	7,364	13,842	6,571	5,883	5,184	9,608	817	13,163	6,084	2,594	13,389	5,360	2,803	5,647	1,072
Shenyang, China	3,854	13,852	6,247	7,648	5,649	9,740	6,543	10,049	10,316	6,778	7,514	8,425	5,579	8,359	6,601	5,380	6,729	6,443	10,836	7,680
Shiraz, Iran	7,993	13,623	9,569	10,521	7,928	11,985	9,222	11,393	10,838	435	4,608	4,503	8,870	2,218	2,573	9,529	488	2,401	10,692	3,995
Sibiu, Romania	10,330	10,603	7,738	8,265	10,776	9,266	12,098	8,533	7,884	3,161	7,588	1,473	11,572	4,197	872	12,020	3,338	1,067	7,669	965
Singapore	2,497	18,734	11,141	12,537	1,672	14,603	2,989	14,943	15,125	6,372	3,619	10,572	2,644	6,797	8,357	3,465	6,205	8,142	15,526	9,906
Sioux Falls, South Dakota	12,974	4,132	3,512	2,156	15,059	806	15,245	336	1,124	11,567	15,857	7,362	14,378	12,676	8,778	13,525	11,726	8,933	1,834	7,572
Skelleftea, Sweden	9,985	9,789	5,622	6,236	11,072	7,504	12,333	6,926	6,445	4,753	9,047	2,168	11,553	6,147	2,000	11,671	4,904	2,122	6,436	1,584
Skopje, Yugoslavia	10,641	10,520	8,126	8,586	10,957	9,469	12,272	8,693	8,002	3,141	7,519	1,430	11,807	3,973	1,277	12,311	3,320	1,445	7,734	1,167
Socotra Island (Tamrida)	7,855	14,680	11,422	12,404	7,167	13,814	8,338	13,149	12,511	1,565	3,005	5,947	8,253	1,189	4,343	9,100	1,423	4,199	12,257	5,593
Sofia, Bulgaria	10,475	10,644	8,073	8,568	10,812	9,502	12,129	8,741	8,065	3,039	7,437	1,528	11,652	3,944	1,112	12,149	3,218	1,277	7,814	1,180
Songkhla, Thailand	2,761	18,245	10,679	12,085	2,388	14,184	3,710	14,413	14,507	5,737	3,518	9,845	3,272	6,319	7,625	4,000	5,576	7,409	14,857	9,171
Sorong, Indonesia	1,080	16,210	10,061	11,238	1,974	12,900	1,998	13,654	14,286	9,173	6,566	12,721	1,056	9,831	10,546	633	9,024	10,340	14,974	11,970
South Georgia Island	14,539	8,152	15,748	14,356	12,558	12,276	11,861	11,919	11,574	12,143	10,569	11,924	12,851	10,399	13,214	13,300	12,141	13,311	10,995	12,581
South Pole	10,783	10,935	17,108	16,184	9,045	14,403	8,088	14,608	14,691	12,914	9,192	15,247	9,056	11,286	15,372	9,363	12,801	15,322	14,339	15,662

Distances in Kilometers

	Davao, Philippines	David, Panama	Dawson, Canada	Dawson Creek, Canada	Denpasar, Indonesia	Denver, Colorado	Derby, Australia	Des Moines, Iowa	Detroit, Michigan	Dhahran, Saudi Arabia	Diego Garcia Island	Dijon, France	Dili, Indonesia	Djibouti, Djibouti	Dnepropetrovsk, USSR	Dobo, Indonesia	Doha, Qatar	Donetsk, USSR	Dover, Delaware	Dresden, East Germany
South Sandwich Islands	13,891	8,895	16,480	15,096	11,873	13,021	11,244	12,646	12,271	11,692	9,848	12,003	12,233	9,920	13,053	12,753	11,673	13,123	11,672	12,608
Split, Yugoslavia	10,988	10,079	7,890	8,273	11,376	9,075	12,694	8,281	7,576	3,587	7,959	987	12,203	4,372	1,534	12,673	3,767	1,729	7,296	862
Spokane, Washington	11,382	5,457	2,262	921	13,461	1,331	13,574	1,995	2,749	11,718	15,438	8,099	12,720	13,164	9,026	11,855	11,850	9,137	3,474	8,115
Spoleto, Italy	11,301	9,800	7,914	8,228	11,679	8,935	12,995	8,116	7,390	3,845	8,183	793	12,514	4,532	1,841	12,987	4,025	2,039	7,082	928
Springbok, South Africa	12,113	11,469	15,860	15,632	10,244	14,762	10,521	13,841	13,010	7,085	6,199	8,623	11,222	5,310	8,818	12,189	7,063	8,829	12,295	8,950
Springfield, Illinois	13,686	3,548	4,186	2,860	15,769	1,313	15,958	390	622	11,589	15,992	7,208	15,098	12,525	8,817	14,240	11,757	8,988	1,215	7,504
Springfield, Massachusetts	14,257	3,854	4,801	3,716	16,221	2,726	16,857	1,743	864	10,427	14,853	5,918	15,887	11,180	7,729	15,194	10,602	7,919	411	6,306
Srinagar, India	5,999	14,728	8,717	9,947	6,366	11,831	7,687	11,543	11,248	2,521	4,591	5,875	7,132	4,064	3,646	7,635	2,448	3,431	11,342	5,188
Stanley, Falkland Islands	15,046	7,067	14,626	13,221	13,285	11,114	12,360	10,900	10,700	13,477	11,941	12,499	13,321	11,770	14,149	13,534	13,492	14,282	10,212	13,225
Stara Zagora, Bulgaria	10,297	10,834	8,126	8,659	10,620	9,639	11,936	8,891	8,225	2,858	7,266	1,712	11,463	3,814	991	11,966	3,037	1,138	7,986	1,318
Stockholm, Sweden	10,313	9,795	6,186	6,718	11,236	7,846	12,529	7,196	6,642	4,424	8,809	1,588	11,811	5,695	1,636	12,017	4,586	1,802	6,553	961
Stornoway, United Kingdom	11,594	8,398	5,872	6,064	12,633	6,817	13,915	6,058	5,412	5,612	10,044	1,432	13,158	6,625	2,905	13,275	5,785	3,101	5,239	1,516
Strasbourg, France	11,395	9,326	7,190	7,472	12,010	8,203	13,332	7,405	6,704	4,410	8,813	248	12,749	5,247	2,001	13,105	4,589	2,216	6,439	511
Stuttgart, West Germany	11,291	9,429	7,198	7,505	11,903	8,266	13,225	7,476	6,783	4,317	8,725	350	12,642	5,179	1,894	13,001	4,495	2,109	6,526	415
Subic, Philippines	1,045	16,428	9,024	10,376	2,661	12,366	3,579	12,856	13,238	7,335	5,821	10,599	2,658	8,321	8,438	2,756	7,206	8,235	13,803	9,846
Suchow, China	3,134	14,850	7,245	8,648	4,754	10,740	5,748	11,038	11,276	6,398	6,587	8,729	4,821	7,834	6,719	4,780	6,320	6,537	11,771	7,971
Sucre, Bolivia	18,247	3,574	11,146	9,759	16,942	7,703	15,871	7,320	7,035	13,410	14,547	10,145	16,734	12,352	12,319	16,539	13,535	12,524	6,530	10,894
Sudbury, Canada	13,517	4,221	4,004	2,887	15,537	2,082	16,058	1,147	491	10,568	14,981	6,195	15,103	11,518	7,801	14,376	10,737	7,975	929	6,481
Suez, Egypt	9,918	11,888	9,557	10,161	9,791	11,132	11,058	10,354	9,648	1,773	5,932	3,047	10,774	2,310	2,063	11,457	1,942	2,052	9,345	2,814
Sundsvall, Sweden	10,239	9,679	5,845	6,395	11,262	7,572	12,537	6,951	6,429	4,684	9,035	1,846	11,782	6,004	1,900	11,934	4,842	2,047	6,377	1,280
Surabaya, Indonesia	2,131	18,358	11,590	12,915	313	14,814	1,623	15,403	15,822	7,707	4,452	11,935	1,421	7,983	9,716	2,380	7,537	9,501	16,375	11,262
Suva, Fiji	6,436	11,268	9,805	9,996	6,895	10,187	5,790	11,163	12,038	14,657	11,435	16,713	5,804	15,178	15,308	4,990	14,513	15,155	12,631	16,111
Sverdlovsk, USSR	7,847	12,024	6,486	7,518	8,794	9,215	10,068	8,832	8,500	3,495	7,196	3,838	9,330	5,239	1,953	9,558	3,581	1,824	8,598	3,079
Svobodnyy, USSR	4,921	12,760	5,163	6,570	6,768	8,672	7,623	8,940	9,191	6,956	8,393	7,798	6,647	8,663	6,224	6,361	6,942	6,097	9,712	7,086
Sydney, Australia	5,276	13,870	12,422	12,958	4,622	13,400	3,306	14,379	15,255	12,555	8,528	16,826	3,843	12,386	14,596	3,573	12,379	14,382	15,844	16,106
Sydney, Canada	14,083	4,690	5,037	4,209	15,825	3,675	16,786	2,714	1,868	9,363	13,778	4,835	15,802	10,092	6,704	15,321	9,540	6,899	1,475	5,247
Syktyvkar, USSR	8,517	11,251	6,031	6,958	9,547	8,554	10,810	8,120	7,754	3,930	7,877	3,276	10,046	5,592	1,775	10,220	4,043	1,728	7,834	2,530
Szeged, Hungary	10,615	10,293	7,641	8,106	11,087	9,034	12,409	8,281	7,615	3,450	7,870	1,161	11,877	4,413	1,143	12,310	3,628	1,349	7,384	711
Szombathely, Hungary	10,841	10,004	7,487	7,901	11,360	8,776	12,682	8,010	7,336	3,740	8,156	877	12,133	4,667	1,378	12,542	3,918	1,590	7,096	473
Tabriz, Iran	8,595	12,621	8,669	9,527	8,803	10,905	10,119	10,294	9,735	1,355	5,711	3,489	9,666	2,951	1,470	10,223	1,503	1,300	9,599	2,926
Tacheng, China	5,984	13,724	7,173	8,438	6,920	10,392	8,181	10,213	10,040	3,669	6,081	5,661	7,437	5,394	3,553	7,695	3,658	3,364	10,252	4,907
Tahiti (Papeete)	9,708	7,919	9,089	8,578	10,278	7,848	9,123	8,713	9,497	17,777	14,655	15,973	9,194	18,511	16,551	8,366	17,683	16,560	9,915	16,005
Taipei, Taiwan	2,037	15,492	7,958	9,332	3,790	11,370	4,691	11,792	12,132	7,067	6,411	9,788	3,743	8,314	7,721	3,677	6,964	7,530	12,680	9,029
Taiyuan, China	3,657	14,650	7,087	8,494	5,157	10,599	6,216	10,815	10,984	5,921	6,508	8,154	5,314	7,424	6,143	5,327	5,854	5,962	11,436	7,395
Tallahassee, Florida	14,781	2,444	5,327	3,979	16,865	2,144	16,845	1,494	1,324	12,079	16,489	7,543	16,085	12,725	9,392	15,160	12,256	9,581	1,254	7,961
Tallinn, USSR	9,944	10,158	6,243	6,861	10,855	8,087	12,148	7,473	6,948	4,168	8,514	1,867	11,433	5,524	1,390	11,651	4,323	1,529	6,886	1,162
Tamanrasset, Algeria	12,721	9,449	9,909	9,916	12,401	10,031	13,575	9,080	8,228	4,516	8,005	2,722	13,459	4,176	3,857	14,220	4,667	4,000	7,704	3,217
Tampa, Florida	15,106	2,161	5,655	4,308	17,188	2,451	17,107	1,822	1,597	12,158	16,527	7,601	16,382	12,712	9,512	15,443	12,336	9,706	1,398	8,052
Tampere, Finland	9,943	10,031	6,005	6,626	10,923	7,872	12,205	7,272	6,766	4,382	8,707	1,978	11,464	5,758	1,616	11,645	4,536	1,746	6,724	1,315
Tanami, Australia	3,026	16,343	12,026	13,073	2,002	14,402	707	15,300	16,073	9,998	6,325	14,218	1,342	10,099	11,989	1,647	9,825	11,774	16,798	13,521
Tangier, Morocco	13,070	8,265	8,212	8,121	13,359	8,256	14,655	7,324	6,493	5,370	9,435	1,562	14,253	5,590	3,601	14,756	5,546	3,804	6,023	2,305
Tarawa (Betio)	5,290	11,607	7,951	8,454	6,498	9,238	5,786	10,200	11,059	13,175	11,199	14,487	5,368	14,300	13,169	4,375	13,073	13,038	11,757	13,874
Tashkent, USSR	6,711	13,788	8,050	9,207	7,253	11,008	8,568	10,668	10,332	2,424	5,398	5,024	7,962	4,167	2,798	8,390	2,421	2,585	10,408	4,313
Tbilisi, USSR	8,733	12,291	8,273	9,111	9,063	10,483	10,384	9,879	9,331	1,778	6,118	3,185	9,884	3,339	1,073	10,390	1,925	889	9,212	2,577
Tegucigalpa, Honduras	15,713	816	6,824	5,419	17,515	3,330	16,713	3,109	3,155	13,595	17,685	9,037	16,408	13,860	11,049	15,407	13,775	11,250	3,004	9,551
Tehran, Iran	8,128	13,150	8,907	9,842	8,279	11,314	9,593	10,741	10,211	1,046	5,243	4,019	9,155	2,794	1,959	9,735	1,151	1,772	10,098	3,448
Tel Aviv, Israel	9,679	11,999	9,336	9,987	9,631	11,042	10,913	10,293	9,613	1,624	5,914	3,033	10,589	2,424	1,819	11,243	1,800	1,788	9,343	2,722
Telegraph Creek, Canada	10,119	6,879	818	708	12,202	2,754	12,518	3,195	3,748	10,673	14,040	7,667	11,592	12,284	8,147	10,820	10,783	8,222	4,444	7,512
Teresina, Brazil	18,736	4,645	10,833	9,690	17,156	8,055	17,124	7,292	6,640	10,558	12,713	7,456	18,035	9,693	9,536	18,763	10,692	9,732	5,942	8,215
Ternate, Indonesia	721	16,571	10,081	11,312	1,708	13,066	2,044	13,767	14,342	8,706	6,171	12,313	1,054	9,374	10,122	1,049	8,557	9,914	15,005	11,567
The Valley, Anguilla	17,071	2,350	7,552	6,329	18,949	4,683	19,319	3,903	3,291	11,298	15,070	6,910	18,612	11,291	9,103	17,707	11,474	9,317	2,632	7,551
Thessaloniki, Greece	10,560	10,679	8,294	8,771	10,824	9,664	12,136	8,887	8,194	2,968	7,334	1,613	11,692	3,779	1,290	12,220	3,148	1,437	7,921	1,358
Thimphu, Bhutan	4,409	15,938	8,989	10,348	4,856	12,404	6,164	12,344	12,234	3,918	4,284	7,433	5,555	5,159	5,203	6,037	3,803	4,990	12,465	6,723
Thunder Bay, Canada	12,982	4,477	3,437	2,249	15,038	1,577	15,453	829	833	10,801	15,140	6,575	14,518	11,888	8,013	13,755	10,963	8,173	1,508	6,786
Tientsin, China	3,651	14,365	6,770	8,176	5,294	10,277	6,283	10,539	10,754	6,305	6,911	8,318	5,349	7,834	6,375	5,271	6,243	6,202	11,239	7,562
Tijuana, Mexico	12,088	4,451	3,834	2,594	14,048	1,344	13,757	2,301	3,172	13,354	17,052	9,441	13,088	14,689	10,614	12,117	13,493	10,740	3,785	9,570
Tiksi, USSR	7,170	10,832	3,661	4,896	8,961	6,958	9,869	7,014	7,120	6,856	9,661	6,097	8,896	8,635	5,118	8,595	6,912	5,070	7,571	5,485
Timbuktu, Mali	13,792	8,629	10,301	10,072	13,291	9,820	14,373	8,842	7,964	5,569	8,717	3,468	14,391	5,006	4,919	15,221	5,712	5,074	7,359	4,086
Tindouf, Algeria	13,737	8,039	8,985	8,762	13,738	8,637	14,970	7,671	6,806	5,731	9,471	2,461	14,733	5,623	4,349	15,369	5,897	4,539	6,252	3,180
Tirane, Albania	10,793	10,407	8,178	8,605	11,090	9,441	12,403	8,650	7,946	3,238	7,595	1,353	11,949	4,004	1,431	12,461	3,418	1,601	7,663	1,177
Tokyo, Japan	3,485	13,429	6,068	7,383	5,544	9,348	6,108	9,871	10,334	8,327	8,488	9,768	5,120	9,856	8,091	4,627	8,269	7,945	10,962	9,048
Toledo, Spain	12,691	8,428	7,837	7,824	13,109	8,103	14,421	7,198	6,393	5,192	9,387	1,102	13,948	5,583	3,223	14,391	5,370	3,431	5,975	1,856
Topeka, Kansas	13,370	3,641	3,979	2,598	15,453	806	15,524	331	1,126	11,948	16,296	7,644	14,703	12,968	9,163	13,812	12,112	9,325	1,738	7,902
Toronto, Canada	13,852	3,916	4,330	3,179	15,876	2,166	16,375	1,189	334	10,710	15,139	6,274	15,428	11,581	7,963	14,683	10,882	8,143	595	6,601
Toulouse, France	12,087	8,876	7,584	7,710	12,581	8,198	13,900	7,335	6,572	4,764	9,068	499	13,381	5,343	2,631	13,792	4,943	2,842	6,220	1,243
Tours, France	11,921	8,807	7,166	7,320	12,553	7,887	13,875	7,050	6,313	4,887	9,257	327	13,291	5,603	2,545	13,633	5,067	2,760	6,004	1,034
Townsville, Australia	3,726	14,598	11,152	11,939	3,601	12,893	2,457	13,852	14,705	11,582	8,115	15,366	2,578	11,854	13,190	2,021	11,417	12,982	15,409	14,612
Trenton, New Jersey	14,370	3,603	4,864	3,719	16,371	2,570	16,915	1,592	732	10,702	15,126	6,187	15,964	11,438	8,007	15,224	10,877	8,196	135	6,581
Tripoli, Lebanon	9,551	11,987	9,077	9,756	9,590	10,864	10,884	10,138	9,480	1,640	6,015	2,939	10,520	2,635	1,558	11,141	1,820	1,515	9,237	2,565
Tripoli, Libya	11,637	10,029	8,990	9,235	11,654	9,759	12,925	8,881	8,096	3,634	7,679	1,743	12,615	3,861	2,509	13,245	3,806	2,658	7,695	2,017
Tristan da Cunha (Edinburgh)	14,624	8,851	15,421	14,388	12,574	12,714	12,429	11,997	11,343	9,582	9,058	9,503	13,327	7,907	10,564	14,135	9,603	10,651	10,635	10,087
Trondheim, Norway	10,518	9,315	5,646	6,124	11,597	7,237	12,862	6,599	6,065	5,027	9,394	1,823	12,087	6,302	2,238	12,201	5,187	2,395	6,009	1,391
Trujillo, Peru	17,317	1,869	9,439	8,034	17,582	5,935	16,261	5,702	5,601	14,305	16,431	10,222	16,735	13,693	12,445	16,035	14,465	12,660	5,246	10,900
Truk Island (Moen)	2,901	13,760	8,239	9,198	4,438	10,597	4,139	11,445	12,192	10,809	8,969	13,122	3,412	11,868	11,305	2,444	10,694	11,135	12,916	12,390
Truro, Canada	14,131	4,488	4,960	4,071	15,933	3,443	16,828	2,476	1,622	9,611	14,030	5,088	15,838	10,348	6,942	15,304	9,788	7,136	1,222	5,494
Tsingtao, China	3,256	14,538	6,933	8,332	4,978	10,419	5,917	10,740	11,005	6,636	6,935	8,756	4,969	8,113	6,804	4,853	6,566	6,630	11,519	8,000
Tsitsihar, China	4,469	13,301	5,705	7,111	6,265	9,213	7,162	9,479	9,719	6,719	7,893	7,964	6,196	8,378	6,250	5,972	6,689	6,106	10,228	7,232
Tubuai Island (Mataura)	9,811	8,093	9,732	9,195	10,176	8,375	8,963	9,208	9,964	18,026	14,343	16,519	9,133	18,154	17,194	8,368	17,892	17,197	10,336	16,612
Tucson, Arizona	12,623	3,951	4,052	2,715	14,604	993	14,327	1,858	2,702	13,228	17,228	9,130	13,655	14,435	10,452	12,686	13,378	10,592	3,277	9,316
Tulsa, Oklahoma	13,562	3,361	4,246	2,851	15,635	891	15,612	634	1,302	12,232	16,602	7,885	14,832	13,205	9,450	13,914	12,398	9,616	1,825	8,166
Tunis, Tunisia	11,745	9,688	8,508	8,727	11,923	9,256	13,217	8,387	7,611	3,936	8,104	1,243	12,835	4,320	2,395	13,397	4,113	2,572	7,231	1,609
Tura, USSR	6,662	11,937	4,957	6,249	8,186	8,262	9,265	8,204	8,181	5,516	8,276	5,638	8,352	7,300	4,169	8,265	5,556	4,071	8,531	4,928
Turin, Italy	11,572	9,361	7,568	7,814	12,065	8,465	13,386	7,638	6,909	4,305	8,661	325	12,858	5,011	2,110	13,274	4,485	2,320	6,602	806
Uberlandia, Brazil	18,541	4,816	11,935	10,651	16,466	8,761	15,902	8,165	7,665	11,739	12,910	9,064	16,893	10,579	11,082	17,259	11,849	11,268	7,029	9,822
Ufa, USSR	8,069	12,009	6,764	7,749	8,914	9,380	10,206	8,947	8,568	3,193	7,048	3,582	9,505	4,915	1,603	9,781	3,290	1,462	8,623	2,825
Ujungpandang, Indonesia	1,513	17,596	11,058	12,336	605	14,151	1,425	14,813	15,327	8,224	5,203	12,252	780	8,641	10,021	1,644	8,060	9,807	15,949	11,542
Ulaanbaatar, Mongolia	4,863	13,696	6,321	7,706	6,319	9,799	7,413	9,887	9,959	5,438	6,992	7,039	6,520	7,109	5,140	6,521	5,410	4,978	10,356	6,285
Ulan-Ude, USSR	5,231	13,258	5,915	7,293	6,741	9,380	7,815	9,453	9,520	5,540	7,364	6,791	6,908	7,255	4,987	6,866	5,527	4,837	9,919	6,044
Uliastay, Mongolia	5,269	13,781	6,677	8,024	6,506	10,077	7,685	10,055	10,025	4,692	6,557	6,469	6,849	6,381	4,477	6,768	4,668	4,303	10,348	5,710
Uranium City, Canada	11,221	6,086	1,681	811	13,278	2,220	13,733	2,252	2,595	10,291	14,209	6,721	12,779	11,721	7,584	12,062	10,427	7,697	3,243	6,693
Urumqi, China	5,498	14,134	7,358	8,665	6,444	10,667	7,964	10,546	10,419	3,883	5,866	6,145	6,948	5,548	4,017	7,209	3,850	3,824	10,662	5,392
Ushuaia, Argentina	14,568	7,131	14,516	13,135	12,965	11,044	11,936	10,949	10,855	14,164	12,217	13,234	12,866	12,426	14,925	12,976	14,167	15,059	10,434	13,968
Vaduz, Liechtenstein	11,343	9,475	7,376	7,673	11,898	8,407	13,220	7,606	6,900	4,234	8,627	341	12,662	5,045	1,904	13,050	4,414	2,118	6,626	531
Valencia, Spain	12,448	8,741	7,977	8,027	12,811	8,376	14,120	7,480	6,683	4,878	9,074	975	13,668	5,276	2,977	14,140	5,056	3,181	6,277	1,693
Valladolid, Spain	12,629	8,373	7,630	7,626	13,120	7,936	14,438	7,039	6,243	5,252	9,493	997	13,929	5,709	3,179	14,336	5,431	3,391	5,842	1,756
Valletta, Malta	11,414	10,089	8,688	8,981	11,535	9,596	12,824	8,742	7,978	3,539	7,709	1,492	12,462	3,941	2,179	13,049	3,715	2,337	7,613	1,684
Valparaiso, Chile	16,631	4,730	12,272	10,866	15,335	8,760	14,205	8,564	8,426	14,411	14,150	11,727	15,059	13,015	13,838	14,924	14,498	14,032	8,003	12,484
Vancouver, Canada	10,925	5,896	1,916	751	13,004	1,780	13,132	2,442	3,169	11,610	15,137	8,200	12,269	13,132	8,977	11,412	11,733	9,074	3,895	8,160
Varna, Bulgaria	10,096	10,980	8,058	8,634	10,446	9,673	11,764	8,946	8,299	2,751	7,175	1,847	11,276	3,800	799	11,769	2,928	935	8,080	1,379
Venice, Italy	11,218	9,719	7,613	7,942	11,695	8,696	13,016	7,895	7,187	3,966	8,347	601	12,490	4,755	1,748	12,917	4,146	1,957	6,907	631

Distances in Kilometers	Davao, Philippines	David, Panama	Dawson, Canada	Dawson Creek, Canada	Denpasar, Indonesia	Denver, Colorado	Derby, Australia	Des Moines, Iowa	Detroit, Michigan	Dhahran, Saudi Arabia	Diego Garcia Island	Dijon, France	Dili, Indonesia	Djibouti, Djibouti	Dnepropetrovsk, USSR	Dobo, Indonesia	Doha, Qatar	Donetsk, USSR	Dover, Delaware	Dresden, East Germany
Veracruz, Mexico	14,607	1,899	5,936	4,534	16,457	2,430	15,833	2,493	2,846	13,800	18,215	9,269	15,388	14,408	11,087	14,385	13,976	11,270	2,970	9,680
Verona, Italy	11,316	9,615	7,589	7,895	11,800	8,622	13,121	7,814	7,101	4,066	8,442	505	12,594	4,834	1,848	13,016	4,246	2,058	6,814	655
Victoria, Canada	10,940	5,858	1,992	844	13,016	1,754	13,123	2,448	3,191	11,702	15,214	8,285	12,267	13,224	9,069	11,403	11,825	9,166	3,917	8,250
Victoria, Seychelles	7,900	15,362	13,300	14,319	6,618	15,651	7,549	14,893	14,164	3,468	1,902	7,573	7,758	2,252	6,208	8,727	3,335	6,079	13,786	7,335
Vienna, Austria	10,823	9,962	7,378	7,796	11,378	8,683	12,700	7,924	7,256	3,806	8,228	856	12,135	4,761	1,377	12,528	3,983	1,591	7,026	369
Vientiane, Laos	2,771	17,034	9,496	10,903	3,254	13,008	4,531	13,204	13,304	5,455	4,340	9,115	3,870	6,414	6,889	4,354	5,318	6,676	13,678	8,396
Villahermosa, Mexico	14,969	1,550	6,190	4,784	16,820	2,678	16,162	2,618	2,857	13,695	18,046	9,139	15,745	14,195	11,026	14,741	13,873	11,215	2,887	9,584
Vilnius, USSR	10,027	10,365	6,770	7,366	10,780	8,526	12,092	7,871	7,303	3,747	8,143	1,635	11,438	5,030	963	11,739	3,910	1,141	7,189	876
Visby, Sweden	10,359	9,853	6,374	6,895	11,226	7,995	12,527	7,329	6,758	4,288	8,689	1,455	11,831	5,527	1,508	12,068	4,453	1,686	6,648	790
Vitoria, Brazil	17,912	5,598	12,457	11,240	15,844	9,439	15,495	8,778	8,206	11,037	12,068	8,758	16,465	9,794	10,647	17,060	11,136	10,820	7,535	9,505
Vladivostok, USSR	4,044	13,327	5,746	7,131	5,979	9,197	6,744	9,577	9,917	7,424	8,189	8,712	5,759	9,038	7,030	5,420	7,383	6,887	10,482	7,987
Volgograd, USSR	8,776	11,834	7,491	8,332	9,353	9,751	10,672	9,187	8,685	2,541	6,788	2,910	10,075	4,121	696	10,473	2,677	497	8,620	2,202
Vologda, USSR	9,091	10,943	6,330	7,134	10,004	8,571	11,292	8,045	7,596	3,742	7,925	2,634	10,571	5,291	1,240	10,800	3,877	1,256	7,599	1,882
Vorkuta, USSR	8,101	11,169	5,288	6,327	9,367	8,077	10,563	7,762	7,513	4,677	8,328	3,973	9,721	6,396	2,678	9,768	4,770	2,630	7,698	3,265
Wake Island	4,637	11,863	6,375	7,203	6,431	8,530	6,206	9,385	10,150	11,513	10,726	12,404	5,457	12,955	11,108	4,507	11,446	10,990	10,875	11,778
Wallis Island	6,820	10,632	9,129	9,247	7,496	9,398	6,456	10,374	11,249	15,000	12,118	16,231	6,378	15,762	15,174	5,502	14,874	15,050	11,846	15,724
Walvis Bay, Namibia	12,480	11,085	15,052	14,828	10,727	14,090	11,127	13,143	12,293	6,666	6,418	7,840	11,760	4,936	8,167	12,749	6,667	8,196	11,588	8,197
Warsaw, Poland	10,372	10,174	6,995	7,513	11,050	8,560	12,368	7,860	7,248	3,773	8,201	1,272	11,747	4,928	1,079	12,082	3,944	1,287	7,086	519
Washington, D.C.	14,410	3,417	4,875	3,682	16,441	2,403	16,892	1,440	636	10,945	15,370	6,432	15,964	11,679	8,246	15,184	11,121	8,434	133	6,825
Watson Lake, Canada	10,181	6,905	707	701	12,258	2,806	12,631	3,158	3,652	10,427	13,884	7,385	11,691	12,022	7,880	10,947	10,540	7,958	4,332	7,231
Weimar, East Germany	11,050	9,548	6,996	7,358	11,725	8,207	13,044	7,446	6,780	4,270	8,697	614	12,432	5,236	1,722	12,761	4,446	1,936	6,560	171
Wellington, New Zealand	7,332	11,694	12,354	12,375	6,853	12,091	5,536	12,993	13,794	14,731	10,498	18,961	6,038	14,287	16,785	5,626	14,551	16,574	14,203	18,202
West Berlin, West Germany	10,851	9,663	6,864	7,271	11,567	8,190	12,884	7,452	6,809	4,220	8,652	834	12,252	5,262	1,590	12,563	4,394	1,801	6,616	165
Wewak, Papua New Guinea	2,322	14,912	9,727	10,717	3,194	12,085	2,661	12,953	13,710	10,538	7,897	13,750	2,074	11,239	11,674	1,073	10,394	11,478	14,435	12,991
Whangarei, New Zealand	6,956	11,750	11,783	11,875	6,677	11,747	5,382	12,680	13,513	14,668	10,605	18,447	5,780	14,449	16,423	5,271	14,492	16,220	13,985	17,708
Whitehorse, Canada	9,831	7,230	436	1,027	11,909	3,116	12,283	3,503	4,002	10,349	13,657	7,501	11,341	11,986	7,869	10,602	10,454	7,935	4,681	7,304
Wichita, Kansas	13,355	3,572	4,034	2,639	15,431	703	15,438	536	1,321	12,152	16,488	7,853	14,643	13,177	9,366	13,734	12,315	9,527	1,906	8,110
Willemstad, Curacao	17,353	1,532	7,855	6,540	19,428	4,678	18,560	4,052	3,617	12,187	15,768	7,821	18,397	12,085	10,013	17,394	12,362	10,227	3,066	8,461
Wiluna, Australia	3,770	16,898	13,132	14,246	2,056	15,616	1,088	16,516	17,274	9,522	5,478	14,001	2,076	9,331	11,840	2,743	9,343	11,628	17,995	13,390
Windhoek, Namibia	12,216	11,346	15,082	14,938	10,476	14,289	10,899	13,334	12,477	6,476	6,150	7,835	11,516	4,731	8,067	12,508	6,471	8,087	11,777	8,163
Windsor, Canada	13,820	3,753	4,275	3,055	15,875	1,864	16,263	882	5	11,022	15,447	6,602	15,343	11,912	8,267	14,553	11,193	8,443	722	6,920
Winnipeg, Canada	12,472	4,795	2,936	1,678	14,546	1,285	14,888	962	1,372	10,971	15,189	6,910	13,968	12,178	8,187	13,181	11,125	8,332	2,079	7,054
Winston-Salem, North Carolina	14,522	3,072	4,979	3,714	16,590	2,206	16,876	1,309	733	11,365	15,788	6,847	15,997	12,079	8,665	15,157	11,540	8,853	537	7,244
Wroclaw, Poland	10,672	9,939	7,071	7,522	11,324	8,477	12,644	7,745	7,105	3,924	8,356	970	12,037	4,980	1,323	12,382	4,098	1,536	6,911	230
Wuhan, China	2,860	15,337	7,734	9,137	4,343	11,231	5,393	11,519	11,740	6,216	6,126	8,864	4,496	7,566	6,782	4,550	6,124	6,590	12,217	8,105
Wyndham, Australia	2,507	16,623	11,660	12,769	1,592	14,237	518	15,088	15,808	9,611	6,128	13,739	813	9,826	11,509	1,264	9,441	11,294	16,522	13,031
Xi'an, China	3,466	15,132	7,592	8,998	4,796	11,104	5,917	11,297	11,436	5,646	5,996	8,223	5,055	7,071	6,133	5,169	5,564	5,941	11,862	7,465
Xining, China	4,070	14,999	7,632	9,023	5,204	11,119	6,395	11,205	11,248	4,979	5,749	7,581	5,584	6,458	5,460	5,782	4,904	5,265	11,610	6,826
Yakutsk, USSR	6,105	11,720	4,213	5,609	7,933	7,713	8,807	7,885	8,073	6,918	9,105	6,926	7,831	8,694	5,640	7,525	6,941	5,551	8,565	6,260
Yanji, China	3,987	13,470	5,877	7,268	5,888	9,342	6,691	9,703	10,022	7,242	8,004	8,625	5,709	8,849	6,904	5,408	7,199	6,757	10,575	7,894
Yaounde, Cameroon	12,613	10,392	12,096	12,079	11,587	11,956	12,493	10,978	10,101	4,803	6,876	4,856	12,726	3,588	5,422	13,679	4,887	5,497	9,490	5,234
Yap Island (Colonia)	1,407	15,117	8,692	9,857	3,239	11,547	3,368	12,279	12,906	9,355	7,522	12,201	2,436	10,344	10,177	1,745	9,230	9,989	13,597	11,443
Yaraka, Australia	4,063	14,777	11,835	12,606	3,550	13,475	2,281	14,447	15,312	11,566	7,828	15,645	2,670	11,644	13,424	2,363	11,394	13,211	16,000	14,912
Yarmouth, Canada	14,247	4,231	4,960	3,999	16,104	3,233	16,925	2,256	1,387	9,895	14,312	5,369	15,935	10,620	7,223	15,346	10,071	7,417	941	5,777
Yellowknife, Canada	10,786	6,527	1,263	817	12,838	2,604	13,321	2,696	3,033	10,071	13,863	6,708	12,359	11,567	7,412	11,664	10,199	7,512	3,669	6,620
Yerevan, USSR	8,753	12,364	8,442	9,274	9,028	10,630	10,346	10,014	9,455	1,626	5,991	3,240	9,869	3,170	1,190	10,398	1,778	1,020	9,322	2,659
Yinchuan, China	3,983	14,735	7,275	8,674	5,297	10,778	6,432	10,913	11,007	5,372	6,166	7,727	5,575	6,886	5,666	5,682	5,305	5,479	11,407	6,968
Yogyakarta, Indonesia	2,358	18,625	11,758	13,098	543	15,028	1,783	15,584	15,960	7,516	4,187	11,801	1,677	7,745	9,592	2,646	7,344	9,377	16,482	11,142
York, United Kingdom	11,636	8,683	6,445	6,649	12,496	7,352	13,805	6,565	5,883	5,175	9,602	846	13,120	6,094	2,570	13,341	5,352	2,778	5,655	1,058
Yumen, China	4,572	14,661	7,449	8,821	5,662	10,897	6,873	10,915	10,904	4,631	5,836	7,080	6,076	6,187	4,967	6,284	4,571	4,774	11,230	6,324
Yutian, China	5,532	14,726	8,248	9,532	6,134	11,495	7,438	11,304	11,099	3,199	4,988	6,190	6,797	4,760	3,971	7,210	3,135	3,760	11,271	5,468
Yuzhno-Sakhalinsk, USSR	4,713	12,428	4,901	6,262	6,735	8,300	7,369	8,734	9,136	8,109	9,139	8,784	6,379	9,791	7,346	5,900	8,087	7,230	9,740	8,102
Zagreb, Yugoslavia	10,938	9,991	7,634	8,027	11,409	8,863	12,730	8,083	7,394	3,715	8,116	858	12,203	4,581	1,466	12,634	3,895	1,673	7,136	607
Zahedan, Iran	7,187	14,268	9,481	10,557	7,188	12,201	8,495	11,711	11,238	1,114	4,259	5,137	8,100	2,702	3,047	8,735	1,034	2,849	11,168	4,560
Zamboanga, Philippines	391	16,824	9,733	11,042	1,880	12,947	2,682	13,531	13,991	7,878	5,733	11,417	1,752	8,663	9,225	1,945	7,734	9,017	14,595	10,672
Zanzibar, Tanzania	9,709	13,591	13,578	14,211	8,386	14,854	9,228	13,930	13,091	3,782	3,676	6,810	9,522	2,013	6,064	10,505	3,727	6,002	12,568	6,792
Zaragoza, Spain	12,362	8,692	7,735	7,798	12,809	8,189	14,125	7,305	6,521	4,932	9,184	786	13,632	5,415	2,897	14,064	5,112	3,106	6,136	1,533
Zashiversk, USSR	6,825	10,863	3,356	4,748	8,721	6,851	9,526	7,028	7,240	7,437	9,927	6,789	8,540	9,222	5,814	8,150	7,481	5,760	7,755	6,188
Zhengzhou, China	3,301	14,936	7,348	8,754	4,806	10,856	5,856	11,107	11,301	6,071	6,362	8,478	4,954	7,511	6,438	4,977	5,993	6,252	11,767	7,719
Zurich, Switzerland	11,413	9,386	7,333	7,613	11,982	8,328	13,304	7,523	6,814	4,324	8,716	253	12,741	5,126	1,983	13,120	4,503	2,198	6,538	567

Distances in Kilometers

	Dubayy, United Arab Emir.	Dublin, Ireland	Duluth, Minnesota	Dunedin, New Zealand	Durango, Mexico	Durban, South Africa	Dushanbe, USSR	East London, South Africa	Easter Island (Hanga Roa)	Echo Bay, Canada	Edinburgh, United Kingdom	Edmonton, Canada	El Aaiun, Morocco	Elat, Israel	Elazig, Turkey	Eniwetok Atoll, Marshall Isls.	Erfurt, East Germany	Erzurum, Turkey	Esfahan, Iran	Essen, West Germany
Dublin, Ireland	5,919	0	5,813	19,143	8,433	9,895	5,759	10,123	13,239	5,574	349	6,393	2,962	4,246	3,799	12,738	1,208	3,848	5,076	926
Duluth, Minnesota	11,382	5,813	0	13,967	2,762	14,831	10,364	14,805	8,371	2,637	5,839	1,692	7,048	10,027	9,378	10,246	6,924	9,350	10,487	6,676
Dunedin, New Zealand	13,902	19,143	13,967	0	11,507	10,681	13,764	10,493	7,159	13,817	18,805	13,155	17,904	15,771	15,987	6,407	18,401	15,891	14,683	18,654
Durango, Mexico	14,142	8,433	2,762	11,507	0	15,609	13,044	15,321	5,686	4,768	8,508	3,359	8,966	12,680	12,114	9,810	9,598	12,098	13,248	9,334
Durban, South Africa	6,627	9,895	14,831	10,681	15,609	0	8,529	460	12,429	15,463	10,043	16,126	7,873	6,587	7,635	14,605	9,167	7,797	7,253	9,308
Dushanbe, USSR	1,945	5,759	10,364	13,764	13,044	8,529	0	8,982	18,730	8,389	5,500	9,798	7,530	3,260	2,564	9,521	4,647	2,371	1,683	4,919
East London, South Africa	7,075	10,123	14,805	10,493	15,321	460	8,982	0	11,969	15,695	10,290	16,213	7,956	6,966	8,026	14,805	9,453	8,193	7,686	9,580
Easter Island (Hanga Roa)	18,492	13,239	8,371	7,159	5,686	12,429	18,730	11,969	0	10,363	13,461	8,949	11,908	16,541	16,846	10,427	14,414	16,976	18,102	14,131
Echo Bay, Canada	9,861	5,574	2,637	13,817	4,768	15,463	8,389	15,695	10,363	0	5,421	1,419	7,913	9,154	8,226	8,380	6,323	8,118	9,021	6,166
Edinburgh, United Kingdom	5,768	349	5,839	18,805	8,508	10,043	5,500	10,290	13,461	5,421	0	6,312	3,293	4,189	3,655	12,412	1,091	3,684	4,907	837
Edmonton, Canada	11,206	6,393	1,692	13,155	3,359	16,126	9,798	16,213	8,949	1,419	6,312	0	8,262	10,308	9,455	8,611	7,318	9,369	10,345	7,119
El Aaiun, Morocco	6,759	2,962	7,048	17,904	8,966	7,873	7,530	7,956	11,908	7,913	3,293	8,262	0	4,694	4,998	15,699	3,343	5,171	6,195	3,187
Elat, Israel	2,065	4,246	10,027	15,771	12,680	6,587	3,260	6,966	16,541	9,154	4,189	10,308	4,694	0	1,087	12,773	3,102	1,287	1,627	3,355
Elazig, Turkey	2,120	3,799	9,378	15,987	12,114	7,635	2,564	8,026	16,846	8,226	3,655	9,455	4,998	1,087	0	11,912	2,591	224	1,304	2,874
Eniwetok Atoll, Marshall Isls.	11,132	12,738	10,246	6,407	9,810	14,605	9,521	14,805	10,427	8,380	12,412	8,611	15,699	12,773	11,912	0	12,546	11,690	11,194	12,635
Erfurt, East Germany	4,711	1,208	6,924	18,401	9,598	9,167	4,647	9,453	14,414	6,323	1,091	7,318	3,343	3,102	2,591	12,546	0	2,641	3,869	285
Erzurum, Turkey	2,085	3,848	9,350	15,891	12,098	7,797	2,371	8,193	16,976	8,118	3,684	9,369	5,171	1,287	224	11,690	2,641	0	1,228	2,926
Esfahan, Iran	894	5,076	10,487	14,683	13,248	7,253	1,683	7,686	18,102	9,021	4,907	10,345	6,195	1,627	1,304	11,194	3,869	1,228	0	4,154
Essen, West Germany	4,993	926	6,676	18,654	9,334	9,308	4,919	9,580	14,131	6,166	837	7,119	3,187	3,355	2,874	12,635	285	2,926	4,154	0
Eucla, Australia	10,040	15,718	16,163	3,889	14,740	8,996	9,959	9,060	11,038	14,220	15,449	14,570	16,333	12,008	12,101	5,962	14,579	12,002	10,797	14,860
Fargo, North Dakota	11,539	6,072	357	13,672	2,630	15,188	10,435	15,162	8,296	2,479	6,081	1,397	7,393	10,259	9,572	9,902	7,160	9,534	10,646	6,918
Faroe Islands (Torshavn)	6,106	968	5,350	18,199	8,074	10,731	5,582	10,987	13,289	4,735	710	5,683	3,902	4,702	4,039	11,798	1,636	4,031	5,221	1,441
Florence, Italy	4,467	1,666	7,477	18,368	10,068	8,397	4,768	8,672	14,459	7,077	1,698	8,009	2,864	2,626	2,401	13,220	803	2,517	3,703	911
Florianopolis, Brazil	12,558	9,853	9,327	10,969	8,299	7,611	14,163	7,217	5,957	11,909	10,201	10,939	7,142	10,903	11,692	16,352	10,479	11,908	12,501	10,302
Fort George, Canada	10,207	4,600	1,216	15,145	3,941	13,916	9,314	13,969	9,439	2,511	4,623	2,255	6,045	8,811	8,177	10,768	5,708	8,157	9,313	5,459
Fort McMurray, Canada	10,833	6,046	1,720	13,478	3,672	15,836	9,446	15,955	9,296	1,099	5,956	378	8,000	9,933	9,076	8,726	6,953	8,991	9,970	6,758
Fort Nelson, Canada	10,685	6,331	2,428	13,111	4,118	16,221	9,161	16,408	9,606	845	6,199	820	8,502	9,996	9,070	8,059	7,134	8,962	9,853	6,965
Fort Severn, Canada	10,346	4,950	1,069	14,711	3,811	14,466	9,295	14,539	9,441	1,961	4,932	1,675	6,594	9,090	8,381	10,166	5,999	8,340	9,453	5,766
Fort Smith, Arkansas	12,578	6,834	1,280	13,082	1,600	14,932	11,639	14,781	7,100	3,748	6,908	2,507	7,573	11,081	10,524	10,460	7,998	10,516	11,685	7,734
Fort Vermilion, Canada	10,698	6,106	2,053	13,375	3,922	15,963	9,251	16,117	9,500	863	5,995	563	8,178	9,892	9,002	8,445	6,963	8,906	9,847	6,781
Fort Wayne, Indiana	11,607	5,814	846	14,108	2,621	14,226	10,801	14,147	7,958	3,452	5,897	2,526	6,626	10,059	9,531	11,000	6,986	9,532	10,719	6,719
Fort-Chimo, Canada	9,405	3,801	2,028	15,896	4,749	13,311	8,580	13,412	10,188	2,658	3,813	2,815	5,456	7,999	7,366	11,038	4,897	7,349	8,513	4,650
Fort-de-France, Martinique	11,841	6,412	4,586	14,107	4,679	11,008	12,155	10,794	6,972	7,074	6,694	6,269	5,140	9,793	9,880	14,445	7,510	10,004	11,167	7,236
Fortaleza, Brazil	10,573	7,003	7,665	13,815	7,787	7,835	11,772	7,596	7,941	9,910	7,351	9,354	4,367	8,627	9,209	17,589	7,668	9,407	10,248	7,476
Frankfort, Kentucky	11,848	6,013	1,123	13,954	2,447	14,147	11,091	14,041	7,675	3,752	6,112	2,769	6,668	10,251	9,759	11,151	7,197	9,768	10,964	6,926
Frankfurt am Main, W. Ger.	4,838	1,090	6,860	18,585	9,513	9,128	4,824	9,404	14,254	6,349	1,024	7,308	3,156	3,173	2,719	12,712	192	2,780	4,007	189
Fredericton, Canada	10,192	4,303	1,953	15,684	4,177	12,887	9,645	12,885	9,177	3,744	4,426	3,411	5,107	8,528	8,082	11,993	5,500	8,107	9,322	5,224
Freeport, Bahamas	12,459	6,546	2,537	13,642	2,617	13,235	12,054	13,043	6,786	5,167	6,722	4,141	6,439	10,621	10,340	12,204	7,753	10,394	11,621	7,469
Freetown, Sierra Leone	7,462	5,012	8,478	15,848	9,778	6,359	8,738	6,334	11,051	9,804	5,333	9,922	2,066	5,533	6,202	17,739	5,212	6,412	7,159	5,111
Frobisher Bay, Canada	8,999	3,639	2,383	15,924	5,144	13,401	8,057	13,552	10,694	2,296	3,592	2,773	5,643	7,727	7,015	10,626	4,646	6,977	8,105	4,421
Frunze, USSR	2,633	5,799	9,984	13,633	12,593	9,205	688	9,660	18,220	7,872	5,511	9,289	7,841	3,817	2,999	8,960	4,768	2,787	2,309	5,024
Fukuoka, Japan	7,190	9,508	10,142	9,680	11,378	12,576	5,473	12,993	14,309	7,531	9,160	8,570	12,266	8,717	7,866	4,058	8,924	7,646	7,154	9,090
Funafuti Atoll, Tuvalu	13,814	15,011	10,600	4,221	9,018	14,570	12,366	14,496	7,753	9,691	14,743	9,316	17,574	15,625	14,807	2,897	15,171	14,585	14,012	15,190
Funchal, Madeira Island	6,954	2,452	6,386	18,407	8,416	8,565	7,503	8,656	11,804	7,212	2,797	7,565	703	4,910	5,048	15,120	3,056	5,198	6,307	2,853
Fuzhou, China	6,356	9,767	11,341	9,498	12,728	11,256	4,888	11,663	15,207	8,706	9,428	9,831	12,232	8,123	7,430	4,781	8,973	7,224	6,501	9,185
Gaborone, Botswana	6,368	9,182	14,075	11,418	15,043	766	8,305	948	12,543	14,757	9,345	15,363	7,108	6,077	7,149	15,210	8,506	7,326	6,908	8,632
Galapagos Islands (Santa Cruz)	15,440	9,674	5,256	10,666	3,135	12,968	15,304	12,581	3,572	7,722	9,889	6,375	8,780	13,419	13,388	11,926	10,862	13,479	14,693	10,577
Gander, Canada	9,262	3,354	2,787	16,647	5,142	12,148	8,831	12,197	10,031	4,021	3,496	4,022	4,287	7,566	7,146	12,400	4,557	7,180	8,402	4,278
Gangtok, India	3,325	7,926	11,796	11,552	14,146	8,811	2,224	9,262	18,245	9,402	7,645	10,795	9,720	5,216	4,724	7,828	6,852	4,550	3,599	7,119
Garyarsa, China	2,550	7,035	11,275	12,471	13,808	8,583	1,294	9,042	18,946	9,044	6,765	10,461	8,786	4,329	3,791	8,588	5,938	3,615	2,703	6,208
Gaspe, Canada	9,864	3,996	2,071	15,942	4,452	12,823	9,290	12,849	9,529	3,585	4,105	3,395	4,985	8,234	7,759	11,910	5,185	7,779	8,989	4,912
Gauhati, India	3,646	8,219	11,915	11,243	14,178	8,963	2,546	9,410	17,924	9,468	7,932	10,844	10,053	5,549	5,056	7,525	7,160	4,882	3,934	7,423
Gdansk, Poland	4,412	1,636	7,051	17,810	9,781	9,404	4,124	9,722	14,860	6,159	1,400	7,261	3,979	3,051	2,333	11,947	637	2,330	3,536	847
Geneva, Switzerland	4,915	1,193	6,999	18,809	9,585	8,787	5,093	9,044	14,066	6,678	1,262	7,566	2,716	3,106	2,823	13,185	641	2,919	4,127	587
Genoa, Italy	4,663	1,487	7,293	18,564	9,875	8,524	4,929	8,790	14,277	6,943	1,541	7,851	2,753	2,822	2,590	13,255	747	2,700	3,893	795
Georgetown, Guyana	12,010	6,953	5,488	13,660	5,312	10,309	12,596	10,059	6,676	7,993	7,259	7,164	5,253	9,946	10,182	15,120	7,973	10,330	11,429	7,713
Geraldton, Australia	8,716	14,546	16,955	5,186	16,095	7,917	0,043	0,050	12,246	14,551	14,322	15,263	14,932	10,639	10,810	6,789	13,358	10,731	9,509	13,643
Ghanzi, Botswana	6,322	8,727	13,532	11,900	14,560	1,303	8,267	1,407	12,493	14,293	8,904	14,839	6,578	5,830	6,914	15,682	8,105	7,101	6,790	8,216
Ghat, Libya	4,528	3,436	8,901	17,102	11,153	6,461	5,657	6,689	14,042	9,010	3,605	9,765	2,349	2,500	3,123	14,969	2,889	3,337	4,109	2,952
Gibraltar	5,841	1,913	6,973	18,871	9,254	8,235	6,389	8,404	12,934	7,315	2,205	7,918	1,241	3,815	3,919	14,576	2,105	4,070	5,179	1,965
Gijon, Spain	5,820	1,091	6,446	19,615	8,891	8,946	6,073	9,141	13,102	6,560	1,389	7,251	1,939	3,906	3,764	13,789	1,506	3,875	5,065	1,296
Gisborne, New Zealand	14,502	18,343	12,994	1,011	10,621	11,686	14,023	11,489	6,733	12,828	18,085	12,144	18,365	16,497	16,468	5,790	18,303	16,325	15,193	18,423
Glasgow, United Kingdom	5,831	307	5,787	18,838	8,451	10,067	5,567	10,310	13,395	5,396	66	6,275	3,264	4,243	3,717	12,438	1,147	3,748	4,971	889
Godthab, Greenland	8,278	2,811	3,127	16,730	5,871	12,608	7,479	12,780	11,301	2,975	2,769	3,593	4,942	6,924	6,251	11,134	3,832	6,228	7,385	3,601
Gomez Palacio, Mexico	13,940	8,227	2,561	11,710	207	15,547	12,862	15,278	5,868	4,618	8,301	3,216	8,787	12,473	11,908	9,890	9,391	11,893	13,045	9,127
Goose Bay, Canada	11,509	7,181	2,620	12,296	3,618	17,039	9,913	17,172	8,881	1,725	7,063	993	9,217	10,880	9,945	7,637	8,012	9,833	10,694	7,839
Gorki, USSR	3,569	3,174	7,869	16,199	10,624	9,628	2,693	10,019	16,138	6,343	2,878	7,651	5,530	3,060	1,994	10,601	2,235	1,836	2,695	2,460
Goteborg, Sweden	4,961	1,245	6,490	18,044	9,222	9,866	4,563	10,167	14,369	5,656	946	6,724	3,926	3,599	2,892	11,869	752	2,883	4,079	767
Granada, Spain	5,682	1,802	7,011	18,933	9,337	8,259	6,202	8,441	13,109	7,266	2,079	7,910	1,429	3,667	3,741	14,417	1,923	3,889	5,007	1,793
Grand Turk, Turks & Caicos	12,261	6,460	3,387	13,874	3,448	12,300	12,163	12,096	6,779	5,971	6,686	5,041	5,864	10,304	10,179	13,149	7,644	10,264	11,482	7,359
Graz, Austria	4,256	1,690	7,457	18,107	10,116	8,661	4,377	8,959	14,775	6,845	1,618	7,857	3,337	2,572	2,143	12,732	542	2,223	3,443	783
Green Bay, Wisconsin	11,428	5,736	408	14,109	2,729	14,503	10,516	14,455	8,230	3,006	5,790	2,100	6,785	9,976	9,385	10,635	6,880	9,371	10,535	6,622
Grenoble, France	4,929	1,255	7,047	18,831	9,614	8,694	5,156	8,946	14,025	6,770	1,350	7,642	2,611	3,089	2,850	13,303	758	2,954	4,154	705
Guadalajara, Mexico	14,427	8,646	3,071	11,344	397	15,351	13,399	15,040	5,331	5,157	8,738	3,751	9,004	12,883	12,369	10,022	9,825	12,364	13,534	9,556
Guam (Agana)	9,332	12,106	11,269	7,062	11,420	13,026	7,875	13,312	12,238	8,969	11,758	9,576	14,924	11,123	10,388	1,914	11,581	10,176	9,503	11,741
Guantanamo, Cuba	12,679	6,844	3,332	13,460	3,066	12,623	12,507	12,397	6,403	5,958	7,058	4,934	6,313	10,737	10,587	12,830	8,036	10,665	11,888	7,751
Guatemala City, Guatemala	14,253	8,337	3,568	11,856	1,813	13,837	13,738	13,527	5,055	6,070	8,507	4,763	8,049	12,397	12,134	11,504	9,545	12,184	13,411	9,262
Guayaquil, Ecuador	14,585	9,119	5,555	11,344	3,953	11,892	14,877	11,528	4,195	8,161	9,377	6,919	7,831	12,523	12,657	13,110	10,256	12,780	13,941	9,977
Guiyang, China	5,118	9,063	11,663	10,282	13,474	10,197	3,768	10,625	16,450	9,056	8,743	10,322	11,261	6,946	6,332	6,032	8,136	6,137	5,319	8,374
Gur'yev, USSR	2,443	4,088	9,029	15,428	11,782	8,778	1,673	9,196	17,258	7,422	3,836	8,763	6,001	2,437	1,392	10,569	2,978	1,170	1,605	3,248
Haifa, Israel	2,143	3,975	9,724	15,982	12,403	6,951	3,106	7,329	16,556	8,798	3,897	9,963	4,653	364	753	12,578	2,807	967	1,557	3,069
Haikou, China	5,646	9,870	12,270	9,485	13,838	10,126	4,474	10,530	15,916	9,638	9,552	10,838	12,000	7,567	7,030	5,623	8,927	6,844	5,948	9,169
Haiphong, Vietnam	5,257	9,588	12,280	9,791	13,997	9,852	4,116	10,265	16,304	9,663	9,276	10,907	11,646	7,184	6,665	6,004	8,616	6,482	5,568	8,864
Hakodate, Japan	7,825	9,005	8,900	10,146	10,107	13,709	5,954	14,144	13,556	6,317	8,661	7,303	11,919	9,054	8,085	3,954	8,635	7,861	7,614	8,752
Halifax, Canada	10,097	4,187	2,220	15,854	4,351	12,614	9,631	12,608	9,214	4,001	4,331	3,691	4,854	8,386	7,980	12,270	5,391	8,015	9,237	5,111
Hamburg, West Germany	4,879	1,078	6,686	18,377	9,380	9,460	4,693	9,748	14,317	6,033	889	7,040	3,496	3,346	2,767	12,333	294	2,797	4,020	309
Hamilton, Bermuda	11,019	5,148	2,826	15,113	4,000	12,210	10,815	12,104	8,103	5,135	5,358	4,504	4,974	9,135	8,912	13,057	6,345	8,981	10,208	6,060
Hamilton, New Zealand	14,258	18,272	13,117	981	10,794	11,650	13,764	11,470	6,989	12,837	17,986	12,207	18,592	16,265	16,212	5,622	18,089	16,068	14,940	18,232
Hangzhou, China	6,333	9,404	10,881	9,839	12,335	11,542	4,750	11,962	15,208	8,244	9,062	9,385	11,954	8,008	7,254	4,809	8,658	7,042	6,401	8,859
Hannover, West Germany	4,850	1,079	6,755	18,444	9,436	9,342	4,722	9,625	14,310	6,146	930	7,139	3,387	3,272	2,732	12,458	179	2,772	3,999	212
Hanoi, Vietnam	5,169	9,525	12,282	9,859	14,032	9,789	4,036	10,205	16,392	9,670	9,214	10,923	11,566	7,098	6,582	6,091	8,546	6,400	5,481	8,795
Harare, Zimbabwe	5,445	8,658	13,948	11,860	15,394	1,331	7,380	1,713	13,463	14,190	8,782	15,008	6,899	5,260	6,314	14,746	7,870	6,481	6,003	8,024
Harbin, China	6,628	8,151	9,077	11,023	10,708	12,729	4,742	13,180	14,711	6,440	7,803	7,618	10,973	7,846	6,892	5,074	7,639	6,668	6,399	7,785
Harrisburg, Pennsylvania	11,230	5,348	1,425	14,660	3,158	13,524	10,607	13,452	8,189	3,848	5,469	3,107	5,950	9,569	9,124	11,664	6,544	9,145	10,357	6,269
Hartford, Connecticut	10,863	4,969	1,644	15,050	3,549	13,224	10,295	13,173	8,517	3,875	5,097	3,276	5,583	9,183	8,752	11,879	6,169	8,779	9,994	5,892
Havana, Cuba	12,980	7,066	2,766	13,124	2,276	13,435	12,547	13,208	6,279	5,399	7,241	4,268	6,900	11,136	10,861	12,018	8,274	10,914	12,141	7,990
Helena, Montana	11,945	6,903	1,519	12,730	2,588	16,335	10,573	16,324	8,171	2,199	6,858	780	8,494	10,944	10,137	8,765	7,899	10,063	11,075	7,682
Helsinki, Finland	4,522	2,032	6,861	17,254	9,621	9,992	3,876	10,333	14,989	5,671	1,715	6,866	4,664	3,484	2,591	11,207	1,343	2,522	3,627	1,478
Hengyang, China	5,685	9,350	11,476	9,952	13,101	10,715	4,260	11,135	15,879	8,844	9,020	10,052	11,687	7,476	6,816	5,454	8,487	6,615	5,851	8,713
Herat, Afghanistan	1,205	5,649	10,661	13,982	13,399	7,824	754	8,274	18,888	8,872	5,429	10,259	7,100	2,622	2,107	10,204	4,475	1,954	999	4,758

Distances in Kilometers	Dubayy, United Arab Emir.	Dublin, Ireland	Duluth, Minnesota	Dunedin, New Zealand	Durango, Mexico	Durban, South Africa	Dushanbe, USSR	East London, South Africa	Easter Island (Hanga Roa)	Echo Bay, Canada	Edinburgh, United Kingdom	Edmonton, Canada	El Aaiun, Morocco	Elat, Israel	Elazig, Turkey	Eniwetok Atoll, Marshall Isls.	Erfurt, East Germany	Erzurum, Turkey	Esfahan, Iran	Essen, West Germany
Hermosillo, Mexico	13,817	8,369	2,558	11,455	839	16,357	12,519	16,103	6,223	4,144	8,396	2,727	9,279	12,582	11,894	9,093	9,480	11,849	12,931	9,233
Hiroshima, Japan	7,350	9,502	9,973	9,678	11,174	12,785	5,608	13,203	14,138	7,371	9,153	8,389	12,294	8,840	7,971	3,943	8,953	7,750	7,291	9,111
Hiva Oa (Atuona)	17,732	13,615	7,803	6,228	5,289	15,491	15,792	15,069	3,652	8,591	13,621	7,425	14,046	17,732	16,800	6,911	14,687	16,668	17,250	14,457
Ho Chi Minh City, Vietnam	5,636	10,521	13,366	8,923	14,879	9,251	4,859	9,630	15,837	10,736	10,225	11,937	12,302	7,669	7,316	6,063	9,479	7,155	6,112	9,741
Hobart, Australia	12,034	17,752	15,413	1,868	13,222	9,663	12,000	9,585	8,992	14,465	17,463	14,229	17,536	13,932	14,123	6,214	16,627	14,035	12,819	16,907
Hohhot, China	5,436	8,004	10,025	11,240	11,913	11,393	3,646	11,844	15,983	7,418	7,663	8,698	10,580	6,875	6,025	5,902	7,266	5,806	5,329	7,463
Hong Kong	5,963	9,873	11,918	9,442	13,394	10,594	4,663	10,998	15,607	9,281	9,545	10,447	12,148	7,829	7,227	5,237	8,988	7,032	6,202	9,218
Honiara, Solomon Islands	11,927	14,982	12,134	4,162	10,981	13,041	10,759	13,100	9,603	10,599	14,643	10,620	17,917	13,905	13,319	2,329	14,597	13,117	12,288	14,737
Honolulu, Hawaii	13,737	11,296	6,481	8,097	5,443	18,718	11,792	18,590	7,481	5,729	11,121	5,177	13,437	14,213	13,130	4,384	11,923	12,943	13,263	11,811
Houston, Texas	13,163	7,358	1,910	12,617	1,121	14,894	12,266	14,686	6,474	4,324	7,451	3,022	7,866	11,597	11,089	10,554	8,538	11,090	12,273	8,269
Huambo, Angola	6,004	7,616	12,394	13,040	13,661	2,462	7,909	2,565	12,646	13,159	7,811	13,672	5,412	5,111	6,193	16,386	7,074	6,398	6,307	7,161
Hubli, India	2,343	8,086	13,007	11,629	15,648	6,888	2,646	7,341	18,617	10,908	7,884	12,327	9,092	4,401	4,359	9,376	6,891	4,267	3,054	7,176
Hugh Town, United Kingdom	5,890	380	6,006	19,499	8,569	9,575	5,874	9,790	13,182	5,905	700	6,674	2,593	4,122	3,777	13,111	1,235	3,848	5,072	956
Hull, Canada	10,747	4,917	1,273	15,010	3,523	13,558	10,052	13,535	8,733	3,399	5,010	2,840	5,812	9,160	8,655	11,452	6,096	8,665	9,864	5,826
Hyderabad, India	2,552	8,128	12,836	11,532	15,410	7,295	2,527	7,746	18,662	10,647	7,907	12,063	9,309	4,616	4,472	8,990	6,949	4,361	3,179	7,233
Hyderabad, Pakistan	1,315	6,780	11,778	12,901	14,488	7,296	1,462	7,755	19,724	9,851	6,571	11,260	7,990	3,324	3,104	9,859	5,591	2,991	1,817	5,876
Igloolik, Canada	8,959	4,078	2,582	15,357	5,266	13,966	7,795	14,168	10,936	1,553	3,960	2,390	6,368	7,922	7,100	9,789	4,936	7,030	8,075	4,748
Iloilo, Philippines	7,236	11,426	12,770	7,882	13,611	10,748	6,146	11,085	14,303	10,181	11,096	11,152	13,670	9,207	8,701	4,333	10,547	8,515	7,598	10,779
Indianapolis, Indiana	11,775	5,975	916	13,958	2,462	14,288	10,966	14,195	7,792	3,548	6,061	2,565	6,740	10,220	9,697	10,979	7,149	9,699	10,887	6,882
Innsbruck, Austria	4,554	1,422	7,220	18,415	9,855	8,765	4,677	9,046	14,467	6,718	1,391	7,683	3,096	2,825	2,446	12,885	414	2,529	3,747	564
Inuvik, Canada	9,597	5,836	3,341	13,482	5,304	15,609	8,003	15,905	10,777	721	5,641	1,960	8,363	9,109	8,121	7,772	6,452	7,992	8,795	6,328
Invercargill, New Zealand	13,738	19,145	14,139	176	11,684	10,536	13,634	10,356	7,306	13,948	18,797	13,309	17,866	15,598	15,828	6,441	18,280	15,737	14,525	18,543
Inverness, United Kingdom	5,863	478	5,699	18,665	8,383	10,224	5,529	10,472	13,407	5,239	184	6,142	3,439	4,328	3,759	12,261	1,225	3,778	4,995	988
Iquitos, Peru	14,044	8,846	5,899	11,694	4,588	11,176	14,578	10,824	4,635	8,535	9,129	7,372	7,293	11,981	12,218	13,863	9,932	12,361	13,471	9,662
Iraklion, Greece	3,094	3,161	8,969	16,895	11,581	7,242	3,870	7,574	15,644	8,327	3,138	9,383	3,737	1,123	1,307	13,145	2,075	1,511	2,459	2,302
Irkutsk, USSR	5,069	6,650	8,917	12,571	11,096	11,540	3,128	12,000	16,058	6,398	6,305	7,762	9,328	6,097	5,121	6,846	5,988	4,897	4,718	6,164
Islamabad, Pakistan	1,965	6,416	10,970	13,128	13,611	8,316	666	8,775	19,239	8,900	6,162	10,317	8,081	3,634	3,084	9,229	5,291	2,911	2,008	5,566
Istanbul, Turkey	2,995	2,959	8,673	16,892	11,365	7,849	3,394	8,200	15,934	7,797	2,858	8,927	4,136	1,383	915	12,480	1,769	1,051	2,215	2,040
Ivujivik, Canada	9,443	4,137	1,956	15,439	4,711	13,869	8,425	14,005	10,316	1,953	4,089	2,285	6,069	8,214	7,483	10,331	5,139	7,439	8,549	4,916
Iwo Jima Island, Japan	8,506	10,804	10,441	8,361	11,092	13,213	6,871	13,575	13,036	7,977	10,456	8,769	13,645	10,128	9,301	2,651	10,308	9,082	8,543	10,458
Izmir, Turkey	3,020	3,036	8,809	16,910	11,468	7,568	3,602	7,911	15,813	8,040	2,971	9,137	3,945	1,218	1,053	12,785	1,884	1,231	2,302	2,137
Jackson, Mississippi	12,663	6,820	1,617	13,177	1,689	14,482	11,867	14,309	6,888	4,193	6,924	3,002	7,308	11,051	10,573	10,938	8,008	10,582	11,778	7,735
Jaffna, Sri Lanka	3,130	8,904	13,704	10,813	16,243	6,827	3,390	7,263	17,836	11,474	8,700	12,885	9,843	5,170	5,174	8,971	7,710	5,085	3,869	7,995
Jakarta, Indonesia	6,566	12,075	15,156	7,498	16,126	8,305	6,316	8,606	14,654	12,519	11,813	13,625	13,290	8,618	8,531	6,444	10,942	8,412	7,240	11,221
Jamestown, St. Helena	8,032	7,674	11,015	13,150	11,611	4,049	9,811	3,875	10,518	12,614	7,965	12,590	4,837	6,663	7,646	18,642	7,591	7,869	8,132	7,567
Jamnagar, India	1,535	7,136	12,130	12,559	14,829	7,140	1,787	7,600	19,484	10,163	6,931	11,576	8,274	3,588	3,436	9,755	5,944	3,332	2,138	6,229
Jan Mayen Island	6,446	1,974	4,940	17,205	7,701	11,619	5,571	11,902	13,209	3,884	1,704	4,975	4,882	5,333	4,513	10,828	2,452	4,455	5,552	2,325
Jayapura, Indonesia	9,673	13,615	12,958	5,609	12,629	11,760	8,625	11,962	11,841	10,769	13,268	11,277	16,126	11,677	11,184	2,846	12,887	10,996	10,078	13,092
Jefferson City, Missouri	12,171	6,440	912	13,455	1,999	14,784	11,247	14,669	7,495	3,476	6,509	2,325	7,276	10,686	10,120	10,541	7,599	10,110	11,279	7,337
Jerusalem, Israel	2,088	4,077	9,836	15,897	12,508	6,834	3,131	7,214	16,578	8,918	4,005	10,083	4,688	247	849	12,622	2,915	1,056	1,548	3,175
Jiggalong, Australia	8,879	14,500	16,101	5,089	15,417	8,734	8,741	8,883	12,246	13,751	14,233	14,411	15,403	10,884	10,912	5,941	13,365	10,805	9,610	13,644
Jinan, China	5,928	8,640	10,317	10,595	11,997	11,597	4,212	12,036	15,554	7,685	8,298	8,897	11,234	7,464	6,644	5,310	7,919	6,427	5,891	8,113
Jodhpur, India	1,781	7,012	11,777	12,613	14,432	7,659	1,417	8,118	19,764	9,721	6,783	11,138	8,383	3,750	3,437	9,380	5,844	3,303	2,188	6,127
Johannesburg, South Africa	6,402	9,415	14,352	11,171	15,286	497	8,329	758	12,562	14,988	9,570	15,629	7,378	6,213	7,276	14,965	8,712	7,446	6,977	8,846
Juazeiro do Norte, Brazil	10,819	7,396	7,923	13,426	7,885	7,724	12,085	7,461	7,685	10,226	7,744	9,615	4,732	8,907	9,526	17,619	8,046	9,728	10,532	7,859
Juneau, Alaska	10,700	6,778	3,078	12,609	4,475	16,653	9,056	16,901	9,750	1,209	6,616	1,405	9,091	10,219	9,240	7,382	7,489	9,112	9,908	7,345
Kabul, Afghanistan	1,686	6,094	10,809	13,473	13,492	8,176	449	8,632	19,178	8,834	5,850	10,244	7,706	3,266	2,709	9,573	4,953	2,538	1,641	5,231
Kalgoorlie, Australia	9,384	15,159	16,639	4,523	15,438	8,423	9,417	8,520	11,631	14,454	14,916	14,982	15,622	11,326	11,466	6,393	13,988	11,378	10,162	14,272
Kaliningrad, USSR	4,336	1,749	7,107	17,685	9,844	9,424	4,010	9,748	14,963	6,160	1,503	7,282	4,099	3,026	2,272	11,841	760	2,258	3,455	972
Kamloops, Canada	11,583	6,941	2,106	12,592	3,250	16,693	10,081	16,771	8,686	1,722	6,850	568	8,826	10,793	9,907	8,143	7,840	9,810	10,740	7,649
Kampala, Uganda	3,686	6,881	12,539	13,507	14,686	3,343	5,620	3,724	14,996	12,278	6,955	13,267	5,721	3,245	4,302	14,320	5,972	4,473	4,101	6,155
Kananga, Zaire	4,955	7,095	12,342	13,461	14,038	2,801	6,861	3,058	13,684	12,664	7,244	13,399	5,300	4,145	5,233	15,577	6,397	5,430	5,270	6,523
Kano, Nigeria	5,122	4,769	9,841	15,886	11,745	5,222	6,612	5,393	13,373	10,311	4,977	10,919	2,822	3,354	4,239	16,126	4,329	4,462	4,950	4,377
Kanpur, India	2,510	7,475	11,858	12,081	14,391	8,154	1,721	8,611	19,056	9,625	7,220	11,040	9,038	4,451	4,053	8,655	6,344	3,899	2,857	6,620
Kansas City, Missouri	12,225	6,546	877	13,321	1,923	14,998	11,241	14,886	7,495	3,351	6,602	2,154	7,460	10,787	10,192	10,324	7,692	10,175	11,331	7,433
Kaohsiung, Taiwan	6,555	10,150	11,659	9,123	12,928	11,165	5,169	11,559	15,014	9,029	9,812	10,120	12,575	8,379	7,725	4,617	9,338	7,523	6,752	9,554
Karachi, Pakistan	1,186	6,734	11,799	12,965	14,522	7,174	1,526	7,634	19,589	9,912	6,532	11,317	7,888	3,212	3,030	10,000	5,540	2,926	1,733	5,825
Karaganda, USSR	3,133	5,228	9,206	14,136	11,820	9,760	1,301	10,208	17,477	7,114	4,920	8,529	7,502	3,912	2,947	8,976	4,285	2,723	2,607	4,520
Karl-Marx-Stadt, East Germany	4,581	1,339	7,035	18,275	9,716	9,113	4,517	9,406	14,548	6,388	1,209	7,402	3,431	2,993	2,462	12,491	134	2,509	3,737	418
Kasanga, Tanzania	4,559	7,704	13,193	12,761	15,030	2,367	6,503	2,741	14,225	13,189	7,807	14,091	6,197	4,226	5,287	14,671	6,866	5,458	5,044	7,031
Kashgar, China	2,493	6,141	10,376	13,320	12,973	8,976	629	9,434	18,551	8,238	5,860	9,657	8,081	3,888	3,158	8,892	5,082	2,956	2,310	5,344
Kassel, West Germany	4,824	1,095	6,819	18,495	9,488	9,236	4,749	9,517	14,305	6,248	982	7,228	3,292	3,208	2,705	12,567	114	2,754	3,982	174
Kathmandu, Nepal	2,998	7,686	11,750	11,816	14,180	8,600	1,949	9,054	18,572	9,417	7,414	10,821	9,414	4,890	4,416	8,151	6,593	4,248	3,276	6,863
Kayes, Mali	7,026	4,338	8,147	16,517	9,692	6,691	8,183	6,716	11,514	9,276	4,655	9,504	1,420	5,035	5,627	17,053	4,527	5,831	6,651	4,424
Kazan, USSR	3,422	3,498	8,079	15,874	10,824	9,640	2,407	10,043	16,395	6,448	3,200	7,784	5,837	3,120	2,035	10,348	2,557	1,853	2,572	2,784
Kemi, Finland	4,999	2,189	6,401	17,001	9,161	10,621	4,129	10,963	14,669	5,069	1,842	6,297	5,028	4,096	3,163	10,753	1,822	3,072	4,109	1,882
Kenora, Canada	11,173	5,730	377	13,989	2,992	14,990	10,083	14,997	8,649	2,260	5,730	1,374	7,149	9,903	9,208	9,974	6,806	9,168	10,280	6,567
Kerguelen Island	8,400	13,426	18,621	6,987	17,133	3,894	9,754	3,869	11,514	18,108	13,477	19,512	11,759	9,401	10,212	11,170	12,441	10,286	9,272	12,655
Kerkira, Greece	3,656	2,500	8,310	17,529	10,921	7,774	4,179	8,084	15,181	7,746	2,486	8,760	3,351	1,769	1,670	13,145	1,442	1,827	2,940	1,653
Kermanshah, Iran	1,280	4,644	10,141	15,137	12,894	7,300	2,000	7,720	17,646	8,800	4,488	10,091	5,743	1,261	852	11,514	3,436	806	462	3,720
Khabarovsk, USSR	7,218	8,147	8,504	11,007	10,025	13,427	5,300	13,880	14,064	5,873	7,801	6,994	11,051	8,298	7,299	4,814	7,765	7,076	6,923	7,882
Kharkov, USSR	3,199	2,920	8,190	16,623	10,947	8,860	2,863	9,234	16,152	6,946	2,692	8,183	4,879	2,273	1,280	11,418	1,784	1,188	2,306	2,057
Khartoum, Sudan	2,600	5,378	11,170	14,872	13,629	5,032	4,359	5,404	15,903	10,623	5,404	11,687	4,884	1,565	2,641	13,731	4,371	2,826	2,700	4,579
Khon Kaen, Thailand	5,017	9,768	12,846	9,671	14,632	9,244	4,122	9,651	16,501	10,247	9,472	11,514	11,604	7,018	6,607	6,422	8,730	6,441	5,433	8,991
Kiev, USSR	3,509	2,524	7,911	17,035	10,658	8,893	3,273	9,249	15,762	6,809	2,310	7,998	4,497	2,349	1,476	11,709	1,374	1,440	2,627	1,649
Kigali, Rwanda	4,059	6,994	12,562	13,443	14,582	3,090	5,989	3,448	14,620	12,460	7,089	13,386	5,646	3,524	4,596	14,654	6,138	4,775	4,454	6,307
Kingston, Canada	10,886	5,045	1,250	14,897	3,400	13,591	10,198	13,556	8,587	3,480	5,144	2,863	5,879	9,286	8,792	11,469	6,228	8,803	10,004	5,957
Kingston, Jamaica	12,962	7,133	3,488	13,176	2,968	12,676	12,796	12,430	6,113	6,124	7,348	5,050	6,553	11,011	10,873	12,769	8,325	10,953	12,174	8,040
Kingstown, Saint Vincent	11,940	6,552	4,713	13,978	4,720	10,945	12,289	10,722	6,854	7,216	6,838	6,393	5,221	9,888	9,995	14,507	7,643	10,122	11,278	7,370
Kinshasa, Zaire	5,420	6,699	11,680	13,934	13,249	3,277	7,259	3,441	13,149	12,259	6,886	12,853	4,638	4,293	5,359	16,309	6,139	5,572	5,608	6,228
Kirkwall, United Kingdom	5,826	660	5,686	18,483	8,390	10,332	5,427	10,589	13,488	5,134	340	6,072	3,621	4,347	3,734	12,081	1,257	3,742	4,950	1,048
Kirov, USSR	3,723	3,439	7,816	15,884	10,552	9,949	2,613	10,350	16,161	6,142	3,125	7,484	5,908	3,415	2,334	10,183	2,585	2,157	2,881	2,790
Kiruna, Sweden	5,294	2,139	6,109	17,024	8,868	10,870	4,394	11,204	14,393	4,789	1,791	6,006	5,044	4,369	3,451	10,699	1,945	3,364	4,405	1,963
Kisangani, Zaire	4,240	6,536	12,009	13,949	13,978	3,415	6,123	3,723	14,356	12,066	6,656	12,912	5,053	3,377	4,464	15,104	5,753	4,660	4,512	5,900
Kishinev, USSR	3,358	2,575	8,138	17,100	10,864	8,514	3,363	8,864	15,774	7,149	2,409	8,306	4,266	2,008	1,253	12,054	1,372	1,276	2,502	1,657
Kitchner, Canada	11,162	5,350	986	14,573	3,086	13,889	10,412	13,840	8,359	3,394	5,438	2,653	6,206	9,595	9,078	11,232	6,526	9,083	10,277	6,257
Knoxville, Tennessee	11,993	6,125	1,381	13,884	2,391	14,012	11,292	13,887	7,482	4,013	6,239	3,010	6,641	10,349	9,893	11,327	7,318	9,909	11,115	7,044
Kosice, Czechoslovakia	3,938	1,984	7,627	17,688	10,331	8,754	3,930	9,077	15,178	6,812	1,838	7,900	3,804	2,425	1,820	12,320	777	1,864	3,092	1,062
Kota Kinabalu, Malaysia	6,796	11,521	13,537	7,868	14,496	9,867	5,963	10,201	14,679	10,916	11,209	11,957	13,450	8,830	8,456	5,113	10,535	8,289	7,267	10,787
Krakow, Poland	4,097	1,834	7,449	17,788	10,156	8,922	4,024	9,241	15,052	6,635	1,672	7,719	3,791	2,607	1,983	12,265	637	2,017	3,244	921
Kralendijk, Bonaire	12,638	7,085	4,442	13,377	4,056	11,566	12,844	11,313	6,220	7,041	7,349	6,072	5,960	10,599	10,645	13,866	8,219	10,760	11,941	7,940
Krasnodar, USSR	2,637	3,363	8,766	16,284	11,519	8,332	2,563	8,718	16,587	7,527	3,170	8,771	5,000	1,755	706	11,557	2,174	599	1,753	2,458
Krasnoyarsk, USSR	4,560	5,828	8,601	13,408	10,982	11,161	2,633	11,615	16,340	6,216	5,486	7,623	8,472	5,360	4,346	7,678	5,134	4,124	4,088	5,314
Kristiansand, Norway	5,194	1,041	6,273	18,200	8,998	9,987	4,799	10,276	14,129	5,513	724	6,547	3,821	3,793	3,117	11,937	823	3,114	4,314	750
Kuala Lumpur, Malaysia	5,532	10,905	14,309	8,644	15,871	8,340	5,147	8,702	15,778	11,694	10,639	12,924	12,291	7,596	7,422	6,737	9,784	7,291	6,147	10,060
Kuching, Malaysia	6,454	11,594	14,221	7,880	15,300	9,070	5,884	9,400	14,926	11,586	11,304	12,686	13,203	8,516	8,269	5,837	10,526	8,124	7,021	10,794
Kumasi, Ghana	6,379	5,190	9,511	15,597	11,028	5,339	7,850	5,392	12,115	10,477	5,462	10,821	2,577	4,590	5,418	17,329	5,049	5,639	6,199	5,027
Kumzar, Oman	163	5,904	11,314	13,890	14,075	6,782	1,783	7,230	18,621	9,748	5,743	11,101	6,829	2,139	2,111	10,989	4,696	2,059	841	4,980
Kunming, China	4,751	8,973	11,910	10,410	13,830	9,767	3,513	10,197	16,819	9,330	8,663	10,627	11,040	6,628	6,070	6,425	7,996	5,883	5,004	8,244
Kuqa Chang, China	3,141	6,464	10,251	12,931	12,736	9,537	1,287	9,997	18,059	7,969	6,162	9,383	8,593	4,531	3,750	8,242	5,476	3,541	2,970	5,723

Distances in Kilometers

	Dubayy, United Arab Emir.	Dublin, Ireland	Duluth, Minnesota	Dunedin, New Zealand	Durango, Mexico	Durban, South Africa	Dushanbe, USSR	East London, South Africa	Easter Island (Hanga Roa)	Echo Bay, Canada	Edinburgh, United Kingdom	Edmonton, Canada	El Aaiun, Morocco	Elat, Israel	Elazig, Turkey	Eniwetok Atoll, Marshall Isls.	Erfurt, East Germany	Erzurum, Turkey	Esfahan, Iran	Essen, West Germany
Kurgan, USSR	3,448	4,446	8,480	14,883	11,149	9,998	1,895	10,429	16,835	6,524	4,129	7,922	6,855	3,748	2,689	9,398	3,566	2,472	2,745	3,783
Kuwait, Kuwait	857	5,095	10,669	14,754	13,414	6,798	2,170	7,225	17,802	9,353	4,961	10,644	5,936	1,262	1,308	11,655	3,890	1,318	505	4,170
Kuybyshev, USSR	3,131	3,663	8,363	15,752	11,110	9,386	2,166	9,793	16,661	6,737	3,378	8,075	5,880	2,904	1,817	10,409	2,659	1,623	2,284	2,903
Kyoto, Japan	7,623	9,556	9,765	9,613	10,895	13,093	5,855	13,509	13,853	7,182	9,208	8,162	12,392	9,071	8,179	3,735	9,058	7,957	7,539	9,205
Kzyl-Orda, USSR	2,353	5,099	9,624	14,368	12,317	8,975	747	9,419	17,995	7,706	4,825	9,105	7,078	3,166	2,274	9,646	4,033	2,056	1,801	4,295
L'vov, USSR	3,832	2,116	7,667	17,495	10,390	8,853	3,731	9,187	15,343	6,750	1,937	7,874	4,039	2,434	1,730	12,092	929	1,748	2,970	1,212
La Ceiba, Honduras	13,894	7,990	3,473	12,232	2,079	13,534	13,478	13,242	5,343	6,044	8,172	4,791	7,632	12,009	11,779	11,850	9,197	11,838	13,066	8,912
La Coruna, Spain	6,040	1,119	6,278	19,715	8,695	9,050	6,282	9,231	12,884	6,478	1,444	7,126	1,849	4,121	3,984	13,856	1,691	4,095	5,286	1,464
La Paz, Bolivia	14,109	9,724	7,409	10,941	5,988	9,966	15,180	9,577	4,407	10,046	10,041	8,884	7,651	12,147	12,638	14,576	10,682	12,818	13,755	10,436
La Paz, Mexico	14,322	8,766	2,987	11,113	573	16,157	13,062	15,853	5,679	4,691	8,814	3,273	9,472	13,003	12,361	9,244	9,903	12,326	13,431	9,648
La Ronge, Canada	10,910	5,894	1,305	13,684	3,450	15,570	9,612	15,654	9,121	1,403	5,830	559	7,704	9,890	9,080	9,124	6,858	9,008	10,034	6,648
Labrador City, Canada	9,707	3,935	1,925	15,891	4,508	13,107	9,008	13,165	9,783	3,124	4,000	3,052	5,236	8,178	7,627	11,480	5,090	7,629	8,821	4,827
Lagos, Nigeria	5,894	5,272	9,909	15,465	11,535	4,986	7,435	5,082	12,598	10,699	5,517	11,146	2,887	4,182	5,071	16,955	4,988	5,295	5,767	5,000
Lahore, Pakistan	1,985	6,659	11,220	12,898	13,849	8,195	921	8,655	19,403	9,125	6,409	10,543	8,267	3,762	3,270	9,161	5,526	3,106	2,138	5,803
Lambasa, Fiji	14,171	15,881	11,212	3,367	9,384	13,870	12,912	13,752	7,366	10,497	15,617	10,032	18,260	16,123	15,432	3,620	16,035	15,218	14,497	16,062
Lansing, Michigan	11,429	5,654	749	14,247	2,779	14,204	10,610	14,142	8,148	3,308	5,731	2,441	6,545	9,901	9,358	10,970	6,821	9,357	10,540	6,555
Lanzhou, China	4,739	8,037	10,696	11,273	12,721	10,528	3,087	10,978	16,750	8,132	7,710	9,454	10,388	6,346	5,596	6,450	7,168	5,386	4,746	7,392
Laoag, Philippines	6,739	10,596	12,100	8,693	13,240	10,962	5,471	11,338	14,828	9,478	10,262	10,534	12,945	8,629	8,035	4,534	9,752	7,839	7,004	9,976
Largeau, Chad	3,822	4,501	10,098	15,943	12,357	5,437	5,308	5,716	14,677	10,032	4,618	10,888	3,467	2,061	3,017	14,828	3,738	3,240	3,639	3,871
Las Vegas, Nevada	13,131	7,971	2,243	11,742	1,680	16,805	11,721	16,641	7,035	3,333	7,954	1,936	9,254	12,090	11,311	8,607	9,016	11,242	12,262	8,788
Launceston, Australia	11,967	17,629	15,351	1,941	13,218	9,755	11,888	9,687	9,087	14,332	17,332	14,130	17,624	13,887	14,045	6,061	16,525	13,951	12,741	16,803
Le Havre, France	5,422	615	6,417	19,189	9,012	9,307	5,441	9,547	13,638	6,158	749	7,005	2,730	3,671	3,309	13,026	794	3,383	4,606	534
Leipzig, East Germany	4,639	1,284	6,969	18,305	9,652	9,174	4,553	9,466	14,502	6,325	1,146	7,337	3,434	3,059	2,520	12,469	98	2,564	3,792	371
Leningrad, USSR	4,307	2,323	7,078	16,980	9,840	9,949	3,591	10,304	15,260	5,784	2,009	7,015	4,901	3,393	2,445	11,019	1,561	2,354	3,413	1,725
Leon, Spain	5,813	1,195	6,514	19,532	8,940	8,853	6,105	9,045	13,088	6,656	1,491	7,337	1,847	3,882	3,770	13,888	1,567	3,887	5,070	1,369
Lerwick, United Kingdom	5,761	820	5,713	18,323	8,432	10,400	5,309	10,666	13,590	5,072	487	6,044	3,778	4,335	3,683	11,926	1,273	3,681	4,880	1,094
Lhasa, China	3,558	7,879	11,534	11,560	13,832	9,163	2,274	9,615	18,002	9,104	7,587	10,488	9,803	5,382	4,821	7,576	6,841	4,638	3,757	7,100
Libreville, Gabon	5,642	6,047	10,859	14,637	12,438	4,054	7,364	4,175	12,872	11,559	6,262	12,072	3,827	4,211	5,217	16,750	5,610	5,439	5,682	5,665
Lilongwe, Malawi	4,930	8,378	13,840	12,089	15,536	1,780	6,864	2,192	13,976	13,850	8,479	14,766	6,817	4,818	5,858	14,443	7,529	6,017	5,501	7,699
Lima, Peru	14,825	9,839	6,687	10,725	4,996	11,041	15,545	10,647	3,769	9,296	10,127	8,048	8,141	12,787	13,119	13,586	10,907	13,274	14,335	10,640
Limerick, Ireland	6,070	175	5,712	19,246	8,311	9,919	5,933	10,135	13,071	5,560	505	6,339	2,857	4,370	3,951	12,842	1,363	4,004	5,232	1,079
Limoges, France	5,285	994	6,730	19,187	9,274	8,904	5,471	9,138	13,684	6,562	1,164	7,381	2,434	3,441	3,201	13,378	922	3,300	4,505	755
Limon, Costa Rica	14,054	8,245	4,167	12,077	2,771	12,879	13,893	12,565	5,002	6,769	8,459	5,540	7,523	12,074	11,976	12,430	9,435	12,060	13,279	9,150
Lincoln, Nebraska	12,139	6,535	757	13,291	2,005	15,190	11,093	15,095	7,640	3,112	6,574	1,893	7,575	10,764	10,132	10,096	7,662	10,106	11,244	7,409
Linz, Austria	4,385	1,546	7,300	18,200	9,964	8,815	4,445	9,110	14,676	6,687	1,462	7,695	3,339	2,728	2,268	12,670	380	2,337	3,561	630
Lisbon, Portugal	6,143	1,640	6,532	19,210	8,832	8,660	6,559	8,819	12,690	6,914	1,962	7,487	1,336	4,150	4,157	14,375	2,085	4,291	5,441	1,894
Little Rock, Arkansas	12,539	6,753	1,337	13,192	1,687	14,728	11,660	14,574	7,085	3,874	6,838	2,669	7,409	10,997	10,470	10,667	7,927	10,468	11,649	7,659
Liverpool, United Kingdom	5,706	216	5,994	19,047	8,630	9,794	5,547	10,033	13,455	5,671	279	6,530	3,034	4,052	3,587	12,677	995	3,633	4,861	715
Lodz, Poland	4,216	1,744	7,293	17,808	10,010	9,110	4,057	9,428	14,981	6,450	1,555	7,541	3,859	2,778	2,113	12,142	593	2,131	3,352	862
Lome, Togo	6,124	5,277	9,770	15,483	11,336	5,098	7,643	5,173	12,368	10,647	5,535	11,045	2,784	4,386	5,254	17,156	5,055	5,476	5,980	5,053
London, United Kingdom	5,476	464	6,274	19,081	8,897	9,513	5,405	9,758	13,636	5,950	532	6,819	2,917	3,782	3,357	12,822	780	3,416	4,644	495
Londonderry, United Kingdom	6,010	199	5,661	18,977	8,302	10,090	5,778	10,320	13,191	5,378	281	6,209	3,128	4,382	3,893	12,571	1,307	3,931	5,157	1,034
Longlac, Canada	10,880	5,281	532	14,491	3,264	14,418	9,925	14,426	8,818	2,552	5,309	1,898	6,585	9,497	8,861	10,509	6,395	8,837	9,985	6,145
Lord Howe Island, Australia	12,676	17,316	13,858	1,870	11,931	11,281	12,135	11,215	8,617	12,858	16,968	12,601	19,130	14,722	14,582	4,776	16,622	14,434	13,322	16,837
Los Angeles, California	13,404	8,327	2,611	11,377	1,725	17,096	11,933	16,897	6,838	3,562	8,304	2,198	9,616	12,425	11,624	8,344	9,361	11,550	12,544	9,136
Louangphrabang, Laos	4,830	9,413	12,487	10,009	14,353	9,395	3,813	9,814	16,717	9,900	9,113	11,186	11,327	6,793	6,330	6,480	8,393	6,156	5,190	8,650
Louisville, Kentucky	11,891	6,066	1,082	13,892	2,386	14,225	11,114	14,118	7,649	3,716	6,162	2,712	6,743	10,307	9,806	11,076	7,248	9,812	11,006	6,978
Luanda, Angola	5,915	7,128	11,887	13,542	13,241	2,978	7,777	3,079	12,678	12,656	7,332	13,155	4,896	4,840	5,907	16,630	6,627	6,119	6,136	6,702
Lubumbashi, Zaire	5,081	7,883	13,188	12,643	14,804	2,047	7,024	2,367	13,689	13,430	8,014	14,225	6,144	4,631	5,706	15,110	7,121	5,887	5,538	7,266
Lusaka, Zambia	5,371	8,302	13,550	12,233	15,032	1,623	7,315	1,952	13,459	13,853	8,436	14,631	6,502	5,027	6,096	15,041	7,545	6,272	5,873	7,690
Luxembourg, Luxembourg	4,999	954	6,756	18,777	9,387	9,139	5,015	9,403	14,072	6,329	942	7,252	2,990	3,293	2,883	12,847	381	2,951	4,176	215
Luxor, Egypt	2,275	4,446	10,257	15,670	12,849	6,148	3,668	6,518	16,259	9,531	4,427	10,641	4,551	485	1,568	13,189	3,358	1,771	1,998	3,591
Lynn Lake, Canada	10,639	5,566	1,276	14,011	3,656	15,256	9,390	15,351	9,341	1,362	5,505	870	7,396	9,578	8,782	9,349	6,537	8,715	9,758	6,325
Lyon, France	5,007	1,162	6,953	18,907	9,523	8,780	5,204	9,030	13,962	6,684	1,263	7,550	2,608	3,177	2,921	13,274	740	3,021	4,225	654
Macapa, Brazil	11,657	7,206	6,537	13,513	6,360	9,251	12,563	8,987	6,919	8,983	7,538	8,223	5,038	9,626	10,035	16,138	8,093	10,209	11,199	7,858
Madison, Wisconsin	11,624	5,926	465	13,930	2,535	14,602	10,702	14,537	8,041	3,102	5,983	2,116	6,926	10,168	9,580	10,590	7,073	9,566	10,730	6,814
Madras, India	2,946	8,623	13,331	11,059	15,864	7,104	3,041	7,546	18,156	11,095	8,408	12,507	9,698	5,006	4,933	8,876	7,438	4,832	3,632	7,722
Madrid, Spain	5,663	1,451	6,788	19,242	9,185	8,563	6,056	8,756	13,190	6,944	1,726	7,626	1,710	3,694	3,658	14,080	1,637	3,789	4,947	1,479
Madurai, India	2,948	8,755	13,649	10,980	16,235	6,694	3,304	7,134	17,945	11,470	8,558	12,886	9,646	4,979	5,008	9,169	7,557	4,925	3,705	7,842
Magadan, USSR	7,918	7,320	6,909	11,825	8,511	14,483	5,983	14,942	13,111	4,283	6,994	5,404	10,281	8,527	7,451	5,419	7,225	7,242	7,420	7,273
Magdalena, Bolivia	13,582	9,200	7,221	11,480	6,043	9,772	14,624	9,404	4,944	9,852	9,521	8,763	7,094	11,603	12,082	14,996	10,140	12,262	13,207	9,897
Magdeburg, East Germany	4,717	1,214	6,871	18,325	9,559	9,280	4,592	9,571	14,445	6,218	1,057	7,230	3,465	3,158	2,601	12,410	139	2,639	3,866	330
Majuro Atoll, Marshall Isls.	12,224	13,298	9,942	5,872	9,102	15,167	10,587	15,275	9,333	8,420	12,996	8,403	16,179	13,826	12,925	1,094	13,289	12,702	12,266	13,338
Malabo, Equatorial Guinea	5,510	5,667	10,534	15,015	12,204	4,409	7,170	4,543	12,990	11,183	5,883	11,716	3,490	3,971	4,947	16,642	5,240	5,170	5,487	5,290
Male, Maldives	3,052	8,970	14,204	10,873	16,897	5,872	3,855	6,308	17,425	12,175	8,811	13,594	9,484	4,944	5,171	9,798	7,762	5,127	3,904	8,045
Manado, Indonesia	7,891	12,442	13,562	6,894	13,981	10,467	7,012	10,751	13,587	11,041	12,116	11,897	14,527	9,925	9,529	4,276	11,519	9,357	8,356	11,761
Managua, Nicaragua	14,147	8,272	3,878	11,993	2,344	13,304	13,827	12,992	5,016	6,447	8,467	5,184	7,745	12,215	12,043	12,022	9,474	12,113	13,339	9,189
Manama, Bahrain	485	5,528	11,096	14,335	13,845	6,546	2,186	6,983	18,042	9,726	5,397	11,035	6,276	1,582	1,743	11,544	4,324	1,748	722	4,603
Manaus, Brazil	12,707	7,998	6,362	12,660	5,691	9,943	13,528	9,633	5,885	8,944	8,315	7,993	6,039	10,667	11,033	15,284	8,968	11,199	12,224	8,718
Manchester, New Hampshire	10,697	4,807	1,680	15,201	3,695	13,163	10,127	13,126	8,685	3,810	4,932	3,275	5,479	9,025	8,587	11,885	6,004	8,612	9,827	5,728
Mandalay, Burma	4,162	8,855	12,343	10,602	14,444	9,021	3,182	9,455	17,389	9,825	8,566	11,167	10,672	6,122	5,674	7,101	7,800	5,505	4,520	8,063
Mangareva Island, Fr.Polynesia	18,963	14,581	8,858	5,479	6,159	13,956	17,190	13,532	2,607	9,993	14,666	8,743	14,191	18,789	18,195	7,838	15,756	18,109	18,771	15,491
Manila, Philippines	6,917	10,968	12,450	8,335	13,473	10,807	5,744	11,167	14,639	9,838	10,636	10,863	13,253	8,853	8,306	4,482	10,100	8,116	7,234	10,329
Mannheim, West Germany	4,832	1,107	6,894	18,614	9,538	9,067	4,851	9,341	14,241	6,408	1,063	7,358	3,095	3,144	2,715	12,781	248	2,782	4,008	242
Maputo, Mozambique	6,173	9,552	14,677	10,992	15,728	457	8,079	904	12,864	15,099	9,685	15,861	7,657	6,149	7,190	14,525	8,783	7,349	6,797	8,934
Mar del Plata, Argentina	13,636	11,259	10,003	9,553	8,449	7,925	15,398	7,487	4,953	12,640	11,606	11,477	8,569	12,165	13,023	15,099	11,906	13,243	13,714	11,728
Maracaibo, Venezuela	13,032	7,435	4,447	13,005	3,798	11,811	13,191	11,538	5,846	7,073	7,691	6,031	6,361	10,997	11,028	13,590	8,581	11,139	12,326	8,301
Marrakech, Morocco	6,156	2,415	7,107	18,419	9,236	7,957	6,841	8,092	12,554	7,670	2,724	8,172	707	4,099	4,326	15,121	2,659	4,492	5,549	2,521
Marseilles, France	4,924	1,407	7,163	18,805	9,699	8,512	5,237	8,758	13,984	6,952	1,532	7,800	2,453	3,034	2,873	13,500	954	2,991	4,172	914
Maseru, Lesotho	6,732	9,721	14,525	10,884	15,263	347	8,653	414	12,260	15,295	9,883	15,870	7,608	6,563	7,626	14,952	9,041	7,797	7,319	9,169
Mashhad, Iran	1,290	5,327	10,380	14,300	13,126	7,909	851	8,354	18,566	8,652	5,108	10,027	6,814	2,416	1,817	10,371	4,154	1,653	835	4,437
Mazatlan, Mexico	14,293	8,614	2,912	11,317	200	15,749	13,149	15,448	5,582	4,835	8,683	3,419	9,166	12,860	12,279	9,653	9,773	12,258	13,399	9,511
Mbabane, Swaziland	6,271	9,535	14,593	11,024	15,590	392	8,183	807	12,745	15,094	9,675	15,814	7,588	6,196	7,245	14,662	8,787	7,408	6,880	8,933
Mbandaka, Zaire	4,861	6,325	11,543	14,253	13,328	3,577	6,683	3,801	13,691	11,899	6,489	12,599	4,507	3,713	4,783	15,852	5,684	4,993	5,026	5,793
McMurdo Sound, Antarctica	13,200	17,287	15,336	3,533	12,603	7,707	14,301	7,407	6,969	16,742	17,554	15,546	14,404	14,112	15,009	9,880	16,857	15,096	14,082	16,961
Mecca, Saudi Arabia	1,638	5,255	11,047	14,815	13,683	5,754	3,355	6,161	16,855	10,121	5,208	11,309	5,381	1,022	1,911	12,759	4,123	2,052	1,706	4,372
Medan, Indonesia	5,219	10,673	14,326	8,904	16,052	8,080	4,915	8,452	16,055	11,738	10,415	13,005	11,976	7,283	7,138	7,059	9,535	7,013	5,855	9,814
Medellin, Colombia	13,672	8,087	4,763	12,350	3,679	11,960	13,840	11,649	5,191	7,400	8,340	6,260	6,970	11,628	11,680	13,336	9,236	11,793	12,977	8,955
Medicine Hat, Canada	11,548	6,549	1,417	13,056	2,934	16,113	10,189	16,147	8,552	1,835	6,493	435	8,244	10,559	9,743	8,831	7,526	9,668	10,678	7,314
Medina, Saudi Arabia	1,588	4,974	10,749	15,057	13,408	6,080	3,163	6,483	16,919	9,788	4,914	10,981	5,264	728	1,577	12,636	3,826	1,721	1,485	4,081
Melbourne, Australia	11,663	17,218	15,314	2,285	13,345	9,857	11,500	9,819	9,444	14,084	16,911	13,991	17,665	13,623	13,716	5,750	16,146	13,611	12,413	16,419
Memphis, Tennessee	12,395	6,583	1,306	13,378	1,871	14,537	11,563	14,391	7,188	3,900	6,676	2,745	7,203	10,824	10,315	10,845	7,762	10,319	11,507	7,493
Merauke, Indonesia	9,918	14,200	13,497	5,049	12,933	11,373	9,023	11,539	11,548	11,385	13,856	11,831	16,552	11,961	11,559	3,281	13,412	11,382	10,396	13,630
Merida, Mexico	13,647	7,731	2,873	12,405	1,585	14,039	13,045	13,774	5,736	5,413	7,882	4,147	7,684	11,864	11,529	11,393	8,938	11,567	12,788	8,656
Meridian, Mississippi	12,577	6,718	1,627	13,292	1,816	14,347	11,817	14,178	6,944	4,230	6,829	3,070	7,171	10,944	10,481	11,068	7,910	10,494	11,695	7,636
Messina, Italy	3,993	2,372	8,174	17,787	10,728	7,701	4,585	7,988	14,801	7,782	2,416	8,728	2,946	2,027	2,061	13,511	1,467	2,227	3,311	1,619
Mexico City, Mexico	14,349	8,489	3,104	11,560	767	14,893	13,469	14,586	5,268	5,365	8,604	3,984	8,667	12,698	12,256	10,481	9,684	12,268	13,464	9,409
Miami, Florida	12,615	6,701	2,559	13,482	2,477	13,337	12,189	13,136	6,643	5,195	6,874	4,132	6,597	10,782	10,497	12,109	7,908	10,548	11,775	7,625
Midway Islands, USA	11,846	10,931	7,440	8,293	7,176	17,266	9,926	17,552	9,492	5,801	10,668	5,834	13,651	12,754	11,686	2,815	11,195	11,474	11,518	11,171
Milan, Italy	4,667	1,417	7,230	18,566	9,828	8,628	4,883	8,896	14,299	6,842	1,451	7,763	2,839	2,860	2,580	13,144	628	2,681	3,884	685

Distances in Kilometers	Dubayy, United Arab Emir.	Dublin, Ireland	Duluth, Minnesota	Dunedin, New Zealand	Durango, Mexico	Durban, South Africa	Dushanbe, USSR	East London, South Africa	Easter Island (Hanga Roa)	Echo Bay, Canada	Edinburgh, United Kingdom	Edmonton, Canada	El Aaiun, Morocco	Elat, Israel	Elazig, Turkey	Eniwetok Atoll, Marshall Isls.	Erfurt, East Germany	Erzurum, Turkey	Esfahan, Iran	Essen, West Germany
Milford Sound, New Zealand	13,682	18,941	14,069	257	11,660	10,673	13,511	10,502	7,401	13,792	18,595	13,189	18,070	15,580	15,756	6,236	18,145	15,655	14,452	18,398
Milwaukee, Wisconsin	11,560	5,839	532	14,030	2,609	14,481	10,670	14,418	8,078	3,156	5,901	2,209	6,809	10,083	9,508	10,704	6,992	9,498	10,668	6,731
Minsk, USSR	3,921	2,218	7,485	17,243	10,235	9,284	3,541	9,631	15,426	6,384	1,970	7,565	4,453	2,770	1,910	11,598	1,167	1,866	3,032	1,411
Mogadiscio, Somalia	2,780	7,382	13,194	12,822	15,681	3,848	4,692	4,297	16,156	12,328	7,374	13,536	6,819	3,235	4,103	12,894	6,304	4,212	3,450	6,538
Mombasa, Kenya	3,657	7,663	13,399	12,665	15,609	2,998	5,590	3,434	15,229	12,904	7,707	13,998	6,644	3,752	4,731	13,660	6,681	4,871	4,256	6,887
Monclova, Mexico	13,719	7,982	2,353	11,963	456	15,388	12,689	15,137	6,042	4,507	8,060	3,122	8,536	12,227	11,676	10,060	9,150	11,664	12,825	8,885
Moncton, Canada	10,070	4,174	2,091	15,824	4,317	12,754	9,552	12,757	9,279	3,815	4,303	3,526	4,964	8,394	7,958	12,094	5,373	7,986	9,203	5,096
Monrovia, Liberia	7,315	5,230	8,840	15,620	10,124	5,997	8,673	5,975	11,187	10,132	5,542	10,276	2,322	5,436	6,164	17,894	5,349	6,379	7,062	5,267
Monte Carlo, Monaco	4,770	1,464	7,253	18,664	9,813	8,496	5,067	8,753	14,150	6,969	1,552	7,849	2,609	2,901	2,709	13,381	851	2,825	4,010	859
Monterrey, Mexico	13,794	8,019	2,453	11,950	475	15,244	12,807	14,985	5,925	4,661	8,107	3,283	8,491	12,261	11,736	10,199	9,195	11,730	12,902	8,928
Montevideo, Uruguay	13,459	10,896	9,734	9,913	8,288	7,953	15,165	7,524	5,098	12,368	11,242	11,242	8,224	11,915	12,744	15,359	11,557	12,962	13,487	11,375
Montgomery, Alabama	12,443	6,563	1,674	13,471	2,022	14,129	11,742	13,967	7,029	4,303	6,684	3,193	6,955	10,776	10,339	11,278	7,760	10,358	11,566	7,484
Montpelier, Vermont	10,665	4,794	1,548	15,180	3,674	13,286	10,049	13,258	8,753	3,643	4,906	3,120	5,566	9,025	8,561	11,732	5,985	8,580	9,789	5,711
Montpellier, France	5,050	1,314	7,048	18,932	9,576	8,591	5,345	8,831	13,865	6,873	1,460	7,704	2,385	3,161	2,994	13,523	982	3,111	4,295	904
Montreal, Canada	10,625	4,777	1,434	15,165	3,669	13,397	9,968	13,378	8,825	3,483	4,878	2,978	5,645	9,018	8,528	11,588	5,962	8,542	9,746	5,690
Moosonee, Canada	10,497	4,844	975	14,940	3,657	14,008	9,618	14,035	9,135	2,658	4,881	2,227	6,157	9,070	8,457	10,810	5,969	8,441	9,604	5,716
Moroni, Comoros	4,291	8,595	14,312	11,746	16,379	2,378	6,162	2,836	14,804	13,801	8,640	14,926	7,457	4,649	5,591	13,396	7,612	5,716	4,988	7,819
Moscow, USSR	3,679	2,802	7,711	16,595	10,472	9,505	3,000	9,880	15,881	6,337	2,518	7,603	5,127	2,918	1,901	10,972	1,832	1,782	2,788	2,061
Mosul, Iraq	1,689	4,230	9,776	15,559	12,521	7,435	2,277	7,841	17,245	8,535	4,082	9,795	5,359	1,072	432	11,738	3,022	430	880	3,305
Mount Isa, Australia	10,424	15,366	14,563	3,967	13,471	10,541	9,861	10,634	10,904	12,655	15,035	12,957	17,168	12,485	12,292	4,349	14,441	12,144	11,039	14,688
Multan, Pakistan	1,684	6,589	11,324	13,008	13,991	7,908	960	8,368	19,658	9,301	6,353	10,716	8,076	3,515	3,092	9,453	5,434	2,942	1,904	5,714
Munich, West Germany	4,570	1,380	7,164	18,402	9,810	8,854	4,648	9,138	14,476	6,631	1,328	7,606	3,167	2,872	2,456	12,795	318	2,531	3,753	493
Murcia, Spain	5,450	1,751	7,130	18,895	9,502	8,220	5,960	8,418	13,349	7,280	2,000	7,974	1,648	3,446	3,500	14,262	1,733	3,647	4,769	1,627
Murmansk, USSR	5,078	2,662	6,405	16,513	9,145	10,959	4,003	11,318	14,755	4,852	2,314	6,143	5,530	4,385	3,391	10,246	2,322	3,270	4,205	2,389
Mururoa Atoll, Fr. Polynesia	18,532	14,719	8,938	5,269	6,288	14,182	16,795	13,771	3,038	9,910	14,774	8,707	14,540	18,964	18,132	7,408	15,862	18,003	18,429	15,609
Muscat, Oman	380	6,275	11,673	13,530	14,434	6,610	1,918	7,064	18,762	10,055	6,115	11,422	7,133	2,439	2,479	10,867	5,067	2,431	1,213	5,350
Myitkyina, Burma	4,221	8,633	11,956	10,789	14,047	9,354	3,054	9,793	17,349	9,429	8,335	10,769	10,581	6,116	5,593	6,958	7,613	5,413	4,496	7,869
Naga, Philippines	7,175	11,172	12,448	8,118	13,358	10,963	5,995	11,313	14,380	9,853	10,838	10,838	13,496	9,110	8,557	4,248	10,324	8,366	7,491	10,549
Nagasaki, Japan	7,169	9,569	10,240	9,623	11,469	12,502	5,469	12,917	14,339	7,629	9,220	8,667	12,313	8,717	7,878	4,056	8,971	7,658	7,148	9,140
Nagoya, Japan	7,719	9,577	9,695	9,584	10,798	13,200	5,944	13,615	13,752	7,119	9,229	8,085	12,428	9,153	8,254	3,663	9,098	8,032	7,627	9,241
Nagpur, India	2,475	7,846	12,430	11,773	14,989	7,640	2,167	8,094	18,930	10,225	7,611	11,641	9,183	4,513	4,268	8,860	6,682	4,139	3,000	6,964
Nairobi, Kenya	3,549	7,247	12,965	13,097	15,175	3,221	5,494	3,636	15,229	12,546	7,299	13,603	6,209	3,418	4,432	13,906	6,286	4,585	4,068	6,485
Nanchang, China	5,962	9,349	11,188	9,925	12,742	11,094	4,454	11,514	15,593	8,551	9,012	9,732	11,789	7,697	6,990	5,170	8,538	6,783	6,078	8,753
Nancy, France	4,970	1,013	6,824	18,793	9,444	9,043	5,029	9,305	14,076	6,425	1,027	7,339	2,916	3,236	2,858	12,936	432	2,934	4,156	313
Nandi, Fiji	14,022	16,049	11,467	3,178	9,639	13,627	12,827	13,518	7,501	10,715	15,774	10,274	18,515	16,006	15,368	3,644	16,132	15,157	14,386	16,177
Nanjing, China	6,165	9,166	10,742	10,079	12,278	11,514	4,547	11,940	15,364	8,105	8,824	9,272	11,718	7,807	7,037	4,992	8,420	6,824	6,207	8,620
Nanning, China	5,365	9,500	12,029	9,854	13,723	10,110	4,128	10,526	16,204	9,408	9,182	10,642	11,647	7,253	6,688	5,842	8,559	6,499	5,630	8,800
Nantes, France	5,515	758	6,465	19,392	9,013	9,139	5,631	9,365	13,488	6,332	975	7,129	2,448	3,694	3,418	13,306	1,008	3,508	4,721	780
Naples, Italy	4,157	2,073	7,883	18,024	10,460	8,014	4,610	8,298	14,699	7,467	2,105	8,415	2,936	2,254	2,147	13,348	1,155	2,289	3,431	1,304
Narvik, Norway	5,423	2,089	5,977	17,065	8,737	10,956	4,526	11,285	14,260	4,681	1,742	5,888	5,015	4,474	3,567	10,714	1,974	3,484	4,533	1,973
Nashville, Tennessee	12,131	6,293	1,260	13,686	2,180	14,269	11,362	14,139	7,400	3,896	6,394	2,830	6,886	10,528	10,041	11,081	7,478	10,051	11,247	7,207
Nassau, Bahamas	12,469	6,569	2,741	13,652	2,765	13,043	12,131	12,845	6,728	5,367	6,757	4,353	6,348	10,600	10,355	12,401	7,774	10,415	11,643	7,489
Natal, Brazil	10,340	7,094	8,066	13,744	8,215	7,406	11,631	7,166	8,162	10,266	7,442	9,751	4,349	8,438	9,077	18,011	7,683	9,281	10,064	7,507
Natashquan, Canada	9,618	3,754	2,255	16,167	4,689	12,684	9,053	12,727	9,769	3,587	3,860	3,498	4,826	7,995	7,514	11,947	4,941	7,533	8,744	4,668
Nauru Island	12,212	14,118	10,887	5,035	9,878	14,268	10,758	14,344	9,358	9,388	13,800	9,369	17,057	14,013	13,231	1,428	13,973	13,013	12,397	14,056
Ndjamena, Chad	4,468	4,948	10,304	15,609	12,351	4,950	6,046	5,180	14,024	10,521	5,110	11,258	3,386	2,822	3,793	15,558	4,326	4,016	4,367	4,422
Nelson, New Zealand	14,109	18,664	13,491	557	11,109	11,229	13,770	11,047	7,060	13,261	18,358	12,620	18,333	16,065	16,133	5,953	18,277	16,009	14,839	18,470
Nema, Mauritania	6,522	4,075	8,295	16,754	10,000	6,580	7,679	6,647	12,022	9,229	4,375	9,568	1,320	4,526	5,126	16,691	4,146	5,332	6,142	4,067
Neuquen, Argentina	14,559	11,822	9,793	8,950	7,946	8,701	16,310	8,253	4,040	12,406	12,162	11,138	9,277	13,064	13,890	14,209	12,579	14,107	14,628	12,378
New Delhi, India	2,203	7,092	11,588	12,471	14,177	8,120	1,350	8,579	19,357	9,427	6,842	10,846	8,655	4,092	3,666	8,933	5,956	3,510	2,486	6,233
New Glasgow, Canada	9,975	4,067	2,265	15,960	4,454	12,578	9,503	12,582	9,341	3,958	4,208	3,697	4,793	8,272	7,859	12,256	5,270	7,892	9,113	4,991
New Haven, Connecticut	10,914	5,017	1,650	15,009	3,510	13,229	10,350	13,174	8,463	3,910	5,147	3,293	5,606	9,228	8,802	11,890	6,217	8,829	10,045	5,940
New Orleans, Louisiana	12,870	7,003	1,876	13,024	1,590	14,405	12,111	14,211	6,649	4,443	7,118	3,232	7,377	11,221	10,771	11,035	8,197	10,786	11,989	7,922
New Plymouth, New Zealand	14,163	18,419	13,288	811	10,949	11,474	13,730	11,295	7,054	13,010	18,121	12,384	18,526	16,153	16,147	5,731	18,140	16,010	14,864	18,306
New York, New York	11,025	5,130	1,603	14,897	3,400	13,300	10,452	13,238	8,358	3,922	5,259	3,263	5,702	9,341	8,914	11,848	6,330	8,940	10,156	6,052
Newcastle upon Tyne, UK	5,648	356	5,978	18,849	8,641	9,905	5,421	10,154	13,557	5,559	144	6,455	3,231	4,052	3,533	12,482	957	3,567	4,792	697
Newcastle Waters, Australia	9,685	14,720	14,737	4,656	13,980	10,206	9,141	10,346	11,643	12,596	14,399	13,072	16,435	11,747	11,555	4,504	13,746	11,409	10,299	14,000
Niamey, Niger	5,700	4,478	9,244	16,257	11,055	5,713	7,065	5,836	12,807	9,918	4,727	10,412	2,196	3,817	4,591	16,487	4,233	4,811	5,440	4,230
Nicosia, Cyprus	2,372	3,683	9,425	16,250	12,107	7,201	3,163	7,571	16,393	8,514	3,601	9,670	4,486	640	652	12,563	2,510	875	1,709	2,773
Niue (Alofi)	15,338	15,947	10,639	3,480	8,531	14,154	14,007	13,943	6,206	10,377	15,761	9,680	17,484	17,254	16,464	4,552	16,457	16,242	15,629	16,396
Norfolk, Virginia	11,470	5,561	1,711	14,507	3,058	13,375	10,923	13,274	7,889	4,209	5,702	3,403	5,950	9,749	9,354	11,896	6,766	9,386	10,606	6,486
Norfolk Island, Australia	13,431	17,265	13,021	1,882	11,035	12,053	12,700	11,952	7,938	12,237	16,937	11,848	19,775	15,494	15,224	4,526	16,905	15,054	14,014	17,058
Noril'sk, USSR	5,352	4,768	7,126	14,400	9,600	11,920	3,616	12,348	15,177	4,843	4,420	6,261	7,636	5,543	4,456	8,194	4,355	4,258	4,667	4,465
Norman Wells, Canada	9,964	5,916	2,920	13,450	4,852	15,780	8,413	16,037	10,357	415	5,747	1,505	8,311	9,374	8,415	7,966	6,617	8,296	9,145	6,472
Normanton, Australia	10,429	15,150	14,204	4,142	13,211	10,871	9,758	10,976	10,947	12,277	14,812	12,588	17,187	12,494	12,233	3,978	14,282	12,075	11,004	14,518
North Pole	7,208	4,092	4,819	15,082	7,343	13,307	5,734	13,660	13,006	2,669	3,805	4,066	6,998	6,734	5,720	8,729	4,354	5,583	6,388	4,302
Nottingham, United Kingdom	5,576	342	6,124	19,017	8,762	9,651	5,439	9,936	13,574	5,772	354	6,647	3,034	3,920	3,457	12,689	866	3,505	4,733	584
Norway House, Canada	10,854	5,609	898	14,027	3,374	15,145	9,672	15,203	9,058	1,740	5,575	1,030	7,272	9,701	8,947	9,621	6,629	8,892	9,966	6,404
Norwich, United Kingdom	5,406	513	6,282	18,926	8,928	9,584	5,284	9,837	13,739	5,880	468	6,780	3,074	3,756	3,287	12,670	695	3,336	4,563	414
Nouakchott, Mauritania	7,335	3,999	7,519	16,869	9,088	7,316	8,334	7,333	11,247	8,713	4,333	8,892	1,043	5,297	5,771	16,725	4,358	5,963	6,880	4,217
Noumea, New Caledonia	13,083	16,501	12,635	2,644	10,888	12,533	12,162	12,475	8,364	11,616	16,173	11,342	19,461	15,138	14,720	3,763	16,178	14,533	13,580	16,316
Novosibirsk, USSR	4,003	5,414	8,711	13,861	11,215	10,627	2,117	11,077	16,751	6,456	5,081	7,874	7,949	4,726	3,712	8,288	4,630	3,489	3,482	4,829
Nuku'alofa, Tonga	14,871	16,309	11,187	3,037	9,126	13,709	13,676	13,530	6,644	10,782	16,087	10,164	18,084	16,865	16,204	4,372	16,648	15,990	15,244	16,635
Nukunono Island, Tokelau Isls.	14,738	14,944	9,981	4,398	8,174	15,042	13,185	14,885	6,832	9,419	14,729	8,852	17,026	16,431	15,510	3,664	15,364	15,287	14,858	15,319
Nuremberg, West Germany	4,650	1,278	7,040	18,428	9,698	9,003	4,663	9,287	14,431	6,483	1,201	7,464	3,231	2,990	2,532	12,691	171	2,596	3,822	365
Nyala, Sudan	3,515	5,346	10,992	15,058	13,241	4,683	5,235	5,000	14,987	10,820	5,438	11,739	4,309	2,200	3,275	14,646	4,497	3,484	3,558	4,659
Oaxaca, Mexico	14,435	8,536	3,325	11,564	1,133	14,552	13,669	14,236	5,079	5,668	8,670	4,303	8,543	12,705	12,325	10,794	9,739	12,350	13,561	9,460
Ocean Falls, Canada	11,402	7,094	2,618	12,376	3,699	16,962	9,808	17,107	8,985	1,622	6,971	963	9,155	10,776	9,840	7,651	7,916	9,726	10,586	7,744
Odense, Denmark	4,936	1,103	6,576	18,262	9,286	9,649	4,658	9,940	14,316	5,854	856	6,883	3,667	3,472	2,838	12,142	493	2,851	4,066	493
Odessa, USSR	3,207	2,730	8,273	16,946	11,005	8,452	3,216	8,809	15,930	7,241	2,561	8,415	4,391	1,913	1,110	11,983	1,528	1,123	2,348	1,814
Ogbomosho, Nigeria	5,724	5,102	9,839	15,621	11,538	5,086	7,242	5,199	12,768	10,558	5,341	11,041	2,798	3,986	4,866	16,759	4,792	5,089	5,577	4,809
Okha, USSR	7,637	7,818	7,730	11,326	9,252	14,040	5,693	14,498	13,536	5,106	7,480	6,209	10,770	8,500	7,454	4,972	7,580	7,236	7,242	7,663
Okinawa (Naha)	7,158	10,138	10,990	9,080	12,107	12,012	5,609	12,406	14,397	8,386	9,792	9,401	12,771	8,865	8,114	3,974	9,452	7,901	7,255	9,641
Oklahoma City, Oklahoma	12,700	7,015	1,332	12,871	1,446	15,211	11,687	15,056	7,046	3,658	7,075	2,362	7,833	11,259	10,669	10,187	8,166	10,652	11,805	7,906
Old Crow, Canada	9,635	6,053	3,551	13,251	5,405	15,767	7,994	16,082	10,803	967	5,848	2,096	8,615	9,228	8,223	7,503	6,633	8,086	8,849	6,518
Olympia, Washington	11,995	7,376	2,330	12,171	3,025	17,069	10,453	17,107	8,327	2,139	7,290	986	9,196	11,236	10,345	7,936	8,284	10,245	11,159	8,091
Omaha, Nebraska	12,068	6,458	686	13,367	2,076	15,135	11,031	15,046	7,702	3,082	6,498	1,886	7,505	10,688	10,058	10,137	7,587	10,033	11,173	7,333
Omsk, USSR	3,620	4,916	8,642	14,391	11,246	10,236	1,861	10,677	16,903	6,540	4,592	7,955	7,370	4,159	3,126	8,896	4,071	2,905	3,010	4,283
Oodnadatta, Australia	10,387	15,771	15,376	3,687	14,045	9,782	10,078	9,848	10,816	13,514	15,464	13,796	16,939	12,412	12,375	5,198	14,723	12,253	11,084	14,990
Oradea, Romania	3,806	2,113	7,796	17,618	10,491	8,567	3,887	8,892	15,262	7,000	1,988	8,086	3,774	2,246	1,687	12,422	907	1,749	2,975	1,187
Oran, Algeria	5,421	2,008	7,977	18,658	9,657	7,977	6,027	8,170	13,335	7,530	2,256	8,206	1,522	3,389	3,527	14,482	1,938	3,687	4,773	1,853
Oranjestad, Aruba	12,772	7,168	4,326	13,272	3,865	11,754	12,925	11,497	6,113	6,938	7,425	5,940	6,119	10,742	10,763	13,674	8,313	10,873	12,062	8,033
Orebro, Sweden	4,885	1,476	6,527	17,790	9,273	9,985	4,389	10,298	14,513	5,571	1,159	6,681	4,182	3,627	2,854	11,621	961	2,825	3,996	1,014
Orel, USSR	3,466	2,793	7,916	16,676	10,676	9,182	2,967	9,555	15,979	6,626	2,537	7,871	4,946	2,597	1,600	11,236	1,727	1,498	2,572	1,981
Orsk, USSR	2,892	4,277	8,791	15,136	11,511	9,377	1,618	9,803	17,151	6,995	3,988	8,370	6,458	3,103	2,053	9,954	3,271	1,834	2,135	3,518
Osaka, Japan	7,611	9,581	9,809	9,588	10,935	13,059	5,850	13,475	13,868	7,225	9,233	8,206	12,413	9,070	8,182	3,730	9,078	7,960	7,534	9,226
Oslo, Norway	5,138	1,269	6,285	17,952	9,026	10,121	4,647	10,422	14,251	5,404	937	6,482	4,071	3,833	3,093	11,691	995	3,072	4,251	971
Osorno, Chile	14,991	12,217	9,857	8,539	7,861	8,987	16,771	8,534	3,640	12,435	12,553	11,122	9,724	13,531	14,361	13,741	13,010	14,578	15,088	12,802
Ostrava, Czechoslovakia	4,187	1,735	7,387	17,906	10,085	8,916	4,142	9,228	14,942	6,624	1,588	7,689	3,676	2,654	2,070	12,361	531	2,113	3,340	816
Ottawa, Canada	10,746	4,916	1,276	15,012	3,524	13,556	10,052	13,532	8,732	3,402	5,009	2,844	5,810	9,159	8,655	11,455	6,095	8,664	9,864	5,825

Distances in Kilometers	Dubayy, United Arab Emir.	Dublin, Ireland	Duluth, Minnesota	Dunedin, New Zealand	Durango, Mexico	Durban, South Africa	Dushanbe, USSR	East London, South Africa	Easter Island (Hanga Roa)	Echo Bay, Canada	Edinburgh, United Kingdom	Edmonton, Canada	El Aaiun, Morocco	Elat, Israel	Elazig, Turkey	Eniwetok Atoll, Marshall Isls.	Erfurt, East Germany	Erzurum, Turkey	Esfahan, Iran	Essen, West Germany
Ouagadougou, Bourkina Fasso	6,113	4,564	9,064	16,216	10,761	5,831	7,457	5,918	12,395	9,896	4,834	10,304	2,042	4,217	4,964	16,824	4,432	5,181	5,843	4,403
Oujda, Morocco	5,546	2,102	7,317	18,609	9,607	7,934	6,181	8,116	13,195	7,590	2,364	8,234	1,362	3,504	3,673	14,631	2,092	3,836	4,911	1,998
Oxford, United Kingdom	5,558	382	6,194	19,121	8,815	9,574	5,475	9,815	13,559	5,890	481	6,748	2,908	3,865	3,439	12,820	859	3,497	4,724	573
Pago Pago, American Samoa	15,085	15,461	10,307	3,922	8,334	14,601	13,633	14,412	6,479	9,906	15,261	9,267	17,289	16,893	16,025	4,127	15,929	15,802	15,287	15,875
Pakxe, Laos	5,364	10,066	12,921	9,357	14,565	9,428	4,452	9,825	16,153	10,301	9,765	11,531	11,946	7,366	6,949	6,116	9,044	6,780	5,780	9,302
Palembang, Indonesia	6,177	11,650	14,880	7,917	16,093	8,285	5,891	8,610	15,069	12,245	11,388	13,402	12,919	8,235	8,122	6,561	10,520	7,999	6,835	10,798
Palermo, Italy	4,182	2,264	8,047	17,948	10,578	7,745	4,770	8,020	14,608	7,728	2,332	8,642	2,759	2,205	2,253	13,635	1,442	2,416	3,504	1,563
Palma, Majorca	5,122	1,673	7,263	18,802	9,708	8,227	5,591	8,450	13,704	7,246	1,868	8,016	2,011	3,145	3,143	13,973	1,427	3,286	4,421	1,364
Palmerston North, New Zealand	14,302	18,554	13,272	741	10,887	11,421	13,908	11,231	6,893	13,083	18,271	12,417	18,337	16,272	16,306	5,904	18,334	16,175	15,018	18,496
Panama, Panama	13,836	8,104	4,359	12,266	3,149	12,487	13,812	12,178	5,136	6,985	8,335	5,802	7,226	11,825	11,788	12,831	9,280	11,883	13,092	8,996
Paramaribo, Suriname	11,771	6,870	5,751	13,778	5,657	9,968	12,445	9,723	6,883	8,216	7,187	7,436	5,028	9,709	9,991	15,466	7,853	10,147	11,219	7,599
Paris, France	5,252	779	6,588	19,065	9,187	9,174	5,302	9,421	13,793	6,290	870	7,158	2,756	3,496	3,142	13,034	667	3,219	4,441	441
Patna, India	2,993	7,854	11,984	11,668	14,414	8,424	2,100	8,877	18,570	9,651	7,588	11,055	9,506	4,936	4,513	8,190	6,746	4,353	3,336	7,019
Patrai, Greece	3,466	2,717	8,526	17,321	11,139	7,600	4,065	7,918	15,340	7,935	2,699	8,963	3,473	1,555	1,526	13,145	1,646	1,698	2,771	1,865
Peking, China	5,845	8,303	9,992	10,924	11,748	11,710	4,063	12,157	15,591	7,365	7,959	8,601	10,935	7,291	6,434	5,488	7,608	6,214	5,746	7,796
Penrhyn Island (Omoka)	16,065	14,480	8,964	5,068	6,857	15,599	14,321	15,310	5,485	8,943	14,358	8,103	15,823	17,363	16,295	4,943	15,244	16,084	15,996	15,105
Peoria, Illinois	11,855	6,118	706	13,771	2,322	14,592	10,960	14,503	7,786	3,337	6,186	2,289	7,002	10,363	9,799	10,669	7,276	9,791	10,963	7,014
Perm', USSR	3,637	3,824	8,031	15,495	10,743	10,016	2,346	10,430	16,400	6,233	3,507	7,602	6,286	3,562	2,475	9,852	2,971	2,279	2,837	3,179
Perth, Australia	9,022	14,881	17,124	4,884	15,974	7,882	9,198	7,988	11,904	14,814	14,666	15,445	15,105	10,917	11,126	6,894	13,687	11,053	9,828	13,972
Peshawar, Pakistan	1,845	6,286	10,908	13,268	13,568	8,255	560	8,713	19,238	8,876	6,036	10,291	7,928	3,483	2,931	9,371	5,154	2,759	1,857	5,430
Petropavlovsk-Kamchatskiy,USSR	8,641	8,133	7,081	11,016	8,337	15,087	6,696	15,546	12,494	4,537	7,815	5,469	11,087	9,367	8,297	4,616	8,087	8,085	8,199	8,127
Petrozavodsk, USSR	4,356	2,554	7,055	16,717	9,813	10,165	3,494	10,529	15,318	5,637	2,227	6,903	5,194	3,587	2,595	10,712	1,859	2,482	3,470	2,011
Pevek, USSR	8,294	6,354	5,499	12,817	7,330	14,889	6,462	15,317	12,443	2,862	6,060	4,077	9,259	8,429	7,348	6,489	6,513	7,165	7,636	6,498
Philadelphia, Pennsylvania	11,154	5,260	1,565	14,769	3,276	13,373	10,572	13,302	8,234	3,948	5,388	3,241	5,809	9,470	9,044	11,808	6,459	9,070	10,285	6,182
Phnom Penh, Kampuchea	5,425	10,342	13,326	9,113	14,933	9,136	4,662	9,523	16,047	10,706	10,049	11,931	12,095	7,459	7,110	6,243	9,290	6,951	5,903	9,554
Phoenix, Arizona	13,371	8,043	2,243	11,726	1,269	16,523	12,032	16,322	6,713	3,651	8,050	2,235	9,148	12,219	11,489	8,920	9,125	11,433	12,490	8,887
Pierre, South Dakota	11,907	6,465	696	13,285	2,290	15,484	10,757	15,430	7,973	2,644	6,473	1,397	7,739	10,650	9,954	9,705	7,551	9,912	11,015	7,310
Pinang, Malaysia	5,275	10,614	14,094	8,930	15,778	8,345	4,857	8,720	16,057	11,495	10,347	12,749	12,033	7,340	7,145	6,840	9,495	7,011	5,875	9,771
Pitcairn Island (Adamstown)	19,489	14,435	8,826	5,715	6,085	13,604	17,696	13,168	2,076	10,158	14,556	8,856	13,781	18,467	18,198	8,377	15,635	18,176	19,147	15,358
Pittsburgh, Pennsylvania	11,393	5,536	1,203	14,441	2,933	13,787	10,703	13,711	8,078	3,707	5,643	2,894	6,211	9,770	9,295	11,421	6,725	9,309	10,513	6,452
Plymouth, Montserrat	11,816	6,295	4,324	14,191	4,489	11,225	12,051	11,020	7,038	6,813	6,569	6,009	5,162	9,782	9,824	14,225	7,413	9,940	11,119	7,137
Plymouth, United Kingdom	5,737	358	6,109	19,367	8,694	9,540	5,708	9,765	13,345	5,931	617	6,735	2,693	3,991	3,622	13,021	1,071	3,690	4,916	791
Ponape Island	10,978	13,171	10,917	5,972	10,420	13,967	9,490	14,152	10,592	9,022	12,835	9,281	16,124	12,747	11,966	671	12,865	11,749	11,134	12,980
Ponce, Puerto Rico	12,118	6,461	3,954	13,961	3,999	11,707	12,216	11,495	6,807	6,501	6,716	5,623	5,546	10,108	10,084	13,745	7,613	10,188	11,386	7,332
Ponta Delgada, Azores	7,583	2,288	5,409	18,403	7,489	9,527	7,862	9,602	11,298	6,342	2,626	6,613	1,654	5,600	5,560	14,493	3,230	5,678	6,857	2,974
Pontianak, Indonesia	6,443	11,678	14,423	7,818	15,496	8,886	5,947	9,211	14,904	11,787	11,394	12,892	13,201	8,508	8,297	5,986	10,593	8,157	7,036	10,864
Port Augusta, Australia	10,826	16,339	15,541	3,163	13,915	9,666	10,615	9,691	10,318	13,894	16,039	14,043	17,170	12,820	12,855	5,522	15,262	12,744	11,555	15,534
Port Blair, India	4,217	9,572	13,520	9,998	15,637	8,046	3,815	8,460	17,136	11,026	9,316	12,371	10,967	6,279	6,066	7,560	8,436	5,933	4,797	8,714
Port Elizabeth, South Africa	7,270	10,150	14,688	10,488	15,105	687	9,185	240	11,751	15,710	10,328	16,144	7,908	7,099	8,166	14,979	9,518	8,338	7,864	9,635
Port Hedland, Australia	8,500	14,090	15,973	5,489	15,572	8,690	8,331	8,867	12,648	13,533	13,822	14,282	15,085	10,517	10,519	5,939	12,959	10,409	9,219	13,237
Port Louis, Mauritius	5,032	10,172	15,977	10,075	18,144	2,872	6,606	3,258	14,585	14,893	10,167	16,220	9,244	6,010	6,788	11,977	9,095	6,861	5,880	9,331
Port Moresby, Papua New Guinea	10,648	14,594	13,092	4,605	12,279	11,932	9,669	12,060	10,839	11,179	14,246	11,468	17,177	12,678	12,223	2,858	13,920	12,039	11,094	14,118
Port Said, Egypt	2,348	3,937	9,727	16,089	12,369	6,765	3,408	7,132	16,298	8,918	3,888	10,046	4,417	318	1,037	12,887	2,804	1,257	1,832	3,052
Port Sudan, Sudan	1,960	5,267	11,077	14,865	13,662	5,514	3,691	5,910	16,534	10,278	5,245	11,426	5,190	1,124	2,122	13,089	4,171	2,284	2,036	4,408
Port-au-Prince, Haiti	12,564	6,791	3,618	13,562	3,402	12,275	12,505	12,047	6,448	6,228	7,022	5,244	6,091	10,587	10,492	13,178	7,970	10,582	11,797	7,686
Port-of-Spain, Trin. & Tobago	12,112	6,798	4,935	13,751	4,797	10,839	12,521	10,599	6,651	7,461	7,087	6,607	5,370	10,053	10,196	14,605	7,875	10,328	11,471	7,605
Port-Vila, Vanuatu	13,108	16,026	12,148	3,126	10,511	13,039	12,034	12,994	8,389	11,078	15,707	10,822	18,949	15,130	14,597	3,301	15,807	14,398	13,529	15,919
Portland, Maine	10,576	4,685	1,745	15,320	3,814	13,089	10,015	13,060	8,801	3,800	4,810	3,312	5,381	8,904	8,466	11,923	5,883	8,491	9,706	5,606
Portland, Oregon	12,162	7,501	2,346	12,062	2,882	17,135	10,622	17,147	8,159	2,304	7,420	1,109	9,269	11,387	10,502	7,949	8,422	10,405	11,325	8,226
Porto, Portugal	6,074	1,366	6,406	19,476	8,770	8,857	6,402	9,028	12,804	6,690	1,689	7,304	1,607	4,116	4,049	14,101	1,863	4,171	5,344	1,655
Porto Alegre, Brazil	12,881	10,209	9,452	10,608	8,275	7,736	14,518	7,329	5,644	12,060	10,556	11,033	7,514	11,259	12,059	16,007	10,849	12,276	12,850	10,670
Porto Alexandre, Angola	6,544	7,856	12,337	12,845	13,379	2,498	8,444	2,499	12,104	13,333	8,074	13,716	5,474	5,598	6,673	16,797	7,400	6,882	6,833	7,467
Porto Novo, Benin	5,968	5,257	9,848	15,488	11,458	5,038	7,499	5,127	12,524	10,665	5,507	11,097	2,836	4,243	5,123	17,016	4,995	5,346	5,832	5,002
Porto Velho, Brazil	13,362	8,754	6,759	11,904	5,727	10,004	14,269	9,656	5,198	9,384	9,069	8,328	6,759	11,344	11,756	14,975	9,724	11,928	12,924	9,475
Portsmouth, United Kingdom	5,530	455	6,265	19,185	8,872	9,472	5,490	9,711	13,563	5,993	590	6,840	2,814	3,808	3,412	12,921	852	3,477	4,703	572
Poznan, Poland	4,402	1,560	7,120	17,967	9,831	9,216	4,229	9,526	14,798	6,323	1,368	7,393	3,760	2,938	2,297	12,187	440	2,317	3,539	692
Prague, Czechoslovakia	4,448	1,471	7,172	18,177	9,854	9,004	4,414	9,302	14,667	6,505	1,347	7,530	3,465	2,856	2,328	12,500	263	2,379	3,607	547
Praia, Cape Verde Islands	8,216	4,524	7,188	16,334	8,472	7,664	9,190	7,617	10,366	8,703	4,870	8,685	1,727	6,178	6,632	17,016	5,054	6,819	7,757	4,882
Pretoria, South Africa	6,354	9,371	14,326	11,212	15,287	534	8,282	808	12,605	14,944	9,525	15,593	7,345	6,162	7,225	14,965	8,665	7,396	6,928	8,799
Prince Albert, Canada	11,122	6,061	1,208	13,538	3,239	15,674	9,826	15,735	8,908	1,587	6,006	514	7,801	10,084	9,282	9,125	7,041	9,213	10,244	6,828
Prince Edward Island	8,147	11,839	16,263	8,765	15,857	1,952	9,919	1,729	11,206	17,412	11,993	17,845	9,652	8,437	9,445	13,528	11,115	9,587	8,884	11,260
Prince George, Canada	11,230	6,758	2,299	12,729	3,645	16,604	9,700	16,738	9,072	1,380	6,646	614	8,784	10,512	9,600	8,000	7,608	9,496	10,397	7,429
Prince Rupert, Canada	11,171	7,011	2,795	12,427	3,979	16,904	9,554	17,091	9,246	1,471	6,874	1,107	9,168	10,606	9,652	7,517	7,793	9,532	10,366	7,632
Providence, Rhode Island	10,783	4,883	1,736	15,147	3,648	13,124	10,238	13,076	8,580	3,924	5,016	3,357	5,478	9,092	8,670	11,963	6,085	8,699	9,916	5,807
Provo, Utah	12,629	7,427	1,734	12,276	1,912	16,459	11,280	16,354	7,463	2,905	7,410	1,487	8,775	11,548	10,780	8,866	8,472	10,716	11,753	8,243
Puerto Aisen, Chile	14,900	12,628	10,388	8,152	8,343	8,679	16,774	8,221	3,823	12,956	12,969	11,629	10,038	13,607	14,504	13,623	13,358	14,726	15,103	13,165
Puerto Deseado, Argentina	14,354	12,537	10,779	8,275	8,846	8,096	16,254	7,638	4,399	13,382	12,884	12,091	9,828	13,152	14,092	14,009	13,169	14,316	14,603	12,998
Puerto Princesa, Philippines	6,892	11,314	13,040	8,030	14,006	10,329	5,896	10,673	14,629	10,427	10,992	11,452	13,425	8,889	8,433	4,762	10,383	8,255	7,294	10,625
Punta Arenas, Chile	14,612	13,232	11,256	7,585	9,152	8,146	16,553	7,686	4,283	13,810	13,579	12,466	10,497	13,610	14,599	13,432	13,839	14,822	14,971	13,676
Pusan, South Korea	7,029	9,303	10,049	9,887	11,363	12,521	5,292	12,945	14,458	7,428	8,955	8,497	12,057	8,529	7,669	4,250	8,715	7,449	6,975	8,881
Pyongyang, North Korea	6,656	8,784	9,786	10,409	11,283	12,406	4,864	12,844	14,789	7,150	8,436	8,287	11,533	8,076	7,191	4,721	8,191	6,969	6,547	8,357
Qamdo, China	4,144	8,112	11,321	11,271	13,469	9,727	2,713	10,176	17,403	8,811	7,803	10,164	10,214	5,908	5,277	6,989	7,136	5,082	4,283	7,383
Qandahar, Afghanistan	1,239	6,099	11,047	13,534	13,767	7,728	821	8,183	19,339	9,172	5,878	10,573	7,508	2,954	2,531	9,957	4,926	2,388	1,337	5,209
Qiqian, China	6,176	7,318	8,597	11,858	10,478	12,555	4,242	13,014	15,026	5,978	6,969	7,249	10,144	7,204	6,207	5,841	6,815	5,984	5,842	6,957
Qom, Iran	1,123	4,874	10,259	14,862	13,020	7,439	1,656	7,868	17,974	8,796	4,698	10,117	6,083	1,606	1,134	11,176	3,669	1,033	230	3,954
Quebec, Canada	10,392	4,544	1,589	15,391	3,900	13,252	9,750	13,249	9,048	3,465	4,644	3,059	5,464	8,785	8,294	11,656	5,728	8,308	9,513	5,456
Quetta, Pakistan	1,276	6,293	11,226	13,345	13,938	7,663	941	8,120	19,532	9,321	6,072	10,726	7,672	3,087	2,707	9,875	5,118	2,570	1,485	5,401
Quito, Ecuador	14,344	8,857	5,374	11,604	3,896	11,879	14,615	11,528	4,452	7,993	9,115	6,776	7,596	12,284	12,402	13,209	9,995	12,524	13,689	9,716
Rabaul, Papua New Guinea	10,906	14,214	12,288	4,947	11,542	12,721	9,727	12,859	10,631	10,420	13,867	10,670	17,034	12,872	12,288	2,063	13,693	12,089	11,253	13,858
Raiatea (Uturoa)	17,102	14,951	9,195	4,778	6,794	14,844	15,428	14,497	4,467	9,596	14,899	8,591	15,587	18,448	17,363	5,978	15,900	17,160	17,108	15,710
Raleigh, North Carolina	11,701	5,797	1,660	14,265	2,818	13,545	11,123	13,430	7,679	4,226	5,934	3,343	6,179	9,990	9,588	11,767	7,000	9,617	10,835	6,721
Rangiroa (Avatoru)	17,371	14,583	8,799	5,186	6,362	15,048	15,593	14,676	4,182	9,316	14,551	8,260	15,141	18,364	17,288	6,245	15,578	17,103	17,246	15,373
Rangoon, Burma	4,334	9,326	12,916	10,170	14,960	8,683	3,594	9,105	17,154	10,385	9,048	11,715	10,987	6,356	6,007	7,129	8,239	5,852	4,795	8,509
Raoul Is., Kermadec Islands	14,787	17,247	12,017	2,103	9,803	12,783	13,903	12,595	6,625	11,721	17,015	11,071	18,511	16,852	16,465	4,989	17,482	16,274	15,323	17,508
Rarotonga (Avarua)	16,425	15,791	10,124	3,845	7,788	14,240	15,022	13,948	5,124	10,293	15,693	9,398	16,581	18,280	17,359	5,508	16,604	17,136	16,676	16,459
Rawson, Argentina	14,313	12,090	10,328	8,710	8,484	8,257	16,153	7,804	4,353	12,945	12,435	11,681	9,434	12,963	13,855	14,272	12,767	14,077	14,475	12,585
Recife, Brazil	10,414	7,320	8,287	13,523	8,361	7,251	11,758	6,999	8,083	10,509	7,668	9,975	4,545	8,543	9,213	18,117	7,885	9,420	10,170	7,715
Regina, Canada	11,389	6,216	1,006	13,425	2,932	15,689	10,124	15,715	8,608	1,902	6,179	698	7,826	10,294	9,519	9,252	7,230	9,456	10,507	7,008
Reykjavik, Iceland	6,892	1,501	4,549	17,829	7,277	11,396	6,265	11,622	12,568	4,074	1,381	4,931	4,158	5,499	4,837	11,608	2,414	4,823	6,003	2,195
Rhodes, Greece	2,858	3,258	9,041	16,721	11,692	7,343	3,568	7,690	15,920	8,276	3,202	9,376	4,022	989	1,004	12,853	2,118	1,207	2,184	2,367
Richmond, Virginia	11,485	5,586	1,584	14,461	2,989	13,495	10,900	13,398	7,903	4,094	5,718	3,276	6,040	9,788	9,373	11,768	6,787	9,400	10,616	6,509
Riga, USSR	4,312	1,960	7,085	17,408	9,838	9,640	3,828	9,977	15,092	5,996	1,677	7,164	4,424	3,160	2,314	11,506	1,082	2,267	3,420	1,267
Ringkobing, Denmark	5,089	981	6,423	18,334	9,132	9,764	4,790	10,050	14,173	5,729	714	6,744	3,642	3,621	2,992	12,137	597	3,004	4,218	522
Rio Branco, Brazil	13,807	9,091	6,734	11,540	5,497	10,306	14,671	9,942	4,759	9,371	9,399	8,251	7,180	11,784	12,177	14,566	10,092	12,344	13,357	9,837
Rio Cuarto, Argentina	14,173	11,097	9,279	9,669	7,636	8,716	15,796	8,282	4,361	11,912	11,437	10,708	8,589	12,536	13,300	14,718	11,873	13,513	14,136	11,667
Rio de Janeiro, Brazil	11,881	9,168	9,146	11,666	8,429	7,325	13,437	6,963	6,622	11,650	9,516	10,807	6,413	10,178	10,951	17,047	9,754	11,166	11,785	9,584
Rio Gallegos, Argentina	14,534	13,028	11,124	7,788	9,069	8,120	16,468	7,660	4,316	13,695	13,375	12,366	10,298	13,472	14,448	13,607	13,641	14,671	14,861	13,475
Rio Grande, Brazil	13,019	10,443	9,609	10,375	8,352	7,729	14,690	7,314	5,518	12,226	10,790	11,171	7,741	11,435	12,252	15,838	11,078	12,470	13,016	10,900
Riyadh, Saudi Arabia	870	5,410	11,083	14,523	13,806	6,258	2,591	6,686	17,629	9,864	5,307	11,135	5,953	1,287	1,710	11,970	4,220	1,770	1,011	4,492
Road Town, Brit. Virgin Isls.	11,918	6,294	4,024	14,147	4,189	11,541	12,052	11,338	6,989	6,536	6,554	5,704	5,331	9,903	9,892	13,907	7,437	10,000	11,194	7,157

Distances in Kilometers	Dubayy, United Arab Emir.	Dublin, Ireland	Duluth, Minnesota	Dunedin, New Zealand	Durango, Mexico	Durban, South Africa	Dushanbe, USSR	East London, South Africa	Easter Island (Hanga Roa)	Echo Bay, Canada	Edinburgh, United Kingdom	Edmonton, Canada	El Aaiun, Morocco	Elat, Israel	Elazig, Turkey	Eniwetok Atoll, Marshall Isls.	Erfurt, East Germany	Erzurum, Turkey	Esfahan, Iran	Essen, West Germany
Roanoke, Virginia	11,655	5,767	1,457	14,260	2,775	13,701	11,021	13,596	7,770	4,026	5,891	3,142	6,263	9,981	9,547	11,587	6,965	9,569	10,781	6,689
Robinson Crusoe Island, Chile	15,523	11,899	9,005	8,790	6,943	9,836	17,078	9,387	3,012	11,552	12,218	10,220	9,659	13,837	14,531	13,383	12,819	14,735	15,453	12,584
Rochester, New York	11,034	5,189	1,211	14,763	3,261	13,654	10,345	13,607	8,439	3,537	5,290	2,859	5,977	9,429	8,939	11,452	6,374	8,951	10,153	6,103
Rockhampton, Australia	11,582	16,151	13,933	3,077	12,468	11,272	10,917	11,297	9,780	12,423	15,804	12,456	18,337	13,646	13,400	4,066	15,385	13,241	12,170	15,606
Rome, Italy	4,326	1,887	7,694	18,206	10,270	8,169	4,721	8,446	14,555	7,306	1,927	8,239	2,851	2,439	2,293	13,337	1,016	2,425	3,586	1,140
Rosario, Argentina	13,830	10,906	9,377	9,878	7,846	8,419	15,469	7,990	4,706	12,015	11,249	10,850	8,335	12,209	12,991	15,052	11,640	13,205	13,804	11,443
Roseau, Dominica	11,828	6,369	4,502	14,140	4,621	11,075	12,117	10,864	6,998	6,989	6,649	6,186	5,141	9,784	9,856	14,377	7,473	9,978	11,146	7,199
Rostock, East Germany	4,773	1,213	6,756	18,224	9,462	9,475	4,550	9,771	14,448	6,033	1,000	7,067	3,636	3,288	2,669	12,212	353	2,688	3,908	453
Rostov-na-Donu, USSR	2,800	3,285	8,586	16,306	11,344	8,581	2,547	8,968	16,524	7,295	3,070	8,552	5,079	2,005	951	11,380	2,120	823	1,907	2,400
Rotterdam, Netherlands	5,175	744	6,506	18,790	9,158	9,421	5,083	9,685	13,956	6,047	673	6,976	3,122	3,528	3,055	12,662	466	3,107	4,335	182
Rouyn, Canada	10,682	4,938	998	14,913	3,508	13,857	9,880	13,855	8,884	3,001	5,001	2,469	6,050	9,181	8,617	11,078	6,091	8,612	9,793	5,829
Sacramento, California	12,929	8,080	2,556	11,554	2,266	17,324	11,399	17,206	7,384	3,068	8,028	1,773	9,603	12,077	11,226	8,032	9,060	11,137	12,084	8,849
Saginaw, Michigan	11,337	5,566	743	14,329	2,868	14,165	10,520	14,111	8,239	3,262	5,641	2,431	6,483	9,812	9,267	10,982	6,731	9,265	10,448	6,466
Saint Denis, Reunion	5,104	10,123	15,912	10,152	17,958	2,646	6,723	3,035	14,450	14,959	10,131	16,257	9,105	5,996	6,806	12,197	9,067	6,888	5,938	9,297
Saint George's, Grenada	12,052	6,684	4,788	13,850	4,713	10,936	12,419	10,704	6,732	7,308	6,970	6,463	5,324	9,997	10,116	14,514	7,772	10,245	11,397	7,500
Saint John, Canada	10,205	4,308	2,016	15,699	4,192	12,819	9,684	12,813	9,145	3,835	4,438	3,492	5,053	8,524	8,093	12,079	5,508	8,121	9,339	5,230
Saint John's, Antigua	11,759	6,236	4,309	14,250	4,513	11,211	11,992	11,010	7,096	6,787	6,510	5,996	5,110	9,726	9,765	14,236	7,354	9,882	11,061	7,078
Saint John's, Canada	9,219	3,301	2,956	16,752	5,246	11,957	8,851	12,000	10,032	4,229	3,463	4,222	4,103	7,486	7,100	12,608	4,508	7,142	8,367	4,227
Saint Louis, Missouri	12,077	6,315	921	13,597	2,119	14,614	11,196	14,503	7,551	3,532	6,391	2,428	7,109	10,561	10,014	10,701	7,481	10,009	11,185	7,216
Saint Paul, Minnesota	11,597	6,006	218	13,794	2,546	14,908	10,581	14,861	8,154	2,790	6,038	1,755	7,168	10,227	9,589	10,240	7,125	9,562	10,703	6,874
Saint Peter Port, UK	5,613	503	6,262	19,357	8,841	9,392	5,628	9,621	13,445	6,077	721	6,889	2,638	3,848	3,501	13,091	982	3,576	4,799	713
Saipan (Susupe)	9,350	11,960	11,056	7,203	11,238	13,202	7,849	13,496	12,218	8,756	11,612	9,364	14,804	11,105	10,344	1,836	11,465	10,129	9,491	11,617
Salalah, Oman	924	6,549	12,176	13,387	14,919	5,746	2,785	6,198	17,990	10,768	6,439	12,098	6,959	2,396	2,805	11,525	5,355	2,826	1,753	5,629
Salem, Oregon	12,229	7,573	2,394	11,991	2,853	17,195	10,682	17,198	8,101	2,373	7,494	1,182	9,332	11,461	10,574	7,914	8,495	10,476	11,394	8,300
Salt Lake City, Utah	12,577	7,394	1,721	12,302	1,973	16,470	11,222	16,373	7,522	2,845	7,374	1,427	8,766	11,507	10,733	8,840	8,434	10,668	11,702	8,206
Salta, Argentina	14,099	10,358	8,369	10,368	6,862	9,255	15,476	8,843	4,394	11,006	10,689	9,834	8,028	12,277	12,915	14,807	11,221	13,114	13,903	10,995
Salto, Uruguay	13,547	10,631	9,311	10,160	7,896	8,267	15,166	7,846	4,979	11,946	10,975	10,823	8,036	11,907	12,683	15,350	11,347	12,897	13,505	11,153
Salvador, Brazil	11,000	7,965	8,499	12,871	8,274	7,344	12,403	7,048	7,492	10,848	8,313	10,190	5,217	9,171	9,869	17,772	8,554	10,078	10,796	8,381
Salzburg, Austria	4,455	1,492	7,270	18,294	9,921	8,786	4,546	9,075	14,586	6,706	1,431	7,695	3,230	2,763	2,341	12,769	383	2,418	3,639	594
Samsun, Turkey	2,495	3,425	9,002	16,335	11,735	7,895	2,776	8,274	16,530	7,898	3,276	9,107	4,754	1,308	380	11,967	2,217	446	1,660	2,500
San Antonio, Texas	13,342	7,584	2,005	12,363	856	15,180	12,366	14,961	6,368	4,290	7,665	2,943	8,163	11,829	11,287	10,272	8,754	11,280	12,449	8,488
San Cristobal, Venezuela	13,273	7,735	4,721	12,725	3,896	11,718	13,493	11,426	5,568	7,355	7,995	6,280	6,564	11,226	11,294	13,636	8,871	11,411	12,588	8,592
San Diego, California	13,539	8,390	2,635	11,337	1,555	16,992	12,091	16,774	6,676	3,712	8,377	2,334	9,604	12,515	11,734	8,457	9,440	11,664	12,673	9,211
San Francisco, California	13,022	8,200	2,672	11,432	2,273	17,423	11,476	17,292	7,314	3,162	8,147	1,883	9,719	12,190	11,334	7,952	9,177	11,243	12,182	8,967
San Jose, Costa Rica	14,144	8,320	4,155	11,991	2,684	12,977	13,950	12,659	4,932	6,746	8,531	5,502	7,631	12,171	12,061	12,322	9,514	12,142	13,363	9,228
San Juan, Argentina	14,538	11,154	8,992	9,584	7,255	9,144	16,090	8,710	3,981	11,615	11,487	10,376	8,755	12,840	13,559	14,379	11,991	13,766	14,454	11,772
San Juan, Puerto Rico	12,046	6,390	3,938	14,034	4,036	11,683	12,144	11,475	6,879	6,474	6,644	5,612	5,479	10,037	10,011	13,768	7,541	10,115	11,314	7,259
San Luis Potosi, Mexico	14,172	8,367	2,847	11,633	431	15,183	13,202	14,892	5,530	5,032	8,464	3,642	8,713	12,600	12,103	10,224	9,550	12,102	13,281	9,280
San Marino, San Marino	4,376	1,723	7,536	18,278	10,139	8,384	4,669	8,665	14,557	7,095	1,737	8,045	2,957	2,550	2,305	13,153	793	2,419	3,607	932
San Miguel de Tucuman, Argen.	14,131	10,540	8,589	10,196	7,046	9,126	15,571	8,709	4,366	11,225	10,874	10,044	8,166	12,348	13,018	14,792	11,384	13,221	13,972	11,162
San Salvador, El Salvador	14,238	8,331	3,678	11,886	1,988	13,664	13,787	13,352	5,021	6,203	8,509	4,909	7,962	12,355	12,122	11,670	9,538	12,179	13,407	9,254
Sanaa, Yemen	1,595	6,074	11,863	14,010	14,499	5,198	3,523	5,628	17,005	10,854	6,025	12,080	6,049	1,836	2,631	12,587	4,939	2,737	2,060	5,190
Santa Cruz, Bolivia	13,656	9,573	7,719	11,135	6,460	9,436	14,850	9,052	4,845	10,353	9,901	9,250	7,337	11,735	12,289	15,105	10,468	12,479	13,356	10,235
Santa Cruz, Tenerife	7,009	2,882	6,729	17,985	8,636	8,176	7,702	8,249	11,686	7,658	3,223	7,966	331	4,947	5,194	15,581	3,386	5,359	6,416	3,206
Santa Fe, New Mexico	12,978	7,501	1,688	12,303	1,297	15,975	11,768	15,810	6,964	3,474	7,525	2,071	8,535	11,710	11,030	9,437	8,608	10,989	12,088	8,362
Santa Rosa, Argentina	14,211	11,424	9,647	9,355	7,940	8,530	15,920	8,089	4,357	12,277	11,766	11,054	8,858	12,666	13,477	14,607	12,165	13,693	14,243	11,967
Santa Rosalia, Mexico	14,037	8,602	2,791	11,226	847	16,443	12,712	16,166	6,035	4,328	8,630	2,915	9,484	12,815	12,124	8,993	9,713	12,077	13,153	9,466
Santarem, Brazil	12,142	7,638	6,566	13,062	6,145	9,468	13,046	9,178	6,430	9,084	7,966	8,233	5,525	10,113	10,523	15,837	8,552	10,696	11,688	8,312
Santiago del Estero, Argentina	14,062	10,584	8,720	10,161	7,188	8,992	15,539	8,573	4,439	11,357	10,919	10,182	8,171	12,304	12,994	14,866	11,408	13,199	13,926	11,191
Santiago, Chile	14,761	11,442	9,143	9,292	7,311	9,210	16,357	8,769	3,772	11,753	11,774	10,486	9,047	13,101	13,836	14,138	12,284	14,045	14,709	12,064
Santo Domingo, Dominican Rep.	12,367	6,637	3,741	13,745	3,652	12,040	12,372	11,820	6,609	6,327	6,877	5,389	5,853	10,376	10,309	13,413	7,806	10,404	11,613	7,522
Sao Paulo de Olivenca, Brazil	13,592	8,544	6,018	12,037	4,933	10,770	14,229	10,432	5,053	8,652	8,838	7,557	6,858	11,534	11,815	14,340	9,595	11,966	13,050	9,331
Sao Paulo, Brazil	12,230	9,363	9,030	11,458	8,186	7,613	13,768	7,241	6,271	11,575	9,711	10,672	6,662	10,511	11,267	16,697	9,995	11,481	12,122	9,816
Sao Tome, Sao Tome & Principe	5,900	5,997	10,657	14,717	12,168	4,218	7,591	4,310	12,607	11,462	6,228	11,916	3,655	4,406	5,388	17,024	5,628	5,610	5,908	5,665
Sapporo, Japan	7,833	8,886	8,751	10,263	9,983	13,788	5,948	14,227	13,527	6,166	8,542	7,158	11,808	9,021	8,040	4,037	8,535	7,817	7,600	8,648
Sarajevo, Yugoslavia	3,915	2,089	7,877	17,814	10,522	8,259	4,202	8,566	15,035	7,260	2,039	8,284	3,381	2,159	1,830	12,873	970	1,941	3,134	1,202
Saratov, USSR	3,024	3,480	8,398	15,982	11,156	9,138	2,287	9,538	16,608	6,887	3,214	8,198	5,587	2,612	1,527	10,741	2,420	1,346	2,148	2,676
Saskatoon, Canada	11,254	6,187	1,205	13,420	3,122	15,769	9,950	15,819	8,785	1,681	6,135	487	7,896	10,217	9,417	9,084	7,172	9,347	10,377	6,958
Schefferville, Canada	9,570	3,845	1,978	15,937	4,619	13,147	8,833	13,221	9,950	2,978	3,893	2,992	5,275	8,080	7,502	11,350	4,983	7,498	8,682	4,725
Seattle, Washington	11,932	7,302	2,277	12,245	3,047	17,001	10,399	17,044	8,378	2,074	7,215	911	9,128	11,164	10,275	7,981	8,209	10,176	11,095	8,017
Sendai, Japan	7,955	9,377	9,216	9,776	10,312	13,635	6,121	14,058	13,472	6,654	9,032	7,599	12,279	9,275	8,331	3,646	8,980	8,108	7,796	9,104
Seoul, South Korea	6,792	8,977	9,885	10,215	11,315	12,449	5,020	12,882	14,670	7,253	8,629	8,365	11,728	8,243	7,368	4,546	8,385	7,146	6,704	8,552
Sept-Iles, Canada	9,875	4,042	1,929	15,852	4,393	12,997	9,242	13,032	9,562	3,380	4,133	3,204	5,145	8,287	7,780	11,707	5,219	7,791	8,995	4,950
Sevastopol, USSR	2,906	3,025	8,569	16,679	11,304	8,248	2,992	8,616	16,203	7,492	2,862	8,685	4,565	1,675	810	11,940	1,820	824	2,051	2,105
Seville, Spain	5,883	1,773	6,841	19,020	9,144	8,383	6,378	8,553	12,916	7,165	2,071	7,773	1,320	3,872	3,932	14,457	2,024	4,076	5,203	1,869
Shanghai, China	6,426	9,375	10,748	9,859	12,186	11,688	4,813	12,108	15,108	8,113	9,032	9,245	11,960	8,073	7,301	4,727	8,652	7,087	6,473	8,848
Sheffield, United Kingdom	5,606	316	6,081	18,996	8,723	9,741	5,451	9,986	13,554	5,722	304	6,598	3,066	3,960	3,487	12,654	896	3,533	4,761	617
Shenyang, China	6,419	8,420	9,584	10,774	11,201	12,338	4,590	12,783	14,987	6,946	8,072	8,127	11,169	7,775	6,870	5,045	7,827	6,647	6,269	7,992
Shiraz, Iran	553	5,379	10,833	14,414	13,593	6,964	1,796	7,403	18,243	9,366	5,222	10,694	6,359	1,702	1,584	11,234	4,171	1,537	351	4,455
Sibiu, Romania	3,590	2,332	8,014	17,425	10,712	8,406	3,725	8,739	15,456	7,184	2,209	8,286	3,882	2,035	1,471	12,407	1,127	1,541	2,764	1,406
Singapore	5,844	11,213	14,457	8,329	15,857	8,435	5,456	8,783	15,461	11,829	10,943	13,021	12,602	7,908	7,739	6,547	10,097	7,608	6,464	10,372
Sioux Falls, South Dakota	11,870	6,324	511	13,465	2,283	15,198	10,797	15,134	7,934	2,826	6,350	1,655	7,490	10,537	9,881	10,009	7,435	9,849	10,976	7,187
Skelleftea, Sweden	5,029	1,988	6,357	17,205	9,118	10,526	4,239	10,859	14,577	5,119	1,642	6,317	4,825	4,036	3,138	10,950	1,639	3,061	4,136	1,687
Skopje, Yugoslavia	3,611	2,411	8,196	17,513	10,845	8,015	3,991	8,334	15,300	7,529	2,357	8,578	3,549	1,837	1,549	12,860	1,278	1,679	2,847	1,520
Socotra Island (Tamrida)	1,403	6,930	12,612	13,056	15,338	5,311	3,221	5,766	17,663	11,249	6,836	12,574	7,141	2,717	3,234	11,668	5,748	3,270	2,230	6,017
Sofia, Bulgaria	3,498	2,479	8,236	17,396	10,904	8,070	3,830	8,397	15,443	7,498	2,401	8,573	3,715	1,791	1,414	12,700	1,312	1,533	2,717	1,570
Songkhla, Thailand	5,206	10,470	13,895	9,058	15,604	8,477	4,717	8,858	16,161	11,296	10,198	12,555	11,956	7,268	7,040	6,778	9,361	6,901	5,781	9,635
Sorong, Indonesia	8,646	13,007	13,419	6,285	13,490	10,953	7,713	11,202	12,842	11,015	12,672	11,729	15,242	10,674	10,249	3,692	12,148	10,072	9,095	12,378
South Georgia Island	12,377	12,253	12,352	8,615	10,818	5,953	14,321	5,494	6,497	14,977	12,590	13,870	9,300	11,535	12,584	14,977	12,483	12,802	12,781	12,402
South Pole	12,799	15,916	15,185	4,919	12,661	6,700	14,272	6,347	6,997	17,334	16,204	15,938	13,010	13,274	14,287	11,272	15,654	14,424	13,619	15,706
South Sandwich Islands	11,880	12,451	13,065	8,413	11,564	5,342	13,819	4,883	7,087	15,674	12,775	14,607	9,492	11,236	12,310	14,819	12,531	12,520	12,361	12,486
Split, Yugoslavia	4,056	1,989	7,793	17,958	10,420	8,259	4,365	8,557	14,877	7,243	1,963	8,240	3,220	2,260	1,982	13,001	925	2,098	3,285	1,130
Spokane, Washington	11,894	7,071	1,910	12,511	2,855	16,672	10,434	16,693	8,325	2,051	7,002	711	8,804	11,018	10,164	8,351	8,018	10,077	11,040	7,815
Spoleto, Italy	4,325	1,832	7,644	18,219	10,233	8,252	4,678	8,532	14,578	7,226	1,859	8,169	2,912	2,465	2,274	13,249	926	2,399	3,572	1,061
Springbok, South Africa	7,275	9,487	13,819	11,197	14,342	1,270	9,218	1,025	11,591	14,986	9,692	15,301	7,108	6,799	7,885	15,829	8,959	8,075	7,764	9,048
Springfield, Illinois	11,941	6,190	801	13,711	2,246	14,585	11,056	14,486	7,691	3,427	6,262	2,359	7,030	10,436	9,881	10,700	7,352	9,874	11,049	7,088
Springfield, Massachusetts	10,833	4,941	1,634	15,074	3,570	13,226	10,259	13,179	8,551	3,847	5,067	3,260	5,574	9,157	8,722	11,864	6,139	8,748	9,962	5,862
Srinagar, India	2,122	6,492	10,954	13,035	13,572	8,443	733	8,902	19,140	8,845	6,231	10,263	8,206	3,784	3,213	9,072	5,378	3,036	2,159	5,651
Stanley, Falkland Islands	13,751	12,595	11,394	8,248	9,551	7,393	15,683	6,934	5,067	14,019	12,944	12,762	9,764	12,709	13,703	14,279	13,092	13,926	14,078	12,951
Stara Zagora, Bulgaria	3,313	2,646	8,380	17,207	11,061	8,021	3,646	8,358	15,636	7,578	2,553	8,678	3,892	1,654	1,223	12,585	1,463	1,340	2,526	1,729
Stockholm, Sweden	4,755	1,633	6,645	17,647	9,396	9,956	4,230	10,277	14,665	5,626	1,319	6,761	4,302	3,549	2,744	11,525	1,030	2,706	3,864	1,119
Stornoway, United Kingdom	6,003	544	5,548	18,614	8,235	10,361	5,637	10,605	13,286	5,102	320	5,994	3,491	4,479	3,902	12,208	1,377	3,918	5,132	1,140
Strasbourg, France	4,856	1,114	6,919	18,681	9,547	8,991	4,920	9,260	14,191	6,480	1,104	7,412	2,987	3,132	2,744	12,894	357	2,819	4,041	323
Stuttgart, West Germany	4,760	1,192	6,986	18,574	9,625	8,975	4,812	9,250	14,296	6,501	1,157	7,453	3,077	3,056	2,645	12,826	280	2,718	3,941	336
Subic, Philippines	6,828	10,899	12,453	8,408	13,514	10,751	5,969	11,114	14,728	9,836	10,568	10,874	13,170	8,764	8,220	4,564	10,024	8,030	7,146	10,254
Suchow, China	5,978	8,878	10,563	10,366	12,190	11,492	4,316	11,926	15,532	7,928	8,536	9,125	11,437	7,575	6,786	5,209	8,135	6,571	5,985	8,334
Sucre, Bolivia	13,911	9,805	7,771	10,895	6,400	9,562	15,111	9,169	4,588	10,408	10,130	9,270	7,595	11,996	12,550	14,876	10,713	12,740	13,617	10,477
Sudbury, Canada	10,926	5,172	851	14,695	3,268	13,981	10,117	13,960	8,645	3,081	5,240	2,430	6,212	9,417	8,859	11,038	6,330	8,855	10,037	6,067
Suez, Egypt	2,301	4,063	9,859	15,983	12,492	6,622	3,447	6,990	16,313	9,064	4,021	10,190	4,458	237	1,145	12,946	2,939	1,360	1,838	3,184
Sundsvall, Sweden	4,993	1,708	6,392	17,505	9,150	10,297	4,338	10,619	14,514	5,296	1,368	6,449	4,509	3,868	3,027	11,272	1,325	2,972	4,098	1,365

Distances in Kilometers	Dubayy, United Arab Emir.	Dublin, Ireland	Duluth, Minnesota	Dunedin, New Zealand	Durango, Mexico	Durban, South Africa	Dushanbe, USSR	East London, South Africa	Easter Island (Hanga Roa)	Echo Bay, Canada	Edinburgh, United Kingdom	Edmonton, Canada	El Aaiun, Morocco	Elat, Israel	Elazig, Turkey	Eniwetok Atoll, Marshall Isls.	Erfurt, East Germany	Erzurum, Turkey	Esfahan, Iran	Essen, West Germany
Surabaya, Indonesia	7,182	12,551	15,028	6,967	15,630	8,821	6,807	9,098	14,095	12,418	12,271	13,416	13,928	9,242	9,104	5,861	11,452	8,974	7,825	11,725
Suva, Fiji	14,134	16,078	11,418	3,161	9,561	13,656	12,935	13,538	7,389	10,710	15,809	10,246	18,465	16,118	15,473	3,728	16,194	15,262	14,497	16,232
Sverdlovsk, USSR	3,534	4,114	8,243	15,210	10,936	10,004	2,122	10,426	16,613	6,368	3,797	7,753	6,549	3,634	2,555	9,642	3,246	2,347	2,774	3,459
Svobodnyy, USSR	6,682	7,643	8,466	11,519	10,194	13,012	4,751	13,469	14,546	5,830	7,295	7,040	10,517	7,710	6,706	5,393	7,211	6,483	6,354	7,337
Sydney, Australia	12,045	17,210	14,606	2,111	12,713	10,568	11,679	10,527	9,168	13,428	16,873	13,286	18,355	14,062	14,029	5,157	16,293	13,901	12,742	16,544
Sydney, Canada	9,783	3,872	2,437	16,162	4,656	12,420	9,338	12,434	9,516	4,018	4,017	3,825	4,614	8,072	7,666	12,350	5,076	7,701	8,924	4,796
Syktyvkar, USSR	4,059	3,421	7,533	15,853	10,255	10,299	2,853	10,698	15,898	5,803	3,092	7,154	6,019	3,755	2,677	9,982	2,677	2,505	3,225	2,854
Szeged, Hungary	3,889	2,043	7,772	17,738	10,450	8,500	4,028	8,817	15,143	7,045	1,943	8,106	3,615	2,257	1,773	12,578	852	1,851	3,071	1,122
Szombathely, Hungary	4,180	1,756	7,507	18,021	10,174	8,658	4,287	8,962	14,861	6,857	1,670	7,884	3,422	2,520	2,065	12,665	583	2,141	3,362	840
Tabriz, Iran	1,656	4,312	9,737	15,412	12,494	7,687	1,964	8,100	17,454	8,377	4,137	9,667	5,618	1,412	621	11,400	3,108	480	772	3,393
Tacheng, China	3,415	6,006	9,631	13,341	12,129	9,958	1,471	10,415	17,577	7,364	5,691	8,781	8,301	4,534	3,641	8,273	5,085	3,421	3,078	5,317
Tahiti (Papeete)	17,319	14,932	9,149	4,837	6,703	14,761	15,637	14,402	4,250	9,639	14,896	8,600	15,436	18,599	17,512	6,195	15,918	17,316	17,314	15,716
Taipei, Taiwan	6,600	9,973	11,364	9,282	12,653	11,399	5,136	11,799	14,965	8,735	9,633	9,825	12,467	8,372	7,677	4,541	9,198	7,471	6,750	9,406
Taiyuan, China	5,524	8,319	10,313	10,933	12,132	11,308	3,796	11,754	15,943	7,696	7,979	8,956	10,860	7,047	6,232	5,727	7,560	6,015	5,475	7,761
Tallahassee, Florida	12,493	6,588	1,935	13,492	2,137	13,885	11,875	13,710	6,913	4,571	6,725	3,479	6,831	10,771	10,379	11,537	7,791	10,408	11,625	7,512
Tallinn, USSR	4,471	2,010	6,912	17,293	9,671	9,910	3,862	10,250	15,015	5,747	1,699	6,935	4,607	3,408	2,524	11,277	1,278	2,460	3,577	1,423
Tamanrasset, Algeria	5,043	3,535	8,751	17,111	10,874	6,432	6,188	6,619	13,516	9,080	3,748	9,732	1,949	3,028	3,649	15,452	3,166	3,861	4,640	3,184
Tampa, Florida	12,589	6,671	2,254	13,460	2,263	13,630	12,062	13,440	6,745	4,892	6,826	3,808	6,740	10,810	10,470	11,808	7,878	10,510	11,733	7,596
Tampere, Finland	4,674	1,995	6,708	17,260	9,469	10,146	3,986	10,485	14,864	5,509	1,666	6,704	4,698	3,646	2,753	11,140	1,406	2,682	3,779	1,513
Tanami, Australia	9,477	14,749	15,209	4,694	14,433	9,725	9,071	9,863	11,787	13,019	14,442	13,537	16,177	11,528	11,414	4,983	13,710	11,281	10,135	13,975
Tangier, Morocco	5,885	1,949	6,965	18,846	9,232	8,226	6,441	8,391	12,885	7,332	2,245	7,924	1,187	3,856	3,969	14,622	2,159	4,121	5,227	2,017
Tarawa (Betio)	12,707	13,943	10,279	5,236	9,183	14,909	11,145	14,955	8,861	8,936	13,646	8,809	16,783	14,400	13,536	1,629	13,958	13,314	12,813	14,005
Tashkent, USSR	2,202	5,585	10,072	13,901	12,741	8,811	312	9,262	18,427	8,078	5,314	9,488	7,479	3,354	2,571	9,420	4,502	2,366	1,838	4,768
Tbilisi, USSR	2,066	3,957	9,319	15,713	12,078	8,047	2,073	8,453	17,168	7,963	3,765	9,247	5,457	1,612	577	11,339	2,764	353	1,173	3,048
Tegucigalpa, Honduras	14,061	8,164	3,653	12,071	2,137	13,492	13,668	13,189	5,157	6,213	8,349	4,946	7,748	12,161	11,949	11,863	9,370	12,011	13,239	9,085
Tehran, Iran	1,211	4,832	10,176	14,881	12,937	7,561	1,574	7,990	17,979	8,687	4,648	10,014	6,110	1,686	1,133	11,089	3,631	1,010	333	3,917
Tel Aviv, Israel	2,140	4,023	9,784	15,952	12,454	6,864	3,159	7,242	16,535	8,877	3,952	10,037	4,640	280	839	12,642	2,862	1,050	1,587	3,121
Telegraph Creek, Canada	10,769	6,710	2,883	12,696	4,313	16,601	9,155	16,826	9,641	1,138	6,558	1,209	8,969	10,228	9,264	7,554	7,453	9,141	9,965	7,301
Teresina, Brazil	11,072	7,323	7,511	13,474	7,434	8,175	12,239	7,912	7,446	9,859	7,669	9,203	4,784	9,116	9,675	17,186	8,048	9,870	10,733	7,845
Ternate, Indonesia	8,179	12,644	13,487	6,673	13,776	10,676	7,271	10,947	13,306	11,006	12,314	11,809	14,795	10,209	9,798	4,029	11,748	9,624	8,634	11,984
The Valley, Anguilla	11,808	6,230	4,150	14,233	4,359	11,375	11,988	11,175	7,075	6,640	6,497	5,835	5,192	9,784	9,796	14,072	7,361	9,908	11,095	7,082
Thessaloniki, Greece	3,445	2,603	8,390	17,343	11,037	7,848	3,902	8,173	15,433	7,709	2,551	8,767	3,628	1,644	1,413	12,884	1,472	1,560	2,700	1,714
Thimphu, Bhutan	3,432	7,977	11,772	11,490	14,095	8,907	2,296	9,358	18,137	9,360	7,693	10,748	9,804	5,314	4,809	7,719	6,913	4,633	3,695	7,177
Thunder Bay, Canada	11,120	5,536	277	14,239	3,023	14,620	10,134	14,612	8,605	2,578	5,563	1,780	6,808	9,751	9,108	10,381	6,649	9,082	10,225	6,399
Tientsin, China	5,920	8,415	10,054	10,812	11,774	11,733	4,152	12,178	15,529	7,423	8,070	8,647	11,047	7,386	6,534	5,391	7,720	6,315	5,835	7,908
Tijuana, Mexico	13,557	8,399	2,640	11,331	1,533	16,978	12,112	16,758	6,654	3,732	8,387	2,352	9,602	12,528	11,748	8,472	9,451	11,679	12,691	9,221
Tiksi, USSR	6,782	5,704	6,483	13,438	8,642	13,394	4,945	13,831	13,942	3,931	5,371	5,297	8,664	7,050	5,963	7,049	5,563	5,767	6,146	5,615
Timbuktu, Mali	6,091	4,067	8,602	16,723	10,400	6,320	7,301	6,419	12,443	9,383	4,345	9,809	1,558	4,115	4,763	16,490	3,997	4,974	5,737	3,949
Tindouf, Algeria	6,260	2,851	7,383	17,985	9,402	7,612	7,076	7,728	12,395	8,063	3,159	8,514	503	4,196	4,530	15,547	3,048	4,709	5,709	2,928
Tirane, Albania	3,717	2,359	8,161	17,614	10,790	7,965	4,141	8,276	15,168	7,560	2,327	8,584	3,396	1,890	1,679	13,008	1,268	1,817	2,970	1,491
Tokyo, Japan	7,948	9,611	9,508	9,546	10,552	13,464	6,152	13,879	13,511	6,951	9,265	7,884	12,493	9,343	8,425	3,509	9,178	8,202	7,833	9,311
Toledo, Spain	5,693	1,507	6,803	19,207	9,184	8,527	6,106	8,716	13,149	6,986	1,786	7,657	1,645	3,716	3,698	14,145	1,701	3,832	4,984	1,544
Topeka, Kansas	12,274	6,615	906	13,242	1,869	15,092	11,267	14,978	7,467	3,326	6,667	2,104	7,552	10,854	10,249	10,235	7,757	10,229	11,380	7,500
Toronto, Canada	11,087	5,266	1,057	14,663	3,172	13,806	10,354	13,761	8,421	3,417	5,357	2,710	6,115	9,510	8,999	11,299	6,444	9,006	10,202	6,175
Toulouse, France	5,247	1,221	6,896	19,119	9,403	8,675	5,533	8,903	13,669	6,795	1,409	7,591	2,249	3,349	3,192	13,603	1,094	3,307	4,493	968
Tours, France	5,349	825	6,590	19,222	9,155	9,078	5,463	9,314	13,658	6,388	986	7,217	2,550	3,542	3,250	13,233	853	3,338	4,553	644
Townsville, Australia	11,052	15,575	13,902	3,667	12,692	11,257	10,330	11,325	10,339	12,177	15,230	12,346	17,805	13,116	12,828	3,800	14,788	12,664	11,613	15,011
Trenton, New Jersey	11,109	5,214	1,576	14,814	3,319	13,349	10,529	13,281	8,278	3,937	5,343	3,247	5,772	9,425	8,998	11,821	6,414	9,024	10,239	6,137
Tripoli, Lebanon	2,131	3,900	9,618	16,014	12,314	7,133	2,971	7,514	16,626	8,638	3,806	9,819	4,717	548	560	12,417	2,717	776	1,477	2,985
Tripoli, Libya	4,159	2,747	8,456	17,604	10,903	7,195	4,995	7,460	14,522	8,270	2,855	9,140	2,615	2,103	2,432	14,103	2,016	2,625	3,582	2,121
Tristan da Cunha (Edinburgh)	9,879	10,031	12,215	10,817	11,779	4,070	11,792	3,669	8,828	14,402	10,338	13,907	7,109	8,869	9,912	17,123	10,016	10,130	10,179	9,984
Trondheim, Norway	5,346	1,478	6,044	17,691	8,799	10,498	4,703	10,804	14,146	5,045	1,130	6,156	4,377	4,152	3,353	11,357	1,385	3,310	4,453	1,348
Trujillo, Peru	14,835	9,606	6,218	10,912	4,518	11,461	15,355	11,077	3,834	8,819	9,879	7,563	8,091	12,775	13,018	13,315	10,709	13,159	14,272	10,436
Truk Island (Moen)	10,321	12,963	11,325	6,188	11,033	13,393	8,899	13,612	11,248	9,259	12,619	9,656	15,856	12,142	11,414	1,226	12,527	11,201	10,520	12,670
Truro, Canada	10,028	4,120	2,225	15,907	4,401	12,616	9,551	12,616	9,291	3,950	4,260	3,669	4,837	8,326	7,912	12,237	5,323	7,945	9,166	5,045
Tsingtao, China	6,232	8,847	10,276	10,376	11,852	11,836	4,515	12,271	15,255	7,638	8,502	8,813	11,484	7,765	6,937	5,008	8,158	6,719	6,195	8,345
Tsitsihar, China	6,407	7,896	9,002	11,283	10,726	12,591	4,507	13,045	14,902	6,367	7,547	7,581	10,705	7,588	6,626	5,347	7,369	6,403	6,155	7,518
Tubuai Island (Mataura)	17,513	15,477	9,668	4,371	7,137	14,116	16,036	13,757	4,038	10,268	15,468	9,200	15,627	19,198	18,121	6,521	16,513	17,915	17,714	16,297
Tucson, Arizona	13,479	8,090	2,279	11,702	1,098	16,408	12,170	16,193	6,572	3,796	8,106	2,378	9,119	12,285	11,575	9,041	9,186	11,524	12,596	8,943
Tulsa, Oklahoma	12,568	6,863	1,221	13,029	1,586	15,078	11,585	14,933	7,150	3,627	6,927	2,365	7,673	11,108	10,528	10,306	8,018	10,514	11,674	7,757
Tunis, Tunisia	4,449	2,236	7,954	18,095	10,431	7,692	5,085	7,948	14,312	7,772	2,352	8,628	2,446	2,438	2,558	13,917	1,577	2,726	3,794	1,647
Tura, USSR	5,399	5,527	7,642	13,650	9,978	12,026	3,528	12,473	15,369	5,216	5,178	6,619	8,363	5,900	4,830	7,529	5,051	4,618	4,821	5,179
Turin, Italy	4,776	1,366	7,171	18,678	9,752	8,625	5,010	8,886	14,178	6,840	1,430	7,737	2,717	2,945	2,696	13,243	706	2,801	4,000	713
Uberlandia, Brazil	12,219	8,966	8,501	11,837	7,746	7,988	13,637	7,634	6,273	11,038	9,312	10,150	6,353	10,408	11,097	16,655	9,660	11,304	12,032	9,467
Ufa, USSR	3,272	3,942	8,360	15,427	11,084	9,671	2,044	10,088	16,720	6,595	3,640	7,962	6,264	3,263	2,182	9,993	3,000	1,976	2,475	3,230
Ujungpandang, Indonesia	7,694	12,760	14,493	6,671	14,872	9,578	7,105	9,845	13,677	11,941	12,456	12,836	14,449	9,758	9,516	5,089	11,731	9,368	8,270	11,992
Ulaanbaatar, Mongolia	5,133	7,141	9,352	12,092	11,438	11,452	3,226	11,911	16,122	6,796	6,798	8,135	9,773	6,334	5,405	6,515	6,441	5,182	4,877	6,627
Ulan-Ude, USSR	5,274	6,830	8,916	12,382	11,032	11,711	3,337	12,171	15,887	6,368	6,484	7,716	9,534	6,326	5,351	6,618	6,192	5,128	4,938	6,363
Uliastay, Mongolia	4,400	6,671	9,495	12,604	11,771	10,813	2,480	11,273	16,786	7,036	6,336	8,421	9,175	5,586	4,674	7,239	5,876	4,452	4,124	6,082
Uranium City, Canada	10,488	5,710	1,789	13,794	3,959	15,537	9,127	15,679	9,611	869	5,613	733	7,735	9,577	8,721	8,865	6,603	8,637	9,622	6,411
Urumqi, China	3,570	6,495	9,970	12,853	12,391	9,982	1,676	10,442	17,616	7,624	6,179	9,032	8,769	4,873	4,035	7,905	5,570	3,818	3,349	5,804
Ushuaia, Argentina	14,403	13,271	11,479	7,557	9,399	7,910	16,348	7,451	4,519	14,045	13,619	12,707	10,491	13,464	14,470	13,506	13,830	14,693	14,790	13,677
Vaduz, Liechtenstein	4,689	1,313	7,122	18,557	9,744	8,798	4,819	9,072	14,324	6,676	1,310	7,616	2,977	2,936	2,583	12,968	439	2,670	3,886	510
Valencia, Spain	5,381	1,605	7,073	18,983	9,485	8,334	5,835	8,541	13,446	7,155	1,841	7,877	1,810	3,399	3,400	14,085	1,558	3,540	4,680	1,450
Valladolid, Spain	5,746	1,304	6,634	19,405	9,048	8,727	6,081	8,919	13,134	6,782	1,590	7,463	1,784	3,798	3,718	13,971	1,590	3,841	5,013	1,409
Valletta, Malta	4,053	2,524	8,296	17,725	10,806	7,480	4,756	7,758	14,687	7,993	2,598	8,906	2,793	2,036	2,207	13,767	1,699	2,386	3,416	1,828
Valparaiso, Chile	14,847	11,454	9,076	9,273	7,223	9,311	16,424	8,870	3,682	11,681	11,784	10,407	9,086	13,172	13,896	14,059	12,310	14,103	14,784	12,087
Vancouver, Canada	11,750	7,188	2,313	12,339	3,229	16,948	10,208	17,021	8,570	1,898	7,092	823	9,079	11,011	10,110	7,934	8,075	10,009	10,916	7,888
Varna, Bulgaria	3,188	2,741	8,426	17,060	11,126	8,097	3,450	8,443	15,805	7,539	2,624	8,668	4,094	1,641	1,076	12,387	1,540	1,172	2,379	1,816
Venice, Italy	4,428	1,603	7,411	18,322	10,032	8,550	4,642	8,833	14,546	6,932	1,594	7,893	3,039	2,649	2,336	13,016	623	2,435	3,640	775
Veracruz, Mexico	14,202	8,311	3,081	11,773	1,033	14,593	13,423	14,294	5,325	5,447	8,440	4,093	8,388	12,494	12,096	10,793	9,512	12,117	13,325	9,234
Verona, Italy	4,530	1,522	7,335	18,427	9,945	8,581	4,746	8,858	14,440	6,895	1,531	7,839	2,951	2,738	2,440	13,073	615	2,541	3,744	729
Victoria, Canada	11,841	7,272	2,341	12,260	3,168	17,015	10,295	17,077	8,486	1,990	7,179	897	9,144	11,102	10,203	7,909	8,164	10,102	11,008	7,975
Victoria, Seychelles	3,306	8,601	14,396	11,536	16,993	3,795	4,974	4,251	16,137	13,164	8,558	14,487	8,160	4,369	5,077	11,950	7,471	5,140	4,146	7,722
Vienna, Austria	4,238	1,686	7,417	18,046	10,092	8,767	4,294	9,071	14,830	6,750	1,585	7,781	3,461	2,610	2,120	12,590	494	2,186	3,411	763
Vientiane, Laos	4,939	9,614	12,684	9,817	14,504	9,318	3,989	9,730	16,594	10,090	9,316	11,365	11,487	6,924	6,489	6,438	8,584	6,319	5,330	8,844
Villahermosa, Mexico	14,120	8,205	3,195	11,927	1,392	14,228	13,465	13,931	5,302	5,651	8,353	4,328	8,132	12,342	12,003	11,156	9,412	12,037	13,257	9,131
Vilnius, USSR	4,088	2,058	7,323	17,380	10,071	9,382	3,702	9,722	15,258	6,259	1,804	7,424	4,362	2,897	2,064	11,639	1,045	2,028	3,200	1,274
Visby, Sweden	4,633	1,614	6,783	17,715	9,528	9,767	4,186	10,088	14,737	5,808	1,323	6,931	4,188	3,377	2,597	11,669	877	2,569	3,746	1,001
Vitoria, Brazil	11,498	8,795	9,064	12,045	8,523	7,168	13,030	6,826	7,000	11,511	9,143	10,742	6,014	9,773	10,539	17,426	9,356	10,753	11,383	9,191
Vladivostok, USSR	7,084	8,594	9,145	10,572	10,594	13,043	5,219	13,486	14,293	6,517	8,246	7,620	11,445	8,347	7,399	4,566	8,120	7,175	6,885	8,259
Volgograd, USSR	2,774	3,514	8,618	16,014	11,379	8,807	2,256	9,206	16,725	7,182	3,272	8,478	5,445	2,279	1,193	10,991	2,392	1,013	1,885	2,663
Vologda, USSR	3,958	2,871	7,468	16,451	10,224	9,905	3,079	10,283	15,739	5,985	2,559	7,276	5,373	3,318	2,284	10,638	2,036	2,149	3,078	2,230
Vorkuta, USSR	4,733	3,915	7,173	15,284	9,812	11,141	3,236	11,551	15,497	5,181	3,568	6,577	6,702	4,639	3,555	9,180	3,386	3,371	3,958	3,516
Wake Island	11,112	11,931	9,290	7,225	9,035	15,415	9,353	15,662	10,399	7,400	11,618	7,642	14,865	12,533	11,579	982	11,866	11,355	11,035	11,923
Wallis Island	14,496	15,476	10,630	3,823	8,799	14,418	13,095	14,280	7,064	10,003	15,238	9,482	17,676	16,351	15,544	3,634	15,775	15,323	14,732	15,764
Walvis Bay, Namibia	6,917	8,685	13,079	12,009	13,867	1,814	8,854	1,726	11,831	14,169	8,898	14,513	6,295	6,208	7,294	16,385	8,196	7,495	7,311	8,274
Warsaw, Poland	4,155	1,831	7,327	17,698	10,052	9,147	3,954	9,472	15,070	6,431	1,626	7,540	3,978	2,770	2,064	12,032	704	2,071	3,285	966
Washington, D.C.	11,351	5,458	1,509	14,571	3,081	13,499	10,750	13,414	8,050	3,977	5,585	3,199	5,983	9,670	9,241	11,728	6,657	9,266	10,480	6,380
Watson Lake, Canada	10,534	6,430	2,800	12,971	4,423	16,320	8,951	16,549	9,833	857	6,277	1,183	8,714	9,957	8,999	7,743	7,172	8,880	9,721	7,019

Distances in Kilometers	Dubayy, United Arab Emir.	Dublin, Ireland	Duluth, Minnesota	Dunedin, New Zealand	Durango, Mexico	Durban, South Africa	Dushanbe, USSR	East London, South Africa	Easter Island (Hanga Roa)	Echo Bay, Canada	Edinburgh, United Kingdom	Edmonton, Canada	El Aaiun, Morocco	Elat, Israel	Elazig, Turkey	Eniwetok Atoll, Marshall Isls.	Erfurt, East Germany	Erzurum, Turkey	Esfahan, Iran	Essen, West Germany
Weimar, East Germany	4,692	1,227	6,939	18,382	9,614	9,161	4,627	9,449	14,434	6,331	1,107	7,328	3,357	3,087	2,573	12,536	20	2,622	3,850	305
Wellington, New Zealand	14,235	18,665	13,392	614	10,995	11,294	13,886	11,105	6,937	13,209	18,373	12,543	18,279	16,189	16,257	5,986	18,366	16,132	14,963	18,546
West Berlin, West Germany	4,624	1,321	6,934	18,201	9,632	9,284	4,471	9,582	14,557	6,226	1,144	7,260	3,578	3,103	2,512	12,315	236	2,542	3,767	454
Wewak, Papua New Guinea	10,015	13,841	12,845	5,365	12,380	11,975	8,947	12,158	11,501	10,740	13,493	11,176	16,427	12,016	11,508	2,649	13,156	11,318	10,413	13,353
Whangarei, New Zealand	14,152	18,046	13,038	1,172	10,776	11,799	13,587	11,633	7,131	12,663	17,752	12,074	18,826	16,182	16,065	5,378	17,852	15,911	14,808	17,989
Whitehorse, Canada	10,429	6,572	3,150	12,795	4,694	16,422	8,790	16,689	10,013	1,034	6,400	1,521	8,946	9,959	8,975	7,429	7,255	8,845	9,637	7,117
Wichita, Kansas	12,474	6,824	1,096	13,036	1,668	15,223	11,444	15,093	7,289	3,427	6,876	2,154	7,737	11,063	10,454	10,137	7,965	10,433	11,580	7,709
Willemstad, Curacao	12,702	7,134	4,415	13,322	3,990	11,630	12,893	11,373	6,164	7,020	7,395	6,039	6,030	10,665	10,704	13,799	8,271	10,818	12,001	7,992
Wiluna, Australia	9,027	14,736	16,404	4,901	15,526	8,521	8,981	8,650	12,041	14,096	14,481	14,721	15,429	11,003	11,087	6,199	13,580	10,991	9,783	13,862
Windhoek, Namibia	6,712	8,707	13,249	11,965	14,115	1,606	8,653	1,573	12,059	14,229	8,907	14,643	6,397	6,078	7,165	16,138	8,170	7,361	7,133	8,260
Windsor, Canada	11,392	5,591	877	14,330	2,844	14,073	10,610	14,009	8,154	3,408	5,676	2,569	6,429	9,836	9,312	11,104	6,764	9,315	10,505	6,497
Winnipeg, Canada	11,249	5,868	508	13,832	2,942	15,179	10,112	15,189	8,619	2,164	5,859	1,196	7,333	10,021	9,305	9,786	6,929	9,260	10,357	6,694
Winston-Salem, North Carolina	11,771	5,877	1,543	14,165	2,697	13,695	11,151	13,579	7,642	4,132	6,006	3,218	6,314	10,083	9,661	11,621	7,077	9,686	10,900	6,800
Wroclaw, Poland	4,330	1,603	7,225	17,984	9,927	9,072	4,226	9,381	14,830	6,462	1,439	7,523	3,678	2,820	2,216	12,302	421	2,250	3,476	700
Wuhan, China	5,770	9,088	11,038	10,188	12,680	11,058	4,221	11,486	15,775	8,405	8,752	9,613	11,530	7,472	6,748	5,367	8,276	6,540	5,858	8,490
Wyndham, Australia	9,085	14,237	14,935	5,182	14,452	9,833	8,591	10,006	12,226	12,635	13,927	13,247	15,831	11,146	10,975	4,802	13,219	10,834	9,710	13,480
Xi'an, China	5,220	8,472	10,786	10,817	12,647	10,824	3,600	11,267	16,294	8,180	8,139	9,456	10,882	6,858	6,110	5,946	7,637	5,900	5,254	7,855
Xining, China	4,568	7,884	10,664	11,434	12,744	10,421	2,904	10,873	16,909	8,119	7,559	9,456	10,213	6,164	5,413	6,629	7,002	5,204	4,566	7,229
Yakutsk, USSR	6,745	6,644	7,383	12,503	9,325	13,333	4,814	13,790	14,237	4,766	6,302	6,054	9,580	7,388	6,321	6,186	6,362	6,108	6,245	6,450
Yanji, China	6,898	8,538	9,261	10,635	10,759	12,849	5,041	13,293	14,487	6,627	8,190	7,754	11,365	8,185	7,247	4,698	8,031	7,024	6,711	8,177
Yaounde, Cameroon	5,241	5,721	10,730	14,927	12,469	4,270	6,933	4,434	13,264	11,270	5,920	11,863	3,683	3,765	4,768	16,370	5,223	4,989	5,250	5,291
Yap Island (Colonia)	8,853	12,273	12,039	6,933	12,263	12,184	7,562	12,469	12,710	9,659	11,925	10,348	14,913	10,750	10,119	2,648	11,604	9,917	9,123	11,795
Yaraka, Australia	11,043	16,000	14,532	3,314	13,140	10,657	10,518	10,704	10,261	12,860	15,665	13,004	17,746	13,098	12,938	4,483	15,096	12,793	11,677	15,340
Yarmouth, Canada	10,311	4,403	2,055	15,633	4,132	12,776	9,820	12,757	9,016	3,964	4,543	3,575	5,047	8,606	8,195	12,176	5,607	8,228	9,448	5,328
Yellowknife, Canada	10,238	5,723	2,236	13,721	4,330	15,611	8,805	15,800	9,941	442	5,596	993	7,912	9,446	8,547	8,541	6,544	8,449	9,387	6,370
Yerevan, USSR	1,936	4,043	9,458	15,659	12,214	7,878	2,095	8,284	17,220	8,127	3,863	9,406	5,444	1,466	483	11,435	2,843	276	1,050	3,128
Yinchuan, China	4,977	7,957	10,386	11,325	12,373	10,870	3,249	11,321	16,476	7,807	7,623	9,118	10,405	6,504	5,706	6,272	7,139	5,491	4,927	7,352
Yogyakarta, Indonesia	6,994	12,451	15,187	7,098	15,888	8,562	6,694	8,843	14,246	12,564	12,180	13,598	13,723	9,048	8,946	6,129	11,332	8,822	7,658	11,608
York, United Kingdom	5,595	341	6,071	18,941	8,721	9,777	5,419	10,024	13,579	5,687	266	6,573	3,122	3,965	3,476	12,598	887	3,519	4,746	614
Yumen, China	4,253	7,385	10,361	11,935	12,564	10,343	2,493	10,801	17,149	7,867	7,061	9,234	9,719	5,747	4,958	7,028	6,500	4,745	4,172	6,727
Yutian, China	2,815	6,701	10,719	12,745	13,231	9,084	1,152	9,543	18,513	8,465	6,414	9,881	8,656	4,390	3,713	8,418	5,656	3,517	2,780	5,915
Yuzhno-Sakhalinsk, USSR	7,815	8,510	8,333	10,635	9,656	13,964	5,898	14,413	13,480	5,736	8,169	6,758	11,449	8,880	7,870	4,337	8,212	7,648	7,518	8,311
Zagreb, Yugoslavia	4,168	1,804	7,587	18,048	10,236	8,514	4,355	8,813	14,828	6,992	1,749	8,001	3,303	2,447	2,065	12,821	683	2,157	3,368	912
Zahedan, Iran	723	5,942	11,133	13,765	13,884	7,292	1,242	7,745	19,043	9,407	5,748	10,788	7,137	2,507	2,233	10,469	4,745	2,127	948	5,030
Zamboanga, Philippines	7,355	11,768	13,173	7,563	13,907	10,494	6,379	10,815	14,157	10,593	11,442	11,543	13,907	9,362	8,915	4,442	10,854	8,737	7,771	11,093
Zanzibar, Tanzania	3,891	7,847	13,554	12,503	15,690	2,758	5,820	3,195	15,018	13,125	7,899	14,201	6,735	3,978	4,965	13,755	6,883	5,107	4,495	7,084
Zaragoza, Spain	5,426	1,361	6,886	19,179	9,336	8,567	5,786	8,778	13,447	6,917	1,597	7,657	1,960	3,482	3,403	13,875	1,383	3,529	4,696	1,247
Zashiversk, USSR	7,324	6,360	6,534	12,784	8,472	13,951	5,435	14,398	13,526	3,909	6,032	5,191	9,322	7,716	6,630	6,380	6,263	6,430	6,738	6,307
Zhengzhou, China	5,651	8,665	10,615	10,595	12,351	11,231	3,994	11,670	15,856	7,988	8,326	9,223	11,171	7,254	6,476	5,533	7,886	6,262	5,661	8,093
Zurich, Switzerland	4,778	1,231	7,042	18,644	9,659	8,848	4,900	9,117	14,237	6,622	1,240	7,551	2,927	3,022	2,673	12,992	447	2,759	3,975	465

Distances in Kilometers

	Eucla, Australia	Fargo, North Dakota	Faroe Islands (Torshavn)	Florence, Italy	Florianopolis, Brazil	Fort George, Canada	Fort McMurray, Canada	Fort Nelson, Canada	Fort Severn, Canada	Fort Smith, Arkansas	Fort Vermilion, Canada	Fort Wayne, Indiana	Fort-Chimo, Canada	Fort-de-France, Martinique	Fortaleza, Brazil	Frankfort, Kentucky	Frankfurt am Main, W. Ger.	Fredericton, Canada	Freeport, Bahamas	Freetown, Sierra Leone
Fargo, North Dakota	15,809	0	5,564	7,738	9,564	1,478	1,482	2,171	1,195	1,291	1,814	1,134	2,272	4,874	7,984	1,372	7,104	2,306	2,760	8,835
Faroe Islands (Torshavn)	15,397	5,564	0	2,347	10,611	4,142	5,320	5,527	4,388	6,486	5,340	5,502	3,329	6,763	7,774	5,744	1,629	4,127	6,504	5,963
Florence, Italy	14,497	7,738	2,347	0	9,977	6,265	7,652	7,874	6,610	8,474	7,684	7,448	5,467	7,487	7,231	7,630	732	5,904	8,026	4,574
Florianopolis, Brazil	13,436	9,564	10,611	9,977	0	9,485	11,041	11,735	9,972	8,473	11,374	8,486	9,673	4,859	2,850	8,206	10,289	8,347	6,804	5,515
Fort George, Canada	16,702	1,478	4,142	6,265	9,485	0	2,063	2,710	603	2,376	2,325	1,491	813	4,626	7,403	1,795	5,644	1,243	3,033	7,668
Fort McMurray, Canada	14,685	1,482	5,320	7,652	11,041	2,063	0	712	1,463	2,695	333	2,566	2,544	6,298	9,319	2,836	6,946	3,269	4,239	9,716
Fort Nelson, Canada	14,006	2,171	5,527	7,874	11,735	2,710	712	0	2,108	3,326	393	3,273	3,084	7,009	10,025	3,537	7,150	3,939	4,930	10,297
Fort Severn, Canada	16,107	1,195	4,388	6,610	9,972	603	1,463	2,108	0	2,347	1,723	1,668	1,187	5,121	7,977	1,988	5,954	1,835	3,350	8,258
Fort Smith, Arkansas	16,018	1,291	6,486	8,474	8,473	2,376	2,695	3,326	2,347	0	3,012	1,028	3,173	4,045	7,253	908	7,913	2,607	1,785	8,672
Fort Vermilion, Canada	14,396	1,814	5,340	7,684	11,374	2,325	333	393	1,723	3,012	0	2,898	2,737	6,627	9,632	3,169	6,968	3,550	4,571	9,941
Fort Wayne, Indiana	16,824	1,134	5,502	7,448	8,486	1,491	2,566	3,273	1,668	1,028	2,898	0	2,234	3,744	6,852	320	6,896	1,586	1,717	7,878
Fort-Chimo, Canada	16,795	2,272	3,329	5,467	9,673	813	2,544	3,084	1,187	3,173	2,737	2,234	0	4,866	7,354	2,514	4,836	1,355	3,602	7,214
Fort-de-France, Martinique	17,861	4,874	6,763	7,487	4,859	4,626	6,298	7,009	5,121	4,045	6,627	3,744	4,866	0	3,211	3,509	7,335	3,517	2,264	5,252
Fortaleza, Brazil	15,864	7,984	7,774	7,231	2,850	7,403	9,319	10,025	7,977	7,253	9,632	6,852	7,354	3,211	0	6,655	7,477	6,166	5,475	3,112
Frankfort, Kentucky	16,880	1,372	5,744	7,630	8,206	1,795	2,836	3,537	1,988	908	3,169	320	2,514	3,509	6,655	0	7,100	1,730	1,415	7,826
Frankfurt am Main, W. Ger.	14,744	7,104	1,629	732	10,289	5,644	6,946	7,150	5,954	7,913	6,968	6,896	4,836	7,335	7,477	7,100	0	5,393	7,621	5,041
Fredericton, Canada	17,943	2,306	4,127	5,904	8,347	1,243	3,269	3,939	1,835	2,607	3,550	1,586	1,355	3,517	6,166	1,730	5,393	0	2,412	6,551
Freeport, Bahamas	17,284	2,760	6,504	8,026	6,804	3,033	4,239	4,930	3,350	1,785	4,571	1,717	3,602	2,264	5,475	1,415	7,621	2,412	0	7,165
Freetown, Sierra Leone	15,342	8,835	5,963	4,574	5,515	7,668	9,716	10,297	8,258	8,672	9,941	7,878	7,214	5,252	3,112	7,826	5,041	6,551	7,165	0
Frobisher Bay, Canada	16,242	2,557	3,025	5,284	10,275	1,256	2,446	2,866	1,368	3,613	2,567	2,746	630	5,488	7,889	3,044	4,609	1,983	4,205	7,508
Frunze, USSR	9,945	10,023	5,492	5,008	14,687	8,995	8,948	8,618	8,919	11,264	8,734	10,485	8,298	12,205	12,163	10,787	4,955	9,444	11,852	9,199
Fukuoka, Japan	7,230	9,924	8,734	9,458	19,333	9,915	8,442	7,762	9,448	11,064	8,110	10,975	9,694	14,536	16,506	11,265	9,111	11,030	12,677	13,979
Funafuti Atoll, Tuvalu	5,785	10,247	14,048	15,927	13,518	11,547	9,574	9,076	10,988	10,236	9,396	11,108	12,118	13,450	15,644	11,117	15,309	12,552	11,633	18,674
Funchal, Madeira Island	16,812	6,727	3,346	2,740	7,460	5,359	7,299	7,799	5,901	6,973	7,476	6,003	4,756	4,887	4,624	6,065	2,863	4,458	5,952	2,699
Fuzhou, China	6,477	11,151	9,129	9,368	18,814	10,978	9,673	9,015	10,562	12,337	9,346	12,156	10,648	15,504	16,593	12,458	9,166	12,003	13,873	13,625
Gaborone, Botswana	9,732	14,431	10,041	7,724	7,337	13,150	15,079	15,490	13,701	14,234	15,217	13,490	12,549	10,385	7,259	13,424	8,456	12,128	12,578	5,614
Galapagos Islands (Santa Cruz)	14,553	5,301	9,734	10,993	5,364	6,129	6,634	7,175	6,282	4,009	6,925	4,649	6,797	3,641	5,781	4,337	10,710	5,663	3,252	8,613
Gander, Canada	18,069	3,121	3,259	4,941	8,498	1,772	3,805	4,402	2,350	3,566	4,036	2,540	1,363	3,855	6,040	2,695	4,443	965	3,248	5,911
Gangtok, India	7,806	11,769	7,632	6,991	15,820	10,934	10,501	10,029	10,766	13,055	10,234	12,404	10,299	14,338	13,843	12,719	7,034	11,514	13,896	10,741
Garyarsa, China	8,685	11,292	6,798	6,056	15,108	10,317	10,138	9,743	10,217	12,553	9,899	11,806	9,632	13,441	12,947	12,111	6,117	10,782	13,190	9,861
Gaspe, Canada	17,803	2,410	3,784	5,617	8,611	1,152	3,214	3,856	1,753	2,864	3,475	1,836	1,063	3,809	6,343	2,017	5,084	358	2,769	6,529
Gauhati, India	7,524	11,869	7,897	7,314	16,100	11,095	10,563	10,064	10,900	13,160	10,286	12,552	10,484	14,627	14,176	12,869	7,342	11,723	14,086	11,072
Gdansk, Poland	14,083	7,256	1,707	1,294	11,116	5,846	6,887	6,991	6,070	8,192	6,860	7,203	5,034	8,038	8,304	7,438	828	5,787	8,114	5,824
Geneva, Switzerland	14,921	7,263	1,945	483	9,857	5,788	7,213	7,461	6,142	7,990	7,257	6,965	4,992	7,104	7,061	7,148	474	5,422	7,561	4,571
Genoa, Italy	14,689	7,557	2,209	198	9,884	6,083	7,496	7,733	6,436	8,282	7,535	7,256	5,287	7,306	7,118	7,436	634	5,709	7,828	4,522
Georgetown, Guyana	17,153	5,767	7,413	7,840	3,942	5,544	7,205	7,915	6,041	4,870	7,535	4,644	5,759	920	2,476	4,397	7,790	4,417	3,088	4,957
Geraldton, Australia	1,410	16,637	14,413	13,182	13,518	17,011	15,275	14,563	16,509	17,202	14,952	17,766	16,737	18,376	15,413	17,939	13,508	18,092	18,687	14,143
Ghanzi, Botswana	10,275	13,888	9,606	7,314	7,064	12,616	14,564	15,001	13,172	13,701	14,715	12,947	12,027	9,888	6,795	12,885	8,044	11,585	12,062	5,070
Ghat, Libya	14,046	9,213	4,309	2,088	8,572	7,754	9,435	9,761	8,208	9,655	9,522	8,651	7,022	7,478	6,142	8,752	2,795	7,068	8,720	3,083
Gibraltar	15,803	7,289	2,880	1,648	8,383	5,840	7,608	8,005	6,317	7,732	7,729	6,722	5,132	6,003	5,599	6,833	1,921	5,138	6,909	3,164
Gijon, Spain	15,857	6,743	2,058	1,363	9,011	5,270	6,924	7,278	5,702	7,322	7,021	6,296	4,517	6,133	6,181	6,444	1,314	4,717	6,714	3,952
Gisborne, New Zealand	4,488	12,689	17,387	18,776	11,223	14,156	12,467	12,109	13,708	12,169	12,366	13,189	14,894	13,688	14,007	13,059	18,483	14,775	12,894	16,480
Glasgow, United Kingdom	15,515	6,031	704	1,737	10,152	4,570	5,920	6,171	4,885	6,851	5,963	5,839	3,762	6,629	7,303	6,053	1,074	4,364	6,658	5,310
Godthab, Greenland	16,387	3,337	2,227	4,457	10,184	1,930	3,258	3,628	2,167	4,301	3,356	3,359	1,129	5,561	7,617	3,631	3,789	2,238	4,625	6,882
Gomez Palacio, Mexico	14,911	2,438	7,869	9,863	8,320	3,736	3,519	3,988	3,614	1,393	3,778	2,415	4,544	4,578	7,714	2,244	9,306	3,974	2,472	9,637
Goose Bay, Canada	13,588	2,290	6,398	8,745	11,648	3,243	1,217	885	2,655	3,185	1,079	3,419	3,761	7,131	10,272	3,626	8,024	4,402	4,928	10,911
Gorki, USSR	12,579	7,999	2,891	2,693	12,666	6,741	7,275	7,182	6,814	9,111	7,159	8,203	5,969	9,571	9,887	8,477	2,428	6,966	9,369	7,246
Goteborg, Sweden	14,505	6,696	1,148	1,553	10,999	5,286	6,351	6,481	5,511	7,635	6,336	6,649	4,474	7,640	8,158	6,888	873	5,250	7,599	5,875
Granada, Spain	15,669	7,322	2,767	1,457	8,571	5,863	7,593	7,971	6,326	7,802	7,704	6,787	5,140	6,167	5,790	6,907	1,741	5,201	7,024	3,324
Grand Turk, Turks & Caicos	17,737	3,646	6,588	7,795	5,946	3,654	5,107	5,811	4,068	2,742	5,440	2,543	4,074	1,307	4,518	2,275	7,492	2,748	958	6,354
Graz, Austria	14,221	7,697	2,177	492	10,462	6,241	7,491	7,661	6,540	8,516	7,497	7,499	5,431	7,818	7,703	7,702	603	5,993	8,203	5,067
Green Bay, Wisconsin	16,527	733	5,345	7,391	8,934	1,225	2,123	2,832	1,276	1,151	2,454	448	2,023	4,179	7,260	749	6,804	1,680	2,162	8,144
Grenoble, France	14,950	7,315	2,041	467	9,752	5,839	7,291	7,549	6,203	8,022	7,340	6,996	5,047	7,057	6,963	7,173	594	5,445	7,559	4,454
Guadalajara, Mexico	14,720	2,967	8,334	10,261	7,954	4,222	4,059	4,514	4,132	1,850	4,313	2,841	5,022	4,521	7,568	2,633	9,731	4,356	2,584	9,696
Guam (Agana)	5,280	10,961	11,275	12,115	17,930	11,479	9,591	8,882	10,910	11,776	9,273	12,095	11,518	15,808	18,872	12,310	11,767	12,712	13,560	16,584
Guantanamo, Cuba	17,303	3,555	6,926	8,212	6,009	3,754	5,035	5,726	4,113	2,530	5,368	2,505	4,252	1,619	4,801	2,209	7,888	2,970	796	6,771
Guatemala City, Guatemala	15,606	3,622	8,255	9,815	6,505	4,464	4,996	5,577	4,595	2,332	5,299	2,976	5,165	3,169	6,005	2,670	9,415	4,129	1,794	8,420
Guayaquil, Ecuador	15,194	5,681	9,343	10,264	4,357	6,208	7,121	7,738	6,485	4,426	7,437	4,818	6,759	2,777	4,598	4,499	10,087	5,488	3,176	7,482
Guiyang, China	6,867	11,534	8,559	8,428	17,581	11,079	10,104	9,506	10,756	12,797	9,793	12,416	10,610	15,263	15,540	12,733	8,327	11,943	14,100	12,476
Gur'yev, USSR	11,631	9,156	3,969	3,165	12,963	7,898	8,390	8,251	7,972	10,270	8,256	9,356	7,122	10,483	10,340	9,626	3,158	8,084	10,473	7,448
Haifa, Israel	12,164	9,948	4,385	2,393	11,072	8,510	9,587	9,640	8,772	10,803	9,541	9,786	7,697	9,700	8,706	9,988	2,891	8,273	10,417	5,638
Haikou, China	6,061	12,112	9,370	9,191	17,725	11,771	10,651	10,019	11,412	13,341	10,330	13,053	11,343	16,060	16,194	13,366	9,117	12,688	14,761	13,090
Haiphong, Vietnam	6,282	12,143	9,126	8,853	17,414	11,711	10,701	10,089	11,383	13,396	10,386	13,040	11,242	15,863	15,811	13,357	8,804	12,573	14,729	12,704
Hakodate, Japan	8,225	8,670	8,138	9,277	18,225	8,757	7,189	6,501	8,259	9,789	6,857	9,740	8,613	13,379	15,791	10,023	8,810	9,918	11,428	13,844
Halifax, Canada	18,213	2,575	4,077	5,760	8,143	1,511	3,547	4,214	2,108	2,804	3,826	1,799	1,532	3,340	5,912	1,909	5,276	280	2,429	6,274
Hamburg, West Germany	14,649	6,914	1,365	1,092	10,609	5,472	6,673	6,845	5,745	7,782	6,679	6,776	4,659	7,466	7,780	6,996	393	5,315	7,604	5,415
Hamilton, Bermuda	18,740	3,161	5,236	6,561	6,844	2,649	4,464	5,172	3,175	2,756	4,780	2,059	2,882	1,994	4,856	1,938	6,201	1,528	1,501	5,916
Hamilton, New Zealand	4,260	12,805	17,305	18,521	11,452	14,262	12,522	12,137	13,796	12,329	12,408	13,344	14,982	13,939	14,247	13,225	18,274	14,930	13,104	16,651
Hangzhou, China	6,920	10,695	8,736	9,092	18,891	10,508	9,220	8,567	10,093	11,892	8,893	11,692	10,182	15,040	16,319	11,996	8,850	11,536	13,409	13,453
Hannover, West Germany	14,671	6,988	1,457	963	10,508	5,540	6,774	6,956	5,825	7,837	6,784	6,827	4,728	7,433	7,685	7,042	261	5,351	7,622	5,293
Hanoi, Vietnam	6,333	12,149	9,072	8,777	17,340	11,697	10,712	10,106	11,377	13,407	10,399	13,037	11,219	15,816	15,723	13,354	8,734	12,547	14,720	12,616
Harare, Zimbabwe	9,699	14,291	9,458	7,113	8,120	12,904	14,683	14,982	13,409	14,336	14,764	13,477	12,226	10,725	7,725	13,466	7,841	12,003	12,814	5,674
Harbin, China	8,582	8,902	7,356	8,227	17,946	8,705	7,435	6,799	8,283	10,122	7,112	9,884	8,410	13,277	15,131	10,189	7,822	9,761	11,601	12,797
Harrisburg, Pennsylvania	17,526	1,762	5,147	6,944	8,063	1,517	3,087	3,799	1,917	1,633	3,410	704	2,074	3,233	6,247	726	6,438	1,045	1,535	7,174
Hartford, Connecticut	17,806	1,997	4,797	6,558	8,069	1,422	3,211	3,916	1,916	2,016	3,523	1,044	1,842	3,212	6,109	1,113	6,059	672	1,782	6,865
Havana, Cuba	16,810	2,934	7,012	8,545	6,685	3,420	4,411	5,078	3,673	1,790	4,739	2,006	4,041	2,430	5,612	1,687	8,143	2,903	521	7,517
Helena, Montana	14,647	1,163	6,266	8,551	10,397	2,465	1,129	1,536	1,981	1,927	1,340	2,236	3,167	5,892	9,062	2,408	7,872	3,449	3,673	9,993
Helsinki, Finland	13,762	7,027	1,707	2,045	11,773	5,690	6,488	6,514	5,832	8,065	6,424	7,118	4,895	8,392	8,939	7,379	1,518	5,814	8,205	6,555
Hengyang, China	6,713	11,319	8,779	8,832	18,166	10,991	9,860	9,232	10,623	12,552	9,540	12,261	10,585	15,363	16,018	12,573	8,679	11,935	13,971	12,995
Herat, Afghanistan	10,107	10,769	5,618	4,460	13,495	9,549	9,895	9,671	9,597	11,915	9,727	11,014	8,780	11,941	11,229	11,287	4,637	9,741	12,120	8,150
Hermosillo, Mexico	14,343	2,328	7,892	10,032	9,138	3,774	3,074	3,426	3,515	1,707	3,282	2,691	4,584	5,358	8,523	2,614	9,418	4,274	3,175	10,302
Hiroshima, Japan	7,328	9,750	8,709	9,506	19,243	9,772	8,268	7,584	9,296	10,879	7,936	10,809	9,571	14,397	16,483	11,096	9,138	10,900	12,506	14,048
Hiva Oa (Atuona)	9,645	7,545	13,061	15,281	9,562	9,015	7,800	7,747	8,690	6,854	7,842	7,881	9,817	9,014	11,101	7,732	14,645	9,458	7,647	14,082
Ho Chi Minh City, Vietnam	5,262	13,212	10,135	9,622	16,833	12,828	11,752	11,118	12,491	14,441	11,431	14,141	12,360	16,898	16,115	14,456	9,662	13,688	15,840	13,047
Hobart, Australia	2,048	15,076	17,287	16,501	12,032	16,450	14,481	13,946	15,900	14,739	14,286	15,740	17,021	15,866	14,807	15,641	16,791	17,315	15,491	15,751
Hohhot, China	8,221	9,896	7,351	7,726	17,687	9,471	8,472	7,886	9,129	11,162	8,164	10,783	9,045	13,827	14,934	11,100	7,458	10,394	12,477	12,175
Hong Kong	6,174	11,745	9,314	9,306	18,190	11,481	10,274	9,628	11,096	12,954	9,950	12,718	11,097	15,896	16,434	13,026	9,179	12,450	14,433	13,361
Honiara, Solomon Islands	4,046	11,778	14,070	15,154	14,895	12,859	10,796	10,178	12,259	12,031	10,549	12,780	13,238	15,537	17,516	12,854	14,779	14,025	13,586	19,282
Honolulu, Hawaii	9,763	6,125	10,419	12,714	12,922	7,398	5,453	5,019	6,843	6,307	5,304	7,063	7,989	10,116	13,206	7,125	11,983	8,427	7,944	14,941
Houston, Texas	15,816	1,904	7,059	8,976	8,067	2,983	3,248	3,840	2,976	630	3,553	1,558	3,767	3,893	7,093	1,346	8,444	3,074	1,666	8,791
Huambo, Angola	11,367	12,748	8,519	6,273	6,853	11,454	13,398	13,846	12,006	12,649	13,552	11,843	10,860	8,995	6,052	11,803	6,997	10,442	11,086	3,978
Hubli, India	7,742	13,067	8,091	6,756	14,093	11,956	11,993	11,625	11,938	14,284	11,767	13,439	11,210	14,183	12,666	13,724	7,040	12,212	14,591	9,602
Hugh Town, United Kingdom	15,814	6,280	1,348	1,499	9,546	4,802	6,334	6,647	5,186	6,976	6,409	5,950	4,018	6,281	6,698	6,131	1,074	4,406	6,571	4,637
Hull, Canada	17,406	1,630	4,644	6,546	8,541	963	2,754	3,454	1,439	1,932	3,061	904	1,495	3,685	6,574	1,103	6,001	710	2,117	7,206
Hyderabad, India	7,645	12,873	8,067	6,872	14,505	11,827	11,740	11,341	11,771	14,117	11,502	13,317	11,104	14,346	13,003	13,612	7,107	12,164	14,567	9,919
Hyderabad, Pakistan	9,012	11,867	6,776	5,503	13,806	10,687	10,907	10,620	10,710	13,042	10,713	12,160	9,926	12,982	11,888	12,437	5,745	10,899	13,275	8,776
Igloolik, Canada	15,396	2,641	3,307	5,648	11,083	1,739	2,019	2,255	1,522	3,862	2,036	3,158	1,413	6,256	8,743	3,476	4,935	2,741	4,770	8,291
Iloilo, Philippines	4,742	12,532	10,838	10,848	17,924	12,570	11,056	10,361	12,105	13,600	10,723	13,611	12,314	17,178	17,806	13,891	10,739	13,662	15,291	14,697
Indianapolis, Indiana	16,756	1,168	5,669	7,606	8,413	1,654	2,629	3,331	1,806	877	2,962	168	2,402	3,708	6,844	207	7,058	1,730	1,621	7,951
Innsbruck, Austria	14,529	7,468	2,003	389	10,235	6,004	7,321	7,522	6,323	8,256	7,342	7,236	5,198	7,512	7,454	7,432	375	5,717	7,907	4,890

Distances in Kilometers	Eucla, Australia	Fargo, North Dakota	Faroe Islands (Torshavn)	Florence, Italy	Florianopolis, Brazil	Fort George, Canada	Fort McMurray, Canada	Fort Nelson, Canada	Fort Severn, Canada	Fort Smith, Arkansas	Fort Vermillion, Canada	Fort Wayne, Indiana	Fort-Chimo, Canada	Fort-de-France, Martinique	Fortaleza, Brazil	Frankfort, Kentucky	Frankfurt am Main, W. Ger.	Fredericton, Canada	Freeport, Bahamas	Freetown, Sierra Leone
Inuvik, Canada	13,542	3,161	4,936	7,235	12,629	3,216	1,712	1,191	2,677	4,405	1,409	4,165	3,290	7,794	10,601	4,461	6,502	4,440	5,876	10,318
Invercargill, New Zealand	3,736	13,842	18,239	18,201	11,011	15,314	13,630	13,252	14,874	13,258	13,521	14,284	16,060	14,242	13,860	14,131	18,458	15,860	13,813	15,801
Inverness, United Kingdom	15,459	5,935	526	1,868	10,295	4,483	5,784	6,021	4,779	6,785	5,820	5,779	3,672	6,694	7,447	6,001	1,177	4,329	6,649	5,488
Iquitos, Peru	15,440	6,068	9,176	9,857	3,717	6,406	7,539	8,190	6,753	4,865	7,864	5,110	6,873	2,435	3,860	4,798	9,754	5,548	3,403	6,797
Iraklion, Greece	13,110	9,218	3,708	1,513	10,408	7,753	9,014	9,154	8,068	9,986	9,008	8,961	6,948	8,750	7,903	9,144	2,114	7,417	9,499	4,903
Irkutsk, USSR	9,606	8,836	5,968	6,518	16,466	8,240	7,489	6,981	7,954	10,125	7,206	9,623	7,751	12,465	13,632	9,942	6,177	9,085	11,272	11,064
Islamabad, Pakistan	9,303	11,024	6,248	5,371	14,473	9,944	9,975	9,647	9,902	12,249	9,763	11,434	9,221	12,800	12,243	11,728	5,465	10,305	12,715	9,165
Istanbul, Turkey	13,011	8,894	3,331	1,487	11,014	7,459	8,553	8,635	7,718	9,766	8,519	8,755	6,646	8,965	8,421	8,965	1,870	7,262	9,470	5,499
Ivujivik, Canada	16,098	2,098	3,514	5,781	10,312	956	1,968	2,435	903	3,217	2,113	2,421	711	5,471	8,053	2,733	5,105	1,965	3,988	7,883
Iwo Jima Island, Japan	6,392	10,166	9,972	10,873	18,993	10,474	8,724	8,014	9,938	11,141	8,395	11,285	10,415	15,021	17,673	11,537	10,492	11,678	12,888	15,415
Izmir, Turkey	13,060	9,043	3,494	1,459	10,737	7,592	8,765	8,874	7,877	9,868	8,744	8,849	6,781	8,866	8,183	9,047	1,956	7,331	9,484	5,224
Jackson, Mississippi	16,358	1,713	6,558	8,427	7,959	2,553	3,166	3,817	2,639	520	3,490	1,073	3,307	3,542	6,753	815	7,908	2,523	1,278	8,288
Jaffna, Sri Lanka	6,929	13,734	8,895	7,568	14,299	12,696	12,571	12,144	12,639	14,984	12,323	14,186	11,969	14,963	13,214	14,479	7,859	13,008	15,398	10,214
Jakarta, Indonesia	3,643	14,964	11,824	10,928	15,436	14,693	13,484	12,814	14,335	16,116	13,155	15,962	14,229	18,405	16,027	16,269	11,112	15,549	17,678	13,419
Jamestown, St. Helena	12,856	11,367	8,642	6,833	4,591	10,367	12,430	13,054	10,968	10,908	12,683	10,302	9,990	6,963	3,834	10,176	7,452	9,179	9,186	2,827
Jamnagar, India	8,670	12,213	7,140	5,837	13,872	11,047	11,228	10,920	11,061	13,397	11,026	12,521	10,288	13,303	12,083	12,800	6,096	11,264	13,638	8,976
Jan Mayen Island	14,956	5,095	1,007	3,230	11,364	3,793	4,599	4,707	3,901	6,167	4,569	5,257	3,023	7,161	8,570	5,535	2,498	4,102	6,511	6,947
Jayapura, Indonesia	3,461	12,631	12,874	13,271	16,530	13,271	11,328	10,626	12,691	13,291	11,019	13,756	13,340	17,290	19,308	13,936	13,079	14,512	15,048	17,077
Jefferson City, Missouri	16,241	997	6,081	8,085	8,615	1,970	2,464	3,130	1,965	407	2,791	662	2,766	4,043	7,227	640	7,516	2,248	1,831	8,465
Jerusalem, Israel	12,093	10,061	4,499	2,484	11,038	8,620	9,707	9,760	8,887	10,908	9,661	9,890	7,808	9,753	8,703	10,089	2,996	8,372	10,503	5,625
Jiggalong, Australia	1,218	15,780	14,205	13,312	14,250	16,245	14,433	13,723	15,711	16,384	14,114	16,908	16,082	19,012	16,267	17,085	13,532	17,414	18,028	14,868
Jinan, China	7,670	10,159	7,966	8,380	18,329	9,860	8,701	8,078	9,477	11,394	8,382	11,107	9,490	14,327	15,586	11,418	8,110	10,845	12,819	12,814
Jodhpur, India	8,737	11,839	6,933	5,818	14,284	10,731	10,797	10,462	10,708	13,053	10,583	12,217	9,993	13,305	12,345	12,506	6,007	11,033	13,433	9,233
Johannesburg, South Africa	9,456	14,708	10,262	7,936	7,482	13,422	15,340	15,735	13,970	14,506	15,470	13,767	12,814	10,639	7,499	13,700	8,668	12,405	12,841	5,891
Juazeiro do Norte, Brazil	15,521	8,233	8,170	7,593	2,458	7,716	9,598	10,307	8,282	7,445	9,916	7,100	7,698	3,403	396	6,888	7,855	6,485	5,661	3,375
Juneau, Alaska	13,325	2,799	5,923	8,256	12,338	3,387	1,384	682	2,786	3,878	1,075	3,920	3,723	7,663	10,703	4,171	7,525	4,619	5,545	10,932
Kabul, Afghanistan	9,631	10,882	5,967	5,010	14,128	9,750	9,893	9,602	9,739	12,082	9,696	11,235	9,009	12,458	11,868	11,523	5,125	10,054	12,458	8,793
Kalgoorlie, Australia	713	16,295	14,947	13,850	13,463	16,964	15,049	14,348	16,401	16,655	14,741	17,376	16,874	18,198	15,644	17,479	14,145	18,178	17,997	14,727
Kaliningrad, USSR	13,969	7,306	1,773	1,389	11,238	5,906	6,907	6,995	6,117	8,258	6,873	7,274	5,095	8,156	8,428	7,513	951	5,871	8,208	5,934
Kamloops, Canada	14,084	1,771	6,209	8,545	11,156	2,803	895	920	2,233	2,685	905	2,899	3,382	6,610	9,751	3,105	7,837	3,926	4,414	10,461
Kampala, Uganda	10,628	12,846	7,596	5,259	9,159	11,378	12,910	13,101	11,801	13,263	12,935	12,275	10,622	10,404	7,920	12,356	5,968	10,699	12,118	5,162
Kananga, Zaire	11,209	12,682	7,936	5,614	7,839	11,285	13,082	13,424	11,789	12,817	13,181	11,912	10,608	9,486	6,759	11,926	6,346	10,406	11,421	4,267
Kano, Nigeria	13,572	10,178	5,686	3,531	7,553	8,778	10,617	11,018	9,290	10,392	10,743	9,447	8,113	7,518	5,486	9,488	4,227	7,915	9,163	2,415
Kanpur, India	8,246	11,878	7,296	6,393	14,996	10,889	10,720	10,317	10,799	13,137	10,479	12,380	10,194	13,850	13,064	12,683	6,516	11,322	13,733	9,954
Kansas City, Missouri	16,033	882	6,153	8,198	8,794	2,019	2,315	2,966	1,946	413	2,637	834	2,826	4,253	7,440	851	7,615	2,403	2,028	8,674
Kaohsiung, Taiwan	6,084	11,457	9,521	9,714	18,776	11,333	9,976	9,307	10,905	12,620	9,646	12,481	11,022	15,883	16,921	12,780	9,531	12,376	14,195	13,902
Karachi, Pakistan	9,077	11,896	6,754	5,431	13,663	10,696	10,962	10,687	10,732	13,058	10,773	12,163	9,929	12,900	11,759	12,437	5,691	10,881	13,246	8,648
Karaganda, USSR	10,573	9,245	4,831	4,638	14,548	8,223	8,184	7,874	8,142	10,486	7,977	9,714	7,537	11,587	11,867	10,017	4,477	8,705	11,106	9,036
Karl-Marx-Stadt, East Germany	14,446	7,266	1,726	796	10,571	5,819	7,035	7,203	6,102	8,116	7,040	7,106	5,007	7,641	7,767	7,319	311	5,625	7,884	5,275
Kasanga, Tanzania	10,246	13,520	8,471	6,124	8,573	12,082	13,749	13,997	12,550	13,759	13,803	12,824	11,363	10,491	7,720	12,859	6,846	11,285	12,413	5,270
Kashgar, China	9,590	10,412	5,865	5,276	14,791	9,391	9,320	8,974	9,313	11,657	9,100	10,882	8,695	12,552	12,363	11,184	5,266	9,836	12,245	9,350
Kassel, West Germany	14,687	7,056	1,545	850	10,421	5,602	6,864	7,055	5,898	7,888	6,879	6,875	4,792	7,406	7,603	7,085	145	5,387	7,640	5,185
Kathmandu, Nepal	8,036	11,741	7,430	6,705	15,507	10,845	10,516	10,072	10,707	13,020	10,259	12,326	10,186	14,095	13,517	12,637	6,772	11,370	13,769	10,413
Kayes, Mali	15,566	8,502	5,294	3,900	6,139	7,253	9,271	9,818	7,830	8,469	9,476	7,610	6,740	5,340	3,600	7,592	4,355	6,197	7,078	687
Kazan, USSR	12,261	8,194	3,191	2,988	12,965	6,970	7,411	7,281	7,017	9,332	7,278	8,442	6,210	9,891	10,199	8,722	2,749	7,239	9,647	7,522
Kemi, Finland	13,823	6,543	1,575	2,586	12,041	5,263	5,919	5,914	5,352	7,635	5,839	6,725	4,491	8,336	9,191	7,001	1,971	5,517	7,927	6,991
Kenora, Canada	15,921	366	5,205	7,395	9,697	1,156	1,362	2,073	829	1,599	1,692	1,211	1,930	4,936	7,984	1,498	6,754	2,112	2,913	8,663
Kerguelen Island	5,243	18,960	14,075	11,782	9,509	17,804	19,197	18,704	18,320	17,969	18,952	17,833	17,135	14,113	10,981	17,621	12,465	16,753	16,288	10,202
Kerkira, Greece	13,696	8,562	3,077	857	10,276	7,095	8,395	8,564	7,418	9,325	8,402	8,301	6,290	8,228	7,646	8,486	1,464	6,760	8,870	4,769
Kermanshah, Iran	11,254	10,315	4,834	3,244	12,164	8,953	9,713	9,640	9,121	11,316	9,610	10,336	8,147	10,705	9,838	10,573	3,568	8,912	11,189	6,765
Khabarovsk, USSR	8,906	8,309	7,292	8,411	17,662	8,220	6,831	6,176	7,764	9,502	6,504	9,326	7,993	12,835	15,004	9,624	7,940	9,328	11,039	12,975
Kharkov, USSR	12,809	8,362	2,926	2,016	11,956	7,009	7,804	7,791	7,167	9,379	7,725	8,415	6,207	9,293	9,243	8,665	1,963	7,048	9,397	6,475
Khartoum, Sudan	11,499	11,444	6,006	3,716	9,958	9,967	11,320	11,455	10,327	12,076	11,315	11,051	9,176	9,964	8,106	11,190	4,390	9,469	11,263	5,037
Khon Kaen, Thailand	6,010	12,725	9,388	8,889	16,838	12,218	11,297	10,698	11,920	13,990	10,986	13,586	11,705	16,150	15,579	13,904	8,914	13,014	15,250	12,474
Kiev, USSR	13,213	8,099	2,597	1,633	11,601	6,717	7,620	7,652	6,907	9,077	7,561	8,099	5,909	8,883	8,864	8,339	1,551	6,699	9,029	6,147
Kigali, Rwanda	10,733	12,880	7,747	5,401	8,794	11,425	13,039	13,271	11,873	13,215	13,084	12,248	10,688	10,196	7,625	12,309	6,121	10,686	11,987	4,944
Kingston, Canada	17,409	1,607	4,784	6,669	8,446	1,083	2,796	3,501	1,526	1,816	3,109	790	1,641	3,596	6,523	969	6,131	798	1,976	7,233
Kingston, Jamaica	17,031	3,690	7,214	8,495	5,892	3,981	5,172	5,852	4,314	2,596	5,503	2,679	4,505	1,721	4,841	2,372	8,176	3,240	965	6,937
Kingstown, Saint Vincent	17,709	4,996	6,915	7,606	4,710	4,777	6,428	7,139	5,267	4,139	6,758	3,870	5,025	161	3,129	3,628	7,467	3,674	2,355	5,265
Kinshasa, Zaire	11,960	12,028	7,593	5,339	7,223	10,675	12,560	12,970	11,206	12,075	12,693	11,201	10,040	8,678	5,974	11,196	6,063	9,731	10,634	3,471
Kirkwall, United Kingdom	15,333	5,912	399	1,950	10,473	4,473	5,710	5,925	4,746	6,795	5,735	5,797	3,659	6,823	7,625	6,027	1,236	4,373	6,716	5,667
Kirov, USSR	12,368	7,922	3,047	3,090	13,050	6,723	7,112	6,972	6,750	9,076	6,975	8,202	5,974	9,790	10,252	8,487	2,777	7,039	9,450	7,655
Kiruna, Sweden	14,008	6,249	1,417	2,733	11,980	4,976	5,628	5,632	5,059	7,347	5,552	6,442	4,209	8,146	9,132	6,721	2,076	5,258	7,669	7,041
Kisangani, Zaire	11,336	12,334	7,332	4,989	8,444	10,892	12,575	12,855	11,359	12,626	12,643	11,667	10,172	9,604	7,102	11,720	5,718	10,114	11,381	4,354
Kishinev, USSR	13,226	8,341	2,791	1,420	11,318	6,932	7,930	7,990	7,154	9,273	7,884	8,278	6,120	8,831	8,622	8,506	1,522	6,834	9,119	5,833
Kitchner, Canada	17,141	1,335	5,057	6,982	8,515	1,160	2,624	3,336	1,484	1,494	2,947	466	1,833	3,694	6,704	690	6,433	1,130	1,885	7,531
Knoxville, Tennessee	16,970	1,616	5,896	7,724	7,953	2,022	3,089	3,786	2,243	952	3,422	576	2,713	3,283	6,449	261	7,214	1,823	1,156	7,723
Kosice, Czechoslovakia	13,822	7,846	2,282	945	10,922	6,415	7,528	7,642	6,669	8,734	7,508	7,729	5,601	8,244	8,171	7,949	924	6,263	8,529	5,501
Kota Kinabalu, Malaysia	4,388	13,319	11,045	10,729	17,123	13,228	11,837	11,154	12,802	14,433	11,505	14,367	12,889	17,707	17,206	14,660	10,722	14,244	16,073	14,186
Krakow, Poland	13,943	7,666	2,102	963	10,925	6,237	7,347	7,465	6,489	8,560	7,328	7,557	5,424	8,138	8,153	7,779	803	6,099	8,378	5,537
Kralendijk, Bonaire	17,228	4,685	7,351	8,246	4,885	4,719	6,158	6,856	5,142	3,680	6,491	3,602	5,097	823	3,733	3,322	8,050	3,750	1,933	6,030
Krasnodar, USSR	12,413	8,944	3,469	2,204	11,943	7,579	8,393	8,372	7,749	9,944	8,311	8,970	6,773	9,647	9,324	9,212	2,332	7,572	9,893	6,429
Krasnoyarsk, USSR	10,305	8,565	5,188	5,660	15,612	7,804	7,315	6,886	7,587	9,853	7,061	9,244	7,241	11,810	12,788	9,562	5,323	8,540	10,826	10,211
Kristiansand, Norway	14,734	6,484	924	1,618	10,851	5,066	6,178	6,330	5,303	7,408	6,173	6,419	4,253	7,415	8,005	6,655	897	5,012	7,358	5,803
Kuala Lumpur, Malaysia	4,813	14,174	10,647	9,806	15,865	13,687	12,727	12,104	13,393	15,421	12,410	15,057	13,155	17,288	15,615	15,376	9,956	14,443	16,720	12,703
Kuching, Malaysia	4,170	14,026	11,228	10,622	16,361	13,805	12,545	11,875	13,422	15,181	12,215	15,034	13,390	17,991	16,564	15,338	10,706	14,732	16,751	13,679
Kumasi, Ghana	14,195	9,864	6,155	4,297	6,314	8,583	10,570	11,079	9,148	9,840	10,754	8,985	8,027	6,549	4,257	8,967	4,910	7,559	8,411	1,299
Kumzar, Oman	10,017	11,464	6,062	4,483	12,704	10,147	10,729	10,568	10,272	12,521	10,588	11,559	9,348	11,890	10,688	11,805	4,828	10,162	12,449	7,576
Kunming, China	6,873	11,801	8,527	8,237	17,153	11,262	10,394	9,815	10,971	13,077	10,089	12,638	10,751	15,280	15,251	12,957	8,184	12,065	14,295	12,160
Kuqa Chang, China	9,322	10,250	6,082	5,750	15,426	9,344	9,064	8,661	9,204	11,523	8,821	10,823	8,696	12,838	12,920	11,135	5,665	9,907	12,290	9,952
Kurgan, USSR	11,384	8,542	4,016	4,002	13,978	7,460	7,565	7,316	7,412	9,758	7,382	8,951	6,754	10,776	11,216	9,250	3,758	7,900	10,306	8,511
Kuwait, Kuwait	10,897	10,851	5,342	3,614	12,046	9,474	10,266	10,192	9,657	11,829	10,163	10,838	8,665	10,993	9,874	11,067	4,008	9,387	11,621	6,769
Kuybyshev, USSR	12,072	8,481	3,417	3,017	12,978	7,247	7,702	7,569	7,302	9,612	7,569	8,716	6,482	10,072	10,247	8,993	2,849	7,492	9,896	7,499
Kyoto, Japan	7,420	9,532	8,737	9,637	19,090	9,612	8,053	7,363	9,120	10,640	7,721	10,606	9,445	14,237	16,491	10,887	9,241	10,761	12,292	14,199
Kzyl-Orda, USSR	10,625	9,701	4,865	4,247	13,963	8,567	8,748	8,495	8,554	10,897	8,565	10,053	7,832	11,511	11,403	10,344	4,218	8,906	11,317	8,459
L'vov, USSR	13,650	7,875	2,318	1,182	11,159	6,460	7,500	7,586	6,691	8,797	7,466	7,801	5,647	8,432	8,405	8,029	1,097	6,360	8,654	5,734
La Ceiba, Honduras	16,011	3,570	7,949	9,441	6,328	4,276	4,995	5,611	4,462	2,300	5,309	2,807	4,939	2,765	5,739	2,491	9,061	3,837	1,450	8,011
La Coruna, Spain	16,078	6,580	2,078	1,583	8,865	5,111	6,806	7,180	5,557	7,132	6,914	6,108	4,371	5,915	6,026	6,250	1,500	4,526	6,500	3,893
La Paz, Bolivia	14,371	7,582	10,215	10,439	2,360	7,861	9,054	9,703	8,237	6,377	9,379	6,611	8,268	3,526	3,536	6,302	10,493	6,919	4,896	6,648
La Paz, Mexico	14,215	2,792	8,337	10,420	8,756	4,199	3,618	3,971	3,987	1,971	3,829	2,996	5,012	5,271	8,350	2,866	9,831	4,578	3,176	10,341
La Ronge, Canada	15,086	1,090	5,223	7,528	10,631	1,700	422	1,135	1,116	2,345	750	2,149	2,261	5,877	8,899	2,425	6,838	2,877	3,834	9,368
Labrador City, Canada	17,329	2,231	3,601	5,588	9,098	809	2,836	3,447	1,379	2,908	3,075	1,904	581	4,286	6,822	2,144	5,007	777	3,097	6,880
Lagos, Nigeria	13,726	10,258	6,222	4,206	6,735	8,932	10,875	11,345	9,481	10,304	11,038	9,421	8,334	7,093	4,789	9,420	4,866	7,957	8,920	1,850
Lahore, Pakistan	9,062	11,270	6,502	5,586	14,537	10,199	10,204	9,863	10,152	12,499	9,987	11,689	9,478	13,033	12,386	11,984	5,698	10,562	12,973	9,294
Lambasa, Fiji	5,357	10,868	14,920	16,776	12,917	12,228	10,311	9,850	11,690	10,719	10,153	11,646	12,847	13,569	15,304	11,619	16,177	13,154	11,968	18,399
Lansing, Michigan	16,841	1,072	5,326	7,295	8,615	1,300	2,456	3,167	1,490	1,180	2,786	191	2,047	3,842	6,917	504	6,733	1,468	1,874	7,847
Lanzhou, China	7,949	10,596	7,494	7,527	17,247	10,043	9,207	8,651	9,750	11,878	8,909	11,418	9,545	14,176	14,743	11,737	7,360	10,870	13,074	11,798
Laoag, Philippines	5,594	11,887	9,988	10,095	18,500	11,807	10,405	9,726	11,369	13,025	10,073	12,928	11,508	16,372	17,242	13,222	9,944	12,862	14,637	14,161
Largeau, Chad	12,879	10,405	5,297	2,960	8,862	8,937	10,545	10,817	9,372	10,866	10,606	9,861	8,189	8,513	6,758	9,962	3,692	8,277	9,893	3,653
Las Vegas, Nevada	14,194	1,931	7,392	9,633	9,921	3,403	2,303	2,578	3,024	1,873	2,472	2,655	4,177	5,855	9,063	2,687	8,976	4,150	3,598	10,513

Distances in Kilometers	Eucla, Australia	Fargo, North Dakota	Faroe Islands (Torshavn)	Florence, Italy	Florianopolis, Brazil	Fort George, Canada	Fort McMurray, Canada	Fort Nelson, Canada	Fort Severn, Canada	Fort Smith, Arkansas	Fort Vermilion, Canada	Fort Wayne, Indiana	Fort-Chimo, Canada	Fort-de-France, Martinique	Fortaleza, Brazil	Frankfort, Kentucky	Frankfurt am Main, W. Ger.	Fredericton, Canada	Freeport, Bahamas	Freetown, Sierra Leone
Launceston, Australia	1,951	15,011	17,134	16,434	12,197	16,362	14,374	13,828	15,803	14,717	14,172	15,709	16,909	15,986	14,974	15,623	16,693	17,272	15,530	15,883
Le Havre, France	15,362	6,681	1,457	1,062	9,805	5,207	6,655	6,926	5,564	7,416	6,710	6,392	4,411	6,717	6,970	6,580	619	4,858	7,038	4,713
Leipzig, East Germany	14,489	7,201	1,660	842	10,571	5,754	6,970	7,139	6,036	8,053	6,975	7,043	4,942	7,603	7,763	7,258	289	5,565	7,829	5,293
Leningrad, USSR	13,467	7,233	1,991	2,206	12,027	5,920	6,637	6,629	6,039	8,296	6,558	7,362	5,132	8,688	9,200	7,628	1,745	6,083	8,479	6,757
Leon, Spain	15,854	6,813	2,162	1,371	8,934	5,342	7,012	7,372	5,781	7,376	7,113	6,351	4,595	6,117	6,108	6,495	1,375	4,770	6,740	3,853
Lerwick, United Kingdom	15,195	5,930	367	2,005	10,639	4,503	5,679	5,872	4,755	6,841	5,693	5,851	3,690	6,964	7,791	6,087	1,278	4,451	6,810	5,820
Lhasa, China	7,879	11,493	7,532	7,029	16,098	10,707	10,201	9,715	10,516	12,783	9,928	12,165	10,095	14,278	14,000	12,482	7,026	11,336	13,697	10,915
Libreville, Gabon	12,790	11,208	6,972	4,809	6,917	9,872	11,792	12,236	10,414	11,244	11,942	10,370	9,258	7,912	5,354	10,364	5,512	8,907	9,821	2,673
Lilongwe, Malawi	9,678	14,173	9,140	6,793	8,565	12,744	14,423	14,663	13,219	14,350	14,474	13,439	12,032	10,913	8,006	13,458	7,513	11,919	12,925	5,760
Lima, Peru	14,435	6,817	10,183	10,792	3,430	7,302	8,255	8,866	7,604	5,560	8,569	5,940	7,815	3,433	4,345	5,622	10,726	6,509	4,271	7,417
Limerick, Ireland	15,892	5,978	1,047	1,768	9,700	4,502	5,997	6,303	4,869	6,713	6,068	5,690	3,709	6,237	6,850	5,883	1,234	4,167	6,391	4,916
Limoges, France	15,301	7,005	1,873	823	9,560	5,527	7,036	7,324	5,909	7,685	7,100	6,658	4,742	6,721	6,746	6,830	731	5,101	7,202	4,365
Limon, Costa Rica	15,952	4,290	8,314	9,590	5,577	4,875	5,733	6,360	5,117	3,039	6,051	3,449	5,481	2,440	5,166	3,129	9,285	4,281	1,882	7,655
Lincoln, Nebraska	15,857	672	6,100	8,195	9,056	1,959	2,063	2,707	1,811	635	2,383	972	2,772	4,504	7,684	1,057	7,593	2,484	2,288	8,848
Linz, Austria	14,324	7,538	2,015	556	10,476	6,083	7,329	7,501	6,379	8,364	7,336	7,348	5,273	7,732	7,699	7,554	456	5,849	8,073	5,114
Lisbon, Portugal	16,158	6,848	2,597	1,793	8,408	5,400	7,180	7,590	5,880	7,302	7,307	6,289	4,695	5,726	5,585	6,404	1,893	4,703	6,521	3,372
Little Rock, Arkansas	16,204	1,399	6,437	8,382	8,292	2,362	2,839	3,485	2,387	208	3,161	941	3,143	3,839	7,046	767	7,836	2,492	1,581	8,479
Liverpool, United Kingdom	15,506	6,247	983	1,497	9,994	4,779	6,178	6,441	5,114	7,030	6,227	6,012	3,975	6,619	7,145	6,215	885	4,509	6,761	5,066
Lodz, Poland	14,000	7,506	1,944	1,079	11,001	6,084	7,168	7,280	6,325	8,416	7,146	7,419	5,271	8,098	8,212	7,646	779	5,976	8,275	5,647
Lome, Togo	13,904	10,122	6,236	4,284	6,522	8,818	10,783	11,273	9,375	10,130	10,957	9,262	8,240	6,868	4,547	9,252	4,925	7,818	8,719	1,619
London, United Kingdom	15,353	6,531	1,238	1,209	9,959	5,060	6,466	6,725	5,401	7,298	6,514	6,277	4,259	6,751	7,117	6,475	639	4,762	6,983	4,917
Londonderry, United Kingdom	15,729	5,914	782	1,828	9,960	4,446	5,860	6,138	4,782	6,702	5,916	5,685	3,642	6,414	7,112	5,892	1,211	4,193	6,467	5,184
Longlac, Canada	16,467	826	4,827	6,946	9,356	687	1,816	2,522	694	1,723	2,130	974	1,500	4,534	7,503	1,294	6,330	1,542	2,667	8,092
Lord Howe Island, Australia	2,857	13,512	16,468	16,902	12,838	14,836	12,848	12,316	14,275	13,341	12,653	14,289	15,388	15,537	15,685	14,246	16,814	15,804	14,428	17,334
Los Angeles, California	13,857	2,297	7,733	9,987	10,022	3,767	2,574	2,772	3,377	2,183	2,711	3,007	4,537	6,104	9,302	3,024	9,324	4,514	3,863	10,846
Louangphrabang, Laos	6,382	12,374	9,015	8,578	16,931	11,839	10,959	10,372	11,550	13,647	10,652	13,217	11,320	15,778	15,402	13,536	8,578	12,628	14,872	12,291
Louisville, Kentucky	16,801	1,317	5,786	7,688	8,254	1,808	2,788	3,485	1,977	835	3,120	318	2,541	3,572	6,724	79	7,152	1,792	1,456	7,905
Luanda, Angola	11,852	12,240	8,041	5,825	6,790	10,938	12,882	13,335	11,490	12,175	13,038	11,351	10,343	8,600	5,748	11,319	6,542	9,935	10,647	3,505
Lubumbashi, Zaire	10,393	13,528	8,695	6,355	8,055	12,128	13,900	14,211	12,628	13,640	13,985	12,749	11,444	10,186	7,316	12,755	7,085	11,250	12,194	5,029
Lusaka, Zambia	10,092	13,894	9,119	6,779	7,961	12,511	14,311	14,632	13,021	13,943	14,402	13,080	11,840	10,375	7,418	13,071	7,509	11,604	12,440	5,290
Luxembourg, Luxembourg	14,928	7,007	1,595	757	10,116	5,540	6,895	7,121	5,868	7,788	6,927	6,768	4,736	7,146	7,297	6,965	192	5,252	7,460	4,901
Luxor, Egypt	12,018	10,507	4,985	2,788	10,503	9,042	10,268	10,369	9,356	11,258	10,246	10,232	8,237	9,687	8,319	10,404	3,403	8,674	10,672	5,209
Lynn Lake, Canada	15,304	1,147	4,902	7,202	10,573	1,432	631	1,300	832	2,438	908	2,095	1,945	5,771	8,733	2,392	6,514	2,644	3,807	9,088
Lyon, France	15,021	7,221	1,958	552	9,749	5,745	7,200	7,461	6,109	7,930	7,250	6,904	4,953	6,997	6,951	7,083	564	5,355	7,476	4,478
Macapa, Brazil	16,498	6,827	7,810	7,820	3,068	6,495	8,245	8,957	7,023	5,957	8,573	5,697	6,619	1,953	1,456	5,461	7,902	5,314	4,174	4,295
Madison, Wisconsin	16,444	721	5,540	7,580	8,869	1,419	2,174	2,876	1,442	957	2,507	416	2,219	4,154	7,268	663	6,995	1,830	2,073	8,245
Madras, India	7,170	13,358	8,578	7,334	14,495	12,335	12,192	11,768	12,269	14,612	11,944	13,826	11,616	14,782	13,231	14,122	7,592	12,678	15,079	10,185
Madrid, Spain	15,695	7,090	2,414	1,289	8,842	5,622	7,302	7,662	6,066	7,629	7,403	6,607	4,880	6,222	6,038	6,743	1,448	5,022	6,943	3,659
Madurai, India	7,100	13,692	8,770	7,398	14,129	12,617	12,564	12,157	12,581	14,928	12,323	14,104	11,879	14,772	13,007	14,393	7,703	12,891	15,270	10,005
Magadan, USSR	10,317	6,713	6,384	7,969	16,157	6,672	5,235	4,585	6,194	7,911	4,908	7,734	6,513	11,298	13,759	8,030	7,373	7,819	9,446	12,327
Magdalena, Bolivia	14,832	7,422	9,719	9,886	2,260	7,575	8,903	9,575	7,988	6,266	9,233	6,400	7,927	3,108	3,012	6,101	9,950	6,572	4,685	6,121
Magdeburg, East Germany	14,538	7,101	1,555	935	10,596	5,656	6,863	7,032	5,934	7,960	6,868	6,952	4,844	7,564	7,780	7,169	309	5,481	7,756	5,346
Majuro Atoll, Marshall Isls.	6,222	9,587	12,333	14,018	15,267	10,641	8,579	7,966	10,042	9,952	8,333	10,623	11,038	13,780	16,725	10,727	13,440	11,811	11,620	18,207
Malabo, Equatorial Guinea	13,062	10,881	6,593	4,440	7,055	9,528	11,430	11,866	10,063	10,964	11,576	10,069	8,902	7,746	5,324	10,075	5,139	8,586	9,589	2,494
Male, Maldives	7,064	14,289	9,105	7,495	13,364	13,104	13,258	12,894	13,136	15,467	13,035	14,564	12,332	14,613	12,484	14,830	7,889	13,223	15,509	9,593
Manado, Indonesia	3,699	13,293	11,879	11,765	17,034	13,491	11,843	11,135	12,992	14,248	11,512	14,408	13,295	18,113	18,170	14,665	11,709	14,629	16,012	15,258
Managua, Nicaragua	15,826	3,974	8,274	9,681	5,990	4,669	5,394	6,003	4,865	2,701	5,706	3,207	5,318	2,742	5,570	2,890	9,333	4,182	1,774	7,988
Manama, Bahrain	10,491	11,274	5,776	4,033	12,155	9,905	10,658	10,561	10,079	12,262	10,546	11,273	9,096	11,366	10,105	11,502	4,441	9,822	12,049	6,994
Manaus, Brazil	16,036	6,607	8,504	8,762	2,967	6,556	8,080	8,778	7,019	5,571	8,412	5,520	6,830	1,965	2,392	5,243	8,780	5,478	3,852	5,348
Manchester, New Hampshire	17,835	2,036	4,628	6,400	8,159	1,326	3,189	3,888	1,851	2,147	3,495	1,151	1,694	3,300	6,143	1,251	5,896	505	1,945	6,805
Mandalay, Burma	6,896	12,269	8,515	7,950	16,416	11,590	10,909	10,368	11,357	13,558	10,617	13,021	11,013	15,259	14,732	13,340	7,983	12,280	14,608	11,620
Mangareva Island, Fr.Polynesia	9,244	8,648	14,207	16,174	8,523	10,069	9,121	9,150	9,834	7,758	9,203	8,772	10,882	9,058	10,514	8,569	15,667	10,284	8,168	13,623
Manila, Philippines	5,192	12,228	10,376	10,417	18,215	12,190	10,746	10,061	11,742	13,340	10,414	13,284	11,903	16,769	17,480	13,573	10,292	13,256	14,984	14,372
Mannheim, West Germany	14,759	7,141	1,683	670	10,231	5,678	6,997	7,207	5,995	7,938	7,022	6,919	4,871	7,313	7,421	7,120	72	5,410	7,626	4,973
Maputo, Mozambique	9,089	15,030	10,365	8,022	7,909	13,698	15,550	15,882	14,227	14,901	15,650	14,128	13,056	11,071	7,942	14,076	8,752	12,724	13,260	6,252
Mar del Plata, Argentina	12,258	10,181	11,986	11,399	1,428	10,382	11,653	12,296	10,797	8,971	11,977	9,195	10,698	5,834	4,263	8,890	11,717	9,345	7,478	6,901
Maracaibo, Venezuela	16,875	4,663	7,666	8,627	4,908	4,833	6,145	6,830	5,217	3,580	6,477	3,621	5,270	1,224	4,000	3,324	8,415	3,941	1,909	6,403
Marrakech, Morocco	15,965	7,437	3,379	2,158	7,840	6,023	7,880	8,322	6,534	7,766	8,025	6,779	5,361	5,695	5,073	6,859	2,476	5,211	6,795	2,618
Marseilles, France	14,962	7,438	2,231	476	9,591	5,960	7,453	7,724	6,339	8,113	7,509	7,085	5,175	7,012	6,815	7,254	798	5,524	7,593	4,263
Maseru, Lesotho	9,317	14,882	10,579	8,260	7,309	13,641	15,596	16,023	14,201	14,593	15,743	13,903	13,059	10,661	7,488	13,816	8,993	12,588	12,889	6,047
Mashhad, Iran	10,428	10,497	5,304	4,149	13,317	9,257	9,660	9,461	9,319	11,627	9,502	10,716	8,483	11,626	10,983	10,986	4,317	9,429	11,803	7,922
Mazatlan, Mexico	14,541	2,763	8,240	10,253	8,379	4,102	3,744	4,160	3,951	1,780	3,982	2,804	4,912	4,851	7,941	2,638	9,691	4,367	2,811	9,969
Mbabane, Swaziland	9,191	14,947	10,360	8,021	7,762	13,633	15,511	15,866	14,170	14,788	15,622	14,029	13,003	10,939	7,803	13,971	8,752	12,642	13,135	6,151
Mbandaka, Zaire	11,959	11,881	7,188	4,891	7,745	10,480	12,285	12,645	10,985	12,051	12,392	11,129	9,804	8,869	6,329	11,154	5,621	9,611	10,715	3,618
McMurdo Sound, Antarctica	5,405	15,233	18,252	16,065	8,133	16,390	15,925	15,903	16,403	14,069	15,998	14,899	17,080	12,560	10,872	14,599	16,794	15,845	13,486	12,338
Mecca, Saudi Arabia	11,151	11,281	5,724	3,615	10,939	9,830	10,932	10,966	10,111	12,086	10,879	11,062	9,020	10,521	8,961	11,245	4,189	9,517	11,540	5,856
Medan, Indonesia	5,048	14,214	10,454	9,530	15,647	13,637	12,790	12,187	13,377	15,482	12,478	15,045	13,069	17,017	15,280	15,364	9,705	14,329	16,663	12,363
Medellin, Colombia	16,221	4,939	8,299	9,280	4,739	5,285	6,415	7,075	5,618	3,759	6,742	3,973	5,785	1,835	4,267	3,661	9,070	4,485	2,269	6,880
Medicine Hat, Canada	14,764	1,083	5,891	8,189	10,551	2,199	745	1,247	1,671	2,094	992	2,214	2,854	5,939	9,066	2,430	7,503	3,267	3,770	9,816
Medina, Saudi Arabia	11,336	10,977	5,415	3,350	11,066	9,533	10,604	10,632	9,802	11,809	10,548	10,787	8,721	10,398	8,986	10,978	3,899	9,254	11,324	5,874
Melbourne, Australia	1,622	14,965	16,696	16,115	12,627	16,243	14,211	13,631	15,663	14,792	13,989	15,752	16,711	16,379	15,391	15,700	16,320	17,265	15,752	16,097
Memphis, Tennessee	16,410	1,421	6,289	8,205	8,198	2,251	2,890	3,554	2,326	398	3,217	788	3,016	3,682	6,883	576	7,668	2,307	1,438	8,275
Merauke, Indonesia	2,835	13,161	13,490	13,740	15,904	13,877	11,903	11,208	13,291	13,731	11,600	14,272	13,978	17,603	18,651	14,430	13,604	15,120	15,446	17,129
Merida, Mexico	16,030	2,947	7,598	9,254	6,956	3,758	4,356	4,966	3,891	1,665	4,668	2,269	4,466	3,102	6,207	1,964	8,816	3,473	1,263	8,272
Meridian, Mississippi	16,497	1,752	6,474	8,318	7,879	2,507	3,220	3,881	2,626	626	3,546	1,017	3,245	3,421	6,631	735	7,807	2,417	1,159	8,148
Messina, Italy	14,020	8,441	3,060	718	9,877	6,965	8,370	8,585	7,322	9,140	8,399	8,113	6,171	7,865	7,238	8,282	1,434	6,552	8,594	4,377
Mexico City, Mexico	15,057	3,055	8,243	10,073	7,532	4,192	4,267	4,773	4,174	1,831	4,542	2,747	4,972	4,080	7,109	2,500	9,579	4,186	2,229	9,280
Miami, Florida	17,124	2,763	6,648	8,186	6,807	3,117	4,245	4,930	3,409	1,728	4,577	1,757	3,709	2,345	5,554	1,446	7,778	2,544	163	7,302
Midway Islands, USA	8,741	7,094	9,970	11,988	15,027	8,044	5,982	5,351	7,442	7,664	5,725	8,185	8,416	11,690	14,898	8,336	11,309	9,241	9,430	15,604
Milan, Italy	14,680	7,489	2,109	249	9,976	6,017	7,406	7,635	6,361	8,232	7,441	7,207	5,218	7,332	7,202	7,392	518	5,668	7,810	4,629
Milford Sound, New Zealand	3,655	13,765	18,033	18,149	11,205	15,230	13,503	13,108	14,774	13,223	13,385	14,247	15,960	14,356	14,053	14,105	18,330	15,830	13,842	16,005
Milwaukee, Wisconsin	16,564	820	5,469	7,489	8,796	1,367	2,252	2,958	1,440	1,018	2,584	317	2,156	4,061	7,164	596	6,911	1,717	2,011	8,124
Minsk, USSR	13,501	7,669	2,191	1,637	11,592	6,294	7,187	7,227	6,475	8,659	7,131	7,687	5,488	8,622	8,807	7,933	1,359	6,311	8,662	6,211
Mogadiscio, Somalia	9,519	13,452	7,926	5,717	10,509	11,982	13,159	13,173	12,303	14,130	13,101	13,105	11,180	11,728	9,353	13,245	6,350	11,524	13,254	6,531
Mombasa, Kenya	9,704	13,694	8,317	6,012	9,635	12,217	13,631	13,743	12,610	14,171	13,619	13,174	11,444	11,288	8,678	13,265	6,698	11,592	13,041	6,036
Monclova, Mexico	15,157	2,254	7,637	9,614	8,264	3,512	3,408	3,912	3,415	1,153	3,680	2,168	4,316	4,394	7,553	1,992	9,063	3,722	2,250	9,412
Moncton, Canada	18,030	2,443	4,019	5,769	8,323	1,330	3,374	4,036	1,929	2,750	3,649	1,731	1,358	3,510	6,098	1,870	5,264	145	2,502	6,423
Monrovia, Liberia	14,980	9,197	6,189	4,676	5,529	8,021	10,065	10,640	8,609	9,032	10,287	8,240	7,556	5,570	3,273	8,188	5,185	6,911	7,513	363
Monte Carlo, Monaco	14,803	7,523	2,236	309	9,742	6,046	7,498	7,751	6,412	8,223	7,545	7,196	5,255	7,179	6,974	7,370	716	5,641	7,735	4,390
Monterrey, Mexico	15,215	2,374	7,700	9,642	8,090	3,591	3,563	4,077	3,520	1,216	3,839	2,210	4,389	4,263	7,409	2,011	9,104	3,740	2,154	9,319
Montevideo, Uruguay	12,614	9,925	11,619	11,063	1,086	10,072	11,402	12,059	10,502	8,735	11,730	8,917	10,367	5,501	3,904	8,616	11,367	9,016	7,201	6,590
Montgomery, Alabama	16,720	1,840	6,349	8,150	7,747	2,453	3,320	3,996	2,625	821	3,650	970	3,163	3,228	6,433	659	7,653	2,260	977	7,923
Montpelier, Vermont	17,687	1,905	4,579	6,403	8,323	1,162	3,028	3,725	1,683	2,104	3,332	1,088	1,566	3,464	6,308	1,228	5,882	503	2,046	6,931
Montpellier, France	15,086	7,326	2,165	594	9,526	5,847	7,359	7,640	6,232	7,991	7,420	6,964	5,065	6,893	6,740	7,131	811	5,400	7,466	4,231
Montreal, Canada	17,548	1,791	4,528	6,400	8,481	1,005	2,878	3,572	1,524	2,084	3,179	1,057	1,446	3,622	6,464	1,236	5,864	543	2,156	7,046
Moosonee, Canada	16,768	1,274	4,418	6,507	9,286	305	2,084	2,764	697	2,082	2,373	1,186	1,092	4,431	7,287	1,491	5,899	1,187	2,754	7,710
Moroni, Comoros	8,928	14,613	9,247	6,945	9,599	13,139	14,557	14,644	13,541	15,024	14,536	14,047	12,371	11,865	9,039	14,117	7,630	12,474	13,769	6,642
Moscow, USSR	12,931	7,861	2,594	2,296	12,264	6,556	7,224	7,181	6,668	8,931	7,130	7,997	5,768	9,211	9,482	8,262	2,025	6,706	9,096	6,859
Mosul, Iraq	11,675	9,962	4,450	2,823	11,911	8,581	9,416	9,378	8,768	10,936	9,328	9,948	7,772	10,291	9,508	10,179	3,151	8,508	10,772	6,461
Mount Isa, Australia	1,613	14,211	14,745	14,626	14,589	15,106	13,074	12,401	14,506	14,554	12,789	15,264	15,286	17,748	17,291	15,361	14,629	16,339	16,087	16,805

Distances in Kilometers

	Eucla, Australia	Fargo, North Dakota	Faroe Islands (Torshavn)	Florence, Italy	Florianopolis, Brazil	Fort George, Canada	Fort McMurray, Canada	Fort Nelson, Canada	Fort Severn, Canada	Fort Smith, Arkansas	Fort Vermilion, Canada	Fort Wayne, Indiana	Fort-Chimo, Canada	Fort-de-France, Martinique	Fortaleza, Brazil	Frankfort, Kentucky	Frankfurt am Main, W. Ger.	Fredericton, Canada	Freeport, Bahamas	Freetown, Sierra Leone
Multan, Pakistan	9,146	11,390	6,486	5,446	14,242	10,273	10,370	10,054	10,254	12,599	10,163	11,759	9,535	12,921	12,142	12,048	5,601	10,579	12,982	9,040
Munich, West Germany	14,523	7,409	1,924	488	10,308	5,948	7,243	7,437	6,259	8,211	7,261	7,192	5,140	7,530	7,521	7,393	304	5,681	7,889	4,977
Murcia, Spain	15,453	7,434	2,701	1,222	8,783	5,967	7,649	8,003	6,413	7,955	7,748	6,935	5,227	6,403	6,014	7,065	1,557	5,349	7,222	3,486
Murmansk, USSR	13,484	6,515	1,957	3,074	12,513	5,315	5,767	5,695	5,340	7,664	5,657	6,799	4,577	8,666	9,663	7,088	2,475	5,692	8,100	7,498
Mururoa Atoll, Fr. Polynesia	8,965	8,709	14,270	16,352	8,951	10,154	9,085	9,065	9,883	7,886	9,144	8,908	10,966	9,400	10,936	8,721	15,791	10,448	8,405	14,042
Muscat, Oman	9,663	11,817	6,432	4,841	12,806	10,510	11,052	10,869	10,627	12,885	10,902	11,927	9,714	12,220	10,903	12,175	5,198	10,534	12,819	7,794
Myitkyina, Burma	7,150	11,877	8,249	7,810	16,639	11,222	10,513	9,970	10,977	13,165	10,220	12,643	10,660	15,010	14,744	12,962	7,799	11,942	14,247	11,643
Naga, Philippines	5,055	12,214	10,560	10,654	18,245	12,239	10,736	10,043	11,775	13,296	10,403	13,287	11,984	16,848	17,737	13,570	10,516	13,331	14,974	14,630
Nagasaki, Japan	7,142	10,022	8,802	9,497	19,410	10,011	8,539	7,860	9,545	11,161	8,208	11,073	9,788	14,632	16,570	11,363	9,159	11,124	12,775	14,006
Nagoya, Japan	7,451	9,459	8,750	9,685	19,022	9,558	7,981	7,288	9,062	10,559	7,648	10,536	9,403	14,181	16,491	10,816	9,280	10,714	12,218	14,252
Nagpur, India	7,898	12,460	7,738	6,655	14,711	11,436	11,319	10,919	11,367	13,711	11,080	12,928	10,724	14,143	13,026	13,226	6,846	11,812	14,221	9,921
Nairobi, Kenya	10,134	13,262	7,920	5,602	9,494	11,787	13,239	13,380	12,189	13,731	13,240	12,734	11,018	10,905	8,379	12,824	6,296	11,152	12,617	5,659
Nanchang, China	6,825	11,018	8,732	8,925	18,499	10,751	9,551	8,913	10,363	12,237	9,229	11,985	10,380	15,205	16,149	12,294	8,731	11,734	13,700	13,189
Nancy, France	14,924	7,078	1,690	671	10,049	5,609	6,982	7,214	5,944	7,846	7,018	6,824	4,807	7,138	7,236	7,017	241	5,300	7,490	4,813
Nandi, Fiji	5,102	11,122	15,084	16,850	12,963	12,476	10,549	10,078	11,935	10,977	10,387	11,904	13,087	13,794	15,423	11,877	16,282	13,410	12,219	18,476
Nanjing, China	7,137	10,567	8,500	8,857	18,708	10,337	9,096	8,453	9,934	11,778	8,772	11,546	9,992	14,842	16,082	11,853	8,612	11,347	13,263	13,233
Nanning, China	6,420	11,886	9,005	8,829	17,646	11,484	10,440	9,824	11,145	13,134	10,123	12,797	11,033	15,710	15,876	13,113	8,749	12,371	14,493	12,784
Nantes, France	15,508	6,741	1,680	1,070	9,532	5,263	6,786	7,086	5,648	7,423	6,856	6,396	4,480	6,540	6,701	6,570	819	4,841	6,961	4,433
Naples, Italy	14,197	8,145	2,745	409	9,966	6,672	8,056	8,269	7,019	8,868	8,084	7,841	5,874	7,737	7,276	8,018	1,119	6,289	8,374	4,496
Narvik, Norway	14,117	6,119	1,325	2,770	11,913	4,843	5,509	5,524	4,928	7,214	5,438	6,309	4,075	8,035	9,067	6,587	2,095	5,127	7,539	7,025
Nashville, Tennessee	16,713	1,452	6,026	7,906	8,114	2,054	2,934	3,620	2,204	696	3,265	563	2,789	3,499	6,680	283	7,380	2,003	1,311	7,982
Nassau, Bahamas	17,364	2,969	6,565	8,020	6,595	3,195	4,447	5,140	3,532	1,996	4,780	1,915	3,735	2,058	5,270	1,618	7,638	2,507	214	7,013
Natal, Brazil	15,528	8,388	7,904	7,198	2,796	7,765	9,706	10,409	8,346	7,677	10,016	7,259	7,681	3,638	430	7,068	7,493	6,524	5,901	2,905
Natashquan, Canada	17,772	2,585	3,540	5,379	8,715	1,243	3,294	3,912	1,832	3,097	3,538	2,070	978	3,949	6,379	2,259	4,841	592	3,002	6,426
Nauru Island	5,285	10,531	13,164	14,648	15,117	11,610	9,549	8,939	11,012	10,833	9,306	11,547	12,010	14,528	17,169	11,634	14,137	12,773	12,449	19,123
Ndjamena, Chad	12,960	10,630	5,810	3,527	8,143	9,194	10,934	11,273	9,674	10,944	11,029	9,972	8,488	8,213	6,178	10,036	4,254	8,412	9,796	3,124
Nelson, New Zealand	4,071	13,186	17,698	18,523	11,252	14,650	12,938	12,560	14,196	12,663	12,828	13,684	15,383	14,032	14,077	13,550	18,469	15,269	13,350	16,316
Nema, Mauritania	15,303	8,646	5,041	3,479	6,617	7,337	9,312	9,821	7,896	8,710	9,496	7,812	6,769	5,761	4,108	7,819	3,982	6,343	7,402	1,109
Neuquen, Argentina	11,988	9,927	12,463	12,136	2,204	10,334	11,359	11,952	10,682	8,666	11,669	9,030	10,756	5,972	4,916	8,714	12,387	9,407	7,333	7,718
New Delhi, India	8,630	11,624	6,931	6,003	14,745	10,589	10,515	10,144	10,523	12,868	10,286	12,080	9,879	13,461	12,716	12,379	6,128	10,981	13,392	9,611
New Glasgow, Canada	18,178	2,617	3,949	5,646	8,227	1,488	3,540	4,197	2,090	2,898	3,812	1,885	1,447	3,438	5,962	2,009	5,156	314	2,556	6,249
New Haven, Connecticut	17,808	2,002	4,849	6,602	8,029	1,465	3,234	3,940	1,951	1,985	3,547	1,026	1,895	3,173	6,085	1,080	6,107	723	1,727	6,871
New Orleans, Louisiana	16,319	1,965	6,769	8,595	7,750	2,798	3,408	4,049	2,897	727	3,729	1,310	3,541	3,421	6,631	1,032	8,092	2,700	1,170	8,279
New Plymouth, New Zealand	4,145	12,977	17,451	18,497	11,406	14,436	12,699	12,313	13,971	12,489	12,584	13,506	15,158	14,017	14,216	13,383	18,330	15,093	13,237	16,541
New York, New York	17,746	1,950	4,958	6,715	8,005	1,507	3,217	3,926	1,968	1,882	3,534	939	1,975	3,153	6,103	975	6,219	834	1,635	6,945
Newcastle upon Tyne, UK	15,377	6,222	837	1,554	10,187	4,762	6,099	6,340	5,074	7,042	6,137	6,029	3,953	6,759	7,338	6,241	883	4,550	6,833	5,260
Newcastle Waters, Australia	1,651	14,399	14,166	13,900	15,023	15,099	13,142	12,444	14,518	14,914	12,837	15,504	15,145	18,454	17,509	15,650	13,932	16,339	16,567	16,290
Niamey, Niger	14,258	9,588	5,431	3,465	7,111	8,224	10,129	10,579	8,758	9,733	10,281	8,809	7,598	6,804	4,875	8,834	4,103	7,302	8,462	1,768
Nicosia, Cyprus	12,410	9,649	4,086	2,120	11,053	8,211	9,294	9,356	8,473	10,507	9,252	9,492	7,398	9,486	8,617	9,696	2,597	7,984	10,146	5,579
Niue (Alofi)	6,241	10,314	15,054	17,258	11,868	11,752	9,999	9,642	11,271	9,972	9,896	10,954	12,457	12,482	14,147	10,880	16,552	12,521	11,046	17,256
Norfolk, Virginia	17,649	2,025	5,419	7,125	7,700	1,899	3,410	4,122	2,292	1,638	3,738	899	2,432	2,890	5,958	773	6,650	1,292	1,170	7,055
Norfolk Island, Australia	3,749	12,680	16,318	17,380	12,637	14,049	12,118	11,631	13,510	12,455	11,948	13,415	14,659	14,755	15,420	13,362	17,091	14,953	13,536	17,728
Noril'sk, USSR	11,685	7,110	3,984	5,035	14,595	6,302	5,931	5,575	6,099	8,391	5,702	7,749	5,742	10,386	11,753	8,066	4,526	7,050	9,323	9,568
Norman Wells, Canada	13,819	2,724	5,053	7,383	12,234	2,899	1,261	752	2,332	3,956	954	3,753	3,072	7,422	10,301	4,043	6,652	4,138	5,457	10,214
Normanton, Australia	1,984	13,855	14,482	14,524	14,892	14,729	12,701	12,025	14,130	14,238	12,415	14,919	14,909	17,641	17,639	15,028	14,472	15,964	15,820	17,074
North Pole	13,512	4,809	3,125	5,156	13,056	4,035	3,711	3,479	3,796	6,085	3,525	5,454	3,560	8,388	10,415	5,773	4,450	4,911	7,069	9,064
Nottingham, United Kingdom	15,397	6,376	1,061	1,372	10,034	4,909	6,293	6,548	5,240	7,162	6,339	6,144	4,104	6,723	7,188	6,347	753	4,641	6,888	5,051
Norway House, Canada	15,583	794	5,003	7,263	10,201	1,234	910	1,617	689	2,084	1,225	1,719	1,874	5,413	8,409	2,014	6,593	2,384	3,429	8,895
Norwich, United Kingdom	15,239	6,531	1,150	1,230	10,118	5,067	6,424	6,664	5,390	7,328	6,463	6,311	4,261	6,875	7,275	6,515	585	4,811	7,058	5,069
Nouakchott, Mauritania	16,188	7,875	4,929	3,819	6,158	6,639	8,668	9,229	7,220	7,844	8,881	6,981	6,146	4,827	3,456	6,965	4,175	5,571	6,481	1,102
Noumea, New Caledonia	3,854	12,284	15,559	16,716	13,336	13,581	11,587	11,057	13,016	12,209	11,392	13,117	14,127	14,961	16,066	13,104	16,360	14,587	13,467	18,481
Novosibirsk, USSR	10,565	8,710	4,856	5,109	15,085	7,823	7,546	7,176	7,667	9,983	7,314	9,295	7,200	11,581	12,298	9,608	4,822	8,452	10,802	9,630
Nuku'alofa, Tonga	5,641	10,857	15,378	17,426	12,144	12,279	10,471	10,077	11,781	10,555	10,349	11,529	12,962	13,059	14,565	11,462	16,771	13,088	11,646	17,636
Nukunono Island, Tokelau Isls.	6,576	9,639	14,020	16,162	12,692	11,018	9,146	8,726	10,494	9,483	9,009	10,407	11,664	12,501	14,672	10,382	15,468	11,919	10,775	17,688
Nuremberg, West Germany	14,569	7,281	1,781	632	10,372	5,823	7,100	7,290	6,127	8,098	7,116	7,081	5,014	7,501	7,572	7,286	188	5,581	7,808	5,074
Nyala, Sudan	12,025	11,296	6,098	3,751	9,045	9,826	11,389	11,624	10,251	11,761	11,433	10,758	9,071	9,259	7,226	10,856	4,474	9,175	10,747	4,193
Oaxaca, Mexico	15,167	3,308	8,345	10,088	7,166	4,360	4,573	5,100	4,389	2,044	4,857	2,885	5,119	3,822	6,796	2,614	9,625	4,244	2,127	9,054
Ocean Falls, Canada	13,608	2,294	6,304	8,651	11,695	3,201	1,159	785	2,609	3,226	999	3,427	3,701	7,149	10,278	3,642	7,930	4,373	4,958	10,867
Odense, Denmark	14,617	6,794	1,231	1,295	10,760	5,364	6,514	6,671	5,619	7,692	6,512	6,694	4,551	7,514	7,925	6,921	599	5,257	7,573	5,604
Odessa, USSR	13,070	8,473	2,930	1,558	11,421	7,069	8,038	8,084	7,284	9,415	7,986	8,422	6,258	8,984	8,741	8,653	1,679	6,985	9,274	5,925
Ogbomosho, Nigeria	13,747	10,186	6,047	4,007	6,924	8,841	10,762	11,218	9,382	10,273	10,918	9,374	8,227	7,148	4,926	9,383	4,673	7,890	8,927	1,930
Okha, USSR	9,546	7,530	6,915	8,281	16,970	7,488	6,050	5,391	7,016	8,716	5,722	8,557	7,306	12,114	14,476	8,852	7,743	8,624	10,267	12,771
Okinawa (Naha)	6,413	10,765	9,417	9,917	19,624	10,773	9,284	8,598	10,305	11,883	8,951	11,826	10,542	15,392	17,118	12,113	9,643	11,882	13,522	14,312
Oklahoma City, Oklahoma	15,742	1,265	6,630	8,664	8,669	2,495	2,582	3,181	2,398	280	2,888	1,245	3,303	4,305	7,515	1,166	8,087	2,831	2,041	8,951
Old Crow, Canada	13,275	3,354	5,141	7,421	12,860	3,474	1,883	1,293	2,927	4,576	1,565	4,383	3,561	8,037	10,865	4,674	6,690	4,702	6,088	10,578
Olympia, Washington	13,834	1,977	6,652	8,986	11,116	3,154	1,334	1,130	2,606	2,695	1,345	3,065	3,775	6,705	9,885	3,235	8,279	4,223	4,468	10,774
Omaha, Nebraska	15,914	625	6,025	8,119	9,057	1,884	2,043	2,697	1,744	669	2,366	912	2,697	4,481	7,655	1,014	7,517	2,411	2,276	8,789
Omsk, USSR	10,967	8,676	4,431	4,519	14,495	7,678	7,609	7,303	7,581	9,923	7,403	9,166	7,006	11,192	11,729	9,472	4,263	8,203	10,592	9,026
Oodnadatta, Australia	788	15,021	15,281	14,769	13,889	15,962	13,923	13,255	15,362	15,257	13,642	16,039	16,139	17,787	16,486	16,105	14,902	17,191	16,641	16,119
Oradea, Romania	13,737	8,019	2,457	912	10,868	6,582	7,714	7,831	6,845	8,893	7,695	7,885	5,769	8,310	8,139	8,100	1,033	6,407	8,654	5,418
Oran, Algeria	15,375	7,637	2,958	1,354	8,624	6,176	7,884	8,248	6,633	8,123	7,988	7,108	5,446	6,420	5,882	7,228	1,770	5,522	7,332	3,274
Oranjestad, Aruba	17,142	4,559	7,404	8,362	5,005	4,651	6,036	6,730	5,056	3,526	6,369	3,491	5,060	996	3,923	3,203	8,148	3,722	1,800	6,221
Orebro, Sweden	14,307	6,718	1,234	1,747	11,255	5,332	6,306	6,403	5,527	7,695	6,275	6,723	4,525	7,844	8,413	6,971	1,103	5,361	7,730	6,125
Orel, USSR	12,926	8,079	2,703	2,088	12,064	6,744	7,493	7,471	6,884	9,118	7,409	8,166	5,947	9,199	9,311	8,422	1,915	6,830	9,200	6,619
Orsk, USSR	11,465	8,884	3,995	3,595	13,516	7,712	8,004	7,807	7,723	10,057	7,844	9,194	6,967	10,683	10,822	9,481	3,461	8,029	10,440	8,011
Osaka, Japan	7,381	9,576	8,766	9,653	19,134	9,654	8,097	7,406	9,163	10,684	7,764	10,649	9,486	14,280	16,523	10,931	9,261	10,803	12,335	14,213
Oslo, Norway	14,553	6,482	974	1,797	11,098	5,086	6,109	6,230	5,294	7,445	6,089	6,469	4,277	7,601	8,250	6,714	1,099	5,100	7,468	6,049
Osorno, Chile	11,689	9,966	12,824	12,586	2,673	10,475	11,365	11,927	10,787	8,688	11,665	9,122	10,944	6,233	5,358	8,804	12,818	9,607	7,450	8,187
Ostrava, Czechoslovakia	14,055	7,610	2,048	861	10,812	6,174	7,318	7,450	6,436	8,488	7,306	7,482	5,360	8,022	8,037	7,700	689	6,013	8,281	5,435
Ottawa, Canada	17,409	1,633	4,644	6,545	8,538	966	2,757	3,457	1,442	1,933	3,064	905	1,496	3,683	6,571	1,104	6,000	707	2,115	7,203
Ouagadougou, Bourkina Fasso	14,532	9,413	5,527	3,689	6,730	8,086	10,037	10,522	8,637	9,486	10,208	8,588	7,495	6,436	4,461	8,595	4,289	7,113	8,155	1,354
Oujda, Morocco	15,469	7,631	3,061	1,517	8,462	6,177	7,918	8,297	6,646	8,085	8,030	7,074	5,459	6,295	5,720	7,186	1,920	5,489	7,253	3,121
Oxford, United Kingdom	15,426	6,451	1,191	1,288	9,928	4,980	6,397	6,661	5,324	7,216	6,447	6,195	4,180	6,682	7,084	6,392	721	4,679	6,901	4,920
Pago Pago, American Samoa	6,408	9,973	14,552	16,729	12,254	11,387	9,575	9,189	10,885	9,718	9,457	10,675	12,065	12,480	14,396	10,624	16,028	12,221	10,899	17,494
Pakxe, Laos	5,739	12,779	9,658	9,220	17,039	12,352	11,332	10,712	12,027	14,026	11,014	13,684	11,873	16,419	15,922	14,000	9,230	13,198	15,372	12,819
Palembang, Indonesia	4,068	14,711	11,400	10,516	15,593	14,349	13,239	12,586	14,017	15,908	12,913	15,665	13,855	18,001	15,883	15,978	10,690	15,162	17,366	13,148
Palermo, Italy	14,205	8,319	2,995	652	9,720	6,842	8,287	8,522	7,211	8,995	8,326	7,967	6,053	7,673	7,064	8,131	1,384	6,401	8,420	4,230
Palma, Majorca	15,149	7,555	2,578	854	9,135	6,080	7,680	7,995	6,498	8,142	7,759	7,117	5,317	6,746	6,378	7,262	1,265	5,536	7,490	3,789
Palmerston North, New Zealand	4,270	12,968	17,589	18,675	11,212	14,434	12,739	12,372	13,985	12,440	12,634	13,462	15,171	13,861	14,022	13,328	18,523	15,047	13,138	16,370
Panama, Panama	16,154	4,510	8,233	9,390	5,243	4,976	5,974	6,619	5,263	3,294	6,297	3,600	5,534	2,104	4,765	3,282	9,124	4,282	1,944	7,283
Paramaribo, Suriname	17,109	6,039	7,381	7,678	3,765	5,742	7,462	8,173	6,258	5,180	7,790	4,910	5,910	1,166	2,133	4,674	7,666	4,583	3,395	4,637
Paris, France	15,207	6,850	1,570	890	9,862	5,377	6,806	7,066	5,729	7,590	6,855	6,566	4,579	6,860	7,035	6,755	480	5,033	7,209	4,707
Patna, India	7,865	11,976	7,622	6,831	15,438	11,073	10,751	10,304	10,939	13,254	10,493	12,556	10,409	14,255	13,551	12,866	6,922	11,584	13,987	10,441
Patrai, Greece	13,503	8,777	3,282	1,073	10,324	7,311	8,597	8,756	7,631	9,543	8,600	8,518	6,506	8,401	7,732	8,703	1,676	6,977	9,078	4,810
Peking, China	8,036	9,843	7,614	8,092	18,068	9,511	8,394	7,783	9,136	11,089	8,079	10,774	9,131	13,962	15,272	11,086	7,799	10,485	12,483	12,568
Penrhyn Island (Omoka)	7,893	8,647	13,678	16,017	11,434	10,100	8,441	8,159	9,644	8,281	8,374	9,263	10,831	11,012	13,185	9,189	15,285	10,833	9,407	16,167
Peoria, Illinois	16,456	898	5,761	7,763	8,666	1,662	2,378	3,069	1,706	725	2,710	377	2,451	3,999	7,147	492	7,193	1,943	1,862	8,249
Perm', USSR	12,002	8,118	3,403	3,455	13,426	6,968	7,235	7,050	6,962	9,301	7,079	8,455	6,237	10,158	10,636	8,746	3,163	7,341	9,753	8,007
Perth, Australia	1,233	16,789	14,774	13,484	13,215	17,302	15,485	14,776	16,775	17,206	15,168	17,894	17,079	18,060	15,224	18,018	13,833	18,432	18,485	14,176
Peshawar, Pakistan	9,435	10,970	6,135	5,225	14,331	9,868	9,945	9,632	9,839	12,185	9,739	11,356	9,138	12,662	12,090	11,648	5,327	10,205	12,614	9,013

Distances in Kilometers

	Eucla, Australia	Fargo, North Dakota	Faroe Islands (Torshavn)	Florence, Italy	Florianopolis, Brazil	Fort George, Canada	Fort McMurray, Canada	Fort Nelson, Canada	Fort Severn, Canada	Fort Smith, Arkansas	Fort Vermilion, Canada	Fort Wayne, Indiana	Fort-Chimo, Canada	Fort-de-France, Martinique	Fortaleza, Brazil	Frankfort, Kentucky	Frankfurt am Main, W. Ger.	Fredericton, Canada	Freeport, Bahamas	Freetown, Sierra Leone
Petropavlovsk-Kamchatskiy,USSR	9,822	6,841	7,185	8,838	16,405	7,022	5,364	4,670	6,495	7,954	5,032	7,924	6,975	11,609	14,318	8,201	8,232	8,223	9,601	13,145
Petrozavodsk, USSR	13,291	7,192	2,123	2,513	12,311	5,919	6,525	6,481	6,003	8,291	6,429	7,380	5,146	8,869	9,477	7,654	2,041	6,154	8,561	7,061
Pevek, USSR	11,733	5,325	5,388	7,305	14,706	5,221	3,866	3,264	4,748	6,561	3,550	6,312	5,078	9,847	12,384	6,614	6,631	6,373	8,028	11,325
Philadelphia, Pennsylvania	17,677	1,906	5,085	6,844	7,968	1,570	3,211	3,922	2,004	1,769	3,532	854	2,076	3,127	6,115	861	6,349	963	1,527	7,023
Phnom Penh, Kampuchea	5,427	13,184	9,972	9,423	16,738	12,750	11,735	11,112	12,430	14,429	11,417	14,088	12,261	16,733	15,912	14,405	9,472	13,579	15,774	12,840
Phoenix, Arizona	14,386	1,971	7,518	9,709	9,516	3,445	2,588	2,928	3,130	1,635	2,788	2,522	4,243	5,528	8,727	2,505	9,074	4,072	3,288	10,307
Pierre, South Dakota	15,553	393	5,953	8,131	9,550	1,869	1,578	2,212	1,574	1,119	1,893	1,296	2,664	4,960	8,119	1,464	7,497	2,635	2,768	9,126
Pinang, Malaysia	5,104	13,973	10,357	9,524	15,920	13,438	12,540	11,931	13,160	15,235	12,226	14,827	12,891	17,002	15,467	15,146	9,668	14,170	16,470	12,506
Pitcairn Island (Adamstown)	9,546	8,642	14,159	15,957	7,983	10,023	9,234	9,321	9,836	7,673	9,341	8,669	10,833	8,674	10,002	8,445	15,524	10,135	7,933	13,113
Pittsburgh, Pennsylvania	17,263	1,527	5,294	7,148	8,203	1,491	2,897	3,609	1,817	1,384	3,224	439	2,131	3,403	6,462	487	6,625	1,245	1,548	7,439
Plymouth, Montserrat	18,008	4,614	6,609	7,425	5,116	4,370	6,036	6,747	4,861	3,803	6,365	3,484	4,624	262	3,450	3,251	7,243	3,271	2,028	5,384
Plymouth, United Kingdom	15,650	6,377	1,304	1,376	9,684	4,901	6,391	6,685	5,270	7,098	6,457	6,073	4,110	6,447	6,838	6,260	912	4,538	6,722	4,722
Ponape Island	5,294	10,573	12,253	13,490	16,384	11,429	9,391	8,721	10,828	11,117	9,108	11,670	11,679	15,078	18,147	11,818	13,040	12,658	12,852	18,064
Ponce, Puerto Rico	17,844	4,226	6,695	7,683	5,408	4,116	5,674	6,381	4,570	3,350	6,005	3,109	4,452	702	3,912	2,855	7,449	3,100	1,566	5,859
Ponta Delgada, Azores	17,608	5,749	2,998	3,161	7,615	4,391	6,359	6,884	4,942	6,016	6,549	5,036	3,816	4,328	4,777	5,109	3,046	3,483	5,095	3,471
Pontianak, Indonesia	4,066	14,230	11,338	10,663	16,154	13,992	12,750	12,081	13,616	15,388	12,420	15,233	13,563	18,089	16,435	15,538	10,771	14,901	16,950	13,602
Port Augusta, Australia	844	15,183	15,872	15,256	13,321	16,268	14,207	13,565	15,666	15,247	13,945	16,119	16,548	17,264	15,977	16,134	15,436	17,450	16,441	16,022
Port Blair, India	6,149	13,459	9,366	8,447	15,627	12,712	12,112	11,572	12,515	14,750	11,821	14,169	12,091	15,931	14,595	14,486	8,606	13,306	15,691	11,548
Port Elizabeth, South Africa	9,186	15,044	11,030	8,730	6,980	13,892	15,904	16,392	14,470	14,612	16,084	14,008	13,361	10,606	7,403	13,891	9,462	12,784	12,862	6,236
Port Hedland, Australia	1,628	15,670	13,796	12,919	14,528	15,997	14,274	13,562	15,490	16,396	13,949	16,804	15,772	19,371	16,366	17,016	13,127	17,120	18,130	14,696
Port Louis, Mauritius	7,142	16,244	10,711	8,506	10,475	14,770	15,843	15,713	15,095	16,800	15,727	15,804	13,972	13,513	10,501	15,893	9,144	14,220	15,527	8,367
Port Moresby, Papua New Guinea	3,104	12,744	13,805	14,321	15,570	13,614	11,581	10,908	13,014	13,189	11,296	13,821	13,825	16,909	18,420	13,946	14,112	14,846	14,844	17,883
Port Said, Egypt	12,320	9,964	4,415	2,310	10,765	8,511	9,672	9,757	8,800	10,771	9,641	9,748	7,700	9,498	8,419	9,937	2,868	8,213	10,303	5,342
Port Sudan, Sudan	11,284	11,325	5,792	3,608	10,607	9,862	11,052	11,120	10,170	12,075	11,015	11,048	9,056	10,323	8,666	11,216	4,221	9,485	11,437	5,569
Port-au-Prince, Haiti	17,442	3,857	6,933	8,102	5,710	3,959	5,332	6,028	4,351	2,867	5,664	2,781	4,404	1,277	4,452	2,496	7,815	3,087	1,105	6,465
Port-of-Spain, Trin. & Tobago	17,443	5,209	7,178	7,816	4,455	5,036	6,654	7,362	5,517	4,308	6,985	4,090	5,297	440	3,005	3,838	7,697	3,945	2,525	5,299
Port-Vila, Vanuatu	4,253	11,795	15,072	16,413	13,616	13,067	11,061	10,524	12,496	11,778	10,862	12,660	13,598	14,755	16,243	12,664	15,982	14,100	13,113	18,970
Portland, Maine	17,881	2,103	4,509	6,279	8,193	1,300	3,213	3,906	1,845	2,260	3,513	1,257	1,612	3,337	6,135	1,368	5,775	384	2,051	6,733
Portland, Oregon	13,820	1,990	6,789	9,118	11,014	3,224	1,469	1,478	2,691	2,626	1,500	3,053	3,868	6,654	9,846	3,207	8,415	4,263	4,407	10,813
Porto, Portugal	16,112	6,715	2,325	1,656	8,653	5,254	6,990	7,381	5,717	7,221	7,107	6,201	4,530	5,833	5,822	6,331	1,671	4,615	6,518	3,646
Porto Alegre, Brazil	13,167	9,674	10,954	10,352	375	9,675	11,156	11,838	10,142	8,544	11,487	8,618	9,902	5,055	3,208	8,329	10,660	8,564	6,918	5,888
Porto Alexandre, Angola	11,490	12,694	8,783	6,598	6,330	11,470	13,469	13,970	12,041	12,479	13,652	11,732	10,926	8,701	5,671	11,664	7,310	10,400	10,850	3,861
Porto Novo, Benin	13,798	10,198	6,210	4,216	6,669	8,879	10,829	11,305	9,430	10,233	10,996	9,354	8,287	7,010	4,707	9,351	4,870	7,896	8,842	1,765
Porto Velho, Brazil	15,325	6,972	9,246	9,508	2,634	7,082	8,454	9,134	7,504	5,845	8,785	5,932	7,423	2,603	2,865	5,637	9,536	6,068	4,222	5,933
Portsmouth, United Kingdom	15,431	6,526	1,300	1,213	9,853	5,053	6,490	6,761	5,405	7,274	6,544	6,251	4,255	6,665	7,011	6,444	697	4,726	6,929	4,819
Poznan, Poland	14,178	7,336	1,772	1,051	10,901	5,909	7,021	7,149	6,157	8,236	7,006	7,237	5,095	7,926	8,098	7,462	632	5,790	8,088	5,587
Prague, Czechoslovakia	14,331	7,403	1,859	744	10,607	5,956	7,163	7,323	6,237	8,255	7,164	7,244	5,144	7,748	7,814	7,457	414	5,762	8,016	5,276
Praia, Cape Verde Islands	16,658	7,546	5,396	4,590	5,424	6,443	8,505	9,121	7,041	7,347	8,751	6,564	6,061	4,040	2,642	6,505	4,865	5,285	5,855	1,325
Pretoria, South Africa	9,476	14,682	10,217	7,889	7,508	13,390	15,302	15,692	13,936	14,492	15,430	13,746	12,779	10,635	7,501	13,682	8,621	12,378	12,833	5,869
Prince Albert, Canada	15,084	951	5,407	7,702	10,514	1,766	533	1,223	1,209	2,171	863	2,052	2,382	5,794	8,853	2,314	7,017	2,901	3,710	9,425
Prince Edward Island	7,594	16,607	12,683	10,348	7,584	15,595	17,637	18,136	16,185	15,892	17,830	15,500	15,101	11,861	8,675	15,325	11,079	14,439	14,109	7,928
Prince George, Canada	13,961	1,990	5,987	8,333	11,480	2,831	786	546	2,237	3,011	651	3,124	3,328	6,862	9,963	3,355	7,616	4,011	4,703	10,495
Prince Rupert, Canada	13,479	2,486	6,196	8,542	11,945	3,284	1,221	684	2,684	3,472	992	3,620	3,729	7,356	10,460	3,848	7,816	4,483	5,186	10,928
Providence, Rhode Island	17,899	2,091	4,726	6,466	8,035	1,450	3,283	3,984	1,964	2,120	3,592	1,150	1,824	3,176	6,042	1,215	5,973	599	1,827	6,765
Provo, Utah	14,589	1,406	6,849	9,089	9,943	2,869	1,835	2,210	2,479	1,607	2,044	2,236	3,636	5,652	8,860	2,316	8,431	3,669	3,390	10,113
Puerto Aisen, Chile	11,192	10,492	13,275	12,884	2,909	11,013	11,880	12,429	11,323	9,210	12,177	9,658	11,479	6,747	5,691	9,339	13,167	10,139	7,987	8,402
Puerto Deseado, Argentina	11,081	10,905	13,254	12,635	2,697	11,326	12,324	12,900	11,675	9,637	12,629	10,021	11,736	6,922	5,540	9,705	12,981	10,383	8,326	8,093
Puerto Princesa, Philippines	4,712	12,818	10,779	10,638	17,631	12,765	11,337	10,651	12,325	13,925	11,005	13,874	12,458	17,313	17,433	14,164	10,573	13,812	15,575	14,342
Punta Arenas, Chile	10,410	11,354	13,952	13,281	3,384	11,883	12,728	13,258	12,195	10,069	13,018	10,529	12,336	7,565	6,232	10,210	13,653	10,991	8,858	8,719
Pusan, South Korea	7,396	9,840	8,534	9,249	19,143	9,789	8,357	7,685	9,332	10,997	8,027	10,878	9,549	14,402	16,303	11,172	8,902	10,890	12,586	13,773
Pyongyang, North Korea	7,838	9,597	8,025	8,729	18,635	9,447	8,121	7,469	9,016	10,795	7,795	10,601	9,161	14,027	15,787	10,903	8,378	10,511	12,317	13,262
Qamdo, China	7,718	11,248	7,679	7,393	16,698	10,581	9,899	9,371	10,337	12,538	9,611	12,003	10,022	14,440	14,486	12,322	7,325	11,310	13,607	11,432
Qandahar, Afghanistan	9,657	11,141	6,057	4,901	13,744	9,952	10,215	9,956	9,980	12,309	10,032	11,425	9,192	12,386	11,581	11,703	5,087	10,175	12,560	8,484
Qiqian, China	9,329	8,457	6,528	7,419	17,133	8,108	7,024	6,436	7,731	9,717	6,715	9,372	7,748	12,602	14,302	9,685	6,997	9,103	11,079	11,993
Qom, Iran	10,973	10,417	5,000	3,534	12,508	9,086	9,742	9,629	9,223	11,459	9,621	10,496	8,287	11,013	10,192	10,743	3,812	9,107	11,417	7,118
Quebec, Canada	17,616	1,941	4,297	6,168	8,549	955	2,931	3,612	1,524	2,311	3,220	1,284	1,270	3,695	6,454	1,470	5,630	365	2,349	6,914
Quetta, Pakistan	9,466	11,316	6,251	5,085	13,823	10,137	10,371	10,099	10,158	12,490	10,182	11,612	9,379	12,571	11,712	11,091	5,279	10,368	12,764	8,609
Quito, Ecuador	15,456	5,514	9,083	10,008	4,403	5,992	6,966	7,596	6,285	4,274	7,286	4,622	6,528	2,523	4,466	4,303	9,826	5,247	2,958	7,299
Rabaul, Papua New Guinea	3,901	11,940	13,357	14,194	15,850	12,830	10,789	10,121	12,229	12,398	10,508	13,018	13,074	16,210	18,550	13,145	13,880	14,057	14,078	18,355
Raiatea (Uturoa)	8,098	8,910	14,271	16,597	10,378	10,388	8,952	8,774	10,004	8,330	8,937	9,350	11,168	10,512	12,325	9,223	15,898	10,936	9,193	15,411
Raleigh, North Carolina	17,448	1,950	5,639	7,365	7,690	2,007	3,378	4,087	2,348	1,430	3,709	818	2,595	2,927	6,047	616	6,886	1,514	1,026	7,246
Rangiroa (Avatoru)	8,544	8,522	13,943	16,242	10,128	10,000	8,627	8,485	9,633	7,908	8,628	8,931	10,787	10,075	11,965	8,797	15,562	10,515	8,747	15,028
Rangoon, Burma	6,403	12,837	9,030	8,336	16,217	12,167	11,465	10,911	11,934	14,125	11,169	13,598	11,585	15,738	14,877	13,918	8,418	12,845	15,183	11,778
Raoul Is., Kermadec Islands	5,067	11,698	16,307	18,206	11,728	13,143	11,386	11,008	12,666	11,295	11,274	12,295	13,851	13,380	14,358	12,200	17,625	13,874	12,229	17,211
Rarotonga (Avarua)	7,092	9,826	15,024	17,370	10,865	11,300	9,747	9,498	10,884	9,308	9,698	10,322	12,062	11,475	13,064	10,206	16,641	11,909	10,199	16,175
Rawson, Argentina	11,577	10,466	12,785	12,267	2,292	10,845	11,901	12,496	11,206	9,207	12,212	9,559	11,243	6,424	5,111	9,244	12,577	9,890	7,856	7,763
Recife, Brazil	15,281	8,607	8,140	7,383	2,597	8,006	9,936	10,641	8,584	7,869	10,249	7,475	7,931	3,825	623	7,278	7,697	6,766	6,089	3,020
Regina, Canada	15,194	699	5,601	7,869	10,251	1,783	830	1,486	1,286	1,865	1,150	1,830	2,473	5,572	8,671	2,071	7,197	2,834	3,448	9,383
Reykjavik, Iceland	15,873	4,764	801	3,078	10,432	3,341	4,574	4,833	3,591	5,692	4,618	4,716	2,529	6,262	7,652	4,966	2,384	3,390	5,792	6,215
Rhodes, Greece	12,894	9,278	3,732	1,656	10,710	7,825	9,004	9,111	8,114	10,092	8,983	9,072	7,014	9,001	8,205	9,266	2,184	7,546	9,678	5,207
Richmond, Virginia	17,537	1,897	5,418	7,162	7,815	1,815	3,286	3,997	2,187	1,538	3,614	770	2,379	3,013	6,087	656	6,675	1,295	1,229	7,170
Riga, USSR	13,773	7,266	1,818	1,722	11,559	5,898	6,787	6,837	6,073	8,266	6,734	7,300	5,094	8,368	8,741	7,551	1,269	5,945	8,312	6,269
Ringkobing, Denmark	14,745	6,643	1,082	1,386	10,709	5,211	6,376	6,543	5,469	7,538	6,379	6,540	4,398	7,392	7,867	6,767	665	5,104	7,425	5,604
Rio Branco, Brazil	15,066	6,923	9,541	9,905	2,805	7,149	8,402	9,065	7,537	5,748	8,730	5,925	7,545	2,816	3,310	5,620	9,906	6,196	4,207	6,381
Rio Cuarto, Argentina	12,694	9,439	11,737	11,453	1,635	9,738	10,899	11,527	10,119	8,208	11,219	8,489	10,117	5,294	4,223	8,178	11,681	8,763	6,776	7,102
Rio de Janeiro, Brazil	13,903	9,412	9,956	9,238	747	9,170	10,866	11,574	9,692	8,410	11,197	8,301	9,275	4,582	2,183	8,041	9,566	7,985	6,675	4,769
Rio Gallegos, Argentina	10,604	11,230	13,748	13,089	3,181	11,726	12,619	13,164	12,050	9,949	12,914	10,387	12,165	7,380	6,028	10,068	13,454	10,818	8,707	8,531
Rio Grande, Brazil	12,948	9,822	11,188	10,574	599	9,861	11,305	11,981	10,320	8,675	11,636	8,778	10,104	5,249	3,441	8,486	10,888	8,762	7,072	6,095
Riyadh, Saudi Arabia	10,725	11,282	5,736	3,853	11,729	9,878	10,757	10,705	10,091	12,209	10,665	11,204	9,065	11,072	9,704	11,417	4,321	9,713	11,876	6,593
Road Town, Brit. Virgin Isls.	18,018	4,308	6,554	7,492	5,379	4,117	5,739	6,449	4,592	3,483	6,069	3,181	4,413	569	3,770	2,941	7,271	3,057	1,708	5,651
Roanoke, Virginia	17,321	1,750	5,572	7,355	7,893	1,842	3,174	3,884	2,159	1,316	3,505	616	2,464	3,129	6,241	446	6,857	1,466	1,198	7,384
Robinson Crusoe Island, Chile	12,211	9,096	12,393	12,507	2,971	9,691	10,473	11,021	9,965	7,810	10,768	8,297	10,213	5,662	5,335	7,977	12,628	8,901	6,657	8,340
Rochester, New York	17,372	1,563	4,933	6,810	8,378	1,191	2,813	3,522	1,596	1,683	3,131	664	1,781	3,537	6,507	824	6,276	924	1,849	7,295
Rockhampton, Australia	2,322	13,576	15,382	15,675	14,008	14,700	12,638	12,020	14,101	13,696	12,391	14,527	15,072	16,576	16,854	14,563	15,577	15,851	15,072	17,630
Rome, Italy	14,365	7,958	2,578	231	9,923	6,484	7,882	8,104	6,835	8,678	7,914	7,652	5,687	7,587	7,207	7,829	959	6,101	8,193	4,481
Rosario, Argentina	12,778	9,554	11,579	11,194	1,306	9,776	11,025	11,669	10,182	8,344	11,349	8,572	10,116	5,262	3,975	8,266	11,449	8,761	6,855	6,800
Roseau, Dominica	17,915	4,791	6,709	7,461	4,943	4,543	6,214	6,925	5,037	3,969	6,543	3,661	4,786	85	3,286	3,427	7,300	3,435	2,190	5,289
Rostock, East Germany	14,508	6,977	1,415	1,149	10,755	5,543	6,698	6,851	5,802	7,866	6,695	6,866	4,730	7,612	7,929	7,090	501	5,418	7,722	5,541
Rostov-na-Donu, USSR	12,460	8,756	3,323	2,244	12,081	7,407	8,173	8,139	7,561	9,778	8,085	8,814	6,606	9,624	9,425	9,063	2,290	7,443	9,785	6,573
Rotterdam, Netherlands	15,030	6,752	1,313	1,037	10,212	5,290	6,617	6,839	5,605	7,558	6,647	6,541	4,482	7,072	7,378	6,747	355	5,043	7,288	5,079
Rouyn, Canada	17,038	1,344	4,581	6,589	8,931	623	2,365	3,061	1,043	1,910	2,668	932	1,304	4,078	6,970	1,211	6,010	971	2,410	7,521
Sacramento, California	13,723	2,210	7,424	9,724	10,537	3,619	2,151	2,252	3,158	2,427	2,239	3,101	4,342	6,449	9,660	3,179	9,038	4,506	4,186	10,978
Saginaw, Michigan	16,872	1,080	5,234	7,208	8,654	1,212	2,432	3,144	1,421	1,268	2,760	281	1,955	3,867	6,923	586	6,644	1,396	1,934	7,807
Saint Denis, Reunion	7,299	16,192	10,691	8,458	10,252	14,714	15,879	15,788	15,063	16,675	15,780	15,694	13,924	13,307	10,281	15,767	9,109	14,116	15,346	8,181
Saint George's, Grenada	17,575	5,066	7,049	7,730	4,610	4,880	6,506	7,216	5,362	4,181	6,837	3,944	5,141	291	3,108	3,695	7,596	3,788	2,397	5,321
Saint John, Canada	18,031	2,370	4,154	5,899	8,260	1,332	3,354	4,026	1,924	2,631	3,636	1,617	1,437	3,432	6,075	1,745	5,398	91	2,370	6,479
Saint John's, Antigua	18,066	4,601	6,552	7,366	5,147	4,338	6,018	6,730	4,834	3,805	6,346	3,470	4,583	289	3,448	3,241	7,183	3,232	2,035	5,348
Saint John's, Canada	18,240	3,294	3,270	4,860	8,333	1,970	4,009	4,610	2,552	3,684	4,243	2,664	1,571	3,737	5,849	2,800	4,387	1,078	3,261	5,707
Saint Louis, Missouri	16,414	1,064	5,978	7,954	8,513	1,894	2,545	3,224	1,940	520	2,875	511	2,676	3,903	7,077	468	7,394	2,096	1,714	8,293
Saint Paul, Minnesota	16,121	358	5,557	7,669	9,215	1,418	1,827	2,523	1,287	1,068	2,160	778	2,231	4,515	7,630	1,015	7,058	2,062	2,412	8,549

Distances in Kilometers	Eucla, Australia	Fargo, North Dakota	Faroe Islands (Torshavn)	Florence, Italy	Florianopolis, Brazil	Fort George, Canada	Fort McMurray, Canada	Fort Nelson, Canada	Fort Severn, Canada	Fort Smith, Arkansas	Fort Vermilion, Canada	Fort Wayne, Indiana	Fort-Chimo, Canada	Fort-de-France, Martinique	Fortaleza, Brazil	Frankfort, Kentucky	Frankfurt am Main, W. Ger.	Fredericton, Canada	Freeport, Bahamas	Freetown, Sierra Leone
Saint Peter Port, UK	15,554	6,532	1,423	1,228	9,674	5,055	6,544	6,834	5,425	7,246	6,608	6,220	4,265	6,528	6,833	6,404	810	4,680	6,848	4,649
Saipan (Susupe)	5,490	10,749	11,116	12,016	18,001	11,266	9,378	8,669	10,697	11,572	9,060	11,883	11,309	15,600	18,662	12,101	11,649	12,500	13,356	16,522
Salalah, Oman	9,619	12,357	6,845	4,992	12,094	10,980	11,723	11,597	11,162	13,329	11,599	12,331	10,170	12,100	10,414	12,551	5,460	10,853	13,012	7,343
Salem, Oregon	13,774	2,038	6,862	9,191	11,009	3,287	1,543	1,544	2,757	2,641	1,573	3,091	3,936	6,675	9,870	3,239	8,488	4,318	4,424	10,866
Salt Lake City, Utah	14,580	1,388	6,809	9,055	9,994	2,844	1,777	2,149	2,445	1,641	1,984	2,244	3,607	5,686	8,892	2,333	8,395	3,662	3,425	10,120
Salta, Argentina	13,572	8,541	10,935	10,880	1,711	8,808	10,010	10,653	9,193	7,327	10,333	7,570	9,189	4,382	3,708	7,262	11,029	7,836	5,855	6,750
Salto, Uruguay	12,984	9,503	11,321	10,892	1,004	9,657	10,981	11,639	10,082	8,316	11,309	8,495	9,964	5,099	3,679	8,194	11,156	8,611	6,779	6,492
Salvador, Brazil	14,880	8,800	8,765	8,057	1,925	8,338	10,189	10,900	8,897	7,953	10,511	7,667	8,337	3,936	1,025	7,442	8,366	7,112	6,170	3,668
Salzburg, Austria	14,412	7,512	2,012	469	10,368	6,053	7,331	7,516	6,359	8,321	7,344	7,303	5,244	7,637	7,590	7,505	410	5,795	8,004	5,012
Samsun, Turkey	12,446	9,199	3,661	2,071	11,581	7,800	8,729	8,743	8,009	10,145	8,663	9,151	6,988	9,559	9,025	9,379	2,349	7,703	9,969	6,070
San Antonio, Texas	15,513	1,943	7,250	9,214	8,251	3,137	3,198	3,752	3,073	764	3,489	1,770	3,936	4,173	7,365	1,591	8,665	3,321	1,964	9,097
San Cristobal, Venezuela	16,579	4,925	7,982	8,895	4,669	5,145	6,407	7,085	5,517	3,804	6,738	3,905	5,593	1,433	3,956	3,602	8,703	4,267	2,188	6,495
San Diego, California	13,909	2,335	7,817	10,053	9,854	3,812	2,706	2,931	3,445	2,115	2,856	2,981	4,593	5,988	9,178	2,978	9,399	4,512	3,759	10,787
San Francisco, California	13,620	2,327	7,541	9,843	10,560	3,739	2,261	2,340	3,279	2,511	2,340	3,206	4,463	6,520	9,730	3,277	9,157	4,621	4,260	11,084
San Jose, Costa Rica	15,860	4,268	8,375	9,678	5,647	4,890	5,703	6,321	5,118	3,008	6,018	3,452	5,509	2,554	5,275	3,132	9,365	4,325	1,919	7,771
San Juan, Argentina	12,770	9,136	11,741	11,617	1,979	9,512	10,582	11,194	9,866	7,887	10,898	8,219	9,933	5,166	4,398	7,904	11,798	8,585	6,516	7,359
San Juan, Puerto Rico	17,916	4,215	6,626	7,611	5,435	4,078	5,657	6,366	4,539	3,359	5,988	3,093	4,404	687	3,898	2,845	7,377	3,050	1,578	5,809
San Luis Potosi, Mexico	15,009	2,769	8,071	9,976	7,878	3,976	3,933	4,425	3,915	1,600	4,202	2,572	4,770	4,286	7,370	2,354	9,454	4,072	2,301	9,432
San Marino, San Marino	14,403	7,794	2,373	99	10,063	6,323	7,685	7,897	6,660	8,543	7,712	7,518	5,522	7,585	7,323	7,703	747	5,979	8,112	4,649
San Miguel de Tucuman, Argen.	13,358	8,757	11,132	11,024	1,651	9,033	10,224	10,864	9,418	7,539	10,547	7,793	9,415	4,604	3,824	7,483	11,191	8,061	6,078	6,833
San Salvador, El Salvador	15,668	3,746	8,276	9,787	6,332	4,542	5,135	5,725	4,694	2,459	5,441	3,059	5,227	3,035	5,921	2,748	9,404	4,157	1,787	8,288
Sanaa, Yemen	10,407	12,094	6,533	4,431	11,058	10,647	11,702	11,699	10,920	12,904	11,633	11,879	9,836	11,171	9,345	12,059	5,007	10,330	12,314	6,288
Santa Cruz, Bolivia	14,378	7,916	10,133	10,167	1,848	8,080	9,397	10,063	8,493	6,748	9,726	6,902	8,425	3,591	3,108	6,601	10,277	7,070	5,186	6,210
Santa Cruz, Tenerife	16,659	7,075	3,795	2,979	7,096	5,740	7,711	8,227	6,295	7,242	7,897	6,298	5,168	4,861	4,284	6,338	3,196	4,784	6,113	2,230
Santa Fe, New Mexico	14,991	1,458	7,021	9,165	9,235	2,903	2,376	2,850	2,649	1,045	2,632	1,908	3,712	5,033	8,244	1,895	8,547	3,466	2,772	9,709
Santa Rosa, Argentina	12,318	9,801	12,085	11,715	1,786	10,121	11,254	11,873	10,497	8,560	11,572	8,862	10,504	5,679	4,499	8,550	11,973	9,150	7,152	7,299
Santa Rosalia, Mexico	14,156	2,560	8,124	10,264	9,124	4,007	3,268	3,592	3,745	1,917	3,465	2,912	4,817	5,469	8,611	2,825	9,651	4,497	3,319	10,468
Santarem, Brazil	16,207	6,836	8,210	8,297	2,859	6,632	8,286	8,994	7,132	5,883	8,617	5,721	6,822	2,011	1,806	5,465	8,362	5,490	4,119	4,757
Santiago del Estero, Argentina	13,275	8,892	11,192	11,033	1,548	9,153	10,360	11,001	9,543	7,676	10,684	7,922	9,525	4,702	3,817	7,613	11,216	8,171	6,206	6,801
Santiago, Chile	12,508	9,274	12,021	11,910	2,214	9,704	10,705	11,301	10,040	8,012	11,016	8,384	10,147	5,414	4,688	8,067	12,091	8,804	6,692	7,635
Santo Domingo, Dominican Rep.	17,633	3,995	6,815	7,913	5,590	4,002	5,460	6,162	4,423	3,058	5,793	2,897	4,402	1,034	4,228	2,625	7,647	3,065	1,276	6,208
Sao Paulo de Olivenca, Brazil	15,692	6,215	8,932	9,478	3,429	6,420	7,696	8,367	6,809	5,062	8,026	5,202	6,824	2,170	3,367	4,900	9,414	5,478	3,486	6,306
Sao Paulo, Brazil	13,872	9,283	10,124	9,504	490	9,120	10,750	11,453	9,624	8,240	11,083	8,185	9,270	4,503	2,360	7,916	9,806	7,958	6,531	5,073
Sao Tome, Sao Tome & Principe	13,033	11,009	6,936	4,832	6,658	9,698	11,646	12,116	10,249	11,003	11,810	10,145	9,106	7,622	5,052	10,130	5,520	8,705	9,553	2,393
Sapporo, Japan	8,376	8,522	8,012	9,187	18,074	8,603	7,042	6,355	8,107	9,647	6,709	9,591	8,460	13,226	15,647	9,874	8,709	9,764	11,281	13,747
Sarajevo, Yugoslavia	13,931	8,120	2,604	577	10,440	6,661	7,917	8,079	6,965	8,923	7,920	7,903	5,852	8,063	7,735	8,100	1,017	6,383	8,557	4,974
Saratov, USSR	12,240	8,534	3,320	2,723	12,665	7,257	7,822	7,725	7,346	9,631	7,705	8,709	6,477	9,890	9,952	8,978	2,607	7,432	9,823	7,176
Saskatoon, Canada	15,038	919	5,538	7,830	10,479	1,854	599	1,256	1,312	2,097	917	2,041	2,492	5,786	8,867	2,291	7,147	2,962	3,675	9,499
Schefferville, Canada	17,159	2,265	3,467	5,506	9,294	798	2,755	3,342	1,320	3,024	2,978	2,037	380	4,488	6,993	2,292	4,907	983	3,289	6,965
Seattle, Washington	13,887	1,926	6,578	8,911	11,109	3,087	1,260	1,249	2,537	2,675	1,274	3,022	3,704	6,675	9,850	3,197	8,205	4,163	4,443	10,713
Sendai, Japan	7,846	8,976	8,517	9,608	18,538	9,110	7,500	6,804	8,604	10,068	7,167	10,059	8,985	13,725	16,180	10,336	9,157	10,281	11,735	14,180
Seoul, South Korea	7,672	9,688	8,214	8,922	18,825	9,575	8,209	7,549	9,134	10,872	7,881	10,705	9,306	14,169	15,979	11,004	8,573	10,653	12,420	13,452
Sept-Iles, Canada	17,599	2,260	3,777	5,678	8,794	954	3,017	3,654	1,554	2,796	3,274	1,772	889	3,978	6,545	1,980	5,125	471	2,835	6,718
Sevastopol, USSR	12,796	8,766	3,229	1,779	11,527	7,367	8,307	8,336	7,576	9,715	8,248	8,723	6,556	9,243	8,892	8,954	1,964	7,286	9,571	6,016
Seville, Spain	15,874	7,156	2,740	1,618	8,456	5,703	7,462	7,856	6,176	7,615	7,581	6,603	4,990	5,969	5,658	6,718	1,836	5,017	6,822	3,282
Shanghai, China	6,999	10,560	8,690	9,102	18,974	10,391	9,083	8,428	9,970	11,752	8,756	11,562	10,076	14,939	16,319	11,865	8,843	11,430	13,279	13,495
Sheffield, United Kingdom	15,410	6,332	1,013	1,419	10,053	4,865	6,245	6,498	5,194	7,123	6,290	6,106	4,060	6,713	7,206	6,310	790	4,607	6,860	5,087
Shenyang, China	8,159	9,411	7,665	8,370	18,272	9,193	7,943	7,307	8,780	10,630	7,621	10,387	8,878	13,743	15,423	10,694	8,014	10,231	12,104	12,911
Shiraz, Iran	10,538	10,995	5,554	3,961	12,468	9,656	10,319	10,196	9,801	12,026	10,195	11,055	8,853	11,389	10,317	11,296	4,302	9,643	11,923	7,212
Sibiu, Romania	13,539	8,235	2,672	1,044	10,939	6,801	7,913	8,017	7,059	9,113	7,888	8,106	5,988	8,494	8,238	8,321	1,248	6,627	8,869	5,462
Singapore	4,507	14,304	10,940	10,122	15,883	13,890	12,842	12,202	13,571	15,528	12,520	15,227	13,384	17,603	15,843	15,543	10,270	14,688	16,916	12,976
Sioux Falls, South Dakota	15,847	370	5,857	7,988	9,284	1,728	1,795	2,459	1,528	927	2,120	993	2,538	4,663	7,816	1,162	7,372	2,383	2,489	8,841
Skelleftea, Sweden	13,990	6,510	1,407	2,415	11,838	5,203	5,939	5,961	5,317	7,578	5,872	6,652	4,420	8,170	8,989	6,922	1,783	5,408	7,815	6,792
Skopje, Yugoslavia	13,639	8,436	2,907	858	10,533	6,979	8,209	8,354	7,278	9,245	8,204	8,225	6,170	8,331	7,875	8,422	1,336	6,706	8,871	5,036
Socotra Island (Tamrida)	9,355	12,803	7,268	5,339	11,886	11,409	12,198	12,078	11,609	13,742	12,077	12,734	10,597	12,270	10,381	12,942	5,843	11,230	13,327	7,358
Sofia, Bulgaria	13,514	8,469	2,920	987	10,702	7,020	8,202	8,328	7,303	9,304	8,188	8,288	6,209	8,472	8,044	8,491	1,392	6,781	8,971	5,202
Songkhla, Thailand	5,251	13,774	10,194	9,410	16,068	13,241	12,344	11,737	12,961	15,038	12,031	14,628	12,698	16,871	15,490	14,947	9,536	13,982	16,274	12,494
Sorong, Indonesia	3,422	13,121	12,375	12,442	16,855	13,515	11,721	11,008	12,975	13,950	11,396	14,254	13,429	17,984	18,784	14,479	12,340	14,715	15,735	16,012
South Georgia Island	10,381	12,552	13,158	11,778	3,115	12,596	14,031	14,688	13,068	11,363	14,359	11,526	12,778	7,971	5,605	11,230	12,321	11,461	9,785	7,295
South Pole	6,491	15,196	16,883	14,852	6,951	15,970	16,292	16,524	16,209	13,920	16,477	14,551	16,446	11,618	9,593	14,232	15,558	15,096	12,937	10,944
South Sandwich Islands	9,827	13,275	13,392	11,785	3,770	13,247	14,757	15,423	13,741	12,100	15,087	12,232	13,371	8,624	6,084	11,941	12,384	12,080	10,528	7,442
Split, Yugoslavia	14,080	8,042	2,557	419	10,289	6,577	7,876	8,057	6,895	8,822	7,888	7,800	5,771	7,906	7,577	7,992	941	6,271	8,425	4,834
Spokane, Washington	14,254	1,557	6,382	8,699	10,799	2,759	1,088	1,289	2,229	2,340	1,198	2,653	3,409	6,317	9,486	2,831	8,004	3,808	4,095	10,359
Spoleto, Italy	14,361	7,904	2,501	166	9,998	6,432	7,811	8,026	6,776	8,639	7,840	7,613	5,633	7,607	7,272	7,794	877	6,067	8,179	4,564
Springbok, South Africa	10,056	14,175	10,401	8,159	6,409	13,047	15,080	15,610	13,632	13,757	15,280	13,138	12,545	9,775	6,584	13,023	8,884	11,923	12,021	5,381
Springfield, Illinois	16,457	976	5,844	7,832	8,589	1,755	2,458	3,145	1,806	646	2,790	408	2,539	3,942	7,101	451	7,267	1,991	1,785	8,250
Springfield, Massachusetts	17,797	1,989	4,763	6,532	8,101	1,388	3,190	3,894	1,887	2,032	3,501	1,052	1,804	3,243	6,131	1,131	6,030	641	1,819	6,868
Srinagar, India	9,227	10,999	6,298	5,479	14,631	9,944	9,924	9,582	9,887	12,234	9,706	11,435	9,231	12,887	12,386	11,733	5,555	10,334	12,746	9,312
Stanley, Falkland Islands	10,741	11,540	13,389	12,487	2,789	11,862	12,980	13,577	12,248	10,286	13,292	10,613	12,210	7,352	5,615	10,301	12,911	10,855	8,903	7,913
Stara Zagora, Bulgaria	13,323	8,607	3,048	1,179	10,849	7,165	8,305	8,411	7,436	9,461	8,282	8,448	6,352	8,664	8,210	8,655	1,556	6,949	9,152	5,342
Stockholm, Sweden	14,145	6,830	1,380	1,793	11,391	5,456	6,385	6,462	5,637	7,823	6,345	6,856	4,651	8,006	8,552	7,107	1,188	5,507	7,881	6,226
Stornoway, United Kingdom	15,549	5,784	424	2,015	10,284	4,332	5,637	5,880	4,627	6,637	5,675	5,633	3,521	6,608	7,439	5,857	1,328	4,190	6,520	5,547
Strasbourg, France	14,809	7,170	1,748	600	10,125	5,703	7,054	7,275	6,031	7,948	7,084	6,927	4,899	7,250	7,319	7,123	184	5,407	7,603	4,860
Stuttgart, West Germany	14,704	7,234	1,778	578	10,217	5,770	7,093	7,302	6,088	8,025	7,117	7,006	4,963	7,357	7,415	7,205	154	5,492	7,699	4,933
Subic, Philippines	5,238	12,235	10,314	10,337	18,194	12,175	10,752	10,070	11,733	13,357	10,421	13,284	11,877	16,741	17,391	13,576	10,216	13,231	14,989	14,283
Suchow, China	7,406	10,399	8,215	8,578	18,475	10,120	8,936	8,306	9,732	11,627	8,615	11,357	9,755	14,593	15,799	11,666	8,326	11,110	13,071	12,974
Sucre, Bolivia	14,191	7,955	10,347	10,421	1,952	8,179	9,431	10,087	8,575	6,763	9,757	6,964	8,553	3,749	3,370	6,658	10,522	7,199	5,246	6,470
Sudbury, Canada	16,986	1,207	4,824	6,821	8,831	828	2,365	3,072	1,151	1,669	2,680	689	1,545	3,995	6,954	975	6,247	1,107	2,226	7,630
Suez, Egypt	12,237	10,099	4,554	2,427	10,719	8,643	9,816	9,903	8,937	10,895	9,786	9,871	7,834	9,557	8,410	10,057	2,999	8,331	10,403	5,322
Sundsvall, Sweden	14,180	6,564	1,246	2,109	11,544	5,216	6,072	6,134	5,370	7,590	6,024	6,640	4,419	7,980	8,697	6,900	1,464	5,338	7,732	6,472
Surabaya, Indonesia	3,184	14,795	12,222	11,489	15,664	14,732	13,317	12,624	14,311	15,846	12,985	15,864	14,363	18,962	16,617	16,151	11,627	15,713	17,555	14,085
Suva, Fiji	5,179	11,075	15,115	16,922	12,862	12,439	10,525	10,064	11,903	10,910	10,368	11,844	13,060	13,692	15,312	11,812	16,341	13,358	12,135	18,371
Sverdlovsk, USSR	11,713	8,318	3,689	3,706	13,683	7,199	7,390	7,175	7,173	9,517	7,222	8,689	6,479	10,447	10,906	8,984	3,439	7,604	10,013	8,239
Svobodnyy, USSR	9,207	8,301	6,815	7,841	17,346	8,070	6,842	6,221	7,655	9,535	6,523	9,265	7,773	12,639	14,575	9,573	7,388	9,123	10,982	12,412
Sydney, Australia	2,101	14,256	16,512	16,415	12,891	15,536	13,512	12,945	14,960	14,122	13,297	15,063	16,029	16,138	15,721	15,026	16,479	16,558	15,193	16,780
Sydney, Canada	18,227	2,786	3,774	5,446	8,249	1,590	3,652	4,296	2,192	3,098	3,914	2,083	1,441	3,499	5,924	2,210	4,960	501	2,730	6,106
Syktyvkar, USSR	12,465	7,627	2,932	3,252	13,154	6,461	6,783	6,631	6,465	8,800	6,640	7,947	5,728	9,695	10,330	8,238	2,865	6,834	9,244	7,826
Szeged, Hungary	13,851	8,002	2,450	755	10,706	6,556	7,735	7,871	6,834	8,851	7,725	7,838	5,744	8,182	7,979	8,047	954	6,345	8,570	5,258
Szombathely, Hungary	14,137	7,743	2,209	569	10,545	6,290	7,517	7,676	6,581	8,574	7,518	7,558	5,480	7,906	7,789	7,765	666	6,059	8,278	5,140
Tabriz, Iran	11,523	9,906	4,451	2,996	12,243	8,555	9,290	9,217	8,711	10,923	9,186	9,952	7,751	10,482	9,811	10,195	3,252	8,550	10,855	6,779
Tacheng, China	9,836	9,632	5,560	5,437	15,311	8,728	8,458	8,069	8,584	10,904	8,220	10,205	8,088	12,323	12,663	10,518	5,276	9,313	11,686	9,797
Tahiti (Papeete)	8,230	8,872	14,284	16,589	10,162	10,350	8,965	8,811	9,982	8,253	8,961	9,277	11,137	10,341	12,114	9,140	15,905	10,860	9,067	15,203
Taipei, Taiwan	6,331	11,163	9,319	9,603	18,999	11,046	9,681	9,012	10,614	12,327	9,352	12,187	10,745	15,609	16,831	12,485	9,390	12,098	13,901	13,874
Taiyuan, China	7,888	10,176	7,677	8,000	17,922	9,784	8,739	8,140	9,431	11,433	8,427	11,081	9,369	14,159	15,222	11,396	7,752	10,719	12,781	12,409
Tallahassee, Florida	16,874	2,118	6,424	8,148	7,461	2,633	3,600	4,279	2,850	1,094	3,931	1,182	3,305	2,951	6,160	862	7,677	2,303	692	7,723
Tallinn, USSR	13,766	7,082	1,727	1,968	11,724	5,737	6,557	6,589	5,887	8,111	6,496	7,160	4,940	8,386	8,892	7,418	1,456	5,844	8,230	6,488
Tamanrasset, Algeria	14,393	9,076	4,458	2,386	8,053	7,642	9,418	9,797	8,129	9,421	9,532	8,436	6,944	7,030	5,609	8,513	3,046	6,867	8,380	2,553
Tampa, Florida	16,984	2,446	6,561	8,196	7,132	2,888	3,928	4,608	3,141	1,401	4,259	1,476	3,524	2,658	5,869	1,159	7,756	2,435	396	7,535
Tampere, Finland	13,840	6,871	1,598	2,139	11,785	5,541	6,325	6,352	5,677	7,917	6,261	6,976	4,749	8,318	8,943	7,239	1,573	5,687	8,083	6,614
Tanami, Australia	1,303	14,873	14,275	13,793	14,739	15,528	13,597	12,896	14,956	15,395	13,289	15,982	15,525	18,736	17,090	16,132	13,892	16,761	17,033	15,851

Distances in Kilometers	Eucla, Australia	Fargo, North Dakota	Faroe Islands (Torshavn)	Florence, Italy	Florianopolis, Brazil	Fort George, Canada	Fort McMurray, Canada	Fort Nelson, Canada	Fort Severn, Canada	Fort Smith, Arkansas	Fort Vermilion, Canada	Fort Wayne, Indiana	Fort-Chimo, Canada	Fort-de-France, Martinique	Fortaleza, Brazil	Frankfort, Kentucky	Frankfurt am Main, W. Ger.	Fredericton, Canada	Freeport, Bahamas	Freetown, Sierra Leone
Tangier, Morocco	15,839	7,283	2,916	1,703	8,329	5,837	7,615	8,018	6,318	7,715	7,739	6,707	5,133	5,957	5,544	6,814	1,974	5,123	6,878	3,117
Tarawa (Betio)	5,913	9,922	12,976	14,687	14,738	11,062	9,012	8,430	10,470	10,168	8,785	10,912	11,514	13,829	16,533	10,985	14,108	12,192	11,762	18,727
Tashkent, USSR	10,136	10,137	5,361	4,677	14,240	9,034	9,136	8,849	9,003	11,349	8,940	10,523	8,308	11,994	11,768	10,816	4,684	9,396	11,808	8,772
Tbilisi, USSR	11,832	9,485	4,051	2,734	12,251	8,141	8,869	8,804	8,291	10,512	8,768	9,547	7,340	10,209	9,725	9,794	2,918	8,162	10,488	6,749
Tegucigalpa, Honduras	15,870	3,742	8,134	9,603	6,218	4,467	5,157	5,765	4,648	2,466	5,469	2,996	5,131	2,818	5,727	2,680	9,233	4,025	1,631	8,070
Tehran, Iran	10,993	10,329	4,935	3,524	12,590	9,008	9,638	9,520	9,136	11,383	9,515	10,425	8,211	11,009	10,246	10,676	3,778	9,049	11,370	7,182
Tel Aviv, Israel	12,147	10,010	4,449	2,429	11,014	8,568	9,662	9,719	8,836	10,855	9,618	9,836	7,756	9,701	8,667	10,035	2,942	8,317	10,447	5,592
Telegraph Creek, Canada	13,503	2,603	5,872	8,212	12,143	3,214	1,195	505	2,612	3,686	893	3,724	3,575	7,468	10,513	3,975	7,482	4,442	5,349	10,789
Teresina, Brazil	15,839	7,816	8,052	7,646	2,564	7,349	9,197	9,908	7,905	7,005	9,518	6,682	7,370	2,967	502	6,464	7,856	6,128	5,220	3,610
Ternate, Indonesia	3,602	13,206	12,052	12,015	17,010	13,480	11,772	11,061	12,964	14,115	11,443	14,330	13,326	18,069	18,436	14,576	11,938	14,645	15,892	15,551
The Valley, Anguilla	18,083	4,440	6,517	7,396	5,286	4,202	5,861	6,573	4,690	3,639	6,190	3,310	4,468	437	3,615	3,078	7,193	3,114	1,869	5,484
Thessaloniki, Greece	13,481	8,630	3,099	1,025	10,554	7,174	8,390	8,535	7,472	9,437	8,390	8,417	6,364	8,469	7,928	8,613	1,530	6,894	9,048	5,044
Thimphu, Bhutan	7,761	11,738	7,667	7,064	15,931	10,925	10,459	9,978	10,748	13,027	10,188	12,391	10,299	14,387	13,941	12,706	7,095	11,524	13,900	10,842
Thunder Bay, Canada	16,324	587	5,077	7,201	9,345	940	1,749	2,461	852	1,505	2,074	879	1,753	4,555	7,581	1,189	6,584	1,733	2,596	8,279
Tientsin, China	7,936	9,899	7,724	8,203	18,178	9,587	8,446	7,828	9,207	11,140	8,128	10,839	9,216	14,054	15,384	11,151	7,911	10,571	12,551	12,675
Tijuana, Mexico	13,915	2,341	7,829	10,063	9,832	3,819	2,724	2,952	3,455	2,108	2,876	2,979	4,601	5,973	9,162	2,973	9,409	4,512	3,746	10,780
Tiksi, USSR	11,458	6,382	4,792	6,309	15,106	5,919	5,021	4,525	5,567	7,667	4,739	7,225	5,552	10,413	12,415	7,542	5,713	6,907	8,915	10,691
Timbuktu, Mali	14,915	8,948	5,033	3,282	6,944	7,602	9,537	10,014	8,146	9,075	9,703	8,155	6,997	6,208	4,512	8,177	3,846	6,656	7,813	1,439
Tindouf, Algeria	15,872	7,721	3,815	2,489	7,488	6,334	8,233	8,696	6,861	7,974	8,390	7,007	5,699	5,643	4,763	7,067	2,870	5,461	6,901	2,192
Tirane, Albania	13,753	8,408	2,903	755	10,378	6,945	8,218	8,380	7,257	9,192	8,221	8,170	6,138	8,201	7,719	8,361	1,304	6,639	8,780	4,882
Tokyo, Japan	7,549	9,264	8,764	9,786	18,818	9,410	7,790	7,093	8,902	10,346	7,457	10,351	9,284	14,023	16,459	10,626	9,357	10,581	12,022	14,360
Toledo, Spain	15,721	7,107	2,471	1,338	8,778	5,641	7,334	7,700	6,090	7,633	7,438	6,612	4,903	6,184	5,975	6,744	1,513	5,026	6,928	3,594
Topeka, Kansas	15,939	874	6,211	8,270	8,852	2,073	2,278	2,919	1,974	422	2,598	925	2,883	4,332	7,523	945	7,682	2,490	2,099	8,769
Toronto, Canada	17,217	1,409	4,981	6,896	8,494	1,131	2,671	3,381	1,491	1,582	2,991	555	1,777	3,663	6,652	762	6,350	1,038	1,904	7,447
Toulouse, France	15,284	7,178	2,119	791	9,389	5,700	7,250	7,550	6,098	7,822	7,320	6,794	4,924	6,697	6,589	6,957	910	5,226	7,274	4,143
Tours, France	15,339	6,861	1,696	917	9,658	5,384	6,870	7,152	5,756	7,563	6,931	6,537	4,595	6,709	6,833	6,715	662	4,988	7,123	4,508
Townsville, Australia	2,266	13,547	14,835	15,083	14,567	14,552	12,494	11,845	13,949	13,809	12,227	14,563	14,834	17,023	17,400	14,639	14,980	15,756	15,310	17,570
Trenton, New Jersey	17,701	1,919	5,040	6,799	7,982	1,546	3,211	3,922	1,990	1,808	3,531	882	2,039	3,137	6,112	900	6,304	918	1,565	6,997
Tripoli, Lebanon	12,170	9,835	4,272	2,355	11,221	8,406	9,442	9,481	8,654	10,715	9,389	9,703	7,592	9,727	8,820	9,911	2,812	8,203	10,379	5,767
Tripoli, Libya	14,067	8,743	3,536	1,218	9,349	7,266	8,792	9,054	7,665	9,341	8,846	8,316	6,492	7,690	6,782	8,459	1,948	6,735	8,632	3,834
Tristan da Cunha (Edinburgh)	11,392	12,524	10,992	9,261	3,549	11,925	13,878	14,582	12,512	11,667	14,189	11,390	11,763	7,667	4,559	11,172	9,874	10,682	9,890	5,043
Trondheim, Norway	14,515	6,224	890	2,188	11,330	4,861	5,781	5,876	5,030	7,233	5,748	6,278	4,060	7,645	8,480	6,535	1,485	4,969	7,364	6,382
Trujillo, Peru	14,700	6,340	9,890	10,652	3,862	6,865	7,773	8,382	7,149	5,079	8,087	5,482	7,403	3,200	4,513	5,163	10,534	6,116	3,832	7,525
Truk Island (Moen)	4,975	10,992	12,087	13,095	16,918	11,727	9,731	9,040	11,133	11,632	9,432	12,110	11,893	15,649	18,814	12,282	12,710	12,968	13,395	17,605
Truro, Canada	18,168	2,577	4,000	5,700	8,214	1,471	3,517	4,178	2,071	2,846	3,792	1,834	1,459	3,417	5,966	1,956	5,210	272	2,507	6,282
Tsingtao, China	7,556	10,102	8,146	8,638	18,608	9,873	8,633	7,994	9,467	11,318	8,310	11,078	9,537	14,395	15,822	11,385	8,349	10,892	12,795	13,096
Tsitsihar, China	8,772	8,840	7,111	7,954	17,716	8,582	7,382	6,763	8,178	10,076	7,064	9,797	8,259	13,123	14,884	10,106	7,553	9,613	11,512	12,524
Tubuai Island (Mataura)	7,935	9,405	14,878	17,143	9,835	10,878	9,568	9,436	10,537	8,714	9,575	9,741	11,676	10,488	11,976	9,584	16,487	11,313	9,396	15,088
Tucson, Arizona	14,448	2,026	7,587	9,755	9,351	3,490	2,725	3,085	3,201	1,570	2,935	2,498	4,294	5,404	8,597	2,459	9,129	4,065	3,176	10,233
Tulsa, Oklahoma	15,894	1,192	6,489	8,510	8,626	2,361	2,564	3,185	2,291	160	2,877	1,084	3,165	4,204	7,411	1,006	7,937	2,670	1,944	8,803
Tunis, Tunisia	14,445	8,238	3,041	779	9,410	6,760	8,281	8,550	7,155	8,860	8,337	7,833	5,983	7,396	6,747	7,984	1,484	6,256	8,213	3,928
Tura, USSR	10,934	7,590	4,756	5,693	15,365	6,905	6,315	5,879	6,649	8,881	6,057	8,315	6,396	11,115	12,521	8,634	5,228	7,727	9,938	10,256
Turin, Italy	14,796	7,435	2,106	319	9,856	5,961	7,383	7,627	6,316	8,158	7,425	7,132	5,165	7,209	7,077	7,313	568	5,586	7,710	4,523
Uberlandia, Brazil	14,392	8,758	9,693	9,214	958	8,581	10,221	10,926	9,086	7,735	10,554	7,656	8,737	3,965	1,993	7,389	9,469	7,422	6,011	4,900
Ufa, USSR	11,828	8,456	3,604	3,406	13,378	7,281	7,593	7,414	7,293	9,626	7,440	8,764	6,538	10,327	10,629	9,051	3,192	7,610	10,022	7,909
Ujungpandang, Indonesia	3,106	14,231	12,318	11,858	16,166	14,353	12,772	12,067	13,878	15,197	12,440	15,338	14,089	18,954	17,389	15,602	11,914	15,441	16,960	14,793
Ulaanbaatar, Mongolia	9,089	9,254	6,475	6,940	16,914	8,714	7,877	7,339	8,410	10,539	7,584	10,076	8,245	12,979	14,103	10,395	6,631	9,584	11,742	11,453
Ulan-Ude, USSR	9,486	8,821	6,129	6,733	16,664	8,276	7,452	6,925	7,971	10,107	7,163	9,637	7,812	12,565	13,823	9,957	6,380	9,153	11,303	11,284
Uliastay, Mongolia	9,366	9,438	6,088	6,319	16,281	8,739	8,133	7,653	8,500	10,729	7,860	10,163	8,193	12,760	13,536	10,483	6,068	9,498	11,768	10,777
Uranium City, Canada	14,805	1,612	4,972	7,308	11,105	1,903	356	810	1,304	2,879	445	2,621	2,292	6,308	9,258	2,912	6,599	3,138	4,326	9,498
Urumqi, China	9,357	9,950	6,040	5,909	15,726	9,110	8,723	8,294	8,937	11,233	8,470	10,576	8,494	12,801	13,126	10,891	5,762	9,742	12,096	10,221
Ushuaia, Argentina	10,279	11,583	14,021	13,245	3,420	12,083	12,965	13,502	12,407	10,300	13,258	10,744	12,518	7,720	6,269	10,426	13,646	11,169	9,065	8,673
Vaduz, Liechtenstein	14,670	7,375	1,947	401	10,119	5,907	7,257	7,473	6,236	8,145	7,286	7,123	5,103	7,369	7,331	7,316	334	5,598	7,776	4,799
Valencia, Spain	15,405	7,372	2,546	1,078	8,949	5,900	7,548	7,888	6,334	7,927	7,639	6,903	5,150	6,487	6,172	7,042	1,381	5,320	7,243	3,663
Valladolid, Spain	15,785	6,934	2,270	1,327	8,895	5,465	7,139	7,498	5,905	7,487	7,239	6,463	4,720	6,163	6,078	6,603	1,399	4,880	6,829	3,768
Valletta, Malta	14,044	8,572	3,262	917	9,650	7,094	8,553	8,788	7,470	9,228	8,593	8,201	6,308	7,789	7,040	8,359	1,648	6,629	8,611	4,141
Valparaiso, Chile	12,623	9,203	12,020	11,947	2,294	9,650	10,630	11,222	9,900	7,930	10,939	0,321	10,104	5,309	4,733	0,004	12,117	0,763	6,634	7,696
Vancouver, Canada	13,862	1,969	6,447	8,786	11,251	3,052	1,143	1,065	2,486	2,797	1,120	3,085	3,637	6,769	9,930	3,275	8,075	4,162	4,551	10,704
Varna, Bulgaria	13,171	8,644	3,080	1,347	11,055	7,213	8,294	8,377	7,465	9,528	8,260	8,520	6,400	8,834	8,416	8,735	1,653	7,039	9,270	5,547
Venice, Italy	14,435	7,664	2,216	206	10,163	6,197	7,532	7,736	6,524	8,434	7,555	7,411	5,392	7,578	7,405	7,602	587	5,882	8,044	4,775
Veracruz, Mexico	15,331	3,070	8,107	9,872	7,285	4,114	4,355	4,895	4,145	1,801	4,643	2,641	4,875	3,763	6,797	2,372	9,400	4,014	1,954	8,967
Verona, Italy	14,540	7,590	2,169	188	10,082	6,121	7,480	7,694	6,455	8,348	7,508	7,324	5,318	7,473	7,317	7,513	547	5,791	7,944	4,710
Victoria, Canada	13,828	1,994	6,535	8,873	11,223	3,110	1,227	1,156	2,550	2,780	1,211	3,100	3,707	6,769	9,938	3,283	8,163	4,207	4,543	10,753
Victoria, Seychelles	8,177	14,622	9,058	6,948	11,151	13,180	14,110	13,991	13,441	15,415	13,993	14,387	12,368	13,003	10,423	14,547	7,539	12,818	14,597	7,763
Vienna, Austria	14,170	7,651	2,110	632	10,593	6,201	7,413	7,569	6,487	8,492	7,412	7,479	5,390	7,886	7,826	7,688	599	5,987	8,220	5,206
Vientiane, Laos	6,172	12,566	9,225	8,756	16,892	12,048	11,144	10,549	11,754	13,835	10,834	13,420	11,534	15,988	15,511	13,739	8,769	12,843	15,081	12,401
Villahermosa, Mexico	15,571	3,224	8,057	9,733	6,949	4,155	4,569	5,139	4,241	1,934	4,868	2,665	4,887	3,419	6,434	2,374	9,292	3,936	1,734	8,642
Vilnius, USSR	13,661	7,510	2,022	1,583	11,504	6,130	7,047	7,100	6,317	8,493	6,997	7,519	5,323	8,466	8,706	7,765	1,237	6,140	8,491	6,155
Visby, Sweden	14,127	6,975	1,477	1,619	11,299	5,588	6,556	6,643	5,784	7,949	6,521	6,974	4,780	8,016	8,467	7,219	1,047	5,600	7,961	6,088
Vitoria, Brazil	14,134	9,345	9,600	8,832	1,160	9,011	10,777	11,488	9,550	8,398	11,105	8,221	9,069	4,479	1,847	7,974	9,169	7,806	6,638	4,355
Vladivostok, USSR	8,294	8,945	7,776	8,720	18,279	8,864	7,465	6,804	8,410	10,127	7,137	9,969	8,628	13,477	15,537	10,266	8,301	9,966	11,681	13,294
Volgograd, USSR	12,208	8,767	3,449	2,595	12,469	7,460	8,101	8,023	7,575	9,836	7,993	8,896	6,670	9,899	9,799	9,156	2,572	7,575	9,947	6,962
Vologda, USSR	12,919	7,600	2,518	2,593	12,514	6,337	6,899	6,827	6,414	8,708	6,792	7,800	5,566	9,237	9,702	8,075	2,227	6,571	8,977	7,168
Vorkuta, USSR	12,244	7,218	3,232	4,042	13,765	6,200	6,219	5,981	6,108	8,453	6,038	7,688	5,537	9,891	10,916	7,995	3,563	6,760	9,132	8,594
Wake Island	6,936	8,950	10,974	12,589	16,330	9,788	7,749	7,079	9,186	9,566	7,466	10,058	10,058	13,592	16,797	10,222	12,019	11,015	11,332	16,932
Wallis Island	5,944	10,288	14,531	16,555	12,784	11,660	9,769	9,331	11,131	10,128	9,624	11,056	12,296	13,044	14,991	11,028	15,898	12,569	11,390	18,094
Walvis Bay, Namibia	10,781	13,436	9,607	7,394	6,306	12,260	14,279	14,797	12,840	13,118	14,472	12,434	11,740	9,218	6,083	12,342	8,113	11,160	11,428	4,609
Warsaw, Poland	13,903	7,534	1,979	1,189	11,119	6,120	7,166	7,264	6,349	8,461	7,137	7,468	5,308	8,201	8,331	7,699	892	6,038	8,349	5,760
Washington, D.C.	17,548	1,835	5,276	7,044	7,932	1,668	3,193	3,905	2,056	1,590	3,519	733	2,225	3,113	6,156	687	6,548	1,159	1,382	7,159
Watson Lake, Canada	13,675	2,545	5,590	7,930	12,108	3,030	1,081	374	2,432	3,690	753	3,646	3,346	7,379	10,379	3,911	7,201	4,268	5,304	10,554
Weimar, East Germany	14,559	7,174	1,647	802	10,494	5,723	6,963	7,142	6,013	8,015	6,973	7,003	4,912	7,530	7,684	7,214	210	5,518	7,772	5,224
Wellington, New Zealand	4,197	13,089	17,697	18,644	11,174	14,557	12,865	12,498	14,110	12,552	12,761	13,574	15,296	13,909	13,993	13,437	18,558	15,159	13,227	16,286
West Berlin, West Germany	14,421	7,158	1,600	986	10,713	5,720	6,891	7,045	5,987	8,035	6,888	7,031	4,907	7,684	7,899	7,251	423	5,570	7,856	5,446
Wewak, Papua New Guinea	3,480	12,510	13,070	13,565	16,323	13,227	11,248	10,553	12,638	13,109	10,946	13,625	13,346	17,057	19,169	13,789	13,348	14,470	14,846	17,420
Whangarei, New Zealand	4,200	12,719	17,079	18,320	11,684	14,164	12,382	11,978	13,682	12,291	12,257	13,299	14,866	14,058	14,470	13,192	18,035	14,882	13,134	16,895
Whitehorse, Canada	13,346	2,893	5,703	8,027	12,455	3,356	1,432	723	2,762	4,023	1,103	3,996	3,633	7,730	10,722	4,260	7,295	4,597	5,651	10,821
Wichita, Kansas	15,784	1,020	6,417	8,479	8,838	2,277	2,358	2,973	2,158	366	2,669	1,114	3,088	4,392	7,595	1,097	7,891	2,689	2,139	8,921
Willemstad, Curacao	17,180	4,654	7,390	8,304	4,913	4,712	6,129	6,825	5,128	3,636	6,462	3,577	5,103	895	3,797	3,293	8,103	3,759	1,898	6,105
Wiluna, Australia	1,014	16,075	14,488	13,483	13,891	16,595	14,756	14,048	16,055	16,598	14,440	17,193	16,441	18,669	15,952	17,348	13,741	17,772	18,140	14,736
Windhoek, Namibia	10,597	13,606	9,615	7,371	6,570	12,396	14,395	14,886	12,969	13,331	14,574	12,623	11,852	9,457	6,335	12,540	8,095	11,318	11,656	4,771
Windsor, Canada	16,974	1,204	5,286	7,225	8,508	1,316	2,575	3,287	1,558	1,251	2,904	223	2,034	3,723	6,788	482	6,673	1,369	1,793	7,717
Winnipeg, Canada	15,730	336	5,319	7,531	9,831	1,321	1,213	1,919	931	1,626	1,546	1,354	2,074	5,093	8,158	1,625	6,882	2,304	3,034	8,855
Winston-Salem, North Carolina	17,301	1,822	5,694	7,457	7,793	1,973	3,263	3,970	2,280	1,283	3,595	697	2,597	3,052	6,185	472	6,967	1,579	1,072	7,395
Wroclaw, Poland	14,160	7,446	1,883	924	10,820	6,012	7,152	7,287	6,271	8,330	7,141	7,326	5,199	7,931	8,028	7,547	601	5,865	8,146	5,479
Wuhan, China	7,066	10,879	8,475	8,666	18,327	10,565	9,421	8,794	10,191	12,113	9,101	11,825	10,174	14,981	15,893	12,137	8,468	11,527	13,536	12,949
Wyndham, Australia	1,802	14,614	13,749	13,336	15,228	15,143	13,277	12,569	14,588	15,262	12,960	15,742	15,079	19,044	17,430	15,926	13,403	16,357	16,986	15,763
Xi'an, China	7,598	10,658	7,889	8,018	17,755	10,214	9,232	8,642	9,882	11,924	8,923	11,540	9,766	14,494	15,243	11,857	7,830	11,108	13,229	12,312
Xining, China	8,075	10,574	7,356	7,353	17,066	9,983	9,200	8,658	9,705	11,860	8,907	11,373	9,468	14,059	14,565	11,693	7,194	10,785	13,016	11,615
Yakutsk, USSR	10,388	7,245	5,768	7,059	16,178	6,916	5,820	5,247	6,525	8,509	5,514	8,160	6,594	11,460	13,464	8,473	6,526	7,947	9,869	11,562
Yanji, China	8,261	9,069	7,736	8,617	18,298	8,949	7,591	6,937	8,506	10,262	7,264	10,079	8,690	13,549	15,508	10,379	8,214	10,034	11,795	13,186

Distances in Kilometers	Eucla, Australia	Fargo, North Dakota	Faroe Islands (Torshavn)	Florence, Italy	Florianopolis, Brazil	Fort George, Canada	Fort McMurray, Canada	Fort Nelson, Canada	Fort Severn, Canada	Fort Smith, Arkansas	Fort Vermilion, Canada	Fort Wayne, Indiana	Fort-Chimo, Canada	Fort-de-France, Martinique	Fortaleza, Brazil	Frankfort, Kentucky	Frankfurt am Main, W. Ger.	Fredericton, Canada	Freeport, Bahamas	Freetown, Sierra Leone
Yaounde, Cameroon	12,815	11,074	6,629	4,421	7,318	9,699	11,566	11,976	10,222	11,200	11,698	10,290	9,052	8,039	5,629	10,307	5,133	8,789	9,857	2,789
Yap Island (Colonia)	4,669	11,741	11,514	12,051	17,888	12,167	10,342	9,630	11,615	12,597	10,019	12,874	12,135	16,610	19,271	13,101	11,795	13,384	14,380	16,282
Yaraka, Australia	1,671	14,175	15,340	15,282	14,044	15,223	13,163	12,520	14,621	14,352	12,900	15,158	15,518	17,163	16,828	15,209	15,493	16,241	16,235	13,425
Yarmouth, Canada	18,136	2,412	4,277	5,980	8,108	1,455	3,451	4,131	2,038	2,590	3,740	1,591	1,595	3,276	5,947	1,692	5,493	241	2,235	6,425
Yellowknife, Canada	14,448	2,056	4,929	7,276	11,545	2,255	658	610	1,671	3,314	460	3,065	2,532	6,736	9,648	3,357	6,555	3,498	4,773	9,739
Yerevan, USSR	11,772	9,629	4,171	2,766	12,175	8,275	9,028	8,969	8,434	10,643	8,930	9,672	7,471	10,251	9,683	9,915	7,331	10,626	12,792	11,897
Yinchuan, China	8,114	10,277	7,369	7,541	17,396	9,765	8,877	8,312	9,456	11,555	8,576	11,120	9,291	13,987	14,772	11,439	11,504	15,765	17,723	13,829
Yogyakarta, Indonesia	3,270	14,968	12,161	11,339	15,487	14,831	13,486	12,800	14,432	16,052	13,154	16,016	14,424	18,826	16,349	16,310	11,792	14,613	16,876	15,143
York, United Kingdom	15,378	6,319	969	1,440	10,107	4,855	6,218	6,465	5,178	7,121	6,260	6,105	4,049	6,749	7,259	6,312	6,692	10,375	12,651	11,156
Yumen, China	8,549	10,293	6,870	6,857	16,643	9,621	8,960	8,451	9,375	11,584	8,678	11,040	9,075	13,594	14,076	11,360	5,841	10,301	12,699	9,888
Yutian, China	9,041	10,728	6,390	5,856	15,281	9,786	9,560	9,162	9,666	11,995	9,319	11,271	9,118	13,108	12,923	11,580	8,380	9,319	10,867	13,421
Yuzhno-Sakhalinsk, USSR	8,823	8,112	7,622	8,886	17,642	8,163	6,630	5,949	7,671	9,256	6,298	9,170	8,014	12,787	15,212	9,457	8,380	9,319	10,867	13,421
Zagreb, Yugoslavia	14,159	7,829	2,319	439	10,412	6,371	7,635	7,808	6,675	8,636	7,643	7,617	5,562	7,863	7,669	7,817	727	6,103	8,295	8,019
Zahedan, Iran	9,876	11,255	5,995	4,634	13,231	9,999	10,422	10,212	10,074	12,372	10,260	11,447	9,217	12,110	11,125	11,711	11,044	14,086	15,685	14,792
Zamboanga, Philippines	4,334	12,928	11,208	11,118	17,516	12,992	11,456	10,757	12,522	13,973	11,123	13,831	11,616	11,292	8,614	13,380	6,895	11,724	13,101	6,041
Zanzibar, Tanzania	9,627	13,856	8,517	6,203	9,480	12,382	13,835	13,962	12,788	14,288	13,831	13,301	11,616	11,292	8,614	13,380	6,895	11,724	13,101	6,041
Zaragoza, Spain	15,466	7,179	2,302	1,021	9,099	5,705	7,324	7,654	6,127	7,768	7,410	6,742	4,945	6,477	6,302	6,890	1,198	5,163	7,141	3,868
Zashiversk, USSR	11,056	6,389	5,430	7,014	15,508	6,116	4,958	4,385	5,700	7,648	4,651	7,320	5,847	10,704	12,930	7,631	6,410	7,188	9,034	11,363
Zhengzhou, China	7,528	10,467	8,032	8,308	18,157	10,115	9,018	8,405	9,750	11,713	8,702	11,392	9,713	14,515	15,537	11,706	8,078	11,065	13,099	12,671
Zurich, Switzerland	14,759	7,296	1,890	459	10,069	5,827	7,193	7,417	6,161	8,061	7,225	7,038	5,025	7,283	7,274	7,230	307	5,510	7,686	4,769

Distances in Kilometers	Frobisher Bay, Canada	Frunze, USSR	Fukuoka, Japan	Funafuti Atoll, Tuvalu	Funchal, Madeira Island	Fuzhou, China	Gaborone, Botswana	Galapagos Islands (Santa Cruz)	Gander, Canada	Gangtok, India	Garyarsa, China	Gaspe, Canada	Gauhati, India	Gdansk, Poland	Geneva, Switzerland	Genoa, Italy	Georgetown, Guyana	Geraldton, Australia	Ghanzi, Botswana	Ghat, Libya
Frunze, USSR	7,743	0	4,902	11,835	7,741	4,445	8,992	15,091	8,689	2,142	1,338	9,086	2,422	4,192	5,278	5,151	12,736	8,929	8,954	6,122
Fukuoka, Japan	9,087	4,902	0	6,942	11,919	1,356	12,770	14,419	10,849	4,045	4,652	10,758	3,801	8,288	9,553	9,541	15,446	7,099	12,987	10,965
Funafuti Atoll, Tuvalu	11,940	11,835	6,942	0	16,872	7,513	15,335	10,062	13,316	10,496	11,335	12,637	10,172	14,633	15,775	15,916	13,718	7,083	15,869	17,848
Funchal, Madeira Island	4,940	7,741	11,919	16,872	0	12,029	7,800	8,509	3,610	9,724	8,787	4,317	10,049	3,688	2,477	2,590	5,134	15,402	7,274	2,768
Fuzhou, China	10,023	4,445	1,356	7,513	12,029	0	11,497	15,773	11,672	3,049	3,828	11,699	2,752	8,343	9,560	9,487	16,356	6,090	11,756	10,543
Gaborone, Botswana	12,651	8,992	12,770	15,335	7,800	11,497	0	12,627	11,383	8,853	8,516	12,059	9,040	8,782	8,097	7,842	9,733	8,617	544	5,747
Galapagos Islands (Santa Cruz)	7,367	15,091	14,419	10,062	8,509	15,773	12,627	0	6,477	17,048	16,428	6,020	17,169	11,289	10,566	10,802	3,672	15,814	12,277	11,112
Gander, Canada	1,849	8,689	10,849	13,316	3,610	11,672	11,383	6,477	0	10,803	10,017	723	11,039	4,875	4,460	4,746	4,684	17,585	10,847	6,139
Gangtok, India	9,710	2,142	4,045	10,496	9,724	3,049	8,853	17,048	10,803	0	937	11,156	335	6,303	7,315	7,153	14,818	6,799	9,000	7,707
Garyarsa, China	9,070	1,338	4,652	11,335	8,787	3,828	8,516	16,428	10,017	937	0	10,423	1,267	5,404	6,387	6,220	13,890	7,615	8,589	6,805
Gaspe, Canada	1,679	9,086	10,758	12,637	4,317	11,699	12,059	6,020	723	11,156	10,423	0	11,367	5,454	5,133	5,423	4,697	17,775	11,520	6,862
Gauhati, India	9,886	2,422	3,801	10,172	10,049	2,752	9,040	17,169	11,039	335	1,267	11,367	0	6,602	7,632	7,474	15,131	6,553	9,209	8,042
Gdansk, Poland	4,703	4,192	8,288	14,633	3,688	8,343	8,782	11,289	4,875	6,303	5,404	5,454	6,602	0	1,268	1,308	8,543	12,924	8,416	3,337
Geneva, Switzerland	4,825	5,278	9,553	15,775	2,477	9,560	8,097	10,566	4,460	7,315	6,387	5,133	7,632	1,268	0	295	7,503	13,628	7,668	2,383
Genoa, Italy	5,116	5,151	9,541	15,916	2,590	9,487	7,842	10,802	4,746	7,153	6,220	5,423	7,474	1,308	295	0	7,672	13,378	7,422	2,161
Georgetown, Guyana	6,375	12,736	15,446	13,718	5,134	16,356	9,733	3,672	4,684	14,818	13,890	4,697	15,131	8,543	7,503	7,672	0	17,460	9,261	7,517
Geraldton, Australia	16,110	8,929	7,099	7,083	15,402	6,090	8,617	15,814	17,585	6,799	7,615	17,775	6,553	12,924	13,628	13,378	17,460	0	9,148	12,636
Ghanzi, Botswana	12,148	8,954	12,987	15,869	7,274	11,756	544	12,277	10,847	9,000	8,589	11,520	9,209	8,416	7,668	7,422	9,261	9,148	0	5,299
Ghat, Libya	6,993	6,122	10,965	17,848	2,768	10,543	5,747	11,112	6,139	7,707	6,805	6,862	8,042	3,337	2,383	2,161	7,517	12,636	5,299	0
Gibraltar	5,166	6,654	11,027	16,913	1,130	11,008	7,489	9,608	4,206	8,604	7,667	4,929	8,931	2,740	1,475	1,521	6,263	14,409	6,996	1,933
Gijon, Spain	4,479	6,248	10,375	16,097	1,557	10,477	8,212	9,633	3,756	8,295	7,367	4,465	8,611	2,133	980	1,175	6,523	14,527	7,735	2,515
Gisborne, New Zealand	14,913	13,768	9,389	3,342	18,517	9,418	12,419	10,108	15,725	11,804	12,740	15,007	11,478	17,673	18,940	18,905	13,391	5,864	12,894	18,111
Glasgow, United Kingdom	3,548	5,576	9,207	14,748	2,759	9,484	9,366	9,823	3,432	7,711	6,831	4,044	7,997	1,466	1,294	1,577	7,197	14,388	8,922	3,624
Godthab, Greenland	828	7,231	9,158	12,666	4,244	9,959	11,866	7,862	1,713	9,279	8,568	1,883	9,486	3,924	3,998	4,288	6,398	15,941	11,373	6,177
Gomez Palacio, Mexico	4,943	12,422	11,337	9,171	8,230	12,682	14,959	3,224	4,938	14,010	13,648	4,247	14,052	9,575	9,379	9,670	5,239	16,253	14,466	10,962
Goose Bay, Canada	3,638	9,339	7,920	8,358	8,516	9,233	16,288	6,747	5,005	10,592	10,397	4,387	10,590	7,876	8,325	8,601	8,003	14,347	15,778	10,600
Gorki, USSR	5,498	2,634	6,765	13,433	5,290	6,739	9,137	12,614	6,139	4,773	3,914	6,613	5,056	1,613	2,826	2,782	10,125	11,525	8,882	4,421
Goteborg, Sweden	4,144	4,565	8,380	14,436	3,540	8,553	9,221	10,799	4,352	6,700	5,822	4,913	6,987	561	1,341	1,494	8,197	13,399	8,833	3,640
Granada, Spain	5,148	6,463	10,842	16,813	1,309	10,817	7,519	9,762	4,259	8,419	7,482	4,980	8,746	2,556	1,289	1,330	6,442	14,282	7,034	1,892
Grand Turk, Turks & Caicos	4,701	12,065	13,501	12,397	5,463	14,626	11,660	3,218	3,383	14,186	13,384	3,093	14,421	8,083	7,357	7,601	2,140	19,020	11,153	8,201
Graz, Austria	5,187	4,576	8,969	15,462	3,166	8,902	8,013	11,256	5,041	6,600	5,671	5,686	6,917	841	717	585	8,219	12,952	7,627	2,496
Green Bay, Wisconsin	2,469	10,169	10,527	10,895	6,138	11,711	13,754	5,007	2,578	12,042	11,478	1,855	12,176	7,052	6,909	7,203	5,083	17,361	13,210	8,716
Grenoble, France	4,894	5,355	9,660	15,894	2,392	9,654	8,000	10,540	4,481	7,379	6,449	5,162	7,698	1,379	120	269	7,441	13,645	7,567	2,277
Guadalajara, Mexico	5,446	12,964	11,741	9,068	8,482	13,094	14,824	2,746	5,320	14,542	14,191	4,650	14,575	10,038	9,778	10,066	5,100	16,106	14,361	11,240
Guam (Agana)	10,985	7,389	2,660	4,511	14,546	3,002	13,527	13,798	12,834	6,007	6,825	12,530	5,690	10,946	12,212	12,200	16,641	5,689	13,942	13,512
Guantanamo, Cuba	4,871	12,374	13,473	11,970	5,908	14,659	12,004	2,832	3,687	14,474	13,704	3,325	14,692	8,457	7,768	8,017	2,358	18,641	11,507	8,649
Guatemala City, Guatemala	5,713	13,457	13,138	10,291	7,630	14,473	13,327	1,689	5,017	15,361	14,781	4,477	15,482	9,893	9,353	9,618	3,639	17,003	12,878	10,381
Guayaquil, Ecuador	7,372	14,833	15,328	11,196	7,643	16,670	11,501	1,186	6,164	16,965	16,135	5,842	17,201	10,754	9,875	10,081	2,604	16,256	11,129	10,119
Guiyang, China	9,982	3,422	2,405	8,719	11,153	1,257	10,366	16,608	11,436	1,798	2,620	11,606	1,495	7,529	8,679	8,567	15,972	6,183	10,586	9,407
Gur'yev, USSR	6,657	1,844	6,552	13,465	5,901	6,255	8,367	13,698	7,228	3,876	2,961	7,734	4,187	2,452	3,450	3,311	10,944	10,491	8,184	4,414
Haifa, Israel	7,407	3,622	8,521	15,456	4,814	7,992	6,436	13,300	7,315	5,151	4,242	7,971	5,486	2,715	2,866	2,591	9,903	10,814	6,182	2,565
Haikou, China	10,714	4,184	2,489	8,169	11,925	1,137	10,389	16,907	12,218	2,352	3,255	12,358	2,019	8,325	9,459	9,335	16,783	5,421	10,670	10,056
Haiphong, Vietnam	10,615	3,856	2,729	8,559	11,592	1,412	10,085	17,110	12,053	1,969	2,881	12,236	1,635	8,023	9,134	9,002	16,532	5,557	10,349	9,676
Hakodate, Japan	8,028	5,305	1,283	6,806	11,457	2,621	13,811	13,177	9,845	4,960	5,391	9,671	4,772	8,020	9,277	9,323	14,298	8,257	13,953	11,042
Halifax, Canada	2,149	9,459	11,226	12,818	4,215	12,167	11,856	5,673	835	11,551	10,794	470	11,772	5,708	5,280	5,563	4,227	18,235	11,313	6,854
Hamburg, West Germany	4,386	4,768	8,782	14,916	3,156	8,890	8,800	10,751	4,384	6,877	5,975	4,992	7,177	576	862	1,019	7,968	13,468	8,399	3,174
Hamilton, Bermuda	3,509	10,710	12,544	12,967	4,461	13,531	11,493	4,532	2,036	12,834	12,030	1,838	13,074	6,757	6,105	6,364	2,903	19,611	10,956	7,228
Hamilton, New Zealand	14,967	13,513	9,166	3,265	18,776	9,172	12,391	10,352	15,871	11,545	12,482	15,149	11,220	17,454	18,717	18,657	13,649	5,643	12,878	18,015
Hangzhou, China	9,556	4,255	1,035	7,617	11,711	470	11,737	15,417	11,217	3,088	3,784	11,233	2,820	8,024	9,259	9,202	15,901	6,558	11,963	10,377
Hannover, West Germany	4,470	4,817	8,886	15,049	3,064	8,973	8,678	10,750	4,413	6,917	6,009	5,033	7,220	635	733	886	7,919	13,470	8,274	3,042
Hanoi, Vietnam	10,593	3,783	2,789	8,647	11,516	1,482	10,016	17,152	12,016	1,883	2,797	12,207	1,548	7,955	9,061	8,927	16,472	5,590	10,276	9,590
Harare, Zimbabwe	12,239	8,066	11,937	15,463	7,565	10,700	926	13,307	11,175	7,971	7,602	11,882	8,171	8,084	7,521	7,250	10,164	8,469	1,056	5,248
Harbin, China	7,791	4,090	1,388	7,959	10,583	2,278	12,742	13,842	9,511	3,919	4,244	9,470	3,778	7,009	8,276	8,291	14,165	8,341	12,833	9,897
Harrisburg, Pennsylvania	2,670	10,360	11,363	11,806	5,342	12,472	12,786	4,732	2,003	12,373	11,696	1,367	12,555	6,821	6,463	6,749	4,150	18,362	12,244	8,027
Hartford, Connecticut	2,461	10,073	11,336	12,146	4,966	12,393	12,478	5,023	1,619	12,117	11,411	1,014	12,313	6,459	6,077	6,362	4,131	18,423	11,934	7,640
Havana, Cuba	4,628	12,324	12,838	11,250	6,434	14,084	12,814	2,769	3,760	14,338	13,661	3,258	14,512	8,631	8,081	8,348	3,159	18,220	12,313	9,201
Helena, Montana	3,267	10,069	9,154	9,119	7,815	10,451	15,574	5,644	4,207	11,559	11,240	3,518	11,599	7,894	8,092	8,383	6,754	15,538	15,033	10,189
Helsinki, Finland	4,478	3,819	7,614	13,883	4,315	7,759	9,402	11,441	4,964	5,960	5,105	5,465	6,238	750	1,984	2,053	8,974	12,715	9,063	4,073
Hengyang, China	9,955	3,856	1,863	8,170	11,531	674	10,912	16,211	11,509	2,375	3,165	11,612	2,079	7,867	9,054	8,961	16,147	6,164	11,147	9,916
Herat, Afghanistan	8,302	1,436	6,177	13,013	7,151	5,503	7,573	15,318	8,872	2,635	1,719	9,393	2,970	4,029	4,838	4,638	12,284	8,897	7,522	5,087
Hermosillo, Mexico	4,882	12,016	10,540	8,560	8,678	11,890	15,740	3,950	5,214	13,426	13,169	4,496	13,432	9,583	9,551	9,846	6,051	15,614	15,232	11,341
Hiroshima, Japan	8,968	5,023	210	6,835	11,926	1,564	12,975	14,210	10,746	4,232	4,819	10,634	3,994	8,318	9,585	9,583	15,311	7,240	13,187	11,057
Hiva Oa (Atuona)	10,042	15,106	10,662	4,597	13,598	11,649	15,860	5,481	10,419	14,678	15,298	9,715	14,397	14,685	14,802	15,097	9,152	11,055	15,959	16,366
Ho Chi Minh City, Vietnam	11,733	4,724	3,501	8,304	12,348	2,156	9,593	17,836	13,143	2,635	3,567	13,348	2,321	8,916	9,950	9,787	17,451	4,455	9,929	10,160
Hobart, Australia	16,761	11,955	8,645	4,913	18,224	8,162	10,428	12,525	18,197	9,827	10,720	17,483	9,535	16,123	16,945	16,697	15,293	3,319	10,958	15,650
Hohhot, China	8,416	3,059	1,844	8,786	10,316	1,778	11,419	15,040	9,973	2,582	2,963	10,069	2,446	6,631	7,874	7,828	14,634	7,706	11,532	9,132
Hong Kong	10,468	4,307	2,028	7,857	12,021	672	10,853	16,445	12,041	2,639	3,500	12,131	2,317	8,372	9,544	9,441	16,686	5,645	11,129	10,298
Honiara, Solomon Islands	12,882	10,343	5,696	2,112	17,416	5,898	13,772	12,165	14,580	8,690	9,590	14,009	8,356	13,966	15,234	15,236	15,828	5,189	14,311	16,396
Honolulu, Hawaii	7,870	11,105	7,086	4,149	12,742	8,318	19,484	7,716	9,167	11,071	11,478	8,494	10,863	11,615	12,358	12,605	10,740	10,898	19,977	14,726
Houston, Texas	4,229	11,894	11,508	10,050	7,303	12,811	14,244	3,405	4,038	13,672	13,182	3,363	13,768	8,761	8,494	8,782	4,647	17,124	13,728	10,034
Huambo, Angola	10,987	8,582	13,061	17,032	6,107	11,966	1,696	11,757	9,687	9,017	8,457	10,365	9,271	7,438	6,597	6,366	8,459	10,181	1,167	4,215
Hubli, India	10,700	3,054	5,878	11,756	9,297	4,724	6,943	17,746	11,343	1,922	1,892	11,862	2,098	6,486	7,180	6,947	14,332	6,468	7,116	6,817
Hugh Town, United Kingdom	3,906	5,962	9,822	15,387	2,110	10,030	8,854	9,637	3,444	8,068	7,161	4,117	8,370	1,770	1,017	1,306	6,774	14,579	8,390	3,115
Hull, Canada	2,089	9,790	10,868	11,862	5,167	11,941	12,803	5,303	1,642	11,793	11,124	932	11,974	6,335	6,062	6,353	4,605	17,948	12,260	7,771
Hyderabad, India	10,571	2,853	5,460	11,423	9,474	4,315	7,359	17,795	11,326	1,517	1,603	11,810	1,681	6,508	7,279	7,059	14,561	6,418	7,534	7,071
Hyderabad, Pakistan	9,436	2,027	5,998	12,502	8,123	5,078	7,180	16,453	10,027	2,031	1,370	10,551	2,343	5,172	5,910	5,689	13,237	7,767	7,231	5,816
Igloolik, Canada	857	7,402	8,290	11,242	5,669	9,282	13,239	7,798	2,705	9,251	8,696	2,473	9,394	4,873	5,222	5,500	7,158	15,366	12,761	7,506
Iloilo, Philippines	11,695	5,840	2,657	6,617	13,574	1,737	11,174	16,224	13,391	4,000	4,918	13,374	3,665	9,932	11,099	10,988	18,068	4,450	11,554	11,704
Indianapolis, Indiana	2,910	10,647	11,058	11,014	6,124	12,254	13,558	4,495	2,689	12,556	11,966	1,991	12,700	7,370	7,123	7,413	4,599	17,761	13,017	8,786
Innsbruck, Austria	4,981	4,862	9,184	15,556	2,888	9,159	8,098	10,950	4,761	6,899	5,971	5,415	7,215	939	417	370	7,919	13,256	7,694	2,477
Inuvik, Canada	2,855	7,444	6,814	9,286	7,671	8,001	14,958	8,333	4,650	8,843	8,554	4,261	8,885	6,206	6,872	7,120	8,714	13,832	14,540	9,245
Invercargill, New Zealand	16,076	13,520	9,643	4,323	18,413	9,425	11,277	10,823	16,823	11,427	12,342	16,117	11,121	17,707	18,651	18,398	13,777	5,023	11,763	16,942
Inverness, United Kingdom	3,432	5,514	9,060	14,567	2,924	9,363	9,527	9,835	3,410	7,653	6,784	4,001	7,935	1,466	1,440	1,716	7,282	14,365	9,087	3,789
Iquitos, Peru	7,499	14,639	15,901	11,889	7,171	17,202	10,765	1,937	6,113	16,772	15,870	5,889	17,060	10,471	9,499	9,683	2,043	16,310	10,384	9,530
Iraklion, Greece	6,719	4,297	9,126	16,039	3,867	8,735	6,641	12,349	6,453	6,006	5,079	7,130	6,340	2,172	1,996	1,708	8,972	11,752	6,307	1,839
Irkutsk, USSR	7,124	2,444	2,942	9,735	9,010	3,167	11,395	14,120	8,612	3,063	2,994	8,750	3,083	5,351	6,613	6,599	13,253	9,032	11,387	8,123
Islamabad, Pakistan	8,688	1,029	5,237	12,011	8,094	4,498	8,170	15,966	9,496	1,640	709	9,949	1,973	4,781	5,716	5,539	13,211	8,177	8,190	6,102
Istanbul, Turkey	6,352	3,743	8,493	15,365	4,147	8,185	7,279	12,480	6,312	5,593	4,656	6,951	5,923	1,668	1,921	1,678	9,280	11,707	6,968	2,489
Ivujivik, Canada	498	8,076	9,068	11,507	5,365	10,078	13,115	7,070	2,073	9,986	9,389	1,724	10,143	5,182	5,323	5,614	6,378	16,157	12,606	7,481
Iwo Jima Island, Japan	9,850	6,323	1,441	5,513	13,247	2,219	13,565	13,863	11,686	5,244	5,956	11,458	4,959	9,676	10,943	10,947	15,929	6,581	13,882	12,405
Izmir, Turkey	6,518	3,990	8,783	15,675	4,008	8,435	6,984	12,425	6,373	5,776	4,842	7,030	6,109	1,884	1,926	1,656	9,139	11,729	6,663	2,187
Jackson, Mississippi	3,809	11,535	11,569	10,578	6,739	12,831	13,802	3,645	3,486	13,404	12,847	2,823	13,529	8,252	7,945	8,231	4,356	17,623	13,276	9,467
Jaffna, Sri Lanka	11,440	3,720	5,779	11,169	10,078	4,520	6,992	18,562	12,151	2,155	2,445	12,656	2,208	7,301	7,996	7,760	15,050	5,649	7,236	7,538
Jakarta, Indonesia	13,603	6,333	5,055	7,980	13,520	3,815	8,814	17,981	14,952	4,192	5,048	15,205	3,932	10,440	11,321	11,112	18,373	2,633	9,253	10,969
Jamestown, St. Helena	10,320	10,436	15,222	17,249	5,505	14,247	3,432	9,428	8,653	11,231	10,571	9,215	11,509	8,125	6,984	6,847	6,303	11,922	2,962	4,843
Jamnagar, India	9,794	2,305	5,978	12,330	8,431	4,986	7,069	16,806	10,391	1,948	1,448	10,916	2,235	5,533	6,251	6,025	13,527	7,413	7,154	6,063
Jan Mayen Island	2,558	5,343	7,971	13,042	4,295	8,515	10,954	9,758	3,388	7,427	6,680	3,743	7,655	2,291	2,880	3,119	7,904	14,197	10,541	5,263
Jayapura, Indonesia	12,810	8,286	4,141	4,307	15,943	3,916	12,383	14,342	14,659	6,484	7,404	14,344	6,149	12,255	13,476	13,397	17,891	4,010	12,875	14,177
Jefferson City, Missouri	3,211	10,884	10,892	10,485	6,660	12,137	14,063	4,345	3,197	12,708	12,181	2,487	12,825	7,787	7,602	7,894	4,904	17,326	13,524	9,313
Jerusalem, Israel	7,521	3,662	8,564	15,492	4,866	8,012	6,324	13,362	7,413	5,146	4,244	8,072	5,481	2,833	2,959	2,682	9,940	10,737	6,074	2,562

Distances in Kilometers	Frobisher Bay, Canada	Frunze, USSR	Fukuoka, Japan	Funafuti Atoll, Tuvalu	Funchal, Madeira Island	Fuzhou, China	Gaborone, Botswana	Galapagos Islands (Santa Cruz)	Gander, Canada	Gangtok, India	Garyarsa, China	Gaspe, Canada	Gauhati, India	Gdansk, Poland	Geneva, Switzerland	Genoa, Italy	Georgetown, Guyana	Geraldton, Australia	Ghanzi, Botswana	Ghat, Libya
Jiggalong, Australia	15,469	8,734	6,388	6,417	15,772	5,477	9,419	15,730	17,141	6,593	7,468	17,145	6,316	12,865	13,724	13,501	18,164	858	9,944	13,059
Jinan, China	8,862	3,658	1,267	8,177	10,966	1,194	11,698	15,128	10,485	2,862	3,399	10,533	2,658	7,282	8,527	8,482	15,167	7,247	11,860	9,760
Jodhpur, India	9,474	1,849	5,529	12,033	8,482	4,599	7,580	16,664	10,192	1,553	936	10,679	1,867	5,385	6,205	5,999	13,612	7,539	7,654	6,249
Johannesburg, South Africa	12,906	9,013	12,652	15,062	8,070	11,361	278	12,801	11,656	8,781	8,482	12,334	8,956	8,970	8,317	8,059	9,974	8,345	821	5,980
Juazeiro do Norte, Brazil	8,243	12,497	16,901	15,425	5,009	16,939	7,183	5,712	6,397	14,115	13,235	6,675	14,446	8,683	7,435	7,485	2,602	15,151	6,739	6,437
Juneau, Alaska	3,449	8,472	7,185	8,500	8,388	8,468	15,959	7,592	5,059	9,713	9,515	4,529	9,717	7,283	7,868	8,129	8,563	13,895	15,502	10,213
Kabul, Afghanistan	8,494	1,042	5,561	12,372	7,727	4,860	7,988	15,701	9,224	2,015	1,086	9,700	2,348	4,460	5,363	5,180	12,850	8,477	7,980	5,727
Kalgoorlie, Australia	16,269	9,456	7,183	6,451	16,100	6,294	9,145	15,181	17,957	7,315	8,165	17,936	7,051	13,527	14,288	14,045	17,353	699	9,683	13,334
Kaliningrad, USSR	4,750	4,070	8,168	14,543	3,813	8,218	8,810	11,392	4,966	6,184	5,287	5,536	6,482	126	1,386	1,414	8,666	12,818	8,453	3,411
Kamloops, Canada	3,333	9,538	8,395	8,755	8,130	9,695	15,930	6,353	4,574	10,910	10,652	3,933	10,929	7,756	8,108	8,391	7,484	14,867	15,404	10,325
Kampala, Uganda	10,519	6,303	10,719	16,218	6,294	9,672	2,857	13,689	9,778	6,681	6,107	10,501	6,946	6,125	5,701	5,415	10,098	9,253	2,690	3,640
Kananga, Zaire	10,636	7,536	12,041	16,992	5,956	10,989	2,110	12,535	9,563	8,004	7,418	10,273	8,268	6,687	5,992	5,734	9,061	9,915	1,735	3,663
Kano, Nigeria	8,179	7,166	12,068	18,936	3,457	11,438	4,475	11,002	7,057	8,442	7,612	7,770	8,766	4,782	3,798	3,593	7,332	12,207	3,986	1,446
Kanpur, India	9,639	1,896	4,846	11,305	9,097	3,876	8,139	16,982	10,535	827	586	10,964	1,137	5,839	6,754	6,567	14,228	7,123	8,253	6,950
Kansas City, Missouri	3,237	10,858	10,723	10,286	6,836	11,980	14,275	4,421	3,341	12,643	12,143	2,624	12,748	7,860	7,715	8,009	5,108	17,109	13,736	9,471
Kaohsiung, Taiwan	10,398	4,759	1,567	7,279	12,392	395	11,452	15,909	12,060	3,231	4,058	12,075	2,917	8,711	9,919	9,837	16,744	5,720	11,741	10,824
Karachi, Pakistan	9,447	2,117	6,142	12,636	8,032	5,220	7,049	16,401	9,999	2,172	1,511	10,535	2,482	5,135	5,844	5,618	13,138	7,818	7,096	5,699
Karaganda, USSR	6,975	779	4,956	11,873	7,323	4,729	9,480	14,334	7,978	2,825	2,096	8,347	3,071	3,674	4,846	4,759	12,179	9,622	9,389	6,010
Karl-Marx-Stadt, East Germany	4,744	4,644	8,837	15,145	3,163	8,866	8,460	10,996	4,684	6,724	5,808	5,309	7,032	552	716	773	8,100	13,224	8,067	2,881
Kasanga, Tanzania	11,321	7,191	11,385	16,014	6,827	10,242	1,878	13,474	10,406	7,348	6,868	11,125	7,584	7,059	6,546	6,268	10,054	8,931	1,764	4,342
Kashgar, China	8,140	396	4,845	11,740	8,015	4,276	8,802	15,487	9,074	1,785	946	9,478	2,081	4,522	5,569	5,427	13,055	8,551	8,796	6,267
Kassel, West Germany	4,547	4,862	8,977	15,165	2,985	9,047	8,569	10,751	4,444	6,952	6,039	5,073	7,258	703	619	768	7,877	13,469	8,162	2,926
Kathmandu, Nepal	9,609	1,942	4,336	10,825	9,432	3,370	8,613	16,973	10,630	329	655	11,012	659	6,057	7,040	6,871	14,542	6,987	8,741	7,384
Kayes, Mali	6,987	8,612	13,333	18,703	2,089	13,055	5,930	8,845	5,482	10,249	9,348	6,137	10,583	5,141	3,886	3,842	5,174	14,272	5,388	2,543
Kazan, USSR	5,720	2,316	6,475	13,200	5,609	6,421	9,179	12,897	6,428	4,457	3,607	6,885	4,737	1,938	3,140	3,085	10,451	11,222	8,949	4,648
Kemi, Finland	4,024	3,962	7,324	13,351	4,604	7,602	10,032	11,179	4,728	6,090	5,289	5,161	6,343	1,317	2,445	2,565	8,986	12,888	9,691	4,653
Kenora, Canada	2,193	9,681	9,768	10,468	6,473	10,964	14,227	5,601	2,863	11,458	10,959	2,170	11,568	6,894	6,921	7,216	5,844	16,627	13,687	8,910
Kerguelen Island	17,064	10,249	10,991	10,677	12,445	9,714	4,659	14,127	16,041	8,719	9,064	16,714	8,668	12,452	12,239	11,949	13,232	4,437	5,196	10,117
Kerkira, Greece	6,074	4,517	9,211	15,994	3,379	8,953	7,142	11,786	5,798	6,376	5,439	6,471	6,706	1,643	1,338	1,053	8,512	12,358	6,774	1,861
Kermanshah, Iran	7,763	2,566	7,459	14,365	5,846	6,873	6,901	14,237	7,983	4,022	3,110	8,585	4,357	3,136	3,673	3,435	10,971	9,958	6,739	3,696
Khabarovsk, USSR	7,388	4,629	1,702	7,644	10,598	2,842	13,415	13,154	9,166	4,618	4,901	9,057	4,485	7,151	8,407	8,455	13,744	8,799	13,481	10,204
Kharkov, USSR	5,810	3,014	7,508	14,276	4,731	7,353	8,333	12,581	6,152	5,071	4,154	6,708	5,381	1,292	2,264	2,146	9,749	11,632	8,055	3,573
Khartoum, Sudan	8,996	5,007	9,774	16,320	5,314	8,952	4,512	13,554	8,511	5,908	5,150	9,221	6,220	4,465	4,185	3,892	9,891	10,088	4,276	2,550
Khon Kaen, Thailand	11,084	3,972	3,351	8,842	11,622	2,013	9,502	17,747	12,429	1,899	2,835	12,668	1,577	8,164	9,208	9,051	16,704	5,159	9,787	9,517
Kiev, USSR	5,542	3,422	7,848	14,536	4,329	7,737	8,331	12,195	5,791	5,483	4,565	6,364	5,793	915	1,857	1,751	9,337	12,023	8,021	3,323
Kigali, Rwanda	10,622	6,671	11,092	16,412	6,246	10,034	2,553	13,404	9,783	7,051	6,483	10,506	7,313	6,329	5,828	5,548	9,849	9,378	2,349	3,671
Kingston, Canada	2,230	9,936	10,969	11,812	5,242	12,055	12,840	5,157	1,750	11,937	11,270	1,053	12,116	6,474	6,186	6,476	4,515	18,030	12,296	7,866
Kingston, Jamaica	5,120	12,657	13,613	11,788	6,165	14,829	12,080	2,542	3,972	14,751	13,989	3,596	14,963	8,747	8,053	8,300	2,372	18,353	11,593	8,895
Kingstown, Saint Vincent	5,647	12,349	14,689	13,429	4,987	15,664	10,333	3,560	4,016	14,478	13,578	3,968	14,770	8,176	7,228	7,426	779	18,224	9,842	7,552
Kinshasa, Zaire	10,127	7,913	12,596	17,738	5,317	11,624	2,524	11,754	8,924	8,598	7,945	9,622	8,879	6,508	5,666	5,433	8,255	10,690	2,035	3,285
Kirkwall, United Kingdom	3,389	5,391	8,882	14,404	3,107	9,197	9,643	9,919	3,470	7,532	6,672	4,040	7,809	1,414	1,546	1,810	7,426	14,269	9,210	3,915
Kirov, USSR	5,469	2,447	6,371	13,011	5,639	6,394	9,482	12,702	6,252	4,585	3,766	6,682	4,851	1,951	3,195	3,170	10,384	11,375	9,245	4,843
Kiruna, Sweden	3,734	4,201	7,375	13,233	4,584	7,717	10,269	10,921	4,489	6,316	5,533	4,901	6,562	1,507	2,543	2,692	8,821	13,114	9,916	4,816
Kisangani, Zaire	10,139	6,792	11,388	17,012	5,664	10,402	2,785	12,868	9,224	7,378	6,742	9,945	7,657	6,000	5,394	5,123	9,279	9,983	2,469	3,153
Kishinev, USSR	5,787	3,589	8,148	14,901	4,158	7,971	7,942	12,232	5,905	5,586	4,656	6,509	5,906	1,086	1,733	1,570	9,234	11,987	7,626	2,951
Kitchner, Canada	2,385	10,124	10,918	11,496	5,572	12,046	13,142	4,982	2,076	12,089	11,453	1,370	12,254	6,753	6,499	6,790	4,610	17,899	12,598	8,198
Knoxville, Tennessee	3,262	11,004	11,523	11,188	6,057	12,719	13,301	4,107	2,783	12,955	12,332	2,134	13,110	7,581	7,242	7,528	4,162	18,111	12,765	8,771
Kosice, Czechoslovakia	5,304	4,111	8,515	15,096	3,634	8,432	8,139	11,634	5,326	6,150	5,225	5,943	6,465	654	1,169	1,055	8,668	12,585	7,782	2,806
Kota Kinabalu, Malaysia	12,261	5,767	3,396	7,181	13,466	2,251	10,308	17,039	13,852	3,744	4,681	13,932	3,418	9,949	11,035	10,887	18,458	3,848	10,701	11,321
Krakow, Poland	5,123	4,176	8,502	15,013	3,586	8,459	8,301	11,499	5,165	6,238	5,317	5,776	6,549	482	1,109	1,040	8,582	12,722	7,938	2,912
Kralendijk, Bonaire	5,727	12,837	14,572	12,661	5,689	15,695	10,987	2,825	4,269	14,979	14,114	4,081	15,248	8,720	7,846	8,060	1,258	18,143	10,511	8,301
Krasnodar, USSR	6,389	2,844	7,563	14,448	4,941	7,274	7,832	13,035	6,660	4,787	3,852	7,238	5,109	1,786	2,546	2,368	10,040	11,186	7,579	3,414
Krasnoyarsk, USSR	6,626	1,957	3,800	10,557	8,164	3,948	10,928	13,857	7,985	3,204	2,866	8,194	3,315	4,496	5,757	5,741	12,553	9,619	10,859	7,294
Kristiansand, Norway	3,937	4,791	8,520	14,444	3,401	8,732	9,329	10,559	4,113	6,928	6,055	4,676	7,212	785	1,337	1,531	7,983	13,637	8,928	3,692
Kuala Lumpur, Malaysia	12,538	5,156	4,498	8,690	12,454	3,157	8,732	18,664	13,796	3,015	3,873	14,091	2,761	9,271	10,184	9,985	17,538	3,793	9,104	10,022
Kuching, Malaysia	12,760	5,795	4,118	7,714	13,318	2,880	9,525	17,730	14,226	3,675	4,590	14,400	3,376	9,977	10,972	10,793	18,450	3,386	9,930	10,967
Kumasi, Ghana	8,219	8,385	13,281	19,790	3,280	12,694	4,575	9,891	6,812	9,701	8,869	7,484	10,024	5,591	4,443	4,306	6,248	12,924	4,037	2,382
Kumzar, Oman	8,931	2,471	7,037	13,688	7,005	6,217	6,528	15,470	9,239	3,194	2,403	9,830	3,517	4,376	4,923	4,676	12,082	8,706	6,484	4,620
Kunming, China	10,129	3,237	2,842	9,069	10,974	1,672	9,929	16,964	11,503	1,427	2,304	11,721	1,106	7,403	8,515	8,385	15,922	6,092	10,148	9,109
Kuqa Chang, China	8,112	758	4,189	11,103	8,476	3,687	9,401	15,472	9,210	1,607	1,083	9,550	1,830	4,883	6,005	5,889	13,416	8,383	9,418	6,873
Kurgan, USSR	6,206	1,547	5,473	12,276	6,621	5,408	9,632	13,545	7,162	3,642	2,885	7,542	3,890	2,938	4,156	4,102	11,386	10,440	9,473	5,575
Kuwait, Kuwait	8,295	2,809	7,629	14,442	6,107	6,930	6,430	14,583	8,447	3,972	3,108	9,066	4,303	3,637	4,066	3,810	11,189	9,568	6,298	3,760
Kuybyshev, USSR	6,000	2,136	6,483	13,282	5,690	6,356	8,940	13,142	6,666	4,267	3,396	7,138	4,556	2,062	3,212	3,130	10,604	11,002	8,724	4,567
Kyoto, Japan	8,850	5,256	517	6,632	11,995	1,859	13,285	13,914	10,649	4,531	5,100	10,506	4,298	8,427	9,695	9,706	15,155	7,400	13,495	11,245
Kzyl-Orda, USSR	7,311	764	5,594	12,536	6,983	5,200	8,679	14,569	8,104	2,828	1,943	8,550	3,128	3,475	4,527	4,393	12,007	9,550	8,583	5,391
L'vov, USSR	5,323	3,892	8,279	14,880	3,859	8,199	8,254	11,787	5,433	5,946	5,024	6,033	6,258	621	1,387	1,288	8,873	12,434	7,911	3,008
La Ceiba, Honduras	5,510	13,236	13,274	10,704	7,219	14,587	12,995	1,858	4,697	15,209	14,571	4,191	15,359	9,564	8,984	9,244	3,276	17,399	12,534	9,967
La Coruna, Spain	4,360	6,448	10,514	16,075	1,405	10,649	8,310	9,412	3,568	8,503	7,577	4,281	8,818	2,309	1,192	1,395	6,315	14,746	7,824	2,651
La Paz, Bolivia	8,897	15,438	17,365	12,126	7,701	18,703	9,659	3,005	7,372	17,351	16,427	7,245	17,686	11,279	10,160	10,290	2,802	14,987	9,348	9,650
La Paz, Mexico	5,348	12,562	10,957	8,467	8,902	12,313	15,608	3,487	5,536	13,958	13,714	4,829	13,955	10,038	9,937	10,230	5,876	15,550	15,130	11,615
La Ronge, Canada	2,257	9,144	8,844	9,875	7,008	10,062	14,807	6,327	3,464	10,776	10,367	2,845	10,854	6,839	7,076	7,364	6,785	15,697	14,281	9,239
Labrador City, Canada	1,207	8,764	10,273	12,355	4,550	11,229	12,341	6,328	970	10,801	10,102	489	10,998	5,299	5,106	5,400	5,179	17,316	11,808	6,982
Lagos, Nigeria	8,480	7,997	12,898	19,510	3,581	12,237	4,220	10,443	7,170	9,219	8,409	7,859	9,538	5,487	4,413	4,242	6,802	12,426	3,693	2,174
Lahore, Pakistan	8,943	1,256	5,206	11,910	8,300	4,404	8,079	16,224	9,752	1,465	576	10,206	1,800	5,024	5,940	5,757	13,426	7,926	8,121	6,246
Lambasa, Fiji	12,715	12,433	7,593	876	17,586	8,024	14,632	10,023	13,978	10,912	11,795	13,276	10,579	15,483	16,645	16,776	13,689	6,723	15,150	18,554
Lansing, Michigan	2,555	10,294	10,838	11,164	5,911	12,005	13,460	4,839	2,408	12,215	11,615	1,694	12,365	7,029	6,811	7,103	4,749	17,703	12,917	8,535
Lanzhou, China	8,920	2,601	2,452	9,279	10,214	1,851	10,572	15,826	10,349	1,721	2,203	10,530	1,577	6,546	7,738	7,651	14,900	7,265	10,704	8,717
Laoag, Philippines	10,885	5,106	1,964	7,076	12,798	883	11,299	16,124	12,552	3,426	4,302	12,563	3,098	9,130	10,320	10,226	17,236	5,237	11,623	11,104
Largeau, Chad	8,119	5,878	10,775	17,631	3,952	10,124	4,768	12,102	7,345	7,135	6,298	8,067	7,461	4,043	3,356	3,088	8,444	11,472	4,377	1,210
Las Vegas, Nevada	4,370	11,193	9,722	8,453	8,608	11,065	16,102	4,814	5,027	12,550	12,315	4,306	12,552	9,047	9,164	9,457	6,624	15,329	15,566	11,143
Launceston, Australia	16,627	11,830	8,480	4,816	18,300	8,006	10,520	12,608	18,123	9,706	10,604	17,420	9,411	16,007	16,868	16,628	15,432	3,256	11,053	15,669
Le Havre, France	4,254	5,557	9,578	15,460	2,346	9,708	8,603	10,100	3,899	7,646	6,732	4,564	7,953	1,379	582	876	7,182	14,114	8,158	2,859
Leipzig, East Germany	4,678	4,671	8,833	15,110	3,152	8,877	8,519	10,946	4,626	6,757	5,844	5,248	7,064	545	726	806	8,070	13,274	8,124	2,929
Leningrad, USSR	4,696	3,524	7,368	13,739	4,575	7,482	9,383	11,720	5,243	5,665	4,814	5,732	5,943	934	2,199	2,237	9,268	12,426	9,064	4,181
Leon, Spain	4,567	6,292	10,455	16,200	1,489	10,541	8,118	9,634	3,811	8,328	7,398	4,523	8,646	2,199	1,016	1,190	6,491	14,513	7,639	2,431
Lerwick, United Kingdom	3,392	5,257	8,715	14,275	3,270	9,035	9,718	10,025	3,562	7,399	6,546	4,113	7,673	1,352	1,625	1,877	7,577	14,152	9,293	4,005
Lhasa, China	9,497	2,081	3,732	10,290	9,768	2,798	9,199	16,789	10,659	354	1,054	10,981	389	6,272	7,330	7,184	14,814	6,931	9,337	7,858
Libreville, Gabon	9,377	7,981	12,814	18,570	4,514	11,974	3,291	11,114	8,114	8,925	8,192	8,806	9,226	6,042	5,086	4,878	7,540	11,511	2,774	2,721
Lilongwe, Malawi	11,995	7,550	11,466	15,462	7,461	10,252	1,443	13,674	11,053	7,478	7,092	11,770	7,686	7,706	7,218	6,939	10,408	8,396	1,523	5,013
Lima, Peru	8,436	15,637	16,352	11,305	8,077	17,707	10,737	1,940	7,108	17,759	16,839	6,857	18,058	11,457	10,453	10,624	2,952	15,320	10,423	10,299
Limerick, Ireland	3,575	5,975	9,658	15,059	2,323	9,933	9,199	9,508	3,213	8,101	7,209	3,866	8,394	1,808	1,287	1,582	6,778	14,712	8,735	3,458
Limoges, France	4,619	5,644	9,837	15,864	2,136	9,893	8,196	10,188	4,136	7,692	6,765	4,822	8,007	1,558	383	626	7,126	14,001	7,747	2,450
Limon, Costa Rica	6,076	13,725	14,033	11,032	7,188	15,346	12,382	1,430	5,061	15,778	15,061	4,639	15,962	9,859	9,154	9,397	2,761	17,242	11,944	9,872
Lincoln, Nebraska	3,140	10,691	10,462	10,139	6,938	11,722	14,458	4,635	3,397	12,439	11,964	2,674	12,536	7,803	7,714	8,008	5,365	16,885	13,916	9,536
Linz, Austria	5,026	4,620	8,946	15,372	3,133	8,913	8,164	11,145	4,899	6,665	5,740	5,539	6,980	738	658	596	8,152	13,068	7,774	2,615
Lisbon, Portugal	4,742	6,776	10,981	16,560	974	11,056	7,910	9,297	3,768	8,783	7,849	4,491	9,105	2,720	1,504	1,631	6,049	14,778	7,412	2,372
Little Rock, Arkansas	3,612	11,304	11,235	10,420	6,818	12,499	14,033	3,922	3,456	13,133	12,604	2,765	13,248	8,140	7,899	8,189	4,667	17,404	13,501	9,516
Liverpool, United Kingdom	3,789	5,596	9,373	15,022	2,561	9,600	9,090	9,891	3,563	7,719	6,825	4,199	8,013	1,423	1,037	1,327	7,150	14,329	8,644	3,345
Lodz, Poland	4,958	4,176	8,417	14,866	3,620	8,412	8,488	11,418	5,050	6,260	5,347	5,649	6,566	294	1,150	1,129	8,566	12,802	8,125	3,076
Lome, Togo	8,408	8,196	13,098	19,669	3,484	12,460	4,333	10,204	7,050	9,449	8,632	7,731	9,769	5,573	4,466	4,308	6,565	12,620	3,799	2,293

Distances in Kilometers	Frobisher Bay, Canada	Frunze, USSR	Fukuoka, Japan	Funafuti Atoll, Tuvalu	Funchal, Madeira Island	Fuzhou, China	Gaborone, Botswana	Galapagos Islands (Santa Cruz)	Gander, Canada	Gangtok, India	Garyarsa, China	Gaspe, Canada	Gauhati, India	Gdansk, Poland	Geneva, Switzerland	Genoa, Italy	Georgetown, Guyana	Geraldton, Australia	Ghanzi, Botswana	Ghat, Libya
London, United Kingdom	4,079	5,491	9,418	15,238	2,501	9,584	8,813	10,082	3,809	7,597	6,691	4,458	7,898	1,298	748	1,037	7,245	14,138	8,372	3,073
Londonderry, United Kingdom	3,462	5,791	9,395	14,817	2,596	9,691	9,379	9,621	3,252	7,926	7,045	3,878	8,213	1,669	1,364	1,655	6,981	14,593	8,924	3,632
Longlac, Canada	1,892	9,573	10,080	11,038	5,913	11,223	13,655	5,599	2,303	11,450	10,881	1,601	11,589	6,531	6,467	6,762	5,451	17,072	13,115	8,388
Lord Howe Island, Australia	15,149	11,909	7,813	3,289	19,629	7,652	12,047	11,914	16,603	9,913	10,849	15,916	9,589	15,995	17,182	17,056	15,284	4,267	12,580	16,902
Los Angeles, California	4,716	11,383	9,655	8,102	8,972	11,007	16,415	4,819	5,394	12,647	12,465	4,673	12,629	9,377	9,519	9,813	6,846	15,022	15,884	11,510
Louangphrabang, Laos	10,699	3,626	3,181	8,995	11,316	1,888	9,612	17,487	12,043	1,607	2,541	12,281	1,274	7,818	8,884	8,735	16,361	5,546	9,868	9,292
Louisville, Kentucky	3,061	10,802	11,222	11,038	6,139	12,422	13,503	4,331	2,756	12,722	12,124	2,072	12,868	7,482	7,205	7,494	4,456	17,865	12,964	8,822
Luanda, Angola	10,474	8,436	13,064	17,546	5,590	12,043	2,212	11,505	9,172	9,041	8,421	9,853	9,312	7,017	6,132	5,909	8,108	10,640	1,684	3,750
Lubumbashi, Zaire	11,455	7,711	11,915	16,177	6,802	10,759	1,448	13,034	10,408	7,881	7,405	11,119	8,114	7,362	6,754	6,487	9,697	9,123	1,252	4,466
Lusaka, Zambia	11,865	8,003	12,055	15,860	7,169	10,854	1,054	13,064	10,779	8,047	7,623	11,485	8,264	7,784	7,176	6,910	9,838	8,853	966	4,881
Luxembourg, Luxembourg	4,533	5,147	9,281	15,404	2,680	9,351	8,456	10,533	4,298	7,225	6,307	4,949	7,534	1,008	378	615	7,598	13,682	8,033	2,757
Luxor, Egypt	8,003	4,252	9,140	16,006	4,839	8,493	5,618	13,327	7,709	5,534	4,674	8,397	5,864	3,385	3,271	2,978	9,773	10,626	5,358	2,261
Lynn Lake, Canada	1,929	8,942	8,881	10,181	6,698	10,067	14,493	6,445	3,178	10,632	10,186	2,584	10,726	6,528	6,749	7,038	6,686	15,829	13,971	8,911
Lyon, France	4,801	5,392	9,659	15,842	2,364	9,673	8,084	10,468	4,391	7,427	6,498	5,070	7,744	1,372	114	355	7,392	13,722	7,649	2,355
Macapa, Brazil	7,213	12,825	16,280	14,394	5,084	16,938	8,699	4,379	5,431	14,759	13,824	5,559	15,091	8,704	7,552	7,674	1,088	16,483	8,244	7,132
Madison, Wisconsin	2,660	10,350	10,605	10,771	6,286	11,807	13,858	4,842	2,746	12,207	11,655	2,024	12,336	7,247	7,097	7,391	5,049	17,350	13,315	8,884
Madras, India	11,080	3,350	5,541	11,182	9,897	4,319	7,233	18,297	11,837	1,801	2,067	12,324	1,881	7,008	7,750	7,523	14,938	5,922	7,451	7,423
Madrid, Spain	4,857	6,280	10,559	16,461	1,462	10,586	7,828	9,777	4,068	8,280	7,345	4,784	8,602	2,274	1,025	1,130	6,553	14,333	7,351	2,144
Madurai, India	11,361	3,669	5,931	11,378	9,889	4,687	6,839	18,388	12,022	2,219	2,427	12,541	2,301	7,161	7,830	7,590	14,845	5,806	7,071	7,337
Magadan, USSR	5,930	5,298	3,254	7,958	9,724	4,439	14,286	11,645	7,756	5,869	5,935	7,570	5,802	6,676	7,846	7,964	12,215	10,339	14,209	9,970
Magdalena, Bolivia	8,555	14,888	17,330	12,636	7,149	18,550	9,410	3,217	6,962	16,798	15,872	6,886	17,133	10,741	9,611	9,738	2,322	15,345	9,066	9,105
Magdeburg, East Germany	4,576	4,694	8,803	15,033	3,162	8,870	8,624	10,885	4,545	6,789	5,880	5,162	7,093	526	775	885	8,043	13,335	8,227	3,022
Majuro Atoll, Marshall Isls.	10,715	10,009	5,114	1,943	15,520	5,875	15,857	10,957	12,368	8,923	9,679	11,791	8,619	12,725	13,913	14,024	14,341	7,250	16,377	15,906
Malabo, Equatorial Guinea	9,010	7,771	12,640	18,840	4,170	11,864	3,649	11,042	7,776	8,820	8,055	8,475	9,129	5,682	4,711	4,506	7,424	11,758	3,139	2,353
Male, Maldives	11,856	4,311	6,731	11,807	9,811	5,459	6,043	18,203	12,306	3,043	3,156	12,886	3,134	7,437	7,953	7,692	14,531	5,699	6,301	7,138
Manado, Indonesia	12,685	6,769	3,600	6,124	14,505	2,786	10,990	16,116	14,416	4,807	5,743	14,358	4,476	10,916	12,047	11,916	19,033	3,522	11,430	12,417
Managua, Nicaragua	5,895	13,608	13,633	10,709	7,370	14,957	12,800	1,485	5,015	15,602	14,945	4,539	15,758	9,865	9,232	9,485	3,142	17,179	12,357	10,091
Manama, Bahrain	8,720	2,860	7,563	14,266	6,479	6,781	6,225	14,977	8,881	3,770	2,957	9,501	4,095	4,071	4,490	4,230	11,526	9,152	6,133	4,045
Manaus, Brazil	7,452	13,734	16,466	13,346	6,024	17,464	9,459	3,390	5,794	15,745	14,808	5,774	16,072	9,559	8,461	8,605	1,117	16,429	9,041	8,179
Manchester, New Hampshire	2,318	9,908	11,239	12,230	4,852	12,278	12,413	5,189	1,459	11,956	11,246	844	12,155	6,291	5,919	6,205	4,217	18,337	11,869	7,509
Mandalay, Burma	10,404	3,056	3,597	9,659	10,682	2,401	9,175	17,541	11,628	959	1,895	11,926	640	7,241	8,271	8,111	15,771	5,959	9,394	8,620
Mangareva Island, Fr.Polynesia	11,202	16,523	11,807	5,152	13,920	12,609	14,332	5,419	11,242	15,638	16,426	10,585	15,318	15,904	15,697	15,976	8,973	10,617	14,461	16,489
Manila, Philippines	11,281	5,414	2,309	6,907	13,135	1,285	11,185	16,250	12,954	3,637	4,540	12,960	3,304	9,482	10,658	10,553	17,638	4,846	11,536	11,342
Mannheim, West Germany	4,653	4,991	9,172	15,381	2,812	9,216	8,393	10,703	4,458	7,063	6,144	5,104	7,373	885	404	564	7,758	13,513	7,979	2,725
Maputo, Mozambique	13,104	8,757	12,243	14,762	8,339	10,940	686	13,241	11,944	8,416	8,159	12,635	8,580	8,998	8,425	8,156	10,417	7,947	1,202	6,128
Mar del Plata, Argentina	11,321	15,982	19,150	12,211	8,882	18,651	7,821	5,329	9,636	16,660	16,149	9,643	16,861	12,544	11,285	11,309	4,960	12,569	7,661	9,924
Maracaibo, Venezuela	5,898	13,157	14,586	12,283	6,087	15,773	11,258	2,425	4,529	15,296	14,450	4,283	15,552	9,071	8,222	8,440	1,540	17,901	10,794	8,702
Marrakech, Morocco	5,460	7,140	11,576	17,343	847	11,525	7,199	9,329	4,319	9,042	8,106	5,039	9,373	3,291	2,024	2,048	5,880	14,555	6,690	1,927
Marseilles, France	5,043	5,462	9,829	16,103	2,279	9,793	7,813	10,528	4,559	7,461	6,528	5,249	7,783	1,563	328	311	7,367	13,635	7,375	2,080
Maseru, Lesotho	13,177	9,335	12,858	14,842	8,304	11,548	539	12,656	11,870	9,040	8,772	12,535	9,204	9,308	8,635	8,380	9,962	8,255	1,032	6,285
Mashhad, Iran	8,014	1,479	6,325	13,208	6,850	5,713	7,621	14,997	8,555	2,908	1,979	9,082	3,242	3,708	4,522	4,325	11,980	9,219	7,540	4,847
Mazatlan, Mexico	5,294	12,684	11,316	8,823	8,616	12,670	15,200	3,159	5,331	14,185	13,879	4,638	14,203	9,946	9,769	10,060	5,467	15,898	14,724	11,352
Mbabane, Swaziland	13,068	8,863	12,387	14,840	8,274	11,087	557	13,092	11,873	8,551	8,284	12,559	8,717	9,017	8,417	8,152	10,278	8,063	1,087	6,105
Mbandaka, Zaire	9,840	7,333	12,048	17,714	5,157	11,115	2,858	12,095	8,761	8,075	7,397	9,473	8,364	6,018	5,247	4,999	8,518	10,637	2,424	2,889
McMurdo Sound, Antarctica	17,643	14,625	12,544	7,709	15,010	11,882	8,353	10,284	16,410	12,630	13,296	16,197	12,435	17,099	16,394	16,166	11,760	5,988	8,752	14,012
Mecca, Saudi Arabia	8,748	4,006	8,776	15,445	5,696	7,990	5,320	14,160	8,553	4,963	4,171	9,232	5,282	4,063	4,098	3,809	10,563	9,758	5,146	3,052
Medan, Indonesia	12,460	4,964	4,677	9,030	12,156	3,324	8,450	18,977	13,640	2,837	3,659	13,974	2,608	9,037	9,918	9,712	17,214	3,965	8,810	9,696
Medellin, Colombia	6,406	13,790	14,822	11,797	6,720	16,088	11,464	1,812	5,129	15,923	15,093	4,835	16,168	9,722	8,877	9,094	1,927	17,296	11,030	9,300
Medicine Hat, Canada	2,910	9,694	8,971	9,351	7,556	10,244	15,348	5,940	3,965	11,225	10,879	3,298	11,277	7,509	7,734	8,024	6,822	15,554	14,812	9,867
Medina, Saudi Arabia	8,437	3,794	8,620	15,387	5,539	7,890	5,633	14,037	8,292	4,891	4,062	8,962	5,217	3,744	3,832	3,546	10,486	9,954	5,446	2,971
Melbourne, Australia	16,366	11,422	8,050	4,720	18,282	7,568	10,621	12,935	18,013	9,306	10,212	17,356	9,007	15,609	16,529	16,305	15,855	2,989	11,160	15,546
Memphis, Tennessee	3,507	11,225	11,315	10,626	6,613	12,563	13,837	3,959	3,271	13,090	12,535	2,589	13,216	7,989	7,722	8,011	4,525	17,598	13,303	9,316
Merauke, Indonesia	13,456	8,733	4,771	4,270	16,458	4,449	12,033	14,322	15,306	6,836	7,769	14,968	6,503	12,786	13,980	13,878	17,988	3,508	12,544	14,447
Merida, Mexico	5,009	12,752	12,634	10,481	7,212	13,943	13,459	2,391	4,387	14,657	14,075	3,814	14,786	9,256	8,784	9,057	3,732	17,440	12,976	9,979
Meridian, Mississippi	3,762	11,499	11,640	10,718	6,606	12,892	13,665	3,657	3,377	13,391	12,816	2,725	13,525	8,165	7,837	8,123	4,244	17,763	13,138	9,337
Messina, Italy	6,000	4,926	9,602	16,333	2,997	9,361	7,040	11,447	5,587	6,777	5,841	6,277	7,109	1,812	1,180	886	8,126	12,662	6,646	1,551
Mexico City, Mexico	5,439	13,077	12,143	9,469	8,171	13,491	14,366	2,414	5,140	14,767	14,344	4,500	14,828	9,938	9,594	9,876	4,643	16,458	13,903	10,938
Miami, Florida	4,305	11,976	12,687	11,489	6,113	13,900	12,689	3,121	3,395	14,008	13,314	2,900	14,191	8,265	7,721	7,988	3,144	18,529	12,176	8,881
Midway Islands, USA	8,097	9,249	4,978	4,080	12,965	6,209	17,681	9,752	9,752	8,987	9,455	9,195	8,766	10,730	11,758	11,938	12,444	9,603	17,962	14,067
Milan, Italy	5,035	5,090	9,445	15,798	2,653	9,408	7,949	10,808	4,706	7,107	6,175	5,377	7,425	1,197	249	118	7,715	13,382	7,532	2,276
Milford Sound, New Zealand	15,947	13,377	9,447	4,145	18,619	9,247	11,418	10,898	16,787	11,298	12,218	16,073	10,988	17,554	18,573	18,343	13,916	4,969	11,910	17,045
Milwaukee, Wisconsin	2,617	10,328	10,671	10,891	6,171	11,862	13,738	4,843	2,639	12,205	11,638	1,919	12,340	7,175	7,006	7,299	4,961	17,456	13,194	8,776
Minsk, USSR	5,112	3,614	7,830	14,370	4,213	7,817	8,706	11,855	5,416	5,720	4,820	5,971	6,020	584	1,746	1,711	9,122	12,352	8,379	3,522
Mogadiscio, Somalia	10,948	5,375	9,427	14,867	7,310	8,310	3,629	15,111	10,565	5,387	4,925	11,273	5,626	6,286	6,195	5,900	11,486	8,114	3,664	4,547
Mombasa, Kenya	11,296	6,276	10,329	15,326	7,209	9,180	2,717	14,457	10,660	6,297	5,852	11,382	6,528	6,760	6,473	6,181	10,936	8,330	2,737	4,524
Monclova, Mexico	4,730	12,266	11,370	9,407	7,976	12,706	14,779	3,268	4,686	13,909	13,511	3,998	13,966	9,343	9,131	9,421	5,082	16,489	14,278	10,707
Moncton, Canada	1,979	9,363	11,049	12,690	4,314	12,001	11,993	5,753	828	11,443	10,700	305	11,658	5,669	5,287	5,574	4,402	18,080	11,451	6,923
Monrovia, Liberia	7,837	9,162	13,999	18,913	2,982	13,557	5,251	8,874	6,261	10,619	9,758	6,885	10,947	5,947	4,712	4,639	5,237	13,787	4,708	3,043
Monte Carlo, Monaco	5,103	5,294	9,681	16,021	2,448	9,631	7,806	10,687	4,677	7,291	6,358	5,361	7,613	1,435	291	144	7,537	13,483	7,378	2,097
Monterrey, Mexico	4,820	12,395	11,545	9,486	7,943	12,882	14,646	3,100	4,705	14,063	13,650	4,027	14,125	9,404	9,159	9,447	4,936	16,567	14,151	10,685
Montevideo, Uruguay	10,988	15,724	19,403	12,485	8,527	18,941	7,803	5,194	9,287	16,585	15,997	9,309	16,816	12,194	10,939	10,969	4,618	12,894	7,611	9,632
Montgomery, Alabama	3,702	11,445	11,757	10,943	6,395	12,992	13,444	3,679	3,214	13,374	12,770	2,580	13,520	8,032	7,670	7,954	4,064	17,987	12,916	9,133
Montpelier, Vermont	2,184	9,815	11,077	12,123	4,930	12,123	12,533	5,278	1,467	11,850	11,153	802	12,043	6,254	5,921	6,209	4,382	18,173	11,990	7,563
Montpellier, France	4,943	5,560	9,887	16,090	2,182	9,874	7,887	10,404	4,435	7,569	6,636	5,128	7,889	1,606	341	416	7,256	13,761	7,444	2,145
Montreal, Canada	2,056	9,720	10,920	12,027	5,000	11,971	12,641	5,371	1,484	11,742	11,057	784	11,930	6,213	5,917	6,207	4,540	18,015	12,098	7,608
Moosonee, Canada	1,561	9,299	10,126	11,454	5,480	11,215	13,244	5,827	1,870	11,233	10,621	1,187	11,391	6,125	6,027	6,322	5,350	17,203	12,706	7,939
Moroni, Comoros	12,229	6,835	10,462	14,660	8,052	9,220	2,328	14,733	11,555	6,526	6,224	12,278	6,713	7,676	7,405	7,113	11,411	7,587	2,536	5,417
Moscow, USSR	5,329	2,997	7,163	13,784	4,885	7,144	8,979	12,328	5,853	5,127	4,250	6,357	5,417	1,215	2,421	2,380	9,746	11,843	8,696	4,079
Mosul, Iraq	7,405	2,781	7,680	14,616	5,441	7,165	6,991	13,815	7,574	4,378	3,454	8,183	4,713	2,745	3,251	3,014	10,571	10,380	6,791	3,380
Mount Isa, Australia	14,789	9,676	6,088	4,464	17,340	5,621	11,259	14,112	16,634	7,637	8,570	16,233	7,317	13,844	14,946	14,790	17,573	2,665	11,796	14,838
Multan, Pakistan	9,017	1,438	5,512	12,182	8,139	4,686	7,779	16,220	9,744	1,701	866	10,225	2,034	4,958	5,818	5,622	13,272	7,970	7,815	6,010
Munich, West Germany	4,913	4,819	9,108	15,459	2,942	9,098	8,190	10,949	4,728	6,867	5,942	5,376	7,181	848	464	462	7,951	13,262	7,788	2,576
Murcia, Spain	5,204	6,226	10,635	16,741	1,551	10,588	7,488	9,991	4,399	8,177	7,240	5,117	8,504	2,359	1,093	1,105	6,683	14,073	7,014	1,796
Murmansk, USSR	4,060	3,752	6,846	12,857	5,095	7,175	10,400	11,345	4,963	5,842	5,090	5,334	6,076	1,788	2,949	3,061	9,353	12,628	10,081	5,124
Mururoa Atoll, Fr. Polynesia	11,248	16,139	11,385	4,725	14,233	12,179	14,604	5,760	11,411	15,207	15,996	10,736	14,888	15,941	15,869	16,157	9,348	10,354	14,767	16,862
Muscat, Oman	9,291	2,598	6,976	13,502	7,333	6,087	6,402	15,819	9,611	3,041	2,325	10,202	3,352	4,748	5,285	5,036	12,383	8,343	6,394	4,890
Myitkyina, Burma	10,047	2,846	3,311	9,596	10,549	2,196	9,479	17,144	11,317	903	1,807	11,590	575	7,037	8,109	7,964	15,580	6,268	9,677	8,605
Naga, Philippines	11,366	5,655	2,327	6,650	13,365	1,437	11,362	16,065	13,069	3,895	4,795	13,045	3,561	9,703	10,888	10,788	17,740	4,781	11,725	11,599
Nagasaki, Japan	9,179	4,905	98	6,933	11,974	1,270	12,705	14,503	10,939	4,003	4,626	10,851	3,754	8,334	9,598	9,582	15,540	7,004	12,928	10,982
Nagoya, Japan	8,812	5,340	624	6,560	12,020	1,962	13,393	13,812	10,618	4,637	5,200	10,463	4,404	8,468	9,736	9,751	15,100	7,455	13,603	11,312
Nagpur, India	10,182	2,448	5,204	11,391	9,305	4,123	7,670	17,470	10,994	1,184	1,181	11,456	1,403	6,216	7,045	6,837	14,428	6,711	7,818	6,999
Nairobi, Kenya	10,883	6,182	10,425	15,717	6,770	9,327	2,841	14,157	10,221	6,380	5,867	10,944	6,629	6,390	6,058	5,768	10,586	8,755	2,774	4,085
Nanchang, China	9,751	4,003	1,486	7,933	11,593	444	11,287	15,842	11,355	2,680	3,421	11,419	2,400	7,910	9,122	9,045	16,028	6,359	11,516	10,106
Nancy, France	4,613	5,177	9,351	15,503	2,625	9,404	8,358	10,546	4,343	7,244	6,323	5,000	7,555	1,068	276	519	7,575	13,665	7,934	2,655
Nandi, Fiji	12,944	12,370	7,565	1,044	17,834	7,942	14,391	10,229	14,229	10,791	11,685	13,530	10,457	15,561	16,755	16,865	13,889	6,470	14,912	18,484
Nanjing, China	9,365	4,039	1,100	7,819	11,473	663	11,680	15,383	11,009	2,956	3,615	11,040	2,704	7,785	9,021	8,966	15,693	6,745	11,888	10,160
Nanning, China	10,404	3,821	2,467	8,451	11,562	1,170	10,331	16,836	11,878	2,047	2,929	12,037	1,720	7,956	9,093	8,973	16,418	5,747	10,586	9,734
Nantes, France	4,364	5,774	9,854	15,714	2,076	9,965	8,425	9,973	3,877	7,845	6,924	4,561	8,156	1,623	601	873	6,975	14,227	7,969	2,679
Naples, Italy	5,692	4,906	9,494	16,128	2,910	9,317	7,351	11,287	5,325	6,821	5,884	6,007	7,149	1,538	884	589	8,041	12,859	6,952	1,800
Narvik, Norway	3,602	4,328	7,439	13,217	4,539	7,804	10,347	10,790	4,364	6,441	5,662	4,770	6,684	1,571	2,557	2,719	8,717	13,237	9,987	4,857

Distances in Kilometers	Frobisher Bay, Canada	Frunze, USSR	Fukuoka, Japan	Funafuti Atoll, Tuvalu	Funchal, Madeira Island	Fuzhou, China	Gaborone, Botswana	Galapagos Islands (Santa Cruz)	Gander, Canada	Gangtok, India	Garyarsa, China	Gaspe, Canada	Gauhati, India	Gdansk, Poland	Geneva, Switzerland	Genoa, Italy	Georgetown, Guyana	Geraldton, Australia	Ghanzi, Botswana	Ghat, Libya
Nashville, Tennessee	3,309	11,049	11,375	10,932	6,295	12,594	13,559	4,091	2,968	12,960	12,369	2,296	13,102	7,721	7,424	7,712	4,365	17,860	13,023	8,998
Nassau, Bahamas	4,345	11,950	12,883	11,771	5,880	14,070	12,393	3,173	3,306	14,014	13,287	2,865	14,213	8,153	7,560	7,823	2,875	18,774	11,880	8,647
Natal, Brazil	8,200	12,058	16,592	15,905	4,673	16,503	6,832	6,155	6,351	13,641	12,767	6,687	13,970	8,320	7,063	7,097	2,905	15,010	6,372	5,976
Natashquan, Canada	1,561	8,858	10,646	12,780	4,149	11,555	11,919	6,254	539	10,937	10,195	246	11,152	5,208	4,896	5,186	4,823	17,606	11,383	6,656
Nauru Island	11,681	10,242	5,371	1,615	16,429	5,898	14,986	11,430	13,341	8,888	9,720	12,760	8,566	13,375	14,610	14,683	14,982	6,372	15,520	16,336
Ndjamena, Chad	8,489	6,632	11,519	18,248	3,971	10,813	4,237	11,713	7,519	7,793	6,987	8,240	8,112	4,696	3,870	3,627	8,041	11,577	3,798	1,512
Nelson, New Zealand	15,384	13,570	9,381	3,676	18,696	9,305	11,969	10,496	16,221	11,546	12,478	15,504	11,226	17,643	18,847	18,697	13,673	5,427	12,454	17,623
Nema, Mauritania	6,963	8,116	12,870	18,884	2,023	12,556	5,814	9,305	5,568	9,740	8,839	6,250	10,074	4,745	3,509	3,437	5,641	13,963	5,280	2,034
Neuquen, Argentina	11,385	16,874	18,265	11,336	9,526	18,425	8,653	4,814	9,827	17,504	17,063	9,731	17,662	13,214	11,977	12,030	5,167	12,503	8,524	10,774
New Delhi, India	9,335	1,604	5,051	11,627	8,708	4,154	8,057	16,644	10,179	1,132	464	10,624	1,461	5,457	6,363	6,176	13,838	7,494	8,137	6,589
New Glasgow, Canada	2,055	9,332	11,140	12,865	4,146	12,066	11,818	5,801	713	11,425	10,666	387	11,647	5,583	5,166	5,450	4,320	18,123	11,276	6,766
New Haven, Connecticut	2,514	10,128	11,378	12,132	4,992	12,439	12,485	4,968	1,665	12,172	11,466	1,067	12,368	6,510	6,122	6,406	4,092	18,460	11,941	7,672
New Orleans, Louisiana	4,054	11,787	11,790	10,560	6,827	13,063	13,744	3,386	3,656	13,662	13,100	3,013	13,788	8,458	8,115	8,399	4,207	17,636	13,225	9,571
New Plymouth, New Zealand	15,143	13,499	9,220	3,422	18,798	9,189	12,216	10,447	16,036	11,507	12,442	15,316	11,184	17,503	18,749	18,650	13,700	5,520	12,703	17,842
New York, New York	2,589	10,224	11,408	12,047	5,092	12,484	12,558	4,870	1,778	12,262	11,562	1,174	12,455	6,621	6,235	6,519	4,073	18,471	12,015	7,778
Newcastle upon Tyne, UK	3,735	5,449	9,178	14,849	2,759	9,416	9,209	9,987	3,614	7,579	6,692	4,231	7,869	1,305	1,121	1,398	7,307	14,228	8,771	3,473
Newcastle Waters, Australia	14,593	8,978	5,651	5,046	16,603	5,047	10,893	14,836	16,432	6,918	7,848	16,165	6,601	13,162	14,232	14,068	18,303	2,296	11,418	14,117
Niamey, Niger	7,717	7,576	12,457	19,371	2,867	11,940	4,952	10,305	6,477	8,996	8,135	7,179	9,325	4,756	3,643	3,486	6,633	12,905	4,436	1,524
Nicosia, Cyprus	7,107	3,634	8,514	15,455	4,608	8,046	6,669	13,068	7,028	5,268	4,346	7,680	5,603	2,418	2,587	2,318	9,721	11,072	6,397	2,496
Niue (Alofi)	12,445	13,489	8,600	1,657	16,941	9,132	14,880	8,893	13,422	12,062	12,932	12,700	11,731	16,016	16,969	17,186	12,547	7,642	15,340	19,346
Norfolk, Virginia	3,038	10,696	11,733	11,874	5,371	12,851	12,652	4,398	2,209	12,728	12,033	1,640	12,916	7,073	6,647	6,928	3,803	18,662	12,112	8,096
Norfolk Island, Australia	14,495	12,397	7,981	2,555	19,407	8,012	12,817	11,115	15,796	10,504	11,439	15,090	10,172	16,269	17,532	17,493	14,605	5,157	13,341	17,781
Noril'sk, USSR	5,124	3,044	4,753	10,926	7,208	5,223	11,536	12,379	6,536	4,670	4,209	6,708	4,804	3,753	4,996	5,061	11,172	11,089	11,349	6,957
Norman Wells, Canada	2,707	7,867	7,223	9,301	7,612	8,429	15,092	7,877	4,434	9,295	8,993	3,988	9,340	6,417	6,997	7,257	8,340	14,193	14,643	9,348
Normanton, Australia	14,416	9,536	5,784	4,240	17,262	5,384	11,581	14,045	16,259	7,539	8,475	15,855	7,213	13,671	14,814	14,679	17,617	2,967	12,114	14,901
North Pole	2,931	5,251	6,284	10,942	6,392	7,115	12,733	10,072	4,579	6,978	6,488	4,592	7,105	3,979	4,886	5,084	9,251	13,185	12,390	7,242
Nottingham, United Kingdom	3,912	5,499	9,337	15,075	2,587	9,537	8,991	10,012	3,694	7,618	6,720	4,332	7,914	1,316	920	1,205	7,241	14,209	8,550	3,251
Norway House, Canada	1,984	9,245	9,257	10,315	6,581	10,446	14,379	6,093	3,006	10,974	10,505	2,366	11,076	6,662	6,800	7,092	6,326	16,176	13,848	8,894
Norwich, United Kingdom	4,056	5,356	9,259	15,109	2,660	9,430	8,891	10,178	3,864	7,468	6,567	4,500	7,767	1,165	797	1,073	7,382	14,042	8,457	3,161
Nouakchott, Mauritania	6,418	8,706	13,269	18,081	1,613	13,141	6,557	8,394	4,871	10,468	9,547	5,517	10,803	4,990	3,722	3,729	4,744	14,878	6,014	2,807
Noumea, New Caledonia	13,900	11,807	7,268	2,039	18,811	7,380	13,298	11,345	15,352	10,007	10,934	14,676	9,672	15,546	16,814	16,808	14,952	5,222	13,834	17,595
Novosibirsk, USSR	6,604	1,478	4,356	11,175	7,682	4,363	10,358	13,943	7,820	3,111	2,595	8,098	3,284	3,995	5,239	5,201	12,268	9,766	10,268	6,681
Nuku'alofa, Tonga	12,912	13,205	8,363	1,523	17,527	8,789	14,452	9,453	13,975	11,649	12,543	13,255	11,315	16,138	17,221	17,395	13,091	7,042	14,937	19,326
Nukunono Island, Tokelau Isls.	11,576	12,613	7,716	989	16,365	8,395	15,795	9,075	12,755	11,413	12,223	12,049	11,094	14,910	15,899	16,101	12,736	7,923	16,293	18,246
Nuremberg, West Germany	4,778	4,811	9,037	15,333	2,974	9,056	8,340	10,891	4,631	6,878	5,957	5,271	7,189	754	516	583	7,942	13,325	7,937	2,719
Nyala, Sudan	8,980	5,866	10,676	17,190	4,827	9,867	4,063	12,781	8,243	6,823	6,063	8,965	7,134	4,724	4,177	3,897	9,109	10,624	3,734	2,107
Oaxaca, Mexico	5,615	13,308	12,508	9,676	8,075	13,855	14,042	2,076	5,183	15,061	14,596	4,572	15,136	10,026	9,613	9,890	4,340	16,577	13,590	10,843
Ocean Falls, Canada	3,564	9,236	7,864	8,418	8,454	9,172	16,215	6,826	4,958	10,500	10,298	4,348	10,501	7,775	8,234	8,508	8,027	14,343	15,709	10,516
Odense, Denmark	4,255	4,701	8,624	14,711	3,302	8,764	8,993	10,745	4,338	6,824	5,932	4,928	7,118	544	1,065	1,226	8,041	13,468	8,596	3,380
Odessa, USSR	5,916	3,455	8,054	14,843	4,298	7,852	7,892	12,389	6,057	5,440	4,508	6,658	5,760	1,224	1,884	1,714	9,382	11,830	7,588	3,005
Ogbomosho, Nigeria	8,355	7,799	12,700	19,470	3,483	12,057	4,322	10,541	7,085	9,049	8,230	7,781	9,370	5,285	4,223	4,046	6,887	12,428	3,802	1,966
Okha, USSR	6,714	5,007	2,432	7,678	10,259	3,624	13,951	12,385	8,524	5,275	5,459	8,367	5,171	6,994	8,216	8,300	13,029	9,524	13,956	10,192
Okinawa (Naha)	9,931	5,115	858	6,760	12,494	837	12,290	15,063	11,676	3,870	4,615	11,605	3,580	8,815	10,063	10,019	16,299	6,243	12,568	11,237
Oklahoma City, Oklahoma	3,708	11,287	10,884	9,962	7,226	12,173	14,515	4,067	3,782	13,021	12,558	3,071	13,110	8,336	8,181	8,473	5,117	16,922	13,982	9,893
Old Crow, Canada	3,124	7,417	6,593	9,046	7,925	7,798	15,137	8,467	4,921	8,745	8,493	4,528	8,774	6,365	7,069	7,312	8,956	13,585	14,734	9,448
Olympia, Washington	3,758	9,893	8,473	8,393	8,506	9,796	16,304	6,157	4,923	11,183	10,973	4,259	11,184	8,200	8,546	8,830	7,555	14,709	15,770	10,749
Omaha, Nebraska	3,069	10,633	10,456	10,204	6,867	11,710	14,401	4,677	3,322	12,393	11,910	2,599	12,493	7,729	7,637	7,932	5,347	16,925	13,859	9,461
Omsk, USSR	6,434	1,348	4,957	11,782	7,127	4,903	9,917	13,800	7,508	3,311	2,641	7,845	3,532	3,440	4,668	4,618	11,832	10,081	9,793	6,073
Oodnadatta, Australia	15,629	9,979	6,787	5,045	17,314	6,182	10,516	14,221	17,478	7,872	8,785	17,092	7,568	14,170	15,149	14,950	17,302	2,051	11,057	14,601
Oradea, Romania	5,481	4,101	8,581	15,220	3,641	8,457	7,954	11,734	5,464	6,110	5,180	6,090	6,429	842	1,209	1,051	8,710	12,480	7,601	2,664
Oran, Algeria	5,439	6,321	10,805	16,994	1,536	10,713	7,242	10,032	4,580	8,233	7,296	5,301	8,563	2,553	1,298	1,265	6,659	13,982	6,765	1,578
Oranjestad, Aruba	5,689	12,896	14,466	12,472	5,832	15,618	11,179	2,678	4,283	15,036	14,185	4,059	15,295	8,804	7,955	8,175	1,447	18,144	10,705	8,463
Orebro, Sweden	4,161	4,362	8,123	14,211	3,797	8,305	9,355	10,948	4,483	6,501	5,635	5,018	6,783	588	1,576	1,708	8,418	13,232	8,980	3,832
Orel, USSR	5,533	3,043	7,379	14,069	4,747	7,296	8,651	12,410	5,952	5,144	4,244	6,486	5,445	1,160	2,270	2,193	9,694	11,789	8,367	3,786
Orsk, USSR	6,457	1,523	5,970	12,846	6,291	5,773	8,993	13,691	7,228	3,659	2,803	7,673	3,944	2,679	3,814	3,718	11,220	10,418	8,827	5,017
Osaka, Japan	8,891	5,254	486	6,627	12,019	1,821	13,255	13,952	10,689	4,510	5,086	10,547	4,274	8,446	9,714	9,723	15,198	7,357	13,469	11,252
Oslo, Norway	3,926	4,609	8,272	14,219	3,650	8,498	9,476	10,687	4,221	6,750	5,889	4,758	7,029	783	1,556	1,729	8,188	13,490	9,087	3,883
Osorno, Chile	11,572	17,343	17,798	10,865	9,954	18,036	8,983	4,753	10,083	17,791	17,459	9,940	17,894	13,642	12,415	12,476	5,465	12,287	8,881	11,244
Ostrava, Czechoslovakia	5,073	4,297	8,613	15,094	3,466	8,577	8,286	11,392	5,076	6,357	5,436	5,693	6,668	503	989	928	8,463	12,827	7,916	2,848
Ottawa, Canada	2,090	9,790	10,870	11,864	5,165	11,943	12,801	5,303	1,640	11,794	11,125	931	11,975	6,335	6,061	6,352	4,602	17,950	12,257	7,769
Ouagadougou, Bourkina Fasso	7,656	7,957	12,822	19,574	2,739	12,338	5,065	9,910	6,323	9,406	8,540	7,012	9,735	4,983	3,820	3,691	6,239	13,205	4,536	1,860
Oujda, Morocco	5,473	6,480	10,967	17,107	1,408	10,875	7,193	9,914	4,555	8,384	7,447	5,278	8,714	2,710	1,450	1,426	6,519	14,070	6,709	1,585
Oxford, United Kingdom	4,004	5,553	9,446	15,211	2,474	9,627	8,871	10,004	3,726	7,664	6,760	4,375	7,964	1,362	821	1,113	7,183	14,216	8,427	3,128
Pago Pago, American Samoa	12,017	13,086	8,185	1,279	16,677	8,791	15,340	8,956	13,093	11,772	12,613	12,377	11,446	15,484	16,452	16,662	12,628	7,789	15,816	18,817
Pakxe, Laos	11,247	4,279	3,213	8,502	11,955	1,857	9,719	17,630	12,651	2,233	3,170	12,857	1,906	8,471	9,532	9,379	17,014	4,947	10,022	9,865
Palembang, Indonesia	13,233	5,909	4,856	8,253	13,127	3,571	8,754	18,307	14,541	3,769	4,623	14,814	3,512	10,015	10,905	10,698	18,094	3,045	9,171	10,613
Palermo, Italy	5,901	5,102	9,752	16,432	2,804	9,532	7,072	11,258	5,436	6,966	6,030	6,131	7,297	1,849	1,076	791	7,933	12,843	6,665	1,489
Palma, Majorca	5,245	5,854	10,290	16,547	1,916	10,222	7,510	10,318	4,577	7,809	6,872	5,286	8,135	2,036	791	750	7,045	13,784	7,054	1,766
Palmerston North, New Zealand	15,184	13,686	9,412	3,544	18,610	9,382	12,157	10,306	15,999	11,685	12,619	15,282	11,363	17,696	18,942	18,835	13,527	5,633	12,637	17,834
Panama, Panama	6,144	13,694	14,339	11,400	6,921	15,631	11,983	1,605	5,005	15,793	15,022	4,638	16,004	9,731	8,966	9,199	2,368	17,370	11,544	9,572
Paramaribo, Suriname	6,517	12,621	15,603	14,037	4,951	16,424	9,387	3,979	4,779	14,669	13,734	4,847	14,989	8,437	7,359	7,515	349	17,251	8,914	7,259
Paris, France	4,413	5,435	9,528	15,522	2,413	9,624	8,475	10,262	4,074	7,513	6,595	4,739	7,822	1,281	414	708	7,309	13,949	8,037	2,740
Patna, India	9,835	2,146	4,440	10,821	9,548	3,418	8,458	17,201	10,834	398	824	11,226	666	6,221	7,178	7,001	14,672	6,792	8,601	7,434
Patrai, Greece	6,285	4,432	9,178	16,015	3,537	8,876	6,978	11,974	6,014	6,247	5,312	6,688	6,579	1,805	1,555	1,268	8,666	12,157	6,621	1,833
Peking, China	8,502	3,474	1,433	8,375	10,648	1,560	11,767	14,883	10,119	2,915	3,355	10,171	2,748	6,971	8,223	8,188	14,801	7,608	11,899	9,536
Penrhyn Island (Omoka)	10,875	13,688	8,890	2,509	15,252	9,724	16,256	7,555	11,741	12,772	13,515	11,019	12,466	14,966	15,619	15,886	11,218	9,281	16,623	17,852
Peoria, Illinois	2,911	10,612	10,819	10,731	6,376	12,035	13,859	4,577	2,885	12,471	11,918	2,171	12,600	7,467	7,280	7,573	4,882	17,453	13,317	9,011
Perm', USSR	5,711	2,111	6,003	12,700	6,026	6,006	9,586	13,002	6,578	4,237	3,444	6,984	4,495	2,338	3,576	3,542	10,763	11,035	9,378	5,148
Perth, Australia	16,454	9,293	7,411	7,000	15,612	6,431	8,599	15,475	17,955	7,166	7,977	18,128	6,922	13,267	13,937	13,681	17,154	371	9,137	12,844
Peshawar, Pakistan	8,612	1,021	5,370	12,159	7,946	4,646	8,092	15,863	9,388	1,792	862	9,850	2,125	4,651	5,573	5,394	13,065	8,297	8,101	5,949
Petropavlovsk-Kamchatskiy,USSR	6,429	6,009	3,111	7,090	10,506	4,421	14,984	11,452	8,278	6,314	6,506	8,009	6,199	7,545	8,703	8,828	12,528	10,014	14,962	10,844
Petrozavodsk, USSR	4,679	3,369	7,079	13,434	4,854	7,224	9,616	11,811	5,344	5,508	4,681	5,799	5,775	1,238	2,499	2,543	9,475	12,295	9,310	4,479
Pevek, USSR	4,509	5,818	4,700	8,704	8,642	5,844	14,486	10,430	6,350	6,862	6,729	6,130	6,859	6,054	7,085	7,257	10,764	11,790	14,258	9,386
Philadelphia, Pennsylvania	2,684	10,339	11,451	11,954	5,204	12,543	12,636	4,753	1,908	12,370	11,677	1,301	12,559	6,749	6,364	6,648	4,046	18,483	12,093	7,897
Phnom Penh, Kampuchea	11,636	4,542	3,561	8,510	12,146	2,207	9,460	17,949	13,010	2,440	3,369	13,236	2,130	8,731	9,755	9,589	17,258	4,581	9,786	9,949
Phoenix, Arizona	4,495	11,522	10,132	8,612	8,521	11,477	15,851	4,404	4,984	12,933	12,671	4,261	12,944	9,195	9,233	9,528	6,274	15,582	15,323	11,122
Pierre, South Dakota	2,940	10,325	9,967	9,922	7,080	11,227	14,735	5,082	3,483	12,013	11,575	2,766	12,096	7,642	7,655	7,950	5,832	16,483	14,192	9,593
Pinang, Malaysia	12,277	4,865	4,403	8,881	12,182	3,050	8,706	18,729	13,512	2,725	3,582	13,817	2,474	8,981	9,899	9,703	17,286	4,080	9,059	9,779
Pitcairn Island (Adamstown)	11,198	17,019	12,344	5,677	13,558	13,147	13,930	5,051	11,081	16,170	16,965	10,452	15,848	15,865	15,494	15,760	8,537	10,893	14,024	16,036
Pittsburgh, Pennsylvania	2,701	10,430	11,237	11,540	5,598	12,376	13,051	4,668	2,210	12,411	11,762	1,540	12,580	6,981	6,665	6,953	4,314	18,158	12,508	8,272
Plymouth, Montserrat	5,247	12,074	14,282	13,332	4,872	15,269	10,591	3,638	3,643	14,213	13,330	3,570	14,494	7,927	7,029	7,240	1,181	18,631	10,089	7,509
Plymouth, United Kingdom	3,974	5,797	9,687	15,351	2,236	9,878	8,826	9,798	3,578	7,902	6,995	4,244	8,204	1,605	893	1,187	6,939	14,420	8,369	3,080
Ponape Island	11,252	8,974	4,117	2,878	15,598	4,640	14,595	12,388	13,043	7,653	8,468	12,568	7,336	12,247	13,506	13,545	15,715	6,123	15,084	15,079
Ponce, Puerto Rico	5,081	12,186	14,018	12,865	5,210	15,084	11,078	3,321	3,598	14,326	13,475	3,424	14,588	8,097	7,268	7,494	1,543	18,808	10,577	7,895
Ponta Delgada, Azores	4,050	7,997	11,732	15,929	978	12,054	8,761	7,857	2,635	10,078	9,156	3,340	10,388	3,812	2,779	2,978	4,743	16,222	8,230	3,665
Pontianak, Indonesia	12,934	5,883	4,324	7,795	13,341	3,082	9,350	17,842	14,371	3,752	4,656	14,565	3,462	10,054	11,024	10,838	18,453	3,229	9,762	10,941
Port Augusta, Australia	16,082	10,540	7,356	5,018	17,655	6,773	10,417	13,782	17,910	8,422	9,327	17,419	8,124	14,725	15,657	15,443	16,722	2,255	10,960	14,891
Port Blair, India	11,499	3,887	4,533	9,816	11,104	3,214	8,290	18,746	12,576	1,795	2,568	12,948	1,618	7,936	8,827	8,627	16,219	5,047	8,574	8,738
Port Elizabeth, South Africa	13,528	9,865	13,233	14,543	8,610	11,903	1,031	12,344	12,122	9,497	9,267	12,762	9,646	9,808	9,090	8,842	9,859	8,207	1,424	6,723
Port Hedland, Australia	15,151	8,323	6,096	6,626	15,419	5,134	9,351	16,111	16,771	6,182	7,057	16,829	5,905	12,455	13,325	13,107	18,470	1,018	9,866	12,736

Distances in Kilometers	Frobisher Bay, Canada	Frunze, USSR	Fukuoka, Japan	Funafuti Atoll, Tuvalu	Funchal, Madeira Island	Fuzhou, China	Gaborone, Botswana	Galapagos Islands (Santa Cruz)	Gander, Canada	Gangtok, India	Garyarsa, China	Gaspe, Canada	Gauhati, India	Gdansk, Poland	Geneva, Switzerland	Genoa, Italy	Georgetown, Guyana	Geraldton, Australia	Ghanzi, Botswana	Ghat, Libya
Port Louis, Mauritius	13,736	7,200	9,749	12,897	9,830	8,410	3,284	15,837	13,281	6,235	6,242	14,001	6,322	9,049	8,982	8,687	12,954	5,814	3,712	7,153
Port Moresby, Papua New Guinea	13,358	9,337	5,087	3,514	16,971	4,959	12,622	13,560	15,185	7,511	8,437	14,747	7,176	13,285	14,517	14,444	17,228	4,015	13,147	15,173
Port Said, Egypt	7,440	3,929	8,829	15,764	4,612	8,292	6,227	13,117	7,251	5,430	4,528	7,922	5,765	2,785	2,791	2,506	9,670	10,954	5,953	2,278
Port Sudan, Sudan	8,814	4,340	9,112	15,751	5,543	8,316	5,051	13,953	8,521	5,283	4,501	9,212	5,600	4,166	4,090	3,797	10,328	9,881	4,856	2,845
Port-au-Prince, Haiti	5,031	12,412	13,757	12,263	5,719	14,912	11,660	2,897	3,731	14,534	13,730	3,435	14,769	8,418	7,670	7,909	2,011	18,677	11,164	8,436
Port-of-Spain, Trin. & Tobago	5,920	12,597	14,951	13,385	5,169	15,940	10,246	3,431	4,295	14,720	13,812	4,242	15,016	8,417	7,447	7,638	563	17,960	9,765	7,686
Port-Vila, Vanuatu	13,363	11,629	6,961	1,553	18,275	7,184	13,803	11,194	14,839	9,932	10,844	14,174	9,597	15,188	16,449	16,480	14,850	5,585	14,342	17,629
Portland, Maine	2,240	9,801	11,199	12,316	4,749	12,222	12,337	5,299	1,338	11,856	11,139	728	12,057	6,171	5,798	6,084	4,251	18,298	11,793	7,398
Portland, Oregon	3,874	10,062	8,586	8,329	8,581	9,915	16,370	6,016	4,988	11,341	11,138	4,314	11,339	8,348	8,675	8,960	7,494	14,732	15,833	10,861
Porto, Portugal	4,546	6,592	10,731	16,310	1,198	10,835	8,112	9,368	3,666	8,625	7,695	4,385	8,944	2,492	1,315	1,479	6,196	14,755	7,621	2,500
Porto Alegre, Brazil	10,512	15,051	19,590	13,157	7,825	18,992	7,504	5,272	8,758	16,109	15,431	8,839	16,377	11,487	10,229	10,258	4,147	13,322	7,259	8,941
Porto Alexandre, Angola	11,105	9,115	13,597	16,975	6,176	12,486	1,760	11,312	9,698	9,552	8,999	10,353	9,803	7,801	6,892	6,676	8,113	10,370	1,222	4,516
Porto Novo, Benin	8,440	8,056	12,958	19,584	3,531	12,308	4,272	10,359	7,115	9,293	8,480	7,801	9,613	5,501	4,415	4,248	6,717	12,503	3,743	2,199
Porto Velho, Brazil	8,051	14,489	16,896	12,789	6,769	18,059	9,594	3,070	6,458	16,478	15,542	6,381	16,809	10,315	9,213	9,354	1,835	15,849	9,219	8,847
Portsmouth, United Kingdom	4,091	5,584	9,524	15,320	2,395	9,688	8,767	10,014	3,770	7,686	6,778	4,427	7,989	1,392	738	1,032	7,152	14,204	8,321	3,023
Poznan, Poland	4,792	4,334	8,508	14,876	3,492	8,536	8,583	11,234	4,863	6,426	5,517	5,464	6,731	243	1,044	1,068	8,405	12,986	8,209	3,101
Prague, Czechoslovakia	4,879	4,558	8,808	15,184	3,224	8,809	8,356	11,119	4,820	6,626	5,707	5,446	6,936	555	753	755	8,195	13,100	7,969	2,812
Praia, Cape Verde Islands	6,423	9,540	13,971	17,468	2,074	13,953	6,926	7,553	4,719	11,341	10,416	5,293	11,676	5,692	4,436	4,480	3,888	15,464	6,384	3,687
Pretoria, South Africa	12,867	8,966	12,622	15,093	8,036	11,333	258	12,822	11,625	8,744	8,440	12,305	8,920	8,921	8,272	8,012	9,976	8,359	799	5,936
Prince Albert, Canada	2,422	9,356	8,973	9,784	7,109	10,206	14,908	6,136	3,538	10,975	10,575	2,896	11,049	7,034	7,247	7,536	6,696	15,758	14,378	9,385
Prince Edward Island	15,273	10,553	12,800	12,798	10,354	11,450	2,658	12,765	13,836	9,643	9,666	14,450	9,706	11,333	10,738	10,476	11,022	6,770	3,136	8,403
Prince George, Canada	3,203	9,150	8,054	8,790	8,083	9,341	15,852	6,742	4,585	10,512	10,257	3,980	10,533	7,491	7,908	8,185	7,751	14,656	15,343	10,171
Prince Rupert, Canada	3,542	8,975	7,605	8,407	8,465	8,907	16,174	7,105	5,019	10,221	10,025	4,436	10,221	7,627	8,135	8,404	8,242	14,159	15,684	10,444
Providence, Rhode Island	2,448	10,025	11,365	12,251	4,861	12,407	12,377	5,075	1,531	12,079	11,363	949	12,280	6,382	5,986	6,270	4,094	18,461	11,833	7,536
Provo, Utah	3,826	10,776	9,652	8,898	8,118	10,974	15,726	5,014	4,521	12,237	11,940	3,804	12,265	8,507	8,620	8,914	6,467	15,643	15,183	10,618
Puerto Aisen, Chile	12,107	17,408	17,650	10,728	10,312	17,613	8,730	5,255	10,600	17,413	17,246	10,471	17,466	13,995	12,748	12,787	5,961	11,759	8,670	11,419
Puerto Deseado, Argentina	12,365	16,911	17,930	11,114	10,157	17,558	8,150	5,731	10,770	16,848	16,665	10,703	16,922	13,806	12,542	12,554	6,090	11,530	8,097	11,053
Puerto Princesa, Philippines	11,833	5,636	2,899	6,992	13,375	1,811	10,746	16,657	13,472	3,712	4,642	13,509	3,377	9,780	10,913	10,786	18,145	4,283	11,123	11,389
Punta Arenas, Chile	12,965	17,238	17,256	10,552	10,842	16,882	8,286	6,094	11,420	16,681	16,704	11,319	16,684	14,475	13,208	13,208	6,752	10,914	8,293	11,626
Pusan, South Korea	8,937	4,712	209	7,138	11,712	1,367	12,690	14,429	10,688	3,920	4,498	10,612	3,688	8,079	9,344	9,332	15,306	7,230	12,890	10,764
Pyongyang, North Korea	8,542	4,262	733	7,617	11,188	1,556	12,510	14,397	10,260	3,667	4,158	10,221	3,470	7,555	8,820	8,810	14,916	7,593	12,667	10,271
Qamdo, China	9,408	2,386	3,120	9,737	10,127	2,226	9,787	16,533	10,703	939	1,603	10,960	771	6,542	7,661	7,537	15,062	6,884	9,938	8,358
Qandahar, Afghanistan	8,701	1,479	5,972	12,720	7,580	5,211	7,532	15,767	9,313	2,263	1,385	9,826	2,598	4,478	5,285	5,081	12,713	8,447	7,522	5,444
Qiqian, China	7,121	3,562	2,207	8,704	9,749	2,902	12,462	13,597	8,786	3,845	3,972	8,796	3,778	6,188	7,454	7,477	13,466	8,990	12,482	9,145
Qom, Iran	7,876	2,244	7,125	14,019	6,170	6,521	7,076	14,512	8,191	3,670	2,757	8,773	4,006	3,320	3,948	3,721	11,300	9,698	6,942	4,050
Quebec, Canada	1,893	9,513	10,841	12,189	4,811	11,863	12,493	5,579	1,263	11,548	10,851	553	11,742	5,980	5,685	5,975	4,608	17,939	11,950	7,397
Quetta, Pakistan	8,885	1,563	5,915	12,613	7,755	5,114	7,491	15,961	9,507	2,132	1,288	10,018	2,464	4,672	5,472	5,265	12,888	8,254	7,498	5,583
Quito, Ecuador	7,144	14,575	15,246	11,377	7,396	16,573	11,461	1,324	5,911	16,708	15,874	5,600	16,950	10,493	9,616	9,825	2,388	16,512	11,072	9,893
Rabaul, Papua New Guinea	12,632	9,321	4,769	3,019	16,661	4,878	13,401	13,058	14,438	7,656	8,555	13,970	7,323	13,056	14,318	14,292	16,663	4,810	13,920	15,361
Raiatea (Uturoa)	11,316	14,801	9,975	3,320	15,144	10,746	15,416	6,920	11,888	13,778	14,566	11,173	13,461	15,745	16,141	16,432	10,579	9,509	15,705	17,912
Raleigh, North Carolina	3,187	10,881	11,757	11,665	5,605	12,905	12,830	4,211	2,444	12,893	12,217	1,856	13,073	7,300	6,887	7,168	3,828	18,555	12,292	8,335
Rangiroa (Avatoru)	10,960	14,942	10,190	3,681	14,699	11,026	15,570	6,495	11,470	14,071	14,820	10,758	13,762	15,475	15,775	16,069	10,161	9,955	15,809	17,466
Rangoon, Burma	10,979	3,544	3,894	9,547	11,049	2,604	8,895	18,084	12,175	1,403	2,301	12,490	1,137	7,700	8,682	8,506	16,177	5,416	9,153	8,850
Raoul Is., Kermadec Islands	13,831	13,522	8,834	2,318	18,177	9,079	13,521	9,740	14,793	11,755	12,682	14,070	11,421	16,918	18,093	18,220	13,262	6,477	14,000	19,092
Rarotonga (Avarua)	12,159	14,467	9,565	2,664	16,151	10,176	14,894	7,856	12,853	13,137	13,993	12,133	12,808	16,322	16,955	17,231	11,488	8,502	15,271	18,918
Rawson, Argentina	11,872	16,773	18,291	11,377	9,735	18,054	8,250	5,353	10,272	17,065	16,740	10,208	17,187	13,405	12,148	12,176	5,592	12,025	8,154	10,772
Recife, Brazil	8,451	12,204	16,805	15,835	4,891	16,643	6,697	6,207	6,602	13,728	12,869	6,933	14,055	8,522	7,261	7,287	3,061	14,790	6,248	6,101
Regina, Canada	2,588	9,662	9,248	9,774	7,141	10,494	14,924	5,821	3,542	11,291	10,886	2,869	11,365	7,249	7,407	7,699	6,466	15,950	14,387	9,494
Reykjavik, Iceland	2,232	6,113	8,902	13,609	3,522	9,450	10,683	9,039	2,577	8,234	7,440	3,039	8,480	2,505	2,640	2,922	6,983	15,032	10,224	4,937
Rhodes, Greece	6,755	3,993	8,828	15,749	4,126	8,431	6,767	12,582	6,586	5,711	4,783	7,249	6,046	2,123	2,131	1,853	9,245	11,550	6,455	2,139
Richmond, Virginia	2,977	10,660	11,622	11,768	5,453	12,749	12,770	4,431	2,232	12,678	11,997	1,634	12,861	7,081	6,683	6,965	3,924	18,533	12,230	8,169
Riga, USSR	4,710	3,840	7,842	14,215	4,120	7,919	9,045	11,525	5,064	5,970	5,089	5,602	6,260	448	1,715	1,750	8,908	12,666	8,703	3,724
Ringkobing, Denmark	4,106	4,818	8,670	14,669	3,250	8,840	9,102	10,602	4,187	6,946	6,059	4,774	7,238	690	1,109	1,299	7,932	13,608	8,698	3,459
Rio Branco, Brazil	8,175	14,860	16,804	12,342	7,168	18,074	9,928	2,705	6,653	16,890	15,953	6,522	17,217	10,673	9,596	9,746	2,140	15,711	9,572	9,289
Rio Cuarto, Argentina	10,746	16,299	18,655	11,888	8,817	19,151	8,579	4,512	9,143	17,356	16,722	9,079	17,593	12,505	11,278	11,341	4,468	13,153	8,390	10,177
Rio de Janeiro, Brazil	9,856	13,948	18,672	14,248	6,753	18,228	6,970	5,660	8,038	15,179	14,422	8,221	15,476	10,391	9,129	9,149	3,666	13,817	6,647	7,829
Rio Gallegos, Argentina	12,795	17,147	17,457	10,722	10,640	17,079	8,235	5,991	11,233	16,735	16,697	11,143	16,758	14,277	13,011	13,014	6,560	11,091	8,225	11,454
Rio Grande, Brazil	10,717	15,238	19,731	12,972	8,057	18,954	7,526	5,314	8,973	16,210	15,567	9,041	16,465	11,715	10,456	10,482	4,346	13,131	7,300	9,139
Riyadh, Saudi Arabia	8,724	3,256	7,988	14,681	6,194	7,205	5,898	14,703	8,761	4,187	3,383	9,404	4,510	4,032	4,323	4,050	11,190	9,363	5,780	3,683
Road Town, Brit. Virgin Isls.	5,040	12,039	14,032	13,077	5,001	15,060	10,902	3,522	3,501	14,181	13,319	3,370	14,450	7,930	7,081	7,303	1,466	18,859	10,397	7,680
Roanoke, Virginia	3,044	10,761	11,557	11,548	5,674	12,710	12,979	4,333	2,418	12,754	12,095	1,792	12,927	7,246	6,875	7,159	4,032	18,370	12,440	8,386
Robinson Crusoe Island, Chile	10,834	17,496	17,320	10,589	9,792	18,084	9,781	3,846	9,459	18,635	18,073	9,245	18,792	13,430	12,269	12,373	4,980	12,955	9,639	11,423
Rochester, New York	2,365	10,079	11,044	11,730	5,347	12,146	12,907	5,016	1,883	12,074	11,413	1,194	12,250	6,622	6,327	6,616	4,456	18,076	12,363	7,986
Rockhampton, Australia	14,689	10,673	6,655	3,468	18,414	6,423	12,021	12,939	16,420	8,700	9,638	15,849	8,373	14,761	15,943	15,824	16,454	3,627	12,565	16,010
Rome, Italy	5,511	4,995	9,525	16,083	2,785	9,386	7,498	11,122	5,136	6,939	6,003	5,818	7,265	1,458	696	401	7,909	13,033	7,092	1,890
Rosario, Argentina	10,742	15,989	18,995	12,211	8,589	19,243	8,263	4,740	9,091	17,015	16,378	9,066	17,259	12,276	11,036	11,088	4,407	13,156	8,064	9,869
Roseau, Dominica	5,408	12,158	14,453	13,418	4,875	15,426	10,448	3,643	3,783	14,293	13,401	3,730	14,580	7,997	7,074	7,279	1,004	18,460	9,949	7,482
Rostock, East Germany	4,439	4,618	8,638	14,820	3,305	8,738	8,825	10,880	4,494	6,730	5,830	5,092	7,029	427	974	1,100	8,118	13,337	8,432	3,237
Rostov-na-Donu, USSR	6,206	2,767	7,409	14,264	4,982	7,169	8,082	12,956	6,543	4,768	3,841	7,104	5,086	1,672	2,547	2,394	10,050	11,261	7,829	3,589
Rotterdam, Netherlands	4,264	5,174	9,173	15,168	2,754	9,300	8,737	10,400	4,097	7,277	6,370	4,732	7,579	984	647	897	7,561	13,821	8,313	3,030
Rouyn, Canada	1,842	9,584	10,483	11,589	5,388	11,574	13,096	5,525	1,794	11,545	10,912	1,074	11,712	6,285	6,107	6,400	4,998	17,552	12,555	7,925
Sacramento, California	4,442	10,836	9,117	8,049	8,936	10,464	16,591	5,383	5,327	12,067	11,897	4,619	12,048	9,027	9,267	9,558	7,232	14,792	16,048	11,363
Saginaw, Michigan	2,466	10,206	10,793	11,216	5,846	11,951	13,419	4,923	2,329	12,132	11,528	1,613	12,284	6,937	6,725	7,017	4,777	17,695	12,875	8,460
Saint Denis, Reunion	13,712	7,328	9,967	13,067	9,702	8,630	3,058	15,613	13,186	6,419	6,401	13,908	6,515	9,044	8,932	8,637	12,737	5,985	3,489	7,049
Saint George's, Grenada	5,764	12,481	14,794	13,368	5,102	15,784	10,334	3,462	4,144	14,610	13,708	4,086	14,902	8,307	7,354	7,551	701	18,117	9,847	7,650
Saint John, Canada	2,063	9,491	11,117	12,614	4,410	12,085	12,061	5,622	958	11,567	10,828	414	11,780	5,805	5,418	5,704	4,330	18,172	11,518	7,034
Saint John's, Antigua	5,206	12,016	14,248	13,371	4,816	15,225	10,574	3,694	3,593	14,154	13,271	3,528	14,436	7,868	6,970	7,182	1,208	18,665	10,069	7,457
Saint John's, Canada	2,045	8,731	11,011	13,507	3,433	11,809	11,791	6,467	209	10,855	10,053	885	11,098	4,853	4,381	4,663	4,548	17,652	10,655	5,995
Saint Louis, Missouri	3,145	10,848	10,984	10,656	6,495	12,215	13,892	4,346	3,051	12,703	12,154	2,346	12,829	7,682	7,471	7,762	4,772	17,489	13,353	9,157
Saint Paul, Minnesota	2,599	10,198	10,267	10,499	6,515	11,483	14,157	5,056	2,931	11,999	11,486	2,209	12,113	7,260	7,189	7,483	5,409	16,990	13,614	9,060
Saint Peter Port, UK	4,129	5,737	9,703	15,464	2,216	9,861	8,680	9,907	3,719	7,831	6,919	4,390	8,136	1,551	744	1,036	7,000	14,307	8,226	2,933
Saipan (Susupe)	10,779	7,347	2,559	4,521	14,405	3,000	13,690	13,666	12,628	6,028	6,828	12,319	5,717	10,831	12,098	12,096	16,440	5,901	14,095	13,466
Salalah, Oman	9,802	3,466	7,538	14,011	7,257	6,764	5,533	15,739	9,901	3,725	3,112	10,541	4,012	5,138	5,464	5,190	12,132	8,243	5,534	4,631
Salem, Oregon	3,946	10,119	8,598	8,268	8,645	9,929	16,431	5,988	5,049	11,384	11,189	4,372	11,378	8,421	8,748	9,033	7,510	14,700	15,892	10,931
Salt Lake City, Utah	3,788	10,717	9,598	8,901	8,107	10,920	15,733	5,074	4,506	12,177	11,879	3,791	12,205	8,464	8,587	8,880	6,505	15,621	15,190	10,596
Salta, Argentina	9,818	15,864	18,205	12,123	8,178	19,534	9,025	3,790	8,237	17,422	16,599	8,154	17,732	11,841	10,655	10,750	3,581	14,079	8,769	9,824
Salto, Uruguay	10,587	15,681	19,203	12,516	8,299	19,364	8,080	4,820	8,904	16,766	16,097	8,908	17,025	11,983	10,740	10,788	4,226	13,302	7,860	9,561
Salvador, Brazil	8,886	12,864	17,467	15,235	5,548	17,290	6,855	5,880	7,041	14,324	13,487	7,310	14,645	9,192	7,932	7,961	3,084	14,563	6,445	6,750
Salzburg, Austria	5,011	4,727	9,053	15,459	3,024	9,023	8,128	11,062	4,842	6,767	5,841	5,489	7,083	828	552	491	8,050	13,148	7,732	2,546
Samsun, Turkey	6,642	3,144	7,947	14,863	4,762	7,589	7,380	13,038	6,768	4,974	4,038	7,379	5,304	1,954	2,475	2,254	9,892	11,169	7,119	3,018
San Antonio, Texas	4,367	11,966	11,347	9,744	7,594	12,665	14,538	3,436	4,285	13,679	13,233	3,597	13,756	8,955	8,731	9,021	4,909	16,818	14,025	10,316
San Cristobal, Venezuela	6,220	13,473	14,847	12,184	6,319	16,060	11,192	2,219	4,855	15,613	14,759	4,610	15,873	9,370	8,498	8,711	1,557	17,574	10,744	8,893
San Diego, California	4,795	11,547	9,829	8,139	8,968	11,181	16,329	4,640	5,407	12,825	12,637	4,684	12,809	9,472	9,582	9,876	6,716	15,101	15,803	11,536
San Francisco, California	4,562	10,907	9,105	7,936	9,054	10,455	16,695	5,376	5,445	12,108	11,955	4,737	12,082	9,141	9,387	9,677	7,295	14,702	16,153	11,484
San Jose, Costa Rica	6,100	13,769	13,973	10,917	7,290	15,293	12,485	1,361	5,119	15,808	15,107	4,683	15,984	9,930	9,240	9,484	2,875	17,164	12,050	9,980
San Juan, Argentina	10,562	16,547	18,239	11,586	8,939	19,048	9,009	4,123	9,021	17,766	17,087	8,910	18,015	12,616	11,413	11,495	4,383	13,323	8,817	10,441
San Juan, Puerto Rico	5,033	12,116	13,986	12,919	5,140	15,042	11,049	3,393	3,536	14,257	13,405	3,372	14,520	8,025	7,196	7,421	1,552	18,862	10,546	7,827
San Luis Potosi, Mexico	5,210	12,788	11,789	9,341	8,189	13,135	14,629	2,771	5,035	14,434	14,038	4,370	14,486	9,774	9,494	9,781	4,896	16,391	14,153	10,946
San Marino, San Marino	5,328	4,911	9,375	15,876	2,838	9,275	7,717	11,088	5,017	6,892	5,957	5,688	7,214	1,244	557	287	7,940	13,091	7,313	2,112
San Miguel de Tucuman, Argen.	10,044	15,987	18,347	12,066	8,335	19,573	8,919	3,955	8,458	17,440	16,654	8,379	17,735	12,007	10,811	10,898	3,796	13,854	8,679	9,914

Distances in Kilometers	Frobisher Bay, Canada	Frunze, USSR	Fukuoka, Japan	Funafuti Atoll, Tuvalu	Funchal, Madeira Island	Fuzhou, China	Gaborone, Botswana	Galapagos Islands (Santa Cruz)	Gander, Canada	Gangtok, India	Garyarsa, China	Gaspe, Canada	Gauhati, India	Gdansk, Poland	Geneva, Switzerland	Genoa, Italy	Georgetown, Guyana	Geraldton, Australia	Ghanzi, Botswana	Ghat, Libya
San Salvador, El Salvador	5,785	13,525	13,307	10,418	7,558	14,639	13,157	1,591	5,028	15,459	14,855	4,508	15,591	9,900	9,329	9,590	3,481	17,054	12,712	10,300
Sanaa, Yemen	9,555	4,207	8,739	15,078	6,417	7,815	4,853	14,786	9,365	4,767	4,088	10,047	5,064	4,860	4,914	4,624	11,134	9,004	4,761	3,700
Santa Cruz, Bolivia	9,053	15,173	17,803	12,592	7,443	19,055	9,116	3,532	7,441	16,950	16,053	7,381	17,283	11,081	9,918	10,028	2,776	14,847	8,801	9,249
Santa Cruz, Tenerife	5,377	7,983	12,295	17,283	468	12,334	7,410	8,501	3,976	9,907	8,971	4,669	10,237	4,023	2,778	2,850	5,015	15,256	6,878	2,652
Santa Fe, New Mexico	4,015	11,303	10,364	9,222	7,910	11,686	15,280	4,332	4,386	12,865	12,511	3,664	12,911	8,714	8,685	8,980	5,818	16,157	14,746	10,525
Santa Rosa, Argentina	11,133	16,467	18,647	11,743	9,114	18,790	8,436	4,807	9,526	17,276	16,742	9,465	17,476	12,800	11,560	11,610	4,848	12,766	8,277	10,358
Santa Rosalia, Mexico	5,112	12,198	10,575	8,378	8,889	11,929	15,853	3,881	5,440	13,561	13,332	4,722	13,554	9,814	9,784	10,078	6,136	15,447	15,355	11,562
Santarem, Brazil	7,431	13,297	16,516	13,941	5,558	17,312	8,953	3,976	5,693	15,246	14,311	5,759	15,578	9,158	8,020	8,148	1,091	16,371	8,519	7,619
Santiago del Estero, Argentina	10,154	15,974	18,482	12,116	8,355	19,624	8,791	4,097	8,553	17,358	16,595	8,486	17,646	12,035	10,829	10,910	3,882	13,745	8,556	9,883
Santiago, Chile	10,777	16,830	18,074	11,325	9,232	18,757	9,108	4,177	9,265	17,928	17,311	9,135	18,146	12,909	11,706	11,788	4,646	13,096	8,938	10,716
Santo Domingo, Dominican Rep.	5,031	12,305	13,858	12,519	5,494	14,978	11,418	3,080	3,650	14,438	13,613	3,404	14,685	8,268	7,488	7,722	1,812	18,779	10,920	8,200
Sao Paulo de Olivenca, Brazil	7,454	14,342	16,125	12,382	6,768	17,358	10,332	2,421	5,966	16,447	15,524	5,808	16,754	10,153	9,137	9,309	1,637	16,421	9,937	9,069
Sao Paulo, Brazil	9,864	14,266	18,855	13,915	6,972	18,580	7,280	5,360	8,067	15,532	14,769	8,210	15,829	10,633	9,376	9,408	3,583	13,880	6,969	8,144
Sao Tome, Sao Tome & Principe	9,250	8,198	13,055	18,783	4,351	12,244	3,453	10,812	7,932	9,196	8,450	8,616	9,500	6,087	5,082	4,888	7,241	11,771	2,923	2,751
Sapporo, Japan	7,875	5,293	1,419	6,873	11,337	2,747	13,871	13,063	9,694	5,018	5,422	9,518	4,838	7,924	9,177	9,229	14,145	8,410	13,998	10,974
Sarajevo, Yugoslavia	5,614	4,465	9,017	15,671	3,302	8,858	7,623	11,559	5,426	6,423	5,487	6,083	6,747	1,170	1,000	760	8,414	12,629	7,249	2,223
Saratov, USSR	6,021	2,348	6,804	13,615	5,421	6,645	8,671	13,053	6,579	4,450	3,555	7,082	4,750	1,853	2,946	2,846	10,390	11,126	8,440	4,234
Saskatoon, Canada	2,548	9,476	9,017	9,693	7,206	10,261	15,003	6,042	3,625	11,079	10,689	2,972	11,149	7,167	7,374	7,663	6,683	15,751	14,470	9,503
Schefferville, Canada	1,002	8,579	10,074	12,307	4,582	11,024	12,382	6,512	1,061	10,607	9,916	683	10,802	5,170	5,025	5,320	5,379	17,111	11,853	6,957
Seattle, Washington	3,684	9,843	8,473	8,460	8,436	9,792	16,235	6,176	4,857	11,149	10,930	4,195	11,153	8,128	8,472	8,756	7,529	14,749	15,703	10,676
Sendai, Japan	8,403	5,490	1,078	6,522	11,829	2,432	13,792	13,341	10,225	4,976	5,474	10,040	4,764	8,360	9,621	9,659	14,645	7,907	13,972	11,330
Seoul, South Korea	8,690	4,426	539	7,439	11,383	1,466	12,577	14,415	10,420	3,754	4,279	10,367	3,543	7,749	9,014	9,003	15,064	7,456	12,750	10,453
Sept-Iles, Canada	1,514	9,018	10,578	12,466	4,471	11,537	12,232	6,079	861	11,071	10,356	205	11,274	5,463	5,195	5,486	4,872	17,623	11,694	6,981
Sevastopol, USSR	6,209	3,278	7,968	14,821	4,511	7,704	7,709	12,673	6,357	5,214	4,278	6,959	5,538	1,523	2,139	1,948	9,619	11,543	7,423	3,030
Seville, Spain	5,019	6,625	10,947	16,767	1,126	10,957	7,637	9,560	4,080	8,597	7,661	4,803	8,923	2,661	1,404	1,478	6,254	14,486	7,145	2,061
Shanghai, China	9,452	4,302	893	7,553	11,701	593	11,877	15,267	11,128	3,200	3,875	11,130	2,939	8,016	9,258	9,207	15,808	6,666	12,099	10,424
Sheffield, United Kingdom	3,865	5,505	9,316	15,031	2,611	9,527	9,041	9,990	3,661	7,626	6,730	4,295	7,921	1,327	968	1,253	7,239	14,230	8,600	3,301
Shenyang, China	8,255	3,970	1,098	7,943	10,823	1,784	12,396	14,332	9,949	3,544	3,960	9,934	3,375	7,191	8,456	8,449	14,621	7,866	12,522	9,935
Shiraz, Iran	8,451	2,459	7,222	14,006	6,510	6,497	6,646	14,952	8,717	3,529	2,671	9,314	3,860	3,861	4,398	4,154	11,609	9,231	6,551	4,202
Sibiu, Romania	5,694	3,968	8,523	15,235	3,784	8,355	7,805	11,939	5,683	5,949	5,016	6,311	6,271	1,028	1,391	1,204	8,876	12,272	7,464	2,628
Singapore	12,763	5,452	4,522	8,421	12,770	3,205	8,858	18,452	14,068	3,310	4,179	14,340	3,046	9,580	10,500	10,302	17,844	3,518	9,248	10,326
Sioux Falls, South Dakota	2,874	10,391	10,221	10,188	6,839	11,466	14,453	4,934	3,260	12,138	11,662	2,538	12,236	7,556	7,509	7,804	5,541	16,787	13,910	9,390
Skelleftea, Sweden	3,975	4,101	7,527	13,532	4,400	7,796	9,924	11,065	4,600	6,235	5,420	5,054	6,494	1,167	2,255	2,385	8,809	13,029	9,572	4,491
Skopje, Yugoslavia	5,923	4,296	8,944	15,701	3,525	8,720	7,395	11,851	5,748	6,204	5,266	6,405	6,531	1,389	1,310	1,052	8,653	12,326	7,038	2,157
Socotra Island (Tamrida)	10,245	3,895	7,992	14,023	7,486	6,951	5,136	15,887	10,272	3,950	3,426	10,927	4,216	5,563	5,817	5,536	12,232	7,962	5,170	4,794
Sofia, Bulgaria	5,944	4,129	8,777	15,549	3,681	8,551	7,462	11,976	5,827	6,044	5,107	6,475	6,371	1,341	1,417	1,175	8,806	12,211	7,115	2,304
Songkhla, Thailand	12,083	4,705	4,236	8,885	12,085	2,881	8,821	18,610	13,334	2,563	3,435	13,630	2,302	8,838	9,777	9,586	17,207	4,254	9,163	9,723
Sorong, Indonesia	12,845	7,435	3,816	5,374	15,173	3,249	11,524	15,401	14,649	5,526	6,458	14,483	5,193	11,532	12,700	12,585	18,795	3,557	11,990	13,169
South Georgia Island	13,371	15,008	17,499	12,284	9,814	16,315	6,053	7,685	11,560	14,705	14,536	11,718	14,804	13,067	11,847	11,761	7,056	10,405	6,056	9,860
South Pole	17,075	14,754	13,719	9,059	13,616	12,887	7,275	9,932	15,428	13,027	13,517	15,414	12,899	16,029	15,123	14,924	10,755	6,818	7,618	12,767
South Sandwich Islands	13,943	14,506	16,810	12,302	10,056	15,583	5,514	8,430	12,107	14,015	13,910	12,319	14,096	13,078	11,911	11,791	7,705	9,755	5,576	9,783
Split, Yugoslavia	5,551	4,628	9,163	15,781	3,138	9,016	7,611	11,410	5,311	6,586	5,651	5,975	6,911	1,216	864	609	8,251	12,771	7,227	2,135
Spokane, Washington	3,435	9,902	8,765	8,792	8,117	10,072	15,906	5,959	4,524	11,301	11,032	3,852	11,323	7,970	8,251	8,538	7,178	15,117	15,370	10,412
Spoleto, Italy	5,447	4,940	9,447	15,990	2,825	9,322	7,584	11,129	5,104	6,899	5,963	5,781	7,223	1,363	649	358	7,942	13,038	7,179	1,985
Springbok, South Africa	12,749	9,906	13,724	15,332	7,811	12,435	968	11,740	11,282	9,821	9,475	11,910	10,007	9,309	8,484	8,254	9,053	9,071	979	6,101
Springfield, Illinois	3,005	10,710	10,900	10,716	6,410	12,121	13,857	4,478	2,940	12,570	12,017	2,230	12,699	7,549	7,349	7,641	4,821	17,488	13,315	9,057
Springfield, Massachusetts	2,424	10,036	11,303	12,150	4,954	12,358	12,479	5,060	1,592	12,080	11,374	980	12,276	6,427	6,051	6,336	4,162	18,393	11,936	7,623
Srinagar, India	8,689	979	5,079	11,858	8,208	4,345	8,308	15,997	9,539	1,517	580	9,977	1,847	4,857	5,816	5,645	13,317	8,120	8,334	6,246
Stanley, Falkland Islands	12,836	16,361	17,886	11,418	10,163	17,151	7,476	6,426	11,158	16,122	15,974	11,159	16,196	13,719	12,453	12,429	6,482	11,061	7,451	10,762
Stara Zagora, Bulgaria	6,073	3,957	8,638	15,449	3,869	8,387	7,427	12,167	5,998	5,858	4,921	6,640	6,185	1,422	1,605	1,367	8,996	12,024	7,095	2,400
Stockholm, Sweden	4,273	4,201	7,990	14,146	3,932	8,156	9,337	11,103	4,634	6,340	5,475	5,163	6,622	556	1,661	1,770	8,578	13,073	8,972	3,867
Stornoway, United Kingdom	3,281	5,605	9,067	14,471	2,952	9,401	9,661	9,715	3,277	7,747	6,885	3,861	8,025	1,599	1,582	1,861	7,212	14,478	9,217	3,918
Strasbourg, France	4,696	5,073	9,279	15,491	2,715	9,314	8,312	10,661	4,452	7,136	6,214	5,106	7,448	992	291	472	7,683	13,550	7,894	2,630
Stuttgart, West Germany	4,747	4,966	9,190	15,445	2,816	9,214	8,302	10,764	4,538	7,028	6,106	5,188	7,340	903	365	484	7,791	13,449	7,890	2,643
Subic, Philippines	11,254	5,332	2,311	6,995	13,056	1,244	11,122	16,314	12,916	3,549	4,452	12,932	3,215	9,408	10,580	10,474	17,600	4,867	11,468	11,254
Suchow, China	9,127	3,789	1,224	8,055	11,187	930	11,623	15,314	10,751	2,829	3,433	10,799	2,600	7,500	8,738	8,684	15,433	6,982	11,808	9,907
Sucre, Bolivia	9,182	15,429	17,776	12,338	7,694	19,100	9,266	3,413	7,604	17,211	16,315	7,517	17,542	11,323	10,168	10,281	2,962	14,716	8,966	9,510
Sudbury, Canada	2,070	9,814	10,595	11,448	5,559	11,712	13,224	5,302	1,988	11,762	11,139	1,265	11,923	6,528	6,338	6,631	4,913	17,619	12,681	8,126
Suez, Egypt	7,578	3,986	8,887	15,812	4,675	8,323	6,087	13,184	7,368	5,434	4,541	8,042	5,769	2,929	2,910	2,622	9,710	10,864	5,818	2,275
Sundsvall, Sweden	4,012	4,251	7,825	13,848	4,096	8,061	9,679	10,972	4,495	6,392	5,552	4,988	6,662	898	1,935	2,071	8,591	13,167	9,314	4,191
Surabaya, Indonesia	13,733	6,762	4,889	7,313	14,126	3,755	9,366	17,322	15,233	4,626	5,520	15,388	4,341	10,923	11,865	11,668	19,033	2,390	9,823	11,618
Suva, Fiji	12,929	12,475	7,663	1,067	17,797	8,049	14,418	10,123	14,187	10,902	11,795	13,484	10,568	15,630	16,812	16,931	13,781	6,553	14,936	18,592
Sverdlovsk, USSR	5,943	1,842	5,756	12,507	6,302	5,727	9,603	13,258	6,852	3,957	3,178	7,246	4,211	2,616	3,844	3,800	11,054	10,756	9,417	5,341
Svobodnyy, USSR	7,154	4,072	1,988	8,235	10,089	2,909	12,946	13,328	8,881	4,246	4,438	8,832	4,150	6,591	7,852	7,890	13,528	8,979	12,979	9,613
Sydney, Australia	15,721	11,524	7,778	4,010	18,911	7,444	11,332	12,564	17,308	9,458	10,385	16,645	9,145	15,701	16,772	16,591	15,762	3,511	11,870	16,143
Sydney, Canada	2,027	9,180	11,111	13,031	3,961	12,005	11,658	5,967	522	11,282	10,512	440	11,510	5,397	4,966	5,250	4,365	18,023	11,117	6,569
Syktyvkar, USSR	5,205	2,614	6,248	12,779	5,706	6,357	9,826	12,493	6,078	4,729	3,949	6,476	4,979	2,040	3,306	3,312	10,326	11,528	9,583	5,086
Szeged, Hungary	5,474	4,254	8,742	15,369	3,490	8,617	7,876	11,628	5,397	6,253	5,321	6,034	6,573	905	1,079	902	8,570	12,580	7,513	2,526
Szombathely, Hungary	5,226	4,486	8,889	15,407	3,256	8,814	8,017	11,339	5,109	6,510	5,581	5,750	6,827	805	807	673	8,309	12,871	7,637	2,536
Tabriz, Iran	7,356	2,446	7,343	14,281	5,666	6,846	7,266	13,956	7,632	4,104	3,173	8,218	4,437	2,764	3,399	3,180	10,799	10,257	7,083	3,696
Tacheng, China	7,500	786	4,225	11,165	8,125	3,931	9,766	14,854	8,638	2,212	1,680	8,957	2,411	4,470	5,648	5,560	12,947	8,949	9,737	6,746
Tahiti (Papeete)	11,306	15,006	10,188	3,533	15,015	10,964	15,311	6,737	11,817	13,995	14,783	11,106	13,678	15,797	16,124	16,417	10,391	9,640	15,579	17,776
Taipei, Taiwan	10,122	4,691	1,280	7,265	12,253	249	11,663	15,659	11,800	3,287	4,075	11,800	2,986	8,566	9,789	9,719	16,481	6,001	11,936	10,791
Taiyuan, China	8,739	3,243	1,680	8,593	10,613	1,453	11,375	15,266	10,305	2,522	3,006	10,396	2,346	6,926	8,161	8,107	14,968	7,379	11,516	9,350
Tallahassee, Florida	3,867	11,603	12,040	11,119	6,291	13,268	13,211	3,500	3,235	13,566	12,934	2,640	13,724	8,090	7,671	7,950	3,780	18,193	12,687	9,045
Tallinn, USSR	4,531	3,821	7,667	13,961	4,268	7,796	9,319	11,461	4,986	5,961	5,099	5,496	6,242	675	1,919	1,981	8,958	12,704	8,979	3,992
Tamanrasset, Algeria	6,974	6,647	11,473	18,290	2,458	11,073	5,693	10,649	5,966	8,239	7,338	6,688	8,573	3,673	2,599	2,420	7,028	12,988	5,214	533
Tampa, Florida	4,103	11,817	12,368	11,279	6,228	13,592	12,971	3,275	3,332	13,814	13,153	2,784	13,982	8,206	7,724	7,998	3,469	18,358	12,453	8,993
Tampere, Finland	4,326	3,904	7,596	13,789	4,325	7,777	9,553	11,324	4,847	6,046	5,202	5,336	6,319	851	2,044	2,134	8,916	12,816	9,209	4,187
Tanami, Australia	14,954	8,959	5,928	5,461	16,430	5,220	10,415	15,099	16,768	6,858	7,777	16,564	6,552	13,151	14,156	13,969	18,324	1,814	10,942	13,834
Tangier, Morocco	5,175	6,708	11,081	16,942	1,081	11,063	7,478	9,565	4,195	8,657	7,719	4,918	8,984	2,793	1,529	1,576	6,213	14,443	6,983	1,945
Tarawa (Betio)	11,230	10,589	5,687	1,290	16,106	6,354	15,641	10,765	12,816	9,385	10,179	12,204	9,071	13,395	14,580	14,694	14,289	7,043	16,180	16,558
Tashkent, USSR	7,778	471	5,362	12,288	7,416	4,859	8,570	15,059	8,599	2,350	1,451	9,040	2,658	3,956	4,977	4,830	12,472	9,054	8,516	5,690
Tbilisi, USSR	6,938	2,452	7,297	14,235	5,450	6,895	7,600	13,626	7,253	4,277	3,340	7,827	4,606	2,378	3,106	2,909	10,572	10,594	7,394	3,679
Tegucigalpa, Honduras	5,701	13,428	13,399	10,636	7,350	14,721	12,973	1,666	4,879	15,399	14,763	4,379	15,547	9,743	9,148	9,406	3,278	17,248	12,521	10,088
Tehran, Iran	7,793	2,145	7,035	13,940	6,180	6,451	7,199	14,485	8,139	3,628	2,707	8,713	3,963	3,264	3,929	3,709	11,313	9,730	7,064	4,108
Tel Aviv, Israel	7,471	3,683	8,584	15,516	4,814	8,042	6,349	13,309	7,358	5,185	4,280	8,018	5,520	2,785	2,904	2,626	9,892	10,792	6,094	2,525
Telegraph Creek, Canada	3,326	8,580	7,378	8,615	8,266	8,658	15,892	7,422	4,902	9,861	9,644	4,360	9,872	7,267	7,815	8,080	8,368	14,088	15,421	10,146
Teresina, Brazil	7,931	12,610	16,773	15,141	4,993	17,012	7,630	5,310	6,095	14,331	13,429	6,334	14,665	8,681	7,454	7,526	2,153	15,555	7,183	6,625
Ternate, Indonesia	12,725	7,011	3,643	5,830	14,752	2,929	11,216	15,832	14,489	5,074	6,009	14,388	4,742	11,138	12,286	12,162	18,973	3,545	11,665	12,703
The Valley, Anguilla	5,093	11,994	14,116	13,241	4,877	15,115	10,734	3,636	3,511	14,135	13,262	3,417	14,410	7,864	6,992	7,209	1,353	18,795	10,229	7,541
Thessaloniki, Greece	6,117	4,236	8,937	15,746	3,639	8,672	7,236	12,008	5,936	6,104	5,167	6,596	6,434	1,558	1,488	1,222	8,772	12,159	6,887	2,103
Thimphu, Bhutan	9,707	2,184	3,935	10,391	9,799	2,939	8,956	17,028	10,825	111	1,018	11,167	250	6,358	7,382	7,224	14,883	6,772	9,105	7,804
Thunder Bay, Canada	2,124	9,768	10,107	10,826	6,140	11,278	13,860	5,434	2,534	11,614	11,068	1,824	11,744	6,780	6,722	7,017	5,467	17,023	13,318	8,635
Tientsin, China	8,588	3,569	1,333	8,275	10,760	1,461	11,804	14,908	10,214	2,951	3,418	10,259	2,773	7,083	8,335	8,299	14,897	7,522	11,944	9,640
Tijuana, Mexico	4,806	11,569	9,851	8,143	8,968	11,204	16,318	4,616	5,409	12,849	12,660	4,686	12,832	9,485	9,591	9,885	6,699	15,110	15,793	11,540
Tiksi, USSR	4,927	4,306	4,231	9,618	8,138	5,096	13,038	11,653	6,630	5,504	5,273	6,604	5,547	5,016	6,186	6,302	11,290	11,186	12,859	8,323
Timbuktu, Mali	7,148	7,761	12,569	19,064	2,245	12,187	5,555	9,757	5,845	9,331	8,439	6,542	9,664	4,570	3,373	3,265	6,092	13,557	5,030	1,645
Tindouf, Algeria	5,831	7,413	11,942	17,751	1,004	11,830	6,850	9,283	4,601	9,253	8,321	5,313	9,587	3,675	2,408	2,401	5,750	14,465	6,332	1,853
Tirane, Albania	5,909	4,451	9,098	15,842	3,382	8,875	7,334	11,736	5,679	6,350	5,413	6,344	6,679	1,450	1,224	952	8,513	12,430	6,966	2,023

Distances in Kilometers	Frobisher Bay, Canada	Frunze, USSR	Fukuoka, Japan	Funafuti Atoll, Tuvalu	Funchal, Madeira Island	Fuzhou, China	Gaborone, Botswana	Galapagos Islands (Santa Cruz)	Gander, Canada	Gangtok, India	Garyarsa, China	Gaspe, Canada	Gauhati, India	Gdansk, Poland	Geneva, Switzerland	Genoa, Italy	Georgetown, Guyana	Geraldton, Australia	Ghanzi, Botswana	Ghat, Libya
Tokyo, Japan	8,701	5,537	890	6,402	12,061	2,222	13,658	13,554	10,521	4,891	5,439	10,339	4,663	8,553	9,818	9,845	14,943	7,608	13,865	11,460
Toledo, Spain	4,889	6,334	10,624	16,518	1,407	10,646	7,790	9,746	4,075	8,329	7,394	4,792	8,652	2,338	1,087	1,183	6,506	14,353	7,310	2,119
Topeka, Kansas	3,281	10,876	10,671	10,191	6,927	11,934	14,370	4,427	3,424	12,642	12,155	2,705	12,742	7,917	7,787	8,081	5,183	17,019	13,830	9,556
Toronto, Canada	2,340	10,073	10,934	11,584	5,480	12,051	13,058	5,028	1,986	12,049	11,404	1,281	12,218	6,676	6,413	6,703	4,580	17,941	12,514	8,106
Toulouse, France	4,823	5,738	10,017	16,111	2,009	10,033	7,962	10,206	4,262	7,757	6,825	4,959	8,076	1,729	472	609	7,066	13,957	7,510	2,215
Tours, France	4,458	5,612	9,733	15,694	2,211	9,821	8,371	10,142	4,025	7,679	6,757	4,703	7,991	1,478	439	721	7,140	14,059	7,924	2,626
Townsville, Australia	14,397	10,078	6,101	3,683	17,819	5,831	11,987	13,417	16,197	8,118	9,055	15,701	7,789	14,166	15,346	15,230	16,998	3,429	12,527	15,530
Trenton, New Jersey	2,650	10,299	11,435	11,986	5,165	12,522	12,610	4,795	1,862	12,331	11,636	1,256	12,522	6,704	6,319	6,603	4,056	18,479	12,067	7,856
Tripoli, Lebanon	7,287	3,468	8,361	15,302	4,848	7,859	6,625	13,309	7,249	5,051	4,133	7,896	5,386	2,587	2,818	2,552	9,957	10,833	6,374	2,687
Tripoli, Libya	6,381	5,393	10,153	16,948	2,809	9,838	6,512	11,318	5,776	7,140	6,213	6,486	7,475	2,422	1,593	1,330	7,865	12,675	6,097	927
Tristan da Cunha (Edinburgh)	12,218	12,465	16,634	14,823	7,729	15,326	3,872	8,913	10,403	12,700	12,267	10,819	12,903	10,553	9,404	9,273	6,804	10,860	3,701	7,258
Trondheim, Norway	3,667	4,602	8,030	13,845	3,917	8,327	9,859	10,605	4,129	6,742	5,910	4,620	7,007	1,114	1,935	2,117	8,276	13,525	9,473	4,273
Trujillo, Peru	8,019	15,377	15,886	11,173	7,971	17,241	11,128	1,507	6,757	17,519	16,640	6,467	17,785	11,236	10,289	10,477	2,844	15,672	10,793	10,314
Truk Island (Moen)	11,417	8,415	3,642	3,502	15,415	4,019	13,987	13,090	13,249	6,998	7,834	12,841	6,676	11,897	13,164	13,171	16,344	5,659	14,456	14,537
Truro, Canada	2,073	9,377	11,154	12,824	4,192	12,088	11,856	5,753	767	11,468	10,712	396	11,688	5,635	5,220	5,504	4,302	18,153	11,314	6,817
Tsingtao, China	8,912	3,956	962	7,880	11,197	1,111	11,958	14,972	10,574	3,141	3,700	10,588	2,925	7,521	8,772	8,735	15,257	7,201	12,133	10,050
Tsitsihar, China	7,636	3,848	1,624	8,230	10,322	2,397	12,573	13,861	9,331	3,788	4,061	9,314	3,669	6,738	8,006	8,019	14,001	8,484	12,645	9,624
Tubuai Island (Mataura)	11,877	15,443	10,563	3,729	15,291	11,238	14,667	6,850	12,276	14,219	15,063	11,577	13,891	16,426	16,667	16,961	10,445	9,336	14,945	17,959
Tucson, Arizona	4,569	11,668	10,302	8,666	8,501	11,647	15,750	4,233	4,989	13,098	12,825	4,266	13,111	9,272	9,277	9,572	6,138	15,669	15,228	11,127
Tulsa, Oklahoma	3,584	11,197	10,914	10,117	7,065	12,192	14,376	4,113	3,622	12,961	12,477	2,912	13,058	8,196	8,026	8,319	5,029	17,057	13,841	9,732
Tunis, Tunisia	5,868	5,420	10,057	16,682	2,515	9,849	7,001	10,996	5,294	7,277	6,341	6,000	7,608	2,056	1,096	852	7,636	13,070	6,574	1,312
Tura, USSR	5,771	2,881	3,986	10,321	7,957	4,462	11,728	12,890	7,260	4,191	3,872	7,392	4,279	4,433	5,692	5,735	11,918	10,391	11,604	7,537
Turin, Italy	4,998	5,218	9,563	15,874	2,524	9,534	7,939	10,694	4,623	7,234	6,303	5,300	7,554	1,301	173	124	7,587	13,491	7,515	2,240
Uberlandia, Brazil	9,333	14,086	18,376	14,003	6,614	18,525	7,609	5,019	7,545	15,544	14,720	7,676	15,860	10,296	9,054	9,106	3,045	14,419	7,265	7,982
Ufa, USSR	6,026	1,889	6,076	12,866	6,049	5,984	9,254	13,273	6,820	4,031	3,199	7,253	4,304	2,384	3,576	3,511	10,895	10,812	9,059	4,983
Ujungpandang, Indonesia	13,467	6,972	4,437	6,608	14,564	3,452	10,134	16,665	15,114	4,884	5,810	15,145	4,572	11,164	12,197	12,027	19,700	2,666	10,594	12,193
Ulaanbaatar, Mongolia	7,617	2,568	2,527	9,412	9,479	2,655	11,369	14,509	9,125	2,781	2,869	9,252	2,752	5,804	7,059	7,030	13,769	8,528	11,407	8,464
Ulan-Ude, USSR	7,183	2,656	2,733	9,506	9,205	3,024	11,584	14,086	8,709	3,151	3,144	8,823	3,147	5,556	6,820	6,811	13,368	8,954	11,587	8,351
Uliastay, Mongolia	7,575	1,816	3,211	10,135	8,931	3,106	10,687	14,738	8,943	2,376	2,258	9,152	2,435	5,243	6,475	6,422	13,485	8,659	10,700	7,756
Uranium City, Canada	2,136	8,643	8,355	9,839	7,033	9,554	14,786	6,862	3,596	10,245	9,851	3,047	10,320	6,532	6,872	7,154	7,223	15,294	14,280	9,112
Urumqi, China	7,896	1,056	3,847	10,785	8,606	3,467	9,847	15,219	9,090	1,829	1,479	9,387	1,990	4,958	6,129	6,035	13,434	8,495	9,860	7,154
Ushuaia, Argentina	13,147	17,034	17,237	10,641	10,861	16,756	8,063	6,334	11,570	16,431	16,459	11,492	16,436	14,461	13,194	13,181	6,892	10,742	8,081	11,539
Vaduz, Liechtenstein	4,901	5,001	9,296	15,610	2,754	9,287	8,124	10,810	4,639	7,041	6,114	5,299	7,356	1,026	278	309	7,777	13,394	7,711	2,464
Valencia, Spain	5,105	6,086	10,466	16,576	1,668	10,434	7,607	10,058	4,364	8,056	7,119	5,078	8,381	2,186	918	947	6,791	14,037	7,139	1,887
Valladolid, Spain	4,693	6,285	10,499	16,314	1,471	10,559	7,992	9,697	3,923	8,305	7,373	4,637	8,625	2,226	1,008	1,154	6,518	14,434	7,514	2,305
Valletta, Malta	6,163	5,123	9,839	16,599	2,903	9,566	6,810	11,395	5,665	6,930	5,997	6,365	7,263	2,075	1,340	1,057	8,013	12,669	6,406	1,281
Valparaiso, Chile	10,732	16,885	17,979	11,254	9,261	18,712	9,209	4,089	9,237	18,026	17,397	9,096	18,247	12,933	11,737	11,822	4,633	13,133	9,039	10,778
Vancouver, Canada	3,586	9,650	8,320	8,502	8,384	9,634	16,184	6,354	4,824	10,959	10,737	4,176	10,966	7,980	8,352	8,633	7,633	14,681	15,658	10,577
Varna, Bulgaria	6,099	3,753	8,434	15,256	4,059	8,180	7,519	12,315	6,094	5,666	4,729	6,725	5,992	1,410	1,749	1,528	9,180	11,887	7,200	2,592
Venice, Italy	5,186	4,860	9,267	15,721	2,881	9,198	7,885	11,053	4,922	6,866	5,934	5,586	7,186	1,088	488	292	7,957	13,141	7,482	2,281
Veracruz, Mexico	5,369	13,064	12,368	9,777	7,905	13,709	14,055	2,282	4,957	14,831	14,354	4,339	14,913	9,791	9,396	9,675	4,329	16,739	13,590	10,673
Verona, Italy	5,122	4,959	9,345	15,757	2,782	9,289	7,910	10,948	4,830	6,970	6,038	5,497	7,289	1,131	385	198	7,853	13,244	7,501	2,274
Victoria, Canada	3,665	9,735	8,356	8,440	8,450	9,674	16,250	6,297	4,882	11,030	10,816	4,229	11,034	8,071	8,437	8,720	7,628	14,668	15,722	10,658
Victoria, Seychelles	12,073	5,226	8,913	13,618	8,653	7,668	3,862	16,193	11,854	5,020	4,814	12,551	5,188	7,371	7,431	7,138	12,685	6,772	4,088	5,888
Vienna, Austria	5,129	4,476	8,835	15,319	3,272	8,782	8,126	11,298	5,040	6,515	5,588	5,675	6,830	703	804	709	8,303	12,916	7,746	2,635
Vientiane, Laos	10,913	3,822	3,265	8,902	11,492	1,942	9,558	17,630	12,259	1,770	2,707	12,497	1,443	8,014	9,069	8,915	16,557	5,330	9,830	9,423
Villahermosa, Mexico	5,411	13,144	12,688	10,091	7,673	14,022	13,691	2,078	4,858	14,988	14,455	4,274	15,093	9,723	9,262	9,535	3,967	16,982	13,227	10,439
Vilnius, USSR	4,952	3,760	7,911	14,385	4,100	7,929	8,791	11,686	5,245	5,874	4,978	5,801	6,171	432	1,647	1,638	8,975	12,519	8,455	3,528
Visby, Sweden	4,418	4,190	8,090	14,313	3,843	8,217	9,147	11,169	4,713	6,323	5,445	5,259	6,611	366	1,517	1,607	8,566	13,024	8,782	3,686
Vitoria, Brazil	9,636	13,536	18,281	14,653	6,369	17,854	6,770	5,861	7,801	14,808	14,033	8,025	15,112	9,993	8,729	8,745	3,578	13,949	6,419	7,417
Vladivostok, USSR	8,019	4,576	1,068	7,450	11,036	2,211	13,106	13,708	9,783	4,254	4,655	9,691	4,082	7,492	8,759	8,781	14,383	8,156	13,229	10,405
Volgograd, USSR	6,236	2,416	7,019	13,877	5,325	6,794	8,338	13,154	6,699	4,462	3,546	7,230	4,773	1,879	2,867	2,735	10,358	11,050	8,107	3,978
Vologda, USSR	5,095	2,980	6,895	13,423	5,083	6,957	9,385	12,225	5,754	5,122	4,280	6,217	5,396	1,399	2,658	2,655	9,819	11,895	9,106	4,452
Vorkuta, USSR	4,959	2,811	5,604	11,928	6,316	5,898	10,696	12,325	6,114	4,764	4,119	6,404	4,964	2,770	4,027	4,076	10,606	11,471	10,468	5,954
Wake Island	9,654	8,738	3,921	3,366	14,247	4,898	15,949	11,403	11,419	7,908	8,570	10,929	7,632	11,296	12,493	12,598	14,331	7,717	16,366	14,492
Wallis Island	12,190	12,571	7,679	737	17,013	8,231	15,176	9,545	13,403	11,191	12,045	12,697	10,864	15,270	16,351	16,522	13,217	7,303	15,684	18,558
Walvis Bay, Namibia	11,934	9,538	13,725	16,148	6,998	12,512	1,177	11,512	10,491	9,715	9,262	11,132	9,935	8,573	7,704	7,481	8,556	9,731	766	5,322
Warsaw, Poland	4,982	4,064	8,299	14,767	3,738	8,293	8,534	11,504	5,118	6,153	5,242	5,708	6,458	281	1,269	1,245	8,676	12,715	8,177	3,164
Washington, D.C.	2,823	10,507	11,498	11,799	5,385	12,615	12,767	4,585	2,107	12,524	11,844	1,492	12,707	6,944	6,564	6,848	4,028	18,462	12,225	8,086
Watson Lake, Canada	3,071	8,388	7,390	8,875	8,011	8,648	15,612	7,506	4,686	9,731	9,479	4,167	9,755	6,988	7,533	7,798	8,286	14,199	15,145	9,866
Weimar, East Germany	4,659	4,749	8,909	15,166	3,073	8,956	8,501	10,882	4,575	6,833	5,918	5,203	7,140	622	653	751	7,993	13,338	8,102	2,890
Wellington, New Zealand	15,311	13,679	9,456	3,657	18,602	9,399	12,031	10,370	16,113	11,662	12,594	15,397	11,341	17,730	18,953	18,814	13,556	5,552	12,511	17,709
West Berlin, West Germany	4,625	4,570	8,689	14,958	3,283	8,747	8,636	10,994	4,638	6,667	5,758	5,247	6,970	405	876	959	8,167	13,226	8,247	3,071
Wewak, Papua New Guinea	12,838	8,594	4,339	3,966	16,207	4,199	12,617	14,010	14,685	6,817	7,734	14,325	6,482	12,521	13,754	13,685	17,594	4,150	13,118	14,516
Whangarei, New Zealand	14,822	13,317	8,931	3,052	18,935	8,957	12,547	10,450	15,809	11,373	12,311	15,086	11,046	17,218	18,484	18,443	13,803	5,597	13,040	18,090
Whitehorse, Canada	3,318	8,208	7,049	8,656	8,245	8,314	15,743	7,798	4,983	9,478	9,263	4,485	9,489	7,036	7,647	7,904	8,637	13,850	15,299	10,002
Wichita, Kansas	3,477	11,042	10,701	10,022	7,117	11,980	14,511	4,304	3,628	12,779	12,312	2,910	12,870	8,123	7,996	8,290	5,226	16,906	13,973	9,757
Willemstad, Curacao	5,732	12,878	14,551	12,586	5,755	15,686	11,054	2,757	4,293	15,020	14,160	4,092	15,285	8,769	7,903	8,118	1,322	18,126	10,579	8,371
Wiluna, Australia	15,828	9,002	6,747	6,508	15,850	5,830	9,221	15,566	17,484	6,860	7,720	17,504	6,591	13,100	13,908	13,675	17,807	604	9,752	13,103
Windhoek, Namibia	12,021	9,339	13,470	16,054	7,099	12,249	929	11,780	10,625	9,468	9,030	11,277	9,684	8,525	7,696	7,465	8,806	9,521	498	5,313
Windsor, Canada	2,563	10,307	10,940	11,289	5,800	12,096	13,330	4,812	2,319	12,247	11,632	1,613	12,403	6,985	6,741	7,032	4,632	17,832	12,787	8,436
Winnipeg, Canada	2,298	9,694	9,644	10,280	6,655	10,855	14,416	5,635	3,046	11,433	10,959	2,357	11,534	7,000	7,060	7,354	5,996	16,458	13,876	9,074
Winston-Salem, North Carolina	3,177	10,893	11,662	11,520	5,735	12,824	12,979	4,200	2,524	12,887	12,228	1,911	13,060	7,364	6,978	7,261	3,948	18,409	12,442	8,458
Wroclaw, Poland	4,907	4,356	8,596	15,007	3,436	8,596	8,438	11,273	4,932	6,433	5,518	5,543	6,741	378	967	958	8,390	12,948	8,063	2,960
Wuhan, China	9,545	3,756	1,557	8,155	11,331	701	11,221	15,801	11,127	2,521	3,222	11,208	2,258	7,647	8,861	8,785	15,791	6,568	11,429	9,867
Wyndham, Australia	14,493	8,458	5,434	5,599	16,017	4,695	10,493	15,441	16,283	6,372	7,297	16,132	6,061	12,650	13,683	13,507	18,838	2,024	11,007	13,512
Xi'an, China	9,137	3,114	1,986	8,767	10,690	1,350	10,916	15,781	10,644	2,083	2,672	10,777	1,876	7,011	8,217	8,139	15,262	7,003	11,079	9,232
Xining, China	8,845	2,418	2,623	9,462	10,046	2,031	10,448	15,831	10,244	1,611	2,040	10,442	1,498	6,383	7,569	7,479	14,767	7,361	10,569	8,534
Yakutsk, USSR	5,973	4,132	3,160	8,897	9,095	4,066	13,112	12,421	7,697	4,890	4,848	7,652	4,871	5,772	6,999	7,079	12,346	10,151	13,033	8,980
Yanji, China	8,076	4,403	1,035	7,589	10,972	2,083	12,910	13,879	9,823	4,058	4,461	9,752	3,888	7,401	8,668	8,682	14,449	8,079	13,033	10,271
Yaounde, Cameroon	9,132	7,545	12,394	18,569	4,349	11,589	3,519	11,347	7,959	8,542	7,789	8,664	8,849	5,635	4,720	4,500	7,727	11,496	3,027	2,339
Yap Island (Colonia)	11,573	7,147	2,780	4,963	14,647	2,704	12,695	14,575	13,409	5,548	6,421	13,174	5,219	10,968	12,212	12,160	17,467	4,934	13,120	13,214
Yaraka, Australia	15,079	10,333	6,631	4,135	17,984	6,237	11,399	13,524	16,881	8,294	9,227	16,374	7,974	14,496	15,603	15,447	16,921	2,955	11,941	15,398
Yarmouth, Canada	2,222	9,635	11,270	12,642	4,415	12,243	12,020	5,485	1,050	11,716	10,971	570	11,931	5,917	5,500	5,783	4,176	18,331	11,477	7,066
Yellowknife, Canada	2,269	8,298	7,910	9,671	7,209	9,107	14,879	7,281	3,875	9,845	9,480	3,376	9,910	6,422	6,859	7,133	7,653	14,875	14,393	9,152
Yerevan, USSR	7,078	2,516	7,386	14,328	5,462	6,950	7,434	13,700	7,356	4,279	3,343	7,939	4,610	2,486	3,155	2,945	10,592	10,517	7,231	3,606
Yinchuan, China	8,664	2,709	2,230	9,130	10,194	1,835	10,899	15,485	10,141	2,059	2,471	10,292	1,929	6,509	7,726	7,656	14,745	7,493	11,019	8,828
Yogyakarta, Indonesia	13,794	6,681	5,046	7,568	13,947	3,871	9,101	17,548	15,232	4,540	5,416	15,431	4,266	10,818	11,726	11,521	18,766	2,363	9,556	11,403
York, United Kingdom	3,845	5,466	9,261	14,979	2,666	9,477	9,079	10,013	3,670	7,589	6,696	4,299	7,884	1,295	997	1,279	7,280	14,206	8,640	3,341
Yumen, China	8,457	1,959	2,982	9,886	9,545	2,517	10,311	15,587	9,802	1,622	1,803	10,028	1,613	5,881	7,068	6,981	14,283	7,793	10,392	8,081
Yutian, China	8,545	904	4,401	11,236	8,595	3,740	8,977	15,912	9,569	1,242	581	9,943	1,518	5,089	6,148	6,007	13,628	8,038	9,018	6,807
Yuzhno-Sakhalinsk, USSR	7,429	5,226	1,813	7,121	10,958	3,101	13,985	12,762	9,248	5,156	5,479	9,071	5,003	7,610	8,852	8,918	13,706	8,849	14,066	10,731
Zagreb, Yugoslavia	5,325	4,578	9,027	15,571	3,164	8,929	7,867	11,326	5,148	6,579	5,647	5,800	6,899	970	763	576	8,244	12,875	7,483	2,370
Zahedan, Iran	8,761	1,928	6,493	13,210	7,255	5,711	7,064	15,603	9,226	2,723	1,884	9,779	3,054	4,354	5,045	4,821	12,376	8,614	7,034	5,007
Zamboanga, Philippines	12,119	6,114	3,077	6,558	13,854	2,143	10,955	16,368	13,809	4,193	5,124	13,798	3,859	10,247	11,389	11,265	18,489	4,027	11,358	11,861
Zanzibar, Tanzania	11,484	6,505	10,502	15,302	7,316	9,334	2,490	14,383	10,801	6,481	6,058	11,524	6,704	6,975	6,658	6,368	10,908	8,266	2,533	4,662
Zaragoza, Spain	4,884	6,007	10,307	16,335	1,734	10,317	7,843	10,017	4,202	8,010	7,076	4,910	8,332	2,019	760	858	6,819	14,116	7,377	2,112
Zashiversk, USSR	5,237	4,771	3,850	8,914	8,775	4,865	13,646	11,560	7,015	5,718	5,610	6,909	5,714	5,721	6,882	7,004	11,604	10,923	13,498	9,031
Zhengzhou, China	9,084	3,477	1,547	8,373	10,942	1,102	11,341	15,484	10,661	2,521	3,107	10,745	2,304	7,254	8,481	8,419	15,327	7,031	11,512	9,599
Zurich, Switzerland	4,829	5,075	9,342	15,611	2,687	9,349	8,169	10,721	4,552	7,121	6,195	5,213	7,436	1,061	212	331	7,697	13,483	7,752	2,491

Distances in Kilometers	Gibraltar	Gijon, Spain	Gisborne, New Zealand	Glasgow, United Kingdom	Godthab, Greenland	Gomez Palacio, Mexico	Goose Bay, Canada	Gorki, USSR	Goteborg, Sweden	Granada, Spain	Grand Turk, Turks & Caicos	Graz, Austria	Green Bay, Wisconsin	Grenoble, France	Guadalajara, Mexico	Guam (Agana)	Guantanamo, Cuba	Guatemala City, Guatemala	Guayaquil, Ecuador	Guiyang, China
Gijon, Spain	822	0	19,387	1,372	3,668	8,689	8,100	3,741	1,999	721	6,441	1,697	6,301	925	9,047	13,018	6,863	8,494	8,907	9,636
Gisborne, New Zealand	19,606	19,387	0	18,089	15,721	10,820	11,288	16,132	17,659	19,795	13,249	18,320	13,158	19,050	10,488	6,730	12,815	11,140	10,915	10,348
Glasgow, United Kingdom	2,191	1,372	18,089	0	2,724	8,244	7,032	2,942	1,011	2,070	6,620	1,672	5,735	1,378	8,679	11,801	6,992	8,442	9,311	8,804
Godthab, Greenland	4,377	3,668	15,721	2,724	0	5,666	4,434	4,847	3,363	4,349	4,969	4,372	3,150	4,066	6,149	11,276	5,208	6,259	7,725	9,759
Gomez Palacio, Mexico	9,058	8,689	10,820	8,244	5,666	0	3,523	10,427	9,016	9,140	3,329	9,909	2,523	9,409	543	11,467	2,960	1,817	3,990	13,392
Goose Bay, Canada	8,804	8,100	11,288	7,032	4,434	3,523	0	8,039	7,364	8,781	5,864	8,541	3,019	8,410	4,013	8,684	5,702	5,251	7,450	9,871
Gorki, USSR	4,291	3,741	16,132	2,942	4,847	10,427	8,039	0	1,933	4,102	9,478	2,205	7,963	2,925	10,940	9,422	9,816	11,084	12,222	5,919
Goteborg, Sweden	2,720	1,999	17,659	1,011	3,363	9,016	7,364	1,933	0	2,552	7,609	1,208	6,493	1,461	9,482	11,019	7,971	9,368	10,317	7,820
Granada, Spain	191	721	19,795	2,070	4,349	9,140	8,781	4,102	2,552	0	6,641	1,915	6,834	1,182	9,459	13,501	7,079	8,767	8,936	9,884
Grand Turk, Turks & Caicos	6,503	6,441	13,249	6,620	4,969	3,329	5,864	9,478	7,609	6,641	0	8,041	2,990	7,336	3,342	14,516	448	2,185	2,781	14,683
Graz, Austria	2,106	1,697	18,320	1,672	4,372	9,909	8,541	2,205	1,208	1,915	8,041	0	7,405	781	10,334	11,627	8,445	9,998	10,587	7,987
Green Bay, Wisconsin	6,784	6,301	13,158	5,735	3,150	2,523	3,019	7,963	6,493	6,834	2,990	7,405	0	6,949	2,999	11,676	2,952	3,321	5,234	11,992
Grenoble, France	1,369	925	19,050	1,378	4,066	9,409	8,410	2,925	1,461	1,182	7,336	781	6,949	0	9,801	12,320	7,751	9,349	9,831	8,762
Guadalajara, Mexico	9,365	9,047	10,488	8,679	6,149	543	4,013	10,940	9,482	9,459	3,342	10,334	2,999	9,801	0	11,682	2,934	1,514	3,599	13,862
Guam (Agana)	13,686	13,018	6,730	11,801	11,276	11,467	8,684	9,422	11,019	13,501	14,516	11,627	11,676	12,320	11,682	0	14,284	13,194	14,972	4,216
Guantanamo, Cuba	6,943	6,863	12,815	6,992	5,208	2,960	5,702	9,816	7,971	7,079	448	8,445	2,952	7,751	2,934	14,284	0	1,737	2,518	14,832
Guatemala City, Guatemala	8,640	8,494	11,140	8,442	6,259	1,817	5,251	11,084	9,368	8,767	2,185	9,998	3,321	9,349	1,514	13,194	1,737	0	2,200	15,083
Guayaquil, Ecuador	8,767	8,907	10,915	9,311	7,725	3,990	7,450	12,222	10,317	8,936	2,781	10,587	5,234	9,831	3,599	14,972	2,518	2,200	0	17,215
Guiyang, China	10,075	9,636	10,348	8,804	9,759	13,392	9,871	5,919	7,820	9,884	14,683	7,987	11,992	8,762	13,862	4,216	14,832	15,083	17,215	0
Gur'yev, USSR	4,810	4,427	15,611	3,903	5,997	11,586	9,089	1,159	2,907	4,620	10,517	2,741	9,122	3,522	12,099	9,139	10,876	12,211	13,207	5,265
Haifa, Israel	3,698	3,714	16,642	3,953	6,611	12,196	10,523	2,702	3,268	3,539	10,145	2,288	9,687	2,860	12,621	10,981	10,572	12,203	12,454	6,843
Haikou, China	10,833	10,422	9,586	9,613	10,529	13,783	10,298	6,718	8,626	10,644	15,409	8,760	12,618	9,538	14,210	3,736	15,520	15,550	17,747	812
Haiphong, Vietnam	10,491	10,103	9,926	9,338	10,384	13,928	10,418	6,423	8,343	10,303	15,316	8,430	12,614	9,210	14,378	4,122	15,465	15,657	17,822	633
Hakodate, Japan	10,717	9,981	9,675	8,698	8,203	10,061	6,638	6,648	7,999	10,545	12,279	8,787	9,292	9,392	10,475	3,159	12,225	11,857	14,051	3,525
Halifax, Canada	4,928	4,541	14,968	4,267	2,308	4,151	4,683	6,943	5,182	4,999	2,663	5,872	1,931	5,297	4,510	12,964	2,923	4,186	5,431	12,056
Hamburg, West Germany	2,274	1,599	18,118	952	3,579	9,173	7,724	2,178	480	2,100	7,538	818	6,655	982	9,617	11,432	7,919	9,391	10,190	8,097
Hamilton, Bermuda	5,407	5,232	14,392	5,292	3,670	3,828	5,446	8,127	6,271	5,524	1,354	6,768	2,429	6,096	4,030	14,053	1,701	3,262	4,131	13,428
Hamilton, New Zealand	19,815	19,361	259	17,998	15,762	10,992	11,331	15,895	17,479	19,908	13,480	18,072	13,296	18,820	10,672	6,508	13,044	11,359	11,168	10,094
Hangzhou, China	10,720	10,155	9,705	9,116	9,504	12,281	8,808	6,433	8,206	10,530	14,157	8,618	11,248	9,357	12,708	3,135	14,194	14,057	16,257	1,378
Hannover, West Germany	2,159	1,506	18,238	990	3,658	9,230	7,834	2,248	613	1,983	7,534	720	6,716	853	9,668	11,539	7,921	9,412	10,167	8,163
Hanoi, Vietnam	10,414	10,031	10,003	9,277	10,351	13,960	10,446	6,358	8,280	10,225	15,292	8,356	12,612	9,136	14,414	4,210	15,449	15,678	17,831	621
Harare, Zimbabwe	7,097	7,759	12,871	8,811	11,425	15,274	15,840	8,308	8,557	7,099	11,947	7,356	13,675	7,433	15,243	12,945	12,330	13,802	12,147	9,534
Harbin, China	9,743	9,055	10,665	7,848	7,807	10,629	7,112	5,553	7,056	9,562	12,348	7,734	9,441	8,388	11,096	3,964	12,384	12,351	14,534	2,766
Harrisburg, Pennsylvania	6,109	5,735	13,777	5,407	3,133	2,957	4,045	7,949	6,280	6,185	2,154	7,038	1,029	6,484	3,319	12,675	2,237	3,135	4,708	12,595
Hartford, Connecticut	5,720	5,344	14,168	5,035	2,844	3,349	4,242	7,623	5,922	5,795	2,256	6,658	1,282	6,096	3,708	12,792	2,410	3,464	4,919	12,437
Havana, Cuba	7,409	7,230	12,386	7,176	5,093	2,159	4,975	9,868	8,113	7,528	1,172	8,724	2,427	8,079	2,182	13,487	813	1,273	2,812	14,418
Helena, Montana	8,292	7,682	11,727	6,815	4,094	2,453	1,259	8,380	7,346	8,305	4,614	8,441	1,882	8,158	2,983	9,916	4,444	4,071	6,255	11,016
Helsinki, Finland	3,436	2,763	16,965	1,777	3,765	9,418	7,396	1,191	795	3,258	8,289	1,584	6,913	2,101	9,911	10,263	8,632	9,942	11,030	7,031
Hengyang, China	10,479	9,993	9,946	9,079	9,806	13,035	9,533	6,254	8,118	10,288	14,638	8,377	11,825	9,143	13,480	3,660	14,734	14,781	16,969	586
Herat, Afghanistan	6,022	5,809	14,371	5,495	7,657	13,207	10,460	2,811	4,526	5,843	12,109	4,126	10,770	4,884	13,729	8,504	12,487	13,870	14,713	4,326
Hermosillo, Mexico	9,411	8,955	10,512	8,344	5,665	834	2,842	10,251	9,023	9,472	4,080	10,015	2,655	9,596	1,208	10,639	3,739	2,642	4,792	12,658
Hiroshima, Japan	11,058	10,390	9,355	9,198	9,063	11,135	7,728	6,815	8,392	10,874	13,341	9,015	10,361	9,698	11,536	2,630	13,302	12,938	15,125	2,609
Hiva Oa (Atuona)	14,524	14,175	5,333	13,573	10,857	5,489	6,867	14,836	14,143	14,618	8,182	15,229	7,901	14,847	5,160	8,804	7,734	5,998	6,600	12,906
Ho Chi Minh City, Vietnam	11,223	10,930	9,179	10,290	11,488	14,837	11,380	7,349	9,282	11,040	16,433	9,235	13,710	10,014	15,239	4,153	16,583	16,627	18,826	1,753
Hobart, Australia	17,568	17,837	2,617	17,528	17,346	13,418	13,266	14,586	16,520	17,484	15,739	16,258	15,644	16,963	13,102	6,248	15,328	13,714	13,149	8,748
Hohhot, China	9,341	8,759	11,083	7,718	8,267	11,816	8,295	5,050	6,805	9,152	13,107	7,246	10,356	7,974	12,307	4,418	13,224	13,461	15,577	1,639
Hong Kong	10,954	10,492	9,470	9,604	10,336	13,344	9,877	6,759	8,637	10,763	15,135	8,859	12,277	9,629	13,762	3,377	15,208	15,126	17,326	895
Honiara, Solomon Islands	16,700	15,979	3,707	14,676	13,438	11,116	9,627	12,461	13,993	16,520	14,417	14,665	12,486	15,345	11,076	3,039	14,006	12,369	13,285	6,995
Honolulu, Hawaii	13,024	12,286	7,101	11,102	8,647	5,538	4,239	11,159	11,196	12,987	8,853	12,402	6,802	12,458	5,641	6,129	8,498	7,122	8,865	9,488
Houston, Texas	8,133	7,778	11,739	7,392	4,897	928	3,588	9,723	8,207	8,217	2,595	9,046	1,761	8,518	1,288	11,999	2,294	1,748	3,901	13,343
Huambo, Angola	5,847	6,601	14,025	7,825	10,219	13,542	14,613	8,090	7,816	5,893	10,214	6,623	12,084	6,492	13,516	14,511	10,597	12,096	10,575	10,731
Hubli, India	8,181	8,118	12,169	7,949	10,098	15,476	12,288	5,258	6,993	8,019	14,530	6,490	13,161	7,208	16,017	7,474	14,927	16,339	16,923	3,497
Hugh Town, United Kingdom	1,533	711	18,709	673	3,081	8,364	7,487	3,363	1,477	1,427	6,419	1,634	5,903	1,047	8,762	12,438	6,818	8,365	9,021	9,279
Hull, Canada	5,839	5,395	14,084	4,950	2,573	3,317	3,819	7,408	5,786	5,898	2,691	6,604	973	6,092	3,730	12,324	2,806	3,687	5,288	12,026
Hyderabad, India	8,350	8,234	12,016	7,973	10,007	15,248	11,975	5,199	6,997	8,182	14,589	6,577	13,015	7,315	15,791	7,094	14,965	16,266	17,117	3,082
Hyderabad, Pakistan	6,995	6,865	13,377	6,637	8,807	14,302	11,360	3,960	5,678	6,824	13,235	5,209	11,904	5,945	14,834	8,033	13,623	15,028	15,757	3,828
Igloolik, Canada	5,770	5,028	14,359	3,928	1,426	5,077	3,105	5,393	4,334	5,727	5,374	5,473	2,792	5,305	5,608	10,130	5,492	6,113	7,941	9,341
Iloilo, Philippines	12,494	12,050	7,928	11,154	11,679	13,620	10,416	8,319	10,194	12,304	16,149	10,408	13,163	11,182	13,922	2,434	16,086	15,424	17,384	2,421
Indianapolis, Indiana	6,860	6,445	13,045	6,003	3,527	2,257	3,432	8,371	6,816	6,928	2,481	7,661	549	7,152	2,677	12,115	2,415	2,818	4,688	12,539
Innsbruck, Austria	1,856	1,396	18,567	1,439	4,160	9,649	8,397	2,435	1,164	1,667	7,736	308	7,155	497	10,066	11,844	8,141	9,702	10,279	8,266
Inuvik, Canada	7,659	6,872	12,524	5,625	3,437	5,169	1,918	6,172	5,744	7,591	6,689	6,951	3,717	6,973	5,699	8,274	6,669	6,706	8,830	8,393
Invercargill, New Zealand	18,752	19,447	1,168	18,838	16,876	11,887	12,443	16,103	17,978	18,795	14,033	17,958	14,284	18,666	11,520	7,039	13,622	12,025	11,486	10,185
Inverness, United Kingdom	2,373	1,553	17,908	182	2,613	8,176	6,886	2,880	967	2,252	6,642	1,762	5,660	1,531	8,621	11,645	7,006	8,427	9,353	8,707
Iquitos, Peru	8,301	8,521	11,361	9,064	7,755	4,604	7,982	12,005	10,074	8,477	2,801	10,216	5,546	9,444	4,254	15,724	2,652	2,788	753	17,480
Iraklion, Greece	2,748	2,785	17,592	3,187	5,902	11,375	10,039	2,736	2,674	2,588	9,201	1,533	8,896	1,972	11,773	11,682	9,631	11,278	11,510	7,638
Irkutsk, USSR	8,088	7,456	12,330	6,358	6,917	10,968	7,529	3,826	5,475	7,902	11,825	6,028	9,216	6,720	11,493	5,602	11,984	12,457	14,438	2,859
Islamabad, Pakistan	6,971	6,695	13,433	6,228	8,128	13,436	10,362	3,358	5,227	6,787	12,829	4,999	11,137	5,773	13,977	7,500	13,174	14,385	15,535	3,312
Istanbul, Turkey	3,019	2,850	17,376	2,916	5,557	11,158	9,520	2,022	2,217	2,838	9,276	1,272	8,643	1,941	11,594	11,087	9,689	11,264	11,742	7,141
Ivujivik, Canada	5,640	4,966	14,428	4,045	1,326	4,513	3,173	5,915	4,624	5,627	4,576	5,681	2,095	5,392	5,026	10,818	4,699	5,396	7,163	10,133
Iwo Jima Island, Japan	12,413	11,727	7,997	10,498	10,071	11,097	7,963	8,183	9,728	12,231	13,809	10,382	10,846	11,054	11,409	1,303	13,665	12,904	14,951	3,470
Izmir, Turkey	2,879	2,801	17,495	3,025	5,711	11,261	9,759	2,350	2,413	2,706	9,242	1,354	8,759	1,925	11,681	11,360	9,663	11,274	11,639	7,366
Jackson, Mississippi	7,565	7,217	12,305	6,864	4,431	1,495	3,704	9,276	7,702	7,650	2,236	8,510	1,369	7,967	1,835	12,287	2,011	1,957	3,968	13,248
Jaffna, Sri Lanka	8,970	8,929	11,372	8,766	10,867	16,089	12,739	6,044	7,805	8,812	15,349	7,308	13,885	8,022	16,630	7,057	15,746	17,125	17,653	3,378
Jakarta, Indonesia	12,402	12,287	7,956	11,879	13,333	16,153	12,947	8,957	10,871	12,238	18,298	10,610	15,520	11,364	16,404	4,724	18,445	17,918	18,837	3,623
Jamestown, St. Helena	5,763	6,584	13,948	7,954	9,709	11,528	13,581	9,246	8,324	5,887	8,251	7,291	10,641	6,864	11,401	16,846	8,580	9,917	8,252	12,995
Jamnagar, India	7,306	7,199	13,059	6,997	9,169	14,646	11,643	4,323	6,040	7,138	13,588	5,554	12,262	6,283	15,180	7,900	13,979	15,393	16,073	3,729
Jan Mayen Island	3,886	3,064	16,383	1,706	1,909	7,501	5,591	2,948	1,773	3,773	6,767	2,964	5,017	2,986	8,004	10,425	7,047	8,168	9,547	8,102
Jayapura, Indonesia	14,917	14,387	5,509	13,319	13,085	12,720	10,341	10,655	12,435	14,726	15,994	12,812	13,360	13,569	12,816	1,825	15,672	14,256	15,497	4,870
Jefferson City, Missouri	7,384	6,951	12,529	6,452	3,894	1,793	3,100	8,707	7,229	7,448	2,764	8,119	745	7,636	2,256	11,764	2,616	2,658	4,685	12,530
Jerusalem, Israel	3,756	3,794	16,576	4,061	6,724	12,301	10,643	2,813	3,385	3,600	10,218	2,393	9,795	2,950	12,723	11,006	10,647	12,287	12,500	6,852
Jiggalong, Australia	14,699	14,675	5,625	14,299	15,431	15,557	13,490	11,366	13,289	14,550	18,788	13,018	16,506	13,759	15,485	4,842	18,341	16,605	16,412	5,734
Jinan, China	9,995	9,409	10,429	8,351	8,772	11,920	8,404	5,704	7,449	9,805	13,514	7,900	10,669	8,628	12,383	3,773	13,589	13,640	15,816	1,482
Jodhpur, India	7,352	7,173	13,032	6,849	8,888	14,256	11,166	4,067	5,867	7,176	13,469	5,495	11,933	6,249	14,795	7,557	13,838	15,144	16,080	3,350
Johannesburg, South Africa	7,741	8,457	12,175	9,593	12,116	15,207	16,545	9,268	9,420	7,767	11,919	8,213	14,031	8,222	15,057	13,311	12,258	13,553	11,690	10,252
Juazeiro do Norte, Brazil	5,969	6,564	13,637	7,696	7,990	7,825	10,514	10,259	8,545	6,159	4,703	8,069	7,516	7,335	7,644	19,189	4,956	6,144	4,526	15,844
Juneau, Alaska	8,523	7,769	11,619	6,594	4,169	4,370	883	7,293	6,801	8,475	6,445	8,002	3,485	7,963	4,872	8,209	6,337	6,053	8,241	9,042
Kabul, Afghanistan	6,602	6,341	13,800	5,916	7,903	13,311	10,347	3,089	4,922	6,419	12,531	4,646	10,956	5,418	13,847	7,862	12,887	14,161	15,208	3,683
Kalgoorlie, Australia	15,106	15,203	5,173	14,982	16,248	15,605	14,023	12,077	13,980	14,977	18,396	13,601	17,027	14,310	15,428	5,491	17,979	16,307	15,727	6,536
Kaliningrad, USSR	2,859	2,258	17,555	1,570	3,980	9,638	7,880	1,488	625	2,675	8,189	922	7,115	1,496	10,106	10,826	8,560	9,983	10,868	7,404
Kamloops, Canada	8,485	7,812	11,581	6,814	4,150	3,136	522	8,056	7,227	8,475	5,346	8,377	2,502	8,186	3,647	9,206	5,192	4,811	7,003	10,285
Kampala, Uganda	5,573	6,109	14,496	6,992	9,691	14,508	13,982	6,295	6,622	5,529	11,424	5,441	12,356	5,628	14,702	12,406	11,860	13,559	12,514	8,423
Kananga, Zaire	5,482	6,161	14,471	7,268	9,830	13,889	14,261	7,175	7,115	5,490	10,621	5,907	12,084	5,896	13,963	13,666	11,035	12,649	11,349	9,742
Kano, Nigeria	3,014	3,752	16,875	4,988	7,391	11,574	11,817	5,785	5,081	3,048	8,477	3,942	9,594	3,686	11,747	14,437	8,918	10,634	9,888	10,223
Kanpur, India	7,968	7,731	12,427	7,287	9,121	14,232	10,957	4,404	6,284	7,788	13,882	6,037	12,057	6,807	14,775	6,827	14,219	15,353	16,593	2,623
Kansas City, Missouri	7,540	7,087	12,384	6,546	3,949	1,718	2,901	8,734	7,300	7,599	2,968	8,216	812	7,753	2,209	11,555	2,806	2,740	4,813	12,406
Kaohsiung, Taiwan	11,358	10,843	9,068	9,869	10,347	12,894	9,486	7,103	8,932	11,167	14,973	9,253	12,035	10,011	13,284	2,777	14,987	14,700	16,881	1,441
Karachi, Pakistan	6,906	6,793	13,461	6,598	8,806	14,333	11,437	3,960	5,647	6,737	13,183	5,147	11,916	5,877	14,862	8,172	13,576	15,009	15,673	3,969
Karaganda, USSR	6,280	5,789	14,146	4,983	6,481	11,647	8,615	2,065	3,983	6,088	11,361	4,174	9,393	4,935	12,188	7,556	11,654	12,687	14,140	3,855
Karl-Marx-Stadt, East Germany	2,190	1,619	18,224	1,267	3,935	9,509	8,083	2,127	769	2,006	7,778	458	6,996	827	9,946	11,495	8,169	9,676	10,388	8,018
Kasanga, Tanzania	6,242	6,854	13,769	7,840	10,498	14,876	14,868	7,279	7,540	6,225	11,624	6,345	12,963	6,463	14,965	12,777	12,039	13,652	12,289	9,020

Distances in Kilometers	Gibraltar	Gijon, Spain	Gisborne, New Zealand	Glasgow, United Kingdom	Godthab, Greenland	Gomez Palacio, Mexico	Goose Bay, Canada	Gorki, USSR	Goteborg, Sweden	Granada, Spain	Grand Turk, Turks & Caicos	Graz, Austria	Green Bay, Wisconsin	Grenoble, France	Guadalajara, Mexico	Guam (Agana)	Guantanamo, Cuba	Guatemala City, Guatemala	Guayaquil, Ecuador	Guiyang, China
Kashgar, China	6,914	6,545	13,504	5,925	7,625	12,803	9,679	2,991	4,915	6,725	12,445	4,860	10,564	5,641	13,346	7,255	12,760	13,853	15,207	3,187
Kassel, West Germany	2,060	1,430	18,341	1,038	3,731	9,281	7,931	2,313	730	1,881	7,533	641	6,772	739	9,714	11,632	7,924	9,432	10,149	8,222
Kathmandu, Nepal	8,309	8,020	12,095	7,479	9,144	14,034	10,668	4,553	6,469	8,125	14,007	6,324	11,978	7,101	14,572	6,334	14,314	15,298	16,772	2,122
Kayes, Mali	2,478	3,270	17,168	4,633	6,322	9,535	10,482	6,582	5,187	2,637	6,337	4,393	7,837	3,769	9,651	15,966	6,771	8,472	7,758	11,945
Kazan, USSR	4,600	4,063	15,825	3,264	5,094	10,629	8,125	326	2,257	4,410	9,779	2,504	8,189	3,236	11,149	9,129	10,110	11,346	12,530	5,593
Kemi, Finland	3,833	3,091	16,543	1,893	3,370	8,962	6,793	1,478	1,116	3,667	8,102	2,156	6,487	2,565	9,469	9,942	8,415	9,618	10,876	6,987
Kenora, Canada	6,993	6,425	13,000	5,681	2,979	2,798	2,337	7,635	6,334	7,018	3,754	7,344	764	6,976	3,324	10,938	3,707	3,915	5,926	11,291
Kerguelen Island	12,003	12,628	7,993	13,519	16,236	17,281	18,783	11,966	12,999	11,996	15,367	11,899	18,228	12,170	16,744	10,101	15,502	15,736	13,573	9,199
Kerkira, Greece	2,249	2,169	18,133	2,533	5,254	10,715	9,445	2,562	2,095	2,072	8,608	905	8,236	1,320	11,117	11,829	9,032	10,656	11,001	7,923
Kermanshah, Iran	4,717	4,606	15,655	4,551	7,023	12,689	10,497	2,458	3,687	4,546	11,030	2,996	10,170	3,697	13,166	9,869	11,439	12,981	13,479	5,713
Khabarovsk, USSR	9,847	9,114	10,545	7,840	7,489	9,952	6,445	5,796	7,130	9,675	11,830	7,922	8,879	8,523	10,409	3,986	11,831	11,695	13,889	3,456
Kharkov, USSR	3,662	3,237	16,763	2,758	5,079	10,744	8,666	874	1,800	3,471	9,375	1,565	8,230	2,341	11,229	10,147	9,750	11,168	12,030	6,422
Khartoum, Sudan	4,385	4,756	15,792	5,448	8,172	13,430	12,340	4,624	4,980	4,293	10,747	3,830	11,050	4,130	13,750	11,908	11,195	12,929	12,479	7,706
Khon Kaen, Thailand	10,501	10,187	9,905	9,536	10,796	14,560	11,046	6,596	8,529	10,317	15,762	8,494	13,167	9,275	15,014	4,514	15,954	16,273	18,401	1,193
Kiev, USSR	3,272	2,827	17,154	2,376	4,788	10,453	8,534	1,109	1,453	3,081	8,983	1,167	7,931	1,937	10,926	10,497	9,363	10,808	11,625	6,824
Kigali, Rwanda	5,591	6,172	14,445	7,122	9,796	14,413	14,145	6,584	6,810	5,562	11,256	5,615	12,356	5,748	14,568	12,739	11,687	13,362	12,223	8,787
Kingston, Canada	5,936	5,506	13,979	5,084	2,719	3,195	3,832	7,554	5,926	5,998	2,573	6,734	917	6,214	3,600	12,380	2,675	3,540	5,150	12,156
Kingston, Jamaica	7,210	7,144	12,542	7,282	5,478	2,879	5,781	10,104	8,261	7,348	707	8,732	3,121	8,034	2,801	14,287	290	1,512	2,255	15,058
Kingstown, Saint Vincent	6,107	6,255	13,578	6,773	5,723	4,626	7,244	9,715	7,783	6,274	1,397	7,944	4,307	7,180	4,549	15,912	1,677	3,167	2,663	15,422
Kinshasa, Zaire	4,966	5,701	14,929	6,902	9,344	13,105	13,765	7,211	6,882	5,000	9,822	5,690	11,400	5,561	13,163	14,395	10,232	11,840	10,571	10,369
Kirkwall, United Kingdom	2,545	1,727	17,746	358	2,578	8,184	6,795	2,760	883	2,419	6,738	1,799	5,662	1,643	8,637	11,463	7,094	8,486	9,463	8,557
Kirov, USSR	4,667	4,084	15,754	3,187	4,867	10,359	7,815	422	2,196	4,479	9,620	2,599	7,937	3,298	10,882	9,031	9,938	11,126	12,386	5,625
Kiruna, Sweden	3,877	3,106	16,482	1,834	3,092	8,669	6,513	1,765	1,203	3,720	7,870	2,331	6,199	2,663	9,178	9,968	8,173	9,347	10,648	7,151
Kisangani, Zaire	5,051	5,667	14,958	6,685	9,319	13,810	13,716	6,417	6,452	5,033	10,653	5,246	11,790	5,307	13,962	13,194	11,085	12,767	11,694	9,146
Kishinev, USSR	3,065	2,713	17,356	2,472	5,011	10,658	8,874	1,470	1,647	2,875	9,013	1,016	8,135	1,793	11,116	10,785	9,407	10,909	11,595	7,009
Kitchner, Canada	6,267	5,831	13,650	5,379	2,943	2,880	3,601	7,790	6,202	6,329	2,588	7,036	615	6,530	3,300	12,214	2,632	3,335	5,053	12,216
Knoxville, Tennessee	6,864	6,509	13,011	6,178	3,818	2,194	3,848	8,662	7,036	6,946	2,031	7,815	1,010	7,263	2,540	12,529	1,951	2,454	4,243	12,992
Kosice, Czechoslovakia	2,576	2,146	17,850	1,899	4,509	10,124	8,527	1,751	1,177	2,385	8,416	470	7,605	1,244	10,570	11,171	8,810	10,321	11,003	7,519
Kota Kinabalu, Malaysia	12,348	12,011	8,060	11,271	12,147	14,503	11,256	8,354	10,277	12,163	16,870	10,325	13,919	11,106	14,807	3,251	16,868	16,309	18,221	2,487
Krakow, Poland	2,554	2,072	17,871	1,734	4,329	9,949	8,350	1,741	996	2,364	8,281	470	7,429	1,197	10,398	11,161	8,671	10,167	10,889	7,571
Kralendijk, Bonaire	6,797	6,885	12,905	7,283	5,926	3,982	6,854	10,209	8,292	6,957	1,074	8,555	4,050	7,806	3,853	15,408	1,152	2,424	2,037	15,684
Krasnodar, USSR	3,831	3,524	16,583	3,235	5,648	11,315	9,245	1,305	2,326	3,643	9,817	1,830	8,796	2,601	11,794	10,160	10,206	11,676	12,411	6,261
Krasnoyarsk, USSR	7,231	6,608	13,187	5,541	6,325	10,834	7,531	2,969	4,636	7,045	11,287	5,170	8,863	5,863	11,373	6,460	11,492	12,169	13,998	3,455
Kristiansand, Norway	2,639	1,883	17,721	787	3,148	8,792	7,211	2,157	240	2,481	7,371	1,332	6,268	1,455	9,254	11,147	7,732	9,128	10,083	8,023
Kuala Lumpur, Malaysia	11,326	11,156	9,049	10,705	12,210	15,835	12,381	7,780	9,696	11,154	17,172	9,469	14,636	10,232	16,224	4,868	17,406	17,629	19,825	2,646
Kuching, Malaysia	12,188	11,952	8,202	11,369	12,556	15,304	12,020	8,426	10,359	12,010	17,454	10,255	14,590	11,030	15,610	4,013	17,533	17,112	18,905	2,797
Kumasi, Ghana	3,284	4,102	16,462	5,456	7,502	10,878	11,786	6,797	5,782	3,388	7,628	4,763	9,208	4,323	10,965	15,694	8,051	9,714	8,745	11,482
Kumzar, Oman	5,887	5,840	14,464	5,807	8,220	13,874	11,387	3,478	4,920	5,724	12,277	4,254	11,370	4,941	14,368	9,198	12,691	14,242	14,645	4,982
Kunming, China	9,877	9,483	10,541	8,726	9,854	13,740	10,217	5,805	7,728	9,688	14,814	7,812	12,224	8,591	14,222	4,584	14,999	15,388	17,457	438
Kuqa Chang, China	7,398	6,968	13,025	6,225	7,672	12,580	9,315	3,291	5,221	7,207	12,592	5,310	10,475	6,086	13,122	6,640	12,870	13,794	15,373	2,678
Kurgan, USSR	5,618	5,070	14,807	4,191	5,684	10,967	8,104	1,331	3,203	5,428	10,544	3,520	8,647	4,254	11,504	8,120	10,841	11,917	13,323	4,618
Kuwait, Kuwait	4,990	4,964	15,357	5,023	7,545	13,209	11,048	3,010	4,194	4,829	11,406	3,419	10,686	4,077	13,675	9,931	11,825	13,415	13,747	5,727
Kuybyshev, USSR	4,651	4,159	15,775	3,444	5,363	10,915	8,411	527	2,433	4,460	10,002	2,545	8,468	3,302	11,433	9,124	10,342	11,607	12,739	5,478
Kyoto, Japan	11,162	10,473	9,246	9,251	8,983	10,860	7,477	6,954	8,474	10,982	13,145	9,145	10,158	9,806	11,253	2,551	13,088	12,668	14,847	2,919
Kzyl-Orda, USSR	5,892	5,501	14,529	4,890	6,733	12,133	9,272	1,975	3,881	5,702	11,453	3,821	9,771	4,601	12,667	8,125	11,787	12,992	14,193	4,185
L'vov, USSR	2,809	2,358	17,617	2,001	4,541	10,183	8,472	1,515	1,180	2,618	8,570	703	7,660	1,467	10,640	10,934	8,958	10,442	11,183	7,294
La Ceiba, Honduras	8,238	8,111	11,535	8,107	6,011	2,046	5,356	10,803	9,048	8,367	1,768	9,638	3,187	8,976	1,829	13,498	1,319	419	2,128	15,097
La Coruna, Spain	844	221	19,265	1,418	3,558	8,494	7,992	3,921	2,135	791	6,221	1,909	6,123	1,142	8,846	13,147	6,643	8,277	8,689	9,827
La Paz, Bolivia	8,801	9,192	10,823	9,979	9,065	6,028	9,470	12,882	10,968	8,990	4,212	10,863	7,050	10,083	5,628	16,485	4,125	4,231	2,038	18,774
La Paz, Mexico	9,698	9,292	10,198	8,760	6,113	704	3,367	10,762	9,477	9,772	4,019	10,431	3,030	9,974	815	10,876	3,639	2,327	4,398	13,132
La Ronge, Canada	7,377	6,724	12,674	5,790	3,084	3,283	1,543	7,342	6,293	7,374	4,692	7,400	1,704	7,147	3,826	10,013	4,630	4,668	6,763	10,455
Labrador City, Canada	5,059	4,522	14,918	3,943	1,534	4,301	4,034	6,357	4,747	5,090	3,513	5,610	1,803	5,147	4,744	12,050	3,711	4,732	6,227	11,172
Lagos, Nigeria	3,406	4,203	16,396	5,519	7,731	11,381	12,091	6,578	5,735	3,482	8,155	4,647	9,622	4,296	11,485	15,226	8,582	10,256	9,296	11,010
Lahore, Pakistan	7,174	6,918	13,226	6,475	8,385	13,676	10,566	3,614	5,475	6,992	13,081	5,223	11,390	5,994	14,217	7,400	13,428	14,642	15,777	3,193
Lambasa, Fiji	17,773	16,963	2,468	15,621	13,465	9,554	9,096	14,217	15,305	17,682	12,645	16,302	11,477	16,765	9,384	5,045	12,203	10,479	11,099	9,180
Lansing, Michigan	6,604	6,159	13,317	5,673	3,173	2,573	3,360	8,016	6,473	6,664	2,669	7,336	342	6,845	3,011	12,018	2,655	3,167	4,995	12,244
Lanzhou, China	9,172	8,673	11,254	7,769	8,676	12,615	9,106	4,934	6,801	8,980	13,615	7,067	11,005	7,828	13,117	4,797	13,785	14,201	16,236	1,088
Laoag, Philippines	11,743	11,258	8,682	10,319	10,839	13,220	9,866	7,518	9,370	11,552	15,437	9,643	12,481	10,409	13,583	2,637	15,431	15,035	17,175	1,703
Largeau, Chad	3,140	3,672	16,938	4,647	7,295	12,167	11,678	4,747	4,458	3,089	9,328	3,250	9,922	3,268	12,434	13,123	9,776	11,512	11,039	8,912
Las Vegas, Nevada	9,216	8,672	10,759	7,908	5,187	1,617	1,962	9,567	8,493	9,251	4,550	9,557	2,471	9,222	2,068	10,023	4,269	3,420	5,606	11,794
Launceston, Australia	17,573	17,783	2,639	17,395	17,195	13,412	13,160	14,458	16,391	17,476	15,814	16,172	15,595	16,892	13,109	6,081	15,397	13,762	13,255	8,604
Le Havre, France	1,550	798	18,789	764	3,426	8,806	7,783	2,992	1,201	1,399	6,882	1,166	6,330	640	9,212	12,219	7,283	8,832	9,468	8,908
Leipzig, East Germany	2,195	1,603	18,216	1,205	3,869	9,445	8,019	2,139	715	2,012	7,729	523	6,931	840	9,884	11,491	8,119	9,620	10,347	8,039
Leningrad, USSR	3,666	3,019	16,743	2,072	4,004	9,639	7,507	901	1,081	3,484	8,577	1,726	7,145	2,312	10,139	10,023	8,916	10,208	11,322	6,740
Leon, Spain	718	104	19,479	1,475	3,758	8,739	8,191	3,802	2,084	619	6,450	1,728	6,363	950	9,091	13,100	6,875	8,515	8,893	9,687
Lerwick, United Kingdom	2,687	1,874	17,614	514	2,593	8,226	6,747	2,632	801	2,557	6,854	1,813	5,703	1,729	8,687	11,297	7,204	8,573	9,590	8,404
Lhasa, China	8,659	8,307	11,755	7,651	9,099	13,700	10,262	4,709	6,642	8,471	14,040	6,620	11,792	7,401	14,228	5,784	14,305	15,102	16,818	1,570
Libreville, Gabon	4,244	5,011	15,609	6,271	8,610	12,290	13,005	6,933	6,361	4,296	9,026	5,205	10,573	4,975	12,367	14,873	9,443	11,081	9,941	10,720
Lilongwe, Malawi	6,906	7,527	13,097	8,512	11,172	15,397	15,538	7,850	8,196	6,892	12,096	7,005	13,598	7,136	15,429	12,598	12,496	14,042	12,501	9,068
Lima, Peru	9,204	9,473	10,444	10,062	8,732	5,054	8,550	13,004	11,072	9,385	3,763	11,169	6,361	10,392	4,623	15,500	3,566	3,304	1,135	18,350
Limerick, Ireland	1,855	1,039	18,368	453	2,748	8,104	7,146	3,349	1,419	1,760	6,293	1,829	5,624	1,337	8,516	12,247	6,679	8,184	8,946	9,236
Limoges, France	1,211	605	19,167	1,177	3,792	9,069	8,175	3,154	1,511	1,041	6,981	1,098	6,621	357	9,456	12,491	7,395	8,992	9,492	9,035
Limon, Costa Rica	8,260	8,234	11,476	8,393	6,506	2,763	6,116	11,200	9,370	8,406	1,797	9,838	3,855	9,132	2,475	14,149	1,402	962	1,391	15,824
Lincoln, Nebraska	7,603	7,120	12,338	6,521	3,881	1,806	2,641	8,622	7,243	7,654	3,225	8,192	820	7,757	2,322	11,304	3,068	2,964	5,059	12,162
Linz, Austria	2,101	1,632	18,324	1,516	4,212	9,757	8,381	2,192	1,059	1,911	7,928	162	7,250	742	10,185	11,606	8,328	9,867	10,495	8,022
Lisbon, Portugal	441	609	19,403	1,937	3,962	8,635	8,380	4,317	2,608	507	6,154	2,200	6,345	1,421	8,952	13,626	6,589	8,269	8,502	10,183
Little Rock, Arkansas	7,599	7,209	12,292	6,780	4,272	1,483	3,375	9,102	7,585	7,674	2,537	8,439	1,144	7,927	1,900	11,980	2,333	2,235	4,288	12,930
Liverpool, United Kingdom	1,929	1,116	18,363	281	2,962	8,423	7,299	2,975	1,056	1,801	6,676	1,488	5,926	1,114	8,847	11,986	7,060	8,552	9,332	8,875
Lodz, Poland	2,619	2,084	17,803	1,619	4,170	9,804	8,165	1,676	820	2,430	8,203	597	7,281	1,250	10,258	11,077	8,588	10,061	10,838	7,552
Lome, Togo	3,389	4,198	16,387	5,533	7,673	11,185	12,000	6,712	5,798	3,478	7,943	4,737	9,475	4,347	11,278	15,454	8,367	10,033	9,055	11,237
London, United Kingdom	1,757	979	18,571	554	3,251	8,691	7,585	2,896	1,041	1,612	6,864	1,232	6,200	826	9,108	12,051	7,256	8,777	9,486	8,814
Londonderry, United Kingdom	2,102	1,281	18,146	216	2,634	8,095	6,990	3,158	1,226	1,996	6,414	1,814	5,595	1,434	8,522	11,979	6,789	8,255	9,099	9,018
Longlac, Canada	6,463	5,923	13,513	5,256	2,610	3,060	2,880	7,389	5,970	6,496	3,422	6,927	596	6,515	3,556	11,403	3,440	3,915	5,792	11,446
Lord Howe Island, Australia	18,499	18,127	1,893	17,012	15,797	12,113	11,634	14,386	16,177	18,322	14,944	16,485	14,128	17,263	11,880	5,211	14,498	12,771	12,781	8,503
Los Angeles, California	9,583	9,037	10,393	8,259	5,535	1,706	2,069	9,849	8,826	9,618	4,804	9,903	2,835	9,579	2,088	9,816	4,501	3,521	5,677	11,794
Louangphrabang, Laos	10,202	9,861	10,210	9,177	10,408	14,271	10,749	6,240	8,172	10,015	15,375	8,173	12,802	8,954	14,740	4,589	15,570	15,949	18,035	879
Louisville, Kentucky	6,902	6,508	12,993	6,102	3,661	2,182	3,561	8,508	6,931	6,975	2,330	7,755	721	7,232	2,579	12,245	2,251	2,658	4,516	12,712
Luanda, Angola	5,341	6,103	14,520	7,344	9,709	13,113	14,097	7,754	7,374	5,391	9,794	6,192	11,583	6,024	13,118	14,723	10,188	11,733	10,319	10,793
Lubumbashi, Zaire	6,314	6,976	13,654	8,041	10,643	14,666	15,063	7,691	7,820	6,316	11,364	6,614	12,928	6,664	14,699	13,236	11,765	13,324	11,852	9,543
Lusaka, Zambia	6,714	7,387	13,244	8,463	11,055	14,906	15,480	8,085	8,244	6,721	11,584	7,038	13,277	7,086	14,896	13,206	11,972	13,477	11,892	9,662
Luxembourg, Luxembourg	1,762	1,126	18,633	985	3,708	9,181	7,990	2,615	981	1,586	7,315	745	6,687	494	9,599	11,935	7,714	9,254	9,900	8,518
Luxor, Egypt	3,786	3,984	16,482	4,476	7,189	12,644	11,254	3,525	3,917	3,656	10,287	2,817	10,179	3,236	13,025	11,494	10,728	12,423	12,370	7,293
Lynn Lake, Canada	7,053	6,396	13,001	5,465	2,756	3,480	1,830	7,070	5,979	7,048	4,627	7,079	1,647	6,820	4,022	10,166	4,599	4,769	6,817	10,399
Lyon, France	1,368	869	19,043	1,290	3,973	9,317	8,321	2,937	1,417	1,184	7,261	827	6,856	94	9,711	12,317	7,674	9,267	9,769	8,793
Macapa, Brazil	6,181	6,592	13,443	7,480	7,124	6,298	9,079	10,317	8,438	6,370	3,222	8,249	6,130	7,472	6,126	17,729	3,445	4,634	3,213	16,228
Madison, Wisconsin	6,951	6,480	12,984	5,927	3,346	2,328	3,003	8,156	6,688	7,004	2,935	7,597	195	7,136	2,804	11,680	2,869	3,154	5,101	12,119
Madras, India	8,779	8,697	11,576	8,474	10,520	15,709	12,371	5,712	7,502	8,615	15,082	7,053	13,518	7,782	16,251	6,964	15,465	16,779	17,529	3,136
Madrid, Spain	496	385	19,770	1,717	4,049	8,985	8,482	3,851	2,228	353	6,616	1,704	6,630	933	9,326	13,215	7,046	8,707	8,999	9,691
Madurai, India	8,784	8,757	11,554	8,623	10,771	16,073	12,775	5,935	7,671	8,628	15,187	7,147	13,816	7,854	16,616	7,255	15,591	17,018	17,448	3,527
Magadan, USSR	9,174	8,375	11,172	7,019	6,142	8,423	4,901	5,632	6,507	9,024	10,249	7,508	7,286	7,966	8,902	5,141	10,238	10,131	12,315	4,970

Distances in Kilometers	Gibraltar	Gijon, Spain	Gisborne, New Zealand	Glasgow, United Kingdom	Godthab, Greenland	Gomez Palacio, Mexico	Goose Bay, Canada	Gorki, USSR	Goteborg, Sweden	Granada, Spain	Grand Turk, Turks & Caicos	Graz, Austria	Green Bay, Wisconsin	Grenoble, France	Guadalajara, Mexico	Guam (Agana)	Guantanamo, Cuba	Guatemala City, Guatemala	Guayaquil, Ecuador	Guiyang, China
Magdalena, Bolivia	8,247	8,646	11,377	9,460	8,669	6,061	9,417	12,348	10,443	8,436	3,925	10,312	6,846	9,533	5,704	16,910	3,895	4,245	2,125	18,263
Magdeburg, East Germany	2,230	1,607	18,175	1,118	3,767	9,352	7,912	2,137	618	2,050	7,669	629	6,837	893	9,793	11,459	8,056	9,546	10,300	8,048
Majuro Atoll, Marshall Isls.	15,200	14,383	5,121	13,011	11,327	9,206	7,411	11,489	12,574	15,065	12,528	13,543	10,305	14,033	9,269	2,978	12,166	10,703	12,143	7,126
Malabo, Equatorial Guinea	3,868	4,632	15,989	5,892	8,238	12,050	12,641	6,614	5,992	3,919	8,821	4,843	10,258	4,599	12,153	14,809	9,246	10,912	9,881	10,618
Male, Maldives	8,747	8,829	11,553	8,874	11,206	16,717	13,549	6,365	7,973	8,607	15,248	7,306	14,325	7,961	17,254	7,890	15,682	17,304	17,063	4,333
Manado, Indonesia	13,399	13,013	7,016	12,175	12,707	14,028	11,084	9,306	11,202	13,211	16,937	11,345	13,965	12,124	14,239	2,562	16,778	15,746	17,291	3,388
Managua, Nicaragua	8,417	8,337	11,338	8,402	6,377	2,340	5,725	11,143	9,358	8,555	1,914	9,900	3,591	9,218	2,048	13,726	1,477	535	1,737	15,497
Manama, Bahrain	5,371	5,376	14,965	5,458	7,975	13,640	11,407	3,387	4,627	5,214	11,816	3,850	11,118	4,498	14,109	9,770	12,239	13,842	14,104	5,553
Manaus, Brazil	7,141	7,487	12,493	8,254	7,507	5,662	8,756	11,159	9,243	7,327	2,979	9,170	5,968	8,389	5,410	17,078	3,062	3,896	2,206	17,056
Manchester, New Hampshire	5,585	5,196	14,310	4,870	2,680	3,494	4,251	7,455	5,754	5,657	2,388	6,496	1,341	5,940	3,862	12,751	2,559	3,633	5,072	12,299
Mandalay, Burma	9,562	9,250	10,845	8,631	10,044	14,337	10,827	5,689	7,621	9,377	15,002	7,556	12,628	8,336	14,839	5,226	15,249	15,890	17,767	1,192
Mangareva Island, Fr.Polynesia	14,996	14,882	4,756	14,609	11,982	6,365	8,283	16,315	15,344	15,137	8,496	16,270	8,880	15,708	5,936	9,631	8,059	6,392	6,373	13,846
Manila, Philippines	12,065	11,605	8,358	10,694	11,241	13,464	10,167	7,869	9,737	11,874	15,806	9,972	12,836	10,743	13,803	2,567	15,781	15,280	17,359	1,992
Mannheim, West Germany	1,858	1,267	18,548	1,111	3,831	9,331	8,080	2,477	945	1,677	7,485	584	6,832	523	9,753	11,829	7,883	9,420	10,068	8,369
Maputo, Mozambique	7,944	8,630	12,001	9,712	12,299	15,645	16,729	9,183	9,471	7,957	12,345	8,269	14,372	8,335	15,504	12,861	12,691	14,001	12,135	9,849
Mar del Plata, Argentina	9,810	10,436	9,796	11,555	11,348	8,516	12,017	14,090	12,420	9,998	6,734	11,886	9,638	11,180	8,067	16,515	6,695	6,767	4,574	18,074
Maracaibo, Venezuela	7,192	7,265	12,513	7,625	6,152	3,741	6,765	10,538	8,631	7,350	1,196	8,929	4,068	8,185	3,568	15,205	1,116	2,099	1,686	15,880
Marrakech, Morocco	556	1,337	19,059	2,705	4,702	9,047	9,090	4,829	3,275	735	6,308	2,631	6,884	1,916	9,314	14,236	6,754	8,477	8,430	10,561
Marseilles, France	1,216	896	19,210	1,556	4,216	9,495	8,582	3,078	1,668	1,025	7,337	893	7,053	209	9,876	12,489	7,757	9,377	9,789	8,878
Maseru, Lesotho	8,019	8,747	11,884	9,905	12,396	15,201	16,810	9,618	9,753	8,051	11,954	8,545	14,189	8,538	15,009	13,369	12,275	13,497	11,569	10,468
Mashhad, Iran	5,722	5,494	14,675	5,174	7,358	12,932	10,265	2,517	4,207	5,541	11,787	3,809	10,480	4,569	13,451	8,709	12,166	13,558	14,395	4,561
Mazatlan, Mexico	9,451	9,083	10,426	8,626	6,030	394	3,621	10,762	9,387	9,533	3,631	10,293	2,898	9,800	426	11,285	3,243	1,923	4,024	13,450
Mbabane, Swaziland	7,903	8,600	12,032	9,701	12,267	15,510	16,700	9,238	9,483	7,921	12,216	8,278	14,282	8,325	15,362	13,006	12,558	13,858	11,986	9,992
Mbandaka, Zaire	4,681	5,371	15,261	6,509	9,038	13,170	13,471	6,654	6,417	4,693	9,952	5,215	11,291	5,147	13,283	13,949	10,377	12,037	10,920	9,858
McMurdo Sound, Antarctica	15,375	16,197	4,369	17,552	18,077	12,796	15,018	16,767	17,572	15,486	13,108	16,365	15,195	16,286	12,273	10,179	12,876	11,930	10,358	12,162
Mecca, Saudi Arabia	4,653	4,845	15,613	5,261	7,946	13,477	11,845	3,888	4,615	4,524	11,151	3,590	10,990	4,072	13,872	10,970	11,593	13,291	13,166	6,755
Medan, Indonesia	11,031	10,886	9,338	10,482	12,091	16,000	12,510	7,573	9,476	10,862	17,023	9,205	14,636	9,962	16,418	5,181	17,299	17,756	19,794	2,686
Medellin, Colombia	7,831	7,918	11,868	8,274	6,715	3,659	6,912	11,179	9,278	7,992	1,751	9,584	4,409	8,838	3,392	15,068	1,537	1,878	1,044	16,364
Medicine Hat, Canada	7,986	7,354	12,049	6,452	3,738	2,787	1,207	7,983	6,962	7,991	4,688	8,067	1,813	7,803	3,324	9,884	4,557	4,331	6,493	10,752
Medina, Saudi Arabia	4,470	4,613	15,818	4,969	7,640	13,201	11,511	3,557	4,298	4,333	10,973	3,298	10,703	3,812	13,610	10,885	11,412	13,091	13,084	6,670
Melbourne, Australia	17,390	17,477	2,876	16,974	16,868	13,533	13,008	14,044	15,974	17,269	16,117	15,822	15,591	16,564	13,265	5,678	15,687	14,014	13,628	8,175
Memphis, Tennessee	7,401	7,020	12,486	6,616	4,143	1,669	3,493	8,983	7,436	7,478	2,387	8,271	1,057	7,748	2,063	12,129	2,210	2,271	4,264	12,952
Merauke, Indonesia	15,387	14,917	5,035	13,909	13,742	13,041	10,877	11,176	12,999	15,196	16,364	13,297	13,893	14,067	13,082	2,474	15,999	14,458	15,425	5,313
Merida, Mexico	8,171	7,960	11,636	7,819	5,568	1,508	4,715	10,403	8,723	8,285	1,919	9,407	2,616	8,788	1,428	12,968	1,506	707	2,772	14,459
Meridian, Mississippi	7,439	7,100	12,427	6,769	4,365	1,625	3,796	9,212	7,617	7,525	2,117	8,409	1,350	7,857	1,948	12,401	1,909	1,973	3,935	13,281
Messina, Italy	1,868	1,880	18,494	2,455	5,173	10,523	9,458	2,911	2,188	1,698	8,291	987	8,075	1,127	10,903	12,228	8,720	10,370	10,634	8,332
Mexico City, Mexico	9,093	8,822	10,739	8,544	6,100	816	4,337	10,933	9,388	9,196	2,929	10,179	2,971	9,609	460	12,141	2,509	1,060	3,187	14,208
Miami, Florida	7,071	6,876	12,732	6,810	4,746	2,337	4,895	9,507	7,747	7,187	1,040	8,361	2,195	7,719	2,432	13,499	807	1,637	3,092	14,164
Midway Islands, USA	12,835	12,017	7,418	10,671	8,731	7,225	4,847	9,859	10,444	12,734	10,384	11,571	7,825	11,874	7,442	4,244	10,099	8,956	10,868	7,377
Milan, Italy	1,602	1,200	18,823	1,490	4,208	9,622	8,505	2,692	1,376	1,412	7,602	513	7,146	275	10,024	12,105	8,014	9,602	10,106	8,500
Milford Sound, New Zealand	18,906	19,484	1,075	18,634	16,736	11,861	12,309	15,944	17,798	18,925	14,099	17,864	14,229	18,606	11,509	6,838	13,681	12,061	11,590	10,026
Milwaukee, Wisconsin	6,843	6,379	13,088	5,845	3,285	2,403	3,108	8,108	6,617	6,898	2,855	7,513	164	7,043	2,867	11,780	2,804	3,158	5,072	12,153
Minsk, USSR	3,213	2,671	17,210	2,036	4,364	10,030	8,110	1,080	1,063	3,024	8,656	1,145	7,511	1,845	10,509	10,490	9,024	10,431	11,336	6,969
Mogadiscio, Somalia	6,429	6,809	13,737	7,423	10,136	15,483	14,045	6,019	6,834	6,344	12,655	5,764	13,093	6,149	15,786	10,980	13,101	14,832	13,942	7,075
Mombasa, Kenya	6,456	6,953	13,638	7,749	10,469	15,430	14,628	6,705	7,284	6,402	12,334	6,141	13,236	6,409	15,624	11,754	12,768	14,452	13,272	7,959
Monclova, Mexico	8,803	8,435	11,075	8,002	5,442	255	3,502	10,223	8,785	8,884	3,128	9,666	2,294	9,159	717	11,601	2,774	1,768	3,964	13,369
Moncton, Canada	4,993	4,576	14,918	4,241	2,178	4,114	4,519	6,869	5,136	5,056	2,793	5,864	1,823	5,309	4,492	12,778	3,034	4,236	5,548	11,910
Monrovia, Liberia	3,348	4,154	16,315	5,522	7,195	9,985	11,264	7,317	6,034	3,498	6,692	5,165	8,506	4,593	10,034	16,547	7,105	8,739	7,729	12,378
Monte Carlo, Monaco	1,377	1,055	19,049	1,582	4,275	9,608	8,614	2,924	1,588	1,186	7,491	729	7,153	209	9,996	12,341	7,910	9,522	9,955	8,710
Monterrey, Mexico	8,791	8,445	11,076	8,049	5,517	320	3,676	10,317	8,848	8,878	3,009	9,707	2,367	9,184	634	11,757	2,644	1,593	3,789	13,542
Montevideo, Uruguay	9,465	10,081	10,141	11,192	10,997	8,345	11,822	13,751	12,062	9,653	6,434	11,548	9,363	10,835	7,913	16,845	6,413	6,572	4,372	18,149
Montgomery, Alabama	7,241	6,917	12,618	6,652	4,272	1,835	3,954	9,116	7,487	7,331	1,929	8,253	1,355	7,687	2,131	12,587	1,751	2,012	3,884	13,336
Montpelier, Vermont	5,634	5,220	14,273	4,845	2,584	3,471	4,100	7,385	5,712	5,700	2,532	6,484	1,228	5,945	3,858	12,585	2,687	3,698	5,193	12,160
Montpellier, France	1,144	771	19,277	1,479	4,116	9,372	8,494	3,148	1,668	956	7,211	984	6,935	227	9,751	12,547	7,631	9,250	9,670	8,971
Montreal, Canada	5,676	5,239	14,243	4,818	2,492	3,464	3,960	7,313	5,667	5,736	2,675	6,467	1,140	5,945	3,868	12,428	2,817	3,773	5,316	12,022
Moosonee, Canada	6,015	5,474	13,962	4,827	2,219	3,452	3,220	7,041	5,565	6,048	3,411	6,499	931	6,074	3,930	11,602	3,489	4,161	5,924	11,349
Moroni, Comoros	7,349	7,871	12,728	8,682	11,402	16,216	15,526	7,538	8,206	7,303	12,995	7,071	14,133	7,340	16,334	11,540	13,413	15,023	13,558	8,057
Moscow, USSR	3,887	3,338	16,536	2,584	4,640	10,272	8,051	405	1,574	3,698	9,164	1,806	7,780	2,520	10,773	9,821	9,513	10,834	11,887	6,313
Mosul, Iraq	4,311	4,186	16,067	4,144	6,652	12,315	10,246	2,224	3,301	4,137	10,608	2,575	9,793	3,276	12,783	10,147	11,018	12,566	13,066	6,033
Mount Isa, Australia	16,210	15,922	4,182	15,093	15,101	13,616	11,975	12,236	14,131	16,032	16,855	14,234	14,937	15,014	13,532	3,826	16,419	14,705	15,048	6,318
Multan, Pakistan	7,009	6,791	13,383	6,419	8,430	13,812	10,777	3,613	5,430	6,830	13,038	5,103	11,476	5,866	14,351	7,677	13,400	14,687	15,686	3,463
Munich, West Germany	1,926	1,431	18,495	1,378	4,093	9,604	8,314	2,367	1,065	1,738	7,733	315	7,104	558	10,025	11,768	8,135	9,683	10,293	8,216
Murcia, Spain	429	726	19,908	1,998	4,394	9,303	8,826	3,884	2,393	242	6,859	1,689	6,966	980	9,634	13,295	7,294	8,974	9,173	9,647
Murmansk, USSR	4,340	3,593	16,036	2,361	3,485	8,951	6,563	1,510	1,623	4,174	8,346	2,629	6,527	3,069	9,472	9,451	8,635	9,740	11,127	6,621
Mururoa Atoll, Fr. Polynesia	15,284	15,107	4,492	14,720	12,045	6,494	8,188	16,170	15,386	15,415	8,783	16,392	8,988	15,892	6,091	9,200	8,341	6,649	6,745	13,415
Muscat, Oman	6,221	6,196	14,122	6,178	8,585	14,234	11,674	3,823	5,291	6,061	12,636	4,620	11,734	5,302	14,732	9,042	13,052	14,612	14,962	4,838
Myitkyina, Burma	9,440	9,084	10,974	8,399	9,710	13,940	10,432	5,460	7,392	9,253	14,677	7,399	12,246	8,180	14,443	5,117	14,906	15,496	17,419	942
Naga, Philippines	12,302	11,829	8,122	10,895	11,357	13,358	10,118	8,090	9,946	12,111	15,823	10,206	12,839	10,974	13,678	2,334	15,769	15,170	17,198	2,236
Nagasaki, Japan	11,072	10,427	9,345	9,268	9,245	11,429	8,015	6,804	8,434	10,887	13,599	9,008	10,625	9,705	11,831	2,619	13,571	13,231	15,419	2,343
Nagoya, Japan	11,201	10,504	9,206	9,272	8,958	10,765	7,391	7,006	8,506	11,021	13,077	9,193	10,088	9,848	11,155	2,529	13,014	12,574	14,751	3,027
Nagpur, India	8,176	8,011	12,202	7,677	9,635	14,828	11,557	4,855	6,689	8,003	14,297	6,335	12,617	7,088	15,371	6,986	14,658	15,889	16,919	2,871
Nairobi, Kenya	6,017	6,520	14,074	7,340	10,056	14,995	14,265	6,421	6,906	5,964	11,927	5,748	12,797	5,991	15,199	11,992	12,364	14,061	12,977	8,088
Nanchang, China	10,567	10,043	9,860	9,069	9,644	12,681	9,189	6,303	8,129	10,375	14,405	8,460	11,545	9,215	13,119	3,426	14,475	14,441	16,636	934
Nancy, France	1,683	1,080	18,717	1,066	3,788	9,238	8,082	2,665	1,076	1,505	7,330	714	6,750	393	9,651	12,007	7,732	9,285	9,898	8,557
Nandi, Fiji	17,955	17,137	2,313	15,781	13,687	9,810	9,333	14,243	15,414	17,850	12,888	16,367	11,734	16,875	9,636	4,983	12,445	10,718	11,293	9,078
Nanjing, China	10,483	9,916	9,942	8,878	9,296	12,216	8,724	6,195	7,966	10,293	13,990	8,382	11,104	9,119	12,656	3,352	14,042	13,975	16,172	1,318
Nanning, China	10,474	10,055	9,947	9,243	10,197	13,655	10,146	6,348	8,257	10,284	15,105	8,396	12,367	9,173	14,104	3,980	15,238	15,387	17,560	448
Nantes, France	1,271	521	19,054	977	3,537	8,808	7,932	3,236	1,481	1,125	6,761	1,287	6,358	605	9,197	12,498	7,170	8,753	9,303	9,144
Naples, Italy	1,784	1,668	18,614	2,145	4,866	10,254	9,143	2,754	1,885	1,601	8,107	699	7,792	845	10,645	12,137	8,531	10,158	10,513	8,325
Narvik, Norway	3,862	3,081	16,488	1,783	2,959	8,538	6,407	1,897	1,225	3,709	7,745	2,382	6,066	2,677	9,046	10,019	8,046	9,215	10,524	7,256
Nashville, Tennessee	7,085	6,711	12,799	6,334	3,908	1,979	3,638	8,755	7,170	7,163	2,227	7,982	933	7,448	2,355	12,309	2,105	2,414	4,304	12,917
Nassau, Bahamas	6,859	6,696	12,931	6,692	4,736	2,629	5,143	9,441	7,646	6,981	752	8,213	2,361	7,554	2,706	13,772	591	1,798	3,027	14,271
Natal, Brazil	5,590	6,218	14,016	7,397	7,887	8,144	10,678	9,878	8,212	5,778	4,945	7,679	7,662	6,959	7,993	19,155	5,231	6,507	4,970	15,381
Natashquan, Canada	4,724	4,241	15,223	3,799	1,677	4,484	4,485	6,374	4,668	4,770	3,292	5,444	2,065	4,926	4,892	12,493	3,539	4,720	6,053	11,425
Nauru Island	15,984	15,186	4,372	13,822	12,278	9,998	8,376	12,015	13,290	15,831	13,325	14,159	11,243	14,729	10,010	2,896	12,938	11,385	12,601	7,107
Ndjamena, Chad	3,357	4,011	16,620	5,130	7,679	12,173	12,108	5,501	5,067	3,351	9,142	3,875	10,086	3,770	12,375	13,799	9,585	11,311	10,600	9,584
Nelson, New Zealand	19,422	19,742	498	18,377	16,183	11,309	11,750	16,044	17,751	19,488	13,667	18,142	13,656	18,923	10,970	6,735	13,239	11,584	11,255	10,169
Nema, Mauritania	2,171	2,988	17,509	4,360	6,255	9,836	10,529	6,140	4,834	2,310	6,702	3,970	8,008	3,390	9,984	15,486	7,142	8,861	8,234	11,438
Neuquen, Argentina	10,514	11,083	9,092	12,107	11,533	8,038	11,561	14,803	13,028	10,704	6,695	12,614	9,458	11,879	7,554	15,734	6,582	6,375	4,245	18,552
New Delhi, India	7,579	7,340	12,817	6,908	8,794	14,010	10,817	4,041	5,908	7,399	13,512	5,647	11,771	6,416	14,553	7,131	13,857	15,044	16,209	2,916
New Glasgow, Canada	4,838	4,436	15,066	4,144	2,188	4,253	4,690	6,815	5,056	4,905	2,785	5,754	1,993	5,185	4,620	12,912	3,049	4,312	5,555	11,941
New Haven, Connecticut	5,754	5,385	14,131	5,085	2,899	3,311	4,255	7,678	5,974	5,831	2,206	6,706	1,281	6,141	3,665	12,819	2,357	3,410	4,865	12,489
New Orleans, Louisiana	7,684	7,364	12,172	7,057	4,661	1,410	3,902	9,508	7,910	7,775	2,116	8,693	1,625	8,133	1,685	12,434	1,850	1,698	3,718	13,499
New Plymouth, New Zealand	19,676	19,508	344	18,136	15,938	11,147	11,508	15,923	17,565	19,731	13,593	18,073	13,463	18,842	10,821	6,566	13,159	11,484	11,242	10,086
New York, New York	5,862	5,496	14,021	5,197	2,994	3,201	4,217	7,782	6,083	5,940	2,151	6,818	1,223	6,253	3,553	12,807	2,284	3,304	4,785	12,554
Newcastle upon Tyne, UK	2,117	1,309	18,189	192	2,912	8,435	7,204	2,821	890	1,983	6,779	1,480	5,926	1,211	8,869	11,788	7,156	8,620	9,456	8,707
Newcastle Waters, Australia	15,473	15,211	4,916	14,459	14,788	14,109	12,118	11,563	13,477	15,296	17,421	13,517	15,132	14,297	14,080	3,635	17,007	15,335	15,788	5,657
Niamey, Niger	2,614	3,410	17,189	4,727	6,957	10,887	11,342	5,938	4,975	2,688	7,765	3,922	8,979	3,525	11,046	14,938	8,205	9,920	9,204	10,754
Nicosia, Cyprus	3,485	3,456	16,871	3,657	6,311	11,900	10,240	2,487	2,970	3,319	9,895	1,994	9,390	2,587	12,328	11,019	10,319	11,935	12,251	6,924
Niue (Alofi)	17,589	16,918	2,470	15,746	13,250	8,715	8,817	15,000	15,705	17,590	11,645	16,856	10,851	17,077	8,482	6,134	11,197	9,462	9,948	10,312

Distances in Kilometers	Gibraltar	Gijon, Spain	Gisborne, New Zealand	Glasgow, United Kingdom	Godthab, Greenland	Gomez Palacio, Mexico	Goose Bay, Canada	Gorki, USSR	Goteborg, Sweden	Granada, Spain	Grand Turk, Turks & Caicos	Graz, Austria	Green Bay, Wisconsin	Grenoble, France	Guadalajara, Mexico	Guam (Agana)	Guantanamo, Cuba	Guatemala City, Guatemala	Guayaquil, Ecuador	Guiyang, China
Norfolk, Virginia	6,199	5,878	13,662	5,639	3,465	2,866	4,315	8,251	6,540	6,287	1,776	7,246	1,304	6,660	3,175	12,980	1,856	2,838	4,335	12,976
Norfolk Island, Australia	19,007	18,300	1,416	16,964	15,212	11,217	10,902	14,717	16,318	18,818	14,078	16,909	13,273	17,637	10,983	5,323	13,630	11,897	12,041	8,976
Noril'sk, USSR	6,429	5,701	13,961	4,464	4,852	9,439	6,301	2,587	3,712	6,258	9,799	4,553	7,375	5,113	9,982	7,339	9,993	10,691	12,495	4,907
Norman Wells, Canada	7,686	6,920	12,469	5,726	3,370	4,716	1,549	6,493	5,931	7,632	6,288	7,130	3,304	7,093	5,247	8,581	6,252	6,252	8,382	8,843
Normanton, Australia	16,141	15,780	4,265	14,868	14,743	13,349	11,609	12,059	13,927	15,957	16,633	14,110	14,583	14,890	13,294	3,467	16,209	14,522	15,036	6,146
North Pole	6,004	5,182	14,282	3,814	2,876	7,173	4,306	3,758	3,604	5,884	7,628	4,789	5,071	5,001	7,716	8,511	7,776	8,384	10,242	7,060
Nottingham, United Kingdom	1,899	1,100	18,414	377	3,085	8,555	7,409	2,886	984	1,761	6,796	1,355	6,057	1,002	8,979	11,959	7,182	8,680	9,442	8,795
Norway House, Canada	7,006	6,384	13,022	5,530	2,806	3,190	2,023	7,292	6,107	7,014	4,255	7,170	1,271	6,864	3,727	10,498	4,222	4,412	6,443	10,773
Norwich, United Kingdom	1,907	1,136	18,432	508	3,231	8,721	7,529	2,752	883	1,757	6,962	1,188	6,220	891	9,147	11,891	7,349	8,850	9,601	8,668
Nouakchott, Mauritania	2,254	2,981	17,360	4,303	5,782	8,928	9,874	6,509	4,962	2,435	5,766	4,305	7,208	3,612	9,060	15,929	6,205	7,922	7,346	12,099
Noumea, New Caledonia	18,280	17,538	2,126	16,200	14,575	11,057	10,372	14,027	15,567	18,101	14,118	16,231	12,923	16,924	10,884	4,608	13,672	11,939	12,351	8,403
Novosibirsk, USSR	6,709	6,125	13,714	5,139	6,215	11,054	7,874	2,420	4,191	6,520	11,178	4,623	8,939	5,340	11,596	7,008	11,422	12,260	13,940	3,704
Nuku'alofa, Tonga	18,078	17,340	2,049	16,080	13,702	9,308	9,274	14,951	15,901	18,047	12,242	16,973	11,413	17,338	9,081	5,815	11,794	10,058	10,488	9,934
Nukunono Island, Tokelau Isls.	16,730	15,975	3,416	14,720	12,354	8,339	7,939	13,923	14,612	16,686	11,495	15,750	10,241	16,012	8,194	5,407	11,059	9,358	10,207	9,623
Nuremberg, West Germany	1,990	1,440	18,425	1,253	3,960	9,491	8,167	2,318	922	1,805	7,673	419	6,986	625	9,918	11,696	8,071	9,602	10,258	8,196
Nyala, Sudan	4,038	4,557	16,046	5,471	8,153	13,053	12,496	5,182	5,185	3,986	10,142	3,982	10,819	4,098	13,304	12,820	10,589	12,323	11,670	8,621
Oaxaca, Mexico	9,033	8,807	10,779	8,608	6,242	1,176	4,689	11,088	9,482	9,145	2,730	10,221	3,153	9,621	804	12,479	2,295	716	2,821	14,559
Ocean Falls, Canada	8,727	8,019	11,369	6,941	4,354	3,601	108	7,932	7,265	8,703	5,888	8,444	3,020	8,320	4,095	8,670	5,736	5,318	7,515	9,796
Odense, Denmark	2,454	1,751	17,930	922	3,457	9,080	7,552	2,086	276	2,283	7,540	992	6,558	1,185	9,533	11,269	7,913	9,354	10,218	7,999
Odessa, USSR	3,199	2,863	17,221	2,625	5,145	10,799	8,967	1,429	1,783	3,009	9,170	1,168	8,275	1,942	11,260	10,684	9,564	11,063	11,750	6,877
Ogbomosho, Nigeria	3,251	4,040	16,566	5,344	7,597	11,379	11,977	6,368	5,541	3,320	8,183	4,444	9,562	4,107	11,501	15,052	8,614	10,302	9,403	10,836
Okha, USSR	9,609	8,837	10,762	7,512	6,879	9,176	5,663	5,779	6,898	9,447	11,073	7,802	8,109	8,335	9,639	4,451	11,061	10,910	13,103	4,222
Okinawa (Naha)	11,532	10,937	8,892	9,843	9,976	12,081	8,720	7,241	8,965	11,343	14,356	9,437	11,377	10,164	12,457	2,275	14,318	13,894	16,056	2,088
Oklahoma City, Oklahoma	7,966	7,536	11,945	7,019	4,425	1,241	2,979	9,201	7,777	8,032	2,999	8,689	1,287	8,217	1,739	11,525	2,768	2,414	4,557	12,680
Old Crow, Canada	7,891	7,099	12,301	5,835	3,697	5,278	1,922	6,257	5,915	7,819	6,916	7,124	3,934	7,172	5,801	8,011	6,883	6,859	9,002	8,229
Olympia, Washington	8,895	8,235	11,160	7,254	4,579	2,934	595	8,482	7,671	8,891	5,417	8,821	2,705	8,624	3,419	9,103	5,225	4,680	6,880	10,458
Omaha, Nebraska	7,528	7,044	12,413	6,445	3,807	1,875	2,657	8,554	7,168	7,579	3,207	8,116	745	7,680	2,388	11,328	3,061	3,001	5,083	12,136
Omsk, USSR	6,132	5,574	14,292	4,652	5,969	11,073	8,052	1,842	3,678	5,942	10,889	4,036	8,838	4,766	11,615	7,603	11,164	12,142	13,669	4,152
Oodnadatta, Australia	16,225	16,123	4,118	15,527	15,894	14,207	12,810	12,597	14,527	16,068	17,258	14,434	15,739	15,198	14,058	4,647	16,809	15,074	15,012	6,734
Oradea, Romania	2,560	2,188	17,865	2,048	4,682	10,284	8,716	1,829	1,362	2,368	8,517	492	7,768	1,269	10,725	11,231	8,917	10,447	11,077	7,518
Oran, Algeria	428	971	19,657	2,255	4,633	9,460	9,067	4,043	2,620	321	6,932	1,838	7,153	1,180	9,776	13,464	7,371	9,067	9,179	9,742
Oranjestad, Aruba	6,933	6,999	12,775	7,359	5,920	3,793	6,706	10,274	8,365	7,091	997	8,661	3,939	7,918	3,659	15,231	1,007	2,229	1,952	15,665
Orebro, Sweden	2,974	2,256	17,409	1,222	3,403	9,068	7,288	1,728	258	2,804	7,775	1,360	6,548	1,696	9,545	10,761	8,128	9,488	10,500	7,588
Orel, USSR	3,713	3,220	16,713	2,603	4,818	10,474	8,345	637	1,611	3,522	9,219	1,609	7,967	2,360	10,966	10,032	9,583	10,958	11,910	6,416
Orsk, USSR	5,238	4,768	15,188	4,053	5,862	11,322	8,620	1,114	3,043	5,047	10,583	3,134	8,923	3,900	11,850	8,589	10,912	12,121	13,334	4,868
Osaka, Japan	11,182	10,495	9,227	9,277	9,021	10,901	7,519	6,969	8,497	11,001	13,188	9,161	10,201	9,825	11,293	2,526	13,131	12,709	14,888	2,890
Oslo, Norway	2,887	2,134	17,478	997	3,158	8,821	7,114	1,977	255	2,726	7,516	1,463	6,299	1,675	9,294	10,897	7,867	9,226	10,246	7,807
Osorno, Chile	10,957	11,509	8,649	12,497	11,774	7,967	11,477	15,240	13,435	11,147	6,870	13,060	9,540	12,318	7,465	15,268	6,723	6,369	4,306	18,454
Ostrava, Czechoslovakia	2,438	1,951	17,987	1,649	4,273	9,879	8,334	1,855	970	2,248	8,174	372	7,360	1,078	10,323	11,272	8,567	10,072	10,776	7,692
Ottawa, Canada	5,837	5,393	14,085	4,950	2,573	3,318	3,822	7,409	5,786	5,896	2,689	6,603	975	6,091	3,731	12,327	2,805	3,686	5,287	12,028
Ouagadougou, Bourkina Fasso	2,661	3,477	17,090	4,828	6,922	10,600	11,254	6,235	5,161	2,761	7,430	4,162	8,781	3,700	10,734	15,332	7,866	9,570	8,801	11,159
Oujda, Morocco	353	1,037	19,561	2,359	4,674	9,411	9,107	4,205	2,764	325	6,832	2,000	7,132	1,334	9,717	13,626	7,274	8,977	9,049	9,901
Oxford, United Kingdom	1,765	972	18,549	496	3,177	8,608	7,519	2,952	1,077	1,626	6,786	1,315	6,118	894	9,025	12,073	7,177	8,695	9,413	8,868
Pago Pago, American Samoa	17,183	16,464	2,923	15,249	12,811	8,509	8,380	14,488	15,177	17,160	11,558	16,324	10,542	16,562	8,317	5,790	11,115	9,389	10,053	9,997
Pakxe, Laos	10,837	10,509	9,572	9,828	10,996	14,507	11,015	6,892	8,824	10,651	15,944	8,819	13,256	9,600	14,938	4,203	16,104	16,264	18,450	1,273
Palembang, Indonesia	12,005	11,872	8,359	11,454	12,937	16,096	12,774	8,532	10,445	11,838	17,906	10,193	15,231	10,949	16,403	4,775	18,100	17,906	19,261	3,271
Palermo, Italy	1,675	1,710	18,684	2,367	5,073	10,374	9,391	3,035	2,182	1,506	8,106	1,009	7,938	1,009	10,747	12,385	8,537	10,192	10,441	8,512
Palma, Majorca	800	821	19,611	1,879	4,423	9,506	8,837	3,531	2,127	612	7,163	1,328	7,122	671	9,857	12,950	7,594	9,256	9,520	9,276
Palmerston North, New Zealand	19,530	19,637	278	18,283	15,989	11,087	11,556	16,117	17,750	19,652	13,468	18,261	13,434	19,034	10,749	6,758	13,037	11,375	11,084	10,274
Panama, Panama	8,011	8,029	11,710	8,269	6,519	3,131	6,421	11,125	9,260	8,163	1,650	9,661	4,023	8,938	2,865	14,544	1,321	1,351	1,232	16,015
Paramaribo, Suriname	6,078	6,382	13,567	7,125	6,489	5,582	8,292	10,034	8,115	6,260	2,440	8,072	5,345	7,292	5,447	16,955	2,683	3,988	2,881	15,927
Paris, France	1,547	855	18,821	895	3,585	8,981	7,926	2,893	1,173	1,383	7,045	998	6,503	485	9,388	12,177	7,448	9,003	9,617	8,801
Patna, India	8,421	8,158	11,979	7,654	9,362	14,269	10,896	4,738	6,645	8,239	14,206	6,461	12,210	7,236	14,806	6,351	14,520	15,529	16,960	2,161
Patrai, Greece	2,408	2,371	17,960	2,747	5,466	10,933	9,638	2,599	2,279	2,236	8,805	1,106	8,453	1,535	11,333	11,779	9,230	10,862	11,172	7,823
Peking, China	9,695	9,091	10,728	8,011	8,406	11,663	8,140	5,406	7,120	9,506	13,163	7,608	10,339	8,326	12,138	4,034	13,248	13,356	15,515	1,731
Penrhyn Island (Omoka)	15,936	15,343	4,063	14,329	11,696	7,037	7,300	14,415	14,533	15,964	10,064	15,741	9,166	15,707	6,828	6,790	9,622	7,900	8,688	10,974
Peoria, Illinois	7,080	6,636	12,840	6,129	3,580	2,115	3,135	8,403	6,909	7,141	2,753	7,796	444	7,315	2,574	11,819	2,658	2,890	4,849	12,369
Perm', USSR	5,046	4,471	15,376	3,569	5,146	10,555	7,073	763	2,582	4,857	9,955	2,966	8,172	3,677	11,005	9,660	10,263	11,401	12,729	5,239
Perth, Australia	14,656	14,818	5,598	14,732	16,307	16,144	14,504	11,884	13,748	14,538	18,661	13,269	17,522	13,949	15,948	5,895	18,307	16,732	15,888	6,548
Peshawar, Pakistan	6,822	6,552	13,582	6,102	8,039	13,390	10,360	3,249	5,103	6,638	12,710	4,856	11,067	5,629	13,929	7,648	13,060	14,298	15,404	3,464
Petropavlovsk-Kamchatskiy,USSR	10,007	9,201	10,329	7,837	6,742	8,277	4,813	6,503	7,363	9,863	10,467	8,379	7,477	8,824	8,716	4,557	10,396	10,054	12,253	5,170
Petrozavodsk, USSR	3,962	3,300	16,444	2,288	4,024	9,614	7,352	823	1,329	3,782	8,703	2,032	7,142	2,613	10,124	9,730	9,028	10,265	11,465	6,516
Pevek, USSR	8,263	7,442	12,034	6,072	4,790	7,218	3,732	5,377	5,763	8,138	8,811	6,892	5,867	7,203	7,727	6,497	8,817	8,840	10,987	6,245
Philadelphia, Pennsylvania	5,983	5,623	13,897	5,326	3,109	3,077	4,185	7,905	6,212	6,063	2,085	6,948	1,173	6,382	3,425	12,802	2,197	3,180	4,688	12,636
Phnom Penh, Kampuchea	11,020	10,735	9,381	10,113	11,368	14,882	11,402	7,171	9,105	10,838	16,327	9,039	13,662	9,818	15,300	4,331	16,500	16,654	18,849	1,675
Phoenix, Arizona	9,189	8,687	10,760	8,000	5,295	1,205	2,358	9,802	8,637	9,237	4,228	9,664	2,406	9,284	1,660	10,383	3,927	3,013	5,195	12,204
Pierre, South Dakota	7,666	7,129	12,306	6,423	3,727	2,106	2,172	8,357	7,082	7,702	3,694	8,089	982	7,707	2,643	10,852	3,554	3,426	5,544	11,681
Pinang, Malaysia	11,053	10,873	9,325	10,413	11,934	15,728	12,242	7,488	9,404	10,880	16,891	9,184	14,413	9,948	16,144	4,951	17,137	17,492	19,645	2,439
Pitcairn Island (Adamstown)	14,659	14,624	5,066	14,496	11,951	6,290	8,472	16,500	15,306	14,811	8,191	16,120	8,814	15,491	5,829	10,165	7,764	6,142	5,950	14,381
Pittsburgh, Pennsylvania	6,350	5,958	13,545	5,583	3,225	2,731	3,817	8,063	6,434	6,422	2,265	7,226	798	6,690	3,113	12,470	2,297	3,037	4,718	12,553
Plymouth, Montserrat	5,976	6,065	13,727	6,503	5,343	4,381	6,875	9,440	7,514	6,135	1,076	7,740	3,918	6,987	4,349	15,555	1,423	3,040	2,847	15,070
Plymouth, United Kingdom	1,588	772	18,690	605	3,147	8,488	7,533	3,201	1,326	1,465	6,579	1,482	6,016	938	8,892	12,310	6,976	8,516	9,187	9,118
Ponape Island	14,943	14,189	5,445	12,866	11,730	10,508	8,307	10,820	12,224	14,773	13,790	12,998	11,306	13,622	10,617	1,646	13,460	12,080	13,574	5,862
Ponce, Puerto Rico	6,293	6,321	13,429	6,649	5,259	3,892	6,461	9,563	7,655	6,445	608	7,971	3,551	7,235	3,861	15,123	933	2,579	2,662	15,019
Ponta Delgada, Azores	1,815	1,805	17,954	2,571	3,413	7,299	7,575	5,414	3,518	1,941	4,704	3,495	5,162	2,730	7,577	14,250	5,140	6,826	7,103	11,331
Pontianak, Indonesia	12,212	12,002	8,172	11,459	12,712	15,504	12,227	8,517	10,448	12,037	17,633	10,308	14,790	11,079	15,803	4,181	17,728	17,309	18,988	2,959
Port Augusta, Australia	16,628	16,618	3,682	16,103	16,416	14,090	13,051	13,166	15,098	16,487	16,921	14,946	15,873	15,698	13,883	5,141	16,480	14,769	14,507	7,320
Port Blair, India	9,975	9,799	10,404	9,382	11,073	15,536	12,019	6,480	8,377	9,802	15,951	8,113	13,790	8,874	16,031	5,645	16,259	17,081	18,691	2,212
Port Elizabeth, South Africa	8,400	9,151	11,477	10,346	12,769	15,066	17,119	10,157	10,240	8,444	11,911	9,032	14,329	8,990	14,817	13,521	12,203	13,306	11,295	10,865
Port Hedland, Australia	14,332	14,282	6,002	13,888	15,069	15,696	13,392	10,955	12,878	14,178	19,016	12,618	16,381	13,363	15,675	4,710	18,596	16,886	16,820	5,344
Port Louis, Mauritius	9,083	9,547	11,029	10,216	12,927	17,993	16,512	8,571	9,603	9,023	14,708	8,556	15,848	8,932	18,034	10,244	15,106	16,586	14,758	7,414
Port Moresby, Papua New Guinea	15,965	15,414	4,461	14,293	13,749	12,399	10,491	11,692	13,442	15,774	15,726	13,859	13,474	14,612	12,404	2,552	15,336	13,743	14,666	5,920
Port Said, Egypt	3,510	3,589	16,809	3,941	6,633	12,163	10,642	2,931	3,325	3,359	9,992	2,270	9,670	2,772	12,569	11,284	10,424	12,080	12,238	7,135
Port Sudan, Sudan	4,530	4,783	15,708	5,295	8,003	13,458	12,003	4,115	4,708	4,413	11,005	3,631	10,999	4,054	13,829	11,290	11,450	13,165	12,930	7,077
Port-au-Prince, Haiti	6,778	6,745	12,964	6,956	5,313	3,302	6,031	9,822	7,948	6,921	348	8,359	3,230	7,645	3,256	14,630	349	1,987	2,433	15,012
Port-of-Spain, Trin. & Tobago	6,294	6,471	13,382	7,023	6,001	4,715	7,440	9,965	8,032	6,464	1,577	8,164	4,531	7,395	4,604	16,081	1,803	3,179	2,475	15,696
Port-Vila, Vanuatu	17,875	17,089	2,504	15,730	14,037	10,673	9,848	13,723	15,158	17,711	13,819	15,921	12,447	16,564	10,532	4,314	13,379	11,660	12,250	8,266
Portland, Maine	5,472	5,077	14,426	4,748	2,577	3,612	4,293	7,340	5,634	5,542	2,462	6,374	1,422	5,819	3,983	12,755	2,648	3,750	5,164	12,222
Portland, Oregon	8,995	8,346	11,052	7,383	4,698	2,798	749	8,645	7,816	8,995	5,360	8,960	2,709	8,750	3,275	9,156	5,154	4,558	6,758	10,595
Porto, Portugal	625	359	19,390	1,664	3,754	8,571	8,183	4,098	2,352	610	6,197	2,026	6,236	1,246	8,906	13,370	6,626	8,283	8,610	9,987
Porto Alegre, Brazil	8,756	9,378	10,851	10,507	10,456	8,308	11,699	13,040	11,363	8,943	6,089	10,837	9,066	10,125	7,918	17,555	6,122	6,500	4,322	17,832
Porto Alexandre, Angola	6,029	6,811	13,804	8,083	10,365	13,275	14,685	8,538	8,149	6,093	9,951	6,973	12,005	6,782	13,204	14,961	10,316	11,749	10,137	11,257
Porto Novo, Benin	3,383	4,185	16,410	5,507	7,696	11,304	12,045	6,610	5,741	3,463	8,075	4,662	9,559	4,297	11,406	15,299	8,501	10,173	9,212	11,083
Porto Velho, Brazil	7,880	8,241	11,750	9,007	8,164	5,729	9,014	11,915	9,998	8,067	3,436	9,921	6,379	9,140	5,406	16,865	3,428	3,915	1,910	17,804
Portsmouth, United Kingdom	1,661	876	18,658	602	3,263	8,666	7,617	2,995	1,146	1,520	6,795	1,277	6,183	803	9,077	12,156	7,191	8,723	9,405	8,913
Poznan, Poland	2,519	1,945	17,897	1,432	3,999	9,625	8,033	1,797	671	2,333	8,020	605	7,103	1,152	10,077	11,168	8,403	9,874	10,661	7,696
Prague, Czechoslovakia	2,224	1,693	18,196	1,405	4,070	9,647	8,204	2,073	865	2,036	7,901	343	7,134	854	10,084	11,468	8,295	9,808	10,500	7,943
Praia, Cape Verde Islands	2,965	3,598	16,641	4,830	5,884	8,326	9,678	7,256	5,596	3,154	5,071	5,064	6,844	4,333	8,405	16,614	5,498	7,183	6,484	12,949
Pretoria, South Africa	7,702	8,415	12,217	9,548	12,075	15,206	16,505	9,218	9,372	7,727	11,913	8,165	14,008	8,177	15,062	13,301	12,255	13,560	11,707	10,221
Prince Albert, Canada	7,511	6,872	12,530	5,965	3,250	3,074	1,502	7,553	6,485	7,513	4,587	7,583	1,615	7,316	3,617	10,069	4,506	4,484	6,595	10,626

Distances in Kilometers

	Gibraltar	Gijon, Spain	Gisborne, New Zealand	Glasgow, United Kingdom	Godthab, Greenland	Gomez Palacio, Mexico	Goose Bay, Canada	Gorki, USSR	Goteborg, Sweden	Granada, Spain	Grand Turk, Turks & Caicos	Graz, Austria	Green Bay, Wisconsin	Grenoble, France	Guadalajara, Mexico	Guam (Agana)	Guantanamo, Cuba	Guatemala City, Guatemala	Guayaquil, Ecuador	Guiyang, China
Prince Edward Island	10,132	10,868	9,763	12,016	14,508	15,896	18,837	11,421	11,807	10,169	13,155	10,605	15,875	10,644	15,489	12,370	13,367	14,086	11,908	10,644
Prince George, Canada	8,369	7,668	11,720	6,614	4,001	3,528	436	7,723	6,972	8,348	5,619	8,140	2,705	7,991	4,042	8,972	5,490	5,185	7,370	9,904
Prince Rupert, Canada	8,689	7,962	11,424	6,847	4,311	3,880	372	7,727	7,128	8,656	6,108	8,316	3,201	8,224	4,375	8,476	5,969	5,590	7,785	9,519
Providence, Rhode Island	5,618	5,247	14,268	4,954	2,801	3,448	4,326	7,562	5,847	5,694	2,257	6,572	1,380	6,004	3,803	12,856	2,431	3,531	4,945	12,429
Provo, Utah	8,695	8,138	11,288	7,363	4,642	1,795	1,749	9,061	7,953	8,726	4,348	9,013	1,997	8,679	2,309	10,175	4,114	3,503	5,703	11,614
Puerto Aisen, Chile	11,278	11,869	8,328	12,914	12,297	8,456	11,951	15,568	13,827	11,467	7,406	13,367	10,074	12,646	7,946	15,023	7,261	6,887	4,841	17,916
Puerto Deseado, Argentina	11,068	11,708	8,540	12,833	12,482	8,949	12,462	15,327	13,696	11,253	7,683	13,125	10,448	12,435	8,450	15,270	7,575	7,330	5,226	17,570
Puerto Princesa, Philippines	12,276	11,878	8,141	11,052	11,760	14,008	10,748	8,172	10,073	12,088	16,392	10,212	13,426	10,991	14,325	2,866	16,371	15,819	17,815	2,254
Punta Arenas, Chile	11,735	12,390	7,875	13,529	13,126	9,273	12,739	15,965	14,382	11,919	8,266	13,773	10,945	13,099	8,755	14,603	8,129	7,741	5,711	17,048
Pusan, South Korea	10,818	10,167	9,598	9,002	8,991	11,315	7,871	6,556	8,172	10,633	13,394	8,760	10,430	9,451	11,731	2,869	13,381	13,106	15,303	2,329
Pyongyang, North Korea	10,294	9,643	10,122	8,484	8,554	11,219	7,726	6,036	7,649	10,109	13,084	8,239	10,156	8,927	11,663	3,392	13,105	12,978	15,176	2,246
Qamdo, China	9,038	8,627	11,383	7,865	9,081	13,353	9,864	4,943	6,867	8,848	14,051	6,962	11,607	7,740	13,866	5,226	14,271	14,870	16,780	1,055
Qandahar, Afghanistan	6,450	6,253	13,939	5,944	8,073	13,578	10,721	3,227	4,971	6,272	12,559	4,574	11,170	5,329	14,108	8,210	12,936	14,303	15,159	4,004
Qiqian, China	8,917	8,223	11,488	7,014	7,074	10,376	6,861	4,762	6,224	8,738	11,762	6,927	8,938	7,567	10,873	4,798	11,843	12,011	14,138	3,080
Qom, Iran	5,040	4,896	15,340	4,762	7,158	12,817	10,473	2,467	3,861	4,865	11,296	3,256	10,309	3,979	13,308	9,519	11,698	13,204	13,790	5,359
Quebec, Canada	5,464	5,015	14,462	4,584	2,282	3,695	4,049	7,090	5,434	5,521	2,812	6,233	1,329	5,714	4,102	12,430	2,982	3,994	5,492	11,874
Quetta, Pakistan	6,625	6,439	13,762	6,138	8,261	13,752	10,854	3,416	5,166	6,448	12,753	4,762	11,353	5,515	14,283	8,107	13,130	14,495	15,346	3,894
Quito, Ecuador	8,518	8,650	11,166	9,049	7,482	3,920	7,341	11,961	10,055	8,686	2,529	10,328	5,044	9,573	3,556	15,047	2,280	2,109	262	17,035
Rabaul, Papua New Guinea	15,793	15,137	4,627	13,908	13,074	11,654	9,690	11,510	13,138	15,606	14,981	13,712	12,670	14,424	11,689	2,119	14,608	13,074	14,208	5,961
Raiatea (Uturoa)	16,047	15,633	3,839	14,860	12,143	6,990	7,892	15,422	15,252	16,129	9,723	16,433	9,332	16,206	6,687	7,771	9,274	7,539	7,988	11,984
Raleigh, North Carolina	6,440	6,120	13,420	5,871	3,652	2,628	4,227	8,459	6,764	6,529	1,745	7,483	1,255	6,901	2,932	12,908	1,765	2,625	4,202	13,080
Rangiroa (Avatoru)	15,612	15,223	4,262	14,508	11,785	6,560	7,600	15,304	14,962	15,699	9,276	16,118	8,924	15,834	6,248	8,076	8,828	7,093	7,576	12,273
Rangoon, Burma	9,921	9,661	10,476	9,113	10,607	14,863	11,343	6,177	8,103	9,741	15,555	7,965	13,204	8,740	15,353	5,223	15,815	16,454	18,332	1,538
Raoul Is., Kermadec Islands	18,983	18,280	1,109	17,011	14,629	9,994	10,196	15,569	16,753	18,978	12,722	17,721	12,216	18,212	9,716	6,202	12,276	10,550	10,680	10,138
Rarotonga (Avarua)	17,039	16,569	2,875	15,661	12,986	7,982	8,630	15,643	15,895	17,109	10,721	17,103	10,283	17,037	7,689	7,175	10,273	8,539	8,885	11,374
Rawson, Argentina	10,675	11,290	8,932	12,383	11,983	8,578	12,100	14,957	13,267	10,862	7,198	12,753	9,990	12,044	8,090	15,647	7,099	6,919	4,785	18,011
Recife, Brazil	5,786	6,430	13,820	7,624	8,140	8,296	10,895	10,069	8,427	5,974	5,131	7,866	7,882	7,156	8,128	19,404	5,403	6,632	5,021	15,488
Regina, Canada	7,599	6,988	12,421	6,135	3,412	2,764	1,618	7,820	6,696	7,611	4,344	7,772	1,411	7,471	3,307	10,267	4,242	4,172	6,291	10,933
Reykjavik, Iceland	3,311	2,515	16,881	1,346	1,427	7,072	5,689	3,578	1,945	3,235	5,953	2,956	4,548	2,722	7,541	11,324	6,264	7,516	8,730	9,007
Rhodes, Greece	3,001	2,977	17,357	3,256	5,947	11,485	9,996	2,510	2,653	2,834	9,413	1,584	8,987	2,122	11,899	11,379	9,838	11,465	11,768	7,336
Richmond, Virginia	6,265	5,927	13,603	5,656	3,431	2,794	4,186	8,236	6,544	6,350	1,883	7,273	1,176	6,699	3,120	12,852	1,942	2,848	4,403	12,893
Riga, USSR	3,186	2,563	17,225	1,743	3,968	9,634	7,721	1,219	735	3,003	8,342	1,248	7,117	1,827	10,116	10,500	8,700	10,071	11,051	7,133
Ringkobing, Denmark	2,444	1,711	17,927	780	3,306	8,926	7,422	2,194	290	2,280	7,400	1,119	6,404	1,227	9,379	11,307	7,771	9,204	10,087	8,096
Rio Branco, Brazil	8,286	8,620	11,349	9,336	8,343	5,515	8,885	12,262	10,336	8,472	3,496	10,308	6,368	9,527	5,158	16,469	3,427	3,700	1,586	18,080
Rio Cuarto, Argentina	9,821	10,373	9,785	11,381	10,854	7,707	11,217	14,103	12,307	10,012	6,085	11,925	8,926	11,181	7,253	16,356	6,007	5,973	3,790	18,892
Rio de Janeiro, Brazil	7,654	8,298	11,954	9,470	9,689	8,425	11,593	11,930	10,292	7,840	5,766	9,725	8,744	9,022	8,110	18,674	5,892	6,617	4,567	16,971
Rio Gallegos, Argentina	11,537	12,188	8,072	13,324	12,941	9,185	12,669	15,776	14,180	11,721	8,100	13,580	10,806	12,902	8,672	14,801	7,971	7,626	5,572	17,203
Rio Grande, Brazil	8,982	9,609	10,625	10,741	10,674	8,393	11,814	13,264	11,595	9,169	6,259	11,060	9,226	10,351	7,989	17,338	6,277	6,593	4,402	17,886
Riyadh, Saudi Arabia	5,102	5,170	15,213	5,366	7,956	13,599	11,566	3,527	4,593	4,954	11,587	3,720	11,077	4,319	14,045	10,190	12,019	13,662	13,782	5,974
Road Town, Brit. Virgin Isls.	6,088	6,129	13,630	6,488	5,181	4,077	6,562	9,412	7,496	6,241	759	7,786	3,618	7,046	4,061	15,239	1,128	2,794	2,825	14,936
Roanoke, Virginia	6,479	6,131	13,393	5,830	3,542	2,578	4,031	8,369	6,704	6,562	1,947	7,457	1,052	6,893	2,916	12,710	1,955	2,718	4,367	12,902
Robinson Crusoe Island, Chile	10,859	11,317	8,754	12,157	11,112	7,051	10,557	15,041	13,141	11,050	6,153	12,955	8,703	12,184	6,546	15,093	5,963	5,483	3,485	19,064
Rochester, New York	6,058	5,639	13,851	5,230	2,866	3,057	3,817	7,702	6,074	6,123	2,480	6,879	849	6,354	3,456	12,404	2,563	3,394	5,025	12,270
Rockhampton, Australia	17,305	16,891	3,107	15,854	15,186	12,628	11,464	13,150	14,968	17,119	15,756	15,249	14,268	16,025	12,490	4,124	15,311	13,580	13,890	7,264
Rome, Italy	1,668	1,495	18,743	1,966	4,684	10,065	8,975	2,767	1,760	1,481	7,936	621	7,603	656	10,456	12,176	8,358	9,979	10,364	8,416
Rosario, Argentina	9,572	10,147	10,034	11,195	10,805	7,908	11,400	13,862	12,101	9,762	6,124	11,671	9,015	10,937	7,468	16,658	6,074	6,149	3,952	18,616
Roseau, Dominica	5,988	6,105	13,707	6,583	5,488	4,518	7,049	9,524	7,594	6,151	1,234	7,787	4,095	7,029	4,469	15,728	1,558	3,131	2,803	15,198
Rostock, East Germany	2,409	1,748	17,988	1,065	3,639	9,256	7,733	2,026	405	2,232	7,670	815	6,735	1,094	9,706	11,290	8,048	9,507	10,331	7,944
Rostov-na-Donu, USSR	3,887	3,526	16,533	3,136	5,478	11,141	9,010	1,055	2,193	3,697	9,745	1,832	8,628	2,612	11,627	10,023	10,125	11,560	12,376	6,188
Rotterdam, Netherlands	1,919	1,202	18,450	721	3,442	8,951	7,709	2,591	804	1,755	7,182	958	6,448	756	9,378	11,817	7,572	9,080	9,808	8,510
Rouyn, Canada	5,993	5,495	13,957	4,944	2,427	3,301	3,455	7,272	5,729	6,038	3,052	6,612	805	6,146	3,753	11,925	3,136	3,873	5,585	11,699
Sacramento, California	9,458	8,859	10,552	7,987	5,270	2,222	1,502	9,398	8,486	9,476	5,142	9,601	2,849	9,335	2,642	9,411	4,875	4,033	6,211	11,226
Saginaw, Michigan	6,529	6,078	13,396	5,584	3,081	2,662	3,362	7,924	6,382	6,587	2,710	7,247	348	6,759	3,102	12,006	2,709	3,254	5,067	12,176
Saint Denis, Reunion	8,982	9,469	11,116	10,178	12,897	17,817	16,607	8,622	9,595	8,928	14,513	8,526	15,761	8,878	17,826	10,470	14,906	16,366	14,531	7,625
Saint George's, Grenada	6,224	6,380	13,459	6,906	5,849	4,625	7,304	9,848	7,916	6,391	1,444	8,070	4,384	7,305	4,531	15,957	1,693	3,128	2,544	15,554
Saint John, Canada	5,106	4,699	14,799	4,376	2,297	3,989	4,483	7,002	5,271	5,172	2,681	5,997	1,731	5,439	4,363	12,803	2,912	4,101	5,429	12,015
Saint John's, Antigua	5,919	6,006	13,785	6,445	5,294	4,403	6,866	9,382	7,455	6,078	1,089	7,681	3,902	6,929	4,377	15,549	1,448	3,080	2,906	15,018
Saint John's, Canada	4,063	3,645	15,852	3,398	1,859	5,044	5,207	6,159	4,341	4,124	3,334	4,981	2,729	4,397	5,411	13,027	3,657	5,044	6,110	11,539
Saint Louis, Missouri	7,230	6,807	12,679	6,334	3,806	1,912	3,231	8,634	7,126	7,296	2,634	7,997	680	7,503	2,356	11,906	2,506	2,658	4,639	12,577
Saint Paul, Minnesota	7,129	6,619	12,828	5,985	3,337	2,345	2,642	8,087	6,699	7,172	3,290	7,657	406	7,234	2,853	11,317	3,208	3,369	5,382	11,834
Saint Peter Port, UK	1,497	700	18,806	720	3,301	8,635	7,684	3,159	1,325	1,362	6,689	1,358	6,167	784	9,036	12,336	7,090	8,643	9,277	9,077
Saipan (Susupe)	13,570	12,887	6,874	11,654	11,078	11,282	8,474	9,324	10,889	13,387	14,311	11,526	11,464	12,208	11,507	213	14,068	13,020	14,834	4,232
Salalah, Oman	6,190	6,300	14,105	6,499	9,052	14,713	12,427	4,448	5,697	6,050	12,692	4,860	12,190	5,459	15,172	9,654	13,128	14,793	14,736	5,507
Salem, Oregon	9,065	8,417	10,981	7,457	4,770	2,774	795	8,715	7,890	9,065	5,379	9,034	2,754	8,823	3,245	9,137	5,167	4,543	6,742	10,622
Salt Lake City, Utah	8,675	8,112	11,312	7,328	4,605	1,855	1,692	9,009	7,911	8,704	4,383	8,975	1,995	8,646	2,370	10,138	4,154	3,559	5,759	11,556
Salta, Argentina	9,233	9,715	10,379	10,630	9,943	6,916	10,393	13,454	11,590	9,424	5,154	11,334	8,011	10,567	6,491	16,628	5,081	5,143	2,943	19,216
Salto, Uruguay	9,273	9,857	10,332	10,922	10,616	7,948	11,413	13,564	11,819	9,463	6,015	11,371	8,940	10,640	7,525	16,967	5,991	6,167	3,967	18,444
Salvador, Brazil	6,458	7,093	13,149	8,268	8,636	8,231	11,067	10,743	9,087	6,645	5,218	8,540	8,091	7,827	8,007	19,678	5,437	6,494	4,705	16,105
Salzburg, Austria	1,991	1,528	18,433	1,483	4,193	9,714	8,394	2,301	1,106	1,801	7,846	200	7,213	633	10,137	11,713	8,249	9,798	10,402	8,130
Samsun, Turkey	3,635	3,430	16,764	3,339	5,875	11,529	9,621	1,763	2,514	3,453	9,824	1,783	9,006	2,509	11,989	10,514	10,228	11,762	12,335	6,530
San Antonio, Texas	8,408	8,035	11,473	7,607	5,064	654	3,433	9,865	8,398	8,488	2,882	9,268	1,914	8,759	1,086	11,745	2,564	1,832	4,022	13,253
San Cristobal, Venezuela	7,433	7,535	12,263	7,929	6,479	3,856	6,985	10,849	8,937	7,596	1,521	9,208	4,349	8,457	3,638	15,315	1,405	2,135	1,385	16,203
San Diego, California	9,606	9,077	10,359	8,330	5,610	1,545	2,244	9,978	8,919	9,646	4,693	9,981	2,835	9,639	1,913	9,954	4,379	3,358	5,506	11,974
San Francisco, California	9,578	8,980	10,431	8,106	5,390	2,240	1,568	9,498	8,601	9,597	5,214	9,718	2,960	9,455	2,642	9,352	4,939	4,055	6,224	11,236
San Jose, Costa Rica	8,359	8,324	11,380	8,465	6,544	2,683	6,060	11,258	9,438	8,504	1,883	9,921	3,851	9,219	2,381	14,048	1,478	872	1,419	15,802
San Juan, Argentina	9,974	10,485	9,635	11,429	10,722	7,333	10,851	14,226	12,381	10,165	5,872	12,080	8,650	11,322	6,868	16,085	5,762	5,623	3,461	19,297
San Juan, Puerto Rico	6,222	6,248	13,501	6,578	5,202	3,926	6,458	9,493	7,584	6,373	621	7,898	3,535	7,163	3,905	15,126	972	2,637	2,733	14,961
San Luis Potosi, Mexico	9,071	8,756	10,780	8,405	5,899	457	3,979	10,708	9,219	9,165	3,083	10,056	2,751	9,516	294	11,848	2,684	1,383	3,539	13,849
San Marino, San Marino	1,744	1,459	18,679	1,780	4,503	9,933	8,770	2,610	1,536	1,553	7,888	421	7,456	554	10,335	12,031	8,303	9,902	10,362	8,331
San Miguel de Tucuman, Argen.	9,379	9,878	10,231	10,816	10,165	7,104	10,591	13,619	11,768	9,570	5,380	11,483	8,232	10,721	6,671	16,577	5,305	5,340	3,143	19,228
San Salvador, El Salvador	8,581	8,457	11,190	8,444	6,311	1,991	5,413	11,120	9,381	8,712	2,099	9,982	3,418	9,322	1,688	13,367	1,652	176	2,037	15,231
Sanaa, Yemen	5,408	5,644	14,836	6,079	8,757	14,294	12,570	4,548	5,415	5,289	11,880	4,407	11,809	4,886	14,683	10,725	12,325	14,042	13,727	6,559
Santa Cruz, Bolivia	8,520	8,966	11,096	9,842	9,151	6,488	9,883	12,694	10,810	8,711	4,430	10,608	7,347	9,835	6,110	17,006	4,397	4,678	2,511	18,595
Santa Cruz, Tenerife	1,331	1,922	18,280	3,189	4,697	8,456	8,927	5,604	3,921	1,523	5,552	3,435	6,461	2,681	8,676	14,940	6,000	7,735	7,576	11,405
Santa Fe, New Mexico	8,592	8,108	11,347	7,473	4,794	1,145	2,457	9,421	8,154	8,644	3,726	9,143	1,811	8,732	1,683	10,823	3,461	2,794	4,993	12,311
Santa Rosa, Argentina	10,095	10,671	9,511	11,712	11,238	8,019	11,537	14,385	12,623	10,285	6,469	12,194	9,298	11,461	7,553	16,155	6,385	6,306	4,136	18,613
Santa Rosalia, Mexico	9,634	9,184	10,285	8,578	5,897	897	2,969	10,469	9,255	9,696	4,206	10,248	2,885	9,828	1,171	10,577	3,850	2,657	4,769	12,734
Santarem, Brazil	6,661	7,056	12,965	7,907	7,401	6,100	9,047	10,769	8,876	6,849	3,193	8,721	6,163	7,942	5,886	17,565	3,353	4,377	2,796	16,687
Santiago del Estero, Argentina	9,389	9,903	10,219	10,862	10,263	7,247	10,733	13,644	11,807	9,581	5,499	11,495	8,362	10,737	6,813	16,626	5,431	5,481	3,284	19,128
Santiago, Chile	10,267	10,778	9,342	11,716	10,960	7,399	10,922	14,519	12,671	10,458	6,078	12,372	8,811	11,615	6,921	15,815	5,949	5,724	3,593	19,205
Santo Domingo, Dominican Rep.	6,563	6,553	13,171	6,811	5,269	3,547	6,200	9,699	7,809	6,709	356	8,182	3,344	7,460	3,511	14,832	587	2,240	2,528	15,007
Sao Paulo de Olivenca, Brazil	7,897	8,157	11,755	8,774	7,643	4,932	8,223	11,715	9,782	8,077	2,768	9,853	5,647	9,076	4,618	16,184	2,701	3,121	1,235	17,401
Sao Paulo, Brazil	7,903	8,524	11,704	9,663	9,741	8,191	11,426	12,189	10,511	8,091	5,643	9,987	8,631	9,272	7,857	18,385	5,741	6,376	4,289	17,325
Sao Tome, Sao Tome & Principe	4,156	4,942	15,669	6,233	8,498	12,024	12,863	7,049	6,380	4,222	8,747	5,247	10,362	4,968	12,089	15,159	9,161	10,790	9,639	10,993
Sapporo, Japan	10,611	9,869	9,777	8,579	8,054	9,935	6,501	6,570	7,892	10,441	12,129	8,697	9,143	9,293	10,353	3,295	12,077	11,727	13,923	3,620
Sarajevo, Yugoslavia	2,193	1,935	18,223	2,090	4,798	10,315	8,961	2,277	1,608	2,004	8,354	428	7,818	1,020	10,733	11,662	8,767	10,350	10,840	7,887
Saratov, USSR	4,366	3,906	16,060	3,280	5,350	10,958	8,579	547	2,276	4,174	9,881	2,262	8,481	3,030	11,466	9,439	10,235	11,559	12,591	5,734
Saskatoon, Canada	7,623	6,990	12,413	6,093	3,376	2,959	1,450	7,685	6,618	7,628	4,565	7,714	1,613	7,442	3,502	10,063	4,470	4,398	6,523	10,703
Schefferville, Canada	5,042	4,477	14,952	3,838	1,354	4,413	3,964	6,192	4,614	5,066	3,718	5,508	1,897	5,070	4,868	11,879	3,912	4,905	6,427	10,967
Seattle, Washington	8,823	8,161	11,234	7,179	4,505	2,952	571	8,415	7,598	8,818	5,390	8,747	2,656	8,549	3,442	9,132	5,204	4,686	6,886	10,442

Distances in Kilometers	Gibraltar	Gijon, Spain	Gisborne, New Zealand	Glasgow, United Kingdom	Godthab, Greenland	Gomez Palacio, Mexico	Goose Bay, Canada	Gorki, USSR	Goteborg, Sweden	Granada, Spain	Grand Turk, Turks & Caicos	Graz, Austria	Green Bay, Wisconsin	Grenoble, France	Guadalajara, Mexico	Guam (Agana)	Guantanamo, Cuba	Guatemala City, Guatemala	Guayaquil, Ecuador	Guiyang, China
Sendai, Japan	11,070	10,343	9,326	9,070	8,589	10,276	6,899	6,959	8,355	10,895	12,602	9,116	9,612	9,736	10,671	2,772	12,530	12,084	14,264	3,440
Seoul, South Korea	10,488	9,837	9,928	8,676	8,717	11,257	7,780	6,229	7,843	10,303	13,202	8,432	10,259	9,122	11,691	3,198	13,211	13,029	15,229	2,262
Sept-Iles, Canada	5,049	4,558	14,901	4,073	1,792	4,186	4,195	6,576	4,916	5,094	3,216	5,728	1,744	5,228	4,607	12,329	3,426	4,508	5,944	11,473
Sevastopol, USSR	3,398	3,113	17,015	2,925	5,442	11,098	9,217	1,498	2,082	3,211	9,455	1,428	8,574	2,188	11,560	10,577	9,852	11,361	12,014	6,696
Seville, Spain	150	683	19,644	2,055	4,229	8,948	8,657	4,229	2,615	205	6,437	2,061	6,657	1,305	9,262	13,604	6,874	8,562	8,739	10,043
Shanghai, China	10,723	10,144	9,702	9,085	9,415	12,133	8,662	6,432	8,185	10,533	14,036	8,624	11,118	9,357	12,558	3,090	14,066	13,911	16,110	1,514
Sheffield, United Kingdom	1,939	1,136	18,370	327	3,039	8,516	7,359	2,887	976	1,803	6,776	1,393	6,017	1,051	8,942	11,935	7,160	8,651	9,429	8,792
Shenyang, China	9,930	9,277	10,485	8,120	8,239	11,126	7,613	5,678	7,283	9,746	12,842	7,879	9,945	8,564	11,587	3,656	12,886	12,856	15,041	2,278
Shiraz, Iran	5,387	5,320	14,971	5,285	7,726	13,390	11,034	3,045	4,409	5,221	11,754	3,727	10,876	4,418	13,875	9,496	12,166	13,716	14,153	5,288
Sibiu, Romania	2,686	2,364	17,735	2,269	4,898	10,505	8,902	1,808	1,565	2,496	8,722	683	7,987	1,440	10,946	11,164	9,125	10,663	11,265	7,390
Singapore	11,643	11,473	8,732	11,009	12,462	15,837	12,436	8,080	9,999	11,471	17,431	9,785	14,798	10,548	16,193	4,702	17,633	17,652	19,615	2,816
Sioux Falls, South Dakota	7,459	6,947	12,498	6,298	3,632	2,087	2,468	8,342	6,995	7,502	3,405	7,968	708	7,556	2,610	11,151	3,279	3,259	5,337	11,881
Skelleftea, Sweden	3,633	2,888	16,741	1,694	3,293	8,918	6,844	1,561	920	3,469	7,965	1,999	6,427	2,375	9,419	10,146	8,286	9,523	10,733	7,166
Skopje, Yugoslavia	2,401	2,219	18,002	2,409	5,110	10,638	9,237	2,269	1,873	2,217	8,653	739	8,140	1,319	11,056	11,571	9,069	10,663	11,108	7,713
Socotra Island (Tamrida)	6,449	6,617	13,822	6,895	9,485	15,132	12,909	4,923	6,123	6,320	12,946	5,240	12,610	5,804	15,573	9,773	13,389	15,086	14,820	5,698
Sofia, Bulgaria	2,560	2,349	17,846	2,456	5,136	10,697	9,212	2,117	1,852	2,375	8,772	789	8,191	1,437	11,123	11,403	9,185	10,764	11,249	7,546
Songkhla, Thailand	10,955	10,753	9,428	10,264	11,748	15,549	12,056	7,333	9,254	10,780	16,710	9,061	14,213	9,829	15,974	4,878	16,947	17,303	19,446	2,241
Sorong, Indonesia	14,086	13,652	6,334	12,728	12,971	13,559	10,854	9,919	11,782	13,896	16,692	12,007	13,826	12,782	13,714	2,177	16,444	15,195	16,562	4,021
South Georgia Island	10,458	11,232	9,187	12,559	13,204	10,896	14,411	14,271	13,167	10,619	9,011	12,257	11,973	11,728	10,431	15,478	9,022	9,165	6,973	15,734
South Pole	14,005	14,826	5,719	16,194	17,131	12,831	15,696	16,249	16,404	14,125	12,378	15,219	14,933	15,008	12,288	11,490	12,230	11,621	9,763	12,943
South Sandwich Islands	10,591	11,392	9,077	12,751	13,698	11,643	15,158	14,121	13,251	10,739	9,704	12,245	12,681	11,791	11,176	15,036	9,733	9,912	7,719	14,988
Split, Yugoslavia	2,029	1,781	18,387	2,012	4,731	10,214	8,936	2,413	1,610	1,840	8,209	402	7,725	873	10,625	11,811	8,624	10,217	10,682	8,049
Spokane, Washington	8,539	7,898	11,502	6,963	4,262	2,741	849	8,348	7,431	8,541	5,038	8,558	2,286	8,324	3,253	9,491	4,863	4,424	6,619	10,677
Spoleto, Italy	1,716	1,497	18,700	1,900	4,621	10,027	8,899	2,686	1,668	1,527	7,936	527	7,558	625	10,424	12,100	8,355	9,967	10,384	8,361
Springbok, South Africa	7,679	8,454	12,165	9,704	12,016	14,286	16,287	9,845	9,699	7,738	11,075	8,501	13,459	8,378	14,081	14,295	11,382	12,568	10,642	11,322
Springfield, Illinois	7,128	6,694	12,786	6,205	3,668	2,039	3,189	8,495	6,992	7,192	2,687	7,870	541	7,382	2,490	11,871	2,580	2,790	4,754	12,463
Springfield, Massachusetts	5,702	5,322	14,188	5,005	2,807	3,370	4,228	7,588	5,889	5,776	2,292	6,630	1,277	6,071	3,732	12,769	2,448	3,498	4,957	12,400
Srinagar, India	7,088	6,796	13,319	6,297	8,145	13,400	10,286	3,407	5,292	6,903	12,884	5,099	11,130	5,876	13,942	7,347	13,221	14,396	15,608	3,164
Stanley, Falkland Islands	10,991	11,687	8,625	12,899	12,869	9,650	13,169	15,144	13,685	11,170	8,208	12,980	11,049	12,340	9,156	15,309	8,135	7,999	5,861	16,931
Stara Zagora, Bulgaria	2,746	2,541	17,657	2,610	5,271	10,854	9,297	2,030	1,955	2,562	8,961	957	8,342	1,628	11,286	11,256	9,373	10,946	11,441	7,371
Stockholm, Sweden	3,085	2,385	17,306	1,382	3,525	9,192	7,347	1,567	397	2,912	7,933	1,376	6,674	1,781	9,672	10,634	8,284	9,635	10,661	7,430
Stornoway, United Kingdom	2,456	1,634	17,808	295	2,461	8,028	6,743	2,974	1,083	2,343	6,529	1,914	5,511	1,670	8,474	11,656	6,888	8,294	9,251	8,770
Strasbourg, France	1,749	1,178	18,660	1,148	3,871	9,341	8,145	2,575	1,054	1,567	7,445	600	6,849	410	9,756	11,937	7,847	9,398	10,011	8,458
Stuttgart, West Germany	1,837	1,283	18,576	1,204	3,925	9,418	8,175	2,476	1,013	1,653	7,547	505	6,922	479	9,838	11,849	7,948	9,493	10,117	8,353
Subic, Philippines	11,984	11,528	8,439	10,626	11,203	13,502	10,188	7,794	9,666	11,793	15,799	9,893	12,836	10,665	13,847	2,650	15,784	15,319	17,413	1,910
Suchow, China	10,201	9,630	10,224	8,591	9,039	12,120	8,611	5,912	7,679	10,011	13,774	8,101	10,918	8,836	12,573	3,610	13,844	13,856	16,041	1,316
Sucre, Bolivia	8,775	9,212	10,842	10,070	9,309	6,439	9,871	12,935	11,044	8,965	4,525	10,860	7,406	10,085	6,042	16,770	4,466	4,639	2,449	18,847
Sudbury, Canada	6,193	5,714	13,747	5,183	2,670	3,061	3,402	7,514	5,972	6,244	2,917	6,849	590	6,375	3,510	11,953	2,972	3,643	5,393	11,874
Suez, Egypt	3,582	3,689	16,725	4,073	6,770	12,286	10,788	3,064	3,468	3,436	10,075	2,403	9,799	2,887	12,688	11,319	10,510	12,175	12,286	7,155
Sundsvall, Sweden	3,313	2,574	17,062	1,424	3,289	8,947	7,019	1,646	598	3,148	7,834	1,709	6,439	2,055	9,437	10,452	8,170	9,465	10,587	7,393
Surabaya, Indonesia	13,002	12,839	7,369	12,337	13,557	15,681	12,662	9,396	11,326	12,832	18,379	11,149	15,416	11,914	15,873	4,215	18,349	17,365	18,283	3,800
Suva, Fiji	17,977	17,163	2,276	15,814	13,679	9,733	9,311	14,328	15,471	17,880	12,796	16,442	11,681	16,932	9,553	5,087	12,352	10,624	11,183	9,188
Sverdlovsk, USSR	5,310	4,749	15,113	3,859	5,397	10,751	7,983	1,019	2,871	5,121	10,231	3,220	8,396	3,943	11,285	8,410	10,535	11,645	13,008	4,949
Svobodnyy, USSR	9,303	8,585	11,095	7,337	7,180	10,104	6,581	5,210	6,592	9,127	11,717	7,350	8,824	7,966	10,586	4,465	11,761	11,792	13,958	3,295
Sydney, Australia	17,877	17,752	2,458	16,928	16,288	12,895	12,306	14,095	15,984	17,726	15,665	16,055	14,888	16,830	12,656	5,285	15,222	13,508	13,361	8,176
Sydney, Canada	4,640	4,235	15,266	3,954	2,084	4,454	4,817	6,647	4,873	4,705	2,913	5,557	2,178	4,984	4,821	12,948	3,195	4,496	5,691	11,843
Syktyvkar, USSR	4,780	4,149	15,635	3,151	4,636	10,065	7,469	710	2,196	4,595	9,458	2,760	7,668	3,415	10,593	8,906	9,761	10,891	12,236	5,657
Szeged, Hungary	2,403	2,054	18,020	2,000	4,668	10,244	8,755	1,988	1,391	2,212	8,413	372	7,732	1,130	10,677	11,393	8,817	10,364	10,953	7,673
Szombathely, Hungary	2,194	1,786	18,233	1,725	4,414	9,967	8,558	2,124	1,208	2,002	8,123	90	7,460	871	10,396	11,546	8,526	10,073	10,674	7,898
Tabriz, Iran	4,536	4,355	15,854	4,201	6,625	12,290	10,076	2,036	3,308	4,358	10,740	2,701	9,775	3,434	12,773	9,822	11,139	12,643	13,259	5,729
Tacheng, China	7,081	6,589	13,345	5,753	7,076	11,970	8,744	2,858	4,762	6,889	12,016	4,975	9,855	5,737	12,512	6,789	12,281	13,175	14,793	3,062
Tahiti (Papeete)	15,948	15,571	3,919	14,854	12,132	6,901	7,927	15,551	15,291	16,039	9,576	16,456	9,274	16,183	6,583	7,988	9,128	7,395	7,795	12,201
Taipei, Taiwan	11,240	10,699	9,186	9,688	10,087	12,615	9,196	6,965	8,766	11,049	14,682	9,134	11,741	9,884	13,012	2,754	14,693	14,418	16,605	1,491
Taiyuan, China	9,624	9,057	10,801	8,034	8,598	12,043	8,519	5,335	7,113	9,434	13,426	7,523	10,651	8,260	12,523	4,176	13,534	13,717	15,856	1,366
Tallahassee, Florida	7,173	6,888	12,668	6,663	4,396	1,963	4,242	9,226	7,552	7,271	1,648	8,273	1,595	7,683	2,195	12,869	1,462	1,864	3,640	13,587
Tallinn, USSR	3,376	2,713	17,027	1,763	3,811	9,469	7,472	1,188	766	3,197	8,301	1,505	6,960	2,034	9,959	10,318	8,647	9,973	11,036	7,054
Tamanrasset, Algeria	1,814	2,521	18,108	3,757	6,176	10,688	10,609	4,865	3,914	1,827	7,811	2,837	8,537	2,483	10,933	14,036	8,259	9,996	9,632	9,941
Tampa, Florida	7,150	6,909	12,672	6,763	4,591	2,108	4,566	9,395	7,677	7,257	1,351	8,346	1,903	7,729	2,264	13,175	1,137	1,694	3,344	13,892
Tampere, Finland	3,478	2,780	16,915	1,727	3,620	9,267	7,234	1,294	786	3,304	8,186	1,692	6,766	2,163	9,762	10,238	8,522	9,813	10,936	7,077
Tanami, Australia	15,310	15,134	5,058	14,505	15,086	14,567	12,589	11,575	13,505	15,142	17,857	13,439	15,605	14,210	14,518	4,050	17,430	15,726	15,973	5,719
Tangier, Morocco	55	859	19,551	2,230	4,390	9,037	8,813	4,346	2,770	246	6,466	2,161	6,772	1,424	9,341	13,739	6,906	8,606	8,720	10,129
Tarawa (Betio)	15,851	15,031	4,461	13,660	11,877	9,305	7,819	12,148	13,241	15,721	12,631	14,212	10,624	14,700	9,312	3,382	12,241	10,686	11,942	7,590
Tashkent, USSR	6,313	5,955	14,104	5,380	7,215	12,561	9,602	2,471	4,371	6,124	11,949	4,265	10,231	5,046	13,099	7,824	12,282	13,472	14,686	3,788
Tbilisi, USSR	4,327	4,078	16,077	3,830	6,212	11,875	9,665	1,628	2,913	4,143	10,408	2,394	9,362	3,153	12,361	9,837	10,799	12,270	12,981	5,826
Tegucigalpa, Honduras	8,379	8,268	11,388	8,284	6,202	2,123	5,489	10,991	9,230	8,512	1,888	9,807	3,372	9,138	1,859	13,541	1,442	361	1,975	15,261
Tehran, Iran	5,050	4,884	15,335	4,713	7,082	12,736	10,361	2,365	3,799	4,873	11,268	3,230	10,232	3,964	13,230	9,446	11,666	13,155	13,786	5,299
Tel Aviv, Israel	3,703	3,739	16,630	4,008	6,673	12,248	10,602	2,790	3,336	3,547	10,164	2,339	9,742	2,895	12,668	11,034	10,592	12,232	12,450	6,886
Telegraph Creek, Canada	8,430	7,686	11,701	6,534	4,064	4,203	760	7,331	6,776	8,388	6,249	7,971	3,290	7,908	4,710	8,400	6,141	5,872	8,057	9,218
Teresina, Brazil	6,005	6,550	13,603	7,618	7,725	7,374	10,090	10,278	8,505	6,196	4,263	8,111	7,104	7,359	7,196	18,774	4,509	5,698	4,125	16,007
Ternate, Indonesia	13,653	13,247	6,764	12,372	12,788	13,830	10,971	9,526	11,409	13,465	16,835	11,588	13,893	12,365	14,021	2,371	16,640	15,521	17,004	3,612
The Valley, Anguilla	5,972	6,034	13,740	6,431	5,204	4,246	6,702	9,362	7,441	6,128	926	7,700	3,743	6,954	4,230	15,384	1,297	2,955	2,895	14,946
Thessaloniki, Greece	2,510	2,376	17,881	2,603	5,304	10,830	9,419	2,321	2,055	2,330	8,816	933	8,333	1,490	11,246	11,551	9,235	10,839	11,246	7,643
Thimphu, Bhutan	8,681	8,362	11,728	7,758	9,288	13,962	10,530	4,818	6,747	8,495	14,208	6,668	12,024	7,448	14,491	5,900	14,489	15,339	16,989	1,688
Thunder Bay, Canada	6,708	6,174	13,264	5,510	2,857	2,821	2,744	7,618	6,219	6,744	3,399	7,181	444	6,770	3,323	11,336	3,382	3,746	5,678	11,548
Tientsin, China	9,807	9,203	10,616	8,123	8,501	11,692	8,172	5,518	7,233	9,618	13,241	7,719	10,403	8,437	12,162	3,925	13,319	13,397	15,565	1,700
Tijuana, Mexico	9,609	9,083	10,354	8,340	5,621	1,524	2,267	9,995	8,932	9,650	4,679	9,992	2,837	9,647	1,890	9,971	4,363	3,337	5,484	11,997
Tiksi, USSR	7,530	6,741	12,824	5,400	4,929	8,509	5,127	4,055	4,848	7,376	9,569	5,850	6,802	6,306	9,038	6,547	9,666	9,996	12,035	5,191
Timbuktu, Mali	2,158	2,978	17,575	4,337	6,410	10,231	10,754	5,892	4,713	2,267	7,132	3,765	8,331	3,253	10,396	15,149	7,574	9,297	8,685	11,048
Tindouf, Algeria	972	1,771	18,664	3,141	5,089	9,218	9,447	5,180	3,688	1,135	6,350	2,975	7,140	2,295	9,454	14,601	6,799	8,533	8,332	10,825
Tirane, Albania	2,256	2,104	18,142	2,377	5,091	10,584	9,262	2,412	1,906	2,073	8,544	727	8,095	1,221	10,994	11,727	8,963	10,570	10,978	7,867
Tokyo, Japan	11,275	10,561	9,126	9,305	8,880	10,523	7,171	7,120	8,567	11,098	12,894	9,294	9,904	9,931	10,907	2,513	12,816	12,335	14,504	3,292
Toledo, Spain	431	430	19,797	1,775	4,083	8,985	8,517	3,913	2,293	296	6,591	1,760	6,640	992	9,321	13,279	7,022	8,689	8,960	9,747
Topeka, Kansas	7,625	7,167	12,302	6,612	4,002	1,666	2,831	8,774	7,357	7,682	3,044	8,283	879	7,827	2,166	11,476	2,872	2,753	4,844	12,377
Toronto, Canada	6,175	5,741	13,741	5,298	2,880	2,967	3,665	7,725	6,126	6,237	2,578	6,953	697	6,442	3,382	12,262	2,639	3,388	5,077	12,201
Toulouse, France	1,011	573	19,390	1,420	3,998	9,200	8,397	3,298	1,733	831	7,014	1,162	6,775	383	9,573	12,675	7,435	9,057	9,473	9,145
Tours, France	1,345	655	19,013	1,000	3,631	8,950	8,005	3,087	1,377	1,185	6,929	1,117	6,490	459	9,345	12,382	7,338	8,916	9,473	8,989
Townsville, Australia	16,718	16,294	3,697	15,282	14,820	12,840	11,356	12,554	14,381	16,531	16,075	14,653	14,262	15,429	12,751	3,626	15,641	13,933	14,409	6,668
Trenton, New Jersey	5,941	5,579	13,940	5,281	3,068	3,120	4,195	7,861	6,167	6,020	2,108	6,903	1,188	6,337	3,470	12,803	2,228	3,224	4,722	12,607
Tripoli, Lebanon	3,725	3,695	16,629	3,864	6,498	12,107	10,363	2,512	3,144	3,560	10,135	2,210	9,592	2,821	12,541	10,841	10,558	12,170	12,491	6,723
Tripoli, Libya	1,736	2,022	18,512	2,884	5,553	10,702	9,916	3,516	2,760	1,609	8,239	1,585	8,321	1,506	11,043	12,753	8,679	10,374	10,426	8,762
Tristan da Cunha (Edinburgh)	8,134	8,949	11,555	10,321	11,747	11,776	14,797	11,629	10,745	8,271	8,943	9,719	11,808	9,284	11,456	16,547	9,138	9,967	7,883	14,234
Trondheim, Norway	3,220	2,441	17,130	1,177	2,932	8,595	6,761	2,010	641	3,067	7,475	1,847	6,082	2,053	9,081	10,632	7,807	9,097	10,232	7,700
Trujillo, Peru	9,101	9,312	10,561	9,814	8,349	4,573	8,065	12,747	10,824	9,277	3,384	11,005	5,898	10,236	4,148	15,218	3,153	2,817	664	17,875
Truk Island (Moen)	14,631	13,926	5,776	12,656	11,817	11,110	8,705	10,404	11,931	14,451	14,346	12,605	11,723	13,276	11,248	1,026	14,041	12,729	14,276	5,217
Truro, Canada	4,889	4,490	15,013	4,197	2,224	4,199	4,662	6,863	5,107	4,957	2,747	5,807	1,947	5,238	4,566	12,909	3,006	4,261	5,514	11,973
Tsingtao, China	10,244	9,641	10,179	8,554	8,861	11,784	8,281	5,954	7,669	10,055	13,525	8,155	10,637	8,875	12,234	3,497	13,575	13,530	15,722	1,665
Tsitsihar, China	9,474	8,790	10,935	7,593	7,622	10,639	7,116	5,279	6,792	9,293	12,234	7,461	9,357	8,117	11,117	4,227	12,288	12,333	14,500	2,757
Tubuai Island (Mataura)	16,304	16,027	3,511	15,422	12,699	7,339	8,551	16,184	15,911	16,419	9,828	17,055	9,768	16,714	6,984	8,238	9,384	7,670	7,842	12,448
Tucson, Arizona	9,194	8,710	10,745	8,055	5,361	1,036	2,528	9,912	8,713	9,247	4,109	9,723	2,414	9,325	1,488	10,525	3,797	2,846	5,026	12,376
Tulsa, Oklahoma	7,805	7,377	12,106	6,871	4,290	1,380	3,029	9,080	7,637	7,870	2,901	8,539	1,144	8,061	1,863	11,616	2,689	2,445	4,560	12,668

Distances in Kilometers	Gibraltar	Gijon, Spain	Gisborne, New Zealand	Glasgow, United Kingdom	Godthab, Greenland	Gomez Palacio, Mexico	Goose Bay, Canada	Gorki, USSR	Goteborg, Sweden	Granada, Spain	Grand Turk, Turks & Caicos	Graz, Austria	Green Bay, Wisconsin	Grenoble, France	Guadalajara, Mexico	Guam (Agana)	Guantanamo, Cuba	Guatemala City, Guatemala	Guayaquil, Ecuador	Guiyang, China
Tunis, Tunisia	1,393	1,540	18,933	2,379	5,041	10,228	9,409	3,324	2,329	1,234	7,867	1,220	7,826	1,002	10,584	12,695	8,301	9,974	10,158	8,829
Tura, USSR	7,144	6,436	13,255	5,224	5,560	9,832	6,528	3,117	4,438	6,968	10,469	5,204	7,920	5,807	10,370	6,589	10,638	11,206	13,113	4,216
Turin, Italy	1,478	1,076	18,946	1,464	4,171	9,546	8,492	2,814	1,440	1,288	7,490	642	7,080	154	9,942	12,223	7,904	9,500	9,983	8,629
Uberlandia, Brazil	7,589	8,171	12,017	9,261	9,227	7,740	10,919	11,879	10,140	7,779	5,115	9,690	8,101	8,954	7,429	18,511	5,224	5,933	3,905	17,334
Ufa, USSR	5,030	4,506	15,396	3,704	5,435	10,894	8,237	773	2,699	4,839	10,185	2,927	8,491	3,670	11,421	8,721	10,507	11,695	12,947	5,146
Ujungpandang, Indonesia	13,435	13,177	6,957	12,520	13,403	14,931	12,031	9,587	11,517	13,256	17,877	11,481	14,893	12,259	15,106	3,475	17,726	16,593	17,748	3,764
Ulaanbaatar, Mongolia	8,532	7,922	11,889	6,851	7,426	11,320	7,840	4,249	5,952	8,344	12,318	6,453	9,662	7,162	11,835	5,176	12,465	12,866	14,894	2,368
Ulan-Ude, USSR	8,294	7,653	12,122	6,536	7,007	10,911	7,447	4,043	5,666	8,109	11,884	6,242	9,224	6,927	11,430	5,392	12,028	12,436	14,456	2,804
Uliastay, Mongolia	7,939	7,375	12,486	6,394	7,284	11,635	8,231	3,649	5,449	7,748	12,245	5,840	9,772	6,574	12,166	5,824	12,445	13,057	14,943	2,503
Uranium City, Canada	7,302	6,605	12,784	5,579	2,937	3,798	1,502	6,927	5,998	7,281	5,159	7,141	2,173	6,952	4,340	9,637	5,121	5,204	7,292	9,925
Urumqi, China	7,554	7,074	12,871	6,241	7,504	12,242	8,926	3,346	5,251	7,363	12,460	5,451	10,212	6,216	12,781	6,363	12,712	13,532	15,229	2,573
Ushuaia, Argentina	11,725	12,400	7,888	13,571	13,281	9,518	12,989	15,913	14,397	11,906	8,454	13,737	11,163	13,083	9,002	14,602	8,328	7,975	5,929	16,845
Vaduz, Liechtenstein	1,737	1,254	18,684	1,353	4,077	9,537	8,345	2,556	1,186	1,548	7,597	450	7,049	368	9,949	11,956	8,003	9,569	10,136	8,402
Valencia, Spain	574	632	19,853	1,842	4,290	9,284	8,718	3,721	2,216	383	6,906	1,532	6,921	807	9,627	13,126	7,338	9,005	9,262	9,506
Valladolid, Spain	615	223	19,606	1,578	3,885	8,847	8,318	3,820	2,142	500	6,523	1,711	6,480	930	9,194	13,150	6,950	8,600	8,940	9,688
Valletta, Malta	1,788	1,920	18,532	2,633	5,335	10,603	9,657	3,171	2,433	1,633	8,268	1,243	8,181	1,269	10,967	12,455	8,703	10,374	10,546	8,516
Valparaiso, Chile	10,302	10,804	9,307	11,726	10,927	7,312	10,835	14,544	12,686	10,494	6,032	12,407	8,746	11,646	6,832	15,750	5,896	5,644	3,523	19,273
Vancouver, Canada	8,740	8,065	11,328	7,058	4,401	3,130	402	8,241	7,455	8,729	5,493	8,611	2,702	8,431	3,625	9,040	5,320	4,850	7,049	10,267
Varna, Bulgaria	2,939	2,703	17,469	2,683	5,306	10,919	9,262	1,853	1,960	2,753	9,103	1,068	8,402	1,782	11,361	11,049	9,511	11,065	11,610	7,168
Venice, Italy	1,811	1,446	18,615	1,639	4,363	9,825	8,611	2,503	1,365	1,619	7,845	299	7,339	521	10,235	11,925	8,256	9,837	10,352	8,275
Veracruz, Mexico	8,846	8,602	10,974	8,378	5,998	1,035	4,512	10,844	9,246	8,955	2,620	9,997	2,907	9,407	771	12,441	2,196	783	2,961	14,376
Verona, Italy	1,719	1,340	18,707	1,574	4,297	9,739	8,567	2,584	1,366	1,528	7,741	387	7,257	415	10,146	12,004	8,153	9,737	10,246	8,372
Victoria, Canada	8,815	8,144	11,249	7,144	4,482	3,073	450	8,333	7,545	8,807	5,488	8,700	2,726	8,516	3,563	9,039	5,307	4,806	7,005	10,321
Victoria, Seychelles	7,757	8,102	12,425	8,611	11,284	16,791	14,812	6,837	7,930	7,666	13,981	6,940	14,337	7,395	17,122	10,061	14,424	16,144	15,007	6,508
Vienna, Austria	2,227	1,781	18,199	1,641	4,319	9,885	8,451	2,073	1,099	2,036	8,080	144	7,375	881	10,318	11,494	8,480	10,014	10,649	7,881
Vientiane, Laos	10,374	10,047	10,035	9,380	10,624	14,428	10,910	6,441	8,374	10,188	15,590	8,356	13,003	9,137	14,888	4,536	15,783	16,127	18,237	1,044
Villahermosa, Mexico	8,642	8,438	11,161	8,290	5,999	1,378	4,802	10,843	9,186	8,759	2,314	9,883	2,977	9,266	1,134	12,806	1,879	451	2,651	14,641
Vilnius, USSR	3,120	2,550	17,299	1,870	4,200	9,866	7,984	1,191	893	2,933	8,489	1,093	7,346	1,751	10,343	10,571	8,856	10,260	11,175	7,100
Visby, Sweden	2,961	2,289	17,438	1,388	3,658	9,323	7,528	1,560	378	2,784	7,984	1,191	6,802	1,634	9,798	10,740	8,343	9,724	10,694	7,460
Vitoria, Brazil	7,254	7,908	12,354	9,098	9,426	8,506	11,566	11,524	9,905	7,440	5,708	9,319	8,658	8,622	8,220	19,083	5,869	6,713	4,735	16,605
Vladivostok, USSR	10,221	9,520	10,184	8,289	8,095	10,530	7,042	6,053	7,522	10,042	12,476	8,228	9,522	8,871	10,973	3,512	12,474	12,293	14,492	2,925
Volgograd, USSR	4,243	3,842	16,181	3,339	5,541	11,179	8,882	844	2,356	4,052	9,958	2,161	8,685	2,940	11,679	9,636	10,325	11,704	12,631	5,833
Vologda, USSR	4,133	3,526	16,285	2,622	4,445	10,027	7,692	403	1,627	3,947	9,105	2,101	7,560	2,765	10,538	9,555	9,436	10,685	11,859	6,194
Vorkuta, USSR	5,479	4,781	14,920	3,619	4,522	9,633	6,783	1,614	2,782	5,302	9,476	3,557	7,362	4,142	10,172	8,237	9,729	10,664	12,245	5,377
Wake Island	13,814	13,006	6,524	11,637	10,180	9,097	6,674	10,071	11,156	13,670	12,286	12,113	9,683	12,613	9,279	2,424	11,996	10,785	12,565	6,148
Wallis Island	17,317	16,534	2,869	15,234	12,957	8,968	8,559	14,137	15,028	17,253	12,084	16,109	10,891	16,467	8,806	5,229	11,644	9,929	10,649	9,426
Walvis Bay, Namibia	6,865	7,645	12,972	8,908	11,199	13,786	15,492	9,214	8,942	6,927	10,500	7,754	12,732	7,595	13,648	14,692	10,837	12,152	10,367	11,330
Warsaw, Poland	2,738	2,200	17,684	1,691	4,200	9,846	8,149	1,557	838	2,549	8,291	702	7,323	1,369	10,306	10,959	8,672	10,132	10,936	7,436
Washington, D.C.	6,175	5,821	13,701	5,523	3,278	2,883	4,124	8,088	6,405	6,256	2,012	7,147	1,105	6,582	3,227	12,773	2,087	2,996	4,555	12,746
Watson Lake, Canada	8,158	7,410	11,977	6,253	3,797	4,302	975	7,076	6,495	8,113	6,184	7,690	3,203	7,626	4,820	8,523	6,099	5,924	8,094	9,158
Weimar, East Germany	2,119	1,524	18,290	1,164	3,846	9,407	8,020	2,218	751	1,937	7,664	530	6,896	769	9,842	11,567	8,056	9,564	10,276	8,118
Wellington, New Zealand	19,431	19,754	402	18,387	16,116	11,195	11,682	16,138	17,813	19,534	13,541	18,254	13,551	19,034	10,853	6,805	13,113	11,459	11,131	10,274
West Berlin, West Germany	2,341	1,729	18,067	1,206	3,822	9,426	7,927	2,013	586	2,160	7,779	624	6,907	992	9,872	11,345	8,164	9,644	10,418	7,923
Wewak, Papua New Guinea	15,206	14,649	5,220	13,542	13,159	12,478	10,225	10,929	12,680	15,015	15,780	13,100	13,242	13,850	12,553	1,886	15,438	13,974	15,160	5,185
Whangarei, New Zealand	19,956	19,137	463	17,766	15,606	10,971	11,184	15,670	17,234	19,773	13,548	17,858	13,232	18,590	10,669	6,272	13,107	11,407	11,296	9,896
Whitehorse, Canada	8,340	7,576	11,813	6,379	4,010	4,582	1,135	7,024	6,560	8,287	6,534	7,764	3,554	7,744	5,091	8,177	6,446	6,236	8,415	8,850
Wichita, Kansas	7,826	7,373	12,098	6,821	4,205	1,466	2,819	8,966	7,563	7,885	3,093	8,492	1,088	8,035	1,975	11,422	2,892	2,643	4,769	12,461
Willemstad, Curacao	6,861	6,943	12,842	7,329	5,944	3,918	6,813	10,252	8,337	7,021	1,061	8,611	4,025	7,864	3,784	15,352	1,110	2,352	1,986	15,698
Wiluna, Australia	14,809	14,843	5,495	14,548	15,779	15,677	13,786	11,629	13,541	14,669	18,741	13,212	16,806	13,937	15,560	5,167	18,299	16,575	16,171	6,060
Windhoek, Namibia	6,915	7,682	12,941	8,920	11,271	14,030	15,611	9,105	8,911	6,968	10,734	7,715	12,910	7,590	13,902	14,428	11,076	12,410	10,635	11,072
Windsor, Canada	6,506	6,074	13,408	5,617	3,154	2,638	3,492	8,001	6,432	6,569	2,563	7,276	473	6,772	3,062	12,145	2,565	3,150	4,935	12,313
Winnipeg, Canada	7,161	6,582	12,838	5,811	3,098	2,754	2,150	7,698	6,441	7,184	3,894	7,469	913	7,118	3,288	10,769	3,830	3,956	6,002	11,214
Winston-Salem, North Carolina	6,557	6,224	13,308	5,943	3,673	2,503	4,092	8,496	6,824	6,644	1,848	7,565	1,143	6,994	2,824	12,775	1,837	2,589	4,237	13,028
Wroclaw, Poland	2,437	1,901	17,983	1,501	4,109	9,720	8,171	1,859	806	2,249	8,055	463	7,201	1,068	10,167	11,256	8,444	9,935	10,676	7,735
Wuhan, China	10,307	9,780	10,120	8,809	9,419	12,611	9,103	6,041	7,867	10,115	14,216	8,200	11,388	8,954	13,062	3,654	14,303	14,347	16,531	861
Wyndham, Australia	14,888	14,663	5,494	13,989	14,587	14,568	12,324	11,066	12,993	14,714	17,897	12,966	15,340	13,743	14,580	3,688	17,512	15,888	16,386	5,196
Xi'an, China	9,660	9,142	10,766	8,197	8,950	12,557	9,033	5,402	7,244	9,468	13,836	7,554	11,115	8,309	13,039	4,282	13,969	14,219	16,339	877
Xining, China	8,998	8,507	11,427	7,618	8,581	12,632	9,134	4,770	6,646	8,807	13,533	6,895	10,966	7,658	13,141	4,980	13,715	14,189	16,187	1,207
Yakutsk, USSR	8,403	7,643	11,973	6,338	5,999	9,213	5,720	4,577	5,687	8,239	10,570	6,580	7,726	7,118	9,722	5,521	10,638	10,813	12,927	4,289
Yanji, China	10,135	9,446	10,273	8,234	8,126	10,692	7,194	5,940	7,447	9,954	12,574	8,124	9,633	8,780	11,140	3,574	12,585	12,446	14,643	2,746
Yaounde, Cameroon	3,971	4,710	15,917	5,933	8,348	12,311	12,770	6,491	5,972	4,007	9,102	4,802	10,465	4,611	12,428	14,521	9,529	11,203	10,187	10,340
Yap Island (Colonia)	13,677	13,090	6,748	11,974	11,783	12,310	9,479	9,387	11,114	13,487	15,332	11,576	12,446	12,312	12,523	844	15,114	14,034	15,758	3,808
Yaraka, Australia	16,854	16,579	3,532	15,721	15,485	13,300	12,012	12,886	14,771	16,679	16,416	14,891	14,880	15,672	13,162	4,243	15,970	14,235	14,423	6,968
Yarmouth, Canada	5,143	4,761	14,750	4,480	2,450	3,931	4,563	7,134	5,388	5,215	2,524	6,090	1,747	5,517	4,290	12,933	2,761	3,981	5,276	12,174
Yellowknife, Canada	7,396	6,668	12,719	5,567	3,021	4,177	1,469	6,699	5,903	7,361	5,599	7,075	2,617	6,945	4,717	9,240	5,566	5,632	7,733	9,485
Yerevan, USSR	4,335	4,119	16,063	3,928	6,345	12,011	9,831	1,796	3,029	4,153	10,481	2,450	9,494	3,195	12,493	9,906	10,878	12,370	13,026	5,861
Yinchuan, China	9,177	8,642	11,249	7,680	8,453	12,269	8,756	4,904	6,732	8,986	13,365	7,071	10,703	7,820	12,769	4,687	13,516	13,872	15,937	1,318
Yogyakarta, Indonesia	12,827	12,695	7,536	12,245	13,578	15,935	12,866	9,312	11,235	12,661	18,484	11,012	15,568	11,771	16,137	4,470	18,519	17,633	18,441	3,824
York, United Kingdom	1,994	1,192	18,318	298	3,019	8,514	7,328	2,846	929	1,857	6,800	1,395	6,011	1,084	8,943	11,880	7,182	8,666	9,460	8,747
Yumen, China	8,501	8,006	11,925	7,121	8,156	12,439	8,982	4,267	6,146	8,310	13,122	6,396	10,645	7,158	12,961	5,431	13,326	13,915	15,826	1,689
Yutian, China	7,493	7,123	12,924	6,479	8,074	13,073	9,818	3,538	5,469	7,304	12,950	5,440	10,933	6,220	13,615	6,734	13,249	14,247	15,726	2,620
Yuzhno-Sakhalinsk, USSR	10,269	9,512	10,112	8,204	7,612	9,598	6,132	6,311	7,550	10,102	11,704	8,400	8,721	8,969	10,032	3,717	11,663	11,375	13,575	3,877
Zagreb, Yugoslavia	2,084	1,731	18,341	1,800	4,509	10,029	8,688	2,262	1,354	1,892	8,114	147	7,530	807	10,450	11,682	8,522	10,089	10,635	7,995
Zahedan, Iran	6,126	5,996	14,248	5,813	8,089	13,688	11,006	3,264	4,875	5,954	12,385	4,348	11,223	5,078	14,203	8,705	12,781	14,243	14,886	4,491
Zamboanga, Philippines	12,758	12,351	7,660	11,501	12,096	13,927	10,788	8,636	10,529	12,569	16,557	10,690	13,568	11,468	14,202	2,588	16,476	15,714	17,551	2,718
Zanzibar, Tanzania	6,595	7,113	13,485	7,940	10,656	15,517	14,848	6,942	7,495	6,547	12,368	6,344	13,378	6,592	15,682	11,857	12,797	14,460	13,197	8,122
Zaragoza, Spain	723	446	19,664	1,598	4,066	9,134	8,489	3,585	2,007	546	6,842	1,432	6,745	663	9,490	12,964	7,268	8,915	9,254	9,419
Zashiversk, USSR	8,207	7,411	12,139	6,058	5,348	8,356	4,877	4,748	5,542	8,058	9,761	6,557	6,883	7,002	8,869	5,997	9,809	9,950	12,069	5,149
Zhengzhou, China	9,939	9,387	10,487	8,382	8,954	12,271	8,750	5,656	7,453	9,748	13,762	7,834	10,959	8,578	12,738	3,914	13,859	13,976	16,139	1,123
Zurich, Switzerland	1,686	1,176	18,732	1,281	4,004	9,452	8,287	2,614	1,177	1,499	7,507	537	6,967	319	9,863	12,002	7,914	9,480	10,050	8,472

Distances in Kilometers

	Gur'yev, USSR	Haifa, Israel	Haikou, China	Haiphong, Vietnam	Hakodate, Japan	Halifax, Canada	Hamburg, West Germany	Hamilton, Bermuda	Hamilton, New Zealand	Hangzhou, China	Hannover, West Germany	Hanoi, Vietnam	Harare, Zimbabwe	Harbin, China	Harrisburg, Pennsylvania	Hartford, Connecticut	Havana, Cuba	Helena, Montana	Helsinki, Finland	Hengyang, China
Haifa, Israel	2,134	0	7,495	7,118	8,802	8,141	3,038	8,944	16,399	7,852	2,972	7,032	5,623	7,600	9,317	8,934	10,935	10,609	3,127	7,357
Haikou, China	6,026	7,495	0	390	3,738	12,814	8,895	14,190	9,330	1,503	8,959	478	9,616	3,220	13,286	13,154	15,035	11,492	7,839	794
Haiphong, Vietnam	5,691	7,118	390	0	3,940	12,684	8,595	14,053	9,669	1,705	8,655	89	9,294	3,307	13,227	13,070	15,040	11,586	7,561	899
Hakodate, Japan	6,703	8,802	3,738	3,940	0	10,134	8,445	11,404	9,481	2,240	8,563	3,990	12,930	1,215	10,164	10,167	11,569	7,875	7,293	3,046
Halifax, Canada	8,045	8,141	12,814	12,684	10,134	0	5,219	1,377	15,133	11,702	5,248	12,653	11,745	9,939	1,195	803	2,936	3,723	5,777	12,072
Hamburg, West Germany	3,020	3,038	8,895	8,595	8,445	5,219	0	6,222	17,924	8,559	133	8,528	8,162	7,476	6,356	5,986	8,124	7,631	1,169	8,425
Hamilton, Bermuda	9,177	8,944	14,190	14,053	11,404	1,377	6,222	0	14,604	13,064	6,226	14,021	11,585	11,287	1,401	1,265	2,006	4,293	6,939	13,449
Hamilton, New Zealand	15,356	16,399	9,330	9,669	9,481	15,133	17,924	14,604	0	9,464	18,038	9,745	12,808	10,453	13,946	14,336	12,599	11,817	16,761	9,695
Hangzhou, China	6,026	7,852	1,503	1,705	2,240	11,702	8,559	13,064	9,464	0	8,648	1,761	10,911	1,811	12,003	11,923	13,629	10,016	7,415	828
Hannover, West Germany	3,050	2,972	8,959	8,655	8,563	5,248	133	6,226	18,038	8,648	0	8,586	8,046	7,586	6,395	6,021	8,142	7,722	1,278	8,501
Hanoi, Vietnam	5,616	7,032	478	89	3,990	12,653	8,528	14,021	9,745	1,761	8,586	0	9,220	3,334	13,213	13,050	15,039	11,608	7,499	945
Harare, Zimbabwe	7,490	5,623	9,616	9,294	12,930	11,745	8,162	11,585	12,808	10,911	8,046	9,220	0	11,838	12,780	12,437	13,119	15,369	8,663	10,093
Harbin, China	5,519	7,600	3,220	3,307	1,215	9,939	7,476	11,287	10,453	1,811	7,586	3,334	11,838	0	10,194	10,123	11,835	8,282	6,309	2,434
Harrisburg, Pennsylvania	9,082	9,317	13,286	13,227	10,164	1,195	6,356	1,401	13,946	12,003	6,395	13,213	12,780	10,194	0	391	1,968	2,905	6,817	12,505
Hartford, Connecticut	8,747	8,934	13,154	13,070	10,167	803	5,986	1,265	14,336	11,923	6,021	13,050	12,437	10,123	391	0	2,255	3,158	6,479	12,383
Havana, Cuba	10,979	10,935	15,035	15,040	11,569	2,936	8,124	2,006	12,599	13,629	8,142	15,039	13,119	11,835	1,968	2,255	0	3,718	8,710	14,241
Helena, Montana	9,505	10,609	11,492	11,586	7,875	3,723	7,631	4,293	11,817	10,016	7,722	11,608	15,369	8,282	2,905	3,158	3,718	0	7,546	10,715
Helsinki, Finland	2,270	3,127	7,839	7,561	7,293	5,777	1,169	6,939	16,761	7,415	1,278	7,499	8,663	6,309	6,817	6,479	8,710	7,546	0	7,323
Hengyang, China	5,688	7,357	794	899	3,046	12,072	8,425	13,449	9,695	828	8,501	945	10,093	2,434	12,505	12,383	14,241	10,715	7,323	0
Herat, Afghanistan	1,663	2,523	4,973	4,597	6,701	9,694	4,571	10,787	14,114	5,405	4,578	4,512	6,650	5,491	10,744	10,406	12,630	11,023	3,928	4,853
Hermosillo, Mexico	11,394	12,275	13,003	13,170	9,270	4,490	9,238	4,408	10,659	11,501	9,310	13,207	15,974	9,893	3,336	3,715	2,928	1,948	9,332	12,272
Hiroshima, Japan	6,643	8,636	2,698	2,939	1,091	11,102	8,802	12,408	9,136	1,244	8,909	2,999	12,139	1,353	11,209	11,191	12,657	8,966	7,634	2,072
Hiva Oa (Atuona)	15,743	17,383	12,534	12,916	9,933	9,640	14,426	9,143	5,513	11,591	14,512	13,002	16,763	11,118	8,446	8,838	7,165	6,800	14,260	12,320
Ho Chi Minh City, Vietnam	6,507	7,664	1,101	1,120	4,776	13,792	9,491	15,157	8,921	2,572	9,537	1,141	8,889	4,320	14,345	14,190	16,131	12,585	8,517	1,893
Hobart, Australia	13,673	14,125	7,936	8,199	9,401	17,539	16,693	16,975	2,430	8,565	16,718	8,258	10,664	10,033	16,366	16,754	14,976	13,995	15,753	8,510
Hohhot, China	4,729	6,676	2,302	2,257	2,429	10,530	7,162	11,906	10,846	1,401	7,253	2,257	10,522	1,337	10,988	10,852	12,783	9,407	6,014	1,543
Hong Kong	6,149	7,733	468	790	3,287	12,593	8,934	13,969	9,217	1,070	9,007	871	10,074	2,842	12,991	12,882	14,677	11,084	7,843	539
Honiara, Solomon Islands	12,140	13,832	6,340	6,721	5,999	14,305	14,428	14,783	3,497	6,114	14,541	6,808	13,655	6,958	13,481	13,768	13,250	10,615	13,264	6,502
Honolulu, Hawaii	11,863	13,860	9,404	9,725	6,117	8,699	11,629	9,054	7,120	8,110	11,754	9,798	19,019	7,234	7,767	8,077	7,692	4,981	10,970	8,927
Houston, Texas	10,881	11,333	13,849	13,929	10,226	3,238	8,332	2,925	11,915	12,377	8,382	13,946	14,461	10,633	2,043	2,434	1,488	2,361	8,662	13,068
Huambo, Angola	7,539	5,441	10,960	10,605	13,825	10,173	7,365	9,893	14,021	12,090	7,236	10,523	1,733	12,632	11,140	10,817	11,386	13,882	8,123	11,314
Hubli, India	4,128	4,484	3,758	3,385	6,868	12,167	7,012	13,233	11,922	4,869	7,007	3,301	6,074	5,841	13,207	12,875	15,102	13,107	6,397	4,076
Hugh Town, United Kingdom	4,202	3,876	10,081	9,786	9,354	4,266	1,194	5,136	18,651	9,680	1,152	9,719	8,355	8,476	5,447	5,062	7,092	7,154	2,271	9,590
Hull, Canada	8,550	8,891	12,728	12,659	9,693	959	5,893	1,739	14,233	11,471	5,940	12,643	12,704	9,667	582	476	2,546	2,789	6,292	11,951
Hyderabad, India	4,099	4,667	3,367	2,990	6,452	12,138	7,051	13,265	11,764	4,453	7,056	2,904	6,492	5,453	13,134	12,819	15,067	12,842	6,363	3,662
Hyderabad, Pakistan	2,819	3,337	4,333	3,943	6,760	10,851	5,704	11,926	13,124	5,090	5,703	3,855	6,260	5,605	11,901	11,565	13,787	12,035	5,086	4,404
Igloolik, Canada	6,541	7,581	10,039	9,973	7,200	2,940	4,655	4,263	14,378	8,813	4,757	9,959	12,735	7,025	3,254	3,120	5,141	3,037	4,510	9,264
Iloilo, Philippines	7,684	9,151	1,672	2,038	3,871	13,844	10,495	15,185	7,673	2,179	10,567	2,122	10,535	3,905	14,020	13,991	15,391	11,673	9,399	2,076
Indianapolis, Indiana	9,523	9,948	13,167	13,162	9,815	1,933	6,941	2,092	13,203	11,792	6,991	13,160	13,571	9,986	793	1,158	1,879	2,224	7,286	12,374
Innsbruck, Austria	3,033	2,556	9,043	8,718	8,954	5,589	706	6,467	18,329	8,865	580	8,645	7,473	7,927	6,762	6,379	8,429	8,245	1,685	8,646
Inuvik, Canada	7,191	8,746	8,951	8,992	5,596	4,690	6,158	5,850	12,504	7,541	6,280	9,002	14,291	5,743	4,569	4,593	6,092	2,716	5,643	8,159
Invercargill, New Zealand	15,302	15,812	9,385	9,685	10,141	16,030	18,280	15,280	1,115	9,775	18,337	9,753	11,706	10,995	14,836	15,227	13,294	12,894	17,184	9,867
Inverness, United Kingdom	3,874	4,029	9,518	9,250	8,534	4,243	997	5,306	17,816	8,989	1,057	9,190	8,961	7,697	5,368	5,001	7,165	6,696	1,699	8,970
Iquitos, Peru	12,909	11,945	18,163	18,113	14,619	5,448	9,897	4,089	11,618	16,757	9,861	18,092	11,398	14,970	4,889	5,043	3,136	6,754	10,823	17,372
Iraklion, Greece	2,578	951	8,328	7,959	9,248	7,269	2,345	8,016	17,351	8,550	2,252	7,875	5,917	8,082	8,456	8,069	10,015	9,973	2,761	8,124
Irkutsk, USSR	3,743	5,838	3,613	3,491	2,964	9,203	5,858	10,578	12,104	2,768	5,957	3,469	10,470	1,777	9,752	9,582	11,627	8,516	4,695	2,900
Islamabad, Pakistan	2,328	3,537	3,962	3,589	5,870	10,294	5,346	11,481	13,174	4,421	5,372	3,505	7,246	4,683	11,259	10,952	13,205	11,097	4,542	3,844
Istanbul, Turkey	1,948	1,055	7,866	7,510	8,561	7,144	1,988	8,024	17,118	7,970	1,928	7,430	6,519	7,408	8,307	7,929	9,991	9,561	2,148	7,597
Ivujivik, Canada	7,074	7,891	10,836	10,766	7,955	2,180	4,877	3,477	14,489	9,609	4,963	10,750	12,724	7,817	2,464	2,322	4,375	2,770	4,929	10,062
Iwo Jima Island, Japan	7,994	9,945	3,229	3,574	1,883	11,911	10,149	13,112	7,783	2,173	10,258	3,654	12,831	2,673	11,793	11,851	12,922	9,221	8,981	2,884
Izmir, Turkey	2,230	942	8,075	7,713	8,876	7,198	2,132	8,019	17,243	8,234	2,055	7,631	6,240	7,716	8,375	7,991	10,004	9,752	2,424	7,836
Jackson, Mississippi	10,428	10,793	13,817	13,855	10,297	2,677	7,809	2,389	12,482	12,382	7,854	13,863	13,962	10,601	1,484	1,874	1,275	2,445	8,187	13,025
Jaffna, Sri Lanka	4,927	5,273	3,452	3,116	6,882	12,971	7,830	14,052	11,127	4,745	7,826	3,041	6,181	5,965	13,990	13,667	15,906	13,660	7,196	3,920
Jakarta, Indonesia	7,988	8,707	2,925	2,990	6,327	15,640	11,006	16,986	7,706	4,275	11,030	3,010	8,303	6,080	16,210	16,060	17,892	14,196	10,147	3,712
Jamestown, St. Helena	9,036	6,920	13,283	12,919	15,718	8,899	7,844	8,246	14,058	14,318	7,712	12,836	3,917	14,508	9,619	9,372	9,392	12,523	8,874	13,581
Jamnagar, India	3,184	3,627	4,174	3,785	6,808	11,215	6,061	12,283	12,808	5,035	6,058	3,696	6,158	5,682	12,266	11,930	14,151	12,354	5,451	4,313
Jan Mayen Island	4,105	4,989	8,903	8,704	7,268	4,124	2,159	5,424	16,299	8,092	2,278	8,661	10,319	6,583	5,038	4,735	6,990	5,629	1,935	8,243
Jayapura, Indonesia	10,125	11,633	4,154	4,523	4,904	14,769	12,793	15,781	5,260	4,234	12,881	4,607	12,004	5,526	14,382	14,539	14,860	11,530	11,647	4,440
Jefferson City, Missouri	9,866	10,405	13,107	13,139	9,628	2,461	7,380	2,574	12,683	11,683	7,437	13,146	14,100	9,895	1,328	1,694	1,949	1,850	7,658	12,314
Jerusalem, Israel	2,217	120	7,494	7,115	8,866	8,237	3,150	9,026	16,337	7,880	3,082	7,029	5,507	7,662	9,416	9,032	11,021	10,727	3,247	7,372
Jiggalong, Australia	10,413	11,016	4,939	5,131	7,500	17,614	13,431	18,885	5,385	5,937	13,454	5,176	9,219	7,680	17,516	17,621	17,666	14,681	12,552	5,635
Jinan, China	5,367	7,279	1,953	2,017	2,117	10,999	7,811	12,369	10,192	770	7,903	2,042	10,827	1,291	11,369	11,264	13,082	9,569	6,660	1,160
Jodhpur, India	2,966	3,736	3,866	3,477	6,318	11,005	5,934	12,138	12,776	4,613	5,944	3,389	6,666	5,179	12,010	11,689	13,934	11,918	5,229	3,926
Johannesburg, South Africa	8,465	6,574	10,244	9,950	13,726	12,133	9,006	11,767	12,142	11,617	8,885	9,882	976	12,687	13,063	12,755	13,069	15,850	9,576	10,790
Juazeiro do Norte, Brazil	10,684	9,001	16,462	16,074	16,177	6,237	8,163	5,136	13,874	16,686	8,067	15,986	7,701	15,527	6,515	6,397	5,761	9,288	9,324	16,343
Juneau, Alaska	8,305	9,857	9,506	9,604	5,912	4,893	7,196	5,848	11,628	8,031	7,314	9,628	15,357	6,298	4,467	4,594	5,657	1,986	6,744	8,730
Kabul, Afghanistan	2,014	3,162	4,339	3,966	6,141	10,031	5,020	11,189	13,541	4,769	5,041	3,882	7,062	4,941	11,027	10,708	12,957	11,020	4,260	4,210
Kalgoorlie, Australia	11,080	11,494	5,746	5,927	8,267	18,401	14,082	19,411	4,950	6,753	14,093	5,969	9,058	8,488	18,055	18,257	17,521	15,150	13,268	6,449
Kaliningrad, USSR	2,339	2,685	8,200	7,898	7,910	5,797	698	6,860	17,334	7,899	760	7,831	8,101	6,892	6,903	6,543	8,724	7,925	663	7,741
Kamloops, Canada	9,143	10,443	10,744	10,847	7,115	4,206	7,559	4,931	11,641	9,263	7,661	10,871	15,571	7,540	3,530	3,737	4,475	760	7,328	9,970
Kampala, Uganda	5,514	3,608	8,723	8,352	11,484	10,476	6,258	10,687	14,378	9,765	6,151	8,268	2,015	10,302	11,631	11,250	12,543	13,775	6,670	9,009
Kananga, Zaire	6,550	4,489	10,021	9,655	12,777	10,154	6,691	10,097	14,418	11,087	6,568	9,572	1,620	11,583	11,223	10,868	11,784	13,749	7,329	10,328
Kano, Nigeria	5,612	3,552	10,767	10,377	12,313	7,669	4,611	7,746	16,864	11,351	4,478	10,289	4,126	11,129	8,772	8,405	9,588	11,243	5,515	10,777
Kanpur, India	3,387	4,414	3,140	2,752	5,700	11,323	6,404	12,531	12,169	3,906	6,428	2,664	7,240	4,603	12,252	11,959	14,213	11,819	5,592	3,202
Kansas City, Missouri	9,893	10,499	12,966	13,009	9,455	2,627	7,467	2,788	12,532	11,530	7,528	13,019	14,300	9,749	1,521	1,877	2,115	1,646	7,705	12,174
Kaohsiung, Taiwan	6,584	8,264	1,072	1,420	2,850	12,544	9,261	13,904	8,820	844	9,343	1,502	10,686	2,629	12,819	12,752	14,384	10,718	8,137	909
Karachi, Pakistan	2,811	3,236	4,467	4,078	6,900	10,826	5,660	11,881	13,209	5,234	5,656	3,989	6,128	5,743	11,889	11,548	13,760	12,090	5,072	4,546
Karaganda, USSR	1,597	3,655	4,653	4,361	5,147	8,732	4,243	10,010	13,898	4,466	4,309	4,297	8,563	3,947	9,603	9,325	11,570	9,308	3,206	4,208
Karl-Marx-Stadt, East Germany	2,849	2,692	8,807	8,494	8,569	5,519	362	6,478	18,002	8,556	280	8,424	7,811	7,561	6,670	6,295	8,405	7,992	1,284	8,375
Kasanga, Tanzania	6,490	4,589	9,219	8,868	12,257	11,042	7,156	11,067	13,682	10,390	7,043	8,788	1,036	11,106	12,146	11,781	12,785	14,530	7,629	9,599
Kashgar, China	2,119	3,727	3,922	3,578	5,352	9,848	5,097	11,091	13,247	4,126	5,140	3,502	7,876	4,145	10,755	10,467	12,718	10,437	4,181	3,659
Kassel, West Germany	3,079	2,916	9,014	8,706	8,667	5,278	251	6,233	18,137	8,727	118	8,637	7,943	7,683	6,432	6,056	8,161	7,803	1,377	8,567
Kathmandu, Nepal	3,615	4,830	2,678	2,294	5,212	11,394	6,629	12,653	11,837	3,395	6,664	2,207	7,721	4,137	12,258	11,987	14,226	11,593	5,744	2,697
Kayes, Mali	6,831	5,107	12,599	12,218	13,161	5,927	4,728	5,735	17,337	12,855	4,606	12,131	5,874	12,127	6,909	6,576	7,473	9,644	5,870	12,442
Kazan, USSR	979	2,773	6,392	6,097	6,401	7,224	2,504	8,426	15,585	6,121	2,573	6,031	8,330	5,286	8,211	7,892	10,142	8,526	1,503	5,931
Kemi, Finland	2,635	3,735	7,799	7,552	6,891	5,511	1,584	6,748	16,365	7,226	1,712	7,497	9,291	5,978	6,484	6,166	8,418	6,996	630	7,222
Kenora, Canada	8,792	9,590	11,894	11,906	8,529	2,390	6,557	3,131	13,107	10,504	6,634	11,909	14,036	8,700	1,737	1,906	3,141	1,348	6,661	11,100
Kerguelen Island	10,840	9,738	8,694	8,617	12,264	16,475	12,711	15,800	7,911	10,157	12,619	8,599	4,913	11,912	17,200	16,982	16,192	19,664	12,803	9,478
Kerkira, Greece	2,701	1,547	8,651	8,295	9,199	6,616	1,723	7,397	17,879	8,726	1,621	8,215	6,462	8,076	7,801	7,414	9,389	9,335	2,315	8,373
Kermanshah, Iran	1,478	1,132	6,364	5,987	7,842	8,818	3,600	9,764	15,402	6,749	3,572	5,902	6,016	6,628	9,951	9,584	11,710	10,803	3,290	6,232
Khabarovsk, USSR	5,909	8,029	3,858	3,976	870	9,525	7,575	10,842	10,351	2,391	7,693	4,008	12,504	710	9,681	9,641	11,242	7,635	6,423	3,088
Kharkov, USSR	1,195	1,909	7,196	6,870	7,474	6,982	1,843	8,050	16,512	7,086	1,863	6,797	7,531	6,350	8,072	7,719	9,912	8,875	1,338	6,817
Khartoum, Sudan	3,926	1,925	8,187	7,798	10,310	9,281	4,647	9,766	15,620	8,933	4,549	7,709	3,702	9,097	10,473	10,082	11,748	12,261	4,985	8,279
Khon Kaen, Thailand	5,762	6,990	887	637	4,574	13,103	8,739	14,456	9,647	2,336	8,786	600	8,733	3,933	13,728	13,545	15,592	12,204	7,765	1,536
Kiev, USSR	1,607	1,989	7,601	7,278	7,756	6,623	1,446	7,664	16,905	7,459	1,458	7,205	7,562	6,657	7,731	7,371	9,546	8,668	1,139	7,210
Kigali, Rwanda	5,839	3,885	9,073	8,705	11,860	10,453	6,428	10,585	14,345	10,133	6,316	8,621	1,760	10,677	11,587	11,212	12,394	13,854	6,903	9,373
Kingston, Canada	8,694	9,020	12,853	12,789	9,786	1,027	6,028	1,674	14,133	11,585	6,073	12,774	12,762	9,779	442	415	2,401	2,770	6,436	12,074
Kingston, Jamaica	11,166	10,850	15,726	15,689	12,352	3,201	8,209	1,991	12,773	14,368	8,210	15,677	12,444	12,561	2,468	2,664	812	4,523	8,920	14,935
Kingstown, Saint Vincent	10,618	9,801	16,219	16,020	13,525	3,499	7,603	2,149	13,830	15,200	7,568	15,972	10,694	13,434	3,372	3,360	2,490	6,001	8,539	15,524
Kinshasa, Zaire	6,730	4,606	10,704	10,329	13,213	9,471	6,431	9,337	14,911	11,683	6,302	10,244	2,277	12,001	10,504	10,160	10,987	13,131	7,198	10,955

Distances in Kilometers

	Gur'yev, USSR	Haifa, Israel	Haikou, China	Haiphong, Vietnam	Hakodate, Japan	Halifax, Canada	Hamburg, West Germany	Hamilton, Bermuda	Hamilton, New Zealand	Hangzhou, China	Hannover, West Germany	Hanoi, Vietnam	Harare, Zimbabwe	Harbin, China	Harrisburg, Pennsylvania	Hartford, Connecticut	Havana, Cuba	Helena, Montana	Helsinki, Finland	Hengyang, China
Kirkwall, United Kingdom	3,782	4,038	9,368	9,105	8,351	4,300	1,001	5,395	17,646	8,820	1,081	9,047	9,059	7,517	5,407	5,045	7,230	6,643	1,572	8,811
Kirov, USSR	1,281	3,064	6,431	6,151	6,230	7,036	2,496	8,266	15,522	6,073	2,579	6,090	8,637	5,143	7,995	7,684	9,938	8,230	1,410	5,932
Kiruna, Sweden	2,923	4,011	7,962	7,727	6,881	5,261	1,683	6,517	16,321	7,328	1,815	7,675	9,543	6,013	6,214	5,902	8,156	6,702	887	7,363
Kisangani, Zaire	5,778	3,724	9,487	9,111	12,062	9,877	6,046	9,982	14,873	10,465	5,928	9,026	2,127	10,858	11,000	10,629	11,788	13,339	6,618	9,732
Kishinev, USSR	1,745	1,658	7,771	7,434	8,106	6,740	1,521	7,717	17,101	7,714	1,497	7,358	7,183	6,989	7,875	7,506	9,639	8,959	1,487	7,422
Kitchner, Canada	8,937	9,324	12,888	12,846	9,711	1,357	6,319	1,851	13,802	11,578	6,368	12,836	13,083	9,767	463	667	2,260	2,494	6,689	12,102
Knoxville, Tennessee	9,805	10,095	13,627	13,617	10,277	1,970	7,126	1,810	13,186	12,257	7,167	13,613	13,384	10,450	779	1,167	1,431	2,615	7,549	12,835
Kosice, Czechoslovakia	2,281	2,103	8,294	7,967	8,368	6,160	953	7,121	17,602	8,150	912	7,893	7,433	7,297	7,306	6,933	9,050	8,522	1,298	7,907
Kota Kinabalu, Malaysia	7,585	8,821	1,676	1,933	4,654	14,397	10,523	15,769	7,802	2,720	10,579	1,997	9,694	4,524	14,717	14,644	16,219	12,508	9,494	2,344
Krakow, Poland	2,362	2,284	8,353	8,032	8,318	6,000	784	6,979	17,630	8,166	756	7,960	7,602	7,264	7,141	6,770	8,898	8,340	1,167	7,947
Kralendijk, Bonaire	11,173	10,495	16,438	16,310	13,342	3,628	8,154	2,256	13,153	15,226	8,131	16,277	11,397	13,419	3,226	3,308	1,924	5,595	9,020	15,681
Krasnodar, USSR	1,022	1,398	7,006	6,660	7,654	7,493	2,292	8,511	16,325	7,048	2,286	6,583	7,008	6,490	8,605	8,244	10,411	9,465	1,925	6,699
Krasnoyarsk, USSR	2,956	5,080	4,250	4,068	3,758	8,632	5,009	9,993	12,960	3,576	5,106	4,031	10,005	2,605	9,291	9,083	11,223	8,398	3,850	3,602
Kristiansand, Norway	3,146	3,470	8,831	8,553	8,098	4,942	529	6,032	17,559	8,376	655	8,491	8,686	7,183	6,043	5,684	7,873	7,157	993	8,310
Kuala Lumpur, Malaysia	6,820	7,652	2,089	2,031	5,775	14,512	9,840	15,832	8,795	3,574	9,867	2,027	8,085	5,306	15,193	14,996	17,062	13,581	8,970	2,872
Kuching, Malaysia	7,549	8,551	2,047	2,173	5,392	14,852	10,552	16,225	7,944	3,342	10,593	2,210	8,936	5,150	15,317	15,198	16,953	13,265	9,601	2,816
Kumasi, Ghana	6,762	4,764	12,021	11,631	13,424	7,291	5,302	7,099	16,546	12,597	5,170	11,542	4,499	12,270	8,284	7,949	8,783	10,999	6,341	12,034
Kumzar, Oman	2,341	2,192	5,524	5,135	7,664	10,074	4,855	11,022	14,217	6,187	4,831	5,047	5,604	6,466	11,197	10,834	12,970	11,845	4,457	5,547
Kunming, China	5,074	6,545	961	620	3,949	12,161	7,976	13,521	10,284	1,816	8,035	552	9,096	3,139	12,772	12,590	14,644	11,337	6,948	1,013
Kuqa Chang, China	2,592	4,354	3,454	3,140	4,691	9,948	5,456	11,244	12,771	3,505	5,514	3,072	8,477	3,488	10,769	10,510	12,736	10,161	4,451	3,100
Kurgan, USSR	1,312	3,439	5,424	5,147	5,474	7,921	3,494	9,192	14,567	5,103	3,571	5,086	8,737	4,324	8,813	8,526	10,777	8,694	2,415	4,931
Kuwait, Kuwait	1,997	1,294	6,322	5,937	8,113	9,281	4,074	10,171	15,112	6,851	4,036	5,849	5,532	6,899	10,430	10,057	12,142	11,354	3,831	6,272
Kuybyshev, USSR	688	2,566	6,269	5,961	6,476	7,470	2,637	8,652	15,529	6,076	2,693	5,893	8,081	5,336	8,472	8,148	10,395	8,817	1,713	5,842
Kyoto, Japan	6,836	8,857	2,995	3,244	866	10,971	8,896	12,256	9,033	1,552	9,006	3,304	12,447	1,420	11,028	11,025	12,424	8,721	7,729	2,380
Kzyl-Orda, USSR	1,083	2,937	4,943	4,610	5,892	8,898	4,050	10,101	14,273	4,995	4,092	4,535	7,764	4,681	9,863	9,553	11,807	9,876	3,166	4,618
L'vov, USSR	2,071	2,095	8,072	7,748	8,139	6,268	1,050	7,263	17,371	7,915	1,038	7,675	7,527	7,063	7,399	7,031	9,174	8,513	1,152	7,678
La Ceiba, Honduras	11,916	11,824	15,627	15,695	11,991	3,873	9,052	2,881	11,758	14,155	9,068	15,707	13,436	12,409	2,878	3,183	937	4,139	9,647	14,843
La Coruna, Spain	4,632	3,932	10,616	10,301	10,085	4,344	1,760	5,015	19,315	10,319	1,676	10,230	7,882	9,183	5,538	5,147	7,015	7,538	2,912	10,175
La Paz, Bolivia	13,601	12,201	19,584	19,293	16,088	6,787	10,707	5,410	11,080	18,269	10,646	19,216	10,398	16,484	6,349	6,468	4,650	8,255	11,754	18,851
La Paz, Mexico	11,911	12,708	13,437	13,624	9,700	4,773	9,670	4,525	10,360	11,938	9,736	13,665	15,966	10,371	3,590	3,978	2,848	2,493	9,818	12,724
La Ronge, Canada	8,476	9,553	11,023	11,059	7,597	3,157	6,586	4,044	12,744	9,606	6,680	11,068	14,473	7,812	2,665	2,794	4,024	1,058	6,490	10,230
Labrador City, Canada	7,497	7,896	11,913	11,804	9,182	954	4,875	2,302	15,037	10,762	4,929	11,779	12,102	8,991	1,600	1,316	3,560	3,268	5,240	11,159
Lagos, Nigeria	6,442	4,385	11,522	11,132	13,141	7,695	5,257	7,580	16,440	12,166	5,124	11,044	4,057	11,960	8,725	8,380	9,304	11,375	6,231	11,571
Lahore, Pakistan	2,573	3,686	3,810	3,431	5,897	10,551	5,588	11,734	12,968	4,354	5,611	3,346	7,157	4,726	11,517	11,209	13,463	11,323	4,796	3,740
Lambasa, Fiji	14,145	16,016	8,561	8,946	7,570	13,408	15,785	13,382	2,400	8,180	15,916	9,033	14,880	8,690	12,330	12,690	11,541	9,771	14,732	8,659
Lansing, Michigan	9,169	9,624	12,889	12,870	9,611	1,697	6,608	2,090	13,467	11,540	6,661	12,865	13,416	9,730	696	985	2,183	2,210	6,935	12,098
Lanzhou, China	4,404	6,188	1,888	1,708	3,248	10,976	7,105	12,346	11,005	1,664	7,180	1,678	9,683	2,203	11,554	11,380	13,423	10,182	6,008	1,321
Laoag, Philippines	6,945	8,539	1,101	1,490	3,236	13,032	9,686	14,389	8,431	1,335	9,764	1,578	10,576	3,106	13,285	13,227	14,802	11,109	8,575	1,266
Largeau, Chad	4,408	2,293	9,468	9,079	11,095	8,064	4,032	8,411	16,818	10,040	3,910	8,991	4,165	9,893	9,237	8,850	10,363	11,352	4,714	9,463
Las Vegas, Nevada	10,690	11,761	12,166	12,318	8,445	4,400	8,756	4,610	10,876	10,664	8,840	12,352	16,132	9,028	3,355	3,695	3,465	1,186	8,722	11,423
Launceston, Australia	13,561	14,070	7,793	8,060	9,234	17,506	16,579	17,023	2,440	8,406	16,610	8,120	10,735	9,868	16,348	16,733	15,019	13,916	15,618	8,359
Le Havre, France	3,772	3,417	9,704	9,398	9,189	4,725	819	5,603	18,647	9,376	745	9,329	8,058	8,257	5,902	5,518	7,559	7,518	1,969	9,243
Leipzig, East Germany	2,883	2,757	8,829	8,518	8,553	5,460	296	6,426	17,999	8,563	216	8,448	7,873	7,551	6,609	6,235	8,350	7,926	1,262	8,390
Leningrad, USSR	2,004	3,031	7,547	7,268	7,087	6,051	1,420	7,226	16,529	7,144	1,519	7,205	8,618	6,078	7,078	6,744	8,982	7,711	296	7,039
Leon, Spain	4,466	3,698	10,470	10,148	10,072	4,589	1,675	5,254	19,465	10,223	1,577	10,076	7,672	9,139	5,783	5,392	7,255	7,761	2,841	10,051
Lerwick, United Kingdom	3,674	4,019	9,215	8,956	8,187	4,388	999	5,508	17,504	8,656	1,095	8,898	9,118	7,350	5,479	5,123	7,322	6,632	1,441	8,653
Lhasa, China	3,880	5,293	2,210	1,844	4,618	11,387	6,848	12,695	11,497	2,799	6,895	1,763	8,312	3,567	12,166	11,925	14,123	11,248	5,885	2,128
Libreville, Gabon	6,609	4,480	11,138	10,754	13,263	8,645	5,894	8,510	15,619	11,974	5,762	10,667	3,108	12,052	9,673	9,329	10,186	12,321	6,764	11,300
Lilongwe, Malawi	7,004	5,182	9,182	8,851	12,435	11,671	7,819	11,626	13,014	10,446	7,707	8,776	517	11,331	12,753	12,395	13,266	15,197	8,257	9,634
Lima, Peru	13,884	12,786	18,833	18,955	15,096	6,424	10,883	5,077	10,702	17,331	10,842	18,966	11,471	15,654	5,792	5,975	3,935	7,373	11,826	18,084
Limerick, Ireland	4,261	4,106	10,043	9,762	9,136	4,044	1,247	4,985	18,323	9,567	1,242	9,699	8,696	8,798	5,212	4,831	6,912	6,831	2,205	9,520
Limoges, France	3,822	3,216	9,819	9,499	9,506	4,948	1,064	5,739	18,987	9,580	953	9,427	7,664	8,539	6,137	5,749	7,722	7,874	2,230	9,399
Limon, Costa Rica	12,272	11,929	16,378	16,431	12,750	4,270	9,321	3,101	11,712	14,912	9,321	16,439	12,891	13,159	3,408	3,663	1,455	4,897	10,021	15,591
Lincoln, Nebraska	9,781	10,467	12,713	12,763	9,193	2,723	7,429	2,991	12,476	11,273	7,495	12,773	14,444	9,495	1,675	2,007	2,376	1,390	7,618	11,923
Linz, Austria	2,795	2,439	8,800	8,476	8,732	5,732	657	6,646	18,084	8,620	558	8,403	7,512	7,695	6,894	6,515	8,595	8,279	1,489	8,400
Lisbon, Portugal	4,940	4,005	10,959	10,630	10,587	4,498	2,201	5,021	19,624	10,743	2,102	10,556	7,532	9,664	5,682	5,292	7,027	7,853	3,367	10,558
Little Rock, Arkansas	10,259	10,726	13,490	13,534	9,963	2,676	7,717	2,563	12,458	12,051	7,768	13,543	14,146	10,273	1,490	1,879	1,608	2,116	8,038	12,699
Liverpool, United Kingdom	3,875	3,775	9,681	9,395	8,904	4,397	862	5,364	18,262	9,244	863	9,331	8,542	8,025	5,554	5,177	7,281	7,056	1,849	9,172
Lodz, Poland	2,386	2,449	8,340	8,026	8,201	5,885	671	6,891	17,570	8,109	672	7,956	7,790	7,163	7,015	6,647	8,794	8,166	997	7,913
Lome, Togo	6,615	4,578	11,757	11,367	13,305	7,552	5,318	7,396	16,449	12,381	5,185	11,278	4,216	12,133	8,564	8,224	9,096	11,249	6,321	11,796
London, United Kingdom	3,732	3,513	9,614	9,317	9,002	4,640	723	5,567	18,439	9,242	683	9,250	8,258	8,087	5,807	5,426	7,504	7,346	1,827	9,133
Londonderry, United Kingdom	4,112	4,101	9,827	9,554	8,864	4,087	1,138	5,090	18,081	9,320	1,161	9,492	8,849	8,032	5,237	4,862	6,986	6,728	1,993	9,290
Longlac, Canada	8,549	9,197	12,094	12,072	8,869	1,820	6,159	2,650	13,631	10,756	6,227	12,067	13,478	8,946	1,301	1,395	2,980	1,919	6,359	11,303
Lord Howe Island, Australia	13,746	14,816	7,726	8,055	8,332	16,059	16,539	15,909	1,635	7,981	16,625	8,130	12,233	9,165	14,965	15,332	13,953	12,400	15,392	8,136
Los Angeles, California	10,960	12,092	12,122	12,295	8,387	4,762	9,098	4,935	10,509	10,620	9,185	12,335	16,484	9,032	3,704	4,049	3,691	1,488	9,034	11,397
Louangphrabang, Laos	5,434	6,746	857	488	4,363	12,716	8,393	14,069	9,951	2,148	8,444	409	8,813	3,645	13,347	13,160	15,223	11,887	7,402	1,323
Louisville, Kentucky	9,658	10,041	13,338	13,334	9,976	1,976	7,045	2,016	13,157	11,960	7,092	13,332	13,545	10,155	798	1,182	1,707	2,338	7,415	12,545
Luanda, Angola	7,277	5,154	11,084	10,717	13,728	9,667	6,916	9,420	14,523	12,128	6,786	10,633	2,171	12,519	10,648	10,320	10,966	13,371	7,716	11,379
Lubumbashi, Zaire	6,949	4,989	9,724	9,377	12,793	10,997	7,414	10,906	13,591	10,916	7,296	9,298	784	11,642	12,057	11,705	12,534	14,592	7,966	10,120
Lusaka, Zambia	7,316	5,387	9,791	9,457	12,993	11,346	7,839	11,195	13,187	11,040	7,720	9,381	398	11,867	12,383	12,039	12,756	14,976	8,383	10,231
Luxembourg, Luxembourg	3,349	3,022	9,308	8,996	8,959	5,128	515	6,031	18,436	9,032	397	8,926	7,863	7,984	6,297	5,916	7,981	7,800	1,675	8,868
Luxor, Egypt	2,921	825	7,882	7,495	9,515	8,514	3,620	9,174	16,268	8,400	3,533	7,407	4,817	8,304	9,707	9,317	11,180	11,250	3,876	7,836
Lynn Lake, Canada	8,211	9,243	10,995	11,012	7,653	2,921	6,267	3,888	13,070	9,606	6,359	11,016	14,147	7,802	2,540	2,626	4,040	1,366	6,194	10,202
Lyon, France	3,563	2,945	9,572	9,248	9,373	5,208	943	6,016	18,825	9,370	817	9,174	7,521	8,378	6,394	6,007	7,996	8,065	2,081	9,168
Macapa, Brazil	10,984	9,642	17,009	16,672	15,230	5,096	8,140	3,850	13,699	16,528	8,069	16,595	9,181	14,928	5,167	5,108	4,244	7,479	9,233	16,556
Madison, Wisconsin	9,314	9,880	12,732	12,738	9,360	2,072	6,849	2,467	13,125	11,346	6,909	12,738	13,807	9,542	1,086	1,381	2,304	1,825	7,108	11,939
Madras, India	4,609	5,083	3,292	2,936	6,607	12,651	7,547	13,766	11,328	4,513	7,548	2,856	6,398	5,655	13,649	13,333	15,580	13,282	6,874	3,697
Madrid, Spain	4,441	3,531	10,464	10,132	10,226	4,834	1,788	5,449	19,702	10,284	1,677	10,057	7,382	9,263	6,027	5,636	7,454	8,047	2,955	10,075
Madurai, India	4,807	5,089	3,632	3,289	7,015	12,846	7,684	13,902	11,310	4,900	7,677	3,212	6,017	6,074	13,884	13,554	15,782	13,663	7,077	4,078
Magadan, USSR	6,098	8,204	5,436	5,526	2,101	8,033	6,984	9,314	11,023	3,985	7,114	5,550	13,362	2,220	8,109	8,089	9,646	6,061	5,926	4,654
Magdalena, Bolivia	13,049	11,651	19,067	18,738	16,052	6,421	10,171	5,048	11,633	18,081	10,107	18,660	10,105	16,272	6,078	6,163	4,497	8,177	11,232	18,466
Magdeburg, East Germany	2,919	2,854	8,841	8,534	8,503	5,380	191	6,361	17,965	8,550	135	8,466	7,979	7,512	6,524	6,152	8,276	7,821	1,211	8,391
Majuro Atoll, Marshall Isls.	11,559	13,613	6,707	7,090	4,871	12,092	13,050	12,665	4,992	5,896	13,180	7,177	15,555	6,041	11,317	11,583	11,364	8,425	11,975	6,549
Malabo, Equatorial Guinea	6,337	4,221	11,076	10,689	13,022	8,328	5,522	8,246	15,996	11,837	5,390	10,601	3,417	11,816	9,376	9,026	9,972	11,983	6,408	11,191
Male, Maldives	5,209	5,116	4,372	4,050	7,837	13,141	7,923	14,056	11,323	5,696	7,898	3,977	5,245	6,907	14,252	13,895	16,031	14,374	7,452	4,870
Manado, Indonesia	8,605	9,911	2,592	2,914	4,735	14,827	11,484	16,134	6,758	3,222	11,550	2,989	10,470	4,908	14,886	14,902	16,007	12,340	10,410	3,102
Managua, Nicaragua	12,243	12,048	16,012	16,091	12,351	4,201	9,342	3,132	11,567	14,532	9,351	16,105	13,294	12,797	3,249	3,539	1,284	4,520	9,977	15,232
Manama, Bahrain	2,322	1,677	6,105	5,716	8,132	9,715	4,509	10,593	14,723	6,736	4,470	5,628	5,312	6,924	10,865	10,492	12,569	11,754	4,249	6,114
Manaus, Brazil	11,910	10,671	17,866	17,581	15,258	5,305	8,986	3,952	12,751	17,003	8,927	17,513	10,025	15,239	5,104	5,135	3,786	7,497	10,029	17,262
Manchester, New Hampshire	8,578	8,774	13,022	12,931	10,083	658	5,820	1,327	14,474	11,808	5,856	12,910	12,349	10,013	544	169	2,422	3,199	6,309	12,255
Mandalay, Burma	4,827	6,077	1,495	1,106	4,689	12,342	7,816	13,664	10,586	2,570	7,860	1,017	8,342	3,822	13,074	12,851	15,009	11,901	6,867	1,759
Mangareva Island, Fr.Polynesia	17,274	18,556	13,321	13,711	11,239	10,418	15,536	9,653	4,985	12,642	15,595	13,799	15,229	12,449	9,240	9,623	7,652	8,058	15,604	13,280
Manila, Philippines	7,257	8,781	1,286	1,669	3,560	13,429	10,043	14,782	8,105	1,737	10,117	1,756	10,499	3,496	13,659	13,611	15,126	11,417	8,942	1,619
Mannheim, West Germany	3,187	2,868	9,158	8,843	8,877	5,289	465	6,200	18,337	8,904	333	8,772	7,782	7,885	6,455	6,075	8,147	7,917	1,585	8,726
Maputo, Mozambique	8,323	6,513	9,818	9,531	13,342	12,457	9,075	12,152	11,951	11,207	8,958	9,465	914	12,332	13,424	13,105	13,500	16,151	9,571	10,379
Mar del Plata, Argentina	14,335	12,366	17,702	17,583	18,409	9,174	12,034	7,817	10,025	19,121	11,935	17,548	8,693	19,079	8,888	8,966	7,248	10,828	13,197	18,475
Maracaibo, Venezuela	11,523	10,889	16,601	16,512	13,331	3,844	8,508	2,495	12,761	15,307	8,489	16,487	11,704	13,496	3,320	3,448	1,791	5,507	9,347	15,824
Marrakech, Morocco	5,298	4,027	11,306	10,955	11,273	4,981	2,830	5,301	19,263	11,249	2,715	10,876	6,881	10,297	6,133	5,751	7,280	8,488	3,992	10,982
Marseilles, France	3,622	2,826	9,647	9,313	9,582	5,366	1,189	6,118	18,965	9,504	1,058	9,238	7,259	8,567	6,557	6,168	8,111	8,303	2,294	9,270
Maseru, Lesotho	8,812	6,924	10,422	10,141	13,966	12,313	9,335	11,878	11,859	11,823	9,213	10,076	1,323	12,955	13,202	12,908	13,088	16,037	9,920	10,995

Distances in Kilometers	Gur'yev, USSR	Haifa, Israel	Haikou, China	Haiphong, Vietnam	Hakodate, Japan	Halifax, Canada	Hamburg, West Germany	Hamilton, Bermuda	Hamilton, New Zealand	Hangzhou, China	Hannover, West Germany	Hanoi, Vietnam	Harare, Zimbabwe	Harbin, China	Harrisburg, Pennsylvania	Hartford, Connecticut	Havana, Cuba	Helena, Montana	Helsinki, Finland	Hengyang, China
Mashhad, Iran	1,361	2,284	5,230	4,859	6,783	9,379	4,250	10,466	14,417	5,592	4,256	4,775	6,703	5,569	10,435	10,095	12,314	10,785	3,618	5,074
Mazatlan, Mexico	11,918	12,580	13,787	13,959	10,051	4,545	9,552	4,200	10,598	12,285	9,611	13,997	15,572	10,684	3,351	3,743	2,460	2,642	9,772	13,061
Mbabane, Swaziland	8,396	6,559	9,966	9,677	13,482	12,373	9,081	12,043	11,988	11,352	8,963	9,611	939	12,465	13,325	13,010	13,368	16,077	9,601	10,524
Mbandaka, Zaire	6,150	4,029	10,229	9,850	12,636	9,361	5,978	9,355	15,215	11,154	5,852	9,763	2,425	11,422	10,445	10,085	11,102	12,944	6,691	10,443
McMurdo Sound, Antarctica	15,618	14,467	11,382	11,542	13,336	15,769	17,151	14,412	4,450	12,324	17,026	11,577	9,019	13,928	15,007	15,263	13,039	14,844	17,590	12,086
Mecca, Saudi Arabia	3,048	1,348	7,277	6,887	9,307	9,364	4,367	10,043	15,400	7,953	4,293	6,799	4,449	8,094	10,554	10,165	12,049	11,957	4,456	7,320
Medan, Indonesia	6,585	7,347	2,218	2,100	5,945	14,380	9,602	15,671	9,085	3,719	9,624	2,081	7,784	5,405	15,129	14,907	17,047	13,686	8,764	2,977
Medellin, Colombia	12,174	11,529	17,026	16,995	13,544	4,412	9,161	3,093	12,117	15,634	9,142	16,983	11,988	13,839	3,770	3,945	2,005	5,669	9,987	16,234
Medicine Hat, Canada	9,108	10,222	11,261	11,335	7,700	3,546	7,255	4,241	12,130	9,801	7,348	11,352	15,079	8,042	2,840	3,051	3,869	397	7,152	10,476
Medina, Saudi Arabia	2,740	1,030	7,227	6,838	9,099	9,109	4,064	9,832	15,595	7,828	3,994	6,750	4,771	7,884	10,295	9,908	11,837	11,635	4,124	7,226
Melbourne, Australia	13,172	13,786	7,364	7,635	8,824	17,522	16,184	17,254	2,655	7,968	16,221	7,667	10,774	9,438	16,422	16,793	15,252	13,840	15,196	7,924
Memphis, Tennessee	10,138	10,558	13,533	13,562	10,048	2,483	7,557	2,359	12,654	12,110	7,606	13,568	13,942	10,321	1,292	1,683	1,524	2,236	7,905	12,740
Merauke, Indonesia	10,577	11,952	4,557	4,907	5,560	15,384	13,337	16,322	4,781	4,796	13,419	4,987	11,737	6,158	14,922	15,106	15,200	12,037	12,206	4,927
Merida, Mexico	11,539	11,648	14,981	15,053	11,352	3,552	8,770	2,764	11,843	13,509	8,798	15,067	13,826	11,763	2,457	2,802	786	3,493	9,274	14,197
Meridian, Mississippi	10,361	10,690	13,864	13,892	10,371	2,563	7,715	2,249	12,606	12,439	7,758	13,897	13,822	10,652	1,374	1,761	1,198	2,537	8,114	13,071
Messina, Italy	3,107	1,856	9,058	8,701	9,559	6,393	1,761	7,108	18,246	9,130	1,640	8,620	6,408	8,449	7,585	7,195	9,109	9,267	2,533	8,782
Mexico City, Mexico	12,090	12,455	14,596	14,744	10,869	4,314	9,491	3,710	10,934	13,094	9,533	14,776	14,794	11,446	3,141	3,521	1,789	3,238	9,864	13,851
Miami, Florida	10,615	10,577	14,810	14,792	11,431	2,571	7,757	1,664	12,941	13,439	7,776	14,785	12,942	11,634	1,636	1,904	366	3,637	8,347	14,018
Midway Islands, USA	10,317	12,439	7,304	7,618	4,065	9,521	10,920	10,243	7,344	5,999	11,053	7,690	16,908	5,231	8,853	9,080	9,289	5,951	10,001	6,815
Milan, Italy	3,253	2,617	9,273	8,943	9,215	5,528	901	6,353	18,580	9,118	768	8,869	7,350	8,189	6,710	6,324	8,331	8,302	1,940	8,888
Milford Sound, New Zealand	15,174	15,778	9,229	9,534	9,936	16,011	18,121	15,322	982	9,592	18,188	9,603	11,826	10,796	14,817	15,208	13,326	12,794	17,006	9,698
Milwaukee, Wisconsin	9,265	9,798	12,776	12,774	9,432	1,956	6,771	2,354	13,232	11,400	6,829	12,773	13,688	9,594	968	1,261	2,266	1,940	7,050	11,983
Minsk, USSR	1,871	2,414	7,761	7,453	7,647	6,245	1,157	7,324	16,975	7,513	1,204	7,384	7,954	6,589	7,336	6,982	9,176	8,233	715	7,322
Mogadiscio, Somalia	5,032	3,574	7,323	6,960	10,304	11,336	6,562	11,771	13,569	8,439	6,479	6,877	2,704	9,169	12,527	12,136	13,719	14,180	6,677	7,658
Mombasa, Kenya	5,794	4,112	8,163	7,809	11,228	11,376	6,958	11,611	13,506	9,330	6,860	7,729	1,791	10,096	12,539	12,156	13,462	14,563	7,236	8,538
Monclova, Mexico	11,382	11,953	13,793	13,920	10,090	3,896	8,934	3,583	11,247	12,295	8,989	13,948	15,062	10,614	2,703	3,094	1,966	2,377	9,200	13,034
Moncton, Canada	7,981	8,141	12,663	12,539	9,952	186	5,192	1,534	15,075	11,535	5,226	12,511	11,861	9,768	1,176	795	3,000	3,326	5,711	11,916
Monrovia, Liberia	7,448	5,567	12,960	12,571	13,951	6,634	5,566	6,276	16,466	13,414	5,440	12,483	5,318	12,867	7,536	7,228	7,858	10,354	6,687	12,912
Monte Carlo, Monaco	3,453	2,682	9,478	9,144	9,454	5,489	1,108	6,264	18,801	9,346	975	9,069	7,231	8,428	6,678	6,290	8,253	8,367	2,176	9,105
Monterrey, Mexico	11,477	11,994	13,968	14,094	10,265	3,904	8,985	3,525	11,254	12,470	9,037	14,122	14,954	10,788	2,710	3,100	1,841	2,544	9,280	13,208
Montevideo, Uruguay	14,035	12,102	17,902	17,732	18,362	8,840	11,680	7,489	10,371	19,394	11,583	17,685	8,654	18,775	8,587	8,653	6,992	10,614	12,842	18,630
Montgomery, Alabama	10,260	10,529	13,941	13,953	10,495	2,390	7,572	2,025	12,801	12,535	7,610	13,955	13,597	10,739	1,216	1,595	1,096	2,697	8,004	13,147
Montpelier, Vermont	8,516	8,767	12,878	12,793	9,918	716	5,794	1,493	14,431	11,653	5,834	12,773	12,449	9,855	569	277	2,509	3,066	6,250	12,107
Montpellier, France	3,722	2,953	9,744	9,413	9,617	5,241	1,194	5,991	19,044	9,579	1,067	9,338	7,346	8,615	6,433	6,043	7,983	8,199	2,325	9,358
Montreal, Canada	8,450	8,752	12,735	12,656	9,759	793	5,763	1,653	14,394	11,502	5,808	12,637	12,537	9,702	640	421	2,605	2,947	6,187	11,963
Moosonee, Canada	8,198	8,774	12,031	11,981	8,948	1,466	5,738	2,477	14,079	10,746	5,802	11,969	13,043	8,939	1,259	1,220	3,128	2,338	5,983	11,248
Moroni, Comoros	6,569	5,004	8,138	7,814	11,483	12,249	7,887	12,389	12,604	9,434	7,790	7,740	1,480	10,425	13,394	13,016	14,152	15,496	8,130	8,614
Moscow, USSR	1,378	2,554	7,110	6,810	7,018	6,668	1,785	7,817	16,300	6,838	1,850	6,744	8,177	5,938	7,708	7,370	9,602	8,312	892	6,655
Mosul, Iraq	1,400	841	6,707	6,335	7,984	8,409	3,193	9,344	15,813	7,016	3,161	6,251	6,129	6,777	9,549	9,179	11,293	10,491	2,951	6,536
Mount Isa, Australia	11,496	12,551	5,519	5,825	6,919	16,614	14,414	17,298	3,924	6,009	14,478	5,895	11,134	7,476	15,955	16,206	15,714	13,055	13,337	6,016
Multan, Pakistan	2,524	3,461	4,053	3,669	6,207	10,554	5,513	11,701	13,126	4,650	5,528	3,582	6,857	5,035	11,553	11,234	13,481	11,494	4,780	4,019
Munich, West Germany	2,996	2,595	8,997	8,674	8,867	5,558	611	6,456	18,262	8,799	488	8,602	7,561	7,845	6,726	6,346	8,410	8,174	1,591	8,590
Murcia, Spain	4,382	3,309	10,405	10,063	10,367	5,155	1,929	5,723	19,708	10,306	1,807	9,985	7,035	9,367	6,346	5,955	7,729	8,394	3,075	10,055
Murmansk, USSR	2,649	4,021	7,430	7,202	6,388	5,713	2,090	6,998	15,859	6,787	2,217	7,152	9,628	5,491	6,618	6,323	8,576	6,870	1,053	6,824
Mururoa Atoll, Fr. Polynesia	17,042	18,654	12,893	13,283	10,841	10,597	15,622	9,901	4,710	12,214	15,693	13,372	15,481	12,054	9,409	9,796	7,895	8,051	15,568	12,849
Muscat, Oman	2,675	2,523	5,335	4,945	7,673	10,446	5,227	11,387	13,878	6,088	5,202	4,857	5,476	6,491	11,569	11,206	13,340	12,172	4,821	5,413
Myitkyina, Burma	4,659	6,044	1,451	1,074	4,356	12,014	7,612	13,350	10,716	2,303	7,663	990	8,630	3,449	12,713	12,501	14,637	11,503	6,626	1,528
Naga, Philippines	7,497	9,037	1,543	1,927	3,548	13,515	10,260	14,854	7,869	1,866	10,337	2,014	10,694	3,576	13,690	13,660	15,086	11,369	9,151	1,836
Nagasaki, Japan	6,572	8,526	2,405	2,652	1,378	11,320	8,832	12,639	9,120	968	8,935	2,713	11,877	1,465	11,461	11,432	12,935	9,251	7,665	1,794
Nagoya, Japan	6,906	8,936	3,099	3,350	802	10,927	8,932	12,204	8,996	1,660	9,043	3,411	12,555	1,460	10,966	10,969	12,344	8,638	7,765	2,488
Nagpur, India	3,782	4,530	3,251	2,864	6,144	11,797	6,768	12,959	11,948	4,220	6,781	2,776	6,787	5,092	12,767	12,460	14,714	12,420	6,031	3,457
Nairobi, Kenya	5,560	3,781	8,344	7,981	11,258	10,935	6,566	11,180	13,944	9,447	6,465	7,898	1,936	10,099	12,099	11,715	13,045	14,149	6,892	8,672
Nanchang, China	5,811	7,560	1,110	1,270	2,671	11,884	8,459	13,257	9,613	450	8,541	1,320	10,463	2,117	12,259	12,155	13,949	10,382	7,335	379
Nancy, France	3,369	2,973	9,345	9,029	9,042	5,171	603	6,054	18,513	9,090	480	8,958	7,769	8,060	6,344	5,962	8,011	7,881	1,754	8,914
Nandi, Fiji	14,112	15,921	8,439	8,822	7,598	13,665	15,892	13,638	2,224	8,116	16,022	8,909	14,625	8,698	12,588	12,948	11,789	10,022	14,813	8,568
Nanjing, China	5,799	7,644	1,575	1,727	2,222	11,508	8,320	12,874	9,701	239	8,410	1,772	10,839	1,665	11,838	11,748	13,500	9,919	7,175	828
Nanning, China	5,664	7,170	370	274	3,669	12,489	8,526	13,863	9,691	1,438	8,590	322	9,530	3,037	13,001	12,854	14,793	11,317	7,469	626
Nantes, France	3,970	3,462	9,935	9,623	9,472	4,692	1,080	5,505	18,926	9,638	991	9,553	7,908	8,536	5,879	5,491	7,481	7,615	2,242	9,490
Naples, Italy	3,068	2,046	9,069	8,721	9,394	6,138	1,449	6,898	18,357	9,067	1,328	8,642	6,723	8,307	7,327	6,939	8,892	8,960	2,274	8,756
Narvik, Norway	3,056	4,116	8,066	7,836	6,920	5,132	1,703	6,393	16,335	7,411	1,836	7,785	9,630	6,071	6,082	5,771	8,025	6,580	990	7,460
Nashville, Tennessee	9,905	10,267	13,530	13,537	10,121	2,171	7,278	2,069	12,969	12,135	7,324	13,537	13,641	10,335	978	1,369	1,506	2,394	7,660	12,736
Nassau, Bahamas	10,533	10,406	14,944	14,902	11,637	2,501	7,635	1,464	13,146	13,605	7,647	14,891	12,648	11,796	1,684	1,900	554	3,887	8,270	14,155
Natal, Brazil	10,258	8,539	15,985	15,596	16,000	6,265	7,814	5,248	14,247	16,279	7,713	15,508	7,310	15,245	6,644	6,495	6,042	9,476	8,981	15,891
Natashquan, Canada	7,492	7,729	12,185	12,052	9,584	632	4,747	2,005	15,359	11,091	4,788	12,022	11,713	9,342	1,613	1,257	3,495	3,669	5,223	11,447
Nauru Island	11,922	13,857	6,574	6,964	5,375	13,053	13,757	13,571	4,213	6,007	13,882	7,052	14,792	6,470	12,245	12,524	12,153	9,368	12,634	6,555
Ndjamena, Chad	5,184	3,067	10,100	9,710	11,868	8,178	4,618	8,354	16,556	10,753	4,490	9,621	3,750	10,664	9,313	8,937	10,235	11,649	5,395	10,146
Nelson, New Zealand	15,401	16,235	9,389	9,714	9,763	15,459	18,163	14,843	425	9,619	18,262	9,787	12,396	10,696	14,267	14,658	12,839	12,216	16,996	9,800
Nema, Mauritania	6,347	4,599	12,090	11,709	12,757	6,080	4,364	6,012	17,646	12,364	4,238	11,623	5,670	11,693	7,119	6,769	7,818	9,768	5,484	11,939
Neuquen, Argentina	15,165	13,252	17,904	17,939	17,570	9,270	12,678	7,894	9,331	18,789	12,589	17,937	9,543	18,592	8,818	8,951	7,032	10,437	13,820	18,667
New Delhi, India	3,006	4,043	3,479	3,094	5,832	10,974	6,020	12,165	12,559	4,149	6,042	3,007	7,145	4,697	11,926	11,624	13,879	11,626	5,226	3,483
New Glasgow, Canada	7,917	8,025	12,702	12,568	10,057	128	5,096	1,488	15,226	11,602	5,126	12,537	11,689	9,845	1,301	912	3,063	3,757	5,649	11,964
New Haven, Connecticut	8,801	8,980	13,204	13,122	10,206	845	6,035	1,236	14,300	11,970	6,070	13,102	12,452	10,169	355	55	2,200	3,161	6,532	12,433
New Orleans, Louisiana	10,658	10,971	14,059	14,104	10,515	2,836	8,005	2,421	12,356	12,616	8,046	14,112	13,949	10,841	1,655	2,038	1,077	2,648	8,410	13,268
New Plymouth, New Zealand	15,339	16,301	9,315	9,648	9,567	15,291	17,996	14,736	177	9,491	18,105	9,724	12,631	10,520	14,103	14,493	12,730	11,993	16,828	9,700
New York, New York	8,907	9,093	13,264	13,188	10,228	957	6,147	1,247	14,192	12,015	6,183	13,170	12,539	10,211	249	162	2,101	3,105	6,639	12,489
Newcastle upon Tyne, UK	3,752	3,762	9,514	9,233	8,705	4,449	772	5,456	18,076	9,057	802	9,170	8,642	7,828	5,593	5,220	7,352	7,001	1,676	8,996
Newcastle Waters, Australia	10,786	11,811	4,850	5,140	6,592	16,596	13,735	17,559	4,658	5,460	13,792	5,207	10,678	7,026	16,160	16,347	16,252	13,268	12,688	5,392
Niamey, Niger	5,919	3,962	11,339	10,951	12,566	7,048	4,495	7,060	17,234	11,814	4,362	10,863	4,703	11,418	8,125	7,765	8,881	10,682	5,505	11,291
Nicosia, Cyprus	2,035	300	7,599	7,227	8,735	7,855	2,739	8,679	16,623	7,884	2,674	7,142	5,871	7,543	9,029	8,647	10,665	10,312	2,845	7,423
Niue (Alofi)	15,115	17,108	9,714	10,101	8,429	12,752	16,172	12,512	2,528	9,257	16,304	10,188	15,335	9,599	11,604	11,984	10,588	9,297	15,285	9,779
Norfolk, Virginia	9,374	9,511	13,669	13,609	10,526	1,375	6,591	1,171	13,844	12,382	6,622	13,594	12,704	10,573	383	628	1,629	3,133	7,105	12,887
Norfolk Island, Australia	14,238	15,548	8,232	8,584	8,322	15,199	16,749	15,013	1,185	8,292	16,859	8,664	13,065	9,273	14,083	14,455	13,065	11,592	15,582	8,554
Noril'sk, USSR	3,169	5,204	5,682	5,532	4,288	7,152	4,158	8,521	13,769	4,800	4,277	5,501	10,651	3,384	7,788	7,583	9,722	7,042	3,014	4,981
Norman Wells, Canada	7,541	9,014	9,393	9,440	5,991	4,398	6,324	5,503	12,469	7,972	6,441	9,451	14,485	6,180	4,189	4,239	5,658	2,264	5,893	8,602
Normanton, Australia	11,369	12,537	5,358	5,680	6,578	16,238	14,235	16,966	4,007	5,757	14,306	5,754	11,422	7,172	15,605	15,846	15,474	12,701	13,132	5,812
North Pole	4,783	6,369	7,784	7,693	5,377	5,057	4,068	6,430	14,184	6,653	4,200	7,675	11,976	4,933	5,544	5,377	7,443	4,839	3,331	7,025
Nottingham, United Kingdom	3,766	3,643	9,599	9,309	8,892	4,527	747	5,487	18,295	9,187	739	9,244	8,434	7,996	5,686	5,308	7,409	7,179	1,779	9,101
Norway House, Canada	8,442	9,375	11,373	11,387	8,024	2,664	6,367	3,555	13,108	9,984	6,453	11,390	14,098	8,180	2,187	2,301	3,662	1,299	6,371	10,579
Norwich, United Kingdom	3,610	3,476	9,470	9,175	8,845	4,698	591	5,655	18,291	9,086	572	9,109	8,318	7,927	5,856	5,478	7,579	7,322	1,672	8,983
Nouakchott, Mauritania	6,885	5,323	12,798	12,428	12,959	5,300	4,526	5,118	17,569	12,895	4,412	12,344	6,501	11,997	6,280	5,946	6,888	9,019	5,690	12,562
Noumea, New Caledonia	13,634	15,136	7,690	8,056	7,568	14,851	16,007	14,886	1,917	7,633	16,121	8,139	13,444	8,539	13,808	14,160	13,032	11,159	14,844	7,950
Novosibirsk, USSR	2,323	4,445	4,515	4,284	4,385	8,516	4,530	9,851	13,479	4,030	4,619	4,235	9,439	3,216	9,272	9,031	11,232	8,654	3,396	3,941
Nuku'alofa, Tonga	14,915	16,776	9,298	9,680	8,311	13,323	16,380	13,111	2,061	8,950	16,513	9,767	14,839	9,446	12,186	12,563	11,188	9,816	15,390	9,420
Nukunono Island, Tokelau Isls.	14,129	16,213	9,107	9,497	7,427	12,172	15,083	12,165	3,418	8,462	15,215	9,586	16,106	8,619	11,091	11,452	10,366	8,555	14,178	9,061
Nuremberg, West Germany	3,002	2,705	8,982	8,665	8,771	5,464	462	6,386	18,202	8,749	338	8,593	7,709	7,762	6,626	6,247	8,330	8,037	1,484	8,559
Nyala, Sudan	4,636	2,523	9,095	8,706	11,168	8,960	4,789	9,275	15,922	9,846	4,674	8,617	3,374	9,953	10,130	9,745	11,206	12,227	5,340	9,194
Oaxaca, Mexico	12,239	12,479	14,959	15,102	11,234	4,349	9,559	3,627	10,984	13,457	9,594	15,133	14,504	11,800	3,205	3,573	1,644	3,568	9,992	14,211
Ocean Falls, Canada	8,982	10,419	10,232	10,347	6,583	4,653	7,628	5,443	11,409	8,745	7,738	10,374	15,751	7,040	4,043	4,230	5,017	1,299	7,292	9,464
Odense, Denmark	2,989	3,154	8,802	8,509	8,264	5,172	207	6,213	17,745	8,425	340	8,444	8,346	7,309	6,294	5,929	8,091	7,486	1,014	8,314
Odessa, USSR	1,612	1,557	7,635	7,295	8,041	6,892	1,674	7,874	16,964	7,602	1,653	7,219	7,121	6,912	8,024	7,656	9,794	9,075	1,571	7,296

Distances in Kilometers	Gur'yev, USSR	Haifa, Israel	Haikou, China	Haiphong, Vietnam	Hakodate, Japan	Halifax, Canada	Hamburg, West Germany	Hamilton, Bermuda	Hamilton, New Zealand	Hangzhou, China	Hannover, West Germany	Hanoi, Vietnam	Harare, Zimbabwe	Harbin, China	Harrisburg, Pennsylvania	Hartford, Connecticut	Havana, Cuba	Helena, Montana	Helsinki, Finland	Hengyang, China
Ogbomosho, Nigeria	6,234	4,183	11,361	10,971	12,932	7,631	5,063	7,565	16,600	11,978	4,930	10,882	4,113	11,753	8,682	8,330	9,323	11,293	6,028	11,393
Okha, USSR	6,068	8,202	4,644	4,755	1,324	8,832	7,362	10,126	10,590	3,176	7,488	4,785	13,027	1,457	8,932	8,907	10,461	6,849	6,247	3,871
Okinawa (Naha)	6,877	8,712	1,902	2,220	2,098	12,075	9,338	13,399	8,655	861	9,433	2,296	11,512	2,169	12,221	12,194	13,666	9,965	8,181	1,502
Oklahoma City, Oklahoma	10,360	10,973	13,198	13,269	9,605	3,040	7,942	3,035	12,099	11,734	8,002	13,284	14,613	9,979	1,885	2,262	2,005	1,730	8,179	12,413
Old Crow, Canada	7,248	8,864	8,768	8,821	5,365	4,954	6,339	6,102	12,274	7,342	6,463	8,834	14,441	5,552	4,807	4,842	6,288	2,828	5,780	7,977
Olympia, Washington	9,560	10,886	10,872	11,000	7,190	4,501	8,003	5,122	11,227	9,377	8,105	11,029	15,990	7,697	3,731	3,973	4,472	830	7,769	10,112
Omaha, Nebraska	9,713	10,391	12,694	12,739	9,189	2,653	7,354	2,943	12,551	11,259	7,419	12,748	14,378	9,478	1,615	1,942	2,382	1,412	7,546	11,903
Omsk, USSR	1,735	3,867	4,962	4,700	4,987	8,242	3,990	9,544	14,054	4,591	4,071	4,644	9,008	3,824	9,078	8,811	11,046	8,733	2,885	4,441
Oodnadatta, Australia	11,745	12,529	5,923	6,189	7,692	17,468	14,745	18,008	3,871	6,600	14,788	6,250	10,460	8,166	16,740	17,018	16,206	13,860	13,750	6,503
Oradea, Romania	2,260	1,929	8,285	7,951	8,468	6,298	1,112	7,233	17,611	8,187	1,058	7,876	7,245	7,381	7,451	7,076	9,175	8,704	1,471	7,920
Oran, Algeria	4,480	3,279	10,489	10,140	10,571	5,320	2,150	5,831	19,588	10,445	2,025	10,061	6,802	9,554	6,506	6,116	7,834	8,613	3,281	10,165
Oranjestad, Aruba	11,256	10,630	16,402	16,295	13,225	3,614	8,240	2,254	13,021	15,149	8,221	16,267	11,593	13,339	3,147	3,252	1,756	5,447	9,083	15,635
Orebro, Sweden	2,750	3,286	8,395	8,118	7,744	5,306	715	6,430	17,225	7,954	843	8,056	8,668	6,798	6,381	6,030	8,241	7,324	557	7,877
Orel, USSR	1,299	2,233	7,203	6,889	7,284	6,776	1,733	7,882	16,468	7,009	1,776	6,819	7,853	6,183	7,846	7,499	9,711	8,569	1,055	6,784
Orsk, USSR	666	2,799	5,656	5,346	6,061	8,020	3,253	9,230	14,939	5,509	3,309	5,277	8,105	4,888	8,989	8,677	10,930	9,130	2,304	5,244
Osaka, Japan	6,842	8,858	2,958	3,209	909	11,012	8,917	12,298	9,013	1,521	9,027	3,270	12,420	1,441	11,071	11,068	12,468	8,764	7,749	2,348
Oslo, Norway	3,011	3,498	8,617	8,345	7,847	5,044	710	6,170	17,312	8,138	843	8,284	8,811	6,933	6,121	5,770	7,979	7,112	791	8,084
Osorno, Chile	15,632	13,722	17,707	17,820	17,196	9,487	13,099	8,112	8,891	18,355	13,014	17,837	9,884	18,315	8,959	9,118	7,116	10,397	14,229	18,401
Ostrava, Czechoslovakia	2,482	2,339	8,473	8,152	8,416	5,911	706	6,876	17,747	8,283	662	8,080	7,600	7,369	7,056	6,683	8,801	8,301	1,226	8,066
Ottawa, Canada	8,550	8,890	12,730	12,661	9,696	956	5,892	1,736	14,235	11,474	5,939	12,645	12,701	9,670	581	473	2,545	2,792	6,292	11,953
Ouagadougou, Bourkina Fasso	6,273	4,351	11,751	11,363	12,880	6,852	4,681	6,781	17,171	12,202	4,549	11,275	4,895	11,750	7,895	7,545	8,560	10,528	5,734	11,693
Oujda, Morocco	4,639	3,406	10,645	10,295	10,726	5,281	2,297	5,752	19,584	10,607	2,173	10,215	6,776	9,713	6,462	6,073	7,752	8,623	3,434	10,326
Oxford, United Kingdom	3,802	3,596	9,670	9,375	9,015	4,557	786	5,487	18,429	9,282	755	9,308	8,322	8,109	5,724	5,343	7,422	7,271	1,869	9,182
Pago Pago, American Samoa	14,655	16,705	9,439	9,828	7,955	12,462	15,646	12,334	2,951	8,888	15,778	9,916	15,736	9,137	11,343	11,715	10,462	8,923	14,753	9,449
Pakxe, Laos	6,082	7,337	728	644	4,465	13,300	9,046	14,664	9,313	2,230	9,096	655	8,972	3,917	13,868	13,705	15,683	12,199	8,053	1,484
Palembang, Indonesia	7,563	8,314	2,612	2,639	6,137	15,243	10,582	16,577	8,107	4,020	10,609	2,652	8,192	5,809	15,865	15,694	17,643	14,010	9,722	3,405
Palermo, Italy	3,277	2,044	9,243	8,887	9,681	6,237	1,735	6,931	18,438	9,296	1,609	8,806	6,463	8,583	7,430	7,040	8,934	9,166	2,585	8,958
Palma, Majorca	4,010	2,986	10,033	9,691	10,056	5,357	1,651	5,997	19,353	9,944	1,523	9,614	7,007	9,036	6,565	6,160	8,001	8,475	2,768	9,685
Palmerston North, New Zealand	15,524	16,434	9,502	9,833	9,751	15,237	18,186	14,632	286	9,685	18,296	9,908	12,598	10,710	14,045	14,436	12,627	12,004	17,019	9,891
Panama, Panama	12,167	11,698	16,622	16,637	13,058	4,243	9,182	2,998	11,952	15,186	9,175	16,635	12,490	13,409	3,477	3,696	1,597	5,186	9,937	15,829
Paramaribo, Suriname	10,809	9,681	16,738	16,457	14,496	4,379	7,863	3,094	13,826	15,981	7,807	16,391	9,815	14,288	4,388	4,343	3,489	7,049	8,900	16,154
Paris, France	3,638	3,242	9,593	9,283	9,172	4,899	747	5,770	18,651	9,300	651	9,213	7,917	8,219	6,077	5,693	7,730	7,679	1,914	9,147
Patna, India	3,773	4,894	2,654	2,266	5,357	11,604	6,791	12,851	11,720	3,475	6,822	2,178	7,573	4,307	12,480	12,205	14,448	11,826	5,929	2,744
Patrai, Greece	2,640	1,343	8,540	8,179	9,210	6,832	1,923	7,602	17,710	8,662	1,825	8,098	6,284	8,071	8,017	7,630	9,596	9,544	2,448	8,285
Peking, China	5,127	7,090	2,280	2,307	2,054	10,636	7,492	12,008	10,494	1,128	7,587	2,323	10,879	1,057	11,022	10,910	12,758	9,287	6,335	1,488
Penrhyn Island (Omoka)	14,926	17,049	10,523	10,911	8,385	11,061	14,950	10,852	4,162	9,732	15,070	10,999	16,875	9,600	9,913	10,292	8,968	7,664	14,321	10,397
Peoria, Illinois	9,560	10,082	12,974	12,986	9,567	2,166	7,058	2,402	12,990	11,576	7,114	12,988	13,855	9,776	1,078	1,421	2,062	1,917	7,345	12,180
Perm', USSR	1,246	3,223	6,046	5,770	5,902	7,350	2,885	8,601	15,142	5,687	2,967	5,709	8,720	4,794	8,278	7,979	10,233	8,361	1,793	5,543
Perth, Australia	10,841	11,105	5,782	5,924	8,548	18,592	13,806	19,952	5,385	6,898	13,804	5,957	8,507	8,672	18,549	18,684	17,984	15,659	13,073	6,520
Peshawar, Pakistan	2,200	3,384	4,116	3,743	5,982	10,190	5,215	11,365	13,323	4,564	5,238	3,659	7,167	4,789	11,168	10,855	13,108	11,070	4,428	3,994
Petropavlovsk-Kamchatskiy,USSR	6,932	9,050	5,506	5,662	1,835	8,458	7,841	9,666	10,188	4,005	7,972	5,701	14,058	2,436	8,378	8,410	9,734	6,043	6,796	4,764
Petrozavodsk, USSR	1,979	3,223	7,326	7,057	6,782	6,138	1,703	7,349	16,234	6,877	1,808	6,997	8,834	5,781	7,130	6,808	9,056	7,616	539	6,796
Pevek, USSR	6,125	8,076	6,787	6,835	3,545	6,591	6,240	7,863	11,926	5,382	6,373	6,849	13,614	3,579	6,665	6,638	8,256	4,787	5,336	5,995
Philadelphia, Pennsylvania	9,032	9,223	13,338	13,262	10,261	1,086	6,277	1,263	14,069	12,074	6,312	13,253	12,631	10,267	151	291	1,984	3,052	6,764	12,561
Phnom Penh, Kampuchea	6,315	7,454	1,104	1,048	4,826	13,675	9,306	15,033	9,122	2,602	9,350	1,054	8,742	4,315	14,265	14,096	16,088	12,594	8,344	1,880
Phoenix, Arizona	10,938	11,902	12,578	12,730	8,856	4,307	8,875	4,391	10,892	11,076	8,952	12,764	15,968	9,439	3,205	3,565	3,117	1,459	8,912	11,835
Pierre, South Dakota	9,511	10,338	12,223	12,278	8,698	2,897	7,304	3,355	12,426	10,779	7,379	12,290	14,637	9,004	1,980	2,262	2,871	945	7,401	11,434
Pinang, Malaysia	6,530	7,388	1,947	1,842	5,671	14,233	9,549	15,547	9,070	3,447	9,577	1,828	8,028	5,142	14,939	14,732	16,833	13,424	8,678	2,711
Pitcairn Island (Adamstown)	17,552	18,336	13,844	14,233	11,758	10,249	15,441	9,398	5,305	13,182	15,485	14,322	14,841	12,964	9,091	9,467	7,413	8,142	15,661	13,817
Pittsburgh, Pennsylvania	9,205	9,510	13,224	13,183	10,022	1,424	6,529	1,636	13,709	11,908	6,572	13,173	13,046	10,097	266	633	1,932	2,658	6,947	12,437
Plymouth, Montserrat	10,377	9,674	15,860	15,678	13,120	3,102	7,358	1,745	13,975	14,803	7,330	15,635	10,907	13,032	2,971	2,953	2,224	5,639	8,256	15,149
Plymouth, United Kingdom	4,035	3,738	9,919	9,623	9,239	4,404	1,029	5,292	18,602	9,531	986	9,556	8,307	8,347	5,581	5,197	7,243	7,232	2,119	9,433
Ponape Island	10,669	12,589	5,368	5,756	4,230	12,934	12,674	13,728	5,255	4,740	12,793	5,845	14,187	5,267	12,335	12,549	12,649	9,435	11,523	5,303
Ponce, Puerto Rico	10,548	9,980	15,781	15,643	12,818	2,967	7,535	1,591	13,671	14,615	7,518	15,609	11,397	12,818	2,656	2,695	1,736	5,215	8,373	15,034
Ponta Delgada, Azores	6,202	5,450	12,132	11,834	11,095	3,242	3,239	3,594	18,183	11,686	3,181	11,767	8,543	10,354	4,384	4,004	5,594	6,842	4,312	11,635
Pontianak, Indonesia	7,616	8,555	2,224	2,330	5,599	15,013	10,628	16,382	7,915	3,543	10,665	2,361	8,775	5,349	15,506	15,378	17,159	13,473	9,697	3,001
Port Augusta, Australia	12,287	12,961	6,509	6,770	8,227	17,730	15,299	17,912	3,445	7,189	15,336	6,829	10,447	8,738	16,820	17,147	15,966	14,024	14,326	7,094
Port Blair, India	5,484	6,316	2,099	1,807	5,721	13,337	8,501	14,596	10,149	3,503	8,524	1,745	7,521	4,960	14,165	13,912	16,126	13,105	7,671	2,680
Port Elizabeth, South Africa	9,358	7,460	10,769	10,505	14,384	12,506	9,812	11,957	11,468	12,202	9,688	10,445	1,869	13,415	13,318	13,049	13,013	16,207	10,433	11,375
Port Hedland, Australia	10,003	10,640	4,555	4,736	7,241	17,299	13,023	18,639	5,759	5,598	13,047	4,779	9,094	7,361	17,357	17,405	17,847	14,611	12,141	5,264
Port Louis, Mauritius	7,472	6,335	7,275	7,020	10,938	14,006	9,350	14,174	10,886	8,723	9,269	6,962	2,794	10,081	15,167	14,785	15,878	16,924	9,378	7,901
Port Moresby, Papua New Guinea	11,177	12,652	5,195	5,559	5,711	15,121	13,815	15,878	4,214	5,262	13,908	5,642	12,391	6,453	14,500	14,730	14,555	11,595	12,660	5,491
Port Said, Egypt	2,428	309	7,778	7,399	9,106	8,069	3,054	8,819	16,574	8,156	2,976	7,313	5,435	7,906	9,254	8,868	10,819	10,670	3,258	7,654
Port Sudan, Sudan	3,328	1,481	7,587	7,197	9,643	9,321	4,429	9,936	15,507	8,284	4,345	7,108	4,197	8,429	10,514	10,124	11,940	12,051	4,607	7,645
Port-au-Prince, Haiti	10,855	10,439	15,727	15,645	12,519	3,008	7,869	1,702	13,199	14,445	7,863	15,623	11,997	12,634	2,448	2,576	1,161	4,774	8,633	14,950
Port-of-Spain, Trin. & Tobago	10,852	9,979	16,495	16,291	13,776	3,774	7,842	2,419	13,637	15,475	7,804	16,242	10,643	13,705	3,614	3,616	2,610	6,191	8,792	15,803
Port-Vila, Vanuatu	13,429	15,083	7,589	7,965	7,173	14,368	15,614	14,491	2,324	7,403	15,734	8,051	13,910	8,189	13,357	13,699	12,701	10,660	14,465	7,783
Portland, Maine	8,462	8,652	12,951	12,854	10,053	544	5,699	1,350	14,589	11,753	5,735	12,831	12,258	9,961	665	288	2,533	3,264	6,193	12,187
Portland, Oregon	9,726	11,038	10,998	11,132	7,304	4,539	8,142	5,111	11,124	9,500	8,243	11,163	16,092	7,832	3,730	3,986	4,392	827	7,924	10,241
Porto, Portugal	4,765	3,948	10,770	10,448	10,320	4,422	1,958	5,024	19,511	10,514	1,866	10,375	7,707	9,406	5,614	5,222	7,029	7,695	3,120	10,349
Porto Alegre, Brazil	13,336	11,433	17,858	17,585	18,333	8,369	10,976	7,048	11,080	19,196	10,877	17,518	8,313	18,254	8,227	8,254	6,766	10,459	12,140	18,405
Porto Alexandre, Angola	8,033	5,919	11,465	11,115	14,366	10,125	7,687	9,734	13,825	12,620	7,557	11,035	2,054	13,172	11,029	10,726	11,117	13,848	8,504	11,838
Porto Novo, Benin	6,490	4,441	11,599	11,209	13,186	7,632	5,262	7,506	16,461	12,233	5,129	11,121	4,123	12,009	8,658	8,314	9,224	11,318	6,247	11,642
Porto Velho, Brazil	12,662	11,367	18,616	18,338	15,631	5,916	9,742	4,544	12,008	17,590	9,684	18,270	10,240	15,784	5,590	5,667	4,062	7,766	10,783	17,965
Portsmouth, United Kingdom	3,818	3,546	9,713	9,414	9,106	4,599	818	5,505	18,534	9,347	769	9,346	8,223	8,192	5,771	5,388	7,450	7,356	1,932	9,235
Poznan, Poland	2,557	2,615	8,488	8,178	8,257	5,698	484	6,706	17,673	8,225	493	8,108	7,901	7,238	6,830	6,462	8,607	8,010	993	8,048
Prague, Czechoslovakia	2,750	2,554	8,728	8,411	8,568	5,654	493	6,605	17,966	8,506	418	8,340	7,698	7,544	6,806	6,431	8,537	8,124	1,304	8,309
Praia, Cape Verde Islands	7,707	6,200	13,662	13,296	13,526	5,005	5,189	4,592	16,875	13,681	5,086	13,212	6,998	12,650	5,861	5,562	6,223	8,707	6,357	13,395
Pretoria, South Africa	8,414	6,524	10,218	9,922	13,691	12,107	8,959	11,751	12,183	11,587	8,838	9,854	926	12,648	13,043	12,733	13,065	15,821	9,526	10,760
Prince Albert, Canada	8,688	9,749	11,181	11,226	7,718	3,181	6,772	3,999	12,607	9,752	6,864	11,237	14,607	7,966	2,607	2,765	3,878	861	6,694	10,390
Prince Edward Island	10,470	8,800	10,336	10,158	14,071	14,158	11,408	13,449	9,742	11,838	11,291	10,116	3,251	13,395	14,846	14,625	14,139	17,732	11,892	11,057
Prince George, Canada	8,796	10,158	10,378	10,472	6,778	4,291	7,322	5,116	11,765	8,904	7,429	10,494	15,415	7,167	3,718	3,890	4,795	1,115	7,034	9,600
Prince Rupert, Canada	8,761	10,247	9,962	10,073	6,325	4,763	7,503	5,611	11,453	8,477	7,616	10,099	15,654	6,765	4,214	4,381	5,261	1,550	7,122	9,192
Providence, Rhode Island	8,682	8,845	13,153	13,062	10,205	708	5,905	1,211	14,438	11,938	5,938	13,041	12,332	10,141	492	106	2,309	3,253	6,413	12,386
Provo, Utah	10,193	11,221	12,047	12,166	8,369	3,927	8,212	4,255	11,401	10,554	8,296	12,193	15,671	8,860	2,939	3,256	3,337	707	8,194	11,282
Puerto Aisen, Chile	15,832	13,827	17,180	17,283	17,311	10,016	13,467	8,640	8,562	17,989	13,375	17,299	9,645	18,514	9,498	9,655	7,652	10,896	14,617	17,899
Puerto Deseado, Argentina	15,454	13,392	16,913	16,950	17,821	10,239	13,305	8,865	8,764	17,995	13,203	16,951	9,066	19,036	9,810	9,939	8,022	11,373	14,470	17,687
Puerto Princesa, Philippines	7,475	8,851	1,456	1,785	4,150	13,978	10,349	15,340	7,884	2,276	10,414	1,862	10,102	4,063	14,242	14,185	15,712	12,000	9,282	2,007
Punta Arenas, Chile	15,983	13,875	16,330	16,416	17,345	10,860	13,984	9,484	8,094	17,308	13,880	16,429	9,211	18,504	10,366	10,519	8,523	11,722	15,151	17,075
Pusan, South Korea	6,351	8,329	2,482	2,696	1,256	11,081	8,573	12,408	9,375	991	8,677	2,751	11,844	1,200	11,249	11,211	12,763	9,097	7,406	1,812
Pyongyang, North Korea	5,857	7,864	2,572	2,715	1,305	10,691	8,049	12,037	9,899	1,098	8,153	2,755	11,636	752	10,930	10,867	12,531	8,925	6,881	1,817
Qamdo, China	4,229	5,795	1,798	1,481	4,024	11,388	7,115	12,732	11,127	2,195	7,174	1,414	8,908	3,009	12,073	11,864	13,996	10,907	6,088	1,568
Qandahar, Afghanistan	2,091	2,892	4,614	4,232	6,586	10,133	5,022	11,235	13,682	5,149	5,029	4,146	6,606	5,390	11,172	10,839	13,069	11,344	4,361	4,550
Qiqian, China	4,819	6,935	3,682	3,686	1,898	9,264	6,648	10,630	11,279	2,438	6,759	3,692	11,540	834	9,618	9,512	11,361	7,959	5,482	2,892
Qom, Iran	1,387	1,486	6,011	5,635	7,538	9,026	3,813	10,013	15,086	6,402	3,796	5,549	6,177	6,323	10,140	9,779	11,936	10,846	3,399	5,879
Quebec, Canada	8,224	8,519	12,598	12,506	9,700	641	5,529	1,705	14,610	11,394	5,574	12,485	12,362	9,602	859	573	2,811	3,084	5,960	11,832
Quetta, Pakistan	2,284	3,042	4,483	4,098	6,569	10,327	5,215	11,429	13,505	5,069	5,221	4,011	6,565	5,383	11,363	11,031	13,262	11,499	4,554	4,448
Quito, Ecuador	12,945	12,209	17,615	17,653	13,964	5,184	9,928	3,876	11,419	16,145	9,906	17,655	12,078	14,395	4,486	4,687	2,617	6,130	10,770	16,826
Rabaul, Papua New Guinea	11,131	12,796	5,306	5,688	5,220	14,334	13,549	15,075	4,399	5,114	13,655	5,774	13,129	6,083	13,696	13,928	13,813	10,791	12,381	5,474
Raiatea (Uturoa)	16,018	18,111	11,477	11,867	9,501	11,132	15,615	10,686	4,002	10,785	15,721	11,955	16,172	10,716	9,944	10,334	8,712	8,049	15,174	11,417

Distances in Kilometers

	Gur'yev, USSR	Haifa, Israel	Haikou, China	Haiphong, Vietnam	Hakodate, Japan	Halifax, Canada	Hamburg, West Germany	Hamilton, Bermuda	Hamilton, New Zealand	Hangzhou, China	Hannover, West Germany	Hanoi, Vietnam	Harare, Zimbabwe	Harbin, China	Harrisburg, Pennsylvania	Hartford, Connecticut	Havana, Cuba	Helena, Montana	Helsinki, Finland	Hengyang, China
Raleigh, North Carolina	9,587	9,750	13,755	13,711	10,535	1,611	6,822	1,337	13,602	12,438	6,855	13,700	12,906	10,627	522	843	1,447	3,020	7,319	12,969
Rangiroa (Avatoru)	16,006	18,004	11,801	12,190	9,640	10,706	15,300	10,242	4,433	11,038	15,400	12,278	16,378	10,854	9,516	9,906	8,265	7,693	14,948	11,699
Rangoon, Burma	5,262	6,347	1,538	1,197	5,058	12,901	8,273	14,210	10,218	2,859	8,309	1,123	8,098	4,279	13,649	13,422	15,586	12,441	7,363	2,032
Raoul Is., Kermadec Islands	15,327	16,876	9,435	9,803	8,939	14,094	17,233	13,723	1,136	9,301	17,364	9,886	13,943	10,016	12,925	13,311	11,744	10,690	16,169	9,669
Rarotonga (Avarua)	15,970	18,072	10,793	11,180	9,275	12,112	16,311	11,693	3,022	10,278	16,430	11,268	15,531	10,473	10,929	11,319	9,718	8,909	15,661	10,831
Rawson, Argentina	15,185	13,180	17,392	17,404	17,903	9,743	12,890	8,370	9,162	18,485	12,793	17,398	9,153	19,048	9,331	9,452	7,565	10,980	14,049	18,173
Recife, Brazil	10,418	8,657	16,059	15,669	16,246	6,509	8,023	5,475	14,048	16,444	7,920	15,580	7,205	15,471	6,868	6,726	6,212	9,685	9,191	16,014
Regina, Canada	8,961	9,964	11,479	11,530	7,987	3,112	6,966	3,831	12,511	10,042	7,053	11,542	14,683	8,262	2,430	2,626	3,594	695	6,935	10,689
Reykjavik, Iceland	4,695	5,184	9,812	9,601	8,165	3,367	2,155	4,600	16,857	9,029	2,238	9,554	10,152	7,514	4,390	4,052	6,291	5,488	2,427	9,167
Rhodes, Greece	2,284	739	8,029	7,661	8,968	7,410	2,369	8,205	17,109	8,246	2,290	7,578	6,014	7,796	8,589	8,205	10,197	9,991	2,649	7,820
Richmond, Virginia	9,364	9,544	13,579	13,525	10,411	1,403	6,607	1,296	13,782	12,281	6,641	13,512	12,812	10,470	306	623	1,665	3,005	7,097	12,795
Riga, USSR	2,176	2,807	7,935	7,642	7,575	5,888	971	7,001	17,008	7,592	1,056	7,576	8,312	6,561	6,964	6,614	8,823	7,830	362	7,455
Ringkobing, Denmark	3,123	3,305	8,901	8,613	8,279	5,021	304	6,070	17,755	8,494	425	8,549	8,466	7,344	6,141	5,776	7,942	7,342	1,081	8,400
Rio Branco, Brazil	13,047	11,802	18,872	18,667	15,523	6,063	10,098	4,687	11,608	17,615	10,045	18,611	10,603	15,808	5,639	5,750	3,991	7,650	11,114	18,130
Rio Cuarto, Argentina	14,528	12,697	18,464	18,390	17,618	8,614	11,964	7,241	10,027	19,486	11,878	18,360	9,433	18,323	8,228	8,337	6,514	10,042	13,100	19,258
Rio de Janeiro, Brazil	12,216	10,338	17,277	16,921	17,883	7,762	9,892	6,523	12,179	18,185	9,789	16,839	7,695	17,312	7,815	7,776	6,624	10,334	11,059	17,554
Rio Gallegos, Argentina	15,827	13,730	16,500	16,572	17,501	10,682	13,783	9,306	8,293	17,508	13,680	16,582	9,159	18,681	10,209	10,354	8,381	11,629	14,950	17,254
Rio Grande, Brazil	13,540	11,616	17,821	17,579	18,449	8,572	11,207	7,243	10,853	19,263	11,107	17,518	8,352	18,478	8,403	8,440	6,904	10,581	12,371	18,438
Riyadh, Saudi Arabia	2,537	1,460	6,515	6,126	8,544	9,590	4,428	10,401	14,979	7,163	4,377	6,037	4,996	7,333	10,759	10,378	12,395	11,833	4,290	6,537
Road Town, Brit. Virgin Isls.	10,382	9,778	15,711	15,555	12,851	2,907	7,365	1,533	13,873	14,592	7,345	15,517	11,205	12,805	2,689	2,696	1,918	5,324	8,222	14,978
Roanoke, Virginia	9,504	9,733	13,570	13,532	10,332	1,596	6,780	1,493	13,569	12,244	6,817	13,523	13,031	10,433	425	799	1,585	2,832	7,240	12,782
Robinson Crusoe Island, Chile	15,660	13,973	18,253	18,491	16,452	8,806	12,863	7,445	9,006	18,192	12,795	18,536	10,665	17,466	8,184	8,373	6,293	9,488	13,930	18,691
Rochester, New York	8,843	9,164	12,960	12,902	9,851	1,136	6,175	1,651	14,008	11,677	6,220	12,889	12,850	9,869	327	434	2,264	2,724	6,585	12,178
Rockhampton, Australia	12,513	13,698	6,489	6,822	7,281	16,130	15,312	16,435	2,849	6,763	15,394	6,898	12,020	8,027	15,230	15,546	14,654	12,417	14,177	6,898
Rome, Italy	3,152	2,225	9,169	8,824	9,387	5,950	1,308	6,719	18,484	9,125	1,182	8,747	6,884	8,316	7,138	6,750	8,711	8,778	2,204	8,836
Rosario, Argentina	14,240	12,377	18,325	18,184	17,898	8,599	11,743	7,233	10,272	19,697	11,653	18,141	9,110	18,455	8,276	8,364	6,621	10,205	12,891	19,083
Roseau, Dominica	10,444	9,686	15,992	15,800	13,295	3,261	7,426	1,912	13,957	14,962	7,394	15,754	10,780	13,196	3,148	3,128	2,366	5,812	8,344	15,292
Rostock, East Germany	2,877	2,972	8,743	8,444	8,314	5,329	153	6,349	17,788	8,409	250	8,376	8,170	7,337	6,458	6,090	8,241	7,671	1,028	8,273
Rostov-na-Donu, USSR	923	1,648	6,947	6,610	7,462	7,373	2,207	8,426	16,277	6,927	2,215	6,534	7,258	6,308	8,469	8,114	10,301	9,252	1,729	6,609
Rotterdam, Netherlands	3,410	3,245	9,308	9,007	8,802	4,930	413	5,880	18,279	8,967	361	8,939	8,145	7,856	6,088	5,711	7,809	7,529	1,561	8,839
Rouyn, Canada	8,424	8,897	12,385	12,331	9,302	1,247	5,872	2,139	14,091	11,105	5,929	12,318	12,950	9,298	902	875	2,801	2,479	6,187	11,603
Sacramento, California	10,489	11,734	11,572	11,735	7,843	4,770	8,787	5,117	10,648	10,069	8,882	11,773	16,501	8,461	3,805	4,117	4,076	1,179	8,638	10,838
Saginaw, Michigan	9,077	9,535	12,827	12,803	9,571	1,631	6,517	2,084	13,544	11,485	6,571	12,797	13,362	9,675	683	942	2,256	2,230	6,843	12,037
Saint Denis, Reunion	7,537	6,328	7,495	7,238	11,150	13,895	9,327	14,015	10,980	8,939	9,242	7,179	2,583	10,280	15,044	14,666	15,684	16,936	9,396	8,116
Saint George's, Grenada	10,748	9,915	16,351	16,153	13,622	3,618	7,734	2,262	13,712	15,320	7,698	16,106	10,713	13,549	3,461	3,460	2,504	6,057	8,672	15,653
Saint John, Canada	8,115	8,273	12,763	12,645	10,007	205	5,327	1,446	14,959	11,618	5,361	12,618	11,946	9,845	1,045	662	2,867	3,518	5,845	12,012
Saint John's, Antigua	10,318	9,617	15,808	15,625	13,090	3,059	7,299	1,707	14,033	14,761	7,271	15,581	10,882	12,992	2,948	2,923	2,244	5,633	8,198	15,100
Saint John's, Canada	7,232	7,243	12,327	12,152	10,022	901	4,347	1,980	16,007	11,357	4,370	12,112	10,998	9,666	2,093	1,703	3,779	4,393	4,976	11,628
Saint Louis, Missouri	9,791	10,285	13,169	13,190	9,725	2,303	7,266	2,404	12,835	11,759	7,321	13,194	13,928	9,964	1,159	1,529	1,871	1,990	7,571	12,376
Saint Paul, Minnesota	9,246	9,928	12,428	12,447	9,016	2,321	6,889	2,818	12,956	11,025	6,957	12,451	14,065	9,226	1,425	1,688	2,609	1,480	7,076	11,634
Saint Peter Port, UK	3,958	3,598	9,875	9,573	9,284	4,543	981	5,411	18,697	9,522	919	9,505	8,156	8,372	5,722	5,337	7,370	7,387	2,109	9,404
Saipan (Susupe)	9,075	10,952	3,789	4,172	2,987	12,752	11,308	13,840	6,625	3,100	11,417	4,259	13,088	3,833	12,462	12,579	13,290	9,708	10,140	3,666
Salalah, Oman	3,346	2,599	5,918	5,532	8,496	10,731	5,556	11,531	13,879	6,810	5,509	5,444	4,607	7,328	11,898	11,519	13,529	12,826	5,333	6,091
Salem, Oregon	9,794	11,111	11,016	11,154	7,316	4,593	8,216	5,149	11,055	9,517	8,317	11,186	16,161	7,857	3,771	4,032	4,400	875	7,996	10,262
Salt Lake City, Utah	10,140	11,179	11,991	12,109	8,316	3,922	8,173	4,271	11,422	10,499	8,258	12,136	15,664	8,802	2,947	3,259	3,380	649	8,147	11,225
Salta, Argentina	14,028	12,387	19,333	19,107	16,963	7,690	11,282	6,316	10,629	19,198	11,207	19,041	9,825	17,443	7,298	7,406	5,609	9,191	12,384	19,709
Salto, Uruguay	13,932	12,072	18,299	18,098	17,996	8,439	11,455	7,083	10,570	19,803	11,363	18,044	8,911	18,362	8,169	8,239	6,570	10,199	12,606	18,981
Salvador, Brazil	11,086	9,298	16,622	16,233	16,816	6,867	8,688	5,737	13,377	17,111	8,587	16,145	7,447	16,115	7,102	7,001	6,228	9,827	9,855	16,647
Salzburg, Austria	2,899	2,483	8,908	8,583	8,834	5,673	674	6,571	18,194	8,729	561	8,510	7,488	7,801	6,840	6,460	8,525	8,270	1,578	8,509
Samsun, Turkey	1,398	945	7,250	6,892	8,087	7,603	2,388	8,548	16,506	7,387	2,355	6,812	6,567	6,911	8,744	8,374	10,490	9,780	2,241	6,993
San Antonio, Texas	11,024	11,556	13,725	13,825	10,064	3,497	8,541	3,229	11,643	12,239	8,595	13,847	14,765	10,520	2,304	2,695	1,753	2,239	8,827	12,951
San Cristobal, Venezuela	11,822	11,131	16,915	16,835	13,583	4,172	8,805	2,822	12,512	15,597	8,782	16,812	11,681	13,788	3,630	3,767	2,016	5,730	9,659	16,134
San Diego, California	11,096	12,187	12,298	12,473	8,562	4,754	9,181	4,871	10,482	10,796	9,265	12,513	16,444	9,212	3,671	4,025	3,567	1,602	9,145	11,574
San Francisco, California	10,585	11,847	11,568	11,738	7,834	4,884	8,904	5,214	10,527	10,065	8,999	11,777	16,618	8,474	3,910	4,226	4,136	1,300	8,747	10,840
San Jose, Costa Rica	12,337	12,023	16,338	16,403	12,690	4,322	9,395	3,174	11,615	14,864	9,398	16,414	13,000	13,120	3,435	3,700	1,472	4,849	10,081	15,554
San Juan, Argentina	14,737	12,983	18,727	18,733	17,191	8,451	12,063	7,075	9,882	19,187	11,983	18,718	9,862	17,962	7,996	8,127	6,227	9,694	13,176	19,481
San Juan, Puerto Rico	10,477	9,908	15,726	15,584	12,792	2,913	7,463	1,537	13,742	14,573	7,445	15,549	11,358	12,778	2,628	2,657	1,768	5,214	8,303	14,983
San Luis Potosi, Mexico	11,867	12,341	14,238	14,385	10,514	4,222	9,346	3,739	10,966	12,736	9,394	14,417	15,011	11,086	3,032	3,421	1,916	2,889	9,664	13,492
San Marino, San Marino	3,067	2,310	9,093	8,755	9,207	5,837	1,086	6,650	18,423	9,002	961	8,679	7,095	8,150	7,020	6,634	8,632	8,595	1,993	8,737
San Miguel de Tucuman, Argen.	14,160	12,471	19,135	18,966	17,132	7,915	11,452	6,541	10,480	19,372	11,374	18,912	9,733	17,659	7,524	7,632	5,827	9,396	12,563	19,814
San Salvador, El Salvador	12,240	12,170	15,711	15,810	12,026	4,201	9,391	3,227	11,413	14,221	9,408	15,830	13,641	12,507	3,180	3,497	1,269	4,225	9,970	14,939
Sanaa, Yemen	3,594	2,148	6,990	6,603	9,417	10,173	5,180	10,813	14,631	7,840	5,108	6,515	3,944	8,222	11,364	10,975	12,817	12,745	5,214	7,141
Santa Cruz, Bolivia	13,330	11,811	19,301	18,913	16,521	6,915	10,517	5,545	11,350	18,586	10,446	18,824	9,850	16,776	6,583	6,667	4,987	8,651	11,604	18,911
Santa Cruz, Tenerife	6,139	4,888	12,159	11,813	11,881	4,530	3,514	4,646	18,527	12,037	3,412	11,734	7,219	10,976	5,621	5,255	6,577	8,183	4,681	11,810
Santa Fe, New Mexico	10,572	11,403	12,756	12,870	9,081	3,697	8,366	3,796	11,485	11,265	8,438	12,895	15,360	9,562	2,592	2,952	2,667	1,314	8,477	11,988
Santa Rosa, Argentina	14,745	12,847	18,097	18,056	17,798	9,000	12,267	7,628	9,749	19,192	12,177	18,036	9,309	18,648	8,610	8,722	6,881	10,377	13,414	18,889
Santa Rosalia, Mexico	11,610	12,507	13,050	13,231	9,313	4,709	9,471	4,590	10,435	11,550	9,543	13,271	16,132	9,972	3,549	3,930	3,043	2,140	9,559	12,332
Santarem, Brazil	11,459	10,132	17,478	17,150	15,388	5,290	8,590	3,987	13,222	16,879	8,523	17,074	9,485	15,203	5,240	5,221	4,124	7,791	9,669	16,983
Santiago del Estero, Argentina	14,157	12,435	18,994	18,826	17,274	8,021	11,483	6,648	10,467	19,512	11,403	18,773	9,610	17,794	7,646	7,749	5,960	9,536	12,602	19,704
Santiago, Chile	15,026	13,252	18,517	18,587	17,121	8,678	12,355	7,302	9,589	18,942	12,276	18,588	9,975	18,004	8,187	8,331	6,384	9,788	13,466	19,217
Santo Domingo, Dominican Rep.	10,713	10,235	15,744	15,638	12,635	2,962	7,714	1,615	13,409	14,508	7,703	15,611	11,745	12,701	2,507	2,597	1,396	4,947	8,508	14,978
Sao Paulo de Olivenca, Brazil	12,571	11,511	18,166	18,018	14,851	5,353	9,578	3,978	12,013	16,894	9,534	17,977	10,941	15,085	4,910	5,023	3,289	6,978	10,546	17,405
Sao Paulo, Brazil	12,516	10,665	17,619	17,268	17,875	7,745	10,122	6,472	11,934	18,517	10,023	17,186	8,020	17,467	7,729	7,712	6,451	10,168	11,286	17,906
Sao Tome, Sao Tome & Principe	6,778	4,660	11,424	11,038	13,459	8,439	5,907	8,260	15,697	12,233	5,774	10,951	3,336	12,252	9,446	9,108	9,910	12,134	6,820	11,570
Sapporo, Japan	6,655	8,763	3,857	4,050	154	9,980	8,341	11,250	9,587	2,356	8,460	4,098	12,983	1,207	10,012	10,014	11,425	7,735	7,193	3,153
Sarajevo, Yugoslavia	2,622	1,889	8,641	8,299	8,919	6,254	1,244	7,105	17,965	8,600	1,147	8,221	6,949	7,829	7,428	7,045	9,078	8,869	1,870	8,306
Saratov, USSR	652	2,266	6,516	6,198	6,810	7,394	2,428	8,537	15,811	6,375	2,471	6,127	7,825	5,667	8,431	8,095	10,328	8,927	1,618	6,116
Saskatoon, Canada	8,819	9,882	11,247	11,299	7,757	3,242	6,903	4,019	12,493	9,810	6,995	11,311	14,719	8,029	2,621	2,797	3,826	728	6,828	10,457
Schefferville, Canada	7,337	7,790	11,707	11,598	8,991	1,152	4,760	2,507	15,060	10,558	4,819	11,574	12,112	8,789	1,780	1,511	3,746	3,258	5,087	10,953
Seattle, Washington	9,496	10,814	10,864	10,987	7,190	4,442	7,929	5,076	11,300	9,371	8,031	11,016	15,917	7,683	3,684	3,921	4,457	790	7,698	10,101
Sendai, Japan	6,959	9,036	3,566	3,801	389	10,501	8,796	11,759	9,128	2,098	8,913	3,859	12,934	1,440	10,502	10,516	11,855	8,146	7,639	2,923
Seoul, South Korea	6,040	8,035	2,525	2,696	1,264	10,837	8,244	12,176	9,705	1,028	8,347	2,741	11,713	909	11,050	10,996	12,620	8,990	7,076	1,796
Sept-Iles, Canada	7,707	8,016	12,217	12,104	9,482	652	5,016	1,994	15,035	11,070	5,063	12,078	12,037	9,299	1,375	1,056	3,310	3,350	5,442	11,464
Sevastopol, USSR	1,449	1,312	7,441	7,094	8,017	7,192	1,973	8,164	16,757	7,472	1,949	7,016	6,918	6,867	8,326	7,957	10,091	9,353	1,824	7,132
Seville, Spain	4,783	3,741	10,808	10,471	10,614	4,811	2,178	5,321	19,903	10,661	2,067	10,395	7,240	9,653	5,995	5,606	7,325	8,152	3,345	10,438
Shanghai, China	6,056	7,910	1,652	1,854	2,090	11,599	8,546	12,958	9,463	150	8,638	1,909	11,048	1,688	11,882	11,808	13,494	9,873	7,396	973
Sheffield, United Kingdom	3,779	3,681	9,597	9,309	8,863	4,495	763	5,464	18,255	9,174	763	9,244	8,484	7,972	5,652	5,274	7,381	7,132	1,771	9,094
Shenyang, China	5,525	7,553	2,711	2,805	1,433	10,403	7,684	11,759	10,263	1,315	7,788	2,834	11,506	509	10,688	10,609	12,342	8,788	6,516	1,927
Shiraz, Iran	1,945	1,707	5,879	5,493	7,750	9,552	4,333	10,496	14,722	6,426	4,307	5,406	5,733	6,538	10,681	10,315	12,444	11,425	3,973	5,836
Sibiu, Romania	2,124	1,713	8,148	7,809	8,455	6,517	1,332	7,444	17,478	8,097	1,279	7,733	7,081	7,349	7,671	7,296	9,390	8,911	1,600	7,805
Singapore	7,130	7,967	2,192	2,188	5,805	14,768	10,149	16,103	8,478	3,640	10,178	2,196	8,242	5,408	15,403	15,224	17,222	13,655	9,269	2,985
Sioux Falls, South Dakota	9,500	10,234	12,444	12,485	8,957	2,638	7,196	3,052	12,627	11,014	7,266	12,494	14,382	9,229	1,683	1,976	2,620	1,249	7,351	11,652
Skelleftea, Sweden	2,704	3,679	7,978	7,726	7,094	5,393	1,393	6,611	16,565	7,424	1,523	7,670	9,199	6,182	6,388	6,064	8,311	7,003	553	7,410
Skopje, Yugoslavia	2,465	1,567	8,453	8,103	8,911	6,574	1,542	7,413	17,743	8,481	1,453	8,024	6,697	7,794	7,750	7,367	9,391	9,172	2,035	8,151
Socotra Island (Tamrida)	3,827	2,957	6,045	5,665	8,814	11,097	5,960	11,833	13,605	7,034	5,906	5,579	4,211	7,667	12,274	11,891	13,839	13,298	5,786	6,284
Sofia, Bulgaria	2,296	1,499	8,288	7,940	8,754	6,656	1,558	7,521	17,588	8,312	1,481	7,861	6,747	7,632	7,826	7,445	9,492	9,181	1,948	7,982
Songkhla, Thailand	6,390	7,305	1,767	1,648	5,499	14,049	9,409	15,371	9,172	3,269	9,439	1,632	8,126	4,952	14,743	14,540	16,634	13,233	8,522	2,523
Sorong, Indonesia	9,278	10,652	3,252	3,598	4,817	14,942	12,092	16,149	6,078	3,641	12,167	3,677	11,068	5,186	14,806	14,886	15,638	12,091	10,987	3,667
South Georgia Island	13,969	11,836	15,302	15,196	18,602	11,252	12,702	9,959	9,357	16,766	12,576	15,167	6,977	18,499	11,152	11,177	9,620	13,228	13,814	16,078
South Pole	15,224	13,638	12,220	12,310	14,625	14,949	15,940	13,576	5,817	13,349	15,808	12,329	8,031	15,070	14,462	14,629	12,562	15,164	16,677	12,978

Distances in Kilometers	Gur'yev, USSR	Haifa, Israel	Haikou, China	Haiphong, Vietnam	Hakodate, Japan	Halifax, Canada	Hamburg, West Germany	Hamilton, Bermuda	Hamilton, New Zealand	Hangzhou, China	Hannover, West Germany	Hanoi, Vietnam	Harare, Zimbabwe	Harbin, China	Harrisburg, Pennsylvania	Hartford, Connecticut	Havana, Cuba	Helena, Montana	Helsinki, Finland	Hengyang, China
South Sandwich Islands	13,667	11,557	14,558	14,448	18,011	11,859	12,774	10,600	9,224	16,029	12,644	14,420	6,440	17,752	11,832	11,836	10,348	13,973	13,828	15,331
Split, Yugoslavia	2,784	2,006	8,804	8,462	9,048	6,136	1,211	6,967	18,129	8,756	1,103	8,385	6,955	7,965	7,314	6,930	8,945	8,812	1,940	8,467
Spokane, Washington	9,451	10,674	11,128	11,236	7,484	4,085	7,742	4,706	11,579	9,643	7,839	11,261	15,635	7,928	3,314	3,553	4,128	425	7,576	10,357
Spoleto, Italy	3,096	2,238	9,117	8,776	9,300	5,921	1,220	6,710	18,442	9,057	1,095	8,698	6,964	8,233	7,107	6,720	8,698	8,714	2,110	8,776
Springbok, South Africa	9,163	7,149	11,317	11,024	14,779	11,644	9,251	11,088	12,178	12,689	9,122	10,956	1,873	13,707	12,447	12,179	12,194	15,337	9,977	11,863
Springfield, Illinois	9,652	10,157	13,064	13,079	9,645	2,207	7,136	2,383	12,939	11,663	7,191	13,082	13,869	9,864	1,090	1,447	1,972	1,961	7,434	12,271
Springfield, Massachusetts	8,713	8,906	13,117	13,033	10,136	781	5,955	1,291	14,355	11,888	5,991	13,013	12,433	10,089	414	38	2,291	3,151	6,444	12,347
Srinagar, India	2,406	3,681	3,824	3,454	5,716	10,330	5,426	11,534	13,060	4,264	5,455	3,371	7,384	4,532	11,278	10,976	13,231	11,043	4,595	3,692
Stanley, Falkland Islands	15,091	12,976	16,346	16,332	18,223	10,691	13,261	9,328	8,833	17,617	13,149	16,322	8,398	19,268	10,355	10,455	8,629	12,059	14,427	17,138
Stara Zagora, Bulgaria	2,132	1,345	8,109	7,758	8,645	6,829	1,694	7,707	17,399	8,155	1,627	7,679	6,694	7,512	7,994	7,615	9,673	9,298	1,975	7,813
Stockholm, Sweden	2,596	3,203	8,237	7,958	7,633	5,455	812	6,587	17,113	7,808	933	7,896	8,634	6,673	6,523	6,176	8,391	7,414	400	7,723
Stornoway, United Kingdom	3,988	4,179	9,581	9,320	8,513	4,109	1,145	5,189	17,729	9,021	1,207	9,261	9,102	7,698	5,227	4,862	7,035	6,545	1,787	9,021
Strasbourg, France	3,261	2,866	9,244	8,927	8,989	5,280	575	6,168	18,445	9,005	443	8,855	7,711	7,995	6,452	6,070	8,125	7,962	1,697	8,820
Stuttgart, West Germany	3,154	2,783	9,139	8,820	8,913	5,369	535	6,267	18,356	8,907	402	8,749	7,689	7,911	6,537	6,156	8,220	8,012	1,622	8,717
Subic, Philippines	7,176	8,693	1,198	1,580	3,571	13,401	9,969	14,758	8,185	1,702	10,042	1,668	10,430	3,475	13,650	13,595	15,140	11,436	8,872	1,548
Suchow, China	5,533	7,404	1,715	1,809	2,218	11,265	8,034	12,635	9,984	527	8,123	1,841	10,766	1,507	11,628	11,526	13,326	9,788	6,888	927
Sucre, Bolivia	13,585	12,073	19,558	19,168	16,496	7,054	10,757	5,679	11,097	18,650	10,688	19,079	10,018	16,847	6,674	6,774	5,021	8,650	11,836	19,108
Sudbury, Canada	8,667	9,136	12,548	12,505	9,397	1,371	6,113	2,100	13,886	11,243	6,169	12,494	13,109	9,433	769	848	2,595	2,364	6,431	11,762
Suez, Egypt	2,529	394	7,785	7,403	9,190	8,184	3,192	8,914	16,495	8,197	3,112	7,317	5,291	7,986	9,371	8,984	10,917	10,811	3,404	7,679
Sundsvall, Sweden	2,746	3,518	8,204	7,941	7,410	5,304	1,073	6,482	16,885	7,697	1,203	7,882	8,975	6,488	6,339	6,001	8,235	7,114	479	7,657
Surabaya, Indonesia	8,479	9,316	3,031	3,180	6,128	15,845	11,496	17,221	7,115	4,225	11,529	3,218	8,898	6,031	16,225	16,144	17,630	13,921	10,578	3,778
Suva, Fiji	14,212	16,030	8,551	8,933	7,682	13,611	15,950	13,561	2,199	8,221	16,081	9,020	14,672	8,787	12,525	12,888	11,702	9,981	14,881	8,677
Sverdlovsk, USSR	1,235	3,308	5,756	5,479	5,702	7,618	3,168	8,878	14,877	5,415	3,248	5,418	8,722	4,574	8,530	8,236	10,489	8,518	2,083	5,258
Svobodnyy, USSR	5,315	7,437	3,811	3,868	1,439	9,302	7,029	10,649	10,895	2,440	7,145	3,886	12,026	638	9,563	9,488	11,228	7,722	5,870	3,019
Sydney, Australia	13,331	14,187	7,377	7,680	8,443	16,819	16,272	16,682	2,212	7,813	16,334	7,749	11,479	9,159	15,743	16,107	14,710	13,129	15,189	7,866
Sydney, Canada	7,743	7,826	12,612	12,467	10,051	315	4,905	1,589	15,426	11,544	4,934	12,433	11,512	9,801	1,503	1,113	3,241	3,916	5,477	11,883
Syktyvkar, USSR	1,621	3,400	6,468	6,207	6,031	6,845	2,550	8,105	15,414	6,014	2,646	6,149	8,985	4,979	7,769	7,470	9,724	7,904	1,402	5,929
Szeged, Hungary	2,411	1,955	8,437	8,102	8,624	6,229	1,089	7,139	17,766	8,348	1,017	8,026	7,183	7,541	7,390	7,012	9,091	8,711	1,579	8,078
Szombathely, Hungary	2,651	2,229	8,670	8,340	8,717	5,941	845	6,847	17,984	8,532	756	8,266	7,349	7,659	7,104	6,725	8,800	8,475	1,539	8,289
Tabriz, Iran	1,102	1,178	6,417	6,050	7,643	8,466	3,252	9,452	15,597	6,688	3,234	5,967	6,392	6,436	9,585	9,222	11,375	10,381	2,879	6,223
Tacheng, China	2,351	4,311	3,865	3,586	4,543	9,362	5,036	10,674	13,097	3,679	5,105	3,525	8,840	3,328	10,161	9,908	12,127	9,560	3,976	3,407
Tahiti (Papeete)	16,186	18,251	11,693	12,082	9,703	11,049	15,637	10,565	4,093	11,002	15,739	12,171	16,092	10,918	9,858	10,249	8,581	8,039	15,251	11,634
Taipei, Taiwan	6,497	8,241	1,276	1,588	2,562	12,269	9,109	13,625	8,941	591	9,194	1,663	10,881	2,343	12,529	12,465	14,090	10,426	7,973	914
Taiyuan, China	4,963	6,864	1,987	1,967	2,439	10,858	7,462	12,234	10,561	1,098	7,551	1,974	10,491	1,459	11,300	11,170	13,076	9,652	6,321	1,216
Tallahassee, Florida	10,361	10,536	14,205	14,208	10,780	2,401	7,614	1,865	12,860	12,809	7,647	14,207	13,395	11,010	1,279	1,631	832	2,985	8,096	13,411
Tallinn, USSR	2,243	3,051	7,860	7,579	7,358	5,801	1,115	6,953	16,820	7,455	1,220	7,517	8,581	6,367	6,851	6,509	8,736	7,612	84	7,353
Tamanrasset, Algeria	4,921	3,098	10,588	10,208	11,508	6,638	3,436	6,904	18,081	10,902	3,303	10,121	5,283	10,379	7,788	7,408	8,847	10,100	4,421	10,448
Tampa, Florida	10,518	10,589	14,520	14,515	11,109	2,498	7,714	1,768	12,873	13,133	7,740	14,512	13,194	11,332	1,458	1,771	534	3,307	8,249	13,727
Tampere, Finland	2,398	3,289	7,887	7,617	7,241	5,655	1,205	6,834	16,719	7,424	1,323	7,556	8,818	6,277	6,684	6,349	8,586	7,385	163	7,356
Tanami, Australia	10,734	11,617	4,908	5,169	6,928	17,008	13,726	18,034	4,805	5,652	13,772	5,229	10,215	7,286	16,633	16,807	16,698	13,747	12,728	5,506
Tangier, Morocco	4,864	3,743	10,887	10,545	10,768	4,911	2,325	5,376	19,768	10,775	2,211	10,468	7,094	9,795	6,090	5,702	7,377	8,291	3,488	10,534
Tarawa (Betio)	12,183	14,207	7,110	7,498	5,516	12,471	13,718	12,916	4,340	6,415	13,848	7,586	15,484	6,671	11,613	11,906	11,459	8,761	12,645	7,023
Tashkent, USSR	1,528	3,169	4,524	4,179	5,776	9,391	4,529	10,597	13,847	4,690	4,567	4,102	7,646	4,561	10,346	10,041	12,295	10,264	3,661	4,251
Tbilisi, USSR	827	1,308	6,546	6,189	7,509	8,086	2,886	9,105	15,819	6,704	2,879	6,109	6,741	6,315	9,193	8,834	11,006	9,958	2,460	6,294
Tegucigalpa, Honduras	12,102	11,981	15,774	15,853	12,117	4,057	9,228	3,043	11,612	14,294	9,242	15,868	13,441	12,559	3,069	3,373	1,123	4,282	9,833	14,994
Tehran, Iran	1,272	1,544	5,962	5,588	7,433	8,972	3,766	9,976	15,079	6,324	3,753	5,503	6,300	6,218	10,079	9,721	11,889	10,745	3,319	5,813
Tel Aviv, Israel	2,216	88	7,532	7,153	8,876	8,182	3,098	8,971	16,390	7,907	3,029	7,067	5,536	7,673	9,361	8,977	10,965	10,679	3,206	7,404
Telegraph Creek, Canada	8,361	9,867	9,691	9,785	6,105	4,718	7,161	5,657	11,717	8,219	7,277	9,807	15,323	6,480	4,275	4,406	5,463	1,802	6,747	8,913
Teresina, Brazil	10,778	9,187	16,681	16,300	15,928	5,887	8,145	4,744	13,848	16,704	8,056	16,213	8,138	15,385	6,111	6,008	5,312	8,859	9,293	16,466
Ternate, Indonesia	8,851	10,191	2,828	3,162	4,729	14,855	11,704	16,128	6,507	3,348	11,773	3,239	10,718	4,980	14,838	14,879	15,852	12,222	10,615	3,294
The Valley, Anguilla	10,316	9,667	15,730	15,559	12,949	2,950	7,297	1,586	13,985	14,649	7,273	15,518	11,035	12,872	2,797	2,784	2,087	5,468	8,175	15,010
Thessaloniki, Greece	2,420	1,380	8,373	8,018	8,944	6,761	1,734	7,585	17,625	8,445	1,647	7,938	6,527	7,812	7,938	7,554	9,568	9,364	2,177	8,092
Thimphu, Bhutan	3,939	5,245	2,253	1,873	4,857	11,566	6,933	12,858	11,470	2,977	6,975	1,787	8,075	3,823	12,373	12,122	14,335	11,510	6,002	2,265
Thunder Bay, Canada	8,777	9,449	12,177	12,170	8,880	2,007	6,411	2,727	13,384	10,814	6,480	12,168	13,705	9,005	1,339	1,499	2,870	1,717	6,598	11,384
Tientsin, China	5,232	7,187	2,216	2,261	2,010	10,725	7,604	12,095	10,382	1,022	7,699	2,281	10,920	1,069	11,097	10,990	12,819	9,327	6,448	1,423
Tijuana, Mexico	11,114	12,200	12,321	12,497	8,585	4,753	9,192	4,864	10,478	10,819	9,276	12,536	16,439	9,235	3,668	4,023	3,551	1,618	9,160	11,598
Tiksi, USSR	4,677	6,708	5,854	5,817	3,389	7,073	5,324	8,434	12,668	4,630	5,453	5,812	12,145	2,882	7,433	7,317	9,228	6,056	4,267	5,072
Timbuktu, Mali	6,022	4,205	11,682	11,299	12,536	6,399	4,236	6,403	17,670	12,016	4,106	11,212	5,347	11,437	7,468	7,110	8,238	10,053	5,318	11,560
Tindouf, Algeria	5,580	4,163	11,551	11,191	11,679	5,219	3,234	5,425	18,843	11,572	3,116	11,109	6,576	10,683	6,344	5,970	7,370	8,796	4,389	11,267
Tirane, Albania	2,620	1,642	8,605	8,254	9,057	6,502	1,544	7,315	17,885	8,637	1,446	8,175	6,652	7,944	7,682	7,297	9,300	9,166	2,125	8,306
Tokyo, Japan	7,066	9,116	3,359	3,614	677	10,801	9,002	12,058	8,923	1,925	9,116	3,675	12,818	1,569	10,798	10,814	12,134	8,421	7,839	2,753
Toledo, Spain	4,494	3,559	10,518	10,186	10,292	4,835	1,854	5,432	19,767	10,345	1,742	10,110	7,352	9,329	6,027	5,636	7,438	8,070	3,020	10,134
Topeka, Kansas	9,933	10,564	12,928	12,978	9,400	2,716	7,530	2,882	12,448	11,486	7,592	12,988	14,394	9,710	1,615	1,969	2,169	1,574	7,753	12,138
Toronto, Canada	8,871	9,240	12,881	12,833	9,733	1,265	6,239	1,796	13,894	11,582	6,287	12,821	12,993	9,772	431	588	2,294	2,570	6,619	12,096
Toulouse, France	3,903	3,147	9,921	9,593	9,716	5,063	1,272	5,797	19,184	9,731	1,153	9,519	7,444	8,732	6,256	5,866	7,792	8,069	2,428	9,524
Tours, France	3,804	3,304	9,778	9,464	9,376	4,843	951	5,670	18,853	9,500	853	9,393	7,835	8,424	6,028	5,641	7,644	7,718	2,120	9,340
Townsville, Australia	11,919	13,152	5,894	6,230	6,782	16,036	14,718	16,564	3,439	6,176	14,799	6,306	11,895	7,480	15,263	15,542	14,933	12,384	13,588	6,301
Trenton, New Jersey	8,988	9,177	13,311	13,240	10,248	1,041	6,231	1,257	14,112	12,052	6,267	13,223	12,600	10,247	180	246	2,026	3,069	6,720	12,535
Tripoli, Lebanon	1,946	194	7,388	7,014	8,623	8,079	2,937	8,915	16,382	7,709	2,877	6,929	5,807	7,424	9,248	8,868	10,899	10,473	2,968	7,229
Tripoli, Libya	3,614	2,038	9,460	9,092	10,157	6,551	2,308	7,132	18,313	9,633	2,181	9,009	5,928	9,032	7,745	7,354	9,137	9,635	3,152	9,238
Tristan da Cunha (Edinburgh)	11,299	9,164	14,196	13,920	17,652	10,416	10,266	9,415	11,683	15,599	10,134	13,855	4,732	16,497	10,803	10,667	9,909	13,556	11,302	14,771
Trondheim, Norway	3,115	3,808	8,512	8,258	7,549	4,936	1,099	6,121	16,978	7,950	1,231	8,201	9,184	6,674	5,971	5,633	7,867	6,805	846	7,944
Trujillo, Peru	13,682	12,744	18,355	18,471	14,623	6,046	10,665	4,721	10,818	16,853	10,633	18,486	11,833	15,168	5,361	5,561	3,476	6,886	11,559	17,598
Truk Island (Moen)	10,158	12,005	4,690	5,079	3,958	13,237	12,361	14,151	5,565	4,161	12,473	5,168	13,528	4,889	12,750	12,931	13,229	9,879	11,195	4,671
Truro, Canada	7,967	8,079	12,732	12,601	10,066	84	5,149	1,458	15,174	11,624	5,179	12,570	11,732	9,864	1,247	858	3,013	3,720	5,698	11,991
Tsingtao, China	5,650	7,578	2,026	2,145	1,873	11,057	8,041	12,420	9,945	645	8,137	2,181	11,095	1,200	11,372	11,285	13,034	9,467	6,884	1,252
Tsitsihar, China	5,250	7,338	3,272	3,326	1,467	9,784	7,209	11,140	10,722	1,928	7,318	3,345	11,663	274	10,082	9,996	11,765	8,263	6,041	2,479
Tubuai Island (Mataura)	16,761	18,872	11,878	12,266	10,170	11,486	16,239	10,897	3,711	11,318	16,335	12,354	15,446	11,382	10,292	10,683	8,895	8,616	15,894	11,898
Tucson, Arizona	11,053	11,972	12,749	12,901	9,026	4,293	8,939	4,319	10,883	11,247	9,014	12,935	15,904	9,611	3,170	3,537	2,985	1,599	9,005	12,006
Tulsa, Oklahoma	10,240	10,824	13,203	13,263	9,638	2,878	7,796	2,889	12,261	11,749	7,855	13,276	14,460	9,983	1,724	2,100	1,946	1,772	8,049	12,415
Tunis, Tunisia	3,594	2,306	9,558	9,201	9,963	6,080	1,862	6,718	18,701	9,611	1,730	9,121	6,432	8,876	7,275	6,884	8,724	9,123	2,804	9,276
Tura, USSR	3,467	5,584	4,971	4,847	3,588	7,844	4,871	9,219	13,054	4,033	4,985	4,823	10,816	2,626	8,411	8,231	10,311	7,392	3,710	4,249
Turin, Italy	3,382	2,711	9,402	9,072	9,321	5,441	960	6,248	18,706	9,242	827	8,998	7,355	8,302	6,626	6,239	8,230	8,265	2,037	9,016
Uberlandia, Brazil	12,291	10,534	17,788	17,408	17,337	7,210	9,770	5,933	12,255	18,306	9,677	17,321	8,306	16,995	7,192	7,174	5,947	9,660	10,925	17,883
Ufa, USSR	894	2,935	5,945	5,651	6,061	7,607	2,951	8,831	15,154	5,691	3,019	5,585	8,381	4,921	8,564	8,255	10,509	8,718	1,934	5,487
Ujungpandang, Indonesia	8,758	9,798	2,956	3,192	5,623	15,615	11,740	16,967	6,700	3,915	11,788	3,249	9,671	5,680	15,788	15,773	16,950	13,288	10,743	3,617
Ulaanbaatar, Mongolia	4,054	6,099	3,107	3,001	2,738	9,707	6,323	11,083	11,658	2,266	6,418	2,984	10,449	1,523	10,229	10,069	12,082	8,875	5,166	2,385
Ulan-Ude, USSR	3,973	6,068	3,535	3,438	2,734	9,280	6,056	10,657	11,898	2,610	6,157	3,422	10,659	1,547	9,792	9,634	11,644	8,461	4,891	2,800
Uliastay, Mongolia	3,342	5,357	3,306	3,112	3,491	9,591	5,785	10,952	12,247	2,784	5,870	3,073	9,763	2,276	10,235	10,034	12,154	9,183	4,654	2,692
Uranium City, Canada	8,046	9,232	10,501	10,531	7,121	3,411	6,323	4,420	12,832	9,095	6,425	10,538	14,359	7,296	3,076	3,156	4,539	1,461	6,133	9,708
Urumqi, China	2,792	4,674	3,376	3,098	4,279	9,801	5,524	11,125	12,621	3,237	5,593	3,039	8,923	3,069	10,565	10,325	12,523	9,807	4,465	2,927
Ushuaia, Argentina	15,860	13,739	16,146	16,214	17,446	11,030	13,986	9,654	8,101	17,196	13,878	16,224	8,989	18,551	10,566	10,709	8,739	11,966	15,155	16,905
Vaduz, Liechtenstein	3,174	2,676	9,181	8,856	9,046	5,466	711	6,331	18,452	8,989	579	8,783	7,515	8,030	6,641	6,258	8,296	8,167	1,762	8,778
Valencia, Spain	4,243	3,245	10,268	9,930	10,191	5,134	1,752	5,748	19,599	10,147	1,630	9,853	7,135	9,194	6,327	5,936	7,753	8,314	2,899	9,907
Valladolid, Spain	4,452	3,623	10,466	10,140	10,138	4,696	1,718	5,339	19,575	10,248	1,614	10,066	7,545	9,192	5,890	5,499	7,342	7,886	2,887	10,060
Valletta, Malta	3,321	1,911	9,230	8,868	9,817	6,459	1,993	7,117	18,301	9,346	1,869	8,786	6,197	8,700	7,653	7,262	9,122	9,427	2,801	8,977
Valparaiso, Chile	15,072	13,318	18,554	18,647	17,020	8,641	12,376	7,266	9,555	18,867	12,299	18,653	10,076	17,909	8,133	8,283	6,320	9,706	13,481	19,218
Vancouver, Canada	9,316	10,659	10,700	10,817	7,038	4,442	7,793	5,130	11,387	9,209	7,897	10,845	15,824	7,511	3,731	3,952	4,584	879	7,538	9,933
Varna, Bulgaria	1,925	1,308	7,909	7,560	8,451	6,927	1,747	7,836	17,210	7,948	1,693	7,481	6,767	7,313	8,084	7,708	9,792	9,304	1,896	7,608
Venice, Italy	3,020	2,394	9,044	8,711	9,075	5,747	917	6,592	18,365	8,916	793	8,636	7,258	8,029	6,925	6,541	8,564	8,451	1,838	8,670

Distances
in
Kilometers

	Gur'yev, USSR	Haifa, Israel	Haikou, China	Haiphong, Vietnam	Hakodate, Japan	Halifax, Canada	Hamburg, West Germany	Hamilton, Bermuda	Hamilton, New Zealand	Hangzhou, China	Hannover, West Germany	Hanoi, Vietnam	Harare, Zimbabwe	Harbin, China	Harrisburg, Pennsylvania	Hartford, Connecticut	Havana, Cuba	Helena, Montana	Helsinki, Finland	Hengyang, China
Veracruz, Mexico	11,996	12,262	14,801	14,930	11,090	4,125	9,328	3,448	11,175	13,302	9,365	14,957	14,477	11,624	2,972	3,344	1,494	3,368	9,751	14,043
Verona, Italy	3,120	2,488	9,143	8,811	9,136	5,654	904	6,490	18,460	9,003	775	8,737	7,295	8,099	6,834	6,449	8,465	8,389	1,880	8,764
Victoria, Canada	9,408	10,751	10,745	10,867	7,074	4,486	7,882	5,150	11,310	9,252	7,985	10,896	15,903	7,562	3,754	3,983	4,565	877	7,631	9,981
Victoria, Seychelles	5,742	4,674	6,590	6,262	9,959	12,642	7,711	13,114	12,248	7,883	7,640	6,188	3,033	8,937	13,836	13,445	15,059	15,200	7,661	7,063
Vienna, Austria	2,647	2,313	8,657	8,331	8,645	5,873	744	6,797	17,955	8,494	662	8,258	7,458	7,596	7,032	6,654	8,742	8,375	1,443	8,264
Vientiane, Laos	5,620	6,887	844	536	4,472	12,932	8,589	14,285	9,777	2,240	8,638	481	8,775	3,799	13,558	13,374	15,426	12,059	7,607	1,426
Villahermosa, Mexico	11,985	12,126	15,100	15,211	11,407	4,023	9,241	3,236	11,370	13,606	9,271	15,234	14,121	11,904	2,910	3,264	1,238	3,626	9,725	14,332
Vilnius, USSR	2,034	2,544	7,895	7,591	7,695	6,074	1,007	7,156	17,070	7,617	1,064	7,523	8,053	6,654	7,166	6,811	9,006	8,087	611	7,444
Visby, Sweden	2,533	3,033	8,265	7,977	7,763	5,539	692	6,644	17,236	7,879	802	7,913	8,446	6,785	6,624	6,271	8,473	7,578	476	7,769
Vitoria, Brazil	11,803	9,930	16,972	16,602	17,626	7,572	9,499	6,376	12,577	17,781	9,395	16,518	7,459	16,946	7,702	7,638	6,626	10,310	10,668	17,182
Vladivostok, USSR	6,027	8,105	3,258	3,405	741	10,160	7,950	11,483	9,976	1,769	8,062	3,444	12,215	509	10,328	10,286	11,876	8,247	6,784	2,507
Volgograd, USSR	586	1,935	6,600	6,270	7,077	7,523	2,441	8,625	15,927	6,545	2,467	6,196	7,493	5,920	8,588	8,243	10,458	9,198	1,778	6,242
Vologda, USSR	1,562	2,955	7,000	6,718	6,688	6,553	1,933	7,752	16,059	6,629	2,019	6,656	8,578	5,636	7,551	7,227	9,474	7,999	846	6,501
Vorkuta, USSR	2,374	4,289	6,183	5,973	5,250	6,816	3,207	8,146	14,718	5,511	3,320	5,927	9,839	4,274	7,611	7,353	9,578	7,348	2,044	5,557
Wake Island	10,197	12,291	5,879	6,238	3,494	11,291	11,631	12,110	6,381	4,821	11,760	6,320	15,357	4,691	10,712	10,915	11,185	7,824	10,547	5,562
Wallis Island	14,200	16,191	8,852	9,241	7,529	12,822	15,507	12,796	2,842	8,345	15,640	9,329	15,458	8,689	11,739	12,100	10,969	9,200	14,524	8,884
Walvis Bay, Namibia	8,619	6,546	11,432	11,108	14,648	10,883	8,486	10,403	12,990	12,708	8,356	11,033	1,817	13,499	11,735	11,450	11,648	14,598	9,261	11,896
Warsaw, Poland	2,282	2,435	8,225	7,912	8,089	5,952	753	6,974	17,451	7,990	769	7,842	7,825	7,047	7,075	6,710	8,867	8,175	915	7,796
Washington, D.C.	9,218	9,422	13,436	13,378	10,294	1,285	6,474	1,330	13,875	12,146	6,510	13,364	12,785	10,337	153	489	1,819	2,963	6,951	12,653
Watson Lake, Canada	8,117	9,597	9,659	9,737	6,128	4,540	6,880	5,530	11,991	8,202	6,995	9,755	15,041	6,441	4,164	4,271	5,448	1,863	6,474	8,875
Weimar, East Germany	2,958	2,791	8,908	8,597	8,623	5,409	299	6,365	18,075	8,642	190	8,527	7,863	7,625	6,562	6,187	8,293	7,911	1,331	8,469
Wellington, New Zealand	15,513	16,361	9,496	9,823	9,817	15,346	18,237	14,719	393	9,709	18,341	9,897	12,472	10,763	14,152	14,544	12,715	12,129	17,068	9,899
West Berlin, West Germany	2,799	2,791	8,717	8,410	8,401	5,473	255	6,468	17,853	8,429	251	8,341	7,978	7,403	6,612	6,241	8,376	7,861	1,109	8,267
Wewak, Papua New Guinea	10,430	11,967	4,481	4,853	5,025	14,735	13,051	15,671	4,974	4,498	13,143	4,938	12,272	5,714	14,270	14,451	14,630	11,391	11,896	4,742
Whangarei, New Zealand	15,161	16,295	9,139	9,482	9,238	15,095	17,681	14,635	245	9,243	17,797	9,560	12,934	10,213	13,917	14,305	12,635	11,709	16,519	9,488
Whitehorse, Canada	8,034	9,597	9,335	9,421	5,784	4,867	6,962	5,876	11,814	7,871	7,081	9,442	15,117	6,120	4,513	4,615	5,789	2,166	6,488	8,554
Wichita, Kansas	10,125	10,772	12,992	13,055	9,425	2,911	7,737	3,018	12,245	11,536	7,800	13,068	14,562	9,772	1,791	2,154	2,156	1,561	7,953	12,205
Willemstad, Curacao	11,222	10,559	16,446	16,326	13,316	3,642	8,204	2,274	13,090	15,217	8,182	16,295	11,467	13,409	3,215	3,306	1,872	5,554	9,063	15,685
Wiluna, Australia	10,649	11,154	5,271	5,451	7,856	17,973	13,661	19,220	5,262	6,291	13,677	5,493	9,066	8,038	17,827	17,957	17,720	14,959	12,819	5,976
Windhoek, Namibia	8,473	6,422	11,166	10,844	14,410	11,042	8,462	10,603	12,947	12,450	8,334	10,769	1,551	13,272	11,922	11,628	11,886	14,764	9,199	11,636
Windsor, Canada	9,151	9,564	12,968	12,941	9,717	1,589	6,556	1,957	13,562	11,630	6,606	12,934	13,294	9,819	561	858	2,127	2,344	6,909	12,178
Winnipeg, Canada	8,852	9,703	11,801	11,825	8,398	2,582	6,676	3,309	12,941	10,397	6,756	11,830	14,215	8,598	1,911	2,092	2,237	1,162	6,746	11,008
Winston-Salem, North Carolina	9,630	9,838	13,692	13,658	10,433	1,698	6,894	1,486	13,488	12,358	6,930	13,649	13,053	10,548	548	908	1,452	2,879	7,365	12,903
Wroclaw, Poland	2,558	2,502	8,522	8,207	8,366	5,767	551	6,750	17,752	8,292	525	8,136	7,758	7,336	6,907	6,536	8,666	8,134	1,125	8,097
Wuhan, China	5,558	7,327	1,233	1,317	2,668	11,671	8,196	13,046	9,873	568	8,278	1,352	10,381	1,998	12,077	11,962	13,803	10,279	7,073	439
Wyndham, Australia	10,247	11,215	4,384	4,651	6,466	16,589	13,225	17,741	5,237	5,130	13,275	4,713	10,219	6,781	16,354	16,480	16,727	13,519	12,212	4,978
Xi'an, China	4,909	6,702	1,582	1,501	2,896	11,232	7,564	12,608	10,519	1,150	7,643	1,497	10,045	1,973	11,731	11,584	13,542	10,159	6,449	890
Xining, China	4,225	6,005	2,016	1,810	3,384	10,885	6,943	12,250	11,178	1,847	7,017	1,772	9,554	2,308	11,491	11,306	13,377	10,192	5,853	1,486
Yakutsk, USSR	4,951	7,074	4,893	4,898	2,370	8,122	6,148	9,474	11,795	3,596	6,272	4,904	12,190	1,819	8,421	8,328	12,002	6,777	5,026	4,102
Yanji, China	5,881	7,947	3,104	3,238	931	10,222	7,868	11,555	10,061	1,630	7,978	3,275	12,019	392	10,422	10,370	12,002	8,391	6,701	2,343
Yaounde, Cameroon	6,159	4,031	10,786	10,399	12,819	8,534	5,510	8,497	15,905	11,573	5,379	10,311	3,218	11,609	9,602	9,246	10,247	12,161	6,349	10,916
Yap Island (Colonia)	8,958	10,650	3,207	3,596	3,581	13,623	11,491	14,784	6,508	2,958	11,586	3,685	12,136	4,163	13,429	13,519	14,322	10,721	10,332	3,303
Yaraka, Australia	12,153	13,178	6,171	6,481	7,385	16,695	15,064	17,099	3,275	6,614	15,130	6,551	11,366	8,018	15,862	16,162	15,325	13,012	13,976	6,653
Yarmouth, Canada	8,242	8,360	12,922	12,803	10,155	221	5,432	1,287	14,916	11,777	5,463	12,776	11,929	10,001	975	583	2,737	3,568	5,973	12,172
Yellowknife, Canada	7,796	9,094	10,056	10,089	6,680	3,765	6,257	4,828	12,747	8,648	6,365	10,098	14,378	6,849	3,503	3,564	4,985	1,771	5,973	9,263
Yerevan, USSR	973	1,177	6,568	6,207	7,627	8,190	2,979	9,188	15,805	6,771	2,965	6,125	6,572	6,428	9,306	8,945	11,103	10,115	2,602	6,340
Yinchuan, China	4,462	6,327	2,078	1,951	2,936	10,744	7,058	12,118	11,005	1,564	7,140	1,933	10,005	1,859	11,280	11,119	13,126	9,842	5,937	1,411
Yogyakarta, Indonesia	8,367	9,133	3,080	3,196	6,299	15,880	11,387	17,248	7,284	4,339	11,415	3,227	8,628	6,149	16,338	16,230	17,841	14,124	10,499	3,847
York, United Kingdom	3,747	3,682	9,553	9,266	8,807	4,504	738	5,485	18,200	9,123	746	9,201	8,517	7,917	5,657	5,281	7,396	7,112	1,723	9,046
Yumen, China	3,741	5,571	2,501	2,269	3,596	10,463	6,441	11,820	11,676	2,297	6,515	2,223	9,401	2,441	11,118	10,916	13,034	9,987	5,354	1,988
Yutian, China	2,699	4,252	3,344	2,998	5,019	10,327	5,664	11,597	12,667	3,622	5,710	2,922	8,056	3,837	11,189	10,917	13,158	10,660	4,722	3,109
Yuzhno-Sakhalinsk, USSR	6,479	8,605	4,185	4,349	600	9,534	8,007	10,808	9,930	2,684	8,129	4,390	13,079	1,243	9,580	9,575	11,026	7,354	6,871	3,450
Zagreb, Yugoslavia	2,736	2,171	8,762	8,427	8,871	5,977	964	6,852	18,088	8,654	862	8,352	7,209	7,806	7,148	6,767	8,816	8,581	1,705	8,396
Zahedan, Iran	2,104	2,487	5,072	4,686	7,103	10,057	4,871	11,089	13,994	5,661	4,863	4,599	6,139	5,905	11,140	10,791	12,985	11,547	4,332	5,046
Zamboanga, Philippines	7,954	9,329	1,931	2,266	4,278	14,267	10,815	15,609	7,403	2,592	10,882	2,344	10,357	4,328	14,436	14,412	15,761	12,047	9,737	2,430
Zanzibar, Tanzania	6,034	4,339	8,301	7,954	11,423	11,502	7,162	11,690	13,360	9,497	7,062	7,874	1,346	10,301	12,655	12,275	13,508	14,750	7,460	8,698
Zaragoza, Spain	4,169	3,304	10,191	9,860	9,998	4,985	1,554	5,653	19,473	10,018	1,437	9,785	7,360	9,020	6,180	5,789	7,656	8,106	2,714	9,804
Zashiversk, USSR	5,317	7,380	5,737	5,754	2,863	7,379	6,019	8,710	11,989	4,396	6,150	5,761	12,738	2,589	7,607	7,534	9,299	5,917	4,973	4,943
Zhengzhou, China	5,238	7,087	1,662	1,684	2,480	11,207	7,795	12,583	10,245	788	7,881	1,702	10,475	1,643	11,629	11,507	13,380	9,905	6,660	876
Zurich, Switzerland	3,251	2,763	9,253	8,931	9,076	5,378	698	6,242	18,505	9,047	565	8,858	7,569	8,069	6,554	6,170	8,207	8,096	1,786	8,844

Distances in Kilometers	Herat, Afghanistan	Hermosillo, Mexico	Hiroshima, Japan	Hiva Oa (Atuona)	Ho Chi Minh City, Vietnam	Hobart, Australia	Hohhot, China	Hong Kong	Honiara, Solomon Islands	Honolulu, Hawaii	Houston, Texas	Huambo, Angola	Hubli, India	Hugh Town, United Kingdom	Hull, Canada	Hyderabad, India	Hyderabad, Pakistan	Igloolik, Canada	Iloilo, Philippines	Indianapolis, Indiana
Hermosillo, Mexico	12,951	0	10,336	5,252	14,040	13,049	11,118	12,557	10,430	4,774	1,515	14,254	15,047	8,551	3,574	14,767	13,981	4,858	12,787	2,559
Hiroshima, Japan	6,320	10,336	0	10,487	3,704	8,695	1,966	2,236	5,653	6,886	11,316	13,245	6,075	9,823	10,721	5,657	6,171	8,163	2,811	10,889
Hiva Oa (Atuona)	16,542	5,252	10,487	0	12,853	7,943	12,346	12,146	6,688	4,010	6,407	16,286	16,273	13,803	8,783	15,898	16,659	9,812	11,126	7,730
Ho Chi Minh City, Vietnam	5,208	14,040	3,704	12,853	0	7,238	3,363	1,503	6,308	10,145	14,944	10,372	3,451	10,685	13,778	3,129	4,345	11,091	1,739	14,258
Hobart, Australia	12,153	13,049	8,695	7,943	7,238	0	9,941	7,976	3,909	9,057	14,343	12,124	9,768	17,862	16,606	9,686	11,051	15,965	6,450	15,607
Hohhot, China	4,367	11,118	1,966	12,346	3,363	9,941	0	2,069	7,446	8,537	11,716	11,413	4,504	8,279	10,427	4,098	4,332	7,738	3,503	10,905
Hong Kong	5,213	12,557	2,236	12,146	1,503	7,976	2,069	0	6,102	8,945	13,445	11,395	4,170	10,106	12,443	3,770	4,658	9,763	1,560	12,824
Honiara, Solomon Islands	11,309	10,430	5,653	6,688	6,308	3,909	7,446	6,102	0	5,730	11,945	15,369	9,740	15,341	13,400	9,436	10,618	12,064	4,701	12,718
Honolulu, Hawaii	12,537	4,774	6,886	4,010	10,145	9,057	8,537	8,945	5,730	0	6,278	18,849	12,956	11,633	7,752	12,538	12,834	7,260	8,519	6,993
Houston, Texas	12,531	1,515	11,316	6,407	14,944	14,343	11,716	13,445	11,945	6,278	0	12,739	14,912	7,477	2,443	14,746	13,664	4,492	13,971	1,392
Huambo, Angola	7,156	14,254	13,245	16,286	10,372	12,124	11,413	11,395	15,369	18,849	12,739	0	7,241	7,269	11,125	7,652	7,090	11,617	12,078	11,923
Hubli, India	2,472	15,047	6,075	16,273	3,451	9,768	4,504	4,170	9,740	12,956	14,912	7,241	0	8,112	12,666	418	1,316	10,432	5,158	13,605
Hugh Town, United Kingdom	5,709	8,551	9,823	13,803	10,685	17,862	8,279	10,106	15,341	11,633	7,477	7,269	8,112	0	5,047	8,180	6,819	4,392	11,665	6,107
Hull, Canada	10,212	3,574	10,721	8,783	13,778	16,606	10,427	12,443	13,400	7,752	2,443	11,125	12,666	5,047	0	12,579	11,367	2,689	13,524	1,060
Hyderabad, India	2,480	14,767	5,657	15,898	3,129	9,686	4,098	3,770	9,436	12,538	14,746	7,652	418	8,180	12,579	0	1,370	10,255	4,810	13,481
Hyderabad, Pakistan	1,158	13,981	6,171	16,659	4,345	11,051	4,332	4,658	10,618	12,834	13,664	7,090	1,316	6,819	11,367	1,370	0	9,226	5,923	12,327
Igloolik, Canada	8,135	4,858	8,163	9,812	11,091	15,965	7,738	9,763	12,064	7,260	4,492	11,617	10,432	4,392	2,689	10,255	9,226	0	10,922	3,307
Iloilo, Philippines	6,633	12,787	2,811	11,126	1,739	6,450	3,503	1,560	4,701	8,519	13,971	12,078	5,158	11,665	13,524	4,810	5,923	10,922	0	13,684
Indianapolis, Indiana	11,182	2,559	10,889	7,730	14,258	15,607	10,905	12,824	12,718	6,993	1,392	11,923	13,605	6,107	1,060	13,481	12,327	3,307	13,684	0
Innsbruck, Austria	4,434	9,778	9,224	15,012	9,534	16,564	7,485	9,133	14,877	12,334	8,778	6,660	6,796	1,336	6,338	6,884	5,517	5,310	10,686	7,396
Inuvik, Canada	8,542	4,616	6,651	8,679	10,052	13,934	6,760	8,585	10,034	5,486	4,959	13,450	10,438	6,189	4,117	10,151	9,456	2,032	9,461	4,255
Invercargill, New Zealand	13,837	11,630	9,646	6,404	8,802	1,706	11,176	9,353	4,175	8,235	12,793	12,908	11,472	19,455	15,186	11,381	12,749	15,492	7,794	14,134
Inverness, United Kingdom	5,486	8,255	9,049	13,469	10,216	17,448	7,593	9,498	14,506	10,937	7,336	7,995	7,948	851	4,898	7,960	6,634	3,784	11,043	5,944
Iquitos, Peru	14,314	5,424	15,707	7,293	19,232	13,431	15,876	17,813	13,957	9,610	4,396	9,822	16,344	8,709	5,455	16,596	15,280	8,143	18,126	4,998
Iraklion, Greece	3,373	11,527	9,220	16,759	8,565	15,052	7,294	8,533	14,626	13,727	10,489	5,411	5,433	3,013	8,059	5,608	4,265	6,995	9,996	9,119
Irkutsk, USSR	3,880	10,364	2,989	12,664	4,609	11,328	1,392	3,437	8,637	8,673	10,718	11,019	4,838	6,940	9,178	4,485	4,244	6,502	4,895	9,757
Islamabad, Pakistan	1,015	13,044	5,392	15,800	4,254	11,347	3,472	4,198	10,295	11,873	12,878	7,956	2,043	6,522	10,700	1,884	1,034	8,392	5,627	11,598
Istanbul, Turkey	3,005	11,221	8,578	16,352	8,205	15,025	6,676	8,034	14,080	13,068	10,307	6,104	5,269	2,899	7,864	5,388	4,019	6,540	9,538	8,918
Ivujivik, Canada	8,706	4,411	8,936	9,549	11,884	16,376	8,534	10,560	12,547	7,412	3,842	11,442	11,071	4,401	1,894	10,921	9,826	798	11,708	2,578
Iwo Jima Island, Japan	7,554	10,265	1,369	9,438	3,975	7,521	3,276	2,784	4,291	6,193	11,471	14,176	6,938	11,138	11,375	6,530	7,260	9,007	2,522	11,333
Izmir, Turkey	3,159	11,365	8,872	16,551	8,367	15,046	6,957	8,260	14,333	13,372	10,393	5,785	5,334	2,934	7,952	5,480	4,119	6,747	9,747	9,011
Jackson, Mississippi	12,087	2,019	11,386	6,972	14,918	14,910	11,610	13,439	12,434	6,731	568	12,254	14,508	6,928	1,918	14,377	13,232	4,159	14,117	905
Jaffna, Sri Lanka	3,280	15,562	5,985	15,756	2,924	8,951	4,644	3,901	9,106	12,838	15,614	7,519	819	8,931	13,439	870	2,129	11,122	4,662	14,350
Jakarta, Indonesia	6,484	15,319	5,238	12,525	1,871	5,688	5,222	3,244	5,869	10,815	16,521	9,978	4,223	12,177	15,646	4,061	5,428	12,958	2,556	16,066
Jamestown, St. Helena	9,081	12,320	15,382	14,150	12,717	12,934	13,446	13,707	16,793	17,039	10,845	2,345	9,538	7,294	9,773	9,941	9,234	11,115	14,416	10,338
Jamnagar, India	1,523	14,301	6,159	16,626	4,102	10,704	4,380	4,526	10,400	12,914	14,020	7,086	953	7,169	11,731	1,044	365	9,572	5,723	12,688
Jan Mayen Island	5,759	7,397	7,924	12,399	9,773	16,616	6,749	8,782	13,124	9,486	6,776	9,477	8,190	2,353	4,482	8,098	6,903	2,594	10,249	5,424
Jayapura, Indonesia	9,118	11,933	4,178	8,904	4,046	4,522	5,633	3,980	2,263	7,186	13,400	13,718	7,479	13,906	14,080	7,173	8,369	11,956	2,486	13,754
Jefferson City, Missouri	11,513	2,029	10,713	7,229	14,207	15,078	10,892	12,736	12,215	6,486	1,020	12,442	13,893	6,590	1,556	13,735	12,643	3,485	13,474	536
Jerusalem, Israel	2,527	12,387	8,682	17,503	7,641	14,043	6,720	7,740	13,834	13,969	11,435	5,344	4,431	3,971	8,994	4,625	3,305	7,700	9,146	10,052
Jiggalong, Australia	8,897	14,861	6,515	10,610	4,079	3,264	7,169	5,101	4,441	10,106	16,376	10,944	6,559	14,600	17,146	6,444	7,814	14,677	3,777	16,905
Jinan, China	4,910	11,178	1,422	11,902	3,053	9,334	654	1,621	6,795	8,211	11,916	11,843	4,755	8,921	10,823	4,338	4,757	8,145	2,930	11,217
Jodhpur, India	1,370	13,865	5,704	16,191	3,928	10,783	3,888	4,184	10,170	12,143	13,681	7,549	1,231	7,079	11,459	1,134	479	9,203	5,471	12,382
Johannesburg, South Africa	7,606	15,996	12,859	15,788	9,421	10,158	11,356	10,710	13,496	19,208	14,506	1,970	6,863	9,091	13,081	7,277	7,161	13,481	10,977	13,835
Juazeiro do Norte, Brazil	11,521	8,644	16,879	10,938	16,280	14,414	15,309	16,734	17,203	13,260	7,248	6,065	12,851	7,088	6,866	13,203	12,134	9,094	18,009	7,082
Juneau, Alaska	9,623	3,716	7,001	7,561	10,599	13,328	7,448	9,099	9,521	4,521	4,346	14,368	11,407	7,112	4,134	11,093	10,495	2,755	9,751	3,967
Kabul, Afghanistan	644	12,967	5,710	16,051	4,621	11,677	3,770	4,571	10,670	12,082	12,708	7,691	2,206	6,187	10,475	2,110	1,017	8,242	6,004	11,400
Kalgoorlie, Australia	9,515	15,008	7,303	10,357	4,857	2,657	7,985	5,916	4,629	10,359	16,499	10,750	7,111	15,218	17,802	7,039	8,399	15,463	4,588	17,332
Kaliningrad, USSR	3,927	9,632	8,200	14,706	8,794	16,007	6,507	8,246	13,849	11,580	8,832	7,487	6,388	1,892	6,411	6,405	5,073	4,897	9,807	7,441
Kamloops, Canada	10,586	2,524	8,206	6,940	11,833	13,667	8,688	10,332	10,099	4,612	3,116	14,237	12,538	7,228	3,322	12,247	11,540	2,904	10,916	2,910
Kampala, Uganda	4,867	14,964	10,900	18,618	8,272	12,026	9,065	9,136	14,120	17,362	13,587	2,350	4,967	6,621	11,405	5,367	4,740	10,903	10,010	12,405
Kananga, Zaire	6,107	14,503	12,220	17,332	9,514	12,277	10,370	10,442	15,027	18,299	13,016	1,050	6,273	6,778	11,112	6,678	6,054	11,169	11,245	12,016
Kano, Nigeria	5,947	12,097	12,187	16,483	10,643	14,783	10,225	11,082	16,900	16,035	10,663	2,851	7,193	4,419	8,623	7,519	6,434	8,775	12,322	9,562
Kanpur, India	1,946	13,743	5,027	15,497	3,265	10,290	3,282	3,453	9,458	11,816	13,765	8,217	1,343	7,576	11,684	1,024	1,206	9,278	4,758	12,540
Kansas City, Missouri	11,532	1,873	10,542	7,102	14,067	14,914	10,769	12,587	12,003	6,274	1,038	12,649	13,884	6,707	1,701	13,711	12,652	3,456	13,291	729
Kaohsiung, Taiwan	5,757	12,089	1,763	11,520	1,957	7,770	2,171	631	5,594	8,334	13,073	12,024	4,801	10,408	12,296	4,400	5,259	9,648	1,343	12,574
Karachi, Pakistan	1,149	14,033	6,315	16,802	4,461	11,110	4,473	4,796	10,742	12,970	13,677	6,948	1,352	6,764	11,360	1,446	144	9,256	6,050	12,331
Karaganda, USSR	1,941	11,256	5,047	14,671	5,315	12,547	3,139	4,703	10,574	10,665	11,116	8,900	3,829	5,428	9,030	3,631	2,747	6,624	6,262	9,874
Karl-Marx-Stadt, East Germany	4,342	9,589	8,869	14,786	9,352	16,494	7,167	8,873	14,518	11,962	8,660	7,047	6,758	1,368	6,218	6,816	5,458	5,017	10,431	7,270
Kasanga, Tanzania	5,758	15,459	11,576	17,718	8,630	11,429	9,827	9,658	14,023	18,295	13,991	1,746	5,523	7,417	11,994	5,938	5,502	11,767	10,344	12,937
Kashgar, China	1,352	12,382	4,981	15,240	4,398	11,611	3,021	4,081	10,161	11,266	12,286	8,491	2,676	6,290	10,185	2,461	1,719	7,795	5,590	11,043
Kassel, West Germany	4,585	9,375	9,003	14,588	9,577	16,735	7,333	9,070	14,640	11,865	8,427	7,122	7,003	1,128	5,985	7,059	5,703	4,850	10,630	7,038
Kathmandu, Nepal	2,320	13,488	4,519	14,985	2,917	10,067	2,806	2,968	9,015	11,329	13,643	8,726	1,725	7,816	11,681	1,343	1,708	9,186	4,322	12,482
Kayes, Mali	7,629	10,143	13,394	14,320	12,656	16,259	11,548	12,837	18,938	14,625	8,654	4,248	9,245	3,961	6,878	9,535	8,331	7,743	14,242	7,699
Kazan, USSR	2,583	10,419	6,531	14,858	7,026	14,264	4,743	6,434	12,168	11,094	9,949	8,202	5,003	3,690	7,663	4,926	3,718	5,571	7,995	8,609
Kemi, Finland	4,290	8,823	7,324	13,660	8,563	15,730	5,830	7,754	12,889	10,342	8,246	8,741	6,729	2,499	5,937	6,653	5,437	3,972	9,291	6,892
Kenora, Canada	10,408	2,689	9,600	7,892	12,990	15,336	9,653	11,541	11,922	6,327	2,224	12,534	12,719	5,946	1,486	12,533	11,510	2,288	12,400	1,292
Kerguelen Island	9,314	17,736	11,175	12,874	7,597	5,779	10,819	9,091	9,251	14,824	17,473	6,355	7,205	13,168	17,383	7,461	8,293	17,311	8,434	17,818
Kerkira, Greece	3,775	10,867	9,285	16,106	8,982	15,671	7,411	8,815	14,840	13,258	9,832	5,809	5,974	2,355	7,399	6,118	4,756	6,378	10,322	8,459
Kermanshah, Iran	1,392	12,621	7,587	17,220	6,560	13,272	5,621	6,602	12,700	13,310	11,894	6,170	3,512	4,628	9,471	3,641	2,279	7,780	8,022	10,503
Khabarovsk, USSR	6,054	9,204	1,581	10,516	4,950	10,198	2,040	3,454	6,866	6,584	9,994	13,209	6,539	8,492	9,175	6,135	6,251	6,588	4,351	9,418
Kharkov, USSR	2,737	10,670	7,573	15,526	7,702	14,855	5,736	7,295	13,181	11,985	9,968	7,232	5,197	3,013	7,568	5,216	3,882	5,842	8,843	8,583
Khartoum, Sudan	3,621	13,706	9,926	18,908	8,017	13,191	7,984	8,531	14,293	15,769	12,509	3,636	4,567	5,165	10,151	4,897	3,878	9,301	9,705	11,199
Khon Kaen, Thailand	4,504	13,806	3,561	13,310	753	7,991	2,829	1,353	6,910	10,288	14,536	10,104	2,963	9,933	13,152	2,596	3,708	10,480	2,227	13,714
Kiev, USSR	3,126	10,420	7,906	15,399	8,114	15,260	6,097	7,693	13,536	12,015	9,655	7,143	5,573	2,605	7,238	5,605	4,262	5,631	9,245	8,266
Kigali, Rwanda	5,236	14,922	11,273	18,246	8,595	12,040	9,441	9,491	14,338	17,701	13,502	1,975	5,321	6,716	11,395	5,724	5,115	11,048	10,332	12,370
Kingston, Canada	10,357	3,476	10,819	8,670	13,908	16,520	10,553	12,564	13,385	7,716	2,313	11,168	12,811	5,170	146	12,726	11,512	2,817	13,626	940
Kingston, Jamaica	12,777	3,682	13,436	7,497	16,802	15,043	13,439	15,397	13,846	8,411	2,290	10,715	15,215	7,105	3,044	15,255	13,913	5,720	16,193	2,576
Kingstown, Saint Vincent	12,064	5,415	14,549	8,964	17,049	15,725	13,989	16,057	15,526	10,162	3,965	8,968	14,283	6,416	3,832	14,456	13,094	6,413	17,335	3,829
Kinshasa, Zaire	6,513	13,745	12,763	16,785	10,256	12,908	10,855	11,109	15,828	17,987	12,245	934	6,945	6,358	10,429	7,340	6,601	10,727	11,993	11,296
Kirkwall, United Kingdom	5,408	8,237	8,869	13,431	10,082	17,304	7,425	9,341	14,323	10,815	7,355	8,126	7,876	1,030	4,924	7,876	6,560	3,700	10,883	5,963
Kirov, USSR	2,847	10,131	6,416	14,545	7,114	14,345	4,681	6,446	12,067	10,798	9,697	8,479	5,237	3,660	7,440	5,140	3,967	5,291	8,005	8,369
Kiruna, Sweden	4,574	8,527	7,364	13,379	8,756	15,871	5,939	7,898	12,877	10,116	7,959	8,945	7,005	2,475	5,663	6,921	5,718	3,677	9,422	6,610
Kisangani, Zaire	5,370	14,332	11,560	18,003	9,075	12,607	9,673	9,889	14,928	17,569	12,902	1,795	5,730	6,241	10,824	6,121	5,390	10,611	10,814	11,787
Kishinev, USSR	3,121	10,668	8,215	15,726	8,221	15,271	6,371	7,890	13,816	12,410	9,836	6,742	5,519	2,596	7,402	5,585	4,223	5,926	9,429	8,444
Kitchner, Canada	10,599	3,144	10,761	8,346	13,960	16,188	10,597	12,578	13,101	7,413	2,013	11,477	13,040	5,484	438	12,937	11,750	2,889	13,572	625
Knoxville, Tennessee	11,468	2,644	11,352	7,678	14,717	15,613	11,360	13,288	12,973	7,244	1,272	11,701	13,916	6,226	1,257	13,817	12,621	3,721	14,145	466
Kosice, Czechoslovakia	3,715	10,174	8,566	15,320	8,784	15,868	6,782	8,390	14,210	12,250	9,285	6,826	6,117	1,998	6,846	6,183	4,821	5,511	9,940	7,894
Kota Kinabalu, Malaysia	6,351	13,671	3,570	11,760	1,162	6,268	3,880	1,811	5,158	9,371	14,829	11,276	4,585	11,715	14,191	4,279	5,507	11,532	886	14,453
Krakow, Poland	3,838	9,994	8,547	15,138	8,869	15,991	6,789	8,436	14,198	12,094	9,114	6,970	6,256	1,871	6,676	6,312	4,955	5,329	9,990	7,722
Kralendijk, Bonaire	12,681	4,794	14,409	8,195	17,411	15,186	14,142	16,188	14,761	9,491	3,410	9,680	14,976	6,984	3,755	15,118	13,749	6,427	17,212	3,529
Krasnodar, USSR	2,305	11,255	7,648	16,095	7,419	14,458	5,746	7,149	13,161	12,462	10,526	6,812	4,722	3,405	8,112	4,775	3,418	6,431	8,673	9,137
Krasnoyarsk, USSR	3,355	10,312	3,846	13,207	5,164	12,100	2,177	4,140	9,495	9,197	10,468	10,383	4,758	6,107	8,710	4,456	3,937	6,087	5,650	9,390
Kristiansand, Norway	4,766	8,812	8,525	13,956	9,502	16,740	6,975	8,832	14,097	11,100	7,977	7,890	7,234	1,308	5,553	7,237	5,918	4,158	10,386	6,585
Kuala Lumpur, Malaysia	5,348	15,031	4,700	13,288	1,002	6,853	4,284	2,504	6,609	10,969	15,938	9,653	3,206	11,016	14,615	2,985	4,331	11,950	2,450	15,184
Kuching, Malaysia	6,170	14,473	4,302	12,311	1,095	6,161	4,347	2,327	5,634	10,142	15,604	10,550	4,152	11,744	14,766	3,901	5,215	12,080	1,689	15,133
Kumasi, Ghana	7,197	11,507	13,389	15,336	11,859	14,976	11,437	12,340	17,983	15,978	10,009	2,884	8,409	4,813	8,245	8,748	7,689	8,927	13,558	9,074
Kumzar, Oman	1,046	13,729	7,196	17,569	5,540	12,023	5,278	5,833	11,820	13,575	13,111	6,166	2,295	5,887	10,706	2,480	1,202	8,871	7,124	11,727
Kunming, China	4,022	13,025	3,046	13,317	1,640	8,808	1,930	1,212	7,287	9,926	13,641	10,301	3,063	9,167	12,196	2,649	3,449	9,525	2,633	12,769
Kuqa Chang, China	2,016	12,087	4,322	14,597	4,066	11,302	2,359	3,557	9,585	10,645	12,149	9,145	2,973	6,649	10,190	2,681	2,241	7,683	5,099	10,978

Distances in Kilometers	Herat, Afghanistan	Hermosillo, Mexico	Hiroshima, Japan	Hiva Oa (Atuona)	Ho Chi Minh City, Vietnam	Hobart, Australia	Hohhot, China	Hong Kong	Honiara, Solomon Islands	Honolulu, Hawaii	Houston, Texas	Huambo, Angola	Hubli, India	Hugh Town, United Kingdom	Hull, Canada	Hyderabad, India	Hyderabad, Pakistan	Igloolik, Canada	Iloilo, Philippines	Indianapolis, Indiana
Kurgan, USSR	2,357	10,636	5,537	14,514	6,123	13,344	3,726	5,442	11,158	10,576	10,387	8,851	4,528	4,665	8,244	4,369	3,348	5,905	7,002	9,114
Kuwait, Kuwait	1,453	13,163	7,770	17,720	6,408	12,887	5,813	6,600	12,652	13,754	12,397	5,802	3,191	5,050	9,963	3,376	2,064	8,329	7,952	11,005
Kuybyshev, USSR	2,303	10,710	6,549	15,122	6,860	14,091	4,716	6,334	12,159	11,321	10,228	8,006	4,737	3,830	7,929	4,672	3,444	5,860	7,892	8,883
Kyoto, Japan	6,575	10,055	310	10,201	3,986	8,708	2,210	2,531	5,539	6,578	11,064	13,539	6,382	9,886	10,553	5,964	6,458	8,032	3,005	10,680
Kzyl-Orda, USSR	1,195	11,817	5,703	15,475	5,446	12,653	3,751	5,070	11,096	11,471	11,523	8,100	3,391	5,242	9,306	3,274	2,172	7,060	6,603	10,219
L'vov, USSR	3,546	10,203	8,330	15,299	8,578	15,697	6,546	8,162	13,973	12,122	9,359	6,977	5,970	2,164	6,926	6,021	4,666	5,488	9,715	7,967
La Ceiba, Honduras	13,567	2,881	13,079	6,415	16,723	14,095	13,462	15,223	12,776	7,467	1,779	11,721	16,039	8,004	3,447	16,001	14,723	5,965	15,658	2,659
La Coruna, Spain	6,026	8,775	10,523	13,983	11,137	18,053	8,921	10,678	16,079	12,196	7,581	6,681	8,339	745	5,209	8,454	7,084	4,937	12,237	6,255
La Paz, Bolivia	14,716	6,827	17,162	7,686	19,171	12,498	17,313	19,327	14,006	10,641	5,894	8,987	16,111	9,519	6,901	16,482	15,424	9,586	18,704	6,504
La Paz, Mexico	13,482	547	10,751	4,886	14,447	12,776	11,616	12,983	10,415	4,873	1,606	14,233	15,593	8,928	3,897	15,312	14,522	5,370	13,107	2,848
La Ronge, Canada	10,024	2,927	8,672	7,850	12,123	14,788	8,819	10,654	11,165	5,735	2,924	13,115	12,198	6,163	2,341	11,966	11,069	1,980	11,466	2,218
Labrador City, Canada	9,159	4,451	10,148	9,702	12,920	17,258	9,618	11,673	13,623	8,207	3,462	10,645	11,615	4,101	1,053	11,535	10,314	1,985	12,895	2,070
Lagos, Nigeria	6,761	11,986	13,019	15,881	11,326	14,649	11,056	11,855	17,433	16,323	10,500	2,526	7,879	4,903	8,653	8,225	7,198	9,147	13,034	9,518
Lahore, Pakistan	1,171	13,269	5,369	15,826	4,050	11,107	3,479	4,069	10,150	11,944	13,128	7,934	1,800	6,759	10,957	1,628	901	8,640	5,465	11,853
Lambasa, Fiji	13,506	9,016	7,505	4,560	8,551	4,224	9,422	8,295	2,245	4,858	10,462	16,316	11,970	16,256	12,450	11,676	12,860	12,049	6,938	11,538
Lansing, Michigan	10,827	2,808	10,674	8,022	13,974	15,848	10,614	12,560	12,796	7,094	1,734	11,802	13,249	5,798	766	13,126	11,972	2,972	13,481	356
Lanzhou, China	3,754	11,941	2,616	13,098	2,818	9,802	869	1,836	7,745	9,365	12,454	10,650	3,643	8,272	10,980	3,233	3,561	8,304	3,393	11,549
Laoag, Philippines	6,017	12,402	2,146	11,440	1,712	7,300	2,647	808	5,295	8,451	13,454	11,996	4,842	10,845	12,768	4,459	5,427	10,130	856	13,016
Largeau, Chad	4,634	12,551	10,901	17,508	9,399	14,439	8,936	9,774	15,704	15,653	11,240	3,410	5,965	4,214	8,980	6,270	5,137	8,573	11,048	9,997
Las Vegas, Nevada	12,194	880	9,521	5,672	13,221	13,180	10,243	11,727	10,173	4,443	1,977	14,489	14,201	8,195	3,443	13,908	13,183	4,213	12,059	2,567
Launceston, Australia	12,057	13,021	8,528	7,949	7,109	167	9,784	7,827	3,761	8,964	14,338	12,217	9,687	17,759	16,563	9,596	10,963	15,823	6,296	15,580
Le Havre, France	5,255	8,970	9,592	14,221	10,272	17,407	7,977	9,750	15,187	11,866	7,926	7,063	7,648	467	5,490	7,721	6,358	4,678	11,311	6,551
Leipzig, East Germany	4,388	9,524	8,863	14,720	9,383	16,537	7,172	8,890	14,509	11,904	8,597	7,102	6,808	1,326	6,156	6,863	5,507	4,952	10,450	7,207
Leningrad, USSR	3,666	9,526	7,393	14,372	8,222	15,458	5,745	7,556	13,036	10,972	8,899	8,157	6,131	2,552	6,547	6,087	4,823	4,683	9,114	7,530
Leon, Spain	5,827	9,016	10,472	14,227	10,963	17,813	8,829	10,547	16,070	12,382	7,826	6,504	8,120	815	5,452	8,243	6,874	5,122	12,104	6,499
Lerwick, United Kingdom	5,310	8,257	8,702	13,428	9,939	17,151	7,262	9,183	14,162	10,733	7,409	8,220	7,781	1,185	4,986	7,772	6,465	3,664	10,723	6,018
Lhasa, China	2,770	13,100	3,915	14,386	2,644	9,877	2,231	2,446	8,538	10,733	13,394	9,330	2,274	8,042	11,584	1,871	2,292	9,007	3,879	12,314
Libreville, Gabon	6,643	12,917	12,962	16,393	10,800	13,711	11,007	11,515	16,617	17,244	11,422	1,610	7,404	5,691	9,604	7,779	6,897	10,013	12,536	10,465
Lilongwe, Malawi	6,135	16,034	11,666	17,260	8,497	10,785	10,020	9,636	13,548	18,549	14,539	1,954	5,593	8,092	12,627	6,011	5,747	12,439	10,172	13,546
Lima, Peru	15,225	5,830	16,144	6,767	19,603	12,436	16,711	18,379	13,295	9,567	5,027	10,028	17,010	9,691	6,367	17,335	16,112	9,041	17,891	5,814
Limerick, Ireland	5,817	8,264	9,649	13,515	10,697	17,927	8,168	10,044	15,101	11,287	7,229	7,614	8,249	345	4,790	8,296	6,945	4,048	11,596	5,850
Limoges, France	5,221	9,272	9,862	14,523	10,326	17,319	8,189	9,895	15,492	12,277	8,174	6,648	7,559	725	5,754	7,661	6,292	5,072	11,452	6,813
Limon, Costa Rica	13,888	3,595	13,838	6,578	17,477	13,942	14,186	15,980	13,136	8,055	2,536	11,206	16,325	8,214	3,989	16,366	15,024	6,595	16,381	3,313
Lincoln, Nebraska	11,408	1,840	10,281	7,091	13,814	14,833	10,527	12,332	11,816	6,094	1,233	12,815	13,730	6,712	1,774	13,541	12,517	3,298	13,029	902
Linz, Austria	4,220	9,857	8,987	15,068	9,299	16,365	7,241	8,888	14,640	12,256	8,898	6,762	6,602	1,511	6,455	6,680	5,315	5,312	10,442	7,511
Lisbon, Portugal	6,243	8,977	10,997	14,112	11,415	17,990	9,351	11,048	16,585	12,607	7,711	6,258	8,473	1,264	5,403	8,620	7,256	5,364	12,603	6,429
Little Rock, Arkansas	11,911	1,873	11,052	6,967	14,591	14,876	11,293	13,110	12,229	6,507	624	12,454	14,305	6,883	1,837	14,154	13,047	3,908	13,786	778
Liverpool, United Kingdom	5,433	8,551	9,372	13,792	10,319	17,544	7,843	9,692	14,894	11,380	7,559	7,545	7,869	452	5,116	7,912	6,563	4,194	11,248	6,174
Lodz, Poland	3,907	9,834	8,457	14,962	8,886	16,047	6,724	8,409	14,110	11,907	8,977	7,153	6,343	1,818	6,542	6,385	5,035	5,151	9,967	7,585
Lome, Togo	6,976	11,804	13,214	15,638	11,568	14,755	11,254	12,086	17,663	16,216	10,311	2,636	8,120	4,904	8,509	8,465	7,430	9,094	13,275	9,355
London, United Kingdom	5,253	8,831	9,426	14,075	10,213	17,400	7,842	9,646	15,001	11,653	7,820	7,281	7,670	472	5,380	7,728	6,371	4,480	11,206	6,438
Londonderry, United Kingdom	5,698	8,218	9,384	13,459	10,506	17,744	7,922	9,816	14,828	11,099	7,235	7,814	8,147	570	4,792	8,177	6,836	3,886	11,364	5,848
Longlac, Canada	10,192	3,089	9,921	8,335	13,177	15,894	9,816	11,769	12,487	6,899	2,344	11,964	12,571	5,475	944	12,420	11,320	2,198	12,732	1,113
Lord Howe Island, Australia	12,480	11,634	7,816	6,789	7,286	1,633	9,380	7,640	2,450	7,437	13,037	13,743	10,333	17,636	15,100	10,155	11,506	14,383	6,084	14,176
Los Angeles, California	12,434	885	9,451	5,328	13,155	12,813	10,276	11,674	9,849	4,125	2,212	14,824	14,356	8,555	3,806	14,045	13,391	4,525	11,917	2,913
Louangphrabang, Laos	4,239	13,537	3,390	13,390	1,120	8,351	2,488	1,278	7,115	10,206	14,204	10,117	2,902	9,587	12,771	2,511	3,515	10,102	2,414	13,347
Louisville, Kentucky	11,318	2,539	11,051	7,668	14,430	15,571	11,077	12,994	12,775	7,046	1,292	11,882	13,749	6,188	1,152	13,632	12,466	3,474	13,843	173
Luanda, Angola	7,028	13,803	13,237	16,329	10,570	12,640	11,351	11,503	15,826	18,333	12,289	517	7,333	6,777	10,621	7,736	7,066	11,111	12,297	11,434
Lubumbashi, Zaire	6,277	15,313	12,108	17,209	9,103	11,432	10,364	10,167	14,279	18,802	13,813	1,277	6,047	7,576	11,955	6,463	6,038	11,961	10,803	12,850
Lusaka, Zambia	6,574	15,592	12,253	16,891	9,110	11,059	10,569	10,243	14,034	19,099	14,080	1,382	6,177	7,993	12,305	6,595	6,265	12,380	10,783	13,175
Luxembourg, Luxembourg	4,821	9,313	9,305	14,552	9,854	16,973	7,638	9,369	14,939	11,993	8,311	6,969	7,215	897	5,870	7,287	5,924	4,892	10,928	6,929
Luxor, Egypt	2,995	12,815	9,270	18,045	7,911	13,874	7,304	8,166	14,197	14,684	11,747	4,627	4,559	4,283	9,328	4,811	3,579	8,250	9,498	10,388
Lynn Lake, Canada	9,778	3,183	8,716	8,166	12,093	15,092	8,760	10,642	11,427	6,045	3,042	12,804	11,996	5,835	2,159	11,778	10,840	1,686	11,522	2,186
Lyon, France	4,945	9,502	9,690	14,754	10,062	17,040	7,984	9,658	15,337	12,377	8,428	6,569	7,279	954	6,001	7,382	6,012	5,216	11,212	7,061
Macapa, Brazil	12,131	7,117	16,176	9,798	17,292	14,916	15,160	17,073	16,446	11,756	5,732	7,507	13,884	6,967	5,584	14,179	12,948	8,032	18,632	5,662
Madison, Wisconsin	10,962	2,475	10,435	7,716	13,827	15,486	10,482	12,383	12,399	6,697	1,570	12,198	13,348	6,089	1,121	13,198	12,094	2,963	13,229	456
Madras, India	2,979	15,188	5,744	15,735	2,884	9,205	4,326	3,726	9,150	12,622	15,241	7,669	607	8,666	13,093	514	1,847	10,750	4,609	13,909
Madrid, Spain	5,740	9,279	10,585	14,474	10,911	17,604	8,897	10,561	16,216	12,671	8,068	6,216	7,985	1,078	5,710	8,125	6,759	5,412	12,112	6,753
Madurai, India	3,152	15,582	6,136	15,964	3,127	9,115	4,746	4,077	9,315	13,003	15,558	7,332	680	8,773	13,340	825	1,995	11,068	4,865	14,269
Magadan, USSR	6,713	7,708	3,103	9,852	6,534	11,364	3,413	5,043	7,693	5,845	8,414	13,637	7,738	7,692	7,618	7,361	7,190	5,100	5,911	7,824
Magdalena, Bolivia	14,163	6,881	17,143	8,150	18,993	13,004	16,935	19,002	14,547	10,925	5,829	8,625	15,646	8,986	6,612	16,001	14,895	9,279	19,247	6,306
Magdeburg, East Germany	4,443	9,424	8,830	14,616	9,411	16,585	7,156	8,894	14,470	11,802	8,507	7,201	6,873	1,282	6,067	6,921	5,568	4,845	10,455	7,117
Majuro Atoll, Marshall Isls.	11,281	8,451	4,986	5,828	7,097	6,048	6,951	6,327	2,218	3,677	9,954	17,272	10,452	13,678	11,198	10,071	10,953	9,921	5,358	10,575
Malabo, Equatorial Guinea	6,463	12,650	12,778	16,419	10,801	14,055	10,816	11,435	16,788	16,880	11,167	1,980	7,374	5,311	9,287	7,736	6,789	9,638	12,528	10,169
Male, Maldives	3,555	16,315	6,938	16,390	3,738	9,010	5,579	4,829	9,706	13,774	16,086	6,641	1,269	8,938	13,742	1,578	2,427	11,648	5,466	14,732
Manado, Indonesia	7,429	13,198	3,729	10,717	2,257	5,409	4,552	2,572	4,075	8,639	14,528	12,124	5,665	12,666	14,428	5,369	6,601	11,890	1,050	14,460
Managua, Nicaragua	13,884	3,170	13,436	6,319	17,103	13,860	13,863	15,601	12,804	7,642	2,164	11,599	16,350	8,268	3,823	16,340	15,035	6,365	15,955	3,060
Manama, Bahrain	1,433	13,580	7,715	17,931	6,117	12,469	5,777	6,409	12,402	13,923	12,831	5,724	2,821	5,478	10,399	3,037	1,785	8,737	7,707	11,439
Manaus, Brazil	13,138	6,496	16,313	8,756	18,335	14,217	15,752	17,801	15,389	10,956	5,236	8,401	14,941	7,796	5,601	15,235	13,991	8,214	19,124	5,450
Manchester, New Hampshire	10,237	3,837	11,098	8,983	14,050	16,885	10,721	12,758	13,814	8,142	2,584	10,744	12,706	4,903	436	12,650	11,396	2,997	13,892	1,278
Mandalay, Burma	3,576	13,659	3,801	14,011	1,680	8,899	2,545	1,865	7,787	10,680	14,148	9,565	2,323	9,010	12,492	1,915	2,847	9,869	3,087	13,163
Mangareva Island, Fr.Polynesia	17,940	6,321	11,654	1,537	13,374	7,324	13,590	13,001	7,068	5,508	7,224	14,928	16,758	14,684	9,666	16,492	17,654	11,095	11,745	8,609
Manila, Philippines	6,258	12,639	2,479	11,351	1,613	6,912	3,043	1,114	5,054	8,538	13,747	11,980	4,922	11,209	13,149	4,555	5,602	10,521	462	13,366
Mannheim, West Germany	4,652	9,452	9,200	14,683	9,694	16,804	7,513	9,224	14,843	12,048	8,465	6,929	7,046	1,066	6,023	7,118	5,755	4,988	10,783	7,081
Maputo, Mozambique	7,371	16,425	12,450	15,946	8,982	9,885	10,997	10,286	13,117	18,846	14,927	2,288	6,494	9,242	13,411	6,905	6,861	13,630	10,530	14,204
Mar del Plata, Argentina	14,683	9,275	19,039	8,604	16,605	10,699	19,040	18,091	13,476	12,318	8,471	7,696	14,764	10,960	9,419	15,181	14,785	12,073	16,980	9,094
Maracaibo, Venezuela	13,051	4,566	14,412	7,800	17,629	14,827	14,299	16,310	14,389	9,207	3,246	9,998	15,367	7,346	3,874	15,499	14,130	6,561	17,178	3,530
Marrakech, Morocco	6,433	9,466	11,610	14,442	11,641	17,513	9,876	11,446	17,255	13,329	8,120	5,527	8,498	2,035	5,920	8,694	7,357	6,118	12,974	6,907
Marseilles, France	4,936	9,705	9,867	14,954	10,094	16,950	8,127	9,751	15,520	12,650	8,597	6,294	7,224	1,158	6,181	7,345	5,976	5,477	11,299	7,240
Maseru, Lesotho	7,935	16,010	13,066	15,444	9,565	9,929	11,620	10,890	13,363	18,975	14,548	2,199	7,118	9,391	13,252	7,529	7,463	13,775	11,079	13,961
Mashhad, Iran	322	12,702	6,459	16,526	5,503	12,474	4,496	5,452	11,554	12,516	12,240	7,113	2,788	5,388	9,907	2,801	1,472	7,869	6,897	10,884
Mazatlan, Mexico	13,523	792	11,111	5,095	14,813	13,025	11,907	13,338	10,793	5,279	1,318	13,840	15,735	8,754	3,707	15,482	14,600	5,389	13,504	2,648
Mbabane, Swaziland	7,471	16,295	12,595	15,872	9,130	9,951	11,131	10,433	13,225	18,954	14,801	2,200	6,630	9,220	13,325	7,041	6,979	13,611	10,678	14,101
Mbandaka, Zaire	5,939	13,748	12,210	17,298	9,842	13,080	10,290	10,622	15,666	17,603	12,279	1,442	6,477	6,000	10,318	6,862	6,065	10,390	11,581	11,238
McMurdo Sound, Antarctica	14,010	12,994	12,609	8,161	10,442	3,936	13,615	11,551	7,569	11,230	13,443	9,800	11,655	16,908	15,584	11,795	12,898	17,852	10,146	14,736
Mecca, Saudi Arabia	2,616	13,603	8,926	18,710	7,201	13,008	6,981	7,599	13,509	14,903	12,590	4,604	3,788	5,114	10,160	4,074	2,945	8,928	8,844	11,221
Medan, Indonesia	5,079	15,215	4,882	13,628	1,187	7,094	4,320	2,658	6,948	11,263	16,027	9,334	2,886	10,770	14,547	2,682	4,039	11,908	2,753	15,179
Medellin, Colombia	13,706	4,493	14,634	7,257	18,109	14,173	14,746	16,681	13,908	8,968	3,328	10,317	16,012	8,001	4,342	16,152	14,783	7,024	17,273	3,861
Medicine Hat, Canada	10,631	2,330	8,788	7,181	12,359	14,251	9,131	10,865	10,762	5,202	2,594	13,651	12,738	6,809	2,644	12,482	11,651	2,645	11,535	2,232
Medina, Saudi Arabia	2,443	13,302	8,763	18,375	7,215	13,229	6,806	7,530	13,514	14,602	12,324	4,862	3,846	4,848	9,888	4,105	2,902	8,604	8,824	10,947
Melbourne, Australia	11,697	13,086	8,102	8,120	6,698	598	9,346	7,392	3,485	8,862	14,460	12,315	9,359	17,373	16,563	9,250	10,620	15,538	5,859	15,635
Memphis, Tennessee	11,794	2,080	11,135	7,157	14,633	15,075	11,313	13,163	12,429	6,705	776	12,252	14,206	6,705	1,667	14,069	12,937	3,846	13,888	620
Merauke, Indonesia	9,465	12,284	4,817	8,842	4,292	3,878	6,197	4,438	2,160	7,511	13,781	13,468	7,654	14,475	14,656	7,380	8,637	12,601	2,893	14,256
Merida, Mexico	13,201	2,330	12,441	6,387	16,076	14,241	12,826	14,577	12,502	7,027	1,133	12,096	15,661	7,782	2,997	15,570	14,358	5,407	15,054	2,111
Meridian, Mississippi	12,022	2,160	11,459	7,095	14,964	15,035	11,642	13,493	12,574	6,869	698	12,114	14,454	6,821	1,831	14,334	13,171	4,141	14,203	853
Messina, Italy	4,169	10,723	9,672	15,974	9,377	15,959	7,809	9,224	15,245	13,383	9,625	5,636	6,325	2,172	7,209	6,484	5,127	6,365	10,730	8,268
Mexico City, Mexico	13,741	1,606	11,939	5,437	15,643	13,356	12,626	14,155	11,497	6,098	1,210	13,070	16,112	8,580	3,603	15,928	14,873	5,680	14,368	2,579
Miami, Florida	12,265	3,057	12,512	7,486	15,897	15,329	12,536	14,472	13,454	7,830	1,558	11,212	14,737	6,729	2,217	14,706	13,421	4,850	15,284	1,649
Midway Islands, USA	10,680	6,401	4,779	5,890	8,089	8,664	6,494	6,842	4,827	2,112	7,806	17,826	10,854	11,307	8,665	10,436	10,824	7,315	6,531	8,163
Milan, Italy	4,609	9,785	9,485	15,033	9,741	16,699	7,740	9,371	15,138	12,495	8,739	6,479	6,939	1,263	6,305	7,042	5,673	5,406	10,922	7,366

Distances in Kilometers	Herat, Afghanistan	Hermosillo, Mexico	Hiroshima, Japan	Hiva Oa (Atuona)	Ho Chi Minh City, Vietnam	Hobart, Australia	Hohhot, China	Hong Kong	Honiara, Solomon Islands	Honolulu, Hawaii	Houston, Texas	Huambo, Angola	Hubli, India	Hugh Town, United Kingdom	Hull, Canada	Hyderabad, India	Hyderabad, Pakistan	Igloolik, Canada	Iloilo, Philippines	Indianapolis, Indiana
Milford Sound, New Zealand	13,738	11,578	9,448	6,373	8,668	1,653	10,993	9,187	3,968	8,090	12,774	13,060	11,398	19,268	15,146	11,294	12,663	15,340	7,627	14,100
Milwaukee, Wisconsin	10,916	2,577	10,503	7,812	13,868	15,599	10,517	12,432	12,519	6,817	1,616	12,078	13,314	5,997	1,008	13,172	12,053	2,955	13,302	392
Minsk, USSR	3,466	9,987	7,873	14,971	8,335	15,540	6,129	7,821	13,525	11,656	9,242	7,468	5,931	2,350	6,835	5,941	4,615	5,196	9,380	7,855
Mogadiscio, Somalia	3,977	15,745	9,617	19,029	6,838	11,142	7,876	7,748	12,755	16,402	14,560	3,656	3,586	7,193	12,204	3,996	3,568	11,155	8,576	13,254
Mombasa, Kenya	4,862	15,865	10,522	18,467	7,601	11,129	8,801	8,599	13,246	17,329	14,508	2,797	4,462	7,427	12,295	4,878	4,495	11,611	9,327	13,307
Monclova, Mexico	13,012	969	11,170	5,744	14,862	13,673	11,775	13,362	11,337	5,727	673	13,332	15,316	8,115	3,069	15,105	14,119	4,895	13,708	2,008
Moncton, Canada	9,636	4,419	10,923	9,600	13,651	17,460	10,374	12,435	14,144	8,562	3,211	10,306	12,108	4,271	854	12,067	10,794	2,761	13,672	1,874
Monrovia, Liberia	8,059	10,657	14,082	14,323	12,854	15,421	12,174	13,253	18,958	15,303	9,145	3,618	9,403	4,851	7,567	9,732	8,630	8,611	14,534	8,313
Monte Carlo, Monaco	4,768	9,801	9,727	15,053	9,924	16,801	7,971	9,585	15,375	12,648	8,715	6,310	7,063	1,250	6,292	7,181	5,812	5,510	11,131	7,352
Monterrey, Mexico	13,114	1,118	11,345	5,743	15,037	13,683	11,946	13,538	11,436	5,853	667	13,222	15,441	8,142	3,103	15,240	14,230	5,011	13,877	2,046
Montevideo, Uruguay	14,468	9,121	19,234	8,747	16,824	11,065	18,764	18,326	13,809	12,370	8,253	7,576	14,726	10,599	9,110	15,145	14,648	11,750	17,323	8,821
Montgomery, Alabama	11,922	2,385	11,580	7,288	15,038	15,231	11,698	13,582	12,798	7,091	911	11,889	14,369	6,655	1,711	14,266	13,076	4,126	14,342	820
Montpelier, Vermont	10,177	3,778	10,934	8,955	13,912	16,826	10,576	12,608	13,679	8,022	2,573	10,859	12,642	4,904	281	12,575	11,335	2,846	13,730	1,228
Montpellier, France	5,052	9,588	9,922	14,836	10,203	17,077	8,198	9,842	15,572	12,581	8,473	6,354	7,347	1,047	6,060	7,466	6,097	5,390	11,392	7,118
Montreal, Canada	10,112	3,736	10,777	8,937	13,775	16,772	10,433	12,462	13,554	7,915	2,581	10,961	12,572	4,901	167	12,495	11,268	2,699	13,574	1,209
Moosonee, Canada	9,851	3,525	9,978	8,775	13,096	16,329	9,735	11,732	12,847	7,308	2,684	11,549	12,260	5,032	745	12,132	10,990	2,018	12,783	1,349
Moroni, Comoros	5,472	16,730	10,664	17,616	7,438	10,252	9,096	8,595	12,649	17,539	15,311	2,992	4,615	8,356	13,181	5,032	4,921	12,537	9,112	14,173
Moscow, USSR	3,037	10,145	7,210	14,899	7,721	14,952	5,454	7,158	12,859	11,342	9,535	7,858	5,505	2,976	7,179	5,473	4,195	5,293	8,718	8,166
Mosul, Iraq	1,745	12,278	7,797	17,058	6,944	13,694	5,836	6,926	13,028	13,255	11,506	6,144	3,933	4,209	9,076	4,057	2,691	7,458	8,373	10,114
Mount Isa, Australia	10,190	12,951	6,147	8,755	5,004	2,566	7,397	5,494	2,525	8,248	14,463	12,844	8,084	15,596	15,794	7,884	9,225	13,932	3,940	15,215
Multan, Pakistan	988	13,442	5,676	16,136	4,227	11,193	3,790	4,330	10,390	12,250	13,226	7,624	1,685	6,669	11,002	1,585	616	8,752	5,695	11,924
Munich, West Germany	4,421	9,722	9,145	14,949	9,501	16,563	7,416	9,080	14,798	12,240	8,737	6,756	6,798	1,320	6,296	6,879	5,513	5,230	10,635	7,354
Murcia, Spain	5,601	9,613	10,672	14,790	10,798	17,307	8,932	10,527	16,324	13,008	8,383	5,885	7,786	1,389	6,040	7,945	6,586	5,751	12,066	7,079
Murmansk, USSR	4,257	8,746	6,840	13,410	8,242	15,330	5,397	7,360	12,387	9,954	8,286	9,165	6,641	2,986	6,055	6,527	5,378	3,893	8,881	6,965
Mururoa Atoll, Fr. Polynesia	17,538	6,384	11,234	1,335	12,965	7,089	13,177	12,571	6,657	5,201	7,375	15,295	16,373	14,852	9,809	16,090	17,226	11,083	11,325	8,749
Muscat, Oman	1,239	14,070	7,143	17,605	5,283	11,662	5,261	5,667	11,584	13,668	13,479	6,154	1,964	6,254	11,076	2,183	1,010	9,215	6,904	12,095
Myitkyina, Burma	3,523	13,265	3,510	13,845	1,892	9,129	2,157	1,742	7,791	10,396	13,753	9,792	2,568	8,806	12,132	2,151	2,916	9,495	3,111	12,783
Naga, Philippines	6,514	12,528	2,483	11,104	1,825	6,729	3,213	1,349	4,797	8,349	13,680	12,197	5,170	11,421	13,194	4,806	5,860	10,591	331	13,363
Nagasaki, Japan	6,167	10,630	295	10,695	3,410	8,570	1,853	1,942	5,657	7,145	11,603	13,020	5,824	9,880	10,964	5,407	5,967	8,384	2,561	11,156
Nagoya, Japan	6,666	9,959	418	10,100	4,084	8,711	2,300	2,634	5,499	6,470	10,977	13,642	6,489	9,911	10,496	6,071	6,559	7,990	3,075	10,609
Nagpur, India	2,210	14,345	5,396	15,765	3,161	9,945	3,758	3,623	9,456	12,253	14,340	7,870	765	7,917	12,206	422	1,193	9,849	4,779	13,090
Nairobi, Kenya	4,751	15,425	10,612	18,700	7,845	11,569	8,830	8,769	13,623	17,286	14,071	2,643	4,604	7,003	11,856	5,012	4,499	11,222	9,580	12,867
Nanchang, China	5,080	11,911	1,693	12,000	2,206	8,557	1,398	733	6,340	8,557	12,740	11,660	4,430	9,606	11,714	4,015	4,699	9,036	2,109	12,092
Nancy, France	4,819	9,381	9,378	14,624	9,876	16,965	7,698	9,412	15,017	12,093	8,363	6,868	7,201	920	5,924	7,280	5,914	4,982	10,971	6,984
Nandi, Fiji	13,401	9,274	7,486	4,780	8,391	3,974	9,383	8,189	2,103	5,098	10,719	16,079	11,795	16,426	12,706	11,510	12,717	12,267	6,803	11,796
Nanjing, China	5,213	11,448	1,299	11,732	2,667	8,798	1,162	1,178	6,343	8,185	12,277	11,972	4,777	9,441	11,300	4,360	4,938	8,633	2,396	11,650
Nanning, China	4,647	12,896	2,677	12,749	1,347	8,304	2,016	605	6,662	9,489	13,663	10,812	3,577	9,711	12,436	3,173	4,057	9,748	2,024	12,916
Nantes, France	5,411	9,008	9,870	14,259	10,477	17,541	8,241	9,993	15,470	12,054	7,915	6,861	7,773	462	5,492	7,864	6,496	4,831	11,553	6,552
Naples, Italy	4,243	10,435	9,555	15,686	9,440	16,171	7,724	9,213	15,170	13,077	9,363	5,932	6,472	1,892	6,938	6,610	5,245	6,050	10,737	7,998
Narvik, Norway	4,707	8,400	7,424	13,271	8,870	15,964	6,026	7,996	12,910	10,045	7,826	9,004	7,139	2,434	5,530	7,053	5,851	3,552	9,514	6,476
Nashville, Tennessee	11,566	2,395	11,201	7,469	14,626	15,391	11,281	13,177	12,714	6,986	1,070	11,960	13,998	6,407	1,386	13,880	12,714	3,709	13,980	404
Nassau, Bahamas	12,171	3,352	12,713	7,719	16,017	15,511	12,654	14,624	13,745	8,125	1,853	10,917	14,638	6,580	2,263	14,632	13,323	4,934	15,501	1,825
Natal, Brazil	11,055	8,953	16,595	11,415	15,805	14,605	14,924	16,266	17,642	13,629	7,522	5,648	12,372	6,772	6,955	12,722	11,654	9,056	17,530	7,255
Natashquan, Canada	9,150	4,715	10,529	9,944	13,161	17,659	9,904	11,970	14,086	8,632	3,604	10,223	11,620	3,880	1,167	11,572	10,309	2,387	13,245	2,227
Nauru Island	11,399	9,275	5,279	6,069	6,784	5,086	7,208	6,250	1,252	4,526	10,789	16,524	10,223	14,495	12,150	9,872	10,903	10,880	5,065	11,491
Ndjamena, Chad	5,354	12,650	11,651	17,193	9,943	14,311	9,685	10,429	16,189	16,228	11,252	2,749	6,492	4,626	9,121	6,825	5,772	9,017	11,633	10,095
Nelson, New Zealand	14,063	11,009	9,364	5,820	8,911	2,146	11,013	9,306	3,765	7,544	12,227	13,596	11,793	19,045	14,580	11,662	13,029	14,802	7,750	13,539
Nema, Mauritania	7,121	10,404	12,939	14,767	12,154	16,232	11,071	12,330	18,430	14,735	8,937	4,118	8,752	3,695	7,038	9,037	7,825	7,681	13,733	7,912
Neuquen, Argentina	15,602	8,748	18,127	7,688	16,838	10,263	19,800	18,141	12,715	11,453	8,117	8,606	15,585	11,552	9,378	15,995	15,695	12,066	16,704	8,910
New Delhi, India	1,559	13,564	5,225	15,712	3,650	10,676	3,403	3,770	9,813	11,930	13,498	8,032	1,482	7,190	11,363	1,249	947	9,006	5,115	12,243
New Glasgow, Canada	9,567	4,575	11,018	9,741	13,675	17,622	10,421	12,486	14,316	8,737	3,343	10,131	12,040	4,151	1,021	12,011	10,724	2,859	13,750	2,023
New Haven, Connecticut	10,460	3,687	11,232	8,799	14,241	16,720	10,902	12,931	13,767	8,070	2,394	10,827	12,929	5,107	513	12,873	11,618	3,169	14,034	1,134
New Orleans, Louisiana	12,318	2,026	11,605	6,843	15,160	14,786	11,861	13,677	12,457	6,782	512	12,228	14,749	7,099	2,125	14,625	13,467	4,416	14,318	1,145
New Plymouth, New Zealand	14,057	10,823	9,196	5,664	8,877	2,281	10,878	9,215	3,572	7,295	12,068	13,847	11,834	18,798	14,397	11,686	13,049	14,553	7,665	13,364
New York, New York	10,567	3,586	11,260	8,689	14,307	16,613	10,962	12,984	13,701	7,996	2,283	10,906	13,035	5,220	544	12,976	11,725	3,225	14,065	1,039
Newcastle upon Tyne, UK	5,332	8,536	9,176	13,763	10,169	17,404	7,656	9,518	14,696	11,254	7,582	7,682	7,780	650	5,139	7,811	6,470	4,102	11,072	6,192
Newcastle Waters, Australia	9,456	13,394	5,734	9,440	4,283	3,121	6,824	4,861	3,004	8,633	14,907	12,408	7,346	14,926	15,896	7,144	8,485	13,746	3,329	15,481
Niamey, Niger	6,438	11,434	12,558	15,785	11,281	15,358	10,616	11,629	17,576	15,582	9,982	3,271	7,840	4,109	8,006	8,152	7,015	8,367	12,932	8,917
Nicosia, Cyprus	2,633	11,976	8,620	17,093	7,817	14,387	6,671	7,817	13,919	13,643	11,040	5,617	4,701	3,593	8,598	4,866	3,518	7,286	9,264	9,655
Niue (Alofi)	14,632	8,269	8,493	3,477	9,721	4,794	10,443	9,434	3,414	4,651	9,640	16,439	13,137	16,282	11,813	12,846	14,025	11,896	8,103	10,827
Norfolk, Virginia	11,032	3,336	11,576	8,332	14,727	16,274	11,371	13,372	13,627	7,898	1,938	11,033	13,502	5,635	954	13,447	12,191	3,636	14,387	922
Norfolk Island, Australia	13,119	10,748	7,952	5,905	7,913	2,403	9,667	8,090	2,325	6,671	12,141	14,508	11,093	17,637	14,245	10,886	12,212	13,786	6,564	13,297
Noril'sk, USSR	4,210	8,984	4,736	12,597	6,641	13,352	3,464	5,518	10,282	8,697	9,012	10,642	6,065	5,099	7,207	5,811	5,059	4,591	6,959	7,896
Norman Wells, Canada	8,933	4,175	7,056	8,388	10,494	14,054	7,212	9,021	10,185	5,380	4,505	13,521	10,874	6,255	3,764	10,593	9,870	1,944	9,861	3,836
Normanton, Australia	10,126	12,662	5,834	8,628	4,919	2,861	7,152	5,301	2,234	7,932	14,177	13,143	8,102	15,402	15,427	7,879	9,200	13,559	3,740	14,875
North Pole	6,202	6,785	6,193	11,085	8,813	14,754	5,485	7,540	11,044	7,643	6,708	11,412	8,305	4,472	4,970	8,080	7,196	2,302	8,818	5,598
Nottingham, United Kingdom	5,314	8,682	9,340	13,921	10,224	17,439	7,786	9,618	14,888	11,474	7,691	7,458	7,746	493	5,249	7,793	6,441	4,304	11,176	6,306
Norway House, Canada	10,033	2,965	9,090	8,059	12,470	15,223	9,134	11,021	11,650	6,168	2,698	12,683	12,294	5,856	1,845	12,090	11,114	1,902	11,895	1,808
Norwich, United Kingdom	5,150	8,840	9,267	14,076	10,080	17,283	7,686	9,497	14,843	11,569	7,859	7,374	7,578	611	5,416	7,628	6,275	4,427	11,056	6,473
Nouakchott, Mauritania	7,834	9,523	13,307	13,839	12,965	16,839	11,543	12,994	18,954	13,999	8,040	4,876	9,611	3,633	6,249	9,875	8,620	7,194	14,466	7,071
Noumea, New Caledonia	12,641	10,511	7,230	5,963	7,475	2,895	8,990	7,510	1,581	6,185	11,965	14,994	10,779	16,872	13,893	10,533	11,816	13,153	6,019	13,015
Novosibirsk, USSR	2,803	10,593	4,418	13,793	5,336	12,442	2,636	4,469	10,046	9,787	10,608	9,761	4,454	5,668	8,691	4,196	3,504	6,147	6,015	9,448
Nuku'alofa, Tonga	14,258	8,849	8,273	4,067	9,236	4,231	10,194	9,045	2,960	5,060	10,232	16,074	12,621	16,666	12,379	12,347	13,569	12,319	7,660	11,405
Nukunono Island, Tokelau Isls.	13,866	7,783	7,590	3,608	9,283	5,442	9,555	8,777	3,092	3,708	9,240	17,438	12,733	15,299	11,214	12,394	13,434	10,961	7,584	10,299
Nuremberg, West Germany	4,462	9,597	9,070	14,817	9,509	16,614	7,362	9,054	14,719	12,091	8,630	6,903	6,858	1,254	6,188	6,928	5,566	5,086	10,612	7,244
Nyala, Sudan	4,507	13,448	10,824	18,261	8,890	13,544	8,874	9,444	15,118	16,302	12,126	2,919	5,440	5,076	9,877	5,784	4,793	9,397	10,593	10,893
Oaxaca, Mexico	13,899	1,972	12,305	5,523	16,009	13,388	12,969	14,519	11,729	6,410	1,415	12,790	16,314	8,605	3,703	16,160	15,045	5,906	14,725	2,718
Ocean Falls, Canada	10,354	2,930	7,674	6,971	11,317	13,323	8,215	9,814	9,662	4,309	3,643	14,545	12,189	7,402	3,801	11,878	11,255	3,016	10,374	3,445
Odense, Denmark	4,573	9,122	8,640	14,285	9,425	16,650	7,026	8,827	14,254	11,432	8,252	7,567	7,029	1,280	5,818	7,052	5,716	4,495	10,387	6,859
Odessa, USSR	2,965	10,798	8,125	15,827	8,074	15,114	6,267	7,760	13,710	12,449	9,981	6,725	5,363	2,753	7,549	5,428	4,066	6,040	9,295	8,589
Ogbomosho, Nigeria	6,573	11,964	12,819	15,999	11,190	14,742	10,857	11,687	17,359	16,215	10,489	2,636	7,740	4,736	8,590	8,080	7,031	9,007	12,890	9,475
Okha, USSR	6,443	8,436	2,284	10,099	5,737	10,700	2,734	4,240	7,164	6,105	9,207	13,545	7,183	8,179	8,437	6,789	6,774	5,894	5,089	8,646
Okinawa (Naha)	6,257	11,268	1,017	10,818	2,794	7,916	2,192	1,439	5,268	7,507	12,306	12,801	5,560	10,431	11,726	5,151	5,893	9,141	1,799	11,906
Oklahoma City, Oklahoma	11,993	1,453	10,695	6,645	14,295	14,500	11,051	12,800	11,751	6,027	666	12,928	14,325	7,170	2,141	14,137	13,107	3,893	13,392	1,107
Old Crow, Canada	8,555	4,691	6,427	8,582	9,869	13,669	6,603	8,393	9,767	5,293	5,115	13,659	10,382	6,410	4,365	10,083	9,438	2,297	9,233	4,467
Olympia, Washington	10,977	2,247	8,278	6,497	11,948	13,299	8,888	10,446	9,814	4,245	3,048	14,607	12,864	7,659	3,586	12,558	11,906	3,348	10,930	3,053
Omaha, Nebraska	11,341	1,916	10,276	7,167	13,795	14,905	10,500	12,316	11,871	6,152	1,280	12,754	13,670	6,635	1,702	13,485	12,453	3,237	13,031	851
Omsk, USSR	2,455	10,681	5,022	14,242	5,708	12,897	3,210	4,959	10,641	10,259	10,552	9,231	4,402	5,149	8,502	4,197	3,316	6,061	6,516	9,325
Oodnadatta, Australia	10,314	13,602	6,864	9,077	5,255	2,014	7,957	5,968	3,259	8,982	15,094	12,142	8,051	15,939	16,625	7,905	9,272	14,773	4,455	15,974
Oradea, Romania	3,636	10,346	8,637	15,503	8,745	15,777	6,828	8,395	14,269	12,432	9,439	6,651	6,013	2,099	6,998	6,092	4,726	5,696	9,939	8,049
Oran, Algeria	5,634	9,792	10,848	14,936	10,842	17,165	9,080	10,628	16,501	13,257	8,536	5,633	7,763	1,645	6,218	7,938	6,588	5,998	12,156	7,249
Oranjestad, Aruba	12,783	4,608	14,299	8,018	17,406	15,095	14,101	16,132	14,570	9,297	3,237	9,876	15,105	7,078	3,689	15,233	13,864	6,371	17,091	3,410
Orebro, Sweden	4,389	9,042	8,134	14,106	9,069	16,307	6,553	8,398	13,737	11,050	8,278	7,983	6,861	1,726	5,873	6,849	5,546	4,295	9,953	6,891
Orel, USSR	2,920	10,379	7,435	15,203	7,761	14,963	5,638	7,275	13,070	11,672	9,713	7,529	5,391	2,925	7,330	5,386	4,075	5,540	8,832	8,334
Orsk, USSR	1,897	11,054	6,050	15,143	6,245	13,478	4,171	5,730	11,614	11,222	10,680	8,201	4,245	4,447	8,435	4,145	2,987	6,245	7,285	9,360
Osaka, Japan	6,568	10,096	282	10,216	3,946	8,675	2,204	2,493	5,520	6,604	11,107	13,520	6,357	9,911	10,595	5,939	6,442	8,074	2,962	10,724
Oslo, Norway	4,651	8,808	8,276	13,904	9,308	16,541	6,737	8,608	13,846	10,943	8,025	8,066	7,123	1,552	5,616	7,110	5,808	4,093	10,159	6,637
Osorno, Chile	16,056	8,642	17,668	7,275	16,701	9,907	19,620	17,862	12,255	11,095	8,117	9,013	15,873	11,958	9,529	16,274	16,090	12,214	16,356	8,994
Ostrava, Czechoslovakia	3,949	9,936	8,656	15,100	8,989	16,102	6,904	8,556	14,308	12,115	9,037	6,935	6,360	1,760	6,597	6,420	5,061	5,299	10,110	7,646
Ottawa, Canada	10,212	3,576	10,724	8,785	13,780	16,609	10,429	12,446	13,403	7,755	2,444	11,123	12,666	5,046	3	12,580	11,367	2,691	13,527	1,062

Distances in Kilometers	Herat, Afghanistan	Hermosillo, Mexico	Hiroshima, Japan	Hiva Oa (Atuona)	Ho Chi Minh City, Vietnam	Hobart, Australia	Hohhot, China	Hong Kong	Honiara, Solomon Islands	Honolulu, Hawaii	Houston, Texas	Huambo, Angola	Hubli, India	Hugh Town, United Kingdom	Hull, Canada	Hyderabad, India	Hyderabad, Pakistan	Igloolik, Canada	Iloilo, Philippines	Indianapolis, Indiana
Ouagadougou, Bourkina Fasso	6,839	11,177	12,917	15,391	11,695	15,494	10,986	12,037	17,985	15,480	9,705	3,370	8,253	4,187	7,810	8,566	7,428	8,343	13,346	8,688
Oujda, Morocco	5,780	9,763	11,009	14,875	10,989	17,215	9,243	10,787	16,662	13,312	8,486	5,569	7,888	1,732	6,190	8,070	6,724	6,052	12,313	7,213
Oxford, United Kingdom	5,329	8,750	9,452	13,996	10,277	17,472	7,881	9,697	15,012	11,598	7,737	7,331	7,749	411	5,297	7,805	6,449	4,414	11,256	6,355
Pago Pago, American Samoa	14,289	8,011	8,069	3,481	9,528	5,107	10,029	9,133	3,240	4,178	9,426	16,936	12,973	15,806	11,511	12,656	13,770	11,437	7,865	10,557
Pakxe, Laos	4,848	13,731	3,421	12,987	493	7,700	2,900	1,185	6,563	10,052	14,550	10,381	3,287	10,240	13,298	2,929	4,056	10,613	1,885	13,805
Palembang, Indonesia	6,067	15,266	5,047	12,827	1,526	6,112	4,889	2,967	6,146	10,900	16,363	9,835	3,835	11,754	15,294	3,657	5,020	12,611	2,483	15,779
Palermo, Italy	4,360	10,590	9,818	15,839	9,568	16,134	7,967	9,404	15,409	13,363	9,472	5,634	6,516	2,041	7,063	6,676	5,320	6,290	10,914	8,121
Palma, Majorca	5,239	9,776	10,332	14,995	10,432	17,061	8,574	10,156	15,985	12,969	8,593	5,948	7,450	1,350	6,216	7,599	6,237	5,740	11,695	7,265
Palmerston North, New Zealand	14,224	10,787	9,387	5,599	9,053	2,363	11,072	9,405	3,760	7,359	12,005	13,773	11,979	18,931	14,357	11,839	13,205	14,619	7,853	13,316
Panama, Panama	13,752	3,965	14,148	6,912	17,722	14,119	14,380	16,247	13,508	8,455	2,832	10,807	16,146	8,050	4,058	16,230	14,868	6,711	16,749	3,475
Paramaribo, Suriname	12,098	6,391	15,481	9,459	17,299	15,344	14,671	16,691	16,144	11,088	4,976	8,111	14,076	6,672	4,819	14,323	13,018	7,318	18,160	4,874
Paris, France	5,101	9,142	9,547	14,391	10,143	17,250	7,903	9,650	15,164	11,988	8,101	6,951	7,485	638	5,665	7,564	6,199	4,821	11,210	6,725
Patna, India	2,407	13,718	4,628	15,060	2,803	9,902	2,971	2,975	8,972	11,469	13,878	8,623	1,537	7,974	11,904	1,141	1,683	9,418	4,272	12,712
Patrai, Greece	3,632	11,084	9,259	16,320	8,841	15,467	7,365	8,717	14,772	13,411	10,049	5,678	5,792	2,571	7,616	5,946	4,588	6,578	10,212	8,677
Peking, China	4,782	10,938	1,549	11,947	3,373	9,690	417	1,972	7,069	8,171	11,623	11,811	4,832	8,590	10,472	4,420	4,723	7,791	3,296	10,887
Penrhyn Island (Omoka)	15,052	6,577	8,739	2,092	10,773	6,482	10,686	10,163	4,611	3,353	7,959	17,509	14,213	14,775	10,124	13,858	14,802	10,405	9,055	9,136
Peoria, Illinois	11,211	2,331	10,645	7,547	14,071	15,376	10,731	12,618	12,414	6,693	1,321	12,218	13,605	6,268	1,243	13,459	12,346	3,227	13,430	310
Perm', USSR	2,668	10,283	6,052	14,501	6,743	13,967	4,298	6,058	11,698	10,667	9,926	8,663	4,989	4,048	7,716	4,867	3,750	5,478	7,617	8,620
Perth, Australia	9,238	15,559	7,546	10,841	4,823	3,020	8,063	5,999	5,177	10,906	17,045	10,199	6,797	14,901	18,210	6,759	8,102	15,694	4,772	17,862
Peshawar, Pakistan	862	13,017	5,523	15,907	4,403	11,480	3,594	4,351	10,448	11,962	12,813	7,845	2,100	6,387	10,611	1,968	1,007	8,334	5,780	11,521
Petropavlovsk-Kamchatskiy,USSR	7,440	7,508	2,925	9,104	6,574	10,685	3,753	5,073	6,921	5,096	8,398	14,466	8,226	8,509	7,934	7,829	7,815	5,577	5,692	7,993
Petrozavodsk, USSR	3,634	9,462	7,101	14,207	8,033	15,255	5,476	7,319	12,738	10,726	8,902	8,424	6,079	2,806	6,587	6,011	4,783	4,605	8,872	7,547
Pevek, USSR	7,121	6,573	4,552	9,628	7,888	12,630	4,622	6,421	8,815	5,784	7,099	13,429	8,611	6,734	6,168	8,275	7,830	3,667	7,358	6,410
Philadelphia, Pennsylvania	10,692	3,475	11,300	8,564	14,389	16,493	11,038	13,052	13,631	7,918	2,158	10,990	13,160	5,349	611	13,097	11,850	3,300	14,108	940
Phnom Penh, Kampuchea	5,003	14,096	3,767	13,052	211	7,415	3,305	1,539	6,518	10,289	14,948	10,204	3,246	10,500	13,694	2,921	4,135	11,012	1,930	14,210
Phoenix, Arizona	12,477	498	9,931	5,574	13,632	13,243	10,648	12,139	10,400	4,684	1,636	14,283	14,550	8,246	3,363	14,269	13,494	4,417	12,452	2,413
Pierre, South Dakota	11,112	1,942	9,785	7,153	13,324	14,718	10,048	11,838	11,509	5,820	1,680	13,064	13,376	6,671	1,940	13,166	12,198	2,978	12,538	1,279
Pinang, Malaysia	5,065	14,941	4,608	13,476	914	7,143	4,076	2,385	6,814	11,014	15,771	9,561	2,963	10,727	14,359	2,724	4,060	11,704	2,518	14,958
Pitcairn Island (Adamstown)	18,450	6,330	12,190	1,937	13,858	7,579	14,121	13,531	7,563	5,946	7,111	14,432	17,187	14,498	9,548	16,955	18,174	11,165	12,253	8,503
Pittsburgh, Pennsylvania	10,868	3,082	11,078	8,219	14,296	16,122	10,934	12,912	13,219	7,502	1,829	11,406	13,320	5,649	655	13,230	12,022	3,224	13,888	529
Plymouth, Montserrat	11,866	5,148	14,142	8,947	16,736	15,982	13,609	15,678	15,401	9,916	3,670	9,175	14,154	6,180	3,426	14,296	12,928	6,008	16,930	3,450
Plymouth, United Kingdom	5,546	8,660	9,691	13,911	10,520	17,697	8,130	9,948	15,233	11,654	7,606	7,258	7,952	166	5,171	8,018	6,657	4,431	11,507	6,232
Ponape Island	10,136	9,721	4,034	7,196	5,685	5,628	5,946	5,021	1,818	4,978	11,195	15,873	9,078	13,534	12,121	8,709	9,678	10,408	3,946	11,647
Ponce, Puerto Rico	12,086	4,662	13,865	8,529	16,740	15,796	13,493	15,549	14,923	9,427	3,191	9,664	14,438	6,378	3,156	14,547	13,179	5,802	16,675	3,058
Ponta Delgada, Azores	7,614	7,719	11,706	12,727	12,709	19,187	10,288	12,154	16,820	11,785	6,371	7,065	9,903	2,052	4,192	10,032	8,664	4,821	13,711	5,161
Pontianak, Indonesia	6,205	14,672	4,509	12,390	1,228	6,075	4,526	2,520	5,703	10,309	15,811	10,403	4,124	11,817	14,951	3,892	5,223	12,263	1,885	15,334
Port Augusta, Australia	10,820	13,553	7,426	8,800	5,817	1,429	8,548	6,559	3,425	9,072	15,004	12,081	8,507	16,488	16,813	8,384	9,754	15,226	5,047	16,031
Port Blair, India	3,990	14,841	4,743	14,376	1,523	8,194	3,725	2,563	7,792	11,500	15,347	8,917	1,948	9,671	13,584	1,667	2,984	11,011	3,257	14,317
Port Elizabeth, South Africa	8,471	15,895	13,443	14,898	9,866	9,642	12,079	11,237	13,217	18,563	14,496	2,553	7,575	9,810	13,423	7,981	7,973	14,170	11,311	14,050
Port Hedland, Australia	8,494	14,961	6,232	10,912	3,675	3,671	6,802	4,733	4,599	10,188	16,464	10,826	6,172	14,193	16,929	6,048	7,418	14,380	3,459	16,824
Port Louis, Mauritius	6,052	18,494	9,959	16,235	6,379	8,498	8,763	7,742	10,937	16,356	17,098	4,518	4,378	9,972	14,920	4,744	5,173	13,887	7,900	15,938
Port Moresby, Papua New Guinea	10,146	11,670	5,100	8,080	5,014	3,705	6,655	5,030	1,402	6,904	13,181	14,123	8,402	14,902	14,308	8,120	9,357	12,503	3,523	13,786
Port Said, Egypt	2,811	12,284	8,945	17,468	7,920	14,249	6,985	8,024	14,118	14,087	11,284	5,179	4,690	3,808	8,848	4,892	3,581	7,657	9,429	9,908
Port Sudan, Sudan	2,953	13,635	9,263	18,850	7,480	13,092	7,318	7,916	13,785	15,191	12,557	4,282	4,049	5,100	10,144	4,351	3,259	9,038	9,140	11,203
Port-au-Prince, Haiti	12,440	4,086	13,590	7,965	16,764	15,423	13,425	15,439	14,316	8,840	2,643	10,265	14,849	6,742	3,000	14,918	13,561	5,688	16,387	2,703
Port-of-Spain, Trin. & Tobago	12,276	5,518	14,807	8,875	17,308	15,476	14,267	16,335	15,492	10,238	4,096	8,925	14,454	6,652	4,087	14,643	13,288	6,682	17,602	4,041
Port-Vila, Vanuatu	12,562	10,092	6,908	5,744	7,473	3,424	8,729	7,371	1,289	5,680	11,567	15,495	10,851	16,403	13,413	10,577	11,813	12,614	5,932	12,565
Portland, Maine	10,120	3,946	11,061	9,101	13,972	16,995	10,651	12,694	13,876	8,219	2,704	10,663	12,590	4,782	478	12,537	11,279	2,940	13,848	1,389
Portland, Oregon	11,146	2,094	8,390	6,345	12,069	13,226	9,032	10,568	9,789	4,181	2,951	14,674	13,029	7,778	3,612	12,721	12,075	3,488	11,021	3,031
Porto, Portugal	6,115	8,880	10,744	14,059	11,260	18,028	9,118	10,846	16,317	12,399	7,652	6,472	8,390	991	5,307	8,521	7,153	5,145	12,403	6,345
Porto Alegre, Brazil	13,840	9,114	19,423	9,270	16,883	11,706	18,062	18,325	14,520	12,725	8,111	7,108	14,335	9,906	8,722	14,751	14,113	11,305	17,767	8,536
Porto Alexandre, Angola	7,691	14,024	13,782	15,745	10,844	12,077	11,955	11,905	15,532	18,786	12,515	542	7,763	7,498	11,064	8,176	7,631	11,782	12,533	11,799
Porto Novo, Benin	6,827	11,913	13,077	15,797	11,408	14,700	11,115	11,930	17,517	16,273	10,425	2,576	7,960	4,887	8,590	8,305	7,273	9,113	13,115	9,450
Porto Velho, Brazil	13,856	6,558	16,718	8,237	18,978	13,470	16,430	18,499	14,772	10,775	5,434	8,695	15,527	8,552	6,119	15,851	14,662	8,780	19,294	5,843
Portsmouth, United Kingdom	5,327	8,820	9,532	14,068	10,305	17,479	7,947	9,747	15,104	11,703	7,790	7,223	7,737	384	5,352	7,800	6,441	4,512	11,307	6,411
Poznan, Poland	4,090	9,663	8,542	14,809	9,049	16,225	6,835	8,548	14,193	11,822	8,794	7,219	6,528	1,645	6,359	6,569	5,220	5,003	10,107	7,402
Prague, Czechoslovakia	4,224	9,726	8,844	14,919	9,257	16,377	7,121	8,803	14,497	12,061	8,797	6,960	6,632	1,485	6,355	6,695	5,335	5,144	10,360	7,408
Praia, Cape Verde Islands	8,706	8,980	13,988	13,022	13,846	16,782	12,306	13,841	19,299	13,627	7,471	5,302	10,484	4,183	5,919	10,754	9,501	7,247	15,333	6,634
Pretoria, South Africa	7,559	15,992	12,828	15,838	9,400	10,191	11,318	10,684	13,514	19,234	14,499	1,939	6,827	9,048	13,055	7,241	7,118	13,438	10,962	13,816
Prince Albert, Canada	10,237	2,714	8,798	7,660	12,282	14,694	8,992	10,806	11,127	5,637	2,738	13,213	12,409	6,323	2,327	12,174	11,282	2,184	11,582	2,107
Prince Edward Island	9,286	16,695	13,004	13,753	9,300	7,904	12,116	10,784	11,567	16,862	15,602	4,289	7,807	11,511	15,036	8,168	8,538	15,895	10,460	15,508
Prince George, Canada	10,216	2,921	7,868	7,226	11,471	13,696	8,302	9,971	10,029	4,675	3,473	14,177	12,143	7,060	3,452	11,850	11,156	2,686	10,603	3,154
Prince Rupert, Canada	10,109	3,210	7,416	7,152	11,048	13,294	7,936	9,546	9,575	4,335	3,905	14,527	11,917	7,330	3,939	11,604	10,997	2,938	10,131	3,648
Providence, Rhode Island	10,340	3,820	11,222	8,937	14,181	16,857	10,852	12,889	13,865	8,178	2,532	10,715	12,810	4,971	532	12,759	11,498	3,128	14,018	1,264
Provo, Utah	11,724	1,240	9,456	6,216	13,126	13,679	10,026	11,623	10,547	4,828	1,882	14,073	13,811	7,654	2,968	13,541	12,742	3,688	12,089	2,171
Puerto Aisen, Chile	16,030	9,111	17,561	7,396	16,163	9,452	19,389	17,363	11,986	11,304	8,634	8,896	15,529	12,352	10,067	15,915	15,900	12,752	15,895	9,529
Puerto Deseado, Argentina	15,503	9,627	17,885	7,948	15,845	9,445	19,207	17,175	12,236	11,876	9,077	8,353	14,953	12,238	10,368	15,342	15,325	13,056	15,822	9,900
Puerto Princesa, Philippines	6,345	13,177	3,069	11,527	1,327	6,514	3,511	1,468	5,035	8,950	14,321	11,646	4,768	11,532	13,727	4,431	5,584	11,085	433	13,957
Punta Arenas, Chile	15,802	9,899	17,230	7,687	15,297	8,750	18,617	16,548	11,579	11,678	9,486	8,667	14,875	12,929	10,934	15,236	15,441	13,621	15,145	10,400
Pusan, South Korea	6,001	10,526	321	10,806	3,523	8,837	1,654	2,031	5,905	7,182	11,455	12,929	5,775	9,616	10,745	5,357	5,852	8,148	2,781	10,965
Pyongyang, North Korea	5,589	10,455	788	11,141	3,660	9,332	1,223	2,161	6,426	7,404	11,285	12,615	5,567	9,095	10,409	5,151	5,525	7,774	3,153	10,698
Qamdo, China	3,286	12,704	3,302	13,775	2,461	9,667	1,676	1,950	8,048	10,132	13,132	9,943	2,847	8,305	11,492	2,435	2,896	8,854	3,458	12,143
Qandahar, Afghanistan	451	13,283	6,126	16,505	4,794	11,703	4,200	4,880	10,953	12,540	12,930	7,242	2,037	6,160	10,635	2,030	735	8,501	6,261	11,592
Qiqian, China	4,995	9,694	2,185	11,555	4,771	10,844	1,450	3,373	7,782	7,581	10,267	12,142	5,727	7,642	9,071	5,344	5,284	6,393	4,605	9,487
Qom, Iran	1,038	12,701	7,255	17,076	6,219	13,003	5,290	6,248	12,346	13,110	12,049	6,424	3,235	4,881	9,644	3,339	1,970	7,845	7,670	10,664
Quebec, Canada	9,886	3,951	10,704	9,163	13,625	16,973	10,297	12,337	13,666	8,063	2,814	10,807	12,348	4,669	380	12,277	11,043	2,580	13,489	1,438
Quetta, Pakistan	644	13,442	6,074	16,501	4,631	11,512	4,167	4,761	10,818	12,565	13,112	7,256	1,844	6,351	10,825	1,836	552	8,675	6,121	11,779
Quito, Ecuador	14,454	4,735	15,047	6,786	18,713	13,410	15,398	17,214	13,474	8,923	3,770	10,478	16,685	8,760	5,064	16,867	15,504	7,728	17,428	4,496
Rabaul, Papua New Guinea	10,273	10,907	4,748	7,615	5,308	4,316	6,468	5,068	1,035	6,134	12,412	14,861	8,753	14,552	13,508	8,437	9,594	11,783	3,673	12,984
Raiatea (Uturoa)	16,150	6,679	9,830	1,546	11,611	6,428	11,785	11,145	5,321	4,267	7,915	16,460	15,057	15,186	10,246	14,738	15,803	10,965	9,936	9,206
Raleigh, North Carolina	11,247	3,116	11,596	8,090	14,826	16,032	11,464	13,444	13,447	7,717	1,700	11,224	13,714	5,875	1,100	13,649	12,405	3,745	14,404	797
Rangiroa (Avatoru)	16,334	6,269	10,036	1,100	11,985	6,861	11,974	11,453	5,718	4,160	7,482	16,453	15,436	14,802	9,829	15,101	16,102	10,645	10,292	8,784
Rangoon, Burma	3,900	14,160	4,103	14,022	1,317	8,426	3,047	1,982	7,596	10,921	14,709	9,422	2,252	9,462	13,067	1,885	3,034	10,446	2,931	13,740
Raoul Is., Kermadec Islands	14,389	9,604	8,769	4,581	9,212	3,445	10,620	9,243	3,187	5,995	10,922	15,133	12,457	17,606	13,169	12,236	13,544	13,255	7,766	12,161
Rarotonga (Avarua)	15,677	7,639	9,444	2,553	10,808	5,438	11,408	10,503	4,503	4,708	8,908	16,220	14,216	16,062	11,213	13,931	15,111	11,733	9,189	10,182
Rawson, Argentina	15,417	9,281	18,209	7,970	16,311	9,924	19,624	17,669	12,608	11,821	8,660	8,316	15,144	11,800	9,886	15,547	15,375	12,572	16,317	9,441
Recife, Brazil	11,165	9,111	16,817	11,398	15,808	14,356	15,106	16,365	17,479	13,751	7,697	5,566	12,397	6,995	7,188	12,757	11,726	9,307	17,545	7,467
Regina, Canada	10,524	2,434	9,071	7,461	12,580	14,668	9,300	11,099	11,196	5,627	2,424	13,229	12,716	6,463	2,213	12,485	11,579	2,433	11,843	1,867
Reykjavik, Iceland	6,355	7,091	8,851	12,274	10,652	17,546	7,681	9,706	13,929	9,799	6,271	9,105	8,823	1,836	3,871	8,776	7,513	2,584	11,183	4,884
Rhodes, Greece	3,081	11,598	8,924	16,790	8,281	14,863	6,994	8,231	14,322	13,581	10,612	5,596	5,188	3,144	8,173	5,349	3,998	6,986	9,699	9,233
Richmond, Virginia	11,025	3,241	11,464	8,271	14,642	16,210	11,283	13,276	13,508	7,780	1,868	11,146	13,491	5,669	888	13,426	12,183	3,553	14,274	797
Riga, USSR	3,808	9,584	7,872	14,576	8,562	15,795	6,196	7,966	13,518	11,330	8,853	7,761	6,279	2,146	6,455	6,271	4,963	4,793	9,526	7,468
Ringkobing, Denmark	4,717	8,970	8,681	14,140	9,540	16,772	7,094	8,917	14,276	11,330	8,097	7,658	7,175	1,191	5,664	7,194	5,861	4,357	10,475	6,705
Rio Branco, Brazil	14,280	6,334	16,612	7,796	19,424	13,155	16,590	18,630	14,325	10,421	5,297	9,089	15,974	8,905	6,187	16,300	15,105	8,869	18,899	5,824
Rio Cuarto, Argentina	15,130	8,460	18,467	8,001	17,364	10,989	19,086	18,790	13,371	11,591	7,691	8,339	15,505	10,831	8,776	15,923	15,391	11,457	17,424	8,379
Rio de Janeiro, Brazil	12,781	9,257	18,665	10,183	16,562	12,638	16,940	17,710	15,636	13,343	8,066	6,318	13,542	8,851	8,252	13,944	13,151	10,688	17,996	8,246
Rio Gallegos, Argentina	15,714	9,827	17,427	7,769	15,455	8,953	18,797	16,731	11,774	11,747	9,373	8,565	14,896	12,726	10,774	15,266	15,407	13,462	15,342	10,260
Rio Grande, Brazil	14,002	9,190	19,524	9,157	16,805	11,473	18,269	18,282	14,300	12,682	8,227	7,195	14,400	10,139	8,906	14,817	14,234	11,503	17,581	8,693
Riyadh, Saudi Arabia	1,843	13,605	8,140	18,257	6,494	12,668	6,199	6,826	12,793	14,274	12,758	5,328	3,142	5,329	10,316	3,389	2,185	8,799	8,105	11,368
Road Town, Brit. Virgin Isls.	11,907	4,837	13,885	8,746	16,639	15,972	13,436	15,500	15,129	9,608	3,354	9,472	14,243	6,202	3,164	14,360	12,991	5,781	16,687	3,142

Distances in Kilometers	Herat, Afghanistan	Hermosillo, Mexico	Hiroshima, Japan	Hiva Oa (Atuona)	Ho Chi Minh City, Vietnam	Hobart, Australia	Hohhot, China	Hong Kong	Honiara, Solomon Islands	Honolulu, Hawaii	Houston, Texas	Huambo, Angola	Hubli, India	Hugh Town, United Kingdom	Hull, Canada	Hyderabad, India	Hyderabad, Pakistan	Igloolik, Canada	Iloilo, Philippines	Indianapolis, Indiana
Roanoke, Virginia	11,166	3,018	11,394	8,060	14,645	15,997	11,282	13,253	13,299	7,570	1,654	11,361	13,627	5,860	972	13,548	12,323	3,575	14,202	609
Robinson Crusoe Island, Chile	16,451	7,720	17,145	6,659	17,410	10,317	18,795	18,222	12,196	10,340	7,229	9,662	16,718	11,682	8,762	17,129	16,736	11,426	16,665	8,162
Rochester, New York	10,506	3,355	10,892	8,536	14,020	16,404	10,662	12,664	13,335	7,649	2,169	11,241	12,959	5,311	294	12,872	11,660	2,930	13,701	807
Rockhampton, Australia	11,293	12,027	6,674	7,602	6,086	2,186	8,163	6,401	1,843	7,468	13,515	13,677	9,246	16,442	15,205	9,035	10,364	13,855	4,845	14,447
Rome, Italy	4,378	10,247	9,580	15,497	9,564	16,348	7,772	9,300	15,213	12,936	9,174	6,058	6,632	1,702	6,748	6,763	5,396	5,879	10,833	7,809
Rosario, Argentina	14,796	8,676	18,801	8,345	17,231	11,135	18,905	18,718	13,652	11,918	7,846	7,998	15,178	10,627	8,813	15,596	15,046	11,478	17,519	8,469
Roseau, Dominica	11,912	5,293	14,314	8,998	16,843	15,910	13,754	15,823	15,499	10,055	3,824	9,049	14,169	6,243	3,601	14,325	12,959	6,175	17,097	3,626
Rostock, East Germany	4,440	9,303	8,660	14,470	9,342	16,549	7,012	8,782	14,291	11,597	8,423	7,412	6,887	1,345	5,987	6,919	5,577	4,679	10,342	7,031
Rostov-na-Donu, USSR	2,364	11,059	7,488	15,853	7,403	14,507	5,605	7,071	13,040	12,213	10,367	7,055	4,813	3,355	7,966	4,844	3,501	6,223	8,607	8,982
Rotterdam, Netherlands	4,933	9,064	9,189	14,294	9,896	17,077	7,568	9,348	14,796	11,713	8,090	7,245	7,355	792	5,648	7,409	6,053	4,612	10,908	6,704
Rouyn, Canada	10,083	3,460	10,334	8,706	13,447	16,410	10,088	12,089	13,063	7,458	2,480	11,409	12,514	5,099	399	12,402	11,230	2,361	13,141	1,100
Sacramento, California	11,922	1,435	8,914	5,658	12,617	12,870	9,699	11,128	9,681	3,963	2,589	14,933	13,789	8,334	3,813	13,471	12,852	4,155	11,437	3,036
Saginaw, Michigan	10,735	2,885	10,631	8,105	13,910	15,919	10,548	12,501	12,829	7,136	1,825	11,756	13,158	5,712	689	13,037	11,880	2,892	13,439	447
Saint Denis, Reunion	6,151	18,381	10,177	16,266	6,605	8,608	8,958	7,963	11,126	16,578	16,939	4,312	4,549	9,912	14,820	4,921	5,302	13,900	8,127	15,822
Saint George's, Grenada	12,188	5,422	14,651	8,883	17,183	15,592	14,116	16,185	15,470	10,156	3,986	8,990	14,396	6,546	3,931	14,573	13,214	6,525	17,445	3,898
Saint John, Canada	9,770	4,307	10,988	9,477	13,758	17,354	10,470	12,528	14,102	8,494	3,083	10,378	12,242	4,402	759	12,200	10,928	2,827	13,747	1,756
Saint John's, Antigua	11,807	5,166	14,109	8,996	16,680	16,041	13,561	15,630	15,436	9,936	3,683	9,149	14,096	6,121	3,397	14,238	12,869	5,970	16,893	3,438
Saint John's, Canada	8,866	5,349	10,912	10,532	13,232	18,368	10,096	12,162	14,788	9,360	4,135	9,496	11,334	3,368	1,776	11,331	10,018	2,902	13,534	2,808
Saint Louis, Missouri	11,443	2,188	10,808	7,370	14,268	15,236	10,938	12,807	12,386	6,657	1,091	12,270	13,841	6,457	1,414	13,695	12,580	3,461	13,580	372
Saint Paul, Minnesota	10,879	2,363	10,094	7,613	13,526	15,277	10,195	12,069	12,080	6,398	1,697	12,485	13,224	6,192	1,363	13,050	11,996	2,796	12,882	810
Saint Peter Port, UK	5,447	8,812	9,712	14,064	10,455	17,600	8,122	9,915	15,282	11,797	7,751	7,119	7,841	278	5,318	7,915	6,551	4,581	11,475	6,378
Saipan (Susupe)	8,492	10,452	2,514	8,745	4,260	6,431	4,348	3,412	3,140	5,977	11,803	14,630	7,541	12,296	12,110	7,155	8,058	9,924	2,558	11,905
Salalah, Oman	2,083	14,663	7,913	18,400	5,708	11,538	6,073	6,289	11,996	14,529	13,888	5,345	2,259	6,470	11,448	2,591	1,745	9,816	7,401	12,496
Salem, Oregon	11,210	2,058	8,400	6,272	12,084	13,163	9,064	10,584	9,740	4,122	2,951	14,735	13,081	7,850	3,663	12,770	12,134	3,561	11,020	3,065
Salt Lake City, Utah	11,668	1,299	9,403	6,254	13,070	13,692	9,966	11,568	10,536	4,821	1,930	14,076	13,751	7,623	2,963	13,481	12,684	3,639	12,041	2,183
Salta, Argentina	14,898	7,697	17,995	7,917	18,247	11,796	18,209	19,721	13,815	11,216	6,832	8,554	15,795	10,117	7,845	16,203	15,392	10,526	18,239	7,464
Salto, Uruguay	14,498	8,731	18,996	8,609	17,234	11,384	18,613	18,737	13,958	12,122	7,839	7,754	14,962	10,347	8,694	15,380	14,777	11,341	17,714	8,399
Salvador, Brazil	11,794	9,060	17,466	10,897	16,238	13,787	15,780	16,963	16,806	13,551	7,714	5,882	12,899	7,646	7,473	13,274	12,306	9,736	17,960	7,640
Salzburg, Austria	4,312	9,827	9,094	15,050	9,402	16,451	7,350	8,997	14,747	12,297	8,850	6,710	6,684	1,435	6,408	6,767	5,401	5,316	10,550	7,465
Samsun, Turkey	2,394	11,523	8,040	16,487	7,588	14,476	6,116	7,423	13,486	12,922	10,709	6,343	4,708	3,412	8,275	4,806	3,436	6,743	8,922	9,317
San Antonio, Texas	12,664	1,212	11,152	6,143	14,812	14,068	11,638	13,309	11,640	5,981	306	13,043	15,005	7,715	2,669	14,815	13,783	4,572	13,766	1,609
San Cristobal, Venezuela	13,333	4,688	14,669	7,656	17,953	14,534	14,615	16,613	14,295	9,256	3,431	9,993	15,614	7,636	4,188	15,766	14,398	6,877	17,399	3,807
San Diego, California	12,583	716	9,624	5,247	13,327	12,808	10,457	11,849	9,918	4,204	2,098	14,764	14,528	8,610	3,802	14,219	13,550	4,635	12,075	2,878
San Francisco, California	12,007	1,436	8,902	5,544	12,606	12,751	9,721	11,121	9,580	3,857	2,648	15,042	13,846	8,454	3,926	13,523	12,926	4,269	11,401	3,138
San Jose, Costa Rica	13,959	3,512	13,776	6,466	17,433	13,857	14,164	15,933	13,021	7,949	2,489	11,318	16,404	8,295	4,015	16,434	15,100	6,604	16,295	3,312
San Juan, Argentina	15,452	8,073	18,045	7,606	17,652	10,989	18,978	18,944	13,154	11,164	7,354	8,750	15,932	10,906	8,555	16,351	15,778	11,243	17,436	8,102
San Juan, Puerto Rico	12,014	4,691	13,835	8,593	16,679	15,869	13,441	15,500	14,972	9,459	3,214	9,625	14,365	6,306	3,120	14,475	13,106	5,759	16,643	3,047
San Luis Potosi, Mexico	13,507	1,261	11,586	5,453	15,289	13,395	12,269	13,798	11,335	5,849	1,014	13,279	15,836	8,478	3,454	15,631	14,624	5,407	14,042	2,406
San Marino, San Marino	4,361	10,092	9,425	15,338	9,523	16,410	7,638	9,210	15,070	12,715	9,049	6,282	6,661	1,573	6,616	6,776	5,406	5,678	10,751	7,676
San Miguel de Tucuman, Argen.	14,970	7,878	18,137	7,929	18,038	11,598	18,429	19,495	13,709	11,305	7,038	8,504	15,743	10,293	8,071	16,155	15,410	10,752	18,048	7,685
San Salvador, El Salvador	13,895	2,817	13,107	6,087	16,792	13,749	13,605	15,290	12,502	7,288	1,888	11,940	16,367	8,348	3,740	16,314	15,052	6,207	15,599	2,904
Sanaa, Yemen	2,771	14,418	8,907	19,305	6,773	12,221	7,018	7,355	13,041	15,295	13,403	4,410	3,322	5,930	10,977	3,663	2,750	9,710	8,473	12,037
Santa Cruz, Bolivia	14,335	7,299	17,609	8,202	18,680	12,597	17,409	19,446	14,412	11,188	6,296	8,440	15,589	9,343	7,117	15,969	14,970	9,782	19,017	6,806
Santa Cruz, Tenerife	7,301	8,949	12,312	13,731	12,509	17,834	10,650	12,285	17,863	13,137	7,536	5,714	9,349	2,527	5,488	9,553	8,222	6,120	13,823	6,411
Santa Fe, New Mexico	12,157	872	10,168	6,117	13,837	13,849	10,712	12,334	10,988	5,262	1,188	13,687	14,356	7,689	2,758	14,113	13,222	4,031	12,788	1,799
Santa Rosa, Argentina	15,225	8,757	18,490	8,010	17,001	10,635	19,428	18,405	13,137	11,702	8,034	8,299	15,379	11,149	9,160	15,795	15,384	11,842	17,054	8,750
Santa Rosalia, Mexico	13,157	233	10,369	5,020	14,070	12,830	11,215	12,599	10,273	4,649	1,677	14,405	15,217	8,783	3,799	14,926	14,175	5,078	12,767	2,777
Santarem, Brazil	12,620	6,930	16,390	9,352	17,777	14,521	15,542	17,511	15,974	11,480	5,603	7,840	14,355	7,411	5,696	14,657	13,435	8,228	19,045	5,669
Santiago del Estero, Argentina	14,924	8,021	18,272	8,019	17,900	11,538	18,515	19,373	13,727	11,427	7,177	8,397	15,632	10,331	8,191	16,046	15,333	10,868	17,987	7,815
Santiago, Chile	15,705	8,119	17,892	7,414	17,476	10,709	19,167	18,679	12,868	11,041	7,465	8,918	16,049	11,197	8,751	16,466	15,979	11,439	17,152	8,262
Santo Domingo, Dominican Rep.	12,280	4,324	13,697	8,208	16,752	15,597	13,443	15,479	14,573	9,084	2,866	10,013	14,668	6,574	3,039	14,754	13,390	5,716	16,505	2,832
Sao Paulo de Olivenca, Brazil	13,919	5,762	15,941	7,787	19,064	13,725	15,869	17,901	14,444	10,058	4,639	9,347	15,872	8,384	5,458	16,141	14,848	8,142	18,539	5,104
Sao Paulo, Brazil	13,120	9,018	18,797	9,830	16,862	12,510	17,226	18,058	15,363	13,020	7,871	6,663	13,891	9,056	8,187	14,295	13,503	10,683	18,190	8,122
Sao Tome, Sao Tome & Principe	6,878	12,666	13,197	16,102	11,098	13,881	11,237	11,795	16,901	17,093	11,164	1,757	7,696	5,634	9,396	8,068	7,166	9,911	12,833	10,236
Sapporo, Japan	6,698	9,147	1,232	9,916	4,903	9,541	2,467	3,410	6,111	6,071	10,088	13,837	6,931	9,237	9,540	6,517	6,789	7,047	4,020	9,667
Sarajevo, Yugoslavia	3,883	10,435	9,077	15,655	9,052	15,947	7,252	8,770	14,697	12,781	9,445	6,269	6,188	1,992	7,005	6,299	4,929	5,899	10,304	8,064
Saratov, USSR	2,314	10,794	6,873	15,350	7,066	14,273	5,025	6,600	12,471	11,603	10,239	7,699	4,780	3,620	7,899	4,747	3,471	5,936	8,153	8,877
Saskatoon, Canada	10,366	2,585	8,840	7,528	12,348	14,599	9,071	10,867	11,063	5,544	2,650	13,307	12,528	6,446	2,369	12,290	11,408	2,318	11,616	2,086
Schefferville, Canada	8,999	4,526	9,951	9,777	12,715	17,220	9,412	11,467	13,518	8,163	3,593	10,687	11,448	4,028	1,219	11,361	10,152	1,791	12,693	2,205
Seattle, Washington	10,919	2,279	8,279	6,569	11,943	13,367	8,866	10,440	9,871	4,312	3,042	14,539	12,820	7,585	3,530	12,516	11,854	3,274	10,941	3,013
Sendai, Japan	6,860	9,472	869	9,827	4,568	9,013	2,521	3,105	5,638	6,099	10,485	13,931	6,859	9,723	10,041	6,442	6,842	7,572	3,557	10,129
Seoul, South Korea	5,739	10,483	604	11,018	3,600	9,148	1,374	2,097	6,233	7,321	11,350	12,732	5,639	9,289	10,535	5,222	5,643	7,913	3,009	10,799
Sept-Iles, Canada	9,369	4,397	10,452	9,633	13,219	17,335	9,923	11,980	13,813	8,320	3,319	10,537	11,833	4,181	877	11,767	10,526	2,289	13,202	1,933
Sevastopol, USSR	2,699	11,090	8,048	16,083	7,844	14,836	6,160	7,584	13,587	12,615	10,282	6,598	5,076	3,036	7,851	5,151	3,785	6,316	9,108	8,890
Seville, Spain	6,030	9,290	10,974	14,422	11,223	17,678	9,277	10,918	16,606	12,875	8,024	5,997	8,220	1,393	5,716	8,379	7,020	5,621	12,464	6,742
Shanghai, China	5,479	11,352	1,100	11,482	2,718	8,616	1,385	1,215	6,089	7,974	12,233	12,210	4,999	9,657	11,354	4,582	5,192	8,702	2,264	11,660
Sheffield, United Kingdom	5,334	8,639	9,318	13,877	10,229	17,450	7,773	9,612	14,858	11,425	7,654	7,507	7,769	508	5,211	7,813	6,463	4,255	11,169	6,268
Shenyang, China	5,325	10,382	1,138	11,353	3,811	9,684	997	2,335	6,787	7,547	11,141	12,407	5,461	8,730	10,156	5,049	5,329	7,502	3,447	10,491
Shiraz, Iran	1,053	13,281	7,368	17,510	5,971	12,547	5,419	6,159	12,209	13,504	12,610	6,124	2,804	5,361	10,195	2,964	1,632	8,426	7,509	11,222
Sibiu, Romania	3,447	10,562	8,586	15,707	8,583	15,575	6,751	8,271	14,197	12,570	9,660	6,536	5,808	2,309	7,219	5,894	4,526	5,897	9,809	8,270
Singapore	5,664	15,019	4,720	13,016	1,092	6,544	4,444	2,575	6,331	10,824	16,016	9,840	3,514	11,328	14,829	3,300	4,647	12,151	2,317	15,347
Sioux Falls, South Dakota	11,121	2,047	10,042	7,293	13,545	14,950	10,244	12,069	11,801	6,102	1,534	12,789	13,432	6,515	1,679	13,241	12,225	3,002	12,807	975
Skelleftea, Sweden	4,366	8,805	7,528	13,707	8,728	15,913	6,026	7,941	13,092	10,461	8,184	8,605	6,819	2,296	5,849	6,756	5,518	3,969	9,481	6,820
Skopje, Yugoslavia	3,632	10,753	9,014	15,965	8,824	15,645	7,154	8,602	14,593	12,995	9,768	6,088	5,899	2,311	7,328	6,022	4,653	6,190	10,122	8,386
Socotra Island (Tamrida)	2,540	15,118	8,175	18,576	5,735	11,226	6,385	6,439	11,961	14,895	14,286	5,069	2,303	6,831	11,843	2,679	2,062	10,281	7,456	12,897
Sofia, Bulgaria	3,483	10,791	8,848	15,980	8,667	15,529	6,985	8,435	14,424	12,918	9,835	6,184	5,772	2,402	7,393	5,886	4,516	6,183	9,957	8,450
Songkhla, Thailand	4,950	14,768	4,442	13,473	774	7,285	3,878	2,212	6,834	10,911	15,577	9,634	2,916	10,591	14,164	2,654	3,970	11,506	2,446	14,759
Sorong, Indonesia	8,157	12,745	3,908	9,971	3,010	4,924	5,025	3,161	3,316	8,076	14,151	12,755	6,424	13,256	14,410	6,127	7,352	12,016	1,602	14,282
South Georgia Island	13,573	11,633	17,645	9,916	14,208	9,230	17,236	15,703	12,776	13,915	10,870	6,481	12,801	11,891	11,647	13,193	13,226	14,191	14,841	11,436
South Pole	13,804	13,218	13,809	8,917	11,191	5,247	14,518	12,463	8,957	12,358	13,296	8,596	11,701	15,536	15,036	11,925	12,810	17,703	11,185	14,406
South Sandwich Islands	13,085	12,376	16,973	10,384	13,465	8,813	16,511	14,963	12,535	14,393	11,614	6,128	12,129	12,078	12,309	12,512	12,638	14,782	14,163	12,148
Split, Yugoslavia	4,044	10,351	9,221	15,585	9,215	16,090	7,404	8,932	14,848	12,803	9,338	6,229	6,338	1,870	6,900	6,453	5,084	5,860	10,467	7,960
Spokane, Washington	10,922	2,139	8,574	6,715	12,215	13,691	9,082	10,713	10,233	4,645	2,743	14,210	12,914	7,341	3,167	12,629	11,895	3,098	11,264	2,646
Spoleto, Italy	4,349	10,198	9,501	15,447	9,526	16,355	7,699	9,244	15,138	12,849	9,140	6,149	6,623	1,664	6,710	6,747	5,378	5,805	10,780	7,771
Springbok, South Africa	8,478	15,104	13,930	14,993	10,483	10,459	12,386	11,784	14,083	18,990	13,668	1,887	7,911	9,134	12,556	8,326	8,132	13,434	12,010	13,181
Springfield, Illinois	11,304	2,284	10,725	7,485	14,162	15,333	10,825	12,707	12,420	6,695	1,229	12,223	13,701	6,336	1,299	13,556	12,440	3,326	13,506	299
Springfield, Massachusetts	10,372	3,728	11,159	8,859	14,152	16,771	10,815	12,847	13,762	8,076	2,457	10,817	12,841	5,035	449	12,783	11,530	3,084	13,958	1,170
Srinagar, India	1,162	12,989	5,234	15,648	4,143	11,267	3,315	4,052	10,152	11,730	12,863	8,110	2,076	6,606	10,714	1,886	1,150	8,373	5,491	11,598
Stanley, Falkland Islands	14,929	10,340	17,915	8,552	15,253	9,244	18,552	16,665	12,330	12,521	9,741	7,780	14,232	12,270	10,899	14,618	14,656	13,572	15,458	10,500
Stara Zagora, Bulgaria	3,291	10,932	8,714	16,097	8,479	15,340	6,838	8,261	14,269	12,940	9,998	6,189	5,581	2,582	7,556	5,693	4,324	6,288	9,778	8,611
Stockholm, Sweden	4,239	9,150	8,005	14,183	8,908	16,146	6,408	8,243	13,619	11,059	8,409	7,991	6,711	1,874	6,012	6,695	5,396	4,380	9,799	7,024
Stornoway, United Kingdom	5,608	8,104	9,050	13,318	10,297	17,517	7,627	9,551	14,468	10,807	7,190	8,119	8,074	924	4,753	8,080	6,759	3,640	11,091	5,798
Strasbourg, France	4,705	9,476	9,309	14,715	9,768	16,851	7,615	9,316	14,953	12,133	8,469	6,838	7,086	1,033	6,029	7,165	5,800	5,049	10,874	7,088
Stuttgart, West Germany	4,599	9,544	9,222	14,777	9,661	16,747	7,519	9,212	14,869	12,137	8,550	6,843	6,983	1,132	6,109	7,061	5,696	5,084	10,770	7,167
Subic, Philippines	6,170	12,678	2,486	11,437	1,542	6,973	2,990	1,036	5,142	8,606	13,771	11,904	4,836	11,138	13,135	4,468	5,513	10,499	528	13,369
Suchow, China	4,996	11,367	1,404	11,886	2,816	9,081	874	1,364	6,614	8,264	12,140	11,841	4,692	9,154	11,083	4,274	4,775	8,407	2,667	11,465
Sucre, Bolivia	14,596	7,239	17,574	7,968	18,759	12,380	17,576	19,645	14,150	11,022	6,290	8,638	15,816	9,580	7,217	16,202	15,224	9,893	18,769	6,861
Sudbury, Canada	10,325	3,241	10,441	8,480	13,618	16,229	10,256	12,240	12,975	7,331	2,236	11,543	12,753	5,328	425	12,637	11,471	2,549	13,251	857
Suez, Egypt	2,829	12,417	9,007	17,610	7,900	14,151	7,044	8,040	14,125	14,223	11,403	5,056	4,638	3,926	8,970	4,852	3,556	7,800	9,429	10,030
Sundsvall, Sweden	4,406	8,877	7,830	13,866	8,922	16,139	6,297	8,184	13,408	10,717	8,185	8,329	6,874	1,999	5,813	6,835	5,564	4,077	9,731	6,808

Distances in Kilometers	Herat, Afghanistan	Hermosillo, Mexico	Hiroshima, Japan	Hiva Oa (Atuona)	Ho Chi Minh City, Vietnam	Hobart, Australia	Hohhot, China	Hong Kong	Honiara, Solomon Islands	Honolulu, Hawaii	Houston, Texas	Huambo, Angola	Hubli, India	Hugh Town, United Kingdom	Hull, Canada	Hyderabad, India	Hyderabad, Pakistan	Igloolik, Canada	Iloilo, Philippines	Indianapolis, Indiana
Surabaya, Indonesia	7,030	14,853	5,055	11,857	2,102	5,201	5,320	3,267	5,201	10,243	16,168	10,592	4,841	12,680	15,696	4,652	6,008	13,026	2,264	15,943
Suva, Fiji	13,511	9,206	7,582	4,678	8,503	4,013	9,484	8,299	2,214	5,073	10,644	16,102	11,906	16,454	12,653	11,621	12,829	12,262	6,915	11,734
Sverdlovsk, USSR	2,506	10,451	5,812	14,518	6,453	13,676	4,031	5,771	11,449	10,629	10,144	8,746	4,767	4,336	7,964	4,629	3,552	5,677	7,330	8,853
Svobodnyy, USSR	5,505	9,392	1,920	11,050	4,912	10,614	1,732	3,453	7,401	7,084	10,061	12,654	6,151	7,980	9,033	5,758	5,766	6,388	4,542	9,371
Sydney, Australia	11,955	12,415	7,808	7,546	6,824	1,058	9,210	7,348	2,852	8,151	13,819	13,026	9,711	17,454	15,860	9,563	10,928	14,914	5,790	14,952
Sydney, Canada	9,390	4,772	10,994	9,943	13,568	17,816	10,341	12,409	14,443	8,896	3,545	9,968	11,862	3,952	1,210	11,839	10,546	2,853	13,702	2,223
Syktyvkar, USSR	3,145	9,815	6,280	14,193	7,203	14,403	4,614	6,453	11,931	10,459	9,424	8,800	5,494	3,673	7,206	5,376	4,245	4,990	8,005	8,113
Szeged, Hungary	3,760	10,325	8,798	15,510	8,887	15,886	6,990	8,551	14,431	12,518	9,389	6,549	6,118	2,003	6,947	6,206	4,838	5,716	10,093	8,001
Szombathely, Hungary	4,039	10,063	8,937	15,268	9,145	16,174	7,162	8,770	14,585	12,393	9,108	6,642	6,407	1,711	6,665	6,492	5,125	5,498	10,319	7,721
Tabriz, Iran	1,487	12,206	7,458	16,827	6,695	13,557	5,498	6,623	12,722	12,965	11,507	6,463	3,791	4,322	9,094	3,881	2,512	7,361	8,087	10,119
Tacheng, China	2,222	11,493	4,331	14,321	4,575	11,783	2,387	3,903	9,793	10,322	11,529	9,366	3,556	6,217	9,581	3,283	2,702	7,064	5,463	10,360
Tahiti (Papeete)	16,361	6,618	10,042	1,424	11,819	6,522	11,996	11,362	5,523	4,391	7,823	16,296	15,262	15,152	10,177	14,947	16,019	10,982	10,148	9,130
Taipei, Taiwan	5,751	11,814	1,480	11,420	2,227	7,978	1,972	810	5,652	8,138	12,783	12,175	4,936	10,242	12,008	4,529	5,318	9,366	1,592	12,279
Taiyuan, China	4,496	11,327	1,828	12,291	3,061	9,613	334	1,738	7,188	8,554	11,977	11,460	4,435	8,589	10,742	4,022	4,370	8,054	3,172	11,199
Tallahassee, Florida	12,023	2,580	11,863	7,351	15,300	15,286	11,951	13,852	13,009	7,320	1,070	11,678	14,484	6,660	1,823	14,402	13,180	4,334	14,630	1,048
Tallinn, USSR	3,898	9,391	7,689	14,334	8,527	15,765	6,056	7,871	13,324	11,054	8,706	8,038	6,369	2,238	6,329	6,340	5,056	4,575	9,429	7,328
Tamanrasset, Algeria	5,620	11,122	11,561	15,993	10,679	15,859	9,647	10,831	16,928	14,807	9,762	4,085	7,315	3,184	7,576	7,579	6,338	7,548	12,234	8,564
Tampa, Florida	12,176	2,788	12,192	7,383	15,613	15,285	12,258	14,173	13,210	7,553	1,275	11,469	14,646	6,722	2,029	14,588	13,334	4,607	14,958	1,355
Tampere, Finland	4,060	9,174	7,609	14,098	8,587	15,814	6,023	7,879	13,224	10,824	8,516	8,260	6,526	2,256	6,155	6,483	5,217	4,349	9,432	7,144
Tanami, Australia	9,333	13,863	6,026	9,778	4,235	3,031	6,983	4,969	3,451	9,108	15,378	11,942	7,134	14,920	16,350	6,960	8,319	14,116	3,483	15,962
Tangier, Morocco	6,073	9,397	11,111	14,499	11,275	17,588	9,396	11,008	16,752	13,036	8,111	5,832	8,226	1,569	5,826	8,397	7,043	5,786	12,549	6,844
Tarawa (Betio)	11,819	8,591	5,571	5,464	7,396	5,533	7,531	6,758	1,869	3,862	10,106	17,214	10,812	14,323	11,549	10,448	11,413	10,459	5,663	10,843
Tashkent, USSR	996	12,210	5,488	15,550	4,979	12,169	3,522	4,680	10,752	11,542	11,977	8,120	2,935	5,719	9,786	2,796	1,773	7,499	6,192	10,687
Tbilisi, USSR	1,732	11,784	7,399	16,451	6,898	13,875	5,458	6,720	12,792	12,652	11,100	6,720	4,129	3,991	8,695	4,189	2,828	6,938	8,218	9,714
Tegucigalpa, Honduras	13,751	2,955	13,203	6,303	16,866	13,936	13,628	15,364	12,719	7,480	1,926	11,736	16,222	8,173	3,638	16,189	14,906	6,153	15,742	2,847
Tehran, Iran	993	12,607	7,163	16,953	6,194	13,027	5,197	6,190	12,291	12,988	11,976	6,540	3,262	4,849	9,578	3,351	1,981	7,750	7,625	10,593
Tel Aviv, Israel	2,563	12,336	8,701	17,459	7,685	14,098	6,740	7,775	13,870	13,948	11,381	5,355	4,483	3,916	8,940	4,674	3,352	7,654	9,185	9,998
Telegraph Creek, Canada	9,708	3,565	7,194	7,538	10,785	13,464	7,619	9,286	9,677	4,600	4,159	14,278	11,535	7,038	3,948	11,228	10,600	2,661	9,946	3,770
Teresina, Brazil	11,710	8,193	16,723	10,602	16,616	14,592	15,306	16,902	17,036	12,816	6,800	6,488	13,168	7,034	6,480	13,506	12,386	8,776	18,307	6,659
Ternate, Indonesia	7,702	13,005	3,757	10,425	2,544	5,237	4,706	2,773	3,782	8,403	14,366	12,384	5,958	12,878	14,403	5,660	6,887	11,915	1,218	14,374
The Valley, Anguilla	11,824	5,005	13,974	8,894	16,629	16,043	13,468	15,536	15,297	9,777	3,520	9,302	14,139	6,126	3,256	14,268	12,898	5,848	16,766	3,276
Thessaloniki, Greece	3,513	10,948	9,013	16,159	8,715	15,477	7,133	8,534	14,560	13,146	9,958	5,954	5,746	2,496	7,519	5,878	4,512	6,378	10,044	8,578
Thimphu, Bhutan	2,726	13,368	4,122	14,567	2,569	9,776	2,486	2,534	8,593	10,966	13,641	9,127	2,020	8,125	11,792	1,612	2,140	9,235	3,907	12,542
Thunder Bay, Canada	10,415	2,835	9,943	8,080	13,267	15,663	9,913	11,839	12,317	6,695	2,132	12,172	12,779	5,730	1,084	12,619	11,538	2,373	12,750	992
Tientsin, China	4,867	10,960	1,457	11,880	3,314	9,582	511	1,894	6,959	8,126	11,668	11,875	4,864	8,702	10,550	4,450	4,785	7,871	3,195	10,951
Tijuana, Mexico	12,602	695	9,646	5,237	13,350	12,807	10,481	11,872	9,927	4,215	2,084	14,757	14,551	8,617	3,803	14,242	13,572	4,650	12,095	2,875
Tiksi, USSR	5,604	7,934	4,145	11,108	6,925	12,786	3,562	5,566	9,281	7,187	8,253	12,139	7,164	6,071	6,879	6,849	6,324	4,197	6,778	7,349
Timbuktu, Mali	6,724	10,776	12,649	15,217	11,718	15,981	10,750	11,937	18,015	14,986	9,325	3,863	8,308	3,689	7,358	8,597	7,398	7,831	13,315	8,261
Tindouf, Algeria	6,626	9,680	11,983	14,528	11,820	17,239	10,214	11,716	17,636	13,686	8,294	5,165	8,591	2,471	6,170	8,811	7,499	6,510	13,222	7,128
Tirane, Albania	3,771	10,719	9,167	15,948	8,968	15,748	7,309	8,756	14,749	13,065	9,707	6,000	6,018	2,236	7,270	6,147	4,781	6,199	10,275	8,330
Tokyo, Japan	6,880	9,713	683	9,859	4,333	8,740	2,517	2,893	5,427	6,208	10,753	13,889	6,750	9,952	10,339	6,332	6,801	7,871	3,269	10,419
Toledo, Spain	5,784	9,287	10,650	14,473	10,960	17,615	8,959	10,618	16,282	12,711	8,066	6,173	8,019	1,131	5,716	8,162	6,798	5,452	12,169	6,757
Topeka, Kansas	11,567	1,790	10,489	7,026	14,029	14,827	10,742	12,545	11,909	6,180	1,031	12,743	13,908	6,780	1,786	13,728	12,684	3,476	13,230	823
Toronto, Canada	10,533	3,236	10,779	8,435	13,948	16,280	10,587	12,577	13,181	7,498	2,095	11,391	12,978	5,397	350	12,880	11,685	2,867	13,590	710
Toulouse, France	5,247	9,429	10,047	14,672	10,391	17,271	8,345	10,012	15,690	12,514	8,297	6,406	7,545	918	5,891	7,664	6,294	5,296	11,565	6,947
Tours, France	5,241	9,138	9,753	14,389	10,312	17,372	8,105	9,841	15,369	12,100	8,061	6,826	7,604	587	5,633	7,694	6,326	4,901	11,400	6,694
Townsville, Australia	10,721	12,186	6,129	8,010	5,513	2,625	7,577	5,804	1,785	7,514	13,695	13,596	8,727	15,856	15,159	8,500	9,815	13,547	4,248	14,502
Trenton, New Jersey	10,648	3,513	11,285	8,608	14,359	16,535	11,010	13,027	13,655	7,944	2,201	10,961	13,115	5,304	584	13,054	11,806	3,272	14,092	973
Tripoli, Lebanon	2,417	12,163	8,474	17,228	7,588	14,150	6,517	7,615	13,717	13,668	11,254	5,635	4,460	3,819	8,811	4,626	3,281	7,441	9,050	9,866
Tripoli, Libya	4,507	10,975	10,232	16,191	9,693	15,895	8,340	9,657	15,736	13,931	9,786	5,058	6,501	2,481	7,416	6,701	5,375	6,811	11,129	8,464
Tristan da Cunha (Edinburgh)	11,039	12,608	16,841	12,423	13,292	10,913	15,224	14,664	14,797	16,277	11,379	3,883	10,806	9,652	11,129	11,223	10,899	13,066	14,651	11,368
Trondheim, Norway	4,774	8,542	8,023	13,581	9,254	16,447	6,554	8,475	13,544	10,556	7,825	8,456	7,243	1,808	5,447	7,202	5,932	3,773	10,014	6,446
Trujillo, Peru	15,111	5,354	15,680	6,593	19,341	12,672	16,237	17,910	13,214	9,198	4,542	10,339	17,113	9,481	5,940	17,385	16,080	8,601	17,648	5,352
Truk Island (Moen)	9,522	10,308	3,589	7,894	4,978	5,594	5,432	4,359	2,069	5,609	11,756	15,193	8,380	13,311	12,484	8,016	9,014	10,562	3,240	12,102
Truro, Canada	9,618	4,525	11,030	9,688	13,709	17,572	10,449	12,513	14,288	8,699	3,290	10,170	12,090	4,205	975	12,060	10,775	2,869	13,768	1,972
Tsingtao, China	5,215	11,026	1,119	11,603	3,124	9,166	922	1,643	6,527	7,938	11,823	12,137	5,021	9,137	10,836	4,603	5,055	8,172	2,819	11,182
Tsitsihar, China	5,258	9,920	1,606	11,333	4,372	10,263	1,227	2,921	7,228	7,421	10,603	12,409	5,706	8,217	9,546	5,306	5,414	6,886	4,067	9,904
Tubuai Island (Mataura)	16,723	7,119	10,430	1,867	11,890	6,128	12,395	11,582	5,588	5,026	8,249	15,704	15,279	15,670	10,645	15,007	16,199	11,588	10,277	9,589
Tucson, Arizona	12,604	349	10,100	5,525	13,801	13,251	10,819	12,309	10,481	4,779	1,514	14,206	14,701	8,284	3,358	14,425	13,632	4,521	12,611	2,380
Tulsa, Oklahoma	11,878	1,615	10,728	6,803	14,302	14,661	11,035	12,812	11,895	6,168	711	12,781	14,227	7,015	1,982	14,049	12,998	3,797	13,445	945
Tunis, Tunisia	4,665	10,481	10,121	15,714	9,874	16,334	8,279	9,721	15,722	13,452	9,318	5,514	6,789	1,969	6,931	6,959	5,609	6,304	11,229	7,983
Tura, USSR	4,207	9,304	3,975	12,431	5,964	12,579	2,717	4,782	9,558	8,448	9,490	11,006	5,762	5,850	7,835	5,464	4,897	5,172	6,199	8,455
Turin, Italy	4,733	9,723	9,601	14,974	9,869	16,810	7,863	9,500	15,254	12,512	8,658	6,451	7,054	1,182	6,229	7,162	5,792	5,390	11,050	7,290
Uberlandia, Brazil	13,030	8,572	18,289	9,744	17,194	12,973	16,927	18,170	15,609	12,726	7,383	6,865	14,030	8,673	7,649	14,420	13,517	10,149	18,682	7,595
Ufa, USSR	2,319	10,636	6,139	14,849	6,586	13,823	4,321	5,989	11,759	10,988	10,249	8,374	4,675	4,136	8,008	4,571	3,418	5,818	7,549	8,930
Ujungpandang, Indonesia	7,414	14,108	4,584	11,184	2,252	5,011	5,144	3,081	4,501	9,472	15,467	11,363	5,376	12,934	15,304	5,142	6,463	12,703	1,784	15,397
Ulaanbaatar, Mongolia	3,978	10,681	2,599	12,602	4,120	10,818	878	2,921	8,215	8,657	11,120	11,131	4,637	7,423	9,659	4,260	4,190	6,976	4,379	10,206
Ulan-Ude, USSR	4,090	10,286	2,773	12,458	4,557	11,175	1,266	3,332	8,425	8,474	10,692	11,236	4,965	7,126	9,222	4,601	4,419	6,537	4,759	9,768
Uliastay, Mongolia	3,233	11,057	3,302	13,331	4,205	11,202	1,409	3,225	8,854	9,363	11,334	10,389	4,108	6,926	9,655	3,761	3,520	7,013	4,762	10,305
Uranium City, Canada	9,563	3,394	8,188	8,155	11,600	14,731	8,287	10,138	10,986	5,739	3,460	13,116	11,694	6,004	2,686	11,452	10,588	1,668	10,991	2,705
Urumqi, China	2,422	11,719	3,967	14,164	4,099	11,297	2,003	3,418	9,348	10,203	11,853	9,570	3,367	6,706	9,984	3,052	2,686	7,422	4,977	10,728
Ushuaia, Argentina	15,599	10,148	17,230	7,890	15,098	8,663	18,446	16,385	11,595	11,889	9,721	8,483	14,625	12,959	11,130	14,985	15,206	13,819	15,021	10,617
Vaduz, Liechtenstein	4,576	9,679	9,332	14,920	9,676	16,704	7,606	9,267	14,984	12,316	8,662	6,663	6,936	1,206	6,224	7,026	5,658	5,251	10,821	7,283
Valencia, Spain	5,494	9,572	10,502	14,774	10,682	17,303	8,770	10,383	16,152	12,884	8,368	6,017	7,710	1,252	6,005	7,859	6,496	5,633	11,926	7,050
Valladolid, Spain	5,787	9,131	10,520	14,336	10,940	17,723	8,857	10,552	16,135	12,508	7,932	6,378	8,060	927	5,565	8,190	6,822	5,249	12,107	6,610
Valletta, Malta	4,307	10,834	9,913	16,079	9,512	15,940	8,037	9,409	15,459	13,622	9,696	5,384	6,395	2,292	7,297	6,572	5,227	6,557	10,902	8,353
Valparaiso, Chile	15,781	8,029	17,795	7,321	17,531	10,709	19,099	18,685	12,817	10,941	7,387	9,015	16,150	11,213	8,700	16,567	16,071	11,387	17,143	8,198
Vancouver, Canada	10,731	2,467	8,128	6,724	11,782	13,414	8,687	10,279	9,864	4,358	3,188	14,491	12,627	7,477	3,547	12,324	11,662	3,140	10,808	3,086
Varna, Bulgaria	3,113	10,971	8,510	16,093	8,290	15,198	6,631	8,057	14,062	12,836	10,075	6,317	5,431	2,702	7,633	5,533	4,163	6,281	9,577	8,685
Venice, Italy	4,363	9,969	9,313	15,209	9,500	16,457	7,545	9,149	14,963	12,546	8,948	6,453	6,694	1,482	6,511	6,796	5,427	5,522	10,696	7,571
Veracruz, Mexico	13,655	1,859	12,167	5,696	15,865	13,588	12,774	14,368	11,811	6,412	1,173	12,753	16,068	8,386	3,464	15,916	14,799	5,663	14,643	2,473
Verona, Italy	4,469	9,891	9,388	15,135	9,604	16,561	7,630	9,245	15,040	12,527	8,859	6,461	6,798	1,388	6,424	6,901	5,532	5,473	10,793	7,484
Victoria, Canada	10,821	2,398	8,162	6,632	11,824	13,351	8,746	10,322	9,821	4,294	3,156	14,556	12,707	7,560	3,584	12,401	11,748	3,228	10,831	3,096
Victoria, Seychelles	4,369	16,949	9,117	17,758	5,924	9,818	7,602	7,045	11,519	15,986	15,877	4,451	3,099	8,442	13,483	3,510	3,599	12,170	7,627	14,541
Vienna, Austria	4,066	9,973	8,880	15,170	9,149	16,212	7,119	8,749	14,531	12,285	9,030	6,749	6,450	1,662	6,588	6,526	5,161	5,394	10,301	7,642
Vientiane, Laos	4,391	13,682	3,475	13,339	911	8,147	2,673	1,299	6,993	10,244	14,386	10,117	2,938	9,784	12,982	2,560	3,626	10,311	2,297	13,549
Villahermosa, Mexico	13,648	2,210	12,489	5,927	16,177	13,764	13,025	14,675	12,140	6,774	1,328	12,401	16,096	8,260	3,436	15,982	14,802	5,763	14,997	2,501
Vilnius, USSR	3,635	9,830	7,949	14,839	8,484	15,697	6,228	7,947	13,602	11,579	9,075	7,524	6,101	2,202	6,666	6,109	4,785	5,051	9,507	7,687
Visby, Sweden	4,160	9,299	8,110	14,356	8,908	16,145	6,480	8,284	13,739	11,249	8,529	7,802	6,630	1,822	6,121	6,627	5,314	4,548	9,843	7,142
Vitoria, Brazil	12,381	9,340	18,295	10,534	16,348	12,960	16,527	17,383	16,043	13,572	8,091	6,024	13,217	8,472	8,114	13,614	12,778	10,478	17,911	8,177
Vladivostok, USSR	5,964	9,765	971	10,674	4,340	9,655	1,697	2,838	6,479	6,840	10,607	13,084	6,171	8,927	9,821	5,758	6,023	7,225	3,706	10,060
Volgograd, USSR	2,172	11,046	7,098	15,675	7,094	14,253	5,218	6,711	12,656	11,936	10,437	7,372	4,644	3,618	8,068	4,641	3,328	6,190	8,254	9,064
Vologda, USSR	3,214	9,860	6,931	14,521	7,672	14,907	5,234	7,016	12,584	10,933	9,320	8,267	5,658	3,091	7,008	5,593	4,362	5,001	8,574	7,968
Vorkuta, USSR	3,691	9,289	5,611	13,374	7,038	14,056	4,121	6,094	11,222	9,575	9,083	9,702	5,849	4,220	7,032	5,664	4,693	4,591	7,607	7,847
Wake Island	10,077	8,280	3,764	6,770	6,491	7,166	5,710	5,449	3,260	3,706	9,704	16,837	9,614	12,309	10,482	9,208	9,905	8,821	4,822	10,045
Wallis Island	13,733	8,425	7,573	4,065	8,928	4,796	9,523	8,555	2,641	4,320	9,874	16,843	12,372	15,841	11,864	12,057	13,181	11,552	7,269	10,947
Walvis Bay, Namibia	8,102	14,575	13,923	15,386	10,695	11,265	12,219	11,889	14,825	19,224	13,092	1,139	7,848	8,329	11,809	8,266	7,896	12,617	12,314	12,488
Warsaw, Poland	3,818	9,861	8,339	14,965	8,777	15,949	6,605	8,292	13,992	11,855	9,026	7,217	6,261	1,920	6,596	6,297	4,951	5,153	9,850	7,634
Washington, D.C.	10,879	3,297	11,343	8,368	14,496	16,301	11,138	13,137	13,507	7,785	1,962	11,132	13,344	5,549	735	13,276	12,037	3,406	14,153	792
Watson Lake, Canada	9,488	3,702	7,212	7,804	10,758	13,706	7,545	9,265	9,895	4,877	4,193	14,005	11,368	6,759	3,805	11,071	10,402	2,388	9,987	3,704

Distances in Kilometers	Herat, Afghanistan	Hermosillo, Mexico	Hiroshima, Japan	Hiva Oa (Atuona)	Ho Chi Minh City, Vietnam	Hobart, Australia	Hohhot, China	Hong Kong	Honiara, Solomon Islands	Honolulu, Hawaii	Houston, Texas	Huambo, Angola	Hubli, India	Hugh Town, United Kingdom	Hull, Canada	Hyderabad, India	Hyderabad, Pakistan	Igloolik, Canada	Iloilo, Philippines	Indianapolis, Indiana
Weimar, East Germany	4,455	9,495	8,939	14,701	9,460	16,607	7,250	8,970	14,583	11,927	8,555	7,072	6,871	1,255	6,113	6,929	5,572	4,946	10,529	7,166
Wellington, New Zealand	14,185	10,902	9,435	5,706	9,028	2,267	11,100	9,408	3,820	7,486	12,112	13,648	11,919	19,043	14,471	11,786	13,153	14,745	7,854	13,428
West Berlin, West Germany	4,331	9,484	8,717	14,659	9,288	16,467	7,036	8,770	14,361	11,782	8,587	7,233	6,765	1,403	6,148	6,809	5,459	4,872	10,330	7,195
Wewak, Papua New Guinea	9,450	11,704	4,361	8,564	4,391	4,376	5,891	4,293	1,918	6,941	13,187	13,995	7,824	14,144	14,001	7,518	8,710	11,981	2,817	13,613
Whangarei, New Zealand	13,960	10,609	8,899	5,511	8,757	2,449	10,620	9,015	3,256	6,960	11,897	14,190	11,811	18,426	14,179	11,640	12,992	14,210	7,477	13,162
Whitehorse, Canada	9,353	3,949	6,869	7,826	10,432	13,446	7,245	8,936	9,606	4,725	4,514	14,177	11,154	6,911	4,148	10,845	10,231	2,586	9,640	4,054
Wichita, Kansas	11,755	1,586	10,515	6,818	14,091	14,629	10,830	12,600	11,766	6,036	899	12,898	14,081	6,989	1,988	13,892	12,866	3,649	13,234	998
Willemstad, Curacao	12,736	4,733	14,386	8,121	17,431	15,135	14,148	16,188	14,687	9,423	3,356	9,751	15,039	7,036	3,749	15,177	13,807	6,426	17,185	3,501
Wiluna, Australia	9,105	15,019	6,874	10,583	4,384	3,050	7,513	5,444	4,590	10,295	16,532	10,780	6,729	14,814	17,485	6,637	8,003	15,036	4,134	17,177
Windhoek, Namibia	7,903	14,813	13,669	15,586	10,427	11,151	11,983	11,624	14,643	19,491	13,321	1,099	7,594	8,357	11,976	8,012	7,667	12,681	12,047	12,683
Windsor, Canada	10,811	2,905	10,778	8,103	14,049	15,952	10,686	12,644	12,928	7,224	1,777	11,674	13,244	5,727	681	13,131	11,960	3,016	13,586	385
Winnipeg, Canada	10,457	2,589	9,473	7,762	12,900	15,154	9,575	11,441	11,730	6,138	2,239	12,723	12,740	6,092	1,676	12,541	11,548	2,323	12,266	1,418
Winston-Salem, North Carolina	11,292	2,974	11,498	7,976	14,769	15,917	11,406	13,372	13,297	7,567	1,576	11,373	13,754	5,964	1,104	13,678	12,449	3,705	14,303	660
Wroclaw, Poland	4,059	9,773	8,633	14,934	9,062	16,208	6,907	8,593	14,286	11,968	8,883	7,073	6,484	1,655	6,444	6,535	5,180	5,133	10,150	7,491
Wuhan, China	4,860	11,855	1,758	12,159	2,332	8,812	1,157	923	6,589	8,643	12,630	11,529	4,322	9,344	11,526	3,904	4,522	13,666	2,363	11,936
Wyndham, Australia	8,881	13,822	5,538	10,034	3,740	3,552	6,456	4,440	3,523	9,048	15,321	11,952	6,745	14,420	16,010	6,548	7,894	13,666	2,958	15,742
Xi'an, China	4,260	11,843	2,162	12,648	2,614	9,399	762	1,428	7,235	8,992	12,476	11,083	3,974	8,719	11,166	3,557	4,013	8,478	2,957	11,663
Xining, China	3,575	11,974	2,783	13,257	2,907	9,945	973	1,992	7,926	9,500	12,443	10,494	3,533	8,114	10,914	3,128	3,404	8,247	3,552	11,508
Yakutsk, USSR	5,540	8,562	3,075	11,029	5,984	11,739	2,653	4,572	8,343	7,022	9,067	12,486	6,697	6,999	7,880	6,340	6,057	5,217	5,723	8,274
Yanji, China	5,784	9,932	976	10,863	4,193	9,669	1,502	2,695	6,566	7,036	10,751	12,896	5,975	8,865	9,908	5,563	5,830	7,293	3,630	10,174
Yaounde, Cameroon	6,218	12,894	12,537	16,719	10,499	13,878	10,579	11,150	16,492	16,993	11,421	1,895	7,076	5,374	9,493	7,441	6,512	9,734	12,228	10,395
Yap Island (Colonia)	8,133	11,482	2,816	9,421	3,450	5,881	4,339	2,921	3,199	6,950	12,836	13,740	6,855	12,575	13,045	6,496	7,539	10,729	1,711	12,903
Yaraka, Australia	10,839	12,692	6,675	8,246	5,660	2,022	8,008	6,136	2,398	8,095	14,185	13,039	8,700	16,242	15,798	8,512	9,861	14,227	4,578	15,086
Yarmouth, Canada	9,895	4,279	11,140	9,421	13,917	17,327	10,630	12,688	14,171	8,535	3,017	10,343	12,367	4,486	783	12,332	11,053	2,982	13,903	1,721
Yellowknife, Canada	9,272	3,719	7,745	8,290	11,156	14,519	7,849	9,692	10,709	5,627	3,885	13,240	11,340	6,037	3,090	11,083	10,268	1,646	10,550	3,151
Yerevan, USSR	1,695	11,932	7,493	16,621	6,889	13,810	5,544	6,756	12,842	12,815	11,227	6,567	4,050	4,062	8,814	4,127	2,760	7,091	8,240	9,839
Yinchuan, China	3,946	11,589	2,378	12,828	3,071	9,919	523	1,948	7,678	9,050	12,125	10,928	3,982	8,208	10,710	3,575	3,839	8,026	3,476	11,249
Yogyakarta, Indonesia	6,887	15,105	5,218	12,100	2,092	5,306	5,381	3,350	5,457	10,511	16,397	10,322	4,651	12,565	15,793	4,480	5,844	13,110	2,452	16,103
York, United Kingdom	5,309	8,629	9,263	13,864	10,190	17,415	7,722	9,565	14,802	11,385	7,655	7,550	7,748	562	5,213	7,788	6,441	4,224	11,122	6,268
Yumen, China	3,196	11,822	3,124	13,525	3,341	10,436	1,184	2,493	8,402	9,675	12,182	10,234	3,489	7,613	10,538	3,106	3,168	7,893	4,053	11,181
Yutian, China	1,786	12,588	4,551	14,951	3,827	11,053	2,621	3,515	9,607	11,047	12,623	8,806	2,470	6,858	10,614	2,182	1,797	8,145	5,014	11,429
Yuzhno-Sakhalinsk, USSR	6,652	8,824	1,639	9,920	5,252	9,966	2,575	3,751	6,475	6,000	9,713	13,807	7,078	8,867	9,103	6,669	6,835	6,600	4,445	9,250
Zagreb, Yugoslavia	4,079	10,145	9,078	15,365	9,213	16,187	7,289	8,871	14,721	12,547	9,162	6,482	6,420	1,724	6,721	6,517	5,148	5,618	10,416	7,779
Zahedan, Iran	551	10,466	11,822	3,124	5,177	11,909	4,722	5,357	11,401	13,026	12,981	6,727	2,146	5,966	10,623	2,239	871	8,630	6,701	11,615
Zamboanga, Philippines	6,826	13,093	3,227	11,119	1,746	6,080	3,895	1,899	4,574	8,714	14,322	11,947	5,197	11,994	13,945	4,873	6,050	11,346	424	14,085
Zanzibar, Tanzania	5,095	15,990	10,697	18,228	7,708	11,001	8,999	8,743	13,243	17,535	14,601	2,669	4,627	7,603	12,430	5,044	4,706	11,817	9,425	13,430
Zaragoza, Spain	5,478	9,399	10,336	14,621	10,643	17,412	8,633	10,289	15,977	12,645	8,223	6,258	7,741	1,012	5,841	7,874	6,506	5,400	11,840	6,891
Zashiversk, USSR	6,128	7,718	3,735	10,513	6,832	12,245	3,514	5,400	8,641	6,551	8,204	12,819	7,483	6,730	7,078	7,140	6,756	4,447	6,475	7,431
Zhengzhou, China	4,671	11,535	1,722	12,208	2,751	9,257	694	1,386	6,903	8,559	12,245	11,524	4,401	8,930	11,074	3,983	4,452	8,388	2,813	11,507
Zurich, Switzerland	4,663	9,598	9,376	14,842	9,755	16,793	7,661	9,335	15,026	12,275	8,576	6,697	7,025	1,117	6,138	7,114	5,746	5,189	10,891	7,198

Distances in Kilometers

	Innsbruck, Austria	Inuvik, Canada	Invercargill, New Zealand	Inverness, United Kingdom	Iquitos, Peru	Iraklion, Greece	Irkutsk, USSR	Islamabad, Pakistan	Istanbul, Turkey	Ivujivik, Canada	Iwo Jima Island, Japan	Izmir, Turkey	Jackson, Mississippi	Jaffna, Sri Lanka	Jakarta, Indonesia	Jamestown, St. Helena	Jamnagar, India	Jan Mayen Island	Jayapura, Indonesia	Jefferson City, Missouri
Inuvik, Canada	6,859	0	13,598	5,457	9,228	8,374	5,803	8,471	7,791	2,580	7,262	8,059	4,867	10,953	11,816	13,144	9,749	4,004	10,083	4,156
Invercargill, New Zealand	18,265	13,598	0	18,675	11,824	16,721	12,517	12,994	16,730	15,594	8,341	16,742	13,353	10,655	7,354	13,076	12,405	17,261	5,551	13,631
Inverness, United Kingdom	1,549	5,457	18,675	0	9,126	3,289	6,226	6,193	2,982	3,928	10,342	3,110	6,815	8,763	11,832	8,135	6,995	1,525	13,181	6,384
Iquitos, Peru	9,912	9,228	11,824	9,126	0	11,016	14,623	15,214	11,311	7,349	15,654	11,179	4,375	17,009	18,906	7,500	15,567	9,494	16,196	5,076
Iraklion, Greece	1,750	8,374	16,721	3,289	11,016	0	6,305	4,371	715	7,213	10,566	387	9,939	6,224	9,655	6,542	4,566	4,447	12,482	9,596
Irkutsk, USSR	6,243	5,803	12,517	6,226	14,623	6,305	0	3,231	5,634	7,288	4,358	5,941	10,531	5,212	6,479	12,757	4,412	5,358	6,967	9,814
Islamabad, Pakistan	5,302	8,471	12,994	6,193	15,214	4,371	3,231	0	3,956	9,043	6,584	4,136	12,495	2,752	5,660	9,991	1,281	6,221	8,112	11,862
Istanbul, Turkey	1,563	7,791	16,730	2,982	11,311	715	5,634	3,956	0	6,837	9,935	328	9,775	6,082	9,447	7,249	4,350	3,954	12,010	9,365
Ivujivik, Canada	5,477	2,580	15,594	3,928	7,349	7,213	7,288	9,043	6,837	0	9,735	7,007	3,459	11,790	13,753	10,676	10,181	2,997	12,639	2,822
Iwo Jima Island, Japan	10,587	7,262	8,341	10,342	15,654	10,566	4,358	6,584	9,935	9,735	0	10,224	11,661	6,681	5,072	16,465	7,190	9,132	3,023	11,057
Izmir, Turkey	1,615	8,059	16,742	3,110	11,179	387	5,941	4,136	328	7,007	10,224	0	9,852	6,139	9,540	6,925	4,437	4,175	12,227	9,472
Jackson, Mississippi	8,237	4,867	13,353	6,815	4,375	9,939	10,531	12,495	9,775	3,459	11,661	9,852	0	15,246	16,624	10,441	13,593	6,329	13,777	719
Jaffna, Sri Lanka	7,614	10,953	10,655	8,763	17,009	6,224	5,212	2,752	6,082	11,790	6,681	6,139	15,246	0	3,450	9,857	1,769	8,958	6,864	14,603
Jakarta, Indonesia	10,918	11,816	7,354	11,832	18,906	9,655	6,479	5,660	9,447	13,753	5,072	9,540	16,624	3,450	0	12,210	5,103	11,564	3,784	15,944
Jamestown, St. Helena	7,205	13,144	13,076	8,135	7,500	6,542	12,757	9,991	7,249	10,676	16,465	6,925	10,441	9,857	12,210	0	9,283	9,646	15,807	10,799
Jamnagar, India	5,861	9,749	12,405	6,995	15,567	4,566	4,412	1,281	4,350	10,181	7,190	4,437	13,593	1,769	5,103	9,283	0	7,265	8,143	13,000
Jan Mayen Island	2,856	4,004	17,261	1,525	9,494	4,447	5,358	6,221	3,954	2,997	9,132	4,175	6,329	8,958	11,564	9,646	7,265	0	12,102	5,762
Jayapura, Indonesia	13,074	10,083	5,551	13,181	16,196	12,482	6,967	8,112	12,010	12,639	3,023	12,227	13,777	6,864	3,784	15,807	8,143	12,102	0	13,346
Jefferson City, Missouri	7,862	4,156	13,631	6,384	5,076	9,596	9,814	11,862	9,365	2,822	11,057	9,472	719	14,603	15,944	10,799	13,000	5,762	13,346	0
Jerusalem, Israel	2,657	8,866	15,725	4,138	11,981	1,017	5,904	3,542	1,170	8,006	9,983	1,042	10,893	5,215	8,654	6,853	3,587	5,108	11,625	10,511
Jiggalong, Australia	13,326	13,037	4,941	14,246	16,642	11,967	8,534	8,085	11,825	15,449	5,774	11,892	16,835	5,753	2,425	12,758	7,476	13,835	3,152	16,482
Jinan, China	8,139	6,999	10,535	8,222	16,215	7,923	1,999	3,972	7,315	8,942	2,666	7,592	11,866	4,775	4,859	13,960	4,760	7,327	4,987	11,154
Jodhpur, India	5,802	9,284	12,467	6,832	15,652	4,647	3,894	822	4,348	9,841	6,782	4,474	13,284	1,980	5,116	9,709	519	6,978	7,930	12,663
Johannesburg, South Africa	8,307	15,163	11,028	9,752	10,959	6,818	11,395	8,164	7,442	13,374	13,396	7,154	14,071	6,874	8,590	3,679	7,034	11,163	12,131	14,339
Juazeiro do Norte, Brazil	7,825	10,925	13,468	7,841	3,777	8,219	14,019	12,536	8,755	8,392	18,057	8,509	6,938	13,359	15,992	3,786	12,312	8,965	18,928	7,443
Juneau, Alaska	7,890	1,120	12,740	6,434	8,734	9,455	6,650	9,491	8,889	3,050	7,367	9,149	4,385	11,858	12,239	13,710	10,773	5,038	9,946	3,724
Kabul, Afghanistan	4,951	8,441	13,336	5,888	14,862	3,994	3,410	377	3,585	8,867	6,924	3,761	12,303	2,964	5,990	9,679	1,338	5,994	8,489	11,689
Kalgoorlie, Australia	13,907	13,749	4,363	14,945	15,881	12,436	9,347	8,755	12,369	16,221	6,500	12,402	17,028	6,294	3,123	12,365	8,050	14,628	3,722	16,842
Kaliningrad, USSR	1,045	6,190	17,583	1,561	10,589	2,184	5,230	4,667	1,647	5,225	9,558	1,880	8,327	7,202	10,326	8,213	5,435	2,307	12,130	7,853
Kamloops, Canada	8,211	2,100	12,745	6,677	7,512	9,895	7,851	10,566	9,418	2,848	8,475	9,638	3,201	13,039	13,436	13,094	11,840	5,465	10,860	2,584
Kampala, Uganda	5,594	12,313	13,339	7,126	11,780	3,953	8,747	5,619	4,522	11,016	11,891	4,255	13,026	5,352	8,276	4,576	4,742	8,395	12,035	12,937
Kananga, Zaire	5,989	12,848	13,311	7,426	10,602	4,573	9,976	6,908	5,238	11,117	13,207	4,931	12,487	6,615	9,330	3,265	6,063	8,844	13,114	12,550
Kano, Nigeria	3,919	10,605	15,749	5,161	9,211	3,080	9,354	6,942	3,785	8,649	13,482	3,461	10,111	7,799	11,058	3,464	6,606	6,663	14,662	10,098
Kanpur, India	6,342	9,126	11,945	7,250	16,250	5,302	3,497	1,059	4,949	9,966	6,068	5,103	13,425	1,860	4,602	10,411	1,132	7,224	7,228	12,763
Kansas City, Missouri	7,965	4,018	13,496	6,472	5,227	9,705	9,718	11,847	9,454	2,827	10,862	9,570	852	14,577	15,778	11,016	13,006	5,795	13,130	217
Kaohsiung, Taiwan	9,515	8,319	9,047	9,750	17,468	9,032	3,561	4,745	8,501	10,442	2,158	8,743	13,121	4,523	3,508	14,338	5,140	8,910	3,560	12,436
Karachi, Pakistan	5,454	9,529	12,811	6,599	15,181	4,170	4,367	1,145	3,944	9,845	7,403	4,034	13,236	2,171	5,507	9,091	407	6,907	8,490	12,658
Karaganda, USSR	4,438	6,709	14,038	4,903	14,007	4,174	2,185	1,792	3,539	7,301	6,397	3,827	10,760	4,498	7,003	10,572	3,049	4,608	8,638	10,106
Karl-Marx-Stadt, East Germany	412	6,501	18,150	1,336	10,062	1,983	5,898	5,159	1,649	5,236	10,227	1,777	8,131	7,577	10,810	7,617	5,811	2,509	12,781	7,717
Kasanga, Tanzania	6,475	13,263	12,600	7,984	11,538	4,889	9,625	6,440	5,483	11,813	12,442	5,207	13,452	5,774	8,345	4,090	5,451	9,309	12,125	13,473
Kashgar, China	5,152	7,795	13,200	5,870	14,987	4,465	2,595	689	3,954	8,471	6,242	4,181	11,931	3,327	5,966	10,430	1,968	5,735	8,057	11,277
Kassel, West Germany	471	6,389	18,379	1,121	9,830	2,172	6,045	5,395	1,880	5,041	10,354	1,990	7,896	7,822	11,049	7,596	6,056	2,385	12,958	7,490
Kathmandu, Nepal	6,625	8,882	11,687	7,429	16,524	5,692	3,152	1,338	5,294	9,904	5,558	5,469	13,346	2,074	4,404	10,923	1,643	7,272	6,803	12,662
Kayes, Mali	4,209	9,756	16,462	4,812	7,110	4,321	10,405	8,644	4,885	7,387	14,762	4,623	8,125	9,905	13,227	3,419	8,557	6,285	16,699	8,227
Kazan, USSR	2,744	6,237	15,777	3,198	12,324	2,912	3,543	3,070	2,201	6,123	7,900	2,527	9,514	5,779	8,645	9,449	4,079	3,187	10,337	8,931
Kemi, Finland	2,207	5,020	16,967	1,763	10,740	3,391	4,465	4,788	2,774	4,450	8,644	3,053	7,797	7,507	10,275	9,411	5,799	1,470	11,426	7,231
Kenora, Canada	7,119	2,964	14,158	5,582	6,276	8,868	8,556	10,678	8,535	1,732	10,086	8,688	1,974	13,397	14,779	11,258	11,858	4,729	12,650	1,259
Kerguelen Island	12,092	17,551	6,825	13,641	13,106	10,367	11,749	9,223	10,784	17,562	10,853	10,592	17,465	6,634	5,937	7,613	7,971	14,719	8,445	18,117
Kerkira, Greece	1,095	7,835	17,358	2,641	10,549	661	6,314	4,737	785	6,569	10,649	640	9,283	6,778	10,179	6,699	5,076	3,863	12,793	8,935
Kermanshah, Iran	3,298	8,620	14,978	4,584	13,013	2,006	4,904	2,405	1,757	8,218	8,868	1,840	11,388	4,325	7,702	7,882	2,599	5,225	10,506	10,910
Khabarovsk, USSR	8,086	5,163	10,998	7,678	14,366	8,428	2,211	5,299	7,733	7,366	2,688	8,052	9,991	6,675	6,656	14,945	6,346	6,444	5,680	9,294
Kharkov, USSR	1,848	6,852	16,496	2,751	11,716	1,862	4,593	3,509	1,148	6,265	8,941	1,476	9,477	6,011	9,167	8,381	4,244	3,273	11,255	8,973
Khartoum, Sudan	4,017	10,629	14,697	5,566	11,821	2,307	7,414	4,537	2,838	9,493	11,106	2,583	11,942	5,189	8,530	5,462	4,013	6,751	12,041	11,707
Khon Kaen, Thailand	8,791	9,586	9,552	9,464	18,542	7,874	3,978	3,531	7,487	11,265	4,104	7,660	14,438	2,585	2,537	12,438	3,498	9,049	4,662	13,719
Kiev, USSR	1,442	6,766	16,907	2,381	11,305	1,733	4,918	3,917	1,054	6,008	9,274	1,362	9,154	6,390	9,573	8,160	4,621	3,040	11,645	8,671
Kigali, Rwanda	5,749	12,533	13,279	7,264	11,483	4,159	9,116	5,994	4,759	11,116	12,252	4,479	12,949	5,683	8,528	4,217	5,114	8,579	12,302	12,906
Kingston, Canada	6,466	4,200	15,074	5,033	5,326	8,182	9,311	10,846	7,996	2,024	11,451	8,080	1,781	13,586	15,775	9,772	11,876	4,628	14,124	1,450
Kingston, Jamaica	8,428	6,829	13,338	7,296	2,439	9,907	12,220	13,462	9,973	4,931	13,733	9,944	2,077	16,035	18,641	8,649	14,268	7,326	15,597	2,725
Kingstown, Saint Vincent	7,638	7,937	14,111	6,839	2,294	8,853	12,626	12,931	9,080	5,626	15,153	8,976	3,632	15,057	18,506	6,906	13,412	7,320	17,346	4,151
Kinshasa, Zaire	5,725	12,527	13,796	7,070	9,827	4,506	10,318	7,384	5,208	10,593	13,838	4,885	11,725	7,340	10,134	2,634	6,650	8,546	13,917	11,827
Kirkwall, United Kingdom	1,611	5,331	18,492	183	9,252	3,332	6,055	6,092	2,987	3,882	10,160	3,132	6,841	8,688	11,717	8,305	6,923	1,370	13,006	6,392
Kirov, USSR	2,815	5,924	15,799	3,105	12,215	3,149	3,429	3,267	2,435	5,862	7,783	2,763	9,273	6,000	8,777	9,666	4,325	2,958	10,304	8,676
Kiruna, Sweden	2,347	4,758	17,006	1,685	10,536	3,631	4,560	5,049	3,033	4,157	8,666	3,304	7,515	7,778	10,492	9,527	6,079	1,186	11,499	6,943
Kisangani, Zaire	5,352	12,196	13,790	6,835	10,961	3,856	9,225	6,203	4,503	10,630	12,616	4,203	12,350	6,152	9,095	3,853	5,430	8,204	12,858	12,323
Kishinev, USSR	1,320	7,130	16,957	2,507	11,232	1,332	5,234	3,983	665	6,263	9,582	963	9,320	6,339	9,603	7,779	4,574	3,333	11,862	8,868
Kitchner, Canada	6,772	4,115	14,750	5,323	5,280	8,495	9,389	11,054	8,294	2,116	11,331	8,386	1,502	13,802	15,813	10,032	12,113	4,850	13,929	1,121
Knoxville, Tennessee	7,539	4,721	14,060	6,134	4,537	9,235	10,197	11,935	9,083	2,969	11,777	9,153	707	14,682	16,530	10,015	12,985	5,727	14,130	786
Kosice, Czechoslovakia	752	6,858	17,549	1,950	10,653	1,519	5,577	4,561	1,048	5,790	9,934	1,237	8,761	6,936	10,195	7,640	5,172	2,939	12,342	8,332
Kota Kinabalu, Malaysia	10,618	10,202	7,758	11,182	18,974	9,717	5,243	5,380	9,336	12,328	3,405	9,508	14,945	3,997	1,693	13,597	5,262	10,570	2,896	14,282
Krakow, Poland	701	6,689	17,657	1,779	10,555	1,692	5,561	4,662	1,229	5,608	9,913	1,418	8,593	7,075	10,309	7,733	5,308	2,760	12,373	8,157
Kralendijk, Bonaire	8,248	7,759	13,521	7,332	1,846	9,544	12,831	13,500	9,730	5,629	14,816	9,646	3,161	15,767	19,161	7,556	14,079	7,647	16,667	3,763
Krasnodar, USSR	2,135	7,416	16,141	3,250	12,045	1,594	4,714	3,172	931	6,848	9,004	1,228	10,027	5,541	8,787	8,123	3,773	3,859	11,129	9,538
Krasnoyarsk, USSR	5,385	5,695	13,349	5,416	14,080	5,490	858	2,904	4,807	6,848	5,214	5,119	10,215	5,262	7,011	11,992	4,169	4,653	7,799	9,512
Kristiansand, Norway	1,234	5,630	18,150	730	9,848	2,837	5,633	5,463	2,415	4,422	9,851	2,595	7,469	8,045	11,103	8,309	6,281	1,633	12,598	7,003
Kuala Lumpur, Malaysia	9,776	11,021	8,505	10,656	19,473	8,591	5,448	4,495	8,335	12,733	4,874	8,449	15,886	2,505	1,178	11,978	4,026	10,408	4,385	15,170
Kuching, Malaysia	10,558	10,880	7,753	11,300	19,561	9,478	5,649	5,257	9,174	12,878	4,208	9,311	15,686	3,475	939	12,850	4,930	10,864	3,410	15,004
Kumasi, Ghana	4,666	10,893	15,500	5,638	8,044	4,189	10,494	8,196	4,865	8,646	14,708	4,554	9,487	8,980	12,126	2,542	7,854	7,161	15,832	9,601
Kumzar, Oman	4,555	9,473	13,728	5,834	14,120	3,139	4,906	1,807	3,002	9,369	8,359	3,045	12,619	3,094	6,516	8,186	1,448	6,374	9,570	12,114
Kunming, China	8,099	8,683	10,304	8,640	17,609	7,369	3,023	3,009	6,905	10,309	3,891	7,114	13,512	2,944	3,484	12,574	3,329	8,135	5,114	12,793
Kuqa Chang, China	5,591	7,471	12,824	6,150	15,258	5,051	2,003	1,232	4,500	8,402	5,597	4,748	11,843	3,509	5,758	11,094	2,426	5,827	7,533	11,161
Kurgan, USSR	3,762	6,186	14,795	4,104	13,191	3,777	2,558	2,491	3,088	6,553	6,904	3,403	10,008	5,238	7,822	10,303	3,681	3,799	9,323	9,371
Kuwait, Kuwait	3,713	9,167	14,589	5,067	13,229	2,242	5,223	2,434	2,151	8,755	9,005	2,163	11,881	3,985	7,413	7,640	2,338	5,766	10,417	11,423
Kuybyshev, USSR	2,805	6,519	15,645	3,390	12,507	2,788	3,573	2,832	2,088	6,407	7,917	2,408	9,788	5,519	8,443	9,330	3,807	3,459	10,269	9,210
Kyoto, Japan	9,343	6,461	9,590	9,096	15,445	9,413	3,138	5,661	8,759	8,796	1,254	9,058	11,151	6,295	5,476	15,650	6,453	7,921	4,187	10,487
Kzyl-Orda, USSR	4,110	7,355	14,249	4,841	13,945	3,557	2,949	1,399	2,985	7,681	7,027	3,240	11,120	4,137	6,991	9,827	2,513	4,825	9,049	10,503
L'vov, USSR	972	6,767	17,362	2,032	10,848	1,613	5,341	4,368	1,054	5,803	9,698	1,293	8,843	6,789	10,015	7,848	5,021	2,900	12,110	8,393
La Ceiba, Honduras	9,339	6,705	12,399	8,099	2,627	10,892	12,390	14,134	10,900	5,223	13,136	10,900	1,861	16,843	18,200	9,573	15,087	7,914	14,628	2,580
La Coruna, Spain	1,606	6,816	19,586	1,595	8,307	3,001	7,606	6,907	3,071	4,842	11,851	3,021	7,018	9,150	12,505	6,571	7,420	3,077	14,553	6,765
La Paz, Bolivia	10,576	10,742	11,043	10,072	1,515	11,348	15,982	15,718	11,786	8,789	16,832	11,588	5,889	16,504	17,438	6,647	15,611	10,682	16,220	6,591
La Paz, Mexico	10,184	5,161	11,289	8,679	5,065	11,926	10,895	13,590	11,658	4,889	10,595	11,785	2,165	16,100	15,595	12,178	14,845	7,884	12,059	2,343
La Ronge, Canada	7,212	2,071	13,842	5,665	7,158	8,931	7,794	10,165	8,507	1,762	9,145	8,702	2,797	12,810	13,876	12,053	11,399	4,572	11,745	2,084
Labrador City, Canada	5,355	3,789	16,063	3,878	6,314	7,094	8,314	9,659	6,857	1,237	10,971	6,963	2,957	12,392	14,786	9,609	10,679	3,438	13,868	2,509
Lagos, Nigeria	4,588	11,065	15,350	5,698	8,591	3,897	10,185	7,748	4,595	8,925	14,307	4,275	9,969	8,437	11,573	2,671	7,349	7,221	15,282	10,050
Lahore, Pakistan	5,528	8,684	12,762	6,442	15,438	4,543	3,345	258	4,155	9,295	6,526	4,323	12,749	2,497	5,419	10,015	1,094	6,479	7,949	12,113
Lambasa, Fiji	16,413	10,122	3,477	15,440	11,744	16,716	10,456	12,492	16,082	12,266	6,152	16,376	11,012	11,310	7,970	16,382	12,645	13,915	4,505	11,002
Lansing, Michigan	7,076	4,024	14,423	5,611	5,274	8,806	9,444	11,243	8,589	2,231	11,180	8,688	1,260	13,995	15,804	10,314	12,333	5,069	13,702	793
Lanzhou, China	7,332	7,500	11,186	7,665	16,416	6,897	1,803	2,791	6,335	9,091	3,800	6,590	12,302	3,778	4,684	12,770	3,574	7,016	5,746	11,584
Laoag, Philippines	9,912	8,764	8,611	10,204	17,823	9,341	4,039	5,002	8,839	10,923	2,266	9,067	13,532	4,478	3,092	14,334	5,274	9,393	3,181	12,857
Largeau, Chad	3,331	10,190	15,777	4,797	10,396	2,020	8,131	5,628	2,729	8,613	12,179	2,402	10,672	6,620	9,982	4,630	5,325	6,187	13,442	10,523
Las Vegas, Nevada	9,346	3,763	11,912	7,800	6,205	11,089	9,487	12,222	10,709	3,879	9,540	10,886	2,332	14,691	14,612	12,773	13,491	6,798	11,449	2,047

Distances in Kilometers	Innsbruck, Austria	Inuvik, Canada	Invercargill, New Zealand	Inverness, United Kingdom	Iquitos, Peru	Iraklion, Greece	Irkutsk, USSR	Islamabad, Pakistan	Istanbul, Turkey	Ivujivik, Canada	Iwo Jima Island, Japan	Izmir, Turkey	Jackson, Mississippi	Jaffna, Sri Lanka	Jakarta, Indonesia	Jamestown, St. Helena	Jamnagar, India	Jan Mayen Island	Jayapura, Indonesia	Jefferson City, Missouri
Launceston, Australia	16,480	13,792	1,786	17,310	13,553	15,004	11,171	11,238	14,951	16,253	7,353	14,984	14,906	8,872	5,582	13,071	10,619	16,450	4,355	15,048
Le Havre, France	870	6,389	19,074	932	9,138	2,570	6,664	6,083	2,433	4,752	10,928	2,474	7,381	8,467	11,730	7,271	6,707	2,442	13,610	7,026
Leipzig, East Germany	454	6,441	18,184	1,272	10,026	2,049	5,896	5,198	1,712	5,170	10,219	1,842	8,069	7,627	10,851	7,652	5,861	2,446	12,791	7,653
Leningrad, USSR	1,868	5,716	16,904	1,995	11,119	2,758	4,439	4,257	2,104	5,136	8,747	2,401	8,433	6,925	9,853	9,009	5,188	2,139	11,378	7,890
Leon, Spain	1,433	6,973	19,372	1,656	8,496	2,763	7,532	6,723	2,855	5,052	11,811	2,794	7,263	8,929	12,299	6,481	7,206	3,168	14,454	7,008
Lerwick, United Kingdom	1,650	5,247	18,328	348	9,390	3,343	5,891	5,975	2,964	3,881	9,994	3,126	6,902	8,590	11,588	8,443	6,829	1,260	12,840	6,436
Lhasa, China	6,913	8,532	11,443	7,584	16,706	6,118	2,738	1,756	5,667	9,754	4,968	5,869	13,147	2,496	4,304	11,520	2,246	7,273	6,363	12,444
Libreville, Gabon	5,198	11,880	14,510	6,446	9,211	4,198	10,308	7,579	4,912	9,832	14,148	4,584	10,898	7,878	10,837	2,457	6,995	7,952	14,608	10,996
Lilongwe, Malawi	7,141	13,900	11,929	8,655	11,748	5,534	9,953	6,730	6,109	12,488	12,408	5,841	14,015	5,735	8,024	4,249	5,650	9,967	11,772	14,081
Lima, Peru	10,868	9,964	10,849	10,127	1,007	11,879	15,542	16,163	12,223	8,255	15,756	12,069	5,103	17,514	17,947	7,683	16,360	10,493	15,557	5,821
Limerick, Ireland	1,550	5,845	19,275	603	8,671	3,274	6,810	6,589	3,101	4,071	10,945	3,165	6,687	9,068	12,248	7,605	7,300	2,043	13,772	6,321
Limoges, France	794	6,803	19,023	1,348	9,118	2,321	6,905	6,096	2,295	5,115	11,211	2,282	7,621	8,374	11,704	6,876	6,632	2,857	13,808	7,302
Limon, Costa Rica	9,533	7,440	12,236	8,406	1,869	10,981	13,070	14,558	11,073	5,831	13,860	11,034	2,577	17,144	18,870	8,987	15,379	8,382	15,132	3,294
Lincoln, Nebraska	7,949	3,771	13,465	6,439	5,484	9,695	9,493	11,688	9,417	2,707	10,601	9,546	1,110	14,404	15,517	11,233	12,866	5,696	12,893	461
Linz, Austria	246	6,798	18,057	1,603	10,139	1,695	6,004	5,075	1,413	5,519	10,351	1,510	8,363	7,421	10,703	7,387	5,662	2,808	12,828	7,966
Lisbon, Portugal	1,917	7,280	19,128	2,115	8,071	3,054	8,058	7,164	3,244	5,211	12,335	3,141	7,144	9,272	12,681	6,060	7,578	3,594	14,971	6,951
Little Rock, Arkansas	8,174	4,543	13,368	6,720	4,706	9,895	10,231	12,278	9,695	3,236	11,334	9,788	334	15,023	16,290	10,701	13,405	6,155	13,498	425
Liverpool, United Kingdom	1,229	5,906	19,014	458	9,053	2,975	6,497	6,203	2,753	4,287	10,686	2,838	7,023	8,688	11,863	7,688	6,919	1,982	13,464	6,634
Lodz, Poland	767	6,501	17,687	1,648	10,523	1,879	5,475	4,703	1,397	5,441	9,820	1,598	8,460	7,161	10,360	7,886	5,392	2,577	12,328	8,013
Lome, Togo	4,661	11,036	15,376	5,714	8,349	4,056	10,356	7,968	4,747	8,845	14,513	4,430	9,785	8,679	11,809	2,557	7,584	7,239	15,524	9,884
London, United Kingdom	958	6,172	18,999	715	9,179	2,697	6,516	6,054	2,504	4,576	10,756	2,573	7,280	8,490	11,712	7,490	6,724	2,219	13,474	6,905
Londonderry, United Kingdom	1,561	5,638	19,002	335	8,848	3,308	6,558	6,439	3,073	3,960	10,676	3,167	6,701	8,964	12,092	7,861	7,195	1,785	13,515	6,305
Longlac, Canada	6,689	3,273	14,662	5,170	6,070	8,438	8,648	10,543	8,146	1,501	10,494	8,279	1,965	13,290	15,012	10,703	11,676	4,449	13,145	1,324
Lord Howe Island, Australia	16,768	12,361	1,831	16,856	13,249	15,762	10,702	11,540	15,484	14,749	6,514	15,621	13,598	9,553	6,110	14,508	11,198	15,556	3,747	13,639
Los Angeles, California	9,695	3,939	11,547	8,148	6,307	11,435	9,587	12,410	11,043	4,222	9,395	11,225	2,616	14,799	14,460	13,049	13,688	7,117	11,190	2,387
Louangphrabang, Laos	8,467	9,247	9,894	9,101	18,157	7,611	3,601	3,246	7,197	10,885	4,062	7,383	14,086	2,633	2,925	12,433	3,337	8,664	4,888	13,367
Louisville, Kentucky	7,487	4,422	14,068	6,049	4,827	9,201	9,929	11,748	9,016	2,740	11,480	9,101	773	14,500	16,235	10,252	12,828	5,563	13,865	561
Luanda, Angola	6,213	12,964	13,412	7,516	9,569	5,042	10,851	7,879	5,747	10,926	14,261	5,423	11,792	7,676	10,305	2,205	7,095	9,009	14,074	11,956
Lubumbashi, Zaire	6,720	13,563	12,490	8,194	11,099	5,208	10,150	6,972	5,835	11,940	12,951	5,544	13,294	6,274	8,723	3,615	5,988	9,573	12,485	13,383
Lusaka, Zambia	7,144	13,987	12,082	8,616	11,140	5,627	10,430	7,226	6,248	12,347	13,018	5,960	13,576	6,342	8,609	3,642	6,189	9,997	12,337	13,704
Luxembourg, Luxembourg	468	6,508	18,648	1,111	9,564	2,213	6,350	5,654	2,018	5,030	10,655	2,082	7,771	8,034	11,298	7,352	6,273	2,510	13,263	7,394
Luxor, Egypt	3,039	9,518	15,494	4,577	11,791	1,289	6,563	3,994	1,734	8,496	10,538	1,504	11,191	5,294	8,739	6,203	3,809	5,677	11,947	10,872
Lynn Lake, Canada	6,888	2,070	14,168	5,340	7,175	8,611	7,688	9,956	8,195	1,434	9,253	8,386	2,853	12,632	13,880	11,799	11,176	4,269	11,923	2,134
Lyon, France	530	6,892	18,744	1,445	9,390	2,062	6,720	5,826	2,015	5,299	11,047	2,008	7,877	8,094	11,427	6,913	6,352	2,910	13,589	7,544
Macapa, Brazil	7,966	9,700	13,601	7,592	2,505	8,759	13,771	13,119	9,171	7,275	16,958	8,982	5,444	14,509	17,483	5,282	13,192	8,437	18,700	5,984
Madison, Wisconsin	7,345	3,806	14,105	5,854	5,435	9,086	9,359	11,321	8,836	2,278	10,882	8,951	1,198	14,067	15,621	10,704	12,451	5,211	13,340	551
Madras, India	7,360	10,577	10,905	8,464	16,946	6,031	4,848	2,395	5,847	11,424	6,510	5,923	14,882	379	3,624	9,993	1,500	8,612	6,893	14,233
Madrid, Spain	1,429	7,255	19,086	1,898	8,574	2,585	7,625	6,659	2,744	5,342	11,935	2,651	7,503	8,789	12,186	6,240	7,084	3,420	14,501	7,265
Madurai, India	7,452	10,966	10,820	8,625	16,801	6,040	5,258	2,680	5,913	11,723	6,860	5,963	15,170	209	3,645	9,667	1,631	8,862	7,073	14,542
Magadan, USSR	7,601	3,569	11,855	6,843	12,772	8,368	2,949	6,167	7,654	5,855	3,934	7,982	8,397	8,007	8,253	14,799	7,362	5,432	6,943	7,698
Magdalena, Bolivia	10,027	10,561	11,578	9,558	1,458	10,793	15,566	15,164	11,230	8,482	17,071	11,032	5,763	16,106	17,632	6,280	15,095	10,226	16,772	6,445
Magdeburg, East Germany	545	6,336	18,213	1,176	9,990	2,154	5,870	5,240	1,806	5,067	10,183	1,944	7,981	7,691	10,897	7,730	5,923	2,340	12,781	7,560
Majuro Atoll, Marshall Isls.	13,658	7,893	5,938	12,830	12,890	14,119	7,818	10,314	13,432	10,355	3,730	13,747	10,395	10,017	7,303	18,980	10,848	11,333	3,554	10,094
Malabo, Equatorial Guinea	4,829	11,500	14,886	6,066	9,163	3,882	10,059	7,422	4,596	9,468	14,005	4,268	10,634	7,889	10,949	2,700	6,910	7,574	14,692	10,702
Male, Maldives	7,602	11,707	10,705	8,899	16,342	6,053	6,060	3,288	6,040	12,252	7,596	6,037	15,636	956	3,872	8,986	2,076	9,313	7,515	15,067
Manado, Indonesia	11,631	10,320	6,797	12,070	18,009	10,800	5,944	6,447	10,399	12,665	3,129	10,582	14,767	5,046	2,177	14,384	6,357	11,300	1,819	14,182
Managua, Nicaragua	9,598	7,105	12,157	8,402	2,276	11,107	12,796	14,487	11,153	5,618	13,435	11,135	2,267	17,164	18,449	9,398	15,397	8,274	14,749	2,985
Manama, Bahrain	4,142	9,513	14,168	5,502	13,559	2,628	5,302	2,326	2,579	9,177	8,906	2,577	12,316	3,600	7,042	7,671	2,018	6,184	10,151	11,856
Manaus, Brazil	8,878	9,665	12,765	8,348	1,472	9,773	14,370	14,109	10,153	7,425	16,705	9,980	5,052	15,558	18,237	6,108	14,242	9,018	17,647	5,678
Manchester, New Hampshire	6,218	4,524	15,377	4,834	5,182	7,912	9,441	10,784	7,766	2,200	11,786	7,831	2,028	13,498	15,921	9,346	11,760	4,569	14,514	1,810
Mandalay, Burma	7,854	9,208	10,481	8,565	17,689	6,949	3,433	2,594	6,550	10,634	4,615	6,727	13,959	2,194	3,328	11,855	2,679	8,240	5,558	13,245
Mangareva Island, Fr.Polynesia	16,000	10,143	5,652	14,540	6,961	17,666	14,086	17,044	17,523	10,726	10,471	17,614	7,763	16,026	12,579	13,010	17,466	13,683	9,328	8,158
Manila, Philippines	10,247	9,121	8,249	10,582	18,056	9,607	4,435	5,246	9,129	11,312	2,408	9,347	13,852	4,490	2,779	14,325	5,424	9,791	2,882	13,188
Mannheim, West Germany	329	6,566	18,482	1,221	9,728	2,077	6,236	5,488	1,855	5,149	10,555	1,930	7,927	7,865	11,130	7,380	6,104	2,562	13,131	7,542
Maputo, Mozambique	8,384	15,204	10,842	9,865	11,405	6,830	11,104	7,876	7,425	13,583	12,956	7,149	14,478	6,472	8,142	4,117	6,714	11,232	11,697	14,716
Mar del Plata, Argentina	11,661	13,339	9,600	11,693	4,114	11,762	17,892	15,599	12,392	11,278	17,709	12,105	8,487	14,750	14,856	5,610	14,772	12,687	15,143	9,190
Maracaibo, Venezuela	8,621	7,785	13,151	7,667	1,606	9,938	13,021	13,851	10,113	5,764	14,710	10,034	3,062	16,162	19,481	7,833	14,463	7,917	16,354	3,707
Marrakech, Morocco	2,395	8,057	18,607	2,885	7,923	3,092	8,635	7,403	3,450	5,917	12,966	3,274	7,553	9,269	12,718	5,269	7,653	4,380	15,422	7,439
Marseilles, France	645	7,166	18,632	1,714	9,382	1,911	6,887	5,844	1,958	5,540	11,229	1,906	8,041	8,034	11,402	6,656	6,308	3,186	13,705	7,731
Maseru, Lesotho	8,634	15,493	10,744	10,066	10,848	7,160	11,703	8,473	7,788	13,637	13,534	7,498	14,139	7,092	8,646	3,704	7,325	11,490	12,107	14,452
Mashhad, Iran	4,116	8,348	14,156	5,166	14,005	3,100	3,906	1,270	2,703	8,424	7,721	2,870	11,788	3,598	6,802	8,967	1,837	5,464	9,382	11,224
Mazatlan, Mexico	10,035	5,349	11,493	8,556	4,677	11,765	11,127	13,705	11,539	4,853	10,989	11,646	1,886	16,302	16,001	11,769	14,936	7,848	12,464	2,175
Mbabane, Swaziland	8,387	15,223	10,877	9,856	11,257	6,853	11,221	7,991	7,458	13,542	13,104	7,178	14,359	6,615	8,286	3,981	6,837	11,239	11,830	14,610
Mbandaka, Zaire	5,272	12,118	14,105	6,672	10,188	3,969	9,734	6,823	4,662	10,319	13,319	4,343	11,740	6,919	9,857	3,174	6,130	8,117	13,626	11,773
McMurdo Sound, Antarctica	16,446	16,694	3,469	17,732	10,324	14,927	14,986	13,677	15,472	17,285	11,457	15,225	13,840	10,926	8,602	9,619	12,545	19,258	8,453	14,464
Mecca, Saudi Arabia	3,835	10,033	14,639	5,348	12,557	2,102	6,424	3,542	2,398	9,234	10,122	2,238	12,038	4,488	7,918	6,466	3,121	6,336	11,247	11,695
Medan, Indonesia	9,513	11,079	8,761	10,440	19,140	8,290	5,422	4,257	8,053	12,681	5,135	8,158	15,926	2,170	1,407	11,666	3,725	10,261	4,726	15,207
Medellin, Colombia	9,276	8,096	12,496	8,313	1,138	10,579	13,520	14,501	10,765	6,234	14,751	10,682	3,258	16,798	19,774	8,077	15,115	8,516	15,991	3,951
Medicine Hat, Canada	7,877	2,395	13,217	6,329	6,958	9,599	8,196	10,720	9,176	2,412	9,122	9,371	2,598	13,309	14,026	12,416	11,972	5,239	11,548	1,941
Medina, Saudi Arabia	3,552	9,698	14,882	5,050	12,501	1,841	6,188	3,407	2,085	8,921	9,989	1,943	11,777	4,580	8,026	6,648	3,114	6,010	11,257	11,414
Melbourne, Australia	16,130	13,513	2,142	16,882	13,952	14,730	10,733	10,856	14,628	16,028	6,942	14,682	15,026	8,548	5,213	13,317	10,281	16,020	3,934	15,099
Memphis, Tennessee	8,003	4,582	13,555	6,561	4,650	9,718	10,223	12,189	9,531	3,150	11,456	9,618	314	14,939	16,368	10,517	13,297	6,036	13,670	426
Merauke, Indonesia	13,571	10,708	4,980	13,778	16,068	12,837	7,552	8,475	12,416	13,273	3,680	12,611	14,199	6,982	3,710	15,413	8,384	12,740	657	13,821
Merida, Mexico	9,117	6,067	12,578	7,794	3,268	10,741	11,780	13,687	10,679	4,689	12,538	10,710	1,257	16,434	17,610	10,027	14,723	7,477	14,214	1,967
Meridian, Mississippi	8,134	4,912	13,468	6,722	4,320	9,830	10,544	12,450	9,676	3,427	11,758	9,748	141	15,202	16,694	10,309	13,533	6,268	13,905	757
Messina, Italy	1,065	7,918	17,612	2,586	10,166	910	6,695	5,138	1,192	6,498	11,039	1,013	9,069	7,122	10,541	6,390	5,440	3,918	13,201	8,757
Mexico City, Mexico	9,901	5,944	11,735	8,498	3,822	11,579	11,747	14,072	11,448	5,048	11,851	11,512	1,686	16,788	16,862	10,942	15,229	7,985	13,269	2,230
Miami, Florida	8,066	5,900	13,652	6,799	3,353	9,660	11,348	12,849	9,628	4,073	12,858	9,644	1,212	15,542	17,714	9,287	13,785	6,638	14,955	1,810
Midway Islands, USA	11,601	5,296	8,386	10,490	11,597	12,589	6,808	9,913	11,877	7,733	4,116	12,204	8,154	10,728	8,962	18,405	10,869	8,965	5,627	7,729
Milan, Italy	262	7,012	18,405	1,623	9,719	1,754	6,503	5,499	1,675	5,532	10,848	1,677	8,191	7,754	11,089	6,964	6,012	3,009	13,321	7,842
Milford Sound, New Zealand	18,171	13,427	207	18,470	11,946	16,702	12,329	12,877	16,665	15,471	8,139	16,698	13,337	10,584	7,254	13,271	12,324	17,057	5,364	13,590
Milwaukee, Wisconsin	7,259	3,865	14,205	5,775	5,390	8,997	9,379	11,293	8,757	2,252	10,969	8,867	1,209	14,042	15,674	10,587	12,411	5,161	13,448	612
Minsk, USSR	1,357	6,357	17,133	2,020	11,054	2,072	4,888	4,199	1,436	5,576	9,239	1,721	8,747	6,744	9,858	8,362	4,978	2,605	11,733	8,253
Mogadiscio, Somalia	5,984	12,191	12,646	7,524	13,212	4,236	7,766	4,542	4,618	11,440	10,523	4,433	13,993	3,923	6,889	5,960	3,496	8,563	10,622	13,760
Mombasa, Kenya	6,324	12,850	12,494	7,871	12,526	4,617	8,682	5,464	5,108	11,793	11,383	4,876	13,946	4,724	7,443	5,133	4,421	9,051	11,223	13,836
Monclova, Mexico	9,404	5,082	12,139	7,938	4,549	11,127	10,884	13,273	10,918	4,309	11,186	11,017	1,240	15,956	16,256	11,354	14,467	7,289	12,898	1,556
Moncton, Canada	5,586	4,504	16,001	4,209	5,587	7,281	9,055	10,213	7,134	1,997	11,726	7,199	2,658	12,907	15,506	9,066	11,158	4,022	14,584	2,392
Monrovia, Liberia	5,008	10,632	15,562	5,702	7,030	4,881	11,114	9,070	5,506	8,220	15,440	5,217	8,645	9,989	13,137	2,524	8,813	7,183	16,847	8,827
Monte Carlo, Monaco	501	7,162	18,494	1,731	9,551	1,780	6,739	5,675	1,795	5,600	11,086	1,755	8,162	7,875	11,237	6,741	6,145	3,168	13,541	7,838
Monterrey, Mexico	9,440	5,244	12,127	7,988	4,375	11,155	11,045	13,398	10,964	4,408	11,355	11,055	1,229	16,095	16,422	11,218	14,580	7,377	13,032	1,623
Montevideo, Uruguay	11,319	13,075	9,962	11,329	3,870	11,470	17,536	15,412	12,088	10,958	17,997	11,806	8,243	14,776	15,126	5,428	14,661	12,321	15,507	8,939
Montgomery, Alabama	7,974	4,996	13,647	6,581	4,232	9,659	10,570	12,382	9,522	3,391	11,916	9,586	366	15,132	16,804	10,095	13,439	6,180	14,111	868
Montpelier, Vermont	6,211	4,357	15,357	4,803	5,320	7,916	9,304	10,703	7,751	2,048	11,619	7,825	2,027	13,428	15,783	9,491	11,700	4,483	14,350	1,750
Montpellier, France	715	7,100	18,759	1,644	9,268	2,038	6,946	5,955	2,080	5,439	11,281	2,033	7,917	8,158	11,522	6,664	6,430	3,133	13,788	7,610
Montreal, Canada	6,197	4,198	15,341	4,769	5,457	7,913	9,169	10,619	7,730	1,901	11,460	7,812	2,046	13,352	15,646	9,626	11,633	4,398	14,196	1,714
Moosonee, Canada	6,256	3,374	15,111	4,746	6,141	8,003	8,518	10,249	7,726	1,249	10,635	7,852	2,248	13,001	14,956	10,364	11,350	4,093	13,377	1,675
Moroni, Comoros	7,256	13,708	11,576	8,804	12,805	5,544	9,165	5,938	6,017	12,726	11,359	5,794	14,759	4,701	7,002	5,306	4,777	9,968	10,771	14,707
Moscow, USSR	2,031	6,220	16,495	2,534	11,646	2,460	4,222	3,665	1,755	5,765	8,577	2,078	9,068	6,304	9,298	8,917	4,559	2,771	11,059	8,526
Mosul, Iraq	2,877	8,394	15,399	4,182	12,611	1,628	5,025	2,746	1,336	7,868	9,104	1,433	10,994	4,747	8,118	7,734	3,017	4,884	10,858	10,530
Mount Isa, Australia	14,529	11,998	3,867	14,980	15,539	13,490	8,777	9,256	13,195	14,576	5,040	13,333	14,959	7,326	3,878	14,461	8,925	14,053	2,018	14,725

Distances in Kilometers	Innsbruck, Austria	Inuvik, Canada	Invercargill, New Zealand	Inverness, United Kingdom	Iquitos, Peru	Iraklion, Greece	Irkutsk, USSR	Islamabad, Pakistan	Istanbul, Turkey	Ivujivik, Canada	Iwo Jima Island, Japan	Izmir, Turkey	Jackson, Mississippi	Jaffna, Sri Lanka	Jakarta, Indonesia	Jamestown, St. Helena	Jamnagar, India	Jan Mayen Island	Jayapura, Indonesia	Jefferson City, Missouri
Multan, Pakistan	5,410	8,882	12,866	6,396	15,301	4,342	3,633	421	3,992	9,385	6,822	4,141	12,826	2,438	5,512	9,710	867	6,520	8,173	12,207
Munich, West Germany	99	6,767	18,258	1,481	9,936	1,810	6,166	5,277	1,587	5,409	10,507	1,657	8,199	7,616	10,904	7,303	5,859	2,765	13,013	7,815
Murcia, Spain	1,452	7,578	18,738	2,178	8,718	2,358	7,694	6,545	2,596	5,689	12,033	2,467	7,817	8,581	12,002	5,987	6,901	3,703	14,494	7,595
Murmansk, USSR	2,700	4,732	16,486	2,218	11,042	3,775	4,019	4,645	3,121	4,450	8,152	3,419	7,867	7,392	9,999	9,905	5,735	1,591	10,963	7,265
Mururoa Atoll, Fr. Polynesia	16,141	10,013	5,444	14,637	7,350	17,865	13,714	16,621	17,600	10,763	10,043	17,746	7,925	15,664	12,229	13,425	17,048	13,677	8,919	8,279
Muscat, Oman	4,920	9,757	13,366	6,206	14,414	3,474	4,998	1,808	3,364	9,725	8,261	3,396	12,989	2,751	6,187	8,248	1,184	6,733	9,326	12,479
Myitkyina, Burma	7,692	8,811	10,674	8,325	17,416	6,886	3,041	2,516	6,446	10,265	4,412	6,643	13,571	2,532	3,636	12,053	2,797	7,930	5,597	12,855
Naga, Philippines	10,478	9,134	8,036	10,780	17,919	9,860	4,603	5,501	9,376	11,377	2,269	9,597	13,812	4,723	2,841	14,541	5,680	9,951	2,634	13,162
Nagasaki, Japan	9,227	6,911	9,584	9,123	15,996	9,143	2,985	5,220	8,515	9,163	1,424	8,802	11,666	5,713	4,958	15,197	5,940	8,045	4,072	10,990
Nagoya, Japan	9,387	6,398	9,568	9,115	15,354	9,482	3,197	5,757	8,824	8,750	1,227	9,125	11,070	6,403	5,559	15,744	6,556	7,924	4,192	10,410
Nagpur, India	6,642	9,729	11,627	7,655	16,471	5,455	4,079	1,509	5,181	10,523	6,340	5,297	13,982	1,274	4,277	10,124	945	7,730	7,198	13,332
Nairobi, Kenya	5,921	12,527	12,927	7,466	12,237	4,232	8,614	5,428	4,751	11,381	11,542	4,506	13,508	4,937	7,788	4,939	4,463	8,677	11,556	13,396
Nanchang, China	8,719	7,858	9,850	8,952	17,086	8,294	2,788	4,081	7,742	9,834	2,564	7,993	12,718	4,295	3,977	13,908	4,627	8,146	4,354	12,012
Nancy, France	419	6,607	18,655	1,199	9,550	2,147	6,417	5,665	1,981	5,111	10,730	2,031	7,821	8,019	11,301	7,254	6,262	2,610	13,318	7,453
Nandi, Fiji	16,498	10,325	3,280	15,599	11,925	16,666	10,454	12,386	16,058	12,500	6,125	16,340	11,269	11,120	7,759	16,258	12,491	14,077	4,350	11,260
Nanjing, China	8,628	7,407	10,014	8,752	16,635	8,331	2,533	4,238	7,745	9,429	2,346	8,012	12,262	4,696	4,416	14,172	4,898	7,864	4,473	11,558
Nanning, China	8,678	8,732	9,755	9,149	17,890	7,990	3,287	3,633	7,516	10,542	3,364	7,730	13,598	3,349	3,210	13,114	3,921	8,549	4,497	12,883
Nantes, France	979	6,590	19,244	1,155	8,950	2,577	6,935	6,265	2,520	4,859	11,208	2,524	7,363	8,590	11,895	7,006	6,840	2,679	13,872	7,039
Naples, Italy	750	7,607	17,851	2,273	10,073	1,132	6,568	5,187	1,238	6,190	10,924	1,138	8,810	7,277	10,671	6,614	5,568	3,605	13,192	8,481
Narvik, Norway	2,382	4,665	17,056	1,626	10,419	3,715	4,643	5,181	3,129	4,026	8,716	3,393	7,382	7,910	10,613	9,540	6,213	1,052	11,569	6,810
Nashville, Tennessee	7,711	4,594	13,862	6,283	4,639	9,419	10,149	11,996	9,246	2,982	11,586	9,326	532	14,748	16,409	10,266	13,076	5,811	13,892	547
Nassau, Bahamas	7,915	6,078	13,821	6,690	3,222	9,480	11,435	12,795	9,476	4,147	13,102	9,479	1,486	15,451	17,866	8,993	13,685	6,608	15,246	2,045
Natal, Brazil	7,444	10,948	13,775	7,549	4,225	7,771	13,670	12,070	8,321	8,386	17,871	8,068	7,179	12,887	15,612	3,410	11,831	8,739	18,986	7,645
Natashquan, Canada	5,174	4,245	16,343	3,756	6,080	6,892	8,574	9,713	6,708	1,675	11,392	6,789	3,067	12,416	15,010	9,144	10,673	3,516	14,314	2,715
Nauru Island	14,313	8,849	5,084	13,643	13,326	14,498	8,231	10,396	13,855	11,326	3,932	14,151	11,256	9,692	6,708	18,018	10,746	12,177	2,928	10,997
Ndjamena, Chad	3,912	10,742	15,456	5,293	9,921	2,765	8,905	6,332	3,479	8,973	12,908	3,151	10,693	7,090	10,350	3,854	5,929	6,746	13,954	10,630
Nelson, New Zealand	18,432	12,927	693	18,196	11,662	17,178	12,306	13,158	17,049	14,903	8,024	17,126	12,792	10,987	7,602	13,669	12,701	16,693	5,390	13,025
Nema, Mauritania	3,807	9,664	16,677	4,541	7,597	3,821	9,955	8,136	4,399	7,387	14,306	4,130	8,395	9,424	12,774	3,604	8,054	6,044	16,194	8,445
Neuquen, Argentina	12,370	13,070	9,016	12,229	3,932	12,610	18,414	16,522	13,217	11,269	16,848	12,941	8,213	15,478	14,982	6,533	15,665	13,056	14,555	8,931
New Delhi, India	5,952	8,957	12,333	6,875	15,859	4,922	3,453	684	4,560	9,677	6,321	4,717	13,135	2,116	4,988	10,180	987	6,890	7,592	12,487
New Glasgow, Canada	5,472	4,640	16,137	4,119	5,566	7,157	9,091	10,166	7,025	2,110	11,845	7,082	2,785	12,844	15,520	8,896	11,089	3,998	14,723	2,547
New Haven, Connecticut	6,426	4,628	15,185	5,051	4,991	8,113	9,634	11,006	7,976	2,371	11,885	8,038	1,832	13,721	16,112	9,366	11,983	4,790	14,561	1,670
New Orleans, Louisiana	8,416	5,113	13,200	7,013	4,140	10,105	10,788	12,742	9,961	3,712	11,845	10,029	259	15,494	16,842	10,357	13,829	6,564	13,880	975
New Plymouth, New Zealand	18,346	12,672	940	17,955	11,675	17,251	12,153	13,131	17,058	14,666	7,848	17,165	12,635	11,034	7,625	13,916	12,728	16,445	5,273	12,845
New York, New York	6,539	4,642	15,073	5,162	4,925	8,225	9,702	11,107	8,089	2,428	11,891	8,150	1,721	13,826	16,177	9,418	12,090	4,889	14,537	1,575
Newcastle upon Tyne, UK	1,249	5,772	18,820	319	9,194	2,996	6,307	6,080	2,726	4,232	10,488	2,834	7,052	8,598	11,736	7,869	6,828	1,819	13,273	6,643
Newcastle Waters, Australia	13,816	11,907	4,546	14,358	16,276	12,749	8,214	8,529	12,460	14,451	4,745	12,595	15,361	6,592	3,148	14,218	8,185	13,550	1,828	15,031
Niamey, Niger	3,841	10,274	16,140	4,907	8,538	3,342	9,643	7,448	4,010	8,170	13,892	3,702	9,435	8,471	11,762	3,369	7,209	6,431	15,320	9,453
Nicosia, Cyprus	2,267	8,476	16,081	3,730	11,764	749	5,771	3,637	755	7,592	9,946	662	10,503	5,500	8,919	7,001	3,822	4,695	11,749	10,109
Niue (Alofi)	16,869	10,120	3,631	15,577	10,582	17,678	11,376	13,621	16,984	11,963	7,169	17,303	10,203	12,465	9,091	15,774	13,815	14,091	5,675	10,294
Norfolk, Virginia	6,962	4,930	14,683	5,611	4,507	8,620	10,131	11,579	8,518	2,844	12,131	8,569	1,371	14,295	16,592	9,416	12,555	5,361	14,654	1,412
Norfolk Island, Australia	17,152	11,803	1,928	16,788	12,563	16,473	10,919	12,143	16,093	14,061	6,601	16,277	12,703	10,333	6,883	14,983	11,923	15,333	4,114	12,761
Noril'sk, USSR	4,692	4,400	14,377	4,312	12,597	5,323	2,081	4,072	4,609	5,346	6,039	4,937	8,734	6,652	8,499	11,800	5,349	3,292	8,890	8,039
Norman Wells, Canada	7,017	456	13,577	5,565	8,791	8,589	6,258	8,895	8,034	2,367	7,613	8,289	4,424	11,400	12,244	13,026	10,169	4,166	10,374	3,715
Normanton, Australia	14,398	11,621	4,055	14,745	15,575	13,462	8,523	9,170	13,124	14,199	4,696	13,282	14,658	7,364	3,936	14,817	8,913	13,755	1,675	14,394
North Pole	4,767	2,416	15,141	3,632	10,419	6,092	4,209	6,272	5,461	3,081	7,259	5,750	6,427	8,934	10,684	11,766	7,517	2,123	10,281	5,731
Nottingham, United Kingdom	1,097	5,995	18,962	538	9,155	2,845	6,448	6,093	2,621	4,410	10,661	2,706	7,155	8,565	11,753	7,646	6,797	2,047	13,413	6,767
Norway House, Canada	6,965	2,447	14,190	5,416	6,797	8,703	8,049	10,251	8,322	1,490	9,609	8,496	2,485	12,948	14,259	11,563	11,456	4,437	12,239	1,766
Norwich, United Kingdom	938	6,084	18,850	643	9,306	2,687	6,358	5,936	2,452	4,553	10,597	2,540	7,324	8,397	11,596	7,626	6,630	2,111	13,317	6,931
Nouakchott, Mauritania	4,085	9,218	16,841	4,477	6,733	4,470	10,327	8,839	4,965	6,805	14,666	4,734	7,507	10,307	13,690	3,928	8,870	5,897	16,951	7,599
Noumea, New Caledonia	16,452	11,143	2,683	16,024	12,932	16,012	10,210	11,642	15,544	13,492	5,871	15,765	12,512	10,058	6,637	15,695	11,552	14,579	3,537	12,481
Novosibirsk, USSR	4,853	5,993	13,788	5,029	13,931	4,868	1,443	2,489	4,192	6,875	5,786	4,500	10,306	5,039	7,135	11,358	3,771	4,438	8,263	9,622
Nuku'alofa, Tonga	17,046	10,477	3,175	15,904	11,102	17,488	11,216	13,243	16,847	12,439	6,923	17,145	10,795	11,927	8,528	15,749	13,338	14,389	5,201	10,871
Nukunono Island, Tokelau Isls.	15,774	9,110	4,531	14,546	10,900	16,639	10,390	12,881	15,930	11,112	6,315	16,256	9,785	12,157	8,958	16,843	13,280	13,039	5,296	9,764
Nuremberg, West Germany	244	6,618	18,293	1,348	9,916	1,942	6,098	5,300	1,682	5,273	10,428	1,773	8,095	7,677	10,941	7,429	5,915	2,616	12,972	7,700
Nyala, Sudan	4,103	10,926	14,890	5,613	10,990	2,579	8,241	5,442	3,235	9,476	12,018	2,930	11,559	6,023	9,286	4,576	4,922	6,945	12,887	11,420
Oaxaca, Mexico	9,935	6,263	11,737	8,572	3,458	11,582	12,062	14,287	11,493	5,245	12,211	11,538	1,812	17,028	17,202	10,629	15,405	8,142	13,560	2,426
Ocean Falls, Canada	8,302	1,811	12,522	6,794	8,039	9,939	7,437	10,259	9,418	3,103	7,931	9,658	3,743	12,645	12,899	13,552	11,540	5,492	10,340	3,127
Odense, Denmark	908	5,966	18,181	929	9,948	2,500	5,708	5,317	2,100	4,743	9,981	2,267	7,736	7,845	10,974	8,049	6,076	1,973	12,658	7,288
Odessa, USSR	1,473	7,206	16,802	2,657	11,383	1,323	5,151	3,832	622	6,390	9,491	941	9,467	6,182	9,448	7,818	4,417	3,446	11,735	9,010
Ogbomosho, Nigeria	4,390	10,909	15,502	5,522	8,706	3,687	9,977	7,565	4,385	8,806	14,113	4,065	9,952	8,314	11,490	2,880	7,190	7,043	15,172	10,009
Okha, USSR	7,932	4,392	11,338	7,341	13,581	8,489	2,569	5,782	7,779	6,659	3,199	8,105	9,207	7,376	7,435	15,024	6,906	6,008	6,221	8,513
Okinawa (Naha)	9,676	7,667	9,027	9,707	16,679	9,409	3,491	5,266	8,823	9,922	1,383	9,091	12,393	5,336	4,233	15,082	5,813	8,707	3,477	11,726
Oklahoma City, Oklahoma	8,435	4,293	13,046	6,947	5,029	10,173	10,054	12,284	9,929	3,288	10,917	10,043	763	14,999	15,925	11,183	13,458	6,266	13,022	585
Old Crow, Canada	7,043	271	13,363	5,665	9,420	8,525	5,691	8,441	7,927	2,850	7,010	8,202	5,049	10,871	11,613	13,405	9,721	4,193	9,818	4,344
Olympia, Washington	8,654	2,450	12,327	7,118	7,429	10,340	8,120	10,919	9,862	3,269	8,450	10,083	3,214	13,328	13,474	13,344	12,198	5,909	10,702	2,662
Omaha, Nebraska	7,872	3,747	13,541	6,363	5,498	9,619	9,456	11,629	9,342	2,639	10,612	9,470	1,124	14,349	15,510	11,187	12,803	5,626	12,928	445
Omsk, USSR	4,276	6,142	14,309	4,556	13,586	4,262	2,052	2,367	3,584	6,748	6,390	3,894	10,206	5,062	7,451	10,767	3,623	4,123	8,816	9,545
Oodnadatta, Australia	14,740	12,854	3,557	15,439	15,381	13,481	9,348	9,441	13,291	15,430	5,825	13,382	15,621	7,256	3,844	13,639	8,946	14,692	2,824	15,465
Oradea, Romania	798	7,046	17,471	2,108	10,708	1,330	5,648	4,507	877	5,968	10,006	1,051	8,912	6,832	10,120	7,505	5,073	3,127	12,359	8,492
Oran, Algeria	1,627	7,833	18,508	2,435	8,700	2,331	7,864	6,596	2,640	5,922	12,212	2,480	7,969	8,549	11,986	5,740	6,895	3,960	14,604	7,769
Oranjestad, Aruba	8,354	7,654	13,418	7,402	1,836	9,678	12,807	13,584	9,848	5,573	14,666	9,771	3,006	15,903	19,227	7,749	14,198	7,669	16,472	3,623
Orebro, Sweden	1,361	5,624	17,729	1,152	10,277	2,759	5,220	5,054	2,247	4,632	9,470	2,472	7,784	7,668	10,682	8,551	5,910	1,707	12,182	7,289
Orel, USSR	1,864	6,528	16,562	2,577	11,630	2,136	4,446	3,626	1,428	5,981	8,803	1,752	9,233	6,199	9,283	8,617	4,439	2,985	11,210	8,712
Orsk, USSR	3,403	6,706	15,029	3,994	13,117	3,194	3,111	2,276	2,530	6,840	7,410	2,831	10,263	5,005	7,843	9,690	3,341	3,953	9,679	9,660
Osaka, Japan	9,361	6,504	9,564	9,123	15,487	9,419	3,150	5,651	8,767	8,838	1,232	9,065	11,194	6,264	5,433	15,641	6,434	7,953	4,154	10,531
Oslo, Norway	1,409	5,489	17,907	908	10,032	2,925	5,390	5,313	2,450	4,402	9,601	2,657	7,528	7,930	10,934	8,538	6,172	1,523	12,356	7,039
Osorno, Chile	12,811	13,074	8,611	12,613	4,076	13,081	18,690	16,956	13,684	11,422	16,378	13,410	8,256	15,687	14,830	6,978	16,035	13,369	14,131	8,975
Ostrava, Czechoslovakia	583	6,693	17,773	1,703	10,437	1,704	5,671	4,779	1,286	5,560	10,021	1,451	8,513	7,179	10,423	7,657	5,414	2,743	12,492	8,086
Ottawa, Canada	6,337	4,120	15,188	4,897	5,453	8,057	9,180	10,700	7,864	1,896	11,378	7,951	1,918	13,440	15,648	9,769	11,731	4,482	14,084	1,558
Ouagadougou, Bourkina Fasso	4,054	10,292	16,114	5,010	8,131	3,696	9,980	7,850	4,347	8,095	14,261	4,047	9,166	8,879	12,150	3,164	7,623	6,533	15,732	9,221
Oujda, Morocco	1,787	7,909	18,470	2,540	8,561	2,461	8,025	6,746	2,791	5,951	12,373	2,623	7,918	8,670	12,112	5,615	7,027	4,065	14,764	7,736
Oxford, United Kingdom	1,041	6,120	19,050	665	9,112	2,778	6,550	6,126	2,587	4,502	10,777	2,656	7,197	8,569	11,784	7,510	6,803	2,181	13,512	6,822
Pago Pago, American Samoa	16,340	9,626	4,065	15,077	10,717	17,192	10,912	13,289	16,488	11,543	6,766	16,811	9,983	12,345	9,045	16,285	13,587	13,581	5,494	10,021
Pakxe, Laos	9,115	9,625	9,241	9,751	18,745	8,219	4,123	3,870	7,825	11,405	3,859	8,002	14,491	2,866	2,356	12,721	3,843	9,283	4,314	13,776
Palembang, Indonesia	10,500	11,551	7,774	11,407	19,236	9,260	6,116	5,236	9,037	13,402	5,002	9,136	16,402	3,077	425	12,109	4,700	11,153	3,998	15,702
Palermo, Italy	1,029	7,886	17,772	2,507	9,973	1,095	6,835	5,327	1,377	6,398	11,186	1,206	8,913	7,312	10,733	6,307	5,632	3,882	13,382	8,614
Palma, Majorca	1,109	7,502	18,629	2,052	9,076	2,038	7,348	6,178	2,235	5,737	11,696	2,120	8,030	8,251	11,660	6,205	6,557	3,562	14,125	7,772
Palmerston North, New Zealand	18,537	12,765	893	18,101	11,507	17,380	12,346	13,305	17,220	14,701	8,038	17,313	12,570	11,176	7,778	13,772	12,880	16,582	5,466	12,803
Panama, Panama	9,354	7,670	12,420	8,293	1,571	10,747	13,210	14,478	10,877	5,932	14,226	10,821	2,808	16,958	19,268	8,586	15,215	8,367	15,527	3,515
Paramaribo, Suriname	7,776	8,935	13,887	7,220	2,273	8,761	13,281	13,045	9,097	6,548	16,181	8,943	4,669	14,775	18,041	5,956	13,297	7,923	18,238	5,199
Paris, France	698	6,505	18,934	1,052	9,276	2,396	6,604	5,941	2,261	4,911	10,891	2,299	7,556	8,304	11,581	7,221	6,546	2,536	13,533	7,200
Patna, India	6,765	9,114	11,536	7,608	16,675	5,774	3,374	1,463	5,402	10,134	5,623	5,566	13,578	1,845	4,225	10,848	1,569	7,484	6,744	12,895
Patrai, Greece	1,309	8,009	17,148	2,853	10,706	444	6,302	4,607	693	6,780	10,619	474	9,499	6,592	10,004	6,648	4,902	4,051	12,689	9,152
Peking, China	7,840	6,687	10,867	7,880	15,884	7,697	1,654	3,881	7,072	8,588	2,870	7,357	11,553	4,917	5,199	13,861	4,757	6,965	5,316	10,839
Penrhyn Island (Omoka)	15,648	8,793	5,230	14,178	9,385	17,070	11,312	14,127	16,391	10,383	7,559	16,705	8,520	13,666	10,473	15,913	14,689	12,793	6,813	8,602
Peoria, Illinois	7,539	4,035	13,947	6,061	5,197	9,273	9,618	11,581	9,043	2,538	11,056	9,149	933	14,328	15,850	10,647	12,704	5,456	13,447	323
Perm', USSR	3,191	5,965	15,411	3,482	12,578	3,409	3,063	2,984	2,699	6,084	7,421	3,024	9,521	5,733	8,425	9,948	4,100	3,244	9,917	8,906
Perth, Australia	13,572	14,099	4,717	14,714	15,940	12,035	9,395	8,532	12,017	16,479	6,837	12,027	17,578	5,978	3,003	11,845	7,746	14,567	4,168	17,384
Peshawar, Pakistan	5,160	8,462	13,132	6,070	15,072	4,217	3,303	154	3,805	8,974	6,724	3,984	12,421	2,831	5,792	9,861	1,288	6,130	8,266	11,795

Distances in Kilometers	Innsbruck, Austria	Inuvik, Canada	Invercargill, New Zealand	Inverness, United Kingdom	Iquitos, Peru	Iraklion, Greece	Irkutsk, USSR	Islamabad, Pakistan	Istanbul, Turkey	Ivujivik, Canada	Iwo Jima Island, Japan	Izmir, Turkey	Jackson, Mississippi	Jaffna, Sri Lanka	Jakarta, Indonesia	Jamestown, St. Helena	Jamnagar, India	Jan Mayen Island	Jayapura, Indonesia	Jefferson City, Missouri
Petropavlovsk-Kamchatskiy,USSR	8,467	3,818	11,056	7,658	12,794	9,238	3,589	6,815	8,524	6,286	3,455	8,852	8,462	8,396	8,162	15,670	7,952	6,212	6,382	7,794
Petrozavodsk, USSR	2,174	5,531	16,649	2,194	11,292	3,015	4,156	4,156	2,342	5,102	8,451	2,649	8,452	6,861	9,700	9,311	5,146	2,126	11,108	7,887
Pevek, USSR	6,918	2,165	12,877	5,890	11,392	8,019	3,802	6,799	7,329	4,411	5,341	7,646	7,030	9,014	9,657	14,025	8,067	4,388	8,318	6,320
Philadelphia, Pennsylvania	6,669	4,669	14,946	5,292	4,845	8,354	9,787	11,227	8,219	2,504	11,906	8,280	1,594	13,949	16,257	9,471	12,215	5,007	14,517	1,473
Phnom Penh, Kampuchea	9,339	10,029	8,991	10,043	19,122	8,357	4,516	4,053	8,001	11,802	4,105	8,161	14,896	2,734	1,970	12,549	3,891	9,632	4,256	14,181
Phoenix, Arizona	9,439	4,119	11,898	7,902	5,799	11,188	9,872	12,551	10,847	4,014	9,932	11,006	2,048	15,066	15,003	12,475	13,812	6,979	11,766	1,878
Pierre, South Dakota	7,861	3,289	13,456	6,327	5,978	9,610	9,039	11,334	9,283	2,473	10,121	9,434	1,605	14,020	15,022	11,596	12,540	5,467	12,475	938
Pinang, Malaysia	9,491	10,830	8,792	10,364	19,301	8,324	5,207	4,205	8,056	12,482	4,872	8,175	15,686	2,292	1,469	11,897	3,761	10,125	4,574	14,968
Pitcairn Island (Adamstown)	15,832	10,363	5,883	14,446	6,510	17,391	14,575	17,582	17,392	10,737	11,011	17,416	7,632	16,419	12,972	12,477	17,960	13,726	9,819	8,078
Pittsburgh, Pennsylvania	6,954	4,427	14,617	5,536	4,943	8,661	9,725	11,349	8,492	2,448	11,618	8,569	1,283	14,092	16,149	9,871	12,386	5,134	14,158	1,065
Plymouth, Montserrat	7,433	7,533	14,332	6,560	2,569	8,723	12,255	12,702	8,908	5,221	14,759	8,823	3,304	14,946	18,351	7,176	13,256	6,974	17,071	3,791
Plymouth, United Kingdom	1,189	6,193	19,301	787	8,875	2,888	6,796	6,356	2,751	4,471	11,012	2,795	7,060	8,771	12,011	7,349	7,008	2,309	13,760	6,709
Ponape Island	13,178	8,402	5,990	12,694	14,321	13,240	7,008	9,137	12,610	10,971	2,675	12,899	11,591	8,608	5,895	18,017	9,540	11,307	2,212	11,205
Ponce, Puerto Rico	7,663	7,222	14,111	6,692	2,517	9,029	12,170	12,876	9,171	5,007	14,392	9,106	2,844	15,245	18,519	7,660	13,518	6,977	16,590	3,365
Ponta Delgada, Azores	3,191	6,847	18,512	2,697	6,721	4,501	8,924	8,492	4,645	4,451	12,953	4,569	5,804	10,708	14,089	6,297	8,994	3,827	15,869	5,695
Pontianak, Indonesia	10,612	11,082	7,687	11,395	19,506	9,489	5,816	5,311	9,206	13,060	4,407	9,333	15,893	3,422	734	12,692	4,929	11,000	3,502	15,210
Port Augusta, Australia	15,254	13,260	3,023	16,020	14,837	13,911	9,939	9,972	13,770	15,837	6,351	13,840	15,555	7,701	4,336	13,393	9,420	15,280	3,331	15,502
Port Blair, India	8,420	10,413	9,857	9,342	18,260	7,249	4,629	3,156	6,978	11,760	5,313	7,096	15,137	1,411	2,506	11,259	2,693	9,213	5,532	14,427
Port Elizabeth, South Africa	9,108	15,962	10,355	10,511	10,594	7,672	12,217	8,989	8,310	13,971	13,805	8,015	14,132	7,502	8,824	3,715	7,823	11,960	12,142	14,514
Port Hedland, Australia	12,926	12,813	5,343	13,835	17,050	11,592	8,159	7,676	11,433	15,163	5,565	11,506	16,876	5,370	2,017	12,735	7,083	13,440	3,106	16,446
Port Louis, Mauritius	8,778	14,594	9,901	10,317	14,034	7,029	9,216	6,189	7,388	14,224	10,344	7,218	16,548	4,119	5,541	6,671	4,910	11,298	9,210	16,466
Port Moresby, Papua New Guinea	14,118	10,535	4,560	14,147	15,316	13,516	7,967	9,145	13,058	13,114	3,844	13,270	13,632	7,739	4,467	15,920	9,114	12,976	1,051	13,319
Port Said, Egypt	2,516	8,898	15,916	4,029	11,710	805	6,142	3,826	1,122	7,929	10,252	922	10,736	5,466	8,911	6,618	3,857	5,075	11,908	10,377
Port Sudan, Sudan	3,858	10,222	14,688	5,393	12,304	2,109	6,753	3,877	2,499	9,306	10,455	2,300	11,998	4,723	8,131	6,128	3,421	6,453	11,523	11,690
Port-au-Prince, Haiti	8,053	6,944	13,719	6,981	2,469	9,491	12,155	13,170	9,587	4,891	13,992	9,544	2,350	15,666	18,633	8,234	13,910	7,115	16,018	2,936
Port-of-Spain, Trin. & Tobago	7,858	8,183	13,881	7,093	2,057	9,035	12,904	13,158	9,283	5,894	15,374	9,169	3,795	15,213	18,655	6,815	13,599	7,594	17,420	4,341
Port-Vila, Vanuatu	16,115	10,605	3,179	15,551	12,872	15,904	9,897	11,551	15,368	12,958	5,540	15,618	12,105	10,164	6,794	16,225	11,573	14,083	3,453	12,034
Portland, Maine	6,097	4,510	15,497	4,713	5,260	7,791	9,363	10,673	7,644	2,145	11,772	7,710	2,148	13,383	15,841	9,296	11,643	4,460	14,527	1,918
Portland, Oregon	8,789	2,619	12,220	7,250	7,318	10,482	8,278	11,087	10,011	3,381	8,531	10,229	3,143	13,488	13,571	13,349	12,366	6,057	10,732	2,619
Porto, Portugal	1,732	7,041	19,375	1,842	8,204	3,005	7,814	7,017	3,133	5,023	12,077	3,057	7,086	9,196	12,580	6,327	7,482	3,324	14,746	6,861
Porto Alegre, Brazil	10,608	12,778	10,653	10,648	3,724	10,778	16,834	14,810	11,387	10,525	18,658	11,109	8,037	14,492	15,364	4,881	14,163	11,689	16,185	8,709
Porto Alexandre, Angola	6,987	13,683	12,723	8,257	9,384	5,831	11,549	8,497	6,534	11,540	14,689	6,211	12,056	8,018	10,356	1,885	7,624	9,762	14,047	12,303
Porto Novo, Benin	4,597	11,040	15,376	5,687	8,507	3,939	10,233	7,817	4,635	8,882	14,370	4,315	9,896	8,520	11,657	2,644	7,426	7,211	15,367	9,981
Porto Velho, Brazil	9,630	10,097	12,008	9,100	1,173	10,484	15,065	14,838	10,885	7,983	16,815	10,703	5,334	16,071	18,067	6,359	14,892	9,732	17,030	6,004
Portsmouth, United Kingdom	991	6,227	19,098	773	9,092	2,714	6,621	6,137	2,548	4,589	10,861	2,604	7,247	8,556	11,793	7,402	6,792	2,291	13,579	6,883
Poznan, Poland	698	6,393	17,852	1,463	10,353	2,005	5,569	4,878	1,560	5,277	9,902	1,744	8,276	7,346	10,537	7,882	5,577	2,442	12,451	7,833
Prague, Czechoslovakia	386	6,608	18,047	1,474	10,165	1,853	5,867	5,052	1,511	5,371	10,206	1,640	8,268	7,451	10,698	7,576	5,687	2,623	12,725	7,855
Praia, Cape Verde Islands	4,821	9,275	16,345	4,993	5,860	5,337	11,042	9,708	5,808	6,754	15,319	5,588	6,964	11,171	14,524	3,934	9,750	6,308	17,816	7,145
Pretoria, South Africa	8,260	15,115	11,069	9,707	10,974	6,768	11,350	8,120	7,392	13,335	13,375	7,104	14,060	6,843	8,583	3,678	6,992	11,116	12,133	14,321
Prince Albert, Canada	7,391	2,234	13,698	5,842	7,007	9,116	7,984	10,377	8,701	1,925	9,233	8,891	2,636	13,017	14,017	12,079	11,612	4,772	11,782	1,931
Prince Edward Island	10,715	17,535	8,627	12,175	11,300	9,163	12,645	9,568	9,744	15,717	12,968	9,476	15,376	7,500	7,904	5,265	8,303	13,567	10,778	15,900
Prince George, Canada	7,989	1,707	12,877	6,470	7,862	9,647	7,454	10,177	9,144	2,737	8,190	9,376	3,521	12,641	13,105	13,189	11,453	5,202	10,664	2,874
Prince Rupert, Canada	8,185	1,574	12,568	6,694	8,301	9,797	7,158	9,996	9,258	3,100	7,704	9,506	3,987	12,367	12,647	13,651	11,277	5,355	10,169	3,355
Providence, Rhode Island	6,291	4,640	15,323	4,922	5,051	7,976	9,572	10,896	7,843	2,331	11,901	7,902	1,970	13,605	16,051	9,281	11,863	4,685	14,610	1,800
Provo, Utah	8,801	3,399	12,445	7,255	6,251	10,544	9,184	11,804	10,169	3,335	9,592	10,343	2,113	14,352	14,640	12,483	13,061	6,266	11,688	1,685
Puerto Aisen, Chile	13,133	13,586	8,215	13,038	4,613	13,256	19,212	16,843	13,893	11,960	16,209	13,603	8,784	15,270	14,293	6,973	15,798	13,859	13,761	9,503
Puerto Deseado, Argentina	12,911	14,035	8,322	12,970	4,255	12,880	19,153	16,281	13,541	12,259	16,517	13,239	9,192	14,717	13,989	6,493	15,217	13,924	13,866	9,911
Puerto Princesa, Philippines	10,497	9,711	7,932	10,951	18,552	9,717	4,894	5,349	9,289	11,879	2,916	9,484	14,438	4,248	2,201	13,982	5,368	10,247	2,788	13,777
Punta Arenas, Chile	13,569	14,426	7,629	13,667	5,479	13,434	19,680	16,452	14,114	12,828	15,869	13,803	9,649	14,527	13,428	6,955	15,278	14,612	13,169	10,367
Pusan, South Korea	8,975	6,713	9,848	8,857	15,851	8,926	2,733	5,072	8,290	8,931	1,645	8,581	11,498	5,707	5,129	15,061	5,843	7,779	4,340	10,814
Pyongyang, North Korea	8,453	6,445	10,369	8,340	15,658	8,435	2,211	4,691	7,790	8,564	2,153	8,085	11,284	5,581	5,371	14,669	5,547	7,286	4,849	10,585
Qamdo, China	7,246	8,203	11,166	7,782	16,814	6,583	2,414	2,276	6,089	9,624	4,368	6,311	12,937	2,974	4,255	12,129	2,858	7,321	5,921	12,223
Qandahar, Afghanistan	4,881	8,807	13,388	5,932	14,748	3,773	3,868	734	3,437	9,094	7,315	3,577	12,497	2,838	6,037	9,257	1,097	6,168	8,741	11,910
Qiqian, China	7,112	5,313	11,830	6,864	14,481	7,352	1,124	4,296	6,664	7,191	3,504	6,979	10,170	5,982	6,603	13,853	5,417	5,772	6,348	9,454
Qom, Iran	3,562	8,577	14,706	4,782	13,340	2,347	4,618	2,051	2,049	8,320	8,527	2,161	11,557	4,052	7,397	8,193	2,304	5,323	10,154	11,053
Quebec, Canada	5,964	4,171	15,567	4,535	5,607	7,682	9,016	10,404	7,495	1,785	11,429	7,579	2,280	13,132	15,496	9,531	11,408	4,183	14,215	1,936
Quetta, Pakistan	5,070	8,944	13,199	6,127	14,925	3,935	3,905	700	3,616	9,274	7,240	3,749	12,684	2,644	5,850	9,308	910	6,356	8,596	12,092
Quito, Ecuador	10,020	8,670	11,746	9,092	704	11,263	14,229	15,273	11,487	6,946	14,951	11,388	3,803	17,432	19,099	8,170	15,824	9,296	15,665	4,517
Rabaul, Papua New Guinea	13,942	9,791	4,930	13,748	14,907	13,596	7,706	9,259	13,063	12,365	3,415	13,309	12,849	8,151	5,035	16,723	9,386	12,468	1,289	12,520
Raiatea (Uturoa)	16,273	9,544	4,952	14,732	8,639	17,916	12,429	15,201	17,313	10,818	8,617	17,598	8,482	14,420	11,066	14,804	15,647	13,479	7,578	8,691
Raleigh, North Carolina	7,200	4,944	14,441	5,840	4,413	8,871	10,247	11,777	8,755	2,962	12,101	8,808	1,134	14,502	16,680	9,562	12,770	5,555	14,550	1,240
Rangiroa (Avatoru)	15,936	9,305	5,361	14,388	8,239	17,636	12,530	15,427	17,096	10,462	8,865	17,355	8,049	14,824	11,494	14,627	15,974	13,190	7,967	8,273
Rangoon, Burma	8,267	9,760	10,041	9,056	18,170	7,250	4,002	2,967	6,902	11,211	4,764	7,057	14,532	1,920	2,795	11,749	2,805	8,789	5,339	13,816
Raoul Is., Kermadec Islands	17,854	11,417	2,247	16,833	11,224	17,761	11,754	13,390	17,264	13,352	7,401	17,503	11,489	11,705	8,256	14,934	13,267	15,312	5,281	11,633
Rarotonga (Avarua)	17,007	10,154	4,016	15,516	9,506	18,369	12,240	14,674	17,661	11,663	8,153	17,987	9,476	13,529	10,126	15,025	14,903	14,153	6,763	9,661
Rawson, Argentina	12,527	13,612	8,763	12,516	4,453	12,608	18,740	16,272	13,248	11,774	16,852	12,956	8,753	14,986	14,466	6,343	15,307	13,436	14,314	9,470
Recife, Brazil	7,638	11,194	13,550	7,778	4,271	7,909	13,873	12,178	8,475	8,634	18,111	8,215	7,367	12,884	15,501	3,292	11,890	8,982	18,741	7,848
Regina, Canada	7,569	2,540	13,588	6,020	6,715	9,304	8,300	10,681	8,912	2,092	9,467	9,093	2,340	13,330	14,299	11,986	11,911	5,005	11,952	1,645
Reykjavik, Iceland	2,758	4,357	17,930	1,212	8,628	4,488	6,290	6,928	4,130	2,725	10,039	4,287	5,778	9,617	12,409	8,988	7,878	938	13,025	5,286
Rhodes, Greece	1,836	8,289	16,551	3,343	11,287	304	6,019	4,074	513	7,245	10,268	240	10,068	5,986	9,404	6,806	4,305	4,414	12,183	9,698
Richmond, Virginia	6,992	4,815	14,637	5,623	4,594	8,670	10,053	11,554	8,544	2,765	12,008	8,601	1,300	14,279	16,504	9,542	12,547	5,333	14,525	1,296
Riga, USSR	1,380	5,988	17,318	1,701	10,803	2,404	4,907	4,492	1,806	5,173	9,228	2,073	8,363	7,087	10,137	8,538	5,327	2,201	11,825	7,860
Ringkobing, Denmark	1,005	5,856	18,265	777	9,826	2,639	5,765	5,450	2,251	4,595	10,015	2,413	7,582	7,990	11,104	8,087	6,222	1,855	12,725	7,134
Rio Branco, Brazil	10,013	10,074	11,651	9,421	912	10,912	15,260	15,254	11,298	8,072	16,537	11,124	5,249	16,506	18,126	6,747	15,339	9,977	16,584	5,939
Rio Cuarto, Argentina	11,675	12,600	9,738	11,503	3,380	12,005	17,695	16,104	12,585	10,659	17,366	12,321	7,734	15,543	15,557	6,157	15,421	12,340	15,268	8,444
Rio de Janeiro, Brazil	9,502	12,369	11,700	9,618	3,864	9,664	15,742	13,771	10,268	9,942	19,518	9,991	7,890	13,829	15,441	4,004	13,242	10,749	17,159	8,506
Rio Gallegos, Argentina	13,374	14,323	7,833	13,462	5,319	13,268	19,568	16,405	13,943	12,668	16,063	13,634	9,522	14,581	13,589	6,811	15,260	14,412	13,374	10,240
Rio Grande, Brazil	10,833	12,942	10,419	10,882	3,832	10,977	17,064	14,960	11,593	10,720	18,485	11,312	8,171	14,518	15,227	5,000	14,269	11,921	15,951	8,851
Riyadh, Saudi Arabia	4,000	9,694	14,352	5,425	13,212	2,389	5,692	2,752	2,453	9,194	9,332	2,397	12,227	3,894	7,344	7,248	2,393	6,220	10,536	11,807
Road Town, Brit. Virgin Isls.	7,478	7,257	14,294	6,535	2,633	8,827	12,098	12,710	8,979	4,989	14,463	8,909	2,984	15,047	18,367	7,491	13,328	6,866	16,753	3,475
Roanoke, Virginia	7,178	4,743	14,436	5,792	4,596	8,865	10,076	11,670	8,727	2,798	11,897	8,790	1,088	14,406	16,493	9,733	12,688	5,450	14,361	1,084
Robinson Crusoe Island, Chile	12,680	12,177	8,884	12,252	3,358	13,225	17,919	17,442	13,755	10,645	16,024	13,516	7,394	16,593	15,560	7,506	16,747	12,818	14,255	8,112
Rochester, New York	6,609	4,258	14,939	5,180	5,215	8,323	9,429	10,992	8,142	2,141	11,497	8,224	1,634	13,733	15,884	9,804	12,025	4,775	14,133	1,327
Rockhampton, Australia	15,530	11,835	3,015	15,713	14,410	14,628	9,504	10,335	14,290	14,374	5,420	14,450	14,046	8,494	5,049	14,952	10,073	14,549	2,537	13,926
Rome, Italy	603	7,460	18,035	2,098	9,936	1,319	6,591	5,310	1,379	6,009	10,948	1,306	8,622	7,440	10,823	6,671	5,723	3,455	13,276	8,292
Rosario, Argentina	11,428	12,713	9,939	11,323	3,486	11,701	17,546	15,764	12,293	10,682	17,703	12,023	7,859	15,242	15,480	5,813	15,078	12,224	15,486	8,563
Roseau, Dominica	7,480	7,710	14,277	6,646	2,481	8,736	12,394	12,764	8,941	5,389	14,937	8,847	3,468	14,954	18,387	7,028	13,283	7,097	17,223	3,964
Rostock, East Germany	760	6,137	18,128	1,091	10,044	2,316	5,711	5,205	1,918	4,927	10,009	2,082	7,904	7,704	10,865	7,942	5,935	2,150	12,643	7,464
Rostov-na-Donu, USSR	2,131	7,174	16,171	3,137	12,037	1,793	4,535	3,178	1,101	6,658	8,849	1,415	9,876	5,630	8,823	8,333	3,861	3,663	11,047	9,372
Rotterdam, Netherlands	718	6,228	18,692	835	9,500	2,466	6,256	5,732	2,219	4,761	10,529	2,311	7,556	8,174	11,390	7,581	6,407	2,233	13,201	7,161
Rouyn, Canada	6,358	3,720	15,088	4,876	5,788	8,096	8,862	10,519	7,857	1,579	10,976	7,966	2,004	13,269	15,310	10,128	11,592	4,327	13,686	1,508
Sacramento, California	9,412	3,396	11,718	7,864	6,820	11,132	9,009	11,861	10,695	3,944	8,918	10,898	2,911	14,220	13,990	13,332	13,141	6,745	10,867	2,544
Saginaw, Michigan	6,988	3,980	14,505	5,520	5,336	8,719	9,371	11,153	8,499	2,147	11,154	8,600	1,352	13,905	15,745	10,293	12,241	4,977	13,701	877
Saint Denis, Reunion	8,740	14,690	9,979	10,285	13,806	6,995	9,383	6,325	7,378	14,204	10,570	7,198	16,397	4,315	5,764	6,450	5,050	11,307	9,423	16,355
Saint George's, Grenada	7,764	8,029	13,983	6,973	2,163	8,968	12,755	13,060	9,202	5,737	15,229	9,095	3,670	15,164	18,614	6,903	13,529	7,452	17,342	4,206
Saint John, Canada	5,718	4,530	15,875	4,344	5,478	7,411	9,158	10,345	7,267	2,053	11,768	7,331	2,528	13,041	15,617	9,098	11,293	4,149	14,602	2,279
Saint John's, Antigua	7,374	7,507	14,391	6,502	2,626	8,666	12,205	12,643	8,850	5,184	14,739	8,765	3,309	14,889	18,292	7,162	13,198	6,920	17,082	3,787
Saint John's, Canada	4,695	4,856	16,929	3,387	6,031	6,368	8,729	9,517	6,253	2,280	11,870	6,301	3,577	12,146	15,022	8,445	10,381	3,463	14,851	3,325
Saint Louis, Missouri	7,737	4,222	13,774	6,270	5,006	9,466	9,838	11,817	9,249	2,774	11,179	9,349	701	14,564	16,028	10,634	12,938	5,687	13,501	172
Saint Paul, Minnesota	7,416	3,484	13,967	5,900	5,745	9,164	9,104	11,186	8,877	2,174	10,523	9,009	1,426	13,917	15,298	11,043	12,348	5,156	12,981	712

Distances in Kilometers	Innsbruck, Austria	Inuvik, Canada	Invercargill, New Zealand	Inverness, United Kingdom	Iquitos, Peru	Iraklion, Greece	Irkutsk, USSR	Islamabad, Pakistan	Istanbul, Turkey	Ivujivik, Canada	Iwo Jima Island, Japan	Izmir, Turkey	Jackson, Mississippi	Jaffna, Sri Lanka	Jakarta, Indonesia	Jamestown, St. Helena	Jamnagar, India	Jan Mayen Island	Jayapura, Indonesia	Jefferson City, Missouri
Saint Peter Port, UK	1,059	6,331	19,256	899	8,951	2,741	6,799	6,272	2,622	4,625	11,041	2,656	7,203	8,660	11,922	7,249	6,900	2,424	13,755	6,858
Saipan (Susupe)	11,737	8,062	7,185	11,495	15,583	11,631	5,498	7,494	11,023	10,609	1,161	11,302	12,084	7,148	4,898	16,972	7,937	10,256	2,032	11,557
Salalah, Oman	5,142	10,518	13,215	6,552	14,107	3,515	5,865	2,656	3,590	10,260	8,969	3,538	13,363	2,918	6,338	7,508	1,778	7,267	9,738	12,925
Salem, Oregon	8,863	2,679	12,149	7,324	7,308	10,556	8,322	11,144	10,084	3,453	8,525	10,302	3,157	13,533	13,572	13,390	12,424	6,131	10,703	2,645
Salt Lake City, Utah	8,765	3,338	12,470	7,218	6,303	10,507	9,123	11,745	10,127	3,296	9,547	10,303	2,149	14,291	14,592	12,504	13,003	6,220	11,659	1,705
Salta, Argentina	11,064	11,700	10,452	10,740	2,472	11,608	16,834	15,911	12,125	9,728	17,331	11,890	6,844	16,006	16,480	6,264	15,502	11,482	15,885	7,548
Salto, Uruguay	11,130	12,652	10,218	11,053	3,451	11,393	17,279	15,473	11,985	10,548	17,998	11,715	7,823	15,071	15,548	5,543	14,821	11,989	15,769	8,518
Salvador, Brazil	8,310	11,551	12,904	8,418	3,954	8,567	14,542	12,803	9,141	9,029	18,698	8,878	7,439	13,329	15,648	3,548	12,449	9,582	18,286	7,977
Salzburg, Austria	137	6,831	18,147	1,580	10,040	1,709	6,111	5,174	1,472	5,506	10,458	1,547	8,312	7,503	10,796	7,302	5,747	2,833	12,937	7,925
Samsun, Turkey	2,088	7,819	16,180	3,379	11,919	1,180	5,134	3,337	619	7,113	9,387	847	10,193	5,526	8,857	7,673	3,776	4,152	11,397	9,740
San Antonio, Texas	9,005	4,898	12,540	7,544	4,555	10,727	10,687	12,963	10,523	3,958	11,255	10,619	855	15,676	16,321	11,132	14,135	6,924	13,117	1,170
San Cristobal, Venezuela	8,900	8,062	12,868	7,975	1,280	10,181	13,345	14,150	10,378	6,081	14,900	10,290	3,291	16,396	19,807	7,784	14,725	8,243	16,342	3,956
San Diego, California	9,768	4,104	11,508	8,223	6,141	11,512	9,765	12,575	11,135	4,304	9,553	11,311	2,527	14,977	14,613	12,943	13,850	7,222	11,303	2,346
San Francisco, California	9,531	3,473	11,597	7,983	6,843	11,249	9,053	11,930	10,809	4,064	8,880	11,013	2,987	14,262	13,951	13,418	13,211	6,858	10,790	2,640
San Jose, Costa Rica	9,616	7,412	12,151	8,475	1,934	11,076	13,066	14,614	11,160	5,845	13,776	11,124	2,555	17,224	18,764	9,094	15,456	8,427	15,019	3,274
San Juan, Argentina	11,818	12,290	9,663	11,541	3,113	12,255	17,630	16,444	12,808	10,446	17,013	12,557	7,425	15,972	15,803	6,546	15,823	12,286	15,142	8,140
San Juan, Puerto Rico	7,590	7,196	14,184	6,621	2,581	8,957	12,115	12,804	9,098	4,964	14,378	9,034	2,856	15,173	18,449	7,634	13,446	6,913	16,614	3,364
San Luis Potosi, Mexico	9,785	5,601	11,809	8,349	4,163	11,488	11,403	13,793	11,319	4,802	11,522	11,400	1,550	16,484	16,557	11,199	14,975	7,766	13,034	2,006
San Marino, San Marino	382	7,241	18,112	1,903	9,956	1,443	6,436	5,272	1,392	5,825	10,792	1,373	8,501	7,474	10,830	6,881	5,741	3,238	13,177	8,153
San Miguel de Tucuman, Argen.	11,217	11,918	10,276	10,928	2,691	11,711	17,048	15,978	12,244	9,954	17,364	12,002	7,058	15,910	16,257	6,234	15,501	11,693	15,740	7,764
San Salvador, El Salvador	9,684	6,846	12,054	8,434	2,615	11,239	12,582	14,439	11,245	5,480	13,080	11,246	2,062	17,164	18,090	9,751	15,417	8,218	14,412	2,772
Sanaa, Yemen	4,654	10,720	13,834	6,164	13,073	2,918	6,651	3,549	3,203	10,039	10,008	3,054	12,849	3,937	7,300	6,486	2,832	7,117	10,790	12,513
Santa Cruz, Bolivia	10,331	11,061	11,225	9,947	1,902	10,987	16,028	15,347	11,464	8,985	17,378	11,248	6,248	15,958	17,138	6,102	15,135	10,674	16,572	6,936
Santa Cruz, Tenerife	3,175	8,129	17,973	3,358	7,058	3,958	9,369	8,269	4,314	5,792	13,647	4,142	6,977	10,110	13,560	5,040	8,514	4,754	16,247	6,947
Santa Fe, New Mexico	8,907	4,026	12,477	7,383	5,539	10,657	9,828	12,323	10,350	3,549	10,284	10,493	1,501	14,947	15,343	11,941	13,555	6,542	12,277	1,264
Santa Rosa, Argentina	11,951	12,959	9,418	11,838	3,752	12,194	18,052	16,167	12,797	11,044	17,253	12,522	8,092	15,348	15,179	6,179	15,381	12,708	14,963	8,805
Santa Rosalia, Mexico	10,011	4,779	11,401	8,488	5,421	11,760	10,498	13,227	11,454	4,640	10,249	11,598	2,201	15,706	15,280	12,424	14,491	7,624	11,826	2,250
Santarem, Brazil	8,435	9,805	13,155	8,013	2,067	9,248	14,150	13,606	9,657	7,454	17,001	9,470	5,364	14,963	17,767	5,569	13,676	8,797	18,235	5,949
Santiago del Estero, Argentina	11,233	12,052	10,238	10,978	2,824	11,688	17,127	15,928	12,233	10,070	17,457	11,985	7,194	15,783	16,129	6,138	15,414	11,769	15,726	7,899
Santiago, Chile	12,111	12,416	9,372	11,827	3,297	12,534	17,876	16,687	13,094	10,644	16,783	12,840	7,560	16,028	15,612	6,746	16,004	12,550	14,848	8,278
Santo Domingo, Dominican Rep.	7,875	7,046	13,899	6,843	2,486	9,286	12,149	13,036	9,400	4,919	14,153	9,348	2,545	15,482	18,600	7,996	13,736	7,039	16,256	3,100
Sao Paulo de Olivenca, Brazil	9,552	9,359	12,159	8,847	496	10,591	14,556	14,848	10,915	7,344	16,025	10,769	4,557	16,520	18,840	7,034	15,122	9,317	16,688	5,237
Sao Paulo, Brazil	9,756	12,296	11,500	9,806	3,603	9,975	15,980	14,113	10,568	9,922	19,212	10,297	7,473	14,168	15,643	4,354	13,595	10,885	17,016	8,356
Sao Tome, Sao Tome & Principe	5,220	11,813	14,597	6,410	8,909	4,320	10,497	7,827	5,033	9,697	14,405	4,706	10,646	8,176	11,137	2,260	7,272	7,927	14,910	10,764
Sapporo, Japan	8,860	5,445	10,262	8,414	14,483	9,190	2,925	5,884	8,498	7,801	2,026	8,815	10,154	6,964	6,470	15,683	6,847	7,136	5,049	9,483
Sarajevo, Yugoslavia	667	7,349	17,652	2,186	10,433	1,105	6,090	4,799	922	6,108	10,446	948	8,904	7,002	10,352	7,059	5,265	3,377	12,745	8,527
Saratov, USSR	2,533	6,704	15,867	3,242	12,323	2,455	3,902	2,951	1,754	6,445	8,240	2,075	9,781	5,578	8,599	8,997	3,835	3,464	10,551	9,226
Saskatoon, Canada	7,520	2,311	13,581	5,972	6,948	9,247	8,079	10,498	8,834	2,051	9,248	9,024	2,573	13,130	14,067	12,134	11,736	4,906	11,762	1,877
Schefferville, Canada	5,260	3,631	16,107	3,765	6,519	7,005	8,108	9,482	6,747	1,061	10,787	6,862	3,101	12,221	14,581	9,714	10,516	3,263	13,700	2,621
Seattle, Washington	8,580	2,398	12,400	7,044	7,429	10,266	8,086	10,869	9,789	3,195	8,466	10,010	3,195	13,291	13,483	13,293	12,147	5,836	10,740	2,632
Sendai, Japan	9,291	5,933	9,768	8,908	14,863	9,521	3,217	5,991	8,843	8,321	1,494	9,153	10,580	6,817	6,050	15,925	6,865	7,653	4,515	9,923
Seoul, South Korea	8,646	6,544	10,176	8,532	15,737	8,617	2,404	4,829	7,975	8,701	1,964	8,268	11,366	5,622	5,276	14,816	5,652	7,469	4,660	10,672
Sept-Iles, Canada	5,464	4,058	16,027	4,021	6,016	7,190	8,615	9,897	6,988	1,529	11,263	7,078	2,793	12,619	15,082	9,413	10,891	3,679	14,141	2,408
Sevastopol, USSR	1,736	7,434	16,531	2,958	11,631	1,253	5,095	3,593	546	6,680	9,408	869	9,768	5,895	9,183	7,794	4,133	3,724	11,564	9,310
Seville, Spain	1,798	7,510	18,902	2,237	8,287	2,790	8,012	6,969	3,026	5,494	12,325	2,901	7,456	9,014	12,437	5,901	7,335	3,746	14,871	7,264
Shanghai, China	8,867	7,408	9,799	8,955	16,617	8,593	2,729	4,502	8,003	9,496	2,083	8,272	12,243	4,886	4,408	14,425	5,146	8,030	4,251	11,547
Sheffield, United Kingdom	1,139	5,945	18,949	488	9,147	2,888	6,432	6,107	2,656	4,362	10,636	2,745	7,119	8,588	11,767	7,688	6,820	2,000	13,398	6,727
Shenyang, China	8,091	6,250	10,734	7,976	15,478	8,102	1,852	4,457	7,450	8,296	2,507	7,748	11,110	5,535	5,575	14,400	5,375	6,936	5,210	10,403
Shiraz, Iran	4,028	9,131	14,253	5,315	13,652	2,644	4,897	2,006	2,478	8,897	8,586	2,530	12,111	3,610	7,017	8,028	1,922	5,900	9,976	11,619
Sibiu, Romania	991	7,212	17,275	2,328	10,884	1,165	5,602	4,336	659	6,180	9,954	857	9,133	6,626	9,931	7,469	4,871	3,319	12,245	8,712
Singapore	10,091	11,144	8,191	10,958	19,600	8,907	5,651	4,806	8,652	12,939	4,795	8,766	16,008	2,798	887	12,150	4,342	10,680	4,123	15,299
Sioux Falls, South Dakota	7,731	3,494	13,638	6,210	5,744	9,480	9,198	11,390	9,182	2,430	10,406	9,319	1,373	14,103	15,272	11,295	12,573	5,425	12,779	672
Skelleftea, Sweden	2,032	5,100	17,170	1,567	10,582	3,286	4,664	4,902	2,693	4,413	8,848	2,960	7,724	7,604	10,425	9,230	5,882	1,417	11,627	7,173
Skopje, Yugoslavia	990	7,594	17,348	2,501	10,682	805	6,037	4,570	634	6,416	10,380	625	9,226	6,711	10,081	6,996	4,984	3,647	12,582	8,850
Socotra Island (Tamrida)	5,513	10,999	12,882	6,957	14,154	3,839	6,262	3,034	3,979	10,709	9,168	3,900	13,750	2,856	6,199	7,297	2,018	7,721	9,720	13,340
Sofia, Bulgaria	1,068	7,544	17,234	2,537	10,831	831	5,873	4,413	504	6,434	10,214	574	9,298	6,585	9,942	7,138	4,850	3,622	12,414	8,906
Songkhla, Thailand	9,366	10,633	8,923	10,211	19,250	8,236	6,009	4,071	7,949	12,286	4,748	8,076	15,488	2,285	1,631	11,976	3,682	9,947	4,583	14,769
Sorong, Indonesia	12,287	10,302	6,201	12,610	17,263	11,530	6,407	7,165	11,106	12,761	3,041	11,301	14,460	5,798	2,778	14,951	7,112	11,717	1,067	13,940
South Georgia Island	12,129	15,691	8,602	12,730	6,498	11,557	17,442	14,223	12,269	13,425	16,729	11,942	10,872	12,598	12,503	5,026	13,090	14,068	13,706	11,568
South Pole	15,241	17,586	4,860	16,376	9,586	13,916	15,795	13,733	14,546	16,924	12,743	14,258	13,577	11,072	9,320	8,242	12,488	17,885	9,721	14,273
South Sandwich Islands	12,154	16,393	8,379	12,928	7,235	11,385	16,882	13,655	12,100	14,040	16,218	11,772	11,606	11,889	11,779	4,954	12,476	14,351	13,224	12,297
Split, Yugoslavia	573	7,353	17,794	2,118	10,272	1,176	6,232	4,962	1,070	6,046	10,589	1,064	8,793	7,151	10,509	6,960	5,418	3,364	12,907	8,429
Spokane, Washington	8,378	2,478	12,670	6,834	7,138	10,086	8,243	10,931	9,637	2,940	8,803	9,844	2,859	13,426	13,795	12,924	12,201	5,685	11,108	2,275
Spoleto, Italy	515	7,374	18,050	2,027	9,965	1,350	6,511	5,273	1,359	5,945	10,869	1,309	8,590	7,433	10,805	6,765	5,709	3,370	13,216	8,251
Springbok, South Africa	8,545	15,323	11,074	9,876	9,919	7,235	12,328	9,112	7,909	13,176	14,456	7,598	13,285	7,945	9,574	2,851	8,030	11,364	12,984	13,649
Springfield, Illinois	7,611	4,122	13,887	6,139	5,108	9,343	9,715	11,678	9,120	2,635	11,122	9,223	834	14,426	15,936	10,625	12,799	5,548	13,487	257
Springfield, Massachusetts	6,352	4,564	15,250	4,970	5,080	8,043	9,544	10,916	7,900	2,286	11,824	7,964	1,898	13,632	16,023	9,382	11,895	4,699	14,519	1,705
Srinagar, India	5,401	8,403	12,904	6,257	15,308	4,505	3,099	158	4,076	9,035	6,426	4,264	12,492	2,755	5,584	10,149	1,369	6,242	7,977	11,850
Stanley, Falkland Islands	12,795	14,690	8,274	13,050	5,503	12,555	18,795	15,639	13,244	12,775	16,605	12,929	9,828	13,990	13,429	6,057	14,528	14,152	13,745	10,543
Stara Zagora, Bulgaria	1,245	7,601	17,046	2,683	11,023	788	5,747	4,225	318	6,560	10,077	462	9,464	6,395	9,749	7,216	4,658	3,713	12,241	9,062
Stockholm, Sweden	1,413	5,657	17,581	1,313	10,439	2,718	5,080	4,896	2,175	4,739	9,346	2,415	7,919	7,517	10,521	8,617	5,761	1,787	12,038	7,416
Stornoway, United Kingdom	1,700	5,331	18,643	152	9,037	3,441	6,255	6,302	3,132	3,777	10,333	3,261	6,671	8,887	11,931	8,218	7,121	1,430	13,197	6,236
Strasbourg, France	310	6,649	18,542	1,271	9,661	2,050	6,342	5,553	1,869	5,193	10,664	1,924	7,928	7,904	11,187	7,269	6,147	2,647	13,230	7,554
Stuttgart, West Germany	235	6,657	18,435	1,316	9,769	1,984	6,251	5,446	1,777	5,244	10,579	1,843	8,011	7,802	11,081	7,316	6,044	2,652	13,130	7,630
Subic, Philippines	10,168	9,120	8,321	10,516	18,101	9,521	4,381	5,159	9,045	11,291	2,463	9,261	13,867	4,409	2,760	14,249	5,335	9,738	2,967	13,199
Suchow, China	8,345	7,238	10,302	8,465	16,462	8,074	2,248	4,035	7,480	9,205	2,558	7,751	12,102	4,664	4,607	14,004	4,756	7,587	4,760	11,393
Sucre, Bolivia	10,581	11,110	10,987	10,173	1,898	11,249	16,209	15,609	11,724	9,096	17,214	11,509	6,270	16,156	17,088	6,307	15,384	10,866	16,311	6,967
Sudbury, Canada	6,593	3,802	14,870	5,116	5,620	8,329	9,048	10,754	8,097	1,781	11,039	8,203	1,761	13,505	15,473	10,194	11,833	4,568	13,692	1,269
Suez, Egypt	2,644	9,044	15,809	4,164	11,746	915	6,227	3,843	1,268	8,068	10,305	1,061	10,854	5,406	8,855	6,530	3,823	5,219	11,903	10,503
Sundsvall, Sweden	1,723	5,317	17,461	1,315	10,403	3,058	4,945	5,004	2,501	4,468	9,156	2,749	7,708	7,671	10,584	8,914	5,929	1,487	11,912	7,183
Surabaya, Indonesia	11,455	11,702	6,832	12,275	18,624	10,260	6,643	6,163	10,018	13,823	4,708	10,127	16,365	4,085	669	12,785	5,696	11,873	3,143	15,736
Suva, Fiji	16,565	10,331	3,269	15,633	11,815	16,770	10,546	12,497	16,156	12,480	6,222	16,441	11,196	11,230	7,864	16,210	12,603	14,109	4,462	11,198
Sverdlovsk, USSR	3,454	6,067	15,124	3,772	12,865	3,569	2,824	2,745	2,868	6,303	7,181	3,189	9,751	5,497	8,142	10,111	3,895	3,502	9,641	9,125
Svobodnyy, USSR	7,522	5,140	11,502	7,180	14,364	7,834	1,636	4,789	7,140	7,180	3,162	7,458	10,006	6,357	6,697	14,351	5,885	6,007	6,095	9,296
Sydney, Australia	16,356	12,882	2,009	16,802	13,768	15,139	10,576	11,057	14,944	15,359	6,576	15,041	14,381	8,915	5,502	13,977	10,605	15,709	3,638	14,416
Sydney, Canada	5,274	4,688	16,338	3,932	5,678	6,956	8,999	10,002	6,829	2,130	11,856	6,884	2,987	12,668	15,402	8,778	10,910	3,856	14,766	2,745
Syktyvkar, USSR	2,948	5,575	15,782	3,050	12,105	3,439	3,312	3,494	2,726	5,583	7,640	3,054	9,014	6,241	8,911	9,924	4,598	2,735	10,247	8,404
Szeged, Hungary	678	7,109	17,587	2,073	10,574	1,284	5,810	4,643	918	5,964	10,167	1,044	8,857	6,936	10,243	7,363	5,182	3,164	12,517	8,452
Szombathely, Hungary	395	6,951	17,872	1,808	10,305	1,500	5,949	4,909	1,204	5,718	10,304	1,302	8,573	7,226	10,523	7,343	5,470	2,974	12,724	8,176
Tabriz, Iran	3,007	8,203	15,258	4,224	12,833	1,911	4,685	2,465	1,522	7,808	8,768	1,674	11,009	4,609	7,932	8,075	2,853	4,812	10,571	10,517
Tacheng, China	5,240	6,882	13,247	5,665	14,722	4,907	1,658	1,668	4,299	7,784	5,662	4,574	11,223	4,120	6,317	11,184	2,933	5,250	7,837	10,541
Tahiti (Papeete)	16,280	9,610	5,013	14,732	8,440	17,965	12,625	15,417	17,398	10,809	8,834	17,669	8,389	14,616	11,246	14,597	15,862	13,518	7,783	8,620
Taipei, Taiwan	9,389	8,024	9,213	9,564	17,179	8,982	3,351	4,746	8,429	10,159	2,002	8,681	12,827	4,703	3,803	14,468	5,220	8,683	3,689	12,141
Taiyuan, China	7,768	7,029	10,866	7,912	16,183	7,514	1,724	3,564	6,912	8,851	3,082	7,186	11,889	4,512	4,911	13,555	4,388	7,081	5,331	11,172
Tallahassee, Florida	7,988	5,269	13,667	6,631	3,964	9,650	10,804	12,522	9,545	3,582	12,205	9,594	599	15,262	17,082	9,843	13,545	6,304	14,375	1,156
Tallinn, USSR	1,612	5,724	17,219	1,693	10,819	2,678	4,743	4,528	2,068	4,985	9,038	2,342	8,228	7,170	10,145	8,796	5,421	1,995	11,689	7,705
Tamanrasset, Algeria	2,767	9,370	16,968	3,931	9,029	2,355	8,611	6,635	2,983	7,451	12,915	2,691	9,197	8,021	11,436	4,454	6,578	5,442	14,704	9,096
Tampa, Florida	8,056	5,592	13,633	6,741	3,646	9,686	11,094	12,716	9,618	3,843	12,528	9,650	888	15,438	17,407	9,582	13,699	6,495	14,652	1,484
Tampere, Finland	1,769	5,485	17,199	1,634	10,744	2,911	4,689	4,652	2,306	4,774	8,950	2,578	8,046	7,321	10,237	8,971	5,582	1,778	11,651	7,511
Tanami, Australia	13,743	12,322	4,569	14,419	16,386	12,564	8,374	8,441	12,327	14,842	5,110	12,438	15,839	6,358	2,911	13,735	8,004	13,732	2,270	15,513

Distances in Kilometers	Innsbruck, Austria	Inuvik, Canada	Invercargill, New Zealand	Inverness, United Kingdom	Iquitos, Peru	Iraklion, Greece	Irkutsk, USSR	Islamabad, Pakistan	Istanbul, Turkey	Ivujivik, Canada	Iwo Jima Island, Japan	Izmir, Turkey	Jackson, Mississippi	Jaffna, Sri Lanka	Jakarta, Indonesia	Jamestown, St. Helena	Jamnagar, India	Jan Mayen Island	Jayapura, Indonesia	Jefferson City, Missouri
Tangier, Morocco	1,911	7,682	18,733	2,411	8,251	2,793	8,142	7,023	3,070	5,647	12,466	2,928	7,544	9,014	12,448	5,726	7,353	3,922	14,972	7,369
Tarawa (Betio)	14,328	8,441	5,309	13,478	12,674	14,753	8,448	10,834	14,075	10,848	4,273	14,387	10,581	10,315	7,396	18,385	11,281	11,973	3,613	10,346
Tashkent, USSR	4,560	7,691	13,778	5,334	14,426	3,876	2,901	913	3,354	8,138	6,778	3,585	11,586	3,663	6,499	9,965	2,093	5,309	8,657	10,959
Tbilisi, USSR	2,702	7,800	15,566	3,843	12,591	1,846	4,545	2,644	1,321	7,388	8,734	1,542	10,607	4,948	8,216	8,220	3,181	4,391	10,693	10,106
Tegucigalpa, Honduras	9,507	6,868	12,237	8,278	2,506	11,047	12,569	14,324	11,066	5,413	13,220	11,061	2,038	17,028	18,261	9,559	15,270	8,104	14,617	2,755
Tehran, Iran	3,537	8,463	14,728	4,729	13,350	2,379	4,507	1,999	2,045	8,233	8,442	2,175	11,488	4,081	7,404	8,295	2,323	5,237	10,110	10,976
Tel Aviv, Israel	2,603	8,829	15,780	4,086	11,933	963	5,913	3,577	1,120	7,957	10,006	988	10,839	5,267	8,706	6,845	3,635	5,063	11,665	10,458
Telegraph Creek, Canada	7,850	1,172	12,831	6,377	8,545	9,438	6,799	9,603	8,887	2,913	7,563	9,141	4,192	12,002	12,432	13,555	10,884	5,007	10,134	3,528
Teresina, Brazil	7,854	10,564	13,531	7,754	3,381	8,370	13,972	12,723	8,872	8,056	17,781	8,642	6,496	13,710	16,435	4,226	12,584	8,803	19,082	7,010
Ternate, Indonesia	11,871	10,287	6,582	12,262	17,718	11,074	6,096	6,714	10,662	12,680	3,048	10,850	14,632	5,339	2,415	14,624	6,645	11,440	1,525	14,071
The Valley, Anguilla	7,392	7,361	14,378	6,483	2,659	8,715	12,120	12,643	8,882	5,059	14,585	8,805	3,143	14,939	18,303	7,325	13,232	6,858	16,916	3,622
Thessaloniki, Greece	1,181	7,764	17,176	2,695	10,806	619	6,047	4,466	511	6,609	10,376	438	9,416	6,555	9,939	6,927	4,838	3,828	12,513	9,042
Thimphu, Bhutan	6,966	8,794	11,368	7,697	16,822	6,095	3,004	1,725	5,674	9,975	5,133	5,861	13,383	2,225	4,157	11,342	2,059	7,445	6,392	12,684
Thunder Bay, Canada	6,943	3,293	14,411	5,424	5,987	8,692	8,774	10,746	8,398	1,712	10,466	8,533	1,790	13,488	15,083	10,856	11,893	4,682	13,055	1,116
Tientsin, China	7,952	6,741	10,755	7,991	15,949	7,801	1,765	3,956	7,178	8,668	2,767	7,462	11,608	4,929	5,129	13,942	4,811	7,070	5,204	10,895
Tijuana, Mexico	9,778	4,126	11,502	8,233	6,119	11,523	9,788	12,596	11,148	4,315	9,573	11,323	2,517	15,001	14,633	12,929	13,872	7,236	11,318	2,342
Tiksi, USSR	5,939	3,340	13,456	5,227	12,315	6,776	2,468	5,298	6,066	4,995	5,265	6,392	8,087	7,628	8,779	13,141	6,573	3,887	8,273	7,369
Timbuktu, Mali	3,633	9,779	16,624	4,519	8,044	3,467	9,681	7,739	4,076	7,590	14,010	3,793	8,777	8,975	12,322	3,629	7,620	6,040	15,763	8,796
Tindouf, Algeria	2,759	8,467	17,907	3,321	7,788	3,256	9,000	7,614	3,685	6,278	13,346	3,479	7,731	9,341	12,788	4,835	7,779	4,816	15,695	7,663
Tirane, Albania	941	7,644	17,446	2,478	10,544	811	6,189	4,716	767	6,404	10,534	704	9,162	6,827	10,208	6,865	5,107	3,676	12,736	8,799
Tokyo, Japan	9,479	6,230	9,533	9,145	15,119	9,638	3,336	5,984	8,970	8,621	1,220	9,276	10,859	6,668	5,776	15,961	6,805	7,914	4,234	10,206
Toledo, Spain	1,488	7,302	19,058	1,957	8,530	2,611	7,689	6,707	2,785	5,372	12,001	2,686	7,501	8,821	12,224	6,180	7,121	3,478	14,561	7,271
Topeka, Kansas	8,034	3,986	13,417	6,536	5,271	9,775	9,704	11,868	9,518	2,862	10,793	9,637	898	14,593	15,726	11,107	13,036	5,839	13,044	309
Toronto, Canada	6,687	4,138	14,839	5,243	5,289	8,409	9,369	10,997	8,212	2,087	11,366	8,302	1,576	13,744	15,806	9,959	12,049	4,789	13,985	1,212
Toulouse, France	879	7,044	18,944	1,593	9,074	2,226	7,080	6,146	2,278	5,318	11,402	2,229	7,739	8,356	11,719	6,632	6,628	3,105	13,948	7,444
Tours, France	810	6,625	19,075	1,170	9,118	2,429	6,808	6,096	2,354	4,955	11,097	2,365	7,511	8,421	11,725	7,041	6,670	2,681	13,732	7,177
Townsville, Australia	14,933	11,554	3,599	15,145	14,959	14,071	8,925	9,755	13,711	14,125	4,907	13,880	14,200	7,992	4,565	15,097	9,532	14,037	1,965	13,999
Trenton, New Jersey	6,623	4,658	14,990	5,246	4,874	8,309	9,756	11,185	8,173	2,476	11,899	8,235	1,638	13,905	16,229	9,454	12,171	4,965	14,524	1,508
Tripoli, Lebanon	2,489	8,575	15,846	3,932	12,000	984	5,659	3,426	949	7,768	9,789	896	10,719	5,258	8,678	7,101	3,583	4,847	11,534	10,315
Tripoli, Libya	1,602	8,448	17,430	3,034	9,907	1,134	7,268	5,505	1,666	6,877	11,593	1,403	9,221	7,273	10,721	5,766	5,663	4,445	13,614	8,972
Tristan da Cunha (Edinburgh)	9,633	15,053	10,762	10,501	7,203	8,900	14,897	11,815	9,613	12,474	17,174	9,286	11,149	10,857	12,104	2,428	10,844	11,986	14,816	11,706
Trondheim, Norway	1,799	5,111	17,669	1,040	10,063	3,283	5,187	5,368	2,773	4,131	9,331	2,998	7,345	8,039	10,934	8,908	6,297	1,182	12,143	6,826
Trujillo, Peru	10,700	9,484	11,045	9,868	801	11,816	15,099	15,998	12,110	7,820	15,366	11,979	4,627	17,725	18,302	7,996	16,363	10,145	15,470	5,345
Truk Island (Moen)	12,810	8,603	6,183	12,492	15,025	12,707	6,578	8,514	12,106	11,182	2,224	12,382	12,121	7,902	5,226	17,417	8,864	11,186	1,659	11,688
Truro, Canada	5,526	4,635	16,083	4,171	5,532	7,211	9,121	10,214	7,079	2,115	11,848	7,136	2,731	12,894	15,557	8,922	11,139	4,041	14,718	2,496
Tsingtao, China	8,388	6,942	10,321	8,421	16,170	8,212	2,197	4,276	7,597	8,968	2,367	7,878	11,800	5,009	4,884	14,264	5,052	7,474	4,770	11,094
Tsitsihar, China	7,656	5,680	11,252	7,443	14,901	7,811	1,508	4,473	7,135	7,681	2,940	7,445	10,546	5,870	6,166	14,251	5,505	6,353	5,765	9,835
Tubuai Island (Mataura)	16,858	10,252	4,547	15,310	8,443	18,582	13,120	15,733	18,042	11,381	9,171	18,306	8,811	14,567	11,135	14,148	15,988	14,141	7,846	9,092
Tucson, Arizona	9,492	4,276	11,876	7,961	5,633	11,242	10,037	12,695	10,917	4,093	10,090	11,069	1,955	15,227	15,160	12,359	13,952	7,070	11,887	1,843
Tulsa, Oklahoma	8,284	4,275	13,205	6,800	5,010	10,019	10,013	12,188	9,783	3,173	10,982	9,893	679	14,914	15,964	11,058	13,351	6,141	13,135	426
Tunis, Tunisia	1,167	7,966	17,919	2,532	9,678	1,355	7,135	5,637	1,691	6,365	11,489	1,507	8,756	7,579	11,010	6,071	5,916	3,968	13,699	8,486
Tura, USSR	5,367	4,688	13,621	5,075	13,269	5,825	1,359	3,871	5,113	5,950	5,292	5,440	9,259	6,268	7,833	12,360	5,147	4,059	8,119	8,550
Turin, Italy	379	7,026	18,513	1,607	9,593	1,831	6,621	5,625	1,787	5,496	10,963	1,775	8,108	7,868	11,211	6,887	6,129	3,029	13,447	7,770
Uberlandia, Brazil	9,445	11,759	11,890	9,398	3,191	9,793	15,613	14,039	10,352	9,386	18,838	10,097	7,216	14,383	16,126	4,526	13,644	10,422	17,438	7,840
Ufa, USSR	3,176	6,329	15,330	3,633	12,757	3,200	3,159	2,696	2,503	6,409	7,507	2,821	9,833	5,432	8,222	9,739	3,772	3,527	9,900	9,228
Ujungpandang, Indonesia	11,782	11,219	6,551	12,437	18,311	10,727	6,517	6,488	10,419	13,491	4,073	10,559	15,715	4,666	1,401	13,556	6,175	11,852	2,383	15,129
Ulaanbaatar, Mongolia	6,679	6,176	12,033	6,724	15,112	6,631	517	3,217	5,980	7,766	3,963	6,277	10,959	4,934	5,991	12,990	4,315	5,875	6,483	10,241
Ulan-Ude, USSR	6,453	5,756	12,333	6,401	14,676	6,535	230	3,415	5,862	7,329	4,141	6,170	10,524	5,306	6,427	12,987	4,575	5,491	6,784	9,806
Uliastay, Mongolia	6,082	6,467	12,530	6,281	15,039	5,918	736	2,518	5,283	7,783	4,652	5,572	11,111	4,508	6,053	12,238	3,679	5,599	7,012	10,401
Uranium City, Canada	6,974	1,554	13,943	5,440	7,675	8,662	7,259	9,667	8,198	1,674	8,717	8,411	3,324	12,291	13,369	12,246	10,912	4,244	11,402	2,609
Urumqi, China	5,720	7,103	12,758	6,152	15,189	5,320	1,558	1,677	4,733	8,160	5,272	4,998	11,575	3,853	5,862	11,481	2,862	5,702	7,363	10,882
Ushuaia, Argentina	13,545	14,667	7,594	13,715	5,676	13,332	19,450	16,222	14,021	13,024	15,884	13,705	9,876	14,276	13,232	6,825	15,038	14,716	13,117	10,594
Vaduz, Liechtenstein	143	6,835	18,406	1,475	9,769	1,848	6,355	5,445	1,695	5,398	10,693	1,733	8,119	7,753	11,061	7,152	6,002	2,831	13,202	7,752
Valencia, Spain	1,286	7,439	18,816	2,021	8,821	2,296	7,525	6,428	2,490	5,594	11,861	2,379	7,804	8,510	11,919	6,158	6,816	3,545	14,344	7,561
Valladolid, Spain	1,423	7,096	19,248	1,760	8,531	2,682	7,571	6,693	2,803	5,179	11,865	2,728	7,368	8,866	12,249	6,376	7,151	3,277	14,475	7,120
Valletta, Malta	1,289	8,148	17,548	2,773	10,056	963	6,941	5,290	1,381	6,661	11,278	1,155	9,136	7,182	10,617	6,120	5,529	4,144	13,381	8,851
Valparaiso, Chile	12,143	12,341	9,356	11,834	3,244	12,592	17,844	16,767	13,145	10,593	16,701	12,894	7,489	16,128	15,663	6,837	16,099	12,535	14,816	8,207
Vancouver, Canada	8,450	2,207	12,492	6,919	7,581	10,126	7,896	10,677	9,638	3,102	8,346	9,863	3,316	13,100	13,343	13,319	11,955	5,689	10,671	2,729
Varna, Bulgaria	1,370	7,538	16,903	2,743	11,202	907	5,546	4,036	259	6,582	9,873	537	9,547	6,248	9,583	7,395	4,502	3,695	12,037	9,127
Venice, Italy	215	7,073	18,163	1,756	9,964	1,558	6,326	5,256	1,434	5,682	10,679	1,452	8,404	7,509	10,843	7,038	5,766	3,070	13,107	8,041
Veracruz, Mexico	9,714	6,051	11,947	8,340	3,569	11,372	11,844	14,042	11,269	5,000	12,123	11,320	1,568	16,784	17,156	10,630	15,160	7,897	13,585	2,181
Verona, Italy	204	7,048	18,266	1,697	9,858	1,639	6,403	5,360	1,536	5,619	10,753	1,546	8,313	7,614	10,949	7,004	5,871	3,044	13,199	7,957
Victoria, Canada	8,538	2,292	12,414	7,006	7,545	10,216	7,967	10,761	9,730	3,180	8,361	9,954	3,300	13,174	13,370	13,353	12,040	5,780	10,658	2,726
Victoria, Seychelles	7,184	12,897	11,360	8,696	14,257	5,440	7,802	4,633	5,728	12,551	9,815	5,587	15,312	3,148	5,692	6,794	3,392	9,590	9,470	15,031
Vienna, Austria	387	6,842	17,903	1,718	10,291	1,602	5,894	4,922	1,277	5,621	10,246	1,392	8,498	7,269	10,549	7,434	5,509	2,866	12,695	8,093
Vientiane, Laos	8,652	9,432	9,700	9,306	18,372	7,763	3,809	3,408	7,363	11,095	4,074	7,542	14,279	2,607	2,709	12,445	3,430	8,880	4,754	13,561
Villahermosa, Mexico	9,594	6,277	12,099	8,262	3,232	11,219	12,046	14,099	11,155	5,069	12,475	11,188	1,609	16,851	17,519	10,267	15,166	7,907	13,943	2,283
Vilnius, USSR	1,275	6,249	17,276	1,851	10,899	2,151	4,969	4,361	1,543	5,419	9,311	1,814	8,578	6,914	10,018	8,358	5,148	2,457	11,843	8,087
Visby, Sweden	1,244	5,844	17,636	1,343	10,451	2,531	5,168	4,850	1,999	4,889	9,457	2,232	8,033	7,440	10,493	8,449	5,678	1,957	12,113	7,543
Vitoria, Brazil	9,099	12,224	12,075	9,250	4,009	9,251	15,341	13,375	9,854	9,749	19,484	9,578	7,878	13,544	15,387	3,691	12,880	10,414	17,474	8,467
Vladivostok, USSR	8,415	5,805	10,551	8,134	14,992	8,591	2,286	5,128	7,916	8,006	2,211	8,225	10,621	6,230	6,019	15,005	6,078	6,968	5,134	9,928
Volgograd, USSR	2,450	7,017	15,888	3,319	12,324	2,172	4,146	2,905	1,488	6,672	8,459	1,799	9,965	5,452	8,565	8,706	3,692	3,678	10,682	9,430
Vologda, USSR	2,293	5,843	16,368	2,545	11,666	2,866	3,955	3,743	2,164	5,514	8,294	2,485	8,873	6,441	9,312	9,295	4,725	2,545	10,862	8,305
Vorkuta, USSR	3,707	4,867	15,243	3,484	12,226	4,340	2,744	3,806	3,628	5,271	6,946	3,955	8,729	6,531	8,840	10,797	5,023	2,735	9,701	8,073
Wake Island	12,231	6,799	7,276	11,457	13,313	12,731	6,458	9,156	12,034	9,352	2,679	12,354	10,057	9,318	7,136	19,139	9,856	9,985	3,726	9,623
Wallis Island	16,174	9,662	3,947	15,056	11,316	16,772	10,466	12,727	16,090	11,732	6,249	16,404	10,422	11,747	8,462	16,608	12,992	13,535	4,894	10,411
Walvis Bay, Namibia	7,782	14,517	11,887	9,081	9,624	6,548	11,982	8,826	7,238	12,364	14,647	6,920	12,669	7,993	9,986	2,258	7,840	10,580	13,552	12,976
Warsaw, Poland	885	6,466	17,579	1,709	10,628	1,908	5,357	4,603	1,388	5,461	9,703	1,610	8,513	7,079	10,261	7,982	5,310	2,569	12,209	8,057
Washington, D.C.	6,868	4,698	14,747	5,487	4,739	8,554	9,904	11,403	8,418	2,616	11,909	8,479	1,397	14,130	16,360	9,569	12,402	5,181	14,465	1,315
Watson Lake, Canada	7,568	948	13,105	6,096	8,555	9,160	6,674	9,414	8,612	2,671	7,643	8,864	4,185	11,860	12,444	13,336	10,693	4,726	10,277	3,502
Weimar, East Germany	413	6,457	18,260	1,240	9,952	2,063	5,973	5,271	1,752	5,152	10,294	1,870	8,025	7,690	10,923	7,597	5,925	2,458	12,870	7,615
Wellington, New Zealand	18,539	12,888	767	18,205	11,543	17,303	12,385	13,276	17,172	14,828	8,090	17,252	12,676	11,113	7,726	13,668	12,826	16,691	5,483	12,916
West Berlin, West Germany	601	6,327	18,089	1,251	10,112	2,123	5,753	5,121	1,739	5,114	10,072	1,894	8,064	7,584	10,779	7,804	5,815	2,343	12,659	7,633
Wewak, Papua New Guinea	13,356	10,068	5,316	13,398	15,855	12,809	7,206	8,442	12,326	12,639	3,144	12,549	13,585	7,206	4,095	16,024	8,486	12,267	345	13,186
Whangarei, New Zealand	18,105	12,312	1,288	17,584	11,765	17,244	11,871	13,008	16,961	14,351	7,544	17,107	12,465	11,024	7,589	14,288	12,683	16,073	5,050	12,637
Whitehorse, Canada	7,658	853	12,923	6,217	8,888	9,207	6,415	9,230	8,635	2,943	7,292	8,898	4,522	11,618	12,104	13,619	10,511	4,803	9,937	3,844
Wichita, Kansas	8,242	4,070	13,211	6,744	5,222	9,984	9,819	12,039	9,726	3,051	10,776	9,846	885	14,754	15,752	11,218	13,216	6,035	12,959	463
Willemstad, Curacao	8,303	7,737	13,466	7,376	1,820	9,608	12,842	13,550	9,789	5,628	14,775	9,707	3,116	15,831	19,209	7,623	14,139	7,675	16,598	3,725
Wiluna, Australia	13,519	13,384	4,746	14,504	16,350	12,101	8,873	8,321	11,997	15,808	6,122	12,046	17,022	5,915	2,672	12,520	7,658	14,154	3,446	16,728
Windhoek, Namibia	7,756	14,543	11,838	9,091	9,891	6,466	11,781	8,608	7,147	12,461	14,379	6,834	12,889	7,729	9,727	2,504	7,603	10,576	13,312	13,177
Windsor, Canada	7,013	4,126	14,506	5,559	5,196	8,737	9,503	11,247	8,533	2,262	11,299	8,626	1,278	13,998	15,887	10,180	12,322	5,057	13,833	879
Winnipeg, Canada	7,250	2,856	13,999	5,708	6,373	8,996	8,504	10,697	8,649	1,822	9,933	8,808	2,036	13,402	14,670	11,449	11,893	4,811	12,472	1,318
Winston-Salem, North Carolina	7,285	4,848	14,341	5,908	4,473	8,966	10,205	11,801	8,836	2,929	11,982	8,896	1,008	14,536	16,614	9,711	12,814	5,580	14,408	1,091
Wroclaw, Poland	592	6,537	17,860	1,547	10,352	1,868	5,654	4,870	1,448	5,394	9,995	1,618	8,360	7,303	10,522	7,750	5,535	2,580	12,512	7,928
Wuhan, China	8,458	7,720	10,112	8,692	16,935	8,051	2,542	3,868	7,491	9,641	2,739	7,746	12,586	4,237	4,144	13,750	4,468	7,900	4,616	11,875
Wyndham, Australia	13,268	11,928	5,063	13,900	16,851	12,156	7,847	7,970	11,883	14,409	4,679	12,010	15,736	5,988	2,543	13,877	7,590	13,205	1,989	15,333
Xi'an, China	7,814	7,521	10,737	8,086	16,621	7,410	2,033	3,285	6,845	9,272	3,299	7,102	12,372	4,012	4,481	13,242	3,997	7,358	5,260	11,654
Xining, China	7,161	7,498	11,345	7,517	16,332	6,714	1,751	2,616	6,154	9,029	3,979	6,408	12,275	3,705	4,765	12,600	3,427	6,898	5,919	11,558
Yakutsk, USSR	6,710	4,108	12,504	6,171	13,270	7,302	1,859	5,027	6,589	6,012	4,227	6,916	8,959	7,045	7,810	13,819	6,249	4,905	7,219	8,242
Yanji, China	8,318	5,920	10,608	8,082	15,126	8,450	2,147	4,940	7,781	8,079	2,281	8,087	10,752	6,040	5,897	14,837	5,882	6,949	5,154	10,055

Distances in Kilometers	Innsbruck, Austria	Inuvik, Canada	Invercargill, New Zealand	Inverness, United Kingdom	Iquitos, Peru	Iraklion, Greece	Irkutsk, USSR	Islamabad, Pakistan	Istanbul, Turkey	Ivujivik, Canada	Iwo Jima Island, Japan	Izmir, Turkey	Jackson, Mississippi	Jaffna, Sri Lanka	Jakarta, Indonesia	Jamestown, St. Helena	Jamnagar, India	Jan Mayen Island	Jayapura, Indonesia	Jefferson City, Missouri
Yaounde, Cameroon	4,809	11,556	14,790	6,104	9,469	3,755	9,862	7,165	4,469	9,599	13,745	4,142	10,883	7,586	10,646	2,899	6,625	7,596	14,387	10,930
Yap Island (Colonia)	11,821	8,951	6,885	11,832	16,511	11,427	5,639	7,118	10,888	11,451	1,723	11,135	13,111	6,373	3,884	16,051	7,369	10,740	1,363	12,571
Yaraka, Australia	15,186	12,238	3,219	15,600	14,892	14,121	9,380	9,911	13,844	14,809	5,503	13,975	14,711	7,929	4,480	14,436	9,555	14,599	2,500	14,570
Yarmouth, Canada	5,808	4,664	15,809	4,454	5,320	7,489	9,317	10,482	7,362	2,204	11,910	7,418	2,457	13,169	15,775	9,018	11,417	4,294	14,726	2,252
Yellowknife, Canada	6,928	1,107	13,862	5,419	8,122	8,578	6,840	9,326	8,076	1,857	8,295	8,306	3,766	11,913	12,922	12,521	10,584	4,132	11,020	3,052
Yerevan, USSR	2,757	7,969	15,508	3,947	12,619	1,785	4,662	2,640	1,316	7,531	8,820	1,507	10,729	4,869	8,168	8,097	3,107	4,536	10,720	10,237
Yinchuan, China	7,326	7,167	11,248	7,568	16,161	6,995	1,541	3,016	6,407	8,817	3,624	6,674	11,987	4,132	4,942	13,006	3,873	6,842	5,751	11,268
Yogyakarta, Indonesia	11,320	11,851	6,958	12,192	18,667	10,081	6,681	6,043	9,861	13,908	4,927	9,960	16,569	3,882	434	12,517	5,524	11,854	3,412	15,923
York, United Kingdom	1,149	5,904	18,897	448	9,183	2,899	6,379	6,075	2,653	4,342	10,581	2,748	7,122	8,567	11,735	7,742	6,798	1,952	13,346	6,724
Yumen, China	6,661	7,275	11,847	7,022	15,909	6,252	1,472	2,288	5,678	8,665	4,381	5,938	11,977	3,776	5,178	12,269	3,243	6,438	6,416	11,264
Yutian, China	5,731	7,973	12,628	6,417	15,542	5,020	2,463	852	4,526	8,851	5,768	4,746	12,302	3,018	5,433	10,835	1,950	6,204	7,485	11,628
Yuzhno-Sakhalinsk, USSR	8,548	5,016	10,640	8,036	14,109	8,976	2,803	5,892	8,275	7,356	2,463	8,596	9,758	7,170	6,866	15,510	6,921	6,729	5,486	9,080
Zagreb, Yugoslavia	389	7,097	17,892	1,896	10,250	1,394	6,089	4,968	1,175	5,819	10,445	1,232	8,622	7,237	10,560	7,178	5,489	3,111	12,834	8,240
Zahedan, Iran	4,655	9,088	13,610	5,820	14,419	3,404	4,354	1,256	3,149	9,177	7,830	3,249	12,518	2,965	6,299	8,735	1,206	6,206	9,170	11,968
Zamboanga, Philippines	10,974	9,873	7,468	11,396	18,304	10,198	5,285	5,831	9,772	12,132	2,851	9,966	14,492	4,642	2,228	14,265	5,827	10,643	2,318	13,861
Zanzibar, Tanzania	6,520	13,081	12,333	8,065	12,447	4,824	8,905	5,683	5,328	11,982	11,527	5,090	14,043	4,854	7,478	5,013	4,621	9,264	11,262	13,962
Zaragoza, Spain	1,159	7,196	19,006	1,777	8,837	2,365	7,369	6,392	2,488	5,375	11,690	2,409	7,661	8,548	11,934	6,393	6,834	3,301	14,232	7,396
Zashiversk, USSR	6,642	3,246	12,810	5,882	12,429	7,475	2,660	5,722	6,764	5,234	4,743	7,091	8,101	7,870	8,644	13,846	6,975	4,492	7,766	7,385
Zhengzhou, China	8,085	7,311	10,525	8,261	16,502	7,769	2,083	3,708	7,183	9,186	2,883	7,450	12,177	4,407	4,586	13,678	4,438	7,441	5,001	11,463
Zurich, Switzerland	230	6,791	18,495	1,409	9,686	1,930	6,402	5,528	1,785	5,327	10,735	1,821	8,032	7,842	11,147	7,150	6,090	2,789	13,265	7,668

Distances in Kilometers	Jerusalem, Israel	Jiggalong, Australia	Jinan, China	Jodhpur, India	Johannesburg, South Africa	Juazeiro do Norte, Brazil	Juneau, Alaska	Kabul, Afghanistan	Kalgoorlie, Australia	Kaliningrad, USSR	Kamloops, Canada	Kampala, Uganda	Kananga, Zaire	Kano, Nigeria	Kanpur, India	Kansas City, Missouri	Kaohsiung, Taiwan	Karachi, Pakistan	Karaganda, USSR	Karl-Marx-Stadt, East Germany
Jiggalong, Australia	10,952	0	6,660	7,527	9,150	15,997	13,051	8,414	817	12,750	14,010	9,846	10,607	12,797	7,028	16,265	5,093	7,882	9,374	13,232
Jinan, China	7,318	6,660	0	4,294	11,609	15,962	7,587	4,294	7,477	7,159	8,829	9,493	10,810	10,818	3,633	11,015	1,587	4,900	3,783	7,819
Jodhpur, India	3,714	7,527	4,294	0	7,549	12,597	10,292	984	8,148	5,280	11,381	5,199	6,517	6,903	730	12,654	4,782	621	2,614	5,711
Johannesburg, South Africa	6,460	9,150	11,609	7,549	0	7,412	16,185	7,998	8,870	8,994	16,196	2,974	2,326	4,728	8,086	14,551	11,300	7,034	9,527	8,662
Juazeiro do Norte, Brazil	8,993	15,997	15,962	12,597	7,412	0	10,981	12,162	15,338	8,806	9,992	8,027	6,826	5,706	13,322	7,654	17,251	12,002	12,224	8,144
Juneau, Alaska	9,977	13,051	7,587	10,292	16,185	10,981	0	9,486	13,668	7,273	1,243	13,404	13,859	11,520	10,074	3,545	8,743	10,576	7,756	7,547
Kabul, Afghanistan	3,169	8,414	4,294	984	7,998	12,162	9,486	0	9,068	4,350	10,522	5,369	6,641	6,586	1,392	11,685	5,113	1,090	1,732	4,821
Kalgoorlie, Australia	11,419	817	7,477	8,148	8,870	15,338	13,668	9,068	0	13,417	14,533	9,926	10,541	12,875	7,696	16,628	5,909	8,456	10,121	13,855
Kaliningrad, USSR	2,803	12,750	7,159	5,280	8,994	8,806	7,273	4,350	13,417	0	7,771	6,131	6,721	4,854	5,726	7,921	8,586	5,039	3,549	669
Kamloops, Canada	10,563	14,010	8,829	11,381	16,196	9,992	1,243	10,522	14,533	7,771	0	13,803	13,965	11,487	11,223	2,387	9,959	11,607	8,794	7,920
Kampala, Uganda	3,492	9,846	9,493	5,199	2,974	8,027	13,404	5,369	9,926	6,131	13,803	0	1,323	2,956	5,874	13,102	9,767	4,597	6,704	5,899
Kananga, Zaire	4,385	10,607	10,810	6,517	2,326	6,826	13,859	6,641	10,541	6,721	13,965	1,323	0	2,507	7,196	12,743	11,073	5,911	7,870	6,352
Kano, Nigeria	3,505	12,797	10,818	6,903	4,728	5,706	11,520	6,586	12,875	4,854	11,487	2,956	2,507	0	7,632	10,281	11,664	6,300	7,185	4,325
Kanpur, India	4,400	7,028	3,633	730	8,086	13,322	10,074	1,392	7,696	5,726	11,223	5,874	7,196	7,632	0	12,727	4,052	1,346	2,666	6,212
Kansas City, Missouri	10,607	16,265	11,015	12,654	14,551	7,654	3,545	11,685	16,628	7,921	2,387	13,102	12,743	10,281	12,727	0	12,272	12,672	10,080	7,807
Kaohsiung, Taiwan	8,278	5,093	1,587	4,782	11,300	17,251	8,743	5,113	5,909	8,586	9,959	9,767	11,073	11,664	4,052	12,272	0	5,398	5,078	9,230
Karachi, Pakistan	3,200	7,882	4,900	621	7,034	12,002	10,576	1,090	8,456	5,039	11,607	4,597	5,911	6,300	1,346	12,672	5,398	0	2,821	5,407
Karaganda, USSR	3,719	9,374	3,783	2,614	9,527	12,224	7,756	1,732	10,121	3,549	8,794	6,704	7,870	7,185	2,666	10,080	5,078	2,821	0	4,170
Karl-Marx-Stadt, East Germany	2,802	13,232	7,819	5,711	8,662	8,144	7,547	4,821	13,855	669	7,920	5,899	6,352	4,325	6,212	7,807	9,230	5,407	4,170	0
Kasanga, Tanzania	4,473	9,609	10,202	5,939	1,989	7,764	14,340	6,220	9,568	7,073	14,644	984	1,005	3,376	6,570	13,657	10,286	5,363	7,635	6,802
Kashgar, China	3,755	8,376	3,583	1,489	8,808	12,684	8,807	816	9,089	4,402	9,892	6,179	7,441	7,240	1,500	11,250	4,568	1,824	1,171	4,955
Kassel, West Germany	3,023	13,472	7,984	5,953	8,778	7,983	7,419	5,059	14,098	828	7,753	6,055	6,459	4,361	6,449	7,584	9,414	5,652	4,369	245
Kathmandu, Nepal	4,824	6,819	3,131	1,229	8,550	13,787	9,786	1,709	7,524	5,939	10,965	6,384	7,706	8,114	512	12,608	3,558	1,850	2,665	6,463
Kayes, Mali	5,104	14,926	12,193	8,775	6,207	3,902	10,433	8,268	14,904	5,252	10,056	5,091	4,363	2,179	9,484	8,428	13,351	8,209	8,410	4,591
Kazan, USSR	2,878	11,050	5,397	3,799	9,298	10,569	7,355	2,816	11,767	1,812	8,168	6,326	7,261	5,985	4,108	8,948	6,783	3,727	1,739	2,446
Kemi, Finland	3,855	12,637	6,460	5,526	10,206	9,583	6,125	4,543	13,392	1,256	6,744	7,296	7,957	6,098	5,813	7,261	7,989	5,438	3,272	1,796
Kenora, Canada	9,703	15,779	9,941	11,490	14,502	8,251	2,734	10,529	16,354	6,943	1,837	12,533	12,419	9,912	11,544	1,187	11,283	11,538	8,903	6,911
Kerguelen Island	9,620	5,294	10,630	8,401	4,385	10,737	18,176	9,306	4,778	12,422	19,304	6,548	6,532	9,035	8,483	18,303	9,434	8,240	11,013	12,349
Kerkira, Greece	1,633	12,531	8,056	5,104	7,333	7,985	8,896	4,365	13,034	1,681	9,281	4,537	5,044	3,258	5,721	9,044	9,275	4,673	4,273	1,363
Kermanshah, Iran	1,140	10,069	6,204	2,643	6,991	10,132	9,740	2,031	10,615	3,062	10,510	4,055	5,151	4,614	3,299	10,972	7,138	2,195	2,739	3,306
Khabarovsk, USSR	8,100	8,090	1,975	5,838	13,370	15,397	5,649	5,535	8,882	7,041	6,886	10,904	12,161	11,504	5,285	9,139	3,156	6,386	4,388	7,700
Kharkov, USSR	2,027	11,591	6,387	4,094	8,479	9,601	7,968	3,178	12,240	1,191	8,629	5,517	6,336	4,918	4,565	9,027	7,698	3,849	2,624	1,654
Khartoum, Sudan	1,811	10,519	8,507	4,356	4,649	8,312	11,727	4,217	10,787	4,463	12,203	1,690	2,626	2,626	5,084	11,842	9,136	3,738	5,268	4,285
Khon Kaen, Thailand	6,974	4,820	2,642	3,268	9,357	15,795	10,225	3,903	5,589	8,042	11,469	7,901	9,185	10,096	2,576	13,598	1,954	3,832	4,564	8,604
Kiev, USSR	2,110	11,997	6,750	4,489	8,492	9,226	7,872	3,583	12,637	828	8,465	5,558	6,290	4,711	4,972	8,735	8,086	4,222	3,008	1,243
Kigali, Rwanda	3,771	10,004	9,868	5,574	2,692	7,717	13,609	5,743	10,039	6,343	13,934	376	955	2,839	6,246	13,080	10,122	4,973	7,060	6,072
Kingston, Canada	9,122	17,214	10,943	11,606	13,117	6,809	4,180	10,622	17,842	6,550	3,330	11,496	11,177	8,695	11,831	1,606	12,407	11,505	9,176	6,351
Kingston, Jamaica	10,924	18,106	13,784	14,128	12,328	4,972	6,447	13,176	17,698	8,851	5,277	12,055	11,192	9,124	14,506	2,903	15,145	13,865	11,933	8,458
Kingstown, Saint Vincent	9,852	18,851	14,488	13,425	10,584	3,306	7,790	12,587	18,037	8,295	6,724	10,424	9,482	7,555	13,979	4,358	16,043	13,011	11,736	7,773
Kinshasa, Zaire	4,516	11,398	11,342	7,075	2,780	6,057	13,468	7,088	11,304	6,559	13,421	1,989	809	1,953	7,777	12,025	11,738	6,458	8,158	6,113
Kirkwall, United Kingdom	4,150	14,124	8,052	6,746	9,863	8,019	6,322	5,794	14,836	1,498	6,601	7,203	7,538	5,300	7,147	6,473	9,585	6,530	4,767	1,356
Kirov, USSR	3,171	11,165	5,334	4,021	9,604	10,629	7,042	3,036	11,899	1,826	7,863	6,631	7,550	6,205	4,288	8,688	6,765	3,983	1,799	2,485
Kiruna, Sweden	4,131	12,834	6,559	5,797	10,449	9,526	5,857	4,813	13,600	1,464	6,456	7,555	8,184	6,261	6,065	6,971	8,107	5,722	3,493	1,937
Kisangani, Zaire	3,618	10,609	10,141	5,861	2,971	7,215	13,241	5,921	10,643	6,026	13,468	822	772	2,239	6,559	12,501	10,518	5,246	7,106	5,698
Kishinev, USSR	1,777	12,018	7,021	4,491	8,107	8,977	8,231	3,631	12,622	1,038	8,786	5,185	5,894	4,323	5,022	8,944	8,310	4,170	3,249	1,239
Kitchner, Canada	9,427	17,056	10,958	11,825	13,420	6,975	4,006	10,841	17,624	6,827	3,090	11,828	11,502	9,023	12,020	1,274	12,387	11,748	9,358	6,647
Knoxville, Tennessee	10,194	17,268	11,679	12,704	13,575	6,674	4,414	11,720	17,601	7,660	3,327	12,350	11,867	9,455	12,901	1,004	13,040	12,616	10,237	7,442
Kosice, Czechoslovakia	2,217	12,612	7,435	5,086	8,323	8,536	7,936	4,214	13,220	671	8,401	5,471	6,050	4,237	5,606	8,416	8,783	4,767	3,704	645
Kota Kinabalu, Malaysia	8,800	3,291	3,399	5,087	10,106	17,314	10,562	5,751	4,105	9,826	11,749	9,294	10,489	11,775	4,414	14,107	1,897	5,622	6,294	10,411
Krakow, Poland	2,398	12,730	7,443	5,208	8,488	8,522	7,764	4,322	13,351	517	8,221	5,645	6,207	4,350	5,713	8,240	8,814	4,905	3,738	504
Kralendijk, Bonaire	10,552	18,447	14,572	14,050	11,230	3,853	7,477	13,171	17,721	8,835	6,342	11,191	10,229	8,327	14,558	3,955	16,045	13,674	12,179	8,351
Krasnodar, USSR	1,509	11,202	6,387	3,676	7,965	9,665	8,534	2,817	11,814	1,702	9,215	4,994	5,879	4,668	4,208	9,597	7,598	3,370	2,608	2,040
Krasnoyarsk, USSR	5,155	9,188	2,814	3,667	10,959	13,172	6,650	2,993	9,991	4,375	7,790	8,180	9,354	8,558	3,433	9,441	4,337	4,042	1,484	5,042
Kristiansand, Norway	3,585	13,519	7,615	6,107	9,534	8,394	6,671	5,160	14,215	860	7,058	6,771	7,220	5,123	6,520	7,077	9,113	5,887	4,196	876
Kuala Lumpur, Malaysia	7,610	3,595	4,028	3,988	8,544	15,696	11,595	4,832	4,301	9,156	12,832	7,696	8,870	10,292	3,441	15,039	2,943	4,422	5,831	9,652
Kuching, Malaysia	8,515	2,983	3,948	4,838	9,318	16,614	11,302	5,613	3,764	9,857	12,505	8,655	9,806	11,268	4,229	14,839	2,569	5,315	6,404	10,397
Kumasi, Ghana	4,726	13,613	12,043	8,159	4,851	4,461	11,663	7,838	13,542	5,682	11,381	3,863	3,011	1,259	8,889	9,803	12,923	7,554	8,353	5,077
Kumzar, Oman	2,145	8,847	5,774	1,658	6,560	10,939	10,572	1,525	9,368	4,296	11,470	3,849	5,116	5,249	2,385	12,162	6,422	1,080	2,979	4,565
Kunming, China	6,548	5,707	1,874	2,973	9,817	15,535	9,375	3,385	6,493	7,279	10,616	8,000	9,317	9,870	2,243	12,679	1,812	3,588	3,745	7,874
Kuqa Chang, China	4,389	8,123	2,932	1,911	9,394	13,255	8,434	1,455	8,872	4,759	9,569	6,823	8,095	7,885	1,657	11,112	4,001	2,364	1,252	5,355
Kurgan, USSR	3,525	10,189	4,380	3,298	9,713	11,586	7,271	2,344	10,938	2,813	8,232	6,790	7,857	6,852	3,441	9,357	5,773	3,397	819	3,458
Kuwait, Kuwait	1,249	9,735	6,363	2,488	6,507	10,144	10,285	2,082	10,239	3,571	11,063	3,608	4,766	4,508	3,194	11,492	7,166	1,955	3,107	3,763
Kuybyshev, USSR	2,666	10,857	5,368	3,541	9,052	10,610	7,636	2,562	11,560	1,939	8,458	6,084	7,050	5,869	3,880	9,231	6,710	3,449	1,633	2,541
Kyoto, Japan	8,907	6,654	1,702	5,993	13,168	16,886	6,767	5,972	7,430	8,311	7,961	11,191	12,510	12,408	5,322	10,312	2,034	6,601	5,242	8,979
Kzyl-Orda, USSR	2,990	9,408	4,371	2,164	8,731	11,739	8,430	1,186	10,107	3,356	9,412	5,897	7,068	6,488	2,432	10,500	5,519	2,216	807	3,907
L'vov, USSR	2,213	12,436	7,199	4,915	8,431	8,771	7,856	4,027	13,060	593	8,364	5,548	6,177	4,429	5,419	8,470	8,551	4,618	3,472	796
La Ceiba, Honduras	11,904	17,024	13,688	14,870	13,229	5,817	6,125	13,891	16,707	9,658	4,893	13,144	12,250	10,216	15,130	2,693	14,841	14,696	12,476	9,328
La Coruna, Spain	4,011	14,895	9,569	7,391	8,558	6,412	7,687	6,555	15,423	2,434	7,690	6,267	6,276	3,838	7,945	6,904	11,019	7,013	5,975	1,809
La Paz, Bolivia	12,208	15,486	17,714	15,880	9,818	3,299	10,239	15,341	14,677	11,403	9,010	11,173	9,893	9,005	16,595	6,742	18,908	15,295	14,947	10,803
La Paz, Mexico	12,817	14,854	11,650	14,411	15,848	8,440	4,246	13,510	14,905	10,092	3,066	15,191	14,594	12,268	14,288	2,222	12,490	14,572	11,801	10,015
La Ronge, Canada	9,671	14,855	9,070	10,986	15,074	9,176	1,804	10,061	15,464	6,868	1,123	12,775	12,859	10,372	10,952	1,950	10,371	11,115	8,373	6,948
Labrador City, Canada	8,002	16,661	10,069	10,412	12,613	7,157	4,111	9,428	17,448	5,372	3,606	10,617	10,483	7,976	10,655	2,611	11,603	10,307	8,012	5,208
Lagos, Nigeria	4,336	13,095	11,645	7,671	4,491	4,978	11,900	7,396	13,058	5,568	11,711	3,313	2,517	834	8,402	10,246	12,449	7,060	8,018	4,999
Lahore, Pakistan	3,684	7,844	3,947	600	8,062	12,668	9,692	577	8,507	4,912	10,781	5,588	6,890	7,036	818	12,096	4,632	1,029	2,029	5,394
Lambasa, Fiji	16,031	6,145	8,793	12,409	14,366	15,027	9,297	12,863	6,054	15,388	9,466	15,975	16,481	18,929	11,692	10,814	7,753	12,985	12,549	16,004
Lansing, Michigan	9,729	16,848	10,946	12,027	13,738	7,174	3,823	11,045	17,360	7,098	2,843	12,167	11,839	9,363	12,189	936	12,335	11,976	9,522	6,940
Lanzhou, China	6,216	6,822	1,196	3,100	10,502	15,088	8,246	3,125	7,625	6,421	9,479	8,300	9,615	9,694	2,455	11,476	2,187	3,705	2,893	7,056
Laoag, Philippines	8,545	4,602	2,077	4,958	11,131	17,536	9,147	5,376	5,417	9,004	10,349	9,797	11,083	11,860	4,229	12,687	492	5,563	5,475	9,640
Largeau, Chad	2,232	11,945	9,518	5,602	4,976	6,997	11,215	5,272	12,167	4,086	11,440	2,442	2,659	1,314	6,330	10,680	10,353	5,005	5,948	3,693
Las Vegas, Nevada	11,878	14,513	10,317	13,039	16,376	9,225	2,837	12,166	14,802	9,082	1,663	14,777	14,553	12,065	12,884	1,840	11,282	13,245	10,443	9,115
Launceston, Australia	13,991	3,161	9,176	10,687	10,249	14,582	13,203	11,572	2,583	15,889	13,570	12,059	12,345	14,847	10,183	14,879	7,614	11,026	12,412	16,392
Le Havre, France	3,514	14,150	8,625	6,625	8,831	7,355	7,357	5,744	14,757	1,504	7,551	6,267	6,507	4,229	7,135	7,137	10,080	6,301	5,053	924
Leipzig, East Germany	2,867	13,274	7,824	5,756	8,723	8,140	7,485	4,862	13,902	667	7,855	5,964	6,411	4,372	6,251	7,743	9,242	5,457	4,187	66
Leningrad, USSR	3,151	12,257	6,393	4,954	9,546	9,583	6,826	3,981	12,975	823	7,462	6,613	7,330	5,613	5,305	7,930	7,858	4,814	2,911	1,485
Leon, Spain	3,776	14,679	9,479	7,188	8,364	6,490	7,865	6,366	15,192	2,324	7,899	6,035	6,071	3,655	7,754	7,146	10,905	6,800	5,844	1,677
Lerwick, United Kingdom	4,132	13,989	7,888	6,640	9,935	8,186	6,253	5,683	14,709	1,426	6,567	7,242	7,610	5,403	7,028	6,512	9,423	6,439	4,624	1,361
Lhasa, China	5,297	6,675	2,529	1,814	9,129	14,289	9,384	2,132	7,419	6,151	10,588	6,987	8,309	8,654	1,114	12,371	3,011	2,435	2,702	6,715
Libreville, Gabon	4,408	12,206	11,547	7,376	3,557	5,481	12,766	7,253	12,131	6,108	12,639	2,575	1,600	1,289	8,098	11,194	12,133	6,755	8,124	5,601
Lilongwe, Malawi	5,065	9,109	10,338	6,156	1,477	8,010	14,988	6,545	9,014	7,715	15,318	1,587	1,533	4,004	6,738	14,271	10,254	5,614	8,051	7,462
Lima, Peru	12,811	15,635	16,942	16,522	10,897	4,171	9,356	15,801	14,875	11,577	8,115	12,162	10,906	9,820	17,171	5,948	17,846	15,998	15,013	11,035
Limerick, Ireland	4,207	14,673	8,803	7,181	9,436	7,244	6,767	6,266	15,329	1,923	6,891	6,946	7,121	4,764	7,647	6,431	10,316	6,897	5,403	1,495
Limoges, France	3,305	14,105	8,841	6,588	8,426	7,124	7,764	5,744	14,664	1,682	7,931	5,902	6,104	3,813	7,135	7,423	10,256	6,225	5,192	1,027
Limon, Costa Rica	11,998	17,094	14,434	15,237	12,603	5,205	6,882	14,280	16,599	9,961	5,651	12,817	11,820	9,956	15,593	3,422	15,599	14,976	12,985	9,569
Lincoln, Nebraska	10,577	16,035	10,765	12,500	14,735	7,903	3,282	11,539	16,430	7,860	2,126	13,174	12,869	10,392	12,549	263	12,013	12,541	9,912	7,775
Linz, Austria	2,545	13,117	7,895	5,590	8,365	8,069	7,846	4,727	13,712	833	8,215	5,601	6,057	4,061	6,119	8,062	9,269	5,256	4,193	299
Lisbon, Portugal	4,071	15,021	10,002	7,592	8,165	5,965	8,119	6,801	15,471	2,844	8,054	6,012	5,916	3,438	8,182	7,104	11,418	7,174	6,349	2,190
Little Rock, Arkansas	10,830	16,590	11,540	13,076	14,304	7,240	4,051	12,100	16,849	8,210	2,870	13,111	12,638	10,225	13,185	525	12,788	13,058	10,527	8,047
Liverpool, United Kingdom	3,879	14,288	8,482	6,796	9,318	7,536	6,870	5,880	14,944	1,538	7,073	6,738	6,994	4,707	7,262	6,736	9,980	6,517	5,034	1,125
Lodz, Poland	2,565	12,784	7,378	5,273	8,676	8,585	7,576	4,370	13,421	337	8,040	5,832	6,394	4,518	5,758	8,091	8,773	4,990	3,706	468
Lome, Togo	4,534	13,301	11,849	7,903	4,606	4,739	11,842	7,613	13,244	5,658	11,608	3,544	2,706	1,032	8,633	10,084	12,677	7,293	8,198	5,073

Distances in Kilometers	Jerusalem, Israel	Jiggalong, Australia	Jinan, China	Jodhpur, India	Johannesburg, South Africa	Juazeiro do Norte, Brazil	Juneau, Alaska	Kabul, Afghanistan	Kalgoorlie, Australia	Kaliningrad, USSR	Kamloops, Canada	Kampala, Uganda	Kananga, Zaire	Kano, Nigeria	Kanpur, India	Kansas City, Missouri	Kaohsiung, Taiwan	Karachi, Pakistan	Karaganda, USSR	Karl-Marx-Stadt, East Germany
London, United Kingdom	3,615	14,136	8,487	6,622	9,039	7,505	7,147	5,722	14,767	1,421	7,361	6,449	6,714	4,450	7,110	7,010	9,959	6,320	4,961	913
Londonderry, United Kingdom	4,206	14,513	8,553	7,055	9,611	7,506	6,581	6,125	15,192	1,776	6,755	7,061	7,290	4,968	7,498	6,405	10,076	6,795	5,199	1,433
Longlac, Canada	9,308	16,241	10,153	11,341	13,931	7,786	3,200	10,366	16,864	6,589	2,392	12,023	11,865	9,359	11,460	1,347	11,559	11,335	8,797	6,506
Lord Howe Island, Australia	14,764	3,871	8,732	11,148	11,774	15,295	11,704	11,906	3,570	15,870	12,041	13,428	13,831	16,310	10,535	13,456	7,284	11,596	12,342	16,510
Los Angeles, California	12,210	14,219	10,312	13,221	16,685	9,447	2,952	12,374	14,477	9,409	1,853	15,143	14,913	12,429	13,026	2,184	11,204	13,459	10,644	9,458
Louangphrabang, Laos	6,736	5,197	2,359	3,058	9,481	15,646	9,917	3,622	5,971	7,695	11,160	7,868	9,169	9,940	2,344	13,251	1,907	3,646	4,198	8,267
Louisville, Kentucky	10,143	17,012	11,388	12,529	13,779	6,955	4,115	11,546	17,401	7,556	3,040	12,429	12,004	9,564	12,697	773	12,741	12,468	10,031	7,370
Luanda, Angola	5,063	11,388	11,820	7,535	2,484	5,794	13,864	7,592	11,223	7,072	13,721	2,371	1,063	2,359	8,226	12,161	12,134	6,922	8,697	6,607
Lubumbashi, Zaire	4,877	9,840	10,737	6,476	1,610	7,338	14,610	6,748	9,735	7,385	14,788	1,441	846	3,352	7,106	13,578	10,793	5,899	8,138	7,067
Lusaka, Zambia	5,274	9,594	10,909	6,689	1,194	7,412	15,034	7,020	9,448	7,806	15,196	1,803	1,233	3,734	7,293	13,903	10,863	6,129	8,460	7,491
Luxembourg, Luxembourg	3,124	13,717	8,290	6,191	8,673	7,677	7,514	5,313	14,323	1,133	7,788	6,016	6,348	4,175	6,704	7,497	9,717	5,868	4,666	503
Luxor, Egypt	720	10,933	7,880	4,028	5,762	8,581	10,620	3,635	11,321	3,375	11,141	2,807	3,665	2,952	4,745	10,986	8,732	3,456	4,381	3,260
Lynn Lake, Canada	9,361	15,000	9,043	10,776	14,759	9,023	1,982	9,839	15,644	6,560	1,438	12,447	12,535	10,050	10,772	2,030	10,388	10,881	8,167	6,628
Lyon, France	3,036	13,826	8,637	6,311	8,307	7,325	7,878	5,472	14,384	1,491	8,095	5,720	5,981	3,757	6,862	7,661	10,032	5,945	4,959	822
Macapa, Brazil	9,661	17,276	15,761	13,373	8,933	1,527	9,615	12,743	16,516	8,829	8,559	9,310	8,189	6,710	14,056	6,190	17,331	12,832	12,377	8,210
Madison, Wisconsin	9,988	16,492	10,780	12,119	14,136	7,515	3,515	11,143	16,974	7,310	2,483	12,522	12,224	9,741	12,234	620	12,124	12,107	9,573	7,189
Madras, India	5,033	5,978	4,493	1,646	7,128	13,401	11,489	2,624	6,553	6,906	12,665	5,447	6,734	7,772	1,482	14,204	4,355	1,906	4,127	7,304
Madrid, Spain	3,602	14,541	9,550	7,091	8,073	6,413	8,153	6,297	15,019	2,396	8,189	5,756	5,781	3,367	7,678	7,408	10,943	6,680	5,868	1,731
Madurai, India	5,029	5,931	4,903	1,887	6,727	13,154	11,892	2,870	6,458	7,064	13,059	5,153	6,420	7,591	1,845	14,524	4,702	2,026	4,448	7,424
Magadan, USSR	8,298	9,596	3,509	6,843	14,311	14,132	4,078	6,315	10,367	6,587	5,320	11,521	12,641	11,386	6,413	7,545	4,750	7,309	4,820	7,191
Magdalena, Bolivia	11,660	15,907	17,417	15,344	9,587	2,798	10,145	14,787	15,090	10,866	8,937	10,754	9,496	8,495	16,054	6,610	18,879	14,768	14,413	10,260
Magdeburg, East Germany	2,964	13,321	7,807	5,810	8,828	8,159	7,379	4,908	13,958	651	7,748	6,070	6,515	4,464	6,295	7,648	9,237	5,521	4,194	172
Majuro Atoll, Marshall Isls.	13,664	6,439	6,375	10,474	15,590	16,666	7,316	10,654	6,756	12,629	7,886	15,368	16,583	17,163	9,749	9,878	5,709	11,095	9,979	13,251
Malabo, Equatorial Guinea	4,155	12,427	11,374	7,267	3,913	5,481	12,391	7,085	12,392	5,750	12,284	2,675	1,854	913	7,995	10,897	12,045	6,649	7,874	5,233
Male, Maldives	5,038	5,961	5,729	2,466	5,921	12,590	12,666	3,407	6,383	7,352	13,806	4,565	5,780	7,200	2,592	15,079	5,444	2,409	5,080	7,632
Manado, Indonesia	9,892	2,788	3,978	6,179	10,764	18,169	10,494	6,821	3,585	10,791	11,599	10,270	11,412	12,843	5,500	13,984	2,392	6,717	7,242	11,400
Managua, Nicaragua	12,124	16,909	14,080	15,206	13,024	5,620	6,506	14,232	16,504	9,962	5,270	13,145	12,185	10,252	15,497	3,096	15,199	15,000	12,852	9,607
Manama, Bahrain	1,615	9,339	6,296	2,240	6,283	10,357	10,627	2,008	9,827	4,004	11,442	3,456	4,677	4,673	2,965	11,923	6,994	1,661	3,260	4,197
Manaus, Brazil	10,694	17,068	16,279	14,407	9,674	2,336	9,398	13,737	16,252	9,683	8,249	10,310	9,147	7,763	15,076	5,866	17,847	13,877	13,222	9,091
Manchester, New Hampshire	8,872	17,561	11,141	11,521	12,691	6,439	4,569	10,540	18,236	6,375	3,752	11,127	10,771	8,298	11,793	1,984	12,640	11,379	9,161	6,130
Mandalay, Burma	6,066	5,691	2,591	2,387	9,065	14,980	9,969	2,967	6,437	7,121	11,202	7,280	8,593	9,277	1,671	13,151	2,492	2,978	3,685	7,672
Mangareva Island, Fr.Polynesia	18,655	10,356	13,073	17,184	14,253	10,275	9,023	17,360	9,929	15,951	8,299	17,151	15,971	15,976	16,454	8,069	12,408	17,788	16,167	15,874
Manila, Philippines	8,781	4,202	2,479	5,140	11,004	17,735	9,469	5,623	5,016	9,357	10,658	9,839	11,103	12,029	4,418	13,013	894	5,733	5,816	9,985
Mannheim, West Germany	2,971	13,548	8,165	6,022	8,606	7,799	7,586	5,146	14,154	1,007	7,889	5,915	6,283	4,156	6,538	7,643	9,580	5,698	4,521	352
Maputo, Mozambique	6,395	8,742	11,226	7,231	449	7,860	16,271	7,730	8,488	9,014	16,428	2,908	2,469	4,943	7,742	14,926	10,871	6,737	9,306	8,724
Mar del Plata, Argentina	12,321	13,206	19,519	15,244	7,910	3,875	12,814	15,289	12,393	12,665	11,576	10,046	8,732	8,816	15,895	9,339	18,289	14,643	15,931	11,998
Maracaibo, Venezuela	10,947	18,090	14,689	14,421	11,494	4,087	7,430	13,528	17,410	9,183	6,262	11,565	10,578	8,715	14,910	3,887	16,102	14,058	12,481	8,714
Marrakech, Morocco	4,071	14,933	10,530	7,736	7,461	5,437	8,870	7,030	15,255	3,410	8,740	5,498	5,262	2,756	8,376	7,608	11,869	7,261	6,796	2,741
Marseilles, France	2,910	13,782	8,781	6,294	8,038	7,184	8,148	5,484	14,308	1,676	8,348	5,476	5,713	3,482	6,868	7,854	10,145	5,902	5,067	1,012
Maseru, Lesotho	6,810	9,075	11,849	7,841	350	7,379	16,498	8,315	8,753	9,334	16,434	3,324	2,646	5,005	8,361	14,667	11,469	7,338	9,861	8,993
Mashhad, Iran	2,299	9,217	5,063	1,691	7,668	11,284	9,440	894	9,836	3,607	10,371	4,863	6,070	5,764	2,248	11,248	5,981	1,454	1,860	4,021
Mazatlan, Mexico	12,686	15,227	11,970	14,527	15,438	8,030	4,488	13,598	15,239	10,007	3,276	14,886	14,230	11,945	14,460	2,087	12,859	14,639	11,913	9,890
Mbabane, Swaziland	6,443	8,863	11,365	7,354	305	7,717	16,276	7,839	8,596	9,035	16,382	2,951	2,442	4,895	7,872	14,821	11,019	6,854	9,402	8,732
Mbandaka, Zaire	3,938	11,297	10,788	6,541	3,092	6,445	13,102	6,521	11,279	6,062	13,165	1,594	805	1,704	7,251	11,962	11,248	5,921	7,573	5,649
McMurdo Sound, Antarctica	14,346	6,452	13,075	12,884	8,152	10,480	15,629	13,860	5,639	17,105	15,093	10,975	10,461	12,602	12,729	14,461	11,489	12,876	15,392	16,813
Mecca, Saudi Arabia	1,230	10,076	7,509	3,416	5,422	9,194	11,150	3,216	10,454	4,033	11,783	2,466	3,572	3,490	4,146	11,800	8,193	2,810	4,298	4,015
Medan, Indonesia	7,302	3,831	4,117	3,713	8,268	15,367	11,703	4,583	4,506	8,924	12,945	7,360	8,541	9,953	3,198	15,089	3,142	4,125	5,662	9,403
Medellin, Colombia	11,585	17,435	15,078	15,076	11,684	4,292	7,637	14,181	16,769	9,834	6,429	12,025	10,971	9,236	15,560	4,109	16,379	14,709	13,101	9,369
Medicine Hat, Canada	10,340	14,697	9,323	11,542	15,620	9,312	1,788	10,637	15,222	7,537	690	13,428	13,460	10,960	11,460	1,758	10,527	11,704	8,930	7,616
Medina, Saudi Arabia	915	10,236	7,353	3,362	5,741	9,235	10,816	3,065	10,646	3,711	11,452	2,777	3,842	3,554	4,087	11,514	8,111	2,774	4,040	3,714
Melbourne, Australia	13,713	2,806	8,738	10,327	10,346	14,999	12,988	11,195	2,297	15,489	13,440	11,989	12,367	14,846	9,804	14,918	7,176	10,688	11,992	16,015
Memphis, Tennessee	10,660	16,776	11,580	12,980	14,109	7,085	4,140	12,001	17,052	8,061	2,981	12,907	12,431	10,018	13,114	597	12,860	12,943	10,450	7,884
Merauke, Indonesia	11,932	2,661	5,559	8,218	11,771	18,272	10,526	8,851	3,151	12,661	11,392	11,978	13,436	14,749	7,540	13,604	4,076	8,751	9,135	13,301
Merida, Mexico	11,737	16,892	13,044	14,455	13,704	6,317	5,479	13,471	16,743	9,343	4,248	13,325	12,538	10,371	14,647	2,066	14,201	14,346	11,981	9,067
Meridian, Mississippi	10,789	16,971	11,911	13,233	13,934	6,820	4,461	12,251	17,168	8,242	3,289	12,891	12,346	9,973	13,392	917	13,188	13,171	10,726	8,034
Messina, Italy	1,927	12,871	8,456	5,486	7,246	7,578	8,954	4,765	13,346	1,875	9,262	4,541	4,932	2,984	6,114	8,877	9,683	5,039	4,673	1,421
Mexico City, Mexico	12,552	15,881	12,736	14,881	14,597	7,185	5,178	13,913	15,769	10,013	3,939	14,332	13,544	11,377	14,930	2,228	13,695	14,887	12,299	9,808
Miami, Florida	10,664	17,894	12,863	13,573	12,950	5,730	5,534	12,596	17,837	8,358	4,384	12,272	11,561	9,316	13,862	1,998	14,216	13,394	11,227	8,039
Midway Islands, USA	12,529	8,753	6,126	10,382	17,504	15,043	4,695	10,161	9,202	10,660	5,344	15,530	16,784	15,512	9,753	7,513	6,236	10,964	8,927	11,192
Milan, Italy	2,711	13,486	8,394	5,974	8,164	7,570	8,025	5,143	14,044	1,305	8,300	5,504	5,840	3,710	6,532	7,953	9,761	5,605	4,683	658
Milford Sound, New Zealand	15,696	4,850	10,350	12,370	11,166	13,663	12,586	13,224	4,299	17,429	12,623	13,421	13,436	15,892	11,832	13,449	8,871	12,730	13,880	18,019
Milwaukee, Wisconsin	9,905	16,598	10,826	12,086	14,015	7,414	3,603	11,108	17,090	7,241	2,588	12,412	12,106	9,625	12,216	710	12,184	12,063	9,552	7,108
Minsk, USSR	2,534	12,282	6,783	4,814	8,874	9,180	7,459	3,881	12,949	469	8,034	5,958	6,645	4,943	5,258	8,313	8,179	4,584	3,118	1,052
Mogadiscio, Somalia	3,455	8,622	8,241	3,992	3,639	9,463	13,311	4,361	8,807	6,259	14,005	1,436	2,699	4,211	4,610	13,890	8,379	3,433	5,912	6,204
Mombasa, Kenya	3,992	8,932	9,156	4,918	2,745	8,750	13,965	5,273	9,002	6,751	14,511	924	1,924	3,878	5,530	13,996	9,228	4,360	6,783	6,596
Monclova, Mexico	12,058	15,778	11,906	14,090	15,032	7,677	4,330	13,136	15,847	9,408	3,088	14,258	13,656	11,327	14,096	1,495	12,933	14,146	11,489	9,268
Moncton, Canada	8,239	17,438	10,836	10,934	12,270	6,422	4,715	9,958	18,219	5,755	4,047	10,554	10,264	7,771	11,236	2,549	12,376	10,773	8,629	5,500
Monrovia, Liberia	5,545	14,521	12,804	9,094	5,528	3,504	11,270	8,702	14,367	6,052	10,817	4,864	3,930	2,213	9,820	9,036	13,814	8,498	9,043	5,403
Monte Carlo, Monaco	2,769	13,620	8,625	6,127	8,026	7,341	8,159	5,315	14,154	1,544	8,393	5,420	5,700	3,519	6,699	7,956	9,982	5,739	4,903	892
Monterrey, Mexico	12,097	15,876	12,080	14,213	14,897	7,526	4,501	13,253	15,912	9,472	3,259	14,211	13,573	11,270	14,236	1,584	13,108	14,252	11,617	9,316
Montevideo, Uruguay	12,062	13,546	19,378	15,116	7,907	3,518	12,598	15,086	12,735	12,317	11,367	9,921	8,601	8,561	15,793	9,095	18,606	14,504	15,626	11,651
Montgomery, Alabama	10,626	17,190	11,988	13,155	13,714	6,630	4,592	12,172	17,393	8,111	3,442	12,676	12,122	9,753	13,341	1,055	13,296	13,071	10,676	7,885
Montpelier, Vermont	8,867	17,394	10,990	11,448	12,811	6,605	4,406	10,466	18,072	6,335	3,604	11,190	10,864	8,382	11,704	1,913	12,483	11,322	9,064	6,110
Montpellier, France	3,037	13,905	8,852	6,412	8,115	7,111	8,072	5,596	14,434	1,723	8,254	5,578	5,791	3,531	6,982	7,734	10,229	6,024	5,151	1,054
Montreal, Canada	8,854	17,234	10,843	11,371	12,918	6,762	4,254	10,388	17,916	6,291	3,468	11,241	10,945	8,456	11,612	1,863	12,331	11,259	8,965	6,085
Moosonee, Canada	8,884	16,408	10,110	11,035	13,519	7,588	3,446	10,054	17,093	6,187	2,753	11,574	11,427	8,920	11,194	1,735	11,565	10,998	8,528	6,082
Moroni, Comoros	4,884	8,245	9,370	5,294	2,263	9,056	14,828	5,801	8,238	7,663	15,432	1,777	2,380	4,649	5,823	14,876	9,210	4,798	7,414	7,525
Moscow, USSR	2,671	11,715	6,108	4,339	9,125	9,855	7,338	3,375	12,412	1,090	8,033	6,163	6,975	5,467	4,720	8,565	7,507	4,182	2,459	1,723
Mosul, Iraq	888	10,490	6,438	3,041	7,100	9,813	9,514	2,369	11,037	2,678	10,232	4,134	5,151	4,390	3,679	10,598	7,445	2,612	2,840	2,893
Mount Isa, Australia	12,507	1,953	6,779	8,859	10,985	16,912	11,721	9,620	2,118	13,719	12,474	11,788	12,555	14,728	8,246	14,510	5,232	9,319	10,172	14,319
Multan, Pakistan	3,452	7,931	4,254	458	7,766	12,415	9,908	526	8,570	4,850	10,974	5,277	6,579	6,761	962	12,200	4,904	734	2,187	5,301
Munich, West Germany	2,699	13,317	8,070	5,791	8,398	7,893	7,801	4,929	13,909	957	8,133	5,674	6,081	4,018	6,321	7,915	9,455	5,453	4,382	314
Murcia, Spain	3,372	14,324	9,586	6,936	7,731	6,380	8,489	6,177	14,766	2,475	8,536	5,412	5,435	3,034	7,546	7,740	10,936	6,500	5,859	1,807
Murmansk, USSR	4,140	12,320	6,018	5,418	10,561	10,057	5,849	4,436	13,095	1,713	6,557	7,619	8,347	6,567	5,637	7,277	7,565	5,395	3,019	2,289
Mururoa Atoll, Fr. Polynesia	18,769	10,052	12,652	16,754	14,507	10,701	8,894	16,944	9,660	15,975	8,240	17,452	16,329	16,404	16,024	8,177	11,977	17,361	15,828	15,973
Muscat, Oman	2,468	8,500	5,723	1,488	6,416	11,139	10,847	1,588	9,009	4,667	11,776	3,812	5,109	5,433	2,217	12,524	6,269	871	3,175	4,936
Myitkyina, Burma	6,043	5,958	2,244	2,442	9,379	15,018	9,572	2,893	6,720	6,914	10,804	7,481	8,800	9,341	1,711	12,759	2,345	3,055	3,424	7,488
Naga, Philippines	9,037	4,105	2,625	5,398	11,174	17,992	9,438	5,878	4,915	9,577	10,612	10,075	11,333	12,286	4,676	12,981	1,042	5,991	6,043	10,211
Nagasaki, Japan	8,567	6,295	1,257	5,496	12,584	16,964	7,282	5,547	7,090	8,214	8,491	10,681	12,004	12,070	4,808	10,821	1,472	6,111	4,977	8,882
Nagoya, Japan	8,987	6,702	1,802	6,095	13,276	16,884	6,688	6,065	7,474	8,352	7,878	11,294	12,612	12,486	5,426	10,233	2,130	6,702	5,314	9,020
Nagpur, India	4,498	6,687	4,042	840	7,600	13,251	10,674	1,771	7,314	6,108	11,825	5,553	6,873	7,546	602	13,303	4,246	1,301	3,226	6,549
Nairobi, Kenya	3,662	9,344	9,222	4,943	2,912	8,471	13,635	5,208	9,430	6,386	14,125	503	1,679	3,457	5,589	13,556	9,400	4,359	6,642	6,205
Nanchang, China	7,581	5,787	892	4,221	11,166	16,495	8,396	4,438	6,604	7,784	9,634	9,344	10,665	11,023	3,505	11,866	803	4,842	4,287	8,430
Nancy, France	3,072	13,716	8,350	6,189	8,576	7,615	7,611	5,320	14,311	1,192	7,876	5,928	6,250	4,073	6,712	7,559	9,768	5,856	4,709	540
Nandi, Fiji	15,929	5,901	8,748	12,272	14,124	15,132	9,517	12,760	5,800	15,462	9,708	15,723	16,224	18,674	11,561	11,072	7,659	12,839	12,519	16,093
Nanjing, China	7,675	6,140	538	4,464	11,569	16,450	7,932	4,581	6,957	7,661	9,169	9,637	10,960	11,155	3,767	11,410	1,054	5,082	4,234	8,318
Nanning, China	7,173	5,288	1,748	3,585	10,200	16,159	9,334	4,009	6,092	7,831	10,577	8,540	9,850	10,486	2,854	12,750	1,229	4,195	4,283	8,439
Nantes, France	3,554	14,305	8,891	6,780	8,658	7,084	7,536	5,919	14,883	1,749	7,681	6,160	6,339	4,017	7,311	7,159	10,334	6,433	5,291	1,130
Naples, Italy	2,129	13,030	8,375	5,583	7,558	7,626	8,640	4,819	13,536	1,612	8,949	4,854	5,241	3,244	6,187	8,597	9,650	5,164	4,601	1,116
Narvik, Norway	4,237	12,948	6,642	5,930	10,530	9,462	5,760	4,946	13,718	1,537	6,343	7,648	8,256	6,301	6,195	6,838	8,196	5,855	3,616	1,976

Distances in Kilometers	Jerusalem, Israel	Jiggalong, Australia	Jinan, China	Jodhpur, India	Johannesburg, South Africa	Juazeiro do Norte, Brazil	Juneau, Alaska	Kabul, Afghanistan	Kalgoorlie, Australia	Kaliningrad, USSR	Kamloops, Canada	Kampala, Uganda	Kananga, Zaire	Kano, Nigeria	Kanpur, India	Kansas City, Missouri	Kaohsiung, Taiwan	Karachi, Pakistan	Karaganda, USSR	Karl-Marx-Stadt, East Germany
Nashville, Tennessee	10,368	17,022	11,578	12,777	13,833	6,897	4,234	11,795	17,343	7,796	3,119	12,589	12,121	9,702	12,943	761	12,906	12,715	10,277	7,601
Nassau, Bahamas	10,489	18,183	13,007	13,498	12,654	5,452	5,757	12,529	18,075	8,250	4,628	12,004	11,275	9,047	13,822	2,242	14,396	13,289	11,212	7,906
Natal, Brazil	8,528	15,866	15,578	12,119	7,071	482	11,089	11,697	15,268	8,442	10,158	7,565	6,380	5,225	12,845	7,859	16,800	11,522	11,814	7,776
Natashquan, Canada	7,831	17,022	10,381	10,440	12,193	6,721	4,578	9,462	17,828	5,290	4,046	10,296	10,100	7,594	10,732	2,846	11,935	10,291	8,123	5,065
Nauru Island	13,888	5,587	6,587	10,431	14,712	16,996	8,288	10,757	5,845	13,269	8,847	14,956	16,030	17,330	9,701	10,783	5,666	11,039	10,325	13,918
Ndjamena, Chad	3,002	12,135	10,257	6,245	4,468	6,387	11,723	5,985	12,255	4,750	11,821	2,335	2,153	711	6,976	10,804	11,023	5,635	6,721	4,298
Nelson, New Zealand	16,161	5,236	10,531	12,707	11,721	13,696	12,053	13,516	4,742	17,519	12,055	14,000	14,003	16,440	12,131	12,881	8,942	13,106	14,007	18,171
Nema, Mauritania	4,596	14,571	11,713	8,267	6,088	4,407	10,410	7,761	14,619	4,851	10,129	4,726	4,107	1,775	8,976	8,639	12,848	7,703	7,932	4,200
Neuquen, Argentina	13,212	13,042	19,507	16,148	8,724	4,545	12,403	16,211	12,226	13,338	11,161	10,956	9,645	9,710	16,777	9,056	18,033	15,553	16,746	12,681
New Delhi, India	4,032	7,412	3,812	485	8,020	12,984	9,937	1,003	8,074	5,345	11,057	5,682	6,999	7,313	391	12,462	4,355	1,091	2,382	5,824
New Glasgow, Canada	8,122	17,524	10,895	10,877	12,095	6,291	4,875	9,904	18,321	5,672	4,220	10,394	10,092	7,602	11,196	2,708	12,445	10,700	8,606	5,398
New Haven, Connecticut	9,078	17,651	11,312	11,743	12,762	6,370	4,617	10,763	18,274	6,594	3,748	11,279	10,887	8,428	12,014	1,856	12,797	11,601	9,380	6,344
New Orleans, Louisiana	11,070	16,885	12,109	13,527	14,008	6,801	4,605	12,545	17,007	8,535	3,406	13,098	12,506	10,165	13,678	1,095	13,347	13,468	11,012	8,322
New Plymouth, New Zealand	16,234	5,285	10,225	12,711	11,966	13,839	11,802	13,494	4,829	17,380	11,818	14,207	14,241	16,688	12,116	12,696	8,831	13,131	13,907	18,044
New York, New York	9,190	17,647	11,364	11,847	12,836	6,382	4,601	10,866	18,240	6,705	3,706	11,381	10,978	8,524	12,112	1,765	12,839	11,709	9,475	6,456
Newcastle upon Tyne, UK	3,869	14,159	8,294	6,690	9,433	7,730	6,753	5,763	14,831	1,414	6,993	6,812	7,107	4,852	7,139	6,738	9,798	6,428	4,873	1,078
Newcastle Waters, Australia	11,768	1,474	6,228	8,121	10,624	17,171	11,763	8,891	1,910	13,038	12,631	11,177	12,024	14,088	7,513	14,814	4,653	8,579	9,499	13,622
Niamey, Niger	3,934	13,507	11,232	7,475	5,217	5,122	11,122	7,082	13,566	4,843	10,979	3,662	3,106	715	8,200	9,641	12,191	6,885	7,514	4,253
Nicosia, Cyprus	415	11,251	7,286	3,897	6,815	8,924	9,584	3,260	11,747	2,389	10,153	3,859	4,688	3,587	4,555	10,202	8,332	3,425	3,599	2,394
Niue (Alofi)	17,138	7,144	9,832	13,571	14,641	13,883	9,170	13,989	6,953	15,945	9,115	16,812	16,941	19,212	12,851	10,124	8,877	14,152	13,526	16,466
Norfolk, Virginia	9,606	17,805	11,751	12,317	12,927	6,212	4,783	11,337	18,250	7,159	3,795	11,662	11,178	8,763	12,584	1,624	13,197	12,172	9,945	6,893
Norfolk Island, Australia	15,510	4,724	9,013	11,826	12,550	15,052	11,052	12,517	4,462	16,148	11,282	14,321	14,675	17,174	11,178	12,582	7,668	12,312	12,742	16,817
Noril'sk, USSR	5,305	10,613	4,034	4,888	11,626	12,148	5,441	4,046	11,425	3,649	6,494	8,683	9,688	8,354	4,793	7,978	5,618	5,136	2,315	4,297
Norman Wells, Canada	9,134	13,382	7,442	9,710	15,315	10,612	873	8,853	14,071	6,410	1,671	12,541	12,989	10,671	9,568	3,573	8,741	9,939	7,124	6,675
Normanton, Australia	12,500	2,208	6,525	8,817	11,308	17,254	11,345	9,539	2,457	13,546	12,110	11,988	12,809	14,904	8,180	14,179	5,000	9,301	9,998	14,164
North Pole	6,488	12,590	5,942	7,095	12,903	10,800	3,536	6,182	13,405	3,938	4,386	9,969	10,656	8,677	7,074	5,672	7,497	7,252	4,480	4,370
Nottingham, United Kingdom	3,746	14,178	8,428	6,679	9,217	7,577	6,969	5,768	14,828	1,434	7,188	6,620	6,892	4,625	7,151	6,868	9,916	6,394	4,949	996
Norway House, Canada	9,491	15,339	9,420	11,069	14,650	8,690	2,294	10,120	15,959	6,701	1,570	12,476	12,479	9,978	11,090	1,673	10,766	11,149	8,467	6,726
Norwich, United Kingdom	3,580	14,021	8,330	6,516	9,113	7,663	7,072	5,608	14,664	1,286	7,318	6,487	6,787	4,553	6,993	7,031	9,806	6,227	4,817	826
Nouakchott, Mauritania	5,336	15,505	12,196	9,045	6,834	3,799	9,854	8,462	15,519	5,108	9,442	5,659	4,980	2,713	9,735	7,799	13,465	8,505	8,430	4,439
Noumea, New Caledonia	15,115	4,670	8,337	11,402	13,024	15,713	10,452	12,019	4,551	15,429	10,783	14,475	15,018	17,425	10,723	12,288	7,051	11,927	12,098	16,098
Novosibirsk, USSR	4,520	9,408	3,289	3,293	10,402	12,674	7,002	2,515	10,193	3,871	8,092	7,581	8,737	7,929	3,179	9,571	4,741	3,594	879	4,530
Nuku'alofa, Tonga	16,786	6,547	9,566	13,127	14,202	14,276	9,573	13,616	6,353	16,052	9,597	16,227	16,458	18,923	12,418	10,697	8,512	13,691	13,319	16,634
Nukunono Island, Tokelau Isls.	16,267	7,304	8,973	12,960	15,538	14,469	8,211	13,231	7,265	14,839	8,284	17,148	17,716	19,692	12,230	9,575	8,184	13,571	12,566	15,367
Nuremberg, West Germany	2,811	13,359	8,015	5,832	8,547	7,948	7,652	4,957	13,965	871	7,989	5,819	6,230	4,159	6,349	7,798	9,418	5,510	4,352	202
Nyala, Sudan	2,428	11,135	9,409	5,271	4,246	7,419	11,983	5,115	11,314	4,749	12,284	1,552	2,004	1,782	5,999	11,578	10,050	4,653	6,070	4,437
Oaxaca, Mexico	12,571	16,063	13,091	15,085	14,269	6,859	5,522	14,108	15,880	10,106	4,281	14,154	13,306	11,206	15,180	2,453	14,060	15,048	12,530	9,866
Ocean Falls, Canada	10,539	13,486	8,332	11,064	16,469	10,526	788	10,243	14,031	7,779	544	13,885	14,177	11,741	10,859	2,931	9,430	11,332	8,511	7,986
Odense, Denmark	3,268	13,398	7,672	5,929	9,197	8,310	7,011	5,000	14,068	650	7,396	6,431	6,885	4,818	6,376	7,369	9,139	5,678	4,150	536
Odessa, USSR	1,677	11,862	6,916	4,335	8,052	9,092	8,311	3,479	12,466	1,167	8,889	5,116	5,859	4,356	4,870	9,083	8,187	4,013	3,137	1,396
Ogbomosho, Nigeria	4,137	13,076	11,449	7,504	4,589	5,127	11,762	7,211	13,070	5,365	11,608	3,258	2,543	632	8,234	10,202	12,276	6,895	7,813	4,801
Okha, USSR	8,285	8,790	2,745	6,389	13,935	14,859	4,863	5,977	9,569	6,893	6,101	11,309	12,512	11,561	5,890	8,355	3,929	6,903	4,645	7,530
Okinawa (Naha)	8,740	5,540	1,538	5,415	12,143	17,498	8,008	5,619	6,339	8,692	9,205	10,508	11,825	12,204	4,696	11,552	847	6,036	5,306	9,354
Oklahoma City, Oklahoma	11,080	16,106	11,259	13,095	14,786	7,701	3,705	12,133	16,376	8,398	2,490	13,511	13,088	10,654	13,143	477	12,446	13,130	10,508	8,282
Old Crow, Canada	8,983	12,784	6,818	9,247	15,333	11,187	1,068	8,426	13,491	6,343	2,168	12,449	13,029	10,821	9,060	4,198	8,110	9,516	6,695	6,677
Olympia, Washington	11,006	13,853	8,988	11,729	16,575	10,105	1,471	10,891	14,324	8,215	445	14,244	14,377	11,888	11,537	2,452	10,040	11,979	9,159	8,364
Omaha, Nebraska	10,501	16,073	10,744	12,440	14,678	7,877	3,282	11,477	16,481	7,787	2,139	13,100	12,801	10,321	12,495	271	12,004	12,477	9,855	7,699
Omsk, USSR	3,946	9,785	3,864	3,189	9,980	12,101	7,198	2,299	10,550	3,315	8,223	7,103	8,220	7,329	3,219	9,515	5,272	3,387	575	3,966
Oodnadatta, Australia	12,470	1,545	7,367	8,951	10,239	16,120	12,576	9,789	1,407	14,049	13,303	11,302	11,947	14,257	8,397	15,255	5,788	9,351	10,545	14,593
Oradea, Romania	2,042	12,531	7,481	5,005	8,137	8,499	8,124	4,154	13,123	857	8,588	5,282	5,867	4,086	5,545	8,579	8,802	4,667	3,728	781
Oran, Algeria	3,334	14,272	9,734	6,953	7,487	6,241	8,739	6,224	14,678	2,665	8,770	5,211	5,198	2,782	7,580	7,920	11,054	6,497	5,985	2,002
Oranjestad, Aruba	10,689	18,358	14,511	14,153	11,421	4,036	7,344	13,261	17,672	8,916	6,197	11,381	10,424	8,510	14,643	3,812	15,959	13,792	12,224	8,446
Orebro, Sweden	3,404	13,094	7,196	5,716	9,547	8,801	6,696	4,759	13,799	601	7,172	6,712	7,255	5,277	6,110	7,351	8,685	5,522	3,761	952
Orel, USSR	2,350	11,707	6,292	4,256	8,799	9,678	7,644	3,313	12,379	1,043	8,313	5,840	6,644	5,160	4,685	8,760	7,651	4,051	2,576	1,605
Orsk, USSR	2,883	10,252	4,819	3,026	9,080	11,180	7,808	2,042	10,964	2,556	8,715	6,147	7,207	6,253	3,307	9,665	6,120	3,012	1,045	3,152
Osaka, Japan	8,907	6,612	1,687	5,977	13,137	16,918	6,810	5,963	7,389	8,329	8,004	11,174	12,493	12,409	5,303	10,355	1,993	6,586	5,247	8,998
Oslo, Norway	3,615	13,343	7,375	5,977	9,675	8,641	6,547	5,020	14,053	823	6,981	6,874	7,370	5,321	6,367	7,104	8,880	5,783	3,995	1,020
Osorno, Chile	13,681	12,779	19,038	16,531	9,038	4,992	12,336	16,656	11,967	13,767	11,102	11,360	10,057	10,179	17,122	9,087	17,656	15,950	17,207	13,115
Ostrava, Czechoslovakia	2,452	12,843	7,558	5,319	8,477	8,406	7,761	4,437	13,459	564	8,196	5,654	6,188	4,290	5,829	8,172	8,933	5,010	3,858	398
Ottawa, Canada	8,993	17,149	10,825	11,460	13,078	6,863	4,138	10,476	17,805	6,411	3,326	11,403	11,109	8,621	11,685	1,703	12,298	11,360	9,031	6,217
Ouagadougou, Bourkina Fasso	4,327	13,836	11,608	7,888	5,336	4,711	11,090	7,483	13,853	5,078	10,868	3,994	3,331	1,093	8,611	9,416	12,595	7,298	7,870	4,463
Oujda, Morocco	3,457	14,381	9,897	7,093	7,442	6,079	8,799	6,374	14,768	2,823	8,799	5,225	5,166	2,723	7,725	7,891	11,215	6,631	6,147	2,158
Oxford, United Kingdom	3,698	14,209	8,525	6,697	9,099	7,472	7,088	5,795	14,844	1,483	7,292	6,521	6,774	4,496	7,182	6,928	10,004	6,399	5,017	992
Pago Pago, American Samoa	16,749	7,231	9,432	13,305	15,093	14,160	8,698	13,648	7,112	15,413	8,700	17,036	17,355	19,743	12,577	9,842	8,557	13,903	13,078	15,936
Pakxe, Laos	7,322	4,563	2,634	3,616	9,564	16,131	10,213	4,242	5,346	8,348	11,454	8,204	9,479	10,437	2,923	13,643	1,738	4,179	4,848	8,919
Palembang, Indonesia	8,264	2,850	4,563	4,700	8,542	15,892	12,034	5,567	3,547	9,901	13,251	8,038	9,138	10,764	4,179	15,550	3,292	5,102	6,583	10,388
Palermo, Italy	2,112	13,060	8,616	5,679	7,283	7,407	8,908	4,954	13,529	1,923	9,182	4,625	4,962	2,933	6,306	8,738	9,858	5,232	4,834	1,414
Palma, Majorca	3,056	14,001	9,228	6,580	7,745	6,742	8,451	5,811	14,471	2,148	8,573	5,305	5,429	3,109	7,183	7,908	10,568	6,154	5,492	1,486
Palmerston North, New Zealand	16,363	5,424	10,419	12,873	11,911	13,645	11,874	13,667	4,946	17,574	11,853	14,218	14,201	16,621	12,286	12,659	9,024	13,284	14,099	18,238
Panama, Panama	11,762	17,334	14,669	15,116	12,206	4,805	7,164	14,181	16,767	9,838	5,945	12,443	11,429	9,603	15,529	3,660	15,904	14,809	12,974	9,414
Paramaribo, Suriname	9,714	18,014	15,230	13,407	9,629	2,274	8,829	12,679	17,224	8,561	7,772	9,766	8,718	7,024	14,044	5,405	16,818	12,914	12,096	7,977
Paris, France	3,339	13,998	8,554	6,472	8,700	7,418	7,485	5,598	14,596	1,407	7,701	6,111	6,375	4,128	6,990	7,311	9,992	6,140	4,949	791
Patna, India	4,881	6,647	3,260	1,212	8,387	13,808	10,014	1,822	7,340	6,105	11,195	6,291	7,613	8,115	487	12,842	3,580	1,821	2,880	6,615
Patrai, Greece	1,425	12,344	8,006	4,947	7,165	8,064	9,077	4,233	12,836	1,833	9,482	4,345	4,888	3,191	5,576	9,261	9,190	4,501	4,227	1,561
Peking, China	7,135	7,026	366	4,273	11,695	15,653	7,310	4,183	7,843	6,848	8,554	9,462	10,770	10,639	3,646	10,705	1,953	4,865	3,533	7,512
Penrhyn Island (Omoka)	17,140	8,725	10,157	14,323	16,055	13,007	7,761	14,449	8,600	14,932	7,547	18,503	18,356	18,530	13,598	8,433	9,551	14,943	13,483	15,293
Peoria, Illinois	10,188	16,598	11,021	12,377	14,136	7,380	3,693	11,399	17,024	7,533	2,613	12,640	12,289	9,822	12,497	462	12,347	12,357	9,835	7,394
Perm', USSR	3,324	10,803	4,951	3,763	9,693	11,011	7,074	2,784	11,546	2,213	7,954	6,729	7,707	6,484	3,981	8,906	6,376	3,779	1,429	2,869
Perth, Australia	11,024	1,064	7,595	7,883	8,325	14,942	14,101	8,828	552	13,163	15,019	9,395	9,992	12,339	7,480	17,169	6,057	8,148	9,989	13,554
Peshawar, Pakistan	3,390	8,217	4,104	869	8,093	12,383	9,493	223	8,880	4,539	10,552	5,513	6,796	6,795	1,190	11,785	4,895	1,104	1,762	5,023
Petropavlovsk-Kamchatskiy, USSR	9,141	9,223	3,689	7,435	14,976	14,670	4,077	6,998	9,955	7,457	5,284	12,291	13,453	12,261	6,937	7,620	4,675	7,942	5,593	8,056
Petrozavodsk, USSR	3,341	12,089	6,122	4,882	9,772	9,862	6,647	3,901	12,823	1,129	7,332	6,823	7,579	5,907	5,191	7,916	7,603	4,783	2,718	1,788
Pevek, USSR	8,185	11,045	4,836	7,564	14,589	12,745	2,858	6,859	11,810	5,989	4,083	11,629	12,550	10,832	7,269	6,179	6,172	7,929	5,182	6,509
Philadelphia, Pennsylvania	9,320	17,644	11,431	11,969	12,913	6,387	4,594	10,988	18,201	6,833	3,671	11,495	11,077	8,630	12,229	1,669	12,895	11,835	9,588	6,586
Phnom Penh, Kampuchea	7,431	4,235	3,035	3,718	9,294	16,083	10,607	4,419	5,004	8,610	11,846	8,085	9,335	10,437	3,059	14,047	2,042	4,250	5,146	9,162
Phoenix, Arizona	12,016	14,787	10,727	13,371	16,118	8,876	3,227	12,479	15,021	9,238	2,027	14,762	14,428	11,969	13,245	1,689	11,691	13,549	10,764	9,230
Pierre, South Dakota	10,451	15,626	10,276	12,152	15,013	8,349	2,789	11,205	16,081	7,690	1,652	13,229	13,035	10,535	12,160	757	11,517	12,232	9,548	7,657
Pinang, Malaysia	7,348	3,886	3,856	3,709	8,527	15,572	11,440	4,544	4,592	8,865	12,681	7,550	8,749	10,091	3,152	14,845	2,869	4,154	5,543	9,364
Pitcairn Island (Adamstown)	18,408	10,690	13,610	17,710	13,870	9,755	9,247	17,891	10,215	15,928	8,444	16,701	15,479	15,449	16,982	8,007	12,942	18,303	16,608	15,760
Pittsburgh, Pennsylvania	9,611	17,303	11,293	12,112	13,328	6,721	4,270	11,128	17,807	7,059	3,299	11,883	11,487	9,033	12,326	1,256	12,715	12,016	9,667	6,849
Plymouth, Montserrat	9,731	19,204	14,097	13,235	10,848	3,652	7,402	12,367	18,406	8,043	6,354	10,520	9,635	7,611	13,757	4,002	15,645	12,852	11,439	7,546
Plymouth, United Kingdom	3,835	14,435	8,774	6,915	9,059	7,228	7,136	6,022	15,056	1,727	7,286	6,546	6,740	4,412	7,411	6,822	10,255	6,603	5,266	1,204
Ponape Island	12,619	5,277	5,322	9,203	14,343	18,095	8,042	9,495	5,722	12,135	8,814	13,951	15,152	16,078	8,473	10,988	4,423	9,816	9,073	12,798
Ponce, Puerto Rico	10,044	19,049	13,940	13,457	11,334	4,095	7,024	12,555	18,381	8,209	5,942	10,980	10,116	8,057	13,935	3,571	15,446	13,112	11,517	7,746
Ponta Delgada, Azores	5,518	16,461	10,920	8,977	9,032	5,173	7,494	8,142	16,918	3,936	7,175	7,247	6,934	4,434	9,533	5,868	12,438	8,589	7,479	3,357
Pontianak, Indonesia	8,515	2,866	4,140	4,861	9,140	16,467	11,510	5,662	3,634	9,936	12,713	8,544	9,677	11,197	4,272	15,046	2,774	5,320	6,509	10,463
Port Augusta, Australia	12,894	1,948	7,956	9,452	10,139	15,600	12,894	10,313	1,557	14,605	13,524	11,455	11,988	14,388	8,921	15,302	6,379	9,826	11,120	15,131
Port Blair, India	6,279	4,931	3,690	2,630	8,148	14,757	11,166	3,483	5,603	7,823	12,402	6,763	8,024	9,137	2,097	14,341	3,167	3,080	4,605	8,304
Port Elizabeth, South Africa	7,346	9,046	12,275	8,341	894	7,259	16,919	8,841	8,661	9,838	16,694	3,865	3,125	5,399	8,841	14,731	11,797	7,850	10,401	9,476
Port Hedland, Australia	10,578	411	6,309	7,124	9,088	16,129	12,099	8,006	1,192	12,341	13,913	9,610	10,429	12,546	6,619	16,231	4,755	7,489	8,965	12,826

Distances in Kilometers	Jerusalem, Israel	Jiggalong, Australia	Jinan, China	Jodhpur, India	Johannesburg, South Africa	Juazeiro do Norte, Brazil	Juneau, Alaska	Kabul, Afghanistan	Kalgoorlie, Australia	Kaliningrad, USSR	Kamloops, Canada	Kampala, Uganda	Kananga, Zaire	Kano, Nigeria	Kanpur, India	Kansas City, Missouri	Kaohsiung, Taiwan	Karachi, Pakistan	Karaganda, USSR	Karl-Marx-Stadt, East Germany
Port Louis, Mauritius	6,219	6,502	8,864	5,406	3,078	10,451	15,662	6,177	6,456	9,013	16,615	3,537	4,106	6,437	5,719	16,622	8,302	5,088	7,906	8,993
Port Moresby, Papua New Guinea	12,638	3,203	6,005	8,929	12,353	18,028	10,228	9,522	3,556	13,161	10,994	12,724	13,677	15,511	8,238	13,102	4,607	9,474	9,685	13,817
Port Said, Egypt	284	11,191	7,587	3,994	6,375	8,710	10,002	3,452	11,640	2,769	10,539	3,426	4,245	3,243	4,682	10,481	8,560	3,474	3,960	2,698
Port Sudan, Sudan	1,361	10,237	7,846	3,733	5,165	8,891	11,335	3,553	10,580	4,146	11,916	2,194	3,256	3,185	4,463	11,806	8,514	3,122	4,618	4,070
Port-au-Prince, Haiti	10,509	18,564	13,817	13,803	11,912	4,608	6,648	12,869	18,077	8,525	5,517	11,579	10,724	8,648	14,224	3,131	15,251	13,505	11,709	8,104
Port-of-Spain, Trin. & Tobago	10,026	18,573	14,765	13,631	10,492	3,153	8,007	12,810	17,758	8,536	6,922	10,461	9,479	7,625	14,201	4,545	16,318	13,200	11,993	8,005
Port-Vila, Vanuatu	15,077	4,975	8,080	11,380	13,528	15,918	9,916	11,928	4,933	15,075	10,266	14,820	15,457	17,771	10,681	11,836	6,876	11,932	11,861	15,739
Portland, Maine	8,750	17,544	11,079	11,406	12,614	6,437	4,587	10,426	18,245	6,255	3,799	11,019	10,676	8,199	11,684	2,088	12,587	11,261	9,056	6,009
Portland, Oregon	11,158	13,878	9,122	11,896	16,644	10,057	1,631	11,060	14,327	8,364	596	14,375	14,476	11,980	11,701	2,406	10,152	12,148	9,328	8,504
Porto, Portugal	4,021	14,949	9,768	7,474	8,363	6,205	7,898	6,659	15,440	2,617	7,870	6,133	6,095	3,638	8,046	7,007	11,201	7,076	6,143	1,974
Porto Alegre, Brazil	11,398	14,027	18,701	14,588	7,636	2,818	12,422	14,470	13,229	11,609	11,218	9,432	8,110	7,906	15,292	8,880	18,834	13,969	14,923	10,942
Porto Alexandre, Angola	5,826	11,162	12,382	8,089	2,036	5,655	14,534	8,230	10,904	7,858	14,272	2,892	1,589	3,099	8,755	12,515	12,534	7,489	9,418	7,384
Porto Novo, Benin	4,395	13,174	11,707	7,746	4,543	4,898	11,865	7,464	13,133	5,584	11,661	3,398	2,591	890	8,477	10,179	12,522	7,136	8,069	5,009
Porto Velho, Brazil	11,384	16,411	16,913	15,094	9,786	2,714	9,719	14,464	15,595	10,439	8,525	10,737	9,516	8,335	15,781	6,176	18,409	14,543	13,979	9,846
Portsmouth, United Kingdom	3,646	14,216	8,592	6,697	8,996	7,399	7,192	5,803	14,839	1,516	7,386	6,430	6,672	4,387	7,192	6,991	10,063	6,387	5,060	986
Poznan, Poland	2,730	12,961	7,488	5,455	8,776	8,475	7,460	4,548	13,603	347	7,897	5,956	6,483	4,546	5,934	7,914	8,900	5,176	3,845	331
Prague, Czechoslovakia	2,664	13,118	7,774	5,594	8,556	8,188	7,659	4,711	13,734	659	8,046	5,778	6,250	4,258	6,103	7,945	9,169	5,282	4,101	138
Praia, Cape Verde Islands	6,215	16,173	12,960	9,925	7,203	3,005	9,777	9,331	16,051	5,814	9,210	6,376	5,566	3,481	10,614	7,354	14,290	9,386	9,226	5,148
Pretoria, South Africa	6,409	9,162	11,575	7,507	51	7,418	16,140	7,952	8,887	8,945	16,161	2,923	2,280	4,688	8,046	14,533	11,276	6,990	9,479	8,615
Prince Albert, Canada	9,866	14,909	9,230	11,199	15,178	9,121	1,870	10,274	15,492	7,065	1,038	12,941	12,990	10,494	11,159	1,785	10,509	11,328	8,585	7,133
Prince Edward Island	8,681	7,627	12,125	8,810	2,424	8,459	18,604	9,513	7,135	11,346	18,358	5,222	4,749	7,122	9,148	16,112	11,246	8,439	11,211	11,059
Prince George, Canada	10,278	13,802	8,455	10,991	16,109	10,221	873	10,140	14,368	7,500	398	13,580	13,829	11,382	10,827	2,688	9,614	11,226	8,409	7,682
Prince Rupert, Canada	10,367	13,306	8,056	10,799	16,419	10,717	511	9,986	13,876	7,626	790	13,749	14,106	11,702	10,585	3,164	9,169	11,076	8,255	7,859
Providence, Rhode Island	8,942	17,675	11,272	11,629	12,654	6,334	4,664	10,649	18,332	6,467	3,823	11,145	10,763	8,299	11,908	1,982	12,769	11,479	9,281	6,211
Provo, Utah	11,338	14,804	10,151	12,625	16,003	9,051	2,578	11,728	15,164	8,544	1,341	14,246	14,073	11,574	12,517	1,469	11,218	12,797	10,016	8,571
Puerto Aisen, Chile	13,776	12,265	18,747	16,310	8,765	5,313	12,818	16,587	11,452	14,119	11,591	11,225	9,946	10,276	16,831	9,612	17,221	15,765	17,429	13,457
Puerto Deseado, Argentina	13,333	12,097	18,751	15,730	8,183	5,151	13,319	16,039	11,280	13,926	12,084	10,671	9,402	9,854	16,249	10,031	17,165	15,191	17,039	13,258
Puerto Princesa, Philippines	8,839	3,672	2,988	5,142	10,552	17,606	10,056	5,726	4,489	9,655	11,241	9,590	10,819	11,950	4,441	13,601	1,437	5,707	6,107	10,264
Punta Arenas, Chile	13,807	11,449	18,074	15,797	8,288	5,841	13,615	16,270	10,633	14,594	12,401	10,934	9,709	10,373	16,212	10,473	16,488	15,317	17,522	13,924
Pusan, South Korea	8,373	6,533	1,101	5,386	12,580	16,698	7,120	5,390	7,332	7,959	8,339	10,583	11,902	11,878	4,712	10,650	1,623	5,996	4,754	8,628
Pyongyang, North Korea	7,913	6,929	813	5,070	12,422	16,180	6,939	4,993	7,736	7,435	8,174	10,265	11,576	11,415	4,426	10,431	1,889	5,667	4,261	8,104
Qamdo, China	5,808	6,540	1,923	2,420	9,710	14,794	8,996	2,642	7,316	6,418	10,220	7,600	8,922	9,212	1,726	12,130	2,471	3,039	2,884	7,015
Qandahar, Afghanistan	2,884	8,448	4,706	921	7,544	11,859	9,869	458	9,064	4,375	10,874	4,916	6,193	6,228	1,530	11,920	5,443	755	2,119	4,793
Qiqian, China	7,006	8,375	1,752	4,900	12,444	14,698	6,006	4,504	9,189	6,073	7,244	9,860	11,097	10,422	4,416	9,326	3,282	5,413	3,294	6,740
Qom, Iran	1,494	9,780	5,866	2,312	7,152	10,486	9,692	1,677	10,346	3,237	10,514	4,252	5,394	4,956	2,955	11,103	6,785	1,897	2,477	3,537
Quebec, Canada	8,621	17,196	10,722	11,151	12,769	6,763	4,293	10,169	17,919	6,059	3,569	11,033	10,763	8,268	11,403	2,079	12,227	11,032	8,762	5,850
Quetta, Pakistan	3,029	8,258	4,653	734	7,494	11,984	9,997	522	8,871	4,570	11,018	4,919	6,209	6,330	1,372	12,100	5,335	591	2,241	4,984
Quito, Ecuador	12,257	16,674	15,668	15,822	11,658	4,416	8,116	14,947	15,987	10,606	6,883	12,366	11,225	9,698	16,332	4,653	16,809	15,422	13,885	10,127
Rabaul, Papua New Guinea	12,799	3,987	5,815	9,143	13,135	18,225	9,444	9,635	4,360	12,935	10,191	13,307	14,342	15,944	8,429	12,303	4,566	9,721	9,580	13,603
Raiatea (Uturoa)	18,212	9,073	11,242	15,328	15,254	12,107	8,462	15,534	8,810	15,733	8,062	18,138	17,414	17,811	14,598	8,549	10,547	15,940	14,599	15,975
Raleigh, North Carolina	9,846	17,701	11,824	12,523	13,104	6,287	4,737	11,540	18,076	7,385	3,706	11,895	11,392	8,988	12,773	1,457	13,242	12,390	10,125	7,127
Rangiroa (Avatoru)	18,117	9,518	11,456	15,624	15,431	11,762	8,208	15,743	9,257	15,475	7,743	18,388	17,461	17,442	14,896	8,136	10,845	16,243	14,672	15,662
Rangoon, Burma	6,325	5,190	3,011	2,612	8,764	15,086	10,493	3,327	5,916	7,582	11,731	7,199	8,490	9,392	1,954	13,719	2,607	3,153	4,208	8,110
Raoul Is., Kermadec Islands	16,849	6,089	9,973	13,140	13,274	14,024	10,512	13,767	5,778	16,819	10,505	15,466	15,554	17,984	12,468	11,471	8,764	13,650	13,756	17,447
Rarotonga (Avarua)	18,125	8,078	10,817	14,655	14,693	12,807	9,117	15,036	7,804	16,284	8,852	17,341	16,998	18,412	13,932	9,512	9,935	15,239	14,420	16,655
Rawson, Argentina	13,130	12,595	19,248	15,807	8,305	4,726	12,944	15,993	11,778	13,527	11,703	10,658	9,364	9,629	16,389	9,597	17,660	15,236	16,782	12,861
Recife, Brazil	8,642	15,645	15,759	12,195	6,930	498	11,320	11,808	15,033	8,643	10,374	7,543	6,334	5,292	12,923	8,061	16,921	11,591	11,984	7,975
Regina, Canada	10,081	15,095	9,530	11,502	15,198	8,926	2,102	10,573	15,640	7,285	1,111	13,083	13,063	10,558	11,471	1,488	10,791	11,622	8,889	7,326
Reykjavik, Iceland	5,298	14,728	8,263	7,643	10,916	8,046	5,279	6,667	15,508	2,567	5,469	8,336	8,595	6,255	7,961	5,355	9,845	7,499	5,411	2,512
Rhodes, Greece	829	11,737	7,622	4,369	6,933	8,523	9,382	3,698	12,228	2,116	9,877	4,024	4,725	3,350	5,016	9,798	8,729	3,907	3,879	2,012
Richmond, Virginia	9,640	17,676	11,655	12,299	13,046	6,340	4,657	11,317	18,128	7,166	3,666	11,747	11,280	8,857	12,551	1,506	13,092	12,168	9,905	6,914
Riga, USSR	2,927	12,556	6,847	5,140	9,221	9,121	7,083	4,189	13,245	336	7,637	6,325	6,969	5,163	5,550	7,917	8,290	4,938	3,282	1,000
Ringkobing, Denmark	3,418	13,527	7,738	6,070	9,309	8,255	6,893	5,136	14,203	790	7,260	6,560	6,992	4,891	6,509	7,215	9,218	5,825	4,252	661
Rio Branco, Brazil	11,820	16,199	17,009	15,533	10,111	3,148	9,624	14,882	15,393	10,796	8,409	11,163	9,930	8,783	16,213	6,099	18,368	14,987	14,319	10,216
Rio Cuarto, Argentina	12,667	13,725	19,596	15,864	8,680	3,861	12,026	15,762	12,907	12,630	10,785	10,680	9,358	9,188	16,553	8,585	18,759	15,247	16,085	11,977
Rio de Janeiro, Brazil	10,308	14,601	17,583	13,630	7,141	1,787	12,211	13,419	13,849	10,512	11,084	8,577	7,268	6,835	14,352	8,698	18,341	13,009	13,802	9,844
Rio Gallegos, Argentina	13,664	11,636	18,272	15,779	8,246	5,638	13,540	16,204	10,819	14,396	12,319	10,850	9,611	10,215	16,226	10,350	16,685	15,280	17,383	13,727
Rio Grande, Brazil	11,579	13,824	18,895	14,707	7,648	3,051	12,553	14,627	13,023	11,837	11,340	9,529	8,207	8,081	15,401	9,018	18,728	14,090	15,131	11,170
Riyadh, Saudi Arabia	1,376	9,597	6,722	2,649	5,971	9,950	10,813	2,431	10,047	3,977	11,567	3,092	4,284	4,256	3,377	11,887	7,414	2,055	3,613	4,099
Road Town, Brit. Virgin Isls.	9,841	19,235	13,902	13,277	11,160	3,970	7,100	12,385	18,515	8,043	6,041	10,767	9,911	7,842	13,769	3,684	15,429	12,922	11,382	7,570
Roanoke, Virginia	9,830	17,513	11,635	12,426	13,254	6,485	4,534	11,442	17,925	7,327	3,510	11,968	11,502	9,079	12,656	1,297	13,046	12,312	10,001	7,091
Robinson Crusoe Island, Chile	13,952	13,361	18,543	17,205	9,856	5,007	11,418	17,090	12,567	13,555	10,187	12,009	10,690	10,505	17,875	8,214	17,787	16,592	17,103	12,936
Rochester, New York	9,266	17,245	11,042	11,753	13,184	6,785	4,197	10,769	17,839	6,699	3,309	11,612	11,271	8,796	11,974	1,497	12,495	11,654	9,318	6,497
Rockhampton, Australia	13,659	3,032	7,520	9,984	11,744	16,459	11,361	10,705	2,984	14,636	11,928	12,866	13,525	15,822	9,348	13,720	6,051	10,463	11,103	15,272
Rome, Italy	2,310	13,192	8,424	5,726	7,709	7,563	8,484	4,944	13,708	1,542	8,775	5,028	5,389	3,336	6,319	8,408	9,726	5,318	4,661	994
Rosario, Argentina	12,345	13,767	19,545	15,519	8,370	3,603	12,191	15,425	12,950	12,400	10,955	10,337	9,015	8,859	16,210	8,712	18,858	14,903	15,811	11,741
Roseau, Dominica	9,740	19,081	14,250	13,278	10,703	3,481	7,580	12,424	18,269	8,115	6,529	10,437	9,529	7,542	13,816	4,173	15,804	12,880	11,535	7,605
Rostock, East Germany	3,085	13,290	7,661	5,800	9,026	8,311	7,187	4,881	13,946	548	7,580	6,250	6,717	4,679	6,263	7,546	9,109	5,535	4,090	366
Rostov-na-Donu, USSR	1,759	11,245	6,251	3,729	8,216	9,773	8,294	2,835	11,878	1,577	8,989	5,244	6,127	4,873	4,226	9,425	7,502	3,463	2,468	1,987
Rotterdam, Netherlands	3,350	13,814	8,216	6,300	8,955	7,763	7,232	5,400	14,447	1,108	7,509	6,294	6,630	4,442	6,788	7,259	9,673	6,004	4,656	598
Rouyn, Canada	9,004	16,747	10,468	11,295	13,373	7,264	3,742	10,312	17,408	6,354	2,968	11,565	11,344	8,843	11,480	1,609	11,924	11,232	8,816	6,208
Sacramento, California	11,854	13,961	9,745	12,667	16,868	9,831	2,382	11,837	14,300	9,051	1,346	14,954	14,889	12,383	12,455	2,329	10,673	12,925	10,105	9,149
Saginaw, Michigan	9,640	16,842	10,886	11,936	13,697	7,185	3,805	10,954	17,375	7,007	2,847	12,094	11,780	9,299	12,101	1,012	12,284	11,884	9,435	6,850
Saint Denis, Reunion	6,211	6,687	9,071	5,551	2,851	10,228	15,772	6,300	6,620	9,012	16,677	3,418	3,929	6,291	5,886	16,519	8,525	5,213	8,024	8,968
Saint George's, Grenada	9,965	18,721	14,611	13,548	10,582	3,269	7,863	12,714	17,908	8,426	6,784	10,483	9,522	7,628	14,106	4,411	16,162	13,129	11,869	7,902
Saint John, Canada	8,371	17,502	10,925	11,068	12,338	6,394	4,706	10,091	18,268	5,891	4,004	10,662	10,353	7,865	11,366	2,440	12,459	10,908	8,756	5,634
Saint John's, Antigua	9,674	19,259	14,052	13,176	10,831	3,656	7,387	12,308	18,457	7,984	6,345	10,479	9,602	7,567	13,698	3,998	15,603	12,793	11,382	7,486
Saint John's, Canada	7,339	17,262	10,619	10,198	11,465	6,208	5,267	9,236	18,074	4,947	4,773	9,631	9,388	6,885	10,561	3,477	12,199	9,986	8,031	4,638
Saint Louis, Missouri	10,390	16,641	11,216	12,612	14,168	7,299	3,831	11,635	17,012	7,751	2,712	12,776	12,380	9,931	12,733	384	12,521	12,590	10,071	7,600
Saint Paul, Minnesota	10,038	16,132	10,475	11,993	14,435	7,877	3,156	11,026	16,630	7,317	2,122	12,701	12,467	9,971	12,069	661	11,794	12,017	9,419	7,236
Saint Peter Port, UK	3,695	14,342	8,769	6,817	8,912	7,220	7,280	5,934	14,950	1,675	7,439	6,391	6,592	4,276	7,325	6,972	10,235	6,494	5,223	1,113
Saipan (Susupe)	10,980	5,055	3,710	7,581	13,477	18,976	7,995	7,852	5,704	10,713	8,996	12,489	13,762	14,436	6,852	11,348	2,800	8,198	7,486	11,382
Salalah, Oman	2,510	8,517	6,502	2,209	5,547	10,612	11,623	2,455	8,933	5,075	12,489	2,995	4,309	4,934	2,904	12,997	6,908	1,603	4,025	5,232
Salem, Oregon	11,231	13,847	9,147	11,952	16,705	10,078	1,677	11,119	14,287	8,437	668	14,449	14,544	12,047	11,751	2,431	10,163	12,208	9,388	8,578
Salt Lake City, Utah	11,295	14,780	10,093	12,566	16,010	9,086	2,518	11,669	15,149	8,501	1,281	14,221	14,063	11,562	12,457	1,488	11,165	12,739	9,957	8,532
Salta, Argentina	12,374	14,632	18,668	15,870	9,159	3,390	11,177	15,542	13,816	11,966	9,943	10,839	9,525	8,992	16,598	7,696	19,401	15,252	15,501	11,334
Salto, Uruguay	12,040	13,941	19,266	15,252	8,197	3,305	12,183	15,130	13,127	12,107	10,954	10,085	8,763	8,557	15,952	8,675	19,020	14,633	15,505	11,447
Salvador, Brazil	9,279	15,399	16,432	12,779	7,068	646	11,569	12,437	14,717	9,313	10,546	7,978	6,724	5,883	13,509	8,184	17,545	12,168	12,656	8,646
Salzburg, Austria	2,587	13,207	8,004	5,681	8,333	7,960	7,871	4,824	13,796	928	8,219	5,591	6,020	3,992	6,216	8,024	9,378	5,340	4,302	337
Samsun, Turkey	1,061	11,250	6,749	3,747	7,520	9,354	8,934	2,967	11,819	1,895	9,568	4,553	5,414	4,228	4,336	9,814	7,899	3,369	2,994	2,087
San Antonio, Texas	11,660	16,074	11,808	13,775	14,799	7,511	4,222	12,811	16,194	9,022	2,982	13,882	13,321	10,963	13,819	1,132	12,913	13,803	11,187	8,874
San Cristobal, Venezuela	11,185	17,797	14,994	14,703	11,420	4,010	7,673	13,823	17,094	9,484	6,489	11,648	10,617	8,840	15,209	4,129	16,380	14,321	12,802	9,004
San Diego, California	12,304	14,309	10,492	13,387	16,596	9,316	3,126	12,533	14,540	9,507	2,011	15,175	14,893	12,422	13,200	2,151	11,375	13,617	10,805	9,539
San Francisco, California	11,966	13,874	9,754	12,734	16,972	9,895	2,443	11,912	14,202	9,164	1,442	15,075	15,008	12,502	12,509	2,426	10,657	13,001	10,180	9,266
San Jose, Costa Rica	12,093	16,993	14,399	15,303	12,705	5,311	6,835	14,342	16,513	10,032	5,601	12,933	11,934	10,070	15,644	3,396	15,539	15,053	13,025	9,647
San Juan, Argentina	12,960	13,846	19,251	16,254	9,110	4,055	11,673	16,091	13,032	12,742	10,430	11,085	9,763	9,506	16,955	8,272	18,700	15,634	16,254	12,101
San Juan, Puerto Rico	9,972	19,122	13,894	13,384	11,306	4,088	7,012	12,484	18,450	8,137	5,938	10,925	10,069	7,999	13,863	3,572	15,406	13,039	11,450	7,674
San Luis Potosi, Mexico	12,442	15,756	12,377	14,608	14,868	7,462	4,822	13,648	15,716	9,844	3,584	14,416	13,699	11,462	14,624	1,976	13,343	14,646	12,011	9,672
San Marino, San Marino	2,403	13,216	8,292	5,720	7,926	7,684	8,270	4,911	13,758	1,334	8,577	5,226	5,607	3,558	6,294	8,263	9,620	5,334	4,546	770
San Miguel de Tucuman, Argen.	12,454	14,411	18,893	15,889	9,045	3,493	11,382	15,614	13,595	12,133	10,145	10,807	9,488	9,043	16,613	7,910	19,297	15,269	15,655	11,495

Distances in Kilometers	Jerusalem, Israel	Jiggalong, Australia	Jinan, China	Jodhpur, India	Johannesburg, South Africa	Juazeiro do Norte, Brazil	Juneau, Alaska	Kabul, Afghanistan	Kalgoorlie, Australia	Kaliningrad, USSR	Kamloops, Canada	Kampala, Uganda	Kananga, Zaire	Kano, Nigeria	Kanpur, India	Kansas City, Missouri	Kaohsiung, Taiwan	Karachi, Pakistan	Karaganda, USSR	Karl-Marx-Stadt, East Germany
San Salvador, El Salvador	12,251	16,697	13,794	15,186	13,382	5,976	6,209	14,204	16,363	9,993	4,969	13,435	12,506	10,521	15,421	2,864	14,870	15,028	12,759	9,670
Sanaa, Yemen	2,033	9,367	7,487	3,227	4,917	9,539	11,841	3,281	9,702	4,824	12,538	2,097	3,361	3,874	3,941	12,619	7,971	2,606	4,633	4,829
Santa Cruz, Bolivia	11,811	15,427	17,914	15,435	9,279	2,839	10,625	14,971	14,610	11,206	9,409	10,638	9,352	8,537	16,161	7,097	19,369	14,836	14,753	10,584
Santa Cruz, Tenerife	4,928	15,711	11,303	8,603	7,682	4,660	8,826	7,897	15,948	4,146	8,528	6,052	5,624	3,151	9,245	7,132	12,687	8,123	7,609	3,484
Santa Fe, New Mexico	11,515	15,345	10,853	13,145	15,552	8,415	3,269	12,217	15,615	8,764	2,026	14,162	13,815	11,356	13,094	1,075	11,930	13,263	10,532	8,717
Santa Rosa, Argentina	12,810	13,341	19,911	15,847	8,522	4,126	12,358	15,843	12,523	12,924	11,115	10,648	9,331	9,312	16,507	8,941	18,395	15,241	16,324	12,266
Santa Rosalia, Mexico	12,620	14,711	11,252	14,047	16,103	8,720	3,849	13,159	14,829	9,862	2,680	15,179	14,687	12,299	13,903	2,099	12,115	14,230	11,442	9,822
Santarem, Brazil	10,149	17,106	16,121	13,861	9,176	1,784	9,636	13,231	16,310	9,283	8,532	9,718	8,565	7,171	14,545	6,147	17,707	13,318	12,832	8,671
Santiago del Estero, Argentina	12,415	14,316	19,013	15,812	8,914	3,478	11,522	15,567	13,498	12,160	10,286	10,707	9,387	8,987	16,532	8,046	19,284	15,190	15,669	11,517
Santiago, Chile	13,226	13,598	19,238	16,451	9,198	4,342	11,758	16,341	12,786	13,034	10,515	11,262	9,941	9,760	17,135	8,403	18,407	15,835	16,547	12,394
Santo Domingo, Dominican Rep.	10,303	18,791	13,860	13,647	11,672	4,396	6,793	12,727	18,236	8,377	5,684	11,324	10,467	8,395	14,093	3,301	15,327	13,330	11,616	7,939
Sao Paulo de Olivenca, Brazil	11,543	16,861	16,279	15,237	10,534	3,292	8,941	14,487	16,068	10,274	7,738	11,286	10,114	8,721	15,864	5,403	17,672	14,743	13,749	9,723
Sao Paulo, Brazil	10,637	14,638	17,876	13,982	7,445	1,968	12,076	13,759	13,866	10,755	10,923	8,929	7,618	7,173	14,705	8,543	18,687	13,361	14,094	10,089
Sao Tome, Sao Tome & Principe	4,593	12,478	11,788	7,645	3,725	5,182	12,665	7,495	12,382	6,159	12,481	2,878	1,874	1,305	8,369	10,965	12,411	7,024	8,313	5,627
Sapporo, Japan	8,830	7,654	2,192	6,352	13,793	16,032	5,769	6,147	8,421	7,815	6,976	11,502	12,788	12,261	5,746	9,311	2,985	6,928	5,110	8,472
Sarajevo, Yugoslavia	1,990	12,741	7,903	5,242	7,817	8,090	8,409	4,436	13,291	1,220	8,802	5,021	5,522	3,654	5,818	8,629	9,196	4,859	4,135	882
Saratov, USSR	2,370	11,022	5,676	3,613	8,792	10,312	7,824	2,652	11,704	1,734	8,601	5,819	6,754	5,535	4,008	9,258	6,993	3,461	1,916	2,296
Saskatoon, Canada	10,000	14,898	9,298	11,320	15,275	9,128	1,881	10,399	15,463	7,198	965	13,065	13,100	10,602	11,273	1,720	10,559	11,455	8,706	7,265
Schefferville, Canada	7,898	16,462	9,863	10,241	12,652	7,332	3,998	9,257	17,253	5,239	3,553	10,583	10,492	7,987	10,472	2,709	11,399	10,148	7,825	5,099
Seattle, Washington	10,934	13,892	8,974	11,680	16,506	10,074	1,437	10,838	14,371	8,142	372	14,170	14,304	11,817	11,495	2,423	10,039	11,925	9,107	8,290
Sendai, Japan	9,095	7,140	2,115	6,388	13,688	16,565	6,200	6,280	7,901	8,249	7,386	11,581	12,889	12,569	5,744	9,744	2,618	6,984	5,385	8,911
Seoul, South Korea	8,083	6,780	894	5,183	12,481	16,373	7,005	5,137	7,585	7,629	8,235	10,382	11,696	11,587	4,527	10,514	1,776	5,786	4,443	8,298
Sept-Iles, Canada	8,119	16,966	10,376	10,639	12,506	6,876	4,326	9,657	17,749	5,540	3,746	10,621	10,424	7,918	10,903	2,532	11,911	10,514	8,272	5,341
Sevastopol, USSR	1,432	11,591	6,804	4,067	7,859	9,235	8,545	3,233	12,183	1,462	9,152	4,906	5,703	4,330	4,620	9,382	8,030	3,728	3,021	1,688
Seville, Spain	3,803	14,753	9,931	7,368	7,889	6,032	8,373	6,602	15,181	2,782	8,340	5,701	5,626	3,162	7,974	7,417	11,311	6,934	6,233	2,115
Shanghai, China	7,941	6,033	736	4,717	11,759	16,692	7,888	4,846	6,847	7,892	9,119	9,881	11,203	11,421	4,015	11,391	946	5,336	4,486	8,551
Sheffield, United Kingdom	3,785	14,192	8,414	6,698	9,267	7,596	6,919	5,783	14,846	1,443	7,139	6,668	6,942	4,674	7,165	6,827	9,906	6,417	4,948	1,025
Shenyang, China	7,606	7,224	796	4,885	12,324	15,816	6,803	4,744	8,035	7,071	8,044	10,060	11,362	11,103	4,270	10,258	2,146	5,470	3,931	7,740
Shiraz, Iran	1,673	9,362	5,955	2,048	6,703	10,586	10,242	1,663	9,892	3,784	11,086	3,871	5,079	4,942	2,751	11,674	6,728	1,529	2,840	4,041
Sibiu, Romania	1,828	12,336	7,402	4,815	7,983	8,593	8,298	3,978	12,919	1,025	8,783	5,106	5,729	4,029	5,367	8,799	8,694	4,465	3,632	1,002
Singapore	7,924	3,289	4,145	4,305	8,660	15,900	11,671	5,145	4,006	9,464	12,900	7,933	9,085	10,570	3,754	15,156	2,956	4,738	6,117	9,965
Sioux Falls, South Dakota	10,345	15,930	10,493	12,203	14,731	8,049	3,057	11,244	16,383	7,610	1,947	13,030	12,789	10,296	12,247	525	11,764	12,252	9,613	7,545
Skelleftea, Sweden	3,799	12,798	6,658	5,626	10,104	9,380	6,197	4,646	13,545	1,120	6,776	7,213	7,839	5,937	5,935	7,210	8,183	5,515	3,426	1,621
Skopje, Yugoslavia	1,667	12,457	7,801	4,980	7,581	8,220	8,666	4,203	12,993	1,416	9,090	4,749	5,305	3,555	5,575	8,950	9,048	4,578	4,019	1,181
Socotra Island (Tamrida)	2,859	8,289	6,778	2,497	5,134	10,553	12,103	2,867	8,657	5,505	12,969	2,731	4,054	4,943	3,148	13,420	7,066	1,925	4,480	5,628
Sofia, Bulgaria	1,605	12,326	7,633	4,835	7,642	8,389	8,624	4,047	12,873	1,354	9,079	4,783	5,381	3,689	5,423	9,002	8,879	4,444	3,851	1,203
Songkhla, Thailand	7,268	4,035	3,664	3,604	8,647	15,614	11,250	4,416	4,753	8,722	12,491	7,587	8,804	10,079	3,024	14,647	2,714	4,069	5,373	9,230
Sorong, Indonesia	10,636	2,736	4,411	6,925	11,285	18,648	10,344	7,541	3,463	11,406	11,375	10,984	12,093	13,597	6,238	13,732	2,861	7,470	7,863	12,033
South Georgia Island	11,752	11,137	17,209	13,607	6,065	5,223	15,214	14,032	10,358	13,167	13,975	8,709	7,512	8,488	14,099	11,724	16,007	13,098	15,381	12,531
South Pole	13,520	7,412	14,061	12,911	7,105	9,208	16,466	13,824	6,598	16,070	15,616	10,039	9,352	11,331	12,931	14,332	12,505	12,754	15,525	15,638
South Sandwich Islands	11,464	10,513	16,461	12,995	5,498	5,716	15,959	13,496	9,752	13,167	14,722	8,261	7,129	8,366	13,446	12,457	15,287	12,516	14,965	12,564
Split, Yugoslavia	2,102	12,894	8,056	5,400	7,811	7,933	8,402	4,599	13,437	1,280	8,764	5,048	5,506	3,575	5,980	8,535	9,356	5,012	4,292	856
Spokane, Washington	10,793	14,260	9,219	11,748	16,180	9,713	1,635	10,878	14,741	7,992	395	13,951	14,017	11,518	11,604	2,070	10,330	11,959	9,153	8,104
Spoleto, Italy	2,327	13,181	8,352	5,702	7,793	7,630	8,402	4,908	13,709	1,448	8,703	5,100	5,474	3,430	6,287	8,364	9,664	5,303	4,595	901
Springbok, South Africa	7,042	9,907	12,664	8,539	1,074	6,462	16,185	8,917	9,531	9,352	15,842	3,667	2,674	4,719	9,106	13,866	12,372	8,000	10,359	8,930
Springfield, Illinois	10,263	16,635	11,111	12,473	14,133	7,330	3,763	11,495	17,038	7,616	2,668	12,683	12,311	9,852	12,596	431	12,431	12,451	9,934	7,470
Springfield, Massachusetts	9,005	17,594	11,228	11,654	12,757	6,420	4,573	10,673	18,238	6,511	3,723	11,236	10,861	8,396	11,922	1,885	12,717	11,514	9,288	6,265
Srinagar, India	3,688	8,008	3,813	882	8,298	12,682	9,412	519	8,688	4,742	10,500	5,771	7,062	7,097	998	11,829	4,594	1,268	1,755	5,248
Stanley, Falkland Islands	12,906	11,685	18,286	15,044	7,497	5,219	14,019	15,426	10,871	13,834	12,779	10,066	8,825	9,486	15,537	10,674	16,775	14,526	16,620	13,167
Stara Zagora, Bulgaria	1,456	12,134	7,483	4,643	7,601	8,552	8,690	3,858	12,684	1,418	9,177	4,715	5,360	3,757	5,232	9,154	8,712	4,252	3,700	1,347
Stockholm, Sweden	3,322	12,933	7,052	5,562	9,524	8,939	6,738	4,603	13,639	535	7,244	6,666	7,243	5,313	5,951	7,474	8,535	5,374	3,601	1,001
Stornoway, United Kingdom	4,289	14,339	8,253	6,950	9,887	7,834	6,299	6,002	15,049	1,689	6,531	7,273	7,562	5,280	7,358	6,323	9,790	6,727	4,982	1,487
Strasbourg, France	2,966	13,602	8,268	6,075	8,527	7,696	7,662	5,208	14,196	1,113	7,946	5,857	6,203	4,057	6,600	7,659	9,677	5,741	4,613	449
Stuttgart, West Germany	2,885	13,496	8,172	5,969	8,514	7,791	7,678	5,101	14,094	1,022	7,984	5,820	6,192	4,077	6,493	7,732	9,576	5,638	4,510	354
Subic, Philippines	8,692	4,235	2,435	5,051	10,943	17,646	9,482	5,535	5,051	9,282	10,676	9,756	11,023	11,940	4,329	13,026	858	5,644	5,740	9,909
Suchow, China	7,438	6,394	267	4,305	11,524	16,169	7,803	4,370	7,211	7,375	9,044	9,497	10,818	10,928	3,624	11,251	1,324	4,919	3,961	8,033
Sucre, Bolivia	12,072	15,265	18,038	15,692	9,422	3,097	10,632	15,233	14,449	11,449	9,407	10,857	9,564	8,791	16,418	7,122	19,321	15,090	14,997	10,830
Sudbury, Canada	9,242	16,791	10,620	11,533	13,502	7,236	3,749	10,550	17,409	6,597	2,902	11,766	11,511	9,016	11,710	1,379	12,056	11,474	9,044	6,448
Suez, Egypt	325	11,117	7,640	3,978	6,234	8,694	10,148	3,472	11,553	2,914	10,684	3,281	4,114	3,181	4,675	10,609	8,584	3,445	4,042	2,835
Sundsvall, Sweden	3,638	12,977	6,933	5,701	9,866	9,087	6,401	4,729	13,707	874	6,926	7,003	7,585	5,637	6,050	7,232	8,445	5,551	3,607	1,313
Surabaya, Indonesia	9,268	1,983	4,882	5,671	9,133	16,544	12,013	6,506	2,756	10,806	13,168	8,937	9,973	11,726	5,114	15,550	3,406	6,095	7,392	11,321
Suva, Fiji	16,039	5,992	8,849	12,384	14,153	15,022	9,510	12,870	5,880	15,533	9,679	15,805	16,277	18,747	11,673	11,011	7,768	12,952	12,618	16,158
Sverdlovsk, USSR	3,403	10,515	4,685	3,537	9,698	11,278	7,167	2,566	11,261	2,491	8,086	6,749	7,771	6,650	3,724	9,119	6,095	3,590	1,142	3,141
Svobodnyy, USSR	7,509	8,317	1,860	5,370	12,919	14,971	5,747	5,006	9,123	6,479	6,990	10,367	11,608	10,910	4,859	9,156	3,264	5,897	3,802	7,141
Sydney, Australia	14,126	3,178	8,579	10,598	11,057	15,325	12,311	11,412	2,812	15,577	12,733	12,645	13,067	15,533	10,025	14,230	7,061	11,008	12,030	16,169
Sydney, Canada	7,923	17,479	10,828	10,705	11,934	6,262	4,970	9,735	18,289	5,487	4,357	10,199	9,912	7,418	11,036	2,903	12,388	10,519	8,460	5,204
Syktyvkar, USSR	3,510	11,274	5,262	4,269	9,951	10,713	6,692	3,289	12,027	1,920	7,525	6,977	7,881	6,471	4,489	8,408	6,736	4,269	1,908	2,590
Szeged, Hungary	2,065	12,649	7,643	5,127	8,065	8,338	8,180	4,288	13,230	940	8,614	5,234	5,783	3,955	5,677	8,544	8,961	4,776	3,888	737
Szombathely, Hungary	2,336	12,932	7,816	5,408	8,214	8,154	8,008	4,557	13,519	876	8,400	5,425	5,913	3,979	5,948	8,271	9,165	5,064	4,086	483
Tabriz, Iran	1,229	10,325	6,104	2,826	7,366	10,122	9,322	2,089	10,901	2,683	10,086	4,412	5,461	4,730	3,433	10,573	7,133	2,447	2,500	2,976
Tacheng, China	4,363	8,651	3,018	2,434	9,780	13,017	7,865	1,783	9,415	4,345	8,982	7,090	8,320	7,862	2,263	10,492	4,277	2,809	802	4,970
Tahiti (Papeete)	18,358	9,223	11,455	15,545	15,160	11,893	8,520	15,749	8,941	15,792	8,079	18,086	17,270	17,598	14,815	8,484	10,765	16,157	14,789	15,999
Taipei, Taiwan	8,261	5,361	1,357	4,839	11,519	17,181	8,450	5,109	6,175	8,441	9,668	9,892	11,206	11,686	4,114	11,978	295	5,459	4,965	9,092
Taiyuan, China	6,902	6,836	417	3,912	11,298	15,592	7,682	3,882	7,652	6,801	8,925	9,110	10,424	10,401	3,269	11,044	1,844	4,513	3,386	7,458
Tallahassee, Florida	10,630	17,426	12,253	13,282	13,478	6,351	4,879	12,298	17,565	8,174	3,730	12,549	11,946	9,611	13,499	1,344	13,576	13,168	10,838	7,919
Tallinn, USSR	3,171	12,554	6,703	5,206	9,493	9,277	6,823	4,242	13,264	583	7,400	6,590	7,245	5,433	5,581	7,754	8,172	5,039	3,221	1,214
Tamanrasset, Algeria	3,094	13,459	10,278	6,774	5,940	5,904	10,289	6,260	13,680	3,759	10,298	3,842	3,668	1,235	7,478	9,266	11,357	6,219	6,517	3,179
Tampa, Florida	10,680	17,648	12,570	13,460	13,235	6,050	5,208	12,478	17,691	8,294	4,055	12,442	11,781	9,492	13,711	1,670	13,903	13,315	11,059	8,008
Tampere, Finland	3,409	12,635	6,666	5,350	9,728	9,331	6,585	4,377	13,360	779	7,165	6,828	7,475	5,631	5,698	7,555	8,158	5,206	3,272	1,361
Tanami, Australia	11,566	999	6,411	7,979	10,146	16,772	12,216	8,793	1,452	13,029	13,103	10,776	11,584	13,708	7,404	15,296	4,825	8,404	9,523	13,582
Tangier, Morocco	3,799	14,740	10,050	7,401	7,732	5,914	8,539	6,654	15,140	2,913	8,491	5,583	5,478	3,004	8,019	7,526	11,413	6,954	6,335	2,244
Tarawa (Betio)	14,251	6,270	6,937	10,937	15,365	16,399	7,798	11,184	6,497	13,298	8,273	15,621	16,724	17,754	10,207	10,134	6,155	11,552	10,595	13,921
Tashkent, USSR	3,205	8,919	4,112	1,704	8,600	12,092	8,745	757	9,613	3,838	9,769	5,853	7,075	6,706	1,936	10,949	5,159	1,838	991	4,374
Tbilisi, USSR	1,390	10,625	6,082	3,100	7,711	10,051	8,921	2,278	11,227	2,291	9,669	4,744	5,740	4,815	3,659	10,159	7,201	2,777	2,370	2,630
Tegucigalpa, Honduras	12,061	16,911	13,842	15,057	13,201	5,790	6,268	14,079	16,561	9,838	5,032	13,217	12,292	10,302	15,322	2,863	14,966	14,877	12,668	9,502
Tehran, Iran	1,561	9,795	5,779	2,304	7,275	10,545	9,577	1,623	10,372	3,178	10,407	4,374	5,512	5,040	2,929	11,024	6,720	1,917	2,360	3,498
Tel Aviv, Israel	55	11,005	7,340	3,758	6,487	8,959	9,939	3,203	11,474	2,757	10,519	3,522	4,401	3,486	4,441	10,554	8,310	3,248	3,728	2,750
Telegraph Creek, Canada	9,987	13,242	7,768	10,408	16,125	10,789	196	9,588	13,855	7,262	1,069	13,391	13,802	11,435	10,207	3,350	8,935	10,678	7,856	7,515
Teresina, Brazil	9,187	16,392	15,953	12,841	7,861	451	10,578	12,347	15,705	8,806	9,569	8,403	7,225	5,988	13,558	7,220	17,359	12,258	12,284	8,152
Ternate, Indonesia	10,173	2,772	4,113	6,461	10,986	18,398	10,411	7,089	3,548	11,013	11,489	10,555	11,687	13,136	5,778	13,868	2,535	7,004	7,464	11,630
The Valley, Anguilla	9,727	19,299	13,948	13,194	10,993	3,821	7,228	12,313	18,528	7,979	6,181	10,605	9,743	7,684	13,701	3,833	15,490	12,826	11,348	7,494
Thessaloniki, Greece	1,478	12,305	7,777	4,850	7,418	8,267	8,840	4,096	12,829	1,576	9,277	4,570	5,153	3,473	5,458	9,144	8,993	4,433	3,995	1,373
Thimphu, Bhutan	5,242	6,550	2,755	1,662	8,881	14,216	9,653	2,101	7,279	6,238	10,854	6,792	8,114	8,548	937	12,615	3,123	2,282	2,850	6,785
Thunder Bay, Canada	9,560	16,178	10,229	11,549	14,137	7,853	3,129	10,577	16,761	6,836	2,242	12,271	12,095	9,591	11,649	1,116	11,605	11,556	8,991	6,759
Tientsin, China	7,231	6,932	274	4,331	11,726	15,766	7,347	4,263	7,749	6,960	8,590	9,525	10,836	10,735	3,695	10,758	1,853	4,928	3,639	7,624
Tijuana, Mexico	12,316	14,320	10,516	13,409	16,584	9,299	3,150	12,554	14,548	9,521	2,032	15,179	14,890	12,421	13,223	2,148	11,397	13,638	10,826	9,551
Tiksi, USSR	6,810	10,555	3,948	6,076	13,120	12,806	4,244	5,345	11,366	4,929	5,411	10,189	11,195	9,750	5,830	7,263	5,471	6,420	3,664	5,530
Timbuktu, Mali	4,196	14,144	11,385	7,845	5,825	4,797	10,579	7,365	14,221	4,670	10,375	4,307	3,758	1,351	8,558	8,986	12,468	7,275	7,615	4,037
Tindouf, Algeria	4,194	14,912	10,867	7,896	7,115	5,116	9,258	7,238	15,159	3,790	9,081	5,297	4,962	2,458	8,558	7,841	12,163	7,394	7,109	3,123
Tirane, Albania	1,736	12,577	7,957	5,114	7,525	8,064	8,707	4,347	13,101	1,489	9,103	4,721	5,237	3,433	5,715	8,905	9,203	4,703	4,175	1,183

Distances in Kilometers	Jerusalem, Israel	Jiggalong, Australia	Jinan, China	Jodhpur, India	Johannesburg, South Africa	Juazeiro do Norte, Brazil	Juneau, Alaska	Kabul, Afghanistan	Kalgoorlie, Australia	Kaliningrad, USSR	Kamloops, Canada	Kampala, Uganda	Kananga, Zaire	Kano, Nigeria	Kanpur, India	Kansas City, Missouri	Kaohsiung, Taiwan	Karachi, Pakistan	Karaganda, USSR	Karl-Marx-Stadt, East Germany
Tokyo, Japan	9,171	6,840	2,046	6,340	13,541	16,847	6,483	6,286	7,601	8,439	7,662	11,539	12,855	12,663	5,677	10,026	2,377	6,944	5,479	9,104
Toledo, Spain	3,628	14,572	9,612	7,132	8,036	6,350	8,195	6,344	15,042	2,460	8,220	5,739	5,748	3,325	7,723	7,415	11,003	6,717	5,926	1,794
Topeka, Kansas	10,672	16,176	10,979	12,678	14,645	7,734	3,489	11,712	16,534	7,978	2,320	13,189	12,836	10,373	12,740	95	12,223	12,705	10,097	7,872
Toronto, Canada	9,343	17,104	10,956	11,766	13,335	6,927	4,054	10,782	17,688	6,751	3,156	11,736	11,411	8,932	11,969	1,366	12,395	11,682	9,309	6,565
Toulouse, France	3,229	14,103	8,999	6,608	8,195	6,964	7,998	5,789	14,631	1,850	8,144	5,705	5,875	3,568	7,176	7,571	10,391	6,222	5,316	1,182
Tours, France	3,397	14,135	8,755	6,610	8,601	7,214	7,588	5,750	14,715	1,603	7,765	6,061	6,278	3,991	7,142	7,294	10,188	6,264	5,138	971
Townsville, Australia	13,118	2,734	6,937	9,425	11,711	17,004	11,173	10,126	2,847	14,040	11,841	12,567	13,333	15,501	8,778	13,787	5,457	9,917	10,506	14,675
Trenton, New Jersey	9,275	17,645	11,406	11,926	12,887	6,386	4,595	10,945	18,214	6,788	3,682	11,456	11,043	8,593	12,187	1,701	12,874	11,790	9,547	6,540
Tripoli, Lebanon	301	11,009	7,125	3,665	6,761	9,122	9,688	3,050	11,508	2,550	10,293	3,792	4,682	3,718	4,329	10,403	8,138	3,186	3,477	2,598
Tripoli, Libya	2,076	12,972	8,981	5,769	6,729	7,106	9,458	5,128	13,370	2,491	9,688	4,140	4,404	2,363	6,433	9,109	10,145	5,274	5,202	1,992
Tristan da Cunha (Edinburgh)	9,082	11,711	15,559	11,337	3,983	4,292	15,261	11,565	11,095	10,641	14,276	6,198	4,931	5,850	11,952	11,911	15,228	10,760	12,749	10,044
Trondheim, Norway	3,927	13,318	7,183	6,069	10,055	8,873	6,176	5,096	14,057	1,126	6,645	7,236	7,754	5,710	6,412	6,879	8,714	5,918	3,944	1,409
Trujillo, Peru	12,779	15,914	16,456	16,453	11,298	4,380	8,870	15,651	15,185	11,353	7,629	12,405	11,180	9,939	17,042	5,469	17,407	15,979	14,713	10,840
Truk Island (Moen)	12,029	4,803	4,791	8,542	13,743	18,801	8,358	8,878	5,326	11,780	9,221	13,244	14,448	15,440	7,811	11,472	3,776	9,151	8,571	12,448
Truro, Canada	8,176	17,541	10,919	10,926	12,133	6,293	4,857	9,952	18,332	5,724	4,190	10,444	10,137	7,648	11,242	2,658	12,466	10,751	8,649	5,451
Tsingtao, China	7,617	6,582	305	4,590	11,863	16,203	7,481	4,599	7,397	7,398	8,720	9,789	11,107	11,119	3,923	10,947	1,489	5,198	4,061	8,062
Tsitsihar, China	7,401	7,843	1,319	4,997	12,529	15,280	6,285	4,720	8,655	6,622	7,529	10,088	11,359	10,862	4,444	9,696	2,764	5,550	3,684	7,290
Tubuai Island (Mataura)	18,970	8,991	11,825	15,742	14,514	11,722	9,158	16,087	8,638	16,426	8,687	17,445	16,651	17,381	15,018	8,968	11,007	16,327	15,301	16,601
Tucson, Arizona	12,085	14,885	10,899	13,517	16,015	8,739	3,395	12,618	15,093	9,317	2,189	14,763	14,384	11,941	13,401	1,666	11,859	13,684	10,907	9,292
Tulsa, Oklahoma	10,931	16,234	11,258	12,997	14,648	7,604	3,729	12,030	16,522	8,259	2,530	13,349	12,930	10,494	13,062	347	12,472	13,018	10,418	8,134
Tunis, Tunisia	2,366	13,316	8,927	5,976	7,222	7,091	8,964	5,264	13,760	2,142	9,177	4,652	4,896	2,752	6,609	8,618	10,175	5,518	5,148	1,574
Tura, USSR	5,674	9,883	3,270	4,653	11,785	12,915	5,648	3,922	10,698	4,322	6,783	8,914	10,010	8,896	4,440	8,470	4,857	4,994	2,267	4,983
Turin, Italy	2,802	13,605	8,517	6,097	8,158	7,447	8,028	5,269	14,156	1,412	8,278	5,530	5,832	3,664	6,657	7,885	9,888	5,723	4,810	753
Uberlandia, Brazil	10,515	15,175	17,579	13,993	7,789	1,621	11,554	13,673	14,400	10,420	10,413	9,069	7,778	7,111	14,723	8,029	18,774	13,378	13,842	9,760
Ufa, USSR	3,030	10,620	4,974	3,455	9,355	10,996	7,437	2,471	11,345	2,259	8,317	6,398	7,404	6,280	3,717	9,235	6,343	3,441	1,292	2,888
Ujungpandang, Indonesia	9,761	2,029	4,632	6,087	9,898	17,303	11,432	6,849	2,846	11,042	12,546	9,669	10,731	12,406	5,470	14,932	3,071	6,562	7,537	11,604
Ulaanbaatar, Mongolia	6,156	8,020	1,500	3,798	11,346	14,485	6,968	3,448	8,834	5,681	8,188	8,818	10,082	9,643	3,317	10,135	3,048	4,321	2,462	6,346
Ulan-Ude, USSR	6,134	8,433	1,841	4,056	11,577	14,211	6,571	3,607	9,248	5,435	7,783	8,956	10,191	9,585	3,629	9,703	3,419	4,544	2,414	6,104
Uliastay, Mongolia	5,412	8,237	2,062	3,161	10,679	13,907	7,350	2,723	9,037	5,118	8,536	8,087	9,340	8,906	2,766	10,318	3,483	3,645	1,746	5,773
Uranium City, Canada	9,351	14,468	8,548	10,489	15,043	9,552	1,483	9,576	15,122	6,552	1,237	12,566	12,766	10,315	10,435	2,482	9,870	10,639	7,875	6,685
Urumqi, China	4,717	8,177	2,610	2,346	9,840	13,474	8,043	1,887	8,947	4,833	9,196	7,256	8,520	8,222	2,031	10,821	3,806	2,809	1,285	5,455
Ushuaia, Argentina	13,666	11,297	17,949	15,556	8,060	5,876	13,864	16,051	10,480	14,578	12,648	10,734	9,522	10,261	15,963	10,703	16,363	15,084	17,366	13,910
Vaduz, Liechtenstein	2,775	13,468	8,260	5,945	8,337	7,703	7,854	5,094	14,047	1,138	8,150	5,653	6,014	3,900	6,486	7,859	9,644	5,595	4,570	478
Valencia, Spain	3,313	14,260	9,424	6,837	7,847	6,541	8,363	6,062	14,726	2,303	8,438	5,478	5,543	3,167	7,437	7,702	10,784	6,413	5,706	1,634
Valladolid, Spain	3,698	14,619	9,509	7,144	8,237	6,457	7,991	6,334	15,117	2,350	8,026	5,913	5,945	3,529	7,719	7,261	10,921	6,746	5,852	1,693
Valletta, Malta	1,968	12,916	8,681	5,602	7,020	7,374	9,173	4,915	13,359	2,141	9,447	4,361	4,700	2,715	6,246	8,978	9,882	5,133	4,899	1,664
Valparaiso, Chile	13,294	13,623	19,137	16,544	9,299	4,391	11,674	16,418	12,812	13,058	10,431	11,357	10,036	9,834	17,231	8,330	18,375	15,927	16,581	12,421
Vancouver, Canada	10,779	13,824	8,802	11,487	16,451	10,162	1,249	10,647	14,327	7,992	255	14,043	14,219	11,742	11,302	2,525	9,887	11,734	8,915	8,154
Varna, Bulgaria	1,425	11,977	7,276	4,471	7,686	8,759	8,634	3,671	12,541	1,388	9,158	4,775	5,468	3,932	5,050	9,213	8,506	4,095	3,493	1,416
Venice, Italy	2,491	13,240	8,198	5,728	8,093	7,770	8,104	4,899	13,801	1,183	8,423	5,381	5,775	3,726	6,287	8,148	9,547	5,359	4,469	600
Veracruz, Mexico	12,355	16,184	12,915	14,840	14,289	6,878	5,334	13,862	16,044	9,871	4,091	14,034	13,230	11,080	14,938	2,211	13,927	14,804	12,286	9,638
Verona, Italy	2,584	13,346	8,283	5,833	8,121	7,683	8,072	5,004	13,904	1,232	8,372	5,431	5,800	3,715	6,392	8,066	9,640	5,464	4,561	615
Victoria, Canada	10,871	13,810	8,853	11,570	16,519	10,166	1,318	10,733	14,302	8,084	332	14,130	14,296	11,815	11,380	2,520	9,923	11,821	9,001	8,243
Victoria, Seychelles	4,562	7,296	7,342	3,910	3,768	10,481	13,989	4,566	7,464	7,326	14,885	2,601	3,664	5,510	4,362	15,145	7,662	3,495	6,270	7,361
Vienna, Austria	2,421	12,963	7,773	5,436	8,323	8,193	7,899	4,574	13,559	780	8,296	5,532	6,022	4,080	5,966	8,186	9,136	5,104	4,058	385
Vientiane, Laos	6,874	4,985	2,508	3,178	9,419	15,740	10,084	3,782	5,757	7,892	11,327	7,893	9,186	10,034	2,475	13,441	1,916	3,753	4,404	8,458
Villahermosa, Mexico	12,216	16,479	13,193	14,880	13,924	6,513	5,606	13,896	16,283	9,807	4,364	13,737	12,898	10,790	15,034	2,346	14,251	14,795	12,370	9,540
Vilnius, USSR	2,664	12,442	6,881	4,982	8,965	9,081	7,346	4,046	13,113	311	7,899	6,064	6,720	4,959	5,420	8,149	8,294	4,754	3,246	939
Visby, Sweden	3,152	12,911	7,127	5,496	9,335	8,852	6,924	4,547	13,603	352	7,419	6,481	7,053	5,131	5,907	7,606	8,593	5,287	3,616	834
Vitoria, Brazil	9,900	14,758	17,169	13,256	6,955	1,455	12,141	13,020	14,032	10,113	11,051	8,250	6,951	6,435	13,982	8,666	18,011	12,636	13,389	9,444
Vladivostok, USSR	8,165	7,454	1,460	5,584	13,034	15,933	6,262	5,401	8,250	7,377	7,494	10,744	12,036	11,637	4,977	9,769	2,514	6,163	4,453	8,044
Volgograd, USSR	2,038	10,990	5,864	3,513	8,459	10,150	8,137	2,581	11,648	1,770	8,892	5,486	6,423	5,250	3,963	9,471	7,131	3,305	2,082	2,263
Vologda, USSR	3,071	11,712	5,885	4,462	9,529	10,082	6,963	3,482	12,435	1,276	7,692	6,563	7,385	5,853	4,783	8,331	7,329	4,363	2,361	1,943
Vorkuta, USSR	4,396	11,103	4,742	4,623	10,810	11,307	5,968	3,685	11,893	2,662	6,894	7,841	8,776	7,355	4,695	8,047	6,289	4,744	2,033	3,319
Wake Island	12,352	6,863	5,185	9,430	15,726	16,920	6,401	9,473	7,349	11,200	7,184	14,570	15,886	15,805	8,728	9,407	4,818	10,048	8,637	11,825
Wallis Island	16,225	6,709	8,913	12,718	14,915	14,748	8,797	13,091	6,639	15,187	8,914	16,551	17,066	19,506	11,992	10,224	7,986	13,312	12,609	15,762
Walvis Bay, Namibia	6,445	10,548	12,576	8,332	1,421	6,008	15,368	8,594	10,226	8,624	15,062	3,234	2,069	3,921	8,952	13,191	12,503	7,757	9,918	8,174
Warsaw, Poland	2,552	12,686	7,259	5,182	8,718	8,704	7,548	4,272	13,330	277	8,034	5,857	6,445	4,603	5,659	8,131	8,654	4,909	3,589	582
Washington, D.C.	9,519	17,609	11,516	12,150	13,044	6,417	4,570	11,168	18,109	7,027	3,606	11,678	11,240	8,802	12,399	1,518	12,961	12,023	9,752	6,783
Watson Lake, Canada	9,717	13,362	7,723	10,224	15,845	10,666	379	9,387	13,998	6,984	1,179	13,113	13,521	11,160	10,048	3,335	8,937	10,476	7,656	7,234
Weimar, East Germany	2,900	13,345	7,902	5,825	8,707	8,062	7,496	4,934	13,968	744	7,850	5,963	6,392	4,331	6,324	7,708	9,321	5,521	4,267	114
Wellington, New Zealand	16,287	5,360	10,448	12,829	11,785	13,613	12,000	13,635	4,868	17,606	11,980	14,096	14,074	16,496	12,251	12,773	9,038	13,231	14,108	18,264
West Berlin, West Germany	2,903	13,204	7,687	5,696	8,836	8,278	7,379	4,790	13,845	530	7,773	6,056	6,530	4,515	6,177	7,718	9,114	5,413	4,070	190
Wewak, Papua New Guinea	11,960	3,297	5,241	8,270	12,360	18,773	9,871	8,819	3,806	12,397	10,740	12,360	13,419	15,005	7,566	12,969	3,852	8,833	8,927	13,053
Whangarei, New Zealand	16,239	5,299	9,966	12,633	12,293	14,100	11,456	13,377	4,900	17,098	11,507	14,451	14,550	17,021	12,014	12,479	8,608	13,082	13,686	17,768
Whitehorse, Canada	9,716	13,015	7,405	10,032	15,962	11,012	271	9,221	13,657	7,024	1,446	13,153	13,638	11,327	9,825	3,674	8,599	10,311	7,490	7,310
Wichita, Kansas	10,881	16,073	11,048	12,851	14,785	7,795	3,516	11,890	16,395	8,183	2,319	13,387	13,013	10,559	12,898	286	12,260	12,890	10,263	8,080
Willemstad, Curacao	10,616	18,398	13,913	14,106	11,296	3,913	7,443	13,222	17,685	8,883	6,302	11,266	10,303	8,401	14,608	3,916	16,033	13,733	12,215	8,404
Wiluna, Australia	11,084	359	7,011	7,735	8,949	15,670	13,372	8,641	476	12,989	14,304	9,796	10,496	12,752	7,263	16,511	5,447	8,065	9,658	13,446
Windhoek, Namibia	6,318	10,331	12,329	8,098	1,185	6,266	15,435	8,383	10,030	8,570	15,199	3,040	1,933	3,938	8,711	13,391	12,237	7,529	9,739	8,142
Windsor, Canada	9,668	16,978	11,028	12,025	13,608	7,047	3,946	11,042	17,494	7,057	2,975	12,064	11,720	9,248	12,203	1,039	12,429	11,961	9,537	6,884
Winnipeg, Canada	9,818	15,607	9,848	11,513	14,691	8,422	2,571	10,559	16,171	7,045	1,647	12,691	12,598	10,090	11,544	1,215	11,168	11,580	8,916	7,032
Winston-Salem, North Carolina	9,935	17,557	11,755	12,555	13,254	6,422	4,615	11,572	17,926	7,447	3,570	12,027	11,536	9,127	12,788	1,307	13,157	12,437	10,133	7,203
Wroclaw, Poland	2,616	12,945	7,560	5,427	8,631	8,402	7,602	4,533	13,574	465	8,030	5,816	6,337	4,405	5,923	8,012	8,957	5,132	3,890	291
Wuhan, China	7,351	6,014	721	4,045	11,110	16,242	8,295	4,221	6,831	7,522	9,536	9,200	10,522	10,806	3,339	11,735	1,065	4,666	4,028	8,168
Wyndham, Australia	11,170	1,166	5,887	7,538	10,231	17,148	11,893	8,327	1,823	12,528	12,844	10,619	11,511	13,510	6,943	15,116	4,300	7,986	9,009	13,092
Xi'an, China	6,730	6,505	782	3,543	10,830	15,593	8,193	3,627	7,317	6,885	9,435	8,737	10,058	10,203	2,866	11,531	1,702	4,156	3,380	7,528
Xining, China	6,034	6,937	1,361	2,947	10,384	14,908	8,269	2,948	7,736	6,257	9,497	8,144	9,457	9,512	2,317	11,456	2,362	3,547	2,723	6,889
Yakutsk, USSR	7,163	9,499	2,952	5,733	13,143	13,857	4,851	5,157	10,307	5,671	6,078	10,345	11,479	10,362	5,356	8,117	4,431	6,172	3,643	6,310
Yanji, China	8,006	7,393	1,273	5,389	12,838	15,904	6,405	5,216	8,195	7,284	7,640	10,553	11,848	11,486	4,781	9,900	2,403	5,970	4,300	7,952
Yaounde, Cameroon	3,960	12,152	11,127	6,990	3,775	5,782	12,479	6,834	12,138	5,696	12,431	2,374	1,622	959	7,716	11,121	11,763	6,370	7,677	5,208
Yap Island (Colonia)	10,660	4,102	3,686	7,073	12,474	19,644	8,965	7,491	4,799	10,844	9,999	11,719	12,943	13,972	6,346	12,365	2,394	7,673	7,418	11,505
Yaraka, Australia	13,130	2,371	7,382	9,503	11,121	16,436	11,850	10,274	2,317	14,371	12,491	12,195	12,858	15,151	8,896	14,362	5,852	9,952	10,822	14,974
Yarmouth, Canada	8,457	17,653	11,084	11,199	12,298	6,262	4,813	10,223	18,410	6,005	4,078	10,685	10,344	7,865	11,506	2,422	12,616	11,030	8,902	5,734
Yellowknife, Canada	9,214	14,057	8,103	10,147	15,124	9,950	1,193	9,252	14,731	6,431	1,361	12,515	12,815	10,408	10,062	2,921	9,423	10,325	7,537	6,616
Yerevan, USSR	1,252	10,570	6,162	3,054	7,543	10,003	9,089	2,269	11,157	2,404	9,832	4,577	5,582	4,708	3,636	10,294	7,248	2,701	2,481	2,710
Yinchuan, China	6,362	7,013	964	3,387	10,835	15,131	7,899	3,332	7,822	6,384	9,134	8,578	9,888	9,858	2,766	11,156	2,203	3,981	2,906	7,031
Yogyakarta, Indonesia	9,082	2,054	4,971	5,522	8,869	16,281	12,199	6,379	2,791	10,702	13,368	8,676	9,706	11,479	4,989	15,742	3,536	5,926	7,331	11,200
York, United Kingdom	3,787	14,160	8,362	6,671	9,304	7,650	6,882	5,753	14,818	1,409	7,112	6,694	6,978	4,719	7,134	6,823	9,857	6,396	4,905	1,014
Yumen, China	5,606	7,398	1,719	2,738	10,267	14,424	8,106	2,590	8,190	5,755	9,316	7,889	9,189	9,101	2,190	11,175	2,857	3,307	2,223	6,387
Yutian, China	4,272	7,831	3,134	1,432	8,958	13,237	8,937	1,160	8,557	4,968	10,072	6,467	7,759	7,730	1,160	11,585	4,018	1,928	1,596	5,530
Yuzhno-Sakhalinsk, USSR	8,678	8,098	2,409	6,415	13,929	15,595	5,378	6,131	8,866	7,505	6,597	11,500	12,759	12,056	5,846	8,912	3,365	6,971	4,973	8,154
Zagreb, Yugoslavia	2,273	12,961	7,943	5,444	8,066	8,032	8,149	4,612	13,530	1,042	8,522	5,295	5,762	3,813	6,000	8,341	9,276	5,082	4,200	604
Zahedan, Iran	2,465	8,681	5,227	1,249	7,088	11,392	10,171	963	9,254	4,261	11,124	4,409	5,678	5,733	1,944	11,997	5,932	799	2,485	4,612
Zamboanga, Philippines	9,316	3,355	3,337	5,613	10,748	17,983	10,140	6,208	4,167	10,122	11,293	9,958	11,159	12,389	4,916	13,674	1,751	6,172	6,573	10,735
Zanzibar, Tanzania	4,219	8,890	9,342	5,123	2,511	8,671	14,195	5,498	8,930	6,968	14,719	1,026	1,856	3,945	5,723	14,127	9,370	4,572	7,019	6,800
Zaragoza, Spain	3,380	14,300	9,287	6,832	8,082	6,675	8,124	6,031	14,798	2,139	8,215	5,677	5,773	3,409	7,414	7,532	10,674	6,429	5,597	1,472
Zashiversk, USSR	7,480	10,236	3,787	6,465	13,709	13,314	4,002	5,811	11,032	5,635	5,222	10,815	11,859	10,458	6,140	7,257	5,218	6,862	4,191	6,232
Zhengzhou, China	7,119	6,480	369	3,983	11,249	15,900	7,927	4,043	7,296	7,129	9,170	9,178	10,498	10,606	3,307	11,329	1,490	4,596	3,678	7,782
Zurich, Switzerland	2,862	13,556	8,315	6,032	8,384	7,647	7,804	5,178	14,136	1,177	8,086	5,717	6,060	3,921	6,570	7,776	9,708	5,684	4,636	509

Distances in Kilometers	Kasanga, Tanzania	Kashgar, China	Kassel, West Germany	Kathmandu, Nepal	Kayes, Mali	Kazan, USSR	Kemi, Finland	Kenora, Canada	Kerguelen Island	Kerkira, Greece	Kermanshah, Iran	Khabarovsk, USSR	Kharkov, USSR	Khartoum, Sudan	Khon Kaen, Thailand	Kiev, USSR	Kigali, Rwanda	Kingston, Canada	Kingston, Jamaica	Kingstown, Saint Vincent
Kashgar, China	7,036	0	5,179	1,565	8,784	2,678	4,345	10,071	9,878	4,736	2,627	4,726	3,309	4,972	3,648	3,721	6,551	10,332	13,044	12,693
Kassel, West Germany	6,943	5,179	0	6,694	4,499	2,636	1,826	6,703	12,535	1,533	3,550	7,797	1,887	4,462	8,827	1,478	6,216	6,116	8,213	7,540
Kathmandu, Nepal	7,071	1,565	6,694	0	9,924	4,243	5,905	11,421	8,695	6,074	3,703	4,828	4,809	5,584	2,193	5,220	6,755	11,826	14,595	14,232
Kayes, Mali	5,341	8,784	4,499	9,924	0	6,863	6,303	8,299	10,577	4,137	6,238	12,291	5,826	4,722	12,039	5,488	4,921	6,921	6,965	5,376
Kazan, USSR	7,309	2,678	2,636	4,243	6,863	0	1,728	7,832	11,819	2,799	2,387	5,556	1,075	4,676	6,273	1,375	6,628	7,809	10,397	10,036
Kemi, Finland	8,257	4,345	1,826	5,905	6,303	1,728	0	6,177	13,352	2,932	3,809	6,024	1,886	5,609	7,818	1,747	7,531	6,082	8,700	8,488
Kenora, Canada	13,233	10,071	6,703	11,421	8,299	7,832	6,177	0	18,863	8,214	9,950	8,127	7,996	11,106	12,476	7,735	12,580	1,495	3,865	5,067
Kerguelen Island	5,775	9,878	12,535	8,695	10,577	11,819	13,352	18,863	0	11,004	9,546	12,545	11,474	8,075	8,007	11,680	6,459	17,385	15,400	13,996
Kerkira, Greece	5,446	4,736	1,533	6,074	4,137	2,799	2,932	8,214	11,004	0	2,478	8,353	1,727	2,930	8,267	1,462	4,716	7,523	9,312	8,338
Kermanshah, Iran	5,024	2,627	3,550	3,703	6,238	2,387	3,809	9,950	9,546	2,478	0	7,115	1,953	2,534	5,873	2,239	4,391	9,609	11,725	10,816
Khabarovsk, USSR	11,738	4,726	7,797	4,828	12,291	5,556	6,024	8,127	12,545	8,353	7,115	0	6,631	9,622	4,608	6,904	11,277	9,279	11,991	12,989
Kharkov, USSR	6,496	3,309	1,887	4,809	5,826	1,075	1,886	7,996	11,474	1,727	1,953	6,631	0	3,830	6,955	412	5,787	7,709	10,040	9,426
Khartoum, Sudan	2,666	4,972	4,462	5,584	4,722	4,676	5,609	11,106	8,075	2,930	2,534	9,622	3,830	0	7,483	3,868	1,960	10,261	11,438	10,024
Khon Kaen, Thailand	8,359	3,648	8,827	2,193	12,039	6,273	7,818	12,476	8,007	8,267	5,873	4,608	6,955	7,483	0	7,367	8,244	13,287	16,196	16,300
Kiev, USSR	6,526	3,721	1,478	5,220	5,488	1,375	1,747	7,735	11,680	1,462	2,239	6,904	412	3,868	7,367	0	5,805	7,378	9,653	9,016
Kigali, Rwanda	731	6,551	6,216	6,755	4,921	6,628	7,531	12,580	6,459	4,716	4,391	11,277	5,787	1,960	8,244	5,805	0	11,478	11,869	10,208
Kingston, Canada	12,069	10,332	6,116	11,826	6,921	7,809	6,082	1,495	17,385	7,523	9,609	9,279	7,709	10,261	13,287	7,378	11,478	0	2,909	3,740
Kingston, Jamaica	12,197	13,044	8,213	14,595	6,965	10,397	8,700	3,865	15,400	9,312	11,725	11,991	10,040	11,438	16,196	9,653	11,869	2,909	0	1,753
Kingstown, Saint Vincent	10,486	12,693	7,540	14,232	5,376	10,036	8,488	5,067	13,996	8,338	10,816	12,989	9,426	10,024	16,300	9,016	10,208	3,740	1,753	0
Kinshasa, Zaire	1,813	7,864	6,188	8,289	3,606	7,340	7,814	11,787	7,130	4,884	5,420	12,527	6,345	2,907	9,889	6,238	1,662	10,486	10,386	8,673
Kirkwall, United Kingdom	8,073	5,751	1,161	7,313	4,991	3,075	1,595	5,556	13,696	2,693	4,548	7,495	2,682	5,622	9,330	2,326	7,351	5,061	7,384	6,971
Kirov, USSR	7,615	2,825	2,654	4,388	6,987	314	1,525	7,561	12,114	2,983	2,701	5,376	1,289	4,974	6,362	1,528	6,930	7,586	10,224	9,938
Kiruna, Sweden	8,510	4,588	1,932	6,141	6,355	2,002	295	5,883	13,646	3,144	4,104	6,018	2,177	5,871	8,015	2,021	7,783	5,809	8,456	8,301
Kisangani, Zaire	1,191	6,713	5,823	7,071	4,317	6,496	7,247	12,044	6,965	4,363	4,382	11,421	5,586	1,854	8,682	5,557	606	10,903	11,270	9,619
Kishinev, USSR	6,148	3,857	1,484	5,309	5,186	1,706	2,111	7,979	11,389	1,094	2,079	7,259	641	3,499	7,483	401	5,424	7,539	9,696	8,957
Kitchner, Canada	12,398	10,520	6,415	11,993	7,232	8,037	6,314	1,280	17,635	7,835	9,889	9,242	7,976	10,587	13,366	7,653	11,810	332	2,843	3,831
Knoxville, Tennessee	12,815	11,400	7,206	12,866	7,517	8,913	7,188	1,757	17,393	8,580	10,715	9,884	8,822	11,237	14,162	8,488	12,287	1,114	2,111	3,398
Kosice, Czechoslovakia	6,407	4,401	890	5,879	4,833	2,043	1,916	7,487	11,823	1,017	2,661	7,507	1,098	3,813	8,041	697	5,676	6,980	9,099	8,373
Kota Kinabalu, Malaysia	9,559	5,466	10,627	4,042	13,813	8,028	9,472	13,162	7,615	10,116	7,713	5,045	8,774	9,150	1,849	9,184	9,599	14,303	17,006	17,868
Krakow, Poland	6,578	4,477	748	5,972	4,863	2,046	1,772	7,307	12,005	1,165	2,818	7,454	1,168	3,991	8,123	756	5,847	6,811	8,960	8,269
Kralendijk, Bonaire	11,231	13,200	8,112	14,761	6,148	10,523	8,907	4,813	14,355	9,006	11,480	12,903	9,994	10,787	16,696	9,588	10,971	3,641	1,121	772
Krasnodar, USSR	5,977	3,084	2,285	4,503	5,810	1,390	2,474	8,578	10,884	1,680	1,375	6,837	590	3,319	6,685	874	5,279	8,252	10,495	9,773
Krasnoyarsk, USSR	9,099	2,218	5,192	3,200	9,550	2,689	3,654	8,258	11,894	5,471	4,217	2,953	3,746	6,749	4,474	4,064	8,538	8,849	11,746	11,970
Kristiansand, Norway	7,677	5,143	769	6,700	5,116	2,478	1,209	6,124	13,187	2,234	3,919	7,231	2,040	5,145	8,749	1,688	6,948	5,691	8,022	7,559
Kuala Lumpur, Malaysia	7,935	4,789	9,889	3,227	12,410	7,467	9,102	13,936	6,606	9,084	6,609	5,947	8,004	7,691	1,473	8,412	7,991	14,752	17,658	17,412
Kuching, Malaysia	8,854	5,456	10,627	3,936	13,380	8,105	9,657	13,844	6,873	9,939	7,479	5,719	8,743	8,664	1,840	9,155	8,942	14,888	17,709	18,139
Kumasi, Ghana	4,004	8,477	5,054	9,372	1,375	7,029	6,870	9,652	9,233	4,235	5,850	12,586	5,954	3,853	11,335	5,693	3,648	8,291	8,226	6,564
Kumzar, Oman	4,721	2,330	4,810	2,866	7,129	3,320	4,921	11,098	8,499	3,684	1,260	7,056	3,144	2,747	4,910	3,468	4,221	10,845	12,975	11,992
Kunming, China	8,586	2,964	8,086	1,756	11,651	5,479	6,952	11,543	8,890	7,690	5,413	3,839	6,251	7,325	956	6,658	8,362	12,331	15,240	15,435
Kuqa Chang, China	7,663	664	5,566	1,503	9,369	2,966	4,520	9,925	10,139	5,274	3,272	4,082	3,745	5,637	3,314	4,148	7,197	10,335	13,145	12,986
Kurgan, USSR	7,757	1,942	3,641	3,474	7,860	1,018	2,454	8,192	11,638	3,756	2,735	4,652	2,037	5,231	5,374	2,377	7,125	8,390	11,122	10,926
Kuwait, Kuwait	4,560	2,792	4,003	3,644	6,290	2,931	4,358	10,485	8,994	2,799	554	7,427	2,493	2,198	5,756	2,758	3,957	10,100	12,107	11,095
Kuybyshev, USSR	7,066	2,482	2,746	4,039	6,851	291	1,993	8,118	11,527	2,742	2,112	5,645	1,025	4,448	6,107	1,384	6,393	8,074	10,630	10,214
Kyoto, Japan	11,878	5,231	9,103	4,816	13,535	6,678	7,391	9,395	11,410	9,451	7,822	1,500	7,732	10,189	3,863	8,052	11,565	10,646	13,212	14,385
Kzyl-Orda, USSR	6,830	1,049	4,130	2,589	7,863	1,677	3,390	9,347	10,455	3,756	1,956	5,159	2,264	4,474	4,697	2,674	6,253	9,452	12,074	11,650
L'vov, USSR	6,496	4,188	1,039	5,679	5,067	1,806	1,780	7,513	11,833	1,182	2,553	7,279	879	3,875	7,833	471	5,767	7,062	9,247	8,563
La Ceiba, Honduras	13,255	13,632	9,083	15,118	8,055	11,075	9,349	3,835	15,699	10,277	12,629	11,772	10,847	12,514	16,290	10,479	12,951	3,301	1,093	2,770
La Coruna, Spain	6,993	6,749	1,608	8,231	3,219	4,244	3,207	6,267	12,768	2,388	4,827	9,221	3,440	4,944	10,393	3,029	6,319	5,318	6,924	6,038
La Paz, Bolivia	10,733	15,715	10,593	17,031	7,112	13,209	11,787	7,786	11,597	11,002	13,329	15,879	12,424	11,609	19,073	12,016	10,833	6,778	3,932	3,366
La Paz, Mexico	15,580	12,929	9,796	14,026	10,239	10,938	9,323	3,158	17,193	11,265	13,107	9,676	11,154	14,047	14,261	10,890	15,108	3,786	3,539	5,291
La Ronge, Canada	13,575	9,523	6,765	10,773	8,945	7,498	5,944	941	19,291	8,297	9,753	7,220	7,820	11,227	11,648	7,611	12,879	2,379	4,774	6,008
Labrador City, Canada	11,295	9,159	4,981	10,673	6,452	6,614	4,887	1,939	16,995	6,433	8,434	8,571	6,521	9,257	12,255	6,197	10,649	1,198	3,972	4,444
Lagos, Nigeria	3,496	8,064	5,006	8,892	1,847	6,789	6,792	10,028	8,873	4,028	5,440	12,325	5,717	3,338	10,817	5,490	3,108	8,707	8,762	7,111
Lahore, Pakistan	6,381	889	5,631	1,149	8,788	3,327	5,046	10,924	8,994	4,933	2,557	5,361	3,747	4,581	3,337	4,154	5,964	11,103	13,716	13,163
Lambasa, Fiji	15,572	12,296	16,033	11,239	18,853	13,968	14,213	11,115	10,001	16,765	14,891	8,422	15,038	16,490	9,153	15,326	16,090	12,385	11,991	13,523
Lansing, Michigan	12,738	10,690	6,710	12,136	7,560	8,254	6,538	1,094	17,889	8,146	10,160	9,180	8,235	10,915	13,411	7,922	12,149	671	2,838	3,972
Lanzhou, China	9,023	2,462	7,247	1,963	11,212	4,611	5,928	10,330	10,059	7,102	5,086	2,909	5,511	7,326	2,175	5,900	8,674	11,114	14,022	14,335
Laoag, Philippines	10,250	4,887	9,831	3,754	13,644	7,196	8,448	11,724	9,029	9,619	7,407	3,608	8,081	9,287	1,898	8,476	10,141	12,877	15,577	16,531
Largeau, Chad	3,204	5,937	3,802	6,806	3,286	4,901	5,336	10,093	8,963	2,405	3,316	10,316	3,875	1,453	8,822	3,748	2,504	9,076	10,011	8,571
Las Vegas, Nevada	15,430	11,551	8,917	12,617	10,265	9,710	8,179	2,251	18,478	10,440	11,987	8,345	10,054	13,349	12,952	9,839	14,806	3,376	4,264	5,934
Launceston, Australia	11,483	11,490	16,631	9,951	16,377	14,134	15,581	15,261	5,865	15,614	13,196	10,031	14,747	13,188	7,862	15,154	12,083	16,482	15,114	15,847
Le Havre, France	7,096	5,874	695	7,387	4,028	3,317	2,298	6,341	12,810	1,909	4,161	8,321	2,578	4,766	9,522	2,167	6,383	5,616	7,570	6,849
Leipzig, East Germany	6,865	4,986	198	6,498	4,609	2,460	1,759	6,846	12,415	1,427	3,362	7,683	1,690	4,351	8,634	1,280	6,136	6,289	8,408	7,736
Leningrad, USSR	7,582	3,887	1,609	5,451	6,075	1,209	718	6,867	12,637	2,373	3,098	6,218	1,168	4,923	7,469	1,056	6,861	6,691	9,205	8,834
Leon, Spain	6,772	6,585	1,496	8,051	3,171	4,123	3,181	6,498	12,547	2,158	4,609	9,204	3,279	4,700	10,223	2,870	6,093	5,561	7,154	6,237
Lerwick, United Kingdom	8,124	5,621	1,186	7,185	5,142	2,943	1,434	5,571	13,710	2,715	4,486	7,330	2,597	5,644	9,188	2,253	7,399	5,125	7,494	7,112
Lhasa, China	7,674	1,762	6,937	604	10,400	4,387	5,973	11,189	9,025	6,452	4,162	4,265	5,071	6,155	1,892	5,482	7,359	11,727	14,576	14,423
Libreville, Gabon	2,599	7,987	5,665	8,605	2,776	7,102	7,359	10,974	7,932	4,471	5,425	12,507	6,060	3,044	10,367	5,895	2,309	9,658	9,607	7,916
Lilongwe, Malawi	675	7,359	7,608	7,223	5,891	7,860	8,883	13,893	5,104	6,104	5,527	11,993	7,092	3,275	8,304	7,143	1,392	12,696	12,632	10,895
Lima, Peru	11,773	15,979	10,807	17,493	7,807	13,325	11,748	7,059	12,446	11,450	13,884	14,996	12,689	12,445	19,519	12,277	11,833	6,233	3,324	3,289
Limerick, Ireland	7,753	6,316	1,250	7,861	4,247	3,674	2,346	5,639	13,494	2,613	4,798	8,281	3,090	5,467	9,944	2,692	7,048	4,917	6,968	6,377
Limoges, France	6,712	5,941	861	7,419	3,677	3,473	2,626	6,671	12,450	1,673	4,050	8,636	2,632	4,441	9,583	2,222	6,006	5,874	7,679	6,846
Limon, Costa Rica	12,814	14,116	9,324	15,649	7,778	11,489	9,781	4,536	14,947	10,398	12,827	12,528	11,151	12,387	17,012	10,765	12,588	3,846	1,112	2,402
Lincoln, Nebraska	13,766	11,080	7,556	12,414	8,580	8,827	7,156	1,011	18,565	9,035	10,898	8,882	8,947	11,866	13,355	8,667	13,169	1,697	3,165	4,612
Linz, Austria	6,503	4,914	481	6,394	4,436	2,499	2,041	7,185	12,061	1,066	3,119	7,865	1,607	3,992	8,556	1,199	5,774	6,586	8,616	7,860
Lisbon, Portugal	6,682	7,057	2,018	8,498	2,698	4,635	3,699	6,552	12,441	2,502	4,979	9,721	3,763	4,800	10,681	3,359	6,032	5,501	6,861	5,839
Little Rock, Arkansas	13,587	11,698	7,816	13,086	8,285	9,331	7,625	1,680	17,798	9,236	11,272	9,660	9,344	11,956	14,121	9,033	13,054	1,713	2,408	3,934
Liverpool, United Kingdom	7,576	5,935	882	7,477	4,386	3,301	2,049	5,901	13,275	2,316	4,430	8,041	2,705	5,213	9,566	2,308	6,862	5,246	7,350	6,759
Lodz, Poland	6,765	4,489	693	6,001	4,969	1,991	1,593	7,146	12,179	1,351	2,937	7,334	1,195	4,175	8,137	787	6,035	6,679	8,877	8,232
Lome, Togo	3,694	8,272	5,068	9,121	1,662	6,932	6,869	9,901	8,991	4,154	5,646	12,480	5,858	3,575	11,056	5,616	3,329	8,559	8,543	6,883
London, United Kingdom	7,289	5,818	669	7,345	4,233	3,222	2,114	6,186	12,986	2,037	4,206	8,136	2,546	4,926	9,462	2,140	6,573	5,508	7,545	6,886
Londonderry, United Kingdom	7,891	6,141	1,195	7,693	4,513	3,480	2,094	5,568	13,602	2,649	4,732	8,010	2,961	5,545	9,753	2,575	7,179	4,923	7,079	6,557
Longlac, Canada	12,695	9,968	6,289	11,383	7,727	7,609	5,915	572	18,294	7,779	9,631	8,409	7,683	10,640	12,613	7,397	12,054	980	3,632	4,672
Lord Howe Island, Australia	12,934	11,629	16,698	10,203	17,884	14,065	15,137	13,747	7,389	16,251	13,783	9,182	14,922	14,353	8,015	15,326	13,493	15,035	14,244	15,437
Los Angeles, California	15,796	11,732	9,263	12,733	10,612	9,982	8,480	2,613	18,177	10,789	12,283	8,338	10,361	13,703	12,932	10,156	15,173	3,737	4,476	6,175
Louangphrabang, Laos	8,380	3,315	8,487	1,919	11,827	5,915	7,443	12,119	8,333	7,980	5,621	4,333	6,625	7,347	387	7,036	8,220	12,906	15,814	15,930
Louisville, Kentucky	12,936	11,199	7,136	12,644	7,671	8,750	7,030	1,458	17,684	8,543	10,617	9,585	8,704	11,256	13,886	8,382	12,383	1,021	2,407	3,689
Luanda, Angola	1,972	8,376	6,670	8,738	3,746	7,886	8,328	12,023	6,869	5,403	5,958	13,058	6,887	3,437	10,249	6,772	2,013	10,666	10,319	8,581
Lubumbashi, Zaire	537	7,563	7,191	7,606	5,173	7,739	8,596	13,264	5,693	5,729	5,495	12,272	6,885	3,067	8,857	6,886	1,112	12,019	11,904	10,170
Lusaka, Zambia	830	7,836	7,615	7,784	5,478	8,125	9,013	13,641	5,302	6,152	5,853	12,515	7,288	3,462	8,914	7,298	1,502	12,364	12,095	10,349
Luxembourg, Luxembourg	6,878	5,458	306	6,962	4,213	2,937	2,095	6,660	12,535	1,555	3,734	8,089	2,154	4,463	9,106	1,742	6,156	5,998	8,002	7,277
Luxor, Egypt	3,782	4,297	3,458	5,206	4,752	3,597	4,497	10,157	9,093	1,947	1,686	8,769	2,717	1,116	7,287	2,753	3,070	9,449	10,993	9,772
Lynn Lake, Canada	13,247	9,325	6,443	10,615	8,652	7,236	5,658	899	18,977	7,975	9,467	7,232	7,528	10,904	11,586	7,310	12,550	2,215	4,762	5,908
Lyon, France	6,553	5,682	708	7,151	3,792	3,252	2,528	6,882	12,263	1,408	3,770	8,503	2,378	4,223	9,320	1,971	5,839	6,123	7,958	7,121
Macapa, Brazil	9,160	13,094	8,008	14,450	4,644	10,642	9,348	6,885	12,161	8,387	10,758	14,594	9,813	9,329	16,631	9,408	9,031	5,507	3,449	1,835
Madison, Wisconsin	13,114	10,744	6,964	12,148	7,955	8,380	6,680	842	18,249	8,425	10,365	8,969	8,425	11,232	13,300	8,127	12,515	1,047	3,023	4,277
Madras, India	5,932	2,956	7,549	1,703	9,841	5,441	7,167	13,022	7,013	6,563	4,092	6,364	5,716	5,148	2,455	6,102	5,790	13,239	15,755	14,884
Madrid, Spain	6,486	6,557	1,583	7,994	2,973	4,165	3,339	6,778	12,261	2,011	4,485	9,357	3,269	4,447	10,178	2,868	5,809	5,816	7,322	6,337
Madurai, India	5,589	3,281	7,670	2,108	9,698	5,677	7,404	13,350	6,638	6,601	4,157	6,783	5,874	4,980	2,772	6,248	5,485	13,486	15,878	14,862
Magadan, USSR	12,454	5,509	7,228	6,019	11,646	5,476	5,403	6,533	14,130	8,128	7,496	1,597	6,506	10,015	6,149	6,679	11,872	7,717	10,395	11,448

Distances in Kilometers	Kasanga, Tanzania	Kashgar, China	Kassel, West Germany	Kathmandu, Nepal	Kayes, Mali	Kazan, USSR	Kemi, Finland	Kenora, Canada	Kerguelen Island	Kerkira, Greece	Kermanshah, Iran	Khabarovsk, USSR	Kharkov, USSR	Khartoum, Sudan	Khon Kaen, Thailand	Kiev, USSR	Kigali, Rwanda	Kingston, Canada	Kingston, Jamaica	Kingstown, Saint Vincent
Magdalena, Bolivia	10,369	15,160	10,052	16,481	6,571	12,675	11,287	7,597	11,703	10,445	12,778	15,724	11,874	11,109	18,591	11,468	10,423	6,497	3,734	2,946
Magdeburg, East Germany	6,971	5,013	177	6,534	4,660	2,460	1,683	6,745	12,520	1,534	3,439	7,633	1,731	4,457	8,661	1,325	6,242	6,200	8,345	7,698
Majuro Atoll, Marshall Isls.	15,631	9,958	13,295	9,245	17,599	11,258	11,469	9,716	11,456	14,051	12,572	5,703	12,334	14,824	7,491	12,593	15,688	11,191	12,064	13,817
Malabo, Equatorial Guinea	2,827	7,797	5,273	8,496	2,515	6,793	6,999	10,639	8,276	4,126	5,206	12,246	5,741	2,913	10,332	5,562	2,451	9,346	9,423	7,759
Male, Maldives	4,896	3,938	7,875	2,911	9,359	6,136	7,843	13,934	5,940	6,661	4,326	7,616	6,180	4,660	3,492	6,524	4,873	13,885	15,955	14,680
Manado, Indonesia	10,450	6,490	11,607	5,113	14,904	8,980	10,325	13,203	7,725	11,182	8,799	5,302	9,783	10,222	2,926	10,190	10,557	14,518	16,817	18,257
Managua, Nicaragua	13,185	14,002	9,361	15,503	8,078	11,421	9,699	4,240	15,309	10,506	12,896	12,155	11,153	12,626	16,691	10,777	12,930	3,677	1,207	2,723
Manama, Bahrain	4,375	2,780	4,437	3,441	6,548	3,282	4,765	10,908	8,594	3,208	959	7,485	2,912	2,211	5,492	3,188	3,819	10,535	12,520	11,464
Manaus, Brazil	10,096	14,030	8,877	15,447	5,701	11,485	10,072	6,731	12,439	9,372	11,778	14,776	10,723	10,384	17,640	10,314	10,017	5,498	2,976	1,806
Manchester, New Hampshire	11,674	10,301	5,892	11,824	6,498	7,724	5,998	1,915	16,959	7,257	9,417	9,541	7,550	9,939	13,399	7,203	11,096	429	2,817	3,451
Mandalay, Burma	7,843	2,720	7,898	1,258	11,155	5,368	6,955	11,986	8,345	7,331	4,954	4,530	6,022	6,692	940	6,434	7,639	12,632	15,513	15,404
Mangareva Island, Fr.Polynesia	16,202	16,590	15,646	15,966	14,036	16,366	15,039	9,010	11,607	17,028	18,748	11,895	16,925	18,471	13,969	16,724	16,799	9,536	7,789	8,972
Manila, Philippines	10,236	5,176	10,181	3,963	13,885	7,545	8,829	12,076	8,708	9,912	7,649	3,978	8,408	9,429	1,959	8,807	10,173	13,256	15,913	16,928
Mannheim, West Germany	6,789	5,299	217	6,799	4,287	2,797	2,043	6,791	12,419	1,423	3,566	8,007	1,992	4,344	8,946	1,580	6,065	6,152	8,171	7,443
Maputo, Mozambique	1,943	8,533	8,855	8,196	6,535	9,190	10,199	14,803	4,106	7,376	6,846	13,024	8,422	4,599	8,933	8,465	2,671	13,455	12,766	11,020
Mar del Plata, Argentina	9,325	16,024	11,848	16,395	7,540	14,386	13,448	10,380	9,008	11,670	13,420	18,462	13,365	11,071	16,949	13,018	9,671	9,305	6,518	5,675
Maracaibo, Venezuela	11,576	13,527	8,473	15,091	6,537	10,848	9,210	4,822	14,416	9,394	11,865	12,947	10,350	11,185	16,947	9,947	11,336	3,750	985	1,164
Marrakech, Morocco	6,086	7,384	2,615	8,739	1,935	5,134	4,387	7,162	11,791	2,666	5,093	10,403	4,172	4,469	10,932	3,790	5,474	6,005	7,009	5,788
Marseilles, France	6,297	5,738	943	7,178	3,579	3,385	2,769	7,104	12,023	1,279	3,712	8,713	2,456	4,007	9,359	2,060	5,586	6,300	8,038	7,131
Maseru, Lesotho	2,340	9,123	9,105	8,818	6,398	9,648	10,550	14,696	4,179	7,670	7,338	13,645	8,828	4,999	9,538	8,839	3,041	13,280	12,328	10,598
Mashhad, Iran	5,781	1,480	4,263	2,600	7,385	2,303	3,995	10,134	9,554	3,479	1,160	6,103	2,416	3,528	4,791	2,804	5,225	10,051	12,456	11,749
Mazatlan, Mexico	15,224	13,059	9,664	14,231	9,887	10,955	9,303	3,127	17,066	11,105	13,051	9,995	11,102	13,824	14,596	10,818	14,781	3,587	3,135	4,888
Mbabane, Swaziland	1,976	8,644	8,858	8,329	6,447	9,252	10,230	14,729	4,171	7,390	6,918	13,155	8,468	4,640	9,080	8,501	2,699	13,366	12,630	10,886
Mbandaka, Zaire	1,712	7,291	5,740	7,762	3,637	6,774	7,312	11,616	7,337	4,381	4,835	11,944	5,792	2,326	9,435	5,702	1,332	10,386	10,552	8,878
McMurdo Sound, Antarctica	10,041	14,229	16,914	12,747	12,994	16,585	18,168	15,594	4,819	15,480	14,365	14,133	16,283	12,642	11,139	16,452	10,772	15,439	12,610	12,399
Mecca, Saudi Arabia	3,442	3,967	4,228	4,635	5,462	3,886	5,052	10,925	8,390	2,761	1,593	8,628	3,184	1,005	6,619	3,318	2,798	10,284	11,856	10,600
Medan, Indonesia	7,612	4,589	9,642	3,024	12,074	7,265	8,924	13,959	6,518	8,795	6,317	6,064	7,761	7,353	1,493	8,166	7,657	14,687	17,567	17,133
Medellin, Colombia	11,955	14,163	9,128	15,729	7,064	11,487	9,834	5,140	14,210	10,042	12,516	13,246	11,004	11,753	17,490	10,601	11,774	4,210	1,307	1,749
Medicine Hat, Canada	14,209	10,065	7,432	11,248	9,435	8,129	6,600	1,160	19,943	8,964	10,406	7,412	8,480	11,893	11,944	8,276	13,521	2,646	4,660	6,057
Medina, Saudi Arabia	3,757	3,785	3,933	4,562	5,442	3,560	4,719	10,619	8,712	2,494	1,309	8,398	2,849	1,228	6,605	2,987	3,099	10,014	11,680	10,484
Melbourne, Australia	11,470	11,087	16,250	9,557	16,535	13,719	15,146	15,188	5,964	15,319	12,871	9,613	14,363	13,024	7,451	14,773	12,039	16,499	15,411	16,245
Memphis, Tennessee	13,380	11,621	7,651	13,032	8,078	9,218	7,505	1,668	17,706	9,060	11,123	9,721	9,203	11,764	14,140	8,886	12,848	1,538	2,307	3,783
Merauke, Indonesia	11,962	8,479	13,489	7,146	16,887	10,855	12,017	13,204	7,915	13,201	10,838	6,331	11,733	12,167	4,965	12,131	12,214	14,691	15,883	17,622
Merida, Mexico	13,542	13,148	8,824	14,591	8,248	10,660	8,933	3,226	16,345	10,105	12,369	11,126	10,520	12,524	15,653	10,170	13,169	2,851	1,385	3,137
Meridian, Mississippi	13,312	11,895	7,798	13,325	7,984	9,455	7,734	1,993	17,388	9,175	11,300	10,050	9,397	11,819	14,468	9,069	12,811	1,691	1,990	3,514
Messina, Italy	5,412	5,145	1,535	6,474	3,738	3,164	3,129	8,101	11,065	409	2,850	8,707	2,101	3,006	8,667	1,803	4,687	7,328	8,997	7,972
Mexico City, Mexico	14,549	13,467	9,571	14,770	9,259	11,159	9,455	3,396	16,517	10,929	13,074	10,768	11,161	13,470	15,377	10,840	14,180	3,465	2,361	4,103
Miami, Florida	12,556	12,370	7,795	13,887	7,225	9,783	8,061	2,936	16,307	9,031	11,344	11,062	9,546	11,425	15,324	9,180	12,137	2,075	929	2,427
Midway Islands, USA	16,320	9,354	11,171	9,256	15,051	9,715	9,414	7,181	13,975	12,289	11,661	4,629	10,731	14,194	8,189	10,873	15,904	8,674	10,072	11,769
Milan, Italy	6,364	5,371	651	6,828	3,948	2,998	2,447	7,146	12,031	1,094	3,429	8,347	2,078	3,966	9,002	1,678	5,642	6,430	8,299	7,455
Milford Sound, New Zealand	12,705	13,064	18,239	11,563	16,663	15,618	16,771	14,074	6,931	17,325	14,908	10,794	16,369	14,740	9,416	16,781	13,374	15,037	13,399	14,228
Milwaukee, Wisconsin	12,998	10,723	6,883	12,140	7,834	8,336	6,630	903	18,144	8,336	10,299	9,028	8,362	11,133	13,329	8,059	12,402	930	2,968	4,187
Minsk, USSR	6,919	3,940	1,254	5,473	5,538	1,396	1,338	7,304	12,115	1,691	2,659	6,784	737	4,272	7,584	435	6,195	6,976	9,314	8,760
Mogadiscio, Somalia	1,961	5,174	6,405	5,110	6,388	5,962	7,264	13,104	6,166	4,890	3,575	9,819	5,382	2,055	6,487	5,541	1,760	12,315	13,320	11,762
Mombasa, Kenya	1,061	6,087	6,773	6,026	5,998	6,685	7,847	13,369	5,770	5,240	4,317	10,746	5,998	2,311	7,307	6,101	1,092	12,390	12,956	11,300
Monclova, Mexico	14,640	12,651	9,040	13,919	9,298	10,431	8,753	2,609	17,379	10,468	12,463	9,946	10,521	13,175	14,548	10,225	14,167	2,945	2,713	4,448
Moncton, Canada	11,140	9,754	5,261	11,294	6,063	7,145	5,426	2,241	16,626	6,625	8,791	9,347	6,935	9,326	12,969	6,583	10,540	943	3,308	3,668
Monrovia, Liberia	4,935	9,292	5,330	10,290	902	7,581	7,149	9,023	9,843	4,800	6,684	13,087	6,521	4,837	12,308	6,211	4,633	7,595	7,265	5,576
Monte Carlo, Monaco	6,258	5,568	858	7,008	3,709	3,228	2,673	7,185	11,962	1,136	3,551	8,585	2,290	3,922	9,189	1,896	5,542	6,413	8,192	7,298
Monterrey, Mexico	14,562	12,782	9,085	14,067	9,222	10,531	8,844	2,724	17,218	10,497	12,532	10,121	10,596	13,171	14,722	10,292	14,108	2,975	2,570	4,313
Montevideo, Uruguay	9,238	15,794	11,497	16,300	7,221	14,051	13,085	10,111	9,237	11,356	13,174	18,234	13,041	10,875	17,095	12,687	9,548	9,000	6,246	5,343
Montgomery, Alabama	13,090	11,842	7,647	13,295	7,760	9,366	7,641	2,048	17,251	9,007	11,164	10,149	9,275	11,624	14,516	8,939	12,592	1,568	1,857	3,325
Montpelier, Vermont	11,757	10,210	5,873	11,724	6,611	7,650	5,923	1,767	17,102	7,259	9,386	9,380	7,504	9,972	13,268	7,164	11,168	313	2,939	3,614
Montpellier, France	6,390	5,839	956	7,287	3,546	3,459	2,778	6,993	12,126	1,406	3,836	8,747	2,549	4,122	9,466	2,149	5,682	6,178	7,912	7,013
Montreal, Canada	11,827	10,115	5,850	11,622	6,714	7,573	5,845	1,634	17,232	7,255	9,348	9,224	7,454	9,995	13,137	7,119	11,229	269	3,064	3,772
Moosonee, Canada	12,250	9,695	5,862	11,147	7,324	7,272	5,563	993	17,900	7,343	9,239	8,436	7,298	10,196	12,496	7,001	11,606	843	3,708	4,577
Moroni, Comoros	1,375	6,599	7,703	6,290	6,690	7,493	8,734	14,293	4,838	6,171	5,107	11,107	6,867	3,241	7,257	6,992	1,812	13,270	13,572	11,858
Moscow, USSR	7,142	3,342	1,912	4,896	6,191	724	1,322	7,495	12,037	2,219	2,491	6,161	646	4,476	6,968	757	6,433	7,324	9,802	9,353
Mosul, Iraq	5,115	2,893	3,136	4,064	5,912	2,206	3,498	9,597	9,858	2,066	422	7,226	1,617	2,526	6,248	1,865	4,450	9,213	11,303	10,403
Mount Isa, Australia	11,560	9,377	14,531	7,921	16,876	11,910	13,221	14,310	6,849	13,962	11,498	7,680	12,685	12,348	5,740	13,095	11,955	15,803	16,216	17,672
Multan, Pakistan	6,073	1,110	5,541	1,375	8,550	3,342	5,070	11,039	8,828	4,762	2,340	5,668	3,670	4,284	3,533	4,070	5,653	11,148	13,690	13,046
Munich, West Germany	6,560	5,114	383	6,596	4,296	2,679	2,109	7,058	12,164	1,161	3,308	7,998	1,806	4,088	8,757	1,397	5,833	6,425	8,422	7,658
Murcia, Spain	6,138	6,485	1,700	7,883	2,799	4,189	3,509	7,123	11,913	1,032	4,307	9,497	3,238	4,126	10,075	2,851	5,462	6,145	7,566	6,511
Murmansk, USSR	8,592	4,145	2,330	5,682	6,810	1,679	507	6,153	13,476	3,362	3,953	5,521	2,120	5,929	7,505	2,069	7,873	6,201	8,914	8,821
Mururoa Atoll, Fr. Polynesia	16,481	16,186	15,756	15,535	14,442	16,185	14,978	9,066	11,617	17,207	18,510	11,513	16,854	18,886	13,550	16,704	17,116	9,684	8,077	9,319
Muscat, Oman	4,637	2,404	5,180	2,717	7,374	3,651	5,275	11,452	8,170	4,034	1,631	7,105	3,512	2,868	4,680	3,839	4,188	11,216	13,336	12,319
Myitkyina, Burma	8,087	2,540	7,707	1,231	11,147	5,136	6,680	11,597	8,743	7,231	4,914	4,158	5,848	6,792	1,140	6,258	7,845	12,271	15,165	15,159
Naga, Philippines	10,455	5,423	10,403	4,221	14,141	7,767	9,022	12,077	8,744	10,159	7,905	4,019	8,642	9,684	2,209	9,039	10,406	13,296	15,884	17,004
Nagasaki, Japan	11,337	4,840	9,025	4,298	13,365	6,512	7,383	9,866	10,894	9,238	7,459	1,797	7,539	9,757	3,271	7,882	11,053	11,065	13,711	14,785
Nagoya, Japan	11,984	5,320	9,141	4,920	13,585	6,733	7,419	9,325	11,490	9,512	7,906	1,489	7,790	10,282	3,968	8,107	11,668	10,588	13,134	14,328
Nagpur, India	6,181	2,054	6,791	962	9,500	4,574	6,295	12,123	7,883	5,931	3,459	5,787	4,926	4,943	2,553	5,324	5,918	12,353	14,947	14,261
Nairobi, Kenya	1,013	6,023	6,375	6,094	5,594	6,421	7,510	12,940	6,181	4,844	4,084	10,727	5,683	1,926	7,506	5,762	755	11,950	12,558	10,923
Nanchang, China	9,953	3,839	8,613	2,995	12,614	5,984	7,193	10,811	9,802	8,509	6,444	2,748	6,910	8,562	1,905	7,295	9,710	11,833	14,664	15,366
Nancy, France	6,786	5,482	376	6,978	4,126	2,985	2,187	6,733	12,453	1,487	3,710	8,172	2,174	4,384	9,129	1,762	6,065	6,051	8,019	7,267
Nandi, Fiji	15,314	12,218	16,137	11,116	19,015	13,983	14,312	11,366	9,753	16,768	14,791	8,457	15,046	16,287	9,009	15,351	15,834	12,642	12,230	13,744
Nanjing, China	10,287	3,921	8,488	3,255	12,630	5,884	6,989	10,365	10,264	8,498	6,547	2,284	6,853	8,763	2,364	7,224	10,007	11,417	14,224	15,003
Nanning, China	9,081	3,567	8,646	2,376	12,276	6,022	7,432	11,655	8,883	8,300	6,038	3,703	6,832	7,928	911	7,236	8,897	12,564	15,456	15,868
Nantes, France	6,963	6,082	923	7,579	3,747	3,559	2,580	6,408	12,708	1,925	4,269	8,604	2,775	4,705	9,730	2,363	6,259	5,613	7,455	6,668
Naples, Italy	5,727	5,148	1,221	6,526	3,839	3,026	2,855	7,803	11,374	501	2,969	8,535	1,990	3,307	8,718	1,651	5,002	7,059	8,810	7,850
Narvik, Norway	8,599	4,716	1,954	6,268	6,340	2,135	424	5,753	13,768	3,213	4,228	6,059	2,296	5,967	8,131	2,128	7,871	5,676	8,329	8,189
Nashville, Tennessee	13,066	11,445	7,367	12,886	7,773	8,998	7,278	1,636	17,592	8,762	10,856	9,754	8,947	11,451	14,097	8,622	12,531	1,251	2,240	3,608
Nassau, Bahamas	12,272	12,341	7,661	13,876	6,945	9,725	8,011	3,116	16,074	8,859	11,205	11,240	9,441	11,194	15,412	9,067	11,862	2,126	786	2,146
Natal, Brazil	7,330	12,234	7,625	13,313	3,450	10,182	9,272	8,379	10,574	7,557	9,668	15,183	9,196	7,831	15,314	8,828	7,260	6,910	5,271	3,558
Natashquan, Canada	10,938	9,249	4,829	10,788	6,011	6,647	4,925	2,324	16,578	6,233	8,339	8,948	6,463	8,996	12,472	6,119	10,309	1,292	3,814	4,109
Nauru Island	15,032	10,133	13,992	9,217	18,455	11,755	12,175	10,671	10,502	14,545	12,756	6,238	12,820	14,756	7,278	13,123	15,229	12,137	12,809	14,545
Ndjamena, Chad	2,891	6,674	4,376	7,465	2,880	5,665	6,006	10,343	8,647	3,083	4,066	11,092	4,627	1,928	9,410	4,477	2,276	9,203	9,799	8,253
Nelson, New Zealand	13,282	13,282	18,345	11,826	16,996	15,725	16,654	13,494	7,508	17,765	15,300	10,631	16,584	15,300	9,649	16,990	13,954	14,474	12,962	13,914
Nema, Mauritania	5,058	8,283	4,127	9,416	509	6,414	5,948	8,420	10,473	3,661	5,730	11,890	5,365	4,251	11,533	5,039	4,586	7,093	7,349	5,805
Neuquen, Argentina	10,214	16,938	12,511	17,264	8,337	15,114	13,991	10,166	9,360	12,473	14,322	17,883	14,135	11,994	17,359	13,768	10,580	9,252	6,369	5,811
New Delhi, India	6,424	1,213	6,062	803	9,127	3,751	5,465	11,284	8,684	5,334	2,922	5,359	4,179	4,798	2,952	4,585	6,057	11,509	14,145	13,589
New Glasgow, Canada	10,973	9,721	5,157	11,268	5,888	7,097	5,383	2,416	16,451	6,503	8,696	9,439	6,856	9,182	12,984	6,498	10,376	1,103	3,328	3,598
New Haven, Connecticut	11,803	10,522	6,104	12,043	6,588	7,947	6,221	1,921	16,974	7,459	9,634	9,684	7,771	10,119	13,598	7,423	11,238	439	2,610	3,320
New Orleans, Louisiana	13,483	12,182	8,085	13,603	8,144	9,751	8,030	2,232	17,243	9,452	11,592	10,226	9,692	12,068	14,690	9,363	13,004	1,985	1,888	3,502
New Plymouth, New Zealand	13,506	13,224	18,197	11,795	17,225	15,609	16,457	13,281	7,735	17,804	15,326	10,435	16,508	15,466	9,609	16,908	14,171	14,295	12,886	13,905
New York, New York	11,898	10,618	6,217	12,135	6,671	8,049	6,323	1,889	17,019	7,572	9,746	9,717	7,880	10,229	13,670	7,533	11,338	442	2,532	3,298
Newcastle upon Tyne, UK	7,665	5,793	847	7,342	4,579	3,145	1,854	5,872	13,333	2,343	4,370	7,843	2,596	5,261	9,416	2,208	6,947	5,272	7,445	6,901
Newcastle Waters, Australia	11,021	8,669	13,840	7,197	16,261	11,237	12,614	14,445	6,677	13,225	10,759	7,301	11,978	11,649	5,024	12,390	11,366	15,932	16,834	18,393
Niamey, Niger	4,026	7,688	4,245	8,667	1,467	6,170	6,048	9,340	9,580	3,376	5,069	11,727	5,095	3,283	10,707	4,834	3,528	8,071	8,409	6,843
Nicosia, Cyprus	4,835	3,771	2,619	4,952	5,022	2,585	3,459	9,290	10,034	1,287	1,257	7,944	1,664	2,169	7,129	1,712	4,123	8,728	10,599	9,592
Niue (Alofi)	16,197	13,383	16,420	12,390	17,686	14,791	14,699	10,602	10,436	17,539	16,003	9,252	15,863	17,620	10,321	16,082	16,832	11,728	10,968	12,424

Distances in Kilometers	Kasanga, Tanzania	Kashgar, China	Kassel, West Germany	Kathmandu, Nepal	Kayes, Mali	Kazan, USSR	Kemi, Finland	Kenora, Canada	Kerguelen Island	Kerkira, Greece	Kermanshah, Iran	Khabarovsk, USSR	Kharkov, USSR	Khartoum, Sudan	Khon Kaen, Thailand	Kiev, USSR	Kigali, Rwanda	Kingston, Canada	Kingston, Jamaica	Kingstown, Saint Vincent
Norfolk, Virginia	12,124	11,090	6,652	12,605	6,833	8,520	6,794	2,050	16,937	7,980	10,191	10,055	8,338	10,580	14,106	7,987	11,596	820	2,090	3,024
Norfolk Island, Australia	13,802	12,154	16,955	10,808	18,389	14,410	15,214	12,933	8,180	16,877	14,468	9,190	15,365	15,233	8,616	15,748	14,377	14,172	13,383	14,668
Noril'sk, USSR	9,658	3,400	4,383	4,631	8,882	2,443	2,610	6,791	13,268	5,102	4,636	3,418	3,461	7,078	5,966	3,644	9,007	7,346	10,245	10,547
Norman Wells, Canada	13,471	8,222	6,546	9,330	9,681	6,576	5,279	2,545	18,007	8,025	8,950	5,588	7,138	10,870	10,036	7,026	12,740	3,838	6,404	7,561
Normanton, Australia	11,808	9,252	14,367	7,832	17,075	11,734	12,982	13,945	7,210	13,901	11,460	7,352	12,550	12,455	5,641	12,957	12,172	15,440	16,026	17,589
North Pole	10,940	5,631	4,317	6,935	8,406	3,823	2,701	4,485	15,488	5,619	6,205	4,627	4,463	8,278	8,184	4,415	10,220	5,103	8,012	8,549
Nottingham, United Kingdom	7,464	5,834	752	7,372	4,368	3,212	2,017	6,029	13,153	2,187	4,302	8,028	2,590	5,088	9,471	2,190	6,748	5,379	7,471	6,861
Norway House, Canada	13,236	9,631	6,531	10,948	8,487	7,472	5,857	521	19,009	8,058	9,657	7,610	7,709	10,978	11,959	7,471	12,556	1,886	4,384	5,547
Norwich, United Kingdom	7,340	5,687	582	7,220	4,384	3,079	1,956	6,183	13,011	2,030	4,131	7,978	2,430	4,941	9,328	2,028	6,621	5,547	7,638	7,012
Nouakchott, Mauritania	5,951	8,913	4,314	10,150	629	6,807	6,068	7,676	11,198	4,190	6,447	12,091	5,811	5,160	12,310	5,446	5,508	6,292	6,410	4,875
Noumea, New Caledonia	14,083	11,590	16,221	10,321	19,113	13,728	14,458	12,507	8,639	16,323	14,020	8,437	14,719	15,142	8,147	15,087	14,587	13,838	13,449	14,896
Novosibirsk, USSR	8,513	1,805	4,697	3,040	8,978	2,121	3,288	8,384	11,654	4,873	3,592	3,587	3,156	6,125	4,611	3,492	7,935	8,834	11,688	11,737
Nuku'alofa, Tonga	15,657	13,063	16,630	11,974	18,158	14,712	14,840	11,136	9,927	17,510	15,647	9,157	15,785	17,043	9,862	16,057	16,267	12,297	11,563	12,997
Nukunono Island, Tokelau Isls.	16,809	12,556	15,333	11,741	17,829	13,729	13,594	9,894	11,207	16,441	15,175	8,226	14,792	17,287	9,804	14,992	17,300	11,148	10,864	12,473
Nuremberg, West Germany	6,708	5,115	236	6,612	4,390	2,635	1,982	6,929	12,302	1,298	3,382	7,902	1,807	4,228	8,763	1,395	5,980	6,318	8,359	7,631
Nyala, Sudan	2,373	5,855	4,572	6,499	3,941	5,284	5,970	10,982	8,093	3,092	3,336	10,451	4,335	915	8,377	4,288	1,651	9,973	10,813	9,305
Oaxaca, Mexico	14,311	13,701	9,626	15,047	9,065	11,326	9,610	3,637	16,199	10,941	13,156	11,126	11,270	13,388	15,733	10,935	13,981	3,561	2,117	3,834
Ocean Falls, Canada	14,775	9,577	7,836	10,574	10,430	8,018	6,688	2,324	18,771	9,348	10,390	6,377	8,561	12,240	10,974	8,430	14,051	3,819	5,820	7,265
Odense, Denmark	7,336	5,040	458	6,583	4,917	2,413	1,389	6,436	12,857	1,894	3,657	7,394	1,836	4,807	8,672	1,456	6,607	5,955	8,203	7,654
Odessa, USSR	6,084	3,718	1,641	5,160	5,283	1,643	2,186	8,109	11,273	1,164	1,927	7,199	567	3,427	7,337	441	5,364	7,686	9,853	9,111
Ogbomosho, Nigeria	3,502	7,871	4,812	8,720	1,850	6,579	6,592	9,947	8,963	3,819	5,246	12,115	5,507	3,185	10,668	5,280	3,074	8,649	8,801	7,171
Okha, USSR	12,194	5,161	7,598	5,459	12,084	5,578	5,782	7,354	13,331	8,332	7,380	786	6,643	9,913	5,385	6,869	11,674	8,537	11,215	12,265
Okinawa (Naha)	11,074	4,986	9,515	4,187	13,708	6,934	7,950	10,617	10,168	9,575	7,607	2,556	7,920	9,758	2,788	8,286	10,870	11,827	14,450	15,545
Oklahoma City, Oklahoma	14,025	11,676	8,057	13,002	8,744	9,411	7,730	1,606	18,129	9,512	11,448	9,346	9,503	12,292	13,873	9,212	13,472	2,034	2,816	4,395
Old Crow, Canada	13,408	7,759	6,573	8,797	10,011	6,306	5,153	3,176	17,418	8,000	8,693	4,957	6,962	10,760	9,422	6,893	12,681	4,445	7,035	8,178
Olympia, Washington	15,076	10,240	8,196	11,256	10,396	8,587	7,182	2,112	19,060	9,725	10,938	7,025	9,066	12,647	11,630	8,906	14,370	3,577	5,283	6,810
Omaha, Nebraska	13,695	11,024	7,480	12,364	8,517	8,760	7,087	952	18,562	8,958	10,825	8,869	8,875	11,790	13,328	8,594	13,096	1,626	3,165	4,591
Omsk, USSR	8,054	1,736	4,143	3,180	8,376	1,533	2,856	8,336	11,588	4,266	3,069	4,179	2,551	5,597	4,965	2,895	7,449	8,647	11,440	11,344
Oodnadatta, Australia	10,972	9,649	14,823	8,130	16,310	12,272	13,717	15,139	6,028	14,021	11,546	8,423	12,939	12,057	6,007	13,350	11,429	16,624	16,564	17,663
Oradea, Romania	6,218	4,377	1,020	5,833	4,757	2,106	2,094	7,661	11,640	845	2,535	7,610	1,105	3,625	8,006	733	5,488	7,131	9,204	8,436
Oran, Algeria	5,917	6,567	1,915	7,934	2,590	4,341	3,734	7,332	11,691	1,860	4,313	9,702	3,361	3,975	10,127	2,986	5,249	6,319	7,639	6,522
Oranjestad, Aruba	11,426	13,264	8,206	14,827	6,332	10,585	8,952	4,699	14,494	9,131	11,601	12,808	10,083	10,957	16,710	9,679	11,163	3,570	947	958
Orebro, Sweden	7,645	4,718	958	6,278	5,438	2,047	870	6,354	13,023	2,214	3,622	6,875	1,694	5,053	8,316	1,385	6,914	6,015	8,417	7,989
Orel, USSR	6,818	3,364	1,819	4,896	5,959	904	1,574	7,713	11,779	1,926	2,243	6,432	325	4,152	7,010	474	6,107	7,473	9,872	9,336
Orsk, USSR	7,117	1,877	3,360	3,440	7,377	804	2,512	8,526	11,208	3,243	2,093	5,257	1,580	4,581	5,492	1,967	6,479	8,581	11,199	10,826
Osaka, Japan	11,856	5,225	9,123	4,796	13,550	6,691	7,415	9,438	11,367	9,462	7,820	1,537	7,743	10,181	3,827	8,066	11,547	10,689	13,255	14,428
Oslo, Norway	7,794	4,968	961	6,530	5,362	2,293	958	6,119	13,234	2,349	3,871	6,980	1,952	5,228	8,556	1,632	7,064	5,757	8,157	7,747
Osorno, Chile	10,592	17,398	12,939	17,586	8,802	15,555	14,370	10,225	9,380	12,938	14,788	17,624	14,591	12,440	17,302	14,219	10,984	9,398	6,495	6,073
Ostrava, Czechoslovakia	6,579	4,597	643	6,090	4,759	2,162	1,816	7,252	12,043	1,144	2,910	7,550	1,287	4,010	8,243	876	5,848	6,731	8,855	8,152
Ottawa, Canada	11,992	10,186	5,984	11,682	6,875	7,664	5,937	1,489	17,380	7,398	9,470	9,178	7,567	10,149	13,154	7,238	11,392	146	3,042	3,830
Ouagadougou, Bourkina Fasso	4,286	8,078	4,433	9,077	1,098	6,480	6,253	9,181	9,720	3,681	5,465	12,031	5,407	3,692	11,121	5,128	3,834	7,867	8,063	6,469
Oujda, Morocco	5,908	6,723	2,065	8,083	2,436	4,504	3,879	7,331	11,676	2,009	4,452	9,857	3,523	4,033	10,276	3,148	5,250	6,287	7,539	6,395
Oxford, United Kingdom	7,357	5,883	747	7,414	4,236	3,279	2,133	6,107	13,060	2,118	4,288	8,149	2,618	5,003	9,525	2,213	6,642	5,425	7,466	6,818
Pago Pago, American Samoa	16,536	13,005	15,895	12,100	17,800	14,289	14,167	10,246	10,823	17,014	15,632	8,766	15,356	17,533	10,092	15,563	17,116	11,435	10,901	12,436
Pakxe, Laos	8,635	3,965	9,140	2,533	12,387	6,568	8,084	12,547	7,997	8,607	6,219	4,570	7,275	7,821	348	7,686	8,542	13,429	16,331	16,572
Palembang, Indonesia	8,166	5,542	10,626	3,979	12,920	8,220	9,854	14,503	6,145	9,775	7,297	6,410	8,743	8,205	2,150	9,150	8,306	15,426	18,328	18,112
Palermo, Italy	5,478	5,326	1,498	6,664	3,583	3,297	3,165	7,983	11,163	592	3,043	8,825	2,245	3,125	8,857	1,927	4,757	7,181	8,812	7,780
Palma, Majorca	6,076	6,114	1,410	7,516	3,105	3,832	3,235	7,233	11,841	1,481	3,959	9,186	2,870	3,935	9,707	2,486	5,382	6,327	7,869	6,857
Palmerston North, New Zealand	13,492	13,408	18,389	11,970	17,055	15,802	16,640	13,278	7,717	17,953	15,479	10,620	16,696	15,523	9,787	17,098	14,167	14,252	12,761	13,746
Panama, Panama	12,421	14,079	9,170	15,634	7,425	11,422	9,734	4,733	14,677	10,182	12,634	12,796	11,022	12,068	17,184	10,628	12,207	3,919	1,042	2,052
Paramaribo, Suriname	9,710	12,927	7,760	14,382	4,878	10,360	8,947	6,100	12,949	8,323	10,765	13,903	9,617	9,600	16,566	9,206	9,513	4,737	2,709	1,048
Paris, France	6,948	5,746	580	7,250	4,020	3,216	2,286	6,508	12,651	1,735	3,994	8,303	2,442	4,599	9,395	2,030	6,233	5,791	7,734	6,991
Patna, India	6,950	1,761	6,849	235	9,970	4,431	6,106	11,655	8,461	6,179	3,774	5,003	4,962	5,557	2,100	5,372	6,660	12,050	14,803	14,389
Patrai, Greece	5,263	4,636	1,740	5,941	4,192	2,817	3,073	8,428	10,795	217	2,310	8,372	1,742	2,725	8,133	1,522	4,533	7,740	9,509	8,510
Peking, China	10,208	3,438	7,670	3,159	11,934	5,104	6,118	9,617	10,923	7,800	6,037	1,765	6,113	8,399	2,917	6,467	9,837	10,594	13,448	14,123
Penrhyn Island (Omoka)	17,827	13,703	15,177	13,094	16,352	14,301	13,694	8,946	12,055	16,609	16,216	9,101	15,271	18,663	11,261	15,343	18,506	10,038	9,411	10,977
Peoria, Illinois	13,198	11,006	7,167	12,413	7,986	8,630	6,925	1,080	18,111	8,613	10,592	9,194	8,657	11,392	13,552	8,352	12,618	1,145	2,798	4,116
Perm', USSR	7,710	2,498	3,041	4,053	7,344	501	1,853	7,761	11,978	3,298	2,721	5,056	1,576	5,103	5,992	1,862	7,043	7,863	10,546	10,307
Perth, Australia	9,022	8,915	13,799	7,351	14,354	11,583	13,254	16,818	4,287	12,651	10,274	9,113	11,974	10,304	5,529	12,362	9,500	18,275	18,017	17,903
Peshawar, Pakistan	6,346	723	5,259	1,489	8,490	2,966	4,689	10,621	9,253	4,586	2,252	5,397	3,375	4,404	3,682	3,782	5,888	10,758	13,349	12,793
Petropavlovsk-Kamchatskiy,USSR	13,199	6,183	8,087	6,503	12,470	6,340	6,265	6,713	14,099	9,003	8,302	1,727	7,376	10,832	6,298	7,554	12,650	8,017	10,519	11,750
Petrozavodsk, USSR	7,798	3,743	1,903	5,308	6,379	1,086	656	6,827	12,732	2,659	3,188	5,913	1,321	5,133	7,282	1,289	7,082	6,732	9,315	9,018
Pevek, USSR	12,610	6,111	6,491	6,951	10,670	5,313	4,737	5,122	15,441	7,645	7,599	3,019	6,215	9,988	7,438	6,286	11,939	6,268	8,986	9,997
Philadelphia, Pennsylvania	12,003	10,734	6,346	12,247	6,760	8,171	6,445	1,869	17,058	7,701	9,875	9,764	8,008	10,353	13,759	7,661	11,448	488	2,438	3,268
Phnom Penh, Kampuchea	8,460	4,210	9,388	2,718	12,446	6,849	8,403	12,952	7,598	8,777	6,352	4,961	7,511	7,811	585	7,922	8,412	13,826	16,731	16,882
Phoenix, Arizona	15,345	11,887	9,023	12,991	10,096	9,961	8,388	2,320	18,218	10,532	12,195	8,756	10,249	13,411	13,364	10,013	14,758	3,281	3,906	5,600
Pierre, South Dakota	13,889	10,710	7,448	12,002	8,816	8,545	6,908	748	19,056	8,954	10,691	8,388	8,738	11,836	12,875	8,480	13,257	1,896	3,658	5,073
Pinang, Malaysia	7,831	4,498	9,600	2,936	12,191	7,176	8,813	13,725	6,776	8,809	6,336	5,798	7,715	7,480	1,249	8,123	7,855	14,497	17,396	17,128
Pitcairn Island (Adamstown)	15,780	17,109	15,522	16,498	13,547	16,597	15,136	9,007	11,522	16,793	18,945	12,396	16,999	17,934	14,473	16,738	16,338	9,413	7,486	8,580
Pittsburgh, Pennsylvania	12,408	10,826	6,613	12,309	7,175	8,317	6,591	1,537	17,433	8,004	10,115	9,566	8,219	10,704	13,702	7,886	11,844	511	2,506	3,536
Plymouth, Montserrat	10,641	12,428	7,308	13,981	5,439	9,758	8,177	4,674	14,370	8,183	10,657	12,583	9,193	10,016	15,995	8,785	10,323	3,335	1,556	407
Plymouth, United Kingdom	7,358	6,124	963	7,650	4,042	3,527	2,368	6,039	13,094	2,228	4,473	8,375	2,847	5,067	9,768	2,439	6,651	5,296	7,264	6,582
Ponape Island	14,203	8,865	12,897	7,981	17,387	10,547	11,111	10,644	10,499	13,318	11,488	5,100	11,601	13,551	6,115	11,921	14,263	12,139	13,386	15,133
Ponce, Puerto Rico	11,122	12,553	7,505	14,117	5,892	9,875	8,245	4,314	14,775	8,467	10,927	12,330	9,378	10,420	16,025	8,976	10,792	3,051	1,078	789
Ponta Delgada, Azores	7,802	8,312	3,135	9,811	2,938	5,741	4,460	5,498	13,414	3,930	6,396	10,266	5,007	6,181	11,960	4,595	7,212	4,269	5,411	4,450
Pontianak, Indonesia	8,717	5,537	10,695	4,001	13,325	8,198	9,771	14,046	6,666	9,965	7,496	5,922	8,809	8,604	1,956	9,220	8,825	15,075	17,910	18,230
Port Augusta, Australia	11,041	10,204	15,365	8,672	16,319	12,842	14,306	15,344	5,829	14,479	12,016	8,975	13,478	12,342	6,570	13,888	11,549	16,785	16,215	17,130
Port Blair, India	7,171	3,506	8,543	1,946	11,190	6,176	7,850	13,168	7,141	7,730	5,258	5,660	6,661	6,512	1,213	7,066	7,094	13,728	16,539	16,053
Port Elizabeth, South Africa	2,881	9,645	9,578	9,287	6,641	10,190	11,063	14,895	3,969	8,166	7,884	14,114	9,360	5,535	9,891	9,362	3,575	13,437	12,230	10,531
Port Hedland, Australia	9,426	7,965	13,065	6,408	14,700	10,639	12,230	15,633	5,393	12,146	9,679	7,797	11,184	10,207	4,414	11,589	9,786	17,013	18,398	19,211
Port Louis, Mauritius	3,117	6,877	9,197	6,087	8,458	8,449	9,931	15,897	3,425	7,684	6,130	10,791	8,050	4,807	6,399	8,258	3,599	15,018	15,233	13,486
Port Moresby, Papua New Guinea	12,672	9,105	13,988	7,827	17,643	11,377	12,407	12,828	8,324	13,841	11,529	6,532	12,305	12,926	5,664	12,693	12,951	14,323	15,197	16,909
Port Said, Egypt	4,399	4,031	2,909	5,108	4,820	3,023	3,878	9,610	9,675	1,453	1,423	8,329	2,106	1,735	7,256	2,134	3,684	8,974	10,698	9,595
Port Sudan, Sudan	3,177	4,304	4,272	4,956	5,197	4,133	5,216	10,974	8,293	2,768	1,897	8,959	3,372	668	6,913	3,470	2,511	10,263	11,707	10,396
Port-au-Prince, Haiti	11,729	12,792	7,859	14,354	6,489	10,124	8,450	3,990	15,183	8,908	11,342	12,099	9,709	10,975	16,101	9,315	11,395	2,876	476	1,329
Port-of-Spain, Trin. & Tobago	10,479	12,937	7,773	14,467	5,449	10,287	8,752	5,293	13,793	8,534	11,010	13,253	9,659	10,130	16,557	9,248	10,231	3,991	1,837	278
Port-Vila, Vanuatu	14,499	11,442	15,839	10,254	19,640	13,436	14,043	12,007	9,146	16,129	13,953	8,043	14,461	15,323	8,112	14,809	14,962	13,364	13,172	14,707
Portland, Maine	11,574	10,194	5,770	11,720	6,416	7,610	5,886	1,963	16,906	7,136	9,296	9,499	7,431	9,822	13,315	7,083	10,992	505	2,910	3,490
Portland, Oregon	15,195	10,407	8,333	11,417	10,449	8,753	7,339	2,152	19,005	9,864	11,101	7,156	9,225	12,789	11,763	9,061	14,493	3,596	5,204	6,756
Porto, Portugal	6,835	6,884	1,789	8,347	2,972	4,419	3,436	6,410	12,605	2,419	4,883	9,455	3,579	4,859	10,521	3,170	6,171	5,411	6,903	5,951
Porto Alegre, Brazil	8,812	15,146	10,791	15,804	6,514	13,340	12,398	9,826	9,428	10,650	12,519	17,891	12,331	10,283	16,980	11,976	9,064	8,621	5,986	4,902
Porto Alexandre, Angola	2,247	9,029	7,440	9,263	4,217	8,665	9,114	12,509	6,362	6,191	6,683	13,744	7,673	4,150	10,602	7,562	2,516	11,094	10,415	8,662
Porto Novo, Benin	3,572	8,127	5,011	8,965	1,771	6,825	6,803	9,970	8,927	4,057	5,503	12,367	5,752	3,416	10,897	5,519	3,190	8,643	8,680	7,027
Porto Velho, Brazil	10,426	14,780	9,633	16,173	6,336	12,242	10,817	7,135	12,130	10,102	12,483	15,256	11,477	10,961	18,357	11,067	10,422	6,005	3,283	2,442
Portsmouth, United Kingdom	7,261	5,908	744	7,432	4,135	3,321	2,219	6,184	12,973	2,053	4,263	8,240	2,628	4,923	9,554	2,221	6,548	5,478	7,479	6,800
Poznan, Poland	6,880	4,652	528	6,171	4,906	2,118	1,552	6,976	12,334	1,443	3,122	7,388	1,370	4,310	8,299	966	6,150	6,495	8,692	8,061
Prague, Czechoslovakia	6,686	4,862	377	6,362	4,595	2,388	1,846	7,048	12,218	1,241	3,173	7,700	1,555	4,157	8,510	1,143	5,956	6,488	8,583	7,879
Praia, Cape Verde Islands	6,563	9,761	4,997	11,024	1,302	7,564	6,674	7,391	11,472	5,026	7,322	12,670	6,601	6,003	13,189	6,223	6,189	5,939	5,682	4,074
Pretoria, South Africa	1,939	8,763	8,731	8,512	6,180	9,247	10,157	14,473	4,417	7,285	6,941	13,330	8,428	4,599	9,331	8,442	2,641	13,093	12,327	10,582
Prince Albert, Canada	13,726	9,734	6,947	10,977	9,020	7,710	6,152	870	19,482	8,479	9,960	7,364	8,025	11,407	11,819	7,812	13,036	2,351	4,640	5,921

Distances in Kilometers

	Kasanga, Tanzania	Kashgar, China	Kassel, West Germany	Kathmandu, Nepal	Kayes, Mali	Kazan, USSR	Kemi, Finland	Kenora, Canada	Kerguelen Island	Kerkira, Greece	Kermanshah, Iran	Khabarovsk, USSR	Kharkov, USSR	Khartoum, Sudan	Khon Kaen, Thailand	Kiev, USSR	Kigali, Rwanda	Kingston, Canada	Kingston, Jamaica	Kingstown, Saint Vincent
Prince Edward Island	4,274	10,256	11,185	9,509	8,366	11,390	12,517	16,522	2,358	9,713	9,007	14,097	10,703	6,908	9,521	10,774	5,004	15,030	13,327	11,759
Prince George, Canada	14,453	9,502	7,525	10,567	10,056	7,824	6,440	1,987	19,037	9,045	10,180	6,521	8,321	11,952	11,091	8,173	13,733	3,476	5,590	6,983
Prince Rupert, Canada	14,659	9,313	7,717	10,296	10,468	7,802	6,512	2,481	18,556	9,218	10,181	6,105	8,375	12,089	10,698	8,258	13,931	3,967	6,061	7,475
Providence, Rhode Island	11,675	10,418	5,971	11,945	6,472	7,833	6,109	1,990	16,893	7,323	9,504	9,667	7,645	9,981	13,529	7,295	11,107	494	2,690	3,326
Provo, Utah	14,925	11,143	8,372	12,281	9,830	9,214	7,659	1,713	18,971	9,895	11,468	8,194	9,529	12,805	12,793	9,306	14,286	2,913	4,149	5,745
Puerto Aisen, Chile	10,409	17,379	13,294	17,254	9,040	15,871	14,801	10,755	8,873	13,171	14,847	17,887	14,863	12,415	16,766	14,510	10,850	9,936	7,033	6,586
Puerto Deseado, Argentina	9,842	16,844	13,114	16,677	8,749	15,612	14,726	11,151	8,410	12,849	14,374	18,459	14,567	11,904	16,383	14,238	10,297	10,243	7,363	6,761
Puerto Princesa, Philippines	9,913	5,363	10,470	4,026	13,915	7,845	9,216	12,667	8,122	10,074	7,727	4,562	8,650	9,328	1,876	9,056	9,909	13,835	16,502	17,474
Punta Arenas, Chile	10,055	17,085	13,788	16,575	9,384	16,237	15,421	11,622	8,036	13,449	14,793	18,124	15,175	12,277	15,895	14,864	10,567	10,804	7,903	7,404
Pusan, South Korea	11,267	4,664	8,768	4,205	13,126	6,267	7,118	9,674	11,057	9,005	7,273	1,570	7,301	9,606	3,327	7,640	10,956	10,849	13,529	14,556
Pyongyang, North Korea	10,996	4,241	8,244	3,930	12,611	5,749	6,598	9,409	11,252	8,498	6,828	1,293	6,788	9,207	3,352	7,123	10,640	10,519	13,273	14,185
Qamdo, China	8,283	2,135	7,226	1,217	10,893	4,617	6,105	10,964	9,348	6,872	4,667	3,715	5,398	6,744	1,728	5,804	7,972	11,631	14,527	14,593
Qandahar, Afghanistan	5,763	1,274	5,035	1,940	7,985	2,983	4,702	10,783	8,989	4,201	1,771	5,989	3,186	3,802	4,103	3,576	5,290	10,780	13,226	12,507
Qiqian, China	10,724	3,689	6,858	4,004	11,318	4,507	5,144	8,223	12,269	7,305	6,024	1,094	5,579	8,537	4,273	5,870	10,230	9,191	12,044	12,762
Qom, Iran	5,206	2,285	3,782	3,352	6,592	2,349	3,879	10,051	9,501	2,793	354	6,828	2,081	2,798	5,528	2,409	4,599	9,785	11,986	11,127
Quebec, Canada	11,635	9,908	5,616	11,422	6,562	7,353	5,625	1,749	17,115	7,022	9,115	9,141	7,223	9,771	12,975	6,887	11,028	502	3,237	3,848
Quetta, Pakistan	5,744	1,315	5,228	1,805	8,122	3,169	4,891	10,959	8,831	4,376	1,930	5,996	3,380	3,867	3,948	3,769	5,294	10,970	13,420	12,691
Quito, Ecuador	12,178	14,947	9,888	16,512	7,556	12,270	10,619	5,747	13,711	10,749	13,227	13,763	11,769	12,277	18,205	11,364	12,084	4,928	2,024	2,412
Rabaul, Papua New Guinea	13,343	9,132	13,746	7,982	17,903	11,208	12,059	12,026	9,127	13,831	11,665	6,071	12,198	13,320	5,890	12,565	13,563	13,521	14,489	16,232
Raiatea (Uturoa)	17,203	14,806	15,815	14,105	15,745	15,338	14,545	9,241	11,641	17,338	17,334	10,219	16,251	19,591	12,162	16,262	17,932	10,140	9,034	10,452
Raleigh, North Carolina	12,344	11,276	6,887	12,780	7,039	8,724	6,997	2,018	17,024	8,221	10,422	10,091	8,561	10,822	14,225	8,213	11,823	957	1,978	3,053
Rangiroa (Avatoru)	17,414	14,983	15,488	14,395	15,333	15,253	14,324	8,858	11,991	17,020	17,404	10,324	16,099	19,930	12,512	16,064	18,122	9,721	8,588	10,017
Rangoon, Burma	7,681	3,188	8,341	1,646	11,360	5,860	7,480	12,558	7,798	7,676	5,244	4,979	6,455	6,775	712	6,867	7,545	13,208	16,082	15,876
Raoul Is., Kermadec Islands	14,806	13,323	17,481	12,070	17,865	15,296	15,660	11,991	9,042	18,027	15,766	9,802	16,342	16,563	9,893	16,671	15,456	13,077	12,023	13,295
Rarotonga (Avarua)	16,516	14,393	16,536	13,465	16,601	15,488	15,037	10,146	10,794	17,964	17,020	10,061	16,515	18,590	11,409	16,639	17,233	11,111	10,028	11,407
Rawson, Argentina	9,873	16,768	12,707	16,853	8,406	15,254	14,276	10,702	8,817	12,532	14,208	18,354	14,232	11,796	16,817	13,886	10,282	9,762	6,892	6,263
Recife, Brazil	7,268	12,367	7,830	13,400	3,593	10,370	9,493	8,604	10,357	7,718	9,783	15,424	9,372	7,880	15,353	9,010	7,230	7,140	5,432	3,738
Regina, Canada	13,835	10,041	7,132	11,291	9,006	7,985	6,405	728	19,583	8,661	10,212	7,652	8,270	11,583	12,126	8,045	13,159	2,219	4,366	5,695
Reykjavik, Iceland	9,185	6,497	2,316	8,055	5,578	3,858	2,152	4,406	14,850	3,847	5,625	7,354	3,700	6,775	9,918	3,385	8,468	4,014	6,549	6,419
Rhodes, Greece	4,979	4,161	2,223	5,400	4,624	2,666	3,278	8,923	10,353	809	1,726	8,154	1,640	2,348	7,585	1,566	4,254	8,301	10,117	9,107
Richmond, Virginia	12,222	11,055	6,674	12,562	6,940	8,501	6,774	1,925	17,066	8,018	10,206	9,947	8,341	10,643	14,030	7,994	11,686	747	2,167	3,146
Riga, USSR	7,280	4,185	1,138	5,737	5,587	1,545	988	6,901	12,519	1,953	3,056	6,706	1,115	4,644	7,809	839	6,552	6,597	8,990	8,510
Ringkobing, Denmark	7,460	5,161	537	6,709	4,917	2,519	1,390	6,285	13,001	2,024	3,810	7,411	1,980	4,944	8,787	1,605	6,731	5,801	8,061	7,533
Rio Branco, Brazil	10,826	15,165	9,998	16,591	6,782	12,588	11,116	7,111	12,221	10,517	12,914	15,232	11,856	11,408	18,784	11,446	10,843	6,066	3,248	2,658
Rio Cuarto, Argentina	10,012	16,422	11,802	17,064	7,700	14,418	13,264	9,655	9,783	11,828	13,796	17,659	13,462	11,576	17,759	13,086	10,308	8,656	5,812	5,133
Rio de Janeiro, Brazil	8,059	14,062	9,699	14,859	5,393	12,226	11,350	9,506	9,613	9,529	11,437	17,160	11,211	9,282	16,412	10,859	8,221	8,170	5,814	4,445
Rio Gallegos, Argentina	9,984	17,020	13,588	16,609	9,194	16,052	15,217	11,492	8,136	13,270	14,667	18,251	14,994	12,163	16,037	14,678	10,480	10,646	7,749	7,218
Rio Grande, Brazil	8,884	15,319	11,020	15,912	6,726	13,562	12,632	9,984	9,295	10,861	12,695	18,081	12,548	10,426	16,958	12,196	9,159	8,802	6,133	5,094
Riyadh, Saudi Arabia	4,033	3,194	4,332	3,859	6,163	3,461	4,839	10,918	8,516	3,006	1,074	7,885	2,958	1,787	5,884	3,186	3,448	10,448	12,294	11,163
Road Town, Brit. Virgin Isls.	10,916	12,403	7,329	13,964	5,678	9,725	8,111	4,377	14,681	8,269	10,734	12,337	9,207	10,204	15,912	8,803	10,580	3,067	1,289	689
Roanoke, Virginia	12,444	11,157	6,853	12,648	7,159	8,628	6,901	1,814	17,221	8,212	10,375	9,893	8,497	10,855	14,053	8,156	11,908	825	2,158	3,256
Robinson Crusoe Island, Chile	11,306	17,688	12,735	18,376	8,904	15,367	13,966	9,368	10,282	12,979	15,090	16,759	14,519	12,925	18,092	14,121	11,636	8,626	5,718	5,505
Rochester, New York	12,172	10,475	6,262	11,966	6,997	7,957	6,230	1,486	17,413	7,665	9,757	9,359	7,858	10,392	13,406	7,527	11,588	149	2,790	3,679
Rockhampton, Australia	12,552	10,400	15,463	8,997	17,886	12,828	13,962	13,741	7,432	15,068	12,627	8,108	13,685	13,510	6,804	14,088	13,004	15,179	15,090	16,500
Rome, Italy	5,893	5,247	1,071	6,647	3,815	3,050	2,766	7,616	11,554	677	3,124	8,524	2,039	3,492	8,837	1,678	5,170	6,870	8,638	7,702
Rosario, Argentina	9,676	16,097	11,573	16,721	7,409	14,172	13,086	9,754	9,635	11,543	13,470	17,840	13,195	11,234	17,547	12,826	9,966	8,697	5,894	5,102
Roseau, Dominica	10,535	12,508	7,369	14,054	5,366	9,844	8,280	4,852	14,195	8,207	10,684	12,753	9,255	9,975	16,097	8,846	10,232	3,511	1,669	239
Rostock, East Germany	7,158	4,949	356	6,483	4,854	2,352	1,473	6,618	12,672	1,714	3,494	7,444	1,707	4,623	8,590	1,315	6,429	6,123	8,338	7,749
Rostov-na-Donu, USSR	6,227	3,033	2,227	4,495	5,942	1,150	2,256	8,390	11,097	1,806	1,562	6,636	399	3,570	6,662	762	5,530	8,107	10,415	9,754
Rotterdam, Netherlands	7,159	5,499	353	7,024	4,392	2,917	1,914	6,402	12,806	1,813	3,901	7,933	2,223	4,732	9,144	1,817	6,437	5,778	7,861	7,208
Rouyn, Canada	12,199	9,980	5,982	11,449	7,166	7,514	5,794	1,143	17,721	7,435	9,415	8,795	7,487	10,245	12,840	7,176	11,577	485	3,360	4,224
Sacramento, California	15,699	11,179	8,966	12,156	10,686	9,514	8,066	2,472	18,515	10,499	11,848	7,770	9,952	13,428	12,371	9,771	15,031	3,766	4,879	6,532
Saginaw, Michigan	12,673	10,602	6,621	12,051	7,511	8,162	6,446	1,071	17,883	8,059	10,068	9,131	8,143	10,834	13,340	7,830	12,081	604	2,899	3,999
Saint Denis, Reunion	2,949	7,014	9,167	6,264	8,288	8,510	9,960	15,853	3,412	7,645	6,171	10,990	8,075	4,748	6,619	8,270	3,460	14,913	15,027	13,277
Saint George's, Grenada	10,525	12,825	7,669	14,362	5,449	10,169	8,622	5,145	13,933	8,458	10,935	13,096	9,556	10,111	16,434	9,145	10,261	3,836	1,746	134
Saint John, Canada	11,237	9,883	5,395	11,420	6,131	7,278	5,557	2,185	16,679	6,756	8,926	9,415	7,070	9,447	13,081	6,718	10,643	835	3,184	3,589
Saint John's, Antigua	10,607	12,370	7,249	13,922	5,396	9,700	8,121	4,657	14,380	8,125	10,599	12,548	9,134	9,966	15,938	8,726	10,285	3,308	1,590	442
Saint John's, Canada	10,242	9,112	4,395	10,673	5,204	6,453	4,769	3,040	15,850	5,716	7,942	9,333	6,137	8,393	12,511	5,768	9,627	1,875	3,945	3,897
Saint Louis, Missouri	13,305	11,242	7,371	12,647	8,055	8,863	7,156	1,287	17,999	8,806	10,811	9,373	8,880	11,562	13,763	8,572	12,742	1,301	2,629	4,014
Saint Paul, Minnesota	13,333	10,590	7,019	11,957	8,237	8,297	6,618	548	18,610	8,504	10,354	8,642	8,404	11,353	13,020	8,123	12,714	1,318	3,351	4,638
Saint Peter Port, UK	7,205	6,057	880	7,574	3,966	3,485	2,398	6,194	12,938	2,082	4,353	8,418	2,766	4,912	9,704	2,355	6,497	5,442	7,377	6,661
Saipan (Susupe)	12,890	7,226	11,512	6,354	15,888	9,034	9,804	10,726	10,312	11,756	9,847	3,824	10,063	11,936	4,589	10,406	12,828	12,167	14,092	15,706
Salalah, Oman	3,784	3,270	5,468	3,415	6,997	4,321	5,845	11,991	7,521	4,143	2,043	7,955	3,996	2,309	5,184	4,265	3,370	11,582	13,399	12,179
Salem, Oregon	15,266	10,463	8,407	11,463	10,507	8,821	7,411	2,208	18,942	9,937	11,171	7,178	9,296	12,862	11,786	9,134	14,566	3,645	5,212	6,775
Salt Lake City, Utah	14,908	11,083	8,335	12,220	9,831	9,161	7,610	1,688	19,027	9,859	11,418	8,137	9,481	12,771	12,735	9,260	14,265	2,911	4,192	5,780
Salta, Argentina	10,281	16,071	11,141	17,096	7,292	13,777	12,489	8,746	10,651	11,348	13,514	16,825	12,895	11,514	18,490	12,501	10,480	7,725	4,892	4,221
Salto, Uruguay	9,446	15,793	11,282	16,464	7,101	13,873	12,815	9,688	9,655	11,235	13,167	17,812	12,891	10,948	17,466	12,524	9,716	8,583	5,824	4,940
Salvador, Brazil	7,616	13,017	8,498	13,996	4,257	11,044	10,145	8,835	10,179	8,387	10,418	16,023	10,046	8,437	15,862	9,684	7,647	7,411	5,424	3,826
Salzburg, Austria	6,483	5,018	467	6,495	4,333	2,609	2,118	7,161	12,069	1,066	3,193	7,966	1,713	3,995	8,659	1,306	5,756	6,537	8,536	7,764
Samsun, Turkey	5,534	3,342	2,330	4,676	5,470	1,859	2,829	8,836	10,568	1,403	1,220	7,278	969	2,870	6,869	1,112	4,830	8,411	10,515	9,677
San Antonio, Texas	14,295	12,355	8,644	13,668	8,959	10,081	8,391	2,286	17,558	10,068	12,081	9,867	10,143	12,777	14,442	9,841	13,802	2,545	2,542	4,240
San Cristobal, Venezuela	11,608	13,840	8,764	15,403	6,666	11,161	9,530	5,098	14,176	9,650	12,126	13,225	10,645	11,349	17,275	10,240	11,404	4,062	1,236	1,343
San Diego, California	15,796	11,898	9,341	12,910	10,571	10,117	8,598	2,664	18,062	10,863	12,405	8,517	10,476	13,768	13,110	10,262	15,190	3,727	4,344	6,055
San Francisco, California	15,820	11,247	9,084	12,202	10,797	9,610	8,172	2,592	18,396	10,617	11,950	7,780	10,059	13,546	12,375	9,881	15,152	3,877	4,936	6,601
San Jose, Costa Rica	12,929	14,161	9,402	15,687	7,892	11,544	9,832	4,522	14,988	10,489	12,912	12,483	11,222	12,497	16,993	10,838	12,704	3,871	1,189	2,517
San Juan, Argentina	10,431	16,707	11,914	17,466	7,936	14,547	13,293	9,366	10,118	12,040	14,096	17,276	13,633	11,937	18,122	13,246	10,715	8,429	5,552	5,005
San Juan, Puerto Rico	11,074	12,483	7,432	14,047	5,836	9,805	8,178	4,297	14,781	8,394	10,854	12,296	9,306	10,355	15,962	8,904	10,739	3,017	1,131	787
San Luis Potosi, Mexico	14,699	13,175	9,439	14,446	9,375	10,924	9,234	3,119	16,858	10,833	12,906	10,409	10,975	13,456	15,017	10,667	14,288	3,323	2,568	4,321
San Marino, San Marino	6,100	5,177	852	6,606	3,978	2,902	2,548	7,449	11,740	783	3,149	8,342	1,922	3,669	8,790	1,543	5,375	6,741	8,587	7,705
San Miguel de Tucuman, Argen.	10,220	16,176	11,306	17,118	7,391	13,940	12,681	8,965	10,442	11,470	13,594	17,031	13,040	11,537	18,333	12,650	10,443	7,951	5,114	4,443
San Salvador, El Salvador	13,508	13,921	9,425	15,385	8,353	11,388	9,661	4,031	15,588	10,623	12,972	11,854	11,181	12,845	16,423	10,815	13,232	3,594	1,410	3,028
Sanaa, Yemen	3,002	4,086	5,045	4,450	5,970	4,503	5,794	11,736	7,603	3,579	2,121	8,812	3,910	1,252	6,258	4,082	2,466	11,100	12,581	11,238
Santa Cruz, Bolivia	10,185	15,417	10,385	16,623	6,706	13,019	11,691	8,096	11,221	10,681	12,943	16,223	12,173	11,123	18,538	11,772	10,294	7,002	4,232	3,430
Santa Cruz, Tenerife	6,526	8,237	3,325	9,606	1,628	5,917	5,005	6,836	12,066	3,532	5,961	11,018	4,993	5,195	11,799	4,601	5,977	5,554	6,244	4,948
Santa Fe, New Mexico	14,732	11,680	8,503	12,889	9,487	9,601	7,979	1,822	18,426	9,998	11,767	8,901	9,814	12,850	13,494	9,556	14,150	2,672	3,475	5,116
Santa Rosa, Argentina	9,938	16,549	12,098	17,008	7,916	14,695	13,601	10,022	9,439	12,052	13,926	17,958	13,713	11,631	17,438	13,347	10,273	9,038	6,187	5,518
Santa Rosalia, Mexico	15,653	12,560	9,608	13,633	10,325	10,634	9,046	2,921	17,537	11,100	12,847	9,278	10,896	13,936	13,868	10,649	15,130	3,698	3,776	5,520
Santarem, Brazil	9,523	13,573	8,466	14,938	5,123	11,094	9,761	6,925	12,176	8,873	11,247	14,815	10,283	9,794	17,121	9,877	9,428	5,607	3,314	1,868
Santiago del Estero, Argentina	10,109	16,150	11,332	17,040	7,368	13,964	12,735	9,097	10,303	11,462	13,554	17,171	13,049	11,464	18,192	12,661	10,342	8,071	5,243	4,541
Santiago, Chile	10,580	16,978	12,207	17,644	8,218	14,840	13,576	9,515	10,012	12,327	14,360	17,301	13,925	12,164	18,013	13,539	10,890	8,623	5,731	5,253
Santo Domingo, Dominican Rep.	11,472	12,680	7,696	14,245	6,234	10,005	8,348	4,108	15,025	8,711	11,157	12,185	9,556	10,735	16,064	9,159	11,138	2,923	732	1,099
Sao Paulo de Olivenca, Brazil	11,055	14,674	9,497	16,177	6,630	12,038	10,505	6,394	12,909	10,145	12,594	14,521	11,376	11,335	18,311	10,964	10,991	5,337	2,530	2,017
Sao Paulo, Brazil	8,401	14,391	9,936	15,211	5,685	12,491	11,551	9,395	9,761	9,822	11,770	17,230	11,490	9,632	16,747	11,131	8,571	8,098	5,646	4,359
Sao Tome, Sao Tome & Principe	2,878	8,217	5,657	8,874	2,537	7,232	7,403	10,786	8,109	4,550	5,635	12,686	6,177	3,300	10,659	5,992	2,609	9,445	9,321	7,624
Sapporo, Japan	12,290	5,352	8,566	5,262	13,063	6,328	6,782	8,380	12,407	9,126	7,817	776	7,403	10,299	4,686	7,679	11,878	9,633	12,207	13,373
Sarajevo, Yugoslavia	5,933	4,721	1,067	6,135	4,317	2,547	2,476	7,768	11,471	486	2,678	8,062	1,516	3,404	8,321	1,173	5,203	7,133	9,051	8,183
Saratov, USSR	6,803	2,669	2,514	4,206	6,532	509	1,997	8,169	11,420	2,413	1,918	5,979	711	4,167	6,315	1,094	6,120	8,044	10,524	10,029
Saskatoon, Canada	13,844	9,853	7,077	11,085	9,103	7,842	6,285	891	19,612	8,609	10,094	7,420	8,159	11,537	11,896	7,946	13,157	2,385	4,596	5,910
Schefferville, Canada	11,284	8,975	4,875	10,483	6,518	6,445	4,719	1,953	17,020	6,345	8,301	8,373	6,378	9,192	12,052	6,062	10,627	1,365	4,172	4,647
Seattle, Washington	15,002	10,191	8,122	11,218	10,332	8,522	7,112	2,053	19,121	9,651	10,871	7,013	8,997	12,574	11,616	8,835	14,296	3,523	5,267	6,782

Distances in Kilometers

	Kasanga, Tanzania	Kashgar, China	Kassel, West Germany	Kathmandu, Nepal	Kayes, Mali	Kazan, USSR	Kemi, Finland	Kenora, Canada	Kerguelen Island	Kerkira, Greece	Kermanshah, Iran	Khabarovsk, USSR	Kharkov, USSR	Khartoum, Sudan	Khon Kaen, Thailand	Kiev, USSR	Kigali, Rwanda	Kingston, Canada	Kingston, Jamaica	Kingstown, Saint Vincent
Sendai, Japan	12,314	5,508	9,015	5,245	13,501	6,702	7,252	8,848	11,979	9,499	8,046	1,231	7,772	10,480	4,427	8,067	11,957	10,130	12,647	13,869
Seoul, South Korea	11,096	4,395	8,438	4,025	12,802	5,941	6,791	9,508	11,179	8,686	6,991	1,381	6,978	9,354	3,332	7,314	10,756	10,643	13,372	14,326
Sept-Iles, Canada	11,264	9,411	5,108	10,935	6,316	6,841	5,114	2,004	16,890	6,530	8,597	8,876	6,703	9,311	12,549	6,368	10,635	1,012	3,691	4,136
Sevastopol, USSR	5,882	3,519	1,933	4,927	5,390	1,660	2,425	8,402	10,995	1,254	1,627	7,187	634	3,217	7,112	687	5,168	7,988	10,140	9,367
Seville, Spain	6,380	6,893	1,972	8,306	2,598	4,541	3,725	6,857	12,144	2,265	4,741	9,745	3,623	4,488	10,496	3,228	5,725	5,815	7,144	6,076
Shanghai, China	10,516	4,187	8,718	3,504	12,887	6,123	7,193	10,371	10,298	8,754	6,813	2,252	7,101	9,024	2,486	7,470	10,250	11,467	14,236	15,099
Sheffield, United Kingdom	7,513	5,842	783	7,382	4,405	3,213	1,994	5,985	13,200	2,230	4,331	7,999	2,606	5,134	9,476	2,209	6,797	5,342	7,449	6,852
Shenyang, China	10,824	3,974	7,879	3,786	12,256	5,393	6,233	9,207	11,404	8,151	6,534	1,178	6,437	8,946	3,434	6,768	10,436	10,270	13,066	13,902
Shiraz, Iran	4,795	2,404	4,285	3,201	6,733	2,918	4,459	10,629	8,921	3,170	735	7,088	2,647	2,568	5,315	2,957	4,232	10,334	12,451	11,495
Sibiu, Romania	6,051	4,232	1,240	5,667	4,810	2,064	2,229	7,876	11,434	771	2,321	7,603	1,017	3,439	7,847	700	5,322	7,352	9,412	8,618
Singapore	8,137	5,089	10,201	3,530	12,699	7,766	9,389	14,082	6,517	9,401	6,926	6,028	8,315	7,977	1,679	8,724	8,220	14,963	17,871	17,728
Sioux Falls, South Dakota	13,660	10,780	7,330	12,112	8,543	8,543	6,880	715	18,772	8,821	10,636	8,624	8,684	11,678	13,073	8,411	13,043	1,624	3,395	4,778
Skelleftea, Sweden	8,166	4,480	1,638	6,042	6,105	1,832	204	6,144	13,346	2,801	3,817	6,226	1,873	5,531	7,981	1,691	7,439	5,994	8,572	8,321
Skopje, Yugoslavia	5,674	4,532	1,380	5,909	4,395	2,512	2,658	8,083	11,169	298	2,388	8,063	1,444	3,112	8,100	1,166	4,944	7,456	9,352	8,447
Socotra Island (Tamrida)	3,443	3,674	5,859	3,656	7,063	4,801	6,309	12,438	7,050	4,484	2,501	8,311	4,449	2,341	5,266	4,704	3,101	11,974	13,650	12,339
Sofia, Bulgaria	5,720	4,367	1,419	5,751	4,563	2,353	2,576	8,114	11,162	446	2,260	7,907	1,283	3,129	7,942	1,022	4,990	7,523	9,469	8,590
Songkhla, Thailand	7,899	4,342	9,465	2,785	12,159	7,019	8,645	13,525	6,969	8,708	6,240	5,611	7,579	7,460	1,050	7,988	7,899	14,301	17,203	17,003
Sorong, Indonesia	11,116	7,173	12,230	5,838	15,662	9,595	10,850	13,078	7,934	11,891	9,534	5,484	10,442	10,979	3,662	10,845	11,260	14,481	16,423	18,089
South Georgia Island	7,819	14,848	12,466	14,526	7,982	14,469	14,283	12,728	6,612	11,721	12,649	19,156	13,406	10,156	14,567	13,183	8,345	11,547	8,866	7,820
South Pole	9,068	14,375	15,692	13,070	11,602	16,184	17,307	15,519	4,518	14,389	13,802	15,375	15,545	11,729	11,819	15,593	9,788	14,903	11,994	11,458
South Sandwich Islands	7,335	14,306	12,529	13,852	8,121	14,279	14,353	13,439	5,872	11,624	12,277	18,415	13,248	9,754	13,820	13,073	7,908	12,216	9,586	8,477
Split, Yugoslavia	5,946	4,884	1,012	6,298	4,173	2,690	2,532	7,693	11,526	523	2,827	8,188	1,670	3,451	8,485	1,315	5,217	7,026	8,907	8,024
Spokane, Washington	14,751	10,260	7,927	11,352	9,989	8,473	7,005	1,696	19,469	9,459	10,793	7,271	8,891	12,389	11,859	8,709	14,057	3,157	4,936	6,426
Spoleto, Italy	5,970	5,198	985	6,609	3,896	2,972	2,671	7,561	11,619	696	3,112	8,437	1,971	3,551	8,797	1,603	5,246	6,834	8,637	7,724
Springbok, South Africa	2,725	9,733	9,008	9,581	5,808	9,920	10,601	14,031	4,832	7,671	7,718	14,376	9,009	5,250	10,431	8,960	3,327	12,569	11,424	9,706
Springfield, Illinois	13,228	11,104	7,242	12,512	7,998	8,724	7,017	1,173	18,052	8,682	10,676	9,279	8,743	11,451	13,647	8,437	12,655	1,193	2,715	4,057
Springfield, Massachusetts	11,772	10,430	6,026	11,950	6,574	7,857	6,131	1,891	16,994	7,388	9,553	9,608	7,686	10,061	13,507	7,339	11,200	397	2,702	3,391
Srinagar, India	6,586	608	5,481	1,226	8,787	3,111	4,820	10,655	9,273	4,859	2,550	5,152	3,595	4,695	3,414	4,005	6,146	10,861	13,509	13,021
Stanley, Falkland Islands	9,207	16,241	13,050	15,956	8,588	15,399	14,767	11,769	7,736	12,601	13,892	19,026	14,327	11,381	15,738	14,036	9,696	10,781	7,938	7,192
Stara Zagora, Bulgaria	5,662	4,188	1,573	5,563	4,710	2,249	2,605	8,250	11,046	574	2,070	7,805	1,173	3,045	7,755	966	4,934	7,687	9,658	8,782
Stockholm, Sweden	7,607	4,557	1,043	6,118	5,539	1,885	795	6,465	12,934	2,199	3,498	6,763	1,559	4,998	8,155	1,269	6,877	6,154	8,573	8,151
Stornoway, United Kingdom	8,128	5,965	1,273	7,527	4,876	3,289	1,801	5,431	13,791	2,793	4,724	7,661	2,878	5,716	9,546	2,514	7,409	4,889	7,178	6,755
Strasbourg, France	6,723	5,376	329	6,868	4,175	2,894	2,155	6,823	12,373	1,392	3,596	8,119	2,067	4,300	9,022	1,655	6,000	6,156	8,134	7,379
Stuttgart, West Germany	6,695	5,269	285	6,761	4,248	2,793	2,099	6,885	12,324	1,329	3,497	8,043	1,959	4,249	8,915	1,548	5,970	6,238	8,235	7,486
Subic, Philippines	10,159	5,092	10,106	3,874	13,797	7,470	8,765	12,078	8,694	9,828	7,562	3,970	8,328	9,341	1,873	8,728	10,091	13,243	15,922	16,900
Suchow, China	10,177	3,688	8,202	3,116	12,364	5,601	6,702	10,186	10,405	8,229	6,315	2,168	6,576	8,570	2,441	6,945	9,870	11,202	14,035	14,754
Sucre, Bolivia	10,382	15,675	10,629	16,883	6,968	13,261	11,910	8,148	11,208	10,940	13,205	16,261	12,425	11,371	18,741	12,023	10,510	7,098	4,286	3,587
Sudbury, Canada	12,380	10,210	6,220	11,671	7,296	7,754	6,036	1,066	17,807	7,668	9,658	8,914	7,732	10,467	13,025	7,419	11,768	433	3,184	4,136
Suez, Egypt	4,255	4,073	3,043	5,110	4,814	3,150	4,024	9,745	9,533	1,572	1,450	8,420	2,246	1,591	7,245	2,279	3,542	9,095	10,782	9,651
Sundsvall, Sweden	7,946	4,620	1,319	6,186	5,784	1,945	520	6,199	13,234	2,541	3,752	6,542	1,799	5,331	8,172	1,554	7,217	5,957	8,458	8,128
Surabaya, Indonesia	8,982	6,412	11,556	4,867	13,895	9,077	10,654	14,655	6,175	10,764	8,287	6,552	9,669	9,194	2,838	10,079	9,184	15,810	18,441	19,094
Suva, Fiji	15,377	12,325	16,196	11,228	18,903	14,072	14,373	11,324	9,789	16,861	14,901	8,539	15,137	16,394	9,121	15,437	15,909	12,587	12,135	13,641
Sverdlovsk, USSR	7,725	2,232	3,319	3,779	7,582	720	2,133	7,964	11,817	3,503	2,707	4,866	1,777	5,152	5,703	2,094	7,073	8,111	10,817	10,597
Svobodnyy, USSR	11,224	4,192	7,247	4,427	11,731	4,967	5,494	8,089	12,485	7,765	6,534	595	6,042	9,050	4,481	6,319	10,738	9,146	11,944	12,797
Sydney, Australia	12,159	11,216	16,385	9,731	17,241	13,768	15,039	14,477	6,674	15,681	13,204	9,264	14,525	13,598	7,569	14,936	12,711	15,800	14,959	16,022
Sydney, Canada	10,786	9,567	4,963	11,118	5,729	6,932	5,225	2,570	16,303	6,303	8,504	9,414	6,673	8,981	12,868	6,312	10,185	1,297	3,478	3,660
Syktyvkar, USSR	7,962	3,003	2,733	4,553	7,151	666	1,365	7,268	12,438	3,226	3,053	5,169	1,579	5,317	6,456	1,764	7,274	7,353	10,044	9,846
Szeged, Hungary	6,160	4,526	963	5,972	4,596	2,267	2,192	7,646	11,632	741	2,625	7,765	1,264	3,590	8,149	895	5,429	7,078	9,103	8,307
Szombathely, Hungary	6,335	4,769	688	6,234	4,468	2,421	2,122	7,389	11,866	889	2,917	7,853	1,475	3,803	8,404	1,079	5,605	6,796	8,813	8,032
Tabriz, Iran	5,388	2,571	3,221	3,796	6,220	1,975	3,389	9,540	9,967	2,289	424	6,887	1,547	2,835	5,987	1,856	4,737	9,234	11,427	10,600
Tacheng, China	7,974	986	5,167	2,123	9,182	2,533	3,988	9,305	10,744	5,048	3,302	3,848	3,422	5,778	3,831	3,809	7,457	9,726	12,553	12,475
Tahiti (Papeete)	17,128	15,016	15,829	14,322	15,549	15,480	14,624	9,208	11,647	17,360	17,527	10,414	16,366	19,711	12,374	16,355	17,849	10,067	8,883	10,278
Taipei, Taiwan	10,445	4,524	9,269	3,610	13,301	6,649	7,802	10,988	9,728	9,196	7,122	2,862	7,589	9,193	2,162	7,971	10,252	12,118	14,850	15,768
Taiyuan, China	9,838	3,167	7,628	2,775	11,793	5,024	6,150	9,939	10,564	7,657	5,788	2,168	5,999	8,098	2,559	6,368	9,485	10,867	13,744	14,321
Tallahassee, Florida	12,924	11,999	7,678	13,475	7,585	9,484	7,757	2,312	16,963	9,003	11,213	10,426	9,348	11,558	14,762	9,002	12,450	1,677	1,573	3,045
Tallinn, USSR	7,547	4,179	1,317	5,741	5,803	1,505	713	6,716	12,737	2,230	3,233	6,488	1,280	4,906	7,774	1,065	6,821	6,473	8,936	8,531
Tamanrasset, Algeria	4,445	6,798	3,185	7,915	2,010	5,107	4,973	8,790	10,192	2,309	4,230	10,660	4,035	2,945	10,042	3,759	3,819	7,661	8,497	7,097
Tampa, Florida	12,769	12,213	7,765	13,709	7,429	9,662	7,935	2,631	16,635	9,047	11,312	10,751	9,476	11,524	15,061	9,120	12,324	1,883	1,245	2,745
Tampere, Finland	7,784	4,272	1,429	5,837	5,928	1,595	483	6,505	12,964	2,450	3,447	6,371	1,496	5,144	7,835	1,301	7,058	6,299	8,810	8,465
Tanami, Australia	10,583	8,632	13,809	7,122	15,866	11,250	12,706	14,911	6,203	13,074	10,597	7,604	11,929	11,329	4,987	12,341	10,952	16,392	17,236	18,635
Tangier, Morocco	6,245	6,967	2,112	8,361	2,431	4,655	3,882	6,989	12,002	2,299	4,766	9,898	3,717	4,409	10,553	3,327	5,598	5,921	7,173	6,061
Tarawa (Betio)	15,729	10,516	13,963	9,711	18,194	11,912	12,138	10,081	11,092	14,708	13,141	6,356	12,987	15,290	7,852	13,254	15,906	11,528	12,110	13,845
Tashkent, USSR	6,753	602	4,601	2,101	8,197	2,172	3,881	9,787	10,063	4,136	2,099	5,094	2,723	4,537	4,233	3,135	6,219	9,933	12,569	12,132
Tbilisi, USSR	5,726	2,640	2,875	3,982	6,160	1,595	2,966	9,119	10,390	2,106	844	6,726	1,133	3,122	6,174	1,464	5,057	8,836	11,088	10,333
Tegucigalpa, Honduras	13,295	13,824	9,257	15,309	8,134	11,264	9,539	4,012	15,547	10,436	12,800	11,917	11,028	12,632	16,454	10,658	13,014	3,492	1,195	2,812
Tehran, Iran	5,329	2,201	3,744	3,313	6,647	2,239	3,788	9,963	9,601	2,801	426	6,717	2,011	2,911	5,496	2,350	4,720	9,719	11,954	11,126
Tel Aviv, Israel	4,502	3,781	2,970	4,863	5,068	2,860	3,817	9,652	9,667	1,578	1,173	8,106	1,995	1,838	7,016	2,070	3,797	9,068	10,869	9,801
Telegraph Creek, Canada	14,315	8,920	7,380	9,928	10,300	7,403	6,132	2,540	18,368	8,869	9,784	5,834	7,988	11,722	10,404	7,879	13,585	3,991	6,252	7,594
Teresina, Brazil	8,175	12,822	7,978	14,006	4,083	10,594	9,511	7,845	11,158	8,094	10,319	15,189	9,662	8,609	16,081	9,276	8,102	6,418	4,522	2,866
Ternate, Indonesia	10,720	6,740	11,833	5,383	15,195	9,201	10,508	13,134	7,828	11,446	9,075	5,337	10,024	10,516	3,202	10,429	10,838	14,486	16,656	18,200
The Valley, Anguilla	10,748	12,353	7,254	13,910	5,517	9,678	8,081	4,500	14,543	8,165	10,634	12,417	9,136	10,060	15,894	8,730	10,416	3,164	1,454	577
Thessaloniki, Greece	5,501	4,457	1,574	5,804	4,416	2,545	2,804	8,277	10,977	282	2,239	8,102	1,470	2,926	7,998	1,238	4,771	7,646	9,517	8,583
Thimphu, Bhutan	7,456	1,837	7,011	435	10,346	4,500	6,119	11,431	8,765	6,457	4,115	4,524	5,134	6,017	1,827	5,545	7,162	11,936	14,763	14,529
Thunder Bay, Canada	12,935	10,162	6,543	11,558	7,930	7,832	6,147	407	18,468	8,033	9,875	8,450	7,925	10,895	12,724	7,643	12,299	1,089	3,558	4,689
Tientsin, China	10,262	3,525	7,783	3,203	12,042	5,216	6,230	9,678	10,878	7,908	6,130	1,770	6,223	8,480	2,878	6,578	9,901	10,670	13,516	14,215
Tijuana, Mexico	15,796	11,920	9,351	12,933	10,566	10,135	8,614	2,672	18,045	10,873	12,421	8,541	10,491	13,776	13,133	10,277	15,192	3,727	4,328	6,040
Tiksi, USSR	11,161	4,609	5,567	5,554	10,006	3,938	3,742	6,116	14,215	6,495	6,137	2,594	4,922	8,588	6,366	5,062	10,515	7,002	9,878	10,572
Timbuktu, Mali	4,684	7,912	3,991	9,005	938	6,152	5,816	8,707	10,202	3,367	5,335	11,676	5,089	3,799	11,106	4,784	4,183	7,420	7,785	6,254
Tindouf, Algeria	5,824	7,638	3,012	8,943	1,506	5,477	4,802	7,459	11,472	2,902	5,260	10,809	4,486	4,396	11,129	4,118	5,243	6,246	7,043	5,724
Tirane, Albania	5,634	4,685	1,363	6,054	4,240	2,660	2,741	8,057	11,173	193	2,509	8,207	1,596	3,103	8,246	1,305	4,904	7,396	9,245	8,316
Tokyo, Japan	12,239	5,531	9,216	5,172	13,685	6,854	7,470	9,140	11,698	9,644	8,102	1,473	7,918	10,500	4,231	8,225	11,914	10,428	12,929	14,167
Toledo, Spain	6,461	6,610	1,647	8,042	2,908	4,226	3,405	6,797	12,236	2,046	4,522	9,423	3,325	4,446	10,227	2,925	5,787	5,822	7,297	6,297
Topeka, Kansas	13,749	11,267	7,649	12,612	8,522	8,985	7,303	1,196	18,361	9,114	11,025	9,095	9,078	11,921	13,570	8,790	13,169	1,693	2,962	4,436
Toronto, Canada	12,307	10,469	6,333	11,949	7,145	7,975	6,250	1,336	17,567	7,749	9,812	9,254	7,903	10,497	13,346	7,577	11,718	240	2,856	3,802
Toulouse, France	6,501	6,022	1,050	7,477	3,456	3,612	2,849	6,849	12,252	1,600	4,034	8,846	2,724	4,277	9,653	2,321	5,799	6,007	7,716	6,817
Tours, France	6,879	5,918	775	7,412	3,821	3,409	2,488	6,524	12,608	1,773	4,101	8,507	2,610	4,583	9,565	2,198	6,170	5,756	7,623	6,837
Townsville, Australia	12,340	9,808	14,867	8,417	17,656	12,232	13,388	13,674	7,496	14,491	12,066	7,593	13,089	13,079	6,224	13,491	12,736	15,152	15,443	16,965
Trenton, New Jersey	11,967	10,693	6,301	12,207	6,729	8,128	6,402	1,874	17,046	7,656	9,829	9,747	7,963	10,310	13,727	7,616	11,410	468	2,471	3,279
Tripoli, Lebanon	4,774	3,587	2,827	4,733	5,222	2,579	3,571	9,475	9,874	1,527	1,031	7,846	1,729	2,113	6,905	1,830	4,073	8,942	10,838	9,832
Tripoli, Libya	4,959	5,581	2,068	6,826	3,222	3,757	3,739	8,416	10,688	958	3,134	9,310	2,685	2,735	9,006	2,411	4,247	7,526	8,946	7,785
Tristan da Cunha (Edinburgh)	5,399	12,370	10,018	12,442	5,701	11,811	11,838	12,541	6,449	9,105	10,010	17,093	10,757	7,486	13,314	10,561	5,823	10,982	9,097	7,555
Trondheim, Norway	8,164	4,975	1,349	6,540	5,697	2,305	725	5,859	13,543	2,724	4,097	6,686	2,148	5,579	8,505	1,878	7,433	5,590	8,094	7,795
Trujillo, Peru	12,078	15,737	10,606	17,292	7,869	13,062	11,441	6,588	12,931	11,349	13,814	14,510	12,493	12,561	19,064	12,083	12,090	5,803	2,899	3,067
Truk Island (Moen)	13,506	8,280	12,571	7,326	16,974	10,117	10,835	11,029	10,085	12,841	10,891	4,819	11,148	12,877	5,420	11,490	13,556	12,517	13,988	15,718
Truro, Canada	11,020	9,766	5,210	11,312	5,926	7,144	5,430	2,381	16,485	6,557	8,749	9,453	6,907	9,234	13,019	6,550	10,425	1,053	3,284	3,577
Tsingtao, China	10,487	3,886	8,220	3,418	12,469	5,651	6,661	9,899	10,720	8,333	6,506	1,836	6,654	8,812	2,780	7,011	10,162	10,952	13,757	14,555
Tsitsihar, China	10,907	3,918	7,415	3,991	11,854	5,012	5,718	8,625	11,944	7,802	6,375	842	6,076	8,855	3,941	6,383	10,462	9,661	12,476	13,282
Tubuai Island (Mataura)	16,482	15,408	16,419	14,548	15,519	16,101	15,268	9,749	11,064	17,951	18,007	10,913	17,008	19,121	12,941	17,001	17,203	10,529	9,125	10,410
Tucson, Arizona	15,316	12,034	9,082	13,153	10,039	10,076	8,489	2,382	18,085	10,584	12,292	8,928	10,342	13,447	13,536	10,099	14,745	3,269	3,767	5,472
Tulsa, Oklahoma	13,865	11,588	7,909	12,933	8,589	9,295	7,608	1,518	18,116	9,359	11,312	9,359	9,369	12,133	13,861	9,075	13,311	1,873	2,753	4,299

Distances in Kilometers	Kasanga, Tanzania	Kashgar, China	Kassel, West Germany	Kathmandu, Nepal	Kayes, Mali	Kazan, USSR	Kemi, Finland	Kenora, Canada	Kerguelen Island	Kerkira, Greece	Kermanshah, Iran	Khabarovsk, USSR	Kharkov, USSR	Khartoum, Sudan	Khon Kaen, Thailand	Kiev, USSR	Kigali, Rwanda	Kingston, Canada	Kingston, Jamaica	Kingstown, Saint Vincent
Tunis, Tunisia	5,468	5,643	1,614	6,973	3,276	3,594	3,361	7,909	11,200	907	3,335	9,104	2,550	3,224	9,165	2,220	4,758	7,044	8,574	7,499
Tura, USSR	9,866	3,182	5,087	4,202	9,574	2,912	3,353	7,291	12,897	5,676	4,870	2,719	3,978	7,383	5,318	4,216	9,257	7,970	10,878	11,276
Turin, Italy	6,377	5,500	710	6,955	3,841	3,122	2,527	7,094	12,066	1,175	3,543	8,452	2,207	4,012	9,131	1,807	5,659	6,352	8,188	7,331
Uberlandia, Brazil	8,611	14,249	9,595	15,217	5,475	12,189	11,154	8,865	10,278	9,590	11,655	16,711	11,220	9,641	16,963	10,847	8,722	7,561	5,139	3,822
Ufa, USSR	7,377	2,261	3,081	3,826	7,258	447	2,096	8,097	11,622	3,156	2,371	5,230	1,435	4,788	5,833	1,777	6,718	8,154	10,793	10,473
Ujungpandang, Indonesia	9,744	6,649	11,828	5,158	14,555	9,262	10,743	14,129	6,780	11,186	8,728	6,134	9,953	9,835	3,001	10,365	9,926	15,403	17,757	19,114
Ulaanbaatar, Mongolia	9,656	2,641	6,502	2,917	10,806	3,953	4,961	8,986	11,377	6,687	5,108	2,086	4,980	7,575	3,511	5,323	9,191	9,790	12,695	13,140
Ulan-Ude, USSR	9,826	2,791	6,247	3,261	10,624	3,763	4,642	8,551	11,796	6,539	5,130	1,986	4,817	7,636	3,950	5,138	9,325	9,352	12,257	12,726
Uliastay, Mongolia	8,942	1,909	5,946	2,438	10,143	3,338	4,530	9,143	11,092	6,009	4,356	2,821	4,327	6,823	3,517	4,688	8,458	9,793	12,695	12,919
Uranium City, Canada	13,414	9,018	6,516	10,247	9,032	7,067	5,565	1,414	18,877	8,045	9,362	6,715	7,450	10,969	11,116	7,265	12,700	2,746	5,276	6,444
Urumqi, China	8,104	1,079	5,653	1,796	9,618	3,021	4,466	9,634	10,486	5,493	3,622	3,648	3,893	6,035	3,358	4,284	7,629	10,126	12,980	12,954
Ushuaia, Argentina	9,845	16,865	13,783	16,323	9,345	16,173	15,457	11,846	7,795	13,376	14,628	18,261	15,103	12,104	15,680	14,807	10,368	11,002	8,107	7,559
Vaduz, Liechtenstein	6,524	5,293	462	6,768	4,116	2,868	2,259	7,028	12,167	1,188	3,436	8,176	1,987	4,095	8,933	1,579	5,800	6,350	8,289	7,495
Valencia, Spain	6,224	6,352	1,524	7,765	2,976	4,028	3,332	7,056	11,997	1,740	4,218	9,321	3,090	4,149	9,954	2,698	5,540	6,113	7,613	6,599
Valladolid, Spain	6,647	6,571	1,527	8,024	3,084	4,138	3,247	6,621	12,422	2,090	4,552	9,270	3,270	4,589	10,202	2,865	5,969	5,673	7,228	6,281
Valletta, Malta	5,211	5,328	1,759	6,622	3,512	3,418	3,392	8,237	10,901	628	2,959	8,967	2,350	2,874	8,811	2,064	4,491	7,413	8,975	7,891
Valparaiso, Chile	10,679	17,043	12,231	17,740	8,274	14,866	13,580	9,447	10,091	12,376	14,429	17,205	13,963	12,249	18,086	13,574	10,985	8,571	5,674	5,229
Vancouver, Canada	14,891	9,998	7,990	11,027	10,305	8,344	6,948	2,062	19,103	9,516	10,698	6,846	8,831	12,433	11,444	8,676	14,179	3,548	5,392	6,879
Varna, Bulgaria	5,733	3,987	1,652	5,373	4,917	2,060	2,524	8,284	11,042	780	1,929	7,613	987	3,093	7,563	826	5,007	7,766	9,796	8,953
Venice, Italy	6,261	5,137	686	6,586	4,099	2,803	2,384	7,317	11,885	899	3,186	8,208	1,854	3,811	8,763	1,461	5,535	6,637	8,540	7,701
Veracruz, Mexico	14,235	13,457	9,399	14,811	8,954	11,081	9,365	3,396	16,409	10,727	12,923	10,956	11,032	13,214	15,557	10,699	13,875	3,323	2,044	3,785
Verona, Italy	6,302	5,238	662	6,690	4,032	2,887	2,410	7,245	11,946	978	3,290	8,269	1,950	3,874	8,866	1,554	5,578	6,549	8,437	7,595
Victoria, Canada	14,975	10,081	8,078	11,101	10,361	8,436	7,041	2,101	19,070	9,605	10,790	6,893	8,924	12,523	11,495	8,769	14,264	3,582	5,374	6,877
Victoria, Seychelles	2,720	5,318	7,577	4,805	7,674	6,716	8,204	14,262	5,149	6,101	4,398	9,632	6,328	3,373	5,711	6,552	2,836	13,601	14,634	13,025
Vienna, Austria	6,443	4,766	604	6,243	4,531	2,376	2,020	7,296	11,966	997	2,970	7,780	1,461	3,907	8,406	1,057	5,713	6,719	8,767	8,013
Vientiane, Laos	8,376	3,504	8,680	2,073	11,953	6,117	7,654	12,315	8,155	8,145	5,766	4,479	6,813	7,429	172	7,224	8,240	13,117	16,026	16,139
Villahermosa, Mexico	13,903	13,540	9,298	14,945	8,649	11,093	9,369	3,530	16,173	10,583	12,841	11,245	10,982	12,986	15,830	10,635	13,566	3,291	1,706	3,436
Vilnius, USSR	7,020	4,091	1,123	5,629	5,477	1,513	1,241	7,145	12,262	1,725	2,824	6,829	908	4,381	7,732	590	6,293	6,806	9,146	8,605
Visby, Sweden	7,420	4,537	904	6,092	5,402	1,884	969	6,611	12,769	2,009	3,368	6,893	1,449	4,815	8,155	1,130	6,690	6,262	8,633	8,159
Vitoria, Brazil	7,770	13,655	9,303	14,485	4,980	11,819	10,971	9,415	9,659	9,116	11,032	16,852	10,801	8,903	16,128	10,450	7,899	8,040	5,814	4,351
Vladivostok, USSR	11,522	4,614	8,161	4,495	12,620	5,789	6,434	8,769	11,924	8,582	7,124	646	6,855	9,578	4,041	7,159	11,119	9,925	12,631	13,632
Volgograd, USSR	6,470	2,703	2,494	4,201	6,330	842	2,225	8,401	11,150	2,194	1,618	6,256	609	3,833	6,348	1,021	5,786	8,211	10,615	10,034
Vologda, USSR	7,544	3,348	2,099	4,913	6,493	674	1,075	7,236	12,348	2,597	2,818	5,825	1,052	4,879	6,919	1,146	6,837	7,153	9,723	9,383
Vorkuta, USSR	8,824	3,205	3,421	4,650	7,910	1,520	1,726	6,873	12,984	4,100	3,849	4,381	2,482	6,195	6,316	2,645	8,146	7,177	9,999	10,048
Wake Island	15,093	8,730	11,874	8,216	16,268	9,847	10,048	9,009	12,125	12,632	11,300	4,303	10,922	13,690	6,734	11,172	14,931	10,504	11,960	13,669
Wallis Island	16,163	12,470	15,758	11,520	18,381	13,913	13,969	10,540	10,566	16,696	15,094	8,360	14,988	16,933	9,495	15,234	16,677	11,798	11,439	13,006
Walvis Bay, Namibia	2,394	9,407	8,241	9,448	5,010	9,316	9,879	13,272	5,593	6,947	7,214	14,125	8,361	4,695	10,549	8,280	2,868	11,830	10,907	9,163
Warsaw, Poland	6,797	4,379	800	5,897	5,083	1,872	1,524	7,172	12,171	1,409	2,877	7,222	1,094	4,192	8,028	693	6,067	6,733	8,962	8,336
Washington, D.C.	12,173	10,902	6,545	12,408	6,912	8,352	6,624	1,836	17,125	7,900	10,071	9,819	8,200	10,548	13,880	7,856	11,625	595	2,316	3,250
Watson Lake, Canada	14,034	8,735	7,098	9,785	10,054	7,155	5,862	2,443	18,353	8,588	9,532	5,812	7,722	11,446	10,349	7,608	13,305	3,858	6,225	7,510
Weimar, East Germany	6,858	5,062	132	6,573	4,539	2,539	1,815	6,820	12,429	1,432	3,417	7,754	1,764	4,360	8,711	1,354	6,130	6,245	8,344	7,662
Wellington, New Zealand	13,367	13,394	18,429	11,943	16,970	15,820	16,708	13,401	7,592	17,891	15,424	10,685	16,692	15,412	9,765	17,097	14,043	14,364	12,836	13,791
West Berlin, West Germany	6,966	4,890	300	6,413	4,761	2,337	1,607	6,801	12,482	1,520	3,345	7,531	1,612	4,430	8,537	1,209	6,236	6,283	8,454	7,819
Wewak, Papua New Guinea	12,426	8,373	13,223	7,138	17,041	10,614	11,652	12,549	8,566	13,107	10,839	5,826	11,549	12,385	5,003	11,935	12,621	14,036	15,346	17,099
Whangarei, New Zealand	13,786	13,059	17,896	11,669	17,581	15,362	16,121	13,012	8,027	17,734	15,269	10,107	16,305	15,629	9,477	16,694	14,435	14,084	12,841	13,955
Whitehorse, Canada	14,095	8,546	7,187	9,545	10,304	7,084	5,867	2,794	18,028	8,655	9,470	5,483	7,705	11,473	10,038	7,614	13,365	4,203	6,568	7,860
Wichita, Kansas	13,934	11,431	7,858	12,758	8,688	9,174	7,498	1,362	18,329	9,323	11,227	9,147	9,279	12,128	13,655	8,993	13,362	1,891	2,962	4,490
Willemstad, Curacao	11,304	13,243	8,164	14,805	6,222	10,565	8,943	4,787	14,392	9,067	11,540	12,886	10,044	10,859	16,722	9,639	11,045	3,632	1,066	846
Wiluna, Australia	9,506	8,638	13,689	7,076	14,844	11,316	12,928	16,093	5,001	12,683	10,240	8,449	11,818	10,554	5,119	12,219	9,934	17,547	18,034	18,508
Windhoek, Namibia	2,169	9,198	8,220	9,204	5,143	9,194	9,821	13,429	5,440	6,890	7,052	13,907	8,259	4,547	10,283	8,195	2,680	12,003	11,151	9,404
Windsor, Canada	12,624	10,703	6,653	12,161	7,434	8,244	6,523	1,214	17,756	8,077	10,119	9,276	8,202	10,830	13,474	7,882	12,041	571	2,758	3,854
Winnipeg, Canada	13,403	10,081	6,828	11,406	8,489	7,887	6,249	192	19,056	8,344	10,036	8,015	8,083	11,246	12,402	7,830	12,745	1,683	3,977	5,221
Winston-Salem, North Carolina	12,485	11,289	6,964	12,781	7,185	8,757	7,029	1,907	17,158	8,314	10,491	10,003	8,618	10,937	14,181	8,275	11,960	958	2,034	3,175
Wroclaw, Poland	6,738	4,665	527	6,173	4,800	2,175	1,694	7,088	12,210	1,298	3,051	7,498	1,364	4,175	8,313	953	6,008	6,579	8,733	8,063
Wuhan, China	9,836	3,602	8,350	2,827	12,368	5,722	6,934	10,662	9,916	8,257	6,215	2,659	6,652	8,370	1,951	7,035	9,569	11,648	14,501	15,142
Wyndham, Australia	10,506	8,138	13,316	6,643	15,687	10,740	12,181	14,617	6,460	12,642	10,171	7,119	11,442	11,049	4,489	11,854	10,821	16,068	17,367	18,995
Xi'an, China	9,429	2,976	7,713	2,360	11,724	5,081	6,335	10,414	10,062	7,609	5,598	2,680	6,003	7,816	2,067	6,388	9,110	11,294	14,109	14,655
Xining, China	8,879	2,279	7,082	1,835	11,030	4,446	5,786	10,301	10,056	6,922	4,904	3,007	5,337	7,153	2,239	5,727	8,519	11,049	13,958	14,217
Yakutsk, USSR	11,277	4,359	6,381	5,001	10,874	4,391	4,571	7,009	13,461	7,120	6,329	1,541	5,447	8,855	5,481	5,659	10,698	7,997	10,834	11,619
Yanji, China	11,328	4,433	8,075	4,299	12,517	5,670	6,368	8,884	11,786	8,456	6,956	760	6,732	9,400	3,874	7,043	10,929	10,015	12,748	13,705
Yaounde, Cameroon	2,570	7,558	5,263	8,219	2,779	6,657	6,951	10,821	8,108	4,047	4,984	12,059	5,617	2,641	10,036	5,460	2,160	9,556	9,710	8,054
Yap Island (Colonia)	12,023	6,962	11,668	5,876	15,745	9,077	10,084	11,699	9,311	11,657	9,521	4,331	10,042	11,376	3,900	10,417	12,038	13,111	15,125	16,722
Yaraka, Australia	11,881	10,034	15,185	8,577	17,220	12,560	13,838	14,319	6,854	14,607	12,137	8,177	13,343	12,875	6,397	13,753	12,331	15,782	15,742	17,071
Yarmouth, Canada	11,240	10,025	5,493	11,566	6,095	7,413	5,695	2,249	16,615	6,836	9,032	9,568	7,188	9,499	13,238	6,832	10,657	833	3,035	3,433
Yellowknife, Canada	13,400	8,667	6,463	9,858	9,243	6,818	5,384	1,860	18,544	7,979	9,150	6,268	7,269	10,883	10,677	7,111	12,676	3,158	5,723	6,874
Yerevan, USSR	5,559	2,681	2,955	3,978	6,106	1,764	3,120	9,263	10,234	2,097	690	6,851	1,268	2,962	6,171	1,576	4,892	8,954	11,166	10,372
Yinchuan, China	9,323	2,620	7,212	2,286	11,292	4,586	5,815	10,018	10,396	7,162	5,244	2,561	5,530	7,548	2,465	5,908	8,953	10,841	13,746	14,147
Yogyakarta, Indonesia	8,714	6,322	11,437	4,766	13,651	8,997	10,601	14,812	5,983	10,598	8,121	6,691	9,552	8,960	2,806	9,960	8,920	15,913	18,645	18,934
York, United Kingdom	7,543	5,805	775	7,348	4,461	3,171	1,939	5,971	13,222	2,242	4,318	7,943	2,579	5,152	9,437	2,183	6,825	5,344	7,472	6,889
Yumen, China	8,669	1,864	6,580	1,765	10,560	3,944	5,298	10,005	10,277	6,441	4,487	3,105	4,841	6,807	2,640	5,229	8,265	10,676	13,578	13,751
Yutian, China	7,275	580	5,752	1,070	9,335	3,220	4,850	10,399	9,643	5,309	3,134	4,465	3,887	5,375	3,076	4,298	6,842	10,759	13,529	13,252
Yuzhno-Sakhalinsk, USSR	12,329	5,323	8,236	5,379	12,734	6,085	6,436	7,960	12,799	8,873	7,705	598	7,160	10,216	4,986	7,416	11,873	9,197	11,800	12,935
Zagreb, Yugoslavia	6,198	4,852	778	6,298	4,322	2,554	2,287	7,478	11,758	760	2,917	8,008	1,579	3,687	8,476	1,195	5,468	6,849	8,808	7,986
Zahedan, Iran	5,272	1,771	4,857	2,395	7,540	3,061	4,737	10,892	8,792	3,885	1,409	6,496	3,075	3,282	4,512	3,439	4,781	10,766	13,070	12,223
Zamboanga, Philippines	10,231	5,844	10,940	4,506	14,381	8,311	9,652	12,804	8,050	10,557	8,206	4,773	9,127	9,764	2,345	9,532	10,266	14,045	16,569	17,758
Zanzibar, Tanzania	923	6,312	6,972	6,215	6,035	6,924	8,074	13,536	5,580	5,441	4,557	10,956	6,229	2,517	7,439	6,326	1,114	12,521	12,975	11,298
Zaragoza, Spain	6,439	6,285	1,337	7,726	3,180	3,899	3,123	6,859	12,209	1,770	4,235	9,128	2,997	4,311	9,908	2,596	5,749	5,952	7,546	6,593
Zashiversk, USSR	11,777	5,038	6,264	5,811	10,681	4,619	4,441	6,158	14,323	7,202	6,760	2,153	5,618	9,241	6,342	5,766	11,150	7,190	9,998	10,860
Zhengzhou, China	9,868	3,367	7,957	2,801	12,068	5,342	6,500	10,239	10,301	7,938	5,994	2,336	6,299	8,242	2,299	6,674	9,551	11,198	14,063	14,676
Zurich, Switzerland	6,582	5,370	447	6,849	4,085	2,928	2,266	6,951	12,238	1,269	3,525	8,207	2,062	4,168	9,012	1,653	5,859	6,264	8,200	7,410

Distances in Kilometers

	Kinshasa, Zaire	Kirkwall, United Kingdom	Kirov, USSR	Kiruna, Sweden	Kisangani, Zaire	Kishinev, USSR	Kitchner, Canada	Knoxville, Tennessee	Kosice, Czechoslovakia	Kota Kinabalu, Malaysia	Krakow, Poland	Kralendijk, Bonaire	Krasnodar, USSR	Krasnoyarsk, USSR	Kristiansand, Norway	Kuala Lumpur, Malaysia	Kuching, Malaysia	Kumasi, Ghana	Kumzar, Oman	Kunming, China
Kirkwall, United Kingdom	7,199	0	2,968	1,507	6,933	2,480	5,345	6,168	1,943	11,035	1,767	7,449	3,199	5,249	643	10,540	11,168	5,801	5,790	8,497
Kirov, USSR	7,608	2,968	0	1,782	6,787	1,892	7,805	8,684	2,154	8,084	2,131	10,397	1,671	2,571	2,402	7,600	8,201	7,218	3,617	5,538
Kiruna, Sweden	8,014	1,507	1,782	0	7,484	2,374	6,035	6,911	2,134	9,638	1,979	8,697	2,766	3,772	1,239	9,323	9,851	6,985	5,215	7,135
Kisangani, Zaire	1,222	6,933	6,787	7,484	0	5,164	11,234	11,692	5,355	10,109	5,518	10,384	5,117	8,590	6,572	8,515	9,476	3,055	4,400	8,731
Kishinev, USSR	5,837	2,480	1,892	2,374	5,164	0	7,825	8,641	598	9,317	742	9,561	816	4,386	1,867	8,457	9,239	5,329	3,335	6,817
Kitchner, Canada	10,805	5,345	7,805	6,035	11,234	7,825	0	881	7,272	14,284	7,101	3,661	8,526	8,963	5,970	14,837	14,906	8,604	11,118	12,411
Knoxville, Tennessee	11,123	6,168	8,684	6,911	11,692	8,641	881	0	8,077	14,918	7,910	3,070	9,362	9,807	6,801	15,634	15,599	8,888	11,956	13,214
Kosice, Czechoslovakia	5,900	1,943	2,154	2,134	5,355	598	7,272	8,077	0	9,866	182	8,968	1,410	4,720	1,368	9,045	9,814	5,132	3,921	7,348
Kota Kinabalu, Malaysia	11,258	11,035	8,084	9,638	10,109	9,317	14,284	14,918	9,866	0	9,940	17,943	8,526	5,917	10,487	1,624	804	12,974	6,701	2,549
Krakow, Poland	6,042	1,767	2,131	1,979	5,518	742	7,101	7,910	182	9,940	0	8,853	1,537	4,703	1,187	9,153	9,908	5,213	4,076	7,412
Kralendijk, Bonaire	9,420	7,449	10,397	8,697	10,384	9,561	3,661	3,070	8,968	17,943	8,853	0	10,377	12,247	8,060	17,988	18,480	7,330	12,681	15,772
Krasnodar, USSR	5,951	3,199	1,671	2,766	5,117	816	8,526	9,362	1,410	8,526	1,537	10,377	0	3,896	2,562	7,641	8,429	5,780	2,594	6,048
Krasnoyarsk, USSR	9,631	5,249	2,571	3,772	8,590	4,386	8,963	9,807	4,720	5,917	4,703	12,247	3,896	0	4,801	5,914	6,241	9,672	4,401	3,529
Kristiansand, Norway	6,956	643	2,402	1,239	6,572	1,867	5,970	6,801	1,368	10,487	1,187	8,060	2,562	4,801	0	9,927	10,582	5,771	5,155	7,940
Kuala Lumpur, Malaysia	9,646	10,540	7,600	9,323	8,515	8,457	14,837	15,634	9,045	1,624	9,153	17,988	7,641	5,914	9,927	0	977	11,447	5,465	2,426
Kuching, Malaysia	10,590	11,168	8,201	9,851	9,476	9,239	14,906	15,599	9,814	804	9,908	18,480	8,429	6,241	10,582	977	0	12,423	6,377	2,729
Kumasi, Ghana	2,238	5,801	7,218	6,985	3,055	5,329	8,604	8,888	5,132	12,974	5,213	7,330	5,780	9,672	5,771	11,447	12,423	0	6,507	11,128
Kumzar, Oman	5,577	5,790	3,617	5,215	4,400	3,335	11,118	11,956	3,921	6,701	4,076	12,681	2,594	4,401	5,155	5,465	6,377	6,507	0	4,621
Kunming, China	9,954	8,497	5,538	7,135	8,731	6,817	12,411	13,214	7,348	2,549	7,412	15,772	6,048	3,529	7,940	2,426	2,729	11,128	4,621	0
Kuqa Chang, China	8,527	6,016	3,048	4,734	7,371	4,333	10,494	11,365	4,842	5,067	4,899	13,427	3,599	1,785	5,438	4,590	5,153	9,115	2,979	2,521
Kurgan, USSR	8,041	3,963	1,007	2,675	7,085	2,678	8,582	9,463	3,057	7,080	3,064	11,361	2,184	1,720	3,408	6,650	7,214	7,953	3,311	4,536
Kuwait, Kuwait	5,105	5,041	3,244	4,653	4,007	2,561	10,386	11,200	3,124	7,569	3,290	11,786	1,908	4,590	4,421	6,361	7,268	5,764	898	5,393
Kuybyshev, USSR	7,158	3,276	596	2,273	6,281	1,666	8,307	9,180	2,076	7,887	2,105	10,722	1,217	2,731	2,662	7,266	7,931	6,948	3,028	5,342
Kyoto, Japan	13,041	8,915	6,548	7,417	11,842	8,373	10,576	11,142	8,702	3,795	8,675	14,207	7,831	3,989	8,598	4,977	4,544	13,595	7,467	3,356
Kzyl-Orda, USSR	7,373	4,730	1,869	3,651	6,306	2,827	9,665	10,545	3,358	6,510	3,431	12,173	2,081	2,288	4,112	5,815	6,502	7,687	2,204	3,992
L'vov, USSR	6,056	2,004	1,920	2,018	5,468	477	7,348	8,166	237	9,653	294	9,147	1,248	4,484	1,394	8,859	9,615	5,348	3,806	7,129
La Ceiba, Honduras	11,442	8,165	10,867	9,085	12,354	10,565	3,125	2,255	9,973	16,536	9,823	2,041	11,342	12,048	8,808	17,715	17,332	9,304	13,890	15,371
La Coruna, Spain	5,791	1,775	4,254	3,204	5,803	2,925	5,644	6,311	2,353	12,213	2,272	6,665	3,738	6,762	2,000	11,373	12,164	4,118	6,061	9,681
La Paz, Bolivia	9,185	10,221	13,163	11,623	10,391	11,859	6,756	6,040	11,327	18,758	11,263	3,171	12,633	15,334	10,762	18,170	18,343	7,759	14,224	18,675
La Paz, Mexico	13,809	8,672	10,654	9,027	14,506	11,124	3,460	2,847	10,614	13,992	10,436	4,621	11,736	10,856	9,260	15,424	14,795	11,583	14,239	13,509
La Ronge, Canada	12,301	5,604	7,207	5,650	12,390	7,902	2,202	2,680	7,469	12,240	7,288	5,746	8,410	7,577	6,106	13,090	12,938	10,262	10,815	10,732
Labrador City, Canada	9,867	3,893	6,395	4,615	10,107	6,374	1,456	2,309	5,827	13,468	5,655	4,525	7,070	7,784	4,515	13,695	13,959	7,776	9,662	11,304
Lagos, Nigeria	1,780	5,851	6,999	6,933	2,511	5,109	9,026	9,353	4,977	12,433	5,077	7,878	5,489	9,383	5,751	10,898	11,873	554	6,027	10,644
Lahore, Pakistan	7,395	6,343	3,525	5,307	6,200	4,207	11,310	12,191	4,790	5,185	4,896	13,741	3,394	3,075	5,712	4,258	5,037	8,294	1,835	2,867
Lambasa, Fiji	17,131	15,279	13,798	14,102	16,692	15,674	12,060	11,661	15,916	7,397	15,845	12,753	15,153	11,295	15,318	8,806	7,836	18,921	14,062	9,495
Lansing, Michigan	11,139	5,625	8,013	6,255	11,574	8,105	340	753	7,560	14,224	7,387	3,735	8,792	9,058	6,244	14,883	14,880	8,933	11,379	12,462
Lanzhou, China	10,147	7,509	4,613	6,081	8,945	6,124	11,191	11,993	6,597	3,562	6,632	14,602	5,423	2,366	6,996	3,647	3,881	10,936	4,586	1,221
Laoag, Philippines	11,783	10,042	7,191	8,573	10,571	8,682	12,849	13,481	9,173	1,438	9,213	16,510	7,950	4,801	9,557	2,648	2,156	13,116	6,613	2,002
Largeau, Chad	2,493	4,898	5,154	5,548	2,038	3,346	9,407	9,979	3,420	10,546	3,569	9,335	3,530	7,363	4,561	9,125	10,094	2,571	3,945	8,562
Las Vegas, Nevada	13,854	7,760	9,413	7,885	14,251	10,119	3,052	2,801	9,664	12,934	9,483	5,385	10,644	9,452	8,296	14,220	13,729	11,639	13,030	12,154
Launceston, Australia	12,988	17,161	14,209	15,718	12,656	15,177	16,150	15,605	15,772	6,128	15,891	15,292	14,363	11,946	16,608	6,743	6,035	15,079	11,952	8,671
Le Havre, France	6,138	1,072	3,315	2,328	5,933	2,136	5,926	6,680	1,540	11,321	1,422	7,432	2,949	5,819	1,093	10,575	11,321	4,749	5,420	8,778
Leipzig, East Germany	6,168	1,290	2,490	1,893	5,759	1,292	6,584	7,382	701	10,438	552	8,310	2,089	5,041	813	9,692	10,432	5,112	4,621	7,898
Leningrad, USSR	7,240	1,867	1,117	1,010	6,604	1,441	6,938	7,803	1,376	9,201	1,276	9,314	1,756	3,589	1,286	8,676	9,305	6,487	4,235	6,654
Leon, Spain	5,605	1,830	4,150	3,201	5,584	2,743	5,887	6,556	2,184	12,051	2,118	6,875	3,550	6,683	1,974	11,174	11,979	3,998	5,837	9,529
Lerwick, United Kingdom	7,290	167	2,827	1,341	6,994	2,432	5,402	6,235	1,916	10,884	1,737	7,581	3,127	5,087	568	10,410	11,027	5,932	5,721	8,349
Lhasa, China	8,886	7,455	4,491	6,188	7,670	5,614	11,865	12,723	6,162	3,705	6,239	14,881	4,828	2,932	6,865	3,138	3,717	9,912	3,419	1,253
Libreville, Gabon	832	6,587	7,346	7,533	1,753	5,498	9,977	10,292	5,473	11,854	5,597	8,673	5,738	9,560	6,409	10,267	11,229	1,413	5,790	10,324
Lilongwe, Malawi	2,294	8,743	8,169	9,142	1,860	6,772	13,023	13,400	7,053	9,349	7,226	11,620	6,557	9,490	8,337	7,730	8,609	4,530	5,089	8,631
Lima, Peru	10,175	10,256	13,220	11,543	11,364	12,185	6,155	5,364	11,615	18,442	11,523	2,849	12,992	15,049	10,848	19,013	18,597	8,601	14,919	18,563
Limerick, Ireland	6,703	786	3,613	2,284	6,579	2,734	5,225	5,989	2,140	11,696	1,994	6,912	3,527	5,991	1,213	11,079	11,769	5,139	6,058	9,147
Limoges, France	5,725	1,488	3,507	2,685	5,543	2,114	6,191	6,916	1,542	11,406	1,467	7,464	2,928	6,053	1,447	10,567	11,352	4,347	5,296	8,879
Limon, Costa Rica	11,013	8,491	11,306	9,530	12,007	10,806	3,715	2,878	10,209	17,266	10,071	1,631	11,607	12,678	9,130	18,461	18,068	8,955	14,073	16,077
Lincoln, Nebraska	12,167	6,431	8,561	6,863	12,598	8,889	1,369	1,237	8,373	13,845	8,196	4,217	9,523	9,236	7,024	14,790	14,579	9,955	12,070	12,442
Linz, Austria	5,828	1,637	2,575	2,203	5,400	1,100	6,887	7,670	515	10,379	455	8,461	1,916	5,146	1,175	9,556	10,329	4,852	4,379	7,857
Lisbon, Portugal	5,386	2,295	4,670	3,709	5,492	3,202	5,832	6,441	2,665	12,519	2,613	6,505	3,997	7,208	2,491	11,579	12,411	3,628	6,179	10,012
Little Rock, Arkansas	11,891	6,737	9,081	7,338	12,462	9,217	1,403	772	8,670	14,612	8,498	3,484	9,902	9,936	7,356	15,563	15,353	9,654	12,487	13,200
Liverpool, United Kingdom	6,622	618	3,251	2,024	6,417	2,359	5,549	6,330	1,769	11,327	1,618	7,297	3,147	5,668	868	10,694	11,389	5,184	5,690	8,779
Lodz, Poland	6,224	1,622	2,049	1,794	5,706	860	6,965	7,781	362	9,943	188	8,801	1,621	4,618	1,022	9,198	9,934	5,359	4,189	7,406
Lome, Togo	1,945	5,872	7,134	6,999	2,736	5,242	8,875	9,178	5,083	12,675	5,176	7,649	5,651	9,547	5,802	11,140	12,114	319	6,256	10,875
London, United Kingdom	6,355	850	3,201	2,129	6,132	2,151	5,814	6,584	1,554	11,245	1,417	7,449	2,954	5,676	906	10,549	11,272	4,971	5,467	8,698
Londonderry, United Kingdom	6,897	516	3,403	2,020	6,726	2,655	5,223	6,011	2,073	11,487	1,914	7,070	3,429	5,745	1,003	10,918	11,585	5,383	5,990	8,941
Longlac, Canada	11,223	5,160	7,353	5,626	11,508	7,617	842	1,549	7,102	13,454	6,924	4,495	8,256	8,277	5,751	14,085	14,093	9,081	10,816	11,664
Lord Howe Island, Australia	14,499	16,674	14,046	15,177	14,082	15,487	14,709	14,269	16,019	6,172	16,074	14,735	14,698	11,542	16,330	7,175	6,312	16,607	12,624	8,673
Los Angeles, California	14,208	8,104	9,681	8,187	14,618	10,445	3,411	3,125	10,000	12,799	9,818	5,597	10,951	9,599	8,633	14,146	13,599	11,987	13,297	12,169
Louangphrabang, Laos	9,847	8,965	5,997	7,637	8,631	7,165	12,989	13,792	7,715	2,152	7,792	16,311	6,375	4,087	8,390	1,848	2,214	11,190	4,714	579
Louisville, Kentucky	11,274	6,073	8,513	6,749	11,795	8,552	729	301	7,997	14,617	7,827	3,371	9,255	9,558	6,698	15,356	15,302	9,045	11,847	12,941
Luanda, Angola	548	7,652	8,153	8,521	1,679	6,371	10,977	11,225	6,418	11,526	6,556	9,309	6,498	10,173	7,438	9,904	10,826	2,376	6,074	10,371
Lubumbashi, Zaire	1,569	8,296	8,040	8,839	1,369	6,499	12,343	12,688	6,715	10,000	6,880	10,900	6,386	9,609	7,941	8,376	9,276	3,807	5,243	9,108
Lusaka, Zambia	1,880	8,719	8,428	9,258	1,793	6,913	12,684	12,991	7,136	9,956	7,302	11,062	6,781	9,921	8,365	8,338	9,211	4,105	5,532	9,225
Luxembourg, Luxembourg	6,037	1,196	2,959	2,178	5,737	1,702	6,304	7,074	1,105	10,914	992	7,864	2,515	5,498	961	10,144	10,897	4,813	4,993	8,376
Luxor, Egypt	3,810	4,614	3,888	4,763	2,899	2,389	9,765	10,484	2,741	9,071	2,921	10,503	2,221	5,837	4,096	7,765	8,706	4,203	2,377	6,957
Lynn Lake, Canada	11,983	5,282	6,949	5,363	12,062	7,595	2,078	2,652	7,155	12,272	6,973	5,693	8,117	7,429	5,790	13,043	12,947	9,960	10,547	10,658
Lyon, France	5,640	1,561	3,304	2,616	5,395	1,843	6,438	7,173	1,282	11,148	1,222	7,742	2,655	5,864	1,398	10,291	11,082	4,374	5,017	8,628
Macapa, Brazil	7,394	7,754	10,627	9,225	8,488	9,240	5,630	5,233	8,715	18,454	8,659	2,328	10,012	12,996	8,246	16,985	17,958	5,539	11,752	16,057
Madison, Wisconsin	11,530	5,857	8,127	6,392	11,944	8,330	724	918	7,799	14,000	7,623	3,984	8,992	9,021	6,463	14,765	14,686	9,327	11,565	12,360
Madras, India	7,435	8,383	5,654	7,435	6,230	6,070	13,448	14,329	6,668	4,002	6,801	15,569	5,264	4,885	7,742	2,600	3,549	8,978	2,892	2,699
Madrid, Spain	5,316	2,066	4,216	3,382	5,297	2,700	6,144	6,796	2,172	12,017	2,129	6,995	3,493	6,770	2,144	11,079	11,907	3,741	5,694	9,514
Madurai, India	7,141	8,554	5,906	7,678	5,950	6,185	13,711	14,589	6,782	4,205	6,923	15,578	5,393	5,271	7,912	2,712	3,683	8,771	2,918	3,091
Magadan, USSR	12,807	6,662	5,222	5,313	11,869	7,073	7,664	8,290	7,164	6,633	7,067	11,321	6,860	3,359	6,549	7,524	7,315	12,266	7,759	5,320
Magdalena, Bolivia	8,766	9,710	12,639	11,132	9,959	11,306	6,504	5,841	10,777	19,191	10,716	2,857	12,078	14,875	10,240	18,104	18,572	7,256	13,693	18,123
Magdeburg, East Germany	6,267	1,189	2,477	1,807	5,865	1,364	6,494	7,296	782	10,457	622	8,263	2,151	5,017	707	9,735	10,464	5,188	4,698	7,915
Majuro Atoll, Marshall Isls.	17,350	12,656	11,068	11,376	16,167	12,958	10,918	10,870	13,162	6,096	13,087	13,116	12,524	8,629	12,608	7,712	6,780	18,287	12,081	7,519
Malabo, Equatorial Guinea	1,148	6,208	7,030	7,168	1,861	5,167	9,667	10,014	5,121	11,883	5,242	8,523	5,441	9,293	6,036	10,320	11,290	1,198	5,653	10,233
Male, Maldives	6,534	8,850	6,391	8,128	5,382	6,403	14,140	14,998	6,987	4,729	7,144	15,436	5,651	6,021	8,211	3,138	4,108	8,321	3,068	3,899
Manado, Indonesia	12,201	11,913	9,008	10,462	11,092	10,347	14,427	14,906	10,880	1,095	10,943	17,927	9,568	6,693	11,401	2,582	1,616	14,021	7,797	3,533
Managua, Nicaragua	11,377	8,476	11,221	9,439	12,342	10,846	3,514	2,649	10,251	16,840	10,106	1,961	11,633	12,450	9,118	18,101	17,643	9,286	14,153	15,776
Manama, Bahrain	5,085	5,476	3,592	5,060	3,937	2,996	10,821	11,635	3,559	7,278	3,725	12,167	2,331	4,727	4,855	6,015	6,938	5,931	583	5,197
Manaus, Brazil	8,365	8,499	11,438	9,917	9,490	10,176	5,552	4,992	9,630	19,490	9,558	1,923	10,965	13,662	9,036	18,006	18,950	6,580	12,799	16,962
Manchester, New Hampshire	10,071	4,878	7,517	5,735	10,516	7,339	734	1,323	6,768	14,528	6,604	3,431	8,076	8,933	5,516	14,847	15,068	7,870	10,667	12,445
Mandalay, Burma	9,247	8,438	5,474	7,167	8,026	6,544	12,749	13,589	7,105	2,786	7,189	15,862	5,745	3,786	7,845	2,170	2,739	10,529	4,044	755
Mangareva Island, Fr.Polynesia	15,589	14,540	16,052	14,748	16,721	16,989	9,234	8,461	16,483	12,217	16,306	8,244	17,513	14,689	15,130	13,553	12,607	14,720	18,826	14,212
Manila, Philippines	11,828	10,422	7,551	8,959	10,629	9,000	13,219	13,830	9,503	1,094	9,549	16,878	8,253	5,188	9,927	2,467	1,859	13,277	6,798	2,239
Mannheim, West Germany	5,995	1,288	2,831	2,148	5,659	1,533	6,456	7,232	937	10,758	827	8,032	2,346	5,381	967	9,978	10,734	4,838	4,826	8,223
Maputo, Mozambique	3,024	9,966	9,500	10,453	3,034	8,089	13,765	13,962	8,346	9,658	8,516	11,672	7,889	10,712	9,599	8,099	8,869	5,167	6,328	9,415
Mar del Plata, Argentina	8,217	11,868	14,476	13,373	9,411	12,726	9,313	8,629	12,344	16,401	12,350	5,665	13,323	17,040	12,267	15,613	15,785	7,607	13,792	17,666
Maracaibo, Venezuela	9,770	7,779	10,712	8,990	10,754	9,930	3,733	3,065	9,336	17,982	9,217	401	10,745	12,475	8,397	18,311	18,637	7,702	13,073	16,004
Marrakech, Morocco	4,682	3,062	5,210	4,425	4,907	3,560	6,336	6,864	3,098	12,781	3,088	6,505	4,301	7,778	3,189	11,679	12,570	2,841	6,216	10,346
Marseilles, France	5,365	1,835	3,460	2,871	5,134	1,881	6,619	7,335	1,363	11,197	1,339	7,773	2,675	6,029	1,664	10,281	11,096	4,115	4,944	8,696
Maseru, Lesotho	3,053	10,181	9,954	10,791	3,309	8,453	13,575	13,678	8,663	10,201	8,826	11,220	8,316	11,286	9,863	8,664	9,405	5,057	6,889	10,035

Distances in Kilometers

	Kinshasa, Zaire	Kirkwall, United Kingdom	Kirov, USSR	Kiruna, Sweden	Kisangani, Zaire	Kishinev, USSR	Kitchner, Canada	Knoxville, Tennessee	Kosice, Czechoslovakia	Kota Kinabalu, Malaysia	Krakow, Poland	Kralendijk, Bonaire	Krasnodar, USSR	Krasnoyarsk, USSR	Kristiansand, Norway	Kuala Lumpur, Malaysia	Kuching, Malaysia	Kumasi, Ghana	Kumzar, Oman	Kunming, China
Mashhad, Iran	6,434	5,089	2,578	4,281	5,320	2,801	10,297	11,163	3,395	6,640	3,517	12,362	1,985	3,319	4,447	5,662	6,476	7,006	1,146	4,274
Mazatlan, Mexico	13,440	8,560	10,679	9,009	14,177	11,031	3,270	2,588	10,502	14,390	10,327	4,213	11,676	11,039	9,164	15,799	15,193	11,221	14,222	13,816
Mbabane, Swaziland	2,964	9,961	9,561	10,481	3,035	8,123	13,672	13,852	8,367	9,805	8,535	11,534	7,941	10,816	9,607	8,247	9,016	5,083	6,426	9,558
Mbandaka, Zaire	585	6,790	7,047	7,523	773	5,301	10,713	11,105	5,397	10,882	5,545	9,640	5,384	9,047	6,506	9,289	10,249	2,326	5,016	9,450
McMurdo Sound, Antarctica	10,733	17,889	16,857	18,459	11,120	16,119	15,262	14,383	16,445	9,742	16,618	12,157	15,694	15,606	17,680	9,723	9,368	12,098	13,289	12,079
Mecca, Saudi Arabia	3,907	5,369	4,196	5,334	2,809	3,003	10,597	11,333	3,445	8,353	3,626	11,340	2,617	5,782	4,813	6,981	7,937	4,744	1,773	6,388
Medan, Indonesia	9,314	10,330	7,411	9,154	8,179	8,197	14,795	15,618	8,788	1,948	8,902	17,754	7,380	5,838	9,710	340	1,317	11,107	5,157	2,416
Medellin, Colombia	10,168	8,422	11,343	9,608	11,206	10,585	4,150	3,399	9,991	18,148	9,872	1,036	11,401	13,022	9,043	18,923	18,932	8,174	13,717	16,535
Medicine Hat, Canada	12,870	6,271	7,834	6,307	13,020	8,570	2,401	2,660	8,139	12,350	7,957	5,702	9,070	8,049	6,776	13,348	13,089	10,776	11,449	11,060
Medina, Saudi Arabia	4,130	5,065	3,869	5,001	3,073	2,677	10,323	11,074	3,133	8,373	3,314	11,213	2,282	5,522	4,500	7,052	7,996	4,812	1,704	6,318
Melbourne, Australia	13,045	16,730	13,786	15,281	12,625	14,816	16,173	15,710	15,407	5,702	15,517	15,662	14,000	11,509	16,188	6,364	5,632	15,196	11,639	8,248
Memphis, Tennessee	11,685	6,582	8,974	7,221	12,255	9,062	1,238	564	8,510	14,702	8,339	3,361	9,758	9,902	7,205	15,594	15,429	9,448	12,347	13,210
Merauke, Indonesia	13,773	13,605	10,841	12,103	12,793	12,321	14,478	14,608	12,828	3,132	12,872	16,879	11,563	8,372	13,172	4,477	3,509	15,835	9,828	5,516
Merida, Mexico	11,737	7,844	10,435	8,659	12,565	10,291	2,634	1,753	9,710	15,925	9,551	2,475	11,042	11,471	8,484	17,069	16,713	9,547	13,625	14,743
Meridian, Mississippi	11,585	6,753	9,217	7,454	12,212	9,229	1,425	595	8,667	15,023	8,499	3,060	9,943	10,210	7,383	15,923	15,755	9,347	12,536	13,536
Messina, Italy	4,703	2,664	3,331	3,314	4,288	1,461	7,647	8,363	1,255	10,515	1,367	8,651	2,087	5,847	2,289	9,458	10,324	3,896	4,030	8,097
Mexico City, Mexico	12,741	8,527	10,906	9,169	13,576	11,004	3,187	2,366	10,442	15,253	10,275	3,399	11,712	11,572	9,155	16,637	16,057	10,557	14,304	14,552
Miami, Florida	10,772	6,864	9,582	7,801	11,531	9,273	1,961	1,185	8,684	16,082	8,532	1,958	10,045	10,918	7,507	16,796	16,780	8,552	12,605	14,371
Midway Islands, USA	17,045	10,331	9,454	9,255	16,030	11,272	8,426	8,516	11,289	7,407	11,168	11,191	11,100	7,445	10,421	8,960	8,200	16,118	11,684	7,815
Milan, Italy	5,546	1,710	3,075	2,573	5,224	1,520	6,741	7,489	982	10,835	952	8,080	2,327	5,645	1,415	9,957	10,755	4,423	4,677	8,325
Milford Sound, New Zealand	13,940	18,287	15,630	16,805	13,895	16,853	14,710	14,044	17,438	7,612	17,535	13,621	16,037	13,163	17,961	8,396	7,627	15,682	13,667	10,154
Milwaukee, Wisconsin	11,410	5,781	8,087	6,344	11,830	8,257	605	857	7,721	14,065	7,547	3,911	8,926	9,027	6,391	14,798	14,742	9,207	11,504	12,387
Minsk, USSR	6,551	1,946	1,459	1,602	5,924	773	7,245	8,088	727	9,376	675	9,303	1,285	4,030	1,303	8,688	9,395	5,858	3,872	6,833
Mogadiscio, Somalia	3,418	7,560	6,276	7,550	2,251	5,230	12,641	13,289	5,658	7,859	5,840	12,533	4,801	7,324	7,025	6,265	7,229	5,238	2,934	6,644
Mombasa, Kenya	2,705	7,932	6,998	8,121	1,686	5,755	12,722	13,266	6,112	8,565	6,291	12,063	5,437	8,216	7,454	6,947	7,886	4,739	3,816	7,525
Monclova, Mexico	12,877	7,947	10,165	8,462	13,565	10,425	2,633	1,939	9,886	14,587	9,712	3,826	11,090	10,719	8,559	15,863	15,384	10,646	13,657	13,704
Moncton, Canada	9,591	4,257	6,950	5,170	9,969	6,712	1,275	1,955	6,138	14,235	5,975	3,776	7,455	8,495	4,898	14,388	14,704	7,423	10,042	12,023
Monrovia, Liberia	3,129	5,879	7,731	7,215	4,050	5,881	7,893	8,084	5,584	13,978	5,633	6,337	6,436	10,267	5,976	12,462	13,438	1,017	7,436	12,044
Monte Carlo, Monaco	5,378	1,837	3,310	2,789	5,104	1,711	6,729	7,457	1,199	11,027	1,183	7,937	2,505	5,881	1,606	10,114	10,927	4,199	4,787	8,527
Monterrey, Mexico	12,788	8,003	10,269	8,554	13,504	10,483	2,670	1,936	9,938	14,756	9,766	3,678	11,160	10,869	8,620	16,039	15,555	10,562	13,737	13,875
Montevideo, Uruguay	8,053	11,504	14,133	13,008	9,259	12,403	9,018	8,355	12,008	16,709	12,010	5,361	13,018	16,689	11,907	15,823	16,062	7,339	13,612	17,719
Montgomery, Alabama	11,360	6,618	9,135	7,364	11,993	9,089	1,330	455	8,521	15,149	8,356	2,900	9,813	10,209	7,252	15,982	15,865	9,122	12,407	13,576
Montpelier, Vermont	10,173	4,840	7,437	5,655	10,592	7,310	642	1,333	6,744	14,373	6,578	3,581	8,037	8,807	5,475	14,721	14,922	7,980	10,630	12,313
Montpellier, France	5,427	1,773	3,524	2,867	5,223	1,984	6,497	7,211	1,452	11,302	1,415	7,652	2,784	6,089	1,645	10,399	11,209	4,126	5,069	8,795
Montreal, Canada	10,263	4,800	7,355	5,575	10,657	7,276	593	1,369	6,715	14,222	6,547	3,730	7,993	8,682	5,432	14,594	14,778	8,080	10,587	12,181
Moosonee, Canada	10,794	4,742	7,026	5,277	11,062	7,209	871	1,722	6,685	13,462	6,508	4,481	7,865	8,095	5,342	13,967	14,059	8,669	10,439	11,541
Moroni, Comoros	3,187	8,863	7,807	9,013	2,410	6,657	13,602	14,098	7,031	8,293	7,212	12,599	6,296	8,791	8,379	6,672	7,559	5,369	4,440	7,619
Moscow, USSR	6,962	2,427	796	1,618	6,227	1,146	7,573	8,436	1,359	8,739	1,340	9,865	1,196	3,364	1,805	8,122	8,792	6,445	3,604	6,192
Mosul, Iraq	5,350	4,152	2,516	3,790	4,378	1,675	9,497	10,316	2,249	8,092	2,410	11,062	1,027	4,291	3,529	7,018	7,879	5,604	1,678	5,751
Mount Isa, Australia	13,341	14,816	11,938	13,336	12,559	13,223	15,547	15,491	13,777	3,911	13,851	16,925	12,423	9,569	14,325	4,899	4,023	15,564	10,362	6,445
Multan, Pakistan	7,088	6,306	3,563	5,340	5,891	4,092	11,367	12,246	4,683	5,375	4,798	13,651	3,276	3,325	5,669	4,366	5,182	8,019	1,537	3,121
Munich, West Germany	5,822	1,535	2,742	2,248	5,441	1,301	6,729	7,503	718	10,579	645	8,260	2,118	5,309	1,140	9,758	10,531	4,763	4,567	8,055
Murcia, Spain	4,979	2,337	4,267	3,577	4,949	2,638	6,474	7,112	2,157	11,921	2,144	7,190	3,403	6,836	2,340	10,915	11,769	3,467	5,491	9,449
Murmansk, USSR	8,244	2,042	1,412	542	7,622	2,458	6,409	7,290	2,349	9,106	2,220	9,198	2,686	3,231	1,710	8,835	9,337	7,366	4,984	6,615
Mururoa Atoll, Fr. Polynesia	15,986	14,621	15,873	14,694	17,090	17,009	9,373	8,629	16,552	11,812	16,371	8,581	17,428	14,345	15,185	13,175	12,221	15,149	18,396	13,782
Muscat, Oman	5,620	6,162	3,944	5,569	4,419	3,707	11,487	12,327	4,291	6,442	4,447	13,018	2,965	4,551	5,527	5,157	6,084	6,686	372	4,458
Myitkyina, Burma	9,428	8,190	5,222	6,881	8,205	6,394	12,380	13,213	6,940	2,926	7,014	15,573	5,610	3,422	7,612	2,501	2,980	10,599	4,092	534
Naga, Philippines	12,063	10,617	7,766	9,145	10,869	9,239	13,244	13,824	9,736	1,151	9,779	16,889	8,497	5,373	10,133	2,631	1,947	13,533	7,056	2,493
Nagasaki, Japan	12,568	8,945	6,412	7,438	11,357	8,179	11,015	11,620	8,553	3,298	8,543	14,670	7,585	3,842	8,577	4,406	4,020	13,289	7,017	2,781
Nagoya, Japan	13,138	8,934	6,598	7,439	11,942	8,430	10,512	11,070	8,753	3,875	8,723	14,137	7,898	4,045	8,626	5,073	4,629	13,667	7,563	3,464
Nagpur, India	7,502	7,564	4,776	6,558	6,280	5,331	12,555	13,437	5,925	4,322	6,046	14,890	4,515	4,035	6,927	3,154	4,023	8,791	2,379	2,451
Nairobi, Kenya	2,415	7,532	6,732	7,779	1,308	5,406	12,282	12,826	5,738	8,844	5,917	11,690	5,135	8,099	7,068	7,237	8,189	4,360	3,711	7,659
Nanchang, China	11,277	8,788	5,963	7,316	10,056	7,527	11,845	12,556	7,991	2,513	8,019	15,463	6,830	3,544	8,312	3,199	3,060	12,276	5,820	1,371
Nancy, France	5,936	1,291	3,017	2,275	5,642	1,698	6,359	7,123	1,106	10,943	1,007	7,863	2,514	5,564	1,062	10,151	10,914	4,714	4,968	8,409
Nandi, Fiji	16,882	15,434	13,826	14,214	16,435	15,686	12,317	11,918	15,963	7,234	15,904	12,975	15,127	11,300	15,440	8,616	7,651	18,771	13,919	9,382
Nanjing, China	11,539	8,583	5,834	7,092	10,323	7,482	11,418	12,114	7,915	2,900	7,929	15,055	6,821	3,338	8,137	3,663	3,491	12,397	6,016	1,753
Nanning, China	10,509	9,000	6,061	7,598	9,289	7,409	12,613	13,373	7,929	2,040	7,986	16,117	6,649	3,900	8,462	2,288	2,363	11,743	5,237	625
Nantes, France	5,942	1,311	3,570	2,610	5,790	2,292	5,929	6,658	1,704	11,540	1,608	7,270	3,108	6,088	1,376	10,748	11,515	4,492	5,521	9,003
Naples, Italy	4,999	2,350	3,168	3,029	4,602	1,354	7,375	8,106	1,034	10,566	1,119	8,511	2,065	5,715	1,978	9,569	10,412	4,099	4,183	8,110
Narvik, Norway	8,072	1,445	1,914	133	7,563	2,473	5,902	6,778	2,208	9,742	2,049	8,578	2,885	3,864	1,235	9,445	9,965	7,000	5,345	7,246
Nashville, Tennessee	11,379	6,310	8,761	6,997	11,939	8,788	972	259	8,231	14,771	8,062	3,243	9,495	9,790	6,938	15,563	15,472	9,145	12,088	13,155
Nassau, Bahamas	10,484	6,763	9,535	7,757	11,256	9,144	2,057	1,361	8,551	16,278	8,403	1,720	9,926	10,971	7,406	16,877	16,946	8,268	12,465	14,456
Natal, Brazil	5,603	7,730	10,257	9,232	6,750	8,566	7,099	6,865	8,142	16,858	8,137	4,162	9,237	12,816	8,072	15,249	16,183	3,979	10,461	15,063
Natashquan, Canada	9,463	3,794	6,448	4,667	9,754	6,263	1,604	2,379	5,698	13,776	5,531	4,259	6,992	8,000	4,431	13,885	14,222	7,347	9,584	11,529
Nauru Island	16,837	13,465	11,599	12,112	15,778	13,459	11,858	11,765	13,743	5,699	13,691	13,808	12,926	9,074	13,351	7,270	6,305	18,589	12,082	7,461
Ndjamena, Chad	1,816	5,413	5,912	6,201	1,705	4,078	9,535	10,021	4,097	11,070	4,234	9,025	4,301	8,140	5,145	9,581	10,557	1,926	4,601	9,218
Nelson, New Zealand	14,488	18,020	15,693	16,636	14,472	17,132	14,146	13,498	17,681	7,817	17,740	13,266	16,329	13,156	17,861	8,719	7,903	16,139	14,081	10,333
Nema, Mauritania	3,393	4,714	6,551	6,020	3,980	4,724	7,413	7,762	4,398	13,313	4,440	6,576	5,326	9,103	4,782	11,928	12,895	1,258	6,624	11,143
Neuquen, Argentina	9,140	12,396	15,165	13,877	10,330	13,503	9,211	8,454	13,080	16,330	13,068	5,659	14,145	17,645	12,854	15,910	15,860	8,488	14,715	18,242
New Delhi, India	7,548	6,775	3,942	5,723	6,337	4,632	11,709	12,590	5,217	4,795	5,325	14,173	3,817	3,289	6,145	3,829	4,619	8,571	2,067	2,558
New Glasgow, Canada	9,417	4,174	6,908	5,133	9,803	6,617	1,435	2,079	6,039	14,292	5,878	3,742	7,368	8,513	4,816	14,389	14,738	7,247	9,950	12,042
New Haven, Connecticut	10,175	5,097	7,739	5,957	10,653	7,556	668	1,125	6,982	14,690	6,819	3,260	8,295	9,137	5,736	15,050	15,248	7,962	10,884	12,643
New Orleans, Louisiana	11,733	7,045	9,512	7,750	12,402	9,520	1,721	879	8,956	15,156	8,789	2,991	10,236	10,474	7,676	16,133	15,907	9,498	12,830	13,766
New Plymouth, New Zealand	14,736	17,781	15,559	16,425	14,697	17,082	13,965	13,340	17,604	7,768	17,645	13,238	16,293	13,007	17,659	8,725	7,888	16,392	14,127	10,266
New York, New York	10,262	5,207	7,840	6,058	10,752	7,667	617	1,013	7,094	14,734	6,931	3,212	8,406	9,214	5,846	15,127	15,305	8,045	10,995	12,715
Newcastle upon Tyne, UK	6,756	449	3,083	1,825	6,515	2,291	5,569	6,365	1,713	11,166	1,551	7,425	3,062	5,481	686	10,564	11,244	5,356	5,626	8,618
Newcastle Waters, Australia	12,824	14,202	11,281	12,750	11,966	12,504	15,719	15,815	13,065	3,213	13,146	17,633	11,700	8,979	13,680	4,159	3,286	15,009	9,622	5,759
Niamey, Niger	2,450	5,062	6,359	6,176	2,924	4,469	8,396	8,790	4,280	12,425	4,367	7,614	4,930	8,817	4,980	10,971	11,946	859	5,817	10,420
Nicosia, Cyprus	4,760	3,739	2,865	3,731	3,930	1,368	9,030	9,806	1,803	8,970	1,984	10,274	1,196	4,991	3,170	7,846	8,730	4,769	2,407	6,643
Niue (Alofi)	17,364	15,446	14,579	14,532	17,387	16,466	11,396	10,884	16,564	8,567	16,450	11,660	16,083	12,187	15,655	9,961	8,996	18,157	15,227	10,640
Norfolk, Virginia	10,438	5,661	8,312	6,530	11,001	8,112	815	692	7,534	15,094	7,373	2,850	8,858	9,663	6,301	15,570	15,699	8,205	11,444	13,150
Norfolk Island, Australia	15,309	16,607	14,339	15,194	14,962	15,975	13,843	13,379	16,441	6,768	16,456	13,939	15,236	11,775	16,420	7,901	6,998	17,303	13,366	9,193
Noril'sk, USSR	9,783	4,132	2,178	2,630	8,919	4,033	7,462	8,309	4,170	7,324	4,094	10,778	3,833	1,503	3,819	7,414	7,704	9,302	5,209	5,015
Norman Wells, Canada	12,613	5,451	6,266	5,006	12,369	7,378	3,730	4,301	7,070	10,617	6,897	7,353	7,712	6,140	5,799	11,467	11,307	10,870	9,844	9,136
Normanton, Australia	13,603	14,577	11,745	13,083	12,773	13,108	15,189	15,167	13,647	3,795	13,710	16,822	12,321	9,329	14,113	4,899	3,986	15,806	10,359	6,299
North Pole	10,480	3,465	3,511	2,475	9,949	4,797	5,190	6,020	4,608	9,340	4,454	8,657	5,015	3,792	3,554	9,652	9,830	9,265	7,090	7,228
Nottingham, United Kingdom	6,533	677	3,173	2,012	6,308	2,233	5,681	6,462	1,641	11,240	1,492	7,407	3,024	5,615	817	10,586	11,290	5,132	5,562	8,692
Norway House, Canada	11,891	5,372	7,192	5,562	12,046	7,739	1,724	2,274	7,276	12,648	7,094	5,319	8,296	7,771	5,908	13,417	13,325	9,817	10,769	11,028
Norwich, United Kingdom	6,446	753	3,051	1,975	6,191	2,064	5,848	6,631	1,471	11,105	1,323	7,565	2,857	5,518	747	10,430	11,143	5,102	5,391	8,557
Nouakchott, Mauritania	4,231	4,659	6,898	6,087	4,902	5,181	6,603	6,892	4,764	14,126	4,769	5,644	5,868	9,469	4,862	12,807	13,763	2,004	7,426	11,840
Noumea, New Caledonia	15,720	15,843	13,638	14,432	15,189	15,347	13,518	13,155	15,771	6,315	15,768	14,138	14,649	11,068	15,661	7,574	6,633	17,867	13,000	8,651
Novosibirsk, USSR	9,001	4,871	2,045	3,447	7,970	3,797	8,979	9,844	4,164	6,190	4,161	12,085	3,274	635	4,375	5,996	6,429	9,054	3,847	3,701
Nuku'alofa, Tonga	16,971	15,758	14,530	14,703	16,838	16,416	11,966	11,472	16,617	8,077	16,531	12,236	15,920	12,050	15,884	9,428	8,470	18,268	14,771	10,240
Nukunono Island, Tokelau Isls.	18,319	14,405	13,504	13,431	17,906	15,382	10,822	10,427	15,458	8,166	15,343	11,702	15,058	11,177	14,572	9,679	8,703	18,929	14,605	9,988
Nuremberg, West Germany	5,969	1,395	2,681	2,112	5,590	1,343	6,619	7,402	747	10,577	640	8,222	2,157	5,241	991	9,788	10,548	4,888	4,642	8,045
Nyala, Sudan	2,096	5,701	5,565	6,206	1,278	3,892	10,304	10,868	4,078	10,009	4,242	10,075	3,895	7,538	5,312	8,511	9,487	2,969	3,659	8,239
Oaxaca, Mexico	12,499	8,612	11,083	9,327	13,379	11,078	3,304	2,448	10,506	15,611	10,342	3,110	11,809	11,859	9,247	17,003	16,414	10,177	14,402	14,897
Ocean Falls, Canada	13,691	6,702	7,707	6,409	13,626	8,771	3,595	3,867	8,427	11,210	8,250	6,886	9,139	7,431	7,114	12,317	11,970	11,727	11,279	10,139
Odense, Denmark	6,633	897	2,381	1,478	6,233	1,585	6,240	7,059	1,052	10,441	873	8,186	2,322	4,864	341	9,803	10,494	5,507	4,905	7,892
Odessa, USSR	5,826	2,626	1,849	2,457	5,121	157	7,970	8,790	755	9,174	897	9,716	662	4,307	2,007	8,303	9,089	5,387	3,182	6,680

Distances in Kilometers

	Kinshasa, Zaire	Kirkwall, United Kingdom	Kirov, USSR	Kiruna, Sweden	Kisangani, Zaire	Kishinev, USSR	Kitchner, Canada	Knoxville, Tennessee	Kosice, Czechoslovakia	Kota Kinabalu, Malaysia	Krakow, Poland	Kralendijk, Bonaire	Krasnodar, USSR	Krasnoyarsk, USSR	Kristiansand, Norway	Kuala Lumpur, Malaysia	Kuching, Malaysia	Kumasi, Ghana	Kumzar, Oman	Kunming, China
Ogbomosho, Nigeria	1,842	5,673	6,789	6,736	2,471	4,899	8,971	9,325	4,771	12,306	4,873	7,940	5,280	9,174	5,560	10,787	11,763	669	5,855	10,475
Okha, USSR	12,787	7,158	5,358	5,734	11,751	7,247	8,487	9,111	7,419	5,810	7,343	12,145	6,924	3,163	6,970	6,732	6,496	12,550	7,474	4,593
Okinawa (Naha)	12,457	9,533	6,869	8,029	11,235	8,552	11,774	12,369	8,972	2,556	8,980	15,425	7,898	4,330	9,124	3,767	3,301	13,453	7,015	2,508
Oklahoma City, Oklahoma	12,350	6,949	9,148	7,439	12,885	9,420	1,705	1,229	8,891	14,235	8,716	3,914	10,074	9,817	7,554	15,285	14,995	10,116	12,636	12,975
Old Crow, Canada	12,733	5,534	5,992	4,898	12,363	7,264	4,350	4,932	7,013	9,986	6,847	7,982	7,518	5,628	5,810	10,845	10,675	11,136	9,505	8,530
Olympia, Washington	13,812	7,043	8,280	6,895	13,897	9,229	3,312	3,436	8,846	11,782	8,666	6,375	9,651	8,107	7,503	12,950	12,556	11,735	11,878	10,808
Omaha, Nebraska	12,101	6,356	8,495	6,794	12,526	8,815	1,299	1,205	8,298	13,842	8,121	4,208	9,450	9,190	6,949	14,768	14,571	9,891	12,000	12,411
Omsk, USSR	8,448	4,407	1,493	3,050	7,449	3,192	8,819	9,696	3,574	6,628	3,579	11,745	2,668	1,229	3,875	6,288	6,802	8,447	3,471	4,097
Oodnadatta, Australia	12,710	15,291	12,340	13,866	12,034	13,419	16,352	16,208	14,002	4,257	14,101	17,021	12,604	10,101	14,741	4,966	4,197	14,948	10,346	6,801
Oradea, Romania	5,728	2,110	2,241	2,317	5,169	524	7,426	8,224	189	9,839	367	9,045	1,337	4,793	1,548	8,978	9,763	5,008	3,796	7,334
Oran, Algeria	4,730	2,592	4,434	3,812	4,726	2,744	6,650	7,266	2,299	11,976	2,303	7,218	3,483	7,005	2,578	10,918	11,791	3,215	5,470	9,529
Oranjestad, Aruba	9,615	7,514	10,451	8,735	10,575	9,663	3,573	2,948	9,068	17,853	8,949	196	10,478	12,245	8,132	18,051	18,448	7,520	12,812	15,773
Orebro, Sweden	7,050	1,038	1,966	986	6,577	1,636	6,282	7,128	1,241	10,051	1,067	8,483	2,249	4,383	436	9,506	10,151	6,009	4,836	7,504
Orel, USSR	6,635	2,491	1,058	1,867	5,898	838	7,733	8,587	1,143	8,808	1,163	9,878	902	3,591	1,851	8,112	8,819	6,161	3,403	6,269
Orsk, USSR	7,396	3,875	995	2,776	6,435	2,205	8,799	9,678	2,664	7,271	2,705	11,324	1,604	2,305	3,269	6,666	7,317	7,383	2,767	4,726
Osaka, Japan	13,028	8,941	6,564	7,443	11,828	8,384	10,619	11,185	8,718	3,752	8,692	14,251	7,839	4,002	8,622	4,936	4,501	13,599	7,456	3,327
Oslo, Norway	7,132	783	2,197	997	6,707	1,861	6,026	6,870	1,420	10,277	1,239	8,232	2,501	4,562	251	9,757	10,392	5,998	5,091	7,734
Osorno, Chile	9,572	12,776	15,592	14,240	10,754	13,961	9,334	8,546	13,528	16,066	13,511	5,860	14,611	18,009	13,254	15,830	15,669	8,958	15,149	18,244
Ostrava, Czechoslovakia	6,005	1,701	2,241	2,010	5,507	841	7,024	7,827	250	10,060	120	8,739	1,645	4,812	1,144	9,269	10,026	5,132	4,170	7,532
Ottawa, Canada	10,427	4,923	7,440	5,663	10,821	7,402	439	1,257	6,845	14,193	6,675	3,753	8,112	8,712	5,552	14,617	14,768	8,242	10,705	12,198
Ouagadougou, Bourkina Fasso	2,619	5,173	6,655	6,363	3,229	4,774	8,188	8,537	4,545	12,837	4,618	7,241	5,273	9,145	5,145	11,376	12,352	629	6,230	10,829
Oujda, Morocco	4,675	2,703	4,596	3,951	4,716	2,906	6,618	7,217	2,462	12,125	2,465	7,097	3,641	7,167	2,714	11,052	11,931	3,099	5,598	9,685
Oxford, United Kingdom	6,407	811	3,251	2,136	6,197	2,230	5,731	6,501	1,634	11,304	1,495	7,376	3,031	5,713	926	10,620	11,338	4,997	5,548	8,756
Pago Pago, American Samoa	17,850	14,941	14,069	14,001	17,703	15,951	11,105	10,648	16,033	8,388	15,918	11,666	15,603	11,712	15,131	9,846	8,871	18,567	14,962	10,345
Pakxe, Laos	10,193	9,613	6,646	8,273	8,992	7,810	13,489	14,260	8,363	1,511	8,442	16,918	7,015	4,671	9,041	1,396	1,582	11,674	5,258	1,148
Palembang, Indonesia	9,934	11,292	8,353	10,074	8,860	9,184	15,485	16,239	9,774	1,597	9,887	18,736	8,367	6,623	10,678	753	794	11,865	6,122	3,104
Palermo, Italy	4,700	2,597	3,452	3,336	4,338	1,604	7,501	8,207	1,336	10,705	1,428	8,460	2,260	5,985	2,263	9,651	10,517	3,796	4,221	8,281
Palma, Majorca	5,027	2,194	3,919	3,326	4,896	2,267	6,652	7,323	1,794	11,552	1,790	7,527	3,032	6,490	2,104	10,564	11,409	3,667	5,157	9,077
Palmerston North, New Zealand	14,671	17,932	15,753	16,601	14,682	17,264	13,923	13,277	17,793	7,948	17,837	13,088	16,471	13,200	17,838	8,885	8,057	16,265	14,270	10,451
Panama, Panama	10,623	8,388	11,256	9,493	11,630	10,646	3,822	3,023	10,048	17,628	9,918	1,283	11,454	12,768	9,021	18,656	18,423	8,582	13,866	16,232
Paramaribo, Suriname	7,913	7,371	10,309	8,796	8,946	9,084	4,851	4,445	8,528	18,387	8,450	1,601	9,882	12,552	7,908	17,276	18,224	5,924	11,848	15,839
Paris, France	6,023	1,176	3,230	2,339	5,791	1,981	6,101	6,855	1,387	11,202	1,279	7,581	2,796	5,755	1,100	10,430	11,185	4,691	5,252	8,663
Patna, India	8,216	7,496	4,586	6,347	6,995	5,445	12,219	13,094	6,022	3,944	6,121	14,937	4,635	3,435	6,878	3,051	3,794	9,371	2,870	1,768
Patrai, Greece	4,757	2,901	3,020	3,295	4,195	1,132	8,053	8,796	1,162	9,981	1,323	9,185	1,619	5,467	2,428	8,919	9,784	4,215	3,499	7,578
Peking, China	11,265	7,708	5,028	6,211	10,079	6,751	10,616	11,348	7,147	3,761	7,147	14,217	6,141	2,485	7,283	4,334	4,295	11,848	5,688	2,087
Penrhyn Island (Omoka)	18,367	14,077	14,025	13,469	19,002	15,742	9,706	9,197	15,603	9,670	15,446	10,205	15,691	12,017	14,422	11,198	10,221	17,428	15,918	11,363
Peoria, Illinois	11,578	6,070	8,380	6,638	12,040	8,547	813	722	8,009	14,214	7,835	3,787	9,220	9,285	6,682	15,015	14,913	9,361	11,799	12,615
Perm', USSR	7,813	3,341	389	2,090	6,938	2,204	8,070	8,951	2,514	7,703	2,502	10,753	1,864	2,206	2,785	7,251	7,832	7,530	3,518	5,159
Perth, Australia	10,753	14,622	11,739	13,482	10,104	12,315	18,098	18,150	12,912	4,196	13,052	17,777	11,518	9,987	13,987	4,162	3,751	12,991	9,017	6,461
Peshawar, Pakistan	7,261	5,972	3,173	4,954	6,085	3,840	10,970	11,851	4,420	5,531	4,525	13,368	3,028	2,939	5,341	4,630	5,400	8,049	1,685	3,162
Petropavlovsk-Kamchatskiy,USSR	13,657	7,479	6,090	6,164	12,684	7,946	7,920	8,453	8,039	6,488	7,940	11,522	7,719	4,112	7,396	7,576	7,227	13,133	8,479	5,561
Petrozavodsk, USSR	7,512	2,051	924	945	6,845	1,686	6,967	7,839	1,673	8,988	1,579	9,473	1,892	3,312	1,513	8,524	9,122	6,792	4,274	6,447
Pevek, USSR	12,518	5,720	5,015	4,572	11,794	6,687	6,223	6,875	6,633	8,064	6,502	9,884	6,679	3,898	5,748	8,861	8,724	11,507	8,146	6,552
Philadelphia, Pennsylvania	10,356	5,336	7,960	6,178	10,860	7,797	589	887	7,224	14,791	7,061	3,152	8,535	9,310	5,974	15,220	15,376	8,135	11,125	12,804
Phnom Penh, Kampuchea	10,071	9,911	6,943	8,600	8,886	8,025	13,890	14,665	8,590	1,372	8,678	17,278	7,221	5,043	9,327	993	1,257	11,655	5,329	1,515
Phoenix, Arizona	13,700	7,874	9,669	8,093	14,184	10,276	2,950	2,585	9,799	13,330	9,618	5,027	10,837	9,814	8,432	14,630	14,127	11,469	13,277	12,562
Pierre, South Dakota	12,366	6,303	8,268	6,613	12,705	8,727	1,595	1,677	8,235	13,351	8,055	4,701	9,321	8,810	6,872	14,303	14,083	10,184	11,828	11,968
Pinang, Malaysia	9,515	10,249	7,310	9,035	8,366	8,171	14,592	15,402	8,758	1,744	8,865	17,696	7,355	5,651	9,636	291	1,190	11,263	5,205	2,189
Pitcairn Island (Adamstown)	15,066	14,466	16,285	14,841	16,218	16,946	9,123	8,318	16,394	12,698	16,224	7,869	17,585	15,143	15,081	13,985	13,055	14,191	19,363	14,743
Pittsburgh, Pennsylvania	10,770	5,568	8,092	6,316	11,259	8,043	337	603	7,481	14,610	7,313	3,337	8,760	9,295	6,199	15,173	15,239	8,550	11,354	12,748
Plymouth, Montserrat	8,829	6,684	9,647	7,980	9,726	8,748	3,432	3,027	8,157	17,489	8,045	823	9,565	11,616	7,285	17,197	17,831	6,676	11,859	15,106
Plymouth, United Kingdom	6,341	957	3,501	2,358	6,187	2,434	5,608	6,360	1,836	11,552	1,707	7,150	3,242	5,961	1,167	10,851	11,578	4,852	5,733	9,004
Ponape Island	15,924	12,511	10,410	11,082	14,759	12,242	11,903	11,991	12,564	4,666	12,527	14,469	11,679	7,859	12,312	6,282	5,350	17,333	10,845	6,230
Ponce, Puerto Rico	9,312	6,804	9,742	8,032	10,193	8,967	3,107	2,619	8,371	17,334	8,249	671	9,781	11,578	7,421	17,341	17,815	7,147	12,151	15,101
Ponta Delgada, Azores	6,289	2,869	5,710	4,372	6,634	4,511	4,600	5,113	3,933	13,760	3,840	5,085	5,325	8,111	3,327	12,961	13,746	4,211	7,614	11,215
Pontianak, Indonesia	10,467	11,268	8,303	9,971	9,366	9,292	15,098	15,799	9,871	1,001	9,970	18,638	8,479	6,391	10,674	920	207	12,335	6,373	2,868
Port Augusta, Australia	12,721	15,875	12,917	14,456	12,149	13,937	16,485	16,196	14,526	4,840	14,634	16,538	13,121	10,692	15,316	5,481	4,748	14,944	10,795	7,380
Port Blair, India	8,751	9,235	6,331	8,087	7,561	7,102	13,871	14,728	7,692	2,638	7,804	16,654	6,286	4,928	8,612	1,358	2,238	10,343	4,140	1,821
Port Elizabeth, South Africa	3,453	10,633	10,495	11,298	3,816	8,973	13,715	13,730	9,167	10,427	9,327	11,111	8,853	11,818	10,341	8,935	9,625	5,335	7,426	10,437
Port Hedland, Australia	11,229	13,713	10,755	12,429	10,388	11,615	16,894	17,224	12,208	2,922	12,324	18,857	10,799	8,799	13,108	3,185	2,580	13,420	8,464	5,307
Port Louis, Mauritius	4,896	10,349	8,753	10,224	4,198	7,976	15,350	15,883	8,434	7,028	8,616	14,191	7,460	9,073	9,803	5,474	6,241	7,117	5,146	6,997
Port Moresby, Papua New Guinea	14,484	13,968	11,335	12,462	13,536	12,913	14,078	14,100	13,390	3,852	13,417	16,151	12,180	8,809	13,595	5,235	4,264	16,586	10,554	6,156
Port Said, Egypt	4,330	4,054	3,306	4,145	3,487	1,772	9,283	10,033	2,148	9,080	2,330	10,301	1,636	5,379	3,513	7,876	8,787	4,456	2,412	6,832
Port Sudan, Sudan	3,573	5,426	4,440	5,492	2,489	3,132	10,581	11,291	3,531	8,627	3,712	11,145	2,824	6,102	4,895	7,225	8,188	4,435	2,100	6,706
Port-au-Prince, Haiti	9,919	7,079	9,967	8,218	10,795	9,337	2,867	2,243	8,739	17,144	8,607	829	10,144	11,627	7,710	17,519	17,765	7,752	12,584	15,151
Port-of-Spain, Trin. & Tobago	8,670	7,227	10,195	8,568	9,649	9,179	4,071	3,601	8,598	18,146	8,498	756	9,993	12,245	7,810	17,618	18,392	6,598	12,170	15,702
Port-Vila, Vanuatu	16,187	15,372	13,322	13,998	15,568	15,099	13,048	12,729	15,474	6,312	15,451	13,938	14,450	10,754	15,235	7,662	6,701	18,379	13,012	8,544
Portland, Maine	9,982	4,757	7,405	5,623	10,413	7,218	826	1,445	6,647	14,471	6,482	3,495	7,956	8,845	5,396	14,757	14,997	7,786	10,546	12,362
Portland, Oregon	13,894	7,178	8,446	7,052	14,011	9,381	3,321	3,399	8,992	11,878	8,811	6,303	9,810	8,272	7,645	13,071	12,657	11,796	12,046	10,949
Porto, Portugal	5,590	2,021	4,443	3,440	5,643	3,039	5,741	6,380	2,484	12,350	2,418	6,597	3,845	6,967	2,227	11,461	12,272	3,881	6,102	9,829
Porto Alegre, Brazil	7,515	10,824	13,423	12,331	8,733	11,694	8,672	8,072	11,297	17,028	11,299	5,019	12,317	15,983	11,212	15,893	16,301	6,671	13,029	17,396
Porto Alexandre, Angola	1,328	8,398	8,935	9,303	2,324	7,161	11,392	11,543	7,206	11,713	7,342	9,352	7,275	10,900	8,207	10,093	10,970	2,900	6,705	10,825
Porto Novo, Benin	1,846	5,842	7,032	6,940	2,594	5,141	8,962	9,282	4,999	12,516	5,096	7,794	5,532	9,428	5,752	10,982	11,957	469	6,101	10,719
Porto Velho, Brazil	8,760	9,249	12,192	10,655	9,928	10,924	6,021	5,378	10,382	19,697	10,312	2,365	11,709	14,384	9,790	18,324	18,995	7,119	13,462	17,719
Portsmouth, United Kingdom	6,300	921	3,303	2,231	6,099	2,218	5,787	6,549	1,620	11,341	1,489	7,368	3,025	5,781	1,011	10,632	11,361	4,887	5,523	8,795
Poznan, Poland	6,287	1,441	2,154	1,728	5,806	1,045	6,782	7,597	513	10,099	331	8,624	1,807	4,712	856	9,373	10,102	5,348	4,375	7,558
Prague, Czechoslovakia	6,026	1,492	2,444	2,005	5,589	1,113	6,784	7,579	516	10,323	390	8,464	1,920	5,009	993	9,543	10,297	5,040	4,433	7,791
Praia, Cape Verde Islands	4,780	5,176	7,631	6,657	5,589	5,983	6,229	6,399	5,531	15,008	5,518	4,846	6,697	10,188	5,468	13,674	14,635	2,560	8,307	12,702
Pretoria, South Africa	2,742	9,818	9,553	10,399	2,922	8,057	13,396	13,559	8,274	10,092	8,439	11,231	7,915	10,912	9,487	8,527	9,305	4,822	6,513	9,785
Prince Albert, Canada	12,414	5,786	7,419	5,857	12,538	8,099	2,149	2,563	7,661	12,368	7,479	5,633	8,615	7,778	6,296	13,254	13,077	10,348	11,027	10,910
Prince Edward Island	5,169	12,284	11,704	12,777	5,363	10,406	15,277	15,124	10,681	9,590	10,851	12,221	10,150	12,471	11,934	8,305	8,799	7,076	8,287	10,258
Prince George, Canada	13,330	6,383	7,517	6,156	13,294	8,504	3,265	3,589	8,141	11,424	7,962	6,636	8,903	7,394	6,813	12,467	12,170	11,355	11,114	10,231
Prince Rupert, Canada	13,654	6,595	7,491	6,237	13,528	8,606	3,760	4,080	8,281	10,961	8,105	7,117	8,948	7,160	6,984	12,048	11,715	11,745	11,046	9,860
Providence, Rhode Island	10,055	4,969	7,629	5,847	10,523	7,425	766	1,263	6,851	14,658	6,688	3,300	8,168	9,062	5,609	14,975	15,199	7,846	10,755	12,575
Provo, Utah	13,397	7,215	8,921	7,364	13,739	9,582	2,598	2,468	9,123	12,948	8,941	5,257	10,118	9,091	7,755	14,127	13,727	11,202	12,533	11,953
Puerto Aisen, Chile	9,516	13,206	15,942	14,689	10,668	14,224	9,872	9,082	13,829	15,556	13,827	6,391	14,823	18,455	13,657	15,294	15,137	9,086	15,062	17,711
Puerto Deseado, Argentina	8,999	13,145	15,724	14,648	10,133	13,925	10,204	9,445	13,576	15,372	13,592	6,640	14,467	18,295	13,545	14,924	14,872	8,693	14,516	17,297
Puerto Princesa, Philippines	11,570	10,797	7,878	9,364	10,397	9,218	13,804	14,421	9,747	508	9,808	17,465	8,445	5,609	10,274	2,018	1,298	13,176	6,786	2,401
Punta Arenas, Chile	9,375	13,842	16,371	15,346	10,461	14,536	10,743	9,953	14,217	14,737	14,242	7,241	15,028	18,920	14,235	14,422	14,283	9,249	14,774	16,841
Pusan, South Korea	12,442	8,679	6,162	7,172	11,240	7,941	10,807	11,430	8,307	3,489	8,293	14,467	7,360	3,591	8,314	4,524	4,190	13,086	6,875	2,763
Pyongyang, North Korea	12,075	8,162	5,641	6,655	10,889	7,429	10,499	11,163	7,787	3,786	7,772	14,156	6,861	3,069	7,791	4,658	4,436	12,609	6,498	2,659
Qamdo, China	9,495	7,641	4,679	6,295	8,280	5,973	11,739	12,572	6,496	3,411	6,556	14,968	5,215	2,782	7,079	3,135	3,557	10,469	4,000	862
Qandahar, Afghanistan	6,654	5,852	3,233	4,983	5,479	3,570	11,016	11,888	4,165	5,944	4,289	13,129	2,755	3,436	5,211	4,905	5,738	7,484	1,079	3,675
Qiqian, China	11,440	6,684	4,347	5,180	10,349	6,213	9,211	9,946	6,496	5,143	6,457	12,820	5,758	1,865	6,350	5,717	5,699	11,526	6,013	3,379
Qom, Iran	5,700	4,734	2,658	4,174	4,630	2,299	10,055	10,896	2,893	7,370	3,040	11,779	1,535	3,960	4,097	6,292	7,150	6,196	1,063	5,060
Quebec, Canada	10,092	4,567	7,138	5,357	10,460	7,042	818	1,601	6,481	14,112	6,313	3,852	7,761	8,511	5,199	14,424	14,644	7,923	10,355	12,021
Quetta, Pakistan	6,694	6,047	3,416	5,170	5,507	3,760	11,204	12,078	4,356	5,784	4,481	13,317	2,946	3,513	5,406	4,721	5,563	7,589	1,123	3,553
Quito, Ecuador	10,439	9,202	12,128	10,393	11,544	11,335	4,841	4,045	10,743	18,294	10,629	1,776	12,151	13,769	9,821	19,678	19,043	8,572	14,400	17,252
Rabaul, Papua New Guinea	15,150	13,565	11,127	12,078	14,128	12,828	13,274	13,303	13,249	4,170	13,251	15,498	12,151	8,562	13,266	5,675	4,699	17,122	10,796	6,252
Raiatea (Uturoa)	17,268	14,662	15,050	14,295	18,173	16,648	9,812	9,185	16,398	10,473	16,225	9,689	16,721	13,129	15,104	11,916	10,945	16,566	16,963	12,355

Distances in Kilometers	Kinshasa, Zaire	Kirkwall, United Kingdom	Kirov, USSR	Kiruna, Sweden	Kisangani, Zaire	Kishinev, USSR	Kitchner, Canada	Knoxville, Tennessee	Kosice, Czechoslovakia	Kota Kinabalu, Malaysia	Krakow, Poland	Kralendijk, Bonaire	Krasnodar, USSR	Krasnoyarsk, USSR	Kristiansand, Norway	Kuala Lumpur, Malaysia	Kuching, Malaysia	Kumasi, Ghana	Kumzar, Oman	Kunming, China
Raleigh, North Carolina	10,646	5,887	8,511	6,729	11,227	8,343	867	478	7,768	15,136	7,606	2,815	9,086	9,802	6,526	15,694	15,771	8,410	11,674	13,269
Rangiroa (Avatoru)	17,183	14,328	14,954	14,063	18,234	16,435	9,394	8,753	16,127	10,856	15,950	9,253	16,609	13,190	14,800	12,323	11,349	16,221	17,223	12,657
Rangoon, Burma	9,185	8,935	5,983	7,700	7,975	6,949	13,327	14,166	7,523	2,475	7,618	16,381	6,139	4,363	8,331	1,623	2,291	10,628	4,233	1,140
Raoul Is., Kermadec Islands	16,035	16,682	15,157	15,550	15,997	16,982	12,745	12,184	17,306	8,056	17,255	12,563	16,348	12,607	16,762	9,257	8,337	17,475	14,715	10,395
Rarotonga (Avarua)	17,134	15,423	15,236	14,820	17,654	17,040	10,781	10,176	16,952	9,653	16,799	10,651	16,858	13,014	15,783	11,029	10,068	17,177	16,312	11,712
Rawson, Argentina	8,907	12,688	15,342	14,187	10,073	13,592	9,731	8,983	13,211	15,869	13,216	6,150	14,178	17,899	13,107	15,373	15,358	8,437	14,473	17,701
Recife, Brazil	5,568	7,959	10,453	9,459	6,735	8,739	7,325	7,072	8,328	16,822	8,328	4,317	9,396	13,017	8,291	15,201	16,116	4,038	10,539	15,155
Regina, Canada	12,458	5,973	7,698	6,109	12,645	8,322	1,984	2,313	7,868	12,640	7,687	5,378	8,859	8,094	6,501	13,557	13,359	10,350	11,297	11,220
Reykjavik, Iceland	8,193	1,157	3,675	1,918	8,027	3,591	4,276	5,128	3,082	11,485	2,903	6,785	4,254	5,569	1,725	11,240	11,747	6,581	6,843	9,021
Rhodes, Greece	4,705	3,369	2,916	3,532	3,991	1,175	8,608	9,368	1,476	9,429	1,657	9,788	1,318	5,210	2,835	8,328	9,205	4,478	2,893	7,070
Richmond, Virginia	10,545	5,668	8,288	6,506	11,093	8,127	705	603	7,553	14,988	7,390	2,956	8,867	9,597	6,307	15,497	15,604	8,313	11,456	13,074
Riga, USSR	6,837	1,606	1,525	1,231	6,260	1,153	6,862	7,710	938	9,573	813	9,026	1,681	4,054	971	8,962	9,635	6,011	4,259	7,024
Ringkobing, Denmark	6,724	743	2,472	1,448	6,349	1,739	6,086	6,905	1,204	10,546	1,026	8,057	2,472	4,926	233	9,932	10,613	5,548	5,058	7,997
Rio Branco, Brazil	9,182	9,564	12,523	10,941	10,357	11,316	6,053	5,359	10,765	19,408	10,689	2,448	12,108	14,626	10,123	18,645	19,053	7,565	13,906	18,062
Rio Cuarto, Argentina	8,790	11,669	14,456	13,150	10,002	12,836	8,638	7,917	12,394	16,998	12,374	5,030	13,507	16,918	12,131	16,388	16,465	7,946	14,322	18,477
Rio de Janeiro, Brazil	6,613	9,798	12,317	11,303	7,835	10,574	8,275	7,797	10,183	17,118	10,189	4,743	11,196	14,885	10,152	15,664	16,317	5,588	12,023	16,564
Rio Gallegos, Argentina	9,257	13,637	16,179	15,141	10,358	14,354	10,591	9,810	14,026	14,920	14,049	7,069	14,861	18,740	14,032	14,566	14,453	9,081	14,696	16,977
Rio Grande, Brazil	7,632	11,059	13,648	12,565	8,846	11,909	8,845	8,228	11,519	16,873	11,523	5,187	12,523	16,211	11,445	15,807	16,166	6,853	13,170	17,448
Riyadh, Saudi Arabia	4,670	5,415	3,775	5,132	3,536	2,946	10,745	11,535	3,476	7,653	3,650	11,881	2,368	5,091	4,812	6,347	7,285	5,514	993	5,614
Road Town, Brit. Virgin Isls.	9,107	6,651	9,600	7,904	9,981	8,786	3,147	2,714	8,192	17,301	8,072	798	9,601	11,486	7,264	17,191	17,726	6,937	11,953	15,000
Roanoke, Virginia	10,764	5,832	8,408	6,629	11,315	8,298	687	384	7,728	14,938	7,564	3,015	9,030	9,644	6,468	15,524	15,579	8,532	11,622	13,099
Robinson Crusoe Island, Chile	10,137	12,401	15,337	13,796	11,346	13,922	8,537	7,723	13,424	16,582	13,377	5,192	14,652	17,437	12,938	16,631	16,328	9,254	15,671	19,044
Rochester, New York	10,572	5,209	7,733	5,956	11,010	7,687	236	964	7,127	14,392	6,958	3,551	8,400	8,977	5,840	14,854	14,990	8,369	10,994	12,451
Rockhampton, Australia	14,281	15,536	12,816	14,028	13,609	14,256	14,881	14,648	14,782	4,956	14,835	15,753	13,477	10,334	15,135	6,051	5,150	16,518	11,515	7,439
Rome, Italy	5,124	2,180	3,174	2,926	4,760	1,416	7,186	7,917	1,020	10,683	1,075	8,356	2,164	5,735	1,837	9,713	10,547	4,143	4,348	8,211
Rosario, Argentina	8,445	11,493	14,226	12,986	9,658	12,565	8,697	8,005	12,138	17,000	12,125	5,058	13,218	16,734	11,933	16,237	16,406	7,620	13,979	18,185
Roseau, Dominica	8,722	6,773	9,739	8,088	9,638	8,799	3,609	3,202	8,211	17,635	8,103	820	9,615	11,744	7,368	17,255	17,937	6,584	11,875	15,221
Rostock, East Germany	6,478	1,072	2,344	1,592	6,060	1,417	6,411	7,225	871	10,372	694	8,296	2,171	4,861	522	9,697	10,404	5,400	4,746	7,825
Rostov-na-Donu, USSR	6,190	3,073	1,424	2,549	5,366	824	8,375	9,220	1,384	8,494	1,487	10,339	250	3,707	2,432	7,667	8,430	5,965	2,745	5,993
Rotterdam, Netherlands	6,313	914	2,908	1,968	6,019	1,837	6,080	6,863	1,243	10,933	1,099	7,771	2,635	5,410	731	10,227	10,952	5,047	5,161	8,387
Rouyn, Canada	10,684	4,886	7,277	5,513	11,018	7,364	544	1,421	6,824	13,821	6,650	4,122	8,045	8,425	5,501	14,310	14,415	8,525	10,631	11,885
Sacramento, California	14,236	7,806	9,208	7,776	14,508	10,078	3,456	3,322	9,663	12,313	9,482	5,999	10,540	9,032	8,304	13,614	13,108	12,056	12,815	11,596
Saginaw, Michigan	11,085	5,534	7,922	6,163	11,507	8,014	279	829	7,470	14,176	7,297	3,779	8,700	8,979	6,153	14,813	14,824	8,883	11,287	12,390
Saint Denis, Reunion	4,712	10,323	8,817	10,252	4,053	7,977	15,245	15,745	8,421	7,255	8,603	13,977	7,486	9,218	9,789	5,701	6,468	6,940	5,223	7,206
Saint George's, Grenada	8,714	7,104	10,072	8,434	9,675	9,084	3,919	3,461	8,500	17,996	8,397	710	9,899	12,102	7,692	17,535	18,273	6,621	12,106	15,569
Saint John, Canada	9,673	4,393	7,081	5,300	10,070	6,847	1,167	1,824	6,273	14,324	6,110	3,675	7,590	8,607	5,033	14,505	14,806	7,495	10,178	12,133
Saint John's, Antigua	8,797	6,626	9,589	7,924	9,688	8,689	3,410	3,020	8,098	17,442	7,986	881	9,506	11,563	7,227	17,138	17,775	6,638	11,801	15,051
Saint John's, Canada	8,741	3,458	6,287	4,538	9,063	5,866	2,205	2,870	5,281	13,972	5,125	4,185	6,633	8,085	4,100	13,858	14,320	6,619	9,201	11,593
Saint Louis, Missouri	11,656	6,282	8,614	6,870	12,157	8,761	976	629	8,219	14,378	8,046	3,647	9,440	9,514	6,898	15,221	15,089	9,429	12,023	12,829
Saint Paul, Minnesota	11,792	5,890	8,034	6,326	12,154	8,346	1,021	1,263	7,832	13,663	7,654	4,333	8,979	8,801	6,481	14,478	14,361	9,606	11,530	12,089
Saint Peter Port, UK	6,200	1,060	3,473	2,407	6,035	2,329	5,755	6,502	1,733	11,498	1,613	7,240	3,142	5,958	1,190	10,765	11,506	4,742	5,611	8,953
Saipan (Susupe)	14,478	11,313	8,927	9,823	13,269	10,703	12,001	12,320	11,074	3,395	11,059	15,212	10,094	6,356	11,012	5,004	4,167	15,689	9,213	4,612
Salalah, Oman	4,873	6,535	4,627	6,140	3,656	4,057	11,875	12,673	4,603	6,844	4,774	12,918	3,413	5,418	5,922	5,419	6,384	6,158	1,061	5,102
Salem, Oregon	13,959	7,252	8,514	7,124	14,083	9,454	3,366	3,427	9,065	11,880	8,885	6,314	9,882	8,323	7,719	13,086	12,661	11,856	12,112	10,978
Salt Lake City, Utah	13,392	7,177	8,867	7,315	13,721	9,538	2,599	2,490	9,082	12,899	8,900	5,298	10,070	9,030	7,713	14,072	13,677	11,202	12,480	11,893
Salta, Argentina	8,879	10,899	13,775	12,351	10,102	12,293	7,711	7,000	11,804	17,918	11,763	4,099	13,020	16,116	11,398	17,250	17,395	7,734	14,234	18,830
Salto, Uruguay	8,178	11,224	13,932	12,722	9,394	12,260	8,598	7,933	11,836	17,126	11,826	4,943	12,910	16,454	11,653	16,232	16,484	7,317	13,695	18,007
Salvador, Brazil	5,989	8,598	11,125	10,102	7,186	9,412	7,565	7,219	9,002	17,141	9,001	4,304	10,064	13,688	8,947	15,525	16,375	4,624	11,130	15,751
Salzburg, Austria	5,776	1,627	2,683	2,270	5,371	1,194	6,840	7,617	618	10,484	564	8,369	2,010	5,253	1,201	9,651	10,429	4,765	4,452	7,963
Samsun, Turkey	5,482	3,353	2,138	3,113	4,654	873	8,698	9,513	1,443	8,717	1,604	10,314	470	4,330	2,737	7,735	8,564	5,364	2,480	6,289
San Antonio, Texas	12,551	7,556	9,820	8,101	13,202	10,035	2,234	1,545	9,493	14,633	9,320	3,663	10,708	10,477	8,171	15,812	15,418	10,315	13,283	13,568
San Cristobal, Venezuela	9,811	8,089	11,029	9,313	10,831	10,213	4,035	3,342	9,621	18,236	9,505	653	11,030	12,803	8,704	18,628	18,938	7,791	13,320	16,331
San Diego, California	14,173	8,184	9,817	8,304	14,625	10,544	3,398	3,065	10,090	12,958	9,908	5,463	11,065	9,771	8,722	14,317	13,759	11,945	13,435	12,349
San Francisco, California	14,352	7,924	9,304	7,883	14,629	10,190	3,566	3,414	9,778	12,279	9,597	6,056	10,646	9,091	8,420	13,600	13,077	12,168	12,907	11,611
San Jose, Costa Rica	11,127	8,558	11,357	9,579	12,122	10,885	3,731	2,884	10,288	17,181	10,149	1,746	11,683	12,690	9,198	18,426	17,984	9,070	14,161	16,065
San Juan, Argentina	9,180	11,702	14,559	13,158	10,396	13,018	8,392	7,643	12,550	17,137	12,518	4,836	13,720	16,924	12,194	16,704	16,684	8,256	14,684	18,899
San Juan, Puerto Rico	9,265	6,734	9,673	7,965	10,139	8,895	3,081	2,612	8,299	17,290	8,177	734	9,709	11,618	7,361	17,272	17,758	7,096	12,070	15,040
San Luis Potosi, Mexico	12,903	8,369	10,663	8,944	13,683	10,849	3,027	2,253	10,299	14,926	10,128	3,643	11,536	11,246	8,990	16,286	15,730	10,696	14,118	14,194
San Marino, San Marino	5,348	1,978	3,010	2,704	4,973	1,323	7,052	7,799	860	10,631	889	8,343	2,105	5,578	1,615	9,707	10,522	4,349	4,390	8,139
San Miguel de Tucuman, Argen.	8,860	11,089	13,948	12,549	10,082	12,431	7,935	7,222	11,953	17,695	11,917	4,325	13,147	16,318	11,580	17,046	17,169	7,786	14,269	18,804
San Salvador, El Salvador	11,697	8,498	11,174	9,393	12,638	10,905	3,401	2,523	10,315	16,485	10,164	2,277	11,680	12,277	9,141	17,794	17,288	9,584	14,233	15,529
Sanaa, Yemen	3,857	6,182	4,817	6,081	2,657	3,787	11,413	12,143	4,251	7,901	4,432	11,994	3,327	6,098	5,618	6,440	7,412	5,088	1,757	6,162
Santa Cruz, Bolivia	8,651	10,104	13,002	11,549	9,861	11,586	7,009	6,340	11,077	18,695	11,027	3,361	12,337	15,310	10,615	17,708	18,076	7,284	13,778	18,356
Santa Cruz, Tenerife	4,954	3,541	5,969	5,000	5,384	4,396	5,880	6,310	3,905	13,648	3,876	5,678	5,153	8,517	3,797	12,538	13,436	2,859	7,073	11,201
Santa Fe, New Mexico	13,090	7,365	9,320	7,684	13,574	9,800	2,340	1,987	9,302	13,652	9,123	4,591	10,397	9,689	7,942	14,838	14,435	10,861	12,896	12,642
Santa Rosa, Argentina	8,799	12,007	14,750	13,495	10,000	13,081	9,017	8,289	12,659	16,612	12,648	5,416	13,724	17,252	12,453	16,035	16,083	8,084	14,365	18,233
Santa Rosalia, Mexico	13,921	8,470	10,344	8,750	14,537	10,899	3,368	2,844	10,406	13,653	10,226	4,879	11,482	10,470	9,044	15,054	14,456	11,684	13,947	13,109
Santarem, Brazil	7,780	8,172	11,070	9,626	8,898	9,716	5,699	5,224	9,186	18,936	9,125	2,204	10,492	13,396	8,680	17,413	18,370	5,984	12,238	16,533
Santiago del Estero, Argentina	8,767	11,141	13,979	12,608	9,989	12,435	8,060	7,352	11,965	17,591	11,933	4,441	13,141	16,380	11,623	16,906	17,046	7,732	14,202	18,695
Santiago, Chile	9,378	11,986	14,851	13,437	10,590	13,310	8,574	7,808	12,842	16,886	12,811	5,055	14,007	17,196	12,483	16,561	16,472	8,513	14,910	18,882
Santo Domingo, Dominican Rep.	9,662	6,947	9,858	8,123	10,539	9,169	2,943	2,379	8,571	17,224	8,443	719	9,979	11,594	7,573	17,445	17,790	7,495	12,392	15,123
Sao Paulo de Olivenca, Brazil	9,337	8,982	11,950	10,316	10,467	10,869	5,325	4,639	10,299	19,423	10,210	1,728	11,676	13,951	9,561	18,982	19,779	7,549	13,674	17,448
Sao Paulo, Brazil	6,965	9,984	12,570	11,491	8,188	10,855	8,186	7,667	10,449	17,334	10,448	4,599	11,495	15,129	10,362	15,940	16,542	5,924	12,371	16,918
Sao Tome, Sao Tome & Principe	1,082	6,557	7,466	7,564	2,056	5,599	9,761	10,051	5,538	12,155	5,654	8,379	5,882	9,734	6,414	10,569	11,532	1,163	6,046	10,601
Sapporo, Japan	13,205	8,231	6,151	6,767	12,065	8,033	9,560	10,129	8,283	4,799	8,229	13,193	7,596	3,703	7,987	5,904	5,534	13,357	7,672	4,039
Sarajevo, Yugoslavia	5,340	2,226	2,691	2,676	4,847	887	7,439	8,206	583	10,164	704	8,820	1,640	5,236	1,750	9,229	10,047	4,557	3,924	7,685
Saratov, USSR	6,844	3,143	812	2,289	5,988	1,347	8,288	9,155	1,791	8,115	1,838	10,562	894	3,063	2,512	7,427	8,125	6,614	2,936	5,578
Saskatoon, Canada	12,516	5,917	7,550	5,991	12,656	8,233	2,168	2,536	7,794	12,410	7,612	5,603	8,749	7,885	6,429	13,325	13,127	10,437	11,159	10,992
Schefferville, Canada	9,893	3,771	6,221	4,444	10,094	6,249	1,602	2,469	5,711	13,262	5,537	4,731	6,933	7,581	4,386	13,493	13,753	7,829	9,522	11,100
Seattle, Washington	13,742	6,969	8,216	6,825	13,823	9,157	3,261	3,402	8,773	11,790	8,592	6,355	9,582	8,064	7,429	12,944	12,562	11,669	11,816	10,788
Sendai, Japan	13,368	8,725	6,543	7,249	12,193	8,408	10,046	10,588	8,690	4,365	8,646	13,658	7,927	4,036	8,459	5,560	5,121	13,707	7,796	3,873
Seoul, South Korea	12,211	8,354	5,834	6,847	11,018	7,619	10,615	11,264	7,980	3,669	7,965	14,275	7,045	3,263	7,985	4,601	4,338	12,786	6,636	2,685
Sept-Iles, Canada	9,783	4,050	6,630	4,848	10,080	6,527	1,308	2,120	5,969	13,775	5,799	4,221	7,242	8,075	4,681	13,983	14,261	7,658	9,836	11,599
Sevastopol, USSR	5,714	2,927	1,904	2,704	4,954	452	8,272	9,091	1,043	8,955	1,193	9,984	435	4,264	2,307	8,045	8,846	5,408	2,883	6,482
Seville, Spain	5,115	2,410	4,598	3,761	5,189	3,038	6,146	6,753	2,531	12,340	2,499	6,756	3,816	7,156	2,526	11,349	12,199	3,429	5,925	9,855
Shanghai, China	11,791	8,784	6,067	7,288	10,574	7,732	11,454	12,126	8,158	2,837	8,169	15,107	7,078	3,550	8,351	3,720	3,473	12,663	6,278	1,952
Sheffield, United Kingdom	6,582	630	3,168	1,982	6,358	2,259	5,643	6,427	1,670	11,241	1,518	7,394	3,047	5,600	799	10,798	11,297	5,177	5,590	8,692
Shenyang, China	11,831	7,799	5,280	6,292	10,659	7,078	10,265	10,955	7,429	4,035	7,412	13,911	6,522	2,709	7,426	4,798	4,648	12,284	6,260	2,665
Shiraz, Iran	5,463	5,275	3,224	4,755	4,333	2,812	10,610	11,443	3,396	7,132	3,553	12,174	2,085	4,310	4,643	5,948	6,844	6,199	526	4,951
Sibiu, Romania	5,618	2,328	2,227	2,466	5,020	384	7,647	8,444	390	9,686	572	9,236	1,164	4,751	1,758	8,794	9,591	4,994	3,581	7,194
Singapore	9,869	10,840	7,893	9,606	8,755	8,772	15,031	15,804	9,359	1,453	9,467	18,289	7,956	6,149	10,230	317	722	11,711	5,779	2,635
Sioux Falls, South Dakota	12,107	6,196	8,274	6,587	12,482	8,643	1,312	1,381	8,136	13,611	7,957	4,422	9,263	8,935	6,780	14,515	14,333	9,914	11,798	12,154
Skelleftea, Sweden	7,675	1,402	1,655	345	7,139	2,035	6,233	7,103	1,789	9,650	1,636	8,753	2,463	3,849	1,005	9,250	9,821	6,688	4,957	7,124
Skopje, Yugoslavia	5,165	2,534	2,690	2,879	4,612	806	7,762	8,528	745	9,948	907	9,096	1,453	5,191	2,032	8,968	9,802	4,528	3,625	7,493
Socotra Island (Tamrida)	4,675	6,948	5,107	6,604	3,453	4,477	12,274	13,053	5,008	6,843	5,182	13,093	3,863	5,851	6,344	5,352	6,327	6,131	1,535	5,280
Sofia, Bulgaria	5,266	2,558	2,538	2,808	4,676	648	7,826	8,603	688	9,788	863	9,232	1,286	5,028	2,027	8,823	9,651	4,681	3,506	7,329
Songkhla, Thailand	9,561	10,093	7,147	8,864	8,399	8,046	14,395	15,203	8,630	1,716	8,734	17,542	7,231	5,458	9,484	462	1,248	11,264	5,130	1,990
Sorong, Indonesia	12,891	12,445	9,600	10,964	11,806	11,022	14,343	14,702	11,539	1,851	11,591	17,539	10,257	7,197	11,968	3,319	2,344	14,766	8,550	4,209
South Georgia Island	7,246	12,913	14,692	14,334	8,275	12,804	11,596	10,971	12,637	14,124	12,714	7,938	13,119	16,864	13,097	13,213	13,441	7,506	12,539	15,367
South Pole	9,529	16,543	16,496	17,533	10,059	15,211	14,815	13,985	15,400	10,663	15,554	11,349	14,992	16,213	16,454	10,352	10,173	10,743	12,917	12,775

Distances in Kilometers	Kinshasa, Zaire	Kirkwall, United Kingdom	Kirov, USSR	Kiruna, Sweden	Kisangani, Zaire	Kishinev, USSR	Kitchner, Canada	Knoxville, Tennessee	Kosice, Czechoslovakia	Kota Kinabalu, Malaysia	Krakow, Poland	Kralendijk, Bonaire	Krasnodar, USSR	Krasnoyarsk, USSR	Kristiansand, Norway	Kuala Lumpur, Malaysia	Kuching, Malaysia	Kumasi, Ghana	Kumzar, Oman	Kunming, China
South Sandwich Islands	6,952	13,108	14,533	14,447	7,900	12,680	12,282	11,684	12,588	13,417	12,685	8,635	12,897	16,434	13,212	12,469	12,718	7,488	12,040	14,625
Split, Yugoslavia	5,297	2,171	2,824	2,718	4,844	1,046	7,335	8,093	686	10,328	777	8,665	1,804	5,377	1,731	9,388	10,208	4,447	4,068	7,848
Spokane, Washington	13,430	6,768	8,171	6,714	13,565	9,017	2,892	3,040	8,608	12,105	8,427	6,014	9,479	8,173	7,253	13,215	12,868	11,333	11,786	11,010
Spoleto, Italy	5,215	2,105	3,091	2,832	4,841	1,355	7,147	7,886	937	10,641	985	8,371	2,117	5,655	1,748	9,690	10,516	4,236	4,344	8,161
Springbok, South Africa	2,821	10,010	10,213	10,814	3,428	8,562	12,845	12,866	8,686	11,132	8,836	10,310	8,545	11,824	9,777	9,591	10,337	4,531	7,436	10,886
Springfield, Illinois	11,594	6,150	8,474	6,731	12,074	8,628	864	659	8,088	14,295	7,914	3,714	9,305	9,384	6,764	15,109	14,998	9,373	11,886	12,711
Springfield, Massachusetts	10,155	5,013	7,648	5,866	10,618	7,475	663	1,192	6,903	14,609	6,739	3,344	8,212	9,045	5,652	14,959	15,162	7,947	10,802	12,552
Srinagar, India	7,542	6,152	3,296	5,076	6,359	4,083	11,062	11,943	4,656	5,261	4,754	13,577	3,277	2,802	5,527	4,414	5,157	8,351	1,965	2,868
Stanley, Falkland Islands	8,476	13,230	15,559	14,734	9,572	13,693	10,766	10,040	13,410	14,905	13,450	7,147	14,149	18,043	13,561	14,301	14,338	8,381	13,914	16,622
Stara Zagora, Bulgaria	5,278	2,695	2,451	2,850	4,643	569	7,987	8,770	777	9,602	959	9,425	1,114	4,907	2,142	8,631	9,460	4,781	3,318	7,149
Stockholm, Sweden	7,060	1,197	1,807	955	6,554	1,546	6,418	7,267	1,202	9,891	1,037	8,644	2,123	4,240	596	9,345	9,989	6,076	4,703	7,344
Stornoway, United Kingdom	7,197	216	3,184	1,698	6,976	2,650	5,178	5,992	2,096	11,249	1,924	7,235	3,384	5,453	843	10,754	11,384	5,731	5,972	8,712
Strasbourg, France	5,905	1,350	2,934	2,257	5,586	1,584	6,463	7,230	994	10,838	899	7,976	2,400	5,487	1,067	10,038	10,804	4,728	4,854	8,307
Stuttgart, West Germany	5,909	1,383	2,838	2,214	5,565	1,479	6,542	7,315	887	10,731	792	8,083	2,294	5,396	1,049	9,931	10,696	4,775	4,756	8,200
Subic, Philippines	11,745	10,356	7,479	8,898	10,545	8,919	13,212	13,833	9,424	1,085	9,471	16,873	8,170	5,127	9,858	2,412	1,833	13,189	6,709	2,152
Suchow, China	11,375	8,296	5,549	6,806	10,165	7,207	11,214	11,928	7,635	3,134	7,647	14,834	6,554	3,050	7,850	3,799	3,691	12,163	5,827	1,732
Sucre, Bolivia	8,873	10,328	13,238	11,762	10,086	11,840	7,091	6,397	11,328	18,554	11,276	3,466	12,595	15,512	10,846	17,761	18,014	7,537	14,034	18,618
Sudbury, Canada	10,838	5,127	7,516	5,754	11,204	7,607	341	1,195	7,065	13,953	6,891	3,991	8,289	8,628	5,744	14,496	14,568	8,661	10,876	12,071
Suez, Egypt	4,215	4,191	3,436	4,291	3,353	1,918	9,406	10,150	2,291	9,061	2,472	10,364	1,765	5,473	3,655	7,833	8,751	4,405	2,374	6,843
Sundsvall, Sweden	7,397	1,165	1,812	625	6,896	1,860	6,210	7,070	1,543	9,870	1,379	8,588	2,380	4,120	696	9,406	10,011	6,372	4,931	7,333
Surabaya, Indonesia	10,779	12,149	9,185	10,853	9,755	10,136	15,793	16,405	10,720	1,509	10,825	19,451	9,320	7,248	11,553	1,683	1,009	12,791	7,124	3,738
Suva, Fiji	16,919	15,470	13,911	14,270	16,508	15,776	12,261	11,850	16,043	7,345	15,980	12,873	15,226	11,391	15,492	8,726	7,761	18,738	14,031	9,493
Sverdlovsk, USSR	7,913	3,632	676	2,362	6,999	2,415	8,311	9,192	2,761	7,412	2,759	11,038	1,993	1,972	3,076	6,969	7,543	7,723	3,406	4,868
Svobodnyy, USSR	11,952	6,998	4,792	5,506	10,860	6,671	9,139	9,834	6,929	5,157	6,881	12,787	6,242	2,359	6,703	5,887	5,772	11,995	6,519	3,637
Sydney, Australia	13,752	16,631	13,794	15,130	13,302	15,039	15,476	15,052	15,608	5,758	15,693	15,362	14,229	11,387	16,172	6,610	5,800	15,907	12,006	8,300
Sydney, Canada	9,244	3,991	6,749	4,979	9,614	6,426	1,629	2,280	5,846	14,218	5,686	3,844	7,181	8,404	4,633	14,259	14,639	7,084	9,760	11,932
Syktyvkar, USSR	7,921	2,900	353	1,589	7,121	2,148	7,561	8,441	2,338	8,135	2,290	10,272	2,004	2,460	2,381	7,739	8,296	7,450	3,949	5,602
Szeged, Hungary	5,622	2,090	2,400	2,404	5,094	668	7,377	8,165	283	9,985	425	8,923	1,471	4,954	1,558	9,105	9,900	4,860	3,884	7,485
Szombathely, Hungary	5,710	1,837	2,521	2,305	5,245	927	7,097	7,880	382	10,234	399	8,642	1,741	5,091	1,346	9,381	10,166	4,819	4,176	7,722
Tabriz, Iran	5,679	4,178	2,289	3,684	4,689	1,737	9,508	10,343	2,332	7,835	2,478	11,240	982	3,956	3,543	6,814	7,653	5,940	1,612	5,458
Tacheng, China	8,685	5,522	2,567	4,186	7,574	4,041	9,880	10,750	4,505	5,518	4,540	12,880	3,372	1,237	4,969	5,158	5,669	9,059	3,253	2,975
Tahiti (Papeete)	17,083	14,670	15,187	14,367	18,038	16,733	9,741	9,094	16,450	10,678	16,274	9,518	16,854	13,315	15,134	12,111	11,141	16,351	17,181	12,572
Taipei, Taiwan	11,850	9,396	6,616	7,909	10,628	8,209	12,096	12,745	8,665	2,188	8,689	15,755	7,516	4,148	8,941	3,220	2,864	12,942	6,461	1,897
Taiyuan, China	10,942	7,745	4,975	6,264	9,746	6,631	10,904	11,656	7,057	3,549	7,070	14,466	5,984	2,496	7,287	3,999	4,028	11,627	5,369	1,699
Tallahassee, Florida	11,175	6,676	9,263	7,485	11,847	9,134	1,482	614	8,559	15,433	8,397	2,612	9,875	10,421	7,315	16,242	16,144	8,939	12,464	13,817
Tallinn, USSR	7,114	1,573	1,430	966	6,534	1,408	6,728	7,586	1,214	9,512	1,084	9,021	1,865	3,896	976	8,967	9,609	6,264	4,409	6,965
Tamanrasset, Algeria	3,179	4,074	5,286	5,111	3,258	3,402	7,993	8,513	3,194	11,840	3,280	7,853	3,913	7,774	3,934	10,515	11,467	1,939	5,139	9,642
Tampa, Florida	11,000	6,796	9,450	7,668	11,719	9,234	1,729	900	8,651	15,762	8,493	2,288	9,991	10,690	7,438	16,533	16,470	8,771	12,569	14,112
Tampere, Finland	7,333	1,495	1,473	728	6,767	1,646	6,549	7,412	1,434	9,548	1,293	8,933	2,084	3,852	955	9,059	9,674	6,434	4,607	7,006
Tanami, Australia	12,380	14,273	11,318	12,862	11,554	12,423	16,188	16,298	13,000	3,238	13,094	17,923	11,610	9,108	13,719	3,992	3,186	14,582	9,425	5,780
Tangier, Morocco	4,955	2,584	4,722	3,924	5,055	3,120	6,253	6,843	2,631	12,401	2,609	6,753	3,885	7,285	2,687	11,374	12,238	3,253	5,932	9,931
Tarawa (Betio)	17,530	13,306	11,727	12,042	16,441	13,615	11,239	11,106	13,829	6,336	13,755	13,110	13,161	9,268	13,272	7,925	6,966	18,940	12,570	7,965
Tashkent, USSR	7,443	5,224	2,357	4,139	6,328	3,260	10,141	11,022	3,809	6,059	3,890	12,663	2,483	2,359	4,604	5,324	6,026	7,931	2,042	3,565
Tbilisi, USSR	5,904	3,789	1,906	3,261	4,968	1,396	9,106	9,947	1,993	8,021	2,127	10,950	595	3,774	3,150	7,079	7,887	5,991	2,012	5,585
Tegucigalpa, Honduras	11,484	8,347	11,057	9,275	12,420	10,739	3,316	2,445	10,146	16,625	9,998	2,065	11,519	12,235	8,990	17,863	17,426	9,366	14,060	15,542
Tehran, Iran	5,811	4,676	2,547	4,083	4,747	2,259	9,987	10,831	2,856	7,341	2,999	11,769	1,479	3,843	4,037	6,290	7,138	6,276	1,139	5,008
Tel Aviv, Israel	4,522	4,099	3,151	4,091	3,636	1,733	9,373	10,140	2,167	8,844	2,348	10,499	1,485	5,159	3,535	7,659	8,563	4,703	2,195	6,584
Telegraph Creek, Canada	13,386	6,271	7,091	5,860	13,201	8,232	3,814	4,218	7,920	10,757	7,746	7,281	8,559	6,778	6,639	11,780	11,495	11,545	10,644	9,548
Teresina, Brazil	6,447	7,929	10,632	9,434	7,587	9,049	6,573	6,245	8,581	17,696	8,554	3,402	9,767	13,140	8,341	16,093	17,029	4,759	11,185	15,732
Ternate, Indonesia	12,479	12,101	9,219	10,636	11,376	10,595	14,377	14,811	11,122	1,383	11,180	17,776	9,822	6,864	11,603	2,871	1,901	14,314	8,083	3,778
The Valley, Anguilla	8,939	6,603	9,560	7,879	9,817	8,704	3,258	2,855	8,111	17,345	7,995	858	9,520	11,492	7,210	17,134	17,722	6,772	11,846	14,994
Thessaloniki, Greece	5,036	2,728	2,742	3,034	4,451	851	7,953	8,717	906	9,846	1,076	9,241	1,399	5,207	2,220	8,835	9,681	4,484	3,464	7,412
Thimphu, Bhutan	8,709	7,574	4,620	6,342	7,489	5,656	12,082	12,944	6,216	3,668	6,301	15,018	4,859	3,174	6,974	2,983	3,619	9,806	3,300	1,323
Thunder Bay, Canada	11,444	5,412	7,573	5,856	11,750	7,866	878	1,450	7,353	13,494	7,175	4,466	8,500	8,429	6,001	14,193	14,155	9,288	11,053	11,781
Tientsin, China	11,340	7,819	5,140	6,321	10,151	6,860	10,687	11,412	7,258	3,674	7,259	14,298	6,248	2,597	7,395	4,281	4,220	11,948	5,763	2,071
Tijuana, Mexico	14,169	8,195	9,836	8,320	14,626	10,558	3,398	3,058	10,102	12,978	9,921	5,446	11,081	9,794	8,734	14,340	13,780	11,940	13,453	12,373
Tiksi, USSR	11,266	5,045	3,660	3,658	10,427	5,460	7,036	7,801	5,517	7,340	5,414	10,624	5,327	2,412	4,897	7,834	7,887	10,605	6,632	5,427
Timbuktu, Mali	3,081	4,685	6,308	5,912	3,579	4,449	7,744	8,132	4,170	12,875	4,229	7,024	5,007	8,835	4,685	11,479	12,447	1,126	6,196	10,742
Tindouf, Algeria	4,345	3,497	5,571	4,849	4,660	3,861	6,576	7,054	3,435	12,973	3,440	6,462	4,569	8,142	3,611	11,792	12,709	2,426	6,332	10,589
Tirane, Albania	5,074	2,523	2,832	2,952	4,555	955	7,705	8,461	826	10,094	973	8,971	1,607	5,342	2,050	9,100	9,941	4,388	3,736	7,645
Tokyo, Japan	13,368	8,962	6,708	7,477	12,178	8,557	10,342	10,878	8,860	4,087	8,823	13,948	8,048	4,173	8,679	5,319	4,851	13,826	7,791	3,729
Toledo, Spain	5,275	2,126	4,279	3,447	5,271	2,753	6,150	6,795	2,229	12,067	2,189	6,960	3,543	6,834	2,209	11,119	11,952	3,684	5,727	9,568
Topeka, Kansas	12,119	6,535	8,722	7,012	12,591	9,002	1,361	1,093	8,478	14,051	8,301	4,023	9,650	9,439	7,135	15,005	14,788	9,897	12,210	12,656
Toronto, Canada	10,716	5,266	7,745	5,973	11,142	7,746	92	938	7,192	14,292	7,021	3,651	8,450	8,933	5,893	14,816	14,904	8,517	11,043	12,391
Toulouse, France	5,485	1,736	3,665	2,918	5,326	2,171	6,328	7,033	1,627	11,486	1,578	7,454	2,974	6,224	1,683	10,594	11,402	4,101	5,267	8,974
Tours, France	5,902	1,311	3,428	2,535	5,712	2,122	6,070	6,807	1,536	11,379	1,442	7,440	2,939	5,958	1,296	10,579	11,348	4,516	5,354	8,844
Townsville, Australia	14,116	14,970	12,222	13,464	13,339	13,663	14,876	14,754	14,186	4,375	14,238	16,202	12,887	9,751	14,552	5,523	4,602	16,343	10,979	6,846
Trenton, New Jersey	10,324	5,290	7,918	6,136	10,823	7,751	595	931	7,179	14,770	7,015	3,174	8,489	9,275	5,929	15,186	15,350	8,104	11,079	12,772
Tripoli, Lebanon	4,799	3,933	2,871	3,849	3,917	1,515	9,242	10,025	1,991	8,743	2,170	10,516	1,207	4,896	3,351	7,608	8,494	4,920	2,166	6,434
Tripoli, Libya	4,123	3,137	3,937	3,914	3,801	2,051	7,852	8,515	1,879	10,847	1,988	8,497	2,595	6,427	2,835	9,686	10,589	3,282	4,221	8,590
Tristan da Cunha (Edinburgh)	4,591	10,677	12,046	11,947	5,673	10,172	11,262	10,950	10,062	13,769	10,158	7,991	10,450	14,222	10,721	12,344	12,967	4,967	10,041	13,798
Trondheim, Norway	7,522	871	2,157	668	7,086	2,154	5,846	6,704	1,766	10,183	1,590	8,240	2,723	4,379	600	9,757	10,345	6,371	5,288	7,654
Trujillo, Peru	10,428	9,987	12,937	11,224	11,595	12,020	5,712	4,906	11,438	18,352	11,336	2,540	12,835	14,644	10,594	19,452	18,760	8,747	14,915	18,120
Truk Island (Moen)	15,217	12,309	10,005	10,837	14,052	11,788	12,304	12,473	12,155	3,961	12,136	15,089	11,177	7,435	12,044	5,578	4,653	16,698	10,192	5,571
Truro, Canada	9,460	4,226	6,955	5,179	9,851	6,670	1,385	2,026	6,092	14,317	5,931	3,711	7,421	8,548	4,868	14,428	14,769	7,287	10,003	12,077
Tsingtao, China	11,644	8,248	5,577	6,748	10,441	7,290	10,952	11,647	7,693	3,360	7,695	14,591	6,668	3,034	7,829	4,115	3,958	12,341	6,078	2,080
Tsitsihar, China	11,761	7,264	4,869	5,759	10,629	6,715	9,662	10,367	7,023	4,648	6,991	13,301	6,218	2,331	6,921	5,345	5,245	11,998	6,244	3,106
Tubuai Island (Mataura)	16,532	15,258	15,813	15,010	17,411	17,378	10,207	9,518	17,078	10,733	16,901	9,667	17,483	13,844	15,745	12,079	11,127	16,125	17,399	12,792
Tucson, Arizona	13,645	7,938	9,787	8,194	14,165	10,355	2,937	2,523	9,869	13,491	9,689	4,887	10,929	9,971	8,504	14,799	14,289	11,410	13,389	12,734
Tulsa, Oklahoma	12,195	6,805	9,035	7,317	12,724	9,279	1,546	1,080	8,746	14,279	8,571	3,840	9,938	9,757	7,412	15,286	15,030	9,962	12,506	12,954
Tunis, Tunisia	4,581	2,642	3,738	3,512	4,307	1,910	7,368	8,048	1,599	11,014	1,670	8,189	2,577	6,283	2,381	9,939	10,813	3,544	4,494	8,597
Tura, USSR	10,190	4,896	2,696	3,390	9,238	4,587	8,060	8,885	4,795	6,592	4,737	11,472	4,269	1,007	4,559	6,782	7,008	9,908	5,245	4,362
Turin, Italy	5,519	1,707	3,194	2,642	5,229	1,648	6,666	7,405	1,110	10,964	1,076	7,959	2,453	5,763	1,460	10,080	10,882	4,346	4,788	8,454
Uberlandia, Brazil	7,085	9,572	12,245	11,077	8,300	10,593	7,650	7,142	10,156	17,804	10,143	4,078	11,270	14,775	9,980	16,328	17,002	5,852	12,352	16,966
Ufa, USSR	7,539	3,505	571	2,353	6,633	2,076	8,370	9,250	2,461	7,582	2,476	10,949	1,619	2,316	2,917	7,045	7,667	7,364	3,154	5,033
Ujungpandang, Indonesia	11,534	12,295	9,334	10,914	10,490	10,466	15,334	15,846	11,033	1,282	11,121	18,874	9,659	7,199	11,733	2,171	1,249	13,507	7,621	3,798
Ulaanbaatar, Mongolia	10,480	6,554	3,865	5,065	9,348	5,621	9,857	10,652	5,995	4,729	5,990	13,333	5,052	1,316	6,117	4,984	5,149	10,815	4,970	2,563
Ulan-Ude, USSR	10,542	6,228	3,643	4,728	9,443	5,457	9,418	10,213	5,793	5,143	5,774	12,903	4,942	1,074	5,819	5,423	5,579	10,723	5,111	3,001
Uliastay, Mongolia	9,729	6,121	3,292	4,673	8,602	4,963	9,898	10,731	5,374	4,979	5,385	13,207	4,353	959	5,632	4,963	5,283	10,091	4,238	2,570
Uranium City, Canada	12,263	5,363	6,769	5,273	12,244	7,575	2,614	3,170	7,174	11,748	6,993	6,222	8,039	7,049	5,825	12,562	12,433	10,311	10,386	10,198
Urumqi, China	8,934	6,008	3,056	4,657	7,790	4,505	10,268	11,129	4,981	5,030	5,021	13,344	3,813	1,409	5,458	4,712	5,194	9,437	3,408	2,490
Ushuaia, Argentina	9,208	13,892	16,326	15,399	10,278	14,467	10,949	10,168	14,173	14,577	14,208	7,421	14,926	18,816	14,261	14,209	14,100	9,158	14,565	16,621
Vaduz, Liechtenstein	5,730	1,551	2,931	2,383	5,390	1,463	6,659	7,420	892	10,758	832	8,105	2,278	5,497	1,228	9,919	10,701	4,611	4,691	8,237
Valencia, Spain	5,106	2,176	4,100	3,401	5,037	2,498	6,440	7,097	2,002	11,798	1,982	7,267	3,274	6,668	2,165	10,821	11,664	3,634	5,417	9,314
Valladolid, Spain	5,479	1,930	4,176	3,277	5,458	2,719	6,000	6,661	2,173	12,035	2,117	6,928	3,522	6,719	2,044	11,132	11,947	3,886	5,773	9,521
Valletta, Malta	4,451	2,863	3,592	3,573	4,072	1,713	7,735	8,429	1,525	10,658	1,635	8,585	2,299	6,097	2,522	9,554	10,437	3,630	4,102	8,269
Valparaiso, Chile	9,470	11,992	14,870	13,436	10,682	13,351	8,517	7,745	12,877	16,907	12,843	5,015	14,055	17,186	12,495	16,627	16,514	8,585	14,995	18,970
Vancouver, Canada	13,676	6,840	8,036	6,663	13,718	9,003	3,299	3,489	8,627	11,652	8,447	6,471	9,415	7,871	7,289	12,783	12,418	11,632	11,633	10,610
Varna, Bulgaria	5,413	2,741	2,273	2,780	4,739	427	8,062	8,858	798	9,409	977	9,588	909	4,709	2,162	8,458	9,278	4,974	3,185	6,949
Venice, Italy	5,518	1,823	2,897	2,536	5,137	1,281	6,946	7,704	766	10,598	766	8,326	2,083	5,468	1,446	9,711	10,511	4,503	4,435	8,093

Distances in Kilometers	Kinshasa, Zaire	Kirkwall, United Kingdom	Kirov, USSR	Kiruna, Sweden	Kisangani, Zaire	Kishinev, USSR	Kitchner, Canada	Knoxville, Tennessee	Kosice, Czechoslovakia	Kota Kinabalu, Malaysia	Krakow, Poland	Kralendijk, Bonaire	Krasnodar, USSR	Krasnoyarsk, USSR	Kristiansand, Norway	Kuala Lumpur, Malaysia	Kuching, Malaysia	Kumasi, Ghana	Kumzar, Oman	Kunming, China
Veracruz, Mexico	12,426	8,377	10,837	9,083	13,271	10,847	3,062	2,211	10,277	15,528	10,112	3,083	11,573	11,628	9,011	16,865	16,331	10,247	14,166	14,705
Verona, Italy	5,527	1,773	2,973	2,551	5,172	1,384	6,859	7,613	857	10,700	843	8,221	2,188	5,545	1,430	9,816	10,616	4,466	4,538	8,193
Victoria, Canada	13,747	6,928	8,128	6,755	13,801	9,094	3,326	3,492	8,718	11,678	8,538	6,459	9,508	7,950	7,379	12,826	12,448	11,693	11,724	10,667
Victoria, Seychelles	4,456	8,712	7,022	8,498	3,411	6,288	13,921	14,606	6,775	6,839	6,955	13,792	5,738	7,536	8,138	5,216	6,142	6,463	3,426	6,070
Vienna, Austria	5,817	1,741	2,464	2,199	5,354	946	7,018	7,807	365	10,232	333	8,615	1,762	5,036	1,240	9,402	10,177	4,907	4,230	7,712
Vientiane, Laos	9,878	9,171	6,203	7,850	8,666	7,346	13,197	13,996	7,901	1,975	7,981	16,527	6,552	4,303	8,593	1,640	2,003	11,279	4,828	786
Villahermosa, Mexico	12,092	8,310	10,861	9,091	12,964	10,762	3,056	2,181	10,183	15,881	10,023	2,725	11,508	11,787	8,948	17,179	16,683	9,927	14,095	14,954
Vilnius, USSR	6,603	1,776	1,548	1,491	6,007	890	7,077	7,918	722	9,517	630	9,142	1,451	4,112	1,133	8,847	9,547	5,842	4,041	6,972
Visby, Sweden	6,871	1,250	1,838	1,143	6,365	1,381	6,531	7,374	1,013	9,910	847	8,670	1,996	4,321	613	9,318	9,984	5,910	4,586	7,361
Vitoria, Brazil	6,274	9,430	11,914	10,933	7,494	10,162	8,165	7,737	9,776	17,026	9,784	4,718	10,783	14,484	9,770	15,499	16,223	5,185	11,638	16,209
Vladivostok, USSR	12,477	7,953	5,641	6,456	11,322	7,493	9,888	10,526	7,794	4,400	7,758	13,549	6,998	3,112	7,642	5,340	5,080	12,779	6,923	3,330
Volgograd, USSR	6,521	3,237	1,144	2,520	5,656	1,180	8,466	9,325	1,698	8,169	1,776	10,595	584	3,321	2,596	7,400	8,135	6,352	2,697	5,652
Vologda, USSR	7,370	2,414	570	1,362	6,637	1,544	7,388	8,260	1,683	8,651	1,632	9,857	1,579	3,099	1,896	8,135	8,756	6,806	3,871	6,104
Vorkuta, USSR	8,825	3,311	1,226	1,818	8,013	3,037	7,344	8,219	3,168	7,857	3,095	10,380	2,897	1,957	2,916	7,696	8,129	8,300	4,606	5,400
Wake Island	16,504	11,280	9,649	9,963	15,286	11,541	10,274	10,408	11,733	5,666	11,657	13,075	11,139	7,247	11,199	7,272	6,436	16,863	10,959	6,570
Wallis Island	17,692	14,905	13,715	13,830	17,280	15,607	11,472	11,070	15,767	7,788	15,673	12,234	15,179	11,284	15,013	9,248	8,273	19,073	14,376	9,765
Walvis Bay, Namibia	2,065	9,219	9,598	10,079	2,842	7,879	12,117	12,201	7,964	11,458	8,107	9,812	7,928	11,400	9,009	9,866	10,681	3,718	7,080	10,893
Warsaw, Poland	6,290	1,672	1,931	1,739	5,749	812	7,016	7,839	395	9,831	253	8,899	1,544	4,499	1,055	9,098	9,828	5,460	4,124	7,292
Washington, D.C.	10,513	5,530	8,137	6,356	11,035	7,993	583	690	7,422	14,858	7,258	3,085	8,729	9,444	6,168	15,346	15,464	8,286	11,320	12,924
Watson Lake, Canada	13,110	5,989	6,844	5,588	12,919	7,958	3,700	4,160	7,642	10,781	7,468	7,230	8,296	6,615	6,358	11,747	11,505	11,287	10,412	9,475
Weimar, East Germany	6,138	1,270	2,569	1,941	5,747	1,352	6,543	7,336	758	10,516	618	8,239	2,154	5,118	828	9,764	10,507	5,055	4,677	7,977
Wellington, New Zealand	14,545	18,033	15,781	16,679	14,556	17,247	14,037	13,383	17,790	7,930	17,844	13,142	16,446	13,237	17,912	8,841	8,023	16,153	14,207	10,442
West Berlin, West Germany	6,299	1,248	2,356	1,747	5,870	1,266	6,574	7,381	699	10,333	529	8,381	2,043	4,900	716	9,616	10,342	5,264	4,601	7,790
Wewak, Papua New Guinea	14,225	13,220	10,570	11,713	13,182	12,161	13,824	13,972	12,631	3,241	12,656	16,395	11,438	8,046	12,836	4,724	3,748	16,170	9,912	5,439
Whangarei, New Zealand	15,070	17,412	15,292	16,077	14,976	16,905	13,753	13,165	17,389	7,629	17,408	13,263	16,143	12,727	17,315	8,662	7,796	16,763	14,105	10,096
Whitehorse, Canada	13,269	6,101	6,771	5,602	13,008	7,975	4,049	4,509	7,689	10,437	7,517	7,578	8,269	6,397	6,436	11,424	11,165	11,512	10,301	9,175
Wichita, Kansas	12,290	6,742	8,909	7,206	12,781	9,208	1,559	1,211	8,685	14,067	8,508	4,044	9,852	9,575	7,341	15,076	14,817	10,063	12,408	12,751
Willemstad, Curacao	9,494	7,492	10,437	8,731	10,459	9,615	3,646	3,040	9,022	17,930	8,906	75	10,431	12,267	8,105	18,032	18,491	7,404	12,744	15,793
Wiluna, Australia	11,276	14,389	11,442	13,133	10,540	12,221	17,372	17,512	12,818	3,633	12,943	18,184	11,409	9,515	13,774	3,849	3,291	13,506	9,003	6,019
Windhoek, Namibia	2,032	9,224	9,482	10,031	2,701	7,796	12,295	12,407	7,906	11,191	8,054	10,060	7,811	11,218	8,988	9,598	10,416	3,825	6,875	10,634
Windsor, Canada	11,016	5,578	8,007	6,242	11,463	8,059	243	707	7,509	14,322	7,337	3,632	8,754	9,102	6,201	14,947	14,968	8,807	11,345	12,523
Winnipeg, Canada	11,971	5,676	7,611	5,955	12,213	8,083	1,458	1,880	7,601	13,039	7,420	4,946	8,667	8,230	6,234	13,856	13,733	9,840	11,169	11,476
Winston-Salem, North Carolina	10,792	5,950	8,538	6,758	11,365	8,413	816	331	7,842	15,048	7,678	2,911	9,149	9,776	6,587	15,653	15,696	8,557	11,740	13,227
Wroclaw, Poland	6,141	1,540	2,230	1,874	5,661	974	6,870	7,677	404	10,122	233	8,639	1,762	4,797	978	9,363	10,107	5,218	4,309	7,587
Wuhan, China	11,116	8,529	5,700	7,060	9,897	7,270	11,671	12,398	7,731	2,730	7,758	15,267	6,577	3,288	8,050	3,310	3,240	12,057	5,624	1,294
Wyndham, Australia	12,317	13,752	10,802	12,335	11,416	11,951	15,896	16,118	12,521	2,718	12,609	18,229	11,142	8,580	13,304	3,565	2,714	14,469	9,025	5,265
Xi'an, China	10,612	7,926	5,067	6,473	9,403	6,621	11,346	12,117	7,084	3,218	7,113	14,857	5,929	2,712	7,432	3,523	3,625	11,448	5,070	1,183
Xining, China	9,981	7,363	4,454	5,946	8,782	5,947	11,135	11,947	6,424	3,692	6,461	14,506	5,243	2,259	6,843	3,704	3,982	10,754	4,415	1,284
Yakutsk, USSR	11,679	5,988	4,158	4,536	10,708	6,041	8,007	8,734	6,199	6,316	6,122	11,635	5,758	2,185	5,767	6,930	6,899	11,331	6,586	4,575
Yanji, China	12,297	7,901	5,531	6,400	11,137	7,371	9,987	10,640	7,685	4,297	7,654	13,647	6,860	2,985	7,573	5,191	4,961	12,639	6,737	3,147
Yaounde, Cameroon	996	6,238	6,903	7,133	1,565	5,062	9,881	10,253	5,054	11,578	5,183	8,820	5,290	9,111	6,030	10,014	10,984	1,490	5,386	9,951
Yap Island (Colonia)	13,699	11,655	9,020	10,148	12,525	10,666	12,966	13,327	11,109	2,465	11,123	16,246	9,977	6,482	11,268	4,089	3,201	15,223	8,731	4,125
Yaraka, Australia	13,620	15,433	12,582	13,940	12,936	13,880	15,495	15,304	14,435	4,569	14,508	16,349	13,079	10,184	14,961	5,531	4,670	15,858	10,986	7,101
Yarmouth, Canada	9,653	4,507	7,219	5,441	10,079	6,953	1,159	1,750	6,375	14,483	6,214	3,516	7,703	8,764	5,149	14,660	14,965	7,463	10,286	12,291
Yellowknife, Canada	12,361	5,326	6,515	5,098	12,252	7,438	3,043	3,617	7,071	11,303	6,893	6,665	7,855	6,657	5,746	12,120	11,986	10,488	10,129	9,764
Yerevan, USSR	5,759	3,900	2,076	3,414	4,810	1,471	9,228	10,064	2,067	8,020	2,210	11,001	702	3,904	3,264	7,040	7,864	5,896	1,891	5,607
Yinchuan, China	10,396	7,407	4,562	5,952	9,204	6,154	10,907	11,696	6,602	3,730	6,625	14,372	5,484	2,193	6,918	3,937	4,108	11,088	4,822	1,525
Yogyakarta, Indonesia	10,512	12,071	9,117	10,809	9,493	10,002	15,917	16,568	10,591	1,650	10,701	19,502	9,186	7,256	11,465	1,548	1,034	12,533	6,942	3,730
York, United Kingdom	6,624	582	3,123	1,926	6,390	2,244	5,644	6,431	1,657	11,198	1,502	7,426	3,027	5,548	747	10,565	11,259	5,229	5,577	8,649
Yumen, China	9,672	6,870	3,953	5,464	8,490	5,455	10,779	11,610	5,926	4,175	5,961	14,070	4,761	1,835	6,344	4,081	4,428	10,332	4,095	1,702
Yutian, China	8,234	6,294	3,343	5,080	7,054	4,438	10,930	11,806	4,980	4,887	5,054	13,739	3,663	2,288	5,694	4,257	4,893	8,976	2,657	2,385
Yuzhno-Sakhalinsk, USSR	13,121	7,853	5,890	6,405	12,018	7,780	9,129	9,713	7,998	5,208	7,935	12,771	7,390	3,524	7,634	6,254	5,928	13,108	7,652	4,282
Zagreb, Yugoslavia	5,550	1,938	2,665	2,468	5,099	995	7,154	7,926	512	10,312	559	8,608	1,796	5,231	1,479	9,426	10,224	4,655	4,171	7,810
Zahedan, Iran	6,132	5,757	3,340	5,027	4,960	3,374	11,021	11,880	3,971	6,336	4,110	12,879	2,580	3,873	5,115	5,200	6,074	6,991	561	4,147
Zamboanga, Philippines	11,926	11,239	8,336	9,792	10,771	9,698	13,986	14,543	10,224	671	10,283	17,613	8,927	6,025	10,727	2,296	1,430	13,604	7,252	2,881
Zanzibar, Tanzania	2,656	8,130	7,236	8,347	1,720	5,977	12,853	13,371	6,325	8,647	6,504	12,055	5,671	8,449	7,661	7,025	7,953	4,750	4,049	7,687
Zaragoza, Spain	5,345	1,933	3,954	3,181	5,255	2,429	6,777	6,954	1,900	11,746	1,859	7,245	3,224	6,514	1,943	10,820	11,642	3,873	5,454	9,242
Zashiversk, USSR	11,956	5,701	4,347	4,346	11,088	6,163	7,184	7,892	6,225	7,113	6,122	10,831	6,008	2,821	5,582	7,785	7,724	11,308	7,169	5,438
Zhengzhou, China	11,050	8,096	5,303	6,618	9,842	6,926	11,227	11,967	7,366	3,195	7,385	14,808	6,260	2,848	7,631	3,709	3,692	11,843	5,500	1,507
Zurich, Switzerland	5,764	1,492	2,983	2,379	5,443	1,547	6,573	7,333	971	10,835	901	8,018	2,363	5,546	1,202	10,004	10,783	4,608	4,780	8,311

Distances in Kilometers	Kuqa Chang, China	Kurgan, USSR	Kuwait, Kuwait	Kuybyshev, USSR	Kyoto, Japan	Kzyl-Orda, USSR	L'vov, USSR	La Ceiba, Honduras	La Coruna, Spain	La Paz, Bolivia	La Paz, Mexico	La Ronge, Canada	Labrador City, Canada	Lagos, Nigeria	Lahore, Pakistan	Lambasa, Fiji	Lansing, Michigan	Lanzhou, China	Laoag, Philippines	Largeau, Chad
Kurgan, USSR	2,067	0	3,206	1,015	5,696	1,183	2,820	11,690	5,247	14,169	11,175	7,721	7,217	7,673	2,743	13,013	8,760	3,611	6,192	5,689
Kuwait, Kuwait	3,455	3,206	0	2,651	8,022	2,303	3,038	13,049	5,184	13,402	13,643	10,303	8,934	5,315	2,534	14,882	10,665	5,206	7,395	3,194
Kuybyshev, USSR	2,821	1,015	2,651	0	6,711	1,454	1,843	11,329	4,349	13,339	11,229	7,789	6,878	6,683	3,087	14,026	8,528	4,526	7,108	4,747
Kyoto, Japan	4,568	5,696	8,022	6,711	0	5,920	8,468	12,820	10,598	16,881	10,464	8,462	10,017	13,241	5,645	7,325	10,476	2,898	2,390	11,132
Kzyl-Orda, USSR	1,518	1,183	2,303	1,454	5,920	0	3,143	12,736	5,703	14,683	12,356	8,899	8,262	7,321	1,656	13,162	9,863	3,351	5,869	5,222
L'vov, USSR	4,619	2,820	3,038	1,843	8,468	3,143	0	10,102	2,561	11,546	10,654	7,458	5,897	5,181	4,601	15,694	7,629	6,366	8,943	3,568
La Ceiba, Honduras	13,619	11,690	13,049	11,329	12,820	12,736	10,102	0	7,893	4,117	2,624	4,643	4,478	9,844	14,392	10,898	2,995	14,163	15,205	11,095
La Coruna, Spain	7,163	5,247	5,184	4,349	10,598	5,703	2,561	7,893	0	8,995	9,103	6,594	4,354	4,250	7,131	16,931	5,974	8,855	11,439	3,826
La Paz, Bolivia	16,158	14,169	13,402	13,339	16,881	14,683	11,546	4,117	8,995	0	6,420	8,673	7,695	8,272	15,886	11,773	6,770	17,696	19,085	10,291
La Paz, Mexico	12,632	11,175	13,643	11,229	10,464	12,356	10,654	2,624	9,103	6,420	0	3,460	4,832	12,085	13,816	8,858	3,135	12,448	12,778	12,824
La Ronge, Canada	9,303	7,721	10,303	7,789	8,462	8,899	7,458	4,643	6,594	8,673	3,460	0	2,494	10,588	10,400	10,588	2,036	9,535	10,805	10,376
Labrador City, Canada	9,194	7,217	8,934	6,878	10,017	8,262	5,897	4,478	4,354	7,695	4,832	2,494	0	8,123	9,916	13,036	1,733	10,102	12,089	8,175
Lagos, Nigeria	8,712	7,673	5,315	6,683	13,241	7,321	5,181	9,844	4,250	8,272	12,085	10,588	8,123	0	7,833	18,822	9,359	10,513	12,621	2,128
Lahore, Pakistan	1,344	2,743	2,534	3,087	5,645	1,656	4,601	14,392	7,131	15,886	13,816	10,400	9,916	7,833	0	12,362	11,498	2,754	4,868	5,723
Lambasa, Fiji	11,685	13,013	14,882	14,026	7,325	13,162	15,694	10,898	16,931	11,773	8,858	10,588	13,036	18,822	12,362	0	11,723	9,841	7,494	17,930
Lansing, Michigan	10,633	8,760	10,665	8,528	10,476	9,863	7,629	2,995	5,974	6,770	3,135	2,036	1,733	9,359	11,498	11,723	0	11,241	12,786	9,744
Lanzhou, China	1,846	3,611	5,206	4,526	2,898	3,351	6,366	14,163	8,855	17,696	12,448	9,535	10,102	10,513	2,754	9,841	11,241	0	2,585	8,385
Laoag, Philippines	4,353	6,192	7,395	7,108	2,390	5,869	8,943	15,205	11,439	19,085	12,778	10,805	12,089	12,621	4,868	7,494	12,786	2,585	0	10,558
Largeau, Chad	6,587	5,689	3,194	4,747	11,132	5,222	3,568	11,095	3,826	10,291	12,824	10,376	8,175	2,128	5,723	17,930	9,744	8,385	10,558	0
Las Vegas, Nevada	11,232	9,854	12,538	10,002	9,248	11,037	9,667	3,603	8,510	7,643	1,410	2,235	4,161	12,075	12,440	9,009	2,716	11,062	11,618	12,335
Launceston, Australia	11,170	13,207	12,822	13,966	8,541	12,534	15,597	14,149	18,002	12,641	12,762	14,689	17,171	14,738	11,000	4,146	15,810	9,655	7,145	14,460
Le Havre, France	6,258	4,312	4,583	3,437	9,675	4,826	1,716	8,472	944	9,902	9,359	6,508	4,527	4,782	6,317	16,336	6,236	7,922	10,504	3,896
Leipzig, East Germany	5,378	3,469	3,822	2,561	8,970	3,937	842	9,274	1,788	10,779	9,951	6,882	5,145	5,041	5,434	15,970	6,877	7,070	9,655	3,752
Leningrad, USSR	4,156	2,123	3,646	1,426	7,497	2,876	1,191	9,918	3,176	12,047	10,019	6,658	5,494	6,351	4,512	14,576	7,177	5,721	8,293	4,749
Leon, Spain	7,016	5,133	4,957	4,213	10,558	5,542	2,400	8,129	245	9,146	9,347	6,808	4,590	4,101	6,943	17,066	6,217	8,732	11,317	3,596
Lerwick, United Kingdom	5,874	3,817	4,989	3,152	8,748	4,605	1,958	8,258	1,930	10,373	8,700	5,588	3,948	5,970	6,227	15,151	5,677	7,353	9,881	4,962
Lhasa, China	1,454	3,520	4,157	4,217	4,211	2,809	5,950	14,973	8,511	17,454	13,629	10,485	10,610	9,443	1,623	10,741	11,978	1,374	3,248	7,342
Libreville, Gabon	8,650	7,897	5,195	6,954	13,217	7,371	5,653	10,676	5,081	8,707	12,994	11,517	9,063	951	7,625	17,923	10,310	10,370	12,235	2,209
Lilongwe, Malawi	7,961	8,240	5,035	7,607	11,973	7,254	7,134	13,660	7,664	10,813	16,100	14,249	11,953	4,048	6,643	14,960	13,362	9,186	10,167	3,878
Lima, Peru	16,265	14,198	14,048	13,502	15,851	14,932	11,816	3,260	9,262	1,079	5,397	7,898	7,267	9,133	16,376	11,052	6,114	17,345	18,018	11,065
Limerick, Ireland	6,639	4,619	5,242	3,839	9,698	5,274	2,279	7,833	1,034	9,550	8,653	5,832	3,821	5,240	6,832	15,924	5,533	8,208	10,765	4,549
Limoges, France	6,365	4,485	4,434	3,560	9,959	4,896	1,753	8,619	812	9,796	9,642	6,876	4,821	4,369	6,321	16,740	6,509	8,081	10,665	3,509
Limon, Costa Rica	14,172	12,181	13,197	11,727	13,576	13,165	10,358	759	8,014	3,358	3,288	5,372	4,979	9,505	14,814	11,129	3,630	14,860	15,959	10,941
Lincoln, Nebraska	10,923	9,203	11,425	9,112	10,049	10,355	8,418	2,935	6,943	6,998	2,241	1,709	2,611	10,387	11,935	10,692	1,031	11,243	12,426	10,741
Linz, Austria	5,347	3,517	3,553	2,560	9,110	3,870	729	9,511	1,838	10,818	10,275	7,238	5,457	4,753	5,303	16,220	7,185	7,086	9,666	3,398
Lisbon, Portugal	7,507	5,648	5,287	4,716	11,082	6,020	2,888	7,872	520	8,663	9,270	6,944	4,618	3,790	7,377	17,402	6,169	9,240	11,824	3,577
Little Rock, Arkansas	11,586	9,787	11,777	9,609	10,817	10,915	8,740	2,171	7,016	6,220	2,100	2,475	2,843	10,123	12,530	10,889	1,112	11,995	13,198	10,726
Liverpool, United Kingdom	6,266	4,258	4,884	3,459	9,434	4,891	1,900	8,206	1,186	9,915	8,955	6,039	4,127	5,240	6,446	15,896	5,850	7,856	10,422	4,379
Lodz, Poland	4,887	3,006	3,421	2,075	8,577	3,440	384	9,723	2,276	11,271	10,281	7,113	5,515	5,236	4,941	15,706	7,247	6,595	9,179	3,754
Lome, Togo	8,917	7,832	5,534	6,835	13,431	7,512	5,293	9,623	4,232	8,034	11,889	10,486	8,010	242	8,057	18,849	9,206	10,725	12,855	2,341
London, United Kingdom	6,179	4,204	4,646	3,360	9,502	4,770	1,707	8,423	1,097	9,987	9,230	6,328	4,399	5,005	6,293	16,114	6,118	7,814	10,391	4,094
Londonderry, United Kingdom	6,442	4,407	5,195	3,659	9,430	5,104	2,188	7,915	1,296	9,764	8,623	5,714	3,797	5,469	6,685	15,686	5,523	7,981	10,528	4,690
Longlac, Canada	9,880	8,053	10,155	7,890	9,734	9,180	7,145	3,771	5,758	7,562	3,512	1,400	1,406	9,460	10,796	11,677	798	10,444	12,017	9,581
Lord Howe Island, Australia	11,178	13,057	13,522	13,975	7,761	12,665	15,797	13,183	18,300	12,691	11,433	13,160	15,644	16,261	11,333	2,650	14,370	9,455	6,870	15,735
Los Angeles, California	11,383	10,083	12,835	10,273	9,170	11,264	9,997	3,742	8,876	7,712	1,341	2,545	4,528	12,428	12,621	8,649	3,074	11,111	11,518	12,701
Louangphrabang, Laos	2,952	5,004	5,537	5,758	3,698	4,362	7,504	15,944	10,064	18,938	14,007	11,302	11,869	10,684	3,068	9,351	13,040	1,800	1,952	8,651
Louisville, Kentucky	11,141	9,267	11,114	9,022	10,840	10,366	8,076	2,491	6,315	6,333	2,797	2,379	2,185	9,498	12,004	11,542	509	11,722	13,181	10,033
Luanda, Angola	9,037	8,588	5,632	7,705	13,521	7,909	6,580	11,347	6,178	8,830	13,811	12,598	10,130	2,010	7,879	16,832	11,304	10,623	12,147	3,025
Lubumbashi, Zaire	8,194	8,230	5,048	7,505	12,410	7,331	6,821	12,938	7,098	10,241	15,369	13,689	11,328	3,336	6,916	15,637	12,679	9,560	10,742	3,398
Lusaka, Zambia	8,454	8,586	5,390	7,886	12,559	7,656	7,240	13,103	7,506	10,201	15,603	14,092	11,708	3,659	7,154	15,277	13,018	9,746	10,779	3,822
Luxembourg, Luxembourg	5,857	3,944	4,164	3,040	9,404	4,410	1,286	8,897	1,309	10,301	9,717	6,773	4,887	4,790	5,887	16,276	6,608	7,548	10,133	3,703
Luxor, Egypt	4,950	4,233	1,566	3,386	9,507	3,623	2,782	12,023	4,191	11,853	13,208	10,202	8,376	3,769	4,100	16,437	10,081	6,744	8,959	1,641
Lynn Lake, Canada	9,132	7,495	10,015	7,526	8,518	8,669	7,148	4,714	6,267	8,685	3,706	328	2,208	10,278	10,196	10,902	1,958	9,450	10,833	10,047
Lyon, France	6,119	4,268	4,156	3,326	9,798	4,640	1,500	8,895	1,083	10,046	9,882	7,055	5,054	4,357	6,049	16,715	6,753	7,851	10,434	3,357
Macapa, Brazil	13,557	11,631	10,888	10,751	16,063	12,067	8,938	4,297	6,402	2,621	6,917	7,823	6,048	6,088	13,301	14,212	5,792	15,239	17,796	7,919
Madison, Wisconsin	10,646	8,831	10,881	8,659	10,225	9,958	7,855	3,035	6,300	6,944	2,840	1,763	1,992	9,751	11,573	11,338	398	11,144	12,563	10,091
Madras, India	3,129	4,875	3,790	5,186	6,054	3,787	6,512	16,515	8,917	16,620	15,728	12,431	12,049	8,442	2,138	11,375	13,635	3,458	4,351	6,558
Madrid, Spain	7,014	5,182	4,806	4,235	10,683	5,522	2,399	8,316	511	9,161	9,601	7,097	4,863	3,826	6,873	17,332	6,476	8,761	11,341	3,316
Madurai, India	3,502	5,171	3,805	5,413	6,446	4,051	6,639	16,718	8,978	16,312	16,125	12,791	12,290	8,229	2,429	11,517	13,914	3,878	4,668	6,413
Magadan, USSR	4,948	4,787	7,915	5,649	2,943	5,626	6,962	10,191	8,437	14,286	8,204	5,624	7,081	12,142	6,292	8,812	7,591	4,253	5,195	10,375
Magdalena, Bolivia	15,614	13,645	12,861	12,798	16,892	14,132	10,998	4,074	8,451	556	6,512	8,508	7,349	7,777	15,334	12,308	6,549	17,213	19,280	9,770
Magdeburg, East Germany	5,394	3,464	3,906	2,574	8,932	3,965	903	9,202	1,784	10,765	9,854	6,777	5,053	5,125	5,478	15,896	6,785	7,071	9,655	3,856
Majuro Atoll, Marshall Isls.	9,303	10,345	12,733	11,346	4,757	10,676	12,943	11,075	14,410	13,507	8,529	8,947	11,408	17,997	10,251	2,760	10,624	7,528	5,612	15,887
Malabo, Equatorial Guinea	8,457	7,613	5,011	6,655	13,023	7,137	5,306	10,502	4,705	8,746	12,753	11,162	8,720	669	7,483	18,277	10,002	10,210	12,177	1,930
Male, Maldives	4,238	5,750	3,889	5,857	7,247	4,588	6,873	16,937	9,048	15,618	16,862	13,453	12,691	7,769	3,055	11,841	14,379	4,711	5,364	6,113
Manado, Indonesia	6,046	8,002	8,663	8,861	3,879	7,524	10,661	16,059	13,208	17,830	13,436	12,262	13,873	13,474	6,260	6,309	14,297	4,406	1,907	11,630
Managua, Nicaragua	14,007	12,061	13,295	11,670	13,171	13,089	10,388	406	8,117	3,745	2,861	5,045	4,844	9,833	14,745	10,848	3,394	14,569	15,548	11,190
Manama, Bahrain	3,442	3,458	435	2,996	7,979	2,456	3,473	13,473	5,596	13,642	14,066	10,706	9,369	5,457	2,383	14,645	11,099	5,117	7,192	3,366
Manaus, Brazil	14,441	12,444	11,928	11,620	16,123	12,987	9,844	3,616	7,286	1,726	6,222	7,667	6,249	7,126	14,303	13,155	5,647	15,998	18,337	8,976
Manchester, New Hampshire	10,349	8,361	9,892	7,980	10,938	9,386	6,865	3,351	5,000	6,596	4,115	2,777	1,157	8,292	11,042	12,790	1,068	11,237	13,118	8,720
Mandalay, Burma	2,435	4,502	4,865	5,192	4,110	3,768	6,898	15,813	9,458	18,266	14,161	11,225	11,541	10,028	2,406	10,023	12,837	1,723	2,595	7,983
Mangareva Island, Fr.Polynesia	15,927	16,050	19,256	16,638	11,389	16,974	16,523	6,782	14,667	6,980	5,871	9,115	10,666	15,205	16,997	4,824	8,936	14,255	12,227	17,271
Manila, Philippines	4,667	6,549	7,606	7,448	2,702	6,177	9,276	15,477	11,789	19,030	12,991	11,151	12,484	12,767	5,096	7,277	13,146	2,938	403	10,738
Mannheim, West Germany	5,705	3,808	3,999	2,892	9,305	4,251	1,120	9,064	1,458	10,454	9,861	6,885	5,034	4,794	5,720	16,249	6,758	7,407	9,992	3,630
Maputo, Mozambique	9,101	9,542	6,364	8,934	12,759	8,520	8,438	13,675	8,745	10,252	16,292	15,315	12,890	4,776	7,761	14,107	14,089	10,137	10,693	5,069
Mar del Plata, Argentina	16,684	15,395	13,234	14,390	18,789	15,295	12,580	6,692	10,287	2,599	8,815	11,271	10,117	7,985	15,611	11,557	9,349	18,345	17,803	10,104
Maracaibo, Venezuela	13,725	11,662	12,179	11,055	14,193	12,508	9,510	1,740	7,045	3,029	4,355	5,742	4,709	8,252	14,095	12,359	3,769	14,811	16,546	9,734
Marrakech, Morocco	7,890	6,151	5,319	5,174	11,717	6,376	3,333	8,066	1,303	8,339	9,711	7,621	5,223	3,029	7,596	18,167	6,676	9,682	12,242	3,122
Marseilles, France	6,200	4,403	4,069	3,437	9,984	4,704	1,594	8,998	1,117	9,979	10,072	7,300	5,254	4,088	6,060	16,973	6,938	7,960	10,536	3,097
Maseru, Lesotho	9,701	10,057	6,851	9,402	13,375	9,067	8,774	13,190	8,842	9,659	15,814	15,312	12,833	4,725	8,364	14,118	13,885	10,760	11,277	5,303
Mashhad, Iran	2,137	2,170	1,331	2,018	6,705	1,066	3,225	13,251	5,711	14,448	13,229	9,775	8,854	6,586	1,454	13,733	10,530	3,931	6,259	4,458
Mazatlan, Mexico	12,803	11,255	13,576	11,243	10,828	12,428	10,557	2,215	8,888	6,054	410	3,541	4,684	11,731	13,940	9,185	2,960	12,725	13,158	12,557
Mbabane, Swaziland	9,218	9,624	6,420	9,000	12,904	8,613	8,464	13,534	8,710	10,104	16,153	15,264	12,824	4,703	7,879	14,170	13,994	10,272	10,842	5,063
Mbandaka, Zaire	7,954	7,461	4,524	6,587	12,484	6,788	5,542	11,629	5,481	9,637	13,873	12,057	9,679	1,798	6,842	17,271	11,051	9,596	11,319	1,977
McMurdo Sound, Antarctica	14,235	16,162	13,814	16,296	12,639	15,046	16,517	12,142	16,190	9,039	12,482	15,893	16,579	12,038	13,423	6,836	15,090	13,249	10,999	13,120
Mecca, Saudi Arabia	4,632	4,327	1,201	3,633	9,187	3,497	3,444	12,890	5,054	12,492	14,019	10,901	9,190	4,257	3,598	15,750	10,907	6,333	8,372	2,204
Medan, Indonesia	4,434	6,479	6,055	7,054	5,168	5,601	8,608	17,782	11,104	17,991	15,631	13,139	13,596	10,558	4,014	9,141	14,865	3,632	2,886	8,790
Medellin, Colombia	14,338	12,283	12,821	11,697	14,389	13,151	10,165	1,616	7,699	2,646	4,204	6,029	5,238	8,727	14,746	11,814	4,137	15,322	16,778	10,300
Medicine Hat, Canada	9,804	8,306	10,958	8,420	8,555	9,489	8,127	4,367	7,217	8,468	2,873	670	3,008	11,131	10,949	10,031	2,154	9,889	10,934	11,017
Medina, Saudi Arabia	4,448	4,030	993	3,311	9,016	3,246	3,124	12,696	4,826	12,522	13,728	10,578	8,906	4,346	3,487	15,758	10,629	6,190	8,314	2,244
Melbourne, Australia	10,754	12,782	12,519	13,558	8,120	12,134	15,223	14,411	17,698	13,070	12,864	14,548	17,042	14,816	10,622	4,114	15,835	9,222	6,708	14,347
Memphis, Tennessee	11,529	9,700	11,623	9,494	10,906	10,817	8,585	2,167	6,826	6,165	2,299	2,510	2,690	9,916	12,442	11,096	970	11,998	13,279	10,525
Merauke, Indonesia	7,990	9,848	10,700	10,768	4,835	9,495	12,600	14,852	15,095	15,844	12,360	12,316	14,497	15,282	8,295	4,328	14,232	6,245	3,661	13,602
Merida, Mexico	13,087	11,213	12,824	10,925	12,184	12,298	9,819	646	7,747	4,762	2,155	4,010	4,047	10,073	13,944	10,757	2,460	13,542	14,573	11,146
Meridian, Mississippi	11,822	9,967	11,789	9,727	11,228	11,070	8,753	1,847	6,900	5,835	2,300	2,841	2,877	9,829	12,705	11,150	1,207	12,322	13,604	10,542
Messina, Italy	5,683	4,138	3,137	3,123	9,833	4,165	1,458	9,983	2,094	10,596	11,097	8,246	6,273	3,724	5,330	17,129	7,965	7,510	10,027	2,273
Mexico City, Mexico	13,292	11,584	13,564	11,438	11,661	12,727	10,528	1,370	8,615	5,223	1,268	3,996	4,643	11,084	14,320	9,753	2,929	13,417	14,007	12,119
Miami, Florida	12,403	10,430	11,779	10,034	12,292	11,450	8,808	1,302	6,662	4,855	3,039	3,845	3,215	9,064	13,106	11,815	1,923	13,149	14,650	10,054
Midway Islands, USA	8,707	9,006	12,023	9,890	4,472	9,725	11,108	9,254	12,001	12,720	6,634	6,364	8,798	16,170	9,954	4,951	8,158	7,298	6,381	14,605
Milan, Italy	5,823	4,016	3,818	3,052	9,605	4,334	1,211	9,232	1,417	10,350	10,175	7,280	5,343	4,360	5,719	16,659	7,053	7,576	10,154	3,191

Distances in Kilometers

	Kuqa Chang, China	Kurgan, USSR	Kuwait, Kuwait	Kuybyshev, USSR	Kyoto, Japan	Kzyl-Orda, USSR	L'vov, USSR	La Ceiba, Honduras	La Coruna, Spain	La Paz, Bolivia	La Paz, Mexico	La Ronge, Canada	Labrador City, Canada	Lagos, Nigeria	Lahore, Pakistan	Lambasa, Fiji	Lansing, Michigan	Lanzhou, China	Laoag, Philippines	Largeau, Chad
Milford Sound, New Zealand	12,674	14,629	14,537	15,495	9,389	14,112	17,242	12,442	19,683	11,198	11,252	13,726	15,993	15,518	12,648	3,306	14,380	11,018	8,439	15,863
Milwaukee, Wisconsin	10,637	8,803	10,811	8,614	10,297	9,924	7,782	3,023	6,198	6,895	2,931	1,837	1,904	9,631	11,546	11,456	277	11,168	12,627	9,983
Minsk, USSR	4,312	2,411	3,184	1,493	8,000	2,893	515	10,111	2,858	11,846	10,460	7,176	5,790	5,696	4,443	15,190	7,509	6,003	8,588	4,059
Mogadiscio, Somalia	5,774	6,184	3,036	5,686	9,918	5,130	5,668	14,413	6,998	12,591	16,101	13,125	11,294	4,684	4,461	14,755	12,967	7,064	8,385	3,361
Mombasa, Kenya	6,695	7,001	3,804	6,421	10,825	5,990	6,158	14,040	7,121	11,780	16,110	13,535	11,474	4,196	5,386	15,053	13,060	7,985	9,202	3,316
Monclova, Mexico	12,450	10,795	12,979	10,716	10,901	11,955	9,949	1,950	8,240	5,998	943	3,148	4,060	11,145	13,516	9,800	2,329	12,559	13,275	11,913
Moncton, Canada	9,838	7,821	9,262	7,395	10,790	8,815	6,238	3,936	4,383	6,941	4,721	2,988	777	7,818	10,471	13,296	1,613	10,833	12,864	8,132
Monrovia, Liberia	9,909	8,556	6,653	7,541	14,252	8,435	5,815	8,333	4,112	6,799	10,688	9,721	7,231	1,569	9,186	18,444	8,210	11,751	14,045	3,493
Monte Carlo, Monaco	6,032	4,246	3,915	3,275	9,843	4,535	1,432	9,145	1,276	10,148	10,177	7,356	5,351	4,150	5,891	16,886	7,046	7,796	10,370	3,066
Monterrey, Mexico	12,593	10,916	13,041	10,814	11,076	12,070	10,007	1,781	8,247	5,823	1,022	3,294	4,111	11,067	13,643	9,859	2,378	12,726	13,448	11,888
Montevideo, Uruguay	16,446	15,064	13,015	14,064	18,938	15,018	12,245	6,475	9,930	2,360	8,678	11,014	9,786	7,733	15,443	11,854	9,067	18,198	18,130	9,859
Montgomery, Alabama	11,792	9,940	11,645	9,634	11,355	10,995	8,613	1,839	6,715	5,745	2,517	2,930	2,764	9,605	12,639	11,371	1,159	12,358	13,722	10,336
Montpelier, Vermont	10,244	8,268	9,867	7,909	10,774	9,306	6,835	3,431	5,029	6,743	4,076	2,617	1,052	8,395	10,961	12,699	982	11,102	12,960	8,773
Montpellier, France	6,294	4,476	4,195	3,519	10,033	4,803	1,680	8,871	992	9,880	9,952	7,200	5,137	4,117	6,173	16,963	6,818	8,045	10,624	3,187
Montreal, Canada	10,137	8,173	9,836	7,835	10,615	9,223	6,800	3,519	5,052	6,888	4,052	2,469	960	8,487	10,876	12,617	928	10,969	12,807	8,817
Moosonee, Canada	9,645	7,765	9,757	7,549	9,808	8,872	6,735	3,976	5,308	7,607	3,934	1,691	957	9,038	10,504	12,108	995	10,320	12,035	9,132
Moroni, Comoros	7,161	7,718	4,572	7,219	10,973	6,644	7,070	14,628	8,034	11,867	16,915	14,467	12,388	4,850	5,821	14,283	13,942	8,246	9,111	4,215
Moscow, USSR	3,673	1,736	3,043	861	7,344	2,307	1,125	10,539	3,520	12,492	10,644	7,262	6,127	6,247	3,917	14,582	7,813	5,335	7,920	4,479
Mosul, Iraq	3,515	2,708	893	1,953	8,020	2,103	2,151	12,211	4,406	12,974	12,754	9,437	8,044	5,223	2,916	15,188	9,774	5,352	7,733	3,119
Mount Isa, Australia	8,965	10,932	11,259	11,785	6,181	10,421	13,564	15,123	16,123	14,908	12,912	13,473	15,779	15,048	9,046	4,226	15,261	7,330	4,775	13,796
Multan, Pakistan	1,630	2,848	2,272	3,087	5,953	1,706	4,505	14,416	7,007	15,659	13,987	10,551	9,955	7,552	311	12,613	11,569	3,060	5,123	5,449
Munich, West Germany	5,543	3,696	3,734	2,748	9,262	4,070	927	9,324	1,636	10,620	10,132	7,139	5,306	4,687	5,505	16,316	7,031	7,274	9,856	3,423
Murcia, Spain	6,971	5,207	4,596	4,233	10,786	5,464	2,391	8,577	857	9,230	9,926	7,445	5,206	3,522	6,750	17,616	6,807	8,749	11,318	2,971
Murmansk, USSR	4,247	2,208	4,507	1,968	6,900	3,256	2,188	9,496	3,704	12,153	9,262	5,833	5,019	7,275	4,902	13,715	6,609	5,547	8,031	5,755
Mururoa Atoll, Fr. Polynesia	15,522	15,775	18,934	16,443	10,972	16,632	16,561	7,048	14,897	7,404	5,961	9,107	10,786	15,636	16,568	4,415	9,066	13,830	11,798	17,694
Muscat, Oman	3,026	3,576	1,235	3,360	7,423	2,432	4,178	14,258	6,416	14,435	14,585	11,149	10,032	6,190	1,782	13,829	11,747	4,527	6,432	4,145
Myitkyina, Burma	2,175	4,234	4,874	4,977	3,818	3,584	6,727	15,428	9,287	18,231	13,770	10,830	11,195	10,113	2,359	10,010	12,460	1,326	2,523	8,036
Naga, Philippines	4,906	6,766	7,864	7,676	2,683	6,419	9,508	15,387	12,011	18,775	12,864	11,145	12,565	13,021	5,353	7,019	13,155	3,157	576	10,996
Nagasaki, Japan	4,187	5,506	7,620	6,514	592	5,604	8,317	13,369	10,569	17,456	11,045	8,942	10,366	12,899	5,184	7,574	10,936	2,431	1,867	10,774
Nagoya, Japan	4,657	5,756	8,112	6,770	108	5,999	8,519	12,730	10,626	16,783	10,364	8,391	9,974	13,320	5,743	7,261	10,409	2,998	2,477	11,214
Nagpur, India	2,259	3,976	3,255	4,328	5,699	2,907	5,753	15,642	8,229	16,550	14,890	11,546	11,167	8,280	1,251	11,700	12,736	2,903	4,352	6,269
Nairobi, Kenya	6,651	6,801	3,595	6,165	10,910	5,839	5,796	13,647	6,686	11,572	15,672	13,130	11,040	3,812	5,373	15,476	12,620	8,037	9,405	2,876
Nanchang, China	3,245	4,973	6,515	5,916	2,002	4,757	7,758	14,518	10,217	18,596	12,358	9,928	10,957	11,827	3,996	8,458	11,827	1,407	1,257	9,708
Nancy, France	5,891	3,996	4,131	3,079	9,479	4,435	1,299	8,924	1,272	10,267	9,779	6,857	4,948	4,689	5,895	16,375	6,666	7,595	10,180	3,607
Nandi, Fiji	11,617	13,012	14,755	14,027	7,317	13,109	15,736	11,137	17,119	11,904	9,114	10,831	13,284	18,598	12,248	258	11,980	9,772	7,384	17,736
Nanjing, China	3,292	4,866	6,663	5,841	1,608	4,774	7,679	14,056	10,080	18,149	11,897	9,476	10,572	11,973	4,182	8,395	11,390	1,461	1,545	9,846
Nanning, China	3,088	5,054	6,016	5,900	2,983	4,582	7,707	15,432	10,248	19,220	13,350	10,802	11,598	11,255	3,492	8,871	12,629	1,534	1,379	9,181
Nantes, France	6,484	4,562	4,667	3,667	9,955	5,034	1,900	8,383	685	9,674	9,379	6,621	4,557	4,543	6,494	16,590	6,247	8,169	10,753	3,759
Naples, Italy	5,659	4,021	3,300	3,013	9,704	4,142	1,257	9,778	1,887	10,573	10,818	7,935	5,989	3,959	5,391	16,950	7,690	7,467	10,011	2,583
Narvik, Norway	4,855	2,799	4,777	2,407	7,470	3,783	2,103	8,953	3,170	11,518	8,899	5,527	4,482	6,960	5,439	14,089	6,121	6,184	8,664	5,614
Nashville, Tennessee	11,382	9,514	11,349	9,270	10,983	10,614	8,312	2,258	6,515	6,150	2,617	2,535	2,427	9,608	12,251	11,411	754	11,937	13,338	10,208
Nassau, Bahamas	12,407	10,407	11,625	9,969	12,501	11,398	8,683	1,425	6,479	4,707	3,330	4,040	3,215	8,783	13,052	12,083	2,066	13,237	14,840	9,810
Natal, Brazil	12,816	11,198	9,670	10,211	16,641	11,305	8,378	6,164	6,077	3,781	8,777	9,288	7,161	4,497	12,198	15,494	7,320	14,656	17,065	6,517
Natashquan, Canada	9,331	7,315	8,821	6,900	10,410	8,315	5,788	4,429	4,060	7,414	5,058	2,942	467	7,708	9,971	13,439	1,923	10,345	12,425	7,859
Nauru Island	9,503	10,789	12,827	11,804	5,098	10,957	13,513	11,776	15,237	13,703	9,306	9,915	12,380	18,094	10,295	2,227	11,557	7,671	5,476	16,018
Ndjamena, Chad	7,330	6,465	3,903	5,517	11,888	5,988	4,262	10,892	4,132	9,685	12,857	10,724	8,405	1,426	6,411	18,278	9,875	9,109	11,198	777
Nelson, New Zealand	12,842	14,713	14,966	15,640	9,277	14,322	17,461	11,974	19,740	11,030	10,691	13,154	15,415	16,019	12,940	2,816	13,814	11,118	8,534	16,442
Nema, Mauritania	8,872	7,402	5,782	6,389	13,092	7,370	4,630	8,442	2,968	7,621	10,536	9,008	6,528	1,614	8,280	19,327	7,747	10,717	13,137	2,805
Neuquen, Argentina	17,593	16,131	14,151	15,151	17,866	16,163	13,315	6,365	10,918	2,488	8,256	11,007	10,183	8,882	16,531	10,715	9,198	19,225	17,559	11,007
New Delhi, India	1,508	3,129	2,843	3,515	5,512	2,076	5,030	14,804	7,555	16,239	14,111	10,728	10,326	8,094	433	12,040	11,889	2,617	4,557	6,004
New Glasgow, Canada	9,823	7,794	9,160	7,342	10,891	8,770	6,145	4,000	4,241	6,897	4,869	3,157	876	7,644	10,423	13,468	1,774	10,860	12,934	7,976
New Haven, Connecticut	10,565	8,581	10,106	8,203	11,065	9,608	7,081	3,129	5,187	6,418	3,944	2,815	1,371	8,396	11,264	12,670	976	11,432	13,272	8,882
New Orleans, Louisiana	12,100	10,257	12,079	10,023	11,366	11,363	9,044	1,605	7,162	5,653	2,104	3,044	3,173	9,991	12,997	10,962	1,500	12,558	13,751	10,773
New Plymouth, New Zealand	12,763	14,593	15,019	15,540	9,100	14,257	17,377	11,880	19,487	11,099	10,519	12,921	15,208	16,275	12,919	2,561	13,631	11,014	8,434	16,648
New York, New York	10,655	8,677	10,218	8,307	11,088	9,709	7,193	3,027	5,298	6,362	3,837	2,797	1,463	8,483	11,365	12,576	905	11,502	13,312	8,988
Newcastle upon Tyne, UK	6,110	4,090	4,837	3,314	9,237	4,754	1,822	8,281	1,384	10,080	8,951	5,974	4,134	5,403	6,325	15,724	5,864	7,682	10,243	4,477
Newcastle Waters, Australia	8,279	10,274	10,519	11,099	5,805	9,716	12,857	15,749	15,418	15,581	13,411	13,556	15,684	14,474	8,316	4,888	15,469	6,693	4,180	13,100
Niamey, Niger	8,315	7,098	5,029	6,091	12,755	6,865	4,494	9,502	3,458	8,410	11,585	9,857	7,416	794	7,562	19,582	8,734	10,149	12,421	1,885
Nicosia, Cyprus	4,380	3,316	1,516	2,399	8,830	2,920	1,799	11,560	3,675	12,084	12,409	9,256	7,600	4,419	3,803	16,064	9,329	6,223	8,625	2,375
Niue (Alofi)	12,753	13,901	16,033	14,896	8,286	14,193	16,370	9,880	16,805	10,612	8,039	10,216	12,541	18,443	13,503	1,170	11,056	10,922	8,638	19,073
Norfolk, Virginia	11,122	9,149	10,655	8,776	11,390	10,181	7,639	2,555	5,674	5,966	3,531	2,988	1,932	8,666	11,837	12,352	962	11,933	13,661	9,302
Norfolk Island, Australia	11,646	13,392	14,261	14,365	7,853	13,160	16,207	12,312	18,382	12,166	10,539	12,405	14,857	17,033	11,953	1,821	13,504	9,855	7,294	16,628
Noril'sk, USSR	3,146	1,922	5,123	2,639	4,788	3,016	3,956	10,555	5,816	13,908	9,531	6,159	6,289	9,129	4,289	11,762	7,562	3,824	6,103	7,332
Norman Wells, Canada	7,912	6,576	9,500	6,862	6,856	7,752	6,996	6,256	6,847	10,306	4,721	1,633	3,532	11,079	9,111	10,115	3,620	7,955	9,180	10,343
Normanton, Australia	8,812	10,742	11,252	11,623	5,856	10,289	13,428	14,938	15,972	15,063	12,647	13,101	15,401	15,277	8,969	4,073	14,910	7,132	4,557	13,908
North Pole	5,441	3,857	6,752	4,106	6,126	5,040	4,482	8,257	5,201	11,828	7,328	3,893	4,134	9,291	6,507	11,818	5,269	6,011	7,988	8,022
Nottingham, United Kingdom	6,176	4,179	4,753	3,364	9,409	4,789	1,776	8,332	1,193	9,998	9,086	6,159	4,259	5,174	6,335	15,951	5,983	7,783	10,354	4,270
Norway House, Canada	9,459	7,777	10,201	7,762	8,890	8,944	7,283	4,346	6,243	8,306	3,470	498	2,040	10,159	10,495	11,007	1,587	9,818	11,210	10,053
Norwich, United Kingdom	6,039	4,055	4,583	3,222	9,343	4,641	1,609	8,502	1,256	10,130	9,249	6,297	4,423	5,124	6,177	15,985	6,148	7,664	10,239	4,154
Nouakchott, Mauritania	9,464	7,820	6,559	6,828	13,416	7,946	5,001	7,503	2,891	6,882	9,631	8,335	5,841	2,463	9,003	18,394	6,930	11,290	13,800	3,708
Noumea, New Caledonia	11,050	12,714	13,880	13,705	7,120	12,569	15,534	12,358	17,617	12,691	10,361	11,901	14,388	17,496	11,470	1,504	13,183	9,231	6,705	16,590
Novosibirsk, USSR	1,541	1,119	3,980	2,133	4,578	1,684	3,927	12,098	6,291	15,070	11,140	7,772	7,717	8,756	2,693	11,899	9,106	2,640	5,182	6,729
Nuku'alofa, Tonga	12,455	13,769	15,612	14,781	8,089	13,935	16,403	10,476	17,256	11,046	8,630	10,708	13,075	18,373	13,106	772	11,626	10,611	8,241	18,489
Nukunono Island, Tokelau Isls.	11,904	12,876	15,313	13,852	7,361	13,277	15,267	9,774	15,897	11,172	7,640	9,403	11,823	19,427	12,798	1,239	10,484	10,112	8,009	18,491
Nuremberg, West Germany	5,528	3,649	3,820	2,720	9,181	4,068	933	9,248	1,636	10,631	10,013	6,999	5,191	4,821	5,532	16,194	6,919	7,241	9,825	3,572
Nyala, Sudan	6,519	5,948	3,065	5,087	11,082	5,292	4,191	11,904	4,717	10,710	13,715	11,237	9,069	2,441	5,493	17,243	10,642	8,232	10,195	898
Oaxaca, Mexico	13,558	11,797	13,629	11,601	12,027	12,923	10,604	1,068	8,596	4,857	1,619	4,286	4,754	10,875	14,539	9,918	3,073	13,750	14,373	12,007
Ocean Falls, Canada	9,216	7,997	10,940	8,303	7,426	9,166	8,370	5,415	7,912	9,531	3,458	1,503	3,988	12,025	10,464	9,164	3,362	9,022	9,815	11,588
Odense, Denmark	5,376	3,386	4,146	2,565	8,728	3,997	1,108	9,023	1,898	10,797	9,562	6,438	4,790	5,464	5,562	15,580	6,522	6,994	9,571	4,226
Odessa, USSR	4,203	2,592	2,416	1,578	8,288	2,693	625	10,720	3,076	11,997	11,258	8,017	6,518	5,151	4,055	15,602	8,249	6,002	8,555	3,342
Ogbomosho, Nigeria	8,517	7,464	5,131	6,473	13,039	7,119	4,974	9,888	4,094	8,425	12,081	10,485	8,032	210	7,654	18,952	9,306	10,323	12,458	1,939
Okha, USSR	4,550	4,766	7,746	5,709	2,139	5,445	7,202	10,986	8,921	15,093	8,916	6,442	7,879	12,356	5,874	8,502	8,415	3,598	4,372	10,451
Okinawa (Naha)	4,366	5,917	7,699	6,903	1,244	5,853	8,736	14,058	11,093	18,066	11,658	9,689	11,122	13,014	5,189	7,319	11,691	2,525	1,148	10,891
Oklahoma City, Oklahoma	11,514	9,798	11,968	9,695	10,451	10,949	8,946	2,430	7,349	6,535	1,759	2,260	3,080	10,577	12,531	10,453	1,377	11,787	12,839	11,104
Old Crow, Canada	7,410	6,204	9,235	6,584	6,230	7,363	6,914	6,874	7,047	10,935	5,232	2,264	4,057	11,297	8,647	9,886	4,248	7,360	8,548	10,370
Olympia, Washington	9,891	8,621	11,491	8,876	8,020	9,797	8,808	4,802	8,108	8,906	2,775	1,518	3,962	12,084	11,128	9,084	3,036	9,700	10,409	11,873
Omaha, Nebraska	10,871	9,142	11,351	9,045	10,047	10,293	8,343	2,962	6,867	7,013	2,316	1,681	2,535	10,321	11,876	10,761	963	11,210	12,420	10,667
Omsk, USSR	1,706	518	3,496	1,527	5,186	1,268	3,337	11,942	5,747	14,627	11,226	7,798	7,495	8,154	2,603	12,507	8,975	3,123	5,698	6,141
Oodnadatta, Australia	9,307	11,336	11,240	12,114	6,923	10,697	13,808	15,491	16,340	14,511	13,505	14,319	16,638	14,464	9,213	4,673	16,053	7,790	5,310	13,473
Oradea, Romania	4,840	3,110	2,983	2,113	8,781	3,342	344	10,094	2,401	11,341	10,781	7,653	5,985	4,838	4,731	16,029	7,717	6,615	9,183	3,243
Oran, Algeria	7,072	5,356	4,572	4,369	10,970	5,558	2,535	8,666	1,080	9,155	10,093	7,673	5,406	3,265	6,793	17,870	6,984	8,868	11,424	2,771
Oranjestad, Aruba	13,469	11,405	11,918	10,790	14,090	12,243	9,242	1,845	6,779	3,216	4,429	5,628	4,494	8,068	13,827	12,574	3,630	14,589	16,415	9,507
Orebro, Sweden	5,004	2,972	4,143	2,240	8,217	3,693	1,193	9,178	2,392	11,198	9,507	6,268	4,827	5,947	5,306	15,076	6,544	6,562	9,126	4,604
Orel, USSR	3,750	1,914	2,789	942	7,580	2,317	907	10,648	3,413	12,408	10,869	7,516	6,280	5,947	3,872	14,853	7,984	5,468	8,050	4,155
Orsk, USSR	2,205	650	2,579	617	6,229	878	2,434	11,860	4,960	13,953	11,586	8,127	7,390	7,080	2,533	13,553	9,004	3,933	6,510	5,065
Osaka, Japan	4,563	5,707	8,016	6,722	43	5,921	8,483	12,862	10,622	16,921	10,503	8,506	10,059	13,242	5,633	7,316	10,520	2,883	2,347	11,131
Oslo, Norway	5,242	3,198	4,388	2,493	8,348	3,947	1,403	8,916	2,250	10,974	9,269	6,057	4,571	5,964	5,565	15,091	6,291	6,773	9,327	4,712
Osorno, Chile	18,057	16,571	14,608	15,602	17,417	16,634	13,763	6,396	11,339	2,711	8,133	11,032	10,379	9,349	16,947	10,244	9,297	19,437	17,202	11,473
Ostrava, Czechoslovakia	5,019	3,180	3,374	2,224	8,781	3,551	411	9,725	2,152	11,143	10,373	7,250	5,581	5,007	5,011	15,931	7,313	6,751	9,332	3,541
Ottawa, Canada	10,192	8,244	9,963	7,929	10,555	9,306	6,925	3,446	5,207	6,899	3,899	2,344	1,053	8,650	10,957	12,453	768	10,982	12,771	8,978

Distances in Kilometers	Kuqa Chang, China	Kurgan, USSR	Kuwait, Kuwait	Kuybyshev, USSR	Kyoto, Japan	Kzyl-Orda, USSR	L'vov, USSR	La Ceiba, Honduras	La Coruna, Spain	La Paz, Bolivia	La Paz, Mexico	La Ronge, Canada	Labrador City, Canada	Lagos, Nigeria	Lahore, Pakistan	Lambasa, Fiji	Lansing, Michigan	Lanzhou, China	Laoag, Philippines	Largeau, Chad
Ouagadougou, Bourkina Fasso	8,700	7,426	5,437	6,414	13,105	7,237	4,765	9,154	3,499	7,997	11,301	9,746	7,277	847	7,969	19,546	8,522	10,538	12,831	2,299
Oujda, Morocco	7,231	5,518	4,700	4,532	11,130	5,717	2,698	8,573	1,116	9,000	10,051	7,697	5,400	3,171	6,941	17,981	6,955	9,029	11,584	2,790
Oxford, United Kingdom	6,238	4,255	4,729	3,421	9,524	4,836	1,784	8,342	1,074	9,930	9,148	6,255	4,317	5,041	6,365	16,086	6,036	7,864	10,439	4,159
Pago Pago, American Samoa	12,363	13,419	15,721	14,404	7,851	13,770	15,842	9,808	16,369	10,865	7,821	9,811	12,185	18,936	13,188	1,091	10,766	10,548	8,349	18,907
Pakxe, Laos	3,603	5,652	6,104	6,411	3,715	5,012	8,153	16,322	10,714	19,366	14,165	11,694	12,431	11,153	3,679	8,807	13,514	2,329	1,616	9,166
Palembang, Indonesia	5,340	7,402	7,020	8,017	5,300	6,565	9,593	18,114	12,091	17,723	15,588	13,621	14,405	11,311	4,996	8,286	15,499	4,315	2,912	9,655
Palermo, Italy	5,859	4,281	3,327	3,269	9,973	4,340	1,553	9,804	1,921	10,410	10,956	8,152	6,139	3,649	5,521	17,246	7,821	7,681	10,206	2,308
Palma, Majorca	6,600	4,848	4,266	3,869	10,452	5,092	2,029	8,864	1,013	9,601	10,112	7,499	5,339	3,669	6,385	17,422	6,980	8,381	10,947	2,878
Palmerston North, New Zealand	12,951	14,786	15,159	15,732	9,290	14,442	17,567	11,766	19,542	10,913	10,469	12,949	15,196	16,171	13,091	2,676	13,591	11,206	8,625	16,659
Panama, Panama	14,188	12,161	12,979	11,649	13,895	13,098	10,208	1,092	7,808	3,083	3,676	5,599	5,009	9,133	14,731	11,471	3,773	15,011	16,285	10,617
Paramaribo, Suriname	13,320	11,315	10,960	10,500	15,344	11,881	8,739	3,624	6,178	2,854	6,222	7,040	5,333	6,478	13,251	13,980	5,007	14,874	17,307	8,158
Paris, France	6,143	4,220	4,412	3,325	9,638	4,698	1,572	8,641	1,028	10,015	9,532	6,665	4,700	4,703	6,173	16,397	6,411	7,827	10,411	3,752
Patna, India	1,735	3,685	3,680	4,220	4,928	2,767	5,827	15,344	8,370	17,082	14,256	11,009	10,892	8,881	1,248	11,206	12,365	2,115	3,745	6,814
Patrai, Greece	5,191	3,747	2,609	2,736	9,434	3,676	1,300	10,481	2,589	11,120	11,482	8,504	6,651	3,979	4,796	16,758	8,363	7,027	9,523	2,268
Peking, China	2,776	4,091	6,229	5,090	1,793	4,161	6,910	13,388	9,247	17,371	11,422	8,757	9,708	11,471	3,881	9,020	10,610	1,196	2,443	9,352
Penrhyn Island (Omoka)	13,039	13,615	16,491	14,490	8,478	14,260	15,473	8,318	15,202	9,728	6,355	8,622	10,878	17,972	14,083	2,581	9,366	11,337	9,423	18,975
Peoria, Illinois	10,910	9,091	11,103	8,908	10,430	10,214	8,072	2,774	6,451	6,709	2,661	1,976	2,186	9,798	11,833	11,270	477	11,400	12,780	10,220
Perm', USSR	2,681	623	3,244	658	6,193	1,599	2,278	11,156	4,643	13,547	10,814	7,356	6,678	7,289	3,241	13,471	8,264	4,224	6,802	5,389
Perth, Australia	8,752	10,808	9,872	11,360	7,697	9,909	12,766	17,115	15,035	14,628	15,447	15,905	17,660	12,509	8,280	6,590	17,861	7,632	5,571	11,664
Peshawar, Pakistan	1,317	2,429	2,288	2,722	5,789	1,306	4,230	14,039	6,765	15,565	13,562	10,126	9,568	7,604	373	12,644	11,166	2,928	5,155	5,482
Petropavlovsk-Kamchatskiy, USSR	5,584	5,620	8,699	6,505	2,693	6,399	7,837	10,170	9,253	14,281	7,967	5,776	7,523	13,016	6,914	7,948	7,801	4,622	5,070	11,241
Petrozavodsk, USSR	3,969	1,912	3,741	1,342	7,200	2,761	1,479	9,990	3,451	12,265	9,966	6,569	5,536	6,651	4,413	14,270	7,193	5,483	8,045	5,019
Pevek, USSR	5,663	4,891	8,092	5,547	4,393	5,942	6,466	8,859	7,465	12,905	7,099	4,236	5,642	11,497	6,973	9,580	6,163	5,398	6,627	10,026
Philadelphia, Pennsylvania	10,764	8,792	10,348	8,429	11,123	9,829	7,322	2,907	5,424	6,291	3,718	2,789	1,575	8,578	11,485	12,474	843	11,589	13,364	9,107
Phnom Penh, Kampuchea	3,896	5,958	6,197	6,679	4,055	5,259	8,386	16,723	10,943	19,098	14,518	12,099	12,816	11,123	3,846	8,761	13,918	2,717	1,840	9,190
Phoenix, Arizona	11,589	10,153	12,741	10,252	9,657	11,335	9,816	3,206	8,516	7,233	1,044	2,463	4,165	11,925	12,775	9,126	2,610	11,464	12,023	12,326
Pierre, South Dakota	10,521	8,862	11,229	8,833	9,555	10,028	8,261	3,417	6,964	7,491	2,417	1,244	2,612	10,592	11,576	10,522	1,288	10,775	11,931	10,787
Pinang, Malaysia	4,303	6,362	6,099	6,975	4,893	5,524	8,571	17,535	11,089	18,266	15,357	12,894	13,426	10,717	3,970	9,025	14,650	3,409	2,618	8,906
Pitcairn Island (Adamstown)	16,449	16,408	19,492	16,881	11,923	17,411	16,469	6,517	14,405	6,466	5,850	9,192	10,572	14,670	17,537	5,319	8,840	14,793	12,753	16,751
Pittsburgh, Pennsylvania	10,813	8,886	10,603	8,583	10,888	9,956	7,567	2,810	5,764	6,422	3,349	2,475	1,708	8,991	11,606	12,067	456	11,527	13,174	9,482
Plymouth, Montserrat	12,691	10,625	10,964	9,947	13,979	11,392	8,340	2,629	5,846	3,729	5,062	5,615	4,043	7,216	12,939	13,489	3,581	13,982	16,132	8,569
Plymouth, United Kingdom	6,485	4,506	4,900	3,666	9,759	5,076	2,000	8,157	846	9,681	9,044	6,231	4,213	4,922	6,593	16,224	5,919	8,114	10,689	4,154
Ponape Island	8,235	9,565	11,570	10,579	3,870	9,692	12,330	12,439	14,276	14,879	9,851	9,792	12,132	16,872	9,043	3,477	11,640	6,403	4,267	14,764
Ponce, Puerto Rico	12,765	10,699	11,262	10,079	13,683	11,532	8,542	2,164	6,100	3,822	4,572	5,255	3,876	7,684	13,121	13,051	3,222	13,935	15,923	8,981
Ponta Delgada, Azores	8,695	6,716	6,726	5,874	11,728	7,264	4,133	6,426	1,588	7,469	7,960	6,054	3,582	4,542	8,718	16,613	4,940	10,319	12,884	4,869
Pontianak, Indonesia	5,257	7,323	7,267	8,017	4,752	6,580	9,677	17,536	12,216	18,156	14,988	13,142	14,129	11,784	5,085	7,889	15,078	4,037	2,364	10,042
Port Augusta, Australia	9,878	11,916	11,683	12,677	7,475	11,249	14,340	15,177	16,838	13,926	13,399	14,584	17,001	14,497	9,738	4,543	16,163	8,379	5,901	13,723
Port Blair, India	3,402	5,418	5,031	5,960	5,049	4,506	7,509	16,976	10,016	17,902	15,330	12,423	12,595	9,807	2,913	10,024	13,982	2,923	3,081	7,913
Port Elizabeth, South Africa	10,214	10,603	7,397	9,946	13,749	9,609	9,284	13,027	9,233	9,339	15,632	15,586	13,092	5,048	8,874	13,779	14,011	11,214	11,572	5,783
Port Hedland, Australia	7,714	9,780	9,355	10,446	6,386	8,997	12,030	17,305	14,502	15,867	15,001	14,697	16,353	12,890	7,436	6,407	16,721	6,433	4,266	11,644
Port Louis, Mauritius	7,303	8,409	5,577	8,159	10,262	7,239	8,428	16,229	9,725	12,833	18,697	15,867	14,063	6,612	6,001	12,495	15,686	7,896	8,090	5,943
Port Moresby, Papua New Guinea	8,585	10,361	11,416	11,315	5,069	10,100	13,157	14,144	15,572	15,188	11,707	11,981	14,300	16,034	8,975	3,573	13,804	6,794	4,232	14,358
Port Said, Egypt	4,661	3,726	1,520	2,830	9,165	3,245	2,175	11,693	3,804	11,924	12,699	9,618	7,871	4,076	3,968	16,313	9,591	6,492	8,828	1,989
Port Sudan, Sudan	4,969	4,620	1,533	3,889	9,524	3,820	3,553	12,758	4,986	12,190	14,027	11,000	9,196	3,939	3,930	16,019	10,898	6,668	8,684	1,919
Port-au-Prince, Haiti	12,940	10,892	11,707	10,346	13,383	11,797	8,897	1,569	6,524	3,902	3,975	4,921	3,848	8,288	13,422	12,466	2,920	13,949	15,706	9,544
Port-of-Spain, Trin. & Tobago	13,242	11,186	11,272	10,461	14,638	11,892	8,792	2,797	6,256	3,090	5,365	6,234	4,716	7,149	13,386	13,434	4,199	14,609	16,805	8,677
Port-Vila, Vanuatu	10,871	12,432	13,869	13,438	6,776	12,384	15,238	12,079	17,146	12,772	9,972	11,381	13,872	17,966	11,396	1,187	12,717	9,033	6,563	16,773
Portland, Maine	10,249	8,255	9,770	7,865	10,906	9,274	6,744	3,464	4,882	6,664	4,230	2,804	1,063	8,203	10,930	12,886	1,164	11,157	13,067	8,608
Portland, Oregon	10,056	8,790	11,654	9,042	8,128	9,966	8,957	4,692	8,215	8,788	2,618	1,622	4,032	12,156	11,296	9,006	3,034	9,848	10,515	11,992
Porto, Portugal	7,316	5,428	5,217	4,512	10,823	5,842	2,700	7,893	247	8,846	9,192	6,767	4,484	4,025	7,236	17,161	6,074	9,030	11,614	3,692
Porto Alegre, Brazil	15,786	14,353	12,389	13,354	19,168	14,332	11,534	6,351	9,230	2,290	8,710	10,752	9,323	7,084	14,864	12,547	8,754	17,595	18,457	9,212
Porto Alexandre, Angola	9,684	9,345	6,328	8,479	14,077	8,622	7,353	11,388	6,872	8,495	13,952	13,157	10,666	2,635	8,476	16,187	11,707	11,190	12,488	3,815
Porto Novo, Benin	8,774	7,716	5,383	6,723	13,297	7,377	5,205	9,762	4,226	8,193	12,008	10,539	8,070	85	7,904	18,852	9,294	10,578	12,698	2,193
Porto Velho, Brazil	15,198	13,198	12,606	12,377	16,485	13,740	10,598	3,708	8,041	972	6,219	8,054	6,845	7,653	15,025	12,528	6,076	16,735	18,859	9,583
Portsmouth, United Kingdom	6,275	4,305	4,695	3,455	9,608	4,860	1,782	8,367	991	9,889	9,212	6,345	4,380	4,931	6,375	16,196	6,094	7,915	10,494	4,061
Poznan, Poland	5,038	3,128	3,605	2,219	8,655	3,603	570	9,536	2,131	11,120	10,107	6,958	5,333	5,246	5,117	15,726	7,066	6,728	9,313	3,833
Prague, Czechoslovakia	5,275	3,404	3,627	2,468	8,961	3,815	684	9,459	1,890	10,885	10,153	7,079	5,347	4,947	5,285	16,036	7,078	6,991	9,575	3,593
Praia, Cape Verde Islands	10,296	8,581	7,440	7,606	14,066	8,778	5,766	6,769	3,468	6,011	9,030	8,138	5,676	3,085	9,876	17,576	6,540	12,106	14,645	4,556
Pretoria, South Africa	9,350	9,663	6,457	9,002	13,138	8,683	8,382	13,233	8,517	9,842	15,851	15,039	12,581	4,458	8,019	14,402	13,716	10,465	11,110	4,929
Prince Albert, Canada	9,509	7,934	10,510	8,001	8,581	9,113	7,653	4,471	6,736	8,522	3,246	214	2,572	10,688	10,612	10,482	1,954	9,717	10,936	10,532
Prince Edward Island	10,717	11,594	8,473	11,119	13,281	10,479	10,768	13,907	10,960	9,871	16,251	17,295	14,806	6,794	9,397	12,034	15,539	11,262	10,916	7,389
Prince George, Canada	9,174	7,860	10,733	8,113	7,630	9,037	8,093	5,252	7,558	9,366	3,463	1,136	3,615	11,656	10,391	9,532	3,047	9,088	10,013	11,257
Prince Rupert, Canada	8,945	7,755	10,730	8,086	7,171	8,919	8,215	5,680	7,865	9,797	3,738	1,607	4,053	12,021	10,199	9,173	3,544	8,742	9,559	11,491
Providence, Rhode Island	10,472	8,479	9,974	8,088	11,061	9,498	6,951	3,242	5,049	6,465	4,081	2,867	1,283	8,275	11,154	12,796	1,087	11,368	13,247	8,747
Provo, Utah	10,860	9,400	12,017	9,506	9,197	10,582	9,128	3,624	7,979	7,728	1,786	1,719	3,637	11,620	12,030	9,486	2,272	10,820	11,584	11,805
Puerto Aisen, Chile	18,039	16,886	14,608	15,886	17,355	16,764	14,066	6,923	11,709	3,233	8,594	11,553	10,913	9,443	16,790	10,059	9,833	18,924	16,749	11,547
Puerto Deseado, Argentina	17,494	16,603	14,102	15,589	17,730	16,318	13,812	7,338	11,562	3,472	9,119	11,981	11,160	9,021	16,217	10,407	10,190	18,453	16,675	11,101
Puerto Princesa, Philippines	4,910	6,871	7,629	7,725	3,290	6,393	9,527	16,035	12,072	18,964	13,510	11,741	13,038	12,647	5,175	7,279	13,735	3,288	958	10,689
Punta Arenas, Chile	17,681	17,200	14,466	16,188	17,107	16,748	14,451	7,788	12,247	4,074	9,373	12,409	11,766	9,546	16,341	9,814	10,705	18,059	16,001	11,585
Pusan, South Korea	4,006	5,266	7,452	6,276	611	5,399	8,070	13,228	10,307	17,337	10,955	8,756	10,128	12,709	5,048	7,795	10,737	2,295	2,051	10,589
Pyongyang, North Korea	3,578	4,751	7,033	5,763	995	4,928	7,551	13,064	9,784	17,172	10,911	8,508	9,742	12,248	4,689	8,292	10,451	1,973	2,360	10,138
Qamdo, China	1,660	3,678	4,705	4,481	3,599	3,146	6,275	14,792	8,823	17,818	13,220	10,208	10,560	10,011	2,178	10,223	11,820	807	2,757	7,898
Qandahar, Afghanistan	1,908	2,650	1,723	2,710	6,394	1,467	3,997	14,006	6,471	15,092	13,821	10,362	9,583	7,028	811	13,171	11,237	3,525	5,677	4,914
Qiqian, China	3,066	3,576	6,346	4,578	2,250	4,069	6,264	12,017	8,350	15,966	10,202	7,376	8,327	11,247	4,384	9,461	9,207	2,246	3,773	9,223
Qom, Iran	2,936	2,562	646	2,062	7,495	1,677	2,763	12,863	5,116	13,680	13,201	9,804	8,599	5,779	2,205	14,537	10,316	4,740	7,053	3,652
Quebec, Canada	9,941	7,966	9,602	7,613	10,551	9,006	6,566	3,731	4,829	7,019	4,277	2,533	749	8,319	10,661	12,796	1,145	10,812	12,708	8,604
Quetta, Pakistan	1,919	2,807	1,840	2,898	6,348	1,626	4,189	14,200	6,657	15,233	13,982	10,525	9,773	7,123	714	13,043	11,423	3,463	5,555	5,018
Quito, Ecuador	15,120	13,067	13,502	12,478	14,777	13,932	10,923	1,991	8,432	2,129	4,365	6,600	5,991	9,124	15,516	11,304	4,795	16,031	17,137	10,832
Rabaul, Papua New Guinea	8,563	10,193	11,622	11,182	4,668	10,078	13,013	13,464	15,266	15,037	10,969	11,186	13,533	16,571	9,115	3,266	13,000	6,729	4,260	14,705
Raiatea (Uturoa)	14,142	14,706	17,598	15,546	9,575	15,378	16,310	7,955	15,454	8,808	6,359	9,069	11,116	17,064	15,139	3,112	9,481	12,411	10,379	19,022
Raleigh, North Carolina	11,290	9,334	10,890	8,983	11,400	10,379	7,870	2,359	5,917	5,890	3,297	2,959	2,119	8,877	12,034	12,130	926	12,050	13,699	9,540
Rangiroa (Avatoru)	14,318	14,702	17,750	15,481	9,771	15,467	16,062	7,509	15,038	8,467	5,936	8,725	10,715	16,739	15,387	3,529	9,064	12,639	10,700	18,588
Rangoon, Burma	2,967	5,027	5,094	5,670	4,411	4,227	7,325	16,388	9,873	18,362	14,648	11,787	12,110	10,107	2,751	9,840	13,415	2,261	2,598	8,125
Raoul Is., Kermadec Islands	12,764	14,306	15,604	15,317	8,618	14,279	17,076	10,961	18,188	10,943	9,339	11,609	13,927	17,475	13,219	1,448	12,407	10,929	8,436	17,883
Rarotonga (Avarua)	13,749	14,693	17,101	15,641	9,219	15,136	16,810	8,954	16,402	9,527	7,340	9,901	12,049	17,581	14,567	2,258	10,446	11,937	9,711	19,625
Rawson, Argentina	17,433	16,263	13,983	15,256	18,004	16,117	13,448	6,907	11,137	2,985	8,785	11,548	10,667	8,796	16,245	10,705	9,725	18,764	17,171	10,902
Recife, Brazil	12,960	11,384	9,765	10,391	16,874	11,455	8,564	6,299	6,294	3,730	8,919	9,518	7,408	4,542	12,298	15,379	7,540	14,805	17,152	6,594
Regina, Canada	9,822	8,231	10,760	8,276	8,848	9,407	7,870	4,165	6,843	8,229	2,958	519	2,591	10,712	10,917	10,445	1,753	10,029	11,213	10,658
Reykjavik, Iceland	6,651	4,593	6,138	4,104	8,840	5,532	3,119	7,227	2,468	9,771	7,536	4,454	2,822	6,715	7,185	14,463	4,538	7,924	10,327	5,989
Rhodes, Greece	4,747	3,502	2,001	2,525	9,120	3,255	1,527	11,086	3,196	11,644	12,015	8,941	7,190	4,173	4,251	16,415	8,913	6,593	9,039	2,238
Richmond, Virginia	11,074	9,113	10,676	8,760	11,275	10,156	7,653	2,581	5,726	6,061	3,451	2,864	1,897	8,770	11,812	12,256	835	11,856	13,554	9,376
Riga, USSR	4,509	2,525	3,585	1,704	7,980	3,148	792	9,760	2,730	11,665	10,058	6,772	5,407	5,887	4,741	15,057	7,121	6,135	8,716	4,353
Ringkobing, Denmark	5,484	3,479	4,300	2,682	8,762	4,121	1,262	8,875	1,845	10,696	9,410	6,295	4,636	5,522	5,696	15,541	6,368	7,083	9,654	4,334
Rio Branco, Brazil	15,553	13,525	13,047	12,735	16,355	14,120	10,977	3,535	8,417	724	5,966	8,012	6,972	8,098	15,447	12,080	6,079	16,992	18,735	10,032
Rio Cuarto, Argentina	17,048	15,434	13,680	14,469	18,163	15,560	12,628	5,916	10,204	1,882	7,997	10,528	9,540	8,370	16,157	11,313	8,650	18,882	18,280	10,498
Rio de Janeiro, Brazil	14,691	13,236	11,338	12,235	18,660	13,220	10,420	6,390	8,158	2,703	8,923	10,447	8,710	6,023	13,848	13,660	8,412	16,523	18,268	8,147
Rio Gallegos, Argentina	17,636	17,025	14,357	16,011	17,297	16,623	14,261	7,661	12,045	3,899	9,306	12,292	11,594	9,386	16,308	9,992	10,560	18,185	16,197	11,437
Rio Grande, Brazil	15,966	14,573	12,550	13,571	19,226	14,526	11,755	6,459	9,461	2,365	8,773	10,905	9,524	7,255	15,005	12,348	8,918	17,751	18,310	9,383
Riyadh, Saudi Arabia	3,857	3,743	541	3,185	8,403	2,806	3,418	13,280	5,387	13,240	14,069	10,778	9,303	5,035	2,809	15,037	11,036	5,543	7,605	2,953
Road Town, Brit. Virgin Isls.	12,632	10,565	11,062	9,925	13,713	11,376	8,366	2,378	5,909	3,885	4,762	5,319	3,834	7,473	12,953	13,268	3,283	13,849	15,911	8,764

Distances in Kilometers	Kuqa Chang, China	Kurgan, USSR	Kuwait, Kuwait	Kuybyshev, USSR	Kyoto, Japan	Kzyl-Orda, USSR	L'vov, USSR	La Ceiba, Honduras	La Coruna, Spain	La Paz, Bolivia	La Paz, Mexico	La Ronge, Canada	Labrador City, Canada	Lagos, Nigeria	Lahore, Pakistan	Lambasa, Fiji	Lansing, Michigan	Lanzhou, China	Laoag, Philippines	Largeau, Chad
Roanoke, Virginia	11,155	9,215	10,852	8,891	11,198	10,275	7,823	2,476	5,931	6,079	3,231	2,755	2,014	8,991	11,928	12,034	722	11,878	13,501	9,594
Robinson Crusoe Island, Chile	18,251	16,344	15,010	15,476	16,853	16,733	13,651	5,533	11,129	2,181	7,212	10,151	9,662	9,694	17,506	10,061	8,476	19,659	17,435	11,818
Rochester, New York	10,473	8,533	10,247	8,222	10,714	9,598	7,210	3,158	5,449	6,676	3,655	2,393	1,346	8,793	11,249	12,290	568	11,232	12,962	9,196
Rockhampton, Australia	9,940	11,823	12,410	12,735	6,647	11,431	14,558	13,999	17,070	13,925	11,926	13,004	15,466	16,042	10,135	3,115	14,563	8,217	5,633	14,953
Rome, Italy	5,744	4,055	3,470	3,056	9,720	4,231	1,253	9,600	1,715	10,469	10,629	7,756	5,800	4,029	5,518	16,920	7,501	7,540	10,095	2,733
Rosario, Argentina	16,731	15,189	13,345	14,210	18,495	15,258	12,373	6,068	9,984	1,972	8,226	10,644	9,536	8,038	15,814	11,621	8,728	18,550	18,366	10,166
Roseau, Dominica	12,786	10,723	10,978	10,027	14,153	11,468	8,397	2,724	5,887	3,595	5,193	5,792	4,205	7,127	12,998	13,549	3,758	14,110	16,293	8,525
Rostock, East Germany	5,305	3,342	3,977	2,486	8,756	3,902	941	9,171	1,911	10,859	9,742	6,623	4,962	5,341	5,447	15,685	6,695	6,953	9,534	4,058
Rostov-na-Donu, USSR	3,514	1,988	2,106	997	7,663	2,004	1,193	11,235	3,736	12,683	11,547	8,199	6,919	5,689	3,409	14,988	8,634	5,318	7,866	3,757
Rotterdam, Netherlands	5,867	3,908	4,351	3,047	9,275	4,451	1,388	8,731	1,353	10,295	9,476	6,499	4,652	5,042	5,970	16,042	6,379	7,518	10,099	3,985
Rouyn, Canada	9,951	8,043	9,922	7,786	10,162	9,133	6,888	3,669	5,321	7,250	3,830	1,957	1,003	8,915	10,775	12,210	748	10,665	12,394	9,127
Sacramento, California	10,817	9,567	12,401	9,803	8,638	10,743	9,643	4,224	8,713	8,248	1,917	2,202	4,412	12,463	12,067	8,658	3,133	10,532	11,002	12,530
Saginaw, Michigan	10,548	8,671	10,574	8,436	10,436	9,773	7,538	3,077	5,894	6,829	3,219	2,010	1,642	9,306	11,409	11,782	92	11,169	12,738	9,669
Saint Denis, Reunion	7,455	8,506	5,618	8,221	10,481	7,342	8,424	16,013	9,641	12,609	18,521	15,878	13,990	6,442	6,143	12,643	15,584	8,091	8,316	5,842
Saint George's, Grenada	13,120	11,060	11,209	10,346	14,483	11,782	8,692	2,737	6,164	3,235	5,283	6,086	4,560	7,169	13,290	13,443	4,051	14,467	16,649	8,659
Saint John, Canada	9,961	7,949	9,396	7,528	10,849	8,947	6,373	3,803	4,506	6,843	4,602	2,961	857	7,897	10,602	13,209	1,506	10,940	12,945	8,244
Saint John's, Antigua	12,633	10,568	10,907	9,888	13,948	11,333	8,281	2,667	5,787	3,780	5,086	5,596	4,002	7,177	12,880	13,534	3,564	13,930	16,091	8,520
Saint John's, Canada	9,269	7,213	8,395	6,685	10,821	8,130	5,398	4,711	3,451	7,261	5,655	3,665	1,173	6,983	9,772	14,159	2,541	10,451	12,691	7,203
Saint Louis, Missouri	11,144	9,327	11,319	9,141	10,587	10,450	8,285	2,552	6,619	6,520	2,485	2,153	2,392	9,879	12,070	11,171	661	11,616	12,948	10,367
Saint Paul, Minnesota	10,458	8,696	10,881	8,581	9,880	9,841	7,875	3,287	6,448	7,258	2,781	1,423	2,098	10,016	11,435	11,092	730	10,877	12,228	10,261
Saint Peter Port, UK	6,433	4,474	4,772	3,612	9,787	5,008	1,907	8,281	812	9,728	9,194	6,386	4,364	4,799	6,507	16,338	6,067	8,084	10,664	4,001
Saipan (Susupe)	6,601	8,031	9,928	9,038	2,414	8,075	10,838	13,317	13,011	16,408	10,698	9,800	11,840	15,236	7,403	5,088	11,805	4,764	2,698	13,122
Salalah, Oman	3,883	4,371	1,508	4,031	8,202	3,261	4,532	14,405	6,515	13,900	15,149	11,782	10,428	5,634	2,602	14,219	12,161	5,306	7,019	3,712
Salem, Oregon	10,108	8,853	11,724	9,110	8,137	10,028	9,031	4,684	8,286	8,774	2,577	1,693	4,095	12,218	11,352	8,941	3,076	9,883	10,522	12,065
Salt Lake City, Utah	10,799	9,342	11,968	9,452	9,145	10,525	9,085	3,676	7,955	7,782	1,846	1,668	3,616	11,616	11,970	9,494	2,275	10,760	11,533	11,781
Salta, Argentina	16,619	14,777	13,491	13,867	17,694	15,101	12,033	5,053	9,533	960	7,263	9,631	8,613	8,207	16,025	11,649	7,729	18,387	19,058	10,305
Salto, Uruguay	16,425	14,890	13,048	13,907	18,687	14,950	12,072	6,061	9,697	1,945	8,297	10,592	9,383	7,738	15,530	11,929	8,645	18,251	18,537	9,866
Salvador, Brazil	13,618	12,058	10,379	11,065	17,500	12,118	9,238	6,195	6,952	3,212	8,815	9,767	7,794	5,108	12,913	14,736	7,750	15,464	17,723	7,193
Salzburg, Austria	5,455	3,627	3,619	2,669	9,215	3,976	836	9,439	1,736	10,711	10,240	7,232	5,416	4,674	5,400	16,310	7,142	7,195	9,775	3,361
Samsun, Turkey	3,902	2,630	1,688	1,682	8,234	2,393	1,350	11,410	3,649	12,405	11,987	8,723	7,247	5,054	3,539	15,538	8,978	5,743	8,229	3,068
San Antonio, Texas	12,185	10,477	12,592	10,363	10,893	11,627	9,559	1,928	7,840	6,037	1,309	2,904	3,666	10,805	13,210	10,161	1,934	12,397	13,279	11,523
San Cristobal, Venezuela	14,047	11,983	12,423	11,364	14,440	12,816	9,799	1,817	7,316	2,721	4,440	6,010	5,034	8,344	14,392	12,215	4,058	15,136	16,811	9,896
San Diego, California	11,555	10,235	12,956	10,408	9,342	11,417	10,093	3,587	8,912	7,540	1,160	2,655	4,559	12,396	12,787	8,666	3,059	11,291	11,686	12,733
San Francisco, California	10,875	9,650	12,503	9,900	8,623	10,825	9,756	4,257	8,834	8,260	1,898	2,319	4,531	12,578	12,134	8,541	3,241	10,558	10,980	12,651
San Jose, Costa Rica	14,204	12,224	13,288	11,785	13,512	13,219	10,435	711	8,104	3,410	3,195	5,346	5,014	9,620	14,871	11,016	3,635	14,851	15,891	11,052
San Juan, Argentina	17,305	15,555	14,011	14,623	17,740	15,793	12,781	5,589	10,308	1,666	7,602	10,221	9,361	8,696	16,515	11,045	8,385	19,142	18,273	10,819
San Juan, Puerto Rico	12,697	10,631	11,190	10,009	13,655	11,462	8,470	2,220	6,028	3,874	4,609	5,238	3,827	7,631	13,049	13,111	3,203	13,877	15,884	8,917
San Luis Potosi, Mexico	12,978	11,311	13,410	11,206	11,309	12,465	10,373	1,650	8,555	5,576	980	3,676	4,476	11,213	14,037	9,669	2,746	13,063	13,662	12,141
San Marino, San Marino	5,654	3,915	3,524	2,926	9,558	4,150	1,096	9,530	1,679	10,537	10,485	7,568	5,653	4,245	5,487	16,720	7,363	7,433	10,000	2,950
San Miguel de Tucuman, Argen.	16,744	14,946	13,549	14,022	17,831	15,226	12,183	5,259	9,699	1,182	7,437	9,847	8,838	8,247	16,079	11,566	7,952	18,549	18,887	10,356
San Salvador, El Salvador	13,882	11,981	13,395	11,645	12,838	13,042	10,441	346	8,239	4,064	2,502	4,801	4,780	10,128	14,696	10,588	3,249	14,335	15,208	11,421
Sanaa, Yemen	4,736	4,802	1,601	4,232	9,187	3,829	4,239	13,635	5,849	12,826	14,837	11,688	10,008	4,561	3,543	15,244	11,724	6,291	8,091	2,689
Santa Cruz, Bolivia	15,917	14,008	12,979	13,124	17,345	14,411	11,302	4,530	8,778	549	6,909	9,004	7,846	7,786	15,494	12,197	7,051	17,610	19,633	9,834
Santa Cruz, Tenerife	8,729	6,934	6,177	5,978	12,393	7,220	4,136	7,319	1,798	7,481	9,141	7,407	4,931	3,194	8,463	17,939	6,218	10,501	13,074	3,786
Santa Fe, New Mexico	11,440	9,875	12,305	9,891	9,908	11,050	9,333	2,912	7,933	7,016	1,343	2,159	3,593	11,313	12,559	9,740	2,000	11,495	12,295	11,732
Santa Rosa, Argentina	17,197	15,712	13,772	14,730	18,210	15,749	12,895	6,264	10,508	2,261	8,282	10,888	9,926	8,486	16,193	11,131	9,025	18,945	17,910	10,613
Santa Rosalia, Mexico	12,250	10,833	13,389	10,925	10,085	12,016	10,434	2,924	9,002	6,797	402	3,137	4,683	12,170	13,449	8,818	3,033	12,046	12,413	12,773
Santarem, Brazil	14,024	12,076	11,376	11,211	16,243	12,541	9,406	4,067	6,862	2,143	6,690	7,866	6,244	6,529	13,790	13,734	5,831	15,675	18,189	8,392
Santiago del Estero, Argentina	16,732	14,973	13,495	14,038	17,965	15,217	12,197	5,399	9,726	1,312	7,579	9,982	8,947	8,187	16,020	11,600	8,080	18,559	18,837	10,301
Santiago, Chile	17,586	15,847	14,259	14,916	17,594	16,078	13,074	5,712	10,600	1,895	7,635	10,354	9,579	8,945	16,745	10,772	8,554	19,430	17,984	11,071
Santo Domingo, Dominican Rep.	12,855	10,797	11,510	10,220	13,501	11,674	8,734	1,822	6,332	3,872	4,225	5,045	3,835	8,031	13,285	12,717	3,024	13,933	15,792	9,300
Sao Paulo de Olivenca, Brazil	14,997	12,941	12,788	12,206	15,699	13,626	10,502	2,908	7,947	1,445	5,433	7,302	6,253	8,097	15,063	12,224	5,355	16,314	18,087	9,914
Sao Paulo, Brazil	15,014	13,506	11,679	12,511	18,714	13,532	10,685	6,167	8,377	2,381	8,668	10,335	8,698	6,365	14,194	13,346	8,305	16,853	18,575	8,487
Sao Tome, Sao Tome & Principe	8,878	8,055	5,427	7,096	13,447	7,572	5,727	10,386	4,999	8,416	12,728	11,358	8,889	772	7,880	18,055	10,091	10,617	12,522	2,371
Sapporo, Japan	4,695	5,413	8,101	6,411	1,016	5,864	8,055	11,856	9,970	15,958	9,582	7,449	9,029	13,085	5,919	7,647	9,460	3,300	3,378	11,054
Sarajevo, Yugoslavia	5,214	3,544	3,067	2,538	9,225	3,702	791	9,983	2,155	10,994	10,846	7,827	6,020	4,395	5,012	16,482	7,743	7,010	9,565	2,874
Saratov, USSR	3,062	1,344	2,469	334	7,038	1,622	1,563	11,265	4,102	13,098	11,303	7,888	6,846	6,349	3,201	14,357	8,523	4,806	7,381	4,421
Saskatoon, Canada	9,621	8,059	10,644	8,133	8,619	9,239	7,786	4,396	6,853	8,462	3,118	344	2,662	10,784	10,732	10,382	1,954	9,804	10,981	10,653
Schefferville, Canada	9,001	7,033	8,807	6,711	9,824	8,087	5,773	4,659	4,316	7,901	4,924	2,433	206	8,162	9,739	13,007	1,859	9,898	11,886	8,142
Seattle, Washington	9,847	8,563	11,424	8,811	8,023	9,740	8,736	4,801	8,035	8,910	2,810	1,446	3,895	12,015	11,080	9,154	2,989	9,675	10,412	11,798
Sendai, Japan	4,844	5,756	8,290	6,765	584	6,108	8,459	12,238	10,451	16,299	9,884	7,912	9,551	13,400	5,999	7,266	9,934	3,292	2,969	11,327
Seoul, South Korea	3,734	4,942	7,187	5,953	836	5,101	7,744	13,128	9,978	17,244	10,929	8,600	9,886	12,419	4,818	8,108	10,559	2,082	2,235	10,305
Sept-Iles, Canada	9,464	7,471	9,088	7,100	10,320	8,499	6,050	4,237	4,379	7,390	4,749	2,652	308	8,025	10,155	13,118	1,617	10,401	12,397	8,183
Sevastopol, USSR	4,033	2,545	2,115	1,543	8,224	2,515	926	11,016	3,329	12,199	11,553	8,295	6,819	5,141	3,809	15,548	8,550	5,853	8,384	3,250
Seville, Spain	7,365	5,558	5,030	4,602	11,073	5,865	2,761	8,163	695	8,822	9,584	7,233	4,924	3,555	7,176	17,625	6,482	9,127	11,703	3,265
Shanghai, China	3,557	5,106	6,928	6,086	1,409	5,036	7,923	14,011	10,305	18,127	11,788	9,471	10,657	12,239	4,443	8,131	11,412	1,727	1,433	10,112
Sheffield, United Kingdom	6,178	4,175	4,786	3,368	9,384	4,798	1,800	8,305	1,222	10,000	9,045	6,111	4,218	5,221	6,349	15,906	5,944	7,777	10,346	4,320
Shenyang, China	3,309	4,400	6,760	5,413	1,311	4,616	7,193	12,917	9,418	16,992	10,854	8,320	9,459	11,936	4,473	8,632	10,232	1,824	2,630	9,835
Shiraz, Iran	3,069	3,044	443	2,628	7,626	2,035	3,285	13,363	5,541	13,845	13,781	10,385	9,154	5,744	2,096	14,439	10,877	4,788	6,953	3,628
Sibiu, Romania	4,715	3,050	2,763	2,041	8,740	3,206	449	10,308	2,580	11,483	11,000	7,858	6,206	4,798	4,555	16,025	7,938	6,508	9,065	3,127
Singapore	4,872	6,936	6,675	7,568	4,986	6,119	9,172	17,792	11,689	18,114	15,383	13,215	13,932	11,160	4,571	8,515	15,058	3,849	2,618	9,416
Sioux Falls, South Dakota	10,621	8,906	11,167	8,829	9,817	10,062	8,173	3,218	6,777	7,259	2,481	1,425	2,426	10,330	11,636	10,772	995	10,952	12,185	10,591
Skelleftea, Sweden	4,676	2,609	4,362	2,085	7,595	3,506	1,673	9,245	3,003	11,608	9,297	5,947	4,796	6,620	5,159	14,396	6,466	6,111	8,639	5,206
Skopje, Yugoslavia	5,051	3,479	2,759	2,465	9,175	3,533	892	10,292	2,440	11,191	11,167	8,128	6,342	4,325	4,775	16,480	8,065	6,869	9,402	2,679
Socotra Island (Tamrida)	4,266	4,847	1,956	4,511	8,470	3,727	4,951	14,687	6,829	13,808	15,594	12,251	10,835	5,593	2,951	14,149	12,567	5,590	7,137	3,788
Sofia, Bulgaria	4,883	3,315	2,651	2,301	9,011	3,365	797	10,398	2,569	11,354	11,214	8,133	6,397	4,468	4,621	16,320	8,125	6,700	9,235	2,774
Songkhla, Thailand	4,130	6,192	6,020	6,822	4,730	5,374	8,440	17,338	10,969	18,424	15,193	12,696	13,236	10,721	3,840	9,057	14,451	3,210	2,486	8,876
Sorong, Indonesia	6,697	8,598	9,411	9,493	4,000	8,195	11,315	15,542	13,838	17,153	12,929	12,143	13,994	14,216	6,986	5,550	14,167	4,987	2,412	12,389
South Georgia Island	15,454	15,273	12,278	14,335	17,788	14,580	12,853	9,091	11,149	4,986	11,151	13,639	12,206	7,695	14,127	11,457	11,668	16,375	15,562	9,591
South Pole	14,564	16,149	13,255	15,900	13,876	14,966	15,526	11,748	14,808	8,178	12,675	16,110	15,872	10,717	13,498	8,183	14,736	13,993	12,014	11,986
South Sandwich Islands	14,879	14,979	11,865	14,109	17,154	14,158	12,790	9,835	11,333	5,725	11,891	14,360	12,808	7,610	13,538	11,445	12,369	15,658	14,854	9,379
Split, Yugoslavia	5,375	3,691	3,205	2,689	9,365	3,865	909	9,846	2,002	10,831	10,754	7,775	5,924	4,301	5,174	16,602	7,642	7,170	9,727	2,850
Spokane, Washington	9,949	8,574	11,347	8,764	8,325	9,756	8,584	4,515	7,764	8,631	2,683	1,178	3,568	11,691	11,149	9,470	2,619	9,874	10,714	11,553
Spoleto, Italy	5,687	3,980	3,470	2,984	9,639	4,177	1,171	9,591	1,717	10,517	10,586	7,690	5,755	4,124	5,483	16,828	7,460	7,477	10,037	2,817
Springbok, South Africa	10,343	10,452	7,274	9,698	14,240	9,554	8,826	12,266	8,520	8,749	14,888	14,745	12,253	4,287	9,029	14,535	13,140	11,540	12,195	5,267
Springfield, Illinois	11,009	9,188	11,186	9,002	10,508	10,311	8,153	2,676	6,508	6,620	2,598	2,060	2,262	9,815	11,931	11,244	538	11,496	12,862	10,267
Springfield, Massachusetts	10,473	8,489	10,027	8,113	10,994	9,517	7,001	3,219	5,125	6,504	3,996	2,774	1,279	8,376	11,173	12,698	986	11,342	13,193	8,834
Srinagar, India	1,096	2,484	2,589	2,882	5,503	1,434	4,460	14,155	7,007	15,850	13,535	10,123	9,678	7,904	281	12,344	11,244	2,633	4,858	5,783
Stanley, Falkland Islands	16,868	16,331	13,573	15,328	17,859	15,847	13,642	7,985	11,561	4,010	9,836	12,624	11,630	8,661	15,555	10,659	10,776	17,739	16,285	10,687
Stara Zagora, Bulgaria	4,713	3,189	2,469	2,176	8,883	3,195	834	10,582	2,761	11,536	11,362	8,246	6,553	4,548	4,431	16,202	8,283	6,535	9,062	2,786
Stockholm, Sweden	4,843	2,813	4,024	2,079	8,092	3,532	1,124	9,328	2,527	11,356	9,621	6,357	4,963	5,998	5,148	15,006	6,676	6,407	8,974	4,599
Stornoway, United Kingdom	6,231	4,178	5,210	3,489	9,090	4,942	2,173	7,970	1,658	10,007	8,529	5,515	3,731	5,804	6,552	15,342	5,464	7,720	10,249	4,938
Strasbourg, France	5,790	3,907	4,018	2,982	9,415	4,329	1,190	9,038	1,375	10,369	9,879	6,934	5,048	4,688	5,783	16,359	6,768	7,501	10,086	3,554
Stuttgart, West Germany	5,685	3,807	3,924	2,878	9,330	4,222	1,082	9,135	1,481	10,475	9,951	6,980	5,123	4,722	5,676	16,311	6,846	7,399	9,983	3,538
Subic, Philippines	4,586	6,475	7,517	7,371	2,716	6,095	9,197	15,508	11,714	19,118	13,037	11,155	12,458	12,679	5,008	7,365	13,144	2,866	369	10,650
Suchow, China	3,049	4,584	6,449	5,562	1,702	4,517	7,399	13,916	9,793	17,967	11,830	9,309	10,334	11,750	3,993	8,647	11,197	1,245	1,812	9,622
Sucre, Bolivia	16,170	14,244	13,239	13,371	17,295	14,666	11,553	4,515	9,023	414	6,833	9,044	7,976	8,036	15,756	11,937	7,118	17,837	19,407	10,089
Sudbury, Canada	10,171	8,275	10,165	8,027	10,260	9,370	7,130	3,448	5,535	7,095	3,600	1,947	1,240	9,064	11,009	12,048	504	10,850	12,520	9,331
Suez, Egypt	4,710	3,832	1,493	2,950	9,232	3,315	2,320	11,785	3,903	11,925	12,828	9,760	7,998	4,012	3,977	16,335	9,715	6,534	8,842	1,908
Sundsvall, Sweden	4,858	2,800	4,287	2,172	7,903	3,619	1,456	9,172	2,695	11,385	9,356	6,057	4,761	6,311	5,259	14,714	6,457	6,350	8,895	4,940

Distances in Kilometers	Kuqa Chang, China	Kurgan, USSR	Kuwait, Kuwait	Kuybyshev, USSR	Kyoto, Japan	Kzyl-Orda, USSR	L'vov, USSR	La Ceiba, Honduras	La Coruna, Spain	La Paz, Bolivia	La Paz, Mexico	La Ronge, Canada	Labrador City, Canada	Lagos, Nigeria	Lahore, Pakistan	Lambasa, Fiji	Lansing, Michigan	Lanzhou, China	Laoag, Philippines	Largeau, Chad
Surabaya, Indonesia	6,141	8,206	8,022	8,893	5,264	7,452	10,531	17,702	13,055	17,376	15,078	13,726	14,937	12,238	5,931	7,303	15,727	4,886	2,944	10,645
Suva, Fiji	11,723	13,105	14,867	14,119	7,410	13,212	15,818	11,043	17,136	11,792	9,039	10,802	13,247	18,609	12,359	214	11,923	9,877	7,494	17,844
Sverdlovsk, USSR	2,393	332	3,208	781	5,961	1,383	2,525	11,408	4,924	13,838	10,987	7,527	6,931	7,463	3,001	13,262	8,498	3,938	6,518	5,521
Svobodnyy, USSR	3,561	4,058	6,859	5,052	1,922	4,580	6,700	11,830	8,700	15,874	9,886	7,212	8,354	11,731	4,868	9,007	9,109	2,584	3,743	9,723
Sydney, Australia	10,820	12,788	12,900	13,641	7,794	12,263	15,402	13,916	17,962	13,051	12,216	13,844	16,338	15,525	10,836	3,417	15,139	9,183	6,615	14,962
Sydney, Canada	9,683	7,646	8,966	7,175	10,877	8,608	5,954	4,178	4,040	6,984	5,069	3,278	899	7,473	10,259	13,647	1,968	10,759	12,878	7,779
Syktyvkar, USSR	3,155	1,089	3,594	944	6,395	2,106	2,111	10,646	4,307	13,121	10,342	6,888	6,169	7,253	3,751	13,584	7,757	4,618	7,177	5,454
Szeged, Hungary	4,995	3,272	3,055	2,275	8,941	3,494	489	10,006	2,269	11,191	10,753	7,663	5,943	4,698	4,864	16,182	7,673	6,774	9,340	3,146
Szombathely, Hungary	5,220	3,436	3,346	2,459	9,069	3,731	617	9,715	1,998	10,953	10,484	7,431	5,667	4,693	5,134	16,243	7,395	6,979	9,554	3,260
Tabriz, Iran	3,185	2,397	977	1,706	7,679	1,761	2,201	12,302	4,574	13,254	12,696	9,332	8,052	5,562	2,650	14,866	9,774	5,026	7,431	3,461
Tacheng, China	620	1,562	3,581	2,435	4,546	1,374	4,274	13,004	6,775	15,730	12,039	8,690	8,592	8,695	1,840	11,809	10,016	2,092	4,673	6,593
Tahiti (Papeete)	14,352	14,875	17,807	15,695	9,787	15,573	16,376	7,809	15,385	8,594	6,282	9,068	11,065	16,847	15,356	3,305	9,412	12,627	10,595	18,834
Taipei, Taiwan	3,933	5,634	7,178	6,589	1,759	5,445	8,431	14,552	10,869	18,641	12,222	10,076	11,325	12,483	4,650	7,775	12,041	2,094	764	10,371
Taiyuan, China	2,516	4,006	5,949	4,984	2,099	3,959	6,821	13,734	9,222	17,636	11,815	9,094	9,942	11,228	3,547	9,204	10,913	815	2,316	9,102
Tallahassee, Florida	11,975	10,059	11,681	9,748	11,640	11,128	8,661	1,644	6,681	5,475	2,661	3,206	2,870	9,431	12,779	11,517	1,364	12,597	14,004	10,242
Tallinn, USSR	4,462	2,436	3,772	1,704	7,787	3,158	1,068	9,673	2,867	11,734	9,874	6,555	5,278	6,151	4,781	14,808	6,978	6,036	8,608	4,630
Tamanrasset, Algeria	7,399	6,055	4,286	5,043	11,741	5,912	3,409	9,579	2,618	9,120	11,359	9,191	6,851	1,822	6,778	19,066	8,333	9,245	11,637	1,518
Tampa, Florida	12,215	10,271	11,764	9,919	11,969	11,318	8,764	1,420	6,699	5,154	2,812	3,532	3,058	9,274	12,973	11,639	1,651	12,891	14,332	10,178
Tampere, Finland	4,521	2,470	3,989	1,820	7,696	3,267	1,299	9,522	2,920	11,704	9,662	6,329	5,102	6,337	4,907	14,644	6,792	6,044	8,602	4,853
Tanami, Australia	8,285	10,315	10,323	11,093	6,119	9,680	12,801	16,144	15,348	15,527	13,866	14,014	16,078	14,054	8,216	5,250	15,944	6,781	4,339	12,775
Tangier, Morocco	7,452	5,673	5,035	4,706	11,215	5,946	2,864	8,203	869	8,748	9,680	7,381	5,053	3,383	7,225	17,799	6,590	9,226	11,798	3,154
Tarawa (Betio)	9,869	10,987	13,266	11,992	5,357	11,274	13,609	11,076	15,050	13,140	8,611	9,362	11,847	18,580	10,754	2,091	10,930	8,067	6,009	16,451
Tashkent, USSR	1,186	1,595	2,339	1,948	5,723	496	3,600	13,222	6,160	15,114	12,753	9,306	8,746	7,536	1,171	12,869	10,332	3,028	5,485	5,414
Tbilisi, USSR	3,209	2,137	1,397	1,341	7,605	1,712	1,841	11,937	4,294	13,107	12,275	8,909	7,650	5,648	2,853	14,875	9,367	5,053	7,526	3,590
Tegucigalpa, Honduras	13,810	11,882	13,214	11,517	12,939	12,926	10,277	192	8,050	3,981	2,667	4,810	4,668	9,909	14,582	10,807	3,184	14,338	15,319	11,206
Tehran, Iran	2,847	2,439	769	1,951	7,400	1,563	2,718	12,819	5,104	13,723	13,111	9,706	8,532	5,866	2,164	14,472	10,245	4,661	6,997	3,741
Tel Aviv, Israel	4,413	3,522	1,298	2,652	8,924	3,005	2,166	11,849	3,956	12,168	12,765	9,624	7,949	4,318	3,722	16,063	9,675	6,243	8,580	2,220
Telegraph Creek, Canada	8,562	7,352	10,332	7,687	6,961	8,518	7,848	5,938	7,598	10,050	4,099	1,614	3,949	11,794	9,808	9,402	3,629	8,412	9,340	11,168
Teresina, Brazil	13,366	11,610	10,366	10,656	16,689	11,847	8,813	5,368	6,385	3,040	7,990	8,775	6,820	5,290	12,871	14,811	6,762	15,172	17,709	7,259
Ternate, Indonesia	6,281	8,214	8,947	9,089	3,884	7,769	10,900	15,848	13,438	17,586	13,224	12,193	13,900	13,766	6,532	6,016	14,228	4,608	2,063	11,923
The Valley, Anguilla	12,599	10,532	10,954	9,872	13,808	11,321	8,289	2,539	5,814	3,862	4,932	5,440	3,887	7,308	12,884	13,423	3,406	13,858	15,975	8,618
Thessaloniki, Greece	4,993	3,489	2,590	2,476	9,183	3,475	1,026	10,466	2,597	11,278	11,361	8,319	6,535	4,258	4,665	16,502	8,257	6,821	9,338	2,545
Thimphu, Bhutan	1,619	3,668	4,073	4,315	4,423	2,883	6,010	15,198	8,569	17,442	13,897	10,738	10,806	9,326	1,558	10,812	12,203	1,622	3,323	7,240
Thunder Bay, Canada	10,055	8,256	10,401	8,115	9,746	9,391	7,395	3,625	6,008	7,489	3,261	1,326	1,654	9,677	10,997	11,453	731	10,562	12,055	9,830
Tientsin, China	2,865	4,202	6,316	5,200	1,709	4,261	7,021	13,437	9,359	17,444	11,440	8,812	9,794	11,566	3,950	8,916	10,677	1,241	2,343	9,446
Tijuana, Mexico	11,578	10,255	12,972	10,426	9,365	11,437	10,106	3,568	8,917	7,517	1,137	2,671	4,564	12,392	12,809	8,667	3,058	11,315	11,708	12,738
Tiksi, USSR	4,195	3,408	6,613	4,145	4,093	4,429	5,321	9,948	6,815	13,780	8,473	5,330	6,132	10,492	5,481	10,474	7,053	4,215	5,959	8,794
Timbuktu, Mali	8,514	7,122	5,364	6,108	12,818	7,024	4,397	8,878	2,992	8,038	10,928	9,252	6,793	1,337	7,875	19,776	8,081	10,359	12,740	2,355
Tindouf, Algeria	8,168	6,491	5,441	5,500	12,101	6,650	3,671	8,117	1,738	8,109	9,896	7,959	5,528	2,649	7,795	18,544	6,915	9,981	12,518	2,993
Tirane, Albania	5,206	3,632	2,862	2,618	9,327	3,688	999	10,196	2,325	11,040	11,124	8,126	6,294	4,195	4,918	16,627	8,012	7,024	9,557	2,597
Tokyo, Japan	4,867	5,891	8,322	6,904	373	6,181	8,628	12,499	10,675	16,533	10,113	8,203	9,850	13,496	5,977	7,122	10,228	3,240	2,707	11,402
Toledo, Spain	7,070	5,243	4,837	4,294	10,749	5,576	2,456	8,296	532	9,107	9,604	7,125	4,879	3,775	6,919	17,387	6,482	8,820	11,400	3,298
Topeka, Kansas	11,119	9,380	11,547	9,268	10,256	10,528	8,529	2,720	6,985	6,784	2,151	1,924	2,682	10,340	12,116	10,721	1,022	11,456	12,634	10,765
Toronto, Canada	10,452	8,530	10,307	8,243	10,597	9,607	7,270	3,170	5,554	6,760	3,550	2,249	1,382	8,937	11,254	12,151	432	11,171	12,859	9,315
Toulouse, France	6,469	4,629	4,392	3,683	10,152	4,983	1,850	8,677	794	9,701	9,786	7,080	4,980	4,121	6,365	16,987	6,651	8,209	10,790	3,297
Tours, France	6,325	4,415	4,502	3,511	9,844	4,871	1,734	8,548	838	9,833	9,515	6,715	4,688	4,544	6,325	16,570	6,385	8,020	10,605	3,676
Townsville, Australia	9,344	11,227	11,870	12,138	6,117	10,837	13,962	14,351	16,474	14,518	12,135	12,879	15,279	15,829	9,559	3,463	14,575	7,621	5,036	14,531
Trenton, New Jersey	10,725	8,752	10,302	8,386	11,110	9,787	7,277	2,949	5,380	6,317	3,759	2,790	1,535	8,545	11,442	12,509	862	11,557	13,345	9,066
Tripoli, Lebanon	4,206	3,248	1,274	2,371	8,691	2,771	1,966	11,796	3,915	12,300	12,605	9,416	7,806	4,551	3,586	15,883	9,537	6,045	8,422	2,472
Tripoli, Libya	6,151	4,710	3,325	3,696	10,403	4,641	2,082	9,973	2,209	10,214	11,312	8,638	6,535	3,099	5,678	17,722	8,181	7,992	10,465	1,763
Tristan da Cunha (Edinburgh)	13,020	12,600	9,674	11,666	17,151	11,960	10,266	9,737	8,914	5,908	12,267	13,458	11,278	5,085	11,773	13,960	11,466	14,405	14,991	6,920
Trondheim, Norway	5,196	3,131	4,628	2,537	8,080	3,981	1,719	8,804	2,536	11,075	9,016	5,748	4,395	6,347	5,624	14,718	6,096	6,646	9,172	5,097
Trujillo, Peru	15,958	13,895	14,026	13,256	15,391	14,703	11,630	2,779	9,097	1,503	4,929	7,419	6,864	9,289	16,227	10,985	5,659	16,899	17,630	11,150
Truk Island (Moen)	7,665	9,115	10,942	10,124	3,469	9,149	11,919	13,076	14,038	15,571	10,469	10,143	12,383	16,211	8,408	4,019	12,063	5,822	3,590	14,129
Truro, Canada	9,865	7,838	9,213	7,390	10,901	8,817	6,197	3,950	4,295	6,869	4,816	3,131	884	7,685	10,471	13,424	1,725	10,893	12,955	8,027
Tsingtao, China	3,234	4,636	6,668	5,632	1,403	4,663	7,456	13,601	9,796	17,684	11,486	9,012	10,118	11,946	4,250	8,504	10,922	1,497	1,980	9,821
Tsitsihar, China	3,266	4,051	6,657	5,063	1,689	4,425	6,789	12,372	8,921	16,407	10,409	7,751	8,840	11,692	4,527	8,964	9,638	2,093	3,249	9,631
Tubuai Island (Mataura)	14,752	15,450	18,167	16,306	10,189	16,062	17,013	8,077	15,829	8,440	6,750	9,655	11,569	16,569	15,638	3,344	9,885	12,969	10,794	18,695
Tucson, Arizona	11,744	10,287	12,835	10,367	9,825	11,468	9,892	3,046	8,535	7,063	895	2,582	4,192	11,874	12,921	9,161	2,598	11,634	12,189	12,334
Tulsa, Oklahoma	11,440	9,700	11,830	9,578	10,488	10,845	8,804	2,432	7,190	6,520	1,917	2,224	2,930	10,421	12,437	10,613	1,219	11,759	12,874	10,942
Tunis, Tunisia	6,176	4,585	3,597	3,574	10,272	4,657	1,825	9,580	1,738	10,096	10,828	8,126	6,035	3,432	5,828	17,514	7,694	7,998	10,523	2,269
Tura, USSR	2,789	2,155	5,307	3,052	4,039	3,055	4,571	11,107	6,559	14,625	9,848	6,585	6,957	9,694	4,057	11,123	8,132	3,149	5,344	7,799
Turin, Italy	5,952	4,140	3,925	3,178	9,719	4,463	1,338	9,128	1,294	10,221	10,107	7,248	5,277	4,297	5,846	16,740	6,980	7,703	10,282	3,192
Uberlandia, Brazil	14,843	13,206	11,612	12,231	18,181	13,335	10,392	5,704	8,013	2,122	8,243	9,805	8,164	6,325	14,145	13,502	7,773	16,686	18,860	8,423
Ufa, USSR	2,522	603	2,888	416	6,298	1,298	2,225	11,438	4,689	13,655	11,165	7,708	6,964	7,096	2,954	13,611	8,574	4,168	6,752	5,145
Ujungpandang, Indonesia	6,297	8,334	8,513	9,105	4,760	7,698	10,829	16,936	13,387	17,477	14,316	13,189	14,670	12,954	6,273	6,656	15,220	4,843	2,582	11,279
Ulaanbaatar, Mongolia	1,996	2,946	5,377	3,955	2,782	3,168	5,759	12,820	8,078	16,491	11,203	8,198	8,811	10,476	3,292	10,102	9,900	1,344	3,524	8,388
Ulan-Ude, USSR	2,184	2,784	5,443	3,798	2,916	3,175	5,558	12,385	7,800	16,067	10,813	7,769	8,379	10,415	3,518	10,230	9,461	1,781	3,902	8,361
Uliastay, Mongolia	1,286	2,321	4,625	3,306	3,505	2,422	5,138	12,959	7,545	16,278	11,593	8,419	8,739	9,739	2,619	10,803	9,980	1,418	3,926	7,643
Uranium City, Canada	8,783	7,242	9,914	7,358	7,986	8,423	7,145	5,175	6,492	9,188	3,934	536	2,638	10,599	9,899	10,592	2,490	9,000	10,311	10,211
Urumqi, China	446	2,050	3,843	2,917	4,201	1,763	4,751	13,383	7,261	16,219	12,262	8,977	9,010	9,053	1,787	11,400	10,388	1,619	4,192	6,935
Ushuaia, Argentina	17,448	17,108	14,285	16,105	17,134	16,578	14,406	8,015	12,265	4,250	9,623	12,642	11,945	9,437	16,105	9,886	10,918	17,833	15,873	11,453
Vaduz, Liechtenstein	5,727	3,886	3,846	2,936	9,447	4,250	1,109	9,205	1,463	10,437	10,079	7,139	5,248	4,551	5,671	16,472	6,965	7,463	10,044	3,361
Valencia, Spain	6,828	5,046	4,525	4,078	10,613	5,325	2,235	8,612	797	9,363	9,898	7,353	5,148	3,676	6,636	17,452	6,771	8,598	11,171	3,040
Valladolid, Spain	7,013	5,151	4,889	4,219	10,611	5,531	2,394	8,211	357	9,153	9,458	6,934	4,709	3,981	6,910	17,182	6,330	8,743	11,326	3,473
Valletta, Malta	5,881	4,383	3,204	3,368	10,079	4,366	1,728	9,981	2,125	10,433	11,193	8,415	6,384	3,454	5,474	17,386	8,058	7,716	10,215	2,044
Valparaiso, Chile	17,642	15,870	14,336	14,948	17,496	16,130	13,108	5,638	10,624	1,865	7,543	10,281	9,537	9,021	16,830	10,709	8,493	19,474	17,966	11,146
Vancouver, Canada	9,654	8,375	11,251	8,632	7,876	9,551	8,585	4,955	7,944	9,068	3,000	1,377	3,856	11,965	10,887	9,211	3,040	9,492	10,266	11,688
Varna, Bulgaria	4,508	2,990	2,355	1,978	8,681	2,990	794	10,706	2,922	11,734	11,412	8,249	6,621	4,730	4,245	16,002	8,353	6,329	8,858	2,925
Venice, Italy	5,597	3,819	3,581	2,842	9,441	4,102	1,000	9,469	1,663	10,582	10,369	7,420	5,537	4,408	5,475	16,570	7,254	7,361	9,935	3,117
Veracruz, Mexico	13,320	11,551	13,400	11,356	11,893	12,677	10,372	1,061	8,392	4,998	1,565	4,059	4,513	10,775	14,294	10,048	2,828	13,546	14,255	11,847
Verona, Italy	5,695	3,904	3,682	2,932	9,512	4,202	1,090	9,368	1,557	10,481	10,287	7,361	5,455	4,384	5,580	16,612	7,168	7,454	10,030	3,145
Victoria, Canada	9,734	8,464	11,343	8,724	7,908	9,639	8,677	4,918	8,022	9,028	2,928	1,446	3,916	12,030	10,970	9,143	3,061	9,554	10,297	11,771
Victoria, Seychelles	5,817	6,718	3,846	6,427	9,426	5,564	6,750	15,727	8,298	13,403	17,367	14,147	12,535	5,914	4,478	13,440	14,239	6,741	7,578	4,704
Vienna, Austria	5,205	3,393	3,410	2,426	9,008	3,724	587	9,660	1,989	10,962	10,397	7,330	5,584	4,788	5,150	16,159	7,314	6,951	9,530	3,368
Vientiane, Laos	3,156	5,213	5,664	5,956	3,779	4,552	7,691	16,134	10,252	19,038	14,144	11,491	12,084	10,766	3,221	9,234	13,245	2,007	1,905	8,753
Villahermosa, Mexico	13,444	11,615	13,300	11,362	12,219	12,717	10,290	696	8,225	4,682	1,930	4,252	4,488	10,460	14,354	10,335	2,856	13,776	14,590	11,598
Vilnius, USSR	4,451	2,521	3,346	1,631	8,069	3,046	547	9,941	2,731	11,710	10,301	7,029	5,621	5,698	4,607	15,215	7,341	6,124	8,708	4,115
Visby, Sweden	4,850	2,844	3,887	2,056	8,205	3,503	945	9,409	2,442	11,332	9,764	6,521	5,076	5,824	5,099	15,170	6,796	6,450	9,025	4,409
Vitoria, Brazil	14,281	12,828	10,941	11,824	18,334	12,807	10,013	6,461	7,772	2,964	9,035	10,356	8,513	5,627	13,458	14,073	8,322	16,117	18,019	7,748
Vladivostok, USSR	3,953	4,832	7,383	5,843	962	5,181	7,561	12,386	9,641	16,500	10,222	7,858	9,207	12,468	5,157	8,184	9,824	2,534	2,962	10,397
Volgograd, USSR	3,156	1,604	2,171	638	7,273	1,661	1,485	11,395	4,046	13,023	11,548	8,153	7,016	6,069	3,146	14,598	8,712	4,945	7,503	4,112
Vologda, USSR	3,605	1,576	3,372	922	7,051	2,351	1,459	10,408	3,693	12,595	10,368	6,956	5,956	6,624	3,999	14,235	7,613	5,182	7,758	4,885
Vorkuta, USSR	3,159	1,346	4,371	1,758	5,693	2,529	2,953	10,468	4,913	13,400	9,829	6,377	6,037	8,127	4,052	12,751	7,497	4,295	6,757	6,356
Wake Island	8,067	8,955	11,522	9,946	3,502	9,366	11,516	11,104	13,050	14,242	8,481	8,150	10,498	16,628	9,128	4,189	10,020	6,373	4,843	14,584
Wallis Island	11,837	13,002	15,152	14,004	7,368	13,273	15,559	10,346	16,475	11,457	8,271	10,035	12,467	19,245	12,618	591	11,134	10,009	7,766	18,317
Walvis Bay, Namibia	10,044	9,926	6,811	9,111	14,230	9,112	8,116	11,819	7,707	8,583	14,432	13,955	11,461	3,470	8,774	15,351	12,422	11,407	12,389	4,549
Warsaw, Poland	4,773	2,887	3,370	1,959	8,461	3,331	341	9,798	2,391	11,385	10,314	7,120	5,564	5,329	4,842	15,602	7,295	6,477	9,061	3,813
Washington, D.C.	10,920	8,960	10,545	8,611	11,158	10,006	7,519	2,733	5,621	6,201	3,529	2,771	1,745	8,736	11,660	12,305	763	11,707	13,425	9,295
Watson Lake, Canada	8,397	7,131	10,081	7,440	6,990	8,302	7,572	5,968	7,324	10,067	4,243	1,503	3,743	11,528	9,624	9,668	3,537	8,321	9,355	10,886

Distances in Kilometers	Kuqa Chang, China	Kurgan, USSR	Kuwait, Kuwait	Kuybyshev, USSR	Kyoto, Japan	Kzyl-Orda, USSR	L'vov, USSR	La Ceiba, Honduras	La Coruna, Spain	La Paz, Bolivia	La Paz, Mexico	La Ronge, Canada	Labrador City, Canada	Lagos, Nigeria	Lahore, Pakistan	Lambasa, Fiji	Lansing, Michigan	Lanzhou, China	Laoag, Philippines	Largeau, Chad
Weimar, East Germany	5,457	3,548	3,872	2,640	9,045	4,014	910	9,216	1,709	10,701	9,918	6,870	5,107	4,992	5,506	16,028	6,837	7,150	9,734	3,733
Wellington, New Zealand	12,949	14,806	15,092	15,741	9,343	14,433	17,568	11,849	19,667	10,921	10,580	13,075	15,317	16,052	13,059	2,792	13,705	11,216	8,633	16,537
West Berlin, West Germany	5,270	3,341	3,818	2,449	8,822	3,842	798	9,303	1,908	10,889	9,919	6,813	5,129	5,189	5,360	15,818	6,862	6,947	9,531	3,872
Wewak, Papua New Guinea	7,840	9,598	10,757	10,555	4,346	9,357	12,398	14,353	14,808	15,888	11,808	11,661	13,857	15,619	8,282	4,160	13,582	6,039	3,489	13,787
Whangarei, New Zealand	12,572	14,344	15,002	15,313	8,794	14,079	17,156	11,810	19,125	11,268	10,327	12,617	14,949	16,636	12,806	2,195	13,415	10,795	8,225	16,881
Whitehorse, Canada	8,181	7,001	10,015	7,365	6,644	8,161	7,605	6,291	7,501	10,397	4,483	1,853	4,051	11,730	9,432	9,465	3,888	8,033	9,013	10,987
Wichita, Kansas	11,269	9,554	11,751	9,458	10,276	10,706	8,735	2,640	7,191	6,732	1,942	2,025	2,890	10,512	12,286	10,540	1,222	11,558	12,661	10,966
Willemstad, Curacao	13,463	11,397	11,849	10,766	14,181	12,217	9,199	1,970	6,723	3,166	4,555	5,719	4,533	7,953	13,791	12,679	3,713	14,618	16,494	9,408
Wiluna, Australia	8,408	10,475	9,884	11,115	7,012	9,662	12,650	16,987	15,064	15,152	14,973	15,177	17,020	13,001	8,077	6,181	17,147	7,149	4,957	11,962
Windhoek, Namibia	9,830	9,775	6,634	8,982	13,976	8,933	8,050	12,073	7,753	8,851	14,682	14,084	11,593	3,542	8,549	15,283	12,605	11,165	12,121	4,486
Windsor, Canada	10,660	8,769	10,620	8,515	10,583	9,862	7,582	2,962	5,887	6,687	3,217	2,154	1,686	9,237	11,503	11,840	134	11,302	12,884	9,646
Winnipeg, Canada	9,915	8,218	10,575	8,175	9,262	9,380	7,620	3,896	6,428	7,886	3,074	800	2,115	10,214	10,942	10,932	1,252	10,268	11,604	10,253
Winston-Salem, North Carolina	11,288	9,347	10,965	9,019	11,298	10,405	7,939	2,343	6,022	5,960	3,167	2,846	2,144	9,022	12,058	11,990	824	12,006	13,610	9,665
Wroclaw, Poland	5,069	3,190	3,523	2,258	8,751	3,617	514	9,592	2,094	11,090	10,211	7,084	5,424	5,109	5,105	15,853	7,157	6,779	9,363	3,686
Wuhan, China	2,999	4,710	6,301	5,655	2,067	4,507	7,498	14,405	9,955	18,426	12,315	9,791	10,750	11,616	3,794	8,694	11,663	1,156	1,514	9,493
Wyndham, Australia	7,775	9,798	9,922	10,590	5,644	9,186	12,317	16,297	14,873	16,050	13,880	13,698	15,643	13,927	7,751	5,477	15,682	6,255	3,814	12,502
Xi'an, China	2,360	4,072	5,709	5,009	2,456	3,862	6,851	14,224	9,319	18,015	12,332	9,581	10,334	11,020	3,235	9,326	11,369	515	2,126	8,893
Xining, China	1,663	3,450	5,026	4,356	3,061	3,170	6,194	14,136	8,690	17,568	12,487	9,521	10,021	10,332	2,586	10,024	11,194	183	2,752	8,204
Yakutsk, USSR	3,824	3,640	6,741	4,541	3,033	4,450	5,984	10,809	7,736	14,762	9,083	6,166	7,175	11,148	5,166	9,724	7,997	3,405	4,915	9,287
Yanji, China	3,770	4,702	7,207	5,715	1,028	5,018	7,451	12,530	9,573	16,639	10,394	7,979	9,270	12,318	4,965	8,311	9,932	2,338	2,863	10,238
Yaounde, Cameroon	8,220	7,448	4,767	6,506	12,788	6,928	5,229	10,792	4,797	9,042	13,014	11,312	8,893	948	7,219	18,097	10,218	9,956	11,886	1,760
Yap Island (Colonia)	6,388	8,060	9,518	9,034	2,833	7,903	10,874	14,341	13,245	17,083	11,718	10,765	12,687	14,714	6,989	5,374	12,787	4,555	2,123	12,675
Yaraka, Australia	9,620	11,577	11,884	12,439	6,686	11,079	14,222	14,654	16,780	14,255	12,597	13,543	15,958	15,374	9,699	3,784	15,184	7,970	5,404	14,310
Yarmouth, Canada	10,111	8,093	9,496	7,661	10,999	9,084	6,480	3,674	4,564	6,684	4,557	3,052	1,015	7,875	10,739	13,218	1,498	11,098	13,102	8,277
Yellowknife, Canada	8,406	6,932	9,704	7,109	7,546	8,115	7,024	5,613	6,571	9,635	4,264	970	2,939	10,744	9,553	10,452	2,931	8,570	9,865	10,214
Yerevan, USSR	3,268	2,285	1,239	1,509	7,704	1,793	1,930	12,031	4,337	13,092	12,420	9,064	7,772	5,542	2,839	14,949	9,493	5,114	7,563	3,468
Yinchuan, China	1,974	3,573	5,399	4,526	2,646	3,438	6,368	13,847	8,816	17,512	12,095	9,211	9,855	10,684	3,004	9,727	10,946	356	2,639	8,557
Yogyakarta, Indonesia	6,081	8,148	7,839	8,803	5,437	7,355	10,407	17,964	12,913	17,312	15,340	13,890	14,992	11,980	5,806	7,542	15,871	4,904	3,088	10,413
York, United Kingdom	6,136	4,130	4,777	3,330	9,329	4,762	1,781	8,322	1,278	10,044	9,039	6,088	4,215	5,270	6,318	15,854	5,942	7,730	10,297	4,352
Yumen, China	1,217	2,948	4,647	3,856	3,382	2,698	5,695	13,830	8,188	17,085	12,349	9,260	9,619	9,927	2,301	10,474	10,857	670	3,253	7,800
Yutian, China	503	2,408	3,237	3,038	4,816	1,624	4,766	14,054	7,326	16,294	13,134	9,793	9,603	8,546	899	11,764	11,080	1,968	4,322	6,419
Yuzhno-Sakhalinsk, USSR	4,677	5,207	8,023	6,188	1,450	5,750	7,775	11,487	9,605	15,601	9,275	7,033	8,583	12,870	5,949	7,919	9,036	3,436	3,777	10,886
Zagreb, Yugoslavia	5,317	3,566	3,326	2,578	9,213	3,819	748	9,726	1,948	10,865	10,557	7,541	5,732	4,527	5,188	16,404	7,456	7,089	9,659	3,106
Zahedan, Iran	2,418	2,902	1,251	2,774	6,916	1,746	3,826	13,918	6,216	14,652	13,992	10,539	9,571	6,526	1,309	13,632	11,262	4,044	6,148	4,421
Zamboanga, Philippines	5,384	7,329	8,101	8,195	3,413	6,872	10,003	15,973	12,544	18,484	13,388	11,868	13,318	13,068	5,655	6,818	13,888	3,732	1,260	11,140
Zanzibar, Tanzania	6,915	7,240	4,045	6,660	11,002	6,226	6,376	14,053	7,277	11,654	16,206	13,730	11,630	4,215	5,600	14,984	13,192	8,177	9,328	3,458
Zaragoza, Spain	6,742	4,915	4,569	3,964	10,440	5,250	2,127	8,528	646	9,433	9,737	7,136	4,963	3,921	6,607	17,211	6,605	8,490	11,070	3,246
Zashiversk, USSR	4,556	4,025	7,217	4,814	3,637	4,980	6,029	9,949	7,475	13,930	8,244	5,307	6,426	11,199	5,883	9,773	7,160	4,266	5,693	9,492
Zhengzhou, China	2,733	4,325	6,123	5,291	2,015	4,212	7,132	14,011	9,555	17,975	12,011	9,381	10,288	11,427	3,666	8,956	11,228	918	1,958	9,299
Zurich, Switzerland	5,799	3,944	3,935	3,002	9,488	4,326	1,183	9,116	1,382	10,364	9,996	7,071	5,165	4,560	5,754	16,477	6,881	7,528	10,110	3,411

Distances in Kilometers	Las Vegas, Nevada	Launceston, Australia	Le Havre, France	Leipzig, East Germany	Leningrad, USSR	Leon, Spain	Lerwick, United Kingdom	Lhasa, China	Libreville, Gabon	Lilongwe, Malawi	Lima, Peru	Limerick, Ireland	Limoges, France	Limon, Costa Rica	Lincoln, Nebraska	Linz, Austria	Lisbon, Portugal	Little Rock, Arkansas	Liverpool, United Kingdom	Lodz, Poland
Launceston, Australia	13,126	0	17,311	16,434	15,324	17,767	17,007	9,750	13,797	10,844	12,561	17,805	17,246	14,018	14,789	16,275	17,983	14,860	17,424	15,941
Le Havre, France	8,584	17,311	0	889	2,232	884	1,188	7,632	5,515	7,769	10,113	706	416	8,678	7,133	1,046	1,407	7,327	487	1,387
Leipzig, East Germany	9,049	16,434	889	0	1,473	1,664	1,295	6,745	5,650	7,526	11,002	1,442	1,017	9,519	7,710	362	2,181	7,984	1,069	497
Leningrad, USSR	8,893	15,324	2,232	1,473	0	3,094	1,734	5,589	6,843	8,198	12,121	2,496	2,469	10,303	7,835	1,652	3,619	8,275	2,136	1,130
Leon, Spain	8,744	17,767	884	1,664	3,094	0	1,976	8,346	4,911	7,444	9,443	1,142	652	8,240	7,183	1,672	526	7,260	1,218	2,138
Lerwick, United Kingdom	7,760	17,007	1,188	1,295	1,734	1,976	0	7,316	6,691	8,791	10,394	951	1,601	8,599	6,462	1,651	2,449	6,788	758	1,581
Lhasa, China	12,222	9,750	7,632	6,745	5,589	8,346	7,316	0	9,186	7,817	17,710	8,054	7,702	15,573	12,161	6,675	8,815	12,868	7,676	6,248
Libreville, Gabon	13,024	13,797	5,515	5,650	6,843	4,911	6,691	9,186	0	3,118	9,646	6,034	5,099	10,284	11,337	5,330	4,650	11,061	5,991	5,770
Lilongwe, Malawi	16,069	10,844	7,769	7,526	8,198	7,444	8,791	7,817	3,118	0	11,878	8,427	7,387	13,159	14,392	7,163	7,346	14,170	8,250	7,413
Lima, Peru	6,670	12,561	10,113	11,002	12,121	9,443	10,394	17,710	9,646	11,878	0	9,664	10,074	2,527	6,193	11,099	9,000	5,423	10,045	11,499
Limerick, Ireland	7,885	17,805	706	1,442	2,496	1,142	951	8,054	6,034	8,427	9,664	0	1,044	8,080	6,427	1,689	1,551	6,627	386	1,910
Limoges, France	8,920	17,246	416	1,017	2,469	652	1,601	7,702	5,099	7,387	10,074	1,044	0	8,778	7,433	1,027	1,164	7,587	897	1,486
Limon, Costa Rica	4,346	14,018	8,678	9,519	10,303	8,240	8,599	15,573	10,284	13,159	2,527	8,080	8,778	0	3,670	9,724	7,928	2,898	8,461	9,989
Lincoln, Nebraska	1,688	14,789	7,133	7,710	7,835	7,183	6,462	12,161	11,337	14,392	6,193	6,427	7,433	3,670	0	8,036	7,165	778	6,720	8,043
Linz, Austria	9,396	16,275	1,046	362	1,652	1,672	1,651	6,675	5,330	7,163	11,099	1,689	1,027	9,724	8,036	0	2,161	8,289	1,340	533
Lisbon, Portugal	8,775	17,983	1,407	2,181	3,619	526	2,449	8,815	4,650	7,346	9,000	1,551	1,164	7,928	7,165	2,161	0	7,171	1,700	2,646
Little Rock, Arkansas	2,077	14,860	7,327	7,984	8,275	7,260	6,788	12,868	11,061	14,170	5,423	6,627	7,587	2,898	778	8,289	7,171	0	6,952	8,358
Liverpool, United Kingdom	8,137	17,424	487	1,069	2,136	1,218	758	7,676	5,991	8,250	10,045	386	897	8,461	6,720	1,340	1,700	6,952	0	1,528
Lodz, Poland	9,313	15,941	1,387	497	1,130	2,138	1,581	6,248	5,770	7,413	11,499	1,910	1,486	9,989	8,043	533	2,646	8,358	1,528	0
Lome, Togo	11,917	14,851	4,808	5,112	6,451	4,095	5,996	9,670	1,114	4,230	8,892	5,237	4,399	9,274	10,231	4,835	3,757	9,947	5,257	5,330
London, United Kingdom	8,424	17,292	223	866	2,101	1,072	965	7,570	5,736	7,962	10,162	597	638	8,655	6,998	1,093	1,585	7,216	290	1,352
Londonderry, United Kingdom	7,805	17,611	796	1,373	2,288	1,385	682	7,867	6,245	8,565	9,846	273	1,186	8,191	6,388	1,663	1,815	6,626	333	1,808
Longlac, Canada	2,755	15,823	5,886	6,441	6,583	5,992	5,189	11,203	10,407	13,349	6,912	5,180	6,199	4,423	1,273	6,770	6,023	1,735	5,462	6,770
Lord Howe Island, Australia	11,659	1,529	17,356	16,525	15,124	18,187	16,508	9,874	15,315	12,312	12,337	17,459	17,535	13,229	13,340	16,525	18,685	13,503	17,186	16,049
Los Angeles, California	367	12,761	8,940	9,392	9,197	9,109	8,100	12,311	13,377	16,433	6,711	8,243	9,279	4,468	2,044	9,741	9,142	2,383	8,490	9,646
Louangphrabang, Laos	12,673	8,219	9,182	8,296	7,107	9,900	8,820	1,554	10,284	8,367	19,135	9,589	9,256	16,654	13,011	8,229	10,367	13,773	9,214	7,800
Louisville, Kentucky	2,608	15,551	6,636	7,308	7,661	6,559	6,131	12,481	10,442	13,536	5,641	5,938	6,889	3,141	981	7,606	6,473	701	6,267	7,692
Luanda, Angola	14,002	12,732	6,584	6,659	7,767	6,004	7,750	9,339	1,099	2,314	9,847	7,121	6,168	10,866	12,322	6,326	5,748	11,983	7,063	6,735
Lubumbashi, Zaire	15,395	11,499	7,285	7,128	7,939	6,889	8,359	8,208	2,397	732	11,291	7,917	6,889	12,454	13,709	6,768	6,750	13,457	7,771	7,068
Lusaka, Zambia	15,734	11,131	7,706	7,552	8,352	7,298	8,783	8,382	2,710	613	11,265	8,335	7,309	12,580	14,046	7,192	7,148	13,756	8,192	7,490
Luxembourg, Luxembourg	8,891	16,878	434	479	1,913	1,191	1,262	7,218	5,463	7,548	10,535	1,085	556	9,110	7,482	615	1,712	7,707	762	971
Luxor, Egypt	12,374	13,844	3,849	3,326	3,808	3,947	4,619	5,723	3,748	4,390	12,551	4,556	3,575	12,027	10,981	2,978	4,155	11,161	4,264	3,102
Lynn Lake, Canada	2,529	14,989	6,181	6,562	6,369	6,481	5,268	10,352	11,203	13,921	7,951	5,504	6,548	5,426	1,810	6,917	6,620	2,545	5,712	6,800
Lyon, France	9,128	16,966	547	828	2,301	903	1,651	7,443	5,046	7,227	10,342	1,243	280	9,058	7,664	772	1,391	7,836	1,023	1,262
Macapa, Brazil	7,709	15,073	7,325	8,190	9,518	6,542	7,915	14,836	6,735	9,461	3,168	7,036	7,193	3,710	6,445	8,210	6,050	5,754	7,384	8,676
Madison, Wisconsin	2,329	15,442	6,518	7,125	7,339	6,541	5,897	11,952	10,701	13,743	6,232	5,812	6,807	3,716	654	7,443	6,514	957	6,117	7,476
Madras, India	14,319	9,120	8,204	7,353	6,600	8,701	8,280	2,147	7,932	5,937	17,571	8,789	8,131	16,867	14,028	7,160	9,064	14,654	8,407	6,879
Madrid, Spain	9,021	17,574	1,055	1,729	3,192	291	2,204	8,314	4,627	7,157	9,504	1,414	725	8,398	7,450	1,675	504	7,509	1,448	2,175
Madurai, India	14,717	9,039	8,308	7,476	6,810	8,755	8,460	2,567	7,673	5,565	17,313	8,918	8,207	16,984	14,360	7,262	9,091	14,958	8,539	7,014
Magadan, USSR	6,835	11,198	7,626	7,159	5,792	8,475	6,507	5,519	12,565	12,847	13,434	7,425	7,996	10,943	7,289	7,414	8,956	8,067	7,261	6,914
Magdalena, Bolivia	7,662	13,150	9,363	10,237	11,523	8,598	9,865	16,898	8,251	10,495	1,410	9,027	9,249	3,320	6,871	10,269	8,112	6,096	9,388	10,727
Magdeburg, East Germany	8,946	16,478	864	107	1,436	1,673	1,189	6,770	5,743	7,633	10,970	1,377	1,036	9,456	7,613	469	2,195	7,893	997	538
Majuro Atoll, Marshall Isls.	8,080	5,912	13,669	13,221	11,816	14,486	12,513	8,669	17,842	15,321	12,542	13,376	14,052	11,591	9,674	13,461	14,927	10,156	13,271	12,946
Malabo, Equatorial Guinea	12,719	14,136	5,136	5,281	6,495	4,533	6,313	9,067	380	3,386	9,652	5,655	4,720	10,146	11,032	4,965	4,277	10,784	5,611	5,413
Male, Maldives	15,469	8,954	8,471	7,688	7,203	8,813	8,773	3,393	7,131	4,812	16,669	9,122	8,318	16,998	14,942	7,437	9,093	15,466	8,756	7,256
Manado, Indonesia	12,559	5,257	12,295	11,422	10,122	13,061	11,755	4,740	12,844	10,173	17,346	12,613	12,410	16,692	13,724	11,389	13,544	14,446	12,258	10,932
Managua, Nicaragua	3,931	13,924	8,734	9,554	10,253	8,350	8,575	15,371	10,633	13,550	2,864	8,112	8,862	427	3,336	9,778	8,066	2,575	8,489	10,012
Manama, Bahrain	12,940	12,407	5,012	4,257	4,056	5,366	5,423	3,986	5,253	4,805	14,343	5,675	4,855	13,603	11,853	3,985	5,682	12,211	5,318	3,856
Manaus, Brazil	7,181	14,362	8,184	9,065	10,321	7,445	8,652	15,789	7,739	10,344	2,121	7,825	8,092	2,936	6,128	9,117	6,974	5,381	8,189	9,559
Manchester, New Hampshire	3,785	16,858	5,358	6,070	6,575	5,245	4,954	11,767	9,242	12,295	6,121	4,669	5,593	3,825	2,099	6,352	5,156	2,018	5,013	6,481
Mandalay, Burma	12,782	8,774	8,593	7,704	6,572	9,285	8,299	984	9,653	7,877	18,693	9,030	8,647	16,464	12,926	7,620	9,742	13,663	8,651	7,207
Mangareva Island, Fr.Polynesia	6,885	7,370	15,141	15,811	15,757	14,907	14,571	15,408	15,429	15,723	6,229	14,450	15,355	6,737	8,110	16,120	14,648	7,831	14,782	16,151
Manila, Philippines	11,876	6,758	10,859	10,002	8,657	11,660	10,262	3,491	12,325	10,110	18,061	11,137	11,008	16,222	12,751	10,002	12,162	13,519	10,791	9,522
Mannheim, West Germany	9,017	16,709	603	341	1,808	1,325	1,336	7,059	5,442	7,457	10,697	1,245	677	9,279	7,624	447	1,841	7,859	908	817
Maputo, Mozambique	16,762	9,968	8,956	8,786	9,520	8,541	10,027	8,767	3,830	1,333	11,330	9,584	8,559	13,052	15,099	8,425	8,374	14,702	9,442	8,704
Mar del Plata, Argentina	10,128	10,861	11,228	11,999	13,453	10,360	12,034	16,995	8,041	9,183	3,467	11,102	10,987	5,939	9,594	11,902	9,834	8,817	11,405	12,427
Maracaibo, Venezuela	5,205	14,929	7,797	8,671	9,640	7,258	7,906	15,178	9,033	11,945	2,583	7,263	7,840	1,253	4,150	8,831	6,895	3,393	7,649	9,160
Marrakech, Morocco	9,345	17,556	2,097	2,747	4,220	1,236	3,210	9,115	3,917	6,736	8,797	2,337	1,767	8,024	7,694	2,637	793	7,618	2,453	3,161
Marseilles, France	9,352	16,890	799	1,031	2,497	898	1,926	7,494	4,771	6,971	10,319	1,471	433	9,130	7,865	886	1,322	8,012	1,284	1,412
Maseru, Lesotho	16,465	10,026	9,141	9,053	9,893	8,653	10,256	9,390	3,805	1,818	10,736	9,736	8,734	12,539	14,863	8,697	8,437	14,388	9,628	9,014
Mashhad, Iran	11,963	12,377	4,934	4,066	3,360	5,514	4,993	3,021	6,517	6,192	14,926	5,495	4,905	13,567	11,130	3,901	5,935	11,619	5,111	3,585
Mazatlan, Mexico	1,664	13,020	9,195	9,826	9,987	9,133	8,599	13,864	12,631	15,724	5,046	8,493	9,461	2,885	2,155	10,141	9,028	1,875	8,809	10,179
Mbabane, Swaziland	16,653	10,036	8,942	8,793	9,557	8,509	10,025	8,901	3,761	1,393	11,182	9,563	8,542	12,907	14,999	8,433	8,331	14,587	9,429	8,723
Mbandaka, Zaire	13,761	13,145	5,746	5,706	6,718	5,280	6,871	8,355	982	2,311	10,599	6,344	5,338	11,256	12,081	5,358	5,113	11,877	6,232	5,729
McMurdo Sound, Antarctica	13,660	4,104	16,818	16,872	17,450	16,093	18,003	12,823	11,314	9,393	9,345	17,224	16,403	11,604	14,594	16,517	15,676	14,052	17,276	16,806
Mecca, Saudi Arabia	13,108	12,976	4,671	4,080	4,338	4,810	5,356	5,192	4,038	3,975	13,263	5,374	4,417	12,882	11,782	3,747	5,023	11,997	5,064	3,795
Medan, Indonesia	14,383	6,989	10,323	9,444	8,472	10,900	10,205	2,994	9,929	7,419	18,963	10,845	10,300	18,491	14,847	9,297	11,294	15,612	10,460	8,953
Medellin, Colombia	5,215	14,274	8,452	9,326	10,279	7,910	8,547	15,788	9,465	12,272	2,030	7,915	8,494	920	4,368	9,486	7,541	3,591	8,301	9,814
Medicine Hat, Canada	1,584	14,164	7,164	7,550	7,316	7,436	6,256	10,920	12,070	14,880	7,620	6,482	7,526	5,118	1,495	7,905	7,549	2,264	6,697	7,782
Medina, Saudi Arabia	12,791	13,190	4,394	3,779	4,004	4,584	5,048	5,101	4,202	4,300	13,248	5,098	4,162	12,725	11,488	3,453	4,825	11,725	4,779	3,480
Melbourne, Australia	13,123	438	16,938	16,053	14,902	17,476	16,575	9,341	13,867	10,848	12,966	17,393	16,911	14,330	14,805	15,916	17,767	14,949	17,017	15,557
Memphis, Tennessee	2,269	15,060	7,153	7,821	8,147	7,070	6,637	12,834	10,854	13,963	5,398	6,454	7,406	2,873	859	8,122	6,975	207	6,783	8,203
Merauke, Indonesia	11,867	3,712	14,156	13,315	11,931	14,977	13,440	6,749	14,518	11,552	15,312	14,361	14,326	15,272	13,377	13,325	15,484	13,938	14,040	12,840
Merida, Mexico	2,998	14,274	8,247	9,009	9,535	7,989	7,924	14,403	10,944	14,001	3,902	7,582	8,432	1,404	2,301	9,271	7,781	1,549	7,943	9,436
Meridian, Mississippi	2,464	15,034	7,275	7,973	8,363	7,145	6,816	13,141	10,758	13,875	5,069	6,584	7,510	2,544	1,178	8,263	7,020	424	6,923	8,369
Messina, Italy	10,343	15,913	1,760	1,480	2,631	1,855	2,712	6,858	4,232	6,080	11,057	2,463	1,455	10,073	8,883	1,129	2,151	9,040	2,211	1,538
Mexico City, Mexico	2,430	13,374	9,038	9,747	10,104	8,859	8,588	14,468	11,952	14,993	4,240	8,352	9,258	2,021	2,387	10,035	8,690	1,831	8,695	10,144
Miami, Florida	3,510	15,368	7,196	7,984	8,620	6,902	6,956	13,802	9,961	13,061	4,198	6,546	7,363	1,772	2,261	8,230	6,684	1,528	6,915	8,427
Midway Islands, USA	5,836	8,531	11,395	11,147	9,918	12,121	10,207	8,655	16,760	16,444	11,642	10,980	11,805	9,915	7,283	11,453	12,497	7,872	10,946	10,997
Milan, Italy	9,384	16,625	817	689	2,129	1,224	1,772	7,131	4,995	7,034	10,666	1,522	621	9,398	7,949	500	1,687	8,142	1,248	1,029
Milford Sound, New Zealand	11,834	1,715	18,932	18,049	16,729	19,439	18,123	11,304	14,665	12,035	10,979	19,069	18,955	12,304	13,408	17,951	19,307	13,340	18,820	17,552
Milwaukee, Wisconsin	2,447	15,556	6,428	7,044	7,284	6,439	5,825	11,956	10,582	13,626	6,199	5,723	6,712	3,692	768	7,360	6,406	995	6,031	7,402
Minsk, USSR	9,403	15,424	1,945	1,070	690	2,729	1,859	5,692	6,163	7,545	12,040	2,391	2,078	10,425	8,241	1,116	3,240	8,619	2,006	596
Mogadiscio, Somalia	15,318	11,145	6,777	6,270	6,547	6,754	7,559	5,712	4,002	2,187	13,592	7,482	6,472	14,164	13,905	5,924	6,849	14,011	7,205	6,013
Mombasa, Kenya	15,619	11,156	7,048	6,662	7,141	6,885	7,955	6,627	3,397	1,275	12,811	7,741	6,703	13,679	14,056	6,303	6,893	14,024	7,507	6,474
Monclova, Mexico	1,657	13,667	8,559	9,205	9,425	8,485	7,992	13,607	12,058	15,170	5,051	7,858	8,819	2,689	1,605	9,514	8,380	1,232	8,179	9,569
Moncton, Canada	4,294	17,417	4,725	5,440	5,982	4,627	4,338	11,272	8,768	11,775	6,556	4,036	4,964	4,362	2,629	5,720	4,559	2,633	4,382	5,855
Monrovia, Liberia	10,874	15,549	4,896	5,426	6,875	4,053	6,028	10,810	2,343	5,413	7,609	5,143	4,531	7,957	9,210	5,224	3,593	8,838	5,270	5,754
Monte Carlo, Monaco	9,430	16,737	849	919	2,367	1,062	1,916	7,324	4,806	6,931	10,489	1,546	541	9,286	7,962	736	1,492	8,126	1,320	1,266
Monterrey, Mexico	1,831	13,682	8,590	9,253	9,510	8,492	8,053	13,764	11,973	15,079	4,876	7,892	8,841	2,517	1,714	9,557	8,372	1,269	8,219	9,625
Montevideo, Uruguay	9,961	11,228	10,872	11,650	13,100	10,006	11,669	16,905	7,834	9,134	3,292	10,739	10,637	5,717	9,352	11,561	9,481	8,575	11,044	12,084
Montgomery, Alabama	2,679	15,233	7,112	7,825	8,258	6,960	6,686	13,134	10,533	13,650	5,015	6,425	7,338	2,501	1,317	8,109	6,824	613	6,770	8,229
Montpelier, Vermont	3,689	16,791	5,355	6,049	6,512	5,273	4,911	11,654	9,346	12,383	6,252	4,660	5,602	3,929	2,009	6,338	5,202	1,989	4,998	6,451
Montpellier, France	9,242	17,016	716	1,066	2,538	777	1,872	7,597	4,819	7,065	10,208	1,368	324	9,004	7,748	961	1,218	7,889	1,203	1,475
Montreal, Canada	3,610	16,729	5,347	6,023	6,445	5,295	4,866	11,541	9,438	12,460	6,383	4,648	5,605	4,037	1,940	6,319	5,241	1,982	4,979	6,416
Moosonee, Canada	3,204	16,253	5,446	6,017	6,216	5,543	4,778	11,003	9,983	12,906	7,025	4,740	5,755	4,583	1,694	6,342	5,575	2,062	5,028	6,358
Moroni, Comoros	16,542	10,288	7,980	7,591	8,022	7,800	8,884	6,872	3,970	1,060	12,934	8,672	7,632	14,170	14,951	7,233	7,788	14,865	8,440	7,392
Moscow, USSR	9,496	14,827	2,594	1,735	636	3,399	2,310	5,077	6,643	7,736	12,641	2,977	2,749	10,905	8,467	1,788	3,912	8,911	2,599	1,271
Mosul, Iraq	11,671	13,618	3,741	2,950	2,781	4,190	4,097	4,498	5,284	5,655	13,496	4,383	3,628	12,405	10,532	2,700	4,565	10,885	4,017	2,535
Mount Isa, Australia	12,690	2,404	15,222	14,344	13,050	15,961	14,655	7,615	14,155	11,048	14,624	15,536	15,317	15,330	14,313	14,291	16,419	14,752	15,186	13,851

Distances in Kilometers	Las Vegas, Nevada	Launceston, Australia	Le Havre, France	Leipzig, East Germany	Leningrad, USSR	Leon, Spain	Lerwick, United Kingdom	Lhasa, China	Libreville, Gabon	Lilongwe, Malawi	Lima, Peru	Limerick, Ireland	Limoges, France	Limon, Costa Rica	Lincoln, Nebraska	Linz, Austria	Lisbon, Portugal	Little Rock, Arkansas	Liverpool, United Kingdom	Lodz, Poland
Multan, Pakistan	12,627	11,092	6,219	5,344	4,503	6,811	6,197	1,893	7,326	6,342	16,210	6,760	6,200	14,796	12,050	5,192	7,230	12,620	6,374	4,856
Munich, West Germany	9,280	16,475	853	355	1,780	1,474	1,568	6,876	5,297	7,225	10,897	1,515	826	9,529	7,895	203	1,968	8,132	1,181	693
Murcia, Spain	9,364	17,289	1,284	1,818	3,291	637	2,465	8,230	4,302	6,809	9,627	1,732	894	8,629	7,786	1,693	705	7,831	1,722	2,219
Murmansk, USSR	8,057	15,177	2,801	2,255	1,018	3,683	1,877	5,698	7,817	9,201	12,046	2,813	3,133	9,973	7,151	2,523	4,200	7,671	2,535	2,049
Mururoa Atoll, Fr. Polynesia	6,894	7,125	15,299	15,907	15,694	15,140	14,637	14,977	15,852	15,961	6,638	14,598	15,545	7,046	8,200	16,236	14,918	7,972	14,913	16,205
Muscat, Oman	13,355	11,593	5,787	4,992	4,595	6,190	6,092	3,295	5,891	4,959	15,180	6,428	5,657	14,430	12,429	4,747	6,522	12,855	6,061	4,561
Myitkyina, Burma	12,387	8,998	8,402	7,516	6,330	9,124	8,048	781	9,792	8,155	18,422	8,809	8,479	16,090	12,533	7,453	9,595	13,272	8,433	7,020
Naga, Philippines	11,784	6,574	11,078	10,226	8,868	11,886	10,456	3,746	12,571	10,314	17,834	11,341	11,235	16,122	12,718	10,232	12,392	13,479	10,998	9,749
Nagasaki, Japan	9,814	8,405	9,631	8,879	7,417	10,506	8,778	3,695	12,799	11,409	16,438	9,720	9,886	14,127	10,559	8,987	11,032	11,332	9,431	8,460
Nagoya, Japan	9,154	8,544	9,706	9,010	7,537	10,590	8,768	4,316	13,307	12,081	15,749	9,718	9,995	13,486	9,970	9,155	11,113	10,737	9,459	8,622
Nagpur, India	13,487	9,847	7,464	6,594	5,751	8,026	7,453	1,529	7,893	6,296	17,299	8,015	7,428	16,051	13,130	6,430	8,424	13,752	7,630	6,109
Nairobi, Kenya	15,190	11,597	6,631	6,270	6,811	6,451	7,559	6,699	3,052	1,444	12,581	7,321	6,280	13,314	13,617	5,910	6,454	13,584	7,094	6,101
Nanchang, China	11,066	8,402	9,277	8,441	7,056	10,105	8,627	2,409	11,595	10,000	17,735	9,516	9,457	15,271	11,612	8,474	10,620	12,389	9,178	7,974
Nancy, France	8,967	16,875	452	527	1,984	1,138	1,361	7,243	5,361	7,457	10,517	1,135	491	9,126	7,548	600	1,654	7,761	832	1,005
Nandi, Fiji	9,266	3,894	16,480	16,063	14,644	17,241	15,301	10,631	17,681	14,703	11,211	16,100	16,876	11,355	10,949	16,295	17,602	11,147	16,052	15,772
Nanjing, China	10,601	8,639	9,137	8,324	6,905	9,984	8,419	2,654	11,806	10,367	17,270	9,329	9,342	14,810	11,155	8,383	10,505	11,933	9,005	7,871
Nanning, China	12,044	8,162	9,335	8,461	7,177	10,104	8,847	1,877	10,910	9,081	18,690	9,674	9,453	16,173	12,502	8,435	10,594	13,275	9,311	7,972
Nantes, France	8,657	17,459	283	1,106	2,499	603	1,440	7,843	5,298	7,637	9,916	790	264	8,558	7,168	1,192	1,128	7,325	697	1,598
Naples, Italy	10,042	16,115	1,465	1,173	2,394	1,657	2,397	6,883	4,506	6,395	10,986	2,171	1,190	9,897	8,597	830	2,011	8,772	1,906	1,278
Narvik, Norway	7,762	15,809	2,312	1,928	1,131	3,177	1,279	6,309	7,577	9,234	11,425	2,229	2,681	9,401	6,732	2,249	3,679	7,205	1,985	1,862
Nashville, Tennessee	2,543	15,378	6,857	7,539	7,908	6,760	6,370	12,716	10,548	13,654	5,433	6,162	7,104	2,922	1,006	7,835	6,659	523	6,495	7,928
Nassau, Bahamas	3,799	15,559	7,047	7,852	8,547	6,718	6,862	13,825	9,675	12,771	4,108	6,411	7,197	1,774	2,502	8,087	6,480	1,793	6,785	8,305
Natal, Brazil	9,492	14,773	7,014	7,776	9,232	6,140	7,896	13,820	5,011	7,599	4,648	6,948	6,764	5,582	8,102	7,687	5,614	7,470	7,223	8,208
Natashquan, Canada	4,498	17,585	4,324	5,003	5,491	4,301	3,868	10,767	8,652	11,588	7,054	3,625	4,588	4,867	2,885	5,296	4,284	3,003	3,956	5,403
Nauru Island	8,964	4,947	14,435	13,896	12,447	15,286	13,314	8,676	17,532	14,628	12,833	14,211	14,795	12,224	10,588	14,098	15,758	11,034	14,070	13,569
Ndjamena, Chad	12,545	14,357	4,366	4,353	5,452	3,922	5,496	8,018	1,438	3,550	10,519	4,970	3,959	10,652	10,896	4,012	3,796	10,786	4,853	4,414
Nelson, New Zealand	11,255	2,180	18,951	18,181	16,745	19,836	17,871	11,522	15,194	12,612	10,721	18,731	19,198	11,882	12,835	18,189	19,660	12,784	18,628	17,713
Nema, Mauritania	10,463	16,332	3,708	4,223	5,675	2,885	4,858	9,892	2,565	5,640	8,308	4,002	3,335	8,201	8,776	4,025	2,456	8,534	4,100	4,556
Neuquen, Argentina	9,621	10,420	11,861	12,675	14,092	11,015	12,558	17,852	8,961	10,041	3,110	11,657	11,657	5,637	9,300	12,614	10,494	8,532	11,986	13,127
New Delhi, India	12,720	10,569	6,746	5,864	4,941	7,364	6,658	1,357	7,830	6,636	16,784	7,264	6,745	15,240	12,293	5,729	7,792	12,907	6,879	5,372
New Glasgow, Canada	4,464	17,583	4,608	5,339	5,924	4,486	4,261	11,263	8,594	11,605	6,545	3,925	4,837	4,398	2,794	5,612	4,405	2,775	4,276	5,761
New Haven, Connecticut	3,680	16,702	5,564	6,284	6,798	5,432	5,174	11,980	9,345	12,415	5,922	4,878	5,793	3,608	1,993	6,563	5,328	1,845	5,225	6,698
New Orleans, Louisiana	2,434	14,790	7,555	8,261	8,659	7,407	7,110	13,406	10,911	14,027	4,854	6,866	7,784	2,328	1,346	8,548	7,269	570	7,208	8,660
New Plymouth, New Zealand	11,048	2,299	18,752	18,047	16,588	19,611	17,636	11,469	15,447	12,838	10,749	18,479	19,057	11,818	12,643	18,100	19,743	12,616	18,394	17,599
New York, New York	3,594	16,597	5,676	6,396	6,904	5,543	5,284	12,066	9,431	12,508	5,849	4,990	5,905	3,517	1,910	6,676	5,436	1,738	5,337	6,809
Newcastle upon Tyne, UK	8,097	17,278	623	1,017	1,967	1,409	574	7,528	6,138	8,337	10,189	530	1,039	8,557	6,712	1,324	1,897	6,970	199	1,442
Newcastle Waters, Australia	13,042	2,968	14,534	13,649	12,397	15,246	14,044	6,908	13,618	10,548	15,350	14,893	14,607	16,016	14,594	13,580	15,693	15,119	14,531	13,154
Niamey, Niger	11,447	15,435	3,995	4,291	5,642	3,307	5,183	9,186	1,662	4,630	9,183	4,447	3,584	9,243	9,764	4,018	3,004	9,561	4,449	4,517
Nicosia, Cyprus	11,463	14,328	3,131	2,459	2,761	3,445	3,719	5,391	4,581	5,440	12,628	3,817	2,943	11,684	10,168	2,144	3,773	10,433	3,482	2,151
Niue (Alofi)	8,396	4,755	16,509	16,417	15,188	17,009	15,351	11,879	17,942	15,535	9,882	15,937	16,923	10,051	10,039	16,734	17,150	10,124	16,026	16,282
Norfolk, Virginia	3,458	16,275	6,096	6,834	7,372	5,919	5,742	12,527	9,607	12,711	5,413	5,418	6,309	3,051	1,821	7,106	5,781	1,463	5,771	7,255
Norfolk Island, Australia	10,803	2,330	17,512	16,814	15,346	18,393	16,451	10,426	16,107	13,170	11,699	17,365	17,812	12,394	12,476	16,908	18,899	12,614	17,199	16,388
Noril'sk, USSR	8,151	13,190	4,906	4,276	2,829	5,790	3,966	4,418	9,520	10,157	13,555	4,913	5,218	11,177	7,782	4,481	6,309	8,463	4,647	3,957
Norman Wells, Canada	3,330	13,920	6,490	6,613	5,986	7,018	5,381	8,985	11,928	14,123	9,516	5,910	6,899	6,994	3,324	6,974	7,291	4,098	6,003	6,710
Normanton, Australia	12,369	2,696	15,050	14,184	12,850	15,827	14,413	7,495	14,407	11,316	14,698	15,316	15,177	15,202	13,975	14,156	16,309	14,439	14,979	13,697
North Pole	5,997	14,588	4,519	4,319	3,359	5,286	3,333	6,721	9,962	11,550	11,335	4,166	4,926	8,897	5,481	4,652	5,717	6,156	4,083	4,268
Nottingham, United Kingdom	8,263	17,323	396	941	2,062	1,198	800	7,580	5,912	8,137	10,144	503	812	8,583	6,851	1,208	1,698	7,084	132	1,407
Norway House, Canada	2,389	15,131	6,224	6,660	6,561	6,465	5,370	10,699	11,096	13,906	7,577	5,535	6,577	5,053	1,466	7,009	6,568	2,181	5,766	6,926
Norwich, United Kingdom	8,413	17,171	358	772	1,948	1,228	850	7,436	5,841	8,012	10,292	671	756	8,750	7,012	1,039	1,743	7,251	301	1,243
Nouakchott, Mauritania	9,636	16,965	3,770	4,446	5,919	2,888	4,817	10,589	3,400	6,511	7,493	3,889	3,462	7,266	7,951	4,323	2,379	7,661	4,076	4,852
Noumea, New Caledonia	10,467	2,789	16,754	16,090	14,617	17,633	15,687	9,899	16,546	13,487	12,131	16,604	17,071	12,536	12,154	16,213	18,134	12,383	16,434	15,685
Novosibirsk, USSR	9,753	12,294	5,348	4,535	3,119	6,193	4,714	2,895	8,925	8,927	14,928	5,582	5,552	12,679	9,382	4,611	6,715	10,046	5,241	4,090
Nuku'alofa, Tonga	8,949	4,185	16,830	16,594	15,255	17,438	15,646	11,489	17,656	15,005	10,366	16,322	17,246	10,635	10,604	16,875	17,650	10,710	16,361	16,379
Nukunono Island, Tokelau Isls.	7,772	5,372	15,476	15,320	14,082	16,073	14,299	11,189	19,019	16,199	10,328	14,955	15,892	10,071	9,454	15,632	16,315	9,656	15,001	15,175
Nuremberg, West Germany	9,147	16,519	793	224	1,687	1,492	1,423	6,877	5,440	7,372	10,883	1,422	840	9,468	7,774	268	2,001	8,022	1,072	646
Nyala, Sudan	13,227	13,567	4,734	4,499	5,331	4,484	5,752	7,070	2,138	3,042	11,570	5,404	4,361	11,698	11,639	4,138	4,475	11,619	5,211	4,430
Oaxaca, Mexico	2,792	13,418	9,068	9,807	10,242	8,839	8,682	14,770	11,724	14,727	3,878	8,392	9,267	1,673	2,635	10,081	8,641	2,010	8,746	10,220
Ocean Falls, Canada	2,051	13,215	7,693	7,922	7,402	8,110	6,652	10,171	12,935	15,443	8,619	7,060	8,087	6,174	2,670	8,284	8,305	3,413	7,209	8,065
Odense, Denmark	8,620	16,529	956	474	1,282	1,832	865	6,782	6,100	7,996	10,940	1,277	1,243	9,315	7,323	834	2,357	7,633	895	725
Odessa, USSR	10,239	15,021	2,293	1,448	1,497	2,891	2,574	5,471	5,512	6,702	12,334	2,890	2,266	10,963	9,026	1,255	3,345	9,361	2,515	1,009
Ogbomosho, Nigeria	12,023	14,826	4,602	4,843	6,145	3,939	5,789	9,267	1,032	4,076	9,270	5,075	4,188	9,570	10,336	4,552	3,644	10,096	5,064	5,032
Okha, USSR	7,572	10,532	8,061	7,505	6,076	8,933	6,998	4,922	12,660	12,511	14,213	7,938	8,407	11,741	8,098	7,726	9,434	8,876	7,735	7,206
Okinawa (Naha)	10,475	7,753	10,149	9,358	7,918	11,010	9,367	3,604	12,790	11,071	16,999	10,296	10,374	14,813	11,290	9,432	11,534	12,060	9,988	8,915
Oklahoma City, Oklahoma	1,594	14,473	7,603	8,218	8,403	7,592	6,988	12,738	11,518	14,620	5,686	6,898	7,883	3,182	596	8,535	7,533	483	7,207	8,568
Old Crow, Canada	3,825	13,526	6,597	6,618	5,839	7,200	5,444	8,427	12,100	14,035	10,134	6,068	7,012	7,616	3,946	6,973	7,517	4,722	6,116	6,659
Olympia, Washington	1,368	13,208	7,987	8,299	7,900	8,321	7,011	10,855	13,020	15,751	7,972	7,324	8,365	5,560	2,203	8,659	8,462	2,893	7,511	8,484
Omaha, Nebraska	1,754	14,861	7,057	7,634	7,765	7,107	6,387	12,117	11,271	14,322	6,218	6,351	7,356	3,693	76	7,960	7,090	796	6,644	7,968
Omsk, USSR	9,870	12,755	4,808	3,975	2,598	5,638	4,256	3,151	8,343	8,502	14,593	5,088	4,992	12,474	9,345	4,031	6,156	9,967	4,733	3,518
Oodnadatta, Australia	13,419	1,871	15,517	14,628	13,455	16,140	15,138	7,898	13,538	10,421	14,404	15,946	15,532	15,555	15,074	14,516	16,523	15,448	15,572	14,131
Oradea, Romania	9,844	15,688	1,634	842	1,530	2,218	2,090	6,135	5,313	6,864	11,660	2,264	1,590	10,312	8,541	589	2,681	8,826	1,902	551
Oran, Algeria	9,567	17,161	1,534	2,019	3,487	876	2,719	8,301	4,047	6,586	9,591	1,988	1,136	8,688	7,974	1,861	825	7,994	1,977	2,393
Oranjestad, Aruba	5,210	15,197	7,529	8,403	9,377	6,993	7,643	14,923	8,866	11,816	2,825	6,996	7,573	1,446	4,074	8,564	6,633	3,332	7,381	8,892
Orebro, Sweden	8,483	16,173	1,458	907	850	2,341	924	6,434	6,551	8,293	11,278	1,648	1,763	9,523	7,282	1,224	2,865	7,654	1,296	880
Orel, USSR	9,751	14,847	2,514	1,630	858	3,272	2,391	5,119	6,325	7,415	12,616	2,966	2,620	10,981	8,673	1,618	3,774	9,089	2,582	1,138
Orsk, USSR	10,306	13,352	4,052	3,174	2,011	4,819	3,745	3,602	7,270	7,611	14,115	4,452	4,167	12,288	9,531	3,158	5,318	10,067	4,074	2,685
Osaka, Japan	9,289	8,508	9,697	8,989	7,517	10,580	8,775	4,192	13,211	11,947	15,889	9,725	9,979	13,619	10,093	9,127	11,104	10,861	9,459	8,595
Oslo, Norway	8,264	16,404	1,343	964	1,087	2,224	663	6,676	6,604	8,449	11,034	1,437	1,689	9,262	7,039	1,313	2,741	7,402	1,107	1,059
Osorno, Chile	9,520	10,060	12,280	13,106	14,507	11,443	12,936	18,144	9,414	10,389	3,183	12,050	12,089	5,690	9,323	13,057	10,925	8,567	12,387	13,565
Ostrava, Czechoslovakia	9,438	16,004	1,308	452	1,356	1,997	1,681	6,358	5,544	7,231	11,405	1,893	1,347	9,966	8,132	337	2,493	8,422	1,521	229
Ottawa, Canada	3,445	16,565	5,489	6,155	6,547	5,450	4,985	11,586	9,601	12,624	6,365	4,789	5,753	3,988	1,777	6,454	5,401	1,838	5,116	6,542
Ouagadougou, Bourkina Fasso	11,238	15,585	4,120	4,496	5,889	3,374	5,303	9,592	1,795	4,864	8,769	4,515	3,719	8,872	9,551	4,246	3,015	9,308	4,555	4,759
Oujda, Morocco	9,559	17,220	1,656	2,174	3,643	937	2,834	8,455	3,975	6,574	9,446	2,070	1,268	8,580	7,952	2,022	787	7,952	2,085	2,553
Oxford, United Kingdom	8,346	17,363	269	943	2,146	1,068	935	7,634	5,781	8,030	10,096	514	683	8,577	6,917	1,176	1,573	7,133	220	1,426
Pago Pago, American Samoa	8,074	5,052	16,010	15,888	14,657	16,559	14,841	11,568	18,469	15,891	10,077	15,461	16,425	10,040	9,739	16,203	16,754	9,880	15,530	15,749
Pakxe, Laos	12,892	7,567	9,835	8,948	7,758	10,547	9,468	2,204	10,688	8,555	19,562	10,241	9,905	17,065	13,395	8,878	11,010	14,168	9,866	8,451
Palembang, Indonesia	14,514	6,005	11,309	10,429	9,429	11,886	11,163	3,886	10,611	7,885	18,338	11,824	11,288	18,859	15,292	10,284	12,275	16,070	11,438	9,937
Palermo, Italy	10,229	16,092	1,648	1,467	2,703	1,679	2,656	7,044	4,197	6,148	10,866	2,344	1,318	9,886	8,750	1,134	1,961	8,891	2,114	1,588
Palma, Majorca	9,483	17,026	1,122	1,505	2,970	768	2,305	7,860	4,394	6,751	9,991	1,692	706	8,943	7,940	1,345	1,022	8,027	1,598	1,876
Palmerston North, New Zealand	11,037	2,393	18,929	18,241	16,780	19,738	17,791	11,651	15,365	12,821	10,575	18,599	19,249	11,686	12,614	18,291	19,575	12,562	18,548	17,793
Panama, Panama	4,695	14,206	8,510	9,367	10,224	8,029	8,504	15,617	9,900	12,760	2,340	7,936	8,587	401	3,915	9,554	7,694	3,137	8,320	9,845
Paramaribo, Suriname	6,951	15,490	7,065	7,950	9,193	6,344	7,525	14,689	7,204	10,060	3,127	6,697	6,987	3,106	5,660	8,014	5,885	4,975	7,062	8,445
Paris, France	8,750	17,158	175	764	2,165	928	1,276	7,506	5,416	7,621	10,246	879	347	8,841	7,306	884	1,454	7,502	629	1,259
Patna, India	12,846	9,789	7,540	6,652	5,638	8,185	7,370	742	8,560	7,080	17,623	8,028	7,558	15,865	12,649	6,537	8,623	13,320	7,643	6,157
Patrai, Greece	10,652	15,413	2,127	1,627	2,484	2,356	2,919	6,335	4,377	5,917	11,595	2,831	1,886	10,592	9,252	1,268	2,681	9,453	2,533	1,511
Peking, China	10,070	9,531	8,303	7,514	6,072	9,164	7,544	2,569	11,424	10,382	16,648	8,463	8,529	14,127	10,457	7,597	9,688	11,230	8,148	7,076
Penrhyn Island (Omoka)	6,721	6,446	15,083	15,233	14,312	15,424	14,013	12,517	18,347	17,152	8,843	14,438	15,473	8,575	8,352	15,590	15,495	8,434	14,598	15,259
Peoria, Illinois	2,278	15,341	6,704	7,330	7,580	6,693	6,115	12,216	10,747	13,816	5,981	5,999	6,981	3,462	599	7,643	6,645	701	6,312	7,691
Perm', USSR	9,538	13,829	3,704	2,875	1,501	4,537	3,196	4,129	7,593	8,240	13,584	3,997	3,893	11,618	8,767	2,949	5,056	9,316	3,637	2,428
Perth, Australia	15,349	2,970	14,434	13,605	12,785	14,798	14,507	7,300	11,580	8,464	14,949	15,046	14,305	16,905	16,964	13,390	15,039	17,400	14,665	13,137
Peshawar, Pakistan	12,203	11,372	5,946	5,062	4,146	6,578	5,857	1,910	7,444	6,650	16,017	6,459	5,954	14,448	11,631	4,934	7,017	12,209	6,073	4,569

Distances in Kilometers	Las Vegas, Nevada	Launceston, Australia	Le Havre, France	Leipzig, East Germany	Leningrad, USSR	Leon, Spain	Lerwick, United Kingdom	Lhasa, China	Libreville, Gabon	Lilongwe, Malawi	Lima, Peru	Limerick, Ireland	Limoges, France	Limon, Costa Rica	Lincoln, Nebraska	Linz, Austria	Lisbon, Portugal	Little Rock, Arkansas	Liverpool, United Kingdom	Lodz, Poland
Petropavlovsk-Kamchatskiy,USSR	6,662	10,522	8,464	8,022	6,666	9,302	7,328	5,960	13,436	13,541	13,331	8,231	8,842	10,929	7,358	8,283	9,773	8,128	8,085	7,785
Petrozavodsk, USSR	8,801	15,116	2,508	1,774	307	3,377	1,906	5,414	7,130	8,403	12,297	2,725	2,761	10,404	7,808	1,959	3,904	8,280	2,378	1,436
Pevek, USSR	5,693	12,467	6,759	6,464	5,279	7,546	5,582	6,530	12,096	13,125	12,120	6,431	7,160	9,600	5,930	6,771	7,982	6,704	6,337	6,327
Philadelphia, Pennsylvania	3,505	16,479	5,806	6,526	7,028	5,669	5,412	12,170	9,525	12,608	5,760	5,120	6,034	3,408	1,825	6,806	5,558	1,619	5,467	6,938
Phnom Penh, Kampuchea	13,265	7,288	10,083	9,194	8,048	10,767	9,770	2,463	10,606	8,342	19,814	10,517	10,132	17,468	13,798	9,106	11,216	14,572	10,138	8,697
Phoenix, Arizona	412	13,201	8,652	9,164	9,096	8,754	7,885	12,609	12,869	15,959	6,257	7,947	8,971	3,944	1,590	9,504	8,751	1,829	8,218	9,454
Pierre, South Dakota	1,550	14,657	7,074	7,592	7,603	7,199	6,319	11,726	11,542	14,536	6,678	6,370	7,396	4,158	496	7,929	7,226	1,273	6,639	7,894
Pinang, Malaysia	14,111	7,033	10,287	9,403	8,385	10,892	10,119	2,853	10,113	7,655	19,221	10,788	10,282	18,261	14,600	9,269	11,300	15,369	10,403	8,909
Pitcairn Island (Adamstown)	6,958	7,637	14,963	15,699	15,847	14,638	14,514	15,945	14,890	15,348	5,744	14,292	15,134	6,410	8,071	15,980	14,337	7,729	14,644	16,087
Pittsburgh, Pennsylvania	3,089	16,100	6,099	6,787	7,202	6,008	5,633	12,191	9,939	13,017	5,819	5,404	6,346	3,385	1,409	7,080	5,921	1,253	5,740	7,183
Plymouth, Montserrat	5,624	16,095	6,624	7,505	8,551	6,054	6,821	14,137	8,052	11,081	3,574	6,121	6,646	2,372	4,252	7,648	5,682	3,596	6,505	7,999
Plymouth, United Kingdom	8,286	17,593	321	1,160	2,397	874	1,101	7,876	5,691	8,032	9,857	401	646	8,373	6,822	1,355	1,357	7,008	344	1,652
Ponape Island	9,259	5,471	13,406	12,782	11,313	14,283	12,352	7,429	16,478	13,919	13,947	13,286	13,733	12,988	10,762	12,952	14,789	11,324	13,091	12,419
Ponce, Puerto Rico	5,153	15,894	6,832	7,702	8,666	6,318	6,932	14,218	8,530	11,568	3,518	6,289	6,887	1,981	3,826	7,870	5,976	3,145	6,675	8,189
Ponta Delgada, Azores	7,631	19,277	2,440	3,327	4,598	1,791	3,034	10,072	5,482	8,438	7,683	2,122	2,397	6,480	5,964	3,418	1,450	5,867	2,463	3,824
Pontianak, Indonesia	13,933	5,954	11,387	10,499	9,402	12,026	11,129	3,813	11,119	8,457	18,501	11,853	11,406	18,267	14,785	10,386	12,448	15,560	11,471	10,002
Port Augusta, Australia	13,465	1,293	16,055	15,168	14,031	16,625	15,723	8,460	13,552	10,455	13,849	16,514	16,040	15,157	15,148	15,037	16,965	15,424	16,136	14,672
Port Blair, India	13,967	8,089	9,225	8,345	7,381	9,816	9,111	2,006	9,279	7,096	18,924	9,745	9,210	17,572	14,121	8,202	10,222	14,848	9,359	7,853
Port Elizabeth, South Africa	16,460	9,748	9,582	9,534	10,414	9,054	10,715	9,849	4,159	2,363	10,409	10,156	9,171	12,344	14,947	9,181	8,809	14,404	10,068	9,514
Port Hedland, Australia	14,544	3,566	13,745	12,868	11,846	14,288	13,578	6,265	12,024	8,953	16,043	14,263	13,708	17,447	15,989	12,714	14,642	16,604	13,878	12,376
Port Louis, Mauritius	18,095	8,526	9,564	9,059	9,214	9,484	10,344	6,586	5,706	2,613	13,904	10,268	9,248	15,656	16,667	8,716	9,517	16,648	9,997	8,784
Port Moresby, Papua New Guinea	11,316	3,538	14,628	13,825	12,396	15,484	13,801	7,402	15,247	12,235	14,589	14,745	14,842	14,532	12,890	13,872	16,005	13,393	14,455	13,368
Port Said, Egypt	11,807	14,203	3,358	2,764	3,188	3,565	4,048	5,581	4,182	5,010	12,533	4,058	3,123	11,765	10,461	2,427	3,838	10,685	3,745	2,506
Port Sudan, Sudan	13,184	13,070	4,669	4,136	4,510	4,741	5,425	5,518	3,702	3,736	12,984	5,376	4,390	12,710	11,801	3,791	4,918	11,975	5,084	3,888
Port-au-Prince, Haiti	4,618	15,504	7,204	8,056	8,921	6,750	7,196	14,387	9,137	12,173	3,422	6,623	7,292	1,490	3,391	8,248	6,439	2,668	7,007	8,533
Port-of-Spain, Trin. & Tobago	6,072	15,603	7,081	7,969	9,088	6,449	7,370	14,674	7,929	10,864	3,042	6,622	7,065	2,357	4,802	8,084	6,039	4,105	7,003	8,466
Port-Vila, Vanuatu	10,005	3,313	16,326	15,724	14,254	17,188	15,220	9,796	17,018	13,924	12,130	16,119	16,669	12,315	11,692	15,884	17,666	11,958	15,975	15,351
Portland, Maine	3,878	16,966	5,236	5,949	6,459	5,127	4,835	11,669	9,154	12,198	6,206	4,547	5,473	3,929	2,194	6,231	5,042	2,134	4,892	6,360
Portland, Oregon	1,215	13,139	8,113	8,439	8,058	8,430	7,148	11,011	13,095	15,869	7,844	7,445	8,488	5,449	2,162	8,799	8,560	2,827	7,638	8,631
Porto, Portugal	8,645	17,998	1,152	1,960	3,378	300	2,175	8,645	4,869	7,502	9,147	1,280	952	7,982	7,056	1,972	274	7,098	1,427	2,437
Porto Alegre, Brazil	9,920	11,870	10,171	10,942	12,395	9,302	10,991	16,401	7,239	8,771	3,332	10,054	9,930	5,594	9,142	10,850	8,776	8,370	10,353	11,374
Porto Alexandre, Angola	14,344	12,182	7,327	7,435	8,556	6,710	8,502	9,867	1,812	2,364	9,546	7,840	6,911	10,837	12,699	7,105	6,422	12,279	7,802	7,521
Porto Novo, Benin	12,009	14,792	4,774	5,049	6,370	4,082	5,963	9,516	1,015	4,121	9,051	5,223	4,363	9,420	10,321	4,765	3,761	10,052	5,229	5,253
Porto Velho, Brazil	7,310	13,613	8,940	9,821	11,076	8,198	9,401	16,537	8,194	10,604	1,485	8,580	8,845	2,967	6,438	9,870	7,723	5,668	8,945	10,314
Portsmouth, United Kingdom	8,426	17,375	166	942	2,205	970	1,045	7,662	5,672	7,934	10,073	562	575	8,589	6,984	1,145	1,481	7,189	323	1,434
Poznan, Poland	9,152	16,116	1,223	342	1,170	2,005	1,407	6,409	5,810	7,533	11,332	1,727	1,357	9,804	7,867	496	2,520	8,177	1,343	187
Prague, Czechoslovakia	9,249	16,279	1,033	203	1,482	1,745	1,492	6,624	5,528	7,345	11,134	1,626	1,092	9,693	7,912	199	2,250	8,185	1,258	397
Praia, Cape Verde Islands	9,192	16,934	4,396	5,147	6,605	3,517	5,340	11,453	3,967	7,073	6,612	4,390	4,137	6,476	7,533	5,065	2,991	7,154	4,635	5,583
Pretoria, South Africa	16,361	10,281	8,786	8,675	9,496	8,322	9,889	9,091	3,523	1,429	10,920	9,392	8,382	12,611	14,715	8,317	8,126	14,291	9,273	8,627
Prince Albert, Canada	2,029	14,601	6,676	7,067	6,865	6,954	5,773	10,682	11,622	14,398	7,730	5,995	7,039	5,206	1,537	7,421	7,075	2,310	6,210	7,306
Prince Edward Island	17,505	8,014	11,255	11,121	11,827	10,773	12,351	9,991	5,899	3,635	10,866	11,856	10,850	13,160	16,359	10,760	10,546	15,689	11,742	11,039
Prince George, Canada	2,058	13,589	7,361	7,618	7,156	7,759	6,340	10,191	12,569	15,125	8,487	6,719	7,751	6,009	2,425	7,980	7,944	3,188	6,879	7,778
Prince Rupert, Canada	2,331	13,180	7,604	7,796	7,221	8,056	6,538	9,891	12,917	15,321	8,892	6,986	8,004	6,439	2,901	8,158	8,272	3,655	7,118	7,919
Providence, Rhode Island	3,799	16,837	5,428	6,152	6,680	5,294	5,049	11,892	9,225	12,290	5,992	4,743	5,656	3,705	2,112	6,429	5,191	1,981	5,092	6,568
Provo, Utah	545	13,619	8,041	8,505	8,371	8,211	7,216	11,921	12,571	15,574	6,801	7,343	8,379	4,381	1,269	8,852	8,254	1,814	7,593	8,772
Puerto Aisen, Chile	9,990	9,608	12,653	13,453	14,885	11,798	13,369	17,762	9,427	10,157	3,720	12,464	12,437	6,222	9,845	13,376	11,275	9,093	12,789	13,896
Puerto Deseado, Argentina	10,506	9,606	12,502	13,261	14,722	11,630	13,310	17,200	8,950	9,579	4,093	12,380	12,253	6,617	10,272	13,150	11,104	9,508	12,684	13,678
Puerto Princesa, Philippines	12,432	6,366	11,159	10,286	8,992	11,926	10,641	3,622	12,126	9,738	18,292	11,487	11,275	16,771	13,339	10,255	12,412	14,105	11,128	9,796
Punta Arenas, Chile	10,778	8,911	13,186	13,930	15,397	12,310	14,007	17,016	9,400	9,728	4,591	13,076	12,928	7,092	10,703	13,805	11,784	9,955	13,376	14,336
Pusan, South Korea	9,698	8,672	9,370	8,624	7,159	10,247	8,512	3,600	12,642	11,368	16,352	9,454	9,629	13,987	10,390	8,737	10,773	11,165	9,167	8,208
Pyongyang, North Korea	9,606	9,168	8,846	8,100	6,635	9,722	7,996	3,330	12,228	11,146	16,272	8,936	9,104	13,820	10,175	8,214	10,248	10,953	8,646	7,685
Qamdo, China	11,825	9,530	7,918	7,039	5,794	8,674	7,494	613	9,781	8,417	17,810	8,286	8,024	15,449	11,907	7,003	9,161	12,641	7,917	6,547
Qandahar, Afghanistan	12,504	11,608	5,705	4,838	4,095	6,270	5,753	2,435	6,845	6,089	15,646	6,267	5,668	14,337	11,788	4,669	6,680	12,313	5,883	4,358
Qiqian, China	8,816	10,679	7,425	6,729	5,255	8,308	6,517	3,494	11,413	11,024	15,274	7,464	7,711	12,747	9,082	6,882	8,832	9,851	7,191	6,349
Qom, Iran	12,032	12,921	4,415	3,590	3,184	4,904	4,661	3,808	5,738	5,679	14,223	5,032	4,328	13,093	11,016	3,370	5,289	11,425	4,658	3,143
Quebec, Canada	3,797	16,923	5,114	5,789	6,220	5,072	4,633	11,353	9,270	12,272	6,545	4,415	5,375	4,231	2,142	6,085	5,027	2,214	4,745	6,182
Quetta, Pakistan	12,654	11,417	5,895	5,031	4,287	6,454	5,947	2,324	6,911	6,048	15,813	6,461	5,855	14,531	11,965	4,859	6,860	12,496	6,077	4,551
Quito, Ecuador	5,529	13,516	9,207	10,086	11,062	8,637	9,329	16,568	9,791	12,416	1,318	8,684	9,233	1,236	4,903	10,235	8,249	4,128	9,070	10,577
Rabaul, Papua New Guinea	10,527	4,153	14,339	13,601	12,137	15,220	13,400	7,503	15,872	12,944	14,297	14,351	14,607	13,910	12,089	13,700	15,745	12,604	14,100	13,177
Raiatea (Uturoa)	6,991	6,426	15,566	15,910	15,209	15,695	14,628	13,545	17,254	16,560	7,995	14,873	15,911	8,088	8,513	16,272	15,625	8,456	15,105	16,038
Raleigh, North Carolina	3,274	16,034	6,335	7,068	7,583	6,161	5,965	12,684	9,815	12,924	5,296	5,655	6,550	2,889	1,672	7,343	6,022	1,246	6,006	7,486
Rangiroa (Avatoru)	6,612	6,862	15,196	15,596	15,008	15,281	14,305	13,821	17,043	16,802	7,624	14,497	15,526	7,648	8,107	15,956	15,194	8,030	14,745	15,765
Rangoon, Burma	13,287	8,307	9,033	8,145	7,068	9,690	8,801	1,516	9,656	7,655	19,126	9,501	9,061	17,041	13,491	8,038	10,128	14,233	9,118	7,648
Raoul Is., Kermadec Islands	9,774	3,423	17,752	17,416	16,000	18,377	16,564	11,645	16,716	14,142	10,395	17,263	18,164	11,021	11,399	17,651	18,543	11,436	17,291	17,128
Rarotonga (Avarua)	7,897	5,430	16,402	16,595	15,633	16,639	15,365	12,944	17,427	15,845	8,794	15,734	16,777	9,065	9,463	16,952	16,610	9,440	15,923	16,614
Rawson, Argentina	10,156	10,084	12,080	12,861	14,309	11,216	12,853	17,418	8,794	9,659	3,650	11,931	11,847	6,176	9,842	12,768	10,691	9,073	12,243	13,293
Recife, Brazil	9,670	14,524	7,227	7,977	9,438	6,350	8,125	13,921	5,009	7,512	4,638	7,176	6,969	5,696	8,306	7,879	5,824	7,663	7,446	8,403
Regina, Canada	1,798	14,583	6,832	7,260	7,114	7,067	5,968	10,998	11,653	14,504	7,425	6,142	7,184	4,904	1,234	7,610	7,161	2,011	6,373	7,516
Reykjavik, Iceland	6,603	17,379	2,094	2,446	2,692	2,616	1,166	8,105	7,523	9,858	9,633	1,491	2,492	7,633	5,299	2,794	2,954	5,648	1,610	2,745
Rhodes, Greece	11,124	14,806	2,688	2,078	2,615	2,964	3,364	5,820	4,437	5,611	12,161	3,384	2,477	11,201	9,776	1,741	3,286	10,010	3,063	1,837
Richmond, Virginia	3,343	16,206	6,127	6,854	7,360	5,971	5,745	12,472	9,713	12,813	5,489	5,445	6,349	3,102	1,698	7,131	5,844	1,369	5,794	7,269
Riga, USSR	8,999	15,670	1,790	991	488	2,633	1,503	5,919	6,407	7,912	11,798	2,135	1,998	10,097	7,842	1,167	3,156	8,229	1,758	652
Ringkobing, Denmark	8,473	16,648	913	597	1,362	1,797	715	6,898	6,177	8,122	10,820	1,157	1,240	9,172	7,170	959	2,320	7,479	782	879
Rio Branco, Brazil	7,117	13,293	9,304	10,189	11,408	8,581	9,713	16,927	8,628	10,981	1,037	8,916	9,225	2,779	6,358	10,252	8,115	5,581	9,287	10,684
Rio Cuarto, Argentina	9,316	11,146	11,146	11,969	13,375	10,306	11,831	17,667	8,532	9,912	2,670	10,932	10,952	5,169	8,836	11,920	9,788	8,060	11,263	12,428
Rio de Janeiro, Brazil	9,988	12,805	9,094	9,846	11,308	8,219	9,964	15,437	6,254	8,112	3,776	9,019	8,839	5,662	8,960	9,742	7,692	8,218	9,301	10,269
Rio Gallegos, Argentina	10,707	9,114	12,984	13,732	15,198	12,109	13,803	17,076	9,261	9,675	4,447	12,872	12,728	6,957	10,584	13,610	11,583	9,831	13,173	14,141
Rio Grande, Brazil	10,008	11,638	10,402	11,170	12,625	9,532	11,225	16,514	7,382	8,818	3,380	10,288	10,159	5,700	9,279	11,075	9,006	8,505	10,586	11,599
Riyadh, Saudi Arabia	13,012	12,616	4,867	4,161	4,122	5,151	5,376	4,409	4,827	4,497	13,968	5,548	4,675	13,360	11,835	3,865	5,434	12,145	5,205	3,796
Road Town, Brit. Virgin Isls.	5,305	16,073	6,653	7,527	8,517	6,124	6,783	14,084	8,323	11,368	3,639	6,121	6,699	2,194	3,935	7,688	5,775	3,276	6,507	8,016
Roanoke, Virginia	3,130	15,989	6,316	7,031	7,500	6,176	5,904	12,538	9,933	13,035	5,468	5,629	6,545	3,037	1,500	7,313	6,057	1,147	5,974	7,439
Robinson Crusoe Island, Chile	8,599	10,460	12,050	12,917	14,221	11,264	12,554	18,976	9,881	11,159	2,398	11,726	11,916	4,849	8,445	12,925	10,764	7,698	12,086	13,401
Rochester, New York	3,284	16,371	5,758	6,435	6,840	5,693	5,273	11,861	9,743	12,794	6,113	5,060	6,013	3,712	1,598	6,731	5,625	1,574	5,391	6,826
Rockhampton, Australia	11,880	2,024	16,131	15,288	13,904	16,948	15,369	8,648	15,111	11,995	13,531	16,307	16,295	14,168	13,555	15,286	17,447	13,882	16,001	14,810
Rome, Italy	9,857	16,289	1,277	1,045	2,345	1,489	2,234	6,991	4,608	6,562	10,858	1,983	1,002	9,728	8,409	725	1,866	8,583	1,722	1,216
Rosario, Argentina	9,523	11,294	10,928	11,736	13,160	10,077	11,657	17,324	8,190	9,586	2,855	10,744	10,718	5,313	8,967	11,672	9,556	8,189	11,065	12,186
Roseau, Dominica	5,783	16,028	6,681	7,566	8,639	6,091	6,913	14,228	7,952	10,963	3,482	6,194	6,691	2,421	4,424	7,700	5,706	3,762	6,577	8,061
Rostock, East Germany	8,805	16,434	971	310	1,272	1,821	1,047	6,698	5,958	7,817	11,030	1,385	1,202	9,450	7,502	661	2,347	7,806	999	557
Rostov-na-Donu, USSR	10,434	14,405	2,909	2,030	1,541	3,560	2,991	4,790	5,962	6,805	12,998	3,453	2,924	11,526	9,344	1,899	4,025	9,743	3,069	1,544
Rotterdam, Netherlands	8,628	16,970	409	547	1,823	1,283	981	7,253	5,731	7,829	10,482	898	717	8,972	7,238	807	1,809	7,482	534	1,030
Rouyn, Canada	3,233	16,350	5,528	6,145	6,430	5,561	4,933	11,323	9,864	12,844	6,680	4,822	5,817	4,255	1,622	6,459	5,554	1,857	5,129	6,507
Sacramento, California	622	12,801	8,695	9,083	8,784	8,938	7,789	11,731	13,414	16,363	7,262	8,010	9,053	4,965	2,135	9,439	9,018	2,635	8,231	9,305
Saginaw, Michigan	2,774	15,879	6,149	6,787	7,085	6,136	5,585	11,896	10,256	13,300	6,183	5,446	6,424	3,706	1,092	7,096	6,093	1,203	5,762	7,156
Saint Denis, Reunion	18,083	8,641	9,513	9,034	9,242	9,403	10,324	6,771	5,528	2,422	13,682	10,215	9,187	15,433	16,581	8,687	9,419	16,514	9,953	8,774
Saint George's, Grenada	5,960	15,716	6,978	7,866	8,968	6,361	7,246	14,556	7,964	10,923	3,156	6,509	6,972	2,336	4,667	7,987	5,959	3,977	6,891	8,362
Saint John, Canada	4,201	17,316	4,857	5,574	6,116	4,750	4,474	11,394	8,848	11,868	6,443	4,169	5,093	4,233	2,529	5,854	4,673	2,510	4,515	5,990
Saint John's, Antigua	5,633	16,154	6,565	7,446	8,493	5,996	6,764	14,080	8,017	11,051	3,632	6,062	6,588	2,421	4,247	7,590	5,624	3,598	6,446	7,940
Saint John's, Canada	5,189	18,305	3,828	4,580	5,260	3,695	3,559	10,721	7,928	10,885	7,031	3,153	4,048	5,044	3,544	4,843	3,628	3,565	3,513	5,016
Saint Louis, Missouri	2,219	15,208	6,896	7,537	7,808	6,862	6,331	12,446	10,824	13,912	5,773	6,193	7,166	3,250	608	7,846	6,797	468	6,511	7,904
Saint Paul, Minnesota	2,097	15,221	6,608	7,171	7,295	6,685	5,920	11,733	10,966	13,975	6,516	5,901	6,914	3,992	544	7,500	6,689	1,135	6,189	7,500

Distances in Kilometers	Las Vegas, Nevada	Launceston, Australia	Le Havre, France	Leipzig, East Germany	Leningrad, USSR	Leon, Spain	Lerwick, United Kingdom	Lhasa, China	Libreville, Gabon	Lilongwe, Malawi	Lima, Peru	Limerick, Ireland	Limoges, France	Limon, Costa Rica	Lincoln, Nebraska	Linz, Austria	Lisbon, Portugal	Little Rock, Arkansas	Liverpool, United Kingdom	Lodz, Poland
Saint Peter Port, UK	8,441	17,503	193	1,075	2,379	797	1,194	7,814	5,557	7,879	9,927	556	492	8,485	6,973	1,239	1,303	7,155	443	1,572
Saipan (Susupe)	9,827	6,264	12,089	11,375	9,904	12,972	11,147	5,794	14,925	12,730	15,402	12,098	12,370	13,977	11,096	11,500	13,496	11,776	11,844	10,970
Salalah, Oman	14,013	11,491	6,008	5,294	5,138	6,277	6,488	4,014	5,226	4,090	14,754	6,689	5,814	14,445	12,932	5,004	6,539	13,271	6,343	4,914
Salem, Oregon	1,180	13,077	8,186	8,512	8,129	8,501	7,222	11,053	13,159	15,940	7,824	7,518	8,560	5,439	2,190	8,872	8,629	2,843	7,711	8,704
Salt Lake City, Utah	583	13,630	8,008	8,466	8,322	8,186	7,177	11,860	12,567	15,560	6,858	7,311	8,348	4,434	1,281	8,814	8,234	1,847	7,558	8,730
Salta, Argentina	8,533	11,948	10,465	11,318	12,669	9,658	11,058	17,646	8,507	10,274	1,868	10,188	10,309	4,297	7,951	11,309	9,152	7,173	10,536	11,795
Salto, Uruguay	9,565	11,544	10,641	11,442	12,873	9,786	11,389	17,063	7,905	9,379	2,902	10,470	10,425	5,303	8,932	11,374	9,263	8,155	10,787	11,889
Salvador, Brazil	9,689	13,954	7,889	8,647	10,105	7,014	8,765	14,534	5,496	7,796	4,186	7,817	7,637	5,538	8,438	8,552	6,488	7,751	8,096	9,076
Salzburg, Austria	9,380	16,363	968	393	1,750	1,567	1,652	6,780	5,265	7,147	10,998	1,629	924	9,642	8,003	110	2,053	8,243	1,292	638
Samsun, Turkey	10,950	14,394	2,946	2,144	2,115	3,442	3,304	5,049	5,277	6,124	12,838	3,578	2,856	11,621	9,755	1,901	3,849	10,090	3,211	1,733
San Antonio, Texas	1,727	14,060	8,159	8,810	9,056	8,085	7,604	13,389	11,728	14,845	5,135	7,459	8,418	2,686	1,275	9,118	7,984	832	7,782	9,178
San Cristobal, Venezuela	5,366	14,640	8,084	8,962	9,953	7,525	8,218	15,501	9,096	11,946	2,255	7,562	8,115	1,213	4,391	9,114	7,148	3,624	7,947	9,453
San Diego, California	426	12,760	9,002	9,473	9,313	9,147	8,185	12,491	13,342	16,420	6,535	8,302	9,335	4,308	2,030	9,820	9,165	2,311	8,557	9,739
San Francisco, California	671	12,684	8,815	9,200	8,891	9,059	7,906	11,770	13,529	16,483	7,265	8,130	9,174	4,994	2,237	9,556	9,138	2,717	8,351	9,419
San Jose, Costa Rica	4,274	13,931	8,759	9,596	10,362	8,331	8,664	15,595	10,399	13,271	2,553	8,156	8,865	115	3,641	9,805	8,023	2,872	8,537	10,064
San Juan, Argentina	8,935	11,142	11,244	12,088	13,458	10,424	11,861	18,066	8,896	10,340	2,329	10,985	11,074	4,850	8,520	12,063	9,913	7,747	11,329	12,559
San Juan, Puerto Rico	5,171	15,966	6,759	7,630	8,596	6,245	6,862	14,151	8,481	11,524	3,582	6,218	6,815	2,050	3,825	7,797	5,904	3,153	6,603	8,117
San Luis Potosi, Mexico	2,072	13,403	8,930	9,610	9,896	8,800	8,422	14,130	12,101	15,178	4,598	8,235	9,169	2,340	2,110	9,908	8,659	1,634	8,569	9,990
San Marino, San Marino	9,684	16,341	1,127	821	2,145	1,469	2,025	6,930	4,832	6,767	10,892	1,832	911	9,683	8,257	507	1,892	8,453	1,548	1,015
San Miguel de Tucuman, Argen.	8,720	11,751	10,634	11,481	12,846	9,818	11,249	17,689	8,515	10,191	2,050	10,372	10,469	4,505	8,164	11,463	9,309	7,387	10,716	11,954
San Salvador, El Salvador	3,591	13,803	8,816	9,615	10,239	8,476	8,589	15,208	10,944	13,888	3,148	8,175	8,965	787	3,093	9,854	8,217	2,352	8,546	10,061
Sanaa, Yemen	13,906	12,196	5,488	4,895	5,076	5,605	6,166	5,041	4,163	3,441	13,688	6,192	5,229	13,573	12,599	4,564	5,793	12,813	5,883	4,597
Santa Cruz, Bolivia	8,098	12,748	9,702	10,566	11,891	8,912	10,262	17,103	8,191	10,263	1,623	9,402	9,565	3,772	7,357	10,575	8,414	6,581	9,755	11,049
Santa Cruz, Tenerife	8,930	17,931	2,720	3,480	4,931	1,841	3,702	9,975	4,138	7,144	7,928	2,762	2,465	7,227	7,248	3,421	1,315	7,078	2,977	3,928
Santa Fe, New Mexico	832	13,810	8,104	8,652	8,677	8,172	7,386	12,557	12,258	15,345	6,095	7,398	8,411	3,670	991	8,985	8,155	1,248	7,681	8,963
Santa Rosa, Argentina	9,620	10,793	11,452	12,260	13,684	10,602	12,170	17,610	8,591	9,799	3,007	11,261	11,243	5,521	9,191	12,195	10,080	8,417	11,586	12,710
Santa Rosalia, Mexico	1,019	12,804	9,203	9,757	9,750	9,244	8,490	13,230	13,096	16,214	5,783	8,497	9,504	3,617	2,072	10,090	9,200	2,075	8,784	10,066
Santarem, Brazil	7,571	14,674	7,779	8,650	9,957	7,008	8,330	15,319	7,146	9,790	2,685	7,467	7,658	3,429	6,407	8,678	6,521	5,685	7,821	9,138
Santiago del Estero, Argentina	8,862	11,692	10,664	11,505	12,883	9,841	11,301	17,619	8,436	10,070	2,193	10,416	10,491	4,644	8,301	11,479	9,329	7,523	10,757	11,975
Santiago, Chile	8,989	10,860	11,536	12,381	13,749	10,717	12,145	18,248	9,120	10,461	2,458	11,273	11,368	4,984	8,647	12,357	10,206	7,879	11,618	12,852
Santo Domingo, Dominican Rep.	4,836	15,685	7,033	7,893	8,799	6,555	7,069	14,307	8,880	11,918	3,465	6,467	7,108	1,698	3,559	8,076	6,232	2,855	6,852	8,374
Sao Paulo de Olivenca, Brazil	6,510	13,855	8,802	9,691	10,842	8,127	9,125	16,423	8,716	11,281	1,316	8,368	8,759	2,169	5,664	9,784	7,686	4,890	8,746	10,188
Sao Paulo, Brazil	9,770	12,676	9,317	10,088	11,541	8,448	10,150	15,787	6,606	8,443	3,458	9,210	9,076	5,429	8,806	9,999	7,922	8,053	9,504	10,521
Sao Tome, Sao Tome & Principe	12,801	13,973	5,485	5,673	6,913	4,841	6,669	9,452	302	3,376	9,349	5,974	5,069	9,987	11,115	5,365	4,549	10,817	5,953	5,823
Sapporo, Japan	8,318	9,373	9,079	8,454	6,991	9,961	8,067	4,673	13,233	12,484	14,976	9,015	9,401	12,615	9,049	8,639	10,474	9,820	8,787	8,109
Sarajevo, Yugoslavia	9,984	15,873	1,529	947	1,959	1,947	2,240	6,468	4,895	6,590	11,365	2,217	1,373	10,151	8,609	590	2,365	8,841	1,893	884
Saratov, USSR	10,113	14,155	3,209	2,323	1,353	3,955	3,031	4,424	6,627	7,358	13,310	3,655	3,304	11,629	9,152	2,289	4,450	9,617	3,271	1,828
Saskatoon, Canada	1,895	14,508	6,802	7,198	6,998	7,072	5,904	10,784	11,720	14,516	7,656	6,120	7,164	5,136	1,467	7,552	7,187	2,244	6,337	7,438
Schefferville, Canada	4,195	17,122	4,444	5,035	5,336	4,548	3,818	10,413	9,096	11,947	7,470	3,738	4,752	5,171	2,690	5,354	4,602	2,971	4,031	5,393
Seattle, Washington	1,401	13,276	7,913	8,225	7,830	8,247	6,936	10,821	12,950	15,677	7,983	7,250	8,291	5,560	2,171	8,585	8,389	2,871	7,436	8,411
Sendai, Japan	8,664	8,845	9,549	8,896	7,427	10,432	8,560	4,643	13,470	12,449	15,275	9,510	9,859	12,994	9,482	9,066	10,950	10,247	9,272	8,534
Seoul, South Korea	9,641	8,983	9,041	8,294	6,829	9,917	8,188	3,423	12,381	11,227	16,311	9,129	9,299	13,886	10,256	8,408	10,443	11,033	8,839	7,879
Sept-Iles, Canada	4,172	17,264	4,620	5,278	5,703	4,620	4,115	10,886	8,971	11,913	6,974	3,918	4,894	4,714	2,564	5,579	4,609	2,711	4,241	5,667
Sevastopol, USSR	10,521	14,747	2,573	1,742	1,719	3,135	2,874	5,260	5,445	6,487	12,571	3,183	2,522	11,249	9,322	1,529	3,572	9,662	2,810	1,310
Seville, Spain	9,083	17,675	1,433	2,116	3,581	580	2,555	8,644	4,393	7,045	9,200	1,711	1,114	8,202	7,477	2,044	314	7,485	1,797	2,553
Shanghai, China	10,516	8,456	9,361	8,557	7,128	10,214	8,619	2,905	12,068	10,580	17,182	9,537	9,574	14,769	11,134	8,622	10,736	11,912	9,218	8,108
Sheffield, United Kingdom	8,218	17,331	445	969	2,056	1,235	756	7,585	5,960	8,186	10,137	484	861	8,561	6,809	1,244	1,730	7,046	100	1,428
Shenyang, China	9,521	9,520	8,481	7,736	6,270	9,357	7,633	3,197	11,949	11,007	16,159	8,572	8,740	13,667	10,004	7,853	9,883	10,781	8,281	7,323
Shiraz, Iran	12,612	12,475	4,893	4,097	3,762	5,319	5,209	3,717	5,593	5,226	14,483	5,533	4,772	13,550	11,590	3,852	5,669	11,987	5,165	3,668
Sibiu, Romania	10,054	15,489	1,842	1,063	1,622	2,388	2,305	5,984	5,234	6,691	11,828	2,481	1,774	10,519	8,759	798	2,834	9,047	2,121	746
Singapore	14,232	6,432	10,888	10,004	8,974	11,491	10,708	3,418	10,508	7,904	18,810	11,387	10,882	18,551	14,903	9,871	11,896	15,680	11,002	9,510
Sioux Falls, South Dakota	1,770	14,896	6,928	7,480	7,564	7,014	6,221	11,861	11,281	14,300	6,473	6,222	7,238	3,947	302	7,811	7,019	1,049	6,505	7,801
Skelleftea, Sweden	8,181	15,766	2,095	1,581	723	2,978	1,243	6,128	7,204	8,800	11,589	2,146	2,428	9,659	7,113	1,876	3,496	7,560	1,845	1,452
Skopje, Yugoslavia	10,294	15,576	1,850	1,247	2,082	2,222	2,541	6,265	4,765	6,326	11,601	2,540	1,675	10,448	8,929	899	2,612	9,164	2,215	1,095
Socotra Island (Tamrida)	14,483	11,189	6,373	5,691	5,599	6,588	6,908	4,260	5,102	3,696	14,722	7,063	6,157	14,662	13,365	5,388	6,818	13,675	6,728	5,329
Sofia, Bulgaria	10,313	15,456	1,936	1,268	1,975	2,357	2,553	6,102	4,886	6,365	11,755	2,614	1,791	10,569	8,974	940	2,760	9,228	2,277	1,049
Songkhla, Thailand	13,933	7,171	10,154	9,268	8,227	10,775	9,961	2,677	10,141	7,743	19,416	10,644	10,159	10,062	14,403	9,143	11,192	15,171	10,260	8,773
Sorong, Indonesia	12,175	4,765	12,909	12,051	10,704	13,706	12,283	5,439	13,559	10,801	16,592	13,175	13,054	16,109	13,480	12,042	14,203	14,155	12,834	11,569
South Georgia Island	12,498	9,397	12,006	12,557	13,983	11,135	13,073	15,058	7,382	7,494	5,862	12,134	11,659	8,336	11,982	12,334	10,635	11,204	12,334	12,853
South Pole	14,006	5,414	15,489	15,690	16,649	14,723	16,675	13,284	10,047	8,457	8,670	15,842	15,082	11,108	14,523	15,356	14,291	13,849	15,925	15,740
South Sandwich Islands	13,243	8,998	12,137	12,597	13,960	11,291	13,262	14,366	7,188	6,956	6,609	12,349	11,765	9,079	12,716	12,340	10,813	11,938	12,507	12,839
Split, Yugoslavia	9,917	16,020	1,413	919	2,050	1,790	2,197	6,632	4,828	6,607	11,203	2,110	1,229	10,005	8,521	557	2,203	8,737	1,800	943
Spokane, Washington	1,291	13,604	7,685	8,038	7,723	7,981	6,745	10,981	12,631	15,425	7,727	7,010	8,054	5,274	1,814	8,396	8,103	2,531	7,213	8,249
Spoleto, Italy	9,799	16,292	1,228	953	2,253	1,497	2,155	6,945	4,702	6,638	10,893	1,934	978	9,730	8,361	631	1,895	8,546	1,662	1,124
Springbok, South Africa	15,617	10,571	8,944	8,985	9,993	8,355	10,106	10,167	3,444	2,386	9,828	9,478	8,528	11,609	14,079	8,643	8,074	13,550	9,424	9,020
Springfield, Illinois	2,268	15,301	6,773	7,407	7,670	6,751	6,197	12,315	10,763	13,840	5,886	6,070	7,047	3,366	609	7,718	6,695	607	6,385	7,772
Springfield, Massachusetts	3,699	16,748	5,490	6,205	6,710	5,370	5,090	11,887	9,325	12,388	6,013	4,802	5,724	3,701	2,012	6,487	5,274	1,897	5,148	6,616
Srinagar, India	12,159	11,155	6,172	5,285	4,307	6,825	6,032	1,615	7,737	6,869	16,268	6,665	6,195	14,599	11,665	5,171	7,272	12,268	6,280	4,789
Stanley, Falkland Islands	11,217	9,409	12,485	13,179	14,652	11,601	13,397	16,473	8,499	8,913	4,726	12,449	12,197	7,252	10,919	13,024	11,078	10,149	12,721	13,557
Stara Zagora, Bulgaria	10,437	15,266	2,115	1,412	1,972	2,550	2,681	5,919	4,930	6,300	11,945	2,785	1,980	10,758	9,121	1,101	2,952	9,388	2,441	1,137
Stockholm, Sweden	8,579	16,013	1,588	964	691	2,467	1,080	6,272	6,580	8,250	11,439	1,806	1,874	9,678	7,401	1,252	2,992	7,785	1,449	849
Stornoway, United Kingdom	7,648	17,374	1,059	1,422	2,082	1,738	368	7,670	6,563	8,799	10,040	634	1,472	8,287	6,288	1,754	2,178	6,574	574	1,789
Strasbourg, France	9,054	16,761	566	447	1,917	1,231	1,409	7,137	5,344	7,392	10,626	1,241	579	9,241	7,645	486	1,742	7,866	925	907
Stuttgart, West Germany	9,111	16,656	665	361	1,834	1,335	1,430	7,030	5,361	7,363	10,734	1,326	682	9,342	7,715	381	1,842	7,945	996	804
Subic, Philippines	11,910	6,821	10,785	9,927	8,586	11,583	10,197	3,404	12,239	10,039	18,139	11,069	10,931	16,256	12,764	9,923	12,084	13,533	10,721	9,445
Suchow, China	10,511	8,923	8,850	8,039	6,618	9,698	8,132	2,511	11,614	10,285	17,159	9,041	9,057	14,665	10,999	8,101	10,220	11,775	8,717	7,588
Sucre, Bolivia	8,053	12,529	9,944	10,811	12,125	9,160	10,484	17,365	8,426	10,441	1,479	9,633	9,812	3,756	7,380	10,825	8,664	6,602	9,989	11,296
Sudbury, Canada	3,051	16,176	5,760	6,384	6,673	5,776	5,176	11,534	10,014	13,019	6,496	5,055	6,044	4,050	1,410	6,697	5,755	1,613	5,365	6,749
Suez, Egypt	11,947	14,109	3,480	2,901	3,333	3,662	4,187	5,595	4,088	4,865	12,555	4,182	3,236	11,842	10,592	2,561	3,921	10,807	3,873	2,649
Sundsvall, Sweden	8,285	15,997	1,779	1,270	748	2,663	1,017	6,303	6,909	8,588	11,409	1,872	2,107	9,555	7,149	1,579	3,183	7,561	1,552	1,191
Surabaya, Indonesia	14,208	5,084	12,245	11,359	10,283	12,858	12,011	4,695	11,493	8,639	17,617	12,726	12,247	18,273	15,287	11,233	13,261	16,036	12,343	10,863
Suva, Fiji	9,211	3,938	16,522	16,127	14,716	17,266	15,339	10,742	17,709	14,760	11,099	16,124	16,922	11,254	10,892	16,366	17,611	11,079	16,087	15,846
Sverdlovsk, USSR	9,689	13,538	3,987	3,150	1,791	4,813	3,486	3,843	7,730	8,234	13,872	4,288	4,167	11,883	8,973	3,210	5,331	9,539	3,927	2,694
Svobodnyy, USSR	8,519	10,447	7,789	7,126	5,657	8,673	6,832	3,893	11,917	11,511	15,088	7,783	8,092	12,574	8,905	7,298	9,193	9,680	7,528	6,766
Sydney, Australia	12,424	910	17,078	16,196	14,904	17,779	16,466	9,455	14,575	11,543	12,815	17,377	17,150	13,916	14,109	16,124	18,182	14,285	17,037	15,701
Sydney, Canada	4,647	17,772	4,410	5,146	5,754	4,285	4,081	11,127	8,423	11,422	6,663	3,728	4,636	4,557	2,984	5,417	4,206	2,976	4,082	5,572
Syktyvkar, USSR	9,086	14,261	3,363	2,585	1,131	4,223	2,749	4,609	7,635	8,520	13,112	3,591	3,594	11,112	8,273	2,716	4,748	8,813	3,246	2,183
Szeged, Hungary	9,842	15,801	1,536	802	1,658	2,079	2,083	6,282	5,190	6,811	11,522	2,187	1,461	10,209	8,512	498	2,533	8,779	1,835	612
Szombathely, Hungary	9,596	16,088	1,244	549	1,669	1,819	1,844	6,529	5,237	6,993	11,259	1,898	1,187	9,920	8,244	210	2,290	8,499	1,550	543
Tabriz, Iran	11,565	13,473	3,857	3,029	2,681	4,366	4,109	4,208	5,624	5,910	13,738	4,471	3,780	12,535	10,494	2,812	4,766	10,884	4,096	2,583
Tacheng, China	10,645	11,645	5,849	4,987	3,683	6,645	5,374	2,025	8,727	8,323	15,728	6,180	5,993	13,567	10,304	4,995	7,151	10,966	5,816	4,507
Tahiti (Papeete)	6,962	6,527	15,545	15,934	15,299	15,628	14,644	13,762	17,044	16,500	7,787	14,846	15,877	7,923	8,457	16,294	15,532	8,374	15,093	16,088
Taipei, Taiwan	11,001	7,820	9,927	9,101	7,698	10,765	9,233	3,042	12,211	10,439	17,599	10,138	10,118	15,311	11,718	9,144	11,282	12,494	9,809	8,640
Taiyuan, China	10,456	9,457	8,279	7,464	6,048	9,125	7,583	2,179	11,135	9,997	16,992	8,484	8,482	14,465	10,799	7,523	9,645	11,568	8,155	7,011
Tallahassee, Florida	2,931	15,299	7,122	7,860	8,357	6,926	6,753	13,336	10,352	13,469	4,766	6,444	7,330	2,267	1,606	8,133	6,764	889	6,797	8,277
Tallinn, USSR	8,787	15,632	1,923	1,195	315	2,790	1,448	5,892	6,681	8,177	11,820	2,184	2,173	10,038	7,670	1,412	3,316	8,082	1,822	916
Tamanrasset, Algeria	10,993	15,899	3,002	3,219	4,556	2,426	4,183	8,391	2,515	5,103	9,782	3,529	2,586	9,444	9,350	2,937	2,249	9,271	3,476	3,431
Tampa, Florida	3,202	15,311	7,187	7,950	8,516	6,941	6,880	13,594	10,183	13,293	4,464	6,522	7,375	1,988	1,932	8,210	6,751	1,200	6,883	8,381
Tampere, Finland	8,562	15,676	1,983	1,333	396	2,863	1,355	5,962	6,887	8,415	11,749	2,165	2,268	9,907	7,465	1,586	3,388	7,892	1,822	1,117
Tanami, Australia	13,523	2,891	14,504	13,615	12,434	15,158	14,121	6,879	13,182	10,096	15,418	14,924	14,537	16,350	15,075	13,515	15,571	15,600	14,550	13,118

Distances in Kilometers	Las Vegas, Nevada	Launceston, Australia	Le Havre, France	Leipzig, East Germany	Leningrad, USSR	Leon, Spain	Lerwick, United Kingdom	Lhasa, China	Libreville, Gabon	Lilongwe, Malawi	Lima, Peru	Limerick, Ireland	Limoges, France	Limon, Costa Rica	Lincoln, Nebraska	Linz, Austria	Lisbon, Portugal	Little Rock, Arkansas	Liverpool, United Kingdom	Lodz, Poland
Tangier, Morocco	9,208	17,596	1,597	2,249	3,719	755	2,728	8,712	4,227	6,908	9,153	1,887	1,262	8,220	7,591	2,156	438	7,580	1,970	2,673
Tarawa (Betio)	8,305	5,406	14,328	13,890	12,485	15,135	13,165	9,151	18,189	15,327	12,228	14,016	14,714	11,530	9,947	14,131	15,563	10,367	13,922	13,615
Tashkent, USSR	11,410	12,051	5,296	4,407	3,372	5,992	5,100	2,354	7,510	7,131	15,408	5,759	5,350	13,659	10,797	4,323	6,461	11,373	5,376	3,909
Tbilisi, USSR	11,143	13,783	3,532	2,680	2,258	4,098	3,714	4,346	5,786	6,267	13,523	4,120	3,489	12,199	10,077	2,492	4,524	10,476	3,741	2,216
Tegucigalpa, Honduras	3,704	13,993	8,640	9,448	10,105	8,285	8,441	15,160	10,728	13,681	3,102	8,006	8,782	643	3,101	9,681	8,018	2,343	8,380	9,899
Tehran, Iran	11,932	12,942	4,386	3,550	3,098	4,895	4,600	3,755	5,839	5,802	14,244	4,993	4,310	13,063	10,933	3,340	5,289	11,351	4,616	3,096
Tel Aviv, Israel	11,829	14,046	3,459	2,814	3,114	3,721	4,082	5,333	4,402	5,097	12,767	4,152	3,250	11,944	10,524	2,492	4,017	10,776	3,825	2,517
Telegraph Creek, Canada	2,689	13,342	7,295	7,452	6,839	7,782	6,207	9,536	12,671	14,971	9,175	6,693	7,699	6,694	3,088	7,814	8,022	3,858	6,808	7,559
Teresina, Brazil	8,777	14,758	7,329	8,144	9,561	6,482	8,094	14,479	5,842	8,438	3,843	7,165	7,127	4,761	7,471	8,099	5,963	6,800	7,475	8,603
Ternate, Indonesia	12,391	5,082	12,517	11,650	10,329	13,297	11,941	4,997	13,130	10,430	17,059	12,814	12,645	16,457	13,611	11,628	13,787	14,316	12,464	11,164
The Valley, Anguilla	5,467	16,150	6,574	7,452	8,470	6,026	6,737	14,049	8,156	11,199	3,667	6,056	6,609	2,331	4,082	7,604	5,667	3,432	6,441	7,943
Thessaloniki, Greece	10,487	15,412	2,037	1,439	2,204	2,374	2,733	6,176	4,661	6,149	11,714	2,730	1,847	10,610	9,123	1,093	2,744	9,356	2,408	1,264
Thimphu, Bhutan	12,490	9,653	7,706	6,817	5,707	8,396	7,439	271	9,035	7,583	17,815	8,152	7,758	15,780	12,408	6,731	8,855	13,108	7,771	6,320
Thunder Bay, Canada	2,508	15,597	6,141	6,694	6,819	6,243	5,440	11,360	10,626	13,586	6,804	5,435	6,454	4,298	1,024	7,024	6,268	1,536	5,717	7,020
Tientsin, China	10,095	9,422	8,416	7,626	6,185	9,276	7,655	2,608	11,509	10,425	16,695	8,575	8,641	14,179	10,509	7,709	9,800	11,283	8,260	7,188
Tijuana, Mexico	439	12,760	9,011	9,485	9,329	9,152	8,196	12,514	13,337	16,418	6,512	8,310	9,342	4,287	2,030	9,831	9,169	2,302	8,567	9,751
Tiksi, USSR	7,064	12,619	5,980	5,497	4,142	6,839	4,886	5,192	10,957	11,646	13,163	5,820	6,343	10,650	7,033	5,754	7,331	7,780	5,631	5,257
Timbuktu, Mali	10,796	16,066	3,642	4,066	5,488	2,874	4,819	9,493	2,270	5,285	8,745	4,013	3,247	8,647	9,112	3,837	2,505	8,903	4,067	4,360
Tindouf, Algeria	9,609	17,304	2,522	3,134	4,607	1,670	3,645	9,347	3,559	6,460	8,626	2,773	2,177	8,021	7,942	2,996	1,225	7,817	2,887	3,527
Tirane, Albania	10,278	15,684	1,781	1,248	2,189	2,102	2,540	6,415	4,654	6,290	11,458	2,480	1,578	10,338	8,890	889	2,478	9,107	2,170	1,158
Tokyo, Japan	8,915	8,572	9,765	9,092	7,619	10,649	8,797	4,568	13,515	12,343	15,493	9,748	10,066	13,253	9,764	9,250	11,169	10,526	9,501	8,717
Toledo, Spain	9,038	17,588	1,120	1,793	3,257	330	2,265	8,365	4,581	7,131	9,457	1,466	790	8,370	7,460	1,734	459	7,511	1,508	2,237
Topeka, Kansas	1,746	14,790	7,208	7,807	7,976	7,226	6,571	12,367	11,288	14,364	5,978	6,502	7,497	3,455	215	8,128	7,189	565	6,805	8,151
Toronto, Canada	3,142	16,242	5,840	6,503	6,870	5,797	5,326	11,829	9,888	12,932	6,174	5,140	6,104	3,748	1,460	6,804	5,741	1,487	5,466	6,886
Toulouse, France	9,100	17,213	663	1,184	2,655	580	1,850	7,781	4,853	7,175	10,018	1,253	249	8,807	7,589	1,124	1,038	7,717	1,139	1,623
Tours, France	8,771	17,289	239	951	2,369	724	1,426	7,679	5,277	7,553	10,082	887	178	8,727	7,298	1,023	1,250	7,469	720	1,438
Townsville, Australia	11,956	2,458	15,537	14,691	13,313	16,350	14,804	8,059	14,932	11,822	14,100	15,735	15,698	14,587	13,601	14,689	16,850	14,004	15,419	14,212
Trenton, New Jersey	3,535	16,520	5,761	6,480	6,984	5,625	5,367	12,133	9,493	12,573	5,792	5,075	5,989	3,447	1,854	6,760	5,516	1,660	5,422	6,893
Tripoli, Lebanon	11,632	14,089	3,356	2,662	2,862	3,685	3,906	5,182	4,665	5,363	12,858	4,037	3,178	11,925	10,364	2,357	4,014	10,644	3,696	2,329
Tripoli, Libya	10,667	15,876	2,137	2,045	3,255	1,965	3,207	7,251	3,621	5,632	10,754	2,806	1,762	9,989	9,139	1,713	2,112	9,225	2,618	2,155
Tristan da Cunha (Edinburgh)	13,327	11,068	9,666	10,079	11,433	8,847	10,822	13,039	4,712	5,222	6,977	9,946	9,280	9,013	12,167	9,815	8,396	11,466	10,063	10,313
Trondheim, Norway	7,968	16,301	1,669	1,354	1,115	2,536	709	6,644	6,993	8,815	11,069	1,630	2,040	9,190	6,800	1,700	3,042	7,201	1,356	1,404
Trujillo, Peru	6,189	12,789	9,916	10,803	11,854	9,289	10,120	17,412	9,858	12,222	486	9,431	9,907	2,052	5,713	10,925	8,868	4,945	9,815	11,298
Truk Island (Moen)	9,797	5,431	13,129	12,440	10,967	14,014	12,145	6,787	15,776	13,241	14,652	13,094	13,425	13,651	11,236	12,575	14,534	11,840	12,860	12,043
Truro, Canada	4,418	17,535	4,662	5,392	5,972	4,539	4,313	11,304	8,636	11,651	6,508	3,979	4,891	4,351	2,747	5,666	4,457	2,722	4,330	5,814
Tsingtao, China	10,173	9,006	8,853	8,064	6,622	9,714	8,083	2,814	11,852	10,610	16,832	9,006	9,079	14,353	10,693	8,146	10,238	11,471	8,694	7,625
Tsitsihar, China	9,049	10,098	7,992	7,281	5,808	8,874	7,097	3,435	11,796	11,153	15,629	8,043	8,271	13,115	9,446	7,423	9,399	10,221	7,766	6,890
Tubuai Island (Mataura)	7,514	6,149	16,085	16,536	15,945	16,074	15,242	14,018	16,604	15,858	7,712	15,380	16,390	8,115	8,958	16,892	15,913	8,821	15,649	16,716
Tucson, Arizona	584	13,214	8,696	9,227	9,194	8,774	7,953	12,774	12,814	15,917	6,086	7,990	9,008	3,782	1,593	9,564	8,757	1,757	8,268	9,526
Tulsa, Oklahoma	1,728	14,635	7,450	8,070	8,275	7,433	6,846	12,683	11,364	14,463	5,692	6,745	7,727	3,176	522	8,386	7,372	365	7,056	8,425
Tunis, Tunisia	10,159	16,303	1,627	1,620	2,943	1,493	2,719	7,358	4,033	6,142	10,563	2,294	1,250	9,638	8,643	1,321	1,712	8,748	2,110	1,816
Tura, USSR	8,445	12,417	5,638	4,967	3,499	6,522	4,730	3,904	10,006	10,308	14,202	5,675	5,934	11,762	8,257	5,145	7,044	8,971	5,399	4,615
Turin, Italy	9,337	16,739	754	776	2,234	1,097	1,780	7,259	4,951	7,049	10,539	1,459	509	9,286	7,885	623	1,558	8,065	1,210	1,146
Uberlandia, Brazil	9,302	13,138	8,957	9,755	11,189	8,100	9,738	15,764	6,657	8,705	3,173	8,808	8,738	4,978	8,291	9,689	7,577	7,545	9,116	10,203
Ufa, USSR	9,896	13,692	3,692	2,903	1,639	4,564	3,369	3,951	7,354	7,897	13,760	4,117	3,914	11,876	9,101	2,931	5,075	9,636	3,746	2,429
Ujungpandang, Indonesia	13,493	4,875	12,523	11,635	10,448	13,208	12,147	4,893	12,235	9,410	17,390	12,935	12,575	17,503	14,672	11,549	13,650	15,395	12,561	11,138
Ulaanbaatar, Mongolia	9,801	10,661	7,134	6,348	4,903	7,995	6,390	2,438	10,533	9,935	16,011	7,303	7,362	13,516	9,904	6,438	8,520	10,653	6,983	5,914
Ulan-Ude, USSR	9,407	11,016	6,859	6,101	4,639	7,730	6,063	2,816	10,537	10,143	15,572	6,988	7,108	13,078	9,473	6,215	8,257	10,219	6,681	5,685
Uliastay, Mongolia	10,183	11,052	6,603	5,780	4,376	7,442	5,962	2,069	9,781	9,247	16,006	6,839	6,797	13,608	10,103	5,838	7,961	10,823	6,498	5,325
Uranium City, Canada	2,644	14,617	6,213	6,619	6,283	6,695	5,330	9,953	11,506	14,087	8,428	5,666	6,702	5,901	2,244	6,979	6,878	3,005	5,838	6,814
Urumqi, China	10,856	11,158	6,337	5,473	4,172	7,129	5,859	1,601	9,030	8,406	16,193	6,669	6,477	13,972	10,622	5,474	7,633	11,306	6,305	4,991
Ushuaia, Argentina	11,028	8,825	13,198	13,918	15,390	12,318	14,058	16,766	9,259	9,506	4,804	13,119	12,925	7,313	10,935	13,777	11,792	10,184	13,408	14,310
Vaduz, Liechtenstein	9,260	16,621	742	503	1,959	1,293	1,603	7,054	5,183	7,192	10,725	1,434	651	9,394	7,847	380	1,782	8,061	1,128	882
Valencia, Spain	9,302	17,274	1,116	1,644	3,117	559	2,301	8,102	4,442	6,897	9,740	1,598	720	8,685	7,741	1,529	763	7,808	1,564	2,051
Valladolid, Spain	8,865	17,684	951	1,686	3,133	127	2,073	8,330	4,787	7,319	9,471	1,260	668	8,310	7,300	1,666	497	7,369	1,315	2,148
Valletta, Malta	10,485	15,905	1,909	1,720	2,901	1,881	2,921	7,024	3,967	5,882	10,929	2,601	1,567	10,039	8,994	1,377	2,114	9,121	2,378	1,805
Valparaiso, Chile	8,899	10,859	11,558	12,407	13,765	10,744	12,150	18,345	9,205	10,562	2,389	11,284	11,395	4,914	8,573	12,389	10,235	7,807	11,632	12,881
Vancouver, Canada	1,591	13,318	7,797	8,089	7,666	8,152	6,803	10,632	12,894	15,565	8,150	7,140	8,179	5,714	2,268	8,450	8,309	2,989	7,317	8,265
Varna, Bulgaria	10,453	15,119	2,235	1,478	1,865	2,717	2,714	5,722	5,089	6,362	12,131	2,887	2,130	10,900	9,172	1,198	3,133	9,461	2,531	1,141
Venice, Italy	9,547	16,381	1,023	651	2,000	1,468	1,864	6,894	5,001	6,927	10,909	1,721	866	9,642	8,137	350	1,921	8,348	1,418	875
Veracruz, Mexico	2,646	13,613	8,848	9,579	9,999	8,636	8,445	14,545	11,639	14,676	4,041	8,169	9,054	1,739	2,398	9,856	8,449	1,764	8,519	9,988
Verona, Italy	9,479	16,485	933	658	2,054	1,363	1,823	6,996	4,995	6,971	10,804	1,635	761	9,538	8,057	404	1,820	8,261	1,343	937
Victoria, Canada	1,519	13,256	7,881	8,178	7,758	8,231	6,892	10,702	12,961	15,650	8,103	7,223	8,263	5,677	2,265	8,539	8,384	2,975	7,403	8,356
Victoria, Seychelles	16,382	9,815	8,008	7,426	7,489	8,053	8,692	5,371	5,145	2,593	14,463	8,714	7,730	15,418	15,132	7,097	8,173	15,310	8,413	7,116
Vienna, Austria	9,499	16,121	1,198	451	1,583	1,819	1,743	6,527	5,340	7,101	11,251	1,833	1,177	9,876	8,156	154	2,302	8,420	1,477	453
Vientiane, Laos	12,824	8,017	9,376	8,488	7,312	10,084	9,028	1,743	10,338	8,339	19,349	9,790	9,442	16,851	13,200	8,415	10,547	13,964	9,413	7,991
Villahermosa, Mexico	2,973	13,798	8,725	9,482	9,982	8,467	8,386	14,717	11,313	14,331	3,752	8,058	8,911	1,385	2,557	9,747	8,255	1,858	8,417	9,906
Vilnius, USSR	9,254	15,579	1,808	948	654	2,612	1,689	5,840	6,192	7,651	11,888	2,232	1,964	10,256	8,078	1,042	3,128	8,452	1,847	509
Visby, Sweden	8,739	16,017	1,498	803	735	2,366	1,151	6,267	6,397	8,064	11,448	1,789	1,754	9,741	7,538	1,072	2,892	7,906	1,418	659
Vitoria, Brazil	10,039	13,127	8,706	9,448	10,913	7,827	9,597	15,056	5,886	7,858	4,020	8,649	8,443	5,753	8,925	9,339	7,301	8,201	8,923	9,866
Vladivostok, USSR	8,916	9,488	8,722	8,033	6,560	9,606	7,786	3,908	12,549	11,715	15,584	8,736	9,013	13,143	9,511	8,186	10,128	10,289	8,475	7,653
Volgograd, USSR	10,384	14,143	3,186	2,298	1,541	3,882	3,138	4,465	6,320	7,028	13,298	3,686	3,237	11,725	9,374	2,211	4,360	9,813	3,300	1,801
Vologda, USSR	9,185	14,773	2,751	1,943	551	3,595	2,278	5,041	7,041	8,132	12,669	3,045	2,957	10,815	8,221	2,059	4,118	8,699	2,682	1,527
Vorkuta, USSR	8,509	13,902	3,983	3,302	1,839	4,865	3,147	4,577	8,532	9,363	13,222	4,072	4,270	11,014	7,883	3,490	5,390	8,493	3,771	2,963
Wake Island	7,737	7,016	12,271	11,796	10,387	13,107	11,132	7,618	16,716	14,986	13,193	12,021	12,646	11,734	9,173	12,032	13,569	9,773	11,889	11,516
Wallis Island	8,422	4,723	15,976	15,721	14,398	16,635	14,789	10,995	18,453	15,549	10,677	15,501	16,390	10,605	10,103	16,006	16,916	10,298	15,514	15,517
Walvis Bay, Namibia	14,991	11,374	8,150	8,227	9,296	7,545	9,320	10,048	2,639	2,262	9,657	8,672	7,734	11,210	13,391	7,891	7,258	12,914	8,627	8,289
Warsaw, Poland	9,327	15,841	1,495	607	1,028	2,255	1,620	6,138	5,849	7,441	11,606	2,000	1,604	10,074	8,078	649	2,764	8,406	1,615	119
Washington, D.C.	3,358	16,290	6,005	6,724	7,214	5,866	5,605	12,318	9,681	12,772	5,639	5,319	6,233	3,256	1,692	7,004	5,752	1,434	5,666	7,135
Watson Lake, Canada	2,837	13,581	7,014	7,171	6,570	7,506	5,925	9,411	12,400	14,691	9,220	6,414	7,419	6,719	3,075	7,533	7,751	3,852	6,527	7,281
Weimar, East Germany	9,029	16,505	814	79	1,547	1,585	1,284	6,822	5,611	7,521	10,926	1,383	939	9,455	7,678	368	2,102	7,944	1,014	574
Wellington, New Zealand	11,159	2,304	19,005	18,271	16,823	19,858	17,889	11,635	15,241	12,696	10,603	18,716	19,288	11,756	12,731	18,295	19,575	12,671	18,647	17,810
West Berlin, West Germany	8,992	16,359	988	154	1,325	1,794	1,233	6,647	5,790	7,624	11,092	1,486	1,154	9,565	7,679	473	2,315	7,971	1,104	424
Wewak, Papua New Guinea	11,253	4,209	13,864	13,060	11,633	14,719	13,054	6,690	14,929	12,056	15,213	13,994	14,078	14,834	12,738	13,110	15,241	13,316	13,697	12,604
Whangarei, New Zealand	10,794	2,442	18,404	17,762	16,291	19,240	17,269	11,316	15,795	13,123	10,863	18,107	18,744	11,794	12,413	17,861	19,561	12,427	18,027	17,342
Whitehorse, Canada	3,073	13,317	7,143	7,249	6,566	7,674	6,028	9,152	12,583	14,739	9,536	6,566	7,553	7,045	3,414	7,609	7,943	4,189	6,657	7,330
Wichita, Kansas	1,594	14,596	7,417	8,015	8,173	7,432	6,777	12,498	11,458	14,544	5,900	6,711	7,706	3,387	351	8,337	7,391	560	7,013	8,358
Willemstad, Curacao	5,330	15,240	7,485	8,362	9,356	6,934	7,622	14,917	8,747	11,692	2,819	6,961	7,520	1,556	4,178	8,516	6,567	3,441	7,346	8,852
Wiluna, Australia	14,726	2,961	14,357	13,491	12,525	14,840	14,259	6,956	12,094	8,982	15,343	14,907	14,288	16,965	16,292	13,317	15,152	16,801	14,522	13,006
Windhoek, Namibia	15,203	11,255	8,159	8,197	9,222	7,583	9,318	9,802	2,672	2,004	9,925	8,701	7,744	11,470	13,585	7,855	7,316	13,128	8,640	8,237
Windsor, Canada	2,838	15,918	6,168	6,822	7,155	6,130	5,633	12,015	10,186	13,245	6,049	5,467	6,434	3,579	1,151	7,126	6,072	1,163	5,789	7,199
Winnipeg, Canada	2,104	15,077	6,480	6,966	6,945	6,657	5,686	11,158	11,159	14,065	7,137	5,781	6,816	4,610	1,008	7,309	6,721	1,728	6,036	7,256
Winston-Salem, North Carolina	3,124	15,915	6,421	7,143	7,626	6,267	6,024	12,671	9,961	13,069	5,340	5,737	6,645	2,905	1,525	7,423	6,138	1,102	6,085	7,555
Wroclaw, Poland	9,271	16,105	1,214	329	1,284	1,954	1,517	6,425	5,666	7,392	11,326	1,765	1,302	9,844	7,970	369	2,462	8,267	1,387	184
Wuhan, China	11,001	8,658	9,015	8,179	6,793	9,843	8,368	2,231	11,410	9,909	17,651	9,255	9,195	15,152	11,484	8,213	10,358	12,260	8,917	7,713
Wyndham, Australia	13,403	3,410	14,012	13,123	11,918	14,692	13,599	6,380	13,095	10,059	15,903	14,412	14,062	16,604	14,881	13,036	15,124	15,469	14,041	12,626
Xi'an, China	10,972	9,248	8,382	7,540	6,167	9,204	7,767	1,756	10,859	9,557	17,473	8,641	8,554	14,948	11,289	7,568	9,716	12,055	8,297	7,071
Xining, China	11,094	9,799	7,760	6,905	5,565	8,565	7,208	1,259	10,195	9,054	17,281	8,056	7,913	14,821	11,226	6,915	9,072	11,972	7,701	6,427
Yakutsk, USSR	7,682	11,571	6,860	6,286	4,854	7,737	5,825	4,552	11,492	11,675	14,062	6,772	7,198	11,535	7,874	6,504	8,244	8,640	6,551	5,983
Yanji, China	9,080	9,503	8,640	7,943	6,470	9,531	7,736	3,711	12,380	11,519	15,743	8,683	8,931	13,286	9,643	8,086	10,055	10,420	8,413	7,554

Distances in Kilometers	Las Vegas, Nevada	Launceston, Australia	Le Havre, France	Leipzig, East Germany	Leningrad, USSR	Leon, Spain	Lerwick, United Kingdom	Lhasa, China	Libreville, Gabon	Lilongwe, Malawi	Lima, Peru	Limerick, Ireland	Limoges, France	Limon, Costa Rica	Lincoln, Nebraska	Linz, Austria	Lisbon, Portugal	Little Rock, Arkansas	Liverpool, United Kingdom	Lodz, Poland
Yaounde, Cameroon	12,932	13,952	5,172	5,259	6,420	4,614	6,336	8,794	450	3,152	9,953	5,719	4,756	10,444	11,248	4,931	4,391	11,024	5,652	5,359
Yap Island (Colonia)	10,861	5,714	12,301	11,510	10,071	13,163	11,489	5,367	14,246	11,807	16,181	12,427	12,526	14,986	12,110	11,577	13,687	12,800	12,129	11,063
Yaraka, Australia	12,523	1,855	15,875	14,999	13,691	16,619	15,270	8,273	14,448	11,331	13,969	16,168	15,975	14,792	14,189	14,948	17,075	14,541	15,825	14,507
Yarmouth, Canada	4,209	17,300	4,944	5,675	6,246	4,809	4,592	11,545	8,826	11,865	6,287	4,261	5,169	4,090	2,527	5,949	4,713	2,459	4,613	6,097
Yellowknife, Canada	2,923	14,396	6,321	6,552	6,102	6,761	5,278	9,546	11,630	14,069	8,868	5,694	6,717	6,342	2,679	6,914	6,982	3,445	5,835	6,709
Yerevan, USSR	11,298	13,723	3,600	2,762	2,409	4,135	3,830	4,363	5,657	6,098	13,538	4,204	3,537	12,276	10,215	2,555	4,548	10,603	3,828	2,309
Yinchuan, China	10,711	9,768	7,877	7,042	5,657	8,706	7,248	1,708	10,585	9,505	17,059	8,125	8,058	14,553	10,920	7,080	9,221	11,676	7,783	6,577
Yogyakarta, Indonesia	14,446	5,195	12,123	11,240	10,205	12,709	11,937	4,629	11,229	8,369	17,665	12,625	12,108	18,543	15,480	11,101	13,099	16,238	12,240	10,746
York, United Kingdom	8,202	17,295	490	956	2,009	1,291	703	7,546	6,005	8,215	10,174	514	907	8,583	6,802	1,243	1,786	7,046	130	1,406
Yumen, China	10,943	10,292	7,258	6,403	5,065	8,063	6,715	1,282	9,838	8,893	16,884	7,557	7,412	14,487	10,954	6,416	8,571	11,683	7,202	5,926
Yutian, China	11,734	10,928	6,447	5,559	4,427	7,164	6,159	1,185	8,413	7,542	16,540	6,876	6,519	14,579	11,400	5,492	7,637	12,052	6,497	5,063
Yuzhno-Sakhalinsk, USSR	7,982	9,798	8,728	8,133	6,682	9,606	7,690	4,805	13,085	12,571	14,651	8,635	9,061	12,246	8,651	8,334	10,114	9,425	8,420	7,807
Zagreb, Yugoslavia	9,695	16,107	1,258	669	1,832	1,755	1,956	6,608	5,072	6,858	11,196	1,936	1,145	9,911	8,320	306	2,207	8,557	1,606	709
Zahedan, Iran	12,723	11,825	5,503	4,663	4,085	6,004	5,671	2,921	6,326	5,623	15,274	6,104	5,426	14,179	11,884	4,458	6,385	12,358	5,726	4,201
Zamboanga, Philippines	12,389	5,930	11,626	10,756	9,449	12,400	11,082	4,105	12,512	10,017	17,861	11,940	11,749	16,675	13,411	10,731	12,889	14,162	11,585	10,268
Zanzibar, Tanzania	15,785	11,034	7,232	6,865	7,369	7,042	8,156	6,814	3,382	1,048	12,696	7,921	6,880	13,661	14,197	6,506	7,033	14,134	7,695	6,687
Zaragoza, Spain	9,108	17,369	878	1,474	2,943	402	2,060	8,042	4,685	7,113	9,771	1,358	497	8,629	7,563	1,405	773	7,654	1,320	1,910
Zashiversk, USSR	6,838	12,078	6,659	6,198	4,850	7,510	5,545	5,385	11,661	12,232	13,205	6,468	7,029	10,678	7,014	6,459	7,994	7,781	6,297	5,965
Zhengzhou, China	10,671	9,101	8,613	7,790	6,385	9,453	7,934	2,196	11,286	9,989	17,271	8,831	8,807	14,751	11,081	7,839	9,971	11,854	8,498	7,331
Zurich, Switzerland	9,185	16,709	653	524	1,994	1,218	1,551	7,131	5,207	7,251	10,644	1,348	571	9,304	7,765	456	1,713	7,975	1,050	938

Distances in Kilometers	Lome, Togo	London, United Kingdom	Londonderry, United Kingdom	Longlac, Canada	Lord Howe Island, Australia	Los Angeles, California	Louangphrabang, Laos	Louisville, Kentucky	Luanda, Angola	Lubumbashi, Zaire	Lusaka, Zambia	Luxembourg, Luxembourg	Luxor, Egypt	Lynn Lake, Canada	Lyon, France	Macapa, Brazil	Madison, Wisconsin	Madras, India	Madrid, Spain	Madurai, India
London, United Kingdom	5,031	0	619	5,743	17,217	8,778	9,116	6,529	6,803	7,487	7,909	491	3,984	6,002	736	7,427	6,390	8,218	1,264	8,336
Londonderry, United Kingdom	5,473	619	0	5,129	17,190	8,159	9,393	5,943	7,326	8,075	8,495	1,095	4,597	5,387	1,341	7,270	5,786	8,676	1,646	8,820
Longlac, Canada	9,331	5,743	5,129	0	14,314	3,122	12,243	1,283	11,453	12,710	13,082	6,224	9,726	1,243	6,422	6,464	778	12,923	6,268	13,223
Lord Howe Island, Australia	16,379	17,217	17,190	14,314	0	11,298	8,324	14,171	14,258	12,987	12,631	17,001	14,801	13,462	17,296	15,302	13,988	9,733	18,187	9,743
Los Angeles, California	12,268	8,778	8,159	3,122	11,298	0	12,671	2,945	14,342	15,753	16,087	9,243	12,718	2,850	9,485	7,924	2,690	14,434	9,387	14,841
Louangphrabang, Laos	10,920	9,116	9,393	12,243	8,324	12,671	0	13,520	10,231	8,890	8,972	8,770	7,085	11,233	8,997	16,365	12,938	2,448	9,864	2,804
Louisville, Kentucky	9,330	6,529	5,943	1,283	14,171	2,945	13,520	0	11,397	12,833	13,149	7,019	10,464	2,355	7,141	5,523	617	14,141	6,808	14,416
Luanda, Angola	2,123	6,803	7,326	11,453	14,258	14,342	10,231	11,397	0	1,591	1,793	6,507	4,356	12,287	6,099	7,192	11,700	7,797	5,718	7,482
Lubumbashi, Zaire	3,511	7,487	8,075	12,710	12,987	15,753	8,890	12,833	1,591	0	424	7,101	4,170	13,364	6,751	8,767	13,065	6,443	6,599	6,092
Lusaka, Zambia	3,820	7,909	8,495	13,082	12,631	16,087	8,972	13,149	1,793	424	0	7,524	4,571	13,767	7,173	8,874	13,409	6,537	7,008	6,169
Luxembourg, Luxembourg	4,840	491	1,095	6,224	17,001	9,243	8,770	7,019	6,507	7,101	7,524	0	3,502	6,448	439	7,711	6,878	7,771	1,280	7,876
Luxor, Egypt	3,981	3,984	4,597	9,726	14,801	12,718	7,085	10,464	4,356	4,170	4,571	3,502	0	9,885	3,328	9,382	10,368	5,165	3,731	5,095
Lynn Lake, Canada	10,179	6,002	5,387	1,243	13,462	2,850	11,233	2,355	12,287	13,364	13,767	6,448	9,885	0	6,728	7,706	1,741	12,253	6,769	12,602
Lyon, France	4,404	736	1,341	6,422	17,296	9,485	8,997	7,141	6,099	6,751	7,173	439	3,328	6,728	0	7,438	7,043	7,851	914	7,927
Macapa, Brazil	5,846	7,427	7,270	6,464	15,302	7,924	16,365	5,523	7,192	8,767	8,874	7,711	9,382	7,706	7,438	0	6,107	14,475	6,545	14,301
Madison, Wisconsin	9,599	6,390	5,786	778	13,988	2,690	12,938	617	11,700	13,065	13,409	6,878	10,368	1,741	7,043	6,107	0	13,699	6,805	14,001
Madras, India	8,684	8,218	8,676	12,923	9,733	14,434	2,448	14,141	7,797	6,443	6,537	7,771	5,165	12,253	7,851	14,475	13,699	0	8,574	421
Madrid, Spain	3,827	1,264	1,646	6,268	18,187	9,387	9,864	6,808	5,718	6,599	7,008	1,280	3,731	6,769	914	6,545	6,805	8,574	0	8,610
Madurai, India	8,471	8,336	8,820	13,223	9,743	14,841	2,804	14,416	7,482	6,092	6,169	7,876	5,095	12,602	7,927	14,301	14,001	421	8,610	0
Magadan, USSR	12,243	7,416	7,154	6,827	10,127	6,863	5,848	7,991	13,354	12,958	13,278	7,488	9,012	5,639	7,925	13,129	7,374	7,666	8,680	8,086
Magdalena, Bolivia	7,537	9,452	9,246	7,328	13,241	7,764	18,396	6,139	8,437	9,893	9,882	9,758	11,318	8,492	9,497	2,066	6,756	16,182	8,609	15,906
Magdeburg, East Germany	5,193	815	1,293	6,343	16,521	9,288	8,319	7,218	6,757	7,233	7,658	483	3,430	6,457	870	8,183	7,030	7,413	1,756	7,542
Majuro Atoll, Marshall Isls.	18,174	13,453	13,115	10,278	4,473	7,780	7,562	10,649	17,602	16,025	15,891	13,554	14,254	9,209	13,991	15,280	10,230	9,939	14,714	10,218
Malabo, Equatorial Guinea	880	5,358	5,866	10,075	15,646	13,075	10,227	10,153	1,473	2,681	3,019	5,088	3,520	10,846	4,669	6,668	10,391	7,920	4,248	7,683
Male, Maldives	8,010	8,528	9,058	13,744	9,830	15,618	3,571	14,865	6,833	5,379	5,422	8,050	4,972	13,241	8,041	13,851	14,516	1,254	8,636	833
Manado, Indonesia	13,717	12,201	12,388	13,586	5,141	12,367	3,202	14,608	12,422	10,857	10,766	11,901	10,166	12,353	12,161	19,548	14,008	5,075	13,046	5,254
Managua, Nicaragua	9,605	8,697	8,205	4,173	13,040	4,045	16,347	2,892	11,248	12,838	12,976	9,163	12,200	5,119	9,140	4,116	3,440	16,852	8,523	17,025
Manama, Bahrain	5,684	5,078	5,630	10,584	13,151	13,231	5,297	11,549	5,596	4,882	5,201	4,595	1,796	10,423	4,578	11,175	11,313	3,425	5,206	3,414
Manaus, Brazil	6,883	8,264	8,039	6,393	14,378	7,349	17,340	5,293	8,124	9,675	9,744	8,588	10,433	7,605	8,348	1,057	5,906	15,531	7,476	15,350
Manchester, New Hampshire	8,140	5,264	4,697	1,379	15,437	4,143	13,014	1,318	10,244	11,611	11,951	5,754	9,164	2,591	5,850	5,176	1,459	13,164	5,492	13,385
Mandalay, Burma	10,263	8,538	8,847	12,050	8,954	12,821	672	13,333	9,650	8,363	8,473	8,174	6,414	11,121	8,383	15,707	12,778	1,944	9,238	2,337
Mangareva Island, Fr.Polynesia	14,975	15,043	14,457	9,382	6,500	6,570	14,143	8,515	15,073	15,712	15,372	15,534	18,742	9,414	15,621	9,393	8,687	16,153	15,098	16,224
Manila, Philippines	13,004	10,752	10,904	12,383	6,527	11,759	2,089	13,529	12,164	10,713	10,724	10,481	9,163	11,190	10,771	18,174	12,912	4,400	11,675	4,687
Mannheim, West Germany	4,853	649	1,238	6,363	16,862	9,367	8,612	7,173	6,473	7,025	7,449	169	3,366	6,561	496	7,859	7,023	7,601	1,389	7,707
Maputo, Mozambique	4,908	9,158	9,745	14,236	11,486	17,084	9,065	14,155	2,790	1,671	1,250	8,770	5,715	14,993	8,422	9,378	14,486	6,736	8,250	6,331
Mar del Plata, Argentina	7,788	11,379	11,359	10,133	11,423	10,147	17,208	8,924	7,732	8,790	8,614	11,542	11,737	11,278	11,176	4,264	9,538	15,029	10,270	14,620
Maracaibo, Venezuela	8,021	7,808	7,413	4,550	14,337	5,394	16,560	3,365	9,641	11,231	11,378	8,231	10,904	5,715	8,119	2,562	3,983	15,957	7,383	15,975
Marrakech, Morocco	2,982	2,299	2,597	6,614	18,804	9,712	10,646	6,931	5,013	6,105	6,490	2,317	4,005	7,302	1,920	5,722	7,041	9,102	1,047	9,076
Marseilles, France	4,138	1,002	1,593	6,633	17,367	9,712	9,045	7,314	5,824	6,487	6,908	703	3,151	6,972	276	7,363	7,238	7,804	820	7,862
Maseru, Lesotho	4,826	9,352	9,917	14,124	11,554	16,752	9,678	13,894	2,716	1,954	1,541	8,994	6,111	15,002	8,622	8,905	14,283	7,358	8,363	6,952
Mashhad, Iran	6,795	4,932	5,376	9,905	12,782	12,212	4,515	11,019	6,958	6,289	6,604	4,500	2,818	9,523	4,629	11,851	10,673	3,300	5,432	3,467
Mazatlan, Mexico	11,530	9,078	8,480	3,421	11,731	1,666	14,328	2,575	13,425	14,992	15,214	9,567	13,035	3,760	9,708	6,507	2,703	15,924	9,379	16,305
Mbabane, Swaziland	4,829	9,147	9,729	14,160	11,558	16,969	9,211	14,050	2,708	1,667	1,243	8,766	5,756	14,944	8,412	9,237	14,391	6,876	8,218	6,472
Mbandaka, Zaire	2,010	5,957	6,521	11,062	14,622	14,123	9,372	11,231	1,128	1,649	2,036	5,610	3,229	11,733	5,230	7,717	11,433	6,988	4,989	6,716
McMurdo Sound, Antarctica	12,019	17,041	17,477	15,786	5,123	13,362	11,526	14,583	10,262	9,752	9,329	16,768	13,738	16,172	16,359	11,132	15,009	11,288	15,839	11,000
Mecca, Saudi Arabia	4,487	4,791	5,395	10,517	13,946	13,440	6,452	11,303	4,431	3,904	4,268	4,303	869	10,591	4,162	10,105	11,181	4,389	4,598	4,285
Medan, Indonesia	10,799	10,306	10,694	14,070	7,473	14,331	1,840	15,351	9,578	8,058	8,030	9,891	7,442	13,073	10,023	16,645	14,775	2,279	10,796	2,377
Medellin, Colombia	8,491	8,462	8,062	4,934	13,704	5,358	17,105	3,690	9,994	11,575	11,685	8,886	11,520	6,039	8,773	2,811	4,299	16,605	8,032	16,607
Medicine Hat, Canada	11,015	6,987	6,371	1,726	12,639	1,882	11,618	2,368	13,136	14,298	14,692	7,435	10,871	989	7,711	7,891	1,798	12,930	7,723	13,305
Medina, Saudi Arabia	4,570	4,510	5,109	10,220	14,098	13,120	6,417	11,034	4,663	4,209	4,580	4,020	714	10,270	3,901	10,081	10,894	4,452	4,384	4,382
Melbourne, Australia	14,949	16,902	17,189	15,758	1,464	12,762	7,804	15,625	12,827	11,524	11,172	16,508	13,613	14,836	16,632	15,510	15,452	8,783	17,315	8,721
Memphis, Tennessee	9,740	7,045	6,459	1,653	13,709	2,581	13,785	517	11,779	13,250	13,550	7,536	10,980	2,553	7,657	5,609	884	14,574	7,317	14,866
Merauke, Indonesia	15,518	14,032	14,110	13,715	3,210	11,587	5,229	14,356	13,865	12,278	12,090	13,791	12,189	12,507	14,094	18,457	13,859	7,054	14,999	7,189
Merida, Mexico	9,861	8,178	7,637	3,209	13,173	3,164	15,312	1,951	11,692	13,271	13,474	8,661	11,928	4,093	8,703	4,790	2,451	16,082	8,198	16,337
Meridian, Mississippi	9,645	7,178	6,603	1,943	13,733	2,752	14,111	705	11,652	13,153	13,436	7,668	11,077	2,882	7,768	5,331	1,190	14,841	7,383	15,121
Messina, Italy	3,834	1,922	2,541	7,643	16,632	10,699	8,383	8,342	5,207	5,656	6,080	1,475	2,122	7,920	1,221	7,983	8,261	6,919	1,675	6,941
Mexico City, Mexico	10,872	8,947	8,377	3,553	12,203	2,492	15,086	2,458	12,680	14,265	14,452	9,437	12,806	4,160	9,521	5,666	2,780	16,411	9,083	16,747
Miami, Florida	8,862	7,139	6,620	2,720	14,268	3,765	14,949	1,479	10,777	12,330	12,570	7,617	10,834	3,833	7,636	4,232	2,094	15,219	7,105	15,416
Midway Islands, USA	16,203	11,172	10,738	7,728	7,068	5,599	8,097	8,262	17,593	16,857	17,030	11,381	13,238	6,612	11,812	13,517	7,776	10,511	12,382	10,891
Milan, Italy	4,427	960	1,579	6,698	16,998	9,738	8,683	7,449	6,024	6,588	7,012	514	3,033	6,954	341	7,736	7,335	7,511	1,191	7,587
Milford Sound, New Zealand	15,550	18,830	18,796	14,588	1,634	11,468	9,753	14,041	13,567	12,609	12,205	18,522	15,499	14,052	18,676	13,768	14,053	10,825	19,176	10,752
Milwaukee, Wisconsin	9,479	6,303	5,701	757	14,105	2,808	12,965	562	11,580	12,947	13,289	6,791	10,277	1,796	6,951	6,014	121	13,676	6,702	13,971
Minsk, USSR	5,806	1,878	2,244	6,973	15,458	9,721	7,240	7,974	7,078	7,265	7,680	1,549	3,161	6,875	1,857	9,260	7,707	6,444	2,771	6,609
Mogadiscio, Somalia	4,921	6,922	7,538	12,662	12,374	15,658	6,473	13,311	3,763	2,496	2,698	6,445	2,947	12,813	6,243	10,733	13,277	4,034	6,502	3,726
Mombasa, Kenya	4,420	7,218	7,836	12,876	12,508	15,981	7,321	13,337	2,970	1,587	1,771	6,765	3,376	13,212	6,502	10,099	13,406	4,873	6,612	4,536
Monclova, Mexico	10,951	8,446	7,852	2,842	12,365	1,797	14,246	1,930	12,896	14,440	14,690	8,936	12,393	3,327	9,068	6,150	2,098	15,577	8,730	15,929
Moncton, Canada	7,680	4,632	4,067	1,669	15,946	4,658	12,582	1,932	9,798	11,108	11,463	5,121	8,536	2,747	5,219	5,278	1,975	12,580	4,879	12,787
Monrovia, Liberia	1,330	5,106	5,408	8,451	17,023	11,207	12,143	8,267	3,148	4,681	4,935	5,054	5,087	9,439	4,624	4,525	8,607	9,978	3,842	9,780
Monte Carlo, Monaco	4,210	1,031	1,642	6,722	17,198	9,787	8,875	7,429	5,847	6,463	6,886	660	3,036	7,029	303	7,531	7,340	7,642	990	7,704
Monterrey, Mexico	10,869	8,482	7,894	2,929	12,406	1,962	14,418	1,955	12,793	14,347	14,586	8,973	12,414	3,464	9,094	5,999	2,172	15,717	8,732	16,063
Montevideo, Uruguay	7,530	11,021	10,995	9,845	11,782	10,000	17,317	8,653	7,582	8,706	8,552	11,191	11,497	11,007	10,830	3,902	9,269	15,034	9,921	14,634
Montgomery, Alabama	9,420	7,021	6,453	1,933	13,947	2,972	14,154	653	11,427	12,929	13,210	7,510	10,899	2,946	7,599	5,150	1,217	14,777	7,194	15,041
Montpelier, Vermont	8,247	5,254	4,678	1,223	15,348	4,050	12,884	1,289	10,356	11,705	12,051	5,744	9,176	2,428	5,855	5,343	1,360	13,089	5,525	13,320
Montpellier, France	4,159	928	1,504	6,518	17,468	9,602	9,149	7,191	5,879	6,571	6,992	689	3,274	6,872	251	7,265	7,119	7,927	720	7,986
Montreal, Canada	8,343	5,240	4,656	1,080	15,267	3,973	12,754	1,289	10,457	11,788	12,139	5,730	9,180	2,274	5,854	5,503	1,287	13,009	5,551	13,248
Moosonee, Canada	8,914	5,307	4,695	449	14,737	3,570	12,119	1,503	11,036	12,272	12,647	5,790	9,290	1,465	5,980	6,326	1,127	12,640	5,819	12,922
Moroni, Comoros	5,056	8,151	8,768	13,792	11,682	16,906	7,333	14,191	3,304	1,723	1,673	7,697	4,291	14,144	7,434	10,490	14,298	4,921	7,524	4,537
Moscow, USSR	6,372	2,506	2,799	7,217	14,789	9,793	6,616	8,296	7,501	7,531	7,934	2,213	3,363	6,979	2,532	9,919	7,975	5,984	3,446	6,185
Mosul, Iraq	5,418	3,789	4,322	9,262	14,188	11,977	5,983	10,225	5,895	5,562	5,937	3,315	1,546	9,144	3,348	10,387	9,988	4,512	4,069	4,579
Mount Isa, Australia	15,253	15,132	15,303	14,854	2,290	12,371	6,062	15,283	13,305	11,778	11,516	14,821	12,617	13,695	15,058	17,449	14,869	7,479	15,915	7,523
Multan, Pakistan	7,777	6,208	6,626	10,885	11,492	12,821	3,285	12,071	7,570	6,608	6,849	5,786	3,836	10,335	5,925	13,098	11,663	2,099	6,727	2,345
Munich, West Germany	4,760	919	1,510	6,633	16,719	9,628	8,430	7,446	6,310	6,809	7,233	431	3,099	6,816	578	8,014	7,296	7,358	1,488	7,456
Murcia, Spain	3,535	1,504	1,949	6,611	18,081	9,731	9,774	7,131	5,390	6,252	6,662	1,415	3,451	7,117	994	6,610	7,140	8,381	348	8,398
Murmansk, USSR	7,357	2,614	2,553	5,942	14,655	8,340	7,125	7,111	8,765	8,955	9,367	2,602	4,812	5,564	3,033	9,766	6,717	7,040	3,846	7,306
Mururoa Atoll, Fr. Polynesia	15,406	15,184	14,582	9,467	6,183	6,565	13,718	8,664	15,463	16,013	15,654	15,673	19,070	9,415	15,802	9,798	8,796	15,770	15,348	15,866
Muscat, Oman	6,423	5,836	6,361	11,177	12,297	13,613	4,508	12,216	6,099	5,168	5,433	5,361	2,631	10,886	5,378	12,012	11,929	2,568	6,041	2,569
Myitkyina, Burma	10,344	8,335	8,615	11,670	9,093	12,431	781	12,953	9,851	8,613	8,744	7,991	6,437	10,729	8,222	15,617	12,394	2,252	9,094	2,660
Naga, Philippines	13,259	10,966	11,104	12,404	6,300	11,653	2,346	13,523	12,391	10,927	10,927	10,704	9,421	11,197	11,001	18,370	12,908	4,642	11,907	4,922
Nagasaki, Japan	13,101	9,473	9,458	10,177	7,755	9,745	3,108	11,320	13,031	11,866	12,000	9,330	9,137	8,979	9,705	16,369	10,703	5,479	10,607	5,867
Nagoya, Japan	13,507	9,531	9,449	9,670	7,741	9,073	3,805	10,768	13,621	12,516	12,666	9,440	9,592	8,451	9,838	16,022	10,154	6,162	10,720	6,554
Nagpur, India	8,518	7,459	7,884	12,021	10,324	13,626	2,405	13,244	7,922	6,712	6,868	7,030	4,751	11,361	7,150	14,131	12,798	902	7,925	1,246
Nairobi, Kenya	4,041	6,805	7,422	12,443	12,945	15,553	7,494	12,896	2,742	1,544	1,823	6,357	3,017	12,804	6,085	9,782	12,967	5,055	6,177	4,742
Nanchang, China	12,048	9,157	9,277	11,036	8,085	11,033	1,702	12,263	11,711	10,477	10,596	8,916	8,073	9,912	9,235	16,540	11,652	4,065	10,147	4,450
Nancy, France	4,740	550	1,165	6,292	17,050	9,320	8,797	7,072	6,405	7,005	7,429	102	3,434	6,531	342	7,671	6,940	7,760	1,208	7,859
Nandi, Fiji	18,652	16,259	15,856	11,930	2,394	8,906	9,218	11,800	16,595	15,381	15,023	16,392	16,296	11,143	16,831	14,377	11,595	11,196	17,497	11,327
Nanjing, China	12,186	9,003	9,082	10,603	8,220	10,571	2,140	11,819	11,993	10,816	10,955	8,793	8,205	9,466	9,132	16,298	11,207	4,448	10,046	4,843
Nanning, China	11,487	9,245	9,458	11,831	8,090	12,021	720	13,088	10,909	9,595	9,685	8,940	7,580	10,759	9,207	16,644	12,489	3,152	10,100	3,517
Nantes, France	4,561	488	955	5,935	17,617	9,017	9,396	6,629	6,375	7,131	7,549	627	3,836	6,293	518	7,086	6,543	8,339	777	8,426
Naples, Italy	4,057	1,618	2,237	7,351	16,722	10,396	8,421	8,077	5,496	5,970	6,394	1,163	2,391	7,610	937	7,954	7,979	7,058	1,516	7,101
Narvik, Norway	7,021	2,108	1,961	5,493	15,230	8,066	7,752	6,616	8,574	8,921	9,340	2,187	4,861	5,238	2,626	9,135	6,259	7,567	3,367	7,811

Distances in Kilometers	Lome, Togo	London, United Kingdom	Londonderry, United Kingdom	Longlac, Canada	Lord Howe Island, Australia	Los Angeles, California	Louangphrabang, Laos	Louisville, Kentucky	Luanda, Angola	Lubumbashi, Zaire	Lusaka, Zambia	Luxembourg, Luxembourg	Luxor, Egypt	Lynn Lake, Canada	Lyon, France	Macapa, Brazil	Madison, Wisconsin	Madras, India	Madrid, Spain	Madurai, India
Nashville, Tennessee	9,435	6,754	6,173	1,513	14,026	2,866	13,733	248	11,483	12,944	13,248	7,245	10,677	2,535	7,358	5,442	799	14,388	7,005	14,665
Nassau, Bahamas	8,578	7,000	6,497	2,854	14,507	4,058	15,031	1,662	10,484	12,040	12,277	7,472	10,635	4,008	7,473	3,962	2,278	15,142	6,912	15,314
Natal, Brazil	4,258	7,174	7,214	7,889	15,606	9,732	15,166	7,137	5,357	6,916	7,008	7,320	8,107	9,114	6,954	1,874	7,675	12,923	6,046	12,681
Natashquan, Canada	7,587	4,216	3,635	1,765	16,066	4,865	12,085	2,313	9,709	10,945	11,318	4,707	8,162	2,664	4,834	5,653	2,240	12,086	4,565	12,300
Nauru Island	18,330	14,227	13,944	11,236	3,531	8,651	7,410	11,556	16,940	15,355	15,156	14,269	14,390	10,180	14,699	15,810	11,161	9,668	15,490	9,899
Ndjamena, Chad	1,658	4,578	5,143	9,805	15,760	12,912	9,266	10,110	2,322	2,967	3,376	4,237	2,381	10,398	3,851	7,419	10,242	7,068	3,632	6,881
Nelson, New Zealand	16,033	18,764	18,479	14,010	1,666	10,889	9,969	13,485	14,098	13,180	12,773	18,651	16,020	13,480	18,961	13,637	13,481	11,208	19,747	11,164
Nema, Mauritania	1,482	3,921	4,259	7,851	17,860	10,818	11,319	7,897	3,604	4,938	5,272	3,853	4,247	8,704	3,421	5,142	8,137	9,351	2,659	9,217
Neuquen, Argentina	8,680	11,993	11,901	9,996	10,808	9,597	17,693	8,738	8,651	9,677	9,484	12,206	12,643	11,060	11,866	4,653	9,335	15,787	10,953	15,369
New Delhi, India	8,323	6,724	7,118	11,175	10,924	12,882	2,704	12,396	8,013	6,961	7,172	6,316	4,403	10,535	6,472	13,680	11,952	1,747	7,288	2,069
New Glasgow, Canada	7,505	4,521	3,966	1,844	16,118	4,827	12,596	2,074	9,623	10,936	11,291	5,010	8,405	2,911	5,095	5,173	2,141	12,523	4,734	12,719
New Haven, Connecticut	8,238	5,474	4,911	1,418	15,309	4,033	13,214	1,151	10,331	11,723	12,055	5,963	9,359	2,653	6,051	5,074	1,374	13,387	5,674	13,608
New Orleans, Louisiana	9,800	7,462	6,890	2,221	13,521	2,693	14,340	1,001	11,777	13,301	13,568	7,951	11,346	3,108	8,044	5,295	1,456	15,132	7,641	15,414
New Plymouth, New Zealand	16,288	18,552	18,230	13,802	1,596	10,681	9,919	13,315	14,351	13,415	13,010	18,501	16,139	13,247	18,861	13,714	13,292	11,242	19,775	11,215
New York, New York	8,323	5,586	5,023	1,405	15,213	3,945	13,287	1,047	10,412	11,813	12,141	6,075	9,472	2,647	6,164	5,067	1,302	13,490	5,785	13,714
Newcastle upon Tyne, UK	5,425	402	367	5,448	16,991	8,447	9,060	6,291	7,205	7,874	8,297	799	4,286	5,649	1,125	7,560	6,118	8,310	1,631	8,453
Newcastle Waters, Australia	14,692	14,457	14,673	14,955	3,027	12,746	5,355	15,574	12,842	11,280	11,049	14,125	11,886	13,743	14,344	18,025	15,093	6,741	15,188	6,790
Niamey, Niger	823	4,218	4,675	8,778	16,935	11,808	10,530	8,911	2,757	3,948	4,306	4,018	3,463	9,542	3,583	6,047	9,118	8,428	3,032	8,263
Nicosia, Cyprus	4,602	3,222	3,807	8,898	15,020	11,795	6,871	9,749	5,307	5,221	5,624	2,732	1,054	8,946	2,670	9,503	9,583	5,296	3,290	5,320
Niue (Alofi)	18,295	16,292	15,749	11,140	3,401	8,029	10,513	10,806	16,909	16,119	15,712	16,594	17,596	10,542	17,001	13,043	10,693	12,539	17,299	12,671
Norfolk, Virginia	8,494	6,014	5,461	1,657	14,959	3,792	13,725	851	10,551	12,002	12,310	6,502	9,861	2,885	6,572	4,835	1,314	13,961	6,151	14,181
Norfolk Island, Australia	17,118	17,322	17,096	13,494	897	10,439	8,898	13,287	15,025	13,830	13,461	17,257	15,618	12,716	17,639	14,783	13,127	10,488	18,537	10,529
Noril'sk, USSR	9,247	4,725	4,647	6,786	12,548	8,339	5,580	8,064	10,328	10,118	10,485	4,672	6,025	5,987	5,090	11,728	7,537	6,272	5,939	6,635
Norman Wells, Canada	11,034	6,279	5,719	2,889	12,451	3,521	9,700	4,001	13,023	13,737	14,161	6,642	9,767	1,662	7,009	9,345	3,384	11,024	7,305	11,410
Normanton, Australia	15,491	14,945	15,074	14,486	2,378	12,056	5,946	14,950	13,593	12,048	11,800	14,663	12,656	13,321	14,928	17,655	14,520	7,495	15,809	7,565
North Pole	9,326	4,296	3,907	4,486	13,493	6,231	7,804	5,767	10,977	11,294	11,709	4,508	7,162	3,699	4,936	10,000	5,232	8,556	5,530	8,904
Nottingham, United Kingdom	5,197	178	463	5,592	17,147	8,616	9,121	6,400	6,980	7,664	8,086	632	4,134	5,833	913	7,456	6,248	8,286	1,410	8,415
Norway House, Canada	10,049	6,055	5,437	906	13,604	2,732	11,603	1,976	12,168	13,317	13,710	6,515	9,986	379	6,771	7,354	1,362	12,571	6,750	12,912
Norwich, United Kingdom	5,156	159	626	5,751	17,060	8,765	8,980	6,567	6,901	7,551	7,974	478	3,976	5,972	808	7,576	6,412	8,120	1,412	8,247
Nouakchott, Mauritania	2,287	3,960	4,161	7,104	18,436	9,984	12,068	7,044	4,375	5,796	6,106	4,015	5,065	8,045	3,619	4,329	7,325	10,214	2,738	10,102
Noumea, New Caledonia	17,630	16,561	16,334	13,077	1,262	10,111	8,402	13,027	15,507	14,182	13,843	16,519	15,338	12,201	16,917	15,277	12,793	10,173	17,793	10,260
Novosibirsk, USSR	8,923	5,221	5,349	8,345	12,009	9,929	4,226	9,613	9,543	9,016	9,339	5,003	5,203	7,595	5,349	12,618	9,109	4,660	6,261	5,020
Nuku'alofa, Tonga	18,302	16,608	16,111	11,681	2,805	8,583	10,075	11,388	16,570	15,621	15,225	16,844	17,146	11,031	17,274	13,534	11,258	12,019	17,725	12,132
Nukunono Island, Tokelau Isls.	19,200	15,255	14,746	10,453	3,887	7,411	9,943	10,305	17,937	16,870	16,501	15,522	16,853	9,722	15,942	13,405	10,101	12,164	16,359	12,365
Nuremberg, West Germany	4,890	826	1,396	6,509	16,694	9,494	8,430	7,339	6,456	6,958	7,382	359	3,229	6,677	623	8,032	7,178	7,412	1,535	7,520
Nyala, Sudan	2,681	4,923	5,530	10,474	14,871	13,593	8,251	10,927	2,642	2,638	3,061	4,506	1,716	10,909	4,189	8,487	10,988	6,009	4,206	5,814
Oaxaca, Mexico	10,658	8,989	8,433	3,745	12,310	2,857	15,437	2,581	12,414	14,004	14,171	9,476	12,783	4,432	9,535	5,347	2,967	16,656	9,052	16,968
Ocean Falls, Canada	11,938	7,494	6,902	2,859	11,690	2,168	10,674	3,578	14,029	14,976	15,394	7,897	11,152	1,780	8,231	9,100	3,011	12,276	8,401	12,679
Odense, Denmark	5,524	820	1,126	6,051	16,405	8,959	8,321	6,968	7,120	7,602	8,026	707	3,764	6,120	1,142	8,246	6,753	7,552	1,964	7,704
Odessa, USSR	5,291	2,308	2,809	7,753	15,345	10,562	7,022	8,698	6,364	6,447	6,858	1,859	2,313	7,712	1,994	9,378	8,470	5,913	2,843	6,029
Ogbomosho, Nigeria	403	4,825	5,299	9,382	16,341	12,380	10,527	9,461	2,120	3,375	3,715	4,600	3,579	10,171	4,169	6,201	9,695	8,309	3,661	8,106
Okha, USSR	12,485	7,862	7,665	7,650	9,558	7,576	5,101	8,812	13,331	12,717	12,997	7,876	8,981	6,462	8,304	13,925	8,195	7,051	9,113	7,472
Okinawa (Naha)	13,232	10,005	10,041	10,936	7,212	10,383	2,705	12,068	12,879	11,589	11,677	9,821	9,253	9,733	10,173	17,097	11,451	5,147	11,085	5,508
Oklahoma City, Oklahoma	10,405	7,479	6,877	1,820	13,081	1,902	13,539	1,090	12,454	13,913	14,220	7,967	11,451	2,389	8,124	6,206	1,093	14,623	7,850	14,956
Old Crow, Canada	11,274	6,379	5,855	3,508	12,101	3,977	9,090	4,632	13,179	13,727	14,149	6,702	9,646	2,289	7,093	9,950	4,015	10,497	7,480	10,892
Olympia, Washington	11,972	7,800	7,192	2,682	11,682	1,494	11,337	3,164	14,092	15,206	15,610	8,229	11,586	1,843	8,532	8,639	2,654	12,959	8,610	13,361
Omaha, Nebraska	10,166	6,922	6,312	1,198	13,409	2,112	12,982	940	12,260	13,642	13,980	7,406	10,905	1,769	7,587	6,425	581	13,974	7,374	14,302
Omsk, USSR	8,318	4,693	4,866	8,241	12,555	10,075	4,588	9,484	8,993	8,543	8,883	4,448	4,640	7,594	4,779	12,116	9,015	4,689	5,693	5,016
Oodnadatta, Australia	14,651	15,467	15,743	15,691	2,327	13,086	6,358	16,026	12,621	11,142	10,851	15,092	12,475	14,547	15,257	16,883	15,657	7,459	16,030	7,441
Oradea, Romania	4,950	1,671	2,214	7,270	16,006	10,181	7,687	8,150	6,248	6,528	6,949	1,202	2,555	7,338	1,319	8,725	7,961	6,572	2,181	6,674
Oran, Algeria	3,280	1,756	2,206	6,812	18,093	9,934	9,836	7,295	5,136	6,019	6,426	1,639	3,358	7,347	1,208	6,536	7,325	8,362	586	8,362
Oranjestad, Aruba	7,839	7,540	7,146	4,400	14,591	5,416	16,323	3,249	9,505	11,096	11,258	7,963	10,655	5,585	7,852	2,510	3,865	15,693	7,120	15,718
Orebro, Sweden	6,016	1,296	1,438	6,012	15,922	8,809	7,956	7,011	7,550	7,942	8,364	1,226	3,971	5,959	1,658	8,679	6,743	7,357	2,482	7,541
Orel, USSR	6,079	2,453	2,813	7,414	14,916	10,054	6,669	8,460	7,175	7,203	7,608	2,107	3,037	7,226	2,384	9,813	8,162	5,892	3,293	6,070
Orsk, USSR	7,247	3,976	4,269	8,336	13,370	10,555	5,141	9,505	7,943	7,586	7,946	3,652	3,586	7,882	3,927	11,360	9,112	4,659	4,832	4,912
Osaka, Japan	13,433	9,526	9,457	9,777	7,735	9,211	3,665	10,884	13,506	12,388	12,534	9,424	9,505	8,561	9,817	16,104	10,268	6,025	10,704	6,417
Oslo, Norway	6,021	1,157	1,210	5,768	16,084	8,594	8,192	6,755	7,621	8,075	8,498	1,186	4,160	5,746	1,624	8,473	6,495	7,619	2,391	7,802
Osorno, Chile	9,148	12,405	12,288	10,095	10,388	9,470	17,667	8,822	9,077	10,055	9,845	12,634	13,108	11,109	12,303	5,022	9,406	16,017	11,390	15,596
Ostrava, Czechoslovakia	5,101	1,311	1,823	6,861	16,195	9,775	7,912	7,749	6,514	6,872	7,294	876	2,953	6,934	1,102	8,538	7,554	6,908	2,010	7,026
Ottawa, Canada	8,506	5,379	4,791	947	15,103	3,808	12,772	1,153	10,618	11,952	12,303	5,869	9,327	2,163	6,000	5,581	1,123	13,093	5,708	13,341
Ouagadougou, Bourkina Fasso	752	4,342	4,757	8,613	17,108	11,594	10,943	8,673	2,853	4,162	4,497	4,188	3,872	9,437	3,749	5,637	8,912	8,839	3,114	8,670
Oujda, Morocco	3,176	1,876	2,298	6,805	18,222	9,926	9,988	7,255	5,068	5,993	6,397	1,784	3,455	7,371	1,357	6,382	7,301	8,489	656	8,482
Oxford, United Kingdom	5,063	83	543	5,662	17,252	8,701	9,178	6,446	6,851	7,551	7,972	574	4,065	5,929	803	7,376	6,308	8,295	1,275	8,416
Pago Pago, American Samoa	18,759	15,790	15,263	10,795	3,623	7,708	10,258	10,548	17,418	16,516	16,123	16,075	17,283	10,134	16,489	13,209	10,392	12,387	16,849	12,554
Pakxe, Laos	11,392	9,769	10,045	12,715	7,683	12,850	653	13,977	10,541	9,126	9,167	9,422	7,635	11,651	9,644	16,977	13,379	2,761	10,507	3,059
Palembang, Indonesia	11,550	11,289	11,667	14,703	6,503	14,391	2,536	15,950	10,136	8,568	8,480	10,877	8,371	13,604	11,011	17,326	15,343	3,231	11,779	3,277
Palermo, Italy	3,749	1,824	2,439	7,516	16,825	10,587	8,571	8,192	5,194	5,703	6,127	1,401	2,278	7,825	1,102	7,796	8,123	7,110	1,491	7,131
Palma, Majorca	3,706	1,344	1,870	6,738	17,718	9,846	9,404	7,326	5,465	6,227	6,643	1,148	3,187	7,171	710	6,981	7,301	8,042	549	8,070
Palmerston North, New Zealand	16,174	18,723	18,361	13,791	1,778	10,671	10,100	13,262	14,272	13,382	12,973	18,693	16,236	13,276	19,054	13,527	13,260	11,390	19,964	11,354
Panama, Panama	8,901	8,501	8,062	4,572	13,500	4,832	16,810	3,303	10,470	12,056	12,180	8,944	11,755	5,630	8,867	3,309	3,899	16,714	8,173	16,783
Paramaribo, Suriname	6,240	7,141	6,911	5,687	15,460	7,179	16,242	4,736	7,761	9,350	9,490	7,474	9,519	6,928	7,247	788	5,320	14,681	6,389	14,568
Paris, France	4,738	341	951	6,057	17,276	9,106	9,058	6,811	6,477	7,146	7,568	288	3,676	6,338	395	7,428	6,692	8,045	1,054	8,144
Patna, India	9,113	7,505	7,867	11,615	10,085	12,959	1,858	12,874	8,654	7,483	7,649	7,112	5,232	10,850	7,288	14,532	12,381	1,475	8,119	1,885
Patrai, Greece	4,116	2,254	2,866	7,995	16,092	11,000	7,853	8,760	5,283	5,558	5,980	1,771	1,731	8,183	1,623	8,512	8,642	6,384	2,197	6,413
Peking, China	11,668	8,160	8,212	9,816	9,057	10,082	2,609	11,059	11,758	10,745	10,939	7,976	7,721	8,719	8,332	15,401	10,454	4,616	9,243	5,032
Penrhyn Island (Omoka)	17,729	14,883	14,290	9,473	5,078	6,354	11,372	9,115	17,819	17,641	17,217	15,272	17,846	8,950	15,619	11,890	9,005	13,657	15,710	13,874
Peoria, Illinois	9,639	6,582	5,982	1,038	13,914	2,630	13,192	427	11,726	13,126	13,457	7,071	10,551	1,978	7,223	5,950	264	13,961	6,953	14,260
Perm', USSR	7,433	3,590	3,784	7,583	13,658	9,790	5,624	8,768	8,360	8,155	8,532	3,346	4,043	7,111	3,686	11,015	8,360	5,379	4,599	5,650
Perth, Australia	12,694	14,466	14,935	17,298	4,071	15,026	5,916	17,940	10,672	9,184	8,896	14,004	10,885	16,060	14,028	16,217	17,485	6,260	14,607	6,130
Peshawar, Pakistan	7,822	5,920	6,312	10,474	11,689	12,400	3,399	11,670	7,759	6,877	7,138	5,516	3,846	9,912	5,683	12,966	11,252	2,481	6,513	2,750
Petropavlovsk-Kamchatskiy, USSR	13,115	8,252	7,961	7,078	9,369	6,634	6,042	8,152	14,204	13,715	14,011	8,342	9,852	5,848	8,780	13,515	7,538	8,079	9,516	8,499
Petrozavodsk, USSR	6,754	2,365	2,502	6,571	14,853	9,095	6,915	7,684	8,041	8,169	8,578	2,205	4,017	6,288	2,600	9,760	7,335	6,525	3,485	6,755
Pevek, USSR	11,549	6,538	6,170	5,390	11,265	5,785	7,109	6,578	13,045	13,051	13,432	6,710	8,900	4,224	7,145	11,686	5,964	8,649	7,785	9,059
Philadelphia, Pennsylvania	8,415	5,716	5,153	1,412	15,106	3,853	13,377	936	10,498	11,910	12,235	6,205	9,599	2,654	6,293	5,053	1,236	13,612	5,910	13,838
Phnom Penh, Kampuchea	11,365	10,028	10,329	13,119	7,488	13,213	967	14,382	10,393	8,938	8,955	9,664	7,700	12,057	9,866	17,082	13,785	2,684	10,712	2,936
Phoenix, Arizona	11,756	8,502	7,885	2,772	11,767	576	13,083	2,427	13,810	15,260	15,574	8,978	12,477	2,733	9,190	7,354	2,243	14,692	9,025	15,084
Pierre, South Dakota	10,449	6,923	6,306	1,207	13,170	1,917	12,535	1,395	12,561	13,881	14,239	7,399	10,899	1,389	7,613	6,908	894	13,642	7,474	13,989
Pinang, Malaysia	10,959	10,260	10,627	13,853	7,447	14,057	1,611	15,130	9,792	8,285	8,267	9,856	7,520	12,835	10,007	16,799	14,547	2,359	10,800	2,501
Pitcairn Island (Adamstown)	14,442	14,888	14,328	9,341	6,866	6,662	14,659	8,397	14,557	15,275	14,955	15,375	18,294	9,479	15,409	8,912	8,619	16,581	14,806	16,608
Pittsburgh, Pennsylvania	8,830	5,997	5,419	1,158	14,704	3,438	13,325	552	10,914	12,322	12,649	6,488	9,919	2,375	6,599	5,349	833	13,743	6,257	13,994
Plymouth, Montserrat	6,994	6,647	6,288	4,272	15,552	5,881	15,617	3,314	8,769	10,351	10,551	7,055	9,695	5,509	6,924	2,214	3,894	14,746	6,173	14,759
Plymouth, United Kingdom	4,932	307	556	5,578	17,497	8,644	9,422	6,316	6,771	7,530	7,949	740	4,164	5,903	844	7,126	6,204	8,504	1,112	8,615
Ponape Island	17,099	13,211	13,014	11,178	4,258	8,989	6,216	11,743	16,175	14,610	14,503	13,188	13,130	10,013	13,603	16,693	11,260	8,547	14,451	8,811
Ponce, Puerto Rico	7,465	6,838	6,438	3,949	15,209	5,403	15,640	2,914	9,257	10,838	11,040	7,266	10,048	5,172	7,167	2,619	3,510	15,017	6,457	15,067
Ponta Delgada, Azores	4,433	2,518	2,367	4,936	19,199	7,996	11,623	5,182	6,549	7,779	8,146	2,854	5,596	5,749	2,671	4,920	5,312	10,488	1,920	10,531
Pontianak, Indonesia	12,024	11,346	11,675	14,289	6,288	13,800	2,337	15,503	10,689	9,131	9,057	10,961	8,683	13,148	11,134	17,854	14,888	3,518	11,945	3,629
Port Augusta, Australia	14,663	16,017	16,319	15,911	2,013	13,118	6,927	16,055	12,577	11,162	10,843	15,625	12,845	14,837	15,762	16,295	15,766	7,924	16,489	7,878
Port Blair, India	10,049	9,206	9,594	13,205	8,525	13,989	1,359	14,485	9,085	7,662	7,707	8,794	6,477	12,313	8,934	15,831	13,947	1,366	9,721	1,611
Port Elizabeth, South Africa	5,127	9,796	10,347	14,326	11,275	16,704	10,054	13,967	3,061	2,477	2,073	9,454	6,644	15,290	9,072	8,784	14,404	7,785	8,766	7,373
Port Hedland, Australia	13,104	13,729	14,102	16,060	4,219	14,270	4,792	16,948	11,252	9,685	9,461	13,312	10,582	14,818	13,429	17,498	16,390	5,587	14,158	5,551

Distances in Kilometers	Lome, Togo	London, United Kingdom	Londonderry, United Kingdom	Longlac, Canada	Lord Howe Island, Australia	Los Angeles, California	Louangphrabang, Laos	Louisville, Kentucky	Luanda, Angola	Lubumbashi, Zaire	Lusaka, Zambia	Luxembourg, Luxembourg	Luxor, Egypt	Lynn Lake, Canada	Lyon, France	Macapa, Brazil	Madison, Wisconsin	Madras, India	Madrid, Spain	Madurai, India
Port Louis, Mauritius	6,809	9,713	10,330	15,447	9,898	18,411	6,579	15,965	4,918	3,345	3,138	9,238	5,740	15,567	9,026	11,953	16,024	4,444	9,219	4,023
Port Moresby, Papua New Guinea	16,267	14,483	14,482	13,366	2,735	11,017	5,908	13,869	14,543	12,965	12,755	14,294	12,923	12,202	14,629	17,756	13,418	7,804	15,543	7,947
Port Said, Egypt	4,270	3,473	4,076	9,197	15,019	12,146	7,020	9,994	4,878	4,779	5,184	2,984	620	9,303	2,861	9,380	9,861	5,293	3,379	5,278
Port Sudan, Sudan	4,171	4,804	5,417	10,546	14,106	13,525	6,756	11,277	4,099	3,622	3,997	4,322	820	10,685	4,146	9,836	11,187	4,644	4,514	4,518
Port-au-Prince, Haiti	8,069	7,190	6,749	3,692	14,694	4,851	15,715	2,544	9,862	11,444	11,643	7,637	10,554	4,875	7,572	3,099	3,159	15,407	6,908	15,500
Port-of-Spain, Trin. & Tobago	6,917	7,123	6,807	4,913	15,255	6,301	16,190	3,897	8,554	10,145	10,307	7,507	9,920	6,144	7,338	1,649	4,493	15,058	6,540	15,015
Port-Vila, Vanuatu	18,121	16,123	15,852	12,578	1,791	9,653	8,341	12,586	16,005	14,632	14,308	16,128	15,382	11,678	16,546	15,298	12,324	10,249	17,379	10,370
Portland, Maine	8,054	5,143	4,576	1,414	15,534	4,237	12,929	1,434	10,161	11,517	11,860	5,632	9,044	2,607	5,729	5,196	1,549	13,051	5,375	13,269
Portland, Oregon	12,038	7,927	7,317	2,724	11,616	1,328	11,474	3,134	14,160	15,309	15,708	8,361	11,732	1,950	8,659	8,581	2,647	13,119	8,719	13,522
Porto, Portugal	4,000	1,322	1,543	5,890	18,484	9,012	10,198	6,397	5,966	6,923	7,327	1,484	4,156	6,441	1,202	6,242	6,409	8,975	425	9,020
Porto Alegre, Brazil	6,874	10,323	10,313	9,511	12,477	9,999	17,115	8,373	7,069	8,288	8,173	10,485	10,853	10,711	10,121	3,331	8,990	14,708	9,213	14,330
Porto Alexandre, Angola	2,697	7,548	8,054	11,937	13,709	14,661	10,628	11,743	790	1,746	1,759	7,268	5,113	12,857	6,855	7,128	12,105	8,179	6,429	7,834
Porto Novo, Benin	160	4,997	5,453	9,402	16,316	12,361	10,762	9,429	2,060	3,406	3,726	4,791	3,834	10,230	4,357	6,003	9,686	8,524	3,809	8,312
Porto Velho, Brazil	7,412	9,021	8,792	6,850	13,630	7,434	18,082	5,678	8,469	9,971	9,993	9,344	11,087	8,027	9,100	1,726	6,295	16,095	8,224	15,865
Portsmouth, United Kingdom	4,953	106	631	5,733	17,323	8,782	9,209	6,499	6,743	7,450	7,871	531	3,997	6,018	710	7,326	6,372	8,287	1,170	8,400
Poznan, Poland	5,331	1,176	1,622	6,595	16,183	9,487	7,959	7,509	6,792	7,171	7,594	821	3,248	6,644	1,152	8,533	7,298	7,064	2,062	7,200
Prague, Czechoslovakia	5,027	1,039	1,569	6,644	16,443	9,591	8,177	7,507	6,524	6,957	7,381	602	3,127	6,760	864	8,285	7,327	7,182	1,778	7,297
Praia, Cape Verde Islands	2,873	4,564	4,662	6,824	18,144	9,523	12,943	6,584	4,830	6,344	6,612	4,692	5,944	7,874	4,326	3,448	6,938	11,086	3,418	10,965
Pretoria, South Africa	4,575	8,994	9,567	13,902	11,806	16,673	9,452	13,761	2,453	1,561	1,144	8,627	5,711	14,723	8,262	8,937	14,113	7,095	8,032	6,695
Prince Albert, Canada	10,579	6,499	5,883	1,384	13,073	2,345	11,478	2,262	12,697	13,825	14,222	6,948	10,390	506	7,223	7,745	1,652	12,638	7,242	12,999
Prince Edward Island	6,873	11,463	12,034	15,968	9,537	17,577	9,772	15,395	4,801	3,995	3,570	11,091	8,021	17,014	10,730	9,935	15,913	7,844	10,483	7,424
Prince George, Canada	11,567	7,165	6,568	2,509	12,063	2,235	10,778	3,295	13,661	14,636	15,052	7,577	10,875	1,407	7,901	8,816	2,711	12,267	8,049	12,662
Prince Rupert, Canada	11,944	7,401	6,817	2,996	11,661	2,441	10,396	3,786	14,015	14,888	15,310	7,791	10,992	1,852	8,137	9,309	3,206	11,999	8,346	12,403
Providence, Rhode Island	8,120	5,339	4,778	1,468	15,438	4,154	13,143	1,286	10,217	11,600	11,935	5,828	9,222	2,691	5,915	5,060	1,484	13,273	5,537	13,489
Provo, Utah	11,472	7,880	7,261	2,232	12,135	901	12,491	2,239	13,576	14,918	15,273	8,347	11,830	2,002	8,585	7,555	1,875	13,976	8,490	14,361
Puerto Aisen, Chile	9,254	12,789	12,710	10,631	10,015	9,925	17,134	9,356	9,003	9,875	9,636	12,988	13,162	11,637	12,638	5,465	9,939	15,615	11,726	15,195
Puerto Deseado, Argentina	8,842	12,655	12,637	10,988	10,145	10,455	16,730	9,728	8,478	9,308	9,063	12,809	12,696	12,043	12,436	5,486	10,323	15,056	11,533	14,635
Puerto Princesa, Philippines	12,888	11,067	11,265	12,970	6,273	12,303	2,107	14,120	11,868	10,370	10,349	10,764	9,163	11,779	11,027	18,457	13,503	4,209	11,915	4,453
Punta Arenas, Chile	9,378	13,343	13,333	11,503	9,454	10,690	16,263	10,227	8,841	9,531	9,251	13,484	13,141	12,500	13,103	6,177	10,808	14,887	12,205	14,473
Pusan, South Korea	12,907	9,211	9,192	9,972	8,019	9,643	3,134	11,130	12,918	11,800	11,951	9,072	8,956	8,783	9,450	16,115	10,513	5,457	10,350	5,853
Pyongyang, North Korea	12,440	8,687	8,675	9,672	8,540	9,580	3,105	10,866	12,567	11,532	11,713	8,548	8,513	8,511	8,926	15,668	10,251	5,303	9,826	5,712
Qamdo, China	10,234	7,836	8,081	11,031	9,524	11,887	1,345	12,314	9,950	8,817	8,986	7,517	6,269	10,101	7,775	15,211	11,757	2,651	8,665	3,071
Qandahar, Afghanistan	7,250	5,704	6,147	10,586	12,050	12,727	3,854	11,732	7,153	6,291	6,562	5,271	3,289	10,127	5,390	12,528	11,360	2,531	6,178	2,716
Qiqian, China	11,408	7,253	7,199	8,412	9,999	8,866	3,937	9,659	11,974	11,252	11,519	7,157	7,675	7,327	7,556	14,166	9,057	5,641	8,436	6,061
Qom, Iran	5,987	4,446	4,950	9,758	13,460	12,315	5,271	10,784	6,234	5,692	6,036	3,984	2,015	9,527	4,048	11,104	10,504	3,803	4,791	3,893
Quebec, Canada	8,181	5,006	4,422	1,180	15,445	4,162	12,590	1,523	10,299	11,608	11,964	5,497	8,949	2,313	5,623	5,544	1,489	12,791	5,330	13,026
Quetta, Pakistan	7,348	5,896	6,341	10,768	11,875	12,871	3,709	11,919	7,184	6,276	6,535	5,461	3,405	10,293	5,577	12,684	11,543	2,337	6,358	2,523
Quito, Ecuador	8,883	9,224	8,837	5,594	13,028	5,619	17,830	4,323	10,206	11,753	11,811	9,640	12,140	6,642	9,511	3,056	4,917	17,289	8,745	17,229
Rabaul, Papua New Guinea	16,812	14,170	14,080	12,567	3,112	10,233	6,086	13,069	15,257	13,669	13,483	14,050	13,171	11,412	14,426	17,412	12,614	8,172	15,329	8,359
Raiatea (Uturoa)	16,831	15,395	14,777	9,722	5,242	6,631	12,311	9,156	16,723	16,861	16,449	15,842	18,931	9,395	16,113	11,126	9,154	14,471	15,956	14,628
Raleigh, North Carolina	8,701	6,251	5,695	1,683	14,729	3,601	13,846	691	10,747	12,212	12,514	6,739	10,104	2,882	6,813	4,880	1,229	14,164	6,394	14,393
Rangiroa (Avatoru)	16,501	15,033	14,414	9,328	5,689	6,256	12,644	8,730	16,653	17,016	16,619	15,492	18,814	9,048	15,740	10,734	8,744	14,858	15,537	15,032
Rangoon, Burma	10,347	8,991	9,328	12,627	8,583	13,307	717	13,910	9,553	8,187	8,261	8,608	6,608	11,689	8,792	15,982	13,353	1,757	9,624	2,095
Raoul Is., Kermadec Islands	17,442	17,529	17,049	12,524	2,222	9,406	10,151	12,129	15,629	14,727	14,323	17,722	16,993	11,934	18,160	13,530	12,052	11,851	18,665	11,901
Rarotonga (Avarua)	17,381	16,211	15,606	10,647	4,237	7,533	11,597	10,138	16,601	16,285	15,861	16,619	18,667	10,229	16,946	11,957	10,110	13,616	16,911	13,734
Rawson, Argentina	8,605	12,226	12,183	10,522	10,579	10,125	17,149	9,269	8,401	9,336	9,119	12,401	12,522	11,597	12,040	5,000	9,869	15,307	11,131	14,887
Recife, Brazil	4,306	7,391	7,444	8,120	15,379	9,903	15,226	7,347	5,298	6,840	6,914	7,525	8,199	9,348	7,153	2,003	7,891	12,938	6,249	12,681
Regina, Canada	10,592	6,662	6,044	1,292	13,061	2,133	11,787	2,014	12,714	13,904	14,292	7,120	10,586	750	7,378	7,526	1,419	12,950	7,352	13,310
Reykjavik, Iceland	6,699	1,896	1,306	4,026	16,379	6,947	9,537	5,005	8,612	9,379	9,799	2,322	5,771	4,130	2,632	7,500	4,744	9,289	2,897	9,502
Rhodes, Greece	4,338	2,794	3,393	8,511	15,503	11,464	7,317	9,321	5,247	5,324	5,739	2,304	1,264	8,625	2,208	9,050	9,179	5,782	2,805	5,806
Richmond, Virginia	8,600	6,041	5,481	1,542	14,871	3,680	13,650	735	10,663	12,106	12,418	6,529	9,908	2,765	6,610	4,960	1,185	13,941	6,207	14,170
Riga, USSR	5,982	1,681	1,957	6,575	15,570	9,318	7,455	7,590	7,355	7,611	8,029	1,444	3,540	6,471	1,819	9,107	7,313	6,779	2,718	6,958
Ringkobing, Denmark	5,575	750	989	5,898	16,467	8,813	8,433	6,814	7,206	7,718	8,142	735	3,908	5,977	1,174	8,157	6,599	7,696	1,950	7,851
Rio Branco, Brazil	7,857	9,376	9,121	6,867	13,236	7,218	18,481	5,655	8,877	10,362	10,369	9,713	11,532	8,009	9,484	2,160	6,269	16,540	8,617	16,301
Rio Cuarto, Argentina	8,157	11,274	11,175	9,443	11,523	9,331	18,027	8,208	8,330	9,480	9,330	11,497	12,138	10,554	11,166	3,927	8,816	15,808	10,252	15,405
Rio de Janeiro, Brazil	5,806	9,254	9,283	9,115	13,531	10,129	16,434	8,096	6,208	7,555	7,501	9,395	9,786	10,352	9,021	2,675	8,700	13,988	8,118	13,647
Rio Gallegos, Argentina	9,215	13,140	13,128	11,359	9,658	10,630	16,400	10,087	8,726	9,457	9,186	13,284	13,006	12,375	12,905	5,976	10,673	14,935	12,006	14,518
Rio Grande, Brazil	7,049	10,555	10,548	9,681	12,244	10,075	17,124	8,528	7,175	8,356	8,226	10,714	11,022	10,873	10,348	3,551	9,145	14,750	9,441	14,363
Riyadh, Saudi Arabia	5,263	4,952	5,526	10,563	13,439	13,319	5,700	11,468	5,186	4,528	4,862	4,463	1,422	10,484	4,404	10,801	11,272	3,749	4,973	3,700
Road Town, Brit. Virgin Isls.	7,254	6,664	6,275	3,989	15,419	5,563	15,529	3,003	9,060	10,638	10,846	7,086	9,838	5,222	6,979	2,520	3,588	14,825	6,258	14,867
Roanoke, Virginia	8,820	6,225	5,658	1,487	14,649	3,464	13,676	524	10,879	12,327	12,637	6,714	10,109	2,680	6,804	5,082	1,030	14,062	6,415	14,303
Robinson Crusoe Island, Chile	9,477	12,146	11,943	9,271	10,582	8,548	18,476	7,990	9,670	10,771	10,594	12,438	13,456	10,243	12,155	4,727	8,561	16,912	11,252	16,492
Rochester, New York	8,640	5,651	5,068	1,005	14,938	3,642	13,026	878	10,742	12,111	12,451	6,142	9,588	2,247	6,263	5,461	958	13,385	5,946	13,634
Rockhampton, Australia	16,225	16,004	16,048	14,310	1,239	11,539	7,103	14,484	14,168	12,714	12,414	15,765	13,787	13,269	16,057	16,540	14,165	8,641	16,953	8,692
Rome, Italy	4,116	1,434	2,053	7,163	16,850	10,212	8,535	7,887	5,614	6,126	6,550	987	2,580	7,431	748	7,848	7,790	7,216	1,365	7,266
Rosario, Argentina	7,827	11,064	10,992	9,514	11,740	9,553	17,780	8,300	7,986	9,145	9,001	11,268	11,807	10,653	10,925	3,788	8,912	15,496	10,012	15,098
Roseau, Dominica	6,903	6,712	6,368	4,449	15,549	6,035	15,723	3,490	8,650	10,235	10,428	7,111	9,684	5,687	6,968	2,036	4,071	14,766	6,200	14,763
Rostock, East Germany	5,408	874	1,260	6,230	16,389	9,144	8,243	7,138	6,969	7,429	7,853	648	3,580	6,305	1,063	8,292	6,929	7,417	1,927	7,560
Rostov-na-Donu, USSR	5,845	2,894	3,336	8,081	14,662	10,736	6,342	9,103	6,736	6,636	7,032	2,478	2,471	7,909	2,658	10,064	8,823	5,340	3,524	5,489
Rotterdam, Netherlands	5,085	322	856	5,975	16,947	8,978	8,800	6,799	6,779	7,383	7,807	282	3,755	6,175	686	7,726	6,640	7,899	1,426	8,022
Rouyn, Canada	8,780	5,402	4,799	576	14,855	3,600	12,462	1,236	10,900	12,189	12,552	5,890	9,378	1,764	6,053	5,982	990	12,913	5,829	13,182
Sacramento, California	12,321	8,521	7,904	3,024	11,303	580	12,104	3,101	14,432	15,735	16,104	8,971	12,400	2,524	9,242	8,319	2,736	13,856	9,222	14,264
Saginaw, Michigan	9,154	6,030	5,434	733	14,431	3,134	12,969	596	11,257	12,621	12,964	6,520	9,995	1,919	6,667	5,814	445	13,545	6,396	13,823
Saint Denis, Reunion	6,635	9,667	10,286	15,384	10,033	18,421	6,794	15,841	4,720	3,154	2,933	9,197	5,709	15,571	8,971	11,732	15,932	4,635	9,134	4,214
Saint George's, Grenada	6,940	7,017	6,690	4,761	15,323	6,194	16,064	3,755	8,611	10,201	10,372	7,406	9,875	5,993	7,246	1,779	4,348	14,998	6,458	14,969
Saint John, Canada	7,756	4,765	4,201	1,616	15,859	4,564	12,694	1,809	9,871	11,196	11,548	5,254	8,664	2,730	5,349	5,224	1,876	12,714	5,000	12,921
Saint John's, Antigua	6,957	6,588	6,230	4,249	15,607	5,892	15,561	3,305	8,741	10,322	10,525	6,996	9,641	5,487	6,865	2,228	3,881	14,688	6,115	14,703
Saint John's, Canada	6,860	3,750	3,211	2,481	16,792	5,555	12,127	2,864	8,982	10,234	10,601	4,236	7,614	3,382	4,308	5,269	2,891	11,839	3,946	12,011
Saint Louis, Missouri	9,713	6,779	6,183	1,274	13,806	2,559	13,405	389	11,784	13,212	13,533	7,269	10,739	2,179	7,411	5,848	499	14,197	7,118	14,496
Saint Paul, Minnesota	9,871	6,468	5,856	731	13,742	2,464	12,664	962	11,982	13,312	13,666	6,951	10,452	1,435	7,141	6,469	363	13,544	6,956	13,864
Saint Peter Port, UK	4,814	285	699	5,731	17,500	8,799	9,363	6,461	6,634	7,380	7,799	627	4,015	6,058	691	7,159	6,354	8,398	1,010	8,501
Saipan (Susupe)	15,460	11,916	11,828	11,189	5,361	9,624	4,646	12,035	14,823	13,357	13,341	11,814	11,487	9,953	12,203	17,528	11,469	7,043	13,094	7,344
Salalah, Oman	5,874	6,092	6,662	11,662	12,381	14,297	5,068	12,600	5,327	4,317	4,571	5,604	2,420	11,502	5,544	11,628	12,385	2,846	6,089	2,713
Salem, Oregon	12,099	8,001	7,390	2,781	11,554	1,276	11,501	3,166	14,221	15,378	15,776	8,434	11,806	2,021	8,732	8,597	2,687	13,165	8,789	13,569
Salt Lake City, Utah	11,470	7,846	7,227	2,213	12,143	932	12,433	2,255	13,576	14,908	15,266	8,311	11,791	1,953	8,553	7,593	1,878	13,915	8,465	14,300
Salta, Argentina	7,979	10,574	10,419	8,520	12,188	8,579	18,636	7,293	8,469	9,765	9,671	10,840	11,925	9,645	10,542	3,152	7,905	16,206	9,635	15,839
Salto, Uruguay	7,526	10,780	10,721	9,424	12,025	9,613	17,659	8,231	7,726	8,918	8,788	10,976	11,507	10,585	10,629	3,553	8,846	15,308	9,717	14,918
Salvador, Brazil	4,876	8,049	8,083	8,385	14,734	9,890	15,773	7,506	5,668	7,158	7,187	8,193	8,813	9,625	7,824	1,996	8,080	13,415	6,918	13,130
Salzburg, Austria	4,753	1,033	1,620	6,739	16,632	9,727	8,333	7,558	6,269	6,740	7,164	546	2,997	6,910	665	8,102	7,405	7,246	1,566	7,342
Samsun, Turkey	5,222	2,987	3,516	8,484	14,871	11,268	6,578	9,425	6,029	5,933	6,332	2,516	1,763	8,422	2,576	9,790	9,201	5,276	3,346	5,364
San Antonio, Texas	10,617	8,047	7,455	2,476	12,742	1,938	14,123	1,529	12,594	14,119	14,385	8,537	11,993	3,054	8,668	5,990	1,719	15,300	8,331	15,635
San Cristobal, Venezuela	8,109	8,100	7,717	4,845	14,105	5,535	16,888	3,640	9,655	11,241	11,367	8,517	11,114	5,994	8,393	2,502	4,256	16,211	7,641	16,204
San Diego, California	12,230	8,844	8,225	3,154	11,312	181	12,850	2,900	14,289	15,728	16,049	9,313	12,798	2,953	9,545	7,791	2,682	14,611	9,422	15,017
San Francisco, California	12,435	8,640	8,024	3,143	11,187	558	12,113	3,198	14,543	15,853	16,221	9,090	12,516	2,642	9,362	8,380	2,844	13,900	9,343	14,311
San Jose, Costa Rica	9,389	8,734	8,264	4,424	13,126	4,388	16,640	3,141	10,980	12,567	12,691	9,191	12,129	5,408	9,144	3,819	3,708	16,938	8,491	17,067
San Juan, Argentina	8,478	11,360	11,219	9,182	11,417	8,939	18,418	7,930	8,728	9,901	9,756	11,611	12,457	10,263	11,300	3,949	8,531	16,238	10,389	15,835
San Juan, Puerto Rico	7,413	6,765	6,366	3,923	15,278	5,424	15,577	2,905	9,215	10,794	11,000	7,193	9,978	5,150	7,094	2,622	3,497	14,944	6,384	14,995
San Luis Potosi, Mexico	11,008	8,828	8,246	3,319	12,172	2,144	14,727	2,302	12,872	14,446	14,656	9,319	12,736	3,853	9,426	5,938	2,557	16,105	9,034	16,454
San Marino, San Marino	4,329	1,263	1,880	7,005	16,803	10,036	8,479	7,760	5,838	6,340	6,764	795	2,724	7,243	636	7,918	7,644	7,238	1,388	7,304
San Miguel de Tucuman, Argen.	8,023	10,748	10,606	8,743	12,025	8,758	18,522	7,514	8,436	9,700	9,592	11,004	11,985	9,865	10,697	3,336	8,125	16,128	9,788	15,750

Distances in Kilometers

	Lome, Togo	London, United Kingdom	Londonderry, United Kingdom	Longlac, Canada	Lord Howe Island, Australia	Los Angeles, California	Louangphrabang, Laos	Louisville, Kentucky	Luanda, Angola	Lubumbashi, Zaire	Lusaka, Zambia	Luxembourg, Luxembourg	Luxor, Egypt	Lynn Lake, Canada	Lyon, France	Macapa, Brazil	Madison, Wisconsin	Madras, India	Madrid, Spain	Madurai, India
San Salvador, El Salvador	9,903	8,766	8,254	4,009	12,847	3,696	16,093	2,741	11,581	13,172	13,319	9,240	12,366	4,893	9,241	4,468	3,255	16,828	8,661	17,046
Sanaa, Yemen	4,802	5,609	6,214	11,334	13,234	14,232	6,141	12,117	4,336	3,511	3,827	5,122	1,660	11,382	4,977	10,581	11,999	3,898	5,383	3,729
Santa Cruz, Bolivia	7,551	9,804	9,629	7,832	12,933	8,184	18,468	6,638	8,289	9,692	9,651	10,087	11,419	8,992	9,805	2,377	7,254	16,084	8,904	15,768
Santa Cruz, Tenerife	3,080	2,892	3,035	6,270	19,453	9,291	11,511	6,413	5,198	6,467	6,822	3,020	4,826	7,102	2,667	4,861	6,601	9,953	1,754	9,915
Santa Fe, New Mexico	11,146	7,962	7,348	2,219	12,381	1,139	13,186	1,816	13,209	14,647	14,966	8,443	11,945	2,382	8,638	6,906	1,641	14,568	8,440	14,938
Santa Rosa, Argentina	8,280	11,586	11,508	9,819	11,217	9,620	17,733	8,578	8,321	9,403	9,229	11,792	12,252	10,921	11,449	4,282	9,184	15,634	10,536	15,223
Santa Rosalia, Mexico	11,984	9,064	8,451	3,322	11,428	941	13,610	2,751	13,962	15,489	15,754	9,546	13,048	3,400	9,735	7,193	2,704	15,336	9,506	15,735
Santarem, Brazil	6,287	7,874	7,695	6,541	14,832	7,763	16,852	5,521	7,550	9,110	9,194	8,171	9,867	7,774	7,906	489	6,122	14,942	7,018	14,755
Santiago del Estero, Argentina	7,964	10,782	10,653	8,870	11,999	8,900	18,387	7,645	8,338	9,586	9,473	11,029	11,934	9,996	10,716	3,386	8,256	16,007	9,805	15,625
Santiago, Chile	8,730	11,651	11,506	9,352	11,124	8,976	18,344	8,090	8,916	10,047	9,886	11,904	12,711	10,408	11,593	4,237	8,685	16,314	10,682	15,903
Santo Domingo, Dominican Rep.	7,812	7,027	6,602	3,779	14,921	5,077	15,677	2,679	9,608	11,188	11,390	7,467	10,332	4,983	7,388	2,899	3,287	15,236	6,705	15,310
Sao Paulo de Olivenca, Brazil	7,855	8,856	8,558	6,140	13,648	6,637	17,946	4,937	9,085	10,623	10,675	9,222	11,330	7,291	9,026	2,012	5,552	16,470	8,190	16,312
Sao Paulo, Brazil	6,146	9,470	9,471	9,028	13,327	9,896	16,780	7,968	6,559	7,896	7,833	9,631	10,125	10,257	9,267	2,651	8,577	14,332	8,359	13,987
Sao Tome, Sao Tome & Principe	887	5,707	6,195	10,216	15,499	13,149	10,570	10,208	1,241	2,649	2,942	5,460	3,952	11,049	5,035	6,433	10,485	8,227	4,561	7,971
Sapporo, Japan	13,245	8,890	8,743	8,718	8,457	8,265	4,466	9,828	13,725	12,826	13,035	8,855	9,486	7,502	9,272	15,076	9,212	6,684	10,120	7,094
Sarajevo, Yugoslavia	4,503	1,625	2,223	7,346	16,336	10,330	8,014	8,154	5,852	6,214	6,637	1,135	2,391	7,507	1,093	8,374	8,009	6,763	1,861	6,835
Saratov, USSR	6,501	3,148	3,492	7,912	14,237	10,396	5,974	9,010	7,391	7,231	7,618	2,799	3,089	7,615	3,059	10,496	8,675	5,258	3,961	5,459
Saskatoon, Canada	10,672	6,626	6,010	1,431	12,982	2,212	11,558	2,236	12,791	13,937	14,332	7,077	10,522	639	7,349	7,739	1,634	12,751	7,359	13,115
Schefferville, Canada	8,055	4,308	3,700	1,449	15,593	4,560	11,666	2,328	10,171	11,334	11,721	4,793	8,291	2,134	4,977	6,241	2,090	11,874	4,826	12,122
Seattle, Washington	11,904	7,725	7,117	2,622	11,749	1,542	11,320	3,127	14,023	15,133	15,537	8,154	11,513	1,770	8,458	8,613	2,610	12,921	8,536	13,321
Sendai, Japan	13,573	9,365	9,239	9,203	7,955	8,587	4,245	10,287	13,869	12,849	13,023	9,309	9,728	7,979	9,719	15,595	9,674	6,561	10,581	6,961
Seoul, South Korea	12,613	8,882	8,867	9,784	8,347	9,605	3,105	10,966	12,697	11,631	11,801	8,743	8,676	8,613	9,120	15,837	10,350	5,355	10,021	5,759
Sept-Iles, Canada	7,901	4,506	3,915	1,441	15,750	4,539	12,162	2,029	10,024	11,270	11,640	4,996	8,464	2,386	5,136	5,748	1,922	12,281	4,886	12,511
Sevastopol, USSR	5,293	2,597	3,107	8,051	15,127	10,841	6,805	9,000	6,256	6,261	6,667	2,140	2,100	7,993	2,246	9,578	8,769	5,631	3,068	5,739
Seville, Spain	3,537	1,635	1,961	6,330	18,509	9,451	10,191	6,786	5,491	6,457	6,858	1,670	3,860	6,909	1,294	6,202	6,826	8,815	390	8,830
Shanghai, China	12,452	9,223	9,286	10,630	7,996	10,471	2,295	11,829	12,241	11,044	11,172	9,024	8,471	9,474	9,368	16,467	11,214	4,650	10,281	5,039
Sheffield, United Kingdom	5,243	228	422	5,550	17,128	8,570	9,124	6,363	7,029	7,714	8,136	675	4,177	5,785	963	7,462	6,208	8,307	1,451	8,439
Shenyang, China	12,123	8,322	8,311	9,446	8,906	9,516	3,155	10,661	12,334	11,360	11,561	8,183	8,219	8,308	8,562	15,339	10,048	5,239	9,462	5,654
Shiraz, Iran	5,965	4,941	5,467	10,329	13,119	12,893	5,094	11,339	5,981	5,300	5,621	4,467	2,007	10,108	4,493	11,326	11,072	3,395	5,181	3,438
Sibiu, Romania	4,921	1,887	2,434	7,488	15,858	10,389	7,534	8,371	6,145	6,373	6,792	1,413	2,357	7,544	1,498	8,864	8,181	6,370	2,331	6,466
Singapore	11,401	10,860	11,223	14,260	6,859	14,136	2,064	15,519	10,108	8,564	8,509	10,458	8,071	13,185	10,607	17,240	14,918	2,907	11,396	3,004
Sioux Falls, South Dakota	10,182	6,786	6,172	1,043	13,422	2,136	12,726	1,094	12,289	13,633	13,984	7,267	10,769	1,511	7,463	6,613	598	13,727	7,285	14,060
Skelleftea, Sweden	6,693	1,911	1,896	5,863	15,341	8,489	7,608	6,954	8,184	8,494	8,912	1,901	4,424	5,655	2,336	9,157	6,621	7,270	3,139	7,496
Skopje, Yugoslavia	4,450	1,948	2,545	7,665	16,108	10,638	7,803	8,477	5,688	5,973	6,395	1,458	2,080	7,809	1,397	8,572	8,331	6,479	2,111	6,540
Socotra Island (Tamrida)	5,835	6,469	7,051	12,093	12,159	14,772	5,189	12,995	5,096	3,979	4,204	5,979	2,664	11,967	5,892	11,653	12,805	2,850	6,385	2,647
Sofia, Bulgaria	4,597	2,019	2,603	7,707	15,953	10,653	7,642	8,544	5,792	6,033	6,453	1,529	2,070	7,816	1,511	8,735	8,383	6,348	2,258	6,417
Songkhla, Thailand	10,963	10,122	10,478	13,654	7,544	13,886	1,411	14,931	9,852	8,361	8,355	9,725	7,463	12,636	9,886	16,788	14,347	2,318	10,690	2,493
Sorong, Indonesia	14,458	12,800	12,936	13,515	4,483	11,950	3,920	14,415	13,081	11,500	11,382	12,529	10,921	12,273	12,813	19,762	13,841	5,833	13,711	6,007
South Georgia Island	7,568	12,206	12,407	12,433	10,378	12,492	14,855	11,270	6,701	7,297	7,013	12,189	11,054	13,621	11,759	6,159	11,887	12,925	10,953	12,504
South Pole	10,682	15,712	16,101	15,519	6,509	13,772	12,200	14,237	9,031	8,714	8,299	15,501	12,846	16,305	15,073	10,007	14,773	11,450	14,478	11,101
South Sandwich Islands	7,510	12,348	12,619	13,122	10,095	13,232	14,108	11,984	6,405	6,828	6,513	12,270	10,751	14,326	11,833	6,767	12,601	12,223	11,084	11,802
Split, Yugoslavia	4,402	1,525	2,133	7,262	16,500	10,266	8,178	8,047	5,802	6,212	6,636	1,038	2,465	7,453	951	8,210	7,915	6,915	1,699	6,982
Spokane, Washington	11,574	7,503	6,890	2,267	12,080	1,513	11,552	2,762	13,696	14,853	15,249	7,943	11,348	1,506	8,231	8,259	2,240	13,051	8,269	13,443
Spoleto, Italy	4,211	1,375	1,994	7,112	16,812	10,152	8,491	7,852	5,707	6,208	6,632	917	2,622	7,364	713	7,897	7,746	7,204	1,391	7,261
Springbok, South Africa	4,344	9,163	9,686	13,464	12,092	15,879	10,555	13,100	2,360	2,226	1,904	8,857	6,325	14,458	8,455	7,989	13,533	8,193	8,071	7,796
Springfield, Illinois	9,653	6,654	6,056	1,136	13,885	2,615	13,288	378	11,734	13,146	13,473	7,143	10,618	2,069	7,290	5,892	364	14,059	7,008	14,357
Springfield, Massachusetts	8,221	5,398	4,832	1,374	15,341	4,055	13,123	1,199	10,319	11,699	12,035	5,888	9,293	2,603	5,981	5,136	1,381	13,297	5,615	13,520
Srinagar, India	8,123	6,138	6,509	10,535	11,427	12,340	3,121	11,751	8,035	7,120	7,369	5,745	4,148	9,921	5,926	13,245	11,312	2,391	6,768	2,696
Stanley, Falkland Islands	8,499	12,657	12,715	11,570	10,104	11,174	16,069	10,328	7,944	8,678	8,414	12,751	12,239	12,666	12,352	5,769	10,933	14,329	11,473	13,908
Stara Zagora, Bulgaria	4,685	2,189	2,764	7,852	15,764	10,774	7,457	8,707	5,810	5,991	6,409	1,701	1,964	7,931	1,700	8,917	8,535	6,156	2,449	6,227
Stockholm, Sweden	6,074	1,436	1,598	6,133	15,781	8,901	7,795	7,146	7,565	7,916	8,337	1,327	3,907	6,052	1,750	8,833	6,869	7,204	2,597	7,391
Stornoway, United Kingdom	5,814	848	363	5,019	16,844	7,996	9,180	5,904	7,637	8,333	8,755	1,259	4,729	5,190	1,582	7,547	5,705	8,585	1,991	8,752
Strasbourg, France	4,746	650	1,258	6,387	16,955	9,406	8,691	7,177	6,379	6,951	7,375	163	3,339	6,610	384	7,770	7,039	7,645	1,283	7,744
Stuttgart, West Germany	4,785	730	1,327	6,454	16,852	9,461	8,584	7,259	6,389	6,932	7,356	241	3,274	6,656	469	7,875	7,113	7,542	1,378	7,643
Subic, Philippines	12,916	10,679	10,837	12,378	6,604	11,797	2,000	13,533	12,084	10,638	10,652	10,405	9,074	11,189	10,693	18,104	12,916	4,315	11,596	4,606
Suchow, China	11,959	8,716	8,794	10,406	8,507	10,496	2,180	11,636	11,841	10,709	10,864	8,508	7,981	9,287	8,849	16,017	11,026	4,397	9,762	4,801
Sucre, Bolivia	7,801	10,042	9,857	7,905	12,685	8,125	18,710	6,692	8,501	9,884	9,830	10,332	11,678	9,046	10,054	2,620	7,306	16,298	9,156	15,971
Sudbury, Canada	8,922	5,637	5,036	550	14,698	3,416	12,648	997	11,038	12,356	12,711	6,125	9,609	1,791	6,282	5,919	765	13,147	6,041	13,420
Suez, Egypt	4,210	3,599	4,204	9,329	14,958	12,286	7,017	10,114	4,762	4,639	5,042	3,111	475	9,445	2,977	9,396	9,989	5,243	3,469	5,215
Sundsvall, Sweden	6,380	1,600	1,634	5,887	15,637	8,602	7,804	6,936	7,901	8,258	8,679	1,580	4,235	5,756	2,015	8,903	6,634	7,347	2,820	7,554
Surabaya, Indonesia	12,473	12,211	12,552	14,961	5,503	14,021	3,217	16,104	10,934	9,346	9,215	11,817	9,379	13,770	11,973	18,065	15,488	4,236	12,762	4,284
Suva, Fiji	18,644	16,300	15,884	11,886	2,448	8,850	9,329	11,736	16,617	15,432	15,069	16,447	16,408	11,116	16,885	14,265	11,540	11,307	17,528	11,436
Sverdlovsk, USSR	7,614	3,876	4,075	7,804	13,379	9,930	5,334	9,003	8,461	8,184	8,552	3,623	4,119	7,291	3,955	11,302	8,582	5,138	4,869	5,421
Svobodnyy, USSR	11,887	7,609	7,513	8,322	9,676	8,546	4,171	9,541	12,486	11,754	12,015	7,542	8,182	7,190	7,950	14,304	8,930	6,027	8,815	6,448
Sydney, Australia	15,659	16,990	17,132	15,047	783	12,065	7,902	14,951	13,537	12,225	11,877	16,672	14,102	14,135	16,882	15,604	14,753	9,119	17,687	9,098
Sydney, Canada	7,338	4,325	3,773	1,998	16,295	5,012	12,481	2,275	9,458	10,757	11,114	4,813	8,204	3,021	4,895	5,187	2,330	12,351	4,533	12,541
Syktyvkar, USSR	7,379	3,229	3,364	7,080	13,994	9,348	6,083	8,260	8,464	8,383	8,774	3,038	4,225	6,636	3,412	10,627	7,856	5,888	4,313	6,157
Szeged, Hungary	4,807	1,591	2,155	7,243	16,155	10,183	7,833	8,099	6,138	6,458	6,880	1,110	2,539	7,346	1,186	8,573	7,925	6,682	2,032	6,775
Szombathely, Hungary	4,787	1,301	1,874	6,977	16,395	9,940	8,082	7,817	6,215	6,612	7,036	819	2,778	7,111	917	8,339	7,652	6,969	1,794	7,065
Tabriz, Iran	5,757	3,886	4,389	9,230	13,965	11,860	5,711	10,237	6,223	5,847	6,214	3,425	1,882	9,047	3,501	10,655	9,970	4,353	4,265	4,452
Tacheng, China	8,886	5,752	5,968	9,260	11,541	10,807	3,455	10,523	9,212	8,496	8,784	5,466	4,983	8,516	5,761	13,174	10,026	3,741	6,670	4,107
Tahiti (Papeete)	16,615	15,381	14,763	9,678	5,378	6,605	12,525	9,074	16,541	16,759	16,353	15,838	19,075	9,392	16,089	10,923	9,093	14,673	15,882	14,823
Taipei, Taiwan	12,707	9,799	9,893	11,267	7,431	10,929	2,072	12,446	12,263	10,959	11,044	9,574	8,741	10,094	9,901	17,118	11,829	4,516	10,814	4,876
Taiyuan, China	11,432	8,148	8,240	10,116	9,077	10,474	2,235	11,371	11,425	10,374	10,559	7,934	7,464	9,044	8,272	15,487	10,772	4,211	9,186	4,628
Tallahassee, Florida	9,241	7,041	6,486	2,156	14,063	3,211	14,396	876	11,223	12,743	13,012	7,528	10,872	3,211	7,595	4,866	1,473	14,915	7,151	15,161
Tallinn, USSR	6,241	1,788	1,979	6,408	15,435	9,100	7,414	7,455	7,632	7,883	8,301	1,617	3,797	6,258	2,017	9,203	7,155	6,851	2,897	7,048
Tamanrasset, Algeria	1,899	3,224	3,733	8,251	17,242	11,360	9,821	8,586	3,594	4,500	4,900	2,976	2,770	8,867	2,549	6,614	8,696	7,919	2,137	7,818
Tampa, Florida	9,077	7,117	6,579	2,449	14,141	3,467	14,691	1,183	11,025	12,563	12,817	7,601	10,886	3,530	7,644	4,557	1,790	15,102	7,156	15,325
Tampere, Finland	6,421	1,826	1,940	6,208	15,391	8,872	7,470	7,273	7,848	8,118	8,536	1,718	4,036	6,033	2,136	9,201	6,960	6,996	2,991	7,205
Tanami, Australia	14,267	14,449	14,721	15,413	3,199	13,224	5,337	16,056	12,382	10,828	10,589	14,083	11,634	14,192	14,265	17,796	15,570	6,534	15,070	6,550
Tangier, Morocco	3,363	1,802	2,137	6,457	18,548	9,576	10,255	6,884	5,325	6,311	6,710	1,813	3,822	7,057	1,422	6,127	6,939	8,824	543	8,828
Tarawa (Betio)	18,785	14,111	13,758	10,651	3,924	7,985	7,958	10,906	17,639	16,054	15,851	14,220	14,810	9,640	14,658	15,140	10,533	10,272	15,369	10,521
Tashkent, USSR	7,737	5,248	5,594	9,639	12,227	11,621	3,907	10,837	7,968	7,269	7,569	4,876	3,784	9,086	5,090	12,494	10,416	3,308	5,960	3,585
Tbilisi, USSR	5,829	3,544	4,024	8,815	14,184	11,439	5,878	9,835	6,451	6,169	6,547	3,098	2,096	8,624	3,213	10,492	9,558	4,675	4,020	4,798
Tegucigalpa, Honduras	9,685	8,595	8,091	3,958	13,056	3,827	16,113	2,679	11,373	12,964	13,116	9,066	12,165	4,887	9,059	4,277	3,218	16,703	8,467	16,901
Tehran, Iran	6,072	4,410	4,904	9,677	13,450	12,212	5,232	10,715	6,346	5,814	6,158	3,953	2,107	9,431	4,031	11,138	10,427	3,823	4,789	3,926
Tel Aviv, Israel	4,514	3,560	4,153	9,255	14,816	12,162	6,777	10,089	5,069	4,902	5,300	3,070	737	9,313	2,981	9,618	9,935	5,084	3,548	5,081
Telegraph Creek, Canada	11,730	7,088	6,515	3,011	11,836	2,822	10,093	3,919	13,770	14,566	14,990	7,466	10,621	1,801	7,822	9,420	3,319	11,631	8,071	12,031
Teresina, Brazil	5,049	7,466	7,420	7,391	15,339	8,998	15,899	6,529	6,203	7,759	7,843	7,673	8,813	8,632	7,342	1,076	7,096	13,731	6,429	13,503
Ternate, Indonesia	14,008	12,417	12,583	13,538	4,898	12,186	3,468	14,516	12,690	11,119	11,020	12,129	10,454	12,299	12,400	19,835	13,924	5,369	13,291	5,548
The Valley, Anguilla	7,089	6,591	6,217	4,098	15,544	5,728	15,514	3,142	8,890	10,468	10,676	7,007	9,711	5,335	6,888	2,388	3,720	14,726	6,154	14,756
Thessaloniki, Greece	4,392	2,139	2,738	7,860	15,992	10,831	7,707	8,667	5,563	5,809	6,230	1,649	1,887	8,000	1,572	8,662	8,524	6,330	2,247	6,381
Thimphu, Bhutan	9,556	7,653	7,973	11,433	9,839	12,581	1,523	12,708	9,152	7,989	8,154	7,287	5,636	10,600	7,494	14,843	12,187	1,877	8,352	2,297
Thunder Bay, Canada	9,543	5,998	5,384	255	14,095	2,875	12,359	1,164	11,663	12,941	13,308	6,479	9,981	1,228	6,677	6,499	592	13,118	6,518	13,427
Tientsin, China	11,765	8,273	8,323	9,884	8,945	10,100	2,579	11,122	11,829	10,799	10,987	8,089	7,813	8,779	8,444	15,507	10,516	4,633	9,355	5,048
Tijuana, Mexico	12,225	8,853	8,234	3,160	11,313	204	12,874	2,895	14,283	15,725	16,044	9,322	12,809	2,967	9,554	7,774	2,683	14,635	9,427	15,041
Tiksi, USSR	10,587	5,774	5,547	6,255	11,682	7,196	6,004	7,522	11,809	11,626	11,990	5,830	7,530	5,236	6,266	12,053	6,934	7,255	7,035	7,653
Timbuktu, Mali	1,263	3,862	4,259	8,142	17,579	11,156	10,901	8,254	3,346	4,598	4,949	3,734	3,819	8,941	3,296	5,582	8,467	8,905	2,620	8,768
Tindouf, Algeria	2,584	2,727	3,033	6,903	18,720	9,974	10,860	7,141	4,650	5,808	6,181	2,720	4,049	7,644	2,309	5,506	7,289	9,197	1,467	9,143
Tirane, Albania	4,315	1,895	2,502	7,630	16,250	10,625	7,951	8,417	5,592	5,920	6,343	1,408	2,100	7,805	1,304	8,422	8,285	6,601	1,979	6,654

Distances in Kilometers	Lome, Togo	London, United Kingdom	Londonderry, United Kingdom	Longlac, Canada	Lord Howe Island, Australia	Los Angeles, California	Louangphrabang, Laos	Louisville, Kentucky	Luanda, Angola	Lubumbashi, Zaire	Lusaka, Zambia	Luxembourg, Luxembourg	Luxor, Egypt	Lynn Lake, Canada	Lyon, France	Macapa, Brazil	Madison, Wisconsin	Madras, India	Madrid, Spain	Madurai, India
Tokyo, Japan	13,678	9,585	9,477	9,500	7,713	8,828	4,070	10,577	13,857	12,772	12,926	9,513	9,787	8,273	9,918	15,895	9,964	6,426	10,789	6,819
Toledo, Spain	3,773	1,328	1,701	6,284	18,239	9,404	9,916	6,810	5,674	6,568	6,976	1,345	3,744	6,798	975	6,491	6,814	8,609	66	8,641
Topeka, Kansas	10,178	7,079	6,473	1,395	13,364	2,090	13,226	867	12,256	13,671	13,998	7,566	11,058	2,018	7,734	6,266	691	14,218	7,489	14,544
Toronto, Canada	8,787	5,729	5,140	872	14,800	3,502	12,968	806	10,891	12,252	12,595	6,220	9,678	2,113	6,351	5,593	814	13,392	6,054	13,650
Toulouse, France	4,151	886	1,417	6,367	17,646	9,461	9,334	7,018	5,924	6,666	7,084	758	3,451	6,752	361	7,089	6,957	8,125	553	8,184
Tours, France	4,572	462	1,015	6,059	17,473	9,130	9,233	6,773	6,346	7,060	7,480	472	3,695	6,387	367	7,240	6,677	8,170	851	8,258
Townsville, Australia	16,033	15,414	15,479	14,232	1,837	11,629	6,517	14,560	14,065	12,550	12,281	15,169	13,283	13,123	15,460	17,135	14,179	8,121	16,357	8,194
Trenton, New Jersey	8,384	5,671	5,107	1,407	15,143	3,884	13,345	974	10,469	11,877	12,203	6,160	9,555	2,649	6,248	5,059	1,257	13,569	5,866	13,794
Tripoli, Lebanon	4,741	3,441	4,019	9,093	14,781	11,959	6,651	9,963	5,347	5,178	5,575	2,952	1,018	9,109	2,903	9,727	9,785	5,055	3,532	5,079
Tripoli, Libya	3,212	2,332	2,933	7,929	16,824	11,029	8,745	8,524	4,615	5,160	5,583	1,944	2,049	8,310	1,595	7,626	8,500	7,105	1,718	7,082
Tristan da Cunha (Edinburgh)	4,983	9,882	10,211	12,061	12,358	13,478	13,457	11,237	4,052	4,862	4,659	9,769	8,389	13,287	9,330	5,722	11,805	11,104	8,621	10,708
Trondheim, Norway	6,400	1,466	1,373	5,535	15,839	8,291	8,134	6,572	8,012	8,453	8,876	1,560	4,498	5,442	1,997	8,624	6,277	7,715	2,724	7,922
Trujillo, Peru	9,047	9,950	9,599	6,456	12,449	6,236	18,699	5,180	10,129	11,611	11,609	10,344	12,575	7,478	10,180	3,233	5,765	17,707	9,371	17,517
Truk Island (Moen)	16,444	12,949	12,822	11,541	4,382	9,545	5,532	12,210	15,478	13,923	13,832	12,871	12,507	10,340	13,267	17,360	11,695	7,845	14,149	8,105
Truro, Canada	7,546	4,575	4,019	1,810	16,074	4,781	12,632	2,021	9,663	10,981	11,334	5,063	8,459	2,889	5,149	5,164	2,094	12,572	4,787	12,770
Tsingtao, China	12,150	8,709	8,753	10,135	8,508	10,154	2,526	11,352	12,120	11,021	11,186	8,526	8,183	9,000	8,882	15,911	10,740	4,737	9,792	5,143
Tsitsihar, China	11,864	7,824	7,779	8,849	9,422	9,068	3,634	10,075	12,283	11,442	11,679	7,716	8,048	7,726	8,109	14,731	9,465	5,550	8,996	5,970
Tubuai Island (Mataura)	16,354	15,935	15,317	10,200	5,120	7,163	12,685	9,521	15,985	16,115	15,707	16,405	19,682	9,976	16,621	10,878	9,583	14,675	16,308	14,769
Tucson, Arizona	11,701	8,551	7,935	2,810	11,796	709	13,255	2,382	13,738	15,210	15,513	9,029	12,531	2,842	9,232	7,215	2,243	14,852	9,042	15,242
Tulsa, Oklahoma	10,250	7,327	6,726	1,693	13,242	2,046	13,521	930	12,304	13,757	14,067	7,816	11,297	2,332	7,969	6,117	949	14,540	7,690	14,865
Tunis, Tunisia	3,517	1,825	2,422	7,426	17,114	10,520	8,882	8,047	5,058	5,662	6,084	1,459	2,460	7,798	1,089	7,483	8,007	7,386	1,271	7,394
Tura, USSR	9,829	5,464	5,411	7,342	11,790	8,595	4,936	8,626	10,737	10,354	10,695	5,383	6,385	6,448	5,790	12,497	8,072	5,891	6,658	6,278
Turin, Italy	4,358	920	1,537	6,639	17,127	9,692	8,812	7,370	5,990	6,590	7,013	519	3,102	6,922	234	7,607	7,267	7,628	1,062	7,700
Uberlandia, Brazil	6,097	9,100	9,064	8,492	13,706	9,444	16,931	7,442	6,715	8,121	8,092	9,289	10,047	9,723	8,943	2,119	8,050	14,512	8,030	14,193
Ufa, USSR	7,250	3,669	3,920	7,905	13,622	10,151	5,473	9,075	8,086	7,829	8,201	3,381	3,748	7,460	3,689	11,088	8,680	5,085	4,601	5,342
Ujungpandang, Indonesia	13,192	12,462	12,736	14,492	5,066	13,290	3,348	15,547	11,700	10,114	9,987	12,106	9,935	13,268	12,309	18,829	14,942	4,771	13,146	4,871
Ulaanbaatar, Mongolia	10,659	6,992	7,054	9,102	10,226	9,879	3,141	10,379	11,002	10,188	10,442	6,808	6,788	8,108	7,167	14,283	9,799	4,581	8,077	4,999
Ulan-Ude, USSR	10,586	6,707	6,734	8,664	10,512	9,496	3,579	9,941	11,073	10,353	10,627	6,552	6,792	7,675	6,926	13,920	9,362	4,946	7,828	5,361
Uliastay, Mongolia	9,926	6,478	6,603	9,192	10,755	10,295	3,130	10,475	10,252	9,471	9,737	6,251	6,037	8,293	6,587	13,873	9,925	4,139	7,500	4,546
Uranium City, Canada	10,515	6,127	5,523	1,778	13,098	2,923	10,769	2,871	12,600	13,578	13,991	6,551	9,915	537	6,861	8,242	2,254	11,912	6,985	12,277
Urumqi, China	9,251	6,241	6,457	9,620	11,058	10,995	2,980	10,893	9,450	8,634	8,897	5,952	5,307	8,820	6,242	13,662	10,378	3,476	7,149	3,863
Ushuaia, Argentina	9,276	13,361	13,380	11,716	9,424	10,941	16,044	10,444	8,671	9,323	9,036	13,481	12,990	12,728	13,090	6,280	11,029	14,636	12,201	14,222
Vaduz, Liechtenstein	4,616	849	1,461	6,590	16,905	9,611	8,608	7,371	6,210	6,756	7,180	369	3,136	6,815	391	7,829	7,239	7,501	1,299	7,590
Valencia, Spain	3,696	1,338	1,804	6,561	17,968	9,667	9,648	7,107	5,525	6,353	6,765	1,238	3,430	7,025	818	6,743	7,097	8,301	302	8,330
Valladolid, Spain	3,978	1,150	1,497	6,113	18,191	9,230	9,883	6,668	5,880	6,762	7,172	1,221	3,851	6,607	895	6,543	6,656	8,644	164	8,691
Valletta, Malta	3,566	2,088	2,702	7,766	16,726	10,844	8,537	8,421	4,949	5,438	5,862	1,667	2,067	8,089	1,362	7,829	8,364	6,994	1,668	6,997
Valparaiso, Chile	8,805	11,670	11,514	9,291	11,099	8,884	18,424	8,026	9,009	10,146	9,986	11,930	12,786	10,339	11,624	4,249	8,619	16,415	10,714	16,004
Vancouver, Canada	11,861	7,606	7,001	2,623	11,789	1,734	11,145	3,207	13,975	15,041	15,450	8,029	11,365	1,693	8,340	8,713	2,670	12,729	8,442	13,130
Varna, Bulgaria	4,872	2,291	2,847	7,900	15,576	10,786	7,263	8,785	5,949	6,077	6,492	1,811	1,992	7,938	1,850	9,115	8,595	6,001	2,629	6,084
Venice, Italy	4,488	1,139	1,751	6,880	16,766	9,898	8,446	7,658	6,009	6,505	6,929	657	2,846	7,096	586	7,965	7,529	7,265	1,421	7,343
Veracruz, Mexico	10,562	8,765	8,205	3,499	12,475	2,739	15,251	2,338	12,363	13,948	14,134	9,253	12,582	4,199	9,320	5,357	2,721	16,413	8,853	16,722
Verona, Italy	4,459	1,060	1,676	6,803	16,866	9,831	8,548	7,569	6,012	6,538	6,962	589	2,924	7,037	481	7,866	7,447	7,370	1,321	7,447
Victoria, Canada	11,923	7,691	7,086	2,666	11,728	1,652	11,199	3,214	14,039	15,120	15,527	8,116	11,456	1,765	8,425	8,710	2,686	12,804	8,521	13,205
Victoria, Seychelles	6,144	8,137	8,744	13,866	11,030	16,681	5,780	14,609	4,688	3,178	3,204	7,651	4,160	13,855	7,487	11,850	14,526	3,372	7,810	2,985
Vienna, Austria	4,879	1,238	1,796	6,888	16,383	9,842	8,081	7,739	6,321	6,721	7,145	766	2,876	7,011	917	8,352	7,567	7,007	1,812	7,111
Vientiane, Laos	11,004	9,312	9,596	12,447	8,146	12,811	216	13,722	10,249	8,879	8,947	8,961	7,204	11,427	9,181	16,522	13,137	2,453	10,044	2,787
Villahermosa, Mexico	10,244	8,654	8,110	3,574	12,716	3,084	15,511	2,351	12,017	13,605	13,783	9,138	12,404	4,367	9,181	4,992	2,801	16,490	8,674	16,766
Vilnius, USSR	5,801	1,730	2,079	6,809	15,577	9,574	7,386	7,806	7,126	7,355	7,772	1,424	3,276	6,726	1,756	9,131	7,542	6,613	2,668	6,779
Visby, Sweden	5,903	1,367	1,603	6,268	15,859	9,064	7,799	7,260	7,378	7,727	8,148	1,200	3,727	6,214	1,610	8,789	6,998	7,133	2,479	7,309
Vitoria, Brazil	5,407	8,869	8,915	8,999	13,905	10,201	16,118	8,033	5,888	7,277	7,245	8,999	9,386	10,241	8,622	2,535	8,627	13,683	7,721	13,356
Vladivostok, USSR	12,642	8,547	8,468	9,054	8,723	8,891	3,790	10,227	12,990	12,059	12,266	8,460	8,803	7,875	8,860	15,214	9,610	5,940	9,738	6,354
Volgograd, USSR	6,228	3,150	3,546	8,124	14,325	10,673	6,019	9,192	7,068	6,897	7,284	2,763	2,757	7,874	2,980	10,409	8,879	5,146	3,863	5,323
Vologda, USSR	6,743	2,633	2,838	6,987	14,607	9,472	6,557	8,105	7,908	7,937	8,339	2,405	3,768	6,681	2,765	10,058	7,753	6,107	3,672	6,334
Vorkuta, USSR	8,244	3,816	3,817	6,765	13,416	8,742	5,931	8,006	9,368	9,258	9,642	3,718	5,114	6,156	4,125	11,042	7,540	6,160	4,995	6,478
Wake Island	16,779	12,059	11,754	9,539	5,683	7,494	6,725	10,149	16,941	15,585	15,599	12,137	12,984	8,371	12,573	15,394	9,646	9,170	13,323	9,505
Wallis Island	19,165	15,753	15,278	11,100	3,237	8,061	9,667	10,951	17,354	16,221	15,854	15,974	16,718	10,352	16,406	13,809	10,751	11,786	16,914	11,955
Walvis Bay, Namibia	3,527	8,370	8,884	12,702	12,898	15,285	10,625	12,420	1,572	1,858	1,671	8,078	5,726	13,662	7,670	7,522	12,819	8,200	7,262	7,825
Warsaw, Poland	5,426	1,452	1,886	6,805	15,931	9,658	7,689	7,745	6,805	7,109	7,529	1,084	3,108	6,809	1,381	8,792	7,518	6,793	2,294	6,934
Washington, D.C.	8,569	5,915	5,351	1,425	14,931	3,701	13,500	764	10,644	12,070	12,389	6,404	9,798	2,658	6,493	5,054	1,138	13,790	6,106	14,022
Watson Lake, Canada	11,468	6,807	6,234	2,880	12,083	2,997	10,028	3,859	13,499	14,284	14,708	7,184	10,346	1,646	7,540	9,326	3,249	11,486	7,794	11,881
Weimar, East Germany	5,060	800	1,325	6,410	16,604	9,374	8,373	7,265	6,626	7,115	7,539	400	3,345	6,549	753	8,111	7,089	7,418	1,652	7,538
Wellington, New Zealand	16,057	18,807	18,473	13,912	1,771	10,793	10,082	13,372	14,148	13,255	12,846	18,735	16,141	13,402	19,066	13,531	13,376	11,333	19,853	11,289
West Berlin, West Germany	5,262	934	1,390	6,407	16,398	9,332	8,196	7,300	6,794	7,238	7,662	604	3,389	6,496	976	8,307	7,101	7,303	1,871	7,436
Wewak, Papua New Guinea	15,860	13,721	13,733	13,060	3,497	10,982	5,224	13,716	14,365	12,774	12,613	13,529	12,289	11,853	13,866	18,357	13,211	7,237	14,780	7,415
Whangarei, New Zealand	16,655	18,197	17,858	13,545	1,487	10,427	9,775	13,123	14,697	13,717	13,318	18,194	16,218	12,941	18,590	13,888	13,065	11,213	19,458	11,210
Whitehorse, Canada	11,681	6,931	6,374	3,227	11,831	3,202	9,723	4,208	13,678	14,376	14,801	7,290	10,364	1,989	7,660	9,676	3,599	11,247	7,961	11,648
Wichita, Kansas	10,347	7,288	6,682	1,596	13,179	1,927	13,317	1,018	12,415	13,846	14,166	7,775	11,267	2,147	7,942	6,313	899	14,378	7,694	14,711
Willemstad, Curacao	7,723	7,500	7,116	4,477	14,668	5,538	16,337	3,341	9,381	10,972	11,133	7,918	10,572	5,670	7,799	2,387	3,956	15,630	7,057	15,644
Wiluna, Australia	13,200	14,356	14,760	16,569	3,804	14,419	5,499	17,273	11,237	9,711	9,448	13,923	11,026	15,332	14,008	16,922	16,780	6,159	14,685	6,086
Windhoek, Namibia	3,617	8,377	8,905	12,857	12,783	15,505	10,362	12,619	1,580	1,636	1,420	8,068	5,598	13,784	7,668	7,778	13,003	7,939	7,297	7,562
Windsor, Canada	9,081	6,054	5,463	875	14,487	3,194	13,102	507	11,178	12,559	12,896	6,545	10,008	2,065	6,681	5,671	529	13,641	6,387	13,912
Winnipeg, Canada	10,088	6,322	5,703	763	13,561	2,463	12,049	1,579	12,210	13,442	13,821	6,792	10,285	817	7,024	7,044	963	13,025	6,938	13,362
Winston-Salem, North Carolina	8,847	6,333	5,770	1,603	14,595	3,452	13,805	545	10,895	12,357	12,660	6,822	10,205	2,782	6,906	5,005	1,102	14,192	6,503	14,431
Wroclaw, Poland	5,196	1,194	1,681	6,699	16,232	9,609	7,978	7,595	6,647	7,027	7,450	793	3,119	6,768	1,078	8,493	7,395	7,026	1,992	7,152
Wuhan, China	11,834	8,894	9,017	10,869	8,348	10,982	1,702	12,108	11,561	10,364	10,498	8,654	7,855	9,763	8,973	16,282	11,501	3,988	9,885	4,383
Wyndham, Australia	14,151	13,948	14,205	15,090	3,612	13,126	4,832	15,854	12,367	10,790	10,580	13,595	11,281	13,854	13,794	18,295	15,326	6,140	14,621	6,186
Xi'an, China	11,234	8,266	8,407	10,571	8,985	10,991	1,730	11,836	11,078	9,963	10,129	8,016	7,252	9,522	8,330	15,677	11,242	3,721	9,242	4,134
Xining, China	10,544	7,654	7,832	10,399	9,622	11,153	1,857	11,680	10,461	9,415	9,609	7,383	6,563	9,427	7,682	15,081	11,108	3,375	8,591	3,796
Yakutsk, USSR	11,272	6,665	6,499	7,202	10,701	7,760	5,139	8,446	12,226	11,781	12,102	6,662	7,872	6,113	7,089	13,124	7,843	6,687	7,909	7,102
Yanji, China	12,496	8,477	8,417	9,157	8,778	9,060	3,615	10,342	12,807	11,865	12,071	8,376	8,637	7,988	8,771	15,251	9,726	5,747	9,655	6,161
Yaounde, Cameroon	1,171	5,390	5,919	10,261	15,449	13,292	9,935	10,384	1,413	2,462	2,821	5,095	3,304	10,993	4,686	6,974	10,603	7,619	4,325	7,379
Yap Island (Colonia)	14,951	12,154	12,167	12,141	5,063	10,657	4,033	13,038	13,987	12,464	12,411	11,974	11,082	10,899	12,323	18,554	12,461	6,316	13,236	6,576
Yaraka, Australia	15,561	15,780	15,928	14,882	1,645	12,186	6,719	15,130	13,523	12,051	11,758	15,477	13,208	13,793	15,716	16,816	14,786	8,097	16,571	8,123
Yarmouth, Canada	7,728	4,858	4,302	1,686	15,867	4,569	12,851	1,759	9,839	11,186	11,531	5,346	8,735	2,833	5,428	5,077	1,880	12,845	5,053	13,047
Yellowknife, Canada	10,676	6,120	5,531	2,202	12,893	3,169	10,333	3,317	12,729	13,605	14,025	6,522	9,806	972	6,857	8,663	2,701	11,534	7,051	11,907
Yerevan, USSR	5,727	3,621	4,117	8,951	14,171	11,597	5,884	9,957	6,305	6,004	6,380	3,166	1,949	8,777	3,259	10,482	9,690	4,605	4,045	4,715
Yinchuan, China	10,890	7,757	7,890	10,148	9,486	10,757	2,101	11,421	10,883	9,860	10,058	7,516	6,917	9,134	7,838	15,160	10,837	3,810	8,751	4,230
Yogyakarta, Indonesia	12,215	12,097	12,460	15,094	5,683	14,267	3,190	16,268	10,664	9,076	8,946	11,692	9,172	13,921	11,832	17,799	15,650	4,050	12,603	4,078
York, United Kingdom	5,294	269	421	5,540	17,074	8,553	9,084	6,364	7,072	7,748	8,170	690	4,188	5,762	997	7,510	6,203	8,284	1,505	8,419
Yumen, China	10,133	7,153	7,335	10,068	10,123	11,030	2,253	11,351	10,167	9,206	9,426	6,881	6,161	9,146	7,181	14,580	10,795	3,422	8,091	3,840
Yutian, China	8,760	6,386	6,695	10,337	11,049	11,886	2,738	11,589	8,730	7,809	8,052	6,033	4,778	9,616	6,261	13,674	11,107	2,639	7,137	3,005
Yuzhno-Sakhalinsk, USSR	13,017	8,534	8,362	8,288	8,847	7,947	4,741	9,412	13,653	12,863	13,100	8,521	9,353	7,078	8,944	14,630	8,795	6,872	9,775	7,288
Zagreb, Yugoslavia	4,622	1,342	1,935	7,056	16,481	10,041	8,160	7,870	6,053	6,467	6,891	852	2,681	7,220	867	8,248	7,721	6,988	1,706	7,073
Zahedan, Iran	6,750	5,525	6,008	10,652	12,374	12,969	4,287	11,746	6,632	5,797	6,079	5,070	2,811	10,286	5,146	12,125	11,417	2,705	5,888	2,814
Zamboanga, Philippines	13,310	11,531	11,714	13,145	5,795	12,232	2,587	14,242	12,197	10,670	10,623	11,235	9,628	11,931	11,503	18,939	13,630	4,627	12,393	4,849
Zanzibar, Tanzania	4,432	7,405	8,022	13,034	12,410	16,149	7,466	13,453	2,878	1,425	1,570	6,957	3,594	13,405	6,685	10,045	13,545	5,019	6,767	4,670
Zaragoza, Spain	3,938	1,098	1,560	6,361	17,915	9,472	9,593	6,953	5,768	6,578	6,993	1,040	3,546	6,808	650	6,818	6,924	8,327	272	8,371
Zashiversk, USSR	11,293	6,450	6,196	6,370	11,064	6,929	6,001	7,602	12,500	12,255	12,606	6,522	8,199	5,261	6,960	12,441	6,996	7,507	7,713	7,918
Zhengzhou, China	11,637	8,486	8,588	10,432	8,744	10,672	2,002	11,679	11,518	10,402	10,564	8,262	7,658	9,342	8,593	15,842	11,076	4,128	9,507	4,537
Zurich, Switzerland	4,621	767	1,383	6,510	16,975	9,537	8,685	7,285	6,240	6,808	7,232	298	3,216	6,746	324	7,758	7,156	7,590	1,237	7,680

Distances in Kilometers	Magadan, USSR	Magdalena, Bolivia	Magdeburg, East Germany	Majuro Atoll, Marshall Isls.	Malabo, Equatorial Guinea	Male, Maldives	Manado, Indonesia	Managua, Nicaragua	Manama, Bahrain	Manaus, Brazil	Manchester, New Hampshire	Mandalay, Burma	Mangareva Island, Fr.Polynesia	Manila, Philippines	Mannheim, West Germany	Maputo, Mozambique	Mar del Plata, Argentina	Maracaibo, Venezuela	Marrakech, Morocco	Marseilles, France
Magdalena, Bolivia	14,129	0	10,225	13,947	8,272	15,264	18,374	3,731	13,110	1,216	6,282	17,725	7,503	19,463	9,909	10,028	2,810	2,780	7,783	9,427
Magdeburg, East Germany	7,086	10,225	0	13,151	5,374	7,765	11,433	9,486	4,341	9,047	5,986	7,733	15,717	10,005	374	8,892	12,023	8,622	2,785	1,091
Majuro Atoll, Marshall Isls.	6,067	13,947	13,151	0	17,733	10,816	5,180	11,200	12,633	14,344	11,619	8,189	6,747	5,539	13,511	15,178	14,054	12,801	15,712	14,238
Malabo, Equatorial Guinea	12,240	8,272	5,374	17,733	0	7,182	12,901	10,481	5,101	7,692	8,934	9,584	15,577	12,291	5,069	4,170	8,227	8,893	3,551	4,394
Male, Maldives	8,912	15,264	7,765	10,816	7,182	0	5,720	17,159	3,464	14,869	13,727	3,150	16,308	5,340	7,884	5,516	13,795	15,837	8,974	7,940
Manado, Indonesia	6,821	18,374	11,433	5,180	12,901	5,720	0	16,274	8,373	19,464	14,817	3,855	11,125	1,509	11,750	10,316	15,954	17,761	13,848	12,227
Managua, Nicaragua	10,578	3,731	9,486	11,200	10,481	17,159	16,274	0	13,712	3,362	3,706	16,218	6,583	15,803	9,332	13,473	6,308	1,609	8,213	9,230
Manama, Bahrain	8,079	13,110	4,341	12,633	5,101	3,464	8,373	13,712	0	12,224	10,327	4,627	19,368	7,380	4,431	6,089	13,281	12,562	5,677	4,483
Manaus, Brazil	13,213	1,216	9,047	14,344	7,692	14,869	19,464	3,362	12,224	0	5,237	16,703	8,338	18,733	8,743	10,123	3,869	1,995	6,708	8,296
Manchester, New Hampshire	7,998	6,282	5,986	11,619	8,934	13,727	14,817	3,706	10,327	5,237	0	12,697	9,783	13,505	5,913	13,032	9,080	3,583	5,629	6,014
Mandalay, Burma	5,957	17,725	7,733	8,189	9,584	3,150	3,855	16,218	4,627	16,703	12,697	0	14,809	2,755	8,014	8,665	16,938	16,153	9,997	8,420
Mangareva Island, Fr.Polynesia	11,351	7,503	15,717	6,747	15,577	16,308	11,125	6,583	19,368	8,338	9,783	14,809	0	12,055	15,689	14,411	7,400	7,843	14,747	15,757
Manila, Philippines	5,557	19,463	10,005	5,539	12,291	5,340	1,509	15,803	7,380	18,733	13,505	2,755	12,055	0	10,337	10,561	17,406	16,891	12,553	10,864
Mannheim, West Germany	7,445	9,909	374	13,511	5,069	7,884	11,750	9,332	4,431	8,743	5,913	8,014	15,689	10,337	0	8,692	11,658	8,399	2,412	727
Maputo, Mozambique	14,042	10,028	8,892	15,178	4,170	5,516	10,316	13,473	6,089	10,123	13,032	8,665	14,411	10,561	8,692	0	8,294	11,939	7,695	8,158
Mar del Plata, Argentina	16,881	2,810	12,023	14,054	8,227	13,795	15,954	6,308	13,281	3,869	9,080	16,938	7,400	17,406	11,658	8,294	0	5,583	9,266	11,017
Maracaibo, Venezuela	11,354	2,780	8,622	12,801	8,893	15,837	17,761	1,609	12,562	1,995	3,583	16,153	7,843	16,891	8,399	11,939	5,583	0	6,905	8,156
Marrakech, Morocco	9,711	7,783	2,785	15,712	3,551	8,974	13,848	8,213	5,677	6,708	5,629	9,997	14,747	12,553	2,412	7,695	9,266	6,905	0	1,751
Marseilles, France	8,172	9,427	1,091	14,238	4,394	7,940	12,227	9,230	4,483	8,296	6,014	8,420	15,757	10,864	727	8,158	11,017	8,156	1,751	0
Maseru, Lesotho	14,631	9,453	9,158	15,503	4,169	6,136	10,811	12,964	6,622	9,603	12,852	9,286	13,908	11,130	8,930	624	7,671	11,466	7,720	8,351
Mashhad, Iran	6,674	13,893	4,122	11,438	6,320	3,849	7,712	13,565	1,408	12,849	9,926	3,858	17,992	6,512	4,332	7,454	14,547	12,731	6,141	4,624
Mazatlan, Mexico	8,498	6,129	9,732	8,930	12,400	16,994	13,845	2,458	14,005	5,816	3,888	14,446	5,984	13,380	9,717	15,883	8,485	3,945	9,436	9,887
Mbabane, Swaziland	14,154	9,880	8,899	15,301	4,107	5,660	10,459	13,328	6,176	9,977	12,941	8,808	14,336	10,709	8,691	148	8,154	11,799	7,643	8,146
Mbandaka, Zaire	12,233	9,197	5,808	16,926	1,131	6,155	11,864	11,600	4,515	8,717	9,984	8,757	16,162	11,388	5,556	3,264	8,776	10,004	4,457	4,958
McMurdo Sound, Antarctica	15,244	9,457	16,976	9,405	11,691	10,472	9,101	11,762	13,412	10,643	15,422	11,886	6,804	10,597	16,727	8,105	6,869	11,926	14,887	16,084
Mecca, Saudi Arabia	9,086	11,974	4,180	13,849	3,884	4,116	9,442	13,063	1,217	11,162	10,010	5,787	19,460	8,540	4,158	5,304	12,073	11,742	4,858	3,998
Medan, Indonesia	7,625	17,852	9,491	8,042	9,980	2,800	2,921	18,183	5,701	17,669	14,752	2,057	13,877	2,736	9,723	7,825	15,498	18,107	11,373	10,005
Medellin, Colombia	11,650	2,509	9,276	12,473	9,352	16,413	17,607	1,344	13,199	2,018	4,091	16,753	7,224	17,074	9,054	12,133	5,243	655	7,531	8,808
Medicine Hat, Canada	5,825	8,359	7,445	8,556	11,725	14,003	12,250	4,757	11,357	7,619	3,070	11,601	8,452	11,257	7,549	15,893	11,057	5,644	8,204	7,952
Medina, Saudi Arabia	8,803	11,993	3,878	13,719	4,021	4,277	9,467	12,887	1,122	11,134	9,751	5,747	19,456	8,502	3,872	5,631	12,241	11,613	4,710	3,751
Melbourne, Australia	10,808	13,582	16,091	5,674	14,190	8,679	4,822	14,210	12,113	14,793	16,901	8,369	7,632	6,321	16,341	10,042	11,297	15,290	17,469	16,582
Memphis, Tennessee	8,125	6,021	7,732	10,348	10,577	15,347	14,575	2,573	12,058	5,270	1,826	13,649	7,999	13,608	7,690	14,503	8,764	3,291	7,416	7,830
Merauke, Indonesia	7,600	16,400	13,312	3,836	14,652	7,549	2,040	14,920	10,402	17,432	15,092	5,889	9,114	3,325	13,652	11,349	14,539	16,523	15,862	14,189
Merida, Mexico	9,545	4,708	8,930	10,680	10,739	16,692	15,526	1,038	13,256	4,187	2,971	15,212	6,926	14,854	8,825	14,145	7,339	2,237	8,056	8,831
Meridian, Mississippi	8,454	5,694	7,886	10,532	10,494	15,565	14,870	2,252	12,224	4,960	1,918	13,967	7,867	13,929	7,826	14,340	8,433	2,975	7,422	7,929
Messina, Italy	8,418	10,040	1,583	14,392	3,875	6,963	11,584	10,197	3,532	8,973	7,042	7,731	16,761	10,320	1,378	7,320	11,276	9,043	2,266	1,029
Mexico City, Mexico	9,238	5,277	9,661	9,719	11,750	17,296	14,698	1,594	14,000	4,954	3,683	15,138	6,103	14,237	9,595	15,044	7,700	3,109	9,011	9,671
Miami, Florida	9,466	4,664	7,910	11,507	9,733	15,667	15,974	1,638	12,207	3,868	2,069	14,704	8,006	14,990	7,783	13,372	7,445	1,901	6,957	7,754
Midway Islands, USA	4,241	12,969	11,059	2,623	16,409	11,667	6,806	9,490	12,108	12,851	9,096	8,568	7,278	6,501	11,381	17,059	14,400	10,966	13,288	12,083
Milan, Italy	7,847	9,799	767	13,909	4,622	7,705	11,858	9,479	4,241	8,659	6,166	8,064	15,945	10,485	450	8,257	11,402	8,458	2,137	387
Milford Sound, New Zealand	11,649	11,736	18,068	5,740	15,039	10,663	6,638	12,210	14,121	12,917	15,355	10,348	5,675	8,080	18,361	10,970	9,792	13,246	18,522	18,603
Milwaukee, Wisconsin	7,434	6,697	6,951	10,349	10,272	14,471	14,092	3,427	11,244	5,831	1,339	12,792	8,766	12,980	6,938	14,365	9,485	3,920	6,928	7,143
Minsk, USSR	6,448	11,305	1,082	12,435	5,818	6,915	10,353	10,420	3,612	10,129	6,813	6,660	16,288	8,933	1,404	8,861	13,018	9,652	3,753	2,002
Mogadiscio, Somalia	10,672	12,183	6,373	13,934	4,071	3,131	8,844	14,462	2,730	11,741	11,994	5,909	17,675	8,413	6,312	3,394	11,286	12,917	6,474	6,040
Mombasa, Kenya	11,572	11,403	6,768	14,659	3,542	3,864	9,496	14,022	3,550	11,068	12,029	6,781	16,944	9,200	6,650	2,541	10,369	12,428	6,406	6,271
Monclova, Mexico	8,400	6,005	9,113	9,401	11,813	16,542	14,158	2,273	13,411	5,551	3,240	14,278	6,607	13,533	9,087	15,465	8,518	3,604	8,793	9,244
Moncton, Canada	7,851	6,582	5,357	11,929	8,446	13,106	14,650	4,275	9,697	5,474	633	12,221	10,416	13,259	5,280	12,587	9,343	3,981	5,066	5,386
Monrovia, Liberia	12,521	6,283	5,485	18,500	2,190	9,337	15,033	8,297	6,855	5,569	7,167	11,476	13,779	14,231	5,115	5,890	6,888	6,704	2,818	4,395
Monte Carlo, Monaco	8,075	9,596	990	14,139	4,432	7,792	12,058	9,381	4,332	8,465	6,134	8,250	15,893	10,697	644	8,134	11,168	8,319	1,905	170
Monterrey, Mexico	8,573	5,831	9,162	9,524	11,735	16,656	14,315	2,100	13,475	5,387	3,251	14,445	6,564	13,705	9,126	15,333	8,343	3,448	8,766	9,263
Montevideo, Uruguay	16,637	2,518	11,673	14,296	8,004	13,821	16,305	6,098	13,086	3,538	8,763	16,970	7,596	17,739	11,310	8,305	367	5,298	8,923	10,675
Montgomery, Alabama	8,553	5,583	7,740	10,751	10,270	15,452	15,037	2,241	12,080	4,812	1,757	13,981	8,029	14,056	7,669	14,118	8,343	2,838	7,215	7,754
Montpelier, Vermont	7,834	6,435	5,963	11,479	9,033	13,683	14,652	3,793	10,303	5,397	167	12,578	9,790	13,346	5,901	13,146	9,235	3,725	5,696	6,026
Montpellier, France	8,176	9,329	1,115	14,242	4,441	8,067	12,327	9,103	4,609	8,192	5,890	8,527	15,630	10,955	742	8,242	10,953	8,034	1,689	127
Montreal, Canada	7,676	6,585	5,935	11,350	9,120	13,632	14,494	3,888	10,271	5,553	327	12,458	9,804	13,191	5,885	13,247	9,387	3,866	5,754	6,031
Moosonee, Canada	6,875	7,336	5,921	10,630	9,646	13,405	13,683	4,370	10,188	6,341	1,154	11,881	9,799	12,413	5,931	13,813	10,145	4,579	6,172	6,189
Moroni, Comoros	12,105	11,555	7,697	14,304	4,182	3,767	9,135	14,548	4,267	11,392	12,897	6,865	16,150	9,051	7,583	1,940	10,149	12,940	7,268	7,201
Moscow, USSR	5,926	11,956	1,736	11,842	6,314	6,568	9,701	10,868	3,445	10,771	7,201	6,053	16,330	8,269	2,073	9,067	13,689	10,202	4,426	2,675
Mosul, Iraq	7,495	12,420	3,030	12,777	5,039	4,740	9,173	12,475	1,326	11,397	9,013	5,321	18,528	7,989	3,148	6,984	13,206	11,447	4,699	3,292
Mount Isa, Australia	8,959	15,445	14,359	4,641	14,380	7,704	2,931	15,069	10,905	16,625	16,225	6,679	8,701	4,399	14,667	10,598	13,265	16,524	16,578	15,098
Multan, Pakistan	6,576	15,111	5,394	10,544	7,190	2,906	6,459	14,755	2,095	14,115	11,066	2,616	17,291	5,338	5,618	7,471	15,302	14,015	7,414	5,921
Munich, West Germany	7,504	10,072	447	13,563	4,928	7,621	11,587	9,588	4,164	8,918	6,184	7,821	15,961	10,194	273	8,472	11,735	8,631	2,469	722
Murcia, Spain	8,889	8,676	1,864	14,946	3,923	8,389	12,970	8,771	4,985	7,569	5,814	9,136	15,353	11,638	1,490	7,905	10,209	7,582	944	807
Murmansk, USSR	4,903	11,668	2,184	10,967	7,461	7,803	9,922	9,861	4,892	10,452	6,157	6,671	14,845	8,419	2,546	10,527	13,911	9,482	4,893	3,272
Mururoa Atoll, Fr. Polynesia	11,029	7,924	15,808	6,318	16,006	16,013	10,722	6,869	18,948	8,741	9,953	14,383	431	11,630	15,820	14,634	7,817	8,180	15,070	15,961
Muscat, Oman	7,895	13,915	5,069	11,962	5,779	2,696	7,536	14,517	858	13,064	11,039	3,843	18,649	6,596	5,194	6,161	13,830	13,412	6,534	5,300
Myitkyina, Burma	5,568	17,675	7,539	8,052	9,700	3,485	3,959	15,833	4,670	16,569	12,349	398	14,743	2,738	7,833	8,988	17,279	15,845	9,895	8,275
Naga, Philippines	5,581	19,244	10,227	5,299	12,541	5,561	1,356	15,698	7,638	18,794	13,560	3,013	11,797	258	10,562	10,729	17,304	16,868	12,795	11,098
Nagasaki, Japan	3,352	17,427	8,851	5,118	12,630	6,664	3,507	13,727	7,546	16,563	11,335	3,535	11,824	2,211	9,219	12,172	19,128	14,684	11,620	9,871
Nagoya, Japan	2,895	16,804	8,971	4,678	13,109	7,355	3,933	13,079	8,073	16,056	10,884	4,218	11,295	2,782	9,344	12,867	18,694	14,116	11,756	10,027
Nagpur, India	6,974	16,039	6,646	9,949	7,825	1,993	5,417	15,994	2,956	15,178	12,292	1,761	16,521	4,487	6,862	7,240	15,479	15,261	8,547	7,130
Nairobi, Kenya	11,457	11,171	6,377	14,935	3,168	4,119	9,804	13,645	3,384	10,771	11,589	6,927	17,165	9,427	6,247	2,769	10,309	12,061	5,966	5,850
Nanchang, China	4,328	18,305	8,436	6,262	11,472	5,246	3,157	14,902	6,378	17,144	12,033	2,123	13,007	1,648	8,781	10,757	18,811	15,578	11,082	9,352
Nancy, France	7,583	9,722	548	13,649	4,986	8,019	11,937	9,186	4,560	8,557	5,801	8,196	15,584	10,525	188	8,675	11,476	8,232	2,239	602
Nandi, Fiji	8,909	12,444	15,994	2,843	18,029	11,630	6,141	11,080	14,500	13,322	13,048	9,890	4,984	7,153	16,354	13,859	11,586	12,580	18,381	17,080
Nanjing, China	3,868	17,911	8,311	6,076	11,659	5,651	3,443	14,438	6,560	16,801	11,630	2,506	12,816	1,948	8,665	11,167	19,269	15,151	11,013	9,268
Nanning, China	5,257	18,697	8,473	6,932	10,831	4,290	2,961	15,826	5,815	17,497	12,718	1,263	13,599	1,617	8,790	9,784	17,857	16,301	10,950	9,284
Nantes, France	7,903	9,131	1,099	13,940	4,918	8,554	12,527	8,632	5,090	7,961	5,335	8,797	15,104	11,104	783	8,799	10,956	7,642	1,816	697
Naples, Italy	8,186	10,018	1,275	14,196	4,144	7,161	11,621	10,005	3,709	8,924	6,783	7,779	16,538	10,318	1,063	7,634	11,377	8,898	2,237	782
Narvik, Norway	5,316	11,031	1,838	11,373	7,209	8,262	10,557	9,308	5,185	9,815	5,603	7,286	14,630	9,052	2,168	10,541	13,300	8,869	4,407	2,885
Nashville, Tennessee	8,157	5,974	7,451	10,615	10,268	15,111	14,714	2,661	11,785	5,164	1,516	13,560	8,289	13,679	7,400	14,221	8,746	3,211	7,097	7,526
Nassau, Bahamas	9,647	4,486	7,782	11,802	9,451	15,514	16,226	1,713	12,050	3,640	2,059	14,748	8,189	15,191	7,640	13,077	7,283	1,707	6,726	7,580
Natal, Brazil	14,016	3,279	7,800	17,112	5,004	12,130	17,772	5,990	9,880	2,768	6,522	14,500	10,755	17,254	7,435	7,515	4,223	4,426	5,050	6,800
Natashquan, Canada	7,485	7,041	4,917	11,870	8,315	12,641	14,242	4,774	9,256	5,912	1,088	11,718	10,827	12,823	4,861	12,482	9,780	4,475	4,852	5,016
Nauru Island	6,812	14,198	13,837	973	17,581	10,408	4,690	11,857	12,658	14,798	12,566	8,068	6,752	5,327	14,207	14,319	13,779	13,465	16,522	14,927
Ndjamena, Chad	11,133	9,181	4,452	16,632	1,154	6,490	12,135	10,940	4,032	8,471	8,821	8,606	16,631	11,352	4,188	4,621	9,356	9,415	3,202	3,579
Nelson, New Zealand	11,368	11,578	18,168	5,367	15,571	11,125	6,800	11,762	14,562	12,727	14,801	10,588	5,192	8,193	18,521	11,534	9,826	12,881	18,928	18,999
Nema, Mauritania	11,330	7,079	4,282	17,371	2,258	8,902	14,405	8,485	6,043	6,198	6,679	10,647	14,536	13,376	3,912	6,386	8,009	6,969	1,665	3,192
Neuquen, Argentina	16,456	2,865	12,688	13,151	9,142	14,536	15,655	5,965	14,204	4,050	9,082	17,604	6,477	17,164	12,334	9,090	923	5,505	9,982	11,729
New Delhi, India	6,397	15,692	5,909	10,026	7,710	2,751	5,878	15,162	2,640	14,694	11,457	2,034	16,761	4,763	6,149	7,696	15,728	14,527	7,991	6,478
New Glasgow, Canada	7,957	6,526	5,258	12,100	8,273	13,017	14,739	4,329	9,594	5,403	759	12,219	10,533	13,332	5,170	12,412	9,272	3,963	4,902	5,256
New Haven, Connecticut	8,130	6,116	6,201	11,586	9,043	13,946	14,941	3,484	10,541	5,092	223	12,906	9,577	13,655	6,122	13,114	8,920	3,397	5,781	6,211
New Orleans, Louisiana	8,633	5,540	8,175	10,456	10,658	15,862	14,936	2,011	12,514	4,862	2,198	14,217	7,586	14,064	8,109	14,425	8,249	2,868	7,651	8,201
New Plymouth, New Zealand	11,140	11,650	18,022	5,125	15,823	11,209	6,735	11,682	14,624	12,782	14,633	10,548	5,100	8,101	18,388	11,774	9,978	12,848	19,160	18,962
New York, New York	8,157	6,069	6,313	11,527	9,133	14,057	14,960	3,385	10,653	5,059	330	12,987	9,464	13,692	6,235	13,192	8,875	3,337	5,884	6,323
Newcastle upon Tyne, UK	7,067	9,556	932	13,084	5,759	8,694	12,086	8,572	5,272	8,354	5,055	8,505	14,800	10,614	920	9,545	11,598	7,771	2,645	1,396
Newcastle Waters, Australia	8,676	16,105	13,670	4,966	13,812	6,994	2,290	15,731	10,166	17,307	16,331	5,961	9,434	3,791	13,967	10,216	13,767	17,234	15,838	14,374
Niamey, Niger	11,430	7,886	4,371	17,427	1,305	7,898	13,503	9,537	5,235	7,103	7,666	9,861	15,389	12,615	4,031	5,474	8,433	8,004	2,257	3,316
Nicosia, Cyprus	8,048	11,531	2,555	13,577	4,303	5,377	10,054	11,792	1,921	10,521	8,485	6,206	18,264	8,882	2,576	6,767	12,375	10,666	3,841	2,563
Niue (Alofi)	9,411	11,144	16,324	3,559	18,310	12,960	7,477	9,796	15,809	11,986	12,104	11,184	3,654	8,433	16,622	14,471	10,553	11,262	17,732	17,277

Distances in Kilometers	Magadan, USSR	Magdalena, Bolivia	Magdeburg, East Germany	Majuro Atoll, Marshall Isls.	Malabo, Equatorial Guinea	Male, Maldives	Manado, Indonesia	Managua, Nicaragua	Manama, Bahrain	Manaus, Brazil	Manchester, New Hampshire	Mandalay, Burma	Mangareva Island, Fr.Polynesia	Manila, Philippines	Mannheim, West Germany	Maputo, Mozambique	Mar del Plata, Argentina	Maracaibo, Venezuela	Marrakech, Morocco	Marseilles, France
Norfolk, Virginia	8,479	5,699	6,753	11,495	9,325	14,509	15,237	2,913	11,089	4,737	797	13,442	9,050	14,032	6,663	13,304	8,509	2,938	6,183	6,721
Norfolk Island, Australia	9,945	12,722	16,782	4,019	16,456	10,665	5,697	12,185	13,913	13,793	14,566	9,550	5,697	6,983	17,152	12,286	11,209	13,538	19,536	17,794
Noril'sk, USSR	3,045	13,485	4,221	8,993	9,197	7,333	8,009	10,955	5,380	12,290	7,435	5,289	14,133	6,502	4,594	11,463	15,962	10,991	6,985	5,307
Norman Wells, Canada	3,992	10,138	6,506	8,008	11,550	12,143	10,697	6,655	9,858	9,267	4,182	9,664	9,825	9,532	6,713	15,399	12,905	7,366	8,053	7,279
Normanton, Australia	8,606	15,609	14,192	4,301	14,613	7,797	2,767	14,915	10,913	16,756	15,860	6,580	8,665	4,194	14,514	10,914	13,544	16,426	16,553	14,989
North Pole	3,395	11,478	4,222	9,210	9,589	9,561	9,837	8,659	7,103	10,350	5,241	7,568	12,558	8,388	4,521	12,877	14,211	8,823	6,503	5,208
Nottingham, United Kingdom	7,278	9,469	874	13,304	5,533	8,627	12,181	8,613	5,187	8,274	5,145	8,552	14,915	10,720	776	9,336	11,450	7,761	2,433	1,180
Norway House, Canada	6,017	8,114	6,557	9,433	10,747	13,528	12,716	4,751	10,616	7,234	2,280	11,482	9,255	11,565	6,636	14,914	10,900	5,337	7,222	7,006
Norwich, United Kingdom	7,268	9,597	707	13,311	5,463	8,457	12,055	8,782	5,017	8,406	5,315	8,406	15,082	10,602	612	9,222	11,537	7,920	2,451	1,082
Nouakchott, Mauritania	11,313	6,330	4,484	17,106	3,128	9,819	15,221	7,547	6,851	5,373	5,869	11,400	13,694	14,077	4,111	7,164	7,581	6,039	1,699	3,441
Noumea, New Caledonia	9,182	13,246	16,051	3,295	16,860	10,491	5,224	12,282	13,568	14,249	14,251	9,067	5,980	6,418	16,424	12,724	11,911	13,738	18,836	17,097
Novosibirsk, USSR	3,942	14,575	4,520	9,252	8,659	5,723	7,041	12,491	4,138	13,360	8,875	3,828	15,291	5,555	4,876	10,174	16,508	12,346	7,248	5,497
Nuku'alofa, Tonga	9,466	11,588	16,510	3,464	18,035	12,390	6,983	10,386	15,351	12,481	12,680	10,747	4,146	8,012	16,842	14,000	10,787	11,837	18,294	17,546
Nukunono Island, Tokelau Isls.	8,314	11,673	15,229	2,605	19,398	12,794	7,112	9,760	15,175	12,359	11,552	10,601	4,225	7,859	15,538	15,308	11,449	11,319	17,024	16,217
Nuremberg, West Germany	7,383	10,086	305	13,445	5,070	7,702	11,574	9,518	4,253	8,923	6,084	7,829	15,853	10,168	190	8,621	11,800	8,589	2,540	811
Nyala, Sudan	10,725	10,218	4,605	15,739	1,997	5,421	11,068	11,972	3,116	9,536	9,615	7,600	17,566	10,329	4,417	4,287	10,177	10,468	4,006	3,939
Oaxaca, Mexico	9,589	4,912	9,724	10,007	11,537	17,444	15,031	1,248	14,063	4,609	3,739	15,468	6,087	14,600	9,638	14,717	7,341	2,801	8,920	9,671
Ocean Falls, Canada	4,826	9,470	7,815	7,444	12,571	13,451	11,055	5,787	11,300	8,793	4,234	10,744	8,390	10,120	7,986	16,644	12,085	6,805	9,019	8,492
Odense, Denmark	6,783	10,266	370	12,849	5,729	7,970	11,386	9,322	4,581	9,073	5,762	7,756	15,433	9,932	671	9,260	12,184	8,534	3,009	1,393
Odessa, USSR	7,054	11,444	1,518	12,901	5,187	6,250	10,207	11,002	2,851	10,319	7,490	6,398	17,116	8,869	1,689	8,023	12,823	10,086	3,687	2,023
Ogbomosho, Nigeria	11,935	7,924	4,929	17,792	696	7,667	13,358	9,889	5,282	7,245	8,238	9,867	15,375	12,612	4,601	4,859	8,184	8,319	2,896	3,898
Okha, USSR	824	14,950	7,443	5,744	12,364	8,304	6,009	11,369	7,856	14,035	8,814	5,264	11,543	4,733	7,813	13,619	17,677	12,176	10,158	8,534
Okinawa (Naha)	4,112	18,132	9,339	5,067	12,668	6,267	2,753	14,403	7,572	17,324	12,096	3,237	11,812	1,463	9,699	11,715	18,612	15,428	12,068	10,319
Oklahoma City, Oklahoma	7,762	6,447	8,123	9,673	11,235	15,534	14,013	2,822	12,399	5,791	2,386	13,483	7,594	13,145	8,114	15,182	9,120	3,796	8,013	8,313
Old Crow, Canada	3,360	10,770	6,514	7,631	11,720	11,648	10,079	7,271	9,570	9,894	4,777	9,076	10,063	8,901	6,755	15,351	13,534	7,998	8,297	7,368
Olympia, Washington	5,489	8,872	8,192	7,614	12,670	14,128	11,553	5,162	11,865	8,258	4,005	11,421	7,864	10,699	8,331	16,831	11,439	6,263	9,136	8,784
Omaha, Nebraska	7,274	6,878	7,537	9,724	10,965	14,878	13,737	3,365	11,780	6,123	2,031	12,889	8,185	12,749	7,548	15,039	9,611	4,149	7,622	7,789
Omsk, USSR	4,427	14,112	3,967	9,856	8,070	5,655	7,526	12,324	3,697	12,904	8,649	4,123	15,764	6,060	4,315	9,780	15,913	12,031	6,666	4,917
Oodnadatta, Australia	9,757	15,016	14,661	5,435	13,797	7,504	3,408	15,364	10,854	16,231	17,051	6,929	8,821	4,916	14,928	9,869	12,623	16,631	16,477	15,244
Oradea, Romania	7,306	10,789	932	13,282	4,965	6,858	10,865	10,365	3,417	9,654	6,911	7,068	16,648	9,507	1,034	8,158	12,285	9,417	3,068	1,362
Oran, Algeria	9,124	8,599	2,073	15,186	3,668	8,319	13,037	8,846	4,949	7,513	5,978	9,190	15,424	11,735	1,701	7,667	10,048	7,613	818	990
Oranjestad, Aruba	11,221	2,932	8,354	12,920	8,714	15,601	17,763	1,768	12,304	2,055	3,381	15,901	8,094	16,775	8,132	11,863	5,742	268	6,653	7,890
Orebro, Sweden	6,271	10,675	823	12,337	6,185	7,872	10,966	9,497	4,573	9,472	5,862	7,415	15,358	9,495	1,174	9,582	12,675	8,815	3,529	1,901
Orel, USSR	6,241	11,864	1,651	12,126	5,999	6,411	9,795	10,965	3,202	10,695	7,330	6,085	16,611	8,389	1,955	8,745	13,484	10,225	4,240	2,497
Orsk, USSR	5,437	13,411	3,189	10,927	6,994	5,414	8,248	12,212	2,855	12,236	8,509	4,579	16,679	6,844	3,502	8,921	14,912	11,651	5,751	4,027
Osaka, Japan	2,985	16,935	8,952	4,757	13,019	7,217	3,837	13,213	7,970	16,167	10,981	4,082	11,398	2,658	9,324	12,728	18,797	14,236	11,736	10,002
Oslo, Norway	6,309	10,456	865	12,372	6,233	8,131	11,179	9,235	4,819	9,249	5,601	7,658	15,128	9,700	1,171	9,725	12,512	8,562	3,438	1,884
Osorno, Chile	16,325	3,144	13,116	12,685	9,601	14,764	15,315	5,991	14,648	4,351	9,256	17,714	6,032	16,819	12,766	9,389	1,374	5,674	10,429	12,173
Ostrava, Czechoslovakia	7,142	10,595	532	13,172	5,186	7,237	11,064	10,005	3,809	9,438	6,518	7,309	16,240	9,669	709	8,514	12,237	9,104	2,974	1,223
Ottawa, Canada	7,621	6,610	6,066	11,202	9,284	13,742	14,431	3,822	10,398	5,598	433	12,493	9,667	13,152	6,022	13,409	9,416	3,871	5,918	6,180
Ouagadougou, Bourkina Fasso	11,654	7,472	4,570	17,705	1,481	8,292	13,914	9,175	5,648	6,692	7,454	10,274	14,975	13,028	4,217	5,623	8,067	7,628	2,235	3,493
Oujda, Morocco	9,263	8,444	2,225	15,320	3,597	8,423	13,189	8,746	5,071	7,364	5,938	9,340	15,317	11,893	1,852	7,632	9,885	7,494	661	1,147
Oxford, United Kingdom	7,410	9,397	888	13,439	5,402	8,610	12,255	8,617	5,161	8,207	5,181	8,603	14,960	10,801	732	9,222	11,346	7,734	2,302	1,064
Pago Pago, American Samoa	8,886	11,384	15,795	3,099	18,840	12,913	7,312	9,757	15,541	12,153	11,826	10,924	3,885	8,170	16,098	14,897	10,973	11,273	17,408	16,765
Pakxe, Laos	6,137	18,929	8,972	7,177	10,660	3,748	2,581	16,714	5,840	17,978	13,564	1,276	13,624	1,638	9,263	9,133	16,993	17,139	11,272	9,688
Palembang, Indonesia	8,005	17,838	10,474	7,466	10,702	3,563	2,289	18,436	6,656	18,211	15,549	2,913	12,949	2,638	10,709	8,093	15,125	19,064	12,333	10,990
Palermo, Italy	8,495	9,853	1,567	14,496	3,834	7,146	11,773	10,014	3,720	8,783	6,887	7,921	16,584	10,502	1,322	7,372	11,124	8,852	2,076	885
Palma, Majorca	8,635	9,047	1,563	14,160	4,015	8,088	12,600	9,071	4,663	7,938	6,013	8,767	15,647	11,267	1,194	7,892	10,560	7,917	1,304	474
Palmerston North, New Zealand	11,307	11,464	18,215	5,279	15,743	11,329	6,919	11,560	14,759	12,600	14,579	10,726	4,984	8,291	18,581	11,732	9,785	12,700	18,986	19,145
Panama, Panama	11,203	2,997	9,309	11,990	9,770	16,710	17,092	818	13,375	2,546	3,852	16,547	6,999	16,566	9,114	12,655	5,680	889	7,750	8,924
Paramaribo, Suriname	12,401	2,340	7,929	14,689	7,095	14,224	19,196	3,489	11,286	1,129	4,418	15,627	9,231	17,708	7,631	10,071	4,859	1,889	5,672	7,207
Paris, France	7,649	9,473	756	13,705	5,038	8,300	12,186	8,902	4,840	8,301	5,533	8,463	15,316	10,761	452	8,817	11,288	7,949	2,101	663
Patna, India	6,224	16,539	6,691	9,284	8,465	2,695	5,025	15,727	3,451	15,545	12,042	1,186	15,972	3,931	6,947	8,026	16,262	15,274	8,839	7,305
Patrai, Greece	8,201	10,564	1,733	14,074	4,041	6,459	11,054	10,706	3,012	9,507	7,473	7,199	17,240	9,808	1,637	7,198	11,706	9,576	2,800	1,485
Peking, China	3,239	17,057	7,494	6,535	11,233	5,864	4,343	13,784	6,191	15,913	10,786	2,765	13,177	2,845	7,855	11,325	19,456	14,342	10,235	8,484
Penrhyn Island (Omoka)	8,845	10,211	15,128	3,849	18,467	14,315	8,625	8,278	16,453	10,848	10,413	12,016	2,918	9,304	15,346	15,971	10,311	9,818	16,041	15,881
Peoria, Illinois	7,598	6,533	7,237	10,268	10,446	14,766	14,184	3,179	11,536	5,710	1,524	13,039	8,481	13,124	7,219	14,501	9,305	3,767	7,147	7,411
Perm', USSR	4,996	13,024	2,864	10,758	7,287	6,175	8,621	11,517	3,559	11,821	7,812	5,113	16,029	7,162	3,216	9,563	14,851	11,060	5,587	3,835
Perth, Australia	10,639	14,995	13,669	7,291	11,843	5,990	3,819	16,869	9,451	16,099	18,623	6,329	10,340	5,177	13,836	7,940	12,232	17,531	14,770	13,930
Peshawar, Pakistan	6,229	15,010	5,106	10,454	7,283	3,329	6,599	14,387	2,192	13,958	10,687	2,745	17,177	5,400	5,350	7,812	15,472	13,722	7,252	5,698
Petropavlovsk-Kamchatskiy,USSR	875	14,219	7,948	5,212	13,113	9,332	6,508	10,537	8,836	13,443	8,339	6,257	10,576	5,394	8,304	14,665	16,781	11,499	10,538	9,030
Petrozavodsk, USSR	5,491	11,748	1,732	11,510	6,785	7,187	9,889	10,334	4,139	10,540	6,639	6,398	15,629	8,414	2,105	9,731	13,736	9,788	4,517	2,800
Pevek, USSR	1,451	12,712	6,376	6,945	11,735	9,853	8,272	9,256	8,346	11,766	6,547	7,119	11,165	6,996	6,703	14,433	15,502	9,932	8,767	7,412
Philadelphia, Pennsylvania	8,198	6,008	6,443	11,466	9,229	14,185	14,989	3,269	10,783	5,015	458	13,087	9,335	13,741	6,365	13,274	8,817	3,263	5,999	6,452
Phnom Penh, Kampuchea	6,534	18,829	9,224	7,283	10,603	3,565	2,467	17,112	5,907	18,125	13,954	1,490	13,584	1,776	9,502	8,857	16,601	17,519	11,435	9,895
Phoenix, Arizona	7,243	7,256	9,063	8,348	12,579	15,819	12,929	3,527	13,152	6,798	3,671	13,184	6,715	12,278	9,111	16,525	9,716	4,833	9,283	9,404
Pierre, South Dakota	6,795	7,366	7,491	9,337	11,222	14,612	13,247	3,816	11,650	6,616	2,322	12,469	8,262	12,257	7,533	15,351	10,087	4,642	7,802	7,830
Pinang, Malaysia	7,363	18,114	9,445	7,837	10,151	2,985	2,758	17,933	5,760	17,842	14,580	1,891	13,796	2,480	9,690	8,085	15,765	18,021	11,414	10,000
Pitcairn Island (Adamstown)	11,789	6,994	15,613	7,287	15,037	16,588	11,604	6,288	19,867	7,861	9,631	15,328	540	12,572	15,537	14,061	6,866	7,471	14,368	15,515
Pittsburgh, Pennsylvania	7,984	6,175	6,700	11,059	9,641	14,396	14,727	3,194	11,038	5,237	765	13,081	9,046	13,541	6,644	13,690	8,982	3,401	6,385	6,769
Plymouth, Montserrat	11,041	3,328	7,462	13,587	7,874	14,647	17,853	2,642	11,347	2,207	3,044	15,121	9,055	16,527	7,223	11,277	6,074	1,216	5,692	6,952
Plymouth, United Kingdom	7,605	9,148	1,116	13,613	5,311	8,788	12,505	8,424	5,330	7,959	5,037	8,844	14,820	11,052	908	9,199	11,101	7,511	2,109	1,071
Ponape Island	5,875	15,343	12,733	1,431	16,442	9,390	3,755	12,589	11,415	15,775	12,555	6,862	7,985	4,156	13,107	13,909	15,034	14,176	15,498	13,810
Ponce, Puerto Rico	10,764	3,478	7,651	13,098	8,344	15,018	17,516	2,210	11,657	2,449	2,807	15,198	8,711	16,305	7,435	11,764	6,273	976	6,044	7,214
Ponta Delgada, Azores	9,216	6,935	3,304	14,739	5,142	10,543	14,717	6,617	7,126	5,747	3,885	11,029	13,199	13,254	3,015	9,310	9,001	5,469	1,751	2,688
Pontianak, Indonesia	7,518	18,366	10,535	6,914	11,191	4,014	1,735	17,841	6,927	18,800	15,245	2,830	12,634	2,065	10,797	8,691	15,586	18,824	12,580	11,139
Port Augusta, Australia	10,274	14,427	15,206	5,640	13,841	7,881	4,000	15,008	11,285	15,642	17,213	7,486	8,428	5,508	15,459	9,794	12,041	16,160	16,808	15,727
Port Blair, India	7,133	17,517	8,391	8,607	9,278	2,285	3,717	17,376	4,702	16,889	13,751	1,204	14,830	3,079	8,626	7,726	15,862	17,006	10,341	8,923
Port Elizabeth, South Africa	15,154	9,171	9,638	15,408	4,532	6,547	10,961	12,771	7,166	9,414	13,008	9,695	13,362	11,398	9,397	1,113	7,248	11,329	8,071	8,799
Port Hedland, Australia	9,328	16,271	12,914	6,511	12,225	5,614	2,507	17,230	8,964	17,406	17,324	5,281	10,716	3,870	13,144	8,668	13,537	18,494	14,587	13,391
Port Louis, Mauritius	12,102	12,643	9,161	12,761	5,944	3,193	7,718	16,069	5,186	12,743	14,659	6,274	15,031	7,940	9,106	2,630	10,670	14,493	9,034	8,815
Port Moresby, Papua New Guinea	7,662	15,743	13,811	3,237	15,397	8,311	2,757	14,191	11,131	16,708	14,741	6,575	8,373	3,929	14,166	11,945	14,158	15,785	16,473	14,752
Port Said, Egypt	8,477	11,376	2,866	13,922	3,918	5,257	10,172	11,902	1,869	10,414	8,710	6,350	18,471	9,065	2,838	6,334	12,057	10,698	3,809	2,716
Port Sudan, Sudan	9,392	11,678	4,239	14,180	3,553	4,295	9,712	12,911	1,551	10,893	9,972	6,094	19,130	8,844	4,185	5,068	11,736	11,547	4,698	3,963
Port-au-Prince, Haiti	10,511	3,638	7,997	12,504	8,949	15,524	17,113	1,655	12,113	2,751	2,713	15,349	8,218	16,065	7,807	12,346	6,446	874	6,560	7,641
Port-of-Spain, Trin. & Tobago	11,705	2,668	7,933	13,870	7,788	14,790	18,496	2,707	11,633	1,533	3,712	15,653	8,822	17,200	7,671	10,932	5,401	1,105	5,956	7,340
Port-Vila, Vanuatu	8,714	13,321	15,676	2,770	17,311	10,665	5,217	12,034	13,590	14,248	13,783	9,011	5,916	6,305	16,049	13,216	12,203	13,543	18,422	16,751
Portland, Maine	7,964	6,341	5,865	11,676	8,842	13,607	14,785	3,816	10,205	5,283	122	12,603	9,905	13,456	5,791	12,951	9,134	3,658	5,522	5,893
Portland, Oregon	5,629	8,765	8,332	7,598	12,749	14,293	11,624	5,047	12,030	8,175	4,025	11,569	7,704	10,799	8,465	16,917	11,310	6,180	9,225	8,908
Porto, Portugal	8,683	8,298	1,966	14,657	4,493	9,057	13,361	8,103	5,621	7,146	5,080	9,582	14,675	11,959	1,623	8,560	10,078	6,982	1,058	1,180
Porto Alegre, Brazil	16,336	2,282	10,966	14,929	7,388	13,546	16,814	5,998	12,487	3,123	8,351	16,646	8,193	18,117	10,602	8,054	1,058	5,011	8,213	9,964
Porto Alexandre, Angola	14,123	8,150	7,531	17,583	2,191	7,125	12,520	11,240	6,259	7,985	10,666	10,085	14,397	12,456	7,241	2,423	7,155	9,653	5,664	6,579
Porto Novo, Benin	12,163	7,696	5,133	18,049	748	7,854	13,558	9,749	5,530	7,042	8,227	10,105	15,131	12,846	4,798	4,834	7,926	8,168	2,996	4,088
Porto Velho, Brazil	13,666	506	9,804	13,965	8,184	15,294	18,764	3,389	12,882	757	5,783	17,431	7,704	19,182	9,498	10,233	3,300	2,313	7,436	9,043
Portsmouth, United Kingdom	7,513	9,354	898	13,545	5,293	8,581	12,301	8,636	5,126	8,167	5,227	8,628	15,010	10,854	697	9,121	11,273	7,729	2,200	965
Poznan, Poland	6,919	10,579	363	12,968	5,448	7,443	11,080	9,826	4,040	9,405	6,295	7,371	15,977	9,660	680	8,815	12,328	8,981	3,068	1,330
Prague, Czechoslovakia	7,226	10,339	304	13,279	5,163	7,499	11,320	9,735	4,061	9,176	6,267	7,577	16,012	9,916	437	8,611	12,034	8,829	2,769	1,023
Praia, Cape Verde Islands	11,733	5,458	5,172	17,083	3,750	10,653	16,102	6,780	7,732	4,492	5,510	12,276	12,817	14,935	4,807	7,571	6,852	5,234	2,433	4,179
Pretoria, South Africa	14,264	9,606	8,780	15,601	3,877	5,890	10,758	13,032	6,234	9,684	12,667	9,033	14,303	10,986	8,559	442	7,944	11,497	7,423	7,993
Prince Albert, Canada	5,767	8,371	6,962	8,911	11,272	13,665	12,357	4,872	10,915	7,556	2,762	11,412	8,913	11,276	7,063	15,135	11,121	5,614	7,740	7,465

Distances in Kilometers	Magadan, USSR	Magdalena, Bolivia	Magdeburg, East Germany	Majuro Atoll, Marshall Isls.	Malabo, Equatorial Guinea	Male, Maldives	Manado, Indonesia	Managua, Nicaragua	Manama, Bahrain	Manaus, Brazil	Manchester, New Hampshire	Mandalay, Burma	Mangareva Island, Fr.Polynesia	Manila, Philippines	Mannheim, West Germany	Maputo, Mozambique	Mar del Plata, Argentina	Maracaibo, Venezuela	Marrakech, Morocco	Marseilles, France
Prince Edward Island	15,507	9,843	11,227	13,783	6,270	6,603	9,893	13,574	8,162	10,366	14,607	9,579	12,253	10,655	11,019	2,337	7,437	12,358	9,814	10,461
Prince George, Canada	4,947	9,276	7,511	7,811	12,206	13,411	11,319	5,634	11,104	8,552	3,887	10,810	8,615	10,331	7,670	16,298	11,943	6,575	8,654	8,160
Prince Rupert, Canada	4,550	9,727	7,689	7,358	12,548	13,177	10,831	6,055	11,082	9,030	4,375	10,464	8,590	9,869	7,873	16,559	12,357	7,047	9,001	8,401
Providence, Rhode Island	8,122	6,151	6,069	11,678	8,921	13,819	14,939	3,592	10,408	5,110	131	12,824	9,713	13,633	5,988	13,002	8,950	3,452	5,647	6,074
Provo, Utah	6,645	7,696	8,402	8,410	12,254	15,079	12,671	3,984	12,423	7,113	3,332	12,543	7,418	11,869	8,472	16,360	10,268	5,119	8,840	8,811
Puerto Aisen, Chile	16,744	3,646	13,471	12,600	9,642	14,370	14,847	6,518	14,599	4,844	9,793	17,218	6,073	16,356	13,112	9,095	1,501	6,210	10,739	12,490
Puerto Deseado, Argentina	17,302	3,820	13,289	13,018	9,181	13,807	14,775	6,936	14,070	4,976	10,068	16,730	6,595	16,273	12,921	8,512	1,278	6,495	10,519	12,267
Puerto Princesa, Philippines	6,145	19,511	10,297	5,780	12,127	5,039	1,136	16,347	7,368	19,263	14,076	2,774	12,098	591	10,614	10,105	16,852	17,481	12,737	11,097
Punta Arenas, Chile	17,386	4,458	13,961	12,478	9,655	13,664	14,096	7,382	14,381	5,635	10,654	16,376	6,262	15,600	13,592	8,581	1,974	7,071	11,184	12,926
Pusan, South Korea	3,146	17,259	8,594	5,299	12,461	6,661	3,747	13,594	7,395	16,345	11,110	3,516	11,974	2,412	8,963	12,177	19,349	14,495	11,367	9,620
Pyongyang, North Korea	2,887	17,000	8,070	5,751	12,030	6,536	4,157	13,444	7,000	15,988	10,758	3,391	12,367	2,747	8,439	12,038	19,713	14,220	10,843	9,097
Qamdo, China	5,043	17,272	7,054	8,081	9,653	3,904	4,387	15,197	4,559	16,100	11,713	1,022	14,827	3,040	7,365	9,340	17,599	15,227	9,516	7,849
Qandahar, Afghanistan	6,768	14,543	4,894	11,044	6,691	3,158	7,028	14,327	1,593	13,546	10,670	3,185	17,779	5,900	5,102	7,280	14,867	13,500	6,849	5,377
Qiqian, China	2,025	15,671	6,688	6,769	11,154	6,888	5,634	12,418	6,421	14,565	9,391	3,966	12,965	4,173	7,061	12,131	18,421	12,939	9,473	7,749
Qom, Iran	7,274	13,129	3,662	12,239	5,528	4,117	8,453	13,143	935	12,120	9,611	4,605	18,610	7,296	3,815	6,982	13,751	12,161	5,427	4,006
Quebec, Canada	7,608	6,699	5,701	11,455	8,947	13,401	14,429	4,095	10,038	5,642	425	12,278	10,038	13,096	5,651	13,088	9,493	4,008	5,554	5,802
Quetta, Pakistan	6,824	14,688	5,087	10,965	6,768	2,979	6,871	14,521	1,669	13,707	10,862	3,038	17,711	5,767	5,292	7,218	14,911	13,690	7,017	5,560
Quito, Ecuador	12,180	2,148	10,039	12,264	9,719	16,892	17,435	1,616	13,864	2,082	4,838	17,526	6,602	17,355	9,808	12,105	4,702	1,424	8,187	9,533
Rabaul, Papua New Guinea	7,071	15,574	13,572	2,458	15,973	8,802	3,105	13,546	11,379	16,364	13,941	6,758	8,081	4,019	13,940	12,720	14,423	15,154	16,338	14,587
Raiatea (Uturoa)	9,922	9,316	15,804	4,889	17,431	14,934	9,395	7,847	17,522	10,069	10,473	12,970	1,863	10,224	15,949	15,261	9,215	9,290	15,987	16,343
Raleigh, North Carolina	8,507	5,645	6,986	11,334	9,538	14,737	15,221	2,727	11,324	4,723	1,012	13,586	8,810	14,063	6,900	13,488	8,452	2,870	6,420	6,963
Rangiroa (Avatoru)	9,919	8,965	15,490	5,151	17,171	15,365	9,786	7,403	17,750	9,680	10,048	13,296	1,618	10,563	15,609	15,480	9,018	8,855	15,542	15,960
Rangoon, Burma	6,452	17,884	8,180	8,201	9,620	2,855	3,569	16,793	4,813	17,018	13,267	578	14,662	2,672	8,445	8,350	16,537	16,689	10,330	8,810
Raoul Is., Kermadec Islands	10,257	11,498	17,343	4,195	17,095	12,039	6,968	10,821	15,271	12,509	13,439	10,815	4,323	8,160	17,697	13,087	10,324	12,162	19,023	18,420
Rarotonga (Avarua)	10,014	10,058	16,490	4,461	17,720	13,978	8,563	8,836	16,894	10,901	11,454	12,268	2,566	9,515	16,700	14,621	9,596	10,251	16,994	17,199
Rawson, Argentina	16,988	3,323	12,883	13,247	9,002	14,053	15,269	6,507	13,993	4,478	9,579	17,079	6,684	16,769	12,520	8,657	868	6,012	10,132	11,883
Recife, Brazil	14,269	3,249	8,004	17,156	5,023	12,103	17,675	6,109	9,960	2,834	6,756	14,567	10,684	17,308	7,637	7,376	4,024	4,564	5,242	6,993
Regina, Canada	6,057	8,090	7,156	8,988	11,311	13,968	12,595	4,564	11,169	7,300	2,641	11,726	8,679	11,547	7,240	15,481	10,827	5,344	7,802	7,613
Reykjavik, Iceland	6,268	9,306	2,344	12,021	7,144	9,871	12,233	7,565	6,570	8,095	3,883	9,081	13,406	10,724	2,431	11,049	11,749	7,074	3,744	2,893
Rhodes, Greece	8,137	11,089	2,180	13,836	4,131	5,853	10,510	11,313	2,403	10,060	8,046	6,657	17,827	9,307	2,156	6,922	12,061	10,180	3,367	2,088
Richmond, Virginia	8,368	5,801	6,772	11,372	9,428	14,518	15,117	2,948	11,111	4,850	791	13,380	9,015	13,923	6,690	13,421	8,610	3,034	6,261	6,764
Riga, USSR	6,261	11,132	962	12,297	6,053	7,289	10,521	10,077	4,011	9,940	6,445	6,896	15,884	9,073	1,329	9,222	12,986	9,365	3,739	2,010
Ringkobing, Denmark	6,761	10,168	490	12,823	5,804	8,122	11,481	9,175	4,735	8,971	5,609	7,874	15,280	10,019	735	9,379	12,129	8,401	2,997	1,436
Rio Branco, Brazil	13,636	546	10,167	13,542	8,624	15,709	18,342	3,188	13,327	1,145	5,876	17,848	7,257	18,945	9,870	10,554	3,270	2,321	7,852	9,437
Rio Cuarto, Argentina	16,103	2,193	11,979	13,636	8,682	14,587	16,373	5,526	13,781	3,352	8,461	17,737	6,899	17,882	11,628	9,074	819	4,908	9,296	11,037
Rio de Janeiro, Brazil	15,786	2,448	9,874	15,954	6,371	12,922	17,315	6,087	11,465	2,839	7,849	15,857	9,209	18,129	9,506	7,582	2,161	4,833	7,107	8,857
Rio Gallegos, Argentina	17,388	4,273	13,762	12,643	9,509	13,702	14,293	7,256	14,287	5,444	10,487	16,482	6,363	15,795	13,393	8,550	1,769	6,906	10,986	12,730
Rio Grande, Brazil	16,508	2,408	11,195	14,768	7,542	13,567	16,608	6,098	12,635	3,305	8,540	16,694	8,047	17,951	10,830	8,059	829	5,163	8,438	10,189
Riyadh, Saudi Arabia	8,430	12,713	4,251	13,059	4,674	3,664	8,747	13,496	427	11,853	10,216	5,031	19,780	7,786	4,304	5,802	12,858	12,280	5,377	4,285
Road Town, Brit. Virgin Isls.	10,782	3,516	7,478	13,282	8,134	14,806	17,574	2,427	11,455	2,440	2,797	15,067	8,920	16,300	7,255	11,588	6,292	1,144	5,833	7,021
Roanoke, Virginia	8,307	5,841	6,947	11,172	9,649	14,677	15,017	2,854	11,287	4,926	961	13,431	8,825	13,863	6,873	13,632	8,646	3,063	6,480	6,962
Robinson Crusoe Island, Chile	15,406	2,698	12,909	12,297	10,025	15,659	15,681	5,127	15,126	3,904	8,519	18,627	5,553	17,108	12,584	10,224	1,982	4,962	10,363	12,063
Rochester, New York	7,790	6,404	6,347	11,149	9,435	14,034	14,578	3,537	10,682	5,423	501	12,762	9,392	13,337	6,297	13,529	9,214	3,647	6,117	6,438
Rockhampton, Australia	9,193	14,477	15,287	4,060	15,376	8,874	3,910	13,922	12,064	15,599	15,607	7,742	7,532	5,288	15,624	11,392	12,608	15,352	17,720	16,135
Rome, Italy	8,128	9,914	1,143	14,161	4,242	7,338	11,731	9,831	3,882	8,807	6,594	7,898	16,354	10,409	899	7,793	11,340	8,741	2,146	602
Rosario, Argentina	16,254	2,201	11,750	13,974	8,343	14,286	16,475	5,685	13,440	3,301	8,481	17,435	7,241	17,963	11,394	8,770	628	4,965	9,040	10,787
Roseau, Dominica	11,214	3,181	7,525	13,722	7,782	14,620	18,029	2,712	11,355	2,044	3,217	15,211	9,062	16,689	7,278	11,134	5,913	1,221	5,688	6,987
Rostock, East Germany	6,877	10,323	216	12,943	5,589	7,812	11,332	9,465	4,412	9,137	5,924	7,668	15,612	9,890	571	9,084	12,181	8,648	2,965	1,296
Rostov-na-Donu, USSR	6,625	12,130	2,081	12,333	5,660	5,783	9,523	11,537	2,521	10,999	7,945	5,725	17,287	8,180	2,311	8,138	13,473	10,701	4,375	2,705
Rotterdam, Netherlands	7,280	9,758	492	13,339	5,354	8,226	11,897	9,009	4,785	8,574	5,547	8,219	15,313	10,456	390	9,053	11,636	8,130	2,473	960
Rouyn, Canada	7,231	6,977	6,051	10,854	9,538	13,633	14,035	4,057	10,356	5,983	828	12,211	9,666	12,771	6,037	13,688	9,786	4,222	6,113	6,249
Sacramento, California	6,287	8,278	8,978	7,550	13,090	15,047	11,942	4,548	12,784	7,802	4,188	12,243	6,973	11,257	9,085	17,221	10,709	5,825	9,634	9,481
Saginaw, Michigan	7,544	6,601	6,695	10,651	9,946	14,287	14,266	3,475	11,008	5,687	1,014	12,760	9,026	13,100	6,670	14,043	9,404	3,822	6,606	6,854
Saint Denis, Reunion	12,282	12,416	9,137	12,972	5,774	3,382	7,941	15,847	5,236	12,517	14,545	6,479	15,011	8,167	9,068	2,403	10,462	14,275	8,916	8,754
Saint George's, Grenada	11,549	2,820	7,828	13,800	7,814	14,770	18,346	2,670	11,575	1,690	3,555	15,537	8,868	17,044	7,571	11,020	5,558	1,088	5,898	7,254
Saint John, Canada	7,908	6,492	5,492	11,890	8,529	13,241	14,716	4,143	9,831	5,394	501	12,340	10,284	13,339	5,413	12,661	9,262	3,872	5,170	5,514
Saint John's, Antigua	11,010	3,375	7,403	13,609	7,836	14,594	17,825	2,687	11,290	2,247	3,012	15,063	9,110	16,487	7,164	11,259	6,116	1,273	5,637	6,893
Saint John's, Canada	7,938	6,840	4,503	12,576	7,594	12,268	14,565	5,018	8,828	5,662	1,551	11,695	11,316	13,093	4,398	11,758	9,490	4,459	4,157	4,465
Saint Louis, Missouri	7,776	6,359	7,444	10,262	10,532	14,998	14,307	2,958	11,753	5,566	1,650	13,263	8,275	13,285	7,419	14,544	9,119	3,606	7,278	7,594
Saint Paul, Minnesota	7,046	7,085	7,074	9,900	10,648	14,422	13,650	3,693	11,309	6,255	1,744	12,534	8,652	12,573	7,091	14,772	9,855	4,319	7,248	7,347
Saint Peter Port, UK	7,680	9,191	1,044	13,705	5,177	8,661	12,465	8,542	5,201	8,008	5,179	8,776	14,960	11,022	797	9,049	11,095	7,605	2,031	915
Saipan (Susupe)	4,948	16,811	11,340	2,918	14,845	7,996	2,746	13,553	9,780	16,912	12,538	5,272	9,614	2,659	11,712	13,028	16,604	15,017	14,122	12,381
Salalah, Oman	8,764	13,411	5,382	12,616	5,159	2,557	7,921	14,605	1,083	12,685	11,356	4,429	18,861	7,138	5,444	5,295	13,040	13,320	6,425	5,419
Salem, Oregon	5,658	8,758	8,406	7,552	12,814	14,343	11,613	5,036	12,099	8,180	4,074	11,602	7,633	10,802	8,539	16,983	11,289	6,185	9,291	8,981
Salt Lake City, Utah	6,587	7,747	8,363	8,394	12,248	15,019	12,630	4,038	12,373	7,158	3,332	12,482	7,463	11,819	8,436	16,363	10,325	5,164	8,824	8,780
Salta, Argentina	15,238	1,275	11,317	13,713	8,603	15,065	17,205	4,672	13,663	2,465	7,530	18,118	6,999	18,699	10,982	9,577	1,644	3,979	8,733	10,441
Salto, Uruguay	16,215	2,096	11,458	14,268	8,051	14,118	16,682	5,688	13,151	3,134	8,350	17,252	7,529	18,141	11,101	8,605	735	4,876	8,740	10,488
Salvador, Brazil	14,778	2,776	8,673	16,718	5,546	12,501	17,795	5,962	10,556	2,605	7,049	15,128	10,099	17,815	8,307	7,518	3,353	4,497	5,915	7,666
Salzburg, Austria	7,501	10,162	495	13,553	4,899	7,506	11,496	9,702	4,049	9,012	6,297	7,722	16,073	10,110	385	8,401	11,794	8,741	2,529	777
Samsun, Turkey	7,329	11,848	2,223	12,952	4,985	5,545	9,780	11,680	2,124	10,772	8,208	5,931	17,835	8,515	2,348	7,455	12,942	10,694	4,069	2,546
San Antonio, Texas	8,299	6,000	8,719	9,658	11,472	16,209	14,286	2,293	13,026	5,459	2,840	14,106	7,003	13,560	8,689	15,222	8,595	3,479	8,406	8,843
San Cristobal, Venezuela	11,630	2,499	8,915	12,804	8,974	16,009	17,875	1,615	12,799	1,815	3,904	16,478	7,629	17,142	8,685	11,868	5,291	328	7,127	8,422
San Diego, California	7,044	7,597	9,370	7,870	13,048	15,791	12,509	3,884	13,356	7,199	4,125	13,001	6,462	11,923	9,440	17,005	9,969	5,253	9,719	9,767
San Francisco, California	6,309	8,300	9,095	7,456	13,206	15,100	11,889	4,574	12,884	7,847	4,299	12,266	6,867	11,229	9,203	17,330	10,705	5,875	9,754	9,601
San Jose, Costa Rica	10,902	3,388	9,533	11,479	10,261	17,101	16,587	343	13,696	3,035	3,864	16,472	6,637	16,146	9,360	13,154	5,982	1,368	8,127	9,219
San Juan, Argentina	15,750	2,065	12,091	13,291	9,033	15,016	16,398	5,193	14,133	3,268	8,258	18,165	6,544	17,898	11,750	9,504	1,233	4,681	9,461	11,187
San Juan, Puerto Rico	10,733	3,524	7,579	13,132	8,292	14,948	17,500	2,274	11,585	2,481	2,766	15,131	8,781	16,268	7,362	11,735	6,314	1,047	5,974	7,142
San Luis Potosi, Mexico	8,879	5,620	9,520	9,496	11,881	17,051	14,409	1,914	13,845	5,261	3,576	14,785	6,215	13,899	9,474	15,312	8,059	3,376	9,021	9,588
San Marino, San Marino	7,919	9,984	919	13,961	4,465	7,407	11,667	9,772	3,944	8,861	6,476	7,850	16,254	10,321	690	8,005	11,484	8,724	2,250	574
San Miguel de Tucuman, Argen.	15,448	1,497	11,482	13,698	8,624	14,962	17,006	4,876	13,704	2,679	7,756	18,062	6,964	18,509	11,143	9,457	1,433	4,204	8,871	10,590
San Salvador, El Salvador	10,286	4,072	9,542	10,860	10,781	17,282	15,917	360	13,819	3,722	3,666	16,014	6,436	15,455	9,407	13,831	6,608	1,942	8,404	9,344
Sanaa, Yemen	9,453	12,338	4,994	13,680	4,086	3,442	8,971	13,783	1,374	11,635	10,821	5,498	19,141	8,212	4,977	4,742	12,067	12,395	5,572	4,807
Santa Cruz, Bolivia	14,627	505	10,560	14,029	8,242	15,069	18,004	4,175	13,196	1,658	6,785	17,813	7,440	19,453	10,233	9,714	2,305	3,283	8,036	9,717
Santa Cruz, Tenerife	10,178	6,925	3,501	15,987	3,806	9,776	14,712	7,440	6,528	5,841	5,151	10,863	13,919	13,396	3,139	7,968	8,523	6,079	869	2,542
Santa Fe, New Mexico	7,345	6,985	8,552	8,909	11,967	15,612	13,342	3,272	12,726	6,424	3,058	13,215	7,190	12,576	8,581	15,946	9,561	4,434	8,676	8,844
Santa Rosa, Argentina	16,435	2,579	12,275	13,541	8,762	14,395	16,004	5,870	13,842	3,733	8,846	17,526	6,840	17,509	11,919	8,903	616	5,290	9,562	11,310
Santa Rosalia, Mexico	7,802	6,874	9,657	8,323	12,836	16,486	13,139	3,189	13,806	6,538	4,055	13,759	6,089	12,636	9,685	16,539	9,210	4,634	9,681	9,937
Santarem, Brazil	13,300	1,591	8,639	14,921	7,096	14,275	19,894	3,848	11,660	596	5,305	16,196	8,913	18,584	8,321	9,625	3,949	2,369	6,207	7,837
Santiago del Estero, Argentina	15,587	1,600	11,509	13,772	8,552	14,833	16,939	5,016	13,640	2,765	7,871	17,946	7,031	18,448	11,167	9,326	1,295	4,327	8,877	10,602
Santiago, Chile	15,822	2,324	12,384	13,054	9,267	15,075	16,118	5,312	14,367	3,534	8,465	18,200	6,313	17,612	12,043	9,582	1,288	4,883	9,753	11,480
Santo Domingo, Dominican Rep.	10,605	3,574	7,837	12,752	8,692	15,304	17,281	1,892	11,912	2,623	2,724	15,278	8,434	16,162	7,636	12,105	6,383	883	6,333	7,449
Sao Paulo de Olivenca, Brazil	12,925	1,208	9,661	13,378	8,668	15,846	18,504	2,592	13,107	977	5,151	17,394	7,428	18,384	9,384	10,982	3,994	1,592	7,501	9,004
Sao Paulo, Brazil	15,777	2,164	10,112	15,604	6,720	13,255	17,401	5,851	11,812	2,679	7,794	16,209	8,861	18,388	9,748	7,882	1,912	4,661	7,361	9,112
Sao Tome, Sao Tome & Principe	12,672	7,956	5,764	18,119	441	7,433	13,147	10,339	5,502	7,437	9,026	9,936	15,179	12,617	5,449	4,021	7,807	8,737	3,796	4,761
Sapporo, Japan	1,948	15,912	8,403	4,934	12,983	7,919	4,888	12,218	8,130	15,107	9,929	4,775	11,242	3,706	8,776	13,415	18,329	13,185	11,167	9,484
Sarajevo, Yugoslavia	7,747	10,440	1,054	13,734	4,541	6,955	11,208	10,232	3,492	9,326	6,884	7,382	16,667	9,879	986	7,863	11,852	9,201	2,676	1,052
Saratov, USSR	5,966	12,552	2,346	11,679	6,325	5,855	9,107	11,594	2,841	11,387	7,926	5,389	16,846	7,714	2,645	8,689	14,072	10,905	4,880	3,155
Saskatoon, Canada	5,825	8,322	7,094	8,850	11,372	13,786	12,375	4,795	11,048	7,526	2,801	11,503	8,779	11,317	7,193	15,539	11,060	5,574	7,846	7,590
Schefferville, Canada	6,890	7,554	4,941	11,307	8,748	12,538	13,674	5,028	9,241	6,452	1,355	11,342	10,776	12,281	4,937	12,916	10,321	4,914	5,231	5,185
Seattle, Washington	5,472	8,869	8,119	7,669	12,600	14,085	11,575	5,165	11,799	8,243	3,951	11,397	7,933	10,705	8,257	16,759	11,450	6,248	9,064	8,709

Distances in Kilometers

	Magadan, USSR	Magdalena, Bolivia	Magdeburg, East Germany	Majuro Atoll, Marshall Isls.	Malabo, Equatorial Guinea	Male, Maldives	Manado, Indonesia	Managua, Nicaragua	Manama, Bahrain	Manaus, Brazil	Manchester, New Hampshire	Mandalay, Burma	Mangareva Island, Fr.Polynesia	Manila, Philippines	Mannheim, West Germany	Maputo, Mozambique	Mar del Plata, Argentina	Maracaibo, Venezuela	Marrakech, Morocco	Marseilles, France
Sendai, Japan	2,473	16,311	8,849	4,601	13,246	7,772	4,388	12,588	8,283	15,579	10,435	4,624	11,085	3,272	9,223	13,288	18,411	13,629	11,626	9,923
Seoul, South Korea	2,977	17,105	8,264	5,583	12,190	6,578	4,002	13,504	7,145	16,126	10,890	3,428	12,223	2,615	8,633	12,090	19,622	14,326	11,038	9,291
Sept-Iles, Canada	7,382	7,041	5,189	11,595	8,635	12,882	14,179	4,594	9,523	5,941	890	11,824	10,542	12,792	5,148	12,800	9,809	4,410	5,178	5,323
Sevastopol, USSR	7,125	11,644	1,815	12,887	5,133	5,951	10,000	11,294	2,550	10,535	7,791	6,173	17,404	8,688	1,971	7,814	12,915	10,357	3,866	2,252
Seville, Spain	9,049	8,268	2,145	15,066	4,018	8,811	13,382	8,350	5,417	7,150	5,469	9,556	14,932	12,031	1,776	8,089	9,884	7,149	664	1,168
Shanghai, China	3,848	17,958	8,541	5,812	11,923	5,838	3,300	14,387	6,823	16,904	11,695	2,706	12,554	1,831	8,898	11,351	19,235	15,180	11,255	9,508
Sheffield, United Kingdom	7,241	9,471	897	13,263	5,581	8,657	12,177	8,588	5,220	8,274	5,111	8,559	14,877	10,713	816	9,385	11,468	7,746	2,470	1,229
Shenyang, China	2,727	16,767	7,705	6,061	11,739	6,485	4,468	13,305	6,747	15,708	10,495	3,368	12,621	3,026	8,074	11,954	19,575	13,996	10,480	8,735
Shiraz, Iran	7,660	13,304	4,174	12,316	5,422	3,591	8,225	13,627	421	12,364	10,149	4,422	18,983	7,162	4,300	6,508	13,633	12,564	5,732	4,424
Sibiu, Romania	7,358	10,930	1,153	13,293	4,893	6,642	10,721	10,576	3,197	9,806	7,132	6,908	16,868	9,381	1,245	7,993	12,349	9,610	3,177	1,512
Singapore	7,617	18,142	10,046	7,500	10,572	3,392	2,337	18,156	6,326	18,232	15,078	2,442	13,248	2,392	10,291	8,213	15,521	18,595	11,994	10,598
Sioux Falls, South Dakota	7,029	7,117	7,381	9,634	10,966	14,649	13,534	3,621	11,594	6,341	2,045	12,631	8,351	12,518	7,405	15,077	9,858	4,376	7,576	7,671
Skelleftea, Sweden	5,591	11,104	1,501	11,657	6,841	7,912	10,512	9,589	4,776	9,891	5,895	7,111	15,058	9,019	1,854	10,109	13,246	9,062	4,186	2,581
Skopje, Yugoslavia	7,831	10,635	1,351	13,758	4,422	6,644	11,003	10,537	3,181	9,542	7,206	7,162	16,989	9,705	1,308	7,611	11,934	9,480	2,853	1,325
Socotra Island (Tamrida)	9,182	13,344	5,782	12,750	5,073	2,344	7,901	14,857	1,544	12,704	11,731	4,575	18,520	7,225	5,823	4,864	12,755	13,494	6,644	5,751
Sofia, Bulgaria	7,698	10,799	1,369	13,606	4,547	6,540	10,841	10,649	3,078	9,701	7,283	7,003	17,059	9,538	1,371	7,660	12,101	9,614	3,018	1,460
Songkhla, Thailand	7,172	18,229	9,308	7,789	10,167	3,026	2,764	17,737	5,691	17,841	14,389	1,708	13,848	2,373	9,559	8,208	15,952	17,854	11,328	9,885
Sorong, Indonesia	6,917	17,708	12,055	4,525	13,632	6,451	759	15,708	9,127	18,704	14,825	4,581	10,367	2,050	12,385	10,842	15,607	17,282	14,553	12,896
South Georgia Island	19,260	5,132	12,619	14,216	7,680	11,672	13,919	8,708	12,163	6,049	11,271	14,701	8,465	15,199	12,251	6,377	2,400	7,906	9,909	11,528
South Pole	16,607	8,528	15,786	10,791	10,419	10,445	10,165	11,346	12,904	9,657	14,765	12,436	7,443	11,614	15,488	7,131	5,796	11,182	13,505	14,800
South Sandwich Islands	19,752	5,853	12,670	14,188	7,513	10,973	13,277	9,453	11,709	6,730	11,921	13,969	8,891	14,502	12,312	5,779	3,145	8,619	10,055	11,586
Split, Yugoslavia	7,842	10,276	1,025	13,848	4,470	7,091	11,371	10,091	3,627	9,163	6,770	7,545	16,553	10,041	901	7,868	11,704	9,046	2,515	893
Spokane, Washington	5,710	8,570	7,933	8,034	12,285	14,183	11,919	4,888	11,734	7,911	3,585	11,597	8,034	11,016	8,052	16,454	11,191	5,919	8,763	8,477
Spoleto, Italy	8,035	9,963	1,052	14,069	4,336	7,346	11,685	9,826	3,886	8,850	6,563	7,857	16,332	10,353	819	7,874	11,416	8,755	2,206	601
Springbok, South Africa	15,180	8,530	9,086	16,278	3,823	6,993	11,735	12,034	7,100	8,673	12,140	10,133	13,486	12,056	8,816	1,502	6,855	10,547	7,316	8,179
Springfield, Illinois	7,683	6,449	7,314	10,283	10,466	14,859	14,250	3,082	11,619	5,636	1,558	13,138	8,404	13,204	7,293	14,503	9,217	3,687	7,186	7,476
Springfield, Massachusetts	8,057	6,198	6,122	11,575	9,021	13,863	14,871	3,575	10,462	5,168	136	12,813	9,650	13,577	6,046	13,104	9,001	3,485	5,737	6,143
Srinagar, India	6,041	15,295	5,324	10,156	7,580	3,334	6,323	14,514	2,485	14,228	10,809	2,475	16,886	5,106	5,580	8,005	15,757	13,922	7,526	5,952
Stanley, Falkland Islands	18,028	4,293	13,220	13,353	8,757	13,080	14,433	7,586	13,502	5,387	10,574	16,023	7,149	15,886	12,847	7,815	1,523	7,036	10,435	12,158
Stara Zagora, Bulgaria	7,641	10,980	1,509	13,507	4,599	6,358	10,657	10,835	2,897	9,887	7,452	6,816	17,219	9,363	1,540	7,605	12,243	9,806	3,197	1,653
Stockholm, Sweden	6,195	10,833	892	12,259	6,217	7,731	10,810	9,649	4,452	9,631	6,007	7,253	15,460	9,341	1,258	9,547	12,813	8,976	3,641	1,982
Stornoway, United Kingdom	6,791	9,498	1,325	12,755	6,184	9,035	12,123	8,277	5,645	8,286	4,695	8,653	14,392	10,630	1,372	10,004	11,675	7,566	2,957	1,849
Strasbourg, France	7,557	9,824	486	13,623	4,970	7,906	11,836	9,300	4,448	8,661	5,909	8,088	15,691	10,429	113	8,620	11,553	8,346	2,302	615
Stuttgart, West Germany	7,502	9,929	417	13,568	4,989	7,811	11,730	9,399	4,355	8,768	5,995	7,980	15,773	10,326	95	8,599	11,645	8,451	2,388	674
Subic, Philippines	5,553	19,531	9,930	5,623	12,204	5,263	1,567	15,839	7,291	18,705	13,487	2,666	12,144	89	10,261	10,500	17,434	16,897	12,471	10,784
Suchow, China	3,727	17,682	8,025	6,285	11,455	5,620	3,716	14,305	6,361	16,546	11,404	2,471	13,011	2,214	8,380	11,132	19,388	14,946	10,732	8,986
Sucre, Bolivia	14,666	643	10,803	13,796	8,485	15,253	17,778	4,148	13,453	1,850	6,897	18,063	7,186	19,193	10,479	9,853	2,232	3,358	8,293	9,970
Sudbury, Canada	7,341	6,838	6,292	10,774	9,693	13,876	14,121	3,840	10,599	5,873	849	12,413	9,427	12,892	6,273	13,828	9,648	4,070	6,297	6,475
Suez, Egypt	8,594	11,380	3,003	13,989	3,832	5,173	10,155	11,987	1,818	10,435	8,827	6,345	18,567	9,071	2,968	6,190	11,997	10,762	3,863	2,824
Sundsvall, Sweden	5,911	10,873	1,186	11,977	6,543	7,931	10,756	9,505	4,710	9,662	5,832	7,286	15,170	9,271	1,535	9,887	12,958	8,907	3,867	2,261
Surabaya, Indonesia	8,136	17,703	11,398	6,682	11,611	4,538	1,655	17,878	7,662	18,614	16,023	3,712	11,941	2,581	11,651	8,687	14,896	19,414	13,338	11,964
Suva, Fiji	8,970	12,333	16,056	2,907	18,064	11,736	6,253	10,982	14,612	13,210	12,990	10,002	4,872	7,265	16,413	13,896	11,488	12,477	18,380	17,139
Sverdlovsk, USSR	4,896	13,314	3,257	10,568	7,434	5,971	8,332	11,774	3,495	12,112	8,070	4,826	16,053	6,876	3,490	9,548	15,105	11,343	5,847	4,097
Svobodnyy, USSR	1,684	15,642	7,080	6,295	11,653	7,280	5,541	12,224	6,932	14,601	9,376	4,276	12,453	4,134	7,454	12,594	18,451	12,871	9,859	8,153
Sydney, Australia	10,357	13,587	16,214	5,008	14,896	9,133	4,789	13,752	12,511	14,771	16,207	8,504	7,180	6,247	16,514	10,753	11,512	14,971	18,066	16,890
Sydney, Canada	7,951	6,599	5,066	12,225	8,098	12,828	14,705	4,501	9,400	5,459	961	12,089	10,732	13,278	4,974	12,245	9,324	4,080	4,711	5,055
Syktyvkar, USSR	4,931	12,608	2,558	10,838	7,311	6,671	9,024	11,008	3,939	11,398	7,303	5,590	15,700	7,547	2,925	9,851	14,581	10,573	5,330	3,589
Szeged, Hungary	7,444	10,638	901	13,432	4,839	6,940	11,015	10,270	3,488	9,507	6,849	7,211	16,609	9,662	944	8,096	12,123	9,298	2,908	1,212
Szombathely, Hungary	7,456	10,402	654	13,483	4,877	7,231	11,254	9,979	3,778	9,260	6,562	7,466	16,330	9,883	653	8,263	11,967	9,015	2,717	982
Tabriz, Iran	7,181	12,699	3,100	12,437	5,380	4,675	8,909	12,582	1,376	11,654	9,055	5,054	18,341	7,696	3,256	7,234	13,544	11,619	4,947	3,470
Tacheng, China	4,532	15,253	4,992	9,303	8,503	4,825	6,449	13,394	3,645	14,004	9,749	2,990	15,741	5,015	5,322	9,513	16,664	13,164	7,594	5,868
Tahiti (Papeete)	10,088	9,104	15,827	5,105	17,216	15,110	9,598	7,691	17,739	9,866	10,391	13,186	1,646	10,438	15,953	15,187	9,004	9,118	15,860	16,310
Taipei, Taiwan	4,455	18,584	9,092	5,635	12,106	5,635	2,632	14,913	7,026	17,574	12,355	2,614	12,366	1,160	9,441	11,094	18,566	15,808	11,760	10,025
Taiyuan, China	3,621	17,267	7,451	6,791	10,959	5,459	4,221	14,133	5,887	16,085	11,040	2,363	13,482	2,711	7,805	10,925	19,155	14,615	10,155	8,409
Tallahassee, Florida	8,829	5,303	7,778	10,988	10,099	15,526	15,325	2,036	12,115	4,523	1,799	14,201	8,026	14,340	7,689	13,888	8,071	2,552	7,121	7,740
Tallinn, USSR	6,004	11,209	1,147	12,050	6,325	7,413	10,436	10,001	4,192	10,008	6,340	6,873	15,670	8,972	1,521	9,490	13,149	9,351	3,931	2,226
Tamanrasset, Algeria	10,345	8,576	3,304	16,350	2,135	7,584	12,935	9,682	4,561	7,664	7,286	9,149	15,991	11,875	2,974	6,132	9,414	8,253	1,657	2,276
Tampa, Florida	9,155	4,977	7,872	11,228	9,943	15,637	15,645	1,794	12,196	4,196	1,940	14,475	7,981	14,669	7,765	13,652	7,749	2,224	7,066	7,775
Tampere, Finland	5,832	11,186	1,270	11,890	6,528	7,592	10,450	9,856	4,406	9,979	6,180	6,945	15,442	8,973	1,641	9,727	13,205	9,255	4,034	2,361
Tanami, Australia	9,024	16,024	13,645	5,445	13,389	6,695	2,433	16,094	9,953	17,240	16,784	5,912	9,680	3,941	13,920	9,740	13,542	17,522	15,627	14,269
Tangier, Morocco	9,218	8,193	2,283	15,240	3,853	8,786	13,452	8,380	5,415	7,089	5,568	9,615	14,957	12,119	1,911	7,938	9,756	7,148	505	1,271
Tarawa (Betio)	6,735	13,614	13,820	670	18,184	11,060	5,351	11,160	13,135	14,145	11,957	8,604	6,257	5,893	14,180	14,984	13,471	12,768	16,353	14,906
Tashkent, USSR	5,717	14,560	4,439	10,473	7,301	4,156	7,089	13,578	2,402	13,435	9,873	3,299	16,987	5,777	4,715	8,359	15,518	13,001	6,782	5,140
Tbilisi, USSR	6,917	12,551	2,744	12,349	5,520	5,060	9,080	12,228	1,799	11,468	8,666	5,235	17,943	7,811	2,928	7,596	13,592	11,322	4,770	3,210
Tegucigalpa, Honduras	10,340	3,960	9,377	11,064	10,563	17,097	16,097	238	13,636	3,556	3,541	15,995	6,632	15,580	9,234	13,649	6,546	1,738	8,195	9,157
Tehran, Iran	7,153	13,170	3,619	12,148	5,625	4,174	8,421	13,104	1,051	12,149	9,553	4,569	18,487	7,246	3,783	7,105	13,843	12,149	5,447	3,998
Tel Aviv, Israel	8,289	11,620	2,912	13,681	4,146	5,092	9,935	12,069	1,668	10,649	8,817	6,107	18,600	8,818	2,917	6,427	12,302	10,895	4,021	2,855
Telegraph Creek, Canada	4,259	9,953	7,345	7,467	12,298	12,798	10,690	6,321	10,682	9,201	4,383	10,134	8,985	9,663	7,542	16,234	12,630	7,235	8,766	8,089
Teresina, Brazil	13,850	2,512	8,155	16,266	5,821	12,969	18,608	5,174	10,602	1,922	6,057	15,227	10,014	17,968	7,803	8,308	3,940	3,636	5,491	7,219
Ternate, Indonesia	6,825	18,139	11,658	4,912	13,190	6,008	294	16,045	8,661	19,171	14,803	4,126	10,835	1,679	11,981	10,539	15,855	17,571	14,111	12,473
The Valley, Anguilla	10,872	3,473	7,406	13,451	7,969	14,673	17,681	2,577	11,342	2,367	2,877	15,032	9,043	16,368	7,175	11,420	6,231	1,231	5,705	6,924
Thessaloniki, Greece	7,918	10,721	1,543	13,803	4,325	6,471	10,909	10,705	3,008	9,643	7,394	7,060	17,178	9,632	1,501	7,440	11,945	9,627	2,940	1,480
Thimphu, Bhutan	5,789	16,888	6,847	8,813	8,929	3,124	4,725	15,593	3,875	15,822	11,963	889	15,531	3,539	7,125	8,515	16,766	15,329	9,123	7,533
Thunder Bay, Canada	6,860	7,277	6,596	10,114	10,297	13,964	13,575	4,029	10,829	6,378	1,510	12,189	9,131	12,414	6,617	14,451	10,074	4,497	6,851	6,887
Tientsin, China	3,272	17,143	7,606	6,442	11,322	5,878	4,241	13,831	6,271	16,008	10,867	2,764	13,097	2,746	7,967	11,352	19,549	14,417	10,346	8,595
Tijuana, Mexico	7,068	7,575	9,382	7,882	13,044	15,814	12,527	3,863	13,372	7,179	4,124	13,025	6,447	11,944	9,450	16,995	9,945	5,234	9,720	9,775
Tiksi, USSR	1,662	13,473	5,424	7,727	10,620	8,422	7,789	10,354	6,849	12,378	7,194	5,895	12,642	6,356	5,784	12,938	16,247	10,752	8,073	6,511
Timbuktu, Mali	11,219	7,500	4,135	17,286	1,933	8,451	13,965	8,928	5,614	6,639	7,013	10,229	14,974	12,968	3,774	6,099	8,316	7,418	1,722	3,048
Tindouf, Algeria	10,142	7,553	3,178	16,148	3,203	8,984	14,055	8,238	5,777	6,518	5,856	10,201	14,694	12,814	2,804	7,367	8,911	6,863	436	2,117
Tirane, Albania	7,955	10,484	1,354	13,899	4,307	6,741	11,152	10,434	3,279	9,395	7,138	7,308	16,920	9,858	1,267	7,566	11,779	9,357	2,701	1,208
Tokyo, Japan	2,772	16,573	9,048	4,501	13,307	7,621	4,090	12,843	8,294	15,870	10,734	4,483	11,074	2,997	9,422	13,132	18,462	13,913	11,831	10,115
Toledo, Spain	8,744	8,555	1,821	14,776	4,203	8,659	13,099	8,500	5,235	7,425	5,493	9,288	15,077	11,732	1,453	8,217	10,206	7,349	982	872
Topeka, Kansas	7,502	6,661	7,712	9,785	10,991	15,110	13,913	3,122	11,977	5,930	2,075	13,137	8,006	12,957	7,711	15,020	9,381	3,947	7,697	7,929
Toronto, Canada	7,680	6,499	6,413	10,995	9,578	14,071	14,455	3,556	10,743	5,534	647	12,719	9,317	13,232	6,372	13,678	9,309	3,733	6,244	6,531
Toulouse, France	8,231	9,150	1,220	14,291	4,474	8,261	12,507	8,907	4,805	8,008	5,713	8,714	15,440	11,126	847	8,334	10,816	7,836	1,565	323
Tours, France	7,842	9,289	952	13,893	4,898	8,390	12,370	8,799	4,927	8,122	5,484	8,631	15,259	10,953	621	8,730	11,084	7,812	1,899	585
Townsville, Australia	8,743	15,071	14,691	3,961	15,160	8,422	3,320	14,311	11,536	16,183	15,580	7,161	8,037	4,690	15,027	11,334	13,179	15,804	17,154	15,541
Trenton, New Jersey	8,182	6,030	6,397	11,486	9,196	14,140	14,978	3,310	10,737	5,032	413	13,052	9,380	13,723	6,319	13,246	8,838	3,290	5,959	6,407
Tripoli, Lebanon	8,010	11,748	2,755	13,446	4,401	5,141	9,829	12,031	1,682	10,748	8,706	5,985	18,472	8,672	2,793	6,694	12,526	10,907	4,077	2,801
Tripoli, Libya	9,043	9,659	2,144	15,005	3,259	7,014	11,932	10,153	3,680	8,644	7,208	8,082	16,726	10,737	1,883	6,831	10,731	8,895	1,998	1,340
Tristan da Cunha (Edinburgh)	17,226	5,760	10,155	16,674	5,018	9,903	14,123	9,438	9,607	6,147	10,696	13,045	11,047	14,790	9,802	4,392	3,961	8,133	7,617	9,077
Trondheim, Norway	5,958	10,570	1,255	12,012	6,622	8,296	11,047	9,137	5,054	9,357	5,464	7,628	14,850	9,553	1,556	10,099	12,732	8,555	3,764	2,262
Trujillo, Peru	12,948	1,728	10,763	12,297	9,837	16,960	17,288	2,381	14,351	2,177	5,712	18,385	6,183	17,735	10,510	11,736	3,953	2,234	8,724	10,177
Truk Island (Moen)	5,785	16,044	12,401	2,135	15,752	8,683	3,068	13,244	10,767	16,472	12,919	6,185	8,642	3,461	12,774	13,302	15,519	14,815	15,186	13,452
Truro, Canada	7,965	6,501	5,311	12,072	8,316	13,070	14,754	4,280	9,647	5,382	706	12,259	10,479	13,352	5,224	12,453	9,251	3,928	4,951	5,310
Tsingtao, China	3,410	17,448	8,044	6,071	11,678	5,964	3,857	13,986	6,601	16,358	11,169	2,816	12,768	2,381	8,405	11,473	19,728	14,684	10,783	9,032
Tsitsihar, China	2,215	16,158	7,243	6,310	11,556	6,803	5,085	12,765	6,692	15,088	9,880	3,760	12,683	3,645	7,616	12,185	18,957	13,395	10,028	8,296
Tubuai Island (Mataura)	10,673	8,970	16,430	5,450	16,830	14,945	9,640	7,921	17,982	9,823	10,832	13,355	1,485	10,601	16,530	14,542	8,610	9,266	16,134	16,821
Tucson, Arizona	7,414	7,091	9,126	8,450	12,532	15,969	13,075	3,362	13,250	6,645	3,649	13,355	6,634	12,441	9,165	16,429	9,544	4,686	9,273	9,441
Tulsa, Oklahoma	7,770	6,416	7,976	9,807	11,079	15,425	14,089	2,830	12,262	5,729	2,224	13,446	7,740	13,187	7,964	15,040	9,112	3,737	7,851	8,157

Distances in Kilometers	Magadan, USSR	Magdalena, Bolivia	Magdeburg, East Germany	Majuro Atoll, Marshall Isls.	Malabo, Equatorial Guinea	Male, Maldives	Manado, Indonesia	Managua, Nicaragua	Manama, Bahrain	Manaus, Brazil	Manchester, New Hampshire	Mandalay, Burma	Mangareva Island, Fr.Polynesia	Manila, Philippines	Mannheim, West Germany	Maputo, Mozambique	Mar del Plata, Argentina	Maracaibo, Venezuela	Marrakech, Morocco	Marseilles, France
Tunis, Tunisia	8,728	9,540	1,712	14,756	3,663	7,381	12,084	9,778	3,981	8,475	6,735	8,231	16,360	10,819	1,416	7,333	10,816	8,583	1,768	829
Tura, USSR	2,632	14,221	4,920	8,379	9,703	7,027	7,248	11,511	5,504	13,036	8,089	4,708	13,952	5,744	5,294	11,572	16,735	11,665	7,700	5,995
Turin, Italy	7,930	9,670	844	13,995	4,577	7,809	11,987	9,371	4,345	8,530	6,082	8,192	15,855	10,613	497	8,260	11,282	8,338	2,016	266
Uberlandia, Brazil	15,241	1,802	9,772	15,568	6,735	13,500	17,939	5,403	11,780	2,164	7,256	16,310	8,880	18,793	9,414	8,232	2,296	4,156	7,058	8,804
Ufa, USSR	5,269	13,122	2,906	10,930	7,060	5,844	8,533	11,792	3,197	11,931	8,088	4,933	16,380	7,100	3,239	9,217	14,794	11,268	5,558	3,814
Ujungpandang, Indonesia	7,687	17,928	11,662	5,912	12,339	5,206	949	17,105	8,178	19,090	15,675	3,932	11,382	2,186	11,945	9,453	15,221	18,670	13,819	12,332
Ulaanbaatar, Mongolia	3,102	16,081	6,326	7,520	10,305	5,819	5,429	13,226	5,411	14,887	9,932	3,033	13,964	3,919	6,688	11,028	18,339	13,514	9,075	7,324
Ulan-Ude, USSR	2,792	15,671	6,072	7,588	10,289	6,171	5,809	12,791	5,516	14,486	9,497	3,457	13,870	4,301	6,440	11,279	18,086	13,080	8,843	7,097
Uliastay, Mongolia	3,683	15,803	5,769	8,257	9,556	5,339	5,795	13,363	4,665	14,588	9,886	2,858	14,712	4,302	6,121	10,380	17,676	13,434	8,471	6,723
Uranium City, Canada	5,120	9,010	6,513	8,772	11,141	12,954	11,816	5,578	10,308	8,137	3,115	10,689	9,476	10,663	6,651	15,235	11,786	6,236	7,590	7,116
Urumqi, China	4,505	15,692	5,479	8,953	8,824	4,623	5,960	13,778	3,854	14,493	10,168	2,542	15,518	4,531	5,807	9,546	17,038	13,619	8,063	6,344
Ushuaia, Argentina	17,627	4,615	13,955	12,576	9,523	13,413	13,974	7,610	14,186	5,778	10,842	16,138	6,450	15,471	13,583	8,347	2,037	7,261	11,171	12,905
Vaduz, Liechtenstein	7,661	9,889	577	13,724	4,812	7,735	11,770	9,462	4,273	8,738	6,098	7,996	15,881	10,381	269	8,424	11,546	8,478	2,281	538
Valencia, Spain	8,713	8,809	1,688	14,772	4,062	8,343	12,841	8,816	4,921	7,692	5,791	9,014	15,394	11,495	1,314	8,011	10,376	7,657	1,110	643
Valladolid, Spain	8,563	8,604	1,703	14,585	4,409	8,735	13,054	8,426	5,294	7,459	5,353	9,263	14,992	11,666	1,345	8,414	10,322	7,313	1,149	851
Valletta, Malta	8,688	9,877	1,822	14,657	3,608	6,979	11,734	10,180	3,583	8,831	7,112	7,880	16,761	10,500	1,587	7,106	11,042	8,980	2,134	1,134
Valparaiso, Chile	15,734	2,311	12,408	12,973	9,349	15,176	16,116	5,237	14,449	3,525	8,419	18,298	6,229	17,602	12,070	9,683	1,389	4,836	9,792	11,514
Vancouver, Canada	5,297	9,017	7,982	7,655	12,539	13,892	11,462	5,324	11,623	8,368	3,973	11,214	8,101	10,564	8,128	16,683	11,617	6,375	8,995	8,594
Varna, Bulgaria	7,477	11,179	1,568	13,316	4,763	6,239	10,461	10,968	2,788	10,080	7,544	6,624	17,281	9,160	1,645	7,675	12,448	9,967	3,397	1,823
Venice, Italy	7,764	10,030	749	13,811	4,633	7,469	11,625	9,719	4,005	8,895	6,381	7,824	16,164	10,262	535	8,170	11,587	8,704	2,333	603
Veracruz, Mexico	9,408	5,026	9,495	10,037	11,441	17,202	15,000	1,312	13,835	4,662	3,509	15,259	6,301	14,497	9,414	14,736	7,508	2,798	8,747	9,461
Verona, Italy	7,801	9,930	749	13,856	4,625	7,569	11,725	9,617	4,106	8,793	6,290	7,927	16,071	10,358	487	8,205	11,507	8,598	2,247	506
Victoria, Canada	5,351	8,984	8,071	7,615	12,608	13,971	11,472	5,283	11,715	8,350	4,008	11,276	8,008	10,592	8,216	16,758	11,570	6,356	9,067	8,679
Victoria, Seychelles	10,749	13,070	7,525	12,922	5,272	2,219	7,748	15,745	3,452	12,809	13,298	5,316	16,739	7,536	7,508	3,396	11,677	14,165	7,815	7,302
Vienna, Austria	7,365	10,413	554	13,399	4,979	7,290	11,245	9,928	3,842	9,264	6,491	7,470	16,250	9,863	597	8,372	12,017	8,985	2,757	1,011
Vientiane, Laos	6,010	18,521	8,513	7,514	10,293	3,530	3,040	16,536	5,411	17,515	13,228	815	14,041	2,001	8,802	8,998	17,072	16,776	10,811	9,225
Villahermosa, Mexico	9,684	4,689	9,403	10,392	11,123	17,159	15,365	962	13,732	4,299	3,432	15,476	6,447	14,842	9,301	14,371	7,217	2,434	8,518	9,309
Vilnius, USSR	6,444	11,171	948	12,457	5,842	7,086	10,486	10,250	3,775	9,990	6,643	6,810	16,138	9,058	1,288	8,962	12,931	9,490	3,666	1,918
Visby, Sweden	6,358	10,803	742	12,418	6,034	7,628	10,845	9,724	4,317	9,607	6,102	7,245	15,615	9,388	1,115	9,360	12,724	9,008	3,517	1,832
Vitoria, Brazil	15,557	2,647	9,477	16,331	5,990	12,655	17,384	6,180	11,077	2,858	7,701	15,520	9,595	17,954	9,109	7,400	2,568	4,845	6,706	8,455
Vladivostok, USSR	2,236	16,365	7,992	5,532	12,318	7,182	4,667	12,763	7,394	15,421	10,185	4,051	11,976	3,332	8,365	12,662	19,036	13,589	10,776	9,053
Volgograd, USSR	6,287	12,472	2,336	11,948	6,025	5,675	9,184	11,712	2,558	11,328	8,074	5,413	17,160	7,823	2,601	8,359	13,863	10,949	4,740	3,046
Vologda, USSR	5,534	12,069	1,922	11,484	6,708	6,768	9,578	10,751	3,759	10,869	7,058	6,024	15,975	8,119	2,283	9,464	13,941	10,179	4,681	2,936
Vorkuta, USSR	4,036	12,926	3,255	9,995	8,204	7,085	8,651	10,852	4,680	11,712	7,194	5,527	14,900	7,145	3,629	10,688	15,174	10,641	6,035	4,332
Wake Island	4,650	14,586	11,727	1,430	16,504	10,205	4,961	11,314	11,479	14,656	10,917	7,293	7,889	4,877	12,090	15,277	15,287	12,833	14,342	12,817
Wallis Island	8,605	11,979	15,637	2,658	18,823	12,325	6,711	10,311	14,957	12,754	12,201	10,335	4,477	7,579	15,970	14,671	11,474	11,845	17,649	16,676
Walvis Bay, Namibia	14,709	8,300	8,326	16,979	3,018	7,061	12,163	11,627	6,687	8,295	11,401	10,140	13,938	12,301	8,045	1,860	6,948	10,081	6,499	7,394
Warsaw, Poland	6,817	10,842	638	12,843	5,494	7,189	10,817	10,091	3,805	9,672	6,543	7,098	16,182	9,405	933	8,738	12,546	9,256	3,280	1,530
Washington, D.C.	8,244	5,935	6,640	11,356	9,390	14,378	15,010	3,101	10,980	4,971	654	13,226	9,136	13,797	6,563	13,411	8,745	3,173	6,185	6,651
Watson Lake, Canada	4,224	9,945	7,064	7,691	12,026	12,635	10,762	6,358	10,436	9,152	4,237	10,041	9,242	9,688	7,260	15,952	12,658	7,203	8,499	7,808
Weimar, East Germany	7,217	10,158	134	13,282	5,241	7,743	11,501	9,494	4,306	8,987	6,022	7,780	15,773	10,082	263	8,776	11,921	8,601	2,672	964
Wellington, New Zealand	11,395	11,470	18,253	5,377	15,619	11,250	6,909	11,637	14,688	12,615	14,688	10,704	5,067	8,295	18,612	11,605	9,747	12,757	18,905	19,119
West Berlin, West Germany	7,005	10,349	124	13,067	5,423	7,669	11,309	9,591	4,254	9,172	6,075	7,610	15,787	9,882	483	8,892	12,140	8,739	2,895	1,185
Wewak, Papua New Guinea	7,027	16,437	13,046	3,283	15,023	7,850	2,163	14,459	10,493	17,303	14,437	5,895	8,984	3,203	13,401	11,931	14,917	16,067	15,720	13,991
Whangarei, New Zealand	10,781	11,822	17,726	4,756	16,170	11,254	6,576	11,634	14,623	12,927	14,438	10,415	5,058	7,905	18,098	12,089	10,257	12,868	19,507	18,747
Whitehorse, Canada	3,900	10,284	7,143	7,412	12,206	12,417	10,412	6,678	10,356	9,501	4,579	9,756	9,292	9,344	7,357	16,031	12,984	7,548	8,702	7,931
Wichita, Kansas	7,558	6,629	7,920	9,660	11,165	15,292	13,886	3,037	12,180	5,937	2,265	13,250	7,799	12,975	7,920	15,168	9,323	3,946	7,892	8,137
Willemstad, Curacao	11,302	2,864	8,314	13,045	8,598	15,508	17,879	1,886	12,232	1,955	3,431	15,897	8,176	16,858	8,086	11,738	5,674	332	6,573	7,832
Wiluna, Australia	9,954	15,562	13,543	6,647	12,332	6,062	3,147	16,827	9,479	16,715	17,905	5,973	10,246	4,557	13,754	8,551	12,850	17,857	15,004	13,947
Windhoek, Namibia	14,546	8,569	8,297	16,770	3,050	6,796	11,904	11,886	6,496	8,558	11,574	9,881	14,119	12,033	8,028	1,615	7,193	10,334	6,569	7,392
Windsor, Canada	7,690	6,456	6,731	10,758	9,881	14,358	14,412	3,356	11,055	5,541	950	12,885	8,994	13,246	6,696	13,961	9,260	3,677	6,569	6,862
Winnipeg, Canada	6,418	7,712	6,865	9,524	10,823	13,967	13,054	4,301	10,995	6,868	2,105	11,937	8,906	11,951	6,921	14,989	10,484	4,943	7,338	7,249
Winston-Salem, North Carolina	8,415	5,728	7,060	11,184	9,682	14,797	15,105	2,721	11,400	4,826	1,074	13,563	8,720	13,970	6,982	13,638	8,531	2,949	6,547	7,060
Wroclaw, Poland	7,050	10,545	390	13,094	5,305	7,377	11,114	9,876	3,958	9,379	6,371	7,382	16,080	9,706	636	8,672	12,247	9,000	2,982	1,234
Wuhan, China	4,218	18,088	8,174	6,457	11,276	5,192	3,409	14,795	6,177	16,908	11,837	2,046	13,204	1,901	8,519	10,709	18,900	15,397	10,823	9,092
Wyndham, Australia	8,566	16,551	13,150	5,371	13,272	6,392	1,909	16,304	9,565	17,767	16,436	5,420	10,038	3,414	13,434	9,810	14,057	17,832	15,240	13,811
Xi'an, China	4,137	17,584	7,536	7,029	10,707	4,963	3,991	14,626	5,609	16,374	11,449	1,860	13,766	2,497	7,879	10,449	10,730	15,031	10,175	9,446
Xining, China	4,307	17,073	6,906	7,707	10,033	4,628	4,558	14,542	4,942	15,859	11,162	1,711	14,428	3,100	7,240	10,025	18,189	14,726	9,507	7,788
Yakutsk, USSR	1,177	14,491	6,225	6,965	11,184	7,912	6,725	11,210	6,902	13,424	8,212	5,126	12,527	5,309	6,596	12,887	17,290	11,739	8,956	7,316
Yanji, China	2,356	16,480	7,905	5,680	12,155	6,991	4,609	12,910	7,212	15,502	10,265	3,863	12,157	3,241	8,277	12,467	19,207	13,700	10,689	8,958
Yaounde, Cameroon	12,124	8,571	5,354	17,464	306	6,877	12,596	10,777	4,840	7,998	9,149	9,295	15,840	11,995	5,064	4,005	8,467	9,191	3,691	4,410
Yap Island (Colonia)	5,655	17,571	11,492	3,651	14,229	7,166	1,718	14,565	9,311	17,907	13,465	4,695	10,115	1,947	11,851	12,025	16,485	16,048	14,207	12,462
Yaraka, Australia	9,379	14,794	15,012	4,605	14,707	8,262	3,580	14,562	11,521	15,969	16,211	7,336	8,105	5,034	15,323	10,759	12,689	15,948	17,198	15,754
Yarmouth, Canada	8,057	6,333	5,594	11,963	8,513	13,352	14,869	4,009	9,931	5,238	443	12,494	10,198	13,496	5,506	12,629	9,104	3,714	5,188	5,587
Yellowknife, Canada	4,673	9,456	6,445	8,506	11,259	12,605	11,385	6,015	10,085	8,578	3,513	10,265	9,660	10,219	6,611	15,275	12,232	6,682	7,718	7,119
Yerevan, USSR	7,070	12,536	2,830	12,454	5,397	4,952	9,085	12,316	1,649	11,469	8,777	5,234	18,111	7,840	2,997	7,427	13,503	11,377	4,763	3,241
Yinchuan, China	3,898	17,067	7,036	7,339	10,410	5,063	4,511	14,251	5,337	15,855	10,980	2,071	14,032	3,015	7,381	10,475	18,614	14,561	9,699	7,961
Yogyakarta, Indonesia	8,282	17,592	11,283	6,952	11,351	4,301	1,908	18,148	7,471	18,406	16,101	3,647	12,146	2,740	11,525	8,422	14,783	19,630	13,148	11,814
York, United Kingdom	7,185	9,516	880	13,209	5,627	8,644	12,131	8,607	5,211	8,318	5,117	8,521	14,877	10,665	823	9,419	11,521	7,776	2,526	1,266
Yumen, China	4,256	16,580	6,404	8,094	9,657	4,660	5,057	14,235	4,598	15,368	10,767	1,983	14,770	3,602	6,739	9,930	17,878	14,308	9,012	7,289
Yutian, China	5,412	15,740	5,585	9,496	8,245	3,736	5,910	14,436	3,164	14,609	10,754	2,154	16,204	4,604	5,874	8,652	16,445	14,055	7,961	6,318
Yuzhno-Sakhalinsk, USSR	1,501	15,521	8,077	5,178	12,815	8,119	5,328	11,856	8,083	14,680	9,489	4,998	11,297	4,117	8,449	13,572	18,085	12,774	10,822	9,164
Zagreb, Yugoslavia	7,621	10,313	776	13,645	4,712	7,215	11,341	9,982	3,754	9,181	6,605	7,537	16,385	9,983	698	8,122	11,833	8,984	2,596	886
Zahedan, Iran	7,225	14,110	4,728	11,557	6,176	3,120	7,427	14,213	1,076	13,158	10,622	3,615	18,299	6,355	4,901	6,841	14,344	13,261	6,496	5,106
Zamboanga, Philippines	6,329	19,036	10,766	5,426	12,531	5,393	674	16,248	7,833	19,536	14,314	3,252	11,641	858	11,086	10,299	16,560	17,553	13,220	11,576
Zanzibar, Tanzania	11,803	11,291	6,972	14,733	3,553	3,973	9,557	14,016	3,788	10,998	12,152	6,939	16,704	9,313	6,846	2,301	10,181	12,413	6,524	6,450
Zaragoza, Spain	8,491	8,882	1,507	14,543	4,306	8,417	12,774	8,744	4,975	7,747	5,641	8,968	15,307	11,403	1,136	8,240	10,527	7,631	1,278	549
Zashiversk, USSR	967	13,685	6,124	7,031	11,326	8,717	7,448	10,349	7,427	12,659	7,426	5,985	12,040	6,079	6,481	13,497	16,495	10,917	8,746	7,208
Zhengzhou, China	3,851	17,622	7,780	6,611	11,128	5,362	3,862	14,407	6,034	16,445	11,380	2,222	13,338	2,352	8,131	10,862	19,156	14,948	10,464	8,723
Zurich, Switzerland	7,669	9,816	584	13,735	4,834	7,825	11,843	9,372	4,363	8,662	6,010	8,076	15,794	10,449	235	8,477	11,496	8,391	2,234	508

Distances in Kilometers

	Maseru, Lesotho	Mashhad, Iran	Mazatlan, Mexico	Mbabane, Swaziland	Mbandaka, Zaire	McMurdo Sound, Antarctica	Mecca, Saudi Arabia	Medan, Indonesia	Medellin, Colombia	Medicine Hat, Canada	Medina, Saudi Arabia	Melbourne, Australia	Memphis, Tennessee	Merauke, Indonesia	Merida, Mexico	Meridian, Mississippi	Messina, Italy	Mexico City, Mexico	Miami, Florida	Midway Islands, USA
Mashhad, Iran	8,003	0	13,256	7,548	5,854	14,283	2,527	5,397	13,386	10,392	2,319	12,015	11,499	9,744	12,892	11,721	3,876	13,450	11,949	10,714
Mazatlan, Mexico	15,405	13,256	0	15,743	13,524	12,473	13,866	15,993	3,799	3,001	13,588	13,145	2,062	12,757	1,751	2,015	10,915	864	2,669	7,042
Mbabane, Swaziland	490	7,548	15,743	0	3,229	8,091	5,367	7,974	11,988	15,831	5,692	10,120	14,390	11,476	14,007	14,221	7,322	14,902	13,245	17,207
Mbandaka, Zaire	3,396	5,854	13,524	3,229	0	11,174	3,328	8,952	10,444	12,656	3,547	13,158	11,669	13,547	11,870	11,600	4,230	12,881	10,860	16,467
McMurdo Sound, Antarctica	7,820	14,283	12,473	8,091	11,174	0	13,134	9,835	11,363	15,241	13,465	4,520	14,146	7,803	12,635	13,883	15,393	12,237	13,374	11,787
Mecca, Saudi Arabia	5,771	2,527	13,866	5,367	3,328	13,134	0	6,652	12,348	11,570	335	12,745	11,819	11,441	12,796	11,927	2,973	13,665	11,703	13,221
Medan, Indonesia	8,399	5,397	15,993	7,974	8,952	9,835	6,652	0	18,752	13,434	6,728	6,619	15,625	4,814	17,146	15,951	9,164	16,812	16,754	9,237
Medellin, Colombia	11,620	13,386	3,799	11,988	10,444	11,363	12,348	18,752	0	5,853	12,232	14,635	3,525	16,066	2,223	3,196	9,687	2,937	2,216	10,834
Medicine Hat, Canada	15,832	10,392	3,001	15,831	12,656	15,241	11,570	13,434	5,853	0	11,247	14,060	2,354	12,081	3,721	2,673	8,907	3,551	3,751	6,029
Medina, Saudi Arabia	6,091	2,319	13,588	5,692	3,547	13,465	335	6,728	12,232	11,247	0	12,942	11,551	11,485	12,573	11,669	2,734	13,420	11,486	12,967
Melbourne, Australia	10,142	12,015	13,145	10,120	13,158	4,520	12,745	6,619	14,635	14,060	12,942	0	15,153	3,287	14,489	15,158	15,640	13,557	15,589	8,297
Memphis, Tennessee	14,198	11,499	2,062	14,390	11,669	14,146	11,819	15,625	3,525	2,354	11,551	15,153	0	14,120	1,570	331	8,858	1,959	1,403	8,044
Merauke, Indonesia	11,716	9,744	12,757	11,476	13,547	7,803	11,441	4,814	16,066	12,081	11,485	3,287	14,120	0	14,503	14,331	13,606	13,523	15,338	6,094
Merida, Mexico	13,693	12,892	1,751	14,007	11,870	12,635	12,796	17,146	2,223	3,721	12,573	14,489	1,570	14,503	0	1,266	9,840	1,011	1,101	8,730
Meridian, Mississippi	14,005	11,721	2,015	14,221	11,600	13,883	11,927	15,951	3,196	2,673	11,669	15,158	331	14,331	1,266	0	8,956	1,775	1,104	8,280
Messina, Italy	7,575	3,876	10,915	7,322	4,230	15,393	2,973	9,164	9,687	8,907	2,734	15,640	8,858	13,606	9,840	8,956	0	10,693	8,756	12,534
Mexico City, Mexico	14,551	13,450	864	14,902	12,881	12,237	13,665	16,812	2,937	3,551	13,420	13,557	1,959	13,523	1,011	1,775	10,693	0	2,071	7,900
Miami, Florida	12,991	11,949	2,669	13,245	10,860	13,374	11,703	16,754	2,216	3,751	11,486	15,589	1,403	15,338	1,101	1,104	8,756	2,071	0	9,346
Midway Islands, USA	17,604	10,714	7,042	17,207	16,467	11,787	13,221	9,237	10,834	6,029	12,967	8,297	8,044	6,094	8,730	8,280	12,534	7,900	9,346	0
Milan, Italy	8,486	4,294	10,011	8,254	5,108	16,278	3,855	9,687	9,112	7,941	3,586	16,292	7,966	13,810	9,033	8,084	966	9,842	7,970	11,820
Milford Sound, New Zealand	10,887	14,055	11,467	11,008	14,234	3,670	14,638	8,659	12,591	13,110	14,871	2,044	13,530	4,799	12,598	13,455	17,605	11,737	13,681	8,200
Milwaukee, Wisconsin	14,163	10,625	2,782	14,271	11,316	15,041	11,094	14,799	4,252	1,902	10,810	15,570	898	13,971	2,453	1,187	8,167	2,825	2,040	7,890
Minsk, USSR	9,219	3,146	10,393	8,894	6,029	16,880	3,749	8,455	10,303	7,841	3,419	15,026	8,475	12,248	9,783	8,665	1,972	10,432	8,810	10,598
Mogadiscio, Somalia	3,962	4,064	15,877	3,494	3,024	10,913	2,227	5,928	13,410	13,795	2,555	11,000	13,819	10,599	14,504	13,868	5,022	15,480	13,414	14,363
Mombasa, Kenya	3,078	4,925	15,810	2,627	2,424	10,365	2,821	6,617	12,858	14,200	3,155	11,074	13,820	11,123	14,242	13,811	5,296	15,251	13,194	15,282
Monclova, Mexico	15,041	12,733	649	15,333	12,931	12,990	13,229	16,008	3,565	2,689	12,955	13,787	1,415	13,237	1,368	1,371	10,272	862	2,120	7,367
Moncton, Canada	12,456	9,322	4,508	12,505	9,468	15,900	9,380	14,266	4,537	3,393	9,119	17,405	2,446	15,199	3,587	2,550	6,414	4,315	2,639	9,352
Monrovia, Liberia	5,685	7,844	10,313	5,789	3,302	12,093	5,693	12,122	7,164	10,174	5,733	15,751	8,635	16,842	8,608	8,504	4,420	9,614	7,649	15,926
Monte Carlo, Monaco	8,344	4,456	9,999	8,126	4,956	16,109	3,876	9,838	8,971	8,012	3,621	16,423	7,946	14,022	8,968	8,051	922	9,799	7,895	12,025
Monterrey, Mexico	14,897	12,831	675	15,199	12,857	12,884	13,256	16,183	3,397	2,849	12,989	13,816	1,438	13,359	1,211	1,352	10,292	704	2,018	7,519
Montevideo, Uruguay	7,684	14,314	8,335	8,162	8,602	7,230	11,872	15,685	4,988	10,827	12,025	11,664	8,513	14,905	7,120	8,184	10,959	7,531	7,175	14,471
Montgomery, Alabama	13,788	11,618	2,221	14,000	11,377	13,942	11,752	15,990	3,100	2,808	11,500	15,367	462	14,545	1,307	225	8,780	1,926	944	8,484
Montpelier, Vermont	12,978	9,868	3,864	13,057	10,073	15,532	10,017	14,634	4,222	2,926	9,752	16,812	1,804	14,931	3,025	1,925	7,054	3,699	2,163	8,946
Montpellier, France	8,426	4,740	9,765	8,227	5,030	16,132	4,123	10,124	8,686	7,851	3,877	16,706	7,707	14,280	8,704	7,804	1,152	9,545	7,627	12,053
Montreal, Canada	13,092	9,805	3,856	13,161	10,151	15,640	10,015	14,514	4,354	2,794	9,745	16,730	1,806	14,779	3,090	1,953	7,060	3,728	2,267	8,808
Moosonee, Canada	13,722	9,558	3,822	13,740	10,624	16,085	10,088	13,924	5,015	2,112	9,795	16,170	1,947	13,968	3,454	2,202	7,201	3,892	2,832	8,055
Moroni, Comoros	2,548	5,581	16,576	2,060	3,054	9,463	3,684	6,360	13,297	15,132	4,019	10,231	14,659	10,591	14,914	14,622	6,229	15,922	13,914	15,428
Moscow, USSR	9,474	2,728	10,618	9,114	6,416	16,856	3,812	7,906	10,847	7,915	3,478	14,418	8,783	11,579	10,165	8,997	2,550	10,740	9,238	10,131
Mosul, Iraq	7,449	1,477	12,682	7,048	4,767	14,670	1,681	6,729	12,098	10,096	1,358	13,292	10,733	11,210	11,959	10,903	2,445	12,678	10,929	11,704
Mount Isa, Australia	10,871	10,493	13,278	10,709	13,250	6,463	11,792	5,205	15,923	13,157	11,904	1,968	14,952	1,360	14,942	15,099	14,346	13,931	15,947	7,130
Multan, Pakistan	8,071	1,297	14,091	7,588	6,536	13,341	3,307	4,105	14,669	11,115	3,208	10,724	12,523	8,498	13,997	12,775	5,153	14,428	13,121	10,264
Munich, West Germany	8,726	4,102	9,989	8,476	5,367	16,540	3,887	9,498	9,286	7,804	3,599	16,117	7,962	13,516	9,092	8,097	1,153	9,867	8,046	11,502
Murcia, Spain	8,023	5,299	9,697	7,874	4,645	15,554	4,320	10,624	8,226	8,071	4,120	17,062	7,638	14,959	8,481	7,695	1,462	9,381	7,385	12,668
Murmansk, USSR	10,908	3,982	9,275	10,567	7,728	18,264	5,301	8,678	10,091	6,473	4,966	14,739	7,566	11,564	9,043	7,815	3,586	9,495	8,226	8,948
Mururoa Atoll, Fr. Polynesia	14,158	17,617	6,106	14,568	16,564	6,853	19,892	13,503	7,570	8,439	19,685	7,365	8,147	8,720	7,152	8,035	16,984	6,291	8,243	6,911
Muscat, Oman	6,738	1,409	14,578	6,266	5,074	12,945	1,944	4,843	14,052	11,777	1,932	11,285	12,716	9,558	13,997	12,907	4,372	14,673	12,975	11,721
Myitkyina, Burma	9,611	3,786	14,051	9,129	8,920	12,224	5,857	2,416	16,425	11,204	5,792	8,584	13,262	5,971	14,821	13,581	7,636	14,740	14,338	8,289
Naga, Philippines	11,290	6,766	13,258	10,877	11,629	10,458	8,797	2,915	16,997	11,224	8,760	6,136	13,577	3,093	14,774	13,895	10,567	14,119	14,970	6,330
Nagasaki, Japan	12,786	6,320	11,406	12,317	12,023	12,464	8,761	4,588	14,918	9,069	8,609	7,975	11,412	4,699	12,729	11,737	9,630	12,233	12,785	5,035
Nagoya, Japan	13,482	6,792	10,730	13,012	12,580	12,645	9,279	5,267	14,304	8,476	9,105	8,125	10,828	4,843	12,096	11,148	9,891	11,564	12,216	4,365
Nagpur, India	7,862	2,530	15,060	7,373	7,003	12,186	4,065	2,875	15,916	12,060	4,059	9,487	13,673	7,450	15,189	13,943	6,309	15,515	14,356	10,164
Nairobi, Kenya	3,257	4,784	15,375	2,836	2,070	10,722	2,536	6,903	12,513	13,791	2,865	11,513	13,381	11,485	13,827	13,374	4,885	14,834	12,771	15,323
Nanchang, China	11,373	5,284	12,699	10,902	10,756	12,223	7,591	3,322	15,951	10,153	7,482	7,964	12,438	4,878	13,872	12,769	8,917	13,496	13,740	6,446
Nancy, France	8,895	4,499	9,625	8,670	5,511	16,667	4,242	9,894	8,887	7,518	3,964	16,513	7,589	13,840	8,698	7,717	1,389	9,483	7,648	11,482
Nandi, Fiji	13,880	13,638	9,440	13,923	17,013	6,673	15,581	8,950	12,027	10,278	15,606	3,857	11,354	4,143	11,005	11,407	17,147	10,002	12,066	5,120
Nanjing, China	11,786	5,392	12,236	11,310	11,002	12,542	7,776	3,788	15,504	9,692	7,644	8,201	11,985	5,035	13,409	12,315	8,902	13,003	13,298	6,078
Nanning, China	10,396	4,897	13,685	9,930	10,019	11,722	7,001	2,369	16,762	11,070	6,937	7,733	13,307	4,914	14,789	13,637	8,708	14,471	14,552	7,379
Nantes, France	8,963	5,092	9,199	8,780	5,568	16,579	4,676	10,488	8,297	7,269	4,417	17,107	7,145	14,410	8,186	7,253	1,718	9,004	7,121	11,642
Naples, Italy	7,886	3,940	10,645	7,636	4,533	15,702	3,228	9,283	9,547	8,597	2,973	15,820	8,593	13,626	9,612	8,700	315	10,447	8,535	12,269
Narvik, Norway	10,871	4,414	8,879	10,567	7,587	18,576	5,444	9,278	9,485	6,185	5,112	15,371	7,088	12,177	8,526	7,320	3,368	9,036	7,670	9,220
Nashville, Tennessee	13,933	11,265	2,373	14,110	11,357	14,336	11,520	15,569	3,504	2,463	11,255	15,472	318	14,361	1,707	457	8,555	2,218	1,312	8,272
Nassau, Bahamas	12,697	11,853	2,956	12,950	10,579	13,364	11,503	16,804	2,093	3,983	11,296	15,800	1,652	15,633	1,337	1,370	8,572	2,331	296	9,633
Natal, Brazil	7,058	10,823	8,368	7,375	5,979	10,673	8,714	14,917	4,679	9,471	8,758	15,176	7,305	18,356	6,636	7,056	7,152	7,534	5,982	15,327
Natashquan, Canada	12,403	8,839	4,874	12,411	9,297	16,400	8,994	13,760	5,039	3,430	8,722	17,486	2,829	14,947	4,059	2,969	6,043	4,744	3,136	9,262
Nauru Island	14,596	11,597	9,697	14,433	16,550	8,548	13,847	7,609	13,066	9,511	13,776	4,702	11,230	3,077	11,436	11,394	14,919	10,448	12,325	3,594
Ndjamena, Chad	4,775	5,194	12,551	4,595	1,379	12,540	2,830	9,242	9,942	11,341	2,926	14,312	10,581	14,038	11,021	10,557	2,888	12,020	9,952	15,350
Nelson, New Zealand	11,436	14,375	10,915	11,569	14,798	4,052	15,153	8,997	12,231	12,534	15,371	2,450	12,976	4,873	12,097	12,912	18,088	11,212	13,188	7,753
Nema, Mauritania	6,306	6,878	10,198	6,309	3,345	13,222	4,966	11,594	7,513	9,533	4,940	16,428	8,326	16,403	8,599	8,255	3,268	9,607	7,553	14,934
Neuquen, Argentina	8,467	15,458	7,958	8,955	9,699	6,596	12,995	15,867	5,064	10,706	13,159	10,857	8,508	13,996	7,003	8,179	12,072	7,226	7,275	13,514
New Delhi, India	8,309	1,858	14,258	7,821	7,009	13,033	3,839	3,582	15,179	11,259	3,760	10,192	12,826	7,916	14,342	13,096	5,728	14,679	13,524	9,897
New Glasgow, Canada	12,281	9,252	4,647	12,330	9,298	15,889	9,253	14,255	4,534	3,567	8,997	17,578	2,584	15,343	3,675	2,673	6,284	4,430	2,698	9,520
New Haven, Connecticut	12,912	10,148	3,705	13,019	10,106	15,208	10,209	14,962	3,892	3,061	9,953	16,769	1,647	15,123	2,750	1,718	7,238	3,475	1,848	9,089
New Orleans, Louisiana	14,060	12,018	1,790	14,301	11,772	13,592	12,199	16,179	3,032	2,821	11,945	14,931	572	14,277	998	296	9,227	1,487	1,077	8,269
New Plymouth, New Zealand	11,684	14,364	10,753	11,811	15,039	4,302	15,270	9,011	12,202	12,306	15,473	2,532	12,810	4,777	11,978	12,758	18,156	11,077	13,074	7,499
New York, New York	12,980	10,256	3,595	13,095	10,199	15,120	10,321	15,044	3,820	3,018	10,065	16,671	1,539	15,092	2,641	1,606	7,350	3,362	1,753	9,043
Newcastle upon Tyne, UK	9,747	5,010	8,817	9,536	6,354	17,440	5,069	10,336	8,421	6,637	4,777	16,864	6,806	13,853	8,000	6,956	2,273	8,731	6,986	10,778
Newcastle Waters, Australia	10,545	9,760	13,793	10,337	12,682	6,906	11,066	4,466	16,648	13,320	11,172	2,532	15,309	1,242	15,505	15,497	13,607	14,498	16,442	7,319
Niamey, Niger	5,468	6,229	11,253	5,412	2,320	12,827	4,089	10,633	8,530	10,420	4,114	15,473	9,354	15,441	9,663	9,296	3,039	10,670	8,614	15,389
Nicosia, Cyprus	7,164	2,369	12,283	6,809	4,191	14,752	1,645	7,548	11,310	9,926	1,330	14,033	10,265	12,093	11,371	10,400	1,623	12,168	10,306	12,288
Niue (Alofi)	14,343	14,843	8,331	14,502	17,731	6,647	16,920	10,295	10,696	9,603	16,926	4,826	10,328	5,487	9,802	10,337	17,816	8,817	10,887	5,285
Norfolk, Virginia	13,045	10,720	3,256	13,198	10,414	14,655	10,718	15,498	3,390	3,108	10,470	16,395	1,256	15,170	2,184	1,241	7,745	2,950	1,283	9,081
Norfolk Island, Australia	12,309	13,407	10,835	12,349	15,475	5,395	14,778	8,212	12,921	11,852	14,907	2,338	12,819	3,678	12,283	12,838	17,281	11,309	13,376	6,524
Noril'sk, USSR	11,972	4,063	9,675	11,544	9,217	17,064	6,217	7,341	11,526	6,674	5,909	12,753	8,420	9,508	9,989	8,724	5,413	10,147	9,415	7,276
Norman Wells, Canada	15,631	8,729	4,901	15,404	12,236	16,495	10,321	11,529	7,662	1,939	9,987	13,670	4,142	10,986	5,616	4,472	8,081	5,489	5,474	5,390
Normanton, Australia	11,204	10,422	13,022	11,028	13,482	6,783	11,849	5,216	15,855	12,795	11,942	2,267	14,636	1,021	14,714	14,797	14,294	13,704	15,686	6,766
North Pole	13,248	5,984	7,433	12,916	9,997	18,607	7,631	9,606	9,312	4,455	7,297	14,190	6,114	10,937	7,683	6,420	5,776	7,856	7,151	6,880
Nottingham, United Kingdom	9,530	4,992	8,941	9,325	6,135	17,212	4,933	10,349	8,414	6,819	4,647	16,921	6,916	13,982	8,073	7,055	2,088	8,827	7,043	11,005
Norway House, Canada	14,873	9,770	3,491	14,854	11,674	15,952	10,720	13,443	5,661	982	10,405	15,010	2,182	12,812	3,731	2,509	7,978	3,840	3,455	6,857
Norwich, United Kingdom	9,429	4,828	9,106	9,214	6,037	17,153	4,770	10,191	8,574	6,959	4,483	16,774	7,083	13,877	8,243	7,224	1,948	8,996	7,213	11,049
Nouakchott, Mauritania	7,021	7,569	9,285	7,075	4,242	13,400	5,826	12,476	6,594	8,815	5,771	17,147	7,455	17,254	7,668	7,366	3,782	8,677	6,630	14,509
Noumea, New Caledonia	12,811	12,913	10,688	12,801	15,792	6,143	14,545	7,898	13,156	11,387	14,625	2,682	12,590	3,184	12,247	12,651	16,732	11,246	13,312	5,849
Novosibirsk, USSR	10,734	2,737	11,290	10,273	8,416	15,714	5,165	5,879	12,928	8,289	4,899	11,861	9,993	8,811	11,554	10,288	5,256	11,755	10,908	8,069
Nuku'alofa, Tonga	13,920	14,492	8,926	14,042	17,261	6,360	16,407	9,759	11,261	10,110	16,450	4,239	10,915	4,969	10,402	10,929	17,856	9,417	11,487	5,463
Nukunono Island, Tokelau Isls.	15,268	14,035	7,976	15,361	18,510	7,707	16,376	10,020	10,819	8,827	16,285	5,351	9,863	5,252	9,588	9,925	16,709	8,578	10,625	4,180
Nuremberg, West Germany	8,875	4,142	9,875	8,624	5,515	16,689	4,008	9,534	9,244	7,666	3,716	16,152	7,854	13,486	9,004	7,995	1,302	9,766	7,965	11,364
Nyala, Sudan	4,586	4,392	13,441	4,298	1,514	12,389	1,900	8,171	11,005	11,885	2,073	13,464	11,417	12,969	11,991	11,428	3,040	12,976	10,906	14,954
Oaxaca, Mexico	14,212	13,600	1,222	14,573	12,667	12,043	13,649	17,176	2,592	3,869	13,419	13,627	2,109	13,788	864	1,879	10,686	366	1,964	8,242
Ocean Falls, Canada	16,739	10,158	3,706	16,619	13,390	15,121	11,740	12,441	6,963	1,214	11,406	13,056	3,526	10,883	4,772	3,833	9,364	4,414	4,929	4,871
Odense, Denmark	9,527	4,252	9,456	9,267	6,176	17,346	4,493	9,573	9,184	7,107	4,183	16,123	7,478	13,213	8,722	7,645	1,953	9,420	7,724	10,713
Odessa, USSR	8,399	2,646	11,170	8,060	5,283	16,023	2,895	8,042	10,741	8,684	2,566	14,661	9,207	12,188	10,444	9,377	1,548	11,152	9,428	11,267

Distances in Kilometers

	Maseru, Lesotho	Mashhad, Iran	Mazatlan, Mexico	Mbabane, Swaziland	Mbandaka, Zaire	McMurdo Sound, Antarctica	Mecca, Saudi Arabia	Medan, Indonesia	Medellin, Colombia	Medicine Hat, Canada	Medina, Saudi Arabia	Melbourne, Australia	Memphis, Tennessee	Merauke, Indonesia	Merida, Mexico	Meridian, Mississippi	Messina, Italy	Mexico City, Mexico	Miami, Florida	Midway Islands, USA
Ogbomosho, Nigeria	4,834	6,394	11,735	4,792	1,791	12,216	4,087	10,447	8,808	11,039	4,168	14,886	9,888	15,200	10,096	9,812	3,517	11,108	9,074	15,981
Okha, USSR	14,231	6,451	9,228	13,743	12,203	14,625	8,942	6,847	12,463	6,626	8,685	10,129	8,938	6,878	10,340	9,267	8,656	9,992	10,286	4,282
Okinawa (Naha)	12,315	6,449	12,031	11,863	11,943	11,771	8,786	3,980	15,632	9,796	8,671	7,318	12,146	4,074	13,425	12,469	9,977	12,875	13,527	5,403
Oklahoma City, Oklahoma	14,872	11,712	1,611	15,068	12,319	14,006	12,270	15,365	3,939	1,937	11,986	14,537	678	13,456	1,785	884	9,339	1,791	1,974	7,396
Old Crow, Canada	15,668	8,372	5,440	15,378	12,310	16,520	10,134	10,914	8,292	2,530	9,800	13,244	4,770	10,441	6,232	5,101	8,097	6,066	6,106	5,040
Olympia, Washington	16,792	10,770	3,026	16,776	13,575	14,653	12,224	13,087	6,376	961	11,893	13,100	3,030	11,207	4,164	3,317	9,704	3,749	4,421	5,122
Omaha, Nebraska	14,810	11,063	2,227	14,940	12,012	14,659	11,705	14,820	4,379	1,497	11,412	14,874	859	13,417	2,332	1,184	8,807	2,444	2,255	7,322
Omsk, USSR	10,319	2,331	11,339	9,870	7,864	15,926	4,658	6,139	12,637	8,355	4,378	12,326	9,895	9,348	11,435	10,175	4,650	11,731	10,708	8,609
Oodnadatta, Australia	10,104	10,629	13,848	9,972	12,682	5,763	11,620	5,240	15,985	13,981	11,775	1,447	15,652	2,174	15,420	15,762	14,376	14,422	16,488	7,963
Oradea, Romania	8,478	3,318	10,664	8,179	5,220	16,257	3,267	8,715	10,072	8,322	2,958	15,333	8,664	12,830	9,844	8,815	1,116	10,590	8,810	11,448
Oran, Algeria	7,777	5,339	9,853	7,634	4,404	15,298	4,225	10,620	8,251	8,295	4,042	16,965	7,798	15,045	8,594	7,845	1,467	9,510	7,495	12,923
Oranjestad, Aruba	11,408	12,463	4,021	11,725	9,832	12,159	11,497	17,840	923	5,564	11,363	15,557	3,216	16,684	2,285	2,909	8,782	3,204	1,813	11,007
Orebro, Sweden	9,884	4,073	9,433	9,599	6,572	17,686	4,634	9,293	9,459	6,936	4,311	15,752	7,511	12,749	8,832	7,703	2,347	9,468	7,876	10,240
Orel, USSR	9,148	2,603	10,827	8,791	6,088	16,594	3,507	7,882	10,875	8,174	3,172	14,450	8,954	11,710	10,300	9,157	2,275	10,913	9,346	10,453
Orsk, USSR	9,426	1,658	11,632	8,999	6,815	15,885	3,682	6,461	12,290	8,737	3,382	12,943	9,963	10,167	11,429	10,210	3,639	11,888	10,573	9,652
Osaka, Japan	13,342	6,700	10,868	12,872	12,472	12,604	9,179	5,128	14,432	8,598	9,009	8,087	10,950	4,801	12,227	11,271	9,845	11,701	12,336	4,497
Oslo, Norway	10,008	4,335	9,188	9,738	6,669	17,827	4,846	9,548	9,204	6,727	4,526	15,980	7,257	12,934	8,572	7,446	2,441	9,213	7,614	10,211
Osorno, Chile	8,768	15,920	7,857	9,257	10,137	6,328	13,444	15,828	5,190	10,688	13,615	10,497	8,558	13,588	7,023	8,232	12,536	7,164	7,381	13,131
Ostrava, Czechoslovakia	8,814	3,628	10,257	8,530	5,515	16,619	3,675	9,016	9,759	7,920	3,367	15,632	8,262	12,992	9,460	8,418	1,312	10,193	8,436	11,224
Ottawa, Canada	13,249	9,907	3,709	13,322	10,316	15,583	10,159	14,549	4,340	2,648	9,887	16,566	1,668	14,660	2,996	1,831	7,208	3,603	2,216	8,668
Ouagadougou, Bourkina Fasso	5,566	6,625	10,959	5,550	2,574	12,725	4,503	11,038	8,144	10,285	4,526	15,662	9,101	15,841	9,338	9,026	3,325	10,348	8,304	15,494
Oujda, Morocco	7,726	5,487	9,804	7,595	4,368	15,193	4,319	10,752	8,128	8,312	4,146	17,045	7,754	15,201	8,516	7,792	1,612	9,442	7,416	13,030
Oxford, United Kingdom	9,410	5,008	8,995	9,209	6,014	17,078	4,873	10,378	8,388	6,913	4,593	16,970	6,962	14,075	8,095	7,095	1,999	8,864	7,057	11,140
Pago Pago, American Samoa	14,806	14,479	8,134	14,937	18,159	7,161	16,709	10,184	10,737	9,214	16,663	5,079	10,086	5,374	9,678	10,120	17,285	8,677	10,744	4,753
Pakxe, Laos	9,731	5,132	14,515	9,281	9,749	10,935	6,963	1,495	17,637	11,957	6,952	7,152	14,200	4,619	15,678	14,530	9,007	15,321	15,435	7,965
Palembang, Indonesia	8,621	6,384	15,987	8,239	9,628	8,998	7,561	987	19,634	13,814	7,657	5,633	16,129	3,987	17,484	16,459	10,140	16,851	17,422	8,983
Palermo, Italy	7,608	4,066	10,766	7,370	4,243	15,417	3,136	9,357	9,496	8,810	2,905	15,824	8,707	13,793	9,668	8,799	193	10,530	8,582	12,579
Palma, Majorca	8,048	4,936	9,900	7,871	4,654	15,699	4,053	10,276	8,563	8,139	3,836	16,767	7,838	14,587	8,743	7,912	1,130	9,622	7,652	12,502
Palmerston North, New Zealand	11,623	14,533	10,693	11,765	14,994	4,168	15,369	9,168	12,052	12,325	15,582	2,650	12,754	4,967	11,882	12,691	18,290	10,994	12,975	7,624
Panama, Panama	12,146	13,431	3,270	12,510	10,875	11,571	12,601	18,603	529	5,387	12,459	14,538	3,089	15,652	1,713	2,758	9,844	2,408	1,862	10,307
Paramaribo, Suriname	9,621	11,800	5,813	9,933	8,184	11,704	10,295	16,944	2,261	7,103	10,230	15,921	4,827	18,300	4,075	4,554	7,931	4,991	3,458	12,778
Paris, France	9,014	4,781	9,370	8,807	5,620	16,728	4,496	10,175	8,605	7,322	4,223	16,793	7,328	14,068	8,420	7,450	1,593	9,213	7,367	11,469
Patna, India	8,649	2,700	14,464	8,160	7,699	12,523	4,627	2,835	15,917	11,482	4,573	9,401	13,264	7,064	14,822	13,556	6,575	15,005	14,107	9,385
Patrai, Greece	7,504	3,342	11,322	7,214	4,243	15,303	2,544	8,625	10,221	9,172	2,278	15,125	9,277	13,081	10,315	9,391	540	11,144	9,239	12,386
Peking, China	11,949	4,913	11,729	11,461	10,702	13,441	7,396	4,405	14,747	9,029	7,222	9,093	11,264	5,898	12,745	11,594	8,196	12,478	12,531	6,112
Penrhyn Island (Omoka)	15,724	15,162	6,657	15,975	18,941	7,904	17,665	11,538	9,305	7,988	17,482	6,514	8,639	6,770	8,182	8,655	16,710	7,183	9,251	4,610
Peoria, Illinois	14,266	10,920	2,498	14,400	11,506	14,752	11,372	15,031	4,063	1,941	11,091	15,377	619	13,947	2,187	927	8,437	2,530	1,870	7,854
Perm', USSR	10,042	2,425	10,862	9,632	7,243	16,643	4,271	7,071	11,686	7,967	3,953	13,405	9,218	10,452	10,703	9,472	3,659	11,132	9,881	9,237
Perth, Australia	8,214	9,559	15,774	8,050	10,733	5,620	10,016	4,330	16,928	15,709	10,223	2,733	17,603	3,629	17,222	17,719	12,944	16,272	18,323	9,709
Peshawar, Pakistan	8,405	1,117	13,667	7,925	6,697	13,750	3,406	4,387	14,373	10,690	3,265	10,993	12,116	8,628	13,603	12,373	4,986	14,012	12,749	10,017
Petropavlovsk-Kamchatskiy,USSR	15,275	7,428	8,297	14,788	13,079	14,490	9,884	7,723	11,711	5,864	9,612	10,152	8,214	7,031	9,527	8,536	9,293	9,092	9,599	3,388
Petrozavodsk, USSR	10,120	3,339	9,953	9,773	6,983	17,550	4,504	8,332	10,421	7,219	4,169	14,689	8,161	11,670	9,582	8,388	2,928	10,111	8,697	9,630
Pevek, USSR	14,937	7,005	7,346	14,513	11,988	16,346	9,169	8,929	10,259	4,509	8,853	12,102	6,746	8,971	8,218	7,077	7,865	8,019	8,057	4,683
Philadelphia, Pennsylvania	13,051	10,381	3,471	13,174	10,301	15,013	10,450	15,144	3,733	2,981	10,195	16,561	1,419	15,062	2,513	1,478	7,479	3,232	1,640	8,998
Phnom Penh, Kampuchea	9,446	5,299	14,876	9,006	9,652	10,565	6,992	1,119	18,035	12,356	7,004	6,880	14,605	4,503	16,077	14,936	9,172	15,694	15,839	8,221
Phoenix, Arizona	16,178	12,234	1,262	16,407	13,650	13,439	13,241	14,795	4,820	1,847	12,932	13,230	2,031	12,160	2,611	2,185	10,411	2,018	3,189	6,173
Pierre, South Dakota	15,170	10,845	2,411	15,262	12,237	14,883	11,671	14,367	4,863	1,003	11,366	14,629	1,351	12,980	2,778	1,673	8,833	2,771	2,748	6,890
Pinang, Malaysia	8,663	5,379	15,719	8,234	9,139	9,997	6,747	274	18,641	13,177	6,808	6,652	15,388	4,698	16,894	15,716	9,186	16,539	16,553	8,979
Pitcairn Island (Adamstown)	13,531	18,462	5,921	13,975	15,636	6,702	18,921	14,302	6,839	8,539	18,987	7,925	7,885	9,580	6,715	7,727	16,482	5,952	7,774	7,771
Pittsburgh, Pennsylvania	13,464	10,562	3,125	13,590	10,708	14,953	10,761	15,128	3,813	2,610	10,497	16,163	1,062	14,687	2,343	1,186	7,797	2,962	1,626	8,608
Plymouth, Montserrat	10,878	11,548	4,665	11,147	9,001	12,768	10,538	16,945	1,859	5,681	10,402	16,474	3,436	17,421	2,923	3,181	7,829	3,915	2,116	11,457
Plymouth, United Kingdom	9,364	5,224	8,877	9,181	5,969	16,949	4,989	10,605	8,165	6,882	4,718	17,207	6,833	14,325	7,928	6,954	2,065	8,717	6,879	11,273
Ponape Island	14,313	10,331	10,258	14,042	15,527	9,381	12,616	6,612	13,882	9,502	12,529	5,141	11,504	2,617	12,005	11,722	13,703	11,072	12,753	3,484
Ponce, Puerto Rico	11,360	11,766	4,176	11,633	9,473	12,826	10,901	17,131	1,626	5,279	10,749	16,243	2,993	16,932	2,434	2,725	8,126	3,430	1,643	10,989
Ponta Delgada, Azores	9,259	7,299	7,688	9,242	6,135	15,547	6,465	12,690	6,120	6,590	6,273	19,204	5,664	16,474	6,358	5,673	3,594	7,290	5,258	12,135
Pontianak, Indonesia	9,222	6,515	15,387	8,837	10,138	9,216	7,901	1,252	19,139	13,296	7,970	5,557	15,635	3,562	16,918	15,961	10,345	16,251	16,982	8,383
Port Augusta, Australia	9,975	11,138	13,715	9,887	12,752	5,190	11,981	5,741	15,507	14,186	12,158	885	15,631	2,674	15,186	15,693	14,817	14,214	16,281	8,225
Port Blair, India	8,335	4,305	15,631	7,873	8,325	10,835	5,729	1,101	17,655	12,806	5,770	7,715	14,825	5,716	16,393	15,137	8,107	16,340	15,801	9,402
Port Elizabeth, South Africa	546	8,544	15,229	1,002	3,844	7,339	6,316	8,687	11,430	16,051	6,635	9,896	14,224	11,705	13,566	14,003	8,055	14,365	12,950	17,751
Port Hedland, Australia	9,034	8,814	15,387	8,794	11,095	6,829	9,730	3,423	17,839	14,593	9,880	3,204	16,777	2,684	17,099	17,007	12,492	16,091	18,018	8,733
Port Louis, Mauritius	3,190	6,254	18,335	2,777	4,824	8,238	4,990	5,209	14,741	16,529	5,305	8,452	16,443	8,952	16,610	16,410	7,805	17,588	15,667	14,431
Port Moresby, Papua New Guinea	12,270	10,416	12,097	12,066	14,283	7,628	12,188	5,572	15,310	11,680	12,222	3,148	13,584	762	13,831	13,768	14,249	12,837	14,724	5,651
Port Said, Egypt	6,724	2,580	12,550	6,374	3,757	14,351	1,320	7,566	11,332	10,287	1,041	13,937	10,511	12,212	11,546	10,628	1,710	12,382	10,465	12,715
Port Sudan, Sudan	5,515	2,861	13,850	5,124	2,993	12,988	337	6,893	12,141	11,670	590	12,860	11,792	11,696	12,699	11,882	2,935	13,597	11,600	13,545
Port-au-Prince, Haiti	11,927	12,118	3,576	12,213	10,078	12,764	11,415	17,371	1,404	4,875	11,247	15,820	2,538	16,333	1,831	2,243	8,583	2,823	1,139	10,448
Port-of-Spain, Trin. & Tobago	10,492	11,963	4,959	10,795	8,899	12,121	10,738	17,325	1,623	6,261	10,634	16,007	3,962	17,627	3,213	3,682	8,161	4,152	2,583	11,900
Port-Vila, Vanuatu	13,323	12,817	10,313	13,297	16,211	6,647	14,638	7,994	12,992	10,879	14,681	3,182	12,165	3,198	11,920	12,245	16,533	10,912	12,963	5,311
Portland, Maine	12,781	9,809	4,006	12,861	9,887	15,519	9,890	14,658	4,177	3,122	9,630	16,999	1,943	15,113	3,090	2,039	6,922	3,805	2,178	9,140
Portland, Oregon	16,848	10,938	2,877	16,856	13,672	14,497	12,378	13,214	6,276	1,025	12,048	13,043	2,973	11,226	4,058	3,251	9,836	3,614	4,354	5,134
Porto, Portugal	8,643	5,803	8,965	8,522	5,296	15,945	5,023	11,184	7,633	7,382	4,808	17,733	6,905	15,274	7,773	6,965	2,094	8,661	6,681	12,240
Porto Alegre, Brazil	7,445	13,669	8,343	7,908	8,048	7,827	11,270	15,701	4,790	10,634	11,405	12,303	8,288	15,569	6,988	7,964	10,252	7,508	6,911	14,837
Porto Alexandre, Angola	2,188	7,643	13,550	2,309	1,892	9,505	5,128	9,782	9,935	13,651	5,378	12,318	12,081	13,747	11,799	11,918	5,990	12,751	10,968	18,344
Porto Novo, Benin	4,773	6,650	11,653	4,759	1,878	12,047	4,331	10,642	8,642	11,077	4,417	14,876	9,845	15,367	9,992	9,755	3,747	11,003	8,986	16,167
Porto Velho, Brazil	9,676	13,573	5,826	10,085	9,158	9,960	11,784	18,023	2,107	7,931	11,778	14,042	5,583	16,732	4,328	5,260	9,701	4,965	4,209	12,770
Portsmouth, United Kingdom	9,306	5,006	9,054	9,108	5,910	16,968	4,812	10,386	8,384	7,001	4,536	16,990	7,016	14,136	8,130	7,143	1,917	8,910	7,086	11,250
Poznan, Poland	9,112	3,768	10,001	8,830	5,804	16,920	3,957	9,131	9,635	7,628	3,645	15,729	8,020	12,973	9,250	8,185	1,586	9,960	8,241	10,966
Prague, Czechoslovakia	8,888	3,903	10,028	8,621	5,555	16,708	3,878	9,291	9,484	7,748	3,577	15,907	8,022	13,235	9,201	8,171	1,325	9,945	8,171	11,256
Praia, Cape Verde Islands	7,346	8,437	8,664	7,468	4,881	13,032	6,698	13,341	5,765	8,550	6,649	17,229	6,951	18,134	6,989	6,824	4,618	8,000	5,995	14,472
Pretoria, South Africa	401	7,620	15,441	304	3,048	8,200	5,372	8,249	11,692	15,589	5,691	10,376	14,095	11,778	13,705	13,923	7,198	14,602	12,943	17,486
Prince Albert, Canada	15,405	9,989	3,329	15,378	12,186	15,684	11,097	13,312	5,882	488	10,775	14,478	2,358	12,340	3,835	2,688	8,419	3,794	3,714	6,347
Prince Edward Island	2,121	9,432	15,912	2,328	5,513	5,769	7,536	8,126	12,301	17,676	7,870	8,179	15,542	10,266	14,524	15,266	9,650	15,093	14,164	16,333
Prince George, Canada	16,374	10,006	3,673	16,268	13,038	15,387	11,489	12,572	6,768	933	11,157	13,429	3,285	11,217	4,606	3,601	9,048	4,329	4,684	5,230
Prince Rupert, Canada	16,707	9,920	3,987	16,546	13,328	15,280	11,558	12,168	7,219	1,420	11,223	13,001	3,760	10,725	5,036	4,072	9,250	4,692	5,162	4,761
Providence, Rhode Island	12,809	10,027	3,842	12,908	9,980	15,297	10,072	14,878	3,962	3,139	9,816	16,899	1,784	15,182	2,875	1,855	7,101	3,610	1,954	9,167
Provo, Utah	16,131	11,483	1,950	16,264	13,275	14,175	12,567	14,259	5,205	1,094	12,251	13,596	1,982	12,144	2,988	2,231	9,800	2,600	3,324	6,062
Puerto Aisen, Chile	8,479	15,937	8,331	8,968	10,092	5,813	13,419	15,296	5,728	11,195	13,618	10,045	9,088	13,193	7,546	8,763	12,777	7,659	7,918	13,285
Puerto Deseado, Argentina	7,896	15,432	8,842	8,386	9,578	5,676	12,906	14,893	6,057	11,657	13,119	10,043	9,490	13,266	7,971	9,161	12,466	8,144	8,268	13,839
Puerto Princesa, Philippines	10,659	6,619	13,905	10,253	11,166	10,105	8,486	2,320	17,643	11,844	8,479	5,933	14,196	3,128	15,420	14,517	10,479	14,767	15,580	6,955
Punta Arenas, Chile	7,980	15,779	9,129	8,463	9,960	5,009	13,265	14,427	6,597	12,032	13,504	9,348	9,954	12,568	8,407	9,630	13,075	8,485	8,789	13,540
Pusan, South Korea	12,796	6,143	11,307	12,321	11,890	12,728	8,606	4,689	14,756	8,903	8,444	8,241	11,239	4,966	12,585	11,565	9,396	12,124	12,601	5,080
Pyongyang, North Korea	12,661	5,713	11,244	12,177	11,512	13,201	8,203	4,786	14,536	8,705	8,026	8,735	11,011	5,469	12,417	11,341	8,886	12,035	12,344	5,327
Qamdo, China	9,963	3,512	13,484	9,476	8,961	12,853	5,771	3,057	15,795	10,598	5,665	9,109	12,627	6,350	14,190	12,945	7,280	14,144	13,697	8,048
Qandahar, Afghanistan	7,863	772	13,884	7,388	6,091	13,629	2,809	4,633	14,155	10,955	2,682	11,249	12,202	9,068	13,628	12,436	4,590	14,139	12,704	10,614
Qiqian, China	12,741	5,029	10,480	12,253	10,856	14,711	7,547	5,766	13,344	7,681	7,311	10,247	9,877	6,976	11,380	10,207	7,670	11,183	11,129	5,687
Qom, Iran	7,496	810	13,170	7,063	5,116	14,312	1,821	6,005	12,814	10,449	1,570	12,585	11,284	10,492	12,576	11,475	3,174	13,241	11,570	11,403
Quebec, Canada	12,953	9,578	4,086	13,006	9,967	15,834	9,783	14,335	4,515	2,906	9,513	16,903	2,039	14,812	3,315	2,187	6,830	3,962	2,466	8,893
Quetta, Pakistan	7,808	965	14,052	7,330	6,136	13,451	2,884	4,447	14,345	11,113	2,778	11,060	12,387	8,911	13,819	12,624	4,762	14,321	12,898	10,613
Quito, Ecuador	11,551	14,136	3,981	11,957	10,772	10,598	12,944	19,531	785	6,354	12,854	13,888	4,093	15,623	2,637	3,763	10,384	3,129	2,882	10,897
Rabaul, Papua New Guinea	13,061	10,519	11,365	12,844	14,892	8,178	12,503	6,015	14,739	10,877	12,495	3,796	12,793	1,393	13,111	12,985	14,237	12,131	13,963	4,848
Raiatea (Uturoa)	14,908	16,273	6,597	15,234	17,851	7,167	18,736	12,253	8,722	8,408	18,591	6,581	8,651	7,439	7,933	8,608	17,315	6,978	9,031	5,703

Distances in Kilometers	Maseru, Lesotho	Mashhad, Iran	Mazatlan, Mexico	Mbabane, Swaziland	Mbandaka, Zaire	McMurdo Sound, Antarctica	Mecca, Saudi Arabia	Medan, Indonesia	Medellin, Colombia	Medicine Hat, Canada	Medina, Saudi Arabia	Melbourne, Australia	Memphis, Tennessee	Merauke, Indonesia	Merida, Mexico	Meridian, Mississippi	Messina, Italy	Mexico City, Mexico	Miami, Florida	Midway Islands, USA
Raleigh, North Carolina	13,212	10,937	3,017	13,379	10,632	14,485	10,960	15,639	3,284	3,025	10,712	16,160	1,039	15,047	1,959	1,002	7,987	2,708	1,118	8,952
Rangiroa (Avatoru)	15,082	16,421	6,166	15,439	17,764	7,432	18,948	12,661	8,292	8,059	18,712	7,023	8,224	7,849	7,487	8,174	16,955	6,534	8,585	5,745
Rangoon, Burma	8,964	4,200	14,950	8,495	8,726	11,320	5,922	1,485	17,304	12,149	5,919	7,912	14,223	5,607	15,782	14,541	8,068	15,670	15,280	8,813
Raoul Is., Kermadec Islands	12,987	14,661	9,604	13,123	16,351	5,439	16,154	9,572	11,547	10,998	16,282	3,549	11,637	4,928	10,967	11,619	18,429	10,015	12,067	6,360
Rarotonga (Avarua)	14,362	15,868	7,590	14,619	17,657	6,542	18,003	11,360	9,666	9,253	18,013	5,577	9,637	6,563	8,940	9,603	18,071	7,984	10,038	5,784
Rawson, Argentina	8,035	15,310	8,492	8,525	9,479	6,173	12,801	15,324	5,588	11,250	12,991	10,521	9,047	13,725	7,545	8,717	12,140	7,767	7,803	13,844
Recife, Brazil	6,905	10,940	8,509	7,235	5,966	10,426	8,782	14,874	4,785	9,689	8,838	14,925	7,502	18,106	6,788	7,246	7,314	7,668	6,165	15,502
Regina, Canada	15,404	10,271	3,026	15,414	12,258	15,423	11,311	13,619	5,594	434	10,993	14,488	2,070	12,494	3,527	2,398	8,584	3,479	3,444	6,455
Reykjavik, Iceland	11,221	6,045	7,442	11,034	7,826	18,496	6,520	11,071	7,690	5,118	6,213	16,952	5,504	13,667	6,847	5,699	3,797	7,462	5,930	9,544
Rhodes, Greece	7,279	2,804	11,872	6,952	4,156	14,990	2,006	8,031	10,824	9,611	1,716	14,516	9,838	12,545	10,910	9,963	1,137	11,724	9,839	12,368
Richmond, Virginia	13,167	10,714	3,186	13,316	10,513	14,702	10,762	15,434	3,471	2,979	10,511	16,313	1,162	15,042	2,180	1,176	7,790	2,911	1,330	8,953
Riga, USSR	9,564	3,491	9,995	9,250	6,329	17,272	4,146	8,741	10,013	7,438	3,818	15,259	8,089	12,366	9,416	8,284	2,179	10,047	8,458	10,356
Ringkobing, Denmark	9,637	4,396	9,302	9,384	6,276	17,450	4,642	9,705	9,051	6,964	4,334	16,237	7,324	13,287	8,571	7,492	2,063	9,266	7,575	10,651
Rio Branco, Brazil	9,984	13,993	5,583	10,406	9,589	9,757	12,232	18,378	1,990	7,842	12,224	13,716	5,514	16,303	4,172	5,185	10,118	4,730	4,176	12,447
Rio Cuarto, Argentina	8,452	14,951	7,669	8,932	9,330	7,293	12,564	16,293	4,518	10,283	12,698	11,583	8,018	14,717	6,562	7,687	11,423	6,891	6,732	13,693
Rio de Janeiro, Brazil	7,005	12,594	8,530	7,433	7,115	8,710	10,252	15,404	4,775	10,445	10,365	13,227	8,103	16,513	6,992	7,796	9,131	7,669	6,700	15,411
Rio Gallegos, Argentina	7,944	15,677	9,052	8,430	9,840	5,201	13,156	14,561	6,443	11,931	13,387	9,551	9,824	12,773	8,285	9,499	12,893	8,392	8,642	13,639
Rio Grande, Brazil	7,445	13,840	8,414	7,914	8,172	7,599	11,418	15,631	4,916	10,768	11,562	12,071	8,427	15,335	7,099	8,102	10,464	7,587	7,060	14,793
Riyadh, Saudi Arabia	6,314	1,786	13,975	5,881	4,097	13,329	790	6,027	12,907	11,438	721	12,342	11,982	10,768	13,107	12,128	3,299	13,899	12,037	12,501
Road Town, Brit. Virgin Isls.	11,194	11,587	4,368	11,458	9,264	12,913	10,689	16,967	1,799	5,371	10,540	16,431	3,116	17,118	2,633	2,861	7,926	3,633	1,798	11,137
Roanoke, Virginia	13,370	10,858	2,971	13,526	10,735	14,616	10,960	15,479	3,464	2,827	10,705	16,092	940	14,865	2,035	968	7,989	2,722	1,275	8,772
Robinson Crusoe Island, Chile	9,601	16,250	6,936	10,088	10,679	6,967	13,909	16,668	4,428	9,786	14,035	10,889	7,700	13,784	6,149	7,378	12,570	6,252	6,576	12,418
Rochester, New York	13,340	10,200	3,449	13,437	10,484	15,299	10,425	14,815	4,094	2,622	10,156	16,402	1,395	14,689	2,703	1,543	7,467	3,318	1,943	8,650
Rockhampton, Australia	11,582	11,589	12,270	11,489	14,261	6,069	12,964	6,363	14,751	12,584	13,074	1,686	14,088	1,975	13,871	14,186	15,462	12,865	14,921	6,669
Rome, Italy	8,034	4,071	10,456	7,793	4,670	15,844	3,416	9,431	9,391	8,417	3,160	15,987	8,404	13,725	9,429	8,512	489	10,260	8,354	12,178
Rosario, Argentina	8,150	14,622	7,888	8,627	8,985	7,373	12,223	16,115	4,616	10,430	12,361	11,732	8,136	14,915	6,714	7,806	11,140	7,093	6,821	14,023
Roseau, Dominica	10,728	11,596	4,794	11,002	8,907	12,631	10,521	16,991	1,845	5,857	10,394	16,417	3,605	17,550	3,047	3,346	7,847	4,030	2,273	11,618
Rostock, East Germany	9,357	4,118	9,632	9,093	6,015	17,178	4,309	9,461	9,300	7,292	4,001	16,036	7,649	13,185	8,880	7,813	1,787	9,588	7,874	10,843
Rostov-na-Donu, USSR	8,566	2,043	11,498	8,191	5,625	15,913	2,860	7,416	11,355	8,856	2,526	14,030	9,602	11,499	10,915	9,796	2,206	11,560	9,935	10,864
Rotterdam, Netherlands	9,275	4,611	9,336	9,048	5,890	17,041	4,544	9,983	8,784	7,163	4,254	16,582	7,315	13,748	8,475	7,456	1,753	9,229	7,443	11,128
Rouyn, Canada	13,559	9,785	3,682	13,607	10,545	15,803	10,193	14,259	4,665	2,301	9,908	16,308	1,718	14,267	3,170	1,941	7,270	3,677	2,495	8,302
Sacramento, California	16,995	11,712	2,225	17,127	14,086	13,777	13,081	13,786	5,837	1,536	12,754	12,759	2,816	11,304	3,620	3,038	10,441	3,027	4,106	5,244
Saginaw, Michigan	13,849	10,438	3,048	13,950	10,990	15,179	10,819	14,791	4,200	2,157	10,540	15,896	1,062	14,239	2,547	1,297	7,880	3,021	1,988	8,173
Saint Denis, Reunion	2,964	6,342	18,144	2,550	4,660	8,208	4,980	5,436	14,517	16,545	5,301	8,581	16,308	9,157	16,407	16,258	7,752	17,376	15,483	14,658
Saint George's, Grenada	10,589	11,874	4,878	10,885	8,930	12,270	10,700	17,253	1,650	6,121	10,588	16,114	3,831	17,586	3,129	3,556	8,089	4,082	2,461	11,792
Saint John, Canada	12,518	9,457	4,383	12,577	9,560	15,783	9,509	14,387	4,421	3,342	9,250	17,321	2,321	15,210	3,452	2,419	6,542	4,183	2,506	9,324
Saint John's, Antigua	10,865	11,490	4,691	11,129	8,964	12,819	10,484	16,886	1,917	5,671	10,348	16,533	3,436	17,444	2,950	3,185	7,771	3,946	2,127	11,463
Saint John's, Canada	11,675	8,547	5,438	11,685	8,587	16,297	8,463	13,691	5,070	4,158	8,209	18,213	3,376	15,500	4,430	3,464	5,493	5,213	3,412	9,960
Saint Louis, Missouri	14,282	11,151	2,299	14,439	11,604	14,516	11,567	15,245	3,876	2,057	11,289	15,265	388	13,982	1,957	707	8,622	2,299	1,706	7,889
Saint Paul, Minnesota	14,594	10,598	2,698	14,683	11,671	15,118	11,246	14,505	4,612	1,436	10,950	15,203	1,121	13,505	2,679	1,447	8,362	2,888	2,422	7,428
Saint Peter Port, UK	9,218	5,127	9,025	9,032	5,822	16,833	4,842	10,515	8,260	7,037	4,574	17,128	6,978	14,310	8,060	7,096	1,911	8,857	7,007	11,389
Saipan (Susupe)	13,544	8,688	11,106	13,174	14,017	10,357	10,986	5,311	14,897	9,673	10,890	5,865	11,924	2,679	12,780	12,198	12,152	11,964	13,296	4,065
Salalah, Oman	5,869	2,206	15,082	5,398	4,352	12,336	1,580	5,087	13,928	12,429	1,720	11,230	13,113	9,893	14,247	13,265	4,423	15,038	13,173	12,556
Salem, Oregon	16,904	11,003	2,844	16,919	13,740	14,425	12,451	13,233	6,272	1,089	12,120	12,994	2,993	11,192	4,053	3,266	9,909	3,590	4,368	5,098
Salt Lake City, Utah	16,144	11,428	2,011	16,269	13,264	14,226	12,525	14,202	5,255	1,037	12,208	13,603	2,012	12,120	3,040	2,265	9,766	2,660	3,361	6,034
Salta, Argentina	8,966	14,670	6,913	9,431	9,381	8,185	12,462	17,115	3,606	9,414	12,546	12,384	7,122	15,397	5,699	6,791	10,939	6,104	5,816	13,325
Salto, Uruguay	7,988	14,321	7,948	8,460	8,712	7,587	11,934	16,084	4,567	10,409	12,067	11,981	8,092	15,188	6,706	7,763	10,833	7,136	6,753	14,233
Salvador, Brazil	7,002	11,578	8,407	7,372	6,428	9,850	9,363	15,213	4,618	9,872	9,437	14,368	7,605	17,629	6,733	7,328	7,984	7,549	6,227	15,449
Salzburg, Austria	8,662	3,993	10,099	8,406	5,313	16,481	3,779	9,390	9,396	7,898	3,490	16,008	8,074	13,434	9,207	8,211	1,088	9,980	8,161	11,524
Samsun, Turkey	7,870	2,089	11,900	7,503	4,915	15,351	2,223	7,458	11,347	9,388	1,890	14,056	9,935	11,798	11,153	10,101	1,809	11,876	10,125	11,569
San Antonio, Texas	14,834	12,380	1,048	15,095	12,583	13,331	12,829	15,925	3,516	2,509	12,557	14,172	1,015	13,488	1,295	991	9,872	1,112	1,850	7,537
San Cristobal, Venezuela	11,374	13,015	4,031	11,725	10,073	11,598	11,942	18,406	406	5,885	11,826	15,009	3,535	16,448	2,373	3,212	9,292	3,178	2,164	11,071
San Diego, California	16,646	12,357	1,489	16,885	14,109	13,242	13,534	14,505	5,202	1,999	13,216	12,776	2,512	11,688	3,018	2,665	10,762	2,322	3,655	5,728
San Francisco, California	17,091	11,800	2,221	17,234	14,205	13,669	13,192	13,779	5,872	1,654	12,865	12,644	2,902	11,220	3,661	3,116	10,561	3,038	4,176	5,170
San Jose, Costa Rica	12,638	13,639	2,794	13,009	11,371	11,573	12,985	18,480	1,021	5,078	12,826	14,238	2,855	15,157	1,357	2,529	10,167	1,930	1,801	9,817
San Juan, Argentina	8,882	15,256	7,281	9,363	9,713	7,395	12,917	16,637	4,248	9,948	13,037	11,578	7,715	14,626	6,231	7,385	11,633	6,517	6,462	13,268
San Juan, Puerto Rico	11,336	11,693	4,214	11,604	9,422	12,885	10,832	17,060	1,698	5,272	10,679	16,316	2,998	16,967	2,477	2,735	8,054	3,476	1,661	11,005
San Luis Potosi, Mexico	14,839	13,223	571	15,173	13,010	12,489	13,586	16,455	3,248	3,210	13,326	13,559	1,789	13,319	1,184	1,659	10,615	359	2,152	7,604
San Marino, San Marino	8,252	4,050	10,322	8,007	4,891	16,065	3,544	9,432	9,377	8,230	3,276	16,020	8,277	13,644	9,338	8,394	688	10,151	8,272	11,957
San Miguel de Tucuman, Argen.	8,843	14,753	7,092	9,312	9,371	7,967	12,496	16,922	3,826	9,623	12,593	12,188	7,338	15,235	5,906	7,007	11,062	6,290	6,037	13,417
San Salvador, El Salvador	13,324	13,580	2,099	13,687	11,904	11,861	13,234	17,911	1,704	4,479	13,042	14,066	2,375	14,602	805	2,068	10,329	1,235	1,635	9,130
Sanaa, Yemen	5,259	2,779	14,683	4,822	3,315	12,379	819	6,104	12,978	12,355	1,118	11,983	12,634	10,917	13,574	12,736	3,780	14,464	12,477	13,441
Santa Cruz, Bolivia	9,125	14,082	6,535	9,566	9,112	8,987	12,027	17,495	2,990	8,842	12,074	13,183	6,510	16,131	5,169	6,183	10,272	5,693	5,161	13,264
Santa Cruz, Tenerife	7,906	7,009	8,836	7,897	4,833	14,546	5,665	12,229	6,695	7,938	5,537	17,991	6,872	16,715	7,361	6,840	3,133	8,342	6,272	13,424
Santa Fe, New Mexico	15,634	11,897	1,382	15,833	13,036	13,823	12,731	14,965	4,499	1,642	12,430	13,843	1,443	12,699	2,279	1,632	9,859	1,923	2,689	6,658
Santa Rosa, Argentina	8,280	15,069	7,965	8,764	9,352	6,914	12,628	15,956	4,889	10,627	12,782	11,231	8,379	14,396	6,908	8,049	11,651	7,203	7,105	13,786
Santa Rosalia, Mexico	16,097	12,912	745	16,405	13,940	12,775	13,836	15,252	4,525	2,528	13,535	12,876	2,282	12,159	2,405	2,342	10,955	1,602	3,194	6,334
Santarem, Brazil	9,125	12,339	6,281	9,481	8,125	10,807	10,583	17,075	2,512	7,880	10,563	15,111	5,556	17,968	4,603	5,261	8,470	5,427	4,157	13,321
Santiago del Estero, Argentina	8,711	14,714	7,235	9,181	9,283	7,878	12,430	16,780	3,957	9,762	12,533	12,130	7,473	15,207	6,045	7,142	11,054	6,433	6,167	13,539
Santiago, Chile	8,958	15,518	7,328	9,442	9,919	7,147	13,150	16,520	4,424	10,055	13,280	11,296	7,856	14,334	6,350	7,527	11,920	6,585	6,632	13,135
Santo Domingo, Dominican Rep.	11,693	11,959	3,827	11,972	9,821	12,808	11,190	17,269	1,486	5,031	11,029	16,014	2,714	16,584	2,084	2,432	8,379	3,079	1,334	10,670
Sao Paulo de Olivenca, Brazil	10,437	13,617	5,037	10,834	9,694	10,448	12,085	18,645	1,311	7,154	12,038	14,266	4,813	16,541	3,529	4,487	9,756	4,174	3,459	12,016
Sao Paulo, Brazil	7,297	12,928	8,280	7,733	7,468	8,602	10,599	15,692	4,557	10,297	10,709	13,105	7,947	16,386	6,780	7,634	9,421	7,422	6,546	15,100
Sao Tome, Sao Tome & Principe	3,954	6,742	12,360	3,943	1,284	11,334	4,285	10,232	9,165	11,896	4,435	14,063	10,611	14,814	10,664	10,506	4,288	11,670	9,691	16,817
Sapporo, Japan	14,039	6,772	9,930	13,554	12,626	13,474	9,298	6,068	13,403	7,556	9,083	8,965	9,904	5,706	11,215	10,227	9,482	10,745	11,284	4,036
Sarajevo, Yugoslavia	8,152	3,573	10,702	7,875	4,848	15,966	3,173	8,954	9,854	8,495	2,886	15,546	8,671	13,196	9,774	8,800	672	10,566	8,716	11,869
Saratov, USSR	9,142	2,009	11,296	8,750	6,275	16,224	3,386	7,202	11,553	8,530	3,058	13,756	9,493	11,038	10,888	9,713	2,799	11,447	9,965	10,207
Saskatoon, Canada	15,495	10,118	3,208	15,479	12,296	15,551	11,230	13,389	5,827	364	10,909	14,394	2,302	12,313	3,757	2,631	8,547	3,689	3,673	6,297
Schefferville, Canada	12,881	8,696	4,792	12,855	9,687	16,774	9,095	13,397	5,441	2,978	8,806	16,965	2,825	14,333	4,215	3,027	6,198	4,783	3,404	8,691
Seattle, Washington	16,726	10,710	3,053	16,705	13,502	14,724	12,153	13,077	6,370	898	11,822	13,165	3,005	11,250	4,162	3,296	9,629	3,766	4,399	5,169
Sendai, Japan	13,908	6,961	10,246	13,432	12,798	12,948	9,475	5,748	13,811	7,987	9,281	8,435	10,340	5,172	11,603	10,660	9,866	11,078	11,731	4,011
Seoul, South Korea	12,712	5,870	11,270	12,231	11,652	13,026	8,351	4,743	14,622	8,779	8,180	8,551	11,098	5,282	12,483	11,426	9,075	12,071	12,442	5,233
Sept-Iles, Canada	12,713	9,060	4,575	12,728	9,622	16,301	9,291	13,876	4,947	3,120	9,015	17,180	2,544	14,764	3,832	2,703	6,349	4,477	2,959	8,996
Sevastopol, USSR	8,208	2,383	11,468	7,856	5,159	15,766	2,632	7,778	11,012	8,961	2,300	14,394	9,509	11,997	10,743	9,678	1,658	11,453	9,725	11,356
Seville, Spain	8,167	5,727	9,341	8,049	4,826	15,516	4,729	11,058	7,792	7,844	4,538	17,473	7,288	15,355	8,083	7,332	1,896	8,997	6,984	12,690
Shanghai, China	11,967	5,658	12,136	11,495	11,257	12,400	8,039	3,867	15,498	9,660	7,909	8,019	11,973	4,855	13,366	12,302	9,157	12,945	13,307	5,864
Sheffield, United Kingdom	9,580	5,012	8,901	9,374	6,185	17,259	4,974	10,363	8,398	6,771	4,687	16,927	6,878	13,970	8,042	7,020	2,135	8,792	7,015	10,960
Shenyang, China	12,578	5,434	11,173	12,090	11,262	13,538	7,941	4,901	14,346	8,550	7,752	9,086	10,830	5,827	12,271	11,160	8,536	11,943	12,139	5,497
Shiraz, Iran	7,042	994	13,745	6,596	4,888	13,732	1,563	5,646	13,210	11,028	1,403	12,158	11,842	10,264	13,103	12,025	3,524	13,797	12,079	11,705
Sibiu, Romania	8,325	3,131	10,884	8,017	5,099	16,080	3,055	8,527	10,265	8,527	2,743	15,141	8,885	12,701	10,062	9,036	1,104	10,810	9,026	11,528
Singapore	8,765	5,978	15,770	8,360	9,527	9,473	7,282	630	19,169	13,440	7,358	6,050	15,725	4,189	17,148	16,056	9,775	16,623	16,980	8,848
Sioux Falls, South Dakota	14,880	10,846	2,424	14,985	11,994	14,882	11,558	14,564	4,622	1,283	11,259	14,884	1,097	13,284	2,589	1,426	8,684	2,687	2,477	7,194
Skelleftea, Sweden	10,445	4,065	9,265	10,136	7,181	18,142	5,009	9,065	9,690	6,608	4,677	15,333	7,435	12,216	8,843	7,657	2,979	9,391	7,952	9,577
Skopje, Yugoslavia	7,920	3,327	11,024	7,629	4,656	15,715	2,852	8,687	10,131	8,796	2,564	15,259	8,993	13,009	10,091	9,123	659	10,888	9,030	11,996
Socotra Island (Tamrida)	5,449	2,679	15,508	4,972	4,185	11,868	1,796	5,014	14,079	12,901	2,004	10,950	13,510	9,826	14,577	13,647	4,737	15,411	13,489	12,879
Sofia, Bulgaria	7,983	3,175	11,081	7,682	4,747	15,758	2,812	8,545	10,267	8,802	2,514	15,130	9,060	12,845	10,184	9,197	825	10,966	9,129	11,877
Songkhla, Thailand	8,791	5,261	15,550	8,356	9,171	10,184	6,704	454	18,461	12,983	6,753	6,785	15,190	4,737	16,698	15,517	9,088	16,363	16,355	8,861
Sorong, Indonesia	11,300	8,434	13,339	10,981	12,578	8,748	10,201	3,659	16,998	12,049	10,224	4,327	14,306	1,311	15,067	14,576	12,296	14,172	15,669	6,352
South Georgia Island	5,767	13,569	10,841	6,254	7,829	5,307	11,083	13,102	7,617	13,453	11,343	9,800	11,142	13,049	9,738	10,813	11,398	10,080	9,796	15,718
South Pole	6,760	14,022	12,570	7,092	10,011	1,394	12,377	10,398	10,694	15,548	12,711	5,812	13,891	9,065	12,322	13,585	14,232	12,148	12,855	13,121

Distances in Kilometers	Maseru, Lesotho	Mashhad, Iran	Mazatlan, Mexico	Mbabane, Swaziland	Mbandaka, Zaire	McMurdo Sound, Antarctica	Mecca, Saudi Arabia	Medan, Indonesia	Medellin, Colombia	Medicine Hat, Canada	Medina, Saudi Arabia	Melbourne, Australia	Memphis, Tennessee	Merauke, Indonesia	Merida, Mexico	Meridian, Mississippi	Messina, Italy	Mexico City, Mexico	Miami, Florida	Midway Islands, USA
South Sandwich Islands	5,184	13,115	11,585	5,664	7,527	4,974	10,690	12,354	8,348	14,192	10,969	9,382	11,872	12,568	10,481	11,544	11,334	10,827	10,514	16,021
Split, Yugoslavia	8,143	3,734	10,602	7,877	4,816	15,963	3,266	9,111	9,699	8,442	2,988	15,697	8,564	13,359	9,647	8,688	597	10,450	8,584	11,940
Spokane, Washington	16,387	10,699	2,884	16,391	13,213	14,838	12,019	13,333	6,064	560	11,692	13,505	2,657	11,620	3,872	2,955	9,418	3,545	4,056	5,539
Spoleto, Italy	8,119	4,040	10,418	7,875	4,758	15,931	3,451	9,410	9,406	8,352	3,188	15,981	8,369	13,672	9,410	8,481	559	10,234	8,339	12,083
Springbok, South Africa	932	8,506	14,480	1,354	3,291	7,912	6,125	9,322	10,690	15,190	6,424	10,735	13,367	12,563	12,779	13,154	7,515	13,623	12,115	18,535
Springfield, Illinois	14,256	11,012	2,424	14,400	11,531	14,655	11,443	15,127	3,974	2,002	11,164	15,347	520	13,979	2,088	829	8,502	2,438	1,788	7,885
Springfield, Massachusetts	12,912	10,061	3,764	13,011	10,077	15,301	10,140	14,870	3,983	3,038	9,882	16,803	1,703	15,087	2,835	1,787	7,171	3,549	1,940	9,067
Srinagar, India	8,605	1,406	13,662	8,122	6,981	13,679	3,700	4,184	14,570	10,669	3,564	10,768	12,184	8,347	13,695	12,451	5,262	14,051	12,877	9,762
Stanley, Falkland Islands	7,203	14,892	9,553	7,691	9,060	5,367	12,372	14,245	6,640	12,331	12,606	9,840	10,119	13,116	8,625	9,789	12,236	8,840	8,856	14,425
Stara Zagora, Bulgaria	7,945	2,984	11,236	7,631	4,748	15,687	2,676	8,352	10,459	8,916	2,370	14,938	9,222	12,665	10,361	9,364	976	11,135	9,311	11,840
Stockholm, Sweden	9,863	3,924	9,554	9,568	6,573	17,640	4,549	9,133	9,619	7,024	4,223	15,593	7,644	12,602	8,977	7,840	2,359	9,603	8,026	10,201
Stornoway, United Kingdom	10,199	5,289	8,408	9,994	6,804	17,829	5,499	10,543	8,209	6,178	5,201	16,942	6,415	13,801	7,658	6,579	2,734	8,355	6,669	10,392
Strasbourg, France	8,849	4,386	9,728	8,617	5,471	16,638	4,141	9,781	9,001	7,597	3,860	16,400	7,694	13,747	8,810	7,824	1,316	9,591	7,761	11,485
Stuttgart, West Germany	8,838	4,280	9,804	8,599	5,467	16,640	4,068	9,674	9,107	7,645	3,784	16,294	7,775	13,644	8,902	7,909	1,283	9,677	7,856	11,455
Subic, Philippines	11,073	6,425	13,423	10,649	11,303	10,642	8,451	2,675	17,099	11,270	8,413	6,384	13,620	3,404	14,882	13,942	10,236	14,279	14,998	6,562
Suchow, China	11,754	5,164	12,157	11,273	10,830	12,810	7,577	3,901	15,326	9,549	7,435	8,485	11,819	5,323	13,270	12,150	8,632	12,936	13,113	6,166
Sucre, Bolivia	9,257	14,344	6,467	9,705	9,341	8,815	12,280	17,578	3,016	8,856	12,331	12,963	6,541	15,878	5,159	6,211	10,532	5,635	5,213	13,110
Sudbury, Canada	13,675	10,027	3,444	13,743	10,715	15,573	10,427	14,456	4,491	2,222	10,145	16,158	1,474	14,258	2,938	1,701	7,498	3,433	2,301	8,246
Suez, Egypt	6,583	2,610	12,675	6,230	3,639	14,205	1,192	7,519	11,392	10,430	927	13,850	10,631	12,193	11,649	10,745	1,809	12,494	10,565	12,830
Sundsvall, Sweden	10,205	4,097	9,304	9,909	6,913	17,973	4,860	9,209	9,543	6,722	4,532	15,568	7,427	12,492	8,796	7,635	2,695	9,386	7,873	9,879
Surabaya, Indonesia	9,166	7,344	15,488	8,828	10,515	8,363	8,566	1,971	19,109	13,795	8,665	4,694	16,146	3,044	17,181	16,457	11,135	16,333	17,546	8,456
Suva, Fiji	13,904	13,747	9,361	13,957	17,071	6,642	15,692	9,060	11,921	10,242	15,718	3,912	11,286	4,253	10,917	11,334	17,236	9,915	11,981	5,147
Sverdlovsk, USSR	10,045	2,286	11,050	9,624	7,338	16,421	4,283	6,793	11,966	8,127	3,975	13,114	9,445	10,171	10,944	9,705	3,876	11,347	10,139	9,132
Svobodnyy, USSR	13,209	5,541	10,182	12,720	11,368	14,529	8,060	5,967	13,229	7,467	7,823	10,022	9,722	6,736	11,186	10,053	8,122	10,918	11,019	5,176
Sydney, Australia	10,852	12,266	12,512	10,830	13,854	4,903	13,239	6,891	14,325	13,350	13,410	711	14,491	3,027	13,933	14,516	16,036	12,972	15,031	7,629
Sydney, Canada	12,127	9,073	4,848	12,166	9,116	16,001	9,052	14,117	4,664	3,713	8,796	17,750	2,786	15,395	3,865	2,874	6,083	4,629	2,875	9,633
Syktyvkar, USSR	10,301	2,888	10,378	9,911	7,364	17,143	4,547	7,565	11,195	7,509	4,219	13,832	8,712	10,804	10,194	8,964	3,554	10,631	9,372	9,151
Szeged, Hungary	8,403	3,443	10,626	8,114	5,122	16,201	3,279	8,839	9,953	8,332	2,977	15,453	8,614	12,985	9,769	8,758	974	10,530	8,727	11,572
Szombathely, Hungary	8,548	3,721	10,350	8,275	5,228	16,365	3,540	9,118	9,670	8,099	3,244	15,735	8,332	13,208	9,479	8,473	1,009	10,245	8,435	11,534
Tabriz, Iran	7,714	1,196	12,648	7,303	5,095	14,787	1,946	6,535	12,273	9,984	1,638	13,131	10,740	10,940	12,017	10,925	2,682	12,695	11,009	11,380
Tacheng, China	10,098	2,255	12,200	9,622	8,104	14,840	4,781	5,019	13,765	9,199	4,559	11,221	10,910	8,333	12,469	11,203	5,451	12,676	11,797	8,464
Tahiti (Papeete)	14,811	16,480	6,508	15,153	17,668	7,114	18,954	12,447	8,542	8,404	18,799	6,696	8,567	7,604	7,805	8,513	17,303	6,861	8,905	5,880
Taipei, Taiwan	11,698	5,962	12,587	11,241	11,346	11,734	8,234	3,409	16,085	10,233	8,137	7,382	12,566	4,233	13,911	12,893	9,603	13,418	13,921	6,033
Taiyuan, China	11,549	4,647	12,118	11,062	10,385	13,281	7,098	4,051	15,049	9,386	6,940	9,019	11,595	5,886	13,094	11,925	8,059	12,856	12,836	6,484
Tallahassee, Florida	13,542	11,714	2,337	13,767	11,214	13,782	11,732	16,226	2,829	3,096	11,490	15,460	749	14,796	1,178	471	8,761	1,934	655	8,751
Tallinn, USSR	9,837	3,586	9,824	9,519	6,606	17,517	4,383	8,758	9,993	7,219	4,052	15,213	7,947	12,244	9,307	8,153	2,450	9,906	8,372	10,084
Tamanrasset, Algeria	6,227	5,380	11,074	6,094	2,868	13,820	3,534	10,186	8,839	9,798	3,474	15,826	9,067	14,959	9,631	9,064	1,958	10,608	8,540	14,355
Tampa, Florida	13,285	11,863	2,460	13,528	11,065	13,556	11,752	16,513	2,509	3,424	11,522	15,503	1,074	15,051	1,061	776	8,789	1,946	330	9,034
Tampere, Finland	10,071	3,752	9,619	9,756	6,830	17,752	4,619	8,860	9,892	6,991	4,287	15,250	7,762	12,220	9,141	7,974	2,655	9,720	8,224	9,882
Tanami, Australia	10,064	9,645	14,244	9,859	12,258	6,676	10,797	4,280	16,900	13,793	10,924	2,470	15,790	1,712	15,939	15,976	13,444	14,928	16,904	7,799
Tangier, Morocco	8,007	5,773	9,430	7,895	4,676	15,340	4,688	11,078	7,786	7,987	4,509	17,421	7,382	15,441	8,141	7,417	1,916	9,066	7,041	12,866
Tarawa (Betio)	15,229	11,994	9,001	15,093	17,214	8,769	14,343	8,262	12,378	8,925	14,240	5,203	10,566	3,777	10,738	10,720	15,055	9,749	11,636	3,146
Tashkent, USSR	8,928	1,010	12,845	8,461	6,863	14,585	3,537	5,107	13,645	9,880	3,323	11,655	11,281	9,080	12,774	11,540	4,544	13,177	11,940	9,709
Tbilisi, USSR	8,061	1,417	12,231	7,660	5,324	15,209	2,293	6,812	11,977	9,562	1,970	13,428	10,335	11,095	11,634	10,525	2,512	12,292	10,639	11,142
Tegucigalpa, Honduras	13,150	13,434	2,260	13,506	11,687	11,951	13,031	17,947	1,541	4,519	12,843	14,263	2,346	14,816	802	2,029	10,137	1,400	1,486	9,300
Tehran, Iran	7,619	740	13,085	7,185	5,227	14,409	1,939	6,008	12,802	10,348	1,683	12,601	11,213	10,458	12,520	11,408	3,188	13,172	11,523	11,287
Tel Aviv, Israel	6,837	2,330	12,632	6,473	3,944	14,388	1,279	7,352	11,533	10,293	966	13,767	10,606	11,976	11,682	10,734	1,873	12,497	10,608	12,523
Telegraph Creek, Canada	16,429	9,517	4,331	16,232	13,035	15,644	11,172	11,884	7,445	1,594	10,837	13,137	3,945	10,710	5,292	4,266	8,915	5,008	5,338	4,850
Teresina, Brazil	7,829	11,460	7,580	8,166	6,814	10,676	9,462	15,760	3,851	8,891	9,484	15,186	6,648	18,468	5,866	6,379	7,685	6,736	5,286	14,593
Ternate, Indonesia	11,021	7,982	13,633	10,681	12,149	8,987	9,734	3,211	17,365	12,151	9,757	4,644	14,454	1,763	15,335	14,740	11,850	14,481	15,843	6,605
The Valley, Anguilla	11,028	11,505	4,538	11,290	9,098	12,899	10,559	16,896	1,885	5,508	10,415	16,518	3,269	17,287	2,802	3,018	7,817	3,802	1,963	11,297
Thessaloniki, Greece	7,759	3,213	11,216	7,460	4,517	15,542	2,658	8,549	10,277	8,988	2,371	15,102	9,184	12,925	10,272	9,311	690	11,075	9,208	12,103
Thimphu, Bhutan	9,138	2,995	14,130	8,650	8,186	12,626	5,070	2,816	15,950	11,179	4,996	9,251	13,069	6,750	14,638	13,373	6,860	14,726	14,008	8,880
Thunder Bay, Canada	14,320	10,132	3,177	14,371	11,294	15,574	10,771	14,194	4,850	1,561	10,473	15,546	1,476	13,611	3,044	1,781	7,898	3,337	2,634	7,586
Tientsin, China	11,976	5,002	11,752	11,490	10,779	13,341	7,478	4,361	14,812	9,074	7,309	8,985	11,320	5,787	12,793	11,651	8,304	12,508	12,597	6,059
Tijuana, Mexico	16,632	12,377	1,466	16,874	14,108	13,226	13,546	14,528	5,182	2,015	13,229	12,777	2,505	11,700	3,000	2,655	10,771	2,300	3,642	5,745
Tiksi, USSR	13,464	5,493	8,683	13,025	10,707	16,722	7,723	7,843	11,183	5,730	7,417	12,204	7,783	8,925	9,320	0,109	6,772	9,281	8,975	5,813
Timbuktu, Mali	6,062	6,489	10,599	6,031	2,977	13,220	4,524	11,144	7,965	9,800	4,505	16,121	8,696	15,955	9,021	8,638	2,988	10,026	7,965	14,993
Tindouf, Algeria	7,364	6,345	9,602	7,308	4,160	14,452	4,878	11,476	7,473	8,526	4,762	17,282	7,612	16,089	8,153	7,597	2,494	9,128	7,061	13,713
Tirane, Albania	7,862	3,468	10,972	7,580	4,573	15,671	2,896	8,817	10,007	8,793	2,618	15,374	8,933	13,161	10,007	9,056	506	10,816	8,940	12,106
Tokyo, Japan	13,748	6,998	10,481	13,277	12,806	12,676	9,496	5,518	14,081	8,269	9,315	8,159	10,622	4,889	11,867	10,940	10,018	11,319	12,016	4,104
Toledo, Spain	8,324	5,476	9,379	8,184	4,954	15,781	4,612	10,835	7,996	7,749	4,402	17,339	7,318	15,057	8,184	7,380	1,703	9,075	7,091	12,438
Topeka, Kansas	14,760	11,286	2,029	14,916	12,054	14,430	11,869	15,062	4,157	1,701	11,581	14,827	662	13,515	2,087	973	8,951	2,204	2,065	7,425
Toronto, Canada	13,492	10,230	3,357	13,587	10,622	15,311	10,510	14,768	4,162	2,468	10,238	16,264	1,319	14,539	2,690	1,495	7,559	3,262	1,986	8,496
Toulouse, France	8,500	4,934	9,593	8,315	5,105	16,155	4,305	10,320	8,489	7,726	4,063	16,904	7,533	14,449	8,514	7,626	1,332	9,361	7,435	12,054
Tours, France	8,910	4,922	9,341	8,715	5,513	16,579	4,529	10,319	8,467	7,367	4,267	16,938	7,290	14,263	8,345	7,402	1,585	9,157	7,283	11,632
Townsville, Australia	11,580	11,013	12,499	11,441	14,031	6,554	12,477	5,842	15,227	12,514	12,569	2,067	14,206	1,382	14,161	14,340	14,889	13,150	15,168	6,515
Trenton, New Jersey	13,028	10,337	3,514	13,147	10,266	15,051	10,405	15,108	3,764	2,993	10,149	16,599	1,460	15,072	2,558	1,522	7,434	3,278	1,680	9,013
Tripoli, Lebanon	7,111	2,163	12,488	6,742	4,223	14,622	1,490	7,308	11,551	10,084	1,163	13,792	10,478	11,869	11,601	10,619	1,865	12,388	10,539	12,246
Tripoli, Libya	7,050	4,234	11,096	6,824	3,673	14,847	2,917	9,377	9,525	9,288	2,737	15,660	9,034	13,970	9,893	9,101	625	10,795	8,795	13,152
Tristan da Cunha (Edinburgh)	3,779	10,993	11,878	4,247	5,176	7,295	8,473	12,109	8,121	13,600	8,714	11,393	11,328	14,221	10,330	11,042	8,809	11,018	9,939	18,313
Trondheim, Norway	10,390	4,464	8,954	10,113	7,058	18,204	5,155	9,564	9,189	6,416	4,831	15,867	7,065	12,738	8,428	7,270	2,828	9,024	7,526	9,826
Trujillo, Peru	11,150	14,801	4,572	11,588	10,824	9,730	13,327	19,449	1,634	7,135	13,283	13,180	4,924	15,297	3,419	4,596	10,967	3,759	3,752	11,252
Truk Island (Moen)	13,740	9,731	10,877	13,440	14,820	9,464	11,958	5,907	14,553	9,910	11,886	5,062	12,011	2,175	12,615	12,248	13,237	11,706	13,306	3,968
Truro, Canada	12,317	9,302	4,593	12,370	9,343	15,853	9,307	14,297	4,496	3,534	9,050	17,536	2,531	15,335	3,623	2,620	6,338	4,376	2,649	9,495
Tsingtao, China	12,095	5,367	11,817	11,614	11,092	12,957	7,814	4,229	15,038	9,235	7,658	8,569	11,521	5,357	12,955	11,851	8,731	12,600	12,831	5,846
Tsitsihar, China	12,805	5,327	10,711	12,315	11,181	14,140	7,854	5,426	13,764	8,009	7,638	9,667	10,261	6,393	11,728	10,592	8,175	11,453	11,552	5,442
Tubuai Island (Mataura)	14,166	16,888	6,946	14,507	17,112	6,480	19,053	12,406	8,662	8,988	19,101	6,357	9,008	7,629	8,134	8,929	17,841	7,227	9,233	6,444
Tucson, Arizona	16,062	12,357	1,093	16,307	13,613	13,332	13,306	14,966	4,662	1,981	13,001	13,256	1,962	12,270	2,458	2,094	10,453	1,847	3,072	6,306
Tulsa, Oklahoma	14,740	11,594	1,756	14,928	12,160	14,115	12,118	15,354	3,908	1,948	11,835	14,698	542	13,579	1,792	786	9,183	1,884	1,888	7,508
Tunis, Tunisia	7,539	4,374	10,622	7,323	4,152	15,314	3,327	9,641	9,224	8,776	3,117	16,057	8,560	14,107	9,468	8,638	500	10,350	8,376	12,767
Tura, USSR	12,122	4,120	10,033	11,667	9,612	16,331	6,463	6,737	12,174	7,046	6,175	11,980	8,947	8,735	10,515	9,262	6,013	10,578	10,021	6,855
Turin, Italy	8,477	4,419	9,936	8,254	5,092	16,251	3,932	9,810	8,992	7,907	3,669	16,411	7,887	13,938	8,937	8,000	1,007	9,754	7,870	11,877
Uberlandia, Brazil	7,664	12,814	7,849	8,084	7,559	9,087	10,581	16,057	4,089	9,780	10,664	13,570	7,433	16,832	6,306	7,124	9,184	6,987	6,031	14,768
Ufa, USSR	9,703	2,068	11,206	9,289	6,964	16,316	3,935	6,850	11,903	8,324	3,621	13,276	9,532	10,413	11,002	9,780	3,536	11,457	10,154	9,507
Ujungpandang, Indonesia	9,924	7,718	14,726	9,593	11,254	8,471	9,150	2,498	18,373	13,195	9,223	4,457	15,524	2,343	16,437	15,819	11,572	15,565	16,923	7,707
Ulaanbaatar, Mongolia	11,640	4,047	11,456	11,152	9,901	14,471	6,573	4,976	13,999	8,569	6,361	10,223	10,654	7,059	12,201	10,978	7,076	12,112	11,813	6,713
Ulan-Ude, USSR	11,882	4,124	11,056	11,398	9,958	14,880	6,644	5,413	13,561	8,150	6,412	10,578	10,219	7,377	11,768	10,542	6,918	11,697	11,374	6,593
Uliastay, Mongolia	10,983	3,295	11,810	10,498	9,149	14,647	5,822	4,898	13,977	8,852	5,608	10,616	10,800	7,555	12,367	11,114	6,405	12,400	11,856	7,449
Uranium City, Canada	15,310	9,324	4,041	15,202	11,973	16,279	10,577	12,607	6,543	1,068	10,249	14,432	3,033	11,994	4,544	3,364	8,025	4,524	4,347	6,160
Urumqi, China	10,147	2,515	12,449	9,663	8,358	14,422	5,031	4,587	14,211	9,457	4,834	10,733	11,261	7,852	12,828	11,562	5,899	12,973	12,201	8,276
Ushuaia, Argentina	7,749	15,589	9,377	8,231	9,793	4,874	13,086	14,206	6,800	12,273	13,332	9,261	10,179	12,505	8,637	9,854	13,009	8,729	8,999	13,723
Vaduz, Liechtenstein	8,660	4,259	9,925	8,423	5,287	16,460	3,942	9,656	9,133	7,802	3,664	16,272	7,888	13,704	8,988	8,015	1,114	9,779	7,934	11,630
Valencia, Spain	8,144	5,189	9,678	7,984	4,757	15,713	4,298	10,534	8,304	7,985	4,086	17,022	7,617	14,818	8,498	7,684	1,389	9,385	7,405	12,507
Valladolid, Spain	8,527	5,476	9,241	8,382	5,153	15,983	4,716	10,854	7,964	7,562	4,495	17,407	7,179	14,987	8,081	7,249	1,772	8,958	6,991	12,234
Valletta, Malta	7,346	4,022	10,996	7,105	3,986	15,158	2,932	9,254	9,618	9,072	2,717	15,656	8,935	13,766	9,864	9,019	270	10,740	8,773	12,802
Valparaiso, Chile	9,059	15,588	7,238	9,543	10,009	7,174	13,233	16,594	4,368	9,976	13,359	11,294	7,786	14,309	6,274	7,458	11,968	6,499	6,571	13,035
Vancouver, Canada	16,687	10,524	3,239	16,637	13,420	14,883	11,994	12,910	6,514	902	11,663	13,192	3,114	11,193	4,314	3,412	9,503	3,942	4,513	5,128
Varna, Bulgaria	8,031	2,803	11,299	7,706	4,875	15,730	2,655	8,183	10,621	8,918	2,339	14,782	9,299	12,465	10,469	9,450	1,182	11,224	9,428	11,687
Venice, Italy	8,420	4,049	10,213	8,172	5,061	16,234	3,653	9,441	9,358	8,084	3,377	16,046	8,175	13,586	9,262	8,299	850	10,061	8,203	11,790

Distances in Kilometers	Maseru, Lesotho	Mashhad, Iran	Mazatlan, Mexico	Mbabane, Swaziland	Mbandaka, Zaire	McMurdo Sound, Antarctica	Mecca, Saudi Arabia	Medan, Indonesia	Medellin, Colombia	Medicine Hat, Canada	Medina, Saudi Arabia	Melbourne, Australia	Memphis, Tennessee	Merauke, Indonesia	Merida, Mexico	Meridian, Mississippi	Messina, Italy	Mexico City, Mexico	Miami, Florida	Midway Islands, USA
Veracruz, Mexico	14,249	13,356	1,156	14,594	12,572	12,288	13,446	17,018	2,647	3,658	13,211	13,810	1,863	13,841	709	1,637	10,479	318	1,793	8,198
Verona, Italy	8,446	4,154	10,128	8,205	5,078	16,253	3,738	9,546	9,253	8,024	3,465	16,152	8,086	13,683	9,165	8,207	891	9,968	8,104	11,805
Victoria, Canada	16,749	10,614	3,174	16,709	13,496	14,791	12,087	12,957	6,484	941	11,755	13,136	3,105	11,173	4,278	3,399	9,590	3,887	4,502	5,100
Victoria, Seychelles	4,019	4,550	17,185	3,531	4,167	9,967	3,350	4,891	14,610	14,804	3,647	9,661	15,123	9,382	15,844	15,190	6,275	16,823	14,756	13,875
Vienna, Austria	8,657	3,747	10,267	8,384	5,337	16,474	3,631	9,143	9,640	7,999	3,332	15,762	8,254	13,187	9,415	8,399	1,115	10,172	8,377	11,433
Vientiane, Laos	9,607	4,673	14,473	9,145	9,415	11,310	6,550	1,648	17,319	11,796	6,527	7,604	13,980	5,074	15,499	14,307	8,546	15,244	15,156	8,140
Villahermosa, Mexico	13,884	13,342	1,521	14,229	12,254	12,235	13,272	17,309	2,287	3,894	13,051	14,019	1,920	12,367	479	1,649	10,318	676	1,571	8,562
Vilnius, USSR	9,309	3,316	10,230	8,991	6,089	17,009	3,885	8,617	10,140	7,696	3,557	15,179	8,307	12,367	9,613	8,496	1,977	10,263	8,639	10,569
Visby, Sweden	9,673	3,842	9,689	9,380	6,383	17,455	4,381	9,098	9,655	7,190	4,057	15,604	7,762	12,666	9,073	7,951	2,172	9,718	8,107	10,381
Vitoria, Brazil	6,840	12,189	8,636	7,252	6,764	9,025	9,866	15,220	4,847	10,396	9,972	13,544	8,074	16,820	7,044	7,777	8,719	7,772	6,674	15,603
Vladivostok, USSR	13,286	6,052	10,555	12,799	11,902	13,577	8,574	5,473	13,878	8,034	8,371	9,064	10,353	5,778	11,740	10,682	8,953	11,346	11,702	4,801
Volgograd, USSR	8,809	1,856	11,525	8,419	5,950	15,966	3,057	7,160	11,601	8,801	2,728	13,756	9,682	11,146	11,043	9,891	2,592	11,640	10,093	10,527
Vologda, USSR	9,878	2,920	10,363	9,513	6,826	17,158	4,194	7,936	10,816	7,602	3,860	14,352	8,580	11,405	10,003	8,809	2,911	10,530	9,114	9,729
Vorkuta, USSR	11,160	3,483	9,914	10,756	8,267	17,394	5,390	7,570	11,227	6,960	5,069	13,464	8,418	10,294	9,957	8,697	4,410	10,269	9,244	8,249
Wake Island	15,762	10,200	8,890	15,421	15,967	10,740	12,688	7,574	12,653	7,873	12,515	6,716	9,944	4,214	10,605	10,182	12,967	9,739	11,247	1,903
Wallis Island	14,655	13,935	8,600	14,728	17,860	7,215	16,114	9,587	11,319	9,467	16,079	4,702	10,505	4,780	10,187	10,561	17,017	9,180	11,238	4,593
Walvis Bay, Namibia	1,476	8,092	14,023	1,724	2,579	8,691	5,627	9,574	10,293	14,425	5,906	11,527	12,723	13,183	12,284	12,534	6,768	13,189	11,534	18,701
Warsaw, Poland	9,058	3,496	10,219	8,759	5,790	16,832	3,782	8,855	9,910	7,789	3,463	15,454	8,253	12,722	9,503	8,424	1,619	10,199	8,501	10,915
Washington, D.C.	13,173	10,569	3,277	13,309	10,467	14,857	10,649	15,281	3,618	2,917	10,394	16,381	1,231	14,994	2,324	1,279	7,677	3,033	1,484	8,914
Watson Lake, Canada	16,150	9,291	4,454	15,950	12,756	15,922	10,906	11,836	7,443	1,602	10,571	13,365	3,925	10,865	5,322	4,251	8,633	5,097	5,303	5,070
Weimar, East Germany	9,036	4,134	9,790	8,781	5,681	16,853	4,108	9,516	9,256	7,537	3,810	16,126	7,779	13,394	8,956	7,928	1,461	9,701	7,927	11,192
Wellington, New Zealand	11,496	14,495	10,801	11,638	14,867	4,058	15,275	9,120	12,106	12,450	15,494	2,575	12,863	4,973	11,974	12,796	18,213	11,092	13,065	7,737
West Berlin, West Germany	9,169	4,009	9,804	8,902	5,831	16,989	4,125	9,373	9,392	7,483	3,818	15,970	7,812	13,189	9,025	7,971	1,602	9,746	8,009	11,002
Wewak, Papua New Guinea	12,321	9,711	12,211	12,062	13,948	8,312	11,592	5,064	15,679	11,429	11,600	3,799	13,494	655	13,962	13,716	13,516	13,002	14,745	5,456
Whangarei, New Zealand	12,017	14,259	10,579	12,131	15,352	4,674	15,352	8,958	12,229	12,012	15,531	2,619	12,625	4,584	11,871	12,591	18,119	10,945	12,971	7,128
Whitehorse, Canada	16,282	9,169	4,714	16,042	12,888	15,874	10,886	11,521	7,780	1,930	10,551	13,085	4,266	10,530	5,645	4,591	8,721	5,384	5,648	4,789
Wichita, Kansas	14,888	11,476	1,825	15,060	12,236	14,246	12,078	15,147	4,121	1,736	11,789	14,640	712	13,414	1,999	985	9,160	2,036	2,088	7,333
Willemstad, Curacao	11,283	12,417	4,147	11,600	9,714	12,138	11,410	17,805	976	5,666	11,281	15,607	3,321	16,805	2,410	3,017	8,714	3,330	1,918	11,131
Wiluna, Australia	8,858	9,426	15,331	8,667	11,208	6,114	10,163	4,066	17,208	14,993	10,338	2,636	16,995	2,922	16,935	17,161	13,009	15,934	17,992	9,014
Windhoek, Namibia	1,280	7,903	14,273	1,482	2,509	8,701	5,460	9,306	10,554	14,575	5,746	11,392	12,934	12,956	12,531	12,753	6,728	13,443	11,765	18,448
Windsor, Canada	13,753	10,512	3,028	13,865	10,934	15,080	10,839	14,920	4,061	2,286	10,564	15,951	1,004	14,365	2,445	1,211	7,890	2,959	1,851	8,292
Winnipeg, Canada	14,887	10,188	3,068	14,916	11,793	15,541	11,042	13,890	5,241	969	10,733	14,999	1,738	13,021	3,277	2,068	8,240	3,387	3,048	6,991
Winston-Salem, North Carolina	13,362	10,983	2,895	13,529	10,774	14,483	11,058	15,610	3,340	2,892	10,806	16,031	895	14,901	1,909	882	8,086	2,617	1,145	8,806
Wroclaw, Poland	8,967	3,738	10,098	8,687	5,657	16,777	3,840	9,115	9,655	7,753	3,531	15,725	8,108	13,024	9,318	8,267	1,440	10,042	8,299	11,108
Wuhan, China	11,328	5,056	12,645	10,852	10,586	12,458	7,392	3,409	15,797	10,038	7,274	8,221	12,301	5,141	13,759	12,631	8,664	13,427	13,582	6,535
Wyndham, Australia	10,177	9,189	14,272	9,936	12,145	7,195	10,461	3,867	17,253	13,531	10,567	2,984	15,647	1,540	16,007	15,867	13,021	15,011	16,877	7,605
Xi'an, China	11,073	4,442	12,634	10,588	10,068	12,956	6,825	3,559	15,496	9,888	6,691	8,812	12,075	5,776	13,588	12,404	8,016	13,369	13,291	6,904
Xining, China	10,647	3,749	12,755	10,158	9,428	13,348	6,158	3,672	15,251	9,891	6,012	9,367	11,969	6,413	13,521	12,291	7,330	13,429	13,096	7,442
Yakutsk, USSR	13,467	5,497	9,339	12,995	11,100	15,671	7,916	6,973	12,133	6,488	7,638	11,152	8,664	7,868	10,174	8,994	7,440	10,012	9,917	5,367
Yanji, China	13,091	5,877	10,723	12,604	11,723	13,577	8,396	5,316	14,006	8,171	8,196	9,075	10,481	5,791	11,884	10,810	8,832	11,508	11,819	4,994
Yaounde, Cameroon	4,048	6,084	12,666	3,951	859	11,675	3,624	9,675	9,564	11,889	3,775	13,986	10,817	14,352	11,018	10,743	3,822	12,029	10,003	16,332
Yap Island (Colonia)	12,527	8,367	12,127	12,170	13,292	9,806	10,482	4,411	15,906	10,671	10,433	5,290	12,944	2,004	13,811	13,223	12,064	12,982	14,324	5,087
Yaraka, Australia	10,974	11,144	12,943	10,860	13,590	5,957	12,370	5,831	15,328	13,159	12,498	1,439	14,746	1,860	14,541	14,852	14,987	13,536	15,594	7,181
Yarmouth, Canada	12,470	9,580	4,325	12,542	9,555	15,629	9,585	14,538	4,266	3,409	9,330	17,332	2,264	15,328	3,340	2,343	6,614	4,095	2,374	9,409
Yellowknife, Canada	15,413	9,045	4,400	15,257	12,035	16,449	10,429	12,169	6,989	1,399	10,097	14,180	3,477	11,623	4,979	3,808	7,989	4,923	4,794	5,385
Yerevan, USSR	7,893	1,388	12,369	7,491	5,177	15,053	2,124	6,767	12,031	9,718	1,802	13,375	10,459	11,109	11,741	10,645	2,499	12,415	10,737	11,290
Yinchuan, China	11,098	4,100	12,375	10,609	9,838	13,460	6,548	3,941	15,050	9,553	6,390	9,332	11,685	6,279	13,220	12,011	7,567	13,073	12,861	6,997
Yogyakarta, Indonesia	8,906	7,204	15,749	8,564	10,251	8,351	8,351	1,809	19,356	13,985	8,459	4,816	16,339	3,303	17,430	16,655	10,963	16,597	17,729	8,713
York, United Kingdom	9,618	4,987	8,899	9,409	6,224	17,308	4,980	10,332	8,428	6,749	4,691	16,887	6,879	13,919	8,053	7,024	2,158	8,797	7,030	10,909
Yumen, China	10,548	3,344	12,591	10,059	9,108	13,778	5,805	4,016	14,857	9,668	5,639	9,861	11,667	6,914	13,231	11,984	6,848	13,219	12,738	7,658
Yutian, China	9,258	1,975	13,300	8,772	7,671	13,814	4,376	4,074	14,683	10,300	4,224	10,522	11,989	7,901	13,539	12,276	5,717	13,776	12,818	9,068
Yuzhno-Sakhalinsk, USSR	14,195	6,700	9,612	13,706	12,537	13,894	9,224	6,402	13,014	7,162	8,991	9,394	9,502	6,143	10,843	9,828	9,216	10,412	10,875	4,032
Zagreb, Yugoslavia	8,399	3,763	10,415	8,132	5,071	16,218	3,462	9,157	9,639	8,209	3,174	15,767	8,387	13,307	9,505	8,520	847	10,288	8,453	11,700
Zahedan, Iran	7,413	763	14,016	6,944	5,569	13,523	2,292	4,910	13,913	11,154	2,180	11,486	12,232	9,467	13,593	12,446	4,258	14,188	12,618	11,123
Zamboanga, Philippines	10,831	7,101	13,790	10,445	11,543	9,739	8,939	2,619	17,585	11,920	8,941	5,494	14,271	2,645	15,386	14,582	10,961	14,654	15,671	6,774
Zanzibar, Tanzania	2,842	5,161	15,889	2,388	2,424	10,144	3,056	6,699	12,823	14,391	3,389	10,966	13,929	11,137	14,283	13,906	5,485	15,294	13,251	15,468
Zaragoza, Spain	8,380	5,168	9,528	8,215	4,991	15,956	4,409	10,540	8,281	7,772	4,183	17,088	7,466	14,728	8,391	7,543	1,455	9,261	7,304	12,265
Zashiversk, USSR	14,047	6,045	8,490	13,593	11,392	16,161	8,352	7,834	11,292	5,625	8,053	11,676	7,809	8,423	9,312	8,139	7,480	9,153	9,077	5,113
Zhengzhou, China	11,486	4,842	12,327	11,003	10,504	12,923	7,250	3,783	15,365	9,651	7,108	8,664	11,888	5,546	13,369	12,218	8,342	13,086	13,149	6,467
Zurich, Switzerland	8,706	4,345	9,840	8,474	5,328	16,497	4,026	9,742	9,046	7,733	3,750	16,359	7,802	13,771	8,899	7,927	1,177	9,691	7,844	11,616

Distances in Kilometers

	Milan, Italy	Milford Sound, New Zealand	Milwaukee, Wisconsin	Minsk, USSR	Mogadiscio, Somalia	Mombasa, Kenya	Monclova, Mexico	Moncton, Canada	Monrovia, Liberia	Monte Carlo, Monaco	Monterrey, Mexico	Montevideo, Uruguay	Montgomery, Alabama	Montpelier, Vermont	Montpellier, France	Montreal, Canada	Moosonee, Canada	Moroni, Comoros	Moscow, USSR	Mosul, Iraq
Milford Sound, New Zealand	18,335	0	14,156	16,987	12,685	12,564	12,115	15,972	15,762	18,452	12,109	10,153	13,639	15,327	18,730	15,303	15,037	11,652	16,339	15,330
Milwaukee, Wisconsin	7,245	14,156	0	7,641	13,180	13,299	2,168	1,862	8,487	7,246	2,234	9,212	1,191	1,243	7,024	1,173	1,068	14,188	7,920	9,918
Minsk, USSR	1,616	16,987	7,641	0	5,973	6,521	9,805	6,198	6,304	1,851	9,875	12,676	8,540	6,768	2,069	6,719	6,580	7,418	675	2,293
Mogadiscio, Somalia	5,965	12,685	13,180	5,973	0	927	15,228	11,381	6,251	5,943	15,220	11,199	13,669	12,027	6,158	12,048	12,222	1,538	5,993	3,801
Mombasa, Kenya	6,261	12,564	13,299	6,521	927	0	15,179	11,447	5,725	6,200	15,134	10,291	13,597	12,087	6,379	12,132	12,427	933	6,631	4,485
Monclova, Mexico	9,374	12,115	2,168	9,805	15,228	15,179	0	3,861	9,762	9,358	175	8,333	1,582	3,219	9,121	3,214	3,224	15,972	10,059	12,086
Moncton, Canada	5,534	15,972	1,862	6,198	11,381	11,447	3,861	0	6,782	5,504	3,878	9,011	2,389	646	5,262	688	1,299	12,329	6,603	8,385
Monrovia, Liberia	4,750	15,762	8,487	6,304	6,251	5,725	9,762	6,782	0	4,512	9,666	6,590	8,279	7,293	4,374	7,407	8,067	6,309	6,938	6,400
Monte Carlo, Monaco	239	18,452	7,246	1,851	5,943	6,200	9,358	5,504	4,512	0	9,381	10,827	7,879	6,142	285	6,144	6,280	7,131	2,522	3,131
Monterrey, Mexico	9,403	12,109	2,234	9,875	15,220	15,134	175	3,878	9,666	9,381	0	8,158	1,552	3,239	9,140	3,244	3,298	15,906	10,145	12,149
Montevideo, Uruguay	11,061	10,153	9,212	12,676	11,199	10,291	8,333	9,011	6,590	10,827	8,158	0	8,085	8,920	10,609	9,074	9,841	10,123	13,349	12,943
Montgomery, Alabama	7,917	13,639	1,191	8,540	13,669	13,597	1,582	2,389	8,279	7,879	1,552	8,085	0	1,779	7,629	1,821	2,150	14,402	8,891	10,764
Montpelier, Vermont	6,166	15,327	1,243	6,768	12,027	12,087	3,219	646	7,293	6,142	3,239	8,920	1,779	0	5,902	160	986	12,963	7,141	8,985
Montpellier, France	471	18,730	7,024	2,069	6,158	6,379	9,121	5,262	4,374	285	9,140	10,609	7,629	5,902	0	5,909	6,074	7,309	2,744	3,415
Montreal, Canada	6,161	15,303	1,173	6,719	12,048	12,132	3,214	688	7,407	6,144	3,244	9,074	1,821	160	5,909	0	828	13,017	7,077	8,950
Moosonee, Canada	6,260	15,037	1,068	6,580	12,222	12,427	3,224	1,299	8,067	6,280	3,298	9,841	2,150	986	6,074	828	0	13,343	6,852	8,863
Moroni, Comoros	7,194	11,652	14,188	7,418	1,538	933	15,972	12,329	6,309	7,131	15,906	10,123	14,402	12,963	7,309	13,017	13,343	0	7,492	5,315
Moscow, USSR	2,289	16,339	7,920	675	5,993	6,631	10,059	6,603	6,938	2,522	10,145	13,349	8,891	7,141	2,744	7,077	6,852	7,492	0	2,199
Mosul, Iraq	3,007	15,330	9,918	2,293	3,801	4,485	12,086	8,385	6,400	3,131	12,149	12,943	10,764	8,985	3,415	8,950	8,863	5,315	2,199	0
Mount Isa, Australia	14,742	3,710	14,987	13,278	10,528	10,878	13,843	16,435	16,451	14,928	13,934	13,632	15,323	16,075	15,206	15,934	15,158	10,198	12,629	11,901
Multan, Pakistan	5,591	12,762	11,630	4,383	4,157	5,082	13,643	10,482	8,923	5,753	13,763	15,138	12,697	10,992	6,037	10,914	10,577	5,532	3,892	2,718
Munich, West Germany	349	18,154	7,211	1,287	6,046	6,397	9,359	5,551	5,099	588	9,399	11,391	7,940	6,173	782	6,157	6,202	7,329	1,962	2,888
Murcia, Spain	1,193	18,834	7,036	2,809	6,181	6,272	9,048	5,205	3,641	961	9,047	9,868	7,504	5,851	753	5,881	6,161	7,182	3,482	3,898
Murmansk, USSR	2,944	16,287	6,677	1,703	7,482	8,118	8,755	5,613	7,656	3,172	8,858	13,546	7,739	6,068	3,284	5,978	5,619	8,982	1,490	3,684
Mururoa Atoll, Fr. Polynesia	16,114	5,451	8,882	16,271	17,767	17,134	6,741	10,583	14,203	16,086	6,710	8,018	8,207	9,948	15,835	9,953	9,894	16,286	16,232	18,389
Muscat, Oman	5,039	13,308	11,870	4,242	2,778	3,686	14,019	10,414	7,637	5,144	14,101	13,673	12,778	11,002	5,425	10,958	10,804	4,246	3,962	2,047
Myitkyina, Burma	7,910	10,532	12,410	6,459	6,138	7,027	13,880	11,888	11,521	8,105	14,047	17,282	13,600	12,226	8,378	12,103	11,510	7,159	5,835	5,261
Naga, Philippines	10,718	7,865	12,979	9,158	8,646	9,424	13,438	13,342	14,489	10,932	13,608	17,650	14,030	13,399	11,188	13,243	12,453	9,254	8,492	8,243
Nagasaki, Japan	9,487	9,389	10,769	7,872	9,380	10,279	11,463	11,143	14,020	9,723	11,638	19,415	11,855	11,173	9,931	11,016	10,223	10,400	7,203	7,685
Nagoya, Japan	9,649	9,366	10,227	8,048	10,023	10,931	10,808	10,746	14,311	9,888	10,983	18,832	11,278	10,719	10,075	10,561	9,751	11,081	7,394	8,099
Nagpur, India	6,813	11,530	12,775	5,641	4,223	5,126	14,688	11,719	9,756	6,964	14,825	15,416	13,882	12,212	7,249	12,127	11,741	5,343	5,146	3,865
Nairobi, Kenya	5,850	13,000	12,860	6,176	1,021	440	14,743	11,007	5,358	5,782	14,700	10,207	13,161	11,646	5,956	11,692	11,994	1,353	6,323	4,216
Nanchang, China	8,967	9,674	11,701	7,380	8,006	8,892	12,686	11,723	13,126	9,190	12,861	19,000	12,853	11,882	9,434	11,734	11,000	8,985	6,707	6,730
Nancy, France	424	18,541	6,852	1,592	6,373	6,683	8,992	5,168	4,963	558	9,026	11,127	7,556	5,794	593	5,783	5,856	7,615	2,261	3,290
Nandi, Fiji	16,750	3,103	11,713	15,240	14,517	14,800	10,056	13,552	18,462	16,982	10,114	11,891	11,628	12,956	17,081	12,873	12,359	14,026	14,616	15,104
Nanjing, China	8,881	9,831	11,258	7,275	8,330	9,230	12,220	11,342	13,200	9,109	12,395	19,457	12,404	11,476	9,342	11,326	10,580	9,366	6,600	6,806
Nanning, China	8,909	9,598	12,527	7,393	7,160	8,020	13,648	12,341	12,666	9,115	13,822	18,005	13,703	12,577	9,380	12,437	11,750	8,050	6,741	6,373
Nantes, France	849	19,142	6,449	2,175	6,736	6,964	8,558	4,705	4,618	800	8,581	10,602	7,082	5,342	585	5,344	5,491	7,893	2,835	3,848
Naples, Italy	658	17,824	7,887	1,761	5,311	5,604	10,005	6,153	4,564	649	10,029	11,051	8,528	6,790	909	6,791	6,911	6,536	2,376	2,554
Narvik, Norway	2,601	16,853	6,210	1,704	7,663	8,225	8,330	5,040	7,207	2,811	8,422	12,934	7,231	5,523	2,876	5,442	5,144	9,120	1,745	3,911
Nashville, Tennessee	7,669	13,840	770	8,216	13,505	13,502	1,725	2,141	8,342	7,644	1,737	8,482	422	1,503	7,403	1,516	1,750	14,342	8,542	10,462
Nassau, Bahamas	7,809	13,859	2,213	8,707	13,167	12,924	2,415	2,588	7,359	7,725	2,310	7,003	1,191	2,171	7,453	2,290	2,922	13,633	9,159	10,787
Natal, Brazil	7,187	13,974	7,570	8,801	9,000	8,302	7,983	6,450	3,025	6,955	7,839	3,876	6,857	6,686	6,733	6,841	7,660	8,638	9,475	9,356
Natashquan, Canada	5,139	16,293	2,138	5,726	11,046	11,171	4,235	506	6,779	5,126	4,267	9,441	2,826	1,047	4,895	1,023	1,331	12,072	6,115	7,938
Nauru Island	14,572	4,880	11,280	13,022	13,533	14,150	10,206	12,893	19,322	14,809	10,318	14,068	11,617	12,430	14,948	12,303	11,595	13,665	12,391	13,018
Ndjamena, Chad	3,738	15,574	10,129	4,765	3,524	3,259	11,922	8,267	2,910	3,580	11,876	9,120	10,341	8,893	3,651	8,955	9,359	4,081	5,220	3,887
Nelson, New Zealand	18,652	579	13,586	17,120	13,245	13,141	11,564	15,413	16,110	18,830	11,562	10,179	13,101	14,767	19,113	14,739	14,459	12,231	16,448	15,718
Nema, Mauritania	3,548	16,869	8,018	5,113	5,978	5,644	9,593	6,204	1,203	3,310	9,527	7,695	8,033	6,781	3,171	6,872	7,432	6,380	5,756	5,406
Neuquen, Argentina	12,116	9,198	9,298	13,723	12,170	11,248	8,073	9,426	7,730	11,887	7,902	1,150	8,120	9,227	11,655	9,370	10,072	10,979	14,398	14,093
New Delhi, India	6,141	12,222	11,928	4,876	4,475	5,402	13,861	10,891	9,487	6,309	13,994	15,595	13,035	11,373	6,592	11,286	10,894	5,762	4,349	3,297
New Glasgow, Canada	5,413	16,114	2,027	6,119	11,237	11,290	3,999	175	6,608	5,378	4,010	8,935	2,504	797	5,132	855	1,470	12,168	6,540	8,287
New Haven, Connecticut	6,369	15,169	1,253	7,034	12,173	12,186	3,056	844	7,234	6,333	3,060	8,608	1,549	330	6,086	470	1,258	13,043	7,424	9,229
New Orleans, Louisiana	8,362	13,192	1,464	8,960	14,111	14,021	1,162	2,830	8,633	8,325	1,116	8,010	447	2,212	8,076	2,245	2,493	14,810	9,294	11,194
New Plymouth, New Zealand	18,586	805	13,398	17,003	13,413	13,338	11,402	15,237	16,344	18,792	11,406	10,328	12,951	14,592	19,057	14,558	14,251	12,434	16,328	15,740
New York, New York	6,482	15,057	1,182	7,143	12,282	12,290	2,946	956	7,307	6,446	2,949	8,567	1,436	412	6,199	533	1,282	13,144	7,530	9,341
Newcastle upon Tyne, UK	1,308	18,624	6,036	1,882	7,232	7,563	8,193	4,425	5,461	1,411	8,238	11,236	6,808	5,032	1,328	5,006	5,019	8,496	2,452	3,961
Newcastle Waters, Australia	14,024	4,399	15,205	12,589	9,877	10,280	14,322	16,410	15,954	14,204	14,429	14,131	15,717	16,169	14,484	16,016	15,201	9,648	11,951	11,162
Niamey, Niger	3,605	16,305	9,000	5,005	4,926	4,581	10,642	7,160	1,624	3,387	10,580	8,153	9,075	7,758	3,339	7,840	8,346	5,330	5,587	4,800
Nicosia, Cyprus	2,338	16,040	9,502	2,130	3,869	4,391	11,658	7,853	5,530	2,415	11,701	12,099	10,241	8,476	2,690	8,460	8,476	5,289	2,310	892
Niue (Alofi)	17,070	3,510	10,805	15,856	15,753	15,900	8,967	12,667	17,364	17,253	9,005	10,829	10,549	12,037	17,219	11,978	11,586	15,043	15,325	16,268
Norfolk, Virginia	6,895	14,679	1,207	7,601	12,627	12,580	2,611	1,404	7,417	6,849	2,593	8,210	1,044	881	6,595	987	1,641	13,407	7,997	9,783
Norfolk Island, Australia	17,408	1,726	13,243	15,795	13,268	13,402	11,470	15,096	17,487	17,637	11,509	11,555	13,052	14,485	17,863	14,412	13,927	12,569	15,120	14,857
Noril'sk, USSR	4,950	14,177	7,538	3,445	8,105	8,923	9,305	7,011	9,699	5,187	9,448	15,595	8,716	7,307	5,336	7,181	6,594	9,635	2,888	4,558
Norman Wells, Canada	7,153	13,416	3,448	6,608	12,506	13,126	4,627	4,213	10,540	7,289	4,788	12,647	4,563	4,015	7,206	3,856	3,029	14,006	6,516	8,705
Normanton, Australia	14,623	3,887	14,637	13,115	10,693	11,087	13,570	16,059	16,729	14,819	13,668	13,911	15,020	15,708	15,091	15,566	14,785	10,439	12,457	11,854
North Pole	4,967	14,939	5,235	4,029	9,775	10,452	7,025	4,896	9,306	5,160	7,162	13,865	6,418	5,100	5,175	4,962	4,319	11,296	3,823	5,981
Nottingham, United Kingdom	1,123	18,777	6,163	1,900	7,076	7,384	8,311	4,513	5,247	1,206	8,351	11,090	6,901	5,130	1,106	5,111	5,159	8,317	2,505	3,888
Norway House, Canada	7,014	14,087	1,418	7,037	12,929	13,272	3,022	2,497	9,250	7,073	3,151	10,629	2,569	2,120	6,901	1,971	1,198	14,204	7,180	9,321
Norwich, United Kingdom	983	18,677	6,327	1,748	6,921	7,241	8,478	4,683	5,253	1,088	8,519	11,179	7,071	5,299	1,023	5,279	5,319	8,174	2,366	3,717
Nouakchott, Mauritania	3,824	17,048	7,205	5,439	6,917	6,574	8,689	5,438	1,418	3,588	8,616	7,244	7,142	5,982	3,385	6,086	6,703	7,291	6,109	6,093
Noumea, New Caledonia	16,713	2,478	12,913	15,098	13,292	13,551	11,303	14,726	18,216	16,949	11,363	12,250	12,872	14,150	17,152	14,059	13,492	12,780	14,428	14,385
Novosibirsk, USSR	5,111	13,610	9,102	3,496	6,780	7,657	10,917	8,393	9,673	5,344	11,058	16,171	10,265	8,760	5,565	8,646	8,122	8,271	2,822	3,657
Nuku'alofa, Tonga	17,276	3,036	11,372	15,892	15,153	15,311	9,561	13,233	17,672	17,487	9,600	11,082	11,143	12,608	17,512	12,545	12,124	14,467	15,306	15,953
Nukunono Island, Tokelau Isls.	15,984	4,383	10,218	14,753	15,837	16,236	8,582	12,062	17,928	16,177	8,648	11,697	10,146	11,461	16,171	11,381	10,887	15,503	14,236	15,379
Nuremberg, West Germany	465	18,175	7,095	1,239	6,176	6,538	9,248	5,452	5,203	695	9,290	11,453	7,841	6,070	853	6,051	6,080	7,469	1,913	2,964
Nyala, Sudan	3,992	14,971	10,881	4,648	2,515	2,418	12,799	9,030	3,969	3,891	12,769	9,972	11,219	9,670	4,037	9,714	10,025	3,319	4,972	3,254
Oaxaca, Mexico	9,862	11,752	2,999	10,536	15,361	15,063	1,194	4,367	9,381	9,806	1,024	7,169	1,996	3,772	9,544	3,817	4,056	15,686	10,876	12,752
Ocean Falls, Canada	8,412	12,386	3,114	8,006	13,939	14,525	3,574	4,487	11,218	8,523	3,748	11,885	3,986	4,081	8,406	3,940	3,188	15,422	7,945	10,139
Odense, Denmark	1,108	18,010	6,677	1,119	6,699	7,117	8,844	5,137	5,760	1,315	8,900	11,828	7,507	5,729	1,393	5,692	5,636	8,041	1,705	3,258
Odessa, USSR	1,668	16,699	8,398	857	5,121	5,665	10,566	6,863	5,963	1,853	10,626	12,504	9,238	7,459	2,129	7,424	7,348	6,561	1,137	1,527
Ogbomosho, Nigeria	4,165	15,665	9,576	5,489	4,604	4,155	11,140	7,750	1,676	3,957	11,067	7,929	9,588	8,336	3,930	8,424	8,955	4,842	6,037	5,022
Okha, USSR	8,187	11,131	8,256	6,693	10,324	11,244	9,165	8,652	12,928	8,422	9,339	17,450	9,370	8,650	8,554	8,493	7,695	11,683	6,113	7,438
Okinawa (Naha)	9,932	8,838	11,520	8,320	9,146	10,014	12,131	11,899	14,274	10,163	12,305	18,979	12,593	11,934	10,389	11,778	10,984	10,033	7,645	7,876
Oklahoma City, Oklahoma	8,420	13,005	1,176	8,789	14,344	14,415	1,023	2,975	9,311	8,419	1,122	8,895	1,090	2,332	8,193	2,298	2,212	15,278	9,036	11,075
Old Crow, Canada	7,202	13,189	4,079	6,491	12,268	12,955	5,204	4,768	10,891	7,359	5,369	13,278	5,193	4,610	7,306	4,450	3,624	13,795	6,324	8,482
Olympia, Washington	8,740	12,209	2,768	8,476	14,445	14,956	2,922	4,351	11,133	8,831	3,097	11,252	3,491	3,866	8,688	3,740	3,073	15,877	8,466	10,665
Omaha, Nebraska	7,872	13,484	697	8,168	13,828	13,981	1,671	2,556	9,152	7,886	1,777	9,365	1,312	1,939	7,671	1,868	1,618	14,877	8,397	10,459
Omsk, USSR	4,531	14,138	8,997	2,922	6,394	7,244	10,917	8,132	9,066	4,761	11,047	15,581	10,131	8,546	4,990	8,442	7,981	7,911	2,247	3,098
Oodnadatta, Australia	14,923	3,436	15,776	13,589	10,131	10,380	14,447	17,291	15,758	15,078	14,518	12,987	15,986	16,906	15,363	16,770	16,007	9,636	12,974	11,962
Oradea, Romania	996	17,373	7,882	858	5,477	5,924	10,045	6,280	5,490	1,193	10,094	11,954	8,666	6,891	1,463	6,865	6,850	6,845	1,450	2,119
Oran, Algeria	1,365	18,621	7,218	2,975	6,024	6,082	9,205	5,377	3,416	1,127	9,197	9,710	7,649	6,021	959	6,057	6,363	6,985	3,643	3,912
Oranjestad, Aruba	8,191	13,513	3,796	9,385	12,718	12,255	3,640	3,756	6,530	8,053	3,491	5,446	2,757	3,527	7,768	3,672	4,405	12,795	9,936	11,182
Orebro, Sweden	1,590	17,546	6,677	964	6,860	7,346	8,841	5,251	6,280	1,810	8,911	12,317	7,581	5,812	1,908	5,760	5,617	8,261	1,389	3,250
Orel, USSR	2,112	16,420	8,103	577	5,702	6,322	10,255	6,721	6,685	2,337	10,334	13,150	9,041	7,277	2,578	7,221	7,036	7,190	330	1,924
Orsk, USSR	3,644	14,880	9,073	2,107	5,585	6,382	11,134	7,938	8,032	3,862	11,243	14,598	10,129	8,431	4,114	8,350	8,016	7,122	1,476	2,058
Osaka, Japan	9,623	9,363	10,340	8,017	9,896	10,802	10,943	10,832	14,262	9,861	11,117	18,958	11,398	10,816	10,052	10,658	9,851	10,945	7,359	8,020
Oslo, Norway	1,611	17,716	6,427	1,219	7,068	7,531	8,593	4,990	6,220	1,815	8,660	12,151	7,323	5,553	1,874	5,501	5,369	8,451	1,647	3,494
Osorno, Chile	12,559	8,789	9,378	14,161	12,540	11,614	8,021	9,636	8,201	12,332	7,853	1,620	8,190	9,396	12,096	9,533	10,202	11,300	14,835	14,563
Ostrava, Czechoslovakia	837	17,653	7,476	782	5,882	6,315	9,640	5,889	5,536	1,070	9,691	11,897	8,272	6,495	1,298	6,466	6,442	7,239	1,452	2,499
Ottawa, Canada	6,304	15,147	1,010	6,834	12,202	12,293	3,070	852	7,564	6,291	3,104	9,108	1,712	278	6,058	165	748	13,179	7,179	9,075

Distances in Kilometers	Milan, Italy	Milford Sound, New Zealand	Milwaukee, Wisconsin	Minsk, USSR	Mogadiscio, Somalia	Mombasa, Kenya	Monclova, Mexico	Moncton, Canada	Monrovia, Liberia	Monte Carlo, Monaco	Monterrey, Mexico	Montevideo, Uruguay	Montgomery, Alabama	Montpelier, Vermont	Montpellier, France	Montreal, Canada	Moosonee, Canada	Moroni, Comoros	Moscow, USSR	Mosul, Iraq
Ouagadougou, Bourkina Fasso	3,807	16,292	8,793	5,271	5,292	4,905	10,359	6,973	1,219	3,581	10,289	7,781	8,804	7,554	3,500	7,644	8,190	5,618	5,874	5,187
Oujda, Morocco	1,525	18,602	7,193	3,137	6,076	6,106	9,156	5,344	3,270	1,287	9,144	9,548	7,593	5,986	1,110	6,027	6,357	7,002	3,805	4,053
Oxford, United Kingdom	1,038	18,874	6,221	1,944	7,002	7,293	8,363	4,549	5,113	1,102	8,399	10,987	6,938	5,171	984	5,157	5,226	8,226	2,565	3,871
Pago Pago, American Samoa	16,546	3,929	10,507	15,328	15,845	16,112	8,759	12,365	17,664	16,733	8,809	11,235	10,337	11,747	16,713	11,678	11,237	15,305	14,807	15,865
Pakxe, Laos	9,329	9,101	13,416	7,893	6,783	7,588	14,513	13,160	12,649	9,518	14,688	17,178	14,594	13,428	9,794	13,292	12,623	7,502	7,269	6,592
Palembang, Indonesia	10,674	7,671	15,388	9,433	6,631	7,231	16,171	15,114	12,880	10,824	16,343	15,375	16,547	15,417	11,110	15,284	14,620	6,845	8,873	7,711
Palermo, Italy	886	17,774	8,028	2,062	5,155	5,400	10,122	6,261	4,285	800	10,138	10,803	8,620	6,903	1,004	6,912	7,073	6,332	2,664	2,638
Palma, Majorca	848	18,672	7,200	2,460	5,988	6,119	9,253	5,395	3,922	610	9,259	10,221	7,727	6,040	460	6,060	6,289	7,060	3,130	3,546
Palmerston North, New Zealand	18,775	797	13,364	17,197	13,467	13,361	11,342	15,190	16,181	18,975	11,341	10,135	12,880	14,545	19,245	14,516	14,240	12,449	16,522	15,895
Panama, Panama	9,208	12,499	3,863	10,305	13,804	13,297	3,042	4,350	7,580	9,084	2,872	5,441	2,685	3,969	8,800	4,089	4,693	13,774	10,813	12,213
Paramaribo, Suriname	7,564	14,035	5,227	9,010	11,161	10,598	5,421	4,558	4,910	7,377	5,277	4,508	4,369	4,584	7,100	4,744	5,563	11,065	9,647	10,371
Paris, France	643	18,810	6,602	1,832	6,606	6,886	8,734	4,900	4,876	692	8,765	10,935	7,287	5,530	597	5,522	5,618	7,818	2,492	3,574
Patna, India	6,961	11,417	12,372	5,638	4,990	5,900	14,154	11,506	10,305	7,136	14,302	16,188	13,524	11,944	7,417	11,843	11,375	6,131	5,073	4,148
Patrai, Greece	1,311	17,120	8,553	1,796	4,675	5,036	10,685	6,842	4,823	1,347	10,714	11,399	9,222	7,476	1,613	7,472	7,560	5,965	2,277	1,905
Peking, China	8,097	10,680	10,497	6,483	8,253	9,175	11,638	10,474	12,574	8,330	11,811	19,154	11,665	10,636	8,551	10,490	9,764	9,441	5,809	6,250
Penrhyn Island (Omoka)	15,785	5,132	9,117	15,000	17,330	17,586	7,288	10,978	16,415	15,909	7,332	10,513	8,870	10,346	15,793	10,290	9,921	16,734	14,641	16,304
Peoria, Illinois	7,520	13,903	295	7,935	13,443	13,535	1,878	2,088	8,611	7,517	1,940	9,041	968	1,451	7,291	1,404	1,364	14,414	8,215	10,210
Perm', USSR	3,449	15,241	8,325	1,834	6,276	7,038	10,370	7,257	8,073	3,684	10,481	14,510	9,399	7,726	3,902	7,638	7,272	7,814	1,161	2,595
Perth, Australia	13,689	4,673	17,597	12,698	8,304	8,471	16,389	18,431	13,816	13,782	16,449	12,562	17,943	18,457	14,057	18,297	17,472	7,697	12,197	10,694
Peshawar, Pakistan	5,355	13,018	11,221	4,070	4,463	5,381	13,222	10,112	8,919	5,529	13,344	15,278	12,300	10,610	5,810	10,528	10,173	5,877	3,547	2,592
Petropavlovsk-Kamchatskiy,USSR	8,711	10,851	7,613	7,323	11,354	12,270	8,290	8,273	13,355	8,937	8,465	16,622	8,662	8,172	9,031	8,013	7,191	12,728	6,800	8,323
Petrozavodsk, USSR	2,434	16,469	7,286	968	6,693	7,319	9,407	6,059	7,182	2,672	9,499	13,380	8,293	6,567	2,839	6,493	6,219	8,186	701	2,900
Pevek, USSR	7,139	12,676	6,018	5,968	11,064	11,892	7,162	6,408	11,570	7,347	7,330	15,229	7,160	6,383	7,390	6,225	5,426	12,586	5,580	7,496
Philadelphia, Pennsylvania	6,611	14,931	1,117	7,271	12,406	12,405	2,822	1,086	7,386	6,575	2,823	8,512	1,306	524	6,327	630	1,329	13,256	7,656	9,470
Phnom Penh, Kampuchea	9,544	8,858	13,822	8,150	6,653	7,427	14,896	13,538	12,648	9,725	15,071	16,799	15,000	13,819	10,005	13,685	13,023	7,283	7,540	6,737
Phoenix, Arizona	9,460	11,833	2,356	9,579	15,423	15,636	1,256	4,217	10,666	9,492	1,428	9,549	2,407	3,592	9,290	3,529	3,218	16,539	9,710	11,863
Pierre, South Dakota	7,882	13,381	1,012	8,049	13,844	14,082	1,941	2,776	9,488	7,915	2,075	9,847	1,805	2,205	7,717	2,105	1,656	14,999	8,228	10,341
Pinang, Malaysia	9,673	8,682	14,575	8,397	6,115	6,826	15,739	14,112	12,275	9,832	15,914	15,956	15,763	14,457	10,117	14,333	13,721	6,595	7,831	6,743
Pitcairn Island (Adamstown)	15,744	5,926	8,690	16,310	17,414	16,601	6,522	10,262	13,259	15,662	6,463	7,059	7,875	9,651	15,388	9,678	9,742	15,876	16,454	18,603
Pittsburgh, Pennsylvania	6,911	14,592	718	7,485	12,759	12,789	2,478	1,384	7,801	6,886	2,495	8,690	1,057	745	6,645	767	1,207	13,649	7,835	9,718
Plymouth, Montserrat	7,262	14,436	3,801	8,511	11,821	11,412	4,189	3,269	5,709	7,116	4,064	5,744	2,983	3,208	6,831	3,365	4,171	12,016	9,087	10,240
Plymouth, United Kingdom	1,134	19,124	6,113	2,184	7,086	7,340	8,240	4,404	4,927	1,145	8,270	10,741	6,791	5,034	969	5,027	5,137	8,271	2,812	4,054
Ponape Island	13,440	5,783	11,374	11,853	12,515	13,228	10,686	12,757	18,115	13,679	10,820	15,330	11,933	12,401	13,847	12,257	11,476	12,888	11,205	11,750
Ponce, Puerto Rico	7,507	14,200	3,424	8,677	12,263	11,879	3,701	3,119	6,188	7,376	3,575	5,958	2,536	2,963	7,091	3,116	3,894	12,496	9,226	10,506
Ponta Delgada, Azores	3,005	18,659	5,197	4,385	8,209	8,156	7,044	3,338	3,791	2,853	7,020	8,636	5,468	3,958	2,567	4,025	4,505	9,013	5,024	5,978
Pontianak, Indonesia	10,804	7,567	14,943	9,471	7,123	7,761	15,587	14,869	13,352	10,970	15,757	15,860	16,070	15,102	11,254	14,959	14,248	7,411	8,878	7,900
Port Augusta, Australia	15,424	2,918	15,887	14,142	10,362	10,532	14,339	17,569	15,661	15,565	14,390	12,405	15,913	17,088	15,850	16,970	16,270	9,740	13,537	12,435
Port Blair, India	8,599	9,751	13,954	7,355	5,334	6,126	15,482	13,233	11,343	8,756	15,649	15,959	15,136	13,645	9,040	13,535	13,009	6,046	6,809	5,664
Port Elizabeth, South Africa	8,951	10,507	14,286	9,737	4,495	3,619	14,932	12,658	5,878	8,800	14,777	7,284	13,794	13,144	8,868	13,268	13,945	3,053	10,006	7,993
Port Hedland, Australia	13,090	5,248	16,489	11,872	8,349	8,704	15,903	17,129	14,358	13,228	16,016	13,870	17,216	17,159	13,513	17,000	16,184	8,055	11,304	10,098
Port Louis, Mauritius	8,755	9,959	15,920	8,693	2,794	2,630	17,755	14,075	8,022	8,725	17,679	10,741	16,190	14,716	8,930	14,758	15,003	1,788	8,620	6,434
Port Moresby, Papua New Guinea	14,366	4,366	13,534	12,772	11,354	11,859	12,606	14,943	17,585	14,589	12,719	14,518	13,988	14,589	14,833	14,446	13,665	11,298	12,097	11,889
Port Said, Egypt	2,545	15,897	9,775	2,543	3,512	3,986	11,916	8,079	5,265	2,584	11,948	11,794	10,460	8,711	2,843	8,705	8,768	4,895	2,752	1,149
Port Sudan, Sudan	3,853	14,702	11,096	3,894	2,134	2,631	13,207	9,347	5,394	3,852	13,223	11,536	11,700	9,988	4,086	9,994	10,111	3,525	4,011	1,940
Port-au-Prince, Haiti	7,913	13,791	3,087	8,992	12,847	12,481	3,120	3,135	6,795	7,797	2,987	6,154	2,076	2,853	7,515	2,993	3,707	13,103	9,505	10,921
Port-of-Spain, Trin. & Tobago	7,670	14,003	4,406	9,000	11,820	11,323	4,549	3,942	5,599	7,508	4,407	5,071	3,501	3,874	7,224	4,031	4,831	11,846	9,600	10,600
Port-Vila, Vanuatu	16,377	2,978	12,444	14,776	13,571	13,902	10,914	14,237	18,738	16,616	10,983	12,531	12,468	13,675	16,789	13,577	12,988	13,170	14,117	14,294
Portland, Maine	6,044	15,473	1,430	6,694	11,877	11,919	3,358	511	7,095	6,013	3,371	8,814	1,878	198	5,769	335	1,152	12,790	7,085	8,892
Portland, Oregon	8,872	12,106	2,762	8,630	14,601	15,099	2,795	4,393	11,173	8,958	2,970	11,128	3,432	3,890	8,811	3,769	3,127	16,023	8,627	10,826
Porto, Portugal	1,519	19,530	6,304	3,026	6,914	7,000	8,316	4,472	3,865	1,348	8,316	9,723	6,775	5,117	1,064	5,148	5,441	7,906	3,695	4,465
Porto Alegre, Brazil	10,350	10,846	8,923	11,966	10,761	9,873	8,267	8,546	5,898	10,116	8,093	711	7,843	8,514	9,899	8,670	9,464	9,793	12,638	12,273
Porto Alexandre, Angola	6,792	12,887	11,984	7,868	4,182	3,307	13,079	10,269	3,499	6,609	12,957	7,038	11,696	10,791	6,629	10,904	11,540	3,422	8,289	6,642
Porto Novo, Benin	4,367	15,546	9,566	5,719	4,769	4,279	11,069	7,757	1,484	4,154	10,990	7,672	9,531	8,331	4,114	8,425	8,981	4,929	6,276	5,280
Porto Velho, Brazil	9,409	12,160	6,232	10,886	12,173	11,437	5,654	6,077	6,124	9,213	5,483	2,998	5,138	5,937	8,941	6,088	6,846	11,663	11,527	12,111
Portsmouth, United Kingdom	965	18,933	6,283	1,970	6,929	7,209	8,419	4,595	5,010	1,011	8,453	10,915	6,983	5,221	881	5,210	5,295	8,141	2,603	3,845
Poznan, Poland	959	17,711	7,222	727	6,171	6,614	9,389	5,669	5,707	1,197	9,444	11,982	8,044	6,266	1,379	6,232	6,181	7,536	1,394	2,719
Prague, Czechoslovakia	647	17,924	7,246	993	6,069	6,468	9,407	5,636	5,394	886	9,454	11,689	8,022	6,247	1,080	6,222	6,220	7,396	1,668	2,759
Praia, Cape Verde Islands	4,566	16,549	6,817	6,177	7,688	7,274	8,097	5,163	1,684	4,336	8,008	6,504	6,599	5,642	4,108	5,763	6,460	7,929	6,852	6,963
Pretoria, South Africa	8,117	11,206	13,993	8,824	3,592	2,697	15,029	12,243	5,507	7,980	14,895	7,939	13,702	12,786	8,070	12,893	13,489	2,223	9,074	7,049
Prince Albert, Canada	7,454	13,588	1,736	7,377	13,319	13,713	2,943	3,018	9,780	7,524	3,091	10,870	2,788	2,607	7,363	2,464	1,720	14,646	7,470	9,642
Prince Edward Island	10,580	8,774	15,802	11,179	5,439	4,716	15,848	14,321	7,576	10,447	15,674	7,577	15,084	14,755	10,539	14,890	15,619	3,902	11,342	9,198
Prince George, Canada	8,091	12,744	2,808	7,745	13,703	14,250	3,474	4,123	10,846	8,196	3,644	11,726	3,741	3,732	8,071	3,588	2,825	15,160	7,715	9,914
Prince Rupert, Canada	8,305	12,425	3,304	7,837	13,742	14,358	3,851	4,592	11,275	8,425	4,024	12,153	4,218	4,218	8,319	4,072	3,297	15,242	7,753	9,941
Providence, Rhode Island	6,233	15,306	1,363	6,908	12,035	12,051	3,194	713	7,127	6,196	3,198	8,634	1,684	288	5,949	446	1,267	12,911	7,305	9,098
Provo, Utah	8,840	12,363	1,996	8,871	14,775	15,080	1,755	3,811	10,476	8,887	1,929	10,075	2,427	3,225	8,701	3,134	2,679	16,006	8,979	11,145
Puerto Aisen, Chile	12,876	8,399	9,912	14,490	12,332	11,406	8,519	10,167	8,387	12,644	8,353	1,823	8,723	9,932	12,421	10,070	10,740	11,025	15,165	14,663
Puerto Deseado, Argentina	12,651	8,514	10,288	14,265	11,757	10,831	9,000	10,399	8,049	12,414	8,831	1,641	9,106	10,215	12,208	10,359	11,065	10,442	14,931	14,219
Puerto Princesa, Philippines	10,726	7,774	13,570	9,217	8,155	8,899	14,086	13,811	14,163	10,928	14,257	17,173	14,645	13,918	11,195	13,765	12,993	8,679	8,565	8,090
Punta Arenas, Chile	13,307	7,822	10,782	14,917	11,915	10,998	9,347	11,014	8,656	13,070	9,184	2,338	9,592	10,796	12,872	10,935	11,611	10,520	15,575	14,683
Pusan, South Korea	9,236	9,653	10,576	7,621	9,307	10,214	11,339	10,905	13,796	9,472	11,515	19,549	11,677	10,949	9,678	10,793	10,006	10,373	6,954	7,489
Pyongyang, North Korea	8,713	10,174	10,307	7,099	9,037	9,955	11,223	10,519	13,294	8,950	11,398	19,517	11,437	10,600	9,154	10,447	9,677	10,182	6,433	7,026
Qamdo, China	7,475	11,014	11,771	5,973	6,322	7,235	13,282	11,464	11,344	7,680	13,446	17,517	12,961	11,589	7,945	11,464	10,869	7,460	5,330	4,981
Qandahar, Afghanistan	5,054	13,291	11,318	3,913	3,906	4,816	13,392	10,072	8,375	5,209	13,500	14,678	12,342	10,606	5,494	10,538	10,255	5,355	3,469	2,150
Qiqian, China	7,374	11,630	9,097	5,783	8,838	9,760	10,330	9,098	12,078	7,613	10,499	18,066	10,270	9,239	7,794	9,091	8,360	10,194	5,140	6,132
Qom, Iran	3,708	14,628	10,442	2,810	3,653	4,443	12,598	8,990	7,036	3,842	12,676	13,511	11,348	9,572	4,128	9,527	9,377	5,191	2,558	729
Quebec, Canada	5,929	15,525	1,379	6,488	11,824	11,920	3,446	502	7,274	5,913	3,477	9,173	2,053	303	5,680	234	848	12,809	6,850	8,717
Quetta, Pakistan	5,240	13,103	11,502	4,107	3,861	4,779	13,567	10,265	8,492	5,393	13,677	14,735	12,532	10,798	5,678	10,728	10,440	5,286	3,662	2,318
Quito, Ecuador	9,848	11,849	4,882	11,075	13,788	13,144	3,877	5,304	7,555	9,699	3,702	4,485	3,700	4,962	9,413	5,087	5,711	13,468	11,626	12,813
Rabaul, Papua New Guinea	14,201	4,728	12,730	12,585	11,902	12,477	11,853	14,157	18,137	14,434	11,972	14,767	13,203	13,789	14,650	13,647	12,873	11,975	11,912	11,994
Raiatea (Uturoa)	16,349	4,900	9,256	15,880	17,570	17,409	7,256	11,080	15,598	16,415	7,256	9,430	8,807	10,434	16,233	10,405	10,169	16,477	15,608	17,408
Raleigh, North Carolina	7,135	14,437	1,134	7,824	12,868	12,813	2,373	1,631	7,607	7,090	2,352	8,162	802	1,074	6,837	1,161	1,731	13,635	8,211	10,016
Rangiroa (Avatoru)	15,993	5,317	8,844	15,662	18,000	17,758	6,815	10,658	15,233	16,042	6,822	9,213	8,371	10,012	15,846	9,987	9,773	16,827	15,453	17,405
Rangoon, Burma	8,466	9,917	13,368	7,117	5,791	6,625	14,816	12,783	11,605	8,641	14,984	16,621	14,558	13,150	8,922	13,031	12,458	6,618	6,530	5,631
Raoul Is., Kermadec Islands	18,104	2,118	12,162	16,586	14,549	14,574	10,249	14,020	17,132	18,333	10,271	10,645	11,824	13,382	18,406	13,333	12,971	13,690	15,951	16,134
Rarotonga (Avarua)	17,133	3,947	10,215	16,322	16,574	16,510	8,237	12,053	16,304	17,242	8,253	9,851	9,805	11,409	17,101	11,373	11,095	15,591	15,909	17,238
Rawson, Argentina	12,268	8,952	9,830	13,884	11,816	10,889	8,615	9,903	7,742	12,034	8,444	1,210	8,655	9,728	11,818	9,873	10,587	10,567	14,556	14,017
Recife, Brazil	7,379	13,750	7,787	8,995	8,979	8,257	8,142	6,694	3,112	7,145	7,995	3,682	7,051	6,921	6,929	7,076	7,897	8,558	9,667	9,480
Regina, Canada	7,620	13,488	1,514	7,610	13,525	13,879	2,629	2,959	9,741	7,680	2,776	10,581	2,509	2,495	7,508	2,362	1,682	14,812	7,726	9,886
Reykjavik, Iceland	2,832	17,743	4,675	2,971	8,716	9,082	6,841	3,291	6,480	2,927	6,907	11,383	5,582	3,823	2,807	3,763	3,620	10,014	3,318	5,244
Rhodes, Greece	1,882	16,516	9,094	1,942	4,194	4,637	11,240	7,413	5,182	1,943	11,276	11,771	9,799	8,042	2,215	8,032	8,083	5,555	2,261	1,337
Richmond, Virginia	6,930	14,628	1,078	7,604	12,693	12,662	2,539	1,415	7,532	6,889	2,528	8,314	990	851	6,639	940	1,548	13,497	7,988	9,800
Riga, USSR	1,641	17,153	7,249	404	6,373	6,908	9,410	5,835	6,388	1,879	9,483	12,635	8,163	6,396	2,054	6,342	6,186	7,809	843	2,695
Ringkobing, Denmark	1,183	18,086	6,523	1,256	6,845	7,254	8,690	4,985	5,771	1,375	8,746	11,771	7,354	5,576	1,423	5,539	5,482	8,182	1,821	3,412
Rio Branco, Brazil	9,797	11,796	6,215	11,248	12,598	11,847	5,461	6,217	6,572	9,607	5,287	3,002	5,083	6,025	9,332	6,170	6,898	12,042	11,880	12,538
Rio Cuarto, Argentina	11,423	9,918	8,770	13,023	11,972	11,066	7,715	8,775	7,139	11,197	7,541	779	7,609	8,611	10,960	8,758	9,487	10,901	13,698	13,535
Rio de Janeiro, Brazil	9,242	11,897	8,616	10,858	9,962	9,115	8,340	7,945	4,786	9,007	8,170	1,830	7,643	8,016	8,796	8,175	8,996	9,164	11,529	11,176
Rio Gallegos, Argentina	13,112	8,026	10,644	14,723	11,862	10,942	9,252	10,838	8,473	12,875	9,087	2,133	9,456	10,631	12,675	10,772	11,457	10,489	15,384	14,544
Rio Grande, Brazil	10,575	10,612	9,081	12,191	10,839	9,942	8,361	8,747	6,096	10,340	8,185	495	7,987	8,701	10,125	8,857	9,645	9,829	12,862	12,457
Riyadh, Saudi Arabia	4,074	14,320	11,196	3,619	2,501	3,264	13,362	9,584	6,446	4,142	13,413	12,660	11,973	10,203	4,412	10,182	10,154	4,035	3,535	1,342
Road Town, Brit. Virgin Isls.	7,318	14,387	3,497	8,511	12,046	11,667	3,881	3,067	5,982	7,183	3,759	5,970	2,664	2,957	6,899	3,113	3,907	12,290	9,069	10,314

Distances in Kilometers

	Milan, Italy	Milford Sound, New Zealand	Milwaukee, Wisconsin	Minsk, USSR	Mogadiscio, Somalia	Mombasa, Kenya	Monclova, Mexico	Moncton, Canada	Monrovia, Liberia	Monte Carlo, Monaco	Monterrey, Mexico	Montevideo, Uruguay	Montgomery, Alabama	Montpelier, Vermont	Montpellier, France	Montreal, Canada	Moosonee, Canada	Moroni, Comoros	Moscow, USSR	Mosul, Iraq
Roanoke, Virginia	7,122	14,423	933	7,761	12,906	12,883	2,323	1,593	7,745	7,086	2,317	8,358	796	993	6,837	1,055	1,558	13,719	8,130	9,973
Robinson Crusoe Island, Chile	12,442	9,045	8,540	13,986	13,267	12,350	7,111	8,943	8,408	12,229	6,944	2,089	7,349	8,650	11,972	8,780	9,408	12,109	14,645	14,801
Rochester, New York	6,571	14,906	839	7,125	12,447	12,510	2,806	1,068	7,658	6,552	2,833	8,912	1,419	423	6,316	412	932	13,385	7,473	9,361
Rockhampton, Australia	15,762	2,829	14,286	14,220	11,653	11,946	12,867	15,975	17,268	15,966	12,940	12,972	14,410	15,481	16,233	15,364	14,680	11,214	13,553	13,022
Rome, Italy	476	18,001	7,698	1,740	5,500	5,785	9,816	5,964	4,565	462	9,840	11,010	8,340	6,601	729	6,601	6,723	6,718	2,378	2,706
Rosario, Argentina	11,174	10,124	8,861	12,782	11,634	10,731	7,904	8,764	6,827	10,944	7,729	467	7,716	8,635	10,714	8,785	9,534	10,581	13,457	13,216
Roseau, Dominica	7,304	14,388	3,978	8,581	11,753	11,323	4,331	3,430	5,609	7,153	4,202	5,581	3,151	3,380	6,867	3,538	4,346	11,909	9,166	10,269
Rostock, East Germany	981	17,969	6,853	1,011	6,514	6,932	9,019	5,298	5,685	1,201	9,073	11,828	7,672	5,894	1,312	5,860	5,814	7,859	1,633	3,091
Rostov-na-Donu, USSR	2,341	16,055	8,761	1,133	5,035	5,681	10,919	7,329	6,594	2,535	10,995	13,161	9,673	7,901	2,807	7,851	7,697	6,535	959	1,244
Rotterdam, Netherlands	796	18,535	6,556	1,560	6,701	7,037	8,708	4,916	5,248	936	8,750	11,281	7,304	5,531	926	5,511	5,544	7,969	2,197	3,487
Rouyn, Canada	6,345	15,030	902	6,762	12,288	12,438	3,062	1,103	7,881	6,349	3,119	9,482	1,864	664	6,130	513	359	13,341	7,066	9,030
Sacramento, California	9,476	11,622	2,856	9,337	15,308	15,735	2,276	4,646	11,341	9,544	2,448	10,554	3,245	4,076	9,377	3,978	3,463	16,668	9,365	11,561
Saginaw, Michigan	6,966	14,460	326	7,417	12,885	12,985	2,419	1,541	8,169	6,960	2,469	9,119	1,244	917	6,733	853	907	13,870	7,721	9,682
Saint Denis, Reunion	8,708	10,043	15,825	8,705	2,765	2,526	17,586	13,971	7,835	8,670	17,500	10,528	16,036	14,608	8,867	14,657	14,938	1,650	8,656	6,462
Saint George's, Grenada	7,580	14,100	4,260	8,891	11,830	11,353	4,453	3,786	5,628	7,422	4,315	5,228	3,371	3,718	7,137	3,875	4,676	11,895	9,485	10,523
Saint John, Canada	5,665	15,850	1,761	6,333	11,502	11,558	3,736	135	6,838	5,633	3,750	8,932	2,256	529	5,390	592	1,270	12,436	6,737	8,520
Saint John's, Antigua	7,203	14,495	3,787	8,452	11,776	11,374	4,209	3,227	5,675	7,058	4,085	5,784	2,985	3,176	6,772	3,334	4,142	11,982	9,028	10,182
Saint John's, Canada	4,629	16,905	2,781	5,403	10,448	10,519	4,791	934	6,057	4,589	4,802	9,139	3,291	1,579	4,341	1,614	2,055	11,407	5,862	7,530
Saint Louis, Missouri	7,712	13,736	527	8,156	13,616	13,678	1,669	2,240	8,655	7,704	1,722	8,861	776	1,596	7,473	1,568	1,593	14,545	8,444	10,427
Saint Paul, Minnesota	7,421	13,902	467	7,697	13,383	13,568	2,136	2,204	8,911	7,441	2,235	9,593	1,513	1,626	7,232	1,529	1,162	14,476	7,927	9,988
Saint Peter Port, UK	988	19,102	6,263	2,123	6,933	7,185	8,387	4,546	4,844	991	8,416	10,737	6,932	5,178	815	5,173	5,290	8,116	2,765	3,933
Saipan (Susupe)	11,998	6,982	11,568	10,386	11,069	11,858	11,413	12,566	16,508	12,236	11,570	16,924	12,382	12,372	12,435	12,215	11,389	11,671	9,720	10,115
Salalah, Oman	5,215	13,188	12,313	4,692	1,908	2,818	14,481	10,724	7,146	5,279	14,539	12,907	13,113	11,340	5,547	11,317	11,262	3,389	4,523	2,400
Salem, Oregon	8,945	12,036	2,803	8,702	14,673	15,172	2,778	4,449	11,226	9,031	2,953	11,111	3,450	3,940	8,884	3,821	3,187	16,096	8,698	10,897
Salt Lake City, Utah	8,806	12,387	1,998	8,825	14,735	15,050	1,814	3,803	10,482	8,855	1,987	10,131	2,459	3,223	8,671	3,129	2,660	15,977	8,929	11,097
Salta, Argentina	10,822	10,622	7,855	12,386	12,209	11,342	6,903	7,850	6,842	10,606	6,728	1,430	6,704	7,680	10,353	7,827	8,557	11,305	13,053	13,203
Salto, Uruguay	10,875	10,405	8,790	12,485	11,400	10,505	7,931	8,608	6,519	10,645	7,755	422	7,663	8,507	10,416	8,660	9,424	10,387	13,160	12,910
Salvador, Brazil	8,052	13,101	7,983	9,668	9,407	8,637	8,100	7,053	3,735	7,818	7,943	3,009	7,146	7,216	7,601	7,374	8,202	8,854	10,340	10,126
Salzburg, Austria	392	18,047	7,320	1,224	5,944	6,305	9,470	5,665	5,125	628	9,510	11,452	8,054	6,286	851	6,269	6,309	7,236	1,897	2,774
Samsun, Turkey	2,236	16,099	9,129	1,547	4,437	5,031	11,296	7,579	6,057	2,380	11,356	12,647	9,959	8,181	2,665	8,148	8,079	5,907	1,611	806
San Antonio, Texas	8,974	12,515	1,782	9,423	14,831	14,801	401	3,461	9,450	8,957	453	8,390	1,210	2,818	8,720	2,814	2,845	15,612	9,691	11,699
San Cristobal, Venezuela	8,731	12,969	4,198	9,952	13,024	12,492	3,738	4,308	6,784	8,587	3,576	5,013	3,090	4,044	8,301	4,184	4,887	12,959	10,509	11,709
San Diego, California	9,804	11,434	2,798	9,827	15,743	16,029	1,650	4,656	11,147	9,847	1,811	9,823	2,887	4,039	9,656	3,969	3,603	16,946	9,914	12,092
San Francisco, California	9,595	11,501	2,965	9,447	15,419	15,854	2,308	4,761	11,446	9,664	2,478	10,556	3,326	4,188	9,498	4,092	3,582	16,786	9,469	11,666
San Jose, Costa Rica	9,485	12,216	3,687	10,494	14,278	13,795	2,616	4,409	8,072	9,375	2,443	5,766	2,496	3,963	9,094	4,068	4,596	14,284	10,968	12,491
San Juan, Argentina	11,571	9,837	8,491	13,152	12,390	11,487	7,350	8,606	7,417	11,350	7,177	1,207	7,318	8,403	11,104	8,546	9,251	11,330	13,823	13,815
San Juan, Puerto Rico	7,434	14,272	3,410	8,606	12,202	11,825	3,732	3,067	6,140	7,303	3,608	5,997	2,542	2,923	7,019	3,077	3,860	12,448	9,155	10,434
San Luis Potosi, Mexico	9,740	11,799	2,614	10,252	15,492	15,339	528	4,207	9,773	9,710	395	7,889	1,840	3,576	9,464	3,590	3,681	16,063	10,531	12,519
San Marino, San Marino	311	18,056	7,555	1,562	5,659	5,969	9,685	5,844	4,745	407	9,714	11,150	8,227	6,477	692	6,472	6,567	6,902	2,215	2,728
San Miguel de Tucuman, Argen.	10,973	10,448	8,076	12,547	12,160	11,282	7,097	8,075	6,912	10,754	6,922	1,242	6,923	7,906	10,504	8,053	8,783	11,213	13,216	13,294
San Salvador, El Salvador	9,578	12,096	3,254	10,444	14,726	14,323	1,937	4,259	8,603	9,491	1,763	6,409	2,090	3,738	9,217	3,820	4,239	14,876	10,862	12,555
Sanaa, Yemen	4,672	13,840	11,913	4,516	1,475	2,203	14,045	10,192	6,081	4,689	14,070	11,909	12,558	10,831	4,932	10,831	10,906	2,992	4,519	2,327
Santa Cruz, Bolivia	10,095	11,391	7,197	11,635	12,051	11,234	6,444	7,078	6,342	9,885	6,270	2,016	6,076	6,938	9,624	7,088	7,841	11,317	12,296	12,605
Santa Cruz, Tenerife	2,927	18,180	6,483	4,524	7,143	6,974	8,206	4,642	2,516	2,706	8,161	8,172	6,625	5,241	2,460	5,321	5,845	7,788	5,199	5,568
Santa Fe, New Mexico	8,917	12,418	1,751	9,125	14,880	15,046	1,064	3,611	10,070	8,938	1,234	9,365	1,847	2,982	8,728	2,923	2,658	15,939	9,300	11,417
Santa Rosa, Argentina	11,697	9,602	9,141	13,305	11,899	10,983	8,036	9,161	7,315	11,467	7,862	757	7,975	8,996	11,237	9,143	9,868	10,764	13,981	13,687
Santa Rosalia, Mexico	10,017	11,351	2,805	10,216	15,976	16,084	1,078	4,641	10,820	10,033	1,207	9,068	2,565	4,000	9,819	3,960	3,758	16,940	10,368	12,506
Santarem, Brazil	8,208	13,318	6,036	9,719	11,148	10,485	5,971	5,467	4,974	8,006	5,813	3,596	5,094	5,470	7,738	5,629	6,441	10,831	10,373	10,875
Santiago del Estero, Argentina	10,987	10,413	8,207	12,569	12,052	11,170	7,239	8,182	6,871	10,765	7,064	1,100	7,056	8,022	10,519	8,170	8,905	11,089	13,240	13,262
Santiago, Chile	11,864	9,545	8,650	13,445	12,541	11,631	7,428	8,830	7,686	11,643	7,257	1,344	7,469	8,608	11,397	8,748	9,437	11,435	14,116	14,086
Santo Domingo, Dominican Rep.	7,729	13,977	3,209	8,845	12,596	12,224	3,360	3,101	6,538	7,607	3,231	6,080	2,253	2,871	7,324	3,017	3,762	12,847	9,374	10,735
Sao Paulo de Olivenca, Brazil	9,351	12,292	5,496	10,734	12,717	12,037	4,855	5,503	6,536	9,174	4,684	3,716	4,376	5,298	8,893	5,443	6,169	12,334	11,345	12,199
Sao Paulo, Brazil	9,498	11,695	8,498	11,114	10,310	9,459	8,115	7,927	5,105	9,265	7,944	1,563	7,490	7,960	9,046	8,119	8,932	9,493	11,787	11,501
Sao Tome, Sao Tome & Principe	5,006	14,761	10,365	6,240	4,304	3,695	11,795	8,567	2,057	4,808	11,706	7,591	10,281	9,134	4,801	9,230	9,798	4,252	6,746	5,475
Sapporo, Japan	9,120	10,056	9,283	7,560	10,342	11,267	9,960	9,798	13,862	9,359	10,135	18,255	10,350	9,764	9,517	9,606	8,795	11,543	6,937	7,950
Sarajevo, Yugoslavia	753	17,586	7,924	1,303	5,338	5,715	10,071	6,252	5,041	885	10,108	11,526	8,640	6,877	1,170	6,865	6,916	6,644	1,901	2,256
Saratov, USSR	2,773	15,726	8,623	1,270	5,487	6,193	10,750	7,329	7,214	2,990	10,841	13,750	9,610	7,864	3,243	7,790	7,555	7,012	726	1,708
Saskatoon, Canada	7,581	13,473	1,724	7,511	13,452	13,842	2,834	3,083	9,856	7,651	2,985	10,814	2,740	2,650	7,488	2,511	1,789	14,774	7,604	9,776
Schefferville, Canada	5,259	16,026	2,010	5,650	11,219	11,429	4,176	979	7,312	5,277	4,234	9,989	2,924	1,243	5,070	1,141	1,004	12,348	5,970	7,915
Seattle, Washington	8,666	12,283	2,723	8,404	14,374	14,882	2,933	4,290	11,072	8,756	3,107	11,258	3,466	3,810	8,614	3,683	3,009	15,804	8,398	10,597
Sendai, Japan	9,553	9,564	9,748	7,973	10,354	11,270	10,317	10,318	14,274	9,792	10,492	18,455	10,791	10,269	9,962	10,110	9,295	11,469	7,335	8,209
Seoul, South Korea	8,907	9,980	10,408	7,293	9,135	10,050	11,268	10,664	13,480	9,144	11,444	19,602	11,529	10,731	9,349	10,577	9,800	10,252	6,626	7,196
Sept-Iles, Canada	5,436	15,973	1,822	5,968	11,358	11,494	3,940	471	7,072	5,430	3,978	9,478	2,572	809	5,203	751	1,013	12,397	6,332	8,201
Sevastopol, USSR	1,913	16,436	8,698	1,121	4,854	5,423	10,866	7,164	6,034	2,082	10,927	12,605	9,539	7,761	2,364	7,725	7,647	6,310	1,273	1,225
Seville, Spain	1,550	19,055	6,719	3,149	6,536	6,580	8,692	4,872	3,475	1,334	8,684	9,536	7,135	5,515	1,083	5,554	5,882	7,477	3,824	4,331
Shanghai, China	9,121	9,614	11,269	7,512	8,563	9,457	12,148	11,431	13,464	9,351	12,323	19,534	12,400	11,539	9,581	11,387	10,626	9,571	6,837	7,072
Sheffield, United Kingdom	1,170	18,760	6,123	1,910	7,120	7,431	8,273	4,479	5,285	1,255	8,314	11,107	6,867	5,094	1,156	5,075	5,116	8,364	2,509	3,918
Shenyang, China	8,352	10,539	10,099	6,738	8,871	9,795	11,115	10,234	12,950	8,589	11,289	19,236	11,247	10,339	8,792	10,188	9,431	10,069	6,074	6,718
Shiraz, Iran	4,152	14,189	11,008	3,368	3,140	3,969	13,168	9,523	7,094	4,266	13,242	13,424	11,893	10,115	4,549	10,074	9,945	4,675	3,137	1,152
Sibiu, Romania	1,165	17,184	8,103	934	5,269	5,732	10,266	6,501	5,518	1,342	10,315	12,024	8,887	7,112	1,620	7,086	7,069	6,649	1,452	1,903
Singapore	10,273	8,081	14,958	8,996	6,508	7,165	15,887	14,639	12,728	10,431	16,061	15,754	16,130	14,947	10,715	14,816	14,164	6,851	8,426	7,335
Sioux Falls, South Dakota	7,741	13,572	718	7,983	13,704	13,898	1,894	2,526	9,203	7,763	2,010	9,609	1,538	1,935	7,556	1,846	1,483	14,805	8,194	10,276
Skelleftea, Sweden	2,267	16,974	6,568	1,266	7,229	7,787	8,704	5,314	6,954	2,489	8,791	12,884	7,557	5,825	2,587	5,752	5,500	8,683	1,355	3,490
Skopje, Yugoslavia	1,061	17,291	8,246	1,398	5,026	5,422	10,393	6,574	5,077	1,164	10,430	11,616	8,961	7,200	1,448	7,187	7,236	6,348	1,922	1,968
Socotra Island (Tamrida)	5,569	12,868	12,729	5,134	1,510	2,435	14,894	11,098	7,136	5,618	14,943	12,645	13,486	11,723	5,877	11,707	11,686	2,942	4,989	2,841
Sofia, Bulgaria	1,171	17,169	8,300	1,286	5,006	5,432	10,454	6,650	5,240	1,295	10,496	11,784	9,039	7,272	1,581	7,255	7,281	6,355	1,779	1,839
Songkhla, Thailand	9,554	8,808	14,376	8,255	6,151	6,883	15,555	13,926	12,273	9,717	15,730	16,136	15,564	14,265	10,001	14,139	13,524	6,683	7,680	6,644
Sorong, Indonesia	12,521	6,031	13,937	10,981	9,565	10,188	13,714	14,758	15,780	12,728	13,861	15,971	14,763	14,658	12,991	14,499	13,672	9,779	10,318	9,902
South Georgia Island	11,874	8,808	11,826	13,363	9,681	8,762	10,908	11,433	7,136	11,640	10,734	2,630	10,711	11,434	11,510	11,591	12,389	8,314	13,940	12,596
South Pole	15,041	5,062	14,769	15,979	10,232	9,556	12,979	15,110	10,703	14,848	12,842	6,142	13,587	14,906	14,834	15,043	15,686	8,712	16,185	14,026
South Sandwich Islands	11,908	8,585	12,536	13,304	9,136	8,230	11,656	12,043	7,242	11,681	11,482	3,365	11,437	12,086	11,582	12,245	13,054	7,718	13,826	12,271
Split, Yugoslavia	615	17,734	7,828	1,412	5,411	5,761	9,968	6,138	4,908	728	10,001	11,375	8,524	6,767	1,013	6,758	6,828	6,692	2,031	2,405
Spokane, Washington	8,452	12,560	2,352	8,275	14,246	14,699	2,694	3,937	10,718	8,532	2,866	10,987	3,119	3,446	8,378	3,321	2,665	15,629	8,307	10,501
Spoleto, Italy	415	18,006	7,655	1,652	5,550	5,849	9,779	5,932	4,651	446	9,806	11,084	8,312	6,567	726	6,565	6,673	6,782	2,296	2,692
Springbok, South Africa	8,366	11,236	13,415	9,305	4,570	3,648	14,135	11,799	5,026	8,197	13,987	6,841	12,942	12,277	8,238	12,402	13,090	3,296	9,648	7,769
Springfield, Illinois	7,589	13,847	388	8,020	13,503	13,581	1,798	2,136	8,612	7,584	1,856	8,955	876	1,495	7,355	1,457	1,455	14,454	8,305	10,293
Springfield, Massachusetts	6,298	15,230	1,261	6,949	12,116	12,141	3,115	766	7,230	6,264	3,123	8,687	1,623	240	6,019	386	1,191	13,003	7,336	9,149
Srinagar, India	5,602	12,783	11,287	4,274	4,682	5,606	13,243	10,245	9,220	5,782	13,372	15,570	12,388	10,725	6,061	10,637	10,249	6,066	3,725	2,883
Stanley, Falkland Islands	12,533	8,474	10,891	14,124	11,098	10,175	9,691	10,858	7,828	12,294	9,521	1,873	9,721	10,727	12,114	10,876	11,614	9,751	14,766	13,781
Stara Zagora, Bulgaria	1,360	16,978	8,454	1,285	4,883	5,338	10,612	6,820	5,370	1,488	10,657	11,929	9,209	7,439	1,773	7,419	7,429	6,255	1,715	1,648
Stockholm, Sweden	1,653	17,400	6,805	840	6,776	7,282	8,967	5,399	6,373	1,881	9,039	12,456	7,721	5,955	1,999	5,900	5,743	8,192	1,231	3,133
Stornoway, United Kingdom	1,770	18,436	5,626	2,143	7,676	8,021	7,790	4,071	5,770	1,872	7,842	11,310	6,440	4,662	1,774	4,626	4,596	8,954	2,638	4,324
Strasbourg, France	364	18,431	6,953	1,499	6,281	6,603	9,095	5,276	5,002	540	9,131	11,204	7,665	5,901	629	5,888	5,953	7,535	2,171	3,176
Stuttgart, West Germany	367	18,323	7,027	1,397	6,219	6,555	9,174	5,362	5,069	576	9,212	11,298	7,751	5,985	705	5,970	6,022	7,488	2,071	3,077
Subic, Philippines	10,406	8,153	12,981	8,857	8,331	9,121	13,567	13,233	14,143	10,617	13,740	17,761	14,065	13,328	10,876	13,175	12,401	8,979	8,194	7,902
Suchow, China	8,599	10,119	11,074	6,992	8,216	9,124	12,113	11,102	12,950	8,828	12,287	19,415	12,231	11,253	9,060	11,104	10,369	9,300	6,317	6,564
Sucre, Bolivia	10,347	11,151	7,253	11,880	12,263	11,435	6,406	7,213	6,599	10,138	6,231	1,973	6,115	7,048	9,876	7,195	7,933	11,491	12,538	12,867
Sudbury, Canada	6,577	14,817	669	7,006	12,513	12,646	2,821	1,248	7,991	6,578	2,877	9,351	1,632	705	6,356	584	533	13,543	7,309	9,273
Suez, Egypt	2,665	15,796	9,902	2,689	3,372	3,840	12,039	8,196	5,234	2,695	12,069	11,740	10,574	8,830	2,950	8,826	8,898	4,750	2,892	1,213
Sundsvall, Sweden	1,953	17,269	6,574	1,119	7,087	7,609	8,727	5,236	6,632	2,173	8,806	12,597	7,524	5,771	2,266	5,708	5,508	8,516	1,369	3,401

Distances in Kilometers

	Milan, Italy	Milford Sound, New Zealand	Milwaukee, Wisconsin	Minsk, USSR	Mogadiscio, Somalia	Mombasa, Kenya	Monclova, Mexico	Moncton, Canada	Monrovia, Liberia	Monte Carlo, Monaco	Monterrey, Mexico	Montevideo, Uruguay	Montgomery, Alabama	Montpelier, Vermont	Montpellier, France	Montreal, Canada	Moosonee, Canada	Moroni, Comoros	Moscow, USSR	Mosul, Iraq
Surabaya, Indonesia	11,639	6,718	15,558	10,340	7,555	8,097	15,813	15,693	13,800	11,797	15,970	15,200	16,603	15,871	12,082	15,722	14,970	7,629	9,754	8,698
Suva, Fiji	16,815	3,096	11,657	15,318	14,611	14,881	9,980	13,501	18,370	17,045	10,036	11,791	11,554	12,900	17,135	12,820	12,317	14,098	14,700	15,212
Sverdlovsk, USSR	3,710	14,956	8,550	2,099	6,224	7,013	10,572	7,522	8,295	3,942	10,687	14,768	9,638	7,981	4,167	7,889	7,504	7,762	1,423	2,627
Svobodnyy, USSR	7,784	11,299	8,979	6,210	9,327	10,252	10,075	9,130	12,513	8,023	10,248	18,138	10,133	9,219	8,192	9,067	8,307	10,662	5,580	6,638
Sydney, Australia	16,555	1,854	14,872	15,133	11,603	11,725	13,147	16,697	16,440	16,722	13,186	11,878	14,730	16,113	17,006	16,026	15,460	10,900	14,487	13,619
Sydney, Canada	5,214	16,315	2,217	5,936	11,036	11,093	4,201	356	6,463	5,177	4,212	8,984	2,704	995	4,930	1,044	1,604	11,974	6,367	8,095
Syktyvkar, USSR	3,210	15,604	7,820	1,617	6,627	7,350	9,876	6,751	7,921	3,449	9,985	14,229	8,890	7,217	3,642	7,128	6,766	8,159	1,007	2,868
Szeged, Hungary	856	17,497	7,844	1,000	5,476	5,897	10,002	6,217	5,332	1,043	10,047	11,792	8,605	6,833	1,317	6,812	6,819	6,821	1,607	2,206
Szombathely, Hungary	603	17,777	7,569	1,071	5,723	6,114	9,724	5,930	5,234	817	9,767	11,630	8,319	6,548	1,074	6,529	6,550	7,042	1,727	2,497
Tabriz, Iran	3,161	15,175	9,906	2,265	3,989	4,715	12,067	8,432	6,725	3,304	12,140	13,279	10,795	9,018	3,590	8,975	8,843	5,518	2,069	342
Tacheng, China	5,484	13,086	10,017	3,918	6,142	7,049	11,837	9,247	9,788	5,704	11,978	16,378	11,175	9,640	5,953	9,531	9,029	7,582	3,256	3,475
Tahiti (Papeete)	16,340	4,970	9,193	15,961	17,655	17,416	7,156	11,003	15,386	16,392	7,161	9,216	8,708	10,358	16,197	10,333	10,124	16,484	15,720	17,582
Taipei, Taiwan	9,639	9,033	11,889	8,044	8,521	9,385	12,650	12,100	13,805	9,864	12,825	18,893	13,002	12,198	10,104	12,045	11,276	9,401	7,370	7,413
Taiyuan, China	8,022	10,685	10,810	6,415	7,879	8,799	12,012	10,701	12,393	8,251	12,184	18,961	11,987	10,894	8,483	10,751	10,045	9,047	5,740	6,023
Tallahassee, Florida	7,920	13,670	1,434	8,611	13,591	13,473	1,718	2,422	8,077	7,870	1,661	7,809	289	1,847	7,613	1,913	2,334	14,254	8,987	10,807
Tallinn, USSR	1,868	17,043	7,096	638	6,606	7,159	9,249	5,739	6,617	2,105	9,327	12,794	8,041	6,283	2,259	6,223	6,029	8,055	868	2,890
Tamanrasset, Algeria	2,538	17,102	8,584	3,920	4,874	4,753	10,435	6,722	2,527	2,330	10,401	9,117	8,853	7,353	2,314	7,410	7,805	5,611	4,508	3,912
Tampa, Florida	7,974	13,649	1,745	8,739	13,538	13,366	1,877	2,543	7,886	7,911	1,793	7,484	616	2,013	7,649	2,099	2,595	14,116	9,141	10,900
Tampere, Finland	2,019	17,015	6,903	876	6,840	7,397	9,050	5,586	6,755	2,251	9,132	12,847	7,867	6,118	2,384	6,053	5,836	8,293	1,024	3,111
Tanami, Australia	13,935	4,441	15,682	12,570	9,504	9,870	14,784	16,823	15,508	14,100	14,886	13,901	16,196	16,620	14,384	16,465	15,644	9,214	11,952	11,009
Tangier, Morocco	1,657	18,892	6,830	3,267	6,451	6,470	8,782	4,978	3,305	1,432	8,769	9,411	7,218	5,619	1,198	5,663	6,010	7,360	3,942	4,360
Tarawa (Betio)	14,578	5,114	10,653	13,102	14,190	14,834	9,516	12,317	19,067	14,808	9,625	13,731	10,944	11,826	14,908	11,706	11,026	14,363	12,504	13,367
Tashkent, USSR	4,776	13,646	10,386	3,373	4,967	5,857	12,390	9,307	8,724	4,971	12,510	15,267	11,470	9,791	5,243	9,706	9,339	6,450	2,799	2,329
Tbilisi, USSR	2,878	15,470	9,495	1,860	4,390	5,092	11,654	8,047	6,722	3,041	11,729	13,308	10,399	8,625	3,324	8,578	8,431	5,912	1,647	612
Tegucigalpa, Honduras	9,396	12,283	3,208	10,293	14,507	14,105	2,047	4,123	8,387	9,306	1,874	6,336	2,027	3,621	9,030	3,710	4,166	14,665	10,725	12,381
Tehran, Iran	3,691	14,645	10,367	2,744	3,773	4,565	12,519	8,933	7,105	3,833	12,599	13,599	11,284	9,511	4,118	9,463	9,301	5,311	2,468	752
Tel Aviv, Israel	2,656	15,751	9,852	2,493	3,502	4,031	12,004	8,185	5,515	2,714	12,043	12,041	10,571	8,812	2,982	8,800	8,831	4,925	2,641	904
Telegraph Creek, Canada	7,978	12,681	3,407	7,462	13,349	13,979	4,156	4,541	11,129	8,106	4,327	12,410	4,397	4,221	8,011	4,069	3,266	14,855	7,363	9,548
Teresina, Brazil	7,605	13,718	6,997	9,199	9,838	9,148	7,226	6,072	3,775	7,381	7,075	3,575	6,191	6,224	7,139	6,382	7,210	9,479	9,873	9,983
Ternate, Indonesia	12,101	6,418	14,014	10,581	9,130	9,774	13,970	14,674	15,326	12,305	14,124	16,213	14,915	14,637	12,571	14,478	13,659	9,397	9,923	9,446
The Valley, Anguilla	7,227	14,476	3,626	8,447	11,890	11,503	4,050	3,115	5,814	7,087	3,928	5,903	2,819	3,040	6,802	3,197	4,001	12,123	9,014	10,216
Thessaloniki, Greece	1,239	17,127	8,439	1,515	4,832	5,234	10,585	6,762	5,070	1,325	10,621	11,633	9,149	7,389	1,606	7,378	7,430	6,160	1,994	1,821
Thimphu, Bhutan	7,176	11,236	12,187	5,776	5,495	6,405	13,866	11,456	10,722	7,363	14,021	16,694	13,360	11,854	7,640	11,744	11,223	6,628	5,176	4,468
Thunder Bay, Canada	6,953	14,339	606	7,217	12,917	13,127	2,607	1,867	8,639	6,977	2,700	9,795	1,797	1,365	6,773	1,237	700	14,042	7,453	9,508
Tientsin, China	8,209	10,568	10,560	6,594	8,304	9,225	11,672	10,562	12,679	8,442	11,845	19,264	11,725	10,716	8,663	10,569	9,838	9,476	5,921	6,347
Tijuana, Mexico	9,813	11,429	2,798	9,842	15,755	16,035	1,631	4,657	11,140	9,856	1,792	9,800	2,877	4,039	9,664	3,969	3,609	16,952	9,930	12,108
Tiksi, USSR	6,185	13,249	6,964	4,807	9,556	10,398	8,419	6,905	10,873	6,414	8,578	15,908	8,151	7,043	6,517	6,896	6,177	11,072	4,317	6,068
Timbuktu, Mali	3,380	16,804	8,349	4,894	5,538	5,228	9,986	6,515	1,434	3,148	9,925	8,013	8,417	7,107	3,046	7,192	7,715	5,987	5,518	5,024
Tindouf, Algeria	2,498	18,097	7,174	4,112	6,353	6,215	8,966	5,317	2,383	2,261	8,928	8,574	7,384	5,934	2,069	6,003	6,466	7,050	4,780	4,882
Tirane, Albania	975	17,399	8,198	1,511	5,047	5,415	10,338	6,506	4,926	1,053	10,371	11,461	8,891	7,136	1,334	7,127	7,197	6,344	2,058	2,091
Tokyo, Japan	9,741	9,330	10,040	8,149	10,278	11,188	10,570	10,618	14,436	9,980	10,745	18,575	11,075	10,569	10,158	10,409	9,594	11,345	7,502	8,284
Toledo, Spain	1,247	19,161	6,710	2,832	6,501	6,599	8,730	4,883	3,778	1,042	8,730	9,858	7,190	5,528	777	5,557	5,834	7,509	3,508	4,107
Topeka, Kansas	8,025	13,368	788	8,366	13,967	14,081	1,450	2,635	9,131	8,030	1,547	9,140	1,124	2,001	7,810	1,949	1,794	14,963	8,610	10,653
Toronto, Canada	6,655	14,801	695	7,171	12,551	12,630	2,718	1,183	7,810	6,642	2,753	9,011	1,391	550	6,409	502	852	13,510	7,504	9,419
Toulouse, France	651	18,924	6,861	2,218	6,320	6,520	8,948	5,087	4,301	483	8,964	10,469	7,448	5,729	198	5,739	5,921	7,446	2,893	3,613
Tours, France	688	18,974	6,584	2,020	6,607	6,854	8,701	4,853	4,682	664	8,727	10,731	7,234	5,488	489	5,487	5,617	7,785	2,685	3,680
Townsville, Australia	15,167	3,417	14,299	13,623	11,294	11,658	13,069	15,866	17,212	15,372	13,157	13,543	14,565	15,439	15,637	15,308	14,569	10,979	12,956	12,456
Trenton, New Jersey	6,566	14,975	1,138	7,226	12,363	12,365	2,865	1,040	7,359	6,530	2,867	8,532	1,352	483	6,282	594	1,311	13,217	7,611	9,425
Tripoli, Lebanon	2,569	15,802	9,706	2,259	3,717	4,278	11,866	8,073	5,706	2,651	11,912	12,258	10,462	8,694	2,928	8,675	8,674	5,164	2,373	694
Tripoli, Libya	1,437	17,474	8,400	2,596	4,789	4,953	10,448	6,593	3,850	1,303	10,451	10,424	8,912	7,238	1,438	7,260	7,482	5,879	3,164	2,762
Tristan da Cunha (Edinburgh)	9,391	10,964	11,705	10,780	7,348	6,424	11,685	10,600	4,803	9,166	11,518	3,931	10,867	10,859	9,080	11,014	11,831	6,194	11,317	9,934
Trondheim, Norway	2,000	17,469	6,216	1,445	7,382	7,873	8,373	4,868	6,564	2,199	8,449	12,368	7,158	5,404	2,245	5,341	5,151	8,788	1,738	3,738
Trujillo, Peru	10,511	11,163	5,736	11,820	13,841	13,099	4,566	6,170	7,741	10,345	4,391	3,772	4,548	5,837	10,062	5,963	6,583	13,282	12,397	13,412
Truk Island (Moen)	13,072	5,978	11,805	11,462	11,808	12,524	11,277	13,055	17,572	13,310	11,418	15,838	12,453	12,759	13,503	12,609	11,804	12,202	10,799	11,172
Truro, Canada	5,467	16,061	1,979	6,170	11,290	11,340	3,946	143	6,642	5,432	3,956	8,916	2,450	746	5,185	808	1,442	12,217	6,590	8,341
Tsingtao, China	8,646	10,133	10,791	7,031	8,526	9,439	11,781	10,890	13,093	8,878	11,956	19,680	11,938	11,014	9,100	10,864	10,114	9,633	6,357	6,737
Tsitsihar, China	7,918	11,054	9,513	6,316	8,982	9,909	10,613	9,614	12,593	8,156	10,785	18,618	10,670	9,725	8,344	9,575	8,824	10,266	5,664	6,616
Tubuai Island (Mataura)	16,894	4,526	9,678	16,606	17,166	16,817	7,592	11,454	15,223	16,920	7,583	8,847	9,115	10,810	16,702	10,797	10,641	15,890	16,363	18,135
Tucson, Arizona	9,507	11,816	2,352	9,666	15,472	15,649	1,097	4,210	10,592	9,532	1,266	9,378	2,318	3,578	9,325	3,522	3,252	16,539	9,811	11,954
Tulsa, Oklahoma	8,266	13,165	1,026	8,653	14,185	14,253	1,152	2,814	9,163	8,263	1,237	8,879	978	2,170	8,036	2,138	2,073	15,116	8,910	10,936
Tunis, Tunisia	966	17,948	7,909	2,325	5,273	5,460	9,975	6,115	3,993	805	9,984	10,494	8,453	6,759	926	6,776	6,979	6,388	2,946	2,935
Tura, USSR	5,628	13,422	8,084	4,071	8,179	9,044	9,722	7,696	10,368	5,866	9,874	16,368	9,273	7,954	6,033	7,820	7,189	9,679	3,463	4,863
Turin, Italy	129	18,452	7,176	1,737	6,023	6,299	9,297	5,451	4,650	148	9,324	10,940	7,831	6,085	342	6,083	6,199	7,232	2,410	3,122
Uberlandia, Brazil	9,191	12,080	7,969	10,799	10,477	9,659	7,654	7,391	4,972	8,962	7,485	1,931	6,975	7,421	8,731	7,580	8,394	9,763	11,474	11,360
Ufa, USSR	3,427	15,171	8,642	1,836	5,918	6,687	10,705	7,521	7,954	3,655	10,813	14,464	9,701	8,007	3,891	7,924	7,585	7,456	1,169	2,268
Ujungpandang, Indonesia	11,985	6,416	15,024	10,585	8,271	8,843	15,074	15,445	14,522	12,162	15,227	15,553	15,985	15,514	12,443	15,357	14,562	8,396	9,964	9,128
Ulaanbaatar, Mongolia	6,938	11,847	9,825	5,322	7,752	8,677	11,251	9,557	11,483	7,172	11,415	17,997	11,015	9,792	7,388	9,655	8,988	9,092	4,650	5,269
Ulan-Ude, USSR	6,714	12,142	9,387	5,101	7,955	8,874	10,835	9,128	11,338	6,951	10,998	17,726	10,577	9,357	7,154	9,218	8,550	9,339	4,437	5,254
Uliastay, Mongolia	6,337	12,353	9,936	4,729	7,060	7,980	11,539	9,454	10,788	6,566	11,696	17,364	11,124	9,758	6,797	9,631	9,027	8,440	4,054	4,524
Uranium City, Canada	7,063	13,811	2,317	6,831	12,803	13,279	3,671	3,232	9,843	7,158	3,820	11,522	3,443	2,950	7,024	2,794	1,975	14,204	6,872	9,063
Urumqi, China	5,962	12,597	10,375	4,403	6,219	7,139	12,123	9,681	10,197	6,180	12,271	16,775	11,546	10,054	6,431	9,940	9,408	7,607	3,743	3,834
Ushuaia, Argentina	13,283	7,790	11,001	14,882	11,692	10,778	9,590	11,187	8,596	13,044	9,426	2,404	9,812	10,986	12,855	11,127	11,815	10,286	15,531	14,535
Vaduz, Liechtenstein	191	18,314	7,152	1,477	6,077	6,397	9,291	5,465	4,926	415	9,325	11,202	7,853	6,093	593	6,082	6,155	7,330	2,152	3,014
Valencia, Spain	1,030	18,886	6,995	2,643	6,204	6,326	9,030	5,177	3,818	803	9,033	10,033	7,496	5,823	580	5,848	6,102	7,241	3,317	3,805
Valladolid, Spain	1,200	19,327	6,554	2,742	6,644	6,765	8,592	4,738	3,961	1,020	8,597	9,970	7,063	5,383	738	5,407	5,664	7,679	3,415	4,134
Valletta, Malta	1,153	17,564	8,268	2,242	4,913	5,141	10,350	6,489	4,173	1,060	10,363	10,729	8,838	7,132	1,248	7,145	7,321	6,072	2,815	2,567
Valparaiso, Chile	11,898	9,527	8,586	13,473	12,640	11,730	7,344	8,791	7,752	11,678	7,172	1,441	7,403	8,560	11,429	8,699	9,382	11,536	14,142	14,151
Vancouver, Canada	8,542	12,369	2,779	8,247	14,212	14,739	3,104	4,285	11,060	8,637	3,277	11,420	3,575	3,828	8,501	3,695	2,994	15,655	8,229	10,428
Varna, Bulgaria	1,510	16,826	8,517	1,188	4,876	5,367	10,681	6,912	5,572	1,655	10,730	12,135	9,300	7,525	1,940	7,501	7,483	6,277	1,557	1,508
Venice, Italy	246	18,090	7,441	1,440	5,788	6,115	9,579	5,749	4,879	436	9,612	11,249	8,135	6,378	703	6,369	6,445	7,048	2,104	2,764
Veracruz, Mexico	9,645	11,957	2,754	10,298	15,206	14,950	1,010	4,139	9,300	9,593	835	7,326	1,760	3,538	9,334	3,580	3,811	15,609	10,634	12,521
Verona, Italy	141	18,195	7,358	1,515	5,862	6,176	9,492	5,657	4,821	343	9,524	11,167	8,043	6,288	602	6,280	6,367	7,108	2,183	2,868
Victoria, Canada	8,628	12,292	2,797	8,339	14,305	14,829	3,053	4,331	11,111	8,723	3,227	11,377	3,566	3,865	8,585	3,734	3,044	15,747	8,322	10,521
Victoria, Seychelles	7,192	11,387	14,437	6,987	1,343	1,753	16,538	12,677	7,462	7,193	16,542	11,665	14,997	13,321	7,423	13,332	13,438	1,553	6,889	4,711
Vienna, Austria	625	17,798	7,486	1,007	5,819	6,218	9,643	5,859	5,307	852	9,688	11,678	8,247	6,474	1,094	6,453	6,463	7,145	1,673	2,552
Vientiane, Laos	8,865	9,561	13,166	7,435	6,487	7,320	14,410	12,798	12,243	9,055	14,583	17,204	14,354	13,097	9,330	12,966	12,327	7,297	6,815	6,135
Villahermosa, Mexico	9,511	12,120	2,818	10,245	14,949	14,647	1,318	4,053	8,971	9,447	1,144	7,023	1,727	3,479	9,182	3,537	3,850	15,278	10,614	12,432
Vilnius, USSR	1,537	17,124	7,475	170	6,112	6,644	9,640	6,027	6,258	1,775	9,709	12,585	8,371	6,598	1,978	6,550	6,415	7,546	789	2,454
Visby, Sweden	1,491	17,464	6,931	714	6,607	7,103	9,096	5,489	6,226	1,722	9,164	12,369	7,827	6,055	1,856	6,005	5,872	8,015	1,196	2,994
Vitoria, Brazil	8,839	12,273	8,538	10,455	9,649	8,820	8,405	7,757	4,374	8,603	8,239	2,241	7,613	7,868	8,395	8,027	8,853	8,915	11,124	10,767
Vladivostok, USSR	8,678	10,349	9,670	7,083	9,573	10,498	10,535	9,984	13,370	8,916	10,710	18,860	10,785	10,024	9,098	9,868	9,082	10,780	6,436	7,280
Volgograd, USSR	2,674	15,760	8,823	1,303	5,174	5,868	10,965	7,467	6,984	2,878	11,050	13,550	9,779	8,020	3,143	7,961	7,755	6,695	907	1,383
Vologda, USSR	2,555	16,198	7,705	960	6,356	7,015	9,821	6,476	7,263	2,793	9,915	13,593	8,714	6,987	2,992	6,914	6,638	7,865	410	2,555
Vorkuta, USSR	3,967	15,049	7,521	2,442	7,402	8,166	9,467	6,697	8,714	4,205	9,592	14,810	8,654	7,086	4,367	6,978	6,504	8,940	1,891	3,710
Wake Island	12,483	7,073	9,757	11,007	13,197	14,040	9,249	11,115	17,160	12,714	9,397	15,482	10,386	10,762	12,824	10,617	9,833	13,926	10,418	11,467
Wallis Island	16,403	3,788	10,868	15,045	15,297	15,631	9,213	12,712	18,251	16,614	9,274	11,748	10,782	12,111	16,646	12,031	11,533	14,871	14,479	15,351
Walvis Bay, Namibia	7,595	12,051	12,699	8,606	4,344	3,422	13,611	11,033	4,250	7,419	13,475	6,881	12,316	11,532	7,448	11,651	12,316	3,294	8,990	7,220
Warsaw, Poland	1,146	17,441	7,445	477	6,005	6,484	9,613	5,918	5,865	1,383	9,672	12,202	8,288	6,509	1,594	6,472	6,397	7,399	1,152	2,480
Washington, D.C.	6,811	14,734	1,024	7,464	12,600	12,590	2,628	1,284	7,521	6,774	2,626	8,446	1,107	702	6,526	787	1,406	13,435	7,842	9,667
Watson Lake, Canada	7,696	12,952	3,331	7,189	13,090	13,708	4,238	4,360	10,891	7,824	4,406	12,425	4,368	4,073	7,730	3,919	3,103	14,590	7,100	9,289

Distances in Kilometers

	Milan, Italy	Milford Sound, New Zealand	Milwaukee, Wisconsin	Minsk, USSR	Mogadiscio, Somalia	Mombasa, Kenya	Monclova, Mexico	Moncton, Canada	Monrovia, Liberia	Monte Carlo, Monaco	Monterrey, Mexico	Montevideo, Uruguay	Montgomery, Alabama	Montpelier, Vermont	Montpellier, France	Montreal, Canada	Moosonee, Canada	Moroni, Comoros	Moscow, USSR	Mosul, Iraq
Weimar, East Germany	633	18,126	7,008	1,149	6,291	6,670	9,166	5,391	5,359	858	9,212	11,573	7,778	6,003	994	5,979	5,985	7,600	1,815	3,004
Wellington, New Zealand	18,765	677	13,479	17,216	13,357	13,241	11,450	15,301	16,090	18,950	11,447	10,099	12,984	14,656	19,230	14,630	14,361	12,329	16,543	15,842
West Berlin, West Germany	842	17,944	7,023	957	6,326	6,739	9,188	5,447	5,579	1,073	9,239	11,791	7,827	6,049	1,217	6,018	5,988	7,666	1,612	2,938
Wewak, Papua New Guinea	13,606	5,125	13,322	12,009	10,951	11,538	12,664	14,551	17,186	13,830	12,794	15,278	13,927	14,276	14,071	14,125	13,315	11,066	11,334	11,187
Whangarei, New Zealand	18,360	1,131	13,174	16,748	13,587	13,566	11,226	15,027	16,708	18,588	11,240	10,602	12,791	14,387	18,816	14,342	13,992	12,674	16,074	15,674
Whitehorse, Canada	7,799	12,763	3,681	7,203	13,042	13,703	4,530	4,686	11,153	7,938	4,700	12,757	4,711	4,414	7,859	4,259	3,440	14,561	7,073	9,247
Wichita, Kansas	8,234	13,163	995	8,569	14,175	14,281	1,258	2,834	9,282	8,239	1,364	9,091	1,165	2,197	8,018	2,150	2,000	15,160	8,806	10,857
Willemstad, Curacao	8,137	13,565	3,884	9,351	12,608	12,137	3,764	3,788	6,412	7,996	3,616	5,374	2,861	3,580	7,710	3,727	4,471	12,672	9,910	11,122
Wiluna, Australia	13,667	4,669	16,890	12,520	8,616	8,875	15,908	17,797	14,383	13,789	15,993	13,189	17,385	17,738	14,072	17,579	16,752	8,154	11,969	10,661
Windhoek, Namibia	7,578	11,996	12,882	8,533	4,107	3,182	13,851	11,188	4,410	7,409	13,718	7,134	12,533	11,701	7,451	11,817	12,463	3,029	8,894	7,073
Windsor, Canada	6,984	14,468	410	7,473	12,884	12,960	2,391	1,514	8,079	6,972	2,431	8,974	1,139	874	6,741	835	1,015	13,837	7,790	9,730
Winnipeg, Canada	7,282	13,911	1,039	7,398	13,232	13,518	2,577	2,433	9,214	7,326	2,702	10,221	2,141	1,958	7,139	1,825	1,176	14,445	7,570	9,689
Winston-Salem, North Carolina	7,225	14,332	1,013	7,882	12,986	12,944	2,248	1,704	7,756	7,185	2,234	8,246	694	1,116	6,935	1,184	1,687	13,772	8,256	10,087
Wroclaw, Poland	854	17,729	7,318	779	6,049	6,481	9,483	5,742	5,592	1,092	9,535	11,903	8,123	6,345	1,294	6,314	6,281	7,405	1,454	2,643
Wuhan, China	8,707	9,936	11,545	7,118	7,882	8,778	12,604	11,512	12,894	8,930	12,779	19,010	12,708	11,688	9,173	11,542	10,819	8,907	6,445	6,495
Wyndham, Australia	13,468	4,927	15,432	12,072	9,300	9,731	14,770	16,404	15,438	13,641	14,887	14,414	16,079	16,269	13,924	16,111	15,284	9,131	11,447	10,577
Xi'an, China	8,061	10,564	11,276	6,477	7,468	8,380	12,523	11,081	12,265	8,283	12,694	18,658	12,458	11,307	8,528	11,167	10,482	8,589	5,805	5,866
Xining, China	7,405	11,179	11,129	5,837	6,922	7,844	12,569	10,745	11,568	7,623	12,735	18,027	12,321	11,029	7,874	10,898	10,264	8,124	5,170	5,169
Yakutsk, USSR	6,966	12,299	7,884	5,473	9,506	10,401	9,154	7,951	11,711	7,202	9,321	16,961	9,057	8,057	7,337	7,907	7,162	10,957	4,902	6,343
Yanji, China	8,580	10,408	9,783	6,979	9,378	10,303	10,692	10,047	13,251	8,819	10,867	18,993	10,909	10,106	9,007	9,951	9,172	10,584	6,326	7,119
Yaounde, Cameroon	4,615	14,935	10,485	5,736	3,766	3,250	12,072	8,647	2,491	4,435	11,999	8,253	10,520	9,243	4,466	9,326	9,828	3,912	6,206	4,837
Yap Island (Colonia)	12,075	6,693	12,557	10,467	10,285	11,020	12,444	13,437	16,166	12,304	12,600	16,846	13,404	13,298	12,536	13,139	12,312	10,754	9,792	9,836
Yaraka, Australia	15,400	3,058	14,907	13,932	10,993	11,274	13,539	16,530	16,649	15,584	13,612	13,055	15,076	16,077	15,863	15,951	15,231	10,542	13,281	12,543
Yarmouth, Canada	5,747	15,792	1,762	6,451	11,554	11,587	3,677	273	6,786	5,710	3,684	8,775	2,170	520	5,462	621	1,368	12,456	6,865	8,624
Yellowknife, Canada	7,036	13,717	2,762	6,681	12,648	13,182	4,065	3,582	10,077	7,148	4,219	11,968	3,890	3,346	7,034	3,188	2,362	14,093	6,672	8,871
Yerevan, USSR	2,921	15,419	9,625	1,985	4,222	4,923	11,787	8,155	6,647	3,074	11,859	13,225	10,516	8,739	3,358	8,695	8,563	5,743	1,804	444
Yinchuan, China	7,575	11,073	10,865	5,982	7,368	8,292	12,217	10,596	11,870	7,800	12,385	18,413	12,053	10,842	8,041	10,705	10,038	8,576	5,309	5,486
Yogyakarta, Indonesia	11,496	6,852	15,715	10,234	7,299	7,832	16,062	15,735	13,540	11,647	16,221	15,075	16,791	15,954	11,933	15,809	15,079	7,360	9,662	8,535
York, United Kingdom	1,192	18,707	6,119	1,877	7,133	7,452	8,272	4,486	5,341	1,286	8,314	11,160	6,873	5,099	1,196	5,077	5,108	8,385	2,469	3,906
Yumen, China	6,906	11,681	10,809	5,335	6,729	7,656	12,356	10,329	11,121	7,125	12,517	17,658	11,998	10,640	7,374	10,514	9,909	8,005	4,668	4,732
Yutian, China	5,951	12,490	11,094	4,508	5,359	6,285	12,939	10,225	9,817	6,148	13,080	16,247	12,238	10,655	6,419	10,553	10,089	6,713	3,899	3,428
Yuzhno-Sakhalinsk, USSR	8,807	10,434	8,864	7,273	10,403	11,330	9,612	9,352	13,557	9,044	9,787	17,943	9,945	9,324	9,191	9,166	8,358	11,668	6,666	7,808
Zagreb, Yugoslavia	531	17,811	7,636	1,223	5,628	5,998	9,785	5,973	5,080	717	9,823	11,498	8,361	6,596	990	6,581	6,626	6,928	1,869	2,495
Zahedan, Iran	4,806	13,529	11,365	3,812	3,451	4,348	13,486	10,010	7,897	4,942	13,581	14,157	12,334	10,572	5,227	10,515	10,297	4,933	3,450	1,820
Zamboanga, Philippines	11,203	7,307	13,705	9,687	8,522	9,235	14,028	14,095	14,600	11,407	14,194	16,901	14,728	14,152	11,674	13,996	13,203	8,962	9,032	8,571
Zanzibar, Tanzania	6,451	12,410	13,436	6,745	1,141	240	15,269	11,579	5,722	6,383	15,215	10,112	13,690	12,215	6,556	12,266	12,585	758	6,864	4,723
Zaragoza, Spain	919	19,042	6,824	2,505	6,364	6,515	8,881	5,021	4,034	719	8,889	10,180	7,360	5,666	448	5,685	5,913	7,435	3,181	3,817
Zashiversk, USSR	6,887	12,604	7,040	5,515	10,103	10,970	8,294	7,203	11,555	7,114	8,461	16,188	8,206	7,267	7,211	7,114	6,350	11,596	5,019	6,715
Zhengzhou, China	8,336	10,346	11,117	6,736	7,907	8,818	12,251	11,049	12,640	8,563	12,424	19,099	12,287	11,232	8,800	11,087	10,372	9,014	6,061	6,248
Zurich, Switzerland	221	18,400	7,068	1,534	6,155	6,467	9,206	5,378	4,903	411	9,239	11,150	7,765	6,006	546	5,996	6,074	7,400	2,209	3,104

Distances in Kilometers	Mount Isa, Australia	Multan, Pakistan	Munich, West Germany	Murcia, Spain	Murmansk, USSR	Mururoa Atoll, Fr. Polynesia	Muscat, Oman	Myitkyina, Burma	Naga, Philippines	Nagasaki, Japan	Nagoya, Japan	Nagpur, India	Nairobi, Kenya	Nanchang, China	Nancy, France	Nandi, Fiji	Nanjing, China	Nanning, China	Nantes, France	Naples, Italy
Multan, Pakistan	9,202	0	5,394	6,588	4,960	16,861	1,472	2,603	5,596	5,488	6,052	1,259	5,064	4,284	5,789	12,491	4,480	3,745	6,384	5,231
Munich, West Germany	14,491	5,394	0	1,528	2,603	16,092	4,934	7,653	10,423	9,151	9,305	6,631	5,997	8,659	403	16,403	8,561	8,631	990	840
Murcia, Spain	15,791	6,588	1,528	0	4,016	15,622	5,830	9,012	11,876	10,678	10,827	7,763	5,836	10,146	1,327	17,763	10,070	10,045	1,026	1,359
Murmansk, USSR	12,794	4,960	2,603	4,016	0	14,742	5,323	6,375	8,603	6,907	6,925	6,151	7,801	6,775	2,693	13,810	6,550	7,068	3,084	3,324
Mururoa Atoll, Fr. Polynesia	8,352	16,861	16,092	15,622	14,742	0	18,226	14,313	11,373	11,401	10,879	16,103	17,403	12,577	15,731	4,582	12,389	13,170	15,288	16,735
Muscat, Oman	10,047	1,472	4,934	5,830	5,323	18,226	0	3,926	6,853	6,949	7,523	2,129	3,625	5,704	5,335	13,674	5,930	5,065	5,885	4,534
Myitkyina, Burma	6,838	2,603	7,653	9,012	6,375	14,313	3,926	0	2,995	3,257	3,926	1,928	7,149	1,868	8,018	9,891	2,211	1,145	8,617	7,663
Naga, Philippines	4,200	5,596	10,423	11,876	8,603	11,373	6,853	2,995	0	2,230	2,755	4,743	9,659	1,829	10,750	6,896	2,088	1,870	11,326	10,561
Nagasaki, Japan	6,011	5,488	9,151	10,678	6,907	11,401	6,949	3,257	2,230	0	698	5,157	10,381	1,418	9,399	7,543	1,050	2,392	9,906	9,527
Nagoya, Japan	6,193	6,052	9,305	10,827	6,925	10,879	7,523	3,926	2,755	698	0	5,805	11,014	2,110	9,517	7,257	1,716	3,090	9,987	9,758
Nagpur, India	8,039	1,259	6,631	7,763	6,151	16,103	2,129	1,928	4,743	5,157	5,805	0	5,228	3,793	7,029	11,548	4,107	3,018	7,620	6,414
Nairobi, Kenya	11,285	5,064	5,997	5,836	7,801	17,403	3,625	7,149	9,659	10,381	11,014	5,228	0	9,017	6,273	15,225	9,332	8,180	6,541	5,194
Nanchang, China	6,028	4,284	8,659	10,146	6,775	12,577	5,704	1,868	1,829	1,418	2,110	3,793	9,017	0	8,968	8,380	466	999	9,532	8,873
Nancy, France	14,853	5,789	403	1,327	2,693	15,731	5,335	8,018	10,750	9,399	9,517	7,029	6,273	8,968	0	16,489	8,851	8,977	601	1,079
Nandi, Fiji	3,990	12,491	16,403	17,763	13,810	4,582	13,674	9,891	6,896	7,543	7,257	11,548	15,225	8,380	16,489	0	8,335	8,757	16,741	16,992
Nanjing, China	6,245	4,480	8,561	10,070	6,550	12,389	5,930	2,211	2,088	1,050	1,716	4,107	9,332	466	8,851	8,335	0	1,454	9,399	8,835
Nanning, China	5,888	3,745	8,631	10,045	7,068	13,170	5,065	1,145	1,870	2,392	3,090	3,018	8,180	999	8,977	8,757	1,454	0	9,567	8,714
Nantes, France	15,448	6,384	990	1,026	3,084	15,288	5,885	8,617	11,326	9,906	9,987	7,620	6,541	9,532	601	16,741	9,399	9,567	0	1,448
Naples, Italy	14,433	5,231	840	1,359	3,324	16,735	4,534	7,663	10,561	9,527	9,758	6,414	5,194	8,873	1,079	16,992	8,835	8,714	1,448	0
Narvik, Norway	13,421	5,472	2,283	3,574	636	14,582	5,699	6,997	9,235	7,503	7,490	6,690	7,878	7,407	2,286	14,207	7,176	7,703	2,592	3,078
Nashville, Tennessee	15,233	12,319	7,672	7,324	7,359	8,445	12,458	13,178	13,664	11,473	10,908	13,491	13,062	12,447	7,296	11,669	12,000	13,288	6,844	8,292
Nassau, Bahamas	16,233	13,050	7,900	7,184	8,199	8,439	12,834	14,392	15,183	12,981	12,428	14,297	12,504	13,890	7,499	12,332	13,455	14,670	6,960	8,361
Natal, Brazil	17,016	11,942	7,516	5,994	9,755	11,181	10,658	14,543	17,511	16,645	16,654	12,770	8,015	16,061	7,253	15,592	16,048	15,687	6,739	7,213
Natashquan, Canada	16,240	9,986	5,134	4,901	5,107	10,975	9,956	11,386	12,917	10,739	10,371	11,220	10,734	11,264	4,760	13,690	10,894	11,859	4,326	5,771
Nauru Island	3,728	10,569	14,223	15,683	11,668	6,323	11,908	7,991	5,072	5,356	5,035	9,813	14,482	6,319	14,360	2,228	6,213	6,847	14,714	14,767
Ndjamena, Chad	14,052	6,128	4,008	3,286	6,445	17,062	4,766	8,687	11,608	11,514	11,972	6,865	2,826	10,407	4,137	18,036	10,566	9,829	4,190	3,183
Nelson, New Zealand	3,909	13,078	18,385	19,413	16,152	4,945	13,731	10,743	7,965	9,331	9,245	11,871	13,577	9,741	18,708	2,633	9,858	9,754	19,232	18,265
Nema, Mauritania	16,503	8,041	3,897	2,443	6,454	14,938	6,871	10,638	13,633	12,898	13,146	8,997	5,228	12,115	3,761	19,520	12,141	11,768	3,434	3,388
Neuquen, Argentina	12,804	16,221	12,437	10,926	14,419	6,895	14,749	17,985	16,992	18,266	17,771	16,322	11,206	18,811	12,148	10,759	19,028	18,184	11,599	12,149
New Delhi, India	8,635	582	5,932	7,157	5,309	16,330	1,940	2,034	5,021	5,020	5,614	847	5,428	3,765	6,323	11,915	3,993	3,179	6,921	5,798
New Glasgow, Canada	16,592	10,426	5,440	5,058	5,587	10,708	10,322	11,892	13,421	11,232	10,849	11,669	10,849	11,779	5,054	13,724	11,406	12,376	4,580	6,027
New Haven, Connecticut	16,213	11,288	6,393	5,993	6,378	9,753	11,256	12,555	13,703	11,474	11,008	12,515	11,745	12,204	6,008	12,928	11,795	12,905	5,536	6,982
New Orleans, Louisiana	14,976	13,069	8,381	7,950	8,109	7,761	13,201	13,829	14,016	11,887	11,283	14,232	13,586	12,958	7,999	11,218	12,500	13,845	7,528	8,974
New Plymouth, New Zealand	3,874	13,069	18,286	19,588	15,952	4,836	13,784	10,688	7,869	9,171	9,065	11,879	13,776	9,628	18,570	2,379	9,729	9,678	19,035	18,293
New York, New York	16,160	11,392	6,506	6,102	6,475	9,640	11,367	12,634	13,735	11,505	11,030	12,616	11,849	12,255	6,121	12,835	11,843	12,968	5,648	7,095
Newcastle upon Tyne, UK	15,012	6,263	1,187	1,892	2,337	14,912	5,998	8,281	10,819	9,237	9,261	7,520	7,155	8,997	884	15,875	8,818	9,144	866	1,961
Newcastle Waters, Australia	740	8,468	13,781	15,055	12,209	9,080	9,308	6,134	3,611	5,568	5,830	7,299	10,674	5,436	14,151	4,661	5,690	5,220	14,750	13,698
Niamey, Niger	15,442	7,299	3,939	2,730	6,538	15,809	6,028	9,898	12,874	12,469	12,824	8,154	4,164	11,513	3,918	19,329	11,606	11,043	3,752	3,250
Nicosia, Cyprus	12,743	3,596	2,304	3,085	3,761	18,355	2,751	6,153	9,136	8,524	8,906	4,707	4,051	7,609	2,685	15,988	7,671	7,266	3,186	1,788
Niue (Alofi)	5,280	13,761	16,770	17,644	14,233	3,245	14,998	11,159	8,175	8,590	8,213	12,869	16,339	9,559	16,695	1,345	9,464	10,017	16,704	17,554
Norfolk, Virginia	16,132	11,862	6,932	6,460	6,947	9,240	11,816	13,085	14,059	11,830	11,327	13,088	12,141	12,641	6,544	12,610	12,219	13,383	6,055	7,498
Norfolk Island, Australia	3,009	12,140	17,081	18,598	14,710	5,360	13,055	9,647	6,741	7,935	7,818	11,021	13,840	8,455	17,330	1,575	8,528	8,587	17,794	17,301
Noril'sk, USSR	10,786	4,482	4,601	6,083	2,113	13,876	5,448	4,925	6,659	4,819	4,812	5,390	8,716	4,861	4,757	11,815	4,572	5,345	5,188	5,204
Norman Wells, Canada	12,248	9,303	6,928	7,637	5,026	9,717	10,138	9,266	9,536	7,321	6,790	10,170	12,784	8,296	6,739	10,329	7,843	9,179	6,674	7,767
Normanton, Australia	378	9,141	14,354	15,715	12,542	8,301	10,056	6,714	3,981	5,710	5,864	8,009	11,485	5,801	14,702	3,848	5,994	5,725	15,289	14,358
North Pole	12,294	6,662	4,669	5,798	2,350	12,420	7,390	7,193	8,493	6,370	6,108	7,663	10,146	6,827	4,610	11,969	6,454	7,477	4,773	5,482
Nottingham, United Kingdom	15,111	6,259	1,048	1,665	2,511	15,044	5,932	8,340	10,930	9,393	9,435	7,514	6,972	9,114	704	16,100	8,948	9,229	640	1,781
Norway House, Canada	13,970	10,623	6,897	7,098	5,794	9,280	11,115	11,091	11,570	9,354	8,822	11,675	12,855	10,290	6,594	11,253	9,845	11,135	6,317	7,672
Norwich, United Kingdom	14,986	6,098	884	1,639	2,457	15,208	5,762	8,199	10,815	9,314	9,373	7,351	6,832	9,003	559	16,125	8,847	9,100	636	1,638
Nouakchott, Mauritania	17,442	8,784	4,162	2,635	6,572	14,082	7,696	11,354	14,328	13,311	13,455	9,805	6,162	12,697	3,937	18,619	12,663	12,459	3,487	3,829
Noumea, New Caledonia	2,794	11,680	16,375	17,903	13,953	5,607	12,716	9,128	6,169	7,226	7,080	10,625	13,977	7,824	16,597	1,249	7,867	8,034	17,037	16,697
Novosibirsk, USSR	9,955	2,907	4,783	6,304	2,919	14,958	4,025	3,500	5,759	4,391	4,639	3,775	7,520	3,938	5,062	11,895	3,791	4,151	5,609	5,138
Nuku'alofa, Tonga	4,696	13,349	16,947	18,054	14,352	3,752	14,519	10,749	7,755	8,345	8,023	12,396	15,749	9,225	16,945	858	9,166	9,615	17,056	17,648
Nukunono Island, Tokelau Isls.	5,360	13,080	15,674	16,687	13,126	3,794	14,441	10,519	7,603	7,717	7,280	12,346	16,645	8,803	15,624	1,497	8,652	9,377	15,694	16,448
Nuremberg, West Germany	14,487	5,429	149	1,605	2,479	15,973	5,011	7,652	10,394	9,082	9,222	6,672	6,139	8,619	367	16,287	8,511	8,615	968	989
Nyala, Sudan	13,026	5,197	4,189	3,863	6,349	17,990	3,783	7,706	10,583	10,661	11,173	5,846	1,979	9,476	4,415	17,015	9,673	8,840	4,616	3,355
Oaxaca, Mexico	14,125	14,629	9,907	9,339	9,675	6,301	14,773	15,070	14,480	12,599	11,930	15,755	14,657	13,857	9,517	10,164	13,392	14,829	9,018	10,452
Ocean Falls, Canada	11,995	10,674	8,218	8,745	6,456	8,294	11,567	10,348	10,070	7,960	7,341	11,459	14,164	9,123	7,990	9,399	8,657	10,076	7,845	9,049
Odense, Denmark	14,317	5,500	811	2,120	1,896	15,502	5,277	7,540	10,146	8,676	8,761	6,758	6,729	8,336	800	15,690	8,186	8,432	1,230	1,644
Odessa, USSR	13,077	3,938	1,456	2,771	2,509	17,122	3,554	6,252	9,109	8,083	8,348	5,175	5,323	7,408	1,854	15,605	7,371	7,274	2,446	1,466
Ogbomosho, Nigeria	15,028	7,375	4,489	3,350	7,073	15,805	6,026	9,945	12,868	12,702	13,117	8,125	3,760	11,645	4,499	18,713	11,784	11,088	4,367	3,755
Okha, USSR	8,238	6,172	7,838	9,290	5,275	11,188	7,565	4,884	4,759	2,529	2,098	6,421	11,182	3,534	7,966	8,569	3,070	4,483	8,343	8,453
Okinawa (Naha)	5,349	5,479	9,607	11,124	7,491	11,382	6,899	3,030	1,470	762	1,329	4,958	10,163	1,196	9,883	7,257	1,079	1,995	10,418	9,905
Oklahoma City, Oklahoma	14,273	12,644	8,387	8,179	7,737	7,706	12,997	13,088	13,093	10,980	10,367	13,725	13,974	12,090	8,028	10,712	11,628	13,004	7,620	9,061
Old Crow, Canada	11,728	8,855	6,950	7,799	4,843	9,917	9,780	8,678	8,908	6,691	6,164	9,662	12,644	7,669	6,802	10,086	7,215	8,558	6,804	7,788
Olympia, Washington	12,234	11,331	8,576	8,958	6,987	7,800	12,178	11,026	10,635	8,568	7,932	12,138	14,569	9,765	8,316	9,329	9,299	10,727	8,114	9,390
Omaha, Nebraska	14,364	11,989	7,819	7,711	7,084	8,276	12,359	12,496	12,719	10,554	9,969	13,074	13,542	11,595	7,471	11,018	11,139	12,480	7,092	8,521
Omsk, USSR	10,453	2,761	4,208	5,722	2,549	15,455	3,694	3,830	6,273	4,989	5,247	3,788	7,076	4,470	4,502	12,503	4,353	4,593	5,062	4,537
Oodnadatta, Australia	859	9,332	14,718	15,837	13,327	8,510	10,007	7,139	4,746	6,705	6,943	8,114	10,803	6,564	15,106	4,422	6,829	6,291	15,706	14,515
Oradea, Romania	13,746	4,612	787	2,135	2,517	16,727	4,165	6,915	9,743	8,616	8,834	5,845	5,550	8,015	1,188	16,066	7,953	7,922	1,775	927
Oran, Algeria	15,811	6,620	1,710	257	4,240	15,712	5,801	9,081	11,977	10,846	11,014	7,773	5,644	10,270	1,547	18,012	10,210	10,133	1,281	1,419
Oranjestad, Aruba	16,759	13,747	8,363	7,322	9,230	8,426	13,152	15,599	16,772	14,564	14,017	14,993	11,880	15,402	7,964	12,798	14,985	16,092	7,375	8,635
Orebro, Sweden	13,892	5,274	1,262	2,641	1,376	15,374	5,205	7,178	9,702	8,177	8,249	6,530	6,977	7,883	1,317	15,180	7,715	8,026	1,738	2,053
Orel, USSR	12,714	3,819	1,806	3,298	1,795	16,532	3,767	5,888	8,618	7,415	7,634	5,078	6,008	6,856	2,142	14,877	6,773	6,835	2,734	2,124
Orsk, USSR	11,171	2,568	3,350	4,816	2,397	16,417	3,062	4,360	7,075	5,995	6,295	3,783	6,170	5,331	3,689	13,535	5,277	5,288	4,279	3,558
Osaka, Japan	6,146	5,940	9,280	10,804	6,925	10,980	7,410	3,792	2,639	557	141	5,676	10,890	1,971	9,499	7,406	1,581	2,949	9,977	9,710
Oslo, Norway	14,099	5,534	1,311	2,580	1,459	15,158	5,461	7,416	9,903	8,329	8,376	6,790	7,154	8,080	1,284	15,208	7,899	8,248	1,626	2,137
Osorno, Chile	12,428	16,637	12,876	11,372	14,780	6,447	15,166	18,111	16,628	17,797	17,325	16,627	11,592	18,456	12,579	10,290	18,590	18,032	12,022	12,607
Ostrava, Czechoslovakia	13,972	4,912	525	2,029	2,277	16,318	4,541	7,134	9,899	8,653	8,828	6,158	5,935	8,137	888	15,995	8,046	8,107	1,489	1,049
Ottawa, Canada	15,797	11,002	6,295	6,039	6,056	9,810	11,076	12,134	13,196	10,967	10,498	12,207	11,854	11,716	5,923	12,709	11,303	12,438	5,491	6,937
Ouagadougou, Bourkina Fasso	15,782	7,708	4,150	2,838	6,751	15,395	6,442	10,308	13,286	12,837	13,171	8,568	4,497	11,909	4,090	19,394	11,992	11,452	3,864	3,511
Oujda, Morocco	15,949	6,764	1,869	375	4,386	15,615	5,925	9,235	12,135	11,007	11,174	7,910	5,667	10,432	1,694	18,135	10,372	10,290	1,394	1,576
Oxford, United Kingdom	15,186	6,282	1,003	1,530	2,630	15,101	5,918	8,397	11,014	9,502	9,552	7,534	6,879	9,202	631	16,236	9,043	9,300	505	1,696
Pago Pago, American Samoa	5,317	13,460	16,241	17,186	13,700	3,461	14,765	10,871	7,912	8,181	7,774	12,645	16,542	9,210	16,177	1,330	9,087	9,726	16,216	17,022
Pakxe, Laos	5,414	3,879	9,078	10,410	7,757	13,206	5,025	1,434	1,883	3,127	3,818	2,898	7,800	1,827	9,447	8,661	2,293	893	10,047	9,054
Palembang, Indonesia	4,252	5,092	10,485	11,601	9,583	12,589	5,799	3,230	2,738	4,760	5,388	3,861	7,559	3,694	10,881	8,082	4,145	2,873	11,476	10,265
Palermo, Italy	14,539	5,345	1,124	1,270	3,635	16,817	4,562	7,822	10,748	9,782	10,030	6,502	4,983	9,088	1,308	17,278	9,066	8,891	1,582	311
Palma, Majorca	15,429	6,227	1,192	371	3,740	15,895	5,501	8,641	11,505	10,332	10,497	7,410	5,708	9,779	1,052	17,541	9,709	9,674	915	997
Palmerston North, New Zealand	4,049	13,237	18,479	19,630	16,134	4,732	13,923	10,870	8,059	9,364	9,255	12,039	13,796	9,820	18,763	2,506	9,922	9,865	19,210	18,448
Panama, Panama	15,649	14,688	9,356	8,390	9,955	7,323	14,215	16,190	16,479	14,435	13,808	15,946	12,938	15,526	8,954	11,693	15,070	16,388	8,376	9,682
Paramaribo, Suriname	17,734	13,083	7,813	6,502	9,333	9,614	12,140	15,464	17,844	15,696	15,295	14,211	10,253	16,068	7,446	14,174	15,764	16,368	6,848	7,861
Paris, France	15,108	6,070	688	1,241	2,793	15,474	5,618	8,279	10,983	9,579	9,672	7,311	6,471	9,191	285	16,530	9,061	9,225	343	1,295
Patna, India	7,798	1,434	6,739	7,997	5,893	15,543	2,692	1,235	4,189	4,397	5,034	788	5,985	3,061	7,125	11,075	3,349	2,374	7,725	6,638
Patrai, Greece	13,806	4,615	1,372	1,999	3,487	17,424	3,844	7,111	10,057	9,201	9,497	5,769	4,643	8,433	1,704	16,743	8,437	8,193	2,140	704
Peking, China	7,132	4,191	7,769	9,290	5,670	12,762	5,663	2,395	2,989	1,446	1,884	4,098	9,216	1,249	8,039	8,986	901	2,045	8,571	8,103
Penrhyn Island (Omoka)	6,805	14,381	15,558	16,058	13,297	2,496	15,810	11,896	9,052	8,907	8,386	13,775	18,023	10,108	15,368	2,824	9,901	10,768	15,227	16,398
Peoria, Illinois	14,907	11,920	7,492	7,284	6,970	8,602	12,165	12,654	13,112	10,916	10,357	13,060	13,095	11,889	7,130	11,527	11,441	12,735	6,718	8,160
Perm', USSR	11,550	3,305	3,120	4,642	1,661	15,811	3,823	4,852	7,377	6,042	6,245	4,490	6,796	5,574	3,402	13,489	5,449	5,676	3,958	3,513
Perth, Australia	2,660	8,318	13,581	14,336	12,998	10,090	8,653	6,639	5,103	7,316	7,748	7,060	8,902	6,709	13,984	6,335	7,089	6,111	14,537	13,151
Peshawar, Pakistan	9,404	425	5,137	6,396	4,561	16,756	1,709	2,669	5,655	5,355	5,884	1,608	5,334	4,227	5,525	12,539	4,379	3,786	6,125	5,038

Distances in Kilometers	Mount Isa, Australia	Multan, Pakistan	Munich, West Germany	Murcia, Spain	Murmansk, USSR	Mururoa Atoll, Fr. Polynesia	Muscat, Oman	Myitkyina, Burma	Naga, Philippines	Nagasaki, Japan	Nagoya, Japan	Nagpur, India	Nairobi, Kenya	Nanchang, China	Nancy, France	Nandi, Fiji	Nanjing, China	Nanning, China	Nantes, France	Naples, Italy
Petropavlovsk-Kamchatskiy, USSR	8,377	7,210	8,370	9,735	5,767	10,238	8,586	5,885	5,373	3,208	2,618	7,466	12,190	4,405	8,438	8,051	3,940	5,388	8,739	9,059
Petrozavodsk, USSR	12,812	4,426	2,085	3,592	799	15,537	4,625	6,142	8,621	7,129	7,239	5,660	7,002	6,801	2,279	14,337	6,638	6,957	2,779	2,697
Pevek, USSR	10,322	7,220	6,819	8,043	4,284	10,917	8,357	6,722	7,028	4,797	4,343	7,862	11,682	5,694	6,810	9,721	5,244	6,573	7,020	7,591
Philadelphia, Pennsylvania	16,104	11,514	6,635	6,226	6,592	9,511	11,497	12,731	13,778	11,548	11,063	12,736	11,965	12,321	6,251	12,732	11,905	13,047	5,777	7,224
Phnom Penh, Kampuchea	5,204	4,020	9,307	10,596	8,090	13,175	5,072	1,724	1,998	3,472	4,155	2,950	7,663	2,213	9,684	8,601	2,679	1,298	10,285	9,237
Phoenix, Arizona	12,924	12,951	9,378	9,364	8,294	6,753	13,612	12,789	12,181	10,224	9,563	13,847	15,200	11,479	9,050	9,384	11,014	12,456	8,707	10,116
Pierre, South Dakota	13,975	11,707	7,801	7,817	6,865	8,319	12,178	12,073	12,226	10,064	9,477	12,749	13,649	11,120	7,471	10,777	10,662	12,016	7,132	8,538
Pinang, Malaysia	5,166	4,082	9,472	10,641	8,550	13,411	4,903	2,232	2,666	4,313	4,992	2,878	7,100	3,053	9,864	8,841	3,519	2,108	10,462	9,291
Pitcairn Island (Adamstown)	9,103	17,830	15,806	15,037	14,997	969	19,138	15,273	12,315	12,363	11,828	17,017	16,771	13,546	15,413	5,469	13,356	14,128	14,894	16,292
Pittsburgh, Pennsylvania	15,699	11,654	6,916	6,579	6,703	9,204	11,725	12,713	13,561	11,335	10,823	12,854	12,348	12,179	6,539	12,325	11,750	12,950	6,086	7,534
Plymouth, Montserrat	17,702	12,840	7,447	6,368	8,494	9,385	12,196	14,857	16,598	14,378	13,922	14,074	11,022	14,979	7,051	13,719	14,609	15,515	6,457	7,689
Plymouth, United Kingdom	15,436	6,504	1,167	1,400	2,861	14,980	6,101	8,642	11,265	9,744	9,785	7,753	6,920	9,452	770	16,385	9,292	9,549	401	1,776
Ponape Island	3,682	9,322	13,092	14,597	10,606	7,554	10,687	6,762	3,908	4,097	3,815	8,619	13,509	5,057	13,272	3,452	4,945	5,623	13,688	13,572
Ponce, Puerto Rico	17,277	13,045	7,670	6,672	8,530	9,026	12,497	14,904	16,345	14,115	13,619	14,295	11,483	14,831	7,270	13,286	14,435	15,454	6,684	7,968
Ponta Delgada, Azores	17,648	8,596	3,215	2,154	4,910	13,474	7,962	10,842	13,460	11,798	11,737	9,815	7,716	11,637	2,834	16,864	11,448	11,763	2,233	3,432
Pontianak, Indonesia	4,002	5,218	10,588	11,796	9,461	12,255	6,071	3,091	2,149	4,227	4,836	4,037	8,073	3,254	10,975	7,698	3,688	2,530	11,575	10,443
Port Augusta, Australia	1,315	9,845	15,239	16,265	13,918	8,139	10,447	7,706	5,336	7,275	7,491	8,613	10,964	7,156	15,632	4,286	7,418	6,876	16,229	14,978
Port Blair, India	6,242	3,010	8,404	9,562	7,624	14,434	3,850	1,602	3,312	4,458	5,155	1,799	6,348	3,059	8,798	9,852	3,499	2,066	9,394	8,213
Port Elizabeth, South Africa	10,771	8,584	9,202	8,431	11,431	13,613	7,268	10,032	11,542	13,157	13,855	8,327	3,803	11,755	9,355	13,550	12,180	10,766	9,392	8,363
Port Hedland, Australia	2,182	7,526	12,915	13,949	11,917	10,402	8,120	5,550	3,789	6,001	6,440	6,284	9,106	5,429	13,313	6,168	5,795	4,900	13,904	12,644
Port Louis, Mauritius	8,449	5,769	8,839	8,884	10,078	15,028	4,845	6,635	8,103	9,670	10,367	5,140	3,071	8,280	9,165	12,237	8,717	7,285	9,512	8,099
Port Moresby, Papua New Guinea	1,493	9,191	14,055	15,543	11,932	7,974	10,292	6,631	3,683	5,026	5,059	8,175	12,228	5,399	14,352	3,393	5,500	5,542	14,895	14,243
Port Said, Egypt	12,771	3,735	2,566	3,136	4,194	18,656	2,725	6,327	9,321	8,834	9,244	4,773	3,634	7,861	2,925	16,212	7,950	7,457	3,378	1,936
Port Sudan, Sudan	11,994	3,636	3,917	4,220	5,491	19,554	2,252	6,174	9,101	9,097	9,616	4,361	2,312	7,920	4,254	15,839	8,110	7,316	4,652	3,209
Port-au-Prince, Haiti	16,691	13,375	8,052	7,142	8,694	8,516	12,940	15,022	16,066	13,854	13,312	14,633	12,082	14,707	7,649	12,704	14,284	15,430	7,076	8,407
Port-of-Spain, Trin. & Tobago	17,519	13,261	7,881	6,703	9,090	9,179	12,490	15,417	17,270	15,047	14,578	14,463	10,956	15,644	7,494	13,649	15,279	16,143	6,894	8,049
Port-Vila, Vanuatu	3,044	11,625	16,031	17,540	13,536	5,522	12,752	9,039	6,051	6,926	6,729	10,634	14,317	7,627	16,214	965	7,631	7,920	16,607	16,451
Portland, Maine	16,268	10,952	6,062	5,697	6,049	10,074	10,918	12,258	13,517	11,295	10,854	12,181	11,479	11,971	5,679	13,143	11,572	12,643	5,214	6,662
Portland, Oregon	12,228	11,500	8,712	9,067	7,149	7,644	12,346	11,174	10,729	8,680	8,039	12,302	14,708	9,892	8,448	9,253	9,426	10,859	8,235	9,523
Porto, Portugal	16,260	7,101	1,774	734	3,935	14,924	6,452	9,424	12,185	10,783	10,853	8,310	6,563	10,401	1,435	17,354	10,275	10,404	879	1,919
Porto Alegre, Brazil	14,269	14,565	10,681	9,157	12,866	8,620	13,118	16,899	18,097	19,687	19,073	14,978	9,751	18,765	10,419	12,591	19,046	17,835	9,899	10,341
Porto Alexandre, Angola	13,018	8,165	7,085	6,108	9,554	14,770	6,696	10,320	12,666	13,555	14,181	8,401	3,174	12,188	7,166	15,967	12,506	11,327	7,109	6,276
Porto Novo, Benin	15,127	7,623	4,696	3,509	7,288	15,562	6,266	10,188	13,100	12,960	13,374	8,359	3,896	11,897	4,690	18,636	12,039	11,330	4,532	3,977
Porto Velho, Brazil	15,869	14,824	9,671	8,309	11,188	8,117	13,709	17,318	19,084	16,993	16,403	15,836	11,176	17,800	9,312	12,680	17,412	18,248	8,717	9,660
Portsmouth, United Kingdom	15,231	6,285	962	1,421	2,719	15,160	5,891	8,429	11,069	9,579	9,637	7,535	6,793	9,260	574	16,345	9,108	9,343	396	1,619
Poznan, Poland	14,003	5,036	610	2,131	2,029	16,040	4,747	7,179	9,884	8,553	8,698	6,290	6,236	8,101	868	15,804	7,987	8,119	1,447	1,304
Prague, Czechoslovakia	14,234	5,187	301	1,828	2,330	16,110	4,804	7,398	10,143	8,851	9,004	6,433	6,079	8,371	620	16,116	8,268	8,361	1,220	1,028
Praia, Cape Verde Islands	18,121	9,661	4,891	3,375	7,168	13,210	8,575	12,223	15,183	14,022	14,093	10,686	6,878	13,510	4,625	17,777	13,445	13,319	4,118	4,640
Pretoria, South Africa	11,001	7,723	8,351	7,690	10,511	14,557	6,370	9,346	11,157	12,554	13,246	7,562	2,862	11,137	8,530	14,158	11,538	10,172	8,614	7,511
Prince Albert, Canada	13,470	10,763	7,319	7,590	6,044	8,910	11,362	11,016	11,263	9,071	8,508	11,755	13,304	10,083	7,031	10,727	9,628	10,966	6,782	8,110
Prince Edward Island	9,204	9,147	10,804	10,144	12,821	12,418	8,048	9,961	10,741	12,709	13,376	8,567	5,020	11,422	10,994	11,804	11,884	10,432	11,081	9,964
Prince George, Canada	12,347	10,587	7,907	8,394	6,232	8,538	11,414	10,412	10,294	8,150	7,549	11,429	13,878	9,268	7,668	9,768	8,804	10,203	7,507	8,733
Prince Rupert, Canada	11,866	10,412	8,100	8,687	6,262	8,481	11,328	10,068	9,825	7,701	7,088	11,185	14,009	8,852	7,885	9,403	8,387	9,801	7,767	8,934
Providence, Rhode Island	16,296	11,174	6,259	5,855	6,274	9,889	11,127	12,476	13,687	11,461	11,006	12,404	11,611	12,163	5,873	13,054	11,760	12,849	5,399	6,845
Provo, Utah	13,046	12,202	8,736	8,835	7,552	7,434	12,865	12,145	11,799	9,746	9,108	13,119	14,653	10,938	8,423	9,741	10,472	11,895	8,116	9,498
Puerto Aisen, Chile	11,993	16,482	13,204	11,684	15,231	6,473	15,035	17,616	16,181	17,626	17,278	16,293	11,419	18,004	12,927	10,085	18,228	17,498	12,387	12,873
Puerto Deseado, Argentina	12,009	15,912	12,988	11,460	15,187	6,987	14,474	17,127	16,130	17,884	17,668	15,715	10,853	17,883	12,741	10,414	18,218	17,191	12,229	12,588
Puerto Princesa, Philippines	4,065	5,390	10,452	11,847	8,827	11,682	6,552	2,843	649	2,801	3,368	4,423	9,156	2,119	10,801	7,133	2,471	1,825	11,391	10,504
Punta Arenas, Chile	11,312	16,051	13,648	12,121	15,884	6,632	14,682	16,772	15,448	17,204	17,056	15,637	11,067	17,231	13,413	9,807	17,536	16,637	12,911	13,213
Pusan, South Korea	6,277	5,355	8,899	10,426	6,641	11,554	6,823	3,215	2,450	267	717	5,089	10,299	1,433	9,142	7,769	1,011	2,429	9,646	9,286
Pyongyang, North Korea	6,768	4,999	8,376	9,903	6,123	11,954	6,471	3,052	2,824	785	1,080	4,850	10,009	1,463	8,618	8,273	998	2,441	9,122	8,771
Qamdo, China	7,305	2,465	7,200	8,609	5,781	14,396	3,893	641	3,288	3,082	3,704	2,121	7,311	1,820	7,551	10,126	2,044	1,436	8,144	7,280
Qandahar, Afghanistan	9,761	570	4,870	6,031	4,645	17,355	1,131	3,163	6,157	5,954	6,489	1,761	4,750	4,800	5,268	13,053	4,969	4,300	5,859	4,675
Qiqian, China	8,281	4,683	7,028	8,547	4,657	12,591	6,088	3,571	4,283	2,277	2,284	4,963	9,711	2,643	7,234	9,481	2,244	3,432	7,705	7,515
Qom, Iran	11,172	1,995	3,564	4,625	3,976	18,302	1,432	4,561	7,552	7,122	7,581	3,138	4,241	6,093	3,967	14,437	6,202	5,684	4,539	3,278
Quebec, Canada	16,005	10,695	5,923	5,662	5,766	10,185	10,726	11,928	13,158	10,937	10,500	11,912	11,481	11,613	5,550	13,051	11,213	12,293	5,113	6,560
Quetta, Pakistan	9,586	432	5,059	6,207	4,826	17,283	1,109	3,034	6,025	5,894	6,445	1,573	4,732	4,709	5,458	12,920	4,895	4,176	6,048	4,853
Quito, Ecuador	15,289	15,426	10,034	8,923	10,874	6,969	14,721	17,186	17,215	15,339	14,683	16,661	12,836	16,508	9,638	11,502	16,046	17,400	9,044	10,260
Rabaul, Papua New Guinea	2,287	9,357	13,869	15,394	11,566	7,665	10,569	6,757	3,762	4,722	4,641	8,440	12,823	5,322	14,121	3,134	5,346	5,627	14,617	14,181
Raiatea (Uturoa)	7,243	15,429	16,195	16,285	14,193	1,432	16,810	12,887	9,968	9,987	9,485	14,710	17,821	11,145	15,926	3,311	10,964	11,745	15,648	17,004
Raleigh, North Carolina	15,962	12,067	7,170	6,702	7,138	8,998	12,046	13,223	14,078	11,855	11,333	13,285	12,375	12,711	6,782	12,388	12,281	13,479	6,296	7,739
Rangiroa (Avatoru)	7,683	15,686	15,863	15,861	14,002	1,204	17,112	13,190	10,309	10,208	9,677	15,048	18,146	11,413	15,573	3,735	11,206	12,056	15,263	16,651
Rangoon, Burma	6,295	2,915	8,240	9,499	7,213	14,247	3,989	961	2,921	3,822	4,518	1,860	6,812	2,410	8,624	9,689	2,839	1,437	9,225	8,140
Raoul Is., Kermadec Islands	4,379	13,426	17,759	18,995	15,161	3,983	14,414	10,876	7,908	8,804	8,564	12,351	15,014	9,522	17,821	1,357	9,529	9,777	17,988	18,322
Rarotonga (Avarua)	6,274	14,833	16,917	17,249	14,624	2,160	16,086	12,234	9,256	9,564	9,138	13,958	16,942	10,597	16,712	2,422	10,476	11,090	16,522	17,757
Rawson, Argentina	12,484	15,934	12,600	11,075	14,727	7,090	14,469	17,467	16,623	18,262	17,925	15,896	10,876	18,380	12,337	10,728	18,712	17,654	11,810	12,243
Recife, Brazil	16,764	12,035	7,711	6,186	9,980	11,112	10,724	14,630	17,562	16,855	16,890	12,823	7,984	16,204	7,456	15,464	16,216	15,775	6,951	7,385
Regina, Canada	13,584	11,065	7,500	7,699	6,314	8,692	11,636	11,330	11,527	9,346	8,773	12,065	13,462	10,378	7,200	10,693	9,922	11,269	6,925	8,278
Reykjavik, Iceland	14,988	7,191	2,686	3,222	2,413	13,472	7,212	8,788	10,887	8,978	8,839	8,431	8,677	9,078	2,408	14,653	8,801	9,455	2,258	3,484
Rhodes, Greece	13,222	4,055	1,883	2,599	3,633	17,975	3,237	6,589	9,559	8,844	9,190	5,184	4,270	7,990	2,249	16,362	8,028	7,690	2,725	1,309
Richmond, Virginia	16,010	11,843	6,960	6,519	6,916	9,197	11,828	13,019	13,946	11,719	11,211	13,062	12,223	12,544	6,573	12,514	12,119	13,297	6,093	7,538
Riga, USSR	13,451	4,700	1,292	2,807	1,411	15,871	4,627	6,675	9,290	7,890	8,020	5,958	6,557	7,488	1,510	15,128	7,353	7,565	2,047	1,928
Ringkobing, Denmark	14,410	5,639	912	2,130	1,896	15,351	5,430	7,653	10,230	8,724	8,793	6,897	6,865	8,415	835	15,659	8,255	8,531	1,195	1,751
Rio Branco, Brazil	15,496	15,253	10,051	8,713	11,467	7,669	14,156	17,704	18,770	16,900	16,265	16,282	11,595	17,898	9,686	12,235	17,469	18,526	9,087	10,069
Rio Cuarto, Argentina	13,531	15,857	11,739	10,237	13,692	7,326	14,403	18,058	17,717	18,695	18,057	16,192	10,975	19,511	11,442	11,374	19,707	18,661	10,887	11,484
Rio de Janeiro, Brazil	15,169	13,559	9,577	8,050	11,830	9,639	12,144	16,035	18,262	18,725	18,645	14,114	8,941	17,843	9,326	13,709	17,982	17,118	8,819	9,222
Rio Gallegos, Argentina	11,516	16,012	13,452	11,925	15,679	6,740	14,619	16,879	15,647	17,406	17,243	15,660	10,997	17,421	13,214	9,989	17,735	16,799	12,709	13,027
Rio Grande, Brazil	14,038	14,703	10,907	9,382	13,100	8,471	13,246	16,968	17,912	19,818	19,120	15,062	9,835	18,813	10,648	12,386	19,166	17,840	10,130	10,558
Riyadh, Saudi Arabia	11,218	2,520	4,033	4,731	5,012	19,374	1,211	5,085	8,044	7,972	8,496	3,338	3,060	6,803	4,419	14,885	6,986	6,230	4,921	3,504
Road Town, Brit. Virgin Isls.	17,494	12,870	7,487	6,469	8,408	9,237	12,298	14,783	16,356	14,128	13,653	14,117	11,270	14,789	7,088	13,503	14,405	15,376	6,499	7,771
Roanoke, Virginia	15,807	11,969	7,144	6,729	7,026	9,000	11,994	13,064	13,876	11,654	11,131	13,177	12,443	12,520	6,760	12,292	12,089	13,298	6,288	7,735
Robinson Crusoe Island, Chile	12,750	17,207	12,732	11,285	14,322	5,981	15,753	19,025	16,876	17,351	16,750	17,451	12,286	18,518	12,397	10,142	18,368	18,621	11,812	12,593
Rochester, New York	15,774	11,295	6,569	6,273	6,347	9,542	11,365	12,399	13,371	11,141	10,653	12,498	12,069	11,932	6,194	12,548	11,512	12,675	5,752	7,199
Rockhampton, Australia	1,172	10,309	15,480	16,877	13,495	7,180	11,206	7,867	5,062	6,591	6,637	9,173	12,365	6,853	15,812	2,869	7,002	6,853	16,385	15,522
Rome, Italy	14,563	5,365	698	1,239	3,246	16,547	4,702	7,772	10,649	9,560	9,772	6,559	5,374	8,943	900	16,978	8,892	8,810	1,259	189
Rosario, Argentina	13,692	15,513	11,495	9,983	13,527	7,667	14,059	17,740	17,831	19,038	18,387	15,856	10,636	19,436	11,209	11,676	19,897	18,458	10,664	11,211
Roseau, Dominica	17,742	12,891	7,497	6,385	8,606	9,400	12,207	14,957	16,766	14,549	14,097	14,116	10,938	15,129	7,104	13,776	14,765	15,644	6,507	7,715
Rostock, East Germany	14,262	5,376	661	2,055	1,976	15,684	5,118	7,462	10,108	8,688	8,793	6,633	6,546	8,307	729	15,785	8,170	8,373	1,229	1,482
Rostov-na-Donu, USSR	12,402	3,314	2,101	3,459	2,449	17,188	3,113	5,570	8,420	7,434	7,727	4,565	5,383	6,725	2,487	14,973	6,697	6,586	3,087	2,149
Rotterdam, Netherlands	14,827	5,886	658	1,609	2,420	15,436	5,532	8,020	10,673	9,225	9,308	7,137	6,631	8,870	379	16,169	8,728	8,938	681	1,440
Rouyn, Canada	15,425	10,837	6,309	6,167	5,877	9,783	10,999	11,844	12,810	10,580	10,104	12,018	12,001	11,358	5,951	12,464	10,938	12,102	5,553	6,989
Sacramento, California	12,182	12,274	9,340	9,569	7,895	6,935	13,119	11,853	11,163	9,208	8,544	13,054	15,325	10,478	9,053	8,912	10,014	11,461	8,795	10,132
Saginaw, Michigan	15,285	11,478	6,942	6,728	6,518	9,153	11,655	12,384	13,113	10,891	10,370	12,648	12,545	11,768	6,578	12,039	11,334	12,564	6,161	7,604
Saint Denis, Reunion	8,629	5,904	8,804	8,796	10,124	15,029	4,933	6,838	8,330	9,889	10,586	5,313	2,965	8,495	9,122	12,386	8,931	7,501	9,451	8,050
Saint George's, Grenada	17,569	13,171	7,785	6,629	8,955	9,218	12,431	15,293	17,114	14,890	14,424	14,383	10,981	15,491	7,395	13,662	15,124	16,001	6,796	7,970
Saint John, Canada	16,426	10,615	5,684	5,324	5,740	10,454	10,550	12,004	13,416	11,211	10,803	11,851	11,118	11,813	5,301	13,465	11,429	12,444	4,834	6,282
Saint John's, Antigua	17,751	12,781	7,388	6,310	8,439	9,439	12,139	14,800	16,561	14,344	13,893	14,015	10,982	14,933	6,992	13,766	14,565	15,463	6,398	7,630
Saint John's, Canada	16,833	9,754	4,667	4,272	5,024	11,497	9,572	11,391	13,214	11,100	10,791	11,007	10,079	11,483	4,276	14,411	11,146	11,983	3,792	5,237
Saint Louis, Missouri	14,895	12,156	7,692	7,445	7,204	8,405	12,390	12,876	13,265	11,082	10,511	13,296	13,238	12,079	7,326	11,429	11,629	12,937	6,904	8,348
Saint Paul, Minnesota	14,534	11,540	7,361	7,296	6,623	8,737	11,889	12,145	12,563	10,365	9,807	12,643	13,132	11,340	7,018	11,348	10,891	12,194	6,650	8,073

Distances in Kilometers	Mount Isa, Australia	Multan, Pakistan	Munich, West Germany	Murcia, Spain	Murmansk, USSR	Mururoa Atoll, Fr. Polynesia	Muscat, Oman	Myitkyina, Burma	Naga, Philippines	Nagasaki, Japan	Nagoya, Japan	Nagpur, India	Nairobi, Kenya	Nanchang, China	Nancy, France	Nandi, Fiji	Nanjing, China	Nanning, China	Nantes, France	Naples, Italy
Saint Peter Port, UK	15,394	6,411	1,046	1,279	2,897	15,126	5,978	8,582	11,239	9,758	9,816	7,656	6,765	9,433	644	16,494	9,283	9,506	259	1,625
Saipan (Susupe)	4,027	7,685	11,659	13,186	9,311	9,183	9,068	5,145	2,435	2,524	2,386	7,033	12,085	3,413	11,888	5,038	3,309	4,017	12,369	12,051
Salalah, Oman	10,212	2,292	5,173	5,834	5,957	18,562	869	4,571	7,391	7,704	8,303	2,668	2,773	6,405	5,560	14,035	6,668	5,684	6,061	4,638
Salem, Oregon	12,185	11,557	8,786	9,137	7,219	7,572	12,412	11,208	10,730	8,692	8,047	12,351	14,782	9,911	8,521	9,189	9,445	10,881	8,307	9,596
Salt Lake City, Utah	13,032	12,143	8,699	8,811	7,499	7,476	12,811	12,085	11,750	9,693	9,056	13,058	14,624	10,882	8,388	9,749	10,416	11,837	8,086	9,464
Salta, Argentina	14,299	15,753	11,119	9,658	12,891	7,430	14,382	18,298	18,486	18,286	17,589	16,381	11,191	19,556	10,794	11,744	19,106	19,355	10,218	10,960
Salto, Uruguay	13,946	15,231	11,198	9,684	13,263	7,956	13,783	17,530	18,035	19,267	18,579	15,622	10,395	19,360	10,916	11,984	19,711	18,366	10,375	10,906
Salvador, Brazil	16,269	12,642	8,383	6,859	10,627	10,530	11,298	15,220	18,053	17,520	17,506	13,370	8,395	16,856	8,125	14,810	16,885	16,363	7,614	8,058
Salzburg, Austria	14,395	5,286	115	1,584	2,605	16,201	4,819	7,558	10,341	9,095	9,260	6,521	5,908	8,583	517	16,389	8,492	8,542	1,099	780
Samsun, Turkey	12,582	3,382	2,093	3,211	3,088	17,807	2,850	5,828	8,764	7,964	8,304	4,584	4,714	7,146	2,496	15,496	7,165	6,901	3,065	1,852
San Antonio, Texas	14,158	13,323	8,962	8,650	8,408	7,140	13,648	13,709	13,482	11,441	10,803	14,403	14,363	12,615	8,593	10,418	12,150	13,556	8,157	9,604
San Cristobal, Venezuela	16,329	14,303	8,912	7,830	9,806	7,976	13,652	16,172	17,100	14,945	14,360	15,543	12,139	15,880	8,516	12,429	15,447	16,621	7,923	9,157
San Diego, California	12,443	12,984	9,703	9,764	8,468	6,468	13,754	12,611	11,814	9,918	9,245	13,800	15,597	11,211	9,388	8,923	10,748	12,199	9,072	10,462
San Francisco, California	12,085	12,345	9,458	9,690	7,997	6,824	13,208	11,876	11,130	9,196	8,528	13,107	15,445	10,477	9,172	8,795	10,014	11,464	8,915	10,251
San Jose, Costa Rica	15,220	14,860	9,611	8,726	10,017	6,943	14,519	16,094	16,040	14,067	13,421	16,112	13,429	15,229	9,208	11,243	14,766	16,142	8,643	9,988
San Juan, Argentina	13,500	16,221	11,877	10,396	13,698	6,973	14,782	18,489	17,697	18,286	17,632	16,612	11,389	19,492	11,562	11,120	19,335	18,992	10,993	11,674
San Juan, Puerto Rico	17,338	12,973	7,597	6,600	8,465	9,095	12,425	14,839	16,313	14,083	13,593	14,223	11,428	14,783	7,197	13,347	14,390	15,398	6,611	7,895
San Luis Potosi, Mexico	13,804	14,158	9,746	9,341	9,252	6,376	14,484	14,387	13,787	11,880	11,214	15,214	14,913	13,138	9,370	9,921	12,672	14,112	8,911	10,359
San Marino, San Marino	14,527	5,347	475	1,318	3,030	16,424	4,749	7,711	10,558	9,413	9,607	6,557	5,562	8,832	716	16,787	8,767	8,732	1,152	373
San Miguel de Tucuman, Argen.	14,113	15,799	11,275	9,802	13,089	7,395	14,402	18,287	18,311	18,421	17,724	16,358	11,145	19,777	10,956	11,653	19,315	19,234	10,384	11,093
San Salvador, El Salvador	14,815	14,730	9,668	8,922	9,795	6,704	14,601	15,623	15,345	13,400	12,745	15,946	13,937	14,601	9,268	10,825	14,136	15,542	8,729	10,124
Sanaa, Yemen	11,146	3,234	4,705	5,094	6,008	19,217	1,764	5,629	8,465	8,711	9,286	3,739	2,011	7,445	5,061	15,047	7,687	6,750	5,489	4,041
Santa Cruz, Bolivia	15,084	15,249	10,382	8,948	12,087	7,868	13,970	17,852	19,204	17,899	17,252	16,064	11,031	18,796	10,045	12,315	18,414	18,978	9,462	10,272
Santa Cruz, Tenerife	17,433	8,283	3,239	1,758	5,502	14,258	7,386	10,756	13,634	12,346	12,423	9,413	6,539	11,894	2,955	18,195	11,799	11,801	2,442	3,093
Santa Fe, New Mexico	13,509	12,709	8,851	8,777	7,924	7,256	13,244	12,817	12,502	10,458	9,819	13,692	14,608	11,646	8,511	9,998	11,181	12,599	8,147	9,569
Santa Rosa, Argentina	13,186	15,886	12,019	10,506	14,037	7,262	14,418	17,880	17,354	18,659	18,109	16,095	10,918	19,125	11,733	11,178	19,430	18,322	11,188	11,727
Santa Rosalia, Mexico	12,788	13,629	9,955	9,839	8,963	6,151	14,285	13,368	12,517	10,664	9,986	14,505	15,644	11,967	9,614	9,076	11,505	12,957	9,240	10,668
Santarem, Brazil	17,019	13,587	8,481	7,090	10,167	9,319	12,495	16,100	18,745	16,609	16,189	14,617	10,182	16,936	8,133	13,896	16,657	17,111	7,544	8,437
Santiago del Estero, Argentina	14,064	15,736	11,292	9,811	13,149	7,461	14,326	18,187	18,263	18,554	17,858	16,259	11,039	19,904	10,979	11,682	19,455	19,095	10,412	11,092
Santiago, Chile	13,213	16,446	12,170	10,688	13,976	6,740	14,993	18,559	17,408	18,109	17,489	16,754	11,550	19,201	11,855	10,842	19,129	18,822	11,286	11,964
Santo Domingo, Dominican Rep.	16,944	13,226	7,878	6,932	8,609	8,739	12,744	14,964	16,179	13,955	13,433	14,482	11,827	14,751	7,476	12,955	14,339	15,434	6,897	8,210
Sao Paulo de Olivenca, Brazil	15,937	14,906	9,582	8,318	10,834	7,821	13,958	17,172	18,290	16,223	15,614	16,041	11,745	17,169	9,203	12,401	16,743	17,840	8,602	9,677
Sao Paulo, Brazil	15,063	13,906	9,828	8,305	12,023	9,291	12,495	16,389	18,484	18,925	18,672	14,467	9,289	18,190	9,565	13,402	18,305	17,468	9,045	9,501
Sao Tome, Sao Tome & Principe	14,423	7,584	5,319	4,246	7,872	15,605	6,158	10,067	12,864	13,043	13,534	8,175	3,354	11,860	5,358	17,827	12,061	11,190	5,257	4,549
Sapporo, Japan	7,064	6,229	8,771	10,266	6,278	10,849	7,690	4,435	3,697	1,515	955	6,201	11,287	2,780	8,940	7,681	2,327	3,778	9,362	9,311
Sarajevo, Yugoslavia	14,055	4,869	714	1,764	2,923	16,806	4,286	7,250	10,119	9,050	9,279	6,079	5,323	8,414	1,083	16,517	8,367	8,282	1,600	478
Saratov, USSR	12,023	3,168	2,483	3,944	2,057	16,681	3,284	5,194	7,945	6,833	7,099	4,423	5,921	6,203	2,831	14,355	6,142	6,149	3,426	2,699
Saskatoon, Canada	13,425	10,886	7,449	7,707	6,176	8,777	11,493	11,107	11,299	9,115	8,544	11,869	13,431	10,146	7,159	10,628	9,689	11,038	6,906	8,238
Schefferville, Canada	15,628	9,783	5,208	5,171	4,839	10,884	9,890	10,994	12,363	10,168	9,781	10,989	10,997	10,752	4,858	13,253	10,367	11,393	4,487	5,909
Seattle, Washington	12,286	11,281	8,502	8,884	6,919	7,870	12,117	11,001	10,644	8,568	7,935	12,096	14,495	9,756	8,242	9,399	9,290	10,715	8,039	9,316
Sendai, Japan	6,531	6,310	9,205	10,713	6,750	10,678	7,781	4,312	3,240	1,163	493	6,155	11,328	2,544	9,391	7,284	2,122	3,536	9,831	9,711
Seoul, South Korea	6,585	5,127	8,570	10,097	6,316	11,807	6,599	3,102	2,679	592	928	4,933	10,115	1,429	8,813	8,087	969	2,422	9,317	8,962
Sept-Iles, Canada	16,028	10,183	5,421	5,223	5,267	10,680	10,207	11,482	12,872	10,672	10,275	11,406	11,057	11,264	5,051	13,370	10,880	11,900	4,631	6,073
Sevastopol, USSR	12,848	3,679	1,728	2,970	2,713	17,391	3,254	6,042	8,931	7,992	8,288	4,907	5,093	7,260	2,129	15,533	7,244	7,084	2,715	1,630
Seville, Spain	16,220	7,018	1,862	434	4,231	15,210	6,263	9,425	12,266	10,995	11,109	8,196	6,141	10,517	1,596	17,810	10,424	10,447	1,151	1,787
Shanghai, China	6,056	4,741	8,799	10,312	6,747	12,126	6,187	2,431	1,945	829	1,517	4,341	9,568	594	9,083	8,073	266	1,587	9,626	9,086
Sheffield, United Kingdom	15,106	6,276	1,088	1,710	2,485	15,004	5,961	8,344	10,922	9,373	9,410	7,532	7,020	9,104	750	16,057	8,935	9,227	684	1,828
Shenyang, China	7,118	4,784	8,013	9,541	5,759	12,213	6,253	3,006	3,122	1,151	1,384	4,727	9,826	1,608	8,254	8,618	1,159	2,534	8,757	8,417
Shiraz, Iran	10,847	1,830	4,040	4,986	4,555	18,590	896	4,431	7,420	7,210	7,718	2,825	3,805	6,084	4,442	14,311	6,242	5,574	4,996	3,668
Sibiu, Romania	13,586	4,428	990	2,257	2,629	16,942	3,950	6,765	9,620	8,555	8,796	5,654	5,363	7,911	1,393	16,046	7,865	7,788	1,970	973
Singapore	4,584	4,682	10,073	11,232	9,113	12,873	5,469	2,755	2,530	4,428	5,078	3,471	7,467	3,291	10,465	8,323	3,749	2,431	11,063	9,886
Sioux Falls, South Dakota	14,274	11,754	7,675	7,626	6,865	8,428	12,155	12,238	12,493	10,318	9,740	12,829	13,462	11,346	7,335	11,028	10,891	12,226	6,974	8,393
Skelleftea, Sweden	13,414	5,171	1,933	3,313	707	15,016	5,316	6,842	9,214	7,586	7,623	6,406	7,441	7,386	1,994	14,500	7,186	7,611	2,378	2,698
Skopje, Yugoslavia	13,820	4,620	1,035	1,975	3,078	17,127	3,984	7,045	9,949	8,972	9,234	5,814	5,036	8,276	1,406	16,491	8,251	8,099	1,910	618
Socotra Island (Tamrida)	10,047	2,647	5,551	6,113	6,431	18,314	1,306	4,756	7,473	7,952	8,574	2,829	2,447	6,615	5,930	13,948	6,907	5,837	6,409	4,971
Sofia, Bulgaria	13,666	4,470	1,099	2,133	2,981	17,174	3,868	6,883	9,782	8,805	9,071	5,671	5,054	8,107	1,486	16,327	8,082	7,933	2,017	781
Songkhla, Thailand	5,258	3,964	9,345	10,539	8,375	13,457	4,838	2,041	2,571	4,147	4,831	2,781	7,145	2,870	9,735	8,878	3,335	1,916	10,334	9,186
Sorong, Indonesia	2,372	7,194	12,236	13,657	10,422	9,963	8,292	4,660	1,836	3,731	4,034	6,171	10,510	3,659	12,572	5,383	3,875	3,613	13,153	12,319
South Georgia Island	11,689	13,830	12,223	10,775	14,790	8,817	12,444	15,083	15,171	17,402	17,828	13,564	8,830	16,412	12,099	11,387	16,875	15,468	11,724	11,604
South Pole	7,707	13,343	15,339	14,210	17,658	7,582	12,616	12,811	11,509	13,632	13,894	12,342	9,862	13,176	15,399	8,032	13,549	12,526	15,236	14,526
South Sandwich Islands	11,211	13,250	12,251	10,872	14,852	9,217	11,913	14,354	14,490	16,712	17,210	12,894	8,336	15,668	12,175	11,346	16,132	14,720	11,861	11,566
Split, Yugoslavia	14,218	5,030	638	1,601	2,992	16,708	4,428	7,413	10,281	9,197	9,418	6,237	5,363	8,573	976	16,646	8,523	8,445	1,464	348
Spokane, Washington	12,654	11,337	8,303	8,617	6,842	7,997	12,100	11,199	10,963	8,861	8,239	12,207	14,299	10,018	8,029	9,718	9,553	10,965	7,799	9,106
Spoleto, Italy	14,529	5,336	609	1,287	3,151	16,515	4,700	7,727	10,593	9,483	9,689	6,537	5,440	8,879	834	16,889	8,823	8,758	1,230	246
Springbok, South Africa	11,641	8,726	8,641	7,746	11,008	13,789	7,329	10,442	12,219	13,656	14,348	8,638	3,727	12,239	8,756	14,316	12,638	11,274	8,735	7,814
Springfield, Illinois	14,920	12,016	7,565	7,338	7,065	8,530	12,253	12,752	13,189	10,997	10,434	13,158	13,141	11,978	7,202	11,503	11,529	12,828	6,784	8,227
Springfield, Massachusetts	16,195	11,199	6,317	5,935	6,286	9,822	11,174	12,463	13,627	11,399	10,938	12,424	11,700	12,120	5,934	12,956	11,713	12,817	5,466	6,913
Srinagar, India	9,147	535	5,374	6,661	4,660	16,463	1,959	2,381	5,361	5,062	5,599	1,494	5,575	3,926	5,758	12,241	4,080	3,491	6,359	5,305
Stanley, Falkland Islands	11,805	15,254	12,879	11,361	15,255	7,524	13,844	16,416	15,781	17,814	17,827	14,996	10,220	17,397	12,674	10,639	17,805	16,588	12,205	12,391
Stara Zagora, Bulgaria	13,476	4,279	1,270	2,320	2,988	17,316	3,681	6,700	9,607	8,665	8,944	5,479	4,969	7,943	1,664	16,199	7,926	7,755	2,203	964
Stockholm, Sweden	13,737	5,118	1,314	2,740	1,292	15,464	5,071	7,017	9,550	8,043	8,126	6,374	6,920	7,732	1,413	15,102	7,569	7,868	1,865	2,075
Stornoway, United Kingdom	15,021	6,512	1,632	2,282	2,237	14,486	6,344	8,406	10,823	9,132	9,107	7,770	7,615	8,994	1,346	15,507	8,784	9,213	1,266	2,422
Strasbourg, France	14,749	5,676	288	1,378	2,659	15,833	5,221	7,913	10,655	9,326	9,454	6,915	6,196	8,878	115	16,466	8,766	8,877	711	1,003
Stuttgart, West Germany	14,642	5,569	190	1,457	2,600	15,909	5,123	7,806	10,552	9,236	9,371	6,809	6,151	8,777	220	16,411	8,669	8,771	819	968
Subic, Philippines	4,468	5,249	10,116	11,557	8,357	11,719	6,507	2,650	347	2,213	2,799	4,399	9,346	1,593	10,449	7,242	1,907	1,531	11,029	10,235
Suchow, China	6,530	4,296	8,278	9,789	6,264	12,586	5,756	2,145	2,364	1,193	1,807	3,999	9,208	631	8,566	8,592	288	1,536	9,113	8,561
Sucre, Bolivia	14,851	15,510	10,631	9,203	12,298	7,614	14,223	18,113	18,942	17,868	17,197	16,309	11,243	18,930	10,291	12,054	18,508	19,239	9,706	10,530
Sudbury, Canada	15,376	11,074	6,546	6,377	6,114	9,547	11,243	12,043	12,922	10,692	10,198	12,251	12,207	11,508	6,185	12,304	11,082	12,272	5,780	7,219
Suez, Egypt	12,722	3,735	2,697	3,216	4,338	18,779	2,676	6,334	9,328	8,890	9,312	4,746	3,488	7,894	3,050	16,224	7,993	7,468	3,492	2,047
Sundsvall, Sweden	13,670	5,251	1,624	2,991	1,027	15,157	5,296	7,031	9,471	7,882	7,932	6,498	7,251	7,645	1,673	14,819	7,458	7,836	2,062	2,406
Surabaya, Indonesia	3,244	6,048	11,436	12,594	10,342	11,583	6,804	3,975	2,581	4,791	5,337	4,837	8,448	3,990	11,826	7,094	4,396	3,361	12,425	11,250
Suva, Fiji	4,088	12,603	16,470	17,804	13,873	4,470	13,786	10,002	7,007	7,641	7,349	11,660	15,308	8,487	16,544	112	8,439	8,867	16,779	17,074
Sverdlovsk, USSR	11,262	3,082	3,385	4,903	1,913	15,808	3,694	4,563	7,092	5,792	6,017	4,245	6,790	5,294	3,677	13,271	5,177	5,386	4,239	3,744
Svobodnyy, USSR	8,067	5,170	7,436	8,944	4,997	12,078	6,587	3,889	4,213	2,071	1,936	5,389	10,211	2,722	7,622	9,037	2,281	3,603	8,071	7,955
Sydney, Australia	1,858	10,969	16,325	17,496	14,591	6,883	11,666	8,681	6,039	7,710	7,787	9,763	12,162	7,862	16,698	3,160	8,051	7,746	17,297	16,172
Sydney, Canada	16,670	10,256	5,243	4,857	5,441	10,909	10,132	11,768	13,375	11,203	10,837	11,503	10,653	11,708	4,856	13,902	11,344	12,280	4,379	5,826
Syktyvkar, USSR	11,945	3,812	2,867	4,393	1,152	15,521	4,269	5,317	7,753	6,294	6,439	5,000	7,083	5,934	3,105	13,626	5,775	6,100	3,630	3,368
Szeged, Hungary	13,890	4,739	683	1,977	2,630	16,709	4,252	7,062	9,899	8,777	8,994	5,967	5,515	8,174	1,085	16,222	8,114	8,075	1,658	770
Szombathely, Hungary	14,143	5,015	391	1,775	2,588	16,444	4,543	7,309	10,117	8,928	9,117	6,248	5,724	8,373	794	16,303	8,296	8,306	1,373	736
Tabriz, Iran	11,675	2,473	3,007	4,116	3,529	18,140	1,984	4,977	7,948	7,349	7,759	3,661	4,466	6,410	3,410	14,788	6,477	6,079	3,986	2,760
Tacheng, China	9,380	2,089	5,184	6,659	3,683	15,361	3,365	2,695	5,241	4,238	4,625	2,861	6,964	3,488	5,510	11,766	3,450	3,495	6,090	5,391
Tahiti (Papeete)	7,411	15,647	16,205	16,204	14,287	1,215	17,027	13,104	10,182	10,201	9,696	14,923	17,812	11,362	15,919	3,499	11,180	11,962	15,613	16,998
Taipei, Taiwan	5,427	4,931	9,327	10,822	7,367	11,935	6,327	2,426	1,276	1,187	1,858	4,348	9,540	688	9,628	7,694	820	1,364	10,186	9,557
Taiyuan, China	7,073	3,855	7,702	9,212	5,722	13,062	5,326	1,990	2,884	1,673	2,197	3,706	8,851	1,065	7,991	9,155	860	1,717	8,541	7,985
Tallahassee, Florida	15,530	12,824	7,959	7,452	7,877	8,223	12,836	13,824	14,317	12,138	11,564	14,027	13,040	13,122	7,570	11,773	12,675	13,960	7,078	8,518
Tallinn, USSR	13,365	4,760	1,519	3,011	1,137	15,639	4,774	6,636	9,183	7,717	7,824	6,013	6,813	7,370	1,693	14,887	7,216	7,491	2,192	2,193
Tamanrasset, Algeria	15,286	6,540	2,866	1,800	5,459	16,376	5,401	9,137	12,131	11,493	11,805	7,517	4,314	10,636	2,875	19,016	10,685	10,267	2,784	2,163
Tampa, Florida	15,720	13,004	8,031	7,447	8,076	8,199	12,941	14,103	14,645	12,466	11,893	14,224	12,938	13,442	7,637	11,893	12,996	14,271	7,127	8,556
Tampere, Finland	13,372	4,899	1,673	3,129	938	15,405	4,970	6,695	9,178	7,649	7,730	6,146	7,052	7,357	1,802	14,732	7,185	7,518	2,260	2,388
Tanami, Australia	1,025	8,347	13,717	14,904	12,326	9,342	9,098	6,117	3,787	5,841	6,151	7,146	10,272	5,586	14,100	5,015	5,875	5,275	14,701	13,560

Distances in Kilometers

	Mount Isa, Australia	Multan, Pakistan	Munich, West Germany	Murcia, Spain	Murmansk, USSR	Mururoa Atoll, Fr. Polynesia	Muscat, Oman	Myitkyina, Burma	Naga, Philippines	Nagasaki, Japan	Nagoya, Japan	Nagpur, India	Nairobi, Kenya	Nanchang, China	Nancy, France	Nandi, Fiji	Nanjing, China	Nanning, China	Nantes, France	Naples, Italy
Tangier, Morocco	16,260	7,060	1,981	483	4,389	15,248	6,265	9,493	12,357	11,126	11,253	8,225	6,030	10,622	1,736	17,986	10,538	10,528	1,316	1,836
Tarawa (Betio)	4,386	11,039	14,233	15,607	11,636	5,826	12,423	8,498	5,643	5,684	5,283	10,361	15,154	6,758	14,316	2,174	6,606	7,362	14,597	14,863
Tashkent, USSR	9,969	1,253	4,524	5,884	3,732	16,607	2,204	3,135	6,023	5,364	5,808	2,421	5,747	4,419	4,897	12,798	4,478	4,168	5,498	4,546
Tbilisi, USSR	11,898	2,714	2,692	3,901	3,112	17,779	2,382	5,125	8,060	7,310	7,679	3,940	4,827	6,454	3,092	14,820	6,485	6,197	3,680	2,544
Tegucigalpa, Honduras	15,033	14,604	9,493	8,723	9,687	6,905	14,427	15,608	15,480	13,494	12,848	15,832	13,719	14,664	9,092	11,043	14,200	15,588	8,548	9,936
Tehran, Iran	11,160	1,967	3,536	4,633	3,875	18,182	1,503	4,514	7,501	7,034	7,485	3,136	4,363	6,021	3,939	14,377	6,121	5,631	4,516	3,280
Tel Aviv, Israel	12,557	3,492	2,645	3,319	4,106	18,719	2,519	6,081	9,074	8,588	9,003	4,544	3,698	7,611	3,018	15,963	7,701	7,209	3,498	2,074
Telegraph Creek, Canada	11,897	10,018	7,762	8,408	5,873	8,869	10,926	9,737	9,633	7,475	6,883	10,808	13,638	8,581	7,561	9,626	8,118	9,516	7,468	8,600
Teresina, Brazil	17,138	12,631	7,916	6,425	9,971	10,435	11,403	15,230	18,224	16,846	16,673	13,527	8,857	16,571	7,617	14,936	16,465	16,356	7,066	7,710
Ternate, Indonesia	2,722	6,735	11,824	13,225	10,095	10,430	7,825	4,217	1,493	3,552	3,931	5,705	10,086	3,320	12,168	5,851	3,576	3,193	12,755	11,880
The Valley, Anguilla	17,647	12,793	7,403	6,358	8,389	9,366	12,188	14,759	16,435	14,212	13,751	14,034	11,108	14,833	7,006	13,657	14,457	15,389	6,414	7,668
Thessaloniki, Greece	13,702	4,500	1,229	2,088	3,211	17,321	3,820	6,955	9,879	8,962	9,244	5,681	4,851	8,228	1,595	16,498	8,218	8,021	2,087	734
Thimphu, Bhutan	7,567	1,801	6,933	8,254	5,862	15,100	3,150	802	3,797	3,893	4,528	1,288	6,490	2,569	7,307	10,693	2,846	1,944	7,908	6,900
Thunder Bay, Canada	14,715	11,094	6,887	6,860	6,161	9,214	11,414	11,806	12,424	10,204	9,679	12,216	12,694	11,107	6,547	11,707	10,667	11,925	6,190	7,606
Tientsin, China	7,023	4,260	7,880	9,402	5,781	12,681	5,732	2,400	2,886	1,343	1,802	4,135	9,273	1,165	8,151	8,880	799	1,996	8,684	8,212
Tijuana, Mexico	12,451	13,006	9,714	9,769	8,486	6,455	13,773	12,635	11,835	9,941	9,267	13,823	15,603	11,234	9,398	8,925	10,771	12,223	9,079	10,471
Tiksi, USSR	10,274	5,719	5,843	7,235	3,241	12,373	6,839	5,500	6,451	4,318	4,082	6,430	10,208	4,839	5,924	10,570	4,441	5,578	6,259	6,533
Timbuktu, Mali	16,066	7,630	3,727	2,359	6,319	15,380	6,437	10,232	13,225	12,592	12,878	8,564	4,807	11,750	3,638	19,886	11,797	11,367	3,380	3,142
Tindouf, Algeria	16,666	7,598	2,839	1,316	5,309	15,042	6,634	10,122	13,061	11,982	12,143	8,691	5,777	11,386	2,637	18,775	11,339	11,202	2,241	2,513
Tirane, Albania	13,961	4,759	999	1,831	3,174	17,078	4,092	7,195	10,103	9,127	9,385	5,946	5,022	8,431	1,347	16,641	8,407	8,251	1,821	472
Tokyo, Japan	6,246	6,287	9,394	10,910	6,972	10,661	7,758	4,188	2,955	962	265	6,063	11,266	2,375	9,593	7,129	1,979	3,354	10,047	9,874
Toledo, Spain	15,963	6,771	1,548	327	3,911	15,333	6,072	9,146	11,964	10,671	10,785	7,965	6,163	10,207	1,272	17,555	10,108	10,155	840	1,553
Topeka, Kansas	14,417	12,226	7,983	7,822	7,311	8,109	12,571	12,744	12,922	10,768	10,176	13,318	13,641	11,826	7,629	10,979	11,369	12,717	7,234	8,670
Toronto, Canada	15,620	11,308	6,645	6,383	6,352	9,459	11,413	12,352	13,261	11,031	10,535	12,501	12,190	11,844	6,274	12,408	11,420	12,602	5,842	7,288
Toulouse, France	15,393	6,231	935	660	3,356	15,652	5,623	8,561	11,357	10,064	10,190	7,445	6,094	9,594	674	17,120	9,493	9,556	465	1,101
Tours, France	15,288	6,215	821	1,055	2,994	15,436	5,718	8,454	11,176	9,784	9,878	7,450	6,434	9,388	436	16,710	9,261	9,410	170	1,305
Townsville, Australia	781	9,740	14,883	16,290	12,928	7,672	10,679	7,278	4,465	6,034	6,112	8,622	12,063	6,260	15,215	3,233	6,415	6,258	15,789	14,939
Trenton, New Jersey	16,123	11,471	6,590	6,183	6,551	9,556	11,451	12,697	13,762	11,532	11,050	12,693	11,925	12,297	6,205	12,767	11,882	13,018	5,732	7,179
Tripoli, Lebanon	12,506	3,371	2,522	3,326	3,846	18,524	2,510	5,940	8,927	8,369	8,768	4,471	3,955	7,424	2,908	15,797	7,498	7,058	3,418	2,028
Tripoli, Libya	14,583	5,473	1,699	1,414	4,204	17,020	4,537	8,019	10,989	10,176	10,465	6,568	4,526	9,396	1,847	17,717	9,409	9,120	2,019	886
Tristan da Cunha (Edinburgh)	12,962	11,463	9,730	8,387	12,333	11,423	10,007	13,351	14,911	16,564	17,258	11,517	6,401	15,148	9,672	13,849	15,551	14,175	9,395	9,040
Trondheim, Norway	13,946	5,618	1,701	2,934	1,184	14,855	5,654	7,365	9,747	8,091	8,104	6,865	7,504	7,918	1,661	14,842	7,712	8,145	1,950	2,525
Trujillo, Peru	14,738	16,098	10,722	9,518	11,715	6,578	15,202	18,058	17,532	15,974	15,291	17,271	12,843	17,252	10,333	11,160	16,786	18,204	9,734	10,872
Truk Island (Moen)	3,397	8,680	12,730	14,255	10,336	8,213	10,021	6,101	3,211	3,609	3,430	7,937	12,802	4,447	12,948	3,960	4,377	4,957	13,411	13,136
Truro, Canada	16,576	10,475	5,494	5,110	5,630	10,654	10,375	11,930	13,439	11,247	10,858	11,717	10,900	11,804	5,108	13,680	11,429	12,407	4,633	6,080
Tsingtao, China	6,604	4,556	8,318	9,838	6,208	12,347	6,024	2,485	2,502	953	1,505	4,318	9,512	919	8,589	8,463	467	1,871	9,121	8,643
Tsitsihar, China	7,701	4,835	7,574	9,097	5,234	12,292	6,281	3,377	3,741	1,694	1,732	4,951	9,898	2,189	7,791	8,972	1,756	3,061	8,271	8,033
Tubuai Island (Mataura)	7,262	15,910	16,790	16,609	14,933	1,097	17,172	13,317	10,343	10,568	10,103	15,044	17,196	11,653	16,481	3,499	11,510	12,172	16,126	17,550
Tucson, Arizona	13,006	13,093	9,433	9,379	8,406	6,684	13,728	12,960	12,342	10,393	9,731	14,003	15,210	11,650	9,099	9,419	11,185	12,628	8,743	10,161
Tulsa, Oklahoma	14,415	12,544	8,236	8,018	7,623	7,857	12,869	13,052	13,141	11,011	10,406	13,640	13,812	12,097	7,876	10,871	11,638	13,001	7,464	8,906
Tunis, Tunisia	14,833	5,648	1,266	1,009	3,843	16,619	4,829	8,136	11,065	10,089	10,326	6,794	5,035	9,405	1,359	17,561	9,381	9,207	1,508	570
Tura, USSR	10,013	4,292	5,279	6,784	2,865	13,647	5,434	4,328	5,895	4,050	4,068	5,042	8,886	4,110	5,463	11,169	3,807	4,646	5,919	5,827
Turin, Italy	14,871	5,716	457	1,073	3,028	16,034	5,148	8,039	10,846	9,606	9,762	6,935	5,885	9,094	419	16,838	9,005	9,038	751	712
Uberlandia, Brazil	15,536	13,871	9,512	8,001	11,615	9,311	12,507	16,433	18,944	18,458	18,136	14,550	9,457	18,087	9,229	13,581	18,071	17,565	8,690	9,241
Ufa, USSR	11,463	2,997	3,113	4,615	1,966	16,152	3,462	4,695	7,323	6,108	6,356	4,205	6,453	5,546	3,427	13,613	5,455	5,575	4,004	3,418
Ujungpandang, Indonesia	2,776	6,426	11,751	13,015	10,385	11,005	7,322	4,129	2,115	4,341	4,822	5,272	9,184	3,759	12,127	6,458	4,114	3,317	12,728	11,657
Ulaanbaatar, Mongolia	8,271	3,595	6,606	8,131	4,523	13,573	5,020	2,636	4,090	2,560	2,852	3,872	8,644	2,272	6,872	10,085	2,029	2,788	7,402	6,967
Ulan-Ude, USSR	8,617	3,811	6,376	7,903	4,188	13,495	5,194	3,061	4,461	2,779	2,973	4,202	8,814	2,661	6,620	10,230	2,378	3,221	7,132	6,789
Uliastay, Mongolia	8,700	2,912	6,016	7,527	4,136	14,324	4,306	2,483	4,502	3,232	3,581	3,352	7,929	2,680	6,307	10,775	2,546	2,950	6,861	6,316
Uranium City, Canada	13,203	10,058	6,896	7,331	5,418	9,440	10,711	10,294	10,667	8,453	7,919	11,031	12,889	9,410	6,639	10,826	8,961	10,274	6,455	7,711
Urumqi, China	8,891	2,075	5,665	7,131	4,147	15,119	3,466	2,229	4,759	3,852	4,285	2,632	7,091	3,023	5,994	11,346	3,013	3,006	6,576	5,850
Ushuaia, Argentina	11,229	15,818	13,627	12,103	15,932	6,812	14,463	16,535	15,330	17,178	17,091	15,386	10,855	17,084	13,407	9,869	17,417	16,443	12,920	13,159
Vaduz, Liechtenstein	14,669	5,553	190	1,340	2,758	16,031	5,056	7,832	10,611	9,340	9,490	6,785	5,991	8,848	300	16,566	8,751	8,815	838	799
Valencia, Spain	15,682	6,482	1,359	177	3,839	15,648	5,761	8,883	11,731	10,510	10,654	7,667	5,892	9,993	1,150	17,594	9,911	9,907	866	1,253
Valladolid, Spain	15,942	6,773	1,472	511	3,752	15,233	6,123	9,110	11,895	10,549	10,645	7,980	6,331	10,122	1,159	17,353	10,010	10,101	668	1,589
Valletta, Malta	14,452	5,285	1,382	1,410	3,853	17,016	4,433	7,798	10,749	9,866	10,139	6,415	4,722	9,122	1,575	17,396	9,120	8,884	1,831	548
Valparaiso, Chile	13,203	16,532	12,201	10,725	13,973	6,657	15,082	18,659	17,391	18,016	17,391	16,854	11,648	19,156	11,882	10,783	19,044	18,872	11,309	12,008
Vancouver, Canada	12,255	11,089	8,370	8,789	6,748	8,031	11,932	10,818	10,508	8,416	7,790	11,904	14,357	9,590	8,118	9,454	9,125	10,546	7,930	9,189
Varna, Bulgaria	13,291	4,099	1,382	2,512	2,883	17,346	3,552	6,503	9,404	8,459	8,743	5,309	5,009	7,736	1,783	15,996	7,720	7,554	2,342	1,161
Venice, Italy	14,503	5,346	306	1,391	2,869	16,319	4,798	7,674	10,497	9,307	9,488	6,567	5,711	8,756	589	16,644	8,680	8,681	1,087	536
Veracruz, Mexico	14,237	14,383	9,684	9,145	9,429	6,506	14,538	14,862	14,387	12,460	11,799	15,511	14,536	13,695	9,295	10,296	13,229	14,658	8,802	10,240
Verona, Italy	14,606	5,451	303	1,303	2,901	16,233	4,901	7,776	10,592	9,385	9,558	6,672	5,769	8,848	512	16,693	8,767	8,779	985	577
Victoria, Canada	12,223	11,173	8,458	8,868	6,840	7,939	12,023	10,880	10,533	8,451	7,821	11,982	14,447	9,636	8,205	9,387	9,170	10,595	8,013	9,276
Victoria, Seychelles	9,218	4,213	7,236	7,495	8,344	16,690	3,142	5,617	7,748	8,850	9,534	3,846	2,104	7,434	7,587	13,197	7,820	6,497	7,993	6,550
Vienna, Austria	14,142	5,038	356	1,813	2,489	16,355	4,599	7,305	10,095	8,875	9,055	6,276	5,829	8,342	754	16,224	8,258	8,292	1,346	836
Vientiane, Laos	5,877	3,427	8,616	9,946	7,338	13,619	4,608	982	2,255	3,187	3,885	2,489	7,508	1,801	8,986	9,094	2,253	803	9,586	8,591
Villahermosa, Mexico	14,541	14,421	9,569	8,956	9,461	6,675	14,467	15,080	14,737	12,781	12,126	15,590	14,241	13,991	9,175	10,580	13,525	14,941	8,664	10,091
Vilnius, USSR	13,414	4,549	1,197	2,725	1,640	16,131	4,411	6,605	9,280	7,954	8,113	5,808	6,293	7,494	1,475	15,275	7,379	7,526	2,046	1,744
Visby, Sweden	13,776	5,057	1,147	2,604	1,456	15,629	4,956	7,020	9,601	8,140	8,241	6,315	6,738	7,790	1,280	15,260	7,640	7,895	1,768	1,891
Vitoria, Brazil	15,464	13,172	9,175	7,647	11,456	10,025	11,769	15,677	18,129	18,326	18,338	13,766	8,628	17,454	8,929	14,122	17,573	16,782	8,429	8,811
Vladivostok, USSR	7,114	5,467	8,332	9,851	5,941	11,576	6,932	3,699	3,375	1,160	985	5,437	10,522	2,151	8,538	8,194	1,686	3,131	9,003	8,807
Volgograd, USSR	12,080	3,080	2,411	3,816	2,336	17,007	3,055	5,242	8,060	7,045	7,338	4,339	5,592	6,350	2,782	14,583	6,315	6,237	3,383	2,524
Vologda, USSR	12,508	4,008	2,214	3,741	1,135	15,856	4,219	5,780	8,333	6,940	7,096	5,245	6,714	6,527	2,467	14,281	6,390	6,630	3,010	2,715
Vorkuta, USSR	11,517	4,180	3,618	5,119	1,276	14,688	4,892	5,204	7,328	5,661	5,726	5,259	7,920	5,500	3,798	12,810	5,275	5,825	4,262	4,202
Wake Island	5,325	9,432	12,136	13,539	9,544	7,471	10,893	7,090	4,672	3,944	3,410	9,018	14,217	5,232	12,232	4,268	4,967	6,037	12,546	12,767
Wallis Island	4,777	12,885	16,075	17,227	13,483	4,055	14,172	10,289	7,322	7,670	7,296	12,049	16,050	8,655	16,075	849	8,550	9,144	16,211	16,792
Walvis Bay, Namibia	12,344	8,465	7,880	6,940	10,304	14,278	7,020	10,414	12,489	13,670	14,337	8,537	3,401	12,263	7,977	15,133	12,625	11,341	7,936	7,061
Warsaw, Poland	13,737	4,762	811	2,337	1,968	16,221	4,496	6,909	9,631	8,342	8,507	6,016	6,116	7,856	1,121	15,665	7,752	7,857	1,711	1,369
Washington, D.C.	15,997	11,694	6,834	6,422	6,763	9,312	11,692	12,866	13,825	11,596	11,095	12,911	12,150	12,405	6,450	12,564	11,983	13,151	5,977	7,423
Watson Lake, Canada	12,075	9,826	7,481	8,131	5,610	9,133	10,700	9,643	9,670	7,488	6,915	10,650	13,364	8,552	7,279	9,890	8,091	9,470	7,188	8,318
Weimar, East Germany	14,422	5,414	316	1,746	2,315	15,877	5,048	7,594	10,306	8,956	9,084	6,663	6,276	8,521	448	16,124	8,403	8,540	1,027	1,151
Wellington, New Zealand	4,025	13,199	18,489	19,505	16,204	4,823	13,857	10,855	8,065	9,406	9,309	11,993	13,677	9,836	18,798	2,617	9,947	9,861	19,288	18,390
West Berlin, West Germany	14,235	5,278	503	1,969	2,102	15,867	4,973	7,415	10,103	8,736	8,861	6,532	6,353	8,313	664	15,909	8,190	8,348	1,223	1,300
Wewak, Papua New Guinea	1,953	8,509	13,293	14,786	11,181	8,574	9,669	5,927	2,952	4,276	4,343	7,542	11,878	4,640	13,587	4,007	4,736	4,820	14,131	13,498
Whangarei, New Zealand	3,774	12,973	18,034	19,543	15,614	4,766	13,772	10,535	7,667	8,886	8,755	11,810	14,005	9,399	18,273	2,009	9,479	9,498	18,684	18,195
Whitehorse, Canada	11,752	9,645	7,568	8,293	5,585	9,160	10,577	9,358	9,323	7,146	6,568	10,426	13,376	8,227	7,387	9,681	7,765	9,153	7,329	8,408
Wichita, Kansas	14,281	12,401	8,192	8,026	7,498	7,901	12,768	12,855	12,930	10,798	10,194	13,480	13,841	11,886	7,838	10,798	11,426	12,792	7,442	8,878
Willemstad, Curacao	16,854	13,704	8,315	7,253	9,230	8,512	13,082	15,603	16,864	14,649	14,110	14,946	11,764	15,461	7,917	12,902	15,049	16,129	7,325	8,572
Wiluna, Australia	2,069	8,150	13,515	14,449	12,624	9,958	8,650	6,252	4,463	6,654	7,059	6,898	9,295	6,135	13,916	5,932	6,493	5,616	14,498	13,184
Windhoek, Namibia	12,148	8,241	7,853	6,969	10,235	14,447	6,804	10,158	12,220	13,413	14,083	8,288	3,180	12,003	7,967	15,057	12,370	11,078	7,953	7,027
Windsor, Canada	15,395	11,567	6,969	6,716	6,607	9,132	11,714	12,511	13,260	11,037	10,516	12,745	12,520	11,911	6,600	12,098	11,477	12,702	6,172	7,618
Winnipeg, Canada	14,121	11,065	7,186	7,284	6,208	8,951	11,519	11,545	11,945	9,741	9,191	12,128	13,092	10,712	6,867	11,183	10,263	11,570	6,554	7,940
Winston-Salem, North Carolina	15,812	12,098	7,252	6,814	7,157	8,901	12,112	13,195	13,978	11,760	11,230	13,308	12,506	12,639	6,867	12,248	12,206	13,422	6,389	7,834
Wroclaw, Poland	14,031	5,014	512	2,040	2,166	16,154	4,680	7,198	9,932	8,639	8,796	6,265	6,100	8,158	823	15,926	8,054	8,155	1,418	1,161
Wuhan, China	6,288	4,087	8,397	9,887	6,518	12,775	5,522	1,754	2,088	1,503	2,175	3,660	8,887	262	8,706	8,620	460	1,044	9,270	8,617
Wyndham, Australia	1,339	7,894	13,238	14,474	11,799	9,685	8,708	5,613	3,264	5,345	5,681	6,712	10,118	5,059	13,616	5,253	5,351	4,752	14,217	13,121
Xi'an, China	6,896	3,536	7,754	9,239	5,934	13,339	4,994	1,483	2,702	1,956	2,560	3,262	8,455	907	8,066	9,257	954	1,270	8,634	7,968
Xining, China	7,485	2,893	7,105	8,575	5,414	14,005	4,363	1,313	3,322	2,604	3,160	2,785	7,888	1,587	7,428	9,955	1,643	1,655	8,005	7,290
Yakutsk, USSR	9,212	5,441	6,617	8,077	4,064	12,201	6,730	4,728	5,394	3,247	3,027	5,937	10,281	3,839	6,751	9,791	3,420	4,646	7,143	7,232
Yanji, China	7,118	5,276	8,236	9,759	5,879	11,755	6,742	3,508	3,299	1,120	1,069	5,241	10,328	1,995	8,452	8,315	1,529	2,964	8,928	8,693

Distances in Kilometers	Mount Isa, Australia	Multan, Pakistan	Munich, West Germany	Murcia, Spain	Murmansk, USSR	Mururoa Atoll, Fr. Polynesia	Muscat, Oman	Myitkyina, Burma	Naga, Philippines	Nagasaki, Japan	Nagoya, Japan	Nagpur, India	Nairobi, Kenya	Nanchang, China	Nancy, France	Nandi, Fiji	Nanjing, China	Nanning, China	Nantes, France	Naples, Italy
Yaounde, Cameroon	14,105	6,923	4,908	3,991	7,402	16,266	5,503	9,418	12,244	12,381	12,877	7,535	2,870	11,202	4,993	17,842	11,400	10,545	4,966	4,104
Yap Island (Colonia)	3,349	7,246	11,754	13,265	9,615	9,688	8,539	4,645	1,692	2,713	2,843	6,434	11,285	3,148	12,036	5,271	3,194	3,501	12,570	12,016
Yaraka, Australia	658	9,852	15,148	16,438	13,399	7,769	10,664	7,495	4,828	6,558	6,689	8,678	11,694	6,652	15,509	3,536	6,851	6,540	16,104	15,082
Yarmouth, Canada	16,525	10,747	5,776	5,373	5,885	10,376	10,658	12,159	13,572	11,364	10,952	11,987	11,146	11,972	5,390	13,475	11,587	12,603	4,912	6,359
Yellowknife, Canada	12,859	9,724	6,845	7,393	5,197	9,596	10,444	9,869	10,225	8,008	7,479	10,662	12,809	8,964	6,614	10,678	8,514	9,832	6,477	7,674
Yerevan, USSR	11,882	2,683	2,753	3,911	3,275	17,949	2,263	5,139	8,090	7,397	7,780	3,892	4,658	6,510	3,155	14,886	6,554	6,223	3,737	2,552
Yinchuan, China	7,413	3,313	7,263	8,759	5,413	13,612	4,785	1,676	3,215	2,221	2,742	3,236	8,330	1,401	7,569	9,671	1,337	1,746	8,132	7,506
Yogyakarta, Indonesia	3,445	5,910	11,303	12,424	10,306	11,795	6,615	3,931	2,761	4,948	5,513	4,684	8,185	4,080	11,697	7,330	4,500	3,394	12,294	11,088
York, United Kingdom	15,059	6,248	1,093	1,762	2,429	14,999	5,948	8,303	10,873	9,319	9,355	7,505	7,042	9,055	769	16,004	8,884	9,183	737	1,848
Yumen, China	7,985	2,612	6,604	8,079	4,936	14,354	4,080	1,603	3,824	2,976	3,475	2,725	7,666	2,073	6,927	10,413	2,080	2,135	7,503	6,800
Yutian, China	8,798	1,203	5,692	7,064	4,614	15,785	2,655	1,961	4,852	4,387	4,910	1,760	6,265	3,309	6,058	11,676	3,427	2,991	6,658	5,725
Yuzhno-Sakhalinsk, USSR	7,502	6,256	8,458	9,935	5,929	10,917	7,699	4,641	4,119	1,910	1,396	6,333	11,318	3,087	8,608	7,968	2,623	4,075	9,010	9,031
Zagreb, Yugoslavia	14,216	5,060	426	1,660	2,754	16,517	4,536	7,389	10,220	9,064	9,263	6,284	5,604	8,487	808	16,461	8,419	8,399	1,353	570
Zahedan, Iran	10,091	1,028	4,654	5,716	4,741	17,873	690	3,626	6,613	6,474	7,012	2,052	4,260	5,305	5,057	13,504	5,484	4,770	5,634	4,374
Zamboanga, Philippines	3,603	5,868	10,927	12,329	9,252	11,228	7,010	3,326	755	2,980	3,480	4,882	9,511	2,497	11,273	6,667	9,402	8,170	7,140	5,794
Zanzibar, Tanzania	10,841	5,297	6,595	6,425	8,349	16,897	3,912	7,195	9,533	10,451	11,108	5,305	601	9,056	6,873	14,729	9,781	9,827	623	1,270
Zaragoza, Spain	15,647	6,464	1,220	406	3,630	15,542	5,804	8,823	11,635	10,353	10,478	7,667	6,083	9,878	960	17,358	9,781	9,827	623	1,270
Zashiversk, USSR	9,782	6,142	6,545	7,922	3,943	11,750	7,350	5,587	6,144	3,942	3,610	6,730	10,805	4,666	6,618	9,873	4,234	5,499	6,937	7,240
Zhengzhou, China	6,721	3,969	8,020	9,523	6,076	15,946	5,146	7,909	10,678	9,387	9,529	6,872	6,059	8,911	218	16,578	8,809	8,887	750	865
Zurich, Switzerland	14,746	5,639	256	1,298	2,768	15,946	5,146	7,909	10,678	9,387	9,529	6,872	6,059	8,911	218	16,578	8,809	8,887	750	865

Distances in Kilometers

	Narvik, Norway	Nashville, Tennessee	Nassau, Bahamas	Natal, Brazil	Natashquan, Canada	Nauru Island	Ndjamena, Chad	Nelson, New Zealand	Nema, Mauritania	Neuquen, Argentina	New Delhi, India	New Glasgow, Canada	New Haven, Connecticut	New Orleans, Louisiana	New Plymouth, New Zealand	New York, New York	Newcastle upon Tyne, UK	Newcastle Waters, Australia	Niamey, Niger	Nicosia, Cyprus
Nashville, Tennessee	6,864	0	1,523	7,098	2,539	11,507	10,263	13,289	8,015	8,536	12,643	2,275	1,332	753	13,125	1,223	6,523	15,564	9,040	9,976
Nassau, Bahamas	7,628	1,523	0	5,696	3,092	12,620	9,690	13,379	7,280	7,154	13,475	2,628	1,845	1,366	13,275	1,761	6,864	16,737	8,343	10,139
Natal, Brazil	9,175	7,098	5,696	0	6,711	17,477	5,905	14,045	3,952	4,940	12,510	6,309	6,473	7,059	14,202	6,494	7,419	17,157	4,646	8,468
Natashquan, Canada	4,537	2,539	3,092	6,711	0	12,842	8,049	15,720	6,105	9,895	10,390	517	1,310	3,258	15,527	1,418	3,987	16,122	7,015	7,437
Nauru Island	12,123	11,507	12,620	17,477	12,842	0	16,674	4,558	18,118	12,922	10,017	13,065	12,525	11,297	4,329	12,461	13,877	4,119	17,818	13,874
Ndjamena, Chad	6,257	10,263	9,690	5,905	8,049	16,674	0	16,146	2,455	10,264	6,668	8,102	8,964	10,763	16,379	9,064	4,975	13,397	1,412	3,151
Nelson, New Zealand	16,661	13,289	13,379	14,045	15,720	4,558	16,146	0	17,270	9,170	12,522	15,558	14,620	12,654	255	14,509	18,434	4,630	16,812	16,481
Nema, Mauritania	6,015	8,015	7,280	3,952	6,105	18,118	2,455	17,270	0	8,818	8,619	6,030	6,786	8,432	17,513	6,875	4,287	15,851	1,064	4,517
Neuquen, Argentina	13,788	8,536	7,154	4,940	9,895	12,922	10,264	9,170	8,818	0	16,633	9,379	8,901	7,963	9,301	8,842	12,171	13,381	9,301	13,247
New Delhi, India	5,854	12,643	13,475	12,510	10,390	10,017	6,668	12,522	8,619	16,633	0	10,846	11,679	13,385	12,506	11,779	6,758	7,903	7,864	4,177
New Glasgow, Canada	5,005	2,275	2,628	6,309	517	13,065	8,102	15,558	6,030	9,379	10,846	0	956	2,949	15,387	1,069	4,327	16,547	6,988	7,739
New Haven, Connecticut	5,825	1,332	1,845	6,473	1,310	12,525	8,964	14,620	6,786	8,901	11,679	956	0	1,993	14,457	113	5,269	16,365	7,785	8,693
New Orleans, Louisiana	7,616	753	1,366	7,059	3,258	11,297	10,763	12,654	8,432	7,963	13,385	2,949	1,993	0	12,505	1,880	7,244	15,414	9,480	10,683
New Plymouth, New Zealand	16,445	13,125	13,275	14,202	15,527	4,329	16,379	255	17,513	9,301	12,506	15,387	14,457	12,505	0	14,348	18,204	4,604	17,067	16,534
New York, New York	5,926	1,223	1,761	6,494	1,418	12,461	9,064	14,509	6,875	8,842	11,779	1,069	113	1,880	14,348	0	5,381	16,333	7,878	8,806
Newcastle upon Tyne, UK	1,787	6,523	6,864	7,419	3,987	13,877	4,975	18,434	4,287	12,171	6,758	4,327	5,269	7,244	18,204	5,381	0	14,364	4,614	3,466
Newcastle Waters, Australia	12,843	15,564	16,737	17,157	16,122	4,119	13,397	4,630	15,851	13,381	7,903	16,547	16,365	15,414	4,604	16,333	14,364	0	14,802	12,003
Niamey, Niger	6,198	9,040	8,343	4,646	7,015	17,818	1,412	16,812	1,064	9,301	7,864	6,988	7,785	9,480	17,067	7,878	4,614	14,802	0	3,946
Nicosia, Cyprus	3,834	9,976	10,139	8,468	7,437	13,874	3,151	16,481	4,517	13,247	4,177	7,739	8,693	10,683	16,534	8,806	3,466	12,003	3,946	0
Niue (Alofi)	14,490	10,647	11,139	14,356	12,894	3,251	19,084	2,940	18,179	9,680	13,193	12,830	11,956	10,121	2,705	11,854	15,891	5,972	18,979	17,113
Norfolk, Virginia	6,398	943	1,309	6,363	1,882	12,406	9,332	14,144	7,072	8,435	12,251	1,496	574	1,490	13,995	472	5,822	16,400	8,099	9,227
Norfolk Island, Australia	15,221	13,137	13,619	15,431	15,257	3,156	16,650	1,443	18,548	10,507	11,562	15,266	14,431	12,624	1,248	14,332	17,002	3,747	17,760	15,724
Noril'sk, USSR	2,687	8,298	9,469	11,861	6,521	9,622	8,088	14,045	8,497	16,339	4,584	7,036	7,637	8,993	13,853	7,713	4,449	10,260	8,450	5,027
Norman Wells, Canada	4,906	4,165	5,661	10,662	3,996	8,975	10,856	12,894	9,625	12,619	9,392	4,359	4,272	4,667	12,641	4,278	5,883	12,202	10,295	8,737
Normanton, Australia	13,163	14,911	15,977	17,380	15,862	3,406	14,214	4,034	16,667	13,046	8,567	16,215	15,854	14,688	3,974	15,804	14,798	816	15,619	12,713
North Pole	2,410	5,999	7,227	10,643	4,440	10,059	8,664	14,573	8,166	14,316	6,838	4,953	5,429	6,686	14,326	5,495	3,907	11,926	8,509	6,111
Nottingham, United Kingdom	1,982	6,627	6,911	7,256	4,089	14,089	4,756	18,642	4,068	12,045	6,767	4,407	5,356	7,340	18,418	5,469	228	14,448	4,386	3,349
Norway House, Canada	5,434	2,157	3,631	8,796	2,476	10,399	10,362	13,510	8,568	10,686	10,843	2,668	2,324	2,741	13,284	2,309	5,718	14,051	9,442	9,076
Norwich, United Kingdom	1,956	6,796	7,080	7,333	4,257	14,078	4,659	18,608	4,066	12,148	6,609	4,577	5,526	7,510	18,400	5,639	325	14,315	4,340	3,182
Nouakchott, Mauritania	6,058	7,148	6,354	3,385	5,396	18,037	3,393	17,290	939	8,325	9,366	5,262	5,959	7,532	17,490	6,042	4,274	16,787	2,000	5,202
Noumea, New Caledonia	14,457	12,903	13,577	16,117	14,817	2,405	16,796	2,204	19,110	11,177	11,098	14,901	14,142	12,465	1,999	14,053	16,238	3,497	18,107	15,273
Novosibirsk, USSR	3,553	9,852	10,931	12,297	7,890	9,674	7,505	13,648	8,521	17,208	2,972	8,393	9,086	10,564	13,514	9,172	5,061	9,330	8,202	4,357
Nuku'alofa, Tonga	14,677	11,233	11,739	14,739	13,442	2,994	18,542	2,484	18,667	9,942	12,773	13,398	12,536	10,716	2,236	12,435	16,207	5,397	19,118	16,833
Nukunono Island, Tokelau Isls.	13,392	10,177	10,900	14,951	12,217	2,534	19,206	3,842	18,175	10,549	12,538	12,233	11,431	9,744	3,592	11,338	14,853	5,977	19,217	16,161
Nuremberg, West Germany	2,143	7,567	7,824	7,577	5,028	14,118	4,156	18,359	4,000	12,487	5,960	5,344	6,295	8,280	18,240	6,407	1,062	13,785	4,069	2,411
Nyala, Sudan	6,285	11,099	10,655	6,938	8,756	15,655	1,071	15,550	3,499	11,098	5,713	8,873	9,776	11,653	15,753	9,882	5,296	12,355	2,476	2,700
Oaxaca, Mexico	9,194	2,334	2,197	7,219	4,818	10,711	11,865	11,243	9,432	6,880	14,912	4,469	3,523	1,582	11,120	3,411	8,792	14,720	10,495	12,198
Ocean Falls, Canada	6,303	3,662	5,172	10,682	4,441	8,412	12,025	11,829	10,470	11,640	10,717	4,657	4,244	3,946	11,585	4,209	7,113	12,124	11,273	10,136
Odense, Denmark	1,496	7,204	7,611	7,969	4,682	13,563	4,819	18,004	4,559	12,810	5,995	5,048	5,979	7,937	17,825	6,090	763	13,649	4,702	2,855
Odessa, USSR	2,560	8,935	9,300	8,677	6,412	13,381	4,084	16,985	4,816	13,610	4,479	6,769	7,706	9,668	16,941	7,818	2,445	12,356	4,528	1,274
Ogbomosho, Nigeria	6,765	9,578	8,795	4,646	7,624	17,934	1,261	16,177	1,564	9,078	7,921	7,577	8,348	9,981	16,432	8,438	5,224	14,434	640	4,214
Okha, USSR	5,756	8,976	10,470	14,704	8,273	6,395	11,224	10,905	11,725	17,161	5,923	8,752	8,948	9,441	10,692	8,977	7,538	7,915	11,696	8,081
Okinawa (Naha)	8,103	12,216	13,729	17,114	11,489	5,149	11,597	8,830	13,220	17,979	4,961	11,986	12,236	12,609	8,690	12,266	9,797	4,865	12,673	8,745
Oklahoma City, Oklahoma	7,307	971	2,250	7,940	3,299	10,552	11,198	12,440	8,980	8,781	12,889	3,128	2,234	928	12,261	2,134	7,211	14,636	10,000	10,676
Old Crow, Canada	4,811	4,797	6,292	11,215	4,514	8,586	10,939	12,696	9,912	13,232	8,906	4,906	4,876	5,291	12,441	4,887	5,978	11,642	10,505	8,599
Olympia, Washington	6,782	3,209	4,681	10,301	4,389	8,564	12,240	11,638	10,490	10,970	11,389	4,526	3,979	3,396	11,404	3,926	7,433	12,439	11,364	10,596
Omaha, Nebraska	6,663	983	2,490	8,071	2,810	10,641	10,823	12,911	8,709	9,326	12,236	2,723	1,929	1,366	12,718	1,848	6,636	14,636	9,695	10,093
Omsk, USSR	3,167	9,728	10,705	11,715	7,626	10,282	6,918	14,206	7,916	16,645	2,948	8,117	8,866	10,460	14,082	8,957	4,560	9,807	7,594	3,767
Oodnadatta, Australia	13,963	15,949	16,752	16,185	17,098	4,496	13,620	3,758	16,014	12,250	8,787	17,450	17,020	15,603	3,783	16,958	15,417	1,144	14,957	12,753
Oradea, Romania	2,393	8,382	8,671	8,098	5,846	13,840	3,928	17,655	4,312	13,038	5,154	6,177	7,124	9,103	17,599	7,237	1,859	13,028	4,153	1,630
Oran, Algeria	3,813	7,483	7,285	5,844	5,089	15,907	3,052	19,198	2,214	10,782	7,193	5,226	6,152	8,094	19,419	6,260	2,146	15,072	2,473	3,072
Oranjestad, Aruba	8,615	3,111	1,590	4,352	4,246	13,613	9,206	13,146	6,755	5,701	14,260	3,732	3,202	2,829	13,110	3,148	7,504	17,459	7,797	10,405
Orebro, Sweden	1,026	7,253	7,785	8,469	4,774	13,044	5,234	17,494	5,078	13,278	5,738	5,179	6,083	7,998	17,309	6,192	1,120	13,245	5,194	2,990
Orel, USSR	1,989	8,704	9,252	9,286	6,242	12,649	4,899	16,582	5,512	14,222	4,305	6,649	7,552	9,453	16,482	7,660	2,454	12,021	5,302	1,984
Orsk, USSR	2,908	9,753	10,521	10,771	7,438	11,326	5,842	15,036	6,904	15,707	2,954	7,893	8,732	10,504	14,943	8,833	3,926	10,483	6,533	2,690
Osaka, Japan	7,496	11,027	12,544	16,669	10,451	5,089	11,886	9,255	13,105	17,875	5,496	10,932	11,108	11,409	9,079	11,131	9,262	5,767	12,760	8,833
Oslo, Norway	1,002	6,997	7,523	8,321	4,513	13,107	5,317	17,611	5,023	13,090	5,996	4,917	5,822	7,741	17,410	5,931	919	13,463	5,199	3,200
Osorno, Chile	14,146	8,610	7,281	5,395	10,117	12,451	10,728	8,741	9,286	471	17,015	9,600	9,067	8,001	8,866	9,001	12,569	13,028	9,772	13,718
Ostrava, Czechoslovakia	2,073	7,982	8,304	8,023	5,448	13,787	4,193	17,860	4,341	12,952	5,440	5,789	6,732	8,706	17,764	6,845	1,463	13,266	4,289	2,039
Ottawa, Canada	5,530	1,387	2,261	6,952	1,166	12,153	9,119	14,581	7,036	9,376	11,364	1,019	510	2,125	14,399	541	5,139	15,899	8,004	8,597
Ouagadougou, Bourkina Fasso	6,376	8,790	8,028	4,235	6,861	18,193	1,803	16,761	776	8,926	8,274	6,799	7,562	9,199	17,015	7,651	4,730	15,162	414	4,323
Oujda, Morocco	3,949	7,438	7,201	5,681	5,071	16,054	3,029	19,162	2,070	10,620	7,339	5,190	6,107	8,037	19,407	6,215	2,260	15,209	2,377	3,206
Oxford, United Kingdom	2,109	6,671	6,919	7,146	4,133	14,222	4,635	18,770	3,934	11,952	6,797	4,438	5,390	7,378	18,550	5,503	362	14,515	4,252	3,306
Pago Pago, American Samoa	13,960	10,403	11,007	14,639	12,558	2,894	19,365	3,372	18,241	10,085	12,903	12,533	11,690	9,920	3,127	11,592	15,388	5,978	19,255	16,677
Pakxe, Laos	8,386	14,178	15,545	15,650	12,669	6,944	9,749	9,323	11,881	17,297	3,297	13,183	13,757	14,738	9,278	13,824	9,713	4,704	11,051	7,474
Palembang, Indonesia	10,195	16,140	17,542	15,483	14,614	6,924	10,053	8,012	12,456	15,311	4,565	15,122	15,747	16,634	8,030	15,817	11,311	3,516	11,460	8,520
Palermo, Italy	3,383	8,402	8,395	6,984	5,899	15,050	2,885	18,270	3,121	11,911	5,919	6,129	7,081	9,067	18,345	7,194	2,190	13,800	2,944	1,815
Palma, Majorca	3,335	7,528	7,460	6,350	5,062	15,400	3,278	19,206	2,719	11,286	6,794	5,254	6,199	8,174	19,284	6,311	1,745	14,695	2,887	2,751
Palmerston North, New Zealand	16,617	13,067	13,169	14,008	15,499	4,496	16,349	222	17,360	9,108	12,676	15,336	14,398	12,434	194	14,288	18,363	4,776	16,965	16,674
Panama, Panama	9,367	3,100	1,799	5,181	4,856	12,615	10,304	12,100	7,857	5,436	15,162	4,369	3,642	2,570	12,050	3,559	8,426	16,350	8,892	11,464
Paramaribo, Suriname	8,696	4,656	3,184	2,562	4,957	15,324	7,735	13,825	5,353	5,134	13,656	4,464	4,307	4,528	13,867	4,296	7,226	18,432	6,331	9,510
Paris, France	2,334	7,032	7,217	7,068	4,499	14,450	4,241	18,909	3,681	11,938	6,601	4,783	5,738	7,730	18,737	5,851	734	14,413	3,920	2,957
Patna, India	6,474	13,116	14,091	13,330	11,000	9,220	7,456	11,696	9,461	17,110	852	11,477	12,261	13,835	11,672	12,355	7,513	7,069	8,686	5,029
Patrai, Greece	3,370	8,979	9,064	7,629	6,450	14,532	2,970	17,574	3,707	12,526	5,191	6,718	7,675	9,667	17,625	7,787	2,557	13,067	3,356	1,093
Peking, China	6,292	11,252	12,668	15,284	10,018	6,802	10,102	10,676	11,462	19,624	3,788	10,532	10,959	11,800	10,533	11,012	7,959	6,588	11,024	7,081
Penrhyn Island (Omoka)	13,397	8,957	9,513	13,487	11,217	3,990	19,203	4,554	16,760	9,390	13,874	11,140	10,264	8,446	4,335	10,162	14,498	7,453	17,816	16,885
Peoria, Illinois	6,505	560	2,071	7,559	2,397	11,185	10,343	13,336	8,189	9,087	12,213	2,247	1,403	1,191	13,154	1,316	6,320	15,172	9,186	9,786
Perm', USSR	2,218	9,016	9,845	10,635	6,753	11,261	6,156	15,306	6,900	15,550	3,648	7,223	8,034	9,765	15,176	8,132	3,468	10,896	6,670	3,053
Perth, Australia	13,605	17,892	18,528	14,833	17,967	6,388	11,728	5,149	14,075	12,147	7,849	18,484	18,713	17,550	5,254	18,702	14,569	2,392	13,026	11,367
Peshawar, Pakistan	5,086	11,918	12,690	11,917	9,613	10,544	6,189	13,303	7,982	16,395	806	10,062	10,910	12,666	13,278	11,012	5,952	8,676	7,298	3,484
Petropavlovsk-Kamchatskiy,USSR	6,162	8,291	9,810	14,618	7,952	5,985	12,002	10,543	12,172	16,158	6,969	8,395	8,446	8,680	10,311	8,459	7,894	8,171	12,301	8,903
Petrozavodsk, USSR	1,078	7,932	8,639	9,517	5,561	12,140	5,731	16,459	5,981	14,357	4,837	6,010	6,862	8,685	16,296	6,966	2,200	12,171	5,946	2,964
Pevek, USSR	4,538	6,756	8,226	12,671	6,054	7,799	10,728	12,310	10,429	15,215	7,170	6,517	6,680	7,274	12,066	6,708	6,156	10,085	10,728	7,864
Philadelphia, Pennsylvania	6,046	1,102	1,661	6,510	1,545	12,395	9,175	14,385	6,972	8,767	11,898	1,198	243	1,751	14,224	130	5,511	16,302	7,980	8,936
Phnom Penh, Kampuchea	8,716	14,584	15,945	15,607	13,044	6,984	9,738	9,109	11,944	16,892	3,444	13,556	14,149	15,142	9,078	14,218	9,991	4,479	11,073	7,609
Phoenix, Arizona	7,967	2,327	3,482	9,157	4,467	9,210	12,484	11,258	10,322	9,214	13,068	4,382	3,544	2,118	11,060	3,451	8,191	13,313	11,329	11,602
Pierre, South Dakota	6,484	1,467	2,982	8,532	2,951	10,269	11,000	12,803	8,977	9,781	11,921	2,949	2,258	1,838	12,597	2,193	6,614	14,209	9,935	10,038
Pinang, Malaysia	9,157	15,343	16,621	15,114	13,609	7,432	9,382	9,000	11,705	16,113	3,541	14,110	14,786	15,937	9,002	14,865	10,273	4,425	10,763	7,577
Pitcairn Island (Adamstown)	14,717	8,163	7,938	10,234	10,696	7,282	16,096	5,476	14,051	5,943	17,296	10,368	9,419	7,439	5,408	9,306	14,683	9,840	14,875	18,077
Pittsburgh, Pennsylvania	6,183	758	1,721	6,864	1,784	11,985	9,569	14,036	7,384	8,875	12,009	1,522	606	1,477	13,868	510	5,771	15,923	8,388	9,220
Plymouth, Montserrat	7,866	3,246	1,826	3,875	3,716	14,358	8,298	14,088	5,844	6,190	13,370	3,203	2,914	3,192	14,061	2,893	6,639	18,371	6,896	9,452
Plymouth, United Kingdom	2,324	6,537	6,733	6,906	4,005	14,414	4,591	18,972	3,758	11,702	7,024	4,287	5,243	7,234	18,737	5,355	539	14,763	4,130	3,452
Ponape Island	11,109	11,745	13,046	18,542	12,599	1,268	15,446	5,554	16,960	14,187	8,778	12,917	12,561	11,681	5,347	12,519	12,893	3,835	16,550	12,607
Ponce, Puerto Rico	7,912	2,824	1,359	4,339	3,596	13,870	8,739	13,815	6,285	6,308	13,553	3,079	2,650	2,720	13,768	2,613	6,796	17,912	7,343	9,747
Ponta Delgada, Azores	4,300	5,346	5,044	4,918	3,174	15,690	4,936	18,350	2,955	9,536	9,142	3,170	4,032	5,906	18,297	4,134	2,641	16,973	3,842	5,211
Pontianak, Indonesia	10,087	15,675	17,143	16,046	14,382	6,412	10,485	7,860	12,846	15,680	4,663	14,898	15,429	16,114	7,853	15,488	11,330	3,263	11,881	8,741
Port Augusta, Australia	14,554	15,942	16,520	15,704	17,469	4,677	13,790	3,287	16,095	11,658	9,310	17,740	17,138	15,500	3,340	17,058	15,986	1,729	15,064	13,198
Port Blair, India	8,213	14,718	15,809	14,282	12,727	8,307	8,433	10,077	10,695	16,436	2,482	13,211	13,967	15,396	10,081	14,056	9,236	5,502	9,788	6,501
Port Elizabeth, South Africa	11,375	13,980	12,661	6,973	12,648	14,465	5,221	11,044	6,593	8,017	8,804	12,484	13,048	14,027	11,294	13,108	10,194	10,503	5,814	7,696
Port Hedland, Australia	12,544	16,992	18,313	15,951	16,689	5,698	11,871	5,622	14,321	13,408	7,005	17,200	17,442	16,961	5,664	17,454	13,749	1,596	13,260	10,870

Distances in Kilometers

	Narvik, Norway	Nashville, Tennessee	Nassau, Bahamas	Natal, Brazil	Natashquan, Canada	Nauru Island	Ndjamena, Chad	Nelson, New Zealand	Nema, Mauritania	Neuquen, Argentina	New Delhi, India	New Glasgow, Canada	New Haven, Connecticut	New Orleans, Louisiana	New Plymouth, New Zealand	New York, New York	Newcastle upon Tyne, UK	Newcastle Waters, Australia	Niamey, Niger	Nicosia, Cyprus
Port Louis, Mauritius	10,345	16,125	15,379	10,080	13,784	12,022	5,862	10,531	8,163	11,361	5,797	13,919	14,815	16,595	10,721	14,918	10,026	7,935	7,116	6,634
Port Moresby, Papua New Guinea	12,523	13,846	15,019	18,296	14,765	2,401	14,800	4,358	17,154	13,528	8,609	15,102	14,740	13,686	4,232	14,694	14,261	1,729	16,202	12,779
Port Said, Egypt	4,244	10,214	10,283	8,245	7,682	14,163	2,763	16,380	4,312	12,944	4,316	7,956	8,912	10,905	16,465	9,025	3,749	12,032	3,657	444
Port Sudan, Sudan	5,597	11,487	11,390	8,410	8,978	14,160	2,514	15,235	4,707	12,658	4,163	9,213	10,165	12,147	15,368	10,277	5,104	11,275	3,801	1,765
Port-au-Prince, Haiti	8,093	2,414	891	4,881	3,636	13,266	9,324	13,372	6,874	6,379	13,854	3,131	2,525	2,196	13,306	2,463	7,113	17,308	7,934	10,194
Port-of-Spain, Trin. & Tobago	8,457	3,803	2,312	3,435	4,386	14,562	8,329	13,705	5,893	5,533	13,810	3,874	3,575	3,650	13,705	3,550	7,147	18,256	6,917	9,777
Port-Vila, Vanuatu	14,015	12,474	13,237	16,353	14,307	1,909	17,095	2,653	19,546	11,430	11,045	14,412	13,685	12,073	2,430	13,599	15,781	3,702	18,482	15,186
Portland, Maine	5,492	1,635	2,159	6,510	970	12,627	8,716	14,918	6,589	9,151	11,346	641	340	2,319	14,748	450	4,933	16,349	7,570	8,364
Portland, Oregon	6,938	3,166	4,619	10,264	4,451	8,541	12,346	11,533	10,556	10,828	11,555	4,568	3,989	3,316	11,301	3,932	7,564	12,453	11,445	10,748
Porto, Portugal	3,409	6,592	6,488	5,862	4,171	15,484	3,959	19,864	2,723	10,724	7,655	4,324	5,260	7,222	19,688	5,370	1,624	15,543	3,235	3,703
Porto Alegre, Brazil	12,262	8,222	6,712	3,167	8,953	14,752	8,486	10,884	6,991	1,832	15,056	8,457	8,212	7,818	11,036	8,182	10,546	14,730	7,475	11,419
Porto Alexandre, Angola	9,354	11,801	10,672	5,257	10,228	16,742	3,109	13,401	4,157	8,064	8,573	10,093	10,732	12,010	13,655	10,803	7,950	12,635	3,418	6,082
Porto Novo, Benin	6,965	9,537	8,704	4,417	7,652	18,172	1,501	16,041	1,553	8,821	8,168	7,583	8,329	9,915	16,296	8,416	5,394	14,556	780	4,471
Porto Velho, Brazil	10,552	5,521	4,019	3,184	6,536	14,307	9,034	11,976	6,840	3,369	15,405	6,021	5,620	5,120	12,035	5,575	9,109	16,551	7,700	11,228
Portsmouth, United Kingdom	2,208	6,722	6,943	7,068	4,187	14,324	4,531	18,867	3,828	11,888	6,805	4,481	5,435	7,425	18,652	5,548	472	14,553	4,142	3,258
Poznan, Poland	1,785	7,745	8,119	8,106	5,219	13,615	4,473	17,841	4,505	13,012	5,549	5,575	6,512	8,475	17,713	6,623	1,255	13,311	4,513	2,315
Prague, Czechoslovakia	2,051	7,738	8,036	7,813	5,202	13,928	4,211	18,108	4,193	12,730	5,714	5,533	6,480	8,458	17,997	6,592	1,216	13,531	4,208	2,256
Praia, Cape Verde Islands	6,612	6,658	5,709	2,628	5,213	18,053	4,182	16,668	1,753	7,550	10,243	4,990	5,566	6,959	16,830	5,636	4,833	17,553	2,770	6,073
Pretoria, South Africa	10,481	13,817	12,647	7,073	12,162	14,728	4,424	11,762	6,057	8,761	7,979	12,067	12,740	14,000	12,006	12,814	9,387	10,636	5,181	6,765
Prince Albert, Canada	5,733	2,403	3,920	9,248	3,009	9,875	10,864	13,013	9,099	10,836	10,938	3,190	2,783	2,879	12,783	2,756	6,150	13,582	9,966	9,452
Prince Edward Island	12,869	15,353	13,897	8,259	14,354	12,819	6,891	9,318	8,335	8,025	9,217	14,149	14,615	15,212	9,567	14,660	11,855	9,031	7,557	9,066
Prince George, Canada	6,045	3,396	4,917	10,362	4,070	8,780	11,677	12,184	10,097	11,545	10,663	4,293	3,906	3,737	11,942	3,876	6,788	12,459	10,907	9,871
Prince Rupert, Canada	6,134	3,882	5,400	10,858	4,513	8,329	11,955	11,876	10,486	11,918	10,447	4,759	4,399	4,195	11,629	4,370	7,014	11,966	11,258	9,968
Providence, Rhode Island	5,716	1,469	1,935	6,425	1,190	12,620	8,832	14,758	6,664	8,951	11,571	820	138	2,129	14,594	250	5,137	16,423	7,660	8,558
Provo, Utah	7,240	2,218	3,599	9,284	3,987	9,320	12,035	11,784	10,005	9,826	12,330	3,983	3,246	2,266	11,573	3,169	7,553	13,347	10,971	10,923
Puerto Aisen, Chile	14,600	9,144	7,819	5,690	10,645	12,283	10,786	8,387	9,510	812	16,785	10,128	9,604	8,529	8,526	9,539	12,976	12,570	9,920	13,853
Puerto Deseado, Argentina	14,573	9,524	8,147	5,490	10,861	12,633	10,332	8,555	9,202	993	16,203	10,345	9,889	8,940	8,713	9,842	12,876	12,538	9,539	13,440
Puerto Princesa, Philippines	9,463	14,270	15,781	17,131	13,365	5,460	11,256	7,934	13,408	16,699	4,808	13,877	14,230	14,648	7,865	14,270	10,959	3,407	12,574	8,978
Punta Arenas, Chile	15,271	10,013	8,689	6,171	11,487	12,034	10,810	7,875	9,825	1,593	16,243	10,970	10,467	9,393	8,038	10,404	13,569	11,848	10,103	13,951
Pusan, South Korea	7,236	11,290	12,790	16,384	10,496	5,572	11,336	9,590	12,664	18,445	4,906	10,992	11,254	11,724	9,428	11,287	8,972	5,829	12,259	8,318
Pyongyang, North Korea	6,722	11,039	12,515	15,861	10,093	6,066	10,893	10,114	12,153	18,829	4,585	10,597	10,912	11,518	9,953	10,952	8,451	6,296	11,774	7,842
Qamdo, China	6,408	12,540	13,753	14,334	10,759	8,122	8,589	11,186	10,387	18,429	1,953	11,267	11,918	13,195	11,113	11,996	7,757	6,621	9,723	5,871
Qandahar, Afghanistan	5,116	11,980	12,615	11,388	9,584	11,105	5,608	13,623	7,477	15,790	1,152	10,006	10,892	12,732	13,622	10,998	5,781	9,024	6,751	3,026
Qiqian, China	5,239	9,856	11,263	14,411	8,653	7,253	9,999	11,527	10,894	18,383	4,435	9,164	9,561	10,420	11,349	9,612	6,994	7,806	10,669	6,854
Qom, Iran	4,303	11,026	11,443	10,022	8,527	12,407	4,395	14,999	6,084	14,658	2,576	8,901	9,830	11,769	15,016	9,941	4,585	10,433	5,420	1,601
Quebec, Canada	5,224	1,751	2,472	6,822	790	12,415	8,757	14,959	6,706	9,505	11,073	676	627	2,478	14,774	714	4,772	16,042	7,660	8,227
Quetta, Pakistan	5,304	12,167	12,809	11,511	9,776	11,000	5,700	13,440	7,613	15,833	1,005	10,200	11,085	12,920	13,442	11,191	5,975	8,848	6,868	3,187
Quito, Ecuador	10,269	4,118	2,802	4,849	5,808	12,754	10,410	11,510	8,027	4,419	15,948	5,308	4,633	3,558	11,495	4,555	9,194	16,027	9,008	12,003
Rabaul, Papua New Guinea	12,125	13,050	14,259	18,640	13,999	1,690	15,238	4,616	17,395	13,700	8,780	14,319	13,937	12,913	4,450	13,890	13,902	2,516	16,589	12,885
Raiatea (Uturoa)	14,207	8,966	9,265	12,588	11,394	4,903	18,489	4,334	16,220	8,297	14,899	11,228	10,298	8,364	4,160	10,189	15,043	7,943	17,172	17,909
Raleigh, North Carolina	6,597	736	1,191	6,458	2,100	12,235	9,562	13,902	7,288	8,344	12,445	1,730	791	1,247	13,753	682	6,055	16,266	8,320	9,466
Rangiroa (Avatoru)	13,968	8,538	8,819	12,244	10,982	5,236	18,143	4,755	15,800	8,095	15,178	10,804	9,870	7,928	4,587	9,760	14,694	8,379	16,777	17,761
Rangoon, Burma	7,821	14,136	15,321	14,604	12,279	7,988	8,703	10,191	10,855	17,116	2,342	12,777	13,477	14,790	10,168	13,560	8,980	5,564	10,010	6,501
Raoul Is., Kermadec Islands	15,535	11,955	12,297	14,455	14,270	3,565	17,689	1,554	18,318	9,535	12,845	14,179	13,279	11,385	1,313	13,174	17,131	5,113	18,261	17,021
Rarotonga (Avarua)	14,752	9,954	10,272	13,283	12,348	4,279	18,865	3,373	17,098	8,702	14,269	12,205	11,284	9,364	3,184	11,176	15,835	6,986	17,928	18,005
Rawson, Argentina	14,107	9,070	7,675	5,086	10,364	12,930	10,143	8,970	8,872	543	16,291	9,849	9,403	8,504	9,118	9,347	12,433	13,025	9,271	13,204
Recife, Brazil	9,404	7,301	5,882	253	6,959	17,431	5,961	13,835	4,088	4,764	12,597	6,554	6,703	7,240	13,997	6,722	7,642	16,915	4,736	8,597
Regina, Canada	5,984	2,137	3,659	9,072	3,005	9,944	10,956	12,910	9,110	10,529	11,247	3,134	2,638	2,580	12,687	2,599	6,323	13,735	10,007	9,666
Reykjavik, Iceland	1,796	5,248	5,867	7,835	2,798	12,910	6,448	17,278	5,397	12,125	7,608	3,239	4,106	5,995	17,022	4,212	1,525	14,488	5,922	4,885
Rhodes, Greece	3,624	9,544	9,667	8,074	7,009	14,200	3,000	16,965	4,125	12,912	4,634	7,295	8,250	10,243	17,020	8,363	3,064	12,482	3,635	486
Richmond, Virginia	6,374	846	1,381	6,492	1,878	12,285	9,419	14,088	7,173	8,524	12,223	1,520	572	1,438	13,934	461	5,840	16,272	8,196	9,258
Riga, USSR	1,323	7,833	8,365	8,763	5,357	12,934	5,035	17,208	5,187	13,645	5,174	5,762	6,667	8,579	17,060	6,775	1,609	12,781	5,169	2,520
Ringkobing, Denmark	1,453	7,050	7,464	7,922	4,529	13,555	4,913	18,037	4,573	12,739	6,129	4,896	5,827	7,783	17,846	5,938	633	13,750	4,752	3,005
Rio Branco, Brazil	10,833	5,480	4,014	3,621	6,691	13,864	9,482	11,590	7,285	3,211	15,834	6,174	5,700	5,021	11,640	5,647	9,446	16,196	8,148	11,658
Rio Cuarto, Argentina	13,062	8,019	6,589	4,273	9,234	13,494	9,777	9,878	8,191	727	16,337	8,719	8,288	7,491	10,003	8,236	11,447	14,105	8,735	12,668
Rio de Janeiro, Brazil	11,242	7,982	6,461	2,080	8,302	15,853	7,439	11,967	5,870	2,950	14,080	7,834	7,740	7,701	12,128	7,729	9,496	15,532	6,376	10,314
Rio Gallegos, Argentina	15,066	9,876	8,535	5,970	11,308	12,215	10,664	8,076	9,639	1,412	16,234	10,791	10,303	9,267	8,238	10,241	13,365	12,049	9,933	13,797
Rio Grande, Brazil	12,496	8,371	6,868	3,395	9,159	14,559	8,650	10,653	7,200	1,638	15,180	8,662	8,397	7,948	10,807	8,364	10,779	14,504	7,664	11,609
Riyadh, Saudi Arabia	5,253	11,698	11,864	9,471	9,160	13,075	3,610	14,789	5,660	13,780	3,059	9,472	10,426	12,413	14,869	10,538	5,177	10,483	4,830	1,736
Road Town, Brit. Virgin Isls.	7,786	2,930	1,507	4,195	3,531	14,065	8,522	14,011	6,069	6,364	13,385	3,015	2,654	2,873	13,968	2,626	6,631	18,123	7,127	9,547
Roanoke, Virginia	6,496	623	1,374	6,650	2,038	12,080	9,640	13,880	7,395	8,527	12,334	1,709	753	1,240	13,723	640	6,015	16,089	8,418	9,445
Robinson Crusoe Island, Chile	13,688	7,770	6,500	5,454	9,437	12,202	11,109	8,916	9,406	1,134	17,683	8,924	8,320	7,137	9,007	8,246	12,254	13,407	10,021	13,919
Rochester, New York	5,823	1,104	2,005	6,898	1,435	12,090	9,313	14,345	7,180	9,144	11,654	1,220	439	1,836	14,169	404	5,418	15,931	8,166	8,872
Rockhampton, Australia	14,094	14,391	15,193	16,720	15,929	3,090	15,167	2,905	17,589	12,027	9,734	16,148	15,538	14,024	2,826	15,463	15,811	1,902	16,527	13,879
Rome, Italy	2,968	8,104	8,181	7,157	5,582	14,761	3,310	18,424	3,378	12,097	5,929	5,838	6,794	8,786	18,435	6,907	1,784	13,832	3,302	1,962
Rosario, Argentina	12,903	8,120	6,662	4,000	9,211	13,813	9,441	10,108	7,895	942	15,993	8,699	8,317	7,622	10,242	8,270	11,253	14,237	8,416	12,355
Roseau, Dominica	7,976	3,418	1,985	3,712	3,871	14,478	8,235	14,056	5,781	6,045	13,427	3,360	3,088	3,350	14,037	3,069	6,715	18,437	6,828	9,470
Rostock, East Germany	1,623	7,373	7,756	7,960	4,847	13,637	4,662	18,017	4,483	12,828	5,880	5,205	6,140	8,103	17,855	6,252	893	13,584	4,586	2,672
Rostov-na-Donu, USSR	2,672	9,346	9,826	9,353	6,859	12,761	4,524	16,311	5,466	14,278	3,838	7,248	8,166	10,091	16,257	8,275	2,969	11,686	5,111	1,440
Rotterdam, Netherlands	1,965	7,028	7,309	7,420	4,489	14,078	4,515	18,552	4,052	12,270	6,402	4,810	5,759	7,742	18,368	5,871	531	14,146	4,265	2,951
Rouyn, Canada	5,380	1,484	2,573	7,350	1,269	11,811	9,313	14,455	7,302	9,718	11,172	1,279	909	2,237	14,259	926	5,135	15,505	8,246	8,601
Sacramento, California	7,659	3,068	4,390	10,087	4,789	8,456	12,812	11,043	10,849	10,172	12,319	4,820	4,109	3,031	10,823	4,033	8,172	12,497	11,798	11,440
Saginaw, Michigan	6,030	843	2,122	7,323	1,839	11,588	9,806	13,893	7,692	9,263	11,800	1,704	938	1,591	13,708	876	5,774	15,477	8,674	9,240
Saint Denis, Reunion	10,371	15,991	15,193	9,859	13,696	12,223	5,731	10,618	8,004	11,162	5,952	13,811	14,693	16,432	10,813	14,795	9,989	8,127	6,963	6,626
Saint George's, Grenada	8,323	3,666	2,185	3,538	4,231	14,511	8,328	13,791	5,885	5,684	13,716	3,718	3,420	3,532	13,784	3,395	7,033	18,298	6,917	9,708
Saint John, Canada	5,170	2,014	2,459	6,434	634	12,851	8,369	15,293	6,283	9,330	11,022	268	710	2,698	15,120	822	4,560	16,430	7,248	7,985
Saint John's, Antigua	7,810	3,241	1,835	3,872	3,672	14,386	8,253	14,147	5,799	6,238	13,311	3,159	2,884	3,201	14,119	2,866	6,580	18,414	6,852	9,395
Saint John's, Canada	4,415	3,067	3,305	6,155	728	13,548	7,358	16,346	5,378	9,704	10,200	792	1,745	3,736	16,170	1,858	3,575	16,613	6,296	6,959
Saint Louis, Missouri	6,737	407	1,927	7,494	2,578	11,167	10,467	13,173	8,274	8,882	12,450	2,392	1,504	960	12,996	1,407	6,524	15,195	9,284	9,990
Saint Paul, Minnesota	6,195	1,112	2,620	8,036	2,406	10,838	10,449	13,325	8,401	9,625	11,801	2,376	1,687	1,684	13,126	1,626	6,177	14,741	9,364	9,629
Saint Peter Port, UK	2,381	6,681	6,856	6,889	4,151	14,492	4,444	19,042	3,667	11,713	6,937	4,427	5,383	7,375	18,821	5,496	621	14,711	4,008	3,315
Saipan (Susupe)	9,871	12,102	13,568	18,964	12,283	2,909	13,812	6,863	15,417	15,798	7,147	12,701	12,605	12,233	6,688	12,594	11,646	3,846	14,914	10,980
Salalah, Oman	6,266	12,833	12,995	10,131	10,296	12,462	4,236	13,669	6,511	13,951	2,690	10,613	11,566	13,552	13,761	11,679	6,310	9,486	5,582	2,878
Salem, Oregon	7,011	3,192	4,636	10,290	4,512	8,493	12,416	11,463	10,617	10,799	11,608	4,624	4,034	3,324	11,231	3,976	7,637	12,417	11,509	10,821
Salt Lake City, Utah	7,191	2,241	3,635	9,316	3,972	9,307	12,018	11,807	10,001	9,885	12,269	3,976	3,250	2,307	11,595	3,175	7,517	13,326	10,962	10,880
Salta, Argentina	12,255	7,110	5,665	3,848	8,313	13,737	9,633	10,524	7,797	1,591	16,301	7,797	7,357	6,605	10,625	7,305	10,712	14,916	8,465	12,314
Salto, Uruguay	12,643	8,059	6,581	3,696	9,045	14,119	9,145	10,399	7,587	1,244	15,721	8,537	8,193	7,591	10,536	8,151	10,976	14,473	8,110	12,048
Salvador, Brazil	10,043	7,434	5,958	875	7,360	16,848	6,534	13,171	4,749	4,091	13,196	6,925	6,973	7,287	13,329	6,979	8,292	16,531	5,356	9,246
Salzburg, Austria	2,311	7,785	8,015	7,578	5,246	14,197	3,961	18,296	3,925	12,505	5,826	5,554	6,507	8,494	18,209	6,620	1,291	13,683	3,934	2,191
Samsun, Turkey	3,225	9,661	9,986	8,915	7,134	13,318	3,841	16,454	4,977	13,785	3,947	7,481	8,423	10,391	16,451	8,535	3,155	11,849	4,521	727
San Antonio, Texas	7,969	1,326	2,145	7,795	3,835	10,488	11,548	11,963	8,930	8,202	13,567	3,599	2,658	818	11,799	2,548	7,797	14,606	10,284	11,262
San Cristobal, Venezuela	9,192	3,475	1,992	4,375	4,803	13,426	9,546	12,619	7,112	5,190	14,824	4,291	3,716	3,083	12,595	3,654	8,073	17,055	8,133	10,915
San Diego, California	8,182	2,806	3,949	9,608	4,882	8,730	12,921	10,856	10,790	9,416	13,052	4,823	4,006	2,589	10,653	3,915	8,520	12,835	11,790	11,889
San Francisco, California	7,766	3,159	4,462	10,158	4,908	8,357	12,933	10,922	10,964	10,153	12,380	4,935	4,216	3,099	10,702	4,140	8,291	12,408	11,915	11,553
San Jose, Costa Rica	9,450	2,918	1,822	5,691	4,913	12,110	10,766	11,789	8,314	5,661	15,295	4,449	3,645	2,303	11,722	3,552	8,630	15,904	9,357	11,776
San Juan, Argentina	13,062	7,733	6,336	4,489	9,078	13,199	10,112	9,759	8,434	824	16,721	8,561	8,077	7,177	9,869	8,018	11,507	14,110	9,027	12,937
San Juan, Puerto Rico	7,846	2,821	1,373	4,324	3,541	13,910	8,678	13,887	6,226	6,359	13,482	3,024	2,613	2,737	13,840	2,578	6,724	17,965	7,284	9,674
San Luis Potosi, Mexico	8,812	2,074	2,431	7,798	4,613	10,254	12,087	11,262	9,703	7,584	14,386	4,333	3,377	1,393	11,114	3,265	8,594	14,339	10,763	12,050
San Marino, San Marino	2,745	7,980	8,107	7,286	5,450	14,579	3,533	18,425	3,551	12,225	5,904	5,723	6,679	8,672	18,398	6,792	1,594	13,801	3,512	2,034
San Miguel de Tucuman, Argen.	12,455	7,329	5,889	3,941	8,537	13,681	9,671	10,364	7,893	1,372	16,333	8,021	7,583	6,818	10,471	7,531	10,894	14,720	8,532	12,408

Distances in Kilometers	Narvik, Norway	Nashville, Tennessee	Nassau, Bahamas	Natal, Brazil	Natashquan, Canada	Nauru Island	Ndjamena, Chad	Nelson, New Zealand	Nema, Mauritania	Neuquen, Argentina	New Delhi, India	New Glasgow, Canada	New Haven, Connecticut	New Orleans, Louisiana	New Plymouth, New Zealand	New York, New York	Newcastle upon Tyne, UK	Newcastle Waters, Australia	Niamey, Niger	Nicosia, Cyprus
San Salvador, El Salvador	9,261	2,500	1,769	6,342	4,749	11,532	11,202	11,628	8,749	6,229	15,103	4,328	3,443	1,803	11,534	3,339	8,620	15,456	9,806	11,906
Sanaa, Yemen	6,196	12,333	12,267	9,058	9,810	13,535	3,171	14,366	5,494	12,987	3,694	10,063	11,018	13,005	14,495	11,130	5,887	10,435	4,536	2,448
Santa Cruz, Bolivia	11,452	6,470	4,987	3,317	7,533	14,186	9,207	11,267	7,215	2,392	15,822	7,019	6,620	6,021	11,355	6,574	9,929	15,715	7,962	11,712
Santa Cruz, Tenerife	4,962	6,555	6,025	4,301	4,514	16,897	3,717	18,344	1,602	9,199	8,859	4,470	5,277	7,047	18,499	5,373	3,176	16,694	2,518	4,707
Santa Fe, New Mexico	7,555	1,728	2,975	8,671	3,876	9,787	11,875	11,845	9,709	9,135	12,882	3,774	2,930	1,614	11,652	2,837	7,665	13,873	10,715	11,104
Santa Rosa, Argentina	13,410	8,387	6,966	4,519	9,620	13,334	9,876	9,584	8,398	422	16,329	9,105	8,673	7,847	9,717	8,620	11,772	13,746	8,891	12,836
Santa Rosalia, Mexico	8,623	2,598	3,489	9,041	4,943	9,131	12,860	10,782	10,595	8,657	13,735	4,797	3,901	2,189	10,598	3,798	8,769	13,249	11,631	12,208
Santarem, Brazil	9,533	5,417	3,905	2,195	5,872	15,393	7,878	13,169	5,624	4,266	14,169	5,377	5,183	5,195	13,241	5,164	7,994	17,642	6,515	9,992
Santiago del Estero, Argentina	12,516	7,462	6,016	3,918	8,641	13,731	9,609	10,342	7,868	1,288	16,262	8,126	7,700	6,955	10,453	7,649	10,937	14,659	8,488	12,379
Santiago, Chile	13,340	7,887	6,517	4,773	9,307	12,936	10,356	9,466	8,714	653	16,926	8,790	8,280	7,310	9,576	8,218	11,796	13,829	9,292	13,212
Santo Domingo, Dominican Rep.	8,001	2,568	1,063	4,657	3,593	13,520	9,073	13,571	6,621	6,359	13,718	3,081	2,548	2,406	13,513	2,497	6,964	17,565	7,680	9,995
Sao Paulo de Olivenca, Brazil	10,204	4,768	3,289	3,735	5,982	13,821	9,430	12,036	7,120	3,932	15,475	5,465	4,973	4,336	12,063	4,918	8,895	16,665	8,051	11,340
Sao Paulo, Brazil	11,424	7,842	6,319	2,313	8,304	15,525	7,783	11,738	6,169	2,652	14,430	7,824	7,674	7,524	11,890	7,656	9,698	15,476	6,704	10,634
Sao Tome, Sao Tome & Principe	7,602	10,307	9,404	4,711	8,470	17,834	1,594	15,273	2,366	8,724	8,095	8,392	9,122	10,652	15,528	9,206	6,108	13,899	1,544	4,744
Sapporo, Japan	6,802	9,974	11,489	15,862	9,431	5,462	11,829	9,875	12,665	17,519	5,867	9,904	10,053	10,373	9,675	10,075	8,589	6,742	12,498	8,689
Sarajevo, Yugoslavia	2,740	8,379	8,559	7,680	5,841	14,291	3,530	17,947	3,866	12,619	5,427	6,137	7,091	9,082	17,929	7,204	1,899	13,327	3,703	1,602
Saratov, USSR	2,420	9,257	9,885	9,907	6,840	12,133	5,189	15,902	6,067	14,846	3,633	7,267	8,149	10,009	15,814	8,255	3,138	11,326	5,757	2,085
Saskatoon, Canada	5,867	2,365	3,886	9,265	3,093	9,811	10,978	12,897	9,191	10,760	11,055	3,256	2,812	2,812	12,669	2,779	6,279	13,554	10,067	9,585
Schefferville, Canada	4,311	2,573	3,411	7,326	615	12,280	8,396	15,447	6,576	10,389	10,147	1,067	1,566	3,324	15,233	1,654	4,029	15,511	7,443	7,493
Seattle, Washington	6,712	3,178	4,657	10,265	4,323	8,620	12,167	11,712	10,423	10,990	11,343	4,464	3,927	3,380	11,477	3,876	7,358	12,483	11,294	10,524
Sendai, Japan	7,290	10,424	11,945	16,388	9,957	5,057	12,096	9,403	13,086	17,512	5,904	10,427	10,553	10,792	9,210	10,572	9,074	6,209	12,853	8,983
Seoul, South Korea	6,913	11,134	12,620	16,055	10,244	5,883	11,057	9,920	12,342	18,699	4,699	10,745	11,040	11,597	9,758	11,078	8,645	6,121	11,954	8,017
Sept-Iles, Canada	4,716	2,262	2,944	6,890	326	12,564	8,375	15,399	6,420	9,878	10,569	584	1,111	2,995	15,204	1,210	4,262	15,963	7,337	7,722
Sevastopol, USSR	2,812	9,237	9,594	8,810	6,714	13,322	4,009	16,749	4,911	13,726	4,229	7,069	8,007	9,970	16,721	8,119	2,744	12,122	4,553	1,048
Seville, Spain	3,743	6,972	6,777	5,661	4,595	15,861	3,497	19,567	2,305	10,574	7,585	4,719	5,641	7,580	19,818	5,749	1,986	15,486	2,764	3,519
Shanghai, China	7,368	12,002	13,476	16,297	10,992	5,947	10,831	9,627	12,401	18,794	4,249	11,501	11,854	12,477	9,494	11,897	9,030	5,521	11,872	7,935
Sheffield, United Kingdom	1,950	6,591	6,885	7,278	4,052	14,052	4,806	18,607	4,108	12,057	6,782	4,375	5,323	7,305	18,380	5,435	182	14,447	4,432	3,387
Shenyang, China	6,360	10,842	12,298	15,495	9,799	6,405	10,596	10,479	11,802	18,995	4,400	10,306	10,655	11,350	10,317	10,700	8,087	6,634	11,444	7,521
Shiraz, Iran	4,883	11,579	11,939	10,113	9,068	12,391	4,327	14,597	6,225	14,554	2,399	9,429	10,366	12,319	14,637	10,477	5,104	10,106	5,470	1,903
Sibiu, Romania	2,550	8,603	8,884	8,183	6,067	13,818	3,832	17,493	4,353	13,121	4,976	6,397	7,344	9,324	17,453	7,457	2,080	12,864	4,136	1,414
Singapore	9,726	15,717	17,085	15,464	14,139	7,025	9,858	8,402	12,221	15,754	4,142	14,646	15,277	16,249	8,408	15,349	10,871	3,844	11,254	8,162
Sioux Falls, South Dakota	6,456	1,180	2,702	8,228	2,735	10,563	10,777	12,996	8,716	9,582	11,993	2,697	1,970	1,619	12,796	1,900	6,490	14,513	9,685	9,935
Skelleftea, Sweden	438	7,201	7,893	9,068	4,816	12,370	5,863	16,857	5,753	13,796	5,582	5,265	6,118	7,953	16,659	6,222	1,651	12,802	5,871	3,397
Skopje, Yugoslavia	2,953	8,701	8,870	7,799	6,164	14,264	3,370	17,683	3,927	12,726	5,185	6,458	7,413	9,404	17,689	7,526	2,218	13,087	3,669	1,282
Socotra Island (Tamrida)	6,729	13,223	13,296	10,075	10,684	12,518	4,234	13,369	6,591	13,652	2,982	10,981	11,937	13,929	13,478	12,050	6,705	9,334	5,619	3,247
Sofia, Bulgaria	2,888	8,771	8,974	7,968	6,232	14,102	3,481	17,542	4,093	12,895	5,032	6,538	7,492	9,480	17,539	7,605	2,265	12,935	3,821	1,205
Songkhla, Thailand	8,985	15,144	16,426	15,150	13,423	7,414	9,371	9,113	11,668	16,311	3,414	13,926	14,594	15,739	9,109	14,672	10,127	4,519	10,742	7,487
Sorong, Indonesia	11,050	14,485	15,945	18,356	14,401	3,972	12,888	6,149	15,163	15,177	6,612	14,870	14,917	14,599	6,066	14,918	12,654	1,842	14,261	10,787
South Georgia Island	14,313	11,105	9,613	5,376	11,812	13,556	8,819	9,039	8,339	2,903	14,072	11,332	11,136	10,639	9,254	11,107	12,531	12,011	8,359	11,959
South Pole	17,598	14,006	12,778	9,364	15,566	9,942	11,344	5,428	11,842	5,690	13,168	15,053	14,577	13,318	5,674	14,511	16,102	8,076	11,499	13,897
South Sandwich Islands	14,445	11,825	10,323	5,814	12,396	13,433	8,621	8,875	8,431	3,636	13,448	11,932	11,797	11,375	9,105	11,774	12,700	11,473	8,323	11,711
Split, Yugoslavia	2,775	8,269	8,423	7,526	5,735	14,422	3,483	18,107	3,728	12,465	5,589	6,020	6,976	8,968	18,092	7,089	1,821	13,490	3,596	1,724
Spokane, Washington	6,597	2,819	4,309	9,899	3,987	8,983	11,892	11,985	10,092	10,767	11,432	4,112	3,559	3,054	11,755	3,507	7,145	12,853	10,980	10,380
Spoleto, Italy	2,875	8,070	8,170	7,227	5,544	14,674	3,401	18,407	3,462	12,167	5,897	5,808	6,764	8,757	18,403	6,877	1,715	13,799	3,396	1,969
Springbok, South Africa	10,878	13,117	11,823	6,154	11,804	15,333	4,633	11,754	5,789	7,685	9,017	11,625	12,178	13,190	12,008	12,238	9,564	11,367	5,069	7,358
Springfield, Illinois	6,598	476	1,996	7,515	2,460	11,195	10,379	13,282	8,208	8,993	12,311	2,292	1,425	1,092	13,102	1,333	6,396	15,200	9,211	9,861
Springfield, Massachusetts	5,735	1,390	1,938	6,516	1,224	12,518	8,925	14,679	6,764	8,988	11,588	887	93	2,065	14,513	194	5,190	16,328	7,758	8,619
Srinagar, India	5,207	11,998	12,830	12,217	9,743	10,242	6,489	13,052	8,279	16,680	649	10,202	11,031	12,741	13,020	11,131	6,153	8,423	7,599	3,775
Stanley, Falkland Islands	14,676	10,134	8,717	5,502	11,300	12,866	9,911	8,582	9,012	1,624	15,511	10,790	10,407	9,579	8,762	10,357	12,918	12,273	9,238	13,056
Stara Zagora, Bulgaria	2,937	8,936	9,158	8,127	6,397	13,979	3,511	17,349	4,235	13,046	4,842	6,710	7,662	9,649	17,348	7,775	2,419	12,744	3,922	1,047
Stockholm, Sweden	1,015	7,389	7,938	8,602	4,918	12,950	5,246	17,369	5,170	13,425	5,579	5,328	6,228	8,136	17,191	6,336	1,277	13,087	5,253	2,910
Stornoway, United Kingdom	1,629	6,139	6,564	7,552	3,615	13,581	5,425	18,121	4,618	12,192	6,985	3,984	4,913	6,870	17,875	5,024	462	14,412	5,012	3,880
Strasbourg, France	2,275	7,402	7,613	7,329	4,865	14,320	4,100	18,619	3,799	12,233	6,211	5,163	6,117	8,107	18,492	6,230	961	14,045	3,923	2,577
Stuttgart, West Germany	2,238	7,484	7,710	7,422	4,946	14,253	4,100	18,517	3,866	12,330	6,104	5,250	6,203	8,192	18,397	6,316	1,014	13,938	3,963	2,492
Subic, Philippines	8,991	13,686	15,194	17,165	12,792	5,415	11,263	8,270	13,288	17,219	4,674	13,302	13,640	14,082	8,180	13,678	10,544	3,852	12,526	8,795
Suchow, China	6,891	11,823	13,260	15,772	10,648	6,454	10,350	10,144	11,878	19,314	3,828	11,161	11,574	12,344	10,013	11,625	8,531	5,971	11,364	7,423
Sucre, Bolivia	11,662	6,515	5,053	3,574	7,676	13,934	9,458	11,019	7,476	2,224	16,081	7,160	6,726	6,038	11,104	6,675	10,160	15,492	8,219	11,974
Sudbury, Canada	5,621	1,245	2,399	7,341	1,476	11,725	9,499	14,245	7,449	9,552	11,404	1,421	869	1,997	14,053	856	5,374	15,499	8,408	8,840
Suez, Egypt	4,390	10,333	10,379	8,227	7,804	14,205	2,678	16,288	4,306	12,890	4,314	8,072	9,028	11,020	16,381	9,141	3,881	11,984	3,619	582
Sundsvall, Sweden	675	7,181	7,799	8,767	4,746	12,692	5,583	17,172	5,432	13,529	5,687	5,176	6,055	7,931	16,977	6,161	1,362	13,043	5,558	3,228
Surabaya, Indonesia	10,968	16,244	17,764	16,194	15,217	6,059	11,019	7,035	13,440	14,889	5,504	15,734	16,191	16,553	7,043	16,239	12,205	2,508	12,430	9,518
Suva, Fiji	14,260	11,601	12,246	15,483	13,648	2,317	18,126	2,613	19,408	10,658	12,026	13,672	12,867	11,142	2,358	12,772	15,913	4,762	19,370	16,096
Sverdlovsk, USSR	2,488	9,251	10,109	10,897	7,017	11,044	6,293	15,031	7,131	15,821	3,399	7,491	8,291	9,997	14,906	8,389	3,758	10,606	6,865	3,161
Svobodnyy, USSR	5,555	9,725	11,174	14,720	8,705	6,813	10,499	11,162	11,321	18,140	4,900	9,208	9,534	10,250	10,973	9,577	7,330	7,639	11,137	7,350
Sydney, Australia	15,204	14,808	15,264	15,563	16,778	4,041	14,977	2,109	17,138	10,986	10,415	16,871	16,086	14,302	2,124	15,990	16,858	2,547	16,172	14,413
Sydney, Canada	4,851	2,476	2,794	6,262	466	13,193	7,912	15,759	5,860	9,459	10,683	202	1,156	3,149	15,587	1,269	4,135	16,581	6,810	7,541
Syktyvkar, USSR	1,715	8,508	9,338	10,358	6,246	11,405	6,205	15,616	6,729	15,221	4,158	6,718	7,525	9,257	15,465	7,623	3,067	11,309	6,593	3,193
Szeged, Hungary	2,474	8,328	8,582	7,936	5,790	13,998	3,816	17,798	4,152	12,876	5,286	6,110	7,060	9,044	17,750	7,172	1,809	13,169	4,006	1,658
Szombathely, Hungary	2,362	8,045	8,290	7,762	5,506	14,090	3,896	18,051	4,042	12,698	5,558	5,822	6,773	8,758	17,983	6,885	1,533	13,427	3,975	1,934
Tabriz, Iran	3,809	10,478	10,881	9,667	7,972	12,687	4,229	15,531	5,716	14,428	3,046	8,342	9,273	11,218	15,536	9,384	4,024	10,939	5,131	1,200
Tacheng, China	4,303	10,764	11,807	12,601	8,742	9,594	7,356	13,206	8,697	17,515	2,076	9,238	9,964	11,480	13,105	10,052	5,650	8,715	8,232	4,290
Tahiti (Papeete)	14,276	8,880	9,134	12,374	11,330	5,119	18,272	4,410	16,029	8,085	15,116	11,148	10,212	8,264	4,246	10,102	15,040	8,116	16,968	18,030
Taipei, Taiwan	7,994	12,611	14,102	16,749	11,663	5,650	11,059	9,080	12,803	18,226	4,397	12,172	12,511	13,054	8,960	12,551	9,624	4,870	12,189	8,295
Taiyuan, China	6,352	11,571	12,961	15,195	10,233	7,001	9,841	10,718	11,310	19,876	3,428	10,749	11,220	12,138	10,589	11,278	7,970	6,495	10,818	6,873
Tallahassee, Florida	7,352	675	905	6,585	2,885	11,841	10,214	13,145	7,875	7,864	13,183	2,521	1,580	559	13,005	1,469	6,846	15,952	8,924	10,253
Tallinn, USSR	1,066	7,700	8,291	8,930	5,253	12,705	5,311	17,047	5,414	13,780	5,212	5,674	6,563	8,449	16,884	6,670	1,654	12,711	5,426	2,768
Tamanrasset, Algeria	5,139	8,749	8,294	5,444	6,495	16,838	1,554	17,661	1,502	10,255	7,119	6,559	7,436	9,285	17,905	7,539	3,625	14,576	1,087	3,027
Tampa, Florida	7,536	998	599	6,296	3,026	12,063	10,113	13,139	7,739	7,556	13,384	2,622	1,717	775	13,012	1,613	6,943	16,181	8,796	10,311
Tampere, Finland	828	7,519	8,151	8,996	5,095	12,566	5,527	16,973	5,552	13,807	5,335	5,527	6,403	8,270	16,795	6,509	1,641	12,733	5,603	3,006
Tanami, Australia	12,962	16,047	17,196	16,720	16,502	4,589	13,028	4,730	15,481	13,225	7,794	16,950	16,828	15,886	4,733	16,800	14,394	482	14,422	11,825
Tangier, Morocco	3,908	7,065	6,827	5,535	4,715	16,029	3,358	19,391	2,130	10,459	7,630	4,822	5,736	7,661	19,642	5,843	2,158	15,522	2,593	3,531
Tarawa (Betio)	12,037	10,848	11,931	16,872	12,302	700	17,166	4,722	18,017	12,581	10,504	12,491	11,903	10,616	4,477	11,835	13,738	4,806	18,082	14,188
Tashkent, USSR	4,270	11,085	11,891	11,647	8,805	10,689	6,165	13,876	7,697	16,417	1,585	9,263	10,096	11,832	13,822	10,196	5,241	9,257	7,129	3,195
Tbilisi, USSR	3,386	10,076	10,521	9,608	7,581	12,666	4,366	15,790	5,664	14,452	3,268	7,961	8,886	10,820	15,772	8,996	3,657	11,169	5,160	1,229
Tegucigalpa, Honduras	9,143	2,445	1,595	6,149	4,617	11,743	10,983	11,821	8,530	6,201	14,994	4,185	3,318	1,781	11,732	3,217	8,457	15,675	9,587	11,720
Tehran, Iran	4,212	10,958	11,400	10,083	8,467	12,331	4,488	15,005	6,140	14,747	2,546	8,847	9,772	11,703	15,014	9,882	4,538	10,423	5,493	1,640
Tel Aviv, Israel	4,196	10,314	10,434	8,495	7,777	13,913	2,992	16,216	4,559	13,191	4,073	8,067	9,023	11,015	16,288	9,136	3,816	11,817	3,907	368
Telegraph Creek, Canada	5,759	4,038	5,561	10,901	4,415	8,440	11,658	12,142	10,289	12,229	10,061	4,702	4,428	4,413	11,892	4,410	6,697	11,948	11,021	9,590
Teresina, Brazil	9,362	6,465	5,010	846	6,393	16,671	6,680	13,703	4,592	4,533	13,207	5,948	5,979	6,356	13,828	5,986	7,665	17,484	5,375	9,091
Ternate, Indonesia	10,727	14,608	16,106	18,027	14,286	4,403	12,428	6,561	14,696	15,499	6,153	14,773	14,915	14,790	6,488	14,927	12,289	2,118	13,797	10,330
The Valley, Anguilla	7,763	3,075	1,670	4,038	3,568	14,235	8,366	14,112	5,912	6,331	13,315	3,054	2,743	3,036	14,076	2,721	6,570	18,288	6,969	9,440
Thessaloniki, Greece	3,112	8,891	9,044	7,839	6,355	14,279	3,253	17,538	3,938	12,752	5,070	6,645	7,600	9,592	17,560	7,713	2,412	12,967	3,625	1,099
Thimphu, Bhutan	6,465	12,945	14,021	13,743	10,950	8,783	7,900	11,476	9,837	17,604	1,236	11,441	12,177	13,642	11,434	12,266	7,628	6,850	9,099	5,358
Thunder Bay, Canada	5,723	1,375	2,792	7,975	1,999	11,067	10,045	13,761	8,065	9,901	11,372	2,042	1,513	2,048	13,555	1,483	5,702	14,852	9,003	9,150
Tientsin, China	6,401	11,314	12,738	15,396	10,108	6,699	10,194	10,563	11,569	19,569	3,847	10,621	11,039	11,853	10,421	11,090	8,071	6,482	11,126	7,181
Tijuana, Mexico	8,197	2,800	3,936	9,592	4,886	8,740	12,923	10,851	10,787	9,392	13,075	4,824	4,004	2,576	10,648	3,913	8,530	12,846	11,788	11,901
Tiksi, USSR	3,667	7,731	9,093	12,612	6,468	8,455	9,537	13,001	9,677	16,247	5,701	6,975	7,366	8,343	12,779	7,419	5,435	9,879	9,772	6,523
Timbuktu, Mali	5,919	8,382	7,697	4,334	6,384	17,907	2,014	17,264	452	9,148	8,206	6,342	7,130	8,824	17,517	7,222	4,245	15,406	659	4,141
Tindouf, Algeria	4,834	7,294	6,817	4,711	5,138	16,954	2,969	18,492	1,231	9,651	8,178	5,148	5,995	7,812	18,728	6,095	3,078	15,933	1,898	4,003
Tirane, Albania	3,020	8,639	8,774	7,643	6,104	14,414	3,271	17,809	3,773	12,571	5,326	6,387	7,343	9,335	17,825	7,456	2,186	13,227	3,529	1,366

Distances in Kilometers

	Narvik, Norway	Nashville, Tennessee	Nassau, Bahamas	Natal, Brazil	Natashquan, Canada	Nauru Island	Ndjamena, Chad	Nelson, New Zealand	Nema, Mauritania	Neuquen, Argentina	New Delhi, India	New Glasgow, Canada	New Haven, Connecticut	New Orleans, Louisiana	New Plymouth, New Zealand	New York, New York	Newcastle upon Tyne, UK	Newcastle Waters, Australia	Niamey, Niger	Nicosia, Cyprus
Tokyo, Japan	7,523	10,711	12,233	16,653	10,256	4,902	12,164	9,186	13,258	17,542	5,857	10,726	10,852	11,069	8,999	10,870	9,302	5,915	12,978	9,077
Toledo, Spain	3,432	7,005	6,895	5,982	4,575	15,554	3,601	19,740	2,596	10,891	7,333	4,737	5,674	7,637	19,834	5,784	1,692	15,235	2,981	3,321
Topeka, Kansas	6,880	848	2,314	7,943	2,926	10,689	10,893	12,799	8,733	9,085	12,479	2,795	1,949	1,131	12,613	1,858	6,804	14,723	9,734	10,266
Toronto, Canada	5,840	1,045	2,070	7,045	1,517	11,936	9,443	14,237	7,324	9,221	11,656	1,342	593	1,791	14,057	553	5,487	15,780	8,306	8,947
Toulouse, France	2,918	7,227	7,260	6,593	4,728	15,023	3,727	19,303	3,102	11,505	6,785	4,954	5,908	7,895	19,221	6,020	1,287	14,673	3,335	2,885
Tours, France	2,526	6,991	7,124	6,863	4,467	14,647	4,134	19,114	3,489	11,738	6,752	4,730	5,686	7,679	18,942	5,799	862	14,587	3,757	3,026
Townsville, Australia	13,534	14,495	15,452	17,227	15,746	3,019	14,818	3,503	17,272	12,615	9,163	16,034	15,543	14,208	3,421	15,480	15,231	1,431	16,215	13,322
Trenton, New Jersey	6,004	1,144	1,696	6,506	1,500	12,418	9,137	14,428	6,938	8,794	11,855	1,153	197	1,796	14,267	84	5,465	16,312	7,945	8,890
Tripoli, Lebanon	3,957	10,191	10,374	8,663	7,653	13,709	3,247	16,240	4,716	13,407	3,953	7,961	8,914	10,903	16,292	9,027	3,674	11,765	4,109	241
Tripoli, Libya	3,962	8,723	8,590	6,665	6,262	15,500	2,310	18,029	2,733	11,551	6,054	6,450	7,392	9,359	18,175	7,503	2,714	13,843	2,423	1,878
Tristan da Cunha (Edinburgh)	11,955	11,163	9,677	4,173	10,817	15,843	6,149	11,312	5,964	4,825	11,822	10,451	10,644	10,981	11,551	10,662	10,251	12,993	5,798	9,286
Trondheim, Norway	643	6,817	7,433	8,572	4,378	12,766	5,707	17,301	5,373	13,266	6,051	4,808	5,686	7,566	17,087	5,793	1,158	13,336	5,578	3,514
Trujillo, Peru	11,103	4,968	3,677	4,847	6,673	12,657	10,646	10,868	8,361	3,588	16,652	6,169	5,507	4,376	10,877	5,430	9,950	15,476	9,280	12,565
Truk Island (Moen)	10,877	12,233	13,596	19,232	12,844	1,891	14,786	5,821	16,502	14,716	8,127	13,207	12,948	12,230	5,636	12,917	12,662	3,416	15,959	12,045
Truro, Canada	5,050	2,221	2,581	6,316	548	13,036	8,150	15,506	6,071	9,351	10,893	54	902	2,895	15,335	1,015	4,380	16,542	7,033	7,792
Tsingtao, China	6,826	11,534	12,988	15,832	10,446	6,294	10,561	10,126	11,993	19,215	4,109	10,957	11,332	12,039	9,983	11,379	8,504	6,076	11,527	7,581
Tsitsihar, China	5,819	10,261	11,703	14,989	9,179	6,745	10,403	10,961	11,419	18,664	4,518	9,687	10,043	10,790	10,787	10,089	7,570	7,235	11,146	7,277
Tubuai Island (Mataura)	14,917	9,316	9,445	12,199	11,808	5,343	17,966	3,988	16,020	7,702	15,350	11,591	10,643	8,668	3,850	10,531	15,611	7,987	16,845	18,669
Tucson, Arizona	8,067	2,266	3,366	9,027	4,478	9,302	12,470	11,243	10,277	9,042	13,219	4,372	3,514	2,007	11,050	3,417	8,247	13,412	11,293	11,672
Tulsa, Oklahoma	7,185	821	2,156	7,835	3,141	10,692	11,036	12,601	8,823	8,795	12,800	2,967	2,073	877	12,422	1,973	7,062	14,766	9,840	10,528
Tunis, Tunisia	3,549	8,251	8,181	6,669	5,773	15,337	2,777	18,480	2,820	11,599	6,224	5,976	6,924	8,900	18,589	7,035	2,213	14,093	2,702	2,094
Tura, USSR	3,453	8,852	10,095	12,620	7,215	8,955	8,569	13,313	9,171	17,084	4,290	7,732	8,283	9,518	13,129	8,354	5,202	9,491	9,050	5,442
Turin, Italy	2,664	7,588	7,706	7,065	5,062	14,671	3,718	18,780	3,448	11,992	6,266	5,327	6,284	8,276	18,715	6,396	1,288	14,151	3,535	2,436
Uberlandia, Brazil	11,005	7,321	5,798	2,032	7,772	15,618	7,751	12,086	5,972	2,925	14,419	7,290	7,136	7,023	12,223	7,118	9,307	15,981	6,592	10,479
Ufa, USSR	2,485	9,323	10,106	10,603	7,019	11,389	5,918	15,284	6,799	15,541	3,371	7,479	8,310	10,074	15,173	8,411	3,588	10,790	6,507	2,785
Ujungpandang, Indonesia	11,020	15,658	17,174	16,965	15,006	5,308	11,696	6,670	14,084	15,066	5,860	15,516	15,815	15,882	6,647	15,844	12,407	2,043	13,101	9,978
Ulaanbaatar, Mongolia	5,150	10,593	11,909	14,121	9,078	7,875	9,155	11,844	10,344	18,931	3,332	9,596	10,121	11,215	11,699	10,187	6,795	7,701	9,973	6,057
Ulan-Ude, USSR	4,807	10,156	11,471	13,870	8,653	8,006	9,134	12,107	10,176	18,535	3,606	9,170	9,685	10,781	11,950	9,750	6,490	8,068	9,872	6,002
Uliastay, Mongolia	4,773	10,703	11,917	13,516	8,959	8,580	8,408	12,401	9,670	18,452	2,717	9,473	10,088	11,370	12,274	10,164	6,318	8,084	9,256	5,325
Uranium City, Canada	5,155	3,041	4,530	9,634	3,103	9,745	10,615	13,250	9,052	11,537	10,219	3,392	3,184	3,574	13,008	3,181	5,756	13,226	9,844	8,939
Urumqi, China	4,772	11,131	12,225	13,050	9,177	9,197	7,687	12,723	9,128	17,923	1,924	9,677	10,380	11,833	12,626	10,465	6,139	8,226	8,622	4,676
Ushuaia, Argentina	15,330	10,233	8,893	6,188	11,654	12,097	10,677	7,867	9,776	1,762	15,999	11,138	10,658	9,620	8,038	10,597	13,603	11,745	10,015	13,825
Vaduz, Liechtenstein	2,410	7,594	7,781	7,326	5,059	14,396	3,920	18,570	3,723	12,247	6,095	5,350	6,304	8,296	18,476	6,417	1,166	13,957	3,794	2,389
Valencia, Spain	3,399	7,305	7,211	6,158	4,858	15,506	3,390	19,446	2,619	11,086	7,047	5,033	5,975	7,943	19,544	6,085	1,729	14,949	2,886	3,010
Valladolid, Spain	3,258	6,867	6,803	6,099	4,417	15,375	3,796	19,851	2,786	10,989	7,329	4,595	5,538	7,510	19,702	5,649	1,502	15,221	3,187	3,375
Valletta, Malta	3,624	8,628	8,580	6,941	6,135	15,171	2,635	18,085	3,034	11,849	5,863	6,353	7,303	9,285	18,188	7,415	2,456	13,712	2,773	1,709
Valparaiso, Chile	13,337	7,821	6,460	4,826	9,270	12,866	10,434	9,438	8,771	731	17,017	8,753	8,232	7,238	9,545	8,168	11,809	13,826	9,360	13,274
Vancouver, Canada	6,551	3,271	4,766	10,340	4,294	8,612	12,075	11,801	10,381	11,168	11,150	4,458	3,961	3,510	11,564	3,915	7,235	12,430	11,234	10,370
Varna, Bulgaria	2,874	9,017	9,282	8,334	6,480	13,778	3,663	17,176	4,440	13,253	4,659	6,807	7,756	9,737	17,165	7,868	2,494	12,561	4,115	1,010
Venice, Italy	2,576	7,880	8,045	7,380	5,345	14,443	3,704	18,412	3,682	12,315	5,896	5,631	6,587	8,579	18,359	6,700	1,451	13,782	3,670	2,110
Veracruz, Mexico	8,949	2,091	2,042	7,223	4,584	10,766	11,729	11,442	9,308	7,071	14,668	4,244	3,295	1,341	11,314	3,183	8,563	14,811	10,372	11,979
Verona, Italy	2,586	7,790	7,944	7,296	5,258	14,501	3,715	18,515	3,621	12,229	6,001	5,539	6,494	8,487	18,458	6,607	1,387	13,886	3,638	2,207
Victoria, Canada	6,643	3,271	4,757	10,351	4,350	8,570	12,153	11,723	10,443	11,111	11,231	4,506	3,990	3,489	11,487	3,943	7,322	12,409	11,303	10,462
Victoria, Seychelles	8,620	14,813	14,508	10,041	12,318	12,397	4,839	11,938	7,285	12,486	4,352	12,539	13,484	15,441	12,096	13,594	8,420	8,587	6,224	4,973
Vienna, Austria	2,254	7,969	8,236	7,806	5,431	14,017	4,003	18,045	4,112	12,739	5,576	5,753	6,702	8,685	17,964	6,815	1,451	13,431	4,065	2,016
Vientiane, Laos	7,964	13,933	15,242	15,258	12,301	7,328	9,353	9,786	11,445	17,513	2,845	12,812	13,427	14,532	9,742	13,500	9,262	5,166	10,636	7,020
Villahermosa, Mexico	8,958	2,103	1,792	6,859	4,519	11,110	11,449	11,620	9,015	6,814	14,743	4,145	3,213	1,358	11,503	3,103	8,472	15,134	10,079	11,849
Vilnius, USSR	1,586	8,047	8,538	8,710	5,556	13,065	4,807	17,234	5,062	13,620	5,040	5,948	6,863	8,791	17,107	6,973	1,719	12,730	4,994	2,257
Visby, Sweden	1,205	7,502	8,011	8,506	5,014	13,095	5,058	17,471	5,023	13,357	5,532	5,413	6,323	8,246	17,305	6,432	1,261	13,114	5,083	2,739
Vitoria, Brazil	10,876	7,934	6,424	1,701	8,092	16,262	7,047	12,358	5,457	3,363	13,700	7,638	7,605	7,702	12,523	7,601	9,119	15,778	5,968	9,903
Vladivostok, USSR	6,508	10,392	11,883	15,679	9,579	5,966	11,167	10,229	12,191	18,285	5,099	10,073	10,329	10,852	10,048	10,363	8,277	6,704	11,926	8,051
Volgograd, USSR	2,649	9,437	9,999	9,734	6,986	12,371	4,883	15,983	5,855	14,664	3,579	7,396	8,296	10,187	15,915	8,404	3,183	11,371	5,498	1,761
Vologda, USSR	1,494	8,353	9,053	9,718	5,979	12,062	5,621	16,246	6,071	14,609	4,424	6,425	7,281	9,105	16,104	7,385	2,515	11,850	5,950	2,716
Vorkuta, USSR	1,907	8,251	9,252	10,988	6,192	10,608	7,105	14,970	7,514	15,695	4,415	6,692	7,408	8,982	14,791	7,497	3,578	10,936	7,447	4,090
Wake Island	9,965	10,167	11,535	17,226	10,965	2,192	15,354	6,740	15,979	14,366	8,959	11,276	10,929	10,170	6,505	10,890	11,699	5,449	16,006	12,229
Wallis Island	13,804	10,820	11,508	15,226	12,864	2,338	18,811	3,266	18,786	10,599	12,323	12,883	12,079	10,375	3,012	11,986	15,354	5,420	19,849	16,193
Walvis Bay, Namibia	10,136	12,457	11,239	5,656	11,017	16,065	3,880	12,566	4,977	7,826	8,816	10,858	11,452	12,597	12,820	11,517	8,772	12,020	4,254	6,734
Warsaw, Poland	1,813	7,982	8,383	8,327	5,462	13,459	4,483	17,595	4,668	13,246	5,273	5,828	6,760	8,716	17,480	6,871	1,519	13,042	4,615	2,137
Washington, D.C.	6,224	913	1,532	6,557	1,737	12,278	9,354	14,188	7,133	8,668	12,071	1,398	442	1,551	14,030	329	5,708	16,230	8,148	9,135
Watson Lake, Canada	5,486	3,994	5,514	10,759	4,210	8,664	11,378	12,416	10,033	12,297	9,890	4,518	4,296	4,415	12,165	4,285	6,415	12,099	10,752	9,319
Weimar, East Germany	1,972	7,496	7,794	7,698	4,958	13,963	4,324	18,260	4,156	12,596	5,936	5,288	6,235	8,215	18,125	6,347	974	13,727	4,238	2,494
Wellington, New Zealand	16,699	13,175	13,255	13,969	15,616	4,584	16,222	126	17,262	9,082	12,642	15,446	14,505	12,537	255	14,395	18,459	4,747	16,846	16,607
West Berlin, West Germany	1,786	7,533	7,885	7,917	5,002	13,742	4,483	18,048	4,376	12,809	5,791	5,351	6,291	8,260	17,906	6,403	1,025	13,546	4,441	2,492
Wewak, Papua New Guinea	11,778	13,728	15,039	18,965	14,311	2,613	14,296	5,122	16,536	14,293	7,928	14,698	14,469	13,675	4,995	14,438	13,505	1,896	15,665	12,079
Whangarei, New Zealand	16,092	12,942	13,185	14,478	15,289	3,970	16,672	625	17,883	9,555	12,402	15,184	14,271	12,348	372	14,164	17,839	4,512	17,427	16,505
Whitehorse, Canada	5,506	4,341	5,862	11,100	4,518	8,383	11,509	12,239	10,263	12,601	9,682	4,841	4,641	4,749	11,986	4,632	6,535	11,761	10,947	9,325
Wichita, Kansas	7,074	955	2,351	8,018	3,132	10,554	11,086	12,594	8,908	9,001	12,643	2,993	2,131	1,090	12,410	2,037	7,012	14,611	9,915	10,474
Willemstad, Curacao	8,611	3,209	1,686	4,226	4,273	13,735	9,099	13,206	6,650	5,654	14,223	3,758	3,257	2,942	13,176	3,207	7,472	17,560	7,688	10,337
Wiluna, Australia	13,249	17,259	18,264	15,560	17,379	5,769	12,107	5,084	14,518	12,698	7,644	17,883	17,985	17,045	5,152	17,973	14,402	1,698	13,456	11,397
Windhoek, Namibia	10,093	12,663	11,469	5,909	11,155	15,874	3,845	12,522	5,083	8,066	8,582	11,013	11,632	12,824	12,775	11,700	8,779	11,805	4,314	6,619
Windsor, Canada	6,109	755	1,979	7,189	1,847	11,690	9,766	13,904	7,625	9,124	11,898	1,671	847	1,507	13,724	773	5,807	15,603	8,615	9,270
Winnipeg, Canada	5,825	1,739	3,240	8,555	2,508	10,479	10,514	13,332	8,607	10,246	11,294	2,608	2,105	2,291	13,115	2,070	6,001	14,263	9,522	9,404
Winston-Salem, North Carolina	6,626	588	1,252	6,597	2,157	12,085	9,696	13,792	7,431	8,403	12,466	1,813	860	1,141	13,639	747	6,128	16,118	8,460	9,552
Wroclaw, Poland	1,931	7,829	8,172	8,027	5,298	13,730	4,327	17,897	4,392	12,944	5,536	5,645	6,586	8,556	17,783	6,698	1,318	13,332	4,380	2,203
Wuhan, China	7,151	12,298	13,722	15,812	11,048	6,542	10,200	10,003	11,871	19,053	3,582	11,564	12,012	12,829	9,889	12,066	8,736	5,691	11,285	7,371
Wyndham, Australia	12,435	15,877	17,173	17,032	16,051	4,575	12,814	5,189	15,265	13,752	7,333	16,519	16,507	15,817	5,176	16,494	13,882	605	14,223	11,411
Xi'an, China	6,570	12,040	13,403	15,166	10,604	7,158	9,612	10,643	11,230	19,423	3,066	11,121	11,635	12,623	10,533	11,698	8,118	6,280	10,663	6,738
Xining, China	6,050	11,899	13,175	14,475	10,254	7,854	8,929	11,285	10,534	19,092	2,463	10,768	11,359	12,532	11,184	11,431	7,529	6,841	9,966	6,040
Yakutsk, USSR	4,566	8,642	10,056	13,644	7,523	7,611	10,055	12,100	10,507	17,172	5,304	8,027	8,375	9,209	11,892	8,422	6,353	8,808	10,478	6,933
Yanji, China	6,456	10,512	11,994	15,631	9,633	6,089	11,006	10,304	12,080	18,481	4,904	10,131	10,414	10,986	10,128	10,451	8,216	6,686	11,790	7,899
Yaounde, Cameroon	7,181	10,506	9,723	5,306	8,498	17,277	991	15,481	2,491	9,385	7,437	8,475	9,265	10,914	15,730	9,357	5,792	13,526	1,487	4,132
Yap Island (Colonia)	10,215	13,114	14,592	19,188	13,113	3,380	13,298	6,677	15,242	15,839	6,679	13,560	13,549	13,264	6,539	13,546	11,936	3,022	14,544	10,724
Yaraka, Australia	14,020	15,046	15,865	16,611	16,426	3,648	14,501	3,252	16,916	12,190	9,286	16,699	16,158	14,694	3,221	16,088	15,647	1,384	15,855	13,377
Yarmouth, Canada	5,311	1,952	2,317	6,311	779	12,920	8,382	15,241	6,261	9,171	11,160	337	624	2,616	15,074	737	4,663	16,554	7,238	8,074
Yellowknife, Canada	4,985	3,487	4,975	10,017	3,407	9,479	10,663	13,170	9,231	11,977	9,860	3,735	3,594	4,015	12,922	3,596	5,737	12,848	9,975	8,806
Yerevan, USSR	3,539	10,198	10,612	9,556	7,694	12,749	4,243	15,758	5,606	14,372	3,247	8,066	8,996	10,939	15,752	9,106	3,751	11,149	5,072	1,128
Yinchuan, China	6,049	11,633	12,960	14,717	10,114	7,533	9,293	11,140	10,804	19,533	2,902	10,630	11,171	12,242	11,023	11,237	7,604	6,800	10,285	6,343
Yogyakarta, Indonesia	10,927	16,419	17,928	15,927	15,249	6,326	10,773	7,188	13,202	14,826	5,376	15,764	16,279	16,766	7,206	16,334	12,108	2,715	12,185	9,342
York, United Kingdom	1,893	6,593	6,902	7,333	4,055	13,996	4,845	18,550	4,163	12,108	6,751	4,383	5,330	7,310	18,325	5,442	133	14,403	4,482	3,387
Yumen, China	5,570	11,577	12,800	13,998	9,832	8,287	8,538	11,787	10,068	18,799	2,257	10,344	10,970	12,236	11,684	11,046	7,030	7,338	9,531	5,592
Yutian, China	5,206	11,833	12,807	12,782	9,719	9,624	7,140	12,702	8,831	17,368	1,009	10,201	10,972	12,557	12,644	11,066	6,351	8,093	8,204	4,314
Yuzhno-Sakhalinsk, USSR	6,435	9,563	11,073	15,438	8,985	5,765	11,663	10,231	12,354	17,374	5,935	9,458	9,615	9,982	10,025	9,638	8,221	7,188	12,249	8,512
Zagreb, Yugoslavia	2,522	8,096	8,301	7,635	5,558	14,245	3,735	18,125	3,891	12,574	5,609	5,860	6,814	8,803	18,076	6,926	1,609	13,495	3,810	1,880
Zahedan, Iran	5,159	11,991	12,505	10,917	9,534	11,598	5,103	13,900	7,032	15,267	1,593	9,931	10,843	12,742	13,920	10,952	5,641	9,351	6,273	2,655
Zamboanga, Philippines	9,887	14,373	15,896	17,521	13,667	5,050	11,690	7,458	13,875	16,314	5,286	14,173	14,455	14,685	7,386	14,485	11,413	2,963	13,024	9,458
Zanzibar, Tanzania	8,449	13,611	12,976	8,230	11,317	14,185	3,350	12,988	5,699	11,054	5,605	11,419	12,303	14,107	13,191	12,406	7,756	10,260	4,639	4,616
Zaragoza, Spain	3,175	7,156	7,118	6,304	4,686	15,292	3,620	19,535	2,839	11,218	7,023	4,882	5,829	7,807	19,504	5,940	1,487	14,921	3,130	3,055
Zashiversk, USSR	4,349	7,794	9,224	13,157	6,797	7,777	10,239	12,332	10,364	16,314	6,057	7,291	7,580	8,351	12,106	7,621	6,103	9,440	10,477	7,203
Zhengzhou, China	6,707	11,874	13,282	15,491	10,584	6,770	10,025	10,391	11,579	19,516	3,505	11,100	11,557	12,424	10,268	11,613	8,315	6,138	11,048	7,110
Zurich, Switzerland	2,401	7,508	7,691	7,274	4,973	14,419	3,958	18,641	3,700	12,189	6,179	5,262	6,217	8,208	18,537	6,329	1,096	14,036	3,798	2,478

Distances in Kilometers	Niue (Alofi)	Norfolk, Virginia	Norfolk Island, Australia	Noril'sk, USSR	Norman Wells, Canada	Normanton, Australia	North Pole	Nottingham, United Kingdom	Norway House, Canada	Norwich, United Kingdom	Nouakchott, Mauritania	Noumea, New Caledonia	Novosibirsk, USSR	Nuku'alofa, Tonga	Nukunono Island, Tokelau Isls.	Nuremberg, West Germany	Nyala, Sudan	Oaxaca, Mexico	Ocean Falls, Canada	Odense, Denmark
Norfolk, Virginia	11,570	0	14,067	8,160	4,542	15,796	5,923	5,902	2,523	6,073	6,207	13,846	9,633	12,160	11,119	6,838	10,189	2,975	4,320	6,540
Norfolk Island, Australia	2,504	14,067	0	12,607	11,842	3,012	13,213	17,202	12,828	17,165	18,733	765	12,298	1,909	3,041	17,017	15,768	11,422	10,965	16,578
Noril'sk, USSR	12,438	8,160	12,607	0	4,823	10,507	2,308	4,624	6,317	4,566	8,674	11,855	1,615	12,447	11,349	4,497	7,723	10,416	6,197	3,976
Norman Wells, Canada	10,030	4,542	11,842	4,823	0	11,870	2,758	6,101	2,034	6,202	9,121	11,213	6,424	10,420	9,055	6,779	11,111	5,808	1,441	6,139
Normanton, Australia	5,165	15,796	3,012	10,507	11,870	0	11,955	14,911	13,599	14,795	17,602	2,700	9,738	4,594	5,164	14,339	13,170	13,916	11,627	14,126
North Pole	12,104	5,923	13,213	2,308	2,758	11,955	0	4,133	4,018	4,170	8,002	12,464	3,901	12,338	11,018	4,524	8,671	8,116	4,199	3,862
Nottingham, United Kingdom	16,115	5,902	17,202	4,624	6,101	14,911	4,133	0	5,891	170	4,077	16,439	5,175	16,435	15,080	940	5,097	8,877	7,318	800
Norway House, Canada	10,583	2,523	12,828	6,317	2,034	13,599	4,018	5,891	0	6,037	7,873	12,348	7,919	11,092	9,807	6,762	10,928	4,099	1,990	6,231
Norwich, United Kingdom	16,198	6,073	17,165	4,566	6,202	14,795	4,170	170	6,037	0	4,116	16,406	5,066	16,496	15,149	771	4,970	9,047	7,437	670
Nouakchott, Mauritania	17,287	6,207	18,733	8,674	9,121	17,602	8,002	4,077	7,873	4,116	0	19,486	8,927	17,833	17,254	4,237	4,432	8,496	9,825	4,701
Noumea, New Caledonia	2,487	13,846	765	11,855	11,213	2,700	12,464	16,439	12,348	16,406	19,486	0	11,608	1,902	2,728	16,299	15,803	11,401	10,428	15,830
Novosibirsk, USSR	12,811	9,633	12,298	1,615	6,424	9,738	3,901	5,175	7,919	5,066	8,927	11,608	0	12,659	11,808	4,726	6,906	12,018	7,772	4,401
Nuku'alofa, Tonga	600	12,160	1,909	12,447	10,420	4,594	12,338	16,435	11,092	16,496	17,833	1,902	12,659	0	1,367	16,814	17,666	9,546	9,351	16,172
Nukunono Island, Tokelau Isls.	1,107	11,119	3,041	11,349	9,055	5,164	11,018	15,080	9,807	15,149	17,254	2,728	11,808	1,367	0	15,534	18,173	8,765	8,012	14,876
Nuremberg, West Germany	16,627	6,838	17,017	4,497	6,779	14,339	4,524	940	6,762	771	4,237	16,299	4,726	16,814	15,534	0	4,337	9,813	8,072	664
Nyala, Sudan	18,266	10,189	15,768	7,723	11,111	13,170	8,671	5,097	10,928	4,970	4,432	15,803	6,906	17,666	18,173	4,337	0	12,847	12,403	4,972
Oaxaca, Mexico	8,947	2,975	11,422	10,416	5,808	13,916	8,116	8,877	4,099	9,047	8,496	11,401	12,018	9,546	8,765	9,813	12,847	0	4,763	9,499
Ocean Falls, Canada	8,899	4,320	10,965	6,197	1,441	11,627	4,199	7,318	1,990	7,437	9,825	10,428	7,772	9,351	8,012	8,072	12,403	4,763	0	7,454
Odense, Denmark	15,966	6,540	16,578	3,976	6,139	14,126	3,862	800	6,231	670	4,701	15,830	4,401	16,172	14,876	664	4,972	9,499	7,454	0
Odessa, USSR	16,428	8,264	15,849	4,010	7,463	12,765	4,856	2,389	7,863	2,220	5,295	15,231	3,710	16,352	15,352	1,500	3,855	11,229	8,863	1,732
Ogbomosho, Nigeria	18,653	8,635	17,139	8,921	10,935	15,243	9,105	4,996	10,064	4,942	2,451	17,556	8,547	18,565	19,597	4,624	2,300	10,909	11,909	5,270
Okha, USSR	9,221	9,302	9,465	3,250	4,812	7,894	4,063	7,738	6,839	7,708	11,812	8,702	3,789	9,201	8,152	7,728	10,691	10,348	5,594	7,170
Okinawa (Naha)	8,398	12,590	7,476	5,440	8,073	5,067	7,100	9,939	10,107	9,847	13,730	6,802	4,825	8,090	7,615	9,551	10,672	13,240	8,669	9,195
Oklahoma City, Oklahoma	9,722	1,911	12,198	8,371	3,840	13,958	6,073	7,339	2,055	7,503	8,118	11,941	9,974	10,302	9,217	8,270	12,000	2,045	3,026	7,845
Old Crow, Canada	9,913	5,164	11,553	4,380	632	11,351	2,503	6,202	2,664	6,287	9,478	10,888	5,954	10,257	8,891	6,800	11,089	6,392	1,818	6,144
Olympia, Washington	8,699	3,963	10,904	6,850	2,045	11,878	4,789	7,627	1,924	7,758	9,776	10,429	8,436	9,190	7,890	8,432	12,721	4,103	684	7,841
Omaha, Nebraska	10,112	1,772	12,546	7,733	3,302	14,024	5,430	6,775	1,419	6,936	7,888	12,221	9,331	10,677	9,523	7,698	11,564	2,687	2,683	7,248
Omsk, USSR	13,415	9,426	12,877	1,761	6,554	10,253	3,905	4,660	7,896	4,542	8,338	12,197	608	13,267	12,405	4,159	6,351	11,967	7,947	3,873
Oodnadatta, Australia	5,624	16,877	3,181	11,401	13,107	1,237	13,050	15,478	14,815	15,334	16,924	3,176	10,429	5,025	5,872	14,740	12,646	14,569	12,833	14,679
Oradea, Romania	16,713	7,673	16,469	4,298	7,259	13,628	4,789	1,771	7,455	1,601	4,714	15,818	4,225	16,743	15,610	847	3,892	10,646	8,615	1,226
Oran, Algeria	17,883	6,606	18,718	6,294	7,889	15,760	6,052	1,919	7,319	1,888	2,467	18,069	6,461	18,308	16,941	1,800	3,667	9,455	8,986	2,346
Oranjestad, Aruba	11,487	2,767	13,785	10,766	7,243	16,646	8,619	7,493	5,209	7,653	5,822	13,968	12,102	12,066	11,515	8,321	10,254	2,914	6,741	8,267
Orebro, Sweden	15,515	6,653	16,061	3,457	5,830	13,683	3,430	1,233	6,104	1,138	5,218	15,311	3,945	15,688	14,415	1,127	5,303	9,576	7,187	521
Orel, USSR	15,628	8,122	15,300	3,198	6,815	12,560	4,138	2,476	7,415	2,325	5,907	14,628	3,024	15,587	14,546	1,780	4,642	11,034	8,239	1,692
Orsk, USSR	14,486	9,305	13,786	2,546	7,079	11,012	4,329	3,980	8,141	3,838	7,386	13,142	1,676	14,318	13,482	3,328	5,302	12,072	8,513	3,180
Osaka, Japan	8,282	11,434	7,833	4,814	6,900	5,822	6,163	9,433	8,933	9,367	13,436	7,100	4,589	8,081	7,362	9,200	11,075	12,067	7,468	8,750
Oslo, Norway	15,463	6,391	16,169	3,568	5,677	13,881	3,359	1,064	5,881	998	5,112	15,412	4,145	15,672	14,373	1,165	5,439	9,318	7,015	504
Osorno, Chile	9,209	8,578	10,063	16,619	12,619	12,655	14,495	12,451	10,740	12,559	8,780	10,724	17,626	9,472	10,083	12,923	11,549	6,829	11,560	13,225
Ostrava, Czechoslovakia	16,509	7,284	16,571	4,181	6,893	13,830	4,482	1,393	7,048	1,223	4,657	15,879	4,274	16,608	15,403	522	4,233	10,256	8,235	818
Ottawa, Canada	11,815	953	14,247	7,209	3,767	15,431	4,971	5,248	1,848	5,415	6,247	13,895	8,692	12,381	11,216	6,187	9,875	3,704	3,804	5,817
Ouagadougou, Bourkina Fasso	18,584	7,848	17,868	8,711	10,283	15,977	8,636	4,503	9,314	4,473	1,674	18,340	8,537	18,834	18,925	4,272	2,872	10,160	11,191	4,885
Oujda, Morocco	17,913	6,551	18,877	6,446	7,954	15,905	6,166	2,034	7,333	2,012	2,304	18,232	6,623	18,371	17,009	1,956	3,688	9,379	9,028	2,491
Oxford, United Kingdom	16,241	5,931	17,329	4,742	6,221	14,995	4,269	136	5,979	200	3,951	16,567	5,264	16,567	15,211	909	4,992	8,906	7,429	870
Pago Pago, American Samoa	532	11,338	2,741	11,919	9,551	5,162	11,578	15,614	10,196	15,690	17,304	2,570	12,340	897	576	16,099	18,329	8,834	8,458	15,440
Pakxe, Laos	9,975	14,249	8,275	6,149	10,071	5,307	8,330	9,774	12,027	9,633	12,657	7,801	4,848	9,514	9,467	9,081	8,712	15,683	10,947	8,974
Palembang, Indonesia	9,422	16,246	7,261	8,117	11,988	4,288	10,324	11,329	13,982	11,172	13,360	6,986	6,730	8,868	9,237	10,520	8,985	17,207	12,720	10,550
Palermo, Italy	17,864	7,583	17,469	5,507	8,035	14,486	5,784	1,995	7,873	1,864	3,609	16,909	5,400	17,954	16,759	1,272	3,106	10,517	9,298	1,934
Palma, Majorca	17,619	6,685	18,234	5,781	7,589	15,347	5,623	1,518	7,176	1,456	2,979	17,557	5,950	17,951	16,598	1,285	3,754	9,596	8,751	1,852
Palmerston North, New Zealand	2,740	13,924	1,437	14,038	12,720	4,156	14,469	18,581	13,299	18,574	17,304	2,184	13,708	2,302	3,666	18,434	15,768	11,027	11,636	18,013
Panama, Panama	10,378	3,106	12,682	11,265	7,230	15,540	9,011	8,438	5,254	8,603	6,927	12,857	12,726	10,956	10,433	9,303	11,356	2,066	6,475	9,188
Paramaribo, Suriname	12,829	4,052	14,821	11,208	8,572	17,826	9,358	7,148	6,573	7,282	4,469	15,205	12,235	13,364	13,052	7,813	8,805	4,689	8,312	7,947
Paris, France	16,622	6,270	17,489	4,885	6,617	14,947	4,589	518	6,386	425	3,790	16,740	5,270	16,920	15,574	641	4,583	9,242	7,835	911
Patna, India	12,364	12,824	10,712	4,866	9,563	7,722	7,170	7,537	11,183	7,382	10,216	10,246	3,273	11,932	11,751	6,760	6,471	15,282	10,801	6,752
Patrai, Greece	17,598	8,195	16,749	5,164	8,208	13,756	5,769	2,403	8,269	2,246	4,278	16,226	4,859	17,517	16,513	1,507	2,920	11,153	9,540	2,088
Peking, China	10,032	11,405	9,312	3,673	7,133	6,872	5,579	8,097	9,096	8,003	11,911	8,624	2,987	9,791	9,139	7,709	9,290	12,828	8,065	7,349
Penrhyn Island (Omoka)	1,692	9,884	4,183	11,858	8,633	6,636	10,996	14,706	8,960	14,821	15,821	4,064	12,649	2,276	1,521	15,409	19,553	7,339	7,389	14,759
Peoria, Illinois	10,586	1,231	13,042	7,802	3,606	14,567	5,496	6,444	1,601	6,609	7,357	12,739	9,373	11,158	10,031	7,377	11,117	2,709	3,151	6,967
Perm', USSR	14,291	8,604	13,961	1,981	6,328	11,356	3,572	3,561	7,371	3,440	7,270	13,266	1,663	14,212	13,231	3,064	5,744	11,324	7,766	2,770
Perth, Australia	7,466	18,784	4,966	11,455	14,446	2,990	13,536	14,542	16,393	14,375	14,971	5,087	10,137	6,867	7,807	13,649	10,802	16,359	14,506	13,811
Peshawar, Pakistan	13,772	11,483	12,295	4,062	8,881	9,320	6,237	5,962	10,202	5,804	8,685	11,795	2,497	13,396	13,025	5,161	5,306	14,219	10,256	5,189
Petropavlovsk-Kamchatskiy,USSR	8,536	8,731	9,134	3,917	4,189	8,012	4,124	8,109	6,215	8,106	12,109	8,374	4,720	8,594	7,439	8,246	11,567	9,453	4,755	7,639
Petrozavodsk, USSR	14,893	7,436	15,052	2,522	5,820	12,601	3,147	2,313	6,498	2,209	6,216	14,319	2,863	14,952	13,788	1,990	5,576	10,265	7,246	1,553
Pevek, USSR	9,964	7,037	10,950	2,969	2,606	9,959	2,265	6,380	4,602	6,406	10,254	10,204	4,346	10,140	8,860	6,681	10,550	8,355	3,643	6,033
Philadelphia, Pennsylvania	11,740	358	14,223	7,808	4,296	15,753	5,579	5,599	2,307	5,769	6,131	13,954	9,276	12,323	11,236	6,537	9,999	3,282	4,181	6,220
Phnom Penh, Kampuchea	9,931	14,646	8,120	6,529	10,474	5,123	8,724	10,041	12,433	9,896	12,754	7,684	5,194	9,447	9,487	9,317	8,686	16,058	11,336	9,244
Phoenix, Arizona	8,449	3,264	10,895	8,488	3,678	12,615	6,298	8,347	2,542	8,502	9,470	10,603	10,096	9,017	7,887	9,249	13,223	2,380	2,444	8,749
Pierre, South Dakota	9,943	2,112	12,328	7,375	2,839	13,626	5,087	6,768	1,084	6,924	8,187	11,954	8,984	10,492	9,289	7,673	11,680	3,048	2,194	7,183
Pinang, Malaysia	10,185	15,313	8,162	7,153	11,279	5,154	9,403	10,296	13,208	10,140	12,573	7,818	5,719	9,660	9,870	9,501	8,313	16,903	12,175	9,512
Pitcairn Island (Adamstown)	4,152	8,874	6,094	14,486	10,020	9,087	12,775	14,775	9,291	14,945	13,230	6,422	15,729	4,622	4,758	15,712	17,026	5,900	8,579	15,362
Pittsburgh, Pennsylvania	11,351	513	13,825	7,792	4,035	15,352	5,525	5,872	2,011	6,041	6,547	13,543	9,302	11,931	10,828	6,812	10,377	3,051	3,818	6,460
Plymouth, Montserrat	12,422	2,628	14,744	10,179	7,160	17,556	8,156	6,612	5,151	6,767	4,906	14,908	11,404	13,007	12,395	7,412	9,335	3,672	6,892	7,398
Plymouth, United Kingdom	16,305	5,775	17,541	4,974	6,274	15,245	4,419	351	5,935	451	3,735	16,777	5,515	16,665	15,301	1,095	5,006	8,747	7,446	1,120
Ponape Island	4,519	12,565	4,112	8,516	8,610	3,310	9,236	13,091	10,289	13,056	17,167	3,350	8,447	4,248	3,761	13,000	14,461	11,375	8,321	12,490
Ponce, Puerto Rico	12,006	2,292	14,375	10,111	6,832	17,101	8,010	6,788	4,806	6,948	5,346	14,492	11,414	12,595	11,938	7,625	9,764	3,194	6,484	7,559
Ponta Delgada, Azores	15,988	4,433	18,430	6,979	6,749	17,438	5,826	2,537	5,618	2,663	2,373	17,941	7,702	16,565	15,388	3,200	5,756	7,221	7,517	3,331
Pontianak, Indonesia	9,043	15,888	6,995	7,862	11,510	3,987	10,005	11,369	13,527	11,219	13,727	6,655	6,562	8,508	8,784	10,609	9,415	16,607	12,177	10,576
Port Augusta, Australia	5,401	16,885	2,905	11,989	13,482	1,677	13,598	16,038	15,073	15,890	16,948	3,043	11,018	4,802	5,771	15,270	12,866	14,323	13,083	15,241
Port Blair, India	11,192	14,521	9,232	6,421	10,868	6,221	8,719	9,248	12,669	9,090	11,541	8,867	4,895	10,684	10,798	8,437	7,375	16,672	11,938	8,473
Port Elizabeth, South Africa	13,917	13,128	11,992	12,519	16,065	11,117	13,764	9,974	15,124	9,880	7,252	12,536	11,273	13,524	14,886	9,351	5,093	14,014	17,062	10,008
Port Hedland, Australia	7,437	17,682	5,055	10,235	13,177	2,387	12,249	13,769	15,170	13,612	15,259	4,953	9,008	6,845	7,539	12,955	10,853	16,301	13,380	12,988
Port Louis, Mauritius	13,275	15,193	10,788	10,221	14,982	8,708	12,234	9,868	15,710	9,714	9,066	10,993	8,675	12,691	13,718	8,969	5,046	17,294	16,405	9,481
Port Moresby, Papua New Guinea	4,735	14,708	3,063	9,836	10,769	1,120	11,049	14,412	12,479	14,325	17,974	2,497	9,291	4,227	4,492	14,010	13,730	13,087	10,508	13,673
Port Said, Egypt	17,414	9,432	15,777	5,463	9,150	12,770	6,543	3,613	9,418	3,450	5,054	15,395	4,744	17,069	16,521	2,688	2,260	12,388	10,539	3,187
Port Sudan, Sudan	17,183	10,660	14,957	6,496	10,495	12,067	7,834	4,954	10,795	4,796	5,584	14,767	5,482	16,649	16,693	4,045	1,565	13,558	11,900	4,567
Port-au-Prince, Haiti	11,438	2,066	13,840	10,136	6,534	16,501	7,953	7,126	4,500	7,291	5,935	13,920	11,524	12,031	11,340	7,995	10,341	2,589	6,062	7,875
Port-of-Spain, Trin. & Tobago	12,319	3,259	14,510	10,824	7,801	17,475	8,825	7,103	5,780	7,251	4,971	14,775	12,007	12,884	12,417	7,859	9,388	3,865	7,465	7,869
Port-Vila, Vanuatu	2,303	13,417	1,252	11,457	10,675	2,887	11,962	15,990	11,833	15,971	19,581	539	11,317	1,771	2,338	15,941	16,057	11,089	9,903	15,428
Portland, Maine	12,211	912	14,667	7,349	4,178	15,900	5,168	5,023	2,307	5,193	5,787	14,342	8,779	12,785	11,648	5,962	9,504	3,860	4,274	5,641
Portland, Oregon	8,596	3,947	10,827	7,019	2,214	11,875	4,957	7,756	2,003	7,889	9,827	10,366	8,603	9,094	7,804	8,569	12,847	3,970	843	7,982
Porto, Portugal	16,983	5,732	18,626	6,046	7,063	16,128	5,447	1,429	6,404	1,480	2,650	17,861	6,484	17,456	16,105	1,792	4,587	8,628	8,105	2,107
Porto Alegre, Brazil	11,505	7,857	12,265	14,937	12,370	14,563	13,331	10,395	10,336	10,481	6,533	12,961	15,460	11,775	12,344	10,744	9,373	7,142	11,752	11,127
Porto Alexandre, Angola	16,147	10,892	14,421	11,108	13,713	13,336	11,753	7,723	12,704	7,652	4,836	14,971	10,275	15,846	17,207	7,230	3,398	12,453	14,627	7,893
Porto Novo, Benin	18,407	8,596	17,079	9,156	11,048	15,358	9,287	5,166	10,107	5,118	2,390	17,557	8,802	18,367	19,356	4,829	2,522	10,793	11,981	5,469
Porto Velho, Brazil	11,358	5,213	13,067	12,984	9,679	16,008	10,973	9,030	7,649	9,163	6,049	13,552	14,102	11,830	11,811	9,677	10,088	4,604	9,063	9,829
Portsmouth, United Kingdom	16,348	5,972	17,425	4,829	6,326	15,047	4,378	245	6,063	265	3,857	16,663	5,325	16,677	15,320	882	4,899	8,946	7,528	924
Poznan, Poland	16,251	7,069	16,488	3,994	6,591	13,842	4,194	1,224	6,763	1,062	4,765	15,772	4,199	16,380	15,146	529	4,533	10,034	7,934	545
Prague, Czechoslovakia	16,536	7,029	16,783	4,307	6,788	14,086	4,454	1,129	6,860	958	4,463	16,075	4,486	16,683	15,434	254	4,324	10,002	8,107	653
Praia, Cape Verde Islands	16,433	5,734	18,057	9,281	9,117	18,361	8,354	4,657	7,655	4,723	881	18,694	9,673	16,962	16,539	4,950	5,240	7,791	9,641	5,348
Pretoria, South Africa	14,684	12,909	12,584	11,576	15,269	11,323	12,853	9,172	14,617	9,067	6,807	13,055	10,354	14,242	15,577	8,500	4,197	14,276	16,429	9,149
Prince Albert, Canada	10,079	2,914	12,301	6,366	1,788	13,102	4,105	6,331	532	6,472	8,405	11,816	7,980	10,580	9,287	7,180	11,398	4,088	1,476	6,626

Distances in Kilometers	Niue (Alofi)	Norfolk, Virginia	Norfolk Island, Australia	Noril'sk, USSR	Norman Wells, Canada	Normanton, Australia	North Pole	Nottingham, United Kingdom	Norway House, Canada	Norwich, United Kingdom	Nouakchott, Mauritania	Noumea, New Caledonia	Novosibirsk, USSR	Nuku'alofa, Tonga	Nukunono Island, Tokelau Isls.	Nuremberg, West Germany	Nyala, Sudan	Oaxaca, Mexico	Ocean Falls, Canada	Odense, Denmark
Prince Edward Island	12,222	14,601	10,245	13,494	17,731	9,566	15,165	11,641	16,815	11,535	8,969	10,799	12,028	11,802	13,157	10,952	6,623	14,728	18,794	11,595
Prince George, Canada	9,250	4,008	11,336	6,105	1,287	11,978	4,025	6,990	1,628	7,113	9,452	10,801	7,700	9,709	8,375	7,762	12,083	4,667	373	7,153
Prince Rupert, Canada	8,958	4,505	10,961	5,940	1,237	11,495	3,980	7,223	2,104	7,337	9,872	10,400	7,508	9,393	8,043	7,952	12,289	5,041	280	7,325
Providence, Rhode Island	12,089	693	14,561	7,564	4,293	15,933	5,372	5,223	2,372	5,393	5,843	14,265	9,000	12,668	11,557	6,161	9,641	3,655	4,313	5,850
Provo, Utah	8,909	3,086	11,290	7,746	2,952	12,711	5,546	7,719	1,847	7,869	9,201	10,926	9,358	9,454	8,252	8,602	12,695	2,946	1,819	8,078
Puerto Aisen, Chile	9,071	9,117	9,744	17,131	13,130	12,236	15,032	12,846	11,269	12,946	9,065	10,431	17,986	9,289	9,998	13,261	11,545	7,329	12,037	13,605
Puerto Deseado, Argentina	9,466	9,427	9,950	17,214	13,582	12,279	15,294	12,728	11,670	12,814	8,827	10,662	17,722	9,644	10,430	13,058	11,050	7,806	12,545	13,458
Puerto Princesa, Philippines	8,447	14,617	6,804	6,973	10,122	3,902	8,925	11,049	12,155	10,922	14,174	6,295	5,928	7,987	7,966	10,438	10,208	15,127	10,702	10,253
Punta Arenas, Chile	8,919	9,985	9,279	17,904	13,970	11,581	15,894	13,418	12,134	13,501	9,487	10,000	18,301	9,060	9,919	13,723	11,457	8,163	12,829	14,140
Pusan, South Korea	8,795	11,621	8,190	4,552	7,129	5,977	6,115	9,130	9,160	9,052	13,060	7,477	4,148	8,565	7,902	8,828	10,505	12,489	7,813	8,416
Pyongyang, North Korea	9,273	11,307	8,714	4,041	6,875	6,475	5,681	8,608	8,890	8,528	12,537	8,000	3,633	9,060	8,355	8,304	10,096	12,395	7,661	7,892
Qamdo, China	11,347	12,445	10,021	4,285	8,659	7,154	6,553	7,829	10,460	7,695	11,045	9,456	2,883	10,980	10,620	7,187	7,658	14,467	9,777	7,030
Qandahar, Afghanistan	14,314	11,465	12,707	4,430	9,211	9,705	6,507	5,765	10,394	5,600	8,215	12,249	2,936	13,912	13,603	4,912	4,708	14,310	10,615	5,022
Qiqian, China	10,325	10,001	10,101	2,551	5,764	7,985	4,216	7,162	7,702	7,094	11,171	9,363	2,497	10,207	9,312	6,942	9,359	11,523	6,779	6,478
Qom, Iran	15,652	10,393	14,131	4,481	8,924	11,126	6,168	4,532	9,736	4,362	6,798	13,672	3,345	15,293	14,840	3,628	3,630	13,343	10,365	3,854
Quebec, Canada	12,180	1,183	14,599	7,012	3,849	15,632	4,816	4,878	2,037	5,046	5,936	14,224	8,459	12,742	11,562	5,817	9,502	4,048	4,022	5,459
Quetta, Pakistan	14,193	11,658	12,541	4,556	9,352	9,535	6,661	5,958	10,565	5,793	8,364	12,095	3,036	13,778	13,509	5,103	4,778	14,496	10,749	5,216
Quito, Ecuador	10,159	4,110	12,280	12,268	8,226	15,267	10,027	9,181	6,267	9,339	7,132	12,576	13,698	10,704	10,389	9,997	11,480	2,764	7,402	9,957
Rabaul, Papua New Guinea	4,431	13,905	3,214	9,453	10,008	1,919	10,465	14,076	11,683	14,010	18,009	2,523	9,090	3,993	4,007	13,803	14,173	12,398	9,708	13,388
Raiatea (Uturoa)	1,974	9,849	4,360	12,907	9,328	7,138	11,851	15,227	9,342	15,367	15,314	4,450	13,760	2,548	2,370	16,051	19,363	7,069	7,990	15,444
Raleigh, North Carolina	11,337	243	13,836	8,299	4,544	15,634	6,042	6,138	2,512	6,308	6,416	13,626	9,791	11,927	10,898	7,074	10,426	2,739	4,238	6,769
Rangiroa (Avatoru)	2,407	9,414	4,807	12,852	9,067	7,572	11,652	14,870	8,979	15,015	14,886	4,889	13,813	2,987	2,708	15,723	19,168	6,623	7,700	15,138
Rangoon, Burma	11,010	14,016	9,226	5,865	10,215	6,226	8,146	9,015	12,051	8,865	11,653	8,790	4,394	10,538	10,513	8,258	7,667	16,008	11,263	8,224
Raoul Is., Kermadec Islands	1,394	12,860	1,376	13,171	11,361	4,358	13,239	17,359	11,977	17,409	17,811	1,749	13,187	941	2,308	17,640	16,989	10,104	10,275	17,028
Rarotonga (Avarua)	1,088	10,845	3,358	13,058	9,990	6,189	12,346	16,036	10,208	16,159	16,231	3,490	13,648	1,602	1,859	16,768	18,883	8,076	8,723	16,121
Rawson, Argentina	9,720	8,948	10,346	16,728	13,162	12,747	14,799	12,292	11,222	12,384	8,448	11,044	17,375	9,936	10,645	12,663	10,918	7,422	12,179	13,035
Recife, Brazil	14,256	6,581	15,233	12,088	10,904	17,127	10,894	7,477	9,026	7,550	3,564	15,932	12,489	14,617	14,898	7,776	6,979	7,346	10,901	8,181
Regina, Canada	9,989	2,714	12,266	6,678	2,091	13,221	4,411	6,497	607	6,642	8,385	11,812	8,292	10,505	9,235	7,364	11,534	3,772	1,612	6,826
Reykjavik, Iceland	14,449	4,679	16,038	4,229	4,420	14,685	2,887	1,721	4,215	1,850	5,135	15,310	5,320	14,832	13,465	2,549	6,817	7,575	5,600	2,030
Rhodes, Greece	17,395	8,778	16,193	5,094	8,522	13,186	5,970	2,931	8,735	2,767	4,770	15,716	4,584	17,188	16,376	2,002	2,722	11,743	9,895	2,505
Richmond, Virginia	11,488	129	13,981	8,094	4,424	15,672	5,846	5,925	2,402	6,095	6,313	13,747	9,578	12,075	11,021	6,863	10,266	2,953	4,191	6,551
Riga, USSR	15,637	7,236	15,823	3,314	6,228	13,266	3,690	1,668	6,633	1,535	5,437	15,099	3,562	15,727	14,530	1,202	4,982	10,158	7,618	868
Ringkobing, Denmark	15,887	6,388	16,601	3,994	6,020	14,211	3,786	701	6,084	593	4,680	15,847	4,477	16,114	14,804	762	5,093	9,346	7,325	154
Rio Branco, Brazil	10,910	5,258	12,650	13,189	9,645	15,614	11,105	9,377	7,631	9,514	6,488	13,119	14,386	11,385	11,364	10,052	10,534	4,365	8,940	10,177
Rio Cuarto, Argentina	10,243	7,846	11,198	15,628	12,158	13,772	13,671	11,324	10,176	11,429	7,655	11,853	16,494	10,542	11,057	11,785	10,666	6,534	11,287	12,093
Rio de Janeiro, Brazil	12,602	7,468	13,364	13,930	12,003	15,493	12,537	9,336	9,991	9,413	5,421	14,071	14,347	12,888	13,403	9,644	8,367	7,308	11,628	10,049
Rio Gallegos, Argentina	9,084	9,827	9,478	17,704	13,868	11,785	15,726	13,215	12,006	13,299	9,290	10,197	18,134	9,236	10,075	13,526	11,332	8,064	12,757	13,939
Rio Grande, Brazil	11,317	8,031	12,038	15,172	12,529	14,330	13,549	10,628	10,497	10,713	6,755	12,738	15,682	11,576	12,174	10,971	9,519	7,222	11,870	11,358
Riyadh, Saudi Arabia	16,205	10,962	14,227	5,662	10,021	11,243	7,278	5,073	10,655	4,904	6,487	13,918	4,490	15,730	15,597	4,133	2,689	13,934	11,459	4,519
Road Town, Brit. Virgin Isls.	12,223	2,337	14,588	10,031	6,877	17,315	7,962	6,618	4,860	6,777	5,130	14,709	11,304	12,812	12,152	7,445	9,547	3,404	6,581	7,394
Roanoke, Virginia	11,267	328	13,759	8,142	4,341	15,473	5,876	6,106	2,309	6,276	6,533	13,525	9,647	11,854	10,799	7,045	10,484	2,781	4,041	6,719
Robinson Crusoe Island, Chile	8,959	7,808	10,141	15,951	11,722	12,929	13,726	12,166	9,878	12,293	8,790	10,741	17,241	9,295	9,732	12,756	12,014	5,921	10,641	12,962
Rochester, New York	11,616	710	14,070	7,474	3,886	15,415	5,222	5,523	1,906	5,692	6,368	13,750	8,968	12,188	11,052	6,463	10,093	3,412	3,808	6,103
Rockhampton, Australia	4,126	15,328	1,851	11,408	12,008	1,168	12,588	15,949	13,486	15,849	18,503	1,641	10,785	3,536	4,297	15,455	14,163	13,032	11,501	15,186
Rome, Italy	17,458	7,311	17,390	5,169	7,611	14,478	5,363	1,599	7,489	1,459	3,772	16,758	5,169	17,594	16,356	846	3,521	10,267	8,882	1,509
Rosario, Argentina	10,563	7,896	11,449	15,516	12,277	13,948	13,650	11,120	10,275	11,220	7,384	12,119	16,270	10,849	11,389	11,547	10,325	6,732	11,466	11,880
Roseau, Dominica	12,469	2,806	14,758	10,316	7,337	17,622	8,311	6,681	5,329	6,834	4,846	14,950	11,520	13,048	12,472	7,467	9,278	3,777	7,067	7,471
Rostock, East Germany	16,109	6,699	16,610	4,028	6,315	14,082	4,009	889	6,415	738	4,662	15,871	4,380	16,295	15,014	521	4,797	9,662	7,635	185
Rostov-na-Donu, USSR	15,888	8,732	15,161	3,592	7,474	12,284	4,770	2,950	8,096	2,786	5,974	14,549	3,092	15,750	14,849	2,123	4,140	11,668	8,904	2,215
Rotterdam, Netherlands	16,322	6,305	17,121	4,515	6,360	14,648	4,250	403	6,247	233	4,159	16,370	4,939	16,588	15,257	540	4,787	9,279	7,616	549
Rouyn, Canada	11,628	1,284	14,020	6,923	3,365	15,055	4,658	5,261	1,459	5,425	6,541	13,627	8,435	12,182	10,979	6,193	10,024	3,816	3,432	5,782
Sacramento, California	8,134	3,950	10,471	7,794	2,991	11,850	5,729	8,353	2,479	8,494	10,057	10,081	9,374	8,664	7,430	9,200	13,406	3,392	1,603	8,637
Saginaw, Michigan	11,126	979	13,568	7,482	3,580	14,931	5,192	5,894	1,551	6,060	6,882	13,238	9,022	11,694	10,544	6,829	10,567	3,164	3,361	6,431
Saint Denis, Reunion	13,395	15,054	10,919	10,337	15,067	8,894	12,312	9,826	15,694	9,674	8,900	11,145	8,806	12,817	13,872	8,937	4,944	17,076	16,500	9,464
Saint George's, Grenada	12,338	3,108	14,562	10,676	7,649	17,501	8,671	6,992	5,630	7,143	4,957	14,804	11,871	12,907	12,406	7,760	9,383	3,804	7,326	7,786
Saint John, Canada	12,563	1,268	15,003	7,119	4,228	16,051	4,988	4,647	2,466	4,817	5,505	14,648	8,512	13,132	11,972	5,585	9,141	4,233	4,454	5,272
Saint John's, Antigua	12,471	2,609	14,798	10,128	7,136	17,599	8,112	6,553	5,130	6,708	4,861	14,957	11,349	13,056	12,436	7,353	9,288	3,706	6,882	7,339
Saint John's, Canada	13,580	2,268	15,974	6,649	4,642	16,460	4,733	3,643	3,204	3,813	4,670	15,545	7,900	14,138	12,933	4,575	8,101	5,240	5,161	4,312
Saint Louis, Missouri	10,456	1,241	12,927	8,033	3,787	14,563	5,726	6,644	1,804	6,809	7,427	12,651	9,607	11,034	9,932	7,579	11,263	2,473	3,255	7,179
Saint Paul, Minnesota	10,491	1,673	12,895	7,330	3,054	14,181	5,023	6,319	1,062	6,479	7,609	12,530	8,918	11,046	9,858	7,238	11,157	3,112	2,649	6,781
Saint Peter Port, UK	16,447	5,913	17,600	5,008	6,418	15,215	4,524	403	6,091	445	3,680	16,838	5,498	16,797	15,435	986	4,852	8,883	7,596	1,097
Saipan (Susupe)	6,158	12,768	5,442	7,197	8,368	3,665	8,325	11,821	10,285	11,757	15,820	4,717	6,915	5,860	5,396	11,583	12,851	12,305	8,460	11,142
Salalah, Oman	15,380	12,104	13,202	6,269	10,881	10,271	8,123	6,211	11,699	6,042	7,390	12,969	4,884	14,844	14,984	5,272	3,193	15,076	12,320	5,639
Salem, Oregon	8,526	3,983	10,763	7,077	2,277	11,834	5,023	7,829	2,069	7,962	9,884	10,306	8,659	9,026	7,738	8,643	12,920	3,948	892	8,056
Salt Lake City, Utah	8,927	3,101	11,301	7,686	2,891	12,695	5,488	7,684	1,806	7,834	9,201	10,930	9,298	9,470	8,261	8,565	12,669	3,005	1,762	8,037
Salta, Argentina	10,523	6,917	11,771	14,753	11,263	14,507	12,745	10,607	9,266	10,725	7,161	12,373	15,769	10,891	11,222	11,150	10,599	5,741	10,458	11,394
Salto, Uruguay	10,868	7,791	11,748	15,276	12,225	14,211	13,477	10,840	10,207	10,936	7,081	12,421	15,977	11,157	11,689	11,251	10,038	6,773	11,475	11,594
Salvador, Brazil	13,629	6,788	14,562	12,730	11,229	16,614	11,440	8,131	9,286	8,208	4,238	15,258	13,162	13,969	14,324	8,447	7,528	7,209	11,084	8,844
Salzburg, Austria	16,801	7,047	17,017	4,578	6,998	14,263	4,708	1,159	6,995	993	4,216	16,321	4,720	16,956	15,701	233	4,115	10,021	8,298	865
Samsun, Turkey	16,510	8,977	15,474	4,302	8,100	12,507	5,432	3,083	8,581	2,912	5,572	14,932	3,702	16,310	15,505	2,163	3,427	11,947	9,516	2,458
San Antonio, Texas	9,348	2,224	11,848	9,040	4,443	13,873	6,746	7,914	2,728	8,080	8,345	11,663	10,646	9,939	8,938	8,851	12,412	1,382	3,495	8,453
San Cristobal, Venezuela	11,100	3,247	13,326	11,318	7,639	16,261	9,144	8,057	5,616	8,216	6,191	13,562	12,673	11,666	11,210	8,875	10,607	2,850	7,029	8,835
San Diego, California	8,017	3,741	10,445	8,503	3,681	12,134	6,380	8,684	2,815	8,835	9,944	10,137	10,096	8,578	7,427	9,570	13,627	2,688	2,341	9,046
San Francisco, California	8,013	4,049	10,353	7,867	3,074	11,755	5,819	8,472	2,599	8,613	10,168	9,967	9,442	8,544	7,312	9,318	13,527	3,403	1,671	8,753
San Jose, Costa Rica	9,940	3,083	12,288	11,190	6,964	15,089	8,904	8,659	5,037	8,826	7,379	12,425	12,704	10,524	9,956	9,548	11,811	1,577	6,121	9,386
San Juan, Argentina	9,953	7,613	11,038	15,549	11,843	13,716	13,493	11,397	9,887	11,512	7,852	11,667	16,568	10,278	10,730	11,913	11,024	6,163	10,924	12,180
San Juan, Puerto Rico	12,069	2,267	14,443	10,054	6,809	17,157	7,960	6,716	4,785	6,876	5,287	14,555	11,351	12,660	11,994	7,552	9,702	3,245	6,479	7,487
San Luis Potosi, Mexico	8,773	2,882	11,275	9,833	5,146	13,558	7,551	8,701	3,544	8,869	8,781	11,169	11,445	9,372	8,474	9,640	13,012	720	4,056	9,265
San Marino, San Marino	17,235	7,204	17,287	4,973	7,397	14,425	5,139	1,420	7,309	1,272	3,906	16,629	5,023	17,382	16,134	624	3,727	10,169	8,676	1,286
San Miguel de Tucuman, Argen.	10,452	7,142	11,630	14,969	11,480	14,329	12,970	10,784	9,486	10,899	7,280	12,246	15,954	10,803	11,180	11,309	10,621	5,928	10,657	11,568
San Salvador, El Salvador	9,558	2,869	11,979	10,792	6,394	14,642	8,487	8,674	4,533	8,843	7,810	12,040	12,352	10,152	9,479	9,591	12,222	888	5,478	9,359
Sanaa, Yemen	16,388	11,521	14,090	6,722	11,032	11,235	8,306	5,751	11,522	5,589	6,394	13,932	5,512	15,829	16,055	4,825	2,120	14,433	12,464	5,301
Santa Cruz, Bolivia	11,046	6,204	12,469	13,948	10,635	15,277	11,972	9,830	8,614	9,952	6,518	13,035	14,976	11,457	11,652	10,404	10,218	5,327	9,939	10,622
Santa Cruz, Tenerife	17,157	5,619	19,616	7,614	8,060	17,420	6,856	2,992	6,970	3,050	1,147	19,272	8,014	17,757	16,702	3,288	4,634	8,221	8,868	3,672
Santa Fe, New Mexico	9,056	2,658	11,508	8,303	3,572	13,193	6,052	7,812	2,129	7,970	8,860	11,217	9,918	9,626	8,501	8,726	12,629	2,257	2,524	8,250
Santa Rosa, Argentina	10,089	8,228	10,926	15,999	12,514	13,436	14,057	11,642	10,543	11,742	7,903	11,599	16,795	10,358	10,944	12,071	10,729	6,849	11,610	12,403
Santa Rosalia, Mexico	8,055	3,536	10,540	9,161	4,343	12,506	6,979	8,915	3,189	9,074	9,708	10,316	10,766	8,638	7,588	9,830	13,669	1,964	3,062	9,354
Santarem, Brazil	12,564	4,890	14,298	12,088	9,429	17,199	10,272	7,897	7,412	8,021	4,817	14,788	13,043	13,051	12,954	8,496	8,942	5,093	9,076	8,691
Santiago del Estero, Argentina	10,494	7,264	11,623	15,051	11,614	14,288	13,078	10,823	9,618	10,935	7,272	12,249	15,997	10,835	11,240	11,330	10,549	6,071	10,799	11,603
Santiago, Chile	9,687	7,804	10,746	15,800	11,966	13,426	13,706	11,687	10,034	11,803	8,141	11,377	16,855	10,003	10,481	12,206	11,253	6,236	10,999	12,471
Santo Domingo, Dominican Rep.	11,683	2,131	14,074	10,111	6,644	16,757	7,960	6,968	4,611	7,132	5,682	14,168	11,465	12,275	11,596	7,826	10,093	2,846	6,227	7,727
Sao Paulo de Olivenca, Brazil	11,059	4,529	12,990	12,495	8,933	15,999	10,384	8,843	6,913	8,988	6,266	13,386	13,747	11,572	11,393	9,570	10,498	3,815	8,274	9,641
Sao Paulo, Brazil	12,275	7,374	13,118	14,107	11,916	15,372	12,607	9,545	9,890	9,629	5,685	13,811	14,609	12,574	13,061	9,890	8,717	7,059	11,466	10,273
Sao Tome, Sao Tome & Principe	17,907	9,369	16,262	9,631	11,839	14,682	9,967	5,880	10,927	5,819	3,165	16,744	9,099	17,694	19,013	5,459	2,387	11,437	12,797	6,114
Sapporo, Japan	8,488	10,374	8,433	4,183	5,841	6,723	5,232	8,778	7,874	8,733	12,849	7,676	4,333	8,384	7,475	8,673	11,149	11,109	6,445	8,158
Sarajevo, Yugoslavia	17,146	7,625	16,859	4,747	7,539	13,960	5,149	1,761	7,598	1,598	4,296	16,233	4,661	17,194	16,040	839	3,577	10,597	8,863	1,409
Saratov, USSR	15,230	8,722	14,657	2,943	7,032	11,873	4,288	3,168	7,834	3,018	6,522	14,008	2,460	15,113	14,185	2,467	4,781	11,591	8,472	2,378
Saskatoon, Canada	9,966	2,916	12,203	6,480	1,860	13,059	4,225	6,459	625	6,601	8,486	11,727	8,094	10,471	9,183	7,311	11,522	3,987	1,433	6,758
Schefferville, Canada	12,550	2,122	14,827	6,085	3,389	15,251	3,928	4,163	1,999	4,325	5,913	14,333	7,520	13,074	11,804	5,090	9,032	4,906	3,912	4,668
Seattle, Washington	8,773	3,921	10,973	6,799	1,988	11,928	4,728	7,552	1,856	7,684	9,712	10,495	8,387	9,263	7,961	8,358	12,647	4,118	653	7,767

Distances in Kilometers	Niue (Alofi)	Norfolk, Virginia	Norfolk Island, Australia	Noril'sk, USSR	Norman Wells, Canada	Normanton, Australia	North Pole	Nottingham, United Kingdom	Norway House, Canada	Norwich, United Kingdom	Nouakchott, Mauritania	Noumea, New Caledonia	Novosibirsk, USSR	Nuku'alofa, Tonga	Nukunono Island, Tokelau Isls.	Nuremberg, West Germany	Nyala, Sudan	Oaxaca, Mexico	Ocean Falls, Canada	Odense, Denmark
Sendai, Japan	8,159	10,859	7,963	4,643	6,318	6,189	5,766	9,258	8,348	9,207	13,317	7,212	4,654	8,016	7,181	9,113	11,354	11,443	6,849	8,618
Seoul, South Korea	9,096	11,426	8,520	4,230	6,968	6,289	5,842	8,802	8,991	8,723	12,731	7,806	3,824	8,876	8,188	8,498	10,247	12,433	7,717	8,086
Sept-Iles, Canada	12,568	1,682	14,935	6,583	3,783	15,650	4,440	4,373	2,177	4,540	5,699	14,504	7,997	13,116	11,894	5,311	9,079	4,567	4,155	4,943
Sevastopol, USSR	16,438	8,564	15,671	4,082	7,703	12,750	5,063	2,683	8,149	2,513	5,437	15,081	3,652	16,311	15,387	1,782	3,701	11,530	9,112	2,033
Seville, Spain	17,447	6,092	18,926	6,327	7,537	16,136	5,665	1,772	6,865	1,787	2,348	18,182	6,642	17,931	16,581	1,917	4,162	8,944	8,580	2,352
Shanghai, China	9,198	12,261	8,287	4,740	7,837	5,796	6,557	9,164	9,853	9,066	12,912	7,619	4,021	8,903	8,387	8,746	9,936	13,308	8,600	8,408
Sheffield, United Kingdom	16,065	5,870	17,170	4,598	6,051	14,903	4,089	50	5,844	205	4,109	16,406	5,166	16,387	15,032	976	5,146	8,844	7,268	803
Shenyang, China	9,597	11,068	9,078	3,681	6,688	6,830	5,372	8,243	8,686	8,163	12,175	8,362	3,281	9,397	8,661	7,941	9,825	12,299	7,542	7,527
Shiraz, Iran	15,591	10,924	13,842	4,965	9,486	10,830	6,728	5,037	10,316	4,866	6,997	13,445	3,718	15,169	14,886	4,116	3,456	13,886	10,926	4,387
Sibiu, Romania	16,768	7,892	16,359	4,331	7,435	13,479	4,930	1,990	7,666	1,820	4,798	15,730	4,168	16,756	15,671	1,061	3,742	10,866	8,801	1,441
Singapore	9,667	15,783	7,588	7,644	11,585	4,588	9,860	10,895	13,561	10,740	13,105	7,269	6,255	9,129	9,410	10,102	8,788	16,988	12,377	10,111
Sioux Falls, South Dakota	10,163	1,887	12,571	7,480	3,051	13,927	5,179	6,635	1,164	6,794	7,914	12,215	9,080	10,719	9,536	7,551	11,487	2,937	2,487	7,084
Skelleftea, Sweden	14,859	6,692	15,416	2,814	5,343	13,178	2,819	1,813	5,841	1,752	5,865	14,660	3,472	15,014	13,755	1,802	5,861	9,535	6,740	1,194
Skopje, Yugoslavia	17,241	7,946	16,686	4,804	7,798	13,741	5,352	2,083	7,906	1,919	4,421	16,099	4,598	17,220	16,144	1,156	3,335	10,916	9,138	1,695
Socotra Island (Tamrida)	15,288	12,464	13,005	6,740	11,362	10,133	8,604	6,595	12,157	6,427	7,495	12,831	5,331	14,727	15,009	5,656	3,168	15,422	12,801	6,052
Sofia, Bulgaria	17,104	8,029	16,520	4,666	7,758	13,583	5,276	2,144	7,923	1,977	4,590	15,930	4,433	17,064	16,012	1,206	3,398	11,003	9,113	1,695
Songkhla, Thailand	10,221	15,118	8,243	6,959	11,082	5,232	9,206	10,154	13,009	10,000	12,524	7,879	5,534	9,705	9,872	9,371	8,305	16,725	11,987	9,367
Sorong, Indonesia	6,719	15,127	4,987	8,432	10,646	2,146	10,099	12,766	12,619	12,650	15,970	4,486	7,594	6,226	6,363	12,214	11,820	14,486	10,837	11,980
South Georgia Island	10,749	10,782	10,478	16,807	15,270	12,034	16,018	12,331	13,243	12,360	8,258	11,242	16,241	10,762	11,822	12,334	9,342	9,725	14,481	12,895
South Pole	7,897	14,083	6,787	17,697	17,244	8,047	20,001	15,875	15,986	15,838	12,006	7,537	16,104	7,663	8,983	15,484	11,337	11,888	15,804	16,146
South Sandwich Islands	10,852	11,467	10,294	16,708	15,984	11,569	16,408	12,488	13,951	12,495	8,462	11,056	15,842	10,795	11,950	12,373	9,037	10,472	15,228	12,975
Split, Yugoslavia	17,225	7,505	17,021	4,856	7,530	14,123	5,184	1,670	7,535	1,511	4,141	16,389	4,807	17,301	16,118	777	3,581	10,474	8,839	1,391
Spokane, Washington	9,051	3,551	11,291	6,860	2,040	12,297	4,719	7,333	1,540	7,469	9,367	10,830	8,464	9,554	8,267	8,162	12,415	3,887	901	7,588
Spoleto, Italy	17,363	7,285	17,330	5,077	7,529	14,436	5,271	1,536	7,427	1,392	3,843	16,689	5,093	17,500	16,262	757	3,598	10,245	8,805	1,419
Springbok, South Africa	14,554	12,259	12,777	12,326	15,364	11,988	13,287	9,339	14,276	9,259	6,413	13,352	11,238	14,213	15,580	8,789	4,677	13,282	16,237	9,452
Springfield, Illinois	10,546	1,212	13,010	7,901	3,691	14,583	5,595	6,517	1,693	6,682	7,369	12,719	9,472	11,122	10,006	7,452	11,164	2,613	3,208	7,047
Springfield, Massachusetts	11,997	664	14,466	7,545	4,213	15,833	5,340	5,279	2,280	5,449	5,945	14,165	8,994	12,575	11,459	6,218	9,729	3,603	4,215	5,897
Srinagar, India	13,471	11,603	12,019	4,008	8,830	9,054	6,230	6,172	10,222	6,017	8,975	11,509	2,412	13,097	12,725	5,393	5,600	14,276	10,183	5,391
Stanley, Falkland Islands	9,796	9,973	10,010	17,363	14,241	12,104	15,733	12,749	12,290	12,816	8,737	10,749	17,413	9,914	10,810	12,965	10,556	8,498	13,250	13,431
Stara Zagora, Bulgaria	17,030	8,203	16,342	4,601	7,828	13,395	5,306	2,309	8,048	2,140	4,754	15,763	4,305	16,955	15,949	1,369	3,366	11,177	9,196	1,818
Stockholm, Sweden	15,483	6,799	15,943	3,346	5,875	13,531	3,424	1,382	6,205	1,279	5,334	15,197	3,794	15,634	14,379	1,188	5,278	9,715	7,246	635
Stornoway, United Kingdom	15,451	5,474	16,733	4,315	5,432	14,778	3,549	670	5,265	788	4,523	15,971	5,082	15,790	14,429	1,499	5,758	8,432	6,651	1,067
Strasbourg, France	16,718	6,653	17,260	4,707	6,789	14,602	4,621	795	6,678	641	4,001	16,534	4,979	16,948	15,638	262	4,351	9,627	8,052	780
Stuttgart, West Germany	16,703	6,742	17,170	4,635	6,806	14,496	4,600	864	6,731	703	4,087	16,450	4,883	16,914	15,617	158	4,323	9,717	8,081	743
Subic, Philippines	8,522	14,024	7,066	6,451	9,533	4,266	8,355	10,649	11,565	10,530	13,991	6,504	5,488	8,100	7,947	10,091	10,241	14,643	10,139	9,860
Suchow, China	9,704	12,009	8,809	4,295	7,679	6,281	6,208	8,661	9,665	8,560	12,387	8,144	3,505	9,419	8,873	8,227	9,477	13,294	8,541	7,899
Sucre, Bolivia	10,787	6,292	12,212	14,127	10,678	15,036	12,108	10,065	8,668	10,190	6,779	12,775	15,198	11,195	11,401	10,652	10,464	5,269	9,931	10,859
Sudbury, Canada	11,439	1,141	13,851	7,127	3,428	15,011	4,851	5,498	1,455	5,662	6,669	13,481	8,651	11,998	10,814	6,431	10,229	3,574	3,387	6,024
Suez, Egypt	17,453	9,544	15,731	5,587	9,296	12,730	6,687	3,741	9,557	3,580	5,067	15,372	4,838	17,082	16,592	2,820	2,136	12,494	10,685	3,327
Sundsvall, Sweden	15,156	6,628	15,733	3,127	5,539	13,445	3,084	1,511	5,921	1,441	5,549	14,978	3,716	15,325	14,055	1,490	5,620	9,513	6,917	873
Surabaya, Indonesia	8,429	16,603	6,253	8,706	12,111	3,283	10,803	12,239	14,145	12,087	14,353	5,982	7,437	7,869	8,290	11,462	9,954	16,653	12,624	11,449
Suva, Fiji	1,235	12,541	1,610	11,889	10,327	3,950	12,006	16,139	11,220	16,168	18,515	1,331	11,988	747	1,439	16,351	17,114	10,074	9,378	15,747
Sverdlovsk, USSR	14,116	8,860	13,698	1,934	6,444	11,070	3,700	3,849	7,562	3,726	7,525	13,011	1,403	14,011	13,071	3,334	5,830	11,548	7,875	3,057
Svobodnyy, USSR	9,845	9,943	9,726	2,884	5,583	7,754	4,304	7,508	7,568	7,450	11,553	8,978	2,994	9,745	8,821	7,343	9,870	11,267	6,504	6,852
Sydney, Australia	4,182	15,742	1,678	12,528	13,016	2,060	13,751	16,966	14,302	16,844	17,847	1,972	11,798	3,587	4,656	16,331	14,093	13,069	12,356	16,174
Sydney, Canada	13,022	1,690	15,449	6,936	4,423	16,292	4,890	4,212	2,795	4,383	5,106	15,069	8,268	13,588	12,413	5,148	8,676	4,664	4,781	4,860
Syktyvkar, USSR	14,319	8,095	14,228	1,886	5,920	11,733	3,164	3,180	6,888	3,073	7,027	13,510	1,995	14,301	13,234	2,790	5,891	10,820	7,362	2,411
Szeged, Hungary	16,846	7,604	16,628	4,444	7,312	13,777	4,878	1,704	7,453	1,534	4,553	15,980	4,386	16,891	15,740	766	3,819	10,579	8,656	1,225
Szombathely, Hungary	16,820	7,315	16,823	4,491	7,137	14,020	4,771	1,418	7,208	1,249	4,387	16,149	4,541	16,922	15,713	478	3,977	10,290	8,460	1,006
Tabriz, Iran	15,935	9,834	14,603	4,272	8,529	11,613	5,787	3,970	9,241	3,801	6,382	14,105	3,323	15,634	15,038	3,068	3,584	12,789	9,968	3,295
Tacheng, China	12,823	10,517	11,943	2,531	7,318	9,201	4,823	5,734	8,841	5,606	9,220	11,306	922	12,581	11,904	5,153	6,626	12,939	8,643	4,937
Tahiti (Papeete)	2,157	9,752	4,503	13,057	9,382	7,314	11,940	15,217	9,326	15,361	15,130	4,620	13,944	2,720	2,586	16,064	19,169	6,941	8,026	15,473
Taipei, Taiwan	8,883	12,906	7,778	5,391	8,446	5,181	7,230	9,749	10,472	9,644	13,382	7,140	4,579	8,540	8,149	9,283	10,108	13,784	9,139	8,980
Taiyuan, China	10,247	11,682	9,387	3,798	7,478	6,834	5,809	8,096	9,420	7,992	11,810	8,721	2,932	9,976	9,390	7,651	8,997	13,204	8,442	7,330
Tallahassee, Florida	10,662	1,026	13,166	8,923	4,838	15,238	6,633	6,928	2,833	7,099	6,973	13,021	10,455	11,259	10,301	7,865	11,117	1,948	4,275	7,559
Tallinn, USSR	15,367	7,135	15,639	3,083	5,971	13,164	3,415	1,747	6,432	1,634	5,630	14,904	3,433	15,469	14,260	1,415	5,257	10,031	7,368	970
Tamanrasset, Algeria	19,389	7,828	18,139	7,364	9,437	15,372	7,484	3,398	8,818	3,333	2,297	18,072	7,167	19,812	18,477	2,999	2,372	10,490	10,530	3,644
Tampa, Florida	10,746	1,144	13,245	9,189	5,163	15,444	6,909	7,013	3,152	7,183	6,825	13,142	10,705	11,345	10,436	7,943	11,043	1,898	4,599	7,669
Tampere, Finland	15,168	6,976	15,547	2,955	5,732	13,158	3,183	1,763	6,213	1,668	5,729	14,803	3,420	15,289	14,061	1,556	5,490	9,853	7,131	1,031
Tanami, Australia	6,302	16,879	3,984	10,442	12,630	1,225	12,212	14,457	14,508	14,315	16,420	3,815	9,419	5,716	6,373	13,734	12,001	15,135	12,593	13,657
Tangier, Morocco	17,588	6,176	19,061	6,480	7,705	16,193	6,041	1,942	7,007	1,952	2,202	18,332	6,763	18,086	16,744	2,044	4,052	9,003	8,737	2,504
Tarawa (Betio)	2,932	11,758	3,404	9,661	8,528	4,076	9,851	13,959	9,837	13,971	17,649	2,706	9,887	2,803	2,047	14,114	16,202	10,011	7,861	13,516
Tashkent, USSR	13,939	10,668	12,755	3,305	8,101	9,849	5,425	5,272	9,372	5,121	8,316	12,190	1,822	13,638	13,077	4,530	5,395	13,383	9,496	4,482
Tbilisi, USSR	15,891	9,450	14,772	3,956	8,121	11,814	5,385	3,617	8,819	3,450	6,274	14,229	3,140	15,647	14,934	2,739	3,812	12,395	9,558	2,916
Tegucigalpa, Honduras	9,774	2,745	12,191	10,743	6,418	14,860	8,443	8,506	4,522	8,676	7,591	12,257	12,288	10,368	9,698	9,419	12,004	1,070	5,550	9,202
Tehran, Iran	15,579	10,336	14,107	4,359	8,812	11,107	6,055	4,491	9,643	4,322	6,841	13,634	3,226	15,231	14,751	3,595	3,738	13,280	10,253	3,801
Tel Aviv, Israel	17,164	9,551	15,558	5,291	9,096	12,548	6,455	3,693	9,442	3,527	5,294	15,159	4,523	16,820	16,282	2,757	2,437	12,516	10,499	3,217
Telegraph Creek, Canada	9,244	4,589	11,169	5,542	854	11,522	3,581	6,910	2,105	7,018	9,716	10,581	7,115	9,659	8,300	7,614	11,950	5,350	656	6,979
Teresina, Brazil	13,651	5,800	15,009	12,036	10,238	17,453	10,566	7,526	8,293	7,623	3,909	15,626	12,675	14,078	14,169	7,960	7,728	6,412	10,104	8,281
Ternate, Indonesia	7,186	15,179	5,431	8,148	10,652	2,534	9,913	12,391	12,656	12,269	15,506	4,945	7,233	6,693	6,819	11,807	11,362	14,807	10,947	11,599
The Valley, Anguilla	12,371	2,453	14,722	10,047	6,986	17,477	8,007	6,550	4,976	6,707	4,974	14,858	11,293	12,959	12,313	7,365	9,395	3,570	6,719	7,331
Thessaloniki, Greece	17,318	8,131	16,602	4,882	7,973	13,634	5,504	2,276	8,099	2,113	4,471	16,042	4,605	17,255	16,230	1,350	3,173	11,100	9,320	1,884
Thimphu, Bhutan	11,961	12,730	10,421	4,649	9,247	7,463	6,956	7,671	10,944	7,523	10,560	9,918	3,104	11,551	11,306	6,941	6,932	15,024	10,439	6,876
Thunder Bay, Canada	10,899	1,665	13,267	6,945	2,889	14,351	4,639	5,847	859	6,006	7,304	12,864	8,518	11,444	10,225	6,763	10,723	3,542	2,731	6,302
Tientsin, China	9,932	11,479	9,200	3,778	7,186	6,762	5,668	8,209	9,157	8,115	12,022	8,513	3,098	9,687	9,045	7,821	9,374	12,860	8,098	7,461
Tijuana, Mexico	8,015	3,735	10,446	8,524	3,703	12,143	6,400	8,694	2,827	8,845	9,939	10,140	10,118	8,576	7,429	9,581	13,632	2,666	2,364	9,058
Tiksi, USSR	11,050	7,816	11,567	1,510	3,794	9,946	2,053	5,641	5,603	5,623	9,703	10,803	2,831	11,123	9,947	5,721	9,222	9,593	5,029	5,124
Timbuktu, Mali	18,624	7,440	18,371	8,317	9,771	16,221	8,150	4,020	8,826	3,997	1,382	18,766	8,240	19,073	18,559	3,842	3,051	9,859	10,689	4,437
Tindouf, Algeria	17,933	6,366	19,617	7,392	8,451	16,690	6,939	2,865	7,547	2,878	1,330	19,205	7,598	18,526	17,351	2,921	3,851	9,014	9,380	3,419
Tirane, Albania	17,366	7,870	16,838	4,935	7,837	13,886	5,426	2,038	7,893	1,878	4,266	16,254	4,750	17,362	16,264	1,131	3,282	10,837	9,164	1,710
Tokyo, Japan	8,049	11,155	7,751	4,860	6,613	5,908	6,049	9,482	8,642	9,426	13,527	7,005	4,779	7,880	7,097	9,307	11,386	11,685	7,123	8,827
Toledo, Spain	17,333	6,147	18,602	6,005	7,349	15,861	5,589	1,472	6,775	1,476	2,672	17,859	6,323	17,768	16,403	1,597	4,190	9,040	8,437	2,029
Topeka, Kansas	10,036	1,718	12,491	7,981	3,539	14,086	5,678	6,936	1,668	7,099	7,894	12,194	9,578	10,608	9,483	7,864	11,663	2,441	2,864	7,429
Toronto, Canada	11,488	801	13,935	7,431	3,759	15,261	5,166	5,598	1,766	5,765	6,516	13,607	8,940	12,058	10,913	6,536	10,212	3,373	3,657	6,162
Toulouse, France	17,163	6,413	17,998	5,430	7,135	15,272	5,175	1,059	6,771	1,005	3,265	17,270	5,710	17,494	16,139	984	4,159	9,357	8,310	1,461
Tours, France	16,746	6,209	17,694	5,089	6,723	15,134	4,754	635	6,421	586	3,585	16,944	5,470	17,069	15,715	803	4,523	9,175	7,916	1,116
Townsville, Australia	4,542	15,411	2,402	10,853	11,764	629	12,130	15,363	13,372	15,260	18,211	2,072	10,194	3,968	4,582	14,858	13,782	13,346	11,383	14,595
Trenton, New Jersey	11,780	397	14,261	7,774	4,288	15,770	5,548	5,553	2,306	5,723	6,101	13,988	9,238	12,362	11,271	6,492	9,958	3,327	4,189	6,174
Tripoli, Lebanon	16,957	9,452	15,490	5,010	8,848	12,479	6,192	3,564	9,249	3,396	5,418	15,051	4,261	16,648	16,041	2,625	2,717	12,424	10,258	3,043
Tripoli, Libya	18,437	7,869	17,586	6,035	8,587	14,575	6,362	2,508	8,337	2,391	3,340	17,147	5,826	18,467	17,330	1,846	2,599	10,752	9,825	2,510
Tristan da Cunha (Edinburgh)	13,372	10,504	12,689	14,205	14,808	13,340	14,106	10,031	12,968	10,023	6,116	13,438	13,590	13,321	14,464	9,856	6,684	10,656	14,813	10,469
Trondheim, Norway	15,073	6,259	15,860	3,292	5,308	13,706	2,969	1,344	5,595	1,313	5,420	15,097	4,007	15,289	13,984	1,556	5,815	9,148	6,661	893
Trujillo, Peru	9,819	4,986	11,763	13,144	9,034	14,775	10,900	9,920	7,105	10,073	7,511	12,143	14,562	10,328	10,188	10,698	11,710	3,397	8,133	10,708
Truk Island (Moen)	5,113	13,009	4,388	8,225	8,853	3,019	9,179	12,845	10,639	12,791	16,885	3,650	7,998	4,790	4,420	12,650	13,783	12,019	8,709	12,189
Truro, Canada	12,781	1,442	15,220	7,069	4,349	16,200	4,977	4,461	2,641	4,631	5,300	14,859	8,432	13,350	12,188	5,398	8,924	4,416	4,630	5,100
Tsingtao, China	9,535	11,753	8,763	4,187	7,379	6,337	6,008	8,644	9,378	8,551	12,457	8,078	3,535	9,276	8,670	8,259	9,714	12,959	8,213	7,898
Tsitsihar, China	9,869	10,462	9,541	3,132	6,123	7,403	4,753	7,735	8,104	7,665	11,727	8,809	2,944	9,719	8,884	7,492	9,705	11,803	7,040	7,043
Tubuai Island (Mataura)	2,175	10,157	4,280	13,667	10,018	7,205	12,586	15,777	9,894	15,928	15,176	4,510	14,478	2,661	2,857	16,652	18,622	7,273	8,651	16,082
Tucson, Arizona	8,459	3,208	10,918	8,637	3,833	12,703	6,436	8,398	2,634	8,555	9,414	10,645	10,247	9,031	7,923	9,306	13,231	2,210	2,613	8,818
Tulsa, Oklahoma	9,884	1,757	12,360	8,302	3,825	14,097	5,999	7,188	1,986	7,352	7,964	12,099	9,900	10,463	9,376	8,121	11,838	2,119	3,071	7,701

Distances in Kilometers	Niue (Alofi)	Norfolk, Virginia	Norfolk Island, Australia	Noril'sk, USSR	Norman Wells, Canada	Normanton, Australia	North Pole	Nottingham, United Kingdom	Norway House, Canada	Norwich, United Kingdom	Nouakchott, Mauritania	Noumea, New Caledonia	Novosibirsk, USSR	Nuku'alofa, Tonga	Nukunono Island, Tokelau Isls.	Nuremberg, West Germany	Nyala, Sudan	Oaxaca, Mexico	Ocean Falls, Canada	Odense, Denmark
Tunis, Tunisia	18,034	7,412	17,780	5,763	8,093	14,788	5,930	2,002	7,825	1,892	3,292	17,226	5,703	18,194	16,940	1,407	3,111	10,322	9,319	2,068
Tura, USSR	11,885	8,789	11,881	774	5,133	9,734	2,870	5,370	6,797	5,305	9,396	11,136	1,411	11,843	10,817	5,185	8,100	10,871	6,428	4,696
Turin, Italy	17,109	6,806	17,531	5,050	7,157	14,751	5,014	1,090	6,973	963	3,706	16,831	5,233	17,339	16,031	553	4,008	9,769	8,401	1,167
Uberlandia, Brazil	12,392	6,839	13,432	13,674	11,380	15,830	12,098	9,164	9,357	9,257	5,412	14,095	14,290	12,736	13,104	9,565	8,727	6,627	10,957	9,911
Ufa, USSR	14,482	8,883	13,983	2,291	6,692	11,287	3,936	3,658	7,715	3,525	7,223	13,311	1,721	14,365	13,443	3,075	5,457	11,641	8,130	2,859
Ujungpandang, Indonesia	7,802	16,148	5,750	8,599	11,608	2,739	10,567	12,469	13,635	12,327	14,973	5,403	7,467	7,261	7,592	11,760	10,626	15,882	12,002	11,669
Ulaanbaatar, Mongolia	11,065	10,610	10,475	2,598	6,631	8,023	4,692	6,931	8,474	6,835	10,758	9,778	1,832	10,868	10,115	6,544	8,430	12,437	7,751	6,180
Ulan-Ude, USSR	11,146	10,172	10,713	2,201	6,211	8,356	4,257	6,636	8,040	6,549	10,537	10,000	1,671	10,988	10,159	6,304	8,466	12,019	7,356	5,904
Uliastay, Mongolia	11,791	10,609	11,071	2,451	6,920	8,481	4,711	6,434	8,646	6,324	10,134	10,399	1,258	11,573	10,856	5,966	7,677	12,703	8,137	5,658
Uranium City, Canada	10,314	3,421	12,390	5,642	1,132	12,827	3,396	5,953	903	6,082	8,437	11,837	7,256	10,776	9,441	6,752	11,050	4,818	1,429	6,162
Urumqi, China	12,441	10,926	11,473	2,843	7,548	8,714	5,151	6,223	9,156	6,095	9,675	10,847	1,294	12,172	11,557	5,637	6,907	13,253	8,828	5,427
Ushuaia, Argentina	9,019	10,184	9,283	17,998	14,211	11,508	16,078	13,445	12,360	13,521	9,472	10,014	18,182	9,138	10,036	13,708	11,297	8,404	13,079	14,149
Vaduz, Liechtenstein	16,882	6,838	17,270	4,774	6,982	14,536	4,778	999	6,883	846	3,975	16,562	4,972	17,086	15,794	279	4,151	9,810	8,252	918
Valencia, Spain	17,529	6,453	18,438	5,907	7,507	15,594	5,634	1,502	7,016	1,469	2,805	17,732	6,140	17,915	16,549	1,432	3,926	9,353	8,635	1,943
Valladolid, Spain	17,135	6,021	18,460	5,853	7,143	15,820	5,391	1,286	6,589	1,302	2,821	17,705	6,221	17,563	16,198	1,503	4,362	8,933	8,237	1,884
Valletta, Malta	18,085	7,798	17,424	5,682	8,300	14,419	6,030	2,260	8,133	2,130	3,586	16,918	5,500	18,121	16,978	1,531	2,840	10,717	9,564	2,190
Valparaiso, Chile	9,619	7,752	10,708	15,773	11,890	13,411	13,659	11,703	9,966	11,820	8,187	11,333	16,863	9,941	10,405	12,235	11,337	6,151	10,913	12,490
Vancouver, Canada	8,861	3,983	11,027	6,607	1,799	11,894	4,544	7,432	1,818	7,560	9,689	10,532	8,194	9,342	8,028	8,226	12,529	4,292	472	7,628
Varna, Bulgaria	16,849	8,302	16,141	4,434	7,778	13,204	5,217	2,400	8,067	2,230	4,961	15,557	4,104	16,758	15,776	1,465	3,467	11,277	9,160	1,850
Venice, Italy	17,066	7,117	17,207	4,829	7,231	14,388	4,969	1,288	7,168	1,134	4,006	16,530	4,922	17,222	15,967	455	3,889	10,087	8,516	1,116
Veracruz, Mexico	9,097	2,752	11,583	10,180	5,595	14,015	7,878	8,651	3,863	8,821	8,376	11,538	11,779	9,698	8,880	9,588	12,696	246	4,583	9,266
Verona, Italy	17,072	7,023	17,295	4,882	7,199	14,489	4,969	1,216	7,103	1,066	3,926	16,611	5,004	17,249	15,977	445	3,930	9,992	8,473	1,108
Victoria, Canada	8,784	3,999	10,961	6,692	1,888	11,864	4,635	7,518	1,876	7,647	9,744	10,472	8,277	9,267	7,957	8,314	12,614	4,239	533	7,718
Victoria, Seychelles	14,414	13,953	11,925	8,573	13,270	9,401	10,514	8,281	14,023	8,120	8,223	11,963	7,080	13,814	14,564	7,358	3,853	16,698	14,705	7,827
Vienna, Austria	16,719	7,248	16,785	4,409	7,028	14,011	4,663	1,346	7,111	1,176	4,436	16,100	4,493	16,831	15,613	412	4,086	10,222	8,353	900
Vientiane, Laos	10,399	13,936	8,735	5,795	9,883	5,770	8,015	9,319	11,798	9,177	12,210	8,254	4,442	9,949	9,858	8,619	8,328	15,598	10,836	8,520
Villahermosa, Mexico	9,359	2,651	11,829	10,320	5,822	14,331	8,013	8,547	4,017	8,717	8,080	11,816	11,905	9,958	9,181	9,479	12,434	417	4,868	9,190
Vilnius, USSR	15,841	7,430	15,886	3,464	6,491	13,244	3,942	1,744	6,884	1,596	5,359	15,178	3,593	15,904	14,736	1,134	4,730	10,366	7,881	956
Visby, Sweden	15,665	6,891	16,058	3,480	6,060	13,581	3,613	1,335	6,361	1,214	5,215	15,319	3,855	15,807	14,561	1,027	5,089	9,822	7,427	547
Vitoria, Brazil	13,011	7,368	13,763	13,562	11,877	15,800	12,251	8,955	9,888	9,028	5,016	14,475	13,940	13,301	13,799	9,244	7,987	7,416	11,595	9,659
Vladivostok, USSR	9,090	10,701	8,800	3,828	6,227	6,797	5,223	8,451	8,252	8,388	12,475	8,060	3,725	8,938	8,112	8,246	10,442	11,706	6,977	7,778
Volgograd, USSR	15,506	8,867	14,796	3,271	7,337	11,950	4,602	3,188	8,081	3,031	6,352	14,173	2,703	15,361	14,475	2,416	4,452	11,770	8,775	2,420
Vologda, USSR	14,942	7,855	14,874	2,505	6,150	12,313	3,437	2,603	6,898	2,482	6,376	14,161	2,599	14,946	13,848	2,142	5,382	10,685	7,585	1,813
Vorkuta, USSR	13,439	7,963	13,543	1,004	5,246	11,267	2,513	3,733	6,446	3,657	7,732	12,801	1,705	13,451	12,347	3,521	6,790	10,497	6,676	3,035
Wake Island	4,950	10,957	5,348	7,564	6,986	4,952	7,867	11,915	8,647	11,913	15,860	4,596	7,877	4,889	3,932	12,020	14,584	10,069	6,685	11,432
Wallis Island	920	11,761	2,394	11,604	9,630	4,604	11,471	15,582	10,446	15,636	17,849	2,091	11,905	873	650	15,942	17,746	9,354	8,629	15,299
Walvis Bay, Namibia	15,338	11,571	13,593	11,751	14,549	12,679	12,543	8,546	13,493	8,471	5,621	14,160	10,790	15,017	16,382	8,026	4,034	12,867	15,438	8,690
Warsaw, Poland	16,197	7,320	16,269	3,852	6,684	13,581	4,213	1,498	6,942	1,336	4,970	15,567	3,971	16,282	15,090	764	4,472	10,280	8,048	781
Washington, D.C.	11,558	236	14,045	7,941	4,313	15,652	5,696	5,797	2,300	5,967	6,284	13,790	9,424	12,143	11,068	6,736	10,187	3,085	4,125	6,415
Watson Lake, Canada	9,522	4,491	11,428	5,345	584	11,699	3,334	6,629	1,978	6,736	9,476	10,830	6,932	9,934	8,574	7,332	11,669	5,430	868	6,698
Weimar, East Germany	16,456	6,784	16,890	4,344	6,623	14,263	4,354	885	6,642	714	4,372	16,164	4,614	16,644	15,362	171	4,490	9,757	7,924	495
Wellington, New Zealand	2,866	14,027	1,495	14,102	12,845	4,144	14,574	18,673	13,424	18,654	17,240	2,251	13,736	2,427	3,791	18,455	15,646	11,121	11,762	18,071
West Berlin, West Germany	16,276	6,846	16,669	4,123	6,507	14,068	4,183	983	6,603	819	4,594	15,942	4,400	16,445	15,177	378	4,605	9,814	7,829	377
Wewak, Papua New Guinea	5,331	14,523	3,816	9,092	10,339	1,586	10,393	13,653	12,157	13,563	17,279	3,218	8,526	4,859	4,956	13,246	13,229	13,285	10,229	12,910
Whangarei, New Zealand	2,412	13,832	954	13,525	12,290	3,838	13,955	18,056	12,993	18,048	17,810	1,675	13,252	1,911	3,252	17,968	15,984	11,008	11,259	17,501
Whitehorse, Canada	9,375	4,841	11,203	5,175	656	11,374	3,267	6,753	2,326	6,853	9,735	10,586	6,741	9,764	8,399	7,419	11,745	5,724	1,035	6,775
Wichita, Kansas	9,841	1,865	12,302	8,127	3,618	13,956	5,828	7,145	1,810	7,308	8,061	12,018	9,729	10,415	9,301	8,073	11,864	2,289	2,860	7,636
Willemstad, Curacao	11,587	2,836	13,870	10,794	7,329	16,749	8,663	7,457	5,295	7,615	5,718	14,065	12,112	12,164	11,627	8,276	10,149	3,039	6,846	8,234
Wiluna, Australia	7,138	18,092	4,679	10,950	13,724	2,365	12,945	14,408	15,665	14,247	15,442	4,688	9,720	6,539	7,367	13,564	11,131	16,084	13,786	13,638
Windhoek, Namibia	15,341	11,769	13,502	11,620	14,600	12,477	12,502	8,554	13,630	8,472	5,760	14,044	10,614	14,990	16,357	8,000	3,924	13,124	15,552	8,664
Windsor, Canada	11,163	837	13,617	7,603	3,727	15,044	5,317	5,921	1,697	6,088	6,804	13,305	9,137	11,735	10,602	6,859	10,543	3,088	3,493	6,474
Winnipeg, Canada	10,432	2,213	12,751	6,775	2,427	13,757	4,474	6,163	459	6,315	7,866	12,319	8,376	10,961	9,713	7,055	11,139	3,642	2,139	6,550
Winston-Salem, North Carolina	11,206	365	13,703	8,274	4,442	15,484	6,006	6,216	2,408	6,386	6,561	13,485	9,780	11,795	10,758	7,155	10,552	2,665	4,105	6,835
Wroclaw, Poland	16,393	7,140	16,569	4,112	6,733	13,879	4,341	1,263	6,882	1,095	4,674	15,863	4,272	16,514	15,288	462	4,389	10,109	8,071	652
Wuhan, China	9,787	12,460	8,714	4,619	8,162	6,063	6,617	8,852	10,141	8,741	12,443	8,080	3,676	9,462	9,013	8,357	9,284	13,785	9,033	8,074
Wyndham, Australia	6,571	16,639	4,349	9,916	12,256	1,407	11,712	13,951	14,186	13,812	16,197	4,100	8,893	5,998	6,544	13,249	11,766	15,251	12,320	13,151
Xi'an, China	10,408	12,113	9,362	4,109	7,972	6,683	6,208	8,228	9,895	8,114	11,794	8,729	3,058	10,096	9,606	7,716	8,724	13,715	8,956	7,446
Xining, China	11,104	11,868	10,030	3,735	7,953	7,292	5,948	7,627	9,792	7,505	11,110	9,409	2,500	10,794	10,292	7,073	8,057	13,758	9,049	6,836
Yakutsk, USSR	10,425	8,802	10,657	2,029	4,561	8,889	3,124	6,547	6,489	6,510	10,623	9,896	2,765	10,419	9,346	6,509	9,588	10,345	5,633	5,958
Yanji, China	9,234	10,798	8,881	3,770	6,347	6,808	5,251	8,385	8,366	8,318	12,389	8,147	3,590	9,069	8,267	8,154	10,269	11,867	7,128	7,700
Yaounde, Cameroon	18,321	9,563	16,281	9,078	11,628	14,330	9,577	5,567	10,909	5,488	3,383	16,639	8,476	17,964	19,313	5,052	1,727	11,822	12,696	5,715
Yap Island (Colonia)	6,515	13,748	5,333	7,532	9,283	3,024	8,948	12,085	11,243	11,996	15,843	4,681	6,975	6,126	5,912	11,701	12,275	13,318	9,460	11,346
Yaraka, Australia	4,774	15,978	2,410	11,362	12,447	857	12,754	15,754	14,033	15,632	17,832	2,299	10,586	4,180	4,970	15,144	13,506	13,699	12,043	14,963
Yarmouth, Canada	12,545	1,159	15,001	7,277	4,354	16,152	5,148	4,744	2,556	4,914	5,467	14,670	8,665	13,119	11,980	5,681	9,173	4,133	4,539	5,382
Yellowknife, Canada	10,252	3,854	12,226	5,276	689	12,481	3,074	5,944	1,346	6,062	8,662	11,638	6,890	10,686	9,334	6,699	11,027	5,226	1,375	6,086
Yerevan, USSR	15,985	9,558	14,782	4,119	8,287	11,808	5,554	3,702	8,968	3,533	6,239	14,258	3,268	15,721	15,046	2,809	3,664	12,511	9,724	3,019
Yinchuan, China	10,782	11,661	9,840	3,605	7,622	7,196	5,742	7,717	9,503	7,605	11,335	9,192	2,543	10,498	9,936	7,221	8,447	13,409	8,674	6,937
Yogyakarta, Indonesia	8,661	16,719	6,452	8,728	12,267	3,504	10,864	12,133	14,298	11,978	14,120	6,203	7,417	8,096	8,543	11,336	9,710	16,920	12,826	11,348
York, United Kingdom	16,023	5,879	17,113	4,543	6,013	14,854	4,037	96	5,826	212	4,165	16,349	5,116	16,340	14,986	976	5,174	8,852	7,237	765
Yumen, China	11,537	11,492	10,524	3,333	7,730	7,794	5,591	7,126	9,503	7,004	10,625	9,897	2,017	11,246	10,692	6,572	7,702	13,533	8,892	6,334
Yutian, China	12,868	11,535	11,577	3,634	8,413	8,672	5,921	6,399	9,939	6,253	9,479	11,021	2,021	12,527	12,080	5,692	6,275	14,035	9,719	5,602
Yuzhno-Sakhalinsk, USSR	8,709	9,944	8,788	3,857	5,417	7,158	4,799	8,416	7,452	8,378	12,492	8,028	4,160	8,641	7,669	8,354	11,041	10,774	6,072	7,819
Zagreb, Yugoslavia	16,985	7,351	16,942	4,652	7,277	14,103	4,930	1,474	7,309	1,309	4,255	16,280	4,675	17,087	15,879	549	3,835	10,324	8,591	1,139
Zahedan, Iran	14,785	11,412	13,070	4,761	9,476	10,058	6,738	5,602	10,532	5,434	7,798	12,651	3,338	14,361	14,106	4,712	4,190	14,324	10,899	4,895
Zamboanga, Philippines	7,988	14,801	6,321	7,357	10,269	3,429	9,238	11,508	12,302	11,384	14,651	5,815	6,368	7,519	7,538	10,911	10,635	15,005	10,749	10,714
Zanzibar, Tanzania	15,787	12,682	13,301	9,162	13,352	11,062	10,686	7,573	13,455	7,432	6,622	13,481	7,892	15,205	16,187	6,737	2,562	15,090	14,746	7,323
Zaragoza, Spain	17,293	6,319	18,288	5,711	7,268	15,537	5,393	1,260	6,807	1,234	2,977	17,558	5,998	17,671	16,306	1,273	4,126	9,241	8,405	1,738
Zashiversk, USSR	10,342	7,987	10,906	2,176	3,698	9,440	2,516	6,313	5,638	6,302	10,356	10,142	3,326	10,417	9,239	6,422	9,900	9,485	4,788	5,818
Zhengzhou, China	10,021	12,011	9,075	4,158	7,757	6,486	6,155	8,437	9,719	8,331	12,107	8,421	3,266	9,728	9,197	7,974	9,149	13,439	8,677	7,667
Zurich, Switzerland	16,856	6,749	17,321	4,800	6,932	14,610	4,756	922	6,810	774	3,931	16,606	5,027	17,077	15,774	307	4,209	9,721	8,194	905

Distances in Kilometers	Odessa, USSR	Ogbomosho, Nigeria	Okha, USSR	Okinawa (Naha)	Oklahoma City, Oklahoma	Old Crow, Canada	Olympia, Washington	Omaha, Nebraska	Omsk, USSR	Oodnadatta, Australia	Oradea, Romania	Oran, Algeria	Oranjestad, Aruba	Orebro, Sweden	Orel, USSR	Orsk, USSR	Osaka, Japan	Oslo, Norway	Osorno, Chile	Ostrava, Czechoslovakia
Ogbomosho, Nigeria	4,941	0	12,146	12,829	10,544	11,138	11,988	10,269	7,945	14,473	4,630	3,093	8,129	5,750	5,737	6,872	13,041	5,771	9,546	4,803
Okha, USSR	7,207	12,146	0	3,290	8,560	4,180	6,245	8,085	4,341	9,015	7,543	9,512	12,045	6,650	6,409	5,403	2,180	6,722	16,962	7,430
Okinawa (Naha)	8,443	12,829	3,290	0	11,694	7,444	9,261	11,287	5,401	6,008	9,016	11,271	15,316	8,710	7,829	6,347	1,201	8,880	17,523	9,095
Oklahoma City, Oklahoma	9,560	10,544	8,560	11,694	0	4,451	2,467	656	9,940	14,979	9,054	8,353	3,755	7,827	9,234	10,121	10,494	7,581	8,783	8,647
Old Crow, Canada	7,334	11,138	4,180	7,444	4,451	0	2,483	3,927	6,134	12,585	7,200	8,055	7,873	5,786	6,637	6,743	6,273	5,661	13,217	6,856
Olympia, Washington	9,331	11,988	6,245	9,261	2,467	2,483	0	2,231	8,592	13,047	9,032	9,188	6,219	7,616	8,749	9,117	8,063	7,426	10,882	8,640
Omaha, Nebraska	8,952	10,269	8,085	11,287	656	3,927	2,231	0	9,288	15,130	8,465	7,898	4,068	7,209	8,601	9,466	10,090	6,966	9,354	8,057
Omsk, USSR	3,103	7,945	4,341	5,401	9,940	6,134	8,592	9,288	0	10,884	3,628	5,873	11,779	3,440	2,431	1,077	5,196	3,656	17,081	3,694
Oodnadatta, Australia	13,267	14,473	9,015	6,008	14,979	12,585	13,047	15,130	10,884	0	13,942	15,801	16,892	14,306	13,013	11,498	6,886	14,534	11,908	14,219
Oradea, Romania	675	4,630	7,543	9,016	9,054	7,200	9,032	8,465	3,628	13,942	0	2,258	9,149	1,430	1,202	2,684	8,795	1,606	13,491	409
Oran, Algeria	2,870	3,093	9,512	11,271	8,353	8,055	9,188	7,898	5,873	15,801	2,258	0	7,356	2,864	3,442	4,941	10,988	2,815	11,233	2,193
Oranjestad, Aruba	9,818	8,129	12,045	15,316	3,755	7,873	6,219	4,068	11,779	16,892	9,149	7,356	0	8,550	9,958	11,388	14,133	8,297	5,886	8,836
Orebro, Sweden	1,759	5,750	6,650	8,710	7,827	5,786	7,616	7,209	3,440	14,306	1,430	2,864	8,550	0	1,471	2,842	8,239	262	13,682	1,070
Orel, USSR	814	5,737	6,409	7,829	9,234	6,637	8,749	8,601	2,431	13,013	1,202	3,442	9,958	1,471	0	1,547	7,594	1,732	14,669	1,282
Orsk, USSR	2,096	6,872	5,403	6,347	10,121	6,743	9,117	9,466	1,077	11,498	2,684	4,941	11,388	2,842	1,547	0	6,237	3,092	16,166	2,825
Osaka, Japan	8,299	13,041	2,180	1,201	10,494	6,273	8,063	10,090	5,196	6,886	8,795	10,988	14,133	8,239	7,594	6,237	0	8,371	17,424	8,798
Oslo, Norway	1,990	5,771	6,722	8,880	7,581	5,661	7,426	6,966	3,656	14,534	1,606	2,815	8,297	262	1,732	3,092	8,371	0	13,486	1,220
Osorno, Chile	14,071	9,546	16,962	17,523	8,783	13,217	10,882	9,354	17,081	11,908	13,491	11,233	5,886	13,682	14,669	16,166	17,424	13,486	0	13,394
Ostrava, Czechoslovakia	998	4,803	7,430	9,095	8,647	6,856	8,640	8,057	3,694	14,219	409	2,193	8,836	1,070	1,282	2,825	8,798	1,220	13,394	0
Ottawa, Canada	7,549	8,588	8,440	11,728	2,143	4,368	3,589	1,704	8,502	16,628	6,997	6,217	3,686	5,873	7,330	8,435	10,598	5,616	9,527	6,596
Ouagadougou, Bourkina Fasso	4,842	788	11,961	13,063	9,756	10,531	11,238	9,484	7,928	15,253	4,429	2,586	7,426	5,390	5,599	6,876	13,112	5,374	9,397	4,533
Oujda, Morocco	3,030	3,005	9,660	11,433	8,318	8,135	9,214	7,877	6,035	15,915	2,420	163	7,237	3,010	3,605	5,103	11,147	2,954	11,071	2,354
Oxford, United Kingdom	2,387	4,863	7,865	10,040	7,397	6,329	7,729	6,840	4,741	15,531	1,753	1,784	7,466	1,330	2,520	4,037	9,548	1,176	12,361	1,389
Pago Pago, American Samoa	15,918	19,144	8,712	8,033	9,459	9,414	8,293	9,811	12,941	5,745	16,185	17,435	11,485	14,984	15,114	14,016	7,849	14,936	9,615	15,977
Pakxe, Laos	7,665	11,006	5,354	2,584	13,893	9,450	11,591	13,372	5,228	5,705	8,332	10,465	16,915	8,607	7,321	5,794	3,678	8,843	17,182	8,562
Palembang, Indonesia	9,029	11,219	7,194	4,059	15,738	11,359	13,320	15,279	7,035	4,254	9,702	11,591	18,805	10,257	8,858	7,418	5,258	10,509	15,185	10,002
Palermo, Italy	1,701	3,445	8,755	10,140	9,197	8,071	9,621	8,674	4,796	14,567	1,216	1,275	8,591	2,358	2,401	3,796	9,986	2,432	12,373	1,360
Palma, Majorca	2,399	3,486	9,006	10,765	8,357	7,714	9,002	7,864	5,365	15,501	1,766	518	7,655	2,366	2,937	4,449	10,470	2,333	11,734	1,678
Palmerston North, New Zealand	17,122	16,335	10,869	8,884	12,218	12,538	11,434	12,690	14,275	3,934	17,784	19,399	12,964	17,495	16,674	15,134	9,270	17,590	8,672	17,956
Panama, Panama	10,802	9,203	12,011	15,137	3,459	7,857	5,876	3,931	12,482	15,817	10,143	8,436	1,111	9,425	10,869	12,226	13,938	9,166	5,523	9,809
Paramaribo, Suriname	9,229	6,567	13,207	16,446	5,432	9,182	7,856	5,639	11,776	17,356	8,560	6,464	1,792	8,344	9,579	11,116	15,386	8,121	5,457	8,330
Paris, France	2,137	4,519	8,064	10,082	7,777	6,709	8,139	7,229	4,721	15,380	1,473	1,483	7,682	1,428	2,394	3,938	9,660	1,344	12,363	1,162
Patna, India	5,295	8,715	5,649	4,244	13,237	9,028	11,484	12,599	3,403	7,981	5,969	8,039	15,010	6,459	5,062	3,627	4,907	6,713	17,410	6,238
Patrai, Greece	1,174	3,769	8,377	9,515	9,729	8,169	9,926	9,175	4,251	13,843	980	2,007	9,313	2,385	1,970	3,209	9,443	2,532	12,993	1,316
Peking, China	6,651	11,272	2,507	1,846	10,962	6,514	8,729	10,434	3,573	7,728	7,200	9,445	14,160	6,867	6,005	4,558	1,787	7,041	19,209	7,261
Penrhyn Island (Omoka)	15,769	18,090	8,866	8,913	8,030	8,617	7,117	8,425	13,207	7,239	15,785	16,275	10,021	14,397	14,971	14,260	8,486	14,278	8,939	15,465
Peoria, Illinois	8,689	9,751	8,417	11,661	902	4,237	2,745	544	9,278	15,673	8,169	7,461	3,661	6,971	8,398	9,366	10,474	6,720	9,152	7,763
Perm', USSR	2,143	7,079	5,080	6,487	9,359	6,013	8,361	8,704	1,104	11,959	2,589	4,804	10,802	2,349	1,389	772	6,207	2,575	15,980	2,614
Perth, Australia	12,158	12,523	9,828	6,557	16,926	13,848	14,830	17,012	10,450	1,957	12,802	14,232	17,774	13,586	12,137	10,779	7,654	13,845	11,925	13,156
Peshawar, Pakistan	3,689	7,419	5,863	5,411	12,226	8,438	10,912	11,571	2,336	9,582	4,364	6,445	13,454	4,935	3,499	2,179	5,779	5,194	16,833	4,641
Petropavlovsk-Kamchatskiy,USSR	7,926	12,810	1,048	3,932	7,772	3,573	5,375	7,355	5,236	9,204	8,181	9,974	11,400	7,130	7,114	6,267	2,736	7,159	15,929	8,014
Petrozavodsk, USSR	1,724	6,445	5,770	7,642	8,384	5,642	7,765	7,740	2,365	13,245	1,821	3,790	9,527	1,082	997	1,884	7,220	1,291	14,764	1,661
Pevek, USSR	6,707	11,303	2,269	5,558	6,436	1,985	4,326	5,908	4,675	11,142	6,800	8,293	9,789	5,557	5,910	5,514	4,435	5,532	15,183	6,552
Philadelphia, Pennsylvania	7,947	8,535	9,019	12,309	2,025	4,910	3,877	1,766	9,068	16,890	7,366	6,383	3,081	6,319	7,787	8,954	11,166	6,058	8,919	6,974
Phnom Penh, Kampuchea	7,877	10,986	5,746	2,886	14,293	9,852	11,976	13,776	5,550	5,439	8,549	10,637	17,287	8,894	7,575	6,065	4,016	9,135	16,784	8,797
Phoenix, Arizona	10,402	11,886	7,983	10,882	1,356	4,195	1,764	1,663	10,190	13,623	9,975	9,556	4,848	8,643	9,952	10,582	9,698	8,416	9,119	9,566
Pierre, South Dakota	8,857	10,526	7,603	10,795	1,015	3,458	1,774	493	8,976	14,765	8,409	8,018	4,561	7,101	8,452	9,222	9,599	6,867	9,794	7,999
Pinang, Malaysia	8,018	10,599	6,581	3,707	15,111	10,662	12,818	14,575	6,004	5,250	8,692	10,648	17,760	9,214	7,822	6,374	4,854	9,466	16,058	8,981
Pitcairn Island (Adamstown)	17,088	14,843	12,019	12,351	7,530	10,303	8,019	8,144	16,168	9,170	16,541	15,083	7,727	15,353	16,704	17,012	11,933	15,109	5,501	16,144
Pittsburgh, Pennsylvania	8,191	8,947	8,808	12,093	1,629	4,658	3,486	1,350	9,132	16,478	7,630	6,743	3,244	6,525	7,984	9,087	10,931	6,267	8,997	7,232
Plymouth, Montserrat	8,903	7,262	11,858	15,139	4,065	7,775	6,454	4,227	11,030	17,844	8,231	6,397	961	7,712	9,087	10,554	14,021	7,465	6,440	7,931
Plymouth, United Kingdom	2,591	4,750	8,077	10,287	7,287	6,410	7,720	6,745	4,992	15,773	1,941	1,657	7,243	1,578	2,759	4,283	9,783	1,415	12,111	1,597
Ponape Island	12,156	16,697	5,355	3,882	10,843	8,132	8,606	10,804	9,053	4,534	12,648	14,800	14,275	11,970	11,448	10,084	3,858	12,063	13,716	12,630
Ponce, Puerto Rico	9,123	7,725	11,586	14,876	3,607	7,455	6,022	3,806	11,078	17,532	8,457	6,719	711	7,840	9,250	10,677	13,726	7,587	6,521	8,138
Ponta Delgada, Azores	4,663	4,452	9,830	12,401	6,266	7,108	7,543	5,893	7,196	17,928	3,988	2,241	5,205	3,759	4,954	6,490	11,757	3,558	9,929	3,722
Pontianak, Indonesia	9,140	11,679	6,701	3,508	15,202	10,879	12,763	14,777	6,921	4,131	9,815	11,809	18,622	10,244	8,895	7,406	4,709	10,489	15,501	10,088
Port Augusta, Australia	13,783	14,532	9,548	6,586	14,976	12,989	13,233	15,210	11,468	592	14,456	16,200	16,426	14,881	13,565	12,062	7,439	15,113	11,316	14,750
Port Blair, India	6,948	9,675	6,414	4,001	14,683	10,280	12,612	14,081	5,104	6,324	7,622	9,571	16,740	8,197	6,781	5,371	5,015	8,452	16,513	7,918
Port Elizabeth, South Africa	8,923	5,175	14,725	12,644	14,884	16,151	17,007	14,900	10,862	9,974	8,982	8,181	11,290	10,379	9,679	9,972	13,715	10,494	8,300	9,310
Port Hedland, Australia	11,459	12,859	8,514	5,241	16,125	12,567	13,788	16,019	9,379	1,895	12,130	13,906	18,761	12,683	11,297	9,841	6,344	12,931	13,157	12,438
Port Louis, Mauritius	7,856	6,615	11,494	9,149	17,045	14,598	17,023	16,591	8,465	7,858	8,256	8,702	14,386	9,612	8,357	7,906	10,227	9,831	11,573	8,664
Port Moresby, Papua New Guinea	12,786	15,957	6,998	4,479	12,910	10,264	10,769	12,936	9,851	2,348	13,409	15,656	15,959	13,187	12,255	10,728	5,039	13,350	13,097	13,535
Port Said, Egypt	1,693	3,875	8,491	9,016	10,951	9,026	10,983	10,385	4,162	12,715	1,966	3,086	10,441	3,367	2,424	3,090	9,166	3,564	13,414	2,370
Port Sudan, Sudan	3,037	3,774	9,264	9,115	12,270	10,334	12,359	11,725	4,966	11,783	3,347	4,106	11,307	4,746	3,697	3,972	9,516	4,946	13,106	3,751
Port-au-Prince, Haiti	9,494	8,326	11,335	14,607	3,110	7,164	5,561	3,381	11,237	17,019	8,837	7,206	710	8,116	9,557	10,928	13,427	7,858	6,543	8,500
Port-of-Spain, Trin. & Tobago	9,331	7,218	12,523	15,808	4,557	8,421	6,992	4,784	11,608	17,438	8,656	6,705	952	8,242	9,576	11,074	14,681	8,001	5,796	8,380
Port-Vila, Vanuatu	14,995	17,999	8,266	6,556	11,506	10,351	9,918	11,757	11,915	3,535	15,542	17,740	13,759	14,907	14,340	12,899	6,760	14,988	10,968	15,557
Portland, Maine	7,369	8,146	8,778	12,056	2,496	4,765	4,063	2,125	8,546	17,102	6,790	5,863	3,451	5,743	7,212	8,397	10,948	5,482	9,332	6,397
Portland, Oregon	9,484	12,064	6,378	9,367	2,389	2,650	169	2,196	8,761	13,032	9,178	9,295	6,143	7,765	8,908	9,285	8,170	7,572	10,734	8,784
Porto, Portugal	3,187	3,873	9,162	11,296	7,445	7,275	8,284	6,981	5,932	16,423	2,515	922	6,718	2,609	3,572	5,119	10,846	2,478	11,150	2,297
Porto Alegre, Brazil	11,796	7,276	17,158	19,565	8,729	13,000	11,152	9,147	14,870	13,590	11,243	8,999	5,127	11,619	12,439	13,891	19,210	11,458	2,303	11,186
Porto Alexandre, Angola	7,152	2,779	14,063	13,320	12,759	13,907	14,612	12,643	9,737	12,275	7,036	5,853	9,547	8,329	7,962	8,697	14,058	8,395	8,471	7,299
Porto Novo, Benin	5,186	258	12,388	13,083	10,507	11,274	12,032	10,256	8,199	14,539	4,862	3,252	7,984	5,955	5,979	7,126	13,298	5,968	9,289	5,024
Porto Velho, Brazil	11,066	7,788	14,489	17,728	6,037	10,310	8,482	6,442	13,655	15,483	10,404	8,246	2,450	10,226	11,451	12,992	16,528	10,002	3,640	10,192
Portsmouth, United Kingdom	2,375	4,753	7,963	10,111	7,459	6,437	7,823	6,908	4,795	15,557	1,729	1,674	7,462	1,402	2,544	4,071	9,631	1,262	12,301	1,380
Poznan, Poland	1,195	5,045	7,236	9,023	8,390	6,557	8,342	7,792	3,636	14,298	694	2,319	8,713	772	1,291	2,833	8,674	919	13,445	302
Prague, Czechoslovakia	1,270	4,746	7,548	9,311	8,420	6,780	8,491	7,837	3,915	14,491	645	2,010	8,561	1,025	1,528	3,075	8,979	1,120	13,168	275
Praia, Cape Verde Islands	6,104	3,119	12,308	14,497	7,627	9,543	9,502	7,475	9,096	17,440	5,498	3,240	5,030	5,854	6,673	8,181	14,089	5,718	7,997	5,402
Pretoria, South Africa	8,001	4,555	13,892	12,118	14,773	15,285	16,542	14,658	9,931	10,258	8,088	7,446	11,423	9,499	8,749	9,030	13,107	9,627	9,077	8,429
Prince Albert, Canada	8,216	10,590	6,582	9,813	2,072	2,414	1,398	1,514	8,010	14,309	7,843	7,815	5,509	6,464	7,722	8,341	8,625	6,251	10,852	7,440
Prince Edward Island	10,333	6,919	14,843	12,058	16,134	17,664	18,559	16,329	11,741	8,375	10,492	9,897	12,383	11,918	11,028	11,015	13,240	12,062	8,191	10,850
Prince George, Canada	8,601	11,541	5,735	8,873	2,833	1,770	764	2,429	7,840	13,189	8,329	8,634	6,497	6,904	8,002	8,353	7,673	6,724	11,493	7,943
Prince Rupert, Canada	8,693	11,897	5,321	8,415	3,280	1,560	963	2,909	7,694	12,711	8,469	8,932	6,975	7,039	8,052	8,280	7,214	6,875	11,840	8,095
Providence, Rhode Island	7,576	8,225	8,938	12,222	2,367	4,891	4,066	2,046	8,770	17,112	6,992	6,014	3,250	5,959	7,429	8,621	11,104	5,698	9,126	6,601
Provo, Utah	9,703	11,558	7,412	10,436	1,350	3,493	1,179	1,325	9,441	13,805	9,302	9,041	5,093	7,946	9,228	9,830	9,239	7,725	9,761	8,895
Puerto Aisen, Chile	14,323	9,645	17,313	17,216	9,300	13,722	11,356	9,878	17,403	11,440	13,777	11,530	6,419	14,078	14,972	16,413	17,353	13,895	538	13,713
Puerto Deseado, Argentina	14,012	9,226	17,894	17,340	9,743	14,187	11,868	10,300	17,115	11,397	13,506	11,290	6,688	13,952	14,708	16,070	17,720	13,790	986	13,483
Puerto Princesa, Philippines	9,080	12,507	5,321	2,053	13,726	9,491	11,274	13,337	6,400	4,503	9,735	11,922	17,364	9,839	8,659	7,112	3,247	10,055	16,395	9,928
Punta Arenas, Chile	14,613	9,754	17,783	16,642	10,152	14,550	12,146	10,738	17,696	10,708	14,137	11,943	7,276	14,639	15,337	16,625	17,092	14,482	1,409	14,135
Pusan, South Korea	7,848	12,510	2,322	994	10,824	6,498	8,432	10,381	4,750	6,967	8,372	10,596	14,367	7,915	7,171	5,766	592	8,066	17,984	8,403
Pyongyang, North Korea	7,338	12,047	2,079	1,431	10,639	6,244	8,301	10,161	4,237	7,438	7,855	10,074	14,071	7,392	6,653	5,262	994	7,544	18,399	7,882
Qamdo, China	5,838	9,831	4,402	3,015	12,468	8,079	10,458	11,869	3,249	7,662	6,487	8,698	14,985	6,644	5,410	3,866	3,579	6,875	18,658	6,677
Qandahar, Afghanistan	3,414	6,847	6,435	5,989	12,377	8,804	11,254	11,723	2,671	9,870	4,084	6,057	13,232	4,830	3,362	2,257	6,384	5,092	16,227	4,399
Qiqian, China	6,145	11,038	1,491	2,942	9,603	5,153	7,455	9,056	3,094	8,949	6,588	8,738	12,759	5,967	5,396	4,170	2,272	6,100	18,336	6,559
Qom, Iran	2,143	5,586	7,122	7,259	11,578	8,635	10,935	10,945	2,851	11,242	2,781	4,641	11,895	3,773	2,344	1,940	7,492	4,029	15,122	3,139
Quebec, Canada	7,190	8,251	8,421	11,697	2,521	4,429	3,861	2,069	8,243	16,852	6,631	5,841	3,804	5,529	6,992	8,132	10,593	5,270	9,681	6,232
Quetta, Pakistan	3,604	6,945	6,466	5,902	12,555	8,935	11,393	11,901	2,802	9,685	4,273	6,229	13,422	5,025	3,557	2,435	6,336	5,286	16,261	4,591
Quito, Ecuador	11,490	9,225	12,977	16,001	4,418	8,849	6,778	4,924	13,418	15,268	10,818	8,932	1,690	10,239	11,648	13,073	14,818	9,985	4,501	10,515
Rabaul, Papua New Guinea	12,716	16,461	6,460	4,279	12,120	9,520	9,965	12,135	9,676	3,135	13,296	15,548	15,303	12,881	12,106	10,623	4,644	13,015	13,246	13,365
Raiatea (Uturoa)	16,701	17,228	9,973	9,951	8,107	9,397	7,619	8,589	14,310	7,535	16,586	16,450	9,518	15,158	15,937	15,354	9,582	15,000	7,842	16,219

Distances in Kilometers	Odessa, USSR	Ogbomosho, Nigeria	Okha, USSR	Okinawa (Naha)	Oklahoma City, Oklahoma	Old Crow, Canada	Olympia, Washington	Omaha, Nebraska	Omsk, USSR	Oodnadatta, Australia	Oradea, Romania	Oran, Algeria	Oranjestad, Aruba	Orebro, Sweden	Orel, USSR	Orsk, USSR	Osaka, Japan	Oslo, Norway	Osorno, Chile	Ostrava, Czechoslovakia
Raleigh, North Carolina	8,494	8,850	9,330	12,611	1,707	5,171	3,848	1,630	9,600	16,685	7,907	6,847	2,717	6,873	8,341	9,505	11,443	6,613	8,471	7,518
Rangiroa (Avatoru)	16,505	16,889	10,027	10,217	7,689	9,172	7,298	8,184	14,339	7,982	16,315	16,019	9,081	14,887	15,778	15,352	9,780	14,713	7,649	15,933
Rangoon, Burma	6,799	9,960	5,733	3,417	14,043	9,620	11,935	13,456	4,667	6,484	7,473	9,535	16,432	7,905	6,540	5,063	4,378	8,153	17,178	7,736
Raoul Is., Kermadec Islands	16,885	17,654	9,925	8,452	11,054	11,196	10,092	11,473	13,790	4,543	17,397	19,249	12,409	16,524	16,198	14,791	8,605	16,537	9,073	17,349
Rarotonga (Avarua)	17,047	17,780	9,935	9,422	9,078	9,980	8,415	9,538	14,238	6,537	17,131	17,430	10,485	15,757	16,234	15,314	9,219	15,640	8,233	16,823
Rawson, Argentina	13,687	8,998	17,670	17,790	9,324	13,775	11,508	9,867	16,780	11,884	13,153	10,915	6,201	13,521	14,352	15,773	18,002	13,350	733	13,104
Recife, Brazil	8,847	4,700	14,953	17,290	8,130	11,460	10,508	8,277	11,902	15,933	8,278	6,029	4,504	8,684	9,470	10,943	16,901	8,540	5,224	8,215
Regina, Canada	8,442	10,623	6,869	10,084	1,758	2,712	1,392	1,217	8,315	14,411	8,049	7,919	5,248	6,686	7,971	8,628	8,892	6,467	10,541	7,643
Reykjavik, Iceland	3,728	6,555	6,885	9,644	5,832	4,584	5,908	5,225	4,960	15,630	3,255	3,476	6,819	2,007	3,459	4,655	8,872	1,754	12,446	2,846
Rhodes, Greece	1,134	3,964	8,234	9,106	10,270	8,429	10,322	9,700	3,981	13,239	1,290	2,591	9,919	2,709	1,932	2,909	9,125	2,896	13,382	1,691
Richmond, Virginia	8,278	8,737	9,191	12,478	1,807	5,047	3,835	1,648	9,382	16,761	7,694	6,669	2,869	6,652	8,120	9,282	11,319	6,391	8,660	7,303
Riga, USSR	1,252	5,683	6,559	8,377	8,393	6,129	8,079	7,769	3,018	13,814	1,110	3,000	9,100	584	888	2,317	7,999	845	14,069	881
Ringkobing, Denmark	1,885	5,330	7,167	9,255	7,691	6,038	7,704	7,095	3,959	14,791	1,376	2,364	8,135	547	1,824	3,296	8,784	452	13,148	967
Rio Branco, Brazil	11,460	8,234	14,452	17,591	5,922	10,276	8,336	6,368	13,968	15,163	10,794	8,658	2,499	10,558	11,817	13,352	16,397	10,328	3,431	10,569
Rio Cuarto, Argentina	12,950	8,559	16,880	18,631	8,346	12,782	10,636	8,856	15,944	12,972	12,360	10,102	5,088	12,556	13,534	15,040	18,187	12,366	1,137	12,257
Rio de Janeiro, Brazil	10,675	6,208	16,561	19,037	8,629	12,615	11,096	8,951	13,754	14,421	10,126	7,887	4,887	10,549	11,324	12,770	18,695	10,400	3,419	10,077
Rio Gallegos, Argentina	14,434	9,593	17,846	16,847	10,039	14,456	12,075	10,617	17,527	10,908	13,949	11,749	7,107	14,436	15,151	16,462	17,283	14,278	1,267	13,941
Rio Grande, Brazil	12,010	7,449	17,332	19,359	8,853	13,160	11,259	9,286	15,090	13,362	11,463	9,222	5,288	11,851	12,660	14,103	19,261	11,691	2,109	11,410
Riyadh, Saudi Arabia	2,811	4,862	8,235	7,997	12,364	9,767	11,999	11,761	4,021	11,126	3,319	4,676	12,026	4,564	3,265	3,119	8,394	4,800	14,226	3,722
Road Town, Brit. Virgin Isls.	8,942	7,512	11,602	14,890	3,745	7,496	6,137	3,912	10,953	17,739	8,274	6,513	877	7,685	9,085	10,526	13,756	7,434	6,593	7,960
Roanoke, Virginia	8,448	8,958	9,131	12,410	1,586	4,969	3,661	1,454	9,470	16,548	7,872	6,882	2,915	6,805	8,270	9,403	11,241	6,546	8,647	7,479
Robinson Crusoe Island, Chile	14,050	9,880	16,063	17,345	7,895	12,313	9,962	8,479	16,808	12,330	13,419	11,181	5,193	13,374	14,536	16,082	16,871	13,153	922	13,257
Rochester, New York	7,834	8,739	8,612	11,902	1,908	4,500	3,540	1,530	8,787	16,584	7,277	6,444	3,474	6,164	7,622	8,728	10,757	5,906	9,284	6,878
Rockhampton, Australia	14,117	16,053	8,556	6,014	13,420	11,565	11,629	13,616	11,323	1,579	14,773	16,927	15,590	14,717	13,676	12,130	6,617	14,893	11,614	14,955
Rome, Italy	1,541	3,828	8,418	9,958	8,872	7,644	9,216	8,332	4,573	14,668	945	1,329	8,477	1,943	2,146	3,617	9,735	2,008	12,552	989
Rosario, Argentina	12,674	8,229	17,054	18,920	8,495	12,906	10,825	8,983	15,703	13,096	12,097	9,841	5,129	12,353	13,280	14,769	18,520	12,172	1,397	12,010
Roseau, Dominica	8,953	7,179	12,030	15,309	4,230	7,952	6,626	4,401	11,135	17,814	8,279	6,407	982	7,797	9,157	10,636	14,196	7,552	6,303	7,987
Rostock, East Germany	1,566	5,145	7,242	9,189	8,022	6,312	8,024	7,427	3,838	14,596	1,043	2,270	8,380	609	1,587	3,103	8,777	655	13,250	634
Rostov-na-Donu, USSR	689	5,479	6,705	7,772	9,900	7,273	9,423	9,272	2,484	12,619	1,345	3,558	10,433	2,093	683	1,439	7,672	2,350	14,741	1,602
Rotterdam, Netherlands	1,993	4,855	7,692	9,740	7,731	6,423	7,951	7,162	4,402	15,148	1,369	1,847	7,862	1,060	2,134	3,663	9,297	972	12,688	996
Rouyn, Canada	7,507	8,843	8,052	11,341	2,078	3,967	3,254	1,546	8,276	16,264	6,984	6,357	4,047	5,797	7,236	8,270	10,205	5,544	9,854	6,578
Sacramento, California	10,187	12,395	7,005	9,861	2,155	3,420	947	2,191	9,538	12,939	9,848	9,785	5,825	8,450	9,639	10,058	8,679	8,247	10,049	9,448
Saginaw, Michigan	8,158	9,250	8,367	11,647	1,460	4,206	3,053	1,022	8,888	16,084	7,627	6,907	3,678	6,452	7,892	8,914	10,480	6,199	9,366	7,223
Saint Denis, Reunion	7,861	6,451	11,686	9,372	16,928	14,706	17,097	16,506	8,578	8,024	8,241	8,608	14,172	9,612	8,386	7,989	10,445	9,826	11,383	8,647
Saint George's, Grenada	9,237	7,234	12,367	15,652	4,434	8,268	6,861	4,648	11,478	17,536	8,562	6,637	903	8,123	9,467	10,958	14,526	7,881	5,943	8,281
Saint John, Canada	6,998	7,833	8,712	11,968	2,860	4,792	4,297	2,457	8,256	17,277	6,415	5,493	3,650	5,386	6,856	8,069	10,891	5,125	9,534	6,023
Saint John's, Antigua	8,844	7,222	11,825	15,104	4,069	7,750	6,450	4,222	10,973	17,902	8,172	6,341	1,016	7,654	9,028	10,496	13,991	7,407	6,490	7,872
Saint John's, Canada	6,020	6,901	8,700	11,833	3,908	5,126	5,117	3,470	7,572	17,673	5,414	4,444	4,208	4,482	5,948	7,256	10,860	4,221	9,970	5,032
Saint Louis, Missouri	8,904	9,838	8,593	11,822	737	4,417	2,808	578	9,514	15,637	8,377	7,617	3,512	7,192	8,623	9,601	10,630	6,940	8,938	7,972
Saint Paul, Minnesota	8,482	9,952	7,865	11,110	1,114	3,685	2,306	471	8,855	15,333	8,000	7,490	4,210	6,738	8,131	9,008	9,924	6,496	9,679	7,591
Saint Peter Port, UK	2,486	4,624	8,137	10,288	7,437	6,545	7,873	6,897	4,966	15,703	1,828	1,535	7,337	1,581	2,694	4,228	9,811	1,441	12,128	1,499
Saipan (Susupe)	10,605	15,057	4,269	2,240	11,322	7,799	8,896	11,120	7,514	4,852	11,139	13,361	15,037	10,631	9,938	8,514	2,392	10,761	15,329	11,168
Salalah, Oman	3,915	5,489	8,429	7,591	13,474	10,558	12,906	12,859	4,528	10,056	4,451	5,762	13,073	5,650	4,285	3,815	8,186	5,894	14,352	4,851
Salem, Oregon	9,557	12,128	6,402	9,374	2,399	2,705	234	2,226	8,821	12,986	9,252	9,365	6,153	7,838	8,980	9,351	8,179	7,646	10,699	8,858
Salt Lake City, Utah	9,659	11,552	7,355	10,385	1,387	3,432	1,125	1,335	9,382	13,795	9,261	9,018	5,135	7,902	9,179	9,775	9,187	7,682	9,821	8,854
Salta, Argentina	12,419	8,380	16,039	18,707	7,479	11,892	9,822	7,967	15,266	13,799	11,793	9,550	4,157	11,831	12,925	14,467	17,729	11,625	1,893	11,644
Salto, Uruguay	12,368	7,928	17,030	19,223	8,479	12,856	10,846	8,945	15,405	13,330	11,794	9,539	5,026	12,071	12,979	14,464	18,718	11,894	1,703	11,711
Salvador, Brazil	9,519	5,276	15,501	17,962	8,201	11,811	10,635	8,416	12,576	15,474	8,952	6,703	4,479	9,344	10,145	11,615	17,530	9,195	4,552	8,888
Salzburg, Austria	1,348	4,474	7,821	9,542	8,496	7,009	8,663	7,926	4,141	14,613	676	1,755	8,473	1,286	1,727	3,267	9,233	1,357	12,947	447
Samsun, Turkey	731	4,846	7,383	8,244	10,290	7,930	10,008	9,681	3,101	12,698	1,316	3,259	10,427	2,482	1,293	2,026	8,240	2,718	14,254	1,693
San Antonio, Texas	10,178	10,793	9,082	12,132	680	5,039	2,874	1,335	10,619	14,789	9,651	8,808	3,486	8,459	9,881	10,796	10,935	8,209	8,179	9,247
San Cristobal, Venezuela	10,369	8,421	12,450	15,681	4,007	8,270	6,469	4,394	12,355	16,376	9,697	7,852	578	9,124	10,526	11,963	14,483	8,872	5,352	9,392
San Diego, California	10,664	12,353	7,756	10,553	1,836	4,147	1,664	2,101	10,234	13,143	10,270	9,963	5,281	8,908	10,171	10,700	9,382	8,690	9,289	9,863
San Francisco, California	10,298	12,511	7,018	9,842	2,236	3,489	1,030	2,295	9,615	12,837	9,963	9,907	5,881	8,563	9,745	10,147	8,664	8,361	10,022	9,563
San Jose, Costa Rica	11,042	9,685	11,696	14,746	3,141	7,583	5,500	3,666	12,509	15,453	10,394	8,787	1,560	9,587	11,049	12,342	13,554	9,326	5,703	10,044
San Juan, Argentina	13,139	8,881	16,507	18,344	8,015	12,463	10,266	8,543	16,052	12,992	12,529	10,275	4,877	12,625	13,681	15,211	17,764	12,422	1,085	12,399
San Juan, Puerto Rico	9,051	7,670	11,554	14,844	3,618	7,431	6,024	3,804	11,012	17,602	8,384	6,648	781	7,769	9,179	10,607	13,699	7,517	6,576	8,065
San Luis Potosi, Mexico	10,994	11,225	9,632	12,527	1,517	5,717	3,390	2,172	11,440	14,341	10,452	9,483	3,450	9,287	10,717	11,638	11,350	9,035	7,518	10,051
San Marino, San Marino	1,460	4,045	8,221	9,828	8,730	7,424	9,019	8,181	4,432	14,671	818	1,443	8,458	1,720	2,001	3,502	9,574	1,784	12,676	793
San Miguel de Tucuman, Argen.	12,555	8,425	16,245	18,746	7,687	12,107	10,017	8,181	15,440	13,598	11,936	9,687	4,383	12,012	13,080	14,616	17,864	11,809	1,691	11,798
San Salvador, El Salvador	11,061	10,177	11,069	14,066	2,554	7,003	4,844	3,128	12,218	15,159	10,437	9,009	2,082	9,507	10,977	12,169	12,880	9,245	6,232	10,067
Sanaa, Yemen	3,671	4,419	9,214	8,637	13,089	10,803	12,976	12,523	5,065	10,912	4,076	4,983	12,159	5,423	4,229	4,179	9,174	5,642	13,410	4,485
Santa Cruz, Bolivia	11,718	7,946	15,446	18,567	6,922	11,267	9,331	7,366	14,488	14,604	11,077	8,854	3,437	11,049	12,185	13,731	17,387	10,838	2,699	10,906
Santa Cruz, Tenerife	4,528	3,112	10,699	12,838	7,503	8,384	8,893	7,179	7,446	17,251	3,891	1,675	5,832	4,178	5,038	6,568	12,416	4,047	9,637	3,758
Santa Fe, New Mexico	9,931	11,273	8,117	11,147	765	4,143	1,891	1,066	9,957	14,222	9,474	8,964	4,421	8,176	9,527	10,262	9,950	7,941	9,085	9,065
Santa Rosa, Argentina	13,188	8,680	17,192	18,400	8,692	13,136	10,952	9,213	16,227	12,609	12,616	10,361	5,472	12,875	13,802	15,285	18,225	12,691	888	12,533
Santa Rosalia, Mexico	11,029	12,153	8,516	11,287	1,670	4,844	2,378	2,148	10,868	13,423	10,578	10,017	4,690	9,272	10,604	11,261	10,124	9,039	8,535	10,169
Santarem, Brazil	9,855	6,650	14,111	17,361	6,119	10,046	8,578	6,393	12,554	16,515	9,199	7,019	2,368	9,114	10,275	11,823	16,285	8,902	4,614	9,005
Santiago del Estero, Argentina	12,556	8,367	16,384	18,834	7,826	12,242	10,159	8,317	15,473	13,532	11,944	9,691	4,502	12,052	13,097	14,627	17,998	11,853	1,635	11,815
Santiago, Chile	13,430	9,132	16,551	18,084	8,128	12,579	10,333	8,673	16,344	12,715	12,821	10,566	5,087	12,914	13,974	15,504	17,614	12,710	820	12,692
Santo Domingo, Dominican Rep.	9,326	8,069	11,429	14,713	3,308	7,272	5,744	3,545	11,157	17,248	8,664	6,990	659	7,984	9,414	10,809	13,544	7,728	6,544	8,334
Sao Paulo de Olivenca, Brazil	11,018	8,212	13,744	16,943	5,248	9,564	7,687	5,671	13,361	15,709	10,345	8,289	1,771	9,994	11,309	12,821	15,742	9,756	4,134	10,091
Sao Paulo, Brazil	10,960	6,549	16,576	19,377	8,451	12,535	10,914	8,801	14,023	14,348	10,398	8,150	4,734	10,767	11,592	13,057	18,754	10,608	3,117	10,335
Sao Tome, Sao Tome & Principe	5,622	905	12,805	13,056	11,279	12,040	12,851	11,051	8,511	13,788	5,385	3,989	8,572	6,579	6,433	7,435	13,442	6,617	9,181	5,595
Sapporo, Japan	7,970	12,876	1,175	2,243	9,465	5,214	7,056	9,045	4,932	7,840	8,386	10,473	13,077	7,638	7,207	6,008	1,060	7,737	17,162	8,326
Sarajevo, Yugoslavia	1,011	4,188	7,993	9,436	9,100	7,516	9,246	8,533	4,061	14,193	452	1,859	8,935	1,733	1,646	3,091	9,239	1,863	13,076	667
Saratov, USSR	1,251	6,139	6,039	7,209	9,727	6,782	9,026	9,083	1,852	12,318	1,813	4,071	10,639	2,107	695	872	7,049	2,368	15,302	1,958
Saskatoon, Canada	8,350	10,689	6,637	9,854	1,984	2,480	1,300	1,450	8,131	14,259	7,976	7,931	5,475	6,598	7,856	8,470	8,662	6,385	10,768	7,573
Schefferville, Canada	6,392	8,064	7,685	10,922	3,183	3,900	3,923	2,614	7,304	16,485	5,872	5,379	4,699	4,686	6,131	7,216	9,865	4,432	10,585	5,466
Seattle, Washington	9,260	11,918	6,232	9,264	2,453	2,438	75	2,197	8,539	13,101	8,959	9,115	6,201	7,544	8,680	9,056	8,065	7,353	10,907	8,567
Sendai, Japan	8,337	13,193	1,710	1,822	9,875	5,696	7,439	9,481	5,260	7,306	8,784	10,913	13,534	8,099	7,593	6,327	625	8,209	17,100	8,746
Seoul, South Korea	7,527	12,219	2,159	1,260	10,709	6,337	8,350	10,244	4,426	7,262	8,047	10,268	14,185	7,586	6,845	5,448	830	7,738	18,253	8,075
Sept-Iles, Canada	6,674	7,943	8,181	11,428	2,990	4,324	4,080	2,488	7,761	16,887	6,121	5,413	4,192	5,010	6,472	7,624	10,361	4,751	10,077	5,720
Sevastopol, USSR	301	4,931	7,236	8,321	9,859	7,554	9,593	9,249	3,044	13,011	941	3,048	10,089	2,048	944	1,998	8,233	2,284	14,191	1,290
Seville, Spain	3,175	3,401	9,494	11,467	7,847	7,742	8,751	7,402	6,071	16,270	2,525	514	6,889	2,871	3,661	5,194	11,094	2,774	11,014	2,381
Shanghai, China	7,623	12,050	3,036	821	11,592	7,207	9,231	11,121	4,591	6,663	8,199	10,455	15,027	7,932	7,015	5,527	1,378	8,111	18,343	8,285
Sheffield, United Kingdom	2,415	5,043	7,704	9,923	7,299	6,153	7,578	6,733	4,654	15,482	1,803	1,964	7,478	1,221	2,486	3,984	9,409	1,044	12,461	1,421
Shenyang, China	6,989	11,733	1,951	1,771	10,487	6,060	8,196	9,986	3,886	7,777	7,499	9,714	13,835	7,026	6,297	4,921	1,317	7,179	18,626	7,521
Shiraz, Iran	2,660	5,562	7,444	7,271	12,149	9,181	11,504	11,519	3,277	10,854	3,270	4,974	12,301	4,333	2,918	2,451	7,619	4,586	15,005	3,645
Sibiu, Romania	514	4,589	7,565	8,934	9,274	7,361	9,228	8,684	3,566	13,760	221	2,361	9,343	1,615	1,171	2,588	8,752	1,804	13,578	627
Singapore	8,618	11,054	6,814	3,757	15,374	10,959	12,995	14,885	6,564	4,650	9,293	11,235	18,341	9,807	8,421	6,965	4,944	10,057	15,644	9,582
Sioux Falls, South Dakota	8,777	10,269	7,842	11,055	896	3,677	2,078	258	9,044	15,059	8,305	7,820	4,286	7,027	8,406	9,240	9,860	6,788	9,612	7,896
Skelleftea, Sweden	2,123	6,422	5,979	8,150	7,682	5,242	7,216	7,043	3,027	13,900	1,972	3,540	8,802	680	1,574	2,629	7,619	754	14,178	1,670
Skopje, Yugoslavia	889	4,116	8,035	9,325	9,422	7,753	9,535	8,853	3,992	13,925	564	2,036	9,215	1,971	1,632	2,982	9,187	2,125	13,188	905
Socotra Island (Tamrida)	4,340	5,463	8,816	7,786	13,897	11,038	13,386	13,291	4,993	9,834	4,850	6,021	13,256	6,087	4,743	4,295	8,451	6,327	14,035	5,254
Sofia, Bulgaria	723	4,258	7,890	9,156	9,475	7,697	9,524	8,899	3,826	13,784	499	2,200	9,348	1,929	1,482	2,814	9,022	2,100	13,357	884
Songkhla, Thailand	7,894	10,598	6,394	3,557	14,916	10,466	12,634	14,377	5,827	5,373	8,569	10,553	17,596	9,060	7,678	6,219	4,691	9,310	16,257	8,850
Sorong, Indonesia	10,887	14,105	6,132	3,023	13,696	10,049	11,279	13,503	8,108	2,985	11,535	13,738	17,352	11,538	10,434	8,887	3,960	11,738	14,797	11,712
South Georgia Island	12,843	7,905	19,927	16,641	11,518	15,902	13,828	11,995	15,693	10,911	12,513	10,552	8,038	13,415	13,642	14,635	17,747	13,344	3,092	12,628
South Pole	15,152	10,904	15,939	12,902	13,931	17,499	15,214	14,574	16,100	6,952	15,219	13,956	11,387	16,578	15,869	15,678	13,839	16,649	5,510	15,526

Distances in Kilometers	Odessa, USSR	Ogbomosho, Nigeria	Okha, USSR	Okinawa (Naha)	Oklahoma City, Oklahoma	Old Crow, Canada	Olympia, Washington	Omaha, Nebraska	Omsk, USSR	Oodnadatta, Australia	Oradea, Romania	Oran, Algeria	Oranjestad, Aruba	Orebro, Sweden	Orel, USSR	Orsk, USSR	Osaka, Japan	Oslo, Norway	Osorno, Chile	Ostrava, Czechoslovakia
South Sandwich Islands	12,699	7,817	19,201	15,957	12,259	16,615	14,576	12,727	15,347	10,404	12,446	10,635	8,742	13,486	13,512	14,329	17,111	13,450	3,798	12,611
Split, Yugoslavia	1,173	4,096	8,105	9,589	9,004	7,525	9,207	8,444	4,208	14,351	584	1,699	8,781	1,756	1,786	3,247	9,379	1,865	12,921	716
Spokane, Washington	9,126	11,599	6,486	9,568	2,130	2,557	420	1,837	8,580	13,467	8,793	8,843	5,864	7,391	8,578	9,041	8,367	7,190	10,707	8,395
Spoleto, Italy	1,484	3,922	8,327	9,887	8,829	7,557	9,145	8,285	4,498	14,649	871	1,391	8,490	1,849	2,068	3,550	9,654	1,917	12,621	897
Springbok, South Africa	8,530	4,430	14,892	13,216	14,032	15,539	16,142	14,032	10,770	10,844	8,508	7,491	10,496	9,861	9,318	9,806	14,209	9,950	8,017	8,806
Springfield, Illinois	8,771	9,771	8,502	11,741	842	4,323	2,786	563	9,377	15,676	8,247	7,513	3,585	7,056	8,486	9,461	10,551	6,805	9,056	7,842
Springfield, Massachusetts	7,626	8,325	8,875	12,161	2,276	4,814	3,964	1,946	8,773	17,010	7,046	6,097	3,288	5,997	7,465	8,641	11,037	5,737	9,156	6,653
Srinagar, India	3,934	7,720	5,643	5,110	12,261	8,366	10,847	11,607	2,327	9,348	4,608	6,716	13,656	5,114	3,699	2,311	5,492	5,371	17,112	4,871
Stanley, Falkland Islands	13,762	8,870	18,599	17,138	10,405	14,856	12,575	10,944	16,815	11,130	13,318	11,169	7,211	13,943	14,510	15,739	17,835	13,811	1,705	13,347
Stara Zagora, Bulgaria	606	4,338	7,809	9,002	9,628	7,747	9,621	9,046	3,697	13,592	594	2,381	9,541	2,009	1,404	2,669	8,893	2,196	13,510	1,000
Stockholm, Sweden	1,661	5,799	6,555	8,569	7,951	5,812	7,688	7,328	3,284	14,146	1,389	2,957	8,711	161	1,323	2,681	8,114	417	13,832	1,058
Stornoway, United Kingdom	2,798	5,631	7,306	9,727	6,798	5,542	6,971	6,213	4,621	15,504	2,256	2,539	7,301	1,250	2,694	4,089	9,118	997	12,569	1,850
Strasbourg, France	1,740	4,496	7,926	9,802	8,129	6,840	8,388	7,569	4,415	14,995	1,074	1,588	8,078	1,286	2,042	3,590	9,434	1,276	12,666	779
Stuttgart, West Germany	1,635	4,528	7,860	9,707	8,203	6,844	8,426	7,639	4,316	14,887	970	1,659	8,184	1,234	1,938	3,485	9,349	1,245	12,765	672
Subic, Philippines	8,787	12,524	4,729	1,474	13,165	8,902	10,723	12,760	5,989	4,975	9,426	11,652	16,774	9,425	8,312	6,766	2,673	9,632	16,880	9,591
Suchow, China	7,097	11,558	2,947	1,346	11,486	7,053	9,192	10,980	4,070	7,108	7,675	9,931	14,772	7,428	6,492	5,002	1,681	7,611	18,868	7,763
Sucre, Bolivia	11,974	8,197	15,478	18,476	6,927	11,308	9,310	7,393	14,721	14,391	11,330	9,112	3,528	11,280	12,432	13,979	17,335	11,066	2,503	11,155
Sudbury, Canada	7,750	8,998	8,163	11,452	1,843	4,042	3,162	1,335	8,502	16,203	7,224	6,563	3,906	6,041	7,480	8,508	10,303	5,788	9,676	6,819
Suez, Egypt	1,838	3,813	8,596	9,056	11,078	9,172	11,128	10,516	4,261	12,646	2,107	3,156	10,507	3,512	2,565	3,193	9,232	3,708	13,358	2,511
Sundsvall, Sweden	1,966	6,113	6,300	8,435	7,707	5,470	7,369	7,077	3,243	14,127	1,730	3,219	8,645	364	1,529	2,749	7,926	447	13,921	1,399
Surabaya, Indonesia	9,982	12,157	7,313	4,038	15,625	11,481	13,158	15,292	7,803	3,285	10,657	12,590	19,354	11,124	9,763	8,284	5,220	11,369	14,676	10,941
Suva, Fiji	15,697	18,738	8,640	7,361	10,646	10,094	9,297	10,962	12,596	4,507	16,149	18,056	12,696	15,239	14,964	13,631	7,400	15,261	10,189	16,069
Sverdlovsk, USSR	2,341	7,253	4,931	6,222	9,566	6,101	8,484	8,911	825	11,668	2,825	5,058	11,085	2,640	1,623	643	5,974	2,866	16,256	2,874
Svobodnyy, USSR	6,609	11,521	1,032	2,796	9,402	4,959	7,171	8,884	3,585	8,775	7,029	9,143	12,710	6,335	5,847	4,662	1,951	6,452	17,985	6,980
Sydney, Australia	14,889	15,592	9,721	7,101	13,861	12,616	12,390	14,177	12,306	1,660	15,563	17,450	15,233	15,742	14,566	13,026	7,763	15,941	10,595	15,812
Sydney, Canada	6,578	7,402	8,739	11,952	3,327	4,955	4,673	2,912	7,978	17,529	5,983	5,026	3,843	5,000	6,471	7,731	10,917	4,738	9,692	5,596
Syktyvkar, USSR	2,123	7,044	5,106	6,788	8,863	5,641	7,939	8,208	1,507	12,391	2,446	4,575	10,316	1,950	1,312	1,258	6,413	2,155	15,631	2,391
Szeged, Hungary	813	4,491	7,691	9,178	9,018	7,269	9,059	8,436	3,790	14,071	162	2,097	9,031	1,486	1,363	2,844	8,956	1,641	13,329	421
Szombathely, Hungary	1,079	4,490	7,741	9,353	8,744	7,121	8,845	8,168	3,953	14,345	404	1,920	8,748	1,344	1,524	3,046	9,084	1,463	13,146	314
Tabriz, Iran	1,582	5,362	7,108	7,549	11,049	8,279	10,514	10,422	2,771	11,774	2,223	4,147	11,352	3,230	1,828	1,748	7,680	3,483	14,899	2,578
Tacheng, China	3,925	8,493	4,222	4,527	10,896	6,830	9,313	10,252	1,135	9,775	4,526	6,782	12,912	4,533	3,378	1,843	4,547	4,759	17,983	4,660
Tahiti (Papeete)	16,796	17,012	10,155	10,168	8,036	9,471	7,635	8,533	14,489	7,682	16,639	16,357	9,349	15,209	16,048	15,524	9,793	15,041	7,630	16,261
Taipei, Taiwan	8,091	12,304	3,635	633	12,153	7,815	9,752	11,709	5,126	6,010	8,693	10,950	15,667	8,517	7,527	6,009	1,719	8,705	17,819	8,807
Taiyuan, China	6,522	11,033	2,903	1,921	11,314	6,863	9,110	10,774	3,493	7,626	7,098	9,354	14,421	6,863	5,914	4,427	2,087	7,051	19,443	7,186
Tallahassee, Florida	9,286	9,423	9,648	12,877	1,355	5,469	3,776	1,599	10,301	16,163	8,698	7,587	2,469	7,658	9,124	10,258	11,684	7,397	7,945	8,309
Tallinn, USSR	1,495	5,947	6,320	8,226	8,229	5,861	7,841	7,598	2,913	13,766	1,387	3,214	9,087	542	1,007	2,302	7,807	790	14,193	1,144
Tamanrasset, Algeria	3,469	1,627	10,611	11,762	9,670	9,587	10,709	9,277	6,559	14,991	3,069	1,551	8,020	4,126	4,229	5,513	11,749	4,145	10,726	3,203
Tampa, Florida	9,387	9,275	9,974	13,206	1,651	5,794	4,092	1,927	10,530	16,307	8,784	7,569	2,142	7,794	9,264	10,444	12,013	7,533	7,646	8,401
Tampere, Finland	1,733	6,135	6,174	8,180	8,029	5,624	7,606	7,394	2,926	13,806	1,611	3,342	8,992	531	1,208	2,399	7,718	730	14,209	1,343
Tanami, Australia	12,272	14,025	8,247	5,116	15,117	12,060	12,917	15,118	9,866	1,022	12,947	14,895	17,767	13,284	11,996	10,477	6,079	13,513	12,898	13,212
Tangier, Morocco	3,253	3,231	9,656	11,587	7,950	7,915	8,900	7,517	6,187	16,268	2,614	467	6,890	3,024	3,768	5,293	11,235	2,935	10,902	2,493
Tarawa (Betio)	13,554	18,387	6,411	5,568	9,887	8,184	7,970	10,002	10,493	5,128	13,947	15,850	12,914	13,005	12,785	11,559	5,355	13,037	12,113	13,841
Tashkent, USSR	3,119	7,339	5,456	5,551	11,392	7,683	10,141	10,736	1,549	10,222	3,780	5,965	12,736	4,186	2,796	1,371	5,721	4,441	16,885	4,010
Tbilisi, USSR	1,239	5,443	6,895	7,563	10,634	7,882	10,099	10,005	2,559	12,045	1,906	3,957	11,055	2,824	1,406	1,493	7,609	3,079	14,923	2,233
Tegucigalpa, Honduras	10,895	9,959	11,131	14,173	2,584	7,034	4,927	3,131	12,134	15,371	10,266	8,807	1,870	9,361	10,831	12,050	12,981	9,099	6,224	9,899
Tehran, Iran	2,103	5,671	7,005	7,182	11,497	8,519	10,826	10,862	2,729	11,247	2,751	4,655	11,882	3,705	2,264	1,818	7,397	3,962	15,213	3,101
Tel Aviv, Israel	1,636	4,118	8,284	8,767	11,027	8,948	10,962	10,449	3,947	12,522	1,992	3,282	10,636	3,358	2,319	2,881	8,924	3,568	13,660	2,401
Telegraph Creek, Canada	8,316	11,661	5,048	8,202	3,516	1,162	1,330	3,087	7,294	12,751	8,109	8,657	7,148	6,679	7,665	7,877	7,005	6,522	12,170	7,740
Teresina, Brazil	9,172	5,428	14,604	17,461	7,259	10,823	9,672	7,446	12,118	16,389	8,558	6,305	3,586	8,757	9,716	11,241	16,724	8,583	4,962	8,436
Ternate, Indonesia	10,457	13,650	6,022	2,813	13,872	10,041	11,425	13,628	7,731	3,254	11,111	13,298	17,601	11,170	10,027	8,479	3,843	11,377	15,141	11,300
The Valley, Anguilla	8,859	7,349	11,690	14,973	3,903	7,602	6,284	4,056	10,929	17,856	8,189	6,396	967	7,634	9,022	10,477	13,851	7,385	6,573	7,881
Thessaloniki, Greece	903	4,048	8,098	9,295	9,615	7,919	9,722	9,047	3,997	13,783	719	2,129	9,363	2,144	1,689	2,967	9,193	2,306	13,217	1,085
Thimphu, Bhutan	5,510	9,155	5,187	3,759	12,988	8,692	11,123	12,363	3,324	7,814	6,179	8,313	15,070	6,546	5,200	3,705	4,401	6,793	17,881	6,420
Thunder Bay, Canada	8,002	9,603	7,684	10,959	1,584	3,517	2,503	951	8,431	15,542	7,522	7,060	4,361	6,258	7,653	8,552	9,789	6,015	9,984	7,113
Tientsin, China	6,759	11,368	2,525	1,734	11,009	6,564	8,758	10,487	3,684	7,622	7,310	9,557	14,238	6,979	6,115	4,666	1,701	7,153	19,124	7,373
Tijuana, Mexico	10,678	12,350	7,780	10,575	1,829	4,169	1,687	2,101	10,255	13,150	10,282	9,968	5,264	8,922	10,186	10,719	9,405	8,703	9,266	9,875
Tiksi, USSR	5,454	10,287	2,124	5,047	7,588	3,243	5,709	6,998	3,163	11,009	5,664	7,467	10,567	4,610	4,640	4,044	4,129	4,654	16,340	5,486
Timbuktu, Mali	4,530	1,240	11,563	12,875	9,342	10,019	10,751	9,043	7,632	15,608	4,068	2,111	7,203	4,948	5,258	6,600	12,829	4,918	9,617	4,138
Tindouf, Algeria	3,978	2,530	10,580	12,403	8,229	8,710	9,468	7,870	7,008	16,453	3,387	1,137	6,620	3,940	4,577	6,064	12,119	3,858	10,105	3,329
Tirane, Albania	1,044	3,986	8,171	9,481	9,374	7,808	9,547	8,813	4,145	14,052	659	1,886	9,092	2,022	1,775	3,138	9,339	2,160	13,032	952
Tokyo, Japan	8,480	13,291	2,001	1,560	10,149	5,992	7,705	9,764	5,387	7,015	8,948	11,104	13,822	8,311	7,751	6,445	405	8,428	17,106	8,926
Toledo, Spain	2,894	3,611	9,179	11,148	7,855	7,528	8,639	7,385	5,754	16,067	2,234	550	7,086	2,548	3,352	4,890	10,769	2,457	11,328	2,070
Topeka, Kansas	9,141	10,296	8,311	11,497	427	4,161	2,374	249	9,531	15,161	8,642	8,003	3,877	7,405	8,808	9,697	10,299	7,159	9,109	8,234
Toronto, Canada	7,892	8,881	8,502	11,791	1,796	4,376	3,386	1,390	8,772	16,430	7,345	6,558	3,567	6,209	7,661	8,740	10,640	5,952	9,350	6,944
Toulouse, France	2,317	3,940	8,631	10,534	8,027	7,255	8,576	7,513	5,140	15,559	1,647	895	7,571	1,982	2,741	4,282	10,171	1,922	11,943	1,458
Tours, France	2,277	4,364	8,264	10,285	7,757	6,834	8,200	7,222	4,918	15,538	1,605	1,302	7,545	1,633	2,576	4,122	9,865	1,542	12,164	1,323
Townsville, Australia	13,525	15,809	8,076	5,439	13,529	11,284	11,575	13,655	10,729	1,477	14,179	16,351	16,028	14,130	13,079	11,533	6,086	14,312	12,206	14,358
Trenton, New Jersey	7,902	8,502	9,003	12,293	2,062	4,900	3,893	1,793	9,029	16,913	7,321	6,340	3,105	6,274	7,742	8,911	11,153	6,013	8,949	6,929
Tripoli, Lebanon	1,404	4,349	8,012	8,569	10,878	8,689	10,734	10,289	3,680	12,512	1,824	3,312	10,646	3,150	2,054	2,610	8,692	3,368	13,878	2,233
Tripoli, Libya	2,120	2,892	9,275	10,487	9,557	8,638	10,123	9,063	5,218	14,508	1,739	1,308	8,641	2,937	2,880	4,183	10,413	3,009	12,019	1,927
Tristan da Cunha (Edinburgh)	10,200	5,292	17,366	16,075	11,905	15,324	14,358	12,146	13,028	12,104	9,922	8,144	8,153	10,975	11,009	11,963	17,119	10,954	5,194	10,084
Trondheim, Norway	2,271	6,155	6,397	8,668	7,354	5,279	7,090	6,728	3,557	14,434	1,955	3,174	8,294	527	1,889	3,108	8,106	390	13,646	1,585
Trujillo, Peru	12,173	9,414	13,727	16,563	5,202	9,651	7,487	5,739	14,263	14,599	11,497	9,501	2,490	11,019	12,396	13,861	15,430	10,770	3,642	11,219
Truk Island (Moen)	11,691	16,045	5,179	3,300	11,364	8,333	9,049	11,272	8,599	4,255	12,223	14,436	14,898	11,674	11,021	9,599	3,451	11,793	14,248	12,244
Truro, Canada	6,822	7,620	8,763	12,001	3,077	4,900	4,492	2,675	8,159	17,433	6,231	5,278	3,698	5,229	6,700	7,940	10,943	4,968	9,569	5,842
Tsingtao, China	7,188	11,751	2,620	1,297	11,172	6,751	8,860	10,676	4,119	7,219	7,744	9,992	14,519	7,415	6,550	5,092	1,387	7,587	18,745	7,809
Tsitsihar, China	6,638	11,485	1,508	2,370	9,943	5,500	7,705	9,425	3,552	8,377	7,107	9,283	13,229	6,534	5,909	4,617	1,709	6,672	18,456	7,096
Tubuai Island (Mataura)	17,442	16,756	10,700	10,469	8,509	10,115	8,242	9,035	15,041	7,446	17,267	16,728	9,509	15,838	16,691	16,095	10,192	15,663	7,238	16,881
Tucson, Arizona	10,483	11,841	8,155	11,048	1,297	4,356	1,934	1,668	10,332	13,691	10,043	9,567	4,707	8,725	10,049	10,708	9,866	8,494	8,949	9,634
Tulsa, Oklahoma	9,419	10,387	8,573	11,732	162	4,442	2,535	569	9,853	15,128	8,908	8,191	3,685	7,690	9,104	10,011	10,531	7,443	8,809	8,501
Tunis, Tunisia	2,012	3,231	9,013	10,454	9,071	8,161	9,612	8,567	5,100	14,835	1,497	979	8,324	2,526	2,693	4,108	10,285	2,571	12,060	1,588
Tura, USSR	4,543	9,484	2,666	4,667	8,834	4,621	7,102	8,214	1,812	10,633	4,906	6,985	11,449	4,181	3,751	2,805	4,063	4,309	17,331	4,832
Turin, Italy	1,795	4,104	8,282	10,055	8,350	7,221	8,717	7,809	4,654	15,047	1,125	1,253	8,072	1,663	2,238	3,772	9,737	1,667	12,434	960
Uberlandia, Brazil	10,707	6,498	16,042	19,104	7,951	11,999	10,417	8,285	13,720	14,846	10,119	7,862	4,218	10,394	11,299	12,798	18,222	10,223	3,372	10,027
Ufa, USSR	1,992	6,886	5,306	6,511	9,691	6,376	8,724	9,036	1,119	11,829	2,510	4,760	11,007	2,484	1,318	431	6,309	2,726	15,986	2,593
Ujungpandang, Indonesia	10,317	12,863	6,867	3,580	14,960	10,985	12,502	14,684	7,893	3,010	10,990	13,039	18,704	11,298	10,012	8,489	4,717	11,530	14,788	11,240
Ulaanbaatar, Mongolia	5,528	10,271	2,591	3,015	10,454	6,047	8,434	9,870	2,430	8,834	6,056	8,291	13,304	5,699	4,856	3,451	2,788	5,876	19,188	6,102
Ulan-Ude, USSR	5,376	10,207	2,371	3,308	10,026	5,633	8,040	9,438	2,279	9,206	5,867	8,076	12,872	5,411	4,665	3,340	2,929	5,575	18,751	5,883
Uliastay, Mongolia	4,860	9,536	3,264	3,598	10,675	6,370	8,820	10,061	1,807	9,193	5,420	7,673	13,204	5,203	4,231	2,767	3,509	5,402	18,883	5,501
Uranium City, Canada	7,682	10,480	5,941	9,205	2,795	1,762	1,680	2,213	7,300	14,059	7,360	7,569	6,111	5,951	7,139	7,670	8,030	5,755	11,567	6,965
Urumqi, China	4,384	8,854	4,105	4,092	11,208	7,031	9,506	10,574	1,610	9,287	4,997	7,249	13,371	5,022	3,859	2,317	4,198	5,247	18,394	5,140
Ushuaia, Argentina	14,537	9,646	17,989	16,575	10,387	14,794	12,395	10,969	17,589	10,603	14,085	11,918	7,461	14,655	15,280	16,512	17,115	14,509	1,623	14,103
Vaduz, Liechtenstein	1,616	4,355	8,007	9,796	8,328	7,023	8,591	7,770	4,398	14,883	941	1,527	8,211	1,400	1,994	3,537	9,465	1,421	12,686	712
Valencia, Spain	2,634	3,502	9,113	10,961	8,146	7,658	8,862	7,665	5,560	15,760	1,988	419	7,395	2,463	3,140	4,665	10,632	2,404	11,530	1,866
Valladolid, Spain	2,866	3,818	9,010	11,042	7,705	7,322	8,447	7,224	5,659	16,093	2,196	750	7,049	2,398	3,277	4,822	10,633	2,293	11,421	1,997
Valletta, Malta	1,790	3,247	8,924	10,197	9,434	8,331	9,886	8,918	4,893	14,437	1,385	1,368	8,721	2,600	2,535	3,870	10,090	2,684	12,314	1,578
Valparaiso, Chile	13,472	9,208	16,458	18,014	8,051	12,502	10,245	8,600	16,362	12,717	12,859	10,606	5,044	12,928	14,006	15,540	17,517	12,721	847	12,724
Vancouver, Canada	9,103	11,862	6,063	9,119	2,584	2,245	246	2,289	8,348	13,078	8,814	9,023	6,321	7,395	8,513	8,871	7,918	7,208	11,090	8,424
Varna, Bulgaria	424	4,520	7,630	8,796	9,688	7,677	9,602	9,097	3,495	13,423	636	2,580	9,701	1,988	1,237	2,464	8,691	2,192	13,717	1,041
Venice, Italy	1,426	4,208	8,075	9,736	8,617	7,255	8,866	8,060	4,335	14,677	760	1,539	8,437	1,551	1,907	3,428	9,457	1,613	12,762	660

Distances in Kilometers	Odessa, USSR	Ogbomosho, Nigeria	Okha, USSR	Okinawa (Naha)	Oklahoma City, Oklahoma	Old Crow, Canada	Olympia, Washington	Omaha, Nebraska	Omsk, USSR	Oodnadatta, Australia	Oradea, Romania	Oran, Algeria	Oranjestad, Aruba	Orebro, Sweden	Orel, USSR	Orsk, USSR	Osaka, Japan	Oslo, Norway	Osorno, Chile	Ostrava, Czechoslovakia
Veracruz, Mexico	10,997	10,802	10,175	13,116	1,811	6,186	3,931	2,448	11,724	14,712	10,419	9,267	2,888	9,338	10,793	11,826	11,935	9,080	7,032	10,027
Verona, Italy	1,530	4,186	8,125	9,821	8,534	7,234	8,814	7,981	4,420	14,783	861	1,461	8,332	1,565	1,995	3,521	9,529	1,610	12,674	732
Victoria, Canada	9,195	11,929	6,112	9,150	2,561	2,325	158	2,289	8,434	13,043	8,905	9,102	6,306	7,486	8,606	8,962	7,950	7,299	11,028	8,514
Victoria, Seychelles	6,162	5,855	10,252	8,482	15,611	12,921	15,300	15,056	6,813	8,795	6,603	7,348	13,982	7,920	6,631	6,192	9,397	8,149	12,782	7,012
Vienna, Austria	1,101	4,586	7,658	9,310	8,660	7,012	8,740	8,081	3,909	14,363	437	1,970	8,717	1,236	1,487	3,020	9,024	1,354	13,183	229
Vientiane, Laos	7,201	10,613	5,253	2,737	13,722	9,271	11,495	13,172	4,800	6,159	7,869	10,003	16,539	8,160	6,863	5,340	3,745	8,397	17,467	8,100
Villahermosa, Mexico	10,914	10,493	10,462	13,448	1,992	6,424	4,229	2,600	11,815	14,982	10,318	9,066	2,529	9,291	10,756	11,854	12,261	9,031	6,797	9,933
Vilnius, USSR	991	5,492	6,714	8,417	8,625	6,389	8,342	8,005	3,028	13,738	880	2,902	9,223	798	735	2,247	8,086	1,050	14,053	722
Visby, Sweden	1,502	5,623	6,703	8,651	8,082	6,000	7,863	7,465	3,328	14,157	1,201	2,814	8,743	257	1,241	2,667	8,226	505	13,772	868
Vitoria, Brazil	10,263	5,810	16,304	18,638	8,628	12,477	11,092	8,912	13,345	14,690	9,717	7,481	4,874	10,163	10,916	12,357	18,364	10,019	3,832	9,673
Vladivostok, USSR	7,418	12,261	1,416	1,916	9,965	5,596	7,615	9,499	4,332	7,835	7,881	10,042	13,453	7,265	6,685	5,397	990	7,391	17,931	7,861
Volgograd, USSR	1,058	5,860	6,341	7,388	9,943	7,100	9,320	9,304	2,096	12,331	1,685	3,924	10,681	2,218	747	1,049	7,282	2,479	15,126	1,895
Vologda, USSR	1,544	6,415	5,745	7,417	8,799	5,940	8,121	8,153	2,060	12,905	1,798	3,920	9,917	1,400	740	1,478	7,068	1,636	15,031	1,733
Vorkuta, USSR	3,021	7,918	4,251	6,224	8,479	4,903	7,289	7,825	1,478	12,058	3,294	5,321	10,397	2,525	2,207	1,840	5,715	2,668	16,052	3,184
Wake Island	11,489	16,418	4,314	4,062	9,298	6,530	6,994	9,210	8,476	6,177	11,855	13,774	12,888	10,917	10,706	9,552	3,510	10,960	13,915	11,742
Wallis Island	15,556	19,431	8,366	7,487	9,862	9,435	8,525	10,172	12,511	5,252	15,901	17,484	12,052	14,815	14,771	13,577	7,364	14,800	10,129	15,746
Walvis Bay, Namibia	7,860	3,615	14,542	13,327	13,397	14,738	15,383	13,339	10,283	11,569	7,790	6,685	10,003	9,114	8,661	9,276	14,205	9,190	8,199	8,070
Warsaw, Poland	954	5,124	7,101	8,796	8,608	6,620	8,478	8,003	3,399	14,024	580	2,510	8,989	862	1,023	2,569	8,478	1,063	13,684	329
Washington, D.C.	8,144	8,697	9,067	12,355	1,852	4,933	3,792	1,637	9,228	16,766	7,564	6,576	3,003	6,510	7,977	9,131	11,201	6,250	6,808	7,172
Watson Lake, Canada	8,044	11,393	5,026	8,225	3,538	989	1,505	3,067	7,090	12,932	7,831	8,380	7,104	6,401	7,400	7,645	7,033	6,242	12,259	7,460
Weimar, East Germany	1,509	4,795	7,571	9,436	8,182	6,637	8,294	7,602	4,054	14,703	889	1,949	8,333	957	1,708	3,253	9,064	995	13,027	511
Wellington, New Zealand	17,101	16,214	10,946	8,915	12,331	12,660	11,560	12,807	14,298	3,882	17,769	19,272	13,021	17,556	16,683	15,139	9,322	17,662	8,650	17,964
West Berlin, West Germany	1,420	4,991	7,351	9,220	8,194	6,500	8,218	7,603	3,844	14,538	862	2,172	8,471	762	1,527	3,064	8,841	840	13,237	453
Wewak, Papua New Guinea	12,037	15,511	6,331	3,716	12,836	9,800	10,561	12,776	9,087	2,794	12,654	14,905	16,199	12,426	11,494	9,970	4,315	12,591	13,861	12,773
Whangarei, New Zealand	16,772	16,790	10,345	8,429	12,056	12,079	11,099	12,488	13,830	3,771	17,408	19,571	13,126	16,981	16,250	14,728	8,774	17,067	9,112	17,524
Whitehorse, Canada	8,053	11,587	4,697	7,881	3,864	798	1,713	3,407	6,930	12,609	7,877	8,545	7,451	6,450	7,380	7,537	6,688	6,306	12,548	7,517
Wichita, Kansas	9,346	10,472	8,361	11,519	245	4,234	2,333	414	9,695	15,011	8,850	8,206	3,890	7,608	9,008	9,880	10,319	7,363	9,011	8,442
Willemstad, Curacao	9,771	8,015	12,126	15,403	3,867	7,959	6,330	4,170	11,777	16,960	9,100	7,282	126	8,526	9,926	11,366	14,224	8,275	5,849	8,792
Wiluna, Australia	12,065	12,996	9,148	5,899	16,318	13,130	14,129	16,334	10,082	1,515	12,728	14,380	18,122	13,354	11,947	10,515	6,970	13,606	12,442	13,053
Windhoek, Namibia	7,769	3,674	14,346	13,062	13,611	14,756	15,536	13,531	10,119	11,384	7,729	6,716	10,253	9,074	8,564	9,125	13,950	9,162	8,433	8,022
Windsor, Canada	8,204	9,185	8,514	11,794	1,463	4,353	3,170	1,085	8,993	16,186	7,664	6,890	3,532	6,509	7,955	9,000	10,626	6,254	9,231	7,261
Winnipeg, Canada	8,211	10,131	7,238	10,489	1,599	3,058	1,920	960	8,346	14,948	7,776	7,496	4,828	6,453	7,795	8,569	9,306	6,222	10,292	7,367
Winston-Salem, North Carolina	8,564	8,993	9,238	12,514	1,560	5,071	3,706	1,484	9,603	16,537	7,984	6,963	2,806	6,927	8,393	9,533	11,342	6,668	8,520	7,592
Wroclaw, Poland	1,129	4,907	7,358	9,097	8,488	6,702	8,475	7,895	3,701	14,303	574	2,219	8,732	918	1,320	2,867	8,769	1,058	13,381	167
Wuhan, China	7,151	11,431	3,439	1,398	11,975	7,538	9,683	11,464	4,208	6,817	7,756	10,012	15,214	7,621	6,595	5,072	2,039	7,818	18,716	7,876
Wyndham, Australia	11,801	13,877	7,779	4,612	14,989	11,670	12,691	14,916	9,345	1,539	12,475	14,483	18,050	12,768	11,499	9,973	5,603	12,996	13,427	12,728
Xi'an, China	6,502	10,832	3,420	2,010	11,811	7,361	9,624	11,261	3,574	7,393	7,108	9,363	14,826	7,001	5,950	4,424	2,437	7,204	19,284	7,232
Xining, China	5,825	10,142	3,676	2,708	11,777	7,365	9,729	11,191	2,968	7,931	6,441	8,692	14,499	6,408	5,299	3,761	3,047	6,622	19,392	6,581
Yakutsk, USSR	6,007	10,939	1,222	3,979	8,401	3,958	6,315	7,847	3,260	9,939	6,325	8,296	11,566	5,437	5,203	4,287	3,067	5,518	17,174	6,208
Yanji, China	7,292	12,112	1,546	1,857	10,105	5,716	7,771	9,629	4,198	7,822	7,768	9,946	13,557	7,190	6,569	5,257	1,049	7,323	18,125	7,759
Yaounde, Cameroon	5,072	933	12,211	12,398	11,470	11,768	12,826	11,180	7,894	13,541	4,891	3,740	9,011	6,155	5,886	6,820	12,783	6,218	9,841	5,135
Yap Island (Colonia)	10,550	14,559	4,904	2,153	12,350	8,694	9,914	12,131	7,546	4,111	11,144	13,402	16,170	10,859	9,967	8,463	2,798	11,023	15,396	11,239
Yaraka, Australia	13,734	15,381	8,692	5,923	14,074	11,967	12,212	14,247	11,094	910	14,403	16,449	16,194	14,529	13,370	11,825	6,653	14,731	11,804	14,629
Yarmouth, Canada	7,105	7,816	8,863	12,122	2,828	4,924	4,358	2,458	8,405	17,370	6,514	5,536	3,491	5,508	6,979	8,206	11,041	5,246	9,375	6,125
Yellowknife, Canada	7,537	10,614	5,495	8,761	3,219	1,318	1,797	2,651	6,962	13,717	7,259	7,638	6,556	5,835	6,952	7,387	7,589	5,655	11,999	6,874
Yerevan, USSR	1,314	5,338	7,035	7,631	10,770	8,051	10,262	10,143	2,695	12,005	1,966	3,956	11,110	2,949	1,553	1,638	7,706	3,202	14,843	2,312
Yinchuan, China	6,040	10,490	3,243	2,416	11,458	7,023	9,350	10,888	3,070	7,914	6,633	8,890	14,348	6,487	5,464	3,951	2,635	6,688	19,768	6,743
Yogyakarta, Indonesia	9,848	11,902	7,459	4,203	15,838	11,636	13,372	15,481	7,760	3,431	10,521	12,412	19,481	11,040	9,658	8,198	5,394	11,289	14,637	10,816
York, United Kingdom	2,398	5,092	7,648	9,870	7,294	6,110	7,551	6,726	4,607	15,442	1,794	2,016	7,509	1,172	2,453	3,945	9,353	991	12,511	1,407
Yumen, China	5,335	9,733	3,701	3,157	11,520	7,161	9,576	10,915	2,469	8,423	5,945	8,199	14,074	5,909	4,798	3,263	3,374	6,125	19,244	6,081
Yutian, China	4,298	8,357	4,977	4,477	11,993	7,913	10,394	11,348	2,112	9,081	4,957	7,144	13,794	5,266	3,935	2,426	4,806	5,512	17,806	5,174
Yuzhno-Sakhalinsk, USSR	7,727	12,660	736	2,656	9,081	4,789	6,696	8,644	4,745	8,283	8,110	10,150	12,659	7,298	6,947	5,821	1,493	7,385	17,073	8,028
Zagreb, Yugoslavia	1,139	4,324	7,902	9,479	8,812	7,270	8,966	8,244	4,083	14,392	477	1,791	8,718	1,501	1,652	3,156	9,229	1,609	13,024	480
Zahedan, Iran	3,217	6,348	6,922	6,497	12,464	9,104	11,519	11,816	3,005	10,143	3,869	5,721	12,995	4,761	3,295	2,417	6,906	5,021	15,705	4,214
Zamboanga, Philippines	9,561	12,935	5,508	2,219	13,758	9,643	11,291	13,416	6,852	4,076	10,214	12,405	17,483	10,293	9,131	7,584	3,370	10,505	15,983	10,403
Zanzibar, Tanzania	5,890	4,186	11,465	10,165	14,537	13,188	15,164	14,123	7,482	10,317	6,137	6,229	12,249	7,562	6,554	6,622	10,978	7,743	11,414	6,526
Zaragoza, Spain	2,572	3,746	8,904	10,823	7,981	7,414	8,642	7,487	5,427	15,778	1,909	659	7,366	2,258	3,023	4,561	10,459	2,186	11,656	1,741
Zashiversk, USSR	6,154	10,995	1,547	4,696	7,538	3,095	5,471	6,987	3,730	10,550	6,372	8,158	10,754	5,307	5,340	4,671	3,676	5,343	16,312	6,193
Zhengzhou, China	6,814	11,236	3,099	1,641	11,585	7,137	9,337	11,058	3,815	7,268	7,401	9,659	14,759	7,205	6,226	4,722	1,996	7,396	19,133	7,502
Zurich, Switzerland	1,701	4,366	8,027	9,851	8,244	6,982	8,527	7,689	4,456	14,967	1,027	1,495	8,124	1,401	2,060	3,605	9,506	1,405	12,627	780

Distances in Kilometers	Ottawa, Canada	Ouagadougou, Bourkina Fasso	Oujda, Morocco	Oxford, United Kingdom	Pago Pago, American Samoa	Pakxe, Laos	Palembang, Indonesia	Palermo, Italy	Palma, Majorca	Palmerston North, New Zealand	Panama, Panama	Paramaribo, Suriname	Paris, France	Patna, India	Patrai, Greece	Peking, China	Penrhyn Island (Omoka)	Peoria, Illinois	Perm', USSR	Perth, Australia
Ouagadougou, Bourkina Fasso	7,808	0	2,470	4,368	18,845	11,466	11,856	3,213	3,042	16,891	8,515	5,933	4,063	9,097	3,679	11,391	17,445	8,965	6,978	13,307
Oujda, Morocco	6,188	2,470	0	1,899	17,485	10,615	11,720	1,420	677	19,339	8,322	6,319	1,615	8,186	2,149	9,608	16,277	7,431	4,966	14,313
Oxford, United Kingdom	5,296	4,368	1,899	0	15,742	9,831	11,361	1,897	1,387	18,715	8,424	7,083	410	7,574	2,335	8,197	14,818	6,500	3,639	14,546
Pago Pago, American Samoa	11,514	18,845	17,485	15,742	0	9,749	9,351	17,332	17,128	3,183	10,385	12,928	16,115	12,093	17,083	9,615	1,495	10,302	13,789	7,641
Pakxe, Laos	13,300	11,466	10,615	9,831	9,749	0	1,998	9,197	10,041	9,457	17,279	16,891	9,710	2,445	8,474	2,938	10,930	13,627	6,272	5,316
Palembang, Indonesia	15,296	11,856	11,720	11,361	9,351	1,998	0	10,333	11,256	8,185	19,196	17,785	11,161	3,800	9,602	4,892	10,757	15,582	8,004	3,415
Palermo, Italy	7,062	3,213	1,420	1,897	17,332	9,197	10,333	0	944	18,474	9,655	7,739	1,488	6,766	733	8,351	16,669	8,295	3,789	13,122
Palma, Majorca	6,214	3,042	677	1,387	17,128	10,041	11,256	944	0	19,417	8,714	6,867	1,034	7,632	1,659	8,936	16,119	7,457	4,291	14,059
Palmerston North, New Zealand	14,359	16,891	19,339	18,715	3,183	9,457	8,185	18,474	19,417	0	11,911	13,689	18,923	11,845	17,767	10,727	4,341	13,114	15,370	5,359
Panama, Panama	4,056	8,515	8,322	8,424	10,385	17,279	19,196	9,655	8,714	11,911	0	2,712	8,669	15,839	10,370	14,349	8,930	3,653	11,583	17,015
Paramaribo, Suriname	4,816	5,933	6,319	7,083	12,928	16,891	17,785	7,739	6,867	13,689	2,712	0	7,186	14,499	8,469	14,865	11,533	5,163	10,693	16,970
Paris, France	5,664	4,063	1,615	410	16,115	9,710	11,161	1,488	1,034	18,923	8,669	7,186	0	7,400	1,952	8,236	15,224	6,878	3,617	14,268
Patna, India	11,905	9,097	8,186	7,574	12,093	2,445	3,800	6,766	7,632	11,845	15,839	14,499	7,400	0	6,039	3,310	13,130	12,645	4,257	7,155
Patrai, Greece	7,615	3,679	2,149	2,335	17,083	8,474	9,602	733	1,659	17,767	10,370	8,469	1,952	6,039	0	7,759	16,764	8,830	3,317	12,447
Peking, China	10,475	11,391	9,608	8,197	9,615	2,938	4,892	8,351	8,936	10,727	14,349	14,865	8,236	3,310	7,759	0	10,270	10,697	4,649	7,957
Penrhyn Island (Omoka)	10,127	17,445	16,277	14,818	1,495	10,930	10,757	16,669	16,119	4,341	8,930	11,533	15,224	13,130	16,764	10,270	0	8,895	13,834	9,124
Peoria, Illinois	1,245	8,965	7,431	6,500	10,302	13,627	15,582	8,295	7,457	13,114	3,653	5,163	6,878	12,645	8,830	10,697	8,895	0	8,616	17,553
Perm', USSR	7,717	6,978	4,966	3,639	13,789	6,272	8,004	3,789	4,291	15,370	11,583	10,693	3,617	4,257	3,317	4,649	13,834	8,616	0	11,401
Perth, Australia	18,213	13,307	14,313	14,546	7,641	5,316	3,415	13,122	14,059	5,359	17,015	16,970	14,268	7,155	12,447	7,957	9,124	17,553	11,401	0
Peshawar, Pakistan	10,612	7,700	6,595	5,992	13,437	4,021	5,368	5,176	6,030	13,451	14,360	12,897	5,802	1,607	4,455	4,005	14,260	11,510	2,902	8,650
Petropavlovsk-Kamchatskiy,USSR	7,937	12,518	10,110	8,242	8,011	6,230	7,967	9,368	9,490	10,473	11,229	12,753	8,495	6,690	9,076	3,492	7,999	7,739	5,856	10,284
Petrozavodsk, USSR	6,587	6,194	3,946	2,405	14,364	7,563	9,277	3,004	3,273	16,488	10,343	9,412	2,450	5,503	2,761	5,797	14,057	7,581	1,291	12,658
Pevek, USSR	6,171	10,879	8,414	6,516	9,432	7,465	9,387	7,901	7,845	12,212	9,835	10,952	6,817	7,174	7,763	4,528	9,063	6,197	4,900	12,090
Philadelphia, Pennsylvania	609	7,748	6,336	5,633	11,484	13,908	15,903	7,321	6,437	14,163	3,460	4,277	5,981	12,467	7,916	11,081	10,049	1,228	8,250	18,686
Phnom Penh, Kampuchea	13,696	11,487	10,783	10,093	9,736	406	1,600	9,363	10,230	9,252	17,684	17,098	9,952	2,599	8,635	3,342	10,974	14,032	6,575	4,951
Phoenix, Arizona	3,366	11,099	9,537	8,423	8,156	13,304	14,915	10,287	9,505	11,037	4,298	6,606	8,821	13,222	10,747	10,479	6,762	2,147	9,811	15,572
Pierre, South Dakota	1,943	9,748	8,009	6,844	9,611	12,908	14,798	8,711	7,943	12,584	4,408	6,121	7,243	12,237	9,169	9,971	8,270	973	8,453	16,598
Pinang, Malaysia	14,361	11,171	10,784	10,331	10,054	1,228	1,044	9,379	10,287	9,164	18,414	17,039	10,142	2,760	8,646	4,149	11,384	14,800	6,961	4,448
Pitcairn Island (Adamstown)	9,549	14,462	14,965	14,805	4,405	14,126	13,354	16,296	15,352	5,277	6,648	8,783	15,136	16,498	16,994	13,709	3,457	8,399	16,313	10,598
Pittsburgh, Pennsylvania	655	8,160	6,703	5,914	11,085	13,826	15,822	7,645	6,776	13,814	3,487	4,565	6,274	12,534	8,220	10,951	9,659	812	8,364	18,315
Plymouth, Montserrat	3,423	6,537	6,278	6,576	12,398	16,251	17,932	7,637	6,704	13,911	2,064	1,427	6,771	14,149	8,362	13,734	10,920	3,741	10,010	18,306
Plymouth, United Kingdom	5,170	4,224	1,757	251	15,819	10,075	11,589	1,943	1,316	18,887	8,212	6,835	496	7,808	2,445	8,444	14,829	6,387	3,890	14,744
Ponape Island	12,124	16,930	14,956	13,218	4,153	5,792	6,043	13,843	14,283	5,528	13,389	16,063	13,397	7,996	13,292	5,543	5,156	11,337	10,060	6,224
Ponce, Puerto Rico	3,153	6,991	6,607	6,763	11,960	16,248	18,095	7,937	6,996	13,627	1,718	1,835	6,986	14,299	8,653	13,582	10,475	3,340	10,094	18,444
Ponta Delgada, Azores	4,189	3,696	2,158	2,463	15,703	12,275	13,676	3,407	2,463	18,163	6,253	4,626	2,566	9,954	4,117	10,577	14,296	5,407	6,097	16,471
Pontianak, Indonesia	14,953	12,284	11,947	11,414	8,935	1,721	601	10,538	11,440	8,019	18,628	18,196	11,249	3,850	9,805	4,484	10,304	15,116	7,938	3,597
Port Augusta, Australia	16,816	15,319	16,300	16,085	5,581	6,275	4,754	15,005	15,947	3,476	15,386	16,766	15,911	8,516	14,292	8,317	7,061	15,743	12,538	2,065
Port Blair, India	13,585	10,200	9,707	9,278	11,026	1,464	2,084	8,300	9,208	10,243	17,579	15,988	9,078	1,745	7,567	3,908	12,293	14,210	5,999	5,409
Port Elizabeth, South Africa	13,420	5,876	8,120	9,851	14,397	10,064	8,833	8,080	8,477	11,223	11,959	9,525	9,461	9,110	8,005	12,394	15,234	14,359	10,587	8,134
Port Hedland, Australia	16,932	13,604	14,020	13,801	7,497	4,161	2,440	12,682	13,621	5,807	17,711	18,270	13,595	6,236	11,962	6,673	8,987	16,524	10,394	1,316
Port Louis, Mauritius	14,918	7,396	8,731	9,792	13,519	6,568	5,470	7,931	8,727	10,753	15,256	12,605	9,394	5,879	7,469	9,029	14,966	16,162	8,663	5,912
Port Moresby, Papua New Guinea	14,311	16,602	15,816	14,516	4,613	5,316	4,748	14,431	15,175	4,425	14,907	17,539	14,559	7,758	13,734	6,325	6,010	13,476	10,949	4,076
Port Said, Egypt	8,847	4,048	3,204	3,555	17,013	7,604	8,524	1,889	2,831	16,586	11,521	9,440	3,183	5,164	1,238	7,398	17,320	10,055	3,486	11,234
Port Sudan, Sudan	10,142	4,215	4,189	4,885	17,004	7,256	7,784	3,085	3,976	15,454	12,415	10,052	4,496	4,942	2,551	7,733	18,002	11,369	4,535	10,126
Port-au-Prince, Haiti	2,998	7,587	7,102	7,113	11,375	16,277	18,249	8,397	7,453	13,176	1,313	2,334	7,364	14,552	9,101	13,470	9,887	2,959	10,302	18,315
Port-of-Spain, Trin. & Tobago	4,084	6,535	6,573	7,056	12,355	16,836	18,288	7,969	7,054	13,543	1,985	879	7,219	14,619	8,700	14,401	10,910	4,322	10,566	17,632
Port-Vila, Vanuatu	13,415	18,785	17,897	16,121	2,277	7,764	7,119	16,695	17,223	2,603	12,656	15,130	16,329	10,197	16,060	8,348	3,761	12,283	12,960	5,478
Portland, Maine	474	7,363	5,825	5,059	11,928	13,485	15,465	6,768	5,894	14,696	3,948	4,444	5,411	11,937	7,352	10,723	10,520	1,627	7,703	18,601
Portland, Oregon	3,615	11,309	9,317	7,856	8,197	11,719	13,426	9,750	9,118	11,327	5,771	7,800	8,266	11,644	10,066	8,867	7,002	2,721	8,528	14,841
Porto, Portugal	5,306	3,264	930	1,306	16,563	10,845	12,169	1,912	972	19,654	7,763	6,046	1,215	8,479	2,610	9,450	15,354	6,551	4,830	15,031
Porto Alegre, Brazil	8,719	7,096	8,837	10,291	11,897	17,144	15,556	10,095	9,509	10,842	5,278	3,995	10,230	15,722	10,697	18,443	11,109	8,778	13,799	13,008
Porto Alexandre, Angola	11,061	3,449	5,774	7,593	16,665	10,872	10,237	5,972	6,206	13,565	10,436	7,764	7,226	9,158	6,073	12,353	17,049	12,101	9,134	10,359
Porto Novo, Benin	8,588	793	3,155	5,031	18,889	11,233	11,396	3,668	3,665	16,189	9,049	6,393	4,698	8,956	4,012	11,529	17,888	9,732	7,325	12,583
Porto Velho, Brazil	6,116	7,286	8,094	8,963	11,561	18,703	18,216	9,512	8,679	11,852	2,617	1,883	9,057	16,258	10,232	16,552	10,320	6,078	12,576	15,501
Portsmouth, United Kingdom	5,351	4,259	1,790	110	15,850	9,862	11,370	1,810	1,278	18,820	8,429	7,045	324	7,590	2,270	8,266	14,917	6,560	3,692	14,530
Poznan, Poland	6,358	4,740	2,477	1,248	15,719	8,611	10,113	1,614	1,801	17,907	9,663	8,288	1,106	6,329	1,617	7,181	15,169	7,511	2,538	13,322
Prague, Czechoslovakia	6,355	4,430	2,169	1,118	16,005	8,827	10,277	1,333	1,493	18,190	9,535	8,066	889	6,511	1,436	7,471	15,398	7,532	2,823	13,428
Praia, Cape Verde Islands	5,916	2,396	3,078	4,542	16,502	13,536	14,209	4,439	3,737	16,636	6,123	3,604	4,443	11,094	5,127	12,659	15,051	6,934	8,010	15,500
Pretoria, South Africa	13,053	5,304	7,401	9,054	15,134	9,540	8,531	7,237	7,701	11,953	12,214	9,631	8,655	8,350	7,116	11,658	16,102	14,116	9,642	8,341
Prince Albert, Canada	2,330	9,843	7,834	6,425	9,683	11,859	13,771	8,322	7,654	12,805	5,443	6,959	6,834	11,212	8,687	8,921	8,471	1,849	7,569	15,949
Prince Edward Island	15,033	7,623	9,844	11,522	12,686	9,608	8,017	9,696	10,167	9,503	12,817	10,715	11,123	9,297	9,534	12,339	13,648	15,815	11,715	6,639
Prince George, Canada	3,456	10,820	8,673	7,099	8,815	11,084	12,905	8,976	8,409	11,989	6,292	8,028	7,506	10,798	9,241	8,174	7,722	2,868	7,596	14,833
Prince Rupert, Canada	3,943	11,194	8,981	7,338	8,505	10,675	12,461	9,191	8,677	11,687	6,735	8,521	7,742	10,524	9,406	7,788	7,484	3,360	7,538	14,338
Providence, Rhode Island	529	7,440	5,971	5,256	11,820	13,695	15,679	6,944	6,061	14,536	3,726	4,299	5,603	12,161	7,538	10,917	10,397	1,526	7,927	18,739
Provo, Utah	2,970	10,778	9,036	7,802	8,573	12,764	14,496	9,687	8,947	11,567	4,701	6,782	8,206	12,513	10,108	9,883	7,241	1,867	9,060	15,702
Puerto Aisen, Chile	10,065	9,560	11,368	12,750	9,505	16,644	14,647	12,623	12,039	8,332	6,060	5,937	12,724	17,055	13,207	19,055	8,943	9,684	16,323	11,397
Puerto Deseado, Argentina	10,366	9,194	11,128	12,623	9,919	16,306	14,318	12,323	11,805	8,520	6,425	6,029	12,558	16,483	12,868	19,117	9,437	10,073	16,090	11,178
Puerto Princesa, Philippines	13,729	12,989	12,077	11,122	8,229	1,528	2,088	10,666	11,476	8,050	17,127	18,159	11,049	3,958	9,953	3,354	9,449	13,714	7,491	4,621
Punta Arenas, Chile	10,932	9,774	11,783	13,312	9,390	15,775	13,777	12,940	12,460	7,846	6,931	6,703	13,237	16,357	13,453	18,436	9,024	10,552	16,726	10,556
Pusan, South Korea	10,748	12,622	10,758	9,239	8,376	3,210	4,914	9,545	10,081	9,621	14,283	15,453	9,320	4,317	8,974	1,239	9,059	10,731	5,794	7,548
Pyongyang, North Korea	10,411	12,131	10,236	8,716	8,842	3,290	5,118	9,032	9,559	10,145	14,089	15,038	8,795	4,066	8,471	811	9,463	10,479	5,274	7,922
Qamdo, China	11,494	10,125	8,856	7,894	11,016	1,980	3,855	7,462	8,238	11,300	15,550	14,977	7,803	1,337	6,770	1,985	11,924	12,018	4,300	7,254
Qandahar, Afghanistan	10,635	7,157	6,201	5,780	13,999	4,449	5,620	4,782	5,672	13,786	14,203	12,520	5,551	2,004	4,051	4,611	14,861	11,612	3,024	8,788
Qiqian, China	9,073	10,987	8,896	7,276	9,847	4,325	6,293	7,797	8,220	11,538	12,956	13,563	7,389	4,204	7,313	1,405	10,193	9,303	4,010	9,333
Qom, Iran	9,644	5,817	4,782	4,527	15,288	5,873	6,988	3,367	4,272	15,173	12,914	11,099	4,252	3,428	2,634	5,707	15,922	10,737	2,626	10,021
Quebec, Canada	379	7,475	5,814	4,923	11,871	13,139	15,125	6,683	5,836	14,736	4,269	4,796	5,289	11,641	7,240	10,366	10,494	1,622	7,425	18,248
Quetta, Pakistan	10,825	7,276	6,371	5,973	13,891	4,295	5,434	4,954	5,850	13,606	14,396	12,690	5,741	1,853	4,222	4,573	14,796	11,795	3,198	8,594
Quito, Ecuador	5,063	8,608	8,803	9,152	10,250	18,293	19,521	10,191	9,268	11,338	1,022	2,678	9,357	16,698	10,922	15,356	8,868	4,668	12,471	16,144
Rabaul, Papua New Guinea	13,511	17,003	15,711	14,192	4,221	5,544	5,272	14,407	15,040	4,643	14,298	17,000	14,295	7,942	13,754	6,104	5,523	12,674	10,751	4,878
Raiatea (Uturoa)	10,248	16,761	16,400	15,320	2,084	11,821	11,393	17,215	16,454	4,111	8,408	10,869	15,728	14,119	17,530	11,368	1,118	9,003	14,888	9,297
Raleigh, North Carolina	1,099	8,063	6,792	6,168	11,110	14,353	16,350	7,825	6,927	13,681	2,970	4,093	6,509	13,002	8,436	11,482	9,652	1,103	8,797	18,622
Rangiroa (Avatoru)	9,831	16,370	15,964	14,957	2,478	12,175	11,815	16,841	16,044	4,532	7,971	10,455	15,362	14,425	17,223	11,560	1,306	8,588	14,827	9,742
Rangoon, Burma	13,068	10,424	9,680	9,059	10,792	1,046	2,374	8,260	9,135	10,340	17,118	15,998	8,896	1,505	7,531	3,226	11,973	13,614	5,630	5,785
Raoul Is., Kermadec Islands	13,171	18,097	19,303	17,493	1,819	9,547	8,629	18,585	18,861	1,364	11,306	13,494	17,828	11,992	17,954	10,235	3,053	11,932	14,809	6,260
Rarotonga (Avarua)	11,214	17,518	17,392	16,143	1,390	11,063	10,469	18,019	17,379	3,151	9,374	11,763	16,552	13,446	18,109	10,993	1,362	9,969	15,000	8,290
Rawson, Argentina	9,883	8,912	10,753	12,191	10,153	16,764	14,787	11,989	11,427	8,924	5,970	5,533	12,144	16,680	12,564	19,612	9,570	9,622	15,718	11,673
Recife, Brazil	7,185	4,329	5,866	7,365	14,561	15,683	15,394	7,150	6,539	13,804	5,296	2,724	7,277	13,407	7,782	15,474	13,456	7,770	10,828	14,606
Regina, Canada	2,217	9,865	7,930	6,586	9,611	12,161	14,062	8,480	7,781	12,699	5,148	6,738	6,994	11,527	8,871	9,224	8,358	1,592	7,856	16,118
Reykjavik, Iceland	3,871	5,965	3,552	1,830	13,970	10,166	11,991	3,713	3,173	17,122	7,582	6,993	2,237	8,258	4,056	7,902	12,989	4,967	4,002	15,400
Rhodes, Greece	8,172	3,994	2,727	2,877	16,920	7,929	9,005	1,329	2,265	17,160	10,978	9,039	2,513	5,486	609	7,398	16,901	9,375	3,157	11,843
Richmond, Virginia	887	7,949	6,618	5,958	11,248	14,166	16,164	7,630	6,738	13,867	3,172	4,176	6,302	12,783	8,233	11,310	9,800	1,106	8,575	18,658
Riga, USSR	6,455	5,409	3,157	1,735	15,106	8,108	9,711	2,238	2,483	17,253	9,992	8,815	1,707	5,911	2,086	6,532	14,682	7,543	1,914	13,017
Ringkobing, Denmark	5,663	4,923	2,503	788	15,364	9,086	10,679	2,033	1,882	18,029	9,049	7,844	897	6,880	2,222	7,411	14,647	6,813	2,860	13,953
Rio Branco, Brazil	6,185	7,734	8,508	9,315	11,113	19,123	18,366	9,928	9,082	11,460	2,465	2,240	9,425	16,686	10,651	16,659	9,876	6,040	12,903	15,352
Rio Cuarto, Argentina	8,774	8,348	9,940	11,232	10,621	17,780	15,855	11,257	10,600	9,810	4,929	4,421	11,227	16,960	11,892	19,247	9,816	8,576	14,843	12,802
Rio de Janeiro, Brazil	8,249	5,991	7,725	9,227	12,978	16,666	15,525	8,974	8,399	11,935	5,298	3,434	9,146	14,810	9,577	17,325	12,106	8,518	12,691	13,544
Rio Gallegos, Argentina	10,772	9,599	11,588	13,109	9,551	15,930	13,933	12,756	12,265	8,045	6,787	6,507	13,037	16,397	13,278	18,635	9,151	10,418	16,538	10,734
Rio Grande, Brazil	8,903	7,289	9,059	10,523	11,718	17,097	15,435	10,309	9,733	10,613	5,395	4,203	10,460	15,818	10,904	18,660	10,965	8,929	14,042	12,812
Riyadh, Saudi Arabia	10,315	5,243	4,790	5,035	15,953	6,231	6,967	3,482	4,425	14,993	13,112	10,940	4,692	3,861	2,800	6,613	16,878	11,485	3,783	9,648
Road Town, Brit. Virgin Isls.	3,162	6,776	6,400	6,590	12,176	16,148	17,942	7,736	6,797	13,825	1,923	1,732	6,805	14,142	8,454	13,541	10,691	3,430	9,956	18,510

Distances in Kilometers	Ottawa, Canada	Ouagadougou, Bourkina Fasso	Oujda, Morocco	Oxford, United Kingdom	Pago Pago, American Samoa	Pakxe, Laos	Palembang, Indonesia	Palermo, Italy	Palma, Majorca	Palmerston North, New Zealand	Panama, Panama	Paramaribo, Suriname	Paris, France	Patna, India	Patrai, Greece	Peking, China	Penrhyn Island (Omoka)	Peoria, Illinois	Perm', USSR	Perth, Australia
Roanoke, Virginia	971	8,171	6,833	6,142	11,026	14,175	16,171	7,831	6,944	13,658	3,136	4,295	6,491	12,873	8,427	11,295	9,578	918	8,687	18,463
Robinson Crusoe Island, Chile	8,760	9,625	11,021	12,093	9,314	17,902	15,941	12,393	11,656	8,817	4,715	5,032	12,155	18,238	13,067	18,493	8,467	8,303	15,723	12,586
Rochester, New York	294	7,955	6,410	5,568	11,331	13,543	15,541	7,317	6,459	14,123	3,793	4,686	5,933	12,190	7,882	10,695	9,925	1,030	8,008	18,297
Rockhampton, Australia	15,208	16,832	17,073	16,045	4,198	6,468	5,418	15,653	16,507	3,012	14,480	16,658	16,043	8,889	14,924	7,853	5,693	14,153	12,427	3,533
Rome, Italy	6,747	3,544	1,490	1,511	16,927	9,171	10,415	427	870	18,599	9,518	7,735	1,108	6,765	886	8,144	16,245	7,971	3,529	13,328
Rosario, Argentina	8,810	8,033	9,678	11,025	10,947	17,610	15,752	10,977	10,344	10,048	5,052	4,332	11,002	16,621	11,601	19,189	10,158	8,679	14,610	12,813
Roseau, Dominica	3,598	6,463	6,283	6,642	12,459	16,362	17,977	7,655	6,727	13,883	2,093	1,249	6,826	14,216	8,383	13,886	10,988	3,917	10,106	18,142
Rostock, East Germany	5,986	4,782	2,420	935	15,580	8,896	10,440	1,777	1,765	18,047	9,316	8,015	893	6,647	1,906	7,343	14,929	7,141	2,733	13,677
Rostov-na-Donu, USSR	7,966	5,445	3,718	2,969	15,399	6,988	8,401	2,369	3,088	16,440	11,388	9,904	2,764	4,638	1,771	5,995	15,448	9,055	1,632	11,600
Rotterdam, Netherlands	5,647	4,420	1,984	397	15,807	9,453	10,966	1,682	1,380	18,553	8,821	7,453	373	7,183	2,026	7,894	14,990	6,838	3,297	14,151
Rouyn, Canada	403	8,069	6,340	5,320	11,303	12,972	14,970	7,133	6,318	14,234	4,353	5,215	5,702	11,676	7,653	10,121	9,949	1,185	7,536	17,810
Sacramento, California	3,816	11,619	9,792	8,446	7,774	12,299	13,895	10,343	9,654	10,830	5,316	7,557	8,855	12,381	10,706	9,509	6,490	2,733	9,299	14,840
Saginaw, Michigan	691	8,467	6,879	5,948	10,831	13,447	15,436	7,737	6,899	13,671	3,843	5,030	6,324	12,280	8,276	10,549	9,437	558	8,174	17,866
Saint Denis, Reunion	14,818	7,234	8,632	9,746	13,656	6,790	5,696	7,873	8,651	10,839	15,033	12,389	9,345	6,059	7,432	9,230	15,087	16,058	8,740	6,073
Saint George's, Grenada	3,929	6,540	6,509	6,949	12,359	16,706	18,228	7,897	6,977	13,625	1,976	998	7,119	14,518	8,628	14,247	10,905	4,181	10,441	17,789
Saint John, Canada	756	7,054	5,458	4,682	12,268	13,268	15,228	6,388	5,518	15,070	4,226	4,495	5,032	11,633	6,972	10,565	10,873	1,978	7,387	18,516
Saint John's, Antigua	3,394	6,494	6,222	6,517	12,443	16,195	17,873	7,580	6,646	13,969	2,117	1,443	6,712	14,090	8,305	13,688	10,964	3,732	9,953	18,345
Saint John's, Canada	1,774	6,135	4,414	3,667	13,261	12,741	14,607	5,337	4,462	16,124	4,970	4,631	4,003	10,873	5,931	10,253	11,895	3,018	6,621	18,020
Saint Louis, Missouri	1,415	9,051	7,582	6,697	10,187	13,830	15,773	8,477	7,628	12,951	3,453	5,062	7,071	12,879	9,023	10,896	8,764	236	8,851	17,553
Saint Paul, Minnesota	1,366	9,173	7,475	6,387	10,170	13,087	15,034	8,232	7,437	13,105	4,196	5,681	6,779	12,191	8,721	10,154	8,812	552	8,248	17,133
Saint Peter Port, UK	5,317	4,113	1,643	272	15,958	10,015	11,500	1,789	1,172	18,983	8,317	6,888	361	7,728	2,298	8,443	14,981	6,536	3,862	14,627
Saipan (Susupe)	12,113	15,301	13,522	11,937	5,797	4,286	4,937	12,305	12,845	6,879	14,371	16,751	12,051	6,380	11,713	3,956	6,752	11,609	8,561	6,109
Salalah, Oman	11,448	5,994	5,866	6,176	15,232	5,519	5,984	4,601	5,541	13,876	14,174	11,858	5,834	3,347	3,934	6,467	16,440	12,604	4,555	8,521
Salem, Oregon	3,666	11,371	9,387	7,929	8,129	11,738	13,433	9,824	9,190	11,256	5,766	7,818	8,339	11,690	10,139	8,894	6,930	2,755	8,595	14,803
Salt Lake City, Utah	2,966	10,773	9,015	7,769	8,587	12,707	14,444	9,655	8,920	11,591	4,752	6,818	8,173	12,452	10,071	9,824	7,262	1,878	9,004	15,685
Salta, Argentina	7,843	8,061	9,390	10,525	10,845	18,606	16,764	10,761	10,028	10,433	4,036	3,565	10,561	17,066	11,439	18,316	9,866	7,669	14,164	13,727
Salto, Uruguay	8,692	7,726	9,376	10,742	11,251	17,572	15,796	10,670	10,043	10,342	5,022	4,129	10,712	16,375	11,293	18,933	10,444	8,619	14,315	12,966
Salvador, Brazil	7,470	4,955	6,540	8,021	13,957	16,177	15,608	7,821	7,212	13,136	5,144	2,779	7,942	13,989	8,449	16,148	12,923	7,933	11,501	14,338
Salzburg, Austria	6,407	4,156	1,915	1,116	16,270	8,982	10,377	1,076	1,238	18,400	9,469	7,910	801	6,636	1,274	7,706	15,623	7,602	3,058	13,467
Samsun, Turkey	8,274	4,876	3,410	3,068	16,041	7,207	8,444	1,995	2,847	16,618	11,440	9,713	2,780	4,786	1,294	6,519	16,160	9,419	2,332	11,489
San Antonio, Texas	2,670	10,009	8,761	7,964	9,129	14,435	16,191	9,721	8,853	11,740	3,007	5,241	8,334	13,904	10,285	11,525	7,665	1,489	10,035	16,741
San Cristobal, Venezuela	4,186	7,749	7,728	8,028	11,136	17,465	19,382	9,100	8,170	12,442	815	1,899	8,234	15,582	9,827	14,650	9,698	4,034	11,380	17,204
San Diego, California	3,805	11,566	9,951	8,766	7,709	13,026	14,552	10,646	9,890	10,637	4,675	7,051	9,169	13,136	11,075	10,262	6,335	2,604	9,933	15,091
San Francisco, California	3,929	11,734	9,913	8,566	7,655	12,295	13,865	10,462	9,775	10,709	5,349	7,621	8,975	12,426	10,823	9,524	6,368	2,836	9,390	14,744
San Jose, Costa Rica	4,014	8,986	8,680	8,655	9,927	17,032	18,778	9,981	9,037	11,592	511	3,220	8,923	15,905	10,684	14,097	8,460	3,451	11,666	16,831
San Juan, Argentina	8,552	8,633	10,113	11,312	10,312	18,099	16,127	11,461	10,763	9,677	4,633	4,372	11,335	17,374	12,117	18,976	9,454	8,286	14,948	12,965
San Juan, Puerto Rico	3,118	6,934	6,537	6,691	12,020	16,187	18,025	7,865	6,924	13,699	1,790	1,835	6,914	14,229	8,581	13,534	10,534	3,331	10,026	18,500
San Luis Potosi, Mexico	3,455	10,456	9,423	8,745	8,604	14,963	16,523	10,458	9,566	11,041	2,718	5,242	9,105	14,681	11,049	12,119	7,116	2,319	10,876	16,239
San Marino, San Marino	6,615	3,745	1,606	1,343	16,704	9,121	10,418	649	948	18,576	9,485	7,777	953	6,732	1,000	8,005	16,029	7,831	3,373	13,395
San Miguel de Tucuman, Argen.	8,069	8,131	9,526	10,700	10,788	18,418	16,545	10,887	10,171	10,279	4,250	3,771	10,726	17,070	11,555	18,542	9,849	7,888	14,337	13,502
San Salvador, El Salvador	3,740	9,452	8,916	8,684	9,497	16,423	18,082	10,150	9,210	11,421	1,178	3,829	8,986	15,614	10,827	13,507	8,011	2,992	11,456	16,769
Sanaa, Yemen	10,976	4,945	5,067	5,692	16,281	6,592	6,967	3,938	4,842	14,584	13,270	10,846	5,313	4,398	3,361	7,422	17,513	12,191	4,839	9,249
Santa Cruz, Bolivia	7,114	7,550	8,696	9,752	11,323	18,817	17,365	10,090	9,319	11,166	3,465	2,758	9,804	16,647	10,786	17,551	10,228	7,029	13,390	14,500
Santa Cruz, Tenerife	5,486	2,347	1,523	2,873	16,958	12,139	13,182	2,943	2,129	18,305	6,937	4,804	2,767	9,708	3,669	10,994	15,493	6,674	6,352	15,433
Santa Fe, New Mexico	2,760	10,486	8,941	7,882	8,768	13,471	15,206	9,729	8,928	11,624	3,992	6,141	8,275	13,124	10,214	10,580	7,367	1,534	9,491	16,165
Santa Rosa, Argentina	9,158	8,514	10,199	11,547	10,487	17,431	15,484	11,490	10,865	9,524	5,292	4,794	11,526	16,878	12,105	19,632	9,757	8,942	15,134	12,416
Santa Rosalia, Mexico	3,801	11,367	9,985	8,983	7,805	13,778	15,250	10,822	10,005	10,560	3,996	6,479	9,375	13,862	11,317	11,022	6,364	2,556	10,490	15,378
Santarem, Brazil	5,693	6,103	6,866	7,821	12,742	17,467	17,674	8,281	7,461	13,055	3,030	916	7,886	15,021	8,999	15,756	11,444	5,946	11,457	16,074
Santiago del Estero, Argentina	8,188	8,089	9,530	10,736	10,839	18,276	16,413	10,881	10,179	10,261	4,386	3,846	10,753	16,982	11,542	18,655	9,924	8,020	14,368	13,396
Santiago, Chile	8,749	8,901	10,405	11,603	10,054	17,943	15,951	11,749	11,055	9,383	4,787	4,645	11,628	17,530	12,402	19,057	9,228	8,436	15,240	12,736
Santo Domingo, Dominican Rep.	3,037	7,332	6,883	6,951	11,627	16,260	18,192	8,192	7,249	13,378	1,479	2,124	7,191	14,437	8,902	13,507	10,139	3,100	10,201	18,409
Sao Paulo de Olivenca, Brazil	5,456	7,643	8,146	8,791	11,204	18,590	19,016	9,563	8,681	11,890	1,818	1,831	8,934	16,309	10,295	15,930	9,879	5,327	12,322	16,058
Sao Paulo, Brazil	8,184	6,315	7,988	9,439	12,643	16,991	15,755	9,261	8,659	11,696	5,075	3,379	9,376	15,163	9,876	17,595	11,755	8,386	12,948	13,591
Sao Tome, Sao Tome & Principe	9,393	1,613	3,906	5,748	18,439	10,981	10,912	4,239	4,364	15,434	9,602	6,904	5,395	8,834	4,471	11,654	18,091	10,522	7,727	11,831
Sapporo, Japan	9,543	12,805	10,627	8,901	8,009	4,585	6,275	9,601	9,958	9,859	12,920	14,342	9,065	5,413	9,142	2,104	8,403	9,419	5,829	8,702
Sarajevo, Yugoslavia	7,004	3,976	2,020	1,708	16,616	8,654	9,940	764	1,393	18,103	9,958	8,248	1,355	6,258	680	7,628	16,130	8,205	3,034	12,937
Saratov, USSR	7,899	6,083	4,233	3,214	14,737	6,626	8,174	2,948	3,577	16,004	11,531	10,273	3,087	4,375	2,404	5,404	14,801	8,919	970	11,479
Saskatoon, Canada	2,372	9,938	7,949	6,552	9,574	11,929	13,830	8,449	7,775	12,689	5,380	6,952	6,961	11,320	8,818	8,992	8,352	1,816	7,698	15,930
Schefferville, Canada	1,219	7,317	5,379	4,227	12,181	12,226	14,202	6,069	5,290	15,230	5,207	5,530	4,616	10,704	6,562	9,503	10,898	2,299	6,499	17,455
Seattle, Washington	3,533	11,170	9,141	7,655	8,365	11,582	13,323	9,547	8,928	11,508	5,873	7,829	8,064	11,447	9,852	8,712	7,192	2,707	8,299	14,875
Sendai, Japan	10,043	13,179	11,070	9,379	7,697	4,290	5,881	9,993	10,396	9,396	13,315	14,852	9,528	5,374	9,501	2,120	8,201	9,874	6,206	8,193
Seoul, South Korea	10,537	12,313	10,429	8,910	8,670	3,250	5,037	9,222	9,753	9,951	14,166	15,195	8,990	4,152	8,657	958	9,314	10,574	5,466	7,781
Sept-Iles, Canada	876	7,178	5,395	4,423	12,233	12,729	14,698	6,207	5,379	15,178	4,731	5,029	4,795	11,152	6,747	10,015	10,891	2,088	6,923	17,968
Sevastopol, USSR	7,850	4,885	3,206	2,677	15,943	7,444	8,766	1,828	2,599	16,897	11,083	9,456	2,414	5,054	1,211	6,552	15,905	8,989	2,156	11,869
Seville, Spain	5,714	2,807	476	1,639	17,036	10,829	12,036	1,704	791	19,650	7,960	6,077	1,442	8,423	2,433	9,626	15,802	6,958	4,980	14,741
Shanghai, China	11,356	12,257	10,618	9,261	8,820	2,379	4,158	9,320	9,952	9,687	15,046	15,899	9,288	3,590	8,695	1,077	9,640	11,442	5,683	7,003
Sheffield, United Kingdom	5,210	4,548	2,078	181	15,565	9,777	11,342	2,043	1,566	18,542	8,419	7,148	568	7,548	2,446	8,082	14,656	6,404	3,556	14,565
Shenyang, China	10,159	11,795	9,875	8,351	9,158	3,411	5,301	8,681	9,198	10,510	13,917	14,728	8,430	3,939	8,128	629	9,731	10,283	4,915	8,201
Shiraz, Iran	10,195	5,878	5,105	5,022	15,284	5,663	6,618	3,716	4,647	14,783	13,348	11,386	4,725	3,237	2,989	5,834	16,104	11,302	3,169	9,543
Sibiu, Romania	7,218	4,428	2,522	1,969	16,244	8,176	9,514	1,234	1,886	17,633	10,344	8,719	1,678	5,798	862	7,130	15,920	8,390	2,557	12,592
Singapore	14,831	11,657	11,368	10,931	9,562	1,545	475	9,968	10,881	8,568	18,814	17,573	10,743	3,359	9,235	4,465	10,930	15,162	7,540	3,888
Sioux Falls, South Dakota	1,681	9,488	7,805	6,705	9,844	13,119	15,034	8,556	7,765	12,776	4,180	5,826	7,099	12,347	9,038	10,181	8,482	670	8,476	16,901
Skelleftea, Sweden	5,849	6,070	3,684	1,929	14,327	8,252	10,003	3,007	3,045	16,841	9,602	8,764	2,086	6,240	2,951	6,317	13,814	6,863	1,999	13,394
Skopje, Yugoslavia	7,327	3,969	2,192	2,031	16,717	8,436	9,671	815	1,609	17,853	10,248	8,476	1,675	6,023	417	7,539	16,348	8,527	3,009	12,630
Socotra Island (Tamrida)	11,842	6,024	6,115	6,553	15,198	5,590	5,867	4,908	5,837	13,581	14,366	11,941	6,198	3,560	4,271	6,769	16,507	13,017	5,036	8,224
Sofia, Bulgaria	7,392	4,127	2,357	2,102	16,584	8,277	9,530	984	1,765	17,706	10,374	8,632	1,764	5,868	510	7,371	16,270	8,583	2,852	12,520
Songkhla, Thailand	14,165	11,152	10,692	10,192	10,074	1,043	1,210	9,281	10,183	9,274	18,217	16,977	10,012	2,618	8,548	3,954	11,381	14,601	6,795	4,623
Sorong, Indonesia	14,413	14,671	13,893	12,849	6,555	3,315	2,957	12,483	13,286	6,254	16,509	19,127	12,811	5,760	11,770	4,766	7,880	13,988	9,211	3,800
South Georgia Island	11,644	8,096	10,405	12,203	11,260	14,594	12,746	11,301	11,057	9,077	8,069	6,877	12,002	14,334	11,673	17,454	11,126	11,664	14,966	10,100
South Pole	15,034	11,372	13,842	15,740	8,423	11,674	9,679	14,225	14,386	5,532	10,994	10,648	15,419	12,835	14,239	14,424	9,005	14,509	16,435	6,467
South Sandwich Islands	12,306	8,101	10,497	12,355	11,377	13,847	12,012	11,258	11,123	8,939	8,806	7,507	12,112	13,652	11,551	16,712	11,415	12,384	14,761	9,463
Split, Yugoslavia	6,899	3,859	1,860	1,607	16,693	8,817	10,097	653	1,229	18,265	9,808	8,084	1,238	6,421	736	7,779	16,143	8,106	3,173	13,077
Spokane, Washington	3,170	10,844	8,863	7,431	8,657	11,840	13,621	9,327	8,676	11,778	5,575	7,474	7,840	11,584	9,664	8,945	7,446	2,340	8,277	15,245
Spoleto, Italy	6,709	3,636	1,553	1,453	16,832	9,130	10,395	515	916	18,573	9,525	7,773	1,056	6,730	910	8,070	16,162	7,929	3,448	13,336
Springbok, South Africa	12,553	5,096	7,418	9,211	15,058	10,635	9,553	7,518	7,825	11,921	11,217	8,715	8,835	9,426	7,529	12,735	15,704	13,490	10,353	9,003
Springfield, Illinois	1,301	8,984	7,480	6,571	10,269	13,720	15,672	8,359	7,515	13,059	3,561	5,104	6,948	12,744	8,900	10,789	8,855	99	8,712	17,573
Springfield, Massachusetts	446	7,540	6,055	5,315	11,726	13,668	15,656	7,016	6,138	14,457	3,734	4,372	5,665	12,168	7,604	10,875	10,306	1,428	7,942	18,658
Srinagar, India	10,715	8,001	6,867	6,208	13,135	3,750	5,159	5,450	6,293	13,196	14,531	13,157	6,032	1,368	4,733	3,723	13,968	11,573	2,999	8,478
Stanley, Falkland Islands	10,897	8,920	11,011	12,635	10,275	15,695	13,733	12,109	11,687	8,573	7,036	6,380	12,520	15,759	12,593	18,625	9,926	10,689	15,896	10,719
Stara Zagora, Bulgaria	7,555	4,239	2,536	2,272	16,517	8,091	9,338	1,146	1,954	17,515	10,565	8,821	1,943	5,679	569	7,227	16,284	8,739	2,749	12,334
Stockholm, Sweden	6,012	5,460	3,106	1,474	14,951	8,446	10,096	2,383	2,452	17,379	9,583	8,502	1,546	6,299	2,359	6,725	14,410	7,099	2,191	13,428
Stornoway, United Kingdom	4,753	5,104	2,639	790	14,955	9,829	11,506	2,652	2,172	18,013	8,180	7,158	1,188	7,709	3,005	7,907	14,038	5,913	3,556	14,829
Strasbourg, France	6,028	4,106	1,739	732	16,196	9,341	10,767	1,248	1,081	18,686	9,069	7,552	400	7,014	1,608	7,959	15,422	7,232	3,318	13,869
Stuttgart, West Germany	6,108	4,156	1,813	814	16,179	9,234	10,661	1,230	1,147	18,591	9,172	7,659	503	6,907	1,544	7,865	15,439	7,307	3,221	13,769
Subic, Philippines	13,138	12,939	11,811	10,729	8,259	1,554	2,606	10,418	11,186	8,370	16,595	17,659	10,686	3,842	9,723	2,801	9,391	13,130	7,090	5,202
Suchow, China	11,085	11,746	10,094	8,756	9,317	2,410	4,317	8,795	9,428	10,207	14,908	15,495	8,775	3,226	8,172	633	10,093	11,265	5,164	7,329
Sucre, Bolivia	7,214	7,808	8,954	9,990	11,067	18,985	17,348	10,349	9,574	10,915	3,470	2,966	10,049	16,904	11,047	17,682	9,984	7,075	13,626	14,363
Sudbury, Canada	428	8,220	6,542	5,554	11,124	13,147	15,144	7,359	6,535	14,023	4,163	5,144	5,934	11,899	7,886	10,276	9,755	946	7,772	17,848
Suez, Egypt	8,969	4,015	3,270	3,681	17,072	7,593	8,472	1,983	2,920	16,497	11,591	9,474	3,305	5,159	1,355	7,459	17,439	10,181	3,608	11,139
Sundsvall, Sweden	5,813	5,752	3,363	1,622	14,625	8,451	10,160	2,713	2,724	17,160	9,479	8,534	1,766	6,376	2,702	6,597	14,068	6,869	2,179	13,528

Distances in Kilometers	Ottawa, Canada	Ouagadougou, Bourkina Fasso	Oujda, Morocco	Oxford, United Kingdom	Pago Pago, American Samoa	Pakxe, Laos	Palembang, Indonesia	Palermo, Italy	Palma, Majorca	Palmerston North, New Zealand	Panama, Panama	Paramaribo, Suriname	Paris, France	Patna, India	Patrai, Greece	Peking, China	Penrhyn Island (Omoka)	Peoria, Illinois	Perm', USSR	Perth, Australia
Surabaya, Indonesia	15,698	12,819	12,721	12,280	8,377	2,590	1,008	11,327	12,244	7,203	18,670	18,692	12,103	4,707	10,596	5,237	9,805	15,693	8,821	2,751
Suva, Fiji	12,656	19,366	18,172	16,275	1,240	8,773	8,190	17,363	17,595	2,477	11,590	14,065	16,577	11,187	16,840	9,085	2,735	11,468	13,577	6,413
Sverdlovsk, USSR	7,965	7,183	5,221	3,926	13,623	5,982	7,721	4,013	4,548	15,100	11,855	10,984	3,897	3,986	3,509	4,388	13,740	8,840	291	11,123
Svobodnyy, USSR	9,036	11,445	9,300	7,626	9,361	4,492	6,415	8,243	8,627	11,161	12,811	13,655	7,763	4,618	7,781	1,564	9,683	9,167	4,467	9,310
Sydney, Australia	15,862	16,370	17,556	17,044	4,405	7,251	5,908	16,227	17,161	2,277	14,164	15,889	16,959	9,594	15,503	8,923	5,860	14,687	13,406	3,300
Sydney, Canada	1,208	6,627	4,991	4,242	12,720	13,076	14,998	5,927	5,052	15,537	4,516	4,494	4,585	11,325	6,518	10,463	11,333	2,442	7,069	18,390
Syktyvkar, USSR	7,207	6,875	4,735	3,270	13,803	6,727	8,491	3,662	4,057	15,658	11,082	10,270	3,295	4,759	3,280	4,941	13,705	8,112	510	11,895
Szeged, Hungary	6,946	4,277	2,260	1,674	16,316	8,477	9,826	1,064	1,607	17,933	10,033	8,417	1,369	6,106	900	7,362	15,871	8,129	2,749	12,899
Szombathely, Hungary	6,664	4,221	2,083	1,384	16,287	8,729	10,105	1,047	1,413	18,171	9,745	8,163	1,079	6,372	1,082	7,525	15,737	7,853	2,886	13,190
Tabriz, Iran	9,094	5,515	4,294	3,966	15,526	6,328	7,520	2,873	3,757	15,699	12,362	10,611	3,695	3,893	2,147	5,912	15,972	10,200	2,330	10,581
Tacheng, China	9,583	8,599	6,944	5,806	12,396	4,098	5,903	5,617	6,291	13,297	13,595	12,876	5,747	2,355	4,990	2,793	12,927	10,290	2,184	9,319
Tahiti (Papeete)	10,178	16,555	16,299	15,305	2,291	12,033	11,579	17,190	16,392	4,188	8,238	10,676	15,710	14,336	17,560	11,579	1,318	8,935	15,038	9,420
Taipei, Taiwan	12,010	12,587	11,112	9,841	8,543	1,975	3,584	9,774	10,456	9,153	15,612	16,569	9,845	3,652	9,121	1,718	9,484	12,052	6,228	6,335
Taiyuan, China	10,744	11,195	9,516	8,189	9,848	2,608	4,586	8,221	8,851	10,783	14,671	15,004	8,202	2,918	7,603	405	10,567	11,019	4,589	7,735
Tallahassee, Florida	1,822	8,641	7,525	6,958	10,471	14,850	16,815	8,596	7,689	12,925	2,429	4,087	7,296	13,701	9,216	11,927	8,992	1,234	9,538	18,107
Tallinn, USSR	6,329	5,658	3,368	1,832	14,835	8,065	9,720	2,504	2,700	17,076	9,950	8,880	1,862	5,924	2,364	6,380	14,406	7,391	1,815	13,061
Tamanrasset, Algeria	7,574	1,373	1,502	3,267	18,985	10,390	11,089	1,858	1,881	17,850	9,131	6,762	2,908	7,963	2,308	10,048	17,699	8,804	5,606	13,173
Tampa, Florida	2,028	8,498	7,498	7,035	10,579	15,159	17,132	8,619	7,699	12,923	2,124	3,781	7,360	13,933	9,259	12,241	9,091	1,557	9,736	18,211
Tampere, Finland	6,155	5,823	3,493	1,861	14,635	8,119	9,812	2,698	2,833	16,984	9,831	8,851	1,942	6,026	2,590	6,336	14,177	7,199	1,848	13,176
Tanami, Australia	16,353	14,769	15,023	14,512	6,342	4,684	3,305	13,636	14,555	4,894	16,658	18,356	14,371	6,978	12,905	6,776	7,827	15,652	10,938	1,916
Tangier, Morocco	5,824	2,631	377	1,809	17,190	10,889	12,051	1,723	854	19,486	7,969	6,026	1,597	8,473	2,456	9,749	15,929	7,066	5,101	14,688
Tarawa (Betio)	11,552	18,373	15,982	14,094	2,498	7,525	7,602	15,162	15,368	4,626	11,921	14,632	14,368	9,732	14,726	7,117	3,414	10,545	11,412	7,044
Tashkent, USSR	9,787	7,514	6,122	5,315	13,544	4,555	6,074	4,725	5,513	14,005	13,594	12,337	5,164	2,274	4,038	3,938	14,159	10,675	2,071	9,413
Tbilisi, USSR	8,695	5,528	4,110	3,622	15,449	6,510	7,799	2,698	3,534	15,944	12,041	10,401	3,375	4,100	1,997	5,865	15,752	9,789	1,986	10,925
Tegucigalpa, Honduras	3,638	9,233	8,712	8,514	9,715	16,476	18,216	9,956	9,015	11,616	1,012	3,627	8,809	15,536	10,638	13,546	8,230	2,956	11,347	16,955
Tehran, Iran	9,578	5,888	4,799	4,490	15,206	5,840	6,993	3,380	4,276	15,175	12,892	11,118	4,224	3,397	2,649	5,614	15,815	10,662	2,508	10,056
Tel Aviv, Israel	8,939	4,299	3,406	3,643	16,769	7,364	8,315	2,058	3,002	16,417	11,709	9,667	3,284	4,922	1,369	7,154	17,133	10,135	3,310	11,079
Telegraph Creek, Canada	3,951	10,978	8,713	7,028	8,778	10,396	12,225	8,863	8,382	11,959	6,974	8,634	7,428	10,157	9,054	7,488	7,807	3,497	7,136	14,291
Teresina, Brazil	6,477	4,961	6,144	7,428	13,895	16,424	16,322	7,508	6,792	13,634	4,361	1,828	7,405	14,044	8,187	15,623	12,685	6,956	11,019	15,331
Ternate, Indonesia	14,406	14,208	13,451	12,469	7,018	2,856	2,554	12,037	12,854	6,674	16,858	19,222	12,413	5,301	11,321	4,475	8,333	14,090	8,831	3,823
The Valley, Anguilla	3,253	6,616	6,280	6,519	12,332	16,141	17,879	7,626	6,689	13,930	2,044	1,601	6,724	14,083	8,348	13,586	10,848	3,568	9,920	18,463
Thessaloniki, Greece	7,518	3,940	2,281	2,222	16,800	8,336	9,532	870	1,730	17,717	10,403	8,587	1,862	5,912	284	7,524	16,499	8,720	3,046	12,459
Thimphu, Bhutan	11,793	9,508	8,465	7,719	11,667	2,156	3,735	7,048	7,885	11,613	15,806	14,739	7,575	506	6,331	2,814	12,662	12,451	4,268	7,140
Thunder Bay, Canada	1,087	8,830	7,051	5,917	10,560	12,813	14,789	7,771	6,990	13,542	4,467	5,717	6,311	11,790	8,250	9,897	9,228	857	7,795	17,222
Tientsin, China	10,552	11,494	9,719	8,309	9,518	2,886	4,828	8,460	9,047	10,615	14,408	14,965	8,349	3,348	7,866	112	10,187	10,758	4,761	7,869
Tijuana, Mexico	3,805	11,563	9,955	8,775	7,709	13,049	14,572	10,654	9,896	10,632	4,655	7,035	9,178	13,159	11,086	10,285	6,332	2,602	9,952	15,099
Tiksi, USSR	6,881	9,992	7,608	5,772	10,521	6,460	8,452	6,842	6,975	12,951	10,824	11,407	5,997	5,784	6,580	3,594	10,365	7,188	3,488	11,527
Timbuktu, Mali	7,356	513	1,986	3,884	18,085	11,454	12,004	2,857	2,586	17,387	8,306	5,803	3,593	9,044	3,391	11,148	17,196	8,531	6,645	13,683
Tindouf, Algeria	6,167	1,833	975	2,732	17,681	11,473	12,417	2,312	1,651	18,561	7,726	5,520	2,517	9,030	3,012	10,581	16,250	7,380	5,941	14,652
Tirane, Albania	7,269	3,824	2,040	1,977	16,839	8,583	9,800	659	1,468	17,985	10,132	8,333	1,606	6,166	379	7,694	16,416	8,477	3,156	12,730
Tokyo, Japan	10,342	13,316	11,262	9,602	7,600	4,076	5,617	10,151	10,586	9,186	13,580	15,152	9,738	5,289	9,637	2,104	8,172	10,162	6,362	7,893
Toledo, Spain	5,714	3,057	607	1,338	16,888	10,558	11,817	1,516	573	19,947	8,143	6,340	1,120	8,166	2,228	9,306	15,734	6,960	4,661	14,625
Topeka, Kansas	1,788	9,509	7,975	6,997	9,751	13,610	15,505	8,813	7,988	12,577	3,701	5,483	7,382	12,847	9,332	10,672	8,345	551	8,936	17,075
Toronto, Canada	351	8,098	6,527	5,646	11,197	13,475	15,472	7,412	6,562	14,014	3,845	4,816	6,015	12,174	7,966	10,611	9,798	905	8,013	18,152
Toulouse, France	5,889	3,473	1,033	928	16,669	9,980	11,306	1,174	459	19,414	8,602	6,913	590	7,608	1,805	8,693	15,690	7,125	4,047	14,251
Tours, France	5,632	3,888	1,429	505	16,247	9,883	11,306	1,459	883	19,127	8,545	7,010	206	7,557	1,989	8,439	15,304	6,856	3,816	14,371
Townsville, Australia	15,162	16,561	16,500	15,457	4,554	5,886	4,917	15,080	15,919	3,608	14,919	17,222	15,447	8,315	14,354	7,272	6,036	14,199	11,833	3,397
Trenton, New Jersey	582	7,715	6,294	5,587	11,521	13,878	15,872	7,277	6,393	14,206	3,495	4,284	5,936	12,427	7,871	11,056	10,089	1,257	8,208	18,692
Tripoli, Lebanon	8,810	4,494	3,444	3,525	16,541	7,251	8,280	2,056	2,992	16,433	11,705	9,743	3,182	4,805	1,335	6,930	16,855	9,992	3,029	11,131
Tripoli, Libya	7,414	2,723	1,409	2,398	17,905	9,352	10,335	579	1,200	18,250	9,730	7,643	1,990	6,907	975	8,735	17,212	8,657	4,255	12,929
Tristan da Cunha (Edinburgh)	11,126	5,585	8,013	9,897	13,894	13,494	12,174	8,731	8,621	11,396	8,647	6,507	9,627	12,302	9,041	15,598	13,790	11,663	12,304	10,665
Trondheim, Norway	5,447	5,745	3,308	1,470	14,547	8,779	10,510	2,821	2,703	17,260	9,118	8,230	1,693	6,733	2,901	6,840	13,895	6,511	2,515	13,887
Trujillo, Peru	5,938	8,869	9,362	9,881	9,976	19,079	18,718	10,774	9,876	10,710	1,890	3,066	10,057	17,455	11,507	16,164	8,683	5,512	13,290	15,302
Truk Island (Moen)	12,487	16,356	14,597	12,965	4,780	5,093	5,357	13,391	13,919	5,825	14,052	16,690	13,100	7,331	12,796	5,041	5,844	11,795	9,641	5,799
Truro, Canada	973	6,841	5,241	4,492	12,486	13,217	15,159	6,182	5,307	15,283	4,326	4,451	4,837	11,522	6,772	10,557	11,091	2,197	7,268	18,511
Tsingtao, China	10,838	11,901	10,154	8,745	9,132	2,734	4,609	8,888	9,483	10,177	14,607	15,343	8,786	3,539	8,287	550	9,852	10,975	5,198	7,542
Tsitsihar, China	9,548	11,477	9,442	7,848	9,405	3,951	5,878	8,309	8,765	10,978	13,350	14,111	7,952	4,170	7,798	1,025	9,848	9,704	4,520	8,820
Tubuai Island (Mataura)	10,646	16,433	16,646	15,856	2,450	12,150	11,493	17,706	16,841	3,768	8,403	10,709	16,255	14,532	18,159	11,978	1,835	9,411	15,648	9,091
Tucson, Arizona	3,360	11,053	9,544	8,470	8,178	13,475	15,077	10,325	9,529	11,021	4,138	6,472	8,866	13,384	10,800	10,650	6,769	2,127	9,936	15,645
Tulsa, Oklahoma	1,983	9,599	8,157	7,245	9,620	13,891	15,762	9,040	8,198	12,378	3,438	5,339	7,624	13,168	9,576	10,956	8,192	746	9,252	17,072
Tunis, Tunisia	6,929	2,949	1,118	1,890	17,507	9,506	10,613	317	728	18,696	9,397	7,437	1,484	7,072	1,033	8,660	16,708	8,169	4,082	13,339
Tura, USSR	7,836	9,335	7,141	5,485	11,378	5,476	7,463	6,122	6,469	13,317	11,881	11,964	5,607	4,436	5,715	2,907	11,466	8,334	2,416	10,754
Turin, Italy	6,228	3,727	1,412	994	16,588	9,457	10,796	904	736	18,903	9,092	7,435	587	7,088	1,391	8,219	15,783	7,449	3,571	13,796
Uberlandia, Brazil	7,646	6,191	7,699	9,064	12,725	17,246	16,209	9,016	8,362	12,029	4,613	2,841	9,026	15,198	9,660	17,260	11,732	7,862	12,629	14,129
Ufa, USSR	8,009	6,830	4,922	3,725	13,992	6,125	7,798	3,679	4,255	15,366	11,823	10,806	3,661	4,021	3,152	4,690	14,114	8,935	364	11,175
Ujungpandang, Indonesia	15,307	13,498	13,180	12,525	7,713	2,695	1,645	11,765	12,653	6,818	17,902	19,430	12,394	5,027	11,033	4,997	9,112	15,125	8,956	2,992
Ulaanbaatar, Mongolia	9,661	10,324	8,453	7,029	10,620	3,639	5,636	7,224	7,779	11,893	13,672	13,798	7,068	3,125	6,660	1,169	11,122	10,056	3,488	8,889
Ulan-Ude, USSR	9,224	10,207	8,237	6,739	10,682	4,076	6,073	7,058	7,560	12,143	13,234	13,409	6,803	3,478	6,529	1,486	11,086	9,619	3,280	9,314
Uliastay, Mongolia	9,657	9,615	7,835	6,522	11,355	3,712	5,666	6,561	7,168	12,468	13,712	13,469	6,521	2,664	5,969	1,791	11,876	10,187	2,905	9,028
Uranium City, Canada	2,689	9,767	7,607	6,058	9,882	11,167	13,104	7,946	7,353	13,054	6,121	7,464	6,467	10,483	8,246	8,231	8,772	2,481	6,900	15,528
Urumqi, China	9,985	8,998	7,410	6,295	12,032	3,618	5,452	6,068	6,763	12,817	14,019	13,365	6,234	2,031	5,426	2,418	12,648	10,642	2,673	8,865
Ushuaia, Argentina	11,128	9,695	11,758	13,335	9,499	15,572	13,575	12,880	12,435	7,847	7,144	6,830	13,242	16,106	13,370	18,316	9,182	10,774	16,668	10,387
Vaduz, Liechtenstein	6,223	3,994	1,685	931	16,357	9,256	10,643	1,053	1,010	18,668	9,214	7,635	568	6,907	1,405	7,958	15,615	7,430	3,310	13,708
Valencia, Spain	6,003	3,005	550	1,367	17,059	10,287	11,515	1,201	260	19,666	8,455	6,617	1,066	7,884	1,918	9,126	15,974	7,248	4,477	14,309
Valladolid, Spain	5,563	3,260	813	1,153	16,686	10,529	11,839	1,593	665	19,858	8,093	6,364	974	8,155	2,282	9,197	15,549	6,807	4,561	14,715
Valletta, Malta	7,296	3,064	1,498	2,160	17,553	9,154	10,223	266	1,121	18,298	9,796	7,806	1,751	6,714	692	8,428	16,933	8,532	3,916	12,939
Valparaiso, Chile	8,698	8,968	10,445	11,621	9,982	18,003	16,008	11,796	11,093	9,353	4,723	4,640	11,652	17,629	12,454	18,965	9,143	8,369	15,259	12,771
Vancouver, Canada	3,550	11,122	9,053	7,537	8,445	11,415	13,174	9,425	8,823	11,600	6,021	7,927	7,946	11,256	9,715	8,536	7,298	2,783	8,115	14,821
Varna, Bulgaria	7,633	4,437	2,736	2,374	16,341	7,898	9,170	1,352	2,143	17,335	10,716	9,009	2,066	5,493	759	7,021	16,169	8,804	2,561	12,202
Venice, Italy	6,510	3,896	1,702	1,220	16,536	9,090	10,428	819	1,030	18,544	9,453	7,803	848	6,718	1,115	7,907	15,863	7,719	3,265	13,450
Veracruz, Mexico	3,464	10,045	9,194	8,682	8,969	15,522	17,124	10,311	9,395	11,225	2,118	4,676	9,022	15,046	10,940	12,645	7,474	2,463	11,078	16,536
Verona, Italy	6,422	3,855	1,622	1,141	16,544	9,193	10,533	838	947	18,644	9,348	7,700	758	6,822	1,196	7,990	15,832	7,635	3,344	13,552
Victoria, Canada	3,587	11,186	9,130	7,622	8,370	11,462	13,208	9,511	8,905	11,521	5,988	7,925	8,031	11,330	9,804	8,591	7,215	2,792	8,206	14,801
Victoria, Seychelles	13,482	6,576	7,405	8,218	14,527	5,963	5,479	6,420	7,285	12,159	15,041	12,349	7,835	4,631	5,884	7,930	16,021	14,710	6,942	6,961
Vienna, Austria	6,587	4,306	2,132	1,320	16,186	8,729	10,130	1,146	1,457	18,154	9,707	8,162	1,038	6,384	1,188	7,479	15,628	7,770	2,834	13,239
Vientiane, Laos	12,984	11,050	10,154	9,375	10,158	464	2,322	8,735	9,578	9,921	17,017	16,429	9,250	1,993	8,014	2,774	11,303	13,390	5,832	5,700
Villahermosa, Mexico	3,436	9,744	8,987	8,571	9,250	15,816	17,475	10,146	9,220	11,406	1,758	4,315	8,898	15,178	10,794	12,913	7,755	2,538	11,119	16,752
Vilnius, USSR	6,665	5,248	3,062	1,793	15,311	8,039	9,593	2,052	2,384	17,301	10,138	8,869	1,704	5,797	1,847	6,576	14,929	7,769	1,930	12,866
Visby, Sweden	6,120	5,297	2,966	1,414	15,133	8,452	10,067	2,200	2,304	17,495	9,634	8,480	1,438	6,268	2,170	6,805	14,600	7,224	2,226	13,375
Vitoria, Brazil	8,111	5,581	7,319	8,843	13,382	16,402	15,430	8,562	7,995	12,330	5,376	3,316	8,753	14,446	9,164	16,913	12,482	8,458	12,286	13,694
Vladivostok, USSR	9,823	12,257	10,200	8,567	8,629	3,978	5,782	9,085	9,524	10,237	13,421	14,536	8,689	4,649	8,579	1,339	9,111	9,833	5,296	8,472
Volgograd, USSR	8,068	5,834	4,085	3,221	15,022	6,668	8,141	2,752	3,445	16,102	11,607	10,224	3,051	4,355	2,161	5,606	15,127	9,119	1,292	11,396
Vologda, USSR	7,008	6,225	4,080	2,682	14,420	7,207	8,888	3,012	3,402	16,298	10,748	9,741	2,671	5,104	2,668	5,572	14,231	8,000	958	12,257
Vorkuta, USSR	7,033	7,711	5,476	3,842	12,918	6,548	8,433	4,504	4,805	14,980	11,040	10,597	3,946	4,876	4,166	4,397	12,803	7,803	1,128	11,842
Wake Island	10,486	16,275	13,913	12,049	4,465	6,460	7,199	13,068	13,282	6,667	12,132	14,669	12,299	8,292	12,663	5,294	4,977	9,736	9,347	7,841
Wallis Island	11,866	19,446	17,570	15,716	601	9,152	8,762	17,100	17,092	3,103	10,956	13,520	16,058	11,507	16,730	9,112	2,033	10,680	13,413	7,177
Walvis Bay, Namibia	11,806	4,279	6,608	8,417	15,849	10,787	9,917	6,761	7,029	12,731	10,811	8,211	8,046	9,317	6,816	12,597	16,380	12,795	9,769	9,689
Warsaw, Poland	6,595	4,862	2,670	1,523	15,666	8,341	9,838	1,679	1,993	17,674	9,935	8,557	1,371	6,054	1,557	6,957	15,208	7,735	2,309	13,053
Washington, D.C.	733	7,910	6,529	5,832	11,308	14,019	16,016	7,520	6,634	13,967	3,324	4,273	6,180	12,629	8,116	11,170	9,868	1,093	8,423	18,622
Watson Lake, Canada	3,809	10,716	8,438	6,747	9,055	10,356	12,219	8,581	8,102	12,235	6,984	8,542	7,146	10,016	8,774	7,432	8,088	3,443	6,898	14,418

Distances in Kilometers	Ottawa, Canada	Ouagadougou, Bourkina Fasso	Oujda, Morocco	Oxford, United Kingdom	Pago Pago, American Samoa	Pakxe, Laos	Palembang, Indonesia	Palermo, Italy	Palma, Majorca	Palmerston North, New Zealand	Panama, Panama	Paramaribo, Suriname	Paris, France	Patna, India	Patrai, Greece	Peking, China	Penrhyn Island (Omoka)	Peoria, Illinois	Perm', USSR	Perth, Australia
Weimar, East Germany	6,112	4,438	2,103	878	15,928	9,025	10,500	1,439	1,437	18,318	9,300	7,872	686	6,726	1,635	7,592	15,249	7,292	2,954	13,667
Wellington, New Zealand	14,473	16,778	19,216	18,805	3,309	9,437	8,136	18,394	19,328	127	11,975	13,710	18,981	11,814	17,700	10,759	4,465	13,228	15,396	5,273
West Berlin, West Germany	6,147	4,649	2,326	1,005	15,746	8,848	10,356	1,600	1,659	18,099	9,422	8,053	880	6,571	1,712	7,375	15,118	7,311	2,742	13,561
Wewak, Papua New Guinea	14,005	16,076	15,066	13,755	5,150	4,655	4,322	13,695	14,419	5,188	15,226	17,937	13,794	7,081	13,008	5,561	6,473	13,304	10,185	4,280
Whangarei, New Zealand	14,181	17,385	19,663	18,189	2,808	9,141	7,985	18,312	19,172	526	12,046	13,990	18,407	11,559	17,579	10,266	4,073	12,940	14,914	5,352
Whitehorse, Canada	4,151	10,930	8,610	6,875	8,895	10,037	11,885	8,680	8,245	12,065	7,316	8,893	7,269	9,773	8,833	7,121	7,990	3,791	6,802	14,072
Wichita, Kansas	1,989	9,684	8,177	7,206	9,562	13,682	15,549	9,022	8,194	12,372	3,651	5,533	7,591	12,993	9,541	10,747	8,150	746	9,117	16,941
Willemstad, Curacao	3,747	7,315	7,162	7,427	11,592	16,938	18,783	8,523	7,589	13,027	1,209	1,667	7,635	14,983	9,247	14,216	10,130	3,756	10,790	17,757
Wiluna, Australia	17,488	13,767	14,481	14,431	7,258	4,872	3,097	13,196	14,139	5,280	17,167	17,656	14,201	6,896	12,490	7,376	8,753	16,868	11,085	728
Windhoek, Namibia	11,973	4,366	6,647	8,427	15,842	10,520	9,653	6,730	7,042	12,693	11,070	8,460	8,048	9,069	6,751	12,357	16,472	12,987	9,639	9,489
Windsor, Canada	682	8,400	6,858	5,972	10,878	13,584	15,575	7,744	6,895	13,681	3,709	4,886	6,343	12,389	8,295	10,690	9,472	577	8,265	17,994
Winnipeg, Canada	1,680	9,366	7,498	6,244	10,071	12,463	14,406	8,125	7,388	13,116	4,821	6,258	6,647	11,641	8,558	9,528	8,780	1,180	7,801	16,640
Winston-Salem, North Carolina	1,103	8,206	6,910	6,250	10,974	14,301	16,295	7,926	7,034	13,571	3,006	4,218	6,596	13,006	8,529	11,416	9,520	962	8,818	18,472
Wroclaw, Poland	6,443	4,613	2,378	1,270	15,861	8,629	10,100	1,471	1,701	17,976	9,695	8,266	1,081	6,325	1,475	7,258	15,315	7,606	2,609	13,280
Wuhan, China	11,529	11,678	10,174	8,940	9,429	1,920	3,843	8,835	9,520	10,082	15,389	15,822	8,928	2,909	8,183	1,055	10,297	11,741	5,312	6,921
Wyndham, Australia	16,013	14,591	14,617	14,010	6,565	4,179	2,912	13,214	14,118	5,344	16,946	18,884	13,883	6,507	12,481	6,252	8,031	15,436	10,421	2,208
Xi'an, China	11,168	11,053	9,525	8,313	10,037	2,144	4,139	8,186	8,872	10,725	15,139	15,264	8,292	2,481	7,537	916	10,849	11,492	4,678	7,364
Xining, China	10,916	10,355	8,853	7,705	10,730	2,415	4,387	7,502	8,207	11,376	14,957	14,733	7,662	1,998	6,846	1,331	11,511	11,366	4,066	7,729
Yakutsk, USSR	7,882	10,740	8,445	6,672	9,911	5,538	7,505	7,535	7,788	12,072	11,742	12,471	6,857	5,219	7,173	2,614	9,977	8,089	3,899	10,486
Yanji, China	9,911	12,126	10,105	8,500	8,779	3,821	5,650	8,967	9,428	10,318	13,556	14,589	8,610	4,453	8,448	1,143	9,285	9,952	5,180	8,401
Yaounde, Cameroon	9,490	1,717	3,682	5,439	18,830	10,362	10,398	3,798	4,054	15,663	10,069	7,398	5,063	8,184	3,946	10,996	18,749	10,667	7,146	11,591
Yap Island (Colonia)	13,048	14,953	13,564	12,188	6,232	3,569	3,950	12,235	12,903	6,733	15,383	17,770	12,235	5,861	11,579	3,999	7,361	12,611	8,637	5,165
Yaraka, Australia	15,801	16,159	16,582	15,832	4,865	6,072	4,866	15,180	16,079	3,394	15,089	17,016	15,763	8,452	14,447	7,729	6,360	14,788	12,194	2,867
Yarmouth, Canada	780	7,034	5,496	4,775	12,262	13,426	15,384	6,457	5,576	15,018	4,077	4,345	5,118	11,778	7,052	10,724	10,854	1,961	7,528	18,673
Yellowknife, Canada	3,093	9,924	7,687	6,056	9,799	10,725	12,658	7,922	7,386	12,982	6,566	7,889	6,461	10,092	8,174	7,787	8,763	2,928	6,621	15,120
Yerevan, USSR	8,814	5,446	4,106	3,701	15,553	6,510	7,753	2,687	3,547	15,919	12,109	10,413	3,440	4,086	1,972	5,953	15,897	9,919	2,152	10,845
Yinchuan, China	10,712	10,666	9,053	7,803	10,389	2,588	4,585	7,733	8,394	11,216	14,719	14,744	7,790	2,449	7,100	886	11,117	11,091	4,174	7,856
Yogyakarta, Indonesia	15,795	12,571	12,539	12,168	8,620	2,584	824	11,155	12,080	7,361	18,939	18,423	11,977	4,597	10,426	5,321	10,055	15,864	8,758	2,731
York, United Kingdom	5,212	4,600	2,131	232	15,521	9,737	11,310	2,070	1,612	18,487	8,445	7,191	604	7,515	2,457	8,030	14,624	6,401	3,510	14,543
Yumen, China	10,539	9,914	8,360	7,204	11,146	2,849	4,788	7,018	7,711	11,876	14,595	14,240	7,160	1,968	6,370	1,594	11,860	11,056	3,565	8,162
Yutian, China	10,615	8,599	7,301	6,450	12,509	3,389	5,010	5,900	6,693	12,827	14,569	13,504	6,321	1,291	5,205	3,031	13,290	11,371	2,997	8,404
Yuzhno-Sakhalinsk, USSR	9,105	12,539	10,301	8,541	8,216	4,910	6,657	9,326	9,638	10,205	12,540	13,899	8,722	5,546	8,901	2,257	8,512	9,007	5,585	9,144
Zagreb, Yugoslavia	6,720	4,059	1,954	1,425	16,453	8,804	10,144	881	1,292	18,259	9,728	8,090	1,086	6,431	963	7,656	15,887	7,917	3,025	13,188
Zahedan, Iran	10,623	6,682	5,858	5,604	14,488	4,860	5,891	4,451	5,366	14,076	14,010	12,164	5,342	2,429	3,719	5,133	15,381	11,661	3,187	8,942
Zamboanga, Philippines	13,947	13,438	12,559	11,584	7,784	1,997	2,209	11,148	11,957	7,572	17,056	18,565	11,519	4,435	10,436	3,703	9,033	13,826	7,948	4,348
Zanzibar, Tanzania	12,428	4,948	6,246	7,480	16,027	7,712	7,281	5,584	6,303	13,207	13,274	10,567	7,071	6,083	5,239	9,369	17,479	13,666	7,278	8,394
Zaragoza, Spain	5,839	3,244	778	1,125	16,818	10,237	11,524	1,278	377	19,693	8,412	6,659	842	7,852	1,963	8,982	15,758	7,081	4,336	14,399
Zashiversk, USSR	7,080	10,694	8,297	6,444	9,814	6,392	8,348	7,550	7,670	12,273	10,891	11,754	6,682	6,033	7,285	3,459	9,682	7,239	4,156	11,247
Zhengzhou, China	11,077	11,432	9,821	8,528	9,638	2,314	4,273	8,507	9,160	10,461	14,972	15,364	8,532	2,919	7,876	624	10,421	11,320	4,916	7,385
Zurich, Switzerland	6,137	3,989	1,651	849	16,333	9,334	10,729	1,106	982	18,730	9,125	7,558	479	6,990	1,486	8,011	15,564	7,346	3,364	13,798

Distances in Kilometers	Peshawar, Pakistan	Petropavlovsk-Kamchatskiy, USSR	Petrozavodsk, USSR	Pevek, USSR	Philadelphia, Pennsylvania	Phnom Penh, Kampuchea	Phoenix, Arizona	Pierre, South Dakota	Pinang, Malaysia	Pitcairn Island (Adamstown)	Pittsburgh, Pennsylvania	Plymouth, Montserrat	Plymouth, United Kingdom	Ponape Island	Ponce, Puerto Rico	Ponta Delgada, Azores	Pontianak, Indonesia	Port Augusta, Australia	Port Blair, India	Port Elizabeth, South Africa
Petropavlovsk-Kamchatskiy,USSR	6,891	0	6,366	1,952	8,483	6,607	7,074	6,863	7,452	11,035	8,223	11,348	8,429	5,112	11,020	9,941	7,434	9,688	7,379	15,773
Petrozavodsk, USSR	4,053	6,366	0	5,007	7,088	7,864	9,021	7,554	8,233	15,757	7,242	8,723	2,655	11,010	8,818	4,840	9,225	13,826	7,248	10,646
Pevek, USSR	6,826	1,952	5,007	0	6,751	7,868	6,085	5,443	8,676	11,519	6,547	9,590	6,676	7,025	9,318	8,020	8,925	11,636	8,321	15,483
Philadelphia, Pennsylvania	11,133	8,483	7,088	6,751	0	14,303	3,351	2,129	14,961	9,176	416	2,865	5,485	12,479	2,567	4,249	15,561	16,970	14,164	13,168
Phnom Penh, Kampuchea	4,201	6,607	7,864	7,868	14,303	0	13,677	13,310	845	14,069	14,227	16,580	10,334	5,876	16,607	12,518	1,371	5,998	1,327	9,760
Phoenix, Arizona	12,526	7,074	9,021	6,085	3,351	13,677	0	1,579	14,523	6,752	2,942	5,305	8,346	9,564	4,827	7,550	14,330	13,629	14,373	16,130
Pierre, South Dakota	11,285	6,863	7,554	5,443	2,129	13,310	1,579	0	14,118	8,264	1,726	4,704	6,769	10,374	4,290	6,102	14,290	14,891	13,668	15,298
Pinang, Malaysia	4,341	7,452	8,233	8,676	14,961	845	14,523	14,118	0	14,237	14,927	16,907	10,561	6,409	17,050	12,677	1,168	5,769	1,079	8,955
Pitcairn Island (Adamstown)	17,712	11,035	15,757	11,519	9,176	14,069	6,752	8,264	14,237	0	8,913	8,687	14,643	8,519	8,366	12,890	13,070	8,748	15,288	12,986
Pittsburgh, Pennsylvania	11,262	8,223	7,242	6,547	416	14,227	2,942	1,726	14,927	8,913	0	3,141	5,779	12,092	2,798	4,637	15,432	16,554	14,196	13,574
Plymouth, Montserrat	12,567	11,348	8,723	9,590	2,865	16,580	5,305	4,704	16,907	8,687	3,141	0	6,346	14,865	490	4,264	17,948	17,354	15,849	10,836
Plymouth, United Kingdom	6,221	8,429	2,655	6,676	5,485	10,334	8,346	6,769	10,561	14,643	5,779	6,346	0	13,432	6,542	2,213	11,651	16,322	9,505	9,792
Ponape Island	9,284	5,112	11,010	7,025	12,479	5,876	9,564	10,374	6,409	8,519	12,092	14,865	13,432	0	14,381	15,045	5,486	4,873	7,202	14,321
Ponce, Puerto Rico	12,748	11,020	8,818	9,318	2,567	16,607	4,827	4,290	17,050	8,366	2,798	490	6,542	14,381	0	4,537	17,968	17,102	16,031	11,308
Ponta Delgada, Azores	8,351	9,941	4,840	8,020	4,249	12,518	7,550	6,102	12,677	12,890	4,637	4,264	2,213	15,045	4,537	0	13,803	18,409	11,604	9,546
Pontianak, Indonesia	5,452	7,434	9,225	8,925	15,561	1,371	14,330	14,290	1,168	13,070	15,432	17,948	11,651	5,486	17,968	13,803	0	4,672	2,240	9,435
Port Augusta, Australia	10,109	9,688	13,826	11,636	16,970	5,998	13,629	14,891	5,769	8,748	16,554	17,354	16,322	4,873	17,102	18,409	4,672	0	6,835	9,798
Port Blair, India	3,286	7,379	7,248	8,321	14,164	1,327	14,373	13,668	1,079	15,288	14,196	15,849	9,505	7,202	16,031	11,604	2,240	6,835	0	8,700
Port Elizabeth, South Africa	8,925	15,773	10,646	15,483	13,168	9,760	16,130	15,298	8,955	12,986	13,574	10,836	9,792	14,321	11,308	9,546	9,435	9,798	8,700	0
Port Hedland, Australia	7,809	8,996	11,679	10,778	17,471	3,829	14,844	15,553	3,476	11,063	17,170	19,597	14,028	5,285	19,428	16,075	2,459	2,337	4,523	9,041
Port Louis, Mauritius	6,179	12,515	9,318	12,966	15,032	6,267	18,215	16,636	5,474	14,934	15,418	13,687	9,870	11,399	14,176	10,784	6,066	7,952	5,221	3,496
Port Moresby, Papua New Guinea	9,299	7,011	12,121	8,963	14,647	5,224	11,584	12,526	5,452	8,847	14,251	16,752	14,762	2,190	16,265	16,795	4,322	2,727	6,459	12,210
Port Said, Egypt	3,673	9,328	3,399	8,308	9,154	7,710	11,928	10,355	7,616	18,168	9,456	9,482	3,678	12,894	9,803	5,288	8,784	13,129	6,550	7,255
Port Sudan, Sudan	3,742	10,197	4,692	9,435	10,405	7,272	13,294	11,718	6,998	18,590	10,730	10,352	4,984	12,936	10,729	6,346	8,144	12,120	5,995	6,057
Port-au-Prince, Haiti	13,050	10,696	9,049	9,080	2,390	16,664	4,276	3,873	17,239	7,899	2,537	1,093	6,903	13,806	607	4,991	17,950	16,644	16,297	11,854
Port-of-Spain, Trin. & Tobago	13,018	11,990	9,276	10,255	3,515	17,136	5,727	5,270	17,339	8,416	3,769	674	6,819	15,216	983	4,668	18,468	16,891	16,261	10,403
Port-Vila, Vanuatu	11,705	7,893	13,951	9,698	13,505	7,683	10,159	11,472	7,891	6,387	13,091	14,675	16,319	2,942	14,235	17,409	6,743	3,470	8,914	13,061
Portland, Maine	10,575	8,321	6,526	6,513	579	13,872	3,772	2,400	14,489	9,752	882	3,083	4,915	12,592	2,863	3,780	15,173	17,286	13,650	12,946
Portland, Oregon	11,080	5,495	7,926	4,481	3,877	12,101	1,616	1,757	12,944	7,855	3,480	6,405	7,842	8,618	5,967	7,614	12,864	13,202	12,757	17,034
Porto, Portugal	6,872	9,499	3,658	7,711	5,494	11,064	8,637	7,096	11,180	14,389	5,845	5,775	1,086	14,517	6,049	1,513	12,317	16,897	10,103	9,025
Porto Alegre, Brazil	14,670	16,498	12,678	14,889	8,139	16,812	9,511	9,637	15,975	7,654	8,354	5,308	10,046	16,018	5,572	7,962	16,094	13,016	15,780	7,090
Porto Alexandre, Angola	8,385	14,964	8,831	13,835	10,878	10,682	14,103	12,987	10,015	13,897	11,293	8,894	7,500	16,240	9,383	7,110	10,815	12,162	9,408	2,435
Porto Novo, Benin	7,672	13,036	6,671	11,500	8,510	11,205	11,856	10,530	10,801	14,597	8,924	7,133	4,909	16,945	7,602	4,489	11,868	14,566	9,889	5,089
Porto Velho, Brazil	14,687	13,796	11,293	12,238	5,517	18,772	6,910	6,933	18,256	7,211	5,694	2,823	8,715	15,387	2,977	6,504	18,788	14,897	17,460	9,427
Portsmouth, United Kingdom	6,002	8,346	2,471	6,624	5,678	10,119	8,497	6,919	10,343	14,844	5,965	6,565	219	13,313	6,761	2,421	11,433	16,105	9,286	9,745
Poznan, Poland	4,745	7,788	1,475	6,287	6,753	8,861	9,287	7,724	9,084	15,905	6,999	7,823	1,479	12,482	8,010	3,663	10,173	14,844	8,030	9,607
Prague, Czechoslovakia	4,915	8,094	1,788	6,574	6,722	9,065	9,366	7,794	9,255	15,897	6,986	7,656	1,323	12,793	7,863	3,452	10,360	15,024	8,193	9,375
Praia, Cape Verde Islands	9,554	12,475	6,893	10,557	5,710	13,635	8,982	7,824	13,444	12,350	6,125	4,145	4,307	17,582	4,605	2,537	14,593	17,300	12,418	7,504
Pretoria, South Africa	8,048	14,932	9,722	14,539	12,892	9,272	16,108	14,989	8,508	13,919	13,307	10,843	9,015	14,346	11,330	9,000	9,129	10,163	8,121	944
Prince Albert, Canada	10,339	5,891	6,778	4,394	2,738	12,262	2,250	1,059	13,064	8,984	2,403	5,533	6,395	9,794	5,160	6,148	13,282	14,551	12,612	15,656
Prince Edward Island	9,542	15,813	12,022	16,367	14,702	9,245	17,098	16,787	8,400	11,979	15,085	12,110	11,482	12,857	12,548	11,284	8,595	8,143	8,437	1,747
Prince George, Canada	10,166	4,943	7,014	3,691	3,853	11,479	2,425	1,936	12,309	8,779	3,502	6,603	7,108	8,669	6,208	7,144	12,377	13,448	12,011	16,690
Prince Rupert, Canada	9,996	4,494	7,056	3,362	4,348	11,065	2,725	2,417	11,902	8,795	3,998	7,097	7,366	8,185	6,699	7,541	11,923	12,986	11,658	17,069
Providence, Rhode Island	10,798	8,456	6,748	6,671	378	14,084	3,671	2,361	14,708	9,552	738	2,920	5,107	12,634	2,678	3,899	15,376	17,249	13,873	12,954
Provo, Utah	11,777	6,553	8,286	5,424	3,090	13,151	753	1,038	13,991	7,477	2,675	5,410	7,744	9,528	4,956	7,140	13,934	13,892	13,742	16,198
Puerto Aisen, Chile	16,738	16,266	15,155	15,674	9,457	16,246	9,593	10,313	15,523	5,554	9,536	6,958	12,501	13,534	7,049	10,344	14,967	10,848	16,014	7,992
Puerto Deseado, Argentina	16,182	16,848	15,008	16,161	9,758	15,901	10,104	10,748	15,134	6,084	9,868	7,147	12,379	13,862	7,284	10,276	14,690	10,809	15,533	7,410
Puerto Princesa, Philippines	5,503	5,983	8,764	7,581	14,322	1,525	12,830	12,845	2,085	12,598	14,128	17,079	11,371	4,362	16,881	13,584	1,500	5,093	2,849	10,901
Punta Arenas, Chile	16,378	16,761	15,687	16,471	10,324	15,376	10,388	11,166	14,653	5,775	10,406	7,784	13,068	13,242	7,895	10,974	14,109	10,119	15,173	7,468
Pusan, South Korea	5,202	3,058	6,870	4,584	11,333	3,570	10,110	9,894	4,415	12,510	11,129	14,151	9,481	4,320	13,899	11,531	4,396	7,538	4,492	13,185
Pyongyang, North Korea	4,815	2,947	6,346	4,289	11,006	3,676	10,018	9,681	4,517	12,899	10,827	13,782	8,958	4,822	13,562	11,019	4,637	8,015	4,456	13,083
Qamdo, China	2,425	5,428	5,590	6,139	12,092	2,312	12,221	11,452	2,869	15,366	12,072	14,274	8,142	6,866	14,297	10,353	3,682	8,238	2,215	10,412
Qandahar, Afghanistan	606	7,455	4,049	7,282	11,123	4,587	12,802	11,477	4,623	18,316	11,290	12,314	5,996	9,851	12,537	8,058	5,769	10,373	3,546	8,390
Qiqian, China	4,381	2,535	4,956	3,173	9,679	4,730	9,218	8,602	5,518	13,457	9,546	12,366	7,513	6,071	12,193	9,526	5,888	9,528	5,160	13,239
Qom, Iran	1,898	8,064	3,240	7,451	10,070	6,012	12,260	10,785	6,016	18,938	10,294	10,958	4,722	11,141	11,214	6,694	7,172	11,722	4,937	8,042
Quebec, Canada	10,311	7,975	6,271	6,158	826	13,529	3,732	2,275	14,160	9,912	1,001	3,442	4,795	12,322	3,222	3,834	14,821	17,091	13,342	13,146
Quetta, Pakistan	603	7,493	4,238	7,380	11,315	4,422	12,958	11,648	4,441	18,251	11,480	12,501	6,188	9,751	12,727	8,243	5,590	10,186	3,363	8,330
Quito, Ecuador	15,143	12,152	11,206	10,832	4,561	18,698	5,121	5,392	19,417	6,187	4,505	2,587	8,925	13,694	2,400	6,846	19,166	14,766	18,429	11,298
Rabaul, Papua New Guinea	9,413	6,370	11,847	8,314	13,842	5,516	10,803	11,722	5,862	8,583	13,447	16,030	14,426	1,402	15,541	16,285	4,788	3,475	6,808	13,011
Raiatea (Uturoa)	15,339	9,086	14,978	10,045	10,067	11,818	6,951	8,520	12,131	2,401	9,708	10,460	15,274	6,125	10,054	14,263	11,001	7,254	13,110	14,385
Raleigh, North Carolina	11,684	8,726	7,641	7,072	555	14,754	3,063	2,075	15,444	8,638	532	2,666	6,014	12,434	2,297	4,671	15,964	16,669	14,684	13,277
Rangiroa (Avatoru)	15,559	9,103	14,797	9,940	9,637	12,190	6,556	8,130	12,532	2,155	9,282	10,019	14,897	6,435	9,611	13,822	11,411	7,700	13,493	14,547
Rangoon, Burma	3,112	6,700	6,908	7,654	13,661	1,108	13,694	13,030	1,337	15,158	13,658	15,616	9,295	6,827	15,724	11,456	2,355	7,027	682	9,345
Raoul Is., Kermadec Islands	13,544	9,395	15,693	11,016	13,056	9,421	9,810	11,323	9,512	4,730	12,678	13,368	17,601	4,750	13,002	17,291	8,344	4,224	10,575	12,585
Rarotonga (Avarua)	14,823	9,148	15,365	10,358	11,055	11,018	7,886	9,440	11,259	3,064	10,689	11,433	16,132	5,542	11,038	15,267	10,109	6,248	12,274	13,873
Rawson, Argentina	16,158	16,647	14,588	15,759	9,276	16,358	9,750	10,323	15,572	6,159	9,394	6,650	11,944	14,178	6,791	9,819	15,173	11,296	15,900	7,570
Recife, Brazil	12,026	14,871	9,727	12,924	6,736	15,615	9,329	8,742	15,082	10,158	7,084	4,067	7,126	18,581	4,524	5,158	15,969	15,451	14,288	6,801
Regina, Canada	10,640	6,155	7,037	4,696	2,569	12,564	1,984	748	13,370	8,733	2,209	5,313	6,543	9,923	4,925	6,172	13,565	14,619	12,927	15,618
Reykjavik, Iceland	6,823	7,011	2,772	5,122	4,337	10,503	6,721	5,153	10,953	13,362	4,525	6,085	1,857	12,123	6,118	2,949	11,874	16,218	10,001	11,646
Rhodes, Greece	3,921	9,004	2,855	7,839	8,493	8,073	11,242	9,669	8,057	17,601	8,787	8,966	3,009	12,940	9,261	4,725	9,220	13,684	6,980	7,799
Richmond, Virginia	11,461	8,613	7,418	6,928	333	14,565	3,156	2,063	15,243	8,850	390	2,751	5,807	12,437	2,409	4,510	15,794	16,783	14,470	13,253
Riga, USSR	4,370	7,133	794	5,695	6,903	8,382	9,175	7,646	8,671	15,908	7,107	8,245	1,985	11,801	8,390	4,198	9,721	14,379	7,643	10,075
Ringkobing, Denmark	5,323	7,611	1,617	5,976	6,067	9,360	8,599	7,033	9,641	15,208	6,306	7,271	1,038	12,501	7,426	3,237	10,698	15,357	8,605	10,113
Rio Branco, Brazil	15,103	13,693	11,614	12,233	5,578	19,220	6,712	6,854	18,631	6,765	5,720	3,013	9,069	14,959	3,098	6,864	18,857	14,584	17,902	9,710
Rio Cuarto, Argentina	15,963	15,964	13,636	14,764	8,168	17,380	8,904	9,326	16,556	6,360	8,303	5,519	10,982	14,762	5,666	8,811	16,275	12,381	16,681	8,042
Rio de Janeiro, Brazil	13,626	16,186	11,595	14,352	7,707	16,429	9,595	9,443	15,666	8,670	7,980	4,844	8,985	17,121	5,192	6,959	16,117	13,873	15,207	6,731
Rio Gallegos, Argentina	16,323	16,810	15,486	16,398	10,163	15,528	10,313	11,052	14,791	5,869	10,254	7,600	12,865	13,429	7,720	10,769	14,277	10,320	15,277	7,438
Rio Grande, Brazil	14,823	16,624	12,909	15,067	8,318	16,748	9,598	9,774	15,905	7,508	8,524	5,500	10,279	15,823	5,752	8,196	15,959	12,788	15,774	7,074
Riyadh, Saudi Arabia	2,618	9,203	4,236	8,632	10,668	6,284	13,198	11,664	6,100	19,705	10,945	11,065	5,187	11,837	11,395	6,884	7,264	11,533	5,055	6,860
Road Town, Brit. Virgin Isls.	12,580	11,067	8,675	9,333	2,590	16,496	4,987	4,391	16,900	8,571	2,848	320	6,366	14,549	217	4,340	17,866	17,296	15,866	11,155
Roanoke, Virginia	11,581	8,523	7,549	6,875	511	14,577	2,937	1,887	15,279	8,670	351	2,868	5,995	12,255	2,500	4,729	15,774	16,562	14,542	13,447
Robinson Crusoe Island, Chile	17,298	15,042	14,444	14,270	8,156	17,529	8,199	8,908	16,879	5,013	8,202	5,844	11,843	13,467	5,862	9,630	16,182	11,745	17,422	9,151
Rochester, New York	10,904	8,072	6,880	6,344	411	13,941	3,175	1,830	14,621	9,267	362	3,276	5,438	12,123	2,974	4,377	15,178	16,720	13,863	13,484
Rockhampton, Australia	10,485	8,500	13,640	10,443	15,381	6,291	12,065	13,286	6,311	7,940	14,965	16,539	16,294	3,456	16,131	18,373	5,144	1,607	7,382	11,401
Rome, Italy	5,161	8,999	2,651	7,496	7,036	9,362	9,929	8,350	9,435	16,116	7,345	7,533	1,587	13,584	7,806	3,272	10,582	15,139	8,356	8,507
Rosario, Argentina	15,625	16,184	13,429	14,876	8,208	17,222	9,111	9,460	16,383	6,701	8,365	5,497	10,776	15,081	5,676	8,626	16,208	12,508	16,423	7,750
Roseau, Dominica	12,627	11,525	8,817	9,763	3,042	16,681	5,459	4,879	16,968	8,683	3,319	178	6,409	15,013	632	4,301	18,041	17,301	15,901	10,678
Rostock, East Germany	5,074	7,737	1,559	6,160	6,381	9,158	8,932	7,366	9,406	15,534	6,627	7,501	1,180	12,544	7,674	3,391	10,481	15,152	8,360	9,841
Rostov-na-Donu, USSR	3,039	7,487	1,659	6,430	8,403	7,208	10,635	9,130	7,379	17,386	8,617	9,532	3,190	11,522	9,732	5,317	8,488	13,147	6,317	9,104
Rotterdam, Netherlands	5,598	8,127	2,100	6,465	6,001	9,709	8,722	7,144	9,937	15,177	6,273	6,970	626	13,025	7,160	2,828	11,025	15,696	8,883	9,734
Rouyn, Canada	10,437	7,537	6,449	5,783	970	13,371	3,199	1,692	14,061	9,582	870	3,818	5,213	11,746	3,535	4,410	14,604	16,486	13,328	13,752
Sacramento, California	11,855	6,074	8,664	5,207	3,956	12,668	1,021	1,873	13,513	7,103	3,541	6,214	8,410	8,690	5,748	7,958	13,312	13,030	13,416	17,039
Saginaw, Michigan	11,076	7,765	7,101	6,112	826	13,851	2,678	1,321	14,578	8,932	466	3,605	5,832	11,653	3,255	4,873	15,021	16,207	13,902	13,983
Saint Denis, Reunion	6,309	12,711	9,356	13,115	14,906	6,492	18,155	16,584	5,700	14,888	15,299	13,485	9,815	11,616	13,974	10,662	6,293	8,102	5,436	3,274
Saint George's, Grenada	12,921	11,839	9,151	10,099	3,361	17,015	5,619	5,133	17,253	8,471	3,619	517	6,712	15,132	842	4,576	18,362	17,000	16,177	10,510
Saint John, Canada	10,244	8,314	6,191	6,462	952	13,648	4,115	2,694	14,231	10,128	1,259	3,188	4,536	12,744	3,022	3,436	14,973	17,527	13,359	12,710
Saint John's, Antigua	12,508	11,323	8,666	9,559	2,840	16,523	5,316	4,697	16,848	8,743	3,122	59	6,287	14,879	516	4,205	17,890	17,413	15,790	10,827
Saint John's, Canada	9,405	8,470	5,373	6,537	1,986	13,094	5,134	3,651	13,572	11,139	2,313	3,532	3,508	13,250	3,514	2,455	14,460	18,116	12,618	11,923
Saint Louis, Missouri	11,746	7,894	7,812	6,386	1,304	14,235	2,048	1,061	15,011	8,184	898	3,649	6,578	11,367	3,230	5,532	15,294	15,674	14,437	14,349
Saint Paul, Minnesota	11,124	7,190	7,272	5,647	1,572	13,492	2,068	579	14,269	8,615	1,182	4,256	6,298	10,911	3,869	5,537	14,564	15,469	13,715	14,734

Distances in Kilometers	Peshawar, Pakistan	Petropavlovsk-Kamchatskiy, USSR	Petrozavodsk, USSR	Pevek, USSR	Philadelphia, Pennsylvania	Phnom Penh, Kampuchea	Phoenix, Arizona	Pierre, South Dakota	Pinang, Malaysia	Pitcairn Island (Adamstown)	Pittsburgh, Pennsylvania	Plymouth, Montserrat	Plymouth, United Kingdom	Ponape Island	Ponce, Puerto Rico	Ponta Delgada, Azores	Pontianak, Indonesia	Port Augusta, Australia	Port Blair, India	Port Elizabeth, South Africa
Saint Peter Port, UK	6,136	8,511	2,647	6,776	5,625	10,267	8,500	6,924	10,477	14,775	5,923	6,433	155	13,489	6,639	2,262	11,575	16,244	9,416	9,649
Saipan (Susupe)	7,641	4,353	9,610	6,296	12,589	4,432	10,190	10,643	5,076	10,151	12,258	15,347	12,171	1,644	14,917	14,083	4,340	5,341	5,738	13,707
Salalah, Oman	2,567	9,453	5,214	9,201	11,809	5,502	14,233	12,733	5,195	19,017	12,081	12,113	6,329	11,284	12,467	7,989	6,338	10,438	4,206	6,400
Salem, Oregon	11,138	5,512	7,997	4,523	3,919	12,119	1,585	1,795	12,963	7,785	3,519	6,427	7,914	8,582	5,986	7,677	12,867	13,150	12,788	17,081
Salt Lake City, Utah	11,718	6,499	8,236	5,363	3,098	13,095	810	1,028	13,935	7,526	2,683	5,443	7,712	9,503	4,991	7,129	13,884	13,888	13,682	16,219
Salta, Argentina	15,760	15,192	12,912	13,865	7,237	18,230	8,121	8,443	17,386	6,464	7,377	4,602	10,274	14,982	4,737	8,072	17,202	13,208	17,301	8,603
Salto, Uruguay	15,332	16,220	13,145	14,807	8,095	17,201	9,153	9,427	16,356	6,989	8,270	5,340	10,494	15,387	5,544	8,356	16,282	12,744	16,302	7,606
Salvador, Brazil	12,653	15,312	10,392	13,390	6,979	16,058	9,325	8,896	15,443	9,568	7,300	4,192	7,780	18,077	4,613	5,772	16,204	14,956	14,741	6,836
Salzburg, Austria	5,032	8,369	2,057	6,841	6,749	9,207	9,481	7,904	9,365	15,920	7,029	7,555	1,282	13,055	7,781	3,319	10,484	15,131	8,296	9,143
Samsun, Turkey	3,187	8,187	2,288	7,141	8,665	7,385	11,122	9,582	7,455	17,818	8,915	9,495	3,256	12,062	9,743	5,232	8,599	13,189	6,377	8,405
San Antonio, Texas	12,906	8,245	9,046	7,016	2,426	14,828	1,365	1,667	15,662	6,911	2,078	3,956	7,840	10,909	3,473	6,656	15,624	14,704	15,310	14,766
San Cristobal, Venezuela	14,019	11,748	10,105	10,216	3,577	17,846	4,983	4,885	18,337	7,241	3,701	1,470	7,802	14,201	1,287	5,734	19,133	15,886	17,306	11,212
San Diego, California	12,562	6,812	9,217	5,964	3,818	13,387	481	1,948	14,231	6,540	3,406	5,768	8,703	9,097	5,287	7,994	13,959	13,156	14,170	16,575
San Francisco, California	11,927	6,077	8,768	5,252	4,060	12,661	1,052	1,986	13,505	7,002	3,645	6,287	8,531	8,607	5,819	8,076	13,279	12,922	13,432	17,119
San Jose, Costa Rica	14,507	10,873	10,459	9,568	3,441	17,433	3,870	4,126	18,240	6,315	3,403	2,482	8,453	12,878	2,086	6,575	18,180	15,061	17,598	12,437
San Juan, Argentina	16,299	15,565	13,706	14,448	7,944	17,693	8,524	9,005	16,892	6,005	8,056	5,380	11,062	14,464	5,487	8,866	16,504	12,400	17,088	8,470
San Juan, Puerto Rico	12,676	10,998	8,749	9,285	2,535	16,544	4,848	4,286	16,981	8,438	2,775	458	6,470	14,407	73	4,464	17,908	17,174	15,960	11,290
San Luis Potosi, Mexico	13,739	8,733	9,889	7,666	3,137	15,337	1,660	2,465	16,183	6,097	2,831	4,105	8,609	10,828	3,616	7,284	15,927	14,173	15,986	14,675
San Marino, San Marino	5,125	8,789	2,451	7,275	6,921	9,324	9,765	8,186	9,426	16,044	7,221	7,522	1,445	13,415	7,779	3,259	10,564	15,160	8,349	8,727
San Miguel de Tucuman, Argen.	15,829	15,382	13,093	14,082	7,463	18,032	8,308	8,656	17,192	6,426	7,601	4,825	10,449	14,936	4,963	8,253	16,978	13,006	17,168	8,469
San Salvador, El Salvador	14,347	10,219	10,304	8,986	3,217	16,814	3,185	3,561	17,649	6,171	3,096	2,916	8,501	12,242	2,464	6,771	17,484	14,836	17,198	13,130
Sanaa, Yemen	3,435	10,204	5,218	9,692	11,258	6,568	14,050	12,484	6,228	18,781	11,575	11,208	5,806	12,357	11,594	7,223	7,355	11,244	5,263	5,804
Santa Cruz, Bolivia	15,194	14,693	12,127	13,213	6,513	18,572	7,690	7,853	17,767	6,918	6,679	3,817	9,502	15,384	3,980	7,293	17,873	14,012	17,354	8,816
Santa Cruz, Tenerife	8,118	10,966	5,217	9,108	5,479	12,303	8,820	7,418	12,276	13,523	5,882	4,873	2,643	16,047	5,247	1,353	13,443	17,498	11,204	8,194
Santa Fe, New Mexico	12,285	7,265	8,623	6,098	2,738	13,860	614	1,076	14,698	7,188	2,328	4,799	7,795	10,090	4,332	6,939	14,641	14,240	14,418	15,633
Santa Rosa, Argentina	16,034	16,239	13,952	15,121	8,551	17,027	9,209	9,679	16,215	6,303	8,682	5,905	11,297	14,601	6,052	9,142	15,894	12,019	16,413	7,850
Santa Rosalia, Mexico	13,204	7,571	9,683	6,700	3,685	14,136	681	2,173	14,977	6,103	3,297	5,267	8,892	9,614	4,778	7,933	14,652	13,359	14,930	15,951
Santarem, Brazil	13,454	13,618	10,192	11,850	5,137	17,567	7,201	6,883	17,246	8,429	5,401	2,272	7,571	16,349	2,612	5,360	18,240	15,924	16,303	8,966
Santiago del Estero, Argentina	15,780	15,524	13,134	14,216	7,583	17,891	8,450	8,793	17,050	6,492	7,726	4,927	10,486	14,991	5,074	8,296	16,853	12,940	17,031	8,333
Santiago, Chile	16,545	15,575	13,996	14,563	8,140	17,539	8,580	9,128	16,766	5,773	8,237	5,622	11,353	14,203	5,712	9,156	16,298	12,123	17,063	8,530
Santo Domingo, Dominican Rep.	12,912	10,821	8,937	9,166	2,435	16,637	4,501	4,034	17,158	8,105	2,621	839	6,736	14,045	351	4,786	17,964	16,853	16,180	11,630
Sao Paulo de Olivenca, Brazil	14,702	13,017	11,031	11,514	4,849	18,884	6,111	6,159	18,812	6,967	4,992	2,343	8,550	14,809	2,386	6,369	19,575	15,147	17,807	10,205
Sao Paulo, Brazil	13,968	16,104	11,824	14,330	7,627	16,738	9,372	9,294	15,958	8,322	7,882	4,763	9,195	16,793	5,085	7,127	16,338	13,786	15,539	7,007
Sao Tome, Sao Tome & Principe	7,690	13,546	7,206	12,136	9,297	10,904	12,632	11,336	10,415	14,639	9,712	7,766	5,643	16,773	8,245	5,308	11,422	13,782	9,577	4,277
Sapporo, Japan	5,993	1,693	6,686	3,391	10,109	4,950	8,729	8,554	5,795	11,757	9,871	12,967	9,124	4,333	12,667	10,963	5,741	8,374	5,823	14,466
Sarajevo, Yugoslavia	4,652	8,622	2,257	7,206	7,334	8,852	10,088	8,512	8,948	16,489	7,621	8,000	1,850	13,094	8,254	3,737	10,087	14,683	7,871	8,646
Saratov, USSR	2,829	6,826	1,343	5,821	8,380	6,880	10,347	8,895	7,136	17,045	8,554	9,775	3,454	10,905	9,929	5,649	8,202	12,872	6,102	9,684
Saskatoon, Canada	10,461	5,926	6,911	4,464	2,755	12,332	2,119	979	13,139	8,851	2,407	5,525	6,520	9,755	5,144	6,242	13,333	14,488	12,705	15,734
Schefferville, Canada	9,393	7,343	5,370	5,453	1,764	12,612	4,221	2,653	13,226	10,696	1,872	4,247	4,134	11,998	4,082	3,623	13,923	16,870	12,402	13,157
Seattle, Washington	10,860	5,371	7,697	4,295	3,829	11,968	1,791	1,734	12,809	8,085	3,440	6,423	7,645	8,652	5,994	7,474	12,769	13,292	12,590	16,947
Sendai, Japan	6,110	2,136	7,124	3,910	10,601	4,634	9,073	8,989	5,474	11,611	10,353	13,465	9,606	3,887	13,150	11,480	5,328	7,839	5,602	14,298
Seoul, South Korea	4,956	2,980	6,540	4,396	11,129	3,628	10,053	9,761	4,472	12,757	10,941	13,922	9,152	4,635	13,690	11,210	4,542	7,837	4,462	13,122
Sept-Iles, Canada	9,802	7,811	5,758	5,940	1,330	13,112	4,144	2,625	13,712	10,425	1,518	3,735	4,302	12,364	3,570	3,495	14,430	17,218	12,865	12,948
Sevastopol, USSR	3,447	7,993	1,917	6,849	8,248	7,644	10,690	9,149	7,761	17,388	8,493	9,168	2,876	12,082	9,398	4,917	8,892	13,519	6,688	8,738
Seville, Spain	6,820	9,880	3,874	8,126	5,871	11,021	9,062	7,534	11,074	14,608	6,234	5,934	1,454	14,836	6,241	1,736	12,229	16,691	9,995	8,549
Shanghai, China	4,643	3,858	6,858	5,251	11,955	2,750	10,928	10,640	3,595	13,094	11,784	14,700	9,510	4,679	14,502	11,652	3,674	7,250	3,651	12,348
Sheffield, United Kingdom	5,976	8,070	2,303	6,337	5,565	10,047	8,303	6,724	10,307	14,741	5,836	6,600	376	13,059	6,773	2,542	11,378	16,044	9,262	10,024
Shenyang, China	4,575	2,897	5,981	4,086	10,759	3,807	9,932	9,513	4,637	13,148	10,596	13,502	8,593	5,167	13,302	10,658	4,846	8,357	4,484	13,021
Shiraz, Iran	1,863	8,420	3,821	7,930	10,606	5,761	12,841	11,364	5,682	19,445	10,842	11,351	5,207	11,137	11,635	7,099	6,848	11,310	4,610	7,586
Sibiu, Romania	4,191	8,233	1,899	6,901	7,587	8,384	10,189	8,624	8,509	16,762	7,851	8,420	2,152	12,610	8,653	4,168	9,639	14,267	7,437	8,835
Singapore	4,942	7,623	8,817	8,979	15,438	1,142	14,639	14,411	601	13,675	15,368	17,507	11,162	6,069	17,634	13,277	627	5,168	1,675	9,012
Sioux Falls, South Dakota	11,334	7,124	7,531	5,657	1,832	13,523	1,740	304	14,320	8,327	1,426	4,407	6,619	10,678	3,998	5,862	14,538	15,173	13,824	14,999
Skelleftea, Sweden	4,798	6,449	746	4,895	6,345	8,565	8,378	6,880	8,960	15,130	6,504	8,016	2,164	11,312	8,094	4,262	9,932	14,487	7,985	10,953
Skopje, Yugoslavia	4,421	8,706	2,365	7,358	7,656	8,621	10,403	8,828	8,689	16,804	7,944	8,274	2,171	13,044	8,539	4,011	9,836	14,403	7,610	8,422
Socotra Island (Tamrida)	2,959	9,849	5,682	9,661	12,179	5,534	14,695	13,182	5,148	18,567	12,467	12,303	6,694	11,381	12,681	8,261	6,264	10,185	4,214	5,974
Sofia, Bulgaria	4,265	8,573	2,251	7,253	7,734	8,465	10,432	8,860	8,543	16,899	8,015	8,412	2,256	12,880	8,669	4,148	9,688	14,269	7,466	8,491
Songkhla, Thailand	4,210	7,272	8,071	8,481	14,766	675	14,345	13,921	199	14,301	14,730	16,765	10,425	6,365	16,888	12,556	1,257	5,900	990	9,094
Sorong, Indonesia	7,318	6,495	10,456	8,353	14,925	3,221	12,522	13,024	3,507	10,848	14,615	17,729	13,100	3,121	17,299	15,295	2,442	3,566	4,476	11,400
South Georgia Island	14,144	18,990	14,289	17,815	11,065	14,201	12,088	12,476	13,367	7,993	11,275	8,227	11,992	14,587	8,498	10,247	13,237	10,379	13,546	5,268
South Pole	13,768	15,877	16,860	17,736	14,427	11,279	13,705	14,917	10,601	7,228	14,481	11,850	15,590	10,765	11,996	14,182	9,998	6,404	11,285	6,244
South Sandwich Islands	13,588	19,388	14,261	18,449	11,738	13,455	12,834	13,211	12,620	8,447	11,966	8,883	12,163	14,351	9,176	10,582	12,513	9,896	12,806	4,666
Split, Yugoslavia	4,815	8,716	2,351	7,268	7,218	9,015	10,012	8,434	9,107	16,358	7,512	7,844	1,734	13,232	8,102	3,580	10,248	14,837	8,030	8,630
Spokane, Washington	10,913	5,656	7,607	4,478	3,459	12,231	1,641	1,368	13,068	8,155	3,070	6,064	7,409	9,022	5,640	7,150	13,076	13,651	12,796	16,589
Spoleto, Italy	5,125	8,905	2,558	7,402	7,006	9,326	9,875	8,297	9,410	16,108	7,311	7,549	1,542	13,500	7,815	3,286	10,554	15,128	8,332	8,594
Springbok, South Africa	9,029	15,914	10,248	15,222	12,298	10,360	15,303	14,427	9,584	13,055	12,703	9,999	9,130	15,176	10,476	8,731	10,154	10,661	9,222	871
Springfield, Illinois	11,607	7,816	7,673	6,285	1,238	14,125	2,119	1,019	14,896	8,317	824	3,686	6,456	11,367	3,278	5,443	15,201	15,732	14,309	14,339
Springfield, Massachusetts	10,820	8,382	6,772	6,606	322	14,059	3,574	2,258	14,694	9,496	648	2,985	5,169	12,535	2,730	3,991	15,341	17,147	13,874	13,057
Srinagar, India	302	6,679	4,195	6,699	11,249	3,944	12,494	11,303	4,124	17,423	11,361	12,783	6,440	8,982	12,947	8,589	5,217	9,884	3,085	9,118
Stanley, Falkland Islands	15,551	17,552	14,952	16,839	10,292	15,290	10,814	11,402	14,495	6,654	10,432	7,589	12,399	14,046	7,770	10,391	14,147	10,553	14,833	6,708
Stara Zagora, Bulgaria	4,076	8,515	2,235	7,241	7,905	8,277	10,566	8,997	8,351	17,076	8,181	8,604	2,434	12,747	8,861	4,340	9,496	14,077	7,273	8,458
Stockholm, Sweden	4,778	7,058	932	5,519	6,463	8,733	8,746	7,211	9,053	15,470	6,665	7,873	1,723	11,862	8,000	3,913	10,083	14,720	8,037	10,363
Stornoway, United Kingdom	6,181	7,598	2,266	5,811	5,153	10,127	7,750	6,175	10,463	14,301	5,393	6,469	882	12,653	6,590	2,674	11,483	16,089	9,447	10,641
Strasbourg, France	5,414	8,415	2,216	6,808	6,359	9,576	9,141	7,563	9,751	15,525	6,645	7,165	882	13,219	7,384	2,943	10,864	15,520	8,685	9,314
Stuttgart, West Germany	5,306	8,363	2,135	6,775	6,446	9,468	9,204	7,626	9,644	15,615	6,728	7,271	977	13,143	7,489	3,050	10,756	15,413	8,578	9,307
Subic, Philippines	5,312	5,406	8,345	6,989	13,730	1,700	12,313	12,269	2,417	12,661	13,535	16,501	10,980	4,242	16,290	13,184	2,040	5,566	2,999	11,346
Suchow, China	4,173	3,863	6,351	5,074	11,690	2,807	10,922	10,508	3,637	13,550	11,548	14,364	9,005	5,186	14,205	11,161	3,884	7,698	3,527	12,165
Sucre, Bolivia	15,456	14,684	12,357	13,270	6,610	18,685	7,643	7,874	17,852	6,662	6,758	3,967	9,739	15,140	4,101	7,529	17,817	13,800	17,537	8,931
Sudbury, Canada	10,674	7,615	6,691	5,897	868	13,549	2,996	1,528	14,252	9,339	678	3,733	5,444	11,708	3,425	4,581	14,759	16,388	13,540	13,848
Suez, Egypt	3,691	9,442	3,543	8,442	9,269	7,690	12,064	10,491	7,576	18,231	9,575	9,546	3,799	12,937	9,875	5,371	8,744	13,051	6,514	7,114
Sundsvall, Sweden	4,893	6,768	889	5,196	6,286	8,754	8,463	6,941	9,115	15,205	6,468	7,835	1,862	11,631	7,935	3,994	10,114	14,710	8,121	10,706
Surabaya, Indonesia	6,301	7,954	10,108	9,571	16,298	2,253	14,581	14,798	1,966	12,347	16,118	18,831	12,514	5,290	18,812	14,643	884	3,809	3,042	9,307
Suva, Fiji	12,649	8,109	14,410	9,763	12,669	8,713	9,323	10,727	8,951	5,357	12,263	13,620	16,418	3,548	13,189	16,822	7,808	4,360	9,963	13,565
Sverdlovsk, USSR	2,671	5,744	1,581	4,892	8,505	6,286	9,974	8,646	6,680	16,373	8,610	10,298	4,177	9,831	10,377	6,386	7,650	12,247	5,725	10,591
Svobodnyy, USSR	4,878	2,078	5,354	2,976	9,635	4,894	8,926	8,416	5,710	12,947	9,471	12,394	7,857	5,657	12,182	9,806	5,969	9,342	5,448	13,698
Sydney, Australia	11,201	9,654	14,660	11,591	15,885	7,018	12,542	13,923	6,891	7,515	15,481	16,185	17,294	4,577	15,882	19,499	5,753	1,261	7,968	10,600
Sydney, Canada	9,896	8,414	5,847	6,519	1,398	13,444	4,573	3,125	13,978	10,564	1,724	3,271	4,089	13,008	3,176	2,984	14,794	17,858	13,063	12,341
Syktyvkar, USSR	3,410	5,803	868	4,676	7,741	7,040	9,349	7,968	7,450	15,938	7,855	9,540	3,521	10,238	9,610	5,708	8,408	12,975	6,498	10,842
Szeged, Hungary	4,499	8,319	1,954	6,914	7,302	8,690	9,963	8,392	8,821	16,478	7,574	8,107	1,849	12,808	8,341	3,857	9,949	14,580	7,749	8,903
Szombathely, Hungary	4,767	8,328	1,974	6,859	7,015	8,949	9,708	8,134	9,096	16,189	7,290	7,827	1,557	12,924	8,056	3,584	10,218	14,859	8,025	9,038
Tabriz, Iran	2,312	8,003	2,766	7,224	9,513	6,490	11,776	10,279	6,535	18,523	9,742	10,420	4,163	11,419	10,667	6,157	7,683	12,264	5,456	8,260
Tacheng, China	1,710	5,228	3,472	5,135	10,159	4,416	10,995	9,905	4,876	16,233	10,201	12,164	6,056	8,333	12,213	8,269	5,786	10,355	4,005	10,624
Tahiti (Papeete)	15,554	9,258	15,078	10,175	9,978	12,026	6,906	8,480	12,329	2,184	9,626	10,294	15,247	6,342	9,894	14,151	11,194	7,386	13,314	14,282
Taipei, Taiwan	4,895	4,384	7,437	5,878	12,605	2,299	11,411	11,223	3,135	12,903	12,423	15,368	10,091	4,393	15,161	12,259	3,069	6,599	3,373	12,038
Taiyuan, China	3,694	3,895	5,784	4,879	11,352	3,013	10,864	10,317	3,801	14,018	11,240	13,940	8,439	5,735	13,818	10,605	4,209	8,218	3,515	11,992
Tallahasee, Florida	12,434	8,947	8,406	7,431	1,341	15,256	2,641	2,093	16,006	7,848	1,174	2,710	6,801	12,190	2,256	5,382	16,348	16,051	15,342	13,534
Tallinn, USSR	4,412	6,874	588	5,420	6,796	8,352	8,973	7,458	8,676	15,720	6,984	8,253	2,083	11,588	8,376	4,283	9,703	14,340	7,664	10,350
Tamanrasset, Algeria	6,482	11,216	4,859	9,676	7,653	10,468	10,939	9,446	10,277	15,524	8,041	7,074	3,178	15,590	7,475	3,405	11,435	15,235	9,244	6,631
Tampa, Florida	12,622	9,276	8,578	7,753	1,490	15,564	2,892	2,421	16,301	7,776	1,403	2,423	6,867	12,455	1,958	5,344	16,673	16,147	15,599	13,258
Tampere, Finland	4,541	6,699	561	5,210	6,634	8,416	8,753	7,245	8,768	15,503	6,810	8,176	2,109	11,470	8,282	4,282	9,774	14,386	7,770	10,583
Tanami, Australia	8,583	8,556	12,225	10,449	16,773	4,422	13,790	14,688	4,271	10,062	16,399	18,720	14,755	4,315	18,301	16,932	3,132	1,602	5,349	10,020

Distances in Kilometers

	Peshawar, Pakistan	Petropavlovsk-Kamchatskiy, USSR	Petrozavodsk, USSR	Pevek, USSR	Philadelphia, Pennsylvania	Phnom Penh, Kampuchea	Phoenix, Arizona	Pierre, South Dakota	Pinang, Malaysia	Pitcairn Island (Adamstown)	Pittsburgh, Pennsylvania	Plymouth, Montserrat	Plymouth, United Kingdom	Ponape Island	Ponce, Puerto Rico	Ponta Delgada, Azores	Pontianak, Indonesia	Port Augusta, Australia	Port Blair, India	Port Elizabeth, South Africa
Tangier, Morocco	6,873	10,051	4,015	8,301	5,964	11,071	9,179	7,659	11,102	14,616	6,332	5,932	1,628	14,993	6,252	1,783	12,261	16,666	10,023	8,385
Tarawa (Betio)	10,978	5,878	12,179	7,589	11,764	7,592	8,540	9,645	8,077	6,794	11,351	13,660	14,263	1,742	13,172	15,277	7,081	5,264	8,918	15,060
Tashkent, USSR	836	6,447	3,255	6,162	10,315	4,788	11,722	10,456	5,033	17,474	10,435	11,880	5,553	9,421	12,025	7,730	6,099	10,770	4,011	9,462
Tbilisi, USSR	2,496	7,755	2,344	6,886	9,125	6,696	11,353	9,858	6,795	18,100	9,345	10,135	3,829	11,403	10,361	5,882	7,930	12,552	5,722	8,605
Tegucigalpa, Honduras	14,228	10,301	10,178	9,019	3,097	16,874	3,302	3,580	17,695	6,357	3,002	2,697	8,327	12,440	2,245	6,571	17,627	15,041	17,162	12,970
Tehran, Iran	1,846	7,945	3,146	7,328	10,011	5,988	12,164	10,696	6,012	18,821	10,229	10,949	4,690	11,064	11,197	6,685	7,164	11,734	4,933	8,164
Tel Aviv, Israel	3,424	9,135	3,308	8,164	9,265	7,476	11,966	10,400	7,397	18,354	9,556	9,679	3,780	12,645	9,991	5,464	8,564	12,948	6,327	7,372
Telegraph Creek, Canada	9,600	4,270	6,669	3,017	4,402	10,791	3,073	2,594	11,622	9,194	4,076	7,207	7,067	8,216	6,828	7,363	11,702	13,061	11,334	16,830
Teresina, Brazil	12,570	14,342	9,831	12,440	5,986	16,413	8,426	7,922	15,953	9,504	6,311	3,219	7,180	17,697	3,655	5,062	16,890	15,845	15,095	7,709
Ternate, Indonesia	6,867	6,469	10,090	8,273	14,948	2,754	12,753	13,141	3,051	11,315	14,666	17,807	12,720	3,491	17,430	14,927	2,013	3,844	4,010	11,153
The Valley, Anguilla	12,511	11,174	8,636	9,422	2,692	16,479	5,152	4,533	16,843	8,687	2,966	175	6,292	14,715	376	4,238	17,850	17,391	15,797	10,993
Thessaloniki, Greece	4,316	8,792	2,479	7,483	7,843	8,511	10,597	9,022	8,558	16,981	8,134	8,419	2,358	13,047	8,692	4,158	9,710	14,253	7,479	8,264
Thimphu, Bhutan	1,878	6,224	5,545	6,799	12,372	2,377	12,876	11,977	2,694	16,064	12,406	14,258	7,959	7,546	14,361	10,141	3,702	8,367	1,792	9,593
Thunder Bay, Canada	10,681	7,074	6,801	5,435	1,467	13,218	2,518	958	13,969	9,095	1,153	4,293	5,833	11,051	3,947	5,163	14,354	15,735	13,356	14,504
Tientsin, China	4,082	3,495	5,909	4,579	11,158	3,289	10,504	10,021	4,103	13,630	11,022	13,824	8,556	5,439	13,666	10,688	4,411	8,211	3,892	12,416
Tijuana, Mexico	12,584	6,836	9,234	5,987	3,815	13,410	473	1,954	14,254	6,524	3,403	5,754	8,711	9,111	5,273	7,994	13,980	13,161	14,193	16,558
Tiksi, USSR	5,318	2,529	3,844	1,518	7,489	6,865	7,438	6,574	7,613	13,016	7,372	10,174	5,975	7,467	9,995	7,713	8,073	11,567	7,095	14,009
Timbuktu, Mali	7,586	12,076	5,795	10,400	7,324	11,508	10,674	9,291	11,257	14,483	7,732	6,287	3,732	16,683	6,725	3,212	12,396	15,722	10,252	6,382
Tindouf, Algeria	7,461	10,972	4,907	9,203	6,206	11,612	9,525	8,078	11,536	14,282	6,601	5,663	2,543	15,908	6,042	1,978	12,703	16,715	10,471	7,697
Tirane, Albania	4,566	8,830	2,478	7,457	7,585	8,765	10,377	8,800	8,823	16,712	7,881	8,149	2,102	13,197	8,420	3,887	9,972	14,524	7,744	8,358
Tokyo, Japan	6,109	2,427	7,318	4,210	10,899	4,409	9,322	9,271	5,244	11,605	10,648	13,763	9,831	3,704	13,446	11,737	5,058	7,553	5,420	14,119
Toledo, Spain	6,560	9,579	3,550	7,845	5,909	10,760	9,037	7,490	10,841	14,780	6,258	6,137	1,171	14,516	6,425	1,891	11,988	16,519	9,762	8,724
Topeka, Kansas	11,809	7,565	7,957	6,145	1,763	14,013	1,597	707	14,815	7,951	1,349	4,082	6,894	10,899	3,648	5,957	14,995	15,208	14,330	14,822
Toronto, Canada	10,913	7,948	6,902	6,236	542	13,875	3,042	1,678	14,569	9,203	362	3,401	5,522	11,970	3,086	4,508	15,095	16,569	13,833	13,638
Toulouse, France	6,002	9,079	2,951	7,406	6,148	10,194	9,139	7,569	10,312	15,193	6,471	6,634	865	13,946	6,893	2,370	11,447	16,047	9,236	8,933
Tours, France	5,956	8,684	2,655	6,991	5,928	10,120	8,829	7,253	10,292	15,056	6,232	6,626	486	13,599	6,853	2,399	11,407	16,059	9,225	9,348
Townsville, Australia	9,906	8,087	13,052	10,039	15,413	5,719	12,175	13,288	5,776	8,463	15,002	16,952	15,706	3,155	16,511	17,832	4,609	1,723	6,840	11,450
Trenton, New Jersey	11,090	8,473	7,045	6,735	46	14,273	3,385	2,150	14,926	9,222	446	2,875	5,440	12,492	2,583	4,209	15,535	17,000	14,125	13,148
Tripoli, Lebanon	3,273	8,858	3,047	7,884	9,157	7,380	11,782	10,223	7,340	18,312	9,436	9,693	3,677	12,441	9,988	5,452	8,504	12,957	6,265	7,647
Tripoli, Libya	5,351	9,918	3,553	8,476	7,628	9,485	10,699	9,132	9,424	16,364	7,972	7,681	2,407	14,266	8,016	3,548	10,591	14,893	8,354	7,515
Tristan da Cunha (Edinburgh)	11,711	18,098	11,734	16,368	10,673	13,190	12,939	12,627	12,379	10,548	11,013	7,923	9,721	16,534	8,341	8,394	12,767	11,704	12,114	3,431
Trondheim, Norway	5,259	6,802	1,233	5,150	5,918	9,089	8,136	6,603	9,466	14,865	6,102	7,495	1,690	11,748	7,585	3,737	10,453	15,021	8,478	10,879
Trujillo, Peru	15,859	12,850	12,013	11,637	5,337	19,447	5,777	6,196	19,700	5,723	5,377	3,311	9,647	13,719	3,196	7,510	18,728	14,065	19,052	10,840
Truk Island (Moen)	8,664	5,092	10,669	7,041	12,889	5,170	10,121	10,823	5,703	9,172	12,519	15,421	13,193	707	14,947	14,998	4,793	4,666	6,497	13,796
Truro, Canada	10,110	8,397	6,058	6,524	1,144	13,591	4,334	2,907	14,150	10,315	1,469	3,180	4,341	12,899	3,049	3,218	14,930	17,712	13,254	12,517
Tsingtao, China	4,409	3,520	6,345	4,778	11,440	3,127	10,585	10,201	3,962	13,305	11,283	14,158	8,992	5,030	13,975	11,117	4,155	7,805	3,875	12,511
Tsitsihar, China	4,575	2,529	5,512	3,517	10,150	4,353	9,457	8,957	5,168	13,194	9,995	12,883	8,086	5,541	12,687	10,108	5,440	8,953	4,922	13,278
Tubuai Island (Mataura)	15,879	9,831	15,723	10,806	10,405	12,101	7,434	9,012	12,316	1,976	10,070	10,467	15,777	6,597	10,097	14,489	11,159	7,100	13,345	13,638
Tucson, Arizona	12,668	7,245	9,125	6,253	3,313	13,848	172	1,635	14,693	6,657	2,908	5,184	8,388	9,681	4,704	7,533	14,491	13,679	14,544	15,997
Tulsa, Oklahoma	12,128	7,804	8,262	6,428	1,864	14,293	1,507	987	15,104	7,670	1,467	3,961	7,133	10,964	3,509	6,104	15,237	15,132	14,642	14,765
Tunis, Tunisia	5,485	9,599	3,248	8,084	7,162	9,668	10,197	8,628	9,669	16,045	7,498	7,368	1,895	14,141	7,678	3,162	10,831	15,256	8,592	7,996
Tura, USSR	3,891	3,467	3,195	2,937	8,442	5,866	8,806	7,824	6,533	14,362	8,395	10,901	5,721	7,815	10,811	7,750	7,174	11,220	5,878	12,664
Turin, Italy	5,481	8,792	2,538	7,199	6,526	9,672	9,406	7,828	9,797	15,642	6,830	7,140	1,064	13,547	7,389	2,881	10,929	15,545	8,773	8,936
Uberlandia, Brazil	13,889	15,570	11,463	13,793	7,090	17,046	8,909	8,778	16,314	8,346	7,348	4,226	8,817	16,864	4,552	6,705	16,802	14,277	15,782	7,404
Ufa, USSR	2,604	6,119	1,482	5,235	8,531	6,411	10,166	8,795	6,754	16,674	8,659	10,190	3,974	10,167	10,297	6,187	7,763	12,400	5,766	10,249
Ujungpandang, Indonesia	6,634	7,420	10,245	9,136	15,882	2,443	13,857	14,193	2,419	11,819	15,642	18,712	12,769	4,517	18,440	14,960	1,252	3,583	3,483	10,050
Ulaanbaatar, Mongolia	3,311	3,637	4,628	4,110	10,269	4,036	10,195	9,440	4,752	14,474	10,194	12,767	7,277	6,633	12,674	9,421	5,318	9,425	4,237	12,136
Ulan-Ude, USSR	3,493	3,400	4,353	3,714	9,832	4,474	9,797	9,012	5,190	14,363	9,755	12,349	6,985	6,786	12,247	9,097	5,751	9,796	4,660	12,391
Uliastay, Mongolia	2,600	4,298	4,121	4,515	10,258	4,084	10,562	9,662	4,704	15,217	10,231	12,569	6,773	7,327	12,537	8,959	5,432	9,783	4,026	11,492
Uranium City, Canada	9,633	5,313	6,173	3,717	3,190	11,572	2,914	1,780	12,363	9,585	2,911	6,046	6,058	9,526	5,707	6,105	12,636	14,374	11,888	15,642
Urumqi, China	1,759	5,138	3,959	5,250	10,569	3,944	11,221	10,206	4,433	16,032	10,593	12,638	6,545	7,931	12,675	8,768	5,315	9,868	3,603	10,659
Ushuaia, Argentina	16,152	16,981	15,686	16,721	10,520	15,170	10,637	11,401	14,435	5,971	10,612	7,943	13,094	13,288	8,070	11,031	13,922	10,016	14,934	7,234
Vaduz, Liechtenstein	5,303	8,524	2,263	6,948	6,547	9,481	9,346	7,767	9,634	15,704	6,837	7,290	1,063	13,273	7,521	3,048	10,755	15,397	8,563	9,129
Valencia, Spain	6,280	9,561	3,417	7,874	6,211	10,481	9,312	7,757	10,545	15,095	6,556	6,444	1,250	14,421	6,737	2,205	11,696	16,206	9,466	8,559
Valladolid, Spain	6,548	9,395	3,421	7,649	5,774	10,742	8,872	7,319	10,851	14,714	6,117	6,106	974	14,356	6,379	1,844	11,990	16,567	9,774	8,928
Valletta, Malta	5,138	9,563	3,198	8,129	7,542	9,305	10,537	8,963	9,286	16,444	7,872	7,764	2,200	13,946	8,078	3,564	10,450	14,855	8,210	7,820
Valparaiso, Chile	16,624	15,479	14,008	14,485	8,089	17,600	8,491	9,053	16,838	5,690	8,180	5,594	11,370	14,132	5,675	9,169	16,343	12,126	17,154	8,631
Vancouver, Canada	10,668	5,214	7,528	4,107	3,875	11,803	1,978	1,812	12,643	8,260	3,494	6,515	7,534	8,605	6,094	7,428	12,625	13,289	12,409	16,939
Varna, Bulgaria	3,888	8,350	2,113	7,112	7,998	8,089	10,594	9,032	8,177	17,174	8,265	8,768	2,549	12,544	9,017	4,507	9,317	13,916	7,100	8,550
Venice, Italy	5,111	8,632	2,307	7,107	6,829	9,303	9,635	8,056	9,427	15,976	7,122	7,508	1,344	13,290	7,753	3,251	10,559	15,178	8,353	8,896
Veracruz, Mexico	13,973	9,296	10,020	8,155	3,053	15,904	2,236	2,819	16,748	6,124	2,813	3,598	8,527	11,387	3,114	7,037	16,528	14,488	16,464	14,076
Verona, Italy	5,216	8,668	2,361	7,122	6,737	9,407	9,561	7,983	9,533	15,877	7,032	7,402	1,254	13,356	7,647	3,145	10,664	15,283	8,459	8,917
Victoria, Canada	10,753	5,253	7,621	4,175	3,899	11,849	1,911	1,819	12,689	8,168	3,514	6,516	7,617	8,580	6,091	7,491	12,655	13,245	12,469	16,989
Victoria, Seychelles	4,599	11,299	7,587	11,423	13,720	5,762	16,564	15,010	5,112	16,667	14,060	13,112	8,324	11,492	13,566	9,546	6,013	9,019	4,503	4,482
Vienna, Austria	4,781	8,236	1,889	6,756	6,945	8,955	9,614	8,042	9,116	16,121	7,215	7,802	1,505	12,858	8,023	3,570	10,233	14,883	8,048	9,147
Vientiane, Laos	3,560	6,178	7,122	7,287	13,589	752	13,235	12,721	1,410	14,550	13,534	15,830	9,619	6,150	15,856	11,815	2,123	6,725	1,273	9,970
Villahermosa, Mexico	14,021	9,603	10,021	8,403	2,974	16,204	2,567	3,007	17,043	6,238	2,780	3,263	8,405	11,748	2,783	6,828	16,882	14,728	16,675	13,713
Vilnius, USSR	4,234	7,318	953	5,921	7,101	8,300	9,425	7,891	8,557	16,149	7,316	8,352	2,037	11,911	8,515	4,243	9,625	14,295	7,517	9,822
Visby, Sweden	4,728	7,223	1,012	5,701	6,560	8,730	8,900	7,358	9,026	15,609	6,771	7,891	1,664	11,993	8,033	3,872	10,072	14,726	8,000	10,174
Vitoria, Brazil	13,229	16,029	11,202	14,144	7,588	16,199	9,655	9,401	15,474	9,056	7,881	4,741	8,604	17,530	5,119	6,607	16,030	14,156	14,938	6,600
Vladivostok, USSR	5,241	2,257	6,260	3,665	10,410	4,361	9,328	9,016	5,204	12,496	10,212	13,226	8,801	4,770	12,976	10,768	5,285	8,396	5,137	13,724
Volgograd, USSR	2,773	7,143	1,585	6,155	8,531	6,902	10,606	9,133	7,110	17,333	8,723	9,797	3,452	11,132	9,975	5,616	8,201	12,871	6,060	9,351
Vologda, USSR	3,637	6,409	421	5,169	7,508	7,499	9,414	7,960	7,844	16,132	7,663	9,098	2,933	10,896	9,206	5,140	8,854	13,481	6,848	10,412
Vorkuta, USSR	3,757	4,910	1,533	3,793	7,605	6,898	8,806	7,529	7,418	15,190	7,659	9,708	4,083	9,480	9,709	6,181	8,265	12,649	6,559	11,703
Wake Island	9,287	3,807	10,081	5,608	10,854	6,650	8,069	8,767	7,333	8,425	10,474	13,360	12,233	1,643	12,890	13,564	6,605	6,504	7,924	15,854
Wallis Island	12,876	7,732	14,096	9,267	11,883	9,136	8,535	9,939	9,455	4,993	11,476	12,952	15,828	3,606	12,506	16,036	8,339	5,133	10,425	14,293
Walvis Bay, Namibia	8,729	15,510	9,562	14,566	11,585	10,552	14,713	13,710	9,824	13,470	11,996	9,428	8,329	15,764	9,914	7,924	10,511	11,417	9,337	1,631
Warsaw, Poland	4,469	7,690	1,333	6,250	7,001	8,589	9,475	7,920	8,808	16,134	7,239	8,099	1,754	12,305	8,285	3,934	9,898	14,569	7,755	9,562
Washington, D.C.	11,310	8,502	7,269	6,802	199	14,417	3,189	2,028	15,092	8,978	308	2,851	5,684	12,398	2,524	4,434	15,653	16,817	14,316	13,275
Watson Lake, Canada	9,407	4,297	6,404	2,925	4,285	10,755	3,206	2,580	11,578	9,441	3,977	7,117	6,787	8,401	6,754	7,116	11,711	13,260	11,244	16,557
Weimar, East Germany	5,134	8,080	1,846	6,510	6,477	9,270	9,139	7,566	9,476	15,653	6,743	7,433	1,091	12,853	7,633	3,250	10,574	15,242	8,417	9,514
Wellington, New Zealand	13,421	10,565	16,534	12,315	14,269	9,226	11,156	12,705	9,122	5,350	13,924	13,964	18,990	5,599	13,690	18,225	7,981	3,412	10,199	11,097
West Berlin, West Germany	4,987	7,870	1,623	6,319	6,532	9,101	9,117	7,548	9,326	15,696	6,785	7,581	1,237	12,630	7,767	3,428	10,414	15,085	8,273	9,654
Wewak, Papua New Guinea	8,596	6,426	11,358	8,373	14,409	4,600	11,557	12,335	4,916	9,476	14,037	16,852	14,002	1,994	16,366	16,067	3,836	3,263	5,877	12,330
Whangarei, New Zealand	13,157	9,947	15,994	11,695	14,044	8,960	10,825	12,343	8,933	5,399	13,674	14,084	18,369	5,011	13,763	18,229	7,774	3,373	10,011	11,638
Whitehorse, Canada	9,229	3,951	6,384	2,637	4,633	10,434	3,457	2,918	11,261	9,518	4,328	7,468	6,929	8,084	7,104	7,368	11,372	12,951	10,956	16,721
Wichita, Kansas	11,982	7,591	8,151	6,219	1,936	14,083	1,415	783	14,896	7,746	1,527	4,147	7,103	10,798	3,701	6,150	15,025	15,040	14,448	14,930
Willemstad, Curacao	13,418	11,493	9,512	9,867	3,144	17,303	4,970	4,663	17,741	7,803	3,320	885	7,201	14,401	699	5,145	18,656	16,481	16,705	11,171
Wiluna, Australia	8,450	9,574	12,366	11,401	17,961	4,534	14,979	15,902	4,141	10,557	17,603	18,881	14,650	5,531	18,832	16,602	3,163	1,819	5,166	8,805
Windhoek, Namibia	8,513	15,330	9,481	14,474	11,771	10,284	14,936	13,890	9,556	13,661	12,184	9,664	8,350	15,524	10,151	8,037	10,247	11,251	9,071	1,511
Windsor, Canada	11,167	7,912	7,177	6,258	709	13,988	2,722	1,422	14,710	8,888	326	3,461	5,850	11,775	3,109	4,830	15,164	16,291	14,021	13,877
Winnipeg, Canada	10,645	6,576	6,895	5,019	2,046	12,868	2,199	659	13,651	8,917	1,702	4,831	6,182	10,457	4,462	5,681	13,936	15,152	13,126	15,087
Winston-Salem, North Carolina	11,711	8,619	7,677	6,985	618	14,703	2,915	1,934	15,409	8,559	482	2,792	6,100	12,287	2,411	4,797	15,892	16,527	14,675	13,426
Wroclaw, Poland	4,733	7,920	1,591	6,431	6,827	8,872	9,401	7,835	9,075	15,992	7,080	7,834	1,490	12,588	8,031	3,647	10,173	14,841	8,016	9,461
Wuhan, China	4,013	4,349	6,540	5,556	12,136	2,318	11,413	10,994	3,145	13,744	12,006	14,759	9,190	5,277	14,626	11,376	3,429	7,409	3,057	11,726
Wyndham, Australia	8,114	8,134	11,706	10,002	16,485	3,932	13,700	14,464	3,835	10,442	16,138	18,923	14,255	4,145	18,441	16,449	2,678	2,125	4,913	10,177
Xi'an, China	3,425	4,407	5,919	5,379	11,777	2,548	11,380	10,809	3,314	14,305	11,683	14,287	8,564	5,890	14,199	10,759	3,797	7,984	2,998	11,505
Xining, China	2,752	4,708	5,331	5,415	11,521	2,795	11,493	10,764	3,458	14,966	11,471	13,870	7,956	6,586	13,837	10,163	4,132	8,519	2,915	11,108
Yakutsk, USSR	5,081	1,980	4,547	1,995	8,485	5,944	8,077	7,396	6,728	12,966	8,341	11,218	6,890	6,546	11,019	8,729	7,091	10,500	6,328	13,997
Yanji, China	5,054	2,427	6,173	3,769	10,502	4,208	9,492	9,148	5,048	12,679	10,313	13,300	8,736	4,880	13,064	10,732	5,164	8,390	4,958	13,531

Distances in Kilometers	Peshawar, Pakistan	Petropavlovsk-Kamchatskiy, USSR	Petrozavodsk, USSR	Pevek, USSR	Philadelphia, Pennsylvania	Phnom Penh, Kampuchea	Phoenix, Arizona	Pierre, South Dakota	Pinang, Malaysia	Pitcairn Island (Adamstown)	Pittsburgh, Pennsylvania	Plymouth, Montserrat	Plymouth, United Kingdom	Ponape Island	Ponce, Puerto Rico	Ponta Delgada, Azores	Pontianak, Indonesia	Port Augusta, Australia	Port Blair, India	Port Elizabeth, South Africa
Yaounde, Cameroon	7,028	12,993	6,704	11,685	9,456	10,301	12,807	11,421	9,846	15,300	9,866	8,163	5,363	16,149	8,632	5,325	10,886	13,604	8,976	4,440
Yap Island (Colonia)	7,271	5,165	9,794	7,065	13,550	3,641	11,223	11,650	4,195	10,637	13,235	16,352	12,434	2,235	15,936	14,511	3,361	4,650	4,968	12,678
Yaraka, Australia	10,058	8,745	13,448	10,697	16,012	5,859	12,718	13,900	5,802	8,491	15,597	17,153	16,083	3,839	16,768	18,288	4,643	1,045	6,880	10,819
Yarmouth, Canada	10,379	8,454	6,326	6,610	865	13,805	4,106	2,722	14,384	10,032	1,207	3,031	4,623	12,842	2,863	3,445	15,132	17,591	13,506	12,649
Yellowknife, Canada	9,299	4,878	5,971	3,271	3,612	11,129	3,228	2,206	11,924	9,801	3,345	6,474	6,077	9,195	6,143	6,306	12,189	14,062	11,467	15,789
Yerevan, USSR	2,489	7,904	2,503	7,052	9,235	6,685	11,505	10,003	6,759	18,256	9,463	10,183	3,902	11,484	10,420	5,923	7,900	12,503	5,682	8,437
Yinchuan, China	3,145	4,269	5,406	5,055	11,320	2,985	11,114	10,448	3,710	14,567	11,244	13,783	8,054	6,265	13,709	10,245	4,274	8,505	3,267	11,556
Yogyakarta, Indonesia	6,178	8,130	10,041	9,708	16,401	2,223	14,824	14,988	1,838	12,541	16,247	18,745	12,399	5,559	18,830	14,499	866	3,935	2,900	9,054
York, United Kingdom	5,945	8,014	2,253	6,284	5,572	10,009	8,290	6,712	10,274	14,748	5,839	6,634	432	13,002	6,802	2,589	11,341	16,006	9,231	10,064
Yumen, China	2,411	4,748	4,834	5,250	11,140	3,213	11,333	10,505	3,821	15,303	11,112	13,412	7,454	7,019	13,399	9,663	4,570	9,009	3,167	11,030
Yutian, China	974	6,018	4,267	6,161	11,177	3,643	12,090	11,005	3,967	16,738	11,244	12,977	6,693	8,358	13,085	8,886	4,980	9,640	3,010	9,764
Yuzhno-Sakhalinsk, USSR	5,991	1,322	6,376	2,947	9,674	5,286	8,394	8,155	6,130	11,798	9,443	12,529	8,759	4,678	12,235	10,554	6,135	8,813	6,089	14,649
Zagreb, Yugoslavia	4,824	8,494	2,137	7,024	7,056	9,016	9,798	8,221	9,142	16,221	7,340	7,791	1,577	13,073	8,031	3,536	10,272	14,896	8,068	8,887
Zahedan, Iran	1,128	7,933	4,082	7,666	11,080	4,967	12,997	11,606	4,927	18,837	11,278	12,057	5,806	10,349	12,313	7,793	6,088	10,623	3,849	7,946
Zamboanga, Philippines	5,984	6,092	9,215	7,777	14,526	1,953	12,776	12,923	2,411	12,136	14,300	17,353	11,834	3,998	17,092	14,045	1,609	4,667	4,667	11,036
Zanzibar, Tanzania	5,603	12,494	7,550	12,132	12,519	7,538	15,784	14,241	6,915	16,362	12,908	11,425	7,520	13,302	11,897	8,272	7,822	10,449	6,249	3,383
Zaragoza, Spain	6,246	9,335	3,239	7,637	6,067	10,444	9,128	7,567	10,540	15,032	6,403	6,423	1,006	14,227	6,697	2,162	11,683	16,248	9,462	8,798
Zashiversk, USSR	5,760	1,825	4,552	1,145	7,678	6,797	7,230	6,534	7,587	12,439	7,516	10,455	6,641	6,823	10,230	8,300	7,919	11,090	7,188	14,589
Zhengzhou, China	3,846	4,055	6,124	5,152	11,684	2,718	11,081	10,595	3,526	13,877	11,563	14,294	8,778	5,502	14,165	10,952	3,877	7,859	3,325	11,909
Zurich, Switzerland	5,386	8,530	2,296	6,937	6,459	9,561	9,268	7,689	9,718	15,614	6,750	7,204	974	13,305	7,433	2,964	10,838	15,483	8,649	9,171

Distances in Kilometers	Port Hedland, Australia	Port Louis, Mauritius	Port Moresby, Papua New Guinea	Port Said, Egypt	Port Sudan, Sudan	Port-au-Prince, Haiti	Port-of-Spain, Trin. & Tobago	Port-Vila, Vanuatu	Portland, Maine	Portland, Oregon	Porto, Portugal	Porto Alegre, Brazil	Porto Alexandre, Angola	Porto Novo, Benin	Porto Velho, Brazil	Portsmouth, United Kingdom	Poznan, Poland	Prague, Czechoslovakia	Praia, Cape Verde Islands	Pretoria, South Africa
Port Louis, Mauritius	6,341	0	9,625	6,296	4,925	14,780	13,437	11,390	14,549	17,191	9,616	10,583	4,841	6,689	12,861	9,718	8,947	8,858	9,672	3,064
Port Moresby, Papua New Guinea	3,297	9,625	0	12,920	12,448	15,660	16,889	2,460	14,780	10,771	15,773	15,212	14,363	16,118	16,036	14,588	13,487	13,765	18,852	12,365
Port Said, Egypt	10,822	6,296	12,920	0	1,382	10,277	9,765	15,360	8,589	11,132	3,801	11,126	5,649	4,133	11,102	3,497	2,660	2,562	5,933	6,325
Port Sudan, Sudan	9,902	4,925	12,448	1,382	0	11,257	10,524	14,887	9,853	12,509	4,937	10,937	4,802	4,014	11,501	4,817	4,042	3,935	6,449	5,114
Port-au-Prince, Haiti	18,872	14,780	15,660	10,277	11,257	0	1,455	13,647	2,792	5,493	6,492	5,836	9,977	8,206	3,158	7,120	8,350	8,226	5,206	11,910
Port-of-Spain, Trin. & Tobago	18,935	13,437	16,889	9,765	10,524	1,455	0	14,614	3,754	6,932	6,160	4,639	8,600	7,064	2,163	7,035	8,296	8,108	4,148	10,492
Port-Vila, Vanuatu	5,226	11,390	2,460	15,360	14,887	13,647	14,614	0	13,869	9,860	17,393	13,241	15,493	18,033	13,585	16,222	15,421	15,730	18,732	13,557
Portland, Maine	17,292	14,549	14,780	8,589	9,853	2,792	3,754	13,869	0	4,088	4,964	8,392	10,593	8,139	5,840	5,106	6,174	6,145	5,444	12,590
Portland, Oregon	13,827	17,191	10,771	11,132	12,509	5,493	6,932	9,860	4,088	0	8,387	11,042	14,662	12,102	8,382	7,949	8,487	8,631	9,532	16,613
Porto, Portugal	14,562	9,616	15,773	3,801	4,937	6,492	6,160	17,393	4,964	8,387	0	9,020	6,652	3,999	7,898	1,217	2,302	2,044	3,245	8,323
Porto Alegre, Brazil	14,324	10,583	15,212	11,126	10,937	5,836	4,639	13,241	8,392	11,042	9,020	0	6,579	7,020	2,705	10,217	11,273	10,979	5,795	7,664
Porto Alexandre, Angola	11,075	4,841	14,363	5,649	4,802	9,977	8,600	15,493	10,593	14,662	6,652	6,579	0	2,670	8,242	7,484	7,575	7,304	5,168	2,018
Porto Novo, Benin	12,971	6,689	16,118	4,133	4,014	8,206	7,064	18,033	8,139	12,102	3,999	7,020	2,670	0	7,571	4,921	5,260	4,958	3,004	4,511
Porto Velho, Brazil	16,777	12,861	16,036	11,102	11,501	3,158	2,163	13,585	5,840	8,382	7,898	2,705	8,242	7,571	0	8,924	10,161	9,931	5,169	9,802
Portsmouth, United Kingdom	13,809	9,718	14,588	3,497	4,817	7,120	7,035	16,222	5,106	7,949	1,217	10,217	7,484	4,921	8,924	0	1,261	1,106	4,458	8,951
Poznan, Poland	12,553	8,947	13,487	2,660	4,042	8,350	8,296	15,421	6,174	8,487	2,302	11,273	7,575	5,260	10,161	1,261	0	313	5,478	8,728
Prague, Czechoslovakia	12,713	8,858	13,765	2,562	3,935	8,226	8,108	15,730	6,145	8,631	2,044	10,979	7,304	4,958	9,931	1,106	313	0	5,187	8,508
Praia, Cape Verde Islands	15,975	9,672	18,852	5,933	6,449	5,206	4,148	18,732	5,444	9,532	3,245	5,795	5,168	3,004	5,169	4,458	5,478	5,187	0	7,183
Pretoria, South Africa	9,096	3,064	12,365	6,325	5,114	11,910	10,492	13,557	12,590	16,613	8,323	7,664	2,018	4,511	9,802	8,951	8,728	8,508	7,183	0
Prince Albert, Canada	14,768	16,070	11,982	9,809	11,191	4,806	6,142	11,301	2,798	1,486	6,904	10,625	13,236	10,637	7,923	6,513	7,149	7,265	8,180	15,145
Prince Edward Island	7,692	3,429	10,682	8,640	7,331	13,026	11,584	11,327	14,559	18,515	10,757	7,588	4,178	6,836	10,200	11,419	11,152	10,947	9,160	2,469
Prince George, Canada	13,680	16,259	10,858	10,267	11,636	5,808	7,191	10,276	3,923	932	7,748	11,555	14,254	11,611	8,855	7,196	7,642	7,805	9,273	16,070
Prince Rupert, Canada	13,184	16,157	10,375	10,377	11,728	6,290	7,681	9,870	4,407	1,121	8,064	12,009	14,641	11,980	9,315	7,439	7,793	7,977	9,725	16,376
Providence, Rhode Island	17,445	14,681	14,817	8,776	10,028	2,583	3,586	13,803	225	4,080	5,122	8,226	10,626	8,209	5,653	5,300	6,382	6,347	5,463	12,632
Provo, Utah	14,794	17,556	11,634	11,264	12,641	4,458	5,907	10,451	3,418	1,070	8,118	9,974	13,968	11,556	7,312	7,882	8,610	8,705	8,800	15,982
Puerto Aisen, Chile	12,639	11,179	12,742	13,519	13,083	7,080	6,308	10,709	9,868	11,205	11,510	2,533	8,356	9,388	4,147	12,684	13,788	13,500	8,313	8,806
Puerto Deseado, Argentina	12,453	10,614	12,880	13,085	12,571	7,369	6,483	10,978	10,135	11,720	11,350	2,333	7,815	8,970	4,325	12,549	13,587	13,288	8,117	8,224
Puerto Princesa, Philippines	3,324	7,476	3,802	9,122	8,775	16,654	17,750	6,241	14,024	11,371	12,226	17,527	12,100	12,728	19,725	11,166	9,944	10,184	15,050	10,536
Punta Arenas, Chile	11,815	10,497	12,188	13,573	12,937	7,943	7,126	10,332	10,727	11,990	12,033	3,024	8,139	9,499	4,963	13,237	14,251	13,949	8,794	8,332
Pusan, South Korea	6,233	9,712	5,291	8,637	8,943	13,657	14,821	7,169	11,068	8,549	10,523	19,446	13,467	12,768	16,808	9,317	8,299	8,599	13,763	12,549
Pyongyang, North Korea	6,610	9,656	5,810	8,172	8,541	13,363	14,455	7,688	10,709	8,428	9,999	18,974	13,156	12,305	16,520	8,793	7,776	8,075	13,239	12,387
Qamdo, China	6,136	7,091	6,970	6,090	6,100	14,394	14,857	9,320	11,623	10,610	8,974	17,008	10,480	10,082	16,857	7,933	6,698	6,934	11,896	9,674
Qandahar, Afghanistan	8,045	5,794	9,760	3,168	3,143	12,890	12,716	12,193	10,553	11,423	6,557	14,078	7,782	7,098	14,254	5,778	4,540	4,674	9,091	7,498
Qiqian, China	8,036	10,079	7,284	7,236	7,877	12,066	13,038	9,003	9,330	7,602	8,574	17,461	12,672	11,291	15,169	7,359	6,419	6,727	11,817	12,401
Qom, Iran	9,386	6,107	11,179	1,776	2,142	11,614	11,326	13,600	9,491	11,100	5,183	12,862	6,944	5,843	12,830	4,509	3,330	3,408	7,672	7,102
Quebec, Canada	16,935	14,543	14,512	8,472	9,765	3,139	4,113	13,736	360	3,899	4,929	8,750	10,765	8,259	6,199	4,977	5,998	5,988	5,645	12,742
Quetta, Pakistan	7,856	5,665	9,610	3,312	3,215	13,084	12,898	12,049	10,746	11,562	6,740	14,150	7,797	7,194	14,409	5,970	4,734	4,866	9,242	7,448
Quito, Ecuador	17,082	14,734	14,862	11,996	12,714	2,181	2,231	12,462	4,928	6,661	8,354	4,391	10,052	9,039	1,875	9,144	10,399	10,240	6,275	11,673
Rabaul, Papua New Guinea	4,054	10,345	804	13,083	12,787	14,941	16,251	2,310	13,982	9,967	15,489	15,477	15,130	16,656	15,780	14,275	13,274	13,570	18,733	13,144
Raiatea (Uturoa)	9,383	14,853	6,681	18,352	19,061	9,498	10,345	4,274	10,589	7,484	15,551	10,043	15,972	16,988	9,480	15,405	15,918	16,097	14,468	15,304
Raleigh, North Carolina	17,618	15,422	14,558	9,673	10,902	2,008	3,276	13,204	1,131	3,823	5,974	7,834	11,070	8,806	5,167	6,210	7,300	7,263	5,923	13,088
Rangiroa (Avatoru)	9,827	15,253	7,089	18,196	19,283	9,053	9,915	4,700	10,164	7,158	15,128	9,804	15,939	16,660	9,109	15,038	15,632	15,789	14,047	15,482
Rangoon, Burma	4,779	5,880	6,323	6,605	6,212	15,903	16,114	8,780	13,172	12,078	9,984	16,398	9,928	10,187	17,695	9,078	7,817	8,008	12,534	8,736
Raoul Is., Kermadec Islands	6,426	11,944	4,245	17,124	16,326	12,475	13,142	1,898	13,550	9,990	18,375	11,353	14,908	17,482	11,805	17,603	17,161	17,472	16,953	13,315
Rarotonga (Avarua)	8,396	13,904	5,815	18,379	18,252	10,490	11,286	3,368	11,568	8,291	16,519	10,509	15,811	17,522	10,269	16,237	16,529	16,760	15,364	14,741
Rawson, Argentina	12,951	10,867	13,313	12,872	12,464	6,886	5,985	11,336	9,645	11,365	10,932	1,919	7,775	8,740	3,828	12,121	13,192	12,898	7,714	8,344
Recife, Brazil	15,743	9,960	18,052	8,360	8,472	5,054	3,602	16,192	6,746	10,467	6,075	2,971	5,157	4,464	3,194	7,285	8,305	8,010	2,834	6,934
Regina, Canada	14,975	16,297	12,104	10,013	11,393	4,549	5,908	11,306	2,691	1,446	7,001	10,352	13,221	10,657	7,648	6,670	7,356	7,459	8,117	15,167
Reykjavik, Iceland	14,327	11,505	13,876	5,209	6,582	6,301	6,691	14,791	3,767	6,039	2,701	10,754	9,326	6,693	8,816	1,928	2,572	2,647	5,468	10,872
Rhodes, Greece	11,356	6,981	13,220	686	2,061	9,710	9,294	15,601	7,924	10,468	3,218	11,080	6,033	4,218	10,775	2,822	1,984	1,877	5,634	6,883
Richmond, Virginia	17,556	15,281	14,582	9,471	10,710	2,165	3,379	13,313	911	3,820	5,789	7,969	11,010	8,701	5,317	6,001	7,083	7,050	5,849	13,027
Riga, USSR	12,145	9,097	12,852	2,924	4,285	8,681	8,757	14,741	6,327	8,232	2,922	11,929	8,144	5,905	10,697	1,781	682	994	6,135	9,172
Ringkobing, Denmark	13,116	9,629	13,732	3,334	4,712	7,736	7,779	15,432	5,488	7,845	2,063	11,073	7,975	5,524	9,727	856	699	786	5,308	9,262
Rio Branco, Brazil	16,584	13,174	15,598	11,540	11,949	3,191	2,384	13,143	5,943	8,227	8,282	2,816	8,626	8,016	448	9,281	10,527	10,305	5,607	10,129
Rio Cuarto, Argentina	14,081	11,481	14,234	12,392	12,230	5,780	4,855	12,082	8,524	10,504	10,013	1,294	7,803	8,304	2,699	11,170	12,308	12,030	6,863	8,713
Rio de Janeiro, Brazil	14,836	10,195	16,250	10,033	9,923	5,570	4,213	14,360	7,870	11,011	7,942	1,121	5,812	5,955	2,704	9,148	10,173	9,876	4,703	7,162
Rio Gallegos, Argentina	11,999	10,523	12,392	13,426	12,825	7,779	6,940	10,525	10,559	11,921	11,832	2,820	8,034	9,338	4,778	13,034	14,054	13,753	8,594	8,290
Rio Grande, Brazil	14,127	10,560	14,978	11,309	11,084	5,998	4,829	13,024	8,583	11,145	9,251	234	6,662	7,192	2,851	10,449	11,500	11,205	6,023	7,678
Riyadh, Saudi Arabia	9,231	5,092	11,503	1,596	1,125	11,873	11,321	13,962	10,095	12,160	5,393	12,060	5,859	5,108	12,499	4,991	3,974	3,961	7,366	5,921
Road Town, Brit. Virgin Isls.	19,633	13,978	16,464	9,598	10,516	815	925	14,451	2,844	6,087	5,853	5,558	9,199	7,391	3,011	6,585	7,837	7,684	4,392	11,155
Roanoke, Virginia	17,420	15,503	14,389	9,665	10,914	2,206	3,479	13,092	1,083	3,639	5,999	8,035	11,219	8,921	5,364	6,187	7,254	7,228	6,062	13,237
Robinson Crusoe Island, Chile	13,756	12,474	13,203	13,673	13,577	5,815	5,234	10,912	8,603	9,813	10,964	2,642	9,123	9,626	3,153	12,047	13,259	13,008	7,956	9,893
Rochester, New York	17,062	15,139	14,301	9,116	10,401	2,775	3,925	13,283	597	3,552	5,539	8,546	11,157	8,728	5,916	5,621	6,642	6,634	5,995	13,161
Rockhampton, Australia	3,312	9,437	1,578	13,927	13,165	15,562	16,354	1,958	15,678	11,595	17,246	13,656	13,769	16,116	14,857	16,109	14,945	15,203	18,885	11,767
Rome, Italy	12,803	8,287	14,327	2,122	3,398	8,238	7,905	16,486	6,474	9,348	1,759	10,299	6,390	4,043	9,548	1,432	1,217	922	4,567	7,662
Rosario, Argentina	14,109	11,207	14,465	12,071	11,889	5,831	4,826	12,365	8,539	10,698	9,787	955	7,463	7,973	2,698	10,959	12,072	11,789	6,608	8,402
Roseau, Dominica	19,449	13,565	16,864	9,487	10,327	1,218	515	14,735	3,254	6,576	5,808	5,138	8,759	7,044	2,676	6,627	7,887	7,713	4,067	10,699
Rostock, East Germany	12,880	9,297	13,666	3,002	4,382	8,002	7,990	15,485	5,803	8,166	2,107	11,123	7,745	5,348	9,894	970	372	473	5,334	8,978
Rostov-na-Donu, USSR	10,838	7,675	12,098	1,882	3,072	10,076	9,981	14,328	7,826	9,583	3,858	12,456	7,515	5,730	11,748	2,972	1,726	1,877	6,789	8,165
Rotterdam, Netherlands	13,406	9,495	14,219	3,223	4,574	7,509	7,444	15,956	5,426	8,084	1,559	10,579	7,538	5,040	9,331	409	854	728	4,800	8,909
Rouyn, Canada	16,533	15,045	13,935	8,874	10,197	3,350	4,476	13,134	848	3,292	5,438	9,106	11,371	8,855	6,487	5,382	6,327	6,346	6,250	13,346
Sacramento, California	13,970	17,961	10,778	11,811	13,193	5,223	6,678	9,600	4,271	778	8,866	10,530	14,834	12,402	7,930	8,533	9,154	9,280	9,666	16,847
Saginaw, Michigan	16,704	15,609	13,822	9,503	10,812	2,968	4,230	12,769	1,104	3,057	5,995	8,798	11,668	9,241	6,126	6,007	6,975	6,988	6,503	13,674
Saint Denis, Reunion	6,535	227	9,824	6,277	4,899	14,576	13,224	11,551	14,437	17,263	9,525	10,363	4,625	6,518	12,634	9,669	8,934	8,834	9,491	2,837
Saint George's, Grenada	19,089	13,506	16,861	9,706	10,492	1,343	157	14,626	3,597	6,803	6,074	4,796	8,674	7,085	2,314	6,930	8,191	8,008	4,147	10,581
Saint John, Canada	17,205	14,187	14,933	8,209	9,473	3,021	3,861	14,164	380	4,334	4,591	8,477	10,330	7,836	5,988	4,727	5,804	5,770	5,208	12,312
Saint John's, Antigua	19,646	13,660	16,782	9,426	10,299	1,123	715	14,720	3,049	6,403	5,717	5,343	8,872	7,095	2,870	6,506	7,764	7,597	4,104	10,826
Saint John's, Canada	16,882	13,145	15,389	7,169	8,421	3,681	4,175	15,035	1,432	5,179	3,538	8,599	9,501	6,926	6,337	3,705	4,830	4,771	4,511	11,435
Saint Louis, Missouri	16,596	16,309	13,485	10,251	11,556	2,818	4,210	12,205	1,759	2,770	6,712	8,615	12,132	9,810	5,911	6,755	7,723	7,738	6,973	14,150
Saint Paul, Minnesota	16,027	16,160	13,075	9,926	11,272	3,506	4,852	12,050	1,822	2,306	6,570	9,330	12,410	9,953	6,630	6,457	7,326	7,374	7,249	14,411
Saint Peter Port, UK	13,937	9,716	14,766	3,533	4,834	7,010	6,893	16,392	5,057	7,996	1,038	10,038	7,368	4,787	8,765	179	1,405	1,224	4,279	8,868
Saipan (Susupe)	4,921	10,406	2,729	11,256	11,309	14,429	15,879	4,402	12,541	8,951	13,237	17,628	15,091	15,307	16,736	12,022	11,056	11,358	16,478	13,467
Salalah, Oman	8,163	4,128	10,646	2,712	1,806	12,967	12,317	13,081	11,234	13,072	6,512	12,388	5,886	5,714	13,270	6,132	5,095	5,095	8,255	5,501
Salem, Oregon	13,801	17,257	10,731	11,205	12,583	5,507	6,948	9,801	4,138	74	8,456	11,033	14,717	12,164	8,379	8,021	8,560	8,705	9,582	16,674
Salt Lake City, Utah	14,766	17,513	11,614	11,224	12,602	4,497	5,944	10,453	3,416	1,021	8,096	10,027	13,976	11,553	7,362	7,849	8,569	8,666	8,808	15,989
Salta, Argentina	14,997	12,092	14,834	12,092	12,140	4,850	3,943	12,536	7,594	9,698	9,360	1,523	8,036	8,133	1,780	10,472	11,660	11,400	6,323	9,186
Salto, Uruguay	14,272	11,082	14,755	11,766	11,601	5,733	4,667	12,671	8,403	10,725	9,497	666	7,222	7,673	2,578	10,674	11,778	11,493	6,309	8,228
Salvador, Brazil	15,558	10,139	17,443	8,998	9,047	5,092	3,646	15,520	7,052	10,577	6,737	2,298	5,432	5,033	2,813	7,943	8,976	8,682	3,501	7,079
Salzburg, Austria	12,805	8,737	13,982	2,459	3,814	8,165	7,986	15,989	6,176	8,800	1,866	10,741	7,047	4,685	9,764	1,077	585	275	4,956	8,285
Samsun, Turkey	10,854	7,146	12,443	1,169	2,404	10,141	9,885	14,773	8,087	10,164	3,726	11,952	6,806	5,100	11,504	3,044	1,916	1,954	6,420	7,469
San Antonio, Texas	16,169	17,400	12,881	11,517	12,806	2,914	4,363	11,263	2,958	2,765	7,918	8,279	12,814	10,730	5,622	8,020	8,998	9,012	7,777	14,793
San Cristobal, Venezuela	18,206	14,455	15,697	10,931	11,735	1,191	1,220	13,394	3,981	6,379	7,245	4,753	9,626	8,259	2,049	8,020	9,275	9,117	5,366	11,427
San Diego, California	14,372	18,520	11,105	12,233	13,609	4,728	6,174	9,688	4,223	1,499	9,042	9,828	14,583	12,327	7,273	8,845	9,577	9,674	9,463	16,586
San Francisco, California	13,891	18,053	10,687	11,925	13,307	5,287	6,742	9,487	4,382	862	8,987	10,545	14,937	12,516	7,960	8,653	9,269	9,396	9,770	16,952
San Jose, Costa Rica	17,343	15,762	14,417	11,861	12,816	1,584	2,473	12,202	3,969	5,387	8,075	5,657	10,946	9,536	3,046	8,668	9,879	9,772	6,590	12,714
San Juan, Argentina	14,218	11,902	14,095	12,681	12,586	5,555	4,727	11,866	8,327	10,131	10,128	1,665	8,216	8,628	2,566	11,257	12,429	12,162	7,036	9,143
San Juan, Puerto Rico	19,497	14,134	16,308	9,732	10,661	657	997	14,295	2,820	5,971	5,976	5,604	9,349	7,549	3,022	6,688	7,938	7,790	4,551	11,301
San Luis Potosi, Mexico	15,934	17,790	12,652	12,286	13,539	3,014	4,389	10,812	3,697	3,255	8,614	7,859	12,982	11,134	5,298	8,796	9,808	9,810	8,136	14,871
San Marino, San Marino	12,823	8,450	14,227	2,235	3,544	8,196	7,914	16,332	6,355	9,153	1,754	10,438	6,614	4,258	9,607	1,273	1,002	702	4,681	7,879
San Miguel de Tucuman, Argen.	14,774	11,949	14,691	12,173	12,171	5,076	4,164	12,425	7,820	9,892	9,521	1,420	7,980	8,176	2,003	10,645	11,823	11,558	6,453	9,074

Distances in Kilometers	Port Hedland, Australia	Port Louis, Mauritius	Port Moresby, Papua New Guinea	Port Said, Egypt	Port Sudan, Sudan	Port-au-Prince, Haiti	Port-of-Spain, Trin. & Tobago	Port-Vila, Vanuatu	Portland, Maine	Portland, Oregon	Porto, Portugal	Porto Alegre, Brazil	Porto Alexandre, Angola	Porto Novo, Benin	Porto Velho, Brazil	Portsmouth, United Kingdom	Poznan, Poland	Prague, Czechoslovakia	Praia, Cape Verde Islands	Pretoria, South Africa
San Salvador, El Salvador	16,992	16,422	13,882	12,039	13,099	1,881	3,030	11,772	3,781	4,724	8,238	6,330	11,588	10,044	3,740	8,710	9,875	9,801	7,061	13,390
Sanaa, Yemen	9,037	4,189	11,675	2,139	878	12,128	11,356	14,085	10,701	13,133	5,807	11,363	4,950	4,642	12,205	5,630	4,763	4,692	7,246	4,868
Santa Cruz, Bolivia	15,784	12,306	15,524	11,527	11,719	4,142	3,152	13,154	6,843	9,220	8,613	1,823	7,946	7,709	1,003	9,703	10,908	10,657	5,660	9,301
Santa Cruz, Tenerife	15,385	9,575	17,293	4,663	5,483	5,785	5,106	18,734	5,054	8,962	1,570	7,465	5,759	3,139	6,571	2,786	3,815	3,531	1,676	7,650
Santa Fe, New Mexico	15,375	17,655	12,146	11,412	12,765	3,808	5,263	10,770	3,160	1,780	8,047	9,263	13,524	11,244	6,605	7,952	8,792	8,854	8,386	15,538
Santa Rosa, Argentina	13,696	11,252	13,941	12,540	12,292	6,163	5,240	11,852	8,910	10,816	10,311	1,418	7,759	8,423	3,085	11,481	12,597	12,313	7,131	8,557
Santa Rosalia, Mexico	14,826	18,715	11,530	12,517	13,868	4,193	5,612	9,904	4,165	2,220	9,106	9,087	14,157	12,096	6,567	9,052	9,896	9,959	9,148	16,102
Santarem, Brazil	17,385	12,229	17,269	9,869	10,310	3,019	1,632	14,812	5,336	8,507	6,708	3,081	7,438	6,446	1,236	7,775	8,992	8,749	3,936	9,184
Santiago del Estero, Argentina	14,674	11,811	14,680	12,135	12,102	5,198	4,263	12,441	7,934	10,034	9,545	1,300	7,871	8,116	2,105	10,679	11,846	11,578	6,453	8,944
Santiago, Chile	13,975	11,928	13,802	12,949	12,817	5,755	4,976	11,580	8,538	10,193	10,421	1,881	8,381	8,878	2,820	11,548	12,722	12,455	7,327	9,232
Santo Domingo, Dominican Rep.	19,121	14,526	15,915	10,068	11,027	257	1,250	13,900	2,793	5,682	6,293	5,733	9,729	7,949	3,083	6,954	8,193	8,059	4,950	11,669
Sao Paulo de Olivenca, Brazil	17,258	13,611	15,794	11,269	11,826	2,462	1,756	13,343	5,219	7,585	7,832	3,482	8,917	8,013	800	8,765	10,023	9,821	5,390	10,547
Sao Paulo, Brazil	14,897	10,485	16,060	10,361	10,271	5,428	4,115	14,080	7,822	10,822	8,166	854	6,154	6,296	2,462	9,365	10,419	10,126	4,941	7,467
Sao Tome, Sao Tome & Principe	12,304	5,976	15,540	4,358	3,951	8,852	7,633	17,234	8,940	12,920	4,778	6,985	1,874	819	7,895	5,638	5,851	5,562	3,698	3,693
Sapporo, Japan	7,394	11,034	5,847	9,066	9,633	12,370	13,624	7,274	9,900	7,171	10,206	18,191	14,377	13,129	15,487	8,994	8,161	8,473	13,404	13,757
Sarajevo, Yugoslavia	12,347	8,131	13,797	1,852	3,206	8,665	8,392	15,976	6,763	9,386	2,232	10,815	6,638	4,417	10,069	1,657	960	757	5,096	7,769
Saratov, USSR	10,611	8,025	11,600	2,520	3,628	10,221	10,270	13,753	7,810	9,190	4,255	13,040	8,167	6,389	12,143	3,239	1,985	2,213	7,311	8,741
Saskatoon, Canada	14,768	16,204	11,940	9,942	11,323	4,775	6,126	11,215	2,843	1,379	7,019	10,583	13,321	10,731	7,879	6,640	7,282	7,396	8,246	15,242
Schefferville, Canada	16,150	13,999	14,157	7,775	9,111	4,052	4,920	13,812	1,264	4,002	4,457	9,522	10,725	8,110	7,050	4,294	5,213	5,237	5,781	12,618
Seattle, Washington	13,823	16,962	10,818	10,911	12,287	5,538	6,966	9,984	4,007	230	8,211	11,150	14,548	11,963	8,476	7,748	8,269	8,417	9,444	16,473
Sendai, Japan	6,890	10,821	5,324	9,342	9,812	12,831	14,116	6,828	10,409	7,546	10,684	18,585	14,472	13,449	15,912	9,469	8,595	8,906	13,900	13,656
Seoul, South Korea	6,468	9,675	5,617	8,344	8,689	13,476	14,595	7,496	10,843	8,473	10,193	19,157	13,272	12,477	16,634	8,988	7,970	8,269	13,433	12,448
Sept-Iles, Canada	16,660	14,104	14,542	7,976	9,282	3,553	4,408	13,998	785	4,138	4,494	9,017	10,534	7,969	6,537	4,479	5,483	5,478	5,489	12,476
Sevastopol, USSR	11,190	7,574	12,614	1,484	2,792	9,777	9,583	14,876	7,670	9,748	3,427	11,901	7,041	5,180	11,278	2,661	1,496	1,559	6,263	7,809
Seville, Spain	14,381	9,204	15,916	3,563	4,616	6,716	6,269	17,758	5,355	8,852	476	8,828	6,179	3,532	7,893	1,537	2,445	2,156	3,033	7,849
Shanghai, China	5,699	8,871	5,270	8,215	8,372	14,321	15,373	7,376	11,641	9,353	10,503	19,305	12,742	12,305	17,472	9,328	8,220	8,505	13,687	11,729
Sheffield, United Kingdom	13,782	9,913	14,394	3,654	4,997	7,106	7,095	15,954	4,989	7,707	1,459	10,414	7,772	5,212	9,031	291	1,244	1,159	4,682	9,222
Shenyang, China	6,895	9,640	6,175	7,861	8,278	13,131	14,175	8,045	10,441	8,329	9,633	18,619	12,949	11,991	16,275	8,428	7,412	7,713	12,873	12,287
Shiraz, Iran	8,976	5,532	10,977	1,950	1,900	12,063	11,678	13,427	10,028	11,670	5,586	12,808	6,656	5,813	13,046	4,997	3,855	3,908	7,878	6,655
Sibiu, Romania	11,937	8,044	13,296	1,761	3,143	9,041	8,835	15,478	7,010	9,375	2,681	11,315	6,935	4,826	10,552	1,942	903	865	5,599	7,934
Singapore	2,879	5,583	4,949	8,190	7,522	17,774	17,935	7,366	14,993	13,109	11,778	15,880	10,267	11,245	18,439	10,944	9,684	9,856	13,969	8,646
Sioux Falls, South Dakota	15,854	16,486	12,828	10,238	11,589	3,593	4,979	11,740	2,128	2,060	6,900	9,380	12,701	10,267	6,676	6,776	7,627	7,682	7,535	14,708
Skelleftea, Sweden	12,390	9,922	12,610	3,807	5,160	8,312	8,584	14,243	5,781	7,372	3,232	12,196	8,968	6,629	10,637	2,016	1,394	1,679	6,470	10,054
Skopje, Yugoslavia	12,066	7,817	13,632	1,532	2,893	8,960	8,650	15,880	7,085	9,677	2,499	10,909	6,477	4,354	10,279	1,979	1,207	1,049	5,245	7,532
Socotra Island (Tamrida)	7,950	3,650	10,586	3,034	1,952	13,205	12,457	12,986	11,609	13,552	6,809	12,163	5,607	5,675	13,246	6,504	5,507	5,490	8,344	5,089
Sofia, Bulgaria	11,933	7,792	13,465	1,496	2,872	9,083	8,796	15,712	7,161	9,668	2,639	11,077	6,582	4,498	10,440	2,058	1,182	1,066	5,413	7,593
Songkhla, Thailand	3,624	5,606	5,486	7,540	6,963	17,057	17,224	7,935	14,299	12,761	11,065	16,136	10,097	10,805	18,320	10,207	8,946	9,124	13,400	8,627
Sorong, Indonesia	2,555	8,286	2,005	10,917	10,471	16,793	18,248	4,462	14,813	11,333	14,005	16,570	13,122	14,301	18,038	12,902	11,708	11,961	16,850	11,283
South Georgia Island	11,414	8,482	12,932	11,547	10,763	8,748	7,561	11,681	11,307	13,694	10,907	2,926	5,966	7,664	5,594	12,105	12,825	12,513	7,766	6,108
South Pole	7,754	7,772	8,952	13,464	12,174	12,053	11,181	8,039	14,838	15,046	14,561	6,676	8,255	10,721	9,034	15,630	15,814	15,554	11,654	7,155
South Sandwich Islands	10,770	7,780	12,530	11,283	10,381	9,451	8,224	11,528	11,950	14,441	11,087	3,615	5,638	7,590	6,306	12,252	12,835	12,528	8,058	5,544
Split, Yugoslavia	12,500	8,204	13,958	1,949	3,285	8,518	8,233	16,124	6,649	9,345	2,073	10,665	6,586	4,321	9,906	1,548	990	745	4,937	7,763
Spokane, Washington	14,187	16,919	11,188	10,754	12,136	5,194	6,615	10,323	3,644	465	7,933	10,852	14,203	11,637	8,166	7,521	8,100	8,233	9,084	16,148
Spoleto, Italy	12,791	8,340	14,267	2,148	3,442	8,241	7,929	16,408	6,442	9,277	1,774	10,373	6,483	4,138	9,592	1,379	1,122	828	4,631	7,746
Springbok, South Africa	9,891	4,117	13,078	6,914	5,835	11,033	9,589	13,882	12,079	16,165	8,302	6,562	1,652	4,321	8,746	9,103	9,093	8,840	6,640	1,103
Springfield, Illinois	16,572	16,210	13,498	10,127	11,436	2,885	4,260	12,267	1,665	2,756	6,604	8,698	12,097	9,748	5,996	6,631	7,591	7,609	6,932	14,114
Springfield, Massachusetts	17,375	14,771	14,717	8,842	10,100	2,613	3,649	13,703	257	3,978	5,202	8,287	10,729	8,310	5,702	5,361	6,431	6,401	5,566	12,734
Srinagar, India	7,598	6,278	9,012	3,972	4,035	13,227	13,251	11,411	10,699	11,015	7,121	14,968	8,651	7,973	14,962	6,222	4,962	5,143	9,842	8,254
Stanley, Falkland Islands	12,019	9,887	12,815	12,675	12,042	7,907	6,917	11,112	10,633	12,430	11,336	2,465	7,249	8,617	4,793	12,551	13,488	13,180	8,093	7,540
Stara Zagora, Bulgaria	11,740	7,663	13,291	1,372	2,754	9,272	8,988	15,558	7,331	9,768	2,832	11,224	6,600	4,581	10,625	2,232	1,288	1,209	5,583	7,552
Stockholm, Sweden	12,522	9,516	13,047	3,297	4,671	8,275	8,403	14,802	5,888	7,838	2,740	11,756	8,348	6,009	10,385	1,541	773	1,055	5,983	9,475
Stornoway, United Kingdom	13,928	10,469	14,150	4,181	5,544	6,869	7,011	15,489	4,574	7,102	1,905	10,634	8,374	5,791	9,035	897	1,606	1,624	5,014	9,842
Strasbourg, France	13,199	9,074	14,266	2,823	4,159	7,764	7,605	16,162	5,787	8,520	1,530	10,496	7,145	4,692	9,416	682	780	516	4,701	8,481
Stuttgart, West Germany	13,093	9,012	14,168	2,748	4,093	7,867	7,712	16,085	5,873	8,561	1,634	10,589	7,158	4,728	9,522	772	684	410	4,794	8,467
Subic, Philippines	3,898	7,882	4,013	8,977	8,755	16,064	17,174	6,393	13,436	10,825	11,882	18,113	12,382	12,757	19,202	10,781	9,584	9,839	14,849	10,924
Suchow, China	6,043	8,728	5,786	7,710	7,912	14,076	15,032	7,901	11,343	9,323	9,989	18,834	12,378	11,814	17,179	8,820	7,702	7,985	13,164	11,491
Sucre, Bolivia	15,632	12,426	15,264	11,788	11,971	4,226	3,309	12,892	6,959	9,194	8,860	1,877	8,139	7,959	1,146	9,942	11,153	10,904	5,920	9,445
Sudbury, Canada	16,604	15,260	13,893	9,109	10,428	3,202	4,381	12,997	902	3,187	5,646	8,995	11,487	9,002	6,353	5,616	6,569	6,586	6,344	13,476
Suez, Egypt	10,751	6,158	12,907	146	1,240	10,357	9,817	15,356	8,706	11,277	3,892	11,077	5,530	4,071	11,116	3,621	2,802	2,700	5,948	6,183
Sundsvall, Sweden	12,567	9,812	12,903	3,623	4,992	8,179	8,386	14,563	5,715	7,521	2,921	11,905	8,682	6,319	10,413	1,705	1,110	1,380	6,163	9,817
Surabaya, Indonesia	1,576	6,116	3,799	9,530	8,785	18,645	19,295	6,129	15,960	13,239	13,145	15,537	10,952	12,323	18,196	12,296	11,036	11,215	15,191	9,128
Suva, Fiji	6,263	12,310	3,504	16,322	15,949	12,609	13,544	1,071	13,087	9,218	17,368	12,490	15,974	18,641	12,568	16,384	15,873	16,185	17,668	14,188
Sverdlovsk, USSR	10,106	8,539	10,676	3,584	4,562	10,579	10,856	12,717	7,962	8,653	5,108	14,057	9,228	7,503	12,866	3,977	2,811	3,091	8,275	9,647
Svobodnyy, USSR	7,999	10,472	6,990	7,737	8,389	12,006	13,068	8,598	9,324	7,312	8,930	17,635	13,184	11,773	15,152	7,714	6,826	7,136	12,163	12,877
Sydney, Australia	3,548	9,116	2,733	14,368	13,381	15,397	15,814	2,472	16,302	12,332	18,070	12,548	13,026	15,585	14,014	17,089	15,857	16,078	17,839	11,086
Sydney, Canada	17,137	13,722	15,186	7,756	9,012	3,261	3,937	14,575	842	4,721	4,124	8,489	9,941	7,413	6,094	4,284	5,385	5,339	4,860	11,906
Syktyvkar, USSR	10,866	9,091	11,265	3,636	4,788	9,806	10,108	13,168	7,194	8,105	4,509	13,523	9,249	7,283	12,149	3,333	2,263	2,566	7,730	9,900
Szeged, Hungary	12,249	8,262	13,567	1,966	3,343	8,731	8,524	15,703	6,727	9,202	2,374	11,081	6,925	4,720	10,256	1,641	722	600	5,338	8,016
Szombathely, Hungary	12,532	8,513	13,772	2,221	3,589	8,442	8,253	15,843	6,440	8,985	2,117	10,919	6,999	4,710	10,011	1,350	577	354	5,149	8,165
Tabriz, Iran	9,929	6,553	11,608	1,487	2,227	11,059	10,805	13,995	8,934	10,677	4,649	12,606	6,966	5,620	12,377	3,949	2,769	2,847	7,246	7,315
Tacheng, China	8,244	7,840	8,885	4,619	5,113	12,363	12,738	11,082	9,650	9,480	6,944	15,683	9,898	8,751	14,759	5,852	4,645	4,902	10,022	9,734
Tahiti (Papeete)	9,540	14,903	6,877	18,472	19,278	9,344	10,165	4,460	10,508	7,496	15,471	9,828	15,799	16,772	9,271	15,387	15,960	16,124	14,278	15,210
Taipei, Taiwan	5,029	8,542	4,729	8,541	8,560	14,958	16,042	6,940	12,304	9,866	11,058	19,110	12,691	12,554	18,116	9,903	8,762	9,037	14,190	11,493
Taiyuan, China	6,471	8,624	6,360	7,171	7,435	13,741	14,599	8,475	10,972	9,250	9,416	18,291	12,001	11,290	16,762	8,252	7,127	7,408	12,587	11,262
Tallahassee, Florida	17,475	16,037	14,223	10,453	11,665	1,788	3,217	12,632	1,919	3,715	6,729	7,559	11,469	9,356	4,855	6,998	8,091	8,054	6,402	13,468
Tallinn, USSR	12,143	9,312	12,705	3,179	4,532	8,644	8,784	14,530	6,223	7,996	3,071	12,091	8,420	6,167	10,763	1,892	918	1,229	6,305	9,444
Tamanrasset, Algeria	13,152	7,379	15,692	2,810	3,306	8,031	7,219	18,151	7,179	10,809	2,428	8,423	4,326	1,830	8,324	3,158	3,432	3,129	3,175	5,899
Tampa, Florida	17,735	15,886	14,456	10,492	11,666	1,468	2,907	12,773	2,056	4,027	6,732	7,231	11,240	9,197	4,527	7,069	8,194	8,142	6,220	13,226
Tampere, Finland	12,224	9,539	12,656	3,418	4,769	8,530	8,722	14,412	6,064	7,761	3,135	12,149	8,635	6,351	10,732	1,932	1,091	1,395	6,378	9,679
Tanami, Australia	1,166	7,486	2,208	11,822	10,989	17,712	18,436	4,067	16,796	12,932	15,448	14,466	12,160	14,135	16,498	14,540	13,283	13,483	17,139	10,158
Tangier, Morocco	14,374	9,097	16,020	3,552	4,563	6,739	6,247	17,922	5,456	8,998	643	8,701	6,009	3,358	7,828	1,705	2,573	2,278	2,910	7,692
Tarawa (Betio)	6,391	12,720	3,096	14,515	14,667	12,568	13,863	2,171	12,024	7,937	15,295	14,387	17,401	18,644	13,689	14,201	13,638	13,948	17,468	15,383
Tashkent, USSR	8,508	6,917	9,706	3,476	3,870	12,293	12,371	12,034	9,762	10,310	6,291	14,602	8,652	7,596	14,183	5,336	4,076	4,278	9,161	8,553
Tbilisi, USSR	10,224	6,974	11,739	1,605	2,550	10,733	10,547	14,076	8,546	10,261	4,388	12,620	7,209	5,699	12,203	3,613	2,402	2,507	7,124	7,661
Tegucigalpa, Honduras	17,209	16,227	14,097	11,845	12,892	1,664	2,819	11,990	3,653	4,813	8,044	6,230	11,389	9,826	3,609	8,537	9,713	9,632	6,842	13,207
Tehran, Iran	9,399	6,213	11,139	1,841	2,259	11,588	11,328	13,551	9,433	10,992	5,176	12,945	7,060	5,928	12,863	4,475	3,283	3,371	7,713	7,225
Tel Aviv, Israel	10,631	6,268	12,679	250	1,401	10,455	9,976	15,116	8,696	11,114	3,967	11,374	5,834	4,376	11,341	3,592	2,680	2,612	6,173	6,437
Telegraph Creek, Canada	13,094	15,756	10,404	10,004	11,348	6,452	7,811	10,046	4,404	1,494	7,805	12,228	14,426	11,757	9,525	7,130	7,438	7,630	9,621	16,081
Teresina, Brazil	16,546	10,895	18,059	8,903	9,168	4,161	2,706	15,775	6,061	9,621	6,190	2,902	6,088	5,208	2,365	7,361	8,483	8,206	3,070	7,866
Ternate, Indonesia	2,527	7,953	2,470	10,454	10,005	16,982	18,411	4,929	14,779	11,489	13,597	16,762	12,770	13,850	18,496	12,518	11,308	11,554	16,386	10,980
The Valley, Anguilla	19,710	13,809	16,633	9,482	10,380	981	836	14,608	2,918	6,237	5,751	5,475	9,029	7,226	2,967	6,510	7,766	7,606	4,230	10,987
Thessaloniki, Greece	11,917	7,623	13,562	1,338	2,699	9,121	8,782	15,848	7,273	9,865	2,645	10,928	6,353	4,290	10,375	2,169	1,386	1,240	5,307	7,369
Thimphu, Bhutan	6,139	6,317	7,422	5,526	5,391	14,556	14,774	9,838	11,863	11,280	8,694	16,220	9,662	9,400	16,559	7,743	6,485	6,689	11,431	8,844
Thunder Bay, Canada	16,023	15,702	13,234	9,451	10,801	3,651	4,921	12,371	1,562	2,534	6,138	9,485	12,132	9,617	6,806	5,988	6,846	6,897	7,000	14,109
Tientsin, China	6,582	9,034	6,212	7,496	7,815	13,545	14,492	8,239	10,805	8,895	9,562	18,554	12,417	11,626	16,639	8,378	7,293	7,583	12,770	11,690
Tijuana, Mexico	14,384	18,533	11,116	12,244	13,621	4,712	6,158	9,692	4,222	1,522	9,046	9,805	14,573	12,323	7,252	8,854	9,590	9,685	9,455	16,574
Tiksi, USSR	10,225	11,482	9,099	6,962	8,005	9,878	10,847	10,350	7,133	5,872	7,058	15,384	12,593	10,510	12,972	5,872	5,259	5,566	10,184	13,070
Timbuktu, Mali	13,885	7,774	16,709	3,913	4,260	7,310	6,344	19,107	6,919	10,825	2,756	7,316	3,958	1,292	7,272	3,776	4,327	4,015	2,205	5,791
Tindouf, Algeria	14,589	8,831	16,743	3,921	4,690	6,583	5,872	18,846	5,753	9,550	1,493	7,863	5,278	2,609	7,230	2,630	3,445	3,140	2,128	7,079
Tirane, Albania	12,188	7,840	13,786	1,578	2,918	8,849	8,517	16,036	7,017	9,687	2,374	10,753	6,380	4,222	10,131	1,918	1,251	1,058	5,090	7,477

Distances in Kilometers	Port Hedland, Australia	Port Louis, Mauritius	Port Moresby, Papua New Guinea	Port Said, Egypt	Port Sudan, Sudan	Port-au-Prince, Haiti	Port-of-Spain, Trin. & Tobago	Port-Vila, Vanuatu	Portland, Maine	Portland, Oregon	Porto, Portugal	Porto Alegre, Brazil	Porto Alexandre, Angola	Porto Novo, Benin	Porto Velho, Brazil	Portsmouth, United Kingdom	Poznan, Poland	Prague, Czechoslovakia	Praia, Cape Verde Islands	Pretoria, South Africa
Tokyo, Japan	6,591	10,630	5,061	9,424	9,833	13,120	14,412	6,636	10,708	7,809	10,906	18,823	14,428	13,548	16,185	9,690	8,785	9,094	14,134	13,511
Toledo, Spain	14,191	9,209	15,604	3,402	4,523	6,881	6,498	17,444	5,377	8,747	415	9,149	6,381	3,757	8,172	1,233	2,125	1,839	3,354	7,995
Topeka, Kansas	16,147	16,705	13,010	10,549	11,878	3,200	4,620	11,742	2,178	2,324	7,090	8,934	12,610	10,273	6,230	7,062	7,974	8,010	7,449	14,627
Toronto, Canada	16,931	15,258	14,147	9,198	10,493	2,864	4,045	13,137	735	3,397	5,649	8,656	11,309	8,873	6,014	5,702	6,703	6,703	6,148	13,312
Toulouse, France	13,711	9,084	14,990	3,031	4,260	7,318	7,029	16,886	5,593	8,696	871	9,760	6,665	4,114	8,758	819	1,512	1,225	3,966	8,151
Tours, France	13,734	9,388	14,760	3,226	4,513	7,245	7,062	16,529	5,363	8,324	1,014	10,026	7,088	4,537	8,877	398	1,293	1,056	4,238	8,556
Townsville, Australia	2,957	9,226	1,081	13,390	12,695	15,919	16,847	2,277	15,636	11,557	16,649	14,220	13,747	15,908	15,446	15,518	14,349	14,606	18,893	11,729
Trenton, New Jersey	17,465	14,993	14,662	9,109	10,360	2,416	3,528	13,537	533	3,895	5,451	8,155	10,853	8,478	5,538	5,632	6,707	6,676	5,685	12,866
Tripoli, Lebanon	10,628	6,463	12,560	483	1,648	10,434	10,016	14,978	8,584	10,888	3,943	11,584	6,113	4,606	11,452	3,480	2,500	2,460	6,292	6,710
Tripoli, Libya	12,612	7,529	14,650	1,811	2,807	8,510	7,953	17,021	7,091	10,248	2,137	9,722	5,393	3,123	9,351	2,302	2,189	1,911	4,203	6,682
Tristan da Cunha (Edinburgh)	11,838	6,927	14,430	8,875	8,145	8,799	7,367	13,941	10,682	14,292	8,668	3,667	3,350	5,063	6,053	9,790	10,311	10,005	5,871	4,013
Trondheim, Norway	12,909	10,127	13,116	3,894	5,272	7,820	8,056	14,658	5,347	7,238	2,773	11,684	8,785	6,349	10,104	1,566	1,284	1,505	5,991	10,007
Trujillo, Peru	16,325	14,331	14,552	12,506	13,065	3,038	2,841	12,099	5,801	7,360	8,998	3,786	9,872	9,206	1,668	9,865	11,126	10,946	6,634	11,320
Truk Island (Moen)	4,766	10,753	1,941	12,307	12,273	14,390	15,825	3,320	12,944	9,076	14,270	16,544	15,582	16,287	16,094	13,054	12,124	12,429	17,482	13,742
Truro, Canada	17,221	13,970	15,085	8,010	9,267	3,092	3,852	14,372	588	4,533	4,377	8,443	10,129	7,624	5,996	4,535	5,628	5,586	5,020	12,106
Tsingtao, China	6,243	9,076	5,775	7,885	8,150	13,818	14,830	7,809	11,112	8,989	10,000	18,983	12,676	12,008	16,951	8,814	7,731	8,021	13,208	11,829
Tsitsihar, China	7,515	9,989	6,704	7,643	8,188	12,528	13,556	8,461	9,825	7,844	9,143	18,040	12,947	11,740	15,663	7,930	6,967	7,273	12,387	12,488
Tubuai Island (Mataura)	9,332	14,377	6,887	19,113	19,217	9,574	10,273	4,431	10,950	8,100	15,887	9,487	15,224	16,503	9,184	15,931	16,582	16,730	14,302	14,564
Tucson, Arizona	14,954	18,255	11,683	11,990	13,350	4,146	5,594	10,209	3,754	1,787	8,649	9,343	14,010	11,803	6,748	8,543	9,358	9,429	8,909	16,006
Tulsa, Oklahoma	16,241	16,883	13,042	10,800	12,115	3,027	4,468	11,662	2,334	2,466	7,285	8,695	12,619	10,351	5,997	7,306	8,246	8,272	7,479	14,634
Tunis, Tunisia	12,944	8,027	14,748	2,127	3,248	8,150	7,683	17,007	6,617	9,736	1,695	9,785	5,826	3,445	9,201	1,793	1,815	1,515	4,122	7,176
Tura, USSR	9,512	10,057	9,071	5,863	6,764	10,801	11,554	10,757	8,009	7,267	6,785	15,710	11,498	9,727	13,717	5,569	4,669	4,981	10,027	11,737
Turin, Italy	13,210	8,810	14,493	2,629	3,921	7,799	7,545	16,487	5,961	8,846	1,392	10,229	6,753	4,302	9,280	911	1,066	758	4,442	8,112
Uberlandia, Brazil	15,436	10,854	16,439	10,234	10,261	4,907	3,579	14,320	7,284	10,330	7,812	1,267	6,375	6,252	2,025	8,994	10,091	9,806	4,626	7,807
Ufa, USSR	10,209	8,300	10,942	3,209	4,207	10,531	10,725	13,034	7,977	8,892	4,862	13,753	8,854	7,136	12,688	3,768	2,561	2,826	7,991	9,305
Ujungpandang, Indonesia	1,684	6,889	3,105	10,032	9,389	18,061	19,385	5,499	15,632	12,572	13,504	15,986	11,724	13,039	18,428	12,555	11,301	11,508	15,835	9,894
Ulaanbaatar, Mongolia	7,646	9,003	7,494	6,406	6,908	12,645	13,418	9,486	9,856	8,588	8,281	17,287	11,668	10,529	15,580	7,097	6,016	6,308	11,494	11,303
Ulan-Ude, USSR	8,063	9,342	7,777	6,372	6,975	12,210	13,004	9,681	9,422	8,196	8,011	17,029	11,767	10,463	15,167	6,813	5,776	6,075	11,244	11,533
Uliastay, Mongolia	7,846	8,485	8,045	5,665	6,156	12,585	13,193	10,136	9,800	8,980	7,735	16,656	10,924	9,794	15,320	6,582	5,442	5,722	10,902	10,635
Uranium City, Canada	14,282	15,492	11,711	9,317	10,697	5,402	6,680	11,307	3,125	1,820	6,681	11,239	13,209	10,555	8,548	6,153	6,668	6,812	8,313	15,003
Urumqi, China	7,772	7,720	8,412	4,983	5,367	12,807	13,218	10,637	10,071	9,670	7,428	16,094	10,107	9,112	15,248	6,341	5,130	5,385	10,487	9,796
Ushuaia, Argentina	11,656	10,246	12,152	13,439	12,760	8,134	7,281	10,362	10,912	12,240	12,046	3,069	7,958	9,393	5,121	13,256	14,233	13,927	8,802	8,105
Vaduz, Liechtenstein	13,068	8,870	14,245	2,625	3,956	7,913	7,715	16,213	5,976	8,724	1,592	10,492	6,979	4,557	9,490	872	792	488	4,701	8,290
Valencia, Spain	13,880	8,927	15,392	3,086	4,212	7,195	6,796	17,363	5,674	8,974	726	9,322	6,251	3,666	8,435	1,257	1,959	1,659	3,536	7,805
Valladolid, Spain	14,231	9,368	15,510	3,481	4,640	6,819	6,489	17,273	5,235	8,556	331	9,264	6,588	3,963	8,210	1,051	2,024	1,752	3,472	8,195
Valletta, Malta	12,545	7,682	14,425	1,726	2,863	8,552	8,071	16,748	6,993	10,015	2,093	10,024	5,731	3,477	9,551	2,072	1,845	1,576	4,435	6,973
Valparaiso, Chile	14,003	12,026	13,768	13,016	12,900	5,707	4,952	11,529	8,493	10,105	10,447	1,966	8,478	8,954	2,802	11,567	12,749	12,485	7,369	9,334
Vancouver, Canada	13,741	16,777	10,779	10,761	12,134	5,651	7,070	10,016	4,024	415	8,124	11,299	14,522	11,915	8,617	7,631	8,125	8,279	9,447	16,416
Varna, Bulgaria	11,581	7,643	13,088	1,382	2,758	9,418	9,163	15,351	7,422	9,752	3,003	11,430	6,738	4,765	10,819	2,342	1,308	1,279	5,788	7,636
Venice, Italy	12,844	8,581	14,155	2,337	3,666	8,157	7,916	16,217	6,260	9,000	1,761	10,538	6,785	4,419	9,644	1,159	845	539	4,766	8,046
Veracruz, Mexico	16,402	17,270	13,154	12,176	13,364	2,507	3,835	11,212	3,630	3,804	8,429	7,275	12,435	10,695	4,698	8,724	9,802	9,774	7,691	14,294
Verona, Italy	12,949	8,654	14,247	2,425	3,744	8,053	7,810	16,288	6,168	8,947	1,657	10,456	6,785	4,394	9,542	1,075	889	577	4,678	8,074
Victoria, Canada	13,734	16,868	10,751	10,852	12,226	5,640	7,065	9,958	4,061	327	8,201	11,266	14,578	11,979	8,589	7,716	8,215	8,368	9,491	16,484
Victoria, Seychelles	7,036	1,735	10,125	4,670	3,341	14,158	13,060	12,262	13,179	15,467	8,226	11,345	4,920	5,998	13,144	8,154	7,286	7,224	8,968	3,733
Vienna, Austria	12,560	8,608	13,741	2,314	3,685	8,401	8,237	15,784	6,369	8,882	2,118	10,967	7,104	4,804	10,016	1,293	471	251	5,188	8,275
Vientiane, Laos	4,580	6,484	5,764	7,157	6,850	15,930	16,398	8,206	13,143	11,630	10,382	17,052	10,622	10,845	18,246	9,405	8,152	8,366	13,087	9,392
Villahermosa, Mexico	16,717	16,915	13,493	12,024	13,172	2,176	3,478	11,506	3,552	4,107	8,249	6,949	12,076	10,379	4,351	8,607	9,720	9,675	7,376	13,929
Vilnius, USSR	12,032	8,841	12,879	2,660	4,021	8,825	8,846	14,842	6,523	8,494	2,908	11,876	7,915	5,718	10,747	1,824	608	897	6,083	8,915
Visby, Sweden	12,500	9,356	13,130	3,120	4,497	8,323	8,407	14,936	5,983	8,013	2,647	11,667	8,162	5,835	10,363	1,470	587	877	5,882	9,286
Vitoria, Brazil	14,963	10,026	16,609	9,625	9,539	5,537	4,136	14,770	7,714	11,017	7,554	1,534	5,531	5,558	2,836	8,763	9,773	9,474	4,311	6,972
Vladivostok, USSR	7,157	10,324	6,029	8,411	8,910	12,743	13,896	7,699	10,142	7,741	9,868	18,530	13,625	12,517	15,901	8,652	7,723	8,031	13,108	12,997
Volgograd, USSR	10,582	7,743	11,733	2,194	3,296	10,294	10,267	13,943	7,956	9,483	4,182	12,844	7,842	6,111	12,080	3,234	1,974	2,164	7,161	8,409
Vologda, USSR	11,301	8,944	11,889	3,159	4,402	9,450	9,638	13,825	6,944	8,283	3,885	12,885	8,697	6,651	11,624	2,735	1,613	1,913	7,090	9,478
Vorkuta, USSR	10,706	9,736	10,683	4,532	5,647	9,823	10,320	12,422	7,094	7,457	5,134	14,123	10,152	8,153	12,441	3,922	3,009	3,321	8,378	10,759
Wake Island	6,832	12,667	3,832	12,597	13,025	12,345	13,793	4,099	10,952	7,015	13,296	16,039	17,331	16,669	14,471	12,153	11,539	11,851	16,064	15,718
Wallis Island	6,959	13,084	4,019	16,498	16,406	11,915	12,932	1,735	12,298	8,443	16,693	12,423	16,667	19,240	12,161	15,826	15,512	15,813	17,079	14,951
Walvis Bay, Namibia	10,499	4,449	13,746	6,293	5,318	10,491	9,072	14,687	11,334	15,420	7,488	6,509	836	3,504	8,458	8,308	8,352	8,089	5,891	1,420
Warsaw, Poland	12,278	8,768	13,249	2,506	3,886	8,622	8,571	15,236	6,422	8,626	2,554	11,492	7,592	5,347	10,428	1,536	276	516	5,702	8,669
Washington, D.C.	17,468	15,215	14,554	9,354	10,603	2,302	3,488	13,348	775	3,783	5,690	8,092	11,008	8,667	5,449	5,877	6,949	6,920	5,842	13,024
Watson Lake, Canada	13,195	15,540	10,584	9,730	11,078	6,402	7,735	10,294	4,251	1,674	7,533	12,211	14,162	11,493	9,506	6,849	7,159	7,349	9,404	15,800
Weimar, East Germany	12,939	9,082	13,904	2,790	4,157	7,990	7,894	15,796	5,901	8,432	1,880	10,865	7,400	4,999	9,743	872	422	245	5,070	8,660
Wellington, New Zealand	5,747	10,636	4,447	16,505	15,354	13,246	13,584	2,685	14,806	11,453	19,738	10,805	13,442	16,071	11,865	18,907	17,934	18,207	16,595	11,826
West Berlin, West Germany	12,796	9,111	13,690	2,815	4,193	8,109	8,055	15,573	5,954	8,359	2,088	11,083	7,572	5,199	9,928	1,020	243	281	5,289	8,789
Wewak, Papua New Guinea	3,291	9,479	765	12,244	11,868	15,780	17,150	3,116	14,459	10,583	15,009	15,968	14,305	15,704	16,687	13,826	12,722	13,002	18,134	12,365
Whangarei, New Zealand	5,665	10,938	4,001	16,486	15,477	13,276	13,769	2,079	14,551	11,000	19,352	11,312	14,011	16,660	12,188	18,293	17,439	17,736	17,103	12,333
Whitehorse, Canada	12,846	15,395	10,262	9,745	11,074	6,750	8,085	10,048	4,590	1,876	7,716	12,553	14,364	11,698	9,849	6,980	7,216	7,421	9,693	15,916
Wichita, Kansas	16,065	16,908	12,891	10,758	12,087	3,228	4,664	11,571	2,370	2,268	7,294	8,908	12,751	10,444	6,209	7,271	8,181	8,218	7,599	14,769
Willemstad, Curacao	18,807	14,261	16,077	10,366	11,216	797	827	13,864	3,498	6,256	6,657	5,041	9,421	7,868	2,376	7,420	8,675	8,517	4,920	11,297
Wiluna, Australia	716	6,390	3,413	11,314	10,307	18,456	18,230	5,028	17,894	14,147	15,100	13,668	10,974	13,079	16,067	14,432	13,186	13,329	16,055	8,963
Windhoek, Namibia	10,272	4,188	13,533	6,176	5,157	10,731	9,318	14,565	11,504	15,581	7,539	6,769	927	3,581	8,725	8,319	8,308	8,053	6,066	1,179
Windsor, Canada	16,846	15,589	13,939	9,525	10,824	2,822	4,084	12,842	1,050	3,169	5,982	8,652	11,576	9,171	5,980	6,028	7,017	7,022	6,409	13,586
Winnipeg, Canada	15,470	16,025	12,640	9,730	11,100	4,121	5,443	11,818	2,154	1,961	6,574	9,952	12,700	10,157	7,255	6,323	7,089	7,168	7,584	14,662
Winston-Salem, North Carolina	17,484	15,558	14,409	9,767	11,007	2,096	3,393	13,060	1,195	3,678	6,085	7,930	11,220	8,951	5,253	6,294	7,369	7,339	6,072	13,237
Wroclaw, Poland	12,539	8,829	13,551	2,537	3,917	8,383	8,295	15,523	6,249	8,619	2,253	11,193	7,430	5,123	10,134	1,271	147	214	5,401	8,583
Wuhan, China	5,651	8,270	5,660	7,630	7,723	14,524	15,420	7,877	11,771	9,815	10,139	18,630	12,061	11,684	17,582	8,998	7,838	8,110	13,252	11,079
Wyndham, Australia	1,144	7,449	2,176	11,433	10,671	17,834	18,859	4,291	16,433	12,720	14,986	14,966	12,213	14,010	17,022	14,042	12,789	12,997	16,987	10,238
Xi'an, China	6,127	8,118	6,306	7,006	7,159	14,160	14,932	8,524	11,375	9,765	9,500	18,095	11,621	11,086	17,088	8,369	7,199	7,467	12,603	10,795
Xining, China	6,545	7,819	6,968	6,309	6,493	13,869	14,490	9,214	11,079	9,879	8,863	17,415	11,035	10,397	16,601	7,755	6,562	6,823	11,929	10,345
Yakutsk, USSR	9,178	11,075	8,070	7,354	8,225	10,868	11,891	9,472	8,157	6,468	7,975	16,454	12,984	11,177	13,995	6,767	6,014	6,327	11,160	13,096
Yanji, China	7,087	10,137	6,070	8,254	8,732	12,848	13,972	7,798	10,220	7,899	9,797	18,581	13,437	12,369	16,006	8,583	7,629	7,936	13,041	12,801
Yaounde, Cameroon	11,943	5,683	15,098	3,733	3,290	9,235	8,087	17,068	9,055	12,912	4,595	7,647	2,177	1,030	8,487	5,331	5,406	5,130	4,032	3,736
Yap Island (Colonia)	3,935	9,414	2,328	10,943	10,789	15,459	16,905	4,483	13,459	9,973	13,449	17,536	14,170	14,793	17,614	12,260	11,174	11,460	16,640	12,466
Yaraka, Australia	2,668	8,766	1,736	13,390	12,557	16,211	16,898	2,631	16,274	12,187	16,917	13,711	13,154	15,449	15,213	15,880	14,658	14,890	18,320	11,142
Yarmouth, Canada	17,361	14,217	15,032	8,290	9,541	2,865	3,704	14,194	334	4,389	4,640	8,323	10,282	7,812	5,829	4,817	5,911	5,870	5,144	12,272
Yellowknife, Canada	13,860	15,267	11,371	9,199	10,570	5,846	7,113	11,103	3,514	1,956	6,772	11,682	13,373	10,706	8,994	6,155	6,573	6,738	8,590	15,082
Yerevan, USSR	10,171	6,816	11,763	1,480	2,383	10,803	10,581	14,122	8,657	10,424	4,421	12,542	7,060	5,595	12,199	3,687	2,496	2,583	7,095	7,493
Yinchuan, China	6,632	8,250	6,792	6,633	6,885	13,694	14,424	8,967	10,903	9,498	9,001	17,759	11,469	10,746	16,574	7,861	6,701	6,974	12,130	10,797
Yogyakarta, Indonesia	1,643	5,848	4,055	9,340	8,564	18,783	19,088	6,365	16,031	13,457	12,993	15,379	10,682	12,065	18,069	12,180	10,921	11,091	14,950	8,864
York, United Kingdom	13,750	9,926	14,340	3,660	5,007	7,132	7,133	15,898	4,995	7,681	1,516	10,467	7,817	5,262	9,074	341	1,221	1,150	4,738	9,259
Yumen, China	7,002	7,847	7,465	5,878	6,142	13,462	14,022	9,691	10,680	9,731	8,361	17,004	10,776	9,989	16,115	7,254	6,060	6,321	11,438	10,227
Yutian, China	7,420	6,806	8,532	4,552	4,712	13,298	13,499	10,883	10,650	10,559	7,463	15,626	9,348	8,612	15,360	6,478	5,224	5,439	10,331	8,915
Yuzhno-Sakhalinsk, USSR	7,835	11,272	6,266	8,903	9,554	11,951	13,188	7,609	9,458	6,817	9,844	17,785	14,341	12,909	15,083	8,636	7,850	8,163	13,017	13,891
Zagreb, Yugoslavia	12,563	8,421	13,884	2,142	3,497	8,429	8,202	15,986	6,484	9,104	2,049	10,787	6,836	4,544	9,929	1,379	739	490	5,028	8,018
Zahedan, Iran	8,286	5,507	10,175	2,745	2,626	12,706	12,418	12,623	10,503	11,688	6,282	13,562	7,267	6,597	13,847	5,591	4,387	4,486	8,678	7,041
Zamboanga, Philippines	3,035	7,672	3,323	9,598	9,223	16,785	18,025	5,768	14,271	11,377	12,700	17,347	12,381	13,151	19,345	11,630	10,414	10,658	15,528	10,735
Zanzibar, Tanzania	8,675	2,514	11,865	4,207	2,860	12,502	11,310	13,849	12,044	15,304	7,149	9,710	3,164	4,297	11,343	7,394	6,825	6,673	7,299	2,464
Zaragoza, Spain	13,913	9,104	15,275	3,166	4,341	7,139	6,799	17,165	5,522	8,756	649	9,471	6,495	3,909	8,495	1,015	1,802	1,513	3,676	8,039
Zashiversk, USSR	9,932	11,852	8,541	7,640	8,643	10,051	11,128	9,678	7,377	5,626	7,721	15,748	13,282	11,217	13,196	6,547	5,964	6,270	10,801	13,661
Zhengzhou, China	6,116	8,495	6,036	7,393	7,585	14,074	14,955	8,191	11,313	9,473	9,746	18,511	12,062	11,491	17,117	8,590	7,451	7,729	12,897	11,214
Zurich, Switzerland	13,155	8,947	14,305	2,710	4,037	7,824	7,632	16,247	5,889	8,659	1,518	10,441	7,006	4,564	9,415	786	834	541	4,647	8,338

Distances in Kilometers

	Prince Albert, Canada	Prince Edward Island	Prince George, Canada	Prince Rupert, Canada	Providence, Rhode Island	Provo, Utah	Puerto Aisen, Chile	Puerto Deseado, Argentina	Puerto Princesa, Philippines	Punta Arenas, Chile	Pusan, South Korea	Pyongyang, North Korea	Qamdo, China	Qandahar, Afghanistan	Qiqian, China	Qom, Iran	Quebec, Canada	Quetta, Pakistan	Quito, Ecuador	Rabaul, Papua New Guinea
Prince Edward Island	17,339	0	18,421	18,816	14,537	17,476	7,771	7,217	10,095	7,069	12,815	12,871	10,467	9,097	13,482	9,090	14,794	8,992	11,978	11,485
Prince George, Canada	1,126	18,421	0	497	3,970	1,734	11,984	12,473	10,917	12,797	7,991	7,811	9,826	10,497	6,856	10,173	3,664	10,638	7,243	10,060
Prince Rupert, Canada	1,616	18,816	497	0	4,460	2,095	12,318	12,825	10,453	13,109	7,550	7,390	9,497	10,363	6,499	10,147	4,140	10,495	7,669	9,579
Providence, Rhode Island	2,845	14,537	3,970	4,460	0	3,359	9,662	9,937	14,204	10,523	11,237	10,887	11,841	10,773	9,521	9,702	556	10,966	4,710	14,015
Provo, Utah	1,509	17,476	1,734	2,095	3,359	0	10,250	10,743	12,441	11,064	9,610	9,475	11,560	12,049	8,583	11,523	3,310	12,206	5,599	10,835
Puerto Aisen, Chile	11,371	7,771	11,984	12,318	9,662	10,250	0	583	15,905	872	17,854	18,344	18,204	16,138	18,769	15,165	10,217	16,143	5,038	12,951
Puerto Deseado, Argentina	11,806	7,217	12,473	12,825	9,937	10,743	583	0	15,768	698	18,139	18,662	17,678	15,586	19,321	14,679	10,491	15,583	5,406	13,162
Puerto Princesa, Philippines	11,867	10,095	10,917	10,453	14,204	12,441	15,905	15,768	0	15,113	2,999	3,319	3,252	5,959	4,713	7,378	13,664	5,811	17,850	4,017
Punta Arenas, Chile	12,224	7,069	12,797	13,109	10,523	11,064	872	698	15,113	0	17,465	17,989	17,384	15,812	19,217	15,075	11,078	15,776	5,910	12,488
Pusan, South Korea	8,889	12,815	7,991	7,550	11,237	9,610	17,854	18,139	2,999	17,465	0	524	2,988	5,805	2,010	6,941	10,709	5,754	15,209	4,978
Pyongyang, North Korea	8,654	12,871	7,811	7,390	10,887	9,475	18,344	18,662	3,319	17,989	524	0	2,729	5,421	1,514	6,501	10,349	5,384	15,055	5,502
Qamdo, China	10,397	10,467	9,826	9,497	11,841	11,560	18,204	17,678	3,252	17,384	2,988	2,729	0	2,985	3,024	4,314	11,291	2,890	16,550	7,015
Qandahar, Afghanistan	10,576	9,097	10,497	10,363	10,773	12,049	16,138	15,586	5,959	15,812	5,805	5,421	2,985	0	4,961	1,426	10,313	194	14,901	9,919
Qiqian, China	7,546	13,482	6,856	6,499	9,521	8,583	18,769	19,321	4,713	19,217	2,010	1,514	3,024	4,961	0	5,741	8,972	4,984	13,969	6,916
Qom, Iran	10,014	9,090	10,173	10,147	9,702	11,523	15,165	14,679	7,378	15,075	6,941	6,501	4,314	1,426	5,741	0	9,295	1,591	13,536	11,311
Quebec, Canada	2,547	14,794	3,664	4,140	556	3,310	10,217	10,491	13,664	11,078	10,709	10,349	11,291	10,313	8,972	9,295	0	10,505	5,259	13,719
Quetta, Pakistan	10,739	8,992	10,638	10,495	10,966	12,206	16,143	15,583	5,811	15,776	5,754	5,384	2,890	194	4,984	1,591	10,505	0	15,088	9,785
Quito, Ecuador	6,438	11,978	7,243	7,669	4,710	5,599	5,038	5,406	17,850	5,910	15,209	15,055	16,550	14,901	13,969	13,536	5,259	15,088	0	14,380
Rabaul, Papua New Guinea	11,183	11,485	10,060	9,579	14,015	10,835	12,951	13,162	4,017	12,488	4,978	5,502	7,015	9,919	6,916	11,311	13,719	9,785	14,380	0
Raiatea (Uturoa)	8,896	12,930	8,293	8,125	10,435	7,532	7,831	8,321	10,307	7,907	10,149	10,564	12,965	15,932	11,310	17,039	10,626	15,853	8,193	6,304
Raleigh, North Carolina	2,868	14,712	3,940	4,435	918	2,925	9,010	9,338	14,651	9,880	11,652	11,355	12,582	11,678	10,077	10,620	1,373	11,870	3,984	13,759
Rangiroa (Avatoru)	8,546	13,169	7,990	7,849	10,007	7,156	7,676	8,186	10,672	7,813	10,356	10,751	13,229	16,161	11,407	17,145	10,209	16,100	7,777	6,686
Rangoon, Burma	11,972	9,118	11,342	10,983	13,393	13,070	16,668	16,202	2,565	15,816	3,841	3,784	1,597	3,481	4,487	4,905	12,850	3,315	18,084	6,582
Raoul Is., Kermadec Islands	11,473	10,867	10,630	10,324	13,415	10,292	8,825	9,119	8,044	8,492	9,041	9,554	11,192	13,996	10,811	15,420	13,541	13,839	10,916	4,201
Rarotonga (Avarua)	9,740	12,291	9,047	8,828	11,421	8,432	8,140	8,573	9,535	8,075	9,754	10,212	12,399	15,378	11,152	16,677	11,590	15,264	9,102	5,519
Rawson, Argentina	11,378	7,508	12,087	12,458	9,449	10,367	649	499	16,266	1,177	18,497	18,993	17,958	15,552	18,923	14,529	10,001	15,573	4,956	13,558
Recife, Brazil	9,474	8,053	10,585	11,082	6,657	9,477	5,501	5,284	17,132	5,960	16,597	16,072	14,450	11,486	14,636	10,136	7,061	11,603	4,914	18,447
Regina, Canada	316	17,248	1,295	1,791	2,713	1,261	11,058	11,497	12,137	11,910	9,169	8,944	10,712	10,869	7,853	10,277	2,472	11,033	6,137	11,302
Reykjavik, Iceland	4,633	13,339	5,269	5,512	3,988	6,059	12,930	12,986	11,173	13,675	8,711	8,221	8,192	6,786	6,707	5,780	3,534	6,979	8,475	13,335
Rhodes, Greece	9,131	9,246	9,614	9,742	8,115	10,581	13,553	13,171	9,423	13,717	8,628	8,139	6,281	3,487	7,074	2,062	7,799	3,652	11,519	13,293
Richmond, Virginia	2,788	14,730	3,880	4,377	702	2,965	9,199	9,517	14,509	10,068	11,512	11,203	12,378	11,455	9,906	10,402	1,150	11,647	4,182	13,780
Riga, USSR	6,973	11,547	7,352	7,453	6,543	8,467	14,431	14,250	9,387	14,921	7,633	7,109	6,162	4,250	5,740	3,196	6,112	4,444	10,790	12,611
Ringkobing, Denmark	6,482	11,712	7,021	7,200	5,698	7,930	13,538	13,405	10,349	14,092	8,462	7,939	7,135	5,165	6,512	4,005	5,305	5,359	9,825	13,427
Rio Branco, Brazil	7,869	10,387	8,754	9,199	5,745	7,158	3,955	4,192	19,320	4,797	16,745	16,519	17,202	14,684	15,257	13,259	6,298	14,842	1,602	15,332
Rio Cuarto, Argentina	10,370	8,255	11,156	11,561	8,330	9,468	1,539	1,628	17,395	2,285	18,773	18,900	18,279	15,372	17,847	14,141	8,881	15,444	3,934	14,372
Rio de Janeiro, Brazil	10,351	7,538	11,378	11,860	7,731	9,947	3,652	3,415	17,613	4,092	18,465	17,941	16,023	13,047	16,481	11,784	8,219	13,134	4,567	16,577
Rio Gallegos, Argentina	12,110	7,100	12,713	13,037	10,356	10,979	739	494	15,303	205	17,666	18,190	17,478	15,747	19,325	14,957	10,911	15,720	5,765	12,688
Rio Grande, Brazil	10,773	7,506	11,684	12,130	8,414	10,080	2,315	2,100	17,364	2,790	19,651	19,207	17,125	14,227	17,693	13,035	8,942	14,293	4,485	15,251
Riyadh, Saudi Arabia	10,983	7,936	11,244	11,253	10,291	12,484	14,187	13,663	7,759	13,993	7,819	7,422	4,984	2,019	6,814	1,182	9,948	2,095	13,548	11,774
Road Town, Brit. Virgin Isls.	5,232	12,428	6,296	6,789	2,670	5,090	7,118	7,333	16,866	7,955	13,906	13,553	14,185	12,356	12,160	11,024	3,204	12,546	2,563	15,730
Roanoke, Virginia	2,665	14,900	3,740	4,236	889	2,762	9,185	9,520	14,452	10,056	11,453	11,159	12,422	11,593	9,890	10,565	1,280	11,784	4,154	13,588
Robinson Crusoe Island, Chile	9,966	9,107	10,579	10,921	8,389	8,846	1,409	1,907	16,812	2,259	17,462	17,743	19,562	16,715	17,414	15,441	8,943	16,792	3,699	13,221
Rochester, New York	2,352	15,055	3,473	3,966	531	2,833	9,822	10,137	13,919	10,691	10,928	10,605	11,758	10,928	9,291	9,933	646	11,118	4,805	13,498
Rockhampton, Australia	12,960	9,731	11,869	11,417	15,646	12,293	11,228	11,330	5,038	10,635	6,857	7,373	8,287	10,873	8,857	12,293	15,489	10,703	14,127	2,130
Rome, Italy	7,930	10,120	8,563	8,772	6,657	9,313	12,832	12,563	10,609	13,199	9,317	8,799	7,375	4,814	7,517	3,426	6,370	4,994	10,109	14,237
Rosario, Argentina	10,493	8,026	11,319	11,737	8,351	9,652	1,726	1,702	17,433	2,389	19,098	19,127	17,936	15,032	17,863	13,814	8,898	15,101	4,077	14,641
Roseau, Dominica	5,710	11,940	6,780	7,274	3,093	5,576	6,818	6,997	17,236	7,638	14,319	13,946	14,383	12,358	12,524	10,990	3,612	12,544	2,546	16,157
Rostock, East Germany	6,811	11,420	7,335	7,504	6,011	8,262	13,617	13,450	10,197	14,128	8,429	7,905	6,963	4,890	6,509	3,698	5,626	5,083	10,069	13,406
Rostov-na-Donu, USSR	8,405	10,396	8,673	8,711	8,040	9,911	14,975	14,638	8,394	15,214	7,204	6,700	5,150	2,815	5,564	1,682	7,620	3,008	12,115	12,039
Rotterdam, Netherlands	6,677	11,373	7,296	7,509	5,626	8,083	13,062	12,909	10,762	13,592	8,965	8,441	7,526	5,383	7,025	4,135	5,277	5,576	9,547	13,936
Rouyn, Canada	1,955	15,392	3,078	3,561	931	2,731	10,392	10,711	13,352	11,262	10,364	10,036	11,203	10,496	8,717	9,569	607	10,683	5,369	13,138
Sacramento, California	2,022	18,118	1,707	1,872	4,219	866	10,505	11,034	11,811	11,270	9,098	9,021	11,307	12,200	8,287	11,859	4,144	12,339	6,140	9,982
Saginaw, Michigan	1,937	15,528	3,040	3,537	1,042	2,319	9,903	10,256	13,688	10,775	10,690	10,399	11,743	11,145	9,145	10,224	1,066	11,332	4,865	13,018
Saint Denis, Reunion	16,076	3,265	16,333	16,260	14,561	17,539	10,997	10,428	7,703	10,326	9,928	9,865	7,285	5,907	10,262	6,163	14,446	5,785	14,507	10,550
Saint George's, Grenada	5,996	11,712	7,049	7,541	3,430	5,784	6,457	6,636	17,595	7,277	14,665	14,299	14,727	12,631	12,882	11,248	3,956	12,814	2,295	16,201
Saint John, Canada	2,981	14,359	4,094	4,567	578	3,725	10,066	10,305	13,895	10,916	10,976	10,595	11,374	10,206	9,184	9,125	437	10,399	5,186	14,142
Saint John's, Antigua	5,517	12,113	6,591	7,086	2,888	5,412	7,007	7,194	17,036	7,832	14,115	13,743	14,219	12,255	12,323	10,899	3,407	12,442	2,646	16,055
Saint John's, Canada	3,736	13,633	4,789	5,225	1,608	4,689	10,483	10,638	13,602	11,294	10,847	10,413	10,783	9,310	8,931	8,160	1,402	9,504	5,854	14,644
Saint Louis, Missouri	2,012	15,752	2,990	3,476	1,635	1,852	9,469	9,865	13,875	10,336	10,902	10,661	12,241	11,845	9,505	10,961	1,794	12,029	4,463	12,686
Saint Paul, Minnesota	1,300	16,267	2,348	2,844	1,786	1,607	10,209	10,608	13,163	11,075	10,179	9,928	11,512	11,265	8,762	10,474	1,704	11,443	5,207	12,271
Saint Peter Port, UK	6,550	11,336	7,259	7,515	5,247	7,899	12,508	12,371	11,330	13,058	9,496	8,973	8,092	5,897	7,539	4,608	4,941	6,088	9,016	14,455
Saipan (Susupe)	9,857	12,575	8,760	8,264	12,642	9,973	15,105	15,376	2,992	14,717	2,767	3,287	5,225	8,210	4,664	9,499	12,217	8,113	14,900	2,256
Salalah, Oman	11,992	7,226	12,142	12,092	11,432	13,500	14,192	13,625	7,020	13,816	7,595	7,270	4,624	1,999	6,948	1,981	11,082	1,964	14,518	11,013
Salem, Oregon	1,554	18,532	999	1,167	4,127	1,069	11,168	11,685	11,373	11,949	8,563	8,448	10,647	11,484	7,637	11,169	3,953	11,622	6,648	9,928
Salt Lake City, Utah	1,458	17,518	1,674	2,037	3,361	61	10,311	10,803	12,392	11,124	9,556	9,419	11,499	11,992	8,523	11,472	3,302	12,148	5,653	10,815
Salta, Argentina	9,478	8,998	10,305	10,727	7,399	8,646	2,379	2,549	18,284	3,183	18,218	18,116	18,182	15,214	16,916	13,868	7,951	15,322	3,062	14,845
Salto, Uruguay	10,448	7,964	11,310	11,741	8,221	9,668	2,013	1,938	17,584	2,634	19,249	19,096	17,672	14,742	17,690	13,511	8,763	14,816	4,073	14,944
Salvador, Brazil	9,703	7,939	10,790	11,286	6,942	9,550	4,827	4,617	17,528	5,297	17,259	16,736	15,079	12,102	15,282	10,771	7,383	12,211	4,631	17,775
Salzburg, Austria	7,413	10,734	7,990	8,176	6,372	8,835	13,267	13,042	10,362	13,698	8,844	8,322	7,110	4,760	6,987	3,450	6,036	4,949	10,143	13,809
Samsun, Turkey	8,924	9,734	9,268	9,335	8,292	10,417	14,436	14,057	8,671	14,599	7,746	7,255	5,476	2,832	6,195	1,474	7,914	3,014	12,079	12,464
San Antonio, Texas	2,707	15,814	3,353	3,764	2,796	1,696	8,688	9,148	14,127	9,530	11,303	11,154	13,097	13,052	10,188	12,222	3,046	13,230	3,908	12,115
San Cristobal, Venezuela	5,876	12,173	6,812	7,276	3,773	5,312	5,889	6,181	17,728	6,751	14,765	14,505	15,554	13,781	13,245	12,428	4,329	13,970	1,124	15,106
San Diego, California	2,451	17,401	2,397	2,616	4,131	969	9,744	10,274	12,463	10,511	9,818	9,758	12,068	12,881	9,047	12,445	4,165	13,028	5,451	10,327
San Francisco, California	2,141	18,130	1,794	1,935	4,328	970	10,472	11,006	11,779	11,230	9,090	9,023	11,338	12,280	8,315	11,957	4,260	12,417	6,159	9,893
San Jose, Costa Rica	5,177	13,231	5,962	6,388	3,745	4,322	6,234	6,637	16,689	7,101	13,931	13,773	15,454	14,407	12,722	13,175	4,266	14,601	1,282	13,795
San Juan, Argentina	10,056	8,653	10,807	11,200	8,127	9,105	1,581	1,814	17,480	2,409	18,346	18,482	18,673	15,719	17,588	14,446	8,681	15,801	3,622	14,171
San Juan, Puerto Rico	5,146	12,544	6,199	6,691	2,637	4,965	7,104	7,333	16,841	7,948	13,865	13,523	14,234	12,464	12,148	11,142	3,179	12,655	2,471	15,578
San Luis Potosi, Mexico	3,471	15,447	3,975	4,334	3,515	2,244	8,010	8,499	14,436	8,833	11,769	11,676	13,795	13,894	10,827	13,056	3,824	14,072	3,475	11,927
San Marino, San Marino	7,744	10,335	8,360	8,562	6,543	9,139	12,971	12,717	10,540	13,360	9,166	8,646	7,296	4,803	7,344	3,437	6,240	4,986	10,105	14,106
San Miguel de Tucuman, Argen.	9,693	8,820	10,510	10,928	7,625	8,843	2,167	2,324	18,070	2,962	18,381	18,318	18,254	15,270	17,142	13,947	8,177	15,370	3,269	14,734
San Salvador, El Salvador	4,620	13,914	5,340	5,749	3,559	3,667	6,753	7,189	15,994	7,610	13,273	13,139	14,993	14,331	12,156	13,203	4,037	14,524	1,939	13,221
Sanaa, Yemen	11,886	6,888	12,230	12,268	10,880	13,367	13,306	12,759	8,089	13,031	8,587	8,232	5,646	2,832	7,764	2,241	10,599	2,851	13,521	12,070
Santa Cruz, Bolivia	8,864	9,409	9,755	10,199	6,655	8,153	3,186	3,331	19,090	3,980	17,745	17,502	17,552	14,689	16,172	13,297	7,202	14,819	2,569	15,447
Santa Cruz, Tenerife	7,500	9,935	8,496	8,888	5,149	8,453	9,973	9,791	13,597	10,470	12,087	11,563	10,365	7,718	10,144	6,295	5,143	7,886	7,336	17,059
Santa Fe, New Mexico	1,947	16,789	2,410	2,797	3,057	712	9,582	10,064	13,145	10,408	10,322	10,184	12,221	12,509	9,266	11,858	3,129	12,675	4,887	11,358
Santa Rosa, Argentina	10,726	7,976	11,491	11,886	8,716	9,791	1,204	1,244	17,012	1,909	18,811	19,102	18,215	15,433	18,228	14,265	9,267	15,487	4,289	14,121
Santa Rosalia, Mexico	2,924	16,645	3,076	3,340	4,035	1,434	8,995	9,520	13,165	9,772	10,569	10,517	12,819	13,483	9,801	12,923	4,177	13,639	4,725	10,775
Santarem, Brazil	7,772	10,017	8,812	9,299	5,183	7,460	5,075	5,136	18,933	5,818	16,367	15,953	15,681	13,018	14,472	11,594	5,692	13,173	2,660	16,957
Santiago del Estero, Argentina	9,829	8,677	10,650	11,069	7,741	8,985	2,093	2,221	17,983	2,870	18,520	18,459	18,198	15,214	17,261	13,906	8,291	15,309	3,408	14,748
Santiago, Chile	10,183	8,631	10,897	11,277	8,334	9,182	1,338	1,638	17,211	2,189	18,205	18,426	18,861	15,957	17,729	14,707	8,890	16,031	3,769	13,883
Santo Domingo, Dominican Rep.	4,939	12,834	5,963	6,450	2,593	4,658	7,078	7,344	16,747	7,935	13,750	13,437	14,344	12,731	12,108	11,435	3,147	12,923	2,271	15,192
Sao Paulo de Olivenca, Brazil	7,164	10,999	8,073	8,528	5,020	6,515	4,664	4,917	18,940	5,513	16,052	15,802	16,610	14,346	14,528	12,927	5,574	14,517	1,137	15,400
Sao Paulo, Brazil	10,229	7,744	11,230	11,706	7,673	9,753	3,380	3,185	17,839	3,873	18,658	18,146	16,371	13,391	16,649	12,117	8,175	13,481	4,303	16,329
Sao Tome, Sao Tome & Principe	11,456	6,023	12,428	12,792	9,004	12,358	9,212	8,746	12,424	9,216	12,879	12,454	10,043	7,094	11,594	5,955	9,068	7,166	9,489	16,172
Sapporo, Japan	7,571	14,193	6,636	6,186	10,051	8,235	17,308	17,836	4,296	17,393	1,380	1,384	4,084	6,595	1,838	7,519	9,546	6,584	13,832	5,345
Sarajevo, Yugoslavia	8,011	10,199	8,562	8,732	6,956	9,440	13,348	13,066	10,084	13,691	8,809	8,293	6,846	4,324	7,038	2,961	6,631	4,508	10,583	13,713
Saratov, USSR	8,098	10,904	8,266	8,263	8,030	9,607	15,571	15,263	7,972	15,857	6,597	6,087	4,721	2,743	4,912	1,920	7,573	2,936	12,329	11,487
Saskatoon, Canada	134	17,398	1,098	1,593	2,879	1,376	11,284	11,725	11,907	12,133	8,938	8,711	10,491	10,703	7,623	10,147	2,605	10,865	6,369	11,139
Schefferville, Canada	2,526	14,882	3,539	3,964	1,482	3,663	11,118	11,366	12,834	11,972	9,929	9,540	10,359	9,419	8,123	8,459	940	9,608	6,192	13,397
Seattle, Washington	1,328	18,521	704	934	4,013	1,183	11,384	11,892	11,282	12,178	8,429	8,292	10,430	11,198	7,431	10,870	3,801	11,338	6,781	10,014

Distances in Kilometers	Prince Albert, Canada	Prince Edward Island	Prince George, Canada	Prince Rupert, Canada	Providence, Rhode Island	Provo, Utah	Puerto Aisen, Chile	Puerto Deseado, Argentina	Puerto Princesa, Philippines	Punta Arenas, Chile	Pusan, South Korea	Pyongyang, North Korea	Qamdo, China	Qandahar, Afghanistan	Qiqian, China	Qom, Iran	Quebec, Canada	Quetta, Pakistan	Quito, Ecuador	Rabaul, Papua New Guinea
Sendai, Japan	8,026	13,864	7,059	6,597	10,556	8,615	17,144	17,610	3,857	17,074	1,113	1,319	4,037	6,717	2,197	7,732	10,057	6,687	14,193	4,842
Seoul, South Korea	8,742	12,851	7,878	7,449	11,018	9,526	18,165	18,468	3,193	17,794	330	195	2,816	5,561	1,696	6,663	10,484	5,518	15,118	5,308
Sept-Iles, Canada	2,708	14,643	3,785	4,238	1,009	3,662	10,610	10,854	13,347	11,463	10,435	10,050	10,849	9,797	8,635	8,776	519	9,989	5,705	13,766
Sevastopol, USSR	8,496	10,111	8,858	8,937	7,877	9,987	14,417	14,077	8,879	14,656	7,764	7,260	5,650	3,146	6,119	1,849	7,492	3,334	11,755	12,579
Seville, Spain	7,368	10,281	8,222	8,540	5,504	8,561	11,344	11,145	12,256	11,817	10,739	10,214	9,011	6,462	8,826	5,058	5,340	6,639	8,488	15,716
Shanghai, China	9,616	11,987	8,761	8,332	11,824	10,408	18,011	18,059	2,383	17,366	842	963	2,297	5,232	2,342	6,468	11,282	5,158	16,001	5,097
Sheffield, United Kingdom	6,284	11,691	6,941	7,174	5,190	7,673	12,859	12,746	11,046	13,437	9,109	8,588	7,830	5,784	7,138	4,558	4,841	5,977	9,167	14,051
Shenyang, China	8,474	12,920	7,673	7,268	10,625	9,361	18,659	19,023	3,583	18,354	890	366	2,614	5,181	1,173	6,213	10,082	5,155	14,903	5,867
Shiraz, Iran	10,595	8,564	10,741	10,703	10,236	12,104	14,979	14,459	7,188	14,788	7,049	6,641	4,271	1,286	6,018	581	9,841	1,398	13,906	11,178
Sibiu, Romania	8,050	10,324	8,519	8,651	7,212	9,513	13,846	13,556	9,594	14,173	8,315	7,801	6,352	3,894	6,567	2,574	6,852	4,081	11,007	13,211
Singapore	13,372	8,300	12,544	12,112	15,208	14,173	15,105	14,762	1,894	14,235	4,565	4,735	3,380	5,221	5,861	6,609	14,654	5,038	19,746	5,411
Sioux Falls, South Dakota	1,263	16,483	2,216	2,703	2,077	1,290	10,136	10,556	13,107	10,995	10,143	9,915	11,611	11,498	8,801	10,747	2,028	11,673	5,176	12,025
Skelleftea, Sweden	6,152	12,435	6,481	6,571	6,003	7,656	14,605	14,525	9,400	15,219	7,322	6,801	6,273	4,786	5,348	3,907	5,530	4,976	10,475	12,263
Skopje, Yugoslavia	8,314	9,947	8,843	9,000	7,278	9,750	13,435	13,124	9,886	13,731	8,737	8,227	6,666	4,068	7,019	2,683	6,954	4,248	10,853	13,592
Socotra Island (Tamrida)	12,459	6,754	12,622	12,573	11,801	13,967	13,840	13,266	7,059	13,420	7,860	7,563	4,873	2,417	7,329	2,457	11,473	2,359	14,618	11,005
Sofia, Bulgaria	8,321	9,994	8,824	8,968	7,357	9,769	13,602	13,289	9,723	13,892	8,571	8,061	6,500	3,920	6,860	2,547	7,022	4,102	10,993	13,423
Songkhla, Thailand	12,867	8,572	12,119	11,714	14,517	13,805	15,723	15,333	2,016	14,852	4,243	4,333	2,676	4,512	5,321	5,915	13,967	4,333	19,226	5,868
Sorong, Indonesia	12,213	10,194	11,130	10,635	14,939	12,346	14,365	14,367	1,817	13,673	3,990	4,454	5,049	7,763	5,964	9,186	14,470	7,610	16,724	2,356
South Georgia Island	13,498	5,123	14,342	14,754	11,146	12,662	2,732	2,152	14,612	2,238	17,611	17,863	15,572	13,574	18,507	12,904	11,664	13,541	7,101	13,474
South Pole	15,899	4,843	15,978	16,022	14,634	14,457	4,973	4,712	11,078	4,111	13,887	14,322	13,452	13,499	15,787	13,839	15,190	13,345	9,979	9,536
South Sandwich Islands	14,224	4,396	15,087	15,502	11,799	13,410	3,402	2,834	13,912	2,804	16,904	17,124	14,860	13,042	17,856	12,504	12,303	12,991	7,844	13,136
Split, Yugoslavia	7,956	10,204	8,533	8,714	6,840	9,373	13,198	12,922	10,247	13,553	8,955	8,438	7,010	4,484	7,171	3,115	6,525	4,667	10,426	13,868
Spokane, Washington	1,028	18,153	790	1,167	3,645	946	11,196	11,689	11,596	12,008	8,713	8,557	10,615	11,221	7,638	10,813	3,445	11,369	6,503	10,384
Spoleto, Italy	7,865	10,203	8,488	8,693	6,628	9,255	12,906	12,642	10,561	13,280	9,239	8,720	7,322	4,787	7,432	3,408	6,333	4,969	10,129	14,166
Springbok, South Africa	14,806	2,557	15,864	16,272	12,084	15,334	7,772	7,193	11,589	7,353	13,649	13,477	10,755	8,460	13,408	7,919	12,284	8,427	10,621	13,878
Springfield, Illinois	1,927	15,773	2,932	3,421	1,552	1,875	9,588	9,979	13,794	10,456	10,814	10,566	12,116	11,706	9,395	10,824	1,680	11,890	4,574	12,697
Springfield, Massachusetts	2,748	14,637	3,873	4,364	103	3,257	9,692	9,975	14,151	10,555	11,178	10,833	11,826	10,804	9,477	9,747	535	10,996	4,724	13,915
Srinagar, India	10,334	9,669	10,110	9,918	10,923	11,749	16,993	16,428	5,220	16,585	4,913	4,534	2,124	893	4,156	2,196	10,424	854	15,346	9,116
Stanley, Falkland Islands	12,456	6,490	13,165	13,529	10,444	11,441	1,297	727	15,341	902	18,081	18,568	16,954	14,969	19,907	14,176	10,992	14,949	6,026	13,191
Stara Zagora, Bulgaria	8,437	9,934	8,913	9,044	7,528	9,895	13,744	13,419	9,541	14,012	8,433	7,926	6,323	3,728	6,749	2,355	7,185	3,910	11,186	13,262
Stockholm, Sweden	6,556	11,881	6,969	7,091	6,106	8,044	14,224	14,088	9,682	14,773	7,783	7,259	6,484	4,679	5,843	3,640	5,670	4,873	10,400	12,753
Stornoway, United Kingdom	5,692	12,311	6,326	6,555	4,784	7,103	13,003	12,950	11,009	13,647	8,865	8,350	7,856	6,054	6,866	4,918	4,393	6,249	8,989	13,731
Strasbourg, France	7,110	10,943	7,733	7,943	5,982	8,510	13,009	12,814	10,700	13,483	9,070	8,546	7,450	5,154	7,172	3,852	5,655	5,344	9,751	14,048
Stuttgart, West Germany	7,158	10,926	7,765	7,968	6,069	8,567	13,104	12,904	10,594	13,572	8,981	8,457	7,344	5,049	7,089	3,751	5,736	5,239	9,857	13,957
Subic, Philippines	11,283	10,622	10,346	9,887	13,615	11,895	16,412	16,317	593	15,648	2,407	2,728	2,957	5,812	4,140	7,208	13,076	5,679	17,402	4,108
Suchow, China	9,466	11,951	8,673	8,267	11,535	10,359	18,515	18,486	2,722	17,812	1,091	929	1,899	4,769	2,014	5,972	10,985	4,704	15,900	5,622
Sucre, Bolivia	8,898	9,459	9,760	10,195	6,766	8,132	3,003	3,186	18,893	3,817	17,742	17,552	17,810	14,950	16,286	13,558	7,317	15,079	2,533	15,185
Sudbury, Canada	1,918	15,456	3,044	3,534	926	2,563	10,214	10,545	13,476	11,085	10,481	10,167	11,401	10,737	8,871	9,813	748	10,924	5,181	13,092
Suez, Egypt	9,951	8,495	10,412	10,523	8,891	11,403	13,451	13,008	9,115	13,485	8,697	8,238	6,113	3,171	7,326	1,801	8,594	3,309	12,047	13,091
Sundsvall, Sweden	6,258	12,220	6,645	6,759	5,936	7,753	14,335	14,236	9,636	14,928	7,619	7,097	6,477	4,838	5,654	3,871	5,481	5,030	10,327	12,570
Surabaya, Indonesia	13,845	8,268	12,863	12,387	16,153	14,297	14,148	13,911	1,992	13,303	4,990	5,295	4,561	6,588	6,632	7,973	15,603	6,405	18,531	4,380
Suva, Fiji	10,694	11,820	9,746	9,387	12,993	9,691	9,987	10,320	7,245	9,717	7,867	8,369	10,236	13,164	9,567	14,547	13,001	13,031	11,393	3,246
Sverdlovsk, USSR	7,741	11,657	7,721	7,640	8,187	9,221	16,587	16,331	7,202	16,951	5,547	5,030	4,010	2,836	3,805	2,574	7,679	3,003	12,751	10,492
Svobodnyy, USSR	7,371	13,845	6,610	6,226	9,505	8,321	18,344	18,926	4,699	18,706	1,812	1,389	3,383	5,463	512	6,253	8,965	5,481	13,808	6,572
Sydney, Australia	13,770	8,878	12,729	12,307	16,212	12,892	10,178	10,239	5,923	9,541	7,978	8,488	9,160	11,514	9,985	12,896	16,195	11,332	13,615	3,288
Sydney, Canada	3,322	14,020	4,414	4,873	1,020	4,161	10,217	10,418	13,814	11,052	10,959	10,553	11,147	9,830	9,106	8,713	851	10,024	5,441	14,410
Syktyvkar, USSR	7,101	12,056	7,175	7,143	7,419	8,599	16,016	15,846	7,902	16,514	6,038	5,514	4,749	3,515	4,168	3,004	6,916	3,693	11,979	11,016
Szeged, Hungary	7,851	10,433	8,363	8,515	6,926	9,299	13,615	13,345	9,886	13,977	8,534	8,016	6,639	4,206	6,746	2,884	6,578	4,394	10,694	13,457
Szombathely, Hungary	7,616	10,600	8,159	8,329	6,639	9,052	13,450	13,204	10,122	13,850	8,680	8,159	6,872	4,487	6,854	3,173	6,295	4,675	10,415	13,629
Tabriz, Iran	9,540	9,415	9,757	9,761	9,145	11,047	15,004	14,560	7,814	15,022	7,150	6,686	4,675	1,915	5,793	562	8,742	2,094	13,003	11,690
Tacheng, China	8,897	11,234	8,588	8,374	9,873	10,262	18,138	17,675	5,316	18,024	4,028	3,554	2,120	2,236	2,777	2,995	9,338	2,295	14,544	8,791
Tahiti (Papeete)	8,890	12,865	8,321	8,170	10,350	7,505	7,626	8,119	10,517	7,713	10,361	10,774	13,182	16,148	11,504	17,239	10,556	16,070	8,003	6,511
Taipei, Taiwan	10,214	11,524	9,321	8,878	12,484	10,931	17,417	17,404	1,720	16,718	1,330	1,599	2,473	5,458	3,015	6,770	11,944	5,360	16,526	4,635
Taiyuan, China	9,263	11,941	8,543	8,164	11,171	10,258	19,065	18,900	3,177	18,285	1,508	1,158	1,588	4,298	1,718	5,450	10,617	4,249	15,686	6,199
Tallahasee, Florida	3,068	14,801	4,029	4,507	1,709	2,701	8,480	8,854	14,930	9,351	11,958	11,712	13,184	12,450	10,529	11,410	2,137	12,641	3,448	13,444
Tallinn, USSR	6,758	11,812	7,108	7,200	6,442	8,258	14,574	14,420	9,307	15,099	7,458	6,934	6,104	4,333	5,541	3,349	5,995	4,526	10,775	12,435
Tamanrasset, Algeria	9,324	8,347	10,175	10,401	7,303	10,401	10,912	10,560	11,916	11,146	11,271	10,773	8,891	5,976	9,614	4,584	7,209	6,113	9,412	15,893
Tampa, Florida	3,396	14,491	4,356	4,833	1,836	3,001	8,183	8,546	15,259	9,054	12,285	12,037	13,462	12,609	10,842	11,523	2,312	12,802	3,146	13,686
Tampere, Finland	6,533	12,050	6,872	6,961	6,285	8,034	14,608	14,481	9,325	15,167	7,388	6,864	6,148	4,489	5,447	3,551	5,826	4,682	10,676	12,357
Tanami, Australia	14,046	8,555	12,924	12,430	16,880	13,830	12,419	12,343	3,500	11,663	6,097	6,544	6,640	8,893	8,043	10,283	16,478	8,712	16,223	2,998
Tangier, Morocco	7,513	10,119	8,378	8,701	5,599	8,689	11,223	11,014	12,330	11,681	10,872	10,348	9,092	6,500	8,970	5,089	5,451	6,674	8,472	15,847
Tarawa (Betio)	9,308	13,374	8,233	7,798	12,005	8,678	11,998	12,397	6,069	11,841	5,878	6,347	8,576	11,557	7,414	12,801	11,830	11,466	12,086	2,389
Tashkent, USSR	9,519	10,223	9,388	9,242	9,986	10,971	16,937	16,441	5,963	16,783	5,175	4,729	2,737	1,128	4,022	1,774	9,491	1,253	14,425	9,725
Tbilisi, USSR	9,117	9,803	9,342	9,355	8,759	10,625	15,077	14,669	7,968	15,174	7,099	6,618	4,773	2,179	5,633	950	8,347	2,368	12,722	11,767
Tegucigalpa, Honduras	4,636	13,802	5,396	5,818	3,430	3,749	6,750	7,171	16,129	7,613	13,358	13,206	14,973	14,191	12,181	13,038	3,922	14,384	1,852	13,433
Tehran, Iran	9,916	9,209	10,063	10,033	9,645	11,425	15,265	14,785	7,339	15,187	6,849	6,406	4,251	1,402	5,629	123	9,231	1,575	13,531	11,256
Tel Aviv, Israel	9,819	8,716	10,236	10,328	8,887	11,289	13,760	13,321	8,880	13,799	8,393	7,930	5,840	2,924	7,012	1,527	8,567	3,070	12,207	12,835
Telegraph Creek, Canada	1,675	18,549	687	402	4,477	2,409	12,656	13,152	10,251	13,460	7,312	7,125	9,156	9,964	6,175	9,747	4,113	10,096	7,929	9,617
Teresina, Brazil	8,713	8,894	9,806	10,302	5,949	8,609	5,324	5,216	17,936	5,913	16,579	16,076	14,952	12,068	14,569	10,673	6,394	12,202	4,003	18,070
Ternate, Indonesia	12,279	10,034	11,222	10,731	14,923	12,525	14,688	14,647	1,377	13,961	3,801	4,235	4,626	7,305	5,730	8,729	14,427	7,149	17,154	2,812
The Valley, Anguilla	5,358	12,279	6,430	6,924	2,752	5,246	7,093	7,293	16,925	7,924	13,986	13,622	14,169	12,273	12,213	10,930	3,277	12,462	2,634	15,900
Thessaloniki, Greece	8,505	9,775	9,027	9,179	7,465	9,943	13,447	13,119	9,798	13,713	8,732	8,225	6,592	3,943	7,048	2,544	7,145	4,120	10,992	13,549
Thimphu, Bhutan	10,936	9,721	10,457	10,160	12,086	12,185	17,492	16,931	3,624	16,746	3,811	3,562	833	2,361	3,764	3,763	11,552	2,232	16,735	7,559
Thunder Bay, Canada	1,273	16,117	2,394	2,887	1,583	1,990	10,518	10,892	13,004	11,388	10,006	9,723	11,168	10,806	8,496	9,997	1,368	10,986	5,487	12,432
Tientsin, China	8,973	12,328	8,213	7,821	10,998	9,917	18,943	19,016	3,261	18,330	1,143	740	2,017	4,688	1,479	5,798	10,448	4,647	15,411	5,993
Tijuana, Mexico	2,466	17,378	2,419	2,639	4,128	980	9,721	10,250	12,484	10,488	9,841	9,782	12,091	12,902	9,071	12,462	4,166	13,048	5,429	10,338
Tiksi, USSR	5,518	14,858	5,013	4,755	7,324	6,734	16,871	17,240	6,906	17,736	4,062	3,631	4,880	5,765	2,198	5,968	6,774	5,866	11,845	8,582
Timbuktu, Mali	9,354	8,128	10,319	10,688	7,005	10,325	9,817	9,483	12,982	10,087	12,365	11,861	10,000	7,069	10,654	5,689	7,016	7,201	8,478	16,986
Tindouf, Algeria	8,070	9,443	9,012	9,372	5,864	9,116	10,395	10,153	12,963	10,809	11,733	11,211	9,774	7,029	9,862	5,603	5,812	7,190	8,097	16,682
Tirane, Albania	8,309	9,903	8,863	9,031	7,207	9,733	13,280	12,972	10,037	13,580	8,891	8,381	6,819	4,204	7,166	2,811	6,895	4,383	10,724	13,748
Tokyo, Japan	8,315	13,617	7,339	6,874	10,855	8,879	17,092	17,515	3,579	16,935	975	1,294	3,957	6,715	2,367	7,781	10,357	6,675	14,442	4,603
Toledo, Spain	7,269	10,444	8,084	8,384	5,536	8,508	11,663	11,469	11,969	12,141	10,415	9,891	8,720	6,220	8,501	4,830	5,337	6,400	8,707	15,393
Topeka, Kansas	1,752	16,193	2,628	3,100	2,075	1,377	9,632	10,057	13,544	10,491	10,600	10,388	12,118	11,953	9,297	11,152	2,162	12,132	4,688	12,212
Toronto, Canada	2,204	15,208	3,323	3,817	684	2,686	9,889	10,214	13,816	10,759	10,821	10,506	11,711	10,952	9,207	9,981	729	11,141	4,862	13,344
Toulouse, France	7,240	10,618	7,971	8,231	5,770	8,560	12,277	12,077	11,374	12,745	9,808	9,284	8,123	5,690	7,907	4,325	5,511	5,874	9,217	14,785
Tours, France	6,880	11,024	7,582	7,831	5,550	8,229	12,523	12,354	11,234	13,032	9,525	9,001	7,985	5,689	7,595	4,370	5,255	5,878	9,213	14,500
Townsville, Australia	12,857	9,835	11,744	11,275	15,637	12,332	11,813	11,902	4,445	11,205	6,301	6,813	7,692	10,306	8,307	11,729	15,405	10,139	14,639	1,765
Trenton, New Jersey	2,742	14,689	3,860	4,354	333	3,117	9,486	9,785	14,303	10,353	11,316	10,986	12,058	11,079	9,654	10,024	786	11,271	4,495	13,858
Tripoli, Lebanon	9,614	8,975	10,002	10,082	8,780	11,093	13,994	13,566	8,758	14,056	8,168	7,699	5,672	2,802	6,753	1,380	8,441	2,959	12,243	12,682
Tripoli, Libya	8,801	9,147	9,497	9,728	7,255	10,128	12,232	11,898	10,852	12,493	9,948	9,444	7,707	4,904	8,264	3,479	7,036	5,063	10,185	14,711
Tristan da Cunha (Edinburgh)	13,410	4,230	14,513	15,009	10,598	13,246	5,028	4,475	14,262	4,792	16,561	16,368	13,638	11,113	16,021	10,284	10,989	11,115	7,903	15,166
Trondheim, Norway	5,946	12,435	6,377	6,515	5,567	7,433	14,077	14,009	9,935	14,705	7,825	7,307	6,802	5,206	5,840	4,227	5,114	5,399	9,973	12,744
Trujillo, Peru	7,250	11,341	8,001	8,406	5,583	6,316	4,177	4,565	18,075	5,048	15,879	15,788	17,424	15,547	14,795	14,141	6,134	15,725	876	14,188
Truk Island (Moen)	10,166	12,429	9,042	8,550	13,008	10,029	14,020	14,297	3,655	13,645	3,850	4,368	6,239	9,219	5,714	10,540	12,650	9,111	14,391	1,287
Truro, Canada	3,161	14,178	4,267	4,735	766	3,939	10,098	10,320	13,899	10,942	11,008	10,615	11,304	10,056	9,186	8,954	637	10,250	5,268	14,300
Tsingtao, China	9,165	12,295	8,352	7,940	11,298	10,030	18,507	18,612	2,921	17,916	799	581	2,204	5,010	1,793	6,169	10,753	4,956	15,590	5,557
Tsitsihar, China	7,911	13,338	7,150	6,763	10,010	8,858	18,723	19,278	4,201	18,778	1,427	939	2,899	5,172	583	6,074	9,466	5,172	14,349	6,347
Tubuai Island (Mataura)	9,472	12,223	8,939	8,800	10,780	8,059	7,188	7,656	10,622	7,210	10,745	11,183	13,463	16,448	12,008	17,684	11,025	16,341	8,066	6,607
Tucson, Arizona	2,368	16,931	2,587	2,894	3,643	892	9,424	9,934	12,991	10,221	10,280	10,189	12,390	12,935	9,388	12,365	3,731	13,093	4,953	10,906
Tulsa, Oklahoma	2,044	16,051	2,860	3,318	2,205	1,449	9,330	9,762	13,771	10,186	10,849	10,652	12,427	12,267	9,588	11,447	2,362	12,446	4,412	12,250

Distances in Kilometers	Prince Albert, Canada	Prince Edward Island	Prince George, Canada	Prince Rupert, Canada	Providence, Rhode Island	Provo, Utah	Puerto Aisen, Chile	Puerto Deseado, Argentina	Puerto Princesa, Philippines	Punta Arenas, Chile	Pusan, South Korea	Pyongyang, North Korea	Qamdo, China	Qandahar, Afghanistan	Qiqian, China	Qom, Iran	Quebec, Canada	Quetta, Pakistan	Quito, Ecuador	Rabaul, Papua New Guinea
Tunis, Tunisia	8,289	9,643	8,989	9,226	6,786	9,620	12,315	12,021	10,979	12,644	9,850	9,336	7,778	5,083	8,085	3,664	6,551	5,254	9,910	14,723
Tura, USSR	6,785	13,433	6,387	6,157	8,219	8,085	17,858	17,983	6,227	18,667	3,783	3,270	3,688	4,347	1,792	4,662	7,664	4,443	12,896	8,707
Turin, Italy	7,419	10,577	8,076	8,299	6,147	8,793	12,754	12,533	10,854	13,192	9,354	8,831	7,604	5,177	7,484	3,825	5,852	5,363	9,726	14,321
Uberlandia, Brazil	9,702	8,222	10,714	11,193	7,135	9,264	3,699	3,573	18,297	4,269	18,195	17,707	16,315	13,335	16,194	12,007	7,637	13,441	3,894	16,615
Ufa, USSR	7,922	11,356	7,960	7,902	8,201	9,415	16,287	16,001	7,398	16,604	5,868	5,354	4,171	2,687	4,163	2,266	7,708	2,865	12,687	10,789
Ujungpandang, Indonesia	13,290	8,946	12,262	11,776	15,801	13,617	14,282	14,125	1,644	13,475	4,565	4,930	4,656	6,985	6,353	8,399	15,273	6,811	17,960	3,639
Ulaanbaatar, Mongolia	8,382	12,422	7,794	7,471	10,063	9,528	19,723	19,479	4,377	19,403	2,320	1,811	2,033	3,903	1,103	4,801	9,507	3,912	14,694	7,263
Ulan-Ude, USSR	7,955	12,769	7,387	7,077	9,628	9,121	19,289	19,361	4,777	19,831	2,524	2,000	2,448	4,065	906	4,842	9,072	4,095	14,255	7,500
Uliastay, Mongolia	8,615	11,913	8,139	7,859	10,015	9,862	19,175	18,726	4,691	18,958	3,008	2,519	1,842	3,180	1,782	4,048	9,463	3,203	14,718	7,877
Uranium City, Canada	730	17,387	1,067	1,437	3,218	2,161	12,089	12,513	11,253	12,945	8,260	7,999	9,672	9,890	6,846	9,394	2,819	10,048	7,126	10,927
Urumqi, China	9,181	11,141	8,799	8,554	10,293	10,500	18,450	17,922	4,826	18,127	3,656	3,206	1,639	2,343	2,622	3,296	9,753	2,362	14,985	8,339
Ushuaia, Argentina	12,459	6,819	13,044	13,358	10,711	11,310	1,091	802	14,968	251	17,443	17,962	17,142	15,594	19,344	14,901	11,265	15,552	6,123	12,483
Vaduz, Liechtenstein	7,316	10,750	7,934	8,141	6,169	8,715	13,014	12,800	10,635	13,461	9,087	8,563	7,383	5,024	7,211	3,701	5,849	5,212	9,877	14,058
Valencia, Spain	7,502	10,264	8,287	8,571	5,837	8,769	11,847	11,629	11,715	12,292	10,257	9,734	8,471	5,927	8,373	4,530	5,626	6,106	9,009	15,228
Valladolid, Spain	7,080	10,646	7,886	8,182	5,400	8,333	11,768	11,589	11,920	12,266	10,291	9,766	8,669	6,228	8,362	4,852	5,185	6,410	8,685	15,267
Valletta, Malta	8,585	9,432	9,243	9,457	7,166	9,943	12,543	12,222	10,639	12,824	9,634	9,126	7,462	4,718	7,926	3,294	6,917	4,885	10,300	14,444
Valparaiso, Chile	10,109	8,726	10,814	11,191	8,288	9,097	1,376	1,704	17,218	2,236	18,108	18,325	18,957	16,039	17,654	14,778	8,844	16,115	3,703	13,834
Vancouver, Canada	1,285	18,576	520	751	4,041	1,349	11,570	12,075	11,143	12,366	8,273	8,128	10,245	11,008	7,249	10,692	3,802	11,148	6,939	9,976
Varna, Bulgaria	8,443	9,997	8,885	9,001	7,623	9,913	13,949	13,621	9,343	14,211	8,228	7,723	6,121	3,554	6,554	2,198	7,266	3,737	11,353	13,056
Venice, Italy	7,598	10,500	8,202	8,400	6,451	9,002	13,068	12,827	10,494	13,476	9,058	8,537	7,246	4,808	7,219	3,462	6,136	4,994	10,094	14,011
Veracruz, Mexico	3,864	14,863	4,474	4,859	3,428	2,764	7,537	8,006	15,036	8,376	12,342	12,232	14,253	14,064	11,326	13,106	3,812	14,250	2,885	12,448
Verona, Italy	7,537	10,532	8,156	8,361	6,358	8,934	12,985	12,750	10,594	13,403	9,136	8,614	7,345	4,914	7,287	3,567	6,048	5,100	9,989	14,094
Victoria, Canada	1,344	18,599	612	813	4,073	1,302	11,505	12,013	11,170	12,297	8,311	8,173	10,310	11,096	7,310	10,784	3,846	11,235	6,899	9,947
Victoria, Seychelles	14,353	4,948	14,536	14,469	13,346	15,855	12,468	11,886	7,195	11,892	8,829	8,655	5,945	4,153	8,775	4,372	13,104	4,045	14,889	10,727
Vienna, Austria	7,516	10,709	8,053	8,221	6,569	8,956	13,496	13,259	10,111	13,909	8,626	8,105	6,859	4,515	6,787	3,218	6,219	4,705	10,389	13,583
Vientiane, Laos	11,664	9,638	10,948	10,560	13,357	12,655	16,932	16,541	1,966	16,060	3,231	3,234	1,559	3,996	4,120	5,418	12,804	3,846	18,038	5,968
Villahermosa, Mexico	4,064	14,532	4,739	5,141	3,341	3,053	7,311	7,763	15,386	8,160	12,656	12,528	14,460	14,070	11,575	13,043	3,765	14,259	2,558	12,796
Vilnius, USSR	7,229	11,286	7,615	7,717	6,738	8,720	14,394	14,185	9,351	14,844	7,702	7,179	6,110	4,082	5,841	2,979	6,318	4,276	10,913	12,673
Visby, Sweden	6,719	11,694	7,148	7,275	6,198	8,202	14,150	13,996	9,714	14,676	7,881	7,357	6,499	4,604	5,957	3,524	5,774	4,798	10,433	12,857
Vitoria, Brazil	10,272	7,514	11,326	11,816	7,587	9,962	4,062	3,814	17,497	4,485	18,072	17,547	15,636	12,654	16,112	11,379	8,056	12,745	4,711	16,973
Vladivostok, USSR	7,998	13,560	7,135	6,708	10,312	8,789	18,049	18,539	3,916	17,998	925	690	3,324	5,845	1,304	6,815	9,784	5,828	14,376	5,625
Volgograd, USSR	8,362	10,582	8,562	8,571	8,174	9,871	15,364	15,028	8,052	15,601	6,814	6,310	4,802	2,616	5,180	1,655	7,733	2,810	12,369	11,658
Vologda, USSR	7,167	11,729	7,365	7,386	7,167	8,675	15,393	15,200	8,447	15,862	6,686	6,163	5,243	3,628	4,826	2,848	6,692	3,817	11,599	11,661
Vorkuta, USSR	6,590	12,841	6,526	6,441	7,317	8,053	16,507	16,452	7,562	17,147	5,398	4,876	4,589	3,996	3,443	3,750	6,783	4,153	12,000	10,356
Wake Island	8,156	14,479	7,030	6,545	10,998	7,962	13,894	14,352	5,255	13,852	4,085	4,489	7,010	9,890	5,382	10,982	10,680	9,836	12,628	3,043
Wallis Island	9,923	12,554	8,995	8,650	12,206	8,902	9,990	10,380	7,631	9,824	7,875	8,354	10,452	13,429	9,427	14,746	12,212	13,316	10,843	3,620
Walvis Bay, Namibia	14,025	3,361	15,065	15,463	11,352	14,658	8,019	7,454	11,884	7,700	13,622	13,377	10,653	8,138	13,093	7,446	11,524	8,129	10,315	14,535
Warsaw, Poland	7,315	11,071	7,767	7,898	6,631	8,788	14,015	13,796	9,681	14,453	8,090	7,567	6,433	4,268	6,235	3,074	6,238	4,462	10,675	13,058
Washington, D.C.	2,704	14,778	3,807	4,304	578	2,960	9,346	9,661	14,381	10,215	11,386	11,071	12,226	11,308	9,766	10,264	999	11,500	4,333	13,750
Watson Lake, Canada	1,597	18,269	781	652	4,337	2,511	12,755	13,236	10,278	13,574	7,315	7,105	9,051	9,755	6,096	9,501	3,949	9,891	7,956	9,803
Weimar, East Germany	7,053	11,109	7,617	7,801	6,103	8,485	13,375	13,184	10,364	13,854	8,700	8,176	7,117	4,906	6,802	3,650	5,745	5,098	10,015	13,678
Wellington, New Zealand	12,931	9,377	12,115	11,814	14,643	11,689	8,302	8,478	8,043	7,801	9,664	10,189	11,294	13,745	11,593	15,123	14,851	13,562	11,387	4,688
West Berlin, West Germany	7,001	11,228	7,529	7,697	6,160	8,449	13,590	13,404	10,173	14,075	8,480	7,955	6,930	4,781	6,579	3,561	5,784	4,974	10,157	13,457
Wewak, Papua New Guinea	11,686	10,914	10,563	10,070	14,527	11,515	13,507	13,638	3,128	12,945	4,542	5,058	6,239	9,076	6,543	10,487	14,159	8,933	15,332	952
Whangarei, New Zealand	12,485	9,905	11,619	11,295	14,408	11,313	8,790	8,999	7,697	8,331	9,140	9,664	10,934	13,533	11,038	14,945	14,553	13,359	11,544	4,166
Whitehorse, Canada	1,947	18,368	1,056	767	4,680	2,787	13,037	13,529	9,933	13,843	6,976	6,775	8,775	9,601	5,799	9,421	4,283	9,731	8,281	9,486
Wichita, Kansas	1,842	16,248	2,648	3,106	2,259	1,271	9,530	9,966	13,559	10,384	10,637	10,440	12,233	12,137	9,382	11,351	2,365	12,314	4,623	12,096
Willemstad, Curacao	5,603	12,269	6,599	7,079	3,300	5,208	6,381	6,638	17,447	7,234	14,448	14,144	14,995	13,184	12,818	11,838	3,853	13,373	1,725	15,425
Wiluna, Australia	15,223	7,346	14,109	13,614	18,016	15,044	11,926	11,748	4,023	11,104	6,892	7,287	6,844	8,654	8,729	9,961	17,548	8,463	16,432	4,209
Windhoek, Namibia	14,163	3,256	15,180	15,560	11,529	14,853	8,241	7,673	11,616	7,900	13,369	13,133	10,406	7,926	12,886	7,274	11,682	7,912	10,581	14,317
Windsor, Canada	2,078	15,405	3,176	3,672	962	2,400	9,768	10,117	13,835	10,640	10,836	10,544	11,870	11,225	9,286	10,282	1,061	11,413	4,731	13,135
Winnipeg, Canada	702	16,712	1,807	2,303	2,177	1,562	10,819	11,228	12,541	11,683	9,554	9,300	10,916	10,825	8,139	10,127	1,941	10,997	5,830	11,838
Winston-Salem, North Carolina	2,749	14,853	3,811	4,306	994	2,776	9,058	9,397	14,559	9,929	11,561	11,272	12,554	11,720	10,011	10,684	1,406	11,911	4,025	13,610
Wroclaw, Poland	7,274	11,009	7,778	7,933	6,455	8,729	13,714	13,500	9,978	14,160	8,386	7,863	6,729	4,510	6,520	3,272	6,080	4,702	10,415	13,357
Wuhan, China	9,950	11,467	9,165	8,759	11,967	10,851	18,254	18,099	2,354	17,463	1,470	1,405	1,629	4,592	2,460	5,866	11,415	4,508	16,387	5,574
Wyndham, Australia	13,747	8,789	12,637	12,141	16,542	13,666	12,947	12,867	2,972	12,188	5,597	6,036	6,126	8,446	7,529	9,849	16,099	8,268	16,628	2,916
Xi'an, China	9,753	11,424	9,051	8,677	11,580	10,770	18,761	18,447	2,896	17,906	1,846	1,594	1,146	4,017	2,208	5,252	11,024	3,947	16,158	6,222
Xining, China	9,706	11,201	9,104	8,768	11,292	10,838	18,928	18,414	3,434	18,082	2,462	2,122	736	3,350	2,288	4,558	10,737	3,293	15,974	6,909
Yakutsk, USSR	6,339	14,503	5,685	5,353	8,342	7,418	17,668	18,143	5,869	18,445	2,992	2,571	4,145	5,607	1,214	6,101	7,797	5,671	12,755	7,590
Yanji, China	8,124	13,387	7,278	6,857	10,393	8,943	18,228	18,697	3,821	18,121	865	534	3,128	5,659	1,224	6,644	9,860	5,639	14,521	5,693
Yaounde, Cameroon	11,429	6,163	12,335	12,659	9,141	12,457	9,864	9,392	11,825	9,847	12,219	11,797	9,384	6,432	10,965	5,301	9,147	6,505	10,024	15,669
Yap Island (Colonia)	10,833	11,552	9,751	9,256	13,576	11,001	15,064	15,207	2,129	14,513	2,980	3,493	4,856	7,799	4,987	9,167	13,122	7,677	15,849	2,175
Yaraka, Australia	13,514	9,180	12,407	11,942	16,260	12,922	11,381	11,422	4,716	10,724	6,826	7,327	7,960	10,408	8,835	11,815	16,059	10,231	14,668	2,448
Yarmouth, Canada	3,063	14,282	4,182	4,660	487	3,745	9,906	10,146	14,053	10,757	11,130	10,752	11,529	10,332	9,343	9,236	520	10,526	5,032	14,238
Yellowknife, Canada	1,147	17,528	1,069	1,295	3,621	2,478	12,518	12,950	10,809	13,371	7,814	7,552	9,252	9,582	6,406	9,161	3,195	9,734	7,569	10,596
Yerevan, USSR	9,271	9,633	9,507	9,522	8,868	10,778	14,980	14,560	7,981	15,053	7,190	6,714	4,806	2,135	5,758	835	8,463	2,320	12,769	11,813
Yinchuan, China	9,390	11,618	8,744	8,393	11,111	10,475	19,230	18,800	3,416	18,359	2,058	1,688	1,159	3,749	1,896	4,905	10,555	3,703	15,741	6,676
Yogyakarta, Indonesia	14,016	8,042	13,055	12,584	16,232	14,520	14,105	13,840	2,149	13,250	5,138	5,422	4,534	6,442	6,723	7,812	15,677	6,256	18,699	4,645
York, United Kingdom	6,262	11,727	6,910	7,140	5,197	7,657	12,910	12,799	11,000	13,491	9,055	8,534	7,787	5,759	7,083	4,541	4,843	5,953	9,198	13,996
Yumen, China	9,452	11,263	8,920	8,612	10,896	10,652	19,018	18,438	3,931	18,295	2,805	2,404	963	3,017	2,238	4,148	10,344	2,984	15,601	7,390
Yutian, China	10,000	10,224	9,676	9,447	10,874	11,359	17,684	17,115	4,783	17,227	4,231	3,842	1,565	1,580	3,487	2,784	10,352	1,550	15,468	8,576
Yuzhno-Sakhalinsk, USSR	7,160	14,506	6,248	5,807	9,611	7,874	17,302	17,867	4,708	17,536	1,743	1,637	4,237	6,585	1,681	7,421	9,104	6,590	13,472	5,742
Zagreb, Yugoslavia	7,724	10,458	8,286	8,463	6,679	9,150	13,320	13,065	10,211	13,706	8,818	8,299	6,964	4,524	7,003	3,186	6,348	4,711	10,377	13,758
Zahedan, Iran	10,752	8,737	10,757	10,657	10,719	12,246	15,623	15,077	6,382	15,327	6,327	5,944	3,486	522	5,457	1,100	10,286	598	14,633	10,370
Zamboanga, Philippines	11,980	10,116	10,987	10,511	14,440	12,441	15,509	15,415	483	14,743	3,204	3,577	3,728	6,437	5,024	7,857	13,912	6,287	17,635	3,565
Zanzibar, Tanzania	13,904	4,481	14,466	14,583	12,170	15,249	11,195	10,619	8,995	10,775	10,392	10,144	7,419	5,042	9,979	4,683	12,057	5,001	13,079	12,503
Zaragoza, Spain	7,288	10,500	8,059	8,338	5,691	8,572	11,988	11,787	11,643	12,456	10,098	9,574	8,393	5,917	8,194	4,536	5,460	6,099	8,999	15,075
Zashiversk, USSR	5,478	15,273	4,828	4,508	7,554	6,563	16,812	17,281	6,651	17,617	3,702	3,333	4,997	6,248	2,069	6,571	7,017	6,332	11,901	7,985
Zhengzhou, China	9,545	11,762	8,792	8,401	11,511	10,496	18,708	18,560	2,818	17,929	1,405	1,175	1,585	4,441	2,021	5,650	10,957	4,377	15,980	5,902
Zurich, Switzerland	7,246	10,800	7,874	8,086	6,081	8,640	12,960	12,753	10,708	13,417	9,133	8,610	7,456	5,111	7,249	3,790	5,763	5,299	9,791	14,107

Distances in Kilometers	Raiatea (Uturoa)	Raleigh, North Carolina	Rangiroa (Avatoru)	Rangoon, Burma	Raoul Is., Kermadec Islands	Rarotonga (Avarua)	Rawson, Argentina	Recife, Brazil	Regina, Canada	Reykjavik, Iceland	Rhodes, Greece	Richmond, Virginia	Riga, USSR	Ringkobing, Denmark	Rio Branco, Brazil	Rio Cuarto, Argentina	Rio de Janeiro, Brazil	Rio Gallegos, Argentina	Rio Grande, Brazil	Riyadh, Saudi Arabia
Raleigh, North Carolina	9,608	0	9,173	14,162	12,621	10,605	8,863	6,670	2,647	4,892	9,017	223	7,457	6,616	5,189	7,772	7,488	9,727	8,001	11,201
Rangiroa (Avatoru)	447	9,173	0	13,221	3,482	1,453	8,294	12,197	8,373	13,178	17,589	9,349	15,291	15,002	8,661	8,511	10,803	7,928	9,661	18,173
Rangoon, Burma	12,866	14,162	13,221	0	10,529	12,098	16,579	14,641	12,285	9,617	6,967	13,955	7,372	8,347	18,139	17,354	15,740	15,930	16,409	5,197
Raoul Is., Kermadec Islands	3,037	12,621	3,482	10,529	0	2,030	9,458	14,295	11,383	15,773	17,464	12,786	16,485	16,986	11,374	10,185	12,474	8,679	11,139	15,596
Rarotonga (Avarua)	1,007	10,605	1,453	12,098	2,030	0	8,786	13,192	9,602	14,315	18,151	10,776	16,023	16,008	9,822	9,232	11,589	8,226	10,333	17,293
Rawson, Argentina	8,462	8,863	8,294	16,579	9,458	8,786	0	4,889	11,072	12,499	12,905	9,040	13,846	12,976	3,703	1,130	3,028	977	1,694	13,575
Recife, Brazil	12,529	6,670	12,197	14,641	14,295	13,192	4,889	0	9,293	8,081	8,213	6,710	8,966	8,137	3,622	4,111	1,869	5,760	3,196	9,547
Regina, Canada	8,735	2,647	8,373	12,285	11,383	9,602	11,072	9,293	0	4,816	9,331	2,586	7,206	6,680	7,583	10,071	10,110	11,797	10,495	11,224
Reykjavik, Iceland	13,520	4,892	13,178	9,617	15,773	14,315	12,499	8,081	4,816	0	4,524	4,670	2,585	1,879	9,074	11,406	9,826	13,475	10,986	6,537
Rhodes, Greece	17,821	9,017	17,589	6,967	17,464	18,151	12,905	8,213	9,331	4,524	0	8,812	2,301	2,651	11,200	12,308	9,966	13,553	11,278	2,199
Richmond, Virginia	9,782	223	9,349	13,955	12,786	10,776	9,040	6,710	2,586	4,670	8,812	0	7,236	6,398	5,354	7,941	7,590	9,912	8,141	10,992
Riga, USSR	15,525	7,457	15,291	7,372	16,485	16,023	13,846	8,966	7,206	2,585	2,301	7,236	0	978	11,044	12,933	10,835	14,723	12,157	4,023
Ringkobing, Denmark	15,314	6,616	15,002	8,347	16,986	16,008	12,976	8,137	6,680	1,879	2,651	6,398	978	0	10,069	12,019	10,002	13,889	11,305	4,673
Rio Branco, Brazil	9,031	5,189	8,661	18,139	11,374	9,822	3,703	3,622	7,583	9,074	11,200	5,354	11,044	10,069	0	2,590	2,981	4,622	2,931	12,945
Rio Cuarto, Argentina	8,750	7,772	8,511	17,354	10,185	9,232	1,130	4,111	10,071	11,406	12,308	7,941	12,933	12,019	2,590	0	2,360	2,093	1,158	13,354
Rio de Janeiro, Brazil	11,070	7,488	10,803	15,740	12,474	11,589	3,028	1,869	10,110	9,826	9,966	7,590	10,835	10,002	2,981	2,360	0	3,891	1,337	11,040
Rio Gallegos, Argentina	8,034	9,727	7,928	15,930	8,679	8,226	977	5,760	11,797	13,475	13,553	9,912	14,723	13,889	4,622	2,093	3,891	0	2,587	13,893
Rio Grande, Brazil	9,890	8,001	9,661	16,409	11,139	10,333	1,694	3,196	10,495	10,986	11,278	8,141	12,157	11,305	2,931	1,158	1,337	2,587	0	12,208
Riyadh, Saudi Arabia	17,948	11,201	18,173	5,197	15,596	17,293	13,575	9,547	11,224	6,537	2,199	10,992	4,023	4,673	12,945	13,354	11,040	13,893	12,208	0
Road Town, Brit. Virgin Isls.	10,270	2,364	9,827	15,583	13,215	11,254	6,837	4,387	5,007	5,995	9,061	2,458	8,230	7,263	3,162	5,708	5,132	7,776	5,744	11,189
Roanoke, Virginia	9,569	203	9,137	14,007	12,568	10,560	9,048	6,864	2,447	4,814	9,003	222	7,389	6,566	5,381	7,961	7,692	9,905	8,201	11,177
Robinson Crusoe Island, Chile	7,408	7,683	7,162	18,075	9,023	7,925	1,607	5,322	9,653	11,924	13,528	7,881	13,827	12,865	2,855	1,351	3,672	2,146	2,507	14,699
Rochester, New York	10,012	825	9,591	13,338	12,959	10,986	9,658	7,126	2,200	4,163	8,444	624	6,746	5,949	5,966	8,555	8,117	10,534	8,724	10,594
Rockhampton, Australia	6,081	15,126	6,522	7,393	3,211	5,106	11,777	16,479	13,018	15,441	14,353	15,218	14,341	15,257	14,455	12,746	14,675	10,839	13,422	12,385
Rome, Italy	16,826	7,552	16,467	8,269	18,326	17,599	12,208	7,335	8,095	3,308	1,486	7,351	1,868	1,607	9,952	11,424	9,181	13,009	10,518	3,684
Rosario, Argentina	9,089	7,835	8,853	17,086	10,468	9,559	1,212	3,827	10,200	11,287	12,004	7,996	12,709	11,812	2,648	345	2,041	2,188	813	13,013
Roseau, Dominica	10,501	2,844	10,063	15,695	13,383	11,467	6,499	3,901	5,489	6,201	8,984	2,929	8,323	7,348	2,882	5,369	4,666	7,454	5,331	11,064
Rostock, East Germany	15,625	6,929	15,322	8,127	17,132	16,291	13,037	8,168	7,011	2,213	2,321	6,712	819	333	10,249	12,115	10,037	13,927	11,353	4,343
Rostov-na-Donu, USSR	16,472	8,956	16,359	6,139	16,224	16,632	14,334	9,518	8,654	4,099	1,529	8,736	1,514	2,362	12,138	13,626	11,335	15,043	12,666	2,584
Rotterdam, Netherlands	15,566	6,540	15,222	8,670	17,482	16,337	12,489	7,632	6,852	2,046	2,539	6,328	1,384	525	9,689	11,555	9,500	13,390	10,810	4,672
Rouyn, Canada	10,136	1,385	9,729	12,788	13,002	11,083	10,232	7,584	1,867	3,791	8,192	1,195	6,373	5,628	6,541	9,130	8,649	11,106	9,287	10,300
Sacramento, California	6,874	3,784	6,524	12,734	9,525	7,730	10,702	10,271	1,873	6,654	11,137	3,829	8,937	8,495	7,733	9,894	10,610	11,210	10,613	12,900
Saginaw, Michigan	9,560	964	9,145	13,337	12,480	10,524	9,789	7,545	1,749	4,446	8,824	854	7,029	6,277	6,135	8,710	8,442	10,629	8,964	10,945
Saint Denis, Reunion	14,924	15,279	15,314	6,092	12,051	13,990	10,673	9,738	16,290	11,480	6,959	15,146	9,107	9,610	12,947	11,271	9,968	10,348	10,342	5,122
Saint George's, Grenada	10,364	3,129	9,931	16,007	13,191	11,314	6,138	3,711	5,765	6,552	9,224	3,229	8,642	7,665	2,525	5,008	4,362	7,092	4,986	11,270
Saint John, Canada	10,961	1,496	10,538	12,904	13,910	11,937	9,811	6,676	2,909	3,424	7,545	1,280	5,970	5,120	6,119	8,684	7,895	10,742	8,676	9,717
Saint John's, Antigua	10,509	2,652	10,069	15,558	13,422	11,485	6,696	4,066	5,299	6,030	8,908	2,732	8,187	7,213	3,064	5,565	4,867	7,648	5,536	11,009
Saint John's, Canada	12,014	2,507	11,592	12,235	14,943	12,986	10,140	6,406	3,733	2,620	6,511	2,302	5,060	4,163	6,545	9,013	7,862	11,105	8,816	8,695
Saint Louis, Missouri	8,840	1,073	8,420	13,837	11,790	9,813	9,419	7,699	1,738	5,186	9,573	1,124	7,765	7,025	5,859	8,381	8,388	10,205	8,761	11,695
Saint Paul, Minnesota	9,017	1,592	8,617	13,105	11,864	9,955	10,162	8,253	1,058	4,756	9,241	1,544	7,298	6,629	6,592	9,122	9,056	10,945	9,481	11,292
Saint Peter Port, UK	15,430	6,152	15,052	9,220	17,730	16,286	11,943	7,105	6,698	2,004	2,867	5,946	1,949	1,034	9,125	10,996	8,969	12,855	10,270	5,051
Saipan (Susupe)	7,752	12,697	8,045	5,294	6,280	7,185	15,737	19,217	10,055	11,149	11,329	12,640	10,384	11,176	16,352	16,398	18,747	14,914	17,419	10,203
Salalah, Oman	17,316	12,342	17,692	4,473	14,579	16,447	13,643	10,171	12,249	7,642	3,337	12,133	5,092	5,793	13,717	13,656	11,465	13,756	12,501	1,142
Salem, Oregon	7,410	3,855	7,084	12,109	9,920	8,218	11,334	10,491	1,507	6,113	10,542	3,856	8,305	7,919	8,218	10,481	11,015	11,882	11,133	12,231
Salt Lake City, Utah	7,563	2,944	7,189	13,011	10,311	8,459	10,426	9,510	1,216	6,020	10,541	2,979	8,421	7,890	7,211	9,526	9,993	11,039	10,134	12,437
Salta, Argentina	8,861	6,845	8,569	17,919	10,651	9,466	2,054	3,733	9,184	10,556	11,911	7,013	12,252	11,307	1,659	931	2,267	2,998	1,532	13,242
Salto, Uruguay	9,380	7,741	9,138	16,950	10,775	9,861	1,464	3,521	10,161	11,051	11,695	7,895	12,419	11,529	2,580	632	1,734	2,431	562	12,724
Salvador, Brazil	11,956	6,851	11,642	15,151	13,624	12,577	4,217	674	9,497	8,668	8,871	6,915	9,635	8,797	3,211	3,444	1,206	5,095	2,524	10,137
Salzburg, Austria	16,281	7,284	15,955	8,138	17,746	16,985	12,660	7,770	7,597	2,782	1,775	7,074	1,263	978	10,147	11,810	9,634	13,503	10,966	3,919
Samsun, Turkey	17,185	9,209	17,059	6,288	16,663	17,318	13,788	9,063	9,156	4,459	886	8,994	1,951	2,612	11,917	13,168	10,836	14,437	12,153	2,083
San Antonio, Texas	7,641	1,989	7,212	14,657	10,639	8,631	8,745	7,965	2,391	6,456	10,841	2,147	9,030	8,299	5,463	7,804	8,278	9,425	8,386	12,969
San Cristobal, Venezuela	9,126	3,169	8,695	17,010	11,952	10,072	5,701	4,497	5,599	7,397	10,429	3,340	9,671	8,704	2,022	4,603	4,636	6,588	4,897	12,504
San Diego, California	6,577	3,542	6,195	13,488	9,388	7,492	9,945	9,775	2,223	7,027	11,549	3,631	9,423	8,898	7,051	9,152	9,970	10,450	9,901	13,433
San Francisco, California	6,755	3,879	6,406	12,750	9,404	7,609	10,681	10,339	1,994	6,772	11,253	3,929	9,047	8,611	7,755	9,888	10,647	11,174	10,625	13,004
San Jose, Costa Rica	7,978	2,915	7,537	17,050	10,916	8,956	6,202	5,803	4,873	7,687	11,293	3,130	10,163	9,243	2,845	5,205	5,746	6,970	5,759	13,457
San Juan, Argentina	8,402	7,525	8,149	17,766	9,970	8,923	1,340	4,345	9,752	11,361	12,559	7,703	13,034	12,097	2,389	431	2,673	2,233	1,556	13,706
San Juan, Puerto Rico	10,119	2,279	9,676	15,656	13,071	11,104	6,840	4,512	4,914	6,052	9,189	2,385	8,319	7,355	3,150	5,713	5,209	7,771	5,785	11,324
San Luis Potosi, Mexico	6,981	2,640	6,542	15,315	10,010	7,983	8,124	7,940	3,157	7,282	11,618	2,829	9,861	9,111	5,074	7,250	8,000	8,742	7,941	13,771
San Marino, San Marino	16,635	7,444	16,288	8,237	18,141	17,386	12,352	7,470	7,915	3,115	1,574	7,240	1,664	1,356	10,003	11,544	9,324	13,169	10,660	3,768
San Miguel de Tucuman, Argen.	8,827	7,070	8,547	17,808	10,535	9,403	1,829	3,814	9,398	10,764	12,015	7,238	12,423	11,484	1,885	705	2,261	2,776	1,398	13,281
San Salvador, El Salvador	7,625	2,664	7,179	16,583	10,625	8,622	6,772	6,464	4,309	7,547	11,432	2,887	10,090	9,210	3,527	5,817	6,441	7,492	6,424	13,626
Sanaa, Yemen	18,356	11,763	18,756	5,547	15,455	17,420	12,723	9,096	12,108	7,331	2,823	11,568	4,918	5,452	12,652	12,644	10,413	12,946	11,486	1,061
Santa Cruz, Bolivia	9,283	6,150	8,955	17,836	11,295	9,968	2,833	3,246	8,580	9,748	11,287	6,306	11,484	10,530	1,001	1,703	2,154	3,792	1,931	12,787
Santa Cruz, Tenerife	15,274	5,848	14,827	11,198	18,241	16,273	9,382	4,510	7,518	3,989	4,235	5,710	4,464	3,633	6,985	8,500	6,378	10,269	7,695	6,216
Santa Fe, New Mexico	7,525	2,463	7,122	13,751	10,411	8,472	9,677	8,854	1,644	6,220	10,726	2,548	8,722	8,099	6,447	8,764	9,252	10,315	9,368	12,739
Santa Rosa, Argentina	8,673	8,151	8,458	17,094	9,957	9,101	745	4,342	10,425	11,773	12,496	8,322	13,233	12,334	2,973	386	2,531	1,714	1,231	13,416
Santa Rosalia, Mexico	6,451	3,312	6,040	14,248	9,385	7,414	9,186	9,192	2,650	7,324	11,831	3,444	9,812	9,203	6,327	8,393	9,271	9,706	9,155	13,834
Santarem, Brazil	10,657	4,908	10,271	16,469	13,041	11,478	4,643	2,280	7,535	7,862	9,539	5,010	9,555	8,597	1,671	3,545	2,581	5,620	3,288	11,284
Santiago del Estero, Argentina	8,893	7,195	8,621	17,675	10,547	9,452	1,723	3,782	9,534	10,838	11,992	7,361	12,454	11,522	2,007	593	2,182	2,680	1,266	13,216
Santiago, Chile	8,166	7,708	7,923	17,744	9,684	8,664	1,196	4,626	9,876	11,629	12,838	7,891	13,326	12,387	2,617	589	2,925	2,023	1,747	13,940
Santo Domingo, Dominican Rep.	9,738	2,102	9,294	15,822	12,706	10,728	6,856	4,835	4,692	6,205	9,510	2,238	8,544	7,590	3,153	5,741	5,418	7,766	5,903	11,663
Sao Paulo de Olivenca, Brazil	9,123	4,461	8,727	17,814	11,666	9,980	4,430	3,788	6,882	8,427	10,868	4,626	10,503	9,525	729	3,319	3,496	5,341	3,615	12,752
Sao Paulo, Brazil	10,723	7,379	10,452	16,082	12,187	11,254	2,773	2,121	9,977	9,954	10,278	7,492	11,074	10,220	2,706	2,034	353	3,670	1,085	11,387
Sao Tome, Sao Tome & Principe	17,021	9,573	16,786	9,947	16,766	17,278	8,574	4,712	11,475	7,457	4,571	9,477	6,467	6,183	8,330	8,279	5,986	9,071	7,134	5,075
Sapporo, Japan	9,520	10,384	9,650	5,156	9,026	9,318	17,880	16,109	7,841	8,029	8,912	10,259	7,479	8,171	15,385	17,526	17,731	17,541	18,315	8,539
Sarajevo, Yugoslavia	16,853	7,864	16,544	7,763	17,843	17,489	12,720	7,856	8,199	3,383	1,170	7,656	1,513	1,542	10,470	11,949	9,696	13,505	11,033	3,337
Saratov, USSR	15,845	8,935	15,762	5,848	15,637	15,967	14,937	10,083	8,364	4,043	2,195	8,712	1,541	2,505	12,512	14,172	11,920	15,681	13,256	2,990
Saskatoon, Canada	8,768	2,859	8,416	12,061	11,360	9,616	11,302	9,489	233	4,763	9,263	2,789	7,107	6,614	7,816	10,303	10,331	12,023	10,727	11,117
Schefferville, Canada	11,171	2,301	10,777	11,912	13,941	12,092	10,872	7,574	2,571	2,679	7,091	2,081	5,263	4,514	7,178	9,746	8,899	11,800	9,724	9,186
Seattle, Washington	7,693	3,810	7,372	11,914	10,165	8,490	11,529	10,473	1,330	5,834	10,249	3,792	8,008	7,631	8,334	10,648	11,081	12,104	11,260	11,931
Sendai, Japan	9,312	10,860	9,475	4,953	8,616	9,037	17,768	16,633	8,288	8,553	9,236	10,742	7,914	8,637	15,773	17,680	18,259	17,243	18,655	8,701
Seoul, South Korea	10,411	11,467	10,606	3,796	9,364	10,043	18,812	16,267	9,028	8,403	8,320	11,319	7,304	8,133	16,611	18,881	18,135	17,995	19,385	7,568
Sept-Iles, Canada	11,076	1,883	10,666	12,391	13,944	12,027	10,360	7,136	2,693	3,016	7,300	1,660	5,593	4,789	6,667	9,233	8,413	11,289	9,218	9,439
Sevastopol, USSR	16,880	8,795	16,714	6,559	16,773	17,139	13,774	8,971	8,726	4,027	1,012	8,579	1,523	2,187	11,679	13,081	10,780	14,483	12,110	2,516
Seville, Spain	15,938	6,334	15,506	9,926	18,842	16,924	10,746	5,862	7,459	3,163	3,033	6,156	3,105	2,336	8,294	9,877	7,730	11,618	9,055	5,158
Shanghai, China	10,700	12,313	10,945	3,005	9,273	10,210	18,540	16,470	9,905	8,967	8,290	12,158	7,581	8,474	17,482	19,441	18,248	17,568	19,399	7,249
Sheffield, United Kingdom	15,180	6,105	14,823	9,024	17,312	15,987	12,308	7,499	6,450	1,672	2,971	5,892	1,669	696	9,375	11,335	9,357	13,234	10,647	5,109
Shenyang, China	10,839	11,126	11,009	3,803	9,907	10,520	19,301	15,707	8,770	7,873	7,809	10,967	6,745	7,573	16,311	18,829	17,575	18,555	18,853	7,165
Shiraz, Iran	17,197	11,154	17,387	4,657	15,175	16,661	14,364	10,206	10,857	6,339	2,387	10,937	3,759	4,540	13,485	14,101	11,765	14,689	12,964	797
Sibiu, Romania	16,756	8,127	16,499	7,303	17,355	17,253	13,216	8,357	8,258	3,471	1,094	7,914	1,241	1,592	10,948	12,453	10,195	13,989	11,531	3,098
Singapore	11,627	15,894	12,038	1,910	8,946	10,731	15,224	15,403	13,669	11,522	8,644	15,704	9,266	10,238	18,688	16,272	15,740	14,386	15,776	6,656
Sioux Falls, South Dakota	8,690	1,771	8,292	13,198	11,535	9,626	10,122	8,439	973	5,056	9,552	1,759	7,582	6,932	6,610	9,107	9,162	10,874	9,523	11,587
Skelleftea, Sweden	14,639	6,898	14,404	7,630	15,844	15,164	14,077	9,289	6,398	2,026	3,189	6,675	887	1,189	10,942	13,070	11,146	15,015	12,429	4,831
Skopje, Yugoslavia	17,124	8,184	16,832	7,526	17,774	17,695	12,798	7,965	8,506	3,691	848	7,977	1,673	1,834	10,687	12,072	9,787	13,550	11,121	3,018
Socotra Island (Tamrida)	17,259	12,704	17,675	4,554	14,376	16,320	13,315	10,095	12,713	8,068	3,687	12,500	5,536	6,206	13,690	13,408	11,287	13,370	12,260	1,533
Sofia, Bulgaria	17,085	8,267	16,812	7,372	17,605	17,605	12,965	8,134	8,520	3,713	811	8,058	1,588	1,840	10,846	12,241	9,956	13,712	11,289	2,934
Songkhla, Thailand	12,155	15,247	12,549	1,165	9,585	11,300	15,770	15,129	13,173	10,781	7,965	15,048	8,521	9,494	18,723	16,746	15,789	14,991	16,073	6,041
Sorong, Indonesia	8,638	15,070	9,030	4,318	6,233	7,804	14,848	18,201	12,423	12,655	11,237	15,001	11,123	12,065	17,602	15,904	17,308	13,876	16,345	9,504
South Georgia Island	10,022	10,753	9,974	14,228	10,031	10,046	2,390	5,126	13,211	13,192	11,811	10,892	13,500	12,899	5,629	3,194	3,523	2,182	2,752	11,786
South Pole	8,150	13,963	8,349	11,858	6,762	7,655	5,207	9,114	15,593	17,121	14,038	14,159	16,318	16,222	8,901	6,336	7,470	4,280	6,458	12,729

Distances in Kilometers	Raiatea (Uturoa)	Raleigh, North Carolina	Rangiroa (Avatoru)	Rangoon, Burma	Raoul Is., Kermadec Islands	Rarotonga (Avarua)	Rawson, Argentina	Recife, Brazil	Regina, Canada	Reykjavik, Iceland	Rhodes, Greece	Richmond, Virginia	Riga, USSR	Ringkobing, Denmark	Rio Branco, Brazil	Rio Cuarto, Argentina	Rio de Janeiro, Brazil	Rio Gallegos, Argentina	Rio Grande, Brazil	Riyadh, Saudi Arabia
South Sandwich Islands	10,335	11,449	10,334	13,487	9,999	10,249	3,113	5,561	13,941	13,526	11,618	11,580	13,492	12,999	6,358	3,941	4,098	2,787	3,456	11,353
Split, Yugoslavia	16,825	7,745	16,499	7,925	17,981	17,505	12,572	7,703	8,138	3,324	1,275	7,539	1,589	1,514	10,306	11,793	9,547	13,365	10,883	3,460
Spokane, Washington	7,898	3,442	7,561	12,126	10,445	8,723	11,309	10,109	983	5,622	10,084	3,423	7,875	7,447	8,039	10,397	10,749	11,924	10,969	11,841
Spoleto, Italy	16,759	7,525	16,406	8,235	18,239	17,518	12,283	7,407	8,033	3,239	1,500	7,323	1,775	1,519	9,994	11,491	9,256	13,090	10,593	3,698
Springbok, South Africa	14,745	12,411	14,835	9,838	13,272	14,371	7,285	5,993	14,756	10,967	7,396	12,384	9,616	9,545	9,059	7,616	6,082	7,294	6,575	6,753
Springfield, Illinois	8,948	1,067	8,530	13,712	11,888	9,918	9,529	7,724	1,664	5,051	9,448	1,090	7,629	6,893	5,954	8,485	8,450	10,323	8,847	11,564
Springfield, Massachusetts	10,353	876	9,926	13,385	13,327	11,337	9,489	6,747	2,613	4,018	8,178	655	6,581	5,745	5,786	8,373	7,805	10,391	8,473	10,350
Srinagar, India	15,043	11,796	15,269	2,867	13,257	14,521	16,426	12,327	10,640	6,966	4,208	11,574	4,557	5,521	15,373	16,261	13,927	16,542	15,119	2,911
Stanley, Falkland Islands	8,808	9,900	8,710	15,508	9,307	8,970	1,081	5,276	12,151	13,218	12,834	10,069	14,167	13,398	4,716	2,129	3,435	786	2,235	13,107
Stara Zagora, Bulgaria	17,144	8,440	16,893	7,182	17,455	17,599	13,104	8,289	8,642	3,845	700	8,230	1,620	1,966	11,032	12,399	10,103	13,835	11,434	2,764
Stockholm, Sweden	15,199	7,018	14,940	7,743	16,452	15,766	13,662	8,815	6,783	2,142	2,650	6,796	444	686	10,718	12,705	10,682	14,571	11,988	4,454
Stornoway, United Kingdom	14,583	5,703	14,237	9,150	16,723	15,373	12,490	7,783	5,869	1,063	3,495	5,485	1,812	914	9,350	11,465	9,615	13,443	10,868	5,572
Strasbourg, France	16,002	6,891	15,655	8,513	17,807	16,772	12,415	7,531	7,283	2,482	2,145	6,683	1,437	835	9,791	11,529	9,399	13,285	10,724	4,309
Stuttgart, West Germany	16,044	6,980	15,704	8,406	17,758	16,794	12,508	7,622	7,335	2,527	2,067	6,770	1,351	817	9,898	11,627	9,490	13,374	10,816	4,222
Subic, Philippines	10,312	14,059	10,651	2,585	8,246	9,604	16,814	17,220	11,556	10,670	9,221	13,916	9,000	9,948	18,999	17,932	18,076	15,842	17,955	7,697
Suchow, China	11,167	12,080	11,397	2,854	9,798	10,706	18,983	15,944	9,764	8,523	7,772	11,913	7,067	7,968	17,267	19,828	17,736	18,009	18,996	6,788
Sucre, Bolivia	9,031	6,227	8,707	18,054	11,034	9,710	2,691	3,499	8,609	9,944	11,549	6,391	11,723	10,766	1,039	1,565	2,330	3,634	1,955	13,043
Sudbury, Canada	9,919	1,208	9,509	12,991	12,806	10,873	10,071	7,571	1,792	4,035	8,429	1,037	6,617	5,870	6,391	8,977	8,575	10,933	9,171	10,541
Suez, Egypt	18,486	9,785	18,340	6,586	17,088	18,450	12,805	8,337	10,153	5,347	823	9,585	3,070	3,474	11,555	12,349	9,990	13,341	11,257	1,520
Sundsvall, Sweden	14,860	6,841	14,606	7,793	16,162	15,425	13,795	8,987	6,492	1,949	2,983	6,619	716	870	10,729	12,804	10,847	14,724	12,138	4,734
Surabaya, Indonesia	10,402	16,643	10,829	3,225	7,621	9,469	14,403	16,063	14,107	12,754	10,001	16,497	10,596	11,572	18,100	15,525	15,778	13,477	15,372	7,975
Suva, Fiji	3,203	12,318	3,629	9,801	1,289	2,311	10,630	15,357	10,656	14,668	16,467	12,447	15,200	15,712	12,122	11,269	13,607	9,898	12,286	14,997
Sverdlovsk, USSR	14,813	9,050	14,779	5,347	14,579	14,866	15,973	11,086	8,033	4,278	3,305	8,828	2,198	3,149	13,194	15,119	12,944	16,768	14,280	3,749
Svobodnyy, USSR	10,800	10,001	10,894	4,768	10,377	10,655	18,671	14,954	7,671	6,932	7,559	9,842	6,144	6,876	15,188	17,740	16,756	18,816	17,853	7,326
Sydney, Australia	6,000	15,512	6,446	8,090	2,966	4,993	10,699	15,320	13,778	16,606	14,899	15,653	15,309	16,265	13,650	11,712	13,539	9,746	12,314	12,775
Sydney, Canada	11,428	1,926	11,005	12,643	14,374	12,404	9,921	6,509	3,281	3,076	7,095	1,718	5,583	4,709	6,261	8,790	7,836	10,870	8,697	9,275
Syktyvkar, USSR	14,718	8,287	14,612	6,116	14,970	14,936	15,439	10,562	7,383	3,506	3,218	8,065	1,596	2,483	12,462	14,502	12,431	16,317	13,753	4,126
Szeged, Hungary	16,640	7,840	16,353	7,610	17,556	17,224	12,991	8,116	8,050	3,243	1,282	7,629	1,219	1,370	10,648	12,199	9,964	13,789	11,301	3,371
Szombathely, Hungary	16,450	7,552	16,143	7,875	17,654	17,098	12,835	7,949	7,808	2,994	1,535	7,341	1,195	1,140	10,398	12,011	9,807	13,658	11,142	3,655
Tabriz, Iran	17,080	10,063	17,099	5,387	15,852	16,897	14,358	9,797	9,793	5,236	1,612	9,845	2,657	3,447	12,797	13,863	11,506	14,884	12,792	1,492
Tacheng, China	14,043	10,682	14,169	3,540	12,979	13,763	17,491	12,765	9,210	6,095	4,607	10,467	4,071	5,035	15,086	16,874	14,565	17,931	15,884	4,039
Tahiti (Papeete)	217	9,510	350	13,078	3,163	1,146	8,254	12,313	8,720	13,522	17,899	9,689	15,598	15,339	8,823	8,534	10,853	7,837	9,675	18,165
Taipei, Taiwan	10,503	12,950	10,785	2,784	8,835	9,928	17,894	16,891	10,496	9,620	8,678	12,800	8,139	9,054	18,075	18,951	18,461	16,918	19,019	7,450
Taiyuan, China	11,655	11,771	11,864	2,834	10,370	11,233	19,371	15,369	9,569	8,013	7,212	11,593	6,494	7,401	16,914	19,414	17,177	18,469	18,480	6,311
Tallahasee, Florida	8,882	791	8,442	14,779	11,911	9,884	8,397	6,776	2,793	5,670	9,802	1,008	8,241	7,407	4,807	7,343	7,354	9,211	7,705	11,988
Tallinn, USSR	15,256	7,351	15,028	7,364	16,243	15,745	14,003	9,138	6,998	2,460	2,568	7,128	277	1,047	11,098	13,062	11,007	14,898	12,322	4,226
Tamanrasset, Algeria	17,528	8,063	17,084	9,372	19,214	18,504	10,266	5,570	9,409	5,020	2,658	7,909	4,084	3,704	8,767	9,652	7,308	10,970	8,623	4,191
Tampa, Florida	8,924	939	8,481	15,053	11,960	9,930	8,086	6,482	3,122	5,823	9,852	1,162	8,378	7,518	4,483	7,026	7,029	8,911	7,377	12,047
Tampere, Finland	15,019	7,189	14,790	7,448	16,086	15,520	14,052	9,210	6,775	2,297	2,805	6,966	507	1,076	11,055	13,085	11,077	14,965	12,381	4,450
Tanami, Australia	8,262	16,747	8,703	5,477	5,360	7,287	12,837	16,483	14,205	14,664	12,309	16,751	12,792	13,769	16,184	13,941	15,200	11,860	14,245	10,250
Tangier, Morocco	16,025	6,417	15,589	9,972	18,980	17,019	10,620	5,732	7,599	3,337	3,047	6,244	3,240	2,493	8,234	9,766	7,600	11,483	8,928	5,143
Tarawa (Betio)	4,394	11,579	4,694	8,564	3,526	3,880	12,647	16,862	9,358	12,636	14,466	11,639	12,966	13,489	13,252	13,103	15,450	12,010	14,212	13,559
Tashkent, USSR	15,273	10,864	15,412	3,744	13,919	14,928	16,303	11,785	9,819	6,026	3,572	10,642	3,637	4,608	14,573	15,862	13,505	16,685	14,784	2,792
Tbilisi, USSR	16,839	9,676	16,808	5,604	15,962	16,784	14,428	9,752	9,370	4,830	1,543	9,457	2,247	3,066	12,613	13,850	11,508	15,024	12,816	1,902
Tegucigalpa, Honduras	7,839	2,550	7,393	16,569	10,834	8,835	6,744	6,276	4,328	7,414	11,244	2,772	9,943	9,054	3,418	5,765	6,303	7,488	6,332	13,436
Tehran, Iran	16,932	10,563	17,030	4,882	15,383	16,594	14,627	10,201	10,180	5,710	2,089	10,343	3,125	3,951	13,289	14,222	11,863	15,067	13,121	1,304
Tel Aviv, Israel	18,198	9,791	18,091	6,369	16,895	18,141	13,113	8,610	10,032	5,247	773	9,585	2,884	3,368	11,777	12,641	10,282	13,655	11,556	1,431
Telegraph Creek, Canada	8,480	4,541	8,214	10,662	10,595	9,158	12,771	11,131	1,905	5,210	9,375	4,463	7,081	6,858	9,433	11,844	12,015	13,382	12,361	10,857
Teresina, Brazil	11,823	5,867	11,463	15,379	13,902	12,567	4,768	935	8,511	7,873	8,672	5,927	9,112	8,215	2,809	3,825	1,972	5,709	3,136	10,202
Ternate, Indonesia	9,102	15,147	9,492	3,853	6,691	8,271	15,137	17,913	12,507	12,377	10,782	15,057	10,737	11,690	18,064	16,223	17,362	14,160	16,547	9,036
The Valley, Anguilla	10,415	2,492	9,973	15,538	13,347	11,395	6,796	4,233	5,139	5,977	8,953	2,576	8,174	7,203	3,142	5,666	5,018	7,742	5,665	11,070
Thessaloniki, Greece	17,301	8,370	17,017	7,412	17,746	17,835	12,806	7,998	8,699	3,885	655	8,164	1,817	2,024	10,788	12,109	9,807	13,535	11,138	2,835
Thimphu, Bhutan	13,670	12,892	13,962	1,363	11,666	13,034	17,158	13,832	11,252	8,260	5,799	12,678	6,019	6,996	16,967	17,465	15,289	16,805	16,321	4,293
Thunder Bay, Canada	9,469	1,654	9,074	12,765	12,280	10,396	10,432	8,202	1,131	4,276	8,765	1,543	6,819	6,149	6,803	9,366	9,133	11,250	9,649	10,812
Tientsin, China	11,283	11,554	11,479	3,211	10,126	10,897	19,506	15,586	9,275	8,007	7,501	11,384	6,644	7,523	16,736	19,325	17,434	18,530	18,769	6,694
Tijuana, Mexico	6,570	3,536	6,186	13,511	9,385	7,487	9,921	9,759	2,236	7,038	11,561	3,626	9,438	8,910	7,029	9,128	9,950	10,427	9,879	13,448
Tiksi, USSR	11,402	7,903	11,342	6,458	11,919	11,595	16,764	12,858	5,833	4,777	6,562	7,725	4,605	5,105	13,065	15,654	14,567	17,607	15,602	7,149
Timbuktu, Mali	16,671	7,661	16,252	10,424	18,528	17,539	9,173	4,456	9,383	5,456	3,770	7,538	5,004	4,467	7,719	8,539	6,199	9,905	7,519	5,227
Tindouf, Algeria	16,072	6,598	15,625	10,504	19,012	17,071	9,778	4,893	8,117	4,170	3,545	6,451	4,122	3,414	7,656	8,976	6,750	10,614	8,085	5,451
Tirane, Albania	17,154	8,110	16,844	7,667	17,929	17,772	12,644	7,809	8,495	3,679	908	7,905	1,764	1,843	10,540	11,916	9,632	13,399	10,966	3,100
Tokyo, Japan	9,276	11,153	9,458	4,783	8,449	8,955	17,733	16,896	8,574	8,819	9,348	11,037	8,105	8,852	16,031	17,797	18,557	17,115	18,856	8,715
Toledo, Spain	15,962	6,389	15,540	9,670	18,707	16,923	11,068	6,184	7,376	2,945	2,836	6,204	2,782	2,015	8,567	10,191	8,054	11,942	9,377	4,997
Topeka, Kansas	8,469	1,549	8,056	13,703	11,385	9,429	9,627	8,144	1,449	5,412	9,866	1,600	7,969	7,276	6,147	8,622	8,764	10,371	9,069	11,947
Toronto, Canada	9,903	879	9,484	13,296	12,837	10,872	9,738	7,272	2,048	4,204	8,523	700	6,789	6,008	6,054	8,641	8,244	10,605	8,831	10,664
Toulouse, France	16,088	6,655	15,694	9,113	18,413	16,979	11,679	6,793	7,377	2,722	2,409	6,458	2,176	1,471	9,147	10,805	8,662	12,547	9,988	4,605
Tours, France	15,760	6,449	15,382	9,057	17,990	16,615	11,940	7,072	7,029	2,319	2,569	6,246	1,909	1,099	9,250	11,028	8,941	12,832	10,256	4,762
Townsville, Australia	6,513	15,229	6,949	6,825	3,736	5,562	12,354	16,979	12,946	14,946	13,791	15,293	13,747	14,669	15,038	13,336	15,217	11,410	13,986	11,869
Trenton, New Jersey	10,110	600	9,680	13,625	13,097	11,097	9,302	6,732	2,578	4,293	8,447	378	6,858	6,022	5,603	8,193	7,716	10,192	8,335	10,623
Tripoli, Lebanon	17,917	9,690	17,816	6,272	16,797	17,898	13,346	8,787	9,834	5,072	728	9,481	2,656	3,195	11,883	12,842	10,484	13,909	11,770	1,511
Tripoli, Libya	17,650	8,111	17,244	8,377	18,895	18,538	11,590	6,814	8,944	4,227	1,431	7,925	2,800	2,604	9,780	10,922	8,602	12,315	9,929	3,385
Tristan da Cunha (Edinburgh)	12,679	10,576	12,604	12,742	12,512	12,715	4,475	3,941	13,218	11,251	9,147	10,632	10,965	10,502	6,304	4,707	3,351	4,684	3,667	9,209
Trondheim, Norway	14,636	6,473	14,361	8,140	16,162	15,257	13,556	8,797	6,172	1,581	3,236	6,251	1,043	826	10,410	12,540	10,646	14,501	11,918	5,063
Trujillo, Peru	7,893	4,858	7,503	18,921	10,429	8,737	4,129	4,862	6,944	9,307	12,088	5,057	11,556	10,582	1,252	3,156	4,159	4,908	3,844	13,997
Truk Island (Moen)	6,789	12,897	7,112	6,132	5,195	6,161	14,652	19,288	10,321	12,049	12,404	12,880	11,449	12,216	15,665	15,331	17,665	13,840	16,333	11,185
Truro, Canada	11,176	1,677	10,751	12,817	14,128	12,153	9,824	6,560	3,101	3,287	7,348	1,466	5,813	4,949	6,145	8,694	7,828	10,764	8,646	9,526
Tsingtao, China	10,937	11,814	11,151	3,203	9,699	10,516	19,082	16,021	9,460	8,413	7,911	11,653	7,082	7,959	17,002	19,481	17,862	18,119	19,189	7,026
Tsitsihar, China	10,965	10,526	11,094	4,241	10,290	10,737	19,176	15,212	8,212	7,287	7,526	10,363	6,291	7,080	15,715	18,279	17,062	18,953	18,270	7,098
Tubuai Island (Mataura)	763	9,915	952	13,184	2,906	1,088	7,828	12,114	9,290	14,104	18,540	10,103	16,239	15,944	8,738	8,199	10,548	7,345	9,320	18,381
Tucson, Arizona	6,924	3,000	6,523	13,865	9,811	7,870	9,578	9,196	2,092	6,788	11,304	3,104	9,262	8,667	6,546	8,732	9,436	10,145	9,428	13,285
Tulsa, Oklahoma	8,267	1,557	7,848	14,010	11,216	9,239	9,337	8,028	1,735	5,692	10,119	1,651	8,258	7,547	5,895	8,345	8,568	10,069	8,824	12,220
Tunis, Tunisia	17,148	7,655	16,750	8,563	18,890	18,027	11,682	6,836	8,432	3,720	1,611	7,464	2,468	2,149	9,619	10,942	8,664	12,458	10,000	3,723
Tura, USSR	12,551	8,912	12,550	5,284	12,518	12,589	17,493	12,844	7,100	4,997	5,572	8,714	3,987	4,725	13,903	16,383	14,693	18,470	15,944	5,833
Turin, Italy	16,314	7,046	15,949	8,593	18,187	17,123	12,148	7,258	7,580	2,810	1,974	6,843	1,747	1,228	9,669	11,298	9,123	12,996	10,454	4,170
Uberlandia, Brazil	10,741	6,848	10,441	16,267	12,423	11,342	3,128	1,883	9,454	9,487	10,097	6,958	10,732	9,850	2,322	2,243	686	4,065	1,500	11,360
Ufa, USSR	15,184	9,081	15,142	5,432	14,908	15,241	15,661	10,787	8,207	4,244	2,933	8,858	1,991	2,964	13,033	14,850	12,636	16,426	13,972	3,428
Ujungpandang, Indonesia	9,767	16,146	10,183	3,522	7,094	8,863	14,624	16,827	13,534	12,767	10,454	16,031	10,803	11,780	18,162	15,753	16,383	13,663	15,797	8,517
Ulaanbaatar, Mongolia	12,238	10,719	12,374	3,589	11,361	11,973	19,206	14,317	8,696	6,806	6,338	10,529	5,364	6,242	15,768	18,209	16,178	19,509	17,512	5,817
Ulan-Ude, USSR	12,204	10,280	12,308	4,018	11,534	12,010	18,914	14,077	8,269	6,426	6,249	10,091	5,111	5,957	15,343	17,830	15,946	19,798	17,261	5,909
Uliastay, Mongolia	12,992	10,743	13,126	3,435	12,025	12,715	18,526	13,697	8,931	6,507	5,622	10,540	4,815	5,735	15,576	17,748	15,535	18,922	16,870	5,068
Uranium City, Canada	9,299	3,415	8,977	11,251	11,696	10,085	12,077	9,870	1,046	4,233	8,650	3,301	6,431	6,025	8,521	11,050	10,889	12,828	11,397	10,404
Urumqi, China	13,758	11,083	13,917	3,103	12,535	13,411	17,824	13,208	9,495	6,561	5,018	10,871	4,561	5,525	15,572	17,318	14,983	18,081	16,286	4,265
Ushuaia, Argentina	8,066	10,084	7,986	15,582	8,542	8,200	1,300	5,971	12,145	13,778	13,610	10,269	14,909	14,108	4,973	2,427	4,109	358	2,834	13,803
Vaduz, Liechtenstein	16,207	7,076	15,860	8,410	17,918	16,968	12,411	7,522	7,488	2,687	1,950	6,869	1,472	996	9,873	11,549	9,388	13,265	10,718	4,125
Valencia, Spain	16,251	6,695	15,834	9,387	18,852	17,197	11,241	6,352	7,620	3,089	2,524	6,508	2,634	1,954	8,836	10,394	8,218	12,095	9,548	4,681
Valladolid, Spain	15,810	6,263	15,394	9,660	18,503	16,758	11,180	6,306	7,191	2,738	2,891	6,074	2,665	1,859	8,598	10,284	8,175	12,066	9,493	5,071
Valletta, Malta	17,474	8,040	17,093	8,198	18,645	18,286	11,904	7,097	8,740	3,979	1,233	7,848	2,448	2,293	9,973	11,208	8,903	12,644	10,234	3,322
Valparaiso, Chile	8,084	7,652	7,838	17,836	9,634	8,592	1,274	4,683	9,801	11,616	12,896	7,836	13,346	12,404	2,584	680	2,999	2,075	1,837	14,023
Vancouver, Canada	7,825	3,883	7,511	11,734	10,251	8,606	11,708	10,553	1,334	5,712	10,102	3,854	7,852	7,493	8,484	10,817	11,206	12,291	11,413	11,760
Varna, Bulgaria	17,068	8,538	16,842	6,997	17,248	17,462	13,309	8,496	8,656	3,880	754	8,325	1,551	2,002	11,225	12,606	10,309	14,035	11,640	2,683
Venice, Italy	16,484	7,357	16,144	8,223	18,000	17,221	12,454	7,567	7,773	2,966	1,665	7,150	1,516	1,217	10,035	11,628	9,426	13,284	10,761	3,847

Distances in Kilometers	Raiatea (Uturoa)	Raleigh, North Carolina	Rangiroa (Avatoru)	Rangoon, Burma	Raoul Is., Kermadec Islands	Rarotonga (Avarua)	Rawson, Argentina	Recife, Brazil	Regina, Canada	Reykjavik, Iceland	Rhodes, Greece	Richmond, Virginia	Riga, USSR	Ringkobing, Denmark	Rio Branco, Brazil	Rio Cuarto, Argentina	Rio de Janeiro, Brazil	Rio Gallegos, Argentina	Rio Grande, Brazil	Riyadh, Saudi Arabia
Veracruz, Mexico	7,240	2,514	6,795	15,806	10,277	8,247	7,613	7,359	3,548	7,335	11,527	2,725	9,919	9,113	4,480	6,705	7,399	8,273	7,362	13,714
Verona, Italy	16,429	7,262	16,081	8,327	18,049	17,187	12,373	7,485	7,709	2,909	1,756	7,057	1,568	1,198	9,933	11,539	9,346	13,209	10,680	3,943
Victoria, Canada	7,737	3,893	7,421	11,793	10,174	8,521	11,650	10,561	1,374	5,798	10,193	3,870	7,944	7,583	8,450	10,768	11,189	12,224	11,377	11,852
Victoria, Seychelles	16,240	14,195	16,678	5,066	13,209	15,237	12,051	9,986	14,595	9,858	5,356	14,014	7,391	7,979	13,540	12,441	10,704	11,884	11,380	3,371
Vienna, Austria	16,343	7,483	16,039	7,886	17,578	16,989	12,884	7,996	7,710	2,897	1,628	7,271	1,104	1,037	10,400	12,048	9,857	13,716	11,190	3,729
Vientiane, Laos	12,221	14,056	12,564	696	10,001	11,486	16,970	15,307	11,973	9,751	7,471	13,861	7,655	8,633	18,660	17,888	16,434	16,201	17,043	5,808
Villahermosa, Mexico	7,474	2,423	7,027	16,034	10,505	8,480	7,357	6,995	3,750	7,299	11,388	2,642	9,874	9,038	4,145	6,421	7,047	8,049	7,043	13,585
Vilnius, USSR	15,784	7,654	15,553	7,272	16,628	16,263	13,795	8,907	7,459	2,804	2,041	7,434	264	1,090	11,105	12,916	10,773	14,649	12,102	3,775
Visby, Sweden	15,386	7,113	15,123	7,725	16,613	15,956	13,578	8,715	6,942	2,258	2,468	6,893	358	636	10,705	12,640	10,584	14,475	11,897	4,307
Vitoria, Brazil	11,457	7,404	11,181	15,439	12,886	11,992	3,436	1,479	10,044	9,499	9,553	7,492	10,438	9,616	3,159	2,768	413	4,285	1,747	10,652
Vladivostok, USSR	10,226	10,737	10,374	4,462	9,516	9,968	18,643	15,911	8,284	7,891	8,305	10,593	7,044	7,809	15,867	18,217	17,717	18,172	18,725	7,807
Volgograd, USSR	16,176	9,085	16,096	5,847	15,838	16,275	14,724	9,902	8,622	4,199	1,900	8,864	1,635	2,558	12,462	14,007	11,722	15,431	13,055	2,684
Vologda, USSR	15,199	8,061	15,050	6,524	15,627	15,503	14,803	9,918	7,431	3,186	2,671	7,838	963	1,903	11,958	13,896	11,786	15,666	13,113	3,878
Vorkuta, USSR	13,824	8,132	13,734	6,087	14,165	14,033	15,999	11,206	6,889	3,630	4,122	7,915	2,327	3,071	12,704	14,968	13,068	16,942	14,357	4,911
Wake Island	6,075	10,838	6,272	7,416	5,622	5,783	14,532	17,392	8,291	10,725	12,456	10,828	10,868	11,411	14,101	14,760	16,908	14,007	15,917	11,903
Wallis Island	2,685	11,539	3,077	10,195	1,777	1,949	10,639	15,140	9,877	14,019	16,484	11,665	14,865	15,242	11,713	11,157	13,517	9,992	12,237	15,366
Walvis Bay, Namibia	15,359	11,736	15,392	9,911	14,077	15,081	7,479	5,521	13,992	10,160	6,729	11,693	8,899	8,777	8,807	7,660	5,881	7,617	6,557	6,311
Warsaw, Poland	16,009	7,550	15,746	7,543	17,019	16,558	13,411	8,522	7,530	2,779	1,847	7,332	560	934	10,796	12,547	10,387	14,258	11,718	3,758
Washington, D.C.	9,874	374	9,443	13,801	12,867	10,863	9,182	6,778	2,515	4,524	8,692	154	7,094	6,262	5,493	8,081	7,694	10,058	8,266	10,867
Watson Lake, Canada	8,759	4,459	8,491	10,578	10,871	9,440	12,840	10,994	1,859	4,930	9,099	4,367	6,807	6,576	9,433	11,884	11,946	13,486	12,352	10,603
Weimar, East Germany	15,909	7,018	15,589	8,219	17,475	16,610	12,783	7,900	7,242	2,427	2,104	6,805	1,067	603	10,111	11,890	9,769	13,655	11,093	4,203
Wellington, New Zealand	4,225	13,784	4,644	10,309	1,490	3,270	8,889	13,761	12,824	17,244	17,091	13,971	17,291	18,096	11,477	9,787	11,892	8,001	10,575	14,914
West Berlin, West Germany	15,819	7,078	15,515	8,059	17,262	16,480	13,001	8,120	7,200	2,396	2,132	6,862	846	519	10,291	12,101	9,989	13,877	11,312	4,174
Wewak, Papua New Guinea	7,234	14,405	7,623	5,682	4,957	6,419	14,075	18,712	11,841	13,180	12,509	14,395	12,087	12,971	16,240	14,998	16,987	13,149	15,734	10,879
Whangarei, New Zealand	3,984	13,592	4,421	10,060	1,021	2,989	9,393	14,281	12,401	16,657	16,988	13,764	16,771	17,510	11,782	10,248	12,413	8,529	11,085	14,895
Whitehorse, Canada	8,710	4,809	8,462	10,286	10,705	9,349	13,143	11,335	2,204	5,075	9,129	4,717	6,829	6,659	9,770	12,204	12,297	13,763	12,692	10,544
Wichita, Kansas	8,263	1,681	7,850	13,812	11,186	9,225	9,544	8,214	1,530	5,618	10,075	1,752	8,171	7,483	6,108	8,555	8,775	10,269	9,037	12,153
Willemstad, Curacao	9,617	2,796	9,180	16,420	12,494	10,580	6,149	4,379	5,345	6,817	9,851	2,941	9,071	8,104	2,445	5,031	4,782	7,063	5,206	11,948
Wiluna, Australia	9,039	17,964	9,486	5,459	6,026	8,037	12,246	15,333	15,398	15,036	11,882	17,964	12,807	13,771	15,869	13,376	14,248	11,290	13,465	9,718
Windhoek, Namibia	15,481	11,939	15,540	9,647	14,049	15,149	7,710	5,778	14,144	10,192	6,636	11,889	8,838	8,756	9,075	7,912	6,149	7,823	6,815	6,127
Windsor, Canada	9,570	818	9,151	13,463	12,508	10,540	9,649	7,410	1,883	4,502	8,849	711	7,087	6,320	5,992	8,568	8,296	10,493	8,818	10,983
Winnipeg, Canada	9,094	2,168	8,716	12,506	11,822	9,991	10,785	8,779	537	4,522	9,045	2,086	6,994	6,401	7,219	9,749	9,654	11,557	10,106	11,016
Winston-Salem, North Carolina	9,490	150	9,056	14,139	12,498	10,484	8,926	6,808	2,521	4,938	9,107	296	7,511	6,683	5,264	7,841	7,604	9,779	8,094	11,285
Wroclaw, Poland	16,058	7,372	15,768	7,819	17,283	16,675	13,112	8,223	7,477	2,682	1,857	7,157	798	803	10,506	12,244	10,089	13,964	11,419	3,879
Wuhan, China	11,345	12,537	11,602	2,390	9,773	10,818	18,592	15,960	10,250	8,830	7,747	12,366	7,226	8,153	17,712	19,697	17,639	17,649	18,720	6,603
Wyndham, Australia	8,543	16,539	8,978	5,002	5,717	7,589	13,361	16,810	13,929	14,136	11,892	16,510	12,284	13,259	16,699	14,467	15,658	12,385	14,748	9,879
Xi'an, China	11,916	12,212	12,153	2,317	10,420	11,427	18,879	15,317	10,061	8,280	7,107	12,028	6,593	7,529	17,293	19,389	17,036	18,069	18,239	6,035
Xining, China	12,588	11,990	12,812	2,266	11,110	12,119	18,675	14,622	10,020	7,801	6,410	11,793	5,974	6,926	16,874	18,700	16,341	18,192	17,574	5,369
Yakutsk, USSR	11,067	8,873	11,080	5,664	11,147	11,101	17,711	13,887	6,648	5,814	7,056	8,705	5,337	5,960	14,059	16,644	15,628	18,389	16,671	7,254
Yanji, China	10,398	10,840	10,552	4,281	9,629	10,124	18,833	15,858	8,413	7,877	8,162	10,691	6,953	7,735	15,992	18,391	17,691	18,303	18,792	7,627
Yaounde, Cameroon	17,682	9,779	17,445	9,323	17,025	17,874	9,229	5,322	11,482	7,210	3,991	9,663	5,991	5,798	8,927	8,941	6,642	9,707	7,795	4,414
Yap Island (Colonia)	8,278	13,690	8,616	4,612	6,376	7,589	15,641	19,253	11,043	11,665	11,123	13,621	10,530	11,404	17,192	16,530	18,517	14,717	17,302	9,722
Yaraka, Australia	6,715	15,781	7,160	6,947	3,786	5,730	11,889	16,360	13,592	15,525	13,858	15,865	14,099	15,053	14,838	12,917	14,660	10,928	13,478	11,823
Yarmouth, Canada	10,915	1,394	10,488	13,056	13,882	11,897	9,652	6,551	2,976	3,557	7,629	1,184	6,091	5,231	5,960	8,525	7,750	10,582	8,521	9,808
Yellowknife, Canada	9,359	3,854	9,059	10,824	11,618	10,098	12,518	10,256	1,461	4,227	8,545	3,735	6,287	5,955	8,968	11,495	11,318	13,258	11,843	10,206
Yerevan, USSR	16,991	9,786	16,969	5,588	15,998	16,901	14,332	9,694	9,523	4,956	1,481	9,567	2,377	3,170	12,614	13,783	11,434	14,906	12,735	1,737
Yinchuan, China	12,205	11,769	12,414	2,599	10,865	11,776	19,117	14,880	9,701	7,762	6,693	11,580	6,087	7,017	16,794	18,990	16,656	18,501	17,939	5,762
Yogyakarta, Indonesia	10,635	16,776	11,064	3,136	7,823	9,693	14,328	15,798	14,285	12,719	9,827	16,619	10,503	11,475	18,030	15,440	15,568	13,419	15,223	7,775
York, United Kingdom	15,157	6,113	14,804	8,989	17,263	15,957	12,361	7,554	6,431	1,644	2,976	5,900	1,628	653	9,417	11,385	9,412	13,287	10,701	5,105
Yumen, China	12,953	11,625	13,153	2,559	11,588	12,533	18,542	14,152	9,768	7,332	5,949	11,423	5,473	6,425	16,403	18,257	15,906	18,357	17,182	5,021
Yutian, China	14,374	11,711	14,586	2,642	12,758	13,899	17,123	12,908	10,312	6,997	4,718	11,493	4,742	5,720	15,743	16,916	14,564	17,202	15,786	3,589
Yuzhno-Sakhalinsk, USSR	9,629	9,958	9,728	5,414	9,321	9,493	17,805	15,687	7,435	7,613	8,707	9,830	7,169	7,825	15,002	17,266	17,284	17,656	17,929	8,482
Zagreb, Yugoslavia	16,579	7,588	16,261	7,935	17,810	17,249	12,701	7,819	7,911	3,095	1,458	7,380	1,361	1,265	10,321	11,891	9,673	13,515	11,008	3,612
Zahedan, Iran	16,446	11,634	16,683	3,861	14,388	15,859	15,033	11,008	11,034	6,753	3,132	11,413	4,177	5,043	14,285	14,856	12,539	15,253	13,708	1,502
Zamboanga, Philippines	9,866	14,813	10,238	3,022	7,563	9,076	15,912	17,492	12,237	11,575	9,904	14,687	9,850	10,808	18,896	17,027	17,649	14,938	17,158	8,219
Zanzibar, Tanzania	17,221	12,913	17,554	6,764	14,442	16,347	10,687	8,176	14,063	9,277	4,853	12,768	7,130	7,459	11,746	10,889	8,977	10,722	9,773	3,504
Zaragoza, Spain	16,077	6,562	15,668	9,357	18,607	17,005	11,390	6,504	7,412	2,848	2,572	6,370	2,465	1,738	8,888	10,519	8,372	12,258	9,698	4,754
Zashiversk, USSR	10,732	8,047	10,690	6,526	11,219	10,897	16,854	13,407	5,786	5,351	7,257	7,886	5,313	5,794	13,236	15,809	15,037	17,541	15,950	7,747
Zhengzhou, China	11,494	12,094	11,724	2,645	10,089	11,027	19,050	15,656	9,848	8,373	7,465	11,919	6,826	7,741	17,256	19,760	17,424	18,115	18,668	6,460
Zurich, Switzerland	16,140	6,988	15,789	8,492	17,925	16,914	12,360	7,472	7,416	2,620	2,037	6,781	1,509	970	9,796	11,490	9,339	13,220	10,667	4,213

Distances in Kilometers	Road Town, Brit. Virgin Isls.	Roanoke, Virginia	Robinson Crusoe Island, Chile	Rochester, New York	Rockhampton, Australia	Rome, Italy	Rosario, Argentina	Roseau, Dominica	Rostock, East Germany	Rostov-na-Donu, USSR	Rotterdam, Netherlands	Rouyn, Canada	Sacramento, California	Saginaw, Michigan	Saint Denis, Reunion	Saint George's, Grenada	Saint John, Canada	Saint John's, Antigua	Saint John's, Canada	Saint Louis, Missouri
Roanoke, Virginia	2,567	0	7,851	683	15,001	7,547	8,028	3,046	6,882	8,894	6,508	1,220	3,625	763	15,368	3,332	1,460	2,854	2,497	913
Robinson Crusoe Island, Chile	5,959	7,851	0	8,504	11,821	12,509	1,695	5,724	13,015	14,738	12,450	9,068	9,128	8,550	12,280	5,372	8,833	5,898	9,365	8,084
Rochester, New York	3,000	683	8,504	0	15,116	7,010	8,603	3,453	6,270	8,256	5,923	575	3,691	514	15,030	3,771	952	3,251	2,001	1,173
Rockhampton, Australia	16,348	15,001	11,821	15,116	0	15,638	12,953	16,571	15,160	13,432	15,723	14,883	11,430	14,604	9,603	16,398	15,926	16,589	16,628	14,098
Rome, Italy	7,611	7,547	12,509	7,010	15,638	0	11,157	7,564	1,355	2,229	1,267	6,799	9,952	7,414	8,237	7,823	6,093	7,475	5,050	8,159
Rosario, Argentina	5,704	8,028	1,695	8,603	12,953	11,157	0	5,340	11,893	13,345	11,337	9,176	10,110	8,784	10,994	4,981	8,679	5,540	8,953	8,492
Roseau, Dominica	489	3,046	5,724	3,453	16,571	7,564	5,340	0	7,571	9,589	7,034	3,994	6,375	3,783	13,360	362	3,351	205	3,667	3,823
Rostock, East Germany	7,506	6,882	13,015	6,270	15,160	1,355	11,893	7,571	0	2,077	566	5,957	8,822	6,604	9,279	7,880	5,433	7,442	4,463	7,353
Rostov-na-Donu, USSR	9,556	8,894	14,738	8,256	13,432	2,229	13,345	9,589	2,077	0	2,572	7,887	10,318	8,542	7,706	9,882	7,464	9,473	6,524	9,279
Rotterdam, Netherlands	6,986	6,508	12,450	5,923	15,723	1,267	11,337	7,034	566	2,572	0	5,654	8,699	6,290	9,458	7,338	5,049	6,911	4,045	7,040
Rouyn, Canada	3,552	1,220	9,068	575	14,883	6,799	9,176	3,994	5,957	7,887	5,654	0	3,553	656	14,962	4,321	1,043	3,790	1,958	1,397
Sacramento, California	5,894	3,625	9,128	3,691	11,430	9,952	10,110	6,375	8,822	10,318	8,699	3,553	0	3,177	18,019	6,562	4,566	6,220	5,503	2,713
Saginaw, Michigan	3,311	763	8,550	514	14,604	7,414	8,784	3,783	6,604	8,542	6,290	656	3,177	0	15,510	4,080	1,438	3,587	2,466	750
Saint Denis, Reunion	13,779	15,368	12,280	15,030	9,603	8,237	10,994	13,360	9,279	7,706	9,458	14,962	18,019	15,510	0	13,295	14,080	13,458	13,044	16,194
Saint George's, Grenada	772	3,332	5,372	3,771	16,398	7,823	4,981	362	7,880	9,882	7,338	4,321	6,562	4,080	13,295	0	3,705	559	4,027	4,072
Saint John, Canada	2,977	1,460	8,833	952	15,926	6,093	8,679	3,351	5,433	7,464	5,049	1,043	4,566	1,438	14,080	3,705	0	3,148	1,055	2,124
Saint John's, Antigua	329	2,854	5,898	3,251	16,589	7,475	5,540	205	7,442	9,473	6,911	3,790	6,220	3,587	13,458	559	3,148	0	3,481	3,643
Saint John's, Canada	3,406	2,497	9,365	2,001	16,628	5,050	8,953	3,667	4,463	6,524	4,045	1,958	5,503	2,466	13,044	4,027	1,055	3,481	0	3,174
Saint Louis, Missouri	3,334	913	8,084	1,173	14,098	8,159	8,492	3,823	7,353	9,279	7,040	1,397	2,713	750	16,194	4,072	2,124	3,643	3,174	0
Saint Paul, Minnesota	3,949	1,393	8,820	1,255	13,863	7,884	9,229	4,432	6,961	8,801	6,704	1,137	2,450	751	16,088	4,708	2,119	4,243	3,092	743
Saint Peter Port, UK	6,460	6,136	11,882	5,583	16,283	1,436	10,783	6,492	1,133	3,099	567	5,364	8,566	5,981	9,661	6,790	4,677	6,374	3,645	6,726
Saipan (Susupe)	15,031	12,499	15,110	12,191	4,294	12,084	16,710	15,520	11,168	9,951	11,689	11,712	9,214	11,794	10,632	15,753	12,591	15,340	12,821	11,698
Salalah, Oman	12,257	12,317	14,996	11,728	11,384	4,820	13,312	12,099	5,466	3,604	5,810	11,421	13,835	12,070	4,191	12,279	10,857	12,059	9,837	12,817
Salem, Oregon	6,109	3,673	9,778	3,598	11,543	9,421	10,679	6,597	8,240	9,654	8,157	3,347	717	3,100	17,331	6,821	4,388	6,426	5,239	2,798
Salt Lake City, Utah	5,123	2,778	8,906	2,834	12,288	9,279	9,708	5,609	8,222	9,862	8,047	2,719	858	2,320	17,500	5,820	3,719	5,444	4,676	1,871
Salta, Argentina	4,784	7,036	1,632	7,626	13,425	10,879	1,017	4,456	11,435	13,107	10,869	8,200	9,128	7,787	11,873	4,094	7,757	4,650	8,113	7,479
Salto, Uruguay	5,560	7,937	1,976	8,494	13,233	10,853	308	5,179	11,604	13,038	11,050	9,065	10,162	8,697	10,866	4,823	8,528	5,381	8,760	8,439
Salvador, Brazil	4,505	7,050	4,676	7,381	15,865	8,009	3,156	4,017	8,834	10,189	8,295	7,872	10,303	7,765	9,913	3,775	7,022	4,202	6,853	7,839
Salzburg, Austria	7,598	7,258	12,817	6,681	15,394	657	11,563	7,605	702	2,000	765	6,419	9,433	7,053	8,704	7,890	5,798	7,496	4,781	7,803
Samsun, Turkey	9,555	9,168	14,359	8,559	13,672	1,983	12,869	9,533	2,288	714	2,682	8,237	10,879	8,887	7,158	9,800	7,714	9,436	6,724	9,634
San Antonio, Texas	3,641	1,930	7,279	2,405	13,210	9,415	7,974	4,106	8,627	10,542	8,311	2,671	2,346	2,024	17,243	4,257	3,336	3,970	4,391	1,275
San Cristobal, Venezuela	1,441	3,360	4,635	3,957	15,157	9,003	4,670	1,445	8,946	10,991	8,423	4,531	5,988	4,114	14,233	1,243	4,198	1,529	4,784	3,863
San Diego, California	5,452	3,413	8,368	3,626	11,588	10,276	9,376	5,920	9,230	10,853	9,050	3,614	760	3,122	18,507	6,070	4,558	5,781	5,563	2,517
San Francisco, California	5,967	3,723	9,101	3,801	11,323	10,071	10,110	6,447	8,938	10,423	8,817	3,669	121	3,287	18,119	6,628	4,681	6,294	5,621	2,810
San Jose, Costa Rica	2,300	3,057	4,853	3,735	14,058	9,818	5,357	2,533	9,523	11,600	9,050	4,272	4,891	3,712	15,538	2,451	4,279	2,532	5,107	3,235
San Juan, Argentina	5,547	7,709	999	8,322	12,651	11,602	756	5,238	12,215	13,823	11,650	8,897	9,506	8,449	11,694	4,877	8,508	5,429	8,902	8,085
San Juan, Puerto Rico	158	2,483	5,923	2,944	16,195	7,733	5,719	613	7,603	9,659	7,087	3,502	5,763	3,234	13,933	851	2,972	477	3,451	3,227
San Luis Potosi, Mexico	3,812	2,627	6,604	3,178	12,771	10,171	7,452	4,231	9,437	11,374	9,101	3,491	2,672	2,837	17,590	4,309	4,077	4,132	5,123	2,096
San Marino, San Marino	7,588	7,432	12,603	6,882	15,577	224	11,284	7,559	1,131	2,146	1,069	6,654	9,766	7,276	8,406	7,828	5,975	7,464	4,938	8,023
San Miguel de Tucuman, Argen.	5,009	7,260	1,514	7,851	13,261	11,016	809	4,678	11,604	13,242	11,039	8,426	9,311	8,011	11,732	4,316	7,982	4,872	8,333	7,697
San Salvador, El Salvador	2,680	2,769	5,352	3,449	13,681	9,946	5,988	3,000	9,509	11,570	9,073	3,943	4,206	3,334	16,201	2,984	4,125	2,958	5,047	2,763
Sanaa, Yemen	11,380	11,768	13,992	11,240	12,316	4,230	12,299	11,178	5,118	3,560	5,362	11,011	13,852	11,637	4,191	11,331	10,321	11,156	9,272	12,384
Santa Cruz, Bolivia	4,013	6,345	2,352	6,909	14,173	10,179	1,697	3,666	10,669	12,407	10,103	7,482	8,709	7,104	12,081	3,305	6,990	3,863	7,314	6,852
Santa Cruz, Tenerife	5,033	5,932	9,528	5,651	18,586	2,991	8,258	4,858	3,659	5,216	3,123	5,732	9,284	6,157	9,436	5,054	4,730	4,820	3,750	6,780
Santa Fe, New Mexico	4,480	2,330	8,175	2,563	12,670	9,381	8,943	4,960	8,432	10,205	8,193	2,611	1,417	2,070	17,572	5,146	3,507	4,807	4,532	1,435
Santa Rosa, Argentina	6,095	8,339	1,368	8,937	12,432	11,675	524	5,754	12,417	13,856	11,861	9,512	10,189	9,086	11,047	5,393	9,070	5,951	9,395	8,745
Santa Rosalia, Mexico	4,959	3,222	7,613	3,576	11,845	10,479	8,619	5,407	9,536	11,285	9,297	3,690	1,516	3,111	18,589	5,521	4,528	5,287	5,573	2,406
Santarem, Brazil	2,553	5,111	4,272	5,547	16,067	8,329	3,435	2,096	8,743	10,540	8,177	6,089	8,189	5,862	12,005	1,782	5,402	2,299	5,543	5,824
Santiago del Estero, Argentina	5,115	7,385	1,540	7,973	13,232	11,019	669	4,777	11,635	13,241	11,071	8,547	9,454	8,138	11,595	4,415	8,091	4,973	8,425	7,830
Santiago, Chile	5,779	7,888	762	8,513	12,359	11,894	934	5,484	12,507	14,113	11,942	9,085	9,548	8,620	11,724	5,123	8,730	5,672	9,151	8,230
Santo Domingo, Dominican Rep.	558	2,303	5,844	2,832	15,809	8,044	5,774	971	7,850	9,918	7,348	3,404	5,436	3,066	14,324	1,127	2,993	867	3,586	2,974
Sao Paulo de Olivenca, Brazil	2,465	4,654	3,501	5,237	14,831	9,546	3,374	2,228	9,726	11,683	9,175	5,812	7,131	5,410	13,384	1,883	5,403	2,398	5,867	5,151
Sao Paulo, Brazil	5,040	7,583	3,331	8,038	14,497	9,455	1,726	4,587	10,269	11,626	9,725	8,581	10,391	8,339	10,259	4,267	7,869	4,791	7,898	8,245
Sao Tome, Sao Tome & Principe	8,039	9,695	9,626	9,526	15,355	4,640	7,938	7,663	5,979	6,100	5,721	9,667	13,208	10,040	5,793	7,670	8,643	7,731	7,743	10,592
Sapporo, Japan	12,698	10,182	16,393	9,699	7,415	9,300	17,795	13,142	8,211	7,400	8,694	9,149	7,718	9,420	11,245	13,469	9,853	12,937	9,871	9,579
Sarajevo, Yugoslavia	8,063	7,844	13,039	7,276	15,117	530	11,680	8,037	1,228	1,699	1,371	7,022	10,029	7,654	8,099	8,306	6,384	7,941	5,358	8,404
Saratov, USSR	9,768	8,852	15,214	8,192	12,998	2,750	13,906	9,848	2,280	666	2,830	7,777	9,944	8,431	8,076	10,160	7,463	9,716	6,586	9,149
Saskatoon, Canada	5,221	2,657	9,878	2,377	12,893	8,058	10,432	5,702	6,943	8,539	6,806	2,007	1,894	1,944	16,210	5,982	3,040	5,511	3,821	1,968
Schefferville, Canada	4,039	2,188	9,866	1,512	15,359	5,720	9,740	4,408	4,843	6,777	4,552	1,115	4,416	1,768	13,935	4,763	1,062	4,205	1,270	2,512
Seattle, Washington	6,107	3,621	9,988	3,488	11,688	9,141	10,834	6,596	7,951	9,354	7,876	3,195	1,003	3,004	17,033	6,834	4,237	6,418	5,051	2,775
Sendai, Japan	13,190	10,657	16,430	10,191	6,896	9,710	17,991	13,641	8,663	7,742	9,159	9,647	8,055	9,897	11,038	13,962	10,371	13,437	10,404	10,025
Seoul, South Korea	13,687	11,270	17,649	10,727	7,182	8,991	19,154	14,088	8,100	6,887	8,635	10,159	9,050	10,508	9,887	14,438	10,738	13,884	10,575	10,752
Sept-Iles, Canada	3,526	1,798	9,368	1,160	15,654	5,884	9,228	3,897	5,111	7,101	4,772	945	4,465	1,531	14,018	4,252	549	3,694	1,043	2,276
Sevastopol, USSR	9,214	8,749	14,219	8,136	13,908	1,731	12,796	9,214	1,867	561	2,286	7,807	10,458	8,459	7,584	9,492	7,299	9,109	6,318	9,205
Seville, Spain	6,038	6,370	10,896	5,938	17,292	1,659	9,633	5,951	2,317	3,862	1,812	5,864	9,320	6,406	9,106	6,194	4,987	5,877	3,941	7,111
Shanghai, China	14,483	12,118	18,107	11,557	6,785	9,140	19,736	14,860	8,396	6,951	8,952	10,985	9,920	11,358	9,087	15,217	11,513	14,658	11,270	11,624
Sheffield, United Kingdom	6,604	6,072	12,169	5,487	15,934	1,646	11,134	6,672	902	2,969	437	5,221	8,306	5,855	9,871	6,984	4,613	6,542	3,612	6,605
Shenyang, China	13,283	10,933	17,864	10,362	7,736	8,442	18,960	13,663	7,540	6,357	8,075	9,790	8,949	10,176	9,844	14,019	10,314	13,461	10,098	10,472
Shiraz, Iran	11,439	11,105	15,436	10,483	11,992	3,830	13,763	11,371	4,225	2,249	4,636	10,130	12,431	10,785	5,593	11,611	9,658	11,294	8,677	11,524
Sibiu, Romania	8,468	8,093	13,539	7,498	14,631	1,032	12,182	8,465	1,259	1,202	1,588	7,204	10,050	7,848	8,032	8,744	6,635	8,361	5,632	8,598
Singapore	17,491	15,718	16,412	15,080	5,738	10,030	16,148	17,569	10,006	7,980	10,538	14,511	13,618	14,992	5,810	17,852	14,753	17,448	14,136	15,361
Sioux Falls, South Dakota	4,095	1,583	8,737	1,548	13,570	8,205	9,230	4,582	7,265	9,079	7,018	1,467	2,144	1,034	16,416	4,840	2,437	4,399	3,419	775
Skelleftea, Sweden	7,957	6,808	13,789	6,142	14,164	2,601	12,888	8,116	1,288	2,256	1,714	5,720	8,089	6,374	9,943	8,455	5,446	7,959	4,633	7,093
Skopje, Yugoslavia	8,346	8,165	13,200	7,599	14,904	746	11,792	8,307	1,511	1,554	1,692	7,344	10,328	7,977	7,789	8,569	6,706	8,216	5,678	8,726
Socotra Island (Tamrida)	12,468	12,690	14,729	12,119	11,218	5,156	13,066	12,275	5,876	4,061	6,196	11,832	14,314	12,477	3,711	12,432	11,230	12,251	10,198	13,226
Sofia, Bulgaria	8,478	8,243	13,368	7,668	14,745	897	11,961	8,447	1,510	1,385	1,746	7,399	10,331	8,036	7,771	8,712	6,783	8,353	5,762	8,786
Songkhla, Thailand	16,744	15,081	17,077	14,425	6,394	9,326	16,568	16,834	9,264	7,248	9,800	13,864	13,338	14,379	5,831	17,130	14,044	16,706	13,398	14,812
Sorong, Indonesia	17,415	14,870	15,064	14,520	3,244	12,420	16,059	17,903	11,940	10,199	12,506	14,011	11,570	14,149	8,506	18,130	14,805	17,720	14,818	14,081
South Georgia Island	8,482	10,952	3,995	11,472	11,376	11,640	3,024	8,054	12,821	13,340	12,374	12,032	13,064	11,716	8,291	7,717	11,372	8,259	11,384	11,488
South Pole	12,044	14,130	6,280	14,783	7,414	14,645	6,356	11,695	15,999	15,237	15,758	15,347	14,274	14,813	7,695	11,336	15,018	11,895	15,274	14,278
South Sandwich Islands	9,149	11,650	4,711	12,148	11,010	11,625	3,768	8,708	12,880	13,131	12,481	12,700	13,805	12,413	7,595	8,379	11,991	8,913	11,922	12,212
Split, Yugoslavia	7,910	7,728	12,878	7,169	15,280	370	11,525	7,880	1,216	1,861	1,291	6,927	9,977	7,554	8,168	8,147	6,270	7,786	5,238	8,303
Spokane, Washington	5,749	3,253	9,792	3,120	12,046	8,929	10,571	6,237	7,772	9,258	7,668	2,838	1,062	2,634	16,963	6,481	3,881	6,058	4,715	2,415
Spoleto, Italy	7,622	7,517	12,567	6,974	15,594	95	11,226	7,582	1,263	2,173	1,194	6,755	9,887	7,374	8,293	7,846	6,062	7,491	5,021	8,119
Springbok, South Africa	10,317	12,579	8,813	12,614	12,262	7,943	7,303	9,844	9,295	8,794	9,132	12,889	16,182	13,113	3,889	9,691	11,847	9,988	11,080	13,483
Springfield, Illinois	3,373	891	8,206	1,071	14,148	8,038	8,591	3,861	7,221	9,142	6,912	1,264	2,740	624	16,101	4,120	2,023	3,678	3,068	140
Springfield, Massachusetts	2,729	827	8,410	428	15,544	6,725	8,399	3,159	6,059	8,081	5,682	848	4,117	940	14,653	3,492	634	2,954	1,679	1,542
Srinagar, India	12,784	11,686	17,598	11,006	10,217	5,424	15,922	12,849	5,283	3,272	5,816	10,524	11,786	11,155	6,419	13,150	10,376	12,725	9,564	11,809
Stanley, Falkland Islands	7,799	10,089	2,626	10,682	11,241	12,390	2,095	7,430	13,399	14,343	12,884	11,256	11,752	10,837	9,702	7,073	10,774	7,631	11,011	10,489
Stara Zagora, Bulgaria	8,670	8,413	13,539	7,832	14,558	1,087	12,115	8,639	1,634	1,232	1,908	7,554	10,441	8,194	7,647	8,905	6,953	8,546	5,937	8,944
Stockholm, Sweden	7,846	6,948	13,531	6,303	14,571	1,977	12,498	7,958	687	1,958	1,184	5,929	8,532	6,584	9,522	8,284	5,534	7,815	4,636	7,321
Stornoway, United Kingdom	6,437	5,652	12,188	5,037	15,722	2,245	11,292	6,558	1,234	3,266	985	4,728	7,714	5,373	10,436	6,889	4,207	6,411	3,260	6,122
Strasbourg, France	7,202	6,869	12,494	6,300	15,717	830	11,293	7,217	684	2,376	437	6,051	9,133	6,680	9,033	7,507	5,409	7,106	4,387	7,429
Stuttgart, West Germany	7,308	6,955	12,598	6,382	15,613	806	11,390	7,324	626	2,268	483	6,125	9,180	6,757	8,975	7,614	5,495	7,212	4,476	7,506
Subic, Philippines	16,280	13,860	17,186	13,327	5,365	10,327	18,001	16,662	9,817	8,098	10,383	12,759	11,292	13,097	8,109	17,018	13,314	16,460	13,053	13,294
Suchow, China	14,167	11,890	18,544	11,301	7,289	8,615	19,773	14,517	7,883	6,427	8,441	10,726	9,932	11,138	8,938	14,877	11,191	14,319	10,885	11,458
Sucre, Bolivia	4,147	6,419	2,106	7,001	13,924	10,436	1,609	3,821	10,910	12,662	10,344	7,575	8,660	7,175	12,203	3,460	7,120	4,014	7,482	6,891
Sudbury, Canada	3,455	1,029	8,877	458	14,781	7,030	9,033	3,910	6,198	8,131	5,892	244	3,400	412	15,171	4,227	1,167	3,708	2,141	1,155
Suez, Egypt	9,669	9,780	13,640	9,236	13,882	2,234	12,025	9,548	3,142	2,013	3,354	9,001	11,954	9,628	6,137	9,761	8,326	9,490	7,283	10,376
Sundsvall, Sweden	7,790	6,761	13,566	6,106	14,449	2,301	12,614	7,928	972	2,195	1,394	5,709	8,222	6,365	9,823	8,262	5,370	7,777	4,513	7,095

Distances in Kilometers	Road Town, Brit. Virgin Isls.	Roanoke, Virginia	Robinson Crusoe Island, Chile	Rochester, New York	Rockhampton, Australia	Rome, Italy	Rosario, Argentina	Roseau, Dominica	Rostock, East Germany	Rostov-na-Donu, USSR	Rotterdam, Netherlands	Rouyn, Canada	Sacramento, California	Saginaw, Michigan	Saint Denis, Reunion	Saint George's, Grenada	Saint John, Canada	Saint John's, Antigua	Saint John's, Canada	Saint Louis, Missouri
Surabaya, Indonesia	18,735	16,444	15,318	15,900	4,410	11,396	15,502	18,920	11,350	9,339	11,889	15,329	13,588	15,680	6,336	19,219	15,790	18,774	15,330	15,844
Suva, Fiji	13,406	12,224	10,035	12,490	2,960	17,055	11,573	13,675	15,846	15,070	16,219	12,416	8,865	11,983	12,456	13,558	13,412	13,667	14,367	11,366
Sverdlovsk, USSR	10,241	8,936	16,013	8,255	12,146	3,769	14,880	10,395	3,016	1,777	3,581	7,774	9,427	8,408	8,625	10,731	7,650	10,241	6,898	9,076
Svobodnyy, USSR	12,168	9,808	17,075	9,238	8,569	7,949	17,836	12,558	6,895	6,042	7,395	8,665	7,970	9,052	10,661	12,911	9,207	12,355	9,037	9,360
Sydney, Australia	16,085	15,431	10,892	15,707	1,166	16,322	11,894	16,160	16,120	14,226	16,685	15,599	12,051	15,198	9,251	15,899	16,617	16,242	17,506	14,584
Sydney, Canada	3,099	1,909	9,034	1,418	16,281	5,638	8,760	3,423	5,016	7,064	4,615	1,442	4,993	1,896	13,616	3,783	467	3,225	591	2,591
Syktyvkar, USSR	9,476	8,177	15,302	7,498	12,776	3,356	14,291	9,641	2,402	1,755	2,954	7,027	8,870	7,667	9,158	9,980	6,880	9,483	6,126	8,347
Szeged, Hungary	8,156	7,810	13,262	7,224	14,924	783	11,936	8,153	1,040	1,493	1,302	6,944	9,862	7,583	8,241	8,432	6,350	8,048	5,341	8,333
Szombathely, Hungary	7,872	7,523	13,044	6,941	15,159	677	11,756	7,875	825	1,742	1,018	6,668	9,632	7,306	8,486	8,159	6,063	7,769	5,051	8,056
Tabriz, Iran	10,479	10,010	15,119	9,382	12,780	2,900	13,547	10,457	3,138	1,151	3,574	9,027	11,424	9,682	6,595	10,722	8,567	10,361	7,599	10,421
Tacheng, China	12,089	10,543	17,899	9,863	10,302	5,456	16,590	12,268	4,883	3,248	5,449	9,337	10,246	9,931	7,982	12,609	9,369	12,108	8,705	10,524
Tahiti (Papeete)	10,110	9,477	7,191	9,937	6,245	16,815	8,873	10,331	15,656	16,604	15,567	10,078	6,868	9,493	14,964	10,188	10,882	10,344	11,937	8,766
Taipei, Taiwan	15,147	12,753	17,836	12,205	6,205	9,624	19,105	15,530	8,958	7,409	9,518	11,635	10,394	11,991	8,764	15,885	12,181	15,328	11,942	12,226
Taiyuan, China	13,764	11,587	18,890	10,973	7,856	8,038	19,195	14,086	7,312	5,853	7,870	10,399	9,900	10,849	8,825	14,448	10,796	13,892	10,429	11,223
Tallahasee, Florida	2,390	857	7,115	1,530	14,583	8,331	7,445	2,875	7,720	9,744	7,331	2,025	3,508	1,442	15,873	3,089	2,287	2,714	3,293	1,056
Tallinn, USSR	8,224	7,274	13,907	6,622	14,216	2,125	12,849	8,338	971	1,674	1,514	6,230	8,708	6,885	9,329	8,665	5,873	8,195	4,994	7,616
Tamanrasset, Algeria	7,259	8,130	10,892	7,774	16,453	2,217	9,346	7,038	3,519	4,078	3,235	7,760	11,260	8,263	7,259	7,190	6,827	7,023	5,808	8,935
Tampa, Florida	2,103	1,060	6,827	1,743	14,731	8,372	7,123	2,584	7,825	9,869	7,415	2,271	3,792	1,723	15,710	2,783	2,408	2,431	3,370	1,384
Tampere, Finland	8,135	7,106	13,883	6,448	14,186	2,308	12,883	8,267	1,074	1,885	1,579	6,044	8,476	6,699	9,558	8,599	5,720	8,118	4,865	7,426
Tanami, Australia	18,518	16,570	13,346	16,397	2,182	13,705	14,045	18,742	13,577	11,616	14,131	15,956	12,979	15,950	7,674	18,517	16,852	18,771	16,937	15,677
Tangier, Morocco	6,046	6,459	10,805	6,042	17,357	1,721	9,517	5,943	2,461	3,942	1,968	5,984	9,455	6,515	8,995	6,177	5,090	5,875	4,050	7,214
Tarawa (Betio)	13,368	11,430	11,779	11,474	3,659	14,829	13,434	13,779	13,611	12,975	14,002	11,224	7,812	10,966	12,920	13,812	12,267	13,688	13,021	10,517
Tashkent, USSR	11,868	10,757	17,100	10,079	10,999	4,646	15,545	11,953	4,383	2,436	4,927	9,606	11,087	10,242	7,033	12,263	9,438	11,821	8,625	10,911
Tbilisi, USSR	10,179	9,618	15,058	8,984	12,977	2,666	13,546	10,180	2,766	734	3,226	8,620	11,005	9,275	7,014	10,458	8,182	10,076	7,227	10,012
Tegucigalpa, Honduras	2,461	2,667	5,356	3,350	13,898	9,759	5,923	2,782	9,349	11,415	8,904	3,860	4,322	3,267	16,008	2,770	3,990	2,739	4,891	2,732
Tehran, Iran	11,010	10,504	15,513	9,868	12,275	3,424	13,896	10,984	3,648	1,612	4,096	9,496	11,751	10,152	6,271	11,247	9,068	10,890	8,111	10,886
Tel Aviv, Israel	9,788	9,775	13,923	9,212	13,708	2,255	12,320	9,688	3,034	1,735	3,297	8,951	11,808	9,586	6,259	9,914	8,316	9,622	7,284	10,336
Telegraph Creek, Canada	6,905	4,339	11,254	4,006	11,519	8,441	12,006	7,384	7,157	8,321	7,183	3,557	2,260	3,611	15,858	7,667	4,529	7,191	5,110	3,635
Teresina, Brazil	3,535	6,066	4,886	6,388	16,544	7,633	3,599	3,047	8,295	9,858	7,738	6,879	9,384	6,776	10,672	2,825	6,037	3,225	5,913	6,868
Ternate, Indonesia	17,511	14,944	15,463	14,538	3,662	11,986	16,348	17,985	11,551	9,771	12,117	14,007	11,777	14,203	8,175	18,271	14,733	17,786	14,646	14,202
The Valley, Anguilla	170	2,694	5,961	3,103	16,495	7,510	5,650	352	7,439	9,481	6,913	3,647	6,054	3,430	13,609	679	3,031	167	3,407	3,478
Thessaloniki, Greece	8,497	8,353	13,260	7,789	14,800	886	11,823	8,447	1,699	1,529	1,885	7,537	10,519	8,169	7,595	8,704	6,894	8,361	5,863	8,918
Thimphu, Bhutan	14,220	12,750	18,737	12,071	8,623	7,015	17,125	14,341	6,785	4,836	7,334	11,539	12,001	12,120	6,504	14,661	11,579	14,200	10,880	12,682
Thunder Bay, Canada	4,001	1,452	9,145	1,079	14,129	7,418	9,451	4,471	6,482	8,322	6,230	764	2,796	692	15,638	4,771	1,802	4,274	2,708	1,089
Tientsin, China	13,628	11,365	18,460	10,770	7,741	8,255	19,294	13,977	7,456	6,103	8,007	10,195	9,530	10,617	9,237	14,338	10,651	13,779	10,349	10,955
Tijuana, Mexico	5,438	3,408	8,344	3,625	11,593	10,285	9,352	5,905	9,242	10,869	9,060	3,617	784	3,122	18,518	6,055	4,559	5,767	5,565	2,513
Tiksi, USSR	9,964	7,720	15,477	7,106	10,667	6,471	15,667	10,334	5,215	5,083	5,626	6,532	6,626	6,986	11,622	10,691	6,989	10,132	6,786	7,402
Timbuktu, Mali	6,508	7,760	9,778	7,513	17,172	3,155	8,234	6,227	4,343	5,161	3,956	7,605	11,158	8,023	7,621	6,334	6,600	6,242	5,661	8,627
Tindouf, Algeria	5,828	6,672	10,084	6,351	17,835	2,447	8,710	5,643	3,365	4,662	2,889	6,385	9,927	6,850	8,701	5,827	5,413	5,610	4,427	7,499
Tirane, Albania	8,226	8,096	13,045	7,538	15,050	616	11,636	8,179	1,529	1,710	1,656	7,297	10,328	7,924	7,806	8,437	6,637	8,091	5,603	8,673
Tokyo, Japan	13,487	10,950	16,501	10,489	6,636	9,881	18,125	13,939	8,866	7,871	9,371	9,945	8,302	10,192	10,849	14,259	10,671	13,736	10,699	10,311
Toledo, Spain	6,226	6,413	11,195	5,950	17,007	1,407	9,950	6,163	1,992	3,577	1,491	5,840	9,244	6,403	9,122	6,418	5,003	6,079	3,949	7,122
Topeka, Kansas	3,764	1,391	8,232	1,581	13,626	8,480	8,753	4,253	7,607	9,475	7,327	1,681	2,236	1,096	16,605	4,488	2,528	4,080	3,562	478
Toronto, Canada	3,120	712	8,560	154	14,964	7,099	8,695	3,578	6,331	8,301	5,997	508	3,542	369	15,153	3,892	1,075	3,377	2,114	1,066
Toulouse, France	6,701	6,658	11,801	6,144	16,409	923	10,564	6,671	1,402	2,992	953	5,969	9,249	6,567	9,017	6,941	5,214	6,575	4,163	7,304
Tours, France	6,669	6,439	11,966	5,896	16,237	1,115	10,801	6,677	1,097	2,919	574	5,686	8,896	6,299	9,331	6,965	4,983	6,567	3,944	7,044
Townsville, Australia	16,727	15,084	12,419	15,108	597	15,050	13,537	17,008	14,567	12,839	15,130	14,808	11,466	14,606	9,405	16,875	15,837	16,997	16,405	14,171
Trenton, New Jersey	2,603	556	8,189	403	15,409	6,991	8,231	3,052	6,336	8,358	5,956	952	3,982	840	14,868	3,373	906	2,850	1,942	1,339
Tripoli, Lebanon	9,789	9,666	14,107	9,087	13,644	2,200	12,525	9,711	2,862	1,458	3,164	8,806	11,591	9,448	6,463	9,948	8,206	9,636	7,184	10,198
Tripoli, Libya	7,808	8,134	12,113	7,658	15,735	1,001	10,628	7,681	2,355	2,744	2,226	7,516	10,814	8,099	7,456	7,895	6,715	7,625	5,660	8,827
Tristan da Cunha (Edinburgh)	8,236	10,775	5,937	11,066	13,078	9,099	4,392	7,748	10,367	10,674	9,991	11,523	13,949	11,476	6,704	7,500	10,592	7,931	10,198	11,569
Trondheim, Norway	7,443	6,394	13,256	5,739	14,677	2,398	12,362	7,592	1,044	2,546	1,327	5,347	7,926	6,003	10,131	7,929	5,002	7,438	4,149	6,735
Trujillo, Peru	3,338	5,025	2,826	5,680	13,610	10,734	3,338	3,239	10,809	12,820	10,272	6,242	6,784	5,730	14,107	2,938	6,053	3,370	6,692	5,301
Truk Island (Moen)	15,102	12,710	14,071	12,515	3,412	13,167	15,635	15,579	12,223	11,036	12,734	12,097	9,210	12,067	10,972	15,730	13,057	15,429	13,452	11,844
Truro, Canada	2,988	1,655	8,889	1,170	16,117	5,892	8,677	3,338	5,258	7,300	4,863	1,241	4,778	1,656	13,862	3,696	219	3,137	846	2,341
Tsingtao, China	13,949	11,622	18,254	11,046	7,307	8,688	19,649	14,317	7,893	6,527	8,444	10,473	9,592	10,866	9,286	14,675	10,974	14,116	10,715	11,164
Tsitsihar, China	12,666	10,334	17,569	9,755	8,276	8,043	18,358	13,044	7,069	6,035	7,591	9,182	8,494	9,581	10,184	13,400	9,695	12,842	9,481	9,898
Tubuai Island (Mataura)	10,309	9,897	6,877	10,393	6,089	17,362	8,532	10,487	16,266	17,235	16,141	10,573	7,453	9,969	14,422	10,311	11,329	10,520	12,383	9,231
Tucson, Arizona	4,868	2,883	8,029	3,157	12,126	9,973	8,939	5,336	9,000	10,730	8,776	3,213	1,187	2,669	18,175	5,489	4,104	5,197	5,133	2,011
Tulsa, Oklahoma	3,641	1,431	7,927	1,747	13,572	8,717	8,485	4,127	7,877	9,768	7,582	1,927	2,275	1,303	16,766	4,341	2,699	3,963	3,748	575
Tunis, Tunisia	7,475	7,669	12,076	7,178	15,956	600	10,663	7,381	1,927	2,684	1,738	7,021	10,302	7,611	7,958	7,615	6,239	7,311	5,184	8,344
Tura, USSR	10,740	8,746	16,595	8,091	10,640	5,810	16,283	11,043	4,735	4,045	5,241	7,528	8,030	8,056	10,196	11,404	7,799	10,852	7,381	8,560
Turin, Italy	7,199	7,036	12,314	6,493	15,891	524	11,050	7,181	1,055	2,470	798	6,277	9,440	6,893	8,759	7,456	5,581	7,082	4,541	7,639
Uberlandia, Brazil	4,503	7,051	3,441	7,501	14,902	9,181	1,983	4,050	9,919	11,384	9,366	8,043	9,924	7,806	10,626	3,731	7,333	4,253	7,378	7,725
Ufa, USSR	10,151	8,977	15,813	8,301	12,385	3,455	14,598	10,278	2,799	1,407	3,364	7,840	9,661	8,483	8,376	10,606	7,652	10,132	6,854	9,169
Ujungpandang, Indonesia	18,469	15,943	15,309	15,473	3,901	11,789	15,792	18,875	11,590	9,651	12,145	14,918	12,878	15,186	7,108	19,228	15,525	18,672	15,241	15,252
Ulaanbaatar, Mongolia	12,606	10,544	18,349	9,905	9,018	7,000	18,046	12,907	6,174	4,889	6,725	9,336	9,298	9,829	9,181	13,269	9,658	12,717	9,243	10,272
Ulan-Ude, USSR	12,182	10,106	17,917	9,467	9,321	6,809	17,705	12,492	5,910	4,762	6,452	8,897	8,916	9,390	9,513	12,854	9,228	12,300	8,832	9,836
Uliastay, Mongolia	12,444	10,581	18,397	9,919	9,529	6,362	17,510	12,695	5,633	4,204	6,195	9,362	9,719	9,903	8,650	13,051	9,565	12,516	9,040	10,413
Uranium City, Canada	5,758	3,212	10,686	2,782	12,828	7,538	11,159	6,223	6,346	7,820	6,272	2,288	2,506	2,453	15,525	6,529	3,226	6,024	3,803	2,669
Urumqi, China	12,555	10,938	18,387	10,261	9,818	5,921	17,020	12,745	5,372	3,702	5,938	9,725	10,425	10,305	7,876	13,088	9,801	12,582	9,163	10,874
Ushuaia, Argentina	8,123	10,263	2,493	10,891	10,589	13,153	2,501	7,795	14,128	15,120	13,601	11,464	11,521	10,987	10,077	7,433	11,092	7,990	11,439	10,560
Vaduz, Liechtenstein	7,336	7,057	12,546	6,493	15,666	631	11,305	7,337	791	2,273	641	6,250	9,338	6,877	8,828	7,621	5,597	7,231	4,570	7,626
Valencia, Spain	6,537	6,716	11,430	6,243	16,750	1,118	10,144	6,467	1,878	3,322	1,434	6,119	9,491	6,691	8,845	6,718	5,298	6,387	4,244	7,414
Valladolid, Spain	6,183	6,281	11,260	5,804	16,952	1,428	10,050	6,139	1,861	3,541	1,339	5,678	9,062	6,250	9,285	6,404	4,859	6,048	3,804	6,974
Valletta, Malta	7,874	8,051	12,375	7,548	15,586	689	10,920	7,775	2,029	2,433	1,949	7,376	10,604	7,974	7,620	8,005	6,614	7,707	5,561	8,711
Valparaiso, Chile	5,746	7,831	677	8,459	12,335	11,935	1,025	5,458	12,528	14,157	11,963	9,031	9,457	8,560	11,823	5,098	8,690	5,645	9,125	8,162
Vancouver, Canada	6,200	3,691	10,172	3,522	11,690	9,016	10,999	6,689	7,811	9,186	7,750	3,199	1,192	3,049	16,853	6,935	4,239	6,508	5,021	2,866
Varna, Bulgaria	8,828	8,505	13,743	7,913	14,365	1,274	12,322	8,807	1,670	1,026	1,997	7,619	10,436	8,263	7,635	9,077	7,046	8,710	6,040	9,012
Venice, Italy	7,564	7,339	12,665	6,780	15,533	395	11,373	7,550	960	2,104	922	6,540	9,620	7,166	8,540	7,826	5,880	7,449	4,850	7,914
Veracruz, Mexico	3,319	2,549	6,128	3,174	13,162	10,054	6,895	3,713	9,431	11,430	9,053	3,572	3,255	2,920	17,059	3,764	4,004	3,630	5,019	2,227
Verona, Italy	7,459	7,247	12,569	6,691	15,632	412	11,286	7,444	964	2,206	863	6,457	9,560	7,081	8,610	7,720	5,789	7,344	4,756	7,829
Victoria, Canada	6,201	3,703	10,109	3,551	11,644	9,103	10,954	6,689	7,901	9,279	7,837	3,242	1,105	3,073	16,944	6,931	4,283	6,511	5,078	2,867
Victoria, Seychelles	13,351	14,224	13,620	13,737	10,329	6,740	12,125	13,034	7,645	5,949	7,894	13,536	16,230	14,154	1,798	13,084	12,802	13,070	11,747	14,896
Vienna, Austria	7,841	7,452	13,064	6,865	15,145	764	11,796	7,853	718	1,747	944	6,585	9,531	7,225	8,583	8,140	5,993	7,743	4,986	7,975
Vientiane, Laos	15,744	13,885	18,263	13,237	6,931	8,708	17,661	15,934	8,440	6,525	8,996	12,671	12,248	13,174	6,702	16,273	12,910	15,773	12,342	13,602
Villahermosa, Mexico	2,991	2,486	5,904	3,142	13,448	9,907	6,599	3,372	9,350	11,378	8,949	3,584	3,588	2,946	16,702	3,411	3,918	3,296	4,905	2,302
Vilnius, USSR	8,350	7,591	13,857	6,955	14,341	1,705	12,680	8,424	858	1,303	1,416	6,594	9,197	7,249	8,850	8,736	6,162	8,294	5,233	7,989
Visby, Sweden	7,874	7,049	13,501	6,411	14,639	1,798	12,425	7,971	552	1,846	1,089	6,049	8,702	6,704	9,358	8,292	5,624	7,833	4,706	7,444
Vitoria, Brazil	5,040	7,607	4,070	7,996	15,031	8,772	2,452	4,563	9,643	10,922	9,110	8,513	10,661	8,346	9,799	4,279	7,715	4,759	7,619	8,341
Vladivostok, USSR	12,981	10,538	17,154	10,006	7,607	8,814	18,439	13,395	7,812	6,816	8,324	9,441	8,331	9,775	10,530	13,739	10,053	13,190	9,946	10,009
Volgograd, USSR	9,806	9,012	15,101	8,361	13,090	2,595	13,729	9,861	2,301	390	2,828	7,964	10,231	8,620	7,788	10,163	7,602	9,738	6,694	9,346
Vologda, USSR	9,059	7,969	14,768	7,301	13,380	2,699	13,672	9,187	1,781	1,334	2,343	6,869	9,030	7,521	8,989	9,517	6,608	9,040	5,779	8,231
Vorkuta, USSR	9,601	7,998	15,552	7,316	12,236	4,170	14,802	9,828	3,070	2,650	3,582	6,800	8,233	7,411	9,824	10,181	6,817	9,654	6,196	8,039
Wake Island	13,040	10,653	13,410	10,491	5,036	12,731	15,104	13,520	11,520	10,939	11,929	10,105	7,146	10,029	12,893	13,688	11,101	13,366	11,627	9,780
Wallis Island	12,722	11,443	9,865	11,701	3,685	16,728	11,479	13,020	15,422	14,990	15,721	11,629	8,078	11,194	13,234	12,932	12,623	12,996	13,581	10,580
Walvis Bay, Namibia	9,742	11,896	8,929	11,883	13,023	7,183	7,330	9,282	8,537	8,174	8,351	12,130	15,520	12,389	4,224	9,161	11,087	9,413	10,291	12,807
Warsaw, Poland	8,113	7,499	13,517	6,881	14,692	1,318	12,305	8,163	627	1,454	1,129	6,553	9,307	7,203	8,763	8,466	6,053	8,040	5,089	7,950
Washington, D.C.	2,564	312	8,032	476	15,238	7,235	8,132	3,029	6,577	8,596	6,200	1,050	3,826	768	15,085	3,336	1,150	2,830	2,186	1,143
Watson Lake, Canada	6,820	4,255	11,348	3,883	11,734	8,159	12,031	7,295	6,876	8,059	6,901	3,410	2,449	3,513	15,633	7,587	4,356	7,099	4,895	3,597

Distances in Kilometers	Road Town, Brit. Virgin Isls.	Roanoke, Virginia	Robinson Crusoe Island, Chile	Rochester, New York	Rockhampton, Australia	Rome, Italy	Rosario, Argentina	Roseau, Dominica	Rostock, East Germany	Rostov-na-Donu, USSR	Rotterdam, Netherlands	Rouyn, Canada	Sacramento, California	Saginaw, Michigan	Saint Denis, Reunion	Saint George's, Grenada	Saint John, Canada	Saint John's, Antigua	Saint John's, Canada	Saint Louis, Missouri
Weimar, East Germany	7,457	6,983	12,838	6,391	15,367	1,014	11,657	7,493	349	2,100	485	6,107	9,071	6,748	9,054	7,792	5,526	7,374	4,527	7,498
Wellington, New Zealand	13,886	13,764	8,813	14,235	3,010	18,549	10,021	13,933	18,094	16,425	18,616	14,352	10,954	13,785	10,721	13,669	15,181	14,023	16,235	13,063
West Berlin, West Germany	7,595	7,035	13,034	6,430	15,163	1,182	11,871	7,645	194	1,967	612	6,125	9,013	6,771	9,091	7,949	5,582	7,522	4,600	7,520
Wewak, Papua New Guinea	16,539	14,221	13,950	14,035	2,316	13,577	15,230	16,995	12,902	11,350	13,455	13,613	10,682	13,587	9,689	17,084	14,559	16,868	14,883	13,345
Whangarei, New Zealand	13,969	13,549	9,210	13,963	2,673	18,307	10,497	14,073	17,546	16,084	18,035	14,020	10,545	13,490	11,040	13,839	14,915	14,140	15,955	12,792
Whitehorse, Canada	7,171	4,606	11,633	4,230	11,440	8,255	12,358	7,646	6,949	8,028	7,008	3,751	2,637	3,863	15,503	7,938	4,686	7,450	5,192	3,943
Wichita, Kansas	3,827	1,537	8,126	1,775	13,466	8,689	8,697	4,315	7,814	9,676	7,535	1,890	2,114	1,299	16,805	4,535	2,725	4,147	3,763	634
Willemstad, Curacao	841	2,995	5,171	3,540	15,683	8,416	5,064	889	8,345	10,391	7,822	4,112	5,944	3,758	14,047	784	3,685	943	4,213	3,612
Wiluna, Australia	18,981	17,786	13,042	17,569	3,071	13,351	13,413	18,743	13,523	11,463	14,035	17,086	14,191	17,147	6,567	18,381	17,861	18,932	17,598	16,893
Windhoek, Namibia	9,976	12,094	9,174	12,060	12,859	7,155	7,584	9,520	8,507	8,058	8,344	12,289	15,719	12,569	3,963	9,405	11,247	9,647	10,427	13,007
Windsor, Canada	3,166	617	8,419	453	14,692	7,428	8,640	3,639	6,646	8,601	6,319	730	3,262	147	15,482	3,935	1,402	3,443	2,446	733
Winnipeg, Canada	4,531	1,965	9,426	1,669	13,549	7,754	9,857	5,009	6,734	8,474	6,532	1,335	2,298	1,237	15,989	5,296	2,377	4,815	3,231	1,368
Winston-Salem, North Carolina	2,487	133	7,721	816	14,979	7,647	7,911	2,969	6,998	9,015	6,619	1,352	3,635	873	15,418	3,247	1,570	2,780	2,597	924
Wroclaw, Poland	7,856	7,330	13,218	6,726	14,993	1,080	12,003	7,894	469	1,701	874	6,420	9,281	7,066	8,813	8,193	5,877	7,775	4,892	7,815
Wuhan, China	14,578	12,349	18,743	11,750	7,116	8,686	19,476	14,907	8,045	6,469	8,608	11,176	10,420	11,602	8,482	15,268	11,605	14,712	11,252	11,937
Wyndham, Australia	18,640	16,349	13,869	16,090	2,507	13,259	14,567	19,016	13,075	11,138	13,632	15,612	12,834	15,677	7,648	18,903	16,447	18,956	16,444	15,489
Xi'an, China	14,131	12,032	19,306	11,406	7,751	8,037	19,049	14,425	7,412	5,820	7,976	10,833	10,417	11,303	8,321	14,785	11,182	14,237	10,758	11,700
Xining, China	13,745	11,822	19,669	11,170	8,383	7,363	18,370	13,995	6,791	5,141	7,357	10,606	10,573	11,121	8,010	14,350	10,854	13,817	10,342	11,585
Yakutsk, USSR	10,998	8,683	16,264	8,094	9,645	7,196	16,692	11,380	6,026	5,531	6,484	7,520	7,180	7,936	11,242	11,735	8,030	11,177	7,855	8,292
Yanji, China	13,062	10,643	17,350	10,099	7,646	8,705	18,595	13,467	7,729	6,682	8,248	9,531	8,498	9,881	10,342	13,815	10,119	13,263	9,982	10,132
Yaounde, Cameroon	8,420	9,885	10,287	9,650	15,120	4,214	8,600	8,074	5,568	5,515	5,366	9,732	13,283	10,159	5,518	8,111	8,734	8,125	7,781	10,760
Yap Island (Colonia)	16,041	13,490	15,395	13,146	3,881	12,080	16,781	16,528	11,342	9,869	11,893	12,646	10,247	12,770	9,639	16,775	13,474	16,342	13,592	12,708
Yaraka, Australia	16,983	15,650	12,102	15,729	673	15,215	13,091	17,168	14,912	13,059	15,477	15,458	12,057	15,221	8,933	16,961	16,494	17,206	17,089	14,742
Yarmouth, Canada	2,818	1,376	8,676	932	15,984	6,171	8,521	3,195	5,540	7,580	5,146	1,110	4,594	1,436	14,103	3,548	159	2,991	1,121	2,092
Yellowknife, Canada	6,189	3,652	11,114	3,202	12,546	7,507	11,606	6,651	6,268	7,628	6,240	2,690	2,699	2,891	15,321	6,961	3,588	6,451	4,084	3,115
Yerevan, USSR	10,235	9,731	15,010	9,103	12,973	2,683	13,474	10,224	2,863	873	3,307	8,746	11,167	9,401	6,853	10,495	8,290	10,124	7,326	10,141
Yinchuan, China	13,634	11,594	19,303	10,956	8,254	7,567	18,696	13,918	6,907	5,364	7,470	10,386	10,179	10,876	8,444	14,278	10,699	13,732	10,251	11,305
Yogyakarta, Indonesia	18,713	16,581	15,318	16,011	4,615	11,239	15,397	18,800	11,244	9,214	11,775	15,437	13,825	15,820	6,068	19,046	15,838	18,686	15,317	16,024
York, United Kingdom	6,635	6,078	12,214	5,489	15,882	1,668	11,186	6,707	872	2,945	437	5,217	8,284	5,853	9,886	7,020	4,620	6,575	3,624	6,603
Yumen, China	13,299	11,463	19,256	10,801	8,885	6,871	17,947	13,532	6,289	4,652	6,855	10,244	10,450	10,781	8,027	13,884	10,441	13,358	9,893	11,280
Yutian, China	12,941	11,582	18,225	10,899	9,820	5,826	16,582	13,062	5,515	3,613	6,069	10,387	11,320	10,994	6,960	13,384	10,351	12,919	9,617	11,606
Yuzhno-Sakhalinsk, USSR	12,263	9,757	16,240	9,265	7,828	9,010	17,500	12,703	7,881	7,183	8,349	8,712	7,391	8,994	11,477	13,033	9,408	12,499	9,426	9,171
Zagreb, Yugoslavia	7,844	7,565	12,942	6,993	15,250	517	11,632	7,834	962	1,819	1,082	6,735	9,743	7,368	8,389	8,111	6,105	7,732	5,084	8,117
Zahedan, Iran	12,124	11,564	16,202	10,915	11,224	4,525	14,515	12,088	4,749	2,684	5,209	10,515	12,463	11,170	5,603	12,343	10,145	11,999	9,207	12,708
Zamboanga, Philippines	17,108	14,610	16,352	14,118	4,560	11,091	17,107	17,521	10,662	8,874	11,228	13,560	11,766	13,849	7,898	17,868	14,171	17,316	13,950	13,971
Zanzibar, Tanzania	11,687	12,990	12,162	12,638	11,890	5,974	10,556	11,330	7,139	5,915	7,231	12,585	15,926	13,119	2,393	11,346	11,687	11,388	10,655	13,802
Zaragoza, Spain	6,501	6,575	11,524	6,085	16,680	1,111	10,276	6,453	1,687	3,253	1,214	5,941	9,284	6,523	9,027	6,716	5,145	6,364	4,090	7,253
Zashiversk, USSR	10,221	7,855	15,405	7,281	10,093	7,177	15,881	10,622	5,914	5,767	6,313	6,709	6,350	7,102	12,009	10,971	7,274	10,418	7,184	7,439
Zhengzhou, China	14,114	11,908	18,866	11,302	7,519	8,338	19,464	14,441	7,644	6,138	8,205	10,727	10,103	11,165	8,702	14,803	11,143	14,247	10,787	11,520
Zurich, Switzerland	7,249	6,969	12,477	6,407	15,736	690	11,248	7,252	793	2,354	578	6,167	9,268	6,793	8,904	7,537	5,510	7,145	4,482	7,541

Distances in Kilometers	Saint Paul, Minnesota	Saint Peter Port, UK	Saipan (Susupe)	Salalah, Oman	Salem, Oregon	Salt Lake City, Utah	Salta, Argentina	Salto, Uruguay	Salvador, Brazil	Salzburg, Austria	Samsun, Turkey	San Antonio, Texas	San Cristobal, Venezuela	San Diego, California	San Francisco, California	San Jose, Costa Rica	San Juan, Argentina	San Juan, Puerto Rico	San Luis Potosi, Mexico	San Marino, San Marino
Saint Peter Port, UK	6,450	0	12,201	6,193	8,069	7,867	10,303	10,498	7,763	1,160	3,138	7,987	7,893	8,857	8,686	8,566	11,086	6,567	8,753	1,299
Saipan (Susupe)	11,106	12,201	0	9,700	8,933	9,935	16,612	17,017	19,513	11,607	10,458	11,551	15,134	9,764	9,156	13,877	16,107	14,920	11,667	11,933
Salalah, Oman	12,388	6,193	9,700	0	13,140	13,450	13,728	13,049	10,705	5,059	3,185	14,092	13,522	14,426	13,931	14,546	14,052	12,397	14,902	4,909
Salem, Oregon	2,349	8,069	8,933	13,140	0	1,022	9,681	10,709	10,594	8,874	10,236	2,758	6,381	1,449	797	5,376	10,106	5,991	3,231	9,226
Salt Lake City, Utah	1,600	7,867	9,935	13,450	1,022	0	8,702	9,723	9,588	8,798	10,372	1,748	5,359	1,009	967	4,375	9,163	4,999	2,304	9,105
Salta, Argentina	8,218	10,303	16,612	13,728	9,681	8,702	0	1,034	3,112	11,201	12,732	6,963	3,676	8,403	9,133	4,343	808	4,785	6,461	10,976
Salto, Uruguay	9,171	10,498	17,017	13,049	10,709	9,723	1,034	0	2,849	11,264	12,561	7,980	4,591	9,437	10,167	5,354	1,003	5,585	7,493	10,982
Salvador, Brazil	8,442	7,763	19,513	10,705	10,594	9,588	3,112	2,849	0	8,443	9,726	7,964	4,378	9,749	10,360	5,638	3,691	4,613	7,846	8,144
Salzburg, Austria	7,468	1,160	11,607	5,059	8,874	8,798	11,201	11,264	8,443	0	1,979	9,073	9,022	9,803	9,551	9,725	11,954	7,708	9,859	434
Samsun, Turkey	9,212	3,138	10,458	3,185	10,236	10,372	12,732	12,561	9,726	1,979	0	10,908	10,965	11,374	10,988	11,704	13,404	9,670	11,722	1,973
San Antonio, Texas	1,787	7,987	11,551	14,092	2,758	1,748	6,963	7,980	7,964	9,073	10,908	0	3,646	1,815	2,397	2,628	7,455	3,498	843	9,285
San Cristobal, Venezuela	4,586	7,893	15,134	13,522	6,381	5,359	3,676	4,591	4,378	9,022	10,965	3,646	0	5,387	6,032	1,325	4,367	1,356	3,468	8,993
San Diego, California	2,477	8,857	9,764	14,426	1,449	1,009	8,403	9,437	9,749	9,803	11,374	1,815	5,387	0	738	4,226	8,759	5,311	1,977	10,105
San Francisco, California	2,563	8,686	9,156	13,931	797	967	9,133	10,167	10,360	9,551	10,988	2,397	6,032	738	0	4,917	9,497	5,835	2,686	9,885
San Jose, Costa Rica	3,976	8,566	13,877	14,546	5,376	4,375	4,343	5,354	5,638	9,725	11,704	2,628	1,325	4,226	4,917	0	4,880	2,155	2,254	9,771
San Juan, Argentina	8,828	11,086	16,107	14,052	10,106	9,163	808	1,003	3,691	11,954	13,404	7,455	4,367	8,759	9,497	4,880	0	5,539	6,876	11,711
San Juan, Puerto Rico	3,857	6,567	14,920	12,397	5,991	4,999	4,785	5,585	4,613	7,708	9,670	3,498	1,356	5,311	5,835	2,155	5,539	0	3,657	7,706
San Luis Potosi, Mexico	2,629	8,753	11,667	14,902	3,231	2,304	6,461	7,493	7,846	9,859	11,722	843	3,468	1,977	2,686	2,254	6,876	3,657	0	10,051
San Marino, San Marino	7,729	1,299	11,933	4,909	9,226	9,105	10,976	10,982	8,144	434	1,973	9,285	8,993	10,105	9,885	9,771	11,711	7,706	10,051	0
San Miguel de Tucuman, Argen.	8,436	10,475	16,575	13,723	9,873	8,899	226	868	3,177	11,354	12,846	7,164	3,900	8,581	9,313	4,548	613	5,011	6,648	11,119
San Salvador, El Salvador	3,484	8,625	13,193	14,751	4,710	3,722	4,980	6,002	6,321	9,783	11,753	1,987	1,968	3,533	4,229	696	5,471	2,523	1,559	9,875
Sanaa, Yemen	12,063	5,659	10,767	1,074	13,205	13,324	12,670	12,027	9,632	4,597	2,973	13,645	12,572	14,331	13,961	13,680	13,028	11,526	14,395	4,361
Santa Cruz, Bolivia	7,581	9,536	16,940	13,401	9,210	8,206	808	1,593	2,697	10,467	12,078	6,458	2,998	8,014	8,727	3,834	1,614	4,025	6,042	10,264
Santa Cruz, Tenerife	6,846	2,607	14,808	7,241	9,025	8,445	7,902	7,963	5,175	3,311	4,933	7,832	6,290	9,277	9,401	7,333	8,645	5,179	8,385	3,075
Santa Fe, New Mexico	1,497	7,948	10,624	13,809	1,774	766	7,936	8,957	8,894	8,956	10,657	985	4,616	1,084	1,488	3,610	8,405	4,347	1,575	9,224
Santa Rosa, Argentina	9,487	11,306	16,216	13,640	10,791	9,849	1,316	823	3,669	12,086	13,367	8,138	4,983	9,441	10,178	5,554	686	6,100	7,562	11,804
Santa Rosalia, Mexico	2,596	9,044	10,395	14,888	2,177	1,491	7,650	8,685	9,118	10,061	11,753	1,371	4,740	760	1,498	3,528	7,999	4,810	1,278	10,325
Santarem, Brazil	6,479	7,610	17,382	12,097	8,518	7,502	2,728	3,223	2,131	8,571	10,276	5,844	2,250	7,620	8,242	3,533	3,533	2,629	5,718	8,395
Santiago del Estero, Argentina	8,569	10,508	16,633	13,635	10,015	9,041	352	729	3,137	11,369	12,831	7,305	4,026	8,724	9,456	4,688	585	5,121	6,791	11,126
Santiago, Chile	8,973	11,378	15,844	14,243	10,165	9,241	1,088	1,216	3,968	12,247	13,687	7,552	4,565	8,795	9,533	5,007	293	5,766	6,944	12,003
Santo Domingo, Dominican Rep.	3,640	6,840	14,629	12,749	5,698	4,694	4,809	5,662	4,896	7,990	9,961	3,143	1,210	4,958	5,503	1,797	5,535	400	3,266	8,008
Sao Paulo de Olivenca, Brazil	5,879	8,618	16,035	13,626	7,581	6,565	2,388	3,294	3,495	9,683	11,528	4,824	1,298	6,476	7,161	2,250	3,109	2,442	4,504	9,577
Sao Paulo, Brazil	8,930	9,186	18,432	11,818	10,822	9,801	1,914	1,418	1,447	9,890	11,143	8,072	4,445	9,734	10,422	5,508	2,332	5,107	7,758	9,591
Sao Tome, Sao Tome & Principe	10,758	5,515	15,207	5,507	12,981	12,356	8,232	7,650	5,206	5,295	5,426	11,470	8,797	13,108	13,321	10,102	8,638	8,197	11,825	4,861
Sapporo, Japan	8,869	9,171	3,121	8,520	7,184	8,181	16,844	17,878	16,672	8,740	8,033	9,929	13,438	8,441	7,712	12,557	17,102	12,640	10,389	9,117
Sarajevo, Yugoslavia	8,075	1,714	11,575	4,479	9,460	9,402	11,409	11,375	8,529	608	1,495	9,672	9,470	10,408	10,146	10,237	12,132	8,181	10,453	478
Saratov, USSR	8,615	3,390	9,357	3,901	9,260	9,555	13,595	13,602	10,756	2,397	1,362	10,388	11,209	10,525	10,043	11,692	14,339	9,858	11,230	2,630
Saskatoon, Canada	1,275	6,675	9,851	12,125	1,445	1,325	9,416	10,393	9,704	7,544	9,058	2,608	5,830	2,317	2,014	5,104	9,984	5,131	3,361	7,872
Schefferville, Canada	2,164	4,286	11,669	10,306	4,067	3,640	8,818	9,586	7,970	5,317	7,122	3,786	5,238	4,600	4,537	5,205	9,567	4,033	4,605	5,567
Seattle, Washington	2,259	7,799	8,925	12,842	300	1,128	9,829	10,851	10,608	8,589	9,937	2,874	6,458	1,709	1,091	5,502	10,281	5,995	3,407	8,945
Sendai, Japan	9,326	9,647	2,603	8,586	7,555	8,564	17,127	18,143	17,205	9,169	8,351	10,311	13,871	8,760	8,040	12,929	17,249	13,126	10,726	9,535
Seoul, South Korea	10,022	9,167	3,094	7,388	8,491	9,471	18,172	19,188	16,930	8,516	7,437	11,212	14,606	9,782	9,049	13,837	18,452	13,653	11,713	8,839
Sept-Iles, Canada	2,080	4,450	12,117	10,571	4,199	3,646	8,306	9,075	7,509	5,532	7,399	3,542	4,736	4,557	4,584	4,753	9,056	3,521	4,332	5,747
Sevastopol, USSR	8,779	2,767	10,507	3,615	9,820	9,942	12,586	12,489	9,641	1,617	434	10,478	10,636	10,945	10,568	11,330	13,289	9,325	11,295	1,679
Seville, Spain	7,000	1,369	13,484	6,255	8,922	8,540	9,273	9,336	6,531	1,934	3,638	8,297	7,396	9,475	9,440	8,299	10,021	6,170	8,969	1,716
Shanghai, China	10,891	9,505	3,045	6,918	9,370	10,353	19,049	19,955	17,141	8,732	7,425	12,094	15,467	10,647	9,916	14,720	19,088	14,461	12,588	9,012
Sheffield, United Kingdom	6,277	442	11,796	6,246	7,780	7,639	10,614	10,854	8,152	1,198	3,112	7,875	8,044	8,639	8,425	8,637	11,405	6,701	8,664	1,466
Shenyang, China	9,734	8,607	3,647	7,069	8,352	9,304	17,951	18,842	16,370	7,960	6,923	11,025	14,290	9,696	8,958	13,628	18,455	13,261	11,583	8,288
Shiraz, Iran	11,048	5,085	9,495	1,405	11,738	12,052	13,930	13,469	10,817	3,926	1,955	12,790	12,816	13,023	12,528	13,637	14,438	11,563	13,620	3,867
Sibiu, Romania	8,219	2,035	11,079	4,230	9,449	9,471	11,909	11,877	9,030	876	1,104	9,872	9,888	10,480	10,165	10,601	12,634	8,581	10,673	946
Singapore	14,618	11,078	4,848	5,716	13,120	14,120	17,165	16,170	15,689	9,966	8,052	15,867	18,919	14,303	13,598	18,495	16,563	17,566	16,280	10,024
Sioux Falls, South Dakota	330	6,772	10,941	12,675	2,097	1,288	8,215	9,188	8,599	7,781	9,505	1,575	4,627	2,147	2,254	3,921	8,796	3,992	2,405	8,047
Skelleftea, Sweden	6,573	2,195	10,008	5,858	7,444	7,608	12,300	12,616	9,941	1,948	2,792	8,337	9,380	8,603	8,197	9,714	13,104	8,026	9,178	2,381
Skopje, Yugoslavia	8,394	2,033	11,494	4,160	9,751	9,711	11,568	11,486	8,636	927	1,238	9,995	9,744	10,718	10,445	10,536	12,273	8,467	10,775	765
Socotra Island (Tamrida)	12,822	6,554	9,834	481	13,620	13,918	13,554	12,816	10,597	5,438	3,610	14,501	13,674	14,898	14,411	14,767	13,816	12,613	15,296	5,260
Sofia, Bulgaria	8,437	2,124	11,326	4,075	9,742	9,730	11,736	11,654	8,805	986	1,089	10,057	9,882	10,738	10,446	10,655	12,442	8,597	10,845	890
Songkhla, Thailand	14,070	10,343	4,996	5,164	12,781	13,748	17,566	16,533	15,515	9,240	7,344	15,471	18,175	14,061	13,333	18,042	17,087	16,820	16,005	9,311
Sorong, Indonesia	13,478	13,072	2,383	8,680	11,313	12,311	16,653	16,305	18,111	12,150	10,488	13,887	17,321	12,079	11,505	15,999	15,862	17,303	13,909	12,345
South Georgia Island	12,217	11,932	15,661	11,579	13,670	12,719	4,039	3,050	4,581	12,240	12,659	10,994	7,631	12,312	13,049	8,381	3,564	8,530	10,440	11,838
South Pole	14,981	15,484	11,676	11,884	14,980	14,515	7,261	6,530	8,568	15,300	14,576	13,258	10,862	13,622	14,184	11,101	6,513	12,046	12,452	14,869
South Sandwich Islands	12,936	12,085	15,232	11,044	14,416	13,467	4,782	3,784	5,071	12,253	12,429	11,740	8,350	13,051	13,788	9,125	4,311	9,205	11,187	11,834
Split, Yugoslavia	7,989	1,593	11,721	4,602	9,419	9,336	11,248	11,221	8,376	545	1,653	9,569	9,314	10,340	10,095	10,092	11,972	8,029	10,343	323
Spokane, Washington	1,889	7,563	9,283	12,793	529	886	9,560	10,575	10,252	8,394	9,817	2,597	6,137	1,661	1,173	5,222	10,040	5,639	3,189	8,737
Spoleto, Italy	7,835	1,393	12,006	4,836	9,351	9,220	10,938	10,923	8,081	564	1,955	9,378	9,019	10,219	10,006	9,819	11,666	7,743	10,139	133
Springbok, South Africa	13,864	8,994	14,472	6,464	16,212	15,354	8,084	7,126	6,074	8,593	8,082	13,946	10,449	15,761	16,267	11,707	8,047	10,455	13,916	8,167
Springfield, Illinois	638	6,604	11,662	12,685	2,788	1,889	7,580	8,533	7,878	7,676	9,501	1,407	3,951	2,582	2,840	3,355	8,194	3,271	2,232	7,900
Springfield, Massachusetts	1,683	5,311	12,555	11,490	4,025	3,259	7,442	8,273	7,026	6,431	8,343	2,716	3,804	4,032	4,226	3,737	8,164	2,691	3,446	6,608
Srinagar, India	11,168	6,360	7,339	2,803	11,070	11,690	16,060	15,630	12,955	5,271	3,458	12,941	14,225	12,506	11,853	14,652	16,600	12,875	13,765	5,380
Stanley, Falkland Islands	11,232	12,372	15,444	12,985	12,397	11,500	3,057	2,257	4,632	12,920	13,714	9,826	6,731	10,993	11,726	7,279	2,404	7,814	9,197	12,562
Stara Zagora, Bulgaria	8,582	2,304	11,183	3,904	9,842	9,854	11,906	11,808	8,959	1,156	897	10,216	10,074	10,863	10,555	10,844	12,606	8,788	11,009	1,082
Stockholm, Sweden	6,857	1,719	10,506	5,531	7,912	7,999	11,985	12,215	9,477	1,325	2,376	8,587	9,285	9,003	8,644	9,742	12,777	7,930	9,417	1,757
Stornoway, United Kingdom	5,750	1,007	11,483	6,698	7,176	7,067	10,690	11,026	8,418	1,732	3,522	7,397	7,876	8,071	7,833	8,354	11,493	6,520	8,204	2,053
Strasbourg, France	7,114	758	11,821	5,451	8,594	8,475	10,889	10,998	8,200	402	2,381	8,697	8,629	9,476	9,251	9,323	11,654	7,312	9,476	633
Stuttgart, West Germany	7,182	858	11,734	5,363	8,634	8,531	10,991	11,095	8,292	305	2,281	8,776	8,735	9,534	9,299	9,424	11,755	7,417	9,559	595
Subic, Philippines	12,578	10,949	2,739	7,050	10,830	11,845	18,766	18,168	17,731	10,032	8,430	13,588	17,154	11,962	11,265	16,182	17,962	16,252	13,939	10,240
Suchow, China	10,717	8,996	3,559	6,514	9,346	10,302	18,925	19,465	16,616	8,210	6,905	12,025	15,249	10,675	9,938	14,627	19,409	14,158	12,577	8,488
Sucre, Bolivia	7,626	9,777	16,712	13,643	9,181	8,186	637	1,553	2,939	10,717	12,339	6,439	3,061	7,952	8,672	3,811	1,422	4,149	5,988	10,518
Sudbury, Canada	956	5,594	11,739	11,663	3,238	2,555	8,049	8,931	7,835	6,656	8,479	2,429	4,374	3,422	3,514	4,064	8,733	3,396	3,247	6,887
Suez, Egypt	10,058	3,653	11,297	2,621	11,350	11,364	12,070	11,721	8,969	2,590	1,301	11,639	10,990	12,372	12,069	11,940	12,646	9,804	12,403	2,354
Sundsvall, Sweden	6,606	1,885	10,317	5,793	7,594	7,707	12,053	12,337	9,642	1,645	2,666	8,352	9,222	8,708	8,333	9,614	12,853	7,866	9,188	2,079
Surabaya, Indonesia	15,144	12,434	4,401	6,988	13,232	14,253	16,455	15,618	16,140	11,329	9,419	15,934	19,438	14,164	13,538	18,160	15,711	18,758	16,055	11,390
Suva, Fiji	11,297	16,530	5,140	14,145	9,153	9,699	11,635	11,881	14,704	16,459	15,598	10,344	12,324	8,865	8,748	11,142	11,014	13,251	9,839	16,861
Sverdlovsk, USSR	8,459	4,147	8,315	4,457	8,718	9,165	14,450	14,583	11,760	3,320	2,453	10,245	11,663	10,078	9,515	11,929	15,231	10,310	11,083	3,621
Svobodnyy, USSR	8,619	7,893	4,317	7,444	7,341	8,262	16,834	17,726	15,579	7,400	6,684	9,961	13,166	8,726	7,990	12,540	17,415	12,142	10,559	7,770
Sydney, Australia	14,498	17,252	5,457	11,690	12,273	12,897	12,452	12,163	14,718	16,225	14,345	13,525	14,718	12,083	11,937	13,817	11,658	15,953	12,949	16,316
Sydney, Canada	2,555	4,228	12,738	10,416	4,778	4,153	7,873	8,589	6,900	5,358	7,289	3,801	4,408	5,011	5,108	4,612	8,644	3,118	4,533	5,523
Syktyvkar, USSR	7,751	3,508	8,793	4,966	8,173	8,544	13,779	14,004	11,231	2,821	2,467	9,538	10,894	9,487	8,965	11,159	14,574	9,543	10,380	3,178
Szeged, Hungary	7,974	1,728	11,301	4,508	9,276	9,259	11,635	11,632	8,790	568	1,411	9,607	9,576	10,267	9,977	10,292	12,369	8,268	10,401	660
Szombathely, Hungary	7,707	1,437	11,447	4,794	9,059	9,014	11,422	11,456	8,623	277	1,702	9,328	9,295	10,021	9,749	10,002	12,167	7,983	10,119	491
Tabriz, Iran	9,951	4,051	9,786	2,458	10,748	10,998	13,512	13,240	10,446	2,894	925	11,687	11,890	11,983	11,526	12,616	14,137	10,594	12,517	2,898
Tacheng, China	9,839	6,017	6,728	4,234	9,533	10,201	16,303	16,282	13,435	5,104	3,731	11,568	13,489	10,977	10,308	13,596	17,054	12,147	12,364	5,344
Tahiti (Papeete)	8,967	15,402	7,969	17,519	7,422	7,537	8,643	9,164	11,739	16,296	17,313	7,554	8,947	6,544	6,750	7,814	8,185	9,960	6,876	16,634
Taipei, Taiwan	11,499	10,078	2,754	6,996	9,878	10,877	19,333	19,301	17,539	9,253	7,834	12,625	16,085	11,101	10,381	15,253	18,805	15,121	13,066	9,510
Taiyuan, China	10,480	8,427	4,117	6,115	9,279	10,199	18,542	18,891	16,042	7,633	6,341	11,889	14,929	10,655	9,917	14,440	19,296	13,768	12,498	7,911
Tallahasee, Florida	1,785	6,938	12,664	13,130	3,732	2,735	6,435	7,387	6,863	8,073	10,001	1,376	2,807	3,118	3,585	2,271	7,059	2,264	1,901	8,228
Tallinn, USSR	7,127	2,067	10,197	5,276	8,068	8,211	12,354	12,563	9,804	1,503	2,172	8,874	9,662	9,210	8,817	10,101	13,144	8,306	9,710	1,915
Tamanrasset, Algeria	8,897	3,043	13,986	5,106	10,878	10,464	9,292	9,038	6,221	2,855	3,530	10,052	8,433	11,371	11,381	9,553	9,912	7,410	10,640	2,429
Tampa, Florida	2,109	7,000	12,972	13,188	4,042	3,037	6,114	7,062	6,553	8,146	10,094	1,575	2,480	3,364	3,864	2,002	6,747	1,971	1,975	8,279
Tampere, Finland	6,924	2,111	10,110	5,490	7,834	7,987	12,353	12,602	9,871	1,670	2,404	8,679	9,569	8,984	8,585	9,966	13,148	8,213	9,516	2,093
Tanami, Australia	15,217	14,688	4,263	9,220	12,897	13,808	14,791	14,262	16,141	13,614	11,725	15,076	17,303	13,311	12,890	16,240	13,984	18,362	14,783	13,694

Distances in Kilometers	Saint Paul, Minnesota	Saint Peter Port, UK	Saipan (Susupe)	Salalah, Oman	Salem, Oregon	Salt Lake City, Utah	Salta, Argentina	Salto, Uruguay	Salvador, Brazil	Salzburg, Austria	Samsun, Turkey	San Antonio, Texas	San Cristobal, Venezuela	San Diego, California	San Francisco, California	San Jose, Costa Rica	San Juan, Argentina	San Juan, Puerto Rico	San Luis Potosi, Mexico	San Marino, San Marino
Tangier, Morocco	7,120	1,539	13,623	6,228	9,067	8,669	9,178	9,218	6,404	2,046	3,687	8,388	7,388	9,597	9,576	8,319	9,919	6,181	9,047	1,798
Tarawa (Betio)	10,219	14,359	3,357	13,026	7,886	8,668	13,255	13,734	16,336	14,223	13,580	9,803	12,733	8,059	7,711	11,415	12,777	13,213	9,557	14,630
Tashkent, USSR	10,289	5,481	7,787	3,065	10,370	10,913	15,475	15,239	12,439	4,427	2,744	12,071	13,308	11,779	11,164	13,712	16,130	11,955	12,906	4,578
Tbilisi, USSR	9,534	3,725	9,787	2,880	10,331	10,575	13,433	13,238	10,412	2,581	704	11,276	11,602	11,560	11,108	12,276	14,096	10,289	12,108	2,635
Tegucigalpa, Honduras	3,465	8,449	13,365	14,556	4,803	3,802	4,910	5,925	6,149	9,608	11,581	2,056	1,780	3,667	4,351	573	5,430	2,305	1,706	9,692
Tehran, Iran	10,392	4,579	9,422	2,085	11,060	11,373	13,931	13,593	10,839	3,424	1,455	12,145	12,419	12,343	11,849	13,143	14,520	11,125	12,981	3,426
Tel Aviv, Israel	9,986	3,640	11,007	2,565	11,187	11,247	12,342	12,015	9,249	2,533	1,032	11,606	11,133	12,255	11,920	12,039	12,931	9,919	12,388	2,347
Telegraph Creek, Canada	2,960	7,213	8,187	11,690	1,546	2,349	10,991	11,994	11,376	7,835	8,951	4,040	7,479	2,993	2,327	6,648	11,494	6,816	4,653	8,229
Teresina, Brazil	7,459	7,184	18,565	10,916	9,641	8,644	3,254	3,314	993	7,990	9,481	7,062	3,563	8,865	9,447	4,868	3,971	3,650	7,012	7,740
Ternate, Indonesia	13,564	12,684	2,564	8,215	11,475	12,486	17,020	16,573	17,967	11,735	10,043	14,115	17,656	12,324	11,720	16,350	16,218	17,421	14,201	11,917
The Valley, Anguilla	4,082	6,382	15,175	12,130	6,260	5,278	4,745	5,497	4,365	7,513	9,463	3,808	1,510	5,618	6,128	2,439	5,518	326	3,981	7,493
Thessaloniki, Greece	8,589	2,218	11,479	3,976	9,939	9,905	11,629	11,515	8,667	1,121	1,129	10,187	9,888	10,912	10,636	10,699	12,322	8,619	10,965	936
Thimphu, Bhutan	11,974	7,890	5,920	3,836	11,322	12,124	17,530	16,877	14,430	6,834	5,055	13,642	15,648	12,760	12,040	15,806	17,877	14,293	14,389	6,964
Thunder Bay, Canada	480	5,986	11,124	11,908	2,587	1,974	8,449	9,373	8,441	6,993	8,732	2,248	4,783	2,904	2,913	4,293	9,093	3,926	3,092	7,260
Tientsin, China	10,213	8,555	3,848	6,530	8,921	9,858	18,395	19,044	16,259	7,818	6,623	11,566	14,723	10,280	9,542	14,146	19,021	13,619	12,149	8,116
Tijuana, Mexico	2,480	8,866	9,782	14,443	1,472	1,021	8,380	9,414	9,731	9,814	11,389	1,800	5,368	24	761	4,205	8,736	5,297	1,956	10,114
Tiksi, USSR	6,663	6,043	6,373	7,685	5,921	6,673	14,723	15,512	13,437	5,840	5,796	8,219	11,063	7,370	6,682	10,638	15,428	9,950	8,939	6,260
Timbuktu, Mali	8,718	3,626	15,095	6,063	10,889	10,318	8,181	7,926	5,106	3,742	4,637	9,626	7,563	11,136	11,274	8,761	8,797	6,665	10,113	3,345
Tindouf, Algeria	7,514	2,462	14,497	6,457	9,615	9,104	8,451	8,407	5,567	2,889	4,301	8,586	7,067	9,972	10,046	8,128	9,161	5,975	9,162	2,576
Tirane, Albania	8,357	1,960	11,649	4,240	9,760	9,696	11,413	11,330	8,480	898	1,380	9,939	9,618	10,701	10,445	10,427	12,117	8,348	10,711	669
Tokyo, Japan	9,615	9,868	2,353	8,546	7,816	8,828	17,326	18,314	17,482	9,354	8,462	10,573	14,150	8,998	8,284	13,185	17,371	13,422	10,970	9,710
Toledo, Spain	6,969	1,071	13,159	6,110	8,817	8,484	9,576	9,654	6,854	1,625	3,389	8,332	7,605	9,437	9,366	8,465	10,329	6,353	9,029	1,437
Topeka, Kansas	689	7,045	11,270	13,053	2,347	1,397	7,737	8,720	8,261	8,091	9,871	1,099	4,184	2,057	2,332	3,426	8,305	3,650	1,941	8,334
Toronto, Canada	1,102	5,668	12,049	11,795	3,444	2,686	7,712	8,592	7,520	6,757	8,619	2,319	4,039	3,490	3,652	3,766	8,400	3,058	3,107	6,966
Toulouse, France	7,077	718	12,559	5,738	8,768	8,531	10,186	10,268	7,464	1,015	2,862	8,547	8,104	9,512	9,370	8,897	10,942	6,821	9,285	889
Tours, France	6,777	331	12,257	5,903	8,397	8,198	10,368	10,510	7,737	929	2,896	8,301	8,093	9,188	9,016	8,811	11,140	6,781	9,060	995
Townsville, Australia	13,856	15,692	3,807	10,900	11,510	12,321	14,022	13,814	16,393	14,797	13,092	13,389	15,633	11,694	11,365	14,475	13,246	16,570	13,023	14,985
Trenton, New Jersey	1,589	5,580	12,590	11,763	3,938	3,124	7,262	8,115	6,980	6,704	8,619	2,468	3,605	3,851	4,087	3,480	7,971	2,551	3,182	6,876
Tripoli, Lebanon	9,823	3,542	10,808	2,652	10,961	11,050	12,511	12,219	9,432	2,408	762	11,471	11,156	12,057	11,702	12,016	13,121	9,916	12,265	2,267
Tripoli, Libya	8,633	2,252	12,688	4,457	10,320	10,099	10,490	10,328	7,478	1,655	2,250	10,048	9,123	11,077	10,935	10,089	11,154	7,945	10,751	1,225
Tristan da Cunha (Edinburgh)	12,167	9,630	16,759	9,170	14,304	13,288	5,187	4,215	3,731	9,730	9,988	11,606	7,961	13,320	13,990	9,096	5,137	8,342	11,350	9,309
Trondheim, Norway	6,257	1,741	10,488	6,135	7,312	7,388	11,766	12,093	9,443	1,746	2,986	7,996	8,872	8,393	8,039	9,248	12,570	7,516	8,830	2,174
Trujillo, Peru	6,044	9,727	15,103	14,861	7,341	6,373	2,345	3,378	4,463	10,827	12,717	4,648	1,912	6,061	6,789	2,073	2,813	3,265	4,117	10,751
Truk Island (Moen)	11,339	13,233	1,086	10,597	9,046	10,000	15,625	15,944	18,737	12,681	11,537	11,478	14,859	9,663	9,135	13,542	15,061	14,967	11,448	13,014
Truro, Canada	2,333	4,481	12,697	10,667	4,588	3,933	7,771	8,516	6,926	5,608	7,534	3,546	4,256	4,776	4,893	4,403	8,532	2,995	4,279	5,777
Tsingtao, China	10,425	8,992	3,426	6,799	9,011	9,973	18,643	19,463	16,695	8,255	7,036	11,702	14,980	10,332	9,596	14,312	19,062	13,931	12,241	8,551
Tsitsihar, China	9,157	8,109	4,099	7,125	7,872	8,799	17,367	18,223	15,860	7,529	6,641	10,501	13,694	9,249	8,511	13,082	17,956	12,645	11,094	7,876
Tubuai Island (Mataura)	9,480	15,930	8,240	17,473	8,026	8,094	8,395	8,831	11,507	16,885	17,947	7,993	9,068	7,093	7,336	8,011	7,876	10,165	7,275	17,197
Tucson, Arizona	2,094	8,541	10,333	14,333	1,757	951	7,950	8,983	9,180	9,538	11,206	1,232	4,830	584	1,212	3,706	8,352	4,727	1,489	9,813
Tulsa, Oklahoma	1,004	7,282	11,412	13,334	2,481	1,482	7,468	8,461	8,113	8,346	10,149	785	3,959	1,986	2,360	3,141	8,020	3,517	1,629	8,577
Tunis, Tunisia	8,133	1,740	12,613	4,828	9,808	9,590	10,444	10,357	7,508	1,244	2,309	9,575	8,826	10,571	10,423	9,734	11,144	7,607	10,293	814
Tura, USSR	7,838	5,748	6,453	6,290	7,319	8,024	15,494	16,047	13,492	5,246	4,733	9,488	11,989	8,766	8,090	11,766	16,281	10,756	10,248	5,624
Turin, Italy	7,360	913	12,115	5,310	8,919	8,760	10,694	10,751	7,931	513	2,356	8,897	8,610	9,755	9,560	9,373	11,444	7,316	9,658	402
Uberlandia, Brazil	8,404	8,817	18,484	11,882	10,333	9,311	1,882	1,687	1,237	9,580	10,944	7,593	3,952	9,285	9,961	5,062	2,462	4,573	7,316	9,304
Ufa, USSR	8,578	3,931	8,633	4,190	8,958	9,360	14,221	14,298	11,461	3,040	2,078	10,365	11,584	10,293	9,753	11,928	14,988	10,227	11,207	3,317
Ujungpandang, Indonesia	14,587	12,706	3,667	7,584	12,561	13,576	16,657	15,956	16,867	11,651	9,807	15,218	18,716	13,428	12,822	17,391	15,864	18,415	15,294	11,759
Ulaanbaatar, Mongolia	9,534	7,274	5,084	5,874	8,627	9,467	17,351	17,770	14,989	6,546	5,452	11,073	13,836	10,058	9,334	13,507	18,145	12,620	11,763	6,855
Ulan-Ude, USSR	9,098	6,991	5,285	6,058	8,237	9,060	16,945	17,449	14,744	6,322	5,364	10,650	13,401	9,675	8,957	13,070	17,728	12,193	11,350	6,652
Uliastay, Mongolia	9,689	6,755	5,747	5,167	9,026	9,801	17,019	17,211	14,371	5,947	4,738	11,322	13,762	10,472	9,766	13,615	17,822	12,477	12,062	6,230
Uranium City, Canada	1,930	6,210	9,424	11,375	1,894	2,105	10,148	11,099	10,157	6,983	8,374	3,436	6,510	3,052	2,616	5,877	10,748	5,686	4,199	7,340
Urumqi, China	10,174	6,505	6,312	4,326	9,720	10,439	16,784	16,712	13,874	5,583	4,152	11,873	13,945	11,169	10,480	13,995	17,523	12,610	12,651	5,815
Ushuaia, Argentina	11,300	13,076	14,726	13,596	12,199	11,371	3,341	2,727	5,314	13,672	14,488	9,769	6,944	10,762	11,481	7,325	2,585	8,120	9,077	13,322
Vaduz, Liechtenstein	7,316	928	11,846	5,266	8,798	8,680	10,932	11,008	8,194	274	2,228	8,892	8,757	9,681	9,457	9,478	11,688	7,449	9,668	428
Valencia, Spain	7,244	1,123	13,015	5,794	9,046	8,743	9,805	9,845	7,024	1,420	3,100	8,631	7,911	9,705	9,612	8,780	10,548	6,665	9,335	1,175
Valladolid, Spain	6,804	883	13,025	6,194	8,627	8,308	9,649	9,757	6,973	1,559	3,397	8,193	7,576	9,267	9,183	8,402	10,410	6,306	8,902	1,426
Valletta, Malta	8,479	2,045	12,383	4,427	10,088	9,912	10,746	10,612	7,766	1,327	1,986	9,950	9,220	10,901	10,724	10,135	11,428	8,006	10,677	907
Valparaiso, Chile	8,904	11,398	15,775	14,336	10,076	9,156	1,097	1,301	4,028	12,279	13,741	7,471	4,516	8,703	9,441	4,935	337	5,729	6,857	12,041
Vancouver, Canada	2,313	7,687	8,832	12,662	479	1,292	9,992	11,011	10,705	8,456	9,776	3,031	6,591	1,902	1,276	5,659	10,453	6,092	3,584	8,817
Varna, Bulgaria	8,631	2,426	10,977	3,816	9,825	9,871	12,111	12,015	9,166	1,267	727	10,287	10,239	10,879	10,550	10,985	12,813	8,944	11,088	1,249
Venice, Italy	7,606	1,205	11,824	4,988	9,074	8,967	11,041	11,072	8,241	266	1,990	9,180	8,978	9,969	9,738	9,727	11,785	7,680	9,953	171
Veracruz, Mexico	2,869	8,664	12,262	14,856	3,785	2,822	5,896	6,925	7,251	9,798	11,716	1,157	2,875	2,575	3,275	1,653	6,342	3,161	602	9,953
Verona, Italy	7,528	1,111	11,900	5,084	9,020	8,899	10,947	10,987	8,159	304	2,096	9,093	8,872	9,900	9,678	9,624	11,692	7,575	9,863	206
Victoria, Canada	2,332	7,770	8,831	12,753	389	1,246	9,948	10,970	10,703	8,544	9,868	2,992	6,568	1,822	1,187	5,620	10,401	6,090	3,528	8,905
Victoria, Seychelles	14,596	8,174	10,179	2,395	15,534	15,808	12,858	11,937	10,333	7,129	5,442	16,138	14,240	16,802	16,326	15,533	12,871	13,508	16,828	6,882
Vienna, Austria	7,619	1,391	11,392	4,866	8,955	8,917	11,446	11,497	8,669	253	1,751	9,248	9,268	9,924	9,647	9,957	12,196	7,951	10,042	564
Vientiane, Laos	12,860	9,557	4,603	5,138	11,655	12,597	18,573	17,564	15,834	8,519	6,744	14,297	17,104	12,990	12,254	16,834	18,263	15,792	14,885	8,657
Villahermosa, Mexico	2,990	8,538	12,627	14,725	4,093	3,109	5,593	6,617	6,886	9,684	11,626	1,388	2,510	2,923	3,613	1,305	6,068	2,833	961	9,816
Vilnius, USSR	7,535	1,982	10,462	4,854	8,567	8,675	12,264	12,385	9,578	1,147	1,697	9,257	9,791	9,678	9,308	10,326	13,035	8,443	10,085	1,514
Visby, Sweden	6,994	1,644	10,616	5,394	8,086	8,158	11,939	12,139	9,380	1,150	2,225	8,713	9,315	9,164	8,814	9,808	12,726	7,962	9,540	1,579
Vitoria, Brazil	8,987	8,584	19,161	11,107	11,026	10,006	2,621	2,145	835	9,231	10,423	8,317	4,673	10,048	10,704	5,842	3,071	5,130	8,092	8,917
Vladivostok, USSR	9,281	8,832	3,370	7,757	7,760	8,734	17,435	18,443	16,540	8,290	7,420	10,472	13,866	9,069	8,334	13,095	17,808	12,941	10,987	8,644
Volgograd, USSR	8,834	3,373	9,562	3,630	9,553	9,820	13,472	13,423	10,574	2,316	1,045	10,597	11,246	10,798	10,332	11,793	14,197	9,903	11,436	2,499
Vologda, USSR	7,686	2,906	9,445	4,828	8,354	8,624	13,207	13,381	10,589	2,165	2,010	9,463	10,493	9,599	9,132	10,872	13,992	9,137	10,305	2,520
Vorkuta, USSR	7,387	4,101	8,107	5,655	7,522	7,996	14,160	14,536	11,863	3,589	3,364	9,159	10,968	8,893	8,319	11,045	14,967	9,646	9,987	3,977
Wake Island	9,292	12,317	2,271	11,631	6,983	7,933	14,653	15,376	17,256	12,125	11,577	9,432	12,917	7,619	7,073	11,631	14,374	12,907	9,458	12,531
Wallis Island	10,508	15,954	5,247	14,631	8,377	8,917	11,414	11,784	14,525	16,086	15,598	9,572	11,716	8,076	7,961	10,491	10,861	12,565	9,089	16,513
Walvis Bay, Namibia	13,138	8,195	14,849	6,173	15,472	14,672	8,014	7,118	5,694	7,837	7,460	13,382	10,017	15,186	15,615	11,314	8,085	9,886	13,453	7,407
Warsaw, Poland	7,535	1,679	10,853	4,868	8,700	8,745	11,913	12,008	9,194	755	1,684	9,224	9,551	9,753	9,421	10,148	12,677	8,212	10,040	1,122
Washington, D.C.	1,489	5,825	12,561	12,007	3,822	2,971	7,152	8,027	6,999	6,948	8,862	2,233	3,481	3,661	3,929	3,284	7,846	2,498	2,938	7,121
Watson Lake, Canada	2,897	6,933	8,309	11,453	1,732	2,450	11,015	12,006	11,263	7,554	8,683	4,095	7,457	3,164	2,525	6,679	11,546	6,738	4,745	7,947
Weimar, East Germany	7,140	1,002	11,451	5,338	8,506	8,447	11,239	11,363	8,570	375	2,198	8,771	8,891	9,453	9,188	9,533	12,008	7,560	9,567	790
Wellington, New Zealand	13,224	19,076	6,930	13,793	11,382	11,713	10,425	10,313	13,095	18,403	16,576	11,849	12,495	10,758	10,833	11,663	9,662	13,762	11,144	18,545
West Berlin, West Germany	7,138	1,167	11,229	5,301	8,433	8,409	11,441	11,578	8,789	525	2,133	8,795	9,033	9,418	9,129	9,641	12,214	7,695	9,600	959
Wewak, Papua New Guinea	12,856	14,004	2,081	10,082	10,551	11,489	15,583	15,519	18,161	13,220	11,715	12,898	16,038	11,089	10,601	14,720	14,854	16,394	12,778	13,472
Whangarei, New Zealand	12,883	18,458	6,387	13,811	10,931	11,333	10,836	10,795	13,609	17,971	16,344	11,620	12,628	10,406	10,425	11,695	10,095	13,834	10,962	18,225
Whitehorse, Canada	3,246	7,072	7,964	11,351	1,926	2,727	11,342	12,339	11,611	7,636	8,671	4,404	7,800	3,375	2,701	7,002	11,859	7,089	5,030	8,039
Wichita, Kansas	879	7,254	11,218	13,257	2,285	1,300	7,680	8,673	8,309	8,300	10,077	924	4,170	1,883	2,204	3,350	8,229	3,707	1,759	8,543
Willemstad, Curacao	4,303	7,293	15,157	12,988	6,266	5,249	4,100	4,954	4,359	8,424	10,372	3,606	601	5,404	6,001	1,671	4,830	766	3,576	8,401
Wiluna, Australia	16,423	14,550	5,380	8,619	14,113	15,023	14,287	13,585	15,064	13,403	11,434	16,227	17,548	14,498	14,100	16,872	13,505	18,903	15,840	13,389
Windhoek, Namibia	13,315	8,212	14,584	5,952	15,636	14,865	8,277	7,375	5,958	7,805	7,345	13,614	10,275	15,412	15,817	11,575	8,338	10,122	13,703	7,378
Windsor, Canada	864	5,997	11,932	12,111	3,211	2,404	7,645	8,552	7,625	7,081	8,932	1,993	3,970	3,175	3,370	3,588	8,309	3,088	2,791	7,295
Winnipeg, Canada	628	6,337	10,557	12,078	2,018	1,532	8,845	9,799	9,001	7,288	8,935	2,275	5,212	2,522	2,419	4,591	9,452	4,446	3,096	7,583
Winston-Salem, North Carolina	1,463	6,240	12,565	12,426	3,710	2,795	6,917	7,824	6,981	7,366	9,282	1,860	3,242	3,394	3,730	2,924	7,586	2,397	2,533	7,535
Wroclaw, Poland	7,430	1,403	11,147	5,005	8,692	8,688	11,612	11,707	8,895	468	1,838	9,090	9,291	9,697	9,397	9,921	12,375	7,959	9,896	869
Wuhan, China	11,195	9,170	3,633	6,242	9,837	10,794	19,361	19,282	16,617	8,322	6,898	12,517	15,705	11,161	10,425	15,115	19,740	14,577	13,068	8,574
Wyndham, Australia	14,966	14,193	3,901	8,881	12,691	13,640	15,319	14,780	16,536	13,137	11,275	15,027	17,659	13,228	12,753	16,490	14,512	18,484	14,828	13,237
Xi'an, China	10,957	8,540	4,250	5,752	9,795	10,711	18,824	18,757	15,978	7,677	6,254	12,393	15,351	11,172	10,434	14,926	19,626	14,145	13,011	7,925
Xining, China	10,849	7,923	4,947	5,149	9,916	10,778	18,223	18,070	15,281	7,025	5,561	12,396	15,052	11,334	10,603	14,816	18,963	13,777	13,078	7,259
Yakutsk, USSR	7,549	6,943	5,355	7,598	6,507	7,358	15,717	16,557	14,482	6,599	6,222	8,997	12,042	7,939	7,218	11,512	16,375	10,976	9,660	6,999
Yanji, China	9,400	8,762	3,441	7,565	7,919	8,887	17,583	18,571	16,499	8,192	7,276	10,621	13,982	9,239	8,503	13,240	17,988	13,027	11,149	8,539

Distances in Kilometers	Saint Paul, Minnesota	Saint Peter Port, UK	Saipan (Susupe)	Salalah, Oman	Salem, Oregon	Salt Lake City, Utah	Salta, Argentina	Salto, Uruguay	Salvador, Brazil	Salzburg, Austria	Samsun, Turkey	San Antonio, Texas	San Cristobal, Venezuela	San Diego, California	San Francisco, California	San Jose, Costa Rica	San Juan, Argentina	San Juan, Puerto Rico	San Luis Potosi, Mexico	San Marino, San Marino
Yaounde, Cameroon	10,851	5,225	14,562	4,868	12,978	12,449	8,883	8,311	5,838	4,871	4,828	11,725	9,275	13,271	13,401	10,559	9,298	8,579	12,153	4,438
Yap Island (Colonia)	12,099	12,438	1,033	9,083	9,957	10,963	17,012	17,076	19,490	11,686	10,290	12,585	16,158	10,796	10,189	14,884	16,344	15,935	12,691	11,960
Yaraka, Australia	14,474	16,045	4,432	10,793	12,137	12,915	13,664	13,354	15,806	15,053	13,233	13,879	15,732	12,240	11,952	14,685	12,869	16,834	13,443	15,183
Yarmouth, Canada	2,143	4,762	12,720	10,949	4,442	3,741	7,598	8,370	6,887	5,891	7,818	3,278	4,041	4,557	4,706	4,139	8,349	2,813	4,002	6,057
Yellowknife, Canada	2,377	6,226	9,027	11,139	2,027	2,419	10,594	11,546	10,562	6,926	8,211	3,847	6,957	3,312	2,800	6,317	11,191	6,120	4,591	7,301
Yerevan, USSR	9,672	3,793	9,861	2,732	10,495	10,729	13,390	13,166	10,350	2,641	700	11,407	11,652	11,717	11,270	12,355	14,039	10,348	12,237	2,667
Yinchuan, China	10,564	8,033	4,638	5,583	9,532	10,415	18,304	18,388	15,548	7,190	5,828	12,062	14,884	10,938	10,204	14,540	19,109	13,654	12,719	7,449
Yogyakarta, Indonesia	15,312	12,313	4,653	6,772	13,452	14,474	16,372	15,496	15,889	11,196	9,267	16,171	19,751	14,412	13,778	18,430	15,650	18,768	16,315	11,241
York, United Kingdom	6,268	497	11,740	6,242	7,755	7,622	10,661	10,906	8,207	1,202	3,100	7,875	8,075	8,623	8,403	8,658	11,454	6,731	8,666	1,484
Yumen, China	10,552	7,422	5,388	4,900	9,773	10,591	17,721	17,640	14,816	6,525	5,091	12,157	14,635	11,209	10,488	14,492	18,473	13,338	12,875	6,763
Yutian, China	10,929	6,629	6,715	3,492	10,611	11,299	16,627	16,284	13,550	5,597	3,912	12,667	14,372	12,058	11,378	14,617	17,230	13,016	13,466	5,757
Yuzhno-Sakhalinsk, USSR	8,455	8,812	3,537	8,545	6,834	7,819	16,514	17,542	16,237	8,432	7,837	9,564	13,034	8,125	7,391	12,192	16,855	12,207	10,054	8,820
Zagreb, Yugoslavia	7,785	1,447	11,586	4,754	9,178	9,113	11,317	11,330	8,493	317	1,713	9,387	9,260	9,606	8,403	8,658	12,055	7,958	10,170	349
Zahedan, Iran	11,350	5,696	8,711	1,547	11,752	12,191	14,725	14,227	11,614	4,542	2,571	13,128	13,527	13,116	12,549	14,259	15,208	12,241	13,971	4,537
Zamboanga, Philippines	13,280	11,795	2,738	7,455	11,373	12,396	17,875	17,294	17,803	10,838	9,153	14,106	17,751	12,385	11,725	16,583	17,068	17,062	14,338	11,020
Zanzibar, Tanzania	13,719	7,365	11,968	3,043	15,378	15,222	11,190	10,335	8,536	6,505	5,262	14,898	12,465	16,189	16,045	13,776	11,312	11,845	15,402	6,162
Zaragoza, Spain	7,061	878	12,848	5,878	8,828	8,545	9,906	9,980	7,174	1,295	3,085	8,481	7,892	9,514	9,405	8,721	10,659	6,625	9,199	1,120
Zashiversk, USSR	6,696	6,715	5,814	8,210	5,668	6,502	14,889	15,772	13,955	6,545	6,478	8,134	11,215	7,108	6,393	10,653	15,523	10,191	8,801	6,966
Zhengzhou, China	10,777	8,764	3,869	6,193	9,499	10,438	18,896	19,158	16,324	7,949	6,603	12,144	15,258	10,852	10,114	14,720	19,600	14,115	12,727	8,217
Zurich, Switzerland	7,235	839	11,889	5,355	8,732	8,606	10,865	10,952	8,143	354	2,317	8,807	8,671	9,606	9,387	9,388	11,624	7,361	9,581	499

Distances in Kilometers	San Miguel de Tucuman, Argen.	San Salvador, El Salvador	Sanaa, Yemen	Santa Cruz, Bolivia	Santa Cruz, Tenerife	Santa Fe, New Mexico	Santa Rosa, Argentina	Santa Rosalia, Mexico	Santarem, Brazil	Santiago del Estero, Argentina	Santiago, Chile	Santo Domingo, Dominican Rep.	Sao Paulo de Olivenca, Brazil	Sao Paulo, Brazil	Sao Tome, Sao Tome & Principe	Sapporo, Japan	Sarajevo, Yugoslavia	Saratov, USSR	Saskatoon, Canada	Schefferville, Canada
San Salvador, El Salvador	5,179	0	13,975	4,507	7,651	2,956	6,153	2,832	4,206	5,320	5,577	2,130	2,945	6,201	10,651	11,895	10,328	11,588	4,537	4,957
Sanaa, Yemen	12,673	13,975	0	12,328	6,348	13,546	12,654	14,651	11,044	12,590	13,233	11,896	12,587	10,766	4,440	9,427	3,991	4,021	12,020	9,913
Santa Cruz, Bolivia	1,021	4,507	12,328	0	7,190	7,441	2,088	7,280	1,935	1,111	1,889	4,079	1,702	1,836	7,902	16,384	10,709	12,864	8,812	8,052
Santa Cruz, Tenerife	8,048	7,651	6,348	7,190	0	8,206	8,783	9,154	5,344	8,060	8,938	5,549	6,634	6,611	3,958	11,764	3,519	5,696	7,593	4,975
Santa Fe, New Mexico	8,134	2,956	13,546	7,441	8,206	0	9,090	1,105	6,789	8,276	8,489	4,020	5,807	9,052	12,024	8,947	9,564	9,961	1,827	3,661
Santa Rosa, Argentina	1,090	6,153	12,654	2,088	8,783	9,090	0	8,680	3,911	980	680	6,125	3,702	2,230	8,349	17,725	12,197	14,424	10,657	10,132
Santa Rosalia, Mexico	7,826	2,832	14,651	7,280	9,154	1,105	8,680	0	6,988	7,969	8,035	4,436	5,776	9,023	12,840	9,194	10,668	11,013	2,794	4,759
Santarem, Brazil	2,922	4,206	11,044	1,935	5,344	6,789	3,911	6,988	0	2,984	3,815	2,849	1,572	2,492	6,844	15,235	8,853	10,962	7,755	6,442
Santiago del Estero, Argentina	143	5,320	12,590	1,111	8,060	8,276	980	7,969	2,984	0	878	5,153	2,736	1,832	8,168	17,160	11,548	13,754	9,767	9,153
Santiago, Chile	903	5,577	13,233	1,889	8,938	8,489	680	8,035	3,815	878	0	5,746	3,327	2,590	8,866	17,046	12,423	14,632	10,106	9,785
Santo Domingo, Dominican Rep.	5,036	2,130	11,896	4,079	5,549	4,020	6,125	4,436	2,849	5,153	5,746	0	2,427	5,291	8,595	12,485	8,479	10,085	4,915	4,041
Sao Paulo de Olivenca, Brazil	2,614	2,945	12,587	1,702	6,634	5,807	3,702	5,776	1,572	2,736	3,327	2,427	0	3,261	8,414	14,709	10,051	12,004	7,114	6,459
Sao Paulo, Brazil	1,908	6,201	10,766	1,836	6,611	9,052	2,230	9,023	2,492	1,832	2,590	5,291	3,261	0	6,337	17,721	9,974	12,201	10,202	8,891
Sao Tome, Sao Tome & Principe	8,244	10,651	4,440	7,902	3,958	12,024	8,349	12,840	6,844	8,168	8,866	8,595	8,414	6,337	0	13,422	4,956	6,765	11,551	8,930
Sapporo, Japan	17,018	11,895	9,427	16,384	11,764	8,947	17,725	9,194	15,235	17,160	17,046	12,485	14,709	17,721	13,422	0	8,838	6,745	7,611	8,838
Sarajevo, Yugoslavia	11,546	10,328	3,991	10,709	3,519	9,564	12,197	10,668	8,853	11,548	12,423	8,479	10,051	9,974	4,956	8,838	0	2,227	8,142	5,922
Saratov, USSR	13,744	11,588	4,021	12,864	5,696	9,961	14,424	11,013	10,962	13,754	14,632	10,085	12,004	12,201	6,765	6,745	2,227	0	8,231	6,687
Saskatoon, Canada	9,630	4,537	12,020	8,812	7,593	1,827	10,657	2,794	7,755	9,767	10,106	4,915	7,114	10,202	11,551	7,611	8,142	8,231	0	2,625
Schefferville, Canada	9,044	4,957	9,913	8,052	4,975	3,661	10,132	4,759	6,442	9,153	9,785	4,041	6,459	8,891	8,930	8,838	5,922	6,687	2,625	0
Seattle, Washington	10,026	4,850	12,906	9,331	8,825	1,894	10,967	2,415	8,557	10,167	10,351	5,719	7,681	10,902	12,783	7,055	9,172	8,960	1,232	3,854
Sendai, Japan	17,276	12,255	9,538	16,762	12,249	9,326	17,797	9,503	15,736	17,414	17,140	12,956	15,122	18,228	13,679	534	9,234	7,098	8,060	9,361
Seoul, South Korea	18,361	13,193	8,362	17,604	11,757	10,237	19,018	10,538	16,110	18,504	18,361	13,557	15,901	18,337	12,612	1,361	8,484	6,276	8,796	9,685
Sept-Iles, Canada	8,531	4,547	10,108	7,539	4,832	3,554	9,619	4,626	5,939	8,640	9,276	3,534	5,949	8,397	8,785	9,329	6,131	7,055	2,788	513
Sevastopol, USSR	12,714	11,356	3,395	11,902	4,719	10,224	13,305	11,320	10,059	12,709	13,577	9,605	11,256	11,075	5,572	7,953	1,209	1,209	8,630	6,692
Seville, Spain	9,422	8,507	5,492	8,552	1,377	8,467	10,157	9,513	6,679	9,436	10,314	6,505	7,890	7,974	4,306	10,507	2,176	4,322	7,481	4,905
Shanghai, China	19,222	14,075	7,942	18,462	12,035	11,119	19,211	11,400	16,803	19,363	18,865	14,389	16,765	18,568	12,323	2,206	8,617	6,390	9,672	10,453
Sheffield, United Kingdom	10,792	8,646	5,792	9,835	3,019	7,769	11,655	8,872	7,902	10,832	11,695	6,951	8,837	9,564	5,928	8,748	1,802	3,177	6,412	4,121
Shenyang, China	18,168	13,012	8,006	17,272	11,198	10,065	19,135	10,456	15,640	18,302	18,468	13,193	15,586	17,783	12,168	1,477	7,939	5,738	8,538	9,256
Shiraz, Iran	13,984	13,706	1,794	13,422	6,594	12,437	14,181	13,503	11,814	13,928	14,682	11,873	13,216	12,108	5,833	7,744	3,400	2,498	10,728	9,018
Sibiu, Romania	12,048	10,651	3,861	11,205	4,015	9,691	12,699	10,795	9,341	12,051	12,926	8,865	10,513	10,474	5,319	8,378	503	1,726	8,183	6,093
Singapore	16,951	17,823	6,729	17,703	12,852	14,885	15,909	15,025	17,648	16,815	16,399	17,718	19,184	15,998	10,810	5,938	9,546	7,733	13,437	13,729
Sioux Falls, South Dakota	8,430	3,385	12,374	7,607	7,167	1,177	9,465	2,280	6,597	8,566	8,928	3,748	5,909	9,020	11,069	8,812	8,388	8,874	1,205	2,487
Skelleftea, Sweden	12,491	9,560	5,764	11,504	4,801	7,955	13,404	9,030	9,573	12,543	13,388	8,205	10,338	11,348	7,241	6,984	2,335	2,057	6,286	4,634
Skopje, Yugoslavia	11,696	10,638	3,670	10,886	3,710	9,882	12,305	10,986	9,055	11,692	12,562	8,771	10,290	10,075	4,847	8,837	323	2,140	8,445	6,243
Socotra Island (Tamrida)	13,530	15,030	1,102	13,291	7,435	14,258	13,363	15,345	12,110	13,434	13,988	12,977	13,664	11,640	5,393	8,847	4,847	4,376	12,593	10,719
Sofia, Bulgaria	11,865	10,743	3,627	11,052	3,873	9,919	12,473	11,024	9,217	11,861	12,731	8,897	10,443	10,244	4,975	8,680	418	1,975	8,453	6,294
Songkhla, Thailand	17,375	17,458	6,208	17,911	12,192	14,511	16,408	14,810	17,247	17,233	16,964	16,984	18,788	16,088	10,441	5,621	8,834	6,990	12,942	13,035
Sorong, Indonesia	16,475	15,359	9,727	17,415	15,410	12,985	15,557	12,662	19,273	16,431	15,572	17,003	17,755	17,294	13,862	4,970	11,893	9,754	12,214	13,806
South Georgia Island	3,832	9,007	10,803	4,636	9,373	11,957	2,879	11,551	5,973	3,693	3,516	8,655	6,338	3,508	7,240	18,752	12,062	14,005	13,444	12,400
South Pole	7,036	11,517	11,701	8,034	13,152	13,952	5,949	13,024	9,734	6,929	6,300	12,046	9,621	7,400	10,041	14,769	14,859	15,719	15,778	16,078
South Sandwich Islands	4,577	9,753	10,336	5,361	9,600	12,705	3,625	12,291	6,616	4,437	4,257	9,347	7,061	4,128	7,081	18,164	12,005	13,791	14,174	12,996
Split, Yugoslavia	11,386	10,192	4,085	10,546	3,356	9,481	12,044	10,584	8,689	11,389	12,264	8,330	9,889	9,822	4,880	8,964	164	2,381	8,086	5,831
Spokane, Washington	9,761	4,583	12,790	9,038	8,498	1,635	10,725	2,303	8,212	9,902	10,123	5,370	7,375	10,578	12,455	7,346	8,985	8,895	917	3,538
Spoleto, Italy	11,077	9,937	4,266	10,234	3,043	9,331	11,746	10,415	8,376	11,082	11,957	8,049	9,580	9,528	4,734	9,212	477	2,681	7,993	5,672
Springbok, South Africa	7,971	12,394	5,727	8,212	7,384	14,786	7,469	15,181	8,199	7,841	8,142	10,804	9,506	6,380	3,525	14,839	8,139	9,411	14,879	12,325
Springfield, Illinois	7,798	2,893	12,261	6,944	6,702	1,505	8,851	2,505	5,880	7,931	8,343	3,032	5,242	8,314	10,535	9,498	8,278	9,010	1,890	2,379
Springfield, Massachusetts	7,668	3,532	10,951	6,702	5,246	2,960	8,758	3,944	5,252	7,784	8,368	2,633	5,059	7,743	9,106	9,983	7,017	8,061	2,781	1,474
Srinagar, India	16,131	14,455	3,704	15,487	8,391	12,281	16,325	13,168	13,731	16,082	16,844	13,099	14,952	14,269	7,985	5,731	4,909	3,017	10,454	9,498
Stanley, Falkland Islands	2,832	7,853	12,162	3,790	9,766	10,754	1,752	10,237	5,469	2,709	2,276	7,861	5,445	3,271	8,317	18,283	12,868	14,995	12,381	11,835
Stara Zagora, Bulgaria	12,033	10,927	3,487	11,229	4,056	10,060	12,625	11,165	9,400	12,027	12,895	9,087	10,633	10,395	5,031	8,575	608	1,846	8,570	6,446
Stockholm, Sweden	12,164	9,656	5,331	11,204	4,307	8,287	13,020	9,380	9,270	12,204	13,067	8,144	10,155	10,904	6,617	7,529	1,725	1,951	6,689	4,819
Stornoway, United Kingdom	10,881	8,304	6,315	9,894	3,395	7,232	11,805	8,337	7,962	10,949	11,778	6,735	8,766	9,796	6,522	8,390	2,338	3,352	5,821	3,616
Strasbourg, France	11,048	9,381	4,960	10,143	3,035	8,606	11,817	9,709	8,234	11,070	11,947	7,590	9,312	9,642	5,347	8,889	977	2,729	7,239	4,956
Stuttgart, West Germany	11,150	9,478	4,887	10,247	3,131	8,673	11,914	9,777	8,339	11,171	12,048	7,694	9,419	9,735	5,372	8,814	897	2,623	7,288	5,027
Subic, Philippines	18,572	15,493	8,125	19,536	13,315	12,604	17,556	12,679	18,524	18,505	17,679	16,155	18,410	18,344	12,531	3,716	9,797	7,635	11,326	12,255
Suchow, China	19,149	14,012	7,518	18,180	11,515	11,064	19,716	11,434	16,383	19,273	19,296	14,121	16,538	18,048	11,862	2,308	8,092	5,865	9,532	10,129
Sucre, Bolivia	862	4,471	12,571	262	7,446	7,420	1,951	7,210	2,168	975	1,685	4,179	1,766	1,998	8,140	16,365	10,965	13,113	8,842	8,182
Sudbury, Canada	8,274	3,717	11,246	7,343	5,890	2,401	9,357	3,470	6,004	8,398	8,915	3,272	5,662	8,494	9,810	9,244	7,259	8,020	1,954	1,358
Suez, Egypt	12,146	12,130	2,010	11,518	4,711	11,546	12,488	12,650	9,884	12,105	12,910	10,144	11,300	10,320	4,270	9,152	1,983	2,645	10,083	7,904
Sundsvall, Sweden	12,239	9,494	5,634	11,262	4,491	8,017	13,132	9,104	9,327	12,286	13,139	8,061	10,142	11,055	6,940	7,302	2,066	2,094	6,392	4,608
Surabaya, Indonesia	16,229	17,529	7,961	17,199	14,189	14,980	15,139	14,790	18,268	16,115	15,486	18,732	18,810	15,936	11,792	6,277	10,912	9,072	13,879	14,731
Suva, Fiji	11,545	10,729	15,155	12,204	18,141	9,937	11,076	9,006	13,784	11,574	10,737	12,859	12,290	13,299	17,841	7,763	16,601	14,448	10,595	13,219
Sverdlovsk, USSR	14,620	11,704	4,810	13,678	6,622	9,673	15,404	10,654	11,746	14,650	15,523	10,481	12,612	13,207	7,874	5,634	3,266	1,114	7,869	6,749
Svobodnyy, USSR	17,055	11,944	8,271	16,147	10,499	9,016	18,094	9,485	14,571	17,186	17,503	12,069	14,462	16,879	12,093	1,361	7,481	5,386	7,439	8,151
Sydney, Australia	12,271	13,576	12,505	13,231	18,685	13,155	11,379	12,209	15,163	12,228	11,369	15,614	14,131	13,378	14,773	8,578	15,838	13,873	13,685	16,268
Sydney, Canada	8,096	4,508	9,862	7,088	4,293	3,966	9,176	4,994	5,409	8,198	8,878	3,198	5,560	7,837	8,225	9,898	5,939	7,093	3,393	1,071
Syktyvkar, USSR	13,961	10,946	5,169	12,993	6,058	9,012	14,814	10,025	11,058	14,002	14,863	9,709	11,863	12,669	7,744	5,945	2,898	1,161	7,231	5,990
Szeged, Hungary	11,778	10,350	4,093	10,922	3,734	9,453	12,455	10,558	9,048	11,785	12,661	8,554	10,206	10,237	5,256	8,541	304	1,973	7,983	5,835
Szombathely, Hungary	11,571	10,058	4,356	10,698	3,523	9,191	12,278	10,296	8,811	11,582	12,460	8,266	9,943	10,070	5,284	8,628	403	2,173	7,748	5,563
Tabriz, Iran	13,608	12,642	2,528	12,899	5,815	11,354	14,021	12,431	11,142	13,579	14,410	10,883	12,433	11,829	5,817	7,609	2,420	1,499	9,673	7,915
Tacheng, China	16,457	13,264	4,993	15,551	8,410	10,832	17,095	11,661	13,626	16,470	17,347	12,288	14,492	14,866	8,935	4,524	4,928	2,715	9,011	8,398
Tahiti (Papeete)	8,610	7,477	18,545	9,067	15,127	7,472	8,459	6,389	10,453	8,676	7,949	9,583	8,923	10,506	16,808	9,721	16,880	15,988	8,761	11,127
Taipei, Taiwan	19,329	14,587	8,050	19,075	12,565	11,643	18,613	11,844	17,470	19,376	18,517	15,036	17,377	18,814	12,483	2,696	9,096	6,880	10,264	11,122
Taiyuan, China	18,762	13,865	7,089	17,743	10,939	10,951	19,708	11,414	15,873	18,849	19,440	13,764	16,191	17,479	11,374	2,497	7,515	5,288	9,338	9,737
Tallahasee, Florida	6,654	1,922	12,531	5,798	6,501	2,100	7,712	2,747	4,807	6,786	7,216	1,968	4,097	7,201	10,094	10,634	8,651	9,709	3,023	3,042
Tallinn, USSR	12,531	9,998	5,144	11,576	4,629	8,534	13,372	9,618	9,643	12,568	13,434	8,516	10,536	11,237	6,737	7,259	1,786	1,593	6,892	5,127
Tamanrasset, Algeria	9,382	9,906	4,142	8,716	2,269	10,333	9,839	11,337	7,099	9,352	10,188	7,790	8,563	7,620	2,487	11,434	2,618	4,711	9,436	6,845
Tampa, Florida	6,335	1,726	12,539	5,472	6,412	2,376	7,396	2,938	4,487	6,466	6,909	1,657	3,770	6,874	9,918	10,963	8,714	9,866	3,352	3,239
Tampere, Finland	12,535	9,844	5,377	11,567	4,702	8,320	13,405	9,401	9,632	12,578	13,437	8,411	10,477	11,296	6,936	7,138	1,997	1,746	6,667	4,947
Tanami, Australia	14,584	15,838	10,136	15,598	16,460	14,353	13,571	13,715	17,480	14,511	13,711	17,966	16,728	15,174	13,458	7,080	13,216	11,301	14,021	15,897
Tangier, Morocco	9,324	8,546	5,440	8,466	1,277	8,580	10,040	9,619	6,608	9,334	10,212	6,523	7,846	7,848	4,136	10,661	2,247	4,420	7,625	5,039
Tarawa (Betio)	13,220	10,833	14,099	13,642	16,567	9,123	12,981	8,443	14,737	13,283	12,528	12,822	13,169	15,108	18,490	5,584	14,399	12,326	9,237	11,762
Tashkent, USSR	15,586	13,526	3,759	14,815	7,636	11,463	16,015	12,402	12,973	15,565	16,406	12,169	14,098	13,828	7,729	5,763	4,120	2,105	9,643	8,569
Tbilisi, USSR	13,544	12,274	2,921	12,782	5,632	10,933	14,047	12,008	10,976	13,526	14,378	10,565	12,210	11,820	5,961	7,465	2,159	1,101	9,250	7,509
Tegucigalpa, Honduras	5,114	219	13,767	4,407	7,438	3,037	6,108	2,984	4,027	5,254	5,548	1,912	2,811	6,072	10,436	11,983	10,147	11,451	4,558	4,850
Tehran, Iran	14,014	13,157	2,363	13,348	6,316	11,767	14,351	12,828	11,627	13,976	14,784	11,413	12,944	12,194	6,053	7,412	2,949	1,818	10,049	8,388
Tel Aviv, Israel	12,423	12,196	2,084	11,774	4,879	11,464	12,787	12,569	10,107	12,385	13,198	10,249	11,496	10,610	4,585	8,838	1,935	2,353	9,952	7,845
Telegraph Creek, Canada	11,197	6,027	11,875	10,434	8,700	3,094	12,178	3,705	9,439	11,336	11,583	6,597	8,748	11,880	12,562	5,962	8,383	7,866	1,685	3,841
Teresina, Brazil	3,383	5,530	9,847	2,624	4,679	7,969	4,122	8,269	1,352	3,387	4,263	3,952	2,890	2,082	5,541	15,779	8,163	10,369	8,716	7,000
Ternate, Indonesia	16,830	15,690	9,264	17,806	14,972	13,185	15,863	12,938	19,730	16,774	15,933	17,168	18,212	17,410	13,432	4,882	11,461	9,342	12,290	13,705
The Valley, Anguilla	4,969	2,837	11,242	3,965	4,898	4,641	6,052	5,128	2,444	5,073	5,756	724	2,460	4,935	7,871	12,796	7,969	9,708	5,351	4,091
Thessaloniki, Greece	11,752	10,812	3,476	10,960	3,804	10,076	12,331	11,181	9,147	11,743	12,609	8,929	10,406	10,101	4,754	8,873	515	2,146	8,637	6,437
Thimphu, Bhutan	17,550	15,441	4,878	17,050	9,988	12,818	17,382	13,499	15,329	17,468	18,036	14,465	16,508	15,642	9,306	4,915	6,497	4,505	11,039	10,612
Thunder Bay, Canada	8,671	3,848	11,587	7,779	6,491	1,964	9,739	3,068	6,553	8,800	9,254	3,755	6,081	9,031	10,430	8,730	7,601	8,143	1,299	1,703
Tientsin, China	18,621	13,550	7,493	17,640	11,106	10,616	19,700	11,041	15,859	18,739	19,070	13,586	16,007	17,707	11,742	2,068	7,738	5,514	9,043	9,589
Tijuana, Mexico	8,558	3,512	14,344	7,992	9,275	1,079	9,417	737	7,602	8,701	8,772	4,943	6,455	9,713	13,103	8,464	10,419	10,542	2,332	4,606
Tiksi, USSR	14,949	10,126	8,205	13,974	8,582	7,366	16,038	8,082	12,322	15,065	15,606	9,913	12,337	14,653	11,045	3,252	6,100	4,443	5,611	5,928
Timbuktu, Mali	8,269	9,188	5,043	7,620	1,873	10,060	8,730	10,972	6,061	8,238	9,074	7,059	7,566	6,508	2,109	12,453	3,617	5,780	9,451	6,827
Tindouf, Algeria	8,580	8,449	5,552	7,779	799	8,914	9,230	9,890	5,995	8,579	9,451	6,347	7,349	7,015	3,420	11,575	2,974	5,197	8,172	5,548
Tirane, Albania	11,541	10,542	3,714	10,733	3,561	9,848	12,149	10,952	8,905	11,537	12,406	8,656	10,149	9,919	4,729	8,981	301	2,294	8,440	6,201

Distances in Kilometers

	San Miguel de Tucuman, Argen.	San Salvador, El Salvador	Sanaa, Yemen	Santa Cruz, Bolivia	Santa Cruz, Tenerife	Santa Fe, New Mexico	Santa Rosa, Argentina	Santa Rosalia, Mexico	Santarem, Brazil	Santiago del Estero, Argentina	Santiago, Chile	Santo Domingo, Dominican Rep.	Sao Paulo de Olivenca, Brazil	Sao Paulo, Brazil	Sao Tome, Sao Tome & Principe	Sapporo, Japan	Sarajevo, Yugoslavia	Saratov, USSR	Saskatoon, Canada	Schefferville, Canada
Tokyo, Japan	17,459	12,506	9,521	17,011	12,474	9,589	17,865	9,737	16,034	17,593	17,234	13,248	15,392	18,526	13,736	827	9,396	7,234	8,347	9,661
Toledo, Spain	9,729	8,641	5,394	8,848	1,692	8,450	10,474	9,514	6,965	9,745	10,623	6,677	8,144	8,295	4,512	10,185	1,908	4,019	7,385	4,845
Topeka, Kansas	7,950	2,880	12,687	7,146	7,224	983	8,976	2,018	6,218	8,087	8,432	3,374	5,454	8,606	11,059	9,257	8,697	9,300	1,681	2,775
Toronto, Canada	7,937	3,452	11,327	7,004	5,789	2,432	9,021	3,459	5,671	8,061	8,585	2,932	5,325	8,159	9,673	9,581	7,355	8,221	2,226	1,534
Toulouse, France	10,340	9,023	5,110	9,452	2,306	8,572	11,088	9,660	7,559	10,357	11,235	7,126	8,702	8,907	4,822	9,613	1,367	3,412	7,363	4,918
Tours, France	10,532	8,893	5,344	9,615	2,562	8,274	11,325	9,370	7,701	10,558	11,433	7,066	8,768	9,172	5,246	9,269	1,435	3,266	7,005	4,613
Townsville, Australia	13,856	14,047	11,861	14,770	18,022	12,768	13,017	12,019	16,661	13,826	12,954	16,173	15,392	15,055	15,198	6,920	14,527	12,401	12,802	15,150
Trenton, New Jersey	7,488	3,260	11,213	6,535	5,442	2,772	8,576	3,724	5,147	7,607	8,168	2,457	4,874	7,638	9,266	10,096	7,289	8,336	2,762	1,725
Tripoli, Lebanon	12,600	12,142	2,274	11,921	4,942	11,292	13,000	12,395	10,216	12,567	13,392	10,236	11,574	10,809	4,841	8,582	1,827	2,072	9,747	7,696
Tripoli, Libya	10,600	10,317	3,682	9,857	2,852	10,126	11,131	11,204	8,115	10,582	11,438	8,292	9,474	8,903	3,668	10,084	1,296	3,367	8,925	6,480
Tristan da Cunha (Edinburgh)	5,065	9,792	8,284	5,389	7,262	12,567	4,578	12,620	5,787	4,934	5,243	8,614	6,846	3,600	4,580	17,688	9,480	11,339	13,420	11,428
Trondheim, Norway	11,958	9,126	5,940	10,970	4,332	7,679	12,877	8,771	9,039	12,010	12,854	7,705	9,812	10,840	7,005	7,434	2,239	2,463	6,080	4,244
Trujillo, Peru	2,532	2,662	13,812	2,025	7,858	5,609	3,492	5,312	2,768	2,675	2,934	3,107	1,245	3,854	9,557	14,501	11,229	13,086	7,174	7,065
Truk Island (Moen)	15,563	12,893	11,671	16,067	15,836	10,623	15,136	10,213	17,040	15,607	14,790	14,621	15,511	17,362	16,072	4,079	12,659	10,442	10,138	12,232
Truro, Canada	7,996	4,277	10,117	6,995	4,514	3,725	9,080	4,746	5,362	8,101	8,760	3,046	5,435	7,814	8,433	9,913	6,191	7,316	3,225	1,080
Tsingtao, China	18,858	13,689	7,788	17,952	11,544	10,737	19,609	11,091	16,246	18,994	18,980	13,875	16,275	18,142	12,093	1,960	8,170	5,944	9,227	9,913
Tsitsihar, China	17,589	12,485	8,002	16,662	10,712	9,555	18,636	10,008	15,024	17,718	18,037	12,584	14,987	17,232	11,993	1,445	7,555	5,394	7,980	8,636
Tubuai Island (Mataura)	8,340	7,736	18,340	8,883	15,340	7,983	8,091	6,887	10,397	8,394	7,624	9,802	8,912	10,208	16,399	10,198	17,482	16,607	9,342	11,644
Tucson, Arizona	8,137	3,019	14,119	7,522	8,790	603	9,037	558	7,054	8,279	8,408	4,374	5,949	9,210	12,573	8,900	10,145	10,456	2,238	4,256
Tulsa, Oklahoma	7,679	2,577	12,936	6,896	7,343	907	8,695	1,832	6,043	7,817	8,141	3,217	5,213	8,397	11,125	9,497	8,949	9,604	1,965	3,036
Tunis, Tunisia	10,570	9,925	4,115	9,774	2,636	9,628	11,177	10,711	7,970	10,564	11,432	7,941	9,264	8,949	4,053	9,880	1,048	3,256	8,413	5,977
Tura, USSR	15,712	11,320	6,875	14,692	8,355	8,687	16,758	9,463	12,850	15,801	16,520	10,791	13,197	14,877	10,143	3,494	5,359	3,379	6,889	6,751
Turin, Italy	10,845	9,474	4,748	9,966	2,800	8,857	11,573	9,955	8,079	10,860	11,737	7,614	9,223	9,377	4,955	9,224	866	2,901	7,546	5,197
Uberlandia, Brazil	1,940	5,757	10,815	1,576	6,276	8,568	2,507	8,588	1,954	1,901	2,743	4,763	2,813	538	6,375	17,183	9,707	11,931	9,678	8,358
Ufa, USSR	14,383	11,744	4,486	13,465	6,351	9,838	15,120	10,845	11,541	14,404	15,281	10,419	12,478	12,908	7,501	5,996	2,942	749	8,051	6,789
Ujungpandang, Indonesia	16,437	16,757	8,589	17,455	14,685	14,283	15,369	14,037	18,956	16,343	15,608	18,225	18,706	16,496	12,535	5,775	11,285	9,316	13,312	14,467
Ulaanbaatar, Mongolia	17,565	12,997	6,727	16,545	9,827	10,189	18,560	10,803	14,665	17,644	18,385	12,646	15,060	16,434	10,739	2,725	6,490	4,277	8,472	8,605
Ulan-Ude, USSR	17,163	12,566	6,860	16,143	9,570	9,775	18,199	10,414	14,288	17,250	17,958	12,213	14,631	16,177	10,727	2,696	6,310	4,127	8,046	8,173
Uliastay, Mongolia	17,209	13,173	5,992	16,220	9,253	10,491	18,033	11,198	14,291	17,255	18,107	12,553	14,907	15,817	9,989	3,477	5,843	3,617	8,716	8,536
Uranium City, Canada	10,366	5,336	11,346	9,508	7,453	2,663	11,413	3,594	8,311	10,499	10,884	5,514	7,806	10,792	11,370	6,971	7,567	7,474	839	2,536
Urumqi, China	16,933	13,629	5,165	16,038	8,885	11,097	17,512	11,875	14,115	16,940	17,814	12,740	14,971	15,294	9,250	4,276	5,392	3,190	9,289	8,813
Ushuaia, Argentina	3,118	7,842	12,829	4,130	10,478	10,652	2,044	10,022	5,936	3,018	2,380	8,119	5,694	3,909	9,083	17,507	13,637	15,772	12,370	12,151
Vaduz, Liechtenstein	11,086	9,550	4,761	10,196	3,049	8,809	11,829	9,912	8,298	11,103	11,981	7,735	9,410	9,639	5,196	8,949	787	2,668	7,445	5,157
Valencia, Spain	9,952	8,958	5,082	9,089	1,904	8,730	10,667	9,800	7,221	9,963	10,840	6,991	8,428	8,470	4,393	10,089	1,634	3,792	7,621	5,107
Valladolid, Spain	9,806	8,558	5,507	8,910	1,799	8,289	10,574	9,359	7,013	9,826	10,703	6,621	8,155	8,410	4,719	10,029	1,903	3,954	7,198	4,670
Valletta, Malta	10,864	10,326	3,724	10,094	3,002	9,976	11,428	11,065	8,316	10,852	11,714	8,342	9,635	9,198	4,019	9,741	942	3,041	8,711	6,318
Valparaiso, Chile	926	5,499	13,323	1,888	8,972	8,405	781	7,943	3,821	916	101	5,702	3,288	2,662	8,950	16,945	12,464	14,668	10,031	9,742
Vancouver, Canada	10,190	5,012	12,741	9,483	8,781	2,056	11,139	2,606	8,669	10,332	10,527	5,826	7,825	11,034	12,735	6,902	9,035	8,785	1,205	3,806
Varna, Bulgaria	12,238	11,050	3,456	11,431	4,253	10,100	12,832	11,204	9,597	12,233	13,101	9,237	10,818	10,601	5,198	8,383	771	1,646	8,576	6,507
Venice, Italy	11,189	9,814	4,472	10,320	3,141	9,099	11,895	10,202	8,439	11,200	12,077	7,974	9,593	9,688	5,029	8,983	514	2,555	7,727	5,447
Veracruz, Mexico	6,088	958	14,236	5,454	8,064	2,065	7,027	1,879	5,125	6,230	6,424	2,764	3,903	7,159	11,357	10,962	10,377	11,348	3,766	4,664
Verona, Italy	11,095	9,713	4,556	10,223	3,047	9,022	11,809	10,124	8,339	11,108	11,985	7,869	9,489	9,606	5,016	9,043	615	2,649	7,666	5,367
Victoria, Canada	10,145	4,968	12,834	9,447	8,844	2,012	11,087	2,532	8,659	10,287	10,472	5,819	7,795	11,012	12,799	6,938	9,124	8,877	1,258	3,869
Victoria, Seychelles	12,765	16,028	2,533	12,854	8,484	16,077	12,290	17,181	12,230	12,641	12,965	13,905	13,773	11,037	5,445	10,026	6,522	6,290	14,487	12,444
Vienna, Austria	11,597	10,002	4,446	10,716	3,552	9,100	12,319	10,206	8,822	11,612	12,490	8,229	9,935	10,116	5,385	8,555	511	2,149	7,648	5,478
Vientiane, Laos	18,432	16,274	6,212	18,527	11,677	13,353	17,577	13,749	17,011	18,293	18,166	15,893	18,153	16,775	10,627	4,580	8,190	6,167	11,743	11,880
Villahermosa, Mexico	5,790	619	14,048	5,126	7,811	2,345	6,752	2,239	4,760	5,932	6,163	2,434	3,553	6,813	11,028	11,277	10,252	11,334	3,974	4,651
Vilnius, USSR	12,428	10,274	4,660	11,508	4,422	8,966	13,204	10,059	9,587	12,453	13,328	8,680	10,584	11,023	6,260	7,604	1,306	1,424	7,363	5,482
Visby, Sweden	12,114	9,740	5,168	11,164	4,206	8,433	12,949	9,529	9,232	12,149	13,017	8,186	10,156	10,813	6,436	7,662	1,535	1,899	6,852	4,937
Vitoria, Brazil	2,634	6,538	10,048	2,416	5,987	9,279	2,944	9,369	2,519	2,564	3,328	5,367	3,606	739	5,613	17,479	9,286	11,509	10,261	8,696
Vladivostok, USSR	17,632	12,455	8,676	16,862	11,438	9,499	18,462	9,828	15,449	17,774	17,783	12,831	15,160	17,826	12,753	769	8,330	6,175	8,051	9,008
Volgograd, USSR	13,611	11,724	3,704	12,762	5,574	10,204	14,242	11,268	10,881	13,614	14,487	10,147	11,985	12,012	6,466	7,017	2,065	334	8,495	6,864
Vologda, USSR	13,381	10,724	4,882	12,433	5,422	9,026	14,196	10,079	10,500	13,414	14,284	9,333	11,392	12,031	7,138	6,601	2,249	935	7,299	5,791
Vorkuta, USSR	14,361	10,742	5,968	13,354	6,703	8,533	15,313	9,487	11,439	14,423	15,243	9,760	12,051	13,275	8,636	5,153	3,743	2,028	6,715	5,843
Wake Island	14,686	10,956	12,653	14,790	14,714	8,560	14,728	8,201	15,162	14,783	14,170	12,570	13,764	16,559	16,936	3,544	12,306	10,280	8,119	10,368
Wallis Island	11,350	10,042	15,681	11,909	17,352	9,149	11,007	8,228	13,342	11,397	10,598	12,168	11,804	13,187	18,537	7,593	16,348	14,338	9,821	12,444
Walvis Bay, Namibia	7,928	11,983	5,331	8,035	6,575	14,161	7,663	14,682	7,781	7,808	8,216	10,252	9,182	6,204	2,710	14,683	7,405	8,811	14,103	11,528
Warsaw, Poland	12,072	10,135	4,579	11,166	4,047	8,992	12,829	10,093	9,253	12,093	12,970	8,466	10,296	10,640	5,907	7,998	955	1,716	7,448	5,438
Washington, D.C.	7,377	3,037	11,457	6,440	5,652	2,578	8,462	3,505	5,117	7,500	8,036	2,367	4,764	7,603	9,449	10,142	7,533	8,566	2,712	1,927
Watson Lake, Canada	11,225	6,075	11,616	10,432	8,449	3,174	12,227	3,855	9,366	11,363	11,647	6,536	8,737	11,826	12,295	5,982	8,102	7,613	1,629	3,625
Weimar, East Germany	11,401	9,557	4,924	10,486	3,402	8,623	12,181	9,728	8,571	11,426	12,301	7,826	9,615	10,011	5,630	8,524	958	2,401	7,184	4,999
Wellington, New Zealand	10,267	11,503	14,486	11,164	18,270	11,741	9,496	10,675	13,062	10,246	9,369	13,446	11,919	11,659	15,312	9,926	18,068	16,007	12,814	15,352
West Berlin, West Germany	11,606	9,643	4,936	10,684	3,619	8,612	12,395	9,717	8,764	11,632	12,507	7,951	9,784	10,229	5,817	8,301	1,035	2,223	7,133	5,013
Wewak, Papua New Guinea	15,446	14,126	11,134	16,252	16,531	12,084	14,706	11,588	17,891	15,438	14,561	16,024	16,346	16,812	15,230	5,166	13,047	10,843	11,659	13,697
Whangarei, New Zealand	10,691	11,468	14,599	11,549	18,738	11,424	9,973	10,387	13,408	10,680	9,802	13,492	12,170	12,165	15,885	9,343	17,780	15,600	12,374	14,962
Whitehorse, Canada	11,550	6,389	11,572	10,770	8,689	3,467	12,542	4,089	9,717	11,689	11,953	6,886	9,077	12,176	12,492	5,638	8,168	7,555	1,976	3,925
Wichita, Kansas	7,890	2,779	12,896	7,109	7,408	801	8,904	1,812	6,245	8,028	8,348	3,414	5,426	8,607	11,226	9,284	8,905	9,494	1,759	2,983
Willemstad, Curacao	4,326	2,204	12,065	3,369	5,747	4,539	5,416	4,815	2,253	4,443	5,046	710	1,722	4,633	8,453	13,167	8,878	10,609	5,571	4,739
Wiluna, Australia	14,066	16,650	9,432	15,079	15,746	15,553	12,991	14,857	16,747	13,968	13,260	18,646	16,543	14,281	12,358	8,010	12,917	11,268	15,207	16,821
Windhoek, Namibia	8,189	12,242	5,133	8,303	6,684	14,375	7,809	14,924	8,042	8,068	8,466	10,490	9,448	6,471	2,773	14,449	7,355	8,687	14,246	11,652
Windsor, Canada	7,868	3,225	11,656	6,960	6,101	2,110	8,944	3,128	5,716	7,995	8,482	2,919	5,266	8,193	9,966	9,567	7,680	8,504	2,082	1,824
Winnipeg, Canada	9,064	4,078	11,851	8,209	7,021	1,731	10,113	2,819	7,074	9,197	9,594	4,247	6,506	9,537	10,973	8,249	7,894	8,236	710	2,119
Winston-Salem, North Carolina	7,141	2,638	11,864	6,231	5,983	2,314	8,218	3,173	5,024	7,267	7,764	2,203	4,537	7,489	9,720	10,283	7,950	8,979	2,735	2,419
Wroclaw, Poland	11,770	9,932	4,649	10,866	3,745	8,901	12,527	10,005	8,956	11,791	12,668	8,221	10,014	10,340	5,710	8,273	815	2,009	7,406	5,308
Wuhan, China	19,584	14,504	7,272	18,566	11,633	11,556	19,323	11,920	16,683	19,667	19,457	14,559	16,984	17,980	11,670	2,766	8,157	5,944	10,017	10,544
Wyndham, Australia	15,113	16,017	9,832	16,126	16,093	14,235	14,096	13,692	18,002	15,039	14,239	18,090	17,218	15,653	13,382	6,619	12,761	10,804	13,734	15,455
Xi'an, China	19,013	14,364	6,756	18,021	10,987	11,461	19,352	11,932	16,096	19,045	19,909	14,167	16,585	17,367	11,110	2,966	7,508	5,296	9,831	10,128
Xining, China	18,377	14,319	6,126	17,456	10,329	11,506	18,779	12,086	15,522	18,382	19,248	13,846	16,209	16,670	10,441	3,430	6,834	4,633	9,795	9,817
Yakutsk, USSR	15,942	10,955	8,276	14,995	9,525	8,090	17,021	8,683	13,386	16,066	16,519	10,919	13,330	15,722	11,622	2,245	6,775	4,866	6,419	6,972
Yanji, China	17,785	12,606	8,488	16,980	11,367	9,651	18,650	9,998	15,504	17,926	17,972	12,929	15,278	17,830	12,589	965	8,215	6,046	8,180	9,069
Yaounde, Cameroon	8,899	11,074	3,797	8,535	4,005	12,194	9,010	13,084	7,402	8,825	9,527	8,978	8,973	6,993	662	12,787	4,479	6,180	11,534	8,912
Yap Island (Colonia)	16,909	14,206	10,157	17,555	14,989	11,656	16,256	11,421	18,408	16,923	16,056	15,655	16,984	18,376	14,542	3,729	11,553	9,331	10,834	12,506
Yaraka, Australia	13,483	14,332	11,698	14,443	18,034	13,321	12,579	12,512	16,374	13,438	12,581	16,454	15,283	14,526	14,696	7,527	14,710	12,679	13,454	15,832
Yarmouth, Canada	7,823	4,000	10,393	6,831	4,722	3,495	8,911	4,498	5,250	7,932	8,571	2,835	5,244	7,721	8,615	10,001	6,472	7,591	3,116	1,221
Yellowknife, Canada	10,812	5,767	11,178	9,955	7,642	3,034	11,857	3,907	8,742	10,945	11,324	5,955	8,253	11,227	11,514	6,530	7,495	7,245	1,239	2,816
Yerevan, USSR	13,496	12,371	2,752	12,754	5,629	11,078	13,960	12,157	10,968	13,474	14,318	10,631	12,228	11,750	5,837	7,586	2,189	1,271	9,405	7,634
Yinchuan, China	18,496	14,010	6,547	17,501	10,501	11,152	19,169	11,693	15,576	18,540	19,389	13,690	16,096	16,970	10,824	2,980	7,041	4,820	9,474	9,650
Yogyakarta, Indonesia	16,146	17,798	7,732	17,087	13,992	15,208	15,057	15,047	18,020	16,026	15,438	18,824	18,757	15,739	11,527	6,445	10,763	8,971	14,056	14,786
York, United Kingdom	10,841	8,662	5,798	9,882	3,075	7,759	11,706	8,862	7,948	10,881	11,744	6,978	8,876	9,618	5,975	8,692	1,807	3,142	6,390	4,115
Yumen, China	17,878	14,035	5,835	16,956	9,831	11,300	18,413	11,950	15,023	17,889	18,765	13,425	15,755	16,225	10,074	3,622	6,342	4,136	9,548	9,416
Yutian, China	16,721	14,328	4,401	15,990	8,816	11,934	17,004	12,752	14,152	16,687	17,489	13,198	15,242	14,900	8,655	5,036	5,300	3,239	10,113	9,414
Yuzhno-Sakhalinsk, USSR	16,702	11,540	9,409	16,003	11,392	8,586	17,514	8,882	14,794	16,844	16,838	12,060	14,315	17,277	13,256	447	8,563	6,522	7,204	8,391
Zagreb, Yugoslavia	11,462	10,070	4,280	10,600	3,415	9,273	12,153	10,378	8,723	11,470	12,348	8,249	9,880	9,940	5,118	8,784	290	2,284	7,855	5,633
Zahedan, Iran	14,773	14,254	2,318	14,229	7,362	12,660	14,912	13,675	12,614	14,712	15,442	12,531	13,994	12,885	6,577	7,111	4,061	2,742	10,882	9,419
Zamboanga, Philippines	17,673	15,889	8,519	18,677	14,079	13,135	16,652	13,061	19,406	17,601	16,789	16,912	18,771	17,811	12,812	4,429	10,565	8,446	12,011	13,117
Zanzibar, Tanzania	11,123	14,325	2,443	11,107	7,066	15,186	10,796	16,204	10,419	11,008	11,449	12,245	11,962	9,318	3,677	11,466	5,918	6,431	14,032	11,590
Zaragoza, Spain	10,058	8,874	5,204	9,177	2,019	8,551	10,800	9,628	7,291	10,074	10,952	6,940	8,457	8,617	4,638	9,894	1,596	3,690	7,408	4,914
Zashiversk, USSR	15,112	10,092	8,795	14,190	9,225	7,230	16,180	7,845	12,667	15,240	15,660	10,113	12,508	15,082	11,752	2,717	6,808	5,119	5,556	6,226
Zhengzhou, China	19,119	14,128	7,193	18,101	11,259	11,195	19,736	11,612	16,232	19,209	19,600	14,103	16,530	17,743	11,535	2,558	7,813	5,589	9,616	10,082
Zurich, Switzerland	11,021	9,460	4,845	10,126	2,990	8,729	11,772	9,831	8,225	11,040	11,917	7,646	9,329	9,587	5,214	8,978	876	2,739	7,374	5,075

Distances in Kilometers	Seattle, Washington	Sendai, Japan	Seoul, South Korea	Sept-Iles, Canada	Sevastopol, USSR	Seville, Spain	Shanghai, China	Sheffield, United Kingdom	Shenyang, China	Shiraz, Iran	Sibiu, Romania	Singapore	Sioux Falls, South Dakota	Skelleftea, Sweden	Skopje, Yugoslavia	Socotra Island (Tamrida)	Sofia, Bulgaria	Songkhla, Thailand	Sorong, Indonesia	South Georgia Island
Sendai, Japan	7,443	0	1,222	9,849	8,300	10,970	1,951	9,230	1,537	7,912	8,763	5,569	9,254	7,455	9,214	8,882	9,054	5,310	4,444	18,217
Seoul, South Korea	8,343	1,222	0	10,194	7,447	10,409	883	8,781	560	6,790	7,992	4,666	10,001	6,994	8,416	7,670	8,250	4,292	4,280	17,779
Sept-Iles, Canada	4,015	9,849	10,194	0	6,976	4,920	10,965	4,335	9,767	9,323	6,342	14,224	2,410	5,015	6,453	10,966	6,517	13,523	14,291	11,903
Sevastopol, USSR	9,522	8,300	7,447	6,976	0	3,385	7,500	2,710	6,918	2,360	749	8,361	9,072	2,377	1,018	4,043	851	7,641	10,691	12,810
Seville, Spain	8,678	10,970	10,409	4,920	3,385	0	10,661	1,810	9,850	5,420	2,662	11,666	7,330	3,524	2,400	6,524	2,555	10,972	14,060	10,573
Shanghai, China	9,225	1,951	883	10,965	7,500	10,661	0	9,150	1,200	6,506	8,115	3,783	10,877	7,391	8,505	7,150	8,336	3,418	3,693	16,904
Sheffield, United Kingdom	7,504	9,230	8,781	4,335	2,710	1,810	9,150	0	8,223	5,066	2,022	10,907	6,592	1,790	2,123	6,632	2,182	10,165	12,757	12,365
Shenyang, China	8,182	1,537	560	9,767	6,918	9,850	1,200	8,223	0	6,378	7,449	4,899	9,737	6,436	7,878	7,382	7,713	4,447	4,792	18,001
Shiraz, Iran	11,440	7,912	6,790	9,323	2,360	5,420	6,506	5,066	6,378	0	3,055	6,263	11,323	4,485	3,102	1,883	2,982	5,598	8,973	12,576
Sibiu, Romania	9,155	8,763	7,992	6,342	749	2,662	8,115	2,022	7,449	3,055	0	9,110	8,523	2,121	473	4,629	353	8,389	11,401	12,488
Singapore	12,993	5,569	4,666	14,224	8,361	11,666	3,783	10,907	4,899	6,263	9,110	0	14,635	9,540	9,285	5,637	9,140	747	3,059	13,128
Sioux Falls, South Dakota	2,038	9,254	10,001	2,410	9,072	7,330	10,877	6,592	9,737	11,323	8,523	14,635	0	6,841	8,707	13,114	8,747	14,122	13,322	12,239
Skelleftea, Sweden	7,146	7,455	6,994	5,015	2,377	3,524	7,391	1,790	6,436	4,485	2,121	9,540	6,841	0	2,534	6,317	2,462	8,794	11,044	14,086
Skopje, Yugoslavia	9,461	9,214	8,416	6,453	1,018	2,400	8,505	2,123	7,878	3,102	473	9,285	8,707	2,534	0	4,525	169	8,580	11,701	12,017
Socotra Island (Tamrida)	13,322	8,882	7,670	10,966	4,043	6,524	7,150	6,632	7,382	1,883	4,629	5,637	13,114	6,317	4,525	0	4,452	5,138	8,654	11,188
Sofia, Bulgaria	9,450	9,054	8,250	6,517	851	2,555	8,336	2,182	7,713	2,982	353	9,140	8,747	2,462	169	4,452	0	8,432	11,537	12,162
Songkhla, Thailand	12,624	5,310	4,292	13,523	7,641	10,972	3,418	10,165	4,447	5,598	8,389	747	14,122	8,794	8,580	5,138	8,432	0	3,519	13,555
Sorong, Indonesia	11,309	4,444	4,280	14,291	10,691	14,060	3,693	12,757	4,792	8,973	11,401	3,059	13,322	11,044	11,701	8,654	11,537	3,519	0	13,794
South Georgia Island	13,841	18,217	17,779	11,903	12,810	10,573	16,904	12,365	18,001	12,576	12,488	13,128	12,239	14,086	12,017	11,188	12,162	13,555	13,794	0
South Pole	15,275	14,236	14,161	15,566	14,944	14,143	13,445	15,920	14,631	13,279	15,078	10,144	14,825	17,190	14,656	11,402	14,732	10,798	9,903	3,990
South Sandwich Islands	14,589	17,652	17,049	12,511	12,629	10,716	16,169	12,526	17,253	12,127	12,394	12,389	12,968	14,166	11,921	10,632	12,054	12,808	13,211	748
Split, Yugoslavia	9,133	9,366	8,630	6,028	1,373	2,012	8,771	1,712	8,083	3,545	662	9,705	8,304	2,382	446	4,961	568	8,994	12,057	11,952
Spokane, Washington	370	7,747	8,615	3,675	9,396	8,397	9,498	7,285	8,432	11,388	8,994	13,277	1,671	7,026	9,281	13,270	9,279	12,879	11,666	13,589
Spoleto, Italy	9,070	9,625	8,912	5,843	1,686	1,699	9,070	1,583	8,363	3,823	972	10,007	8,155	2,507	725	5,180	867	9,299	12,370	11,731
Springbok, South Africa	16,084	14,754	13,542	12,098	8,376	7,829	12,831	9,388	13,364	7,520	8,381	9,695	14,129	10,472	7,944	6,080	8,030	9,709	12,209	5,115
Springfield, Illinois	2,750	9,950	10,660	2,154	9,071	7,008	11,529	6,478	10,372	11,388	8,467	15,254	721	6,954	8,600	13,096	8,658	14,696	14,043	11,580
Springfield, Massachusetts	3,911	10,485	10,962	1,019	7,926	5,587	11,773	5,245	10,574	10,284	7,266	15,187	1,974	6,028	7,339	11,864	7,417	14,502	14,859	11,209
Srinagar, India	10,798	5,835	4,671	9,921	3,701	7,082	4,345	6,184	4,301	2,162	4,441	4,723	11,366	4,939	4,687	3,173	4,528	3,984	7,037	14,360
Stanley, Falkland Islands	12,598	17,923	18,389	11,322	13,788	11,083	17,718	12,773	18,900	13,904	13,339	14,162	11,198	14,563	12,887	12,608	13,046	14,692	14,115	1,440
Stara Zagora, Bulgaria	9,548	8,940	8,114	6,679	683	2,744	8,182	2,345	7,580	2,793	394	8,948	8,890	2,505	346	4,288	193	8,240	11,356	12,241
Stockholm, Sweden	7,616	7,985	7,453	5,151	1,944	2,986	7,788	1,372	6,893	4,203	1,560	9,646	7,144	624	1,943	5,973	1,887	8,899	11,385	13,508
Stornoway, United Kingdom	6,896	8,889	8,541	3,877	3,099	2,317	8,983	620	7,988	5,454	2,477	11,054	6,059	1,611	2,653	7,104	2,688	10,307	12,650	12,766
Strasbourg, France	8,313	9,335	8,741	5,155	2,015	1,669	9,000	839	8,182	4,328	1,278	10,353	7,430	1,966	1,299	5,823	1,376	9,623	12,475	12,138
Stuttgart, West Germany	8,352	9,257	8,651	5,234	1,911	1,761	8,903	906	8,093	4,230	1,177	10,246	7,497	1,914	1,220	5,739	1,288	9,516	12,371	12,203
Subic, Philippines	10,729	3,290	2,601	12,766	8,605	11,951	1,802	10,642	2,999	7,074	9,300	2,347	12,528	8,954	9,622	7,139	9,455	2,306	2,124	15,204
Suchow, China	9,180	2,169	958	10,642	6,976	10,141	525	8,647	1,000	6,033	7,589	3,906	10,729	6,898	7,980	6,772	7,811	3,447	4,159	17,002
Sucre, Bolivia	9,313	16,712	17,635	7,669	12,160	8,805	18,514	10,070	17,351	13,682	11,460	17,720	7,637	11,725	11,144	13,523	11,310	18,011	17,168	4,602
Sudbury, Canada	3,106	9,735	10,285	1,157	8,050	6,067	11,121	5,458	9,930	10,374	7,445	14,690	1,281	5,963	7,581	12,073	7,637	14,055	14,063	11,921
Suez, Egypt	11,056	9,420	8,407	8,100	1,626	3,640	8,259	3,783	7,931	1,930	1,904	8,145	10,371	3,953	1,664	2,928	1,634	7,504	10,903	11,442
Sundsvall, Sweden	7,297	7,770	7,291	4,963	2,239	3,205	7,668	1,491	6,732	4,442	1,897	9,702	6,885	322	2,285	6,242	2,228	8,955	11,304	13,765
Surabaya, Indonesia	13,174	5,820	5,178	15,242	9,726	13,028	4,344	12,249	5,540	7,616	10,475	1,367	15,070	10,815	10,651	6,860	10,507	2,091	2,171	12,620
Suva, Fiji	9,366	7,371	8,183	13,327	15,630	17,829	8,177	16,095	8,713	14,423	16,134	8,432	10,975	14,559	16,581	14,056	16,419	8,989	5,495	11,317
Sverdlovsk, USSR	8,424	5,996	5,221	7,180	2,322	5,247	5,414	3,845	4,674	3,093	2,779	7,257	8,679	2,284	3,220	4,937	3,059	6,512	8,925	15,112
Svobodnyy, USSR	7,152	1,770	1,540	8,661	6,594	9,205	2,321	7,481	1,125	6,530	7,018	6,003	8,633	5,698	7,476	7,818	7,319	5,516	5,802	18,951
Sydney, Australia	12,455	8,057	8,298	16,470	14,644	17,928	7,847	16,960	8,848	12,514	15,391	6,293	14,181	15,236	15,577	11,445	15,434	7,005	4,204	10,210
Sydney, Canada	4,611	10,424	10,705	644	6,878	4,520	11,446	4,180	10,256	9,238	6,202	14,523	2,879	5,102	6,260	10,782	6,341	13,797	14,868	11,345
Syktyvkar, USSR	7,875	6,356	5,709	6,414	2,208	4,701	5,991	3,170	5,151	3,566	2,459	8,025	7,983	1,525	2,929	5,447	2,786	7,281	9,588	14,947
Szeged, Hungary	8,985	8,942	8,208	6,070	1,061	2,372	8,361	1,738	7,660	3,358	313	9,421	8,282	2,060	486	4,896	470	8,700	11,688	12,365
Szombathely, Hungary	8,771	9,044	8,352	5,789	1,342	2,149	8,539	1,454	7,800	3,649	599	9,697	8,018	1,970	698	5,178	731	8,972	11,917	12,317
Tabriz, Iran	10,447	7,867	6,857	8,224	1,288	4,547	6,742	3,996	6,377	1,103	2,018	7,131	10,230	3,401	2,154	2,920	2,010	6,427	9,630	12,925
Tacheng, China	9,267	4,744	3,728	8,865	3,794	7,035	3,706	5,732	3,243	3,242	4,425	5,432	10,002	4,154	4,802	4,650	4,633	4,697	7,064	15,792
Tahiti (Papeete)	7,709	9,518	10,622	11,015	16,990	15,844	10,916	15,170	11,047	17,410	16,817	11,820	8,642	14,710	17,164	17,444	17,137	12,356	8,840	9,841
Taipei, Taiwan	9,751	2,341	1,483	11,634	7,946	11,188	672	9,737	1,867	6,744	8,593	3,243	11,469	7,997	8,961	7,176	8,792	2,974	3,056	16,301
Taiyuan, China	9,091	2,477	1,273	10,248	6,404	9,564	1,102	8,084	1,029	5,542	7,013	4,148	10,519	6,345	7,406	6,404	7,237	3,604	4,701	17,060
Tallahasee, Florida	3,752	11,077	11,806	2,654	9,586	7,073	12,675	6,896	11,517	11,945	8,918	16,391	1,823	7,665	8,971	13,487	9,056	15,807	15,044	10,434
Tallinn, USSR	7,770	7,703	7,129	5,476	1,752	3,287	7,439	1,741	6,569	3,921	1,516	9,268	7,405	628	1,951	5,727	1,864	8,521	11,019	13,741
Tamanrasset, Algeria	10,636	11,806	10,958	6,821	3,517	1,958	10,947	3,447	10,434	4,728	3,059	10,816	9,226	4,799	2,598	5,242	2,754	10,227	13,689	9,444
Tampa, Florida	4,070	11,406	12,132	2,821	9,686	7,056	13,000	6,982	11,838	12,046	9,002	16,701	2,152	7,834	9,031	13,525	9,123	16,102	15,347	10,108
Tampere, Finland	7,535	7,592	7,059	5,309	1,987	3,381	7,402	1,750	6,499	4,126	1,748	9,356	7,198	390	2,175	5,945	2,094	8,609	11,013	13,889
Tanami, Australia	12,961	6,551	6,376	16,366	12,023	15,338	5,725	14,461	6,871	9,923	12,771	3,675	14,992	12,886	12,959	9,040	12,814	4,383	2,119	11,679
Tangier, Morocco	8,827	11,121	10,542	5,040	3,452	176	10,778	1,981	9,984	5,434	2,740	11,690	7,450	3,682	2,453	6,484	2,613	11,004	14,140	10,410
Tarawa (Betio)	8,029	5,233	6,173	12,013	13,532	15,715	6,340	13,918	6,667	12,840	13,953	7,688	9,935	12,325	14,417	13,115	14,263	8,049	4,647	13,548
Tashkent, USSR	10,087	5,961	4,892	8,986	2,917	6,293	4,743	5,281	4,440	1,996	3,632	5,630	10,501	4,000	3,930	3,509	3,765	4,885	7,775	14,562
Tbilisi, USSR	10,031	7,754	6,796	7,828	967	4,324	6,747	3,641	6,295	1,515	1,715	7,395	9,811	2,979	1,927	3,343	1,769	6,677	9,785	13,142
Tegucigalpa, Honduras	4,930	12,356	13,267	4,427	11,189	8,307	14,150	8,480	13,067	13,534	10,479	17,922	3,388	9,433	10,456	14,827	10,564	17,500	15,554	8,946
Tehran, Iran	10,761	7,631	6,569	8,712	1,814	5,065	6,387	4,516	6,115	681	2,548	6,607	10,662	3,820	2,679	2,563	2,538	5,907	9,150	13,021
Tel Aviv, Israel	10,891	9,107	8,101	8,065	1,395	3,750	7,966	3,731	7,621	1,720	1,777	7,973	10,294	3,758	1,613	2,914	1,552	7,316	10,678	11,754
Telegraph Creek, Canada	1,290	6,395	7,194	4,158	8,556	8,281	8,076	6,860	6,986	10,302	8,287	11,859	2,861	6,197	8,645	12,171	8,608	11,431	10,539	15,029
Teresina, Brazil	9,642	16,313	16,263	6,532	9,333	6,056	16,689	7,541	15,717	10,809	8,665	16,310	7,623	9,310	8,315	10,881	8,483	15,983	19,088	5,479
Ternate, Indonesia	11,449	4,370	4,071	14,203	10,256	13,633	3,415	12,385	4,558	8,508	10,971	2,622	13,432	10,699	11,262	8,194	11,099	3,058	467	13,905
The Valley, Anguilla	6,253	13,293	13,760	3,579	9,128	5,925	14,544	6,537	13,345	11,335	8,381	17,440	4,235	7,923	8,248	12,333	8,383	16,694	17,557	8,395
Thessaloniki, Greece	9,649	9,239	8,413	6,645	974	2,519	8,474	2,316	7,880	2,944	582	9,152	8,901	2,689	194	4,337	230	8,453	11,615	11,953
Thimphu, Bhutan	11,089	4,869	3,647	11,078	5,288	8,673	3,089	7,678	3,443	3,630	6,021	3,273	12,107	6,267	6,281	4,061	6,121	2,527	5,440	14,792
Thunder Bay, Canada	2,446	9,206	9,829	1,673	8,298	6,576	10,685	5,804	9,509	10,570	7,740	14,356	788	6,098	7,920	12,341	7,960	13,770	13,469	12,399
Tientsin, China	8,743	2,057	874	10,102	6,659	9,738	967	8,194	607	5,917	7,239	4,406	10,235	6,429	7,647	6,826	7,479	3,909	4,658	17,433
Tijuana, Mexico	1,732	8,782	9,805	4,560	10,960	9,479	10,670	8,648	9,719	13,040	10,492	14,325	2,150	8,618	10,729	14,915	10,749	14,084	12,096	12,288
Tiksi, USSR	5,668	3,776	3,790	6,440	5,552	7,409	4,526	5,606	3,331	6,430	5,727	8,005	6,740	3,930	6,199	8,144	6,072	7,413	8,047	17,950
Timbuktu, Mali	10,682	12,850	12,048	6,703	4,601	2,303	12,059	4,063	11,516	5,808	4,088	11,771	9,037	5,628	3,644	6,140	3,807	11,123	14,724	8,498
Tindouf, Algeria	9,397	12,027	11,404	5,462	4,135	1,093	11,586	2,902	10,849	5,867	3,477	12,103	7,840	4,603	3,117	6,642	3,285	11,461	14,779	9,486
Tirane, Albania	9,473	9,362	8,570	6,398	1,174	2,259	8,661	2,081	8,031	3,216	606	9,418	8,672	2,609	156	4,595	325	8,716	11,852	11,883
Tokyo, Japan	7,711	300	1,160	10,149	8,431	11,179	1,782	9,456	1,568	7,933	8,918	5,317	9,539	7,674	9,363	8,823	9,201	5,084	4,145	17,926
Toledo, Spain	8,566	10,647	10,085	4,896	3,116	325	10,343	1,513	9,526	5,215	2,382	11,436	7,299	3,205	2,153	6,401	2,301	10,733	13,767	10,888
Topeka, Kansas	2,346	9,687	10,468	2,610	9,439	7,502	11,347	6,895	10,218	11,724	8,862	15,117	507	7,255	9,018	13,479	9,068	14,618	13,653	11,769
Toronto, Canada	3,334	10,071	10,624	1,225	8,194	6,054	11,460	5,560	10,268	10,534	7,566	15,015	1,398	6,167	7,677	12,191	7,742	14,372	14,384	11,581
Toulouse, France	8,501	10,065	9,479	5,039	2,556	933	9,729	1,107	8,920	4,746	1,811	10,911	7,402	2,653	1,646	6,064	1,778	10,195	13,165	11,434
Tours, France	8,126	9,732	9,195	4,769	2,545	1,238	9,490	683	8,635	4,829	1,800	10,894	7,099	2,288	1,748	6,255	1,851	10,166	13,001	11,803
Townsville, Australia	11,630	6,395	6,623	15,498	13,320	16,701	6,201	15,350	7,174	11,446	14,039	5,214	13,582	13,589	14,320	10,760	14,159	5,850	2,647	11,854
Trenton, New Jersey	3,844	10,590	11,110	1,288	8,203	5,829	11,934	5,519	10,737	10,561	7,541	15,406	1,854	6,301	7,610	12,134	7,689	14,732	14,922	11,081
Tripoli, Lebanon	10,663	8,861	7,872	7,935	1,146	3,760	7,763	3,601	7,385	1,662	1,605	7,924	10,127	3,521	1,510	3,032	1,423	7,251	10,565	12,026
Tripoli, Libya	10,049	10,457	9,631	6,578	2,184	1,813	9,668	2,557	9,100	3,745	1,712	10,000	8,960	3,583	1,247	4,713	1,403	9,343	12,664	10,779
Tristan da Cunha (Edinburgh)	14,333	17,663	16,445	11,024	10,151	8,267	15,741	10,072	16,219	10,006	9,876	12,399	12,330	11,655	9,403	8,841	9,540	12,522	14,383	2,673
Trondheim, Norway	7,017	7,916	7,499	4,596	2,554	3,100	7,915	1,314	6,942	4,795	2,142	10,050	6,540	535	2,490	6,579	2,453	9,304	11,575	13,672
Trujillo, Peru	7,497	14,812	15,830	6,576	12,423	9,086	16,704	9,910	15,673	14,450	11,675	19,189	5,994	11,291	11,480	14,877	11,629	19,900	16,530	6,348
Truk Island (Moen)	9,090	3,588	4,176	12,636	11,592	14,539	4,114	12,817	4,726	10,504	12,164	5,370	11,128	11,038	12,580	10,683	12,412	5,658	2,467	14,756
Truro, Canada	4,431	10,434	10,762	586	7,122	4,771	11,522	4,428	10,326	9,482	6,450	14,684	2,652	5,312	6,512	11,035	6,592	13,966	14,876	11,322
Tsingtao, China	8,849	1,839	619	10,426	7,082	10,176	558	8,629	692	6,260	7,670	4,210	10,428	6,860	8,075	7,070	7,906	3,775	4,245	17,328
Tsitsihar, China	7,687	1,710	1,117	9,148	6,594	9,385	1,818	7,712	620	6,302	7,075	5,464	9,173	5,922	7,520	7,475	7,358	4,974	5,393	18,461
Tubuai Island (Mataura)	8,316	9,961	11,022	11,499	17,634	16,217	11,244	15,731	11,474	17,734	17,451	11,776	9,158	15,352	17,777	17,280	17,763	12,365	8,883	9,292
Tucson, Arizona	1,960	9,241	10,225	4,157	10,773	9,069	11,099	8,354	10,104	12,946	10,258	14,806	1,770	8,475	10,462	14,791	10,495	14,516	12,658	11,916
Tulsa, Oklahoma	2,516	9,915	10,727	2,834	9,718	7,686	11,608	7,148	10,492	12,016	9,128	15,386	823	7,556	9,271	13,753	9,326	14,907	13,791	11,506

Distances in Kilometers

	Seattle, Washington	Sendai, Japan	Seoul, South Korea	Sept-Iles, Canada	Sevastopol, USSR	Seville, Spain	Shanghai, China	Sheffield, United Kingdom	Shenyang, China	Shiraz, Iran	Sibiu, Romania	Singapore	Sioux Falls, South Dakota	Skelleftea, Sweden	Skopje, Yugoslavia	Socotra Island (Tamrida)	Sofia, Bulgaria	Songkhla, Thailand	Sorong, Indonesia	South Georgia Island
Tunis, Tunisia	9,538	10,281	9,526	6,086	2,145	1,437	9,634	2,052	8,983	3,996	1,535	10,255	8,460	3,192	1,130	5,115	1,299	9,575	12,796	11,045
Tura, USSR	7,058	3,929	3,460	7,257	4,572	7,048	3,970	5,346	2,909	5,083	4,914	6,996	7,958	3,557	5,382	6,741	5,233	6,335	7,661	17,382
Turin, Italy	8,643	9,661	9,025	5,363	2,038	1,423	9,245	1,139	8,469	4,264	1,290	10,397	7,681	2,343	1,166	5,658	1,283	9,679	12,649	11,781
Uberlandia, Brazil	10,403	17,690	17,891	7,862	10,842	7,650	18,311	9,181	17,354	12,049	10,210	16,416	8,500	10,953	9,831	11,743	10,000	16,426	17,812	4,042
Ufa, USSR	8,662	6,349	5,544	7,201	1,957	4,974	5,697	3,659	5,002	2,805	2,447	7,341	8,811	2,221	2,878	4,672	2,714	6,593	9,149	14,737
Ujungpandang, Indonesia	12,523	5,290	4,791	14,978	10,080	13,444	4,015	12,472	5,212	8,092	10,823	1,868	14,478	10,918	11,045	7,493	10,892	2,493	1,398	13,063
Ulaanbaatar, Mongolia	8,404	2,941	1,999	9,113	5,449	8,461	2,235	6,916	1,471	5,021	5,995	5,176	9,612	5,158	6,417	6,242	6,251	4,552	5,900	17,404
Ulan-Ude, USSR	8,008	2,987	2,194	8,682	5,322	8,216	2,562	6,618	1,638	5,113	5,824	5,614	9,181	4,843	6,261	6,449	6,098	4,991	6,251	17,637
Uliastay, Mongolia	8,783	3,690	2,698	9,032	4,761	7,878	2,785	6,424	2,197	4,272	5,343	5,193	9,804	4,719	5,748	5,552	5,580	4,509	6,337	16,740
Uranium City, Canada	1,606	7,445	8,096	2,845	7,952	7,155	8,962	5,904	7,803	9,972	7,559	12,693	1,957	5,584	7,857	11,849	7,849	12,165	11,738	14,141
Urumqi, China	9,465	4,447	3,370	9,289	4,240	7,512	3,274	6,221	2,920	3,471	4,889	4,978	10,320	4,635	5,254	4,711	5,085	4,250	6,578	15,900
Ushuaia, Argentina	12,427	17,152	17,769	11,640	14,565	11,812	17,265	13,466	18,325	14,596	14,111	14,029	11,226	15,254	13,661	13,194	13,821	14,634	13,579	2,027
Vaduz, Liechtenstein	8,517	9,386	8,757	5,351	1,878	1,673	8,989	1,043	8.201	4,165	1,132	10,234	7,633	2,078	1,109	5,633	1,196	9,510	12,422	12,055
Valencia, Spain	8,788	10,538	9,928	5,177	2,843	542	10,151	1,548	9,371	4,907	2,120	11,139	7,573	3,136	1,862	6,086	2,015	10,439	13,520	10,952
Valladolid, Spain	8,373	10,496	9,961	4,736	3,101	486	10,242	1,325	9,401	5,256	2,358	11,449	7,133	3,045	2,169	6,498	2,309	10,737	13,708	11,057
Valletta, Malta	9,812	10,121	9,314	6,446	1,878	1,837	9,376	2,308	8,779	3,607	1,365	9,870	8,804	3,240	907	4,717	1,068	9,196	12,456	11,131
Valparaiso, Chile	10,264	17,040	18,261	9,234	13,624	10,347	18,783	11,710	18,370	14,761	12,967	16,459	8,856	13,393	12,608	14,084	12,777	17,036	15,557	3,609
Vancouver, Canada	193	7,297	8,182	3,991	9,362	8,594	9,064	7,383	8,012	11,261	9,008	12,837	2,114	6,986	9,321	13,142	9,307	12,456	11,214	14,011
Varna, Bulgaria	9,530	8,743	7,910	6,756	477	2,933	7,975	2,433	7,377	2,659	415	8,775	8,934	2,438	545	4,214	380	8,063	11,158	12,420
Venice, Italy	8,791	9,406	8,730	5,639	1,667	1,769	8,923	1,332	8,177	3,910	920	10,027	7,923	2,215	829	5,350	930	9,308	12,293	11,985
Veracruz, Mexico	3,943	11,310	12,276	4,331	11,298	8,754	13,154	8,617	12,125	13,652	10,639	16,873	2,700	9,291	10,697	15,210	10,781	16,565	14,484	9,899
Verona, Italy	8,739	9,471	8,807	5,553	1,773	1,674	9,009	1,261	8,253	4,014	1,025	10,132	7,846	2,236	927	5,443	1,032	9,414	12,392	11,936
Victoria, Canada	121	7,328	8,224	4,046	9,455	8,670	9,106	7,469	8,062	11,352	9,099	12,876	2,122	7,078	9,411	13,234	9,397	12,504	11,214	13,961
Victoria, Seychelles	15,237	9,930	8,717	12,623	5,874	7,861	8,021	8,323	8,559	3,799	6,387	5,423	14,906	8,201	6,202	1,916	6,160	5,183	8,436	9,737
Vienna, Austria	8,667	8,975	8,298	5,711	1,376	2,175	8,499	1,380	7,745	3,704	649	9,717	7,928	1,865	798	5,256	819	8,990	11,901	12,401
Vientiane, Laos	11,480	4,337	3,222	12,377	6,981	10,366	2,389	9,323	3,303	5,222	7,713	1,850	12,916	7,818	7,973	5,237	7,814	1,211	3,768	14,701
Villahermosa, Mexico	4,236	11,636	12,579	4,284	11,214	8,556	13,460	8,516	12,408	13,575	10,537	17,205	2,856	9,284	10,569	15,055	10,661	16,855	14,848	9,613
Vilnius, USSR	8,270	8,026	7,373	5,799	1,267	3,050	7,613	1,753	6,816	3,535	992	9,155	7,822	1,149	1,438	5,293	1,342	8,413	11,107	13,344
Visby, Sweden	7,791	8,112	7,552	5,255	1,791	2,868	7,863	1,333	6,992	4,081	1,376	9,622	7,284	807	1,753	5,830	1,700	8,876	11,435	13,360
Vitoria, Brazil	11,073	18,013	17,742	8,221	10,367	7,333	17,838	8,977	17,183	11,371	9,784	15,604	9,113	10,767	9,375	10,945	9,543	15,582	17,491	3,779
Vladivostok, USSR	7,607	932	745	9,513	7,375	10,128	1,626	8,426	710	7,014	7,853	5,409	9,257	6,638	8,299	8,080	8,138	5,021	4,876	18,521
Volgograd, USSR	9,253	7,355	6,497	7,214	951	4,210	6,568	3,203	5,967	2,236	1,563	7,711	9,101	2,261	1,937	4,100	1,768	6,972	9,850	13,702
Vologda, USSR	8,054	7,015	6,357	6,178	1,682	4,057	6,619	2,599	5,800	3,428	1,827	8,432	7,942	1,163	2,300	5,300	2,164	7,685	10,168	14,309
Vorkuta, USSR	7,229	5,595	5,069	6,310	3,111	5,384	5,473	3,712	4,510	4,283	3,329	7,959	7,585	1,927	3,802	6,136	3,665	7,234	9,146	15,805
Wake Island	7,036	3,258	4,337	10,725	11,488	13,685	4,714	11,876	4,769	11,128	11,870	7,119	9,071	10,238	12,338	11,845	12,188	7,243	4,464	15,646
Wallis Island	8,596	7,251	8,176	12,542	15,545	17,167	8,284	15,535	8,679	14,713	15,930	8,966	10,186	14,142	16,401	14,600	16,253	9,474	5,954	11,600
Walvis Bay, Namibia	15,322	14,691	13,469	11,317	7,727	7,015	12,842	8,595	13,215	7,099	7,675	10,005	13,417	9,740	7,227	5,836	7,323	9,929	12,701	5,477
Warsaw, Poland	8,405	8,420	7,761	5,722	1,255	2,672	7,989	1,516	7,206	3,606	753	9,409	7,832	1,394	1,140	5,289	1,078	8,671	11,452	12,958
Washington, D.C.	3,747	10,629	11,190	1,512	8,445	6,064	12,025	5,763	10,832	10,802	7,785	15,555	1,726	6,527	7,855	12,379	7,933	14,896	14,913	11,017
Watson Lake, Canada	1,455	6,431	7,182	3,964	8,286	8,008	8,062	6,579	6,949	10,061	8,009	11,840	2,830	5,924	8,366	11,934	8,330	11,385	10,643	15,053
Weimar, East Germany	8,220	8,968	8,371	5,236	1,801	2,039	8,635	915	7,812	4,152	1,109	10,077	7,450	1,634	1,265	5,731	1,297	9,342	12,130	12,492
Wellington, New Zealand	11,634	9,459	9,994	15,295	16,868	19,565	9,715	18,635	10,554	14,722	17,610	8,524	12,895	16,910	17,806	13,492	17,665	9,235	6,253	8,999
West Berlin, West Germany	8,144	8,745	8,150	5,271	1,719	2,259	8,421	1,004	7,591	4,079	1,081	9,927	7,443	1,431	1,318	5,707	1,321	9,188	11,931	12,711
Wewak, Papua New Guinea	10,603	4,637	4,866	14,120	11,872	15,154	4,506	13,635	5,422	10,315	12,545	4,459	12,639	11,855	12,891	10,062	12,723	4,927	1,409	13,598
Whangarei, New Zealand	11,171	8,885	9,470	14,963	16,576	19,818	9,239	18,017	10,027	14,603	17,285	8,345	12,553	16,321	17,577	13,555	17,417	9,030	5,887	9,601
Whitehorse, Canada	1,674	6,084	6,849	4,281	8,284	8,191	7,730	6,703	6,627	9,971	8,048	11,511	3,173	5,942	8,421	11,832	8,376	11,069	10,293	15,382
Wichita, Kansas	2,311	9,703	10,514	2,817	9,644	7,704	11,396	7,104	10,281	11,924	9,069	15,175	651	7,452	9,227	13,685	9,276	14,700	13,598	11,718
Willemstad, Curacao	6,311	13,629	14,260	4,230	10,039	6,820	15,097	7,443	13,902	12,236	9,292	18,330	4,386	8,791	9,156	13,164	9,291	17,583	17,477	7,957
Wiluna, Australia	14,171	7,495	7,138	17,325	11,787	14,873	6,388	14,424	7,580	9,523	12,529	3,551	16,206	13,084	12,625	8,368	12,500	4,298	3,081	10,779
Windhoek, Namibia	15,473	14,443	13,221	11,459	7,625	7,064	12,584	8,603	12,977	6,910	7,606	9,739	13,600	9,690	7,165	5,605	7,254	9,660	12,449	5,670
Windsor, Canada	3,123	10,044	10,654	1,549	8,505	6,386	11,503	5,883	10,320	10,839	7,884	15,129	1,127	6,447	8,002	12,512	8,065	14,511	14,291	11,569
Winnipeg, Canada	1,860	8,711	9,395	2,189	8,502	7,024	10,263	6,118	9,106	10,707	7,990	13,992	706	6,223	8,208	12,529	8,234	13,452	12,915	12,844
Winston-Salem, North Carolina	3,668	10,754	11,381	1,923	8,865	6,450	12,231	6,183	11,049	11,222	8,204	15,845	1,631	6,935	8,271	12,794	8,351	15,211	14,940	10,845
Wroclaw, Poland	8,401	8,701	8,057	5,567	1,426	2,370	8,291	1,287	7,501	3,786	790	9,676	7,734	1,539	1,067	5,412	1,050	8,941	11,752	12,702
Wuhan, China	9,672	2,580	1,406	11,056	7,006	10,256	682	8,842	1,492	5,873	7,654	3,424	11,213	7,126	8,021	6,469	7,852	2,955	3,920	16,510
Wyndham, Australia	12,729	6,094	5,871	15,939	11,560	14,907	5,205	13,953	6,358	9,512	12,305	3,249	14,768	12,362	12,513	8,731	12,363	3,935	1,650	12,148
Xi'an, China	9,605	2,894	1,671	10,637	6,358	9,611	1,219	8,220	1,524	5,288	7,005	3,689	11,006	6,524	7,372	6,014	7,203	3,116	4,537	16,543
Xining, China	9,702	3,441	2,239	10,317	5,673	8,955	1,909	7,621	1,953	4,611	6,331	3,918	10,933	5,968	6,690	5,441	6,521	3,260	5,149	16,301
Yakutsk, USSR	6,286	2,752	2,724	7,483	6,051	8,292	3,485	6,515	2,285	6,483	6,352	7,075	7,591	4,770	6,824	8,023	6,681	6,530	6,976	18,836
Yanji, China	7,761	1,090	628	9,577	7,242	10,045	1,492	8,362	514	6,835	7,734	5,269	9,385	6,572	8,176	7,886	8,014	4,863	4,851	18,396
Yaounde, Cameroon	12,755	13,030	11,953	8,820	5,000	4,119	11,662	5,616	11,514	5,171	4,805	10,267	11,171	6,800	4,339	4,773	4,456	9,863	13,326	7,831
Yap Island (Colonia)	9,941	3,195	3,302	12,977	10,407	13,616	2,955	12,067	3,856	9,075	11,050	3,904	11,946	10,286	11,422	9,157	11,253	4,140	1,380	15,022
Yaraka, Australia	12,268	6,996	7,140	16,173	13,503	16,869	6,653	15,747	7,683	11,477	14,243	5,215	14,189	14,033	14,471	10,605	14,319	5,899	2,993	11,237
Yarmouth, Canada	4,300	10,518	10,894	708	7,405	5,027	11,671	4,711	10,472	9,765	6,733	14,909	2,455	5,581	6,793	11,316	6,874	14,198	14,948	11,222
Yellowknife, Canada	1,727	7,007	7,649	3,171	7,797	7,247	8,515	5,894	7,357	9,734	7,450	12,248	2,396	5,420	7,775	11,617	7,754	11,726	11,323	14,587
Yerevan, USSR	10,194	7,866	6,890	7,945	1,026	4,338	6,818	3,728	6,396	1,383	1,767	7,357	9,952	3,127	1,939	3,190	1,787	6,645	9,798	13,001
Yinchuan, China	9,326	3,003	1,815	10,156	5,909	9,124	1,598	7,708	1,504	4,992	6,538	4,125	10,631	6,005	6,918	5,884	6,749	3,511	5,051	16,730
Yogyakarta, Indonesia	13,386	6,000	5,312	15,294	9,586	12,859	4,463	12,145	5,652	7,440	10,335	1,238	15,254	10,757	10,495	6,631	10,354	1,982	2,440	12,476
York, United Kingdom	7,477	9,173	8,727	4,336	2,695	1,865	9,098	56	8,168	5,053	2,015	10,873	6,583	1,735	2,128	6,631	2,183	10,131	12,709	12,421
Yumen, China	9,544	3,704	2,547	9,910	5,190	8,456	2,343	7,121	2,173	4,245	5,839	4,314	10,657	5,477	6,204	5,228	6,035	3,626	5,651	16,286
Yutian, China	10,350	5,139	3,982	9,865	4,097	7,473	3,693	6,405	3,605	2,823	4,812	4,551	11,098	4,994	5,109	3,849	4,944	3,804	6,594	15,023
Yuzhno-Sakhalinsk, USSR	6,692	978	1,660	8,883	7,729	10,159	2,536	8,384	1,635	7,685	8,115	6,305	8,408	6,636	8,580	8,897	8,428	5,951	5,417	19,192
Zagreb, Yugoslavia	8,891	9,196	8,491	5,846	1,381	2,048	8,664	1,514	7,940	3,645	633	9,742	8,098	2,133	610	5,127	679	9,022	12,012	12,155
Zahedan, Iran	11,460	7,238	6,083	9,767	2,930	6,150	5,747	5,626	5,702	808	3,666	5,517	11,602	4,798	3,783	1,996	3,647	4,833	8,172	13,090
Zamboanga, Philippines	11,305	3,956	3,433	13,626	9,361	12,736	2,682	11,504	3,869	7,660	10,075	2,115	13,197	9,839	10,369	7,475	10,205	2,372	1,335	14,422
Zanzibar, Tanzania	15,090	11,457	10,235	11,641	5,651	6,722	9,626	7,620	9,991	4,208	5,947	7,234	14,049	8,011	5,629	2,650	5,643	6,979	10,237	8,541
Zaragoza, Spain	8,568	10,349	9,768	5,002	2,799	644	10,017	1,305	9,210	4,938	2,061	11,137	7,388	2,925	1,854	6,186	1,997	10,428	13,439	11,162
Zashiversk, USSR	5,439	3,251	3,467	6,732	6,246	8,084	4,276	6,276	3,081	7,006	6,434	7,924	6,732	4,627	6,906	8,655	6,778	7,390	7,634	18,533
Zhengzhou, China	9,321	2,460	1,239	10,594	6,684	9,882	825	8,426	1,158	5,706	7,310	3,843	10,805	6,694	7,692	6,455	7,523	3,332	4,350	16,857
Zurich, Switzerland	8,452	9,419	8,804	5,266	1,965	1,616	9,045	967	8,246	4,255	1,220	10,319	7,553	2,081	1,197	5,721	1,285	9,594	12,492	12,036

Distances in Kilometers

	South Pole	South Sandwich Islands	Split, Yugoslavia	Spokane, Washington	Spoleto, Italy	Springbok, South Africa	Springfield, Illinois	Springfield, Massachusetts	Srinagar, India	Stanley, Falkland Islands	Stara Zagora, Bulgaria	Stockholm, Sweden	Stornoway, United Kingdom	Strasbourg, France	Stuttgart, West Germany	Subic, Philippines	Suchow, China	Sucre, Bolivia	Sudbury, Canada	Suez, Egypt
South Sandwich Islands	3,600	0	11,910	14,336	11,719	4,610	12,301	11,867	13,784	2,107	12,111	13,561	12,982	12,200	12,254	14,501	16,255	5,337	12,600	11,166
Split, Yugoslavia	14,824	11,910	0	8,939	313	8,105	8,178	6,903	5,073	12,735	760	1,763	2,270	876	808	9,960	8,246	10,802	7,161	2,074
Spokane, Washington	15,283	14,336	8,939	0	8,861	15,723	2,385	3,544	10,868	12,385	9,386	7,471	6,685	8,104	8,148	11,037	9,432	9,030	2,742	10,898
Spoleto, Italy	14,737	11,719	313	8,861	0	8,034	7,997	6,694	5,384	12,474	1,059	1,883	2,176	757	725	10,272	8,545	10,489	6,987	2,264
Springbok, South Africa	6,721	4,610	8,105	15,723	8,034	0	13,470	12,187	9,252	6,528	8,021	9,863	9,998	8,725	8,730	11,997	12,587	8,351	12,981	6,781
Springfield, Illinois	14,410	12,301	8,178	2,385	7,997	13,470	0	1,456	11,671	10,597	8,815	7,185	5,992	7,304	7,380	13,210	11,355	6,988	1,023	10,252
Springfield, Massachusetts	14,666	11,867	6,903	3,544	6,694	12,187	1,456	0	10,940	10,490	7,586	6,142	4,831	6,042	6,128	13,561	11,490	6,810	830	8,958
Srinagar, India	13,776	13,784	5,073	10,868	5,384	9,252	11,671	10,940	0	15,780	4,341	4,955	6,363	5,648	5,540	5,019	3,877	15,749	10,758	3,991
Stanley, Falkland Islands	4,273	2,107	12,735	12,385	12,474	6,528	10,597	10,490	15,780	0	13,157	14,066	13,049	12,736	12,818	15,917	18,028	3,683	11,105	12,585
Stara Zagora, Bulgaria	14,702	12,111	760	9,386	1,059	8,021	8,815	7,586	4,341	13,157	0	1,953	2,833	1,552	1,461	9,279	7,657	11,487	7,793	1,514
Stockholm, Sweden	16,584	13,561	1,763	7,471	1,883	9,863	7,185	6,142	4,955	14,066	1,953	0	1,410	1,371	1,309	9,271	7,282	11,437	6,173	3,443
Stornoway, United Kingdom	16,460	12,982	2,270	6,685	2,176	9,998	5,992	4,831	6,363	13,049	2,833	1,410	0	1,420	1,467	10,565	8,497	10,116	4,969	4,315
Strasbourg, France	15,388	12,200	876	8,104	757	8,725	7,304	6,042	5,648	12,736	1,552	1,371	1,420	0	108	10,352	8,482	10,390	6,286	2,950
Stuttgart, West Germany	15,408	12,254	808	8,148	725	8,730	7,380	6,128	5,540	12,818	1,461	1,309	1,467	108	0	10,249	8,385	10,494	6,361	2,877
Subic, Philippines	11,647	14,501	9,960	11,037	10,272	11,997	13,210	13,561	5,019	15,917	9,279	9,271	10,565	10,352	10,249	0	2,169	19,278	12,883	8,983
Suchow, China	13,795	16,255	8,246	9,432	8,545	12,587	11,355	11,490	3,877	18,028	7,657	7,282	8,497	8,482	8,385	2,169	0	18,300	10,876	7,758
Sucre, Bolivia	7,898	5,337	10,802	9,030	10,489	8,351	6,988	6,810	15,749	3,683	11,487	11,437	10,116	10,390	10,494	19,278	18,300	0	7,428	11,780
Sudbury, Canada	15,154	12,600	7,161	2,742	6,987	12,981	1,023	830	10,758	11,105	7,793	6,173	4,969	6,286	6,361	12,883	10,876	7,428	0	9,235
Suez, Egypt	13,320	11,166	2,074	10,898	2,264	6,781	10,252	8,958	3,991	12,585	1,514	3,443	4,315	2,950	2,877	8,983	7,758	11,780	9,235	0
Sundsvall, Sweden	16,924	13,847	2,100	7,160	2,207	10,203	6,957	5,967	5,052	14,256	2,289	342	1,379	1,647	1,597	9,204	7,170	11,487	5,953	3,769
Surabaya, Indonesia	9,200	11,921	11,071	13,506	11,373	10,087	15,770	16,108	6,074	13,412	10,314	10,963	12,364	11,714	11,607	2,583	4,619	17,090	15,462	9,478
Suva, Fiji	7,995	11,286	16,727	9,682	16,965	14,322	11,441	12,896	12,351	10,552	16,293	15,164	15,538	16,524	16,472	7,353	8,695	11,943	12,253	16,335
Sverdlovsk, USSR	16,307	14,865	3,409	8,418	3,692	10,395	8,936	8,199	2,751	16,102	2,944	2,482	3,847	3,590	3,492	6,804	4,893	13,914	8,009	3,699
Svobodnyy, USSR	15,698	18,241	7,609	7,382	7,862	13,897	9,257	9,453	4,646	19,601	7,214	6,219	7,171	7,566	7,487	4,112	2,098	16,227	8,804	7,829
Sydney, Australia	6,250	9,848	15,998	12,795	16,300	11,436	14,660	16,115	10,956	10,110	15,241	15,588	16,828	16,591	16,484	6,318	8,338	12,994	15,451	14,295
Sydney, Canada	15,116	11,930	5,821	4,262	5,608	11,486	2,489	1,089	10,041	10,845	6,514	5,151	3,799	4,965	5,053	13,245	11,095	7,237	1,599	7,871
Syktyvkar, USSR	16,843	14,822	3,020	7,837	3,269	10,548	8,207	7,433	3,509	15,739	2,715	1,799	3,114	3,032	2,943	7,478	5,488	13,221	7,264	3,768
Szeged, Hungary	15,130	12,308	425	8,811	709	8,412	8,205	6,983	4,747	13,160	611	1,461	2,224	970	872	9,581	7,836	11,176	7,182	2,104
Szombathely, Hungary	15,237	12,297	413	8,587	586	8,517	7,928	6,696	5,009	13,053	891	1,350	1,959	679	580	9,804	8,016	10,950	6,906	2,357
Tabriz, Iran	14,220	12,588	2,577	10,370	2,876	8,062	10,285	9,191	2,596	14,120	1,818	3,101	4,360	3,295	3,193	7,609	6,233	13,161	9,271	1,554
Tacheng, China	15,182	15,278	5,086	9,358	5,391	10,686	10,390	9,871	1,565	17,146	4,476	4,374	5,737	5,414	5,311	4,939	3,182	15,793	9,556	4,688
Tahiti (Papeete)	8,061	10,168	16,840	7,902	16,753	14,613	8,877	10,269	15,258	8,614	17,209	15,257	14,582	16,001	16,048	10,527	11,382	8,815	9,858	18,611
Taipei, Taiwan	12,773	15,582	9,254	10,040	9,559	12,593	12,136	12,431	4,593	17,046	8,629	8,369	9,599	9,540	9,441	1,133	1,104	19,054	11,765	8,572
Taiyuan, China	14,194	16,321	7,669	9,318	7,968	12,343	11,112	11,134	3,406	18,296	7,084	6,716	7,949	7,906	7,809	2,657	578	17,907	10,563	7,224
Tallahassee, Florida	13,372	11,157	8,530	3,406	8,307	12,686	1,147	1,663	12,535	9,460	9,229	7,801	6,493	7,680	7,769	14,349	12,498	5,841	1,805	10,564
Tallinn, USSR	16,593	13,749	1,858	7,645	2,031	9,893	7,479	6,475	4,584	14,367	1,892	381	1,786	1,633	1,555	8,901	6,929	11,810	6,473	3,326
Tamanrasset, Algeria	12,525	9,408	2,510	10,352	2,311	5,953	8,844	7,394	6,779	10,293	2,867	4,179	4,049	2,870	2,901	11,786	10,429	8,978	7,950	2,805
Tampa, Florida	13,096	10,830	8,587	3,727	8,353	12,417	1,472	1,806	12,735	9,146	9,301	7,941	6,607	7,749	7,841	14,678	12,816	5,518	2,063	10,597
Tampere, Finland	16,825	13,922	2,059	7,413	2,213	10,119	7,288	6,315	4,700	14,462	2,127	396	1,710	1,754	1,686	8,904	6,898	11,796	6,288	3,564
Tanami, Australia	7,791	11,114	13,376	13,330	13,680	10,885	15,681	16,788	8,343	12,030	12,621	13,124	14,487	13,990	13,883	3,994	6,149	15,393	15,960	11,764
Tangier, Morocco	13,968	10,547	2,083	8,541	1,770	7,660	7,113	5,684	7,140	10,938	2,799	3,136	2,492	1,802	1,891	12,039	10,256	8,721	6,182	3,623
Tarawa (Betio)	10,150	13,520	14,514	8,387	14,738	15,919	10,551	11,902	10,678	12,708	14,160	12,928	13,399	14,291	14,236	5,980	6,829	13,398	11,124	14,574
Tashkent, USSR	14,581	14,081	4,284	10,123	4,597	9,474	10,772	10,005	940	15,900	3,587	4,026	5,436	4,789	4,682	5,693	4,235	15,074	9,842	3,527
Tbilisi, USSR	14,622	12,846	2,321	9,950	2,630	8,370	9,876	8,802	2,760	14,277	1,581	2,691	3,977	2,977	2,872	7,726	6,229	13,043	8,864	1,702
Tegucigalpa, Honduras	11,562	9,691	10,010	4,651	9,751	12,223	2,858	3,409	14,346	7,823	10,749	9,512	8,150	9,206	9,304	15,614	14,066	4,383	3,639	11,935
Tehran, Iran	13,952	12,625	3,105	10,708	3,402	8,041	10,749	9,689	2,140	14,288	2,345	3,569	4,863	3,824	3,722	7,158	5,889	13,610	9,741	1,874
Tel Aviv, Israel	13,553	11,472	2,047	10,748	2,272	7,062	10,209	8,950	3,723	12,900	1,404	3,277	4,236	2,912	2,831	8,730	7,462	12,035	9,188	315
Telegraph Creek, Canada	16,421	15,773	8,370	1,463	8,360	16,074	3,567	4,385	9,527	13,847	8,680	6,727	6,240	7,615	7,635	9,676	7,986	10,443	3,560	10,150
Teresina, Brazil	9,442	6,012	8,003	9,283	7,695	6,913	6,903	6,033	12,864	5,352	8,653	8,901	7,735	7,704	7,803	17,880	16,179	2,886	6,842	8,897
Ternate, Indonesia	10,090	13,284	11,624	11,799	11,938	11,940	14,152	14,850	6,588	14,342	10,916	11,015	12,309	12,069	11,964	1,746	3,855	17,569	14,080	10,439
The Valley, Anguilla	12,000	9,053	7,815	5,893	7,523	10,153	3,514	2,815	12,721	7,743	8,575	7,796	6,389	7,120	7,226	16,344	14,215	4,109	3,560	9,550
Thessaloniki, Greece	14,504	11,835	626	9,471	880	7,801	8,792	7,527	4,587	12,859	300	2,108	2,847	1,490	1,412	9,548	7,950	11,219	7,774	1,470
Thimphu, Bhutan	13,049	14,097	6,661	11,246	6,973	9,924	12,550	12,085	1,598	16,204	5,936	6,384	7,789	7,199	7,092	3,451	2,721	17,310	11,753	5,532
Thunder Bay, Canada	15,365	13,101	7,516	2,085	7,367	13,638	956	1,484	10,734	11,490	8,105	6,378	5,273	6,642	6,709	12,413	10,479	7,842	661	9,583
Tientsin, China	14,335	16,688	7,889	8,981	8,181	12,772	10,849	10,954	3,799	18,557	7,334	6,837	8,018	8,072	7,977	2,704	540	17,764	10,349	7,555
Tijuana, Mexico	13,602	13,027	10,350	1,681	10,228	15,745	2,579	4,030	12,528	10,969	10,875	9,017	8,082	9,486	9,544	11,984	10,698	7,930	3,424	12,383
Tiksi, USSR	17,949	18,093	6,191	5,800	6,376	13,836	7,284	7,281	5,204	17,762	6,028	4,533	5,187	5,896	5,841	6,328	4,211	14,090	6,695	7,088
Timbuktu, Mali	11,859	8,538	3,488	10,361	3,244	5,607	8,555	7,104	7,884	9,252	3,936	5,027	4,609	3,662	3,718	12,879	11,540	7,881	7,763	3,899
Tindouf, Algeria	13,069	9,623	2,817	9,086	2,516	6,927	7,414	5,958	7,743	10,045	3,456	4,046	3,393	2,693	2,773	12,730	11,062	8,038	6,559	3,960
Tirane, Albania	14,582	11,797	370	9,285	608	7,863	8,548	7,270	4,833	12,740	496	2,006	2,630	1,246	1,175	9,775	8,136	10,991	7,531	1,704
Tokyo, Japan	13,953	17,352	9,532	8,019	9,797	14,613	10,237	10,784	5,826	17,748	9,080	8,193	9,131	9,534	9,453	3,018	2,064	16,947	10,032	9,496
Toledo, Spain	14,419	11,020	1,745	8,296	1,436	8,025	7,014	5,616	6,817	11,407	2,493	2,662	2,048	1,347	1,441	11,653	9,824	9,100	6,051	3,490
Topeka, Kansas	14,326	12,504	8,604	1,996	8,436	13,957	525	1,977	11,848	10,705	9,219	7,527	6,386	7,728	7,801	12,971	11,213	7,167	1,454	10,678
Toronto, Canada	14,840	12,263	7,250	2,966	7,061	12,768	955	582	11,007	10,769	7,904	6,345	5,098	6,378	6,458	13,223	11,213	7,090	340	9,320
Toulouse, France	14,834	11,529	1,210	8,258	923	8,285	7,188	5,842	6,251	12,001	1,970	2,084	1,713	738	829	11,047	9,210	9,702	6,193	3,137
Tours, France	15,254	11,920	1,302	7,892	1,079	8,706	6,923	5,615	6,191	12,314	2,037	1,752	1,294	544	651	10,877	8,975	9,860	5,915	3,343
Townsville, Australia	7,871	11,449	14,691	11,995	15,004	12,319	14,205	15,535	9,635	11,789	13,974	13,983	15,162	15,119	15,016	4,767	6,703	14,521	14,735	13,352
Trenton, New Jersey	14,457	11,752	7,173	3,475	6,961	12,278	1,270	277	11,207	10,316	7,859	6,419	5,108	6,314	6,401	13,711	11,666	6,633	860	9,224
Tripoli, Lebanon	13,816	11,750	1,954	10,529	2,205	7,342	10,069	8,839	3,567	13,158	1,256	3,060	4,081	2,798	2,711	8,585	7,254	12,183	9,046	585
Tripoli, Libya	13,646	10,709	1,212	9,816	1,092	6,943	8,716	7,332	5,638	11,643	1,521	2,960	3,175	1,800	1,793	10,651	9,145	10,119	7,735	1,867
Tristan da Cunha (Edinburgh)	5,902	2,527	9,383	13,981	9,193	2,912	11,609	10,689	11,966	3,899	9,605	11,043	10,572	9,691	9,741	14,745	15,494	5,500	11,513	8,770
Trondheim, Norway	17,039	13,804	2,248	6,866	2,307	10,339	6,598	5,599	5,415	14,073	2,536	610	1,077	1,660	1,633	9,488	7,425	11,191	5,591	4,039
Trujillo, Peru	9,105	7,095	11,068	7,241	10,762	10,234	5,417	5,599	16,087	5,207	11,820	11,180	9,773	10,445	10,552	17,804	16,673	1,914	6,052	12,540
Truk Island (Moen)	10,823	14,421	12,805	9,458	13,088	14,631	11,832	12,913	8,362	14,398	12,268	11,554	12,469	12,884	12,800	3,548	4,633	15,818	12,083	12,341
Truro, Canada	15,029	11,925	6,074	4,077	5,862	11,657	2,241	833	10,249	10,768	6,764	5,379	4,037	5,217	5,304	13,323	11,185	7,134	1,378	8,126
Tsingtao, China	13,994	16,582	8,321	9,106	8,614	12,923	11,063	11,250	4,118	18,262	7,759	7,273	8,445	8,509	8,415	2,347	348	18,041	10,615	7,940
Tsitsihar, China	15,249	17,727	7,691	7,920	7,960	13,535	9,794	9,961	4,324	19,506	7,239	6,407	7,447	7,726	7,641	3,618	1,561	16,753	9,326	7,725
Tubuai Island (Mataura)	7,416	9,586	17,428	8,497	17,309	13,984	9,348	10,705	15,578	8,112	17,845	15,891	15,158	16,569	16,624	10,690	11,729	8,626	10,346	19,248
Tucson, Arizona	13,568	12,662	10,066	1,800	9,922	15,178	2,091	3,548	12,641	10,643	10,632	8,831	7,810	9,193	9,257	12,477	11,094	7,474	3,003	12,125
Tulsa, Oklahoma	14,005	12,244	8,852	2,182	8,675	13,908	682	2,114	12,169	10,416	9,480	7,815	6,652	7,977	8,052	13,204	11,489	6,908	1,691	10,926
Tunis, Tunisia	14,079	11,025	916	9,303	694	7,401	8,230	6,861	5,762	11,821	1,463	2,569	2,671	1,324	1,332	10,735	9,108	10,033	7,242	2,208
Tura, USSR	17,134	17,134	5,479	7,165	5,721	12,581	8,433	8,193	3,779	18,119	5,146	4,062	5,082	5,406	5,328	5,696	3,532	14,863	7,721	5,976
Turin, Italy	14,995	11,826	720	8,423	482	8,338	7,517	6,213	5,729	12,423	1,474	1,736	1,750	393	429	10,534	8,723	10,218	6,507	2,745
Uberlandia, Brazil	7,909	4,666	9,551	10,074	9,250	6,737	7,791	7,204	14,191	3,731	10,159	10,536	9,379	9,311	9,408	18,731	17,790	1,788	7,957	10,206
Ufa, USSR	16,071	14,491	3,090	8,638	3,380	10,036	9,030	8,219	2,724	15,744	2,592	2,323	3,720	3,334	3,233	7,025	5,174	13,707	8,078	3,325
Ujungpandang, Indonesia	9,436	12,396	11,447	12,867	11,756	10,841	15,193	15,741	6,383	13,703	10,702	11,137	12,510	12,019	11,912	2,214	4,365	17,286	15,019	9,994
Ulaanbaatar, Mongolia	15,311	16,763	6,637	8,583	6,924	12,321	10,152	10,032	3,073	18,843	6,115	5,556	6,755	6,793	6,700	3,864	1,742	16,724	9,516	6,481
Ulan-Ude, USSR	15,747	17,051	6,452	8,177	6,729	12,522	9,716	9,597	3,279	19,016	5,973	5,273	6,425	6,547	6,457	4,250	2,097	16,313	9,077	6,457
Uliastay, Mongolia	15,293	16,154	5,995	8,927	6,290	11,628	10,285	9,997	2,381	18,149	5,436	5,052	6,329	6,221	6,123	4,236	2,263	16,435	9,560	5,737
Uranium City, Canada	16,608	14,853	7,527	1,444	7,466	14,836	2,569	3,132	9,621	13,152	7,951	6,029	5,294	6,709	6,747	10,665	8,789	9,556	2,325	9,462
Urumqi, China	14,854	15,324	5,551	9,580	5,858	10,787	10,741	10,287	1,542	17,310	4,923	4,863	6,223	5,898	5,795	4,454	2,754	16,281	9,938	5,041
Ushuaia, Argentina	3,928	2,568	13,502	12,254	13,237	7,135	10,678	10,746	16,353	777	13,934	14,784	13,702	13,473	13,558	15,515	17,684	3,978	11,290	13,346
Vaduz, Liechtenstein	15,230	12,095	677	8,309	554	8,550	7,501	6,231	5,544	12,696	1,377	1,466	1,624	206	180	10,303	8,468	10,445	6,485	2,751
Valencia, Spain	14,375	11,047	1,470	8,528	1,157	7,884	7,304	5,915	6,541	11,535	2,205	2,563	2,129	1,202	1,283	11,415	9,629	9,343	6,333	3,173
Valladolid, Spain	14,617	11,202	1,744	8,107	1,444	8,231	6,864	5,477	6,798	11,547	2,501	2,519	1,846	1,245	1,345	11,588	9,725	9,159	5,892	3,576
Valletta, Malta	13,979	11,064	861	9,591	774	7,266	8,595	7,239	5,419	11,981	1,201	2,618	2,918	1,514	1,494	10,414	8,852	10,355	7,600	1,807
Valparaiso, Chile	6,346	4,348	12,305	10,038	11,997	8,243	8,275	8,320	16,924	2,355	12,942	13,082	11,782	11,975	12,077	17,671	19,198	1,675	8,858	12,979
Vancouver, Canada	15,459	14,759	9,000	457	8,944	16,083	2,832	3,940	10,606	12,778	9,402	7,464	6,773	8,187	8,223	10,586	9,010	9,470	3,124	10,906
Varna, Bulgaria	14,791	12,275	931	9,378	1,238	8,135	8,882	7,678	4,150	13,353	207	1,916	2,891	1,669	1,572	9,077	7,450	11,689	7,859	1,527
Venice, Italy	15,039	11,990	389	8,588	303	8,337	7,790	6,514	5,360	12,687	1,117	1,591	1,906	493	440	10,182	8,399	10,573	6,774	2,462

Distances in Kilometers	South Pole	South Sandwich Islands	Split, Yugoslavia	Spokane, Washington	Spoleto, Italy	Springbok, South Africa	Springfield, Illinois	Springfield, Massachusetts	Srinagar, India	Stanley, Falkland Islands	Stara Zagora, Bulgaria	Stockholm, Sweden	Stornoway, United Kingdom	Strasbourg, France	Stuttgart, West Germany	Subic, Philippines	Suchow, China	Sucre, Bolivia	Sudbury, Canada	Suez, Egypt
Veracruz, Mexico	12,126	10,647	10,256	3,699	10,031	13,324	2,367	3,374	14,031	8,692	10,954	9,476	8,199	9,405	9,494	14,536	13,122	5,407	3,329	12,284
Verona, Italy	15,039	11,954	483	8,531	332	8,347	7,705	6,422	5,464	12,620	1,220	1,616	1,846	427	394	10,279	8,486	10,475	6,690	2,547
Victoria, Canada	15,368	14,709	9,089	452	9,031	16,130	2,837	3,972	10,689	12,719	9,493	7,555	6,859	8,274	8,311	10,615	9,059	9,431	3,160	10,997
Victoria, Seychelles	9,493	9,097	6,613	15,185	6,782	4,825	14,777	13,423	4,743	11,177	6,017	7,818	8,847	7,488	7,417	7,462	7,762	13,034	13,768	4,540
Vienna, Austria	15,345	12,388	521	8,484	671	8,625	7,846	6,625	5,019	13,119	969	1,244	1,869	639	535	9,784	7,976	10,966	6,824	2,450
Vientiane, Laos	11,989	13,954	8,354	11,719	8,666	10,493	13,486	13,336	3,287	15,889	7,628	7,998	9,386	8,879	8,772	1,913	2,316	18,750	12,856	7,149
Villahermosa, Mexico	11,991	10,361	10,125	3,976	9,889	12,959	2,439	3,297	14,099	8,438	10,838	9,434	8,125	9,287	9,378	14,878	13,408	5,089	3,347	12,127
Vilnius, USSR	16,066	13,308	1,399	8,135	1,614	9,373	7,854	6,779	4,434	14,066	1,364	680	1,974	1,387	1,290	8,983	7,094	11,751	6,838	2,806
Visby, Sweden	16,395	13,397	1,576	7,642	1,703	9,674	7,309	6,238	4,915	13,951	1,770	190	1,455	1,227	1,157	9,316	7,353	11,400	6,293	3,266
Vitoria, Brazil	7,756	4,307	9,137	10,731	8,848	5,910	8,395	7,665	13,530	3,801	9,690	10,293	9,251	9,001	9,091	17,888	17,324	2,616	8,454	9,583
Vladivostok, USSR	14,779	17,794	8,465	7,875	8,730	14,074	9,917	10,253	4,975	18,809	8,019	7,143	8,128	8,476	8,394	3,324	1,611	16,890	9,560	8,490
Volgograd, USSR	15,406	13,471	2,225	9,178	2,535	9,078	9,208	8,210	2,988	14,727	1,620	2,069	3,439	2,675	2,567	7,742	6,043	13,015	8,208	2,316
Vologda, USSR	16,571	14,218	2,367	7,977	2,612	10,058	8,092	7,192	3,785	15,081	2,112	1,240	2,629	2,389	2,296	8,047	6,104	12,669	7,111	3,298
Vorkuta, USSR	17,493	15,717	3,853	7,232	4,079	11,438	7,901	7,316	3,782	16,466	3,606	2,400	3,510	3,741	3,663	7,085	4,988	13,561	7,025	4,662
Wake Island	12,134	15,601	12,419	7,406	12,639	16,673	9,771	10,900	8,998	14,739	12,095	10,835	11,392	12,203	12,145	4,951	5,137	14,592	10,072	12,677
Wallis Island	8,530	11,656	16,447	8,906	16,633	15,020	10,654	12,108	12,575	10,695	16,161	14,762	14,947	16,076	16,041	7,668	8,788	11,652	11,464	16,543
Walvis Bay, Namibia	7,465	5,063	7,362	14,968	7,274	817	12,783	11,455	8,975	6,835	7,327	9,125	9,201	7,951	7,960	12,234	12,535	8,202	12,234	6,166
Warsaw, Poland	15,795	12,935	1,029	8,250	1,226	9,080	7,817	6,678	4,686	13,672	1,147	810	1,848	1,024	922	9,328	7,468	11,412	6,795	2,651
Washington, D.C.	14,309	11,700	7,417	3,376	7,206	12,405	1,091	518	11,422	10,209	8,104	6,654	5,348	6,558	6,645	13,789	11,774	6,528	905	9,469
Watson Lake, Canada	14,668	15,709	8,089	1,570	8,078	15,812	3,519	4,248	9,343	13,920	8,403	6,449	5,959	7,333	7,354	9,698	7,948	10,453	3,430	9,876
Weimar, East Germany	15,654	12,538	916	8,029	923	8,957	7,369	6,157	5,358	13,105	1,447	1,023	1,391	370	290	10,006	8,118	10,732	6,346	2,925
Wellington, New Zealand	5,426	8,850	18,228	11,904	18,530	11,798	13,173	14,565	13,169	8,518	17,472	17,436	18,121	18,713	18,613	8,373	10,232	10,915	14,140	16,412
West Berlin, West Germany	15,825	12,750	1,026	7,964	1,089	9,115	7,389	6,211	5,204	13,328	1,449	812	1,398	593	513	9,807	7,905	10,927	6,366	2,954
Wewak, Papua New Guinea	9,608	13,151	13,207	10,972	13,515	13,182	13,338	14,432	8,305	13,555	12,551	12,285	13,407	13,502	13,404	3,289	5,021	15,991	13,603	12,241
Whangarei, New Zealand	6,046	9,465	17,943	11,458	18,256	12,361	12,892	14,322	12,890	9,074	17,231	16,870	17,503	18,208	18,121	7,986	9,761	11,294	13,821	16,416
Whitehorse, Canada	16,735	16,122	8,165	1,841	8,171	16,016	3,866	4,592	9,152	14,221	8,439	6,489	6,085	7,435	7,449	9,354	7,627	10,786	3,777	9,891
Wichita, Kansas	14,176	12,457	8,813	1,974	8,645	14,070	707	2,164	12,016	10,623	9,427	7,730	6,594	7,937	8,009	12,992	11,278	7,121	1,662	10,886
Willemstad, Curacao	11,343	8,657	8,723	5,972	8,431	10,372	3,681	3,342	13,625	7,151	9,484	8,687	7,278	8,031	8,137	16,855	14,831	3,469	3,977	10,430
Wiluna, Australia	7,058	10,157	13,066	14,541	13,346	9,671	16,897	17,933	8,250	11,329	12,309	13,194	14,603	13,802	13,698	4,589	6,744	14,921	17,119	11,233
Windhoek, Namibia	7,506	5,231	7,319	15,124	7,245	789	12,979	11,632	8,755	7,043	7,250	9,079	9,214	7,937	7,941	11,966	12,284	8,469	12,400	6,046
Windsor, Canada	14,688	12,267	7,576	2,753	7,390	13,006	623	861	11,251	10,695	8,226	6,643	5,413	6,704	6,783	13,243	11,281	7,031	494	9,648
Winnipeg, Canada	15,530	13,561	7,822	1,504	7,697	14,223	1,266	2,078	10,670	11,856	8,367	6,561	5,556	6,956	7,015	11,955	10,090	8,254	1,255	9,867
Winston-Salem, North Carolina	13,999	11,545	7,833	3,302	7,618	12,559	922	939	11,817	9,969	8,522	7,070	5,768	6,976	7,063	13,968	12,008	6,302	1,157	9,881
Wroclaw, Poland	15,667	12,703	844	8,229	986	8,947	7,684	6,506	4,957	13,387	1,166	919	1,693	723	620	9,629	7,771	11,113	6,662	2,677
Wuhan, China	13,386	15,763	8,315	9,924	8,621	12,179	11,832	11,926	3,712	17,572	7,689	7,470	8,735	8,616	8,515	1,843	492	18,724	11,331	7,666
Wyndham, Australia	8,290	11,561	12,922	13,097	13,229	11,031	15,476	16,456	7,867	12,542	12,172	12,609	13,965	13,507	13,400	3,467	5,624	15,921	15,640	11,383
Xi'an, China	13,795	15,804	7,667	9,828	7,972	11,883	11,586	11,547	3,128	17,799	7,041	6,848	8,134	7,975	7,874	2,430	763	18,224	11,005	7,047
Xining, China	14,056	15,593	6,994	9,892	7,301	11,415	11,463	11,269	2,458	17,690	6,356	6,253	7,575	7,334	7,231	3,026	1,422	17,688	10,795	6,351
Yakutsk, USSR	16,878	18,605	6,884	6,472	7,105	14,002	8,182	8,293	4,907	18,773	6,606	5,339	6,146	6,709	6,642	5,284	3,208	15,094	7,466	7,466
Yanji, China	14,751	17,658	8,353	8,024	8,622	13,878	10,038	10,336	4,786	18,882	7,891	7,065	8,081	8,387	8,303	3,228	1,436	17,022	9,657	8,331
Yaounde, Cameroon	10,432	7,630	4,419	12,449	4,307	3,772	10,690	9,239	7,323	8,946	4,494	6,178	6,227	4,969	4,981	11,908	11,200	8,776	9,895	3,639
Yap Island (Colonia)	11,053	14,495	11,710	10,296	12,013	13,452	12,667	13,493	6,971	15,107	11,090	10,719	11,844	11,954	11,858	2,035	3,476	12,790	12,690	10,961
Yaraka, Australia	7,248	10,806	14,872	12,631	15,182	11,685	14,787	16,157	9,803	11,256	14,128	14,376	15,635	15,406	15,299	5,105	7,137	14,206	15,373	13,335
Yarmouth, Canada	14,858	11,844	6,355	3,940	6,141	11,783	1,999	562	10,515	10,615	7,047	5,657	4,319	5,499	5,587	13,471	11,349	6,961	1,205	8,404
Yellowknife, Canada	16,929	15,297	7,468	1,656	7,430	15,018	3,015	3,538	9,273	13,594	7,844	5,901	5,276	6,677	6,706	10,220	8,343	10,003	2,744	9,344
Yerevan, USSR	14,454	12,695	2,349	10,110	2,653	8,208	10,005	8,913	2,763	14,153	1,596	2,821	4,083	3,040	2,937	7,754	6,303	13,015	8,990	1,570
Yinchuan, China	14,261	16,014	7,198	9,529	7,501	11,867	11,187	11,082	2,858	18,092	6,591	6,336	7,615	7,479	7,379	2,949	1,080	17,706	10,565	6,683
Yogyakarta, Indonesia	9,139	11,767	10,920	13,713	11,219	9,828	15,943	16,193	5,961	13,317	10,161	10,879	12,286	11,584	11,478	2,735	4,711	16,999	15,581	9,285
York, United Kingdom	15,972	12,581	1,722	7,261	1,603	9,432	6,476	5,252	6,151	12,828	2,343	1,324	586	853	914	10,595	8,596	10,116	5,455	3,790
Yumen, China	14,413	15,618	6,501	9,710	6,808	11,273	11,154	10,878	2,132	17,721	5,873	5,753	7,082	6,833	6,730	3,528	1,833	17,190	10,441	5,927
Yutian, China	14,084	14,424	5,464	10,451	5,777	9,927	11,470	10,880	697	16,453	4,765	5,104	6,509	5,953	5,846	4,519	3,211	16,250	10,611	4,585
Yuzhno-Sakhalinsk, USSR	15,203	18,604	8,683	6,972	8,920	14,949	9,087	9,544	5,743	18,437	8,333	7,195	8,007	8,562	8,491	4,123	2,562	16,002	8,811	8,997
Zagreb, Yugoslavia	15,078	12,131	256	8,701	429	8,359	7,991	6,739	5,073	12,903	857	1,512	2,048	697	612	9,903	8,140	10,853	6,971	2,273
Zahedan, Iran	13,268	12,578	4,215	11,456	4,508	7,981	11,752	10,758	1,414	14,472	3,455	4,617	5,950	4,942	4,839	6,266	5,288	14,489	10,759	2,733
Zamboanga, Philippines	10,764	13,749	10,728	11,634	11,042	11,762	13,900	14,380	5,702	15,037	10,023	10,136	11,449	11,173	11,068	906	3,072	18,452	13,667	9,589
Zanzibar, Tanzania	9,322	8,002	5,961	14,898	6,040	3,429	13,708	12,261	5,823	9,957	5,553	7,500	8,215	6,795	6,751	9,236	9,303	11,302	12,788	4,061
Zaragoza, Spain	14,615	11,270	1,434	8,312	1,130	8,127	7,140	5,766	6,500	11,713	2,189	2,365	1,885	1,027	1,118	11,324	9,497	9,428	6,159	3,262
Zashiversk, USSR	17,486	18,793	6,898	5,617	7,083	14,477	7,331	7,500	5,614	17,927	6,732	5,234	5,834	6,593	6,540	6,061	4,037	14,274	6,848	7,764
Zhengzhou, China	13,848	16,111	7,968	9,560	8,270	12,306	11,412	11,471	3,550	18,005	7,367	7,056	8,300	8,230	8,132	2,297	327	18,260	10,887	7,438
Zurich, Switzerland	15,252	12,087	762	8,242	619	8,585	7,417	6,143	5,626	12,659	1,467	1,476	1,557	143	167	10,371	8,525	10,375	6,401	2,835

Distances in Kilometers	Sundsvall, Sweden	Surabaya, Indonesia	Suva, Fiji	Sverdlovsk, USSR	Svobodnyy, USSR	Sydney, Australia	Sydney, Canada	Syktyvkar, USSR	Szeged, Hungary	Szombathely, Hungary	Tabriz, Iran	Tacheng, China	Tahiti (Papeete)	Taipei, Taiwan	Taiyuan, China	Tallahassee, Florida	Tallinn, USSR	Tamanrasset, Algeria	Tampa, Florida	Tampere, Finland
Surabaya, Indonesia	10,997	0	7,200	8,533	6,664	4,927	15,641	9,291	10,787	11,061	8,497	6,668	10,585	3,697	4,995	16,891	10,583	12,091	17,219	10,657
Suva, Fiji	14,878	7,200	0	13,361	9,120	3,219	13,852	13,706	16,305	16,379	14,896	11,867	3,390	7,801	9,257	11,696	14,956	19,123	11,812	14,797
Sverdlovsk, USSR	2,469	8,533	13,361	0	4,274	13,118	7,340	773	2,987	3,138	2,338	1,894	14,973	5,951	4,317	9,784	2,105	5,810	9,988	2,139
Svobodnyy, USSR	6,010	6,664	9,120	4,274	0	9,714	9,166	4,593	7,186	7,280	6,300	3,288	10,993	2,979	1,939	10,401	5,933	10,073	10,720	5,824
Sydney, Australia	15,505	4,927	3,219	13,118	9,714	0	17,041	13,792	15,700	15,965	13,424	11,238	6,129	7,240	8,893	14,843	15,219	16,464	14,914	15,217
Sydney, Canada	5,006	15,641	13,852	7,340	9,166	17,041	0	6,566	5,914	5,626	8,153	9,103	11,349	12,118	10,671	2,716	5,500	6,367	2,810	5,357
Syktyvkar, USSR	1,736	9,291	13,706	773	4,593	13,792	6,566	0	2,599	2,688	2,642	2,629	14,850	6,571	4,919	9,028	1,441	5,512	9,226	1,427
Szeged, Hungary	1,803	10,787	16,305	2,987	7,186	15,700	5,914	2,599	0	292	2,329	4,686	16,682	8,853	7,259	8,630	1,495	2,921	8,708	1,711
Szombathely, Hungary	1,687	11,061	16,379	3,138	7,280	15,965	5,626	2,688	292	0	2,617	4,887	16,479	9,047	7,438	8,342	1,458	2,889	8,418	1,652
Tabriz, Iran	3,345	8,497	14,896	2,338	6,300	13,424	8,153	2,642	2,329	2,617	0	3,134	17,260	7,095	5,688	10,853	2,825	4,227	10,963	3,034
Tacheng, China	4,358	6,668	11,867	1,894	3,288	11,238	9,103	2,629	4,686	4,887	3,134	0	14,245	4,168	2,613	11,360	3,996	7,261	11,603	4,031
Tahiti (Papeete)	14,921	10,585	3,390	14,973	10,993	6,129	11,349	14,850	16,682	16,479	17,260	14,245	0	10,720	11,868	8,775	15,332	17,367	8,807	15,094
Taipei, Taiwan	8,266	3,697	7,801	5,951	2,979	7,240	12,118	6,571	8,853	9,047	7,095	4,168	10,720	0	1,654	13,281	8,011	11,321	13,608	7,988
Taiyuan, China	6,612	4,995	9,257	4,317	1,939	8,893	10,671	4,919	7,259	7,438	5,688	2,613	11,868	1,654	0	12,244	6,360	9,869	12,554	6,334
Tallahassee, Florida	7,618	16,891	11,696	9,784	10,401	14,843	2,716	9,028	8,630	8,342	10,853	11,360	8,775	13,281	12,244	0	8,130	8,746	329	7,963
Tallinn, USSR	522	10,583	14,956	2,105	5,933	15,219	5,500	1,441	1,495	1,458	2,825	3,996	15,332	8,011	6,360	8,130	0	4,342	8,278	239
Tamanrasset, Algeria	4,489	12,091	19,123	5,810	10,073	16,464	6,367	5,512	2,921	2,889	4,227	7,261	17,367	11,321	9,869	8,746	4,342	0	8,672	4,522
Tampa, Florida	7,772	17,219	11,812	9,988	10,720	14,914	2,810	9,226	8,708	8,418	10,963	11,603	8,807	13,608	12,554	329	8,278	8,672	0	8,120
Tampere, Finland	352	10,657	14,797	2,139	5,824	15,217	5,357	1,427	1,711	1,652	3,034	4,031	15,094	7,988	6,334	7,963	239	4,522	8,120	0
Tanami, Australia	13,108	2,310	5,112	10,647	7,909	2,622	16,966	11,373	13,081	13,350	10,805	8,754	8,427	5,061	6,651	16,428	12,744	14,271	16,651	12,785
Tangier, Morocco	3,363	13,049	18,004	5,365	9,354	17,917	4,624	4,833	2,458	2,248	4,587	7,135	15,923	11,295	9,679	7,148	3,429	1,811	7,122	3,530
Tarawa (Betio)	12,645	6,751	2,237	11,217	6,946	4,515	12,630	11,501	14,097	14,152	13,029	9,900	4,612	6,109	7,353	11,163	12,720	17,013	11,378	12,560
Tashkent, USSR	4,115	6,968	12,904	1,835	4,533	11,802	9,101	2,581	3,928	4,175	1,999	1,246	15,477	5,106	3,696	11,609	3,653	6,218	11,803	3,763
Tbilisi, USSR	2,928	8,761	14,924	2,031	6,133	13,682	7,775	2,258	2,028	2,308	423	3,072	17,003	7,141	5,671	10,465	2,407	4,200	10,584	2,614
Tegucigalpa, Honduras	9,358	17,723	10,947	11,599	11,986	13,781	4,361	10,837	10,176	9,884	12,476	13,195	7,689	14,679	13,896	1,835	9,859	9,692	1,611	9,709
Tehran, Iran	3,793	7,972	14,487	2,453	6,141	12,899	8,660	2,892	2,859	3,147	530	2,890	17,131	6,700	5,362	11,351	3,271	4,641	11,470	3,469
Tel Aviv, Israel	3,594	9,318	16,074	3,394	7,515	14,179	7,868	3,488	2,012	2,283	1,244	4,378	18,338	8,291	6,924	10,575	3,130	3,058	10,624	3,368
Telegraph Creek, Canada	6,392	12,209	9,616	7,238	5,924	12,454	4,801	6,743	8,160	7,980	9,365	7,987	8,531	8,641	7,857	4,684	6,825	10,207	5,012	6,586
Teresina, Brazil	9,027	16,994	14,825	11,294	14,802	15,449	5,930	10,692	8,398	8,198	10,281	13,084	11,612	17,243	15,606	5,911	9,251	6,093	5,608	9,288
Ternate, Indonesia	10,949	1,855	5,963	8,543	5,609	4,575	14,751	9,223	11,263	11,497	9,178	6,668	9,305	2,757	4,377	15,201	10,644	13,222	15,516	10,649
The Valley, Anguilla	7,748	18,731	13,559	10,206	12,235	16,197	3,128	9,445	8,068	7,786	10,388	12,065	10,253	15,211	13,798	2,547	8,174	7,115	2,265	8,092
Thessaloniki, Greece	2,449	10,517	16,593	3,243	7,512	15,440	6,446	2,998	665	891	2,028	4,768	17,346	8,915	7,378	9,156	2,093	2,567	9,213	2,322
Thimphu, Bhutan	6,430	4,579	10,804	3,986	4,159	9,393	11,301	4,756	6,323	6,578	4,190	2,214	13,888	3,178	2,419	13,557	6,005	8,335	13,808	6,085
Thunder Bay, Canada	6,128	14,995	11,660	8,012	8,387	14,836	2,205	7,295	7,496	7,231	9,472	9,435	9,424	11,312	10,208	2,039	6,649	8,491	2,346	6,447
Tientsin, China	6,709	5,156	8,980	4,500	1,607	8,812	10,555	5,054	7,472	7,636	6,009	2,895	11,495	1,613	429	11,989	6,493	10,152	12,305	6,448
Tijuana, Mexico	8,723	14,182	8,866	10,098	8,750	12,085	5,012	9,506	10,279	10,032	11,999	10,999	6,536	11,123	10,678	3,107	9,225	11,373	3,351	8,999
Tiksi, USSR	4,251	8,829	10,631	3,442	2,251	11,830	6,925	3,345	5,798	5,800	5,779	3,642	11,550	5,197	3,868	8,398	4,346	8,688	8,701	4,171
Timbuktu, Mali	5,308	12,989	19,805	6,864	11,097	16,824	6,166	6,508	3,912	3,830	5,341	8,367	16,479	12,436	10,978	8,268	5,244	1,115	8,143	5,398
Tindouf, Algeria	4,283	13,425	18,758	6,195	10,258	17,939	4,962	5,706	3,225	3,057	5,149	7,902	15,926	12,069	10,484	7,271	4,325	1,480	7,193	4,438
Tirane, Albania	2,348	10,783	16,731	3,370	7,621	15,708	6,188	3,065	549	704	2,289	4,958	17,181	9,117	7,562	8,895	2,040	2,454	8,948	2,259
Tokyo, Japan	7,986	5,533	7,219	6,142	1,976	7,794	10,722	6,535	9,107	9,220	7,942	4,809	9,485	2,110	2,433	11,362	7,901	11,945	11,690	7,798
Toledo, Spain	2,885	12,802	17,584	4,930	8,881	17,725	4,536	4,377	2,084	1,850	4,307	6,728	15,885	10,875	9,248	7,144	2,962	2,097	7,145	3,057
Topeka, Kansas	7,282	15,486	10,919	9,146	9,120	14,138	2,990	8,439	8,608	8,337	10,625	10,500	8,405	11,929	11,014	1,412	7,803	9,354	1,735	7,602
Toronto, Canada	6,140	15,801	12,352	8,256	9,143	15,566	1,537	7,504	7,295	7,014	9,433	9,839	9,831	12,104	10,895	1,530	6,658	7,901	1,765	6,480
Toulouse, France	2,332	12,277	17,167	4,316	8,297	17,200	4,753	3,770	1,504	1,253	3,786	6,118	16,044	10,261	8,633	7,429	2,366	2,339	7,461	2,475
Tours, France	1,968	12,256	16,754	4,094	7,968	17,134	4,530	3,499	1,488	1,203	3,817	5,938	15,732	10,044	8,402	7,233	2,067	2,763	7,286	2,147
Townsville, Australia	13,869	3,912	3,333	11,551	8,036	1,679	16,141	12,186	14,331	14,563	12,207	9,705	6,688	5,615	7,268	14,764	13,626	16,000	14,946	13,601
Trenton, New Jersey	6,242	16,277	12,704	8,464	9,613	15,922	1,353	7,699	7,257	6,970	9,468	10,121	10,022	12,586	11,325	1,386	6,751	7,614	1,533	6,590
Tripoli, Lebanon	3,370	9,278	15,906	3,115	7,254	14,172	7,764	3,209	1,865	2,146	1,022	4,145	18,058	8,108	6,710	10,478	2,894	3,219	10,540	3,130
Tripoli, Libya	3,291	11,341	17,813	4,461	8,722	16,147	6,249	4,170	1,599	1,618	3,043	5,964	17,592	10,084	8,577	8,865	3,070	1,351	8,860	3,269
Tristan da Cunha (Edinburgh)	11,337	12,496	13,795	12,441	16,533	11,969	10,385	12,320	9,783	9,770	10,267	13,247	12,492	15,468	15,217	10,582	11,224	6,882	10,267	11,400
Trondheim, Norway	368	11,336	14,893	2,803	6,172	15,762	4,639	2,053	2,004	1,842	3,695	4,682	14,684	8,526	6,874	7,250	883	4,529	7,403	719
Trujillo, Peru	11,128	17,873	11,048	13,574	14,603	12,975	6,297	12,806	11,365	11,094	13,632	15,395	7,690	17,147	16,512	4,304	11,559	9,808	4,008	11,473
Truk Island (Moen)	11,351	4,636	4,063	9,397	5,341	4,573	13,276	9,863	12,384	12,526	10,848	7,809	7,006	3,770	5,196	12,718	11,255	15,061	12,999	11,159
Truro, Canada	5,225	15,763	13,628	7,535	9,226	16,829	255	6,763	6,163	5,875	8,395	9,279	11,095	12,192	10,777	2,468	5,724	6,608	2,570	5,576
Tsingtao, China	7,142	4,860	8,563	4,936	1,814	8,383	10,899	5,491	7,905	8,072	6,401	3,305	11,150	1,227	720	12,209	6,930	10,566	12,530	6,884
Tsitsihar, China	6,226	6,150	9,061	4,300	542	9,402	9,636	4,708	7,267	7,386	6,176	3,079	11,165	2,486	1,407	10,937	6,099	10,105	11,255	6,012
Tubuai Island (Mataura)	15,557	10,487	3,387	15,567	11,500	5,839	11,792	15,480	17,301	17,084	17,799	14,705	646	10,990	12,241	9,158	15,975	17,472	9,163	15,737
Tucson, Arizona	8,552	14,729	9,356	10,103	9,098	12,573	4,565	9,470	10,027	9,769	11,875	11,149	6,873	11,580	11,035	2,541	9,065	10,930	2,781	8,846
Tulsa, Oklahoma	7,576	15,688	10,806	9,464	9,399	14,021	3,165	8,754	8,870	8,595	10,915	10,821	8,195	12,179	11,303	1,253	8,097	9,508	1,561	7,899
Tunis, Tunisia	2,888	11,612	17,642	4,311	8,525	16,492	5,775	3,936	1,339	1,274	3,179	5,932	17,100	10,091	8,534	8,417	2,725	1,617	8,426	2,906
Tura, USSR	3,864	8,002	11,248	2,281	2,160	11,757	7,641	2,460	5,059	5,136	4,549	2,220	12,720	4,624	3,050	9,496	3,773	7,972	9,777	3,667
Turin, Italy	2,026	11,763	16,900	3,833	7,891	16,681	5,127	3,324	983	732	3,281	5,612	16,297	9,765	8,146	7,829	1,967	2,478	7,878	2,109
Uberlandia, Brazil	10,668	16,450	13,474	12,897	16,389	13,807	7,306	12,320	9,958	9,775	11,679	14,632	10,523	18,773	17,213	6,686	10,880	7,452	6,360	10,925
Ufa, USSR	2,362	8,644	13,705	376	4,637	13,322	7,319	829	2,672	2,842	1,989	2,086	15,341	6,213	4,596	9,831	1,942	5,458	10,020	2,015
Ujungpandang, Indonesia	11,131	773	6,567	8,665	6,318	4,575	15,457	9,399	11,130	11,391	8,899	6,773	9,957	3,345	4,811	16,273	10,757	12,685	16,593	10,804
Ulaanbaatar, Mongolia	5,434	6,138	10,181	3,234	1,576	10,078	9,507	3,772	6,217	6,372	4,928	1,806	12,441	2,845	1,208	11,255	5,211	8,963	11,551	5,168
Ulan-Ude, USSR	5,129	6,565	10,322	3,045	1,417	10,403	9,084	3,515	6,028	6,163	4,913	1,871	12,400	3,198	1,599	10,817	4,941	8,837	11,112	4,881
Uliastay, Mongolia	4,970	6,291	10,873	2,632	2,283	10,540	9,364	3,253	5,581	5,755	4,183	1,054	13,194	3,324	1,686	11,344	4,690	8,263	11,620	4,677
Uranium City, Canada	5,717	13,243	10,806	7,060	6,691	13,741	3,487	6,443	7,383	7,166	8,938	8,172	9,315	9,575	8,564	3,715	6,202	9,109	4,038	5,970
Urumqi, China	4,843	6,196	11,450	2,382	3,120	10,749	9,548	3,112	5,155	5,363	3,497	489	13,965	3,707	2,197	11,742	4,485	7,675	11,995	4,519
Ushuaia, Argentina	14,956	13,127	9,781	16,878	18,855	9,480	11,214	16,493	13,927	13,812	14,872	17,819	7,876	16,605	18,121	9,568	15,098	11,068	9,268	15,180
Vaduz, Liechtenstein	1,763	11,599	16,630	3,575	7,616	16,499	5,151	3,053	820	538	3,148	5,372	16,206	9,516	7,891	7,864	1,692	2,729	7,928	1,836
Valencia, Spain	2,814	12,503	17,637	4,740	8,768	17,420	4,832	4,222	1,833	1,620	4,013	6,507	16,180	10,666	9,052	7,453	2,835	1,932	7,457	2,952
Valladolid, Spain	2,728	12,815	17,381	4,835	8,734	17,742	4,393	4,259	2,053	1,801	4,319	6,654	15,740	10,785	9,150	7,025	2,833	2,300	7,036	2,915
Valletta, Malta	2,952	11,223	17,487	4,127	8,381	16,093	6,151	3,820	1,245	1,271	2,826	5,670	17,444	9,810	8,281	8,806	2,718	1,694	8,820	2,920
Valparaiso, Chile	13,148	15,523	10,677	15,544	17,416	11,355	8,845	14,875	12,700	12,495	14,473	17,382	7,868	18,469	19,355	7,151	13,450	10,249	6,846	13,449
Vancouver, Canada	7,142	13,049	9,424	8,239	6,976	12,485	4,598	7,695	8,843	8,633	10,274	9,075	7,845	9,597	8,914	3,863	7,611	10,552	4,184	7,376
Varna, Bulgaria	2,243	10,142	16,090	2,749	7,022	15,068	6,612	2,547	701	992	1,652	4,269	17,147	8,423	6,878	9,328	1,815	3,065	9,409	2,053
Venice, Italy	1,911	11,393	16,715	3,519	7,639	16,311	5,433	3,052	614	384	2,915	5,270	16,488	9,431	7,822	8,143	1,762	2,590	8,202	1,933
Veracruz, Mexico	9,272	16,641	10,208	11,303	11,081	13,239	4,440	10,574	10,354	10,066	12,554	12,701	7,117	13,647	13,016	1,726	9,790	10,332	1,698	9,611
Verona, Italy	1,928	11,499	16,762	3,602	7,702	16,416	5,339	3,120	717	476	3,020	5,363	16,427	9,521	7,908	8,048	1,806	2,563	8,105	1,969
Victoria, Canada	7,234	13,067	9,357	8,329	7,031	12,428	4,648	7,787	8,934	8,723	10,367	9,155	7,756	9,634	8,970	3,853	7,704	10,628	4,172	7,468
Victoria, Seychelles	8,104	6,348	13,288	6,830	9,221	10,260	12,337	7,361	6,624	6,889	4,821	6,301	16,340	7,850	7,532	14,928	7,598	6,216	14,881	7,822
Vienna, Austria	1,580	11,080	16,298	3,091	7,209	15,973	5,558	2,620	359	109	2,660	4,860	16,373	9,014	7,399	8,274	1,363	2,980	8,355	1,552
Vientiane, Laos	8,011	3,004	9,206	5,542	4,338	7,712	12,697	6,293	8,014	8,266	5,869	3,666	12,435	2,107	2,409	14,598	7,618	9,951	14,895	7,676
Villahermosa, Mexico	9,246	17,006	10,489	11,354	11,349	13,471	4,337	10,611	10,245	9,955	12,485	12,824	7,342	13,968	13,277	1,634	9,760	10,080	1,538	9,590
Vilnius, USSR	975	10,496	15,350	2,203	6,259	15,271	5,766	1,674	1,004	1,028	2,432	4,044	15,859	8,154	6,519	8,441	528	3,907	8,569	765
Visby, Sweden	532	10,949	15,325	2,514	6,343	15,632	5,232	1,866	1,271	1,163	2,978	4,399	15,442	8,434	6,784	7,899	425	4,005	8,031	529
Vitoria, Brazil	10,465	15,781	14,020	12,537	16,413	13,884	7,628	12,033	9,555	9,400	11,096	14,152	11,240	18,096	16,764	7,325	10,614	6,895	7,004	10,688
Vladivostok, USSR	6,947	5,906	8,283	5,079	962	8,752	10,043	5,470	8,040	8,154	6,938	3,822	10,429	2,219	1,737	11,063	6,845	10,886	11,389	6,748
Volgograd, USSR	2,257	9,062	14,679	1,410	5,662	13,917	7,218	1,493	1,840	2,070	1,195	2,867	16,321	7,033	5,468	9,867	1,739	4,468	10,010	1,921
Vologda, USSR	1,273	9,735	14,360	1,246	5,250	14,363	6,260	658	1,948	2,030	2,394	3,135	15,314	7,176	5,531	8,826	861	4,867	8,998	924
Vorkuta, USSR	2,221	9,138	12,886	1,200	3,825	13,319	6,564	904	3,440	3,493	3,455	2,555	13,962	6,091	4,446	8,826	2,108	6,361	9,058	2,004
Wake Island	10,559	6,597	4,334	9,166	4,897	6,108	11,369	9,413	12,004	12,054	11,125	8,001	6,286	4,680	5,593	10,653	10,622	14,924	10,937	10,464
Wallis Island	14,452	7,793	789	13,226	8,953	4,007	13,063	13,472	16,045	16,060	15,017	11,903	2,891	7,982	9,328	10,931	14,604	18,941	11,057	14,421
Walvis Bay, Namibia	9,462	10,542	15,139	9,838	13,598	12,231	10,713	9,924	7,686	7,775	7,530	10,324	15,206	12,695	12,221	12,073	9,177	5,152	11,823	9,397
Warsaw, Poland	1,150	10,760	15,740	2,575	6,653	15,589	5,640	2,068	668	641	2,514	4,390	16,066	8,521	6,892	8,340	832	3,529	8,449	1,043
Washington, D.C.	6,473	16,367	12,498	8,676	9,707	15,712	1,598	7,913	7,501	7,214	9,708	10,313	9,784	12,670	11,449	1,148	6,984	7,837	1,313	6,820
Watson Lake, Canada	6,115	12,250	9,882	7,008	5,869	12,689	4,608	6,497	7,880	7,700	9,111	7,814	8,809	8,643	7,794	4,652	6,551	9,931	4,981	6,313

Distances in Kilometers	Sundsvall, Sweden	Surabaya, Indonesia	Suva, Fiji	Sverdlovsk, USSR	Svobodnyy, USSR	Sydney, Australia	Sydney, Canada	Syktyvkar, USSR	Szeged, Hungary	Szombathely, Hungary	Tabriz, Iran	Tacheng, China	Tahiti (Papeete)	Taipei, Taiwan	Taiyuan, China	Tallahassee, Florida	Tallinn, USSR	Tamanrasset, Algeria	Tampa, Florida	Tampere, Finland
Weimar, East Germany	1,320	11,432	16,187	3,229	7,198	16,274	5,094	2,662	836	569	3,089	5,066	15,928	9,181	7,543	7,809	1,265	3,170	7,897	1,397
Wellington, New Zealand	17,227	7,158	2,592	15,123	11,221	2,231	15,647	15,696	17,914	18,163	15,654	13,306	4,298	9,173	10,807	13,025	17,123	17,724	13,017	17,040
West Berlin, West Germany	1,123	11,278	15,974	3,020	6,975	16,090	5,159	2,442	850	631	2,999	4,868	15,849	8,970	7,331	7,869	1,043	3,368	7,968	1,179
Wewak, Papua New Guinea	12,145	3,446	4,119	9,912	6,265	3,449	14,755	10,501	12,813	13,013	10,897	8,128	7,438	3,967	5,596	14,184	11,941	15,043	14,449	11,895
Whangarei, New Zealand	16,641	6,987	1,990	14,651	10,652	2,122	15,381	15,178	17,565	17,772	15,446	12,885	4,087	8,724	10,338	12,862	16,580	18,218	12,889	16,477
Whitehorse, Canada	6,151	11,903	9,678	6,895	5,556	12,418	4,925	6,421	7,936	7,768	9,053	7,609	8,771	8,305	7,487	4,996	6,568	10,093	5,325	6,329
Wichita, Kansas	7,482	15,480	10,736	9,324	9,190	13,954	3,189	8,622	8,817	8,545	10,826	10,651	8,198	11,966	11,096	1,447	8,003	9,549	1,760	7,801
Willemstad, Curacao	8,628	19,438	12,799	11,075	12,778	15,300	3,863	10,308	8,980	8,698	11,298	12,912	9,445	15,742	14,470	2,572	9,064	7,925	2,247	8,974
Wiluna, Australia	13,252	2,283	6,019	10,800	8,675	3,077	17,835	11,563	12,841	13,127	10,512	8,947	9,180	5,717	7,181	17,599	12,817	13,480	17,785	12,906
Windhoek, Namibia	9,418	10,287	15,069	9,698	13,389	12,099	10,863	9,812	7,631	7,732	7,378	10,125	15,338	12,430	11,978	12,295	9,115	5,173	12,050	9,339
Windsor, Canada	6,430	15,826	12,040	8,502	9,196	15,258	1,867	7,757	7,616	7,336	9,737	10,043	9,498	12,136	10,988	1,320	6,950	8,227	1,593	6,767
Winnipeg, Canada	6,288	14,526	11,141	7,997	7,992	14,288	2,760	7,313	7,765	7,512	9,623	9,297	9,065	10,873	9,857	2,413	6,803	8,962	2,737	6,589
Winston-Salem, North Carolina	6,886	16,551	12,179	9,067	9,924	15,377	2,012	8,308	7,920	7,633	10,128	10,677	9,395	12,864	11,710	731	7,399	8,193	927	7,232
Wroclaw, Poland	1,257	11,031	15,997	2,877	6,933	15,879	5,453	2,356	585	431	2,710	4,691	16,098	8,823	7,194	8,164	1,046	3,297	8,260	1,229
Wuhan, China	7,384	4,190	8,726	5,031	2,580	8,123	11,489	5,672	7,916	8,113	6,172	3,230	11,562	940	823	12,973	7,108	10,396	13,290	7,095
Wyndham, Australia	12,587	1,905	5,356	10,130	7,407	3,088	16,517	10,851	12,613	12,877	10,361	8,236	8,718	4,539	6,123	16,334	12,230	13,973	16,592	12,267
Xi'an, China	6,774	4,613	9,363	4,396	2,453	8,741	11,031	5,051	7,267	7,466	5,540	2,581	12,131	1,589	517	12,710	6,482	9,759	13,016	6,477
Xining, China	6,202	4,989	10,060	3,779	2,653	9,340	10,662	4,468	6,599	6,806	4,842	1,921	12,803	2,275	966	12,554	5,880	9,062	12,844	5,892
Yakutsk, USSR	5,091	7,816	9,863	3,772	1,184	10,804	7,982	3,895	6,472	6,519	6,024	3,375	11,239	4,151	2,931	9,316	5,099	9,392	9,629	4,955
Yanji, China	6,878	5,806	8,405	4,956	953	8,783	10,096	5,371	7,928	8,049	6,778	3,654	10,603	2,110	1,541	11,185	6,759	10,756	11,510	6,669
Yaounde, Cameroon	6,510	11,309	17,890	7,281	11,468	14,688	8,296	7,194	4,772	4,831	5,177	8,286	17,469	11,829	10,713	10,355	6,266	2,191	10,206	6,475
Yap Island (Colonia)	10,577	3,371	5,380	8,369	4,733	4,998	13,576	8,940	11,305	11,491	9,526	6,625	8,492	2,461	4,053	13,688	10,379	13,747	13,998	10,328
Yaraka, Australia	14,297	3,862	3,625	11,906	8,593	1,213	16,813	12,580	14,546	14,801	12,323	10,028	6,873	6,037	7,689	15,253	14,006	15,820	15,403	14,006
Yarmouth, Canada	5,499	15,949	13,419	7,793	9,364	16,633	534	7,022	6,446	6,158	8,677	9,520	10,831	12,338	10,955	2,185	6,000	6,845	2,289	5,850
Yellowknife, Canada	5,578	12,799	10,666	6,767	6,245	13,504	3,815	6,181	7,294	7,092	8,727	7,800	9,389	9,129	8,123	4,162	6,046	9,186	4,485	5,810
Yerevan, USSR	3,066	8,723	14,991	2,190	6,260	13,649	7,878	2,428	2,079	2,365	280	3,162	17,158	7,197	5,749	10,576	2,547	4,131	10,688	2,758
Yinchuan, China	6,257	5,105	9,774	3,893	2,228	9,255	10,536	4,538	6,793	6,984	5,154	2,116	12,418	2,064	550	12,297	5,971	9,350	12,596	5,963
Yogyakarta, Indonesia	10,928	270	7,435	8,473	6,777	5,084	15,660	9,236	10,647	10,925	8,344	6,624	10,815	3,829	5,060	17,077	10,500	11,869	17,406	10,584
York, United Kingdom	1,437	12,213	16,043	3,799	7,426	16,912	4,190	3,121	1,735	1,453	3,980	5,687	15,151	9,687	8,033	6,904	1,695	3,493	6,994	1,699
Yumen, China	5,707	5,437	10,518	3,278	2,670	9,841	10,231	3,972	6,104	6,308	4,400	1,421	13,166	2,757	1,303	12,221	5,380	8,605	12,500	5,395
Yutian, China	5,151	5,858	11,785	2,719	3,970	10,640	10,054	3,492	5,106	5,349	3,115	1,103	14,588	3,989	2,723	12,412	4,724	7,339	12,642	4,806
Yuzhno-Sakhalinsk, USSR	6,955	6,695	8,046	5,407	1,171	8,993	9,451	5,664	8,263	8,334	7,471	4,445	9,823	3,072	2,661	10,227	6,940	11,174	10,556	6,808
Zagreb, Yugoslavia	1,848	11,108	16,538	3,272	7,433	16,024	5,662	2,840	327	166	2,636	4,999	16,600	9,164	7,562	8,377	1,624	2,724	8,445	1,818
Zahedan, Iran	4,811	6,879	13,616	3,039	5,961	11,799	9,747	3,651	3,977	4,265	1,648	2,705	16,663	5,957	4,820	12,418	4,294	5,535	12,552	4,472
Zamboanga, Philippines	10,082	1,876	6,780	7,659	4,965	5,460	14,124	8,350	10,365	10,600	8,296	5,779	10,074	2,010	3,562	15,016	9,763	12,386	15,343	9,776
Zanzibar, Tanzania	7,829	8,126	14,807	7,253	10,468	11,627	11,224	7,589	6,106	6,319	4,954	7,276	17,216	9,534	8,990	13,555	7,383	4,867	13,435	7,621
Zaragoza, Spain	2,604	12,503	17,399	4,604	8,581	17,430	4,680	4,059	1,760	1,522	4,006	6,399	16,016	10,547	8,921	7,327	2,653	2,174	7,343	2,758
Zashiversk, USSR	4,946	8,620	9,932	4,090	1,956	11,259	7,261	4,039	6,506	6,508	6,416	4,054	10,886	4,931	3,787	8,468	5,052	9,394	8,784	4,875
Zhengzhou, China	6,959	4,650	9,001	4,640	2,184	8,546	11,024	5,258	7,562	7,749	5,918	2,891	11,709	1,314	360	12,548	6,698	10,123	12,862	6,676
Zurich, Switzerland	1,763	11,683	16,639	3,632	7,649	16,579	5,063	3,097	908	624	3,237	5,438	16,135	9,577	7,949	7,775	1,719	2,739	7,838	1,853

Distances in Kilometers	Tanami, Australia	Tangier, Morocco	Tarawa (Betio)	Tashkent, USSR	Tbilisi, USSR	Tegucigalpa, Honduras	Tehran, Iran	Tel Aviv, Israel	Telegraph Creek, Canada	Teresina, Brazil	Ternate, Indonesia	The Valley, Anguilla	Thessaloniki, Greece	Thimphu, Bhutan	Thunder Bay, Canada	Tientsin, China	Tijuana, Mexico	Tiksi, USSR	Timbuktu, Mali	Tindouf, Algeria
Tangier, Morocco	15,356	0	15,890	6,366	4,380	8,343	5,100	3,747	8,445	5,950	13,707	5,929	2,561	8,734	6,701	9,861	9,600	7,575	2,127	925
Tarawa (Betio)	5,272	15,890	0	11,048	12,962	11,044	12,715	14,271	7,939	16,044	5,068	13,538	14,457	9,277	10,471	7,020	8,068	8,396	17,954	16,788
Tashkent, USSR	9,208	6,366	11,048	0	2,043	13,412	1,677	3,228	8,843	12,224	7,341	11,811	3,856	2,411	9,845	4,032	11,800	4,644	7,333	7,037
Tbilisi, USSR	11,060	4,380	12,962	2,043	0	12,114	886	1,389	8,959	10,183	9,342	10,094	1,830	4,356	9,056	5,967	11,577	5,466	5,312	5,005
Tegucigalpa, Honduras	16,057	8,343	11,044	13,412	12,114	0	12,995	12,006	6,083	5,342	15,876	2,619	10,628	15,387	3,809	13,593	3,647	10,123	8,970	8,237
Tehran, Iran	10,281	5,100	12,715	1,677	886	12,995	0	1,591	9,633	10,724	8,695	10,918	2,546	3,719	9,915	5,706	12,360	5,845	5,749	5,634
Tel Aviv, Israel	11,617	3,747	14,271	3,228	1,389	12,006	1,591	0	9,949	9,150	10,216	9,674	1,423	5,280	9,508	7,251	12,268	6,795	4,162	4,147
Telegraph Creek, Canada	12,403	8,445	7,939	8,843	8,959	6,083	9,633	9,949	0	10,385	10,606	7,032	8,822	9,803	2,936	7,526	3,016	4,379	10,468	9,148
Teresina, Brazil	17,117	5,950	16,044	12,224	10,183	5,342	10,724	9,150	10,385	0	18,847	3,390	8,375	14,428	7,449	15,735	8,849	12,596	5,002	5,198
Ternate, Indonesia	2,313	13,707	5,068	7,341	9,342	15,876	8,695	10,216	10,606	18,847	0	17,633	11,171	4,990	13,514	4,370	12,341	7,860	14,257	14,327
The Valley, Anguilla	18,672	5,929	13,538	11,811	10,094	2,619	10,918	9,674	7,032	3,390	17,633	0	8,396	14,177	4,119	13,675	5,604	10,019	6,353	5,691
Thessaloniki, Greece	12,827	2,561	14,457	3,856	1,830	10,628	2,546	1,423	8,822	8,375	11,171	8,396	0	6,184	8,114	7,631	10,923	6,296	3,637	3,182
Thimphu, Bhutan	6,798	8,734	9,277	2,411	4,356	15,387	3,719	5,280	9,803	14,428	4,990	14,177	6,184	0	11,594	2,848	12,784	5,454	9,429	9,339
Thunder Bay, Canada	15,318	6,701	10,471	9,845	9,056	3,809	9,915	9,508	2,936	7,449	13,514	4,119	8,114	11,594	0	9,962	2,909	6,359	8,364	7,134
Tientsin, China	6,673	9,861	7,020	4,032	5,967	13,593	5,706	7,251	7,526	15,735	4,370	13,675	7,631	2,848	9,962	0	10,304	3,674	11,254	10,692
Tijuana, Mexico	13,322	9,600	8,068	11,800	11,577	3,647	12,360	12,268	3,016	8,849	12,341	5,604	10,923	12,784	2,909	10,304	0	7,393	11,133	9,972
Tiksi, USSR	10,159	7,575	8,396	4,644	5,466	10,123	5,845	6,795	4,379	12,596	7,860	10,019	6,296	5,454	6,359	3,674	7,393	0	9,558	8,501
Timbuktu, Mali	15,042	2,127	17,954	7,333	5,312	8,970	5,749	4,162	10,468	5,002	14,257	6,353	3,637	9,429	8,364	11,254	11,133	9,558	0	1,321
Tindouf, Algeria	15,676	925	16,788	7,037	5,005	8,237	5,634	4,147	9,148	5,198	14,327	5,691	3,182	9,339	7,134	10,692	9,972	8,501	1,321	0
Tirane, Albania	13,092	2,307	14,559	4,083	2,073	10,357	2,811	1,681	8,681	8,160	11,412	8,126	272	6,429	7,884	7,802	10,712	6,318	3,494	2,962
Tokyo, Japan	6,253	11,327	5,118	6,007	7,849	12,613	7,683	9,186	6,678	16,604	4,070	13,591	9,380	4,783	9,500	2,028	9,021	4,046	13,006	12,226
Toledo, Spain	15,111	478	15,430	6,012	4,066	8,446	4,830	3,574	8,111	6,368	13,345	6,120	2,286	8,402	6,533	9,418	9,442	7,099	2,562	1,402
Topeka, Kansas	15,205	7,611	10,039	10,974	10,209	2,887	11,071	10,619	3,295	7,299	13,794	3,914	9,212	12,612	1,157	10,724	2,055	7,245	9,079	7,931
Toronto, Canada	16,247	6,161	11,320	10,084	9,032	3,362	9,914	9,289	3,863	6,527	14,410	3,227	7,868	12,043	931	10,684	3,489	7,027	7,654	6,484
Toulouse, France	14,578	1,064	14,955	5,427	3,518	8,836	4,315	3,174	7,931	6,982	12,748	6,605	1,803	7,827	6,621	8,805	9,519	6,576	3,005	1,963
Tours, France	14,534	1,394	14,553	5,333	3,510	8,713	4,347	3,342	7,525	7,204	12,600	6,584	1,927	7,743	6,314	8,552	9,196	6,192	3,412	2,316
Townsville, Australia	1,793	16,771	3,654	10,408	12,395	14,266	11,707	13,165	11,340	17,118	3,068	16,884	14,221	8,039	14,074	7,161	11,702	10,171	16,830	17,311
Trenton, New Jersey	16,782	5,922	11,788	10,273	9,079	3,139	9,966	9,220	4,403	5,987	14,940	2,703	7,797	12,334	1,470	11,133	3,848	7,463	7,289	6,167
Tripoli, Lebanon	11,585	3,771	14,045	3,020	1,122	11,957	1,427	281	9,701	9,298	10,106	9,681	1,331	5,143	9,344	7,028	12,071	6,514	4,331	4,232
Tripoli, Libya	13,631	1,773	15,664	4,987	2,945	10,115	3,513	2,027	9,408	7,245	12,207	7,686	1,221	7,229	8,182	8,841	11,084	7,396	2,417	2,127
Tristan da Cunha (Edinburgh)	12,547	8,093	16,016	12,001	10,472	9,653	10,397	9,083	15,072	4,709	14,256	8,095	9,323	12,805	12,140	15,645	13,300	15,569	6,036	7,181
Trondheim, Norway	13,420	3,266	12,675	4,476	3,281	8,990	4,151	3,881	6,156	8,793	11,232	7,405	2,665	6,777	5,778	6,951	8,407	4,310	5,283	4,191
Trujillo, Peru	15,596	9,052	12,027	15,190	13,386	2,618	14,150	12,731	8,688	4,018	16,994	3,385	11,605	17,557	6,341	16,210	6,038	12,699	8,806	8,585
Truk Island (Moen)	3,884	14,684	2,432	8,850	10,861	13,087	10,468	12,057	8,541	18,392	2,812	15,263	12,564	6,892	11,436	4,933	9,678	7,303	16,173	15,569
Truro, Canada	16,950	4,873	12,459	9,310	8,013	4,135	8,899	8,121	4,683	5,947	14,784	3,029	6,699	11,483	2,004	10,645	4,777	6,996	6,386	5,195
Tsingtao, China	6,282	10,298	6,636	4,412	6,373	13,748	6,081	7,639	7,665	16,169	3,973	14,005	8,055	3,034	10,200	438	10,356	3,985	11,671	11,127
Tsitsihar, China	7,481	9,527	6,942	4,318	6,050	12,527	5,968	7,411	6,463	15,152	5,170	12,726	7,539	3,696	8,918	1,065	9,272	2,712	11,163	10,412
Tubuai Island (Mataura)	8,258	16,272	4,904	15,912	17,586	7,942	17,588	18,958	9,165	11,479	9,350	10,442	17,965	14,115	9,945	11,887	7,083	12,164	16,457	16,129
Tucson, Arizona	13,887	9,182	8,627	11,861	11,452	3,139	12,270	12,035	3,239	8,289	12,896	5,034	10,656	13,041	2,555	10,676	570	7,600	10,636	9,505
Tulsa, Oklahoma	15,248	7,789	10,030	11,293	10,502	2,593	11,368	10,878	3,538	7,164	13,955	3,796	9,464	12,930	1,463	11,005	1,979	7,552	9,183	8,068
Tunis, Tunisia	13,918	1,438	15,424	5,042	3,012	9,728	3,682	2,313	8,909	7,190	12,350	7,361	1,186	7,359	7,679	8,770	10,578	7,070	2,573	1,996
Tura, USSR	9,681	7,196	9,041	3,232	4,289	11,290	4,540	5,668	5,773	12,808	7,381	10,765	5,438	4,154	7,482	3,011	8,789	1,427	8,964	8,099
Turin, Italy	14,061	1,533	14,664	4,905	3,002	9,291	3,811	2,747	7,977	7,478	12,230	7,107	1,338	7,304	6,894	8,331	9,764	6,269	3,291	2,383
Uberlandia, Brazil	15,694	7,534	15,133	13,668	11,635	5,618	12,075	10,485	11,358	1,644	17,946	4,398	9,871	15,651	8,498	17,372	9,265	14,148	6,338	6,734
Ufa, USSR	10,807	5,084	11,576	1,786	1,666	11,628	2,147	3,021	7,500	11,029	8,754	10,107	2,891	4,070	8,121	4,800	10,312	3,801	6,522	5,894
Ujungpandang, Indonesia	1,988	13,485	5,996	7,231	9,126	16,952	8,385	9,809	11,628	17,754	1,104	18,550	10,926	4,820	14,494	4,904	13,446	8,541	13,633	13,953
Ulaanbaatar, Mongolia	7,858	8,586	8,134	3,039	4,830	12,995	4,696	6,169	7,126	14,457	5,584	12,631	6,414	2,708	9,219	1,281	10,082	2,872	10,050	9,428
Ulan-Ude, USSR	8,242	8,348	8,219	3,116	4,775	12,562	4,731	6,143	6,725	14,153	5,952	12,211	6,273	3,086	8,781	1,595	9,698	2,440	9,905	9,212
Uliastay, Mongolia	8,190	7,993	8,863	2,286	4,100	13,143	3,944	5,426	7,493	13,924	5,981	12,447	5,733	2,327	9,334	1,899	10,496	3,128	9,360	8,806
Uranium City, Canada	13,671	7,311	9,229	8,819	8,517	5,344	9,291	9,306	1,314	9,164	11,762	5,872	8,045	10,206	1,761	8,287	3,069	4,794	9,263	7,952
Urumqi, China	8,267	7,609	9,534	1,523	3,475	13,572	3,200	4,737	8,176	13,553	6,180	12,535	5,212	1,815	9,785	2,514	11,192	3,799	8,786	8,363
Ushuaia, Argentina	11,544	11,672	11,931	16,587	15,043	7,841	15,015	13,661	13,708	5,969	13,850	8,087	13,635	16,496	11,606	18,215	10,738	17,962	10,023	10,788
Vaduz, Liechtenstein	13,886	1,791	14,393	4,701	2,845	9,372	3,678	2,720	7,810	7,727	12,008	7,250	1,297	7,107	6,845	8,070	9,691	5,999	3,563	2,653
Valencia, Spain	14,813	629	15,434	5,752	3,784	8,762	4,533	3,259	8,286	6,578	13,092	6,430	1,987	8,131	6,802	9,238	9,711	7,058	2,529	1,490
Valladolid, Spain	15,120	656	15,237	5,976	4,061	8,365	4,846	3,643	7,908	6,459	13,294	6,082	2,314	8,375	6,363	9,309	9,273	6,923	2,763	1,579
Valletta, Malta	13,527	1,832	15,318	4,730	2,689	10,130	3,318	1,915	9,129	7,494	12,004	7,759	904	7,015	8,020	8,535	10,909	7,042	2,739	2,324
Valparaiso, Chile	13,717	10,247	12,452	16,467	14,434	5,473	14,853	13,266	11,499	4,302	15,925	5,726	12,658	18,135	9,190	18,974	8,680	15,546	9,134	9,495
Vancouver, Canada	12,905	8,745	8,033	9,896	9,859	5,087	10,583	10,736	1,099	9,734	11,343	6,344	9,507	10,900	2,463	8,569	1,925	5,476	10,629	9,336
Varna, Bulgaria	12,446	2,992	13,967	3,385	1,392	10,875	2,182	1,376	8,631	8,858	10,719	8,736	503	5,742	8,152	7,129	10,892	5,874	4,139	3,660
Venice, Italy	13,690	1,866	14,481	4,540	2,632	9,634	3,445	2,436	8,065	7,815	11,871	7,473	1,014	6,936	7,135	8,018	9,979	6,103	3,488	2,676
Veracruz, Mexico	15,238	8,817	10,067	13,138	12,158	1,106	13,042	12,300	5,159	6,428	14,787	3,487	10,882	14,796	3,297	12,680	2,554	9,376	9,730	8,854
Verona, Italy	13,796	1,774	14,525	4,642	2,737	9,533	3,551	2,529	8,029	7,724	11,970	7,368	1,108	7,039	7,058	8,101	9,909	6,140	3,438	2,597
Victoria, Canada	12,885	8,821	7,986	9,983	9,952	5,047	10,675	10,828	1,174	9,735	11,350	6,345	9,597	10,971	2,500	8,622	1,844	5,553	10,695	9,405
Victoria, Seychelles	8,198	7,781	13,080	5,280	5,243	15,809	4,479	4,613	14,067	10,887	8,024	13,191	6,008	5,119	14,120	7,960	16,818	9,911	6,851	7,695
Vienna, Austria	13,362	2,282	14,068	4,174	2,338	9,830	3,188	2,368	7,872	8,230	11,485	7,758	989	6,581	7,142	7,590	9,935	5,708	3,909	3,107
Vientiane, Laos	5,138	10,426	7,890	4,092	6,047	16,300	5,383	6,916	10,262	16,010	3,311	15,727	7,874	1,693	12,560	2,738	13,013	6,203	11,022	11,016
Villahermosa, Mexico	15,551	8,612	10,411	13,188	12,099	746	12,985	12,160	5,426	6,063	15,152	3,158	10,750	14,961	3,390	12,953	2,902	9,581	9,443	8,606
Vilnius, USSR	12,719	3,175	13,125	3,528	2,029	10,122	2,913	2,621	7,345	9,091	10,711	8,287	1,572	5,928	7,055	6,688	9,693	4,795	4,858	4,035
Visby, Sweden	13,135	3,013	13,087	3,994	2,574	9,592	3,458	3,106	6,911	8,826	11,057	7,818	1,920	6,371	6,514	6,917	9,177	4,696	4,870	3,916
Vitoria, Brazil	15,419	7,200	15,845	13,095	11,095	6,387	11,457	9,874	11,945	1,706	17,476	4,916	9,394	14,918	9,033	17,022	10,028	14,261	5,786	6,344
Vladivostok, USSR	6,992	10,273	6,162	5,048	6,822	12,526	6,711	8,177	6,450	15,757	4,711	13,061	8,319	4,153	9,094	1,310	9,092	3,175	11,941	11,167
Volgograd, USSR	11,320	4,297	12,588	2,115	784	11,579	1,563	2,022	8,175	10,228	9,428	9,738	1,918	4,525	8,359	5,714	10,815	4,774	5,551	5,036
Vologda, USSR	11,883	4,187	12,149	2,846	1,977	10,596	2,750	3,042	6,994	10,075	9,788	9,015	2,384	5,162	7,216	5,684	9,616	3,916	5,853	5,052
Vorkuta, USSR	11,063	5,531	10,662	2,930	3,099	10,660	3,631	4,377	6,038	11,236	8,820	9,593	3,883	4,769	6,957	4,508	8,913	2,441	7,322	6,433
Wake Island	5,925	13,857	2,099	9,208	11,003	11,137	10,883	12,364	6,574	16,469	4,743	13,200	12,389	7,797	9,416	5,211	7,635	6,308	15,862	14,777
Wallis Island	5,798	17,335	2,018	13,022	14,972	10,261	14,669	16,249	8,894	14,491	6,418	12,880	16,456	11,088	10,874	9,012	8,078	10,260	19,199	17,993
Walvis Bay, Namibia	11,539	6,845	16,682	9,087	7,808	11,797	7,565	6,459	15,257	6,455	12,392	9,575	7,093	9,822	12,886	12,647	15,174	13,254	4,790	6,110
Warsaw, Poland	13,010	2,792	13,512	3,802	2,139	9,975	3,023	2,504	7,535	8,722	11,048	8,042	1,300	6,212	7,055	7,069	9,766	5,163	4,467	3,644
Washington, D.C.	16,706	6,155	11,638	10,490	9,318	2,924	10,204	9,464	4,376	6,009	14,956	2,677	8,042	12,524	1,445	11,244	3,656	7,582	7,490	6,385
Watson Lake, Canada	12,547	8,173	8,176	8,639	8,704	6,119	9,389	9,678	282	10,271	10,691	6,943	8,543	9,676	2,827	7,476	3,187	4,232	10,205	8,885
Weimar, East Germany	13,691	2,173	13,951	4,483	2,744	9,389	3,612	2,847	7,460	8,065	11,729	7,381	1,459	6,893	6,664	7,704	9,464	5,556	4,005	3,061
Wellington, New Zealand	4,852	19,392	4,727	13,989	15,910	11,696	15,128	16,341	12,085	13,613	6,668	13,987	17,663	11,591	13,662	10,647	10,753	13,034	17,277	18,473
West Berlin, West Germany	13,522	2,395	13,737	4,317	2,638	9,479	3,516	2,852	7,350	8,276	11,534	7,524	1,507	6,725	6,660	7,488	9,429	5,344	4,220	3,284
Wewak, Papua New Guinea	2,364	15,261	3,305	8,973	11,011	14,334	10,441	12,000	10,055	18,823	1,869	16,706	12,827	6,724	12,956	5,449	11,103	8,410	16,106	16,007
Whangarei, New Zealand	4,680	20,003	4,106	13,661	15,651	11,670	14,934	16,291	11,550	14,064	6,320	14,086	17,471	11,296	13,301	10,154	10,403	12,424	17,889	19,087
Whitehorse, Canada	12,206	8,359	7,913	8,479	8,652	6,440	9,306	9,679	384	10,618	10,340	7,293	8,594	9,419	3,177	7,161	3,398	3,996	10,417	9,097
Wichita, Kansas	15,093	7,812	9,898	11,148	10,410	2,800	11,270	10,828	3,325	7,356	13,756	3,981	9,420	12,746	1,355	10,796	1,879	7,355	9,259	8,121
Willemstad, Curacao	17,854	6,817	13,037	12,709	11,006	1,992	11,827	10,564	7,247	3,462	17,721	911	9,302	15,057	4,444	14,296	5,387	10,623	7,098	6,532
Wiluna, Australia	1,216	14,847	6,441	9,170	10,826	16,857	9,982	11,138	13,563	16,057	3,128	19,003	12,467	6,822	16,495	7,283	14,508	10,912	14,102	14,949
Windhoek, Namibia	11,325	6,897	16,509	8,892	7,667	12,054	7,394	6,334	15,335	6,712	12,135	9,808	7,025	9,574	13,048	12,405	15,400	13,128	4,873	6,190
Windsor, Canada	16,077	6,491	11,062	10,335	9,333	3,152	10,212	9,614	3,752	6,636	14,347	3,286	8,194	12,237	838	10,759	3,174	7,124	7,962	6,804
Winnipeg, Canada	14,730	7,158	9,889	9,813	9,201	4,070	10,038	9,767	2,377	8,012	12,979	4,657	8,402	11,403	595	9,586	2,531	6,053	8,891	7,639
Winston-Salem, North Carolina	16,600	6,536	11,430	10,888	9,738	2,535	10,624	9,880	4,419	6,000	15,026	2,619	8,458	12,883	1,555	11,485	3,388	7,844	7,802	6,730
Wroclaw, Poland	13,291	2,492	13,763	4,084	2,355	9,767	3,229	2,565	7,579	8,420	11,346	7,781	1,249	6,494	6,951	7,369	9,709	5,391	4,205	3,350
Wuhan, China	5,835	10,361	6,966	4,178	6,208	14,556	5,792	7,380	8,477	16,311	3,577	14,616	7,976	2,410	10,948	986	11,184	4,647	11,510	11,130
Wyndham, Australia	528	14,937	5,272	8,719	10,602	16,235	9,842	11,219	12,084	17,526	1,801	18,810	12,388	6,308	15,018	6,150	13,241	9,659	14,817	15,329
Xi'an, China	6,396	9,715	7,559	3,543	5,566	14,389	5,173	6,757	8,367	15,664	4,176	14,153	7,328	1,976	10,672	917	11,196	4,316	10,874	10,481
Xining, China	6,920	9,053	8,247	2,845	4,871	14,313	4,478	6,060	8,432	14,997	4,764	13,749	6,641	1,517	10,524	1,385	11,357	4,193	10,176	9,803
Yakutsk, USSR	9,088	8,452	7,633	4,544	5,776	10,975	5,980	7,158	5,012	13,659	6,791	11,060	6,892	4,822	7,284	2,682	7,963	1,071	10,341	9,373
Yanji, China	6,960	10,187	6,304	4,874	6,670	12,673	6,542	8,019	6,592	15,750	4,666	13,137	8,191	3,957	9,203	1,115	9,262	3,198	11,820	11,074

Distances in Kilometers	Tanami, Australia	Tangier, Morocco	Tarawa (Betio)	Tashkent, USSR	Tbilisi, USSR	Tegucigalpa, Honduras	Tehran, Iran	Tel Aviv, Israel	Telegraph Creek, Canada	Teresina, Brazil	Ternate, Indonesia	The Valley, Anguilla	Thessaloniki, Greece	Thimphu, Bhutan	Thunder Bay, Canada	Tientsin, China	Tijuana, Mexico	Tiksi, USSR	Timbuktu, Mali	Tindouf, Algeria
Yaounde, Cameroon	13,108	3,959	17,888	7,074	5,337	10,856	5,400	3,954	12,394	6,124	12,885	8,256	4,230	8,652	10,488	11,083	13,269	10,522	2,136	3,365
Yap Island (Colonia)	3,391	13,732	3,957	7,552	9,593	14,382	9,106	10,694	9,159	19,505	1,531	16,179	11,376	5,446	12,091	3,887	10,814	6,925	14,855	14,527
Yaraka, Australia	1,574	16,903	4,255	10,626	12,552	14,548	11,806	13,180	12,016	16,608	3,363	17,123	14,350	8,224	14,715	7,619	12,246	10,766	16,501	17,246
Yarmouth, Canada	16,983	5,126	12,326	9,576	8,295	3,860	9,181	8,402	4,633	5,901	14,883	2,873	6,980	11,729	1,856	10,810	4,556	7,147	6,587	5,419
Yellowknife, Canada	13,284	7,409	8,991	8,495	8,309	5,780	9,054	9,171	1,058	9,569	11,336	6,300	7,959	9,803	2,200	7,843	3,332	4,372	9,415	8,096
Yerevan, USSR	11,028	4,386	13,061	2,091	170	12,207	789	1,255	9,127	10,146	9,351	10,147	1,827	4,361	9,193	6,054	11,733	5,628	5,245	4,984
Yinchuan, China	6,916	9,232	7,897	3,158	5,150	14,019	4,818	6,386	8,066	15,179	4,694	13,652	6,882	1,964	10,259	948	10,962	3,903	10,462	10,015
Yogyakarta, Indonesia	2,484	12,873	7,019	6,867	8,620	17,990	7,816	9,133	12,394	16,730	2,117	18,675	10,356	4,498	15,141	5,244	14,430	8,915	12,750	13,221
York, United Kingdom	14,420	2,036	13,864	5,246	3,621	8,497	4,498	3,734	6,824	7,594	12,338	6,570	2,322	7,641	5,795	8,142	8,633	5,550	4,116	2,958
Yumen, China	7,409	8,556	8,654	2,402	4,407	14,012	4,061	5,630	8,260	14,503	5,265	13,296	6,160	1,552	10,206	1,673	11,233	3,939	9,719	9,313
Yutian, China	8,062	7,547	10,034	1,180	3,208	14,246	2,712	4,302	9,065	13,387	6,161	12,897	5,030	1,280	10,518	3,108	12,081	4,697	8,452	8,211
Yuzhno-Sakhalinsk, USSR	7,527	10,318	5,839	5,691	7,299	11,620	7,310	8,683	5,569	15,335	5,326	12,358	8,628	5,058	8,305	2,242	8,148	2,842	12,165	11,237
Zagreb, Yugoslavia	13,404	2,138	14,314	4,254	2,347	9,893	3,167	2,219	8,118	8,084	11,588	7,754	804	6,650	7,311	7,767	10,129	5,966	3,672	2,925
Zahedan, Iran	9,189	6,174	12,063	1,518	1,985	14,097	1,118	2,508	10,255	11,617	7,709	12,030	3,641	2,825	10,881	5,210	13,135	6,149	6,615	6,649
Zamboanga, Philippines	3,089	12,811	5,678	6,445	8,451	16,044	7,819	9,357	10,336	18,352	898	17,189	10,281	4,106	13,158	3,604	12,405	7,200	13,446	13,445
Zanzibar, Tanzania	9,841	6,606	14,875	6,089	5,331	14,109	4,805	4,257	14,206	9,076	9,831	11,521	5,442	6,588	13,285	9,417	16,194	10,637	5,292	6,317
Zaragoza, Spain	14,810	776	15,204	5,688	3,755	8,682	4,532	3,325	8,050	6,696	13,019	6,400	1,997	8,082	6,613	9,094	9,520	6,839	2,764	1,682
Zashiversk, USSR	9,754	8,252	7,699	5,146	6,120	10,114	6,448	7,467	4,159	13,070	7,490	10,293	7,001	5,654	6,442	3,521	7,131	708	10,255	9,177
Zhengzhou, China	6,291	9,994	7,153	3,919	5,923	14,169	5,568	7,144	8,105	15,934	4,020	14,151	7,657	2,413	10,517	579	10,876	4,196	11,235	10,785
Zurich, Switzerland	13,968	1,740	14,403	4,779	2,931	9,283	3,767	2,807	7,758	7,666	12,080	7,163	1,384	7,187	6,765	8,123	9,615	6,008	3,551	2,614

Distances in Kilometers

	Tirane, Albania	Tokyo, Japan	Toledo, Spain	Topeka, Kansas	Toronto, Canada	Toulouse, France	Tours, France	Townsville, Australia	Trenton, New Jersey	Tripoli, Lebanon	Tripoli, Libya	Tristan da Cunha (Edinburgh)	Trondheim, Norway	Trujillo, Peru	Truk Island (Moen)	Truro, Canada	Tsingtao, China	Tsitsihar, China	Tubuai Island (Mataura)	Tucson, Arizona
Tokyo, Japan	9,513	0	10,855	9,967	10,367	10,267	9,943	6,127	10,888	8,946	10,600	17,524	8,144	15,037	3,365	10,734	1,754	1,843	9,905	9,489
Toledo, Spain	2,019	10,855	0	7,497	6,059	614	917	16,413	5,865	3,563	1,722	8,559	2,789	9,328	14,215	4,789	9,855	9,061	16,302	9,053
Topeka, Kansas	8,974	9,967	7,497	0	1,453	7,647	7,367	13,693	1,795	10,466	9,188	11,987	6,930	5,498	11,386	2,746	10,908	9,661	8,893	1,577
Toronto, Canada	7,620	10,367	6,059	1,453	0	6,240	5,984	14,954	541	9,160	7,762	11,211	5,775	5,735	12,365	1,293	10,954	9,664	10,296	3,029
Toulouse, France	1,531	10,267	614	7,647	6,240	0	425	15,812	6,103	3,124	1,568	9,039	2,279	9,868	13,621	5,008	9,243	8,463	16,535	9,171
Tours, France	1,662	9,943	917	7,367	5,984	425	0	15,641	5,883	3,257	1,924	9,441	1,884	9,902	13,306	4,784	8,989	8,158	16,256	8,869
Townsville, Australia	14,468	6,127	16,413	13,693	14,954	15,812	15,641	0	15,436	13,089	15,190	13,401	14,107	14,161	3,003	16,010	6,728	7,724	6,576	12,252
Trenton, New Jersey	7,540	10,888	5,865	1,795	541	6,103	5,883	15,436	0	9,112	7,585	10,670	5,874	5,370	12,898	1,099	11,418	10,127	10,449	3,349
Tripoli, Lebanon	1,600	8,946	3,563	10,466	9,160	3,124	3,257	13,089	9,112	0	2,105	9,354	3,669	12,800	11,866	8,015	7,422	7,161	18,677	11,856
Tripoli, Libya	1,106	10,600	1,722	9,188	7,762	1,568	1,924	15,190	7,585	2,105	0	8,184	3,399	10,705	13,771	6,503	9,262	8,758	18,022	10,726
Tristan da Cunha (Edinburgh)	9,276	17,524	8,559	11,987	11,211	9,039	9,441	13,401	10,670	9,354	8,184	0	11,318	7,410	16,359	10,462	15,826	16,285	11,958	12,782
Trondheim, Norway	2,533	8,144	2,789	6,930	5,775	2,279	1,884	14,107	5,874	3,669	3,399	11,318	0	10,780	11,504	4,857	7,381	6,417	15,312	8,221
Trujillo, Peru	11,343	15,037	9,328	5,498	5,735	9,868	9,902	14,161	5,370	12,800	10,705	7,410	10,780	0	14,426	6,130	16,346	15,144	7,667	5,606
Truk Island (Moen)	12,735	3,365	14,215	11,386	12,365	13,621	13,306	3,003	12,898	11,866	13,771	16,359	11,504	14,426	0	13,194	4,510	5,158	7,231	10,246
Truro, Canada	6,441	10,734	4,789	2,746	1,293	5,008	4,784	16,010	1,099	8,015	6,503	10,462	4,857	6,130	13,194	0	10,979	9,707	11,537	4,322
Tsingtao, China	8,230	1,754	9,855	10,908	10,954	9,243	8,989	6,728	11,418	7,422	9,262	15,826	7,381	16,346	4,510	10,979	0	1,291	11,521	10,757
Tsitsihar, China	7,670	1,843	9,061	9,661	9,664	8,463	8,158	7,724	10,127	7,161	8,758	16,285	6,417	15,144	5,158	9,707	1,291	0	11,637	9,629
Tubuai Island (Mataura)	17,781	9,905	16,302	8,893	10,296	16,535	16,256	6,576	10,449	18,677	18,022	11,958	15,312	7,667	7,231	11,537	11,521	11,637	0	7,390
Tucson, Arizona	10,432	9,489	9,053	1,577	3,029	9,171	8,869	12,252	3,349	11,856	10,726	12,782	8,221	5,606	10,246	4,322	10,757	9,629	7,390	0
Tulsa, Oklahoma	9,222	10,192	7,695	322	1,636	7,869	7,602	13,675	1,901	10,732	9,398	11,826	7,221	5,210	11,476	2,916	11,179	9,941	8,666	1,454
Tunis, Tunisia	974	10,444	1,286	8,696	7,278	1,060	1,412	15,386	7,118	2,333	512	8,499	2,961	10,479	13,698	6,030	9,199	8,602	17,566	10,227
Tura, USSR	5,521	4,131	6,724	8,464	8,036	6,137	5,813	10,083	8,410	5,391	6,627	14,718	4,048	13,770	7,493	7,762	3,416	2,369	13,298	8,964
Turin, Italy	1,070	9,851	1,119	7,958	6,579	523	598	15,296	6,480	2,669	1,430	9,312	2,052	10,386	13,186	5,381	8,768	8,031	16,839	9,449
Uberlandia, Brazil	9,675	17,988	7,968	8,094	7,623	8,582	8,824	15,474	7,101	10,666	8,694	4,035	10,436	3,528	17,503	7,280	17,808	16,774	10,275	8,750
Ufa, USSR	3,030	6,489	4,662	9,267	8,311	4,048	3,853	11,788	8,488	2,741	4,112	12,065	2,714	13,489	9,718	7,525	5,234	4,647	15,940	10,290
Ujungpandang, Indonesia	11,185	4,994	13,192	14,861	15,357	12,634	12,563	3,358	15,868	9,743	11,836	13,175	11,450	17,511	3,864	15,537	4,560	5,831	9,908	14,000
Ulaanbaatar, Mongolia	6,571	3,020	8,140	10,117	9,840	7,528	7,271	8,436	10,239	5,927	7,633	15,011	5,684	15,558	6,169	9,625	1,719	1,281	12,900	10,363
Ulan-Ude, USSR	6,412	3,109	7,893	9,686	9,401	7,285	7,007	8,746	9,802	5,889	7,494	15,116	5,362	15,119	6,363	9,199	2,020	1,277	12,892	9,964
Uliastay, Mongolia	5,903	3,759	7,562	10,311	9,870	6,948	6,720	8,937	10,224	5,188	6,945	14,271	5,253	15,594	6,833	9,507	2,327	2,032	13,651	10,725
Uranium City, Canada	7,867	7,739	7,019	2,458	2,649	6,919	6,535	12,654	3,185	9,086	8,455	13,806	5,426	7,950	9,832	3,374	8,495	7,229	9,920	3,045
Urumqi, China	5,410	4,486	7,207	10,823	10,230	6,598	6,423	9,221	10,532	4,517	6,396	13,449	5,165	15,844	7,387	9,717	2,905	2,839	14,389	11,379
Ushuaia, Argentina	13,513	16,991	12,136	10,722	10,962	12,736	13,036	11,152	10,548	13,922	12,418	4,619	14,749	5,265	13,664	11,111	17,821	18,823	7,360	10,470
Vaduz, Liechtenstein	1,047	9,577	1,359	7,928	6,574	746	668	15,069	6,502	2,614	1,614	9,578	1,810	10,557	12,916	5,403	8,507	7,759	16,774	9,396
Valencia, Spain	1,723	10,736	316	7,782	6,350	483	884	16,159	6,167	3,252	1,418	8,560	2,759	9,620	14,082	5,086	9,674	8,924	16,610	9,332
Valladolid, Spain	2,044	10,709	207	7,341	5,909	549	768	16,355	5,731	3,615	1,855	8,749	2,615	9,326	14,073	4,648	9,747	8,926	16,178	8,891
Valletta, Malta	760	10,269	1,685	9,054	7,646	1,407	1,714	15,023	7,498	1,947	355	8,539	3,073	10,856	13,469	6,406	8,959	8,426	17,942	10,573
Valparaiso, Chile	12,452	17,136	10,655	8,358	8,530	11,266	11,458	12,931	8,118	13,457	11,492	5,344	12,858	2,862	14,726	8,723	18,879	17,948	7,549	8,320
Vancouver, Canada	9,336	7,568	8,474	2,452	3,368	8,393	8,012	11,613	3,887	10,505	9,934	14,435	6,868	7,664	9,026	4,427	8,681	7,512	8,457	2,146
Varna, Bulgaria	699	8,880	2,674	9,275	7,981	2,137	2,174	13,780	7,953	1,193	1,723	9,776	2,513	11,999	12,062	6,861	7,553	7,040	17,790	10,666
Venice, Italy	759	9,586	1,475	8,218	6,861	891	921	14,938	6,784	2,338	1,395	9,466	2,004	10,756	12,902	5,685	8,454	7,756	17,061	9,686
Veracruz, Mexico	10,620	11,557	8,842	2,201	3,132	9,148	8,958	13,456	3,098	12,203	10,558	10,749	8,907	3,557	12,019	4,190	12,791	11,619	7,465	2,068
Verona, Italy	849	9,654	1,376	8,136	6,774	787	821	15,037	6,691	2,436	1,406	9,432	2,000	10,651	12,976	5,592	8,537	7,826	16,992	9,611
Victoria, Canada	9,425	7,597	8,552	2,445	3,397	8,476	8,097	11,575	3,913	10,598	10,018	14,431	6,959	7,617	9,010	4,473	8,729	7,566	8,367	2,080
Victoria, Seychelles	6,243	9,798	7,811	15,216	13,833	7,594	7,854	9,991	13,676	4,787	6,091	7,734	8,428	14,789	10,791	12,592	8,098	8,795	15,906	16,642
Vienna, Austria	811	9,154	1,870	8,251	6,936	1,264	1,177	14,548	6,899	2,224	1,720	9,862	1,733	11,078	12,469	5,806	8,026	7,323	16,981	9,677
Vientiane, Laos	8,120	4,149	10,094	13,414	13,177	9,516	9,422	6,348	13,557	6,798	8,896	13,386	8,343	18,901	5,460	12,848	2,658	3,799	12,574	13,407
Villahermosa, Mexico	10,485	11,888	8,660	2,350	3,119	8,993	8,823	13,762	3,020	12,079	10,367	10,398	8,879	3,265	12,382	4,093	13,081	11,889	7,662	2,402
Vilnius, USSR	1,539	8,208	2,731	8,202	7,002	2,117	1,896	13,745	7,056	2,395	2,601	10,782	1,289	11,662	11,535	6,000	7,125	6,382	16,501	9,510
Visby, Sweden	1,816	8,314	2,544	7,660	6,457	1,954	1,644	14,048	6,515	2,895	2,776	10,877	775	11,202	11,671	5,464	7,355	6,517	16,075	8,982
Vitoria, Brazil	9,220	18,300	7,657	8,736	8,128	8,263	8,548	15,560	7,593	10,075	8,189	3,289	10,273	4,374	18,078	7,635	17,449	16,689	10,947	9,500
Vladivostok, USSR	8,448	1,067	9,803	9,723	9,900	9,211	8,895	7,074	10,393	7,930	9,538	16,921	7,120	15,101	4,411	10,087	1,265	781	10,884	9,500
Volgograd, USSR	2,093	7,482	3,918	9,516	8,397	3,323	3,218	12,495	8,486	1,741	3,134	11,032	2,621	13,099	10,648	7,447	6,140	5,647	16,937	10,710
Vologda, USSR	2,429	7,193	3,736	8,372	7,323	3,125	2,871	12,787	7,464	2,771	3,531	11,703	1,631	12,397	10,517	6,473	6,122	5,364	15,955	9,521
Vorkuta, USSR	3,932	5,796	5,060	8,066	7,298	4,472	4,152	11,663	7,567	4,096	5,031	13,205	2,444	12,860	9,155	6,732	4,937	4,009	14,587	8,940
Wake Island	12,476	3,202	13,386	9,320	10,339	12,881	12,490	4,782	10,866	12,115	13,582	18,033	10,606	12,861	2,067	11,257	4,881	4,954	6,706	8,200
Wallis Island	16,536	7,135	16,963	10,131	11,563	16,638	16,214	4,005	11,918	16,038	17,639	14,183	14,417	10,577	4,213	12,838	8,616	8,960	3,028	8,570
Walvis Bay, Namibia	7,138	14,597	7,215	13,285	12,037	7,489	7,912	13,046	11,562	6,741	6,182	3,005	9,581	10,027	15,162	10,892	12,855	13,298	14,598	14,604
Warsaw, Poland	1,217	8,602	2,356	8,190	6,938	1,742	1,553	14,095	6,955	2,307	2,240	10,408	1,389	11,401	11,926	5,880	7,506	6,775	16,698	9,551
Washington, D.C.	7,784	10,925	6,105	1,612	566	6,347	6,127	15,292	245	9,356	7,825	10,708	6,105	5,208	12,826	1,344	11,517	10,227	10,207	3,145
Watson Lake, Canada	8,401	6,719	7,835	3,287	3,744	7,651	7,244	11,538	4,284	9,432	9,126	14,933	5,877	8,734	8,702	4,501	7,634	6,410	9,442	3,368
Weimar, East Germany	1,256	9,165	1,716	7,773	6,461	1,108	871	14,770	6,432	2,700	2,014	10,023	1,386	10,729	12,514	5,342	8,142	7,356	16,525	9,200
Wellington, New Zealand	17,933	9,246	19,821	12,692	14,127	19,416	19,187	3,606	14,313	16,366	18,143	11,299	17,342	10,748	5,882	15,393	10,209	11,029	3,869	11,139
West Berlin, West Germany	1,335	8,942	1,936	7,781	6,494	1,330	1,074	14,567	6,487	2,686	2,179	10,231	1,226	10,884	12,291	5,403	7,925	7,133	16,459	9,183
Wewak, Papua New Guinea	13,045	4,364	14,841	12,881	13,885	14,227	13,996	1,771	14,419	11,866	13,940	14,871	12,364	15,126	1,520	14,688	5,012	5,961	7,503	11,673
Whangarei, New Zealand	17,723	8,680	19,523	12,394	13,845	18,945	18,609	3,257	14,085	16,265	18,266	11,919	16,735	10,964	5,325	15,133	9,717	10,483	3,740	10,823
Whitehorse, Canada	8,465	6,371	8,004	3,624	4,092	7,789	7,377	11,228	4,631	9,426	9,234	15,271	5,933	9,050	8,371	4,826	7,309	6,097	9,410	3,622
Wichita, Kansas	9,182	9,980	7,702	209	1,651	7,855	7,576	13,549	1,971	10,674	9,394	12,026	7,131	5,417	11,300	2,943	10,967	9,731	8,684	1,384
Willemstad, Curacao	9,031	13,918	7,021	3,983	3,638	7,513	7,495	16,129	3,167	10,579	8,563	8,039	8,279	2,500	15,023	3,725	14,584	13,294	9,597	4,829
Wiluna, Australia	12,739	7,196	14,712	16,420	17,425	14,270	14,328	2,840	17,965	11,157	13,074	11,393	13,599	15,644	5,085	17,900	6,936	8,200	8,915	15,068
Windhoek, Namibia	7,082	14,344	7,253	13,485	12,213	7,501	7,921	12,860	11,747	6,615	6,154	3,242	9,551	10,295	14,913	11,048	12,606	13,076	14,719	14,831
Windsor, Canada	7,947	10,338	6,392	1,128	333	6,572	6,313	14,708	728	9,481	8,095	11,338	6,067	5,597	12,196	1,620	11,010	9,724	9,964	2,704
Winnipeg, Canada	8,185	9,002	6,958	1,209	1,518	6,999	6,667	13,483	2,052	9,585	8,566	12,713	5,953	6,662	10,847	2,573	9,797	8,530	9,614	2,272
Winston-Salem, North Carolina	8,200	11,047	6,499	1,400	843	6,754	6,541	15,080	663	9,774	8,221	10,709	6,519	4,896	12,754	1,759	11,738	10,452	9,807	2,854
Wroclaw, Poland	1,107	8,887	2,053	8,074	6,790	1,439	1,257	14,396	6,782	2,394	2,046	10,178	1,427	11,130	12,219	5,698	7,807	7,064	16,716	9,470
Wuhan, China	8,177	2,439	9,946	11,699	11,667	9,333	9,125	6,522	12,110	7,189	9,148	15,091	7,659	17,165	4,678	11,590	829	2,040	11,867	11,584
Wyndham, Australia	12,650	5,795	14,665	15,029	15,947	14,116	14,051	2,030	16,487	11,172	13,244	12,871	12,896	16,054	3,645	16,525	5,762	6,971	8,592	13,810
Xi'an, China	7,528	2,811	9,301	11,503	11,334	8,689	8,488	7,155	11,748	6,560	8,503	14,777	7,058	16,999	5,307	11,150	1,058	1,924	12,463	11,551
Xining, China	6,846	3,399	8,649	11,438	11,113	8,039	7,855	7,786	11,489	5,862	7,810	14,268	6,503	16,847	6,005	10,802	1,664	2,180	13,150	11,662
Yakutsk, USSR	6,957	3,009	7,974	8,089	8,005	7,419	7,058	9,134	8,462	6,881	8,060	16,202	5,203	13,585	6,323	8,046	2,957	1,669	11,811	8,246
Yanji, China	8,326	1,189	9,721	9,856	9,996	9,124	8,816	7,104	10,483	7,774	9,412	16,726	7,061	15,258	4,497	10,147	1,094	663	11,051	9,663
Yaounde, Cameroon	4,232	13,081	4,284	11,214	9,790	4,513	4,934	14,886	9,422	4,216	3,219	5,160	6,608	10,141	15,455	8,519	11,432	11,352	17,047	12,766
Yap Island (Colonia)	11,578	2,905	13,298	12,288	13,008	12,684	12,438	3,321	13,547	10,528	12,538	15,759	10,797	15,947	1,530	13,562	3,449	4,404	8,673	11,366
Yaraka, Australia	14,610	6,721	16,618	14,268	15,576	16,050	15,944	684	16,038	13,138	15,200	12,719	14,562	14,093	3,673	16,673	7,194	8,253	6,686	12,784
Yarmouth, Canada	6,722	10,818	5,054	2,512	1,068	5,283	5,063	15,918	820	8,297	6,771	10,475	5,131	5,899	13,169	283	11,132	9,853	11,266	4,088
Yellowknife, Canada	7,796	7,302	7,089	2,893	3,074	6,942	6,545	12,339	3,605	8,940	8,451	14,180	5,308	8,390	9,473	3,722	8,049	6,784	10,008	3,370
Yerevan, USSR	2,080	7,954	4,089	10,345	9,153	3,554	3,567	12,395	9,190	997	2,902	10,333	3,415	13,416	10,931	8,119	6,455	6,164	17,733	11,602
Yinchuan, China	7,074	2,974	8,812	11,133	10,890	8,198	7,987	7,660	11,290	6,176	8,071	14,716	6,539	16,601	5,711	10,661	1,269	1,740	12,788	11,284
Yogyakarta, Indonesia	10,624	5,716	12,641	15,682	15,920	12,129	12,124	4,132	16,377	9,102	11,150	12,266	11,272	17,967	4,905	15,797	4,966	6,256	10,702	14,974
York, United Kingdom	2,090	9,400	1,568	6,890	5,561	1,154	729	15,299	5,526	3,599	2,589	10,127	1,258	9,944	12,761	4,437	8,576	7,658	15,716	8,343
Yumen, China	6,360	3,698	8,150	11,164	10,752	7,539	7,353	8,288	11,106	5,422	7,339	14,067	6,011	16,477	6,456	10,380	2,023	2,263	13,544	11,499
Yutian, China	5,261	5,135	7,190	11,594	10,884	6,602	6,494	9,228	11,138	4,121	6,143	12,660	5,500	16,279	7,756	10,245	3,439	3,633	14,937	12,245
Yuzhno-Sakhalinsk, USSR	8,721	1,274	9,840	8,860	9,149	9,279	8,924	7,343	9,660	8,420	9,827	17,690	7,072	14,171	4,466	9,466	2,216	1,422	10,329	8,565
Zagreb, Yugoslavia	585	9,369	1,758	8,408	7,070	1,178	1,185	14,656	7,011	2,101	1,452	9,605	1,992	11,042	12,666	5,914	8,202	7,533	17,196	9,855
Zahedan, Iran	3,909	7,237	5,926	12,037	10,951	5,425	5,465	10,669	11,035	2,421	4,522	10,602	5,176	15,219	9,708	9,982	5,532	5,683	16,938	13,120
Zamboanga, Philippines	10,519	3,666	12,448	13,611	14,005	11,851	11,706	3,965	14,511	9,237	11,333	14,329	10,373	17,705	3,292	14,192	3,235	4,489	10,162	12,932
Zanzibar, Tanzania	5,618	11,367	6,752	14,214	12,761	6,692	7,034	11,622	12,480	4,507	5,124	6,229	8,089	12,998	12,602	11,469	9,621	10,117	16,607	15,788
Zaragoza, Spain	1,726	10,553	329	7,611	6,187	290	651	16,085	6,023	3,296	1,576	8,790	2,534	9,634	13,908	4,935	9,532	8,751	16,472	9,152
Zashiversk, USSR	7,025	3,537	7,777	7,228	7,187	7,265	6,875	9,620	7,657	7,186	8,105	16,275	4,991	12,726	6,699	7,305	3,767	2,479	11,492	7,397
Zhengzhou, China	7,848	2,372	9,568	11,296	11,221	8,954	8,731	6,929	11,658	6,939	8,847	15,206	7,225	16,787	4,939	11,127	621	1,643	12,054	11,253
Zurich, Switzerland	1,132	9,613	1,299	7,846	6,488	684	580	15,138	6,414	2,703	1,657	9,574	1,791	10,473	12,957	5,315	8,560	7,799	16,698	9,317

Distances in Kilometers

	Tulsa, Oklahoma	Tunis, Tunisia	Tura, USSR	Turin, Italy	Uberlandia, Brazil	Ufa, USSR	Ujungpandang, Indonesia	Ulaanbaatar, Mongolia	Ulan-Ude, USSR	Uliastay, Mongolia	Uranium City, Canada	Urumqi, China	Ushuaia, Argentina	Vaduz, Liechtenstein	Valencia, Spain	Valladolid, Spain	Valletta, Malta	Valparaiso, Chile	Vancouver, Canada	Varna, Bulgaria
Tunis, Tunisia	8,912	0	6,394	940	8,700	3,982	12,062	7,530	7,356	6,871	7,945	6,384	12,589	1,153	970	1,392	402	11,479	9,423	1,669
Tura, USSR	8,780	6,394	0	5,733	14,447	2,657	7,860	1,866	1,451	1,853	6,055	2,416	18,772	5,458	6,609	6,579	6,278	16,485	6,865	4,965
Turin, Italy	8,195	940	5,733	0	9,067	3,552	12,112	7,058	6,831	6,461	7,042	6,089	13,170	275	907	1,071	1,169	11,771	8,521	1,629
Uberlandia, Brazil	7,892	8,700	14,447	9,067	0	12,616	17,029	16,091	15,796	15,527	10,258	15,083	4,328	9,322	8,161	8,070	8,973	2,800	10,531	10,366
Ufa, USSR	9,581	3,982	2,657	3,552	12,616	0	8,819	3,549	3,384	2,913	7,256	2,574	16,521	3,303	4,456	4,578	3,782	15,309	8,479	2,394
Ujungpandang, Indonesia	15,037	12,062	7,860	12,112	17,029	8,819	0	6,002	6,409	6,260	12,733	6,288	13,326	11,924	12,907	13,181	11,686	15,627	12,410	10,518
Ulaanbaatar, Mongolia	10,421	7,530	1,866	7,058	16,091	3,549	6,002	0	439	753	7,662	1,562	19,171	6,796	7,965	8,029	7,315	18,347	8,217	5,911
Ulan-Ude, USSR	9,992	7,356	1,451	6,831	15,796	3,384	6,409	439	0	899	7,233	1,738	19,582	6,563	7,734	7,771	7,166	17,915	7,820	5,773
Uliastay, Mongolia	10,625	6,871	1,853	6,461	15,527	2,913	6,260	753	899	0	7,886	841	18,716	6,206	7,366	7,465	6,636	18,108	8,592	5,230
Uranium City, Canada	2,759	7,945	6,055	7,042	10,258	7,256	12,733	7,662	7,233	7,886	0	8,452	13,178	6,912	7,226	6,822	8,211	10,812	1,479	7,939
Urumqi, China	11,143	6,384	2,416	6,089	15,083	2,574	6,288	1,562	1,738	841	8,452	0	17,893	5,852	6,981	7,136	6,111	17,855	9,272	4,717
Ushuaia, Argentina	10,419	12,589	18,772	13,170	4,328	16,521	13,326	19,171	19,582	18,716	13,178	17,893	0	13,442	12,276	12,268	12,754	2,433	12,615	14,129
Vaduz, Liechtenstein	8,175	1,153	5,458	275	9,322	3,303	11,924	6,796	6,563	6,206	6,912	5,852	13,442	0	1,171	1,286	1,318	12,012	8,390	1,507
Valencia, Spain	7,986	970	6,609	907	8,161	4,456	12,907	7,965	7,734	7,366	7,226	6,981	12,276	1,171	0	441	1,369	10,876	8,690	2,392
Valladolid, Spain	7,545	1,392	6,579	1,071	8,070	4,578	13,181	8,029	7,771	7,465	6,822	7,136	12,268	1,286	441	0	1,784	10,732	8,279	2,674
Valletta, Malta	9,277	402	6,278	1,169	8,973	3,782	11,686	7,315	7,166	6,636	8,211	6,111	12,754	1,318	1,369	1,784	0	11,764	9,690	1,407
Valparaiso, Chile	8,066	11,479	16,485	11,771	2,800	15,309	15,627	18,347	17,915	18,108	10,812	17,855	2,433	12,012	10,876	10,732	11,764	0	10,441	13,148
Vancouver, Canada	2,639	9,423	6,865	8,521	10,531	8,479	12,410	8,217	7,820	8,592	1,479	9,272	12,615	8,390	8,690	8,279	9,690	10,441	0	9,379
Varna, Bulgaria	9,543	1,669	4,965	1,629	10,366	2,394	10,518	5,911	5,773	5,230	7,939	4,717	14,129	1,507	2,392	2,674	1,407	13,148	9,379	0
Venice, Italy	8,464	978	5,489	370	9,391	3,225	11,743	6,752	6,539	6,138	7,186	5,744	13,443	290	1,237	1,439	1,076	12,113	8,662	1,264
Veracruz, Mexico	1,880	10,123	10,642	9,554	6,715	11,395	15,875	12,227	11,805	12,479	4,593	13,019	8,616	9,590	9,155	8,731	10,515	6,341	4,113	11,050
Verona, Italy	8,381	963	5,549	265	9,304	3,312	11,847	6,833	6,615	6,224	7,135	5,838	13,373	222	1,145	1,336	1,101	12,020	8,612	1,369
Victoria, Canada	2,622	9,508	6,944	8,607	10,512	8,570	12,421	8,284	7,888	8,666	1,565	9,350	12,546	8,477	8,770	8,358	9,777	10,385	93	9,471
Victoria, Seychelles	15,456	6,563	8,486	7,261	11,290	6,578	7,091	7,673	7,958	7,067	13,759	6,255	11,649	7,288	7,509	7,946	6,189	13,067	15,056	5,978
Vienna, Austria	8,512	1,363	5,062	752	9,814	2,803	11,398	6,322	6,107	5,714	7,062	5,338	13,876	527	1,653	1,809	1,375	12,523	8,528	1,055
Vientiane, Laos	13,707	9,045	5,147	8,994	16,962	5,676	3,150	3,345	3,783	3,345	10,959	3,192	15,844	8,793	9,824	10,065	8,695	18,241	11,307	7,435
Villahermosa, Mexico	2,036	9,945	10,814	9,415	6,362	11,425	16,240	12,445	12,019	12,661	4,787	13,164	8,396	9,466	8,974	8,558	10,341	6,083	4,401	10,945
Vilnius, USSR	8,489	2,299	4,110	1,653	10,698	1,958	10,732	5,412	5,179	4,834	6,692	4,531	14,819	1,385	2,556	2,632	2,247	13,354	8,114	1,289
Visby, Sweden	7,945	2,392	4,184	1,580	10,455	2,328	11,146	5,636	5,365	5,111	6,201	4,889	14,678	1,307	2,428	2,410	2,432	13,034	7,640	1,739
Vitoria, Brazil	8,557	8,253	14,321	8,720	848	12,227	16,436	15,771	15,548	15,123	10,777	14,571	4,492	8,986	7,816	7,782	8,490	3,400	11,188	9,896
Vladivostok, USSR	9,982	9,377	3,084	8,789	17,321	5,427	5,490	2,016	2,056	2,768	7,356	3,544	18,058	8,516	9,677	9,662	9,205	17,682	7,443	7,821
Volgograd, USSR	9,816	3,066	3,688	2,803	11,765	1,035	9,345	4,499	4,374	3,815	7,750	3,327	15,504	2,590	3,673	3,870	2,821	14,529	9,080	1,415
Vologda, USSR	8,678	3,282	3,112	2,670	11,694	1,092	9,898	4,405	4,163	3,852	6,549	3,624	15,836	2,401	3,571	3,625	3,179	14,302	7,882	1,960
Vorkuta, USSR	8,387	4,762	1,666	4,071	12,880	1,485	9,139	3,246	2,918	2,879	5,895	2,985	17,177	3,796	4,943	4,919	4,678	15,236	7,043	3,443
Wake Island	9,409	13,327	6,956	12,571	16,363	9,532	5,837	6,199	6,227	6,947	7,884	7,688	13,964	12,299	13,363	13,201	13,233	14,080	6,981	11,907
Wallis Island	10,022	17,327	11,020	16,466	13,290	13,588	7,121	10,148	10,237	10,872	10,059	11,521	9,918	16,213	17,076	16,757	17,286	10,528	8,659	15,973
Walvis Bay, Namibia	13,265	6,629	12,078	7,562	6,499	9,470	11,310	12,040	12,190	11,316	14,028	10,481	7,500	7,781	7,081	7,422	6,514	8,316	15,308	7,454
Warsaw, Poland	8,466	1,915	4,504	1,264	10,322	2,311	11,029	5,795	5,568	5,206	6,811	4,874	14,425	1,001	2,170	2,267	1,888	12,999	8,257	1,129
Washington, D.C.	1,693	7,359	8,564	6,725	7,067	8,707	15,917	10,381	9,943	10,388	3,195	10,717	10,415	6,746	6,407	5,971	7,740	7,983	3,801	8,196
Watson Lake, Canada	3,547	8,628	5,608	7,696	11,299	7,263	11,694	7,019	6,610	7,357	1,130	8,020	13,820	7,528	8,008	7,632	8,847	11,566	1,263	8,356
Weimar, East Germany	8,034	1,579	5,039	714	9,677	2,982	11,711	6,425	6,177	5,859	6,614	5,552	13,843	444	1,571	1,607	1,695	12,327	8,085	1,522
Wellington, New Zealand	12,491	18,601	13,375	18,894	12,000	15,381	6,788	11,927	12,184	12,492	13,180	12,824	7,797	18,675	19,561	19,958	18,207	9,341	11,726	17,298
West Berlin, West Germany	8,048	1,765	4,816	930	9,892	2,782	11,539	6,208	5,957	5,648	6,539	5,354	14,066	657	1,794	1,822	1,849	12,531	8,005	1,494
Wewak, Papua New Guinea	12,955	14,012	8,325	13,732	17,202	10,180	2,695	6,730	7,017	7,281	11,341	7,657	12,903	13,482	14,633	14,746	13,701	14,524	10,543	12,347
Whangarei, New Zealand	12,217	18,598	12,811	18,484	12,480	14,933	6,549	11,428	11,664	12,024	12,686	12,412	8,341	18,223	19,390	19,341	18,205	9,767	11,252	17,037
Whitehorse, Canada	3,878	8,743	5,393	7,806	11,649	7,166	11,344	6,744	6,342	7,110	1,465	7,794	14,091	7,626	8,163	7,799	8,944	11,870	1,483	8,380
Wichita, Kansas	213	8,904	8,594	8,166	8,100	9,450	14,834	10,223	9,794	10,436	2,561	10,965	10,618	8,137	7,988	7,547	9,262	8,272	2,431	9,483
Willemstad, Curacao	3,795	8,253	11,484	8,017	4,115	10,989	18,823	13,343	12,912	13,226	6,198	13,374	7,415	8,161	7,329	6,988	8,649	5,005	6,429	9,646
Wiluna, Australia	16,453	13,441	10,225	13,783	14,818	10,891	2,379	8,360	8,775	8,561	14,801	8,477	10,949	13,660	14,397	14,772	13,039	13,288	14,111	12,159
Windhoek, Namibia	13,475	6,613	11,921	7,550	6,767	9,333	11,056	11,824	11,986	11,106	14,132	10,269	7,696	7,762	7,105	7,458	6,479	8,566	15,448	7,369
Windsor, Canada	1,303	7,611	8,184	6,909	7,660	8,570	15,332	9,963	9,524	10,029	2,599	10,422	10,851	6,900	6,683	6,242	7,978	8,422	3,173	8,299
Winnipeg, Canada	1,528	8,058	7,255	7,233	9,008	8,141	13,985	8,925	8,492	9,103	1,302	9,615	11,911	7,161	7,214	6,780	8,381	9,524	1,870	8,396
Winston-Salem, North Carolina	1,408	7,760	8,876	7,138	6,959	9,107	16,035	10,672	10,233	10,713	3,312	11,071	10,137	7,163	6,804	6,370	8,144	7,706	3,744	8,616
Wroclaw, Poland	8,343	1,680	4,779	968	10,021	2,613	11,313	6,095	5,863	5,508	6,799	5,175	14,136	701	1,871	1,964	1,701	12,697	8,259	1,201
Wuhan, China	11,976	9,151	3,873	8,833	17,842	5,284	3,988	2,025	2,423	2,418	9,268	2,768	17,307	8,587	9,733	9,860	8,872	19,403	9,502	7,483
Wyndham, Australia	15,108	13,503	9,157	13,595	16,180	10,296	1,489	7,330	7,715	7,662	13,324	7,748	12,066	13,410	14,374	14,661	13,119	14,246	12,659	11,992
Xi'an, China	11,796	8,502	3,390	8,188	17,197	4,641	4,497	1,525	1,954	1,805	9,049	2,119	17,713	7,943	9,086	9,219	8,225	19,862	9,427	6,834
Xining, China	11,744	7,819	3,079	7,532	16,505	4,002	4,971	1,324	1,753	1,302	8,985	1,444	17,848	7,293	8,425	8,574	7,535	19,298	9,517	6,150
Yakutsk, USSR	8,382	7,791	1,491	7,062	15,219	4,148	7,495	2,120	1,741	2,592	5,635	3,387	18,696	6,787	7,900	7,810	7,707	16,447	6,100	6,431
Yanji, China	10,119	9,262	3,015	8,693	17,341	5,300	5,413	1,851	1,919	2,600	7,472	3,365	18,160	8,421	9,586	9,584	9,082	17,872	7,595	7,691
Yaounde, Cameroon	11,312	3,649	9,558	4,579	7,020	6,906	12,035	10,092	10,091	9,340	11,268	8,595	9,707	4,802	4,122	4,488	3,560	9,611	12,686	4,650
Yap Island (Colonia)	12,437	12,552	6,762	12,199	18,763	8,649	2,634	5,168	5,449	5,739	10,366	6,168	14,469	11,944	13,105	13,194	12,269	16,009	9,843	10,884
Yaraka, Australia	14,225	15,470	10,589	15,528	14,977	12,113	3,426	8,879	9,214	9,329	13,329	9,540	10,652	15,327	16,333	16,599	15,084	12,568	12,259	13,944
Yarmouth, Canada	2,666	6,300	7,958	5,661	7,184	7,790	15,681	9,817	9,387	9,722	3,337	9,953	10,932	5,685	5,353	4,915	6,679	8,530	4,309	7,144
Yellowknife, Canada	3,190	7,945	5,658	7,025	10,692	6,982	12,297	7,235	6,808	7,478	447	8,064	13,606	6,877	7,277	6,888	8,189	11,251	1,566	7,817
Yerevan, USSR	10,635	2,999	4,439	3,043	11,577	1,828	9,106	4,934	4,892	4,199	8,676	3,552	14,916	2,899	3,800	4,092	2,662	14,377	10,023	1,418
Yinchuan, China	11,433	8,048	2,900	7,701	16,747	4,150	5,011	1,051	1,489	1,287	8,676	1,676	18,145	7,453	8,603	8,724	7,783	19,376	9,144	6,384
Yogyakarta, Indonesia	15,895	11,435	8,039	11,619	16,245	8,568	1,042	6,181	6,613	6,296	13,398	6,159	13,066	11,463	12,339	12,662	11,043	15,481	13,257	9,993
York, United Kingdom	7,145	2,086	5,291	1,166	9,233	3,616	12,432	6,864	6,565	6,374	5,876	6,177	13,520	1,058	1,598	1,380	2,335	11,758	7,355	2,427
Yumen, China	11,475	7,334	2,725	7,033	16,030	3,500	5,450	1,159	1,536	883	8,725	951	18,046	6,792	7,928	8,074	7,057	18,803	9,355	5,666
Yutian, China	11,916	6,216	3,292	6,080	14,786	2,790	6,077	2,393	2,628	1,731	9,275	917	16,987	5,871	6,932	7,150	5,897	17,562	10,157	4,564
Yuzhno-Sakhalinsk, USSR	9,107	9,597	3,204	8,907	16,740	5,776	6,208	2,682	2,580	3,419	6,549	4,244	17,687	8,632	9,758	9,678	9,480	16,739	6,533	8,145
Zagreb, Yugoslavia	8,662	1,111	5,292	657	9,652	2,968	11,455	6,506	6,305	5,881	7,286	5,471	13,664	520	1,512	1,726	1,106	12,384	8,756	989
Zahedan, Iran	12,344	4,742	4,746	4,925	12,843	2,831	7,323	4,410	4,556	3,679	10,086	2,848	15,115	4,796	5,625	5,951	4,363	15,525	11,273	3,297
Zamboanga, Philippines	13,816	11,462	6,601	11,332	18,325	7,864	1,361	4,769	5,156	5,122	11,398	5,290	14,613	11,111	12,195	12,397	11,121	16,789	11,177	9,825
Zanzibar, Tanzania	14,375	5,634	9,281	6,486	9,533	6,927	8,879	8,892	9,096	8,200	13,485	7,360	10,553	6,590	6,484	6,922	5,323	11,549	14,950	5,586
Zaragoza, Spain	7,822	1,095	6,422	790	8,294	4,333	12,879	7,817	7,575	7,235	6,999	6,878	12,447	1,030	245	319	1,479	10,984	8,467	2,365
Zashiversk, USSR	7,521	7,777	1,926	6,968	14,559	4,455	8,257	2,966	2,569	3,378	4,777	4,133	17,866	6,700	7,747	7,598	7,750	15,586	5,252	6,576
Zhengzhou, China	11,580	8,822	3,409	8,462	17,519	4,909	4,454	1,567	1,959	2,011	8,854	2,451	17,771	8,210	9,365	9,475	8,559	19,499	9,148	7,160
Zurich, Switzerland	8,092	1,183	5,490	263	9,266	3,365	12,004	6,847	6,610	6,263	6,849	5,919	13,401	90	1,126	1,217	1,372	11,947	8,327	1,597

Distances
in
Kilometers

	Venice, Italy	Veracruz, Mexico	Verona, Italy	Victoria, Canada	Victoria, Seychelles	Vienna, Austria	Vientiane, Laos	Villahermosa, Mexico	Vilnius, USSR	Visby, Sweden	Vitoria, Brazil	Vladivostok, USSR	Volgograd, USSR	Vologda, USSR	Vorkuta, USSR	Wake Island	Wallis Island	Walvis Bay, Namibia	Warsaw, Poland	Washington, D.C.
Veracruz, Mexico	9,869	0	9,774	4,063	16,548	9,996	15,418	365	10,129	9,584	7,491	11,544	11,528	10,441	10,253	10,044	9,478	12,878	10,047	2,855
Verona, Italy	106	9,774	0	8,699	7,080	511	8,730	9,643	1,446	1,445	8,941	8,590	2,542	2,462	3,893	12,427	16,377	7,582	1,052	6,936
Victoria, Canada	8,750	4,063	8,699	0	15,147	8,618	11,360	4,355	8,206	7,732	11,176	7,487	9,172	7,974	7,133	6,960	8,589	15,360	8,348	3,821
Victoria, Seychelles	6,998	16,548	7,080	15,147	0	6,978	5,747	16,284	7,139	7,664	10,444	9,268	6,009	7,210	8,029	12,412	13,995	4,845	7,092	13,916
Vienna, Austria	433	9,996	511	8,618	6,978	0	8,266	9,890	951	1,058	9,451	8,089	2,063	1,962	3,414	11,969	15,967	7,882	559	7,143
Vientiane, Laos	8,627	15,418	8,730	11,360	5,747	8,266	0	15,685	7,582	8,001	16,136	3,922	6,206	6,761	6,146	6,720	9,564	10,591	7,881	13,711
Villahermosa, Mexico	9,740	365	9,643	4,355	16,284	9,890	15,685	0	10,075	9,533	7,133	11,843	11,498	10,442	10,339	10,409	9,771	12,514	9,971	2,782
Vilnius, USSR	1,380	10,129	1,446	8,206	7,139	951	7,582	10,075	0	545	10,372	7,144	1,469	1,018	2,465	11,027	15,049	8,663	394	7,293
Visby, Sweden	1,416	9,584	1,445	7,732	7,664	1,058	8,001	9,533	545	0	10,192	7,260	1,988	1,269	2,518	10,992	14,936	8,937	624	6,752
Vitoria, Brazil	9,021	7,491	8,941	11,176	10,444	9,451	16,136	7,133	10,372	10,192	0	17,375	11,310	11,386	12,685	17,206	13,924	5,653	9,984	7,588
Vladivostok, USSR	8,521	11,544	8,590	7,487	9,268	8,089	3,922	11,843	7,144	7,260	17,375	0	6,428	6,128	4,744	4,187	8,180	13,915	7,538	10,466
Volgograd, USSR	2,443	11,528	2,542	9,172	6,009	2,063	6,206	11,498	1,469	1,988	11,310	6,428	0	1,201	2,362	10,558	14,605	8,481	1,698	8,720
Vologda, USSR	2,393	10,441	2,462	7,974	7,210	1,962	6,761	10,442	1,018	1,269	11,386	6,128	1,201	0	1,503	10,057	14,108	9,400	1,411	7,689
Vorkuta, USSR	3,837	10,253	3,893	7,133	8,029	3,414	6,146	10,339	2,465	2,518	12,685	4,744	2,362	1,503	0	8,566	12,608	10,824	2,855	7,761
Wake Island	12,382	10,044	12,427	6,960	12,412	11,969	6,720	10,409	11,027	10,992	17,206	4,187	10,558	10,057	8,566	0	4,067	17,116	11,413	10,781
Wallis Island	16,352	9,478	16,377	8,589	13,995	15,967	9,564	9,771	15,049	14,936	13,924	8,180	14,605	14,108	12,608	4,067	0	15,832	15,423	11,714
Walvis Bay, Namibia	7,577	12,878	7,582	15,360	4,845	7,882	10,591	12,514	8,663	8,937	5,653	13,915	8,481	9,400	10,824	17,116	15,832	0	8,354	11,703
Warsaw, Poland	986	10,047	1,052	8,348	7,092	559	7,881	9,971	394	624	9,984	7,538	1,698	1,411	2,855	11,413	15,423	8,354	0	7,196
Washington, D.C.	7,028	2,855	6,936	3,821	13,916	7,143	13,711	2,782	7,293	6,752	7,588	10,466	8,720	7,689	7,761	10,781	11,714	11,703	7,196	0
Watson Lake, Canada	7,783	5,230	7,747	1,347	13,837	7,591	10,202	5,483	7,070	6,634	11,858	6,437	7,920	6,734	5,809	6,761	9,165	14,995	7,257	4,272
Weimar, East Germany	620	9,530	616	8,174	7,456	479	8,565	9,430	1,027	868	9,371	8,107	2,372	2,020	3,374	11,857	15,771	8,195	685	6,675
Wellington, New Zealand	18,528	11,321	18,630	11,648	12,052	18,153	9,901	11,497	17,326	17,545	12,285	10,293	16,093	16,331	15,036	6,759	3,225	12,608	17,692	14,073
West Berlin, West Germany	790	9,584	805	8,094	7,465	524	8,390	9,496	824	650	9,592	7,883	2,216	1,803	3,151	11,642	15,572	8,361	518	6,729
Wewak, Papua New Guinea	13,396	13,320	13,487	10,525	9,786	12,981	5,093	13,674	12,115	12,366	17,330	5,303	10,981	11,124	9,927	3,568	4,549	13,778	12,485	14,344
Whangarei, New Zealand	18,155	11,194	18,245	11,177	12,257	17,737	9,604	11,400	16,839	16,994	12,813	9,735	15,727	15,826	14,476	6,141	2,660	13,175	17,223	13,852
Whitehorse, Canada	7,873	5,530	7,842	1,557	13,719	7,659	9,894	5,792	7,092	6,676	12,209	6,104	7,868	6,696	5,696	6,447	8,976	15,200	7,299	4,622
Wichita, Kansas	8,427	2,054	8,345	2,416	15,425	8,460	13,502	2,227	8,405	7,864	8,761	9,770	9,713	8,565	8,234	9,233	9,949	13,412	8,396	1,777
Willemstad, Curacao	8,384	3,014	8,278	6,415	13,867	8,670	16,552	2,655	9,190	8,715	4,762	13,532	10,645	9,898	10,407	13,013	12,160	9,877	8,950	3,072
Wiluna, Australia	13,422	16,226	13,527	14,093	7,280	13,163	5,286	16,497	12,683	13,163	14,410	7,813	11,222	11,982	11,419	7,135	6,756	10,334	12,911	17,910
Windhoek, Namibia	7,549	13,132	7,559	15,504	4,581	7,840	10,326	12,768	8,597	8,890	5,922	13,680	8,356	9,304	10,708	16,852	15,784	268	8,298	11,894
Windsor, Canada	7,188	2,844	7,101	3,195	14,164	7,257	13,307	2,855	7,305	6,759	8,202	9,921	8,686	7,598	7,516	10,154	11,251	12,290	7,249	632
Winnipeg, Canada	7,449	3,405	7,378	1,909	14,371	7,417	12,243	3,559	7,241	6,711	9,571	8,654	8,475	7,301	6,891	8,823	10,358	13,464	7,279	2,004
Winston-Salem, North Carolina	7,444	2,435	7,351	3,753	14,309	7,562	14,013	2,364	7,712	7,170	7,526	10,648	9,136	8,097	8,131	10,693	11,399	11,886	7,616	420
Wroclaw, Poland	718	9,687	771	8,349	7,176	326	8,169	9,790	685	732	9,687	7,824	1,972	1,702	3,122	11,665	15,648	8,206	303	7,024
Wuhan, China	8,496	13,614	8,587	9,551	7,360	8,081	1,829	13,900	7,231	7,528	17,241	2,093	6,093	6,265	5,244	5,389	8,879	12,168	7,594	12,225
Wyndham, Australia	13,225	15,327	13,330	12,646	8,022	12,885	4,637	15,661	12,218	12,624	15,853	6,500	10,833	11,369	10,535	5,710	6,000	11,643	12,517	16,444
Xi'an, China	7,849	13,525	7,941	9,484	7,062	7,436	1,912	13,781	6,592	6,900	16,630	2,220	5,444	5,634	4,667	5,899	9,496	11,798	6,952	11,882
Xining, China	7,188	13,549	7,282	9,582	6,629	6,780	2,068	13,769	5,959	6,292	15,934	2,662	4,768	5,024	4,170	6,544	10,191	11,266	6,310	11,643
Yakutsk, USSR	6,853	10,142	6,903	6,166	9,641	6,436	5,326	10,381	5,492	5,484	15,311	2,105	5,177	4,529	3,031	5,535	9,580	13,543	5,879	8,566
Yanji, China	8,419	11,702	8,490	7,641	9,073	7,986	3,751	11,996	7,045	7,177	17,332	196	6,293	6,027	4,665	4,348	8,322	13,721	7,438	10,562
Yaounde, Cameroon	4,608	11,722	4,608	12,758	4,974	4,935	9,999	11,408	5,771	5,993	6,266	12,107	5,872	6,606	8,093	16,283	18,674	2,984	5,435	9,621
Yap Island (Colonia)	11,874	13,283	11,962	9,845	9,302	11,452	3,948	13,648	10,567	10,803	18,799	3,774	9,492	9,569	8,359	3,254	5,646	13,863	10,944	13,534
Yaraka, Australia	15,160	13,832	15,263	12,218	9,664	14,800	6,535	14,114	14,066	14,420	14,981	7,634	12,737	13,151	12,124	5,464	4,357	12,429	14,393	15,878
Yarmouth, Canada	5,966	3,908	5,873	4,350	12,861	6,089	13,066	3,810	6,280	5,743	7,574	10,207	7,725	6,742	6,716	11,200	12,630	11,031	6,163	1,064
Yellowknife, Canada	7,142	5,005	7,098	1,658	13,533	6,986	10,521	5,211	6,550	6,079	11,197	6,909	7,533	6,332	5,586	7,558	9,937	14,203	6,698	3,625
Yerevan, USSR	2,675	12,275	2,780	10,116	5,086	2,402	6,048	12,208	2,152	2,698	11,022	6,934	952	2,142	3,267	11,118	15,065	7,651	2,239	9,430
Yinchuan, China	7,368	13,208	7,458	9,205	7,079	6,950	2,301	13,444	6,094	6,391	16,244	2,211	4,983	5,127	4,146	6,142	9,864	11,713	6,458	11,432
Yogyakarta, Indonesia	11,250	16,903	11,355	13,277	6,084	10,948	2,975	17,269	10,393	10,858	15,555	6,047	8,948	9,660	9,121	6,859	8,039	10,277	10,646	16,483
York, United Kingdom	1,346	8,625	1,278	7,441	8,330	1,376	9,284	8,526	1,718	1,289	9,032	8,370	3,173	2,554	3,658	11,821	15,487	8,639	1,491	5,770
Yumen, China	6,691	13,314	6,784	9,424	6,552	6,281	2,469	13,510	5,457	5,791	15,495	2,857	4,277	4,523	3,704	6,884	10,620	11,063	5,808	11,271
Yutian, China	5,717	13,795	5,818	10,236	5,341	5,345	2,929	13,908	4,657	5,092	14,162	4,278	3,282	3,882	3,587	8,315	11,961	9,666	4,952	11,339
Yuzhno-Sakhalinsk, USSR	8,681	10,618	8,737	6,573	10,176	8,257	4,870	10,924	7,307	7,335	17,037	952	6,807	6,316	4,844	3,762	7,829	14,718	7,698	9,711
Zagreb, Yugoslavia	287	10,102	392	8,845	6,812	268	8,340	9,983	1,189	1,326	9,265	8,302	2,162	2,183	3,653	12,216	16,226	7,615	805	7,255
Zahedan, Iran	4,561	14,083	4,666	11,363	3,819	4,305	4,417	14,051	3,983	4,521	12,149	6,363	2,555	3,666	4,231	10,412	13,912	7,637	4,122	11,270
Zamboanga, Philippines	10,973	14,988	11,073	11,197	7,510	10,588	2,442	15,298	9,819	10,173	17,615	4,129	8,530	8,905	7,982	5,008	7,184	12,111	10,153	14,568
Zanzibar, Tanzania	6,311	14,988	6,368	15,040	1,811	6,423	7,458	14,675	6,866	7,320	8,691	10,697	6,105	7,249	8,406	14,171	15,568	3,234	6,700	12,701
Zaragoza, Spain	1,149	9,038	1,049	8,548	7,657	1,540	9,773	8,869	2,406	2,239	7,974	9,498	3,591	3,414	4,757	13,140	16,832	7,324	2,029	6,264
Zashiversk, USSR	6,808	9,281	6,843	5,320	10,355	6,414	6,187	9,518	5,503	5,399	14,763	2,782	5,447	4,620	3,136	5,617	9,552	13,925	5,871	7,751
Zhengzhou, China	8,132	13,259	8,221	9,201	7,482	7,712	2,159	13,532	6,843	7,120	17,013	1,829	5,757	5,863	4,800	5,463	9,105	12,234	7,212	11,777
Zurich, Switzerland	373	9,501	294	8,414	7,370	606	8,871	9,376	1,435	1,324	8,939	8,553	2,667	2,447	3,826	12,312	16,204	7,811	1,057	6,658

Distances in Kilometers	Watson Lake, Canada	Weimar, East Germany	Wellington, New Zealand	West Berlin, West Germany	Wewak, Papua New Guinea	Whangarei, New Zealand	Whitehorse, Canada	Wichita, Kansas	Willemstad, Curacao	Wiluna, Australia	Windhoek, Namibia	Windsor, Canada	Winnipeg, Canada	Winston-Salem, North Carolina	Wroclaw, Poland	Wuhan, China	Wyndham, Australia	Xi'an, China	Xining, China	Yakutsk, USSR
Weimar, East Germany	7,179	0	18,350	223	13,139	17,838	7,261	7,981	8,291	13,560	8,168	6,781	6,943	7,095	401	8,259	13,200	7,620	6,984	6,352
Wellington, New Zealand	12,361	18,350	0	18,135	5,211	621	12,190	12,487	13,082	5,209	12,569	13,794	13,239	13,676	17,994	10,098	5,309	10,740	11,385	12,145
West Berlin, West Germany	7,069	223	18,135	0	12,926	17,615	7,140	7,988	8,432	13,428	8,327	6,810	6,918	7,149	296	8,051	13,026	7,414	6,782	6,132
Wewak, Papua New Guinea	10,211	13,139	5,211	12,926	0	4,759	9,877	12,786	16,323	3,569	13,544	13,715	12,368	14,261	12,788	4,900	2,153	5,547	6,214	7,367
Whangarei, New Zealand	11,822	17,838	621	17,615	4,759	0	11,636	12,193	13,198	5,193	13,124	13,514	12,843	13,473	17,522	9,658	5,098	10,305	10,968	11,551
Whitehorse, Canada	351	7,261	12,190	7,140	9,877	11,636	0	3,665	7,547	13,344	15,255	4,007	2,642	4,693	7,359	8,117	11,865	7,995	8,052	4,632
Wichita, Kansas	3,335	7,981	12,487	7,988	12,786	12,193	3,665	0	4,000	16,304	13,618	1,323	1,354	1,531	8,281	11,766	14,938	11,590	11,546	8,178
Willemstad, Curacao	7,199	8,291	13,082	8,432	16,323	13,198	7,547	4,000	0	18,144	10,127	3,612	4,919	2,889	8,691	15,267	18,155	14,866	14,524	11,629
Wiluna, Australia	13,689	13,560	5,209	13,428	3,569	5,193	13,344	16,304	18,144	0	10,124	17,279	15,917	17,816	13,162	6,360	1,479	6,842	7,260	9,857
Windhoek, Namibia	15,067	8,168	12,569	8,327	13,544	13,124	15,255	13,618	10,127	10,124	0	12,473	13,621	12,089	8,162	11,912	11,416	11,550	11,026	13,374
Windsor, Canada	3,656	6,781	13,794	6,810	13,715	13,514	4,007	1,323	3,612	17,279	12,473	0	1,377	729	7,106	11,744	15,812	11,440	11,252	8,077
Winnipeg, Canada	2,292	6,943	13,239	6,918	12,368	12,843	2,642	1,354	4,919	15,917	13,621	1,377	0	2,051	7,202	10,569	14,443	10,337	10,244	6,926
Winston-Salem, North Carolina	4,343	7,095	13,676	7,149	14,261	13,473	4,693	1,531	2,889	17,816	12,089	729	2,051	0	7,444	12,470	16,397	12,157	11,951	8,803
Wroclaw, Poland	7,299	401	17,994	296	12,788	17,522	7,359	8,281	8,691	13,162	8,162	7,106	7,202	7,444	0	7,897	12,802	7,255	6,611	6,136
Wuhan, China	8,437	8,259	10,098	8,051	4,900	9,658	8,117	11,766	15,267	6,360	11,912	11,744	10,569	12,470	7,897	0	5,307	649	1,338	3,667
Wyndham, Australia	12,211	13,200	5,309	13,026	2,153	5,098	11,865	14,938	18,155	1,479	11,416	15,812	14,443	16,397	12,802	5,307	0	5,868	6,394	8,589
Xi'an, China	8,298	7,620	10,740	7,414	5,547	10,305	7,995	11,590	14,866	6,842	11,550	11,440	10,337	12,157	7,255	649	5,868	0	698	3,415
Xining, China	8,333	6,984	11,385	6,782	6,214	10,968	8,052	11,546	14,524	7,260	11,026	11,252	10,244	11,951	6,611	1,338	6,394	698	0	3,420
Yakutsk, USSR	4,916	6,352	12,145	6,132	7,367	11,551	4,632	8,178	11,629	9,857	13,374	8,077	6,926	8,803	6,136	3,667	8,589	3,415	3,420	0
Yanji, China	6,572	8,017	10,371	7,795	5,335	9,821	6,242	9,906	13,633	7,752	13,485	10,026	8,773	10,754	7,727	1,922	6,462	2,028	2,465	2,127
Yaounde, Cameroon	12,119	5,223	15,537	5,396	14,717	16,065	12,284	11,392	8,894	12,066	2,988	10,098	11,003	9,922	5,261	11,010	12,981	10,449	9,780	11,045
Yap Island (Colonia)	9,265	11,588	6,762	11,372	1,568	6,285	8,917	12,241	16,191	4,441	13,601	12,911	11,535	13,561	11,245	3,401	2,976	4,050	4,735	5,865
Yaraka, Australia	12,216	15,077	3,368	14,888	2,361	3,132	11,908	14,113	16,280	2,399	12,254	15,315	14,127	15,634	14,687	6,913	1,967	7,529	8,127	9,716
Yarmouth, Canada	4,466	5,625	15,127	5,687	14,676	14,881	4,799	2,705	3,526	18,011	11,764	1,385	2,441	1,478	5,981	11,764	16,587	11,341	11,012	8,187
Yellowknife, Canada	815	6,553	13,108	6,462	10,972	12,586	1,111	2,989	6,641	14,396	14,286	3,037	1,749	3,754	6,709	8,823	12,923	8,611	8,559	5,196
Yerevan, USSR	8,871	2,823	15,880	2,728	11,042	15,645	8,820	10,547	11,057	10,762	7,508	9,456	9,347	9,850	2,440	6,267	10,576	5,628	4,931	5,924
Yinchuan, China	7,979	7,121	11,234	6,913	6,031	10,787	7,689	11,231	14,384	7,347	11,474	11,011	9,951	11,721	6,761	1,138	6,388	520	451	3,065
Yogyakarta, Indonesia	12,426	11,312	7,312	11,164	3,714	7,164	12,081	15,685	19,522	2,327	10,021	15,965	14,690	16,693	10,912	4,268	2,110	4,658	4,998	7,917
York, United Kingdom	6,543	905	18,579	983	13,582	17,962	6,665	7,098	7,474	14,395	8,646	5,883	6,103	6,190	1,270	8,793	13,912	8,172	7,575	6,459
Yumen, China	8,141	6,482	11,886	6,280	6,708	11,465	7,877	11,283	14,092	7,716	10,833	10,908	9,960	11,594	6,110	1,817	6,884	1,168	502	3,270
Yutian, China	8,899	5,636	12,814	5,462	7,804	12,480	8,684	11,748	13,779	8,101	9,443	11,102	10,394	11,715	5,240	3,082	7,565	2,474	1,789	4,303
Yuzhno-Sakhalinsk, USSR	5,578	8,201	10,277	7,980	5,595	9,685	5,237	8,894	12,747	8,454	14,497	9,141	7,833	9,859	7,966	3,041	7,066	3,158	3,548	1,869
Zagreb, Yugoslavia	7,837	672	18,241	771	13,127	17,884	7,911	8,617	8,665	13,147	7,573	7,394	7,604	7,673	594	8,228	12,938	7,580	6,915	6,681
Zahedan, Iran	10,033	4,725	14,024	4,623	9,509	13,861	9,902	12,229	12,938	8,864	7,430	11,239	10,948	11,687	4,339	5,102	8,762	4,534	3,871	6,056
Zamboanga, Philippines	10,384	10,835	7,566	10,642	2,661	7,216	10,035	13,607	17,582	3,712	11,846	13,996	12,668	14,710	10,451	2,745	2,562	3,319	3,884	6,146
Zanzibar, Tanzania	13,934	6,872	13,086	6,946	11,572	13,428	13,933	14,412	12,129	8,820	2,988	13,089	13,689	13,047	6,691	8,948	9,721	8,564	8,039	10,633
Zaragoza, Spain	7,771	1,398	19,660	1,619	14,513	19,233	7,923	7,818	7,305	14,453	7,347	6,520	7,014	6,666	1,727	9,617	14,356	8,972	8,320	7,694
Zashiversk, USSR	4,057	6,256	12,361	6,045	7,878	11,747	3,778	7,316	10,821	10,595	13,788	7,245	6,072	7,973	6,097	4,506	9,272	4,275	4,276	863
Zhengzhou, China	8,053	7,869	10,483	7,658	5,273	10,025	7,740	11,371	14,810	6,825	11,984	11,306	10,152	12,030	7,515	466	5,764	441	1,096	3,233
Zurich, Switzerland	7,476	456	18,744	677	13,542	18,273	7,578	8,054	8,074	13,748	7,796	6,815	7,085	7,075	755	8,649	13,491	8,006	7,359	6,808

Distances in Kilometers	Yanji, China	Yaounde, Cameroon	Yap Island (Colonia)	Yaraka, Australia	Yarmouth, Canada	Yellowknife, Canada	Yerevan, USSR	Yinchuan, China	Yogyakarta, Indonesia	York, United Kingdom	Yumen, China	Yutian, China	Yuzhno-Sakhalinsk, USSR	Zagreb, Yugoslavia	Zahedan, Iran	Zamboanga, Philippines	Zanzibar, Tanzania	Zaragoza, Spain	Zashiversk, USSR	Zhengzhou, China
Yaounde, Cameroon	11,940	0	13,931	14,449	8,723	11,366	5,208	10,163	11,049	5,660	9,414	7,994	12,636	4,667	5,915	12,228	3,268	4,363	11,225	10,873
Yap Island (Colonia)	3,792	13,931	0	3,860	13,612	9,956	9,642	4,512	3,626	12,014	5,218	6,411	4,172	11,612	8,271	1,794	11,109	12,972	6,441	3,743
Yaraka, Australia	7,650	14,449	3,860	0	16,567	13,020	12,533	8,043	4,050	15,699	8,629	9,456	7,956	14,873	10,729	4,250	11,217	16,302	10,239	7,340
Yarmouth, Canada	10,274	8,723	13,612	16,567	0	3,707	8,401	10,858	15,997	4,720	10,598	10,498	9,557	6,196	10,263	14,327	11,711	5,205	7,429	11,302
Yellowknife, Canada	7,026	11,366	9,956	13,020	3,707	0	8,471	8,243	12,953	5,862	8,309	8,902	6,106	7,221	9,804	10,958	13,396	7,044	4,336	8,411
Yerevan, USSR	6,779	5,208	9,642	12,533	8,401	8,471	0	5,223	8,576	3,710	4,475	3,241	7,428	2,392	1,904	8,464	5,161	3,783	6,280	5,993
Yinchuan, China	2,015	10,163	4,512	8,043	10,858	8,243	5,223	0	5,139	7,659	757	2,173	3,097	7,102	4,271	3,839	8,488	8,483	3,927	776
Yogyakarta, Indonesia	5,939	11,049	3,626	4,050	15,997	12,953	8,576	5,139	0	12,111	5,432	5,778	6,857	10,966	6,715	2,081	7,859	12,348	8,733	4,722
York, United Kingdom	8,306	5,660	12,014	15,699	4,720	5,862	3,710	7,659	12,111	0	7,075	6,367	8,328	1,518	5,606	11,458	7,642	1,357	6,220	8,376
Yumen, China	2,665	9,414	5,218	8,629	10,598	8,309	4,475	757	5,432	7,075	0	1,438	3,678	6,419	3,539	4,383	7,861	7,820	4,105	1,519
Yutian, China	4,089	7,994	6,411	9,456	10,498	8,902	3,241	2,173	5,778	6,367	1,438	0	5,054	5,432	2,102	5,264	6,499	6,865	5,049	2,885
Yuzhno-Sakhalinsk, USSR	1,135	12,636	4,172	7,956	9,557	6,106	7,428	3,097	6,857	8,328	3,678	5,054	0	8,493	7,092	4,857	11,537	9,556	2,283	2,777
Zagreb, Yugoslavia	8,195	4,667	11,612	14,873	6,196	7,221	2,392	7,102	10,966	1,518	6,419	5,432	8,493	0	4,283	10,690	6,200	1,434	6,673	7,869
Zahedan, Iran	6,177	5,915	8,271	10,729	10,263	9,804	1,904	4,271	6,715	5,606	3,539	2,102	7,092	4,283	0	6,856	4,578	5,635	6,664	4,960
Zamboanga, Philippines	4,053	12,228	1,794	4,250	14,327	10,958	8,464	3,839	2,081	11,458	4,383	5,264	4,857	10,690	6,856	0	9,319	12,121	6,899	3,202
Zanzibar, Tanzania	10,501	3,268	11,109	11,217	11,711	13,396	5,161	8,488	7,859	7,642	7,861	6,499	11,537	6,200	4,578	9,319	0	6,678	11,207	9,000
Zaragoza, Spain	9,412	4,363	12,972	16,302	5,205	7,044	3,783	8,483	12,348	1,357	7,820	6,865	9,556	1,434	5,635	12,121	6,678	0	7,524	9,240
Zashiversk, USSR	2,845	11,225	6,441	10,239	7,429	4,336	6,280	3,927	8,733	6,220	4,105	5,049	2,283	6,673	6,664	6,899	11,207	7,524	0	4,081
Zhengzhou, China	1,642	10,873	3,743	7,340	11,302	8,411	5,993	776	4,722	8,376	1,519	2,885	2,777	7,869	4,960	3,202	9,000	9,240	4,081	0
Zurich, Switzerland	8,461	4,830	12,000	15,404	5,597	6,818	2,987	7,514	11,548	985	6,858	5,948	8,656	610	4,885	11,183	6,659	972	6,707	8,269